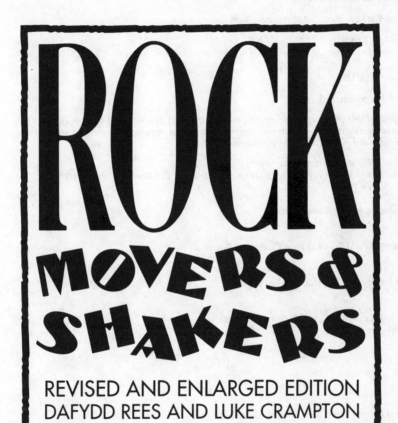

ROCK
MOVERS & SHAKERS

REVISED AND ENLARGED EDITION
DAFYDD REES AND LUKE CRAMPTON

BILLBOARD BOOKS
AN IMPRINT OF WATSON-GUPTILL PUBLICATIONS/NEW YORK

A **Banson** Production
3 Turville Street
London E2 7HR
UK

Compiled by Dafydd Rees and Luke Crampton

Edited by Jane Lyons, Ben Barkow, Reet Nelis, Austin Guest

Designed by Jim Wire Graphic Design

Typeset by Quantum

Printed by The Bath Press, Bath, UK

Copyright © 1991 Banson Marketing Ltd

This edition first published 1991 in the United States and Canada by
Billboard Books, an imprint of Watson-Guptill Publications, a division of BPI Communications, Inc.,
1515 Broadway, New York, NY 10036.

Library of Congress Cataloging-in-Publication Data

Rees. Dafydd.
    Rock movers & shakers / Dafydd Rees and Luke Crampton.–Rev. and
enl. ed.
        p.   cm.
    British   ed. published under title: The Guinness book of rock
stars.
    ISBN 0-8230-7609-1
    1. Rock musicians.   I. Crampton, Luke. II. Title. III. Title:
Rock movers and shakers.
ML394.R43 1991
782.42166'092'2–dc20
    [B]   91-22879
                                                  CIP
                                                  MN

Simultaneously published in the United Kingdom by Guinness Books,
library edition published in the United States and Canada by ABC-CLIO.

First Printing, 1991

1 2 3 4 5 6 7 8 9 / 96 95 94 93 92 91

Front cover illustrations (from left to right): Frankie Avalon, Chuck Berry, Elvis Costello, Bob Dylan, The Everly Brothers, Connie Francis, Marvin Gaye, Whitney Houston, Billy Idol, Michael Jackson, Kiss, Cyndi Lauper. Back cover: Madonna, Willie Nelson, Roy Orbison, Prince, Suzi Quatro, David Lee Roth (Van Halen), Bruce Springsteen, Tina Turner, U2, Ritchie Valens, Tom Waits, XTC, Neil Young, Frank Zappa.

Photographs: *John Beecher/Flair Photography*: Everly Brothers; *London Features International Ltd*: Janis Joplin; *Pictorial Press Ltd*: The Grateful Dead; *Q Magazine*: Abba, Dire Straits, Led Zeppelin, The Mamas And The Papas, Elvis Presley, Otis Redding, Van Halen; *Q/Greg Freeman, S.I.N.*: Guns N' Roses; *Q/Robert Ellis/Repfoto*: The Walker Brothers; All others courtesy of MRIB/MIRO.

Thanks to: Peter Compton, Barry Lazell, Pete Frame, John Tracy, Charles, Barry and Rachel and the MRIB/MIRO team.

Dedications and apologies to Linda, Christiaan and Elaine.

INTRODUCTION

This book has been compiled as an entertaining reference work which identifies the most influential and popular artists of the past 40 years and documents the events of their musical careers and personal lives chronologically.

The number of acts in the line-up of this rock 'n' rollcall is clearly restricted. Included are: the major acts who made rock happen; acts who have had a formative influence but maintained little chart impact; acts with a lengthy chart career but limited biography; and artists popular in either the United States or the United Kingdom. Many entries have been added for this second edition as artists have developed, been reassessed or shown significant potential since the first edition.

The length of the entries varies, depending on how long each act has been recording and performing. Also, the history of some of the artists is intrinsically more interesting and vital than others and requires greater documentation.

Only objective information is presented on these major players in the modern music arena, allowing rock history to speak for itself.

THE ENTRIES

The acts are presented alphabetically and the group line-up (with instrument played) is either the original or the best known.

Singles and EPs are in italics (*Rock Around The Clock*), albums (including cassette, 8-track, LPs and CDs) are in bold italics (***It's Only Rock'N'Roll***).

All relevant UK and US pop singles and albums chart peaks are given in each entry. Additional reference to specialist charts (R&B, Independent, Country etc) or other national chart surveys (Australia, Germany etc) is included where notable.

Magazines, newspapers, books and other literary references are presented in bold (**Rolling Stone**). Television and radio programs, films, videos, tours and events are shown in quotation marks ("Top Of The Pops").

All US locations are presented by town and (abbr.) state (Los Angeles, CA) while town and county (abbr.) (Blackpool, Lancs.) are listed for the UK. For the rest of the world, city and country are given (Tokyo, Japan).

All dates are as accurate as can be determined, though extensive research still leaves some conflicting information, particularly for birth dates where post-fame publicity often seems to make rock stars younger.

If you are included in this book (or think you ought to be!), and would like to correct, corroborate or contribute further information for subsequent editions, please write to the publishers.

SOURCE MATERIAL

Among a myriad of newspapers and magazines, the following proved particularly useful during research: US: **Billboard, Circus, Discoveries, Entertainment Weekly, Goldmine, People, Performance, Premiere, Radio & Records, Rolling Stone, TV Guide, USA Today.** UK: **Kerrang!, Melody Maker, Music & Media, Music Collector, New Musical Express, Q, Record Business, Record Collector, Record Mirror, Smash Hits, Time Out, Vox.**
Books: **Guinness British Hit Singles** and **Hit Albums, The Billboard Book Of Top 40 Hits, Top 40 Albums** and **Book Of Number One Hits.**

ABBA

Benny Andersson (keyboards, synthesizer, vocals)
Bjorn Ulvaeus (guitar, vocals)
Agnetha Faltskog (vocals)
Frida Lyngstad (vocals)

1966 Andersson (b. Goran Bror Benny Andersson, Dec.16, 1946, Stockholm, Sweden), former piano player with The Hep Stars, a group which sells more records than The Beatles in Sweden, and Ulvaeus (b. Bjorn Christian Ulvaeus, Apr.25, 1945, Gothenburg, Sweden), having formed folk band The West Bay Singers with friends from school in 1963, meet at a party in Vastervik, Sweden, and begin a songwriting partnership forming publishing company Union Songs.

1969 Having been spotted by Stig Anderson (b. Stikkan Anderson) and brought to Stockholm, changing their name to The Hootenanny Singers, they are signed by Anderson as the first act on his Polar label. On a Swedish TV show, Ulvaeus meets Faltskog (b. Agnetha Ase Faltskog, Apr.5, 1950, Jonkoping, Sweden), signed as a soloist to CBS Sweden at 17, having a Swedish #1 in 1968 with *I Was So In Love* then playing Maria Magdalena in the Swedish production of "Jesus Christ Superstar" followed by a summer folk circuit tour throughout Sweden.

Aug Andersson becomes engaged to Lyngstad (b. Anni-Frid Synni Lyngstad, Nov.15, 1945, Narvik, Norway), whose German father was thought to have been killed before Lyngstad is born when his ship sinks during World War II and whose mother dies shortly after her birth, has moved to Eskilstuna, southwest of Stockholm at age 2 to be brought up by her grandmother. At 10 she has entered a local amateur singing contest, and when 11 sings at a Red Cross soiree and in her teens fronts her own dance band, The Anni-Frid Four, winning a television talent contest in Sept.3, 1967 on "Hyland's Corner" with *A Day Off*, which leads to a contract with EMI, and she is already a veteran of song festivals in Japan and Venezuela.

1971 **Feb** [14] After Faltskog and Lyngstad have sung backing vocals on *Hey Old Man* for Andersson and Ulvaeus' forthcoming album *Happiness*, they decide to perform together so as not to spend time apart, making their first appearance as a group as The Engaged Couples at the Festfolk Quartet nightclub in Gothenburg, but, unhappy with their performance, they abandon plans to continue as a group.

July [7] Ulvaeus and Faltskog marry in Verum, Sweden. Andersson is organist at the wedding.

Oct Andersson and Ulvaeus become producer partners at Polar Music.

1972 **Feb** They submit *Better To Have Loved*, sung by Lena Andersson, as the Swedish entry in the Eurovision Song Contest. It comes third but will go on to top the Swedish chart.

June *People Need Love* is released in Sweden under the name Bjorn, Benny, Agnetha & Frida, and hits #2. Anderson begins calling the foursome Abba, after their initials, then realizes it is the name of the largest fish-canning company in Sweden. He negotiates with company to use the name. They send a carton of tuna as a gesture of goodwill.

Nov With *She's My Kind Of Girl* selling over 250,000 copies in Japan, Bjorn & Benny are invited to take part in the World Popular Song Festival in Tokyo.

1973 **Jan** Andersson, Ulvaeus and Anderson are asked to submit a song for the Swedish heat of the Eurovision Song Contest. They produce *Ring Ring*, which the quartet records and agrees to perform.

Feb [10] *Ring Ring* fails to be chosen as Swedish Eurovision entry (it comes in third, as had *Better To Have Loved* the previous year) but is recorded in Swedish, German, Spanish and English (with lyrics provided by Neil Sedaka and Phil Cody) for a single on which they are credited as Abba for the first time.

[23] Linda Ulvaeus, daughter of Bjorn and Agnetha, is born in Stockholm.

Apr *Ring Ring*, in Swedish, tops all Scandinavian charts as the group embarks on its first Swedish tour. An English version becomes #1 in Austria, Holland, Belgium and South Africa.

Oct *Ring Ring* is released in UK, as Abba begins recording its first album at Metronome studios in Stockholm.

1974 **Feb** [9] New Andersson/Ulvaeus/Anderson song *Waterloo*, sung in English, wins heat to represent Sweden in the Eurovision Song Contest.

Apr [6] *Waterloo* wins the Eurovision Song Contest held in Brighton, E.Sussex. (Stig Anderson has bet $40 to win on the 20/1 odds.)

May [4] *Waterloo* tops UK chart.

June [1] Debut album *Waterloo* reaches UK #28.

July [27] *Ring Ring*, reissued in UK, makes #32.

Aug [6] *Waterloo* hits US #6. Abba makes its first US promotion trip, appearing on TV's "Mike Douglas Show".

Sept *Waterloo* peaks at US #145.

Oct [26] *Honey Honey* reaches US #27.

Nov Group begins its first European tour at the Falkontheater, Copenhagen, Denmark, playing dates outside Sweden for the first time, in Denmark, Germany, Austria and Switzerland, as *So Long* is issued in UK, but does not chart, and *Abba* peaks at US #174.

1975 **Aug** [2] *I Do, I Do, I Do, I Do, I Do* makes UK #38, 3 months after its release.

Oct [25] *S.O.S.*, already recorded by Agnetha on her solo album *Eleven Women In One Building*, hits UK #6.

Nov [8] *S.O.S.* reaches US #15, as Abba makes second promotional US visit.

1976 **Jan** [31] *Mamma Mia* tops UK chart, ending 9-week reign of Queen's *Bohemian Rhapsody*, as parent album *Abba* reaches UK #13.

Apr [24] *Greatest Hits* tops UK chart, becoming the first of 8 consecutive UK #1 Abba albums.

May [1] *I Do, I Do, I Do, I Do, I Do* reaches US #15.

[8] Latin-flavored *Fernando*, already recorded by Frida on her album *Frida Alone*, hits UK #1. (It also tops the chart in Australia, where they have 4 other singles in the same Top 30 as they begin a tour. Their popularity will perhaps be greater there than anywhere else. According to record company figures, 1 in 4 Australians will own a copy of *Greatest Hits*.)

June [18] They give a Royal Performance in Stockholm for Sweden's King and his Queen-to-be, on the eve of the Royal Wedding.

July [4] *Mamma Mia* makes US #32.

Sept [4] *Dancing Queen* becomes their third consecutive UK #1, and sells over 850,000 copies.

Nov [20] *Fernando* reaches US #13, as Abba visits for extensive TV appearances.

[27] *Greatest Hits* makes US #48.

Dec [11] *Money Money Money*, taken from the album, climbs to UK #3. Tickets go on sale for Abba's forthcoming show at London's Royal Albert Hall, and 3½ million applications arrive for only 11,000 seats.

1977 **Jan** [1] *Arrival* tops UK chart.

[28] Group begins a tour of Europe and Australia at the Ekeberghallen, Oslo, Norway.

Feb [14] Abba performs 2 sell-out concerts at the Royal Albert Hall during its first UK tour.

Mar "Abba – The Movie" is filmed at the end of the tour in Australia.

Apr [2] *Knowing Me, Knowing You* tops UK chart.

[9] *Dancing Queen* hits US #1, having climbed the chart since Dec. It is Abba's biggest US seller and only chart-topper and becomes the group's first US gold disk.

[16] *Arrival* reaches US #20.

July [23] *Knowing Me, Knowing You* reaches US #14.

Nov [5] *The Name Of The Game* tops UK chart.

[19] *Money Money Money*, belatedly issued in US, peaks at #56.

1978 **Jan** [21] *The Album* enters UK chart at #1.

Feb [4] A cappella-introed *Take A Chance On Me* tops UK chart, completing a second consecutive #1 hat-trick.

[16] "Abba – The Movie", chronicling the group's 1977 Australian tour and featuring many of the songs on *The Album*, premieres in London.

Mar [11] *The Name Of The Game* reaches US #12.

May Abba's Polar studio in Stockholm, one of the most advanced in the world, is completed. Group's US management team The Scotti Brothers declares May "Abba Month".

June [12] *The Album* sells its millionth copy in UK.

July [8] *Take A Chance On Me* hits US #3, earning a gold disk for 1 million sales.

[22] *The Album* reaches US #14.

Oct [6] Andersson and Lyngstad marry in Sweden (both have been married before).

[7] *Summer Night City* hits UK #5.

Dec [24] Ulvaeus and Faltskog separate and announce they are filing for divorce.

1979 **Jan** [9] The "Music For UNICEF Concert", to celebrate the International Year Of The Child, takes place in the General Assembly Hall of the United Nations in New York. Abba sings *Chiquitita*, donating their royalties from the song to UNICEF.

[10] NBC TV airs "A Gift Of Song – The Music For UNICEF Concert".

Feb [10] *Chiquitita* hits UK #2.

May [5] *Voulez Vous*, the group's first album to be recorded at Polar studios, tops UK chart and sells over a million copies in 5 weeks.

[12] *Does Your Mother Know?* hits UK #4.

July [21] *Does Your Mother Know?* reaches US #19.

Aug [11] Double A-side *Angeleyes/Voulez Vous* hits UK #3.
Sept [1] *Voulez Vous* makes US #80 as parent album *Voulez-Vous* reaches US #19.
[13] Abba begins 18-date North American tour, their first, in Edmonton, Canada. The tour will end at the Maple Leaf Gardens in Toronto, Canada on Oct.7.
Oct [13] *Voulez Vous* B-side, *Angeleyes*, peaks at US #64.
[19] Group begins month-long tour of 9 European countries in Gothenburg. The tour, highlighted by 6 sell-out performances at Wembley Arena, London, before a combined audience of 48,000 people, will end on Nov.15 at the R.D.S. Main Hall, Dublin, Eire.
Nov [10] *Gimme Gimme Gimme (A Man After Midnight)* hits UK #3.
[17] *Greatest Hits Vol.2* tops UK chart, as Abba is listed as the biggest-selling group in recording history in the new edition of the **Guinness Book Of World Records**.
Dec [22] *I Have A Dream*, with the choir of the International School of Stockholm, hits UK #2.
1980 **Jan** [12] *Chiquitita* reaches US #29.
[19] *Greatest Hits Vol.2* makes US #46.
Aug *The Winner Takes It All* is first Abba UK #1 hit for 2½ years.
Nov [22] *Super Trouper* tops UK chart.
[29] *Super Trouper* also tops US chart.
1981 **Jan** Ulvaeus marries Lena Kallersjo, in Stockholm.
Feb [14] Andersson and Lyngstad announce divorce proceedings, after he reveals his love for Swedish TV personality Mona Norklit.
Super Trouper reaches US #17.
Mar [14] *The Winner Takes It All* hits US #8, their first US Top 10 hit for 2½ years.
May [23] *Super Trouper* makes US #45.
July [11] *On And On And On* stalls at US #90.
[25] Disco-styled *Lay All Your Love On Me*, released in UK as a 12" only single aimed at the disco market, hits #7.
Dec [19] *One Of Us* hits UK #3, as *The Visitors* tops UK chart.
[31] Andersson marries Norklit.
Polydor International rewards the group with its Golden Gramophone award, an honor usually given in the classical field.
1982 **Jan** [1] Abba makes its last live appearance in Stockholm.
[3] Emma Ulvaeus, daughter to Bjorn and Lena Kallersjo, is born.
[10] Ludvig Andersson, son of Benny and Mona Norklit, is born.
Feb [13] *The Visitors* reaches US #29.
Mar [13] *When All Is Said And Done* reaches US #27.
[20] *Head Over Heels* reaches UK #25.
May [22] *The Visitors* peaks US #63.
Aug. The first concrete sign that Abba members are going their separate ways in music as well as their personal lives is when Lyngstad moves to London and releases solo album *Something's Going On*, produced by Phil Collins and Russ Ballard-penned *I Know There's Something Going On* single.
Sept [4] *I Know There's Something Going On* makes UK #43.
[18] *Something's Going On* debuts at its peak position of UK #18.
Oct [30] Abba's *The Day Before You Came*, subsequently a 1984 UK #22 hit for UK duo Blancmange, reaches UK #32.
Nov [27] Double anthology *The Singles: The First Ten Years* completes the group's run of UK #1 albums, and is a huge Christmas seller.
Dec [25] *Under Attack* charts at UK #26. Also included on *The Singles*, this is the final Abba recording.
1983 **Jan** *The Singles: The First Ten Years* makes US #62.
Mar [26] *I Know There's Something Going On* reaches US #13.
Something's Going On makes US #41.
June [4] After making her acting debut in Swedish film "Rakenstam", Faltskog begins a solo hit-making career with *The Heat Is On*, which makes UK #35. No official notice that Abba is over comes from the 4 members (but from now on both female vocalists will pursue solo work, while Andersson and Ulvaeus, still writing and producing at Polar studios, will begin a collaboration with UK lyricist Tim Rice that results in the musical "Chess", in 1985).
[18] Faltskog's *Wrap Your Arms Around Me*, produced by Mike Chapman, reaches UK #18.
Aug [20] Title ballad *Wrap Your Arms Around Me* makes UK #44.
Sept *Wrap Your Arms Around Me* makes US #102.
Oct [22] Extracted *Can't Shake Loose*, like Frida's chart debut written by Russ Ballard, peaks at UK #63.
Nov [5] *Can't Shake Loose*, reaches US #63.
[26] Abba's last UK chart single, appropriately titled *Thank You For The Music*, the old airplay and stage favorite from *Abba – The Album* in 1978, makes UK #33.

Thank You For The Music reaches UK #17.
1984 **Jan** [7] *Time*, a Frida/B.A. Robertson duet, makes UK #45.
Oct [20] Frida's *Shine*, produced by Steve Lillywhite, spends a week on UK chart at #67.
1985 **Jan** Murray Head's *One Night In Bangkok*, from the forthcoming "Chess", reaches UK #12.
Feb [9] Elaine Paige and Barbara Dickson's duet *I Know Him So Well*, also from "Chess", begins a 4-week tenure at UK #1.
May [4] Agnetha's *Eyes Of A Woman*, produced by Eric Stewart, debuts at UK #38.
[18] *One Night In Bangkok* hits US #3.
1986 **Jan** The group reunites to appear on Swedish TV's "This Is Your Life" tribute to Stig Anderson, singing *Tivedshambo* accompanied by Andersson's accordian.
Apr [7] *I Know Him So Well* is named Best Selling A-Side of 1985 at the annual Ivor Novello Awards lunch at the Grosvenor House, London.
1988 **Mar** [12] Faltskog's *I Stand Alone*, recorded in Malibu, CA, with producer Peter Cetera, spends a week on UK chart at #72.
Apr [30] Faltskog/Cetera duet, *I Wasn't The One (Who Said Goodbye)*, from the album makes US #93.
Nov Retrospective *Absolute Abba* peaks at UK #70.
1990 **Dec** [15] Faltskog marries Swedish surgeon Tomas Sonnenfeld.
1991 As Andersson and Ulvaeus await the outcome of a lawsuit filed against Stig Anderson to collect unpaid royalties, they prepare for the scheduled Nov.1992 premiere in Stockholm of new musical "The Immigrants".

ABC

Martin Fry (vocals)
Mark White (guitar)
Stephen Singleton (saxophone)
Mark Lickley (bass)
David Palmer (drums)

1980 Band is formed in Sheffield, S.Yorks., when Fry (b. Mar.9, 1958, Manchester, Gtr.Manchester), who at age 18 has gone to Sheffield University to study English Literature, joins White (b. Apr.1, 1961, Sheffield) and Singleton (b. Apr.17, 1959, Sheffield) after interviewing them for his fanzine **Modern Drugs**, which he has launched in 1977 focusing on local bands and fashions, about their group Vice Versa. Fry is asked to join as lead singer and at their first gig they are showered with beer bottles. David Robinson (drums) and Lickley (bass) round out the quintet.
Dec First live performance as ABC is in Sheffield. The name is chosen because "the first 3 letters of the alphabet are known the world over".
1981 They sign to Phonogram Records, for releases via their own Neutron label in UK and Mercury in US.
Nov [28] Debut *Tears Are Not Enough* reaches UK #19.
1982 Robinson soon leaves and is replaced by Palmer.
Mar [20] *Poison Arrow* hits UK #6.
June [12] *The Look Of Love* hits UK #4.
July [3] *The Lexicon Of Love*, produced by Trevor Horn, enters UK chart at #1 and reaches US #24 during an 8-month chart stay. ABC tours UK, then begins a world trek, during which they make a 60-min. documentary movie "Man Trap" with director Julien Temple.
Sept [25] Lush ballad *All Of My Heart* hits UK #5.
1983 **Jan** [8] *The Look Of Love*, their US chart debut, reaches #18, aided by MTV video promotion.
Mar [26] *Poison Arrow* reaches US #25.
May Palmer leaves.
Nov [12] *That Was Then But This Is Now*, produced by Gary Langan, reaches UK #18. Co-self-produced album *Beauty Stab*, reflecting Fry's and White's view of the current state of Great Britain, reaches UK #12.
1984 **Jan** [28] *S.O.S.* makes UK #39.
Feb [18] *That Was Then But This Is Now* stalls at US #89, as *Beauty Stab* climbs to US #69.
Nov [17] *(How To Be A) Millionaire* makes UK #49. It is produced by Fry and White, now the only full members as Singleton and Lickley have left and been replaced by session players for recordings. Fry and White will move to New York and recruit 2 new members, David Yarritu and Eden, who, despite the fact that neither can play any instruments or even sing, are added for dramatic and visual effect.
1985 **Apr** [13] *Be Near Me* reaches UK #26.
June [15] *Vanity Kills* spends a week on UK chart at #70.
Oct *How To Be A Zillionaire*, with help from Brad Lang on bass and Palmer returning to play drums, reaches UK #28 and US #30.

Nov [9] *Be Near Me* gives ABC its first US Top 10 hit, at #9. A disco remix of it proves a huge US club favorite, and a Dance chart-topper.

986
Jan *Ocean Blue* makes UK #51.
Mar [22] *(How To Be A) Millionaire* reaches US #20.
May [24] *Vanity Kills* stalls at US #91.

987
After Fry has been seriously ill and recuperated, he and White start writing and recording again.
June *When Smokey Sings*, a tribute to Smokey Robinson, first release from sessions with US producer Bernard Edwards, reaches UK #11.
Sept [19] *When Smokey Sings* hits US #5.
Oct *The Night You Murdered Love* climbs to UK #31. *Alphabet City*, with rhythm section David Clayton on keyboards, Lang on bass and Graham Broad on drums, hits UK #7 and makes US #48.
Dec *King Without A Crown* makes UK #44.

989
June *One Better World* makes UK #32.
Sept Fry guests on *Mythical Girl*, from producer Arthur Baker's album.
[23] *The Real Thing* peaks at UK #68.
Oct [28] *Up* makes UK #58.

990
Apr [14] *The Look Of Love (1990 Mix)* peaks at UK #68.
[21] Greatest hits compilation *Absolutely* hits UK #7.
May [7] BBC TV documentary "That Was Then, This Is Now" airs.

PAULA ABDUL

984
Of Syrian-Brazilian/French Canadian ancestry, Abdul (b. June 19, 1963, Los Angeles, CA), the second daughter of Harry (once a livestock trader and now owner of a sand and gravel business) and Lorraine (a former assistant to Billy Wilder), has grown up in North Hollywood, CA, where she has, at age 7, performed in community theater groups, spent summers touring in US theatrical productions and begun studying jazz and tap dance techniques from age 10 to win a scholarship to study under Joe Traime at the Bell Lewitzky Company. Attending Van Nuys High, then Cal State-Northridge college, Abdul has majored in TV and radio studies and has successfully auditioned for (and subsequently choreographed) Los Angeles dance troupe The Laker Girls, earning $50 per game during her freshman year. She decides to take up a full-time career in dance and has already been asked to choreograph a Jacksons/Mick Jagger video for their single *Torture*. This has brought her firmly into the pop dance arena where she is now asked by A&M Records A&R head John McClain to choreograph for another Jackson (Janet), resulting in the hugely successful generic dance visuals for the Jackson hits *When I Think Of You*, *Nasty* and *What Have You Done For Me Lately*.

987
Abdul has established a reputation as the leading American pop dance choreographer, her talent commissioned for video clips promoting Z.Z. Top (she creates the Velcro Fly dance step), Duran Duran, Debbie Gibson and even Warren Zevon and Dolly Parton, among others.

988
Aug [13] Having been signed by Virgin America, debut release *Knocked Out*, setting the trend of all the releases from her debut recordings – commercial pop dance cuts boosted by predictably perfect-timing dance-step promotion videos – makes US #41.
Nov [12] *(It's Just) The Way That You Love Me* stalls at US #88.

989
Feb [11] *Straight Up* tops US chart, as her debut album, *Forever Your Girl*, with songs written by Elliot Wolff and Jerry Leiber's son Oliver, begins US chart climb.
Apr *Forever Your Girl* hits UK #5.
[19] Abdul participates in Prince's Trust Gala at the London Palladium with Erasure, Debbie Gibson, T'Pau, Wet Wet Wet and others.
May *Straight Up* hits UK #3.
[20] Title cut *Forever Your Girl* tops US chart.
June Abdul embarks on 40-city "Club MTV Live" tour with Tonë Loc, Was (Not Was), Milli Vanilli and Information Society. *Forever Your Girl* reaches UK #24.
Aug *Knocked Out* makes UK #45, as UK chart career appears to stall.
Sept [2] *Cold Hearted* tops US chart, her third consecutive #1.
[6] She wins Best Dance, Best Female Video and Best Choreography awards for *Straight Up* video at the sixth annual MTV Music Video Awards ceremony at the Universal Amphitheater, Los Angeles. She is also a performing highlight of the show.
[17] Abdul wins Best Choreography for the "Tracey Ullman Show" at the annual Emmy awards.
Oct [7] *Forever Your Girl*, after over 14 months on chart, hits US #1, where it will stay for 10 weeks, becoming Virgin America's biggest-selling album.
Dec [2] Reissued *(It's Just) The Way That You Love Me* now hits US #3

and peaks at UK #74.
[17] Abdul participates in "America Has Heart" benefit at the Universal Amphitheater, Los Angeles, to raise money for the Red Cross Disaster Relief Fund, depleted by Hurricane Hugo and the San Francisco earthquake.
[23] Abdul wins Top Pop Album Artist, Female in **Billboard**'s The Year In Music, one of 3 #1 feats in this year's round-up.

1990
Jan [22] Abdul wins Favorite Pop/Rock Female Vocalist and Favorite Dance Artist categories at the American Music Awards. She performs *The Way That You Love Me* at the ceremonies. On returning home to her Studio City condominium, she discovers thieves have stolen $3,400 worth of jewelry.
Feb [3] *Forever Your Girl* returns to US #1 after 81 weeks on chart.
[10] *Opposites Attract*, credited with The Wild Pair and including a rap from The Soul Purpose's Derrick Delite, helped by inventive real life/cartoon-integrated video, tops US chart.
Mar [8] Abdul's latest awards include Best Female Singer, Best New Female Singer, Best Dressed Female Rock Artist, Sexiest Female Rock Artist in **Rolling Stone** 1989 Readers' Picks.
[26] She choreographs the dance routines at the annual Academy Awards in Los Angeles, the latest commission in her parallel choreographic career which has also now included a scene in Kevin Costner movie "Bull Durham", "Coming To America", George Michael's "Monkey" video and other awards shows, including 4 MTV ceremonies. *Opposites Attract* achieves gold status, as *Forever Your Girl* reaches 6 million sales in US. (It becomes the only debut album to have featured 4 #1s.)
May [5] *Opposites Attract* hits UK #2.
[12] *Forever Your Girl* re-enters UK chart at #3.
[16] Elliot Wolff wins Song Of The Year award for *Straight Up* at the seventh annual ASCAP pop awards dinner at the Regent Wilshire hotel, Beverly Hills, CA.
June [9-10] Abdul participates in the making of a video for the Take It Back Foundation to promote recycling, co-founded by Quincy Jones' daughter Jolie. With Kenny Loggins, Randy Newman, Alice Cooper and B.B. King, she films "Yakety Yak, Take It Back", a new version of The Coasters' classic *Yakety Yak*, with new lyrics.
July Abdul is lensed with her idol and dance icon Gene Kelly, by Annie Leibovitz for **Vanity Fair** magazine. Abdul's megastar status now includes lucrative sponsorship and advertising deals with Diet Coke and Reebok.
[28] Shep Pettibone remix *Knocked Out* reaches UK #21.
Oct [6] *Cold Hearted* makes UK #46.
Nov [10] *Shut Up And Dance (The Dance Mixes)* peaks at UK #40.
Dec [9] Driving her Jaguar, Abdul rear ends another car on Laurel Canyon Boulevard, Los Angeles. She is taken to the North Hollywood medical center.
[22] Abdul wins Top Pop Album Artist, Female in **Billboard**'s The Year In Music survey.

1991
Feb [20] "Opposites Attract" wins Best Music Video, Shortform at the 33rd annual Grammy awards at Radio City Music Hall, New York.
Apr Abdul contributes *Goodnight My Love* to an all-star Disney album *For Our Children*, released to benefit the Pediatric AIDS Foundation.
May Abdul releases *Spellbound*.

AC/DC
Angus Young (guitar)
Malcolm Young (guitar)
Bon Scott (vocals)
Mark Evans (bass)
Phillip Rudd (drums)

1973
Dec [31] Angus Young (b. Mar.31, 1959, Glasgow, Scotland) and brother Malcolm (b. Jan.6, 1953, Glasgow), debut the group at the Chequers club in Sydney, Australia (where the family emigrated in 1963), with Rob Bailey, Peter Clark and singer Dave Evans.
1974
July Group records its first single, *Can I Sit Next To You*, for Albert Productions, run by producers Harry Vanda and George Young (both ex-Easybeats; Young is also older brother of Angus and Malcolm). The original line-up disbands shortly thereafter and the Young brothers, now relocated to Melbourne, Australia, recruit the group's roadie, fellow immigrant, and veteran of bands The Spectors, The Valentines, Fraternity and Mount Lofty Rangers since the mid-60s, Scott (b. Ronald Scott, July 9, 1946, Kirriemuir, Scotland) on vocals. (Scott's convictions on some minor criminal offenses and a rejection by the Australian Army on the grounds that he is "socially maladjusted", further endear

him to the Youngs.) Drummer Rudd (b. May 19, 1954, Melbourne) and bassist Evans (b. Mar.2, 1956, Melbourne), ex-Buster Brown, complete the line-up. (Original singer Evans will form Rabbit, releasing 2 albums for CBS in Australia, before joining Hot Cockerel in 1984 and then releasing *David Evans And Thunder Down Under* in 1986.)

Dec After touring solidly since the summer and building a live following for its exuberant hard rock style, AC/DC signs to Albert Productions and begins work on its debut album.

1975 **Feb** Resultant *High Voltage* is released in Australia.

Dec After touring Australia for much of the year, the group's second album *TNT* is released.

1976 **Jan** On signing to Atlantic Records, the band moves base to UK, where early dates are at London's Marquee and other clubs.

Apr First UK single, *It's A Long Way To The Top*, is released.

May [11-12] AC/DC begins UK tour, supporting Back Street Crawler, at the Marquee, as UK album *High Voltage* is released, with tracks from earlier Australian albums. The 9-date tour will end at Reading Town Hall, Berks.

June [11] Group begins its first headlining UK tour, the 19-date "Lock Up Your Daughters" package, at the City Hall, Glasgow. The tour will end at the Lyceum, London, on July 7. Their visual image, with Angus Young as a short-trousered, naughty schoolboy, helps build their following, and will be their most enduring and identifiable image.

July Band begins a tour of Europe, supporting Rainbow.

Aug AC/DC appears at the Reading Rock Festival, Berks., during a second UK tour which accompanies release of second single *Jailbreak*.

Oct Group visits US for the first time, playing clubs to promote recently released *High Voltage*.

Dec *Dirty Deeds Done Dirt Cheap* is released in UK, but does not chart. Band returns to Australia for a 26-date year-end tour, and stays for the recording of next album in Sydney with Vanda and Young.

1977 **Feb** [18] Group begins 25-date UK tour, playing material from the yet-to-be released album, at Edinburgh University, Scotland. The tour will end on Mar.21 at the Pavilion, Hemel Hempstead, Herts.

June [11] Tired of touring, Evans leaves and Cliff Williams (b. Dec.14, 1949, Romford, Essex), ex-Bandit and Home, is chosen from 50 replies from a **Sounds** ad. (Evans will join Finch, which name-changes to Contraband, then play with a variety of bands, including Swanee, Heaven, Best, Hellcats, Headhunters and Boss, before joining The Party Boys.) Williams' first gigs with the band will be a major European tour supporting Black Sabbath.

July AC/DC begins its second US tour.

Oct [15] *Let There Be Rock* climbs to US #154.

Nov [5] *Let There Be Rock* reaches UK #17.

1978 **Jan** New album recordings are made at Albert studios in Sydney.

May [6] *Powerage* makes UK #26, as they begin UK "Powerage" tour.

July "Powerage" tour is punctuated by sessions for the next album.

[15] *Rock'N'Roll Damnation* is first UK hit single, reaching #24.

Sept [23] *Powerage* makes US #133.

Oct [21] *If You Want Blood, You've Got It*, recorded live in Glasgow during the "Powerage" tour, reaches UK #13.

1979 **Jan** *Highway To Hell* recording begins. New producer Robert John "Mutt" Lange is brought in to the sessions midway.

Feb [17] *If You Want Blood, You've Got It* makes US #113.

July "Highway To Hell" year-ending tour of UK, US and Europe begins.

Aug [4] *Highway To Hell* hits UK #8.

[18] AC/DC supports The Who at Wembley Stadium, London, on a bill with Nils Lofgren and The Stranglers.

Sept [15] *Highway To Hell* peaks at UK #56.

Nov [10] *Highway To Hell*, helped by touring as support for Cheap Trick, Ted Nugent and UFO, reaches US #17, where it becomes the band's first million-seller.

Dec During the European leg of the tour, a gig in Paris, France, is filmed and will be released in France as "Let There Be Rock".

[12] *Highway To Hell* makes US #47.

1980 **Jan** *Touch Too Much* reaches UK #29.

Feb [19] While recording in UK, Scott and musician friend Alistair Kennear spend evening at the Music Machine in Camden Town, London, watching groups Protex and The Trendies while consuming a large amount of alcohol. Kennear drives Scott back to his house in East Dulwich, South London, leaving him asleep in the car.

[20] Kennear returns to the car to find Scott unconscious, and drives him to nearby King's College Hospital, where he is pronounced dead. The coroner will record a verdict of death by misadventure, stating that Scott had "drunk himself to death".

Mar Band announces that Brian Johnson (b. Oct.5, 1947) (former lead singer of UK band Geordie) will replace Scott.

Apr Band begins recording album *Back In Black* at Compass Point studios in the Bahamas with Lange.

June Reissued *Dirty Deeds Done Dirt Cheap* (#47), *Whole Lotta Rosie* (#36), *High Voltage (Live Version)* (#48), *It's A Long Way To The Top (If You Wanna Rock'N'Roll)* (#55) all chart in UK.

July After preliminary warm-up gigs in Belgium and Holland, AC/DC embarks on "Back In Black" world tour in US. The tour will include Europe, a first visit to Australia since 1977 and a first visit to Japan.

Aug [9] *Back In Black* tops UK chart.

Sept *You Shook Me All Night Long* makes UK #38.

Oct [19] Group begins 20-date UK tour at the Colston Hall, Bristol, Avon, ending Nov.12 with 3 dates at London's Hammersmith Odeon.

Nov [8] *You Shook Me All Night Long* makes US #35 – their first US Top 40 hit single.

Back In Black hits US #4, and in next decade will sell 10 million copies in US.

Dec [13] *Rock'N'Roll Ain't Noise Pollution* reaches UK #15.

1981 **Feb** [21] *Back In Black* makes US #37.

May [23] Belatedly issued in US, *Dirty Deeds Done Dirt Cheap* hits #3.

High Voltage makes US #146.

Aug [22] AC/DC headlines the Monsters Of Rock Festival at Castle Donington, Leics., before a crowd of 65,000.

Dec [5] *For Those About To Rock (We Salute You)* hits UK #3.

[26] *For Those About To Rock (We Salute You)* tops US chart, selling more than 1 million copies.

1982 **Feb** [20] *Let's Get It Up* reaches UK #13 and US #44.

July [10] *For Those About To Rock (We Salute You)* reaches UK #15.

1983 **Aug** Rudd leaves, like Evans, exhausted by touring, and is replaced by ex-Tytan and A To Z, Simon Wright (b. June 19, 1963), who like Williams has responded to an ad in **Sounds**. (Rudd will take up helicopter flying in New Zealand.)

Sept *Flick Of The Switch* hits UK #4 and reaches US #15.

Oct [22] *Guns For Hire* peaks at US #84.

Nov [5] *Guns For Hire* makes UK #37.

1984 **Aug** [11] *Nervous Shakedown* hits UK #35.

[18] AC/DC headlines the Monsters Of Rock Festival at Castle Donington for the second time, before a crowd of 65,000.

Mini-album *'74 Jailbreak*, reprising tracks recorded in Australia almost a decade earlier, makes US #76.

1985 **Jan** [19] Group takes part in the Rock In Rio festival at Barra da Tijuca in Rio de Janeiro, Brazil, headlining a bill featuring Ozzy Osbourne, The Scorpions and Whitesnake, before an estimated crowd of 342,000.

July [13] *Fly On The Wall* hits UK #7.

[20] *Danger* makes UK #48.

Sept [7] *Fly On The Wall* reaches US #32, as the band undertakes corresponding "Fly On The Wall" tour of US to promote it.

1986 **Jan** [16-17] Group performs at Wembley Arena, London, during European leg of "Fly On The Wall" tour.

[25] *Shake Your Foundations* reaches UK #24.

May [31] *Who Made Who*, containing old and 3 new AC/DC songs used on the soundtrack of Stephen King movie "Maximum Overdrive", reaches UK #11 and makes US #33.

June [7] Extracted *Who Made Who* reaches UK #16.

Aug [30] *You Shook Me All Night Long* makes UK #46.

1987 **Dec** After a lengthy silence, AC/DC completes new recordings with producers Vanda and Young for *Blow Up Your Video*.

1988 **Jan** [23] *Heatseeker*, from the album, reaches UK #12.

Feb [13] *Blow Up Your Video* hits UK #2 and will reach US #12.

Apr [9] *That's The Way I Wanna Rock'N'Roll* makes UK #22.

Group begins major tour to promote the album. Cousin Steve Young replaces Malcolm on "Blow Up Your Video" tour. Rumors are rife that Malcolm is endeavoring to kick a dependency habit, but it is also rumored that he wishes to look after his ailing son.

1989 During an AC/DC sabbatical, Wright is asked to play on Dio's album *Lock Up The Wolves* and subsequently leaves to join him permanently. Veteran Chris Slade (b. Oct.30, 1946), ex-Manfred Mann's Earthband, Firm and Gary Moore, joins in his place.

1990 **Apr** Group begins recording *The Razor's Edge*, with producer Bruce Fairbairn, in Vancouver, Canada.

Sept [29] *Thunderstruck*, issued via new US sideways contract with Atco, reaches UK #13.

Oct [6] *The Razor's Edge* enters UK chart at #4, its peak position.

[27] *The Razor's Edge* hits US #2, AC/DC's highest charting US album

since 1981.

Nov [2] 34-date US leg of "The Razor's Edge" world tour begins at Worcester Centrum, MA. The tour will end at Long Beach Arena, CA. Line-up now includes Paul Greg on bass.

[11] 21-year-old David Gregory is killed outside AC/DC's Brendan Byrne Arena, East Rutherford, NJ, concert. A New Jersey state trooper will be cleared of criminal wrongdoing.

Dec [1] *Moneytalks* makes UK #36.

1991
Jan [18] Teenagers Curtis Child, Jimmie Boyd and Elizabeth Glausi are killed during a crush in a crowd of 13,294 at the band's Salt Palace Arena, Salt Lake City, UT, concert. (Glausi will die after her parents request her life-support be turned off.)

Feb [9] *Moneytalks* reaches US #24.

JOHNNY ACE

1949
June Following wartime service in the US Navy, Ace (b. John Marshall Alexander, Jr., June 9, 1929, Memphis, TN), the son of a local preacher, returns to Memphis and joins R&B/blues band run by Adolph Duncan, as a pianist, then joining B.B. King's band. When King moves west to Los Angeles, CA, and the group's singer Bobby Bland goes into Army, Ace takes over vocal duties and renames the band The Beale Streeters.

1952 He signs with Duke Records, owned by a DJ based in Houston, TX. Still known by his given name, Alexander adopts the name Johnny Ace.

Aug Don Robey, a Houston-based entrepreneur who runs the Texas chitlin circuit, buys Duke.

Sept [27] Ace's first single for the label, *My Song*, credited to Johnny Ace with The Beale Streeters, tops US R&B charts for 9 weeks. It sets a style followed by subsequent releases: sensitive baritone vocal with subdued jazz small-group backing, highly popular with black US audiences of the time. (Aretha Franklin will score with it in 1968.)

1953
Feb *Cross My Heart* hits #3 on US R&B chart.

July [18] His third single, *The Clock*, tops US R&B chart for 5 weeks; he then goes solo with Robey backing him with The Johnny Otis Band.

1954
Feb *Saving My Love For You* hits US R&B #2.

June *Please Forgive Me* hits US R&B #6.

Oct *Never Let Me Go* hits US R&B #9.

Dec After constantly touring the South throughout the year, mainly on a bill with Willie Mae "Big Mama" Thornton, Ace is named Most Programmed Artist Of 1954, following a national DJ poll organized by US music trade weekly, **Cash Box**.

[25] Backstage at a concert at a "Negro Christmas Dance" at the City Auditorium in Houston, Ace fatally shoots himself with a .32 pistol. (To embellish what is perhaps the first rock'n'roll fatality, stories abound that Ace was playing Russian roulette or that a hired killer had climbed through his dressing room window. Robey seeks to color the story by stating that Ace died on Christmas Eve as midnight neared.)

1955
Jan [2] An estimated 5,000 people attend Ace's funeral at the Clayborn Temple AME church in Memphis.

Feb [12] Posthumously released *Pledging My Love*, with The Johnny Otis Orchestra, is his most successful ever, at US R&B #1 for 10 weeks.

Mar [19] *Pledging My Love* reaches US #17. It becomes a standard rock ballad. (Ironically, Elvis Presley's version is on the B-side of his current single at the time of his death, nearly 23 years later. The original *Pledging My Love* will resurface in the mid-80s film "Christine".)

Aug *Anymore*, with The Johnny Board Orchestra, hits US R&B #7.

ADAM & THE ANTS

Adam Ant (vocals)
Marco Pirroni (guitar)
Kevin Mooney (bass)
Terry Lee Miall (drums)
Merrick (drums)

1976
June [30] Weekly music paper **Melody Maker** appears with ad "Beat On A Bass With The B-Sides" in classified section, placed there by recent Hornsey School of Art, London, leaver Ant (b. Stuart Leslie Goddard, Nov.3, 1954, London), who has been in his first band Bazooka Joe & His Rhythm Hot Shots while there.

July [3] Ant meets Andy Warren, who has phoned him 2 days earlier in response to the ad, outside the Marquee club. They form The B-Sides, rehearsing in South Clapham, London, throughout the rest of 1976 and into early 1977 with various personnel, including Lester Square (guitar), Paul Flanagan, Bob Hip and David Tampin (drums), Bid (occasional guitar and vox) and with Warren (bass) and Ant (guitar

and vocals). They record a punk version of *These Boots Are Made For Walking*, and then disband.

1977
Apr [23] The Ants, comprising Ant, Warren, Square and Flanagan, make their debut at the Roxy club in Neal Street, London, as The Banshees play their last concert there.

May [8] Square leaves the group.

[10] Mark Ryan (aka Mark Gaumont) joins as The Ants make their first appearance at the ICA restaurant, London.

[11] They support X-Ray Spex at the Man In The Moon in Chelsea, which will lead to a headlining gig there 2 weeks later.

June [2] The Angel's drummer Dave Barbe joins The Ants as they support Desolation Angels at Ant's alumni, Hornsey College of Art.

[20] Group supports The Slits in Cheltenham, Glos.

July [5] They film an appearance for Derek Jarman's movie "Jubilee", with Banshees drummer Kenny Morris standing in.

[11] Group plays the opening of punk venue the Vortex club with The Banshees and The Slits.

[14] They record *Plastic Surgery* and *Beat My Guest* at Chappells studios.

[18] Ant dislocates his knee while filming *Plastic Surgery* at London's Drury Lane theater for "Jubilee".

1978
Jan [23] Band makes its radio debut on BBC Radio 1's "The John Peel Show", performing *Deutscher Girls*, *Lou*, *It Doesn't Matter* and *Puerto Rican*.

[24] They record *Deutscher Girls* and *Plastic Surgery* for Derek Jarman's film "Jubilee" at AIR studios with new drummer Johnny Bivouac.

May [14] Bivouac and Jordan quit after a gig at the Roundhouse, London, with X-Ray Spex.

[15/19] They record demos of *Young Parisians*, *Lady* and *Catch A Falling Star* at Virtual Earth studios and Chelsea College of Art, London.

June [6] Matthew Ashman makes his debut with the band at a debutante's party at the Hard Rock Café, London.

July [10] Group records its second "John Peel Session", performing *Physical*, *Zerox* and *Friends & Cleopatra*.

[29] They sign a 2-single deal with Decca Records.

Sept [9] Group begins European tour in Leopoldsburg, Belgium. The tour will end on Oct.21 at the Titan club, Rome, Italy.

Nov [14] Group records a demo of *Kick* at RAK studios with Snips producing.

1979
Jan Decca single *Young Parisians* fails, and band signs to Do It Records.

[11] Group begins its first major UK tour at Brannigans in Leeds, W.Yorks. The tour will end on Feb.19 at the Civic Hall, Bishops Stortford, Herts.

[26] Group makes its third "John Peel Session" appearance, performing *Ligotage*, *Tabletalk*, *Animals & Men* and *Never Trust A Man With Egg On His Face*.

July [6] *Zerox/Whip In My Valise*, recorded at London's Roundhouse studios, is released by Do It Records.

[13] 17-date UK "Zerox" tour begins at the Porterhouse, Retford, Notts. It will end with a sell-out date at the Lyceum, London, on Aug.5.

Aug [1] Ant splits his head open at a Plymouth Woods gig, Devon, and requires 6 stitches.

[12-24] Group records debut album *Dirk Wears White Sox* at Sound Development studios, London.

Sept [28-29] They play 2 sell-out shows at London's Electric Ballroom.

Oct [3] Warren leaves to join Square in The Monochrome Set, and is replaced by Lee Gorman. Malcolm McLaren becomes the group's manager, who temporarily introduces Jordan, a girl acquaintance of his, on additional vocals. *Dirk Wears White Sox* is released.

1980
Jan [1] Band plays a sell-out New Year's Day gig at the Electric Ballroom, with Gorman making his debut. (It will be his only gig with the band.)

[14] The UK Independent labels chart is launched in UK, with *Dirk Wears White Sox* at #1.

[24] At the urging of McLaren, The Ants split from Adam to become "more autonomous". McLaren will pair Ashman, Gorman and Barbe with girl singer Annabella Lwin as new act Bow Wow Wow.

[28] Ant and ex-Models and Siouxsie & The Banshees guitarist Pirroni meet in a cake shop in Covent Garden and agree to establish a songwriting partnership to create "antmusic". They team up with new manager Falcon Stewart, and recruit drummer/producer Chris Hughes (later known as Merrick).

Feb [18] Ant, Pirroni and Hughes re-record *Cartrouble* and *Kick!* at Rockfield studios, Monmouth, S.Wales.

Apr [19] The Ants begin recording the first fruits of the Ant-Pirroni partnership at Matrix studios, London.

May *Cartrouble* completes Do It contract, after which Ant and Pirroni sign a publishing deal, having recruited Mooney on bass and Miall (who had been with Pirroni in The Beastly Cads, later known as The Models, before forming The Music Club), as a second drummer.

[22] 14-date UK "Ants Invasion" tour, promoting new flamboyant visual image and a drum/percussion oriented sound, begins with a sell-out date at the Electric Ballroom. The tour will end on July 8 at the Empire Ballroom, London, with special guest 60s singer Dave Berry.

July [16] Group signs to CBS, and begins recording at Rockfield studios.

Aug CBS debut *Kings Of The Wild Frontier* makes UK #48.

Nov [8] *Dog Eat Dog*, helped by the band's first BBC TV "Top Of The Pops" appearance, hits UK #4, the group's first Top 10 hit.

1981 **Jan** [17] Percussion-heavy *Antmusic* hits UK #2.

[24] *Kings Of The Wild Frontier* tops UK chart.

Feb [7] *Young Parisians*, reissued by Decca, hits UK #9, as Do It reissue *Zerox*, already an Indie chart-topper, makes UK #45.

[14] Other Do It Indie chart-topper *Cartrouble* makes UK #33.

Mar [7] *Dirk Wears White Sox* reaches UK #16.

[14] *Kings Of The Wild Frontier* is reissued, and this time hits UK #2.

May [9] *Stand And Deliver*, with hugely popular "Dandy Highwayman" video, enters UK chart at #1.

June [6] *Kings Of The Wild Frontier* makes US #44.

Sept [19] *Prince Charming* hits UK #1, as the group embarks on sell-out "Prince Charming Revue Tour".

Nov [14] *Prince Charming* hits UK #2. Mooney soon leaves, later forming Wide Boy Awake, and is replaced by Gary Tibbs, fresh from Roxy Music.

Dec [26] *Prince Charming* makes US #94.

1982 **Jan** [9] *Ant Rap* hits UK #3. (Ant will decide to go solo, dismantling the band, but keeping Pirroni as his writing partner.)

Feb [24] *Kings Of The Wild Frontier* wins Best British Album at the first BRIT Awards at the Grosvenor House, Mayfair, London.

Mar [6] Polydor label reissues old track *Deutscher Girls* from "Jubilee" film soundtrack; it reaches UK #13.

[20] EP *The Antmusic EP (The B-Sides)*, of old Do It tracks, makes UK #46.

Apr [29] Ant and Pirroni are named Songwriters Of The Year and *Stand And Deliver* is honored as Best Single A-Side at the annual Ivor Novello Awards lunch at the Grosvenor House.

June [12] First release as Adam Ant, *Goody Two-Shoes*, tops UK chart.

Oct [2] *Friend Or Foe* hits UK #9.

[23] *Friend Or Foe*, produced by Ant and Pirroni, hits UK #5.

Dec [4] *Desperate But Not Serious* breaks the run of UK Top 10 hits by only reaching #33.

1983 **Feb** [12] *Goody Two-Shoes* provides long-awaited US hit, reaching #12.

Mar [26] *Desperate But Not Serious* is a minor US follow-up success, at #66. *Friend Or Foe* reaches US #16.

May [16] Ant appears on US TV as special guest in "Motown 25th Anniversary", alongside many Motown legends.

Nov [12] *Puss'N Boots*, produced by Phil Collins hits UK #5, and *Strip*, on which Ant and Pirroni are helped by Richard James Burgess, who plays keyboards, drums, percussion and produces, reaches UK #20.

Dec [17] *Strip*, also produced by Collins, stalls at UK #41 after being withdrawn when Ant is asked by BBC TV to change the lyrics of the song and to tone down the accompanying video, and refuses. *Strip* makes US #65.

1984 **Mar** [24] *Strip* makes US #42.

Oct [6] *Apollo 9* reaches UK #13.

Ant records *What's Going On* for "Metropolis" soundtrack.

1985 **July** [13] Ant opens UK segment of "Live Aid" at Wembley Stadium, London, before embarking on UK tour, which is cancelled after 3 dates, when Ant is unable to get himself insured.

[20] *Vive Le Rock* makes UK #50.

Sept *Vive Le Rock*, produced by Tony Visconti, reaches UK #42. It is Ant's last chart entry before he moves to US and into film and TV acting, where his most noted roles will be in "Slam Dance" and in "The Equalizer" TV series.

Nov *Vive Le Rock* makes US #131.

1986 **Sept** CBS releases compilation album *Hits*, but it does not chart. Ant's only other recording during the year is a collaboration with Stewart Copeland on the theme song to movie "Out Of Bounds". (His recording career will go on hold until a comeback in 1990, while he will live in US making more movies and TV shows.)

1990 **Mar** *Room At The Top*, his recording return on MCA, peaks at UK #13, while parent album, *Manners And Physique* makes UK #19 despite

spending only 3 weeks on the survey. It is produced by Andre Gymone and features longtime cohort Pirroni.

Apr [28] *Can't Set Rules About Love* makes UK #47.

May [5] *Room At The Top* reaches US #17 as parent album *Manners And Physique* makes US #57.

1991 **Mar** *Give Peace A Chance*, a remake of John Lennon's classic anti-war hymn, by The Peace Choir, an all-star line-up including Ant, begins US chart rise.

BRYAN ADAMS

1977 Adams (b. Bryan Guy Adams, Nov.5, 1959, Kingston, Ontario, Canada, the son of English immigrants) forms a writing partnership with Jim Vallance, former drummer with Prism and has arranged with Vallance tracks *You Walked Away* and *Take It Or Leave It* for Prism's 1980 album *Armageddon*, and after signing with Rondor publishing, they begin providing hit songs for acts including Loverboy, Bachman-Turner Overdrive, Kiss and Bonnie Tyler.

1981 Adams and Vallance make demos which get scant response from record companies, until A&M offers to record 4 songs for $1. Debut single *Let Me Take You Dancing* is promoted as a dance record, but does not catch on, before **Bryan Adams**, with support from Keith Scott (guitar), Dave Taylor (bass) and Vallance (drums), is released.

1982 **Mar** *Lonely Nights* makes US #84 as parent album *You Want It, You Got It*, produced by Bob Clearmountain, climbs to US #118. Adams will spend much of the year gaining a live reputation by playing support on US tours by The Kinks, Foreigner and fellow Canadians Loverboy.

1983 **May** [28] *Straight From The Heart* is first hit single, at US #10.

June *Cuts Like A Knife*, with Mickey Curry taking over from Vallance as Adams' drummer, is similar breakthrough, hitting US #8.

Aug [6] Extracted title track and AOR ballad *Cuts Like A Knife* reaches US #15.

Oct [29] *This Time* makes US #24.

1985 **Jan** [19] Rock-driven *Run To You* hits US #6.

Feb [9] *Run To You* is Adams' first UK hit, reaching #11.

Mar *Reckless*, produced by Adams and Clearmountain, with Pat Steward joining Adams' band on drums, hits UK #7.

Apr [6] *Somebody* reaches US #11 and UK #35.

June [1] *Heaven*, featured some 2 years earlier on soundtrack album *A Night In Heaven*, makes UK #38.

[22] *Heaven*, only released as a single after pressure from US radio, tops US chart and is his first million-selling single.

July [13] Adams opens US segment of the Live Aid concert at the JFK Stadium, Philadelphia, PA. (Adams and Vallance compose Northern Lights all-star recording *Tears Are Not Enough* as Canada's contribution to raise money to combat the famine in Ethiopia.)

Aug [10] *Reckless* hits US #1 in its 38th week on chart, helped by Adams' exposure as support on Tina Turner's world tour. *You Want It, You Got It* makes US #78.

[31] Yesteryear yearning *Summer Of '69* hits US #5 and makes UK #42.

Nov [9] *One Night Love Affair* reaches US #13.

Dec A duet with Tina Turner on *It's Only Love* reaches UK #29. Seasonal *Christmas Time* peaks at UK #55.

1986 **Jan** [18] *It's Only Love* reaches US #15.

Mar *This Time*, from 1983, reissued in UK, makes #41 while *Cuts Like A Knife* reaches UK #21.

June [4] Adams begins 2-week Amnesty International's "A Conspiracy Of Hope" US tour, featuring U2, Sting, Peter Gabriel and Lou Reed at the Cow Palace, San Francisco, CA.

July Another UK 1983 reissue, *Straight From The Heart*, peaks at US #51.

1987 **Feb** *Rock For Amnesty*, on which Adams is featured with Dire Straits, Paul McCartney, Sting and others, makes US #121.

May *Into The Fire*, produced by Adams with Clearmountain and Curry on drums, hits US #7 and UK #10, a million-plus seller.

[16] *Heat Of The Night* hits US #6 after making UK #50.

June [3] He records live version of Christmas oldie *Run Rudolph Run* at London's Marquee club, for donation to a charity album.

[5-6] Adams takes part in the fifth annual Prince's Trust Rock Gala, with Elton John, George Harrison, Ringo Starr and others, at the Wembley Arena, London.

Aug [8] *Hearts On Fire* reaches US #26 and UK #57.

Oct [3] *Victim Of Love* reaches US #32 and peaks at UK #68.

Dec Special Olympics charity album *A Very Special Christmas*, which includes Adams' *Run Rudolph Run*, makes US #20 and UK #40.

1988 **June** [11] Adams takes part in "Nelson Mandela's 70th Birthday

Party" at Wembley Stadium, London.

1989 **Mar** [6] Greenpeace album *Rainbow Warriors*, which features Adams and other artists, is released in the Soviet Union on Melodiya label.
June Adams takes part in Roskilde Festival '90 in Rosiled, Denmark.

1990 **July** [21] Adams takes part in Roger Waters' performance of "The Wall" at the Berlin Wall in Potzdamer Platz, Berlin, Germany. The event is broadcast live throughout the world, and raises money for the Memorial Fund For Disaster Relief.
Dec Adams guests on title track of David Foster's *River Of Love*.

1991 **Mar** Adams, having not released an album for 4 years due not least to unsatisfactory separate recording sessions with producers Steve Lillywhite, Robert John "Mutt" Lange and Bob Clearmountain, prepares for what is now effectively a comeback, as new project approaches completion.

AEROSMITH

Steven Tyler (vocals)
Joe Perry (guitar)
Brad Whitford (guitar)
Tom Hamilton (bass)
Joey Kramer (drums)

1970 Tyler (b. Steven Talarico, Mar.26, 1948, New York, NY), spending his summers at family-owned Trow-Rico resort in Sunapee, NH, meets Perry (b. Sept.10, 1950, Boston, MA), working in local ice-cream parlor the Anchorage during his vacation. Perry, playing in The Jam Band, invites Tyler, a veteran of Chain Reaction and The Strangeurs, to a gig at local Barn club. They decide to form a Cream-style trio with other Jam member Hamilton (b. Dec.31, 1951, Colorado Springs, CO) with Tyler its drummer. Ray Tabano joins, but is soon replaced by Whitford (b. Feb.23, 1952, Winchester, MA), ex-Justin Tyme, Earth Inc. and The Cymbals Of Resistance, and then Kramer (b. June 21, 1950, New York) completes the line-up. Group moves into an apartment at 1325 Commonwealth Ave. in Boston, and begins to build a local reputation as a hard-rock act, playing its first gig at Nipmuc Regional high school.

1972 **Aug** Clive Davis sees band at Max's Kansas City club, New York, and signs them to CBS/Columbia Records for a reported $125,000.

1973 **Oct** *Aerosmith*, produced by Adrian Barber and released to moderate US success, climbs to #166, as the band embarks on US tour as support to The Mahavishnu Orchestra.
Dec [1] *Dream On*, from the album, peaks at US #59.

1974 Group spends most of the year touring US, supporting The Kinks, Mott The Hoople and Sha Na Na.

1975 **July** [19] *Sweet Emotion* makes US #36, as the group plays Schaefer Music Festival in New York's Central Park.
Sept [13] Jack Douglas-produced album *Toys In The Attic*, boosted by the band's reputation from considerable live work, is US breakthrough, reaching #11 and spending over a year on chart.
Oct [18] *Get Your Wings* makes US #74, 18 months after it first enters the chart.

1976 **Apr** [3] Debut *Aerosmith* also re-ascends US chart, peaking at #21.
[10] Reissued *Dream On* hits US #6, the group's first million-seller.
June [26] *Rocks* hits US #3 and is also a million-seller.
Aug [7] *Last Child*, taken from *Rocks*, reaches US #21.
Oct [16] *Home Tonight* makes US #71.

1977 **Jan** [29] *Walk This Way*, from *Toys In The Attic*, hits US #10. Band rests from touring for first extended period in almost 5 years, to write and prepare the next album.
May [7] *Back In The Saddle* makes US #38.
Nov [19] *Draw The Line* makes US #42.

1978 **Jan** [28] *Draw The Line* reaches US #11, but is regarded by many fans and critics as a disappointment.
Mar [18] Aerosmith performs at the California Jam 2 festival in Ontario, CA, before a crowd of 250,000, together with Heart, Jean-Michel Jarre, Frank Marino & Mahogany Rush, Dave Mason, Ted Nugent and Santana.
Apr [1] *Kings And Queens* makes US #70.
July Band appears as villains in movie "Sgt. Pepper's Lonely Hearts Club Band", starring The Bee Gees and Peter Frampton. Their musical contribution is a revival of Lennon/McCartney's *Come Together*.
[4] Group participates in the Texxas World Music Festival. (Their performance will be seen in video release as "Aerosmith's Live Texxas Jam '78" in 1989.)
Sept [30] *Come Together*, from *Sgt. Pepper* soundtrack, reaches US #23.

1979 **Jan** [13] Double live album *Live! Bootleg* reaches US #13.
Feb [3] From the album, *Chip Away The Stone*, recorded at the Civic

Auditorium, Santa Monica, CA, in Apr.1978, makes US #77.
Apr [7] Aerosmith takes part in the California Music Festival, at the Memorial Coliseum, Los Angeles, before a crowd of 110,000, with Van Halen, Cheap Trick, Ted Nugent and The Boomtown Rats.
July [28] Group appears at the "World Series Of Rock" concert at the Municipal Stadium, Cleveland, OH, with Journey, Ted Nugent and Thin Lizzy.
Dec Perry leaves, citing musical and personality conflicts with Tyler, and is replaced on guitar by Jimmy Crespo, from New York band Flame. (Perry forms The Joe Perry Project with Ralph Morman (vocals), David Hull (bass) and Ronnie Stewart (drums) and will release albums *Let The Music Do The Talking* (1980) and *I've Got The Rock'N'Rolls Again* (1981), before breaking up the band in 1982.)

1980 **Jan** [19] *Night In The Ruts*, produced by the band with Gary Lyons, reaches US #14.
Feb [9] An unlikely revival of The Shangri-Las' 1964 US #5 *Remember (Walkin' In The Sand)* peaks at US #67. Whitford leaves to form his own Whitford-St. Holmes Band with ex-Ted Nugent-axeman Derek St.Holmes, Dave Hewitt and Steve Pace. He is replaced by Rick Dufay.

1981 **Jan** [24] *Aerosmith's Greatest Hits* makes US #53.
Tyler is hospitalized after a motorcycle accident.

1982 **Oct** [16] *Rock In A Hard Place* reaches US #32.

1984 **Feb** [14] Perry and Whitford see Aerosmith backstage at the Orpheum theater, Boston, and they agree to re-form.
Mar After a long, silent absence, the original Aerosmith line-up regroups and announces its intention to go on US tour circuit in the summer. They begin rehearsals at a Howard Johnson's in Boston, with new manager Tim Collins. Band will then embark on major US "Back In The Saddle" reunion tour, but in typical dramatic Aerosmith style, Tyler will collapse during a show in Springfield, IL.

1985 **Nov** Newly signed to Geffen Records, band releases its first new recording for 3 years, Ted Templeman-produced *Done With Mirrors*, recorded at Fantasy studios in Berkeley, CA.

1986 **Jan** *Done With Mirrors* reaches US #36.
May *Classics Live!* makes US #84.
Sept [27] Run D.M.C.'s *Walk This Way*, an innovative mix of rap and heavy metal with Tyler and Perry's contribution significantly updating 1977 original, hits US #4, having attracted heavy US MTV rotation.

1987 **Sept** [5] *Permanent Vacation*, recorded in Vancouver, Canada, with producer Bruce Fairbairn, becomes first UK chart success, making #37.
Oct [31] *Dude (Looks Like A Lady)* makes UK #45.
Nov *Permanent Vacation* climbs to US #11, after band recaptures its onstage reputation on "Permanent Vacation" tour which lasts for 12 months, covering over 150 shows in 42 US states, Japan and Canada.
Dec [12] *Dude (Looks Like A Lady)*, reaches US #14.

1988 **Apr** *Angel* peaks at UK #69.
[30] *Angel*, confirming major singles comeback, hits US #3.
Aug [20] *Rag Doll* reaches US #17.
Dec *Toys In The Attic* (5 million) and *Rocks* (3 million) are awarded multiplatinum status by RIAA. Retrospective *Gems* peaks at US #133.

1989 **Feb** Whitford produces fourth album for Boston rock trio The Neighborhoods, winners of first WBCN "Rock'N'Roll Rumble" in 1979.
Mar [6] Chelsea Anna, daughter of Steven and Theresa Tyler, is born.
Aug [19] Tyler and Perry join Bon Jovi on stage at the Milton Keynes Bowl, Bucks., to sing *Walk This Way*.
Sept [12] Group donates instruments and stage clothing for wall display at the Hard Rock Café in Boston, called the Aerosmithsonian, in the presence of Mayor Ray Flynn.
[30] *Love In An Elevator* reaches UK #13 as parent album *Pump*, produced by Fairbairn, hits UK #3.
Oct [28] *Love In An Elevator* hits US #5, spurred by traditionally risqué "sex in an elevator" teasing promo clip.
Nov [14] Group embarks on first European tour in 12 years. David Coverdale will join them on stage at Hammersmith Odeon, London, duetting on *I'm Down* during 9-date UK leg of the tour.
Pump hits US #5.
Dec During extensive North American dates, fans bring canned foods to a hometown Boston Garden concert, which group passes on as a 20-ton food parcel to the Boston Food Bank.

1990 **Feb** [10] *Janie's Got A Gun* hits US #4.
[17] Group, music guests on NBC TV's "Saturday Night Live", takes part in "Wayne's World" skit with Mike Myers and Dana Carvey, singing the title song, which becomes an in-demand bootleg item.
Mar [3] *Dude (Looks Like A Lady)*, reissued in UK, now reaches UK #20.
[6] Aerosmith are inducted into Hollywood's Rock Walk on Sunset Boulevard.

AEROSMITH cont.

[8] Band is voted Best Heavy Metal Band in **Rolling Stone** 1989 Critics Award.

Apr [19] At Boston's SKC Music Awards, Perry is voted Outstanding Guitarist, Hamilton voted Outstanding Bassist, *Pump* Outstanding Pop/Rock Album, *Janie's Got A Gun* Outstanding Song/Songwriter and Aerosmith Outstanding Pop/Rock Band.

[21] *Rag Doll* makes UK #42.

May [5] *What It Takes* hits US #9.

June [29] They play the first of 2 heavy metal bills, with Metallica, Warrant and The Black Crowes at the Skydome, Toronto, Canada. (Second gig will be played next day at Silver Stadium, Rochester, NY.)

July [28] Aerosmith performs at the Capital Center, Landover, MD, on the final date of the US part of another world tour.

Aug [18] Group takes part in the Monsters Of Rock Festival at Castle Donington, Leics., with Whitesnake, Poison, The London Quireboys and Thunder, before a crowd of 72,500. Jimmy Page joins them on stage for *Train Kept A-Rollin'*, as *The Other Side Of Me* reaches US #22.

[20] Page joins the band on stage again at their London Marquee club gig, playing a blues jam which ends with *Immigrant Song*.

[31] Group participates in Winterthurer Musikfestwochen festival at Winterthur, Switzerland.

Sept [1] *The Other Side* debuts at peak UK #46, as the band performs at Super Rock '90 festival in Mannheim, Germany, with Whitesnake, Poison, Dio and others.

[8] Aerosmith headlines the opening night of the Las Vegas, NV, Hard Rock Café, before heading back for Far East/Australia leg of marathon "Pump" tour, which will resume in Japan on the 12th.

Oct 163-date "Pump" tour ends in Australia. In all, 3 million fans have seen the band in 15 countries.

[28] *Love In An Elevator* hits US #5.

Nov *Pump* is certified by RIAA with over 4 million sales, while career album sales have now topped 25 million over 20 years.

Dec [22] *What It Takes* wins Top Album Rock Tracks category in **Billboard**'s The Year In Music.

1991 Jan [28] Aerosmith wins Favorite Pop/Rock Band, Duo Or Group and Favorite Heavy Metal/Hard RockArtist at the 18th annual American Music Awards at the Shrine auditorium, Los Angeles.

Feb [20] They win Best Rock Performance By A Duo Or Group with Vocal for *Janie's Got A Gun* at the 33rd annual Grammy awards at Radio City Music Hall, New York. Band also performs *Come Together* as part of a tribute to Grammy Living Legend John Lennon.

Mar [3] Tyler and Perry present the 20th annual Juno Awards at the Queen Elizabeth theater, Vancouver, for the second year running.

[7] Aerosmith is named Best Band in the annual **Rolling Stone** Readers' Picks music awards.

May Group begins works on new album with producer Fairbairn in Vancouver.

A-HA

Morten Harket (lead vocals)
Mags Furuholmen (keyboards, vocals)
Pal Waaktaar (guitar, vocals)

1977 Living in Oslo suburb Manglerud, Furuholmen (b. Magne Furuholmen, Nov.1, 1962, Oslo, Norway), his father having been in The Bent Solve Orchestra, and Waaktaar (b. Sept.6, 1961, Oslo), who have been playing together since childhood, form part-time band, Spider Empire, influenced by The Doors and Jimi Hendrix.

1979 Oct Spider Empire evolves into a 4-man Doors-like band named Bridges, with Furuholmen, Waaktaar, Viggo Bondi (bass) and Oystein Jevanord (drums).

1980 Oct *Fakkeltog (Torchlight Procession)* is issued on own label, Vakenatt, with only 1,000 copies pressed.

1981 While working on their second release, Waaktaar and Furuholmen meet Harket (b. Sept.14, 1959, Konigsberg, Norway), singing with Mercy, Laelia Anceps and then soul group Souldier Blue. They discuss ideas for making a more commercial form of music, and Bridges ceases.

1982 Recognizing Norwegian market as an ineffectual launching pad for major success, Waaktaar and Furuholmen travel to UK to sell their ideas, but return without success. (Through a misunderstanding, Harket does not come to London with them.) Furuholmen coins the name A-ha, easily memorized as it is familiar in many languages.

1983 Jan Trio moves to London, to share a flat and work on songs.

June Their song *Lesson One* impresses John Ratcliff, studio manager at Rendezvous studios, where they are making demos. Ratcliff plays the track to former record company executive Terry Slater, who becomes

their manager, and arranges auditions for record companies in a London rehearsal studio.

Dec They go to Norway for Christmas, having been signed by WEA Records for international releases.

1984 Jan *Lesson One*, now rewritten as *Take On Me*, is recorded in London with producer Tony Mansfield.

Oct *Take On Me* is issued in UK after successful Norwegian release, but sells an approximate 300 copies.

1985 Apr *Love Is Reason*, their follow-up in Norway, does not chart.

May Slater has A-ha remake *Take On Me* with Alan Tarney as producer, but it fails again.

June Disillusioned, the trio splits up to spend the summer in Oslo.

July US Warner label issues *Take On Me*, and decides to spend $100,000 on a ground-breaking (and later award-winning) semi-animated video by Steve Barron to help catch promotion time on MTV.

Sept A-ha flies to Los Angeles, CA, for promo visit, and *Take On Me* is given its third UK release.

Oct [19] *Take On Me* tops US chart. After finally succeeding in UK, *Take On Me* hits #2, behind Jennifer Rush's *The Power Of Love*.

Nov *Hunting High And Low* is issued, and hits UK #2 and US #15.

1986 Jan [25] *The Sun Always Shines On TV* tops UK chart.

Feb [22] *The Sun Always Shines On TV* reaches US #20.

Mar Group begins recording second album in London.

Apr [19] *Train Of Thought*, remixed from debut album, hits UK #8.

May [7] They feature in the Montreux Pop Festival, Switzerland.

June A 120-date world tour begins in Perth, Australia.

[28] Extracted ballad *Hunting High And Low* hits UK #5.

July A-ha tours Japan, and goes to Hawaii to complete work on its second album.

Oct [18] *I've Been Losing You* hits UK #8 as *Scoundrel Days* debuts at UK #2.

Nov [15] *Scoundrel Days* makes US #74.

1987 Jan [10] *Cry Wolf*, accompanied by another startling video using state-of-art visual trickery, hits UK #5, as the group plays 3 nights at the Royal Albert Hall, London.

Feb World tour ends at home in Oslo.

Mar [14] *Manhattan Skyline* reaches UK #13 (the group's first single to miss the Top 10) as *Cry Wolf* makes US #50.

July [18] *The Living Daylights*, theme from the new James Bond movie, with lyrics by Waaktaar and music by John Barry, hits UK #5.

1988 Apr [2] *Stay On These Roads*, title track from A-ha's forthcoming album, hits UK #5.

May [21] *Stay On These Roads* hits UK #2.

June [25] *The Blood That Moves The Body* reaches UK #25.

July [2] *Stay On These Roads* peaks at US #148.

Sept [10] *Touchy!* reaches UK #11.

1989 Jan *You Are The One* reaches UK #13.

Feb [11] Harket marries Camille Malmquist in Stockholm, Sweden. Before year's end, Harket will record anti-pollution single with Bjorn Eidsvag and star in movie "Kamilia And The Thief".

1990 Nov [3] *Crying In The Rain*, remake of The Everly Brothers' 1962 US #6, reaches UK #11.

[10] *East Of The Sun*, with 10 tracks written by Furuholmen and Waaktaar and produced by Chris Neil and Ian Stanley, reaches UK #12.

Dec [15] After 13 consecutive Top 30 singles, *I Call Your Name* stalls at UK #44.

1991 Feb [26] A-ha plays the Hammersmith Odeon, London, during a short UK tour.

THE ALARM

Mike Peters (guitar, vocals)
Dave Sharp (guitar)
Eddie MacDonald (bass)
Nigel Twist (drums)

1981 After playing together for 4 years in Rhyl, Wales, first as punk band, The Toilets, and then as mod group, 17 (recording *Don't Let Go* backed with *Bank Holiday Weekend* on Vendetta label), the quartet, comprising Peters (b. Feb.25, 1959, Prestatyn, Wales), Sharp (b. Jan.28, 1959, Salford, Lancs.), MacDonald (b. Nov.1, 1959, St. Asaph, Wales) and Twist (b. July 18, 1958, Manchester, Gtr. Manchester) makes a fresh start as The Alarm, after Dexy's Midnight Runners fire them as support band on a UK tour because they are not good enough and when Peters is inspired by seeing U2 at the Marquee, deciding to embrace a similar "emotionally honest" attitude to their own material.

Sept Group records *Unsafe Buildings* in a Manchester studio for their own White Cross label, pressing 2,000 copies to sell at gigs and to use as demos for audition.

Oct They move to London in search of a deal and live work.

1982 Aug After supporting The Jam, U2 and The Beat and gaining music press support and industry interest, Alarm signs to IRS Records.

Oct *Marching On* is their first IRS single; good reviews but no hit.

1983 Sept Chart debut *68 Guns* reaches UK #17, helped by the group's first UK TV appearance on "Top Of The Pops".

Nov Group records its second album at Abbey Road and Good Earth studios in London with producer Alan Shacklock.

1984 Feb *Where Were You Hiding When The Storm Broke* repeats success, climbing to UK #22.

Mar [3] Debut album *Declaration* hits UK #6.

Apr *The Deceiver* peaks at UK #51.

[14] *Declaration* makes US #50 as *The Alarm* peaks at US #126.

Nov *The Chant Has Just Begun* is another minor UK hit at #48.

1985 Mar *Absolute Reality* reaches UK #35.

Oct *Strength*, produced by Mike Howlett, reaches UK #18, while extracted title track *Strength* makes UK #40.

1986 Feb *Spirit Of '76*, an affectionate time-warp hymn to punk music, reaches UK #22.

[8] *Strength* makes US #61 with parent *Strength* set to peak at US #39 a week later.

May *Knife Edge* makes UK #43.

June Alarm joins The Bangles, The Go-Go's, Bob Marley, R.E.M., Sting and others, contributing unreleased live and studio tracks to *Live! For Life* to raise funds for the AMC Cancer Research Center.

July [5] *Live! For Life* makes US #105.

[11-12] Alarm supports Queen for 2 nights at Wembley Stadium, London.

1987 Oct First fruits of fresh recording period, *Rain In The Summertime* makes UK #18.

Nov *Eye Of The Hurricane*, produced by John Porter, reaches UK #23 and makes US #77.

Dec *Rescue Me*, taken from the album, charts fleetingly at UK #48.

1988 Jan [16] *Rain In The Summertime* peaks at US #71.

Feb *Presence Of Love (Laugherne)* makes UK #44.

Apr [16] *Presence Of Love* stalls at US #77.

July Group embarks on 2½-month US tour with Bob Dylan.

Nov [5] *Electric Folklore Live*, recorded at The Wang Center For The Performing Arts, Boston, MA, on Apr.26, 1988, makes UK #62.

[12] *Electric Folklore Live* peaks at US #167.

1989 Sept [23] *Sold Me Down The River* makes UK #43.

[30] *Change*, produced by Tony Visconti, reaches UK #13. (Band also records a Welsh-language version, *Newid*, only available in Wales.)

Nov *Change* makes US #75. *A New South Wales*, with The Morriston Orpheus Male Voice Choir, with B-side *The Rock*, makes UK #31.

[14] Band begins substantial US tour with first of 2 Los Angeles, CA, concerts. It will end in New York on Dec.14.

[25] *Sold Me Down The River* makes US #50.

1990 Feb *Love Don't Come Easy* makes UK #48.

[5] "No Frontiers" UK tour ends at the Brixton Academy, London.

Oct [27] *Unsafe Building 1990* peaks at UK #54.

Nov [24] Compilation album *Standards* debuts at UK #47.

Dec Group releases a cover version of John Lennon's seasonal *Happy Xmas (War Is Over)*.

1991 Feb Sharp cuts solo album *Hard Travlin'* at the Hit Factory in New York with producer Bob Johnston and plays selected acoustic gigs throughout the Northeastern US.

Apr [16] 20-date UK tour includes appearance at the Town & Country club, London.

May Alarm releases *Raw*, a new studio album for IRS.

THE ALLMAN BROTHERS BAND

Duane Allman (guitar)
Gregg Allman (keyboards, guitar, vocals)
Dickey Betts (guitar, vocals)
Berry Oakley (bass)
Butch Trucks (drums)
Jaimoe Johanson (drums)

1966 Aug Veterans of Miami, FL-based bands, The Y-Teens, The Shufflers, The Escorts, The House Rockers, and now The Allman Joys, playing teen dances at the YMCA and then Daytona clubs like the Martinique, brothers Duane (b. Howard Duane Allman, Nov.20, 1946, Nashville, TN) and Gregg Allman (b. Dec.8, 1947, Nashville), sons of an Army sergeant murdered on Christmas leave during the Korean War, relocated to Daytona Beach, FL, from Lebanon, TN, in 1958, bassist Bob Keller and drummer Maynard Portwood record demos of *Spoonful*, *Crossroads* and *Shapes Of Things* at Bradley's Barn in Nashville, after singer J.D. Loudermilk has seen the band at The Briar Patch in Nashville, and recommended them to Buddy Killen at Dial Records.

1967 The Allman Joys disperse, with Duane and Gregg moving to Decatur, AL, where they join The Five Minutes, which includes Paul Hornsby (piano/guitar), Pete Carr (bass) and Johnny Sandlin (drums). Band moves to St. Louis, MO, reverting to The Allman Joys name and then Almanac.

June Almanac moves to Los Angeles, CA, at the suggestion of Bill McEuen, who has seen them in a St. Louis club. Group signs with Liberty Records, renaming to Hour Glass.

Aug Group begins recording its debut album *Hour Glass* at Liberty Sound studios, Los Angeles.

Oct [19-21] Hour Glass supports Eric Burdon & The Animals at the Fillmore West, San Francisco, CA.

1968 Jan Group records its second album *Power Of Love*.

Apr Third projected Hour Glass album is recorded at Rick Hall's Fame studio in Muscle Shoals, AL, but is rejected by Liberty, and Hornsby, Sandlin and Carr, disillusioned with the label, quit.

June The brothers return to Jacksonville, playing informally with The 31st of February, a band run by Trucks (b. Jacksonville, FL), who has known the Allmans since touring with The Allman Joys when a member of The Bitter End, sitting in with them from time to time, and recording demos with them (later issued as *Duane And Gregg* in 1973).

Sept The 31st Of February, also comprising guitarist Scott Boyer and bassist David Brown, record at TK studios in Hialeah, FL. Trucks asks them to help record the group's second album, uncredited as they are still signed to Liberty.

Nov Hall, impressed by Duane's guitar playing, invites him back to Fame as a salaried session man. His contributions to tracks by Wilson Pickett (it is Allman's idea that Pickett record Lennon/McCartney's *Hey Jude*), Arthur Conley, King Curtis and Clarence Carter for Atlantic prompt label's Jerry Wexler to have him back Aretha Franklin and record material of his own for a projected solo album. (Wexler buys out Duane's contract from Hall for $15,000.) Duane and Gregg are unable to record under their names as they still owe Liberty an album so Gregg returns to Los Angeles to honor the contract and cut solo album.

1969 Mar Phil Walden, about to form Atlantic-distributed Capricorn Records, suggests to Duane that he form a band. Allman hires Johanson (b. John Lee Johnson, July 8, 1944, Gulfport, MS), with whom he has worked at Fame and who has toured with Percy Sledge, Otis Redding, Joe Tex and Clifton Chenier, and they go to Jacksonville and recruit old friend Oakley (b. Apr.4, 1948, Chicago, IL), who has toured with Tommy Roe's back-up band The Romans, to form a Hendrix/Cream-style trio. While there, they begin playing free concerts with Oakley's band Second Coming, which also includes Betts (b. Dec.12, 1943, West Palm Beach, FL). With Trucks now joining, Walden's hoped-for trio becomes a quintet. Duane, against the wishes of the others, insists on Gregg becoming the group's vocalist. Walden relocates the band to Macon and puts them on the road throughout the year. (Over the next 2½ years, the group will play over 500 US dates. Their first major gig is on a Blood, Sweat & Tears headlining bill at the Fillmore East, New York.)

Sept They make their first recordings at Atlantic's New York studios, before becoming the first act to record in Capricorn's own studio.

1970 Feb Debut album *Allman Brothers Band*, on Atlantic's Atco label, reaches US #188, but is more popular in the South, where the band starts extensive touring. Duane continues session work between bookings.

Mar [11] King Curtis' *Games People Play*, on which Duane is featured guitarist, wins Best R&B Instrumental Performance at the 12th annual Grammy awards.

July [3] Band plays the second annual Atlanta International Pop Festival, alongside Jimi Hendrix, Jethro Tull, B.B. King and others.

Aug [26] Duane starts recording as part of Derek & The Dominoes at Miami's Criteria studios. Clapton has invited him to join after seeing him play with The Allman Brothers, at the recommendation of producer Tom Dowd. A double album is finished in less than 10 days. Clapton will later say that Allman was "the catalyst" of this whole project, which will become the *Layla* album, and Allman's guitar duetting with Clapton on the title track will become his most famous work outside the brothers' band.

Sept Dissatisfied with recording results from Capricorn studios, they

move to Atlantic's New York studios, with Adrian Barber producing.
Dec Dowd-produced *Idlewild South*, named after their Macon farmhouse base, makes US #38.

1971 Jan [9] First charting single *Revival (Love Is Everywhere)* makes US #92.
Mar [12-13] They play the Fillmore East in New York, on a bill with Elvin Bishop and Johnny Winter.
[22] The entire band is arrested in Jackson, AL, for possession of heroin and marijuana.
June [27] The Allmans headline the last night at the Fillmore East, on a bill with Albert King, The J. Geils Band, The Beach Boys and Mountain.
Aug [17] Duane, and musicians he has worked with on Herbie Mann's *Push*, play at the funeral of King Curtis, murdered in New York days earlier.
Sept Capricorn-released *At Fillmore East*, recorded on Mar.12 and 13, reaches US #13.
Oct [29] Returning from wishing Oakley's wife, Linda, a happy birthday, Duane crashes his motorbike in an effort to avoid a truck. After 3 hours of emergency surgery he dies in Macon Medical Center.
Nov [1] Band performs at Duane's funeral, joined by Thom Doucette (harmonica), Dr. John (guitar), Bobby Caldwell (drums) and Delaney Bramlett (vocals).

1972 Apr [2] Group plays the Mar Y Sol Festival, Vega Baja, Puerto Rico.
May *Eat A Peach*, which includes the last 3 tracks recorded by Duane, hits US #4.
[13] *Ain't Wastin' Time No More* peaks at US #77.
Duane & Gregg Allman makes US #129.
Aug [19] *Melissa* stalls at US #86.
Nov [11] Oakley is killed when his motorbike collides with a bus, only 3 blocks from the site of Duane Allman's death a year before in Macon. He is buried in Macon's Rose Hill cemetery, where Allman also lies.
Dec [23] *One Way Out* peaks at US #86.
Duane's An Anthology reaches US #28.

1973 Jan Lamar Williams, a friend of Johanson's, replaces Oakley on bass.
Apr First 2 albums repackaged together as *Beginnings* makes US #25.
July [28] The Allman Brothers Band takes part in the largest ever rock festival before a 600,000 crowd with The Grateful Dead and The Band at Watkins Glen Raceway in upstate New York.
Aug [25] Trucks crashes his car in Macon, but escapes with a broken leg.
Sept [8] *Brothers And Sisters*, dedicated to Oakley, tops US chart for 5 weeks, and is the group's UK chart debut at #42.
[26] Group plays The Winterland, San Francisco, with The Marshall Tucker Band.
Oct [13] *Ramblin' Man* hits US #2, behind Cher's *Half-Breed*.
Nov Gregg Allman's solo album *Laid Back*, produced by Johnny Sandlin, reaches US #13.
Early Allman, released on Dial label, peaks at US #171.

1974 Jan [12] Group begins 12-date European tour at the Odeon theater, Birmingham, W.Midlands, ending in Amsterdam on Feb.11.
Feb [16] Instrumental *Jessica* peaks at US #65, highlighting the playing of Betts, who begins to guide the band's direction.
[23] Gregg Allman's solo single *Midnight Rider* reaches US #19, as he embarks on a solo tour.
Aug Betts makes solo album *Highway Call* as Richard Betts, reaching US #19. He tours US with country and bluegrass musicians.
Duane's An Anthology Vol 2 reaches US #49, while Chuck Leavell, Williams and Johanson form jazz trio We Three, playing local clubs and colleges followed by a 6-week tour.
Dec Gregg Allman's *The Gregg Allman Tour* makes US #50, having been recorded live by the spin-off Gregg Allman Band, which features most of Brothers Band (but not Betts).

1975 Jan Gregg meets Cher at end of solo tour and forms a romantic union.
Feb Allman testifies against his former road manager and bodyguard John "Scooter" Herring, on trial for drug trafficking. Herring is sentenced to 75 years in jail, and Allman is ostracized by other band members, who claim he has betrayed their former fraternal loyalty, and vow not to work with him again, despite the fact that Allman has been threatened with a Grand Jury indictment unless he testifies.
June [30] Allman marries Cher, 4 days after her divorce from Sonny Bono. They will separate acrimoniously after only 10 days, followed by a 3½ year on-off-on-off marriage.
Oct *Win, Lose Or Draw* hits US #5.
Nov [22] *Nevertheless/Louisiana Lou And Three Card Monty John* peaks at US #67.
[25] Group plays a benefit concert for Jimmy Carter's Presidential Campaign Fund at the Civic Center, Providence, RI.

1976 Jan [24] Double album *The Road Goes On Forever*, a compilation of their best work to date, reaches US #43.
Mar [6] *The Road Goes On Forever* makes UK #54.
July [16] Band goes its separate ways: Allman recording with Cher (*Allman And Woman*) and then returning to his own Gregg Allman Band; Betts will form Great Southern, Trucks will study music at college, while the others, already playing as We Three, form Sea Level with guitarist Jimmy Nalls.
Dec [25] *Wipe The Windows, Check The Oil, Dollar Gas*, compiling previously unreleased live recordings, makes US #75.

1977 Jan Allman and Betts mend rift during Jimmy Carter Inauguration celebrations.
Apr Betts signs with Arista, after a financial dispute with Capricorn, and forms Great Southern, with Dan Toler from Melting Pot, who had opened for the Allmans. Toler in turn recommends fellow Melting Pots Ken Tibbets (bass) and Jerry Thompson (drums).
[23] *Sea Level* makes US #43.
May [28] *Dickey Betts & Great Southern* reaches US #31.
July [10] Elijah Blue is born to Gregg and Cher, who also release *Two The Hard Way*, credited as Allman & Woman.
[23] *Playin' Up A Storm* by Gregg Allman Band makes US #42.
Nov While Betts is recording second album with a new band comprising Toler, drummer Doni Sharbano, bassist David "Rook" Goldflies, keyboardist Michael Workman and drummer/percussionist David Toler, Allman tells Walden that he wants to get The Allman Brothers Band back together.

1978 May [20] Great Southern's *Atlanta's Burning Down* makes US #157.
July Band re-forms with rifts healed after Allman, Trucks and Johanson join Great Southern on stage at a Central Park, New York concert. Great Southern's Dan Toler (guitar) and Goldflies (bass) complete the new line-up.
Aug Re-formed group plays the Capricorn Annual Barbecue in Macon.
Nov Allman Brothers Band, minus Leavell and Williams (still with Sea Level, Johanson has quit to join the re-formed Allmans) return to Criteria studios with Dowd.

1979 Jan [16] Allman and Cher are divorced.
Apr [14] Reunion album *Enlightened Rogues* hits US #9.
May [5] *Crazy Love* reaches US #29.

1980 Jan [18] Capricorn Records announces bankruptcy, leaving the band without a label.
July They sign to Arista Records.
Sept [9] They play first of 3 UK dates at Apollo theater, Manchester. They will then play London's Rainbow theater, with a line-up including Allman, Betts, Johanson, Trucks, Goldflies and Dan Toler.
Oct [4] First Arista album *Reach For The Sky*, produced by the group with Mike Lawler and Johnny Cobb, climbs to US #27.
[11] *Angeline* makes US #58.

1981 Sept [19] *Straight From The Heart* makes US #39. *Brothers Of The Road*, from which it is taken, reaches US #44 and garners poor reviews. Leavell rejoins them shortly after, but with their style now less fashionable, band has little more to offer collectively, and splits again.
Nov *The Best Of The Allman Brothers Band* peaks at US #189.

1982 Dec Betts, Leavell and Trucks team with Wet Willie's Jimmy Hall to form the BHLT Band. They embark on US tour, augmented by Goldflies on bass and Danny Parks on fiddle.

1983 Jan [25] Band's ex-bassist Williams, a Vietnam veteran, succumbs to Agent Orange-related cancer in Los Angeles.

1984 The BHLT Band splits. Trucks quits to work for a studio and sound company, Leavell does session work with The Rolling Stones, The Fabulous Thunderbirds, Dave Edmunds and others, and Betts moves to Nashville, where he will form a country band, play on a Hank Williams Jr. album, and co-write Mickey Gilley's country hit *Your Memory Ain't What It Used To Be*.

1986 After a substantial number of club dates across the country, Betts' new band signs with Epic, and will perform gigs during the year with Allman's outfit.
July The Allmans reunite to play at Charlie Daniels' "Volunteer Jam".
Oct [31] Group plays the "Crackdown On Crack" benefit at Madison Square Garden, New York.

1987 May After a 4-year break, Gregg Allman returns, signed to Epic Records, with The Gregg Allman Band and a solo album *I'm No Angel* which reaches US #30.
[9] *I'm No Angel* makes US #49.

1988 Aug Gregg Allman Band's *Just Before The Bullets Fly* peaks at US #117.

Nov The Dickey Betts Band's *Pattern Disruptive*, recorded at Trucks' Pegasus recording studios in Tallahassee, FL, with tracks co-written with Don Johnson, peaks at US #187.

1989 The Allman Brothers re-form with Allman, Betts, Johanson, Trucks and new members Johnny Neel (keyboards), Warren Haynes (guitar) and Allen Woody (bass).
June [28] Group embarks on 13-date US tour at Chautauqua Amphitheater, NY, ending July 15 at Civic Arena, Pittsburgh, PA.
July Boxed set compilation *Dreams*, produced by Bill Levenson, makes US #103.
Aug [18] *Seven Turns*, The Allman Brothers' first studio album in 9 years, peaks at US #53.
Sept [19] US tour ends at Merriweather Post Pavilion, Columbia, MD.
1991 **Feb** [23] Group plays American Airlines "Celebrity Ski For Cystic Fibrosis" charity concert at Crested Butte, CO.
Mar [7] The Allmans are named Comeback Of The Year in the annual **Rolling Stone** Readers' Picks music awards, as they wrap new album with producer Dowd.

HERB ALPERT

1958 After serving in the US military, as a trumpeter in the 6th Army band for 2 years at The Presidio in San Francisco, CA, Alpert (b. Mar.31, 1935, Los Angeles, CA), the son of a Russian immigrant and Hungarian mother, who have encouraged his trumpet playing since age 8, starts in the record industry as a writer in partnership with insurance salesman Lou Adler. They have early success when they take 4 demos to Keen, where Bumps Blackwell invites them to start an A&R training program at $42 a week and then hires them as staff writers. This leads to writing with Sam Cooke, for whom they write 4 consecutive hits, *Love You Most Of All*, *Everybody Likes To Cha Cha Cha*, *Only Sixteen* and *Wonderful World*, under the collective pseudonym Barbara Campbell, Cooke's wife's real name.
1959 Keen rejects Alpert and Adler's song *Baby Talk*, which they then take to Dore Records, who will have a Top 10 US hit with the song as recorded by Jan And Dean. Alpert also records as a vocalist without success for RCA as Dore Alpert, and secures bit parts in some Hollywood films, notably playing drums in the scene when Moses comes down from the mountain in "The Ten Commandments".
1962 **Mar** Alpert splits with Adler, and joins Jerry Moss, who produced him for RCA and is one of the industry's top independent promotion men, to form Carnival Records, which they swiftly change to A&M (based on their surnames). The label initially operates from Alpert's garage at home and funds itself with $1,000 secured when Dot Records picks up national distribution for one of Dore Alpert's singles.
Oct Alpert experiments with Sol Lake's tune *Twinkle Star*, re-arranging it as *The Lonely Bull*, by double-tracking the trumpet part, thereby creating his trademark sound. He records the track for $65 and releases it on A&M under the name of The Tijuana Brass.
Dec [8] Latin-flavored jazz instrumental *The Lonely Bull* hits US #6, selling over 700,000 copies and establishing both Alpert and A&M.
1963 **Jan** *The Lonely Bull* is released, reaching US #24, as single *The Lonely Bull* reaches UK #22.
Mar [30] *Marching Thru Madrid* makes US #96.
1964 **Feb** [17] The Tijuana Brass, a group of musicians put together by Alpert to play in concert, which will grow into one of the top-grossing live attractions in US in mid-60s, is launched in concert in San Francisco, CA. Band comprises Bob Edmundson (trombone), Lou Pagani (keyboards), John Pisano (rhythm guitar), Tonni Kalash (second trumpet), Nick Ceroli (drums) and Pat Senatore (bass).
Apr [18] *Mexican Drummer Man* makes US #77, as *Tijuana Brass Vol.2* reaches US #17.
July [18] *The Mexican Shuffle*, penned by *Lonely Bull* writer Sol Lake, makes US #85.
Dec BBC Radio program "Newly Pressed" adopts Alpert's *Up Cherry Street* as its theme tune.
1965 **Feb** *South Of The Border* hits US #6.
May [8] *Whipped Cream* peaks at US #68.
Oct [2] *The 3rd Man Theme*, B-side of *Taste Of Honey*, makes US #47.
Nov [27] Already on chart for 6 months, *Whipped Cream And Other Delights* tops US chart. *A Taste Of Honey*, his first Top 10 single for 3 years, hits US #7.
1966 **Jan** *Spanish Flea*, written by Julius Wechter from labelmate The Baja Marimba Band, hits UK #3, re-establishing Alpert in UK, as *Going Places* hits UK #4. *Herb Alpert's Tijuana Brass Vol.2* reaches US #17.
Feb [5] *Tijuana Taxi*, *Zorba The Greek*'s B-side, makes US #38.

[26] *Zorba The Greek* reaches US #11.
Mar [5] *Going Places* tops US chart for 6 weeks. *Tijuana Taxi* makes UK #37.
[13] Alpert makes one-off UK appearance at the Hammersmith Odeon, London. (The concert will be televised by the BBC on Aug.4 and 11.)
[15] *A Taste Of Honey* wins Record Of The Year, Best Instrumental Performance, Non-Jazz, Best Instrumental Arrangement and Best Engineered Recording of 1965 at the 8th annual Grammy awards.
[25] The Tijuana Brass performs at the White House Correspondents' Dinner in Washington, DC.
Apr Group performs at Carnegie Hall, New York.
[16] *Spanish Flea*, used as the theme for US TV show "The Dating Game", reaches US #27.
[23] *What Now My Love*, A-side of *Spanish Flea*, reaches US #24.
May [28] *What Now My Love* tops US chart for 9 weeks, and *Whipped Cream And Other Delights* hits UK #2.
June *What Now My Love* reaches UK #18.
July [18] The "Herb Alpert & The Tijuana Brass Show" opens at the Greek theater, Hollywood.
[23] *The Work Song* reaches US #18.
Sept [19] Alpert performs at Monaco Palace for Princess Grace.
Oct [1] *Flamingo* reaches US #28.
[7] Group completes European tour at the Royal Albert Hall, London.
Dec [17] *Mame* reaches US #19.
1967 **Jan** *S.R.O.* hits US #2 and UK #5.
Mar [2] *What Now My Love* wins Best Instrumental Performance (Other Than Jazz) and Best Instrumental Arrangement Of 1966 at the 9th annual Grammy awards.
Apr [1] *Wade In The Water* makes US #37.
May *Casino Royale*, the theme tune to spoof James Bond movie, reaches US and UK #27.
June [17] *Sounds Like* tops US chart, then climbs to UK #21.
Aug [5] *The Happening*, an instrumental version of the film theme which has topped US chart in a vocal version by The Supremes 3 months earlier, makes US #32.
Oct [14] *A Banda* makes US #35.
1968 **Jan** *Herb Alpert's 9th* hits US #4, then makes UK #26.
Feb [10] *Carmen* makes US #51.
Apr [22] Alperts stars in his own CBS TV special.
May [25] *Cabaret* makes US #72.
June [22] Softly swaying ballad *This Guy's In Love With You*, sung by Alpert to his wife Lani Hall on his TV special, tops US chart for 4 weeks, becoming Alpert's first vocal hit, his first #1, A&M's first #1 and songwriters Bacharach and David's first #1. It will be his last chart-topper for more than a decade.
July [27] *The Beat Of The Brass* tops US chart and hits UK #4.
Aug *This Guy's In Love With You* hits UK #3.
Sept [21] *To Wait For Love* is his second vocal hit, but much less successful, reaching US #51.
1969 **Jan** [11] *My Favorite Things* makes US #45.
Apr [19] *Zazueira* stalls at US #78.
June [21] A vocal version of the Nilsson song *Without Her* peaks at US #63 and will make UK #36. Subsequent releases will revert to trumpet-led instrumentals.
Aug *Warm* reaches US #28 and UK #30.
Nov [4] The Tijuana Brass performs at the Royal Festival Hall, London. (The show is recorded and will air on ITV on New Year's Eve.) After selling more than 45 million albums, Alpert decides to give up performing, partly due to a tired lip, and will concentrate on his executive responsibilities at A&M.
1970 **Jan** Alpert is impressed by demo tapes from a brother/sister act, The Carpenters, whom he signs to the label. (They will score 12 million-selling singles for A&M over the next 5 years.)
Mar *The Brass Are Comin'* makes US #30 and UK #40.
June *Greatest Hits* hits UK #8 and US #43.
[27] *Down Mexico Way* peaks at UK #64.
Nov [7] *Jerusalem* peaks at US #74.
1971 **Jan** *Jerusalem* makes UK #42.
July *Summertime* makes US #111.
Nov [13] *America* makes UK #45.
1972 **June** *Solid Brass* peaks at US #135.
1973 **Apr** [28] *Last Tango In Paris* peaks at US #77.
Dec *Foursider* makes US #196.
1974 **Apr** [19] Alpert begins his first major concert tour in years at Harrah's, Lake Tahoe, NV.
June [15] *Fox Hunt* stalls at US #84, as *You Smile The Song Begins*,

Alpert's first album in 3 years, makes US #66.

1975 **Apr** *Coney Island Number* reaches US #88.

1977 **Oct** [29] *40 Greatest* makes UK #45.

1978 **Mar** [25] *Herb Alpert/Hugh Masekela*, a collaboration with South African trumpeter, reaches US #65.

1979 **Oct** [20] *Rise*, written by Andy Armer and Alpert's nephew Randy Badazz and featuring contemporary disco rhythm far removed from the traditional Alpert feel, and boosted by its exposure in TV's "General Hospital", tops US chart, toppling Michael Jackson's *Don't Stop 'Til You Get Enough*. It is a million-plus-selling single.

Nov [24] *Rise* reaches UK #13 as parent album, produced by Alpert with Badazz, makes UK #37.

Dec [1] *Rise* hits US #6.

1980 **Jan** [19] *Rotation*, also penned by Armer and Badazz, hits US #30, and will make UK #46.

Feb [27] *Rise* wins Best Pop Instrumental Performance Of 1979 at the 22nd annual Grammy awards.

July [26] *Beyond* makes US #50.

Aug [23] *Beyond* reaches US #28.

1981 **Sept** [19] *Magic Man* stalls at US #79, as parent album *Magic Man* makes US #61.

1982 **Aug** [14] *Route 101* makes US #37.

Sept [4] *Fandango* makes US #100.

1983 **Sept** [3] *Garden Party* makes US #81, as *Blow Your Own Horn* makes US #120.

Dec [24] *Red Hot* makes US #77.

1984 **Aug** *Bullish* makes US #75.

Sept [15] *Bullish* makes US #90.

1985 **Sept** *Wild Romance* peaks at US #151.

1987 **Jan** Alpert plays cameo trumpet on UB40's UK hit *Rat In Mi Kitchen*.

Apr *Keep Your Eye On Me*, mainly produced by Jimmy Jam and Terry Lewis at Flyte Tyme studios in Minneapolis, MN, signals another commercial return. It reaches US #18 and UK #79. The title track also makes UK #19.

[4] *Keep Your Eye On Me*, with vocal by Lisa Keith and Terry Lewis, makes US #46.

June [20] Dance-styled *Diamonds*, also from the album and featuring Janet Jackson and Lisa Keith on vocals, tops US R&B chart and hits US #5 and UK #27.

Sept [5] Ballad *Making Love In The Rain*, from the album once again, with Jackson and Keith on vocals, peaks at US #35. Alpert meanwhile continues to co-run A&M, now just past its 25th birthday, and grown into one of the biggest and most successful independent labels in the world.

1988 **Jan** [31] Alpert performs the American National Anthem at Super Bowl XXII between the Washington Redskins and the Denver Broncos at San Diego Jack Murphy Stadium, San Diego, CA.

1989 **Oct** Having recently launched his own "Listen" perfume, Alpert and Moss sell A&M Records to PolyGram conglomerate for $460 million.

1990 **Sept** Alpert sings *This Guy's In Love With You* with Bacharach at a benefit for AIDS Project Los Angeles at Wiltern theater, Los Angeles.

1991 **Mar** New album *North On South St.* is released.

AMEN CORNER

Andy Fairweather-Low (vocals, guitar)
Blue Weaver (organ)
Neil Jones (guitar)
Clive Taylor (bass)
Mike Smith (tenor sax)
Alan Jones (baritone sax)
Dennis Bryon (drums)

1966 Group forms in Cardiff, Wales, its 7 members veterans of local Welsh bands – lead singer Fairweather-Low (b. Aug.8, 1950, Ystrad Mynach, Hengoed, Wales) having been a member of local R&B band The Taffbeats, is in The Sect Maniacs with Alan Jones (b. Feb.6, 1947, Swansea, Wales); Taylor (b. Apr.27, 1949, Cardiff) and Neil Jones (b. Mar.25, 1949, Llanbradach, Caerphilly, Wales) are from The Dekkas; Weaver (b. Derek Weaver, Mar.3, 1949, Cardiff) and Bryon (b. Apr.14, 1949, Cardiff) are from The Witnesses; and Smith (b. Nov.4, 1947, Neath, Wales) is in Lot 13 – gaining a reputation as a strong live R&B band, the twin saxes giving a "fatter", more American sound than most UK beat groups of the time. They record a version of Georgie Fame's *Bidin' My Time* at an independent studio in Monmouth, Wales, but EMI turns it down.

1967 **May** Group signs to Decca's Deram label.

Aug [19] Their debut, slow and bluesy *Gin House* reaches UK #12.

Oct *World Of Broken Hearts*, with a more mainstream commercial pop sound, reaches UK #26.

Nov [14] Band begins a 15-date twice-nightly UK package tour, with The Jimi Hendrix Experience, The Move, Pink Floyd, The Nice, and others, at the Royal Albert Hall, London, ending Dec.5 at Green's Playhouse, Glasgow, Scotland.

1968 **Feb** [17] Group covers American Breed's major US hit *Bend Me, Shape Me* in brasher form, and hits UK #3.

Mar First album *Round Amen Corner* reaches UK #26.

Apr [5] They begin a 28-date twice-nightly UK tour with Gene Pitney, Status Quo, Don Partridge, Simon Dupree & The Big Sound and others, at the Odeon cinema, Lewisham, London, ending May 7 at the Granada cinema, Walthamstow, London.

May [10] With 2 days rest, they begin a 10-date twice-nightly UK tour, with billtoppers Herman's Hermits, Dave Berry, The Paper Dolls, John Rowles And The Echoes, at Birmingham Town Hall, W.Midlands. It will end May 19 at the Theatre Royal, Nottingham, Notts.

Sept [14] *High In The Sky*, another brash dance single, hits UK #6. (Soon after, the band signs a recording deal with Immediate Records.)

Dec [31] Group takes part in the "Giant New Year's Eve Gala Pop & Blues Party" at Alexandra Palace, London, with Joe Cocker, John Mayall's Bluesbreakers, The Small Faces and others.

1969 **Feb** [14] More than 300 fans are injured at an Amen Corner/Love Affair show at the Ice Rink, Paisley, Scotland.

[15] Immediate debut, *(If Paradise Is) Half As Nice* (a cover of *Il Paradiso Belavista*, an Italian hit for La Ragazza 77, with English lyrics by Jack Fishman) tops UK chart, jumping from #19 the previous week.

July [1] Amen Corner headlines "Pop Proms" concert at the Royal Albert Hall, London, with Marmalade, The Equals and others.

[19] *Hello Suzie*, penned by Roy Wood and featured on his album *Shazam*, is the group's last UK hit, at #4.

Aug Group plays in a club scene in Christopher Lee, Peter Cushing and Vincent Price horror picture "Scream And Scream Again".

Oct [5] After many months of rumors that Fairweather-Low is leaving the group to pursue a solo career, Amen Corner makes its final appearance at the Gliderdrome in Boston, Lincs.

Nov [1] *Explosive Company* reaches UK #19.

1970 Group's last single is a cover of The Beatles' *Get Back*. Fairweather-Low, Weaver, Bryon, Taylor and Neil Jones regroup as Fair Weather; Alan Jones and Smith form the nucleus of Judas Jump with Andy Bown.

Aug [29] Fair Weather's *Natural Sinner* hits UK #6, as the group makes its live debut at Scene Two in Scarborough, N.Yorks, but the group splits by the year's end. (Fairweather-Low will have solo success in the mid-70s, charting with *Reggae Tune* and *Wide Eyed And Legless*, while Weaver and Bryon, with guitarist Alan Kendall, will become The Bee Gees' rhythm section throughout that group's glory days in the late 70s and early 80s.)

1976 **Feb** [28] Reissued *(If Paradise Is) Half As Nice* makes UK #34.

AMERICA

Dewey Bunnell (vocals, guitar)
Gerry Beckley (vocals, guitar)
Dan Peek (vocals, guitar)

1967 Bunnell (b. Jan.19, 1951, Yorkshire), Beckley (b. Sept.12, 1952, Texas) and Peek (b. Nov.1, 1950, Panama City, FL) meet at Central high school, Bushey Park, London, all sons of US Air Force officers stationed in UK.

1970 **Oct** Completing school, they form acoustic folk-rock quintet Daze in London. Soon becoming a trio, they audition for Roundhouse venue promoter Jeff Dexter, who books them frequently as opening act for several major bands. Warner Bros. sign the trio, beating out Atlantic and DJM and, as America, they begin recording debut album with producers Ian Samwell and Jeff Dexter at Trident studios in London.

Dec America plays its first major gig at the Roundhouse on the "Elton John/Who Christmas Party".

1971 **Sept** [21] America is featured on the first edition of BBC2 TV show "The Old Grey Whistle Test".

1972 **Jan** *A Horse With No Name* is instant UK chart success, hitting #3, as debut album *America*, though not including the single, reaches UK #14.

Feb Group goes "home" to build on its success, making its first concert appearance in the lunchroom of an Ontario college, before embarking on a major North American tour, supporting The Everly Brothers.

Mar [25] Released in US on the strength of UK success, *A Horse With No Name* shoots to US #1, dislodging Neil Young's *Heart Of Gold* as debut album *America* tops US chart.

July [1] *I Need You* hits US #9.

Dec [9] *Ventura Highway*, recorded in Los Angeles, CA, with producer George Martin and Joe Osborn (bass) and Hal Blaine (drums), hits US #8 and makes UK #43.

1973 **Jan** Aptly titled *Homecoming*, hits US #9 and UK #21.
Mar [3] *Don't Cross The River* makes US #35, as America wins Best New Artist Of 1972 at the 15th annual Grammy awards.
May [26] *Only In Your Heart* peaks at US #62.
[29] Group begins recording its third album at the Record Plant in Los Angeles, with help including Joe Walsh, Carl Wilson and Tom Scott.
Sept [22] Willis Alan Ramsey-penned *Muskrat Love*, the trio's first non-original, peaks at US #67. (It will hit US #4 in 1976 for The Captain & Tennille.)
Nov *Hat Trick* reaches US #28 and UK #41.

1974 **Apr** [17] Back in London, America begins work with producer Martin at Air studios on forthcoming *Holiday*.
Nov [9] Extracted single, *Tin Man*, hits US #4, as *Holiday* hits US #3.

1975 **Jan** [6] Work begins on third collaboration with Martin, and regular sidemen David Dickey (bass) and Willie Leacox (drums), at the Record Plant studios in Los Angeles and San Francisco, CA.
Mar [8] *Lonely People*, also from *Holiday*, hits US #5.
June [14] *Sister Golden Hair* tops US chart for 1 week, as parent album *Hearts* hits US #4.
Sept [27] *Daisy Jane* breaks US Top 10 hits run, reaching #20.
Dec [20] *History: America's Greatest Hits*, the hits to date, hits US #3.

1976 **Jan** [17] *Woman Tonight* makes US #44.
Feb [7] *History: America's Greatest Hits* peaks at UK #60.
[16] Once again with Martin at the helm, America begins recording new album at the Caribou Ranch studios.
June [5] *Hideaway* reaches US #11.
July [10] *Today's The Day*, from *Hideaway*, reaches US #23.
Sept [11] *Amber Cascades* peaks at US #75.

1977 **Mar** *Harbor*, recorded at Ka Lae Kiki studios in Kauai, HI, with Martin, reaches US #21, but does not include any hit singles.
May Peek leaves (later to become a born-again Christian and record solo religious material).

1978 **Jan** *Live* makes US #129.
Oct [13] Signed to the Lamb & Lion label, Peek scores his only US pop hit with *All Things Are Possible*, which makes #78.

1979 **Mar** [19] Now signed to Capitol Records, sessions begin on first studio album without Peek. Beckley and Bunnell are now backed by Dickey and Leacox with recent additions Mike Woods (lead guitar), Jim Calire (keyboards, sax) and Tom Walsh (percussion).
Apr [21] *California Dreamin'*, from the film "California Dreaming", peaks at US #56.
July [28] *Silent Letter* makes US #110. (It will be the final collaboration with Martin.)

1980 **Sept** [20] *Alibi*, recorded with new production team of Matthew McCauley and Fred Mollin and with help from Timothy B. Schmit, J.D. Souther and Steve Lukather among others, peaks at US #142.

1982 **Oct** [16] The duo makes a chart comeback with Russ Ballard's *You Can Do Magic*, which hits US #8. It is their first non-original Top 10 hit.
[30] Parent *View From The Ground*, with support from Carl Wilson, Christopher Cross, Timothy B. Schmit, Jeff Porcaro, Steve Lukather and others, makes US #41. (Beckley and Bunnell are now writing songs with Bill Mumy, best known to TV audiences as William Robinson in 60s series "Lost In Space".)
Nov [13] *You Can Do Magic* peaks at UK #59.

1983 **Jan** [15] *Right Before Your Eyes*, produced by Bobby Colomby, makes US #45.
July *Your Move*, produced by Ballard, makes US #81.
Aug [6] *The Border*, with the distinctive sax of Raphael Ravenscroft, makes US #33, after which America's chart successes cease.

1984 **Nov** *Perspective*, using 3 different producers and with material penned with Journey's Steve Perry and Jimmy Webb (for whom Beckley and Bunnell have been featured vocalists on his soundtrack for animated feature "The Last Unicorn"), peaks at US #185.

1985 **June** [1] A performance at the Arlington theater, Santa Barbara, CA, is recorded for future *America In Concert* release. It will be America's last album, but they will continue regular US tours, their soft-rock sound remaining in vogue in the live arena.

LAURIE ANDERSON

1972 After years studying violin and playing in Chicago Youth Symphony, graduating with degree in art history from Barnard College and earning her master of fine arts in sculpture from Columbia University,

multi-media artist Anderson (b. June 5, 1947, Chicago, IL), begins giving public performances of her work, combining music with mime, speech, graphics, film, sculpture and slides, making her debut performance with "Automotive" on the town green at Rochester, VT, with the townsfolk beeping car, truck and motorcycle horns.

1974 She performs on the 59th Street Bridge in New York, playing the violin while wearing skates embedded in blocks of ice.

1976 She reaches international audiences via museum, festival and concert performances in Europe.

1981 **May** She records 8-min. monotone-backed *O Superman* (an extract from 7-hour work "United States"), selling an initial 1,000 copies by mail order from her Canal Street loft, then as a limited edition of 5,000 for New York independent label, One Ten.
Aug *O Superman* is picked up by Warner Bros., which then signs her to an album contract.
Oct [24] Despite *O Superman*'s length, its odd electronically-treated vocal and atmospheric style secure it UK airplay and it quickly charts, hitting #2. Similar success follows around Europe, though mainstream US radio finds it too alternative.

1982 **May** *Big Science* is released, making UK #29 and US #124.

1983 **Feb** "America", 7 hours long and in 4 parts, premieres in US. (Anderson continues with her avant-garde work, but rarely surfaces in the mainstream rock scene.)

1984 **Mar** *Mister Heartbreak*, a collaboration with Peter Gabriel, peaks at UK #93 and US #60.

1985 **Jan** *United States Live*, recorded at the Brooklyn Academy of Music in Feb.1983, makes US #192.

1986 **May** *Home Of The Brave*, the soundtrack from an Anderson performance film, with contributions from William Burroughs, Bill Laswell and Nile Rodgers, peaks at US #150.

1989 **Nov** *Strange Angels* peaks at US #171, Anderson having recently premiered "Empty Places" at the Brooklyn Academy of Music and embraced the mainstream, filming an ad for Reebok shoes.

1990 **Feb** [7] She embarks on "Strange Angels" North American tour in Tempe, AZ.

THE ANIMALS
Eric Burdon (vocals)
Alan Price (keyboards)
Hilton Valentine (guitar)
Chas Chandler (bass)
John Steel (drums)

1962 Burdon (b. May 11, 1941, during an air-raid in Walker, Newcastle, Tyne & Wear) joins The Alan Price Combo, Newcastle-based group playing R&B and rock'n'roll. Price (b. Apr.19, 1941, Fairfield, Durham) has formed the band in 1960 as The Alan Price Trio with Chandler (b. Bryan James Chandler, Dec.18, 1938, Heaton, Tyne & Wear), with whom Price has briefly played in The Kansas City Five, before they name-change to The Kontors, and Steel (b. Feb.4, 1941, Gateshead, Tyne & Wear), who has worked in the DeHavilland Aircraft factory in the South, before heading back to Newcastle to join the band. Price had sat in with Burdon's group The Pagans formed at Newcastle's College of Art & Industrial Design. Valentine (b. May 21, 1943, North Shields, Tyne & Wear) from Whiteley Bay's The Wild Cats is invited to complete the line-up. They gain a regular slot at Newcastle's Downbeat club and legend has it that local fans call them "the animals" because of their notoriously wild stage act. (Claims are also made that the group in fact gets its name from an army veteran known as "Animal Hog", who ran a gang, which Burdon and Steel were on the fringes of.)

1963 **May** Group begins 2-month stint at Hamburg's Star club, Germany.
Dec They record a demo EP for fans, pressing 500 copies which are all sold. The disk is heard in London, leading to work offers in the capital.
[27] Group makes its first radio broadcast on BBC's "Saturday Club".
[30] At one of the group's last appearances at Newcastle's Club A-Go-Go, they back US bluesman Sonny Boy Williamson. (In earlier times they have backed John Lee Hooker and Memphis Slim.)

1964 **Jan** Group moves to London, and signs with emerging record producer Mickie Most, who has seen them at Club A-Go-Go and interests EMI Records in them.
May [2] First single *Baby Let Me Take You Home*, an R&B adaptation of blues *Baby Don't You Tear My Clothes*, is released in UK on EMI's Columbia label, and reaches #21.
[9] They begin a 21-date twice-nightly UK tour, with Chuck Berry, The Swinging Blue Jeans, The Nashville Teens, Karl Denver and others, at

Finsbury Park Astoria, London, ending May 29 at the Odeon cinema, Southend, Essex.

June [2] Group begins a 10-day tour of Japan.

July [11] *House Of The Rising Sun*, a Price rearrangement of a traditional folk-blues, is almost not issued when EMI argues that its length (4½ mins.) will prevent radio play, but Most and the group prevail. It knocks Roy Orbison's *It's Over* off the top spot, where it stays for 1 week.

Sept [5] *House Of The Rising Sun* is issued (in shortened form) in US by MGM Records, and shoots to hit #1 in 5 weeks, replacing The Supremes' *Where Did Our Love Go*, and selling over a million copies.

[14] Group begins its first US tour in York, PA.

[26] *Baby Let Me Take You Home*, previously unsuccessful in US, is reissued after *Rising Sun*'s success, but it is B-side *Gonna Send You Back To Walker*, a cover of Timmy Shaw's US R&B #41 *Gonna Send You Back To Georgia* retitled geographically to signify Burdon's birthplace, which becomes a US chart entry, peaking at #57.

Oct [10] *I'm Crying*, penned by Price and Burdon, hits UK #8.

[18] Group makes its debut on US TV's "Ed Sullivan Show".

[19] They begin 28-date twice-nightly tour with Carl Perkins, The Nashville Teens and Elkie Brooks, at the Odeon cinema, Liverpool, Merseyside, ending Nov.15 at Bournemouth's Winter Gardens, Dorset.

Nov [7] *I'm Crying* reaches US #19.

Debut album, *The Animals* hits UK #6 and US #7 while *House Of The Rising Sun* is voted Best Disc Of The Year in **New Musical Express** poll.

Dec Group plays a 9-day tour behind the Iron Curtain.

1965 Jan [9] Released in US as a single, a revival of John Lee Hooker's *Boom Boom* makes #43.

[22] As the group prepares to go on stage at the Harlem Apollo to record planned live album *The Animals At The Apollo*, the US Immigration Department orders the cancellation of the shows.

[30] They guest in the first afternoon edition of UK BBC Light Programme's "Top Gear".

Feb [27] A cover of Nina Simone's *Don't Let Me Be Misunderstood*, hits UK #3. Their interpretation does not please Ms. Simone, however.

Apr [3] *Don't Let Me Be Misunderstood* reaches US #15.

[11] Band participates in the **New Musical Express** annual Poll Winners Concert at the Empire Pool, Wembley, London.

[16] Group begins a Caribbean tour in San Domingo.

[18] Film "Pop Gear" with The Beatles, Billy J. Kramer & The Dakotas, Herman's Hermits and The Rockin' Berries goes on general UK release.

[29] A 7-day tour of Scandinavia begins, without Price, who is ill.

May [5] Due to growing musical disagreement with Burdon, and a dislike of flying which has made US tours anathema to him, Price announces he is leaving.

[7] A cover of Sam Cooke's *Bring It On Home To Me* hits UK #7.

[8] Band returns from the Scandinavian tour, where Mickey Gallagher, previously with The Unknowns, has filled in for Price. Dave Rowberry (b. Dec.27 1943, Newcastle), from The Mike Cotton Sound, takes Price's place full-time.

[30] Group appears on CBS TV's "Ed Sullivan Show" at conclusion of 10-day US trip.

June *Animal Tracks* hits UK #6.

[12] *Bring It On Home To Me* makes US #32 as US-only *The Animals On Tour* peaks at #99.

July [16] The Alan Price Combo, comprising Boots Slade (bass), Roy Mills (drums), John Walters (trumpet), Terry Childs (baritone sax), Steve Gregor (tenor sax) and Pete Kirtley (guitar), takes up residency at Newcastle's Club A-Go-Go, and signs with Decca.

Aug [7] *We've Gotta Get Out Of This Place*, an original Barry Mann/Cynthia Weil song, hits UK #2.

[8] The Animals play the last day of the fifth annual Jazz & Blues Festival at the Athletic Ground, Richmond, London.

[12] Burdon and Chandler both collapse while performing on "Ready Steady Go!".

[27] Price debut single, *Any Day Now*, credited to The Alan Price Set, is released on Decca.

[25] *We've Gotta Get Out Of This Place* reaches US #13.

Oct *Animal Tracks* makes US #57.

Nov [13] *It's My Life* hits UK #7.

1966 Jan [1] *It's My Life* reaches US #23.

Burdon refuses to re-sign the group's contract with Mickie Most and EMI because of unhappiness over the material on offer. Group switches to new producer Tom Wilson, and Decca Records. The US agreement with MGM is unaffected.

Feb Decca debut *Inside Looking Out*, based on a Mississippi prison

song, and aired on "Ready Steady Go!" under the title *Rosie* (Burdon and Chandler will subsequently rewrite the lyrics) reaches UK #12. Steel announces his intention to leave the band, returning to Newcastle where he will become a successful businessman. Newspaper reports say names being suggested as his replacement are The Who's Keith Moon, Viv Prince, formerly with The Pretty Things and The Nashville Teens' Barry Jenkins. Jenkins (b. Dec.22, 1944, Leicester, Leics.) gets the job, earning £100 a week for 3 months and then a percentage.

[28] The Animals headline at the opening of Tiles club in London's Oxford Street.

Mar Compilation *The Best Of The Animals* hits US #6, the group's best-selling US album, remaining charted for 113 weeks.

[5] Steel makes final appearance with the group at Birmingham University, W.Midlands.

[15] Jenkins debuts with The Animals at the Paris Olympia, France.

Apr [2] *Inside Looking Out* makes US #34.

[13] Group's fifth US tour opens at the Washington Boat Show, Washington, DC, ending May 4 at Indianapolis State Fair, IN.

May *The Most Of The Animals*, released in UK by EMI, anthologizes the Mickie Most-produced singles up to *It's My Life*. It hits #4.

June Gerry Goffin/Carole King song *Don't Bring Me Down* hits UK #6. *Animalisms* hits UK #4.

[4] Scheduled to fly to Spain, the group stays in UK to resolve differences which threaten a split.

July [1] Group begins a US tour, with Herman's Hermits, Jerry Lee Lewis and Lou Christie, in Honolulu, HI.

[2] *Don't Bring Me Down* reaches US #12.

Sept A widening split between Burdon and the others (he is getting heavily involved with LSD, they are not) prompts the group to split at the end of a US tour. Jenkins remains with Burdon to form the nucleus of a new group, while the others go their separate ways.

Oct [20] The Animals, now comprising Burdon, Jenkins, John Weider, ex-Family, (b. Apr.21, 1947, London) on lead guitar, Danny McCullough (b. July 18, 1945, London) on bass and Tom Parker on organ, embarks on 16-date twice-nightly UK tour as special guests, with Georgie Fame & The Georgie Fame Band, Chris Farlowe, Geno Washington & The Ram Jam Band and The Butterfield Blues Band, at Finsbury Park Astoria, London. Tour ends Nov.6 at the Odeon cinema, Leicester, Leics.

[22] The last single by the original group, but credited to Eric Burdon & The Animals, *See See Rider*, reviving Ma Rainey's 1925 hit, is only issued in US, and ironically is one of their biggest hits, hitting #10. *Animalization* (also not issued in UK) reaches US #20.

Nov *Help Me Girl*, credited to Eric Burdon & The Animals (though it is actually recorded by Burdon in New York with session players, led by jazzman Benny Golson), reaches UK #14.

Dec [31] *Help Me Girl* reaches US #29.

1967 Jan The original group's final album *Animalisms*, partly recorded on the last US tour (and mostly featuring blues and R&B standards) is belatedly released in US and reaches #33. Meanwhile, Burdon relocates to California with his new Animals, with Vic Briggs, ex-Brian Auger & The Trinity (b. Feb.14, 1945, Twickenham, London), joining on guitar but without Parker. This group is signed to MGM for the UK and US.

Feb [10] North American tour starts at Hunter College, New York.

Mar [1] Fans stage a riot at the Coliseum, Ottawa, Canada, while waiting over an hour for the group to appear. Band fails to play at all.

Apr A Burdon solo album, *Eric Is Here*, recorded at the same time as *Help Me Girl*, is issued in US, and reaches #121.

[11] Group embarks on tour of New Zealand, Australia, Singapore and Hong Kong, with Dave Dee, Dozy, Beaky, Mick & Tich and Paul & Barry Ryan, in Christchurch, New Zealand. (The Mothers Of Invention's Roy Estrada fills in for McCullough, who is unable to play after breaking his wrist.)

May [6] First release by the new group, with producer Tom Wilson, is *When I Was Young*, which eschews the traditional Animals R&B sound in favor of psychedelic-flavored hard rock, showing the influence on Burdon of the burgeoning US West Coast scene, and reaching US #15.

[25] Band attends premiere of James Mason/Bobby Darin film "Stranger In The House", in which they perform *Ain't That So*.

June *When I Was Young* makes UK #45.

July Compilation *The Best Of Eric Burdon & The Animals, Vol.2* makes US #71.

Sept [16] *San Franciscan Nights*, celebrating Burdon's new lifestyle, hits US #9; *Good Times*, berating his hard-drinking past, makes UK #20.

[24] Group makes its cabaret debut at the Stockton Fiesta.

Nov *San Franciscan Nights* hits UK #7, while *Winds Of Change*, a

968 Jan [13] *Monterey*, a tribute to the 1967 Monterey Pop Festival, reaches US #15.

Feb 2-part single *Sky Pilot*, a controversial attack on the complacency of religion in the face of war (and on which Weider experiments with electric violin), makes UK #40.

Apr [27] *Anything* climbs to US #80.

May *The Twain Shall Meet* makes US #79.

June Briggs and McCulloch leave, replaced by ex-Big Roll Band and Dantalian's Chariot members, Zoot Money (keyboards) and Andy Summers (guitar). The band becomes Eric Burdon & The New Animals.

July [27] *Sky Pilot* reaches US #14.

Sept *Every One Of Us* reaches US #152.

Dec [28] *White Houses*, the band's final US chart single, peaks at #67 as Burdon announces, at the end of US and Japanese tours, that they will disband after a Christmas concert in his home city of Newcastle. (Weider and Jenkins announce they will form Bicycle with members of The Grass Roots, but nothing comes of it. Jenkins joins Heavy Jelly with Jackie Lomax. Briggs and McCulloch make *Mr. Moon And Mr. Sun*.)

969 Jan As group winds up, a revival of Johnny Cash's *Ring Of Fire* gives it a further UK chart entry, at #35.

Feb Double album *Love Is* peaks at US #123 after the group has split.

Apr Compilation *The Greatest Hits Of Eric Burdon & The Animals* makes US #153.

970 Jan Now in Los Angeles, CA, with more interest in looking for movie parts than forming another band, Burdon (at producer Jerry Goldstein's suggestion), teams up with Night Shift, a heavy funk band from Long Beach, CA, which changes its name to War. They record together, and tour US.

971 Jan Eric Burdon & War begin a European tour, only to have Burdon, suffering from exhaustion, quit midway through and return to US. War continues the tour without him (and will quickly develop into one of the most successful US funk bands of the 70s). When he recovers, Burdon devotes his energy to fulfilling an ambition, and records *Guilty* with blues singer Jimmy Witherspoon. (They will team up again in 1976 for *Black & White Blues*, released on MCA.)

Oct Retrospective budget album *Most Of The Animals* makes UK #18.

972 Oct *House Of The Rising Sun* is reissued in UK on Mickie Most's RAK label, and is a best-seller again, reaching #25.

973 Aug [23] Burdon performs at Reading Festival, Berks., with a new back-up trio comprising Aaron Butler (guitar), Randy Rice (bass) and Alvin Taylor (drums).

The Best Of The Animals peaks at US #188.

974 Oct Still living in California, Burdon and wife Rose have a daughter, Mirage, born in Palm Springs.

975 Jan With Burdon now signed to Capitol Records with his recent live group as The Eric Burdon Band, *Sun Secrets* reaches US #51.

Aug Second Eric Burdon album *Stop* (with a different line-up) sells less well, peaking at US #171, and the band splits.

976 Jan The original 5 Animals get together to play for fun at Chandler's house; their rapport is such they hire a mobile studio to cut an album.

977 Mar Chandler produces Burdon solo *Survivor*, mostly co-written by the singer and ex-New Animals keyboard player Zoot Money, for Polydor in Germany. Released in UK the next year, it will not chart.

Aug *Before We Were So Rudely Interrupted*, credited to The Original Animals, is taken from the previous year's reunion session, is issued on Chandler's Barn label. It fails to chart in UK, but climbs to US #70, where it is issued on the Jet label.

982 Oct [23] *House Of The Rising Sun* has its second, and still more successful, reissue in UK, reaching #11.

983 July The original quintet regroups again for *Ark* on IRS Records. It does not chart in UK.

Aug Group embarks on a lucrative worldwide tour. The liaison is not intended as a permanent arrangement, but as a series of reunions because of proven popular appeal.

Sept [24] *The Night*, from *Ark*, makes US #48 while album reaches #66.

Dec [31] *Rip It To Shreds : The Animals Greatest Hits Live* is recorded at Wembley Arena, London, by the reunited line-up, but fails to chart in UK, and only reaches US #193. The Animals split again after this (though will reunite sporadically for specific live commitments, particularly in US.)

986 Burdon's autobiography **I Used To Be An Animal, But I'm Alright Now** is published.

990 Burdon tours US with The Doors' Robby Krieger during the summer, after an active period, releasing his own *Wicked Man* in 1988, guesting on Paul Shaffer's *Coast To Coast*, singing *Sixteen Tons* in the opening

scene of Tom Hanks/Meg Ryan movie "Joe Versus The Volcano" and making a cameo appearance on ABC TV's "China Beach".

PAUL ANKA

1956 July Already an experienced part-time entertainer, he has made his first public appearance at age 10 and earned $35 impersonating Johnnie Ray in an amateur talent contest in 1953 at Ocean Beach club in Gloucester, MA, and budding songwriter while still at high school, Anka (b. July 30, 1941, Ottawa, Ontario, Canada), son of Lebanese immigrant restaurateurs Andy and Camy Anka, spends the summer vacation away from his family's restaurant, staying with his uncle Maurice in Los Angeles, CA, working at the Civic Playhouse in an attempt to break into show business.

Sept He takes his composition, *I Confess*, to nearby Modern Records, whose A&R chief Ernie Freeman records it, backed by the label's *Stranded In The Jungle* hitmakers The Cadets. The disk sells 3,000 copies.

Oct Back at Fisher Park high school in Ottawa, he forms The Bobby-soxers vocal trio with 2 classmates, and begins work on *Diana*, a song inspired by the family's 18-year-old babysitter Diana Ayoub, for whom the 15-year-old Anka has a passion.

1957 Apr He wins an Easter trip to New York in a grocery store contest in which he collects more Campbell's Soup can labels than anyone else. Impressed by the city, he borrows $100 from his father to make a return visit with 4 songs he has committed to tape. Staying with friends The Rover Boys (who are signed to Paramount Records), he visits, at their suggestion, Don Costa at ABC Records who signs him to Parmount, impressed by his (then rare) singer/songwriter abilities.

Aug [30] *Diana* is an immediate UK hit, topping the chart within a month of release, and staying there for 9 weeks. Worldwide sales will top 9 million and it becomes one of the top 5 selling records of all time.

Sept [1] Anka begins "The Biggest Show Of Stars For 1957" package tour with Buddy Holly & The Crickets, Chuck Berry, The Drifters, Frankie Lymon & The Teenagers, The Everly Brothers, Clyde McPhatter and others, at the Brooklyn Paramount theater. The tour will end on Nov.24 at the Mosque, Richmond, VA. (The white artists on the bill are unable to play on several dates because of segregation laws which forbid black and white acts on the same stage.)

[9] *Diana* tops US chart, replacing Debbie Reynolds' *Tammy*.

Nov *I Love You Baby* hits UK #3, helped by a successful "Sunday Night At The London Palladium" TV spot, and a UK, Europe and Australia tour. Its B-side, *Tell Me That You Love Me*, reaches UK #25.

Dec [7] Anka begins his first UK tour at London's Trocadero theater.

[16] *I Love You Baby* peaks at US #97.

1958 Jan Anka begins 6-day tour of Australia, playing Melbourne, Sydney and Brisbane, with Buddy Holly & The Crickets and Jerry Lee Lewis.

Feb [24] *You Are My Destiny* hits US #7 and UK #6.

Mar He visits UK for second time.

May [5] *Crazy Love* makes US #15.

[19] B-side *Let The Bells Keep Ringing* reaches US #18.

[30] *Crazy Love* reaches UK #26.

Aug [18] *Midnight* peaks at US #69.

Sept [26] *Midnight* reaches UK #26.

Oct Anka gives *It Doesn't Matter Anymore* to Buddy Holly, who has expressed interest in recording an Anka song. It will become a 1959 posthumous UK #1 and US #14 for Holly.

[20] *Just Young* peaks at US #80.

1959 Jan [5] *The Teen Commandments*, with George Hamilton IV and Johnny Nash, reaches US #29, while Anka tours UK again.

Feb [2] Standard *(All Of A Sudden) My Heart Sings*, originally a hit for both Johnnie Johnson and Martha Stewart in 1945, reaches US #15. *(All Of A Sudden) My Heart Sings* hits UK #10.

Mar He makes his first Hollywood movie, "Girls Town", with Mamie Van Doren and Mel Torme and will go on to make others including "The Private Lives Of Adam & Eve", "Look In Any Window" and "The Longest Day", writing song themes for them all.

Apr [27] *I Miss You So* makes US #33.

July [13] Self-penned *Lonely Boy*, from "Girls Town", tops US chart for 4 weeks.

Lonely Boy hits UK #3.

Aug Anka makes his first nightclub appearance, at Sahara hotel, Las Vegas, NV.

Oct [5] *Put Your Head On My Shoulder* is a million-seller, hitting US #2 and UK #7.

Dec [28] *It's Time To Cry* hits US #4.

1960 Feb [26] *It's Time To Cry* reaches UK #28.

PAUL ANKA cont.

Apr [4] *Puppy Love*, written about Annette Funicello, hits US #2, behind Percy Faith's *Theme From A Summer Place*, and makes UK #33.
[11] *Adam And Eve*, the B-side of *Puppy Love*, peaks at US #90.
June He becomes the youngest performer to star at New York's Copacabana nightclub.
[27] *Something Happened, My Home Town* B-side, makes US #41.
July [4] *My Home Town* hits US #8, as *Paul Anka Sings His Big 15* makes its chart bow. It will hit US #4, during a 140-week chart-stay.
Sept [5] *Hello Young Lovers* reaches US #23.
[12] B-side *I Love You In The Same Old Way* makes US #40.
[19] *Hello Young Lovers* makes UK #44.
Oct [31] *Summer's Gone* reaches US #11.
Dec *Anka At The Copa* reaches US #23.

1961 Feb [20] *The Story Of My Love* peaks at US #16.
May [1] *Tonight My Love, Tonight* reaches US #13.
July [10] *Dance On Little Girl* hits US #10.
Aug Anka tapes TV spectacular for UK Granada TV.
Sept [11] *Kissin' On The Phone* makes US #35.
Oct [9] *Kissin'* B-side, *Cinderella* peaks at US #70.
Paul Anka Sings His Big 15, Vol.2 makes US #72.
Nov [13] ABC Paramount agrees to terminate his contract early. A week later he will sign a million-dollar contract with RCA.

1962 Apr [7] First RCA release *Love Me Warm And Tender* reaches US #12, and restores Anka to UK chart at #19.
May *Young, Alive And In Love!* makes US #61.
July [7] *A Steel Guitar And A Glass Of Wine* makes US #13 and UK #41.
Aug [25] Paramount single, *I'm Coming Home*, stalls at US #94.
Sept [22] *Every Night (Without You)* makes US #46 as *Let's Sit This One Out* climbs to US #137.
Oct [2] NBC TV airs the first "Tonight" show, for which Anka writes the theme, with host Johnny Carson.
[12] "The Longest Day", for which Anka writes the theme and in which he is one of the many stars, opens at the Leicester Square theater, London.
Dec [8] The Bossa Nova craze is briefly acknowledged with Latin-tempoed *Eso Beso (That Kiss)*, a US #19.

1963 Feb [16] Anka marries Marie Ann Alison DeZogheb, daughter of Count Charles DeZogheb, a Lebanese businessman, in a chapel at Orly Airport, near Paris, France. (They met in Puerto Rico.)
[16] *Love (Makes The World Go 'Round)* reaches US #26.
May [25] Anka-penned *Remember Diana*, sequel to his first hit, peaks at US #39.
June [29] *Hello Jim* stalls at US #97.
July [6] *Paul Anka's Golden Hits*, a re-recorded version of his ABC Paramount hits, begins a 33-week US chart stay, although never reaching higher than #65.
Dec [7] The Beatles, appearing on BBC TV show "Juke Box Jury", vote Anka's new single *Did You Have A Happy Birthday?* a miss.
[14] *Did You Have A Happy Birthday?* stalls at US #89.

1964 May [17] Anka guests on the "Ed Sullivan Show".
Nov [9] He arrives in London with his wife for a 2-week stay to meet UK songwriters and TV producers.

1965 Jan [16] Anka returns to UK, a day after the release of the Burt Bacharach-penned *To Wait For Love*, his first single recorded in UK. His UK TV appearances include ITV's "The Eamonn Andrews Show" and BBC TV's "Juke Box Jury".

1969 Feb [22] Following a quieter 3-year period during which he can assess his favorable financial position in between selected cabaret and film work, *Goodnight My Love* reaches US #27.
Mar *Goodnight My Love*, Anka's first chart album in 5 years, makes US #101.
Apr [19] *In The Still Of The Night* peaks at US #64.
May [10] Frank Sinatra reaches US #27 with *My Way*, a Claude Francois original called *Comme D'Habitude* onto which Anka has transposed English lyrics. It becomes Sinatra's new signature tune, even though the first attempt at over-writing English lyrics on the French standard was actually made by David Bowie.
My Way hits UK #4.
June [21] *Sincerely* reaches US #80.
Dec [6] *Happy* stalls at US #86.
[27] *Life Goes On* makes US #194 during a 2-week chart stay.

1971 Jan Anka's *She's A Lady*, is a UK #12 hit for Tom Jones, and hits US #2 where it sells a million.
Nov [27] Anka, newly signed to Buddah Records peaks at US #53 with *Do I Love You?*

1972 Jan Buddah album debut *Paul Anka* climbs to US #188.

May [6] *Jubilation*, from his forthcoming album, peaks at US #65.
June *Jubilation* makes US #192.

1973 June [20] Anka sings *Put Your Head On My Shoulder* on "American Bandstand's 20th Anniversary Special".

1974 Feb [16] *Let Me Get To Know You*, a one-off hit on the Fame label, stalls at US #80.
Aug [24] *You're Having My Baby*, a duet with protegee Odia Coates, whom Anka had met when producing The Edwin Hawkins Singers' *Oh Happy Day*, tops US chart, and is a million-seller. (Written about his wife's pregnancy, it nonetheless brings the ire of the National Organization Of Women, who present him their "Keep Her In Her Place" award.)
Anka hits US #9, and is his first RIAA certified gold album.
Oct [26] *You're Having My Baby* hits UK #6.
Dec *Paul Anka Gold*, a Sire release of original ABC Paramount hits, makes US #125.

1975 Jan [25] *One Man Woman/One Woman Man*, a second duet with Coates, hits US #7.
May [24] Solo *I Don't Like To Sleep Alone* hits US #8. Parent album *Feelings* reaches US #36.
Sept [27] Third duet with Coates, *(I Believe) There's Nothing Stronger Than Our Love*, reaches US #15.

1976 Feb [7] Solo *Times Of Your Life* hits US #7, helped by exposure as the tune to a Kodak TV commercial, and is Anka's final Top 10 hit.
[28] *Times Of Your Life*, featuring the hit and 9 tracks from his previous 2 United Artists albums, makes US #22.
May [15] *Anytime (I'll Be There)* reaches US #33.
Dec [25] *The Painter* makes US #85.

1977 Jan [22] *Happier* peaks at US #60.
May [7] *My Best Friend's Wife* stalls at US #80.
June *The Music Man* climbs to US #195.
Aug [6] *Everybody Ought To Be In Love* peaks at US #75.

1978 Dec [2] Now re-signed to RCA, Anka makes US #35 with *This Is Love*, from upcoming album *Listen To Your Heart*.
[9] *Listen To Your Heart*, David Wolfert-produced, peaks at US #179.

1981 May [23] *I've Been Waiting For You All Of My Life* makes US #48.
June *Both Sides Of Love* climbs to US #171.

1983 Sept [3] Signing to CBS/Columbia Records brings Anka a latter-day US success with *Hold Me 'Til The Mornin' Comes*, penned with compatriot David Foster and with backing vocals by Peter Cetera, reaching US #40.
Parent album *Walk A Fine Line* makes US #156.
Based in Las Vegas, with his wife and daughters, Anka will continue playing cabaret dates there and at Lake Tahoe, NV.

1990 Jan [17] Anka inducts the late Bobby Darin into the Rock'N'Roll Hall Of Fame at the fifth annual dinner at the Waldorf Astoria, New York.
Aug [30] Anka receives his certificate of US citizenship with 54 other people during a federal court ceremony in Las Vegas. (He parks his car in a US Immigration and Naturalization Service parking bay and has it towed away.)

1991 Feb [10] Anka joins with 100 celebrities in Burbank, CA, to record *Voices That Care*, a David Foster and fiancee Linda Thompson Jenner composed and organized charity record to benefit the American Red Cross Gulf Crisis Fund.

ANTHRAX

Joey Belladonna (vocals)
Dan Spitz (guitar)
Scott "Not" Ian (guitar)
Frank Bello (bass)
Charlie Benante (drums)

1981 July Band is initially formed in New York with Dan Lilker on bass and Neil Turbin handling vocals. The members are drawn together by their mutual interest in hardcore thrash heavy metal music, comics and skateboarding. (Spitz' older brother David played in Black Sabbath and Bello (b. July 9, 1965) came to live with Benante's family.)

1982 Hectic small-town touring throughout US occupies most of the year.

1983 May Band meets Johnny Z, who signs them to his Megaforce label and releases *Soldiers Of Metal*. They tour further, supporting Manowar and Metallica.

1984 Feb *Fistful Of Metal* is released on Megaforce in US, and licensed to Music For Nations in Europe. The album is notable for some of the fastest metal riff music ever heard, but is not successful.
As they tour continuously in US, Ian forms the concurrent splinter group Stormtroopers Of Death (SOD), to play even faster thrash. SOD's

Speak Of English Or Die is released. Lilker leaves, later joining Nuclear Assault, and the group's roadie Bello becomes their permanent bassist.
Aug [12] Working on EP *Among The Living* in Ithaca, NY, Ian fires singer Turbin. He is temporarily replaced by Matt Fallon, who is in turn replaced by Belladonna (b. Oct.30, Oswego, NY), singer with Bible Black from Oswego, and his range and power give a new polished focus to their recordings.

985 Feb *Armed And Dangerous*, a 5-track mini-album recorded at Pyramid studios in New York, includes a revival of The Sex Pistols' *God Save The Queen*, and inspires interest from Island Records' US division, which signs the band to record its second album, with producer Carl Canedy, again in New York.

986 Feb *Spreading The Disease* is released, with Music For Nations again picking up the European license. *Madhouse*, taken from it, is reissued several times in the ensuing months.
June Band makes its UK debut at London's Hammersmith Palais supporting Onslaught, followed by a European and Scandinavian tour supporting Metallica.
Spreading The Disease makes US #113.
Nov [16-17] They play 2 sell-out shows at the Hammersmith Odeon, London.
The latter part of the year and early 1987 is spent in Miami and the Bahamas recording a third album with producer Eddie Kramer.

987 Feb [15] Group plays a sell-out date at Hammersmith Odeon.
Mar *I Am The Law*, first release from the new album, is their UK chart debut at #32.
May *Among The Living* receives critical acclaim, charting at UK #18, and will make US #62, the group's first gold album.
June *Indians* makes UK #44.
Nov 2 sell-out dates at London's Hammersmith Odeon confirm Anthrax as a major international force in heavy metal rock.
Dec *I'm The Man* reaches UK #20.

988 *I'm The Man*, 3 tracks of which are live recordings from a gig in Dallas in July 1987, makes US #53.
Aug Group takes part in annual Monsters Of Rock Festival at Castle Donington, Leics.
Sept *Make Me Laugh* reaches UK #26 as parent album *State Of Euphoria* reaches UK #12 and US #30, the group's second gold album.
Dec [8] US tour begins at Meadowlands, East Rutherford, NJ, set to end Dec.27 at the Arizona Veterans Memorial Coliseum & State Fairgrounds, Phoenix, AZ.

989 Mar [8] Group begins 6-date UK tour at the Apollo theater, Manchester, Gtr.Manchester, ending at London's Hammersmith Odeon, as *Anti-Social* makes UK #44.

990 Jan [24] Band's rehearsal studios in Yonkers, NY, catch fire, causing more than $100,000 worth of damages to the group's equipment.
Aug [27] Group begins tour of Australia at Thebarton, Adelaide.
Sept [8] *Persistence Of Time* debuts UK chart at #13, its peak position.
[22] *Persistence Of Time* reaches US #24.
Oct [21] Anthrax supports Iron Maiden on the latter's "No Prayer On The Road" tour beginning in Barcelona, Spain. They stay with the tour through to London's Wembley Arena concert on Dec.18.

991 Jan [12] *Got The Time* reaches UK #16.
[13] 33 US tour dates, again supporting Iron Maiden, begin at the Metro center, Halifax, Canada, set to end at the Cow Palace, San Francisco, CA, on Mar.14, though Anthrax continues for further concerts without Iron Maiden. (During the tour, Belladonna will sing the national anthem at the US Hot Rod Mud & Monster Truck Racing Championships at Madison Square Garden, New York.)
Feb [20] *Persistence Of Time* is nominated for Best Metal Performance at 33rd annual Grammy awards at Radio City Music Hall, New York.

HE ARCHIES

rchie Andrews (vocals, lead guitar)
ughead Jones (bass guitar)
eronica Lodge (organ)
etty Cooper (tambourine)
eggie (drums)
ot Dog (mascot)

967 CBS TV commissions Filmation studios to create animated Saturday morning show featuring The Archies, a fictional rock group based on the comic book characters originated by John Goldwater in 1942. Don Kirshner is recruited to supervise the music. He hires Jeff Barry to produce, who recruits his wife Ellie Greenwich, Toni Wine, Andy Kim, Tony Passalacqua and Ron Dante (b.Carmine Granito, Aug.22, 1945,

Staten Island, New York, NY). Archie comic books publish **The Music Man** showing the group auditioning for Kirshner. (Cartoonist Bob Montana claims The Archies are his invention and based on people he studied with at Haverhill high school, MA.)

1968 Sept The first "Archies" song, *Bang-Shang-A-Lang* (which launches the cartoon show) is recorded with Dante on lead vocals. His voice becomes identified as The Archies' sound, even though he is never actually seen performing. Greenwich joins in on vocals.
[14] "The Archies" airs for the first time on US TV. (The second series will be renamed "The Archies Comedy Hour".)
Dec [7] Jeff Barry-penned *Bang-Shang-A-Lang* released on Calendar label, reaches US #22, as parent album **The Archies** makes US #88.

1969 Feb [1] *Feelin' So Good (Skooby-Doo)*, written by Barry with Kim and with the same vocal pairing as its predecessor, peaks at US #53.
Sept [20] *Sugar Sugar*, also written by Barry and Kim and sung by Dante with Wine, tops US chart for 4 weeks, displacing The Rolling Stones' *Honky Tonk Women*. It will become the biggest worldwide seller of 1969, with over 6 million copies sold. Parent album *Everything's Archie* makes US #66.
Oct [25] Despite Archie cartoons being unknown in UK, *Sugar Sugar* is released; it tops UK chart for 8 weeks, selling over 900,000 copies.

1970 Feb [7] *Jingle Jangle*, the first single on the Kirshner label, once again written by Barry and Kim and sung as a duet by Dante and Wine, hits US #10 and is another million-seller. *Jingle Jangle* makes US #125.
Mar Princess Anne presents Don Kirshner with Carl-Alan award for *Sugar Sugar* as Best Tune Of 1969.
[28] *Who's Your Baby*, penned by Barry and Kim, makes US #40.
July [4] Wilson Pickett's version of *Sugar Sugar* reaches US #25.
Aug [1] *Sunshine*, penned by Barry, peaks at US #57, as *Sunshine* makes US #137.
Nov *The Archies Greatest Hits* reaches US #114.

1971 Last Barry-penned single, *A Summer Prayer For Peace*, is released. The cartoon series continues as "Archie's TV Funnies" with no music at all. (Dante, having formed his own studio group The Cuff Links, hitting both US and UK Top 10 with *Tracy*, will have his greatest successes in the 70s, producing several Barry Manilow albums, before becoming a successful Broadway theater producer, most notably with "Ain't Misbehavin'" and "They're Playing Our Song". In 1975 he will release a new version of *Sugar Sugar*, produced by Manilow.)

1978 Jan The cartoon series ends. During the height of "Archiemania", the Post Cereal group issued Archies records on the back of cereal boxes and an "Archies" restaurant opened in Joliet, IL, serving pre-teens.

1987 Aug *Sugar Sugar* is rediscovered as a dance novelty by UK clubs and re-charts at #91. It will remain a popular oldie.

JOAN ARMATRADING

1969 Having taught herself to play piano and guitar as a child, writing her first song, "When I Was Young", aged 14, but intending to follow a career in law, Armatrading (b. Dec.9, 1950, Basseterre, St. Kitts, West Indies), the family settling in Birmingham, W.Midlands, in 1958, meets fellow immigrant Pam Nestor (b. Apr.28, 1948, Berbice, Guyana) and begins a songwriting and performing partnership.

1974 A deal with Cube Records results in Gus Dudgeon-produced album *Whatever's For Us*, but Nestor soon leaves, unhappy with her part in the arrangement.

1975 Armatrading signs solo to A&M Records, and begins to write her own lyrics, previously supplied by Nestor.
Apr Peter Gage-produced *Back To The Night* is issued.
Nov [13] Armatrading embarks on 30-date UK tour with Supertramp at Bristol's Colston Hall, Avon. The tour ends Dec.20 at the Kursaal, Southend, Essex.

1976 Oct [23] A collaboration with producer Glyn Johns results in *Joan Armatrading*, which reaches UK #12.
Nov [13] Extracted *Love And Affection*, with distinctive Jimmy Jewel sax solo, hits UK #10.

1977 June [18] *Joan Armatrading* makes US #67.
Oct [1] *Show Some Emotion*, again overseen by Johns, hits UK #6.
Dec [24] *Show Some Emotion* makes US #52.

1978 Controversy rages over Armatrading's decision to write and perform the theme for "The Wild Geese", an action-adventure film about white mercenaries in South Africa.
Oct [28] *To The Limit*, on which Armatrading is backed by labelmates The Movies, reaches UK #13, and introduces a harder, rockier style.
Dec [9] *To The Limit* peaks at US #125.

1980 Jan [19] US-only issued mini-album *How Cruel* makes #136.

JOAN ARMATRADING cont.

Feb *Rosie* makes UK #49.

May [24] Armatrading begins a 17-date UK tour at the Gaumont cinema, Southampton, Hants, to promote new album *Me, Myself, I*. The tour ends June 25 at the Dublin National Stadium, Eire.
[31] Richard Gottehrer-produced *Me, Myself, I* hits UK #5.

Aug [2] Extracted title track, *Me, Myself, I* reaches UK #21.
[9] *Me, Myself, I* reaches US #28.

Sept *All The Way From America* peaks at UK #54.

1981 **Sept** [19] Steve Lilleywhite-produced *Walk Under Ladders* hits UK #6, as extracted *I'm Lucky* makes UK #46.

Nov *Walk Under Ladders* makes UK #88.

Dec [13] 11-date UK tour ends at Hammersmith Odeon, London.

1983 **Jan** [30] *No Love* makes UK #50.

Feb *Drop The Pilot* reaches UK #11.

Apr Lilleywhite-produced *The Key* hits UK #10 and makes US #32.

June [25] *Drop The Pilot* stalls at US #78.

Nov Retrospective greatest hits collection, *Track Record* reaches UK #18 and US #113.

1985 **Feb** Mike Howlett-produced *Secret Secrets* (UK #14, US #73) brings her back to the charts after a lengthy recording absence.

Mar *Temptation* peaks at UK #65.

1986 **May** *Sleight Of Hand*, Armatrading's first self-produced effort, makes UK #34.

June Armatrading performs at the 10th anniversary of the Prince's Trust at Wembley Arena, London.

Aug *Sleight Of Hand* makes US #68.

1988 Armatrading returns to the studio to record new album *The Shouting Stage*, helped by Mark Knopfler and Big Country's Mark Brzezicki.

June [11] She performs at "Nelson Mandela's 70th Birthday Party" concert at Wembley Stadium, London.

Aug She embarks on short US tour.

Sept *The Shouting Stage* reaches UK #28 and US #100.

1990 **May** [26] *More Than One Kind Of Love*, from forthcoming *Hearts And Flowers*, spends a week at UK #75.

June [16] Self-produced *Hearts And Flowers*, recorded at her own home studio, reaches UK #29.

July [8-9] Armatrading plays the Hammersmith Odeon, London, during UK tour to promote new album.
[19] *Hearts And Flowers* peaks at US #161.

Aug [6] Armatrading begins 14-date US tour at SPAC in Saratoga, NY.

1991 **Mar** [4] A second greatest hits compilation, *The Very Best Of Joan Armatrading*, is issued by A&M.

THE ART OF NOISE

Anne Dudley (keyboards)
J.J. Jeczalik (keyboards, programmer)
Gary Langan (engineer)

1984 **Jan** Having met through their individual work as part of Trevor Horn's early 80s production team (creators of hits for ABC, Dollar, Frankie Goes To Hollywood and Malcolm McLaren), the original 3 members, all noted arrangers and producers in their own right, first get together after working on a strenuous session with Yes. (Only Dudley, who was a pianist on BBC TV's "Play School" after leaving college, has had chart success as an artist, teaming with actress Joanne Whalley as Cindy & The Saffrons on a remake of The Shangri-Las' *Past, Present And Future* (UK #56 in Jan.1983). The initial idea (consistently adhered to) is to release original sound, normally instrumental-only, in a faceless almost groupless guise. The name, coined by ZTT Records' Paul Morley, comes from an Italian futurist manifesto.

Apr First release *Beat Box* reaches US #101, but is a US dancefloor favorite and, released on Island, climbs to #10 on R&B chart.

Aug *Close (To The Edit)* stalls at US #102, but again does well on the R&B chart (#23), and climbs to US #4 on the Dance chart.

Nov *(Who's Afraid Of) The Art Of Noise*, released on Horn's ZTT label, reaches UK #27.

1985 **Feb** First UK hit single is *Close (To The Edit)*, an original, quirky non-vocal, which hits #8.

Apr *Moments In Love/Beat Box* reaches UK #51 (the former later used by Madonna at her wedding to Sean Penn).

Aug *(Who's Afraid Of) The Art Of Noise* makes US #85.

Nov *Legs*, on the new China label in UK, makes UK #69.

1986 **Apr** A collaboration with guitar legend Duane Eddy, on an update of his 1959 classic *Peter Gunn*, hits UK #8. *In Visible Silence*, reaches UK #18, and includes offbeat collaboration with TV character Max Headroom on *Paranoimia*. Extracted as a single, it makes UK #12. (Its

success leads to the group's creation of the theme for Headroom's second UK TV series, and to further involvement with UK TV theme work ("Krypton Factor 2" and "The Return Of Sherlock Holmes") and ads for Revlon, Britvic, Bols, Bazique, Martini, Swatch, Barclays Bank, Fabergé, BP, Mars and Brylcream.)

June *In Visible Silence* makes US #53.

July Band's first live concerts take place in Japan, US and a single date in UK. All are sold out.
[5] *Peter Gunn* makes US #50.

Oct [4] *Paranoimia* reaches US #34.

1987 **Jan** *Legacy* is released in UK, but does not chart.

Feb [24] *Peter Gunn* wins Best Rock Instrumental Performance (Orchestra, Group Or Soloist) For 1986 at the 29th annual Grammys. (*Peter Gunn* won 2 Grammys for Henry Mancini at the 1st annual awards in 1959.)

July *Dragnet* peaks at UK #60, as ZTT Records issues a compilation album of early material, entitled *Daft*, which fails to chart.

Oct [10] Third album *In No Sense? Nonsense!* makes UK #55 (without Langan, who subsequently becomes a floating group member).

Nov Band completes work on theme music for Dan Aykroyd's film "Dragnet", to be included on the soundtrack album and released as a UK and US single. *In-No-Sense? Nonsense!* peaks at US #134.

1988 **Feb** Work is completed on a soundtrack contribution to The Fat Boys' film "Disorderlies".

Mar *Dragnet '88* reaches UK #94, issued to coincide with the movie's UK release.

Nov *Kiss* featuring Tom Jones and reviving Prince's 1986 US #1, hits UK #5.

Dec *The Best Of The Art Of Noise* makes UK #55.

1989 **Jan** [14] *Kiss* makes US #31, as *The Best Of The Art Of Noise* makes US #83.

Aug *Yebo*, featuring Mahlathini & The Mahotella Queens, peaks at UK #63. (Individually, the band members' careers also blossom. Dudley's successes as producer/writer/arranger/player include hits by Lloyd Cole, Moody Blues, Tom Jones, Rush, Boy George, k.d. lang, A-ha, McCartney, New Edition, Five Star and Phil Collins, with whom she will combine for successful soundtrack to movie "Buster". Other film theme work includes "Wilt", "Say Anything", and "Mighty Quinn", with TV music scored for "Jeeves And Wooster" and "Rory Bremner". Jeczalik's production and mixing credits include The Pet Shop Boys, Godley & Creme and McCartney; Langan's talents are on hand for Spandau Ballet, ABC, Billy Idol, Public Image Ltd., and many others.)

1990 **May** [5] Dudley conducts the orchestra at Yoko Ono-organized tribute concert to John Lennon held at the Pierhead, Liverpool, Merseyside.

July Previously issued material is collectively released as *The Ambient Collection* by China.

Sept Dudley combines with ex-Killing Joke frontman Jaz Coleman to release album *Songs From The Victorious City*.

ASIA

John Wetton (lead vocal, bass)
Steve Howe (guitar, vocals)
Geoff Downes (keyboards, vocals)
Carl Palmer (drums, percussion)

1981 **Jan** Having folded UK, Roxy Music and King Crimson veteran Wetton (b. July 12, 1949, Derby, Derbys.), talks to Howe (b. Apr.8, 1947, London), who has just left Yes, about forming a new band, since Geffen Records in US is keen to sign such a new project. They approach former Emerson, Lake & Palmer drummer Palmer (b. Mar.20, 1947, Birmingham, W.Midlands), and Yes/Buggles keyboards player Downes, and form Asia.

1982 **Mar** After much preparation, debut album *Asia*, produced by Mike Stone, is lambasted by UK critics as staid and stale, though it is received more kindly elsewhere, not least by US rock fans.

May [15] *Asia* tops US chart, where it reigns for 2 months, but stalls by comparison in UK, at #11.

June [26] *Heat Of The Moment*, taken from the album, hits US #4.

July [17] *Heat Of The Moment* makes UK #46, as the band begins stadium-filling live work in US and around the world.

Sept [18] Second single *Only Time Will Tell* reaches US #17 and UK #54 a week later.

1983 **Feb** Asia begins recording its second album in Canada, at Le Studio in Quebec and Manta Sound in Toronto.

Aug Second album *Alpha*, released at end of world tour, hits UK #5 and US #6.

Sept [17] *Don't Cry*, taken from the album, climbs to US #10 and UK #33. Wetton leaves, and is replaced by Greg Lake (b. Nov.10, 1948, Bournemouth, Dorset), Palmer's earlier partner in ELP.
Nov [26] Second US extract from *Alpha* is *The Smile Has Left Your Eyes*, which makes US #34.
Dec [6] "Asia In Asia", a live TV concert from Budokan theater, Tokyo, Japan, has an audience of over 20 million in US (via MTV), and is also heard on 285 US radio stations. It is Lake's first appearance with the band and proves the peak of its career.

985 Howe quits, and is replaced by Krokus guitarist Many Meyer.
Dec [14] Wetton rejoins Asia for much less successful third album *Astra*, which peaks at UK #68 and US #67 in early 1986.

986 Jan [18] *Go* makes US #46. Asia eventually disbands as the members follow other projects.
July [12] GTR, a 5-piece UK rock band with Howe, ex-Genesis Steve Hackett and Max Bacon, reaches US #14 with *When The Heart Rules The Mind. GTR* peaks at US #11.
Sept [6] GTR's *The Hunter* makes US #85.
Dec Live video "Asia In Asia" is released by Vestron Video.

990 Sept [15] Now re-formed with new guitarist Pat Thrall, from Go and Automatic Man, Asia returns to US chart with partly retrospective *Then And Now*, peaking at #114, and only spending 10 weeks on the survey.
Oct [27] *Days Like These* peaks at US #64.

THE ASSOCIATION
erry Kirkman (vocals, keyboards)
im Yester (vocals, guitar)
ary Alexander (vocals, guitar)
uss Giguere (vocals, guitar)
arry Ramos, Jr. (vocals, guitar)
rian Cole (vocals, bass)
ed Bluechel, Jr. (vocals, drums)

965 Nov Kirkman (b. Dec.12, 1941, Salina, KS), a veteran of California's folk circuit and Alexander (b. Sept.25, 1943, Chattanooga, TN), old friends now working as arrangers in Los Angeles, CA, join a loose band of musicians who congregate to sing and play on Monday nights after closing at the Troubadour club. Bluechel (b. Dec.2, 1942, San Pedro, CA), Cole (b. Sept.8, 1942, Tacoma, WA) and Bob Page become part of this group calling itself The Inner Tubes. In time, their number is pared down to 13 and they become The Men, securing a proper date to play the Troubadour. During subsequent rehearsals several members depart. With an upcoming date at the Icehouse, Giguere (b. Oct.18, 1943, Portsmouth, NH), who is working the lights at the club and has been part of The Inner Tubes, replaces Mike Whalen, who has left to replace Barry McGuire in The New Christy Minstrels. Page leaves during rehearsals, replaced by Yester (b. Nov.24, 1939, Birmingham, AL), who, fresh out the Army, joins within a week of returning to Los Angeles. After 6 months rehearsing, The Association (coined by Kirkman's wife Judy after browsing through a dictionary – the name The Aristocrats had been an earlier suggestion) makes its stage debut at Pasadena's Ice House. *Babe I'm Gonna Leave You* is recorded for Jubilee label in a one-off deal.

966 Band signs to Valiant Records, having auditioned at the Troubadour, and releases a version of Bob Dylan's *One Too Many Mornings*.
May Sessions with producer Curt Boettcher for debut album begin at G.S.P. (Gary Paxton's home studio) and Columbia studios in Hollywood, CA.
June [4] Originally cut as a demo for Davon Music, with Alexander on bass, and given by its writer Tandyn Almer to the group on a 6-month exclusive, *Along Comes Mary* enters the Hot 100 at #79, after garnering immediate US radio play despite some interpreting it as a drug hymn.
July [16] *Along Comes Mary* hits US #7.
Aug *Cherish*, a soft ballad in contrast to *Mary*, recorded by The New Christy Minstrels, but refused a release by writer Kirkman, is issued with debut album *And Then ... Along Comes The Association*, as group embarks on first national tour at San Francisco's Fillmore West.
Sept [24] *Cherish* tops US chart for 3 weeks, displacing The Supremes' *You Can't Hurry Love*, and becomes a million-seller.
Nov [19] *And Then ... Along Comes The Association* hits US #5, and becomes the group's first gold record.
Dec [24] Alexander's *Pandora's Golden Heebie Jeebies*, in stark contrast to *Cherish* and without strong radio support, makes US #35.

967 Feb [25] *No Fair At All*, written by Yester, peaks at US #51, but hits #1 in the Philippines.
Mar [18] Produced by Yester's brother, *Renaissance* makes US #34.

Apr Warner Bros. buys Valiant Records, and with it the group's recording contract. Alexander leaves to study meditation in India, and is replaced by New Christy Minstrel Ramos (b. Hilario Directo Ramos Jr., Apr.19, 1942, Waimea, Kauai, HI).
June [16] Band opens the Monterey International Pop Festival, CA, with *Enter The Young*.
July [1] *Windy*, written by group friend California teen Ruthann Friedman tops US chart for 4 weeks, preventing The Music Explosion from achieving its only chart-topper with *Little Bit O' Soul*.
Sept [2] *Insight Out*, produced by Bones Howe, hits US #8, and is the group's second certified gold disk, as *Requiem For The Masses*, B-side of *Never My Love*, spends 2 weeks at anchor position on US Hot 100.
Oct [7] *Never My Love*, penned by Don and Dick Addrisi, returns to the soft style of *Cherish*, and hits US #2 for 2 weeks, unable to dislodge The Box Tops' *The Letter*, but goes on to be a million-seller.
Nov The Association is voted #1 Group Of The Year in US by Bill Gavin Radio-Record Congress, displacing The Beatles after 3 years.

1968 Mar [2] Kirkman's *Everything That Touches You* hits US #10.
May [1] Group arrives in UK to promote *Time For Livin'*. They appear on BBC TV's "Top Of The Pops" and make 2 live appearances at London's Tottenham Royal and at the annual **New Musical Express** Poll Winners Concert at Empire Pool, Wembley, London, helping *Time For Livin'* become their only UK hit, reaching #23. They also play dates in Europe at Bremen, Amsterdam, Brussels and Antwerp.
June [15] *Birthday*, also produced by Howe, reaches US #23.
[22] *Time For Livin'*, penned by the Addrisi brothers, makes US #39.
Sept [14] *Six Man Band*, an uncharacteristic (and autobiographical) heavy rock track penned by Kirkman, is their last US Top 50 single, peaking at #47. Soon after, Alexander rejoins, now using his other forename Jules, and they become a 7-man band.

1969 Feb [8] *Greatest Hits!* hits US #4, and will go platinum in 1971.
Mar [15] *Goodbye Columbus*, title theme to Richard Benjamin/Ali MacGraw movie, makes US #80.
Sept [6] *Goodbye Columbus* soundtrack, including 3 Association originals, makes US #99. (Yester's title song will receive a Golden Globe nomination for Best Song.)
Nov [1] *The Association*, produced by the group with John Boylan, reaches US #32.

1970 July Giguere leaves to record solo album *Hexagram 16* and will subsequently form The Beechwood Rangers with Bill Martin and Warren Zevon and then Hollywood, and is replaced by Richard Thompson (b. San Diego, CA) (ex-Cosmic Brotherhood, John Klemmer and Richard Thompson Trio), on keyboards.
Aug [22] *The Association Live*, recorded Apr.3, 1970 at University of Utah, Salt Lake City, makes US #79.

1971 Aug [21] *Stop Your Motor* peaks at US #158.
1972 June [10] A new recording deal with Columbia Records in US produces *Waterbeds In Trinidad*, with material by John Sebastian, John Stewart, Gerry Goffin and Carole King, but is the group's least successful album, peaking at US #194.
Aug [2] Cole dies in Los Angeles from an apparent heroin overdose.

1973 Mar Group signs to Mums label, a subsidiary of Columbia, releasing a one-off Albert Hammond-produced single *Names Tags Numbers Labels*, which stalls at US #91.

1975 Group, with Bluechel, Ramos and Yester the only original members and new recruits Maurice Miller (percussion), David Vaught (bass), Dwayne Smith (keyboards) and Art Johnson (guitar), signs a 1-single deal with RCA, which releases Jack Richardson-produced *One Sunday Morning*. Alexander invites Giguere to join Bijou, with other founding member Kirkman now writing TV jingles.

1981 Feb [14] Following the success of an HBO TV special, original group reunites (with Ric Ulsky in Brian Cole's place) with producer Bones Howe and signs a singles deal with Elektra. *Dreamer* peaks at US #66. (Band will continue to perform around US regularly until the "Happy Together" tour in 1984, when only Giguere and Ramos remain, taking rights to The Association name with them. With new line-up featuring Donni Gougeon (keyboards), Paul Holland (bass), Bruce Pictor (drums), and Del Ramos (backing vocals), they will play more than 100 dates a year into the 90s.)

1990 Sept To celebrate its 50th anniversary, BMI announces its most played songs over the last half-century. *Never My Love* and Paul McCartney's *Yesterday* are the only 2 songs to have received over 5 million plays.

RICK ASTLEY

1983 Brought up in Newton-le-Willows, Merseyside, where his early interests include choir singing and playing piano and drums, Astley (b. Feb.6, 1966, Warrington, Cheshire), joins his first band, Give Way, at school, as a drummer.

1984 He joins FBI as lead singer, a new band whose numbers are increasingly influenced by music heard on visits to Wigan's legendary soul music club, the Pier Casino. (The group receives a grant from the UK Government as part of the Enterprise Allowance Scheme.)

1985 Feb Astley is spotted at the Monks sports and social club, Warrington, by Pete Waterman, of the Stock/Aitken/Waterman writing and production hit factory, who offers him solo work in London.

1986 Astley sings an uncredited duet on O'chi Brown's *Learning To Live Without Your Love.*

1987 **July** [27] Following 18 months of rehearsal, grooming and styling with the SAW team at PWL studios in London, while also employed as a tape operator, Astley is launched in the UK.

Aug [29] Debut single *Never Gonna Give You Up* tops UK chart for 5 weeks, and becomes UK's biggest-selling single of the year, before moving on to repeat its chart-topping status in 15 other countries worldwide, including US, Australia and Germany.

Nov *Whenever You Need Somebody* hits UK #3, and marks the start of a 6-month non-stop worldwide promotion trek.

[28] Debut album ***Whenever You Need Somebody*** enters UK Album chart at #1, and will sell over a million copies in 6 months.

Dec *When I Fall In Love*, a faithfully-styled revival of Nat "King" Cole's 1957 classic ballad, hits UK #2. The reissue of Cole's original halts its progress to the top, so the single is flipped to give joint promotion (and additional sales) to double A-side coupling, *My Arms Keep Missing You.*

1988 **Feb** [8] *Never Gonna Give You Up* is named Best British Single at the seventh annual BRIT Awards at London's Royal Albert Hall.

Mar [12] After a 3-month climb, *Never Gonna Give You Up* tops US chart for 2 weeks, knocking George Michael's *Father Figure* off the top. *Together Forever*, from debut album, hits UK #2.

Apr Astley undertakes promotional tour of the Far East and Australia.

June [6] Astley performs *Never Gonna Give You Up* at the Prince's Trust concert at the Royal Albert Hall, London.

[18] *Together Forever* becomes Astley's second US chart-topper, again dislodging George Michael, this time with *One More Try*, as parent album ***Whenever You Need Somebody*** climbs to US #10.

Sept [17] *It Would Take A Strong Man* hits US #10.

Oct *She Wants To Dance With Me* hits UK #6.

Dec *Take Me To Your Heart* and parent album ***Hold Me In Your Arms*** both hit UK #8. Astley embarks on his first world tour, playing 70 shows in 15 countries including UK, US, Japan and Australia.

1989 **Feb** Ballad *Hold Me In Your Arms*, one of 6 Astley-penned cuts from the parent album, hits UK #10.

[25] *She Wants To Dance With Me* hits US #6, as ***Hold Me In Your Arms*** reaches UK #19.

May [27] *Giving Up On Love* makes US #38, as Astley prepares for 3-month US tour.

Aug [26] Temptations-covered *Ain't Too Proud To Beg* stalls at US #89.

1990 **Mar** Astley begins recording third album which will be co-produced in the Isle of Man, UK, Copenhagen, Denmark, and Los Angeles, CA, by Gary Stevenson.

1991 **Jan** After a lengthy period off the scene, having extricated himself from his involvement with Stock/Aitken/Waterman, amid much rancor, Astley returns with gospel-tinged *Cry For Help*, which hits UK #7 and begins US chart rise. It is taken from album ***Free*** (to be released on Feb.11), mainly written with Level 42's Mark King and Climie Fisher's Rob Fisher, and including keyboard help from Elton John and Michael McDonald track *Name Of Love*.

Mar [2] ***Free*** debuts at UK #9 peak.

ASWAD

Brinsley Forde (vocals)
Tony Gad (guitar)
Angus "Drummie" Zeb (drums)

1975 The band forms in UK (Aswad is Arabic for black), with Forde (former child star of 1971 BBC-TV children's series "Here Come The Double Deckers"), and Zeb, plus Donald Benjamin (guitar), Courtney Hemmings (keyboards) and Ras George Levi (bass).

1976 They sign to Island Records, the first UK reggae act to secure a major deal, and release Back To Africa, which tops UK Reggae chart, and Aswad, equally popular in specialist reggae circles.

1978 Group moves to independent label Grove Muzic and supports popular Rock Against Racism cause. They embark on extensive summer tour of West Africa, becoming the first reggae band to perform in Senegal.

1979 Grove licenses its Aswad releases to Island, including second album Hulet, as Gad replaces Hemmings.

1980 They contribute music to UK film "Babylon", dealing with pressures of young black life in contemporary London, in which Forde has a major acting role. Soundtrack album, containing their tracks, is released by Chrysalis Records. Meanwhile Aswad signs to CBS Records.

1982 July [31] Not Satisfied on CBS is their first UK chart success, at #50.

1983 Dec Aswad re-signs to Island, and Live And Direct charts at UK #57.

1984 Mar Chasing For The Breeze, recorded in Jamaica, becomes their first UK chart single, peaking at #51.
Oct 54-46 (Was My Number) makes UK #70.
Nov Aswad tours UK, promoting Rebel Souls, which makes UK #48.

1985 They tour on and off for the next 2 years, their status now confirmed as Britain's premier reggae act.

1986 Feb [12-14] Aswad hosts a 3-day careers course at London's Camden Centre.
June To The Top on own independent Simba label peaks at UK #71. With a change of management and a reduction of the group to 3, they re-sign to Island via Mango label.

1987 Aswad tours, rehearses and records new material for 1988 release.

1988 Mar [26] Don't Turn Around, a reggae re-styling of an Albert Hammond/Diane Warren song first recorded by Tina Turner, tops UK chart for 2 weeks.
Apr Parent album Distant Thunder hits UK #10.
June Follow-up, another Hammond/Warren song, Give A Little Love reaches UK #11.
Aug Don't Turn Around makes #45 on US R&B chart.
Sept Distant Thunder makes US #173.
[24] Set Them Free peaks at UK #70.

1989 Mar [6] Greenpeace album Rainbow Warriors, which features Aswad, is released in USSR on Melodiya label.
Apr A reggae adaptation of The Temptations' Beauty Is Only Skin Deep makes UK #31.
June [16-17] Group takes part in "Cliff Richard – The Event", performed over 2 days to sold-out 72,000 capacity crowds at London's Wembley Stadium. They duet with Richard on Share A Dream With Me.
Aug On And On, reviving US singer/songwriter Stephen Bishop's lilting Caribbean-styled ballad, substituting "puts on Sinatra and starts to cry" line with "puts on Marley and starts to cry", reaches UK #25.
Dec Aswad's 6th chart album, Renaissance, makes UK #52. Group contributes vocals to When The Stone Begins To Turn, a track from Jackson Browne's World In Motion.

1990 Apr [16] Aswad participates in "Nelson Mandela – An International Tribute To A Free South Africa" concert at Wembley Stadium.
June [22-24] Group performs at Glastonbury Festival Of Contemporary Performing Arts near Glastonbury, Somerset.
Sept [8] Next To You reaches UK #24.
[29] Too Wicked makes UK #51.
Nov [24] Smile, featuring Sweetie Irie, peaks at UK #53.

1991 Feb [16] Group begins 27-date US tour at Municipal Auditorium, Eureka, CA, ending at Respectable Street Café, West Palm Beach, FL.
Mar Cover version of The Eagles' Best Of My Love, as part of Too Wicked EP begins UK chart rise.

AVERAGE WHITE BAND

Hamish Stuart (vocals, guitar)
Alan Gorrie (vocals, bass)
Onnie McIntyre (guitar)
Roger Ball (alto, baritone saxophone)
Malcolm "Molly" Duncan (tenor, soprano saxophone)
Robbie McIntosh (drums)

1972 The band is founded by Gorrie (b. July 19, 1946, Perth, Scotland) with musician friends who have helped him on solo recordings the year before. McIntosh (b. 1950, Scotland) has earlier been with Oblivion Express, while Stuart (b. Oct.8, 1949, Glasgow, Scotland), Ball (b. June 4 1944, Dundee, Scotland), Duncan (b. Malcolm Duncan Aug.24, 1945, Montrose, Scotland) and McIntyre (b. Sept.25, 1945, Lennox Town, Scotland) have played with various Scottish bands since mid-60s.
July After playing the European club circuit and US military bases,

Average White Band, a name given to them by Bonnie Bramlett, makes its first appearance at the Lincoln Festival, Lincs.

Oct Chuck Berry's double-entendre *My Ding-A-Ling,* on which McIntyre and McIntosh both play, tops US chart for 2 weeks.

1973
Jan [13] They support Eric Clapton at his comeback concert at London's Rainbow theater. The band's blue-eyed R&B/funk style interests MCA Records, which signs them for album *Show Your Hand,* and they visit US for a less than successful tour.

1974
July Now signed to Atlantic Records, the band relocates to US and records second album *Average White Band* with producer Arif Mardin.
Sept [23] McIntosh dies at a Los Angeles, CA, party from a strychnine-based heroin overdose when he believes he is snorting cocaine. Corrie is saved by the alertness of Cher, who keeps him conscious. McIntosh is replaced by former Bloodstone drummer Steve Ferrone (b. Apr.25, 1950, Brighton, Sussex).

1975
Feb [22] Funk dominated soul *Average White Band,* and extracted instrumental *Pick Up The Pieces,* hit US #1 in the same week.
Mar [15] *Average White Band* hits UK #6.
[22] *Pick Up The Pieces* hits UK #6.
Apr Original MCA album is reissued in US as *Put It Where You Want It* and reaches #39.
May [3] *Cut The Cake* makes UK #31.
June [21] *Cut The Cake* hits US #10.
[28] *Cut The Cake,* dedicated to McIntosh, reaches UK #28 and will hit US #4.
Sept [27] *If I Ever Lose This Heaven* makes #39 in US, where the band is now based.
Dec [27] *School Boy Crush* makes US #33.

1976
May [14] Group embarks on 9-date UK tour at the Odeon theater, Edinburgh, Scotland, ending on May 29 at the Odeon theater, Birmingham, W.Midlands.
July [31] *Soul Searching* peaks at UK #60.
Aug [28] *Soul Searching* hits US #9.
Oct [16] *Queen Of My Soul,* taken from it, makes US #40.
[30] *Queen Of My Soul* reaches UK #23.

1977
Mar [5] *Person To Person* reaches US #28.
Sept [10] *Benny And Us* makes US #33, with most lead vocals performed by soul singer Ben E. King. Its success predates band members' later work as session players with many artists including Chaka Khan.

1978
May [6] Now signed to RCA, sarcastically titled label debut *Warmer Communications,* their last with Mardin, reaches US #28.

1979
Mar [10] *Feel No Fret,* recorded at Compass Point studios in the Bahamas, charts at UK #15, where it is their best-selling album since *Average White Band.*
Apr [28] The album yields a soulful remake of Bacharach/David's *Walk On By,* which makes UK #46 and US #92.
May [19] *Feel No Fret* reaches US #32.
Sept [1] *When Will You Be Mine* makes UK #49.

1980
June [7] The band takes part in "The Summer Of 80 Garden Party" at the Crystal Palace Concert Bowl, London, with Bob Marley & The Wailers, The Q-Tips and Joe Jackson.
July *For You For Love* makes UK #46.
[12] *Shine* makes US #116.
[19] Disco-styled *Let's Go Round Again* makes US #53 and will reach UK #12.
[21] *Shine* reaches UK #14.
Aug [4] Group begins 6-date tour at the Theatre Royal, Nottingham, Notts., their first in UK for some time, before embarking on further dates in Europe.
Sept [27] *Volume VIII* stalls at US #182.

1983 2 Stuart compositions are featured on George Benson's *In Your Eyes.*
1988 Stuart, Gorrie and Ferrone team with Renee Geyer as Easy Pieces on A&M.
1989
Jan Now signed to Track, *The Spirit Of Love* makes US R&B #47, as parent album *Aftershock* makes #69 also on US R&B survey.
1990
Dec Stuart contributes lead vocals to David Foster's *River Of Love.* He ends year as an integral part of Paul McCartney's world touring band.

AZTEC CAMERA
Roddy Frame (vocals, guitar)
Eddie Kulak (keyboards)
Gary Sanford (guitar)
Paul Powell (bass)
Dave Ruffy (drums)

1980
Jan Frame (b. Jan.29, 1964, East Kilbride, Scotland) forms the band, which will always revolve around his creativity, with Dave Mulholland (drums) and Campbell Owens (bass).
Dec After playing their innovative brand of melodic rock in Scottish towns, they sign to Glasgow independent label Postcard.

1981
Apr Debut single *Just Like Gold* is immediately successful on UK Independent chart, hitting #10.
Aug *Mattress Of Wire* also hits UK Independent chart, at #8. The rest of the year will be spent touring England for the first time.

1982
June A new independent label deal is signed with Rough Trade Records in London. Ruffy is the band's fifth and most permanent drummer. Bernie Clarke also joins (temporarily) on keyboards, co-producing early material with John Brand.
Oct *Pillar To Post* is another UK Independent chart hit, at #4.

1983
Mar *Oblivious* becomes their first UK pop chart entry, at #47.
May Highly-rated debut album *High Land, Hard Rain* makes UK #22. Band is signed via a US deal to Sire Records, as album reaches US #129.
June *Walk Out To Winter* peaks at UK #64.
Aug Band begins a 3-month tour of major US venues supporting Elvis Costello. Frame, only 19, has to lie about his age in several US states.
Oct In mid-year, they sign a new UK record deal with WEA Records.
Nov WEA reissues *Oblivious,* which is the band's first Top 20 hit, at UK #18, as Frame prepares songs for a new album.

1984
Sept *All I Need Is Everything* (with an acoustic version of Van Halen's *Jump* on the B-side) reaches UK #34.
Oct *Knife,* produced by Mark Knopfler, reaches UK #14 and US #175, and the band, now comprising Frame, Owens, Ruffy and Malcolm Ross on guitar, begins an extensive world tour to promote it.
Nov *Still On Fire* does not chart, and after the tour Frame retreats to write new songs for a third album.

1985
Apr US-only released 10" album *Aztec Camera,* including live tracks recorded at the Dominion, London, in Oct.1984, makes #181.

1986
Mar Aztec Camera, now a vehicle for a solo Frame with help from session musicians (including Marcus Miller, Steve Jordan and System's keyboardist David Frank), begins recording new project in New York, and Boston, MA, with producers Russ Titelman, Tommy LiPuma, David Frank, Michael Jonzun, Rob Mounsey and Frame himself.

1987
June Band begins UK tour in advance of forthcoming releases.
Oct *Deep Wide And Tall,* from the simultaneously-released album *Love,* does not chart, while the album initially peaks at UK #49.
Nov Band tours US to promote *Love.*
Dec *Love* peaks at US #193.

1988
Jan They return to UK for more live dates, before touring Australia.
Mar After an absence of more than 4 years from UK Top 30, *How Men Are* reaches #25.
June *Somewhere In My Heart* hits UK #3, their biggest hit to date. It revives UK sales interest in *Love,* which now peaks at #10 and earns a platinum award. A major UK tour culminates in 2 sold-out dates at London's Royal Albert Hall.
Aug *Working In A Goldmine* makes UK #31.
Oct *Deep And Wide And Tall,* now reissued, peaks at UK #55.

1990
June [16] *Stray,* recorded at Dave Edmund's Rockfield studio, Wales, and at the Power Plant, London, produced by Frame with Eric Calvi and introducing a new Aztec Camera, comprising Powell on bass, Gary Sanctuary on keyboards and Frank Tontoh on drums, enters UK chart at #22. Paul Carrack, Mick Jones and Edwyn Collins also make guest appearances.
[19] Aztec Camera plays the Hammersmith Odeon, London, the highlight of a 21-date UK tour. The support act is Frame himself, performing a short acoustic opening to each show.
July *The Crying Scene* stalls at UK #70.
Nov *Good Morning Britain,* co-written and performed by Aztec Camera with Big Audio Dynamite frontman Mick Jones makes UK #19, as band finishes 6-month world trek.
Dec Aztec Camera's contribution to the *Red Hot & Blue* AIDS awareness album, *Do I Love You,* an update of a Cole Porter song, misses UK Top 75.

THE B52'S

Cindy Wilson (guitar, vocals)
Kate Pierson (organ, vocals)
Ricky Wilson (guitar)
Fred Schneider (keyboards, vocals)
Keith Strickland (drums)

1976 **Oct** Friends, Pierson (b. Apr.27, 1948, Weehawken, NJ), playing in folk-protest band The Sun Donuts, Schneider (b. July 1, 1951, Newark, GA), a veteran of bands Bridge Mix and Night Soil, studying forestry at University of Georgia and working in vegetarian restaurant called Eldorado, Ricky Wilson (b. Mar.19, 1953, Athens, GA) and Strickland (b. Oct.26, 1953, Athens), working at local bus stations and Ricky's sister Cindy (b. Feb.28, 1957, Athens) making shakes at the Whirly-Q luncheonette, having dined together at an Athens Chinese restaurant and shared a tropical drink called Flaming Volcano, on their way home decide to form a band, taking its name from the Southern US nickname for a bouffant hairstyle adopted by its 2 female members.

1977 **Feb** [14] Group makes its first live performance, at a Valentine Day's houseparty in a greenhouse in Athens.
Dec [12] Having gone to New York with fellow Athens band The Fans and dropped off a tape at Max's Kansas City, the band plays its first gig at the new wave venue in front of an audience of 17. Despite the poor turn-out they are invited back, and quickly developing a highly visual stage act featuring boots, mini-skirts and the girls' B52 hairdos, they become cult favorites at the club.

1978 **Aug** They finance their own recording of *Rock Lobster* and *52 Girls*, with a loan from local record store owner Danny Beard, quickly selling the 2,000 copies pressed, which brings them to the attention of Island Records' boss, Chris Blackwell.

1979 **June** They visit Nassau to record their debut album for Island, and sign to Warner Bros. for US.
July [8] The B52's perform UK debut, supported by pre-Eurythmics The Tourists, at the Lyceum Ballroom, London, at the beginning of a short album-supporting tour.
[21] *The B52's* reaches UK #22.
Aug *The B52's* makes US #59.
[18] *Rock Lobster* (the band's self-financed original reissued by Island) makes UK #37.

1980 **Apr** Group begins recording *Wild Planet*, co-self-produced with Rhett Davies, again at Compass Point studios in the Bahamas, following a US tour and dates in Japan and Australia.
May [24] *Rock Lobster* peaks at US #56.
Aug *Give Me Back My Man* peaks at UK #61.
Sept Confirming their quirky musical approach, *Wild Planet* reaches both US and UK #18.
Nov [8] *Private Idaho* peaks at US #74.
Dec Band makes second visit to UK for 3 gigs at the Hammersmith Odeon, London, among others.

1981 In between recording breaks for new album *Mesopotamia*, Strickland, Pierson and Cindy Wilson record 2 cuts with Adrian Belew and Japanese group The Plastics under one-off studio name, Melon, though these tracks will only ever appear in Japan.
July [18] Mini-album *The Party Mix Album*, featuring dance-oriented remixes from first 2 albums, makes UK #36.
The Party Mix Album makes US #55.
Nov *Give Me Back My Man* is included in **New Musical Express** as a free promotional cassette.

1982 **Feb** [27] Mini-album *Mesopotamia*, produced by David Byrne of Talking Heads, reaches UK #18, helped by debut UK TV appearance on Channel 4's "The Switch".
Mar [13] *Mesopotamia* makes US #35.

1983 **May** *Future Generation* peaks at UK #63 as *Whammy!* reaches UK #33.
July [30] *Legal Tender* stalls at US #81.
Whammy! reaches US #29.

1984 As a group, The B52's remain quiet but Schneider releases solo project through Warner Bros. under the group name Shake Society, while he, Pierson and Cindy Wilson also make guest appearance in The Ramones' Live Aid spoof video for "Something To Believe In".

1985 **Jan** Group takes part in Rock In Rio festival in Rio de Janeiro, Brazil.
Oct [12] Ricky Wilson dies from AIDS.

1986 **May** Double A-side reissue of *Rock Lobster* with another early favorite *Planet Claire*, yields their biggest-ever hit, reaching UK #12. *Bouncing Off The Satellites*, dedicated to the memory of Ricky Wilson and produced by Tony Mansfield, makes US #85.

1987 **Aug** *Bouncing Off Satellites* peaks at UK #74. A quiet period ensues,

not least due to financial wrangles, during which Schneider writes a book of poetry.

1989 **Mar** Group participates in a "Rock Against Fur" benefit at The Palladium, New York.
May They perform at "Don't Bungle The Jungle" benefit at the Brooklyn Academy of Music, New York, on a bill with Madonna. Band also makes cameo appearance in similarly styled Julien Temple-directed movie "Earth Girls Come Easy".
June Group embarks on "Cosmic Thing Tour", its first for 5 years, set to end in late Aug. Augmented stage line-up includes Sara Lee (bass), ex-Gang Of Four and now Raging Hormones, Pat Irwin (keyboards), ex-Raybeats and Zach Alford (drums).
July [29] *Cosmic Thing*, The B52's debut for Reprise/Warner Bros., and their first since Ricky Wilson's death, featuring Strickland on guitar, initially peaks at UK #75 and begins US chart rise.
Oct [31] Group begins another major US tour in Atlanta, GA, ending Feb.7 at Radio City Music Hall, New York.
Nov [18] *Love Shack*, written about a "liberal" night club in Atlanta, hits US #3, as parent album *Cosmic Thing* hits US #4, benefiting also from current exhaustive US tour.

1990 **Mar** [8] *Love Shack* is voted Best Single Of 1989 in **Rolling Stone** magazine's Music Awards and the band is voted Comeback Of The Year in the magazine's Critics Awards.
[10] *Roam* hits US #3.
[31] *Cosmic Thing* hits UK #9, peaking the next week at #8.
Apr *Love Shack* hits UK #2, becoming one of the year's Top 20 best-sellers.
[22] Group participates in "Earth Day" festivities in Central Park, New York, with Daryl Hall & John Oates and others.
June *Roam* reaches UK #17.
[2] *Deadbeat Club* reaches US #30.
[14] *Best Of B52's Dance This Mess Around*, a remixed collection of earlier Island highlights, enters UK chart at peak #36.
[15] 40-city "Summer Of 1990" tour opens in Middletown, NY. The tour will end on Aug.18 at the Aztec Bowl, San Diego, CA.
Aug *Channel Z* stalls at UK #61.
[13] At a Forum, Los Angeles, CA, concert, they raise $300,000 for various AIDS organizations.
[27] Group begins 19-date tour of Australia and Japan at the Entertainment Centre, Melbourne.
Sept Pierson duets with Iggy Pop on the latter's Don Was-produced single *Candy*, set to make UK #67.

1991 **Feb** [23] US remix album *Party Mix – Mesopotamia* makes US #184, as they contribute track to the Animal Rights album *Tame Yourself*.

BACHMAN-TURNER OVERDRIVE

Randy Bachman (guitar, vocals)
Blair Thornton (guitar)
C.F. (Fred) Turner (bass, vocals)
Robbie Bachman (drums)

1972 After leaving Guess Who (Canada's most successful band of the 60s) in 1970 and releasing solo *Axe*, Randy Bachman (b. Sept.27, 1943, Winnipeg, Canada) embarks on new venture, Brave Belt, with brother Robbie Bachman (b. Feb.18, 1953, Winnipeg), C.F. (Fred) Turner (b. Oct.16, 1943) and Chad Allan (also a former member of Guess Who), playing unsuccessfully for 2 years and recording 2 non-charting albums for Reprise, before forming Bachman-Turner Overdrive with Tim Bachman replacing Allan, its new name partly derived from trucking industry magazine **Overdrive**, with the band appropriately developing a blue-collar image and lyrical inclination.

1973 **Aug** After 24 record company rejections of their no-frills, solid-rock approach, the band signs to Mercury Records and *Bachman-Turner Overdrive* is released. Promoted by regular US touring (the band's hallmark), it climbs to US #70, but Tim Bachman leaves shortly after, replaced on guitar by Thornton (b. Vancouver, Canada).
Dec [29] First US chart single *Blue Collar* peaks at US #68.

1974 **Apr** [27] *Let It Ride* reaches US #23.
Aug [10] *Takin' Care Of Business* is the group's first Top 20 single, reaching US #12, as *Bachman-Turner Overdrive 2* hits US #4.
Oct [19] *Not Fragile* tops US chart for a week.
Nov [9] *You Ain't Seen Nothing Yet*, a song only included on *Not Fragile* as an afterthought, replaces Stevie Wonder's *You Haven't Done Nothin'* to hit US #1 for a week and become a million-plus seller. Written by Randy for his brother Gary, who has a stutter, and sung appropriately, it is based on Dave Mason's instrumental *Only You*

Know And I Know.

Dec *You Ain't Seen Nothing Yet* is the band's UK chart debut, and hits #2, while *Not Fragile* reaches UK #12.

1975 Mar [1] *Roll On Down The Highway* reaches US #14. It also reaches UK #22 where it is the group's last chartmaker.
A former Brave Belt album is reissued by Reprise Records as *Bachman-Turner Overdrive As Brave Belt*, but its appeal is mostly esoteric, and it only makes US #180.
July [5] *Hey You* reaches US #21, while *Four-Wheel Drive* hits US #5.

1976 Jan [3] *Down To The Line* makes US #43.
Mar [6] *Head On* reaches US #23.
[13] *Take It Like A Man*, extracted from *Head On*, makes US #33.
May [15] *Lookin' Out For #1* peaks at US #65.
Oct [2] *Gimme Your Money Please* peaks at US #70.
[9] Compilation *The Best Of BTO (So Far)* reaches US #19.

1977 Apr Randy Bachman leaves to go solo, and is placed by Jim Clench on *Freeways*, which makes US #70.

1978 Mar *Street Action*, on which the band's name is shortened to BTO, makes US #130. Bachman's solo album *Survivor*, recorded with Burton Cummings (keyboards), Ian Gardiner (bass) and Jeff Porcaro (drums), fails to chart.

1979 Mar [31] *Heartaches*, taken from forthcoming *Rock'N'Roll Nights*, peaks at US #60 used is the band's final hit single.
Apr *Rock'N'Roll Nights*, also as BTO, stalls at US #165.
May Randy Bachman re-emerges with new band Ironhorse, which signs to Scotti Brothers and has a minor US chart success with *Ironhorse*, making #153. More successful is extracted *Sweet Lui-Louise*, which makes US #36 and UK #60.

1980 May Ironhorse has another US hit with *What's Your Hurry Darlin'* at #89, from second album *Everything Is Grey*. (After this, the band will break up, and Randy Bachman will work solo again for a while, before re-forming BTO in 1984 with Turner and Tim Bachman.)

1984 Sept A hoped-for comeback album, on the Compleat label, simply titled *Bachman-Turner Overdrive*, makes US #191. (The reunion holds, however, and the trio works as a touring attraction in US and Canada, much as in the early 70s, but there will be no more hit records.)

BAD COMPANY

Paul Rodgers (vocals)
Mick Ralphs (guitar)
Boz Burrell (bass)
Simon Kirke (drums)

1973 Aug Left without a band after the break-up of Free, Kirke (b. July 28, 1949, Wales) and Rodgers (b. Dec.17, 1949, Middlesbrough, Cleveland) join up with Ralphs (b. Mar.31, 1948, Hereford, Hereford & Worcs.), who has just left Mott The Hoople. Band's name is taken from title of a 1972 film starring Jeff Bridges.
Nov Former King Crimson bassist Burrell (b. Raymond Burrell, 1946, Lincoln, Lincs.) joins the others, who have spent 2 months in rehearsal.

1974 Mar [8] Band makes live debut, at Newcastle-upon-Tyne's City Hall.
Apr They sign to Island Records in UK, and to Led Zeppelin-owned Swan Song in US, and record *Bad Company* in 10 days in Ronnie Lane's mobile studio.
June [8] Debut album *Bad Company* hits UK #3.
[15] Guitar-driven *Can't Get Enough*, taken from it, reaches UK #15.
Sept [28] *Bad Company* tops US chart.
Nov [2] *Can't Get Enough* hits US #5.

1975 Mar [1] Follow-up *Movin' On* hits US #19.
Apr [12] *Good Lovin' Gone Bad* makes UK #31.
[19] *Straight Shooter* hits UK #3 and US #3.
May [10] *Good Lovin' Gone Bad* makes US #36.
Sept [20] *Feel Like Makin' Love*, showcasing both Rodgers' distinctive vocals and Ralphs' memorable hard rock guitar hook, hits US #10.
[27] *Feel Like Makin' Love* reaches UK #20.

1976 Feb [7] *Run With The Pack* hits UK #4.
Apr [10] *Run With The Pack* hits US #5.
May [22] *Young Blood*, a remake of The Coasters' 1957 US #8, reaches US #20.
Aug [7] *Honey Child* peaks at US #59.

1977 Mar [1] *Burnin' Sky*, their first not to reach Top 10, climbs to UK #17.
Apr [23] *Burnin' Sky* reaches US #15.
June [11] Title track *Burnin' Sky* stalls at US #78.

1979 Mar [10] *Desolation Angels*, updating basic 4-piece rock sound with synthesizer and strings and released amid (unfounded) rumors about band splitting up, hits UK #10.

May [19] *Desolation Angels* hits US #3.
June [16] *Rock'N'Roll Fantasy* is last major US hit single, reaching #13.
Aug [25] *Gone, Gone, Gone* peaks at US #56.

1982 Aug [28] After 3-year silence, band returns with *Rough Diamonds*, reaching UK #15.
Oct *Rough Diamonds* reaches US #26.
[16] Extracted *Electricland* stalls at US #74.
By year's end, Rodgers will have quit the line-up.

1983 July After months of inactivity, apart from hints that Kirke and Burrell are each putting together new bands, Bad Company officially announces its break-up. (Rodgers will form The Firm with Jimmy Page, while Ralphs tours with David Gilmour.)
Dec [8] Rodgers plays alongside Eric Clapton, Jimmy Page and many others in the Ronnie Lane ARMS Appeal concert at New York's Madison Square Garden.

1986 Jan *10 From 6* compilation from previous albums makes US #137.
Nov [1] *This Love* makes US #85.
Fame And Fortune, featuring new vocalist, and Ted Nugent band member, Brian Howe, makes US #106.

1988 Oct *Dangerous Age* makes US #58.
1989 Apr [29] *Shake It Up*, from *Dangerous Age*, stalls at US #82.
1990 Mar *Can't Get Enough* enjoys the dubious distinction of becoming the first reissued song used for a UK TV Levi jeans commercial not to concurrently make UK chart.
July [17] First leg of US tour with Damn Yankees, begins in Burlington, VT, including latest band members Paul Cullen (bass) and Geoffrey Whitehorn (guitar), alongside veterans Kirke and Howe.
[28] *Holy Water* makes US #89.
Aug [4] Parent album *Holy Water* reaches US #35.

1991 Mar The Law, a new band put together by Rodgers with former Who drummer Kenney Jones, releases debut album *The Law*.
[2] *If You Needed Somebody* reaches US #16.

BADFINGER

Pete Ham (guitar, piano, vocals)
Tom Evans (bass, vocals)
Joey Molland (guitar, keyboards, vocals)
Mike Gibbins (drums)

1968 July After performing locally in Welsh clubs for a couple of years, and being seen by semi-professional musician Bill Collins, who becomes the group's manager, Ham (b. Apr.27, 1947, Swansea, Wales), Gibbins (b. Mar.12, 1949, Swansea), Ron Griffiths (bass), David Jenkins (rhythm guitar) and Terry Gleeson (drums), having auditioned for The Kinks' Ray Davies, are backing UK vocalist David Garrick, playing on his hit *Dear Mrs. Applebee*, when Collins gives a demo tape to Beatles assistant Mal Evans, who in turn gives it to Paul McCartney who signs them to Apple Records as The Iveys. Evans (b. June 5, 1947, Liverpool, Merseyside), who has been in Liverpool group The Calderstones, has replaced Jenkins, who has left to join another band.
Nov The Iveys' debut single *Maybe Tomorrow*, produced by Tony Visconti, is released.
Dec Griffiths is asked to leave after an argument with Evans and is replaced by Molland (b. June 21, 1948, Liverpool), formerly with The Profiles, The Masterminds, The Merseys and Gary Walker & Rain. Evans switches to bass.

1969 Mar [15] *Maybe Tomorrow* peaks at US #67.
July Proposed *Maybe Tomorrow* is withdrawn from UK and US release schedule, while *No Escaping Your Love* is a Europe-only issue.
Sept Band, now renamed Badfinger, records Paul McCartney's *Come And Get It* and 3 other tracks in a McCartney-produced session for upcoming Peter Sellers/Ringo Starr movie "The Magic Christian".

1970 Jan *Come And Get It* hits UK #4, taken from parent album *Magic Christian Music*, which incorporates some *Maybe Tomorrow* cuts.
Apr [18] *Come And Get It* hits US #7, as *Magic Christian Music* makes US #55.
Oct Group begins an 8-week US tour.
Dec [5] *No Matter What* hits US #8, as *No Dice* reaches US #28.

1971 Jan *No Matter What* hits UK #5.
Aug [1] Badfinger plays in George Harrison's benefit concert for Bangladesh at Madison Square Garden, New York.

1972 Jan *Day After Day* hits UK #10, but parent album *Straight Up* flops.
Feb [5] *Day After Day* hits US #4, 1 place in front of Nilsson's cover of Pete Ham/Tom Evans' *Without You*, which will go on to top US chart 2 weeks later, for a month. *Day After Day* becomes the group's first million-seller, and *Straight Up* reaches US #31.

BADFINGER cont.

Mar [11] *Without You* tops UK chart, for 5 weeks.
Apr [29] *Baby Blue* reaches US #14.

1973 **Dec** *Ass* is the group's last Apple release, making US #122.

1974 **Mar** Now signed to Warner Bros., *Badfinger*, produced by Chris Thomas climbs to US #161, but goes no further after Warner Bros. withdraw all copies from the stores and initiate a lawsuit against Badfinger Enterprises. (Group's business manager Stan Polley will be accused, amid much bitterness, of mishandling their affairs.) Ham quits the band, and is replaced by Bob Jackson. Ham rejoins a few days later.
Nov *Wish You Were Here*, released during US tour, makes US #148. Frustration over management and financial problems sees Molland leave at the end of UK tour with Man; Ham becomes deeply depressed.

1975 **Jan** Group begins work on tentatively titled *Head First*, with producers Kenny Kerner and Richie Wise.
Apr [23] Plagued mainly by the group's ongoing problems, Ham commits suicide, hanging himself in the garage of his London home. The other members drift apart. Gibbins moves back to Wales. (Years later he will reappear, playing drums on Bonnie Tyler's worldwide hit, *It's A Heartache*.) Molland forms Blue Goose, then Natural Gas releasing an eponymously-titled album and opening for Peter Frampton at the height of his *Frampton Comes Alive!* success. Evans and Jackson join The Dodgers, releasing a handful of singles.

1978 Molland, laying carpet in Los Angeles, CA, and Evans, insulating pipes in the UK, re-form Badfinger, with Joe Tanzin on guitar and Kenny Harck on drums, and sign to Elektra Records to record *Airwaves*. Session drummer Andy Newmark replaces Harck midway through the sessions, and by the time the project is completed, Tanzin has also left. When the record is released Molland and Evans are the only credited band members.

1979 **Mar** *Airwaves* makes US #125.
Apr [21] *Love Is Gonna Come At Last* peaks at US #69.

1981 **Mar** Group, now comprising Molland, Evans, Tony Kaye (ex-Yes), Glenn Sherba and Richard Bryans, signs with Radio Records.
[21] *Hold On* peaks at US #56, as parent album *Say No More* reaches US #155.

1983 **Nov** After the band splits once again at the end of a US tour, Evans, fighting a continuing battle to receive a fair royalty deal for his songs, especially the multi-million-selling *Without You*, commits suicide in identical circumstances to Ham.

1985 Molland, now living in Minneapolis and with solo *After The Pearl* to his credit, and Gibbins, living in Royal Oak, MI, successfully sue to recover royalties from the group's Apple recordings and re-form Badfinger.

1989 Still touring US intermittently, Molland forms Independent Records, releasing *Timeless* with Randy Anderson (guitar), A.J. Nicholas (bass) and Gibbins (drums).

1990 Rhino releases *The Best Of Badfinger, Volume II*, comprising Warner Bros. material, while Rykodisc releases *Day After Day*, a live album of a 1974 concert.

JOAN BAEZ

1958 **July** Raised in California, New York, Iraq and Massachusetts, where her father is working at MIT, Baez (b. Joan Chandos Baez, Jan.9, 1941, Staten Island, New York, NY), the second of 3 daughters of a Mexican father and Scottish mother, studying at Boston University's School of Drama, having played local coffee houses Club Mt. Auburn 47, the Ballad Room and the Golden Vanity in Cambridge, MA, and cut demos which will emerge in 1964 as *Joan Baez In San Francisco* and participated in a recording for local Veritas Records, *Folksingers 'Round Harvard Square*, performs before a crowd of 13,000 as Bob Gibson's special guest at the first Newport Folk Festival in Newport, RI. (Her performance will be featured on compilation album *Folk Festival, Vol.2*.)

1960 She signs to Vanguard Records as a folk singer, and releases her eponymous debut album (which will chart at US #15 in 1962 and UK #9 in 1965).

1961 **Apr** Baez meets Bob Dylan for the first time, at Gerde's Folk City in Greenwich Village, New York.
Oct *Joan Baez, Vol.2* is released, becoming first chart entry at US #13.

1962 **Oct** *Joan Baez In Concert* is released, and climbs to hit US #10.

1963 **May** [17] She headlines the first Monterey Folk Festival, Monterey, CA, alongside protege Bob Dylan.
July Baez appears at Newport Folk Festival (the first to be held since she debuted there) and also introduces Bob Dylan. (She is featured on compilation albums *Newport Broadside*, the only time Baez and Dylan will appear together on record, and *Evening Concerts At Newport Vol.1*.)
Aug [28] She sings *We Shall Overcome* at a Civil Rights march on Washington, DC.
Nov [9] Baez' debut chart single *We Shall Overcome*, recorded live at Miles college in Birmingham, AL, peaks at US #90.
Dec Early recordings made at 1959 Newport Folk Festival, with Bill Wood and Ted Alevizos, are released on *The Best Of Joan Baez*, for Squire Records, which reaches US #45.

1964 Live *Joan Baez In Concert, Vol.2* hits US #7, and 6 months later will become her UK chart debut at #8.
Apr Baez refuses to pay 60% of her income tax in protest at US Government expenditure on armaments. She joins a picket line in Texas supporting youngsters opposing racial discrimination in employment. She also refuses to appear on ABC TV's "Hootenanny", because the program refuses to book blacklisted acts.

1965 **Jan** *Joan Baez No.5* reaches US #12.
May [23] Baez performs at the Royal Albert Hall, London.
[28] During her stay in London, she leads a Vietnam protest march with Donovan from London's Marble Arch to Trafalgar Square, where the Committee Of 100 stages a rally against US policy in Vietnam. She and Donovan sing in Trafalgar Square.
June *Joan Baez No.5* hits UK #3, and is her most successful UK album. Baez founds the Institute For The Study Of Non-Violence, in Carmel, CA, with political mentor, Ira Sandperl, and withholds a further 10% of taxes from the US Government. *We Shall Overcome* becomes her first UK hit single, reaching UK #26.
July *Joan Baez* hits UK #9.
Aug Phil Ochs' song *There But For Fortune* hits UK #8.
Sept Dylan's song *It's All Over Now Baby Blue* takes her to UK #22.
[29] Baez begins a UK tour at Fairfield Hall, Croydon, London, which will include a performance at the Royal Albert Hall, London, on Oct.18.
Oct [9] *There But For Fortune* makes US #50.
Dec She films segment for "TNT Awards Show", with Bo Diddley, The Byrds, Ray Charles, Lovin' Spoonful, The Ronettes, Ike & Tina Turner, Roger Miller, Petula Clark and Donovan, singing *You've Lost That Lovin' Feelin'*. *Farewell Angelina*, another Dylan song, makes UK #35.

1966 **Jan** [20] *Farewell Angelina* makes UK #49, as parent album *Farewell Angelina* hits US #10 and UK #5.
July [28] *Pack Up Your Sorrows*, written by Baez' brother-in-law Richard Farina, who has died in a motorcycle crash 2 months earlier, makes UK #50.
Oct [8] She takes part in a peace festival with The Grateful Dead and Quicksilver Messenger Service at the Outdoor theater in Mt. Tamalpais State Park, CA.
[16] Baez is one of 124 anti-draft demonstrators arrested for blocking the entrance to the Armed Forces' Induction Center at Oakland, CA, and jailed for 10 days.

1967 **Aug** Because of her strident opposition to the Vietnam War, the Daughters Of The American Revolution refuse to allow Baez to perform live at Constitution Hall, Washington, DC.
Sept *Joan* reaches US #38.

1968 **Mar** Baez marries draft resister David Harris, leader of Peace & Liberation Commune in Palo Alto, CA, who will spend half of their 3-year marriage in jail for draft evasion, in New York.
Baez' memoirs **Daybreak** are published in US.
Aug *Baptism* makes US #84.

1969 **Jan** *Any Day Now*, consisting wholly of Bob Dylan songs and recorded in Nashville, TN, is released and will reach US #30.
May [10] *Love Is Just A Four-Letter Word* stalls at US #86.
June She releases *David's Album*, a collection of songs dedicated to her imprisoned husband; it reaches US #36.
July Compilation album *Joan Baez On Vanguard* peaks at UK #15.
Aug [17] Baez performs at the Woodstock Festival.
Dec Son Gabriel is born.

1970 **May** *One Day At A Time* stalls at US #80. (She is also featured on compilation albums *Woodstock* and *Celebration At Big Sur*.)
Aug [30] Baez plays the final day at the Isle of Wight Pop Festival.
Oct *Daybreak* is published in UK. Compilation album *The First 10 Years* makes US #73.

1971 "Carry It On", a film in which she appears with husband Harris, is released. She also releases her final album for Vanguard, and is featured on *Woodstock Two* and *Sacco And Vanzetti*.
Mar [15] Harris is released from jail.
Apr [3] *The First 10 Years* makes UK #41, her last UK chart album.
Oct [2] Her cover of The Band's Civil War story-song *The Night They*

Drove Old Dixie Down, hits US #3, becoming a million-seller, and will hit UK #6. Taken from *Blessed Are*, it returns her to US Top 20 at #11.

Dec [18] A revival of The Beatles' *Let It Be* makes US #49.

972 Jan *Carry It On* peaks at US #164.

May After more than a decade with Vanguard, Baez signs to A&M Records and releases *Come From The Shadows*, recorded in Nashville with co-producer Norbert Putnam, reaching US #48. (She is also featured on albums *Silent Running*, *A Tribute To Woody Guthrie, Part 2*, *Earl Scruggs: His Family & Friends* and *One Hand Clapping*.)

Sept [2] *In The Quiet Morning*, written by her sister Mimi Farina in tribute to Janis Joplin, peaks at US #69.

Dec Baez travels to Hanoi, N.Vietnam, through the auspices of the Liaison Committee to distribute Christmas gifts and mail to US prisoners of war.

[12] *The Joan Baez Ballad Book* peaks at US #188.

973 May Indicating that her political stance has not relaxed, Baez devotes one side of album *Where Are You Now, My Son?* to a sound documentary of US bombing in Vietnam. It makes US #138.

July *Hits/Greatest & Others* makes US #163.

974 Baez releases *Gracias A La Vida!*, with Joni Mitchell duetting on track *Dida*.

975 July [26] *Diamonds And Rust*, featuring songs by Jackson Browne, Janis Ian and John Prine, her biggest-seller for 4 years, reaches US #11. (She is also featured on *The Earl Scruggs Revue: Anniversary Special Vol.1*.)

Aug [2] *Blue Sky* peaks at US #57.

Oct [29] Baez joins Dylan as part of his "Rolling Thunder Revue" tour of US, which launches in Plymouth, MA.

Nov [15] Title track *Diamonds And Rust*, an autobiographical song concerned with Baez' early romantic involvement with Dylan, is her last US chart single, reaching #35.

976 Mar [20] Live album *From Every Stage* reaches US #34.

Dec [11] *Gulf Winds* makes US #62.

977 Aug [6] *Blowin' Away*, recorded in Los Angeles with Wilton Felder, Joe Sample, Larry Knechtel, Donald "Duck" Dunn, Jeff "Skunk" Baxter, Tom Scott and others, and the first result of signing to Portrait Records, makes US #54. (She is also featured on compilation album *Banjoman*.)

978 Jan [7] A&M compilation *The Best Of Joan C. Baez* peaks at US #121.

Feb She appears opposite Bob Dylan in his film, "Renaldo And Clara".

979 May Baez is one of 84 signatories of the open letter to the Socialist Republic of Vietnam, calling for an end to torture in Vietnam and release of political prisoners. Baez lobbies President Carter to rescue Vietnamese boat people from drowning. The President will send the 7th Fleet to expedite Baez' plea.

Aug [25] *Honest Lullaby*, produced by Barry Beckett at Muscle Shoals Sound studios in Alabama, on Portrait, reaches US #113, and is Baez' last chartmaking album.

980 Baez is featured on *Bread & Roses Festival Of Acoustic Music* and guests on *The Amazing Rhythm Aces*.

981 Aug On tour in South America, she is greeted with bomb threats and general harassment, having been vocal in opposition to the right-wing coup in Chile. (She also records an album with Grateful Dead, but it will never be released.)

982 June Still a tireless campaigner in peace causes, Baez (with Jackson Browne, Linda Ronstadt and others) performs for 1 million people in Central Park, New York, at the end of a peace rally.

983 During the year, Baez embarks on an 18-city US tour which will end with 2 shows at Beacon theater, New York.

984 She tours Europe with Dylan and Santana, but drops out of tour midway amidst arguments. (She is also featured on *The Earl Scruggs Revue: Super Jammin'* and *Hard Travellin'*.)

985 July [13] Baez performs at Live Aid in Philadelphia, PA.

986 June Baez takes part in the Amnesty International concert performing with The Neville Brothers, on a bill also featuring Sting, Peter Gabriel, Bryan Adams, Joni Mitchell and Lou Reed.

987 A second autobiography **And A Voice To Sing With** is published. She signs to Gold Castle Records and releases *Recently*, featuring her interpretations of Peter Gabriel's *Biko* and U2's *MLK* amongst others. It is her first album in 5 years.

989 Apr *Diamonds & Rust In The Bullring*, recorded live in Bilbao, Spain, in 1988, is released.

July [18-19] Baez takes part in the seventh annual Prince's Trust Rock Gala, with Alexander O'Neal, Van Morrison, Level 42 and others, at the NEC, Birmingham, W.Midlands.

Dec [16] Baez ends a US tour at Universal Amphitheater, Los Angeles.

990 *Speaking Of Dreams*, featuring a version of George Michael's *Hand To Mouth*, is released.

Aug [11] Baez performs at Ben & Jerry's Newport Folk Festival at Fort Adams State Park, RI, during a short 7-date tour of Northeastern US.

ANITA BAKER

1980 As lead singer of Chapter 8, Baker (b. Dec.20, 1957, Detroit, MI) records *I Just Want To Be Your Girl* which collects strong R&B airplay, but neither it nor *Chapter 8* achieve chart success. Baker quits the group and settles into an office job in Detroit.

1983 Jan She is offered a solo recording contract by US independent R&B music label, Beverly Glen Records.

June First solo release is double-A-sided ballad *No More Tears*, paired with *Will You Be Mine*, which makes #49 on US R&B chart.

Oct *Angel* hits US R&B #5, but despite sales does not cross over.

Nov *The Songstress*, which contains the singles, having already reached #12 on R&B album survey, crosses over to US #139.

1984 Feb *You're The Best Thing Yet* is another R&B chartmaker (#28). Baker now falls out with Beverly Glen, and will spend time in legal efforts to break free from her contract.

1985 With problems resolved, Baker signs to Elektra Records, and teams with producer (and former Chapter 8 keyboardist) Michael Powell to record a series of songs (her own and some covers) over which they have total creative control.

1986 Apr Later to be regarded as a soul classic, *Rapture* hits first in UK, eventually making #13.

July [26-27] Following UK acclaim for the album, Baker visits London and plays 2 sell-out shows at Hammersmith Odeon, to unanimous critical euphoria.

Sept [20] *Rapture* tops US R&B chart, having reached US #11.

Nov [1] *Sweet Love*, co-written by Baker, finally gives her a major US hit single, hitting #8.

Dec *Sweet Love* peaks at UK #13.

1987 Feb [14] A remix of *Caught Up In The Rapture* (originally from the album) reaches US #37.

[24] Baker wins Best R&B Vocal Performance, Female, for *Rapture* and Best R&B Song for *Sweet Love* at the 29th annual Grammy awards. *Caught Up In The Rapture* makes UK #51, as Baker concentrates on follow-up to her multi-platinum Elektra debut.

Oct The Winans' *Ain't No Need To Worry*, with lead vocals by Baker, reaches US R&B #15.

1988 Mar [2] Baker wins Best Soul Gospel Performance By A Duo, Group, Choir Or Chorus with The Winans for *Ain't No Need To Worry* at the 30th annual Grammy awards.

May [23] *Same Ole Love (365 Days A Year)* makes US #44.

Oct *Giving You The Best That I Got* makes UK #55.

[24] *No One In The World* makes US #44.

Nov [12] *Giving You The Best That I Got* tops US R&B chart.

[19] *Giving You The Best That I Got* hits US R&B #1 and UK #9.

Dec [17] Title ballad *Giving You The Best That I Got* hits US #3.

[24] Baker marries long-time beau Walter Bridgeforth as *Giving You The Best That I Got* hits US #1, achieving multi-platinum status.

1989 Feb [22] Baker wins Best R&B Vocal Performance, Female and Best R&B Song for *Giving You The Best That I Got* at the 31st annual Grammy awards.

Apr [1] *Just Because* reaches US #14.

May [11] Baker co-hosts The Songwriters' Hall Of Fame 20th Anniversary.

1990 Jan [22] Baker wins Favorite Soul/R&B Female and sings *Good Love* at 17th annual American Music Awards.

Feb [21] Baker wins Best R&B Vocal Performance, Female for *Giving You The Best That I Got* at the 32nd annual Grammy awards at the Shrine Auditorium, Los Angeles, having won the Singles category for the title cut a year earlier.

Mar Melba Moore's *Lift Every Voice And Sing*, on which Baker guests with Bobby Brown, Howard Hewett, Freddie Jackson, Jeffrey Osborne, Dionne Warwick and Stevie Wonder, is released.

Apr [16] Baker participates in the "Nelson Mandela – An International Tribute To A Free South Africa" concert at Wembley Stadium, London.

June [15-16] European dates are highlighted by sell-out concert at the Wembley Arena, London.

[30] Baker begins extensive "Compositions" tour at Pine Knob Music theater, Clarkston, MI, as *Talk To Me* peaks at UK #68.

July [14] *Compositions*, mainly recorded live without overdubs using a rhythm section comprising Greg Phillinganes (keyboards), Nathan East (bass) and Steve Ferrone and Ricky Lawson (drums), enters UK chart at peak position #7.

[28] *Talk To Me* makes US #44.

Aug [25] *Compositions* hits US #5 in its sixth week of release.

Oct [13] *Soul Inspiration* peaks at US #72.

Nov [3] *Rubáiyát*, Elektra's 40th anniversary compilation, to which Baker contributes a cover of *You Belong To Me*, makes US #140.

Dec [1] Baker wins Best Female Artist for *Compositions* at the 23rd annual NAACP Image awards at the Wiltern theater, Los Angeles.

1991 **Jan** *Fairy Tales*, the third single from *Compositions*, fails to chart as Baker begins further US live dates.

[20] Baker wins Best R&B Vocal Performance, Female for *Compositions* at the 33rd annual Grammy awards at Radio City Music Hall, New York.

HANK BALLARD

1953 **May** Raised by an aunt and uncle in Bessemer, AL, Ballard (b. Henry Ballard, Nov.18, 1936, Detroit, MI) leaves Ford car factory to join the Detroit-based Royals, a doo-wop group signed to Federal Records, taking over as lead singer from Henry Booth. Later the name is changed to The Midnighters to avoid confusion with label-mates The Five Royales.

1954 **Mar** First single under new name is *Work With Me Annie*, written by Ballard. Ripe with sexual innuendo and widely radio-banned, it still becomes a #1 US R&B chart hit.

July *Sexy Ways* continues the *Annie* saga, hitting #3 on US R&B chart.

1955 The theme continues with *Annie Had A Baby* and *Annie's Aunt Fanny* during the year, also prompting answer records like Etta James' *Roll With Me Henry*.

1959 **Jan** After a long spell without hits, they switch to King label (Federal's parent), with name amended to Hank Ballard & The Midnighters.

Mar [23] *Teardrops On Your Letter* is an R&B chart smash (#4), and makes US pop chart at #87. The B-side is Ballard composition *The Twist*, which Ballard claims is lifted from The Drifters' 1953 *Whatcha' Gonna Do?* and given to him by The Nightingales, with Ballard making some minor changes.

May [11] *Kansas City* peaks at US #72, though eclipsed by Wilbert Harrison's #1 version.

1960 **Aug** [15] *Finger Poppin' Time*, a Ballard song about a dance, is the long-awaited pop chart triumph, hitting US #7, one place above Chubby Checker's fast-climbing cover of *The Twist*, and ultimately selling over a million copies.

Sept [19] Checker's *The Twist*, with massive national TV promotion behind it, tops US chart, as Ballard's version, selling well in Checker's wake, reaches US #28.

Nov [21] Follow-up million-seller *Let's Go, Let's Go, Let's Go* hits US #6.

1961 **Jan** [30] Dance-themed *The Hoochi-Coochie-Coo* reaches US #23.

Mar [20] *Let's Go Again (Where We Went Last Night)* makes US #39.

May [15] *The Continental Walk*, using another new dance fad, reaches US #33.

June [19] *The Float* climbs to US #92.

July [24] New dance novelty *The Switch-A-Roo* reaches US #26.

Aug [28] *Nothing But Good* makes US #49.

Sept [11] B-side *Keep On Dancing* peaks at US #66, but the dance gimmick is about to run out of momentum.

1962 **Feb** Chubby Checker tops US chart again with *The Twist* during the dance's worldwide revival.

Mar [10] Ballard counters with *Do You Know How To Twist?* It makes US #87, but is his last hit. The Midnighters discover Islam and, as black Muslims, refuse to play to white audiences. He splits with band, stays on King label as a soloist and begins to work with James Brown band.

1968 After a long period with few releases, Ballard becomes a full-time member of the James Brown tour revue.

1972 **Nov** After a spell with Silver Fox Records, the first of several label switches which will bring no hits and increasing obscurity, Ballard returns to work with James Brown for a period. His recitation on Brown's *Get On The Good Foot* praises him for rescuing Ballard from a self-destructive spiral.

1974 He tries a novelty revival of his *Let's Go* hit as topical *Let's Go Streaking*, but finds no success.

1986 **Dec** After years playing his old hits on the US soul club circuit, he visits UK to perform London Christmas show organized by Charly Records, licensee of his King hits in UK. The show is recorded for a UK live album which gains critical favor, and Ballard belatedly earns R&B legend status in the UK, where he never had a hit.

1989 Ballard, Checker and Joey Dee play at Lulu's Roadhouse, Kitchener,

Canada, for reunion to be part of feature length documentary on the Twist.

1990 **Jan** [17] Ballard is inducted into the Rock'N'Roll Hall Of Fame at the fifth annual dinner at the Waldorf Astoria hotel, New York. He breaks down during his induction speech as he pays tribute to his wife and manager Theresa McNeil, a fatal victim of a hit-and-run driver in New York 3 months earlier.

AFRIKA BAMBAATAA

1976 After 2 years as a teenage lieutenant in a Bronx, New York, street gang called The Black Spades, Bambaataa (b. 1958, South Bronx, New York, NY) forms Zulu Nation, a Bronx-based grouping of cultural/political street people. The music of turntable DJs and rappers at block parties and in clubs is central to the group and Bambaataa's reputation as a DJ and Emcee grows as the momentum of the rap/electro/hip-hop genre he is helping to pioneer develops.

1980 Bambaataa makes his first venture into recorded hip-hop for producer Paul Winfield, with different versions of *Zulu Nation Throwdown* by 2 rap groups in his collective, Cosmic Force and Soulsonic Force. Thereafter, Bambaataa joins forces with fledgling New York street dance label Tommy Boy, run by Tom Silverman.

1982 **Feb** Debut Tommy Boy release is *Jazzy Sensation* (based on Gwen Guthrie's *Funky Sensation*) by another Zulu Nation rap group, The Jazzy Five, co-produced by Bambaataa and Arthur Baker.

Sept [11] *Planet Rock*, credited to Afrika Bambaataa & The Soul Sonic Force (Emcee G.L.O.B.E., Mr. Biggs and Pow Wow), produced by John Robie and Arthur Baker, and fusing rap with the electronic music of European groups like Tangerine Dream and Kraftwerk (whose *Trans-Europe Express* is a primary inspiration for the track), is a huge street-level, 12" single hit in New York and other US urban areas. Lack of airplay restricts it to US #48, but it still earns it a gold disk for a million-plus sales. In UK it reaches #53. (It will have a huge dance record influence on both sides of the Atlantic with its bass line used on at least 70 American releases in 1983.)

1983 **Mar** Bambaataa, Baker and Soul Sonic Force follow up with *Looking For The Perfect Beat*, a US and UK Dance chart smash, which he features in film "Beat Street". (The track will subsequently evolve into Bomb The Bass' smash *Beat Dis*.)

1984 **Mar** *Renegades Of Funk*, Bambaataa's last Tommy Boy release, cements his position as the most influential producer/arranger/catalyst in the new musical style, and also reaches UK #30.

June Switching to New York label Celluloid, Bambaataa releases first album *Shango Funk Theology*, co-produced with bassist Bill Laswell and featuring Shango – a studio line-up of rappers and funk musicians.

Sept Tom Silverman teams Bambaataa with soul veteran James Brown on *Unity (Part 1 – The Third Coming)*, which charts at UK #49.

1985 **Feb** The liaison with Laswell continues on *World Destruction* by Time Zone, which pairs Bambaataa and Public Image Ltd (and ex-Sex Pistols' singer John Lydon. It makes UK #44.

Dec [14] Artists United Against Apartheid, comprising 49 artists including Bambaataa, makes US #38 and UK #21 with *Sun City*.

1986 He severs connection with Soul Sonic Force, following the prosecution of 2 of its members for armed robbery in the late 70s.

1987 Signed to The Family, he releases *Bambaataa's Theme* and *Beware (The Funk Is Everywhere)*.

1988 Now with EMI, he records *The Light With The Family*, with Bill Laswell returning to co-produce some tracks, with guests Boy George, Nona Hendryx and UB40.

Mar *Reckless*, with UB40 and Family, reaches UK #17.

BANANARAMA

Sarah Dallin (vocals)
Keren Woodward (vocals)
Siobhan Fahey (vocals)

1981 **Jan** Dallin (b. Dec.17, 1961, Bristol, Avon) and Woodward (b. Apr.2, 1961, Bristol), former Bristol schoolfriends and now living in a flat in London's Tin Pan Alley above a rehearsal hall with Fahey, leave their day jobs (Woodward working at the BBC, Fahey working in the Decca Records press office and Dallin attending the London School of Fashion) to perform as an unaccompanied vocal trio in pubs and clubs.

June DJ Gary Crowley (Fahey's former Decca colleague) helps them make some demos, leading to a one-off deal with Demon Records.

Sept First recording *Ai A Mwana*, with production by ex-Sex Pistol

Paul Cook, appears in UK on Demon and enters the Independent chart, attracting London Records which signs the trio, reissuing the same cut.
Oct UK trio Fun Boy Three asks the trio to back them on a new single.

'82 **Mar** [13] *It Ain't What You Do, It's The Way That You Do It* by Fun Boy Three With Bananarama, hits UK #4.
May [1] Trio's revival of The Velvelettes' oldie *Really Sayin' Somethin'*, with Fun Boy Three now backing them, hits UK #5.
July Bananarama team with producers Tony Swain and Steve Jolley, who present them with a song called *Big Red Motorbike*. They rewrite the lyrics, and the song re-emerges as *Shy Boy*, which hits UK #4.
Dec [11] *Cheers Then*, a ballad which departs from the now-familiar jaunty trio sound and produced by Barry Blue, is a comparative UK flop, only reaching #45.

'83 **Mar** A revival of Steam's 1969 US #1 *Na Na Hey Hey Kiss Him Goodbye*, climbs to UK #5. Debut album *Deep Sea Skiving* hits UK #7.
July [16] *Shy Boy* provides US chart debut peaking at #83, as parent album *Deep Sea Skiving* climbs to US #63.
Aug *Cruel Summer*, continuing mostly synchronized dance step routine promo video clip in Bananarama tradition, hits UK #8.

'84 **Mar** *Robert De Niro's Waiting* is their biggest UK hit at #3.
Apr *Bananarama* reaches UK #16.
May [26] *Robert De Niro* stalls at US #95, but the actor himself loves the song and contacts the band to arrange a meeting.
June *Rough Justice* reaches UK #23. (During its recording, the band's personal and professional friend Thomas Reilly was shot dead in Belfast – they attend his funeral.)
July [29] *Cruel Summer*, released in US after being featured in movie "The Karate Kid", becomes their first major US chart success, at #9. *Bananarama* benefits accordingly, reaching US #30.
Nov [25] Bananarama gathers with 35 other artists in SARM studio, Notting Hill, London, to record historic *Do They Know It's Christmas?*
Dec [8] Though not issued in UK, *The Wild Life*, from film of the same title, makes US #70.
UK release *Hotline To Heaven* disappoints commercially, peaking at #58.

'85 **Aug** *Do Not Disturb*, their only release of 1985, peaks at UK #31.
'86 **May** First link with the production team Stock/Aitken/Waterman results in a recording of Shocking Blue's 1970 hit *Venus*.
July *Venus* hits UK #8. *True Confessions* follows, peaking at UK #46.
Aug *More Than Physical* makes UK #41.
Sept [6] *Venus* tops US chart. (This is the fourth occasion that a remake of a #1 has topped the Hot 100. Shocking Blue's original hit the top spot on Feb.7, 1970.)
True Confessions reaches US #15.
Nov [8] *More Than Physical* makes US #73.
Dec [30] Keren Woodward and her husband David have a son.

'87 **Jan** [24] *A Trick Of The Night* stalls at US #76.
Feb BBC TV's "In At The Deep End" shows the making of an amateur promo video, lensed by host Chris Searle, for new Bananarama single *A Trick Of The Night*. It is mysteriously replaced by a completely new clip when shown to promote the UK #32 hit.
Apr Bananarama is in the line-up of Stock/Aitken/Waterman's *Let It Be* single by Ferry Aid, a benefit record for the Zeebrugge Disaster Fund. This enters UK chart at #1.
July *I Heard A Rumour* reaches UK #14.
Aug Siobhan Fahey marries Dave Stewart of Eurythmics.
Sept Fourth album *Wow!* reaches UK #27 and US #44.
[26] *I Heard A Rumour* hits US #4.
Oct *Love In The First Degree* peaks at UK #3, its funky Stock/Aitken/Waterman-contrived B-side, *Mr. Sleeze*, contributing strongly to sales.

'88 **Jan** [9] *I Can't Help It* makes US #47.
I Can't Help It reaches UK #20.
Feb [8] Group performs *Love In The First Degree* at the seventh annual BRIT Awards at London's Royal Albert Hall, in what will be Fahey's last performance with group. Now living in Los Angeles, Fahey retires from the group to enjoy married life in California, before starting new duo Shakespear's Sister with Marcella Detroit. A friend, Jacqui Sullivan, one-time vocalist with The Shillelagh Sisters, takes her place.
Apr *I Want You Back* hits UK #5.
[23] *Love In The First Degree* makes US #48.
Oct *Love, Truth And Honesty* reaches UK #23.
The Greatest Hits Collection, featuring 18 cuts on CD, hits UK #3.
Dec [3] *Love, Truth & Honesty* stalls at US #89.
Nathan Jones, updating The Supremes' 1971 US #16, reaches UK #15.
The Greatest Hits Collection peaks at US #151.

'89 **Jan** Shakespear's Sister performs in Leningrad, USSR.
Mar *Help*, with La Na Nee Nee Noo Noo, a parody of Bananarama

both vocally and stylistically and featuring Bananarama themselves, comprising comediennes Dawn French, Jennifer Saunders and Kathy Burke, hits UK #3, with profits from the record going to Comic Relief.
June *Cruel Summer* remix reaches UK #19.
Aug Shakespear's Sister's *You're History* hits UK #7.
Sept Shakespear's Sister's debut album *Sacred Heart* hits UK #9.
Oct Extracted single, *Run Silent*, peaks at UK #54.

1990 **Aug** [4] *Only Your Love* reaches UK #27, co-written and produced by Youth.
1991 **Jan** [19] Bananarama's self-written *Preacher Man*, again produced by Youth, reaches UK #20.
Apr After long period of silence, Bananarama returns with *Poplife* and extracted single, a revival of The Doobie Brothers' *Long Train Running*.

THE BAND

Robbie Robertson (guitar, vocals)
Richard Manuel (piano, vocals)
Garth Hudson (organ)
Rick Danko (bass, vocals)
Levon Helm (drums, vocals)

1964 Helm (b. May 26, 1942, Marvell, AR), playing in local Marvell band The Jungle Bush Beaters, joins Ronnie Hawkins & The Hawks, and after extensive touring in Canada, in Ontario and Quebec, and US cities near the Canadian/US border, decide to settle in Toronto, Canada in 1959. 15-year-old Robertson (b. Jaime Robertson, July 5, 1944, Toronto), already a veteran of local bands Robbie & The Robots, Thumper & The Trombones and Little Caesar & The Consuls, joins on bass, taking over on guitar from Fred Carter Jr., when he decides to return to US. Danko (b. Dec.9, 1943, Simcoe, Canada) joins after opening for Hawkins in 1961, replacing Rebel Paine. Manuel (b. Apr.3, 1945, Stratford, Canada), from Stratford rock band The Rockin' Revols, joins that summer. Hudson (b. Aug.2, 1937, London, Canada), leader of Paul London & The Capers, joins just before Christmas 1961, only after Hawkins agrees to pay him for giving the other band members music lessons. The Hawks, also comprising vocalist Bruce Bruno and saxophonist Jerry Penfound, split from Hawkins dissatisfied with the financial set-up. Calling themselves The Levon Helm Sextet, which soon is changed to Levon Helm & The Hawks, they work for the next 18 months in southern Ontario and colleges and bars in Arkansas, Missouri, Oklahoma and Texas. Now without Bruno and Penfound, group records its first single *Leave Me Alone* for Toronto-based Ware label, under the name The Canadian Squires.

1965 They record a one-off single, Robertson-penned *The Stones I Throw*, for Atlantic subsidiary, Atco. Albert Grossman's secretary Mary Martin suggests that The Hawks might be the band that Grossman's act Bob Dylan is looking for to back him on his proposed electric world tour. Dylan sees them during a 4-month residency at Somers Point, NJ.
Apr [30] Dylan's "Don't Look Back" tour with The Band begins in England.
Sept After his first electric gigs at Forest Hills, NY, and the Hollywood Bowl, Los Angeles, CA, where Dylan has used an electric band comprising Robertson, Helm, Al Kooper and Harvey Brooks, he begins rehearsals with The Hawks in Toronto.

1966 **May** Dylan's world tour culminates in a concert at London's Royal Albert Hall. (Helm has not been with the tour since near its start, unhappy with the nightly booing Dylan's folk fans shower on each night's concert. Mickey Jones takes his place.)

1967 After the tour Dylan moves to Woodstock, NY, to begin work on assembling a documentary of the tour. Group is placed on a weekly retainer with Danko and Manuel helping Dylan with the film. Danko finds a rambling house, painted pink, in nearby West Saugerties, NY. Dylan and the group members begin writing and rehearsing material, with Helm being asked back into the band, the results first becoming the celebrated original rock bootleg *Great White Wonder*, released officially by CBS in 1975 as *The Basement Tapes*. Grossman signs a deal for them with Capitol (on the contract they are called The Crackers) and they begin work with producer John Simon.

1968 **Aug** The Band's debut album *Music From Big Pink* (named after the house), including some Dylan compositions (*Tears Of Rage*, *This Wheel's On Fire* and *I Shall Be Released*) plus their own originals, reaches US #30.
Sept [28] *The Weight*, featured in film "Easy Rider", makes UK #21 and US #63, though versions by Aretha Franklin, The Supremes, The Temptations and Jackie DeShannon all go higher in US chart than The Band's original.

1969 Group embarks on live dates, their first since Danko's recovery from a bad auto accident. The Band makes its live debut at the Winterland, San Francisco, CA. (Robertson is so nervous that he becomes ill and can only perform under hypnosis.)

Aug [31] They perform on the second day of Isle of Wight Festival Of Music with Bob Dylan.

Oct *The Band*, recorded in Hollywood Hills, CA, in a house rented from Sammy Davis Jr., hits US #9 and UK #25. It includes *The Night They Drove Old Dixie Down*, later a big hit for Joan Baez (US #3/UK #6).

1970 **Jan** [3] *Up On Cripple Creek* reaches US #25.

Mar [14] *Rag Mama Rag* peaks at UK #57.

May *Rag Mama Rag* reaches UK #16.

Sept *Stage Fright*, the title track written about the group's experience returning to performing, recorded at Woodstock Playhouse, engineered by Todd Rundgren and mixed by Glyn Johns, hits US #5 and UK #15.

Oct [31] Extracted *Time To Kill* is a minor US chart single, at #77.

1971 **Oct** *Cahoots*, the first record to be made at Bearsville studios in Woodstock, reaches US #21, and includes *Life Is A Carnival* on which Allen Toussaint guests and arranges the horn parts, and *4% Pantomime* on which Van Morrison (who co-writes with Robertson) guests.

Nov [13] *Life Is A Carnival* peaks at US #72.

[27] *Cahoots* makes UK #41.

Dec [31] The Band plays 3 concerts at New York's Academy of Music.

1972 **Sept** Double live album *Rock Of Ages*, recorded at the earlier Academy of Music concerts, hits US #6.

Nov [4] Extracted *Don't Do It*, reviving Marvin Gaye's 1964 US #27, makes US #34.

1973 **July** [28] Group plays its first concert since New Year's Eve 1971 in the Watkins Glen Festival with The Allman Brothers Band and The Grateful Dead, at the Watkins Glen racetrack in upstate New York. The Band begins recording *Moondog Matinee*, a collection of oldies. (Title is taken from Alan Freed's Cleveland radio show, which the group members would pick up north of the border in the late 50s.)

Dec [22] *Ain't Got No Home*, the first single to be released from the upcoming oldies album and originally recorded by Clarence "Frogman" Henry, peaks at US #73.

1974 **Jan** [3] Dylan and The Band begin a 6-week tour at Chicago Stadium. In addition to backing Dylan, The Band also has its own set.

Feb The Band, again with Dylan, works on his album *Planet Waves*, and releases its own *Moondog Matinee*, which reaches US #28.

July The Band tours with Dylan, and a live double album *Before The Flood* results, which will hit US #3 and UK #8.

1976 **Jan** [31] *Northern Lights-Southern Cross*, recorded in the group's own Shangri-La studio in Zuma Beach, CA, reaches US #26.

Apr [3] *Ophelia*, the title inspired by Minnie Pearl's real name, peaks at US #62.

Oct [16] *The Best Of The Band* makes US #51, as the group decides to stop touring, and despite good intentions over the next 2 years, split as a band.

Robertson produces Neil Diamond's *Beautiful Noise*.

Nov [25] The Band concludes its career in the grandest style, hosting "The Last Waltz", a remarkable final concert on Thanksgiving Day at San Francisco's Winterland auditorium, the site of their first gigs in the spring of 1969. They invite Paul Butterfield, Bobby Charles, Eric Clapton, Neil Diamond, Bob Dylan, Emmylou Harris, Ronnie Hawkins, Dr. John, Joni Mitchell, Van Morrison, The Staples, Ringo Starr, Muddy Waters, Ron Wood and Neil Young, to the event which is recorded and filmed by Martin Scorsese.

1977 **Apr** [23] *Islands*, recorded to honor the group's contract with Capitol, reaches US #64.

Nov [4] Scorsese-lensed "The Last Waltz", critically acclaimed and revered as one of rock's finest films, premieres in New York.

1978 **Feb** [4] Solo album *Danko* makes US #119.

Apr [29] Warner Bros.' released triple box set *The Last Waltz*, from their farewell concert, makes UK #39.

May The film is released.

June [24] *The Last Waltz* reaches US #16. (Each member of the group will continue to perform in the music arena; Danko and Helm make solo albums, as does Robertson (in 1987), though Hudson and Manuel are rarely heard. Helm forms Levon Helm & The RCO Allstars with Steve Cropper, Dr. John and Paul Butterfield making 3 albums for ABC between 1977 and 1980.)

1980 Helm stars in "The Coalminer's Daughter". Robertson stars in "Carney".

1986 After a number of attempted reunions over the past 5 years, the latest, with James Weider replacing Robertson, reconvenes for live work.

Mar [6] Manuel, apparently in a fit of depression, hangs himself after

a gig in Winter Park, FL. (Robertson will dedicate future solo cut, *Fallen Angel* to him.)

1987 *Robbie Robertson*, his long-awaited debut solo album peaks at US #38 Co-produced with Daniel Lanois, it includes cameo help from U2, Maria McKee and Rick Danko among others.

Dec *Robbie Robertson* reaches UK #24.

1988 **Aug** Though Robertson's *Fallen Angel*, with guest vocals by Peter Gabriel has failed, *Somewhere Down That Crazy River* reaches UK #15. Promotion for his parent album in US has included his first TV appearance for 12 years on NBC TV's "Saturday Night Live".

1989 **Mar** With most ex-members increasingly active, Danko and Helm guesting on Ringo Starr's US tour, Robertson contributing to the Greenpeace-supporting *Rainbow Warriors* album and new *Beauty* album by Japanese artist Ryuichi Sakamoto, The Band is inducted into the Canadian Hall Of Fame at the Juno Awards in Toronto, with Robertson, Danko and Hudson performing together.

During the year, Capitol Records issues double package retrospective *To Kingdom Come*, including previously unreleased material.

1990 **July** [21] The Band takes part in Roger Waters' performance of "The Wall" at the site of the Berlin Wall in Potzdamer Platz, Berlin, Germany. The event is broadcast live throughout the world, and raises money for the Memorial Fund For Disaster Relief.

While Robertson records a second album for Geffen with help from Aaron Neville, Blue Nile, Toni Childs and others, The Band, now comprising Danko, Helm, Hudson and Stan Szelest, on piano, and Weider continues to work on the first of 4 albums, part of a new contract with Columbia.

BAND AID

1984 **Nov** Bob Geldof of The Boomtown Rats sees a graphic BBC TV report on famine in Ethiopia and determines to raise funds to help the situation. With Ultravox's Midge Ure, he writes a song and devises the idea of an all-star record from which nobody (from artists to manufacturer to record shops) takes any profit. Intensive calls around the UK record industry start up the project, with all parties agreeing to donate to the cause. Geldof sets aside his musical career and The Boomtown Rats effectively cease to be.

[25] 36 artists gather in the SARM studio, Notting Hill, London, to record the historic *Do They Know It's Christmas?*, including Geldof and Ure with members of their bands, plus: Bananarama, Phil Collins, Culture Club (Boy George and Jon Moss), Duran Duran, Heaven 17 (Glenn Gregory and Martin Ware), Kool & The Gang (Robert Bell, James Taylor and Dennis Thomas), Marilyn, George Michael, Spandau Ballet, Status Quo (Rick Parfitt and Francis Rossi), Sting, U2 (Bono and Adam Clayton), Jody Watley, Paul Weller and Paul Young.

Dec [7] The record is launched with an Ethiopia Benefit concert at London's Royal Albert Hall, organized by the Save The Children Fund

[15] *Do They Know It's Christmas?* enters UK chart at #1. It stays there for 5 weeks, selling more than 3 million copies to become the biggest-selling ever UK single.

1985 **Jan** [19] *Do They Know It's Christmas?* reaches US #13, and sells over a million copies. With phenomenal success, the official Band Aid Trust is established as a permanent charity to ensure the swift collection of funds and aid to Africa.

[28] Geldof participates in the recording of USA For Africa's *We Are The World*.

Mar The first shipment of relief supplies paid for by Band Aid reaches Ethiopia, accompanied by Geldof.

July [13] At 12.01, Status Quo begins the Live Aid concert extravaganza, staged as a follow-up to the Band Aid project. Held alternately between Wembley Stadium, London, in the presence of the Prince and Princess of Wales, and the JFK Stadium, Philadelphia, PA, the world's biggest rock acts participate in a worldwide fund-raising event. The 16-hour mega-concert includes appearances by Paul Weller Bob Geldof and The Boomtown Rats, Adam Ant, INXS, Ultravox, Spandau Ballet, Elvis Costello, Nik Kershaw, B.B. King, Sade, Sting, Howard Jones, Bryan Ferry, Paul Young, Alison Moyet, Bryan Adams U2, The Beach Boys, Dire Straits, Tears For Fears, Queen, Simple Minds, David Bowie, The Pretenders, The Who, Santana, Pat Metheny Elton John, George Michael, Madonna, The Thompson Twins, Paul McCartney, Tom Petty, Cars, Neil Young, Power Station, Led Zeppelin Duran Duran, Cliff Richard, Daryl Hall & John Oates, Tina Turner, Bo Dylan, The Rolling Stones, Lionel Richie, Harry Belafonte and Patti LaBelle. Phil Collins makes rock history by playing a set at Wembley and flying immediately to Philadelphia to appear later in the day.

Organized by Geldof again, the event is seen as a major synthesis of the rock era. It is watched by an estimated 1½ to 2 billion people, with telethons in 22 countries, and raises $70 million.

Dec *Do They Know It's Christmas?* re-charts in UK, hitting #3, now with special Christmas messages collected on the B-side by artists including Bowie and McCartney. (It will continue to be reissued every Christmas from now on as a perennial reminder.)

1986 June Geldof receives an honorary knighthood from the Queen, in recognition of his humanitarian activities, and is henceforth Bob Geldof KBE. During a heady period, when suggestions are made that he should be honored with the Nobel Peace Prize, Geldof speaks to the United Nations in New York.

1989 Dec [23] Stock/Aitken/Waterman-conceived re-recording of *Do They Know It's Christmas?*, with Kylie Minogue, Jason Donovan, Chris Rea, Matt Goss, Marti Pellow, Cliff Richard, Sonia and Lisa Stansfield, and credited to Band Aid II, enters UK chart at #1.

THE BANGLES
Susanna Hoffs (guitar, vocals)
Vicki Peterson (guitar, vocals)
Michael Steele (bass, vocals)
Debbi Peterson (drums, vocals)

1981 Dec After playing in Los Angeles, CA, as The Colours, Vicki Peterson (b. Jan.11, 1958, Los Angeles, CA), having formed her first band in ninth grade, and needing a drummer, buys a drum kit and recruits sister Debbi (b. Aug.22, 1961, Los Angeles) to play it (the Peterson sisters have already played in The Fans from 1979-1980), and Hoffs (b. Jan.17, 1957, Newport Beach, CA), graduating from the University of California, Berkeley, CA, and placing ad in **The Recycler** – "Band members wanted: Into the Beatles, Byrds and Buffalo Springfield", become The Supersonic Bangs and then The Bangs. With bassist Annette Zilinskas, they release *Getting Out Of Hand* on their own independent label, Downkiddie, with minimal sales.

1982 Jan They are forced to alter their name to The Bangles because a New Jersey group already records as The Bangs. Gigging in Los Angeles area leads to local DJ Rodney Bingenheimer including Bangles song *Bitchin' Summer* on his third *Rodney On The ROQ* compilation album on Posh Boy Records. Miles Copeland signs them to a management deal and books them as opening act for The English Beat.
June 5-song mini-album *The Bangles* is issued on IRS' subsidiary Faulty Products label.

1983 Group signs to CBS Records. Zilinskas leaves and joins Blood On The Saddle and is replaced by Steele (b. June 2, 1954), the original lead singer of all-girl group The Runaways. (Zilinskas will re-surface in 1991 as a member of The Ringling Sisters.)

1984 Aug [4] *All Over The Place*, produced by David Kahne, debuts on US chart, climbing to #80 during a 30-week stay.
Sept *Hero Takes A Fall* is released in US and UK, but does not chart.

1985 Mar [16] *All Over The Place* stalls at UK #86.

1986 Jan Group embarks on world tour.
Feb [1] 6-date UK mini-tour begins at Portsmouth polytechnic, Hants, set to end at Warwick University, W.Midlands on Feb.8.
Mar *Manic Monday*, written by Prince under the pseudonym Christopher and marking the group's chart debut, hits UK #2. *Different Light* is released. It will hit US #2 and UK #3 in Jan.1987 after many months on chart.
Apr [19] *Manic Monday* hits US #2, unable to displace its writer who is at #1 with *Kiss*. Prince will join the band on stage at a concert in San Francisco, CA, for an encore of *Manic Monday*.
May *If She Knew What She Wants*, inked by Jules Shear, makes UK #31.
June [22] The Bangles support Simple Minds at the Milton Keynes Bowl pop festival, Bucks. (and will open for Queen at a concert in Eire).
July Continuing their 60s-tinged musical and visual style, *Going Down To Liverpool*, originally recorded by Katrina & The Waves and featuring Leonard Nimoy in the video, reissued in UK, makes the chart at #56, as the group performs its own sell-out dates in London.
[12] *If She Knew What She Wants* reaches US #29.
Aug Band embarks on major US tour.
Sept Hoffs acts in her debut movie, starring in her film-maker mother Tamara's "The Allnighter", while Steele takes a sabbatical in Australia.
Nov Written by Liam Sternberg in 1983 and rejected by Toni Basil, *Walk Like An Egyptian*, from *Different Light*, hits UK #3.
Dec [20] *Walk Like An Egyptian* is the group's biggest US hit, topping the chart for 4 weeks, toppling Bruce Hornsby's *The Way It Is*. It is aided by fun-time "King Tut" aping video.

1987 Jan *Walking Down Your Street*, the fourth single from *Different Light*, reaches UK #16.
Feb [9] They win Best International Group at the sixth annual BRIT Awards at the Grosvenor House, Mayfair, London.
Apr *Following* peaks at UK #55.
[18] *Walking Down Your Street* reaches US #11.
May [1] "The Allnighter" premieres in US.

1988 Feb [6] Bangles' revival of Simon & Garfunkel's 1966 US #13 *Hazy Shade Of Winter*, produced by Rick Rubin for soundtrack to film "Less Than Zero", and issued as a US single on Rubin's Def Jam label, hits #2, behind Tiffany's *Could've Been*.
Mar *Hazy Shade Of Winter* reaches UK #11.
Nov *In Your Room* makes US #5.
Dec *Everything*, produced by Davitt Sigerson and with contributions from David Lindley and Vinnie Vincent, reaches US #15 (earning a gold disk) and UK #5.

1989 Jan [7] *In Your Room* hits US #5.
Apr [1] Ballad *Eternal Flame* becomes Bangles' second US chart-topper.
[15] *Eternal Flame* tops UK chart.
June [6] Peterson marries group production manager Steve Botting.
[9] Reissued *Walk Like An Egyptian* peaks at UK #73.
[16] *Bangles' Greatest Hits* hits UK #4, but only climbs to US #97.
[24] *Be With You* reaches US #30 and UK #23.
Aug [9] 15-date US tour begins in Wilkes Barre, PA, and will end Sept.2 in Santa Clara, CA.
Sept [21] Group breaks up due to "irreconcilable differences", not least to Hoffs consideration of a solo career.
Oct [14] *I'll Set You Free* peaks at UK #74.

1991 Mar [2] Always the focal point of The Bangles, Hoffs' solo debut album, produced by David Kahne, *When You're A Boy*, makes US #83.
[23] *My Side Of The Bed*, written by Hoffs with Tom Kelly and Billy Steinberg, reaches US #30, having already made UK #44, despite steamy bedroom video.

BAUHAUS
Peter Murphy (vocals)
Daniel Ash (guitar, vocals)
David Jay (bass, vocals)
Kevin Haskins (drums)

1978 Band forms in Northampton, Northants., after the Haskins brothers have played in punk group The Submerged Tenth, and the trio without Murphy has played as The Craze. The quartet's first name is Bauhaus 1919 (taken from the German art movement which began that year).
Dec [31] First public gig as Bauhaus is at a Wellingborough, Northants., pub.

1979 Aug A one-off deal with Small Wonder Records in London produces 12" single *Bela Lugosi's Dead*, which does not chart but will sell consistently in UK for years, a seemingly permanent fixture on the UK Independent chart.
Nov After a concert at London's Rock Garden, and a session for John Peel's BBC Radio 1 show, Beggars Banquet Records signs them to 4AD, its independently-distributed subsidiary label.

1980 Jan *Dark Entries*, a remake of the B-side of *Bela Lugosi*, is released, reinforcing their brooding, sonorous style.
Apr Group embarks on its first European tour, of Germany, Holland and Belgium.
June *Terror Couple Kill Colonel* (inspired by a newspaper headline) is released, again dominating the UK Independent chart.
Sept Bauhaus begins its first US tour.
Oct A revival of T.Rex's *Telegram Sam* continues UK Independent chart success.
Nov [15] Debut album *In The Flat Field* makes UK #72 and tops UK Independent chart for 2 weeks.

1981 Apr [25] *Kick In The Eye*, released on main Beggars Banquet label and the group's first UK national chart single, makes #59.
July *The Passions Of Lovers*, written and recorded within a day, makes UK #56.
Oct [31] *Mask* is a major success, reaching UK #30.
Nov Jay (b. David Haskins) teams with poet/painter Ren Halkett (student of original Bauhaus movement) on *Nothing*. Murphy appears in a highly-rated UK TV ad for Maxell Tapes.

1982 Jan Group makes its first UK TV appearance, on BBC2's "Riverside". Band films a scene for David Bowie/Catherine Deneuve film "The Hunger", performing *Bela Lugosi's Dead* at Heaven nightclub, London.
Mar [20] EP *Searching For Satori* (which includes a remixed version of

Kick In The Eye), makes UK #45.

June [26] *Spirit* makes UK #42, though Bauhaus are publicly unhappy about its arrangement and production.

Oct Group sets out on a UK tour in preparation for new album, supported by Southern Death Cult.

[30] A revival of David Bowie's *Ziggy Stardust*, a tongue-in-cheek issue after a BBC radio session including their version, creates interest, reaches UK #15, helped by an appearance on BBC TV's "Top Of The Pops", and is their biggest hit. *The Sky's Gone Out* benefits accordingly and hits UK #4.

1983 **Jan** *Lagartija Nick* makes UK #44.

Feb Murphy contracts pneumonia, and misses much of recording *Burning From The Inside*.

Apr *She's In Parties* reaches UK #26.

June On its return from dates in Japan, the band begins another UK tour to promote the new album.

July *Burning From The Inside*, a compilation of individual rather than band work, reaches UK #13.

[5] Bauhaus' final UK tour date in London ends with lengthy encores and farewells from the band, and a later press release confirms their dissolution. (Murphy will pursue a largely unsuccessful solo career; Ash and Haskins will work as Tones On Tail then regroup with Jay as Love And Rockets.)

Nov *The Singles 1981-1983* peaks at UK #52.

1985 **Nov** *1979-1983* makes UK #36.

1987 Love And Rockets' *Express* makes US #72.

1989 **May** *Love And Rockets* reaches US #14.

Aug [5] Love And Rockets' *So Alive* hits US #3, aided by heavily rotated stocking clad steamy video clip, as Bauhaus' *Swing The Heartache – The BBC Sessions* makes US #169. (*So Alive* will fail to hit in UK, despite 3 separate releases.)

Sept [30] Love And Rockets' *No Big Deal* climbs to US #82.

1990 **Apr** Murphy undertakes small venue US tour in support of his third solo album *Deep*, still on Beggars Banquet in UK and licensed to RCA in US.

Dec [22] Murphy's *Cuts You Up* wins Top Modern Rock Tracks category in **Billboard**'s The Year In Music.

1991 **Jan** Ash's solo *This Love*, from forthcoming *Coming Down*, is released in US.

Apr [6] *Coming Down* peaks at US #109.

THE BAY CITY ROLLERS

Eric Faulkner (guitar)
Stuart "Woody" Wood (guitar)
Leslie McKeown (vocals)
Alan Longmuir (bass)
Derek Longmuir (drums)

1967 Group is formed at Tynecastle school, Edinburgh, Scotland, by brothers Alan (b. June 20, 1953, Edinburgh) and Derek (b. Mar.19, 1955, Edinburgh) Longmuir, who invite Gordon "Nobby" Clarke to be lead vocalist. Tam Paton, resident bandleader at the Edinburgh Palais, sees them and realizing their potential quits his job to manage them. He picks the group name by sticking a pin in a map of the US, and finding it in Bay City, UT.

1969 Group begins a 12-month Saturday residency as a Top 20 covers band at the Top Storey club, Edinburgh.

1970 **Apr** After Neil Henderson (b. Glasgow, Scotland), having played in several semi-pro bands, and Archie Marr (b. 1953, Edinburgh) join on lead guitar and organ respectively, Eric Manclark (b. 1954, Edinburgh) is recruited.

1971 **June** Group signs with Bell Records in UK which releases first single, a revival of The Gentrys' 1965 US #4 hit *Keep On Dancing*, produced by Jonathan King.

Sept *Keep On Dancing* hits UK #9.

1972 **Mar** Follow-up *We Can Make Music*, fails to chart.

June *Maana* is released, featuring new guitarist Faulkner (b. Oct.21, 1955, Edinburgh). It wins Radio Luxembourg Grand Prix Song Contest.

1973 **Jan** *Saturday Night* fails in UK. Early members John Devine and Clarke leave, replaced by Wood (b. Feb.25, 1957, Edinburgh) and McKeown (b. Nov.12, 1955).

1974 **Feb** *Remember (Sha La La)*, the first of several hits to be written and produced by Bill Martin and Phil Coulter, hits #6, restoring UK success.

May Helped by strong TV exposure, *Shang-A-Lang* hits UK #2.

Aug With group image now firmly aimed at teenage girls, *Summerlove Sensation* hits UK #3.

Oct [12] First album *Rollin'* tops UK chart. *All Of Me Loves All Of You* is released and hits UK #4. A 26-date UK tour follows, with scenes of teenage girl fan mania everywhere. National UK press coins "Rollermania" for the craze, and picks up on the group's tartan stage uniforms as a clothing fad.

1975 **Mar** [22] *Bye Bye Baby*, produced by Phil Wainman and reviving an old Four Seasons' song, becomes their biggest UK hit, topping the charts for 6 weeks.

Apr [1] "Shang-A-Lang" TV series, featuring the group, premieres on ITV. (The series will air until Aug.17, 1977.)

May [3] *Once Upon A Star*, an immediate hit, enters UK chart at #1.

July [19] *Give A Little Love* tops UK chart for 3 weeks.

Sept [20] Group is launched in US via a live appearance on Howard Cosell's "Saturday Night Variety Show" on ABC TV, appropriately singing *Saturday Night*.

Dec [6] *Money Honey* hits UK #3 as parent album *Wouldn't You Like It* hits UK #3.

1976 **Jan** [3] *Saturday Night* tops US chart for a week. (At the height of the group's US success, they sign a deal to have their faces on cereal boxes.)

[24] *Bay City Rollers* reaches US #20.

Apr [3] *Money Honey* hits US #9.

[14] Faulkner almost dies after taking a drug overdose at Tam Paton's house, while in a state of exhaustion.

May [1] *Love Me Like I Love You* hits UK #4.

[8] US-only *Rock'N'Roll Love Letter* reaches US #31.

June [12] Unreleased in UK, *Rock And Roll Love Letter*, an earlier album track for its writer Tim Moore, reaches UK #28. Alan Longmuir leaves, and is replaced by guitarist Ian Mitchell (b. Aug.22, 1958, Scotland), with Wood switching to bass.

Sept [25] Group's revival of Dusty Springfield's *I Only Want To Be With You* hits UK #4, as does parent album *Dedication*.

Oct [23] *I Only Want To Be With You* reaches US #12.

Nov [13] *Dedication* makes US #26.

1977 **Jan** [8] *Yesterday's Hero* peaks at US #54.

Mar [26] *Dedication* peaks at US #60.

May [28] *It's A Game* reaches UK #16.

July [30] *It's A Game* is the band's last charting album, at UK #18.

Aug [6] *You Made Me Believe In Magic* is the Rollers' final single to chart in UK, making #34. It sells better in the US, hitting #10.

[27] *It's A Game* reaches US #23. (Mitchell leaves to form The Ian Mitchell Band, replaced by guitarist Pat McGlynn (b. Mar.31, 1958, Edinburgh).)

1978 **Jan** [1] *Greatest Hits* makes US #77.

[7] *The Way I Feel Tonight* fails in the UK, but makes US #24.

Oct [28] *Strangers In The Wild* makes US #129 but fails to chart in UK, and it is clear that the Rollers have gone out of fashion. Faulkner leaves to go solo and will have success in Japan. (Group will prevail into the 80s pushing the nostalgia aspect of its hits and costumes in minor UK and US venues and clubs.)

1982 **May** [6] Group's former manager, Paton, is convicted of a gross indecency charge and sentenced to 3 years in jail.

1989 With the band now only popular in Japan, where various ex-members reunite annually for touring, a comprehensive Japanese-only CD collection, *Memorial*, is issued by Arista Records.

1990 A group claiming to be The Bay City Rollers embarks on club tour of US. Faulkner says band is doing so under false pretences.

THE BEACH BOYS

Brian Wilson (bass, keyboards, vocals)
Mike Love (vocals)
Carl Wilson (guitar, vocals)
Al Jardine (guitar, vocals)
Dennis Wilson (drums, vocals)

1961 Keen music and radio listener Brian Wilson (b. Brian Douglas Wilson, June 20, 1942, Inglewood, CA), son of Murry Wilson (owner of the ABLE (Always Better Lasting Equipment) machine shop, a small company importing lathes and drills from England, and his wife Audree, who have already taken Brian to audition for a group trying to sign to Art Laboe's Original Sound label, living in Los Angeles, CA-suburb Hawthorne, with his brothers Dennis (b. Dennis Carl Wilson, Dec.4, 1944, Inglewood) and Carl (b. Carl Dean Wilson, Dec.21, 1946, Hawthorne), invites cousin Love (b. Michael Edward Love, Mar.15, 1941, Baldwin Hills, CA) (his mother Emily is Murry Wilson's younger sister) and Jardine (b. Alan Charles Jardine, Sept.3, 1942, Lima, OH) (Brian's classmate at El Camino junior college who has broken quarterback Brian's leg during a Hawthorne Cougars football game) to form a singing quintet. Brian is entranced by the close harmony vocals of The Four Freshmen and other similar acts. They perform some early dates, including one at local Hawthorne high school talent show, as Carl & The Passions, subsequently changing to The Pendletones, playing instruments (not least with money left for the Wilson brothers by Murry and Audree for food, while their parents vacation in Mexico).

Sept [15] Jardine has arranged for the group to meet publisher Hite Morgan, for whom he has already auditioned as a past member of a folk group. Morgan and his wife Dorinda, who are coincidentally friends of the Wilson parents, invite The Pendletones to their home studio to record a song called *Surfin'*, written by Brian and Love at the prompting of keen surfer Dennis. They also record *Laura*, written by Morgan's son Bruce, and a third cut *Lavender*. Morgan signs *Surfin'* to his own Guild publishing company.

Oct [3] Group re-records *Surfin'* and *Laura* at World Pacific studio.

Dec [8] Morgan releases *Surfin'* on his own X label. When RCA threatens suit over the use of X as a label-name, Morgan takes the record to Era's Herb Newman, who picks up distribution through the larger Candix distribution. Candix A&R man Joe Saraceno plays the song to Russ Regan, working at Candix's Buckeye Record Distributors, and between them they coin The Beach Boys. (Group wants to be called The Pendletones, which the label does not like, and Candix wants to dub them The Surfers, a name already used by another group, as pointed out by Regan.)

[29] Group plays the Rendezvous Ballroom, on a bill with Dick Dale, The Surfaris and The Challengers, performing 2 songs during the intermission.

[31] Local radio station K-FWB, where Brian Wilson heard The Four Freshmen for the first time, hires them for a show where they debut under their new name The Beach Boys on the bill of Ritchie Valens' Memorial Dance at Municipal Auditorium, Long Beach, a date for which they earn $300.

1962
Feb Jardine, discouraged by the lack of money the group has made from *Surfin'* (about $200 each), leaves to study dentistry, and is replaced by David Marks (b. Newcastle, PA), who lives across the street from the Wilsons, on rhythm guitar, with Brian switching to bass. Dennis, originally marginally involved, settles as drummer.

[8] Now gigging regularly at the Rainbow Gardens and Cinnamon Cinder clubs in Los Angeles, the group records *Surfer Girl, Surfin' Safari, Judy* and *Karate* (aka *Beach Boy Stomp*) at World Pacific.

Mar [25] *Surfin'* peaks at US #75.

May Under-funded Candix label folds. Murry Wilson, who has assumed the role of manager, takes their recordings to Dot, Decca and Liberty Records in search of a new deal, finally interesting Capitol Records' producer Nick Venet with demo *Surfin' Safari*.

June [4] Capitol releases *409* backed with *Surfin' Safari*.

Oct Group begins a week's engagement at Pandora's Box in Sunset Boulevard.

[13] Initial B-side *Surfin' Safari* now reaches US #14, while A-side *409*, a hot rod song, makes US #76.

Nov *Surfin' Safari*, a mixture of oldies and Brian Wilson songs (mainly written with neighbor Gary Usher) is released, peaking at US #32.

1963
Jan [5] *Ten Little Indians*, from the album, makes US #49.

May [25] *Surfin' USA* returning to the surf theme and their first Top 10 record, hits US #3. It is Brian Wilson's adaptation of the lyrics of Chuck Berry's *Sweet Little Sixteen*, and is the first single to highlight the vocal harmonies that become the group's trademark.

June [22] *Shut Down*, another hot-rodding song, on B-side of *Surfin' USA*, makes US #23.

July [6] *Surfin' USA* hits US #2. Meanwhile, Jan And Dean top US chart with *Surf City*, a song written for them by Brian.

Aug *Surfin' USA*, the group's UK chart debut, makes #34. Jardine, who has finished his dental studies, is invited back because Brian has been missing so many live dates. Sensing that Murry Wilson wants him out, Marks quits. (Months later he will form David Marks & The Marksmen, signing to A&M, before joining Casey Kasem's Band Without A Name and doing sessions with The Turtles. After a long battle with drugs, Marks will enrol at Berklee School of Music, Boston, MA, and then the New England Conservatory of Music.)

Sept [14] *Surfer Girl*, slow harmony ballad on a surf theme, hits US #7.

[28] B-side *Little Deuce Coupe*, by now predictably a car/hot rod song, is again a US hit in its own right, reaching #15.

Oct *Surfer Girl* and *Little Deuce Coupe* are released within 4 weeks of each other, the former showcasing surf numbers, the latter hot rod and

car songs. They are the first Beach Boys albums produced by Brian Wilson. Despite near-simultaneous release, both are major sellers: *Surfer Girl* hits US #7, and *Little Deuce Coupe* hits US #4.

Dec [21] *Be True To Your School*, from *Little Deuce Coupe*, hits US #6, as B-side ballad *In My Room* reaches US #23.

1964
Jan Group makes it first overseas tour, a week-long trip to Australia opening in Sydney. On their way home, they play a concert in Hawaii.

Mar [21] *Fun Fun Fun* hits US #5, as band's clean cut all-American visual style is firmly established.

Apr At a recording session at Western studios for *I Get Around*, Brian fires Murry after they have a fight.

May *Shut Down Vol. 2* reaches US #13.

June Carl Wilson graduates.

July [1] Group headlines "A Million Dollar Party", presented by K-POI, at the International Center Arena, Honoulu, HI, with Jan And Dean, Jimmy Clanton, The Kingsmen, The Rivingtons, Ray Peterson, Jody Miller, Bruce & Terry, Jimmy Griffin, Mary Saenz and Peter And Gordon.

[4] *I Get Around*, the group's first US #1, tops the chart for 2 weeks and sells over a million. B-side *Don't Worry Baby*, written for The Ronettes but rejected by Phil Spector, peaks at US #24.

Aug *All Summer Long* hits US #4, while *I Get Around* is their second UK chart entry and climbs to #7.

Sept Group begins its first major US tour, set to end in Worcester, MA.

[27] They make their debut on CBS TV's "Ed Sullivan Show".

Oct [17] *When I Grow Up (To Be A Man)* hits US #9.

[28-29] The Beach Boys record the "TAMI Show" (Teen Age Music International Show) at the Civic Auditorium in Santa Monica, CA, with The Barbarians, Chuck Berry, James Brown, Marvin Gaye, Gerry & The Pacemakers, Lesley Gore, Jan And Dean, Billy J. Kramer & The Dakotas, Smokey Robinson & The Miracles, The Rolling Stones and The Supremes. (The show will open in UK at the Futurist, Birmingham, W.Midlands as "Gather No Moss" on Aug.7, 1966.)

Nov [1] Group arrives in London for its first UK promotional visit.

[6] They perform *I Get Around, When I Grow Up (To Be A Man)* and *Dance Dance Dance* live on ITV's "Ready Steady Go!", and will also make TV appearances on BBC TV's "Top Of The Pops" and ITV's "Thank Your Lucky Stars" in the next few days.

[14] 2 tracks from EP *Four By The Beach Boys, Wendy* and *Little Honda*, reach US #44 and US #65 respectively, while in UK *When I Grow Up (To Be A Man)* reaches #27, as they set out on second tour of Australia.

Dec [5] *The Beach Boys Concert*, recorded live in Sacramento, CA, and their first #1 album, tops US chart for 4 weeks.

[7] Brian marries Marilyn Rovell at Los Angeles' city courthouse.

[19] *Dance Dance Dance* hits US #8 as *The Beach Boys Christmas Album* is released for the seasonal market.

[23] Brian Wilson suffers a nervous breakdown, the first of 3 in the next 18 months, on a flight from Los Angeles to Houston, TX, at the start of a 2-week tour. Suffering also from partial deafness in one ear, he decides to retire from live performance with the group, and concentrate on writing and producing the records.

1965
Jan Glen Campbell (b. Apr.22, 1936, Delight, AR) joins as temporary replacement for Brian on live gigs. *Dance Dance Dance* reaches UK #24.

Mar [25] 22-year-old secretary, Shannon Harris, files a paternity suit against Love before Superior Court Commissioner Frank B. Stoddard. (Her 3-month-old daughter Shawn will marry Dennis in 1983.)

[27] *Please Let Me Wonder* peaks at US #52.

Apr [9] Bruce Johnston (b. June 27, 1944, Peoria, IL), former member of Bruce & Terry and The Rip Chords, who had met The Beach Boys in 1963 when working as a producer at Columbia, replaces Campbell to become a full-time Beach Boy, making his debut at a gig in New Orleans, LA.

[10] Group's revival of Bobby Freeman's *Do You Wanna Dance*, and A-side of *Please Let Me Wonder* reaches US #12.

May [29] Traditionally Brian-produced *Help Me Rhonda* tops US chart for 2 weeks, while *The Beach Boys Today!* hits US #4.

June *Help Me Rhonda* reaches UK #27.

Aug [28] *California Girls*, on which Brian begins to show the influence of Phil Spector's production style, hits US #3, and *Summer Days (And Summer Nights!!)* hits US #2.

Sept *California Girls* reaches UK #26.

[8] Group begins the first of 4 days recording sessions for *Party* album.

Oct *Surfin' USA* is the group's UK album chart debut, reaching #17.

[15] Love marries Suzanne Belcher in Las Vegas, NV.

[23] The Sunrays' *I Live For The Sun*, written by Murry Wilson, peaks at US #51.

1966 Jan [1] *The Little Girl I Once Knew,* another more complex production, reaches US #20. By contrast, *Beach Boys Party* is the raw result of impromptu "live in the studio" sessions with friends, and hits US #6.
[18] Brian begins work on what will be regarded as his recording zenith, the *Pet Sounds* project.
[29] *Barbara Ann,* a revival of The Regents' 1961 hit and taken from *Party,* with guest lead vocal by Dean Torrence (of Jan And Dean), hits US #2. The Beach Boys tour Japan.
Feb [3] Carl Wilson marries Annie Hinsche.
[4] Jardine marries Linda at El Segundo's Episcopal Church.
[18] Brian lays down first track of *Good Vibrations* at Gold Star studios.
Mar *Barbara Ann* and parent album *Beach Boys Party* both hit UK #3.
Apr [30] Brian Wilson's *Caroline No,* the first solo single by a Beach Boys member, makes US #32.
May [7] *Sloop John B,* the revival of 1927 traditional Caribbean tune, hits US #3 and UK #2, and sells over a million.
Belatedly released in UK, *The Beach Boys Today!* hits #6. Painstakingly produced and richly-textured *Pet Sounds,* the result of many months of Brian's work, sets new standards for the group, and is critically acclaimed as its best work yet. It hits US #10 and UK #2, behind The Beatles' *Revolver.* Brian has begun the *Pet Sounds* project having been inspired to creatively match the heights of Beatles opus *Rubber Soul.*
June [25] "The Beach Boys' Summer Spectacular", with The Lovin' Spoonful, Percy Sledge, The Byrds and Chad & Jeremy, takes place at the Hollywood Bowl, CA.
Aug Released in UK a year after its US success, *Summer Days (And Summer Nights!!)* peaks at #4 while *Pet Sounds* rests 2 places higher.
[27] Ballad *God Only Knows* hits UK #2, and will become one of The Beach Boys' most covered hits.
Sept [1] Recording of *Good Vibrations* is completed at United Western studios.
[17] *Wouldn't It Be Nice* hits US #8.
[24] *Wouldn't It Be Nice* B-side, *God Only Knows* makes US #39.
Oct Brother Records is formed with David Anderle overseeing the operation.
[24] Compilation *Best Of The Beach Boys* hits US #8.
Nov [6] Group begins a 7-date twice-nightly UK tour, with Lulu, David & Jonathan and others, at the Astoria theater, Finsbury Park, London. The tour will end on Nov.13 at the Birmingham theater, W.Midlands.
[10] A fire breaks out near Gold Star studios on Santa Monica Blvd., the evening that Brian Wilson has been recording a string segment for the track *Fire.* He thinks he is responsible for it, and places the tapes in a vault out of harm's way.
Dec [10] *Good Vibrations,* a track which Brian has been working on for 6 months, using 17 sessions at 4 different studios, tops US chart and is a US million-seller. (It has already topped UK chart on Nov.17.) It will be critically rated the group's best-ever recording.
The Beach Boys displace The Beatles as World's Best Group in the annual **New Musical Express** poll, while *Best Of The Beach Boys* (a different compilation from earlier US release) hits UK #2, and will remain charted for 142 weeks.

1967 Jan Brian begins working on sessions for an album to further develop the music created on *Pet Sounds.* First working title for the project is *Dumb Angel,* later changed to *Smile.* Stresses begin to tell on the group, and on Brian in particular, while this work is in progress. There is heavy drug use, while Brian's ideas and modes of work (such as standing a grand piano in a huge sandbox) become increasingly eccentric as his stability deteriorates.
[3] Carl Wilson, having received a US Army draft notice refuses to be sworn in, saying he is a conscientious objector.
Mar Group files suit in Los Angeles Superior Court against Capitol Records, for alleged non-payment of royalties, and seeking termination of their recording contract. (Brian has already filed a $275,000 lawsuit there against Capitol for not paying him producer's royalties.)
[2] *Good Vibrations,* nominated in the Best Contemporary (Rock'N'Roll) Recording category, loses to New Vaudeville Band's *Winchester Cathedral* at the ninth annual Grammy awards.
Apr *Surfer Girl,* never previously released in UK, appears instead of a new album, and reaches UK #13.
Carl is arrested in New York by the FBI, and held in custody for 5 days for refusing to take the Oath of Allegiance and avoiding military call-up. He refuses to report for induction to military service, citing his opposition to the war and is granted Conscientious Objector status, but refuses to report for assigned alternative civilian duty as a bedpan changer at Los Angeles' Veterans' hospital. In refusing, he cites that the

job would not make use of his talents. (He will be arraigned for trial in June 1967, but the case will drag on for years until community service in lieu is settled.)
[13] Group opens 2-week US tour in Starkville, MS, which will end on Apr.29 in Schenectady, NY.
May [2] They begin an 8-date twice-nightly UK tour at the Adelphi theater, Dublin, Eire, with Helen Shapiro, Simon Dupree & The Big Sound, and Terry Reid with Peter Jay's Jaywalkers. The tour will end on May 10 at ABC theater, Edinburgh, Scotland, as the *Smile* sessions finally cease in disarray, and will become increasingly notorious in their commercial absence.
June Lacking new material, Capitol Records in UK extracts the cover version of The Crystals' *Then He Kissed Me* (retitled *Then I Kissed Her*) from *Summer Days (And Summer Nights!!),* and it hits UK #4. The group pulls out of the Monterey International Pop Festival, CA, purportedly because of Carl's draft trial, although there is speculation that they are concerned how they will be received by the crowd. Otis Redding will takes the group's place and Carl will be acquitted on draft evasion charge.
Aug Group creates its own label, Brother Records, distributed by Capitol (cause of much rancor between the 2 camps) for the release of *Heroes And Villains,* a track created in similar fashion to *Good Vibrations.* (Brother's first 2 signings are Redwood and Amy. Redwood's scheduled first single is a 1963 Brian Wilson song *Thinkin' 'Bout You Baby,* originally recorded by Sharon Marie and now re-written as *Darlin'.* The record is never released, and Redwood leaves Brother to become Three Dog Night.)
[25] Brian Wilson makes his first concert appearance with the group in over 2 years at the International Center, Honolulu, HI.
[26] *Heroes And Villains,* penned with Brian's new writing partner Van Dyke Parks, reaches US #12 and UK #8.
Sept Compilation *Best Of The Beach Boys, Vol.2* peaks at US #50. (A version with different track listing will hit UK #3 in Nov.)
Nov *Smiley Smile,* first release on Brother through Capitol, peaks disappointingly at US #41, while hitting UK #9. It contains parts of the abandoned *Smile,* plus some lighter-weight later material, and is carried by the already familiar *Good Vibrations* and *Heroes And Villains.*
Dec [2] *Wild Honey,* a return to a simpler R&B/rock sound, makes US #31 and UK #29.
[15] The Beach Boys play a UNICEF benefit concert in Paris, France, and there meet Maharishi Mahesh Yogi who introduces them to transcendental meditation.

1968 Jan R&B-flavored *Wild Honey* reaches US #24 and UK #7.
Feb [3] Extracted *Darlin',* already recorded by Redwood, returns the group to both US and UK Top 20, at #19 and #11 respectively.
Apr [4] Band is scheduled to open a US college tour, with Buffalo Springfield and Strawberry Alarm Clock in Nashville, TN, but when word comes that Martin Luther King has been assassinated in nearby Memphis, they cancel the show and subsequently the tour.
[29] Brian and Marilyn Wilson become parents to a daughter Carnie.
May [4] Group begins a 18-day US tour with the Maharishi at the Singer Bowl, New York, scheduled to end in San Diego, CA, on May 21, but the concerts are poorly attended and several dates are cancelled. Their live show, based around an old-fashioned greatest hits presentation, is an increasing anachronism in an era of progressive rock concerts. Jardine will comment "if anybody benefits from this tour, it'll be the florists".
[18] *Friends,* a song inspired by their transcendental meditation conversion, makes US #47 and UK #25.
[23] Christian Love is born.
July *Friends,* again heavily influenced by T.M., is their poorest-selling US album yet, peaking at #126.
Aug [28] *Do It Again,* a celebratory return to the group's early sound, tops UK chart for a week.
Sept [14] *Do It Again* reaches US #20.
Oct *Friends* fares better in UK, reaching #13, while compilation *Best Of The Beach Boys, Vol.3* hits UK #9 after stalling at US #153.
Dec [1] Group tours UK and plays the London Palladium, where onstage recordings are made which will later appear as a live album.
[28] Johnston's first Beach Boys production, *Bluebirds Over The Mountain,* a revival of an oldie by Ersel Hickey, peaks at US #61.

1969 Jan *Bluebirds Over The Mountain,* with lead guitar by Ed Carter, makes UK #33.
Feb Group begins a 5-city tour of Texas.
Mar Taken from new album *20/20, I Can Hear Music,* another of the group's revivals (originally by The Ronettes), hits UK #10.

The Association

Abba

Aswad

The Beach Boys

The Beatles

Apr [1] Group sues Capitol Records for over $2 million, claiming unpaid royalties and production fees, plus other losses incurred through general mismanagement on Capitol's part. *20/20* climbs to US #68 and hits UK #3.

[26] *I Can Hear Music* reaches US #24.

May Group holds a press conference to announce the impending end of its Capitol contract, a poor financial situation, and a quest for a new and better label deal.

July Last single for Capitol, *Break Away*, which Brian co-writes with Murry, who uses the pseudonym Reggie Dunbar, hits UK #6.

Aug [2] *Break Away* peaks at US #63.

[3] Carl Wilson is indicted in Los Angeles for failing to appear for community service work (as an orderly in a hospital) in lieu of the military. (A mutually acceptable form of community service is found – which means free Beach Boys' concerts at hospitals, prisons, and so on.) US-only album *Close Up* makes #136.

Oct [16] Brian and Marilyn Wilson have a second daughter Wendy.

Nov Murry Wilson sells the "Sea Of Tunes" catalog, comprising all of Brian's songs, to Irving/Almo Music for $700,000.

1970
Jan Group resurrects its Brother Records label as part of a new deal with Warner/Reprise Records. (The first 2 signings to Brother are The Flames and Amy, the 15-year-old daughter of a record company vice-president.)

Apr [4] US-only, *Add Some Music To Your Day*, peaks at #64.

June Capitol in UK remixes *Cottonfields*, from *20/20*, with Red Rhodes on pedal steel, and resulting stronger track hits UK #5. It is not released in US.

Oct *Sunflower*, their first album for Brother/Reprise, peaks at US #151. In UK, the album remains with EMI (owner of US Capitol) on the Stateside label, and reaches #29, while UK-only compilation *Greatest Hits* on Capitol hits UK #5.

In US the group's live shows take on a new lease of life as the hip rock crowd re-discovers them in an event-stealing appearance at the Big Sur Folk Festival, Monterey, CA, with Kris Kristofferson, Linda Ronstadt, Country Joe McDonald and organizer Joan Baez.

Nov [5] During a 4-night stint at the Whiskey A-Go-Go, Los Angeles, Brian joins the group on stage for only the second time in 5 years. His recurring ear problem has caused further damage, and he will not play with the band again for some time.

Dec Dennis records a solo single, *Sound Of Free*, written with Daryl Dragon, under the name Dennis Wilson And Rumbo, released only in UK. Shrouded in obscurity, it does not chart.

1971
Jan Former journalist and radio DJ Jack Rieley takes over the group's management, encouraging it to finish *Surf's Up*, a Brian Wilson song from the abandoned *Smile* sessions, of which Brian himself has recently performed a solo version on a Leonard Bernstein-hosted CBS TV special "Inside Pop: The Rock Revolution".

Feb Group plays a sell-out concert at New York's Carnegie Hall, to rave reviews. Rieley has prompted a long overdue update of the group's live image, dropping its stage uniforms and lengthening the song sets.

Apr [27] The Beach Boys jam with The Grateful Dead at the Fillmore East, New York, on a rendition of *Johnny B. Goode*, cementing new-found favor with the progressive rock audience.

May [1] They perform at a May Day anti-war demo in Washington, DC, before an estimated crowd of 500,000 people. (Later in the year they will play benefit for The Berrigan Brothers defense fund.)

June [11] Dennis accidentally puts his right hand through a window pane and severs some nerves. He is replaced for live work by Ricky Fataar, former drummer with South African group Flame, whom The Beach Boys have earlier signed to Brother Records and used for some time as a support band. (Carl Wilson had produced their 1970 debut.)

Oct An album originally to be titled *Landlocked* because of its ecological theme, but renamed *Surf's Up* after the addition of that track, reaches US #29 and UK #15.

Nov [20] Extracted *Long Promised Road*, penned by Carl with manager Rieley, reaches US #89.

Dec Group begins 4-month recording sessions at Brother studios, while Dennis also appears in "Two Lane Blacktop" movie with James Taylor and Warren Oates.

1972
Jan Johnston leaves after 7 years, citing personality clashes with Rieley. His place is taken by Fataar's former Flame colleague, Blondie Chaplin.

Feb Group makes a TV special in Amsterdam, Holland, and plans to record there.

[24] They perform at Grand Gala Du Disque, Holland.

May Group visits UK, appearing at Lincoln Festival, London's Royal Festival Hall, and Crystal Palace where they are joined on stage by Elton John and The Who's Keith Moon.

June *Carl And The Passions/So Tough*, with the title evoking one of the group's pre-Beach Boys names, reaches US #50 and UK #25. In US, it is jointly packaged with a reissue of *Pet Sounds*, US rights to which have reverted to the group from Capitol. After its release, the group has a demountable recording studio transported from Los Angeles to Baambrugge, Holland, at considerable expense, and members take up temporary Dutch residence while the next album is planned.

Dec [31] Carl and Annie Wilson become parents to a son Dennis.

1973
Mar [1] The New York's Joffrey Ballet makes its debut performance of the "Deuce Coupe Ballet", set to the music of The Beach Boys. *Holland,* the result of sessions in that country (costing an estimated $250,000), plus Los Angeles-recorded track *Sail On Sailor* (added at the insistence of Reprise Records executives, who feel album lacks commerciality without it), reaches US #36 and UK #20. It contains a free EP, *Mount Vernon And Fairway*, a musical fairy tale written by Brian Wilson.

[17] *Sail On Sailor* is extracted as a US single but stalls at #79. *California Saga (On My Way To Sunny Californ-i-a)* makes UK #37.

June [2] *California Saga (On My Way To Sunny Californ-i-a)* stalls at US #84. Shortly after the album's release, Rieley is fired as manager, and replaced by Love's brother, Steve.

[4] Murry Wilson, father of Brian, Carl and Dennis, and their original manager, dies from complications following a heart attack.

1974
Jan [26] Double live *The Beach Boys In Concert*, recorded during the group's 1972 winter and 1973 summer tours, reaches US #25, but fails in UK. After its release, Chaplin and Fataar leave, and a recovered Dennis, who had considered staying out of the group to try solo projects, returns on drums. James William Guercio, producer of Chicago and Blood, Sweat & Tears and owner of Caribou studios, CO, a long-time fan of the group, joins on bass and takes over some management duties.

July [27] Elton John's *Don't Let The Sun Go Down On Me*, on which Carl Wilson and Bruce Johnston contribute backing vocals, hits US #2.

Sept Double re-package of *Wild Honey* and *20/20* reaches US #50.

[28] *Surfin' USA* is extracted and re-hits to make US #36.

Oct [5] Double album compilation *Endless Summer*, put together by Capitol to satisfy nostalgia for the group's 60s classics, tops US chart for a week (only the second #1 of the group's career), during a 155-week residence.

Nov Double re-package of *Friends* and *Smiley Smile* reaches US #125.

[30] Chicago's *Wishing You Were Here*, on which Jardine and Carl and Dennis Wilson sing at the invitation of Guercio, reaches US #11.

1975
May Guercio pairs The Beach Boys and Chicago for a 12-city US tour during which 700,000 will pay $7.5 million to see the bands perform.

[31] *Sail On Sailor* is reissued in US 2 years after first charting and peaks at #49.

June [21] Group plays Wembley Stadium, London, to a rousing reception from 72,000 people, second on the bill to Elton John, who finds it difficult to follow the group successfully on stage.

[28] Capitol's second US-only double nostalgia compilation *Spirit Of America* hits #8.

Aug [30] Compilation album, *Good Vibrations – Best Of The Beach Boys* (of later tracks on Brother/Reprise), reaches US #25.

1976
Jan [2] Dennis Wilson is arrested for carrying a .38 revolver which he has taken from his girlfriend. He is released after charges are dropped.

[30] Group begins recording at Brother studios in Santa Monica with Brian, who having dropped out of a largely non-productive deal to work with Bruce Johnston and Terry Melcher's Equinox Records, nominally returns as producer on *15 Big Ones*, a title which refers to the group's 15th anniversary and the number of tracks on the album (which mostly contains nostalgic revivals of other acts' oldies).

May [21] Dennis marries Karem Lamm in Kauai, HI.

June [20] Brian films a segment for forthcoming NBC special on The Beach Boys in which he is arrested by "Saturday Night Live" alumni Dan Aykroyd and John Belushi, posing as the Surf Police, for not being able to surf.

July [2] Scheuled 44-date US tour begins at the Oakland Stadium, CA. Tour will end Oct.3 at the Tulsa State Fair, OK.

[3] Brian plays on stage with The Beach Boys for the first time in 7 years at Anaheim Stadium, CA.

[10] Having not promoted either *Endless Summer* or *Spirit Of America*, Capitol/EMI in UK puts together its own Beach Boys compilation album, TV-advertised *20 Golden Greats*. It tops UK chart for 10 weeks, as new album *15 Big Ones* makes UK #31.

[24] Extracted *Good Vibrations* reaches UK #18 as a revival of Chuck Berry's *Rock And Roll Music*, from *15 Big Ones*, makes UK #36.

Aug [5] NBC TV special "The Beach Boys: It's OK" airs.

[14] *Rock And Roll Music* hits US #5, and becomes the group's first US Top 10 hit since *Good Vibrations* a decade earlier.

[28] *15 Big Ones* hits US #8.

Sept [18] Brian is a presenter and nominee at "Don Kirshner's Rock Music Awards" on a US TV show devoted to the event.

Oct [2] *It's OK*, a Brian Wilson-Mike Love original from *15 Big Ones* which features sax work by Wizzard's Roy Wood, reaches US #29.

Nov [27] Brian sings and appears in sketches on NBC TV's "Saturday Night Live".

Dec [31] Group, with Brian again in the line-up, plays a show to commemorate the 15th anniversary of their first gig, at Los Angeles Forum.

1977 Jan [8] Live tracks recorded at the Finsbury Park Astoria on Aug.12, 1968 and the London Palladium on Dec.1, 1968 released by Capitol in US as *Beach Boys '69: Live In London*, makes UK #70.

Feb [19] Johnston wins Song Of The Year for *I Write The Songs* at the 19th annual Grammy awards.

Mar Group signs to Caribou Records, having just completed an album for Reprise, and owing the label one more.

May [7] *The Beach Boys Love You*, produced by Brian Wilson, reaches UK #28.

[21] *The Beach Boys Love You* makes US #53.

July [30] Group plays an exclusive gig for UK CBS Records' (distributors of Caribou Records) annual sales conference in London, having abandoned plans to do a Wembley concert.

Sept Dennis is the first Beach Boy to release a solo album, *Pacific Ocean Blue* on Caribou Records, which climbs to US #96.

1978 Feb [3] ABC TV's "Dead Man's Curve" biopic, starring Bruce Davison and Richard Hatch as Jan And Dean, in which Love makes a cameo appearance, airs in US.

June [24] Title song from film "Almost Summer", written by Love, Jardine and Brian, and performed by Celebration, featuring Love, reaches US #28.

Sept [30] Buddy Holly's *Peggy Sue*, from forthcoming *M.I.U.*, peaks at US #59.

Oct [28] *M.I.U. Album*, recorded at the Maharishi International University, Fairfield, IA, with Jardine and Ron Altbach producing, and released to fulfill the Reprise contract, makes US #151.

1979 Jan [23] Brian and Marilyn Wilson divorce after 15 years of marriage.

Apr [7] *Here Comes The Night*, with a strong disco flavor, first release by the group on Caribou, makes US #44.

[21] *Here Comes The Night* reaches UK #37.

[28] *L.A. (Light Album)* makes UK #32. Johnston returns to the group both as its producer (with Curt Becher) and as a performer.

May [12] *L.A. (Light Album)* climbs to US #100.

June [9] *Good Timin'*, from the album, makes US #40.

July [21] *Lady Lynda*, written by Jardine about his wife, also from *L.A. (Light Album)*, is The Beach Boys' first UK Top 10 hit since 1970, at #6.

Oct [13] *Sumahama*, from the album, reaches UK #45.

1980 Jan [13] They play a Los Angeles benefit concert for the people of Kampuchea, along with Starship and The Grateful Dead.

Apr [12] *Keepin' The Summer Alive* makes UK #54.

[19] *Goin' On* stalls at US #83.

[26] *Keepin' The Summer Alive* makes US #75.

June [6-7] Group plays 2 concerts at Wembley Arena, London.

[20] They top the bill at the Knebworth Festival, Herts.

July [4] Group gives a free performance to half a million people in Washington, DC, on Independence Day. The July 4 concert will become a regular feature of The Beach Boys' calendar during the decade.

1981 May Carl reaches US #185 with his solo *Carl Wilson*, and leaves (to tour with his own Carl Wilson Band). Englishman Adrian Baker, a long-time admirer and professional emulator of The Beach Boys' sound, is called in to fill out group harmonies on live work, while Dennis will fully return to the line-up over the next few months.

Sept [12] Following the medley craze sparked in US and UK by the Star Sound hit *Stars On 45*, Capitol puts together *The Beach Boys Medley* which links excerpts from their 60s classics, and makes UK #47.

Oct Love's solo *Looking Back With Love* is released, but does not chart. (His 2 other solo albums, *First Love* and *Country Love*, remain unreleased.) He tours with his own group, The Endless Summer Beach Band.

[3] *The Beach Boys Medley* reaches US #12, the group's first US Top 20 hit for 5 years.

1982 Jan [30] Double compilation *Ten Years Of Harmony (1970-1980)* climbs to US #156, as extracted *Come Go With Me*, a revival of The Del Vikings' oldie, reaches US #18.

Feb Love records in UK with Adrian Baker, who remains close to the group.

Apr Carl returns to The Beach Boys, and his own manager Jerry Schilling becomes group's manager.

July [17] Further compilation *Sunshine Dream* peaks at US #180.

Sept [2] Dennis and Shawn Wilson become parents to son Gage (Gage was Murry's middle name).

Nov [5] Brian is fired from group by the other band members.

1983 June [4] Carl's solo *What You Do To Me* peaks at US #72.

Aug [6] A second UK TV-advertised double album compilation from Capitol, *The Very Best Of The Beach Boys* tops UK chart.

Dec [28] Dennis drowns while swimming from his boat in the harbor at Marina Del Rey, CA. (Special dispensation is granted, with the help of President Reagan, who sends his condolences to the Wilson family, for a burial at sea – normally reserved for Naval personnel – of the only genuine surfer in The Beach Boys.)

1984 The Beach Boys make a one-off recording with Frankie Valli & The Four Seasons, *East Meets West*, written by Bob Crewe and Bob Gaudio. It is released on The Seasons' own FBI label in US, but does not chart.

1985 June [22] *The Beach Boys* (with Stevie Wonder on his own *I Do Love You*), produced in London by Steve Levine, makes US #52 and UK #60.

[29] Extracted *Getcha Back*, Love/Melcher-penned, reaches US #26.

July [13] Group plays the Live Aid concert in Philadelphia, PA.

Aug [17] *It's Gettin' Late*, also from the album, makes US #82.

1986 July [19] *Rock'N'Roll To The Rescue*, written by Love and Melcher, peaks at US #68. It trailers double compilation *Made In The USA* which reaches US #96. It is released by Capitol in celebration of the group's 25th anniversary, which contains 20 1962-68 Capitol tracks; plus later hits *Rock And Roll Music*, *Come Go With Me* and *Getcha Back*, and 2 new Beach Boys' recordings produced by Terry Melcher.

Oct [25] Also from the album, a revival of The Mamas And The Papas' *California Dreamin'*, with electric 12-string guitar played by Roger McGuinn of The Byrds, peaks at US #57 as Joan Jett & The Blackhearts' *Good Music*, with backing vocals by The Beach Boys, makes US #83.

1987 Jan Brian Wilson inducts Leiber and Stoller into the Rock'N'Roll Hall Of Fame at the second annual induction dinner, at which Seymour Stein approaches him to record a solo album for Sire.

Sept Group is invited to co-perform on a remake of *Wipe Out* by rap act The Fat Boys, which hits UK #2 and US #12.

1988 Jan [20] Elton John inducts The Beach Boys into the Rock'N'Roll Hall Of Fame at the third annual induction dinner at the Waldorf Astoria, New York. Love in accepting the honor proceeds to upset the assembled multitude with a rambling and nonsensical speech.

June [12] The Beach Boys and The Four Tops take part in a sing-off at half-time during the NBA championship game between the Los Angeles Lakers and the Detroit Pistons. The Beach Boys sing for The Lakers, and The Four Tops for The Pistons.

July Now taking a daily 6-mile jog along Pacific Coast Highway, Brian releases his first solo album *Brian Wilson* on relaunched Reprise label. Partly co-produced and co-written with his therapist Eugene Landy, who he claims has successfully rehabilitated The Beach Boys using the "milieu" therapy program, it makes US #54 but fails in UK despite intense promotion. Extracted *Love And Mercy* fails to chart.

Sept The Beach Boys, without Brian, undertake an 8-date US tour. Brian contributes *Goodnight Irene* to the Woody Guthrie/Leadbelly tribute album *Folkways: A Vision Shared*.

Oct During a UK promotion visit, Brian unexpectedly visits the 10th Annual Beach Boys Convention at the Parish Centre, Greenford, London.

Nov [5] The Beach Boys, again without Brian, hit US #1 with *Kokomo*, a Caribbean-flavored pop ditty written by John Phillips, Scott McKenzie, Mike Love and Terry Melcher and featured in Tom Cruise movie "Cocktail". It is over 24 years since their first hit – the longest span ever achieved in the rock era.

[16] Former manager Stephen Love, Mike's brother, is sentenced to 5 years' probation for embezzling more than $900,000 from the group. (Stephen Love and brother Stan are also sued by Mike Love and a business associate Michael Seeman alleging that they kidnapped, assaulted and beat Seeman and extorted $40,000 from him.)

Dec *Kokomo* reaches UK #25.

1989 Apr [17] Dr. Eugene Landy surrenders his license to practice therapy after an investigation by the California State Board of Medical Quality Assurance of alleged improprieties.

May [27] The Beach Boys and Chicago begin their first tour together since 1975 at Pacific Amphitheater in Los Angeles. Brian sits in on 3 songs.

June [20] Band, with Brian, begins 6 major US dates co-headlining with Chicago.

Aug [26] *Still Cruisin'*, from Mel Gibson/Danny Glover "Lethal Weapon 2", makes US #93.

Sept Brian files $100 million civil suit at Los Angeles Superior Court to recover copyrights to songs his father sold to A&M Records and Irving Music for $700,000 in 1969.

Oct *Still Cruisin'*, an album of old and new Beach Boys tracks featured in movies, reaches US #46.

1990 Apr [29] "Summer Dreams: The Story Of The Beach Boys", based on Stephen Gaines 1986 biography **Heroes & Villains: The True Story Of The Beach Boys**, airs on US TV. (Irving Music will sue producers Leonard Hill for lying about their intent for requesting the licensing of The Beach Boys' music.)

May [2] Stan Love files suit in California Superior Court in Santa Monica seeking control of Brian Wilson's personal and financial affairs.

[7] Brian Wilson breaks in to press conference in Burbank, CA, called by Stan Love, as he is about to announce his intention to become legal overseer of Brian Wilson's estate and life.

June Various artists compilation *Smiles, Vibes, And Harmony – A Tribute To Brian Wilson*, an album of cover versions by Sonic Youth, Das Damen, Original Sins, Handsome Dick Manitoba and others, is released on DeMilo Records.

[2] *Wouldn't It Be Nice* peaks at UK #58.

[7] Brian Wilson files his reply to Stan Love's suit, alleging him to be "a violent thug" motivated by "insatiable greed".

[9] Brian's daughters Wendy and Carnie top US chart with *Hold On*, exactly 25 years after The Beach Boys' *Help Me Rhonda* was at #1.

[16] *Pet Sounds*, part of a widely-praised re-mastering of the complete Beach Boys works available for the first time on CD, makes US #177.

[17] Brian Wilson files $100 million suit against law firm Irell & Manella and attorney Werner Wolfen for fraud and negligence, saying the company helped A&M's publishing company Almo defraud him of his publishing rights by making him sign documents when he was incapacitated by a mental breakdown and drug and alcohol problems.

[22] Brian Wilson files suit against Stan Love, alleging he is seeking to do little more than become Wilson's prison guard at a lucrative salary.

[23] Third TV-advertised UK Beach Boys collection *Summer Dreams*, released by Capitol, hits UK #2.

July [21] *Problem Child*, written and produced by Melcher from movie "Problem Child", is released.

1991 Jan [28] Brian Wilson plays a solo set at Hollywood's China club.

THE BEASTIE BOYS

King Ad-Rock (Adam Horovitz) (vocals)
MCA (Adam Yauch) (vocals)
Mike D (Michael Diamond) (vocals)

1981 Yauch (b. Aug.15, 1967, Brooklyn, New York, NY), adopting the name MCA (Master Of Ceremonies Adam), and Diamond (b. Nov.20, 1965, New York) team up as a hardcore rock band, with 2 others, to play at MCA's 15th birthday party. Horovitz (b. Oct.31, 1966, Manhattan, New York) son of playwright and screenwriter Israel Horovitz, with The Young & The Useless, who have released 1 single *Real Men Don't Use Floss*, soon joins, and the 3 record an 8-song EP *Polly Wog Stew* for New York independent label, Rat Cage Records.

1983 Aug *Cookie Puss*, more a harangue than a song, is backed by *Beastie Revolution*, a snatch of which is used on a British Airways commercial, resulting in the group getting a $40,000 pay-off from the airline.

Oct They begin to rap as part of their stage act, notably on *Cookie Puss*, which is otherwise difficult to "perform" live. As the rap portion of their show expands and the hard rock portion shrinks, they add DJ Double RR (Rick Rubin) to scratch on turntables behind them.

1984 July The trio supports Madonna on US tour.

Oct Group signs to Rubin's new Def Jam label (in association with CBS), and releases its first full rap single *Rock Hard*.

Nov They perform *She's On It* in the rap movie "Krush Groove", with L.L. Cool J., Kurtis Blow, The Fat Boys and other rising rap stars.

1986 Sept On a UK visit as part of the "Raisin' Hell" tour, their outrageous stage act and apparently similar behavior offstage begins a love/hate relationship with UK press.

1987 Mar [7] Band's debut album *Licensed To Ill* is the first rap album to top US chart, holding at #1 for 7 weeks, as single *(You Gotta) Fight For*

Your Right (To Party) hits US #7.

Apr *(You Gotta) Fight For Your Right (To Party)* reaches UK #11.

May [30] On tour in UK, Horovitz is arrested in Liverpool on a charge of Actual Bodily Harm, when he allegedly hits a girl fan during a riot following their Royal Court theater concert. (He will be acquitted in Nov. when the case goes to court.) The tabloid press invents lurid stories about their supposed anti-social behavior, such as laughing at mentally handicapped children. The Volkswagen medallions worn by the trio also attract trouble as, throughout UK, fans emulate the style by stealing them from cars.

June *No Sleep Till Brooklyn* makes UK #14 as *Licensed To Ill* hits UK #7.

Aug *She's On It* hits UK #10.

Oct Double A-side *Girls/She's Crafty* makes UK #34.

1988 Apr [25] *Brass Monkey* makes US #48.

While members consider their future as The Beastie Boys, Horovitz follows a cameo performance in TV series "The Equalizer" with his first major role in movie "Santa Ana Project".

1989 Aug *Paul's Boutique*, named after Brooklyn store and produced by The Dust Brothers (Matt Dike, John King and Mike Simpson), reaches US #14 and UK #44.

Sept [2] *Hey Ladies* makes US #36.

Oct [26] Out on US video, Horovitz and Donald Sutherland star in Hugh Hudson's "Lost Angels" movie.

1990 Mar [8] Group wins Best Album Cover for *Paul's Boutique* in **Rolling Stone** magazine's 1989 Critics Awards.

THE BEATLES

John Lennon (vocals, rhythm guitar)
Paul McCartney (vocals, bass)
George Harrison (vocals, lead guitar)
Ringo Starr (vocals, drums)

1957 July [6] The Quarry Men Skiffle Group, after auditioning for Carroll Levis' "TV Star Search Show" at the Empire theater, Liverpool, Merseyside, a month earlier, are playing the Woolton Parish Church Garden Fête, Liverpool, when Ivan Vaughan, who had been in The Quarry Men when they were known as The Black Jacks, introduces the group's lead singer Lennon (b. John Winston Lennon, Oct.9, 1940, Liverpool) to McCartney (b. James Paul McCartney, June 18, 1942, Liverpool), at the end of the band's set. McCartney impresses Lennon with his ability to tune a guitar and his knowledge of rock'n'roll lyrics.

Aug [7] The Quarry Men make their Cavern club debut in Liverpool, but without McCartney who is at a scout camp in Hathersage, Derbys.

Oct [18] McCartney makes his debut with the group at the New Clubmoor Hall Conservative club in Broadway, Liverpool.

1958 July [15] Lennon's mother, Julia, dies in a road accident in Liverpool.

Aug Harrison (b. Feb.25, 1943, Liverpool), who has been at school with McCartney at Liverpool Institute High, joins The Quarry Men and the group, now comprising Lennon, McCartney, Harrison, Colin Hanton and John Lowe, cuts its first record. They pay 17s 6d to record a demo of Buddy Holly's *That'll Be The Day* backed with a Harrison/McCartney composition *In Spite Of All The Danger*.

1959 Aug [29] On the day of the opening of the Casbah coffee club in West Derby, Liverpool, run by Mona Best, Les Stewart and Ken Brown of the scheduled band The Les Stewart Quartet, argue, with Stewart walking out. Brown asks Harrison if he knows anyone who can help out, and he brings in Lennon and McCartney. This performance leads to a regular Saturday night spot at the Casbah, until Oct. when Brown is fired.

Nov [15] Lennon, McCartney and Harrison, now calling themselves Johnny & The Moondogs, participate in the final round of judging for Carroll Levis' "TV Star Search" at the Hippodrome theater, Ardwick, Manchester, Gtr.Manchester.

1960 Jan Lennon's art school friend Stuart Sutcliffe (b. Stuart Fergusson Victor Sutcliffe, June 23, 1940, Edinburgh, Scotland) joins on bass. (They will continue without a regular drummer until the summer.)

May [20] Group, having failed an audition for Larry Parnes to be Billy Fury's backing band, begin a 7-date tour of Scotland at Alloa Town Hall, as The Silver Beetles (after a brief spell as The Beatals) backing Johnny Gentle, another singer from the Parnes talent stable. (Tommy Moore has been added to the line-up on drums. For the tour, McCartney uses the pseudonym Paul Ramon, Sutcliffe calls himself Stuart da Staël and Harrison adopts the forename Carl.)

Aug [12] Pete Best (b. 1941), the son of Casbah club owner Mona Best, passes an audition at the Wyvern Social club, and joins the group as its drummer in time for its first visit to Germany.

[17] They arrive in Hamburg, Germany, and play at the Indra club,

before moving to the larger Kaiserkeller club, making 106 appearances in total, playing their last gig Nov.30.

Oct [15] Starr (b. Richard Starkey, July 7, 1940, Liverpool), drummer with Rory Storm & The Hurricanes, fills in for Best as the group backs Rory Storm guitarist Wally Eymond on a recording of Gershwin's *Summertime* at the Akustik studio in Hamburg.

Dec [27] Group plays a gig at the Litherland Town Hall, Hatton Hill Road in Liverpool, to scenes which hint at the adulation they will receive in the future. (Chas Newby substitutes for Sutcliffe, who has stayed behind in Germany.)

1961 Feb [21] The Beatles make their Cavern club debut, at the first of many lunchtime sessions.

Mar [27] They begin a second spell in Hamburg, playing 98 nights at the Top Ten club, through to July 2.

Aug German Polydor releases *My Bonnie*, by Tony Sheridan & The Beat Brothers. (The name The Beatles is considered too risque in Germany, as it sounds like the word "peedles", German slang for penis.) Recorded under the auspices of orchestra leader Bert Kaempfert at Harburg Friedrich Ebert Halle in Hamburg, the session also featured 2 other numbers backing Tony Sheridan plus an old Eddie Cantor original, *Ain't She Sweet* with a Lennon vocal, and a Shadows instrumental parody, *Cry For A Shadow* penned by Lennon and Harrison.

Oct [15] Group appears on the same bill as comedian Ken Dodd at a St. John's Ambulance Brigade star fundraiser at the Albany cinema, Maghull, Liverpool.

[19] The Beatles and Gerry & The Pacemakers combine forces as 1 group when they play at Litherland Town Hall.

[28] Raymond Jones calls at Brian Epstein's NEMS record store in Liverpool to enquire about the availability of The Beatles' German release. Epstein (b. Sept.19, 1934, Liverpool), unable to trace the record, promises to investigate further. (Beatle historians will question whether Epstein already knew of The Beatles at this time.)

Nov [9] Following up on Jones' enquiry, Epstein sees the group for the first time at a Cavern lunchtime session.

Dec [9] The Beatles play their first gig in the South of England at the Palais Ballroom, Aldershot, Hants, on a program with Ivor Jay & The Jaywalkers, billed as a "Battle Of The Bands – Liverpool v. London". Only 18 people turn up.

1962 Jan [1] Group auditions for Decca Records at the company's West Hampstead, London, studios prior to Brian Poole & The Tremeloes, who are chosen in preference to The Beatles because they are based in the South of England.

[4] The Beatles top the first-ever **Mersey Beat** group popularity poll.

[24] Epstein signs the group and begins to direct their image away from leather jackets towards a smarter stage presentation, with matching suits and respectful bows to the audience.

Feb [1] The Thistle Café in West Kirby, Merseyside, is christened "The Beatles Club" for one night to mark Epstein's debut booking for the group. He reduces his usual commission to 10% on their earnings for the night (£18) to mark the occasion. (Ironically they never play at the venue again.)

Mar [8] BBC radio broadcasts "Teenager's Turn (Here We Go)", featuring The Beatles in their first ever radio appearance. (Over the next few years they will have their own series and various specials on BBC radio, performing many songs not featured on their albums.)

Apr [10] Sutcliffe, still living in Hamburg dies of a brain hemorrhage, in the arms of his fiancee Astrid Kirchherr.

[13] Group returns to Germany for 48 nights at Hamburg's new venue, the Star-Club. They will end their stint there May 31.

May [8] During a trek around London, visiting UK record companies Oriole, Phillips and Pye, Epstein visits the HMV record store in Oxford Street, which has a facility to transfer tape to acetate. Ted Huntly, the engineer who carries out the job of converting the Beatles' demo tape recorded for Decca to record, sees potential in the songs. He sends Epstein to publisher Ardmore & Beechwood director Sidney Coleman, who arranges meeting with EMI producer George Martin for next day.

June [4] Having aroused Martin's interest sufficiently, The Beatles sign a provisional contract with EMI to record demos.

[6] Group makes its debut session at EMI's Abbey Road studios to record a test for Parlophone, under the direction of Martin's assistant Ron Richards. They perform *Besame Mucho* and impress Martin with 3 self-penned compositions *P.S. I Love You*, *Ask Me Why* and *Love Me Do*.

[9] The Beatles play "Welcome Home" night at the Cavern, in front of an attendance-breaking 900 people.

Aug [14] Long dissatisfied with Best's role in the group, a decision is

made by Epstein and the other 3 Beatles to fire him. Rory Storm drummer Starr, currently playing at Butlin's holiday camp in Skegness, Lincs., is asked to replace him, after Epstein's choice, Johnny Hutchinson of The Big Three, has turned down the invitation.

[15] Best plays his last gig with the group at the Cavern.

[16] Best is dismissed from the group. (Hutchinson fills in for 1 gig at the Riverpark Ballroom, Chester, Cheshire.)

[18] Starr makes his Beatles debut at the Horticultural Society Dance, Hulme Hall, Port Sunlight, Merseyside.

[23] Lennon marries Cynthia Powell at Mount Pleasant Register Office, Liverpool, with McCartney as best man and spends his wedding night playing with The Beatles at the Riverpark Ballroom.

Sept [4] Group's first proper recording session at Abbey Road takes place. They are asked to record Mitch Murray's *How Do You Do It*, which they reluctantly perform. (Gerry & The Pacemakers will hit UK #1 with it the following year.) When they insist on performing their own material Martin challenges them to come up with a song as good. They record Lennon/McCartney's *Love Me Do*, featured at their audition, which Martin decides has the potential to be their first single.

[11] Martin, not happy with the results of the previous week's session, has the group return to Abbey Road to re-record *Love Me Do*, with session drummer Andy White taking over from Starr. (They will also record an early version of *Please Please Me* at this session.)

Oct [2] Epstein signs the group to 5-year management contract.

[5] The Beatles' debut single, *Love Me Do*, is released.

[6] Group makes the first of many personal appearances signing copies of *Love Me Do*, at Dawson's Music Shop, Widnes.

[12] The Beatles play at the Tower Ballroom, New Brighton, Merseyside, on a bill headed by Little Richard with Billy J. Kramer & The Contours, The Big Three, The Dakotas and other local groups.

[17] Group makes its TV debut on "People And Places", live from Granada's Manchester studios, singing *Love Me Do* and *Ooh! My Soul*.

[28] Group makes its first major stage appearance at the Liverpool Empire, on a bill headed by Little Richard with Craig Douglas, Jet Harris, Kenny Lynch and Sounds Incorporated.

Nov [1-14] The Beatles plays a run of 14 nights at the Star-Club.

Dec [18] Group begins its fifth and final club stint in Germany with 13 nights at the Star-Club, supporting Johnny & The Hurricanes. Ted Taylor of Liverpool group King Size Taylor & The Dominoes records their final performance on New Year's Eve. (It will be released commercially in 1977.)

[27] *Love Me Do* reaches UK #17. (It is later alleged that Epstein purchases 10,000 copies of the record for his NEMS shop to boost its chart position.)

1963 Jan [3] Group begins its first headlining tour – 4 nights in Scotland commencing at the Two Red Shoes Ballroom, Elgin, Morayshire, after the first night has been cancelled because of bad weather. (At one date they are billed as "The Love Me Do Boys – The Beatles).

[19] They make their first national TV appearance on "Thank Your Lucky Stars", performing *Please Please Me*.

Feb [2] The Beatles begin their first nationwide tour at Bradford's Gaumont cinema, on the bill headed by Helen Shapiro with Danny Williams and Kenny Lynch. Their payment for the tour is £80 a week shared by all 4 members.

[8] The Beatles, with Helen Shapiro and Kenny Lynch, are asked to leave the Carlisle Golf club dance at the Crown & Mitre hotel, because they are wearing leather jackets and causing a disturbance.

[11] They complete 10 new tracks for their debut album **Please Please Me** in one session at Abbey Road studios in 15 mins. short of 10 hours. Lennon's vocal for their cover of The Isley Brothers' *Twist And Shout* is recorded in 1 take as an afterthought to complete the album's tracks.

[23] *Please Please Me* hits UK #2. (It will top the chart on 3 of the 4 UK published record charts.)

Mar [3] The Helen Shapiro headlining tour ends at the Gaumont cinema, Hanley, Staffs.

[7] Group joins Gerry & The Pacemakers, The Big Three, Billy J. Kramer & The Dakotas and other local groups for a one-night stand package "Mersey Beat Showcase" at the Elizabethan Ballroom, Nottingham, Notts. (There will be 5 more of these through to June 16, when all the acts are available at the same time.)

[9] The Beatles begin a 21-date twice-nightly UK tour supporting Tommy Roe and Chris Montez at the Granada cinema, East Ham, London. With their fame rapidly spreading, they eventually top the bill. (Lennon misses 3 dates because of a heavy cold, and the band plays on as a trio.) Tour will end Mar.31 at the De Montfort Hall, Leicester, Leics.

Apr [4] At the request of schoolboy Dave Moores, the group appears at Roxburgh Hall, Stowe School, Bucks., for a fee of £100.
[8] John Charles Julian Lennon is born to John and Cynthia at Sefton General hospital, Liverpool.
[14] The Beatles see The Rolling Stones at the Crawdaddy.
[21] Group performs at the annual **New Musical Express** Poll Winners Concert at the Empire Pool, Wembley, London, before 8,000 fans.
May [4] *From Me To You* (the title inspired by the **New Musical Express**' letters column "From You To Us") tops UK chart for 7 weeks, selling over 250,000 copies. It begins a record-breaking run of 11 consecutive #1s from 11 consecutive releases.
[11] *Please Please Me* tops UK chart.
[16] The Beatles make their BBC TV debut on "The 625 Show", a program showcasing new talent.
[18] Group begins its third UK tour, supporting Roy Orbison with Gerry & The Pacemakers, at the Adelphi cinema, Slough, Berks. Due to audience reaction, The Beatles again become bill-toppers. The 21-date tour will close June 9 at King George's Hall, Blackburn, Lancs.
[19] 3 girls are taken into police custody after climbing through a dressing room window 100' above ground level by way of a metal ladder at the group's Hanley Gaumont show. They are released after getting the group's autographs.
June [4] The first in a regular series of radio programs, "Pop Go The Beatles", is broadcast on BBC radio.
[8] *My Bonnie*, credited to Tony Sheridan & The Beatles, charts for a week at UK #48.
Aug [1] A magazine devoted to the group, **Beatles Monthly**, is published for the first time. (It will continue until Dec.1969, selling 350,000 copies a month at its peak.)
[3] Group plays its final gig at the Cavern after 274 appearances.
Sept [10] Group is honored with Top Vocal Group Of The Year award at the Variety Club of Great Britain luncheon at London's Savoy hotel.
[14] *She Loves You* tops UK chart. (With a reported advance order of 310,000 copies, it will sell 1.6 million in UK alone and remain Britain's best-selling single until *Mull Of Kintyre* by Wings overtakes it in 1977.) It is replaced at #1 by Brian Poole & The Tremeloes' *Do You Love Me*, followed by Gerry & The Pacemakers' *You'll Never Walk Alone* (but will return to the top slot 8 weeks later).
Oct [4] Group makes its first live appearance on new ITV show "Ready Steady Go!"
[9] BBC TV airs "The Mersey Sound" documentary.
[13] Group makes its debut, topping the bill, on ITV's "Sunday Night At The London Palladium". Press reports scenes of hysteria amongst fans outside the Palladium and the term "Beatlemania" is coined.
[17] Group records its first Christmas record for its fan club members.
[25] A 5-date Swedish tour begins in Karlstad.
Nov [1] Group's first official headlining trek, "Beatles' Autumn Tour", a 33-date twice-nightly package with Peter Jay & The Jaywalkers, The Brook Brothers, The Vernons Girls and others, opens at the Odeon cinema, Cheltenham, Glos., as Beatlemania begins to grip UK. Tour will end Dec.13, at the Gaumont cinema, Southampton, Hants.
[4] Group receives a royal seal of approval from the Queen Mother, Princess Margaret and Lord Snowdon when it plays the Royal Variety Performance at London's Prince of Wales theater. Lennon creates major headlines when he asks the audience, "Will the people in the cheaper seats clap your hands. All the rest of you, rattle your jewellery."
[5] The **Daily Mirror** headlines an editorial, "Yeah! Yeah! Yeah!" which continues: "You have to be a real sour square not to love the nutty, noisy, happy, handsome Beatles. If they don't sweep your blues away, brother, you're a lost cause. If they don't put a beat in your feet, sister, you're not listening."
[16] Clark's Grammar school in Guildford, Surrey, sends boys who have Beatle haircuts home.
[21] In the House of Commons, a Member of Parliament questions the cost of police protection for The Beatles during their tour.
[30] *She Loves You* returns to #1 for 2 weeks, having passed the 1 million mark on Nov.27, and with advance orders of 270,000, **With The Beatles** tops UK chart, displacing *Please Please Me*. (Combined they will hold the top spot on the chart continuously for 51 weeks from May 1963 to May 1964.) *With The Beatles* becomes the first million-selling album in UK. All 4 Beatles appear on BBC TV show "Juke Box Jury". They vote the record that they will knock off the top in the US in 8 weeks time, Bobby Vinton's *There! I've Said It Again*, a miss.
Dec [14] *I Want To Hold Your Hand* tops UK chart for 5 weeks. (After an initial advance order of 940,000, it will sell 1.5 million copies in UK and worldwide sales will total 15 million.) It dethrones *She Loves You*,

the first time an act has replaced itself at #1. (Lennon will posthumously equal this in 1981 when *Woman* replaces *Imagine* at #1.)
[20] Group wins World Vocal Group and British Vocal Group categories in the **New Musical Express** poll for 1963.
[22] "The Beatles Come To Town" Pathé News documentary opens in cinemas throughout the UK.
[24] "The Beatles Christmas Show", with Rolf Harris, The Barron Knights, Tommy Quickly, The Fourmost, Billy J. Kramer & The Dakotas and Cilla Black, mixing music and pantomime, opens at London's Finsbury Park Astoria. It will run until Jan.11.
[27] **The Times** music critic William Mann hails Lennon and McCartney as the outstanding English composers of 1963.

1964

Jan [3] Group is seen for first time on US TV when NBC's "Jack Paar Show" airs a clip of *She Loves You* from the BBC's "The Mersey Sound".
[15] Band makes its French debut at the Cinéma Cyrano in Versailles, before embarking on a 20-date stint at the Paris Olympia with Trini Lopez and Sylvie Vartan.
[18] The Beatles make their US chart debut with *I Want To Hold Your Hand*, which enters at #45.
Feb [1] *I Want To Hold Your Hand*, described in **Billboard** review as a "driving rocker with surf on the Thames sound" and first played on WWDC in Washington, tops US chart displacing Bobby Vinton's *There! I've Said It Again*. (The first #1 by a UK act to top the US charts since The Tornados' *Telstar* on Dec.22, 1962, it is the first of 3 consecutive chart-toppers and 20 US #1s and becomes the fastest-ever UK million-seller in the US. The Beatles will stay at #1 until May 9, when *Hello Dolly* topples *Can't Buy Me Love*.)
[3] The RIAA certifies *I Want To Hold Your Hand* and **Meet The Beatles** gold.
[7] Pan-Am flight PA 101 touches down at 1:20EDT at New York's John F. Kennedy international airport, bringing The Beatles to US where they experience near riotous scenes thanks to major publicity built up by Capitol Records. (Capitol originally turned down Epstein and the group's first 4 singles were released in US by Vee-Jay Records.)
[9] Group makes its live CBS TV debut on the "Ed Sullivan Show" watched by an estimated 73 million viewers. (The crime rate in US cities is reported to have dropped dramatically during the show's broadcast time.) They sing *All My Loving, Till There Was You, She Loves You, I Saw Her Standing There* and *I Want To Hold Your Hand*, and are paid $2,400. Also appearing on the show are Georgia Brown and the children's chorus from the Broadway show "Oliver" (including future Monkee Davy Jones), Tessie O'Shea and Frank Gorshin.
[11] The Beatles' US concert debut takes place at the Washington Coliseum, Washington, DC, with Tommy Roe, The Chiffons and The Caravelles.
[12] Band makes its New York debut at Carnegie Hall. (The New Street Music record store in New York, located next to a barber shop, offers to send buyers of the Beatles album next door for a free Beatle haircut.)
[15] **Meet The Beatles!** tops US chart for 11 weeks.
[16] A second "Ed Sullivan Show" is broadcast direct from Miami's Deauville hotel.
[18] In Miami, FL, for a concert, the group visits Cassius Clay, preparing for his World Heavyweight bout with Sonny Liston, at his training camp.
[22] Group arrives back from the US at Heathrow airport. BBC sports program "Grandstand" screens their early morning return during its afternoon broadcast later in the day.
[29] *Introducing ... The Beatles* hits US #2 for 9 weeks, unable to dislodge *Meet The Beatles!*
Mar [2] Work begins on their first feature film at Pinewood studios, based around a typical day in the life of the group.
[14] *Please Please Me* hits US #3 as *My Bonnie* reaches US #26.
[16] Leeds University Law Society elects Starr its vice-president.
[19] Prime Minister Harold Wilson presents The Beatles with their award for Show Business Personalities Of The Year For 1963 at the Variety Club of Great Britain luncheon at London's Dorchester hotel.
[20] Group appears live on UK TV show "Ready Steady Go!", bringing the show its highest ever audience rating.
[21] *She Loves You* tops US chart; while *I Saw Her Standing There* reaches US #14.
[23] Lennon's book of nonsense verse and rhyme, **In His Own Write**, is published in the UK as the group receives 2 Carl-Alan awards from the Duke of Edinburgh at the Empire Ballroom, Leicester Square, London. It is announced that The Beatles have won 3 Ivor Novello awards – the Most Broadcast Work Of The Year (*She Loves You*), the Highest Certified British Sales (*She Loves You*) and the Special Award

For Outstanding Services To British Music, shared with Brian Epstein and George Martin. (*I Want To Hold Your Hand* has the second highest sales, and *All My Loving* comes second in the Year's Outstanding Song category.)

[25] Group makes its first appearance on BBC TV's "Top Of The Pops" singing *Can't Buy Me Love.*

[28] The Australian chart published this week reads – #1 *I Saw Her Standing There*, #2 *Love Me Do*, #3 *Roll Over Beethoven*, #4 *All My Loving*, #5 *She Loves You* and #6 *I Want To Hold Your Hand.*

Apr [4] *Can't Buy Me Love* tops UK chart, after selling a record 1,226,000 copies in its first week, and tops US chart, making a record leap in US from a #27 chart debut vaulting over *Twist And Shout* which moves up 1 place to hit #2, and selling 2 million copies in its week of release, after advance orders of 1,700,000. Its advance orders of 1 million are the largest in UK record history. *From Me To You* and *Roll Over Beethoven* reach US #41 and #68 respectively. The **Billboard** chart for this week ending reads: #1 *Can't Buy Me Love*, #2 *Twist And Shout*, #3 *She Loves You*, #4 *I Want To Hold Your Hand*, #5 *Please Please Me.*

[11] *You Can't Do That* and *There's A Place* make US #48 and #74 respectively.

[18] *Why* peaks at US #88, while **The Beatles With Tony Sheridan And Their Guests** and **Jolly What! The Beatles & Frank Ifield** make US #68 and #104 respectively.

[23] On the occasion of Shakespeare's 400th birthday Lennon is guest of honour at a Foyle's Literary Lunch at London's Dorchester hotel. His speech consists of, "Thank you very much. You've got a lucky face."

[25] Peter & Gordon's Lennon/McCartney-penned *World Without Love* knocks *Can't Buy Me Love* off the top of UK chart, as *All My Loving* makes US #45. (The group has a record 14 singles on US chart.)

[26] The Beatles make their second appearance at the annual **New Musical Express** Poll Winners concert at the Empire Pool, Wembley.

[27] Lennon's **In His Own Write** is published in the US. (It receives rave reviews with **Newsweek** magazine calling him "an unlikely heir to the English tradition of literary nonsense".)

May [2] *The Beatles Second Album* replaces *Meet The Beatles!* at US #1, where it will stay for 5 weeks.

[6] Jack Good-directed "Around The Beatles" airs on ITV.

[9] *Do You Want To Know A Secret* hits US #2 as *Thank You Girl* makes US #35.

[16] *I Want To Hold Your Hand* re-enters UK chart at #48.

[18] McCartney is interviewed on BBC TV's "A Degree Of Frost".

[30] *Love Me Do* tops US chart. Recently made Madame Tussaud's waxworks of The Beatles are seen on BBC TV's "Juke Box Jury".

June [3] Ringo is rushed to University College hospital, London, after collapsing at a photo session in Barnes, London, suffering from tonsilitis and pharyngitis.

[4] Group begins its first world tour at K.B. Hallen, Copenhagen, Denmark, with Jimmy Nicol of The Shubdubs (and once of Georgie Fame & The Blue Flames) deputizing for Ringo for the first 5 dates.

[6] *P.S. I Love You* hits US #10.

[11] Ringo is discharged from hospital, and flies out to Australia to join the tour on June 15 at the Festival Hall, Melbourne.

[14] In Melbourne, 250,000 people – the largest collection of Australians ever assembled in 1 place – gather to meet the group. Meanwhile, thousands of miles away in Sunderland, Tyne & Wear, 12-year-old Carol Dryden is found by an observant railway clerk in a tea chest addressed to The Beatles.

[27] Peter & Gordon's *World Without Love* tops US chart, becoming Lennon/McCartney's first non-Beatle US #1, while EP *Four By The Beatles* (#92) and *Sie Liebt Dich* (#97) both make a brief US showing and *Ain't She Sweet* reaches UK #29.

July [6] "A Hard Day's Night" receives its world premiere at the London Pavilion. (It receives 2 Academy award nominations.)

[10] 200,000 people pack the route from Speke airport to Liverpool city center as group arrives in its home town for a civic reception at the Town Hall and to attend Northern premiere of "A Hard Day's Night".

[23] Group participates in "The Night Of A Hundred Stars" midnight charity revue at the London Palladium.

[25] *A Hard Day's Night* tops UK chart. **A Hard Day's Night** tops UK and US charts and is unique in being the only album comprised entirely of Lennon/McCartney songs. **The American Tour With Ed Rudy** reaches US #20.

Aug [1] *A Hard Day's Night* tops US chart as *I'm Happy Just To Dance With You* makes US #95.

[15] *I Should Have Known Better* peaks at US #53.

[19] Second North American tour, with The Righteous Brothers, Jackie

De Shannon, The Exciters and Bill Black's Combo, opens at the Cow Palace, San Francisco, CA. The 26-date tour ends with a charity performance at the Paramount theater, New York on Sept.20. (They will be paid a world record fee of $150,000 for a concert at the Municipal Stadium, Kansas City, MO.)

[22] *Ain't She Sweet* reaches US #19, as **Something New** hits US #2 for weeks, behind **A Hard Day's Night**.

[29] *I'll Cry Instead* reaches US #25.

Sept [5] *And I Love Her* reaches US #12 as *If I Fell* peaks at US #53.

[15] Police inspector Carl Bear of Cleveland's Juvenile Bureau stops a Beatles show after screaming fans invade the stage at Cleveland's Public Hall.

Oct [3] Group tapes an insert for ABC TV's "Shindig" at the Granville theater, Fulham, London.

[9] The Beatles begin their only UK tour of 1964, a 27-date twice-nightly UK package, with Mary Wells, Tommy Quickly, Sounds Incorporated and others, at the Gaumont cinema, Bradford, W.Yorks. The tour will end Nov.10 at the Colston Hall, Bristol, Avon.

[10] *Slow Down* reaches US #25.

[13] CBS TV's "The Entertainers" airs hour-long documentary on The Beatles' North American tour.

[17] *Matchbox* reaches US #17, as **The Beatles Vs The Four Seasons** peaks at US #142.

Dec [2] Ringo has his tonsils removed at London's University College hospital.

[5] **Song, Pictures And Stories Of The Fabulous Beatles** makes US #63.

[12] *I Feel Fine* tops UK chart, with advance orders of 750,000, and is their fourth consecutive UK million-seller.

[19] **Beatles For Sale** hits UK #1, displacing **A Hard Days' Night** which has been at the top for 21 weeks.

[24] "Another Beatles Christmas Show" opens at London's Hammersmith Odeon, with Freddie & The Dreamers, The Yardbirds, Elkie Brooks, Jimmy Savile, Mike Haslam, Mike Cotton Sound, Sounds Incorporated and Ray Fell. The show will end Jan.16.

[26] *I Feel Fine* tops US chart as *She's A Woman* hits US #4, completing run of 30 US hits for the year.

1965 Jan [2] **The Beatles' Story** hits US #7.

[9] Lennon guests on Peter Cook and Dudley Moore's BBC2 TV show "Not Only ... But Also", as **Beatles '65** begins a 9 weeks run at the top of US chart.

Feb [24] Filming of the second, as yet untitled, Beatles' feature begins in The Bahamas.

Mar [13] *Eight Days A Week* hits US #1, knocking The Temptations' *My Girl* off the top.

[20] *I Don't Want To Spoil The Party* makes US #39.

[27] *4 By The Beatles* peaks at US #68.

Apr [11] The Beatles make their third appearance at the **New Musical Express** annual Poll Winners' Concert at the Empire Pool, Wembley, before appearing on UK commercial TV's "The Eamonn Andrews Show" that evening.

[13] The Beatles win Best Performance By A Vocal Group for *A Hard Day's Night* and Best New Artist Of 1964 at the 7th Grammy awards.

[24] *Ticket To Ride* tops UK chart. Epstein writes to music paper **Melody Maker** informing it that McCartney plays lead guitar on the record and wins an award for writing the letter of the week.

May [15] *Yes It Is* makes US #46.

[18] Group appears on "The Best On Record", an NBC TV special featuring the Grammy winners.

[22] *Ticket To Ride* knocks Herman's Hermits' *Mrs. Brown, You've Got A Lovely Daughter* off the top in US.

June [7] BBC airs "The Beatles (Invite You To Take A Ticket To Ride)", the group's final radio session.

[12] **The Early Beatles** makes US #43, as it is announced that The Beatles have been included in the Queen's Birthday honors list, receiving the MBE (Member Of The British Empire). (Protests pour in to Buckingham Palace along with returned medals. Colonel Frederick Wragg returns 12 medals and former Canadian MP Hector Dupuis MBE claims, "The British house of royalty has put me on the same level as a bunch of vulgar numbskulls.")

[20] A 9-date European tour begins at the Palais Des Sports, Porte de Versailles, Paris, France.

[24] Lennon's second book **A Spaniard In The Works** is published in UK, as the band makes its Italian debut at Milan's Velodromo Vigorelli.

July [1] **A Spaniard In The Works** is published in US.

[3] European tour ends at the Plaza de Toros Monumental, Barcelona, Spain.

[10] *Beatles VI* tops US chart.

[13] Lennon and McCartney win 2 Ivor Novello Awards. *Can't Buy Me Love* wins the Most Performed Work Of 1964 and the Highest Certified British Sales categories. (*A Hard Day's Night* is runner-up in the Most Performed Work category, *I Feel Fine* is the runner-up in the Highest Certified British Sales category and *A Hard Day's Night* is the runner-up in the Year's Outstanding Theme From Radio, TV Or Film category.) McCartney, the only Beatle to attend the awards ceremony at the Savoy hotel, London, says "Thanks. I hope nobody sends theirs back now."

[29] "Help!" premieres at the London Pavilion.

Aug [7] *Help!* takes over the UK #1 spot from The Byrds' *Mr. Tambourine Man*.

[9] Brian Epstein-managed Silkie record a cover of *You've Got To Hide Your Love Away*, with McCartney on guitar, Harrison on tambourine and Lennon producing. (It will makes UK #28 and US #10.)

[11] "Help!" premieres in New York.

[14] *Help!* tops UK chart.

[15] Third North American tour begins at Shea Stadium, Flushing, Queens, New York, before a record crowd of 55,600. (With a security force of 2,000 men, the show grosses $304,000, a world record for a pop concert.)

[27] Group meets Elvis Presley for the first and only time at his Bel Air, CA, home on Perugia Way. Lennon, McCartney and Presley join forces on an impromptu version of *You're My World*.

[31] Tour ends at San Francisco's Cow Palace.

Sept [4] *Help!* tops US chart.

[11] *Help!* tops US chart for 9 weeks.

[12] The Beatles appear on the first "Ed Sullivan Show" of a new season, Sullivan's 18th, singing *I Feel Fine*, *I'm Down*, *Act Naturally*, *Ticket To Ride*, *Yesterday* and *Help!* Also featured on the bill are Cilla Black, Soupy Sales and Allen & Rossi.

[25] "The Beatles" cartoon series premieres on ABC TV. The half-hour series features 2 stories each week. The first program features "I Want To Hold Your Hand" in which the group, exploring the ocean floor in a diving bell, encounters a lovesick octopus and "A Hard Day's Night", in which the band rehearses in a haunted house.

Oct [9] *Yesterday* tops US chart. (Over 2,500 cover versions will make it one of the most recorded songs in the history of popular music. When McCartney uses the song in his 1984 film *Give My Regards To Broad Street* he has to apply to the publishers for its use as he no longer holds the copyright.)

[23] *Act Naturally* makes US #47.

[26] The Queen presents The Beatles with their MBEs in the Great Throne Room at Buckingham Palace, London, with 182 other recipients. (They later admit to having smoked marijuana in the lavatories.) When the Queen asks Starr, "How long have you been together now?" he replies, "40 years."

Nov Pete Best asks the Manhattan Supreme Court to assume jurisdiction over an $8 million defamation of character suit he has brought against The Beatles and **Playboy** magazine.

Dec [3] Group's final UK tour, a 9-date twice-nightly package, with The Moody Blues, The Koobas and Beryl Marsden, opens at Glasgow's Odeon cinema. The tour will finale on Dec.12 at the Capitol cinema, Cardiff, Wales.

[13] Band scraps plans to make a third feature film, based on Richard Condon's book **A Talent For Loving**.

[16] "The Music Of Lennon-McCartney", a 50-min. tribute featuring Peter Sellers, Marianne Faithfull, Cilla Black, Peter & Gordon, Lulu, Billy J. Kramer, Esther Phillips and Richard Anthony, airs on ITV in London. (The rest of the UK will see the program the following night.) The Beatles perform *We Can Work It Out* with Lennon playing the harmonium used by Ena Sharples at the Glad Tidings Mission in TV soap "Coronation Street", which is brought in from an adjoining studio as they are unable to supply their own.

[18] *Day Tripper/We Can Work It Out* tops UK chart, as The Beatles spend their third successive Christmas at #1.

[25] *Rubber Soul* tops UK chart.

[26] McCartney, spending Christmas with his father on the Wirral, Merseyside, suffers a 5" cut to his mouth when he falls off a moped he is riding.

1966 **Jan** [3] Band records spot for NBC TV show "Hullabaloo".

[8] *We Can Work It Out* and **Rubber Soul** top US charts. Peter Sellers becomes the first artist to chart in UK with a cover of a Beatles' single when his comic version of *A Hard Day's Night* (featuring his impression of Sir Laurence Olivier reciting the song as Richard III) reaches UK #14.

[21] Harrison marries Patti Boyd, whom he met on the set of "A Hard

Day's Night", at Esher Register Office, Surrey. McCartney is best man.

[22] *Day Tripper* hits US #5.

[28] The Cavern club closes down with debts of £10,000.

[29] The Overlanders' version of *Michelle* tops UK chart, becoming Pye Records fastest seller since Lonnie Donegan's *My Old Man's A Dustman*.

Mar [1] "The Beatles At Shea Stadium" receives its TV world premiere on BBC1.

[4] Lennon, interviewed by Maureen Cleave in London's **Evening Standard** newspaper, states "We're more popular than Jesus now." (The remark raises little interest in UK but has severe repercussions for the group when reprinted in US before their summer tour.)

[19] *What Goes On* makes US #81.

[26] *Nowhere Man* hits US #3 as Peter & Gordon's *Woman*, penned by McCartney under the pseudonym Bernard Webb, reaches UK #22.

May [1] The Beatles give their last UK concert at the annual **New Musical Express** Poll Winners Concert at the Empire Pool, Wembley. Actor Clint Walker presents them with their award.

June [25] *Paperback Writer* tops UK and US charts, as its promotional film is shown on final broadcast of "Thank Your Lucky Stars".

[26] During a 4-city tour of Germany, the group returns in triumph to Hamburg in an 8-car motorcade escorted by a dozen motorcycle police, playing to a sell-out crowd of more than 7,000 at the Ernst Merck Halle. (It is the band's first visit to the city since leaving after the final Star-Club date on Dec.31, 1962.)

[30] They play the first of 3 concerts at the Nippon Budokan Hall, Tokyo, Japan.

July [4] Group performs 2 shows before a crowd of 80,000 at the Rizal Memorial football stadium, Manila in The Philippines.

[5] After an administrative mix-up which results in The Beatles failing to appear at a Presidential reception at the Malacanang Palace with President Ferdinand Marcos and his wife the day before, the group flees an angry crowd at Manila Airport.

[9] *Rain* makes US #23.

[12] The Beatles win 2 more Ivor Novello awards. *We Can Work It Out* has the Highest Certified British Sales Of 1965 and *Yesterday* wins the Outstanding Song Of 1965 category.

[30] *Yesterday ... And Today* tops US chart but its notorious "butcher" cover (the band posing in white coats amongst bloody cuts of meat and dismembered dolls) is hastily withdrawn, becoming a collector's item.

[31] 2 days after US **Datebook** magazine publishes Lennon's interview with Maureen Cleave, citizens of Birmingham, AL, publicly burn Beatles' records and memorabilia, amidst general anger in the Southern states.

Aug [8] The South African Broadcasting Corporation (SABC) bans all Beatles records in response to Lennon's remarks.

[11] The 3 US TV networks air The Beatles press conference held at the Astor Towers hotel in Chicago, IL, shortly after the group's arrival for its US tour. Lennon publically apologises for his "Jesus" remarks.

[12] Band's fourth and final 14-city North American tour, with The Cyrkle, The Ronettes, The Remains and Bobby Hebb, begins at the Chicago's International Amphitheater.

[13] *Revolver* tops UK chart. Its closing track, *Tomorrow Never Knows*, signals their first departure from the 3-min. pop song formula and makes use of backward tapes and sitars.

[20] Double A-side *Yellow Submarine*, featuring Starr on lead vocal, coupled with *Eleanor Rigby*, tops UK chart.

[22] New York police talk teenagers Carol Hopkins and Susan Richmond down from the 22nd floor ledge of the Americana hotel, after they threaten to jump unless they can get to meet The Beatles. The girls are taken to Roosevelt hospital for observation.

[29] The final Beatles' concert takes place at Candlestick Park, San Francisco, CA. Their final number after 9 years of gigging is Little Richard's *Long Tall Sally*. In UK, BBC Light radio program broadcasts "The Lennon And McCartney Songbook".

Sept [5] Lennon flies to Celle, Germany, to begin filming the role of Private Gripweed in "How I Won The War".

[10] *Revolver* tops US chart.

[17] *Yellow Submarine* hits US #2, as McCartney-produced *Got To Get You Into My Life* hits UK #6 for Cliff Bennett & The Rebel Rousers.

[24] *Eleanor Rigby* reaches US #11.

Nov [9] Lennon meets Yoko Ono for the first time at a private preview for the "Unfinished Paintings And Objects" exhibition at the Indica Gallery in Mason's Yard, London.

[26] Group starts work on new album at Abbey Road studios.

Dec *A Collection Of Beatles' Oldies* hits UK #7.

[18] Hayley Mills/Hywel Bennett-starring film "The Family Way", for

which McCartney has written the score, premieres in London.

[26] Lennon guests as a mens room attendant on Peter Cook and Dudley Moore's BBC TV show "Not Only ... But Also".

[31] Harrison is refused admission to Annabel's nightclub in London for not wearing a tie, so he, and his party, including wife Patti, Brian Epstein and Eric Clapton see in the New Year at Joe Lyons' Corner House in Coventry Street in the West End of London.

1967 Jan [27] The Beatles sign a 9-year contract with EMI Records.
Feb [9] Film clips for *Penny Lane* and *Strawberry Fields Forever* are shown on "Top Of The Pops".

[10] *A Day In The Life* is recorded for *Sgt. Pepper's Lonely Hearts Club Band*. In an unprecedented move in pop, the group uses 40 session musicians to create the track's orchestral sound.

Mar [2] *Michelle* wins Song Of The Year, *Eleanor Rigby* wins Best Contemporary (Rock'N'Roll) Solo Vocal Performance and *Revolver* wins Best Album Cover, Graphic Arts Of 1966 at the 9th annual Grammy awards.

[11] *Penny Lane/Strawberry Fields Forever* hits UK #2. A run of 11 consecutive UK #1s is stopped by Engelbert Humperdinck's *Release Me*.

[18] *Penny Lane* tops US chart.

[25] The Beatles win 2 more Ivor Novello awards, for *Michelle,* as Most Performed Work Of 1966 and *Yellow Submarine* as Highest Certified British Sales For 1966.

[30] A photo session for *Sgt. Pepper's Lonely Hearts Club Band*'s sleeve, a montage design created by pop artist Peter Blake, with Michael Cooper as photographer, takes place at Chelsea Manor studios in Flood Street, London. EMI insists that permission must be granted for use of their photographs by the many famous people selected by the group as an imaginary audience and all those known to be alive are contacted. Mae West rejects the idea of being in a lonely hearts club but is won over by a personal request from the group. Some of Lennon's choice of audience-members (including Jesus Christ, Gandhi and Adolf Hitler) are removed from the final shot. Bob Dylan and Dion are the only 2 singers featured on the sleeve.

Apr [1] *Strawberry Fields Forever* hits US #8.

[5] Paul joins Jane Asher in Denver, CO, for her 21st birthday.

May EMI announces total Beatles' record sales currently top 200 million worldwide.

[18] Lennon and McCartney turn up for a Rolling Stones recording session at Olympic studios in Barnes, London. They contribute backing vocals to *We Love You*.

[20] BBC announces a ban on *Sgt.Pepper*'s closing cut, *A Day In The Life,* citing that it may encourage drug-taking.

June [8] *Sgt. Pepper's Lonely Hearts Club Band* hits UK #1. It sets new standards in modern music, costing £25,000 to produce and involving 700 hours of studio time. It will be critically revered as perhaps the "best" album in rock history, and will be seen by others at the climax of the group's career. The sleeve is the first to print lyrics and one of the first gatefold covers. The inner sleeve has a psychedelic design instead of being plain white. At the group's insistence the album is issued concurrently all over the world and is the first release in US by Capitol to match a Beatles' UK disk exactly.

[19] Having admitted in **Life** magazine that he has taken LSD, McCartney reiterates his claim during a ITV newscast and creates a media furore as intense as that experienced by Lennon the year before.

[25] The recording of *All You Need Is Love* at Abbey Road studios is transmitted worldwide as part of the first global TV link-up, "Our World", to an estimated audience of 400 million. The song features excerpts from the Brandenburg concertos, "La Marseillaise", "Greensleeves" and *She Loves You*. Martin also uses a segment of Glenn Miller's *In The Mood,* thinking it is out of copyright. (He is later successfully sued for a royalty settlement by Miller's publishers.) In addition to 13 session musicians, friends on backing vocals are Mick Jagger, Keith Richard, Marianne Faithfull, Eric Clapton, Keith Moon, Jane Asher, McCartney's brother Mike McGear, The Walker Brothers' Gary Leeds and Graham Nash and his wife Rose.

July [1] *Sgt. Pepper's Lonely Hearts Club Band* tops US chart.

[22] *All You Need Is Love* tops UK chart.

[24] All 4 Beatles and Epstein sign a petition calling for the legalization of marijuana which is published in **The Times** newspaper.

Aug [12] *Baby You're A Rich Man* reaches US #34.

[19] *All You Need Is Love* tops US chart, and Maureen Starr gives birth to a second son, Jason, at Queen Charlotte's hospital, Hammersmith, London.

[25] Group attends a conference of the Spiritual Regeneration League at Normal college, Bangor, Wales, to study transcendental meditation

with Indian guru Maharishi Mahesh Yogi.

[27] Epstein is found dead in bed at his London home of an apparent drug overdose after a long period of depression. **The New York Times** calls him "the man who revolutionized pop music in our time."

[31] Group announces that it will now manage its own affairs.

Sept [11] Shooting of TV film "Magical Mystery Tour" begins in Teignmouth, Devon.

[27] The Beatles form Apple Publishing Limited.

Oct [7] New York concert promoter Sid Bernstein offers the group $1 million to perform live again. They reject his offer.

[18] The Beatles attend the world premiere of "How I Won The War" at the London Pavilion.

Nov [26] The promotional clip of *Hello Goodbye* airs on the "Ed Sullivan Show", but is not shown on UK TV due to a Musicians' Union agreement banning miming.

[28] Group records its last fan club record, *Christmas Time Is Here Again!,* with all 4 members taking part, at Abbey Road.

Dec [1] Ringo flies to Rome to begin filming "Candy".

[7] The Apple Boutique opens at 94 Baker Street, London.

[9] *Hello Goodbye* tops UK chart for 7 weeks.

[11] Apple Music publishing company signs its first act Grapefruit.

[23] *I Am The Walrus* reaches US #56 with vocal contributions from The Mike Sammes Singers and a section from a UK BBC radio production of "King Lear", broadcast at the time of recording.

[25] McCartney announces his engagement to Jane Asher.

[26] "Magical Mystery Tour" airs on BBC TV and is castigated by critics who slur the film's absence of plot and direction. The **Daily Express** TV critic claims never to have seen "such blatant rubbish".

[30] *Hello Goodbye* tops US chart, as double EP *Magical Mystery Tour* hits UK #2.

1968 Jan [6] *Magical Mystery Tour* tops US chart.

[7] Harrison begins writing the score for the film "Wonderwall".

[20] *Magical Mystery Tour* import album makes UK #31.

[22] Apple Corps Ltd opens its offices at 95 Wigmore Street, London. (They will later move to 3 Savile Row).

Feb [6] Starr guests on Cilla Black's BBC TV show "Cilla", for which McCartney has penned the theme tune *Step Inside Love*.

[15] The Harrisons and Lennons fly to India, to study meditation with the Maharishi in Rishikesh. (McCartney and Jane Asher and the Starrs leave 4 days later. Starr soon becomes bored however, returning to London on Mar.1, comparing the retreat center to a Butlins holiday camp. The rest of group depart after the Maharishi has purportedly made amorous advances to actress Mia Farrow, although it seems more likely that this is a mischievous rumor.)

[29] *Sgt. Pepper* wins Album Of The Year, Best Contemporary Album, Best Engineered Recording and Best Album Cover, Graphic Arts Of 1967 at the 10th annual Grammy awards.

Mar [23] Grapefruit's debut single, *Dear Delilah* reaches UK #21.

[30] *Lady Madonna* tops UK chart as *The Inner Light* makes US #96.

Apr [20] *Lady Madonna* hits US #4. The group's company, Apple Corps Ltd, begins operation in London. (Future Beatles releases will be made on the Apple label.)

May [4] Mary Hopkin wins her heat on commercial TV talent show "Opportunity Knocks". McCartney sees her and makes her the first signing to the Apple label.

[15] Lennon and McCartney appear on NBC TV's "The Tonight Show" with Joe Garagiola sitting in for Johnny Carson, at which they announce the setting up of Apple.

[17] "Wonderwall" premieres at the Cannes Film Festival.

[23] Apple Tailoring opens at 161 New Kings Road, London.

June McCartney meets future wife Linda Eastman on US business trip.

[18] The National Theatre's production of "In His Own Write" opens at London's Old Vic theater.

July [17] Animated feature *Yellow Submarine* premieres at the London Pavilion. The Beatles make a cameo appearance at the film's end but do not supply their own voices for their characters.

[20] Appearing on BBC TV's "Dee Time", Asher announces that her relationship with McCartney is over.

[31] The Apple Boutique in Baker Street closes down, with the remaining stock being given away.

Aug Starr quits during sessions for the band's new album, but returns a few days later. The incident is kept hidden from the press.

[22] Cynthia Lennon sues John for divorce, citing Yoko Ono.

Sept [8] Band performs *Hey Jude* on UK TV show "Frost On Sunday".

[14] *Hey Jude* tops UK chart, longest-playing #1 ever (7 mins. 10 secs.).

[21] *Revolution* makes US #12. Madame Tussaud's give The Beatles'

waxworks their fifth change of clothes and hair in 4 years.

[28] *Hey Jude* tops US chart for 9 weeks.

[30] Hunter Davies' authorized biography **The Beatles** is published.

Oct [18] Lennon and Ono are taken to Paddington Green police station and charged with obstructing the police in execution of a search warrant, when cannabis is discovered in the apartment where they are staying.

[19] Lennon and Ono are remanded on bail at Marylebone Magistrates Court and their case adjourned until Nov.28.

Nov [8] Cynthia Lennon is granted a divorce because of Lennon's adultery with Yoko Ono.

[28] Lennon pleads guilty to cannabis possession. He is fined £150.

Dec [7] Double *The Beatles* tops UK chart. It is referred to as the *White Album* because of its plain white sleeve (a reversal from *Sgt. Pepper's* lavish one). For the first time The Beatles work separately on some of the songs on the album, as cracks begin to appear in the partnership.

[11] Lennon, Ono and Julian Lennon take part in The Rolling Stones' never-to-be shown TV extravaganza "Rock And Roll Circus".

[28] *The Beatles* tops US chart.

1969 Jan [2] Filming begins at Twickenham Film studios of the group rehearsing for a back-to-the-roots album (which will evolve into the film and record *Let It Be*).

[10] Harrison walks out on the band, albeit temporarily.

[18] A scheduled Beatles concert at the Roundhouse in London does not materialize.

[30] Group, with Billy Preston guesting on organ, performs for 42 mins. on the roof of the Apple building in London's Savile Row, before police bring it to a halt. Stephen King, chief accountant of nearby Royal Bank of Scotland rings the police to complain about the noise.

Feb *Yellow Submarine* hits UK #3.

[3] Allen Klein is appointed The Beatles' business manager.

[4] The Beatles appoint New York lawyers Eastman & Eastman as general counsel to Apple.

[7] Harrison enters University College hospital, London to have his tonsils removed.

Mar [1] *Yellow Submarine* hits US #2 for 2 weeks, behind The Supremes & The Temptations' *TCB*.

[12] McCartney marries Linda Eastman at Marylebone Register Office, London.

[20] Lennon marries Yoko Ono in the British Consulate building in Gibraltar.

[25] Lennon and Ono participate in a 7-day "bed-in" promoting world peace at Amsterdam's Hilton hotel, ending Mar.31.

[31] George and Patti Harrison are fined £250 for cannabis resin possession. (They had been arrested on McCartney's wedding day.)

Apr [22] Lennon changes his middle name by deed-poll from Winston to Ono in a ceremony on top of the Apple building. The commissioner of Oaths is Senor Bueno de Mesquita.

[24] Dispelling rumors, McCartney reveals from his farm in Campbeltown, Scotland, that he is not dead.

[26] *Get Back* tops UK chart, the only Beatles single to debut in UK at #1. On it, Billy Preston receives a label-credit as "The Beatles with ...", the only artist ever to do so.

May [22] *Hey Jude* wins Ivor Novello Award.

[24] *Get Back* tops US chart as *Don't Let Me Down* makes US #35.

[26] John and Yoko begin another "bed-in", in Room 1742 of Hotel La Reine Queen, Montreal, Canada, until June 2.

June [14] *The Ballad Of John And Yoko*, with only Lennon and McCartney playing on the track, tops UK chart. It is the first stereo single release by the group and its last UK #1.

July [1] The Lennons are taken to Lawson Memorial hospital after a car crash in Golspie, Scotland. John receives 17 stitches for a facial wound, Yoko 14 stitches, Kyoko 4, while Julian suffers from shock.

[12] *The Ballad Of John & Yoko* hits US #8, plagued by radio censorship problems through its use of the word "Christ".

Aug [8] The photo of the group on the zebra crossing outside Abbey Road studios is taken at 10am for use on the sleeve of forthcoming *Abbey Road*. A policeman holds up traffic as the picture is taken.

[20] The Beatles are together for the last time in a recording studio as they complete *I Want You (She's So Heavy)* for *Abbey Road*.

[28] Linda McCartney gives birth to daughter, Mary, at the Avenue Clinic, London.

Sept [20] Klein negotiates a new deal with EMI/Capitol for an increased royalty rate.

[23] Illinois University newspaper **Northern Star** prints a story, headlined "Clues Hint At Beatle Death", which speculates that McCartney had been killed in a car crash in Scotland on Nov.9, 1966 (despite the fact that he and then-girlfriend Jane Asher were vacationing in Kenya at the time) and been replaced by former Beatle-look-a-like competition winner William Campbell, having undergone plastic surgery. (The rumor will mushroom when Detroit radio station WKNR-FM DJ Russ Gibbs breaks the story on air, which will lead to major print articles, which further fuel the story. **Sunday People** journalist Hugh Farmer tracks McCartney down to his farm in Scotland, and is greeted with the comment "Do I look dead? I'm as fit as a fiddle.")

Oct [4] *Abbey Road* tops UK chart for 11 weeks.

Nov [1] *Abbey Road* tops US chart for 11 weeks.

[29] Originally charting separately, *Come Together/Something* tops US chart.

Dec [6] *Something/Come Together* hits UK #4. It is the first Beatles' disk not to make either UK #1 or #2 since *Love Me Do* in 1962, and the first from an already issued album. *Something* is also the first Beatles' single not penned by Lennon/McCartney, but by Harrison. Frank Sinatra calls it the greatest love song of the last 50 years.

For the first time a Beatles song is licensed for use on a non-Beatles album: *Across The Universe* features on World Wildlife Fund charity *No One's Gonna Change Our World*. The falsetto harmonies are performed by teenage Beatles' fans Lizzie Bravo and Gayleen Pease, selected from fans waiting for the group outside Abbey Road studios.

Beatles Monthly ceases publication after 77 issues as The Beatles rapidly begin to lose their collective identity and refuse to co-operate for promotion.

1970 Jan [16] The police shut down an exhibition of Lennon's erotic lithographs at a London gallery, for alleged obscenity.

Mar [11] *Abbey Road* wins Best Engineered Recording Of 1969 at the 12th annual Grammy awards.

[21] *Let It Be* hits UK #2, held off top by Lee Marvin's *Wand'rin' Star*.

[23] Legendary record producer Phil Spector is called in to remix **Let It Be** as the sound is considered too raw for commercial release. (Spector has long wanted to work with the group and, left alone with the master tapes, proceeds to impose his style on the album. He particularly upsets McCartney by adding strings and choir to *The Long And Winding Road*. What began as a back-to-the-roots project finishes with one of their most lavishly produced sets, involving many hours of mixing.)

[28] Compilation *Hey Jude* hits US #2 for 4 weeks, behind Simon & Garfunkel's *Bridge Over Troubled Water*.

Apr [1] The last session for a Beatles' album takes place with only Starr in attendance. He records drums on 3 tracks for forthcoming Spector-produced *Let It Be*.

[9] With a rift growing, both financially and artistically, between McCartney and the rest of the group, he quits The Beatles, releasing his debut solo *McCartney* almost simultaneously with the group's *Let It Be*. With Lennon enjoying hits with the Plastic Ono Band and Starr about to release his debut solo *Sentimental Journey*, The Beatles are no more. The decision is unanimous amongst the 4 but when the story breaks the following day, McCartney is blamed by the press as the "man who broke up The Beatles".

[11] *Let It Be* tops US chart, having debuted at #6, the highest position ever for any single in its first week of release.

May [13] "Let It Be" premieres in New York.

[20] "Let It Be" opens simultaneously at the London Pavilion and Liverpool Gaumont without any of the group attending. It documents the making of the album and outlines the discontent amongst The Beatles during its recording.

[23] *Let It Be* tops UK chart. **New Musical Express** calls it a "cardboard tombstone" and a "sad and tatty end to a musical fusion".

June [13] *The Long And Winding Road/For You Blue* tops US chart. *Let It Be* also tops US chart as *The Beatles Featuring Tony Sheridan – In The Beginning (Circa) 1960*, a compilation of early Polydor material recorded in Germany, makes US #117.

Nov [11] Ringo and Maureen's daughter Lee Starkey is born at Queen Charlotte's hospital, London.

Dec [31] McCartney files suit against the rest of the group to dissolve The Beatles & Co. partnership and seeks the appointment of a receiver to handle the group's affairs. He also ends links with Allen Klein who now handles the affairs of the other 3.

1971 Jan [16] *A Hard Day's Night* re-charts at UK #30.

[19] The case to dissolve the Beatles' partnership begins in London's High Court. Under oath, Ringo says "Paul behaved like a spoilt child."

Mar [3] The South African Broadcasting Corporation lifts its ban on Beatles' music.

[12] Judge declares in McCartney's favor.

Apr [15] *Let It Be* wins an Oscar for Best Film Music (Original Song Score) at the annual Academy Awards.

July *Help!* makes UK #33.

Aug [3] McCartney announces the formation of his new group, Wings.

1972 Feb [8] The Beatles Fan Club shop is liquidated.

Mar [14] Group is honored at the 14th annual Grammy awards, receiving NARAS' Trustees Award "for their outstanding talent, originality and music creativity that have done so much to express the mood and tempo of our times and to bridge the culture gap between several generations".

[31] The Official Beatles Fan Club closes down.

May [21] BBC's Radio 1 begins airing "The Beatles Story".

1973 Apr [27] Double album *The Beatles 1967-1970* hits UK #2.

May [12] Double album *The Beatles 1962-1966* hits UK #3.

[19] *The Beatles 1962-1966* hits US #3.

[26] *The Beatles 1967-1970* tops US chart, a record 15th US chart-topping album.

1974 July [26-28] The Strawberry Fields Forever Fan Club holds the first Beatle Convention in Boston, MA.

Aug [14] Willy Russell's play "John, Paul, George, Ringo & Bert" opens at Liverpool's Royal Court theater.

1975 Jan [9] The Beatles & Co. partnership is dissolved at a private hearing in the London High Court.

1976 Jan [26] The Beatles' 9-year contract with EMI expires. Shortly thereafter US promoter Bill Sargent offers the group $30 million to reunite for 1 concert.

Apr [3] *Yesterday*, released in UK for the first time, hits #8, having been a US hit 11 years earlier. The entire back catalog of Beatles' singles is re-promoted: *Hey Jude* makes UK #12, *Paperback Writer* reaches UK #23, *Penny Lane/Strawberry Fields Forever* makes UK #32, *Get Back* reaches UK #28 and *Help!* reaches UK #37. As nostalgia increases, **Beatles Monthly** begins a reissue series from magazine #1.

June [19] *Rock'N'Roll Music* reaches UK #11.

July [10] *Rock'N'Roll Music* hits US #2.

[24] *Back In The USSR* reaches UK #19, while *Got To Get You Into My Life* hits US #7.

Aug [7] *The Beatles Tapes* reaches UK #45.

Sept [20] Sid Bernstein, the promoter of The Beatles' New York concerts from 1964 to 1966, takes out full-page advertisements asking the group to reunite for a charity concert.

Nov [20] With Harrison guesting on the show, "Saturday Night Live" producer Lorne Michaels offers The Beatles the union minimum payment to reunite on the show. Ironically McCartney is staying with Lennon in New York, and both see the show.

Dec [11] *Ob-La-Di, Ob-La-Da* makes US #49.

[18-19] Europe's first Christmas Beatles Convention, held at Alexandra Palace in North London, is a commercial disaster.

1977 Jan [10] All oustanding litigation between The Beatles, Apple, Klein and his company ABKCO is settled.

May [26] "Beatlemania", a musical tribute, opens at the Winter Garden theater, New York.

June [4] *The Beatles At The Hollywood Bowl* tops UK chart. It is a record-breaking 12th UK chart-topping album, created by joining together performances at the Hollywood Bowl from Aug.23, 1964 and Aug.30, 1965.

[11] *The Beatles At The Hollywood Bowl* hits US #2.

July [30] *The Beatles Live! At The Star-Club In Hamburg, Germany: 1962* reaches US #111.

Oct [18] To celebrate the Queen's Silver Jubilee, the BPI hold a ceremony at Wembley Conference Centre, honoring the best in British music since 1952. The Beatles win the Best British Pop Album, 1952-1977 category with *Sgt. Pepper's Lonely Hearts Club Band* and Best British Pop Group, 1952-1977 category.

Dec [10] Double *Love Songs* reaches US #24.

[17] *Love Songs* hits UK #7.

1978 Mar [27] "All You Need Is Cash", an affectionate parody of the group's career featuring The Rutles, airs on BBC TV.

Sept [30] *Sgt. Pepper's Lonely Hearts Club Band/With A Little Help From My Friends* peaks at US #71, as Robert Stigwood's film fantasy of the album starring The Bee Gees, Peter Frampton and others opens in cinemas.

Oct [21] *Sgt. Pepper's Lonely Hearts Club Band/With A Little Help From My Friends* peaks at UK #63.

1979 May [19] McCartney, Harrison and Starr reunite at a party to celebrate the wedding of Eric Clapton and Harrison's ex-wife Patti.

Sept [21] United Nations secretary general Kurt Waldheim asks the group to reunite to aid the Vietnamese boat people.

Oct [18] "Beatlemania" opens at the Astoria theater, London.

Nov [3] *Rarities* makes UK #71.

1980 May [31] *Rarities* reaches US #21.

Sept [17] *Beatles Ballads* makes UK #17.

Dec [8] Lennon, returning from a recording session, is gunned down in the courtyard of the Dakota building in New York, Lennon's home for the past decade. He dies from loss of blood shortly thereafter at the Roosevelt hospital.

1982 May [8] *The Beatles' Movie Medley* reaches US #12, while *Reel Music* makes US #19.

July [3] *The Beatles' Movie Medley* hits UK #10.

Sept [10] The Beatles' Decca audition is released as *The Complete Silver Beatles*.

Oct [30] *Love Me Do* hits UK #4 on its 20th anniversary of original release. All their singles will be subsequently re-released on their matching dates, the majority receiving respectable chart placings.

Nov [6] Continuing to repackage past hits, *20 Greatest Hits* makes UK #10 and US #50.

1983 Jan [29] *Please Please Me* makes UK #29.

Feb [8] The Beatles are honored for their Outstanding Contribution To British Music at the second annual BRIT Awards at Grosvenor House, London.

Apr [30] *From Me To You* reaches UK #40.

Sept [10] *She Loves You* makes UK #45.

Nov [26] *I Want To Hold Your Hand* peaks at UK #62.

1984 Mar [31] *Can't Buy Me Love* peaks at UK #53.

Apr [9] The Beatle City exhibition center opens in Liverpool.

July [28] *A Hard Day's Night* peaks at UK #52.

Dec [8] *I Feel Fine* peaks at UK #65.

1985 Apr [20] *Ticket To Ride* peaks at UK #70.

Aug [10] Michael Jackson pays $47.5 million for ATV Music and with it the entire Lennon/McCartney catalog.

1986 Aug [30] *Yellow Submarine/Eleanor Rigby* peaks at UK #63.

Sept [27] *Twist And Shout*, through its exposure in the films "Ferris Bueller's Day Off" and "Back To School", reaches US #23.

Oct [11] *The Early Beatles*, originally charting in 1965, makes US #197.

1987 Feb *Penny Lane/Strawberry Fields Forever* peaks at UK #65.

Mar [7] As the group's back catalog is systematically released on CD, The Beatles' timeless popularity is underlined as they return to the charts: *Please Please Me* (UK #32), *With The Beatles* (UK #40), *A Hard Day's Night* (UK #30), *Beatles For Sale* (UK #45).

May [9] The second batch of Beatles' albums is released on CD: *Help!* (UK #61), *Rubber Soul* (UK #60), *Revolver* (UK #55).

June [1] Granada TV airs "It Was Twenty Years Ago Today", a documentary of the making of *Sgt. Pepper* and its cultural significance at the time.

CD *Sgt. Pepper's Lonely Hearts Club Band* hits UK #3 on a wave of media nostalgia for the 20th anniversary of the album, widely regarded as the most important record of the rock era.

July *All You Need Is Love* makes UK #47.

Sept [5] CD *The Beatles* reaches UK #18 while CD *Yellow Submarine* makes UK #60.

Oct [3] CD *Magical Mystery Tour* makes UK #52.

[31] CD *Abbey Road* reaches UK #30 and CD *Let It Be* makes UK #50.

Dec [5] *Hello Goodbye* peaks at UK #63.

1988 Jan [20] The Beatles are inducted into the Rock'N'Roll Hall Of Fame at the third annual dinner at the Waldorf Astoria, New York. McCartney does not show, citing business differences with Harrison and Starr.

Mar [19] *Past Masters Vol. 1* reaches UK #49 and *Past Masters Vol. 2* makes UK #46.

[26] *Lady Madonna* peaks at UK #67.

Apr [9] *Past Masters – Volume One* makes US #149.

[16] *Past Masters – Volume Two* makes US #121.

May [17] A New York appellate court reinstates punitive damages and claims of fraud and theft against Capitol records in a 9-year-old $80 million breach of contract suit brought by Harrison, Starr, Ono and Apple Records. A $40 million suit which claims Capitol has deliberately stalled release of Beatles' CDs is dismissed in Manhattan district court.

July [22] Worldwide release of *The Beatles Decca Sessions* is prevented by lawyers acting on behalf of the remaining members of the group and Yoko Ono.

Sept [10] *Hey Jude* peaks at UK #52.

[23] Acknowledged Beatles' authority Mark Lewisohn's book **The Complete Beatles Recording Sessions**, a day-by-day detailed account of the group's studio activity, is published in the UK. It is a companion study to his exhaustive **The Beatles Live**, detailing every live performance by the group, and first published in 1986.

Oct [1] BBC Radio 1 airs the first program in a 14-part series called "The Beeb's Lost Beatles Tapes". (It will win the Sony National Radio Award for 1988 as the Best Rock & Pop program on British radio.)

[26] Apple releases "Magical Mystery Tour" on video in the US.

'89   Apr [22] *Get Back* peaks at UK #74.

June [24] Rosanne Cash's version of *I Don't Want To Spoil The Party* (B-side of The Beatles' 1965 *Eight Days A Week*) becomes the first Lennon/McCartney composition to hit US C&W #1.

[30] McCartney, Harrison, Starr and Yoko Ono seek injunctions against EMI and Dave Clark, banning sale of videos of "Ready Steady Go!" featuring The Beatles. The case is settled out of court.

Nov [8] All outstanding lawsuits between The Beatles and EMI/Capitol are settled amicably.

'90   Apr [12] Asteroids 4147-4150, discovered in 1983 and 1984 by Brian A. Skiff and Dr. Edward Bowell, of the Lowell Observatory in Flagstaff, AZ, are now named Lennon, McCartney, Harrison and Starr, announced by the International Astronomical Union's minor planet center in Cambridge, MA.

EFF BECK

'65   Mar [26] After playing with Screaming Lord Sutch and in groups The Nightshifts and The Tridents, guitarist Beck (b. June 24, 1944, Wallington, Surrey) replaces Eric Clapton in The Yardbirds.

'67   Mar After a successful period with The Yardbirds, he launches a solo career with *Hi-Ho Silver Lining*, which features him on lead guitar, and as lead vocalist, a role he will rarely undertake again. (Rod Stewart sings lead on B-side.) It reaches UK #14, but will be unrepresentative of all future work.

Aug Follow up, *Tallyman*, written by Graham Gouldman (later of 10cc) reaches UK #30. Stewart is not allowed by producer Mickie Most to sing lead vocal.

[13] Beck plays the seventh National Jazz & Blues Festival at the Royal Windsor Racecourse, Windsor, Berks.

'68   Feb Third single, *Love Is Blue*, an instrumental version of a song from the Eurovision Song Contest, is recorded at Most's behest (Beck will later claim he was forced to cut it against his better judgement) and reaches UK #23.

June The Jeff Beck Group makes its US debut at the Fillmore East, New York.

July Beck guests on *Barabajagal* by Donovan which reaches UK #12 and US #36. Plans for Beck and Stewart to form a group with Tim Bogert (bass) of Vanilla Fudge, and Carmine Appice (drums) are dropped after Beck is hospitalized following a car accident.

Aug The Jeff Beck Group – lining up as Beck, Stewart, Ron Wood (bass) and Mickey Waller (drums) – releases debut album, *Truth*, which reaches US #15 but fails in UK. Waller is replaced by Tony Newman, and Nicky Hopkins joins on keyboards.

Beck returns to the eighth National Jazz & Blues festival with Rod Stewart.

Oct [11] US tour opens in Chicago, IL.

'69   July [3] Beck plays the Fillmore East with Jethro Tull, before taking part in the annual Jazz Festival in Newport, RI.

Sept [13] *Beck-Ola*, makes UK #39 and US #15. Stewart and Wood leave to join The Faces.

'70 Beck forms a new group, with Cozy Powell (drums), Clive Chaman (bass), Max Middleton (keyboards) and Bobby Tench (vocals).

'71   Nov *Rough And Ready* reaches US #46, while his current UK tour heads up to Scotland.

'72   May *Jeff Beck Group* (often known as the "orange" album since it pictures one on the sleeve), produced by Steve Cropper of Booker T. & The MG's, reaches US #19.

Nov *Hi-Ho Silver Lining*, reissued on RAK, reaches UK #17.

'73   Jan Bogert and Appice resurrect the idea of forming a group with Beck and "supergroup" Beck, Bogert And Appice is born.

Apr *Beck, Bogert & Appice* reaches US #12 and UK #28. Produced by Don Nix, it includes a version of Stevie Wonder's *Superstition*. During a world tour, they cut a live double album in Japan, where it will be exclusively released.

May *I've Been Drinking*, originally the B-side of *Love Is Blue* from 1968, is re-issued, credited to Jeff Beck and Rod Stewart, and reaches UK #27.

'74   Jan [26] Beck, Bogert And Appice continue touring, including UK dates throughout the month, highlighted by 2 performances at the Rainbow theater, London.

'75   Apr Declaring himself tired of working with vocalists, Beck forms a totally instrumental group of himself, Max Middleton, Philip Chen (bass) and Richard Bailey (drums). This line-up plays on Beck's solo album *Blow By Blow*, produced by George Martin, which hits US #4, and establishes the guitarist among the most respected of his era.

'76   June Beck begins a year-long US tour with The Jan Hammer Group.

July [10] *Wired*, featuring Middleton, Bailey, Jan Hammer (ex-Mahavishnu Orchestra, drums/synthesizer), Wilbur Bascomb (bass), and Narada Michael Walden (drums/keyboards), who also writes half the tracks on it, and with Martin producing, makes UK #38.

Aug [7] *Wired* reaches US #16.

'77   May [14] *Jeff Beck With The Jan Hammer Group Live* reaches US #23.

'80   July After a long rest period and search for new collaborators, Beck records *There And Back*, assisted by Simon Phillips (drums), Mo Foster (bass), Tony Hymas (keyboards) and Jan Hammer. It reaches US #21 and UK #38.

'81   Sept Beck plays a set with Eric Clapton at "The Secret Policeman's Other Ball" in London, in aid of the Amnesty International Benefit Concert, and contributes to the resulting album, *The Secret Policeman's Other Ball*, which will make UK #69 in Dec.

'82   Oct [23] Second reissue of *Hi-Ho Silver Lining* peaks at UK #62.

'83   Mar [17] Beck participates in the second annual Prince's Trust Rock Gala benefit gala concert at the Royal Albert Hall, London, with fellow axemen Eric Clapton, Jimmy Page, Bill Wyman, Carmine Appice, Andy Fairweather Low and Ronnie Lane.

Sept [20-21] Beck joins Clapton, Page, Steve Winwood, Wyman, Charlie Watts, Joe Cocker, Paul Rodgers, Kenney Jones, Low, Ray Cooper and Lane (himself a sufferer) in a benefit concert at the Royal Albert Hall, London, in aid of ARMS (Action for Research into Multiple Sclerosis.) The second show will be performed in the presence of the Prince and Princess of Wales.

Dec [8] Beck, Clapton, Page and Ry Cooder give another ARMS benefit concert at Madison Square Garden, New York.

'85   July After a brief tour with Stewart, and a collaboration with him on single reviving Curtis Mayfield's *People Get Ready* (US #48), Beck releases his second album of the 80s, *Flash*. Credited producers include Nile Rodgers (of Chic) and Arthur Baker, while performers include Stewart, Hammer, Appice, Hymas, and vocalist Jimmy Hall.

Aug [17] *Flash* charts at UK #83 and US #39. Beck works on Mick Jagger's solo album, *She's The Boss*.

'86 Beck releases his version of The Troggs' *Wild Thing*.

Feb [25] Beck wins Best Rock Instrumental Performance for *Escape*, from *Flash*, at the 28th annual Grammy awards.

'87 Beck works on Jagger's second solo album, *Primitive Cool*. A reported collaboration with ex-Sex Pistols' manager, Malcolm McLaren, has yet to produce commercial results.

'88   Jan [20] Beck inducts Les Paul into the Rock'N'Roll Hall Of Fame at the third annual dinner at the Waldorf Astoria, New York.

'89   Oct New album *Jeff Beck's Guitar Shop With Terry Bozzio And Tony Hymas* on Epic, makes US #49.

[25] Beck teams with Stevie Ray Vaughan on US arena tour dubbed "The Fire And The Fury" starting at Northrop Memorial Auditorium, Minneapolis, MN. The only time they have previously met was at CBS Convention in Hawaii in 1984.

'90   Feb [21] *Jeff Beck's Guitar Shop With Terry Bozzio And Tony Hymas* wins Best Rock Instrumental Performance at the 32nd annual Grammy awards at the Shrine Auditorium, Los Angeles.

THE BEE GEES

Barry Gibb (vocals, guitar)
Maurice Gibb (vocals, bass)
Robin Gibb (vocals)

1958 Barry Gibb (b. Sept.1, 1947, Douglas, Isle of Man) and his twin brothers Robin, older by an hour, and Maurice (b. Dec.22, 1949, Douglas) emigrate from their semi-detached home in Keppel Road, Chorlton-cum-Hardy, Gtr.Manchester, to Australia with their parents, soon after the birth of latest arrival, Andy, having performed at Saturday morning picture shows since 1956 at the Manchester Gaumont, Whalley Range Odeon and the Palentine theater, singing the hits of the day, with Paul Frost and Kenny Oricks, and known as The Rattlesnakes, name-changing later as Wee Johnnie Hayes & The

Bluecats. (Their father Hugh is leader of Mecca-contracted Hughie Gibb Orchestra, their mother Barbara a singer.)

1960 Performing at Brisbane's Speedway Circus, they meet race-track organizer Bill Good who introduces the group to DJ friend Bill Gates, who plays Gibb tapes on his radio show "Clatter Chatter" on station 4KQ. (When interest is shown in the brothers' music, Good names them The B.G.'s after his and Gates' initials, and not because of the Brothers Gibb initials as popularly believed.) This leads to a TV debut on "Anything Goes" and then regular appearances on BTQ7 TV's "Cottie's Happy Hour" show, followed by a 6-week residence at Surfer's Paradise, Beachcomber Hotel, Brisbane.

1962 Relocating to Sydney, they play Sydney Stadium on a Chubby Checker headliner, now billing themselves as The Bee Gees. They begin writing, their first composition being *Let Me Love You*, and enjoy their first composing success for Col Joye with his Australian chart-topper *Starlight Of Love*.

1963 **Jan** Brothers sign to Festival Records, following an 18-month residency as house band at a club in Queensland, and release debut single *Three Kisses Of Love*, on Leedon, a Festival subsidiary.

1965 First group hit *Wine And Women* hits #10 in Australia. They link with Bill Shepherd (musical director) and Ozzie Byrne (producer) and sign to Spin Records.

1966 **Aug** Following 10 singles of varying chart success, they record their eleventh single, *Spicks And Specks*.

1967 **Jan** [3] Group returns to UK on a 5-week boat trip, with *Spicks And Specks* now at #1 in Australia.
Feb [24] The Bee Gees sign a 5-year management contract with Robert Stigwood (who is in partnership with Brian Epstein) at NEMS Enterprises, following an audition at the Saville theater, having been turned away by the Grade Organization.
Mar Colin Petersen (b. Mar.24, 1946, Kinearoy, Queensland, Australia), who, as a child actor, has already appeared in "Cry From The Streets" with Max Bygraves, "Smiley" and "The Scamp" and played in Australian band Steve & The Board, is recruited on drums. Melouney (b. Aug.18, 1945, Sydney, Australia), whose first Australian chart success has come with The Vibratones' cover of The Shadows' *Man Of Mystery*, formed a new band with group's rhythm guitarist Tony Barber called Vince & Tony's Two and another called Vince Melouney, before joining Billy Thorpe & The Aztecs, who have 7 Australian #1s, has been working in UK at Simca Motors for 4 months, when the Gibbs ask him to complete the line-up.
May Immediate success comes with the group's first UK-recorded single *New York Mining Disaster 1941* which reaches UK #12 and is a global million-seller.
[11] Band makes its "Top Of The Pops" TV debut singing *New York Mining Disaster*, showcasing their instantly appealing 3-part harmonies led by Barry's distinctive falsetto.
June [29] Group begins a 2-week promotional visit to the US.
July [1] *New York Mining Disaster 1941* reaches US #14.
Aug *To Love Somebody*, written for Otis Redding but performed by The Bee Gees themselves, makes UK #25.
[26] *To Love Somebody* reaches US #17, as parent album *Bee Gees 1st* hits UK #8 and US #7.
Oct [11] *Massachusetts*, written in New York during the band's first promotional US trip, hits UK #1, as Home Secretary Roy Jenkins rescinds Melouney and Petersen's expulsion orders, due to come into effect Nov.30, when their work permits expire. Jenkins cites the group's value to UK during its balance-of-payments crisis.
Nov [5] Robin, returning from a weekend in Hastings, Sussex, is traveling on a train back to London which crashes just outside Hither Green in South-East London, killing 49 and injuring 78. Gibb suffers shock.
[11] *Holiday* reaches US #16.
[17] Group turns on festive illuminations in Carnaby Street, London.
[19] The Bee Gees perform at the Saville theater with The Flowerpot Men and The Bonzo Dog Doo Dah Band.
Dec *World* hits UK #9.
[9] *Massachusetts* reaches US #11.
[24] Group's Christmas special "How On Earth", filmed at Liverpool Cathedral, Merseyside, airs on ITV.

1968 **Jan** [27] Group makes its US concert debut at the Convention Center, Anaheim, CA, and will guest on NBC TV's "Rowan & Martin's Laugh-In" and CBS TV's "The Smothers Brothers Show".
Feb Ballad *Words*, despite 6-day halt in sales following grant of an ex-partia injunction, hits UK #8. *Horizontal* makes UK #16 and US #12.
[8] Group flies to Scandinavia to begin a tour. (They currently have 4

singles in the Danish Top 20.)
Mar [2] *Words* reaches US #15.
[17] They make their debut on CBS TV's "Ed Sullivan Show" singing *Words* and *To Love Somebody*.
[27] Group embarks on 26-date UK tour with Grapefruit, Dave Dee, Dozy, Beaky, Mick & Tich and The Foundations, at the Royal Albert Hall with a 67-piece orchestra.
Apr [20] *Jumbo* peaks at US #57 and, backed with *The Singer Sang His Song*, makes UK #25.
July [27] Robin collapses as group prepares to fly to US for its first tour. (He is admitted to a London nursing home the next day, suffering from nervous exhaustion.)
[31] He moves from the nursing home to a health farm in Sussex.
Aug [10] Group begins its re-scheduled US tour in impressive style at Forest Hills Stadium, New York, receiving 13 curtain calls at the end of their performance.
Sept [7] *I've Gotta Get A Message To You*, a fictional account of a man on death row about to be electrocuted, hits UK #1.
[8] Group arrives back in UK at the end of a US tour. Barry announces he will be leaving the group to pursue solo career in movies.
[9] Band flies to Brussels to film Jean Christophe Averti-directed TV spectacular.
[28] *I've Gotta Get A Message To You* hits US #8, as *Idea* hits UK #4 and US #17.
Oct [31] Group begins 18-date tour of Germany and Austria in Bremen.
Nov [18] The tour is cancelled after a concert in Munich, with 6 dates remaining, when Barry and Robin are ordered to bed, suffering from acute tonsilitis. (Melouney announces that he is thinking of quitting the band to write and produce. Maurice states that he thinks it "very probable The Bee Gees will be non-existent in 2 years from now.")
Dec *Rare, Precious & Beautiful*, a compilation of pre-fame tracks cut in Australia, reaches US #99.

1969 **Feb** [8] *I Started A Joke* hits US #6, as band tours Japan.
Mar Despite immense fame, the group is prone to internal strife, exacerbated not least by intoxicants, including fame. *First Of May* (UK #6) and *I Started A Joke* (US #6) are the last Bee Gees' hits on which Melouney and Petersen appear, while Robin Gibb leaves his brothers for a solo career. (Melouney will leave to form Ashton, Gardner & Dyke, working as its writer and producer.)
[19] Stigwood sues Robin for leaving group.
Apr [5] Double album *Odessa*, released in a suede sleeve, hits UK #10. *Odessa* reaches US #20.
[18] Maurice marries singer Lulu, at Gerrards Cross, Bucks., with Bee Gee Robin Gibb as best man.
[19] *First Of May* makes US #37.
June Barry and Maurice continue as The Bee Gees, charting with *Tomorrow Tomorrow* at UK #23.
[14] *Tomorrow Tomorrow* peaks at US #54.
July Robin's debut solo, dramatic ballad *Saved By The Bell* hits UK #2.
Aug [11] Barry and Maurice begin filming "Cucumber Castle", with guest stars Lulu, Frankie Howerd, Vincent Price, Spike Milligan and others. Barry plays the King Of Cucumber, while Maurice plays the King Of Jelly.
Sept Petersen is fired from The Bee Gees, and will sue, citing a 5-year contract he signed with the group and Stigwood on July 4, 1967.
[20] *Don't Forget To Remember*, from "Cucumber Castle", hits UK #2.
[27] *Don't Forget To Remember* peaks at US #73.
Best Of The Bee Gees, the first of many compilations, hits UK #7 and US #9. Barry produces P.P. Arnold, and goes solo, leaving Maurice as the sole representative of The Bee Gees.

1970 **Feb** Robin's *August October* makes UK #45. Maurice opens in stage musical "Sing A Rude Song" at Greenwich theater, playing Bernard Dillon, a jockey who wins the 1910 Derby and the lover of Marie Lloyd played by Barbara Windsor.
Mar [28] Barry and Maurice's *I.O.I.O.* makes UK #49. A second volume of Australian material, *Rare, Precious & Beautiful Vol. 2* climbs to US #100.
Apr [4] The Bee Gees' *If Only I Had My Mind On Something Else* stalls at US #91.
[18] With The Bee Gees at a disparate low, Maurice's solo debut *Railroad*, written with brother-in-law Billy Lawrie, is released.
May [9] *Cucumber Castle* makes US #57 and UK #94.
July [11] *I.O.I.O.* climbs to US #94.
Nov [14] Engelbert Humperdinck makes US #47 with Gibb-penned *Sweetheart*.

[20] Tin Tin's *Come On Over Again*, produced by Moby Productions (Maurice and Billy Lawrie), is released.

Dec The brothers settle their differences, but have lost much of their UK popularity, evidenced by *Lonely Days* only reaching UK #33. About their reunion, Robin tells **Time** magazine: "If we hadn't been related, we would probably never have gotten back together."

1971 Jan [30] US popularity has been less affected by squabbles, and *Lonely Days* hits US #3, while fully regrouped album *2 Years On* and *Trafalgar* chart at #32 and #34, but fail in UK.

Aug [7] Plaintive ballad *How Can You Mend A Broken Heart*, written by Barry and Robin when they reconcile after a 15-month period apart, hits US #1 for 4 weeks, and is a million-seller.

Nov [20] *Don't Wanna Live Inside Myself* peaks at US #53.

1972 Feb *My World*, written backstage at ITV's "The Golden Shot" on which they were appearing, reaches UK #16.

[26] *My World* reaches US #16.

Aug *Run To Me* hits UK #9, their first UK Top 10 single for 3 years.

Sept [23] *Run To Me* reaches US #16.

Dec [16] *Alive* makes US #34.

To Whom It May Concern reaches US #35.

1973 Mar *Life In A Tin Can* and *Best Of The Bee Gees Vol. 2* chart in US (at #69 and #98).

Apr [7] *Saw A New Morning* climbs to US #94.

June [24] They perform at the London Palladium.

1974 Jan *A Kick In The Pants Is Worth Eight In The Head* is rejected by RSO Records (to which group is now signed in UK after previous releases on Polydor, and Atco (RSO's US distributor and previous Bee Gees' US label). Group starts to use Arif Mardin as producer at Stigwood's suggestion, but *Mr. Natural* makes only US #178.

Mar [23] Extracted *Mr. Natural* climbs to US #93, and, at a career low, The Bee Gees will perform at the Batley's Variety Club in Batley, W.Yorks, before year ends.

1975 Apr Still with Mardin, The Bee Gees assemble a regular back-up group of Alan Kendall (guitar), Dennis Bryon (drums) and Blue Weaver (keyboards), and record *Main Course*, at Atlantic's New York studios and Criteria studios in Miami, which reaches US #14.

Aug [2] Funky and stuttered *Jive Talkin'*, a major new musical direction for the band from *Main Course*, hits UK #5.

[9] *Jive Talkin'* tops US chart.

Oct [17] Maurice Gibb marries Yvonne Spencely.

Dec [13] *Nights On Broadway*, also from the album, hits US #7.

1976 Mar [20] *Fanny (Be Tender With My Love)* reaches US #12, as parent album *Main Course* reaches US #14.

Aug [28] No holds barred *You Should Be Dancing* hits UK #6.

Sept [4] *You Should Be Dancing* tops US chart. Their third US chart-topper, it is co-produced with Albhy Galuten and Karl Richardson at Criteria studios in Miami, an arrangement and location which will prove long-term.

Nov [13] *Children Of The World*, on which they were unable to use Atlantic house producer Mardin, so combined with Galuten and Richardson, after sessions with Richard Perry proved unproductive, hits US #8.

[20] Ballad *Love So Right* hits US #3 and makes UK #41.

Dec [2] The Bee Gees perform at a Madison Square Garden concert, donating the proceeds to the Police Athletic League of New York.

1977 Jan [21] Compilation *Bee Gees Gold Volume One*, reaches US #50.

Mar [12] *Boogie Child* reaches US #12.

Stigwood, still head of his own RSO Records and manager of The Bee Gees, produces disco music film "Saturday Night Fever". He contacts the group, who are recording at the Chateau d'Heronville studios in France, urgently requesting 4 songs for the soundtrack to his film project. They finally record 5 and donate 2 others. (*Stayin' Alive, How Deep Is Your Love, Night Fever, More Than A Woman, Jive Talkin', You Should Be Dancing, If I Can't Have You* (to be recorded by Yvonne Elliman) and *More Than A Woman* (for Tavares).)

July [30] Double album *Here At Last ... Bee Gees ... Live* hits US #8 as Andy hits US #1 with Barry-penned *I Just Want To Be Your Everything*.

Sept [3] *Edge Of The Universe* reaches US #26.

Dec [2] Ballad featured in John Travolta smash movie "Saturday Night Fever", *How Deep Is Your Love* hits UK #3.

[24] *How Deep Is Your Love* tops US chart, displacing Debby Boone's *You Light Up My Life* after 10 weeks at the top. It spends 17 consecutive weeks in US Top 10, a **Billboard** Hot 100 record.

1978 Jan [21] Soundtrack double album *Saturday Night Fever*, containing the 7 Bee Gees songs, tops US chart. It will eventually sell over 30 million copies worldwide, and remain the best-selling soundtrack ever.

Feb [4] *Stayin' Alive*, featured in the movie's opening sequence while character Tony Manero struts down New York City sidewalks, tops US chart for 4 weeks, displacing Player's *Baby Come Back*, which in turn had taken over from *How Deep Is Your Love*.

[23] Bee Gees win Best Pop Vocal Performance By A Duo, Group Or Chorus for *How Deep Is Your Love* at the 20th annual Grammy awards.

Mar [4] *Stayin' Alive* hits UK #4 as Andy Gibb's *(Love Is) Thicker Than Water*, co-written by Barry, replaces *Stayin' Alive* at US #1.

[18] Now at the peak of their commercial career, disco classic *Night Fever* replaces *(Love Is) Thicker Than Water* at US #1, where it will stay for 8 weeks. It is RSO's fifth consecutive US chart-topper, and, in its first week at #1, *Stayin' Alive* is still alive at US #2. Bee Gees-penned and produced *Emotion* by Samantha Sang hits US #3. (Such is their current success, many are convinced that Sang does not exist and that the record is The Bee Gees slowed down.)

Apr [29] *Night Fever* tops UK chart.

May [6] *Saturday Night Fever* tops UK chart as Tavares' *More Than A Woman* makes US #32.

[12] The Bee Gees are honored with the Special Award as *How Deep Is Your Love* wins Best Pop Song and Best Film Music Or Song at the annual Ivor Novello Awards lunch.

[13] Elliman's *If I Can't Have You* tops US chart, replacing *Night Fever*.

[27] *If I Can't Have You* hits UK #4 as *More Than A Woman* makes US #7.

[31] Group appears on premiere edition of NBC TV's "Headliners With David Frost", live from New York with fellow guests John Travolta and former CIA chief Richard Helms.

June [17] Andy's *Shadow Dancing*, written with The Bee Gees and produced by regular Barry Gibb/Galuten/Richardson team, tops US chart for 7 weeks.

July [29] *Sgt. Pepper's Lonely Hearts Club Band* makes UK #38.

Aug Group acts and sings in film, "Sergeant Pepper's Lonely Hearts Club Band" (based on the celebrated Beatles' album), which is critically mauled, though its slamming will not affect The Bee Gees as much as their co-star Peter Frampton.

[19] *Sgt. Pepper's Lonely Hearts Club Band* hits US #5.

[26] Frankie Valli's *Grease*, Barry Gibb-penned title tune for Stigwood-produced John Travolta/Olivia Newton-John film, tops US chart.

Sept [30] *Grease* hits UK #3.

Oct [7] *Oh Darlin'* by Robin Gibb, from *Sgt. Pepper*, reaches US #15.

Nov Bee Gees begin recording *Spirits (Having Flown)*, at Criteria studios, Miami, with their band Blue Weaver, Dennis Bryon and Alan Kendall (guitars). Chicago's James Pankow, Walter Parazaider and Lee Loughnane provide horn assistance.

Dec [9] Airy ballad *Too Much Heaven* hits UK #3.

[16] Andy's *(Our Love) Don't Throw it All Away*, written by Barry with Blue Weaver, hits US #9. (By the year's end, Barry Gibb will have spent 25 weeks at #1 on the Hot 100 as a writer.)

1979 Jan [6] *Too Much Heaven* tops US chart.

[9] The Music For UNICEF Concert, to celebrate the International Year Of The Child, takes place in the General Assembly Hall of the United Nations in New York, to be broadcast the following day on NBC TV as "A Gift Of Song – The Music For UNICEF Concert". The Bee Gees sing *Too Much Heaven*, donating their royalties from the song to UNICEF.

[12] They are presented with a star on the Hollywood Walk Of Fame.

Feb [15] The Bee Gees win Album Of The Year and Best Pop Vocal Performance By A Duo, Group Or Chorus for *Saturday Night Fever*, Best Arrangement For Voices for *Stayin' Alive* and Best Producer Of The Year at the 21st annual Grammy awards.

Mar [3] Uptempo *Tragedy* tops UK chart, as disco-molded parent album *Spirits (Having Flown)* tops US and UK charts.

[24] *Tragedy*, again highlighting Barry's falsetto, tops US chart.

May [4] *Stayin' Alive* is named International Hit Of The Year and *Night Fever* is named Most Performed Work and Best Selling A-side at the annual Ivor Novello Awards lunch.

[5] *Love You Inside Out* reaches UK #13.

June [9] *Love You Inside Out* hits US #1, and is the group's sixth consecutive chart-topper.

Nov [27] The Bee Gees deny US press reports that they are to split.

1980 Jan [12] Compilation *Bee Gees Greatest* tops US chart and hits UK #6.

[26] The title track of *Spirits (Having Flown)* reaches UK #16.

Mar [29] The Bee Gees are sued by songwriter Ron Selle, who claims they stole *How Deep Is Your Love* from an unpublished song he had written years earlier. He loses the case.

Oct [25] Barbra Streisand's *Woman In Love*, written and produced by Barry, tops US chart, and will also hit UK #1. (His collaboration with Streisand will produce her US and UK #1 album *Guilty*, and further duetted hit single *Guilty* which will hit US #3 and UK #34.)

Dec [6] *Help Me*, a Robin solo, makes US #50.

1981 **Jan** [10] *Guilty* hits US #3.

Feb [25] Barry wins Best Pop Performance By A Duo Or Group With Vocal with Streisand for *Guilty* at the 23rd annual Grammy awards.

Mar [21] *What Kind Of Fool*, by Barry and Streisand, hits US #10.

May [19] *Woman In Love* wins Best Song Musically Or Lyrically category at the annual Ivor Novello Awards lunch.

Oct [24] *He's A Liar*, from forthcoming *Living Eyes*, reaches US #30.

Nov [14] *Living Eyes*, with back-up from Jeff Porcaro, Richard Tee, Steve Gadd, Don Felder, Russ Kunkel and Ralph McDonald, peaks at UK #73, a dramatic reversal of fortune after mid-70s dizzy heights.

Dec [5] *Living Eyes* makes US #45.

[12] *Living Eyes* makes US #41.

1982 **Oct** Barry produces *Heartbreaker* for Dionne Warwick, which contains hit singles *Heartbreaker* and *All The Love In The World*.

1983 **Jan** The Bee Gees contribute songs to the soundtrack of movie "Stayin' Alive", a sequel to "Saturday Night Fever", though the disco backlash prevents repeat success for both the film and its music.

June [18] Extracted ballad *The Woman In You*, from *Stayin' Alive*, reaches US #24. Robin releases second solo album *How Old Are You?*, and extract, *Another Lonely Night In New York*, peaks at UK #71.

Aug *Stayin' Alive*, from the soundtrack, reaches US #14 and US #6.

Sept [17] Extracted ballad *Someone Belonging To Someone* makes US and UK #49.

Oct Band's success is increasingly eclipsed by Barry's writing and production projects; he now works with Kenny Rogers on *Eyes That See In The Dark*, which yields *Islands In The Stream*, a Rogers' duet with Dolly Parton, which hits UK #7 and US #1.

1984 **July** Robin releases his third solo album *Secret Agent*.

[21] Extracted, *Boys (Do Fall in Love)*, makes US #37.

Oct [6] Barry's first solo single *Shine Shine* makes US #37, as parent album *Now Voyager* makes US #72 and UK #85, despite a complete parallel video package simultaneously released both featuring a ballad duet with Olivia Newton-John.

1985 Barry, with Karl Richardson and Albhy Galuten, begins work producing *Eaten Alive* for Diana Ross. Robin releases solo album *Walls Have Eyes* which fails to chart in UK or US.

1986 **Mar** [8] Extracted Ross' single *Chain Reaction*, written by the Gibb brothers, hits UK #1, but only climbs to US #66.

Barry releases *We Are The Bunburys* under the alias of The Bunburys, co-masterminded with cricket-mad entrepreneur David English about a group of cricket-playing rabbits, and featuring the help of cricket icon Ian Botham. Ken Kragen becomes the group's new manager.

1987 **Apr** [15] *Chain Reaction* is named Most Performed Work at the annual Ivor Novello Awards lunch.

Oct [3] *You Win Again* peaks at US #75, as parent album *E.S.P.* climbs to US #96.

[17] The Bee Gees return triumphantly to UK chart, hitting #1 with *You Win Again*, becoming the only band to chart-top in each of 3 decades. *E.S.P.*, dedicated to first producer Ozzie Byrne, hits UK #5.

Dec Extracted title track *E.S.P.* peaks at UK #51.

1988 **Mar** [10] Andy Gibb dies in the John Radcliffe Hospital, Oxford, Oxon, 5 days after his 30th birthday.

Apr [7] *You Win Again* wins Best Contemporary Song category as The Bee Gees are honored for their Outstanding Contribution To British Music at the annual Ivor Novello Awards lunch. They are unable to attend the ceremony, mourning the death of their younger brother.

May [14] Group performs at Madison Square Garden as part of Atlantic Records' 40-year Anniversary Party celebration concert.

June [5-6] The Bee Gees participate in the sixth Prince's Trust Rock Gala with Eric Clapton, Phil Collins, Peter Gabriel, Elton John and others, at the Royal Albert Hall, London.

[11] Band makes a further live appearance at "Nelson Mandela's 70th Birthday Party" at Wembley Stadium, London.

Sept The soundtrack to Timothy Dalton-starring "Hawks", featuring material written and performed by Barry, fails to lift the fortunes of either the film or the record.

Still persisting with The Bunburys, Barry enlists the help of his brothers and Clapton among others to record *Fight (No Matter How Long)* for just released 1988 Summer Olympics album *One Moment In Time*.

1989 **Apr** *Ordinary Lives* peaks at UK #54, as parent *One* reaches UK #29.

June [24] *One* peaks at UK #71.

July [31] The Bee Gees begin a US tour in Chicago, IL, with a line-up comprising Vic Martin on keyboards, George Perry on bass, Chester Thompson on drums and Phyllis St. James percussion.

Aug *One* makes US #68.

Sept [30] Almost unrivalled in their capacity to bounce back, The Bee Gees hit US #7 with *One*, their first US Top 10 appearance in a decade.

1990 **Apr** Group contributes *How Can You Mend A Broken Heart?*, recorded at the National Tennis Center, Melbourne, during concerts on Nov.17/18, 1989, to the **Nobody's Child** anthology, dedicated to raising funds and awareness to the plight of Romanian orphans.

Dec [8] Another career anthology, UK-issued *The Very Best Of The Bee Gees* hits UK #8.

1991 **Feb** [27] 34-date European tour opens in San Remo, Italy, set to conclude July 6 at Wembley Arena, London.

Apr [6] *Secret Love*, from forthcoming *High Civilization*, hits UK #5.

PAT BENATAR

1977 Having studied classical singing in New York, Benatar (b. Patricia Andrzejewski, Jan.10, 1953, Brooklyn, New York, NY), marrying her high school sweetheart Dennis Benatar and moving for a while to Richmond, VA, has been singing in cabaret at New York's Catch A Rising Star and being managed by its owner Rick Newman, when she is spotted by Chrysalis Records talent scouts, and is signed to the label (keeping her husband's name although they will later divorce).

June She recruits Neil Geraldo, ex-Derringer, who assembles a backing band comprising Scott St. Clair Sheets (guitar), Roger Capps (bass) and Glen Alexander Hamilton (drums) and begins recording debut album *In The Heat Of The Night* with producers Mike Chapman and Peter Coleman at MCA Whitney studios in Glendale, CA, after earlier pairing with Ron Dante does not work out.

1980 **Mar** *In The Heat Of The Night* reaches US #12.

[15] Extracted *Heartbreaker*, originally recorded by UK singer Jenny Darren, reaches US #23.

June [14] Geraldo-penned *We Live For Love* reaches US #27.

Aug [30] *You Better Run*, a revival of The Young Rascals' 1966 US #20, makes US #42. Her second album *Crimes Of Passion*, produced by Keith Olsen, with Myron Grombacher replacing Hamilton on drums, is released.

Dec [20] Rock-driven *Hit Me With Your Best Shot* hits US #9, and is a million-seller.

1981 **Jan** *Crimes Of Passion* hits US #2.

Feb [25] Benatar wins Best Rock Vocal Performance, Female for *Crimes Of Passion* at the 23rd annual Grammy awards.

Mar [14] *Treat Me Right* reaches US #18.

Aug [1] *Precious Time*, her UK chart breakthrough, reaches UK #30.

[15] *Precious Time* tops US chart for a week.

Sept [5] *Fire And Ice* reaches US #17.

Oct [31] *Promises In The Dark* makes US #38.

1982 **Feb** [20] Benatar marries her guitarist/producer Geraldo, on the island of Maui in Hawaii.

[24] Benatar wins Best Rock Vocal Performance, Female for *Fire And Ice* at the 24th annual Grammy awards.

Nov *Get Nervous*, produced by Geraldo with Peter Coleman, with Charlie Giordano joining on keyboards in place of Sheets and Geraldo switching from keyboards to guitar, peaks at UK #73.

Dec [11] *Shadows Of The Night*, written by D.L. Byron, reaches US #13.

1983 **Jan** *Get Nervous* hits US #4.

Feb [23] Benatar wins Best Rock Vocal Performance, Female for *Shadows Of The Night* at the 25th annual Grammy awards.

Mar [26] *Little Too Late* reaches US #20.

May [28] *Looking For A Stranger* makes US #39.

Oct Performance album *Live From Earth*, recorded in France and California during the group's US and Europe tour of 1982 and 1983, makes UK #60.

Dec [10] *Love Is A Battlefield*, aided by Bob Giraldi video, takes her back into US Top 10, hitting #5, while *Live From Earth* makes US #13.

1984 **Feb** [28] Benatar wins Best Rock Vocal Performance, Female (for the fourth successive year), for *Love Is A Battlefield* at the 26th annual Grammy awards, which also becomes her first UK chart single, at #49.

Nov *Tropico* reaches UK #31.

1985 **Jan** [5] *We Belong* hits US #5. It is taken from *Tropico* which reaches US #14. *We Belong* reaches UK #22.

Feb [16] *Ooh Ooh Song* makes US #36.

Apr *Love Is A Battlefield*, reissued in UK, reaches #17.

June *Shadows Of The Night*, not previously a UK hit, is reissued and makes #50.

Aug [24] *In The Heat Of The Night* charts for 1 week at UK #98.

Sept [14] *Invincible*, the theme from Helen Slater-starring film "Legend

Of Billie Jean", hits US #10. *Invincible* peaks at UK #53.
Dec *Seven The Hard Way* reaches US #26 and UK #69.
[14] Artists United Against Apartheid, comprising 49 artists including Benatar, makes US #38 and UK #21 with *Sun City*.

1986 **Jan** [18] *Sex As A Weapon* makes US #28.
Feb *Sex As A Weapon* peaks at UK #67.
Mar [8] *Le Bel Age* peaks at US #54.

1987 **Nov** In the absence of new material from Benatar (who is now mother of a small child), compilation album *Best Shots* featuring her hit singles is released in UK, and will hit #6, her best performing UK album.

1988 **Aug** *All Fired Up* reaches US #19 and UK #19, as parent album *Wide Awake In Dreamland* reaches US #28 and UK #11.
Oct *Don't Walk Away* makes UK #42.

1989 **Jan** *One Love* peaks at UK #59.
Nov *Best Shots* makes US #67.

1990 **Dec** Benatar records Charles Brown seasonal standard *Please Come Home For Christmas* for the coalition troops serving in the Gulf War.

1991 First single from blues-directed new album *True Love*, is B.B. King's *Payin' The Cost To Be The Boss*.

GEORGE BENSON

1963 Having played guitar since age 8, sung with R&B bands on the chitlin and gravy circuit in Pittsburgh, PA, since leaving school, then graduated to guitar session work and some small-label recording, Benson (b. Mar.22, 1943, Pittsburgh, PA) moves to New York on the recommendation of jazz artist Grant Green to become a session musician and joins jazz organist Brother Jack McDuff's group, recording for Prestige Records.

1966 He signs to Columbia Records as a jazz soloist, making early albums under his own name.

1969 **Aug** Now signed to A&M Records, his first US success is *Tell It Like It Is*, with guitarwork influenced by the style of labelmate Wes Montgomery, whose jazz guitar album *A Day In The Life* made US Top 20 in 1967. Benson's album peaks at US #145.

1970 He joins veteran jazz producer Creed Taylor's CTI label, whose workshop approach has resident virtuoso players backing each other on "solo" efforts. First CTI album is *Beyond The Blue Horizon*, which does not chart.

1974 **Feb** As a staff musician at CTI Records, he plays guitar on the album sessions of almost every act on the label, but scores in his own right with *Bad Benson*, which makes US #78.

1975 **Nov** [22] Benson' first chart single (and only one for CTI) *Supership*, on which he is credited as George "Bad" Benson, reaches UK #30.

1976 **Jan** [6-8] Signed to Warner Bros., Benson records his debut for the label at Capitol Records studio, Hollywood, CA.
July [31] He shoots spectacularly to US #1 with *Breezin'*. The album sells over a million, and it starts a permanent shift of emphasis in Benson's records: albums have showcased chiefly his guitar playing, but now his Warner Bros. output with producer Tommy LiPuma focuses on his vocals.
Aug [21] Earlier-recorded *Good King Bad* on CTI makes US #51.
[28] Benson's first US chart single, a cover of Leon Russell's *This Masquerade*, extracted from *Breezin'*, hits #10.
Sept [4] Similarly earlier-recorded album *The Other Side Of Abbey Road* on A&M collects further spin-off success from *Breezin'*, making US #125. The latter, originally from 1969, is a jazz guitar version of the entire Beatles *Abbey Road* album.
Nov [13] Bobby Womack-penned Warners album title track *Breezin'* peaks at US #63.
[27] CTI album *Benson And Farrell* (a collaboration with jazz flautist Joe Farrell) makes US #100.

1977 **Feb** [19] Benson wins Record Of The Year for *This Masquerade*, Best Pop Instrumental Performance and Best-Engineered Non-Classical Recording for *Breezin'* and Best R&B Instrumental Performance for *Theme From Good King Bad* at the 19th annual Grammy awards.
Mar [12] CTI album *George Benson In Concert: Carnegie Hall*, recorded live in 1975, reaches US #122.
[19] Warner album, *In Flight* hits US #9, and is another million-seller.
Apr [23] *In Flight* peaks at #19 - his first UK charted album.
June [25] A revival of Nat King Cole/Bobby Darin hit *Nature Boy* makes UK #26.
July [23] *Gonna Love You More* peaks at US #71.
Oct [8] *The Greatest Love Of All*, theme from the Muhammad Ali biopic "The Greatest" and released as a one-off by Arista Records (which has soundtrack rights), reaches US #24. (The song will be revived as a US

#1 in 1986 by Whitney Houston.)
[22] *The Greatest Love Of All* reaches UK #27.

1978 **Feb** [4] Double album *Weekend In L.A.* makes UK #47.
Apr [15] *Weekend In L.A.* hits US #5, and is Benson's third million-selling album.
June [10] A revival of The Drifters' *On Broadway*, taken from *Weekend In L.A.*, hits US #7.

1979 **Feb** [15] Benson wins Best R&B Vocal Performance, Male for *On Broadway* at the 21st Grammy awards.
Mar [17] Double album, *Livin' Inside Your Love*, reaches UK #24.
Apr [21] *Livin' Inside Your Love*, hits US #7.
[28] *Love Ballad* reaches US #18.
May [5] *Love Ballad* reaches UK #29.

1980 **Sept** *Give Me The Night*, Benson's first successful collaboration with UK songwriter Rod Temperton and produced by Quincy Jones, hits UK #7. Parent album *Give Me The Night* hits US #3, is another million-seller and also hits UK #3.
[27] *Give Me The Night* is Benson's biggest US chart single, hitting #4.
Nov *Love X Love*, also penned by Temperton, peaks at US #61, but is more popular in UK, where it hits #10.

1981 **Feb** [21] *What's On Your Mind* makes UK #45.
[25] Benson wins Best R&B Vocal Performance, Male for *Give Me The Night*, Best R&B Instrumental Performance for *Off Broadway* and Best Jazz Vocal Performance, Male for *Moody's Mood* at the 23rd annual Grammy awards.
Sept [26] Benson's duet with Aretha Franklin on *Love All The Hurt Away* makes US #46.
Nov [21] Double compilation *The George Benson Collection* makes UK #19.
Dec [5] Uptempo *Turn Your Love Around* reaches UK #29.

1982 **Jan** [30] *The George Benson Collection* makes US #14.
Feb [6] *Turn Your Love Around* restores him to US Top 10 at #5.
[20] Similarly-styled *Never Give Up On A Good Thing* reaches UK #14.
Apr [10] *Never Give Up On A Good Thing* peaks at US #52.

1983 **June** [10] *Lady Love Me (One More Time)* reaches UK #11.
[18] *Inside Love (So Personal)* makes US #43. Both are taken from new Arif Mardin-produced album *In Your Eyes*, which reaches US #27, and is one of his most successful UK albums, hitting #3 and staying on chart for 53 weeks.
Aug *Feel Like Makin' Love*, a revival of Roberta Flack's 1974 US #1, reaches UK #28.
Sept [10] *Lady Love Me (One More Time)* reaches US #30.
Oct Lush ballad and title track *In Your Eyes* hits UK #7 - his last Top 10 single.
Dec *Inside Love (So Personal)* is belatedly issued in UK, though makes only #57.

1984 **Feb** [28] Benson wins Best Pop Instrumental Performance for *Being With You* at the 26th annual Grammy awards.

1985 **Jan** [26] *20/20* makes US #48.
20/20 reaches UK #29. It is taken from album of the same title, which climbs to US #45 and UK #9.
Apr Revival of Bobby Darin hit *Beyond The Sea (La Mer)* makes UK #60.
Oct [26] UK-compiled TV-advertised album *The Love Songs*, featuring all his major hit singles, tops UK chart for 2 weeks.

1986 **Aug** *Kisses In The Moonlight* peaks at UK #60.
Sept *While The City Sleeps ...*, mainly produced by Narada Michael Walden, reaches UK #13.
While The City Sleeps ... makes US #77.
Dec *Shiver* is Benson's biggest UK hit single for over 3 years, at #19.

1987 **Feb** *Teaser* makes UK #45.
July Jazz guitar-returning *Collaboration*, with Earl Klugh, makes US #59 and UK #47.

1988 **Sept** *Let's Do It Again*, reviving The Staple Singles 1975 US #1, peaks at UK #56. *Twice The Love* reaches UK #16.
Oct *Twice The Love* peaks at UK #76.

1989 **July** *Tenderly*, continuing Benson's lean towards his jazz roots, makes UK #52.
Aug *Tenderly* makes US #140.
Sept [2] *Tenderly* tops US Jazz chart.

1990 **Jan** [17] Benson inducts Charlie Christian into the Rock'N'Roll Hall Of Fame at 5th annual induction dinner at the Waldorf Astoria, New York.
Aug [17] Benson performs at the JVC Jazz Festival, Fort Adams State Park, Newport, RI, with B.B. King, Miles Davis and others.
[25] 14-date US tour starts at the Amphitheater, Chautauqua, NY, and will end Sept.30 at County Park, St. Louis, MO.
Oct *Big Boss Band*, featuring the Count Basie Orchestra, and reviving

GEORGE BENSON cont.

such standards as *I Only Have Eyes For You*, *Walkin' My Baby Back Home* and *Skylark*, is released.

Nov [14] Benson starts short 6-date UK concert visit at Wembley Arena, London.

1991 Feb [20] Benson wins Best Jazz Instrumental Performance, Big Band with the Count Basie Orchestra for *Basie's Bag* at the 33rd annual Grammy awards at Radio City Music Hall, New York, having also played on Quincy Jones' multi Grammy-winning album *Back On The Block*, guesting on the tracks *Jazz Corner Of The World*, *Birdland* and *Setembro (Brazilian Wedding Song)*.

BROOK BENTON

1957 After singing with The Camden Jubilee Singers gospel quartet before moving to New York in 1948 to join the Bill Landford Spiritual Singers, singing R&B with The Sandmen and recording unsuccessfully as a soloist on Epic, Benton (b. Benjamin Franklin Peay, Sept.19, 1931, Camden, SC) is working as a truck driver in New York when he meets music publisher and Mercury Records A&R chief Clyde Otis (the first black in such a position with a major label) and joins him as a studio demo singer, also forming a songwriting team with Otis and arranger Belford Hendricks.

1958 Mar He has his first minor US hit (#82) with *A Million Miles From Nowhere*, while signed to RCA subsidiary Vik Records.

May Nat King Cole has a US hit with Benton's *Looking Back*, hitting #6.

Dec Benton has a second major success as a writer when Clyde McPhatter hits US #6 with *A Lover's Question*.

1959 Jan Otis persuades Mercury Records to sign Benton as a vocalist, with himself and Hendricks producing and arranging his recordings.

Apr First Mercury release *It's Just A Matter Of Time*, written by all 3, hits US #3, tops US R&B chart for 10 weeks, and is a million-seller. A lush, deep-voiced ballad, it also sets the style for Benton's hit career. (B-side *Hurtin' Inside* climbs to US #78.)

June *Endlessly* reaches US #12 and its B-side *So Close* makes #38.

July [13] *Endlessly* is his UK chart debut, reaching #28.

Aug *Thank You Pretty Baby* makes US #16 and tops R&B chart for 4 weeks. (B-side *With All Of My Heart* climbs to US #82.)

Nov *So Many Ways* hits US #6, also topping the R&B chart for 3 weeks.

Dec *This Time Of The Year* peaks at US #66.

1960 Mar *Baby (You Got What It Takes)*, a duet with Dinah Washington, hits US #5, tops R&B chart for 8 weeks, and is a million-seller.

Apr [18] *Hither And Thither And You* peaks at US #58.

May [9] *Hither's* A-side, *The Ties That Bind*, makes US #37.

June Second duet with Washington, *A Rockin' Good Way (To Mess Around And Fall In Love)*, hits US #7, and tops R&B chart for 5 weeks.

Sept *Kiddio* hits US #7 and is R&B #1 for 9 weeks. B-side *The Same One* reaches US #16.

Nov *Kiddio* makes UK #41.

Dec [5] *Fools Rush In*, penned by Johnny Mercer, reaches US #24.

[26] B-side *You'll Want Me To Want You* stalls at US #93.

1961 Feb [20] *Fools Rush In* makes UK #50.

Apr *Think Twice* makes US #11, and B-side *For My Baby* makes #28.

June His first album to chart in US is the compilation *Brook Benton Golden Hits*, which reaches US #82.

July A revival of the traditional *The Boll Weevil Song* is another million-seller, and is Benton's highest US chart single hitting #2 for 3 weeks, unable to dislodge Bobby Lewis' chart-topping *Tossin' And Turnin'*, while peaking at UK #30 – his final UK chart entry.

Sept Another traditional song *Frankie And Johnny* reaches US #20.

Oct *Frankie's* B-side *It's Just A House Without You* makes US #45, as **The Boll Weevil Song & 11 Other Great Hits** climbs to US #70.

1962 Jan *Revenge* reaches US #15 and B-side *The Last Penny* makes US #77.

Feb *Shadrack*, a remake of 1931 song *Shadrack, Meshack, Abednigo* reaches US #19. *If You Believe* stalls at US #77.

Mar Film theme, *Walk On The Wild Side* makes US #43.

June *Hit Record* only climbs to US #45. Benton quickly eschews its gimmick-laden style and goes back to blues-ballads.

Oct *Lie To Me*, in more familiar style, reaches US #13.

Dec B-side *Still Waters Run Deep* stalls at US #89 as **Singin' The Blues – Lie To Me** makes US #40.

1963 Jan *Hotel Happiness*, his biggest seller for nearly 2 years, hits US #3 – but will be his last US Top 10 entry for 7 years.

Mar *Dearer Than Life* peaks at US #59.

Apr *I Got What I Wanted* reaches US #28, as **Brook Benton's Golden Hits, Volume 2** makes US #82.

July *My True Confession* reaches US #22.

Oct *Two Tickets To Paradise* reaches US #32.

[13] Benton makes his UK TV debut, second on the bill behind The Beatles, on "Sunday Night At The London Palladium".

[19] He begins "Greatest Record Show Of 1963" tour with Dion, Lesley Gore, Trini Lopez and Timi Yuro at London's Finsbury Park Astoria.

1964 Feb *Going Going Gone* makes US #35. Benton continues to tour US with great success, earning $25,000 for a week-long stint at the Apollo theater in Harlem, New York.

June *Too Late To Turn Back Now/Another Cup Of Coffee* is his last Mercury single to make US Top 50 – the 2 almost equally popular sides make #43 and #47 respectively.

Aug *A House Is Not A Home* scrapes US #75, its sales split with those of Dionne Warwick's version which climbs to US #71 in the same week.

Oct *Lumberjack* is his last Mercury hit of any consequence, at US #53.

Dec *Do It Right* peaks at US #67.

1965 July Benton leaves Mercury as his last release, *Love Me Now*, spends a week at US #100, and signs to RCA Records.

Dec *Mother Nature, Father Time* reaches US #53, but is his only RCA release to chart.

1967 Sept After 2 barren years and another label change, he has one US chart success on Frank Sinatra's Reprise Records: *Laura (Tell Me What He's Got That I Ain't Got)* makes US #78. Benton regards it as one of his own favorite recordings.

Oct *Laura (What's He Got That I Ain't Got)* makes US #156.

1968 Oct He signs to Atlantic subsidiary label Cotillion, where he records in a laid-back soul idiom which updates his earlier style, beginning with *Do Your Own Thing*, a minor return to US chart at #99.

1969 July *Do Your Own Thing* peaks at US #189.

Aug *Nothing Can Take The Place Of You* reaches US #74.

1970 Feb *Brook Benton Today* is released and reaches US #27.

Mar Benton has his first million-seller for almost a decade with what becomes widely regarded as the definitive version of Tony Joe White's soul ballad *Rainy Night In Georgia*. It hits US #4 (and R&B #1), though does not sell in UK because of poor promotion.

May A version of Frank Sinatra's *My Way* proves an inappropriate follow-up, reaching only US #72.

June His strong interpretation of Joe South's *Don't It Make You Want To Go Home* makes US #45.

Aug [22] *Home Style* makes US #199.

1971 Jan He duets with The Dixie Flyers on *Shoes*, which makes US #67, but is his last hit for Cotillion and also proves his US chart swan song. (His moves to MGM, Stax, All Platinum and Olde Worlde later in the 70s, plus a brief tie-up with the Brut perfume company when it tries to move into music, bring some well-reviewed records but little sales action. For the next 17 years of his life he will achieve little as a record seller, but because his relaxed style and wide repertoire of past hits have enduring appeal, he will remain in demand on the US club circuit as a ballad singer.)

1988 Apr [9] Benton dies in hospital in New York at 56, following an illness.

CHUCK BERRY

1952 Berry (b. Charles Edward Anderson Berry, Oct.18, 1926, San Jose, CA, though Berry will state in his autobiography that he is born in St. Louis, MO), after spending 3 years in the Algoa Reform school following a robbery conviction and having made his first public appearance at age 16 at Gleeson's Show Place, Cleveland, OH, joins club trio The Johnnie Johnson Trio in St. Louis, MO, with himself on guitar, Johnson on piano and Ebby Harding on drums. They play evening gigs while Berry, with a degree in cosmetology and tonsorial skills at the Poro School of Beauty Culture, works by day as hairdresser and beautician.

1955 May Berry meets Muddy Waters, who had seen him at East St. Louis' Cosmopolitan club and who puts him in touch with Chess Records, which takes interest in Berry's demos of his own songs, one of which is traditional country tune *Ida Red*, and signs him to a record deal.

[21] Berry records self-penned *Ida Red*, now rewritten as *Maybellene* in Chicago with Johnnie Johnson on piano, Willie Dixon on bass, Jasper Thomas on drums and Jerome Green playing maracas, laying down his basic style: uptempo blues-based with a country rockabilly infusion, driven by a guitar rhythm – a legendary style which will inspire thousands of artists over the following 30 years.

Aug [31] *Maybellene* hits US #5, also topping R&B chart for 9 weeks.

Nov [12] Berry is named Most Promising R&B Artist in *Billboard's* annual DJ poll.

1956 June After 2 unsuccessful singles, *Roll Over Beethoven* makes US #29.

Dec He appears in film "Rock Rock Rock", singing *You Can't Catch Me*.

1957 **May** *School Day* hits US #3, is a million-seller and tops R&B chart.
June *School Day* is his US chart debut, at #24.
July Berry appears on ABC TV's "The Big Beat", hosted by Alan Freed.
Aug *Oh Baby Doll*, with Lafayette Leake on piano, Willie Dixon on bass and Fred Below on drums, a line-up which will play on many of Berry's classic singles, peaks at US #57.
Sept He appears in film "Mr. Rock And Roll", which stars rock DJ Alan Freed.
Dec *Rock And Roll Music* hits US #8, and continues to confirm Berry's pioneering role in the genre of which he sings.

1958 **Mar** *Sweet Little Sixteen*, self-penned like the majority of his output, hits US #2 and tops R&B chart for 3 weeks, becoming another million-seller and his biggest hit to date.
May *Sweet Little Sixteen* reaches UK #16.
June *Johnny B Goode*, his song later most covered by other artists, hits US #8 and UK #27.
July Berry appears at the Newport Jazz Festival; his performance of *Sweet Little Sixteen* will be seen some months later in "Jazz On A Summer's Day", the documentary film of the event made by Bert Stern.
Aug *Beautiful Delilah* stalls at US #81.
Sept *Carol* reaches US #18.
Nov [17] *Joe Joe Gun*, B-side of still-climbing *Sweet Little Rock And Roller*, stalls at US #83.
Dec [1] *Sweet Little Rock And Roller* makes US #47. Both sides of a special seasonal single make US chart – *Run Rudolph Run* at #69 and *Merry Christmas Baby* at #71.

1959 **Mar** *Anthony Boy* peaks at US #60.
May *Almost Grown* makes US #32. Its B-side *Little Queenie* (which itself makes #80) is from film "Go Johnny Go", in which Berry also sings *Memphis Tennessee* and has a small acting role.
July *Back In The USA* makes US #37.
Dec [1] After performing in El Paso, TX, Berry meets 14-year-old Apache Indian Janice Norine Escalanti who is, unknown to Berry, working as a waitress and prostitute.
[23] Berry is arrested and charged with violating the Mann Act, after he takes Escalanti to work as a hat-check girl in the nightclub he owns in St. Louis, although in the opinion of the police he has transported a minor across a State Line for immoral purposes. Berry allegedly fires her when she is suspected of working as a prostitute. After she reports him to the police, Berry is initially convicted and sentenced to the maximum penalty of 5 years in jail and fined $2,000. (However, after racist comments by case authority judge George H. Moore Jr. are made public, Berry is freed, prior to a retrial.)

1960 **Mar** *Too Pooped To Pop* makes US #42, with B-side *Let It Rock* peaking at US #64.

1962 **Feb** Berry is finally convicted on the Mann Act charge, and begins a 3-year sentence in the Indiana Federal Penitentiary in Terre Haute. (He will serve 2 years, and be released in 1964.)

1963 **June** New interest in Berry's music hits UK as the R&B boom takes hold, with hundreds of groups across the country using his songs as basic repertoire. A compilation album of oldies, simply titled *Chuck Berry*, is issued to capitalize on this boom, and climbs to UK #12.
July *Go Go Go*, an earlier US single, is released in UK and makes #38. The Rolling Stones also enter UK chart with their first single, a revival of Berry's *Come On*, which reaches #21.
Aug Renewed interest hits US, where The Beach Boys and Lonnie Mack have just had Top 5 hits with revivals of *Sweet Little Sixteen* (re-written as *Surfin' USA*) and *Memphis Tennessee* (instrumentally, as *Memphis*). With Berry still in jail, Chess Records puts his versions of these songs, plus others, on an album which has audience noise dubbed on and is released as *Chuck Berry On Stage*.
Oct *Chuck Berry On Stage* reaches US #29 (his first charted album), and hits UK #6.
Nov Another reissued oldie, *Memphis Tennessee*, backed with *Let It Rock*, eclipses a cover version by Dave Berry to become Berry's first-ever UK Top 10 single, hitting #6.
Dec *Run Rudolph Run* is a UK Christmas release, making #36. Compilation *More Chuck Berry* hits UK #9.

1964 **Jan** Out of prison and in demand (as another boost, The Beatles have just included *Roll Over Beethoven* on their second album), Berry returns to Chess Records' Chicago studio to record new material.
Mar Newly-recorded *Nadine (Is It You?)* reaches US #23 and UK #27.
May [9] He begins his first UK tour at the Astoria, Finsbury Park, London, a 21-date twice-nightly package supported by The Animals, The Swinging Blue Jeans, The Nashville Teens, Karl Denver and others. It will end May 29 at the Odeon theater, Southend, Essex.

[23] Berry appears on ITV show "Thank Your Lucky Stars".
June *No Particular Place To Go*, which updates *School Day*'s melody with new car-cruising lyrics, hits US #10 and UK #3. *His Latest And Greatest* hits UK #8 while *Chuck Berry's Greatest Hits* makes US #34.
Sept *You Never Can Tell* reaches US #14 and UK #23.
Oct UK-only *You Never Can Tell* reaches #18.
Nov *Little Marie*, a lyrical sequel to *Memphis Tennessee*, peaks at US #54.
Dec [12] *Promised Land* makes US #41.

1965 **Jan** US-only *St Louis To Liverpool* climbs to #124.
[8] Backed by The Five Dimensions, Berry begins 24-date twice-nightly UK tour, with Long John Baldry and The Moody Blues, at the Odeon theater, Lewisham, London. It will close Jan.31 at the Regal theater, Edmonton, London.
[9] He records several tracks with The Five Dimensions at Pye studios in London, which will appear on *Chuck Berry In London*.
[30] *Promised Land* reaches UK #26.
Apr [3] *Dear Dad* stalls at US #95.
June [17-20] Berry takes part in the First New York Folk Festival at Carnegie Hall, New York.

1966 **June** He leaves Chess to sign to Mercury Records for a $50,000 advance, but his time with this label will produce no hits. (He also continues to receive income from his 42-acre Berry Park theme project, featuring a guitar-shaped swimming pool, located in Wentzville, MO.)
Aug [7] "Gather No Moss", filmed before a live audience in Santa Monica, CA, premieres in UK at Birmingham's Futurist cinema.

1967 **Feb** [19] Near the end of a London Saville theater concert, 2 fans get on stage, at which point the safety curtain is brought down, almost hitting Berry. Brian Epstein later fires house manager Michael Bullock. Berry will return to play a further concert the next week on Feb.26.
May *Chuck Berry's Golden Decade* stalls at US #191.
Sept He records live album *Live At The Fillmore* at the Fillmore West, San Francisco, with The Steve Miller Band.

1969 **Jan** [30] Berry begins a 4-day stint at the Fillmore West, San Francisco, on a bill with Mike Bloomfield, Mark Naftalin and Nick Gravenites.
July [4-5] Berry plays 2 dates at the Royal Albert Hall, London, during current UK tour.
Sept [13] He appears at the "Toronto Rock'N'Roll Revival Concert" at the Varsity Stadium of Toronto University, Canada, along with Little Richard, Gene Vincent, Jerry Lee Lewis, Bo Diddley, The Doors, Alice Cooper and John Lennon's Plastic Ono Band.

1970 **Feb** Berry re-signs to Chess and records *Back Home*, which includes *Tulane*, later a UK hit for The Steve Gibbons Band.

1972 **Feb** [3] Berry appears at the Lanchester Arts Festival at Coventry Locarno, W.Midlands.
June Tracks made in a London studio with members of The Faces backing him, together with a live show recorded, unknown to Berry, at the Lanchester Arts Festival while on UK tour, are packaged as *The London Chuck Berry Sessions*. It will eventually hit US #8, and become his biggest-selling album.
Oct The double-entendre audience participation novelty number *My Ding-A-Ling*, backed by Onnie McIntyre and Robbie McIntosh of Average White Band, Dave Kafinetti and Nic Potter and taken from the live portion of the album, tops US chart for 2 weeks, becoming a million-plus seller and ironically Berry's most successful single ever.
Nov [25] *My Ding-A-Ling* tops UK chart for 4 weeks, in spite of efforts by public morality campaigner, Mary Whitehouse, to have it banned. Double compilation *Chuck Berry's Golden Decade*, originally issued in 1967, is reactivated by the success of *My Ding-A-Ling*, and climbs to US #72. *St. Louie To Frisco To Memphis* stalls at US #185.

1973 **Feb** *Reelin' And Rockin'*, also a live album extract, reaches US #27 and UK #18, but will be Berry's last hit single in either country. *Chuck Berry's Golden Decade, Vol.2* makes US #110.
Sept *Bio*, blues-based like most of his 70s Chess recordings and backed by Elephant's Memory, makes US #175.

1975 **Feb** [19] Berry begins a 9-date UK tour at the Lewisham Odeon, London. The tour will end on Mar.2 at the Birmingham Odeon.
Mar *Chuck Berry '75*, on which he duets for the first time on some tracks with his daughter, Ingrid Berry Gibson, is released.

1977 **Feb** [5] A compilation album of hits *Motorvatin'*, aided by TV advertising, hits UK #7.

1978 **Mar** Berry plays himself in the film "American Hot Wax", which chronicles the story of DJ Alan Freed.

1979 **June** [7] He performs at the White House by special request of President Jimmy Carter.
July [10] Berry is sentenced to 5 months in jail, for income tax evasion in 1973.

CHUCK BERRY cont.

Oct *Rockit*, with Johnnie Johnson on piano, is released, the only fruit of a new recording deal with Atlantic Records.

Nov [19] He is released from jail after serving his sentence in Lompoc Prison Farm, CA.

1980 Berry will continue to tour throughout US and Europe over the next 4 years, though recorded output will be minimal and unsuccessful.

1985 **Feb** [26] Berry is honored by the NARAS at the 27th annual Grammy awards with a Lifetime Achievement Award, noting him to be "one of the most influential and creative innovators in the history of American popular music, a composer and performer whose talents inspired the elevation of rock'n'roll to one of music's major art forms".

1986 **Jan** [23] Keith Richards inducts Berry into the first annual Rock'N'Roll Hall Of Fame dinner at the Waldorf Astoria, New York.

Oct [16] A special concert at the Fox theater in St. Louis, organized by The Rolling Stones' Keith Richards (who leads the backing band), is held to celebrate Berry's 60th birthday and to form the basis of a documentary film.

1987 During the year, Berry is given his star on the Hollywood Walk Of Fame at 1777 N. Vine.

1988 **Jan** *Chuck Berry: The Autobiography* is published, a revealing account of his personal and musical life, mostly written during his 1979 incarceration.

Feb Taylor Hackford's film "Hail! Hail! Rock'N'Roll" is released, documenting the 1986 birthday concert. Among Richards' hand-picked band sharing stage and screen is Berry's original pianist, Johnnie Johnson.

Mar In UK to promote both book and film, Berry plays a London concert at Hammersmith Odeon, sings *Memphis Tennessee* on UK TV chat show "Aspel", and tells a magazine interviewer he may retire "soon".

[2] *Maybellene* is inducted into the NARAS Hall Of Fame at the 30th annual Grammy awards.

Nov MCA releases an anthology of historic Berry recordings made for Chess between 1955 and 1973.

1989 **June** Berry becomes one of the first 10 people to be inducted into the St. Louis Walk Of Fame.

Aug [27] *Johnny B. Goode* is featured on Voyager Interstellar Record. Berry sings the song at JPL party after Voyager 2 has encountered the Neptune system.

Nov [3] Berry participates in the 20th anniversary "Rock'N'Roll Revival Concert" with The Coasters, Jay & The Americans, The Five Satins, The Skyliners, Bo Diddley and others.

Dec [26] A suit is filed that Berry made videotapes "created for the improper purpose of the entertainment and gratification" of Berry's "sexual fetishes and predilections", after he purportedly filmed women using a restroom at a Wentzville, MO, restaurant.

1990 **Feb** [21] *Roll Over Beethoven* is inducted into the NARAS Hall Of Fame at the 32nd annual Grammy awards. *Chuck Berry – The Chess Box* wins Best Historical Album for its producer Andy McKaie.

June [30] St. Charles County drug enforcement agents raid Berry's Berry Park estate and seize several plastic bags of marijuana, an unspecified quantity of hashish, 2 rifles, a shotgun, $122,500 in cash, homemade videos of suspected pornography and a box of 8mm films depicting bestiality. The DEA has been surveying Berry since Dec.1988 after an informant's tip that he was trafficking in cocaine.

July [30] Berry surrenders to police in St. Charles, MO, and is charged with possession of a controlled substance and 3 counts of child abuse. He is released after posting $20,000 bond.

Nov [20] Berry is cleared of felony child abuse charges. He pleads guilty to 1 misdemeanor count of marijuana possession and is placed on 2 years unsupervised probation, given a 6-month jail sentence and ordered to donate $5,000 to a local hospital.

BIG AUDIO DYNAMITE

Mick Jones (guitar, lead vocals)
Don Letts (effects, vocals)
Dan Donovan (keyboards)
Leo Williams (bass)
Greg Roberts (drums)

1984 The day after he leaves The Clash, Jones (b. June 26, 1955, Brixton, London) begins recruiting members for his new musical project, Big Audio Dynamite. Still signed to CBS in UK, he negotiates a new Columbia contract in US.

1985 **Sept** After 18 months of recruitment, writing and recording, first single *The Bottom Line* is released, but does not chart.

Nov *This Is Big Audio Dynamite* is released, set to make US #103.

1986 **Apr** After extensive UK touring, their first chart single (and the first rock hit to feature a sampling technique with lines taken from the Mick Jagger film "Performance") *E=MC²* climbs to UK #11, and revives sales of the debut album, which now makes UK #27.

June *Medicine Show* sampling Clint Eastwood lines from "A Fistful Of Dollars" reaches UK #29.

July During the recording of a second album in Soho, London, ex-Clash co-founder Joe Strummer wanders into the studio, resulting in him co-producing and co-writing many of the band's new tracks – a reunion which receives considerable press interest.

Nov *No.10 Upping St* (a mock reference to the Prime Minister's London residence) makes UK #11, and *C'mon Every Beatbox*, taken from it, peaks at UK #51. *No.10 Upping St* makes US #119.

1987 **Feb** *V Thirteen* reaches UK #49. (The rest of the year will be spent touring UK, Europe and US, where their live achievements will include a record 5 sell-out nights at the Roxy in Los Angeles, CA, and 9 at Irving Plaza in New York.)

June Band supports U2 on a major European stadium tour. Planet Bad a "nightclub" hosted by group members, becomes a feature in some of the cities where they play.

Aug On their first visit to South America, they play 7 nights in Brazil.

1988 **Jan** Band spends time writing and recording new songs at its Notting Hill, London, base.

June *Just Play Music*, which hits out at the over-sampling on current singles (a trend the band helped launch), peaks at UK #51.

July *Tighten Up, Vol. '88* (featuring a cover painting by ex-Clash colleague Paul Simenon), reaches UK #33 and US #102.

1989 **Sept** *Megatop Phoenix* reaches UK #26.

1990 Jones, who was hospitalized for several months during the previous year with life-threatening viral pneumonia and chicken pox, re-emerges, fully recovered, with new line-up comprising Nick Hawkins (guitar), Gary Stonedage (bass) and ex-Sigue Sigue Sputnik Chris Kavanagh (drums). Roberts, Williams and Letts form their own band, while Donovan (recently separated from his wife Patsy Kensit) takes up session work.

Nov [2] Second phase Big Audio Dynamite II releases *Kool Aid*, which makes UK #55.

THE BIG BOPPER

1954 As a DJ on K-TRM radio in Beaumont, TX, J.P. Richardson (b. Jiles Perry Richardson, Oct.24, 1930, Sabine Pass, TX) nicknames himself The Big Bopper after his ample size. (During his 4 years at the station, he breaks the record for non-stop dee-jaying when he broadcasts for 5 days, 2 hours and 8 mins.)

1957 A prolific spare-time songwriter, he sends some songs to "Pappy" Dailey, Mercury Records' Houston representative, which results in a contract to record C&W. 2 hillbilly-style C&W singles, *Beggar To A King* and *Teenage Moon*, appear in US credited to Jape Richardson, but neither charts.

1958 **June** He writes a novelty rock song *The Purple People Eater Meets The Witch Doctor*, parodying the current hits by Sheb Wooley and David Seville. Initially released on Bopper's own Texas-based D label, this is quickly taken up by Mercury when B-side, *Chantilly Lace*, gets airplay.

Aug *Chantilly Lace* hits US #6, selling over a million, and remaining on chart for 6 months.

Dec Both sides of next single *The Big Bopper's Wedding/Little Red Riding Hood* chart in US, at #38/#72.

1959 **Jan** *Chantilly Lace* reaches UK #12. Bopper, who has put together a stage act based on his hits and comic radio persona, joins "The Winter Dance Party", a multi-artist rock one-nighter tour of Minnesota, Wisconsin and Iowa cities.

Feb [2] After a tour date at Clear Lake, IO, Bopper persuades Waylon Jennings to give him his seat on a light aircraft being chartered by Buddy Holly to the next venue, since his bulk makes sleeping on a tour coach uncomfortable, and he has developed a heavy cold, for which he wishes to consult a doctor.

[3] Just before 1am the plane leaves nearby Mason City Airport in falling snow, then crashes within minutes, killing the pilot and its passengers The Big Bopper, Holly, and Ritchie Valens.

1960 **Jan** [18] Posthumous success as a songwriter comes when *Running Bear*, written for fellow Texan Johnny Preston, tops US chart.

Mar [21] *Running Bear* repeats its US success, hitting UK #1 for 2 weeks.

BIG COUNTRY

Stuart Adamson (guitar, synthesizer, vocals)
Bruce Watson (guitar)
Tony Butler (bass)
Mark Brzezicki (drums)

1981 June Adamson (b. William Stuart Adamson, Apr.11, 1958, Manchester, Gtr. Manchester), disillusioned with his involvement in UK punk-pop outfit, the Skids, returns home to Dunfermline, Scotland, to form a new band with old friend Bruce Watson (b. Mar.11, 1961, Ontario, Canada) who quits his job as a cleaner aboard nuclear submarines. They pair with The Jam's Rick Buckler to demo for Virgin Records, at the London Townhouse, performing *Heart & Soul* and *Angle Park*.
July Virgin Records passes on signing the band.
Sept Adamson and Watson form Big Country with Pete Wishart, later of Runrig, his brother Alan and Clive Parker, ex-Spizz Oil.
Nov Ensign offers the band a singles-only deal.

1982 Feb Group's first major gig is supporting Alice Cooper at the Brighton Centre, Brighton, E.Sussex. After the second night at the Odeon, Birmingham, W. Midlands, they are dropped from the tour.
Apr Adamson fires the rhythm section and enters the studio with Watson to record demos for Phonogram, the latest in a line of interested UK labels. They are assisted by studio regulars Brzezicki (b. June.21, 1957, Slough, Bucks.) and Butler (b. Feb.13, 1957, Ealing, London). The foursome combine as a permanent unit.
May Big Country signs to Phonogram's Mercury label, and performs at the 101 club, Clapham, London.
Aug Group plays its first US gig, supporting The Members at The Peppermint Lounge, New York.
Sept Debut single *Harvest Home*, produced by Chris Thomas and introducing the band's unique twin-guitar based sound, sells 6,000 copies.
Oct Band completes a tour of Scottish clubs.
Nov They support A Certain Ratio at the Lyceum Ballroom in London.
Dec Big Country makes its UK TV debut on Channel 4's "Whatever You Want", in front of a live audience at Brixton's Ace Club, London and supports The Jam for 6 nights at Wembley Arena, London.

1983 Jan They open for The Popsicles at The Venue, London.
Feb Group supports U2 at the Hammersmith Palais, London, and then embarks on "Dingwalls UK Tour" playing Sheffield, S.Yorks., Liverpool, Merseyside, Hull, Humberside and Newcastle, Tyne & Wear.
Mar Group records session for BBC Radio 1's "John Peel Show".
Apr [16] *Fields Of Fire (400 Miles)*, produced by Steve Lillywhite, hits #10. They complete a 16-date UK tour including a headlining spot at the Lyceum. The band makes its first appearance on BBC TV's "Whistle Test".
May Big Country begins recording debut album *The Crossing* with Lillywhite at The Manor and RAK studios.
June [11] Self proclaiming *In A Big Country* reaches UK #17. Band starts its first full headlining UK tour, taking in 34 dates including London's Hammersmith Palais.
Aug [6] *The Crossing* enters UK chart at #4, hits #3, subsequently remaining on the chart for 80 weeks. It will earn platinum status in UK, gold in US and double platinum in Canada. Band is featured in a live TV broadcast from Sefton Park, Liverpool.
Big Country appears on the same bill as U2, Simple Minds, Eurythmics and Steel Pulse at Phoenix Park, Dublin, Eire. They appear as special guests of The Stranglers at the Reading Rock Festival, Berks.
Sept Band journeys to New York for a promotional tour, performing 2 nights at the Ritz club.
Group appears on a live ITV special from Shepton Mallet, Somerset, and makes its directing debut on a documentary for Channel 4's "Play At Home" series.
Oct [1] *Chance* hits UK #9, as the band embarks on a European tour.
Nov *The Crossing* is their US chart bow, peaking at #18 as their first North American tour kicks off in Vancouver, Canada.
Dec [3] *In A Big Country*, their US singles debut, reaches #17 as they appear on NBC TV's "Saturday Night Live".

1984 Jan [28] *Wonderland* hits UK #8.
Feb [25] *Fields Of Fire (400 Miles)* peaks at US #52.
[28] Big Country performs at the 26th annual Grammy awards in Los Angeles, CA, where they are nominated in the Best New Group and Best Single categories.
May Band completes a Japanese tour and performs at The Pink Pop Festival in Holland.

June [ ] *Wonderland* climbs to US #86, while mini-album *Wonderland* makes US #65.
July Big Country plays Wembley Arena, London, as the special guest of Elton John.
Aug Group enters Polar studios, Stockholm, to record Steeltown, with Lillywhite again producing.
Oct [6] *East Of Eden* reaches UK #17.
[27] *Steeltown* enters UK chart at #1 and achieves gold status.
Dec [8] *Where The Rose Is Sown* reaches UK #29, while *Steeltown* makes US #70.
[13-14] Band plays 2 sell-out gigs at Wembley Arena and Birmingham NEC, W.Midlands, supported by the Cult.
[24] Group's Christmas Eve gig at the Edinburgh Playhouse, Scotland, airs live on BBC2 TV.

1985 Jan [26] *Just A Shadow* reaches UK #26.
May Butler and Brzezicki perform on Roger Daltrey's solo album, *Under A Raging Moon*, with Watson also guesting on one track.
July [13] Big Country participates in the Live Aid supergroup finale at Wembley Stadium.
Dec Recording of *The Seer* begins, with Robin Millar producing. Group supports Roger Daltrey at Madison Square Garden, New York.

1986 Feb Band contributes the title track to movie soundtrack of "Restless Natives".
Mar "The Seer" tour begins in Holland and their performance on German TV's "Rock Palace" is broadcast throughout Europe. Group sells out 2 nights at Hammersmith Odeon on the UK leg of the trek.
Apr After a lengthy chart absence, *Look Away* becomes their biggest UK hit single, at #7. (The theme to "Restless Natives" is available on the 12" format.) Band plays the Montreux Golden Rose Festival in Switzerland and headlines the Seinejoke Festival in Finland.
June [20] Group takes part in the fourth annual Prince's Trust Rock Gala concert, with Eric Clapton, Phil Collins, Elton John, George Michael, Rod Stewart, Paul Young and others, at the Wembley Arena, and headlines Lochem Festival in Holland. *The Teacher* makes UK #28.
July *The Seer* hits UK #2, achieving gold status. Band headlines the Brittany Festival and the 3-day Roskilde Festival in Denmark.
Aug Big Country, along with Status Quo and Belouis Some, supports Queen at Knebworth, Herts., in front of a 200,000 crowd. As part of "The Seer" American tour they play to 7,000 at The Pier in New York and make TV appearances on "American Bandstand" and "Solid Gold". *The Seer* makes US #59.
Sept "The Seer" tour returns to Europe. *One Great Thing* reaches UK #19, the group's 10th consecutive Top 30 hit.
Oct A performance at Limehouse studios, London, is broadcast live to US college TV stations.
Nov *Hold The Heart* peaks at UK #55.
Dec [11-12] Group performs 2 sell-out shows at Wembley Arena.

1987 June Big Country supports David Bowie on his UK "Glass Spider" tour, including 2 dates at Wembley Arena, Cardiff Arms Park, Wales, and Slane Castle, Dublin.
Dec "Under Wraps" tour takes the band to UK clubs and colleges.

1988 Jan Recording of fourth album *Peace In Our Time*, begins in Los Angeles, CA, with Peter Wolf producing.
June [5-6] Brzezicki drums alongside Phil Collins at the 6th annual Prince's Trust Rock Gala concert at the Royal Albert Hall, London.
[11] Brzezicki plays in the all-star backing band for the Nelson Mandela 70th birthday tribute at the Wembley Stadium.
July Band shoots videos for *King Of Emotion* and *Broken Heart* in Australia with director Richard Lowenstein. They also top the bill with Bryan Adams at the Peace Festival in East Berlin, Germany, in front of 140,000.
Aug 200,000 see the group perform at the Soviet Peace Festival in Tallinn, Estonia, with Public Image Ltd.
King Of Emotion reaches UK #16. Big Country plays a live set at the Soviet Embassy in London after announcing their plans to make a full tour of Russia. The event is broadcast live on BBC Radio 1 and reported on ITV's "News At Ten".
Oct *Peace In Our Time* hits UK #9. Big Country performs in front of the first ever standing crowd in a Moscow Sports Stadium. These are the first Russian concerts to be organized by a private promoter.
Nov Band shoots the video for *Peace In Our Time* in Moscow and Washington. *Broken Heart (Thirteen Valleys)* makes UK #47. *Peace In Our Time* climbs to US #160.
Dec Stuart Adamson is made an Honorary Patron of the Scottish Prince's Trust.

1989 Jan 3 sell-out gigs at Hammersmith Odeon conclude the UK leg of

BIG COUNTRY cont.

their European tour.

Feb *Peace In Our Time* makes UK #39.

Mar Watson joins Fish at the Lockerbie Disaster benefit concert in Scotland.

May Relentless touring continues in Europe including concerts in Munchengladbach, Germany, and St. Gallen, Switzerland.

July Brzezicki quits the band.

Sept Adamson performs an acoustic set of Big Country numbers at Wet Wet Wet's free concert in Glasgow.

Oct Watson joins Fish's solo tour for his Glasgow Barrowlands gig.

Nov Adamson appears at Jerry Lee Lewis' Hammersmith Odeon concert with Brian May, Van Morrison, John Lodge, Dave Edmunds and others.

1990 **Feb** Pat Ahern joins Big Country on drums.

Mar *Save Me* is recorded in London with producer Tim Palmer.

May [19] *Save Me* makes UK #41.

[23-24] Group plays 2 concerts at the Hammersmith Odeon, London during UK tour.

[26] Retrospective package *Through A Big Country – Greatest Hits* hits UK #2, behind The Carpenters' retrospective *Only Yesterday*.

July [18] Group takes part in the eighth annual Prince's Trust Rock Gala concert at the Wembley Arena.

[21] *Heart Of The World* makes UK #50.

CILLA BLACK

1963 **Jan** [25] After working as a cloakroom attendant and occasionally guesting with groups (notably Kingsize Taylor & The Dominoes, The Big Three and Rory Storm & The Hurricanes) usually billed as "Swinging Cilla", Black (b. Priscilla Maria Veronica White, May 27, 1943, Liverpool, Merseyside), employed at the BICC cable firm, makes her debut as a vocalist at Liverpool's Cavern club, with Rory Storm & The Hurricanes.

July [25] She makes a recording test for EMI, whose George Martin has spotted her while checking out Gerry & The Pacemakers in Liverpool, and is signed to the company's Parlophone label.

Aug [26] Black makes her first major concert appearance during a week-long residency at the Odeon cinema, Southport, Merseyside, on a bill headed by The Beatles.

[28] She records her debut session for EMI.

Sept [6] Black formally signs a management contract with The Beatles' manager Brian Epstein at her 380 Scotland Road home in Liverpool. She had auditioned for Epstein in a Birkenhead club backed by The Beatles. (She becomes Black rather than White after a misprint in **Mersey Beat**.)

[27] Her debut *Love Of The Loved*, an unrecorded song donated by Paul McCartney, is launched with her TV debut on UK TV's "Ready Steady Go!".

Oct *Love Of The Loved*, on EMI's Parlophone label, makes UK #35.

Dec [24] She begins a 3-week season in "The Beatles' Christmas Show" at Finsbury Park Astoria, London, with The Beatles, Billy J. Kramer, The Fourmost and Rolf Harris. The show will finale Jan.11.

1964 **Feb** [29] A cover of Dionne Warwick's US hit *Anyone Who Had A Heart*, tops UK chart for 4 weeks, selling over 900,000 copies in UK – one of the all-time UK best-selling singles by a female singer, and the first by a British girl since Helen Shapiro with *Walkin' Back To Happiness*. (The week's Top 10 is also the first to feature only British acts.) She begins a UK tour with Gene Pitney, Billy J. Kramer & The Dakotas and The Swinging Blue Jeans, at the Odeon cinema, Nottingham, Notts.

May [6] Black is featured on UK TV show "Around The Beatles".

[30] *You're My World*, adapted from the Italian ballad *Il Mondo*, becomes Black's second UK #1, topping the chart for 3 weeks, as she opens an 8-month season in the "Startime Variety Show" at the London Palladium with The Fourmost, Frankie Vaughan and Tommy Cooper.

July [1] Black, accompanied by the Joe Loss Orchestra, plays at a charity ball at London's Mansion House in the presence of Princess Margaret and the Lord Chief Justice.

Aug [29] *It's For You*, another McCartney song not recorded by The Beatles and featuring McCartney on piano, hits UK #7, while *You're My World* is her US chart debut and biggest hit, reaching #26.

Oct [3] *It's For You* climbs to US #79.

Nov [2] Black performs in the "Royal Variety Show" at the London Palladium.

Dec She has a cameo role in Gerry & The Pacemakers' film "Ferry Cross The Mersey", singing *Is It Love?*

1965 **Jan** A cover of The Righteous Brothers' *You've Lost That Lovin' Feelin'*, hits UK #2 outselling the original for its first 2 weeks, until the Brothers visit UK for TV promotion and leap to #1.

[29] Black begins a 22-date twice-nightly UK tour, with P.J. Proby, The Fourmost, Tommy Roe, Tommy Quickly and Sounds Incorporated, at the ABC cinema, Croydon, London. It will end Feb.21 at the Liverpool Empire.

Mar Debut album *Cilla* hits UK #5.

[8] She starts 17-day Australian tour with Freddie & The Dreamers.

Apr [4] Black makes her US CBS TV debut on the "Ed Sullivan Show".

[11] She performs at the annual **New Musical Express** Poll Winners Concert at the Empire Pool, Wembley, London, with a host of others.

[18] She makes her "Sunday Night At The London Palladium" UK TV debut.

May *I've Been Wrong Before*, penned by new US writer Randy Newman, reaches UK #17.

July [26] Black makes her New York debut as she begins a 3-week residency at the Plaza hotel's Persian Room, finishing Aug.14.

Oct [2] She represents UK at the Grand Gala Du Disque at the Congresscentrum, Amsterdam, Holland.

[8] Black begins 18-date twice-nightly "Star Scene 65 Tour" in association with Radio London, with billtoppers The Everly Brothers, Billy J. Kramer & The Dakotas and Paddy Klaus & Gibson, at the Granada cinema, Bedford, Beds. The package tour ends Oct.28 at the ABC cinema, Wigan, Gtr.Manchester, and will be Black's last.

Dec [16] "The Music Of Lennon-McCartney", a 50-min. tribute featuring Black and many other artists, airs on UK commercial TV in London. (The rest of the UK sees the program the following night.)

[27] Black makes her stage acting debut in the title role of Christmas pantomime "Little Red Riding Hood" at the Wimbledon theater, London, through to Feb.5.

1966 **Feb** [5] *Love's Just A Broken Heart* hits UK #5.

Apr [16] *Alfie*, written by Burt Bacharach and Hal David after seeing the Michael Caine movie of the same name, with Bacharach on piano, hits UK #9.

[18] Black opens a cabaret season at London's Savoy hotel.

June *Don't Answer Me* hits UK #6, as *Cilla Sings A Rainbow* hits #4.

Sept *Alfie* climbs to US #95, in competition with a #32 cover version by Cher and is her US chart swan song.

Nov [3] Black and comedian Frankie Howerd open in "Way Out In Piccadilly" revue, written by Ray Galton and Alan Simpson with Eric Sykes, at London's Prince of Wales theater. (She will leave July 1967.)

[12] *A Fool Am I* reaches UK #13.

1967 **Jan** [30] Black begins filming "Work ... Is A Four-Letter Word", based on Henry Livings' play "Eh?", with David Warner, Alfred Marks and director Peter Hall.

May [27] Epstein celebrates Cilla's 24th birthday with greetings illuminated at Piccadilly Circus, London, and Birmingham, Bristol and Manchester.

June *What Good Am I* makes UK #24. Shortly afterwards, claiming inattention to her career, Black splits from Epstein's management agency. The disagreements resolved, she returns to him, and is reportedly devastated by his death 2 months later.

Dec *I Only Live To Love You* makes UK #26.

1968 **Jan** [30] Her UK BBC television series is launched, with new McCartney song, *Step Inside Love*, as the theme tune.

Feb [6] Ringo Starr guests on the TV show, duetting with Black on *Act Naturally*.

Apr *Step Inside Love* is released as a single and hits UK #8, her first Top 10 hit for nearly 2 years.

May *Sher-oo* hits UK #7.

June *Where Is Tomorrow* sells disappointingly, making UK #39.

Dec Compilation album *The Best Of Cilla Black*, with all her A-side hits to date, reaches UK #21.

1969 **Mar** *Surround Yourself With Sorrow*, penned by Bill Martin and Phil Coulter, hits UK #3. Black marries her personal manager, Bobby Willis (a marriage still going strong in the 90s).

Aug *Conversations* hits UK #7.

1970 **Jan** *If I Thought You'd Ever Change Your Mind*, a cover of Kathe Green's John Cameron-original, reaches UK #20.

Aug *Sweet Inspiration* makes UK #42.

1971 **Dec** Roger Cook/Roger Greenaway's *Something Tells Me (Something's Gonna Happen Tonight)*, theme from her new UK TV series, hits UK #3.

1974 **Feb** *Baby We Can't Go Wrong*, the theme from her third UK TV series, makes UK #36, but proves to be her final UK hit single. Having moved sideways to a "family entertainer" role (the perfect vehicle for her engaging and gregarious Liverpool personality), she will henceforth concentrate on cabaret and TV work quite divorced from the rock field.

83 **Feb** TV-advertised retrospective album *The Very Best Of Cilla Black* returns her to UK chart after almost a decade, reaching #20. (She has let her career wane during the late 70s and early 80s while raising her family, but she now returns to UK public view with a vengeance via TV, occasionally still singing, but mainly hosting top-rated shows "Surprise Surprise" and "Blind Date", in the process becoming the UK's first female game show hostess.)

HE BLACK CROWES

ris Robinson (vocals)
ch Robinson (guitar)
f Cease (guitar)
nny Colt (bass)
ve Gorman (drums)

84 Brothers Chris (b. Christopher Robinson, Dec.20, 1966, Atlanta, GA) and Rich Robinson (b. Richard Robinson, May 24, 1969, Atlanta), the sons of 1959 US #83 *Boom-A-Dip-Dip* hitmaker Stan Robinson, who after 4 years on the road has settled in Atlanta, GA, to set up a clothing business with his wife Nancy (nee Bradley), a Nashville country singer, make their debut in punk band Mr. Crowe's Garden in Chattanooga, TN. The $50 cheque they are paid for their services bounces. Always based in Atlanta, Chris will also enrol at Georgia State University.

8 After running through 6 bass players, Colt (b. May 1, 1966, Cherry Point, NC) becomes a permanent fixture. The Robinsons also meet drummer Gorman (b. Aug.17, 1965, Hopkinsville, KY), who is playing for another band in an adjacent studio to Mr. Crowe's Garden, who are recording demo sessions, and invite Gorman to join. Band then recruits Cease (b. June 24, 1967, Nashville, TN), in a desire to play harder rock with a 2-guitar attack, at a party following a Nashville gig featuring Mr. Crowe's Garden and Cease's current band.

89 **May** With a settled line-up, dedicated to a no-compromise rock stance and to recording mainly Robinson brothers' songs, they name-change to The Black Crowes, are signed to Def American by A&R man George Drakoulias, and begin debut recordings with considerable help from ex-Allman Brothers Band member Chuck Leavell. Recorded in Atlanta and Los Angeles, CA, all but 1 of the songs are written by the Robinsons, while the project is produced by Drakoulias.

0 **Mar** [24] Having built up solid cult following through incessant US touring and benefiting from promising early reviews, *Shake Your Money Maker* enters US chart at #174, but will go on to multi-platinum US sales and a lengthy chart tenure.
June [23] Debut single *Jealous Again* stalls at US #75.
[29] They play the first of 2 heavy metal bills, with Aerosmith, Metallica and Warrant at the Skydome, Toronto, Canada. (The second gig will be played June 30 at the Silver Stadium in Rochester, NY.)
Aug [7] During a year when they will be on the road for 11 out of 12 months, Black Crowes set off on Heart-supporting North American tour in Winnipeg, Canada. They have already opened for Aerosmith and completed a European club tour.
Sept [22] *Hard To Handle*, a remake of Otis Redding's 1968 US #51 original, is UK Singles chart debut, peaking at #45.
Oct [9] Group makes its US network TV debut on NBC TV's "Late Night With Letterman".
Dec [15] As the group ends the year (after supporting Robert Plant) with a 2-month round of 1,000-2,000 seaters in US, *Hard To Handle* makes US #45.

1 **Jan** [4] The Black Crowes join the Z.Z.Top tour in New Orleans, LA, augmented by keyboardist Eddie Harsch.
[19] *Twice As Hard* makes UK #47, though parent album remains uncharted in UK.
Feb [20] They play an impromptu gig with borrowed equipment at the Ritz, Detroit, MI, to benefit the Delta Blues Museum. Finishing their set, they are told that they have been beaten for Best New Artist at the 33rd annual Grammy awards by Mariah Carey. Rich Robinson says "I'm relieved. If we'd won, it'd be much too respectable."
Mar [7] Group is named Best New American Band in the annual **Rolling Stone** Readers' Picks and Critics' Picks 1990 music awards. Chris Robinson is named Best New Male Singer in the Critics' Picks.
[16] Band guests on NBC TV's "Saturday Night Live".
[25] Following continual comments at the top of their live set by Chris Robinson about commercial sponsorship of tours, and repeated warnings to desist, Z.Z.Top's management drop the group from the tour after a show in Atlanta.

Apr [6] *Shake Your Money Maker* finally peaks at US #4 after over a year on the chart. Taking 54 weeks to reach the Top 5, it is the slowest to do so since Jimi Hendrix's 1968 59-week chart-climbing *Are You Experienced*. Extracted third single *She Talks To Angels* stands at US #55 on its way towards US Top 40.
May [4] Black Crowes perform at the Memphis In May Beale Street Music Festival in Memphis, TN.

BLACK SABBATH

Tony Iommi (guitar)
"Geezer" Butler (bass)
Ozzy Osbourne (vocals)
Bill Ward (drums)

1967 Schoolmates Iommi (b. Feb.19, 1948, Birmingham, W.Midlands), Ward (b. May 5, 1948, Birmingham), Butler (b. Terry Butler, July 17, 1949, Birmingham) and Osbourne (b. Dec.3, 1948, Birmingham), form a blues band, first named Polka Tulk but soon changed to Earth.

1968 Playing a jazz-blues fusion, they tour exhaustively in UK then to the rest of Europe, and break The Beatles' long-held house attendance record at the Star-Club, Hamburg, Germany.

1969 **Jan** Big Bear Ffolly, combining local groups Earth, Bakerloo (of which Spencer Davis Group's Pete York is a member), Tea & Symphony and Locomotive, makes its debut at Birmingham's Opposite Lock.
Feb [6] Big Bear Ffolly makes its London debut at the Marquee. Prompted by manager Jim Simpson, Earth switches name to Black Sabbath (the title of an early song originated by Butler's abiding interest in popular black magic novelist Dennis Wheatley) and changes to a suitably matching macabre image.
Dec After a year's constant touring to build a huge live following, the group signs to Philips Records' subsidiary, Fontana.

1970 **Jan** Debut release is *Evil Woman (Don't Play Your Games With Me)*, a cover of a US hit by Crow, but it fails to chart.
Apr *Evil Woman* is reissued (again without success) on Philips' new "progressive rock" label Vertigo, alongside their first album *Black Sabbath*, recorded in 2 days for £600 with producer Rodger Bain. Filled with occult imagery, it climbs to hit UK #8, staying 5 months on chart.
May [24] Group plays at the Hollywood Music Festival near Newcastle-under-Lyme, Staffs.
Oct [10] Second album *Paranoid*, which features many of their early stage favorites like *War Pigs*, tops UK chart for 2 weeks, and the title track hits #4. Both will become their most enduring records, and be regarded as classics of early heavy metal rock.
Dec Following a US college tour, *Black Sabbath*, released in US on Warner Bros., climbs to #23 (eventually staying on chart for 65 weeks), while *Paranoid* reaches US #61.

1971 **Mar** *Paranoid* is issued in US, reaches #12 and also spends 65 weeks on chart. Their US and UK popularity thus cemented, they become synonymous with the "hard rock lifestyle": a mixture of drink, drugs, groupies and exhausting schedules.
Sept *Master Of Reality* hits UK #5 and US #8.

1972 **Mar** *Iron Man*, belatedly taken from *Paranoid* in US, charts at #52.
Oct *Black Sabbath Vol.4* hits UK #8 and US #13. Band changes management, replacing Simpson with Patrick Meehan, and releases *Tomorrow's Dream*, first UK single since *Paranoid*.

1974 **Jan** Fifth album *Sabbath Bloody Sabbath*, with keyboard help from Rick Wakeman, hits UK #4 and US #11, while Meehan is replaced as manager by agent Don Arden. The disgruntled Simpson takes action over what he considers an unfairly broken contract with the band and Osbourne is handed a subpoena as he walks on stage at a US tour date, precipitating an almost 2-year enforced hiatus for Sabbath, as legal battles over management rage. Osbourne begins to drift away from the others because of his even harder drinking lifestyle and unwillingness to move away from Sabbath's established musical formula.

1975 **July** Group makes its Madison Square Garden, New York, debut.
Sept With legal matters finally settled and their UK contract and back-catalog moved to NEMS Records, they return with major UK tour.
[13] *Sabotage* hits UK #7 and will reach US #28.

1976 **Jan** [31] Double compilation album *We Sold Our Souls For Rock'N'Roll* reaches UK #35.
Apr [10] *We Sold Our Souls For Rock'N'Roll* makes US #48.
Oct [23] *Technical Ecstasy*, which returns the band to Vertigo, reaches UK #13. It appears after crises in its recording, as Iommi wants to experiment with more complex arrangements, overdubs and even a horn section, all against Osbourne's will.
Nov [27] *Technical Ecstasy* makes US #51.

BLACK SABBATH cont.

1977 Nov Osbourne finally quits after more internal friction. He is replaced on some live dates by ex-Savoy Brown singer, Dave Walker.

1978 Jan Osbourne rejoins, but relations with rest of the band are strained.
June [24] First UK hit single since *Paranoid*, *Never Say Die*, a taster of the forthcoming album, reaches UK #21.
Oct [7] *Never Say Die*, recorded at Sounds Interchange in Toronto, Canada, reaches UK #12.
[21] *Hard Road*, taken from it, climbs to UK #33.
Dec [2] *Never Say Die* makes US #69.

1979 Jan The basic conflicts between Osbourne and the band still unresolved, he now leaves permanently to form Blizzard Of Oz and embark on a successful solo career.
Mar Sabbath attempts to shed business and legal problems by signing a new management deal with Don Arden. Former Rainbow vocalist Ronnie James Dio (b. c.1950, NH) is recruited to replace Osbourne as lead singer.
July Butler leaves, replaced for live work by Geoff Nicols from Quartz, but he decides to return in time for the next album recording sessions.

1980 May [7-10] Group plays 4 nights at the Hammersmith Odeon, London, during current UK tour, as *Heaven & Hell*, introducing Dio's mythology-influenced lyrics, hits UK #9.
July *Neon Knights* is their third consecutive UK hit single at #22, while *Heaven And Hell* reaches US #28.
Black Sabbath: Live At Last, a previously unheard onstage recording made in 1975 by the original line-up, is released by NEMS. Though the current line-up disowns it, the album climbs to hit UK #5.
Sept [27] Encouraged by this success, NEMS reissues *Paranoid*, which re-charts in UK at #54 almost 10 years after its original success. It tops UK Independent chart, sitting oddly among current new wave records.
Nov Following a successful US tour, Bill Ward leaves, his departure forced by recurring bad health, and is replaced on drums by Vinnie Appice, younger brother of Carmine Appice of Vanilla Fudge fame.
Dec [13] *Die Young* makes UK #41.

1981 Nov [14] *Mob Rules* reaches UK #12, while the extracted title song reaches UK #46. Sabbath experiences more personal bickering as Iommi voices his growing resentment at Dio's influence on the album. *Mob Rules* reaches US #29.

1982 Feb [13] *Turn Up The Night* makes US #37.
Nov Dio quits after Iommi accuses him of tampering with the mix of the band's forthcoming live album in order to highlight his vocals. He takes Appice with him to form his own group, Dio. Dave Donato replaces Dio.

1983 Jan Double live album *Live Evil*, recorded on the road in Dallas, TX, San Antonio, TX, and Seattle, WA, reaches UK #13 and US #37, though when it appears the band lacks coherence and seems destined to fold.
June Personnel problems are solved when Ward returns, and Ian Gillan, former vocalist with Deep Purple and his own band Gillan, is persuaded to join.
Aug Black Sabbath headlines the Reading Festival, Berks., with its new line-up. Bev Bevan of ELO plays drums when Ward is forced by illness to withdraw again.
Oct *Born Again*, recorded at the Manor studios, Shipton on Cherwell, Oxon, with Ward back on drums, hits UK #4 and US #39.

1984 Mar [10] Gillan leaves to join the re-forming Deep Purple.

1985 July [13] Original Black Sabbath line-up including Osbourne, re-forms strictly as a one-off to play at the Live Aid concert, Philadelphia, PA.

1986 Mar *Seventh Star*, credited to "Black Sabbath with Tony Iommi" (he being the only remaining member of the old band), playing with former Deep Purple vocalist Glenn Hughes and newly-recruited musicians, Geoff Nichols (b. Birmingham), Dave Spitz (b. New York, NY) and Eric Singer (b. Cleveland, OH) reaches UK #27 and US #78, but the incarnation shows little sign of maintaining the fan following or success which Black Sabbath achieved in earlier years.

1987 Nov [28] *The Eternal Idol* makes UK #66.

1988 Jan *The Eternal Idol* peaks at US #168.

1989 Neil Murray leaves Vow Wow to join Black Sabbath tour line-up.
Apr [15] Now signed to IRS, *Headless Cross* peaks at UK #62.
[29] Parent album *Headless Cross* reaches UK #31.
May *Headless Cross* makes US #115.
June [27] Group begins 16-date US tour in Daytona, FL, ending July 16 in Sacramento, CA. Line-up is now Iommi, Powell, Murray and vocalist Tony Martin.

1990 Sept [1] Second IRS released album *TYR* debuts at peak UK #24.

BOBBY BLAND

1952 Jan A Memphis, TN, resident since his teens, and a gospel and blues vocalist since school days, then becoming B.B. King's valet in 1949 and Roscoe Gordon's chauffeur, Bland (b. Robert Calvin Bland, Jan.27, 1930, Rosemark, TN) has been part of a loose musical aggregation, The Beale Streeters (which includes Johnny Ace, Gordon, Earl Forrest and Little Junior Parker) for some 3 years when he makes his first recordings in Memphis with Ike Turner, for the Los Angeles, CA-based Modern label. (*Crying All Night Long* and *Good Lovin'* will be released to instant obscurity.) He signs to James Mattis' Duke label, but is drafted into US Army service after one release, ironically titled *Army Blues*.

1957 Aug Post-military service, Houston, TX-based entrepreneur Don Robey who has bought the label from Mattis, pairs him with bandleader Joe Scott. His bluesy vocal styling gains him the name-tag Bobby "Blue" Bland, which sticks with him for 2 decades. After a handful of releases, Bland scores in US pop chart when *Farther Up The Road* (a #5 R&B hit) makes #43 and stays charted for 5 months. This breaks him into the nationwide R&B live circuit with Junior Parker as "Blues Consolidated", backed by Parker's band and later by his own 12-piece road band led by horn player Joe Scott (who arranges Bland's material), and featuring Wayne Bennett, who plays lead guitar on most shows. For the next 5 years, the package will play 300 shows a year. Most of his hits will be written by these and others of Bland's musicians, under the communal pen-name "Deadric Malone".

1960 Feb *I'll Take Care Of You*, his highest-placed entry yet on R&B chart (#2), makes US #89. (For much of the next decade, most of Bland's singles will be US Top 100 entries as well as specialist hits.)
Nov *Cry Cry Cry* reaches US #71.

1961 Mar *I Pity The Fool* reaches US #46, also topping R&B chart for a week.
Aug *Don't Cry No More* makes US #71 (R&B #2).

1962 Jan *Turn On Your Love Light* is first US Top 30 entry, at #28 (R&B #2).
Mar *Ain't That Loving You* stalls at US #86.
Apr *Who Will The Next Fool Be?* makes US #76.
Sept *Yield Not To Temptation* reaches US #56, while *Here's The Man* is his first album seller (an area where Duke Records is never to become heavily involved), making US #53.
Oct *Stormy Monday Blues* makes US #43, staying charted for 3 months.

1963 Feb Double A-side *Call On Me/That's The Way Love Is* is Bland's biggest US hit single, some estimates putting its sales over a million. (Because Duke does not let its sales figures – and thereby its royalty payments be known, this is never confirmed.) Topping R&B chart, the 2 sides march independently up the Hot 100 to reach #22 and #33 respectively.
Aug *Sometimes You Gotta Cry A Little* peaks at US #56, while *Call On Me/That's The Way Love Is* (containing both hits) is Bland's one major album seller during the 60s. It makes #11, remaining on chart 26 weeks.
Dec *The Feeling Is Gone* stalls at US #91.

1964 Apr *Ain't Nothing You Can Do*, his second-biggest hit, makes US #20.
July *Share Your Love With Me* makes US #42.
Aug *Ain't Nothing You Can Do* reaches US #119.
Nov *Ain't Doing Too Bad* makes US #49.

1965 Jan *Blind Man/Black Night* is another double-sided hit, reaching US #78/#99 (*Blind Man* is in competition with fellow bluesman Little Milton's version, which peaks at #86).
Apr [24] *Ain't No Telling* stalls at US #93.
Oct *These Hands (Small But Mighty)* makes US #63.

1966 Feb *I'm Too Far Gone (To Turn Around)* peaks at US #62.
June *Good Time Charlie* reaches US #75.
Oct *Poverty* climbs to US #65.

1967 Apr [22] *You're All I Need* stalls at US #88.

1968 Mar A revival of Charles Brown's blues classic *Driftin' Blues* makes US #96. Joe Scott and guitarist Wayne Bennett leave Bland.

1969 Jan *Rockin' In The Same Old Boat* is Bland's strongest seller for over 4 years: peaking at US #58, it remains on chart for 10 weeks.
June [14] *Gotta Get To Know* stalls at US #91.
Oct *Chains Of Love* peaks at US #60.

1970 Feb [14] *If You've Got A Heart* stalls at US #96.
Dec *Keep On Loving Me (You'll See The Change)* makes US #89.

1971 June [19] *I'm Sorry* stalls at US #97.

1972 Mar His biggest seller since *Rockin' In The Same Old Boat* is *Do What You Set Out To Do*, which reaches US #64. It is also his last release for the Duke label which, following Don Robey's death, is bought by ABC Records, along with its back catalog and artist contracts. Bland is moved to ABC's Dunhill label.

1974 Jan Results of his first West Coast recordings for Dunhill (with producer Steve Barri and musical director Mel Jackson, veteran of US

West Coast rock, who widens Bland's repertoire without eroding his roots or style) are on his *California Album*, which makes US #136. Taken from it is *This Time I'm Gone For Good*, his first US Top 50 entry for 9 years, peaking at #42 and charting for 13 weeks.

Mar A revival of the blues standard *Goin' Down Slow* makes US #69.

Aug *Ain't No Love In The Heart Of The City* reaches only US #91, but becomes a classic of Bland's later repertoire, and will be a hit cover in 1978 for heavy rock band Whitesnake. *Dreamer* peaks at US #172.

Nov *I Wouldn't Treat A Dog (The Way You Treated Me)* is his final US hit single, at #88, as Dunhill pushes him as a sophisticated soul album act.

Dec Bland is teamed with his long-time friend (and one-time employer) B.B. King, also an ABC artist, for *Together For The First Time ... Live*, which charts for 20 weeks in US, peaking at #43 and earning a gold disk for a half million sales.

75 Sept ABC phases out Dunhill and moves Bland to the main label for C&W-styled *Get On Down With Bobby Bland*, which makes US #154.

76 Aug [28] Success of first Bland/King collaboration prompts release of a similar second set, *Together Again ... Live*, which makes US #73. Perhaps to emphasize both men's artistic roots, it is issued on ABC's jazz label, Impulse.

77 May *Reflections In Blue* reaches US #185.

78 July *Come Fly With Me* also makes US #185.

79 Oct By the time *I Feel Good, I Feel Fine* is released, ABC has been bought by MCA Records, which retains Bland and moves him to the main label. Nevertheless, this is his final US Album chart entry, reaching #187. (He will have 5 R&B chart albums on MCA, up to *You've Got Me Loving You* in 1984.)

82 Bland tours UK for the first time: a country where he has never charted, but where a specialist following of 20 years acclaims his visit.

85 Dec Signed in a new deal to Malaco Records, he records *Members Only*, which will reach Top 50 on US R&B chart in 1986. Malaco, based in Jackson, MS, is a fiercely independent, R&B-oriented label, an 80s equivalent of the musical environment in which Bland first succeeded. This album and its 1986 sequel *After All* confirm the singer's artistry to be intact even when retired from the pop chart mainstream.

88 Mar *Blues You Can Use* makes US #71 on US R&B chart.

89 Once again credited as Bobby "Blue" Bland, he has his biggest chart success in years when *Midnight Run* spends 70 weeks on US R&B chart, reaching #26.

LIND FAITH

ic Clapton (vocals, guitar)
eve Winwood (vocals, keyboards)
ck Grech (bass)
nger Baker (drums)

59 Feb Eric Clapton (b. Eric Patrick Clapp, Mar.30, 1945, Ripley, Surrey) and Ginger Baker (b. Peter Baker, Aug.19, 1939, Lewisham, London), remaining together after the demise of Cream in Nov.1968, join with Steve Winwood (b. May 12, 1948, Birmingham, W.Midlands) who has just quit Traffic. Rick Grech (b. Nov.1, 1946, Bordeaux, France) is invited to complete the band, and he leaves Family during a US tour to do so. The music press dubs the line-up an "instant supergroup".

June [7] After recording an album, the band plays live debut, and only ever UK date, in London's Hyde Park. Donovan joins them on stage.

July [12] Promoted as "The Ultimate Supergroup", Blind Faith makes its US concert debut at Madison Square Garden, New York. It is the start of a sell-out US stadium tour which, despite being financially rewarding, convinces band members that Blind Faith is musically unsatisfying, and that they should split when the tour is complete.

Sept [20] *Blind Faith* tops both US and UK charts for 2 weeks. The original UK sleeve with a picture of a nude 11-year-old girl (Baker's daughter) holding a "phallic" model airplane is considered too controversial for use in US. No single is released from the album. Band completes US tour; Clapton has already lost interest, and carries on touring with Delaney & Bonnie. Blind Faith does not play together again, despite manager Robert Stigwood's assertions that the group members will reunite in Jan. (Grech will stay with Baker in Airforce at the end of 1969, while Winwood will work solo before reforming Traffic early in 1970.)

72 Feb *Blind Faith* is reissued and makes US #126.

BLONDIE

Deborah Harry (vocals)
Chris Stein (guitar)
Jimmy Destri (keyboards)
Gary Valentine (bass)
Clem Burke (drums)

1974 Aug Group forms in New York, the original line-up pairing former Playboy bunny waitress Harry (b. July 1, 1945, Miami, FL) with the backing musicians from her earlier girl vocal group The Stilettos. Previously, Harry has recorded as a member of folk-rock band Wind In The Willows (who had an eponymous album on Capitol in July 1968) but other original members Stein (b. Jan.5, 1950, Brooklyn, New York, NY), a graduate of New York's School of Visual Arts, bassist Fred Smith and drummer Billy O'Connor have only played in local bands. With 2 girl back-up singers, and a repertoire based on the girl group sounds of the 60s, the group begins to play at noted New York punk birthplace, CBGBs.

Oct Czechoslovakian refugee Ivan Kral joins on guitar, and Tish and Snookie replace Julie and Jackie as back-up singers.

1975 Jan Kral, bored, leaves to join the Patti Smith Group.

May Ex-Sweet Revenge drummer Burke (b. Clement Burke, Nov.24, 1955, New York) replaces O'Connor when the latter goes to law school.

Aug Smith leaves to join Television, and is replaced by Valentine, a friend of Burke's.

Oct Ex-Knickers member Destri (b. Apr.13, 1954) joins on keyboards.

1976 Group signs to small Private Stock label, and makes debut single *X-Offender* and *Blondie* with producer Richard Gottehrer (once a member of The Strangeloves).

1977 Jan They make their US West Coast debut at the Whisky A-Go Go in Los Angeles, CA, with an image firmly focused on platinum blonde Harry, then tour nationally supporting Iggy Pop.

Feb *Blondie* is released in UK, where it attracts attention as being more accessible than other new wave acts such as New York Dolls and Sex Pistols. Shortly after, the band visits UK as support to Television.

July Valentine leaves to form his own group, The Know. Temporary replacement on bass is Frank Infante (ex-World War III) for recording of second album *Plastic Letters*, again produced by Gottehrer.

Aug Chrysalis Records buys Blondie's contract from Private Stock, also acquiring previously-recorded material.

Oct *Plastic Letters*, is released by Chrysalis, which also reissues the debut album.

Nov Infante moves to rhythm guitar, and UK bass player Nigel Harrison (ex-Silverhead) joins.

1978 Mar [18] Blondie breaks through in UK as *Denis (Denee)*, a remake of Randy & The Rainbows' 1963 US #10 *Denise*, hits #2, while *Plastic Letters* hits UK #10.

Apr [15] *Plastic Letters* makes US #72.

May [27] *(I'm Always Touched By Your) Presence Dear*, also from the album, hits UK #10. Group records a third album, switching producer to Mike Chapman (who as half of the Chinnichap production team has made numerous UK hits for Mud, The Sweet, Smokie and others.)

Sept [23] *Picture This*, first single from the Chapman session, reaches UK #12, and reflects a more deliberate commercial approach.

Dec [2] *Hanging On The Telephone*, second single from *Parallel Lines*, hits UK #5.

1979 Feb [3] *Heart Of Glass*, a disco-flavored third single (a far cry from Blondie's new wave beginnings) from *Parallel Lines*, tops UK chart for 4 weeks, and sells over a million copies in UK alone, making it band's biggest UK success. *Parallel Lines* tops UK chart for 4 weeks. [24] *Blondie* peaks at UK #75.

Apr [28] Group makes major US breakthrough as *Heart Of Glass* hits US #21, while parent album *Parallel Lines* hits US #6.

May [26] *Sunday Girl* also from album tops UK chart for 3 weeks.

Aug [4] *One Way Or Another*, from the same album, reaches US #24.

Sept Bomp Records in US and London Records in UK release *Little GTO*, by "The New York Blondes featuring Madame X". The latter is actually Harry, who is clearly heard on vocals. Chrysalis threatens legal action, and the single is withdrawn. [29] *Eat To The Beat* tops UK chart, remaining charted 9 months.

Oct [6] *Dreaming* from fourth album *Eat To The Beat*, produced by Chapman, hits UK #2.

Nov [24] *Eat To The Beat* reaches US #17.

Dec [1] *Dreaming* reaches US #27. [15] *Union City Blue*, a song connected with Debbie Harry-starring feature film "Union City", reaches UK #13.

BLONDIE cont.

1980 **Feb** [2] *The Hardest Part* stalls at US #84.
Mar [1] *Atomic*, from *Eat To The Beat*, tops UK chart for 2 weeks.
Apr [19] *Call Me*, a track written and produced by Giorgio Moroder for the soundtrack of Richard Gere movie "American Gigolo", to which Harry has written lyrics to fit Moroder's existing backing track, tops US chart, and is a million-seller.
[26] *Call Me* tops UK chart.
June Harry stars with Meat Loaf in the film "Roadie". The soundtrack includes Blondie's version of Johnny Cash's *Ring Of Fire*.
July *Atomic* makes US #39.
Nov [15] *The Tide Is High*, a light reggae number written by John Holt and previously recorded by The Paragons, hits UK #1 for 2 weeks, while *Autoamerican*, a return to Chapman's production, hits UK #3.
1981 **Jan** [31] *The Tide Is High* also tops US chart for a week (selling over a million), as *Autoamerican* hits US #7.
Feb Stein/Harry-penned *Rapture*, highlighted by an innovative Harry rap also excerpted from *Autoamerican*, with Tom Scott strongly featured on sax, hits UK #5. Harry announces that she is to record a solo album, produced by Nile Rodgers and Bernard Edwards of Chic.
Mar [28] *Rapture* tops US chart for 2 weeks, keeping John Lennon's *Woman* from #1 and becoming another million-seller.
Aug [8] Harry solo single *Backfired* makes UK #32.
[15] Parent album *Koo Koo* hits UK #6.
Sept [19] *Backfired* makes US #43, as *Koo Koo* reaches US #25.
Oct [31] Compilation *The Best Of Blondie* hits UK #4 and will reach US #30.
Nov [7] Second Harry solo single *The Jam Was Moving* stalls at US #82.
1982 **Jan** Infante sues the band, claiming he is being excluded from group activities. Following an out-of-court settlement, he remains a member.
June [5] Blondie's final album *The Hunter*, again a Chapman production, hits UK #9.
[12] Extracted *Island Of Lost Souls* reaches UK #11.
July [3] *Island Of Lost Souls* makes US #37, their last US chart single.
[10] *The Hunter* makes US #33.
[31] *War Child*, taken from *The Hunter*, is their final UK hit, making #39. A projected UK tour is cancelled due to insufficient advance audience interest.
Oct Group splits. (Subsequently, Stein will launch his own label, Animal Records, through Chrysalis, before becoming seriously ill. Harry will nurse him back to health and take occasional film acting roles (notably "Videodrome" with James Woods, and in John Waters' "Hairspray") before eventually relaunching her own solo singing career. The duo will also write a book, **Making Tracks: The Rise Of Blondie**. The others will mainly move into production or work with new groups: Burke eventually drums with Eurythmics. Destri releases solo album *Heart On The Wall*.)
1983 **Apr** [20] Harry stars as a wrestler with Andy Kaufman in the comedy "Teaneck Tanzi: The Venus Flytrap" at the Nederlander theater, New York. The show ignominiously closes after its opening night. She then retires to look after Stein, who is seriously ill.
1986 **Dec** Harry returns to UK chart with *French Kissin' (In The USA)*, which hits #8, and parent *Rockbird*, which climbs to US #97 and UK #31.
1987 **Jan** [10] *French Kissin' (In The USA)* peaks at US #57.
Mar Another Harry solo, *Free To Fall*, makes UK #46.
May *In Love With Love*, third single from *Rockbird*, makes UK #45.
July [25] *In Love With Love* peaks at US #70.
1988 **Dec** *Denis* (remix) makes UK #50. It is included on *Once More Into The Bleach*, an album of inexplicably updated remixes of earlier Blondie hits which peaks at UK #50.
1989 **Feb** *Call Me* remix peaks at US #61.
Mar Harry appears in and performs *Bright Side* in CBS TV's "Wiseguy".
July [12] Disney press conference announces Harry will play The Old Woman Who Lived In A Shoe in Disney Channel's Shelley Duvall-produced "Mother Goose Rock'N'Rhyme", with Paul Simon, Bobby Brown, Art Garfunkel, Little Richard and Cyndi Lauper among others.
Oct [3] Harry makes her live UK comeback, after a 7-year absence, at the small Borderline club in London.
Nov Harry comeback single, still via Chrysalis but now known as Deborah Harry, *I Want That Man*, reaches UK #13, as parent album, produced by old stalwart Chapman and The Thompson Twins' Tom Bailey, *Def, Dumb And Blonde* reaches UK #12 and US #123. Meanwhile Harry undertakes US concert tour with a backing band including Stein (guitar), Leigh Fox (bass), Jimmy Clark (drums), Carla Olla (rhythm guitar) and Suzy Davis (keyboards).
1990 Harry's live performances during the year will include US dates in Feb., supporting Tears For Fears and another UK visit including June 2-3 at the Brixton Academy, London.
Apr Also from *Def Dumb And Blonde*, *Sweet And Low* peaks at UK #5?
Oct Harry and Iggy Pop contribute *Well Did You Evah* to *Red Hot + Blue*, an anthology of Cole Porter songs to benefit AIDS education.
1991 **Jan** [19] *Well Did You Evah* peaks at UK #42.
Mar [23] A second Blondie retrospective *The Complete Picture – The Very Best Of Deborah Harry And Blondie* hits UK #3.

BLOOD, SWEAT & TEARS

David Clayton-Thomas (lead vocals)
Steve Katz (guitar, harmonica, vocals)
Jim Fielder (bass)
Bobby Colomby (drums, percussion, vocals)
Fred Lipsius (piano, alto saxophone)
Dick Halligan (keyboards, trombone, flute, vocals)
Chuck Winfield (trumpet, flugelhorn)
Lew Soloff (trumpet, flugelhorn)
Jerry Hyman (trombone, recorder)

1967 **Dec** [16] CBS launches new signing Blood, Sweat & Tears at the Scene in New York.
1968 **Apr** Envisioned by Al Kooper (b. Feb.5, 1944, Brooklyn, New York, NY), Katz (b. May.9, 1945, New York), Colomby (b. Dec.20, 1944, New York) and Fielder (b. Oct.4, 1947, Denton, TX) as an experimental rock quartet with a horn section, comprising Lipsius (b. Nov.19, 1944, New York), Halligan (b. Aug.29, 1943, Troy, NY), Randy Brecker (b. Nov.27, 1945, Philadelphia, PA) and Jerry Weiss, recruited from the New York session scene, accommodating jazz and serious music forms and players, the band debuts with *The Child Is Father To The Man*, on CBS/Columbia Records, which wraps Kooper's songs and some pop cover versions in tight brass and string arrangements. It reaches US #47, but Kooper and 2 horn players, Brecker and Weiss soon leave.
July [13] *The Child Is Father To The Man* makes UK #40.
1969 **Mar** [29] A new line-up fronted by Clayton-Thomas (b. David Thomsett, Sept.13, 1941, Surrey), with horn recruits Winfield (b. Feb.5, 1943, Monessen, PA), Soloff (b. Feb.20, 1944, Brooklyn, New York) and Hyman (b. May 19, 1947, New York), produces *Blood, Sweat & Tears*, which tops US chart for 7 weeks and sells over 2 million copies by the end of the year, while laying the ground rules for most of the 70s rock/jazz fusion boom.
Apr [12] A revival of old Motown ballad *You've Made Me So Very Happy* hits US #2, the first of 3 million-sellers from the album.
[30] *You've Made Me So Very Happy* reaches UK #35 (the band's only UK hit single), while *Blood, Sweat & Tears* makes UK #15.
July [5] *Spinning Wheel*, written by Clayton-Thomas, hits US #2, as the band plays Atlanta Pop Festival before 140,000 people.
Nov Laura Nyro-penned *And When I Die* hits US #2, and becomes the third million-selling single from *Blood, Sweat & Tears*, the first time in RIAA history that 3 singles from one album have all gone gold.
1970 **Mar** [11] *Blood, Sweat & Tears* wins Best Album, Best Arrangements Accompanying A Vocalist (Lipsius for *Spinning Wheel*) and Best Contemporary Instrumental Performance (*Trios Gymnopedies On A Theme By Erik Satie*) at the 12th annual Grammy awards.
June Group embarks on a US State Department-sponsored cultural tour of East Europe, taking in Romania, Poland and Yugoslavia.
Aug [8] *Blood, Sweat & Tears 3* tops US chart for 2 weeks and reache UK #14.
[29] Extracted single, a cover of Goffin-King's *Hi-De-Ho*, makes US #1
Nov [7] *Lucretia MacEvil* reaches US #29.
1971 **Feb** Band scores and plays music for the film "The Owl And The Pussycat", the soundtrack album of which reaches US #186.
Aug *B, S & T; 4*, recorded in San Francisco, CA, made with new horn player Dave Bargeron (b. Sept.6, 1942, Massachusetts), who has replaced Hyman, hits US #10.
[28] Extracted single, *Go Down Gamblin'*, makes US #32.
Nov [27] *Lisa, Listen To Me* peaks at US #73. Group plays its first concert with full symphony orchestra in New Orleans, LA.
Dec [31] Clayton-Thomas and Lipsius make their last appearances with the band at the Anaheim Convention Center, Anaheim, CA.
1972 **Jan** Blind singer Bobby Doyle (b. Houston, TX), once leader of The Bobby Doyle Trio, which included Kenny Rogers, Georg Wadenius from Swedish band Made In Sweden and saxophonist Joe Henderson join the group. The new line-up fails to gel, and the band reorganizes with Jerry Fisher (b. 1943, DeKalb, TX), who takes over on vocals, Lou Marini Jr. (b. Charleston, NC) and Larry Willis (b. New York, NY)

joining, while original member Halligan leaves.

Apr Compilation *Greatest Hits* reaches US #19.

Nov [25] *So Long Dixie* reaches #44 in US, and *New Blood*, produced by Colomby, peaks at #32.

1973 **Aug** [25] *No Sweat* peaks at US #72. After Katz, Winfield and Marini leave, the band's personnel becomes extremely fluid, varying from concert to concert, although Jerry LaCroix takes over vocal/harmonica duties briefly and Tom Malone becomes a permanent member.

1974 **July** [13] *Tell Me That I'm Wrong*, with Clayton-Thomas back on vocals, after cutting solo albums for Columbia and RCA, peaks at US #83.
Sept *Mirror Image* stalls at US #149.

1975 **July** [12] A revival of The Beatles' *Got To Get You Into My Life* peaks at US #62, as parent album *New City* makes US #47.

1976 **Aug** [7] *More Than Ever*, with guest vocalists Chaka Khan and Patti Austin, is another disappointing seller (US #165), after which the band is dropped by Columbia.

1977 **Nov** Signed to ABC records with line-up now Clayton-Thomas (vocals), Dave Bargeron (trombone), Randy Bernson (guitar), Larry Willis (b.New York, NY) (keyboards), Tony Klatka (trumpet), Bill Tillman (saxophones, flute), Forrest Buchtel (trumpet, flugelhorn), Mike Stern (guitars), Danny Trifan (bass), Roy McCurdy (drums) and Colomby (percussion), they record *Brand New Day*, produced by Bobby Colomby and Roy Halee, but it is not a major seller. (Personnel changes will continue to be made with Chris Albert (trumpet), Gregory Herbert (saxophone) and Neil Stubenhaus (bass), all spending some time with the group.)

1980 **Mar** *Nuclear Blues*, produced by Jerry Goldstein, is their second and last ABC release, but fails to chart. Line-up is Clayton-Thomas, Robert Piltch (guitar), Bruce Cassidy (trumpet, flugelhorn), Richard Martinez (keyboards), Bobby Economou (drums), Earl Seymour (saxophones, flute), David Piltch (bass) and Vernon Dorge (saxophones, flute). (After this, the band fades from view for most of the next 8 years, although Clayton-Thomas and Colomby (who jointly own the name Blood, Sweat & Tears) occasionally put together an aggregation for live work.)

1988 **July** Clayton-Thomas and a re-formed Blood, Sweat & Tears play live dates in the US.

1990 Clayton-Thomas sues the writers of Milli Vanilli's *All Or Nothing* for not giving him credit (and royalties) for its similarity to *Spinning Wheel*.

MIKE BLOOMFIELD

1965 Bloomfield (b. July 28, 1944, Chicago, IL), who learned blues guitar as a teenager from Chicago giants like Muddy Waters, joins The Paul Butterfield Blues Band, after acoustic gigs with Nick Gravenites on vocals and Charley Musselwhite on harmonica. The Butterfield Band backs Dylan at the Newport Folk Festival. Bloomfield plays lead guitar on *Highway 61 Revisited* sessions.

1967 **Apr** After leaving Butterfield, Bloomfield forms Electric Flag. Band has Bloomfield on guitar, Barry Goldberg (keyboards), Buddy Miles (drums), Nick Gravenites (vocals), Harvey Brooks (bass), Marcus Doubleday (trumpet), and Peter Strazza and Herbie Rich (saxes). Bloomfield intends to combine blues with varied musical elements from the others' backgrounds.
June [16] Electric Flag debuts live at Monterey Pop Festival, CA. Album debut is *The Trip*, the soundtrack to an underground Peter Fonda film, which is a cult but not a chart hit.

1968 **Apr** First official Electric Flag album is *A Long Time Comin'*, which reaches US #31. Bloomfield quits the squabbling line-up while the album is on chart, leaving Miles to organize one more Electric Flag album *The Electric Flag*, which reaches US #76 in Feb.1969 before they all drift apart. Miles teams up with Hendrix, and Gravenites joins Big Brother & The Holding Company.
Bloomfield joins Al Kooper on *Super Session*, which reaches US #12.

1969 **Feb** First joint project success prompts an onstage recording of double *The Live Adventures Of Mike Bloomfield And Al Kooper* at the Fillmore, San Francisco, CA. It reaches US #18.
Apr Bloomfield plays live in Chicago with original idol Muddy Waters, the results being released on *Fathers And Sons*.
Nov Bloomfield solo *It's Not Killing Me* makes only US #127.

1970 Bloomfield writes the score for movie "Medium Cool". (He also pens soundtracks to "Steelyard Blues" in 1973 and Andy Warhol's "Bad".)

1973 **June** He collaborates on *Triumvirate* with John Paul Hammond and Dr. John. It reaches US #105.

1974 Bloomfield reunites with Miles, Goldberg and Gravenites with Roger Troy (bass), as Electric Flag for Atlantic label. *The Band Kept Playing* does not sell, and the group splits again.

1976 **June** He plays on *KGB*, debut album by KGB, which also includes Goldberg (keyboards), Ray Kennedy (vocals), Rick Grech (bass) and Carmine Appice (drums). It struggles to US #124, and Bloomfield leaves before the second (and last) KGB album *Motion*, never to play as a member of a band again.

1977 *If You Love These Blues, Play 'Em As You Please* is released in association with magazine **Guitar Player** as a virtuoso primer for blues guitarists, and is nominated for a Grammy award. He signs to small Takoma label, and records a series of uncommercial blues/roots albums over the next 4 years, including *Analine, Between The Hard Place And The Ground* and *Michael Bloomfield*.

1978 *Count Talent And The Originals*, on the Clouds label, reunites him with Gravenites and Naftalin.

1981 **Feb** [15] Bloomfield is found dead in his car in San Francisco of an apparently accidental drug overdose, just after the release of final album, ironically titled *Living In The Fast Lane*.

KURTIS BLOW

1976 After studying voice at the High School of Music and Art, and communications at New York City College, Blow (b. Kurt Walker, Aug.9, 1959, New York, NY) begins rapping as a DJ in Harlem, New York clubs. He will hone his art over 3 years at New York venues like Small's Paradise, working with Grandmaster Flash, among others.

1979 **Nov** He signs to Mercury Records just as Sugarhill Gang's *Rapper's Delight* is becoming the first international rapping pop hit.
Dec Debut release is the seasonal *Christmas Rappin'*, which fails to chart in US, but reaches UK #30.

1980 **Sept** *The Breaks* makes US #87, but with huge specialist-market sales, particularly in New York, is a certified million-seller, and hits #4 on the R&B chart. It marks Blow's record debut with partner Davy D. on backing tracks. It makes UK #47.
Oct *Kurtis Blow*, produced by J.B. Moore and Robert Ford Jr., makes US #71.

1981 After finding wider performing success around US with Davy D. accompanying him at the turntables, he tours Europe and UK.
Aug *Deuce* makes US #137.

1982 **Oct** *Tough* peaks at US #167.

1984 **Oct** *Ego Trip* makes US #83.

1985 **Mar** [16] *Party Time* peaks at UK #67.
Apr Novelty rap *Basketball* makes US #71.
June René & Angela's *Save Your Love (For Number 1)*, which features Blow, peaks at UK #66.
Dec [14] Artists United Against Apartheid, comprising 49 artists including Blow, makes US #38 and UK #21 with *Sun City*.

1986 **Feb** *If I Ruled The World* is his biggest hit single, reaching UK #24.
Nov *I'm Chillin'* peaks at UK #64, after which Blow's profile drops as his flow of recordings stops.

1987 **May** *Rap's Greatest Hits Volume 2*, featuring Blow with Run DMC, Whodini and others, makes US #167.
Dec [13] *Kingdom Blow* stalls at US #196.

1988 **Sept** *Back By Popular Demand* makes #84 on US R&B chart, but Blow's career as a rap innovator and as one of the genre's founding fathers dissipates.

BLUE NILE

Paul Buchanan (vocals, synthesizer)
Robert Bell (synthesizer)
Paul Moore (synthesizer)

1983 Buchanan, Bell and Moore, all native Scots, form Blue Nile in their home town Glasgow, Scotland. Dedicated to crafting synthesizer-based easy-flowing musical collages around Buchanan's songs, they release *Tinseltown In The Rain*. A subsequent demo tape is used by a UK hi-fi equipment manufacturer, Linn, to test record cutting technology. Linn offers £250 worth of speakers to the band and will form its own Linn Records offshoot to specifically and uniquely sponsor and release future Blue Nile material.

1984 **May** Debut album *Walk Around The Rooftops*, recorded entirely in East Lothian, Scotland, and offering an impressionist musical landscape, which deeply impresses record reviewers, makes UK #80, licensed via Virgin Records.

1988 Trio, unimpressed by the demands or potential rewards of the record industry, has spent nearly 5 years on a follow-up album, meticulously writing and re-recording Buchanan's songs, with access to Linn's technological recording advances made available to them in their remote East Lothian studio.

1989 Oct Promoted with earnest trade and press ads, quoting enthusiasm for the band from the likes of Phil Collins and Sting, Blue Nile's second album *Hats*, again released on Linn, debuts at UK peak #12, while the slowly crescendoed *Downtown Lights* has recently made UK #67. Produced by the band, the 7-track, all Buchanan-penned set again wows reviewers, though in interviews the reluctant trio insist on the unimportance of it all.

1990 Apr [7] *Hats* peaks at US #108 during a 14-week chart visit, as several cuts including *Downtown Lights* and *Saturday Night* become popular modern and college radio items. Band makes a short spring visit to US to perform its debut live dates, with some trepidation.

Sept [13] After long-time champion of the band, Rickie Lee-Jones, has enticed Buchanan and Moore on stage earlier in the year on her US tour, to help them overcome stage nerves, Blue Nile finally begins its first, 6-date, UK tour, at the Free Trade Hall, Manchester, Gtr.Manchester, set to end Sept.23 at the Royal Concert Hall, Glasgow. Band, augmented by 3 additional musicians, insists on a no frills, no dry-ice, no T-shirt merchandising event, so that the audience can fully concentrate on the group's emotive music.

[29] Second album extract, *Headlights On The Parade*, stalls at UK #72. Having recently recorded a duet cover version of *Easter Parade* with Jones, Buchanan, with Moore and Bell, feature on Robbie Robertson's long-awaited second solo album.

1991 Jan [19] Released 16 months after its parent album, *Saturday Night* makes UK #50, as band retreats for another extended recording period.

BLUE ÖYSTER CULT

Eric Bloom (lead guitar, keyboards, "stun guitar")
Donald "Buck Dharma" Roeser (lead guitar, vocals)
Albert Bouchard (drums, vocals)
Allen Lanier (rhythm guitar, keyboards)
Joe Bouchard (bass, vocals)

1970 Band forms in Long Island, New York, out of The Stalk-Forrest Group, which itself has developed from 3 bands, The Cows, Soft White Underbelly and Oaxoa, a band originally launched at Stony Brook University by Roeser, Lanier, and Al Bouchard, along with **Crawdaddy** magazine writer Sandy Pearlman and Richard Meltzer. From its early beginnings, Pearlman has had a major influence on the band, and as its producer/manager, he is tagged as a Svengali figure.

1971 Oct After Elektra has rejected 2 albums from the group (first as Soft White Underbelly, then as The Stalk-Forrest Group), with vocalist Les Bronstein, and with Joe Bouchard and Bloom joining, they sign as Blue Öyster Cult to Columbia Records and begin recording debut album at the Warehouse with producers Murray Krugman and Sandy Pearlman.

1972 June Debut album *Blue Öyster Cult* encapsulates their trademark sound: fast, loud and heavy. It is a fair seller in US, reaching #172, and they begin extensive US touring as regular support to Alice Cooper.

1973 Apr *Tyranny And Mutation* climbs to US #122. Like the first album, it features some lyrics by non-member rock writer Meltzer.

1974 June *Secret Treaties*, which reaches US #53, includes songs written by Patti Smith, who becomes Lanier's girlfriend.

1975 Apr Live *On Your Feet Or On Your Knees*, recorded in Long Beach, New York, Phoenix, Portland, Seattle and Vancouver and Capitol theater, New Jersey, achieves the band's highest US Album chart placing, at #22.

1976 Aug *Agents Of Fortune*, contains the band's only sizeable hit single, the uncharacteristically mellow and Byrds-influenced *(Don't Fear) The Reaper*. This reaches US #12, while the album peaks at US #29 and UK #26, and is eventually awarded a platinum disk for a million-plus sales.

1977 Dec *Spectres* reaches US #43.

1978 Feb [4] *Spectres* makes UK #60, while in the US the band embarks on a massive 250-date tour, promoting the previous album and recording for a planned live release.

June 2 years after its US success, *(Don't Fear) The Reaper* becomes the band's only UK hit single, climbing to #16.

Oct Live *Some Enchanted Evening*, recorded in Atlanta, GA, Columbus, GA, Little Rock, AR and Newcastle, Tyne & Wear, reaches US #44 and UK #18.

1979 Aug *Mirrors*, produced by Tom Werman, makes US #44 and UK #46.

Sept Strings-arranged *In Thee*, taken from *Mirrors*, peaks at US #74.

1980 Aug *Cultosaurus Erectus*, produced by Martin Birch, reaches US #34 and UK #12, where it is their highest chart-placed album. Fantasy novelist Michael Moorcock co-writes one of its tracks, *Black Blade*.

1981 Aug *Fire Of Unknown Origin* reaches US #24 and UK #29. Moorcock again co-writes one track, while the band's previously most prolific songwriter, Al Bouchard, leaves after the climax of a UK tour at the Castle Donington Monsters Of Rock Festival. He is replaced by Rick Downey, for many years the band's crew chief on the road.

Oct *Burnin' For You*, from *Fire Of Unknown Origin* makes US #40.

Dec [15] Robbie Krieger joins the band on stage at the Country club in Reseda, CA, playing lead on The Doors' *Roadhouse Blues*.

1982 June Third live album *ETL (Extra-Terrestrial Live)*, recorded in Hollywood, FL, Long Island, NY, Philadelphia, PA, Reseda, CA, and Poughkeepsie, NY, reaches US #29 and UK #39.

Oct Roeser releases solo *Flat Out*, for Portrait Records, as Buck Dharma. It does not chart in US or UK.

1983 Dec *The Revolution By Night*, produced by Bruce Fairbairn, peaks at US #93 and UK #95.

1984 Feb *Shooting Shark*, taken from the album and written by Roeser and Patti Smith, makes US #83.

1986 Mar Group, now comprising Bloom, Joe Bouchard, Roeser and new recruits Jimmy Wilcox on percussion and Tommy Zvoncheck on keyboards, returns with *Club Ninja*, which makes US #63.

1988 Sept *Imaginos* peaks at US #122.

1989 Mar [7] Group begins a 13-date UK tour at the Manchester Apollo, ending Mar.20 at the Royal Café, Nottingham, Notts. (New band Deadringer, which includes Joe Bouchard with Neil Smith (ex-Alice Cooper), Dennis Dunaway, Charlie Huhn and Jay Johnson releases *Electrocution Of The Heart*.) Group, without support to embark on major arena tours, settles into a successful second-phase career playing club gigs, as many of the newer bands reflect the influence of the Blue Öyster Cult.

1990 CBS releases retrospective collection *Career Of Evil – The Metal Years*.

MICHAEL BOLTON

1979 Bolton (b. Michael Bolotin, Feb.26, 1953, New Haven, CT), youngest son of local Democratic Party official George Bolotin, and raised on the sounds of Motown and the blues, having auditioned for Shelter Records in Los Angeles, CA, has formed hard rock combo Blackjack with Bruce Kulick, Jimmy Halsip and Sandy Germarro, which releases debut set *Blackjack*, making US #127. A second album with the band, *Worlds Apart*, will fail to score and Bolton will secure a solo deal with CBS/Columbia. (Performing in Connecticut bars at age 15, Bolton has already recorded unsuccessful solo albums prior to joining Blackjack, helped by David Sanborn and Andy Newmark.)

1983 May [15] *Fools Game* peaks at US #82 as parent album *Michael Bolton* makes US #89. Aimed toward the hard rock market, the Gerry Block/Bolton co-produced project includes guest appearance by Aldo Nova and is dedicated to Bolton's father.

Oct [8] Bolton has his first major success as a writer when Laura Branigan reaches US #12 with *How Am I Supposed To Live Without You*.

1984 Bolton devotes himself to composition, building up songwriting relationships with the likes of Diane Warren, Eric Kaz, Desmond Child and Barry Mann and Cynthia Weil for acts including The Pointer Sisters, Irene Cara and Starship (who will cover his *Desperate Heart* cut from his unsuccessful 1985 album *Everybody's Crazy*.)

1987 Dec [12] Co-penned with Eric Kaz, breakthrough solo hit, soul-tinged ballad *That's What Love Is All About* reaches US #19 (Bolton has recently performed the song and his revival of Otis Redding's *(Sittin' On) The Dock Of The Bay* on US syndicated TV show "It's Showtime At The Apollo"), while parent album *The Hunger* climbs the US Album survey featuring title cut co-written with Journey's Jonathan Cain, who appears on the album with fellow Journeyman Neal Schon. Produced by Keith Diamond, and 2 cuts separately helmed by Journey's Cain and Susan Hamilton, album guests include James Ingram, Neal Schon and The Hawkins Singers. Highlighting the full virtuosity of Bolton's 4-octave vocal range, it will make US #46 during a 41-week run.

1988 Jan Bolton-penned and produced *I Found Someone* hits UK #5 for Cher

Mar [26] *(Sittin' On) The Dock Of The Bay*, reviving Redding's 1968 US chart-topper, reaches US #11. In a personal letter from widow Zelma Redding, she has recently called it "my all-time favorite version of my husband's classic".

Apr Bolton receives Best Male R&B Vocalist Of The Year at the annual New York Music Awards.

June [25] *Wait On Love* stalls at US #79, while Bolton is midway through a 2-month cross-country US tour with Heart.

Oct Bolton travels to Moscow, USSR, as a member of a US songwriting team (including Warren, Mann, Weil, Cyndi Lauper, Holly Knight,

Brenda Russell, Tom Kelly and Billy Steinberg) to collaborate on album *Glasnost*, written and performed with USSR counterparts.

Dec Bolton performs 4 songs (including *I Found Someone*) in front of an audience of his peers, including Lamont Dozier, Carole King, Jimmy Webb and Brian Wilson, at the VH1 broadcast "Fourth Annual Salute To The American Songwriter" at the Wiltern theater, Los Angeles.

1989
June [22] Bolton sings *Georgia On My Mind* and *Yesterday* and duets with Jeffrey Osborne on *You've Lost That Lovin' Feelin'* at the Songwriters Hall Of Fame, held at Radio City Music Hall, New York, (subsequently broadcast on CBS TV).

July *Soul Provider* is released set to hit US #3 during a year's chart stay. Co-produced with Peter Bunetta, Michael Omartian, Desmond Child and Susan Hamilton, it features an airplay-attracting mix of soul, rock and power ballads, variously co-written with Mann and Weil, Andy Goldmark, Warren, Kaz and others, and showcasing Bolton's awesome vocal power.

Aug Bolton receives 2 airplay awards at the annual ASCAP Awards for *I Found Someone* and *That's What Love Is All About*.

Sept [16] Title cut *Soul Provider*, featuring Kenny G on saxophone, reaches US #17.

1990
Jan [20] Power ballad *How Am I Supposed To Live Without You*, reviving Laura Branigan's 1983 US #12, tops Hot 100.

Feb [21] Bolton wins Best Pop Vocal Performance, Male for *How Am I Supposed To Live Without You* at the 32nd annual Grammy awards at the Shrine Auditorium, Los Angeles.

Mar [3] UK debut *How Am I Supposed To Live Without You* hits #3.

Apr [21] Co-written with Paul Stanley, Kiss ballad *Forever* hits US #8, while Bolton features on newly released benefit album *Requiem For The Americas For Save The Children* (US #166).

May [5] Further power ballad *How Can We Be Lovers* hit US #3.

June [2] *How Can We Be Lovers* hits UK #10.

Aug [4] *When I'm Back On My Feet Again*, Warren-penned, hits US #7.

[25] Reissued *The Hunger* makes UK #44, while *Soul Provider* is on its way to hit UK #4 and double platinum status (triple in US).

Oct [6] Remake of Ray Charles' classic *Georgia On My Mind* makes US #36, while soaring *When I'm Back On My Feet Again* makes UK #44.

Dec [28-31] Bolton ends his most successful career year to date with 4 performances at the Universal Amphitheater, Universal City, CA. His US trek is also named Tour Of The Year by **Pollstar**.

1991
Feb [10] Bolton joins nearly 100 celebrities in Burbank, CA, to record *Voices That Care*, a David Foster and fiancee Linda Thompson Jenner composed and organized charity record to benefit the American Red Cross Gulf Crisis Fund.

Apr [20] *Love Is A Wonderful Thing*, written with Andy Goldmark and from forthcoming album *Time, Love & Tenderness* (featuring regular writing partners Diane Warren and Desmond Child as well *Steel Bars*, written with Bob Dylan and a duet with Patti LaBelle), enters Hot 100 at US #36. Bolton performs the single on NBC TV's "Saturday Night Live" prior to a 5-month US tour. He also participates in an all-star spoof charity troupe, Musicians For Free Range Chickens (in which he is the only genuine all-star).

BON JOVI
Jon Bon Jovi (vocals)
Richie Sambora (guitar)
David Bryan (keyboards)
Alec John Such (bass)
Tico Torres (drums)

1983
Mar Band is formed in Sayreville, NJ, by Bon Jovi (b. John Bongiovi, Mar.2, 1962, Sayreville, NJ), his mother Carol, an ex-Playboy bunny and his father a hairdresser, and Bryan (b. David Rashbaum, Feb.7, 1962, New Jersey) who have played together in high school and later in local cover version bands. They recruit Sambora (b. July 11, 1959) and Such (b. Nov.14, 1956), ex-Phantom's Opera, who have disbanded their own club act Message in 1982 and Torres (b. Oct.7, 1953), whose musical past has included stints with Franke & The Knockouts and performances in strip bars. Bon Jovi, who after leaving high school has swept the floor for his cousin Tony Bongiovi who was working at the Record Plant, New York, where Bon Jovi subsequently cuts a demo, has already played in a number of bands including a 10-piece R&B group The Rest (who at one point supported Hall & Oates), The Wild Ones, Johnny & The Lechers, The Raze and Atlantic City Expressway, who opened for Bruce Springsteen, The Asbury Jukes and Squeeze among others.

July [1] Band signs to Phonogram's Mercury label and begins building solid live reputation on the hard rock circuit, including future slots for Z.Z. Top, and starts work on its debut album.

1984
Apr *Runaway*, a track first recorded by Bon Jovi as a solo effort which has won inclusion on radio station WDHA-FM's compilation album of unsigned acts, becomes the band's debut chart single, making US #39. *Bon Jovi* reaches US #43 and UK #71.

July [14] *She Don't Know Me* makes US #48.

Oct During the band's first UK tour, 1 gig is broadcast by BBC Radio 1.

1985
May [25] *Only Lonely* peaks at US #54.

7800° Fahrenheit makes US #37, is the group's first gold album and also reaches UK #28.

Aug [17] *In And Out Of Love* peaks at US #69.

[31] *Hardest Part Is The Night* is their UK Singles chart debut for 1 week at #68.

1986
Sept UK chart breakthrough, the hard rocking but melodic *You Give Love A Bad Name*, reaches UK #14.

Oct [25] *Slippery When Wet*, recorded at Vancouver's Little Mountain studios with Bruce Fairbairn, tops US chart for 8 weeks and will go on to sell 8 million copies by the end of 1987. It also hits UK #6.

Nov [29] *You Give Love A Bad Name* tops US chart, becoming their first million-selling single worldwide.

Dec *Livin' On A Prayer* hits UK #4. *Bon Jovi* re-charts at US #77.

1987
Jan *Slippery When Wet* returns to US #1, where it will stay for a further 7 weeks.

Feb [14] *Livin' On A Prayer* tops US chart for 3 weeks.

Apr Rock ballad *Wanted Dead Or Alive* reaches UK #13.

June [6] *Wanted Dead Or Alive* hits US #7.

Aug [22] Bon Jovi tops the bill of annual Monsters Of Rock Festival at Castle Donington, Leics., climaxing a year in which it has become the most popular heavy rock band in the world.

Never Say Goodbye reaches UK #21.

Dec Group ends year having played 130 shows in the "Tour Without End", grossing $28,400,000.

1988
Apr [25] As the group takes a rest, its manager, Doc McGee is convicted of drug offenses in connection with the 1982 seizure of nearly 40,000lb. of marijuana, smuggled into North Carolina from Colombia, and sentenced to a $15,000 fine, a 5-year suspended prison term and extensive community service.

Oct [1] *New Jersey* hits US #1.

[15] *New Jersey* tops US chart for 4 weeks.

Bad Medicine reaches UK #17.

Nov [19] *Bad Medicine* tops US chart.

Dec *Born To Be My Baby* reaches UK #22.

1989
Feb [18] *Born To Be My Baby* hits US #3.

Mar Bon Jovi is charged with trespassing after being caught on the ice at New York's City Wollman skating rink at 3.30am with girlfriend Hurley and another couple.

[15] At Meadowlands, East Rutherford, NJ, homecoming concert, the Mayor of Sayreville hands the group the keys to the city in honor of Bon Jovi Day.

Apr Bon Jovi gives away childhood home in MTV promotion.

[29] Bon Jovi marries childhood sweetheart Dorothea Hurley on the steps of the Graceland Chapel, Las Vegas, NV, in the presence of Reverend George Colton.

May Rock ballad *I'll Be There For You* reaches UK #18.

May [13] *I'll Be There For You* tops US chart.

June Sambora begins a romantic relationship with Cher, later announcing that "Cher's very cool".

July [10] David F. Pearsall, 18, of Manchester, NH , is charged with theft and released on $1,000 bail, after allegedly stealing Sambora's $2,000 white Kramer guitar at a July 8 concert at Riverfront Park.

[29] *Lay Your Hands On Me* hits US #7.

Aug [11] *New Jersey* is released in USSR. Bon Jovi is paid the maximum allowable license fee $9,600 from the Russian record company, Melodiya.

[12-13] Group headlines the Moscow Music Peace Festival at Lenin Stadium with Ozzy Osbourne, Motley Crue, The Scorpions, Cinderella, Skid Row, Drum Madness and from USSR Gorky Park, Nuance, CCCP and Brigada S. All proceeds go to programs that fight drug and alcohol abuse in US and USSR.

[19] Group headlines a bill, which includes Europe, Vixen and Skid Row, at the Milton Keynes Bowl, Bucks. Aerosmith's Steve Tyler and Joe Perry join them for an encore of *Walk This Way*.

Sept [6] Bon Jovi and Sambora perform at MTV Music Video Awards at the Universal Amphitheater, Los Angeles, CA.

Lay Your Hands On Me reaches UK #18.

Oct [15-16] Torres participates in the first World Music Invitational pro/am celebrity golf tournament at Stonebridge Ranch in Dallas, TX.
Dec Bon Jovi contributes to the hard rock compilation album *Stairway To Heaven/Highway To Hell*, produced by Bruce Fairbairn, for the Make A Difference Foundation – Rockers Against Drug And Alcohol Abuse, with Skid Row, The Scorpions and others.
Living In Sin makes UK #35.
[16] *Living In Sin* hits US #9.

1990 **Feb** At the end of another massive world trek, Bon Jovi's 16-month 237-date world tour ends.
Apr Bon Jovi and Bobby Bandiera play at one of 3 benefits for 8-year-old Tishna Rollo, daughter of producer/engineer John Rollo, battling Wilm's Tumor, at the Stone Pony, Asbury Park, NJ. Sambora's solo *The Wind Cries Mary* is featured in Andrew Dice Clay movie "The Adventures Of Ford Fairlane".
July Bon Jovi makes a cameo appearance in "Young Guns II" and writes theme *Blaze Of Glory* and entire soundtrack for the movie with contributions from Little Richard, Jeff Beck and Elton John. During a sabbatical from the group, he also writes with Aldo Nova and tours with Southside Johnny.
Aug [25] *Blaze Of Glory/Young Guns II* hits UK #2.
Sept [8] *Blaze Of Glory*, Bon Jovi's first solo success, hits US #1, aided by mountain-top located promoclip, heavily rotated on MTV, and reaches UK #13. Parent album *Blaze Of Glory/Young Guns II* hits US #3 in only its third week of release.
Nov [15] Bon Jovi is honored with the Silver Clef Award at the third annual Nordoff-Robbins Therapy Centre lunch at Roseland, New York.
Dec [22] *Miracle* reaches US #12, having made UK #29.
[23] Group reassembles for a charity concert to benefit the Monmouth County Arts Council and Holmdel's Sisters Of The Good Shepherd at the Count Basie theater, Red Bank, NJ. It is the group's first gig of 1990.
[31] They play at the Tokyo Dome, Japan, with Cinderella, The London Quireboys and Skid Row at start of 15-date overseas tour.

1991 **Jan** [19] *Blaze Of Glory* wins Best Original Song at the Golden Globe film awards.
[28] *Blaze Of Glory* wins Pop/Rock Single at the 18th annual American Music Awards at the Shrine Auditorium, Los Angeles.
Mar [25] Bon Jovi performs the Oscar-nominated *Blaze Of Glory* at the annual Academy Awards.

GARY U.S. BONDS

1959 The son of a college professor and music teacher, Bonds (b. Gary Anderson, June 6, 1939, Jacksonville, FL) has been performing in Norfolk, VA, where his father is a college professor and his mother a music teacher, with his doo-wop group The Turks when he signs to Frank Guida's local LeGrand Records as a soloist. The studio is a poorly-equipped room behind Guida's record store, Frankie's Birdland, but the odd acoustics and makeshift effects combine to create a unique "outdoor" sound.

1960 **Sept** First single *New Orleans* is issued nationally after local interest. Guida names Anderson as U.S. Bonds because "buy U.S. Bonds" proves an effective promotional tag. Anderson is not aware of his new identity until he hears it on the radio.
Nov *New Orleans* hits US #6, but quickly-released follow-up *Not Me* does not chart.

1961 **Feb** *New Orleans* reaches UK #16.
June *Quarter To Three*, with a Guida lyric on Gene Barge's earlier instrumental *A Night With Daddy G* and which Bonds later recalls making while he and the band were drunk, tops US chart for 2 weeks and is a million-seller.
Aug *Quarter To Three* hits UK #7. The song will become involved in a lawsuit in 1962, because of Chubby Checker's alleged plagiarism of it on his hit *Dancin' Party*.
Sept *School Is Out* hits US #5, but fails to chart in UK, as will the balance of Bonds' LeGrand label US hits. From this record on, his billing is adapted to Gary U.S. Bonds, at the request of both himself and the United States Bonds authorities.
Oct *Dance Till Quarter To Three* hits US #6.
Nov *School Is In* is an answerback part 2 of the previous single, and reaches US #28.

1962 **Feb** *Dear Lady Twist* exploits the year's big dance craze, hitting US #9.
Apr [21] Bonds begins a 23-date twice-nightly UK tour with Johnny Burnette, Gene McDaniels, Mark Wynter, Danny Rivers and others, at St. Andrew's Hall, Glasgow, Scotland. Tour will end at the Granada cinema, Walthamstow, London on May 13.

May Same craze-oriented *Twist, Twist Señora* hits US #9.
July *Seven Day Weekend* reaches US #27.
Sept Unique sound formula proves to have worn thin on *Copy Cat*, which stalls at US #92. (Bonds' hit run stops, though he continues recording for LeGrand for 4 or 5 more years – in 1963 turning down *If You Wanna Be Happy*, which label-mate Jimmy Soul then takes to US #1. He will continue US live dates in the 60s and 70s, but spend more time songwriting with Jerry "Swamp Dogg" Williams and producing Doris Duke, Z.Z. Hill, Johnny Paycheck and others, than recording.)

1969 **Nov** [29] Bonds takes part in Richard Nader's second "Rock'N'Roll Revival" concert with Jackie Wilson, Bill Haley & His Comets and a host of other late 50s/early 60s acts, at Madison Square Garden, New York. He will be a regular performer on Nader's bill through the years.

1975 **Mar** Now signed to Prodigal, Bonds records *Grandma's Washboard Band*, but it fails to restore his chart status.

1978 Playing New Jersey club the Red Baron, he invites audience member Bruce Springsteen on stage, a long-time fan who has performed *Quarter To Three* live frequently. They become friends and Springsteen suggests Bonds works with him and his guitarist Miami Steve Van Zandt on a comeback album, *Dedication*, as a shared production.

1981 **Apr** *Dedication*, released by EMI America Records, reaches US #22.
June *This Little Girl*, from the album and penned by Springsteen, reaches US #11 and UK #43.
Aug A revival of oldie *Jolé Blon* peaks at US #65 and UK #51. *Dedication* makes UK #43.
Nov The Lennon/McCartney song *It's Only Love* makes UK #43.

1982 **June** [12] Bonds takes part in a rally for nuclear disarmament in Central Park, New York, with Jackson Browne, Linda Ronstadt, Bruce Springsteen and James Taylor, before an audience of 750,000.
July *On The Line*, again produced by Springsteen with Van Zandt, with The E. Street Band providing most of the back-up, makes US #52 and UK #55.
July A revival of The Box Tops' *Soul Deep* peaks at UK #59.
Aug Springsteen-written *Out Of Work* reaches US #21.

1984 **Aug** Bonds puts together new backing group, The American Men, and signs to Phoenix Records, releasing *Standing In The Line Of Fire*. (After this, his chart success will wane again, but the comeback generated by the Springsteen association and its hits will maintain his high profile as a live performer.)

BONEY M

Bobby Farrell (vocals)
Marcia Barrett (vocals)
Liz Mitchell (vocals)
Maisie Williams (vocals)

1976 Writer/producer Frank Farian, working as a producer with Peter Meisel's Munich, Germany-based Hansa label, records *Baby Do You Wanna Bump?*, using sessions singers and musicians. (This causes a furore in 1990, when it is revealed that his creation, Milli Vanilli, have not performed on their debut album.) After *Baby Do You Wanna Bump?* begins selling well in Holland, Farian puts together a group to perform in clubs and discos to promote the record further. Although all its members are of West Indian origin, the quartet is already working individually in Germany, Farrell (b. Oct.6, 1949, Aruba, West Indies) as a club DJ, Mitchell (b. July 12, 1952, Clarendon, Jamaica) in the German cast of "Hair", taking over from Donna Summer, who by now has achieved worldwide fame with her debut *Love To Love You Baby*, and Barrett (b. Oct.14, 1948, St. Catherine's, Jamaica) and Williams (b. Mar.25, 1951, Montserrat, West Indies), both doing session work. Their role is to sing vocals on Farian's electronic disco-style productions, and also to provide a focus for live and TV performances of the records.

1977 **Feb** *Daddy Cool*, with electronic dance beat and stylized female/bass male vocals, sets the basic style and sound of the group. It reaches UK #6 and US #65.
Apr A revival of Bobby Hebb's 1966 hit *Sunny* hits UK #3. *Take The Heat Off Me* is issued, climbing to UK #40.
July *Ma Baker* hits UK #2, but only makes US #96.
Aug [6] *Love For Sale* makes UK #60.
Dec *Belfast*, with a "socially aware" lyric, hits UK #8.

1978 **May** [13] An adaptation of The Melodians' reggae standard, *Rivers Of Babylon*, shoots to #1 in UK and stays at the top for 5 weeks.
Aug *Rivers Of Babylon* reaches US #30, and is their biggest US hit.
Sept When *Rivers Of Babylon* finally fades, UK radio starts playing the B-side, the traditional *Brown Girl In The Ring*, and the single takes off

again with this as the featured side, re-hitting UK #2. Total UK sales are eventually just short of 2 million, making it the country's #2 all-time best-selling single (behind only Wings' *Mull Of Kintyre*).

[9] *Night Flight To Venus*, containing both sides of the mega-single, hits UK #1 for 4 weeks, staying on chart for 65 weeks. The album also makes US #134.

Oct *Rasputin*, taken from the album, and with a disco arrangement parodying Cossack dance music, hits UK #2.

Dec **[9]** A revival of Harry Belafonte's 1957 hit *Mary's Boy Child* is released for Christmas, arranged by Farian in a medley with his own *Oh My Lord* (which ensures him half the writing/publishing royalties). It rapidly tops UK chart, staying for 4 weeks and selling over 1 million copies, putting it in the UK all-time Top 5 singles sellers. In US it reaches #85, and is their last US chart entry.

979 **Mar** A revival of *Painter Man*, originally by the mid-60s UK band Creation, hits UK #10.

May Calypso-styled *Hooray! Hooray! It's A Holi-Holiday* hits UK #3.

Sept *Gotta Go Home/El Lute* reaches UK #12.

[29] *Oceans Of Fantasy* tops UK chart.

980 **Jan** *I'm Born Again* is their first single not to make the UK Top 30, peaking at #35.

May Another revival, The Smoke's 1967 UK hit *My Friend Jack*, reaches UK #57.

[17] Hits compilation *The Magic Of Boney M* is UK #1 for 2 weeks.

981 **Feb** **[21]** *Children Of Paradise* peaks at UK #66.

Nov **[28]** *We Kill The World (Don't Kill The World)*, with an ecological message, revives UK chart fortunes by climbing to #39, but it will be their final hit record, witnessing the group's subsequent rapid demise.

986 **Sept** Compilation album *The Best Of 10 Years* reaches UK #35.

988 **Dec** *Megamix/Mary's Boy Child* peaks at UK #52. (With interest renewed from the reissue of original Boney M music, the group re-forms for the club and cabaret circuit.)

HE BONZO DOG DOO-DAH BAND

ivian Stanshall (vocals, trumpet)
eil Innes (vocals, piano)
odney Slater (sax, trumpet)
oger Ruskin Spear (sax, kazoo, mechanical objects)
ernon Dudley Bohay-Nowell (guitar, banjo)
am Spoons (percussion)
Legs" Larry Smith (drums)

965 Group is formed by a group of art students at Goldsmith's College, Lewisham, London, as a whimsical, 20s-inspired outfit (originally The Bonzo Dog Dada Band). Led by Slater (b. Nov.8, 1944, Lincolnshire) and Spear (b. June 29, 1943, London) but with an otherwise fluid personnel of up to 30, the number is reduced to a stable 7, comprising Innes (b. Dec.9, 1944, Essex), Stanshall (b.Mar.21, 1943, Shillingford, Oxon), Smith (b. Jan.18, 1944, Oxford, Oxon) and Spoons (b. Martin Stafford) when they start playing London pub gigs.

966 **Apr** They move to the club and cabaret circuit, where Spear's job is mainly to manage the considerable number of props and gadgets involved in their stage act. They also sign to EMI's Parlophone label, releasing *My Brother Makes The Noises For The Talkies*, which fails.

Sept They revive The Hollywood Argyles' *Alley Oop*, again without success.

967 **Oct** Moving to Liberty Records, the group shows its increasingly diversified musical approach, and skills at parody, on debut album *Gorilla*, but neither this nor the extracted *Equestrian Statue* chart.

Dec They appear in The Beatles' TV musical film "Magical Mystery Tour", performing *Death Cab For Cutie*.

968 **Jan** They begin a residency on the ITV satirical comedy series "Do Not Adjust Your Set", indulging their musical and comic talents through 13 weekly shows.

Apr When the TV series ends, Spoons and Bohay-Nowell leave, and Dennis Cowan (b. May 6, 1947, London) joins on bass in preparation for album recording sessions.

Dec *I'm The Urban Spaceman*, an Innes song produced by Paul McCartney pseudonymously as Apollo C. Vermouth, hits UK #5.

969 **Jan** **[18]** *The Doughnut In Granny's Greenhouse* makes UK #40.

Mar *Mr. Apollo* is released but does not chart.

Aug **[30]** *Tadpoles* reaches UK #36, as the band plays on the opening day of Isle of Wight Festival of Music.

Nov *Keynsham* (named after the district of Bristol, Avon, plugged incessantly on Radio Luxembourg by football pools' entrepreneur Horace Bachelor) does not chart; nor do *I Want To Be With You* and *You*

Done My Brain In, extracted from it in quick succession.

1970 **Jan** Group breaks up, despite being a consistently popular club and touring attraction. Smith joins Bohay-Nowell and Spoons in Bob Kerr's Whoopee Band, while Spear becomes a solo novelty act.

Aug Compilation album *The Best Of The Bonzo Dog Doo-Dah Band* is released in UK, without charting. Meanwhile, most of the individual members pursue solo projects. (Stanshall and Innes will keep the highest profiles through into the 80s: the former as a TV and radio personality, creator of movie "Sir Henry At Rawlinson End", Master of Ceremonies for Mike Oldfield's *Tubular Bells*, and lyricist for Steve Winwood's *Arc Of A Diver*; the latter as a composer, songwriter, TV performer, ad jingle singer, and collaborator with Eric Idle on "Rutland Weekend Television" and The Beatles' spoof, The Rutles).

1971 **Nov** Stanshall, Innes and Cowan revive Bonzo Dog name, and with help from Bubs White (guitars), Andy Roberts (guitars, fiddle), Dave Richards (bass), Dick Parry (saxophone, flute) and Hughie Flint (drums) start recording *Let's Make Up And Be Friendly* in Oxfordshire.

1972 **May** *Let's Make Up And Be Friendly* makes US #199.

1974 **June** **[22]** Double compilation album *The History Of The Bonzos* reaches UK #41.

1990 **Apr** **[27]** Double album retrospective *Bestiality Of Bonzo Dog Doo Dah Band* is released on Liberty label.

BOOKER T. & THE MG'S

Booker T. Jones (keyboards)
Steve Cropper (guitar)
Lewis Steinberg (bass)
Donald "Duck" Dunn (bass)
Al Jackson Jr. (drums)

1962 **May** Jones (b. Dec.11, 1944, Memphis, TN), Cropper (b. Oct.21, 1941, Willow Springs, MO), Jackson (b. Nov.27, 1935, Memphis) and Steinberg are all working as regular session musicians in Stax Records' Memphis studio (as well as recording as part of The Mar-Keys) when they record 2 impromptu tracks at the end of a session backing Billy Lee Riley. (The MG's stands for The Memphis Group.) Stax owner, Jim Stewart, likes the bluesy instrumental *Behave Yourself*, and releases it in US on subsidiary label Volt Records.

July After DJs begin playing the B-side, *Green Onions*, a rhythmic organ/guitar instrumental, Stax reissues it as A-side.

Sept *Green Onions* hits US #3 and becomes a million-seller. It is not a hit in UK at this time, but helps build a UK cult following.

Dec Parent album *Green Onions* reaches US #33.

1963 **Jan** **[12]** Second single *Jellybread* stalls at US #82.

Sept **[14]** *Chinese Checkers* makes US #78.

1964 **Feb** **[22]** *Mo-Onions* spends a week on US chart at #97.

Mar Steinberg is asked to leave because of unpunctuality for studio sessions, and is replaced by Dunn (b. Nov.24, 1941, Memphis), also a former Mar-Keys member.

Aug *Green Onions* is belatedly released in UK and is their first success, reaching #11.

[15] *Soul Dressing* stalls at US #95.

1965 **July** **[17]** After some lesser-selling records (during which time they also provide backing on hits by most other Stax acts), *Boot-Leg* returns them to US chart, peaking at #58.

1966 **Sept** **[3]** *My Sweet Potato* stalls at US #85.

1967 **Mar** **[17]** Band begins the 13-date "Soul Sensation '67 UK Tour" at London's Finsbury Park Astoria, alongside Otis Redding, Sam And Dave, Eddie Floyd, Arthur Conley, Carla Thomas and The Mar-Keys. The tour will end Apr.8 at London's Hammersmith Odeon.

June **[3]** *Hip Hug-Her* returns them to US Top 40 success, making #37.

[16] Group plays Monterey International Pop Festival, CA, also backing Otis Redding at the event.

Aug *Hip Hug-Her* reaches US #35. *Back To Back* makes US #98.

[26] *Slim Jenkin's Place* (originally titled *Slim Jenkin's Joint*, but changed to avoid possible controversy), B-side of still climbing *Groovin'*, peaks at US #70.

Sept **[23]** An instrumental cover of The Young Rascals' vocal hit *Groovin'* reaches US #21.

1968 **May** *Doin' Our Thing* peaks at US #176.

Aug **[31]** *Soul Limbo* reaches US #17.

Oct *Soul Limbo* makes US #127.

Nov *The Best Of Booker T. & The MG's* peaks at US #167.

1969 **Jan** *Soul Limbo* is their first UK Singles chart entry, reaching #30. The Caribbean-flavored tune will be widely known in later years in UK as regular theme to BBC TV's "Test Match Special" cricket coverage.

Feb [8] *Hang 'Em High*, theme from the Clint Eastwood movie, returns them to US Top 10, hitting #9.

May [3] *Time Is Tight*, from Booker T.'s own score for the film "Up Tight", hits US #6. Their soundtrack from the movie makes US #98.

June *Time Is Tight* hits UK #4, where it is their biggest hit.

July [12] An instrumental revival of Simon & Garfunkel's *Mrs. Robinson* makes US #37.

Aug *The Booker T. Set* reaches US #53.

Oct [4] *Slum Baby* stalls at US #88.
UK prefers *Mrs. Robinson*'s B-side *Soul Clap '69*, which makes #35.

1970 **May** *McLemore Avenue* makes US #107. The album contains instrumental covers of all songs on The Beatles' *Abbey Road*, and the sleeve photo is also similar, showing the MG's walking across the street outside their studio.

July [11] *McLemore Avenue* peaks at UK #70.

Aug [15] *Something*, from *McLemore Avenue*, makes US #76.

Nov *Booker T. & The MG's Greatest Hits* peaks at US #132.

1971 **Apr** *Melting Pot* reaches US #43.

May [22] *Melting Pot* is their last US hit single, making #45 but stays on the Hot 100 for 4 months. Tired of the strain of working with the band and a punishing session schedule at the Stax studios, Jones quits soon afterwards, leaves the band, and goes to live and work in Los Angeles, CA. (He will marry singer Priscilla Coolidge, sign to A&M Records, and begin a solo career as songwriter and soul vocalist.)

Aug Cropper also leaves Stax to open his own TMI recording studio and label in Memphis and work as a producer and session player, free from previous pressures.

1973 Dunn and Jackson make *The MG's* for Stax, with Bobby Manuel (guitar) and Carson Whitsett (keyboards) taking up the 2 vacant roles, but it raises little interest.

1975 **Oct** [1] Jackson is shot dead when he disturbs an intruder at his Memphis home.

1976 *Union Extended*, consisting of previously unreleased Booker T. & The MG's tracks, is released in UK only.

1977 **Feb** [4] Jones, Cropper and Dunn reunite as part of an all-star band to play on the 25th birthday show of US TV's "American Bandstand". The trio stays together, adding drummer Willie Hall (b.Aug.8, 1950), to record *Universal Language* for Asylum Records which has poor reviews and sales, after which group splits again.

1978 Jones has his biggest success as a producer when he oversees Willie Nelson's *Stardust*.

1980 **Jan** Due to its inclusion on soundtrack of The Who film "Quadrophenia", *Green Onions* becomes popular again in UK, and finally charts 17 years after its US Top 10 success, hitting #7.

June Cropper and Dunn feature in movie "The Blues Brothers", as members of the starring duo's backing band. (They will continue into the 80s as respected freelance players and producers, working with many other acts. Jones continues to have a mildly successful career as a soul vocalist, but is heard of less as the 80s progress.)

1990 With nostalgia increasingly in vogue, the band once again reunites, this time for US and European tours.

THE BOOMTOWN RATS

Bob Geldof (vocals)
Johnnie Fingers (keyboards, vocals)
Gerry Cott (guitar)
Pete Briquette (bass, vocals)
Gerry Roberts (guitar, vocals)
Simon Crowe (drums, vocals)

1975 Having interviewed the likes of Elton John and Little Richard for the **New Musical Express** and other papers as a music journalist, Geldof (b. Oct.5, 1954, Dublin, Eire), forms The Boomtown Rats (originally named The Nightlife Thugs) in Dun Laoghaire, Eire, with Fingers (b. Johnny Moylett), his cousin Briquette (b. Patrick Cusack), Cott, Roberts and Crowe.

1976 **Oct** They move to England and are signed to Ensign Records at the start of the new wave of punk music in UK.

1977 **Sept** *Looking After No.1* is issued after weeks of UK touring, including support dates with Tom Petty. It reaches UK #11, and album debut *The Boomtown Rats* climbs to UK #18.

Dec *Mary Of The Fourth Form* reaches UK #15.

1978 **May** *She's So Modern* reaches UK #12.

July *Like Clockwork* is the group's first Top 10 record, hitting UK #6, while *A Tonic For the Troops*, produced by Robert "Mutt" Lange, hits UK #8 and remains charted for 44 weeks.

Nov [18] Dramatic and different *Rat Trap* tops UK chart for 2 weeks.

1979 **Jan** [29] San Diego, CA, schoolgirl Brenda Spencer shoots and kills several of her schoolmates. Pressed for a reason, she says: "I don't like Mondays," which inspires Geldof to write a song.

Mar *A Tonic For The Troops* makes US #112.

Apr [7] Their first American tour includes the California Music Festival, with Ted Nugent, Aerosmith, Cheap Trick and Van Halen.

May US tour ends at the Palladium, New York.

July [28] *I Don't Like Mondays*, produced by Phil Wainman, hits UK #1 in its second week on chart, remains top for 4 weeks, and (aided by a striking promo video), becomes the Rats' biggest-selling single.

Nov *The Fine Art of Surfacing*, chiefly the work of Geldof and Fingers, hits UK #7.

Dec *Diamond Smiles* reaches UK #13. **The Fine Art Of Surfacing** makes US #103.

1980 **Feb** *Someone's Looking At You* hits UK #4. After promoting it, band sets off on a lengthy world tour, covering Europe, US, Japan and Australia.

Mar Despite attempts by Brenda Spencer's parents to have *I Don't Like Mondays* banned in US, and with many US radio stations refusing to program it, the single becomes their sole US hit, peaking at #73.

Dec A switch to Mercury Records sees release of reggae-tinged *Banana Republic*, which hits UK #3.

1981 **Feb** *Mondo Bongo*, produced by the band and Tony Visconti, hits UK #6, while extracted *The Elephants' Graveyard (Guilty)* reaches UK #26. *Mondo Bongo* makes US #116. Cott leaves soon after, and the band continues as a quintet.

Dec *Never In A Million Years* peaks at UK #62, their first single not to breach the Top 30.

1982 **Apr** *House On Fire*, with an offbeat arrangement, rekindles interest reaching UK #24. Parent album *V Deep* makes UK #64.

June *Charmed Lives* is the group's first single not to chart in UK.

Aug Geldof has a starring role in "The Wall", a movie based on the 1979 Pink Floyd album of the same title.

1984 **Feb** [18] *Tonight* peaks at UK #73.

May *Drag Me Down* makes UK #50, and is the last Boomtown Rats UK chart single.

Nov Geldof sees a graphic BBC TV report on famine in Ethiopia and determines to raise funds to help the situation. It is the start of Band Aid. Geldof sets aside his musical career and The Boomtown Rats effectively cease to be.

[25] 36 artists gather in the SARM studio, Notting Hill, London, to record the historic *Do They Know It's Christmas?*, including Geldof and members of The Boomtown Rats.

1985 **Jan** [28] Geldof participates in the making of the US equivalent of the Band Aid record, USA For Africa's *We Are The World*.

July [13] The Boomtown Rats, still close to Geldof's heart, play in the UK leg of the Live Aid concert at Wembley Stadium, London.

1986 **June** Geldof receives an honorary knighthood from the Queen, in recognition of his humanitarian activities, and is now Bob Geldof KBE.

Aug Geldof marries his long-time girlfriend, UK TV presenter and writer, Paula Yates in Las Vegas, NV, witnessed by Eurythmics' Dave Stewart and Annie Lennox. They already have a daughter, Fifi Trixiebelle.

Nov Geldof launches a solo recording career on Mercury Records with *This Is The World Calling*, which reaches UK #25. Solo *Deep In The Heart Of Nowhere*, mainly produced by Dave Stewart, makes US #130.

Dec [6] *Deep In The Heart Of Nowhere* spends a week at UK #79.

1987 **Jan** [10] *This Is The World Calling* peaks at US #82.

Feb *Love Like A Rocket* reaches UK #61. Geldof continues his efforts for the Band Aid charity, and will also write a best-selling autobiography and star in a series of milk commercials.

1988 **May** [14] Geldof performs Graham Parker's *You Can't Be Too Strong* at Atlantic Records' 40th birthday celebration in New York.

1989 **Mar** [13] Mr and Mrs Geldof have a second daughter, Peaches.

1990 **July** [7] *The Great Song Of Indifference*, from forthcoming *The Vegetarians Of Love*, makes UK #15.

Aug [4] Well-received *The Vegetarians Of Love*, produced by Rupert Hine, reaches UK #21.

BOSTON

Tom Scholz (guitar, keyboards)
Brad Delp (guitar, vocals)
Barry Goudreau (guitar)
Fran Sheehan (bass)
Sib Hashian (drums)

1975 While a product designer for Polaroid, Scholz (b. Mar.10, 1947, Toledo, OH), an MIT graduate with a master's degree in mechanical engineering, makes sophisticated rock demos with musician friends in his spare time, using a self-constructed basement studio in Boston, MA.

1976 His demos sufficiently impress US Epic label to gain a recording contract. The debut album, mostly featuring Scholz's basement originals, is completed in Los Angeles, CA, studio sessions with producer John Boylan. Scholz recruits local musicians, Delp (b. June 12, 1951, Boston, MA), Goudreau (b. Nov.29, 1951, Boston), Sheehan (b. Mar.26, 1949, Boston) and Hashian (b. Aug.17, 1949, Boston), to tour to promote the project. They are named Boston after their home base.
Dec [12] *Boston* hits US #3 and eventually sells over 6 million copies. *More Than A Feeling*, subsequently regarded as an adult-oriented rock classic, hits US #5.

1977 **Jan** *More Than A Feeling* reaches UK #22.
Feb *Long Time* climbs to US #22. *Boston* makes UK #11.
June *Peace Of Mind* makes US #38.
Sept *Don't Look Back* hits UK #9.
Oct Title cut *Don't Look Back* hits US #4 and makes UK #43.

1978 **Sept** *Don't Look Back* tops US chart.
Nov [4-5] Band plays live in Boston itself for the first time; 2 sell-out shows at Boston Garden.

1979 **Jan** *A Man I'll Never Be* makes US #31.
Apr *Feelin' Satisfied* makes US #46.

1980 **Oct** Goudreau's solo album, *Barry Goudreau*, released on Portrait, makes US #88.

1981 **Apr** [4] *Boston* re-charts, making UK #58.

1982 Goudreau leaves Boston to form Orion The Hunter.

1984 **June** Orion The Hunter's eponymously-titled album makes US #57.

1986 **Nov** [1] *Third Stage*, on MCA Records, tops US chart for 4 weeks, as new-look Boston, with Scholz and Delp now joined by Gary Phil (guitar) and Jim Masdea (drums), resurfaces after a 7-year absence. It reaches UK #37. *Boston* and *Don't Look Back* both re-chart at US #98 and US #146, respectively.
[8] *Amanda* tops US chart.

1987 **Feb** [14] *We're Ready* hits US #9, restoring Boston to the large-venue US live circuit it attained in the 70s.
Apr [18] *Can'tcha Say (You Believe In Me)/Still In Love* reaches US #20.

1989 With news that he and Delp are working on an album together, Goudreau sues Scholz for hurting his livelihood. An out-of-court settlement is reached.
Aug [15] Delp cameos on *Get Back* at Ringo Starr's Great Woods, Mansfield, MA, concert.

1990 **Feb** [13] A lawsuit between CBS Records and Scholz begins in US Federal Court, White Plains, NY. CBS is suing Scholz for reneging on a contract which required 10 albums in 5 years. Scholz is countersuing, claiming millions in royalties.
Mar [20] After a 7-year legal battle, CBS loses $20 million lawsuit against Scholz. Jury decides against CBS, which must pay Scholz back royalties.

DAVID BOWIE

1964 **Jan** Bowie (b. David Robert Jones, Jan.8, 1947, Brixton, London), while working at an advertising agency, forms The King Bees with school friend George Underwood. While attending Bromley technical school, where Peter Frampton is also studying, Underwood has formed George & The Dragons while Bowie has fronted The Kon-Rads.
June Group releases one-off UK single *Liza Jane*, on Decca's Vocalion label, with little success.
Dec Using his real name, David Jones, he moves to new London-based group The Manish Boys.

1965 **Mar** The Manish Boys sign to Parlophone label at EMI, and release *I Pity The Fool*.
[8] His first TV appearance is on "Gadzooks! It's All Happening" with The Manish Boys, who are almost barred from playing because of the length of Bowie's hair.
June The Manish Boys disband. Jones forms The Lower Third, playing

summer gigs in UK seaside towns.
Aug The Lower Third records *You've Got A Habit Of Leaving* for Parlophone. It is attributed to Davy Jones.
Sept After seeing The Lower Third at London's Marquee club, Ken Pitt becomes Jones' manager.

1966 **Jan** The Lower Third signs to Pye Records, and he adopts the surname Bowie for the first time after Pitt learns that another Davy Jones has been signed for new US TV group The Monkees.
[14] *Can't Help Thinking About Me*, by David Bowie & The Lower Third, is released in UK by Pye and in US by Warner Bros. Airplay on major pirate station Radio London makes it his best seller yet, though still non-charting.
Feb The Lower Third splits up, and Bowie continues as a soloist.
Apr First solo single *Do Anything You Say* is released.
Aug He plays "The Bowie Showboat", a regular Sunday afternoon slot at Marquee club, London, backed by The Buzz and broadcast by sponsor Radio London. *I Dig Everything* is released unsuccessfully by Pye, which then drops Bowie's contract.
Sept Pitt persuades Denny Cordell at Decca Records' new progressive Deram label to sign Bowie.
Dec *Rubber Band* is first Deram single, again a non-charter.

1967 **Apr** [14] *The Laughing Gnome*, a novelty song in Anthony Newley-style, is released, but is not a success at this time.
June Debut album *David Bowie* is released by Deram, garnering good reviews but unimpressive sales.
July Extracted *Love You Till Tuesday* is released in UK.
Aug Bowie meets fringe theatrical artist Lindsay Kemp and begins mime and dance lessons with him.
Dec Bowie works on tracks for BBC "Top Gear" radio show with producer Tony Visconti, the start of a long working partnership. He appears in Kemp's mime production "Pierrot In Turquoise", in Oxford.

1968 **Apr** [24] Apple Records turn down Bowie.
July He forms a trio named Feathers, with his girlfriend Hermione Farthingale and bassist John Hutchinson; they record privately but never professionally, and play live at London's Middle Earth and other clubs and colleges.

1969 **Feb** Feathers disband, and Bowie and Pitt make a 30-min. film intended for TV, based around songs from the first album and a new number, *Space Oddity*.
May Bowie co-founds the Beckenham Arts Lab, a performance club in a South London pub backroom where he tries out new material.
June He meets Angela (Angie) Barnet at a reception at the Speakeasy club, London, for King Crimson. Calvin Lee of UK Mercury label at Philips Records has heard *Space Oddity* and, convinced it will be a hit, offers Bowie a new record deal.
[20] Bowie signs to Philips and the same day is in Trident studio, London, re-recording *Space Oddity* with producer Gus Dudgeon.
July [11] Innovative astronomical-themed epic *Space Oddity*, featuring memorable song character "Major Tom", is released in UK (to be released on Mercury in US), initially without sales interest.
Aug [5] Bowie's father dies.
Bowie wins song festivals in Malta and Italy with *When I Live My Dream*. He organizes and plays in the Beckenham Free Festival, Kent, which 5,000 attend at a recreation ground; it is later commemorated in his song *Memory Of A Free Festival*.
Sept Following strong airplay and helped by BBC TV using it as its US moon landing coverage theme, *Space Oddity* is his first UK chart entry, hitting #5.
Oct As an acoustic solo act, he supports Humble Pie on a UK tour.
Nov Bowie and Angie Barnet move into a flat in Haddon Hall, Beckenham. *David Bowie*, produced by Visconti, is released in UK on Philips, and in US as *Man Of Words, Man Of Music* on Mercury. Bowie receives Ivor Novello Award from UK Songwriters Guild for *Space Oddity*, recognizing outstanding originality.

1970 **Feb** He forms new backing band, Hype, with Visconti on bass, John Cambridge on drums and Mick Ronson on guitar, which makes its live debut at the Roundhouse, Camden Town, London.
Mar *The Prettiest Star*, written for Angie, is issued as a UK single.
[20] Bowie and Angie Barnet are married at Bromley Register Office, London.
June *Memory Of A Free Festival* is issued as a UK single, re-recorded with new band Hype, with Mick "Woody" Woodmansey on drums.
Aug Bowie and Pitt part amicably. Tony DeFries, originally brought in to handle financial affairs, becomes his new manager. Bowie plays sax on Dib Cochran & The Earwigs' *Universal Love*, a group featuring Visconti, Rick Wakeman and Mickey Finn.

Nov *The Man Who Sold The World* is released in US before UK, but makes no impression. US Mercury Records arranges a promotional trip there to push the album to DJs and the media.

1971 Jan Single *Holy Holy* is released.

[27] Bowie arrives in US for his first visit. He does not perform live because of work permit problems, but gets plenty of publicity when he wears dresses in Texas and Los Angeles.

Mar Bowie works with Arnold Corns, a group based around his protege dress designer Freddi Burretti (renamed Rudi Valentino). He plays and sings on single *Moonage Daydream*, but after it fails to sell, Arnold Corns disbands.

Apr *The Man Who Sold The World* is released in UK, but with a different sleeve showing Bowie in a dress. This is later withdrawn and copies of the original will become high-priced collectors' items. Demo recordings are made for what will become album *Hunky Dory*. Visconti is no longer available to play bass, and Trevor Boulder is recruited.

May [28] Son Duncan Zowie Haywood is born in Bromley hospital.

June Peter Noone (of Herman's Hermits) reaches UK #12 with Bowie song *Oh You Pretty Thing*. DeFries negotiates the signing of Bowie to RCA Records worldwide, on the strength of *Hunky Dory* demo tapes and commercial success of *Oh You Pretty Thing* in UK.

[20] He plays a solo acoustic set at hippy-attended UK Glastonbury Fayre festival, Somerset.

July Tracks for what will become *Ziggy Stardust* are recorded.

Dec *Hunky Dory* is released, with no immediate success.

1972 Jan *Changes* is first RCA-issued Bowie single. It has no UK chart success but gives him a US chart debut at #66. Bowie declares his bisexuality in an interview in **Melody Maker.**

Feb Lengthy UK tour starts with a slot in the Lancaster Arts Festival, Lancs. On tour the band, led by guitarist Ronson with Boulder on bass and Woodmansey on drums, acquires the name The Spiders.

Apr [5] Bowie plays Oakland Coliseum, CA, as *Hunky Dory* makes a belated US chart showing at #93, the first Bowie Album chart entry anywhere. *Starman* is released as a single.

June *The Rise And Fall Of Ziggy Stardust And The Spiders From Mars*, providing a theatrical pseudonym basis for Bowie and the band, proves UK Album chart breakthrough, at #5, and also reaching US #75.

July *Starman* hits UK #10 and US #65.

[8] Bowie walks on stage at London's Royal Festival Hall, at a concert to benefit Save The Whale campaign, and proclaims "I'm Ziggy". Lou Reed joins him during the set.

Sept [7] Lengthy UK tour finally ends in Hanley, Stoke-on-Trent. *John I'm Only Dancing* is released in UK, and reaches #12. *Hunky Dory* charts in the wake of *Ziggy Stardust*, hitting UK #3. (Mott The Hoople's *All The Young Dudes*, written by Bowie, hits UK #3.)

[22] Debut US tour by Bowie & The Spiders begins in Cleveland, OH.

[28] Bowie sells out his first-ever New York show at Carnegie Hall.

Nov RCA reissues *The Man Who Sold The World* and the first Philips/Mercury album, now retitled *Space Oddity*, in both UK and US. They now chart at UK #26, US #105, and at UK #17, US #16 respectively. *The Jean Genie*, written on the road in US and recorded in New York, hits UK #2 but stalls at US #71.

Dec [24] Bowie, having returned to UK by sea at the end of US tour, plays a Christmas Eve concert at the Rainbow, London.

1973 Jan *Space Oddity* single is reissued by RCA in US, this time charting at #15 – his first US Top 20 hit.

[25] Always a fearful flier, he departs aboard the QE2 on a 100-day world tour, opening in US.

Feb [14] Bowie performs the opening concert of the US leg at Radio City Music Hall, New York.

Mar *Images 1966-1967*, comprising material recorded while signed to Deram and produced by Mike Vernon, makes US #144.

Apr [7] *The Rise & Fall Of Ziggy Stardust (Spiders From Mars)* makes US #75.

[8] Japanese leg of tour, which includes a performance at Hiroshima, opens in Tokyo.

[28] Lou Reed's *Walk On The Wild Side*, produced by Bowie and Ronson, reaches US #16 and will hit UK #10.

May [5] *Aladdin Sane*, with songs written on first US tour, tops UK chart and goes on to reach US #17. *Drive-In Saturday* hits UK #3. With a new visual image unveiled with each of his album releases, Bowie's reputation as an innovating musical, theatrical and video force is strengthened with every incarnation.

[12] A week after completing the world tour, he plays to 18,000 fans at Earls Court, London.

July *Life On Mars*, issued on the strength of its onstage popularity, hits

UK #3, his third space themed UK smash.

[3] UK tour closes at Hammersmith Odeon, London, with Jeff Beck joining him on stage. Bowie announces he is to retire from live performing. Although he is tired and genuinely wants several years' rest, it eventually transpires that the Ziggy Stardust fantasy stage persona is being retired, not Bowie.

Oct *The Laughing Gnome*, a novelty reissued by Deram, hits UK #6.

[18] Bowie films US TV show "The Midnight Special" at the Marquee, London, with guests The Troggs and Marianne Faithfull.

Nov [3] *Pin-Ups*, featuring Twiggy on the sleeve and containing revivals of Bowie's favorites by other acts from the 60s, is released, tops UK Album chart and reaches US #23. A revival of The Merseys' *Sorrow* from the album, hits UK #3.

Dec RCA announces that Bowie has sold 1,056,400 albums and 1,024,068 singles in UK alone since it signed him.

1974 Feb Lulu revives *The Man Who Sold The World* and it hits UK #3. Bowie produces and sings backing vocals on it.

Mar [2] Rolling Stones-sounding *Rebel Rebel* hits UK #5.

Apr He travels to US, where he will live and work for almost 2 years.

May [11] *Rock And Roll Suicide* makes UK #22.

[25] *Diamond Dogs*, recorded in London and Hilversum, Holland, with Tony Newman and Aynsley Dunbar on drums, Herbie Flowers on bass and Mike Garson on keyboards, with a controversial sleeve painting by Belgian artist Guy Peellaert and featuring songs *1984* and *Big Brother* from a musical version of "1984", which George Orwell's widow refuses to sanction, hits UK #1 and US #5. *Rebel Rebel* is released as a US single, and peaks at #64.

June [14] "Diamond Dogs" tour, a highly choreographed and theatrical stage performance drawing on concepts from the album, opens in Montreal, Canada.

July [13] *Diamond Dogs* reaches UK #21.

[20] Tour closes at Madison Square Garden, New York. Plans to take it to London prove financially unsound.

Oct [12] A revival of Eddie Floyd's *Knock On Wood* hits UK #10.

Nov *David Live*, recorded at the Tower, Philadelphia, on the "Diamond Dogs" tour, hits UK #2, held off the top by The Bay City Rollers' *Rollin'*, and US #8.

1975 Jan Bowie initiates legal action to break from manager DeFries, and looks towards a new deal with Michael Lippman.

[26] BBC TV "Omnibus" program broadcasts "Cracked Actor", a documentary film about Bowie.

Feb Nicolas Roeg signs him to star in movie "The Man Who Fell To Earth".

[1] *Changes*, a belated US single release, makes #41.

Mar [8] *Young Americans*, co-written with Luther Vandross, reaches UK #18.

[29] *Young Americans*, highlighting new soul-based style, hits UK #2, behind Tom Jones' *20 Greatest Hits*. It is recorded in Philadelphia with Main Ingredient guitarist Carlos Alomar, Willie Weeks on bass and Vandross on backing vocals. John Lennon plays on 2 tracks.

Apr [12] *Young Americans* hits US #9.

May [10] *Young Americans* reaches US #28.

July Bowie begins filming "The Man Who Fell To Earth".

Sept [6] *Fame*, co-written with Lennon and Alomar and extracted from the album, reaches UK #17.

[20] *Fame* is his most successful US single, hitting #1 for 2 weeks.

Nov [8] *Space Oddity*, reissued in UK on a 3-track single with *Changes* and previously unreleased *Velvet Goldmine*, tops UK chart for 2 weeks.

1976 Jan [10] *Golden Years* from forthcoming album, hits UK #8 and US #10.

[31] *Station To Station* hits UK #5.

Feb [2] World tour opens in Vancouver, Canada. Bowie sues manager Lippman after firing him.

[28] *Station To Station* hits US #3.

Mar [18] Premiere of "The Man Who Fell To Earth" in London is not attended by Bowie, who is on tour in US.

[21] Bowie is arrested with Iggy Pop and others at a Massachusetts hotel on suspicion of marijuana possession, and bailed for $2,000. (The case is adjourned and will be dropped a year later.)

[26] US leg of the world tour ends in New York. He sails for Europe.

Apr [27] After a trip to Moscow, Bowie is detained for hours on a train at the Russian/Polish border by customs officers who take exception to Nazi books and mementoes found in his luggage. It is apparently research material for a film on Goebbels.

May [3-8] He plays 6 shows at Wembley, London, his first UK gigs for almost 3 years.

June [5] *TVC 15* makes UK #33 and US #64, as Bowie and Iggy Pop vacation at Château d'Herouville, France, and go into studio to work on what will be Pop's *The Idiot*.

July [10] *Changesonebowie*, a compilation of past hits selected by Bowie, hits UK #2.

[17] *Changesonebowie* hits US #10.

Oct He moves to West Berlin, Germany, to live semi-reclusively for 3 years.

Nov [16] Final mix of *Low* is completed at Hansa studios in Berlin.

'77 Jan *Low* is released, introducing synthesized "European" sound, and hits UK #2 and US #11.

Mar *Sound And Vision*, from the album, hits UK #3 but stalls at US #69.

Sept [9] He appears on Marc Bolan's ITV show "Marc", singing *Heroes* and a duet with Bolan titled *Standing Next To You*. After the show they tape demos which will not develop as Bolan dies a week later.

[11] Bowie records guest appearance on seasonal TV show "Bing Crosby's Merrie Olde Christmas", duetting with Crosby on *The Little Drummer Boy*. (Crosby will die a month later, before the show is screened, but the duet will be a UK hit 5 years later.)

[20] Bowie attends Bolan's funeral and will set up a Trust Fund for Bolan's son, Rolan.

Oct Single *Heroes* reaches UK #24. French and German-language versions are also released.

[22] *Heroes*, with major contributions from Brian Eno and Robert Fripp, hits UK #3.

Dec [10] *Heroes* makes US #35.

'78 Feb [4] *Beauty And The Beast*, from *Heroes*, makes UK #39. Bowie and wife Angie agree to split. He begins filming David Hemmings-directed "Just A Gigolo" in Berlin, with Sydne Rome and Marlene Dietrich.

Mar [29] 1978 world tour starts at the Sports Arena, San Diego, CA, following rehearsals in Dallas, TX, with tour musicians Alomar (guitar), Roger Powell and Sean Mayes (keyboards), George Murray (bass), Dennis Davis (drums) and Simon House (violin).

May [9] US leg of tour ends at Madison Square Garden, New York.

[14] European tour section begins in Hamburg, Germany.

June [10] RCA's new version of Prokofiev's *Peter And The Wolf*, on which Bowie narrates with Eugene Ormandy conducting The Philadelphia Orchestra, makes US #136.

[14] UK leg of his European tour starts in Newcastle, Tyne & Wear.

July [1] First leg of UK tour closes at Earls Court, London.

Sept 1964 King Bees' single *Liza Jane* is reissued in UK, to no success.

[30] Double live album *Stage*, recorded at the Spectrum, Philadelphia, on Apr.28-29, hits UK #5.

Nov [11] World tour recommences in Adelaide, Australia.

[16] World premiere of "Just A Gigolo" screens in West Berlin.

Dec [2] *Stage* makes US #44.

[6] Japanese tour begins in Osaka.

[9] EP *Breaking Glass* makes UK #54.

[12] World tour ends in Tokyo, and Bowie and son Zowie stay for Christmas in Japan.

'79 Apr [23] *Boys Keep Swinging* premieres on BBC TV's "Kenny Everett Video Show".

May *Boys Keep Swinging* hits UK #7.

June [2] *Lodger* hits UK #4.

July [14] *Lodger* reaches US #20.

Aug *D.J.* reaches UK #29.

Dec Unissued 1975 version of *John I'm Only Dancing (Again) (1975)/ John I'm Only Dancing (1972)* appears as a single, making UK #12.

[31] He sings new acoustic version of *Space Oddity* on UK TV's "Kenny Everett New Year TV Show".

'80 Feb [8] Divorce becomes final between Bowie and Angie. He gains custody of son Zowie, now known as Joe. Angie gets £30,000 settlement.

Mar Brecht/Weill's *Alabama Song* is revived on a UK single, coupled with acoustic *Space Oddity*. It climbs to #23, with little exposure.

June Bowie researches the history of John Merrick, the Elephant Man, in London, prior to portraying him on stage in US.

July [29] He opens in Denver, CO, in title role of "The Elephant Man", breaking venue's box office record and pleasing critics.

Aug [5] "The Elephant Man" moves from Denver to Chicago, IL, for 3 weeks.

[23] *Ashes To Ashes*, a continuation of the "Major Tom" saga, from *Space Oddity*, accompanied as ever by a visually striking and innovative video, is Bowie's second UK #1 single.

Sept [23] He opens in "The Elephant Man" on Broadway, New York.

[27] *Scary Monsters And Super Creeps* hits UK #1 and makes US #12.

Oct He films a cameo appearance for German movie, "Christiane F".

Nov [22] *Fashion* hits UK #5.

1981 Jan [3] He plays his final night in "The Elephant Man" on Broadway.

[10] *Fashion* restores Bowie to US Singles chart at #70.

[24] TV-advertised *The Very Best Of David Bowie* hits UK #3, while *Scary Monsters (And Super Creeps)* reaches UK #20.

Reissues of *Hunky Dory* and *The Rise And Fall Of Ziggy Stardust* reach UK #32 and #33 respectively.

Feb [24] He receives #1 Male Singer award in the annual UK Rock & Pop Awards.

Apr [4] *Up The Hill Backwards* makes UK #32.

July At Montreux, Switzerland, where he is now based, Bowie records vocal for Giorgio Moroder's theme for film "Cat People", and also joins Queen in the studio, where they record *Under Pressure*.

Aug He takes the title role in Bertolt Brecht's "Baal", in a production being filmed by BBC TV.

Nov [21] *Under Pressure* by Queen and Bowie hits UK #1.

Dec [12] RCA-issued *Wild Is The Wind* reaches UK #24.

1982 Jan [9] *Under Pressure* reaches US #29.

[16] Compilation *Changestwobowie* makes UK #24 and US #68.

Feb "Christiane F", a huge box office hit in Germany, is shown in US, having premiered in UK in Dec.

Mar [2] "Baal" is shown on BBC TV.

[13] *Baal's Hymn*, a 5-song EP of songs from the play reaches UK #29.

Aladdin Sane reissue makes UK #49.

He starts filming "The Hunger", a fantasy about vampirism co-starring Catherine Deneuve and Susan Sarandon.

Apr [10] *Christiane F* soundtrack with 9 Bowie cuts makes US #135.

[24] *Cat People (Putting Out Fire)*, the movie theme with Bowie vocal, makes UK #26.

May [8] *Cat People (Putting Out Fire)* peaks at US #67.

Sept He begins filming "Merry Christmas Mr. Lawrence" in the Pacific, with co-stars Tom Conti and Ryuichi Sakamoto.

Nov Work ends on "Merry Christmas Mr. Lawrence" and he flies to New York for album recording sessions.

Dec [25] His 1977 duet with Bing Crosby, *Peace On Earth-Little Drummer Boy*, hits UK #3.

1983 Jan [27] He signs a new 5-year recording contract in New York with EMI America Records, reportedly worth $10 million.

Rare reissue reaches UK #34.

Apr [23] *Let's Dance*, produced with Nile Rodgers and featuring Stevie Ray Vaughan and Tony Thompson among others, hits UK #1 and US #4.

Reissued *Pin-Ups* and *The Man Who Sold The World* make UK #57 and #64 respectively.

May [9] First EMI single *Let's Dance* hits UK #1 and stays there for 3 weeks. It tops US chart in May, to become the first Bowie single to be #1 in both UK and US. It is his first million-selling single since *Fame*.

Diamond Dogs reissue makes UK #60.

[30] Prior to touring, he tops bill of "US 83 Festival" in San Bernardino, CA, being paid a record fee of $1 million.

June [2] "Serious Moonlight 83" UK tour opens at Wembley Arena, London. Each show is sold out on the day of announcement.

China Girl, an older song co-penned with Iggy Pop, hits UK #2 despite BBC ban on its video (which has a brief nude sex scene). It hits US #10. Reissued *Heroes* and *Low* make UK #75 and #85 respectively.

July [12] "Serious Moonlight 83" North American tour opens in Montreal, Canada.

Aug RCA compilation *Golden Years* makes UK #33 and US #99.

Oct *Modern Love* hits UK #2 and US #14.

Nov [24] Pacific leg of the tour opens in New Zealand.

Ziggy Stardust – The Motion Picture, the album of Bowie's final tour as Ziggy Stardust, reaches UK #17 and US #89. RCA's *White Light, White Heat* makes UK #46.

Dec [12] Final date of "Serious Moonlight 83", in Bangkok, Thailand.

1984 Feb [21] Bowie wins Best British Male Artist at the third annual BRIT Awards at the Grosvenor House, Mayfair, London.

Mar [10] *Without You* peaks at US #73.

Apr *Fame And Fashion*, more RCA greatest hits, makes UK #40 and US #147.

[19] *Let's Dance* is named both International Hit Of The Year and Best Rock Song at the annual Ivor Novello Awards lunch at the Grosvenor House, London.

May Reissued Deram album *Love You Till Tuesday* makes UK #53.

Sept [28] 22-min. film "Jazzin' For Blue Jean" airs on Channel 4's "The Tube".

Oct [6] *Tonight*, despite generally lukewarm reviews, tops UK chart

DAVID BOWIE cont.

and will reach US #11.

Blue Jean, boosted by a Julien Temple video, hits UK #6.

Nov [3] *Blue Jean* hits US #8.

Dec [22] *Tonight*, penned with Pop, charts at #53 in both UK and US.

1985 Feb Bowie links with highly-rated jazz group, The Pat Metheny Band, on *This Is Not America*, theme for movie "The Falcon And The Snowman" (in which he does not appear). It reaches UK #14.

[26] "David Bowie" wins Best Video, Short Form at the 27th annual Grammy awards.

Mar [23] *This Is Not America* makes US #32.

June *Loving The Alien* reaches UK #19.

July [13] He appears in Live Aid concert at Wembley Stadium, London, shown worldwide on TV, and records a version of Martha & The Vandellas' *Dancing In The Street* with Mick Jagger, introduced via video at Live Aid, with promise that all royalties will go to the appeal.

Sept [7] *Dancing In The Street* enters UK chart at #1 where it stays for a month.

Oct [12] *Dancing In The Street* hits US #7.

1986 Mar His theme from Temple movie "Absolute Beginners", in which Bowie has a character part, hits UK #2.

Apr "Absolute Beginners" opens in UK, to mixed reception.

May [3] *Absolute Beginners* peaks at US #53.

July *Underground*, the theme from "Labyrinth", spectacular children's fantasy film in which Bowie plays the Goblin King, reaches UK #21.

Nov He sings the theme for full-length cartoon film "When The Wind Blows", which deals with nuclear holocaust.

1987 Apr *Day In-Day Out* reaches UK #17 and US #21. UK BBC TV bans the promo video claiming it "contains disturbing images". Meanwhile, Bowie flies round the world with his new live band (including one-time schoolfriend Peter Frampton on guitar), holding a series of press conferences/performances to announce dates and venues of his forthcoming world tour (to cover Europe, UK, US, Australia and Japan, and to be named after *Glass Spiders*, a track on his imminent album).

May *Never Let Me Down* hits UK #6 and US #34, while "Glass Spider" 1987 world tour, featuring Frampton as lead guitarist, begins in Rotterdam, Holland.

[23] *Day-In Day-Out* reaches US #21.

June Guest acts on individual "Glass Spider" tour dates in UK cities include Alison Moyet, Big Country, and Terence Trent D'Arby.

July *Time Will Crawl*, taken from the album, peaks at UK #33.

Sept [26] *Never Let Me Down* makes UK #34.

Never Let Me Down reaches US #27.

Oct [9] Wanda Lee Nichols alleges that Bowie sexually assaults her "in a Dracula-like fashion" in a Dallas, TX, hotel room after a "Glass Spider" tour concert.

1988 Apr Bowie plays a benefit gig at the ICA, London, with guitarist Reeves Gabrels.

May "Glass Spider 1" and "2" videos are released chronicling performances from Bowie's last major tour.

Aug Bowie appears as Pontius Pilate in Martin Scorsese's controversial movie "The Last Temptation Of Christ".

1989 Apr Bowie selects small Massachusetts label Rykodisc to reissue his 18 back-catalog albums on CD.

May Bowie enthusiastically returns to a 2-guitar, bass and drums line-up for his new band, Tin Machine, and enlists Gabrels, Tony and Hunt Sales (with whom he worked in 1977 on an Iggy Pop album). Tin Machine's eponymous debut album hits UK #3 and begins its US rise to #28. It includes a version of John Lennon's *Working Class Hero*.

[31] Tin Machine makes its live debut at the first International Music Awards in New York playing *Heaven's In Here*.

June Bowie is confirmed as musical director of forthcoming film, starring Kylie Minogue, "The Delinquents", though his actual involvement will diminish. Tin Machine tour dates begin at the Kilburn National Ballroom, London, while *Tin Machine* peaks at UK #28.

[14] Tin Machine makes its US stage debut at the World Ballroom, New York.

July [1] Hinting at commercial failure for the Tin Machine project, extracted *Under The God* stalls at UK #52.

Sept [9] Tin Machine's *Tin Machine*, twinned with live cover version of Bob Dylan's *Maggie's Farm* stalls at UK #61.

Oct First Rykodisc collection, *Sound + Vision*, anthologizing past hits and unreleased rarities peaks at US #97.

1990 Jan [23] Bowie holds a London press conference to announce his forthcoming, and final, global concert tour, "The Sound And Vision World Tour 1990", during which, and via local radio stations who will add up the votes, Bowie will invite audiences to request past hits for

inclusion in this "greatest hits" sojourn.

Feb [12] Sexual assault suit by Nichols against Bowie is dismissed by a Dallas Federal judge (Bowie admits spending the night with her).

[21] *Sound + Vision* wins Best Album Package at the 32nd annual Grammy awards at the Shrine Auditorium, Los Angeles.

Mar [19] UK leg of world tour begins.

[31] Not to be confused with earlier volumes, a new retrospective hits collection, *Changesbowie*, debuts at UK #1, and will remain charted for 26 weeks, also set to make US #39.

Apr Fashionably updated *Fame 90*, included on multi-platinum selling *Pretty Woman* soundtrack album and remixed by Jon Gass, and featuring Queen Latifah, reaches UK #28.

[4] Released in batches, Bowie's RCA albums are made available on CD, now licensed to EMI in UK but to Rykodisc in US. Demand for them and the original artwork vinyl albums, also now re-available, returns most titles to the chart, *Hunky Dory*, *The Man Who Sold The World* and *Space Oddity* making UK #39, #66 and #64 respectively.

May Adrian Belew and Bowie's *Pink Rose*, penned by Bowie, is released in US on Atlantic.

June The most in-demand UK reissue proves to be *The Rise And Fall Of Ziggy Stardust*, which makes UK #25.

[21] Bono joins Bowie onstage at the Richfield Coliseum, singing *Gloria*.

July [14] Reissued *The Rise And Fall Of Ziggy Stardust* makes US #93.

[28] Reissued *Aladdin Sane* makes UK #43 for 1 week, while *Pinups* peaks at UK #52.

Aug [4-5] Further UK dates include 2 open air concerts at Milton Keynes Bowl, Bucks. By the tour's end, Bowie will have played 110 shows in 15 countries.

Oct [27] Reissued *Diamond Dogs* makes UK #67.

THE BOX TOPS/BIG STAR

Alex Chilton (guitar, vocals)
Gary Talley (guitar)
John Evans (organ)
Bill Cunningham (bass, piano)
Danny Smythe (drums)

1967 After high school, Chilton (b. Dec.28, 1950, Memphis, TN), Talley (b. Aug.17, 1947, Memphis), Cunningham (b. Jan.23, 1950, Memphis), Evans and Smythe form as a white soul group in Memphis, and come to the attention of producer/writer Dan Penn, who works with them at the city's American Recording studios.

July Group is signed to Bell Records' Mala label, debuting with *The Letter*, produced by Penn.

Sept [23] *The Letter* tops US chart for 4 weeks, selling a million-plus.

Oct *The Letter* hits UK #5.

Nov *The Letter/Neon Rainbow* makes US #87.

Dec *Neon Rainbow* reaches US #24.

1968 Apr *Cry Like A Baby*, featuring a distinctive electric sitar sound, hits US #2 and UK #15, and is their second million-seller. *Cry Like A Baby* makes US #59. Evans and Smythe leave the group to go back to college and are replaced by Rick Allen (b. Jan.28, 1946, Little Rock, AR) and Tom Boggs (b. July 16, 1947, Wynn, AR).

June *Choo Choo Train* reaches US #26.

Oct Gospel-flavored, *I Met Her In Church*, makes US #37.

Dec *The Box Tops Super Hits* makes US #45.

1969 Feb *Sweet Cream Ladies, Forward March* reaches US #28.

May Bob Dylan-inked *I Shall Be Released* peaks at US #67. Jerry Riley joins on guitar, replacing Talley.

Aug Group returns to US Top 20 with *Soul Deep* (#18); it is also their third and last hit at UK #22.

Sept *Dimensions* makes US #77.

Nov *Turn On A Dream* peaks at US #58.

1970 Mar They move to Bell label for final chart hit *You Keep Tightening Up On Me* (US #92). Cunningham leaves, and Swain Scharfer (piano) and Harold Cloud (bass) join.

1972 Group having lost impetus, Chilton leaves to form Big Star. He and songwriting partner, guitarist Chris Bell (b. Jan.12, 1951, Memphis), recruit bassist Andy Hummel (b. Jan.26, 1951, Memphis) and drummer Jody Stephens (b. Oct.4, 1952) and work on combining Beatles-style harmonies and punch guitars, later termed "power pop".

Apr They sign to Terry Manning's Memphis-based Ardent label, associated with Stax, and make *#1 Record*. Stax, oriented to R&B music, finds the album hard to promote.

1973 After serious studio disagreements with Chilton, Bell leaves to continu songwriting in Memphis (then to pursue a minor solo acoustic career that will take him to UK in l975).

974 **Feb** *Radio City* is released to critical approval. Meanwhile, Tommy Cogbill, who produced later Box Tops' Mala hits, revives the group one last time with *Willobee And Dale* on Stax. However, its name now means little commercially and the single and The Box Tops disappear.

975 After recording third album with the aid of guitarist Steve Cropper and other session men, Big Star splits with the disk unreleased, and Chilton goes to New York for a solo career which will regularly find critical interest and a cult following, but no chart success.

978 **July** *#1 Record/Radio City* is released in UK for the first time, as a double package. Previously unavailable *Third Album* also belatedly appears on UK Aura label. (Chilton will subsequently release 2 solo albums, *One Day In New York* and *Like Flies On Sherbert*, and play occasional club dates.)
Dec [27] Bell is killed in a car crash in Memphis.

BOY GEORGE AND CULTURE CLUB

Boy George (vocals)
Jon Moss (drums)
Roy Hay (guitar, keyboards)
Mikey Craig (bass)

978 George (b. George O'Dowd, June 14, 1961, Eltham, Kent), the third of 6 children, his brothers boxers and his father a boxing club manager, having spent his early teens idolizing rock stars Marc Bolan and David Bowie, is a regular at Billy's, a club run by Steve Strange (later of Visage) and Rusty Egan which will spark the London club boom of the early 80s. He has a flamboyant style, with his elaborate clothes and make-up, and becomes friends with budding pop media figure Marilyn (aka Peter Robinson), a cross-dresser with a penchant for the blonde bombshell look, and Martin Degville (later of Sigue Sigue Sputnik), with whom he shares an apartment in Birmingham, W.Midlands, for a year. When the crowd moves to Blitz and Hell (centers for the dressy New Romantic fashion) George attracts media attention. Malcolm McLaren, ex-manager of The Sex Pistols, working with the group Bow Wow Wow, invites George to appear at the band's London Rainbow concert as Lieutenant Lush. The alliance soon dissolves, but George forms a band after meeting ex-DJ Mikey Craig (b. Feb.15, 1960, Hammersmith, London). They call themselves In Praise Of Lemmings, changing to Sex Gang Children when guitarist John Suede joins. George's friend Kirk Brandon (of Theatre Of Hate) introduces them to Moss (b. Jonathan Aubrey Moss, Sept.11, 1957, Wandsworth, London), a professional musician who has had brief associations with The Clash, The Damned and Adam & The Ants.

981 George renames the band Culture Club. Suede leaves, to be replaced by Hay (b. Aug.12, 1961, Southend, Essex), from Russian Bouquet and a veteran of other semi-pro Essex bands. Group debuts in an Essex club and approaches young producer Steve Levine to oversee their first demos. They record *White Boy* and *I'm Afraid Of Me* at EMI studios, but the label turns them down.

982 **May** Virgin Records signs them, releasing *White Boy*, which flops.
June *I'm Afraid Of Me* again fails to chart. George's striking image attracts increasing media interest, particularly in the fashion pages (many outfits are designed by Sue Clowes). BBC Radio 1 DJ Peter Powell asks the band to record 4 songs for his show. It only has 3 ready so hastily writes a fourth, *Do You Really Want To Hurt Me*.
Oct *Do You Really Want To Hurt Me* tops UK chart for 3 weeks as debut album *Kissing To Be Clever* (named after an early song that never made it past the demo) is released. It contains versions of all 3 singles and hits UK #5.
Dec *Time (Clock Of The Heart)* hits UK #3.

983 **Jan** *Kissing To Be Clever* makes US #14; it will chart for 88 weeks.
Mar *Do You Really Want To Hurt Me* hits US #2. (It entered the chart in Dec.1982 and will spend 25 weeks on it.) With Virgin yet to establish a full US operation, the record is distributed by Epic.
Apr *Church Of The Poison Mind*, with Helen Terry on vocals, hits UK #2. *Time (Clock Of The Heart)* also hits US #2.
July A US-only release, a remix of *I'll Tumble 4 Ya*, hits US #9.
Sept *Karma Chameleon* tops UK chart for 6 weeks and is a million-seller, with a striking video filmed on a Mississippi steamboat.
Oct *Colour By Numbers* tops UK chart while *Church Of The Poison Mind* hits US #10.
Dec *Victims*, backed with a grandiose video featuring full orchestra, hits UK #3.

984 **Feb** *Colour By Numbers* hits US #2 where it stays for 6 weeks, unable

to dislodge Michael Jackson's *Thriller*. *Karma Chameleon* tops US chart for 3 weeks.
[21] Culture Club wins Best British Group and *Karma Chameleon* wins Best British Single at the third annual BRIT Awards at Grosvenor House, London.
[28] Culture Club wins Best New Artist Of 1983 at the 26th annual Grammy awards.
Mar *It's A Miracle* hits UK #4 as *Miss Me Blind* hits US #5.
May *It's A Miracle* reaches US #13.
Oct *The War Song* hits UK #2. George moves away from his braids and baggy clothes and puts on a black wig as the first in a succession of new looks.
Nov *Waking Up With The House On Fire* hits UK #2 but only US #26. Group tours US with a million-dollar production and extended band including horn section and backing singers Ruby Turner and Mo Birch.
Dec *The Medal Song* peaks at UK #32. *Mistake No.3* peaks at US #33.

1985 After a UK tour the band agrees to take a break. (Craig and Hay head for tax exile, although Hay will shortly return with new band This Way Up, Moss for production work, later forming Heartbeat UK, and George for club dancefloors and associated hedonism.)

1986 **Apr** *Move Away* hits UK #7.
May *God Thank You Woman* reaches UK #31. George appears in an episode of US TV series "The A Team".
[31] *Move Away* reaches US #12. Parent album *From Luxury To Heartache*, produced by Arif Mardin, hits UK #10 and US #32.
July George makes a brief appearance at an anti-apartheid concert on London's Clapham Common. He has lost his familiar chubbiness, arrives inexplicably covered in flour and introduces himself as "your favorite junkie". Within a week, his brother, fearing for George's life, leaks the story of George's heroin addiction to the press. The pop star who had publicly denounced drugs, is now himself an addict.
[12] The police arrest George, Marilyn and several others. No sooner have the headlines slipped off front pages than New York keyboardist Michael Rudetski (who played on the last Culture Club album and was signed up for the next) dies of a drug overdose in George's home. (Rudetski's parents later take unsuccessful legal action against George for contributing to their son's death.) George is arrested for possession of cannabis. He tells the court he will undertake Dr. Meg Patterson's electronic "black box" treatment to cure his addiction.

1987 Publicly stating he is cured on BBC TV chat show "Wogan", George confirms Culture Club's split and new ambitions of a solo career.
Mar George's remake of Bread's *Everything I Own*, a copy of Ken Boothe's 1974 reggae-style chart-topper, hits UK #1.
Apr *This Time* hits UK #8.
June *Keep Me In Mind* makes UK #29. George's solo *Sold* peaks at UK #29 in its week of entry.
July Title track from *Sold* reaches UK #24.
Aug *Sold* makes US #145.
Nov Fourth track from the album, *To Be Reborn*, co-written with Lamont Dozier, climbs to UK #13.

1988 **Feb** [20] *Live My Life*, from the film "Hiding Out", makes US #40.
Mar *Live My Life* peaks at UK #62.
June *No Clause 28*, a song about UK Government's decision to ban promotion of homosexuality by local authorities, peaks at UK #57.
Oct *Don't Cry* peaks at UK #60.

1989 **Mar** *Don't Take My Mind On A Trip* peaks at UK #68.
Nov George's new band Jesus Loves You makes UK #68 with *After The Love*, on his own recently formed label, More Protein.

1990 George, reportedly now a member of the Hare Krishna movement, records album with Asha Bhosle in Bombay, India.

1991 **Feb** [23] With Krishna-promoting sleeve and lyrics, *Bow Down Mister* enters UK chart at #69.

BILLY BRAGG

1977 Following 4 years of dead-end jobs after leaving school, Bragg (b. Steven William Bragg, Dec.20, 1957, Barking, Essex) forms punk/R&B band Riff Raff. They record unsuccessful EP *I Wanna Be A Cosmonaut* for Chiswick Records.

1981 Riff Raff splits, and unemployed Bragg signs up for the British Army. Posted to a tank division, he finds army life unsuitable and buys himself out after 90 days.

1982 He begins to tour UK as a solo singer/songwriter, keeping on the road via bus and train.

1983 He is given 3 afternoons of studio time to record demos of his songs for music publisher Chappell.

July The song demos are collected as mini-album *Life's A Riot With Spy Vs Spy*, released on Utility, a subsidiary of Charisma Records, and are well reviewed.

[27] First radio session is for BBC Radio 1's "John Peel Show".

Oct Bragg signs to Go! Discs Records, which takes over the album from Charisma.

1984 Jan *Life's A Riot With Spy Vs Spy* reaches UK #30, and tops UK Independent chart for 2 months. He follows the success with more touring, including dates throughout Europe.

Aug Bragg embarks on a well-received first tour of US.

Sept He emphasizes his political colors in UK by playing "Food For The Miners" benefit shows.

Oct [19] He is arrested with others during an anti-apartheid sit-down outside South Africa House, Trafalgar Square, London.

Brewing Up With Billy Bragg reaches UK #16.

1985 Feb [23] Kirsty McColl's version of Bragg's song *A New England*, originally featured on *Life's A Riot*, hits UK #7.

Mar [23] EP *Between The Wars* is his own UK singles chart debut, making #15.

1986 Jan *Days Like These* makes UK #43.

Bragg forms Red Wedge, a politically active group of musicians, to raise funds in support of the Labour Party. Group embarks on the "Red Wedge Tour" with The Style Council and The Communards.

July *Levi Stubbs' Tears* reaches UK #29.

Oct *Talking With The Taxman About Poetry*, a title from Soviet poet Mayakovsky, hits UK #8.

Nov [2] He is arrested and charged with criminal damage after cutting an air base fence in Norfolk, UK, in an anti-nuclear demonstration.

Greetings To The New Brunette makes UK #58.

1987 June Double album *Back To Basics*, with tracks from *Life's A Riot* and EP *Between The Wars*, climbs to UK #37.

1988 May [21] With a cover version of The Beatles' *She's Leaving Home* Bragg, with featured pianist Cara Tivey, enjoys a surprise chart-top as one side of a double A-side charity record with Wet Wet Wet's version of *With A Little Help From My Friends*. Both songs are featured on compilation album *Sergeant Pepper Knew My Father*.

Sept *Waiting For The Great Leap Forwards* peaks at UK #52.

Oct *Workers Playtime* reaches UK #17.

Nov [5] *Workers Playtime* spends a week on US chart at #198.

1989 Feb [22] Bragg makes his US network TV debut on NBC's "Late Night With David Letterman".

1990 Apr [21] Bragg takes part in an "Earth Day" benefit concert at the Merriweather Post Pavilion, Columbia, MD.

May [12] *The Internationale* peaks at UK #34.

June Bragg tours Eastern Europe with 10,000 Maniacs' Natalie Merchant and R.E.M.'s Michael Stipe.

July *The Internationale* is released as an EP in US on Utility, through Elektra.

Sept Bragg and Merchant record as The Lemon Jeffersons at Fort Apache studios in Boston, MA.

Nov [3] *Rubáiyát*, Elektra's 40th anniversary compilation, to which Bragg contributes a cover of *Seven & Seven Is*, makes US #140.

1991 Apr [20] Bragg takes part in the "Earth Day 1991 Concert" at Foxboro Stadium, MA, with Jackson Browne, Rosanne Cash, Bruce Cockburn, Bruce Hornsby & The Range, Indigo Girls, Queen Latifah, Ziggy Marley, Willie Nelson and 10,000 Maniacs.

BREAD

David Gates (keyboards, vocals)
James Griffin (guitar, vocals)
Robb Royer (guitar, vocals)
Mike Botts (drums)

1968 Griffin (b. Memphis, TN), who already has solo *Summer Holiday* to his credit, hires Gates (b. Dec.11, 1940, Tulsa, OK) a songwriter, producer and session musician, who has first recorded with Leon Russell for Lee Hazlewood's East West label in the late 50s before moving to Los Angeles, CA, in the early 60s as an arranger on recommendation of Royer who, as a member of The Pleasure Fair with Michele Cochrane, Tim Hallinan and Steve Cohn, has released eponymously-titled album for Uni, produced by Gates. They harmonize, join forces, and take their demos to Elektra Records, a folk label which has moved into rock with acts like The Doors but has not previously signed a pure pop band.

Oct Band, now named Bread, chosen after they were stuck behind a Wonder bread truck in traffic, releases debut album *Bread*, which reaches US #127, but fails to chart in UK, despite critical acclaim. Session man Jim Gordon plays drums on the album.

1970 Aug *Make It With You*, from second album *On The Waters*, tops US chart and hits UK #5. The album reaches US #12 and UK #34.

Nov Further ballad *It Don't Matter To Me*, from *Bread*, is reissued and hits US #10.

1971 With plans to take Bread on tour, they recruit full-time drummer Botts (b. Sacramento, CA).

Feb *Let Your Love Go*, from third album, *Manna*, reaches US #28.

Mar *Manna* reaches US #21. Griffin and Royer's lyrics to the song *For All We Know* from movie "Lovers And Other Strangers" win them an Oscar for Best Film Song Of 1970, with Griffin using the alias Arthur James and Royer being credited as Robb Wilson.

May *If*, from *Manna*, hits US #4. Royer leaves and is replaced by multi-instrumentalist Larry Knechtel (b. Bell, CA), a former member of Duane Eddy's Rebels but now a legendary Los Angeles session player. (He has played bass on The Byrds' *Mr. Tambourine Man*, piano on Simon & Garfunkel's *Bridge Over Troubled Water*, and been part of a session trio comprising Joe Osborn (bass) and Hal Blaine (drums), which has played on million-selling records by The Beach Boys, The Monkees, The 5th Dimension, Johnny Rivers, The Association, Paul Revere & The Raiders and countless others.)

Aug *Mother Freedom*, the first disk to include Knechtel, makes US #37.

Nov Title track from the still unissued album *Baby I'm-A Want You* is released and hits US #3 and UK #14.

1972 Mar *Baby I'm-A Want You* is finally released, hitting US #3 and UK #9, as further single from it, *Everything I Own*, hits US #5 and UK #32.

June *Diary*, also from the album, reaches US #15.

Sept Title track from their fifth album, *Guitar Man*, reaches US #11 and UK #16, the guitar solo played by Knechtel.

Oct *Best Of Bread* is released in UK, and hits #7.

Nov *Guitar Man* reaches US #18.

Dec *Sweet Surrender*, from *Guitar Man*, reaches US #15.

1973 Mar *Aubrey*, the third single from *Guitar Man*, reaches US #15. Group disbands amid rumors of disagreement between Gates and Griffin over whose songs should be released as singles. (Gates has composed the majority of Bread's hits. An early agreement was that their songs would alternate as singles.)

May Compilation *Best Of Bread* hits US #2 enjoying a 2-year chart residency. Gates and Griffin embark on solo careers, Botts works with Linda Ronstadt and Knechtel returns to sessions, before illness forces him to retire for a time.

Oct Gates' debut solo album, *First*, very much in Bread style, is released set to make US #107. It includes the Aug.1973 US mini-opus *Clouds*, an ambitious 7 min. single.

Nov Gates' *Sail Around The World* stalls at US #50.

1974 July Compilation *Best Of Bread Vol. 2* reaches US #32 and UK #48.

1975 Feb Gates' *Never Let Her Go* peaks at US #29, as parent album, similarly titled, makes US #102.

1977 Jan After relatively unsuccessful solo careers Gates and Griffin bury the hatchet, and Bread re-forms with the same line-up as before. *Lost Without Your Love* reaches US #26 and UK #17, while the title track hits US #9 and UK #27.

May *Hooked On You*, from the album, peaks at US #60.

Nov [26] TV-advertised 20-track compilation album, *The Sound Of Bread*, sells prodigiously in UK, achieving double platinum status and topping chart for 3 weeks, knocking The Sex Pistols' *Never Mind The Bollocks – Here's The Sex Pistols* from the top spot. A similar US compilation fails to chart. Group drifts apart again into solo work. (Griffin later records an album with Terry Sylvester of The Hollies, but Gates is the most successful with his songwriting, topping UK chart in 1974-75 with covers of *If* (by actor Telly Savalas) and *Everything I Own* (by Ken Boothe), which is also revived as a chart-topper in 1987 by Boy George.) Griffin sues Gates when the latter tours using the name, which they co-own. A Judge orders group not to record, perform or collect royalties until case is resolved. (Litigation finally ends in 1984.)

1978 Feb Gates' title theme song to Neil Simon hit movie "Goodbye Girl" reaches US #15.

Aug Opportunist album *Goodbye Girl*, including previously released Gates material, sneaks to US #165 and contains US #30 (and UK #50) *Took The Last Train*.

1980 Feb Gates' Elektra swan song *Where Does The Lovin' Go?* makes US #46

1981 Oct Now signed to Arista, Gates, still recording in familiar Bread style releases unsuccessful album *Take Me Now*, including US #62 title cut.

1987 Nov [28] *The Very Best Of Bread* peaks at UK #84.

1991 Griffin, who has moved to Nashville, TN, and initially formed group

Dreamer, teams with ex-Eagle and Poco Randy Meisner and *I Can Help*-hitmaker Billy Swan as Black Tie, scoring a US Country hit with a revival of Buddy Holly's *Learning The Game* on indie Bench label. Meanwhile the other slices of Bread are less visible, with Gates now running an 800-acre ranch in Northern California, Knechtel, after 14 years on a neighboring cattle ranch, moving to Nashville, cutting new age album *Mountain Moods*, and playing in Elvis Costello's band, and Botts writing jingles, doing sessions and working on children's albums.

BOBBY BROWN

1985 Brown (b. Robert Baresford Brown, Feb.5, 1969, Roxbury, MA), having first performed at age 3, when his mother pushed him on stage during the intermission of a James Brown concert in Boston, MA, has already earned his musical spurs as one fifth of smash R&B pop teen act New Edition, which he co-founded in 1981, and following the act's current *All For Love* platinum album, becomes the first member of the unit to decide on a solo career, signing to MCA in his own right.

1986 Dec As extracted *Girlfriend* tops US R&B chart, his debut album *King Of Stage*, produced by Bobby Louil Siolas Jr., enters US chart, set to reaches #88.

1987 Jan [24] *Girlfriend* peaks at US #57.
Mar Follow-up *Girl Next Door*, makes US R&B #31.

1988 Jan Brown completes recording his second album, mainly helmed by hot hitmaking writing/production duo L.A. Reid & Babyface, but also with hip-hop specialist Gene Griffin and soul ballad producer Larry White, enabling Brown to display his full range of funk, R&B, rap, dance, soul and ballad qualities.
July [23] Lead-off cut *Don't Be Cruel* tops US R&B chart.
Aug *Don't Be Cruel* makes UK #42.
Oct [15] *Don't Be Cruel* hits US #8 as follow-up *My Prerogative* tops US R&B chart.

1989 Jan [14] *My Prerogative*, boosted by feverish Brown dance-displaying hotly rotated video clip, hits US #1 and UK #6.
[21] Having already topped US R&B Album chart for 11 weeks, *Don't Be Cruel* hits US #1, during a 97-week chart tenure, which will accrue 6 platinum sales awards in US alone. It will also hit UK #3, its mix of light hip-hop fused with aggressive dance and soul numbers proving popular worldwide.
[25] Wowing fans with his non-stop dancing antics, Brown is arrested at the Municipal Auditorium, Columbus, GA, for an overtly sexually suggestive performance. He will be fined $652 under the Anti-Lewdness Ordinance for giving a "sexually explicit performance harmful to minors on city property, whether the performers are clothed or not".
Mar [18] *Roni* hits US #3, his third US Top 10 single in a row.
Apr Reissued *Don't Be Cruel* reaches UK #13.
[25] Brown wins Act Of The Year, R&B Act, Top Male Vocalist, Top Rock Single (*My Prerogative*) at the third SKC Boston Music Awards at the Wang Center in his hometown Boston.
May Having recently cancelled 20 concerts on the final leg of his US tour, amid much criticism, *Every Little Step* hits UK #6.
June [10] Once again helped by up-beat precision-timed dance-busting video, *Every Little Step* hits US #3. (His trademark dancing abilities will bridge the gap between Michael Jackson and next year's hot-foot sensation, MC Hammer.)
Aug [5] Trailering MCA synergized movie project "Ghostbusters II", Brown's *On Our Own*, from the soundtrack, hits US #2, having already hit UK #4, while reissued *King Of Stage* now makes UK #40.
[12] At a Walt Disney press conference, it is announced that Brown will play the Three Blind Mice in their cable channel's Shelley Duvall-produced "Mother Goose Rock'N'Rhyme", alongside Paul Simon (Simple Simon), Art Garfunkel (Rhymeland bartender), Little Richard (Old King Cole), Deborah Harry (the old woman who lived in a shoe) and Cyndi Lauper (Mary).
Sept [6] Brown performs at the annual MTV Music Video Awards at the Universal Amphitheater, Universal City, CA.
Nov [4] Remixed *Rock Wit'Cha* hits US #7, having peaked at UK #33.
Dec While a belated UK release of *Roni* climbs to UK #21, a remix album of hit extracts from *Don't Be Cruel, Dance ... Ya Know It!* fills between studio projects, hitting US #9 and UK #26.
[23] He wins Top Pop Singles Artists – Male, Top Pop Album Artists – Male and Top Black Artists categories in **Billboard**'s The Year In Music statistical round-up.

1990 Jan [12] Brown is scheduled to be presented with the Martin Luther King Jr. Musical Achievement Award in Boston at Symphony Hall

during a Tony Bennett/Count Basie Orchestra concert, but fails to show up.
[27] MCA Music Video issues eponymously titled collection of video hits, from the past 18 months.
Feb [21] *Every Little Step* wins R&B Vocal Performance, Male at the 32nd annual Grammy awards at the Shrine Auditorium, Los Angeles.
Mar [8] Brown wins Best New Male Singer and Best R&B Artist in **Rolling Stone**'s Readers Picks for 1989 and Best R&B Artist in the Critics Awards.
Apr [19] He also wins Outstanding Male Vocalist and Outstanding R&B Act at the fourth annual SKC Boston Music Awards at the Wang Center, Boston.
June [5] Brown plays the first of 8 sell-out nights at the Wembley Arena, London, during his current world tour, as MCA UK-issued *Free Style Mega-Mix* reaches UK #14.
July [21] Glenn Medeiros-featuring Bobby Brown duet *She Ain't Worth It* tops US chart and will also reach UK #12.

1991 Feb [10] Brown joins with nearly 100 celebrities in Burbank, CA, to record *Voices That Care*, a David Foster and fiancee Linda Thompson Jenner-composed and organized charity record to benefit the American Red Cross Gulf Crisis Fund.
Apr Having already established his own Bosstown recording studio in Atlanta, GA, where he is now based, Brown forms the Bosstown label and continues recording the follow-up to *Don't Be Cruel* with production assistance once again from L.A. Reid & Babyface and others, including Teddy Riley.

JAMES BROWN

1954 After delinquent teenage years in Augusta, GA, including a 4-year hard labor stretch at age 16 for petty theft in a state corrective institution (he had originally been sentenced to serve 8 to 16 years), and later singing on tour with gospel groups and learning to play drums and organ, Brown (b.May 3, 1933, Barnwell, SC, various birthdates and places will be listed in print, the confusion arising from Brown's use of fake I.D. on occasion), who has been raised by an aunt, joins Atlanta-based Gospel Starlighters before forming an R&B vocal group, The Famous Flames, in Macon, GA, and begins to play live gigs around Georgia, in a style which blends gospel with raucous jump blues-based R&B. Brown has also previously formed The Swanees in 1952 with Bobby Byrd, Sylvester Keels and Nafloyd Scott, which will become The Famous Flames. Early gigs include a stint as house band at Clint Brantley's Two Spot club in Macon.

1956 Jan With The Famous Flames, Brown is signed by Ralph Bass to Federal, a subsidiary label of King Records, Cincinnati, OH.
Feb [4] He records *Please, Please, Please* (originally cut as a demo for Bass the previous Nov., at radio station WIBB in Macon).
Apr *Please, Please, Please*, credited to James Brown & The Famous Flames, creeps on to R&B chart, mainly from regional sales from Georgia and bordering states, where it benefits from the group's rapidly-growing touring popularity. (It will continue to sell steadily for 2 years, wherever Brown takes his live show, but will never cross over to US Top 100.)

1959 Jan After further regional hits in Southeastern states, *Try Me*, a song from Brown's gospel roots, is his first national hit, reaching #48 and topping R&B chart for a week. He signs to Universal Attractions booking agency and its owner Ben Bart takes a special interest in the young star. With Bart's guidance, not least on the business side, Brown takes a unique and unprecedented show on the road, mixing calculated hysteria with absolute musical precision. (This will break box office records in all the major R&B venues around the US between 1959 and 1962.)

1960 June *Think*, his second US crossover hit, reaches #33.
[27] *You've Got The Power* stalls at US #86. (Brown begins to put out singles at a rate of 1 every 2 or 3 months – a practice he will continue for the next 10 years, and which satisfies the demand fuelled by constant touring. Most of them are medium-sized pop hits, including: *This Old Heart* (#79 – his last for Federal), *The Bells*, reviving Billy Ward & His Dominoes' death song (#68 – his first hit on parent King label), *Bewildered* (#40), *I Don't Mind* (#47), *Baby You're Right* (#49) and *Lost Someone* (#48). Though none are UK hits, many pass into repertoires of groups spearheading the UK beat boom in the mid-60s.)

1962 May *Night Train*, a personalization of the old Jimmy Forrest hit on which Brown name-checks his regular tour venues, hits US #35. Follow-up chartmakers in 1962 are *Shout And Shimmy* (#61), *Mashed Potatoes USA* (#82) and *Three Hearts In A Tangle* (#93).

Oct [24] The legendary stage act at Harlem's Apollo theater, New York, is taped for a live album.

1963 Feb [9] *Every Beat Of My Heart* spends a week at US #99.

June Brown's first US Top 20 revives the schmaltzy but intense ballad *Prisoner Of Love*, a hit for Perry Como, Billy Eckstine and The Ink Spots in 1946, which reaches #18. *Live At The Apollo*, recorded the previous Oct., is released and sells quite unprecedentedly for an R&B album, (over a million within the year) peaking at US #2.

Aug *These Foolish Things*, another old standard updated with gospel fervor, peaks at US #55.

Oct *Prisoner Of Love* makes US #73.

Dec *Signed, Sealed And Delivered* reaches US #77.

1964 Feb [15] Reissued *Please, Please, Please* stalls at US #95.

Mar *Oh Baby Don't You Weep*, a major seller, reaches US #23.

Apr Restricted by arrangements at King, and determined to build upon the huge audience crossover success of such hits as *Live At The Apollo*, Brown and Bart form their own production company, Fair Deal, and, ignoring King, send a set of new recordings to Mercury subsidiary Smash. King issues live *Pure Dynamite! Live At The Royal* (recorded at the Royal theater, Baltimore), which hits US #10.

May The first 2 releases on Smash, *Caldonia* and *The Things That I Used To Do*, only reach US #95 and #99 respectively, but third live album *Showtime* makes #61. Third single *Out Of Sight* climbs to US #24, pioneering a whole new Brown style, with hard, rhythmic, dance-funk base and stripped-down phrase-shouting song structure. Brown quickly develops this "funk" sound into a blend which will revolutionize the whole R&B idiom, and power his own next few hits.

Oct [28-29] James Brown records the "TAMI Show" (Teen Age Music International Show) at the Civic Auditorium in Santa Monica, CA, with The Barbarians, Chuck Berry, The Beach Boys, Marvin Gaye, Gerry & The Pacemakers, Lesley Gore, Jan And Dean, Billy J. Kramer & The Dakotas, Smokey Robinson & The Miracles, The Rolling Stones and The Supremes. (The show will open in UK at the Futurist, Birmingham, W.Midlands as "Gather No Moss" on Aug.7, 1966.)

Dec After the success of *Out Of Sight*, King Records accedes to Brown's demands for greater creative and marketing freedom and he returns to the label, with *Have Mercy Baby* which reaches US #92. The new deal also allows him to continue sending productions to Smash (but only instrumentals, normally with Brown at the organ).

[18] Brown tries to attend the funeral of Sam Cooke in Chicago but fans rush the limousine and he drives away rather than cause further disruption.

1965 May Instrumental album *Grits And Soul* on Smash reaches US #124.

Sept Teamed with new band leader Nat Jones, Brown develops his *Out Of Sight* rhythm pattern with *Papa's Got A Brand New Bag*. It gives him his first US Top 10 at #8, tops R&B chart for 8 weeks, and is a million-seller. It is also his UK chart debut, reaching #25.

Oct *Papa's Got A Brand New Bag* reaches US #26.

Dec *I Got You (I Feel Good)* hits US #3 and spends 6 weeks at R&B #1, selling over a million. An instrumental version of *Try Me* reaches US #63; it comes from Smash label instrumental *James Brown Plays James Brown Yesterday And Today*. It also has a non-vocal version of *Papa's Got A Brand New Bag*, which makes US #42.

1966 Mar *I Got You (I Feel Good)* reaches UK #29, while album of the same title makes US #36.

[11] UK ITV's "Ready Steady Go!" is entirely devoted to Brown's music, following which, he performs 2 London gigs the same evening.

[15] Brown wins Best R&B Recording Of 1965 for *Papa's Got A Brand New Bag* at the 8th annual Grammy awards.

Apr *Ain't That A Groove* makes US #42.

May The slow, intense, orchestra-backed ballad *It's A Man's Man's Man's World* hits US #8, and R&B #1 for 2 weeks, another million-seller. Instrumental *James Brown Plays New Breed* makes US #101.

July *It's A Man's Man's Man's World* reaches UK #13.

[10] Civil disturbance occurs, when fans are unable to get in to Brown's Los Angeles Sports Arena concert.

Aug *Money Won't Change You* peaks at US #53.

Oct *It's A Man's Man's Man's World* reaches US #90.

Nov *Don't Be A Drop-Out* recorded to support the US "Stay In School" campaign reaches US #50.

Dec *Handful Of Soul* makes US #135.

[21] Band begins a 1-week stint at the Westbury Music Fair, Long Island, New York.

1967 Feb *Bring It Up* reaches US #29.

Mar A revival of Wilbert Harrison's *Kansas City* peaks at US #55.

Apr *Think*, a duet with backing singer Vicki Anderson, revives

Brown's own 1960 hit and just makes US #100. (Brown will later return to this song as a soloist.)

May *Raw Soul* peaks at US #88, while *Let Yourself Go* reaches US #46.

June [2] Brown begins a 1-week engagement at the Apollo theater, Harlem.

July *Live At The Garden* reaches US #41, as *James Brown Plays The Real Thing* makes US #164.

Aug Alfred Ellis replaces Jones as The Famous Flames' leader and Brown's chief musical collaborator. The 2 define their musical path in a new direction unrelated to any other R&B or pop trend, building a funk genre with the rhythm section (usually highlighting "funky drummer" Clyde Stubblefield and guitarist Jimmy Nolan), with vocals and lyrics used as rhythmic addenda rather than focal point of the recordings. First example *Cold Sweat* hits US #7, with 3 weeks at R&B #1, and tops a million.

Oct *Cold Sweat* reaches US #35.

Nov *Get It Together* reaches US #40.

By year's end, Brown has bought radio station W-JBE, Knoxville, TN, and will purchase W-EBB, Baltimore, MD, and W-RDW, Augusta, GA.

1968 Jan *I Can't Stand Myself (When You Touch Me)* reaches US #28.

Feb B-side *There Was A Time* charts in its own right, reaching US #36.

Apr [4] After the assassination of Martin Luther King and riots in 30 US cities, Brown makes a national TV appeal from the Boston Garden, urging restraint and more constructive channelling of justified anger. Its calming effect results in an official commendation from Vice President Hubert Humphrey.

I Got The Feelin', another million-seller, peaks at US #6 and tops R&B chart for 2 weeks.

May *I Can't Stand Myself* climbs to US #17.

June *Licking Stick, Licking Stick*, the epitome of funk minimalism combined with mesmeric appeal, reaches US #14. Released at the same time (and reaching US #52) is contrasting *America Is My Home*, another spoken narration which affirms Brown's social conscience and patriotism. (Much of US black youth now looks to him as an important figurehead: a deprived individual who has fulfilled the classic American dream via raw talent.)

July *I Got The Feelin'* reaches US #135.

Aug *I Guess I'll Have To Cry, Cry, Cry*, the last hit to be credited to James Brown & The Famous Flames, peaks at US #55. Hereafter Brown is listed alone though original band remains intact and on the road. *James Brown Plays Nothing But Soul* makes US #150.

Oct *Say It Loud – I'm Black And I'm Proud*, provides another million-seller, reaching US #10 and tops R&B chart for 6 weeks. *Live At The Apollo, Vol.2* makes US #32 and stays charted for 9 months.

Dec *Goodbye My Love* makes US #31.

1969 Jan Brown begins US tour in San Bernardino, CA. The tour will end on Feb.10 at Dallas Memorial Auditorium, TX.

Mar *Give It Up Or Turnit A Loose* climbs to US #15, and spends 2 weeks at R&B #1.

May *I Don't Want Nobody To Give Me Nothin' (Open Up The Door, I'll Get It Myself)* reaches US #20, while *Say It Loud – I'm Black And I'm Proud* peaks at #53.

July [3] Brown plays the Newport Jazz Festival, alongside several rock and blues acts like Blood, Sweat & Tears and Johnny Winter.

[23] Los Angeles declares James Brown Day, in honor of his sell-out concert at the Los Angeles Forum. Mayor Sam Yorty is late to hand Brown the proclamation, so the singer walks out (though the concert goes ahead).

Gettin' Down To It peaks at US #99.

Aug Brown inaugurates a dance, the Popcorn. *Mother Popcorn (You Got To Have A Mother For Me)* is a million-seller, reaching US #11 and R&B #1 for 2 weeks, while wholly instrumental *The Popcorn* makes #30.

Sept [6] At the end of a Memphis, TN, concert Brown announces his intention to retire from the road after next Independence Day. (In fact, he will cut down touring in 1975, but never give it up completely.) Instrumental *Lowdown Popcorn* reaches US #41, and (also instrumental) *James Brown Plays And Directs The Popcorn* makes US #40.

Oct *World* reaches US #37 and *It's A Mother* peaks at #26.

Nov *Let A Man Come In And Do The Popcorn (Part 1)* climbs to US #21.

Dec Largely instrumental *Ain't It Funky Now* reaches US #24.

1970 Jan *Let A Man Come In And Do The Popcorn (Part 2)* reaches US #40.

Mar *It's A New Day* reaches US #32.

Apr *Funky Drummer* makes US #51, while instrumental *Ain't It Funky* reaches US #43.

May *Brother Rapp* reaches US #32.

June *Soul On Top*, recorded by Brown with The Louie Bellson

Orchestra, climbs to US #125. The Famous Flames break up and Brown reorganizes his band, The JB's, incorporating many younger musicians, like Bootsy Collins, and more experienced players, like Fred Wesley and Alfred Ellis.

July *It's A New Day So Let A Man Come In* peaks at US #121.

Aug *Get Up, I Feel Like Being A Sex Machine*, one of his most distinctive and enduringly influential releases, reaches US #15 and is Brown's first million-seller of the decade.

Oct *Get Up, I Feel Like Being A Sex Machine* restores him to UK chart after 4 years, reaching #32.

Nov *Super Bad*, another million-seller, reaches US #13 and tops R&B chart for 2 weeks. Live *Sex Machine* reaches US #29.

[19] Brown marries Deirdre Jenkins at her home in Barnwell.

1971 Jan *Get Up, Get Into It, Get Involved* makes US #34.

Mar *Soul Power* reaches US #29. Instrumental *Spinning Wheel* makes US #90, and live *Super Bad* US #61.

May *I Cried* makes US #50, *Sho Is Funky Down Here* makes US #137.

July *Escape-ism*, a spoken monologue by Brown over The JB's rhythm track, reaches US #35. The first release on his own People label, following a decision to split from King, it fills the gap while negotiations over a worldwide deal proceed with Polydor.

Aug Brown turns the summer's fashion craze into dancefloor number *Hot Pants (She Got To Use What She Got To Get What She Wants)*, on People. It reaches US #15, tops R&B chart, and is another million-seller. After this, he signs to Polydor with full creative control, bringing to the label his entire back-catalog of recordings from the previous 2 decades. He also parts from many of The JB's, including Ellis who is replaced by Wesley as leader, and Collins, who moves with other JB members to George Clinton's Parliament/Funkadelic collective.

Sept His Polydor debut *Make It Funky* reaches US #22 and tops R&B chart for 2 weeks.

Oct *Hot Pants* reaches US #22.

Nov *My Part: Make It Funky Part 3*, a variation on the previous single, peaks at US #68.

Dec *I'm A Greedy Man* makes US #35. *Hey America* reaches UK #47.

1972 Feb Double live album *Revolution Of The Mind – Live At The Apollo, Vol.3* reaches US #39. The JB's single *Gimme Some More* reaches US #67. Written and produced by Brown (and possibly featuring him on keyboards) it is released on People.

Mar *Talking Loud And Saying Nothing* reaches US #27 and spends a week at R&B #1. *King Heroin*, a harrowing anti-drug message narrated by Brown, makes US #40.

June *There It Is* makes US #43, while *Pass The Peas* by The JB's (featuring Brown uncredited) creeps to US #95.

July Brown's revival of Bill Doggett's 1956 million-seller *Honky Tonk* climbs to US #44.

Aug *James Brown Soul Classics*, a compilation of previous hits, reaches US #83 and *There It Is*, with new material, reaches #60.

Sept *Get On The Good Foot* puts him back in US Top 20 at #18, and is R&B #1 for 4 weeks, his first million-seller for over a year.

Dec [11] After a concert in Knoxville, TN, Brown is arrested while talking to fans about drug abuse and charged with "Disorderly Conduct", when an informant tells police that he is trying to incite a riot. Brown threatens Knoxville with a million-dollar lawsuit, and the incident is hastily written off as a "misunderstanding". *I Got A Bag Of My Own* makes US #44.

1973 Jan Brown duets with his new protegee Lyn Collins on *What My Baby Needs Now Is A Little More Lovin'*, which climbs to US #56.

Feb *I Got Ants In My Pants (And I Want To Dance)* reaches US #27, while double album *Get On The Good Foot* makes US #68.

Mar Brown and Wesley of The JB's score the movie "Black Caesar", starring Fred Williamson. Soundtrack album by Brown (now billed on album sleeves as "The Godfather Of Soul") reaches US #31. *Down And Out In New York City*, extracted from it, makes US #50.

June Brown's oldest son Teddy is killed in a car accident in upstate New York. *Think*, a revival of his 1960 hit, also a duet with Vicki Anderson in 1967, climbs to US #77.

July *Doing It To Death*, credited to Wesley & The JB's, but written and produced by Brown (playing incognito), reaches US #22 and tops R&B chart for 2 weeks, selling over a million.

Aug In another marketing move that only Brown would contemplate, he releases yet another (different) recording of *Think*, which peaks at US #92.

Sept Brown and Wesley's score for a second movie, "Slaughter's Big Rip-Off" (starring Jim Brown – no relation) is released on album and makes US #92. Extracted *Sexy, Sexy, Sexy* makes US #50.

1974 Jan *Stoned To The Bone* peaks at US #58.

May *The Payback* reaches US #26, spending 3 months on chart, and hits R&B #1 for 2 weeks. It sells over a million, while double album of the same title reaches US #34, and is also a gold disk winner (for a half-million sales).

Aug *My Thang* climbs to US #29, and tops R&B chart for 2 weeks.

Sept Double album *Hell* reaches US #35.

Oct *Papa Don't Take No Mess* reaches US #31, and spends a week at R&B #1.

Dec Double A-side *Funky President (People It's Bad)/Coldblooded* peaks at US #44.

1975 Mar *Reality* reaches US #80, while album of the same title makes #56. Brown's billing is now "Minister Of New New Super Heavy Funk". (This fails to impress US Treasury Department, which is claiming that "the hardest working man in show business" has been working overtime and owes $4.5 million in unpaid taxes.)

May *Sex Machine, Part 1* (an updated re-recording of *Get Up I Feel Like Being A Sex Machine*) makes US #61.

June *Sex Machine Today* reaches US #103.

Oct *Everybody's Doing The Hustle And Dead On The Double Bump* limps to US #193.

1976 Sept *Get Up Offa That Thing* reaches UK #22 (his first UK hit for almost 5 years).

[11] Album of the same title makes US #147.

Oct [9] *Get Up Offa That Thing* makes US #45.

1977 Feb *Body Heat* makes US #88 and UK #36. This will be his last US Top 100 entry for nearly 9 years. Album of the same title reaches US #126.

Sept [29] The JB's, frequently rumored to be at odds with Brown over peremptory treatment and disputed wages, walk out in mid-tour in Hallandale, FL, complaining of underpayment. (Most will later return.)

1978 Jan Brown is forced to sell W-JBE to help restore his financial position.

Sept [2] *Jam/1980s* makes US #121 remaining charted for 22 weeks.

1979 Sept [1] *The Original Disco Man* (the title a jibe at the style which has supplanted his own as US dancefloor mainstay) makes US #152. Richmond County Superior Court finds Brown guilty of unpaid rent, breach of contract and punitive damages regarding a property in Augusta.

1980 Apr Radio station W-RDW is sold by auction.

June Brown makes a cameo appearance in the film "The Blues Brothers", playing a manic singing and dancing preacher.

Aug Double live album *James Brown ... Live/Hot On The One*, recorded in Tokyo, Japan, reaches US #170.

Nov *Live And Lowdown At The Apollo, Vol.1* peaks at US #163.

1981 Jan [17] He returns to UK chart with *Rapp Payback (Where Iz Moses?)*, recorded for Florida's TK Records, and leased in UK to RCA. It is hugely popular on UK dancefloors and reaches UK #39.

1982 Apr Brown records track for projected Island album at Compass Point, The Bahamas with Sly Dunbar and Robbie Shakespeare.

1983 July *Bring It On ... Bring It On*, another independent production, for Augustasounds in his native Georgia, makes UK #45.

Dec [18] Jimmy Nolan, Brown's former lead guitarist, dies in Atlanta from a heart attack, aged 47.

1984 Sept New York's Tommy Boy label teams Brown on a one-off recording project with electro-rapper Afrika Bambaataa. *Unity (The Third Coming)* reaches UK #49.

1985 May With Brown's old hits starting to become cult favorites in UK clubs, Polydor in UK commissions from top club DJ Froggy a spliced medley of snatches from 12 of them. *Froggy Mix* reaches UK #50 and is unique in being entirely by Brown, but one he has not actually recorded.

June *Get Up, I Feel Like Being A Sex Machine*, reissued in UK after 15 years, reaches #47.

1986 Jan Brown in inducted into the Rock'N'Roll Hall Of Fame at the first annual dinner at the Waldorf Astoria, New York.

Feb *Living In America*, written and produced by Dan Hartman, is the theme from film "Rocky IV", recorded by Brown at the specific request of Sylvester Stallone. It is his first million-seller in 13 years, hitting US #4 and UK #5.

Mar *Get Up, I Feel Like Being A Sex Machine* re-enters UK chart, this time peaking at #46.

Oct [18] *Gravity* peaks at UK #65 and US #93, as *Gravity*, with duets from Alison Moyet and Steve Winwood, makes US #156 and UK #85.

1987 Feb [24] Brown wins Best R&B Performance, Male for *Living In America* at the 29th annual Grammy awards.

Oct TV-advertised hits compilation *The Best Of James Brown – Godfather Of Soul* reaches UK #17.

1988 **Jan** *She's The One*, recorded in the early 70s but not issued at the time, is released by Polydor to satisfy UK demand for new Brown material. Remixed by Tim Rogers, it makes UK #45.

Mar [7] Brown visits UK to be presented with a special award for 20 years of innovation in dance music, by the assembled delegates to the World DJ Convention at London's Royal Albert Hall. (Brown's influence is extended to a new generation of dance music enthusiasts as his archive material becomes the most extensively used, albeit in sound-bite form, in increasingly successful DJ practice of scratching, mixing and sampling.) His unannounced and dramatic stage entrance to accept the award earns a 5-min. standing ovation.

Apr [7] Brown turns himself in to authorities in Aiken County, SC. He is charged with assault with intent to murder and aggravated assault and battery. He is released on $15,000 bond. His wife announces she will file for a legal separation.

[9] Wife Adrienne is arrested at Bush Field Airport, Augusta, GA, after allegedly receiving nasal spray bottles containing PCP from a courier. She is released on $1,550 bond.

[28] Adrienne files a request to drop the assault charges and also the legal separation.

May *The Payback Mix*, a sampled medley (by mixing team Coldcut) of snippets from Brown oldies and some by former associates like The JB's and Bobby Byrd, reaches UK #12.

[10] Adrienne is charged with criminal mischief and arson in a Bedford, NH, hotel room. Brown claims his wife set fire to some of his clothes. PCP is also confiscated from her.

[19] Brown is released on $24,000 bond after spending the night in jail, following a car chase in Aiken County, SC, near his home. He is charged with assault, possession of PCP and illegal weapons and resisting arrest. It is his fifth arrest in 10 months. (Brown is a member of the President's Council Against Drugs.)

[20] Adrienne is arrested again at Bush Field. More PCP is found in her possession.

[25] Adrienne pleads innocent in Merrimack District Court to causing the Bedford hotel fire.

[30] Brown announces, despite loving her, that he is divorcing his wife.

June *I'm Real*, recorded by Brown with production team Full Force, reaches UK #31. It fails to make US Top 100 but achieves US R&B #2. Album of the same title, containing new material, makes UK #27 but only US #96.

[3] Adrienne's attorney asks for dismissal of a Richmond County, GA, traffic misdemeanor charge, citing diplomatic immunity. (US Representative D. Douglas Bernard Jr. on James Brown Appreciation Day in 1986 called Brown "our number 1 ambassador".)

[7] Adrienne is indicted in Augusta, on 2 counts of PCP possession.

[16] Adrienne is arrested at her Beech Island home. After waiving extradition, she is jailed in Richmond County.

[20] Adrienne is released from jail after posting $30,000 total property bond, on condition she remains in 4-county area and submits to drug tests and counseling.

July Brown, back from a European tour, is sentenced on charges of resisting arrest, carrying a pistol and drug possession.

[21] Brown pleads no contest to PCP possession and guilty to carrying a gun and resisting arrest in Aiken circuit court. He receives 2-year suspended sentence and $1,200 fine.

I Got You (I Feel Good), backed with Martha & The Vandellas' *Nowhere To Run*, reissued because of their exposure in film "Good Morning Vietnam", peaks at UK #52.

Aug [5] Brown is admitted to Crawford Long Hospital, Atlanta, for lower jaw surgery to correct degenerative disorder.

He guests with Aretha Franklin on *Gimme Your Love*, which makes US R&B #41.

Dec [15] As a climax to months of conflict with law regulators, not least involving a car chase through 2 states, Brown is finally sentenced to a 6-year jail term.

1989 **July** [19] Brown is moved from minimum security State Park Correctional Facility in Columbia, SC, to medium-security Stevenson Correctional Institution after having $40,000 in checks and cash discovered in his prison cell.

1990 **Jan** [19] Brown becomes eligible for work release.

Apr [12] Having already served 15 months of his term, Brown is transferred from State Park to Lower Savannah Work Center, Aiken County. He will earn at least the minimum $3.80 an hour counselling youths about drug abuse.

May [15] Brown sings medley of hits and lectures students in the Job Training Partnership Act on the importance of education at Jack's Beauty College in North Augusta, SC. It was his first appearance as a community liaison and counselor with the Aiken-Barnwell Counties Community Action Commission in a prison work-release program. The singer was transferred to the minimum-security Lower Savannah Work Release Center after serving 15 months of his 6-year sentence.

Aug [31] Brown is interviewed for Channel 4 program "The Word".

Dec [25] While on a 72-hour furlough from the work center, he plays 2 3-song sets (*I Got You*, *Please Please Please Me* and *Living In America*) for the troops at Fort Jackson, Columbia, SC.

1991 **Feb** [27] Brown is released from Lower Savannah Work Center on parole 8 days prior to his eligibility date. (Brown's parole term is scheduled to end on Oct.23, 1993, at which point he will begin a 5-year period on probation.) Following an intended 2-week vacation at his Beech Island, SC, home, Brown announces he has plans for albums, concert tours, movies and documentaries to reinstate his hardworking reputation. On being released, Brown is quoted as saying: "I feel good."

May [7] Career box-set *Star Time*, a 72-song collection from his 35-year career, is released.

JACKSON BROWNE

1966 **Apr** Having become a proficient pianist, folk-oriented singer, songwriter and guitarist, Browne (b. Oct.9, 1948, Heidelberg, Germany, of US Army parents) becomes an active member of the folk-rock fraternity at Los Angeles, CA, Paradise club. Invited to join The Nitty Gritty Dirt Band, he does not stay long but leaves 2 of his songs, *Melissa* and *Holding* for inclusion on their 1967 debut album.

1967 **Jan** Signed as a songwriter to Nina Music, publishing arm of Elektra Records, he picks up a number of gigs on the New York club circuit including playing guitar for Nico, who takes 3 of his compositions for her in-progress *Chelsea Girl*. Songs cut as demos for his publishers will later appear illicitly on bootleg albums.

1968 Signed to Elektra, he returns to Los Angeles, but the results of his attempts to record an album at Paxton Lodge ranch studio, CA, are never issued. The label lets him go, signing instead Steven Noonan, to whose debut album Browne contributes 5 songs. His songs are also recorded by acts like Tom Rush, who cuts *Shadow Dream Song* on his *The Circle Game* for Elektra.

1971 **Oct** He signs with record entrepreneur David Geffen's fledgling Asylum label. Browne has sent a demo tape and an 8" x 10" photo of himself to the company. Impressed, Geffen's secretary urges her boss to visit Browne at his Echo Park, Los Angeles, home (where he will also meet Longbranch Penny Whistle, which he will sign as The Eagles).

1972 **Mar** Debut album *Jackson Browne* (sometimes called *Saturate Before Using* – a legend printed on the sleeve) is recorded with assistance from Russ Kunkel (drums), Leland Sklar (bass) and Craig Doerge (keyboards) along with David Crosby (harmony vocals) and Albert Lee and The Byrds' Clarence White (guitars). It peaks at US #53.

May Debut single *Doctor My Eyes*, from the album, hits US #8. (It is not a UK hit, but a cover version by The Jackson 5 will reach UK #9 in 1973.) Browne supports Joni Mitchell on a US tour and later accompanies her on some European dates.

Sept Browne tours US with The Eagles, and *Rock Me On The Water* makes US #48. The Eagles' *Take It Easy*, co-written by Browne with member Glenn Frey, reaches US #12. Browne's own version will appear on his second album.

1973 **Nov** *For Everyman* sees the addition of multi-instrumentalist David Lindley. It reaches US #43, while excerpted *Redneck Friend* (said to concern masturbation), peaks at #85. Browne appears on the sleeve of Eagles album, *Desperado*, for which he co-writes *Doolin' Dalton*.

1974 **Jan** Second single from the album, coupling *Ready Or Not* and *Take It Easy* is not a hit. Browne co-writes *James Dean* for third Eagles album *On The Border*.

Dec Third album *Late For The Sky*, with a sleeve in the style of French painter Magritte, reaches US #14. It features his friend Lindley (guitar, violin), plus Jai Winding (keyboards), Doug Haywood (bass, vocals) and Larry Zack (drums). Extracted US singles *Walking Slow* and *Fountain Of Sorrow*, fail.

1976 **Mar** [25] Browne's wife Phyllis commits suicide.

Dec [18] *The Pretender*, with help from Bonnie Raitt, Lowell George, David Crosby and Graham Nash, hits US #5 and is a million-seller. It also marks his UK chart debut, reaching #26.

1977 **Mar** *Here Come Those Tears Again*, from the album, makes US #23.

June Title track, *The Pretender* reaches US #58.

1978 **Feb** The unique live "road" album *Running On Empty*, chronicling his US summer tour and recorded on stage, in hotel rooms, dressing rooms, and on the tour bus, is a second US million-selling album, hitting #3; it reaches UK #28.

Apr Title track *Running On Empty*, recorded at the Merriweather Post Pavilion, Columbia, MD, reaches US #11.

Aug *Stay*, taken from *Running On Empty*, and a revival of the 1960 Maurice Williams & The Zodiacs hit, reaches US #20 and UK #12.

979 **Aug** [4] Browne joins Emmylou Harris, Nicolette Larson, Michael McDonald, Bonnie Raitt, Linda Ronstadt and members of Little Feat in a benefit concert for Lowell George's widow at the Forum, Los Angeles. The 20,000 crowd raises over $230,000.

980 **Jan** Triple-album set *No Nukes*, a compilation recorded live at Madison Square Garden concert organized by Browne and Raitt's MUSE (Musicians United For Safe Energy), reaches US #19. Produced by Browne, John Hall and Raitt, it features US stars such as James Taylor, The Doobie Brothers and Tom Petty, and has 3 of Browne's tracks: one with his own band, and the others duets with Graham Nash and Bruce Springsteen (another version of *Stay*).

Sept [13] *Hold Out*, dedicated to his wife Lynne Sweeney, tops US chart and is another million-seller, while also making UK #44. *Boulevard*, taken from it, reaches US #19.

Nov *That Girl Could Sing*, extracted from *Hold Out*, reaches US #22.

982 **June** [12] Browne takes part in a rally for nuclear disarmament in Central Park, New York, with Ronstadt, Springsteen, Gary U.S. Bonds and Taylor, before an audience of 750,000.

Oct *Somebody's Baby*, from the soundtrack of movie "Fast Times At Ridgemont High", becomes Browne's biggest US hit to date at #7.

983 **Sept** Now without Lindley (replaced by Rick Vito, later with Fleetwood Mac), but retaining a long-standing band including Russ Kunkel, Craig Doerge, Bob Glaub and Doug Haywood, Browne hits US #8 with *Lawyers In Love*, his album first for 3 years. It makes UK #37, and extracted title track peaks at US #13.

Nov *Tender Is The Night*, also from the album, reaches US #25.

984 **Feb** *For A Rocker*, third single from *Lawyers In Love*, peaks at US #45.

985 **Dec** [14] Artists United Against Apartheid, comprising 49 artists including Browne, makes US #38 and UK #21 with *Sun City*.

986 **Jan** [18] He duets with Clarence Clemons, Springsteen's sax player, on *You're A Friend Of Mine* (with additional vocals by Browne's girlfriend, actress Daryl Hannah), which reaches US #18.

Apr Browne expresses his criticism of US foreign policy and support of Amnesty International in *Lives In The Balance*, which reaches US #23 and UK #36.

[19] *For America* reaches US #30.

July [5] *In The Shape Of A Heart*, from the album, makes US #70.

Oct *In The Shape Of A Heart* reaches UK #66 – the first instance of a record by Browne scoring better in UK than US, boosted by his well-received "Lives In The Balance" UK tour.

988 **June** [11] Browne appears in "Nelson Mandela's 70th Birthday Tribute" at Wembley, London, (an event shown on TV throughout the world), leading a star band on a song specially written for the occasion. On his return to US, Browne embarks on a 6-week tour in support of the Christic Institute, a non-profit organization whose lawsuit against a group of US covert operatives is currently on appeal.

989 Browne sings *For America* at "Steal This Wake", for Abbie Hoffman, in Los Angeles.

June [17] *World In Motion*, dedicated to his mother Bea Koeppel, who has died of cancer in 1988, reaches UK #39.

July [28] A 16-date US tour begins at the Mud Island Amphitheater, Memphis, TN, as *World In Motion* makes US #45. Tour will end Aug.27 at the Open Air theater, San Diego, CA. (During a concert at Bally's Grandstand Under The Stars, Atlantic City, NJ, Browne is joined on stage by Springsteen for encore of *Stay*, and then sings *Running On Empty* and *Sweet Little Sixteen*.) A few days later Browne joins Neil Young and others at the Paha Sapa Music Festival on South Dakota's Pine Ridge Reservation to benefit the Oglala Lakota Sioux.

990 **Aug** [31] Browne joins Stevie Wonder and Bonnie Raitt to sing *Amazing Grace* at the memorial service for Stevie Ray Vaughan at Laurel Land Memorial Park, Dallas, TX.

Nov [16-17] Browne joins Springsteen and Raitt in 2 all-acoustic benefit concerts at the Shrine Auditorium, Los Angeles, the proceeds of which will again go to the Christic Institute to finance a lawsuit claiming that the US Government sanctioned illegal arms sales and drugs trafficking to finance covert operations during the Iran-Contra affair.

Dec [16] Browne and Raitt perform at a concert in Sioux Falls, ND, to commemorate the 100th anniversary of massacre at Wounded Knee.

THE BUCKINGHAMS

Dennis Tufano (guitar, lead vocals)
Carl Giammarese (guitar)
Nick Fortune (bass)
Marty Grebb (keyboards)
Jon-Jon Poulos (drums)

1965 Giammarese (b. Aug.21, 1947, Chicago, IL) and Fortune (b. Nicholas Fortuna, May 1, 1946, Chicago), members of The Centuries, playing the Chicago dance circuit and teen clubs and having already recorded *Love You No More* for local Spectra-Sound label and Tufano (b. Sept.11, 1946, Chicago) and Poulos (b. Mar.31, 1947, Chicago), members of The Pulsations, team up together retaining the name The Pulsations, adding Dennis Miccilos on keyboards. Group auditions for "All Time Hits", a variety show on local TV station WGN, and secures a 13-week contract. (A security guard at WGN suggests The Buckinghams because the station wants a name with a British sound.) They revive The Drifters/Searchers' hit *Sweets For My Sweet* on Spectra-Sound, before signing to larger local USA label; meanwhile building a large following in the Chicago area.

1966 **Dec** [31] After 3 singles, *I'll Go Crazy*, *I Call Your Name*, and *I've Been Wrong*, have failed to catch on nationally, *Kind Of A Drag* captures radio attention around US and enters Hot 100 at #90.

1967 **Feb** [18] *Kind Of A Drag*, written by Jim Holvay of fellow Chicago group The Mob, tops US chart for 2 weeks, knocking The Monkees' *Daydream Believer* from #1, and becomes a million-seller. Group's contract is bought from USA by CBS Records, which teams them with producer/manager Jim Guercio, whom The Buckinghams have met through his cousin Burt Jesperson, one of the group's roadies. (At the time Guercio is brought in to the produce the band, he is in Los Angeles, CA, playing bass for UK duo Chad And Jeremy.)

Mar Grebb (b. Sept.2, 1946, Chicago) replaces Miccolis, who has been fired at the beginning of the year.

Apr [8] Lloyd Price-revived classic *Lawdy Miss Clawdy*, released by USA as by The Falling Pebbles but subsequently credited to The Buckinghams, to compete with debut on new label, makes US #41.

[23] *Kind Of A Drag*, compiled by USA from earlier recordings, makes US #109.

May [13] *Don't You Care*, on Columbia, adds a fuller, brassier sound to the smooth vocal/keyboard blend introduced on *Kind Of A Drag*, and hits US #6. It is again written by Holvay, along with fellow Mob player Gary Beisbier, and produced by Guercio.

Aug [4] Group begins its only nationwide US package tour in Hartford, CT, with Gene Pitney, Buffalo Springfield, The Easybeats, The Happenings and The Music Explosion.

[12] Taken from *Time And Charges*, *Mercy Mercy Mercy*, a brass-backed vocal version of jazzman Cannonball Adderley's early 1967 US #11 instrumental original, hits US #5.

[19] *Time And Charges* makes US #58.

Oct [14] *Hey Baby (They're Playing Our Song)*, another Beisbier/Holvay original, reaches US #12.

1968 **Jan** [27] *Susan*, with topical cacophonous psychedelic bridge, reaches US #11.

Mar [30] *Portraits* makes US #53.

June [29] *Back In Love Again*, written by Grebb and with new producer Jimmy Wisner, peaks at US #57 – their first hit single. Disillusioned with CBS over musical differences and producer selection (Guercio has left over publishing and management differences), the band continues, fulfilling outstanding commitments, without support from the label. (Guercio goes on to develop The Buckinghams' brass-rock sound, with even greater success, with fellow CBS acts Chicago and Blood, Sweat & Tears.)

Oct [12] Appropriately-titled *In One Ear And Gone Tomorrow*, mainly self-penned, makes US #161.

1969 **July** [19] Compilation *Greatest Hits* is their US chart swan song, at #73, as Grebb leaves, going on to form The Fabulous Rhinestones with Kal David and Harvey Brooks. He is replaced by John Turner.

1970 The Buckinghams call it a day, as Tufano and Giammarese team as a duo, Poulos goes into management and Fortune becomes a session player in Chicago. (After The Fabulous Rhinestones break up, Grebb becomes an integral part of Bonnie Raitt's band.)

1973 **June** [2] Tufano and Giammarese, now signed to Ode Records, return to US chart with Lou Adler-produced *Music Everywhere*, making #68.

1980 **Mar** [26] Poulos dies of drug-related heart failure.

July Tufano, Giammarese and Fortuna (reverting to his given name), at the behest of Chicago's WLS program director John Guerin, re-form

The Buckinghams for the annual ChicagoFest, adding John Cammelot (keyboards) and Tom Osfar (drums). (They will play the festival again the following summer, and begin playing dates in the Chicago area.)

1985 **Apr** Group, now comprising Giammarese, on lead vocals, Fortuna , Cammelot and Tom Scheckel (b. Nov.19, 1954, Chicago) on drums (Tufano has decided to pursue an acting career in Los Angeles, CA), joins the "Happy Together Tour" with The Turtles, The Grass Roots, Gary Lewis and The Mamas And The Papas at the Abbey, Lake Geneva, WI, as local Red label releases *Veronica* and parent album *A Matter Of Time*. (Band continues playing more than 100 dates a year throughout US, with Giammarese, Fortuna, Scheckel, Bruce Soboroff (b. Aug.31, 1952, Chicago) (keyboards) and Bob Abrams (b. Feb.24, 1955, Ohio) (lead guitar).)

TIM BUCKLEY

1966 After performing with California C&W bands and as a solo singer and guitarist in Los Angeles, CA, folk clubs, and being spotted by Frank Zappa's manager, Herb Cohen, Buckley (b. Timothy Charles Buckley III, Feb.14 1947, Washington, DC) is signed to Elektra Records.
Oct His debut album *Tim Buckley*, produced by Jac Holzman, introduces an individual folk/rock style which garners good reviews, though it does not chart.

1967 **Nov** After a spell in New York playing with ex-Velvet Underground singer Nico and others, he releases *Goodbye And Hello*, produced by Jerry Yester of The Lovin' Spoonful. This contains his best-known and most-covered (notably by Blood, Sweat & Tears) song *Morning Glory*, but it sells disappointingly, reaching only US #171.

1968 **Mar** [8] Buckley plays on opening night of the Fillmore East, New York, with Albert King and Big Brother & The Holding Company.
Oct He tours UK, appearing on several TV shows, and recording a 6-song session for BBC Radio 1's "Top Gear" show.

1969 **May** *Happy Sad*, more jazz-oriented, and produced by both Yester and Zal Yanovsky of The Lovin' Spoonful, reaches US #81.

1970 **Feb** He moves to Cohen and Zappa's Straight Records for *Blue Afternoon*, which is a minor US chartmaker at #192.
Oct *Lorca*, recorded for Elektra to fulfill contractual obligations, contains material in an experimental free-form jazz style, rendering it wholly uncommercial.

1971 **Jan** *Starsailor* further develops Buckley's jazzy, avant-garde experimentations. It fails to sell, but does introduce his second best-known number *Song To The Siren*, later revived in UK by This Mortal Coil. However, disillusioned by its poor reception, he withdraws from music for over a year.

1972 **Oct** After working as a chauffeur and taxi driver, he records *Greetings From L.A.* for Warner Bros. in unaccustomed funk-rock style, produced by Jerry Goldstein (ex-Strangeloves). More accessible than his previous 2 albums, and well reviewed, it still fails to chart.

1973 **Dec** *Sefronia*, on Frank Zappa and Herb Cohen's new label Discreet Records, combines new songs with revivals of oldies like The Jaynettes' 1963 hit *Sally Go Round The Roses*.

1974 **Aug** He tours Europe, playing at Knebworth Festival in UK and on BBC TV's "Old Grey Whistle Test".
Nov *Look At The Fool*, another funk-based set, is less well received.

1975 **Apr** Buckley returns to live work in US, touring Texas and California, and begins planning a retrospective double album of his work, to be recorded live on stage.
June [29] He dies in hospital in Santa Monica, CA, from an overdose of heroin and morphine, having taken the drug cocktail at a friend's house, apparently believing it to be cocaine.

1990 *Dream Letter: Live In London*, recorded during his Oct.1968 visit, is released.

BUCKS FIZZ

Cheryl Baker (vocals)
Jay Aston (vocals)
Mike Nolan (vocals)
Bobby G (vocals)

1981 **Mar** Group is formed from experienced session singers in London, to represent UK in the Eurovision Song Contest with the purpose-written *Making Your Mind Up*. Baker (b. Rita Crudgington, Mar.8, 1954, London) has entered in 1978 with Co-Co, which lost the contest, but had a #13 UK hit with its entry *Bad Old Days*. Aston (b. May 4, 1961, London), Nolan (b. Dec.7, 1954, Dublin, Eire) and G (b. Robert Gubby,

Aug.23, 1953, London), a self-employed builder who auditions after placing an ad in **The Stage** in a last ditch attempt for a career in showbiz, have no previous chart pedigree. They sign to RCA Records.
Apr [4] Band wins Eurovision Song Contest, and *Making Your Mind Up* shoots to #1 in UK, where it stays for 3 weeks. This success ensures the group will stay together, rather than return to session work.
June *Piece Of The Action* reaches UK #12.
Sept *One Of Those Nights* is a slower, smoother sound but less popular, reaching UK #20. Debut album *Bucks Fizz*, reaches UK #14.

1982 **Jan** [16] *The Land Of Make Believe* tops UK chart for 2 weeks.
Apr [17] *My Camera Never Lies* also hits UK #1: the group's third and last chart-topper.
May Second album *Are You Ready?* hits UK #10.
July Ballad *Now Those Days Are Gone*, highlighting their close-harmony talent, hits UK #8.

1983 **Jan** Penned by songwriter/production team Andy Hill and Nichola Martin, who provide the hitmaking backbone for the group, *If You Can't Stand The Heat* hits UK #10.
Mar *Run For Your Life* reaches UK #14.
Apr *Hand Cut* reaches UK #17.
June Richly-produced Abba pastiche *When We Were Young* hits UK #10.
Oct *London Town* breaks their run of UK Top 20 successes at #34. They perform in the presence of Queen Elizabeth the Queen Mother at the Royal Variety Performance, London.
Dec *Greatest Hits*, including the singles to date, reaches UK #25.

1984 **Jan** *Rules Of The Game* peaks at UK #57.
Sept *Talking In Your Sleep*, a cover of 1983 US #3 hit by Detroit group The Romantics, makes UK #15.
Nov *Golden Days* peaks at UK #42, while *I Hear Talk* reaches UK #66.
Dec Bobby G makes UK #65 with self-penned theme song for UK TV series "Big Deal", issued on BBC's own label. Shortly after leaving a gig at Newcastle, Tyne & Wear, the Bucks Fizz tour bus crashes in icy conditions and the group and entourage suffer various degrees of injury. Most serious is Nolan, who is taken comatose to hospital and believed brain-damaged. (He will regain consciousness and eventually return to performing.)

1985 **Jan** Title track from *I Hear Talk* makes UK #34.
July *You And Your Heart So Blue* makes UK #43.
Sept *Magical* peaks at UK #57.
Nov Bobby G's *Big Deal* theme is reactivated due to new TV series and now peaks at UK #46.
Aston leaves amidst much rancor, selling the story of her affair with producer Andy Hill to a national newspaper. Shelley Preston (b. May 14, 1960), who has been working in night clubs in Sri Lanka, is chosen from over 1,000 auditioning girls to replace her.

1986 **July** A label switch from RCA to Polydor is followed by the euphoric, tribal-sounding *New Beginning (Mamba Seyra)*, sung partly in Swahili, which hits UK #8: the group's first Top 10 hit for 3 years.
Sept A brisk revival of Stephen Stills' *Love The One You're With* makes UK #47.
Nov *Keep Each Other Warm* makes UK #45, their last disk for Polydor.
Dec Aptly-titled *The Writing On The Wall* climbs to UK #89.

1988 **Nov** Group, now back with RCA, returns to UK chart with *Heart of Stone* (a worldwide hit for Cher in 1990), which makes #50. Thereafter, the band dissolves, reuniting for occasional live projects. Most prominent among ex-members, Baker successfully pursues a career in television, hosting a number of UK kids and games shows.

BUFFALO SPRINGFIELD

Stephen Stills (vocals, guitar)
Neil Young (vocals, guitar)
Richie Furay (vocals, guitar)
Bruce Palmer (bass)
Dewey Martin (vocals, drums)

1966 **Mar** [3] Group forms with members who have been variously linked in other projects: Stills (b. Jan.3, 1945, Dallas, TX) and Furay (b. May 9, 1944, Yellow Springs, near Dayton, OH) in New York folk group The Au Go Go Singers (an East Coast answer to The New Christy Minstrels); Young (b. Nov.12, 1945, Toronto, Canada) and Palmer (b. 1946, Liverpool, Canada) in The Mynah Birds. Prime mover Stills invites them all to Los Angeles, CA, to investigate teaming up, where they are joined by ex-Dillards' drummer Martin (b. Sept.30, 1942, Chesterville, Canada) and (briefly) by bass player Ken Koblun, a former colleague of Young's in The Squires, who returns to Canada.
1967 **Jan** Signed to Atco Records, and adopting a name seen on a

steamroller during local road repairs, Buffalo Springfield releases its eponymously-titled debut album, which includes 7 songs written by Stills and 5 by Young. Initial sales are slight.

Mar Stills is inspired to write a song about unrest among Los Angeles youth, who have been subjected to police oppression in the name of law and order. This song, *For What It's Worth*, will become an anthem of the era, and is the group's only major hit, at US #7. The album, which does not include the hit, makes US #80. In UK (where *For What It's Worth* does not chart), the album sleeve and label both suggest the hit is included. In fact, the album omits it but features Stills' *Baby Don't Scold Me* (later something of a collector's item as it is replaced by *For What It's Worth* on all subsequent pressings).

May Palmer, a Canadian, is deported from US for visa infringement, but will rejoin the group at intervals, his bass slot on stage otherwise being filled by Koblun or Jim Fielder (later in Blood, Sweat & Tears). Second album *Stampede* is recorded but never released (although it appears as a bootleg). It includes Koblun, Fielder and guitarist Doug Hastings, who is recruited for a short period when Young (who rarely sees eye to eye with Stills) leaves the group.

June [16] Without Young and Palmer, but with Hastings on guitar and additional guest vocalist David Crosby from The Byrds, the band plays the Monterey Pop Festival, CA.

Aug [4] They begin US tour in Hartford, CT, with Gene Pitney, The Buckinghams, The Easybeats, The Happenings and The Music Explosion.

[25] *Bluebird*, written by Stills, peaks at US #58. This includes participation from Bob West on bass and Charlie Chin (later in Cat Mother & The All Night Newsboys) on banjo.

Sept Young rejoins to work on a new album (though he will in-out more than once again); group recording engineer Jim Messina (b. Dec.5, 1947, Maywood, CA) takes over as a more permanent bass player.

Oct *Rock'N'Roll Woman*, another Stills' song, peaks at US #44.

Dec *Buffalo Springfield Again* reaches US #44. Its sleeve lists people who have inspired or influenced the group, including Hank B. Marvin of The Shadows (the inspiration for Young's early guitar playing).

1968 Jan [20] From the album, Young's song *Expecting To Fly* makes US #98, but the group de-stabilizes as it attempts to record another album.

May [5] Group finally implodes after a last gig in Los Angeles, and the members quickly fan out to launch other projects: Stills to form Crosby, Stills & Nash (after assisting Al Kooper to complete the album *Super Session*); Young and Palmer to solo careers (the latter briefly before fading from sight; the former with major success after signing to Reprise Records); and Furay to plan the formation of Poco. Martin will attempt to form a new Buffalo Springfield 6 months later, but is prevented from using the name, and drops out of view soon after.

Sept Third Buffalo Springfield album to be released, *Last Time Around*, assembled after the split by Messina from the later sessions, makes US #42.

Oct [26] *On The Way Home*, taken from the album, stalls at US #82, by which time Messina has joined Furay in newly-launched Poco.

1969 Apr Compilation *Retrospective/The Best Of Buffalo Springfield*, which includes their chart singles, equals their highest US Album chart placing by peaking at #42.

1973 Dec Double compilation *Buffalo Springfield* reaches US #104 in the wake of the success achieved by Stills, Young, Furay and Messina in their various post-Springfield projects.

JIMMY BUFFETT

1969 Having majored in history and journalism at the University of Southern Mississippi and become a freelance journalist for a while (including a stint at **Billboard** magazine), Buffett (b. Dec.25, 1946, Mobile, AL) moves to Nashville, TN, to attempt to secure a deal as a country singer.

1970 Sept Signed to Andy Williams' Barnaby label, he releases debut album *Down To Earth*, which reputedly sells only 324 copies.

1971 Tapes of Buffett's second album *High Cumberland Jubilee* are misplaced by Barnaby, delaying its release indefinitely. He leaves the label and Nashville shortly afterwards.

1972 Buffett settles in Key West, FL, after a gig falls through at a Miami club. He cannot afford to go back to Nashville, and begins hanging out with Jerry Jeff Walker. In time he buys a 50-foot ketch and makes it his home and begins the lifestyle for which he will later become famous and which will influence much of his songwriting. By night, he plays local bars the Green Parrot and Ernest Hemingway's old haunt Sloppy Joe's.

1973 He signs to ABC/Dunhill Records. *A White Sport Coat And A Pink*

Crustacean (a play on the title of an old Marty Robbins hit) does not chart but introduces the wryly humorous and buccaneering style which will permeate subsequent hits.

Oct Buffett records *Living And Dying* at Woodland Sound studio in Nashville, with producer Don Gant.

1974 Apr *Living And Dying In 3/4 Time* reaches US #176. He appears in the movie "Rancho Deluxe", for which he writes the music (and contributes 6 tracks to the non-charting soundtrack album, on United Artists).

July [13] Reassuring *Come Monday*, his first US hit single, reaches #30.

1975 Buffett forms his Coral Reefer Band with Roger Bartlett (guitar), Greg Taylor (harmonica), Harry Dailey (bass) and Phillip Fajardo (drums).

Apr *A1A* (the designation of a beach access road off US Route 1 in Florida) makes US #25.

1976 Mar [27] *Havana Daydreamin'*, on ABC Records, reaches US #65. Following this success, the previously unissued second Barnaby album is released, under the title *High Cumberland Jubilee*, but fails to chart.

1977 July Nautical-themed *Changes In Latitudes, Changes In Attitudes* climbs to US #12 and earns a platinum disk as Buffett's first million-seller.

[23] Extracted *Margaritaville* hits US #8.

Nov [5] Extracted title track *Changes In Latitudes, Changes In Attitudes* makes US #37.

1978 May He makes a cameo appearance in film "FM", singing *Livingston Saturday Night*, which is included on the soundtrack album, which hits US #5 and UK #37.

[20] *Son Of A Son Of A Sailor*, produced by Norbert Putnam, hits US #10, and is a second million-seller.

June [17] *Cheeseburger In Paradise*, taken from the album, makes US #32. Jay Spell joins the Coral Reefer Band on keyboards.

Sept [9] *Livingston Saturday Night* peaks at US #52.

Dec [9] *Manana* peaks at US #84.

[16] Live double *You Had To Be There*, recorded at the Fox theater, Atlanta, GA, and the Maurice Gusman Cultural Center, Miami, makes US #72.

1979 May [1-17] Buffett records forthcoming *Volcano* at Air studios, Montserrat, West Indies.

Oct [13] *Volcano*, his first for MCA after ABC label has been phased out, reaches US #14 and sells a million copies.

Nov [3] Extracted *Fins* makes US #35.

1980 Jan [19] Extracted title track *Volcano* peaks at US #66.

Mar [29] *Survive* climbs to US #77.

1981 Mar [28] *It's My Job* peaks at US #57 (and is Buffett's last hit single). *Coconut Telegraph* makes US #30. By now, his touring has become less frequent as he spends much time at sea in the Caribbean on his latest ketch, Euphoria II.

1982 Feb [13] *Somewhere Over China* reaches US #31. Buffett opens a store in Key West, named Margaritaville, in which he sells the tropical shirts which have become an essential part of his image. He launches **The Coconut Telegraph**, a regular newsletter for his fans which mails out a consistent 4,000 copies.

1983 Nov *One Particular Harbor* makes US #59.

1984 Oct *Riddles In The Sand* makes US #87. His range of "Caribbean Soul" tropical shirts is put into retail outlets across US.

1985 Aug *Last Mango In Paris* makes US #53. A competition accompanies its release, offering a trip on Buffett's ketch as the prize. 100,000 people enter and 5 winners receive a free cruise. Meanwhile, Buffett's song *Turning Around* is used on the soundtrack of the film *Summer Rentals*.

Dec Compilation retrospective *Songs You Know By Heart – Jimmy Buffett's Greatest Hit(s)*, with chart singles and favorite album tracks, peaks at US #100. A video is made for *Who's The Blonde Stranger*, in which Florida Governor Bob Graham makes a guest appearance. Buffett completes the script for a projected movie to be titled *Margaritaville*. (Buffett becomes campaign singer for Tony Tarracino in his bid to become mayor of Key West, which he does.)

1986 July *Floridays*, recorded variously in Memphis, Fort Lauderdale and Los Angeles, and co-produced by Buffett with Mike Utley, reaches US #66.

1987 He divides his time between music and other pursuits: writing a children's book **The Jolly Man** with 8-year-old daughter Savannah Jane (who also plays mini-conga on *Floridays*), editing **The Coconut Telegraph** and running the "Margaritaville" restaurant and clothing stores. He becomes chairman of the Save The Manatee committee, dedicated to the protection of the endangered marine animal.

1988 July *Hot Water*, recorded at Buffett's own Shrimpboat Sound studios in Key West, is released to coincide with a major 31-city US tour from late June to mid-Aug. It peaks at US #46. *Homemade Music* is extracted and promoted via an offbeat "outrageous" video.

1989 **June** [30] He embarks on 18-date US tour at Auburn Hills, MI, which will end on July 27 in Birmingham, AL.

July *Off To See The Lizard* peaks at US #57.

Aug Buffett is on organizing board of the "Earth Day 1990", set for Apr.22, 1990, to heighten people's awareness of the environment.

Oct As his novel "Tales From Margaritaville" hits the **New York Times** Best Seller book list, Buffett continues his "Off To See The Lizard Tour '89" with The Coral Reefer Band and The Neville Brothers in support. He has also become an investor in a Florida Minor League baseball team.

1990 **Jan** [21] As "The Lizard" tour continues at Barton Coliseum, Arkansas State Fairgrounds, Little Rock, AR, in between touring and recording commitments, Buffett will team with Glenn Frey to write a musical, "Rules Of The Road".

June "Jimmy's Jump Up" US tour begins.

Aug [19] Tour ends at the Performing Arts Center at Saratoga Springs, NY.

Dec [1] *Feeding Frenzy* makes US #68.

1991 **Feb** [10] Buffett joins nearly 100 celebrities in Burbank, CA, to record *Voices That Care*, a David Foster and fiancee Linda Thompson Jenner-composed and organized charity record to benefit the American Red Cross Gulf Crisis Fund.

Mar As he prepares for release of new live album *Feeding Frenzy*, Buffett encounters 4 Cuban exiles who have swum up to his house in Florida, seeking political asylum. He hands them over to local authorities after offering them refreshments.

SOLOMON BURKE

1955 **Dec** A former boy preacher, Burke (b. 1936, Philadelphia, PA), broadcaster on "Solomon's Temple", and soloist in his family's own Philadelphia church, the House Of God For All People, signs to Apollo Records in New York after being discovered by Kae Williams, the wife of a local DJ, and makes his first recording, *Christmas Presents From Heaven*. (This and subsequent singles on Apollo and Singular Records 1956-59 will feature him trying to mold a distinctive secular style from his gospel roots, and will not sell.)

1960 **Dec** He signs to Atlantic Records, at the suggestion of **Billboard** magazine's Paul Ackerman.

1961 **Nov** Second Atlantic release, C&W song *Just Out Of Reach (Of My Two Empty Arms)* climbs to US #24 – one of the first country/R&B hybrids, and one of the first definable hits in the 60s soul genre in which Atlantic is to be a prime mover.

1962 **Mar** *Cry To Me*, written by Burke's new producer Bert Berns, reaches US #44, and will be covered by The Rolling Stones and others.

July Double A-sided *Down In The Valley/I'm Hanging Up My Heart For You* charts in US at #71/#85.

Sept Country song *I Really Don't Want To Know* makes US #93.

1963 **June** *If You Need Me* is a song given to Burke while on tour, by its co-writer and fellow R&B singer, Wilson Pickett. In US chart competition with Pickett's own version, Burke's single reaches #37 against Pickett's #64. It also hits R&B #2.

Aug *Can't Nobody Love You* makes US #66.

Dec *You're Good For Me* reaches US #49.

1964 **Feb** Another C&W oldie, *He'll Have To Go*, climbs to US #51.

June *Goodbye Baby (Baby Goodbye)* reaches US #33.

Aug Gospel-like *Everybody Needs Somebody To Love* (later used by Burke as a fund-raiser march in his church) peaks at US #58.

Oct *Yes I Do* stalls at US #92.

Dec *The Price*, which Burke writes about his own disintegrating marriage, makes US #57.

1965 **Apr** His biggest US hit is *Got To Get You Off My Mind*, reaching #22 and also spending 4 weeks at R&B #1.

June [14] Burke arrives in UK for a promotional visit; during it he will appear on "Ready Steady Goes Live!" and "Thank Your Lucky Stars".

July *Tonight's The Night*, written with Don Covay and coupled with a cover of Bob Dylan's *Maggie's Farm*, is his last US Top 30 entry, at #28 (and reaching R&B #2).

Aug Compilation *The Best Of Solomon Burke* is one of only 2 albums during his entire career to make US chart, reaching #141.

Sept With the rise to chart status of other solo soul singers with styles approximating his own (many also on Atlantic), Burke's sales reduce, as *Someone Is Watching* peaks at only US #89. (His next 3 singles, *Only Love (Can Save Me Now)*, *Baby Come On Home* and *I Feel A Sin Coming

On, will only reach #94, #96 and #97 respectively, through 1965-66.)

1967 **Feb** *Keep A Light In The Window Till I Come Home* is his best-seller for 2 years, reaching US #64.

July *Take Me (Just As I Am)*, recorded at Stax in Memphis, continues his resurgence, making US #49.

1968 **June** Burke makes US #68 with *I Wish I Knew (How It Would Feel To Be Free)*. He soon finds out, as Atlantic lets him go.

1969 **June** Signing a new recording deal with Bell Records, he covers Creedence Clearwater Revival's *Proud Mary*, only 3 months after the original has been a million-seller, but it climbs to US #45. It is, however, his only hit for Bell, and he finds it hard to maintain with other labels the consistency he managed at Atlantic.

July *Proud Mary* tops his only other Album chart entry by one place, reaching #140.

1971 **May** Signed now to MGM Records, he re-charts in US after 2 years' absence, with *The Electronic Magnetism (That's Heavy, Baby)*, which climbs to #96.

1972 **Apr** Also on MGM (where his releases vary greatly in quality, much of the material offered him being sub-standard), *Love's Street And Fool's Road*, a song from movie "Cool Breeze", reaches US #89.

1975 **Mar** After 3 years and a brief spell on the Dunhill label, Burke has switched labels again to Chess Records when he returns with Barry White-styled *You And Your Baby Blues*, reaching US #96. Shortly after this, he semi-retires from secular performing and recording to concentrate on his religious duties as bishop of his church. (This will remain his foremost activity through into the late 80s, with most album releases being gospel or inspirational led, though he will make occasional US tours as part of "The Soul Clan", an aggregation of soul soloists who first made their names on the Atlantic labels during the 60s, which also includes Eddie Floyd, Joe Tex, Ben E. King and Wilson Pickett.)

DORSEY AND JOHNNY BURNETTE

1952 After attending high school with Elvis Presley, Johnny Burnette (b. Mar.25, 1934, Memphis, TN) works for a while as a Mississippi bargeman and attempts to earn additional living as a boxer and a singer. He persuades older brother Dorsey (b. Dec.28, 1932, Memphis) and neighbor Paul Burlison (b. Feb.4, 1929, Brownsville, TN), a member of local band The Memphis Four, to form a trio.

1953 With Johnny on guitar and lead vocals, Dorsey on stand-up bass and Burlison on lead guitar, they begin to play Memphis dates and become regulars at the Hideaway club. First single *You're Undecided* for Von Records in Boonsville, MS, fails to score.

1955 When friend Elvis Presley becomes successful on local Sun label, the trio auditions there for Sam Phillips, but he finds their sound too Elvis-like and rejects them.

1956 **Mar** Seeing Presley on TV, they decide to drive to New York, take temporary jobs (Dorsey and Burlison as electricians, Johnny in a factory), and join auditions for TV's "Ted Mack Amateur Hour".

Apr The trio becomes the show's winners for 3 successive weeks, earning a tour and spot in Sept. finals. They also attract New York record companies, and sign to Coral.

May [7] They record *Tear It Up* (soon issued), and other tracks, at Pythian Temple studio, New York.

July [2-5] They record extensively at Bradley's Barn studio, Nashville, TN. *Oh Baby Babe* and *The Train Kept A-Rollin'* emerge, but are not hits.

Sept Narrowly failing to win "Amateur Hour" final, they join a 3-month tour of Northeast US, with Carl Perkins and Gene Vincent.

Nov Dorsey drops out of live work with trio, and is replaced on stage dates by Tony Austin. New line-up films a spot in Alan Freed movie "Rock Rock Rock", singing *Lonesome Train*, which is their next (unsuccessful) single.

1957 **Sept** After record company apathy and poor promotion see 2 more singles fail to hit, the trio splits. Burlison retires into business in Memphis, and the Burnettes head for Los Angeles, CA.

Dec They have their first songwriting success with *Waiting In School* for Ricky Nelson (US #18). They will write later hit *Believe What You Say* for Nelson, while Johnny pens *Just A Little Too Much* and Dorsey writes *It's Late* and *A Long Vacation*.

1958 They record *My Honey* for Imperial Records as The Burnette Brothers, but it fails to chart.

Oct Johnny signs as a solo singer to Freedom Records, a new subsidiary of the successful Liberty label. His 3 singles on Freedom fail to sell, but when the label is closed, Johnny is transferred to Liberty and to producer Snuff Garrett.

1959	**Dec** Dorsey signs to Era Records as a soloist.
1960	**Mar** *Tall Oak Tree*, an ecology-slanted song written for Ricky Nelson but turned down, reaches US #23 in Dorsey's own version on Era. **July** Johnny's first single with Garrett, *Dreamin'*, climbs to US #11. **Aug** Dorsey's *Hey Little One* makes US #48. **Oct** Johnny's *Dreamin'* hits UK #5. **Dec** Johnny's *You're Sixteen* hits US #8 and is a million-seller.
1961	**Feb** *You're Sixteen* hits UK #3. **Mar** *Little Boy Sad* reaches US #17 for Johnny. **May** *Little Boy Sad* reaches UK #12. **June** First ballad for Johnny after 3 uptempo hits, *Big, Big World*, is less successful, only reaching US #58. It is not released in UK. **Sept** Johnny's *Girls*, released only as a UK single, reaches #37. **Nov** *God, Country And My Baby*, a mock-patriotic song, is Johnny's final US chart entry, at #18. Meanwhile Dorsey moves to US Dot label and switches style towards country music.
1962	**Apr** [21] Johnny embarks on 23-date twice-nightly UK package tour with Gary U.S. Bonds, Gene McDaniels, Mark Wynter, Danny Rivers and others, at St. Andrews Hall, Glasgow, Scotland. Tour will end May 13 at the Granada cinema, Walthamstow, London. **May** *Clown Shoes*, written by P.J. Proby, is Johnny's final UK hit, at #35. **July** He moves to Chancellor Records, but *I Wanna Thank Your Folks* and *Remember Me* are unsuccessful. Meanwhile Dorsey changes labels again, this time to Reprise.
1963	Johnny switches labels to Capitol in search of new success formula, but *All Week Long* and *Sweet Suzie* do not sell. **Nov** [1] Johnny begins UK tour in Birmingham, W.Midlands.
1964	Johnny records briefly for small Sahara label, then decides to form his own label, Magic Lamp, to pursue new projects. **Aug** [1] Before Magic Lamp can get into stride, Johnny falls from his boat while fishing on Clear Lake, CA, and is drowned.
1968	Dorsey signs to Liberty Records (on which Johnny Burnette had solo hits) as a country singer.
1969	**Feb** *The Greatest Love* returns him to US pop chart at #67.
1972	He signs to Capitol Records and begins a 4-year spell of country hits, with 10 C&W chart singles and the albums *Here And Now* and *Dorsey Burnette*. He will also have success as a writer for Jerry Lee Lewis and Glen Campbell.
1973	He is voted Year's Most Promising Newcomer by Academy Of Country Music, despite a 20-year career.
1975	He joins Motown's country label Melodyland, and has a C&W hit with *Molly (I Ain't Gettin' Any Younger)*.
1977	He signs to the Calliope label for country album *Things I Treasure*.
1979	**Aug** [19] Dorsey dies of a heart attack at Canoga Park, CA. (The Burnettes' sons will continue their musical heritage – Dorsey's son Rocky (b. June 12, 1953, Memphis, TN) scores a major UK hit with *Tired Of Toein' The Line*, while Johnny's son Billy (b. May 8, 1953, Memphis) joins Fleetwood Mac when Lindsay Buckingham leaves the band.)

KATE BUSH

1974	While still at St. Joseph's Convent grammar school, Bush (b. Catherine Bush, July 30, 1958, Bexleyheath, Kent) signs recording and publishing contracts with EMI, after Dave Gilmour of Pink Floyd has heard her songs and a friend of her parents, Ricky Hopper, has paid for demo studio recordings. The company decides to wait before launching her, encourages her writing and sees that she takes voice, dance (with Lindsay Kemp) and mime (with Adam Darius) classes which are to hone her eventual style. Meanwhile, she gains live experience playing South London pub gigs with her K.T. Bush Band, comprising brother Paddy and future boyfriend Del Palmer.
1976	**July** EMI Records advances Bush £3,000, and a further £500 by EMI Publishing.
1978	**Jan** *Wuthering Heights*, with lyrics inspired by Emily Bronte's novel, is released in UK with a major artist launch publicity campaign, despite EMI's concern that the record is not commercial. **Mar** *Wuthering Heights* tops UK chart for 4 weeks. **Apr** Andrew Powell-produced *The Kick Inside*, written during the previous 3 years and recorded in 1977, including work by Gilmour, hits UK #3 on its way to a million-plus UK sales. **July** Ballad *The Man With The Child In His Eyes*, the lyrics she had written when she was 14, hits UK #6. **Nov** *Hammer Horror* proves a UK chart disappointment, reaching #44. **Dec** Follow-up album *Lionheart* hits UK #6.
1979	**Mar** After initial US failure with *Wuthering Heights*, *The Man With The Child In His Eyes* peaks at US #85.
	Apr [3] She plays her first major live show at the Empire theater, Liverpool, Merseyside, introducing the 28-date "Tour Of Life", a 2½ hour-long act strong on dance, image and theatrical choreography (including 17 costume changes), which will play throughout UK and then across Europe. After this she will not tour again. *Wow* is re-recorded from second album and makes UK #14. **May** [12] Bush, with Steve Harley, Peter Gabriel and other friends, headlines a benefit concert at Hammersmith Odeon, London, for the family of her lighting director Billy Duffield, killed in a stage accident. **Oct** EP *Kate Bush On Stage*, featuring 4 live tracks from the benefit show, hits UK #10. Bush devises and records a 30-min. special, including guest appearance by Gabriel, for UK BBC2 TV broadcast.
1980	**Mar** Bush sings guest back-up vocals on Gabriel's *Games Without Frontiers*, which hits UK #4 and makes US #48. **May** *Breathing*, a song about nuclear fallout in a ruined world, climbs to UK #16. **June** *Babooshka* hits UK #5, her first Top 5 hit since *Wuthering Heights*, aided by a dramatic video. With her visual leanings, Bush is one of the first major UK acts to embrace the booming promo video medium. **Sept** *Never For Ever*, self-produced with Jon Kelly and with the unlikely help of animal impressionist Percy Edwards and Australian singer/painter Rolf Harris, enters UK chart at #1. **Oct** *Army Dreamers* reaches UK #16. **Dec** Seasonal *December Will Be Magic Again* climbs to UK #29.
1981	**Aug** *Sat In Your Lap* reaches UK #11. **Oct** Video "Live At The Hammersmith Odeon" is issued.
1982	**Aug** Title song from forthcoming *The Dreaming* makes a small impact as a single, reaching UK #48. **Sept** *The Dreaming*, co-produced with Palmer (bassist and long-time beau) hits UK #3. **Nov** *There Goes A Tenner*, from the album, is her first UK chart failure.
1983	**June** Bush begins upgrading her home studio at her 350-year-old South London farmhouse, resulting in a self-contained 48-track facility. **July** US-only issued mini-album *Kate Bush* reaches US #148. **Dec** Video collection "The Single File" is released by EMI.
1985	**Aug** After 2 years out of the public eye, Bush returns with popular *Running Up That Hill*, which hits UK #3, and is her second biggest-seller after *Wuthering Heights*. **Sept** *Hounds Of Love*, launched by EMI with a party at the London Planetarium, enters UK chart at #1 and remains on top for a month. **Nov** *Running Up That Hill* finally gives Bush her US breakthrough, making #30. *Cloudbusting*, also from the album, reaches UK #20. The promo video co-stars Bush with actor Donald Sutherland. **Dec** *Hounds Of Love* reaches US #30.
1986	**Mar** *Hounds Of Love*, the title track from the album, reaches UK #18. **May** *The Big Sky* charts briefly at UK #37. **June** Video "Hair Of The Hound" is issued. **Nov** *Experiment IV*, promoted with a self-directed video, reaches UK #23. She duets with Gabriel on *Don't Give Up*, making UK #9.
1987	**Jan** *The Whole Story*, anthologizing her best-known work, hits UK #1, and becomes her best-selling album. A video version is also a #1 success on UK Video charts. The album makes US #76. **Feb** [9] Bush wins Best British Female Artist at the sixth annual BRIT Awards at the Grosvenor House, London. **Mar** [28] Bush makes a rare live appearance performing *Running Up That Hill* and *Let It Be* with Gilmour and Gabriel at "The Secret Policeman's Third Ball", London. **Apr** [25] *Don't Give Up* peaks at US #72.
1988	A new Bush song is included by producer John Hughes in his film "She's Having A Baby".
1989	**Oct** Bush returns with *The Sensual World*, which hits UK #2, and extracted title track which reaches UK #12. **Dec** Second single from album, *This Woman's Work*, reaches UK #25.
1990	**Mar** *Love And Anger* peaks at UK #38. **Oct** [26] Bush has been 16 years old with EMI, which issues a career box set comprising all of her recordings to date, titled *This Woman's Work*. **Nov** Currently recording her eighth album, Bush appears at her fan club convention and announces that she hopes to tour (she has not done so since 1979), following the album's 1991 release.

JERRY BUTLER

1957	A resident of Chicago, IL, since age 3, Butler (b. Dec.8, 1939, Sunflower, MS) has spent several years in church choirs, notably the Northern Jubilee Gospel Singers, and sung with local doo-wop group The Quails, when he and close friend Curtis Mayfield (introduced in Mayfield's

mother's church), singing with The Alphatones, meet a Tennessee R&B group named The Roosters in Chicago, and join forces with them.
Dec Renamed The Impressions, with Butler as lead singer, the group auditions for Ewart Abner's Falcon Records, a subsidiary of leading Chicago R&B label Vee-Jay, and is signed.

1958 **Apr** First recording session produces the group's own ballad composition *For Your Precious Love*, the song which most impressed Abner at the audition. He decides to release it as a single.
July *For Your Precious Love* reaches US #11, though the group is disconcerted to find Abner has credited "The Impressions Featuring Jerry Butler" on the record label, in clear emphasis of the soloist.
Sept 2 more singles follow, neither charting, and both with soloist-plus-group billing at the label's insistence. Butler, sensing the others' antagonism, decides to leave. Abner then decides to retain him as a solo act, and drops the group, which promptly disbands (though Mayfield remains at Vee-Jay studios as a session musician and writer, and 3 years later will re-form The Impressions as a trio, with original member Sam Gooden and previous Roosters member Fred Cash, finding major US chart success in the 60s).

1960 **Dec** After several solo records, 2 hits on R&B chart, and a move to Vee-Jay after the subsidiary labels close, Butler is reunited with Mayfield on *He Will Break Your Heart*, a major US hit (#7) which they co-write and on which Mayfield supplies backing vocals and guitar.

1961 **Apr** *Find Another Girl*, a similar collaboration, reaches US #27.
Aug *I'm A-Telling You*, again with Mayfield's back-up, makes US #25.
Dec Sensing the chance to broaden his audience appeal, Butler records *Moon River*, Henry Mancini's song from movie "Breakfast At Tiffany's", which reaches US #11, 2 weeks in advance of the composer's original. This success launches him as a purveyor of (usually R&B-oriented) sophisticated ballads throughout the 60s, and ensures him regular lucrative live engagements in US supper-club field.

1962 **Sept** *Make It Easy On Yourself*, a Burt Bacharach/Hal David song which becomes another standard (and a hit for The Walker Brothers in 1965), reaches US #20.
Nov *You Can Run (But You Can't Hide)* reaches US #63.
Dec *Theme From Taras Bulba (The Wishing Star)* stays a week at US #100.

1963 **Apr** *Whatever You Want* peaks at US #68.

1964 **Jan** *Need To Belong*, a Curtis Mayfield song, climbs to US #31.
Apr *Giving Up On Love* reaches US #56.
July *I Don't Want To Hear It Anymore*, one of the earliest hits written by Randy Newman, stalls at US #95, but many radio DJs play the B-side, Butler's own song *I Stand Accused*, which makes US #61 (much covered, it will be a US Top 50 hit for Isaac Hayes in 1970).
Nov After hearing the ballad *Let It Be Me* in the Bahamas, Butler records it as a duet with Vee-Jay girl, Betty Everett, and it becomes his biggest US hit to date, at #5. Their album of duets, *Delicious Together*, reaches US #102.

1965 **Jan** *Smile*, a second ballad duet with Everett, reaches US #42.
Mar Solo *Good Times* peaks at US #64.
June [25] He stars on UK TV's "Ready Steady Go!"
July [3] He appears on UK TV's "Thank Your Lucky Stars".

1966 **Mar** A revival of *For Your Precious Love* peaks at US #99, but Vee-Jay is in no position to promote it, since the company crashes almost immediately afterwards with major debts.
Aug Now dubbed "The Ice Man" by Philadelphia DJ George Woods (a tag which stays with him hereafter), because of his super-cool stage presence and un-histrionic vocal style, Butler signs a new contract with Mercury Records.

1967 **Feb** First Mercury release, *I Dig You Baby*, reaches US #60.
Nov *Mr. Dream Merchant* is his first solo US Top 40 for 4 years, at #38.

1968 **Jan** *Lost* reaches US #62.
Feb *Mr. Dream Merchant* is his first solo album to chart in US, at #154.
Mar *Jerry Butler's Golden Hits Live* reprises many earlier singles in onstage versions, and reaches US #178. While performing at Prep's nightclub in Philadelphia, Butler meets songwriting/production team Kenny Gamble and Leon Huff, and they agree to work together.
July First fruit of the Philadelphia recording sessions is *Never Give You Up*, a Gamble/Huff/Butler composition which makes US #20.
Nov *Hey, Western Union Man*, another of the trio's compositions, is a bigger hit still, peaking at US #16, and topping R&B chart.

1969 **Jan** Gamble/Huff-produced *The Ice Man Cometh* (with the 2 recent hits) reaches US #29. *Are You Happy?* is also extracted, making US #39.
Apr *Only The Strong Survive*, last single from *The Ice Man Cometh*, hits US #4 (topping R&B chart for 2 weeks) and is a million-plus seller, attracting cover versions from Elvis Presley and others.
July From new Philadelphia sessions, *Moody Woman* reaches US #24.

Oct *What's The Use Of Breaking Up* makes US #20.
Dec *Don't Let Love Hang You Up* reaches US #44, while Butler's second Gamble/Huff-produced album, *Ice On Ice*, containing this and the 2 previous hits, makes US #41.

1970 **Jan** 2 more *Ice On Ice* tracks are US chart singles: *Got To See If I Can't Get Mommy (To Come Back Home)* (#62), and *I Could Write A Book* (#46).
July Compilation *The Best Of Jerry Butler*, rounding up Mercury singles to date, reaches US #167. This also marks the end of Butler's Philly period, as Gamble and Huff, thanks largely to their huge success with him, have launched their own Philadelphia International label, and major companies are sending artists like Wilson Pickett and Archie Bell & The Drells to work with the duo. With his own credibility at an all-time high, Butler establishes the Songwriters' Workshop in Chicago, backed by music publisher Chappell, and giving creative opportunity to young writers like Chuck Jackson, Marvin Yancy, Terry Callier and Brenda Eager – who will in turn provide Butler with a fund of material for future recordings.
Aug *Where Are You Going*, recorded for the soundtrack of film "Joe", charts briefly at US #95, while *You And Me* peaks at #172.

1971 **Jan** Duet with fellow Chicago artist Gene Chandler, *You Just Can't Win (By Making The Same Mistake)*, credited to Gene & Jerry, makes US #94.
Mar Solo single *If It's Real What I Feel* reaches US #69. It is taken from *Jerry Butler Sings Assorted Sounds* (most of them courtesy of the Songwriters' Workshop), which makes US #186.
Apr Again duetted with Chandler, *Gene & Jerry – One & One* reaches US #143.
July *How Did We Lose It Baby* stalls at US #85.
Oct Another Workshop-originated album, *The Sagittarius Movement* is released, peaking at only US #123, but becoming a steady seller, on chart for 22 weeks. Single *Walk Easy My Son* makes US #93.

1972 **Mar** *Ain't Understanding Mellow*, a duet with young protegee Brenda Lee Eager (found in the Chicago choir run by Rev. Jesse Jackson, to whose charitable endeavors in the city Butler is a regular contributor), reaches US #21, staying charted for almost 5 months and becoming his second certified million-selling single. Eager becomes a member of his vocal backing group, Peaches.
June A revival of *I Only Have Eyes For You*, from *The Spice Of Life*, reaches US #85, while the album peaks at US #92.
Sept A second duet with Eager, *(They Long To Be) Close To You*, and solo *One Night Affair* are his final Mercury chart entries, peaking at US #91 and #52 respectively. He then concentrates on the Workshop, his music publishing activities and the running of 2 small talent-showcase labels, Fountain and Memphis, in Chicago.

1975 **Jan** Butler's contract with Mercury expires, and he is approached by Abner, who first recorded him, now President of Motown Records.
Apr Butler signs to Motown, but first album, *Love's On The Menu*, fails to chart.

1977 **May** *Suite For The Single Girl* reaches US #146, while from it comes *I Wanna Do It To You*, which makes US #51.
July Motown teams him with Thelma Houston, in anticipation of repeating past duetting successes; *Thelma And Jerry* reaches US #53, but there are no hit singles from it.

1979 **Jan** He is reunited with Gamble and Huff, signing to their Philadelphia International label. The renewed liaison does not repeat earlier chart triumphs, but *Nothing Says I Love You Like I Love You* reaches US #160. It is his last US chart entry outside the R&B field; after this Butler concentrates on his businesses and still-lucrative live performances.

1983 He reunites with Mayfield and various members of The Impressions, for a 30-city "Silver Anniversary" (the 25th birthday of *For Your Precious Love*) US tour, sponsored by Budweiser beer. (Its success leads Butler and other erstwhile Impressions to reunite semi-regularly for live dates in the next few years, billed as The Love Reunion.)

1985 Butler is seen on US TV in an ad with Aretha Franklin, on which they duet promoting McDonald's new lettuce and tomato hamburger.

1986 Butler wins political office in Chicago, devoting most of his time to his duties, although he will occasionally tour US.

PAUL BUTTERFIELD BLUES BAND

1965 Vocalist and harmonica player Butterfield (b. Dec.17, 1942, Chicago, IL) forms a racially integrated R&B band, The Paul Butterfield Blues Band, in Chicago. Personnel include the ex-rhythm section of a band previously fronted by bluesman Howlin' Wolf, who are Smokey Smothers (guitar), Jerome Arnold (bass) and Sam Lay (drums), plus Butterfield's former University of Chicago classmate, Elvin Bishop (b. Oct.21, 1942, Tulsa, OK) (guitar). Signed to Elektra Records, Smothers leaves and they bring in Mike Bloomfield on guitar, and Mark Naftalin joins on keyboards during recording of the first album.

July [25] Amongst their first live gigs outside Chicago is a spot on the Newport Folk Festival, RI, where their electric blues set is ill-received by many acoustic folk music purists. But they impress Bob Dylan, who invites them to back him on stage later the same day. This, Dylan's first-ever non-acoustic set, proves equally controversial.

1966 Jan *The Paul Butterfield Blues Band*, recorded in New York, makes US #123.

June Band contributes 5 tracks to a seminal Elektra various artists album, *What's Shakin'* alongside The Lovin' Spoonful, Eric Clapton, Tom Rush and Al Kooper.

Oct [20] They begin a 16-date twice-nightly tour at London's Finsbury Park Astoria, with Georgie Fame, Chris Farlowe, Geno Washington and special guests The Animals. It will end Nov.6 at the Leicester Odeon, Leics. While on tour they record with John Mayall.

Dec With Billy Davenport replacing Lay on drums, *East West*, the title track of which lasts over 13 mins. and includes Eastern instrumental influences, peaks at US #65. Bloomfield leaves after its release to form Electric Flag.

1967 Jan Butterfield cuts EP *Bluesbreakers With Paul Butterfield* with John Mayall, released in UK by Decca Records.

1968 Feb A considerably changed band, with only Butterfield, Bishop and Naftalin from previous line-ups, is heard on *The Resurrection Of Pigboy Crabshaw*, (a title that refers to Bishop's nickname), which reaches US #52. In addition to a fresh rhythm section, the group now includes 3 horn players.

Aug [15] Band appears at the Woodstock Festival, and will later be heard briefly on the 3-album set *Woodstock*.

Sept *In My Own Dreams*, by the same line-up (with Naftalin credited as Naffy Markham), reaches US #79.

1969 Nov After further personnel changes, Butterfield is the only original group member still heard on his band's fifth album *Keep On Moving*, produced by Jerry Ragovoy, which peaks at US #102.

1971 Feb Double album *Live*, produced by Todd Rundgren and recorded at the Troubadour in Los Angeles, CA, after yet more personnel changes, reaches US #72.

Sept A final studio album for Elektra, *Sometimes I Just Feel Like Smilin'* reaches US #124, after which, tired of touring, Butterfield breaks up the band, and moves to Woodstock.

1972 June Retrospective double album *Golden Butter – The Best Of The Paul Butterfield Blues Band* peaks at US #136.

An Offer You Can't Refuse, featuring Butterfield's earliest recordings from 1963 with Smokey Smothers' band in Chicago, is released by specialist UK blues label, Red Lightnin'.

1973 Feb After a quiet period in Chicago, Butterfield forms a new group, Better Days, and signs to Bearsville Records. New line-up includes Geoff Muldaur and guitarist Amos Garrett, plus guests like Bobby Charles (writer of Bill Haley's *See You Later, Alligator*), sax player David Sanborn (b. July 30, 1945, Tampa, FL), and Muldaur's wife Maria. These changes do not improve Butterfield's chart fortunes, as *Better Days* peaks at only US #145.

Nov Second Better Days' album *It All Comes Back* reaches US #156, after which this group also splits up.

1976 Feb *Put It In Your Ear*, featuring Butterfield accompanied mainly by session musicians including Levon Helm and produced by Henry Glover, is released by Bearsville.

Nov [25] He makes a guest appearance in The Band's spectacular farewell concert in San Francisco, and is later seen in Martin Scorsese's movie of the event, "The Last Waltz". (He duets on *Mystery Train* with Helm, plays harmonica for Muddy Waters on *Mannish Boy*, and joins an all-star cast on *I Shall Be Released*.)

1981 After a long absence during which he has attempted without much success to work with Helm and Rick Danko (ex-members of The Band) in both the RCO All-Stars and the Danko-Butterfield Band, Butterfield tries to restart his recording career. During the recording of *North South* for Bearsville, recorded in Memphis with producer Willie Mitchell, he is stricken with peritonitis, entailing 2 operations which long delay the album's completion. He returns to live work after its release, but the album fails to sell and he will not regain lost popularity.

1986 A lengthy recording silence is broken by US release of *The Legendary Paul Butterfield Rides Again* on Amherst Records. This, however, has both poor reviews and sales.

1987 May [4] Butterfield is found dead in his North Hollywood, CA, apartment.

THE BUZZCOCKS
Pete Shelley (guitar, vocals)
Howard Devoto (vocals)
Steve Diggle (guitar, bass)
John Maher (drums)
Steve Garvey (bass)

1976 July [20] The Buzzcocks, formed by philosophy student and Iggy & The Stooges fan Devoto (b. Howard Trafford), after traveling to see The Sex Pistols at High Wycombe, Bucks, in Feb., and then promoting a Pistols gig in Manchester, Gtr. Manchester, 2 months later, and Shelley, already playing in The Jets Of Air, whom Devoto has met at the Bolton Institute of Higher Education, Lancs., with Diggle, seen at a Manchester gig and Maher, recruited from a **Melody Maker** ad they had placed, makes its debut supporting The Sex Pistols and The Damned at Manchester Free Trade Hall.

Aug Group makes its London debut at Screen On The Green, Islington, London, with The Sex Pistols and The Clash.

Sept [21] Band plays in 100 Club Punk Festival with The Damned and The Vibrators, and receives widespread UK rock press recognition.

Oct Group enters Stockport studio and records an 11-track demo.

Dec [28] Having played some gigs on the "Anarchy In The UK Tour", The Buzzcocks begin recording with producer Martin Hannett at Indigo Sound studio.

1977 Jan EP *Spiral Scratch* is released on own independent label New Hormones, with £500 borrowed by Devoto and Shelley.

Mar Having played just 11 gigs with the group, Devoto leaves, forming Magazine by the year's end. Diggle switches from bass to guitar, and Shelley brings in Garth Smith, from Jets Of Air, as bassist. They make their first appearance with this line-up supporting The Clash at the Coliseum, Harlesden, London, before embarking on The Clash's "White Riot" tour as support band.

Aug [16] They sign to EMI's United Artists label on the day Elvis Presley dies.

Oct First UK single *Orgasm Addict*, produced by Martin Rushent, is released.

Nov Smith is fired for extreme unreliability during their first UK tour as headliners, and is replaced on bass by Steve Garvey.

1978 Feb [25] *What Do I Get*, the group's first UK hit, makes #37.

Mar [18] *Another Music In A Different Kitchen* reaches UK #15.

May [13] *I Don't Mind* peaks at UK #55, as the group plays throughout UK with The Slits and then Penetration on "Entertaining Friends" tour.

July [22] *Love You More* makes UK #34.

Sept [30] *Love Bites* reaches UK #13.

Nov [4] Biggest UK hit *Ever Fallen In Love (With Someone You Shouldn't Have)* (later to be successfully covered by The Fine Young Cannibals) reaches #12, as the group embarks on "Beating Hearts" tour with The Subway Sect.

Dec [16] *Promises* reaches UK #20.

1979 Jan During a break from recording and touring, Shelley produces Alberto Y Los Trios Paranioas while Maher assists Patrick Fitzgerald with his debut album.

Mar [17] *Everybody's Happy Nowadays* reaches UK #29, as the group plays concerts in Europe and a 5-date UK tour.

Aug [4] *Harmony In My Head*, a Diggle song premiered on BBC Radio 1's "John Peel Show", makes UK #32.

Sept [15] EP *Spiral Scratch*, by the original line-up, is reissued to meet fans' demand in UK, and this time charts at #31. Group embarks on its first US tour, promoting *Going Steady*, a compilation of UK singles.
[29] *A Different Kind Of Tension* reaches UK #26, in a 3-week stay on chart, while the band tours UK with Joy Division.

1980 May Band makes its first live appearance of the year at Manchester polytechnic.

Sept [13] *Are Everything/Why She's A Girl From The Chainstore* stalls at UK #61, exacerbated by UK "Tour Of Instalments" dissolving after only a few dates.

1981 Feb After 2 non-charting singles and a loss of career momentum, the band splits when each member receives a solicitor's letter stating that Shelley wishes to sever all commitments to The Buzzcocks. (Shelley will start a solo career with Garvey backing, while Diggle and Meyer will launch a new band, Flag of Convenience, in Sept.)

1987 July *Singles – Going Steady* is released on CD.

1989 Diggle's band FOC tours Europe, only to discover that posters promoting the gigs are using The Buzzcocks name. Diggle name-changes to Buzzcocks FOC for the group's next single. This leads to Diggle and Shelley deciding to re-form the group, providing it with

THE BUZZCOCKS cont.

the original line-up. Garvey, now living in New York, and Maher, owner of a Volkswagen repair shop in Manchester, agree, and the group embarks on its first dates since 1980.

Nov [7] The Buzzcocks plays its first US date in a decade in Providence, RI.

1990 *Product*, a boxed set of the group's 4 studio albums and last 3 singles, is released.

THE BYRDS

Roger (Jim) McGuinn (vocals, guitar)
Gene Clark (vocals, percussion)
David Crosby (vocals, guitar)
Chris Hillman (vocals, bass)
Michael Clarke (drums)

1964 Jim McGuinn (b. James Joseph McGuinn III, July 13, 1942, Chicago, IL), who has worked with The Limeliters, The Chad Mitchell Trio (with whom he tours South America for the State Department), Judy Collins and Bobby Darin (the latter as a writer at New York's Brill Building) and Clark (b. Harold Eugene Clark, Nov.17, 1941, Tipton, MO), at 13 forming his own band The Sharks, playing with The Surf Riders before joining The New Christy Minstrels, meet at the Troubadour club in Los Angeles, CA, where McGuinn has opened for Hoyt Axton and Roger Miller, and start working as a duo at the Folk Den. Crosby (b. David Van Cortland, Aug.14, 1941, Los Angeles) ex-Les Baxter's Balladeers, sees them and persuades them to let him sing harmony with them. Crosby introduces McGuinn and Clark to producer Jim Dickson, for whom he has already recorded solo, and he records *The Only Girl I Adore* with them. Shortly thereafter they form a trio as The Jet Set, cutting *You Movin'* and *The Only Girl*, with session players Hal Blaine and Larry Knechtel. Drummer Clarke (b.June 3, 1944, New York, NY), whom Crosby has been playing with Dino Valenti in Big Sur, CA, and bluegrass prodigy Hillman (b.Dec.4, 1944, Los Angeles), ex-Scottsville Squirrel Barkers, The Golden State Boys who become The Blue Diamond Boys, and finally The Hillmen with Vern and Rex Gosdin and Don Parmley, who has just made some recordings with Dickson, are recruited. Elektra boss Jac Holzman shows interest, and newly-formed group records a series of demos (which will emerge in 1969 as *Preflyte* and reach US #84) including *Please Let Me Love You*, which Holzman releases on Elektra as by The Beefeaters.

Nov [10] McGuinn, Hillman and Crosby sign to CBS/Columbia Records, after Miles Davis recommends them to the label.
[19] They name-change to The Byrds on Thanksgiving Day.

1965 Jan [20] Now resident at Los Angeles club Ciro's, band records *Mr. Tambourine Man*, produced by Doris Day's son Terry Melcher (ex-The Rip Chords and Bruce & Terry with Beach Boy Bruce Johnston) and producer of CBS' act Paul Revere & The Raiders, with Blaine (drums), Knechtel (bass), Jerry Cole (rhythm guitar), Leon Russell (electric piano) and McGuinn (lead guitar) at Columbia's Hollywood studios.

May [11] The Byrds make their network TV debut on NBC's "Hullabaloo".

June [26] *Mr. Tambourine Man* recorded in a harmony-rich arrangement with McGuinn's distinctive 12-string Rickenbacker guitar, considerably different from Dylan's original, tops US chart, and is a global million-seller.

July [24] *Mr. Tambourine Man* tops UK Chart, dislodging The Hollies' *I'm Alive*.

Aug *Mr. Tambourine Man* hits US #6 and UK #7.
[4] Group arrives in UK for a 14-day stay of TV, radio and ballroom dates, touring with Them and Kenny Lynch, but much of it is cancelled when McGuinn contracts a viral infection.
[17] The Byrds scheduled show at Portsmouth Guildhall, Hants, is called off because of lack of support. 250 fans who bought tickets are given their money back in 4,000-seater theater.
[21] *All I Really Want To Do*, another Dylan song, hits UK #4, and US #40 (where Cher's version is the bigger hit).

Dec [4] After quickly recording second album, *Turn! Turn! Turn!*, group releases the title track as its third single. Adapted by folk singer Pete Seeger from a passage in the Book of Ecclesiastes, it tops US chart and reaches UK #26.
The Byrds film a segment for the "TNT Award Show", alongside Joan Baez, Bo Diddley, Ray Charles, The Lovin' Spoonful, The Ronettes, Ike & Tina Turner, Roger Miller, Petula Clark and Donovan.

1966 Feb [26] Double A-side *Set You Free This Time* (written by Clark)/*It Won't Be Wrong* (co-written by McGuinn) is a minor US hit, the former reaching #79, and the latter #63.

Mar [1] Clark announces his decision to leave the group, reportedly (although he later partially denies it) due to his fear of flying. He is not replaced, as the group still includes 3 vocalists. (Clark will go on to form The Gene Clark Group with The Grass Roots' Joel Larson, The Leaves' Bill Reinhardt and The Modern Folk Quartet's Chip Douglas.) *Turn! Turn! Turn!*, with Jim Dickson producing, is released and peaks at US #17 and UK #11.

May [21] *Eight Miles High* runs into some airplay bans from broadcasters who "hear" drug connotations, though group insists the song is about the experience of being at 40,000' in an aircraft. Written by McGuinn, Crosby and Clark, it has been recorded before the latter's departure, and reaches US #14 and UK #24.

June [22] The Gene Clark Group plays Hollywood's Whisky A Go-Go.
[25] The Byrds play "The Beach Boys Summer Spectacular", with The Lovin' Spoonful, Percy Sledge and Chad And Jeremy.

July [30] *5D (Fifth Dimension)*, written by McGuinn, makes US #44.
Sept *Fifth Dimension*, with Allen Stanton producing, makes US #24. Clark rejoins for a 12-day stint at the Whisky A Go-Go.
Oct [1] *Fifth Dimension* reaches UK #27.
[29] *Mr. Spaceman*, extracted from the album and again written by McGuinn, makes US #36.
Nov [28] Group begins recording for fourth album with producer Gary Usher and guests Clarence White and Vern Gosdin on guitars and Hugh Masekela on trumpet.
Dec Clark's debut solo single *Echoes* is released in US.

1967 Feb Band performs at a concert sponsored by CAFF (Community Action For Facts & Freedom) with Peter, Paul & Mary, Buffalo Springfield and The Doors at the Valley Center, and will also undertake a UK tour which will include an appearance at their fan club gathering at the Roundhouse, London.
Mar [4] *So You Want To Be A Rock'N'Roll Star*, co-written by McGuinn and Hillman and said to have been inspired by the overnight success of The Monkees, with a standout trumpet solo by Masekela, reaches US #29. McGuinn, now a follower of the Subud religious cult, decides he wishes to be known henceforth as Roger McGuinn.
[10] Clark plays the Ash Grove folk club, Hollywood, with Clarence White and The Gosdin Brothers.
May [6] *My Back Pages* marks a return to the Dylan songbook, and takes the group to US #30, while parent album, Usher-produced *Younger Than Yesterday* climbs to US #24 and UK #37.
June [17] The Byrds take part in the Monterey International Music Festival at Monterey, CA.
[18] Crosby joins Buffalo Springfield on stage at Monterey.
July [1] From the same album, *Have You Seen Her Face* (written by Hillman), reaches US #74. B-side *Don't Make Waves* is the theme to a movie starring Tony Curtis as a swimming pool salesman. In UK it will appear as B-side to their next release.
Aug [19] *Lady Friend*, written by Crosby, peaks at US #82.
Oct Crosby leaves, unhappy that the group has chosen to record Goffin/King's *Goin' Back* in preference to his *Triad*. (*Triad* will appear on Jefferson Airplane's *Crown Of Creation* in 1968.) He agrees to be bought out, spending his proceeds on a yacht. After numerous discussions with McGuinn, Clark is briefly re-recruited to replace Crosby. *Greatest Hits* hits US #6.
Nov After 3 days recording, Clark leaves again.
Dec [2] *Goin' Back*, 1966 UK #10 for Dusty Springfield, makes US #89. Clarke also decides to quit to Hawaii, much of his work on the forthcoming album having already been done by session drummer Jim Gordon, leaving McGuinn and Hillman to complete the project.

1968 Jan McGuinn and Hillman re-sign with CBS, and hire Hillman's cousin, ex-Rising Sons Kevin Kelley (b. 1945, CA), as the trio embarks on a tour of the US college circuit.
Feb Singer/guitarist Gram Parsons (b. Cecil Connor, Nov.5, 1946, Winter Haven, FL), ex-The Shilohs and International Submarine Band, is recruited to play keyboards.
[15] The Byrds perform the Grand Ole Opry, Nashville, TN.
Apr *The Notorious Byrd Brothers* makes US #47 and UK #12. The sleeve shows McGuinn, Hillman and Clarke looking out of the windows of a stable while a fourth window, which contains a horse, is rumored to represent the way McGuinn regards Crosby. By this time the quartet (of McGuinn, Hillman, Kelley and Parsons) is joined by occasional members, pedal steel guitarist Sneaky Pete Kleinow and banjo player Doug Dillard. The next album will feature contributions from John Hartford (banjo, guitar) and ex-Kentucky Colonels Clarence White (guitar).
June [8] *You Ain't Going Nowhere*, from forthcoming album, peaks at

US #74 and UK #45 – the group's first UK hit for over 2 years.
July On the eve of the South African leg of the group's world tour, Parsons, refusing to play to segregated audiences, checks out of his London hotel and quits the band and is replaced for the tour by ex-Byrds roadie, Carlos Bernal.
Aug [4-5] Group plays the Newport Pop Festival in Costa Mesa, CA, alongside The Grateful Dead, Steppenwolf, Sonny & Cher, Canned Heat, Jefferson Airplane and many more.
Sept *Sweetheart Of The Rodeo* appears, having been delayed because Parsons (who has influenced the group towards country-rock music and sung lead on many original tracks) is threatened with legal action if his voice can be heard on the album. (He still owes an International Submarine Band album.) It has to be erased and either Hillman's or McGuinn's vocal substituted. Album reaches US #77, but fails in UK (though it is later regarded as one of the most influential albums of the 60s, pointing the way towards the early 70s country-rock boom).
Oct On their return from tour, McGuinn finds himself the only remaining Byrd, as Hillman retires, although he will soon team up with Gram Parsons to form The Flying Burrito Brothers, as will Kleinow. Kelley and the other occasional group members also depart, Kelley joining Tim Buckley's band. McGuinn recruits Clarence White (b. June 6, 1944, Lewiston, ME), who has been in Nashville West and the second incarnation of The Gene Clark Group, on guitar. He recommends Nashville West veterans, Gene Parsons (b. Apr.9, 1944) (who has also played with White in Cajun Gib & Gene) on drums and John York, a member of Clark's group, completing sixth incarnation of The Byrds.

1969 Feb Clarke joins The Flying Burrito Brothers.
[6-9] The Byrds play the Fillmore West, San Francisco, with Mike Bloomfield, Pacific Gas & Electric, Nick Gravenites and Mark Naftalin.
Mar New line-up's debut *Bad Night At The Whiskey* fails to chart. (Its B-side *Drug Store Truck Driving Man*, co-written by McGuinn and Parsons prior to the latter's departure, will become better known.)
Apr *Dr. Byrds & Mr. Hyde*, Bob Johnston-produced, makes US #153.
May [24] *Dr. Byrds & Mr. Hyde* reaches UK #15.
June A version of Dylan's *Lay Lady Lay*, coupled with *Old Blue*, from *Dr. Byrds*, fails to chart.
[12-15] The Byrds headline a bill comprising Pacific Gas & Electric, Joe Cocker & The Greaseband at the Fillmore West.
Aug [31] The Byrds play the New Orleans Pop Festival at the Louisiana International Speedway, Gonzales, LA.
Sept Double A-side *I Wasn't Born To Follow* (performed on the soundtrack of movie "Easy Rider"), and *Child Of The Universe* (from *Dr. Byrds* and also the "Candy" movie soundtrack) is released.
York leaves to join the Sir Douglas Quintet.
Oct Skip Battin, formerly half of Skip & Flip with Gary "Flip" Paxton, takes York's place.
Dec [6] *The Ballad Of Easy Rider* peaks at US #65.

1970 Jan *The Ballad Of Easy Rider*, with producer Melcher, reaches US #36. A version of the title track credited solely to McGuinn has previously appeared on *Easy Rider* soundtrack album, alongside *I Wasn't Born To Follow* and McGuinn solo, *It's Alright Ma (I'm Only Bleeding)*.
[7] *Jesus Is Just Alright*, from *The Ballad Of Easy Rider*, spends 1 week at US #97, but fails in UK.
[14] *The Ballad Of Easy Rider* makes UK #41.
Nov With the group's most stable line-up assembled, double album *Untitled* is released and reaches US #40 and UK #11.

1971 Feb *Chestnut Mare*, written with New York psychologist Jacques Levy for "Gene Tryp", a C&W musical version of Henrik Ibsen's "Peer Gynt" from the album, makes UK #19 but fails in US (where The Byrds will have no more hit singles).
May *I Trust (Everything Is Gonna Work Out Right)*, from forthcoming *Byrdmaniax*, is released as group undertakes a UK tour.
Aug *Byrdmaniax* reaches US #46, but fails in UK.
Oct *Glory Glory*, also from *Byrdmaniax*, fails to chart.

1972 Jan *Farther Along* peaks at US #152, but single taken from it, *America's Great National Pastime* (co-written by Battin and Kim Fowley), fails.
July Last Byrds sessions take place at Columbia. 3 of the recorded songs will eventually appear on McGuinn's first solo album.
Aug Parsons quits for a solo career (and will eventually join The Flying Burrito Brothers, signing to Warner/Reprise).
Sept Battin is fired, and is replaced by ex-session drummer John Guerin, before a major re-shuffle brings in temporary drummers Daryl Dragon (ex-Beach Boys) and Jim Moon.
Dec Compilation album *Best Of The Byrds – Greatest Hits Vol. 2* peaks at US #114.
Clark releases solo album *Roadrunner* via A&M, which features all 5

original Byrds on 2 tracks, and adds to his 1971 album *White Light*.

1973 Jan Original group of McGuinn, Hillman, Crosby, Clark and Clarke re-forms for a new album to be released on Asylum label. The reunion is shortlived, but produces *Byrds*, which reaches US #20, and unsuccessful single *Things Will Be Better*.
Feb [24] The Byrds (current version) makes its final live appearance at the Capitol theater in Passaic, NJ, after which McGuinn dissolves the band. McGuinn and White are the only remaining members, Battin having left to make a solo album. Hillman returns for the date, and Joe Lala from Manassas fills in on drums.
Apr [14] *Byrds* makes UK #31.
May [19] Retrospective double album *History Of The Byrds* makes UK #47, as McGuinn makes his post-Byrds solo debut at New York's Academy of Music.
July [14] White is killed by a drunk driver while loading equipment after a gig in Palmdale, CA.
McGuinn's debut solo album *Roger McGuinn* makes US #137.
Sept [8] Reissued by CBS, *Preflyte*, the album of demos which reached US #84 when released by Together Records in 1969, makes US #183.
[19] Gram Parsons dies of heart failure in mysterious circumstances in Joshua Tree, CA.

1974 Ex-Byrds members remain active. Crosby will work solo and in varying combinations of the Crosby, Stills, Nash & Young family. Clark's solo album *No Other* makes US #144. (He will work with Doug Dillard in Dillard & Clark and record a number of solo albums for Takoma Reacords in the 80s.) McGuinn also concentrates on a solo career and his *Peace On You* makes US #92.

1975 McGuinn joins Bob Dylan's touring "Rolling Thunder Revue". His solo albums include *Roger McGuinn Band* which makes US #16 and Mick Ronson-produced *Cardiff Rose* (1976) and *Thunderbyrd* (issued in 1977 including a version of Tom Petty's *American Girl*).

1976 Hillman's solo album *Slippin' Away* makes US #153.

1977 Hillman's *Clear Sailin'* makes US #188.
May McGuinn, Clark & Hillman re-link for a package tour of Europe, on which each plays as a soloist.

1979 The trio reunites for *McGuinn Clark & Hillman* which makes US #39, and extracted *Don't You Write Her Off* which reaches US #33. They also tour, during which they are joined on stage in San Francisco by Crosby.

1980 The trio's *City* makes US #136, while McGuinn and Hillman complete *McGuinn/Hillman*.

1984 Hillman, in addition to the various reunions with McGuinn and Clark, having quit The Flying Burrito Brothers and joined Stephen Stills' Manassas, has formed The Souther Hillman Furay Band with J.D. Souther and Richie Furay for 2 late 70s albums, forms successful country act, The Desert Rose Band, with Herb Pedersen, Jaydee Maness, John Jorgensen, Bill Bryson and Steve Duncan, (which will continue to be popular to the end of the decade).

1987 Clark distances himself from his ex-colleagues by siding with Clarke for a dubious folk album with Carla Olson. Meanwhile Clarke is sued by Crosby, McGuinn and Hillman for illegally using The Byrds name. He has spent many years in The Flying Burrito Brothers before having later success with Firefall.

1988 McGuinn and Hillman link with Crosby to make an impromptu performance at the Ash Grove, Los Angeles. (In between the McGuinn, Clark and Hillman projects, McGuinn has made occasional tours with his wife, and manager, Camilla, and guested on other artists' records including The Beach Boys' 1986 version of The Mamas' & The Papas' *California Dreamin'*. He will guest on Elvis Costello's forthcoming 1989 album *Spike*.)

1989 Jan Crosby, McGuinn and Hillman play 3 California club dates as The Byrds to establish their legal right to the band's name and to keep Gene Clark and Michael Clarke from touring with that name. McGuinn and Hillman contribute *You Ain't Going Nowhere* to The Nitty Gritty Dirt Band's Grammy winning album *Will The Circle Be Unbroken Volume Two*. The track, when released as a single, will hit US C&W #6.
Feb [20] Arista Records president Clive Davis announces the signing of Roger McGuinn at a pre-Grammy dinner at the Beverly Hills Hotel. McGuinn plays a short set for the assembled multitude.
Apr [7] McGuinn joins Crowded House on *Mr. Tambourine Man*, *Eight Miles High* and *So You Want To Be A Rock'N'Roll Star* in concert in Los Angeles. The tracks will be released under the name Byrdhouse on a CD EP.

1990 Feb [24] McGuinn, Crosby and Hillman sing *He Was A Friend Of Mine*, *Turn! Turn! Turn!* and *Mr. Tambourine Man*, the latter with Dylan, at the "Roy Orbison All-Star Tribute", Universal Amphitheater, Los Angeles.
Aug [6-8] McGuinn, Crosby and Hillman record 4 songs, including

THE BYRDS cont.

McGuinn's *He Was A Friend Of Mine*, Dylan's *Paths Of Victory* and Julie Gold's *From A Distance* at Treasure Isle Recorders in Nashville, TN.
Nov [17] Definitive 90-track 4-CD set *The Byrds* makes US #151.

1991 **Jan** [16] The Byrds are inducted into the Rock'N'Roll Hall Of Fame at the sixth annual dinner at the Waldorf Astoria in New York. During the dinner, Crosby announces "an airstrike has just started on Baghdad".
Mar [9] McGuinn's *Back From Rio*, his first solo album in 13 years, with contributions from Elvis Costello, Michael Penn, Tom Petty and Dave Stewart reaches US #44.

CAMEO

Larry Blackmon
Thomas Jenkins
Nathan Leftenant

1976 Band is formed as The New York City Players by native New Yorker Larry Blackmon, who has already been in a number of groups, including The Mighty Gees, Concrete Wall and East Coast. The name is soon changed to the more manageable Cameo, whose reputation is then established by brute force, via 200-gig-a-year touring. The original nucleus is Blackmon with vocalists Jenkins and Leftenant, but the group numbers as many as 13 in its early stages.

1977 Taking their Blackmon-produced debut album, *Cardiac Arrest*, to Casablanca Records, they sign to its Chocolate City subsidiary.
Aug Cameo is invited to support Parliament/Funkadelic Mothership's 1977-78 tour and begins to build its own following.
Sept [10] *Cardiac Arrest* gives the band its first chart success, reaching US #116.

1978 **Apr** [22] *We All Know Who We Are* , also produced by Blackmon, who will continue as producer on all Cameo projects, spends 23 weeks on US chart, peaking at #58.
Dec [16] *Ugly Ego* makes US #83.

1979 **Sept** [29] Band makes its US Top 50 debut when *Secret Omen* climbs to #46.

1980 **Aug** [16] *Cameosis* reaches US #25, and is their biggest-selling record to date during a 6-month chart-stay.

1981 **Jan** *Feel Me* makes US #44.
July *Knights Of The Sound Table* also makes US #44. It is their first UK album release, though their seventh in US (the previous 6 have all been hot UK imports).

1982 **May** [15] *Alligator Woman* reaches US #23.

1983 **June** Group switches to Blackmon's own label Atlanta Artists for *Style*, which makes US #53, their first album since *Ugly Ego* not to receive a gold disk in US.

1984 **May** [5] *She's Strange*, helped by Amos Poe video, gives the group its first R&B/dance/pop crossover hit in US making #47 and is the group's UK chart debut at #37. *She's Strange* reaches US #27 and recaptures their gold disk status.
June Following its breakthrough there, Cameo makes a short UK tour, to wildly enthusiastic cult following.

1985 **July** [13] *Attack Me With Your Love*, from the forthcoming *Single Life*, peaks at UK #65.
Sept *Single Life* makes US #58, and peaks at UK #66.
Oct Extracted title track *Single Life* becomes Cameo's first Top 20 entry, reaching UK #15. It also spends longer at the top of UK Dance chart than any other record in 1985. It hits US R&B #2, but fails to cross over.
Dec Cameo returns to UK for a full headlining tour, which includes 3 sell-out shows at the Hammersmith Odeon, London. *She's Strange* is reissued as a UK single, and this time climbs to #22.

1986 **Mar** Atypical ballad *A Goodbye* peaks at UK #65.
May Blackmon trims the group to a trio (himself on drums and vocals, plus Jenkins and Leftenant), bringing in other players when needed.
Oct *Word Up* hits UK #3, and will be their biggest international smash.
[4] *Word Up* tops US R&B chart.
[25] *Word Up!* tops US R&B chart.
Nov *Word Up!*, the group's 12th and most successful album, hits US #8 and UK #7.
[22] *Word Up* hits US #6.
Dec A UK tour gains a high profile, not least because of the prominent red codpiece, made by Jean-Paul Gaultier, which forms part of Blackmon's stage garb. *Candy*, from *Word Up!*, reaches UK #27.

1987 **Jan** [31] *Candy* tops US R&B chart for 2 weeks.
Mar [21] *Candy* reaches US #21.
May *Back And Forth*, also from the album but remixed for single release, reaches UK #11.
[30] *Back And Forth* makes US #50.

Nov Blackmon makes a surprise appearance as guest vocalist on Ry Cooder's *Get Rhythm*. (He continues to work in his own Atlanta Artists studio with several protege acts and on material for the next Cameo album.) *She's Mine*, last single from *Word Up*, reaches UK #35.

1988 **Oct** [29] *You Make Me Work* peaks at UK #74.
Nov [19] *You Make Me Work* stalls at US #85.
[26] *Machismo* makes UK #86.
Dec *Machismo* reaches gold status as it climbs to US #56.

1989 Blackmon produces tracks for Eddie Murphy's *So Happy*.
June *Pretty Girls* peaks at US R&B #52.

1990 **July** [21] *Real Men Wear Black* makes US #84 but fails in UK.

GLEN CAMPBELL

1960 Campbell (b. Apr.22, 1938, near Delight, AR) having left school in 1953 to join a band in Wyoming, but ending up having to sell his guitar and hitchhike home, joining his uncle's The Dick Bills Band in Albuquerque, NM, in 1954 and gaining live touring experience, before forming his own group, Glen Campbell & The Western Wranglers in 1958, is on the road for 18 months. Having married Billie Campbell in Carlsbad, NM, he decides to settle in Los Angeles, CA, and seeks session work as a guitarist. He also becomes a studio and stage member of The Champs for a while, when the group's leader Dave Burgess drops out.

1961 **Dec** [25] His debut *Turn Around, Look At Me*, for the small Los Angeles label Crest, written by Eddie Cochran's former partner Jerry Capehart, peaks at US #62.

1962 **Sept** [1] Campbell charts with *Too Late To Worry – Too Blue To Cry*, which makes US #76, on Capitol. He records an album which the company takes 6 months to issue, losing the momentum gained by the single.

1963 He plays on 586 sessions this year (later reckoning that only 3 hit singles emerge from them).
Oct The Folkswingers, an instrumental quartet of session players with Campbell on guitar, makes US #132 with *12 String Guitar!*

1965 **Jan** Still playing sessions and being a regular player on ABC TV's "Shindig" music show, he joins the stage line-up of The Beach Boys, replacing Brian Wilson, but leaves when Bruce Johnston joins the group on a permanent basis. (It is Campbell's lead guitar which has been heard on most of The Beach Boys' hits).
Oct [30] A cover of Donovan's *The Universal Soldier* outsells original and puts Campbell on US chart after 3-year absence, peaking at #45.

1966 Campbell demands that Capitol gives him a chance to record and release on his own terms. Within months he has a Country chart hit with a revival of Jack Scott's *Burning Bridges*.

1967 **Aug** [5] A cover of John Hartford's *Gentle On My Mind* makes US #62.
Dec [16] *By The Time I Get To Phoenix*, written by 21-year-old Jimmy Webb, gives Campbell his first US Top 30 hit, reaching #26. (It will win a Grammy award for Best Male Vocal Performance of 1967.) *Gentle On My Mind* is his first US Album chart entry, and will eventually hit #5 on the back of later successes. (It is voted Album Of The Year by the Academy of Country Music.)

1968 **Jan** *By The Time I Get To Phoenix* quickly peaks at US #15. These album successes help him become a regular US TV music guest on CBS' "The Smothers Brothers Comedy Hour".
Feb [24] *Hey Little One* peaks at US #54.
[29] Campbell wins Best Vocal Performance, Male and Best Contemporary Male Solo Vocal Performance for *By The Time I Get To Phoenix* and Best C&W Recording and Best C&W Solo Vocal Performance, Male for *Gentle On My Mind* at the 10th annual Grammy awards. (*Gentle On My Mind*'s writer John Hartford also wins Grammys for Best Folk Performance for his version of the song and Best C&W Song.)
May [25] *I Wanna Live* makes US #36. *Hey Little One* makes US #26, his third album to achieve a gold disk for a half million sales.
June [23] Campbell hosts "The Summer Brothers Smothers Show", the summer replacement for "The Smothers Brothers Comedy Hour". (The show will air until Sept.8.)
Aug [10] *Dreams Of The Everyday Housewife* makes US #32. *A New Place In The Sun* reaches US #24.
Nov [2] Reissued *Gentle On My Mind* makes US #39.
[23] His first duet with labelmate Bobbie Gentry, *Mornin' Glory*, peaks at US #74.
Dec Duetted *Bobbie Gentry And Glen Campbell* reaches US #11.
[21] *Wichita Lineman* tops US chart for 5 weeks and achieves gold status.

1969 Jan [11] Extracted *Wichita Lineman*, a further collaboration with writer Webb, hits US #3 and earns a gold disk for million-plus sales.
[29] "The Glen Campbell Goodtime Hour" debuts on CBS. (The program will run for 3 series until June 13, 1972.)
Mar [8] Another duet with Gentry, reviving The Everly Brothers' *Let It Be Me*, makes US #36.
[12] *By The Time I Get To Phoenix* wins Album Of The Year and *Wichita Lineman* wins Best Engineered Recording at the 11th annual Grammy awards.
[15] *Wichita Lineman* is his UK chart debut, hitting #7.
Apr [12] *Galveston*, penned by Webb as an anti-war song some 6 years earlier, hits US #4 and is another million-seller.
May [31] *Where's The Playground, Susie*, also written by Webb, reaches US #26, as *Galveston* reaches UK #14. *Galveston* hits US #2, earning another gold disk.
June He issues a lawsuit against Starday Records for releasing demos, which he had recorded in the early part of his career.
Aug Campbell breaks new ground when he stars alongside John Wayne in movie "True Grit".
[23] *True Grit*, the movie's title song, makes US #35.
Nov [29] *Try A Little Kindness* reaches US #23 as *Glen Campbell – Live* makes US #13.
1970 Jan [24] A revival of The Everly Brothers' *All I Have To Do Is Dream*, duetted with Gentry, hits UK #3.
[31] Campbell makes his UK album debut with *Glen Campbell – Live* which will climb to #16.
Feb [14] *Try A Little Kindness* makes UK #45.
[28] *Honey Come Back*, also by Webb, reaches US #19.
Apr [4] Gentry duet *All I Have To Do Is Dream* reaches US #27. *Try A Little Kindness* reaches US #12 as Campbell makes his Las Vegas, NV, cabaret debut at the International hotel.
May [5] Campbell co-stars with The 5th Dimension in a US TV special.
[9] A revival of Edwin Hawkins' gospel song *Oh Happy Day* makes US #40, trailing an inspirational album of the same title, which reaches US #38.
June [6] *Honey Come Back* hits UK #4 as *Try A Little Kindness* makes UK #37.
July Soundtrack album from movie "Norwood" (Campbell's second film role, playing Norwood Pratt) climbs to US #90.
Aug [15] *Everything A Man Could Ever Need* peaks at US #52.
Oct [31] A remake of Conway Twitty's *It's Only Make Believe* hits US #10 as *Everything A Man Could Ever Need* makes UK #32.
Nov *The Glen Campbell Goodtime Album*, based on his TV show, reaches US #27.
[18] Campbell appears at a Royal Command Performance in London.
Dec *It's Only Make Believe* hits UK #4 as *The Glen Campbell Album* reaches UK #16.
1971 Apr [17] A revival of Roy Orbison's *Dream Baby* makes US #31 and will be his last UK chart single in 4 years at UK #39.
May *Glen Campbell's Greatest Hits* makes US #39.
July [24] *The Last Time I Saw Her* peaks at US #61, followed by an album of the same title which stalls at US #87.
Nov [6] Capitol teams Campbell with labelmate Anne Murray on an Al De Lory arrangement blending *I Say A Little Prayer* and *By The Time I Get To Phoenix* (sung by Murray and Campbell respectively) which climbs to US #81. Companion album, *Anne Murray/Glen Campbell*, released to coincide with a US tour by the duo, peaks at US #128.
Dec [18] *Glen Campbell's Greatest Hits* hits UK #8 – his first UK Top 10 album (and longest chart stayer at 113 weeks).
1972 Sept [30] *I Will Never Pass This Way Again* peaks at US #61.
Dec *Glen Travis Campbell* makes US #148.
1973 Jan [20] *One Last Time* climbs to US #78.
May [19] *I Knew Jesus (Before He Was A Star)* makes US #45.
June *I Knew Jesus (Before He Was A Star)* makes US #154.
1974 Mar [2] *Houston (I'm Comin' To See You)* peaks at US #68.
Nov *Reunion* (composed mostly of new Webb songs) makes US #166.
1975 Sept [6] After a 14-year chart career, *Rhinestone Cowboy*, a cover of Larry Weiss' original, gives Campbell his first US #1, selling over a million. (Sylvester Stallone/Dolly Parton film "Rhinestone" will be based on the song.)
Oct [18] *Rhinestone Cowboy*, produced by Dennis Lambert and Brian Potter, reaches US #17 and earns a gold disk.
Nov [8] *Rhinestone Cowboy* returns him to UK chart, hitting #4 as *Rhinestone Cowboy* makes UK #38.
1976 Jan [17] *Country Boy (You Got Your Feet In LA)*, written by Lambert and Potter, reaches US #11.

May [8] A medley covering Hamilton, Joe Frank & Reynolds' *Don't Pull Love* and The Casinos' *Then You Can Tell Me Goodbye* reaches US #27.
[15] *Bloodline* makes US #63.
Nov [27] TV-advertised compilation *20 Golden Greats* tops UK chart for 6 weeks.
Dec [11] US equivalent *The Best Of Glen Campbell* makes US #116.
1977 Apr [23] Allen Toussaint-penned *Southern Nights* reaches UK #28 as parent album *Southern Nights* makes UK #51. (These are his final UK hits, although he will remain a popular live performer in UK.)
[30] *Southern Nights* hits US #1 and is another million-seller.
May [21] *Southern Nights* reaches US #22.
Aug [20] *Sunflower* makes US #39.
1978 Jan [21] *Live At The Royal Festival Hall*, with the Royal Philharmonic Orchestra, peaks at US #171.
Dec [9] *Can You Fool* makes US #38.
[23] *Basic* makes US #164.
1980 June [28] A duet with Rita Coolidge on *Somethin' 'Bout You Baby I Like* makes US #42.
1981 Feb [14] *I Don't Want To Know Your Name* peaks at US #65.
Mar *It's The World Gone Crazy* makes US #178, following which Campbell leaves Capitol after 20 years.
Aug [29] *I Love My Truck*, for new label, Mirage, reaches US #94, as Campbell turns to mainstream country music.
1982 Weekly 30-min. "The Glen Campbell Music Show" airs on US syndicated TV.
1983 Campbell signs to Atlantic America, a country division set up by R&B/rock-oriented Atlantic Records. His 1983 Country chart successes for the label, *I Love How You Love Me*, *On The Wings Of My Victory* and *Old Home Town* fail to cross to wider success.
1984 2 Top 10 Country chart hits, *Faithless Love* and *A Lady Like You*, fail to make the pop chart. Like several other country-rooted stars who made big crossovers in the 60s and/or 70s, Campbell finds a faithful audience and consistent sales in US country market of the 80s.
1988 *Still Within The Sound Of My Voice*, his first album via 1987 deal with MCA Records, celebrates 1 year on US Country chart. In the past 18 months Campbell has scored a number of hits on the US Country survey, including *The Hand That Rocks The Cradle*, (#6, a duet with Steve Warner), Webb-penned *Still Within The Sound Of My Voice*, (#5), a revivial of Frank Ifield's *I Remember You* (#32), *I have You* (#7), *Light Years* (#35) and second MGA album, *Light Years* (#58).
1989 July *The Complete Glen Campbell*, a UK-only compilation on Stylus label, makes UK #47.
1990 Jan [9] He holds a benefit concert for 5-month-old Tommie Tenuta of Phoenix, AZ, who needs a liver transplant.
Walkin' In The Sun, released on Capitol Nashville label continues Campbell's success on the US country chart.
1991 Jan Campbell embarks on "The Goodtime Glen Campbell Music Show" US tour with John Hartford, Nicolette Larson and others, as *Unconditional Love* is released.

CANNED HEAT

Bob "The Bear" Hite (vocals, harmonica)
Al "Blind Owl" Wilson (guitar, harmonica, vocals)
Henry Vestine (guitar)
Larry Taylor (bass)
Frank Cook (drums)

1966 Evolving from a jug band, the group, taking its name from a Tommy Johnson song, begins to play electric blues and boogie in Los Angeles, CA, through the influence of its joint lead singers, Hite (b. Feb.26, 1945, Torrance, CA), a 300lb. (hence his nickname) blues expert and archivist and Wilson (b. July 4, 1943, Boston, MA) with Vestine (b. Dec.25, 1944, Washington, DC), Cook and ex-Kaleidscope Stuart Brotman completing line-up. (Brotman does not stay long, and is briefly replaced by Mark Andes, before Taylor (b. Samuel Taylor, June 26, 1942, Brooklyn, New York, NY), once playing piano with Chuck Berry under the name Lafayette Leake and at 14 with Jerry Lee Lewis, becomes group's permanent bass player.
1967 June [16] An appearance at Monterey Pop Festival, CA, leads to a contract with Liberty Records.
Oct Debut album *Canned Heat* reaches US #76.
1968 Feb *Boogie With Canned Heat* is released, and will eventually climb to US #16 in a 12-month chart stay.
Sept *On The Road Again*, originally recorded by The Memphis Jug Band in the late 20s, reaches US #16 and hits UK #8. Band tours UK

and Europe, with Fito de la Parra (b. Adolpho de la Parra, Feb.8, 1946, Mexico City, Mexico) replacing Cook on drums. (Cook has been on vacation in Mexico, where he meets de la Parra and tells him he can take his place in the band.)

[2] Band plays London's Revolution club at start of its first UK visit.

Oct *Boogie With Canned Heat* hits UK #5 after 21 weeks on chart.

1969 Jan *Going Up The Country* reaches US #11 (band's biggest US hit) and UK #19.

Feb Double *Living The Blues* makes US #18. Half is live and half is dominated by long *Refried Boogie*. De la Parra is arraigned in Southfield, Detroit, MI, after the arrest of 28 people on narcotics charges.

Apr *Time Was*, from the double album, peaks at US #67.

Aug [1-2] Band plays the Fillmore East, New York, with Jefferson Airplane, before playing Woodstock Festival in Bethel, NY.

Sept Harvey Mandel (b. 1946, Detroit, MI) replaces Vestine on guitar for *Hallelujah*, which makes US #37.

1970 Jan *Vintage Canned Heat*, compiling early pre-Liberty tracks, reaches US #173, while more contemporary compilation *Canned Heat Cookbook (The Best Of Canned Heat)* makes US #86.

Feb A revival of Wilbert Harrison's *Let's Work Together* hits UK #2.

Mar *Canned Heat Cookbook* becomes a major UK seller, hitting #8.

July Live *Canned Heat '70 Concert* reaches UK #15, while a revival of Cleveland Crochet's oldie *Sugar Bee* makes UK #49.

Sept [3] Wilson dies, aged 27, of a drug overdose, having suffered from heavy depression. He is found in the garden of Hite's house in Topanga Canyon, CA.

[13] Despite Wilson's death, the band begins its planned European tour at the Free Trade Hall, Manchester, Gtr.Manchester. Joel Scott Hill joins the group in Paris, France.

Oct *Future Blues* reaches US #59 and UK #27, and is the band's last UK chart album.

Nov *Let's Work Together* climbs to US #26.

1971 Apr *Hooker'N'Heat*, pairing the band with blues legend John Lee Hooker, reaches US #73.

July *Canned Heat Concert*, recorded live in Europe, scrapes US #133.

1972 Apr *Rockin' With The King*, with Little Richard guesting on piano and vocals, stalls at US #88. *Historical Figures And Ancient Heads* reaches US #87.

1974 *Many Rivers To Cross*, produced by Barry Beckett and Roger Hawkins at Muscle Shoals, is released by Atlantic. (As the blues boom abates, band falls from wide audience favor, and by the end of the decade, it is mainly performing in bars and minor clubs and festivals. Taylor and Mandel are by now playing with John Mayall's band.)

1981 Apr [5] Hite dies from a heart attack, aged 36, in Venice, CA.

1989 With line-up comprising de la Parra, Taylor, Junior Watson (guitar) and James Thornbury (flute, guitar, harmonica), the band embarks on 60s revival tour "An Evening Of California Dreamin'".

Sept The group guests on John Lee Hooker's *The Healer*.

THE CAPTAIN & TENNILLE

Daryl Dragon (keyboards)
Toni Tennille (vocals)

1971 Sept Dragon (b. Aug.27, 1942, Los Angeles, CA), son of conductor Carmen Dragon, meets Tennille (b. May 8, 1943, Montgomery, AL) at Marines Memorial theater, San Francisco, CA, where she is appearing in musical "Mother Earth" which she has co-written. Dragon (a regular in The Beach Boys' stage band) is keyboard player in the house band.

1972 After "Mother Earth" closes, the duo tours with The Beach Boys – Dragon on keyboards and Tennille on back-up vocal harmonies. Mike Love dubs Dragon "Captain Keyboard" because of the naval officer's cap he invariably wears on stage.

1973 Sept After the tour ends, the duo is performing regularly at the Smoke House restaurant in Encino, CA, when, unable to interest any record labels in their material, they organize and pay for the recording of their own first single *The Way I Want To Touch You* (a ballad written by Tennille while on The Beach Boys tour.) They also spend $250 to have 500 copies pressed on their own label, Butterscotch Castle.

1974 Feb [14] They are married in Virginia City, NV, on St. Valentine's Day, while driving through 22 states promoting the single. A&M Records becomes interested and signs them to a recording contract, re-releasing the single.

1975 June [21] Their first hit, Neil Sedaka/Howard Greenfield-penned *Love Will Keep Us Together*, hits US #1 for 4 weeks and sells over 2 million.

Aug [2] *Love Will Keep Us Together* hits US #2.

[16] *Love Will Keep Us Together* makes UK #32.

Sept [13] Spanish-sung version, *Por Amor Viviremos*, makes US #49.

Nov [29] *The Way I Want To Touch You* is re-released as follow-up, hitting US #4 and selling over a million.

1976 Feb [7] *The Way I Want To Touch You* reaches UK #28.

[28] *Love Will Keep Us Together* wins Record Of The Year at the 18th annual Grammy awards. It will also win Best International Single at the Juno awards (Canada's equivalent of the Grammys).

Mar [27] *Lonely Night (Angel Face)* hits US #3 and is million-plus seller.

May [1] *Song Of Joy* hits US #9.

July [10] *Shop Around*, a revival of The Miracles' first major chart success, hits US #4 and sells over a million.

They are invited to sing at White House dinner in honor of the Queen.

Sept [20] The duo's prime time musical variety show "The Captain And Tennille" premieres on ABC TV.

Nov [20] *Muskrat Love* hits US #4, another million-seller.

1977 Mar [14] "The Captain And Tennille" airs for the last time on ABC TV.

May [7] *Can't Stop Dancin'* reaches US #13.

[28] *Come In From The Rain* reaches US #18.

July [2] Extracted title track, *Come In From The Rain*, peaks at US #61.

1978 Feb [4] *Captain & Tennille's Greatest Hits* package makes US #55.

May [20] *I'm On My Way* peaks at US #74.

Aug [26] *Dream* climbs no higher than US #131, despite spending 30 weeks on chart.

Nov [11] *You Never Done It Like That* peaks at UK #63.

[18] *You Never Done It Like That* hits US #10.

1979 Jan [27] *You Need A Woman Tonight* makes US #40. By mutual consent, the duo leaves A&M and signs a new deal with Casablanca.

1980 Feb [9] *Make Your Move* reaches US #23.

[16] *Do That To Me One More Time*, penned by Tennille, tops US chart and will prove to be the duo's final million-selling single.

Mar [15] *Do That To Me One More Time* hits UK #7.

[29] *Love On A Shoestring* peaks at US #55, as *Make Your Move*, the duo's only UK chart album, makes #33.

June [7] *Happy Together (A Fantasy)* peaks at US #53 and is the duo's last hit single. It is followed by a period of re-assessment during which Tennille decides on a solo career.

1984 Tennille releases *More Than You Know* on Mirage label, and tours to promote it.

1986 Tennille album *Moonglow* also fails to score.

1987 Dec [26] Third Tennille album *All Of Me*, released through Gaia label and featuring standards from 1929 to 1948, charts briefly at US #198.

CAPTAIN BEEFHEART & THE MAGIC BAND

Captain Beefheart (vocals)
Alex St Clair (guitar)
Jeff Cotton (guitar)
Jerry Handley (bass)
John French (drums)

1964 Having appeared regularly as a child on TV, displaying a prodigious talent for clay sculpting, Van Vliet (b. Jan.15, 1941, Glendale, CA), a high school friend of Frank Zappa with whom he formed an unsuccessful band, The Soots, adopts the name Captain Beefheart, from his idea for a movie "Captain Beefheart Meets The Grunt People", and forms the first Magic Band.

1966 In Los Angeles, CA, Beefheart and the band sign to A&M Records, where they are produced by David Gates (later of Bread). (The complete recordings appear 20 years later as *The Legendary A&M Sessions*, but originally just 2 singles, *Diddy Wah Diddy* and *Frying Pan/Moonchild* are released, unsuccessfully, before A&M drops them.)

May [20-22] Band joins Love and Big Brother & The Holding Company to perform at the Avalon Ballroom, San Francisco, CA.

1967 Apr *Safe As Milk* is recorded for Buddah Records with a band that includes Ry Cooder and Antennae Jim Semens (Jeff Cotton) on guitars. During the recording, Beefheart (with a multi-octave vocal range) destroys a high-quality studio microphone by singing into it. Cooder leaves soon after (causing plans to appear at Monterey Pop Festival to be abandoned), but Semens becomes a regular Beefheart sideman.

1968 Dec *Strictly Personal* is released by Blue Thumb Records (and on Liberty in UK), but the quality is marred for Beefheart by unauthorized post-production work from Blue Thumb's Bob Krasnow.

1969 Oct Signed to Straight Records, and now assuming artistic control over recording, he produces double album *Trout Mask Replica*, which, despite not charting in US, is destined for cultural landmark status. It features the first assemblage of the definitive Magic Band, including Zoot Horn Rollo (Bill Harkleroad) on guitar, Rockette Morton (Mark

Boston) on guitar and bass, and The Mascara Snake on clarinet.

Nov Beefheart is featured on Zappa's *Hot Rats*.

Dec [6] *Trout Mask Replica* reaches UK #21.

971 Jan *Lick My Decals Off, Baby* is another UK chartmaker, at #20.

Feb Beefheart & The Magic Band make their New York live debut at Ungano's.

May [29] *Mirror Man*, featuring the remaining material recorded for, but not released by, Buddah in 1968, and featuring Semens, Handley, Drumbo and St.Clair, much to Beefheart's displeasure, makes UK #49.

972 Feb After falling out with Zappa, *The Spotlight Kid* appears on Reprise, and is Beefheart's US chart debut, reaching #131.

[19] *The Spotlight Kid*, recorded by Beefheart with Rollo (ex-surf band The Nightbeats), Taj Mahal, Ed Marimba, Rockette, Bassus Ophelius, Winged-Eel Fingerling, John "Drumbo" French, Ted Cactus and Rhys Clark, makes UK #44.

973 Dec *Clear Spot*, now adding latest Magic Band recruits Marimba, Orejon, Milt Holland and Russ Titelman, reaches only US #191, and fails to chart in UK.

974 Mar *Too Much Time*, from *Clear Spot* is released in UK, to no success.

May *Unconditionally Guaranteed* charts at US #192 and is Beefheart's last album with the existing Magic Band as Rollo and Morton leave to form their own group, Mallard. A new deal is signed with Virgin Records in UK, and with Mercury in US.

Nov *Blue Jeans and Moonbeams*, is poorly received despite new line-up: the Captain, Jeff Morris Tepper, Bob West, Mark Gibbons, Michael Smotherman, Gene Pello, Jimmy Caravan and Ty Grimes.

975 July Beefheart supports Pink Floyd at Knebworth Festival, Herts.

Nov Back with Zappa, singing with The Mothers Of Invention, he tours and contributes to *Bongo Fury*. Afterwards, Beefheart temporarily retires, returning to the Mojave Desert, CA, to paint.

978 Nov *Shiny Beast (Bat Chain Puller)*, released by Warner Bros. in US, breaking a long silence, has no chart success. UK release is delayed until Virgin wins a suit to enforce its own rights to Beefheart material. The Magic Band has changed once more, now including Tepper, Bruce Malbourne Fowler, Eric Drew Feldman, Richard Redus, Robert Arthur Williams and Art Tripp III.

980 Sept *Doc At the Radar Station*, recorded with Drumbo, Gary Lucas, Redris and Tripp, is released internationally on Virgin, coinciding with a successful tour of US and Europe by Beefheart, and unprecedented US TV appearance on NBC TV's "Saturday Night Live".

982 Sept [25] *Ice Cream For Crow*, featuring Hatsize Snyder, Cliff Martinez, Williams, Lambourne Fowler and mainstay Drumbo, returns him to UK chart, at #90. Issued via Epic Records in US, it fails to chart.

986 After a long silence, and an eventual announcement that he is leaving music to concentrate on painting, Beefheart exhibits in London.

987 Virgin issues the majority of its licensed Beefheart material on CD.

MARIAH CAREY

988 Singing since age 4, Carey (b. Mar.22, 1970, New York, NY), whose mother Patricia (having named her daughter after *They Call The Wind Mariah*, from Lerner and Loewe musical "Paint Your Wagon", from which *Wand'rin Star* by Lee Marvin was UK #1 the day Carey was born) has been a vocal coach and former New York City opera singer, has begun writing songs with Ben Margulies in high school at 16. While working as a waitress in New York, she wins an audition to be back-up singer for Brenda K. Starr, who passes Carey's demo tape to CBS Records President Tommy Mottola, who now signs her.

989 Carey spends much of the year commuting between the Tarpan studios, San Rafael, CA, and the Sky Line and the Hit Factory studios in New York, recording tracks for her debut release.

990 Apr Columbia launches Carey with an invitation-only soiree in New York, where she sings 3 songs accompanied by Richard Tee on piano.

June Carey makes TV appearances on NBC TV's "Tonight" and Fox TV's "Arsenio Hall" shows. (She has already taken a stir by singing the national anthem before the first game of the NBA finals.)

[30] Debut album *Mariah Carey* enters US chart at #80. Co-produced by Narada Michael Walden, Rhett Lawrence, Ric Wake and Carey, reviews of the 10-track Carey co-written project indicate that Columbia has firmly pitched her between Whitney Houston and Anita Baker.

Aug [4] Hot airplay cut *Vision Of Love*, co-penned with Margulies, tops US chart for 4 weeks.

Sept [15] *Vision Of Love* hits UK #9 as parent album *Mariah Carey* debuts at peak UK #6.

Oct [27] Carey is musical guest on NBC TV's "Saturday Night Live".

Nov [10] Ballad follow-up *Love Takes Time* tops US chart for 3 weeks.

Dec [1] *Love Takes Time* makes UK #37.

1991 Feb [2] House remixed version of uptempo *Someday* makes UK #38.

[20] From 5 nominations, Carey wins Best Pop Vocal Performance, Female for *Vision Of Love* and Best New Artist at the 33rd annual Grammy awards at Radio City Music Hall, New York.

[23] "Mariah Carey: The First Vision" enters US and UK video charts, a mini-collection of video clips from her debut project.

Mar [2] *Mariah Carey*, after 36 weeks on chart, hits US #1, and is on its way to 5 platinum RIAA US sales awards.

[7] Carey is named Best New Female Singer in the annual **Rolling Stone** Readers' Picks music awards.

[9] *Someday* becomes Carey's third consecutive US #1.

[12] Carey wins Best New R&B/Urban Contemporary Artist, Best R&B/Urban Contemporary Single, Female and Best R&B/Urban Contemporary Album, Female for *Mariah Carey* at the fifth annual Soul Train Awards at the Shrine Auditorium, Los Angeles.

Apr Another extract, ballad *I Don't Wanna Cry*, is released.

BELINDA CARLISLE

1985 May [10] After 3 successful albums, including multi-platinum *Beauty And The Beat* and 7 US hit singles, including million-seller *We Got The Beat*, The Go-Gos hold a press conference to announce the break-up of the band. Carlisle (b. Aug.16, 1958, Hollywood, CA) remains signed to IRS Records, and prepares a solo career and album with assistance of ex-Go-Go colleague Charlotte Caffey.

1986 May [9] Carlisle plays her first solo concert in Cleveland, OH.

Aug [9] *Mad About You* hits US #3, while parent album *Belinda* reaches US #13.

Oct [11] *I Feel The Magic*, also from the album, reaches US #82. Carlisle tours US as support to Robert Palmer, followed by a 3-month club tour of her own.

1987 Oct Second album *Heaven On Earth* is released. Although now signed to MCA in US, Virgin Records picks up release rights for UK. Collaborators on this follow-up project include Thomas Dolby, Charlotte Caffey, Ellen Shipley, and Michelle Phillips, one-time member of The Mamas And The Papas.

Dec [5] *Heaven Is A Place On Earth*, taken from the album, tops US chart for a week. Its success is aided by the impact of a promo video directed by actress Diane Keaton.

1988 Jan [16] *Heaven Is A Place On Earth* tops UK chart for 2 weeks, while *Heaven On Earth* makes US #13 and hits UK #4, attaining platinum status in both countries.

Mar [19] *I Get Weak*, also from the album, hits US #2 and UK #10.

May Carlisle sets out on her first major solo headlining tour, starting in US and Canada.

June [18] She visits Japan, while *Circle In The Sand*, from *Heaven On Earth*, hits US #7 and UK #4.

Aug Debut US release *Mad About You* is re-issued by IRS in UK and climbs to #67.

[13] *I Feel Free*, reviving Cream's 1967 UK #11, stalls at US #88.

Sept She plays her first UK tour, including 3 sold-out dates at London's Hammersmith Odeon. *World Without You*, released to tie in with the tour, makes UK #34.

Dec *Love Never Dies* peaks at UK #54.

1989 Mar [6] *Greenpeace Rainbow Warrors* album is released, featuring a contribution from Carlisle.

Oct *Leave A Light On* hits UK #4.

Nov *Runaway Horses*, with fellow Go-Gos Caffey, Valentine and Schock guesting on *Shades Of Michaelangelo* and contributions from George Harrison and Bryan Adams, hits UK #4 and will remain on chart for over 18 months.

Dec [9] *Leave A Light On* reaches US #11 and will climb to UK #38.

[16] Parent album *Runaway Horses* makes US #37.

1990 Mar [3] *Summer Rain* reaches US #30.

[10] *Runaway Horses* makes UK #40.

[28] The Go-Gos regroup for a one-off benefit concert at the Universal Amphitheater in Los Angeles for the California Environmental Protection Initiative of 1990. (This event will lead to a reunion later in the year.)

May [2] Carlisle announces she is pulling out of $35,000 appearance at the Frontier Days Rodeo in Cheyenne, WY, on July 23, citing maltreatment of livestock at such events.

June [2] *Vision Of You* peaks at UK #41.

Nov [3] *(We Want) The Same Thing* hits UK #6.

1991 Jan [26] *Summer Rain* peaks at UK #23.

ERIC CARMEN

1970 Carmen (b. Aug.11, 1949, Cleveland, OH), classically trained at Cleveland Institute of Music and ex-Cyrus Erie and The Quick, joins as lead singer of 1968 *It's Cold Outside* chartmakers The Choir, formed by Wally Bryson and Dave Smalley on guitar and Jim Bonfanti on drums, out of previous group The Outsiders.

1972 Group becomes The Raspberries and signs to Capitol Records.
May *Don't Want To Say Goodbye* makes US #86. Debut album *The Raspberries* climbs to US #51.
Oct *Go All The Way* hits US #5.
Dec *Fresh* makes US #36.

1973 **Jan** *I Wanna Be With You* reaches US #16.
June *Let's Pretend* makes US #35.
Sept *Tonight* peaks at US #69.
Nov *Side 3* reaches US #128. Smalley and Bonfanti leave to form Dynamite and are replaced by Mike McBride, ex-Cyrus Erie on drums, and bassist Scott McCarl.
Dec *I'm A Rocker* makes US #94.

1974 **Nov** *Overnight Sensation (Hit Record)*, penned by Carmen, like all previous chart singles, reaches US #18.

1975 **Apr** The Raspberries split after poor sales of their album *Starting Over* and Carmen moves to a solo career, signing to Arista Records.
Nov First solo album *Eric Carmen* is issued and climbs to US #21.

1976 **Mar** *All By Myself*, based on a Rachmaninoff melody, hits US #2 and is a million-seller.
May *All By Myself* reaches UK #12. Carmen visits UK for TV and radio promotion. *Eric Carmen* spends 1 week on UK chart at #58.
June *Raspberries' Best Featuring Eric Carmen* makes US #138.
July *Never Gonna Fall In Love Again* makes US #11. (Irish singer Dana's version has already made UK #31 in Mar.)
Sept *Sunrise* makes US #34.
Oct He begins recording second album in London, with producer Gus Dudgeon.

1977 **Feb** Disagreements lead Dudgeon to quit and Carmen completes the album alone.
Oct *Boats Against The Current* climbs to US #45.
Nov *She Did It* peaks at US #23.
Dec *Boats Against The Current* reaches US #88.

1978 **Dec** *Change Of Heart* makes US #19, but album of the same name reaches only US #137.

1979 **Feb** Carmen's remake of The Four Tops' 1964 smash *Baby I Need Your Lovin'* makes US #62.

1980 **July** *It Hurts Too Much* reaches US #75 and parent album *Tonight You're Mine* makes US #160.

1985 **Mar** After 5-year absence, he signs to Geffen records. *I Wanna Hear It From Your Lips* reaches US #35. Second album titled *Eric Carmen* makes US #128.
Apr *I'm Through With Love* makes US #87.

1988 **Feb** [13] *Hungry Eyes*, from movie "Dirty Dancing", hits US #4.
June Arista Records releases compilation *The Best Of Eric Carmen* which rises to US #59. Carmen embarks on "Dirty Dancing The Concert Tour" with Bill Medley, Merry Clayton and The Contours.
Aug [13] *Make Me Lose Control* hits US #3, taking his record sales to over 15 million worldwide.
Oct [15] *Reason To Try*, used by NBC TV for coverage of 1988 Summer Olympics and taken from *One Moment In Time*, peaks at US #87.

THE CARPENTERS

Karen Carpenter (vocals, drums)
Richard Carpenter (keyboards, vocals)

1967 Richard Carpenter (b. Oct.15, 1946, New Haven, CT) and sister Karen (b. Mar.2, 1950, New Haven), having relocated from New Haven to Downey, CA, form a jazz trio with tuba/bass player Wes Jacobs. They release 2 singles for local Magic Lamp label, before winning a Battle Of The Bands contest at the Hollywood Bowl, Hollywood, CA. They perform *The Girl From Ipanema* and *Iced Tea* and are spotted by RCA A&R chief Neely Plumb who signs them to the label as The Richard Carpenter Trio. They cut 4 tracks which are never released.

1968 When Jacobs leaves to study music, Karen and Richard form Spectrum with John Bettis, a friend of Richard's from California State college. Despite support gigs at Disneyland, the Troubadour and the Whiskey A-Go Go, the band is short-lived, but the duo perseveres and records some tracks in the home of top Los Angeles session bassist Joe Osborn,

which reach A&M label boss Herb Alpert.

1969 **Apr** [22] The Carpenters sign with A&M Records.
Nov Debut album *Offering* is released.

1970 **May** Debut single, a cover of The Beatles' *Ticket To Ride*, makes US #54.
July *(They Long To Be) Close To You*, an unknown Bacharach/David song recorded by Dionne Warwick 7 years earlier, is US #1 for 4 weeks.
Sept *Close To You* enters US chart, starting an 87-week chart run, which will see it hit #2.
Oct Helped by a TV ad for a bank targeting newlyweds, *(They Long To Be) Close To You* hits UK #6. Paul Williams/Roger Nichols penned *We've Only Just Begun* hits US #2.

1971 **Jan** *We've Only Just Begun* makes UK #28. *Close To You* makes UK #23.
Mar *For All We Know*, from film "Lovers And Other Strangers" hits US #3. (It will subsequently win an Oscar for Best Song Of The Year.) Debut album *Offering*, retitled *Ticket To Ride* peaks at US #150.
[16] Duo wins Best Contemporary Vocal Performance By A Group for *Close To You* and Best New Artist Of 1970 at the 13th annual Grammy awards.
June *Rainy Days And Mondays* hits US #2. *Carpenters* enters US chart and will hit #2.
July [20] Having spent the first half of the year touring the world, The Carpenters launch their own NBC TV series "Make Your Own Kind Of Music". Featuring regulars Al Hirt and Mark Lindsay (ex-Paul Revere & The Raiders), it will run until Sept.7.
Sept [24] Duo performs at the Royal Albert Hall, London.
Oct *Superstar/Bless The Beasts And Children* (the latter from film of same name), hits US #2/#67. *Superstar*, written by Leon Russell, backed with *For All We Know*, reaches UK #18.
Nov *The Carpenters* reaches UK #12.

1972 **Jan** *Merry Christmas Darling* makes UK #45.
Feb Originally recorded by Ruby & The Romantics, *Hurting Each Other* hits US #2.
Mar [14] The Carpenters win Best Pop Vocal Performance By A Group for *The Carpenters* at the 14th annual Grammy awards.
Apr *Ticket To Ride* reaches UK #20.
June *It's Going To Take Some Time* reaches US #12.
July *A Song For You* enters US chart, hitting #4.
Aug *Goodbye To Love* hits US #7.
Sept The Carpenters tour US.
Oct *Goodbye To Love* is double A-side with *I Won't Last A Day Without You* in UK where it hits #9. *A Song For You* reaches UK #13.

1973 **Apr** *Sing* hits US #3.
June *Now And Then* is released and features the novel idea of one side comprising 8 segued pop classics. It hits #2 in both US and UK.
July *Yesterday Once More* also hits US and UK #2.
Dec Carpenter-Bettis penned *Top Of The World* tops US chart and hits UK #5. *The Singles 1969-1973* featuring 12 hits, is released (and will eventually top both US and UK charts).

1974 **Mar** Cajun standard *Jambalaya (On The Bayou)*, backed with *Mr Guder* reaches UK #12.
May [1] Duo performs, at the request of President Nixon, at a White House state dinner honoring West German Chancellor Willy Brandt. *I Won't Last A Day Without You*, also penned by Paul Williams and Roger Nichols, reaches US #11. Reissued in UK, it makes #32.

1975 **Jan** *Please Mr Postman*, a cover of The Marvelettes 1961 chart-topper, hits US #1 and UK #2.
May *Only Yesterday* hits US #4 and UK #7.
June *Horizon* reaches US #13.
July *Horizon* tops UK chart.
Aug Reissued *Ticket To Ride* makes UK #35.
Sept *Solitaire* reaches US #17 and UK #32.
Dec Following 5 years of constant recording and touring Karen, now weighing only 90lbs., takes 2 months off to recuperate. She sends Christmas greetings to her UK fans in the form of *Santa Claus Is Comin' To Town* which makes UK #37.

1976 **Apr** A cover of Herman's Hermits 1967 smash, *There's A Kind Of Hush (All Over The World)* reaches US #12 and UK #22.
July *I Need To Be In Love* reaches US #25 and UK #36. *A Kind Of Hush* makes US #33 and hits UK #3.
Sept Originally a hit for Wayne King in 1931, *Goofus* peaks at US #56, breaking a run of 17 consecutive Top 30 hits.

1977 **Jan** *Live At The Palladium* reaches UK #28.
July *All You Get From Love Is A Love Song* makes US #35. Richard Carpenter receives substantial damages in High Court for a **Daily Mail** article alleging that the duo could not write their own songs.
Oct *Passage* makes US #49, but reaches UK #12.

Uncharacteristic *Calling Occupants Of Interplanetary Craft (The Recognized Anthem Of World Contact Day)* makes US #32, but hits UK #9.

8 **Apr** *Sweet Sweet Smile* makes US #44 and UK #40.

Dec *I Believe You* stalls at US #68. ***The Singles 1974-78***, a UK-only release, hits #2. ***Christmas Portrait*** makes US #145.

9 Karen, having taken a rest from The Carpenters, records a solo album with Phil Ramone. The album is not finished as she rejoins Richard to commence work on a new album titled ***Made In America***.

1 **Aug** *Touch Me When We're Dancing* returns the duo to US Top 20, reaching #16. ***Made In America*** makes US #52, but reaches UK #12.

Oct *(Want You) Back In My Life Again* stalls at US #72.

2 **Jan** *Those Good Old Dreams* peaks at US #63.

May *Beechwood 4-5789*, a remake of another Marvelettes smash, stalls at US #74. (It will be the duo's last US chart entry.)

Dec [17] Karen makes her last singing appearance at Buckley school in Sherman Oaks, where her godchildren attend.

3 **Feb** [4] Found unconscious at her parents' Downey home, Karen is rushed to Downey community hospital where she dies, aged 32, of cardiac arrest at 9.51am Pacific Standard Time. The Los Angeles coroner gives the cause of death as "heartbeat irregularities brought on by chemical imbalances associated with anorexia nervosa".

June [25] Karen Carpenter is remembered in a tribute at the First Congregational Church of Long Beach.

Oct *Make Believe It's Your First Time* stalls at UK #60.

Nov *Voice Of The Heart* makes US #46 and UK #6.

4 **Oct** *Yesterday Once More*, UK-only TV-advertised album, hits UK #10.

5 **Jan** *An Old-Fashioned Christmas* spends a week on US chart at #190.

June [26] Richard starts work on solo ***Time***. (He will sing lead vocals on the majority of the tracks. Dusty Springfield will guest on *Something In Your Eyes* and Dionne Warwick on *In Love Alone*.)

7 **Oct** *Time* is released, but fails to chart in either US or UK.

9 **Jan** [1] CBS TV movie "The Karen Carpenter Story", with Cynthia Gibb in the title role, tops US ratings.

0 **Jan** [13] Reissued *The Singles 1969-1973* and *The Singles 1974-1978* re-chart in UK, reaching #24 and #42 respectively. Box set CD ***Lovelines*** makes UK #73.

Apr [7] New TV-advertised compilation, ***Only Yesterday***, tops UK chart for 2 weeks, enjoying a 3-month stay in the Top 10.

Dec [29] Re-released *Close To You*, now paired with the festive *Merry Christmas Darling* reaches UK #25.

1 **Jan** [5] Seasonal ***Christmas Portrait*** returns to US chart, making #159.

HE CARS

: **Ocasek** (vocals, guitar)
njamin **Orr** (vocals, bass guitar)
iot **Easton** (guitar)
eg **Hawkes** (keyboards)
vid **Robinson** (drums)

76 Ocasek (b. Richard Otcasek, Mar.23, 1949, Baltimore, MD) and Orr (b. Benjamin Orzechowski, Cleveland, OH), having been songwriting and performing partners for almost a decade in Cleveland, New York, Woodstock, NY, and Ann Arbor, MI, and now resident in Cambridge, MA, team with Hawkes, who in 1970 has played on album by Milkwood, a folk group fronted by Ocasek and Orr, then Easton (b. Elliot Shapiro, Dec.18, 1953, Brooklyn, New York, NY), who in 1974 has joined with Ocasek and Orr in Boston, MA-based Cap'n Swing and ex-Modern Lovers and DMZ drummer Robinson. They decide upon the name The Cars.

Dec [31] Group makes its live debut at a New Year's Eve show at Pease Air Force Base, Portsmouth, NH.

77 **Feb** They begin playing regularly at Boston club, the Rat, and are noted by Fred Lewis, who becomes their manager.

Mar Lewis arranges a spot opening Bob Seger's concert at Boston's Music Hall, and a demo tape of *Just What I Needed* becomes Boston's WCOZ-FM and WBCN-FM radio stations' #1 request. Supporting dates for The J. Geils Band, Foreigner and Nils Lofgren soon follow.

Nov They sign to Elektra Records after being seen at Holy Cross College, Boston.

78 First album *The Cars* is recorded in just 2 weeks, with producer Roy Thomas Baker, in England.

Sept [16] Debut single *Just What I Needed* reaches US #27.

Nov Group makes a mini-tour of UK, Belgium, France and Germany.

[25] *My Best Friend's Girl*, the first picture disk single available commercially in UK, hits #3.

Dec [23] *My Best Friend's Girl* makes US #35.

[27] *The Cars* is certified platinum by the RIAA.

1979 **Jan** The Cars are voted Best New Band Of The Year in **Rolling Stone** magazine.

Feb [15] A Taste Of Honey beats out The Cars, among others, to win Best New Artist at the 21st annual Grammy awards.

Mar [24] *The Cars* reaches US #18, 39 weeks after its chart debut. It will spend 139 weeks on chart, becoming a million-seller.

[31] *Just What I Needed* reaches US #17.

Apr [14] *The Cars* reaches UK #29.

May [12] *Good Times Roll* makes US #41.

July [14] *Candy-O* reaches UK #30.

[28] *Let's Go* peaks at UK #51.

Aug Band plays to an audience of 500,000 in Central Park, New York.

[25] *Candy-O* hits US #3.

Sept [8] *Let's Go* reaches US #14.

Nov [24] *It's All I Can Do* makes US #41.

1980 **Sept** [20] *Panorama* hits US #5.

Oct [18] *Touch And Go* reaches US #37.

1981 Band buys Intermedia studio, Boston, and relaunches it as Synchro Sound, recording there itself. All band members involve themselves with other projects – Ocasek produces Suicide, New Models, The Peter Dayton Band, Bebe Buell and Romeo Void; Robinson produces singles for The Vinny Band and Boys Life, while Easton produces The Dawgs.

1982 **Jan** [9] *Shake It Up*, recorded at Synchro Sound, hits US #9.

Feb [27] *Shake It Up* hits US #4.

May [8] *Since You're Gone* makes US #41.

June [12] *Since You've Been Gone*, the band's first UK chart success in 3 years, makes #37.

Sept [3-5] The Cars play the US Festival, financed by Apple Computers founder Steven Wozniak, in San Bernardino, CA, to 400,000 people, along with Jackson Browne, Fleetwood Mac, The Grateful Dead, Eddie Money, Police, Santana, Talking Heads and many others.

1983 **Mar** Ocasek releases solo album, ***Beatitude*** on Geffen Records, which reaches US #28.

[19] Extracted *Something To Grab For* makes US #47. (Ocasek produces Bad Brains, while Easton will do the same for The Peter Bond Set and Jules Shear during this period.)

1984 **Apr** [28] *You Might Think* hits US #7. (Its computer-generated video will win first prize in the First International Music Video Festival in St. Tropez, France.) *Heartbeat City*, produced by Robert John Lange, hits US #3.

July [7] *Magic* reaches US #12.

Sept [29] Ballad *Drive*, with lead vocal by Orr, is The Cars most successful US single yet, a #3 hit and eventual million-seller.

Oct [13] *Drive* hits UK #5, their first UK Top 10 for 6 years, as *Heartbeat City* reaches UK #25.

Dec [22] *Hello Again* reaches US #20.

1985 **Mar** [30] *Why Can't I Have You?* makes US #33.

Apr [6] Easton's solo ***Change No Change*** makes US #99.

Aug [31] Repromoted in UK after its use during Live Aid providing mood backing for African famine film footage, *Drive* re-charts and hits #4. Ocasek gives all his royalties to the Band Aid Trust.

Nov Compilation *The Cars' Greatest Hits* reaches UK #27 and US #12.

1986 **Jan** [11] *Tonight She Comes* hits US #7.

Mar [22] *I'm Not The One* makes US #32.

Nov [15] Ocasek has a solo US hit with *Emotion In Motion*, reaching #15, as parent album ***This Side Of Paradise*** makes US #31.

1987 **Jan** [24] Ocasek's *True To You* peaks at US #75.

Feb [14] Orr's *Stay The Night* reaches US #24 as his debut solo album ***The Lace*** makes US #86.

Sept [5] *Door To Door* peaks at UK #72.

Oct [24] The Cars' *You Are The Girl* reaches US #17 as parent album ***Door To Door*** reaches UK #26.

Nov [21] *Strap Me In* stalls at US #85.

1988 **Feb** [1] The break-up of The Cars is publicly announced.

[13] *Coming Up You* peaks at US #74.

1989 **Jan** Ocasek's son Christopher releases solo album, before going on to form Glamour Camp.

Aug [23] Ocasek marries long-time belle, Czechoslovak model Paulina Porizkova, on the Caribbean island of St. Bart's.

1990 **Apr** [22] Ocasek makes his first solo public appearance at the "Earth Day" festivities in Central Park, New York, with The B52's, Hall & Oates and others.

JOHNNY CASH

1950 An avid country music fan since childhood, having written his first song at age 12, Cash (b. Feb.26, 1932, Kingsland, AR), son of a cotton farmer, raised on a Federal Government resettlement colony in Dyess, AR, joins US Air Force after graduating from high school and is stationed in Germany, where he learns to play guitar and write songs for it, and forms group called The Landsberg Barbarians, with 5 other servicemen who have backgrounds in country music.

1953 Cash's first published song is "Hey Porter", printed in the service newspaper **Stars And Stripes**.

1954 **July** [3] He leaves US Air Force and moves to Memphis, TN.
Aug Working around Memphis as a door-to-door salesman, and enrolled in a radio announcers' course part-time, Cash meets The Tennessee Three, a trio of part-time musicians who work as mechanics at the same garage as Cash's brother, Roy, and have played with him in The Delta Rhythm Ramblers. He begins to rehearse and play small local gigs with them: Marshall Grant (guitar), Luther Perkins (guitar) and Red Kernodle (steel guitar). (Although Kernodle will soon leave.)
[7] Cash marries Vivian Liberto, whom he met 3 weeks before entering the service and with whom he corresponded daily through his German posting.

1955 Encouraged by Elvis Presley's success at Sam Phillips' Sun Records, Cash and the duo try to audition for Phillips as a gospel act. Phillips insists they can only succeed commercially singing country. Grant moves to bass while Perkins switches from acoustic to electric guitar. Sun signs the remaining trio, largely on the strength of Cash's voice and his songs "Hey Porter" and "Cry Cry Cry".
May [24] Daughter Rosanne is born. (During the 80s, she will become a major country artist in her own right, having done back-up singing and solo spots in her father's stage show during the 70s.)
June [21] First single, *Hey Porter/Cry Cry Cry*, is released.
Sept *Cry Cry Cry* hits #1 in Memphis, and the group supports Elvis Presley on local gigs and features in a 15-min. radio show on KWEM, Memphis (sponsored by Cash's employer).
Nov *Cry Cry Cry* makes US national Country chart #14 for 1 week.
Dec Cash plays a guest slot on the "Louisiana Hayride" show in Shreveport, LA, (becoming a weekly regular the following month), and plays live gigs around the Mid-South with Carl Perkins, supporting Presley, George Jones and others.

1956 **Jan** Cash leaves his day job to concentrate on performing.
Mar Double-sided *So Doggone Lonesome/Folsom Prison Blues* hits #5 on Country chart. Bob Neal, ex-manager of Presley, becomes Cash's manager.
May *I Walk The Line* is released. Written by Cash and originally performed on "Louisiana Hayride" as a slow ballad, Phillips insists on speeding up the tempo and it becomes Cash's first crossover success.
July [7] He appears on the "Grand Ole Opry" in Nashville, TN.
Nov [10] *I Walk The Line* reaches US #17, having hit #2 on Country chart for several weeks.
Dec [4] Carl Perkins and his group are recording a session at Sun studios, with Jerry Lee Lewis guesting on piano. Cash is also present but his wife draws him away to go shopping. Presley, in Memphis for Christmas, arrives and the 3 of them settle down to an impromptu session, mostly singing gospel songs and recent hits.

1957 **Jan** *There You Go* hits #2 on Country chart. Cash is in demand for live appearances all over US, having toured Florida, Colorado, California, and even some dates in Ontario, Canada.
[19] He appears on CBS TV's "Jackie Gleason Show", having already been seen regularly on "The Jimmy Dean Show".
July [1] *Next In Line* makes US #99 and #9 on Country chart.
Sept Cash undergoes throat surgery in a Memphis hospital and is ordered not to sing for a month.
Oct [21] *Home Of The Blues* reaches US #88 and #5 on Country chart.
Johnny Cash With His Hot & Blue Guitar, the only album released by Sun while Cash is with the label (there will be 6 more after he leaves), does not chart.

1958 **Mar** [31] Pop-oriented *Ballad Of A Teenage Queen* reaches US #14 and tops Country chart. Produced and written by Jack Clement, whom Phillips has paired with Cash to widen the singer's appeal to a teenage audience, the original trio recording has dubbed male and female back-up voices added to give the pop/rock feel.
June [30] *Come In Stranger*, B-side of *Guess Things Happen That Way*, peaks at US #66.
July [28] *Guess Things Happen That Way* reaches US #11 and tops Country chart.

Aug [1] Cash's Sun contract expires, and he and The Tennessee Two sign to CBS/Columbia Records. He ends his residency on the "Grand Ole Opry" and moves with family, band and manager Neal from Memphis to Los Angeles.
Sept [15] *The Ways Of A Woman In Love*, penned by Charlie Rich and released by Sun upon Cash's departure, reaches US #24.
Nov [10] First CBS/Columbia single, *All Over Again* makes US #38.
[24] B-side *What Do I Care?* peaks at US #52.
Dec [15] Sun single *I Just Thought You'd Like To Know*, B-side of *It's Just About Time*, climbs to US #85.

1959 **Jan** Debut CBS/Columbia album *The Fabulous Johnny Cash* is his first US Album chart entry, reaching #19.
[12] *It's Just About Time* makes US #47.
Feb [16] *Don't Take Your Guns To Town* reaches US #32.
June [1] *Frankie's Man Johnny* peaks at US #57.
Aug [10] *Katy Too* (on Sun) makes US #66.
Sept [21] Double A-side *I Got Stripes* and *Five Feet High And Rising* reach US #43 and #76 respectively.
Oct [4] "The Rebel", for which Cash supplies the theme *The Ballad Of Johnny Yuma* each week, premieres on ABC TV.
Dec [28] Seasonal *The Little Drummer Boy* peaks at US #63. (Cash recruits his own drummer boy, signing up W.S. Holland, who will remain with Cash for 30 years.)

1960 **Jan** [1] Cash plays the first of many free jailhouse shows in San Quentin prison. Country cohort Merle Haggard is part of the captive audience.
Mar [14] *Straight A's In Love* (on Sun) peaks at US #84.
July [25] *Second Honeymoon* climbs to US #79 while double A-side on Sun *Down The Street To 301/Honky-Tonk Girl* makes US #85/#92.

1961 **Jan** [9] *Oh Lonesome Me* climbs to US #93.
Constantly on the road, and beginning to rely heavily on drink and pills, Cash becomes estranged from his family, which by now includes 4 daughters. He spends time on the bohemian folk scene in New York Greenwich Village.
Dec [11] *Tennessee Flat-Top Box* makes US #84.

1962 **Sept** [15] *Bonanza!* climbs to US #94.

1963 **May** *Blood, Sweat And Tears* reaches US #80, his second chart album in almost 5 years.
July [27] *Ring Of Fire*, a brass-flavored Mexican/western arrangement climbs to US #17. It is co-written by Merle Haggard and June Carter (b. June 24, 1929), an established country performer. Carter and Cash begin playing as a duo.
Sept *Ring Of Fire – The Best Of Johnny Cash* reaches US #26.
Nov [30] *The Matador*, styled similarly to *Ring Of Fire*, makes US #44.

1964 **Mar** [21] *Understand Your Man* makes US #35. Cash becomes an erratic and unreliable performer and he and his band start to miss gigs.
Aug *I Walk The Line*, featuring 6 newly-recorded versions of his old Sun hits, reaches US #53.
Nov [28] A version of Bob Dylan's *It Ain't Me Babe* peaks at US #58.
Dec *Bitter Tears (Ballads Of The American Indian)*, a collection of Indian protest songs penned with Peter La Farge, makes US #47.

1965 **Mar** [13] *Orange Blossom Special* climbs to US #80.
Apr *Orange Blossom Special* makes US #49.
June [12] *It Ain't Me Babe* is Cash's first UK chart entry, reaching #28.
[17-20] Cash takes part in the first New York Folk Festival at Carnegie Hall, New York.

1966 **Mar** [26] *The One On The Right Is On The Left*, a tongue-twisting novelty, makes US #46.
May [7] Cash begins a 10-date UK tour at the Empire theater, Liverpool, Merseyside, with The Statler Brothers and June Carter.
[22] Tour ends at Granada cinema, Walthamstow, London.
July [9] *Everybody Loves A Nut* makes US #96, as parent album *Everybody Loves A Nut* peaks at US #88.
[23] *Everybody Loves A Nut* reaches US #28.

1967 Cash is found one night near death in a small Georgia town and a policeman has to revive him. Vivian divorces him.
Aug Compilation *Johnny Cash's Greatest Hits, Volume 1* reaches US #82 and will stay on chart for 71 weeks.

1968 **Jan** [27] *Rosanna's Going Wild* peaks at US #91.
Feb [29] Cash and Carter win Best C&W Performance Duet, Trio Or Group (Vocal Or Instrumental) for *Jackson* at the 10th annual Grammy awards.
Mar Cash marries June Carter, having proposed to her on stage.
May [4] *From Sea To Shining Sea* makes UK #40. Cash starts a 13-date UK tour at Manchester Free Trade Hall, Gtr.Manchester.
[19] Tour ends at Newcastle Odeon, Tyne & Wear.

July [6] A new version of *Folsom Prison Blues*, originally recorded in mid-50s for Sun, is issued to trailer *Johnny Cash At Folsom Prison* and climbs to US #32. *Old Golden Throat* makes UK #37.

Aug Live *Johnny Cash At Folsom Prison*, a recording of a concert in the jail, is a major crossover success for Cash. It reaches US #13 (spending 122 weeks on chart) and hits UK #8 (53 weeks on chart).

Oct [21] Cash wins Best Album for *Johnny Cash At Folsom Prison* at the Country Music Awards.

[25] Further UK dates begin at the Manchester Odeon as twice-nightly soirees with Perkins, The Statler Brothers, Carter and The Tennessee Three, set to end at Birmingham Empire, W.Midlands, Nov.3.

69 Feb [17] Cash records a session in Nashville with Bob Dylan. *Girl From The North Country*, included on Dylan's *Nashville Skyline* (for which Cash writes the liner notes), is the only duet released from the session.

[22] *Daddy Sang Bass* makes US #42.

Mar [12] Cash wins Best Country Vocal Performance, Male for *Folsom Prison Blues* and Best Album Notes for *Johnny Cash At Folsom Prison* at the 11th annual Grammy awards.

Apr *Then Holy Land*, gospel music with a narration, reaches US #54.

June [7] Cash begins his own ABC TV series, "The Johnny Cash Show", with regulars The Carter Family, The Statler Brothers, Carl Perkins and The Tennessee Three (Bob Wotton replaces Luther Perkins, who perishes in a house fire).

Aug Live *Johnny Cash At San Quentin*, soundtrack to ITV documentary of the same title, focusing on a Cash concert in the prison, tops US Album chart for 4 weeks and is later a million-seller.

[23] Extracted *A Boy Named Sue*, a tongue-in-cheek narrative song written by Shel Silverstein, hits US #2 and is also a million-seller.

Oct [18] *A Boy Named Sue* hits UK #4. *Johnny Cash At San Quentin* hits UK #2 (and will stay charted for 114 weeks).

Dec [6] Double A-side *Blistered/See Ruby Fall* makes US #50, as *Get Rhythm*, original 1956 B-side of *I Walk The Line*, is reissued by Sun and peaks at US #60. *Greatest Hits, Volume 1* reaches UK #23 and stays on chart for 6 months.

70 Feb [28] A version of Tim Hardin's *If I Were A Carpenter*, duetted with Carter, makes US #36 as *Rock Island Line* on Sun climbs to US #93.

Mar *Hello, I'm Johnny Cash* hits both US and UK #6.

[11] *A Boy Named Sue* wins Best Country Vocal Performance, Male and Best Country Song (for its writer Shel Silverstein) and Cash's annotation for Dylan's *Nashville Skyline* wins Best Album Notes at the 12th annual Grammy awards.

Apr [17] Cash plays the White House at the invitation of President Nixon. (The Commander-in-Chief supposedly makes a special request for *Okie From Muskogee*, but Cash respectfully declines and sings *A Boy Named Sue* instead.)

May He wins 4 awards at first UK CMA ceremonies held at the Royal Lancaster hotel, London.

[23] *What Is Truth?* reaches US #19.

June [27] *What Is Truth?* reaches UK #21.

July *The World Of Johnny Cash* climbs to US #54 and hits UK #5.

Oct [3] *Sunday Morning Coming Down*, penned by Kris Kristofferson, makes US #46.

Dec *The Johnny Cash Show* reaches UK #18.

71 Jan [9] *Flesh And Blood*, from *I Walk The Line* soundtrack album, makes US #54.

Mar [16] Cash and Carter win Best Country Performance By A Duo Or Group for *If I Were A Carpenter* at the 13th annual Grammy awards.

Apr [3] *The Man In Black*, an archetypal Cash narrative song, peaks at US #58.

May "The Johnny Cash Show" airs for the last time on ABC TV. The Cashes travel to Israel to film "Gospel Road", about Christianity and modern-day life in the Holy Land.

June [10] *Kate* peaks at US #75.

Aug *Man In Black*, which included a duet with evangelist Billy Graham, makes US #56.

Sept *Man In Black* reaches UK #18.

[17] Cash performs the first of 3 UK gigs at Manchester Belle Vue.

Nov Documentary "In The Footsteps Of Jesus" airs on US TV. *The Johnny Cash Collection (His Greatest Hits, Volume II)* reaches US #94 as *Johnny Cash* makes UK #43.

72 After appearing with Kirk Douglas in western "A Gunfight", Cash will guest-star on NBC TV's "Columbo", among a half-dozen guest roles.

May *A Thing Called Love*, with The Evangel Temple Choir, hits UK #4, while album of the same title reaches US #112 and UK #8.

Oct Compilation *Star Portrait* reaches UK #16. *Johnny Cash: America (A 200-Year Salute In Story And Song)* reaches US #176.

1973 Mar *Any Old Wind That Blows* reaches US #188. Cash joins evangelist Graham on stage and sings a duet with Cliff Richard at Wembley Stadium, London.

1976 May [29] Novelty song *One Piece At A Time* reaches US #29.

July [24] *One Piece At A Time* makes UK #32 as parent album *One Piece At A Time* makes US #185, his final solo US pop chart entry.

Aug Cash starts a new 4-week summer series, "The Johnny Cash Show", on CBS TV, originating from Grand Ole Opry in Nashville, and with country music guest stars.

[14] *One Piece At A Time* makes UK #49.

Oct [9] Compilation *The Best Of Johnny Cash* makes UK #48.

1978 Sept [2] *Itchy Feet – 20 Foot-tapping Greats*, Cash's last chart album, reaches UK #36.

1980 Oct [13] Cash is inducted into the Country Music Association Hall Of Fame.

1981 Apr [23] Carl Perkins and Jerry Lee Lewis, in Germany appearing in different music festivals, join Cash on stage in Stuttgart. Their performance is recorded and later released as *The Survivors*.

1985 Sept [28] Cash teams with Waylon Jennings, Willie Nelson and Kris Kristofferson for *The Highwayman* which tops US Country chart, and makes US #92. (Extracted title track *The Highwayman*, penned by Jimmy Webb and recorded nearly a decade earlier by its writer, has topped US Country singles chart on Aug.17.)

1986 Feb [25] *The Highwayman* wins Best Country Song at the 28th annual Grammy awards.

July Cash joins Jerry Lee Lewis, Carl Perkins and Roy Orbison for *Class Of '55 (Memphis Rock & Roll Homecoming)*. It makes US #87.

1987 Feb [24] *Interviews From The Class Of '55 Recording Sessions* wins Best Spoken Word Or Non-Musical Recording at the 29th annual Grammy awards.

Mar *1958-1986: The CBS Years* anthologizes a selection of hits.

May Cash debuts for Mercury with *Johnny Cash Is Coming To Town*.

1988 The Country Music Foundation organizes an exhibition to commemorate Cash's career.

Dec [17] *Water From The Wells Of Home*, featuring a cast including Paul McCartney, The Everly Brothers, Waylon Jennings, Emmylou Harris, Hank Williams Jr., daughter Rosanne Cash, and son John Carter Cash, enters US Country chart on its way to peaking at #48. Extracted *That Old Wheel*, a duet with Hank Williams Jr., reaches #21 on US Country chart. *Classic Cash*, featuring re-recordings of several of his best-known hits, is released.

[19] Cash is admitted into a Nashville hospital for double bypass open heart surgery.

UK label Red Rhino releases *'Til Things Are Brighter*, a various artists tribute of Cash material to benefit AIDS research, featuring Michelle Shocked, Brendan Croker, The Mekons and others.

1989 Mar *Ballad Of A Teenage Queen*, with daughter Rosanne and The Everly Brothers, makes #45 on US Country chart, as Cash is bestowed with the Aggie Award, the highest honor awarded by the Songwriters Guild Of America.

1990 Nov [21] Cash sings *A Love Song To America*, written by Sgt. Jeffrey Grantham serving with the 831st Supply Squadron in the Persian Gulf, on TNN TV's "Nashville Now".

1991 Mar [27] Cash, on a promotion visit to UK, performs 2 songs on morning broadcast TV AM, as his new album *The Mystery Of Life* is issued via current record deal with Mercury.

DAVID CASSIDY

1970 Sept [25] "The Partridge Family", in which Keith Partridge is played by Cassidy (b. Apr.12, 1950, New York, NY), son of actor Jack Cassidy and stepson of actress Shirley Jones, with a part on Broadway in "The Fig Leaves Are Falling" and small TV drama roles in "Adam 12", "Bonanza" "The FBI", "Ironside", "Marcus Welby MD" and "The Mod Squad" to his credit, premieres on ABC TV. The Partridge Family, comprising Shirley (Shirley Jones), Keith (Cassidy), Laurie (Susan Dey), Danny (Danny Bonaduce), Christopher (Jeremy Gelbwaks) and Tracy (Suzanne Crough), is loosely based on real-life family singing group The Cowsills.

Oct The Partridge Family signs to Bell Records, and debuts in US with Tony Romeo-penned *I Think I Love You*, with Cassidy the featured lead singer, backed by top Los Angeles, CA, session singers Ron Hicklin, Jackie Ward and Tom and John Bahler. *The Partridge Family Album*, produced by Wes Farrell, is issued, and hits US #4. (As with The Archies, Farrell will recruit top writing talent, including Neil Sedaka, Barry Mann and Cynthia Weil and Tommy Boyce and Bobby Hart.)

Nov [21] *I Think I Love You* tops US chart for 3 weeks, ultimately selling over 5 million copies.

1971 Mar [27] *Doesn't Somebody Want To Be Wanted* hits US #6, and is another million-seller. With TV show not yet shown in UK to promote it, *I Think I Love You* reaches #18. **The Partridge Family Up To Date** is released, hitting US #3.

June [12] *I'll Meet You Halfway* hits US #9.

Sept [25] *I Woke Up In Love This Morning* reaches US #13. Third album, **The Partridge Family Sound Magazine**, hits US #9.

Oct First Cassidy solo single released in US, is a revival of The Association's #1 hit *Cherish*.

Dec [25] *Cherish* hits US #9 and is a million-seller.

1972 Jan [8] Family album *Up To Date* makes UK #46.

[22] Family single *It's One Of Those Nights (Yes Love)* reaches US #20.

Mar As "The Partridge Family" reaches UK TV, *It's One Of Those Nights (Yes Love)* boosts The Family chart fortunes, peaking at UK #11.

Apr [1] Cassidy's second solo single *Could It Be Forever* peaks disappointingly in US at #37.

[22] **The Partridge Family Shopping Bag** enters UK chart and climbs to #14 and will reach US #18.

[29] Partridge Family's *Am I Losing You* peaks at US #59.

May Cassidy is launched as soloist in UK with *Could It Be Forever*, using *Cherish* as the B-side, and hits UK #2, while parent album *Cherish* reaches US #15.

[11] He is featured bare-chested on the cover of **Rolling Stone**.

June Solo album *Cherish* hits UK #2.

July [1] Cassidy's solo revival of The Young Rascals' *How Can I Be Sure* reaches US #25.

Aug [19] Family's revival of Sedaka's *Breaking Up Is Hard To Do* hits UK #3 at the height of TV show's UK popularity, and makes US #28.

Sept [30] *How Can I Be Sure* tops UK chart for 2 weeks. Huge media coverage confirms him as a major teenage idol in UK.

Oct [14] R&B-flavored solo *Rock Me Baby*, a deliberate attempt to harden his teeny-bop musical image makes US #38, his last solo US hit single for 18 years. Meanwhile, **Greatest Hits** by The Partridge Family reaches US #21.

Dec The unexpected style of *Rock Me Baby* puzzles some UK teenage fans, but it climbs to #11.

[9] Seasonal **Christmas Card** makes UK #45, and is The Partridge Family's final charting UK album.

1973 Jan [27] Family revival of Gene Pitney's *Looking Through The Eyes Of Love* makes US #39 and will hit UK #9.

Solo *Rock Me Baby* hits UK #2 after peaking at US #41.

Apr Cassidy from now on concentrates his solo recording career in UK, where his fan following is strongest. Ballad *I Am A Clown*, backed with *Some Kind Of A Summer*, hits UK #3.

[21] The Partridge Family US chart swan song is *Friend And Lover*, a lowly #99.

June Final Family UK hit revives The Ronettes' *Walking In The Rain*, and sees the group out with a major hit at UK #10.

Oct [27] Double A-side *Daydreamer/The Puppy Song* tops UK chart, boosted by Cassidy's arrival at Heathrow airport, lip-synching to the song as he walks down the plane's steps on live TV.

Dec [15] **Dreams Are Nothin' More Than Wishes**, a US non-charter, is Cassidy's most successful UK solo album, topping the chart for a week. (Produced by Rick Jarrard, the album features songs by Nilsson, Michael McDonald and Kim Carnes, who, with husband Dave Ellingson, is a member of Cassidy's live band.)

1974 May [26] Tragedy occurs during a UK concert at White City, London, when in the frenzied crowd over 1,000 people have to be treated by ambulance workers. 6 girls are taken to hospital, and 14-year-old Bernadette Wheelen dies 4 days later from heart failure. Cassidy admits he is shaken by the tragedy and feels some responsibility.

June [1] *If I Didn't Care* hits UK #9.

Aug [10] A revival of Lennon/McCartney's *Please Please Me* ("The Beatles wrote the soundtrack to my youth" is Cassidy's most notable quote of the time) climbs to UK #16. Solo **Cassidy Live** hits UK #9.

[31] "The Partridge Family" airs for the last time, leaving Cassidy free to pursue his solo career.

1975 Feb He signs a worldwide solo recording contract with RCA, which will bring no US chart success, but will bear fruit internationally.

Aug [9] First RCA single *I Write The Songs*, backed with *Get It Up For Love*, reaches UK #11, as parent album **The Higher They Climb** with help from members of The Beach Boys, The Turtles and America reaches UK #22.

Nov [22] A revival of The Beach Boys' *Darlin'* hits UK #16. (2 more

unsuccessful RCA albums, **Home Is Where The Heart Is** and **Gettin' It In The Street**, are released.)

1978 Cassidy stars in a production of John Van Druten's "Voice Of The Turtle" at West Point, NY, with his wife actress Kay Lenz. He is nominated for Best Actor In A Television Drama for his role in "A Chance To Live".

Nov [2] Cassidy returns to series TV (he has guest-starred on "The Love Boat" and "Fantasy Island"), starring as policeman Dan Shay in NBC TV's "David Cassidy – Man Undercover". (The show will air until Aug.2, 1979.)

1981 May He stars in West Coast run in George M. Cohan's musical "Little Johnny Jones". (When show reaches Broadway, Donny Osmond has taken over the role.)

1983 Mar Cassidy replaces Andy Gibb on Broadway in Tim Rice and Andrew Lloyd Webber's "Joseph And His Amazing Technicolor Dream Coat", until the show closes on Sept.4.

May [2] Cassidy plays George M. Cohan in "Parade Of Stars Playing The Palace" at the Palace theater in New York, an all-star benefit for the Actors' Fund Of America.

1984 After completing a road tour of "Jesus Christ Superstar", Cassidy retreats with his new wife Meryl Tanz (he and Lenz had divorced in 1981) to his Santa Barbara, CA, home to breed horses.

1985 Mar [16] A new recording deal with MLM/Arista Records and producer Alan Tarney sees comeback single *The Last Kiss*, with vocal help from George Michael, hit UK #6.

June [8] *Romance (Let Your Heart Go)* peaks at UK #54.

[15] *Romance* reaches UK #20.

1986 *David Cassidy – His Greatest Hits Live*, recorded at a Royal Albert Hall, London, concert in Oct.1985 is released in UK on Starblend label.

1987 He takes over role of The Rock Star from Cliff Richard in the West End production of Dave Clark's musical "Time" at the Dominion theater, London. On his return to US, Cassidy makes 2 feature films "Instant Karma" and "Spirit Of '76".

1988 June [21] Cassidy is named in a Los Angeles paternity suit.

1989 Apr [12] DJs Mark Thompson and Brian Phelps, the morning drive team at Los Angeles station K-LOS, are wondering out loud what has happened to Cassidy on his 39th birthday, when their studio rings with Cassidy on the other end to tell them. They invite him to the studio and he sings 3 new songs on air. Cassidy then hears from 3 companies, one of which, Enigma, signs him.

1990 Sept [15] Asia's **Then And Now**, featuring Cassidy/John Wetton-penned *Prayin' For A Miracle*, makes US #114.

Oct [11] Cassidy makes his first ever live TV appearance on Fox TV's "Arsenio Hall" show.

Nov [17] Second recording comeback, *Lyin' To Myself* reaches US #27 as parent **David Cassidy** makes US #136.

1991 Feb [10] Cassidy joins with nearly 100 celebrities in Burbank, CA, to record *Voices That Care*, a David Foster and fiancee Linda Thompson Jenner-composed and organized charity record to benefit the American Red Cross Gulf Crisis Fund.

Mar "Spirit Of '76", in which Cassidy plays a time traveler destined for 1776, but instead returning to 1976 and the disco boom, is released in cinemas throughout US.

[7] Cassidy is named Most Unwelcome Comeback in the annual **Rolling Stone** Readers' Picks music awards.

CHAD & JEREMY

Chad Stuart (vocals, guitar)
Jeremy Clyde (vocals, guitar)

1963 Stuart (b. Dec.10, 1943, UK) and Clyde (b. Mar.22, 1944, UK) meet at the Central School of Drama in London. They both play guitar and decide to form an acoustic folk-pop duo, with Stuart handling the musical side of their songs and Clyde the lyrics.

Dec Duo signs to UK independent label Ember Records and, after appearing on UK TV's "Ready Steady Go!", releases *Yesterday's Gone*, part-written by Stuart, which makes UK #37 – their only UK success.

1964 July In the euphoria for UK acts following The Beatles' success in US, *Yesterday's Gone*, licensed by World Artists Records, climbs to US #21.

Oct *A Summer Song* hits US #7 after failing in UK. (When previewed on BBC TV's "Juke Box Jury" it had been voted a miss, but panellist Ringo Starr predicted that "it will do well in the States".) Chad & Jeremy move to Hollywood, realizing that their best chance of success may lie in US. They embark on "Memphis Special" tour with Johnny Rivers.

Nov Debut album *Yesterday's Gone*, with both hits, reaches US #22.

Dec They record guest spot for US TV's "Dick Van Dyke Show".

65 Jan Standard revival *Willow, Weep For Me* makes US #15, after well-received appearances on US TV shows like "Hullaballoo".
Apr *Chad & Jeremy Sing For You* reaches US #69. *If I Loved You*, revived from the musical "Carousel", makes US #23.
[23] Duo cancels one-nighter US tour with Gene Pitney, when Stuart is stricken with glandular fever.
May *What Do You Want With Me* peaks at US #51 and duo signs to CBS/Columbia Records.
June *Before And After*, written by Van McCoy, makes US #17.
[1] Duo flies to US to begin 4-week tour of one-nighters.
July Duo's version of Lennon/McCartney's *From A Window*, issued by World Artists, peaks at US #97 while Billy J. Kramer's makes US #23.
Aug Columbia follow-up, *I Don't Wanna Lose You Baby*, reaches US #35. First Columbia album, *Before And After*, makes US #37.
[24] Clyde opens in the musical "Passion Flower Hotel" at London's Prince of Wales theater.
Nov Another standard ballad, *I Have Dreamed*, from musical "The King And I", makes US #91.
Dec *I Don't Wanna Lose You Baby* reaches US #77.

66 Jan Duo reaches the final of the San Remo Song Festival.
Apr [3] Movie "The Great St. Trinian's Train Robbery", in which Clyde has a cameo role, goes on general release.
May *The Best Of Chad & Jeremy* and *More Chad & Jeremy*, compiling their early Ember/World Artists tracks, are issued in US on Capitol, and chart at US #49 and #144. *Distant Shores* makes US #30.
June [25] They play "The Beach Boys Summer Spectacular", with The Byrds, The Lovin' Spoonful and others, in Anaheim, CA.
Oct *Distant Shores* climbs to US #61. *You Are She* makes #87 and is their final US chart entry.
Dec Chad & Jeremy appear in an episode of "Batman". Catwoman steals their voices and threatens to use her voice eraser machine unless her demands of $22.5 million for their return are met.

67 Nov *Of Cabbages And Kings*, which makes US #186, is a 5-movement piece scored and arranged by Stuart. The critics praise it but Chad & Jeremy announce a final split. (Stuart begins to write musicals and Clyde immerses himself in acting, his most prominent early stage role is in "Conduct Unbecoming" in London's West End. He will continue to be seen in UK TV roles throughout the 70s and 80s.)

THE CHAMBERS BROTHERS

George Chambers (bass, vocals)
Willie Chambers (guitar, vocals)
Lester Chambers (harmonica, vocals)
Joe Chambers (guitar, vocals)
Brian Keenan (drums)

54 The Chambers family moves from Mississippi to Los Angeles, CA, where George Chambers (b. Sept.26, 1931, Flora, MS), home after a tour of US Army duty in Korea, organizes brothers Willie (b. Mar.3, 1938, Flora), Lester (b. Apr.13, 1940, Flora), and Joe (b. Aug.24, 1942, Scott County, MS) into a gospel group. George has sung professionally, but they play almost exclusively to church congregations for several years.

61 George meets Ed Pearl, owner of Los Angeles' famous Ash Grove coffee house and, after an audition, they make their club debut at Ash Grove. Inevitably, the Chambers are influenced by the coffee house folk scene, and begin to add folk numbers to their gospel set.

65 July Favorites in the folk field, they get a wild reception at Newport Folk Festival. They are beginning to add pop and blues songs to their repertoire, with Lester being taught harmonica by blues legend Sonny Terry, and the rest of the band picking up rock guitar styles.
Aug Signing to Vault Records in Los Angeles, they record *People Get Ready*, a set of rough soul-blues, highlighted by the title track and *Your Old Lady*.

66 *The Chambers Brothers Now* is issued. For it the brothers have brought in ex-Manfred Mann drummer Keenan (b. Jan.28, 1944, New York, NY), who has played in London groups from age 17 after being sent to school in UK, returning to New York on his 20th birthday.

67 Oct Columbia Records sees promise in the group and signs it.
Dec Debut Columbia album, *The Time Has Come*, is issued in US. It picks up rock and "progressive" FM airplay, and will eventually hit US #4, earning a gold disk by Dec.1968.

68 Now selling-out clubs and auditoriums around the country, they play in a network TV showcase for new performers, and are invited back. Their cross-cultural influences and "black hippie" image make them highly popular with the new white counter-culture.
Aug [4-5] They appear at Newport Pop Festival in Costa Mesa, CA,

alongside The Byrds, Jefferson Airplane, Steppenwolf and many others.
Sept *The Time Has Come Today*, from album of the same title, reaches US #11.
Dec *A New Time – A New Day* climbs to US #16, while the extracted revival of Otis Redding's *I Can't Turn You Loose* makes #37.

1969 Jan Vault Records issues one of its older tracks, the group's update of The Isley Brothers' *Shout*, which reaches US #83.
July *Wake Up*, used on the soundtrack of movie "The April Fools", makes US #92.

1970 Feb *Love, Peace And Happiness*, a double set of which one record has been recorded live at New York's Fillmore East, peaks at US #58. The title track is their last US chart single, making a brief entry at #96.
Aug [28] Group begins its second tour of Europe.
Dec Double album of material recorded 1965-66, *The Chambers Brothers' Greatest Hits*, released by Vault, charts fleetingly at US #193.

1971 Mar *New Generation* reaches US #145.
Dec Columbia issues its own version of *The Chambers Brothers' Greatest Hits*, which makes US #166.

1972 Mar Group has temporarily broken up by the time the album *Oh My God!* is released. Drummer Keenan joins Genya Ravan's band.

1974 The Brothers re-form to record *Unbonded* in a deal with Avco Records.

1975 *Right Move* is released, the group by now the hitmaking sales are behind them, and they will dissolve and re-form more than once again between ad hoc recording projects.

1989 Nov The Chambers Brothers participate in Earthquake Relief alongside Bonnie Raitt, Neil Young, Los Lobos and others in San Francisco, CA.

GENE CHANDLER

1959 After 2 years US Army service in Germany, Chandler (b. Eugene Dixon, July 6, 1937, Chicago, IL), who had led The Gaytones vocal group at Englewood high school, rejoins R&B vocal quintet The Dukays (originally formed in 1957) in Chicago.

1961 July Signed to Nat Records, they make US #64 with *The Girl's A Devil*.
Nov Nat sells gimmicky *Duke Of Earl*, intended as the follow-up, to Vee-Jay Records (which already owns the publishing), where A&R man Calvin Carter is convinced it will be a hit. Vee-Jay signs him as a soloist but he remains a member of The Dukays for Nat. He also becomes Gene Chandler, taking the name from his favorite actor, Jeff Chandler.

1962 Feb *Nite Owl*, the official Dukays follow-up, reaches US #73, but *Duke Of Earl*, credited to Gene Chandler, tops US chart for 3 weeks and is a million-seller. Chandler changes his name to "The Duke Of Earl" and appears on stage in top hat, cape and monocle. He has a cameo role in the movie "Don't Knock The Twist".
Apr *The Duke Of Earl* and single *Walk On With The Duke*, both credited to "The Duke", are not hits, the album reaching US #69 and the single only #91, prompting a name change back to Gene Chandler.
Dec *You Threw A Lucky Punch* (an "answer" disk to Mary Wells' US hit *You Beat Me To The Punch*) reaches US #49.
May *Rainbow*, B-side of *Lucky Punch* climbs to US #47.
Sept *Man's Temptation* reaches US #71: Chandler's final hit for Vee-Jay.

1964 May He moves to Ewart Abner's newly-formed Constellation Records. He debuts with *Soul Hootenanny (Pt.1)*, which peaks at US #92, followed with a rush of US chart singles.
Aug *Just Be True* makes US #19.
Nov *Bless Our Love* reaches US #39.

1965 Jan *What Now* makes US #40.
Mar *You Can't Hurt Me No More* climbs to US #92.
June *Nothing Can Stop Me* makes US #18.
Aug *Good Times* stalls at US #92.

1966 Jan *Gene Chandler – Live On Stage In '65* reaches US #124, but extracted *Rainbow '65* (a live treatment of his 1962 hit) makes #69.
Mar *(I'm Just A) Fool For You* charts at US #88 and Chandler leaves Constellation.

1967 Jan *I Fooled You This Time*, recorded for Checker in Chicago, makes US #45, but Chandler signs a long-term deal with Brunswick Records and 3 chart singles follow.
Apr *Girl Don't Care* makes US #66.
June *To Be A Lover* reaches US #94.
Sept *There Goes The Lover* peaks at US #98.

1968 June *Nothing Can Stop Me*, reissued in UK by Soul City label, gives him a UK chart entry at #41.
Sept *There Was A Time* makes US #82.
Nov A duet with Barbara Acklin, *From The Teacher To The Preacher*, reaches US #57.

1969 Dec Chandler moves into label management with Bamboo Records, signing Mel & Tim, and producing their *Backfield In Motion*, which hits US #10 and sells over a million. He also launches Mr. Chand Records to showcase his own productions, but less successfully.

1970	**Sept** He recaptures his initial chart form with *Groovy Situation*, for Mercury. It reaches US #12, his second million-seller.
Nov *Simply Call It Love* makes US #75, while **The Gene Chandler Situation** reaches only US #178.

1971	**Jan** Chandler teams with Jerry Butler for *You Just Can't Win (By Making The Same Mistake)* which makes US #94, his last chart single for 8 years.
Apr Duetted *Gene & Jerry – One & One* reaches US #143.

1979	Now a vice-president of Chi-Sound Records, after a spell in prison for drug offenses, he records **Get Down** for the label, with producer Carl Davis. The album spends nearly 6 months on US chart peaking at #47. The title track from it reaches US #53.
Mar *Get Down* becomes a huge UK dance floor hit at UK #11.
Oct *When You're #1* stops 98 places short at US #99, while album of the same title reaches US #153. The single fares better in UK, making #43.

1980	**July** *Does She Have A Friend For Me* fails in US; it later reaches UK #28.
Aug **Gene Chandler '80** spends 5 months on chart but climbs to only US #87. (Chandler will continue as an executive of Chi-Sound and does not give up recording even when hits cease. Albums such as **Here's To Love** (1981) and **I'll Make The Living (If You'll Make The Loving Worthwhile)** (1982) will continue to keep his name alive in the US R&B market of the 80s. He signs to independent Fastfire label.)

HARRY CHAPIN

1971	**June** A member of the Brooklyn Heights Boys Choir and a musical act before college with his brothers, Chapin (b. Dec.7, 1942, Greenwich Village, New York, NY, son of a big band drummer), after several years making film documentaries (including 1969 Oscar-nominated "Legendary Champions", made with Jim Jacobs), advertises in **Village Voice** for help to perform narrative songs he has written. He is joined by John Wallace (Brooklyn choirboy friend) on bass, Ron Palmer on acoustic guitar, and Tim Scott adding an unusual blend on cello.
June [29] Group, having rehearsed for a week, debuts at the Village Gate supporting his brothers The Chapins, and establishes a live reputation performing Chapin's "story songs".
Dec After interest from several record companies, Chapin signs a 9-album deal worth $600,000 plus a $40,000 advance with Elektra and free studio time at the label's Los Angeles, CA, studios.

1972	**June** Debut album *Heads And Tales* reaches US #60, staying charted for 6 months,
[3] *Taxi*, extracted despite its near 7-min. length, makes US #24.
Nov [18] *Sunday Morning Sunshine* peaks at US #75 as parent *Sniper And Other Love Songs* climbs to US #160.

1974	**Mar** [23] *W-O-L-D*, the story of a radio station DJ, climbs to US #36, while Chapin's third album *Short Stories* peaks at #61.
June [1] *W-O-L-D*, his only UK chart success, makes US #34.
Dec Chapin dismantles his band as he starts work on musical "The Night That Made America Famous". He retains Wallace and Masters for the show, adding Doug Walker (electric guitar) and Howie Fields (drums), with brothers Tom, Steve and Jim.
[21] *Cat's In The Cradle*, based on a poem by his wife about a neglectful father, tops US chart and is a million-seller. (The song will garner Chapin a Grammy nomination for Best Pop Vocal Performance, Male.)

1975	**Jan** Boosted by its success, *Verities And Balderdash*, hits US #4 and earns a gold disk.
Feb [26] Chapin's musical revue "The Night That Made America Famous" opens at the Ethel Barrymore theater on Broadway, New York. (It will close on Apr.6 after 75 performances. The show will receive 2 Tony nominations.)
Mar [29] *I Wanna Learn A Love Song* reaches US #44. Chapin wins an Emmy Award for his music on the US ABC TV children's series "Make A Wish", hosted by his brother Tom. He co-founds WHY (World Hunger Year), raising funds to combat international famine. It will receive over $350,000 from benefit concerts in its first year.
Nov [15] *Portrait Gallery* reaches US #53.

1976	**May** [29] Double live **Greatest Stories – Live**, recorded in San Diego, Santa Monica and Berkeley during a major West Coast tour in 1975, makes US #48 and is Chapin's second gold album.
July [10] *Better Place To Be (Parts 1 & 2)* reaches US #86. Increasingly active politically, he is a delegate at the Democratic Convention.
Sept CBS TV airs "Ball Four", for which Chapin writes theme.
[15] Chapin is honored for Outstanding Public Service at the third Annual Rock Music Award show, during a year in which he is also

honored with Broadcast Excellence from the International Radio Programming Forum for his Hungerthons, a Humanitarian Award from the Music & Performing Arts Lodge of B'nai B'rith, 1977 Man Of The Year from both Junior Achievers of New York and the Long Islan Advertising Club, and named one of the 10 most outstanding young men in America by the US Jaycees.
Nov [20] **On The Road To Kingdom Come** reaches US #87.

1977	**Oct** [8] Double album *Dance Band On The Titanic*, produced by his brother Steve, reaches US #58.

1978	**Feb** [3] Chapin briefs President Jimmy Carter at the White House on the need for a Presidential Commission On Hunger.
July [29] *Living Room Suite* reaches US #133.

1979	**Nov** Scholes quits the band in mid-concert in Dallas, TX. Yvonne Cab takes over. Scholes stays with the band, organizing their travel needs.
[10] Double live album *Legends Of The Lost And Found – New Greatest Stories Live* reaches US #163.

1980	**Oct** Chapin is inducted into Long Island Hall Of Fame.
Dec Chapin signs to Boardwalk Records, and *Sequel*, his only album for the label, peaks at US #58.
[13] 6-min. title track from it (a sequel to *Taxi*) climbs to US #23.

1981	**Jan** [9] Chapin plays his 200th performance at the Bottom Line.
July [16] Scheduled to begin a summer tour with a benefit concert at the Lakeside theater, Eisenhower Park, Long Island, New York, Chap is killed on the Long Island Expressway near Jericho, New York, whe a tractor-trailer runs into the back of his car while he is driving to a business meeting, rupturing the gas tank and exploding. The exact cause of death is unknown, but the autopsy reveals Chapin has had a heart attack either before or after the crash. At a memorial service hel in Brooklyn, New York, the Harry Chapin Memorial Fund is announced, launched with a $10,000 donation from Elektra Records.
Aug [17] A benefit concert for the fund is held at Nassau Coliseum, Long Island, headlined by Kenny Rogers. It is estimated that during h career Chapin has raised over $5 million from benefit performances fo the causes to which he was committed.

1987	**Dec** [7] "The Gold Medal Celebration" memorial concert takes place on what would have been Chapin's 45th birthday at Carnegie Hall, New York. Senator Patrick Leahy, one of his strongest supporters, presents the Special Congressional Gold Medal to his widow Sandy. The show, which is hosted by Harry Belafonte, features contributions from The Hooters (*One Light In A Dark Valley*), Richie Havens (*W-O-L-D*), Judy Collins (*Cats In The Cradle*), Pat Benatar (*Shooting Sta* Bruce Springsteen (*Remember When The Music*), Graham Nash (*Sandy*) and others (an album, **Tribute**, documenting the event, will emerge in 1990 on the Relativity label).

TRACY CHAPMAN

1982	Having started writing songs at age 8, Chapman (b. 1964, Cleveland, OH) graduates from Wooster school, CT, and goes to Tufts University Medford, MA, where she majors in anthropology and African studies (During her sophomore year at Wooster, school chaplain the Reverend Robert Tate takes a collection to buy Chapman a new guitar – he will receive a thank-you credit on the liner notes of her debut album.)

1986	Chapman joins an African drum ensemble at college, but develops he own folk guitar playing and performs self-written acoustic songs on t Boston folk circuit. She records demos at Tufts campus radio station W-MFO. Fellow student Brian Koppelman recommends her to his father, Charles, president of SBK Publishing, who in turn introduces her to producer David Kershenbaum and also to Elektra Records whe she links up with manager, Elliott Roberts.

1987	She records her debut album with Kershenbaum producing, after several other producers turn her down.
Mar Chapman visits London, performing 3 nights at the Donmar Warehouse, with Natalie Merchant from 10,000 Maniacs.
May She plays 2 nights at the Bitter End club in New York.

1988	**Apr** *Tracy Chapman* immediately attracts critical favor and rapid success, particularly in UK. Chapman tours US and plays some select UK dates supporting her labelmates, 10,000 Maniacs.
June [11] She appears at televised "Nelson Mandela's 70th Birthday Party" at Wembley Stadium, London, and is called back after her initi slot to fill in for Stevie Wonder who is unable to go on after a comput program of his is stolen. Her appearance results in *Tracy Chapman* selling 12,000 copies 2 days later.
July [2] *Tracy Chapman* tops UK chart, and *Fast Car*, extracted from it hits UK #5.
Aug [27] *Tracy Chapman* tops US survey as *Fast Car* reaches US #20

Sept [2] Together with Peter Gabriel, Bruce Springsteen, Sting and Yossou N'Dour, Chapman performs at Wembley Stadium, London, at the start of a 6-week "Human Rights Now" world tour for Amnesty International. The superstar trek will end Oct.15 in Buenos Aires, Argentina.

Oct [10] *Talkin' 'Bout A Revolution* peaks at US #75.

Dec [24] *Baby Can I Hold You* makes US #48.

'89 Jan [30] Chapman wins Pop New Artist category at the American Music Awards.

Feb [13] Chapman is named Best International Artist, Female and Best International Newcomer at the eighth annual BRIT Awards at London's Royal Albert Hall.

[22] She wins Best Pop Vocal Performance Of 1988, Female for *Fast Car*, Best Contemporary Folk Recording of 1988 for *Tracy Chapman* and Best New Artist Of 1988 at the 31st annual Grammy awards.

Apr [25] Chapman collects Female Vocalist, Top Song (*Talkin' 'Bout A Revolution*) and Rock Album (*Tracy Chapman*), at the third SKC Boston Music Awards at Wang Center For The Performing Arts, Boston, MA.

May She participates in the AIDS benefit concert at the Oakland Coliseum with The Grateful Dead and John Fogerty.

Sept *Crossroads* peaks at UK #61.

Oct [14] *Crossroads* tops UK chart, but fails to repeat multi-platinum status of her debut album.

Nov [4] *Crossroads* stalls at US #90, as parent *Crossroads* hits US #2.

'90 Mar [30] The 3 winners of "Crossroads In Black History", a high school essay contest and education program initiated by Chapman, receive college scholarships.

May Chapman embarks on major summer tour of US.

AY CHARLES

46 Charles (b. Ray Charles Robinson, Sept.23, 1930, Albany, GA), who has lived in Greenville, FL, where he sings in the Shiloh Baptist church and the Red Wing cafe where proprietor Wylie Pittman lets him play the piano, since age 2, and been blind since suffering from glaucoma at age 7, after witnessing his younger brother George fall into a washtub and drown in the family's backyard, having studied music (classical piano and clarinet) at St. Augustine's School for the Deaf and Blind in Orlando, FL, moves to Jacksonville, FL, after his mother's death where he begins playing for his living with various bands, including The Florida Playboys, Henry Washington's Big Band and Joe Anderson's band.

48 Moving to Seattle, WA, after being orphaned a year earlier, he enters a talent contest on his first night in town, and is immediately offered a job playing at the local Elks club. 17-year-old R.C. Robinson (as he is billed) forms The McSon Trio with G.D. McGhee on guitar and Milton Garred on bass, to play light jazz and blues modelled on the Nat "King" Cole Trio style at The Rockin' Chair. He also plays regularly at The Washington Social club, The 908 club and The Black & Tan.

49 Trio signs to Jack Lauderdale's Downbeat Records and releases Charles' own composition *Confession Blues*. He alters his billing to his 2 forenames to avoid confusion with boxer/singer Sugar Ray Robinson. Downbeat becomes Swingtime Records and releases a string of singles by Charles, including *See See Rider* and *I Wonder Who's Kissing Her Now?* (used 38 years later as soundtrack for a UK TV Volkswagen car ad). Charles will spend much of the next 2 years touring as Lowell Fulson's musical director.

51 Jan First US R&B chart entry is *Baby Let Me Hold Your Hand*, followed by *Kiss-A-Me Baby*, recorded with The McSon Trio.

52 June Atlantic Records buys Charles' contract from Swingtime for $2,500, releasing *Roll With My Baby*.

53 *Mess Around*, later an R&B standard, is written for Charles by Atlantic owner Ahmet Ertegun, and is one of the first uptempo numbers in his previously jazz-ballad repertoire. He plays on Guitar Slim's *The Things I Used To Do*, and then forms his own band with saxophonist David "Fathead" Newman.

54 Mar *It Should Have Been Me*, his first major seller for Atlantic, hits US R&B #7. (Over the next 3 years R&B chart successes follow: *Don't You Know, I've Got A Woman* (R&B #2), *This Little Girl Of Mine* (R&B #2), *Drown In My Own Tears* and *Hallelujah I Love Her So*.)

57 July His first album *Ray Charles* is released.

Nov [25] Charles' first crossover success is *Swanee River Rock (Talkin' 'Bout That River)*, which makes US #34.

58 July [5] Charles appears at the Newport Jazz Festival, his performance is recorded by Atlantic for a live album.

Dec [28] *Rockhouse* reaches US #79. *Ray Charles At Newport*, from the summer's festival, is released.

1959 Feb [9] *(Night Time Is) The Right Time* reaches US #95. *Soul Brothers*, recorded with jazz vibist Milt Jackson, is released.

May Charles plays an outdoor festival at Herndon Stadium in Atlanta, GA, with B.B. King, Ruth Brown, The Drifters, Jimmy Reed and other major R&B names. His performance is recorded by Atlantic for future album release.

June [26] Charles records *I'm Movin' On*, impressing rival label ABC-Paramount.

Aug [17] Self-penned gospel-style rocker *What'd I Say* tops US R&B chart for 2 weeks and hits US #6, his first million-seller. (Jerry Lee Lewis, Bobby Darin and Elvis Presley will all have 60s hits with revivals of the song.)

Nov Charles signs to ABC Paramount Records on a 3-year contract. (Atlantic is unable to match the offer of a large advance and ownership of his own material.) He also establishes his own Tangerine publishing company.

Dec [14] *I'm Movin' On* (a cover of Hank Snow's C&W number), on Atlantic, makes US #40.

[29] Charles begins his first recording session with producer Sid Feller in Hollywood, CA.

1960 Jan [25] *Let The Good Times Roll*, on Atlantic, makes US #78.

Feb [15] B-side *Don't Let The Sun Catch You Cryin'* stalls at US #95.

Mar *The Genius Of Ray Charles*, on Atlantic, makes US #17, his first US chart album.

Aug [8] ABC debut *Sticks And Stones* reaches US #40, while Atlantic album *Ray Charles In Person*, recorded at Herndon stadium in May 1959, reaches US #13.

Nov [14] A revival of Hoagy Carmichael's *Georgia On My Mind*, recorded after Charles' chauffeur constantly sang it on trips, tops the US chart and is his second million-seller.

Dec *Georgia On My Mind* is his UK chart debut, at #24.

[5] Similarly-styled *Come Rain Or Come Shine*, a 1959 recording issued by Atlantic, makes US #83. *Hard-Hearted Hannah*, the B-side of the still climbing *Ruby*, peaks at US #55. Debut ABC album, *The Genius Hits The Road*, from which *Georgia* is taken and which has US place names as the themes of its songs, hits US #9, his first Top 10 album.

[31] *Ruby* reaches US #28.

1961 Feb [6] *Them That Got* peaks at US #58.

Apr [12] Charles wins Best Vocal Performance Single Record Or Track – Male and Best Performance By A Pop Single Artist for *Georgia On My Mind*, Best Vocal Performance Album, Male for *The Genius Of Ray Charles* and Best R&B Performance for *Let The Good Times Roll* for 1960 at the 3rd annual Grammy awards.

Dedicated To You reaches US #11.

May [1] Instrumental *One Mint Julep*, released on ABC's subsidiary jazz label Impulse, hits US #8. It is taken from Charles' largely instrumental big band album *Genius + Soul = Jazz*, arranged by Quincy Jones, which includes a guest line-up of jazzmen. The album hits US #4.

June [26] *I've Got News For You* peaks at US #66 as B-side *I'm Gonna Move To The Outskirts Of Town* makes US #84.

Sept *What'd I Say*, of earlier Atlantic material, makes US #20, while on the same label, relaxed instrumental album *The Genius After Hours* reaches US #49.

Oct [9] *Hit The Road Jack*, written by Charles' friend, R&B singer Percy Mayfield, tops US chart for 2 weeks, his third million-seller. Album of duets, *Ray Charles And Betty Carter*, climbs to US #52.

Nov *Hit The Road Jack* hits UK #6.

Dec Atlantic album *The Genius Sings The Blues* reaches US #73.

[5] Charles is charged with possession of narcotics after being arrested in a downtown hotel in Indianapolis, IN. (He has been a heroin addict since age 16.)

1962 Jan [13] *Unchain My Heart* hits US #9.

[20] B-side *But On The Other Hand, Baby* peaks at US #72. Atlantic issues *Do The Twist!* (which has nothing to do with the current dance craze, but is a compilation of early material with tempos to suit twisting). It makes US #11, his highest-placed Atlantic album.

Mar [10] Charles and Carter duet, *Baby, It's Cold Outside*, peaks at US #91. Charles launches his own label, Tangerine Records.

May [5] *Hide Nor Hair* reaches US #20.

[12] B-side *At The Club* makes US #44.

[29] Charles wins Best R&B Recording for *Hit The Road Jack* at the 4th annual Grammy awards.

June Charles records outstanding country music songs in his own style for *Modern Sounds In Country And Western Music*. It tops the US chart for 14 weeks and is his only million-selling album.

[2] Taken from it, a revival of Don Gibson's *I Can't Stop Loving You* sells over 2 million copies and tops US chart for 5 weeks. It will be certified as the year's best-selling single.

[30] B-side *Born To Lose* makes US #41.

July Charles is fined by a court in Atlanta, GA, after refusing to perform at a segregated dance where blacks were only spectators.

[14] *I Can't Stop Loving You* tops the UK chart.

Aug *Modern Sounds In Country And Western Music* hits UK #6, his first UK chart album.

[11] *Careless Love*, B-side of *You Don't Know Me*, peaks at US #60.

Sept [8] Second single from the country album, *You Don't Know Me*, hits US #2 and is another million-seller. Double album *The Ray Charles Story* an Atlantic compilation of his 50s work, reaches US #14, while ABC compilation *Ray Charles' Greatest Hits*, containing the more recent hits prior to *I Can't Stop Loving You*, hits US #5.

Oct *You Don't Know Me* hits UK #9.

Dec Charles follows up his successful country experiment and album, *Modern Sounds In Country And Western Music, Vol.2* hits US #2.

[22] From it, *Your Cheating Heart* reaches US #29.

[29] *Your Cheating Heart*'s A-side, *You Are My Sunshine* written by Jimmie Davis, the racist former Governor of Louisiana, hits US #7 as *Your Cheating Heart* reaches UK #13.

1963 Mar *Modern Sounds In Country And Western Music Vol.2* reaches UK #15. Charles opens his own studios and offices in Los Angeles, CA.

[16] *The Brightest Smile In Town* makes US #92.

[30] Its A-side, *Don't Set Me Free* reaches US #20 and UK #37.

May [15] Charles wins Best R&B Recording for *I Can't Stop Loving You* at the 5th annual Grammy awards.

[25] *Take These Chains From My Heart*, extracted from the second country album, hits US #8.

June *Take These Chains From My Heart* hits UK #5 (his fourth and last in UK Top 10).

July [20] Double A-side *No One/Without Love (There Is Nothing)* makes US #21 and #29.

Aug Compilation album *Ray Charles' Greatest Hits* reaches UK #16.

Oct [19] *Busted*, a return to bluesy big band style, hits US #4 and is another million-seller. *Ingredients In A Recipe For Soul* hits US #2, while *No One* reaches US #35.

Nov *Busted* makes UK #21.

1964 Jan [18] A revival of *That Lucky Old Sun* reaches US #20. The song is featured (with 8 other Charles numbers) in film "Ballad In Blue", in which he stars with Dawn Addams and Tom Bell.

Mar [21] *Baby Don't You Cry* makes US #39.

Apr [4] *My Heart Cries For You*, the flip of *Baby Don't You Cry*, makes US #38.

Sweet And Sour Tears hits US #9.

May [12] Charles wins Best R&B Recording for *Busted* at the 6th annual Grammy awards.

[18] Charles begins filming "Light Out Of Darkness" in Madrid, Spain.

June [27] *My Baby Don't Dig Me* peaks at US #51.

July [7] Charles begins his second UK concert tour, for 3 weeks.

Aug [2] He performs at legendary Star-Club in Hamburg, Germany.

[22] Double A-side *No One To Cry To/A Tear Fell*, peaks at US #55 and #50 respectively, as Charles begins a 10-day tour of Japan.

Oct *No One To Cry To* makes UK #38. *Smack Dab In The Middle* peaks at US #52, as parent *Have A Smile With Me* makes US #36.

[31] Charles is seized by Customs agents after landing at Logan airport, Boston, MA, for a concert at the Back Bay theater. He is arraigned before US Commissioner Peter J. Nelligad, charged with possession of narcotics. (Agents claim to have found a small quantity of heroin and marijuana, a hypodermic needle and a spoon.)

1965 Jan [16] A revival of *Makin' Whoopee* reaches US #46 and UK #42.

Mar [13] Another revival, of Johnnie Ray's *Cry*, peaks at US #58. *Ray Charles Live In Concert* makes US #80.

May [1] From it, a revival of his own *Gotta Woman* makes US #79.

Aug [7] A version of Joe Barry's *I'm A Fool To Care* makes US #84.

Sept *Country And Western Meets Rhythm And Blues* makes US #116.

1966 Feb [12] *Crying Time* makes UK #50.

[19] After a string of middling charters, *Crying Time* hits US #6.

Apr [2] *You're Just About To Lose Your Crown*, B-side of the still climbing *Together Again*, makes US #91.

[23] Charles' revival of Buck Owens' country ballad *Together Again* makes UK #48.

[30] *Together Again* reaches US #19. *Crying Time* makes US #15.

July [16] Bluesy *Let's Go Get Stoned* makes US #31. It is the first single

to give a full co-credit to Charles' own Tangerine Records with ABC.

Oct [8] *I Chose To Sing The Blues* makes US #32, while *Ray's Moods* climbs to US #52.

Dec [3] Charles is convicted on charges of possessing heroin and marijuana. He is given a 5-year suspended prison sentence, a $10,000 fine, and put on probation for 4 years. Random drug tests showing that he has refrained from drug use since his original arrest, keep him out of jail. (He has gone cold turkey in 92 hours while in St. Francis hospital in Lynwood, CA.)

[10] *Please Say You're Fooling* makes US #64.

[17] B-side *I Don't Need No Doctor* peaks at US #72.

1967 Mar [2] *Crying Time* wins Best R&B Recording and Best R&B Solo Vocal Performance , Male Or Female Of 1966 at the 9th annual Grammy awards.

[18] *I Want To Talk About You* makes US #98.

Apr Double compilation *A Man And His Soul* reaches US #77 and stays on chart for 62 weeks, earning a gold disk for a half million sales.

[22] Charles plays the Royal Festival Hall, London, during a UK tour.

July [8] *Here We Go Again*, a return to country soul, makes UK #38.

[15] *Here We Go Again* reaches US #15.

Aug *Ray Charles Invites You To Listen*, the first album to carry the ABC-Tangerine Records dual logo, reaches US #76.

[12-13] Charles headlines New York's first Jazz Festival at the Downing Stadium.

Sept [30] Charles' dramatic deep soul theme song, written by Quincy Jones, from Rod Steiger/Sidney Poitier movie "In The Heat Of The Night" makes US #33.

Dec [9] His re-working of The Beatles' *Yesterday* makes US #25.

1968 Jan *Yesterday* makes UK #44.

[27] Atlantic reissue *Come Rain Or Come Shine* makes US #98.

Mar [30] *That's A Lie* peaks at US #64.

May *A Portrait Of Ray* reaches US #51.

July [27] Another Lennon/McCartney cover, *Eleanor Rigby*, makes US #35.

Aug *Eleanor Rigby* makes UK #36.

[17] Its B-side *Understanding* makes US #46.

Oct *Ray Charles' Greatest Hits, Vol.2*, compiled for UK, makes US #24.

[5] *Sweet Young Thing Like You* climbs to US #83.

[19] B-side *Listen, They're Playing My Song* makes US #92.

1969 Feb [8] Charles' duet with Jimmy Lewis on *If It Wasn't For Bad Luck* peaks at US #77.

Apr *I'm All Yours – Baby!* climbs to US #167.

May [24] *Let Me Love You* makes US #94.

June [13] He appears with Aretha Franklin, Sam And Dave, The Staple Singers and many more, at Soul Bowl '69 at Houston Astrodome, TX, promoted as the biggest-ever soul music festival.

Aug *Doing His Thing* makes US #172.

1970 Mar [21] *Laughin' And Clownin'* stalls at US #98.

July Instrumental *My Kind Of Jazz*, on Tangerine, reaches US #155.

Aug *Love Country Style* peaks at US #192.

Oct [25] Charles plays the Hammersmith Odeon, London, during a UK tour, having played the Royal Festival Hall the previous night.

1971 Jan [2] *If You Were Mine* makes US #41, staying on chart for 18 weeks.

Apr [24] *Don't Change On Me* makes US #36.

May [22] *Booty Butt*, an R&B instrumental credited to The Ray Charles Orchestra (allowing it to be issued on Tangerine, independent of ABC) makes US #36.

July *Volcanic Action Of My Soul* reaches US #52, his biggest-selling album for over 3 years.

Oct [9] *Feel So Bad* peaks at US #68.

Dec Double album *A 25th Anniversary In Show Business Salute To Ray Charles* is a collaboration between ABC and Atlantic with an album of Charles' hits on each label. It is released on Atlantic worldwide, but on ABC in US, where it reaches US #152.

1972 Jan [29] Revival of Chuck Willis' *What Am I Living For?* makes US #54.

[20] Charles guests on Emmy-winning "Carol Burnett Show".

June *A Message From The People* climbs to US #52.

Aug [5] A cover of Melanie's *Look What They've Done To My Song, Ma* peaks at US #65.

Dec Last ABC album, *Through The Eyes Of Love*, climbs to US #186.

1973 Charles leaves ABC, taking his Tangerine Records operation and the rights to all his ABC releases. Tangerine becomes new label Crossover Records, which will release both Charles' new recordings and reissues.

June Atlantic double album *Ray Charles Live*, comprising the 2 earlier live albums from Newport in 1958 and Herndon Stadium in 1959, makes US #182.

[16] Charles' last ABC single, *I Can Make It Thru The Days (But Oh Those Lonely Nights)*, climbs to US #81.

Sept [7] He headlines the second Ann Arbor Jazz and Blues Festival, Ann Arbor, MI.

Dec [15] His first Crossover single is *Come Live With Me*, at US #82.

'74 Debut Crossover album *Come Live With Me* is released but fails.

'75 **July** Second Crossover album *Renaissance* peaks at US #175.

Sept [27] A cover of Stevie Wonder's *Living For The City*, taken from *Renaissance*, makes US #91.

'76 **Feb** [28] Charles wins Best R&B Vocal Performance, Male for *Living For The City* at the 18th annual Grammy awards.

Dec Charles and UK jazz singer Cleo Laine record a double album of Gershwin's *Porgy And Bess*, released by RCA, which makes US #138.

'77 **Feb** [28] He is attacked, while performing, by a man who rushes on stage with a rope and tries to strangle him.

Mar [15] John Ritter-sitcom "Three's Company", for which Charles sings the theme with Julia Rinker, airs for the first time on ABC TV.

Nov [19] *True To Life*, a one-off return to Atlantic with a Crossover Records production, climbs to US #78. (He divorces his second wife, Della, after 22 years of marriage.)

'78 **Feb** [24] Charles guests on US TV's "The Second Barry Manilow Special".

'80 **June** Charles appears as the streetwise owner of a musical instrument store in movie "The Blues Brothers".

July [26] TV-advertised compilation album of Charles oldies, *Heart To Heart – 20 Hot Hits*, reaches UK #29.

Oct Charles teams with Clint Eastwood to release *Beers To You*, from Eastwood-starring film "Any Which Way You Can".

'83 He signs to CBS/Columbia's Nashville division to concentrate on country-based music. First album *Wish You Were Here Tonight*, recorded in Nashville, a US Country chart success, does not cross over.

June He appears in the 30th annual Kool Jazz Festival in New York, co-headlining with Miles Davis and B.B. King.

'85 **Jan** [28] Charles takes a major role in the recording of USA For Africa's *We Are The World*, leading the gospel-like climax.

Apr [13] *We Are The World* tops both US and UK charts.

[23] *Seven Spanish Angels*, from current *Friendship* project, a duet with Willie Nelson, tops US Country chart.

May [4] *Friendship*, featuring Charles in 10 duets with major country music stars including Mickey Gilley and Hank Williams Jr., makes US #75, his first US album chart entry since 1977.

Dec Charles produces country soul-styled seasonal album *The Spirit Of Christmas*.

'86 **Jan** Quincy Jones inducts Ray Charles into the Rock'N'Roll Hall Of Fame at the first annual dinner at the Waldorf Astoria in New York.

Dec [26] Charles is honored at the ninth annual Kennedy Center ceremony in Washington, DC.

'87 **Feb** [2] *A Little Bit Of Heaven* makes #76 on US country chart.

Apr [25] Charles guests with Billy Joel on his *Baby Grand*, which reaches US #75.

(Charles will remain quiet on the recording scene but will continue to play live throughout the world, often in a big band environment. He will act, guesting in TV series "Moonlighting", "St. Elsewhere" and "Who's The Boss", in which he sings *Always A Friend* and will become a regular celebrity in TV advertising campaigns, including American Express, Kentucky Fried Chicken and, most notably, Pepsi Cola.)

'88 **Mar** [2] Charles is honored by the NARAS at the 30th annual Grammy awards with a Lifetime Achievement Award, noting that he is "The father of soul, whose unique and effervescent singing and piano-playing have personified the true essence of soul music in all his recorded and personal performances of basic blues, pop ballads, jazz tunes and even country music".

'89 **May** [11-12] Charles performs "A Fool For You" with the New York City Ballet at the Lincoln Center.

June He undertakes a 16-date US tour including dates in New York (June 28) and Little Rock, AZ (July 26).

Oct [3] Another set of US concerts opens in Valdosta, GA, the first of 18 performances set to finale on Dec. 15 in San Francisco, CA.

Nov Charles is named chairman of the Washington, DC-based Rhythm & Blues Foundation.

'90 **Jan** [27] *I'll Be Good To You*, a track from Quincy Jones' forthcoming *Back On The Block* which sees Charles duet with Chaka Khan, reaches US #18. (It is Charles first US Top 30 hit since 1967.)

Feb [3] *I'll Be Good To You* reaches UK #21.

[21] *I've Got A Woman* is inducted into the NARAS Hall Of Fame at the 32nd annual Grammy awards. Charles also contributes to a tribute to

Paul McCartney, being honored with a Lifetime Achievement Award by NARAS, singing *Eleanor Rigby* at the ceremonies.

Mar [1] 7-date mini-tour starts at Morton H. Myerson Symphony Center, Dallas, TX.

[24] *The Ray Charles Collection* debuts at UK #36.

May [5] Charles sings *Let It Be* for the "John Lennon Tribute Concert" organized by Yoko Ono at the Pier Head Arena in Merseyside.

Sept [29] Charles embarks on world tour with B.B. King in Taiwan. The tour will end in New York on Nov.10.

1991 **Feb** [20] Charles and Khan wins Best R&B Performance By A Duo Or Group With Vocal for *I'll Be Good To You* at the 33rd annual Grammy awards. (It is Charles' 11th Grammy.)

[21] Charles is honored with the Rhythm & Blues Foundation's Legend Award at a ceremony at Tatou in New York.

CHEAP TRICK

Robin Zander (vocals, guitar)
Rick Nielsen (vocals, guitar)
Tom Petersson (vocals, bass)
Bun E. Carlos (drums)

1961 Nielsen (b. Dec.22, 1946, Rockford, IL) begins playing in several bands (which will include The Phaetons, Boyz and The Grim Reapers) in his hometown of Rockford. (He also begins collecting rare and bizarre guitars which will number over 100 within 20 years.)

1969 He forms a new band Fuse with Petersson (b. May 9, 1950, Rockford, IL) and Carlos (b. Brad Carlson, June 12, 1951, Rockford) and they release an unsuccessful album on Epic.

1971 Band moves to Philadelphia, PA, and changes name to Sick Man Of Europe.

1973 After a European tour, they return to Rockford where they form new combo Cheap Trick, with folk vocalist Zander (b. Jan.23, 1953, Rockford). (Group will gig incessantly, completing more than 200 concerts a year, including support slots for The Kinks, Santana, Kiss, Boston and many others.)

1977 **Jan** Debut *Cheap Trick* is released on Epic. It sells 150,000 copies in US but fails to chart. In Japan it is immediately popular and goes gold.

Oct [22] Second album *In Color* peaks at US #73 on the strength of continued touring. Once again it goes gold in Japan.

1978 **Feb** First visit to Tokyo sees unexpected "Trickmania". Their dates at Budokan Arena sell out within 2 hours. A live recording of the gigs is made, capturing their live expertise and fanatical Japanese reaction.

July [8] Third album *Heaven Tonight* makes US #48 and achieves platinum status in Japan.

Sept [2] Debut chart single *Surrender* peaks at US #62.

1979 **Feb** [24] *Cheap Trick At Budokan* begins 1-year US chart stay.

Mar [10] *Cheap Trick At Budokan* reaches UK #29, as the group makes its first UK tour.

Apr [7-8] Cheap Trick plays the California Music Festival at the Memorial Coliseum, Los Angeles, CA, with Van Halen, Aerosmith and Ted Nugent.

June [2] From the live album, *I Want You To Want Me* reaches UK #29.

July [14] *Cheap Trick At Budokan* hits US #4, and becomes the group's first US platinum-selling album.

[21] *I Want You To Want Me* hits US #7. In Japan, the album achieves triple platinum.

Sept [29] Follow-up *Ain't That A Shame*, live cover of Fats Domino standard, makes US #35. Band plays the Reading Festival, Berks.

Oct [13] Studio album *Dream Police* reaches UK #41.

[27] *Dream Police* hits US #6.

Nov [24] *Dream Police* reaches US #26.

1980 **Feb** [2] *Voices* makes US #32 as UK-only released *Way Of The World* peaks at #73. Nielsen, Zander and Carlos contribute to John Lennon's *Double Fantasy* sessions in New York.

June *Voices* is featured in the soundtrack to current Debbie Harry/Meat Loaf movie "Roadie".

July [5] *Everything Works If You Let It* makes US #44. A 10" mini-LP, *Found All The Parts*, featuring songs recorded 1976-79, makes US #39.

Aug [26] Petersson leaves to form a group with his wife Dagmar. He is replaced first by Pete Comita and then by Jon Brant (b. Feb.20, 1954).

Oct [16] Group begins a 7-date UK tour at the Mayfair, Newcastle, Tyne & Wear. It will end Oct.24 at the Hammersmith Odeon, London.

Dec [6] *Stop This Game* makes US #48.

[13] George Martin-produced *All Shook Up* reaches US #24.

1981 Epic rejects an entire album as the band returns to the studio to record

CHEAP TRICK cont.

1982 **June** [5] *One On One* is released by Epic, climbs to US #39 (Oct.9) and makes UK #95 for 1 week.
July [24] Taken from it, *If You Want My Love* makes US #45.
Aug [7] *If You Want My Love* peaks at UK #57. (In Japan, all 8 albums have topped the chart.)
Oct [23] *She's Tight* peaks at US #65.
1983 **Oct** *Next Position Please* makes US #61.
1985 **Oct** [12] *Tonight It's You* makes US #44. *Standing On The Edge* peaks at US #35.
1986 **Nov** The Doctor makes US #115.
1988 **Apr** Band travels to Switzerland to play the Montreux Rock Festival.
June With the group using outside writers and Petersson rejoining the line-up, *Lap Of Luxury* is a return to form.
July [9] Richie Zito-produced ballad *The Flame*, tops US chart, after a 14-week climb. Cheap Trick is currently on US tour, begun in Louisville, KY, as Robert Plant's special guests.
Aug Single's success spurs sales of *Lap Of Luxury*, making US #16.
[28] 29-date North American tour ends at the Forum, LA.
Oct [8] Cheap Trick's version of *Don't Be Cruel* hits US #4, becoming first Elvis Presley cover to hit US Top 10 since his death.
Dec [24] *Ghost Town* makes US #33.
1989 **Mar** [4] *Never Had A Lot To Lose* peaks at US #75.
1990 **Mar** [11] *Surrender To Me*, Zander's duet with Heart's Ann Wilson, from movie "Tequila Sunrise", hits US #6.
Aug [25] *Busted* makes US #48.
Sept [22] *Can't Stop Falling Into Love* reaches US #12, as group tours North America as support to Heart.
Nov [24] US tour ends in Buffalo, NY.
Dec [1] *Wherever Would I Be* makes US #50.

CHUBBY CHECKER

1958 **Dec** Checker (b. Ernest Evans, Oct.3, 1941, South Carolina), signed under his real name to Cameo-Parkway Records in Philadelphia, PA, after Henry Colt, his boss at a chicken market, impressed by his singing, brought him to the attention of Cameo's Kal Mann, attracts the attention of Dick Clark ("American Bandstand") and wife Bobbie with his ability to imitate other acts' styles when the Clarks visit Cameo to commission a novelty recording as a Christmas greeting. He records *The Class*, written by Mann, and Cameo changes his name after Bobbie Clark notes his resemblance to a teenage Fats Domino (Fats = Chubby; Domino = Checker). The Clarks send it out as their Christmas card.
1959 **June** Cameo releases *The Class* on Parkway label and it climbs to US #38. It features Checker imitating Fats Domino, The Coasters, Elvis Presley and The Chipmunks.
July Dick Clark on "American Bandstand" is bombarded with requests for *The Twist*, a Hank Ballard & The Midnighters' 18-month-old B-side, because of nationwide teen enthusiasm for the dance. He suggests Philadelphia act Danny & The Juniors cover it but they decline, so Clark phones Cameo and suggests the song for Checker, who records it with vocal group The Dreamlovers, in a 35-min. session.
1960 **Aug** [6] Checker debuts *The Twist* on ABC TV's "The Dick Clark Saturday Night Show". (First time that Checker performs the song is before 3,000 teenagers at the Ice House, Haddonfield, NJ.)
Sept Checker's cover enters US chart 2 weeks after Ballard's original which peaks at US #28, but the exposure given to Checker's cover by "American Bandstand" takes it to top of US chart for a week. It sells over a million copies and reaches UK #44.
Nov *The Hucklebuck*, reviving a 1949 Tommy Dorsey dance hit, in new musical idiom, reaches US #14. The B-side, reviving Jerry Lee Lewis' *Whole Lotta Shakin' Goin' On*, makes US #42 in its own right.
Dec *Twist With Chubby Checker* hits US #3. He stars in Clay Cole's "Christmas Rock'N'Roll Show" at the Paramount theater, Brooklyn, New York, with Neil Sedaka, Bobby Vee, The Drifters, Dion, Bo Diddley and others.
1961 The New York State Safety Council announces that of 54 cases of back trouble reported in a single week, 49 were due to too much Twisting.
Feb *Pony Time* hits US #1 for 3 weeks and is Checker's second million-seller, setting off a new dance craze for the Pony. The song is a re-write of *Boogie Woogie*, written and recorded by Clarence "Pinetop" Smith in 1928, but the record is a cover of Don Covay & The Goodtimers' original (which peaks at US #60).
Apr *Pony Time* reaches UK #27.
May *Dance The Mess Around* peaks at US #24 and is a minor dance craze. B-side *Good Good Lovin'* makes US #43.

June *It's Pony Time* peaks at US #110.
July Checker features in Dick Clark's "Caravan Of Stars", a summer rock stage show in Atlantic City, NJ, with Duane Eddy, Fabian, Freddy Cannon, Bobby Rydell and others.
Aug On the first anniversary of *The Twist*, *Let's Twist Again* is released to catch the beginning of a new wave of interest in the dance, spreading from teen hops to adult clubs and from US to other countries. It hits US #8 and reaches UK #37, earning Checker a third gold disk.
Oct [22] As the Twist reaches fashionable nightspots like New York's Peppermint Lounge, Checker appears on US TV's "Ed Sullivan Show" singing *The Twist* and demand for it is sparked again. *Let's Twist Again* reaches US #11.
Nov *The Fly*, a Twist variation with arm movements to approximate a buzzing fly, hits US #7.
Dec Checker's revival of Bobby Helms' seasonal hit *Jingle Bell Rock*, as duet with labelmate Bobby Rydell, makes US #21. He features in film "Twist Around The Clock", based around New York DJ Clay Cole.
[11] *Twistin' USA* peaks at US #68.
1962 **Jan** *The Twist* is re-released in US and tops chart again for 2 weeks – the only single ever to hit US #1 on 2 separate occasions. *For Twisters Only* hits US #8. Compilation album (of tracks from his previous 4 albums), *Your Twist Party*, hits US #2.
Feb *The Twist* and *Let's Twist Again* are reissued in UK as the dance craze hits the country for the first time. Checker makes a UK promotion visit, demonstrating the dance movements on TV. *The Twist* reaches US #14 but *Let's Twist Again* becomes UK's Twist anthem, hitting #2. *Twist With Chubby Checker* reaches UK #13. *Bobby Rydell/Chubby Checker* collection of duets hits US #7.
Mar *For Twisters Only* reaches UK #17.
[17] B-side of *Slow Twistin'*, *La Paloma Twist*, climbs to US #72.
Apr *Slow Twistin'*, a duet with (uncredited) labelmate Dee Dee Sharp, hits US #3 and UK #23. Another Rydell duet, *Teach Me To Twist*, makes UK #45.
May *For Teen Twisters Only*, which includes the hits *The Fly* and *Slow Twistin'*, climbs to US #17.
[29] Checker wins Best Rock And Roll Recording Of 1961 for *Let's Twist Again* at the 4th annual Grammy awards.
June *Twistin' Round The World* peaks at US #54. Checker features in movie "Don't Knock The Twist" and sings 6 songs. They appear on soundtrack album *Don't Knock The Twist* which makes US #29.
July *Dancin' Party* reaches US #12. Sounding much like Gary U.S. Bonds' 1961 hit *Quarter To Three*, it prompts Bonds to sue for plagiarism for £100,000. (The case is settled out of court.)
Sept *Dancin' Party* reaches UK #19.
[3] Checker begins 14-date twice-nightly UK tour with Brook Brothers, The Kestrels and others, at Colston Hall, Bristol, Avon. Tour ends Sept.21 at Granada cinema, East Ham, London.
Nov Double A-side *Limbo Rock* and *Popeye (The Hitchhiker)*, each side promoting a different current dance craze, becomes Checker's biggest 2-sided US chart success. *Popeye* peaks first, hitting #10.
Dec *Limbo Rock* (a Champs instrumental US chart hit earlier in the year) hits US #2 and reaches UK #32. Checker-Rydell duet *Jingle Bell Rock* makes UK #40 and US chart again at #92. *All The Hits (For Your Dancin' Party)*, which includes *Limbo Rock*, reaches US #23 and *Down To Earth*, a selection of duets with Dee Dee Sharp, makes US #117.
1963 **Feb** *Limbo Party* peaks at US #11 and compilation *Chubby Checker's Biggest Hits* makes US #27.
Mar [2] Checker hosts "The Limbo Party", a stage show at the Cow Palace, San Francisco, with guests including Marvin Gaye, The Crystals, Lou Christie and The Four Seasons.
Let's Limbo Some More peaks at US #20.
Apr B-side of *Let's Limbo*, *Twenty Miles*, becomes a bigger US hit than its A-side, at #15. *Let's Limbo Some More* makes US #87.
June *Birdland*, plugging yet another dance craze, the Bird, climbs to US #12. B-side *Black Cloud* makes US #98.
Aug Checker moves in on The Beach Boys/Jan And Dean-led surfing fad with *Surf Party* but it reaches only US #55 and is overtaken by the back-to-1962 *Twist It Up*, which reaches US #25, at a time when Twist songs are thought to be dead. *Beach Party* makes US #90.
Oct Live *Chubby Checker In Person* reaches US #104.
Nov *What Do Ya Say*, recorded in London with producer Tony Hatch, reaches UK #37 after Checker's UK promotional visit and TV slots, but it will be his last UK hit for 12 years.
Dec *Loddy Lo* climbs to US #12.
1964 **Feb** *Hooka Tooka*, B-side of *Loddy Lo*, is another double-sided US hit for Checker when it replaces its A-side in the Top 20 to peak at #17.

Apr *Hey, Bobba Needle* reaches US #23.

[12] Checker marries Dutch beauty queen (Miss World 1962), with whom he will have a long marriage and 3 children.

July *Lazy Elsie Molly* makes US #40.

Sept *She Wants T'Swim*, following Bobby Freeman's US Top 5 *C'mon And Swim*, peaks at US #50 but the Swim is a short-lived dance craze.

5 Jan *Lovely, Lovely* peaks at US #70.

May *Let's Do The Freddie*, a cash-in on Freddie & The Dreamers' stage act "dance" which becomes a US craze, makes US #40, but is outsold by the group's own (different) song *Do The Freddie*.

6 July *Hey You! Little Boo-Ga-Loo* is his final hit single on Parkway, reaching US #76.

9 Apr Signed to Buddah Records, Checker makes a minor US chart comeback with a cover of The Beatles' **White Album** track *Back In The U.S.S.R.* (#82).

0 June [23] Checker is arrested with 3 others in Niagara Falls, after police discover marijuana and other drugs in their car.

3 Jan Double compilation album of his chart singles **Chubby Checker's Greatest Hits** makes US #152, his first US album chart entry since 1963.

Apr [29] An oldies edition of US TV's "Midnight Special", hosted by Jerry Lee Lewis, features Checker among the guest performers.

5 Dec Capitalizing on an unexpected revival of the Twist in UK discos (and an opportunistic UK revival of *Let's Twist Again* by John Asher which makes #14), double A-side reissue of *Let's Twist Again* with *The Twist* hits UK #5.

2 Mar Signed to MCA Records, Checker returns to US Top 100 for the first time in 13 years, at #91, with *Running*, which also makes Top 40 Dance chart. **The Change Has Come** reaches US #186.

8 May The Fat Boys team with Checker to record a new version of his most famous hit, this time titled *The Twist (Yo' Twist)*.

June [11] Checker and the group perform the song at "Nelson Mandela's 70th Birthday Party" at London's Wembley Stadium. The record takes off in the UK 3 weeks later, hitting #2.

Aug *The Twist (Yo' Twist)* peaks at US #16.

9 Checker, Hank Ballard and Joey Dee play at Lulu's Roadhouse, Kitchener, Canada, for a reunion to be part of a feature length documentary on the Twist.

Oct [26] Checker, supported by his band the Wild Cats, begins his first UK tour in several years at the Swansea Leisure Centre, Wales.

HER

3 Cher (b. Cherilyn Sarkasian La Pierre, May 20, 1946, El Centro, CA), having moved to Los Angeles, CA, to attend acting classes, meets Sonny Bono (b. Salvatore Bono, Feb.16, 1935, Detroit, MI), who is working for Phil Spector, and through him begins doing back-up vocals for Spector on singles by The Ronettes and others.

4 Sonny and Cher marry in Tijuana. Spector uses Cher as the soloist on novelty single *Ringo I Love You*, released on Spector's minor label, Annette, to cash in on Beatlemania, and credited to "Bonnie Jo Mason".

5 While Sonny & Cher are experimenting with early duo recordings, Sonny interests Imperial Records in signing Cher as a soloist. First release, *Dream Baby*, under her full name Cherilyn, fails to sell.

Aug With Sonny & Cher signed to Atco as a duo, Imperial changes the billing to Cher on her solo material.

[21] Sharing in the publicity generated as the duo's *I Got You Babe* tops US chart, her cover of Bob Dylan's *All I Really Want To Do* reaches US #15. (The Byrds' version makes US #40.)

Sept Duo's *I Got You Babe* tops UK chart while *All I Really Want To Do* hits UK #9. (The Byrds' version hits UK #4.)

Oct Debut solo **All I Really Want To Do**, produced by Sonny from Spector experience, reaches US #16 and hits UK #7.

Nov [13] *Where Do You Go*, written and produced by Sonny in a style similar to debut album, reaches US #25.

6 Apr [23] *Bang Bang (My Baby Shot Me Down)*, Cher's first solo million-seller, hits US #2. Produced by Sonny, it combines stark melodrama, racing gypsy violins and arresting tempo changes.

[30] *Bang Bang (My Baby Shot Me Down)* hits UK #3.

June **The Sonny Side Of Cher** reaches US #26 and UK #11.

Aug Cher covers Cilla Black's movie title track *Alfie*.

[27] When the film opens in US, Cher's version is added over the credits and reaches US #32. Cilla Black's makes only US #95 (but was a Top 10 hit in UK, where Cher's is not released). *I Feel Something In The Air*, a slightly controversial Sonny song about unmarried pregnancy, reaches UK #43. (Released in US as *Magic In The Air*, it failed to chart.)

Oct Cher's cover of Bobby Hebb's (US #2 and UK #12) hit *Sunny* – in

her case, with an implied "o" in the word rather than "u" – is released only in UK and makes #32. (Georgie Fame's cover makes UK #13.)

Nov *Cher* reaches US #66. *Behind The Door* charts briefly at US #97. Its B-side, another slightly controversial lyric, *Mama (When My Dollies Have Babies)*, is promoted in UK, but gains no airplay and fails to chart.

1967 Sept [9] After a recording gap with Sonny & Cher engaged on film "Good Times", Cher's *Hey Joe* makes US #94.

Dec [23] *You Better Sit Down Kids*, written by Sonny about family break-up, hits US #9. **With Love – Cher** makes US #47. Both fail to hit in UK, despite good airplay for the single, and mark the end of Cher's Imperial recording contract.

1968 She signs to Atco (to which Sonny & Cher are still contracted) on which her *Yours Until Tomorrow*, flops in US and is not released in UK.

1969 Aug **3614 Jackson Highway** (named after Muscle Shoals Sound studio address, where it is recorded with producers Jerry Wexler, Tom Dowd and Arif Mardin) makes US #160. Other Atco singles released in US and UK fail to chart. Cher has an acting role in film "Chastity", produced, written and scored by Sonny. She also sings the theme song, *Band Of Thieves*. (Chastity is also the name of the Bonos' daughter.)

1971 May Both the duo and Cher as a soloist are signed to a new recording deal with Kapp Records, but Cher's first single *Put It On Me* flops.

Aug [1] Sonny & Cher start "The Sonny And Cher Comedy Hour" on prime time CBS TV (which will follow a successful short summer run with 3 long, high-rating series). The routines, in a variety of characterizations, serve to hone Cher's acting skills for later film work.

Nov [6] *Gypsies, Tramps And Thieves*, produced by Snuff Garrett (the Bonos' next-door neighbor in Bel Air, CA), a dramatic story-song written for her by Bob Stone, hits US #1 for 2 weeks. It is her second solo million-seller. Album of the same title makes US #16.

Dec *Gypsies, Tramps And Thieves* hits UK #4.

1972 Feb Double Imperial compilation **Cher Superpak**, makes US #92.

Mar [25] *The Way Of Love*, a ballad taken from **Gypsies, Tramps And Thieves**, hits US #7.

June [24] *Living In A House Divided* reaches US #22. The Bonos' marriage is starting to shake despite their successful professional relationship.

Sept *Foxy Lady* reaches US #43.

Oct [21] *Don't Hide Your Love* makes US #46.

1973 Jan Garrett stops working with the Bonos after selecting *The Night The Lights Went Out In Georgia*, a Bobby Russell story-song of jealousy and murder, for a Cher single, which Sonny vetoes unknown to Cher at the time. (The song hits US #1 by Vicki Lawrence 3 months later.)

May **Bittersweet White Light** reaches US #140.

Oct [6] *Half Breed*, written specifically for Cher by Mary Dean and Al Capps, and produced by Garrett who knows it to be a smash, is Cher's first release for MCA. It tops US chart for 2 weeks and sells over a million, but makes no chart impression in UK. Album of the same title peaks at US #28.

1974 Feb [20] The Bonos separate, with Cher filing for divorce.

Mar [2] *Dark Lady*, written by The Ventures keyboards player Johnny Durrill, makes UK #36 (it will be her last chart entry for over a decade).

[23] *Dark Lady* hits US #1 and is Cher's fourth solo million-seller.

May Sonny & Cher's US TV series finishes.

June [26] Cher is divorced from Sonny Bono, at Santa Monica Supreme Court, CA.

[29] *Train Of Thought* reaches US #27.

[30] She marries Gregg Allman of The Allman Brothers Band, in Los Angeles. (It will be a stormy liaison and 9 days later she will announce that she wants a divorce.)

July *Dark Lady* peaks at US #69.

Sept [14] *I Saw A Man And He Danced With His Wife* peaks at US #42.

Dec Compilation album **Greatest Hits** reaches US #152, and marks the end of Cher's MCA recording deal. She signs to Warner Bros., and is reunited with her first producer, Phil Spector.

1975 Feb [16] CBS TV series "Cher", a weekly hour of music and comedy, airs for first time, with guests Bette Midler, Elton John and Flip Wilson. Spector produces a highly-rated single, coupling *A Woman's Story* (later revived by Marc Almond) and *Baby I Love You*. The first release on the Warner-Spector label, it fails to chart.

Apr A Spector-produced duet with Harry Nilsson of revival *A Love Like Yours* also flops. Cher does not continue working with Spector.

May **Stars**, produced by Jimmy Webb, is Cher's only Warner Bros. album to chart, reaching US #153.

Nov [8] David Bowie makes his US TV debut on "Cher", singing *Fame* and duetting with the hostess.

1976 Jan [4] The last "Cher" airs on US TV. (It will be replaced for a while

by less successful, "Sonny And Cher" series. The Bono reunion is purely professional.)
Oct *I'd Rather Believe In You* teams her with producers Steve Barri and Michael Omartian, but raises little interest.
1977 **Jan** [22] *Pirate* makes US #93.
Nov *Allman And Woman: Two The Hard Way* is recorded with husband Gregg Allman but does not chart.
1979 **Jan** [16] Cher's divorce from Allman is finalized.
May [12] Signed to predominantly disco-oriented Casablanca Records, Cher hits US #8 with *Take Me Home*. It is another US million-seller but fails in UK. Album of the same title makes US #25 and earns a gold disk. (She is now making the gossip columns as "constant companion" of another Casablanca artist, Gene Simmons of Kiss, but the relationship will not be long-lived.)
July [7] *Wasn't It Good* makes US #49.
Oct [13] *Hell On Wheels*, her last hit for Casablanca, makes US #59 and is her final US chart entry for several years.
1980 **Aug** [30] She makes an unannounced appearance as vocalist with Black Rose, a band formed by current boyfriend Les Dudek, in New York's Central Park.
Nov *Black Rose* is released, with Cher on vocals, but does not sell.
1982 **Feb** Cher duets (uncredited) with Meat Loaf on *Dead Ringer For Love* (which hits UK #5, but fails to chart in US), and appears with him in mini-movie promo video.
[14] Cher takes part in the "Night Of 100 Stars" at Radio City Music Hall, New York.
[18] Cher opens in her Broadway acting debut in "Come Back To The Five And Dime, Jimmy Dean, Jimmy Dean", directed by Robert Altman, at the Martin Beck theater, New York. (She will reprise her role in Robert Altman's film version.)
Mar She signs to CBS/Columbia Records. Debut *Rudy* fails.
Nov *I Paralyze* on CBS/Columbia, but fails to chart.
1984 **Mar** She is nominated for an Oscar as Best Supporting Actress in movie "Silkwood", which stars Meryl Streep.
1985 **Mar** Cher gives another critically-rated performance, in a leading role in Peter Bogdanovich's film "Mask". She is also honored by Harvard University's Hasty Pudding club as "Woman Of The Year".
1987 She co-stars with Jack Nicholson in "The Witches Of Eastwick" and later in the year appears in comedy "Moonstruck".
Oct *I Found Someone*, produced by Michael Bolton, on Geffen Records, hits UK #5 after an almost 14-year chart absence.
Nov [14] Sonny & Cher sing *I Got You Babe* for the first time in 10 years on NBC TV's "Late Night With Letterman".
1988 **Jan** *Cher*, made with several producers, makes UK #26.
Mar [5] *I Found Someone* hits US #10.
Apr [11] Cher wins an Academy Award as Best Actress for her work in "Moonstruck". Second single from *Cher*, *We All Sleep Alone*, co-written and co-produced by Jon Bon Jovi, reaches UK #47.
May *Cher* makes US #32, earning a gold disk.
June [11] *We All Sleep Alone* reaches US #14.
Aug [20] *Skin Deep*, third single from *Cher*, peaks at US #79.
1989 **May** [13] *After All*, Cher's duet with Peter Cetera from the film "Chances Are", hits US #6.
July *Heart Of Stone* US #10.
Aug *Heart Of Stone* reaches UK #15.
[16-20] To promote Cher's performances at Sands Casino hotel in Atlantic City, NJ, 28-year-old Renee Sohile showcases her collection of Cher memorabilia assembled over the last 21 years in her Rochester, NY, apartment. In return Sohile receives 30 opening night tickets and an audience with her idol for the first time.
Sept [6] Cher performs at MTV Video Music Awards held at the Universal Amphitheater, LA.
[23] *If I Could Turn Back Time* hits US #3, promoted via risque US Navy battleship location video.
Oct *If I Could Turn Back Time* hits UK #6, as Cher continues filming "Mermaid".
Dec [23] *Just Like Jesse James* hits US #8.
1990 **Feb** [24] *Just Like Jesse James* reaches UK #11 as parent album *Heart of Stone* hits UK #7.
Mar [8] Cher wins Worst Dressed Female Rock Artist **Rolling Stone** 1989 Music Awards and Worst Video (*If I Could Turn Back Time*) **Rolling Stone** 1989 Critics Awards.
Apr [14] *Heart Of Stone* (written by Pete Sinfield and Andy Hill originally for Bucks Fizz) reaches US #20.
[21] *Heart of Stone* makes UK #43.
June [14-19] Cher's summer dates include 6 nights in Las Vegas, NV,

and a performance at the Milwaukee Summerfest, WI, a bill shared with, among others, Anita Baker, Crosby, Stills & Nash, Depeche Mode, Fleetwood Mac, Richard Marx and others.
Aug [18] *You Wouldn't Know Love* makes UK #55.
1991 **Jan** [19] *The Shoop Shoop Song (Its In His Kiss)* makes US #33.
[26] Cher hosts a specially made 2-hour video in her Malibu, CA, home, featuring 22 clips including such artists as Janet Jackson, John Fogerty, Van Halen, Bonnie Raitt and Paul Simon, for the troops involved in Operation Desert Storm in the Gulf War.
Apr [20] *The Shoop Shoop Song (Its In His Kiss)* reaches UK #23.

NENEH CHERRY

1980 Cherry (b.Oct.10, 1964, Stockholm, Sweden), her mother Swedish artist Moki and father African percussionist Ahmadu Jah, after being educated in Manhattan and Sweden, and raised by Moki and stepfather, jazz trumpeter, Don Cherry, moves to London, having dropped out of school 2 years earlier, before visiting her real father's family in Africa.
1981 She works with all-girl group The Slits, before joining Float Up C.P., which in time becomes Rip, Rig & Panic (whose only success will be *I Am Gold*, which makes UK #67 in June 1982).
1982 An A&R man sees her rapping in a London club, and invites her to cut *Stop The War* and *Give Sleep A Chance*, both songs about the war in the Falkland Islands. She soon begins writing with her beau/producer Cameron "Booga Bear" McVey, of production team Dynamik Duo and subsequent band, Morgan McVey.
1986 **Nov** Cherry duets with Matt Johnson on *Slow Train To Dawn* from The The's *Infected*.
1988 **Dec** Part hip-hop dance smash, *Buffalo Stance* hits UK #3.
1989 **Mar** Daughter Tyson Cherry Kwewanda McVey is born. (Cherry already has another daughter born in 1983.)
June *Manchild* hits UK #5.
[17] *Raw Like Sushi* enters UK chart. It hits #2.
[24] *Buffalo Stance* hits US #3, as parent album *Raw Like Sushi* enters US chart, beginning a climb to #40.
Aug *Kisses On The Wind* reaches UK #20.
Sept [6] Cherry collapses after an MTV show suffering from Lyme disease. She pulls out of a major US tour as support to Fine Young Cannibals, apparently suffering from exhaustion.
[30] *Kisses On The Wind* hits US #8.
1990 **Jan** [6] *Heart* peaks at US #73.
[20] *Inna City Mamma* makes UK #31.
Feb [18] Cherry wins Best International Newcomer and Best International Artist at the ninth annual BRIT Awards at the Dominion theater, London.
Mar [8] She wins Best New Female Singer award in **Rolling Stone**'s 1989 Critics Awards.
Oct [13] *I've Got You Under My Skin*, Cherry's contribution to *Red Hot + Blue*, an anthology of Cole Porter songs to benefit AIDS education, reaches UK #25, and proves to be the most successful single cut from the project.
Dec Cherry marries long-time boyfriend McVey.

CHIC

Nile Rodgers (guitar)
Bernard Edwards (bass)
Tony Thompson (drums)
Alfa Anderson (vocals)
Luci Martin (vocals)

1972 After playing together in various New York clubs since meeting in 1970, Edwards (b. Oct.31, 1952, Greenville, NC) and Rodgers (b. Sept.19, 1952, New York, NY) team with Thompson to form The Big Apple Band, a rock-fusion trio.
1976 Band, despite steady club work and tours, backing soul acts New York City and Carol Douglas, and switching to the newly-emerging disco genre, name-changing to Allah & The Knife-Wielding Punks, feels it is going nowhere. It adds Norma Jean Wright (for whom it produces and writes an early album on the Bearsville label) as female lead voice.
1977 **June** Group adopts the name Chic, and self-produces several dance-oriented tracks in an unsuccessful attempt to win a recording deal. Tom Cossie and Mark Kreiner buy Chic's masters of the already-recorded tracks, and form M.K. Productions.
Sept Group signs to Atlantic Records (which earlier turned it down)

after the personal intervention of company president Jerry Greenberg.

'78 **Jan** [14] Debut *Dance Dance Dance (Yowsah Yowsah Yowsah)* hits UK #6.
Feb [25] *Dance Dance Dance (Yowsah Yowsah Yowsah)* hits US #6, becoming a million-seller.
Mar [4] *Chic*, recorded in just 3 weeks, reaches US #27. Wright leaves and Martin and Anderson are recruited as joint lead vocalists.
May [13] *Everybody Dance* hits UK #9.
June [17] *Everybody Dance* makes US #38.
Dec [9] Seminal dance cut *Le Freak* hits US #1 for 6 weeks. One of the biggest-selling singles of the decade, it tops 4 million in US, becoming Atlantic's best-selling single.
[16] *Le Freak* hits UK #7.
[23] *C'Est Chic*, containing *Le Freak*, hits US #4 and is also a million-seller, later to be regarded as a landmark dance album.

'79 **Apr** [7] *I Want Your Love* hits UK #4 as *C'Est Chic* hits UK #2, kept off top by German bandleader James Last's *Last The Whole Night*.
[14] A Rodgers/Edwards production for Sister Sledge's *He's The Greatest Dancer* hits UK #6. (Sister Sledge's album and single *We Are Family* will follow, with further hit singles and a second album, all successfully guided by Chic organization.)
May [5] *I Want Your Love* hits US #7 and is another million-seller.
[12] *He's The Greatest Dancer* hits US #9.
July [21] *Good Times* hits UK #5. (Built around a distinctive bass line, it will be one of the most imitated in popular music in succeeding years. The Sugarhill Gang's *Rapper's Delight* will be found guilty of plagiarizing the arrangement and give joint composer credits to Rodgers and Edwards.)
Aug [18] *Good Times* tops US chart and is the group's third consecutive million-seller.
Sept [1] *Risque* reaches UK #29.
[22] *Risque* hits US #5.
Nov [3] *My Forbidden Lover* reaches UK #15 and US #43.

'80 **Jan** [5] *My Feet Keep Dancing* (featuring a unique tap dance solo) reaches UK #21, while compilation album *Les Plus Grands Succés De Chic: Chic's Greatest Hits* makes UK #88.
[19] Same compilation, but retitled *The Best Of Chic*, reaches UK #30.
Feb [2] Rodgers/Edwards' production of *Spacer* by Sheila B. Devotion makes UK #18.
Aug [9] Diana Ross' *Upside Down*, produced by Rodgers/Edwards, hits UK #2. It is taken from *Diana*, also produced by the duo, though remixed by Ross without their cooperation because she feels her vocals have been sublimated to their production.
[30] Chic's *Real People* reaches UK #30.
Sept [6] *Upside Down* tops US chart.
[20] Group's *Rebels Are We* peaks at US #61.
Nov [22] Double A-side *Real People/Chip Off The Old Block* reaches only US #79.

'81 **Aug** [15] Debbie Harry's *Koo Koo*, produced by Rodgers and Edwards, hits UK #6.
Sept [19] *Koo Koo* reaches US #25.

'82 **Jan** [23] Chic's *Take It Off* makes US #124.
June [26] *Soup For One*, theme from the film of the same title with score by Rodgers and Edwards, is Chic's last US hit single, at #80.
Aug [7] Rodgers/Edwards-created *Why*, from *Soup For One* by Carly Simon, peaks at US #74.
Oct [2] *Why* hits UK #10.
Dec [11] *Tongue In Chic* peaks at US #173 and does not chart in UK.

'83 **Mar** [12] *Hangin'* is Chic's last UK chart appearance, peaking at #64. (As the group fades, Rodgers and Edwards branch out in new directions. Rodgers will produce a prodigious body of work throughout the remainder of the decade, including David Bowie's *Let's Dance*, Madonna's breakthrough album, *Like A Virgin*, and other projects for artists including Duran Duran, Aretha Franklin, Jeff Beck, Mick Jagger, Al Jarreau, Grace Jones, Johnny Mathis and Spanish Language single, Ole-Ole. He will also briefly join The Honeydrippers with Robert Plant, Jimmy Page and Jeff Beck.)

'85 Rodgers releases solo album *B-Movie Matinee*. Both Edwards and Thompson join Power Station, with Robert Palmer and members of Duran Duran. This will lead Edwards into successful production of Palmer's solo albums.

'87 Rodgers teams up with Phillipe Saisse and Felicia Collins to form the trio Outloud.
Sept [13] *Jack Le Freak*, a Stock/Aitken/Waterman up-dated segued medley, reaches UK #19.
Dec *Freak Out*, a compilation comprising Chic and Sister Sledge material, peaks at UK #72.

1989 **Nov** Rodgers hosts "New Visions" on VH1.
1990 **July** [14] *Megachic – Chic Medley* peaks at UK #58.
Chic re-forms and signs to Warner Bros., as Rodgers prepares to form a new label with former cohort Tom Cossie in New York for 1991 launch.

CHICAGO

Peter Cetera (vocals, bass)
Robert Lamm (vocals, keyboards)
Terry Kath (guitar)
Danny Seraphine (drums)
James Pankow (trombone)
Lee Loughnane (trumpet)
Walter Parazaider (saxophone)
Laudir de Oliveira (percussion)

1966 Parazaider (b. Mar.14, 1945, Chicago, IL) after studying at DePaul University, Chicago, where he meets fellow students Loughnane (b. Oct.21, 1946, Chicago), Pankow (b. Aug.20, 1947, Chicago), and Seraphine (b. Aug.28, 1948, Chicago), has been playing in Jimmy & The Gentlemen with Kath (b. Jan.31, 1946, Chicago), when the 2 of them begin auditioning for music jobs, one of which is for a group called The Executives, for which Seraphine is also auditioning. The 3 of them decide to form their own band The Missing Links, recruiting Loughnane and Lamm (b. Oct.13, 1944, New York, NY), whom they have met while he is studying at Roosevelt University, Chicago. Cetera (b. Sept.13, 1944, Chicago), who has been a member of highly-rated local band The Exceptions, completes the line-up, now calling itself The Big Thing. Fellow Chicagoan James William Guercio, now living in Los Angeles, CA, and making a name for himself in the music business, offers to manage the group providing it changes name to Chicago Transit Authority.

1967 **May** [22] Band makes its debut as Chicago Transit Authority, with a 2-week residency at the Stardust Lounge, Rockford, IL.
Nov [1-5] They make their hometown debut, playing 5 nights at the Club Laurel in Chicago.

1968 **June** [18] Relocated to Los Angeles by Guercio, where he pays their rent, group plays the Kaleidoscope.
Sept [12-14] Group makes its debut at the Fillmore West in San Francisco, CA.

1969 **Jan** Through Guercio's influence at CBS/Columbia Records (he is currently working with Blood, Sweat & Tears and has guided The Buckinghams), group signs a worldwide contract. (Guercio will produce all the material.)
Feb [21] Group makes its Fillmore East debut in New York.
May [17] Debut *Chicago Transit Authority* begins a 3-year stay on the US chart. Unusually for a first effort, it is a double album. Containing a popular fusion of jazz pop ballads and rock (and protest chants from 1968 Democratic Convention), it will reach US #17 and hit UK #9. Touring to promote the album, the group supports Janis Joplin and Jimi Hendrix.
July After legal threats from the Chicago mayor Richard Daley, Guercio persuades the band to shorten its name to Chicago.
Aug [1] Group takes part in the Atlantic City Pop Festival, NJ.
[23] First single from debut album, Robert Lamm-penned *Questions 67 And 68*, peaks at US #71.
[30-31] Group participates in the Dallas Pop Festival, TX.
Sept [13] Chicago performs at the "Toronto Rock'N'Revival Show" in the Varsity Stadium at the University of Toronto, Canada, on a bill which includes Chuck Berry, Cat Mother & The All Night Newsboys, Alice Cooper, Bo Diddley, Fats Domino, The Doors, Kim Fowley, Doug Kershaw, Jerry Lee Lewis, Little Richard, Screaming Lord Sutch, Gene Vincent, Tony Joe White and The Plastic Ono Band.
Dec [4] Chicago begins 14-date European tour at the Royal Albert Hall, London. The tour will end on Dec.21 in Newcastle, Tyne & Wear.

1970 **Jan** [8-11] Group plays 4 dates at the Fillmore West, at the start of an 11-month US tour.
Feb [14] A cover of Spencer Davis Group's *I'm A Man* hits UK #8. Follow-up double album *Chicago* begins a 134-week US chart stay, eventually hitting #4 and UK #6.
June [6] *Make Me Smile*, written by Pankow, hits US #9.
July [28] Group performs at the Expo '70 exhibition in Montreal, Canada.
Aug [28] Chicago plays the Isle of Wight Festival in UK, during a break in its North American tour.
Sept [5] *25 Or 6 To 4*, written by Lamm, becomes a worldwide smash, hitting UK #7.

[12] *25 Or 6 To 4* hits US #4.

Nov [26] Group plays its 162nd, and last, concert of the year at the Auditorium theater, Chicago.

1971 **Jan** [2] Re-released from debut album, *Does Anybody Really Know What Time It Is?* hits US #7. Third double album, *Chicago III* hits US #2.
[20] Group begins 72-date North American tour at the Warehouse, New Orleans, LA. The tour will end on May 23 at Millett Hall, Miami University, Oxford, OH.
Apr [3] *Free* reaches US #20 as *Chicago III* makes UK #31.
[5-10] Chicago becomes the first rock group to play Carnegie Hall in New York, with 6 sell-out concerts, recorded for 4-album set *Chicago At Carnegie Hall*.
May [20] Cetera, attending a baseball game, is beaten up by a gang and undergoes hours of emergency surgery.
June [1] Group begins 15-date world tour at London's Royal Albert Hall. It will cover Germany, France, Denmark, Sweden, Italy, Greece, Thailand and Japan, ending June 19 at H.I.C. Arena, Honolulu, HI.
[12] *Lowdown* makes US #35.
July [12] Chicago begins another major US tour at the Santa Clara Fairgrounds, San Jose, CA.
Aug [14] Double A-side, *Beginnings/Color My World* from the first album, hits US #7.
Nov [20] Another re-issue, previously charted *Questions 67 And 68* coupled with previous UK hit *I'm A Man*, reaches US #24. An argument between some band members and Guercio precedes release of *Chicago At Carnegie Hall*. Guercio insists it should be released but Chicago feels the recordings are of poor quality. It hits US #3, the highest charting 4-album box set.

1972 **Feb** Chicago undertakes successful tours of Japan and Australia, beginning a world trek which will include dates in Yugoslavia, Poland and Czechoslovakia.
Aug [19] New studio album, and their first 1-disk set, *Chicago V* hits US #1, for 9 weeks.
Sept [23] *Saturday In The Park*, from *Chicago V*, hits US #3. In UK, the album climbs to #24. Guercio writes and directs film "Electra Glide In Blue", which features performances from 4 Chicago members.
Dec [9] *Dialogue (Part I & II)* reaches US #24.

1973 **Feb** Chicago records at Guercio's newly-built studio, Caribou, with Oliveira on percussion. (He will become full-time member in 1974.)
July [28] *Chicago VI* hits US #1 for 5 weeks.
Aug [18] *Feelin' Stronger Every Day*, written by Cetera and Pankow, hits US #10. Japan-only release, *Chicago Live In Japan* sells over 1 million copies in the Far East.
Dec [8] *Just You'N'Me*, written by Pankow, hits US #4.

1974 **Apr** [27] Another double album, *Chicago VII*, tops US chart.
May [1] *(I've Been) Searchin' So Long*, from *Chicago VII*, hits US #9.
Aug [10] Second single from the album, Loughnane-penned *Call On Me*, hits US #6. Keyboardist Lamm releases solo album *Skinny Boy*, the title track of which, with vocals from The Pointer Sisters, is also included on *Chicago VII*.
Nov [30] Taken from seventh album, *Wishin' You Were Here*, featuring backing vocals from Al Jardine and Carl and Dennis Wilson of The Beach Boys, whom Guercio is managing, reaches US #11.

1975 **Apr** [5] *Harry Truman*, written by Lamm, reaches US #13.
May [3] *Chicago VIII*, tops US chart. Group embarks on 12-city US tour with The Beach Boys, with more than 700,000 paying a total of $7.5 million to see the bands.
June [7] *Old Days*, written by Pankow, hits US #5.
Sept [20] *Brand New Love Affair (Part I & II)*, also penned by Pankow, peaks at US #61.
Dec [13] *Chicago IX – Chicago's Greatest Hits* hits US #1 for 5 weeks.

1976 **May** Chicago's Mayor Richard Daley awards the group the city's "Medal Of Merit".
Aug [7] *Another Rainy Day In New York City*, written by Lamm, makes US #32 as parent *Chicago X* hits US #3, during a 44-week chart stay.
Oct [23] Ballad *If You Leave Me Now*, written by Cetera and featuring a distinctive Jimmie Haskell arrangement, tops US chart.
Nov [13] *If You Leave Me Now* tops UK chart, becoming Chicago's biggest worldwide smash.
Dec [4] *Chicago X* reaches UK #21.

1977 **Jan** Chicago undertakes another world tour beginning with sell-out dates in UK and Europe.
Feb [19] *If You Leave Me Now* wins Best Pop Vocal Performance By A Duo, Group Or Chorus at the 19th annual Grammy awards.
Apr [30] *You Are On My Mind*, written by Pankow, makes US #49.

June Guercio, increasingly involved in other projects, stops managing Chicago. Band appears at Geraldo Rivera "One To One" benefit show.
Nov [12] *Chicago XI*, the last album produced by Guercio, hits US #6
[19] *Baby, What A Big Surprise*, written by Cetera with a backing vocal from Carl Wilson, makes UK #41.
Dec [3] *Baby, What A Big Surprise* hits US #4.

1978 **Jan** [23] Founder and lead guitarist Kath, an avid gun collector for 6 years, accidentally shoots himself in the head while playing with what he believes is an unloaded gun at a friend's house in Woodland Hills, CA. Johnny Carson's TV bandleader Doc Severinsen visits the group after Kath's funeral and persuades it to continue as Chicago.
Apr [1] *Little One*, written by Seraphine and David "Hawk" Wolinski and with a featured lead vocal from Kath, makes US #44.
June [3] *Take Me Back To Chicago*, Seraphine/Wolinski-penned and featuring Chaka Khan on backing vocals, peaks at US #63.
Aug Group signs a management deal with Wald-Nanas Associates, and will begin recording 13th album with Phil Ramone at Criteria studios in Miami, FL. Donnie Dacus is recruited from the Stephen Stills Band to replace Kath.
Dec [2] *Alive Again*, penned by Pankow, reaches US #14, as parent album *Hot Streets*, their first not to feature "Chicago" in the title, reaches US #12 and is supported by a "comeback" US tour.

1979 **Mar** [3] *No Tell Lover* reaches US #14.
Apr [28] *Gone Long Gone*, written by Cetera, peaks at US #73.
Sept [1] *Must Have Been Crazy*, the first (and only charting) single from new album *Chicago 13* written and sung by Dacus, climbs to US #83.
[29] *Chicago 13*, breaking the sequence of roman numerals (UK title: *Street Player*), reaches US #21. Dacus will leave the band shortly thereafter. (Chris Pinnick will be replace him.)
Dec [21-22] Chicago joins The Eagles and Linda Ronstadt for 2 benefit concerts at San Diego's sports arena and Los Angeles' Aladdin theater, which raise almost $500,000 for the presidential campaign of California governor Jerry Brown.

1980 **Sept** [13] *Chicago XIV*, produced by Tom Dowd and recorded at The Record Plant in Los Angeles, makes US #71 and is the group's least successful album.
[20] *Thunder And Lightning* written by Lamm and Seraphine makes US #56. Band begins its longest period of silence as careers are re-assessed.

1981 CBS/Columbia drops Chicago, releasing an end of year album *Chicago – Greatest Hits, Volume II*, which makes US #171. Cetera releases solo album *Peter Cetera* on Full Moon label, which will make US #143.

1982 Chicago signs to Full Moon and Bill Champlin (ex-Sons Of Champlin), and a successful solo artist (his album *Runaway* makes US #178 in Feb.) joins as additional vocalist.
Sept [11] Chicago ballad *Hard To Say I'm Sorry*, written by Cetera with new producer David Foster, also used in Daryl Hannah-starring movie "Summer Lovers", tops US chart for 2 weeks.
[18] *Chicago 16* hits US #9, their first Top 10 album in 5 years.
Oct [9] *Hard To Say I'm Sorry* hits UK #4.
[23] Parent album *Chicago 16* makes UK #44.
Dec [4] *Love Me Tomorrow* reaches US #22.
[25] UK-only TV-advertised compilation *Love Songs* makes UK #42.

1983 **Jan** [29] *What You're Missing* stalls at US #81.
1984 **June** [23] *Stay The Night* reaches US #16. It is taken from new album *Chicago 17*, released on Full Moon, which will hit US #4.
Oct [20] *Hard Habit To Break*, again with Foster, hits US #3.
Nov [24] *Hard Habit To Break* hits UK #8.
Dec *Chicago 17* reaches UK #24.

1985 **Jan** [19] *You're The Inspiration* hits US #3.
Feb [23] *You're The Inspiration* reaches UK #14. Cetera leaves amidst some bitterness to pursue a solo career. He is replaced by Jason Scheff, son of Jerry Scheff, Elvis Presley's bass player for many years. Recent recruit Pinnick also quits.
Apr [20] *Along Comes A Woman* reaches US #14.

1986 **Aug** [2] Cetera's theme from film "The Karate Kid II", *The Glory Of Love* tops US chart. It will also hit UK #3. His second solo album *Solitude/Solitaire* reaches US #23.
Sept [27] Chicago's new version of its 1970 hit *25 Or 6 To 4* makes US #48, as Cetera's *Solitude/Solitaire* peaks at UK #56.
Dec [6] Cetera teams with Christian singer Amy Grant for *The Next Time I Fall* which hits US #1.

1987 **Feb** [14] Cetera's *Big Mistake* peaks at US #61.
[21] *Will You Still Love Me?* hits US #3 during a 23-week run, as parent album *Chicago 18*, produced by Foster, reaches US #35. Cetera co-writes and produces former Abba star Agnetha Faltskog's *I Stand Alone* duetting with her on the title track.

May [30] Chicago's *If She Would Have Been Faithful* reaches US #17. (Champlin duets with Patti LaBelle on *The Last Unbroken Heart*, featured in NBC TV's "Miami Vice".)

July [18] *Niagara Falls* stalls at US #91.

1988 Mar [6] "In The Heat Of The Night", which features Champlin giving his best Ray Charles impression, premieres on NBC TV.

Apr [30] Cetera/Faltskog duet, *I Wasn't The One (Who Said Goodbye)*, peaks at US #93.

Aug *Chicago 19*, produced by Ron Nevison, makes US #37.

[27] *I Don't Wanna Live Without Your Love* hits US #3.

Sept Third Cetera album *One More Story*, produced by Madonna's musical director, Patrick Leonard, makes US #58.

Oct [1] Cetera's *One Good Woman* hits US #4. Lamm announces a solo project with co-producer Randy Goodrum, as group reveals plans to take part in Amnesty International's 25th anniversary.

Dec [3] Cetera's *Best Of Times* peaks at US #59.

[10] *Look Away* tops US chart.

1989 Mar [25] *You're Not Alone* hits US #10.

May [13] Cetera and Cher's *After All*, from Cybil Shepherd/Robert Downey Jr. film "Chances Are", hits US #6.

[27] Chicago begins its first tour with The Beach Boys since 1975 at the Pacific Amphitheater in Los Angeles.

June [17] *We Can Last Forever* peaks at US #55.

[20] Band plays the first of 6 major US dates co-headlining with The Beach Boys.

Dec Compilation album *The Heart Of Chicago* reaches UK #15.

[23] *Look Away* wins Top Pop Singles category in **Billboard**'s The Year In Music.

1990 Feb [10] *Greatest Hits 1982-1989* makes US #37.

[24] *What Kind Of Man Would I Be?* hits US #5.

Aug [18] *Hearts In Trouble*, from Tom Cruise movie "Days Of Thunder", peaks at US #75. Seraphine leaves Chicago a quarter of a century after joining.

1991 Mar [9] *Chasin' The Wind*, written by Diane Warren, makes US #39, as parent album *Twenty 1* peaks at US #66.

Feb [10] Cetera joins nearly 100 celebrities in Burbank, CA, to record *Voices That Care*, co-written by him and David Foster and fiancee Linda Thompson Jenner, to benefit the American Red Cross Gulf Crisis Fund.

THE CHIFFONS

Judy Craig (lead vocals)
Barbara Lee (vocals),
Patricia Bennett (vocals)
Sylvia Peterson (vocals)

1960 The group, all from New York, forms while still at high school, singing during lunchbreaks and in the neighborhood after school. Ronnie Mack, a local songwriter and pianist, drafts them to rehearse and perform some of his songs for a demo tape.

Sept Mack sells *Tonight's The Night*, featuring guitar work by Butch Mann (later of The Drifters) to local label Big Deal, resulting in a minor US hit which reaches #76.

1962 After making the industry rounds with his demos, Mack interests Brooklyn quintet The Tokens (of *The Lion Sleeps Tonight* 1961 US #1 fame), now producing under the name Bright Tunes, who sign Mack and The Chiffons.

Dec *He's So Fine* is recorded (with The Tokens playing back-up instruments) at Mirror Sound studios, Manhattan, NY, where the session engineer, impressed by the "doo-lang" chant with which the group accompanies the song, suggests that it should form the introduction.

1963 Jan Capitol Records, with which The Tokens have a first-refusal deal, reject *He's So Fine*, but smaller label Laurie buys it.

Mar *He's So Fine* tops US chart for 4 weeks, selling over a million.

May Mack collapses in the street, and is hospitalized in New York with Hodgkins' Disease. At his hospital bed, he is presented with a gold disk for his #1 song by The Tokens, but dies shortly afterwards. *He's So Fine* reaches UK #16.

June *He's So Fine* peaks at US #97.

July Follow-up, *One Fine Day*, hits US #5. Composers Goffin and King, having originally recorded this song with Little Eva on lead vocal for The Tokens, take it to The Chiffons' producers, who buy the whole production and erase Little Eva's voice track, substituting The Chiffons'. The Tokens also record The Chiffons under the pseudonym The Four Pennies on *My Block*. Released on Laurie subsidiary label

Rust, it reaches US #67.

Aug *One Fine Day* makes UK #29.

Oct *A Love So Fine*, the third consecutive Chiffons release with the word "fine" in the title, peaks at US #40, but fails in UK (as will their next few singles).

Nov *When The Boy's Happy (The Girl's Happy Too)* by The Four Pennies is released. It charts briefly at US #95, but the pseudonym is abandoned after this.

1964 Jan *I Have A Boyfriend* reaches US #36.

June Group supports The Rolling Stones on first US tour.

Aug *Sailor Boy* peaks at only US #81. Group sues to extricate itself from the contract with Bright Tunes – a deal from which they earned little, since the producers financed all their studio time by deductions from The Chiffons' royalties. A court eventually frees them on grounds of having been minors when signing the original agreement. Other labels are now wary of them, so they return to Laurie and sign a direct deal.

1965 *Nobody Knows What's Going On* reaches US #49.

1966 June *Sweet Talkin' Guy* restores them to US Top 10 after 3 years, hitting #10. It also climbs to UK #31.

Aug *Out Of This World*, a near-clone of *Sweet Talkin' Guy*, makes US #67.

Oct *Stop, Look and Listen* stalls at US #85, and is the group's last US hit.

1969 Craig quits the group which, despite hitless years, is still performing in New York and touring US on a regular basis.

1972 Apr *Sweet Talkin' Guy* is reissued in UK, and becomes a surprise smash hit, at #4.

1976 Aug [31] US district court judge Richard Owen finds George Harrison guilty of "subconscious plagiarism" of Ronnie Mack's song *He's So Fine* when writing his 1970 million-seller *My Sweet Lord*. Earnings from the song, frozen since the suit was filed in 1971, go partly to the inheritors of Mack's estate. Taking advantage of the publicity surrounding the trial and verdict, The Chiffons record their own version of *My Sweet Lord*, but it fails to sell.

1989 Group goes on "The Royalty Of Doo-Wop" US tour with The Belmonts, The Diamonds, The Flamingos and The Silhouettes.

THE CHI-LITES

Eugene Record (lead vocals)
Marshall Thompson (drums)
Robert "Squirrel" Lester (vocals)
Creadel Jones (vocals)
Clarence Johnson (vocals)

1960 Group forms in Chicago, IL, as an R&B quintet, The Hi-Lites, initially led by Thompson, who backed R&B acts at Chicago's Regal theater and, with Jones, is ex-The Desideros; Record, Johnson and Lester are ex-The Chantours. Rival band called The Hi-Lites claims original title use, so they become Marshall & The Chi-Lites. (Marshall is Thompson's forename and C is added as a location identify of their home town Chicago.) They sign to Mercury, and release *Pots And Pans*, which fails.

1967 After passing through several R&B labels including Blue Rock, Daran and Ja Wes labels and gaining local success, Marshall & The Chi-Lites sign to Dakar label, through MCA.

1969 Apr [12] Now known as The Chi-Lites and signed to another MCA subsidiary, Brunswick, group's *Give It Away* reaches US #88. It is written by Record, who is establishing himself as a successful songwriter (particularly for fellow Brunswick artiste Barbara Acklin, whom he also marries).

Aug [16] *Let Me Be The Man My Daddy Was* peaks at US #94.

Sept *Give It Away* spends 3 weeks on chart, peaking at US #180.

1970 Sept [12] *I Like Your Lovin' (Do You Like Mine)* peaks at US #72, after topping US R&B chart.

1971 Jan [23] *Are You My Woman? (Tell Me So)* also climbs to US #72.

May [29] With Record now singer/writer/producer, his *(For God's Sake) Give More Power To The People* reaches US #26. Album of the same title will later climb to US #12.

Aug [21] *We Are Neighbors* peaks at US #70.

Sept *(For God's Sake) Give More Power To The People* makes UK #32.

Nov [27] *I Want To Pay You Back (For Loving Me)* peaks at US #95.

Dec [11] During a 14-week chart stay, Record ballad *Have You Seen Her* hits US #3 (it will become popularly covered, not least by MC Hammer in 1990).

1972 Feb *Have You Seen Her* hits UK #3.

May [27] Group, now at the height of its pop and R&B success, tops US chart with harmonica-laden *Oh Girl*, breaking a 6-week top spot residence by Roberta Flack's *The First Time Ever I Saw Your Face*.

June *Oh Girl* reaches UK #14. (It too will re-hit in 1990 as a worldwide cover smash for Paul Young.) *A Lonely Man* hits US #5 and goes gold (no album will make the UK chart).

Sept [2] *The Coldest Days Of My Life* peaks at US #47.

Oct [21] *A Lonely Man/The Man And The Woman (The Boy And The Girl)* peaks at US #57 as *The Chi-Lites Greatest Hits* begins 6-month US chart stay.

Dec [30] *We Need Order* peaks at US #61 as the group completes its most successful year.

1973 **Apr** [14] *A Letter To Myself* climbs to US #33. Album of the same title makes US #50. Record is made a senior executive at Brunswick.

June [30] *My Heart Just Keeps On Breakin'* reaches US #92.

Sept [22] *Stoned Out Of My Mind* reaches US #30 and tops R&B chart as *Chi-Lites* peaks at US #89.

Dec [29] *I Found Sunshine* peaks at US #47.

1974 **Mar** [23] *Homely Girl* peaks at US #54.

May [4] *Homely Girl* hits UK #5 as the group begins a UK tour.

July [20] *There Will Never Be Any Peace (Until God Is Seated At The Conference Table)* peaks at UK #32.

Aug [3] *I Found Sunshine* makes UK #35. *Toby* peaks at US #181 (their lowest album showing in 5 years, and their last for 6 more.)

Sept [7] *You Got To Be The One* peaks at US #83.

Nov [30] *Too Good To Be Forgotten* hits UK #10.

1975 **Apr** [12] *Toby/That's How Long* reaches US #78. Rumors persist of Record's dissatisfaction with their current form.

June Re-released double A-side *Have You Seen Her/Oh Girl* hits UK #5.

Oct [18] Another Record pop/soul ballad *It's Time For Love* hits UK #5.

Nov [22] *It's Time For Love* stalls at US #94 (and is the final group US chart single). Record announces his decision to leave The Chi-Lites and pursue a solo career, as *Half A Love* fails to sell. Danny Johnson will replace him. Jones will also leave, making way for David Scott.)

1976 **Sept** [11] *You Don't Have To Go* hits UK #3. The remaining members sign a new deal with Mercury, who will release their unsuccessful *Happy Being Lonely*. 2 compilation albums are also released: *Very Best Of The Chi-Lites* (Brunswick) and *Chilitime* (London).

1977 Without Record, The Chi-Lites release *The Fantastic Chi-Lites*, on Mercury, which fails to chart. Still a Brunswick executive, Record issues *Greatest Hits Volume 2* in US only.

1979 **Aug** With other Chi-Lites now inactive, Record signs to Warner Bros. as a solo act and releases *Magnetism* and *Welcome To My Fantasy*. Both fail beyond the disco market in US and UK.

1980 **Nov** Record reunites The Chi-Lites and establishes the label Chi-Sound. *Heavenly Body* makes US #179 but has no hit singles.

1982 **May** [1] Another Chi-Sound album *Me And You* makes US #162.

1983 **Aug** Now established on US label Larc and licensed in UK through specialist dance label Red Bus, *Bottom's Up*, led by Record, climbs to US #98.

[20] Taken from it, *Changing For You*, peaks at UK #61. (The Chi-Lites will remain popular on the soul cabaret circuit, particularly in UK where compilation albums will periodically appear including *The Chi-Lites Classic* (1984) and *20 Golden Pieces Of The Chi-Lites* (1985).)

1986 **May** The Chi-Lites back Donnell Pitman on *Your Love Is Dynamite* which makes #82 on US R&B chart.

CHINA CRISIS

Gary Daly (vocals)
Eddie Lundon (guitar)
Brian MacNeil (keyboards)
Gazza Johnson (bass)
Kevin Wilkinson (drums)

1979 After leaving school at age 17, Daly and Lundon join forces in Kirkby, Merseyside, and become (and will remain) the core of China Crisis. Band plays locally and develops a following as an integral part of the early 80s Mersey music scene.

1982 **Aug** Signed to Liverpool independent label, Inevitable, group releases *African And White*.

[14] Picked up by Virgin Records, it climbs to UK #45, and band signs a long-term contract with the label.

1983 **Feb** [19] With new members Johnson and Wilkinson, second single *Christian* reaches UK #12 as parent *Difficult Shapes And Passive Rhythms* climbs to UK #21. Band begins a European tour supporting Simple Minds.

June [11] *Tragedy And Mystery* peaks at UK #46.

Oct [22] *Working With Fire And Steel* makes UK #48.

Nov *Working With Fire And Steel – Possible Pop Songs Vol.2* reaches UK #20.

1984 **Jan** [28] Taken from the album, *Wishful Thinking* hits UK #9.

Mar [17] *Hanna Hanna* makes UK #44.

1985 **Jan** Group's car turns over on an icy road in UK during an early morning journey home from the recording studio. Daly has a broken arm and Johnson a broken upper jaw but the others escape without serious injury.

Apr [27] Steely Dan-influenced *Black Man Ray*, recorded at sessions with ex-Steely Dan Walter Becker producing, reaches UK #14.

May [11] Becker-produced *Flaunt The Imperfection* debuts at UK #9. Band tours UK and Ireland.

June [29] Extracted from the album, *King In A Catholic Style (Wake Up)* reaches UK #19.

Flaunt The Imperfection makes US #171, as the band tours US, with limited success.

Sept *You Did Cut Me* peaks at UK #54.

1986 **Jan** China Crisis becomes the first major rock band to play in Gibraltar.

July Group teams with producers Clive Langer and Alan Winstanley to record a new album.

Sept Lundon and Daly play a few UK pub dates under the name Kirk Douglas & The Long Coats From Hell.

Nov *Arizona Sky*, taken from forthcoming album, peaks at UK #47.

Dec Fourth album *What Price Paradise?* peaks at UK #63.

1987 **Feb** *Best-Kept Secret*, also from the album, reaches UK #36.

Mar *What Price Paradise?* peaks at US #114.

1989 **May** [13] *Diary Of A Hollow Horse* makes UK #58.

1990 **Sept** [15] *China Crisis Collection*, chronicling the band's singles career to date debuts at UK #32 as Virgin reviews its commitment to the group.

THE CHRISTIANS

Garry Christian (vocals)
Russell Christian (vocals)
Henry Priestman (vocals)
Roger Christian (vocals)

1984 Having flirted musically with The Yachts in late 70s and It's Immaterial in early 80s, Priestman, main songwriting and creative force in the band, meets the 3 Christian brothers (part of a family of 11 Christian offspring) in Pete Wylie's Liverpool, Merseyside, studio. As a soul a cappella trio, they have previously called themselves Equal Temperament, The Gems and even Natural High – the name used for their appearance in 1974 on UK TV talent show "Opportunity Knocks".

1985 The Christian brothers begin to concentrate on Priestman's material – songs that will become the core of the band's career. They play a live concert, The Liver Aid Ethiopian Famine benefit in Liverpool. Much time is spent in Priestman's 8-track studio, recording a demo tape of what will later become their first 3 UK singles.

1986 **Mar** A day before signing to independent label Demon, band is snapped up by Island Records on the strength of its demo. First recording efforts, with Clive Langer producing, are fruitless, but a later link-up with Laurie Latham suits both group and record company.

Sept *Forgotten Town*, *Hooverville* and *When The Fingers Point* are cut with Latham, but as the group embarks on a UK mini-tour Roger Christian becomes irritated by the attentions being focused on the more photogenic Garry, and also strongly objects to touring.

Nov Relations become strained and Priestman himself threatens to leave on 3 occasions if the family bickering continues.

1987 **Feb** Band makes its debut as a trio without Roger on UK Channel 4 TV's "Saturday Live."

Mar Debut single *Forgotten Town* reaches UK #22.

Apr They tour UK and complete work on their first album.

July *Hooverville (They Promised Us The World)* reaches UK #21.

Oct *When The Fingers Point* makes UK #34.

[31] *The Christians* debuts at UK #2, behind Fleetwood Mac's *Tango In The Night*, becoming Island's best-seller by a debuting group.

1988 **Jan** *Ideal World* reaches UK #14. Group undertakes an extensive European tour, establishing itself as a major UK act.

Mar *The Christians* peaks at US #158.

May *Born Again* is the fifth hit single to be extracted from the debut album, and reaches UK #25.

June Group opens for Fleetwood Mac on selected UK dates.

Oct A cover of Isley Brothers' classic *Harvest For The World* hits UK #8.

1989 **May** [20] *Ferry Cross The Mersey*, on which The Christians join with Paul McCartney, Gerry Marsden, Holly Johnson and Stock/Aitken/Waterman to aid the relatives of those who lost their lives in the Hillsborough soccer disaster, enters UK chart at #1.

Sept Roger Christian makes his solo chart debut at UK #63 with *Take It From Home*.

Dec [30] The Christians' *Words* reaches UK #18.

990 Jan *Colours* enters UK chart at #1.

Apr [7] *I Found Out* peaks at UK #56.

May [5] The Christians sing *Revolution* at the "John Lennon Tribute Concert" at the Pier Head Arena in Merseyside, to celebrate his songs.

Sept [22] *Greenbank Drive* peaks at UK #63.

LOU CHRISTIE

962 Oct Having won a State Scholarship at Moon Township high school, to study classical music and voice training, and sung on unsuccessful releases by The Classics (1960) and Lugee & The Lions (1961), Christie (b. Lugee Alfredo Giovanni Sacco, Feb.19, 1943, Glenwillard, PA) records his first solo *The Gypsy Cried*, highlighting his trademark falsetto, for CO&CE Records in Pittsburgh, PA. It is his first recorded composition with Twyla Herbert, a clairvoyant 15 years older than himself, with whom he has written since 1958.

963 Mar *The Gypsy Cried* is picked up by Roulette and climbs to US #24.

June Four Seasons-like *Two Faces Have I* is his first US Top 10 hit, at #6.

Aug *How Many Teardrops* peaks at US #46.

Sept *Lou Christie* climbs to US #124.

964 After touring the US with Dick Clark's "Caravan Of Stars" package, Christie is called up for US Army reserve duty and spends 6 months stationed at Fort Knox.

965 Out of the army, he signs a management deal with Bob Marcucci (former mentor of Fabian and Frankie Avalon), and a recording deal with MGM. Christie and Herbert write *Lightnin' Strikes*, which MGM hates but is pressured into releasing.

966 Feb *Lightnin' Strikes* tops US chart and becomes a million-seller.

Mar *Lightnin' Strikes* is Christie's UK chart debut, reaching #11. In US its success prompts labels owning earlier recordings to release them: *Big Time* on Colpix charts at only #95, while *Outside The Gates Of Heaven* on CO&CE reaches #45.

Apr Official follow-up to *Lightnin' Strikes* is similarly-arranged *Rhapsody In The Rain*, which is banned by many US radio stations for suggestive lyrics. Despite this, it climbs to US #16 and makes UK #37. *Lightnin' Strikes* peaks at US #103.

[16] He returns home to US during UK tour, missing 5 appearances. Promoter Mervyn Conn considers action for alleged breach of contract.

July *Painter* reaches US #81, but *Painter Of Hits* does not chart.

[1] Christie begins US tour in Honolulu, HI, with Herman's Hermits, The Animals and Jerry Lee Lewis.

967 May He moves to CBS/Columbia Records. *Shake Hands And Walk Away Cryin'* makes US #95.

969 Oct After 2 quiet years, Christie signs to Buddah Records for *I'm Gonna Make You Mine*, which provides a major chart comeback. It hits US #10 and UK #2. He tours UK for promotion and appears on BBC TV's "Top Of The Pops". (He will be resident in UK for some years during the 70s, having married an English girl, former beauty queen, Francesca Winfield. He also has highly successful Five Arts company, managing other acts and making TV ads.)

970 Jan *She Sold Me Magic*, his last UK hit, reaches US #25. *Are You Getting Any Sunshine?* peaks at US #74.

974 Mar Christie's last US hit at #80 is a revival of 30s standard *Beyond The Blue Horizon*, for independent Three Brothers label. (He will undertake unsuccessful recording spells with Midsong International, Lifesong, Elektra and Three Brothers and rely increasingly on oldies revival tours and club engagements for the remainder of his career.)

CLANNAD

Maire Ni Bhraonain (lead vocals, harp)
Pol O. Braonain (guitar, keyboards, vocals)
Ciaran O. Braonain (bass, synthesizers, vocals)
Noel O. Dugain (guitar, vocals)
Padraig O. Dugain (mandola, guitar, vocals)

976 The daughter and sons of Irish band leader Lee O. Braonain and their uncles form Clannad (Gaelic for "family") with the main intention of entering local Irish folk festivals.

979 Clannad sells out 5 nights at New York's Bottom Line, supported strongly by the local Irish community.

980 Sister Enya Ni Bhraonain joins the band on vocals and keyboards. (She will play on 2 Clannad albums and leave in 1982, before finding success

in 1988 as Enya with UK hit *Orinoco Flow*.)

1982 After 6 popular Irish tours and some local releases, Clannad is commissioned to score the music for "Harry's Game", an ITV drama series about the troubles in N.Ireland.

Nov [20] *Theme From Harry's Game*, released on RCA Records, hits UK #5. Its haunting melodic style attracts critical media praise.

1983 May [5] Group wins Best Theme From A Television Or Radio Production for *Theme From Harry's Game* at the annual Ivor Novello awards at the Grosvenor House, London. Debut UK album *Magical Ring* reaches UK #26, going gold after a 21-week run.

July [2] *New Grange* peaks at UK #65.

Sept Clannad sets off on a lengthy European tour.

1984 Jan Group begins work composing and recording everything for a 26-part ITV series "Robin Of Sherwood".

May Selected excerpts from the score are released on *Legend*, which reaches UK #15 during a 40-week chart stay. From it, the main theme *Robin (The Hooded Man)* makes UK #42.

June [2] *Magical Ring* is reissued and charts for 1-week at UK #91.

1985 Feb Clannad receives a British Academy Award for Best Soundtrack Of The Year for the "Robin Of Sherwood" project, the first Irish group to achieve this. Meanwhile U2 begins using *Theme From Harry's Game* to close every concert, giving Clannad's music worldwide exposure.

Mar Group spends 6 months recording new non-theme songs in Dublin, London and Switzerland.

Nov Resultant *Macalla* (Gaelic for echo) makes UK #33.

1986 Jan An uncredited duet from the album featuring U2's Bono and Maire, *In A Lifetime*, reaches UK #20. Clannad begins a 23-date sell-out UK tour.

Apr *Macalla* makes US #131.

1987 Feb Band, writing and recording a new album in Wales, aims for a more commercial outlook and enlists production help from Russ Kunkel and Greg Ladanyi, who in turn invite contributions from Bruce Hornsby, Steve Perry and J.D. Souther.

Nov *Sirius* peaks at UK #34.

1988 Feb Following a 2-year hiatus, Clannad begins a world tour, which will take in UK, Europe, Australia, US and Canada with all dates sold-out. It includes 7 sell-out concerts in native Dublin to celebrate the city's millennium.

Mar *Sirius* makes US #183, as group tours US.

July Clannad returns to Ireland to work in a studio on new 3-part BBC TV series, "The Atlantic Realm".

1989 Feb [1] *Atlantic Realm* makes UK #41.

May [6] Compilation album *Pastpresent*, the latest and most prominent of a number of retrospectives hits UK #5.

June Reissued *In A Lifetime* reaches UK #17.

1990 Oct [20] *Anam* debuts at its UK #14 peak. (Pol Braonain is no longer in the band.)

ERIC CLAPTON

1962 Educated at Ripley primary school and St. Bede's secondary modern, Clapton (b.Eric Patrick Clapp, Mar.30, 1945, Ripley, Surrey), is given his first guitar by his grandparents, Rose Clapp and her second husband Jack, who raised him after his parents separated. After 2 years of mild interest in blues, R&B and rock'n'roll, he learns guitar licks from the records of old blues masters like Blind Lemon Jefferson and Son House. While studying stained glass design at Kingston College of Art, he makes his first public performance as a busker. Later that year he works on a building site by day and plays with local amateur bands by night.

1963 Jan Clapton joins The Roosters, a London R&B band which includes Tom McGuinness (later of Manfred Mann and McGuinness Flint).

Aug Clapton and McGuinness leave to join Merseybeat-style band Casey Jones & The Engineers.

Oct Clapton is asked to replace lead guitarist "Top" Topham in R&B group The Yardbirds, who have just taken over The Rolling Stones' residency at the Crawdaddy club in Richmond, London. He becomes the group's focal point with his playing ability and his suitably sharp dressing. Group's manager, Giorgio Gomelsky, gives him the nickname "Slowhand".

Dec Group records live, backing Sonny Boy Williamson on UK tour.

1964 Feb Gomelsky takes demos to various labels. Decca turns them down, feeling it already has too many R&B bands. Group signs to EMI's Columbia label and cuts 3 songs at its first recording session.

[28] They play the first Rhythm & Blues Festival at Birmingham Town Hall, W. Midlands.

June Debut single, a revival of Billy Boy Arnold's *I Wish You Would*, fails to chart but gets exposure on TV and in the pop press.

Oct Despite a BBC ban, a revival of Don & Bob's R&B standard *Good Morning Little Schoolgirl* makes UK #44.

Dec Debut album, recorded live at the Marquee club in London, is *Five Little Yardbirds*.

[24] Band opens "Another Beatles Christmas Show" at the Hammersmith Odeon, London.

1965 Mar Opposing the group's shift from R&B to mainstream pop, Clapton leaves. (2 weeks later, The Yardbirds hit UK #3 with *For Your Love*.) John Mayall invites him to join his Bluesbreakers.

Aug After a brief spell with The Bluesbreakers, Clapton sets off in a large American car with a group of musicians known variously as The Glands and The Greek Loon Band. The intention is to play their way around the world, but at Athens some members have to return to UK. The remaining musicians step in for a Greek club band and the club owner tries to blackmail Clapton into staying. He is forced to flee minus his clothes and new Marshall amplifier.

Nov Clapton rejoins The Bluesbreakers. His first recording with the band, *I'm Your Witchdoctor* (produced by Yardbird Jimmy Page), is issued on Immediate label. Clapton earns his first session fee on Champion Jack Dupree's *From New Orleans To Chicago*. Producer Mike Vernon invites Clapton and Mayall to record for his Purdah label, resulting in *Lonely Years*, an authentic-sounding set of Chicago blues. Vernon is invited to produce The Bluesbreakers' eponymous album, which features Clapton's first recorded lead vocal on Robert Johnson's *Ramblin' On My Mind*.

1966 Clapton and fellow musicians Jack Bruce, Paul Jones, Peter York and Steve Winwood cut 3 tracks for Elektra Records as The Powerhouse. They are included on compilation *What's Shakin'*.

June Drummer Ginger Baker sits in on a Bluesbreakers' performance in Oxford and later suggests to Clapton that they form a group. Clapton proposes Bruce as bass player/singer. (Bruce had joined and left The Bluesbreakers to join Manfred Mann.) The 3 begin secret rehearsals, but UK music paper **Melody Maker** runs a speculative scoop.

July Clapton plays his last Bluesbreakers gig at the Marquee before Mayall fires him in favor of Peter Green, later of Fleetwood Mac. Meanwhile Clapton's new group, Cream, is already signed to Robert Stigwood's Reaction label. As the group's popularity soars, "Clapton Is God" graffiti appear on buildings in London.

Nov First UK Cream release is the atypical and low-key *Wrapping Paper* which peaks at #34.

1967 Jan *I Feel Free*, co-written by Bruce and Pete Brown, climbs to UK #11. Debut *Fresh Cream* hits UK #6 and sets the tone for the group's sound: blues/jazz solos and general instrumental fireworks, with a pop tinge.

Apr Cream tours US, where the music press has already built a strong following. Live shows feature considerable improvisation by all members as Clapton's lead guitar playing secures a growing cult following. Clapton guests on Frank Zappa And The Mothers Of Invention's *We're Only In It For The Money*.

June *Strange Brew* climbs to UK #17, and confirms Cream as a mainstream success. *Fresh Cream* debuts the band on US chart. It reaches US #39 during a 92-week chart run.

Oct Cream tours US, and the mainstream press (such as *Time* magazine) becomes interested in the band's spreading reputation.

Dec Cream's *Disraeli Gears* hits UK #5, and is their US breakthrough, hitting #4.

1968 Feb In spite of triumphant appearances in UK, US and Europe, rumors are rife that Cream plans to split. *Sunshine Of Your Love*, taken from *Disraeli Gears*, is Cream's first US chart single, reaching #36.

June *Anyone For Tennis*, an uncharacteristic Cream track used as theme for the film "The Savage Seven", reaches UK #40 and US #64.

July [10] Clapton announces that Cream will break up after a brief farewell tour in the fall.

[25] Clapton plays lead guitar on George Harrison's *While My Guitar Gently Weeps* on *The Beatles* (aka *The White Album*). He also plays on Harrison's solo album, *Wonderwall Music*.

Aug Cream double album *Wheels Of Fire*, combining a studio-recorded set and a live one from the Fillmore West in San Francisco, CA, tops US chart for 4 weeks. In UK the album is marketed both as a double, which hits #3, and as a single album with just studio recordings, hitting UK #7.

[31] In US, the album's success re-boosts sales of *Sunshine Of Your Love*, which now hits US #5, selling over a million.

Sept It is announced that Cream will split after a farewell US tour and some final UK dates.

Oct *Sunshine Of Your Love* is released in UK and reaches #25. The farewell US tour begins.

Nov [9] *White Room* hits US #6.

[25-26] 10,000 ecstatic fans attend the group's last 2 live shows, at London's Royal Albert Hall (supported by Yes and Taste), but thousands more miss out on tickets. The members explain that the band's music has gone as far as it can. Cream disbands.

Dec [10] Clapton takes part in The Rolling Stones TV show "Rock And Roll Circus", filmed in a London studio, with The Who, John Lennon and others. (The show is never transmitted.)

1969 Jan *White Room* reaches UK #28.

Feb Clapton and Baker, with Steve Winwood, form a new group, eventually named Blind Faith. First Cream album *Fresh Cream* is reissued in UK and hits #7.

Mar Cream's *Goodbye* tops UK chart and hits US #2.

May Rick Grech, bass player and violinist with Family, joins Blind Faith.

June [7] Blind Faith makes its debut in a free concert in London's Hyde Park before an audience of 36,000. When the group announces its first US tour, advance promotion bills it as "The Ultimate Supergroup".

July [12] US live debut at Madison Square Garden, New York, is start of sell-out US stadium tour which earns a fortune, yet convinces members that Blind Faith is musically unsatisfying, and that it will split when tour is over. Delaney & Bonnie open for Blind Faith on the tour.

Aug Group's first and only album, *Blind Faith*, is released amid controversy over a naked 11-year-old girl pictured on the sleeve.

Sept Blind Faith completes the US tour but Clapton has already lost interest, and carries on touring with Delaney & Bonnie.

[13] After rehearsing on the plane trip, Clapton appears with The Plastic Ono Band, at its debut at the "Toronto Rock'N'Roll Revival Show" in the Varsity Stadium at the University of Toronto, Canada, which is recorded for Lennon's *Live Peace In Toronto*. A few weeks later in UK, he plays on Lennon's *Cold Turkey*.

[20] *Blind Faith* tops both US and UK charts for 2 weeks. Clapton spends hours jamming with Blind Faith's US support act, Delaney & Bonnie. Cream's *The Best Of Cream* hits US #3.

Nov *The Best Of Cream* hits UK #6.

Dec Clapton appears with Lennon as part of the Plastic Ono Supergroup in a UNICEF benefit concert at the London Lyceum.

1970 Jan Blind Faith splits and Clapton joins (and helps finance) the "Delaney & Bonnie And Friends" US tour. As well as the Bramletts, tour band includes George Harrison, Rita Coolidge, Dave Mason, Bobby Keyes and others. A tour album, *Delaney And Bonnie On Tour*, is released on Atlantic.

Mar Clapton records his first solo album, *Eric Clapton*, in Los Angeles, CA, with members of the touring band and Leon Russell.

June He plays a charity concert for Dr. Benjamin Spock's civil liberties fund. His band, having fallen out with Delaney Bramlett and available to tour, is Carl Radle (bass), Bobby Whitlock (keyboards), Jim Gordon (drums) with Dave Mason of Traffic on guitar. Mason plays only 1 concert, but the others stay with Clapton to become Derek & The Dominoes. They set out on a summer club tour in UK. Band also plays on George Harrison's *All Things Must Pass*, with producer Phil Spector. (Although Clapton's role is uncredited. His own sessions for the year include work on Leon Russell's debut album, Vivian Stanshall and Neil Innes' *Labio-Dental Fricative* and as a member of an all-star band for gospel singer Doris Troy's Apple Records album.) Spector also cuts a Derek & The Dominoes single, *Tell The Truth*, which is withdrawn soon after release.

[15] Derek & The Dominoes debut at the Lyceum, London.

Aug Clapton heads for Miami, FL, to work on a new album.

[26] Derek & The Dominoes start recording at Criteria studios in Miami. Clapton invites Duane Allman to join its recording after seeing him play nearby with The Allman Brothers. A double album is finished in less than 10 days. After finishing, the band begins a US tour.

[29] *Eric Clapton* reaches US #13.

Sept *Eric Clapton* reaches UK #17, while *Live Cream* hits UK #4 and US #15.

Nov Derek & The Dominoes' *Layla And Other Assorted Love Songs* is released. Clapton refuses to have his name printed on the sleeve in an attempt to escape his guitar-hero image. It fails in UK, making US #16.

[5] Band record their network TV debut in Nashville on the "Johnny Cash Show".

Dec [12] Clapton's version of J.J. Cale's *After Midnight*, from his first album, reaches US #18.

1971 Apr Recordings begin on a second Derek & The Dominoes album in England, but are scrapped when band's personal problems, mainly with drugs, get in the way. Clapton retires to his Surrey home, his drug dependency worsening, and will stay a virtual recluse for the year, except to make occasional appearances, including at Harrison's "Bangladesh" concert at Madison Square Garden, New York.

Aug George Harrison persuades Clapton to play in his group for the "Concert For Bangladesh", which includes Leon Russell, Billy Preston, Ringo Starr, Klaus Voorman and others. (Later in the year Clapton plays some tour dates with The Dominoes and works on sessions for Harrison, Dr. John, a reunited Bluesbreakers and as part of the all-star band on Howlin' Wolf's *The London Sessions*.)

Dec He guests in Leon Russell's concert at London's Rainbow theater.

1972 Apr With Clapton inactive, compilation album *History Of Eric Clapton* hits US #6 during its 42-week chart run. It features his work with The Yardbirds, The Bluesbreakers, Cream, Blind Faith, Derek & The Dominoes and Delaney & Bonnie.

June Vault-searching Polydor Cream album *Live Cream Vol.2* reaches UK #15 and US #27.

Aug Derek & The Dominoes' *Layla*, written with Jim Gordon about George Harrison's wife Patti and inspired by Persian poet Nizami's **The Story Of Layla And Majnun**, hits UK #7 as *History Of Eric Clapton* peaks at UK #20.

Oct Polydor releases *Eric Clapton At His Best*, a collection of songs from albums *Eric Clapton* and *Layla*, which reaches US #87.

Dec [2] *Let It Rain*, written with Bonnie Bramlett, makes US #48.

1973 Jan [13] The Who's Pete Townshend gets Clapton back on a stage after his heroin addiction, organizing an all-star comeback concert for him at London's Rainbow theater. Townshend also recruits Ron Wood, Steve Winwood, Jim Capaldi and others. The concert is recorded and released as *Eric Clapton's Rainbow Concert*. Despite these efforts, Clapton retreats once again.

Feb Polydor's second retrospective album, *Clapton*, reaches US #67.

Mar RSO Records releases *Derek & The Dominoes In Concert* which reaches US #20 and UK #36.

[10] *Bell Bottom Blues* makes US #78.

Sept *Eric Clapton's Rainbow Concert* enters UK and US charts, reaching #19 and #18 respectively.

Nov Clapton begins electro-acupuncture treatment for his addiction. He follows 2 months' treatment with a period of convalescence on a friend's farm in Wales. Cream's *Heavy Cream* stalls at US #135.

1974 Apr When Clapton informs label boss Stigwood that he is ready to return, Stigwood throws a party at a Chinese restaurant in London's Soho district and invites producer Tom Dowd to oversee a forthcoming project. Clapton goes to Miami to record. He has only 2 songs in mind: Charles Scott Boyer's *Please Be With Me* and his own *Give Me Strength*. Band assembled is Radle, Jamie Oldaker (drums), Dick Sims (keyboards), George Terry (guitar) and Yvonne Elliman and Marcy Levy (vocals). (They will form the basic line-up for his next 4 albums.)

Aug [17] First product of the comeback sessions, a version of Bob Marley's *I Shot The Sheriff*, hits US #9.

[1] Clapton is joined on stage in Atlanta, GA, by Pete Townshend and Keith Moon, during which Townshend hits Clapton over the head with a plastic ukelele.

[17] *461 Ocean Boulevard*, named after the Miami studio address, tops the US chart for 4 weeks and hits UK #3.

Sept [14] *I Shot The Sheriff* tops US chart.

Dec [4] Clapton plays the Hammersmith Odeon, London.

[7] *Willie And The Hand Jive* makes US #26 as Clapton tours Japan.

1975 Apr [19] *There's One In Every Crowd* reaches UK #15 and US #21.

June [7] His interpretation of the spiritual *Swing Low Sweet Chariot* reaches UK #19. Clapton tours Australia and Hawaii before touring US.

Aug [30] A cover of Bob Dylan's *Knockin' On Heaven's Door* makes UK #38, as live album *E.C. Was Here* reaches UK #14. With Clapton still the reluctant guitar player, Terry handles most of the lead guitar work.

Oct [18] *E.C. Was Here* reaches US #20.

1976 July Clapton plays at the Crystal Palace Rock Festival, London, with Freddie King.

Sept [18] *No Reason To Cry*, with guest appearances from Dylan and The Band, hits UK #8.

Nov [13] *No Reason To Cry* reaches US #15.

[25] Clapton performs *Further On Up The Road* at The Band's "The Last Waltz" farewell concert on Thanksgiving Day. (Clapton's live band now includes South American percussionist Sergio Pastora. Session appearances include Joe Cocker's *Stingray*, Stephen Bishop's *Careless* and Ringo Starr's *Rotogravure*.)

Dec [11] *Hello Old Friend* reaches US #24.

1977 Feb RSO reissues Cream albums *Disraeli Gears* and *Wheels Of Fire* which make US #165 and #195 respectively.

Apr [28] Current dates include London's Hammersmith Odeon.

June Pastora leaves the group to return to South America.

Aug [5] Clapton and the band play Ibiza bullring.

Dec [3] *Slowhand* reaches UK #23. (During the year Clapton also contributes to Ronnie Lane and Pete Townshend's *Rough Mix* and Roger Daltrey's *One Of The Boys*.)

1978 Jan [21] *Lay Down Sally* makes UK #39.

Apr [1] *Lay Down Sally* hits US #3 as *Slowhand* hits US #2 behind *Saturday Night Fever*.

July [15] Clapton's ballad *Wonderful Tonight*, written for his wife Patti, reaches US #16.

Nov Clapton embarks on a 2-month European tour with Radle, Oldaker and Sims.

[18] *Promises* makes UK #37.

Dec [9] *Backless* reaches UK #18.

1979 Jan [13] *Backless* hits US #8.

[20] *Promises* hits US #9.

Mar Clapton begins a world tour with an all-new UK band, featuring Albert Lee (guitar), Chris Stainton (keyboards), Dave Markee (bass) and Henry Spinetti (drums). In Japan, a live album is recorded at the Budokan. *Watch Out For Lucy*, original B-side of *Promises*, makes US #40.

1980 May [2] Clapton begins 13-date UK tour at the New Theatre, Oxford, Oxon. The tour, featuring Clapton's 1979 band with new recruit Gary Brooker, formerly with Procol Harum, on keyboards and vocals, will end on May 18 at the Civic Hall, Guildford, Surrey.

[17] Live Budokan album, *Just One Night* hits UK #3.

[30] Radle dies.

June [21] *Just One Night* hits US #2, where it stays for 6 weeks.

Aug [16] *Tulsa Time*, backed with J.J. Cale's *Cocaine* reaches US #30.

Nov [22] *Blues Power* reaches US #76.

1981 Mar [7] *Another Ticket* reaches UK #18.

[14] Clapton goes into hospital in St.Paul, MN, with bleeding ulcers. A 60-date US tour has to be cancelled.

Apr [22] Clapton is hospitalized with injuries from a car-accident.

May [2] *I Can't Stand It* hits US #10, as parent album *Another Ticket* hits US #7.

Clapton contributes to Phil Collins' debut album, beginning a long-running cooperative arrangement between them.

June [20] *Another Ticket* reaches US #78.

Sept Clapton leaves RSO to set up his own WEA-distributed label, Duck Records. He plays a set with Jeff Beck at "The Secret Policeman's Other Ball" in London, in aid of Amnesty International. (The 2 will be featured on the concert album.)

1982 Apr [3] Reissued *Layla*, now established as a rock classic, hits UK #4.

May [1] A history of Clapton's solo career, *Time Pieces – The Best Of Eric Clapton* reaches UK #20.

June [12] *Time Pieces* makes US #101, as *I Shot The Sheriff* re-enters UK chart at #64.

1983 Feb *Money And Cigarettes* makes US #16 and UK #13.

Mar [17] Clapton joins Carmine Appice, Jeff Beck, Andy Fairweather-Low, Ronnie Lane, Jimmy Page and Bill Wyman at the second Prince's Trust Rock Gala at the Royal Albert Hall, London, to benefit the ARMS (Action for Research into Multiple Sclerosis) charity.

[26] Clapton's first Duck Records release, *I've Got A Rock'N'Roll Heart*, reaches US #18.

Apr [23] *The Shape You're In* peaks at UK #75.

Sept [20] Clapton participates in the Ronnie Lane Benefit Concert for ARMS charity, at the Royal Albert Hall, London.

Dec [8] Clapton joins Jeff Beck, Jimmy Page, Ry Cooder and others to play a third ARMS benefit, at Madison Square Garden.

Clapton is awarded the Silver Clef by the Nordoff-Robbins Music Therapy Centre.

1984 June Compilation album *Backtrackin'* reaches UK #29.

July Clapton joins Dylan on stage at Wembley Arena , London.

1985 Mar [23] *Behind The Sun* debuts at UK #8.

[16] *Forever Man* peaks at UK #51.

Apr [26] *Forever Man* reaches US #26.

May [25] *Behind The Sun* makes US #34.

July [6] *See What Love Can Do* climbs to US #89.

Sept During his current world tour, Clapton leaves his wife of 6 years for a young photographer and TV actress, Lori Del Santo, whom he meets at a party in Italy. She will give birth to Clapton's son, Conor.

Oct [21] Clapton, and friends George Harrison, Dave Edmunds and others, join Carl Perkins for a Channel 4 TV special at Limehouse studios, London.

1986 Jan Clapton and Michael Kamen write the score for BBC TV nuclear thriller "Edge Of Darkness". The theme peaks at UK #65.

Apr Clapton makes a cameo appearance in Michael Caine-starring film "Water".

June [20] Clapton takes part in the fourth annual Prince's Trust Rock Gala concert, with Phil Collins, Elton John, Paul McCartney, George Michael, Rod Stewart, Tina Turner and others, at Wembley Arena.

Oct [16] Clapton joins Keith Richards, Linda Ronstadt, Etta James, Julian Lennon and others, on stage at the Fox theater in St. Louis, MO, for Chuck Berry's 60th birthday concert performance, featured in Taylor Hackford's documentary film "Hail! Hail! Rock'N'Roll".

Dec *August*, produced by, and featuring, Phil Collins, hits UK #3.

1987 Clapton receives a special award at BPI annual ceremony in London.

Feb Yellow Magic Orchestra original *Behind The Mask*, co-written by Greg Phillinganes, who joins Clapton's band, makes UK #15.

Mar *August* makes US #37. He again teams with Kamen to write the score for Mel Gibson movie "Lethal Weapon".

Apr [27] Clapton plays a sell-out night at Madison Square Garden, part of a 1-month US tour.

June [5-6] Clapton takes part in the fifth annual Prince's Trust Rock Gala concert, with George Harrison, Elton John, Ben E. King, Ringo Starr and others, at Wembley Arena.

July Clapton and Tina Turner's *Tearing Us Apart* peaks at UK #56.

Sept *The Cream Of Eric Clapton* begins a 79-week UK chart run, hitting UK #3.

Nov Clapton embarks on a tour of Japan.

1988 Apr A 4-CD boxed set *Crossroads*, a major career retrospective, fails to chart in UK, but makes US #34.

May [14] *Crossroads* tops US CD chart.

June Clapton's wife Patti files for divorce, ending their 9-year union.

[5-6] Clapton takes part in the sixth annual Prince's Trust Rock Gala concert, with The Bee Gees, Leonard Cohen, Peter Gabriel and others, at the Royal Albert Hall, an event which will raise over £3 million. He is backed by Elton John and Mark Knopfler on his performance of *Cocaine*.

[11] Clapton joins Dire Straits on stage at "Nelson Mandela's 70th Birthday Party" concert at Wembley Stadium, London.

July He completes the soundtrack for new Mickey Rourke movie "Homeboy".

Sept Enlisting Knopfler again, Clapton embarks on major US dates backed by Buckwheat Zydeco.

1989 Feb He completes work with Michael Kamen on the soundtrack for Mel Gibson-starring sequel "Lethal Weapon 2".

May [31] Clapton attends the first International Rock Awards held in Lexington Avenue Armory, New York. He is awarded an "Elvis" as Best Guitarist.

Aug [1] Clapton finishes a world tour with a free concert for the King's Trust, before more than 100,000 fans in Mozambique, Africa.

Oct Clapton joins The Rolling Stones on stage at Shea Stadium, New York, playing lead guitar on *Little Red Rooster*.

Nov *Journeyman* hits UK #3 and reaches US #16.

Dec [12] *Pretending* peaks at US #72.

1990 Jan [18] Clapton begins an 18-night stand at the Royal Albert Hall, with 4 different programs, 3 different bands, Robert Cray & Buddy Guy and a 60-piece orchestra. The stand will end on Feb.18.

Feb [17] *Bad Love*, written with Foreigner's Mick Jones, reaches UK #25 as *Journeyman* hits UK #2, behind Phil Collins' *But Seriously*.

Mar "The Cream Of Eric Clapton" video collection is issued in US.

[8] Clapton wins Best Guitarist in **Rolling Stone**'s 1989 Readers Poll.

[10] *Bad Love* debuts at US #88.

[28] Clapton begins first leg of 56-date US tour in Atlanta, GA (set to end on May 5 at the Shoreline Amphitheater, San Francisco, CA), with band comprising Phil Palmer (guitar), Steve Ferrone (drums), Alan Clark and Greg Phillinganes (keyboards), Nathan East (bass), Ray Cooper (percussion), Tessa Niles and Katie Kissoon (backing vocals).

Apr [21] *No Alibis* peaks at UK #53.

June [6] Clapton is named Living Legend Of The Year at the second International Rock Awards in New York. After the ceremonies, he performs *Sweet Home Chicago* as part of an all-star band, comprising Billy Joel and Steve Tyler.

[30] Clapton joins Phil Collins and Genesis, Pink Floyd, Robert Plant, Paul McCartney, Cliff Richard and The Shadows, Status Quo, Elton John, Mark Knopfler and Tears For Fears, all previous Silver Clef winners, on a star-studded bill at Knebworth Park, Herts., in aid of Nordoff-Robbins Music Therapy Centre.

July [23] Clapton begins second leg of US tour at the Arena, Miami. The tour will end at the Coast Coliseum, Biloxi, MS, on Sept.2.

Aug [27] 3 members of Clapton's entourage (tour manager Colin Smythe, bodyguard Nigel Browne and agent Bobby Brooks) are killed in a helicopter crash near Troy, WI, following a concert at the Alpine Valley Music theater by Clapton, Robert Cray and Stevie Ray Vaughan, who also dies.

Dec [22] Clapton wins Top Album Rock Tracks Artists in **Billboard**'s The Year In Music statistical round-up.

1991 Feb [5] Clapton begins a 24-date stand at the Royal Albert Hall. Now divided into 5 segments, Clapton plays with a 4-piece band comprising Phillinganes, East and Phil Collins, a second 4-piece band, with Steve Ferrone taking Collins' place, a 9-piece band, a blues band with guitarists Albert Collins, Robert Cray, Buddy Guy and Jimmie Vaughan and a 9-piece band with orchestra conducted by Michael Kamen. The series will end on Mar.9.

[20] Clapton wins Best Rock Vocal Performance, Male for *Bad Love* at the 33rd annual Grammy awards at Radio City Music Hall, New York. (It is his second Grammy, having won his first as part of *The Concert For Bangla Desh* Album Of The Year in 1972.)

Mar [20] Clapton is devastated by the death of his 4-year-old-son Conor, who has walked out of an open window and plunged 700' from the 53rd floor apartment, Manhattan, New York, where his mother Lori Del Santo has been staying. Clapton, who has only been in New York for 24 hours staying in a nearby hotel, is taken to hospital severely traumatized.

[26] He issues a statement asking those who wish to express sympathy over the tragedy to make a donation to the Great Ormond Street, London, children's hospital.

THE DAVE CLARK FIVE

Mike Smith (vocals, keyboards)
Dave Clark (drums)
Lenny Davidson (guitar)
Denis Payton (saxophone)
Rick Huxley (guitar)

1958 Clark (b. Dec.15, 1942, Tottenham, London) and bassist Chris Walls advertise in **Melody Maker** for musicians to form a band. They are joined by Huxley (b. Aug.5, 1942, Dartford, Kent) on rhythm guitar, Stan Saxon as singer and sax player and Mick Ryan on lead guitar. The Dave Clark Five featuring Stan Saxon makes its debut at South Grove youth club, Tottenham.

1961 After several personnel changes and experience gained on the live circuit, the band, still semi-professional, signs a long-term contract with the Mecca ballroom chain. Line-up is Clark, a film stuntman, on drums, Huxley, a lighting engineer, switched to bass, Davidson (b. May 30, 1944, Enfield, London), a progress clerk, on guitar and backing vocals and Payton (b. Aug.11, 1943, Walthamstow, London), an electrical engineer, replacing tenor saxophonist Jim Spencer. New focal point of the group is Smith (b. Dec.12, 1943, Edmonton, London), a classically-trained pianist, who has been in The Impalas with Davidson and takes over vocals permanently when Saxon fails to turn up for a gig, having stood-in before when Saxon's voice has given way.

1962 Jan Band makes its live debut at South Grove youth club, Tottenham, where the group was formed.

Clark, who controls the group's recordings, sells the master of *Chaquita*, an instrumental modelled on The Champs' *Tequila*, to Ember Records.

June Pye Records signs the group to its Piccadilly label and releases first vocal record, *I Knew It All The Time*. The disk is released on Congress label in US. *Chaquita*, credited to The Dave Clarke Five, is issued on Ember 8 weeks later.

Dec The Piccadilly deal is wound up with release of *First Love*, another instrumental, which again fails to chart.

1963 Jan Band is playing its home venue, the Tottenham Royal, when an A&R man from EMI's Columbia label sees and later signs it.

Mar A rock version of nursery rhyme *The Mulberry Bush* is the group's Columbia debut, but fails to chart.

Oct Band covers The Contours' *Do You Love Me*, which (helped by a publicity stunt involving the Duke of Edinburgh's supposed criticism of the lyrics) makes UK #30. Brian Poole & The Tremeloes' simultaneous version tops UK chart.

Dec Group wins the Mecca Gold Cup as the ballroom circuit's best band of 1963.

1964 Jan [12] They complete their residency at Basildon's Locarno, Essex, where they have played for the last year. They then play a few nights a week at the Tottenham Royal before going professional in Mar.

[18] *Glad All Over*, written by Smith and Clark (as will be most of the group's major hits) tops UK chart, replacing The Beatles' *I Want To Hold*

Your Hand and prompting "London Topples Liverpool"-type stories in UK tabloid press. Its eventual UK sales are over 870,000. 4-track EP *The Dave Clark Five*, featuring *Do You Love Me*, makes UK #28.

[25-26] ABC Pathé films them in action at the Tottenham Royal for a 7-min. perfect pictorial at a weekend.

Feb [9] They top bill on ITV's "Sunday Night At The London Palladium".

TV appearances include "Thank Your Lucky Stars" (Feb.15), "Scene At 6:30" (Feb.20), "Ready Steady Go!" (Feb.21) and "Top Of The Pops" (Feb.19/26).

Mar *Bits And Pieces* hits UK #2, selling 590,000 copies in UK. It is banned by many ballroom managers who fear damage to wooden dancefloors since its "stomping" break encourages dancers to stamp their feet in time with it.

[7] Band makes its radio debut on BBC's Light Programme "Saturday Club", joining The Crystals and Adam Faith.

[14] Group turns professional and signs to the Harold Davidson Organization in a deal which guarantees it £50,000 a year for live performances. First professional engagement is a week at Liverpool Empire, Merseyside.

[29] They begin a 6-week UK tour, with The Hollies, The Kinks, The Mojos and Mark Wynter, at the Coventry theater. Tour will end at the Granada theater, Tooting, London, on May 13.

Apr [25] *Glad All Over* hits US #6.

[26] Group appears in the **New Musical Express** Poll Winners concert at the Empire Pool, Wembley, London, with The Beatles and others.

May *A Session With The Dave Clark Five* hits UK #3.

[2] *Bits And Pieces* hits US #4 and *Glad All Over* (first of a long series of US albums unissued in UK) hits US #3.

[30] Group plays New York's Carnegie Hall.

[31] Band appears on CBS TV's "Ed Sullivan Show". (Group's first US tour is a huge success, but Huxley suffers facial injuries when the Five are mobbed by fans in Washington, DC. Over the next 3 years, the Five will visit US constantly, maintaining a high chart profile by ready availability for live and TV work.

June *Can't You See That She's Mine* hits UK #10.

[6] *Do You Love Me* reaches US #11. *I Knew It All The Time* on Congress Records (licensed from UK Piccadilly 2 years earlier) peaks at US #53.

[15] Group performs at Croydon's Fairfield Hall with The Applejack and The Mojos.

[18] Group begins 3-week tour of Australia and New Zealand.

[20] Dave Clark Five summer season begins at the Blackpool Winter Gardens, Lancs.

June Plane with the group as passengers is involved in a runway collision at San Francisco airport, CA.

July [18] *Can't You See That She's Mine* hits US #4 and *The Dave Clark Five Return!* hits US #5.

Aug *Thinking Of You Baby*, featured in MGM film "Get Yourself A College Girl" in which they co-star with The Animals, reaches UK #26.

Sept [12] *Because*, the group's first ballad written by Clark and Smith, hits US #3.

Oct *American Tour* reaches US #11.

Nov *Any Way You Want It* reaches UK #25.

[7] *Everybody Knows* makes US #15.

1965 Jan [9] *Any Way You Want It* reaches US #14. *Everybody Knows* makes US #37.

[18] Band embarks on an Australian tour.

Feb *Coast To Coast* hits US #6.

[8] Group begins filming its first feature film, directed by John Boorman from a Peter Nichols screenplay, on location in London and the West of England.

Mar A revival of Chuck Berry's *Reelin' And Rockin'* peaks at UK #24.

[20] Ballad *Come Home* makes US #14.

May [22] Australasian tour starts, set to end June 12. *Reelin' And Rockin'* reaches US #23 and *Weekend In London* makes US #24.

June *Come Home* reaches US #16.

[18] Band appears at New York's Academy of Music, the beginning of a 6-week US tour.

July [8] "Catch Us If You Can" premieres at the Rialto cinema in London's West End.

[17] Group guests on 200th edition of ITV's "Thank Your Lucky Stars".

Aug *Catch Us If You Can* hits UK #5 as soundtrack album *Catch Us If You Can* hits UK #8.

[7] A revival of Chris Kenner's *I Like It Like That* hits US #7. Smith suffers 2 broken ribs when he is pulled off stage by fans at a show in Chicago, IL, on the first day of a further US trek.

Sept "Catch Us If You Can" is released in US as "Having A Wild Weekend".

[25] *Catch Us If You Can* hits US #4. Soundtrack album *Having A Wild Weekend* reaches US #15.

Oct Group appears on ABC TV's "Shindig!" performing *Having A Wild Weekend*.

Nov [8] Band appears at the Royal Variety Performance in London, in the presence of the Queen and Prince Philip, performing a version of Jim Reeves' *Welcome To My World*.

A remake of Bobby Day's *Over And Over* makes UK #45.

Dec [25] *Over And Over* hits US #1 and is a million-seller. (It will be the group's only US chart-topper.)

1966 Jan *I Like It Like That* reaches US #32.

Mar [12] *At The Scene*, unreleased in UK, reaches US #18.

Apr Compilation *The Dave Clark Five's Greatest Hits* hits US #9. "The Swingin' Set", in which the Five feature with Nancy Sinatra and The Animals, opens in London's West End as B-feature to Elvis Presley's "Frankie & Johnny".

May [7] R&B-flavored *Try Too Hard* climbs to US #12.

[16-17] Band films guest spot for "Lucy Looks At London" TV special.

[21] *Look Before You Leap* makes UK #50.

June [12] Group makes its 12th appearance on CBS TV's "Ed Sullivan Show" – a record for any UK act.

July [9] *Please Tell Me Why* reaches US #28 and *Try Too Hard* US #77.

Sept [3] *Satisfied With You* makes US #50.

Oct *Satisfied With You* climbs to US #127.

Nov [19] *Nineteen Days* makes US #48.

Dec Compilation album *The Dave Clark Five: More Greatest Hits* peaks at US #103.

1967 Jan Group forms its own film company, Big Five Films, to make "low-budget features and documentaries". (The first documentary, "Hold On – It's The Dave Clark Five", a profile of the group itself, will be sold to US TV.)

Feb [11] *I've Got To Have A Reason* makes US #44.

Apr *5 By 5* reaches US #119. A revival of Marv Johnson's *You Got What It Takes* makes UK #28.

May [13] *You Got What It Takes* hits US #7.

June [16] Group begins US tour in Boston, MA. It will end in New Jersey on July 23.

July [1] A rocked-up revival of oldie *You Must Have Been A Beautiful Baby* reaches US #35.

Aug [26] *A Little Bit Now* peaks at US #67 and *You Got What It Takes* reaches US #149. (The Five's last album to chart in US.)

Nov [25] *Red And Blue* reaches US #89.

Dec *Everybody Knows* (not the Five's 1964 hit but a ballad written by Les Reed and Barry Mason, with Lenny Davidson on lead vocal) hits UK #2 behind The Beatles' *Hello Goodbye*.

1968 Jan [20] *Everybody Knows* peaks at US #43, their final US chart entry.

Mar Ballad *No One Can Break A Heart Like You* makes UK #28.

Oct A cover of Raymond Froggatt's *Red Balloon* hits UK #7.

Dec The football chant-styled *Live In The Sky* peaks at UK #39.

1969 Nov Now retired from major touring, the group begins a series of successful oldie revivals with Jackie DeShannon's *Put A Little Love In Your Heart*, which makes UK #31.

1970 Jan Medley *Good Old Rock'N'Roll*, a cover of US hit by Cat Mother & The All-Night Newsboys (and featuring rock oldies like *Long Tall Sally*, *Lucille* and *Blue Suede Shoes*) hits UK #7.

Apr *Everybody Get Together*, a cover of The Youngbloods' US hit *Get Together*, hits UK #8.

July Another revival, Jerry Keller's *Here Comes Summer*, makes UK #44.

Aug Group announces its break-up. Clark and Smith continue until 1973, to complete a 10-year contract with EMI, though Clark has already begun an acting course at Central School of Speech and Drama.

Nov *More Good Old Rock'N'Roll*, a medley made by Clark and Smith on the lines of the earlier hit, reaches UK #34 and is the group's final UK chart single.

1971 *Southern Man* and *Won't You Be My Lady* are released, without success. (Clark and Smith will release singles under the name Dave Clark & Friends until 1973 – mostly covers of US hits like Tommy James' *Draggin' The Line* and The Stampeders' *Sweet City Woman*. None will chart. Smith will collaborate with ex-Manfred Mann Mike D'Abo, releasing an eponymous album in 1975 which they will promote on tour as support to Sailor, before moving to sessions (he sings on the original *Evita* album), commercial jingle writing and promotion. Clark will concentrate on business activities, including music publishing and showbiz involvement with proteges like John Christie. Davidson will move to antique dealing, Payton to real estate and Huxley to musical equipment retailing.)

1978 **Apr** [1] *25 Thumping Great Hits*, compiled by Clark from original group recordings (all of which have remained his property) and licensed to Polydor, hits UK #7.

1985 **June** Several compilation editions of 60s program "Ready Steady Go!" are shown on Channel 4 TV, leased by Clark who purchased the tapes and rights to the series following its demise. The new compilations are by Clark and frequently feature his former group (including some US concert footage not from the programs).

Aug [24] Smith makes UK #82 with *Medley*, featuring a newly recorded version of snippets of classic group hits, on Proto.

1986 **Apr** [9] The musical "Time", devised, co-written and produced by Clark, premieres at the Dominion theater in London with Cliff Richard in the leading role. (It will have a long and moderately successful run and David Cassidy will take over the lead.)

May *Dave Clark's Time – The Album*, an all-star package of songs from the musical, reaches UK #21. It features Cliff Richard, Freddie Mercury, Dionne Warwick, Leo Sayer, Ashford And Simpson and Stevie Wonder. Most of the material is new but *Because*, sung on the album by Julian Lennon, is a revival of The Dave Clark Five's 1964 hit.

1990 **Nov** Mooncrest releases Smith's *It's Only Rock'N'Roll*.

Dec [24] Dave Clark, through his company Right Time Production, takes out double page ads in the world's media press thanking those who helped him win a major court action against Rank Theatres Limited, claiming that Rank "had failed to run an efficient box office at the Dominion theater, London, being responsible for the premature closure of the "Time" musical and loss of box office revenue."

PETULA CLARK

1942 Encouraged by her father into a showbiz career (her first "paid" job is for a bag of candy from the management of Bentalls department store in Kingston-upon-Thames, Surrey, when she sings with the resident band in the store's entrance while shopping), Clark (b. Nov.15, 1932, Epsom, Surrey) is launched into wartime entertainment in UK as a child performer, finding radio stardom on "It's All Yours" at the Criterion theater and playing over 150 shows in her first 2 years on the stage, and on "Variety Band Box" and "The Children's Hour". (Nicknamed "The Forces Girl", she performs 500 shows for the troops.)

1943 She signs with the Rank organization, and makes "Murder In Reverse", the first of more than 2 dozen films over the next decade. (Her films through her teens and into the mid-50s, will include "Vice Versa", "The Card", "London Town", "I Know Where I'm Going", "White Corridors", "Romantic Age", "Drawn Daggers".)

1946 **July** [17] "Cabaret" airs for the first time on BBC TV. The show will run until Nov.2. (She will also be a regular on BBC radio, appearing in programs "Cabin In The Cotton", "Calling All Forces" and "Guest Night".)

1949 Her first record, *Put Your Shoes On Lucy*, is released on EMI's Columbia label.

1950 She signs to the newly-formed Polygon label on the recommendation of its musical director Alan Freeman (and will stay with the label until 1971, seeing it change name to Nixa and then Pye Records in the 50s). *You Are My True Love* is released.

Nov [24] "Pet's Parlour" airs for the first time on BBC TV. (The show will run until July 24, 1953.)

She wins an award as Most Outstanding Artist On UK TV, partly for her popular Sunday afternoon show "Pet's Parlour".

1952 **Dec** Seasonal children's novelty *Where Did My Snowman Go?* just misses the published UK Top 12.

1954 **July** Another children's song, *The Little Shoemaker* (recorded while she is still partly in shock following a car accident on the way to the studio) hits UK #7.

1955 **Feb** *Majorca* reaches UK #12.

Sept [30] "Pet's Parade" airs for the first time on BBC TV. The show will run until Feb.14, 1957.

Dec Her version of much-covered ballad *Suddenly There's A Valley*, her first single on Nixa, hits UK #7.

1957 Clark ends her management relationship with her father, and moves out of the family home into an apartment in Stratton Court in London's West End.

Sept Clark's cover of Jodi Sands' US hit *With All My Heart*, hits UK #4.

Dec Her cover of *Alone* hits UK #8, ahead of The Shepherd Sisters' original US version at UK #14 and The Southlanders' at UK #17.

1958 **Mar** *Baby Lover* makes UK #12 (her last UK success for 3 years).

Nov Clark gives her first French-language show at the Alhambra theater, Paris, France, after Leon Cabat, president of the Vogue label, France's Nixa counterpart, unhappy that Clark's UK hits are being covered in France by Dalida, encourages her to sing French language versions. She also appears on French radio show "Musicarama".

1959 In Paris for a Pye recording (initially phonetic, as she does not speak the language), she meets Vogue promotion man Claude Wolff, and they become romantically attached. She signs to Vogue.

1961 **Feb** [27] *Sailor*, Norman Newell's English adaptation of Lolita's German hit *Seeman*, hits UK #1 for a week despite a competing Top 10 version by Anne Shelton.

Apr *Something Missing* makes UK #44.

June [8] Clark marries Wolff in Paris.

Aug *Romeo*, a remake of the 1925 hit *Salome*, hits UK #3. It is a huge hit in Europe and tops a million sales internationally.

Dec *My Friend The Sea* hits UK #7.

[11] Clark gives birth to daughter, Barbara.

1962 **Feb** *I'm Counting On You* makes UK #41.

July *Ya Ya Twist*, a rocking adaptation of Lee Dorsey's US R&B hit, sung in French and intended for the European market, reaches UK #14. Another period without major UK hits follows but *Monsieur* and *Chariot*, sung in French, and *Casanova*, in German, are all European million-sellers. (English version of *Chariot*, *I Will Follow Him* is a hit for Little Peggy March. *Monsieur* wins the Grand Prix Du Disque, France's equivalent of the Grammy.)

Freeman takes an executive role at Pye, leaving Tony Hatch to take over as Clark's producer.

[29] Clark guests on ITV's "Thank Your Lucky Stars" with Cliff Richard, The Shadows, Helen Shapiro, Frank Ifield, Karl Denver, Craig Douglas, and Ronnie Carroll.

1963 **May** *Casanova/Chariot*, a UK double A-side featuring the original foreign language versions, makes UK #39.

1964 **Jan** [12] Clark returns to UK to record a segment for ITV's "Big Night Out", followed by a BBC TV taping of "Language Of Love" with Amanda Barrie and Richard Briers, due to air on Feb.13. Further TV appearances during the next few months will include ITV's "Ready Steady Go!" with The Rolling Stones on Apr.24 and BBC TV's "A Swinging Time" on June 11.

Dec Tony Hatch, who has been producing French sessions for Clark, interests her in his song *Downtown*, originally written with The Drifters in mind. Completed in only its second studio take, it hits UK #2 behind The Beatles' *I Feel Fine*. (Warner Bros. A&R executive Joe Smith on vacation in London, hears the song and signs Clark to the label in US.)

[14] Clark returns to London, not least to record ITV's "Ready Steady Go!", airing on Dec.18, a BBC TV "Top Of The Pops" appearance and a cameo in new ITV series "The Ladybirds" on Dec.31.

[27] While in London, Clark guests on ITV's "Sunday Night At The London Palladium".

1965 **Jan** [23] *I Feel Fine* fails to hold off *Downtown* in US, where it hits #1 for 2 weeks and sells over a million. She becomes the first UK female to top the US charts since Vera Lynn in 1952.

Mar *Downtown* reaches US #21.

[14] On her first visit to the US, Clark sings *Downtown* and *I Know A Place* on CBS TV's "Ed Sullivan Show".

Apr *I Know A Place* makes UK #17.

[13] Clark wins Best Rock And Roll Recording Of 1964 for *Downtown* at the 7th annual Grammy awards.

May [1] *I Know A Place* hits US #3 and Clark becomes the only female vocalist to chart her first 2 singles in the US Top 3. (This achievement will stand until Cyndi Lauper repeats the feat in 1984.)

[16] Clark appears on CBS TV's "Ed Sullivan Show".

June *I Know A Place* peaks at US #42, coinciding with her first North American tour dates.

Aug *You'd Better Come Home* makes UK #44.

[21] *You'd Better Come Home* makes US #22.

Oct *Round Every Corner* makes UK #43, while Clark again guests on CBS TV's "Ed Sullivan Show".

Nov Clark co-penned *You're The One* makes UK #23 but is not released as a single in US. (The Vogues' cover of it makes US #4.) *Petula Clark Sings The World's Greatest International Hits* makes US #129. Clark is offered the chance to co-star with Elvis Presley in "Paradise Hawaiian Style", but declines.

[13] *Round Every Corner* reaches US #21.

[15] She begins a season at Manhattan club Copacabana in New York.

Dec Clark films a segment for the "TNT Award Show", alongside Joan Baez, Bo Diddley, Ray Charles, Lovin' Spoonful, The Ronettes, Ike &

Tina Turner, Roger Miller, The Byrds and Donovan.

966 **Feb** [5] *My Love*, recorded in New York in Nov. during her engagement at the Copa, a track Clark dislikes and tries not to have released, tops the US chart for 2 weeks and is her second US million-seller. (Clark becomes the first UK female singer to have 2 US #1s.) It hits UK #4.

Mar [15] Clark wins Best Contemporary (Rock'N'Roll) Vocal Performance, Female for *I Know A Place* at the 8th annual Grammy awards.

Apr [23] *A Sign Of The Times* makes UK #49 and US #11.

May *My Love* reaches US #68.

June [6] Clark opens in cabaret at the Savoy hotel, London.

[16] 6-week BBC TV series "This Is Petula Clark" airs for the first time.

July *I Couldn't Live Without Your Love* (the first co-credited Hatch/Trent song) hits UK #6, as album of same title makes UK #11.

Aug *I Couldn't Live Without Your Love* hits US #9.

Oct *I Couldn't Live Without Your Love* makes US #43.

[9] Clark appears live on CBS TV's "Ed Sullivan Show".

[13] She opens at the Copacabana, New York, for 2-week residency.

Nov Clark makes her Las Vegas, NV, cabaret debut with Woody Allen.

[26] *Who Am I* reaches US #21.

967 **Jan** [21] *Color My World* reaches US #16.

Feb [18] Clark's version of Charlie Chaplin-penned *This Is My Song*, recorded in Reno, NV, (from his movie "Countess From Hong Kong" starring Sophia Loren) tops the UK chart for 2 weeks, selling over 500,000 copies, and beating a rival version by Harry Secombe which hits #2. Clark's recording is produced by Claude Wolff with Ernie Freeman arranging. She premieres the song before release on "The Hollywood Palace". Compilation album *Petula Clark's Hit Parade* reaches UK #18 and *Colour My World* hits UK #16.

Mar *Color My World/Who Am I* makes US #49.

[3] Clark appears at the London Palladium in the presence of Princess Margaret.

Apr *This Is My Song* hits US #3.

[28] She performs before President Johnson as a star cabaret guest at the annual White House Press Correspondents' dinner.

July *Don't Sleep In The Subway*, a song created by Tony Hatch from unfinished segments of 3 others, reaches UK #12 and hits US #5.

Sept [30] *The Cat In The Window (The Bird In The Sky)*, written by Gary Bonner and Alan Gordon, reaches US #26.

Oct *These Are My Songs*, produced by Sonny Burke, reaches UK #38 and US #27.

968 **Jan** *The Other Man's Grass (Is Always Greener)* charts at #20 in UK and #31 in US.

Mar [6] *Kiss Me Goodbye*, penned by Les Reed and Barry Mason, makes UK #50.

Apr *The Other Man's Grass Is Always Greener* reaches UK #37 and US #93.

[6] *Kiss Me Goodbye* reaches US #15.

[8] NBC TV special "Petula" airs. The show is part-sponsored by Chrysler, for whom Clark has recorded TV ads for the company's Plymouth range to the tune of *The Beat Goes On* the previous year.

Aug [24] *Don't Give Up* makes US #37.

Oct Having turned down 2 previous straight acting film roles, she plays the role of Sharon McLonergan in a movie adaptation of "Yip" Harburg's 1947 musical "Finian's Rainbow", at the invitation of Quincy Jones, head of Warner Bros. music department, with Fred Astaire and Tommy Steele, and directed by Francis Ford Coppola. The soundtrack album reaches US #90, while Clark's own *Petula* peaks at US #51.

969 **Jan** Compilation *Petula Clark's Greatest Hits, Vol.1* makes US #57. Clark splits with Hatch and Trent after 2 unsuccessful single releases.

June *Portrait Of Petula* reaches US #37.

Aug She co-stars with Peter O'Toole in "Goodbye Mr Chips", a remake of 1939 Robert Donat/Greer Garson film. Soundtrack album charts at US #164.

Oct Clark's performance at London's Royal Albert Hall is recorded for subsequent album release and also becomes the first show broadcast in color on BBC TV.

Nov *Record Retailer* announces Clark will play a nude bedroom scene in forthcoming film "Stanyan Street".

970 **Jan** *Just Pet* peaks at US #176.

Feb Clark records Les Reed songs in London with Tony Hatch.

Aug *Memphis*, cut in Memphis with Chips Moman, makes US #198.

971 **Mar** *The Song Of My Life* reaches UK #32.

Apr *Warm And Tender*, produced by Arif Mardin, peaks at US #178 (her last US chart album).

1972 **Jan** [15] Clark's version of Rice/Lloyd Webber's *I Don't Know How To Love Him* from "Jesus Christ Superstar", recorded in Miami while she is appearing at the Diplomat hotel, makes UK #47. She leaves Pye in UK and Warners in US, signing to Deutsche Grammophon, which releases her on Polydor in UK, and on MGM in US. (No big sellers will emerge from this deal, though 5 Polydor albums are released over 4 years.)

1977 **Feb** [12] TV-advertised compilation album *20 All-Time Greatest* reaches UK #18. This comes between a short recording return to Pye (which produces a disco version of *Downtown*) and a signing to CBS, neither being productive in commercial terms.

1979 **Apr** She co-stars with Paul Jones in ITV musical drama "Traces Of Love". By now, Clark has semi-retired to her Geneva chateau where she devotes much time to her husband and 3 children.

1981 After initial reluctance to follow in Julie Andrews' footsteps, Clark stars as Maria in a stage revival of "The Sound Of Music" at London's Apollo Victoria theater, which runs successfully for 14 months.

1982 **Mar** [6] *Natural Love*, on Scotti Brothers, peaks at US #66.

1983 After making feature film "Never Never Land", she takes a non-singing stage role in a short run of George Bernard Shaw's "Candida".

Feb Clark performs with the London Philharmonic Orchestra at London's Royal Albert Hall (to be released as a live double album).

1985 Clark starts work with Dee Shipman on "Someone Like You", a musical about the US Civil War, which will premiere in 1987 at the Arts theater, Cambridge.

1987 **July** Clark performs residence at Caesar's Palace, Atlantic City, NJ.

1988 **Dec** *Downtown '88*, a typically fashionable 80s update of a 60s classic, hits UK #10, and sees Clark return to TV appearances, including BBC TV's "Top Of The Pops".

THE CLASH

Joe Strummer (vocals, guitar)
Mick Jones (guitar)
Paul Simonon (bass)
Nicky "Topper" Headon (drums)

1976 **June** After 9 abortive months with seminal punk outfit London SS, Jones (b. June 26, 1955, Brixton, London) forms The Clash in Shepherds Bush, London, with Simonon (b. Dec.15, 1955, Brixton) who has never played before, but learns bass guitar. Bernie Rhodes from Malcolm McLaren's London Sex boutique becomes their manager. Guitarist Keith Levene (later of Public Image Ltd) and drummer Terry Chimes join, and Strummer (b. John Mellors, Aug.21, 1952, Ankara, Turkey) is persuaded to leave R&B group The 101ers.

Aug [13] The Clash gives its first public performance in a London rehearsal hall.

[29] Formal debut gig (after an unannounced support slot behind The Sex Pistols in Sheffield, S.Yorks.) is at Screen On The Green, Islington, London.

Sept [20] Band plays the 100 Club Punk Festival, London, but club owners are wary of potential punk violence and gigs generally prove hard to find. Levene leaves after only 5 shows.

Dec [6] Band lands a spot on The Sex Pistols' highly controversial "Anarchy In The UK" tour (the first 3 gigs have been cancelled because of venue bans).

1977 **Jan** [1] The Clash plays the opening night of the Roxy club in London's Covent Garden.

Record companies now show interest in the genre, and The Clash signs to CBS worldwide, negotiated by Rhodes. Debut album is recorded over 3 weekends. Chimes leaves and is replaced by "Topper" Headon (b. May 30, 1955, Bromley, Kent).

Apr [9] Debut single *White Riot* makes UK #38.

[30] *The Clash*, produced by Mickey Foote, reaches UK #12.

May [1] The "White Riot" UK tour starts at the Roxy, with The Jam and The Buzzcocks as support bands (The Jam will pull out on May 29). *Remote Control* is released, but does not chart.

June [10] Strummer and Headon are each fined £5 in London for spray-painting "Clash" on a wall.

[11] Duo are detained overnight in prison in Newcastle, Tyne & Wear, having failed to appear at Morpeth magistrates court on May 21 to answer a robbery charge relating to the theft of a Holiday Inn pillowcase. They are fined £100. The tour which starts a few days later is wryly named "Out On Parole".

Oct [8] *Complete Control*, recorded with reggae producer Lee "Scratch" Perry, makes UK #28.

1978 **Feb** Strummer is hospitalized for 11 days with hepatitis.

Mar [4] *Clash City Rockers* makes UK #35. Band is involved in a feature film with Ray Gange. Debut album, still not released in US (where CBS deems it unsuitable for radio play) sells more than 100,000 on import, making it the biggest-selling imported album ever in US.

[30] Simonon and Headon are arrested in Camden Town, London, for criminal damage, after shooting down racing pigeons with air guns. Fines this time total £800.

Apr [30] Band headlines the Anti-Nazi League Carnival in London, organized by Rock Against Racism.

July [1] *(White Man) In Hammersmith Palais* makes UK #32. With some work already done for a second album, they meet Blue Öyster Cult producer Sandy Pearlman, and complete the album with him.

[8] Strummer and Simonon are arrested and fined (£25 and £50) for being "drunk and disorderly" after a show at the Apollo in Glasgow, Scotland.

Oct [21] Rhodes is fired as manager after both band and CBS find him increasingly hard to deal with. He is replaced by one of the Clash's early champions, **Melody Maker** journalist Caroline Coon.

Nov [1] Rhodes, who has a contract giving him 20% of the band's income, is granted a court order stating that all Clash earnings are to be paid directly to him.

[25] Second album *Give 'Em Enough Rope* debuts at UK #2.

Dec Band begins "Sort It Out" UK tour.

1979 Jan [6] *Tommy Gun* reaches UK #19, their biggest-selling single yet.

[31] Group begins North American tour in Vancouver, Canada, with Bo Diddley as support.

Feb [17] US leg of the tour, dubbed "Pearl Harbor '79", opens at New York Palladium.

Mar [24] *English Civil War (Johnny Comes Marching Home)* makes #25 on UK chart.

Apr [7] *Give 'Em Enough Rope* makes US #128.

June [23] 4-track EP *The Cost Of Living*, headed by a revival of Bobby Fuller's *I Fought The Law*, reaches UK #22. Coon is fired as manager.

Aug Group records 12 songs in 3 days with veteran producer Guy Stevens.

Sept Second US tour, with The Undertones supporting, is dubbed "The Clash Take The Fifth" (a reference to temporary fifth member Mickey Gallagher, of Ian Dury's Blockheads, on keyboards). US support acts include R&B stalwarts Sam And Dave, Screamin' Jay Hawkins and Lee Dorsey, plus "new wave" country-rocker Joe Ely, and psychobilly band The Cramps.

Oct [6] *The Clash*, belatedly released in US, makes #126.

Nov A new album, completed with Stevens, is announced as a double set retailing at single album price.

Dec [22] Double album *London Calling* (originally to have been *The New Testament*) debuts at peak UK #9.

[27] Group co-headlines (with Ian Dury) second of 4 benefit concerts for the people of Kampuchea, at the Hammersmith Odeon, London.

1980 Jan [19] Extracted title track *London Calling* reaches UK #11. In need of management, the band signs to Blackhill, run by Peter Jenner and Andrew King (former Pink Floyd and currently Ian Dury managers).

Mar [15] "Rude Boy", a fictionalized documentary film of a Clash roadie (played by Ray Gange) made by Jack Hazan and David Mingay, opens at the Prince Charles cinema in London. Much of it has been filmed behind the scenes on the road over previous 18 months.

[22] *London Calling* reaches US #27.

May [24] *Train In Vain (Stand By Me)*, the band's first US chart single, reaches #23.

[21] Strummer is arrested at a much-troubled gig in Hamburg, Germany, after smashing his guitar over the head of a violently demonstrative member of the audience. He is released after an alcohol test proves negative.

June Band tours US and Europe. Jamaican DJ Mikey Dread with whom they record *Bankrobber*, plays on some European dates.

Aug They start recordings for self-produced album at Electric Ladyland studios, New York, with tensions between Jones and the others affecting some sessions. Jones also produces an album by US singer Ellen Foley, his current girlfriend.

Sept [6] *Bankrobber*, released in UK by CBS after a flood of Dutch imports, reaches UK #12.

Nov 10" mini-album *Black Market Clash*, customized for US market, peaks at US #74.

Dec [6] *The Call Up*, an anti-draft song, makes UK #40.

[20] Triple album set *Sandinista!*, issued at the band's insistence at double album price and with mixed reactions due to its sprawling contents, reaches UK #19.

1981 Jan Strummer, dissatisfied with recent temporary management arrangements, meets Bernie Rhodes by chance in London and within 2 months Rhodes is back as manager.

[31] *Hitsville UK* peaks at UK #56.

Mar *Sandinista!* makes US #24.

May [2] Dance-oriented *The Magnificent Seven* reaches UK #34.

Dec [5] *This Is Radio Clash* makes UK #47. Work starts on new album.

1982 Jan With the project unfinished, The Clash makes its first tour of the East, taking in Japan, New Zealand, Australia, Hong Kong and Thailand.

Mar Group returns to UK and finishes recording, with Glyn Johns completing the final mixing.

Apr [26] On the eve of the UK "Know Your Rights" tour, Strummer disappears, and the dates are postponed. (It is later revealed to be a Rhodes publicity stunt.)

May [8] *Know Your Rights* makes UK #43.

[22] *Combat Rock* hits UK #2 in its first week, and will remain charted for 23 weeks.

[24] Strummer returns to the band on the same day that Headon leaves (officially because of "a difference of political direction"). Chimes returns temporarily to play drums on the band's US tour, its most extensive yet. This exposure will lead to record US sales.

July [2] Headon is remanded on bail in London, charged with stealing a bus stop and receiving stolen property.

Aug [7] *Rock The Casbah* reaches UK #30.

Sept [22] After US tour, band accepts an invitation to support The Who on their farewell US tour: 8 major shows, including 2 at Shea Stadium, New York.

[18] *Should I Stay Or Should I Go?/Straight To Hell* makes US #45.

Oct [23] *Should I Stay Or Should I Go?/Straight To Hell* reaches UK #17.

Dec Band appears at the Jamaican World Music Festival.

1983 Jan *Combat Rock*, produced by Johns, becomes their biggest US album, hitting #7 and selling over a million.

[22] *Rock The Casbah* hits US #8.

Feb Chimes leaves.

Mar [26] *Should I Stay Or Should I Go?* is reissued in US, and re-enters the chart, reaching #50.

May Pete Howard joins on drums.

[28] Group appears on the first of the 3-day "US '83 Festival" in San Bernardino, CA. They co-headline the day's bill with Men At Work and The Stray Cats.

Sept A CBS "Clash Communique" reads: "Joe Strummer and Paul Simonon have decided that Mick Jones should leave the group. It is felt that Jones has drifted apart from the original idea of The Clash." Jones goes (and will re-emerge with hitmaking band Big Audio Dynamite).

1984 Jan Guitarists Vince White and Nick Sheppard are added, and Strummer declares in interviews that "a whole new Clash era is underway".

1985 Nov *Cut The Crap* reaches UK #16 after being savaged by critics, while extracted *This Is England* makes UK #24. A "Busking Tour" of UK does not impart the new credibility that Strummer claims for the band, and he and Simonon call it a day.

1986 Jan *Cut The Crap* reaches US #88, by which time the band has broken up. (Simonon will fade from view and Strummer will devote most of the next 2 years to acting in films made by Alex Cox – notably "Straight To Hell". Headon will sign as a soloist to Mercury Records, releasing the album *Waking Up*, but his career will fall apart in Nov.1987 when he is jailed on heroin offenses.)

1988 Mar Reissued in UK as a single to trail the forthcoming album, *I Fought The Law* climbs to UK #29.

Apr Retrospective double *The Story Of The Clash, Volume 1* hits UK #7 and will go on to make US #142.

May Another spin-off from the compilation, reissued *London Calling*, makes UK #46.

June After scoring 2 movie soundtracks, "Walker" and "Permanent Record", Strummer embarks on "Rock Against The Rich" UK tour. (Now based in Los Angeles, CA, Strummer plays on Bob Dylan's *Down In The Groove* and records and tours with his own band the Latino Rockabilly War.)

1989 May [13] "Lost In Space", a 3-episode picture written and directed by Jim Jarmusch, in which Strummer appears as Johnny, is shown at the Cannes Film Festival.

Oct [27] *London Calling* tops **Rolling Stone**'s "Top 100 Albums Of The 80s."

1990 Mar Strummer's *Earthquake Weather*, with new band members Zander Schloss (guitar), Jack Irons (drums) and others, is released.

The Bee Gees

David Bowie

Jon Bon Jovi

Chuck Berry

Dire Straits

Sam Cooke

Cher

Deep Purple

July [21] *Return To Brixton* peaks at UK #57.
Rock The Casbah is the first record to be broadcast on Armed Forces radio in the Persian Gulf.

1991 Feb Simonon's new band, Havana 3 A.M., releases its eponymously titled debut album on IRS.

Mar [2] *Should I Stay Or Should I Go*, reissued through its use in a Levi's TV commercial, returns at UK #5, hitting #1 a week later, the group's first UK chart-topper. Strummer and Jones are reported to disagree over the song's sponsorship of the product. Jones' view has clearly predominated, as Columbia Records include the BAD (Big Audio Dynamite) II cut *Rush*, at his insistence, on the B-side. The single's success will spur sales of 3-year-old retrospective *The Story Of The Clash, Volume 1*.

JIMMY CLIFF

1962 Cliff (b. James Chambers, 1948, St. Catherine, Jamaica) having quit college and moved to Kingston, Jamaica, to pursue a musical career, which includes fronting local band Shakedown Sound, teams up with local Chinese/Jamaican musician and producer Leslie Kong, who has been impressed by Cliff's *Dearest Beverley*, a song about an ice-cream parlor, and has a #1 local hit in Jamaica with *Hurricane Hattie*, inspired by the storm which swept across the Caribbean.

1965 On a US tour organized by the Jamaican government, with Prince Buster and Byron Lee's Dragonaires, he meets Chris Blackwell of Island Records, who persuades him to sign to the label and move to UK, where he initially works as a back-up singer before recording in his own right and performing live (a mixture of ska and R&B) in UK and Europe.

1966 Jan [7] Cliff's UK debut *Call On Me* is released on Fontana.

1967 July *Give And Take* receives radio interest but just fails to chart.

1968 He represents Jamaica in an international song festival in Brazil with his own song *Waterfall*. It is a prize-winning entry and a hit in South America.

1969 Nov After 5 Island singles, *Wonderful World, Beautiful People*, his debut for Trojan Records, hits UK #6 as reggae music becomes popular in UK.

1970 Jan [24] *Wonderful World, Beautiful People* reaches US #25.
Feb *Vietnam*, a self-penned reggae protest song, makes UK #46.
Mar [28] *Come Into My Life* climbs to US #89.
Sept Cliff writes *You Can Get It If You Really Want*, a UK #2 hit for Desmond Dekker. *Wild World*, a reggae adaptation of a Cat Stevens song from Stevens' *Tea For The Tillerman*, hits UK #8. (It is not released in US, where the original version is a Top 20 hit.)

1971 Cliff records *Another Cycle* at Muscle Shoals studio, AL. It consists entirely of R&B/soul material.
Sept The Pioneers hit UK #5 with the Cliff-penned *Let Your Yeah Yeah Be Yeah*.

1972 He stars in the semi-autobiographical lead role in Perry Henzell's Jamaican-made film "The Harder They Come", which receives critical acclaim. Cliff has 4 self-penned songs on the soundtrack album.

1973 He signs to EMI in UK and Warner/Reprise in US (but will have no further UK chart success). He has a conversion of faith to Islam after meeting Black Muslims in Chicago while on a US visit. It has a profound effect on his songwriting and prompts him to visit Africa, a trip which is mostly concerned with his roots and the lifestyle of his ancestors.

1974 He makes his first full US tour, premiering at New York's Carnegie Hall. *Struggling Man* is well reviewed but not does not chart.

1975 Mar Soundtrack album *The Harder They Come* makes US #140, following the cult movie's belated US release.
Nov [8] *Follow My Mind* makes US #195.

1978 *Give Thankx* fails to chart, though Cliff rates it as his best effort yet.

1980 Cliff signs a new deal with MCA Records, though neither of the resulting albums, *I Am The Living* or *Give The People What They Want*, are notably successful. He plays a concert in Soweto, South Africa, to a racially-mixed audience of 75,000 – his condition for the show. He is now a much-toured artist around the African continent, having played in Nigeria, Senegal, Cameroon, Zambia and South Africa. During the year, he will also feature in the movie "Bongo Man".

1982 July He signs to CBS/Columbia Records.
Aug [14] First album for the label, *Special*, produced in Jamaica by Chris Kimsey, peaks at US #186. He follows it with a 6-week US tour, accompanied by his new band Oneness and shares the bill with Peter Tosh. It closes with 2 sell-out dates at New York's Felt Forum.
Oct Cliff co-headlines the World Music Festival at the Bob Marley Center in Montego Bay, Jamaica.

1983 Aug Cliff returns to Africa for a month-long tour, playing concerts in Lesotho and Zimbabwe.
Oct *The Power And The Glory*, mostly recorded with Oneness in Jamaica, includes 2 tracks cut with Kool & The Gang in their New Jersey studio.

1985 Feb [26] Cliff is nominated in the first Best Reggae Recording category, for *Reggae Night*, one of the tracks recorded the previous year with Kool & The Gang, at the 27th annual Grammy awards. Black Uhuru's *Anthem* wins.
May Cliff's composition *Trapped* is recorded by Bruce Springsteen as his contribution to USA For Africa album *We Are The World*. Springsteen has also been playing it live for several months, having been said to have first heard Cliff's original version over an airport P.A. system in Europe.
Aug *Cliff Hanger*, much of which is again recorded with Kool & The Gang again, is another critical, if not chart, success.
Dec [14] Artists United Against Apartheid, comprising 49 artists including Cliff, makes US #38 and UK #21 with *Sun City*.

1986 Feb [25] Cliff wins Best Reggae Recording for *Cliff Hanger* at the 28th Grammy awards.
July Cliff stars in movie "Club Paradise" with Robin Williams, Peter O'Toole and a host of US comedy talent. He has 7 tracks on the soundtrack album, including a duet with Elvis Costello, *Seven Day Weekend*, which is released as a single.
Aug He embarks on a worldwide tour with Oneness, as support to Steve Winwood.

1988 Mar *Hanging Fire*, produced by Kool & The Gang's Khalis "Ronald Bell" Bayyan and partly recorded in The Congo, is released.

1989 Sept He forms his own Cliff Records, releasing *Images*, produced with Ansel Collins.
[22] Bruce Springsteen joins Jimmy Cliff on stage at the Stone Pony, Asbury, NJ, to sing *Trapped*.

PATSY CLINE

1954 Sept Starry-eyed C&W aspirant, Cline (b. Virginia Patterson Hensley, Sept.8, 1932, Winchester, VA), after singing on local radio at age 14 and serving an apprenticeship in local beerjoints and taverns, signs with Four Star Records of Pasadena, CA.

1955 June She makes her debut on prestigious Nashville, TN, stage/radio show "Grand Ole Opry" singing *A Church A Courtroom And Then Goodbye*. It is an appropriate choice: her sexual notoriety soon causing as many ripples in the C&W fraternity as her music. The wife of her manager Bill Peer cites Cline as co-respondent in their divorce, and Cline's own marriage soon dissolves when she meets Charlie Dick, who becomes her second husband. She becomes a regular on Jimmy Dean's weekly "Town And Country Jamboree" appearing in fringed dude-cowboy regalia.

1956 Nov *Walkin' After Midnight*, written for and rejected by Kay Starr years earlier, is foisted on Cline. With other songs, she cuts it with Nashville producer Owen Bradley.

1957 Jan [21] In New York for the first time, Cline appears on nationally networked CBS TV show "Arthur Godfrey's Talent Scouts". She sings *Walkin' After Midnight* and wins. Decca, now marketing her records after a deal with Four Star, rush-releases the song as her fifth single.
Apr [6] *Walkin' After Midnight* crosses over from C&W chart to peak at US #12. She makes her second "Grand Ole Opry" appearance, this time as guest star, and on Alan Freed's stage show she successfully confronts a rock'n'roll audience.
Despite 9 releases in the next years, Decca's failure to find an equally incisive follow-up restricts her to the Country scene, where her elevation to superstardom is swift and sure.

1961 June [14] Cline sustains a fractured hip and near-fatal head injuries when thrown through the windshield in an automobile collision in Madison, TN.
Sept [4] Establishing Bradley's lavish settings and Cline's sophisticated weepie style, both at variance with current Nashville tradition, *I Fall To Pieces*, written by Hank Cochran and Harlan Howard, restores her to the pop chart at US #12.
Oct [23] *Who Can I Count On*, B-side of still climbing *Crazy* spends a week at US #99.
Nov [27] Distinctive Willie Nelson ballad *Crazy*, recorded with Cline on crutches, becomes her biggest seller, hitting US #9.

1962 Feb [17] *Strange* makes US #97.
Mar [31] A-side *She's Got You* reaches US #14, as *The Patsy Cline Showcase* climbs to US #73.

Apr [26] *She's Got You* makes UK #43.
May [19] *Imagine That* climbs to US #90.
June [16] *When I Get Through With You* peaks at US #53.
Aug [25] *So Wrong* makes US #85.
Nov [17] *Heartaches* climbs to US #73 and gives Cline her second UK chart success, reaching #31.

1963 **Feb** [23] An established "Grand Ole Opry" headliner and America's highest-ranked female Country star, 30-year-old Cline continues to make the transition from C&W to pop chart, with *Leaving On Your Mind* peaking at US #83.
Mar [5] Returning from a Kansas City, MO, benefit concert for widow of disk jockey Cactus Jack Call, who had died in a road accident, the single-engined Piper Commanche carrying Cline and fellow stars Hawkshaw Hawkins and Cowboy Copas crashes near Camden, TN, killing all 3 and the pilot (also her manager) Randy Hughes.
[10] Over 25,000 mourners attend Cline's funeral.
June [15] Cline's version of Don Gibson's *Sweet Dreams* becomes a posthumous hit, making US #44.
Sept [7] For the last time, Cline's name appears on the pop chart as *Faded Love* climbs to US #96 and her album *The Patsy Cline Story* makes #74.

1964 Regular releases, like *When You Need A Laugh, He Called Me Baby* and *Anytime* reach the C&W chart and sustain Cline's following.

1973 **Oct** [15] Cline becomes the first female solo performer to be inducted into the Country Music Hall Of Fame.

1977 Loretta Lynn releases a tribute album, while a new generation of Nashville stars acknowledges Cline's influence.

1981 Tapes of Cline and Jim Reeves, re-arranged and mixed to simulate duet performances, are released as *Greatest Hits*. Issued as singles, *Have You Ever Been Lonely* and *I Fall To Pieces* become C&W hits.

1985 "Sweet Dreams", a Hollywood movie based on Ellis Nassour's biography with Jessica Lange in the title role, revives interest in the Cline legend. Soundtrack album reaches US #29.

1988 **July** *Live At The Opry*, recordings from 1956 to 1962, makes #60 on US Country chart.
Aug [19] The Amusement & Music Operators Association announces that *I Fall To Pieces* is the second all-time most played jukebox song.

1989 **Sept** [16] *20 Golden Hits*, released on the DeLuxe label, makes #70 on US Country chart.

1991 **Jan** [12] *Crazy* reaches UK #14, reviving UK interest in the Country legend which will also see 2 albums, *Sweet Dreams* and *Dreaming* make UK #18 and #55 respectively.

GEORGE CLINTON

1955 Clinton (b. July 22, 1940, Kannapolis, NC), the first of 9 children, now living in Newark, NJ, forms doo-wop group The Parliaments, as an extension to his gang The Outlaws, with Audrey Boykins and her brother Eugene, Glen Carlos, Charles "Butch" Davis and Herbie Jenkins. They play local hops and dances and sing on street corners, working by day at Newark barber shop, the Uptown Tonsorial Parlor.

1956 The Parliaments, now comprising Clinton, Jenkins, Robert Lambert, Danny Mitchell and Grady Thomas, record *The Wind* and *A Sunday Kind Of Love* on acetate in a Newark record booth. Clinton, attending Clinton Place high school, begins work as foreman of the New Jersey Wham-o hula-hoop factory.

1958 **Apr** The Parliaments, already in their third incarnation with Clinton, Lambert, Thomas, Calvin Simon and the returning Davis, record *Poor Willie* and *Party Boys* for Hull label.

1959 **June** ABC-Paramount picks up the Hull recordings to release on its Apt subsidiary, as the group, now with Clinton, Davis, Simon, Thomas and Johnny Murray, records *Lonely Island* and *Cry* for Flipp label.

1963 Clinton, after working for a year in New York as a staff writer for Jobete Music, takes The Parliaments, now Clinton, Thomas, Clarence "Fuzzy" Hawkins and Raymond Davis, to Detroit, MI, to audition for Motown. Although not signed, The Parliaments will cut several demos for the label. Clinton will also produce for it. While working for Motown, Clinton will team with fellow ex-Jobete writer Sidney Barnes and Motown sax session man Mike Terry to form Geo-Si-Mik production team, signing with Ed Wingate's recently founded Golden World and Ric Tic record labels. Clinton commutes to Detroit every week, working at his New Jersey barber shop weekends.

1966 Clinton continues to write and produce for Geo-Si-Mik, including The Parliaments' *Heart Trouble* and *My Girl*, which is released on Golden World, but dissatisfied and disillusioned with the record business, returns to Newark to work full-time at his barber shop.

1967 **Sept** [2] The Parliaments' *I Wanna Testify*, recorded in late 1966 for Revilot label, reaches US #20. Clinton reassembles the group adding a rhythm section comrprising Eddie Hazel (guitar), Lucius Ross (guitar), Billy Nelson (bass), Mickey Atkins (organ) and Ramon Fulwood (drums).
Nov [25] *All Your Goodies Are Gone* makes US #80.

1969 Clinton temporarily loses the rights to the name The Parliaments, after Motown buys out Golden World, while LeBaron Taylor leases *A New Day Begins* to Atco. To remain active, Clinton, using The Parliaments rhythm section, assembles Funkadelic, soon adding Bernie Worrell on keyboards. They sign to Armen Boladian's new Westbound label, releasing debut single *Music For My Mother* and album *Funkadelic*.
Nov [1] Funkadelic's *I'll Bet You* peaks at US #68.

1970 **Mar** Clinton relaunches The Parliaments as Parliament, on Invictus, with debut album *Osmium*.
Apr [4] Funkadelic's *I Got A Thing, You Got A Thing, Everybody's Got A Thing* makes US #80, as *Funkadelic* climbs to US #126. Funkadelic continues to record for Westbound. Keyboardist Bernie Worrell joins the Parliament-Funkadelic (P. Funk) family.
Sept [12] Funkadelic's *I Wanna Know If It's Good To You?* makes US #81.

1971 **Apr** *You And Your Folks, Me And My Folks* reaches US #91.
Sept *Can You Get To That* peaks at US #93.

1972 Bassist Bootsy Collins, ex-James Brown's backing band The JB's, joins in time for Funkadelic album *America Eats Its Young*.

1973 Guitarist Gary Shider joins in time for Funkadelic album, *Cosmic Slop*.

1974 Funkadelic's *Standing On The Verge Of Getting It On* is released. Following the collapse of Invictus, Clinton signs Parliament to Casablanca, despite interest from Westbound. Westbound releases *Funkadelic's Greatest Hits*.
Aug Parliament's *Up For The Down Stroke* makes US #63.

1975 **May** *Chocolate City* peaks at US #91.
June *Chocolate City* stalls at US #94.
Nov Funkadelic's *Better By The Pound* reaches US #99.

1976 **Feb** Parliament's *Mothership Connection* climbs to US #13.
May *Tear The Roof Off The Sucker (Give Up The Funk)* reaches US #15. Collins releases *Stretchin' Out*, made with Parliament/Funkadelic members. (Other in-house projects released in the next 2 years will include The Horny Horns (P. Funk horn section Fred Wesley, Maceo Parker, Rick Gardner and Richard Griffith; Wesley and Parker, like Collins, having come to Clinton via James Brown's JB's), Parlet (P. Fun vocalists Mallia Franklin, Jeanette Washington and Shirley Hayden) and The Brides Of Dr. Funkenstein (P. Funk vocalists Lynn Mabry and Dawn Silva).)
Oct Parliament's *The Clones Of Dr. Funkenstein* climbs to US #20.

1977 **Jan** [19] Parliament/Funkadelic/Bootsy play Los Angeles's Forum to an audience of more than 18,000.
May *Parliament Live/P. Funk Earth Tour* makes US #29. Bootsy Collins releases *Ahh ... The Name Is Bootsy Baby*. The Horny Horns release *A Blow For Me, A Toot For You*.
Dec Parliament's *Funkentelechy Vs. The Placebo Syndrome* reaches US #13. Clinton now tours with some 40 musicians. His stage show incorporates separate sets from Parliament/Funkadelic, Parlet, Collins Rubber Band, The Brides Of Dr. Funkenstein and The Horny Horns.

1978 **Feb** Parliament's *Flash Light* makes US #16. Parlet releases *The Pleasure Principle* and The Brides Of Dr. Funkenstein release *Funk Or Walk*.
Apr [15] Collins' *Player Of The Year*, produced by Clinton, makes US #16.
July [8] *Bootzilla* makes UK #43.
[21] At a dinner sponsored by The Rod McGrew Scholarship Fund, Inc, Communicators With A Conscience, Clinton and Collins are challenge to do something more ambitious and less superficial with their music. (Clinton pledges to donate 50 cents for every ticket sold for his Aug. and Sept. concerts to the United Negro College Fund.)
Sept Funkadelic's *One Nation Under A Groove* reaches US #28. Group signs to Warner Bros.
Nov [25] *One Nation Under A Groove* reaches US #16.
Dec P. Funk plays rapturously-received concerts in London. The adventurous stage show includes a lifesize flying saucer. Funkadelic's *One Nation Under A Groove* hits UK #9 as Parliament's *Motor Booty Affair* makes US #23.
[16] *Brides Of Funkenstein* reaches US #70.

1979 **Feb** Parliament's *Aqua Boogie (A Psychoalpha Disco-Betabioaqua-Doloop)* peaks at US #89.
[3] Funkadelic's *One Nation Under A Groove* makes UK #56.

Oct Funkadelic's *(Not Just) Knee Deep* climbs to US #77.

Nov [10] *Underjam* reaches US #18.

Dec Parliament's *Gloryhallastoopid (Pin The Tale On The Funky)* makes US #77.

980 Clinton's release schedule is halted by protracted legal disputes with a number of record companies. Issues include disputed royalty payments and use of the names Parliament and Funkadelic.

981 **Jan** A breakaway trio of P. Funk musicians, using the name Funkadelic, releases *Connections And Disconnections*, which peaks at US #151.

Feb The official Funkadelic releases *The Electric Spanking Of War Babies*, featuring Sly Stone.

982 Clinton signs as a solo artist to Capitol. (He will record for the label with the P. Funk family, but will not use the names Parliament or Funkadelic.)

Dec *Computer Games* makes US #40 as *Loopzilla* reaches UK #57.

983 *Atomic Dog* tops US R&B chart. Its accompanying video clip wins a **Billboard** award for video animation.

984 **Jan** *You Shouldn't Nuf Bit, Fish!* peaks at US #102.

Apr *Do Fries Go With That Shake* makes UK #57.

985 **June** *Some Of My Best Friends Are Jokes* is released. One track is written with Thomas Dolby, with whom Clinton will collaborate on *May The Cube Be With You.*

986 **Apr** *Do Fries Go With That Shake* peaks at UK #57.

989 **Sept** After a long hiatus, Clinton returns with *The Cinderella Theory*, recorded at Prince's Paisley Park studios. It makes US #192.

990 Clinton stars as himself in Prince's film "Graffiti Bridge".

991 **Jan** [6] Clinton guests at Prince's Glam Slam club gig in Minneapolis.

THE COASTERS

Carl Gardner (lead tenor)
Leon Hughes (tenor)
Billy Guy (baritone)
Bobby Nunn (bass)

955 **Oct** Gardner (b. Apr.29, 1927, Tyler, TX) and Nunn (b. Birmingham, AL) leave The Robins, an R&B vocal group whose most celebrated recording was *Smokey Joe's Café*, made under the direction of songwriters/producers Leiber and Stoller, to start The Coasters (the name reflecting their West Coast roots) with Hughes and Guy (b. June 20, 1936, Attasca, TX).

Nov Leiber and Stoller sign a deal whereby their masters will be released on Atlantic subsidiary, Atco. One of their acts is the newly constituted black vocal quartet, The Coasters, the perfect vehicle for Leiber and Stoller's studio genius.

956 **Jan** Group cuts 4 tracks at Hollywood Recorders in Los Angeles, CA: *Brazil, Down In Mexico, One Kiss Led To Another* and *Turtle Dovin'.*

Mar Debut *Down In Mexico* enters US R&B chart and hits #4.

Sept *One Kiss Led To Another*, their first pop chart entry, makes US #73.

957 **Feb** Hughes is replaced by Young Jessie, ex-The Flairs.

May Cranky, funky *Searchin'* hits US #5/R&B #1 and UK #30. Their first million-seller, it establishes The Coasters as one of the most amusing, innovative and influential vocal groups of the rock'n'roll era. Particularly revered by British fans, their songs will soon be revived by The Beatles, The Stones and almost every UK beat group of the early 60s. B-side *Young Blood* also makes the Top 10, hitting US #8.

Oct Of 6 titles recorded, only *Idol With The Golden Head* reaches the chart, peaking at US #64.

958 **Mar** The Coasters, and Leiber and Stoller, move to New York. Jessie and Nunn, loath to travel, are replaced by ex-Flairs lead singer Cornelius Gunter (b. Nov.14, 1938, Los Angeles, CA) (second tenor) and ex-Cadets Will "Dub" Jones (bass). Legendary "fifth Coaster" King Curtis, whose sax playing will add piquancy to their work, also joins.

May *Yakety Yak* rockets up the chart to hit US #1 and becomes their second UK hit, reaching UK #12. It epitomizes Leiber and Stoller's "Coaster style", which takes the form of "a white kid's view (Lieber's) of a black person's conception of white society."

Dec [11] Group records *Charlie Brown* in New York.

959 **Feb** *The Shadow Knows* does not chart. The uproarious exploits of incorrigible schoolkid *Charlie Brown* hits US #2 and UK #6, and is a million-seller. It contains speeded-up voices on one line as a sardonic nod to *The Chipmunk Song* which is heading towards US #1.

May Conceived as 3-minute comic operas, and scripted like radio plays, Coasters' records are hailed as pop masterpieces. *Along Came Jones*, mocking the cliches of TV westerns, hits US #9.

Aug *Poison Ivy* reaches US #7 and UK #15 and is the group's fourth

and last million-seller. (The Rolling Stones will cut the most famous of some 20 cover versions.) B-side *I'm A Hog For You* reaches US #38.

Dec Double-sided *Run Red Run/What About Us* peaks at US #36/#47.

1960 **May** A revival of *Besame Mucho*, a million-seller for Jimmy Dorsey in the early 40s, reaches only US #70.

June *Wake Me Shake Me*, written by Guy, recounting the miseries of a recalcitrant garbage man, fails to climb beyond US #51.

Oct Adapted from the half-remembered *Clothesline* by Kent Harris, *Shopping For Clothes* stalls at US #83.

1961 **Feb** Atco attempts to reverse The Coasters' slide with *Wait A Minute*, by Bobby Darin/Don Kirshner. Cut and shelved over 3 years earlier, it makes US #37.

Apr *Little Egypt*, about a tattooed burlesque dancer who ends up marrying the singer, lifts them to US #23.

Aug *Girls Girls Girls* rises no higher than US #96. As Leiber and Stoller's Atlantic workload increases (The Drifters, Ben E. King, Ruth Brown, LaVern Baker, The Isley Brothers), they are able to devote less time to The Coasters.

1964 **Mar** After a long chart absence, *T'Aint Nothing To Me* reaches US #64. Group continues recording for Atco, without success, until 1966.

1967 CBS subsidiary Date signs The Coasters. Former Cadillacs frontman Earl Carroll (b. 1937, New York, NY) replaces Gunter and a reunion with Leiber and Stoller yields *Down Home Girl* (covered by The Stones), *D.W. Washburn* (covered by The Monkees) and a revival of The Clovers' hit *Love Potion Number Nine*, which (when leased to King Records) creeps into the chart 4 years later, reaching US #76. (Gunter joins Dinah Washington's revue, before forming his own Coasters. He will be sued in 1971 by H.B. Barnum, manager of the legitimate group.)

1980 **Apr** Bass singer Nathaniel "Buster" Wilson is shot, his dismembered body dumped near Hoover Dam and in a canyon near Modesto, CA.

1986 **Nov** [5] Bobby Nunn dies.

1987 **Jan** Group is inducted into the Rock'N'Roll Hall Of Fame at the annual dinner at the Waldorf Astoria hotel, New York.

1988 **May** The Coasters, with Gardner, Guy, Jones and Gunter and relative newcomer Tom Palmer, participate in Atlantic's 40th birthday concert at New York's Madison Square Garden.

1990 **Feb** [27] Gunter, in Las Vegas, NV, to perform with the latest variation of the group at the Lady Luck hotel, is gunned down in his car.

EDDIE COCHRAN

1955 **Jan** Having lived in Bell Gardens suburb of Los Angeles, CA, since age 12 and become a proficient guitarist in his early teens, Cochran (b. Ray Edward Cochran, Oct.3, 1938, Albert Lea, MN), joins (unrelated) Hank Cochran as his guitar accompanist, after being introduced to him by Bob Bull, a member of Richard Ray & The Shamrock Valley Boys whom Cochran had joined on stage at an American Legion club gig in Bell Gardens in Oct.1954.

Apr Hank and Eddie, now working as The Cochran Brothers, are signed to American Music Corp. agency, which leads to appearances on live TV shows, "Town Hall Party" and "Hometown Jamboree".

May They audition for Ekko Records' Charles Matthews at Sunset Recorders in Hollywood. Duo's first single for the label is *Mr. Fiddle*, backed with *Two Blue Singin' Stars*, but after playing the "Big D Jamboree" in Dallas, TX, a few days after Elvis Presley, and hearing about the singer from stage staff at the event, they decide to change from their hillbilly style to a harder rock style.

Oct Cochran, buying guitar strings in Bell Gardens music center, meets aspiring songwriter Jerry Capehart.

1956 **Jan** The Cochran Brothers become regulars on KVOR TV's "The California Hayride". They relocate to Napa, CA, to be near Stockton, CA, TV station.

May They spend a week in Hawaii, opening for C&W star Lefty Frizzell.

July During a session at Master Recorders in Los Angeles, the Cochrans decide to part company. (Hank Cochran will move to Nashville, where he will become a successful songwriter.) Cochran and Capehart, now good friends, cut *Skinny Jim*, a song they have written together as an answer record to *Long Tall Sally*. Capehart places the song through his contacts at American Music's record label, Crest. It does not sell, but Capehart uses it as a demo to circulate to major record companies.

Aug [14] Cochran, spotted by movie producer Boris Petroff while recording some backing music with Capehart for a Petroff low-budget picture, films a role for Jayne Mansfield-starring "The Girl Can't Help

It", in which he sings *Twenty Flight Rock*, at 20th Century Fox studios.

Sept [8] Cochran signs a 1-year deal with Liberty Records.

Dec Cochran films "Untamed Youth" with Mamie Van Doren, in which he performs *You Ain't Gonna Make A Cotton Picker Out Of You*, on location in Bakersfield, CA.

1957 **Apr** Cochran embarks on a major tour to promote his chart debut, a cover version of Johnny Dee's (actually John D. Loudermilk of later songwriting fame) *Sittin' In The Balcony*, backed by The Johnny Mann Singers. He plays a week at the Mastbaum theater in Philadelphia, PA, on a package show which also features Gene Vincent.
[27] *Sittin' In The Balcony* reaches US #18, outselling the original version which makes US #38.
Aug Cochran embarks on tour of Eastern and Mid-West states.
Sept [23] *Drive-In Show* makes US #82.
Oct Cochran begins a tour of Australia with Gene Vincent and Little Richard. On his return he joins the second stage of "The Biggest Show Of Stars For '57" package tour.
Nov [24] Tour ends at the Mosque, Richmond, VA.
Dec After a show at the Paramount theater, New York, before Christmas, Phil Everly introduces his girlfriend Sharon Sheeley to Cochran.

1958 **Mar** [10] *Jeannie Jeannie Jeannie* makes a 1-week at US #94, while Cochran helps with backing vocals on Gene Vincent studio sessions.
Sept [29] *Summertime Blues*, co-written with Capehart, is his breakthrough hit and only US Top 10 entry, hitting #8 and gaining a gold disk for a million-plus sales.
Nov *Summertime Blues* is Cochran's UK chart debut, reaching #18.
Dec He appears in Alan Freed's 10-day New York "Christmas Rock'N'Roll Spectacular" with The Everly Brothers, Chuck Berry, Jackie Wilson, Dion & The Belmonts and others at Loew's State theater.

1959 **Jan** [5] *C'mon Everybody* makes US #35. Cochran begins filming Hal Roach/Alan Freed-produced "Go, Johnny Go!", in which he sings *Teenage Heaven*. His role forces him to withdraw from the "Winter Dance Party Tour" of Northwestern US states, alongside close friend Buddy Holly.
Feb He is deeply affected by the deaths of Holly, Valens and The Big Bopper and records a version of John D. Loudermilk's tribute song *Three Stars* (which will not be released until several years after his own death). He tries to avoid all flying but begins US tour which will last much of the year, punctuated by returns to Los Angeles for recording sessions. The Kelly Four (from Cochran's Irish ancestry), comprising Gene Ridgio (drums), Jim Stivers (piano), Mike Henderson (sax) and Dave Schreiber (bass), is formed to back him on the road.
Mar [16] *Teenage Heaven* makes US #99 for a week.
Apr *C'mon Everybody* hits UK #6.
Sept [7] *Somethin' Else* peaks at US #58 (his last US hit). Its writer, Sharon Sheeley, becomes Cochran's fiancée soon afterwards.
Oct *Somethin' Else* reaches UK #22.

1960 **Jan** [8] Cochran makes what will be his final recording at Goldstar studios in Hollywood. One of the tracks is *Three Steps To Heaven*.
[9] He flies to UK to co-headline (with Gene Vincent) a 10-week Larry Parnes package tour which includes Billy Fury, Joe Brown and Georgie Fame. The tour is a huge success, with ecstatic fan fervor, creating newspaper headlines.
[16] Cochran makes his UK TV debut on Jack Good's live rock show "Boy Meets Girls", the first of 4 appearances while on tour.
[24] Tour starts at the Gaumont theater, Ipswich, Suffolk.
Feb A revival of Ray Charles' *Hallelujah I Love Her So* makes UK #22.
[21] Cochran, backed by The Wildcats, performs at the **New Musical Express** Pollwinners Concert, at the Empire Pool, Wembley, London.
[22] He makes his UK radio debut on BBC's "Parade Of The Pops".
Mar Cochran invites Sheeley to UK to join him on tour, and to celebrate her forthcoming 20th birthday on Apr.4.
[5] He makes the first of 2 appearances on BBC radio show "Saturday Club", where he sings *What'd I Say*, *Milk Cow Blues*, his current release *Hallelujah I Love Her So*, and *C'mon Everybody*.
Apr The tour has proved so successful, Cochran and Vincent are offered an extension from the end of Apr. They accept, but return to US for the intervening 2 weeks, Cochran specifically to do some recording.
[16] Tour comes to end at the Hippodrome, Bristol, Avon, on Easter Saturday. Arrangements are made to catch a late train to London after the show for their transatlantic flight next morning, but Cochran, Vincent and Sheeley hire a taxi instead.
[17] En route to London on the A4, near Chippenham, Wilts., the Ford Consul in which they are traveling, skids into a roadside lamp post. Tour manager Pat Thomkins and 19-year-old driver George Martin,

both in the front of the car, are uninjured, but Vincent, Sheeley and Cochran, on the back seat all suffer injuries. Vincent breaks his collarbone and ribs and Sheeley breaks her pelvis, but Cochran is thrown head-first through the windshield. Rushed to Bath hospital, he dies 16 hours later, without regaining consciousness, from brain lacerations. One of the local policemen called to the accident is 16-year-old police cadet David Harman (later Dave Dee of Dave Dee, Dozy, Beaky, Mick & Tich); he salvages Cochran's hardly-damaged Gretsch guitar from the road, and will occasionally play it at the police station before it is returned to Cochran's mother 2 months later.
[25] Cochran is buried at a private ceremony at Forest Lawn cemetery in Glendale, CA.
June [25] Ironically-titled, *Three Steps To Heaven* tops UK chart and is his biggest UK seller, but never charts in US.
July [30] *Singing To My Baby*, his first chart album reaches UK #19.
Oct *Sweetie Pie* makes UK #38, while commemorative *The Eddie Cochran Memorial Album* hits UK #9.
Nov *Lonely*, the other side of *Sweetie Pie*, peaks at UK #41.

1961 **July** *Weekend* reaches UK #15 during a 4-month chart run.
Dec *Jeannie Jeannie Jeannie* makes UK #31.

1963 **Jan** *Cherished Memories* reaches UK #15.
May Reissued *The Eddie Cochran Memorial Album* makes UK #11 and stays charted for 18 weeks. Previously unissued *My Way* climbs to UK #23.
Sept [14] Heinz' tribute disk *Just Like Eddie* hits UK #5.
Oct [19] A reissue of Cochran's first album *Singing To My Baby* reaches UK #20.

1964 **Aug** *My Way*, with further previously unissued material, is released in UK, but does not chart.

1968 **May** A UK revival fad for 50s rock'n'roll sees reissue of *Summertime Blues*, alongside re-releases of Buddy Holly's *Peggy Sue* and Bill Haley's *Rock Around The Clock*. It climbs to UK #34.

1970 **May** Compilation *The Very Best Of Eddie Cochran* charts at UK #34.

1979 **Sept** [15] Further retrospective *The Eddie Cochran Singles Album* makes UK #39.

1980 **Mar** The 20th anniversary of his death is marked in UK by release of a limited-edition boxed set, **20th Anniversary Album**.

1987 **Jan** [21] Mick Jones inducts Eddie Cochran into the Rock'N'Roll Hall Of Fame at second annual dinner at the Waldorf Astoria in New York.

1988 **Mar** *C'mon Everybody* is used as the soundtrack to a UK TV ad for Levi's 501 jeans (the ad theme based on Sharon Sheeley's story of how she wore her Levi's to the party at which she first met Cochran. Sheeley appears uncredited in a party scene in the ad). Reissued and boosted by TV exposure, it makes UK #14, 29 years after its first success.
Apr Compilation *C'mon Everybody*, which makes Cochran's music available on CD, reaches UK #53.

JOE COCKER

1960 Cocker (b. John Robert Cocker, May 20, 1944, Sheffield, S.Yorks.), having left school, buys a cheap drumkit and forms a skiffle group with schoolfriends. He takes a day job as a fitter with the Gas Board and plays in brother Victor's skiffle group The Cavaliers at night, making his first public appearance at the Minvera Tavern in Sheffield.

1963 When The Cavaliers change their name to Vance Arnold & The Avengers, Cocker steps out front and sings, changing his forename to Joe, after Cowboy Joe. He also sits in with local bands like Dave Berry & The Cruisers.

1964 After an audition for producer Mike Leander in Manchester, Gtr. Manchester, Cocker is offered a contract with Decca Records. He takes leave of absence from the Gas Board and travels to Decca's studio in London. He debuts with a version of Lennon/McCartney's *I'll Cry Instead*. Despite a good performance and session help from guitarist Big Jim Sullivan and The Ivy League on backing vocals, it flops and Cocker reportedly only receives 10 shillings in royalties. He joins his first professional band, The Big Blues, on a brief UK tour with Manfred Mann and The Hollies and then tours US army bases in France. When he returns to the UK he no longer has a recording contract, so takes up his Gas Board job again and plays only an occasional local gig. Band splits and Cocker teams with Chris Stainton to write and record *Marjorine* and form The Grease Band.

1965 The Grease Band, with Cocker on vocals, Stainton on bass, Tommy Eyre on keyboards, Kenny Slade on drums and Alan Spenner and Henry McCullough both on guitars, plays soul material in clubs and pubs across the North of England. Its first recording, a live version of blues standard *Saved*, is on a free flexidisk with the Sheffield

University magazine **Twikker**.

967 Cocker and Stainton send a demo tape to promotion man Tony Hall, who gives it to producer Denny Cordell, who arranges a recording session in London.

968 **May** [22] *Marjorine*, credited to a solo Joe Cocker and issued on EMI's Regal Zonophone label, makes UK #48.

Oct [18] Following an appearance at the National Jazz & Blues Festival in Aug., Cocker embarks on a 10-date UK tour starting at the Newcastle Rutherford, Tyne & Wear. Including a Dec.8 gig with The Who and Arthur Brown.Tour will end Dec.20 at the Redcar Jazz club, Yorks.

Nov [6] Cocker's distinctive cover of The Beatles *With A Little Help From My Friends* hits UK #1 for a week. The Beatles are impressed with his version and send him a congratulatory telegram and place music press ads praising the record. Subsequent TV exposure introduces a wider audience to Cocker's flailing, tortured stage movements. Some find his performance distasteful and when he appears on the "Ed Sullivan Show", he is obscured by dancers as he sings.

Dec [14] *With A Little Help From My Friends* peaks at US #68.

969 **Feb** [8] Cocker begins 27-date twice-nightly UK tour, with bill-topper Gene Pitney, The Marmalade, The Iveys and others, at the Lewisham Odeon, London. The tour will end on Mar.9 at the ABC cinema, Blackpool, Lancs.

Apr [27] Cocker makes his major US TV debut on CBS TV's "Ed Sullivan Show" with The Grease Band, before embarking on 2-month US tour.

May Debut album *With A Little Help From My Friends* consists mainly of interpretations of other people's songs, but includes several Cocker/Stainton originals. It fails to chart in UK but reaches US #35.

July [19] *Feeling Alright* peaks at US #69.

Aug Stainton moves to keyboards after Eyre and Slade leave The Grease Band. With Alan Spenner on bass and Bruce Rowlands on drums, band tours US, highlighted by its performance at Woodstock Festival, NY, captured on album and in film "Woodstock". Cocker also meets Leon Russell.

[30] Cocker plays the Isle of Wight Festival Of Music.

Oct [30] Cocker plays the Royal Albert Hall, London, on a bill with Tiny Tim, The Bonzo Dog Doo Dah Band and Peter Sarstedt.

Nov [8] Cocker's recording of Russell's *Delta Lady* hits UK #10 and peaks at US #69. Russell and Cordell set up Shelter Records and supervise the recording of Cocker's next album at A&M (Cocker's US label) studios in Los Angeles. *Joe Cocker!*, which reaches US #11, is the last to feature The Grease Band. Group breaks up after Cocker cancels a US tour. (Stainton will stay with Cocker while the others will take up session work.)

970 **Feb** [7] Another distinctive cover of The Beatles' *She Came In Through The Bathroom Window* reaches US #30 and earns a gold disk. With no band and a commitment to play US dates, Cocker assembles, with the assistance of Cordell and Russell, a disparate collection of 21 musicians who will be known as Mad Dogs And Englishmen. The "Mad Dogs And Englishmen" tour clocks up 65 concerts in 57 days, leaving Cocker so exhausted that he temporarily retires to recuperate in California and then in Sheffield.

May [30] Cocker's cover of The Box Tops' hit *The Letter* hits US #7.

July *The Letter* makes UK #39.

Oct "Mad Dogs And Englishmen" tour provides basis for double *Mad Dogs And Englishmen* which reaches UK #16 and hits US #2, and a feature film.

Nov [14] *Cry Me A River*, recorded live at the Fillmore East, New York, in Mar.1970, reaches US #11.

971 **July** [17] Double A-side *High Time We Went/Black-Eyed Blues* reaches US #22. *Cocker Happy*, a compilation of his early hits, is released. Cocker joins "Mad Dogs" veteran Rita Coolidge on stage at the Sheffield City Hall as part of a Byrds package tour.

972 Cocker reunites with Stainton for US tour as 12-piece Joe Cocker & The Chris Stainton Band. Cocker is in poor physical shape, sometimes unable to remember his words and in Australia is arrested for possession of marijuana, which prevents him from obtaining a visa to tour US. Group returns to UK and splits.

Feb [12] Reissued *Feeling Alright* makes US #33.

May Double-pack album *Joe Cocker/With A Little Help From My Friends* reaches UK #29.

Oct [28] *Midnight Rider*, taken from *Something To Say*, which consists of studio cuts and live recordings from the year's tour, reaches US #27.

Dec *Joe Cocker* makes US #30.

973 **Jan** [6] *Woman To Woman*, B-side of *Midnight Rider*, peaks at US #56.

Mar [17] *Pardon Me Sir* makes US #51.

1974 Cocker moves to Los Angeles after Stainton joins Tundra.

July [27] *Put Out The Light* makes US #46.

Aug *I Can Stand A Little Rain*, produced by Jim Price, climbs to US #11. Released in UK on Cube Records, it fails to chart.

1975 **Mar** [29] Billy Preston/Jim Price-penned ballad *You Are So Beautiful*, listed as double A-side with *It's A Sin When You Love Somebody* during its first 5 weeks on chart, hits US #5.

Oct [4] *Jamaica Say You Will*, produced by Price, reaches US #42.

1976 **June** [19] *Stingray*, produced by Rob Fraboni and backed by soul-funk outfit Stuff, makes US #70. With A&M releasing Cocker's records in UK as well, Cube cashes in with *Live In Los Angeles*.

Oct [2] Cocker appears on NBC TV's "Saturday Night Live" duetting with John Belushi on Traffic's *Feelin' Alright*, with the latter doing his famous Cocker impersonation.

1977 **Dec** [24] *Joe Cocker's Greatest Hits* reaches US #114.

1978 **Nov** [4] *Luxury You Can Afford*, Cocker's first on Asylum label, is produced by R&B legend Allen Toussaint. It makes US #76.

Dec [27] *Fun Time* makes US #43.

1981 **Oct** [3] The Crusaders' *I'm So Glad I'm Standing Here Today*, on which Cocker guests on lead vocals, makes US #97 and UK #61. The track and *This Old World's Too Funky For Me*, which also features Cocker, are from the group's *Standing Tall*.

1982 Cocker signs to Island Records, who fly him to Compass Point studios in Nassau, Bahamas, to record *Sheffield Steel* with Blackwell producing and Sly & Robbie providing the rhythm section.

Nov [6] Cocker's duet with Jennifer Warnes on Jack Nitzsche, Buffy Saint-Marie, Will Jennings-penned ballad *Up Where We Belong*, from the soundtrack of Taylor Hackford's film "An Officer And A Gentleman", spends 3 weeks on top of US chart. Cocker's critically well-received *Sheffield Steel*, including covers of songs by Steve Winwood, Bob Dylan and Jimmy Webb, makes US #105.

1983 **Feb** [12] *Up Where We Belong* hits UK #7. Cocker makes an extensive US tour before playing Europe, with a triumphant return to Sheffield on his first major UK concert in more than 10 years.

[23] *Up Where We Belong* wins Best Pop Performance By A Duo Or Group With Vocal at the 25th annual Grammy awards.

Apr [11] *Up Where We Belong* wins Best Film Song at the annual Academy Awards.

1984 **June** [30] Signed to Capitol Records, Cocker's *Civilised Man* reaches the anchor position on UK Top 100 and makes US #133.

Nov [17] *Edge Of A Dream*, "Teachers" film theme, peaks at US #69.

1986 **Mar** [15] *Shelter Me* makes US #91. Cocker performs Randy Newman's *You Can Leave Your Hat On* in Adrian Lyne's film "9½ Weeks".

May *Cocker* makes US #50.

1987 **Nov** With new production team of Dan Hartman and Charlie Midnight, Cocker releases *Unchain My Heart* which reaches US #89. Extracted title track *Unchain My Heart*, a cover of Ray Charles' 1961 smash, reaches UK #46. He contributes *Love Lives On* to film "Harry And The Hendersons" (UK title: "Bigfoot And The Hendersons").

1988 **June** UK re-release of *You Don't Love Me Anymore* fails to chart despite tour dates.

[5-6] Cocker takes part in the sixth annual Prince's Trust Rock Gala concert, with Eric Clapton, Phil Collins, Peter Gabriel, Elton John and others, at the Royal Albert Hall, London.

[11] Cocker contributes to a soul supergroup including Ashford & Simpson and Al Green performing at "Nelson Mandela's 70th Birthday Party" at Wembley Stadium, London.

1989 **Jan** [21] Cocker takes part in a "Celebration For Young Americans" concert during one of President-Elect George Bush's inauguration parties at the Convention Center in Washington, DC.

Sept [16] *One Night Of Sin*, title track a remake of a 1956 Smiley Lewis song, makes US #52.

Nov Cocker performs at the Berlin Wall.

1990 **Jan** [13] *When The Night Comes*, co-written by Bryan Adams, peaks at UK #65.

[20] *When The Night Comes* reaches US #11.

May [5] Cocker sings *Come Together* and *Isolation* at the "John Lennon Tribute Concert" held at the Pier Head Arena in Merseyside to celebrate the songs of Lennon.

June [8] He begins 28-date North American "The Power And The Passion Tour" with Stevie Ray Vaughan & Double Trouble at the Shoreline Amphitheater, Mountain View, CA, set to end July 22 in Vancouver, Canada. His band includes Phil Grande (guitar), T.M. Stevens (bass), Steve Holley (drums), Deric Dyer (sax), Jeff Levine (keys), Chris Stainton (keys), Maxine Green (vocals) and Cydney Davis (vocals).

[30] *What Are You Doing With A Fool Like Me* spends a week on Hot 100 at US #96.

[31] Cocker teams with Pat Benatar for a benefit concert in his home town Santa Barbara to help those whose houses have been destroyed in the recent fire.

July [7] *Joe Cocker Live* makes US #98.

Oct [7] Cocker joins Richie Havens and others to play a free rock concert in the Old Town Square in Prague, Czechoslovakia.

1991 Jan [18] Cocker performs at Rock In Rio II festival at Maracana soccer stadium in Rio de Janeiro, Brazil, before an estimated crowd of 60,000.

THE COCTEAU TWINS

Elizabeth Fraser (vocals)
Robin Guthrie (bass, guitar, drum programing, keyboards)
Simon Raymonde (bass, piano, keyboards)

1981 Nov The original Cocteau Twins – Fraser, Guthrie and Will Heggie – travel from their native Falkirk, Scotland, to London, armed with 2 demo tapes. One is given to BBC Radio 1 DJ John Peel (for whom they will record 2 radio sessions), the other to Simon Raymonde, a shop assistant (and son of 60s arranger/producer Ivor Raymonde) working in an outlet beneath the 4AD record company office. After listening to it, 4AD label manager Ivo Watts-Russell offers to help.

1982 June First album, *Garlands*, is released, having cost just £900 to record in 9 days. It is an instant UK Independent chart hit, at #2. The Twins resist all offers of management as well as overtures from major record labels, electing always to release material in their own time through 4AD. (For the remainder of 1982 and into 1983, they will support OMD on a 50-date European tour.)

Oct 12" EP *Lullabies* is released, beginning a series of records which are big Independent chart successes, but fail to cross to mainstream appeal.

1983 Nov *Head Over Heels* finally charts at UK #51, remaining on chart for 15 weeks. Fraser and Guthrie appear as part of Watts-Russell's occasional 4AD conglomerate group This Mortal Coil on its debut single, a revival of Tim Buckley's *Song To The Siren*. This reaches UK #66 (and will remain on Independent chart for over a year). Heggie leaves, replaced by Raymonde.

1984 May *Pearly-Dewdrops' Drops* is their first pop crossover, reaching UK #29. While this is on chart, they turn down an appearance on BBC TV's "Top Of The Pops".

Nov *Treasure* reaches UK #29.

1985 Mar EP *Aikea Guinea* makes UK #41.

Nov 2 12"-only EPs, *Tiny Dynamine* and *Echoes In A Shallow Bay* are released with *Tiny Dynamine* and *Echoes In A Shallow Bay* charting at #52 and #65 respectively.

1986 Jan The Twins release a US CD-only compilation, **The Pink Opaque**.

Apr Fourth album *Victorialand* hits UK #10.

Oct *Love's Easy Tears* makes UK #53 and is their last single release for almost 2 years.

Nov All the members individually collaborate with 4AD's new signing, pianist Harold Budd, on Independent chart album **The Moon And The Melodies**. They also complete a sell-out UK tour.

1988 Oct After a 2-year hiatus, new studio album *Blue Bell Knoll* reaches UK #15 and US #109.

1990 Sept *Iceblink Luck* peaks at UK #38. Critically praised as ever, **Heaven Or Las Vegas**, written and produced by The Cocteau Twins and recorded at September Sound studios, London, hits UK #7.

Nov [9] Group embarks on first ever North American concert tour at the Music Hall, New Orleans, LA. Tour will end San Diego, CA, Dec.9.

1991 Feb [10] Fraser is nominated in Best Female Singer category at UK record industry Brit Awards.

LEONARD COHEN

1951 Cohen (b. Sept.21, 1934, Montreal, Canada) forms C&W band, The Buckskin Boys, while studying at McGill University and begins attracting attention as a student poet.

1956 Starting in 1955 he publishes 2 collections: **The Spice Box Of Earth** and **Let Us Compare Mythologies**, which wins a national poetry prize.

1962 **Parasites Of Heaven** is published. The anthology contains several poems that become Cohen songs, including *Suzanne* and *Avalanche*.

1963 Cohen publishes his first novel, **The Favorite Game**.

1964 After a brief spell at Columbia University, New York, Cohen publishes a controversial poetry collection, **Flowers Of Hitler**.

1966 He has been writing and singing songs for several years when Judy Collins becomes the first artist to cover one (*Suzanne*), on her album *In*

My Life. Cohen publishes his second novel, **Beautiful Losers**. He performs at the Newport Folk Festival, CA, and is signed to CBS/Columbia by talent scout John Hammond.

1967 The Canadian National Film Board produces a documentary film, "Ladies & Gentlemen ... Mr. Leonard Cohen". He joins Judy Collins on stage at her summer concert in New York's Central Park.

1968 Jan Debut album *The Songs Of Leonard Cohen*, produced by John Simon, is released by CBS/Columbia.

Apr *The Songs Of Leonard Cohen* reaches US #83 (but is more successful in UK in the fall, reaching #13 and remaining on chart for 71 weeks). *Suzanne*, extracted from it, does not chart. (Cohen will never have a hit single in US or UK.) He appears in and scores another Canadian NFB film, "The Ernie Game".

1969 May *Songs From A Room* reaches US #63 and UK #2.

1970 May [10] Cohen plays the Royal Albert Hall, London.

Aug [30] He takes part in the Isle of Wight Festival in UK.

1971 May *Songs Of Love And Hate* reaches US #145 and hits UK #4. Cohen's songs are used as an integral part of Robert Altman's film "McCabe And Mrs Miller" starring Warren Beatty.

1973 June *Live Songs*, recorded on stage in Paris in 1970, reaches US #156.

1974 Oct *New Skin For The Old Ceremony*, with a soft-rock feel, fails to chart in US but makes UK #24. (He retires to a Greek island, returning to live performance in 1976.)

1977 Dec In a move away from the folky acoustic feel of earlier albums, Phil Spector is brought in to produce Cohen. Problems develop when Spector takes to using armed guards in the studio to enforce his will. The end product, *Death Of A Ladies' Man*, makes only UK #35.

1979 Sept *Recent Songs*, co-produced by Henry Lewy and with vocal arrangements and duets with Jennifer Warnes, returns to the spirit of earlier albums but includes unusual instrumental flourishes, such as the use of a Mariachi band.

1984 "I Am A Hotel", a half-hour feature film written, scored and directed by Cohen, wins first prize at the Festival International De Télévision De Montreux, Switzerland.

1985 Feb *Various Positions* marks a change of direction for Cohen, with its use of modern musical technology and a more upbeat theme, and a change of label to Passport Records. Cohen embarks on a worldwide tour to promote the album. It reaches UK #52 while *Dance Me To The End Of Love* is released as a single and complemented by a video. Cohen wins a Canadian Juno Award for Best Movie Score for his collaboration with Lewis Furey on rock-opera "Night Magic".

1986 Cohen makes a cameo appearance as head of Interpol in NBC TV's "Miami Vice".

1987 June His long-time backing singer Jennifer Warnes releases *Famous Blue Raincoat*, a collection of Cohen's songs which includes *First, We Take Manhattan*.

1988 Mar Cohen releases *First, We Take Manhattan*, extracted from *I'm Your Man*, which is his best-received in years. He performs 3 nights at London's Royal Albert Hall following its UK release.

July Special UK BBC TV documentary focusing on Cohen excites chart entry for *I'm Your Man* at UK #48 and *Greatest Hits*, first released in 1975, which enters at UK #99.

1990 Cohen guests on *Elvis' Rolls Royce* from Was (Not Was)' *Are You O.K.?*, as he is inducted into the Juno Canadian Hall Of Fame.

LLOYD COLE & THE COMMOTIONS

Lloyd Cole (vocals, guitar)
Neil Clark (guitar)
Lawrence Donegan (bass)
Blair Cowan (keyboards)
Steven Irvine (drums)

1983 July Cole (b. Jan 31, 1961, Scotland) meets Cowan in the Tennants Bar in Glasgow, Scotland, both on their way to a Ramones concert. They decide to form a band and team up with Clark (b. July 3, 1955).

1984 Jan Irvine (b. Dec.16, 1959), a former Scottish lightweight boxing champ, and Donegan (b. July 13, 1961), recently released from jail, are recruited to form Lloyd Cole & The Commotions. Local gigging and demo tapes lead to a record deal with Polydor.

July [7] First single *Perfect Skin* immediately appeals to the rock fraternity and climbs to UK #26.

Sept [15] *Forest Fire*, extracted from forthcoming debut album, makes UK #41.

Oct [12] *Rattlesnakes* is released, ultimately reaching UK #13, during a 30-week chart stay. A sell-out European tour follows.

Nov Extracted title track *Rattlesnakes* peaks at UK #65.

85 **Oct** *Brand New Friend*, from forthcoming album, is first Top 20 hit, reaching UK #19.

Nov Second album *Easy Pieces* is released, produced by Clive Langer/Alan Winstanley team, and hits UK #5. It achieves significant sales worldwide, but an increasingly disillusioned Cole gives his gold and platinum award disks to his local cafe where they are used as tea-trays. *Lost Weekend* reaches UK #17.

86 **Jan** *Cut Me Down* makes UK #38.

June Sandie Shaw records a cover version of *Are You Ready To Be Heartbroken*, a track from *Rattlesnakes*, which peaks at UK #68. Session tapes, produced by Chris Thomas for a new album, are recorded in between touring but are shelved.

87 **Jan** Cole teams with Ian Stanley, ex-collaborator with Tears For Fears and Peter Gabriel, and invites him to produce new album.

Oct First fruit of this liaison is *My Bag* which makes UK #46. Cowan leaves the group. A UK tour commences and is a sell-out, including 2 nights at London's Brixton Academy.

Nov Third album *Mainstream* hits UK #2.

88 **Jan** Group begins an extensive European tour as *Jennifer She Said* makes UK #31. A 12" version features covers of Bob Dylan's *I Don't Believe You* and Elvis Presley's classic *Mystery Train*.

Apr [17] They play the final tour date at Wembley Arena, London.

[23] While preparing for their first visit to Japan, EP *From The Hip* peaks at UK #59.

89 **Apr** Compilation album *1984-1989* reaches UK #14, as the band announces its intention to split.

90 **Feb** [10] *No Blue Skies*, marking the beginning of a solo career for Cole, now based in New York, makes UK #42.

Mar [3] *Lloyd Cole*, very similar in style and content to his efforts with The Commotions, debuts at UK #11, during a 6-week chart stay.

Apr [14] *Don't Look Back* peaks at UK #59.

June [15] Cole begins 25-date US tour in Atlanta, GA, which will end July 20 in Los Angeles, CA.

Oct [4] Cole plays benefit in New York for IMPACT NYC, which develops educational and recreational programs for homeless children.

NATALIE COLE

62 The second of Nat "King" Cole's 5 children, who all grow up in affluent Los Angeles suburb Hancock Park, Cole (b. Feb.6, 1950, Los Angeles, CA) appears on stage for the first time with her father.

65 Following her father's death, Cole becomes one of only 200 black students at the 20,000 student University of Massachusetts, Amherst, MA, where she studies for a BA in psychology. She becomes politically active as a committed pacifist and a member of the Black Panther Party. She also forms a student band which plays gigs off campus.

72 Although she feels artistic leanings to follow her father as a vocalist, she collects a degree in child psychology.

73 Having begun singing in clubs, she tries to hide her background from nostalgic promoters keen to hear her perform her father's work.

Feb Playing at the Executive Inn in Buffalo, NY, she meets Canadian promoter Kevin Hunter who becomes her manager and secures bookings on TV and at larger venues.

74 **Dec** R&B writer/producers Chuck Jackson and the Reverend Marvin Yancy invite her to record demos in Curtis Mayfield's Curtom studio.

75 **June** After major labels turn her down, she eventually signs to Capitol (the same company for which her father recorded).

July At Yancy's behest, Cole is re-baptized before beginning her first major US tour.

Oct [25] *This Will Be*, taken from *Inseparable*, makes UK #32.

Nov [22] *This Will Be* hits US #6.

[29] *Inseparable* reaches US #18, earning a gold disk.

76 **Feb** [28] Cole wins Best New Artist Of The Year and Best R&B Vocal Performance, Female for *This Will Be* at the 18th annual Grammy awards.

Mar [27] *Inseparable* makes US #32.

Apr Cole opens for Bill Cosby at the Hilton hotel, Las Vegas, NV.

July [17] *Natalie* reaches US #13, earning Cole her second gold disk.

[31] Cole secretly marries Marvin Yancy in Chicago, IL.

Aug [7] *Sophisticated Lady (She's A Different Lady)* reaches US #25.

Oct [30] *Mr. Melody* makes US #49.

77 **Feb** [14] She announces publicly, on Valentine's Day, that she was married in 1976 and is now pregnant.

[19] Cole wins Best R&B Vocal Performance, Female for *Sophisticated Lady* at the 19th annual Grammy awards.

Apr [23] Third album *Unpredictable* hits US #8 and earns Cole her

first platinum disk.

[30] Extracted *I've Got Love On My Mind* hits US #5, and is her first gold single. Cole guests on US TV specials "Sinatra And Friends" and "Paul Anka ... Music My Way".

Aug [13] *Party Lights* peaks at US #79.

Oct [14] Cole gives birth to a son, Robert Adam.

Dec Cole is voted Best Female Vocalist by the National Association For the Advancement Of Colored People (NAACP).

1978 **Jan** [14] She performs on TV "Super Bowl" celebration special.

[16] She co-hosts the annual American Music Awards.

Mar [30] Cole begins 4 days of concerts at Long Island's Westbury Music Fair.

Apr [8] *Thankful* reaches US #16, Cole's second platinum album.

[15] *Our Love* hits US #10, having already topped US Soul chart, and is her second gold single.

June "The Natalie Cole Special" airs on US TV.

Sept [9] Double album *Natalie ... Live!*, recorded in New Jersey and Los Angeles, reaches US #31.

1979 **Feb** [8] Cole makes her cabaret debut at MGM Grand in Las Vegas.

May [5] *I Love You So* peaks at US #52. (Cole wins the Grand Prize at the Tokyo Music Festival.)

1980 **Mar** [1] *We're The Best Of Friends*, an album of Cole duets with Peabo Bryson, makes US #44. From it, *Gimme Some Time* (#8) and *What You Won't Do For Love* (#16) are both R&B hits.

July [26] *Don't Look Back* climbs to US #77.

Sept [20] *Someone That I Used To Love* reaches US #21.

1981 **Oct** *Happy Love* peaks at US #132. *The Natalie Cole Collection* is her final release on Capitol.

1982 **Feb** She signs worldwide to Epic Records. *I'm Ready* reaches US #182.

1983 **Sept** Cole joins Johnny Mathis on *Unforgettable – A Tribute To Nat "King" Cole*.

1985 **June** [8] *Dangerous*, Cole debut for Modern Records, peaks at US #57.

July [20] *Dangerous* peaks at US #140.

Sept [21] *A Little Bit Of Heaven* climbs to US #81.

1986 **Sept** Cole signs to EMI subsidiary Manhattan.

1987 **Aug** *Everlasting* is released. (On it Cole covers *When I Fall In Love*, which will give her father a posthumous UK #4 at Christmas.) *Jump Start* makes UK #44.

Oct [3] *Jump Start* reaches US #13.

1988 **Jan** *Over You*, a duet with Ray Parker Jr., makes UK #65.

Feb [6] *I Live For Your Love* reaches US #13.

May [7] A re-working of Bruce Springsteen's *Pink Cadillac* (originally B-side of his *Dancing In The Dark*) hits US #5. *Pink Cadillac* also hits UK #5. Re-sleeved and re-mastered *Everlasting* makes US #42 and peaks at UK #62 (her first UK chart album).

June [11] She makes a rare live appearance, at "Nelson Mandela's 70th Birthday Party" at Wembley Stadium, London, as part of a soul supergroup with Ashford & Simpson, Joe Cocker, Al Green and others.

July *Everlasting* reaches UK #28.

Aug [27] *When I Fall In Love* climbs to US #95.

Sept *Jump Start*, reissued at US #36. Cole begins a US tour.

Nov *I Live For Your Love* makes UK #34.

Dec Cole plays 2 shows at Hammersmith Odeon, London, during a short UK visit. (She is featured on the soundtrack of Bill Murray film "Scrooged").

1989 **Jan** [14] Cole wins Best Female Artist at NAACP's 21st Image Awards.

May Michael Masser co-written ballad *Miss You Like Crazy* hits UK #2, as parent album *Good To Be Back* hits UK #10.

June [3] *Miss You Like Crazy* tops US R&B chart.

July [8] *Miss You Like Crazy* hits US #7 as *Good To Be Back* makes US #59.

Best Of The Night peaks at UK #56.

Dec *Starting Over Again* peaks at UK #56.

1990 **Apr** [14] Uptempo *Wild Women Do*, featured in Richard Gere/Julia Roberts hit movie "Pretty Woman", makes US #34.

[16] Cole participates in the "Nelson Mandela – An International Tribute To A Free South Africa" concert at Wembley Stadium.

May [5] Cole sings *Lucy In The Sky With Diamonds* and *Ticket To Ride* at the "John Lennon Tribute Concert", held at the Pier Head Arena in Merseyside, to celebrate the songs of Lennon, as *Wild Women Do* reaches UK #16.

Sept [15] Talent show "Big Break", with Cole as host, airs for the first time on US syndicated TV.

Dec Cole provides guest vocal on David Foster's seasonal single *Grown-Up Christmas List*.

JUDY COLLINS

1954 Collins (b. May 1, 1939, Seattle, WA), daughter of blind Denver radio personality and musician Chuck Collins, after studying piano in Denver, CO, with acclaimed pianist/conductor Dr. Antonia Brico and making her public debut at age 13 with the Denver Businessmen's Symphony Orchestra, gradually turns to the folk guitar.

1957 She drops out of college in Jacksonville, IL, and returns to Denver to marry her teacher boyfriend Peter Taylor. They live in a cabin in the Rockies and have a son, Clark.

1959 Collins begins singing professionally with first engagements early in the year in Boulder, CO, and the couple moves to Chicago, IL.

1960 She lands a regular gig at Chicago's Gate Of Horn, billed second to poet Lord Buckley.

1961 Collins signs to Elektra Records after owner Jac Holzman hears her performing on the New York folk circuit.
Oct First album, *A Maid Of Constant Sorrow*, features traditional folk songs and prompts growing reputation on the specialist scene.

1962 **July** *Golden Apples Of The Sun* is released to wide critical approval.
Sept She debuts at New York's Carnegie Hall.
The pressures of new-found fame and the break-up of her marriage take their toll. By the end of the year she is seriously ill with tuberculosis and spends 6 months in hospital.

1963 **Dec** When she returns to the folk scene, it has become more contemporary and third album, *Judy Collins #3* (with arrangements by Jim McGuinn, soon to find fame with The Byrds) contains overtly political material. (She will become active in the protest movement.)

1964 **Apr** *Judy Collins #3* reaches US #126.
Oct Live *The Judy Collins Concert*, featuring songs by Bob Dylan, Tom Paxton and Phil Ochs, is released but does not chart.

1965 **Nov** *Fifth Album*, produced by Joshua Rifkin, climbs to US #69.

1967 **Jan** *Hard Lovin' Loser* is her first US single chart entry, reaching #97.
Feb *In My Life* is recorded in London and includes *Suzanne* and *Dress Rehearsal Rag*, the first recordings of songs by Leonard Cohen, and some numbers from Peter Weiss' stage production of "The Marat/Sade", with orchestral backing. It peaks at US #46.
July Collins introduces a visibly nervous Cohen on stage during a concert in Central Park, New York.
Dec [9] Collins performs at Carnegie Hall, New York.
[31] She guests on New Year's Eve broadcast of CBS TV's "The Smothers Brothers Show".

1968 **Jan** *Wildflowers* contains first of her own songs and broadens her style to interpret songs by Jacques Brel, Brecht/Weill and newer writers Joni Mitchell and Randy Newman. On chart in US for nearly 18 months, it will hit #5, earn a gold disk, and become her all-time best-seller.
[20] She appears with Bob Dylan, The Band and others in a concert at Carnegie Hall, New York, commemorating folk singer Woody Guthrie, recently deceased.
Mar [14] Collins arrives in UK for first professional visit, which will include UK TV debut on "Whole Scene Going" and dates in London, Nottingham, Norwich and Birmingham.
Dec [21] A version of Joni Mitchell's *Both Sides Now* from *Wildflowers* is her biggest chart single, hitting US #8. It will win a Grammy award for Best Folk Performance of 1968.

1969 **Jan** *Who Knows Where The Time Goes* reaches US #29 and earns a gold disk. Her backing band for this includes short-term beau Stephen Stills who is subsequently inspired to write *Suite: Judy Blue Eyes*, recorded by Crosby, Stills & Nash on their debut album.
Mar [8] *Someday Soon* peaks at US #55.
[12] Collins wins Best Folk Performance Of 1968 for *Both Sides Now* at the 11th annual Grammy awards.
July [15] Collins opens in the New York Shakespeare Festival production of Ibsen's "Peer Gynt" at Delacorte theater in Central Park, New York. She plays Solveig, in a cast which includes Stacy Keach, Estelle Parsons and Olympia Dukakis. The play will close Aug.2.
Aug [23] *Chelsea Morning*, another Joni Mitchell song, makes US #78.
Nov [14] Collins performs at Royal Albert Hall, London, while *Recollections*, a compilation of early material, reaches US #29.
Dec [27] A revival of The Byrds' *Turn! Turn! Turn!* peaks at US #69.

1970 **Jan** [23] Collins, testifying at the trial of the "Chicago Seven", is denied permission to sing her testimony.
Both Sides Now marks her UK chart debut at #14.

1971 **Jan** *Whales And Nightingales* makes US #17 and earns a gold disk. It includes *Farewell To Tarwathie*, a traditional Scottish whaling song arranged around real recordings of the song of the humpback whale.
Feb [20] An arrangement of traditional *Amazing Grace*, recorded in St.

Paul's Chapel at Columbia University and taken from *Whales And Nightingales*, reaches US #15 and hits UK #5. It is her biggest UK hit and one of the longest runs in UK chart history. (Initially on chart for 32 weeks and continuing via constant re-entries in the lower part, it moves up to #20 in mid-1972 and finally exits in Jan.1973, after 67 weeks.)
Apr *Whales And Nightingales*, her first UK chart album, makes #37.

1972 **Jan** [29] *Open The Door (Song For Judith)* climbs to US #90. *Living* makes US #64. Collins takes a year off to write prose and begin work co-directing "Antonia: A Portrait Of The Woman", a film about her former piano teacher Antonia Brico (which will later be nominated for an Academy Award).
May She joins other artists in campaigning through benefit concerts for George McGovern's US presidential bid.
July Compilation album *Colors Of The Day/The Best Of Judy Collins* climbs to US #37.

1973 **Mar** *True Stories & Other Dreams*, notable for its original songs, including *Ché* and *Song For Martin*, reaches US #27.
[31] *Cook With Honey*, taken from it, makes US #32.

1975 **June** *Judith*, produced by Arif Mardin, reaches US #17 and becomes her biggest-selling UK album, at #7.
May [31] *Send In The Clowns*, taken from Stephen Sondheim's musical "A Little Night Music", hits UK #6.
Aug [2] *Send In The Clowns* makes US #36.

1976 **Oct** [16] *Bread And Roses* reaches US #25.

1977 **Oct** [22] Compilation *So Early In The Spring: The First 15 Years* peaks at US #42.
Nov [26] *Send In The Clowns* climbs to US #19 in a second chart run, and completes 27 weeks on the Hot 100.

1979 **Mar** [31] *Hard Times For Lovers*, her last US hit single, climbs to #66.
Apr [28] *Hard Times For Lovers* peaks at US #54.

1980 **May** [17] *Running For My Life* makes US #142.

1982 **Apr** [10] *The Times Of Our Lives* climbs to US #190, during a 5-week stay on chart.

1985 **Dec** UK-only TV-advertised compilation *Amazing Grace* makes #34.

1987 After an 18-month break from recording, Collins returns on new label, Gold Castle, with *Trust Your Heart*. It includes a new recording of *Amazing Grace*. Collins' book **Trust Your Heart: An Autobiography** is published.

1988 **Sept** It is announced that a live album *Grace's Sanity* is to be released shortly.

1989 **Feb** Collins launches Judy Collins Harmonics cosmetics line. First product is Liposome Eye Gel.

1990 **June** [21] Collins sings *Amazing Grace* at the Nelson Mandela rally at Yankee Stadium, New York.
Now signed to CBS/Columbia, Collins returns with *Fires Of Eden*, her best received work in years. The album, produced by Joel Dorn and Lucy Simon, includes interpretations of *The Air That I Breathe* and future Grammy winner *From A Distance*.

PHIL COLLINS

1981 **Jan** Having been a child actor, as the Artful Dodger in London stage production of "Oliver" and an extra in The Beatles film "A Hard Day's Night" among other roles, a member of art-rock band Flaming Youth in the early 70s (releasing 1 album *Ark 2*) and later of part-time jazz-rock outfit Brand X, Collins (b. Jan.30, 1951, Chiswick, London), already a major international star as drummer and lead singer of Genesis, after Peter Gabriel's 1975 departure, signs to Virgin in UK and Atlantic in US for a parallel solo career.
Feb [7] *In The Air Tonight*, from forthcoming *Face Value*, hits UK #2, behind John Lennon's *Woman*.
[21] *Face Value*, which Collins claims to have been motivated by his divorce from his first wife, enters UK chart at #1, eventually selling over 900,000 copies in UK and spending 274 weeks on chart
Mar [21] *I Missed Again*, second single from the album, makes UK #14.
May [23] *I Missed Again*, Collins' first US solo single, reaches US #19. B-side features demo versions of the first 2 hits.
June [27] Heart-broken ballad *If Leaving Me Is Easy* peaks at UK #17.
July [11] *Face Value* hits US #7, earning a gold disk for half a million sales.
Aug [15] *In The Air Tonight* reaches US #19.

1982 **Apr** [29] *In The Air Tonight* wins International Hit Of The Year at the Ivor Novello Awards.
July [21] Collins takes part in the first Prince's Trust Rock Gala at the Dominion theater, London. He plays drums for Ian Anderson.
He plays drums on Robert Plant's *Pictures At Eleven*, which hits UK # and US #5.

Sept Collins produces solo album *Something's Going On* for former Abba vocalist Frida, which makes UK #18 and US #41.

Oct [30] *Thru' These Walls* peaks at UK #56.

Nov [13] Second album *Hello, I Must Be Going* hits UK #2, spending 160 weeks on chart.

'83 Jan [15] A revival of The Supremes' 1966 million-seller *You Can't Hurry Love*, taken from the album, gives Collins his first UK #1 single (for 2 weeks). It is accompanied by nostalgic video.

Feb [5] *You Can't Hurry Love* hits US #10 as parent album *Hello, I Must Be Going* hits US #8.

Mar [26] *I Don't Care Anymore* makes US #39. Ballad *Don't Let Him Steal Your Heart Away* makes UK #45.

May [5] Collins, with the other members of Genesis, wins the Outstanding Contribution To British Music Award at the annual Ivor Novello Awards at Grosvenor House, Mayfair, London.

[28] *I Cannot Believe It's True* climbs to US #79.

Dec [17] Adam & The Ants' *Strip*, an unlikely production credit for Collins, makes UK #41.

'84 Apr [21] *Against All Odds (Take A Look At Me Now)* tops US chart for 3 weeks and is a million-seller, and also hits UK #2. Collins had been asked by director Taylor Hackford to write a song for his movie "Against All Odds". He uses an out-take from *Face Value* titled *How Can You Sit There?*, rewriting it as *Against All Odds*. (It will be nominated for an Oscar at the following year's Academy Awards.)

June [8] Collins takes part in the annual Prince's Trust Rock Gala at the Royal Albert Hall, London.

Aug [4] Collins marries Jill Tavelman.

Oct *In The Air Tonight* receives further airplay through exposure on NBC TV series "Miami Vice", in which Collins guests as game show host Phil The Shill, and also in Tom Cruise film "Risky Business". It bubbles under the Hot 100 at US #102.

Nov [25] He drums and sings at the recording session for Band Aid's *Do They Know It's Christmas?* which will become UK's all-time best-selling single.

'85 Feb [2] *Easy Lover*, jointly-credited uptempo dance number with Earth, Wind & Fire's Philip Bailey, hits US #2 and is another million-seller.

[9] *Sussudio*, a taster from his next album, reaches UK #12.

[26] Collins wins Best Pop Vocal Performance, Male for *Against All Odds* at the 27th annual Grammy awards.

Mar [2] *No Jacket Required*, with help from Sting, Nathan East, Greg Phillinganes and others, debuts at UK #1, where it will remain for 5 weeks, and stay charted for 175 weeks.

[13] *Against All Odds (Take A Look At Me Now)* wins Best Song Musically And Lyrically at the annual Ivor Novello Awards at London's Grosvenor House.

[23] *Easy Lover* hits UK #1, topping the chart for 4 weeks.

[30] Sax-laden ballad *One More Night* spends 2 weeks at US #1 and will sell over a million, as *No Jacket Required* begins a 7-week run at the top of US chart.

Apr [27] *One More Night* hits UK #4.

July [6] *Sussudio* tops US chart for a week, Collins' third consecutive US #1, and is another million-seller.

[13] Uniquely, Collins performs on the same day at Wembley Stadium, London, and JFK Stadium, Philadelphia, PA, both Live Aid venues, jetting the Atlantic on Concorde between appearances. Amongst his guest slots at the event, he plays drums behind Jimmy Page and Robert Plant in a Led Zeppelin reunion.

Aug [24] *Take Me Home* reaches UK #19.

Sept [28] *Don't Lose My Number* hits US #4.

Oct Collins, at the suggestion of Atlantic president Doug Morris, records *Separate Lives*, written by Stephen Bishop in 1982 and to be featured as love theme in Mikhail Baryshnikov/Gregory Hines film "White Nights", with singer Marilyn Martin.

Nov [30] *Separate Lives* hits US #1 and is Collins' fifth US million-seller from his last 6 releases.

Dec *Separate Lives* hits UK #4.

'86 Feb [10] Collins wins Best British Male Artist and *No Jacket Required* wins Best British Album at the fifth annual BRIT Awards.

[25] Collins wins Best Pop Vocal Performance, Male and Album Of The Year for *No Jacket Required* at the 28th annual Grammy awards.

Mar He produces Howard Jones' *No One Is To Blame* (UK #16, US #4).

Apr [7] *Easy Lover* wins Most Performed Work category at the annual Ivor Novello Awards.

May [10] *Take Me Home* hits US #7.

June [20] Collins takes part in fourth annual Prince's Trust Rock Gala concert, with Paul McCartney, Elton John, Tina Turner, Dire Straits and

others, at the Wembley Arena, London.

Nov He joins Greg Phillinganes (keyboards) and Nathan East (bass) to become Eric Clapton's band for his new album *August*. Collins will also be part of lengthy world tour to promote it.

Dec Clapton's *August*, also produced by Collins, hits UK #3.

1987 EP *12"ers*, remixes of previous singles, is released only on CD. In US it is also released as an album.

1988 June [5-6] Collins takes part in the sixth annual Prince's Trust Rock Gala concert, with Clapton, Joe Cocker, Elton John, Howard Jones and others, at the Royal Albert Hall, London.

[11] He drums in an all-star band put together by Midge Ure for the "Nelson Mandela's 70th Birthday Party" concert at Wembley Stadium.

July Remixed version of debut single *In The Air Tonight*, released through its exposure on a Mercury Communications TV commercial, hits UK Top 10 again at #4.

Sept *Groovy Kind Of Love*, a remake of The Mindbenders' 1966 UK #2 and featured in forthcoming film "Buster", tops UK chart. (Collins stars in the title role as former Great Train Robber, now flower-seller, Buster Edwards. He also compiles the film's soundtrack album of 60s songs.)

Oct [22] *Groovy Kind Of Love* tops US chart.

Dec Co-written and produced by Lamont Dozier and accompanied by a dated 60s-era video featuring Collins in the roles of 4 mock band members, follow-up *Two Hearts* hits UK #6.

1989 Jan [21] *Two Hearts* tops Hot 100, and is Collins' seventh US #1.

Feb [13] He wins Best British Male Artist and *Buster* wins Best Film Soundtrack at the eighth annual BRIT Awards at the Royal Albert Hall.

[15] Collins describes the Queen as a "pretty good jiver" as she dances at Prince Charles's 40th birthday.

[22] *Two Hearts* wins Best Song Written Specifically For A Motion Picture Or Television at the 31st Grammy awards.

Mar [18] Collins' wife Jill gives birth to their first child, a daughter Lily Jane.

Apr [4] *Two Hearts* wins Best Film Theme Or Song at the annual Ivor Novello Awards. Dozier accepts the award as Collins has 'flu. (Collins has also recently been awarded a Golden Bug in Sweden and a Genie in Canada, both acting honors for "Buster".)

May [11] Collins performs at the Songwriters Hall Of Fame 20th anniversary in New York.

Aug [24] Collins plays the part of Uncle Ernie in a benefit performace of Pete Townshend's "Tommy" at Universal Amphitheater, Los Angeles, with Elton John as The Pinball Wizard, Steve Winwood as The Hawker, Patti LaBelle as The Acid Queen, and Billy Idol as Cousin Kevin. (The show will be broadcast on the Fox network on Sept.13.)

Nov Plight of urban homelessness themed ballad, *Another Day In Paradise* hits UK #2.

Dec [2] *But Seriously* debuts at UK #1, spending 15 weeks at the top. It is the fastest selling album in UK chart history and will become one of its biggest.

[23] *Another Day In Paradise* tops US chart.

1990 Jan [6] *But Seriously* tops US Album chart.

Feb [10] *I Wish It Would Rain*, featuring Clapton fret work, hits UK #7.

[18] Collins wins Best British Male Artist at the ninth annual BRIT Awards at the Dominion theater, London.

Mar [8] He wins Best Drummer award in **Rolling Stone** 1989 music awards.

[31] *I Wish It Would Rain* hits US #3.

May [5] *Something Happened (On The Way To Heaven)* reaches UK #15.

[31] US tour dates include 3 concerts at the Nassau Coliseum, Uniondale, NY.

June [30] *Do You Remember?* hits US #4 as Collins joins Genesis, Pink Floyd, Robert Plant, Paul McCartney, Cliff Richard And The Shadows, Status Quo, Eric Clapton, Elton John, Mark Knopfler and Tears For Fears, all previous Silver Clef winners, on a star-studded bill at Knebworth Park, Herts., in aid of Nordoff-Robbins Music Therapy Centre.

Aug [4] *That's Just The Way It Is* reaches UK #26.

Sept [8] CBS TV special "Seriously, Phil Collins" airs.

Oct [2] Collins closes a 127-show, 9-month, 16-country, 59-city tour at Madison Square Garden, New York.

[6] *Something Happened On The Way To Heaven* hits US #4.

[13] *Hang In Long Enough* makes UK #34.

Nov [17] *Serious Hits ... Live!*, a double-set collecting the best recordings from Collins recent "But Seriously World Tour", debuts at UK #2, behind *The Very Best Of Elton John*.

[26] Collins wins Top Adult Contemporary Artist, Top Worldwide Album and Top Adult Contemporary Single categories at the 1990

PHIL COLLINS cont.

Billboard Music Awards Shows in Santa Monica, CA.
Dec [15] *Do You Remember (Live)* peaks at UK #57.

1991 **Jan** [12] *Hang In Long Enough* reaches US #23.
[28] Collins wins Favorite Pop/Rock Album for *... But Seriously* and Favorite Pop/Rock, Male Artist at the 18th annual American Music Awards at the Shrine Auditorium, Los Angeles. (While in US, Collins films a minor role in Steven Spielberg's Robin Williams/Dustin Hoffman-starring "Hook", a modern day adaptation of "Peter Pan".)
Feb [2] *Serious ... Hits Live!* reaches US #11.
[5] He plays drums for the opening series of 24 Eric Clapton concerts at the Royal Albert Hall, London.
[16] *Who Said I Would* peaks at US #73.
[20] *Another Day In Paradise* wins Record Of The Year at the 33rd annual Grammy awards at Radio City Music Hall, New York. (It is Collins' seventh Grammy.)
Mar [7] Collins is once again named Best Drummer in the annual **Rolling Stone** Readers' Picks music awards.
May [4] Collins receives an honorary Doctorate of Music degree from the Berklee College of Music, Boston, MA.

THE COMMODORES

Lionel Richie (vocals, keyboards)
William King (trumpet)
Thomas McClary (lead guitar)
Milan Williams (keyboards, trombone, guitar, drums)
Ronald LaPraed (bass, trumpet)
Walter "Clyde" Orange (vocals, drums)

1967 The Mighty Mystics are formed at Tuskegee Institute, AL, when 6 students including McClary (b. Oct.6, 1950) and Richie (b. June 20, 1949, Tuskegee) combine and enter a talent contest to impress girls. The Mystics later link with another campus group, The Jays, which includes King (b. Jan.30, 1949, Alabama) and Willams (b. Mar.28, 1948, Mississippi). The Commodores name is decided by the toss of a dictionary and a finger-point from King.

1968 Having become local favorites in Montgomery, AL, The Commodores are sent by the Tuskegee Institute to play a benefit at New York's Town Hall. Local entrepreneur Benny Ashburn handles publicity.

1969 The band members return to their studies at the Institute having aroused popular support on New York's club scene. During the summer, they return to New York and contact Ashburn, who secures them an audition at Small's Paradise, Harlem's best-known club.
Sept Orange (b. Dec.10, 1947, Florida) replaces Andre Callahan as the group's drummer. Bassist Michael Gilbert is drafted and replaced by LaPraed (b. 1950, Alabama). Ashburn and the band form Commodores Entertainment Corp., harnessing the group's business qualifications.

1970 Ashburn, now their full-time mentor and manager, secures The Commodores dates on the European club circuit. They travel on board the S.S. France, and become local favorites in St. Tropez and other French resorts. While on tour, they meet a vacationing Ed Sullivan.

1971 Searching for an exciting opening act for Motown Records' biggest stars, The Jackson 5, Motown's Creative Vice President, Suzanne de Passe, sees the group perform at New York's Turntable and books them for the tour. They sign to the label, having released Swamp Dogg-produced *Keep On Dancing* on Atlantic earlier in the year. (It will be 3 years before Motown releases their first album.) Group begins its first Far East tour.

1974 **June** Instrumental *Machine Gun*, written by Williams, crosses over from R&B chart to US #22 and UK #20. (It will be played after the national anthem at closedown on Nigerian TV and radio stations.)
Aug *Machine Gun* peaks at US #138. It fails in UK, but achieves gold in Japan and Nigeria, where it is the biggest selling international album.
Nov UK follow-up *The Zoo (Human Zoo)* reaches #44. *I Feel Sanctified* peaks at US #75.

1975 **Mar** Second album *Caught In The Act* is released. During a 33-week chart stay, it will peak at US #26.
June Taken from the album, *Slippery When Wet* makes US #19 and wins the Bronze Prize at the Tokyo Music Festival. Following their own headlining tour, The Commodores are invited to support The Rolling Stones on their world tour.
Dec Richie ballad *Sweet Love* hits US #5. *Movin' On* climbs to US #29. Despite international tours and sales, most band members are still completing degree courses, studying while on the road and returning to university for mid-term and final exams.

1976 **July** During a tour supporting The O'Jays, *Hot On The Tracks* peaks at US #12.

Oct Second Richie ballad, *Just To Be Close To You* hits US #7.

1977 **Feb** Follow-up from the album, *Fancy Dancer* peaks at US #39.
The Commodores begin their own headlining world tour.
Apr Fifth album, *Commodores*, is released. It will hit US #3 and spend over a year on chart.
June Band appears with Donna Summer in disco movie "Thank God It's Friday", and contributes to its soundtrack.
Aug *Easy* hits US #4 and UK #9, written by Richie, as are most of their biggest hits. Band is on a 70-city US tour which will gross $6 million.
Sept *Brickhouse*, a dance anthem, hits US #5.
Oct Released as double A-side with revived *Sweet Love*, *Brickhouse* climbs to UK #32. During a UK visit, LaPraed's wife dies of cancer. (The next 2 albums will be dedicated to her.)
Dec *Too Hot Ta Trot* makes US #24. The Commodores complete their most successful year to date with sell-out US dates. Live double *Commodores Live!* hits US #3.

1978 **Mar** Double A-side *Too Hot Ta Trot/Zoom* makes UK #38.
Apr Group performs in the Congressgebouw, The Hague, Holland, at the start of a 21-date European tour.
May *Commodores Live!* makes UK #60: their UK Album chart debut.
July *Flying High* makes UK #37.
Aug [12] Richie ballad *Three Times A Lady* hits US #1, displacing The Rolling Stones' *Miss You*. Dedicated to his wife, the song was inspired by Richie's parents' 37th wedding anniversary. The disk will later go double platinum. (Richie will receive a Country Songwriter award by ASCAP in Nashville.)
[19] *Three Times A Lady* begins a 5-week chart stay at UK #1, becoming Motown's biggest selling single. A worldwide smash, it spurs *Natural High* to hit US #3 and UK #8.
Nov *Flying High* makes US #38 while *Just To Be Close To You* peaks at UK #62, as group ends a 4-month US tour in Louisville, KY.
Dec *Greatest Hits* peaks at US #23 and UK #19.

1979 **Aug** The Commodores participate in Saarbrucken Festival, Germany, at the start of a 19-date European tour.
Oct While new studio album *Midnight Magic* hits US #3 and UK #15, Richie-composed country/soul ballad *Sail On* hits US #4 and UK #8. It focuses on the failing marriage of friend William Smith and is passed on the chart by another Richie ballad, *Still*.
Nov *Still* hits US #1, replacing The Eagles' *Heartache Tonight*. It also hits UK #4.

1980 **Jan** *Wonderland* makes US #25 and UK #40.
Apr [25] LaPraed marries Jacqueline Echols in Tuskegee. They will spend their honeymoon on the group's 95-date US tour.
June Spiritually inspired *Heroes* is released. It hits US #7 but makes only UK #50. From it, *Old-Fashion Love* makes US #20.
Oct Title cut *Heroes* peaks at US #54. Their current tour is less successful than any in recent years.

1981 **Jan** The Commodores perform the title theme in movie "Underground Aces". Richie, thinking of a solo career, duets with Diana Ross on self-penned *Endless Love*. The group's *Lady (You Bring Me Up)* hits US #8 and makes UK #56. Richie's final album with the group, *In The Pocket*, climbs to US #13 and UK #69.
Nov Final Richie ballad for the group *Oh No* hits US #4 and UK #44.

1982 **Feb** Last group single featuring Richie vocals, *Why You Wanna Try Me* peaks at US #66. He leaves to write and produce for himself and other
Aug UK K-Tel compilation *Love Songs* hits UK #5, their most successful UK album (and not on Motown).
Aug [17] Manager Ashburn dies of a heart attack in New Jersey.
Dec *Painted Picture* peaks at UK #70. Richie's solo *Truly* hits US #1. US compilation on Motown, *All The Greatest Hits* makes US #37.

1983 **Apr** The Commodores record the theme for US TV show "Teachers Only", called *Reach High*. It fails to chart. McClary quits to record solo *Thomas McClary* and single *Thin Walls* for Motown, both with limited success.
June Another compilation, *Commodores Anthology* peaks at US #141.
Sept *Only You* makes US #54.
Nov First album since Richie's departure, *Commodores 13* reaches US #103. (As live interest also wanes, group will spend the next year re-assessing with no activity. Urgently needing a new vocalist, they recruit ex-Heatwave UK singer, J.D. Nicholas (b. Apr.12, 1952, Watford, Herts.), who has recently sung for Diana Ross.)

1985 **Jan** Composed by Orange as a tribute to Marvin Gaye and Jackie Wilson, *Nightshift* hits both US and UK #3. It features co-lead vocals by Orange and Nicholas and is taken from *Nightshift* which makes US #12 and UK #13.
June *Animal Instinct* reaches US #43 and UK #74.

Sept *Janet* peaks at US #87.

Nov Another UK TV compilation, on Telstar, *The Very Best Of The Commodores* makes UK #25. Motown drops the group after 11 years.

1986 Feb [25] *Nightshift* wins Best R&B Performance By A Duo Or Group With Vocal at the 28th annual Grammy awards, which helps them sign a new recording deal with Polydor Records. Band also signs a management deal with Natalie Cole's manager Dan Cleary.

Nov First Polydor single *Goin' To The Bank* reaches US #65 and UK #43, as the band begins a tour of Belgium, Holland, Germany and UK.

Dec *United* makes US #101, but fails to chart in UK.

[6] *Goin' To The Bank* makes US #65.

1988 Sept Used extensively as the theme to UK Halifax Building Society TV ad, *Easy* re-enters UK chart making #15.

Oct *Rock Solid* is released together with single *Solitaire*. The Commodores have sold over 40 million records worldwide, with 24 platinum and gold disks.

RY COODER

1969 Having started out as a member of Jackie DeShannon's backing group, played in Los Angeles, CA, in 1966 with Taj Mahal in blues group The Rising Sons, with Captain Beefheart's Magic Band in 1967 on *Safe As Milk*, and as a studio session guitarist, working with The Everly Brothers, Paul Revere & The Raiders, Randy Newman and a host of others, Cooder (b. Ryland Peter Cooder, Mar.15, 1947, Los Angeles) visits London, with arranger/producer Jack Nitzsche and meets The Rolling Stones. Tipped to join the band in Brian Jones' place, he does not do so, but plays mandolin on The Stones' *Let It Bleed*, works with Nitzsche and Newman on the soundtrack for Mick Jagger/James Fox film "Performance", playing dulcimer and bottleneck guitar, and works on "Candy" film soundtrack.

1970 Cooder signs to Reprise Records as a soloist.

Dec He plays extensively on Little Feat debut album.

1971 Jan Debut album *Ry Cooder* fails to chart, though is critically well-rated for its authentic folk-blues approach. He plays on The Rolling Stones' *Sticky Fingers*.

1972 Mar *Into The Purple Valley*, his US chart debut, reaches #113.

Nov *Boomer's Story* is released, but fails to chart.

1974 June *Paradise And Lunch* makes US #167.

1976 Nov *Chicken Skin Music* reaches US #177. Cooder tours with "The Chicken Skin Revue", with Hawaiian steel guitarist Gabby Pahinui, Tex-Mex accordionist Flaco Jiminez, and gospel vocal back-up trio led by Bobby King, who all played on the album.

1977 Sept Live *Show Time*, recorded at the Great American Music Hall, San Francisco, CA, with "The Chicken Skin Revue", peaks at US #158.

1978 June *Jazz* revives late 40s big band music with sidemen from the era and arrangements by Joseph Byrd. Cooder reunites with Captain Beefheart to work on "Blue Collar" film soundtrack.

1979 Sept *Bop Till You Drop* (the first rock album to be recorded using digital process) reaches US #62 and marks Cooder's UK chart debut at #36. He performs at Cambridge Folk Festival, Cambs.

1980 June He scores Walter Hill's movie "The Long Riders", drawing on US hillbilly-folk styles, and Hill's film "Southern Comfort", but no soundtrack recording is made available.

Sept [26] Cooder plays Dublin Stadium, Eire, as European tour starts.

Nov *Borderline* peaks at US #43 and UK #35.

1982 Feb He scores film "The Border", starring Jack Nicholson. The soundtrack album has Sam The Sham and Freddy Fender guesting.

June *The Slide Area* reaches US #105 and UK #18, but Cooder, unhappy with the album and its UK sales, backs out of tours and retreats to work at home in Santa Monica, CA, on movie soundtracks.

1983 June Cooder plays club dates in San Francisco, CA, in a small band put together by Duane Eddy.

Dec [8] He plays with Eric Clapton, Jeff Beck, Jimmy Page and others in the Ronnie Lane Benefit Concert for ARMS, at New York's Madison Square Garden.

1985 Jan Cooder scores Wim Wenders' modern-day western "Paris, Texas".

May Album of soundtrack for Louis Malle's "Alamo Bay", which includes contributions from John Hiatt and Los Lobos, is released on independent Slash Records, but does not chart.

1986 May *Crossroads* makes US #85.

1987 Cooder, now primarily an in-demand film writer, scores "Blue City" and blues movie "Crossroads", the latter including collaborations with Sonny Terry and The Frank Frost Blues Band from Mississippi.

Dec *Get Rhythm*, made with his current band (including Van Dyke Parks on keyboards and Jim Keltner on drums), guest vocalists Larry

Blackmon (of Cameo) and actor Harry Dean Stanton (who starred in "Paris, Texas"), re-activates his non-movie recording career, peaking at US #177 and UK #75.

1988 May *Get Rhythm*, a revival of a Johnny Cash song, and from album of the same title, becomes his first chart single at UK #93.

June *Pecos Bill*, with Cooder playing music to Robin Williams' narrative, is released in US on Windham Hill label.

1989 Feb [22] *Pecos Bill* wins Best Recording For Children at the 31st annual Grammy awards.

1990 July [12-15] Cooder, consistently popular in UK live arena, plays 4 nights at the Hammersmith Odeon, London with David Lindley.

SAM COOKE

1951 Cooke (b. Samuel Cook, Jan.22, 1931, Chicago, IL) one of Reverend Charles S. Cook's 8 children, having performed in church with 2 of his sisters and a brother as The Singing Children and moved to adult gospel singing with R.B. Robertson's Highway QCs and The Pilgrim Travelers, becomes lead tenor with star gospel group The Soul Stirrers, replacing R.H. Harris and quickly developing a distinctive vocal style.

1956 Specialty Records' (to whom The Soul Stirrers are signed) A&R man Robert "Bumps" Blackwell, sensing pop potential in Cooke's voice, records several non-gospel tracks with him and releases *Lovable*, a reworking of The Soul Stirrers' *Wonderful* with Cooke thinly disguised as "Dale Cooke" so as not offend his gospel fans, but the pseudonym is seen through and Art Rupe, safeguarding his label's large stake in the gospel market, refuses to release any more pop records by Cooke.

1957 Blackwell and Cooke are freed from their contracts at Specialty in exchange for relinquishing outstanding royalties and sign with Bob Keene's Keen Records. Gospel-styled but purely secular ballads (*I Love You*) *For Sentimental Reasons* and *Lonely Island* are Cooke's first 2 releases for Keen.

Dec [1] Cooke appears on CBS TV's "Ed Sullivan Show" (Buddy Holly & The Crickets also debut), singing *You Send Me*.

[2] *You Send Me*, written by his brother Charles, tops US chart for 2 weeks and sells 1.7 million copies.

1958 Jan [17] *You Send Me* makes UK #29 for 1 week.

Feb [10] Specialty releases a 1956 taboo Cooke pop number, *I'll Come Running Back To You*, which reaches US #18. (*I Love You*) *For Sentimental Reasons*, released by Keen in 1957, makes US #17.

Mar [31] *You Were Made For Me*, released immediately prior to *You Send Me*, makes US #39, while debut album *Sam Cooke* makes US #16.

Apr [5] Irvin Feld's "Greatest Show Of Stars" begins a 40-date tour at Norfolk, VA, with Cooke headlining, alongside The Everly Brothers, Clyde McPhatter and a host of rock and R&B names.

[14] *Lonely Island*, flip side of *You Were Made For Me*, reaches US #26.

Sept [15] *Win Your Love For Me* reaches US #22.

Nov [10] Cooke and Lou Rawls, a member of his tour backing group The Pilgrim Travelers Quartet, suffer minor injuries in a car crash in Marion, AR, in which Cooke's driver Edward Cunningham is killed.

Dec [28] *Love You Most Of All* reaches US #26.

1959 Apr [20] *Everybody Likes To Cha Cha Cha*, released to cash in on a novelty dance craze, makes US #31.

July [13] *Only Sixteen*, written by "Barbara Campbell" (a collective pseudonym for Cooke and friends Lou Adler and Herb Alpert, and Cooke's wife's maiden name), reaches US #28.

Aug *Only Sixteen* reaches UK #23 but Craig Douglas' cover version tops UK chart for 4 weeks.

Nov [9] RCA Records, aware that Cooke's contract with Keen is close to expiry, offers him a $100,000 guarantee.

[23] *There, I've Said It Again* makes US #81. Cooke and manager J.W. Alexander (ex-Pilgrim Travelers) form Kags publishing company.

1960 Jan [22] Cooke signs to RCA, which acquires his Keen back catalog and pairs him with producers Hugo Peretti and Luigi Creatore.

Mar [14] Cooke's first West Indies tour opens in Montego Bay, Jamaica. He is a sell-out sensation in the Caribbean. (This visit and 2 later ones are significant because Cooke's style will have a major influence on a generation of Jamaican artists-to-be, including Bob Marley and Jimmy Cliff.)

Apr [4] RCA debut *Teenage Sonata* makes US #50.

June [27] Belatedly issued on Keen, *Wonderful World* (a perennial favorite for later cover versions by Herman's Hermits, Art Garfunkel and others) climbs to US #12.

July *Wonderful World* reaches UK #27.

Oct [3] Gospel-styled *Chain Gang* hits US #2 and UK #9 and is his second million-seller.

Dec [19] *Sad Mood* reaches US #29.

1961 Jan Cooke launches his own SAR record label, one of the early artist-owned labels, with J.W. Alexander and his manager Roy Crain, using their initials. (It will find chart success later in the year with The Simms Twins' *Soothe Me* and in 1962-64 with several singles by The Valentinos, made up of the Womack brothers.)

Mar [27] *That's It, I Quit, I'm Movin' On* makes US #31.

July [24] *Cupid* makes US #17. (It will bring US and UK chart success later to Johnny Nash, The (Detroit) Spinners and Tony Orlando & Dawn.)

Sept *Cupid* hits UK #7.

Oct [23] *Feel It* peaks at US #56.

1962 Mar [24] Self-penned, like most of Cooke's material, *Twistin' The Night Away*, an infectious tribute to the worldwide dance craze, hits US #9, eventually selling 1.5 million copies.

Apr *Twistin' The Night Away* hits UK #6.

July [14] Another dance-styled release, *Having A Party*, reaches US #17 as *Twistin' The Night Away*, Cooke's first US chart album in 4 years, makes #72.

Aug [25] *Bring It On Home To Me*, a mid-tempo ballad gospel-style duet with Lou Rawls, and the other side of *Party* reaches US #13.

Nov [17] *Nothing Can Change This Love* reaches US #12.

[24] Gospelly B-side *Somebody Have Mercy* peaks at US #70.

Dec Compilation **The Best Of Sam Cooke**, with most of his biggest successes from *You Send Me* to *Bring It On Home To Me*, reaches US #22.

1963 Feb [23] Revival of Little Richard's *Send Me Some Loving* makes US #13.

Apr *Mr Soul* climbs to US #92.

May [25] *Another Saturday Night*, penned on the road during Cooke's UK tour, hits US #10 and reaches UK #23.

July His youngest son Vincent drowns in the family swimming pool.

Sept [7] *Frankie And Johnny*, a smooth R&B version of an old folk song, reaches US #14 and UK #30.

Oct *Night Beat* makes US #62.

Dec [14] Cooke's version of Willie Dixon's familiar blues *Little Red Rooster*, recorded in an all-star session with Ray Charles on piano and Billy Preston on organ, reaches US #11.

1964 Feb [15] Cooke announces he is to revise his live concert schedule, cutting his previous 8 months on the road to 2, to devote more time to developing his record label.

[24] After "whupping" Sonny Liston in their World Heavyweight Championship bout in Miami Beach, FL, Cassius Clay announces, among many other things, that "Sam Cooke is the world's greatest rock'n'roll singer – the greatest singer in the world."

Mar [14] *(Ain't That) Good News* reaches US #11.

Apr Cooke shows his appreciation of Clay's endorsement by duetting with him on US TV.

June *Ain't That Good News* reaches US #34. It includes Cooke's protest civil rights composition *A Change Is Gonna Come*.

[24] Cooke begins a 2-week engagement at Manhattan's Copacabana club, New York, with a 20'x100' billboard in Times Square announcing "Who's The Biggest Cook In Town?", followed days later by another billboard which says "Sam's The Biggest Cooke In Town".

July [4] *Tennessee Waltz*, still active *Good Times*' B-side, makes US #35.

[18] *Good Times* reaches US #11.

Sept [16] Cooke stars in the first edition of ABC TV's Jack Good-produced pop show "Shindig", with The Righteous Brothers and The Everly Brothers.

Nov [7] The boisterous *Cousin Of Mine* makes US #31, while more soulful B-side *That's Where It's At* peaks at US #93. Live album *Sam Cooke At The Copa*, recorded earlier in the year at the Copacabana club, reaches US #29 (and will stay charted in US for over a year).

Dec [11] Cooke is shot dead at the $3-a-night Hacienda motel at 9137 S.Figueroa, Los Angeles, CA, by its manager Bertha Franklin, after spending the previous night at PJs nightclub and checking in with 22-year-old Elisa Boyer. Franklin claims that Cooke had attempted to rape Boyer, and then tried in anger to assault Franklin herself when his intended victim fled to phone the police. The coroner's office returns a verdict of justifiable homicide.

[18] Cooke's funeral is held in Chicago, where his body is laid in a glass-topped coffin at the A.R. Leak Funeral Home prior to burial. A reported 200,000 fans file past to pay their respects, and as the sheer numbers get out of hand, the glass doors of the establishment are smashed. The service, attended by many of his musical contemporaries and friends, becomes chaotic despite Ray Charles singing *Angels Keep Watching Over Me*.

1965 Feb [27] *Shake*, the first posthumous single release, hits US #7. (Rod Stewart will cover it, as will Otis Redding – who will often dedicate it to Cooke when he sings it in concert.)

Mar [6] B-side *A Change Is Gonna Come* makes US #31, as *Shake!* reaches US #44.

May [8] Extracted *It's Got The Whole World Shakin'* makes US #41.

June [26] *When A Boy Falls In Love* peaks at US #52.

Aug *The Best Of Sam Cooke, Volume 2*, a compilation from his later hits, climbs to US #128.

Sept [4] *Sugar Dumpling* makes US #32.

Nov *Try A Little Love* peaks at US #120.

1966 Feb [26] A reissue of a minor 1961 hit *Feel It* makes US #95.

Apr [30] *Let's Go Steady Again*, first released in 1959 as B-side of *Only Sixteen*, is final posthumous US chart entry, spending a week at #97.

1985 July [20] **Live At The Harlem Square Club**, recorded in Miami, Jan.12, 1963, makes US #134.

1986 Jan [23] Cooke is inducted into the Rock'N'Roll Hall Of Fame at the first annual dinner at the Waldorf Astoria in New York.

Apr *Wonderful World*, once again familiar from its exposure in Harrison Ford/Kelly McGillis film "Witness" and reissued after a similar cover version use in a UK TV advertising campaign, hits UK #2. *The Man And His Music* makes US #175.

May [10] Follow-up UK reissue of *Another Saturday Night* peaks at US #75 as double compilation **The Man And His Music** hits UK #8, his only UK chart album.

1989 Jan [18] The Soul Stirrers are inducted into the Rock'N'Roll Hall Of Fame at the fourth annual dinner at the Waldorf Astoria, New York.

ALICE COOPER

Alice Cooper (vocals)
Glen Buxton (guitar)
Michael Bruce (guitar, keyboards)
Dennis Dunaway (bass)
Neal Smith (drums)

1965 Cooper (b. Vincent Damon Furnier, Feb.4, 1948, Detroit, MI), raised in Phoenix, AZ, son of a preacher, forms The Earwigs with schoolmates at Cortez High, playing mainly Rolling Stones and Who covers.

1966 Now known as Spiders, with Buxton, Bruce, Dunaway, Smith, and Cooper on vocals, they have a #1 in Phoenix with *Don't Blow Your Mind*, on local Santa Cruz label. They begin making periodic visits to play in Los Angeles, CA.

1968 Looking for the big break, they move permanently to Hollywood, CA, name-changing to The Nazz. Discovering another Nazz on the East Coast, with Todd Rundgren a member, they name-change for a final time to Alice Cooper. The name is soon applied to Furnier himself as well as the band. (Legend has it that the name came from a spirit called up at a ouija board session.) First break is meeting Frank Zappa and manager Shep Gordon, recently graduated from University of Buffalo, who has seen them at the Cheetah club in Los Angeles; they sign to their Straight label, saviour of many an unorthodox artist of the time.

1969 July *Pretties For You* captures the sound of a musically unremarkable garage band, but is a minor US hit, at #193.

Sept [13] Group takes part in the Toronto Rock'N'Roll Festival at Varsity Stadium, University of Toronto, Canada, with Bo Diddley, Chicago Transit Authority, Jerry Lee Lewis, Chuck Berry, Gene Vincent, Little Richard, Fats Domino and The Plastic Ono Band.

1970 May *Easy Action* is much like the first album. Now with a reputation as one of the worst bands in Los Angeles, they eventually pack up and move to Detroit.

June Band appears as group cameo in movie "Diary Of A Mad Housewife", starring Richard Benjamin.

1971 July Under the guidance of producer Bob Ezrin, **Love It To Death** surpasses earlier recordings, and the group is signed by Warner Bros.

Apr [24] *Eighteen*, taken from the album, climbs to US #21, while the album follows it to peak at #35. Stage sets can now become more elaborate and expensive to match the theatricality of the performance, and the group becomes a top box-office draw.

1972 Jan *Killer* consolidates the new success by reaching US #21.

[29] Extracted *Under My Wheels* peaks at US #59.

Feb *Killer* is the group's UK chart debut at #27.

Apr [22] *Be My Lover* makes US #49.

July [29] *School's Out* hits US #7.

Aug [12] *School's Out* tops UK chart for 3 weeks, cementing the group's success, and becoming an international teen anthem. Parent album *School's Out* hits US #2 and UK #4.

Sept *Love It To Death*, reissued in UK, reaches #28.

Nov [11] *Elected* reaches US #26 and will hit UK #4.

73 Mar *Hello, Hurray* makes US #35 and hits UK #6.

[24] *Billion Dollar Babies*, with contributions from Marc Bolan, Donovan and Harry Nilsson, sees the group at its peak of popularity, entering UK chart at #1 – displaying its nadir of gleeful bad taste with songs like *I Love The Dead*. The highly theatrical live show based around the album is massively successful, and equally gory.

Apr [21] *Billion Dollar Babies* tops US chart.

June [2] *No More Mr. Nice Guy* reaches US #25 and hits UK #10.

Sept [1] Extracted title track *Billion Dollar Babies* peaks at US #57.

74 Jan *Muscle Of Love* hits US #10 and UK #34.

[26] Extracted single *Teenage Lament '74* makes US #48.

Feb [16] *Teenage Lament '74* reaches UK #12. Following this, Cooper fires his original band and brings in Dick Wagner and Steve Hunter (guitars), Prakash John (bass), Penti Glan (drums) and Joseph Chrowski (keyboards). The first 2 have played anonymously on previous Cooper album sessions, while all have played with Lou Reed.

Oct Compilation album *Alice Cooper's Greatest Hits* hits US #8.

75 Apr *Welcome To My Nightmare*, which hits US #5 and UK #19, features actor Vincent Price. The accompanying stage show is more full of props and gore than ever, and is documented in film. Cooper makes a guest appearance on *Flash Fearless Vs. The Zorg Women Pts. 5 And 6*, a comic concept album.

June [21] Uncharacteristically melodic *Only Women Bleed*, from *Nightmare*, reaches US #12, and will later be covered by other artists (including a 1977 UK #12 hit version by Julie Covington).

[23] In Vancouver, Canada, with his "Welcome To My Nightmare" tour, Cooper falls from the stage and breaks 6 ribs.

Oct Cooper raises $200,000 for charity in 30 cities during his Halloween charity drive.

Nov [22] Title track *Welcome To My Nightmare* makes US #45.

76 Aug [14] *Alice Cooper Goes To Hell* reaches UK #23.

Dec [18] *Alice Cooper Goes To Hell* reaches US #27.

77 Jan [8] *I Never Cry*, while failing to chart in UK, reaches US #12, topping a million sales.

May [28] *(No More) Love At Your Convenience* is Cooper's first UK hit single in over 3 years, peaking at #44, as parent album *Lace And Whiskey* debuts at UK #33.

June [5] Cooper's boa constrictor, long a co-star of his live act, suffers a mortal bite from the rat it is being fed for breakfast. The distraught artist holds a public audition for a new performing boa, and a snake named Angel gets the gig.

July [2] *Lace And Whiskey* makes US #42.

Aug [13] *You And Me*, from the album, hits US #9.

78 Jan [14] Live album *The Alice Cooper Show*, the first to feature Cooper's new band (Dick Wagner and Steve Hunter on guitars, Prakash John on bass, Fred Mandel on keyboards and Pentti "Whitey" Glan on drums) on record, makes US #131, but Cooper is in a psychiatric hospital receiving treatment for chronic alcoholism. He will, however, be featured in a cameo role in movie "Sergeant Pepper's Lonely Hearts Club Band".

Dec [9] *From The Inside*, based on his hospital experience with relevant album packaging, and produced by David Foster with lyrics by Bernie Taupin, makes US #40.

[23] *How Are You Gonna See Me Now?*, dedicated by Cooper to his wife, reaches US #12 and UK #61.

79 Jan [27] *From The Inside* makes US #60. He is, however, not yet back to full health.

July [27] Cooper's Indian art store in Scottsdale, AZ, is mysteriously fire-bombed with the destruction of $200,000-worth of stock, including some of his own gold disks.

80 May [24] *Flush The Fashion*, produced by Roy Thomas Baker, makes UK #56.

July [5] *Clones (We're All)* makes US #40 as parent album *Flush The Fashion* climbs to US #44, while Cooper makes an appearance in movie "Roadie", starring Meat Loaf.

81 Sept [12] *Special Forces*, produced by Richard Podolor, reaches US #125 and UK #96.

'82 Mar [13] A live cover of Love's *Seven And Seven Is* makes UK #62.

May [8] Double A-side *For Britain Only/Under My Wheels* peaks at #66 on UK chart.

Sept *Zipper Catches The Skin*, self-produced with Erik Scott, fails to chart (possibly because the title makes potential buyers squirm).

83 Nov [12] *Dada* makes UK #93.

86 June [26] Reviving *School's Out*, Swiss band Krokus makes US #67.

Oct After time in the musical wilderness, a link-up with movie "A Nightmare On Elm Street 2" provides *He's Back (The Man In The Mask)*, which makes UK #61 and prompts a new contract with MCA Records.

[28] Cooper begins "The Nightmare Returns" tour in Lansing, MI.

Nov [1] *Constrictor* charts briefly in both US and UK, reaching #59 and #41 respectively, as musical climate revives, with many new glam-shock metal groups citing him as a major influence.

1987 Cooper has a cameo role in John Carpenter's movie "Prince Of Darkness".

Nov *Raise Your Fist And Yell* climbs to UK #48, but stalls at US #73.

1988 Apr Cooper's new controversial live show is taken to Europe and UK. It involves one moment when he slashes open the belly of a female dummy and pulls out a baby. *Freedom* makes UK #50 during the tour.

[7] Cooper accidentally hangs himself in a rehearsal. His safety rope snaps and he dangles for several seconds before a roadie saves him.

1989 Cooper signs with Epic Records and begins recording new album with producer Desmond Child.

Aug *Poison* hits UK #2, as parent album *Trash*, featuring Jon Bon Jovi, Richie Sambora, Kip Winger and all Aerosmith members except Brad Whitford, hits UK #2.

Oct *Bed Of Nails* makes UK #38.

Nov [25] *Poison* hits US #7 as parent album *Trash* reaches US #20.

Dec *House Of Fire* peaks at UK #65.

1990 Feb *House Of Fire* peaks at US #56.

Mar [18-21] Cooper plays his hometown Detroit at the Fox theater, with his new touring band, Al Pitrelli (guitar), Pete Friezzin (guitar), Tommy "T-Bone" Caradonna (bass), Derick Sherinian (keyboards), Jonathan Mover (drums) and Devon Meade (backing vocals), during a major North American tour.

May [5] *Only My Heart Talkin'* makes US #89.

1991 Cooper prepares for his role as Freddy Krueger's father in the sixth and final "Nightmare On Elm Street" movie, titled "Freddy's Dead: The Final Nightmare".

ELVIS COSTELLO & THE ATTRACTIONS

Elvis Costello (vocals, guitars)
Steve Nieve (keyboards)
Bruce Thomas (bass)
Pete Thomas (drums)

1971 Son of bandleader Ross McManus, Costello (b. Declan McManus, Aug.25, 1955, London) is already writing songs in his early teens in Liverpool, Merseyside, when he leaves school at age 16 to become a computer operator at an Elizabeth Arden cosmetics factory in Liverpool. (During the next 5 years he will play solo as D.P. Costello (Costello is his mother's maiden name) at local folk clubs.)

1976 He fronts the country-rock band Flip City and sends demos, recorded at Pathway studios while moonlighting from his day job, to record companies. One reaches Jake Riviera's newly-formed Stiff Records and Riviera, seeing potential in the patchy demo (which will be available on bootleg album *5,000,000 Costello Fans Can't Be Wrong*) contacts him.

1977 Riviera signs him and suggests he renames himself Elvis Costello. While a backing band is assembled, US West Coast group Clover, currently in UK, is brought in to provide backing on an album, with Nick Lowe producing.

Apr Debut single *Less Than Zero*, written about Fascist leader Oswald Mosley, is released on Stiff but fails to chart.

May Ballad *Alison* also fails to chart. A line from its chorus will provide the title for Costello's first album.

[27] He makes live debut as Elvis Costello at the Nashville in London.

July [9] He quits his day job at Elizabeth Arden.

[14] Costello and his backing band The Attractions play their first gig together as support to Wayne County at the Garden, Penzance, Cornwall. The line-up is bassist Thomas (ex-Sutherland Brothers & Quiver), keyboardist Nieve and drummer Thomas (ex-Chilli Willi & The Red Hot Peppers).

[26] Seeking a US record deal, Costello performs outside the London Hilton where there is a CBS sales conference in progress. He is arrested and subsequently fined £5 for obstruction, although it is thought the incident is nothing more than an imaginative Stiff PR exercise.

Aug [20] *My Aim Is True*, produced by Nick Lowe, reaches UK #14. Extracted *Red Shoes* is released.

Sept [10] Costello plays at the Crystal Palace Bowl, London, on a bill headed by Santana.

Oct [3] "Stiffs Live" UK tour with Costello, Lowe, Ian Dury, Wreckless Eric and Larry Wallis begins.

Nov [5] At the end of the tour, Riviera takes Costello, Lowe and The Yachts with him to the newly-formed Radar Records, leaving Stiff to Dave Robinson.

[15] Costello begins his first US tour, ending Dec.16 in New York.

Dec [17] Deputizing for The Sex Pistols on NBC TV's "Saturday Night Live", Costello stops in the middle of performing *Less Than Zero* and says, "I'm sorry ladies and gentlemen, there's no reason to do this song", and launches into *Radio Radio*, which he had previously been told not to sing.

[24] *Watching The Detectives*, Costello's last for Stiff and his first Singles chart entry, reaches UK #15.

1978 Jan Costello returns for further North American dates.

Mar [18] *My Aim Is True* reaches US #32, after 36 weeks on chart. Unlike the UK edition, it includes *Watching The Detectives* and is licensed for release to CBS/Columbia for North America.

Apr [1] *This Year's Model*, issued with The Attractions, hits UK #4.

[15] *(I Don't Want To Go To) Chelsea* reaches UK #16.

May [20] *This Year's Model* makes US #30, again with a different track listing to UK version.

June [17] *Pump It Up* reaches UK #24.

Nov [4] *Radio Radio*, a lament about the state of the nation's airwaves, reaches UK #29.

Dec Costello leaves his wife and young son. (They will be reunited a year later.)

1979 Jan [20] *Armed Forces* hits UK #2.

Feb [15] A Taste Of Honey beats out Costello, among others, to win Best New Artist at the 21st annual Grammy awards.

Mar [10] *Oliver's Army* hits UK #2, as parent album *Armed Forces* hits US #10, helped by a US tour. In a much-publicized incident in a bar at the Holiday Inn in Columbus, OH, Costello has an argument with Stephen Stills and Bonnie Bramlett, who is so angered by his racist remarks about Ray Charles and James Brown that she starts punching him, which is explained by Costello as "bringing a silly argument to a quick end ... and it worked too." Incident turns US media against him.

June [16] *Accidents Will Happen* reaches UK #28. He produces the first Specials album while Riviera sets up new label, F-Beat, following the collapse of Radar.

Dec [22] Costello performs at the first of 4 benefit concerts for the people of Kampuchea at Hammersmith Odeon, London.

1980 Feb F-Beat is launched with *Get Happy!*, produced by Lowe, which hits UK #2.

Mar [8] *I Can't Stand Up For Falling Down*, Costello's cover of an old Sam And Dave song, hits UK #4.

Apr [12] *Get Happy!* reaches US #11. (Linda Ronstadt, who has already recorded *Alison* on her 1978 album *Living In The USA* covers 3 Costello tunes (*Party Girl*, *Girls Talk* and *Talking In The Dark*) on *Mad Love*, much to Costello's displeasure.)

[26] *Hi Fidelity* reaches UK #30.

June [14] *New Amsterdam* makes UK #36.

Aug [17] Costello performs at the Playhouse theater during the Edinburgh Rock Festival.

Nov *Taking Liberties*, a US-only compilation of out-takes, demos and unreleased UK 45s, reaches US #28. (It features *Hoover Factory*, written by Costello to help save the historic Hoover vacuum cleaner manufacturing site, located on the A40 motorway outside London.) A similar album is released in UK with different track-listings in cassette form only, called *Ten Bloody Mary's And Ten How's Your Fathers*.

[30] Elvis Costello and Squeeze play a joint benefit concert at the Top Rank club in Swansea, S.Wales, for the family of boxer Johnny Owen, who has died from injuries received during a title bout in the US.

Dec [20] *Clubland* peaks at UK #60.

1981 Jan [31] *Trust* debuts at UK #9.

Feb *Trust* reaches US #28 as Costello tours US, with Squeeze as opening act.

May [18-29] Costello & The Attractions record a country album with producer Billy Sherrill at CBS studios in Nashville, TN.

June [20] Squeeze's Costello-produced *East Side Story* makes UK #19.

Nov [7] *Almost Blue*, recorded in Nashville, hits UK #7. Extracted *A Good Year For The Roses* (originally recorded by George Jones, with whom he records *Stranger In The House* on a Jones album) hits UK #6.

[8] ITV's "South Bank Show" airs a documentary on Elvis Costello, concentrating on the *Almost Blue* sessions. *Almost Blue* makes US #50.

1982 Jan Costello & The Attractions play London's Royal Albert Hall with the Royal Philharmonic Orchestra.

[16] A cover of Patsy Cline's *Sweet Dreams*, from *Almost Blue*, makes UK #42.

Apr [10] *I'm Your Toy*, recorded live with the RPO, peaks at UK #51.

June [26] *You Little Fool* makes UK #52.

July [10] *Imperial Bedroom* debuts at UK #6.

Aug [7] Extracted single *Man Out Of Time* peaks at UK #58.

Sept [25] *Imperial Bedroom* reaches US #30.

Oct [2] *From Head To Toe* makes UK #43.

Dec *Party Party*, from the teenage film soundtrack album *Party Party*, makes UK #48.

1983 May While a change of distribution is negotiated for F-Beat, Costello releases a single as The Imposter, creating his own Imp label. *Pills And Soap* makes UK #16.

Aug [6] *Everyday I Write The Book* reaches UK #28 and makes US #36. *Punch The Clock*, with backing vocals from Afrodiziak, hits UK #3 and reaches US #24. (The sleeve has a half-smile from Costello, which he later describes as a "welcoming" look.)

Sept [17] *Let Them All Talk* peaks at UK #59.

1984 June [18] Another Imposter single, *Peace In Our Time* (the only one on the Imposter label), makes UK #48.

I Wanna Be Loved/Turning The Town Red, helped by a video by Godley & Creme, reaches UK #25.

July *Goodbye Cruel World* hits UK #10 and makes US #35.

Aug [25] *The Only Flame In Town*, recorded with Daryl Hall, makes UK #71 and US #56. Costello spends the rest of the year touring mainly college venues in US with singer-songwriter T-Bone Burnette. He also tours with The Attractions.

1985 Costello appears in Alan Bleasdale's ITV drama "Scully", for which he has written the theme *Turning The Town Red*. He produces second album *Rum, Sodomy And The Lash* by Anglo-Irish band The Pogues.

Apr TV-advertised *The Best Of Elvis Costello – The Man* hits UK #8.

May [18] Early cut *Green Shirt* peaks at UK #68.

July Costello and Burnette release *The People's Limousine* as The Coward Brothers. (It is Costello's only new release of the year.)

Dec *The Best Of Elvis Costello & The Attractions* makes US #116.

1986 Feb Costello's remake of The Animals 1965 UK #3 *Don't Let Me Be Misunderstood*, credited as The Costello Show with backing by a group of US musicians, The Confederates, makes UK #33.

May *The King Of America* for which Costello reverts to his given name, reaches UK #11 and US #39. Produced by T-Bone Burnette, it covers a wide musical vista, reflecting his interests in Tex-Mex, country, cajun and Irish music. The players are drawn from Hall & Oates, Tom Waits, Los Lobos and the James Burton/Jerry Scheff/Ron Tutt axis which backed Elvis Presley in the late 60s. The Attractions play on only 1 track. (Nieve and Thomas are soon to be recruited for house band on Channel 4 TV show "The Last Resort".)

[16] He marries The Pogues' bassist Caitlin O'Riordan in Dublin, Eire.

Aug Costello makes his acting debut as a bungling magician in film "No Surrender".

[30] *Tokyo Storm Warning*, on Imp label, peaks at UK #73.

Oct *Blood & Chocolate*, a reunion with Nick Lowe, reaches UK #16 and US #84.

1987 Nov Costello signs a worldwide deal, excluding UK, with Warner Bros. Records. He insists on a clause which states that Warners may not release his product in South Africa while apartheid remains. Paul McCartney elicits the help of Costello to write *Back On My Feet*, B-side of McCartney's *Once Upon A Long Ago*. This will lead to further McCartney/Costello collbaorations for respective solo albums, an experience which McCartney will later compare to working with John Lennon.

1988 Costello, still using his real name, writes score for film "The Courier".

Aug He finishes work on a new album in Los Angeles, CA, after a month's recording in Dublin. He also records in New Orleans with The Dirty Dozen Brass Band and co-writes 2 tracks with Ruben Blades on the latter's first English-language album *Nothing But The Truth*.

1989 Feb Warner Bros. debut *Spike* hits UK #5.

Mar *Veronica*, written with McCartney, makes UK #31.

May [14] Costello plays the first of 4 concerts titled "A Month Of Sundays" at the London Palladium, in the midst of a UK tour.

[20] EP *Baby Plays Around* peaks at UK #65.

June [24] *Veronica* reaches US #19 as *Spike* makes US #32.

July Costello embarks on a major US tour, with a band comprising Jerry Scheff, Pete Thomas, Larry Knechtel, Marc Ribot, Michael Blair and Steven Soles. On the West Coast leg of the trip, he will jam with Jerry Garcia and James Burton at the Sweetwater club in San Francisco, CA, at a concert to celebrate the 21st anniversary of the Village Music record store in Mill Valley.

Sept [6] Costello wins Best Male Video for "Veronica" at the sixth annual MTV Video Awards at the Universal Amphitheater, Los Angeles.

Oct [28] *Girls Girls Girls*, a comprehensive retrospective compilation released on Demon, makes UK #67, as Costello plays the Montreux Jazz Festival with Squeeze's Chris Difford and Glen Tilbrook.

990 Mar [8] Costello is named Best Songwriter in **Rolling Stone**'s 1989 Critics Awards.

991 May Costello releases *Mighty Like A Rose* on Warner Bros.

COUNTRY JOE & THE FISH

ountry Joe McDonald (guitar, vocals)
ruce Barthol (bass)
arry Melton (guitar, vocals)
avid Cohen (keyboards)
ary "Chicken" Hirsch (drums)

964 After 4 years' US Navy service, McDonald (b. Jan.1, 1942, El Monte, CA) and Melton arrive as students in Berkeley, CA. They become involved in the local folk music scene and form the Instant Action Jug Band. McDonald begins writing the politically conscious lyrics that will typify his work.

965 Dec After almost a year as an acoustic band, they decide to go electric and form Country Joe & The Fish. Line-up is McDonald and Melton, with Cohen, Barthol, John Gunning (drums) and Paul Armstrong (bass). Band fails to secure a recording deal but cuts 2 limited-edition EPs for **Rag Baby** folk magazine.

966 Nov Ed Denson, editor of **Rag Baby** and the band's manager, arranges a recording deal with specialist folk label Vanguard. Gunning and Armstrong have left, Barthol has switched to bass and Hirsch has joined on drums.

967 June Band plays the Monterey Pop Festival, CA.
July Debut album *Electric Music For The Mind & Body*, a definitive psychedelic album, despite lack of airplay climbs to US #39. *Not So Sweet Martha Lorraine* is a particular favorite.

968 Jan *I Feel Like I'm Fixin' To Die* peaks at US #67. The title track, a light but barbed Vietnam war commentary, becomes an anthem.
Feb Band plays London's Roundhouse on its first European tour.
Aug McDonald pulls the group out of Jerry Rubin's hippie "Festival Of Love", which coincides with the Chicago Democratic Convention. *Together* makes US #23.
Sept Barthol leaves to avoid the draft and is replaced by Mark Ryan.
Dec [28] Band performs before 100,000 people at Miami Pop Festival in Hallendale, FL.

969 Jan Ryan, Hirsch and Cohen quit the line-up.
Feb McDonald recruits Mark Kapner (keyboards) and, from Big Brother & The Holding Company, Peter Albin (bass) and David Getz (drums). They begin recording and McDonald invites in a surprising array of session players, including members of Count Basie's band and the Oakland Symphony Orchestra.
Apr New line-up undertakes a European tour.
July *Here We Are Again* is released but the line-up which recorded it has already broken up, with Albin and Getz re-forming Big Brother & The Holding Company.
Aug [16] McDonald brings in Doug Metzner (bass) and Greg Dewey (drums) to perform at the Woodstock Festival, Bethel, NY.
Sept [22] Group plays the Royal Albert Hall, London at the start of a European tour.
Dec McDonald releases solo *Thinking Of Woody*, a tribute to folk singer Woody Guthrie.

970 Mar Second solo album *Tonight I'm Singing Just For You* is released. [18] McDonald is convicted of obscenity and fined $500 for leading an audience in his "Gimme an F..." Fish Cheer.
May *C. J. Fish*, made by the whole band, peaks at US #111.
June McDonald disbands the group and goes solo.

971 Apr *Hold On, It's Coming*, recorded in London with a collection of English musicians including Spencer Davis, is released but fails to chart. McDonald joins Jane Fonda and Donald Sutherland's "Free The Army" anti-war revue and tours US Army bases, but quits after a public row with Fonda.
Aug *War War War*, based on Robert W. Service's World War I book of poetry **Rhymes Of A Red Cross Man**, is played, sung and produced by McDonald and reaches US #185.
Nov Double compilation *The Life & Times Of Country Joe & The Fish From Haight-Ashbury To Woodstock* charts briefly at US #197.

972 Feb Live solo *Incredible! Live! Country Joe!* reaches US #179.
Dec McDonald, still a major concert draw, puts together Country Joe &

His All-Star Band, a large (and fluid) group for club and touring work.

1973 Sept *Country Joe LP Paris Sessions* is released without charting.

1974 Jan The All-Star Band faces financial collapse and splits.
Feb McDonald forms a duo with old friend Melton. Based mostly in Paris, they clock up around 150,000 miles on tour.

1975 Apr Solo *Country Joe* is released. He returns to Berkeley and joins Energy Crisis, a band formed by Phil Marsh and Bruce Barthol.
June Energy Crisis is now being called Country Joe & His Band and even Country Joe & The Fish. Group tours heavily, even to Australia and Japan.
Nov McDonald, now a solo artist with Fantasy Records, has his last US chart entry with *Paradise With An Ocean View*, which makes US #124.

1976 Apr Heavily involved in the Save The Whale campaign, McDonald records his own song *Save The Whales*, a hit single in several countries.
June Original group line-up for the first 3 albums re-forms for the Cardiff Castle Festival in Wales. Fantasy issues a group album, *Reunion*, which fails to sell.
Aug *Love Is A Fire* is released, unsuccessfully.
Dec McDonald leaves the original Fish, which fails to release an album without him and breaks up.

1977 Apr He plays a 3-day rally in Tokyo, Japan, with Jackson Browne, Richie Havens and others, to raise $150,000 for an international effort to save whales and dolphins from industrialized fishing. (He spends most of the year touring solo.)

1978 May *Rock'N'Roll Music For The Planet Earth* is released.
Aug McDonald reunites again with Melton for European gigs.
Sept McDonald returns to California to join The Barry Melton Band, which has been playing Melton's songs and old Fish material, and the group becomes yet another Country Joe & The Fish. They tour California and Texas.

1982 May McDonald appears in a benefit concert at the Moscone Center in San Francisco, CA, with The Grateful Dead, Boz Scaggs and Jefferson Starship, in aid of the Vietnam Veterans' Project.

1989 Aug [4-6] McDonald takes part in 13th annual Maine Arts Festival at Deering Oaks Park, Portland, ME.

1991 Jan McDonald returns to the recording scene with *Superstitious Blues*, released on the Rykodisc label.

COWBOY JUNKIES

Margo Timmins (vocals)
Michael Timmins (guitar)
Alan Anton (bass)
Peter Timmins (drums)

1979 Toronto, Canada-based Michael Timmins forms Hunger Project with Anton, playing music mainly influenced by Velvet Underground and Siouxsie & The Banshees. They audition for a female vocalist and one of Timmins' 3 sisters, Margo, offers but is rejected.

1983 Having relocated to New York and eventually London in search of underground sympathy, they regroup as Germinal, playing improvisational and experimental material. Band fails to impress and Timmins ends up working at the Record & Tape Exchange in Notting Hill, London.

1985 Having returned to Canada, Timmins and Anton are now based at 547 Crawford Street, and put together Cowboy Junkies with Timmins' younger brother Peter on drums, older brother John, who soon leaves the line-up, on guitar and sister Margo who passes the second audition. They write and perform in a sparse, quiet and natural style, and after 3 months of Canadian club gigging, decide to record their debut album with the help of engineer friend Peter Moore.

1986 Recorded on 1 Caltrec Ambiosonic microphone in 6 hours, *Whites Off Earth Now!!*, is released on Cowboy Junkies own Latent label and sells 3,000 copies regionally.

1987 Nov [27] Focusing more on a mellow country blues mix, and splashing out $162, Cowboy Junkies record their second album *The Trinity Session* in a day at Church of The Holy Trinity, Toronto. Dominated by Margo and Michael Timmins' compositions, it is again released initially on Latent, but will ultimately make a reasonable financial return, accumulating over 1 million worldwide sales.

1988 Aug As band begins an 18-month solid touring schedule, taking in US, Europe and Japan, *The Trinity Session* has attracted considerable record company interest and the band signs with RCA.
Dec In US, RCA reissues the album and an understated slow cover version of Lou Reed's *Sweet Jane*, which hits US #5 on **Billboard**'s Modern chart, while Reed is quoted as saying that the single is "the best and most authentic version I've heard".

COWBOY JUNKIES cont.

1989 **Jan** [28] *The Trinity Session* enters US chart set to reach US #26, during a 29-week residence. Its sales are boosted mainly through the heavy rotation on MTV of the *Sweet Jane* Junkies' video.
Mar During UK dates, the group performs at the Cambridge Corn Exchange, while *The Trinity Session*, which UK Independent label Cooking Vinyl has licensed prior to the RCA deal, achieves UK #1 Independent Album chart success.
Apr Back in Northern Ontario, Canada, the band records *Sharon In Quaker Meetinghouse*, which remains unreleased.
Dec They record *The Caution Horses* sessions at Eastern Sound, Toronto.

1990 **Mar** [24] Third album, recorded by candlelight over 3 arduous days, *The Caution Horses*, released worldwide by RCA, debuts at UK peak #33. Once again featuring mainly Margo and Michael Timmins songs, it takes a greater retro country roots direction than its predecessors.
Apr [21] *The Caution Horses* peaks at US #47. Clearly an albums oriented act, extracted singles will merely remain hot alternative and college airplay hits.
[27] They perform on NBC TV's "Late Night With Letterman" singing *'Cause Cheap Is How I Feel*.
May [1] Following a 5-month tour lay-off, Cowboy Junkies begin another lengthy North American sojourn at New Haven, CT, set to climax with 3 dates in hometown Toronto, July 5-7.
Sept On major US tour supporting Bruce Hornsby, they have to cancel several gigs, after Margo Timmins contracts pneumonia.

1991 **Jan** In preparation for their next Toronto recording sessions Margo takes voice control classes as part of a possible move to sing louder.
Feb RCA reissues *Whites Off Earth Now!!*

THE COWSILLS

Bill Cowsill (guitar, vocals)
Bob Cowsill (guitar, vocals)
Barbara Cowsill (vocals)
Sue Cowsill (vocals)
Paul Cowsill (keyboards, vocals)
Barry Cowsill (bass, vocals)
John Cowsill (drums)

1965 Bill (b. Jan.9, 1948, Newport, RI) and Bob Cowsill (b. Aug.26, 1949, Newport) form a duo, using a guitar brought home by their father, Navy chief petty officer William "Bud" Cowsill, on leave. With brothers Barry (b. Sept.14, 1954, Newport) on bass and John (b. Mar.2, 1956, Newport) on drums, they begin playing local frat parties near their Newport home as The Cowsills. Following his retirement after 20 years in US Navy, Bud Cowsill begins managing the family band, incorporating 7-year-old Susan (b. May 20, 1960, Newport) as a singer and brother Paul (b. Nov.11, 1952, Newport) on keyboards. Under the father's disciplined management, the group becomes a slick club entertainment unit, and at talent agents' suggestion, mother Barbara (b. 1928, Newport) is drafted as a further vocalist. Remaining brother Richard (b. Aug.26, 1950, Newport) becomes The Cowsills' road manager and sound engineer. Playing regularly at a local club, they are seen by a producer of the NBC TV "Today" morning program and booked to appear on the show.

1966 While struggling financially with investment, equipment and transport debts, Bud Cowsill meets writer/producer Artie Kornfeld, who is impressed with the group's stage act.

1967 Moving to New York, and with Kornfeld's aid, the family signs to Leonard Stogel's management company and to MGM Records.
Dec Debut single *The Rain The Park And Other Things*, co-written and produced by Kornfeld, hits US #2 and is a million-seller. MGM sends the family on a 22-city US West Coast tour at a cost of $250,000, to promote the hit and *The Cowsills*, which climbs to US #31.
[28] A major showcase concert at New York's Town Hall theater is highly rated; the group is billed as "America's First Family Of Music" (and becomes the inspiration for TV's "The Partridge Family").

1968 **Feb** *We Can Fly* reaches US #21.
Apr *In Need Of A Friend* peaks at US #54. *We Can Fly* reaches US #89.
July *Indian Lake* hits US #10.
Sept *Captain Sad And His Ship Of Fools* peaks at US #105.
Oct *Poor Baby*, taken from the album, reaches US #44.
Dec Now relocated to Santa Monica, CA, where they are offered their own TV series, based on their lives (they reject it, however, when it is suggested that Shirley Jones play their mother), The Cowsills appear on NBC TV in their own special. Susan dedicates *What The World Needs Now Is Love* to brother Richard, now with the armed forces in Vietnam.

1969 **Feb** Compilation *The Best Of The Cowsills* makes US #127.
Mar The American Dairy Association launches promotion, offering 3 unreleased Cowsills tracks, *All My Days*, *Nothing To Do* and *The Fun Song*, for 69 cents.
May Group's version of the title song from rock musical "Hair" hits US #2 and is a second million-seller.
June Live *The Cowsills In Concert* which includes *Hair*, makes US #16.

1971 **May** With Bill now pursuing a solo career (he had been fired by his father for smoking marijuana), group leaves MGM and signs to London Records for *On My Side*, which makes only US #200 and no hit singles.

1972 Group disbands, after an unsuccessful tour of US bases in Europe, as the family declares bankruptcy. Several of the band will battle drugs, alcohol and depression, before turning the corner and pursuing further education or alternative careers.

1985 **Jan** [21] Barbara Cowsill dies of emphysema, aged 56, in Tempe, AZ, estranged from her children.

1990 **July** Bob, Susan, John and Paul reunite to play the Paradise nightclub in Boston, MA. (Barry continues to work as a musician, living in Monterey, CA, and Bill, now living in Vancouver, Canada, pursues a career in country music.)

RANDY CRAWFORD

1967 Crawford (b. Veronica Crawford, Feb.18, 1952, Macon, GA), having sung in church and school choirs and worked in local night clubs in Cincinnati, OH, where she was raised, performs for 3 months in St. Tropez, France, during her summer break on a trip to Europe. Returning to Cincinnati, she sings on a regular club basis and is signed by an agent.

1972 She makes her debut New York performance on the same bill as George Benson at jazz/soul club Nico's.

1975 **Nov** Crawford performs in Los Angeles, CA, with Benson and Quincy Jones at the World Jazz Association tribute concert to the late Cannonball Adderley. 2 of her songs are recorded live for inclusion on her debut album.

1976 *Everything Must Change* is released in US only by Warner Bros. Featuring Crusader Joe Sample and other noted jazz/soul musicians, it has good reviews but limited sales.

1977 **May** Crawford's vocals are featured on ex-Genesis member Steve Hackett's second solo album, *Please Don't Touch*.
Nov Crawford features on jazz musician Harvey Mason's *Marching In The Streets*.

1978 Second album *Miss Randy Crawford*, released in US only, attracts only specialist interest.

1979 *Raw Silk*, including songs written by Allen Toussaint, Ashford & Simpson and Oscar Brown, is released (in US only) but fails to chart.
Sept The Crusaders, a popular jazz combo, invite Crawford to sing vocal lead on the 11-min. title track for their album *Street Life*, which will top US Jazz chart for 20 weeks.
[15] *Street Life* hits UK #5.
Nov [10] *Street Life* makes US #36.

1980 **June** [28] *Now We May Begin* on which The Crusaders co-write, play on or produce most of the selections, reaches US #180, as extracted *Last Night At Danceland* peaks at UK #61.
Sept Ballad *One Day I'll Fly Away* hits UK #2 as parent album *Now We May Begin* hits UK #10. (Her success prompts WEA UK to release her first 3 albums as catalog items.)

1981 **Mar** *Love Theme The Competition* is released by MCA as part of soundtrack to Richard Dreyfuss movie "The Competition".
July [18] *You Might Need Somebody* makes UK #11. *Secret Combination* hits UK #2 (spending over a year on the chart) and reaches US #71.
Sept [12] Her cover version of Brook Benton's *Rainy Night In Georgia* climbs to UK #18. She adapts it to *Rainy Night In London* during her sell-out stint at the Theatre Royal Drury Lane, London, on a UK tour.
Nov [7] *Secret Combination*, with a live recording of *Street Life* on the flip, makes UK #48.

1982 **Jan** [30] Her cover version of John Lennon's *Imagine* peaks at UK #60.
Feb [24] Crawford wins Best Female Artist at the first annual BRIT awards at the Grosvenor House, Mayfair, London.
June [12] Ballad *One Hello*, written by Carole Bayer Sager and Marvin Hamlisch, makes UK #48.
[19] *Windsong*, produced by Tommy LiPuma, hits UK #7.
Aug [7] *Windsong* makes US #148.

1983 **Feb** *He Reminds Me* peaks at UK #65.
May Crawford duets with Al Jarreau on 5 cuts on *Casino Nights*, recorded at the Montreux Jazz Festival.

Oct *Nightline* makes UK #37 and US #164. Title track reaches UK #51.

'84 Oct UK compilation *Miss Randy Crawford – The Greatest Hits*, released on TV-advertising label K-Tel, hits UK #10. Crawford completes a successful European tour.

Dec [8] Crawford's duet with Rick Springfield, *Taxi Dancing*, from his album *Hard To Hold*, peaks at US #59.

'86 June *Abstract Emotions* reaches UK #14.

Aug *Abstract Emotions* makes US #178.

'87 Jan Characteristic Crawford-penned ballad *Almaz*, championed by UK DJ Steve Wright, hits UK #4.

Oct UK compilation album *The Love Songs*, TV-advertised by Telstar Records, peaks at UK #27.

'88 Aug Crawford is invited to perform in 2 concerts with the London Symphony Orchestra as part of its summer season at London's Barbican Centre. Consistent with her continuing UK popularity, they are both sell-outs.

'89 Oct [21] *Rich And Poor* peaks at UK #63, going on to make US #159. Crawford's interpretation of *Knockin' On Heaven's Door*, heard in Mel Gibson/Danny Glover movie "Lethal Weapon 2", features Eric Clapton on guitar and David Sanborn on saxophone.

OBERT CRAY

'73 Cray (b. Aug.1, 1953, Columbus, GA), the son of a serviceman, having been a long-time admirer of blues singer/guitarist Albert Collins who performs at a graduation dance at Cray's high school, where he has already formed his own One Way Street blues band, meets his bass player Richard Cousins and, through him, joins Collins' West Coast touring band.

'75 After completing a 2-year "apprenticeship" with Collins, Cray and Cousins strike out independently to form what will become The Robert Cray Band, featuring Cray (guitar and vocals), Cousins (bass), Peter Boe (keyboards) and David Olson (drums).

'78 First album *Who's Been Talkin'* is cut during constant touring in US. (It will be shelved for 2 years and released in US by short-lived Tomato label. Later, Atlantic will reissue it in US and blues/R&B specialist label Charly Records in UK.)

'83 After almost a decade of regular live West Coast performances, Cray records *Bad Influence*, released on Hightone in US and Demon in UK. (It will take 4 years to chart, but wins 4 prestigious W.C. Handy Awards For The Blues, including Best Contemporary Album.)

'84 The Robert Cray Band makes its first tour of UK and Europe. Critics acclaim their contemporary blues style.

'85 Oct [12] *False Accusations*, his first chart entry, peaks at UK #68 and tops UK Independent chart. In US, it wins the Best Blues Album award from the National Association Of Independent Record Distributors (NAIRD). Cray collaborates with Albert Collins and guitarist Johnny Copeland on *Showdown!* for Alligator Records.

'86 Cray signs to major label Mercury and begins recording *Strong Persuader* with Hightone's producers Bruce Bomberg and Dennis Walker. Ceaseless touring will mean the band plays 170 engagements through the year, including its seventh European tour since 1984.

Mar *Showdown!* makes US #124.

May *False Accusations* makes US #141.

Oct [16] Cray joins Keith Richards of The Rolling Stones, along with Eric Clapton and others, on stage in St. Louis, MO, for Chuck Berry's 60th birthday concert performance, featured in the film "Hail! Hail! Rock'N'Roll".

Nov Cray makes his network TV debut on NBC TV's "Late-Night With Letterman".

[16] He wins a record 6 Handy Awards at America's seventh National Blues Awards, hosted by B.B. King and Carl Perkins.

Dec Cray tapes a special for UK TV with Tina Turner, to be shown on HBO in US the following year.

'87 Feb [24] *Showdown!* wins Best Traditional Blues Recording at the 29th annual Grammy awards.

Mar Cray begins a US arena tour, supporting Huey Lewis & The News, as *Bad Influence*, originally released on Hightone in 1983, peaks at US #143.

Apr *Strong Persuader*, Cray's Mercury debut, reaches US #13, the first blues album to make Top 20 since Bobby Bland's *Call On Me* in 1972.

[18] *Smoking Gun* is Singles chart breakthrough reaching US #22.

[27] Cray backs Eric Clapton on a sell-out night at Madison Square Garden, New York, part of a 1-month US tour supporting Clapton.

May He supports Tina Turner in Europe, including 7 sell-out performances at the Wembley Arena, London.

[30] *Right Next Door (Because Of Me)* climbs to US #80.

June *Right Next Door (Because Of Me)* makes UK #50.

July *Strong Persuader* reaches UK #34.

Nov Cray begins tour of Japan, once again supporting Eric Clapton.

1988 Mar [2] Cray wins Best Contemporary Blues Recording for *Strong Persuader* at the 30th annual Grammy awards.

June He begins a headlining US tour.

Sept *Don't Be Afraid Of The Dark*, recorded in Los Angeles, CA, with producers Bromberg and Walker and David Sanborn guesting on sax, reaches UK #13 and makes US #32.

Oct [8] *Don't Be Afraid Of The Dark* peaks at US #74.

1989 Feb [22] Cray wins his second Best Contemporary Blues Recording for *Don't Be Afraid Of The Dark* at the 31st annual Grammy awards.

1990 Jan [18] Cray opens at the Royal Albert Hall, London, on the bill of Eric Clapton's 18-night stand, having recently added fret work to Clapton's current *Journeyman* album.

Aug [27] Following a concert at East Troy, WI, featuring Cray, Clapton and Stevie Ray Vaughan, the latter is killed along with 3 members of Clapton's entourage in a helicopter crash.

Sept [29] *Midnight Stroll* debuts at UK #19.

Oct [27] *Midnight Stroll* makes US #51 as Cray plays the Beacon theater, New York, during a major North American tour.

1991 Jan [9] Cray begins new world trek at the Club Quattro, Tokyo, Japan.

[24-27] He plays on Eric Clapton's Hammersmith Odeon, London, bill.

CREAM

Eric Clapton (vocals, guitar)
Jack Bruce (vocals, bass)
Ginger Baker (drums)

1965 Nov Having had successful stints in The Yardbirds and John Mayall's Bluesbreakers, Clapton (b. Eric Patrick Clapp, Mar.30, 1945, Ripley, Surrey) returns from a trip to Greece with holiday combo "The Greek Loon Band" and rejoins Bluesbreakers which includes singing bass player Bruce (b. John Bruce, May 14, 1943, Glasgow, Scotland). Clapton is impressed by Bruce who leaves to join Manfred Mann in search of better money.

1966 June After attending a Bluesbreakers gig in Oxford, Baker (b. Peter Baker, Aug.19, 1939, Lewisham, London) suggests forming a new group with Clapton, who nominates Bruce, with whom Baker has played in Alexis Korner's Blues Incorporated in 1962 and The Graham Bond Organization in 1963, for bass player.

July After Bruce has agreed to leave Manfred Mann, Cream is born. The players' reputations quickly win a UK recording contract with Robert Stigwood's Reaction Records and with Atlantic in US. The original idea is for a purist blues trio, but Cream emerges as a rock-blues band.

[31] Billed under their individual names, trio plays its first major concert at the sixth annual Jazz & Blues Festival at Windsor, Berks.

Nov First UK release is the atypical and low-key Jack Bruce/Pete Brown-penned *Wrapping Paper* which peaks at #34.

1967 Jan *I Feel Free*, co-written by Bruce and Pete Brown, climbs to UK #11. Debut album *Fresh Cream* hits UK #6 and sets the tone for their sound: blues/jazz solos and general instrumental fireworks, with a pop tinge.

Mar [28] Group features in Murray The K's "Music In The Fifth Dimension" week-long stage show at the RKO theater, Manhattan, New York.

Apr Cream tours US, where the music press has already built a strong following. Live shows feature much improvisation by all members, as Clapton's lead guitar playing finds growing cult following.

June *Strange Brew* reaches UK #17, and confirms Cream as a mainstream success. *Fresh Cream* debuts the band on US chart. It reaches US #39 during a 92-week chart run.

July [2] Trio plays the Saville theater, London, with The Jeff Beck Group and John Mayalls' Bluesbreakers.

Aug [13] Cream performs on the final day of the seventh annual Jazz & Blues Festival at Windsor, Berks.

[22] A second US tour begins with a 2-week stint at the Fillmore West, San Francisco, CA.

Dec *Disraeli Gears* hits UK #5, and is their US breakthrough, at #4.

1968 Feb In spite of triumphant appearances in UK, US and Europe, rumors are rife that they plan to split. *Sunshine Of Your Love*, taken from *Disraeli Gears*, is their first US chart single, making #36.

June *Anyone For Tennis*, an uncharacteristic track used as the theme for "The Savage Seven" film, reaches UK #40 and US #64.

Aug Double album *Wheels Of Fire*, combining a studio-recorded set and a live one from the Fillmore West in San Francisco, tops US chart for 4 weeks. In UK the album is marketed both as a double, which hits #3, and as a single album with just the studio recordings, which hits UK #7. In US, the album success re-boosts sales of *Sunshine Of Your Love*, which now hits US #5, selling over a million.

Sept It is announced that Cream will split after a farewell US tour and some final UK dates.

Oct *Sunshine Of Your Love* is released in UK and reaches #25. The farewell US tour begins.

[19] *White Room* hits US #6.

Nov [1] Band plays Madison Square Garden, New York, at the end of the farewell tour.

[25-26] 10,000 ecstatic fans attend the group's last 2 live shows, at London's Royal Albert Hall (supported by Yes and Taste), but thousands more miss out on tickets. The members explain that the band's music has gone as far as it can.

1969 **Jan** *White Room* reaches UK #28.

Feb Clapton and Baker form Blind Faith, with Rick Grech (ex-Family) on bass and Stevie Winwood (ex-Traffic) on keyboards and vocals. Bruce heads for a solo career which will continue into the 80s. The first Cream album *Fresh Cream* is reissued in UK and hits #7.

Mar *Goodbye* tops UK chart and hits US #2.

Apr *Badge*, taken from *Goodbye*, reaches UK #18 and US #60.

Aug After the group breaks up, re-cycling of material begins in earnest. *The Best Of Cream* hits US #3.

Nov *The Best Of Cream* hits UK #6.

1970 **July** *Live Cream* hits UK #4 and reaches US #15.

1972 **June** *Live Cream – Volume 2* continues the release of old music from the vaults, reaching UK #15 and US #27.

Nov Compilation *Heavy Cream* makes US #135, as reissued *Badge* makes UK #42.

1977 **Feb** *Disraeli Gears* and double *Wheels Of Fire* are reissued in US by Clapton's current label RSO Records, and re-chart at #165 and #197.

1987 **Sept** [26] TV-advertised *The Cream Of Eric Clapton* chronicles solo Clapton hits with those of Cream and begins an initial 79-week UK chart run during which it will hit #3.

CREEDENCE CLEARWATER REVIVAL

John Fogerty (vocals, guitar)
Tom Fogerty (rhythm guitar)
Stu Cook (bass),
Doug "Cosmo" Clifford (drums)

1959 John Fogerty (b. May 28, 1945, Berkeley, CA) forms a rock'n'roll band with his Portola junior high school, El Cerrito, CA, friends: bass player Cook (b. Apr.25, 1945, Oakland, CA) and drummer Clifford (b. Apr.24, 1945, Palo Alto, CA). Fogerty, a singer and guitarist, is also teaching himself to play piano, tenor sax, drums, dobro, harmonica and a number of other instruments. Trio plays local parties before John's brother Tom (b. Nov.9, 1941, Berkeley) also a multi-instrumentalist, joins on rhythm guitar and becomes co-lead vocalist.

1963 Having left school, the group plays Bay Area clubs and bars as Tommy Fogerty & The Blue Velvets. Tom Fogerty becomes a packing and shipping clerk at Berkeley-based Fantasy Records.

1964 Group auditions as an instrumental band for Fantasy, which was recently the subject of TV documentary "Anatomy Of A Hit" (relating the story of The Vince Guaraldi Trio's 1963 US Top 30 success *Cast Your Fate To The Wind*). Fantasy's Hy Weiss signs them, but encourages their UK-style beat music over their instrumentals. They adopt the name The Visions, but Weiss prints labels for their debut single as The Golliwogs, to make them sound British. Band dislikes but accepts the name.

Nov *Don't Tell Me No Lies*, released in Fantasy has Tom on lead vocals.

1965 Band continues to record as The Golliwogs with UK-style rockers *Where You Been* and *You Can't Be True*, but with little success.

1966 **Jan** Fantasy establishes new subsidiary label Scorpio Records for teen-oriented releases, and The Golliwogs are moved to it. *Brown-Eyed Girl* becomes a moderate local hit, selling 10,000 copies around Northern California. (It is also the group's first UK release, on Vocalion). Hopes of promoting it nationally are thwarted when John Fogerty and Clifford are drafted for national service. Follow-up *Fight Fire* does little.

Dec *Walking On The Water* is the final Golliwogs release.

1967 **July** With both draftees back in the band, they spend 6 months rehearsing a tougher rock blend than their UK-influenced sound, with John on lead vocals. They also decide on a new name: Creedence comes from an old friend's name, Clearwater from a beer commercial and

Revival is a statement of intent.

Nov *Porterville* is first Creedence Clearwater Revival disk on Scorpio.

1968 Band builds a live reputation, and cuts a demo of its version of Dale Hawkins' *Suzie Q*, which is played by a local radio station. Strong reaction urges Fantasy's new owner Saul Zaentz to relaunch the group on the main label as Creedence Clearwater Revival. *Suzie Q* is re-recorded in the studio in a lengthy version which is split into Parts 1 and 2 on both sides of a single.

June Group releases debut album *Creedence Clearwater Revival*, which includes *Porterville*, *Suzie Q*, some soul and R&B revivals and a few John Fogerty originals.

Oct *Suzie Q (Part 1)* makes US #11. *Creedence Clearwater Revival* reaches US #52 (and will spend 17 months on chart).

Dec From the album, a revival of Screamin' Jay Hawkins' *I Put A Spell On You* makes US #58.

1969 **Mar** *Proud Mary*, an exuberant tale of a Mississippi steamboat, written by John Fogerty on the morning he was discharged from the US Army hits US #2 (behind Tommy Roe's *Dizzy*). It is the group's first million-seller (and will be the most-covered Creedence song, with a 1971 million-selling version by Ike & Tina Turner, covers by Solomon Burke and Sonny Charles & Checkmates Ltd.; Elvis Presley will also include it on an album in 1970). *Bayou Country*, developing their "swamp-rock" idiom and fulfilling Fogerty's musical fantasy/odyssey hits US #7 and is their first million-selling album.

June Million-seller *Bad Moon Rising* hits US #2 (behind Henry Mancini's *Love Theme From Romeo And Juliet*). B-side *Lodi* makes US #52.

[2] Creedence Clearwater Revival plays the Newport 69 Pop Festival in Northridge, CA, to 150,000 people, with Jimi Hendrix, Jethro Tull, The Byrds and others.

[27] Group plays Denver Pop Festival in the city's Mile High Stadium, with Jimi Hendrix, Frank Zappa's Mothers Of Invention and other acts.

July *Proud Mary*, the group's first UK chart debut, hits #8.

[4] Group performs at the Atlanta Pop Festival to 140,000 people, with Led Zeppelin, Canned Heat, Johnny Winter, Joe Cocker and others.

Aug [1] Creedence plays the Atlantic City Pop Festival, NJ, alongside Jefferson Airplane, The Byrds, Little Richard, Santana and others.

[15] Group plays the Woodstock Festival, NY, but does not consent to its performance being used on the movie or album.

Sept A third million-seller, *Green River* hits US #2 (behind The Archies' *Sugar Sugar*), while B-side *Commotion* climbs to US #30.

[20] *Bad Moon Rising* tops UK chart for 3 weeks.

Oct *Green River*, another million-seller, hits US #1 for 4 weeks, deposing **Blind Faith** and then yielding to The Beatles' *Abbey Road*.

Nov Group has another million-seller with its biggest double A-side US hit as *Down On The Corner* hits #3 and *Fortunate Son* makes US #14. (The latter song will be included in **Rolling Stone** magazine's all-time Top 100 singles, chosen in 1988.)

1970 **Jan** *Green River* makes UK #19. *Willy And The Poorboys* (the title taken from a phrase in *Down On The Corner*, which is included) hits US #3 and is another million-seller.

Feb *Down On The Corner* peaks at UK #31, while *Green River* reaches UK #20.

Mar *Travelin' Band*, a Little Richard pastiche by John Fogerty, is another million-seller and hits US #2 (behind Simon & Garfunkel's *Bridge Over Troubled Water*). B-side *Who'll Stop The Rain*, an allegory about the Vietnam War, makes US #13.

Apr *Willy And The Poor Boys* hits UK #10.

[14-15] Band plays the Royal Albert Hall, London, on a European tour.

May *Up Around The Bend* hits US #4 and is a million-seller. B-side *Run Through The Jungle* reaches US #48. *Travelin' Band* hits UK #8 and *Bayou Country* has a belated 1-week stay at UK #62, aided by the London concert (which is recorded by Fantasy), supported by Booker T. & The MG's.

July *Up Around The Bend* hits UK #3.

Aug *Cosmo's Factory* tops US chart for 9 weeks, selling over a million.

Sept *Cosmo's Factory* is the band's only UK chart topper, for 1 week. Taken from it, country-rocker *Lookin' Out My Back Door* hits US #2 and is their seventh US million-selling single. B-side *Long As I Can See The Light* makes US #57, but is promoted as UK A-side and reaches #20.

1971 **Jan** Tom Fogerty leaves the band to spend more time with his family (but will return to record *Goodbye Media Men* and several solo albums on Fantasy). Group's *Pendulum*, which still features him, hits US #5 (the band's last US Top 10 album) and gains a gold disk. It also makes UK #23.

Mar *Have You Ever Seen The Rain?* hits US #9 and is another million-seller. B-side *Hey Tonight* charts briefly at US #90.

Apr *Have You Ever Seen The Rain?* reaches UK #36.

Aug *Sweet Hitch-Hiker* is the group's last million-selling single, hitting

US #6 and making UK #36. Band begins first US tour as a trio.
Sept Group starts its second European tour, at Amsterdam Concertgebouw. Clifford collapses following show with scarlet fever.
Oct Arco Industries, which holds the copyright of Little Richard's *Good Golly Miss Molly*, files a suit against John Fogerty and his publishing company Jondora Music, alleging that *Travelin' Band* partially plagiarizes the 50s hit. (The suit is dropped.)

972 May *Mardi Gras*, highlighted by the previous year's *Sweet Hitch-Hiker*, makes US #12 and earns another gold disk, Extracted, country-styled *Someday Never Comes* reaches US #25. The album is produced by all 3 members, the result of a demand for group democracy after a long period of Fogerty domination, but the band's strength and unerring commercial aim are dimmed. Rock critic Jon Landau calls it "the worst album I have ever heard from a major band". It fails to chart in UK.
June Tom Fogerty's eponymous debut solo album reaches US #180. (It will be his only success.)
Oct [16] Band announces its decision to split. John Fogerty continues recording, adopting a bluegrass/country-rock style which he will market under the name The Blue Ridge Rangers.

973 Jan The first of several Creedence compilation albums, *Creedence Gold*, reaches US #15 and earns a gold disk.
Feb The Blue Ridge Rangers' (Fogerty's) revival of Hank Williams' *Jambalaya (On The Bayou)* makes US #16.
May *Hearts Of Stone* by The Blue Ridge Rangers reaches US #37.
June *The Blue Ridge Rangers* peaks at US #47.
Aug Second compilation album, *More Creedence Gold*, reaches US #61.
Dec Fantasy, with which Fogerty is increasingly at odds, releases Creedence album *Live In Europe*, recorded live on the world tour in Sept.1971. It peaks at US #143.

975 Oct John Fogerty's eponymous solo album is released on Asylum, with all instruments played by him. Self-penned *Rockin' All Over The World*, taken from it, reaches US #27 (and will be a UK #3 hit when covered by Status Quo).
Dec *Almost Saturday Night*, also from *John Fogerty*, peaks at US #78 (and will be a UK hit for Dave Edmunds' cover).

976 Jan Group's version of *I Heard It Through The Grapevine*, first heard on *Cosmo's Factory*, is belatedly released as a single and reaches US #43. The 11-min. track receives US airplay when circulated as a 12" single.
Mar A Creedence double compilation album, *Chronicle (The 20 Greatest Hits)*, makes US #100, while Clifford and Cook appear in The Don Harrison Band, recording for United Artists.
May John Fogerty's *You Got The Magic* peaks at US #87. His album *Hoodoo* is planned but withdrawn a week before release. (Disillusioned by the record industry, Fogerty quits the music business for many years, and retires with his family to a farm in Oregon. His brother Tom will re-emerge with the band Ruby in 1978, but will later go to Hawaii to work in real estate. Cook becomes a producer, while Clifford forms a trio with Chris Solberg (ex-Santana) and Louis Ortega (ex-Doug Sahm), to no notable success.)

979 July Compilation *Greatest Hits* reaches UK #35.

980 Tom Fogerty re-marries; the band reunites to play at his nuptial party.

981 Jan Live *The Concert* makes US #62. This is originally released as *The Royal Albert Hall Concert*, until Fantasy realizes that the wrong tape has been used and that it contains a show recorded at Oakland Coliseum in 1970 rather than London.

983 Creedence re-forms for a school reunion in El Cerrito.

985 Jan [31] John Fogerty makes his first public live appearance in years, playing in an A&M soundstage show with Albert Lee and Booker T. Jones, singing mainly R&B covers.
Mar John Fogerty makes a comeback with solo *Centerfield* on Warner Bros., which is released to much critical praise and hits US #1, selling over a million and earning a platinum disk. In UK, it makes #42. (Fogerty chooses the title after attending the 1984 All-Star Baseball game at Candlestick Park and sitting in centerfield.) Fogerty includes *Zaentz Kan't Dance* to vent his feelings about his former label boss, who threatens legal action. The track is retitled *Vance Kan't Dance*. *The Old Man Down The Road*, extracted from the album, hits US #10, helped by an acclaimed video.
Apr Also from *Centerfield*, *Rock'N'Roll Girls* makes US #20.
June Title track from *Centerfield* (and B-side of *Rock'N'Roll Girls*) climbs to US #44.
Oct A UK TV-advertised compilation, *The Creedence Collection*, reaches UK #68.

986 Aug [27] Fogerty begins his first tour in 14 years.
Sept [20] *Eye Of The Zombie* by Fogerty reaches US #81.
Oct Fogerty's *Eye Of The Zombie* climbs to US #26. (He will continue

making occasional live appearances in US.)
Creedence's *Chronicle*, originally charting in 1970, makes US #165.

1987 July [4] Fogerty performs at the "Welcome Home" benefit for Vietnam War veterans in Washington, DC, singing a selection of Creedence classics.

1988 Jury finds in favor of Fogerty over suit brought by Fantasy that *Old Man Down The Road* infringed *Run Through The Jungle* copyright, but it costs him $400,000 in legal fees.

1989 May He plays in the AIDS benefit concert in Oakland with The Grateful Dead and Tracy Chapman. The band is Jerry Garcia, Bob Weir, Randy Jackson, Steve Jordan, joined on encore by Clarence Clemons.
Nov John Fogerty takes part in "Earthquake Relief" with Bonnie Raitt, Neil Young, Aaron Neville, The Chambers Brothers, Los Lobos and Santana in San Francisco, CA.

1990 Feb [24] He takes part in the "Roy Orbison All-Star Benefit" concert at the Universal Amphitheater, Universal City, CA, singing *Ooby Dooby*.
Sept [6] Tom Fogerty dies in Scottsdale, AZ, of respiratory failure after a lengthy battle with tuberculosis.

JIM CROCE

1963 Croce (b. Jan.10, 1943, Philadelphia, PA), while studying at Villanova University, PA, begins broadcasting a folk program on campus radio and develops his songwriting skills, having bought his first guitar 2 years earlier, while working part-time in a Philadelphia toy store.

1965 He tours Africa and the Middle East as part of a US State Department-sponsored tour.

1966 Newly-married Croce and his wife Ingrid teach at summer camp in Pine Grove, PA. He composes the score for Emmy award-winning documentary "Miners' Story".

1967 They move to New York at the suggestion of college friend Tommy West. Croce plays the local folk circuit, which leads to a recording contract for him and his wife with Capitol Records. *Approaching Day* is released but fails to chart.

1970 Having returned to Pennsylvania, Croce has various temporary jobs including truck driver and telephone lineman. He records 6 new compositions and sends them to West, who has linked with producer Terry Cashman. They invite Croce back to New York to cut demos at the Hit Factory studios.

1972 July ABC Records signs Croce and issues *You Don't Mess Around With Jim*, which will top US chart and stay on chart throughout 1973 and into 1974.
Sept *You Don't Mess Around With Jim* hits US #8.
Dec *Operator (That's Not The Way It Feels)* peaks at US #17.

1973 Feb *Life And Times* enters US chart (and will stay on chart throughout 1973, hitting #7.)
Mar *One Less Set Of Footsteps* makes US #37.
July [21] Produced by Cashman and West, *Bad Bad Leroy Brown* (inspired by a character Croce met in Fort Dix, NJ, while working as a lineman) hits US #1 after an 11-week climb.
Sept [12] TV movie "She Lives", starring Desi Arnaz Jr., concerning the death of a woman from cancer, uses a track from *You Don't Mess Around With Jim* as its theme: *Time In A Bottle* will gain considerable radio play. The night of the telecast, Croce completes recording of his third album *I Got A Name*.
[20] Having performed at Northwestern Louisiana University, Natchitoches, LA, Croce is due to perform his second concert that day 70 miles away in Sherman, TX. His chartered aircraft hits a tree on take-off, killing Croce, aged 30, and 5 others including his longtime guitarist, Maury Muehleisen.
Nov Posthumously-released *I Got A Name*, featured in film "The Last American Hero", hits US #10. *Time In A Bottle* enters chart same week.
Dec *I Got A Name* enters US chart. It will hit #2 and earn a gold disk.
[29] Recorded over 2 years earlier, *Time In A Bottle* hits US #1, overtaking Charlie Rich's *The Most Beautiful Girl*.

1974 Jan *It Doesn't Have To Be That Way* makes US #64.
Apr *I'll Have To Say I Love You In A Song* hits US #9.
May Frank Sinatra's version of *Bad Bad Leroy Brown* makes US #83.
July *Workin' At The Car Wash Blues* reaches US #32.
Oct Compilation *Photographs & Memories – His Greatest Hits* enters US chart (and will hit #2, becoming Croce's fourth gold disk).

1975 Nov *The Faces I've Been*, a retrospective of early recordings on Cashman and West's Lifesong label, reaches US #87.

1976 Feb *Chain Gang Medley* makes US #63.

1977 Feb *Time In A Bottle – Jim Croce's Greatest Love Songs*, a collection of material already released, reaches US #170.

CROSBY, STILLS, NASH & YOUNG

David Crosby (vocals, guitar)
Stephen Stills (vocals, guitar)
Graham Nash (vocals, guitar)
Neil Young (vocals, guitar)

1968 **June** After the break-up of Buffalo Springfield, Stills (b. Jan.3, 1945, Dallas, TX) is working out future plans with Atlantic when Crosby (b. David Van Cortland, Aug.14, 1941, Los Angeles, CA), ex-The Byrds, takes Nash (b. Feb.2, 1942, Blackpool, Lancs.), who is touring US with The Hollies and to whom he was introduced 2 years earlier by Mama Cass Elliot, to meet Stills at his Los Angeles Laurel Canyon home. The trio, all with experience and a history of success, embarks on a creative jamming session and decides to form a group.

Aug David Geffen, on behalf of Atlantic Records, begins the legal and contractual process necessary to unite them on the label. Crosby, Stills & Nash travel to UK, to compose and rehearse in London (and Nash to serve The Hollies 1 month's notice).

Dec [8] Nash leaves The Hollies after a charity concert at the London Palladium.

1969 **Jan** [15] The new trio, having rehearsed in Moscow Road, London, until the New Year, and in John Sebastian's house in Long Island, NY, signs to Atlantic after the label agrees "to assign to CBS all right, title, etc., to the exclusive services of Richard Furay" in exchange for acquiring the rights to Graham Nash, who is still signed to Epic through The Hollies. (This releases Furay to record for Epic as part of Poco.) They fly to California to begin recording.

June Debut album *Crosby, Stills & Nash* is released. (It will sell over 2 million copies in US in 12 months, but will never hit higher than US #6 during a 2-year residence). The trio, about to tour US for the first time, needs to find musicians to back the vocal/acoustic line-up (on the album, Stills and Clear Light's drummer Dallas Taylor have played most instrumental parts). Atlantic boss Ahmet Ertegun suggests Young (b. Nov.12, 1945, Toronto, Canada), who agrees to join initially on a casual basis as lead guitarist and occasional vocalist, provided his separate work with Crazy Horse is unaffected. He brings with him ex-Buffalo Springfield bassist Bruce Palmer, who soon leaves and is replaced by session man Greg Reeves. (Young becomes a full-time member, but his arrival will start a trend of group splits and reunions over the next 20 years, always sparked by the independent spirits of the 4 personalities).

July [25] Group's first live performance is a gig at New York's Fillmore East with Country Joe McDonald.

Aug [16] Group performs its second live gig at the Woodstock Festival, NY, opening as the acoustic Crosby, Stills & Nash, and then being joined by Young and the band for an electric set.

[18] Band plays the Greek theater, Los Angeles. Buffalo Springfield's Bruce Palmer joins them on stage.

[23] *Marrakesh Express*, a Nash song which The Hollies had failed to finish recording in Apr.1968, makes US #28. A lengthy US tour begins.

Sept *Crosby, Stills & Nash* peaks at UK #25, *Marrakesh Express* at #17.

[30] Crosby's girlfriend Christine Hinton is killed in a car crash in San Francisco, CA, on the day the album is certified gold in US.

Nov [29] From the album, *Suite: Judy Blue Eyes* (penned by Stills for girlfriend Judy Collins), makes US #21. The label credit is still to Crosby, Stills & Nash.

Dec [6] Crosby, Stills, Nash & Young guest on The Rolling Stones concert at Altamont Speedway, CA. After their act, the event turns into violent tragedy when a murder occurs during The Stones' set.

1970 **Jan** They tour Europe and UK, ending at London's Royal Albert Hall, and then split for 3 months to pursue individual work. Stills buys a house from Ringo Starr and settles in UK, taking guitar lessons from Jimi Hendrix, and working on his first solo album.

Mar [11] Group wins Best New Artist at 12th annual Grammy awards.

May [9] *Woodstock*, a Joni Mitchell song celebrating the festival, is the first Crosby, Stills, Nash & Young release, and peaks at US #11.

[16] First CSN&Y album, *Deja Vu*, tops US chart, having been certified gold after its first week on release. All 4 members contribute songs to it (totalling 800 hours' work in the studio). Group tours US again after its 3-month sabbatical, replacing Reeves and Taylor with Calvin "Fuzzy" Samuels and John Barbata (ex-Turtles). *Deja Vu* hits UK #5.

June Young, watching the TV report of the killing of 4 students at the Kent State University riots, writes *Ohio* the same night. Group records it the next morning, and it is released 8 days later.

July [25] Nash's song *Teach Your Children* makes US #16.

Aug [8] *Ohio* reaches US #14. (The week before *Teach Your Children*

and *Ohio* have stood at #16 and #17 respectively on the Hot 100.)

[14] While on tour, Stills is arrested on suspected drugs charges at a San Diego motel, after being found crawling along a corridor in an incoherent state. He is freed on $2,500 bail. (At the end of the US tour, at New York's Carnegie Hall, the group splits, following internal dissent, mainly between Young and the others.)

Oct [31] *Our House*, another Nash song from *Deja Vu*, peaks at US #30 and is the final CSN&Y single released.

Dec Stills' solo album *Stephen Stills*, recorded in London in May, with contributions from Crosby and Nash, Eric Clapton, Jimi Hendrix and others, hits US #3 and UK #30, as he embarks on a 52-date North American tour to promote the album. He begins work on a second album in London with his new Stephen Stills Band (which includes former CSN&Y sidemen Samuels and Taylor).

1971 **Jan** [30] *Love The One You're With* by Stills, taken from his album, reaches US #14 (and UK #37 2 months later).

Apr [3] *Sit Yourself Down*, from Stills' album, makes US #37.

May [1] Crosby's *Music Is Love* climbs to US #95. It is from his album *If Only I Could Remember My Name*, with help from Jerry Garcia, Joni Mitchell, Nash, Young and others, which reaches both US and UK #12.

[12] Stills is a guest at Mick and Bianca Jagger's wedding at St. Tropez, France.

Nash compiles live double album *4-Way Street* from recordings made at the group's Chicago, Los Angeles and New York gigs. Already certified gold on ship-out, it hits US #1 and UK #5, confirming CSN&Y as the most popular ex-band after The Beatles (they are currently voted Best International Group in UK **Melody Maker** poll). Young's parallel solo career, with the Top 10 success of his album *After The Gold Rush*, makes any group reunion unlikely in the short term.

July [24] Final single from Stills' first album, *Change Partners*, makes US #43, while Nash releases solo album *Songs For Beginners*, reaching US #15 and UK #13. His extracted *Chicago* peaks at US #35.

Aug Solo album *Stephen Stills 2* (recorded with the 1970 line-up of The Stephen Stills Band, before its split after a long US tour) hits US #8 and makes UK #22.

Sept [25] From his solo album, Stills' *Marianne* makes US #42.

Oct [2] Nash's *Military Madness* peaks at US #73.

[4] Stills joins Crosby and Nash on stage at a Carnegie Hall concert in New York.

While recording in Miami, Stills, joined by Chris Hillman and Al Perkins from The Flying Burrito Brothers, Taylor, percussionist Joe Lala, bassist Kenny Passarelli and keyboard player Paul Harris, forms new group Manassas.

Dec [4] Crosby and Nash, on a tour of Europe, perform at the Royal Albert Hall, London, then head to Stockholm, Sweden for a concert on Dec. 6.

1972 **May** Double album *Manassas* hits US #4 and UK #30, while Crosby and Nash unite on *Graham Nash/David Crosby* which hits US #4 and peaks at UK #13.

June [17] Their extracted single *Immigration Man* makes US #36, as Stills' *It Doesn't Matter* peaks at US #61. Crosby and Nash begin to play regular gigs together around US.

July [22] Stills' follow-up (with Manassas), *Rock And Roll Crazies*, reaches US #92.

[29] Young and Nash, backed by Young's new band The Stray Gators, produces one-off single *War Song* which makes US #61.

Aug [12] Stills plays alongside Jefferson Airplane and James Brown at the "Festival Of Hope" benefit concert at Roosevelt Raceway, New York, as *Southbound Train* by Nash and Crosby peaks at US #99.

1973 **Jan** Crosby and Nash join Young on some dates of his US tour with The Stray Gators. Stills marries French singer Veronique Sanson.

May Second Manassas album *Down The Road* reaches US #26 and makes UK #33.

June [2] Extracted single *Isn't It About Time* peaks at US #56. Crosby, Stills, Nash & Young come together in Hawaii to play, and then rehearse at Young's La Honda, CA, ranch. Projected album *Human Highway* does not materialize, but they plan to play an Oct. tour (which will not come about when Young pulls out).

Sept Hillman, Perkins and Harris leave Manassas to form the Souther Hillman Furay Band with J.D. Souther and Richie Furay. Stills replaces them with Donnie Dacus (guitar), Jerry Aiello (keyboards) and Russ Kunkel (drums).

Oct [4] Crosby and Nash join Stills and Manassas on stage at Winterland, San Francisco, followed later by Young. It results in a 50-min. CSN&Y set.

Dec [22] Stills loses a paternity suit brought by Harriet Tunis of Mill Valley, CA.

1974 **Feb** Nash's solo album *Wild Tales* reaches US #34.

May The quartet reunites to rehearse for live work, and Stills disbands Manassas.

July [9] A CSN&Y US 30-date tour opens in Seattle, WA, where they perform a 4-hour set to 15,000 people, backed by Kunkel and Lala from Manassas and bassist Tim Drummond. Personnel conflicts continue as Young throughout travels separately from the other 3.

Sept [11] Group returns to UK, playing (with The Band and Joni Mitchell) at Wembley Stadium, London, to 80,000 people.

Nov Nash-compiled anthology album *So Far*, with the quartet's best-known material, tops US chart (the third CSN&Y #1 in 3 releases) and reaches UK #25.

Dec [14] Crosby and Nash play as a duo at a San Francisco joint benefit concert for the United Farm Workers and for Project Jonah, devoted to whale protection.

1975 **Jan** Group tries to record again, at the Record Plant in Sausalito, CA, with Russ Kunkel, Lee Sklar and Bill Kreutzmann. A major row between Nash and Stills over a single harmony note prompts Young to leave the studio, vowing never to return. Stills signs a new recording deal with CBS/Columbia, and forms a new band with Lala, Dacus, Aiello, George Perry on bass, and Ronald Ziegler on drums.

July [26] Stills' Columbia debut *Stills* reaches UK #31.

Aug [9] *Stills* reaches US #19.

[23] Extracted single *Turn Back The Pages* makes US #84. He plays a 6-week US tour with his new band (plus Rick Roberts from Firefall).

Nov [29] Signed to ABC label, Nash and Crosby's *Wind On The Water* hits US #6.

Dec [6] From it, *Carry Me* peaks at US #52.

1976 **Jan** [25] Stills appears with Bob Dylan (and stages a guitar duel with Carlos Santana) on the all-star bill of the "Night Of The Hurricane 2" benefit concert for imprisoned boxer Hurricane Carter, at Houston Astrodome, TX.

Feb [14] *Stephen Stills – Live* on Atlantic, with tracks mainly recorded by Stills and Manassas before it was disbanded, makes US #42.

July [3] Stills' *Illegal Stills*, on CBS/Columbia, makes US #31 and UK #54. He links again with Young to record an album as the Stills/Young Band and tours US (the band is basically Stills' current outfit, with new drummer Joe Vitale, plus Young as co-lead vocalist and guitarist). The Stills/Young Band tour is almost halted when Young pulls out after the first few dates with throat problems. Chris Hillman deputizes to allow Stills to complete the tour.

Aug [21] Crosby and Nash's *Out Of The Darkness* makes US #89.

Sept [18] Parent album *Whistling Down The Wire* reaches US #26.

Oct [16] The Stills/Young Band *Long May You Run*, released on Young's current label, Reprise, reaches UK #12.

Nov Stills plays a solo, mainly acoustic, US tour, before talking to Crosby and Nash about another reunion.

[17] *Long May You Run* reaches US #26 and is certified gold for a half million US sales.

[25] Young and Stills appear with The Band at its "Last Waltz" farewell concert at San Francisco's Winterland.

Dec Crosby and Nash make a brief UK concert visit.

1977 **Jan** [29] Compilation album *Still Stills – The Best Of Stephen Stills*, peaks at US #127.

Mar Crosby, Stills & Nash re-form in studio to record new material.

June [2] CS&N begin a month's tour at Pine Knob Music theater, Clarkston, MI.

July [23] The trio's album *CSN* reaches UK #23.

Aug [13] *CSN* hits US #2, and is certified platinum as a million-selling album in US.

[27] From it, *Just A Song Before I Go* hits US #7. A major US tour begins.

Nov [12] *Fair Game*, also taken from *CSN*, makes US #43.

Dec [17] *Crosby/Nash Live*, released by ABC, climbs to US #52.

1978 **June** CS&N embark on another US tour, this time playing an acoustic-only set.

Nov [4] Greg Reeves sues CSN&Y, claiming $1 million back royalties.

[11] Retrospective *The Best Of Crosby/Nash*, on ABC, reaches US #150.

[18] Stills' solo album *Thoroughfare Gap* reaches US #83.

1979 **Jan** Stills plays a lengthy US tour with a new band comprising Dallas Taylor, George Perry, Mike Finnigan and Jerry Tolman, with Bonnie Bramlett (ex-Delaney & Bonnie) on back-up vocals.

Mar [2] Stills plays the Havana Jam Festival, alongside Billy Joel and Kris Kristofferson.

Sept Crosby, Stills & Nash come together again to play at New York's Madison Square Garden anti-nuclear benefit concerts organized by Musicians United For Safe Energy (MUSE).

1980 **Mar** [29] Nash's solo album *Earth And Sky*, on Capitol, reaches US #117. Crosby is attempting to find a label for his solo projects.

June [14] Stills and Nash perform as soloists in a "No Nukes" benefit concert at the Hollywood Bowl, CA, headlined by Bruce Springsteen.

July [16] Documentary film "No Nukes" premieres in New York, and includes CS&N's set from the Sept.1979 concert.

1981 **Jan** Compilation album *Replay*, with tracks from both CS&N and Stills' solo albums, peaks at US #122.

Sept Nash rejoins The Hollies to appear on BBC TV's "Top Of The Pops" with UK #29 hit *Holliedaze*.

1982 **Mar** [28] Crosby is arrested in Los Angeles for driving while under the influence of cocaine, possessing quaaludes and "drug paraphernalia", and carrying a concealed .45-caliber pistol.

Apr [13] Crosby is arrested again when police find him preparing cocaine in his dressing room at Cardi's nightclub in Dallas, TX, with a concealed gun nearby.

June Crosby, Stills & Nash play "Peace Sunday" anti-nuclear concert at the Rose Bowl in Pasadena, CA, alongside Bob Dylan, Joan Baez, Stevie Wonder and others.

Aug [14] *Daylight Again*, another CS&N reunion with most of its songs written by Stills, hits US #8 and collects their second platinum award for million-plus US sales.

[21] From it, *Wasted On The Way* hits US #9.

Nov [20] *Southern Cross*, also from *Daylight Again*, reaches US #18.

1983 **Feb** [12] CS&N's *Too Much Love To Hide* peaks at US #69.

July [30] A remake of The Supremes' *Stop! In The Name Of Love*, which sees Nash rejoin The Hollies again, reaches US #29 as parent album *What Goes Around* makes US #90. This line-up of The Hollies (Nash, Allan Clarke, Tony Hicks and Bobby Elliott) tours US before disbanding once more. Live CS&N album *Allies*, and extracted *War Games* both peak at US #43.

Aug [5] Crosby is convicted in Texas on charges of possessing cocaine and carrying a gun into a bar. He is sentenced by Judge Pat McDowell to 5 years in the Texas State penitentiary (but remains free while the sentence is appealed).

1984 **Sept** [15] Back on Atlantic as a soloist, Stills peaks at US #61 with *Stranger* as *Right By You* makes US #75.

Dec Judge McDowell allows Crosby to enter a drug rehabilitation program in lieu of serving time in jail.

1985 **Jan** Crosby enters a drug-treatment program at Fair Oaks hospital, Summit, NJ.

Mar [7] He is returned to jail in Dallas, after "eloping" from Fair Oaks.

July [13] Crosby, out on an appeal bond, joins Stills, Nash and Young to play the Live Aid concert in Philadelphia, PA, as part of a major US CS&N tour.

Dec [12] Crosby, after spending 17 days as a fugitive from justice, turns himself in to the FBI in Florida to face charges.

1986 **May** [17] Nash's *Innocent Eyes*, on Atlantic label, makes US #84 as parent album *Innocent Eyes* climbs to US #136. Crosby, now serving time in Texas State penitentiary, joins an inmates' rock group.

1987 **Feb** CS&N are prevented from taking part in a Greenpeace benefit in Vancouver, Canada, when Crosby is not allowed into the country.

May [15] Crosby marries long-time girlfriend Jan Dance in Los Angeles. Nash and his wife Susan renew their wedding vows at the ceremony. Crosby celebrates by signing a solo deal with A&M.

1988 **Jan** Young is prevented from rejoining CS&N by label boss David Geffen.

May [14] CS&N open Atlantic Records' 40th anniversary concert in New York's Madison Square Garden.

Sept CSN&Y return to the studio to cut their first tracks together in 14 years.

Dec [11] Nash attends Roy Orbison's memorial service with Don Henley, Tom Petty, and Bonnie Raitt among others.

1989 **Jan** CSN&Y's comeback album *American Dream* reaches US #16 and UK #55.

Feb [25] Extracted single *Got it Made* peaks at US #69.

Mar Crosby's solo album *Oh Yes I Can* makes US #104.

Nov [21] CS&N give a 20-min. performance of *Teach Your Children*, *Long Time Gone* and *Carried Away* in the Tiergarten Park in front of the Brandenburg Gate, Berlin, Germany.

1990 **Mar** [31] CSN&Y play a benefit for their erstwhile drummer Dallas Taylor, in need of a liver transplant, at Santa Monica Civic Auditorium. Don Henley and The Desert Rose Band also play on the bill.

Apr [1] Group plays another fund-raiser for the California Environmental Protection Initiative.

[16] Crosby guests on NBC TV's "Shannon's Deal".

CROSBY, STILLS, NASH & YOUNG cont.

[17] Taylor has liver transplant at Cedars-Sinai medical center, Los Angeles.
July [21] CS&N's *Live It Up* makes US #57.
[25] CS&N embark on lengthy US tour at Binghamton, NY, set to end Aug.29 in Park City, UT.
Sept Crosby and Nash contribute vocals to Michael Hedges *Taproot*.
Oct [14] "The Inside Track", a weekly 1 hour one-on-one interview show with music presented by Nash, airs on the A&E network.
Nov [17] Crosby breaks his left leg, ankle and shoulder when he comes off his Harley Davidson motorbike near his home.
1991 Feb [10] Stills joins nearly 100 celebrities in Burbank, CA, to record *Voices That Care*, a David Foster and fiancee Linda Thompson Jenner-composed and organized charity record to benefit the American Red Cross Gulf Crisis Fund.
[20] Crosby provides harmony vocal to Phil Collins' *Another Day In Paradise* at the 33rd annual Grammy awards at Radio City Music Hall, New York.

CHRISTOPHER CROSS

1971 The son of an Army officer, Cross (b. Christopher Geppert, May 3, 1951, San Antonio, TX) joins, as singer and guitarist, a local hard rock band, Flash, which establishes a live reputation and opens for many rock acts including Led Zeppelin, Jefferson Airplane and Deep Purple.
1973 He quits Flash to concentrate on pop/ballad songwriting.
1975 After spending 2 years working at pre-med studies, he joins a Top 40 covers band, begins sending demo tapes to record companies and forms a backing band for his compositions which features keyboardist Rob Meurer, bassist Andy Salmon and Tommy Taylor on drums.
1976 Having built up a local live reputation, Cross and the band are spotted by Tim Neece, a manager, and Michael Brovsky, who take the music into the studio for more professional demo work.
1978 Oct After a special performance arranged for Warner Bros. A&R chief Michael Ostin at Alamo Roundhouse in Austin, TX, Cross signs to the label, establishes his own publishing company, Pop'N'Roll and moves to Los Angeles with his band.
1979 Producer Michael Omartian is brought in to work on Cross' songs for debut album. Local singers, including Michael McDonald, J.D. Souther, Don Henley and Nicolette Larson, give vocal backing.
1980 Jan Cross contributes guitar parts to Carole King's *Pearls – Songs Of Goffin And King*, recorded at Pecan Street studios in Austin.
Feb Debut album *Christopher Cross* is released in US. (It will spend over 2 years on chart and peak at US #6.) Extracted *Ride Like The Wind*, featuring McDonald on backing vocals, hits US #2.
Apr *Ride Like The Wind* is released in UK and makes #69 for 1 week.
Aug Follow-up US single, ballad *Sailing*, tops US chart.
Nov *Never Be The Same* peaks at US #15. Cross and his backing band play major US dates.
1981 Feb *Sailing* rises to UK #48 and debut album *Christopher Cross* begins a 77-week run on chart. It will peak at UK #14 and earn a gold disk.
[22] Cross sweeps the 23rd annual Grammy awards, winning in 5 categories (beating the previous best by Frank Sinatra and Barbra Streisand) – Record Of The Year (*Sailing*), Album Of The Year (*Christopher Cross*), Song Of The Year (*Sailing*), Best New Artist and Best Arrangement Accompanying Vocalist (*Sailing*).
Apr *Say You'll Be Mine* reaches US #20.
Oct Burt Bacharach, responsible for the music score for Dudley Moore/Liza Minnelli movie "Arthur", invites Cross to co-write and sing the theme. *Arthur's Theme (Best That You Can Do)*, co-written with Bacharach, Carole Bayer Sager and Peter Allen, tops US chart for 3 weeks but reaches only UK #56.
1982 Jan *Arthur's Theme*, reissued in UK after the success of the film, hits UK #7. Cross visits UK for selected sell-out dates.
Apr *Arthur's Theme* wins an Oscar for Best Song From A Film.
June Co-produced by Cross, Alessi brothers' *Long Time Friends* fails to chart. *Put Away Your Love* peaks at US #71.
1983 Feb Second album *Another Page* is released. Produced by Omartian and featuring backing vocals by Art Garfunkel, Karla Bonoff and Carl Wilson, it makes US #11 and hits UK #4. Extracted *All Right* climbs to US #12 and UK #51.
June *No Time To Talk*, also from *Forever*, makes US #33 but fails in UK.
1984 Jan After a slow start, third single from the album, *Think Of Laura*, hits US #9. It benefits from character use in US ABC TV's "General Hospital" soap series.
June Released on special 23rd Olympiad celebration album, Cross' *A Chance For Heaven* is chosen as the official swimming theme. It sinks at US #76.

1985 Oct As a prelude to forthcoming album, single *Charm The Snake* is released, but reaches only US #68.
Nov *Every Turn Of The World*, featuring songs co-written with Bobby Alessi, Will Jennings and producer Omartian, makes only US #127 and fails to chart in UK.
1986 July Cross adds the cut *Loving Strangers* to Tom Hanks/Jackie Gleason movie "Nothing In Common" soundtrack album.
1988 Aug After a long lay-off, Cross releases his fourth album *Back Of My Mind*, through reactivated Reprise label. Featuring vocal backing from Michael McDonald again, its limited sales indicate that his style, briefly fashionable, is no longer popular and it fails to chart. First single from it, a duet with Frances Ruffelle, *I Will (Take You Forever)*, is released.

THE CRYSTALS

Barbara Alston (vocals)
Mary Thomas (vocals)
Dee Dee Kennibrew (vocals)
Lala Brooks (vocals)
Pat Wright (vocals)

1961 Group forms at high school in Brooklyn, New York, just for fun, meets songwriter Leroy Bates (whose daughter Crystal gives it its name) and works on demos of his songs for publisher Hill And Range Music.
May After meeting at the publisher's New York office, producer Phil Spector signs The Crystals as the first act on his new Philles label and records *Oh Yeah, Maybe Baby*, backed with *There's No Other (Like My Baby)*, at Mirasound studios, New York.
Dec US DJs first reject the single, then start to play the B-side; after 2 months, *There's No Other (Like My Baby)*, a Spector re-working of a Bates original, charts at US #20.
1962 May *Uptown* (written for Tony Orlando until Spector persuades writers Barry Mann and Cynthia Weil that it should have a female vocal) reaches US #13, with Alston as lead vocal.
Aug *He Hit Me (And It Felt Like A Kiss)* fails to reach US Top 100, suffering airplay problems because of the apparent masochism in the lyrics. Spector allows it to die when he hears Gene Pitney's demo of *He's A Rebel* and recognizes it as a potential smash.
Nov *He's A Rebel* tops US chart for 2 weeks and is a million-seller. Lead vocal on it is by Darlene Love, backed by Fanita James and Jack Nitzsche's wife Gracia (fellow members of The Blossoms). The bona fide Crystals are holed up in New York while Spector is hurriedly recording in Los Angeles, CA, to beat a rival version of the song by Vikki Carr onto the market. Group reduces to a quartet when Thomas leaves to get married.
1963 Jan *He's A Rebel* reaches UK #19.
Feb *He's Sure The Boy I Love*, featuring Darlene Love and The Blossoms in the real Crystals' absence, reaches US #11.
Mar *He's A Rebel* is the quartet's only album chartmaker, at US #131.
June *Da Doo Ron Ron*, featuring Brooks on lead vocal, hits US #3 and is another million-seller.
July *Da Doo Ron Ron* hits UK #5, and is the group's first major international hit.
Sept *Then He Kissed Me* hits US #6 and is regarded as the first fully-fledged landmark of the Phil Spector "Sound". Relations between group and producer are progressively more strained: the group feels its creative input to be minimal and not career-enhancing; Spector is concerned about production to the exclusion of the artists' position.
Oct *Then He Kissed Me* hits UK #2.
Nov Philles seasonal compilation *A Christmas Gift For You*, on which the group is featured, singing *Santa Claus Is Comin' To Town* and *Rudolph The Red-Nosed Reindeer*, is released.
Dec Frances Collins replaces Wright, who returns to college.
1964 Feb *Little Boy* sells disappointingly (US #92). Spector halts its UK release and switches it to the B-side of newly-recorded track *I Wonder*.
[14] Group performs on UK TV's "Ready Steady Go!" with The Rolling Stones, Dusty Springfield and others.
[16] They embark on UK tour, with Manfred Mann (backing the group on the 6-week tour), Johnny Kidd, Heinz and Joe Brown, at the Coventry theater, W.Midlands.
Mar *I Wonder* makes UK #36.
Aug *All Grown Up*, the group's US chart swan song, crawls to #98.
Nov [13] Group embarks on Dick Clark's "Caravan Of Stars" tour with Johnny Tillotson, The Drifters, The Supremes, Brian Hyland, Bobby Freeman, The Hondels, Dee Dee Sharp, Lou Christie and others, in New Haven, CT. Tour will end Dec.6 in Chattanooga, TN.
1965 The dissatisfied group buys itself out of the Philles contract and signs to United Artists.

Oct *My Place*, the United Artists debut, suffers from a lack of the group's identifiable sound and fails to chart.

1966 Feb *Are You Trying To Get Rid Of Me, Baby?* also fails to sell. United Artists takes the title literally and drops The Crystals, who continue to perform live for a while but then retire to domestic life.

1971 June Group re-forms to play the now-burgeoning US oldies live circuit, and appears in one of Richard Nader's major "Rock'N'Roll Revival" concerts in New York.

1974 Nov *Da Doo Ron Ron* is reissued in the UK and charts at #15.

THE CULT

Ian Astbury (vocals)
Billy Duffy (lead guitar)
Jamie Stewart (rhythm guitar)
Kid Chaos (bass)
Les Warner (drums)

1982 Band, formed in Bradford, W.Yorks., as Southern Death Cult, fronted by American Indian-costumed and coiffured vocalist Astbury (b. May 14, 1962, Heswall, Merseyside), using the name Ian Lindsay, plays a non-nihilistic development of punk-rock which endears it to UK rock press. Strong word-of-mouth "buzz" precedes the band's shift to London, where its debut gig at the Heaven club attracts more people than the venue can hold.

1983 Jan Signed to independent label Situation 2, band's debut *Fat Man* makes UK #50 and tops UK Independent chart. Band supports Bauhaus on a UK tour.
Feb [26] Southern Death Cult's final gig is at Manchester polytechnic, Gtr.Manchester, and the band splits.
Apr Lindsay, deciding to form a band free from the hype which had overwhelmed the first line-up, recruits Duffy (ex-Theatre Of Hate), Stewart and drummer Ray Mondo (both ex-Ritual). Group name is shortened to Death Cult.
June *Southern Death Cult*, anthologizing single, demo, live and radio session tracks by the original band, makes UK #43.
July Remaining with Situation 2, Death Cult debuts with eponymously-titled 4-track 12" EP, which does not chart. Lindsay reverts to his real surname of Astbury and Death Cult debuts live in Oslo, Norway, followed by other European dates.
Sept [18] Group plays the Futurama Festival in Leeds, S.Yorks, as the climax to debut UK tour.
[21] Mondo quits; Nigel Preston, ex-Sex Gang Children, joins on drums.
Oct *God's Zoo* is released but fails to chart. Band plays further UK tour.

1984 Jan Band amends its name to The Cult and appears on Channel 4 TV's "The Tube".
May *Spiritwalker*, promoted on a UK tour, tops Independent chart but does not cross over.
Aug The Cult makes its live US debut.
Sept *Dreamtime*, initially coupled with live album recorded at London's Lyceum on May 20, reaches UK #21. It is released on Beggars Banquet, the WEA-distributed parent label of Situation 2. *Go West* on the same label does not chart.
Dec Following a further UK tour, an appearance on BBC TV's "Whistle Test" and a Wembley Arena, London, appearance supporting Big Country, the band makes UK #74 with *Resurrection Joe*. The **Zig Zag** magazine poll votes The Cult Best Group and Best Live Act of 1984.

1985 May Band tours Europe, followed by further UK gigs, after which Preston leaves.
July *She Sells Sanctuary* reaches UK #15. On recordings for a new album, Mark Brzezicki of Big Country fills the still-vacant drum seat.
Sept Band tours Japan with Warner (b. Feb.13, 1961) as temporary drummer. He soon joins permanently.
Oct *Rain* makes UK #17. Group plays another nationwide UK tour.
Nov *Love*, which completes band's metamorphosis from punk beginnings to a Led Zeppelin-inflected heavy rock group, hits UK #4 and makes US #87.
Dec *Revolution*, remixed from the album, reaches UK #30.

1986 Jan Band plays a European tour, supported by The Sisterhood (soon to become The Mission), beginning a 3-month period spent playing gigs in US, Canada and Europe.
June [28] The Cult plays its only London concert of the year at the Academy, Brixton. (Other UK gigs are arena concerts at Ibrox Stadium, Glasgow, Scotland, and Milton Keynes Bowl, Bucks.)
Aug Recording sessions at Manor studios in Oxfordshire for a new album prove unsatisfactory and are not completed.
Nov Astbury and Duffy remix album tracks at Def Jam's New York

studios with label chief Rick Rubin and decide to re-cut the album completely.

1987 Mar From the New York sessions, *Love Removal Machine* reaches UK #18. Band plays its first UK tour for over a year. Ex-Zodiac Mindwarp bassist Chaos joins and Stewart switches from bass to rhythm guitar.
Apr *Electric*, produced by Rubin, hits UK #4, and will make US #38.
May *Lil' Devil*, taken from the album, reaches UK #11.
Aug *Wild Flower*, a double-single package which includes 2 live tracks recorded at Brixton in March, reaches UK #24. By the year's end, the band will have supported Billy Idol on UK tour, and headlined themselves with Guns N' Roses opening.

1988 Band relocates to Los Angeles, CA, splitting with its UK management and firing drummer Warner, who is offered £2,000 and a drum kit as compensation. While The Cult remains inactive for an extended period, the aggrieved Warner plans legal action against the band. Matt Sorum is recruited as the new drummer.

1989 Apr [22] *Sonic Temple* hits UK #3.
[29] *Sonic Temple* enters US chart as it climbs to hit #10.
Extracted *Fire Woman* reaches UK #15. Group supports Metallica on North American "Damaged Justice" tour, following which they will embark on their own "The Prayer Tour".
July [8] *Fire Woman* makes US #46.
Edie (Ciao Baby) makes UK #32.
Sept [6] Group performs at the annual MTV Video Music Awards from Los Angeles Universal Amphitheater.
[30] *Edie (Ciao Baby)* makes US #93.
Nov [18] *Sun King*, with *Edie (Ciao Baby)* on the B-side, makes UK #39.

1990 Jan [9] Further US tour dates begin at Tempe, AZ, set to extend to Mar.25 in Huntsville, AL.
Mar [10] *Sweet Soul Sister* makes UK #43.
Apr Stewart who is quitting to concentrate on writing, producing and spending time with his wife, plays his last gig with band at Los Angeles Universal Amphitheater.
Oct [6-7] Astbury organizes A Gathering Of The Tribes Festival held at the Shoreline Amphitheater, Mountain View, CA, and the Pacific Amphitheater, Costa Mesa, CA, with The Cramps, Ice-T, The Indigo Girls, Public Enemy, Queen Latifah, The Charlatans UK and others.

THE CURE

Robert Smith (guitar, vocals)
Michael Dempsey (bass)
Lol Tolhurst (drums)

1977 Apr Having recently left school, Smith (b. Apr.21, 1959, Crawley, Sussex), Tolhurst, Dempsey and Porl Thompson see ad in **Melody Maker** headed "Wanna Be A Recording Star?", stating that German record giant Hansa is looking for new bands. Now called Easy Cure, after being Obelisk at Notre Dame middle school and Goat Band then Malice at St. Wilfrid's middle school, they gather in Smith's parents' dining room with singer Peter O'Toole, where they make a rough tape for Hansa. Within a month the band has auditioned for Hansa and signed for £1,000, using the money on equipment, enabling them to play at local Crawley venues like the Rocket. O'Toole soon quits to join a kibbutz, leaving Smith to take over lead vocals.
Oct Group makes the first of 2 visits to London's SAV studios to record their first demos.

1978 Mar Hansa drops the band, after they have refused to comply with the label's request to record cover versions instead of their own material. Thompson soon quits, leaving the band as a trio. While Dempsey finds work as a psychiatric hospital porter and Tolhurst works in a chemical job, and with Smith refusing to find work, they name-change to The Cure, and raise £50 to record 4 tracks in nearby Chestnut studios.
July After being turned down by most labels, Chris Parry, A&R man at Polydor and shortly to set up his own Fiction label, signs them.
Sept Group starts recording at Morgan studios in North London. They also secure a spot on a Gen X tour, but are dropped when Tolhurst walks in on Billy Idol and a young lady in a compromising position.
Dec Debut single *Killing An Arab*, inspired by a passage in Albert Camus' novel **The Stranger**, is released in a one-off deal with UK independent label Small Wonder, after Polydor have refused to release any product until the New Year.

1979 Jan With only 1 single release, **Sounds** magazine features the band as a cover story.
Feb The National Front causes a riot at a gig at the Nashville, London, over the controversial *Killing An Arab*.
Apr Group begins a month residency at London's Marquee. (Smith

sets up his own Dance Fools Dance label, its first release being The Obtainers' *Yeah Yeah Yeah*.)

June [9] Debut album *Three Imaginary Boys* makes UK #44, as the group embarks on extensive UK tour. Extracted single *Boys Don't Cry* receives excellent reviews but fails to chart.

Aug The Cure plays the Reading Festival, Berks.

Sept Smith meets The Banshees' Steve Severin at a Throbbing Gristle gig and is invited to support Siouxsie & The Banshees on UK tour. Prior to the date in Aberdeen, Scotland, McKay and Morris quit The Banshees and Smith will be invited to join the band. He agrees, providing he can continue with The Cure on the tour.

[18] Tour resumes at Leicester's De Montfort Hall, with Smith playing both sets.

Nov At the end of the tour, friction with Smith causes Dempsey to leave, joining labelmates The Associates, to be replaced on bass by Simon Gallup, a friend of Smith's from the band Lockjaw. An acquaintance from Crawley, Mathieu Hartley, a part-time hairdresser and keyboard player in local band The Magpies, also joins on keyboards. New line-up makes its debut at Eric's, Manchester, playing until the year's end with The Associates and The Passions on the "Future Pastimes" tour.

Jumping Someone Else's Train is well-reviewed but fails to chart.

Dec Smith and Tolhurst issues *I'm A Cult Hero* under the joke name of The Cult Heroes, with Gallup and Horley, Sussex postman Frank Bell on vocals.

1980 Mar As The Cult Heroes they support The Passions at the Marquee.

Apr Smith participates in a benefit concert at the Rainbow theater, London, for jailed Stranglers' guitarist Hugh Cornwell.

May [10] Debut album *17 Seconds*, produced by Mike Hedges, reaches UK #20.

[17] Extracted single *A Forest* makes UK #31, the group making its BBC TV "Top Of The Pops" debut to promote it. Tours of US and Australasia follow.

July World tour starts in Holland, and will take in New Zealand, Australia, US, Scandinavia, Germany, Belgium, France, Spain and Italy.

Sept Hartley quits, after a gruelling 24-date club tour in Australia and New Zealand, before the recording of the next album, leaving the band to continue as a trio.

Nov [6] Group embarks on UK tour which will end on Nov.18 at the Hammersmith Palais, London.

1981 Jan The Cure provides the instrumental soundtrack to a short film "Carnage Visors", which will prelude the band's own performance on its summer "Faith" tour.

Apr [25] *Primary* makes UK #43 as *Faith* debuts at UK #14. (The cassette version of the album contains the soundtrack music for "Carnage Visors".)

Oct *Charlotte Sometimes*, with singularly innappropriate Mike Mansfield video, makes UK #44.

Nov They begin work on new album at the Windmill studio in Surrey.

1982 Jan The initial sessions are scrapped, with the band going into RAK studios to record with new producer Phil Thornalley.

Apr "Fourteen Explicit Moments" tour begins to promote forthcoming album *Pornography*.

May [15] Band finally breaks the Top 10 barrier when *Pornography*, produced by Phil Thornalley, debuts at UK #8.

[27] While on tour, a fight breaks out in Strasbourg, France, between Gallup and Smith. (When the tour ends, Gallup is no longer with the band. He leaves for 18 months to form The Cry and will return for *The Head On The Door*. Smith goes camping in Wales and Tolhurst travels to France and Spain.)

July [31] *Hanging Garden* makes UK #34 while band still tours UK. Steve Goulding joins on bass, with Tolhurst switching to keyboards.

Nov Smith is asked to rejoin The Banshees, replacing John McGeoch, who is suffering from nervous exhaustion. (Tolhurst meanwhile produces And Also The Trees.)

Dec *Let's Go To Bed*, which Smith dislikes so much he tries to release it under the pseudonym The Recur, makes UK #44. Smith steps in to play guitar for Siouxsie & The Banshees again on a tour of the Far East, following John McGeoch's departure (and he will stay with them between Cure commitments through most of 1983).

1983 Feb Smith is approached by Nicholas Dixon, a choreographer with the Royal Ballet, to write the music for "Les Enfants Terribles". After experimenting with *Siamese Twins* and an accompanying dance sequence on BBC TV show "Riverside", he shelves the plan.

Apr The Cure, no longer officially together, are offered a slot on BBC TV "The Oxford Roadshow". Smith recruits Tolhurst, Brilliant's Andy

Anderson on drums and SPK's Derek Thompson on bass to perform *100 Years* and *Figurehead*. Smith decides to re-form The Cure.

May The Cure headlines the Elephant Fayre Festival in St. Germain's, Cornwall, with Phil Thornalley, who had played bass for the band on "Top Of The Pops", agreeing to stay along with Anderson.

July *The Walk*, produced by Steve Nye, is the group's first Top 20 single, reaching UK #12.

Aug Smith records *Like An Animal*, with Steve Severin of The Banshees and vocalist Jeanette Landray, under the name The Glove, which climbs to UK #52.

Sept Low-priced compilation *Boys Don't Cry*, featuring early material, charts at UK #93 (re-entering at #77 months later). Mini-album *The Walk*, compiled for US release by Sire Records, enters US chart at #179.

Nov Group achieves its biggest UK hit at #7 with *The Love Cats*, recorded at the Studio Des Dames in Paris.

1984 Jan Mini-album *Japanese Whispers*, compiling recent singles tracks, reaches UK #26.

Mar *Japanese Whispers*, an expanded version of the UK release, reaches US #181.

Apr *The Caterpillar* makes UK #14 while the band is again on UK tour, Oxford and London (Hammersmith Odeon) concerts being recorded.

May *The Top* hits UK #10 and reaches US #180. (Thompson, invited to play sax on the album, rejoins.)

June Scheduled to tour with Siouxsie & The Banshees, Smith is forced to pull out suffering from exhaustion after The Cure's own recent stint on the road. (He retreats to Wales and the Lake District, only to resurface when The Cure plays the "Rock Around The Dock" show at Glasgow Barrowlands.)

Sept On tour in the Far East, Anderson's increasingly bizarre behavior comes to a head when he attacks the other 4 band members.

Oct Smith fires him, and the band arrives in US to tour, but without a drummer. Vince Ely, Psychedelic Furs' original drummer, fills in for 11 dates, before Boris Williams, who Thornalley knows through his work with The Thompson Twins and Kim Wilde, completes rest of tour.

Nov *Concert – The Cure Live* reaches UK #26.

[19] Group participates in a charity concert for MENCAP at Camden Palace, London, in part broadcast live on BBC TV's "Whistle Test". Williams takes up Smith's offer of a full time role in the band.

Dec Thornalley leaves to pursue a solo career.

1985 Jan Smith patches up his differences with Gallup, who is pursuing a less than successful career with Cry and then Fools Dance, and asks him to rejoin.

Aug [17] *In Between Days (Without You)* reaches UK #15.

Sept *The Head On The Door* hits UK #7, becoming the band's most successful album to date. It will also make US #59 a few weeks later.

Oct *Close To Me* makes UK #24, complemented by an acclaimed claustrophobic video by Tim Pope, their regular visual collaborator.

1986 Feb [15] *In Between Days (Without You)*, released the previous summer, makes US #99.

May Band's new, updated version of *Boys Don't Cry* climbs to UK #22. Line-up has re-stabilized as a quintet with Smith and Tolhurst, with Gallup back on bass, Paul Thompson on guitar and Boris Williams on drums. They play a benefit concert for Greenpeace at the Royal Albert Hall, London.

[31] Retrospective album of their successes to date *Standing On A Beach – The Singles* achieves their highest-ever chart hit at UK #4. A video collection is simultaneously released. *Standing On A Beach* makes US #48.

June Band plays the annual Glastonbury Festival, Somerset.

July [27] Concert-goer Jon Moreland, having been jilted by his girlfriend, clambers on to the stage at a Cure concert in Los Angeles, CA, and stabs himself repeatedly. The 18,000 crowd cheer enthusiastically, thinking it to be part of the show.

Aug Band tours Spain and France, at the end of which, they will record at Miraval studios, located in a vineyard in Southern France.

Dec The Cure re-signs with Fiction.

1987 Jan They finish recording new album in Brussels, Belgium, after recording the bulk of it at Compass Point in the Bahamas.

Mar Band tours South America, playing major dates in Argentina and Brazil.

May *Why Can't I Be You?* reaches UK #21, as they play at the Golden Rose Festival in Montreux, Switzerland.

June Double album *Kiss Me, Kiss Me, Kiss Me* hits UK #6 and reaches US #35.

July *Catch*, taken from the album, reaches UK #27. The Cure embarks on US tour, with Psychedelic Furs' Roger O'Donnell on keyboards.

Aug [8] *Why Can't I Be You?* peaks at US #54.

Oct *Just Like Heaven* reaches UK #29.

Dec A major European tour ends at the Wembley Arena, London, as Zomba prepares to publish **10 Imaginary Years**, The Cure's autobiography.

1988

Jan [9] *Just Like Heaven* makes US #40.

Feb *Hot! Hot! Hot!* makes UK #45.

Apr [9] *Hot! Hot! Hot!* peaks at US #65.

Aug [13] Smith marries childhood sweetheart Mary Poole at the Benedictine Monastery, Worth Abbey, Sussex. Best man is fellow band member Gallup.

Dec Group re-assembles with Smith, Gallup, Thompson, Williams and now full-time member O'Donnell to work on a new album.

1989

Feb Smith fires Tolhurst, feeling that he is no longer making a contribution.

Apr *Lullaby* hits UK #5.

May [13] *Disintegration* debuts at UK #3, as group embarks on "The Prayer Tour" of Europe. Tour ends with 3 nights at Wembley Arena. *Disintegration* reaches US #12.

June [17] *Fascination Street*, from film "The Lost Angels", charts in US at #46.

Aug They set sail on the QE2 in preparation for biggest US tour yet.

Sept *Lovesong* hits UK #8.

[6] The Cure performs at the annual MTV Video Music Awards from Universal Amphitheater, Los Angeles, CA.

Oct [21] *Love Song* hits US #2, behind Janet Jackson's *Miss You Much*.

Dec [16] *Lullaby* peaks at US #74.

1990

Feb [18] Group wins Best Music Video category at ninth annual BRIT Awards at Dominion theater, London.

Apr [14] *Pictures Of You* reaches UK #24.

May [19] *Pictures Of You* peaks at US #71.

June [22-24] The Cure participates in Glastonbury Festival Of Contemporary Performing Arts, Somerset. O'Donnell quits after the gig, and is replaced by one-time roadie Perry Bamonte.

Sept [1] Group broadcasts 4-hour on-air session pirate radio show from a secret central London location to premiere their new album of remixes **Mixed Up**. The show features interviews, unreleased recordings, news, weather, traffic reports and commercials, all presented in Cure style.

Oct [6] *Never Enough* reaches UK #13.

Nov [3] **Rubáiyát**, Elektra's 40th anniversary compilation, to which band contributes a cover of The Doors' *Hello I Love You*, makes US #140.

[10] **Close To Me**, remixed by Paul Oakenfold from the compilation album **Mixed Up**, and originally released in 1985, reaches UK #13.

[17] *Never Enough* peaks at US #72 as **Mixed Up** debuts at UK peak #8.

[24] **Mixed Up** reaches US #14.

1991

Jan [26] *Close To Me* makes US #97.

Feb [10] The Cure wins Best British Group at the 10th annual BRIT Awards at the Dominion theater, London, and perform live to close the ceremony.

Apr [6] The Cure's **Entreat** hits UK chart peak #10.

THE DAMNED

Dave Vanian (vocals)
Brian James (guitar)
Captain Sensible (bass)
Rat Scabies (drums)

1976

May Band forms as a trio in UK from the same London punk scene as The Sex Pistols, with Sensible (b. Ray Burns, Apr.23, 1955, UK), who has played in various bands since 1970, James (b. Brian Robertson), ex-proto-punk outfit London SS, and Scabies (b. Chris Miller, July 30, 1957, Kingston-upon-Thames, Surrey) ex-Rot and London SS. After 2 gigs in Nick Kent's Subterraneans, the trio recruits Vanian (b. David Letts), who is working as a gravedigger, to form The Damned. Andy Czezowski becomes the band's manager.

July [6] Group debuts at London's 100 club, supporting The Sex Pistols.

Aug [21] Fifth gig is at the Mont De Marsan punk festival in the South of France. On the outward bus trip, Scabies has a fight with Nick Lowe, which leads to a working friendship.

Sept The band splits from Czezowski, signs to Stiff and Stiff's Jake Riviera becomes its manager.

[21] It plays at London's 100 club punk festival, with The Buzzcocks and others.

Nov Debut single is James' *New Rose*, with Lennon/McCartney's *Help*

on the B-side. Produced by Nick Lowe and regarded as the first ever "punk" release, it does not chart but is Stiff's biggest seller to date and helps the label to a distribution deal with Island.

Dec [6] Band supports The Sex Pistols on the "Anarchy In The UK" tour, but is fired in mid-trek for trying to play a gig without the bill-toppers.

1977

Apr [8] The Damned, the first UK punk group to play US dates, opens at CBGB's, home of New York punk scene, on a US tour organized by Stiff's Advancedale Management.

[16] **Damned, Damned, Damned**, produced by Lowe and recorded and mixed in only 8 hours makes UK #34. *Neat Neat Neat*, another James song, is paired with Scabies' *Stab Your Back* as the first Stiff single issued through Island.

May They tour UK, supported by The Adverts.

Aug James insists on a second guitarist and previously unemployed Lu Edmunds joins. This heightens tensions within the band. Problems arise recording the next album, so producer Shel Talmy is dropped and Pink Floyd's Nick Mason is recruited.

Sept *Problem Child*, recorded with Mason, does not chart.

Oct [1] Scabies leaves during a European tour. Jon Moss (later of Culture Club) replaces him on drums.

Nov *Music For Pleasure* does not chart. A UK tour with US band The Dead Boys fails to excite.

Dec Group leaves Stiff after *Don't Cry Wolf*, which does not chart.

1978

Feb [28] Group splits. James forms his own band Tanz Der Youth; Sensible switches to guitar and joins The Softies, then forms a band called King; Vanian joins The Doctors Of Madness; Moss and Edmunds go into The Edge.

Apr [8] The Damned re-forms for a farewell gig at London's Rainbow theater, smashing the equipment after the final encore.

Sept [5] Vanian, Scabies and Sensible play a reunion gig, as "Les Punks", at London's Electric Ballroom, with Lemmy of Motorhead on bass, and decide to re-form. While acquiring the rights to "The Damned" name from its legal owner James, the trio plays for 2 months as The Doomed, with temporary bass player Henry Badowski.

1979

Jan [7] Having regained The Damned name, new line-up with Alistair Ward ex-The Saints on bass, debuts at Croydon Greyhound, London. The band is signed to Chiswick Records.

May [26] *Love Song* reaches UK #20.

Oct [27] *Smash It Up* makes UK #35.

Nov [17] **Machine Gun Etiquette**, produced by the band with Roger Armstrong, reaches UK #31.

Dec [8] *I Just Can't Be Happy Today* makes UK #46. With 3 consecutive hit singles, the band is a leading live attraction.

1980

Feb Ward leaves to join heavy metal band Tank and is replaced by Paul Gray, ex-Eddie & The Hot Rods. Band continues to tour exhaustively.

Oct [18] *The History Of The World Part 1* peaks at UK #51.

Nov [29] Double **The Black Album** reaches UK #29, but seasonal *There Ain't No Sanity Claus* does not chart.

1981

Jan Band leaves Chiswick after differences but continues to tour.

Mar US tour follows non-charting US release of **The Black Album**.

June Band tours Europe, while Chiswick unsuccessfully issues extracted *Wait For The Blackout* in UK, coupled with *Jet Boy Jet Girl* by Captain Sensible and The Softies.

July They play a fifth anniversary gig at the Lyceum in London.

Nov They sign to NEMS Records.

Dec [5] EP *Friday The 13th*, their only NEMS release, with *Disco Man* and a version of The Rolling Stones' *Citadel*, makes UK #50, as **The Best Of The Damned**, with live versions of the Stiff singles, on Chiswick's Big Beat label, reaches #43. Band plays the Christmas On Earth festival in Leeds, S.Yorks.

1982

May The Damned signs to Bronze Records, while Captain Sensible makes a solo deal with A&M.

July [3] Sensible's first solo release *Happy Talk*, a remake from the musical "South Pacific", tops UK chart for 2 weeks, setting the record for the biggest jump (from #33) to the pole position.

[17] The Damned's *Lovely Money* makes UK #42.

Sept [11] *Wot* by Captain Sensible reaches UK #26 as his solo album **Women And Captains First** peaks at #64. Meanwhile, The Damned's *Dozen Girls* does not chart.

Oct [23] **Strawberries**, packaged with a strawberry-smelling lyric sheet, reaches UK #15. Roman Jugg joins on keyboards for both the album and subsequent tour.

1983

Apr Bronze drops the band and Gray leaves.

1984

Apr [14] Sensible's *Glad It's All Over* (backed by a medley of The

THE DAMNED cont.

Damned oldies titled *Damned On 45*), hits UK #6.

June [16] *Thanks For The Night*, on the Damned label, makes UK #43.

Aug [11] Sensible solo *There Are More Snakes Than Ladders* peaks at UK #57. He leaves to concentrate on solo work and acting, including a Weetabix TV commercial, which prompts a personnel shuffle: Jugg moves from keyboards to guitar and Bryn Merrick joins on bass.

Oct The Damned, with the new line-up, signs worldwide to MCA.

1985 Apr [6] *Grimly Fiendish*, the MCA debut, reaches UK #21, with a new mainstream pop direction evident.

July [6] *The Shadow Of Love* reaches UK #25.

[27] *Phantasmagoria*, produced by Jon Kelly, enters UK chart at #11, and is followed by extensive international touring.

Sept *Is It A Dream* makes UK #34.

1986 Feb A remake of Barry Ryan's 1968 hit *Eloise* gives the band its biggest seller, hitting UK #3.

Nov *Anything* makes UK #32.

Dec *Anything* charts briefly at UK #40.

1987 Feb *Gigolo* reaches UK #29.

May A revival of Love's *Alone Again Or* reaches UK #27.

Nov [28] *In Dulce Decorum* stalls at UK #72.

Dec [12] Definitive "best of" compilation **Light At The End Of The Tunnel**, released through MCA, spends a week on UK chart at #87.

1989 July Group decides to quit and begins another farewell tour of UK. Sensible, now married to a Dolly Mixture, contributes *Sporting Life* to benefit album **The Liberator – Artists For Animals**. He will continue to record for a number of UK independent labels.

DANNY & THE JUNIORS

Danny Rapp (lead vocals)
Dave White (first tenor, backing vocals)
Frank Mattei (second tenor, backing vocals)
Joe Terranova (baritone, backing vocals)

1955 Rapp (b. May 10, 1941, Philadelphia, PA) forms the group with friends as The Juvenairs while they are still in high school in Philadelphia.

1957 Out of school, they are introduced by singer friend Johnny Medora to his vocal tutor Artie Singer, a music entrepreneur who offers to manage them. White (b. David White Tricker, Sept.1940, Philadelphia), Medora and Singer write *Do The Bop* for the group to record on Singer's new Philadelphia-based label, Singular Records. DJ Dick Clark hears the song and persuades Singer it would be more commercial if revised to *At The Hop*, which is how it is finally recorded.

Nov With 7,000 copies of *At The Hop* sold in Philadelphia on Singular, it is picked up for national distribution by ABC-Paramount Records.

1958 Jan *At The Hop* tops US chart for 7 weeks, selling over a million copies.

Feb *At The Hop* hits UK #3.

Mar *Rock And Roll Is Here To Stay*, written by White, reaches US #19.

July *Dottie* makes US #39.

1960 Nov After a period without hit records, but in which much live tour work is done, the group (minus White, who has been replaced by Bill Carlucci) signs to Swan Records. Topical dance song, *Twistin' USA* makes US #37.

1961 Mar *Pony Express* peaks at US #60.

Oct *Back To The Hop*, updating the original hit, stalls at US #80.

1962 Jan They team with labelmate Freddy Cannon for another Twist cash-in, *Twistin' All Night Long*, which peaks at US #68.

Apr *Doin' The Continental Walk* stalls at US #93.

1963 Jan Group switches to another Philadelphia label, Guyden Records, and another dance craze for its final US hit *Oo-La-La-Limbo*, which creeps to #99. Shortly after, it breaks up. (White will have subsequent success, co-writing Len Barry's 1965 US #2 *1-2-3*, and releasing solo album **David White Tricker**.)

1975 Danny & The Juniors assist former Shirelle Shirley Alston on her version of *Sincerely* from her **With A Little Help From My Friends**.

1976 July *At The Hop* is reissued in UK, and makes #39.

1983 Apr [5] Rapp is found dead in Parker, AZ, having apparently shot himself.

TERENCE TRENT D'ARBY

1979 Son of a Pentecostal preacher, the Reverend James Benjamin Darby and a teacher, Frances, D'Arby (b. Mar.15, 1962, New York, NY), having moved during his childhood from New York to Chicago, IL, and Florida and been the regional Golden Gloves boxing champ, is studying journalism at the University of Central Florida.

1980 Apr He quits university and enlists in US Army. After initial post at Fort Sill, OK, he is sent to join Elvis Presley's old regiment, the Third Armored Division, near Frankfurt, Germany.

1982 Attracted by German night life, he joins a local 9-piece funk outfit, Touch, as a singer. Setting his sights on going AWOL from the army (as he will later claim), he links up with Klaus Pieter Schleinitz, known as K.P., press officer for European record label, Ariola International.

1983 Apr D'Arby is officially discharged from the army. He will continue to romanticize the episode for years and devotes full energies to Touch.

1984 Jan He leaves the disintegrating band and heads for London with K.P., now his full-time manager.

1986 June After successfully recording a demo of his own songs, crafted over 2 years, D'Arby secures a worldwide recording contract with CBS/Columbia and is based in London, which he makes his base.

1987 Apr Debut single *If You Let Me Stay* hits UK #7. D'Arby begins a deliberately outspoken relationship with the press. He makes an impressive appearance on Channel 4 TV's "The Last Resort" when he sings *What A Wonderful World*. (He will make a point of interpreting classic soul songs in future live performances.)

D'Arby performs in an Artists Against Apartheid concert at the Royal Albert Hall, London, while touring UK, supporting Simply Red.

July *Wishing Well* hits UK #4.

[25] *Introducing The Hardline According To Terence Trent D'Arby*, produced by Martyn Ware of Heaven 17, and highlighting D'Arby's distinctive soul vocal talent, tops UK chart. Following his own short "Hardline Introduction" UK tour (with shows in Glasgow, Birmingham, Bristol and London) to launch the album, he supports David Bowie on UK dates.

Sept D'Arby visits US on a promotional trip, his first visit to his home country (which he frequently denounces in more interviews) since joining the US Army.

[30] He makes his US live debut at a Roxy, Los Angeles, CA, concert.

Oct *Dance Little Sister* reaches UK #20.

Nov [10] D'Arby cancels a concert in Vienna, Austria, in protest over Kurt Waldheim's confirmation as the new President of Austria.

[21] *If You Let Me Stay* peaks at US #68.

1988 Jan Ballad *Sign Your Name* hits UK #2.

Feb [8] D'Arby wins Best International Newcomer at the 7th annual BRIT Awards, defeating Los Lobos, L.L. Cool J., Bruce Willis and The Beastie Boys. In a speech he asks the authorities for a UK passport.

Mar *Introducing The Hardline* is certified quadruple platinum, having sold 1,200,000 copies in UK alone. D'Arby embarks on a major US tour.

Apr He causes media alarm by releasing an Easter promotion picture of himself naked and crucified.

[30] *Introducing The Hardline* tops US R&B chart.

May [7] *Wishing Well* tops US chart for a week and *Introducing The Hardline* hits US #4. D'Arby emerges as one of the major international stars of the late 80s.

June In an article in **Rolling Stone**, D'Arby claims it will definitely be his last ever interview.

Aug [13] *Sign Your Name* hits US #5. He contributes vocals to Brian Wilson's critically acclaimed solo debut album.

Oct [22] *Dance Little Sister* reaches US #30.

Dec [31] D'Arby becomes a father when his girlfriend Mary Vango gives birth to a daughter, Seraphina.

1989 Feb [22] D'Arby wins Best R&B Vocal Performance, Male for *Introducing The Hardline* at the 31st Grammy awards.

Nov Critically slammed second album **Neither Fish Nor Flesh** reaches UK #12, and will stall at US #61. It will fade from view with ferocious speed despite efforts from concerned CBS executives worldwide.

1990 Jan [27] *To Know Someone Deeply Is To Know Someone Softly* peaks at UK #55.

Apr [16] D'Arby participates in the "Nelson Mandela – An International Tribute To A Free South Africa" concert at Wembley Stadium, London.

May [5] D'Arby sings *You've Got To Hide Your Love Away* at the "John Lennon Tribute Concert" at the Pier Head Arena in Merseyside to celebrate the songs of Lennon.

1991 Jan D'Arby contributes to The Peace Choir, an all-star remake of Lennon's *Give Peace A Chance*.

Feb Asked for a comment by a reporter at the opening of Mick Fleetwood's new Los Angeles blues club, Fleetwool's, D'Arby is quoted as saying "Every time I open my mouth, I ruin my career."

Mar D'Arby's former management company sues him for £76,000 in unsettled royalties for his first album.

BOBBY DARIN

1956
Mar Having dropped out of Hunter College, where he had won a scholarship, after 1 term to pursue acting, recording and songwriting with mentor/manager Don Kirshner (with whom he has doubled as a bus boy/singer on the Borscht Belt), Darin (b. Walden Robert Cassotto, May 14, 1936, The Bronx, New York, NY) records a cover of Lonnie Donegan's hit *Rock Island Line* on Decca but it fails to chart.

1957
May Darin signs with Atlantic subsidiary Atco, but 3 singles, produced by Herb Abramson, go nowhere.

1958
June Departing radically from his usual black R&B fare, Atlantic boss Ahmet Ertegun produces *Splish Splash*, a pop novelty co-written in 10 mins. by Darin and DJ Murray The K's mother. It hits US #3, establishes Darin as Atlantic group's first white star and is his first gold disk. It makes UK #18, where Charlie Drake's comedy cover will hit #7.
July Frustrated by his lack of success on Atco, Darin has cut 2 of his songs *Early In The Morning/Now We're One* as The Ding Dongs for Brunswick but Atlantic objects and secures rights to the single, which reaches US #24 under a new pseudonym The Rinky Dinks. Brunswick recruits Buddy Holly to cover both sides and his single scores #32.
Oct Teen-oriented *Queen Of The Hop* hits US #9, his second million-seller, but only UK #24. Ruth Brown reaches US #24 with Darin's song *This Little Girl's Gone Rockin'*.

1959
Feb *Plain Jane*, written by Pomus and Shuman of Brill Building, peaks at US #38.
Apr *Dream Lover*, his own composition, hits US #2 and UK #1 and is his third million-seller.
Aug Darin records a jazzy selection from Brecht and Weill's "Threepenny Opera", which is playing in New York. *Mack The Knife* hits US #1 where it remains for 9 weeks, earning Darin a fourth gold disk. The single also hits UK #1.
Oct *That's All*, the album from which *Mack The Knife* was taken, climbs to US #7 and UK #15.
Nov [29] Darin wins Record Of The Year for *Mack The Knife* and Best New Artist Of 1959 at the 2nd annual Grammy awards.

1960
Jan Brassy, swinging arrangements of standards become his forte, with *La Mer (Beyond The Sea)* (a 1945 hit for French composer Charles Trenet) hitting US #6 and UK #8, earning Darin a fifth gold disk. He hits the night club/cabaret circuit, starting with the Sahara in Las Vegas.
Mar Darin's update of Gold Rush ballad *Clementine* reaches US #29 but hits UK #8. His second album *This Is Darin* reaches US #6 and UK #4 (his last UK album hit for 25 years).
May A revival of jazz standard *Bill Bailey* makes US #19 and UK #34. B-side *I'll Be There*, a Darin original, reaches US #79 and 5 years later will provide a hit for Gerry & The Pacemakers.
Sept *Beachcomber*, a piano solo, reaches only US #100.
Oct Double-sided *Artificial Flowers/Somebody To Love* makes US #20/#45. Live *Darin At The Copa* hits US #9.
Dec Darin marries film star Sandra Dee. *Christmas Auld Lang Syne/Child Of God* becomes a short-lived seasonal hit, at US #51/#95. He appears in movie "Pepe" (starring Mexican comedian Cantinflas) and "Heller In Pink Tights" (with Sophia Loren and Anthony Quinn). He is voted American Variety Club's Personality Of The Year.

1961
Feb A reworking of Hoagy Carmichael's *Lazy River* reaches US #14 and UK #12.
May Greatest hits compilation *The Bobby Darin Story* makes US #18.
June Darin reprises Nat King Cole's 1948 hit *Nature Boy*, making US #40 and UK #24.
Sept Another revival, *You Must Have Been A Beautiful Baby* hits US #5 and UK #10. Fifth album *Love Swings* makes only US #92.
Oct *Come September*, an instrumental credited to The Bobby Darin Orchestra, charts at UK #50. Tune is title theme from his latest movie (co-starring Rock Hudson and wife Sandra). Darin features in 2 other movies this year: "State Fair" with Pat Boone and "Too Late Blues" with Stella Stevens and Fabian. (While filming "State Fair" in Dallas, TX, Hurricane Carla strikes: Darin, Frankie Laine and Alice Faye put on charity concert at the Majestic theater, raising $65,000.)
Dec Double-sided *Irresistible You/Multiplication* reaches US #15/#30. B-side only hits UK #5.

1962
Jan *Twist With Bobby Darin* exploits the dance craze, making US #48.
Mar *What'd I Say* climbs to US #24.
May Parent album *Bobby Darin Sings Ray Charles* scrapes US #96.
July Darin begins a month-long season at the Flamingo, Las Vegas, NV, before embarking on an open air tour with Count Basie and The Tarriers. His own composition *Things* hits US #3 and UK #2 and is his sixth and last million-seller.

Sept After 5 years on Atco, Darin signs with Capitol. His self-penned title song from his latest film "If A Man Answers" (co-starring his wife) reaches US #32 and UK #24. During the year Darin also gets star billing in "Pressure Point" with Sidney Poitier and "Hell Is For Heroes" with Steve McQueen. Atco releases his version of the standard *Baby Face* which reaches US #42 and UK #40.
Oct An Atco compilation *Things And Other Things* charts at US #45.
Nov His first Capitol album *Oh! Look At Me Now* hits US #100.
Dec Old Atco recording *I Found A New Baby* climbs to US #90.
[1] Darin cancels a lucrative one-nighter to celebrate his second wedding anniversary.

1963
Jan *You're The Reason I'm Living* hits US #3 as Darin embraces C&W and folk idioms. His night club guitarist during this period is Jim (Roger) McGuinn, later instigator of The Byrds.
Mar *You're The Reason I'm Living* makes US #43.
May *Heart! (I Hear You Beating)* by Wayne Newton at US #82 is first hit for Darin's new publishing/recording venture, TM Music Inc. *18 Yellow Roses* hits US #10 and returns Darin to UK chart at #37.
Aug His night club career thrives but recording success declines: *Treat My Baby Good* stalls at US #43 and *18 Yellow Roses* makes only US #98.
Nov *Be Mad Little Girl* climbs to only US #64.
Dec Darin's role in "Captain Newman MD" attracts an Oscar nomination for Best Supporting Actor.

1964
Feb Darin is voted National Heart Ambassador for the American Heart Association.
Mar Darin's revival of *I Wonder Who's Kissing Her Now* makes US #93.
May Atco releases Darin's version of Edith Piaf classic *Milord* which reaches US #45.
Oct *The Things In This House* peaks at US #86. Darin feels Capitol is neglecting his interests in favor of their youth-market roster, which includes The Beatles, The Beach Boys and Peter & Gordon.
Dec *From Hello Dolly To Goodbye Charlie* makes only US #107.

1965
Jan He sings at President Johnson's Washington, DC, inaugural gala.
Feb His last Capitol chart single, show tune *Hello Dolly*, makes US #79.
July *Venice Blue* reaches US #132.
Aug Title song from his latest movie "That Funny Feeling" (co-starring Sandra Dee) fails to chart.
Sept Darin returns to Atlantic: his first 2 singles make no impact.

1966
Apr *Mame*, borrowed from the current Broadway musical, returns Darin to the charts at US #53.
Sept Publishers Charles Koppelman and Don Rubin encourage Darin to investigate contemporary material. Their folk-rock production of Tim Hardin's *If I Were A Carpenter* gives Darin a Top 10 comeback, hitting US #8 and UK #9, but his last UK chart entry.
Dec *The Girl That Stood Beside Me* stalls at US #66.

1967
Jan *Lovin' You* written by John Sebastian makes US #32. During the year he stars in 2 movies, "Gunfight In Abilene" and "Cop Out" (with James Mason). He and Sandra Dee are divorced.
Feb His only Atlantic album to chart, *If I Were A Carpenter*, reaches US #142.
Apr *The Lady Came From Baltimore*, a Tim Hardin song, makes US #62.
July A revival of The Lovin' Spoonful hit *Darling Be Home Soon* reaches US #93.

1968 After working tirelessly for Bobby Kennedy's presidential campaign, Darin leaves Atlantic to launch his own label, Direction. His first album ***Born Walden Robert Cassotto ("Written, Arranged, Produced, Designed And Photographed By Bobby Darin")*** features poetry and protest material.
Aug Darin sells his publishing company for $1 million.

1969
Feb *Long Line Rider* is the only one of 5 Direction singles to chart, reaching US #79. "The Happy Ending", with Jean Simmons, is his first film in over a year.
Aug Having denied Tim Hardin a hit with his own *If I Were A Carpenter*, Hardin's only US chart hit at #50, *Simple Song Of Freedom*, is written by Darin.

1971 Darin signs with Motown, who issue 5 non-chart singles and 2 non-chart albums. He has surgery to insert 2 artificial valves in his heart which it is thought were weakened by a childhood attack of rheumatic fever.

1973
Jan Nationally syndicated television series, "The Bobby Darin Show", begins weekly transmission, running until April. The previous summer he had hosted an NBC TV variety series.
May His last film is "Happy Mother's Day" with Patricia Neal.
Dec [20] Darin dies in the Cedars Of Lebanon hospital, Hollywood, CA, following surgery to repair a heart valve. At 37, he had outlived his early conviction that he wouldn't reach 30.

1979 **Apr** [14] *Dream Lover/Mack The Knife* on picture disk peaks at UK #64.

1985 **Oct** Atlantic compilation *The Legend Of Bobby Darin – His Greatest Hits* makes UK #39.

1989 **Oct** [9] Darin's son files suit against McDonald's Corp for infringing the rights to *Mack The Knife* for their Mac Tonight commercials, as film director Barry Levinson plans to make a biopic on Darin.

DAVE DEE, DOZY, BEAKY, MICK AND TICH

Dave Dee (lead vocals, tambourine)
Dozy (bass)
Beaky (guitar)
Mick (drums)
Tich (lead guitar)

1961 Group is formed (semi-professionally at first) in Salisbury, Wilts., as Dave Dee & The Bostons with Dee (b. David Harman, Dec.17, 1943, Salisbury), an ex-police cadet (who was among the police called to the scene of Eddie Cochran's fatal car crash), Dozy (b. Trevor Davies, Nov.27, 1944, Enford, Wilts.), Beaky (b. John Dymond, July 10, 1944, Salisbury) and Tich (b. Ian Amey, May 15, 1944, Salisbury). Several drummers come and go before Mick (b. Michael Wilson, Mar.4, 1944, Amesbury, Wilts.) joins at the end of the year.

1962 After building a live reputation around the UK West Country, group turns professional for a residency at the Top Ten club in Hamburg, Germany, where an act is developed fusing rock'n'roll and uptempo R&B (in gradually-honed 4-part harmony vocals) with comedy patter and carefully-choreographed "casual" clowning.

1964 Group plays as the ballroom rock band at Butlin's Clacton-on-Sea, Essex, holiday camp for the summer season.
Sept Group supports The Honeycombs on a one-nighter at Swindon, Wilts., and impresses their managers Ken Howard and Alan Blaikley with its highly professional act.
Oct They sign the group to a management contract, change its name to Dave Dee, Dozy, Beaky, Mick and Tich, and negotiate a recording contract with Fontana.

1965 **Jan** [29] Debut single *No Time* is released, but does not chart despite appearances on UK TV "Gadzooks! It's All Happening" (their TV debut) and "Ready Steady Go!". It is written by Howard and Blaikley (who will write all the singles) and produced by Steve Rowland (who will produce most later releases).
July *All I Want*, a ballad, also flops.

1966 **Jan** *You Make It Move*, in a thumping, uptempo style which will be a trade mark of the group's early hits, reaches UK #26.
Feb [12] Group begins 14-date twice-nightly tour, with Gene Pitney, Len Barry and others, at the Gaumont cinema, Ipswich, Suffolk. Tour ends Feb.27 at the ABC cinema, Southampton, Hants.
Apr *Hold Tight*, an audience-raising stomping chant adapted from The Routers *Let's Go* and subsequently used as a chant by soccer fans at the World Cup during the coming summer, hits UK #4. Group begins to adopt garish but fashionable (and ever-changing) stage attire, building the act from a comedy routine to a blend of color and drama.
May [1] Group takes part in the annual **New Musical Express** Poll Winners Concert at the Empire Pool, Wembley, London.
July *Hideaway* hits UK #10. Group's first (eponymous) album makes UK #11.
[23] While traveling by train to Liverpool, the group has breakfast with Prime Minister Harold Wilson and his wife Mary.
Oct *Bend It*, a *Zorba's Dance*-styled accelerating-tempo song about a supposed dance, but with lyrics open to double entendre (particularly with Dee's wry vocal delivery), hits UK #2. Its bouzouki sound is created on an electrified mandola. The single is widely banned by US radio, prompting a re-recorded US version which de-emphasizes the apparent salaciousness, but it fails to chart in US.
[1] Group opens 33-date UK tour, with The Walker Brothers and The Troggs, at the Granada cinema, East Ham, London. Tour will close Nov.13 at Finsbury Park Astoria, London.
Dec *Save Me* hits UK #4.
[5] Group starts tour of Germany with The Spencer Davis Group at the Circus Krone, Munich.

1967 **Jan** *If Music Be The Food Of Love (Prepare For Indigestion)* charts at UK #27.
Apr *Touch Me, Touch Me* reaches UK #13.
[1] Group begins a tour of New Zealand, Australia, Singapore and Hong Kong, with Eric Burdon & The Animals and Paul & Barry Ryan, in Christchurch, New Zealand.
June *Okay!*, with Tich playing balalaika, hits UK #4.

Nov *Zabadak*, a highly experimental song with gibberish vocal and a percussive mock-Caribbean arrangement, hits UK #3.

1968 **Jan** *Zabadak* peaks at US #52, the group's only US chart success.
Mar *The Legend Of Xanadu* a story song with dramatic Latin arrangement, tops UK chart for a week and is group's biggest UK seller. It features a distinctive whipcrack sound (achieved in the studio with 2 pieces of plywood slapping and an empty bottle sliding on guitar strings), which leads to Dee brandishing a bullwhip on stage – an effective (audience-approved) addition to the flamboyant live act.
[27] Group begins 26-date UK tour supporting The Bee Gees with Grapefruit at London's Royal Albert Hall. Tour will end Apr.28 at Granada cinema, Tooting, London.
Aug *Last Night In Soho* hits UK #8 and is another story song with a chorus and additional musicians added to the backing.
Sept [29] Group plays City Hall, Vienna, Austria, with Ray Charles and Diana Ross & The Supremes (ending Oct.1).
Oct *The Wreck Of The Antoinette*, the group's third mini-musical drama, reaches UK #14.

1969 **Mar** *Don Juan*, a dramatic *Xanadu*-style song and arrangement, reaches UK #23.
June *Snake In The Grass*, without the dramatics but with a subtle arrangement far removed from the sledgehammer beat of early hits, reaches UK #23 – the last in a run of 13 consecutive UK Top 30 hits, all Howard/Blaikley compositions.
Aug Dee leaves the group for a solo vocal career (having already done solo work on TV, both acting and singing), while the others continue as D,B,M and T. (Dee forms record production company Avenue Artists Production, with agents Bob James and Len Cannon. First releases from the company are *Do It Yourself* by The Chances and *Daffodillo* by The Nite People.)

1970 **Mar** Dee's solo ballad *My Woman's Man* reaches UK #42.
Aug D,B,M and T's *Mr. President* reaches UK #33. (The group will go on to record the unsuccessful **Fresh Ear**, before breaking up.)

1973 Having found only minor success as an actor, Dee moves to the backroom of the record industry, becoming head of A&R (Artists & Repertoire) at WEA's UK division.

1974 **Oct** Dee and the group re-form for a one-off single, *She's My Lady*, on Antic label under Dee's own auspices through WEA. It fails to sell, and the reunion does not last. (Dee will go on to form his own Double D record label.)

1982 **Sept** [21] Group has another one-off reunion in an all-star concert at London's Hammersmith Odeon, organized by Dee as UK record industry charity committee member. Celebrating 15 years of UK BBC Radio 1, and featuring acts including Billy Fury, Dave Berry, The Troggs and Herman's Hermits, the show is a benefit for the industry's charity, The Nordoff Robbins Music Therapy Centre. The group's live revival of *The Legend Of Xanadu* appears on the souvenir compilation *Heroes And Villains*. They stay together long enough to tour Germany, where interest in the group is still strong, and where D,B,M and T have been playing regularly for many years.

1988 D,B,M and T, with a new "Mick", still play live, based in their own club in Marbella, Spain.

THE SPENCER DAVIS GROUP

Steve Winwood (guitar, keyboards, vocals)
Spencer Davis (guitar)
Muff Winwood (bass)
Pete York (drums)

1963 **Aug** Former Birmingham University student Davis (b. July 17, 1942, Swansea, Wales), a teacher and part-time blues musician in Birmingham, W.Midlands and ex-London skiffle group The Saints, forms the group after meeting York (b. Aug.15, 1942, Redcar, Cleveland) and the Winwood brothers: Steve (b. May 12, 1948, Birmingham) and Muff, named after TV puppet Muffin The Mule, (b. Mervyn Winwood, June 14, 1943, Birmingham), at the Golden Eagle, a Birmingham pub. He has been playing there as a folk/blues soloist, and they as trad group The Muff-Woody Jazz Band; together, they quickly evolve as a tough R&B quartet, appropriately called The Rhythm & Blues Quartet.

1964 **June** [1] Group is spotted and signed by Chris Blackwell, who owns the fledging Island Records. As yet lacking full resources to promote his acts, Blackwell licenses the group's output to Philips Records' Fontana label. First Fontana single revives John Lee Hooker's *Dimples*, but is not a hit.
Nov *I Can't Stand It* is UK chart debut, at #47.

'65 Mar Revival of Brenda Holloway's *Every Little Bit Hurts* makes UK #41.
June *Strong Love* peaks at UK #44.
Aug [8] Group plays on the last day of the fifth annual National Jazz & Blues Festival at the Athletic Ground, Richmond, London.
Sept [24] They begin a 24-date twice-nightly UK tour, with The Rolling Stones, Unit 4 + 2 and others, at Finsbury Park Astoria, London. Tour will end Oct.17 at Granada cinema, Tooting, London.
'66 Jan *Keep On Running*, penned by Blackwell's Jamaican protege Jackie Edwards and originally a B-side, is their breakthrough hit, topping UK chart after deposing The Beatles' *We Can Work It Out*.
Feb *Their First LP* (originally released in July 1965) and new *The Second Album* are simultaneous UK hits, at #6 and #3 respectively.
Mar *Keep On Running* peaks at US #76.
Apr [14] *Somebody Help Me* hits UK #1 for 2 weeks, as UK tour with The Who opens at the Gaumont cinema, Southampton, Hants.
May [1] Group takes part in the annual **New Musical Express** Poll Winners Concert at the Empire Pool, Wembley, London.
July [11] They begin shooting "The Ghost Goes Gear" film on location in the Windsor, London, area and Chiddingstone Castle, Kent, with Dave Berry.
[29] They play on the first day of the sixth annual National Jazz & Blues Festival at Windsor, Berks.
Aug [22] Group makes its cabaret debut for a week at the Fiesta, Stockton, Cleveland and the Franchi, Jarrow, Tyne & Wear.
Sept *When I Come Home* reaches UK #12.
Oct *Autumn '66* hits UK #5.
[1-2] Group represents UK in the annual Grand Gala Du Disque in Amsterdam, Holland.
Nov *Gimme Some Lovin'*, written by Winwood, hits UK #2, kept from #1 by The Beach Boys' *Good Vibrations*.
Dec "The Ghost Goes Gear" is released in UK as support to "One Million Years BC".
[5] A German tour with Dave Dee, Dozy, Beaky, Mick and Tich opens at the Circus Krone, Munich.
'67 Feb *I'm A Man*, another Winwood song (written with producer Jimmy Miller) originally written as background music for a US documentary film on Swinging London, hits UK #9. *Gimme Some Lovin'*, in remixed form with added instrumentation and female chorus, hits US #7, becoming their biggest US success.
Mar [11] They begin a 21-date UK tour with The Hollies, The Tremeloes and Paul Jones, at the Granada cinema, Mansfield, Notts. Tour will close Apr.2 at the Empire theater, Liverpool, Merseyside.
[20] They win Carl Alan Award for Most Outstanding Group Of 1966.
Apr [2] Having given lengthy notice of intention, both Winwood brothers leave (Steve to form new band Traffic, and Muff to move into record production and eventual executive heights in UK record industry with CBS).
May *I'm A Man* hits US #10, and *Gimme Some Lovin'* makes US #54.
[7] New line-up of Davis, York, organist Eddie Hardin (b. Edward Harding, Feb.19, 1949) and lead guitarist Phil Sawyer (b. Mar.8, 1947), debuts at the annual **New Musical Express** Poll Winners Concert at the Empire Pool, London.
July *Somebody Help Me*, belatedly released in US, reaches #47, while *I'm A Man* reaches #83. Group opens US tour in Lake Geneva, WI.
Aug Psychedelia-tinged *Time Seller*, recorded by the new line-up, reaches UK #30, though the group has lost its distinctive sound, based around Winwood's vocals.
Nov Group makes a cameo appearance in a dancehall sequence in movie "Here We Go Round The Mulberry Bush", for which they also write 6 songs.
'68 Jan Last UK hit is *Mr. Second Class*, which reaches #35.
Aug [11] Group takes part in the eighth National Jazz & Blues Festival.
Oct Hardin and York leave to work on their own, recording *Tomorrow Today* for Bell Records as Hardin & York.
Nov North American tour begins with a new line-up comprising Dee Murray (bass) and Dave Hynes (drums). (Hynes will shortly be replaced by Nigel Olsson.)
'69 July Davis breaks up the band (Murray and Olsson moving on to accompany Elton John), and moves to California to work as a soloist. (He will continue to play and record, mostly in US, through the 70s.)
'71 Davis teams up with Peter Jameson.
'73 Davis briefly re-forms the group with Hardin for US and UK tours but reunion does not last and band finally quits. Davis will eventually assume an executive post at Island Records, Los Angeles, CA.
'90 Davis forms new Spencer Davis Group with Don Kirkpatrick and Ed

Tree (guitars), Rick Seratte (keyboards), Charlie Harrison (bass) and ex-Wang Chung Bryan Hitt (drums). (Hitt's tenure will not be long as he accepts an invitation to join REO Speedwagon.) York now lives in Germany hosting TV show "Super Drummers".

BOBBY DAY

1957 Sept Day (b. Robert James Byrd, July 1, 1930, Fort Worth, TX), having moved to Watts, Los Angeles, CA, as a youngster, and later served an R&B apprenticeship under Johnny Otis at the Barrelhouse club, is active both as a songwriter and member of vocal group The Hollywood Flames. Over a period of time the group goes through a variety of name-changes settling on The Satellites when Day releases *Little Bitty Pretty One* as Bobby Day & The Satellites for songwriter/producer Leon Rene's Class Records.
Dec A cover version of *Little Bitty Pretty One* by Thurston Harris on Aladdin Records, helped by an appearance on "American Bandstand", hits US #6 while Day's original peaks at #57. Day is also climbing US chart as one of The Hollywood Flames, with their sole US pop hit *Buzz Buzz Buzz*, backed with *Crazy*.
1958 Feb *Buzz Buzz Buzz*, which has Earl Nelson (later Bob & Earl of *Harlem Shuffle* fame) on lead vocals, reaches US #11. Despite this group success, Day concentrates on his solo career from this time onward.
Oct *Rockin' Robin*, penned by Jimmie Thomas and with a distinctive Plas Johnson flute riff, hits US #2 (including 1 week at #1 on the R&B chart), becoming a million-seller and staying on chart for 5 months. Sales are aided by B-side *Over And Over*, which makes US #41.
Nov *Rockin' Robin* reaches UK #29 where it is Day's only hit.
1959 Jan *The Bluebird, The Buzzard And The Oriole*, continuing the lyrical theme of *Rockin' Robin* is less successful, peaking at US #54.
2 later singles, *That's All I Want* and *Gotta New Girl* will only spend a week each at the bottom of US Top 100, ending his chart career. (Day will continue recording, without great success, through the 60s for RCA, Rendezvous, Sureshot and other labels, but his songs will prove far more enduring. The Dave Clark Five will have a US #1 and million-seller with *Over And Over* in 1965, while Michael Jackson will hit US #2 and UK #3 in 1972 with *Rockin' Robin*. *Little Bitty Pretty One* will have US Top 30 hit revivals by Clyde McPhatter in 1962 and The Jackson 5 in 1972. He will also have success through 2 companies Byrdland Attractions and Quiline Publishing. He will return to live work in the nationwide tour "Thirty Years Of Rock'N'Roll" with Donnie Brooks and Tiny Tim. He will also work with Jewel Akens.)
1990 July [27] Hospitalized since July 15, Day dies of cancer.

DEACON BLUE

Ricky Ross (vocals)
Lorraine McIntosh (vocals)
Graeme Kelling (guitar)
James Prime (keyboards)
Ewan Vernal (bass, keyboard bass)
Douglas Vipond (drums, percussion)

1982 Ross (b. Dec.22, 1957, Dundee, Scotland), former youth club leader and teacher, joins Woza, a local band in Glasgow, Scotland, providing keyboards and vocals. He continues to work part-time as a teacher for children with behavioral difficulties in the Maryhill district. The outfit will remain together for a year, supporting bands including Friends Again and The Waterboys throughout the region.
1983 Ross concentrates on songwriting and unsuccessfully sends an 11-track solo demo tape to publishers in London. He is advised to form a band to showcase his composing talent.
1985 Ross forms Deacon Blue (inspired by a Steely Dan song from their *Aja* album), initially a 5-piece featuring Prime (b. Nov.3, 1960, Kilmarnock, Scotland) on keyboards, Vipond (b. Oct.15, 1966, Johnstone, Scotland) on drums, Kelling (b. Apr.4, 1957, Paisley, Scotland) on guitar and fellow ex-Woza, Vernal (b. Feb.27, 1964, Glasgow) on bass.
1986 Following interest by Gordon Charlton of CBS London's A&R department, his boss, Muff Winwood, signs the band after a gig in Glasgow. No other label has shown interest.
Nov Deacon Blue begins 2 months of recording at AIR studios, London. Ross' girlfriend McIntosh (b. May 13, 1964, Glasgow), although not yet a member of the band, lends considerable vocal assistance to many tracks, all of which are penned by her beau.
1987 Mar Debut release *Dignity* does not chart, despite constant UK touring.
May *Raintown* is released to critical approval and spends 2 weeks on

UK album chart at #82, helped considerably by strong regional sales in the Glasgow area. 2 further single releases fail to chart.

1988 **Feb** Re-release of *Dignity*, now remixed by Bob Clearmountain, together with 4 previously unissued bonus tracks on the CD single format, sees their UK Singles chart debut peak at UK #31.

Apr Reissue of *When Will You Make My Telephone Ring*, featuring the backing vocals of soul veterans Jimmy Helms, Jimmy Chambers and George Chandler (who will form Londonbeat), makes UK #34, but fails in US, where it is their debut release.

June Re-promotion of *Raintown* activates UK chart peak at #14.

July Deacon Blue embarks on its first major venue headlining UK tour, supported by fellow Scots Fairground Attraction, while *Chocolate Girl* makes UK #43.

Aug To further spur album sales, CBS issues a 10,000 limited edition of *Raintown*, now twinned with a bonus album collection of B-sides and rarities under the title *Riches*.

Oct Their first new A-side recording since 1986, *Real Gone Kid* proves their major breakthrough, hitting UK #8. With McIntosh as a full band member, Ross has written the song about ex-Lone Justice vocalist Maria McKee, inspired by an onstage performance by her earlier in the year.

1989 **Mar** *Wages Day*, which includes a B-side cover version of Julian Cope's *Trampolene*, reaches UK #18.

Apr [15] Second album *When The World Knows Your Name* debuts at UK #1, supplanting Madonna's *Like A Prayer*.

May [1] Band embarks on 18-date headlining tour at Dublin Stadium, Eire. It will incorporate 2 nights at the Hammersmith Odeon, London, and end at the Hippodrome, Bristol, Avon, May 28.

June *Fergus Sings The Blues*, packaged as a "souvenir from Scotland" boxed single, reaches UK #14.

Aug [1] 6-date US promotional tour, which will end at the Paradise, Boston, MA, Aug.9, starts at Slims in San Francisco, CA.

Sept *Love And Regret* reaches UK #28.

Dec [12] 8-date sell-out UK mini-tour begins at the Mean Fiddler, London.

1990 **Jan** [13] Appropriately timed *Queen Of The New Year*, the fourth single from *When The World Knows Your Name*, reaches UK #21.

May 250,000 attend Glasgow's Big Day, Scotland's largest free open-air festival headlined by Deacon Blue.

[5] Group sings *A Hard Day's Night* at the "John Lennon Tribute Concert" at the Pier Head Arena in Merseyside to celebrate the songs of Lennon.

June [22-24] Band takes part in the 3-day Glastonbury Festival of Contemporary Performing Arts, Somerset.

Sept [1] Departing from his own songwriting, Ross elects to record 4 Burt Bacharach/Hal David hits from the 60s. Led by the main radio choice *I'll Never Fall In Love Again*, the *Four Bacharach & David Songs (EP)*, produced by Jon Kelly, becomes Deacon Blue's biggest hit at UK #2, held from the top spot by Bombalurina's *Itsy Bitsy Teeny Weeny Yellow Polka Dot Bikini*.

[4] Now elevated to the UK's largest venues, Deacon Blue plays the first of 8 sell-out shows, including 3 at the Wembley Arena, London, at the Aberdeen Exhibition Centre, Scotland. World dates will follow in the US, Germany, Spain and Holland.

[22] Billed as a collection of B-sides, film tracks and miscellaneous sessions, *Ooh Las Vegas*, immediately hits UK #3.

1991 **Jan** Group begins recording its fourth album at Guillaume Tell studios in Paris, France, with producer Kelly and engineer Steve Jackson. Ross masterminds charity album *The Tree And The Bird And The Fish And The Bell*, a collection of Glasgow songs by Glaswegian artists including Deacon Blue, Wet Wet Wet and Big Dish.

June Deacon Blue releases *Fellow Hoodlums*.

CHRIS DE BURGH

1974 **Sept** Having graduated from Trinity College, Dublin, Eire, toured Eire with Horslips at the end of 1973 and honed his writing and singing skills entertaining guests at his family's 12th-century castle hotel in Ireland, De Burgh (b. Christopher Davidson, Oct.15, 1948, Argentina), the son of a diplomat, signs to A&M Records in UK after meeting producer/songwriters Doug Flett and Guy Fletcher.

Nov On his first UK gigs, he supports A&M stablemates Supertramp on their "Crime Of The Century" tour.

1975 **Feb** Debuts, *Hold On* and *Far Beyond These Castle Walls*, produced by Robin Geoffrey Cable, attract critical attention but do not chart.

July Second single *Flying* is released. It meets with scant sales in UK but will go on to top the Brazilian charts for 17 weeks.

Nov *Spanish Train And Other Stories* is released.

1976 2 further singles, *Lonely Sky*, released in Jan., and *Patricia The Stripper*, also fail to chart.

Dec *A Spaceman Came Travelling*, taken from *Spanish Train And Other Stories*, is released without chart success, but becomes his most popular song for many years and a festive favorite at Christmas.

1980 **July** After successful live work all over the world (notably in South Africa, South America and Europe), and 2 more non-charting albums, *At The End Of A Perfect Day* and *Eastern Wind* is issued, De Burgh's first with a backing band which now accompanies him on stage. Still not a hit in UK or US, it is a smash in Norway – selling 125,000 copies and making it the country's second best-selling album after The Beatles *Abbey Road*.

1981 **Sept** [19] Compilation album *Best Moves* released at the suggestion of A&M's Canadian office, with De Burgh's own pick of his earlier songs and one new number, is his UK chart debut at #65.

1982 **Oct** [30] *Don't Pay The Ferryman*, remixed from new album *The Getaway*, makes UK #48.

Nov [6] *The Getaway*, which sees De Burgh teamed with producer Rupert Hine, reaches UK #30.

1983 **July** [2] *Don't Pay The Ferryman* is his US breakthrough, making #34. *The Getaway* makes US #43 and stays on chart for 5 months.

Sept [10] *Ship To Shore* peaks at US #71.

1984 **May** [19] *Man On The Line* debut at UK #11.

[26] *High On Emotion* makes UK #44.

Aug [25] *High On Emotion* makes US #44, with *Man On The Line* peaking at US #69.

1985 **Feb** [6] TV-advertised compilation *The Very Best Of Chris De Burgh* introduces him to a wider UK audience, and hits UK #6 during a 70-week stay on the chart.

Aug [2] Early album *Spanish Train And Other Stories* belatedly charts in UK at #78.

Dec [19] He takes part in Carol Aid, a London benefit performance supporting the Band Aid Appeal, with Cliff Richard, Lulu and others.

1986 **Aug** [2] Ballad *The Lady In Red*, written for and about his wife and De Burgh's 24th single release, tops the UK chart for 3 weeks as parent album *Into The Light* hits UK #2. Both are De Burgh's biggest sellers to date. Press reports state that Prince Andrew and his wife Sarah Ferguson take a copy with them on their honeymoon.

Oct *Fatal Hesitation* makes UK #44 as another early album, *Crusader*, shows briefly at UK #72.

1987 **Jan** A festive reissue of *A Spaceman Came Travelling*, a double A-side with *The Ballroom Of Romance*, makes UK #40.

May [23] *The Lady In Red* is his biggest US hit at #3 and takes combined UK/US sales well over a million.

June *Into The Light* reaches US #25.

1988 **Jan** [2] *The Simple Truth (A Child Is Born)* peaks at UK #55.

July *Love Is My Decision*, theme to film "Arthur 2: On The Rocks", sung by De Burgh, is released in the US.

Oct [15] De Burgh's studio album *Flying Colours* debuts at UK #1.

Nov Sentimental ballad *Missing You* hits UK #3.

1989 **Jan** *Tender Hands* makes UK #43.

Oct *This Waiting Heart* peaks at UK #59.

Nov *From A Spark To A Flame – The Very Best Of Chris De Burgh* hits UK #4.

1990 **Sept** [29] *High On Emotion – Live From Dublin* reaches UK #15, and continues De Burgh's 15-year association with A&M.

1991 **May** [12] De Burgh appears live in "The Simple Truth" concert for Kurdish refugees at Wembley Arena, London, to which he also contributes the title song.

JOEY DEE AND THE STARLITERS

Joey Dee (vocals)
Carlton Latimer (keyboards)
Willie Davis (drums)
Larry Vernieri (back-up vocals)
David Brigati (back-up vocals)

1960 **Sept** After playing in clubs and at dances in New Jersey for a couple of years and being the resident band at the Riviera club, Dee (b. Joseph DiNicola, June 11, 1940, Passaic, NJ) And The Starliters become the house band at the Peppermint Lounge, a socialite-favored New York club on West 45th Street. Dee has sung back-up in Brigati's doo-wop group The Hi-Fives in the late 50s.

1961 **Sept** As Chubby Checker's *The Twist* becomes popular at the Peppermint Lounge, The Starliters are noted in local media as an integral part of the dance craze. This attention leads to a recording contract with Roulette Records.

Oct Dee and Roulette producer Henry Glover write *Peppermint Twist*, tying the dance to the venue.

'62 **Jan** *Peppermint Twist* tops US chart for 3 weeks, replacing Checker's *The Twist* after its second spell at US #1. *Doin' The Twist At The Peppermint Lounge* hits US #2, equalling Chubby Checker's *Your Twist Party* as the highest-placed Twist album ever on US chart.

Feb Dee and The Starliters feature in "Hey Let's Twist", a quickly-made exploitation movie which also stars Jo-Ann Campbell and Teddy Randazzo. *Peppermint Twist* reaches UK #33, outdone by Danny Peppermint & The Jumping Jacks' version, which reaches UK #26. It will be Dee's only UK chart entry.

Mar *Hey Let's Twist*, from the film, makes US #20.

Apr Soundtrack album *Hey Let's Twist* climbs to US #18.

May A revival of The Isley Brothers' *Shout* hits US #6 - the only version of this R&B classic to reach US Top 40.

July *Back At The Peppermint Lounge, Twistin'* reaches US #97.

Oct Dee appears in second movie "Two Tickets To Paris" with Gary Crosby and others. A Dee solo song from the film, *What Kind Of Love Is This?* (written by Johnny Nash), reaches US #18.

Dec *I Lost My Baby* breaks the US Top 20 run by making only #61.

'63 **June** Group reaches US #36 with *Hot Pastrami And Mashed Potatoes*, a dance-oriented follow-up to The Dartells' US Top 20 hit *Hot Pastrami* a month earlier.

July *Dance Dance Dance* closes group's US chart career, reaching #89.

'64 Dee opens his own New York club, the Starliter, and plays there with a new group line-up which includes Felix Cavaliere, Gene Cornish and Eddie Brigati (younger brother of original Starliter David), who will go on to form The Young Rascals later in the year. (Dee will later sell his club and begin touring, continuing to work regularly - eventually on the US oldies circuit - right through into the 80s, when his band will include his son, Joey Dee Jr. The Peppermint Lounge does not fare so well. It loses its liquor license in 1965 and by 1971 is a topless club.)

'87 Dee establishes the Starlite Starbrite Foundation For The Love Of Rock'N'Roll in Florida to help rock stars who have fallen on hard times. The aim is to raise $20 million for a retirement community in Clearwater, FL, and health insurance for needy musicians.

'89 Dee, Hank Ballard and Chubby Checker play at Lulu's Roadhouse, Kitchener, Canada, for a reunion to be part of a feature length documentary on the Twist.

DEEP PURPLE

Ian Gillan (vocals)
Ritchie Blackmore (guitar)
Jon Lord (keyboards)
Roger Glover (bass)
Ian Paice (drums)

'67 Chris Curtis (b. Christopher Crummy, Aug.26, 1941, Oldham, Lancs.), ex-The Searchers drummer, approaches London businessman, Tony Edwards, a textile company boss, to manage him. Edwards invites John Coletta, an advertising consultant, both of whom have no experience of the music business, to invest in Curtis and the group Edwards wants him to put together. Curtis recruits his flat-mate Lord (b. June 9, 1941, Leicester, Leics.), ex-Artwoods and currently playing with The Flowerpot Men, who in turn invites Blackmore (b. Apr.14, 1945, Weston-Super-Mare, Avon), ex-Outlaws, Screaming Lord Sutch and Neil Christian & The Crusaders, and now living in Germany, to form a new band. Musicians are auditioned from a **Melody Maker** ad in Deeves Hall, a country house in Hertfordshire.

'68 **Feb** Group forms as Roundabout. The line-up is Lord, Blackmore, Curtis (vocals), Dave Curtis (bass) and Bobby Woodman (drums).

Mar After unpromising rehearsals, the line-up is changed. Woodman and both Curtises are replaced by Paice (b. June 29, 1948, Nottingham, Notts.) and singer Rod Evans (b. 1945, Edinburgh, Scotland), both ex-MI5 and ex-Maze, and bassist Nick Simper (b. 1946, Southall, London), ex-Johnny Kidd & The Pirates (who survived the car crash which killed Kidd).

Apr [20] Group makes its live debut in Tastrup, Denmark, and changes its name to Deep Purple (after rejecting Concrete God), using US group Vanilla Fudge as its model.

May Deep Purple records an album (in an 18-hour session) and is signed to EMI in UK and Bill Cosby's Tetragrammaton label in US.

Aug [10] Group's first major UK performance is at the Sunbury festival.

Sept [21] First single, a revival of Joe South-penned Billy Joe Royal hit *Hush* hits US #4.

Oct *Shades Of Deep Purple* reaches US #24, again without a UK placing. Group begins a North American tour, but Blackmore contracts hepatitis and after one gig in Quebec with Randy California deputizing, they cancel the tour.

Dec [7] A revival of Neil Diamond's *Kentucky Woman*, makes US #38.

1969 **Feb** *The Book Of Taliesyn* reaches US #54.

[8] Taken from it, a revival of Ike & Tina Turner's *River Deep, Mountain High* reaches US #53.

July *Deep Purple* reaches US #162. Evans and Simper both leave (Evans to US to join Captain Beyond). US Tetragrammaton label folds, leaving Deep Purple with no product outlet.

Aug Glover (b. Nov.30, 1945, Brecon, Wales) and Gillan (b. Aug.19, 1945, Hounslow, London), join from UK group Episode Six, playing their first gig with the band at London's Speakeasy club.

Sept [15] Deep Purple perform *Concerto For Group And Orchestra*, composed by Lord, with The Royal Philharmonic Orchestra conducted by Malcolm Arnold, at London's Royal Albert Hall.

1970 **Jan** *Concerto For Group And Orchestra*, originally recorded for the BBC at the Royal Albert Hall concert, reaches UK #26 (the group's UK chart debut) and US #149 (on Warner Bros.).

Feb [7] UK tour begins at Leicester University, Leics.

Aug *Deep Purple In Rock* hits UK #4, during a 68-week stay on the chart, and will make US #143.

Oct *Black Night* is the group's first UK singles hit at #2, behind Freda Payne's *Band Of Gold*.

[27] Gillan plays the role of Jesus in Tim Rice and Andrew Lloyd Webber's "Jesus Christ Superstar", in a live performance at St Peter's Lutheran Church, New York.

Nov Studio cast recording of *Jesus Christ Superstar* is released and eventually hits UK #6 and tops US chart.

Dec [26] *Black Night* peaks at US #66.

1971 **Mar** *Strange Kind Of Woman* hits UK #8.

July Group tours US with The Faces.

Sept [25] *Fireball* tops the UK chart for 1 week, and will reach US #32.

Oct They form Purple label, marketed by EMI.

[25] A concert in Hamilton, Canada, is cancelled after Gillan is admitted to a New York hospital suffering from exhaustion.

Nov Band begins rehearsals for 3 weeks at Clearwell Castle, Glos., before heading for Montreux to record.

Dec Extracted title track, *Fireball*, reaches UK #15.

[3] Deep Purple is recording in Montreux Casino, Switzerland, when it burns down during a set by Frank Zappa's Mothers Of Invention. The group immortalizes the incident in *Smoke On The Water* on next album.

1972 **Apr** [22] *Machine Head* tops the UK chart for 3 weeks, aided by a TV advertising campaign. (It will later hit US #7.) *Never Before* reaches UK #35. Lord releases *Gemini Suite*, with the London Symphony Orchestra.

June Band performs on the first night at the re-opened Rainbow theater, London.

Aug Group tours Japan, and concerts are recorded for album release.

Oct *Purple Passages*, a compilation on Warner of tracks from the group's 3 Tetragrammaton albums, reaches US #57. Gillan informs the group he is to leave after existing tour commitments. (Former Marbles singer Graham Bonnet will replace him briefly.)

Dec Group plays its last gig of the year, having been on the road for 44 weeks during 1972.

1973 **Jan** Live album *Made In Japan*, recorded during the group's 1972 summer tour, reaches UK #16.

Mar *Who Do We Think We Are* hits UK #4 and US #15.

Apr *Made In Japan* begins a climb to hit US #6.

June [29] Gillan quits after a show in Osaka at the end of a tour of Japan. Glover also leaves, initially to be Purple label's A&R man, and to begin a solo career with the label. (Both reportedly leave over differences with Blackmore.)

July [28] *Smoke On The Water*, from *Machine Head* about the Montreux Casino fire, is belatedly released in US and hits #4, selling a million and earning the group its only gold disk for a single.

Sept Vocalist, ex-The Government, David Coverdale (b. Sept.22, 1949, Saltburn-by-the-Sea, Cleveland), working in a menswear shop called Gentry in Redcar, Yorks., playing semi-pro with The Fabuloser Brothers (who have supported Deep Purple at Bradford University in 1972), answers an ad placed by Purple, as does ex-Trapeze bassist Glenn Hughes (b. Penkridge). Coverdale, asked to supply a photo of himself, sends the only one in his possession - taken as a boy in scout uniform. He also sends a tape with 2 Fabuloser Brothers tracks and 2 acoustic solo numbers, including *Everybody's Talkin'* and *Dancing In The Street*. They both join as replacements for Gillan and Glover, who sign solo deals with Oyster and Island respectively.

Oct [20] *Woman From Tokyo*, issued as a US single, peaks at #60.

1974 **Mar** [9] *Burn*, with the new line-up, hits UK #3 and will hit US #9.

[30] *Might Just Take Your Life* makes US #91.

May [22] Band plays at the Kilburn State Gaumont during UK tour which has started in Scotland and is set to end at Southend in June.

Nov *Stormbringer*, recorded in Germany, hits UK #6 and makes US #20.

[13] An imposter posing as Blackmore borrows a Porsche in Iowa City, IA, and wrecks it, having already conned food and shelter from several Deep Purple fans. (Blackmore is in US at the time, but in San Francisco, CA, with the band.) The imposter is arrested and charged with misrepresentation.

1975 **Apr** [7] Blackmore quits to form own band Rainbow, and is replaced by ex-James Gang guitarist Tommy Bolin (b. 1951, Sioux City, IA).

Aug [23] Compilation album *24 Carat Purple* reaches UK #14.

Oct [16] Glover's *The Butterfly Ball*, released late in 1974, is performed at London's Royal Albert Hall, with Gillan as lead vocalist.

Nov *Come Taste The Band*, featuring Bolin on guitar, reaches UK #19. Group begins a world tour, taking in the Far East, Australasia, US, Europe and UK. **Guinness Book of Records** lists them as the "world's loudest band".

1976 **Jan** [10] *Come Taste The Band* makes US #43.

July [19] Group splits at the end of the UK tour dates in Liverpool, Merseyside. (Coverdale begins a solo career before forming Whitesnake, Lord and Paice team with Tony Ashton to form Paice, Ashton and Lord, Hughes rejoins his former band Trapeze, and Bolin returns to US to form The Tommy Bolin Band.) Gillan's *Child In Time* makes UK #55.

Nov [13] *Deep Purple Live* reaches UK #12.

Dec [4] Bolin dies from a heroin overdose at the Newport hotel in Miami, FL.

[11] *Made In Europe*, US version of *Deep Purple Live*, makes US #148.

1977 **May** [7] Belated UK release, *Smoke On The Water*, reaches #21.

Oct [22] EP *New Live And Rare*, including an unheard live version of *Black Night*, makes UK #31.

1978 **Oct** [14] Compilation EP *New Live And Rare II* makes UK #45.

1979 **Apr** [14] *The Mark II Purple Singles*, compiling A and B-sides made by the Gillan, Lord, Glover, Blackmore, Paice line-up, reaches UK #24.

Oct Gillan's *Mr. Universe* reaches UK #11.

1980 A bogus Deep Purple, fronted by Rod Evans, plays a US tour. (Blackmore and Glover will take legal action to prevent Evans from using the name.)

June [21] Gillan's *Sleepin' On The Job* peaks at UK #55.

July Rumors insist that Blackmore has bought the house featured in the film "The Amityville Horror".

Aug [2] TV-advertised hits-compilation *Deepest Purple* tops the UK chart for a week.

[30] *Black Night*, reissued in UK to tie in with the album, makes #43. Gillan's *Glory Road* hits UK #3 and makes US #183.

Oct [11] Gillan's *Trouble* reaches UK #14.

Nov Compilation EP *New Live And Rare III*, including *Smoke On The Water*, makes UK #48. *Deepest Purple/The Very Best Of Deep Purple* reaches US #148.

Dec [13] Live album *In Concert*, featuring tracks recorded between 1970-72, makes UK #30.

1981 **Feb** [14] Gillan's *Mutually Assured Destruction* peaks at UK #32.

Apr [25] Gillan's *Future Shock* hits UK #2.

May [2] Gillan revives Freddy Cannon's 1960 hit *New Orleans*, reaching UK #17.

July [4] Gillan's *No Laughing In Heaven* makes UK #31.

Oct [31] Gillan makes UK #36 with *Nightmare*.

Nov [7] Gillan's *Double Trouble*, makes UK #12.

1982 **Jan** Gillan reaches UK #25 with *Restless*.

Sept *Deep Purple Live In London*, originally recorded for BBC radio in 1974, reaches UK #23.

[11] Gillan's *Living For The City* reaches UK #50.

Oct [9] Gillan's *Magic* climbs to UK #17.

1983 **Sept** Gillan joins Black Sabbath for *Born Again*.

1984 **Nov** Amid rumors that each member is offered $2 million to re-form, the group begins a world tour. Line-up is Blackmore, Gillan, Glover, Lord and Paice. Deep Purple signs to Polydor Records (Mercury in US) and releases *Perfect Strangers*, which hits UK #5 and US #17.

1985 **Jan** [26] *Knocking At Your Back Door* peaks at US #61.

Feb [2] Title track *Perfect Strangers* makes UK #48.

June [15] *Knocking At Your Back Door*, backed with *Perfect Strangers*, peaks at UK #68.

July [6] Double compilation album *The Anthology* makes UK #50.

1987 **Feb** *The House Of Blue Light* hits UK #10 and US #34. Band tours Europe, and causes a controversy when Blackmore repeatedly refuses to play *Smoke On The Water*.

1988 **June** A re-recording of the band's original hit *Hush* makes UK #62.

July *Nobody's Perfect*, recorded live during 1987, reaches UK #38, as the group embarks on 2-month "Nobody's Perfect" US tour in Saratoga, NY.

Aug *Nobody's Perfect* makes US #105.

1989 **July** [29] Gillan quits the group citing "musical differences".

Dec Gillan collaborates with Brian May, Bruce Dickinson and Robert Plant as Rock Aid Armenia with a remake of *Smoke On The Water*, which makes UK #39, with all profits from the record going to the victims of the Armenian Earthquake disaster.

1990 Deep Purple, now comprising Blackmore, Lord, Glover, Paice and Joe Lynn Turner, signs with RCA Records.

Oct [20] *King Of Dreams* peaks at UK #70.

Nov [3] *Slaves & Masters* debuts at peak UK #45.

[17] *Slaves & Masters* makes US #87.

DEF LEPPARD

Joe Elliott (vocals)
Phil Collen (guitar)
Steve Clark (guitar)
Rick Savage (bass)
Rick Allen (drums)

1977 Group is formed in Sheffield, when ex-schoolboys Pete Willis and Elliott (b. Aug.1, 1959, Sheffield, S.Yorks.) leave their own fledgling group to join heavy metal band Atomic Mass led by British Rail apprentice Savage (b. Dec.2, 1960). Elliott abandons his guitar playing ambitions to take lead vocals and Savage switches to bass, allowing Willis to play guitar. The name is changed to Def Leppard (from Elliott's initial suggestion of Deaf Leopard). Clark (b. Apr.23, 1960, Hillsborough, S.Yorks.), an acquaintance of Willis' at Stannington College in Sheffield, joins on second guitar.

1978 **Jan** [29] During Clark's first rehearsal with the band, now comprising Elliott, Willis, Savage and drummer Tony Kenning, at a rehearsal room in Bramall Lane, Sheffield, he plays the guitar solo from Lynyrd Skynyrd's *Freebird*, and is immediately asked to join the band full-time.

July Group's live debut is at Westfield school, Sheffield, for a £5 fee. Small pub gigs follow with a series of drummers (none of whom proves suitable).

Nov Group records a 3-track EP with stand-in drummer Frank Noon in the small Fairview studios in Kingston-upon-Hull, Humberside, and forms its own Bludgeon Riffola label with a loan from Elliott's father. It recruits Derbyshire drummer Allen (b. Nov.1, 1963), who at 15 is the youngest in a young band (Elliott is the oldest at 19).

1979 **Jan** 3-track EP *Getcha Rocks Off* is released in an initial pressing of 1,000. It is picked up first by local Radio Hallam's rock show, for which the band records 6 songs. A session for BBC Radio 1's John Peel show follows and music press identifies the band with the emergent new wave of British heavy metal. The record is picked up and re-pressed by Phonogram Records and sells 24,000 copies. Sheffield record retailer Peter Martin notes the demand for the record and during the summer he and promoter Frank Stuart Brown become the group's first managers.

Aug Def Leppard signs Bludgeon Riffola to Phonogram's Vertigo label and begins recording with producer Tom Allom. An album is completed in only 18 days.

Nov [17] Vertigo debut *Wasted* peaks at UK #61.

1980 **Mar** [8] Follow-up, *Hello America*, makes UK #45.

[29] Debut *On Through The Night* makes UK #15. Band supports Sammy Hagar and AC/DC on UK tours and meets Peter Mensch, an employee of AC/DC's New York-based Leber/Krebs management. He becomes the group's new manager, directing it towards the US market.

July [5] *On Through The Night* reaches US #51.

Aug [22-24] Group participates at "Reading Rock '80" in Reading, Berks., with Gillan, Iron Maiden, Krokus, Magnum, Ozzy Osbourne, UFO and Whitesnake. UK fans react against the band's new US market orientation, showering them with a hail of bottles which forces the band to leave the stage. (US audiences will be more enthusiastic when

'81 Group records with a new producer, Robert "Mutt" Lange, under whose guidance *High'N'Dry* takes 3 months to complete and the smoother, tighter result is aimed particularly at US FM rock radio.
Aug [1] *High'N'Dry* reaches UK #26.
Sept [12] *High'N'Dry* makes US #38, with the help of US tour co-headlining with Blackfoot. Willis finds himself increasingly out of step with the rest of the band and considers leaving.
Dec By the end of the year the group, exhausted by the demands of non-stop touring, slips into a period of inactivity.
'82 Band spends several months in the studio working on an album, again with Lange producing. During the sessions, Willis' alcohol problem and incompatability with the rest of the group comes to a head and he is fired. Collen (b. Dec.8, 1957), ex-glam-rock band Girl, replaces him.
'83 **Feb** [5] *Pyromania* spends a 92-week US chart run, during which time it will spend 2 weeks at #2, behind Michael Jackson's *Thriller*.
[19] Extracted single, *Photograph*, peaks at UK #66.
Mar *Pyromania* reaches UK #18. Group begins a world tour to promote it, starting in UK, then Europe, and by the time it reaches US the album is in the Top 10. With live support, it continues selling and will eventually sell more than 6.5 million copies in US alone. The US tour is followed by Japanese and Australian dates.
May [21] *Photograph* reaches US #12.
Aug [13] *Rock Of Ages* reaches US #16.
Sept [3] *Rock Of Ages* makes UK #41.
Nov [5] *Foolin'* reaches US #28.
'84 **Jan** Group sweeps the annual American Music Awards.
Group takes an 8-month break before teaming up to record with Lange. But pre-production in Dublin, Eire, indicates that Lange has been overworked and is too tired to work effectively (he had followed *Pyromania* with *Heartbreak City* for The Cars and Foreigner's 4).
June [30] A remix of *Bringin' On The Heartbreak* from *High'N'Dry* peaks at US #61. *High And Dry* reissued with the remix and new track *Me And My Wine* re-charts to make US #72.
Aug Recording begins at Wisseloord in Holland with producer/writer Jim Steinman (of Meat Loaf and Bonnie Tyler fame).
Dec Recording is halted for a Christmas break and the group decides to fire Steinman and produce the album itself.
[31] Driving from Sheffield to Derbyshire, Allen is involved in a serious auto accident. The impact of the crash tears off his left arm and badly damages his right. Surgeons sew the arm back on only to be forced to remove it 3 days later when infection sets in.
'85 **Jan** [2] The rest of the group returns to Holland to continue recording. Allen affirms by phone that he wants to return to the band.
Apr Allen rejoins the group. Little progress is made in the studio, even with the services of Lange's engineer Nigel Green. It is decided to scrap the tapes and wait until Lange is ready to work. Meanwhile, Allen learns to play in spite of his disability. He works with a Fairlight computer to create drum sounds and uses it to record most of the album's drum tracks on his own. He has a sophisticated Simmons electronic drumkit custom-built, with an SD57 computer to store sounds and fills. By summer, Lange is ready to record.
'86 **Aug** [17] Allen makes his first public appearance since his accident as Def Leppard plays the first of 3 "Monsters Of Rock" festivals, including Castle Donington, in UK and Europe. Receptions, especially for Allen, are warm and the experience gives them fresh motivation in the studio.
'87 **Aug** AOR-driven *Animal*, the first extract from forthcoming *Hysteria*, is released, hitting UK #6.
[29] *Hysteria*, 3 years in the making, debuts at UK #1, and will go on to spend 95 weeks on the chart. A highly successful UK tour follows.
Sept [5] *Women* stalls at US #80.
Oct *Pour Some Sugar On Me* reaches UK #18, as the group embarks on a major world tour.
Dec *Hysteria* makes UK #26.
[26] *Animal* reaches US #19.
'88 **Feb** [15] Group cancels a show in El Paso, TX, after threats to disrupt the concert, following a Sept.7, 1983, gig when Elliott referred to El Paso as "the place with all those greasy Mexicans".
Mar [26] *Hysteria* hits US #10.
Apr *Armageddon It* reaches UK #20.
July [23] *Pour Some Sugar On Me* hits US #2; *Love Bites* makes UK #11.
[16] Road crew technician Steve Cayter dies of a brain hemorrhage on stage before a show at the Alpine Valley Music theater, East Troy, WI.
[23] After 49 weeks on the US charts, *Hysteria* finally climbs to the top. (Only Fleetwood Mac's and Whitney Houston's eponymous albums have taken longer.) Band becomes the first to have sold more than 5

million copies of 2 consecutive albums in US.
Oct [8] *Love Bites* tops US chart, as the band's 14-month worldwide tour ends at the Memorial Arena in Seattle, WA.
1989 **Jan** [21] *Armageddon It* hits US #3.
[30] Group wins Favorite Heavy Metal Artist and Favorite Heavy Metal Album for *Hysteria* at the American Music Awards.
Feb Fifth single from *Hysteria*, *Rocket* reaches UK #15.
[13] Group performs live at eighth annual BRIT awards at the Royal Albert Hall, London.
[25] Elliot is hit in the face by a coin thrown by a fan at a gig in Spain.
Apr [29] *Rocket* reaches US #12.
Sept [6] Def Leppard performs live at the annual MTV Video Music Awards at the Universal Amphitheater, Los Angeles.
1991 **Jan** [8] Clark, after a night's drinking with friend Daniel Van Alphen, is found dead by his girlfriend in his Chelsea flat in London. Group will announce its intention to continue, with a fifth album, produced by Mike Shipley, scheduled for 1991 release.

DESMOND DEKKER

1963 Having lived in the St. Thomas township and worked as an engineering welder before joining studio group The Aces, Dekker (b. Desmond Dacris, July 16, 1942, Kingston, Jamaica) records his first Jamaican single, *Honour Your Mother And Father*, for Yabba label. (With The Aces, he will have hits in Jamaica with *Generosity* (1964), *Get Up Adinah* (1964), *King Of The Ska* (1965), *007 (Shanty Town)* (1966), *Jezebel* (1966), and *Rock Steady* (1966).)
1966 After a variety of producers, Dekker & The Aces start recording for Leslie Kong (they will continue to be produced exclusively by Kong until his death in 1971).
1967 **Aug** *007 (Shanty Town)*, a chart-topper in Jamaica, is a celebration of the Kingston "rude boy" lifestyle. It is an underground club hit in the US for 6 months before it reaches #14. Its release in UK on Pyramid achieves #14.
1969 **Apr** Dekker becomes first Jamaican artist to hit UK #1, with *The Israelites*, which tops the chart for 3 weeks.
June *The Israelites* hits US #9.
July *It Miek* hits UK #7 and *This Is Desmond Dekker* reaches UK #27.
Sept *Israelites* reaches US #153.
[21] Dekker plays at the Caribbean Music Festival at the Empire Pool, Wembley, London, with Johnny Nash, Jackie Edwards, Jimmy Cliff, Max Romeo and others. (Dekker wins the Golden Trophy for Best Song Of Year in Jamaica. It is his fifth consecutive award.)
1970 **Jan** *Pickney Gal* climbs to UK #42.
Oct Dekker almost scores a second UK #1 with *You Can Get It If You Really Want*, missing out at #2. Written by Jimmy Cliff, it is the first non-original song Dekker has recorded.
1971 After his producer Kong dies of a heart attack, Dekker, who has visited the UK regularly since the success of *007 (Shanty Town)*, moves to London. But by this time, the ska phenomenon is being replaced by reggae, with a new generation of Jamaican artists emerging, spearheaded by Bob Marley & The Wailers. Dekker fails to enjoy further mainstream chart success with new recordings.
1975 **June** *The Israelites*, reissued in UK by Cactus reggae label, hits #10.
Sept *Sing A Little Song* reaches UK #16.
1980 Dekker performs and records on a sporadic basis from London, updating versions of his old hits on Stiff album *Black And Dekker*, backed with The Rumour.
1981 *Compass Point* is produced by Robert Palmer but fails to impress.
1985 **Jan** [6] Dekker performs with fellow reggae artists Dennis Brown, Smiley Culture, Lee Perry and others, at an Ethiopian benefit concert at Brixton Academy, London.
1990 *The Israelites* is used as theme song for award-winning Maxell Tapes TV ad which misinterprets the lyrics of the original song to become "My ears are alight".

DELANEY & BONNIE

Delaney Bramlett (guitar, vocals)
Bonnie Lynn Bramlett (vocals)

1967 Delaney Bramlett (b. July 1, 1939, Pontotoc Co., MS) and Bonnie Lynn (b. Nov.8, 1944, Acton, IL) meet in Los Angeles, CA, on Jack Good's rock TV show "Shindig". He is in resident band The Shindogs, while she is a session singer (formerly with Ike and Tina Turner's Ikettes). They marry within a week of meeting.

DELANEY & BONNIE cont.

1968 They record *Home* with Booker T. & The MG's for Stax Records in Memphis, but it is not released at this time.

1969 **July** They sign to Elektra, releasing *The Original Delaney And Bonnie - Accept No Substitute*, which makes a US chart showing at #175.
Sept Delaney & Bonnie & Friends (the latter a frequently-changing aggregation of session men) are hired as opening act on US tour by Blind Faith, which leads to immediate friendship with Eric Clapton, who admires their music and joins in inter-date jam sessions on the tour bus.
Dec [15] Delaney & Bonnie appear as guest musicians with John Lennon's Plastic Ono Band for the "War Is Over" concert at the Lyceum, London, at the end of a UK tour.

1970 **Jan** After Blind Faith folds, Clapton joins Delaney & Bonnie's Friends as guitarist on a 2-month US tour of their own, which he has agreed to co-finance. *Comin' Home*, credited jointly to the group and Clapton, is released by Atco Records, reaching US #84 and UK #16. It is their only UK hit single. The Bonnie-sung ballad *Groupie (Superstar)* on the B-side will become a million-selling song when covered and revised to *Superstar* by The Carpenters in 1971.
Apr Clapton departs at tour's end to work on his first solo album, on which the Bramletts will both guest, and many of the Friends (Jim Gordon, Carl Radle, Bobby Keys, Bobby Whitlock, Jim Price and Rita Coolidge) also leave to become part of "Mad Dogs And Englishmen" touring group with Joe Cocker.
June *Delaney & Bonnie & Friends On Tour With Eric Clapton* reaches US #29 and UK #39.
Sept *Soul Shake*, the B-side of *Free The People* which stalls at US #75, makes US #43.
Nov *To Bonnie From Delaney* reaches US #58.

1971 **May** *Motel Shot* peaks at #65 in US.
July *Never Ending Song Of Love* is their biggest US hit single, reaching #13. It is quickly covered and taken to UK #2 by The New Seekers.
Nov *Only You And I Know* makes US #20.

1972 **Feb** *Move 'Em Out* climbs to #59 in US.
Apr *Where There's A Will There's A Way* ends their singles chart career (US #99), before a label switch to CBS/Columbia Records sees *D & B Together* climb to US #133, but the title proves ironic, as the couple divorce and split professionally soon afterwards. (Both will record solo through the later 70s, without great success.)

1979 **Mar** [16] Bonnie Bramlett makes rock headlines when, singing back-up vocals with Stephen Stills in Columbus, OH, she gets into a fierce argument with a less-than-serious Elvis Costello (staying at the same Holiday Inn) about racial matters relating to music, and punches him in the face.

1990 Rhino releases a retrospective of Delaney & Bonnie's best work.

JOHN DENVER

1965 Denver (b. Henry John Deutschendorf, Dec.31, 1943, Roswell, NM), having studied architecture at Texas Tech in Lubbock, TX, travels to California to pursue his interest in folk music. While working as a draughtsman in Los Angeles, CA, he plays the folk scene at night, eventually recording demos, and adopting a performing surname after his favorite city. He joins folk group The Chad Mitchell Trio, replacing Mitchell himself, having auditioned with 250 others.

1967 Denver marries Ann Martell, whom he met at a trio concert in 1966 at her college, Gustavus Adolphus in Minnesota.

1968 After 3 years in the trio, during which he has been developing his songwriting skills, Denver signs as a solo artist to RCA Records.

1969 **Nov** His first solo album *Rhymes And Reasons*, produced by The Chad Mitchell Trio's arranger Milton Okun, makes US #148.
Dec [20] It features his composition *Leaving On A Jet Plane* which, covered by Peter, Paul and Mary, hits US #1 to become a million-seller.

1970 **May** *Take Me Tomorrow* reaches US #197.

1971 **Aug** [28] *Take Me Home, Country Roads*, his debut chart single, hits US #2 and becomes a million-seller. It is credited to Denver with Fat City (Bill Danoff and Taffy Nivert, the writers of the song) and taken from *Poems, Prayers And Promises*, which makes US #15 and is his first gold album, selling over a half million copies, in an 80-week chart stay.
Dec [18] *Friends With You* makes US #47. *Aerie* peaks at US #75.

1972 **Mar** [18] A revival of Buddy Holly's *Everyday* reaches US #81.
Aug [19] *Goodbye Again* makes US #88.
Nov *Rocky Mountain High* is his first US Top 10 hit album at #4 and earns another gold disk. It is dedicated to Denver's favorite environment – the Colorado mountains – where he and his wife have settled in Aspen.

1973 **Mar** [3] Extracted title track, *Rocky Mountain High*, hits US #9.
Apr [29] Denver begins a weekly live BBC TV special "The John Denver Show", from the company's Shepherds Bush Green studios.
June Denver makes a dual UK chart debut with the albums *Poems, Prayers And Promises* and *Rhymes And Reasons*, which reach #19 and #21 respectively.
July [21] *I'd Rather Be A Cowboy* peaks at US #62.
Sept *Farewell Andromeda* reaches US #16 (earning a gold disk).
[29] *Farewell Andromeda (Welcome To My Morning)* makes US #89.

1974 **Jan** [12] *Please, Daddy* peaks at US #69.
Mar [30] Compilation album *John Denver's Greatest Hits* tops the US chart for 3 weeks, and will sell 5 million copies during a chart tenure of over 3 years, as *Sunshine On My Shoulders* (written with Dick Kniss and Mike Taylor) also hits US #1. It will be used as the theme song to NBC sitcom "Sunshine", starring Cliff DeYoung and Elizabeth Cheshire, which will premiere on Mar.1975.
July [27] *Annie's Song*, a love ballad for his wife Ann, inspired by a temporary rift in their marriage, tops the US chart for 2 weeks and earns a gold disk for million-plus sales. It was written by Denver in 10 mins. while riding on a ski-lift. (At the height of this success, Denver will play 7 concerts at the Universal City Amphitheater in Los Angeles, which were sold out in 24 hours.)
Aug [10] *Back Home Again* is his second consecutive US album chart-topper, and another million-seller.
Oct [12] *Annie's Song* tops the UK chart for a week. (It is Denver's only UK solo hit single.) *Back Home Again* and compilation album *The Best Of John Denver* hit UK #3 and #7 at the same time.
Nov [9] Extracted title track *Back Home Again* hits US #5, becoming Denver's second million-selling single from the album. Denver is proclaimed as the state's poet laureate by Governor John Vanderhoof of Colorado for his promotion of the Rocky Mountains.

1975 **Feb** [15] *Sweet Surrender*, from Walt Disney film "The Bears And I", reaches US #13.
Apr [12] Double live album *An Evening With John Denver*, recorded at the Universal City Amphitheater, from 1974's sell-out US tour, hits US #2 (another gold disk) and makes UK #31.
May [19] ABC TV "An Evening With John Denver" wins Outstanding Special – Comedy/Variety Or Musical at the 27th Emmy awards.
June [7] *Thank God I'm A Country Boy*, written by Denver's long serving back-up guitarist John Sommers and originally on live album *Back Home Again*, is extracted in a new version and hits US #1 (his third US #1 and fifth million-selling single).
Sept [20] Denver guests on the premiere edition of ABC TV show "Saturday Night Live With Howard Cosell".
[27] *I'm Sorry* is another US chart-topper and million-seller. After it drops to #2, its B-side *Calypso*, a tribute to marine explorer Jacques Cousteau and titled after his ship, picks up major airplay in its own right, giving it a double A-side credit, which keeps its at #2 for 4 further weeks.
Oct [18] *Windsong*, after debuting 2 weeks earlier behind Pink Floyd's *Wish You Were Here*, hits US #1 for 2 weeks. (Denver will shortly launch his own record label, named Windsong after this album. Its most successful act will be The Starland Vocal Band, including former Fat City members and *Take Me Home, Country Roads* writers Bill and Taffy Danoff, whose *Afternoon Delight* will hit US #1 in 1976.)
Dec [27] Seasonal album *Rocky Mountain Christmas* reaches US #14 and earns another gold disk.

1976 **Jan** [3] Seasonal *Christmas For Cowboys* peaks at US #58.
[24] *Fly Away*, with vocal back-up from Olivia Newton-John (who had a UK hit with a cover of *Take Me Home, Country Roads* in 1973), reaches US #13 as seasonally-packaged double *The John Denver Gift Pack* (comprising both the Christmas album and *Windsong*) makes US #13.
Mar [29] Denver begins a week's residence at the London Palladium, which is recorded for future release. His band comprises John Sommers and Steve Weisberg (guitars), Dick Kniss (bass), Hal Blaine (drums) and Lee Holdridge (arrangements).
Apr [3] *Looking For Space* reaches US #29 as *Windsong* belatedly reaches UK #14.
May [22] *It Makes Me Giggle* peaks at US #60.
[29] UK-only release album, *Live In London*, recorded earlier in the year, hits UK #2.
July Denver plays a week of concerts in Los Angeles (he donates the proceeds to more than 30 different charities).
Sept [25] *Spirit* hits US #7, earning a platinum disk, and UK #9.
Oct [2] Extracted *Like A Sad Song* makes US #36.
Dec Newsweek proclaims Denver "the most popular singer in

America", and the Country Music Association (CMA) votes him Entertainer Of The Year.

1977
Jan [29] *Baby, You Look Good To Me Tonight* peaks at US #65.
Mar [22] Johnny Cash, Glen Campbell and Roger Miller join Denver in his ABC TV special "Thank God I'm A Country Boy".
Apr [2] A second compilation album, *John Denver's Greatest Hits, Volume 2* hits US #6, earning another platinum disk.
[9] *Best Of John Denver Vol.2* hits UK #9.
[21] Denver guests in "Sinatra And Friends" US TV special.
May [14] *My Sweet Lady* (originally B-side of *Thank God I'm A Country Boy*) makes US #32.
Oct He makes his starring film debut in comedy "Oh, God", with George Burns.

1978
Jan [14] *How Can I Leave You Again* makes US #44 as parent album *I Want To Live* reaches US #45.
Feb [18] *I Want To Live* makes UK #25.
[23] Denver emcees the 20th annual Grammy awards, taking over from Andy Williams.
Mar [8] He plays a week of concerts at South Lake Tahoe, NV, as his annual Pro/Am Ski tournament takes place.
Apr [1] *It Amazes Me* peaks at US #59.
May [13] *I Want To Live* makes US #55.
[15] Denver's 2-month US tour ends at the Forum, Los Angeles.
July Irish flautist James Galway hits UK #3 with an instrumental version of *Annie's Song*.

1979
Jan [9] The "Music For UNICEF" concert, to celebrate the International Year Of The Child, takes place in the General Assembly Hall of the United Nations in New York. Denver sings *Rhymes & Reasons*, donating the royalties from it to UNICEF. (Denver is increasingly involved in social and environmental causes including a 2-year commitment to the Presidential Commission On World And Domestic Hunger, and supporting the Wilderness Society Friends Of The Earth and the World Wildlife Fund.)
[10] NBC TV airs "A Gift Of Song – The Music For UNICEF Concert".
Mar [3] *John Denver* reaches US #25.
Apr [21] *John Denver* makes UK #68.
June [11-21] Denver records *Autograph* at Filmways/Heider studios, Hollywood, CA, with his regular studio and live band – James Burton (guitar), Glen D. Hardin (keyboards), Emory Gordy Jr. (bass), Hal Blaine (drums), Jim Horn (horns), Herb Pedersen (banjo), Denny Brooks (acoustic guitar) and Danny Wheetman (mandolin, harmonica).

1980
Jan [5] *A Christmas Together*, recorded with The Muppets, reaches US #26 and is a million-seller. Denver also guests on a Muppets Christmas TV special.
Apr *Autograph* peaks at US #52.
[19] *Autograph* makes US #39.
June *Dancing With The Mountains* stalls at US #97.
Denver co-produces TV special "The Higher We Fly", which will be honored by the Houston Film Festival and wins the coveted Earl Osborn Award from the Aviation/Space Writer's Association.

1981
Aug *Some Days Are Diamonds (Some Days Are Stone)* makes US #36, as parent *Some Days Are Diamonds*, recorded at the Sound Emporium, Nashville, TN, with producer Larry Butler, reaches US #32. Denver's performance in Tokyo, Japan, is attended by the Crown Prince of Japan (his first pop concert).
Nov [21] *The Cowboy And The Lady* peaks at US #66.
Dec [26] Denver's duet with opera singer Placido Domingo on *Perhaps Love* makes UK #46.

1982
Feb [13] *Perhaps Love* peaks at US #59.
May [2] *Seasons Of The Heart* makes US #39. (It is his first self-produced album, with help from Barney Wyckoff, and his last to earn a gold disk.)
[22] Extracted *Shanghai Breezes* makes US #31.
Aug [21] Extracted title track *Seasons Of The Heart* stalls at US #78.

1983
Oct *It's About Time*, recorded at Criteria studios, Miami, FL, with help from The Wailers and The I-Threes, makes US #61 and UK #90. Shortly after their 15th anniversary, Denver and his wife Ann separate, and later divorce.

1984
Feb He writes and performs *The Gold And Beyond*, theme song for the 1984 Winter Olympics, singing it for US TV on the slopes of Mount Sarajevo. He opens an exhibition of his photographs (a 15-year legacy of Rocky Mountain landscape and wildlife) at New York's Hammer galleries in Manhattan.
Sept Denver travels to Africa on a fact-finding trip for The Hunger Project. He records *Africa Sunrise* in Burkina Faso and Mozambique, which will be included on *Dreamland Express*.

Nov [24] He plays an informal concert at the US Embassy in Moscow, and teams with French singer Sylvie Vartan for *Love Again*, which makes US #85 (his last US Hot 100 entry).
Dec *The John Denver Collection*, a TV-advertised compilation album on Telstar, makes UK #20.

1985
Sept [7] *Dreamland Express*, Roger Nichols-produced, makes US #90. Denver embarks on a 12-day concert tour of the Soviet Union.

1986
June [10] Denver joins with a host of other singers and groups to celebrate The Nitty Gritty Dirt Band's 20th anniversary at the Red Rocks Stadium, Denver.
July [30] RCA Records drops Denver from his contract. Industry insiders speculate that RCA's new owner General Electric, a top military contractor, takes exception to his recording *Let Us Begin (What Are We Making Weapons For?)*, which he had made with top Soviet singer Alexandre Gradsky in Moscow's Melodiya studio.
Aug *One World* makes UK #91.

1987
Dec Denver ends the year appearing in special Christmas TV shows with Julie Andrews and The Muppets and his own "A Rocky Mountain Christmas". During the past 12 months, he has also filmed "Rocky Mountain Reunion", a documentary about endangered species (which wins 6 awards including the American Film Festival's New York City Blue Ribbin' Award For Best Educational Production), another documentary "John Denver's Alaska: The American Child", has become a member of the National Space Institute and the European Space Agency, become further involved in the charity works of Human/Dolphin Foundation, The Hunger Project, has been presented with the Presidential World Without Hunger Award by Ronald Reagan, funded his own Windstar Foundation and taken part in an annual Celebrity Pro/Am Ski Tournament.

1988
Aug *Aviation Week & Space Technology* magazine, under the headline "Ural Mountain High", says that Denver has asked the Soviet Union to launch him to the Mir Space Station. The Soviets are reported to be considering it, with a price tag of $10 million.
[12] Denver marries Australian singer/actress Cassandra Delaney.
Oct *Higher Ground*, his first in 3 years on new Windstar label, enters the US Country chart.
Dec Denver records *And So It Goes* with The Nitty Gritty Dirt Band, for inclusion of the group's *Will The Circle Be Unbroken Volume Two*.

1989
July [5] Denver hosts NBC TV special "In Performance At The White House", the first of 3 concerts filmed before President and Mrs. Bush.

1990
Denver releases his second album on Windstar, *The Flower That Shattered The Stone*, dedicated to his year-old daughter Jesse Belle.
Oct UK group New Order settles out of court with Denver's publisher Cherry Lane Music, for allegedly infringing the copyright of *Leaving On A Jet Plane*, on their song *Run*. New Order's Steven Morris says "It's New Order's contribution to sending John Denver into space."

DEPECHE MODE
Dave Gahan (vocals)
Martin Gore (synthesizer)
Andy Fletcher (bass synthesizer)
Alan Wilder (synthesizer)

1980
May Vince Clarke (b. July 3, 1960, Basildon, Essex), ex-No Romance In China, and one-half of a gospel duo, teams with former schoolfriends, bank clerk Gore (b. July 23, 1961, Basildon), ex-The French Look and Norman & The Worms, and insurance clerk Fletcher (b. July 8, 1960, Basildon) to form a trio in Basildon. They call themselves Composition Of Sound, after rejecting such colorful suggestions as Peter Bonetti's Boots, The Lemon Peels, The Runny Smiles and The Glow Worms. They play their first gig, as an all-guitar line-up, at Scamps in Southend, Essex, and are then spotted, headlining a Saturday night electronic showcase at Croc's in Rayleigh, Essex, by Some Bizzare Records' supremo Stevo, who includes their track *Photographic* on his compilation album *Some Bizzare Album*, but does not sign them. With Clarke unhappy in his singing role, they look for a singer, and spot Gahan (b. May 9, 1962, Epping, Essex), who is studying window design at Southend technical college. He joins the band and they make their first appearance as a 4-piece at Fletcher and Gore's old school, St. Nicholas in Basildon. (It is Gahan, thumbing through a French fashion magazine, who comes up with the name Depeche Mode after seeing the phrase (meaning "fast fashion").)
Oct Group, now with Fletcher playing synthesizer, records a 3-song demo. They send the tape to every club and promoter they know of, which leads to a booking at the Bridgehouse in Canning Town, London, on a regular "Futurist" night.

Dec Demo tapes sent to several labels evoke no response, but they are approached at the Bridgehouse gig by independent Mute label's owner Daniel Miller, whose act Fad Gadget they are supporting. (Miller apparently had heard their demo, describing it as "bloody awful".) He finances the recording of a first single and album, although they will not sign a proper contract with Mute until 1986, despite overtures from larger companies.

1981 Apr [11] Debut *Dreaming Of Me*, written by Clarke and produced by Miller, peaks at UK #57.

Aug [8] *New Life* reaches UK #11, as the band makes its BBC TV "Top Of The Pops" debut to promote the record.

Oct [17] Continuing the band's synthesized electronic pop, *Just Can't Get Enough* hits UK #8.

Nov [14] Debut album *Speak And Spell* hits UK #10, as the group ends its first UK tour at the Lyceum, London.

Dec [1] Clarke, the chief songwriter, but a studio addict who is unwilling to tour, announces he is leaving the band to form Yazoo with Alison Moyet. (After his departure, virtually all the band's material will be written by Gore.)

1982 Jan Clarke is replaced by vocalist and synth player Wilder (b. June 1, 1959), ex-The Dragons and The Hitmen, who responds to **Melody Maker** ad – "Name band. Synthesizer. Must be under 21", despite being 22. He initially joins for their first US trip, but remains permanently.

Feb *Speak And Spell* is the group's US debut, at #192.

Mar [13] *See You*, recorded between Clarke's departure and Wilder's arrival, hits UK #6 while the band is making its US debut at The Ritz Club in New York.

May [15] *The Meaning Of Love* reaches UK #12.

Sept [25] *Leave In Silence* reaches UK #18.

Oct [16] *A Broken Frame*, recorded as a trio, hits UK #8 and the group embarks on its biggest UK tour yet.

Dec [18] *A Broken Frame* climbs to US #177.

1983 Mar [5] *Get The Balance Right* reaches UK #13, as the band embarks on a major tour of Canada, US, Japan and Hong Kong.

Aug [20] Introducing a starker tone, *Everything Counts* hits UK #6.

Sept *Construction Time Again* hits UK #6.

Oct [22] *Love In Itself* reaches UK #21, after 7 consecutive Top 20 hits.

1984 Apr [14] *People Are People* hits UK #4.

Aug *People Are People* climbs to US #166. (It will however re-chart in 1985 and go on to peak at US #71.)

Sept [22] *Master And Servant* hits UK #9.

Oct *Some Great Reward* hits UK #5.

Nov [17] Double A-side *Somebody/Blasphemous Rumours* makes UK #16. (Gore moves to Berlin during the year to be with his girlfriend. He will live there until 1986.)

1985 June [8] *Shake The Disease* reaches UK #18.

Aug [3] *People Are People*, their US chart debut, reaches #13 after a 3-month climb.

[17] *Some Great Reward* makes US #51.

Sept [14] *Master And Servant* climbs to US #87.

Oct *It's Called A Heart* reaches UK #18. Compilation *The Singles 1981-85*, the gatefold sleeve of which contains a collage of the group's bad reviews, hits UK #6. Released in US as *Catching Up With Depeche Mode*, the album will make #113 in early 1986.

1986 Jan Group starts work on a new album at the Hansa studios in Berlin, Germany.

Mar Using a guitar for the first time on a single, Depeche Mode reaches UK #15 with *Stripped*.

Apr *Black Celebration* debuts at UK #4, and will make US #90.

May *A Question Of Lust* reaches UK #28.

Aug Band completes a lengthy tour and begins an 8-month sabbatical, during which they will write material for a new album.

Sept *A Question Of Time* reaches UK #17.

1987 Feb Group starts work on new album at Guillaume Tell studio in Paris, France, with engineer/producer Dave Bascombe.

May *Strangelove* reaches UK #16.

Aug [22] *Strangelove* stalls at US #76.

Sept *Never Let Me Down* reaches UK #22.

Oct *Music For The Masses* hits UK #10.

Nov *Music For The Masses* makes US #35.

1988 Jan *Behind The Wheel* reaches UK #21. Group has had 7 years of consistent UK hits and has become a major hit in Europe, particularly in France and Germany, through constant tours.

Feb [13] *Never Let Me Down Again* peaks at US #63.

May [21] *Route 66/Behind The Wheel* climbs to US #61.

[28] Import *Little 15* peaks at UK #60.

June [18] Sell-out world tour ends in a 75,000 attendance at the Rose Bowl, Pasadena, CA, part of UK festival with Orchestral Manoeuvres In The Dark (OMD). (The concert is filmed by famed D.A. Pennebaker and subsequently released on video as "Depeche Mode 101".)

Sept [7] Depeche Mode features a re-release of *Strangelove* on the annual MTV awards show in US, as *Music For The Masses* tops 2 million sales worldwide.

Oct [22] A remixed version of *Strangelove* makes US #50.

1989 Feb *Everything Counts* reaches UK #22.

Mar *101*, a live recording of the band's 1988 Rose Bowl concert, hits UK #5.

Apr [25] "101" movie premieres in Los Angeles, as related album *101* makes US #45.

June [24] Gore's solo album *Counterfeit EP* spends 1 week on UK chart, at #51.

Sept *Personal Jesus* reaches UK #13.

1990 Feb [24] *Enjoy The Silence* hits UK #6, aided by "monarch with a deck-chair" video starring central character, Gore.

Mar [3] *Personal Jesus* reaches US #28.

[20] 5 fans are treated for minor injuries at the Cedars-Sinai Medical Center, Los Angeles, after thousands of fans seeking autographs at a promotion at Wherehouse Records are crushed. Group is there to sign copies of new album *Violator*. (Wherehouse agree to pay $25,000 to the City of Los Angeles to compensate for the facilities provided by the Police and Fire Departments.)

[31] *Violator* hits UK #2, behind David Bowie's *Changesbowie*.

May [5] *Violator* hits US #7, group's first US million-seller.

[26] *Policy Of Truth* peaks UK #16.

[29] Group begins 43-date North American leg of "World Violation Tour" at the Civic Center, Pensacola, FL. The tour will end on Aug.5 at Dodgers Stadium, Los Angeles.

July [14] *Enjoy The Silence* hits US #8, after worldwide Top 10 success.

Oct [13] *World In My Eyes* reaches UK #17.

[20] *Policy Of Truth*, remixed by Francis Kevorkian, reaches US #15.

Dec [22] *World In My Eyes* peaks at UK #52 as group wins Top Modern Rock Tracks Artists in **Billboard**'s The Year In Music.

DEXY'S MIDNIGHT RUNNERS

Kevin Rowland (vocals, guitar)
Al Archer (guitar)
Pete Williams (bass)
Pete Saunders (organ)
Andy Growcott (drums)
"Big" Jimmy Patterson (trombone)
Steve "Babyface" Spooner (alto sax)
Jeff "J.B." Blythe (tenor sax)

1977 Nov Rowland (b. Aug.17, 1953, Wolverhampton, W.Midlands, of Irish parents), having made his playing debut in Lucy & The Lovers, is guitarist in Birmingham UK-based punk band The Killjoys on its only single *Johnny Won't Get To Heaven* on Raw Records. Rowland and the band's rhythm guitarist Archer leave to form their own band in the 60s soul mold.

1978 July Dexy's Midnight Runners is formed (named after dexedrine, a widely-used pep pill, though the band itself abides by a strict "no drink or drugs" code), with Rowland, Archer, Saunders, Spooner, Patterson, Williams, J.B. and Bobby Junior on drums. They adopt a visual image taken from characters in Robert De Niro movie "Mean Streets".

1979 Bernie Rhodes, ex-manager of The Clash, signs the band after seeing it play and negotiates a recording deal with EMI, after they have finished a nationwide tour with The Specials.

1980 Feb [9] *Dance Stance*, a Rowland comment on anti-Irish prejudice, makes UK #40.

May [3] Horn-laden *Geno*, a tribute to 1960s UK soul singer Geno Washington, tops the UK chart for 2 weeks.

July [20] "Intense Emotion Revue" tour ends at the Metro Marquee, Ashington, Northumberland.

[26] Debut album *Searching For The Young Soul Rebels* hits UK #6. It is only released after Rowland had seized the master tapes from producer Pete Wingfield and refused to return them until more favorable contract terms were granted.

Aug [2] *There There My Dear* hits UK #7. (Rowland will be given a suspended prison sentence after a fight with members of another band during the filming of the single's promo video.)

Sept [25] Group begins extensive tour of Europe.

Oct *Keep It Part Two*, released as a single at Rowland's insistence but against the wishes of the rest of the band and EMI, who protest its uncommerciality, fails to chart and acrimony breaks out in the band.
Nov [7] Band splits into 2: Rowland and Patterson remain as the nucleus of Dexy's Midnight Runners and recruit Micky Billingham (keyboards), Steve Wynne (bass), Billy Adams (guitar), Paul Speare (tenor sax), Brian Maurice (alto sax) and Seb Shelton (drums); the others leave to form The Bureau.

81 Mar [28] *Plan B*, recorded by the new band but released by EMI unwillingly, during rock-bottom relations between Rowland and the label, peaks at UK #58. The 2 parties will separate shortly afterwards.
Aug [8] Now signed to Phonogram's Mercury label, Tony Visconti-produced *Show Me* reaches UK #16.
Oct Bass player Wynne leaves and is replaced by Giorgio Kilkenny. *Liars A To E*, an eccentric single with string accompaniment, fails.
Nov Band appears live at the Old Vic, London, in "The Projected Passion Review" and gains positive reviews from a press previously alienated by Rowland.

82 Mar Band takes a new direction with a fusion of its traditional soul style with Irish folk, and adds a three-piece fiddle section (Helen O'Hara, Steve Brennan and Roger MacDuff) which shares billing on records as The Emerald Express. The visual image also changes: the original "Mean Streets" look and the later anoraks and sports gear are discarded for dungarees and gypsy-like accoutrements.
[27] *The Celtic Soul Brothers*, resulting from the new collaboration, makes UK #45.
June Surviving original group member Patterson leaves, followed by the 2 sax players, who feel their new role is too insignificant.
Aug [7] *Come On Eileen*, featuring a populist easy-chant title chorus, 5tops the UK chart for 4 weeks and sells over a million copies in UK as parent album *Too-Rye-Ay* hits UK #2.
Oct [9] A revival of Van Morrison's *Jackie Wilson Said* hits UK #5. The band is billed as Kevin Rowland & Dexy's Midnight Runners, which Rowland explains is a basic nucleus of himself, Adams and Shelton, augmented by hired musicians in various combinations as necessary. When the band appears playing the hit on BBC TV's "Top Of The Pops", an apparent misunderstanding on the part of the TV production staff leads to the display of a photo of darts player Jocky Wilson as a studio backdrop, not the intended soul legend Jackie Wilson picture.
Dec [25] *Let's Get This Straight (From The Start)/Old* reaches UK #17.

83 Feb [8] *Come On Eileen* wins Best British Single at the second annual BRIT awards at the Grosvenor House, London.
Mar [26] *Geno*, an EMI compilation, makes UK #79.
Apr [16] A new version of *The Celtic Soul Brothers*, giving Rowland lead billing, reaches UK #20. A tour by the augmented band follows, after which it splits up, and the nucleus musicians retreat into silence.
[23] *Come On Eileen* tops the US chart for 1 week, replacing Michael Jackson's *Billie Jean*, and is itself replaced by Jackson's *Beat It*, as parent album *Too-Rye-Ay* reaches US #14.
May [5] *Come On Eileen* is awarded Best Selling A-Side Of 1982 at the annual Ivor Novello Awards lunch.
June [11] US follow-up *The Celtic Soul Brothers* peaks at US #86.

85 Sept After a long silence, ***Don't Stand Me Down*** reaches UK #22. At Rowland's insistence no single is taken from it.
Nov [1] Group begins a 10-date "Park Street South" UK tour at the Playhouse, Edinburgh, Scotland, after a 6-night warm-up at the Paris Olympia, France. The tour, which will end at the Dominion theater, London, is not well received and the band splits again.

86 Dec After 3 years out of the UK singles chart, the band (now basically a solo Rowland) returns with *Because Of You*, the theme tune to UK BBC TV's "Brush Strokes" comedy series, which reaches UK #13.

88 May Rowland returns as a soloist (though still with Mercury and billed as Kevin Rowland Of Dexy's Midnight Runners) with *Walk Away* and *The Wanderer*, but neither charts.

EIL DIAMOND

52 At New York University as a pre-med major and on a fencing scholarship, Diamond (b. Noah Kaminsky, Jan.24, 1941, Brooklyn, New York, NY), who has become interested in songwriting while at Erasmus high school, when folk singer Pete Seeger visits his winter holiday group at Surprise Lake camp, before graduating from the Abraham Lincoln high school 2 years after Neil Sedaka, and teaming with friend Jack Parker as an Everly Brothers-style duo, Neil & Jack, cutting 2 unsuccessful singles, *What Will I Do* and *I'm Afraid* on small New York label Duel Records, drops out 6 months before graduation to become

an apprentice songwriter at a small publishing company, Sunbeam Music, earning $50 a week.
1965 He will have several "production line" songwriting jobs for 2 years, until he sets up on his own in a tiny Manhattan office above a jazz club, releasing one-off solo single, *Clown Town*, for CBS/Columbia Records. He continues to perform as well as write, mainly in Greenwich Village coffee houses, when he is seen by songwriters Jeff Barry and Ellie Greenwich, who, impressed by his style and material, sign him to their writing and publishing organization.
1966 With his songs starting to earn money with hitmaking acts: Jay & The Americans reach US #18 with *Sunday And Me*; Cliff Richard records *Just Another Guy* (B-side of his UK #1 hit *The Minute You're Gone*) and further songs cut by Jimmy Clanton, Bobby Vinton and The Angels among others. Barry and Greenwich arrange an audition with Atlantic Records, which recommends Diamond to Bert Berns at Atlantic-distributed New York label Bang Records. He signs to Bang with Barry and Greenwich as his producers.
July [2] Bang debut, the introspective *Solitary Man*, peaks at US #55.
Oct [15] *Cherry Cherry* is his first major hit at US #6.
Nov Parent album *The Feel Of Neil Diamond* makes US #137.
Dec [17] *I Got The Feelin' (Oh No No)* makes US #16.
[31] The Monkees follow-up to US chart-topping debut is Diamond's *I'm A Believer* (placed with them by Jeff Barry), with advance orders of 1,051,280 on the day of release, tops the US chart for 7 weeks and UK chart for 4, selling an additional 750,000 copies in UK to add to total US sales of over 3 million.
1967 Mar [4] *You Got To Me* reaches US #18.
Apr [29] The Monkees hit US #2 and UK #3 with another Diamond song, *A Little Bit Me, A Little Bit You*, another multi-million seller.
May [27] *Girl, You'll Be A Woman Soon* hits US #10. Although Diamond's records are not yet charting in UK, his songs are: Lulu's cover of one of his B-sides, *The Boat That I Row*, hits UK #6 and Cliff Richard's double A-side, *I'll Come Running* and *I Got The Feelin' (Oh No No)* reaches UK #26.
Aug [26] Gospel-influenced *Thank The Lord For The Night Time* reaches US #13.
Oct *Just For You* makes US #80.
Nov [18] *Kentucky Woman* reaches US #22.
1968 Feb [3] A revival of Gary U.S. Bonds' *New Orleans*, his first non-original single, peaks at US #51.
Apr [20] *Red Red Wine* (revived later as an international hit by UB40) peaks at US #62. Diamond leaves Bang, partly through frustration over its refusal to issue *Shilo* as a single, which he considers his best song to date, and signs to MCA Records' new Uni label, moving from New York to Los Angeles, CA, in the process.
June [1] First Uni release, the autobiographical *Brooklyn Roads*, produced by Chip Taylor, makes US #58. *Velvet Gloves And Spit* fails to chart. One of its songs, the anti-drug and naive *Pot Smoker's Song*, alienates him from the drug-tolerant rock mainstream of the late 60s (and Uni will remove it from re-pressings of the album).
Aug [3] *Two-Bit Manchild* peaks at US #66. Diamond makes a guest appearance in Hollywood in TV detective series "Mannix".
Sept Bang label compilation album *Greatest Hits* reaches US #100.
Nov [23] *Sunday Sun* peaks at US #68.
1969 Apr [26] *Brother Love's Traveling Salvation Show* peaks at US #22. ***Brother Love's Traveling Salvation Show***, on Uni, climbs to US #82.
Aug [16] *Sweet Caroline* hits US #4, Diamond's first million-plus seller.
Dec [27] *Holly Holy*, his second million-seller, hits US #6.
1970 Jan ***Touching You, Touching Me*** makes US #30.
Mar [7] A cover of Buffy Saint-Marie's *Until It's Time For You To Go*, extracted from the album, reaches US #53.
Apr [25] Bang Records issues the disputed *Shilo* in competition to Diamond's current material and it climbs to US #24.
May [30] Percussive, African-styled *Soolaimon*, a foretaste of Diamond's *African Trilogy* suite, makes US #30.
Sept [12] Bang reissues *Solitary Man*, which peaks at US #21.
Oct [10] *Cracklin' Rosie* is Diamond's first US chart-topper (for 1 week), and his third million-seller. *Gold*, his first live album, recorded at the Troubadour in Hollywood, hits US #10 while *Shilo*, a Bang assemblage of early tracks, makes US #52.
Dec *Cracklin' Rosie* hits UK #3. ***Tap Root Manuscript***, which includes the experimental *African Trilogy*, reaches US #13.
[19] Diamond's early revival of The Hollies' *He Ain't Heavy He's My Brother* climbs to US #20, and another Bang reissue, *Do It*, originally the B-side of *Solitary Man*, makes US #36.
1971 Mar *Sweet Caroline*, is reissued in UK as follow-up to *Cracklin' Rosie*

and hits UK #8. *Do It*, another Bang compilation, makes US #100.

Apr *Tap Root Manuscript* and *Gold* chart simultaneously in UK, making #19 and #23 respectively.

May [8] The autobiographical *I Am ... I Said* (which Diamond will later claim to have been his hardest major song to write) hits US and UK #4 and is another million-seller.

June [19] Its B-side, *Done Too Soon*, concerning prominent names who died young, charts at US #65.

July [31] Diamond's own version of his song for The Monkees, *I'm A Believer*, is reissued by Bang and hits US #51.

Dec [18] *Stones* reaches US #14 as parent *Stones* climbs to US #11.

1972 **Jan** *Stones* reaches UK #18.

Mar [16] Diamond performs at the Royal Albert Hall, London, during a UK tour.

July [1] *Song Sung Blue* tops the US chart for a week and is another million-seller. It climbs to UK #14.

Aug *Moods* hits US #5 and UK #7.

[24] A concert at Los Angeles' Greek theater is recorded for live album *Hot August Night*.

Oct [5] Having just played 2 performances at the Grand Ole Opry, Diamond begins a 20-night series of sold-out concerts at New York's Winter Garden theater, after which he announces he will take a break from live work to spend time with his family and friends. (This sabbatical will last for more than 3 years.)

[7] *Play Me* reaches US #11.

Dec [30] *Walk On Water*, taken from *Moods*, reaches US #17. It is his last release on Uni, which is absorbed by parent MCA label.

1973 **Jan** Live double album *Hot August Night* hits US #5. It will remain charted for 78 weeks and reach UK #32.

Mar Double compilation album *Double Gold*, another Bang anthology, makes US #36.

May [5] A live version of *Cherry Cherry*, taken from *Hot August Night*, reaches US #31.

June His MCA contract expired, Diamond signs to CBS/Columbia Records in a 10-album deal guaranteeing $5 million.

[20] Diamond sings *Cherry Cherry* on ABC TV's "American Band 20th Anniversary".

Sept *Rainbow* makes US #35.

Dec Soundtrack album *Jonathan Livingston Seagull* hits US #2.

[1] *Be*, on CBS/Columbia single, is taken from his soundtrack for movie "Jonathan Livingston Seagull" and makes US #34.

1974 **Jan** *Hot August Night* makes UK #32.

Feb [16] *Jonathan Livingston Seagull* reaches UK #35.

Mar [2] Diamond wins Album Of Best Original Score Written For A Motion Picture for *Jonathan Livingston Seagull* at the 16th annual Grammy awards. (His score will also snare a Golden Globe award.)

[9] *Rainbow* makes UK #39.

[30] *Skybird*, from the film soundtrack, peaks at US #75.

July [13] Compilation album *His 12 Greatest Hits*, on MCA, reaches US #29 and UK #13.

Nov [23] *Longfellow Serenade*, Diamond's first US Top 10 single for over 2 years, hits #5.

Dec *Serenade*, produced by Tom Catalano, hits US #3 and UK #11.

1975 **Mar** [1] *I've Been This Way Before* makes US #34.

1976 **Jan** Diamond makes his first concert appearance since Oct.1972 when he begins a tour of Australia and New Zealand.

June [30] Diamond is subject to a minor drug bust when police, entering his California home on a search warrant (ostensibly checking a report of intruders), find less than one ounce of marijuana.

July [4] Diamond's first US live performance after his lay-off opens the new Aladdin theater for the Performing Arts in Las Vegas, NV.

[17] *Beautiful Noise*, produced by friend and near neighbor, The Band's Robbie Robertson, hits UK #10.

Aug [7] *If You Know What I Mean*, a trailer for his new album, climbs to US #11.

[14] *Beautiful Noise* hits US #4, Diamond's first million-selling album.

[21] *If You Know What I Mean* makes UK #35.

Oct [2] *Don't Think ... Feel*, with Dr. John adding Hammond organ, makes US #43.

[30] MCA compilation *And The Singer Sings His Song* peaks at US #102.

Nov [13] Extracted title song *Beautiful Noise*, issued as a UK single, reaches #13.

[25] Diamond appears in an all-star guest line-up in The Band's "Last Waltz" farewell concert at the Winterland, San Francisco, CA, which is also filmed (for later cinema release as "The Last Waltz") by Martin

Scorsese. He sings *Dry Your Eyes*, written with Robertson, and joins an all-star cast in *I Shall Be Released*.

1977 **Feb** [21] Diamond stars in a NBC TV special about his music, taped at Los Angeles' Greek theater in front of a celebrity audience in Sept.197▢

Apr [9] Second live double album *Love At The Greek*, again recorded at the Greek theater and produced by Robertson, hits US #8, and is another million-seller.

Aug [6] *Love At The Greek* hits UK #3.

Dec [24] *Desiree* makes UK #39.

1978 **Jan** [28] *I'm Glad You're Here With Me Tonight*, produced by Bob Gaudio of The Four Seasons, reaches UK #16.

Feb [11] *Desiree* makes US #16.

[18] *I'm Glad You're Here With Me Tonight* hits US #6, selling over a millio▢

Dec [2] A duet with Barbra Streisand, *You Don't Bring Me Flowers*, to the US chart for 2 weeks, returning to the top after dropping to #3 aft▢ its first week at #1, and sells over a million. (It was recorded by the d▢ and produced by Gaudio after CBS/Columbia heard of the spliced "duet" of their individual versions in the same key played by a DJ at W-AKY in Louisville, KY, which had huge listener response.)

[9] Compilation album *20 Golden Greats*, a UK-originated anthology of Uni/MCA material, hits UK #2 and stays charted for 6 months. *You Don't Bring Me Flowers* hits UK #5.

1979 **Jan** [20] *You Don't Bring Me Flowers*, which includes the duet, reaches US #15.

[27] *You Don't Bring Me Flowers*, produced by Gaudio, hits US #4, and sells over a million.

Mar [24] *Forever In Blue Jeans* reaches US #20.

Apr [21] *Forever In Blue Jeans* reaches UK #16.

June [16] *Say Maybe* peaks at US #55. Diamond begins work on a remake of the 1927 Al Jolson movie "The Jazz Singer", taking the lead role opposite Laurence Olivier and providing the soundtrack songs. His contract will guarantee Diamond a place in movie history, as he receives the largest salary ever paid for a debut film role.

1980 **Feb** [9] *September Morn*, again produced by Gaudio, reaches UK #1

[16] *September Morn*, another million-seller, hits US #10.

Mar [1] Extracted title track *September Morn*, written with Gilbert Becaud, reaches US #17.

Apr [26] *The Good Lord Loves You* peaks at US #67.

Dec [27] *Love On The Rocks*, from *The Jazz Singer*, reaches UK #17.

1981 **Jan** [10] *Love On The Rocks* hits US #2, and sells over a million copies

Feb [7] Soundtrack album *The Jazz Singer*, released (like its spin-off singles, for contractual reasons) on Capitol, hits US #3 and is a million-seller. (The film is successful, though not a blockbuster: much of its popularity is the result of the hit songs and album.)

[21] *Hello Again*, taken from the movie soundtrack, peaks at UK #51.

Mar [7] MCA compilation *Love Songs* makes US #43.

[21] *The Jazz Singer* hits UK #3.

[28] *Hello Again*, taken from the movie soundtrack hits US #6.

June [13] *America*, the third and last extract from *The Jazz Singer*, hits US #8 but fails to chart in UK. With its patriotic immigrant theme, it becomes Diamond's most played and requested song in US.

Dec [19] *On The Way To The Sky* makes UK #39.

[26] *The Jazz Singer* wins Top Soundtrack Album category in **Billboard**'s The Year In Music.

1982 **Jan** [9] *Yesterday's Songs* reaches US #11.

[16] *On The Way To The Sky* reaches US #17, another million-seller.

Mar [27] Extracted title track *On The Way To The Sky* hits US #27.

June [26] Compilation album *12 Greatest Hits, Volume II*, a collectio▢ of both CBS/Columbia and Capitol material, reaches UK #32.

July [3] *Be Mine Tonight* makes US #35.

His Twelve Greatest Hits, Volume II makes US #48.

Nov [13] *Heartlight*, inspired by movie "E.T." and written with Burt Bacharach and Carole Bayer Sager, hits US #5.

[20] *Heartlight* makes UK #43.

[27] *Heartlight* makes UK #47 as parent album *Heartlight* hits US #9, and is another million-seller.

1983 **Feb** [19] *I'm Alive*, written with David Foster, makes US #35.

May [21] *Front Page Story*, another collaboration with Bacharach and Sager, peaks at US #65.

July *Classics – The Early Years*, a compilation of Bang material released on Columbia, makes US #171.

Dec *The Very Best Of Neil Diamond*, a K-tel TV-advertised compilation, makes UK #33.

1984 **Aug** *Primitive* hits UK #7.

Sept [8] *Turn Around* peaks at US #62 as parent album *Primitive* makes US #35.

'86 May *Headed For The Future* makes UK #36.
June [28] *Headed For The Future* makes US #53.
Headed For The Future reaches US #20, and is another million-seller.

'87 Jan [25] Diamond sings the American national anthem for Super Bowl XXI between the New York Giants and the Denver Broncos at the Rose Bowl, Pasadena, CA.

'88 Jan Diamond's third double live album, *Hot August II*, recorded at Los Angeles' Greek theater again, makes US #59 and UK #74.
Dec [18-20] Diamond finishes US tour at the Miami Arena, FL.

'89 Mar *The Best Years Of Our Lives* makes US #46, on its way to platinum status, and UK #42.
Oct [13] He begins a European tour in Dublin, Eire. The tour will end at the Wembley Stadium, London, on Nov.22.

'90 Jan [22] Diamond is honored with the American Music Award Of Merit at the 17th American Music Awards.

THE DIAMONDS

Dave Somerville (vocals)
Mike Douglas (vocals)
John Felton (vocals)
Evan Fisher (vocals)

'55 Group forms in Toronto, Canada, originally with Somerville and Douglas, joining fellow Canadians Ted Kowalski and Bill Reed.

'56 Jan Signed to Mercury Records in US, and with Californians Felton and Fisher now replacing Reed and Kowalski, they release a cover version of Frankie Lymon & The Teenagers' *Why Do Fools Fall In Love?*
Apr *Why Do Fools Fall In Love?* reaches US #16, the least successful of 3 US Top 20 versions (Lymon hits #7; Gale Storm #15.)
May A cover of The Willows' *Church Bells May Ring* this time eclipses the original. The Diamonds reach US #20, and The Willows only #62.
July Their cover of The Clovers' *Love Love Love* climbs to the same US chart peak as the original (#30) almost simultaneously.
Sept *Ka-Ding-Dong/Soft Summer Breeze* is a double-sided hit, the titles reaching US #35 & #34 independently. Another cover of *Ka-Ding-Dong* by The Hilltoppers reaches US #38, while original by The G-Clefs peaks at #53. There is a bigger US hit version of *Soft Summer Breeze* by Eddie Heywood (#12).

'57 Apr *Little Darlin'* is their biggest and most enduring hit, selling over a million, hitting US #2 for 8 weeks, and spending 6 months on chart. The original version is by The Gladiolas, and reaches US #41.
July *Little Darlin'* hits UK #3, and proves to be their only UK hit.
Sept *Zip Zip* reaches US #45.
Nov *Silhouettes* hits US #10, while The Rays' original hits #3.

'58 Feb Chuck Willis-penned *The Stroll* is their second-biggest seller and hits US #5, popularizing the dance of the same name.
May *High Sign*, a rare Diamonds original, reaches US #38.
July Another non-cover, *Kathy-O*, makes US #45.
Nov *Walking Along* reaches US #29.

'59 Mar *She Say (Oom Dooby Doom)* is their last US Top 20 hit, peaking at #18. Although they are imitators of the 50s R&B doo-wop vocal tradition rather than a part of the genre, their records fall from chart success as the vocal group sound rapidly loses commercial favor at the close of the 50s.

'61 Aug Following several personnel changes, and 2 years playing nightclubs rather than the rock packages with which they toured between 1956 and 1958, the group returns with a revival of The Danleers' 1958 hit ballad *One Summer Night*, which reaches US #22. After this, they slide into obscurity and split up.

'73 Apr [27] After a decade apart, group reunites to appear on US TV in a "Midnight Special" show devoted to oldie hitmakers, alongside Little Richard, Little Anthony & The Imperials and Jerry Lee Lewis.

'89 Group embarks on "The Royalty Of Doo-Wop" US tour with The Belmonts, The Chiffons, The Flamingos and The Silhouettes.

BO DIDDLEY

'51 Diddley (b. Otha Ellas Bates, Dec.28, 1928, McComb, MS, but given the surname McDaniel in infancy on adoption by his mother's first cousin Gussie McDaniel) begins playing regularly as an electric blues/R&B act (his sister Lucille buying him his first guitar) at the 708 club on the south side of Chicago, IL, where he has lived since age 8. He has already been a street corner performer since school days as part of The Hipsters with Roosevelt Jackson, Samuel Daniel and Jerome Green, name-changing to The Langley Avenue Jive Cats, when Clifton James

and Billy Boy Arnold are added. (Diddley has gained his professional name from the nickname given him in his teens whilst training as a Golden Gloves boxer.)

1955 Mar [2] Diddley, with Green on maracas, Frank Kirkland on drums, Lester Davenport on harmonica and Otis Spann on piano, demos *Bo Diddley, I'm A Man* and *You Don't Love Me*..
June Diddley is signed to Chess Records subsidiary label, Checker, and debuts with the demo which had secured them their deal of double A-sided *Bo Diddley/I'm A Man*, which hits #2 on US R&B chart.
Aug [20] He appears at the Apollo theater, Harlem, New York, with a band which will play with him regularly through the 50s: Spann on piano, Arnold on harmonica, Kirkland on drums and Green on bass, maracas and general onstage banter with Diddley.
Nov [20] He appears on CBS TV's "Ed Sullivan Show" in a 15-min. segment with other R&B artists, and plays *Bo Diddley*, despite having rehearsed *16 Tons*.

1956 June His first UK release is EP *Rhythm & Blues With Bo Diddley*, which arouses little interest outside esoteric R&B circles.
July *Who Do You Love*, subsequently another of his most-covered numbers, is released in US but does not make the Top 100.

1959 July *Crackin' Up* is his first US pop chart entry, peaking at #62.
Oct *Say Man*, a semi-comic jive talk repartee between Diddley and Jerome Green over an archetypal Bo Diddley rhythm track, is his biggest US hit, reaching #20.

1960 Mar [21] *Road Runner*, also much-covered, peaks at US #75.

1962 Sept [29] *You Can't Judge A Book By The Cover* makes US #48.
Dec *Bo Diddley* reaches US #117 – his only US album entry.

1963 Sept [22] Diddley arrives in London for UK tour and immediately records a spot for ITV's "Thank Your Lucky Stars".
[29] He begins his first UK tour (with "The Duchess", a guitarist by the name of Norma Jean Wofford, who he had heard play in a support act on a bill in Pittsburgh, on guitar and back-up vocals, and Green) jointly supporting The Everly Brothers with The Rolling Stones (who are also on their first UK tour, and drop all of Diddley's songs from their own act out of respect), at the New Victoria theater, London. The tour will end at the Hammersmith Odeon, London, on Nov.3. While in London, Diddley will play the capitol's only R&B club, the Scene, 3 times.
Oct *Pretty Thing* makes UK #34, while *Bo Diddley* reaches #11, both on the strength of tour success.
[9] *Bo Diddley Is A Gunslinger* reaches UK #20.
[23-24] During mid-tour, Diddley tapes TV appearances for BBC's "Saturday Club" and ITV's "Scene At 6.30".
Nov [30] *Bo Diddley Rides Again* reaches UK #19.

1964 Feb *Bo Diddley's Beach Party* reaches UK #13.
June *Mona (I Need You Baby)* makes UK #42.
Sept He releases the album *Two Great Guitars*, on which he duets with Chuck Berry on 2 lengthy guitar jams.

1965 Mar *Hey Good Lookin'* makes UK #39.
Sept [25] Diddley begins a 21-date tour at the Imperial theater, Nelson, Lancs.
Oct [2] Diddley fails to show for a gig at the Birdcage, Portsmouth, Hants., after his car breaks down. 2,000 fans get their money returned.
Dec Diddley films segment for TNT Award Show, alongside Joan Baez, The Byrds, Ray Charles, Lovin' Spoonful, Ronettes, Ike & Tina Turner, Roger Miller, Petula Clark and Donovan.

1967 Feb [11] *Ooh Baby* climbs to US #88 – his first US chart single for 5 years, but also his final one.
Apr [16] Diddley, on a UK tour, plays the Saville theater, London, supported by Ben E. King.

1968 With Muddy Waters and Little Walter, Diddley records the critically-acclaimed album *Super Blues Band*.

1969 Sept [13] He performs at the "Rock'n'Roll Revival" concert, alongside Chuck Berry, Jerry Lee Lewis, Little Richard and John Lennon and The Plastic Ono Band, among others, at the Varsity Stadium, University of Toronto, Canada. (He will also be seen in D.A. Pennebaker's movie of the event, released in 1970 as "Sweet Toronto" and in revised form in 1972 as "Keep On Rockin'".)

1970 June [6] Diddley tops bill at Hampden Scene 70 in Glasgow, Scotland, also featuring Chuck Berry, Blue Mink, Radha Krishna Temple, Atomic Rooster, Taste, The Pretty Things, Beggars Opera and Spiggy Topes.

1971 June [11] Diddley appears in the sixth "1950s Rock & Roll Revival Concert" with a host of 50s and 60s rock legends at Madison Square Garden, New York. (He will appear in a further half-dozen of these regular concerts over the next 10 years.)
Oct *Another Dimension* attempts to set Diddley within prevailing "politically conscious" lyricism, but his old fans are unimpressed.

BO DIDDLEY cont.

1973 Diddley is featured in the film "Let The Good Times Roll", along with contemporaries Fats Domino, Bill Haley, Little Richard and others.
July *The London Bo Diddley Sessions* is released, including 6 tracks recorded with UK musicians in London (including Roy Wood of The Move and Wizzard).

1976 **Apr** With the demise of the Checker label, Diddley signs to RCA Records for the *The 20th Anniversary Of Rock'N 'Roll*, featuring Joe Cocker, Alvin Lee, Leslie West, Elvin Bishop, Keith Moon, Billy Joel, Roger McGuinn and Carmine Appice. His career as rock'n'roll/R&B elder statesman continues, and he maintains a busy live performance schedule, both as a headliner in his own right and as a support artist.

1979 **Jan** [20] Never shying from working with younger, emergent acts, he opens for The Clash on their first US tour.

1983 He appears in Dan Aykroyd/Eddie Murphy movie "Trading Places".

1986 Diddlley records the album *Hey Bo Diddley* live in concert, with Dick Heckstall-Smith's Mainsqueeze as his backing band, during a UK and European tour.

1987 **Jan** [21] Diddley is inducted into the Rock'N'Roll Hall Of Fame at the second annual dinner at the Waldorf Astoria, New York.
Nov [4] Diddley and Ron Wood, collectively known as The Gunslingers, open a North American tour at the Newport Music Hall, Columbus, OH. The tour will end Nov.25 with a show at the Ritz, New York, which is recorded and will be released as *Live At The Ritz* on JVC label in Aug.1988.

1988 **Mar** [2] Diddley begins a 2-week tour of Japan with Ron Wood.

1989 **Jan** [21] Diddley performs at the "Celebration For Young Americans" at President Bush's inauguration at the Washington Center with Dr. John, Willie Dixon and others.
Apr [27] He has his hands and name set in stone at Sunset Boulevard's Rock Walk with Willie Dixon.
July [11] Bo Jackson Nike TV commercial, with Diddley saying "Bo, you don't know diddley", airs for the first time during Major League Baseball's All-Star game.
Diddley releases *Breakin' Through The B.S.* on Triple X label, through his own Bad Dad Productions, his first US studio album in 15 years.

1990 **May** [4] US tour begins in New Orleans, LA, set to end with 5 nights at Anton's club, Washington, DC, on Nov.4
Diddley states, after appearing in the Nike TV commercial, "You work your buns off all these years – going up and down the highway, riding those raggedly airplanes and stuff like that. Then I make a commercial with Bo Jackson and all I say is Bo, you don't know Diddley. All of a sudden I'm back up at the top again. I ain't figured it out yet."

1991 **Jan** Diddley combines with Ben E. King and Doug Lazy to remake The Monotones' *Book Of Love*, featured in the movie of the same name.

DION & THE BELMONTS

Dion DiMucci (lead vocals)
Fred Milano (tenor vocals)
Carlo Mastrangelo (bass vocals)
Angelo D'Aleo (tenor vocals)

1957 **Sept** Having made his first public appearance 6 years earlier on "Paul Whiteman's Teen Club", and after recording 4 songs for his mother as a St. Valentine's Day gift, DiMucci (b. July 18, 1939, Bronx, New York, NY), records *The Chosen Few*, credited as Dion & The Timberlanes, for Mohawk Records, and subsequently picked up by the larger Jubilee label. Backed by a group of singers he has never met before, Dion feels he can find better singers from his own neighborhood and rounds up the best street corner singers he knows in The Bronx, including Milano (b. Aug.26, 1940, Bronx), Mastrangelo (b. Oct.5, 1939, Bronx) and D'Aleo (b. Feb.3, 1941, Bronx). New group rehearses on the 6th Avenue "D" train to Manhattan.

1958 Group's name is changed to Dion & The Belmonts, taken from Belmont Avenue which cuts through their corner of the Bronx. *We Went Away* on Mohawk follows and after a third single, *Tag Along*, fails, its writer Gene Schwartz sets up his own Laurie label to record Dion.
June [30] Laurie debut *I Wonder Why*, a doo-wopping upbeater, reaches US #22.
Oct [3] Dion begins 19-date "The Biggest Show Of Stars For 1958 – Autumn Edition" tour with Frankie Avalon, Bobby Darin, Bobby Freeman, Buddy Holly & The Crickets, Clyde McPhatter, The Coasters and others, at the Auditorium, Worcester, MA. The tour will end Oct.19 at the Mosque, Richmond, VA.
[13] *No One Knows* reaches US #19. It is written by Ernie Maresca, whose name will appear under several Dion hits.

1959 **Jan** [5] *Don't Pity Me* makes US #40.

[23] Dion begins 24-date "Winter Dance Party" tour, with Buddy Holly, The Big Bopper, Ritchie Valens and Frankie Sardo at George Devine's Million Dollar Ballroom, Milwaukee, WI. The tour will end on Feb.15 at the Illinois State Armoury, Springfield, IL. (Midway through the tour, Holly, Valens and The Big Bopper will all perish in a plane crash near Mason City, IA.)
May [18] New York songwriters Doc Pomus and Mort Shuman provide the classic *A Teenager In Love* which hits US #5 and is a million-seller.
June *A Teenager In Love* makes UK #28, despite covers by Marty Wilde (#2) and Craig Douglas (#13), which scoop the major UK sales. Group becomes fan-mag pin-ups, discussing in print their penchant for clothes (collegiate sweaters, mostly) and revealing such unlikely interests as skindiving. D'Aleo is conscripted into the US Navy on national service and the group continues as a trio.
Oct [5] *Every Little Thing I Do* makes US #48.
[19] Maresca-penned B-side *A Lover's Prayer* peaks at US #73.

1960 **Feb** [8] A richly-harmonized, saxophone-propelled reworking of 1937 Rodgers and Hart number, *Where Or When*, hits US #3 and is a second million-seller.
May [23] Group revives a song first heard in the 1940 Walt Disney movie, "Pinocchio", *When You Wish Upon A Star*, which makes US #30.
Aug [15] Revived Cole Porter's *In The Still Of The Night* makes US #38
Oct Group splits. Dion stays with Laurie as a soloist and The Belmonts sign to the Sabina label.
Dec [19] Returning to teen-oriented material, Dion's solo debut, *Lonely Teenager*, reaches US #12, with its B-side *Little Miss Blue* showing briefly at US #96.

1961 **Jan** *Lonely Teenager* makes UK #47.
Mar [6] Dion's *Havin' Fun* peaks at US #42.
May [15] Dion's *Kissin' Game* peaks at US #82.
July [10] The Belmonts, minus Dion, release *Tell Me Why*, which reaches US #18.
Sept [18] The Belmonts revive *Don't Get Around Much Anymore* which peaks at US #57.
Oct [23] Dion hits US #1 for 2 weeks with the million-selling *Runaround Sue*, a whooping rocker with an exuberance which belies its tale of woe, with uncredited vocal backing from The Del Satins. Co-written with Maresca, it is derived from Gary U.S. Bonds' recent US chart-topper *Quarter To Three*. (Some 20 years later, the song will become a US hit for Leif Garrett and a UK success for Racey.)
Nov *Runaround Sue* takes Dion to UK #11.

1962 **Jan** [14] Movie "Teenage Millionaire", in which Dion appears with Jimmy Clanton and features songs by Chubby Checker and Jackie Wilson, goes on general release in the UK. (Dion also appears in "Ten Girls Ago" with Buster Keaton, Bert Lahr and Eddie Foy Jr, in which he sings 3 songs and "Don't Knock The Twist".)
[20] The Belmonts peak at US #75 with *I Need Someone*. Dion's *Runaround Sue* makes US #11.
Feb [24] Dion's *The Wanderer* hits US #2 and is a million-seller. The B-side, *The Majestic*, makes US #36. He sings both songs in the movie "Twist Around The Clock".
Mar *The Wanderer* hits UK #10. (It will be his last UK hit until it returns to #16 in 1976. Status Quo will revive it for a UK Top 10 hit in 1984.)
May [19] Maresca leaves the demo studio to write a smash of his own. *Runaround Sue*-inflected *Shout Shout (Knock Yourself Out)* hits US #6.
[26] Dion's *(I Was) Born To Cry* makes US #42.
June [9] B-side *Lovers Who Wander* hits US #3.
Aug [18] A Dion original, *Little Diane* (with a prominent kazoo in the backing) hits US #8. His album *Lovers Who Wander* reaches US #12.
Sept [15] The Belmonts reach US #28 with *Come On Little Angel* (co-written by Maresca).
[16] Dion begins his first UK tour with Del Shannon, Buzz Clifford, Joe Brown and The Angels.
Dec [15] The Belmonts' *Diddle-Dee-Dum (What Happens When Your Love Is Gone)* peaks at US #53.
[22] *Love Came To Me*, self-penned by Dion, hits US #10. He leaves Laurie to sign a major contract with CBS/Columbia.

1963 **Jan** *Dion Sings His Greatest Hits*, which has only 2 solo cuts and 10 with The Belmonts, makes US #29. After years of gruelling package tours, Dion graduates to the live supper club circuit.
Feb [23] Dion's Columbia debut, a revival of Leiber and Stoller's *Ruby Baby* (originally a hit for The Drifters in 1955), climbs to hit US #2 and sells over a million.
Apr His first Columbia album, also titled *Ruby Baby*, reaches US #20.
[20] Laurie joins the lucky streak with girls' names and issues *Sandy*, which climbs to US #21.

May [4] The Belmonts' girl-name single, *Ann-Marie*, makes US #86.
[18] Dion's *This Little Girl* reaches US #21.
July [13] Dion's revival of The Del Vikings' *Come Go With Me*, his last on Laurie and originally on one of his albums, reaches US #48. A Laurie compilation, ***Dion Sings To Sandy (And All His Other Girls!)*** makes US #115.
Aug [3] On CBS/Columbia, the offbeat and downbeat *Be Careful Of Stones That You Throw*, a morality tale about not taking people at face value, makes US #31.
Oct [19] Dion begins UK "Greatest Record Show Of 1963" tour with Brook Benton, Lesley Gore, Trini Lopez and Timi Yuro at London's Finsbury Park Astoria.
[26] Yet another girl song (and yet another by Maresca), Dion's *Donna The Prima Donna* hits US #6.
Nov [2] During the tour, Dion appears live on ITV's "Ready Steady Go", singing *Donna The Prima Donna*, but becomes irritated by the dancing audience around him and walks out despite being scheduled to perform another song.
Dec [28] Dion hits US #6 with *Drip Drop* (another Leiber/Stoller Drifters oldie from 1958), completing a run of 18 Hot 100 hits in 3 years.
Apart from a minor hit with Chuck Berry's *Johnny B Goode* (US #71), the British Invasion and a developing narcotic problem combine to move Dion out of the public eye and he becomes involved in blues. His other singles are pure blues: Muddy Waters' *I'm Your Hoochie Coochie Man* and Willie Dixon's *Spoonful*. With little US airplay, they fail to chart. Dion experiments with folk and blues material but CBS/Columbia refuses to make much of it public.
With folk-rock hitting the charts, CBS/Columbia issues 3 folk-oriented singles billed as Dion & The Wanderers, but they receive little promotion. By the end of the year, artist and label have parted.
May Released on ABC Paramount, ***Together Again*** is a surprise reunion of Dion with all 3 Belmonts on a collection of material which owes much to their R&B vocal group roots. 2 singles, *Berimbau* and *Movin' Man* are extracted, but only collectors show interest.
June Dion is featured on the sleeve of *Sgt Pepper*. (Dylan is the only other non-Beatle singer included.)
Schwartz invites Dion, now living in Miami, FL, to record once again for Laurie, which he does in the folk style he has been honing since the passing of his blues passion, it completes what Dion will later describe as a watershed year in his life and career. (He finally kicked his heroin habit in the spring.)
Dec [14] He hits US #4 with Dick Holler's later much-covered martyr memorial song *Abraham Martin And John* and earns another gold disk.
Jan After an absence of 5 years on the US Album chart, ***Dion***, featuring the hit single and several adventurous selections, makes #128.
Feb [8] A folk-styled reworking of Jimi Hendrix's *Purple Haze* peaks at US #63.
Apr [26] Only months after Judy Collins' version leaves the Top 10, Dion's version of Joni Mitchell's *Both Sides Now* reaches US #91.
June As a singer/songwriter bent over his acoustic guitar, Dion enters another phase of his career and signs to Warner Bros.
July [4] A candid allusion to his heroin addiction, *Your Own Back Yard* peaks at US #75 (to become his last chart single). 2 albums, ***Sit Down Old Friend***, featuring just Dion and guitar, and ***You're Not Alone***, with a small group accompaniment, fail.
Jan [1] ***Sanctuary*** (which contains live versions of *The Wanderer* and *Ruby Baby* from the Bitter End club, with newer acoustic material) makes US #200 for 2 weeks.
June [2] Dion & The Belmonts reunite again for a one-off at the ninth "Rock & Roll Spectacular" at Madison Square Garden, New York.
Dec ***Suite For Late Summer***, a concept album with orchestral accompaniment produced by Russ Titelman, reaches US #197.
Mar The Dion & The Belmonts' performance from Madison Square Garden is released as live album ***Reunion***, which reaches US #144.
Apr ***Dion's Greatest Hits***, collating 10 of his hits, reaches US #194 (and will be his last US chart appearance).
Oct Dion's ***Born To Be With You*** for which Phil Spector oversees production (Phil Gernhard and Cashman & West share the actual producing) is released on the Phil Spector International label, in the UK only. Meanwhile, The Belmonts assist former Shirelle Shirley Alston on her version of *Where Or When* from her album ***With A Little Help From My Friends***.
June [26] *The Wanderer*, reissued in UK, reaches #16.
Aug Production team of Steve Barri and Michael Omartian fails to bring success for Dion with ***Streetheart*** and he leaves Warner Bros.
Return Of The Wanderer, produced by Terry Cashman and Terry West

on Lifesong Records, with Dion returning to his Bronx roots, is released.

1980 **May** [17] ***Dion And The Belmonts' 20 Golden Greats***, a K-Tel TV-advertised compilation, reaches UK #31. Dion will begin a long-term association with the Christian Dayspring label, releasing a handful of inspirational albums through the 80s, as part of his commitment to the born-again faith which has redirected his life.

1983 **Mar** [4] Dion participates in the 22nd "Rock & Roll Revival Spectacular" at Madison Square Garden.

1986 During the summer Dion sings at anniversary concert for New York oldies station W-CBS.

1989 **Jan** [17] Arista Records host a tribute to their recently signed act at the Hard Rock Café in New York.
[18] Lou Reed inducts Dion into the Rock'N'Roll Hall Of Fame at the fourth annual induction dinner at the Waldorf Astoria in New York.
Aug [26] *And The Night Stood Still*, written by Diane Warren, peaks at US #75, as *King Of The New York Streets* makes UK #74. Parent album *Yo Frankie*, produced by Dave Edmunds and with guest appearances from Bryan Adams, k.d. lang, Lou Reed and Paul Simon, makes US #130 as The Belmonts prepare to go on "The Royalty Of Doo-Wop" tour with The Chiffons, The Diamonds, The Flamingos and The Silhouettes.

1990 **Jan** [17] Dion joins Frankie Valli on stage at the fifth annual Rock'N'Roll Hall Of Fame dinner to sing *Goodnight Sweetheart*.
Feb Dion contributes *Mean Woman Blues* to charity album of Elvis Presley covers ***The Last Temptation Of Elvis***.
Dec [5] Dion joins Frankie Valli, Graham Nash, Ben E. King, Keith Sweat, Johnny Gill, Eddie Kendricks and Dennis Edwards in a rendition of *The Longest Time*, to honor its writer Billy Joel, being inducted as a NARAS Grammy Living Legend at the Royale theater, New York. (Dion remains in the limelight, his theme to CBS TV sitcom "Lenny" being heard every week.)

DIRE STRAITS
Mark Knopfler (guitar, vocals)
John Illsley (bass)
Hal Lindes (guitar)
Pick Withers (drums)
Alan Clark (keyboards)

1977 **July** Former **Yorkshire Evening Post** journalist Knopfler (b. Aug.12, 1949, Glasgow, Scotland), an English graduate part-time teacher, pub-rock player and songwriter, having spent 2 months with Northern band Brewer's Droop before forming Café Racers, is sharing a flat with fellow group members in Deptford, London, his social worker and guitarist brother David (b. 1951), and sociology undergraduate and bank manager's son Illsley (b. June 24, 1949, Leicester, Leics.), where they frequently jam and rehearse Knopfler's own material. They are joined by session drummer Withers and a friend of his notes their financial plight and dubs them "Dire Straits". Band scrapes together £120 to record a 5-song demo tape at London's Pathway studios.
Aug A copy is given to DJ Charlie Gillett, who features songs from it on his weekly UK BBC Radio London show "Honky Tonk".
Oct Phonogram Records' A&R man John Stainze, one of many impressed by the broadcast demos, tracks the band down and, after strong competition, signs it to Phonogram's Vertigo label.
Dec NEMS agent Ed Bicknell hears the band's tape when Stainze enquires about an agency deal for it and, after seeing the band live at Dingwalls club in London, he asks to manage it and an informal agreement is reached, which will prove a lasting union.

1978 **Jan** [20] Group begins a 16-date UK tour supporting Talking Heads.
Feb [14] Dire Straits begins recording its first album at Basing Street studios, London, with producer Muff Winwood. (The project will cost £12,500 to complete.)
Mar Band secures a short residency at the Marquee, London, and gains strong reviews.
May Group supports The Climax Blues Band on a UK tour and Styx in Europe (Paris, Hamburg and The Hague). Debut single *Sultans Of Swing* (originally a song on the demo) is released in UK with good reviews but does not chart.
June Band plays its first UK headlining tour, as Bicknell secures a US deal with Warner Bros.
Sept [2] Debut album ***Dire Straits***, released in June, makes UK #38. Knopfler visits Muscle Shoals studios in US, meeting producer Jerry Wexler and playing on a Mavis Staples session. A deal is struck with Wexler and Barry Beckett to produce Dire Straits' second album.

Oct *Dire Straits* is released in US and gains heavy airplay. Band plays sell-out tours in Holland, Belgium and Germany. The album tops charts in Australia and New Zealand.

Nov Group flies to The Bahamas to record a follow-up at Compass Point studios, Nassau, before returning to UK for Christmas.

1979 Feb [23] Dire Straits begins its first North American tour, comprising 51 sold-out shows over 38 days, at the Paradise club, Boston, MA.

Mar Bob Dylan attends a Los Angeles, CA, concert and invites Knopfler and Withers to play on his next album.

Apr [7] *Sultans Of Swing* hits UK #8 and US #4.

[14] *Dire Straits* hits US #2.

[21] Boosted by the success of *Sultans Of Swing*, *Dire Straits* now hits UK #5. (The album will eventually be a million-seller in both countries, and spend 104 weeks on UK chart.)

May [1-12] Knopfler and Withers work with Dylan in Muscle Shoals on his forthcoming *Slow Train Coming*.

June [30] *Communique*, coinciding with another sell-out UK and European tour, hits UK #5.

Aug [4] *Communique* makes US #11.

[11] *Lady Writer* peaks at UK #51.

[25] *Lady Writer* makes US #45.

Sept Band begins it second US tour.

Dec After major Dublin and Belfast dates, and 4 London concerts (following a Nov. tour of Scandinavia), the band calls a 6-month work break and to work on material for a third album .

1980 July [25] After a month's recording sessions with new producer Jimmy Iovine, David Knopfler quits the band to pursue a solo career. New York session man Sid McGinnis replaces him temporarily.

Sept Following auditions, Lindes (b. June 30, 1953, Monterey, CA), ex-Darling and Clark (b. Mar.5, 1952, Durham, Durham) are recruited on guitar and keyboards respectively.

Oct [20] Band begins a 2-week North American tour as *Making Movies* is released.

Dec [19-20] A 1-month UK tour is punctuated by 2 dates in Dortmund, Germany, with Roxy Music and Talking Heads, which are televised across Europe to a multi-million audience.

1981 Jan *Making Movies*, with E. Street Band's keyboardist Roy Bittan, reaches US #19.

[31] *Skateaway*, taken from it, peaks at US #58.

Feb [14] *Making Movies*, assisted by the still climbing *Romeo And Juliet*, hits a belated UK chart peak of #4.

[21] Knopfler-penned ballad *Romeo And Juliet* hits UK #8.

Mar [18] Recently returned from a successful appearance at the San Remo Song Festival in Italy, Dire Straits embarks on its first tour of Australia and New Zealand. (The concert in Auckland will be the highest-grossing in the band's career to date.)

Apr [11] *Skateaway* makes UK #37.

May [3] Group begins sell-out tour of Germany, Sweden, Denmark, Norway, Finland, Holland, France, Switzerland, Italy, Belgium and Luxembourg, which will end on July 6.

Oct [17] *Tunnel Of Love* peaks at UK #54.

1982 Feb Knopfler is invited by film producer David Puttnam to compose and perform the soundtrack score of movie Bill Forsyth's "Local Hero".

Mar [1] Band begins recording its fourth album.

July "Local Hero" soundtrack music is recorded, after Knopfler visits location shooting in Scotland.

Sept [18] Despite its 7-min. length, half-whispered *Private Investigations* hits UK #2, behind Survivor's *Eye Of The Tiger*.

Oct [2] *Love Over Gold* hits UK #1 for 4 weeks.

Nov [13] *Love Over Gold* reaches US #19. Withers leaves and is replaced on drums by Terry Williams, ex-Man and Dave Edmunds' band Rockpile.

1983 Jan [22] *Industrial Disease* peaks at US #75.

Feb [5] EP *Twisting By The Pool* reaches UK #14.

[8] Dire Straits wins Best British Group at the second annual BRIT awards at the Grosvenor House, London.

Mar [12] Knopfler's solo single *Going Home*, theme from "Local Hero", debuts at UK #56.

Apr Marketed as a mini-album, *Twisting By The Pool* makes US #53.

May Knopfler's *Local Hero* soundtrack album reaches UK #14.

[5] *Private Investigations* wins Outstanding British Lyric at the annual Ivor Novello Awards lunch in London.

Nov Knopfler produces Dylan's *Infidels*, and marries Lourdes Salomon at Kensington Register Office, London.

1984 Feb [25] Double A-side *Love Over Gold/Solid Rock* (both live versions) makes UK #50.

Mar Double album *Alchemy – Dire Straits Live* hits UK #3.

Apr [19] *Going Home* wins Best Film Theme Or Song at the annual Iv Novello Awards lunch in London.

May *Alchemy – Dire Straits Live* makes only US #46.

Oct Knopfler's album of soundtrack music for film "Cal" reaches UK #65. He writes score for "Comfort And Joy", his second for director B Forsyth. (Illsley releases solo album *Never Told A Soul* on Vertigo.)

1985 Mar [23] Tina Turner hits US #7 with Knopfler-penned *Private Dance*

May [4] *So Far Away* reaches UK #20.

[25] *Brothers In Arms* debuts at UK #1 and holds the top slot for 3 weeks. Shortly after, Lindes leaves the band.

June Dire Straits is awarded the 1985 Silver Clef for outstanding services to British music by the Nordoff-Robbins Music Therapy Centre.

July [13] After 10 consecutive nights' concerts at Wembley Arena, London, the band plays at Live Aid at Wembley Stadium. (This will b followed by the 12-month "Brothers In Arms" world tour, ending in Australia in mid-1986. Clark leaves and Guy Fletcher joins on keyboards for the tour.)

Aug [10] *Money For Nothing*, from *Brothers In Arms*, hits UK #4.

[31] *Brothers In Arms* tops US chart for 9 weeks.

Sept [21] Aided by an innovative animated promo video which gets heavy MTV and other US TV exposure, *Money For Nothing* tops the U chart for 3 weeks, the band's biggest US hit and its first million-selling single. (Sting guests on vocals, and by his inclusion of a Police melod line, winds up sharing 50/50 writing credit with its writer, Knopfler.)

Dec Extracted title track, *Brothers In Arms* reaches UK #16.

1986 Jan [25] Uptempo *Walk Of Life* hits US #7.

Feb *Walk Of Life* hits UK #2.

[10] Dire Straits wins Best British Group, for the second time, at the fifth annual BRIT Awards at the Grosvenor House.

[25] They win Best Rock Performance By A Duo Or Group With Voc for *Money For Nothing*. *Brothers In Arms* wins Best Engineered Recording (Non-Classical) and Knopfler wins Best Country Instrumental Performance with one of his original guitar heroes, Che Atkins, for *Cosmic Square Dance* from *Stay Tuned* at the 28th annual Grammy awards.

Apr [26] *So Far Away* reaches US #19.

May *Your Latest Trick* reaches UK #26.

Knopfler, his guitar-maker Steve Phillips and Brendan Croker play th Grove, a small Leeds folk club, a prelude to a more formal forthcomin collaboration.

June [20] Knopfler and Illsley take part in the fourth annual Prince's Trust Rock Gala concert, with Eric Clapton, Phil Collins, Paul McCartney, Elton John, Tina Turner and others, at the Wembley Arer

Sept [5] *Money For Nothing* wins Best Video and Best Group Video a the annual MTV awards. (The song's opening Sting-sung lyric "I Wan My MTV" becomes the cable station's catch-phrase.)

Oct [25] Knopfler breaks his collarbone in an accident in a celebrity race before the Australian Grand Prix,

1987 Jan Knopfler guests at Eric Clapton's concert at the Royal Albert Hal London.

Feb [9] *Brothers In Arms* wins Best British Album at the sixth annua BRIT Awards at the Grosvenor House.

[24] "Dire Straits Brothers In Arms" wins Best Music Video, Long Form at the 29th annual Grammy awards.

Mar Knopfler duets with Chet Atkins, at "The Secret Policeman's Third Ball" at the London Palladium, in aid of Amnesty International

Nov *Brothers In Arms* sells its 3-millionth copy in UK, becoming the UK's all-time best-selling album and its second-biggest-selling recording of any kind. (Only Band Aid's *Do They Know It's Christmas?* has a higher UK sales total.)

Dec Knopfler writes and performs the soundtrack music for Rob Reiner-directed film "The Princess Bride", also released on album.

1988 Apr Knopfler works with Dylan on the latter's *Down In The Groove*.

June [11] Band headlines "Nelson Mandela's 70th Birthday Party" concert at Wembley Stadium, televised worldwide, with Eric Clapton guesting as second guitarist. The show helps album *Brothers In Arms* back into the UK Top 20 after 162 weeks on chart.

July Knopfler guests on Joan Armatrading's *The Shouting Stage*.

Sept Knopfler contributes and part-produces Randy Newman's *Lan Of Dream* and accompanies Clapton on his US tour as guitarist and vocalist.

[15] After much spectaculation, Knopfler announces the official end Dire Straits.

Oct Randy newman's latest album, *Land Of Dream*, featuring production and performance by Knopfler is released.

[29] Greatest hits compilation *Money For Nothing* debuts at UK #1. A multi-platinum success in UK, in US its track listing is criticised and it stalls at #62.

Nov [5] Extracted single *Sultans Of Swing* peaks at UK #62.

'89 Mar Dire Straits are featured on Greenpeace-supporting album *Rainbow Warriors* initially launched in Russia.

Apr [4] Knopfler and Illsley (as Dire Straits) are honored with Outstanding Contribution To British Music at the annual Ivor Novello Awards lunch in London.

Sept [11] Jim Hensons's "The Ghost Of Faffner Hall", on which Knopfler is one of many guests, airs on HBO TV.

'90 Mar [17] The Notting Hillbillies' *Missing ... Presumed Having ...* debuts at UK #2. Knopfler has formed the band in a deliberate non-celebrity move to return to more low-key performing act with old friend Phillips (whom he met in 1965 to form the Doulian String Pickers), Croker, who has teamed with Phillips in 1976 in Nev & Norris, and Guy Fletcher with whom Knopfler has been producing Croker and Phillips at Knopfler's Notting Hill, London, home studio.

Apr [19] Knopfler appears with David Gilmour, Mark King, Lemmy and Gary Moore, as witnesses in a comedy courthouse sketch on BBC TV's "French And Saunders" and end sketch jamming together.

[21] *Missing ... Presumed Having ...* makes US #52.

May [19] A modest venue Notting Hillbillies UK tour ends. They then appear on NBC TV's "Saturday Night Live". The live line-up is augmented by Nashville-based Paul Franklin (pedal steel) and Marcus Cliff, of Croker's Five O'Clock Shadows, (bass).

June [30] Knopfler joins Phil Collins and Genesis, Pink Floyd, Robert Plant, Paul McCartney, Cliff Richard and The Shadows, Status Quo, Elton John, Eric Clapton and Tears For Fears, all previous Silver Clef winners, on a star-studded bill at Knebworth Park, Herts., in aid of Nordoff-Robbins Music Therapy Centre.

Nov [24] *Neck And Neck*, a Mark Knopfler/Chet Atkins guitar laden duet album, debuts at UK #41.

Dec [1] *Neck And Neck* makes US #127.

'91 Feb While recording for new Dire Straits album project, Knopfler contributes guitar solo to *Voices That Care*, a David Foster and fiancee Linda Thompson Jenner-composed and organized charity record to benefit the American Red Cross Gulf Crisis Fund.

[20] Knopfler and Atkins win Best Country Vocal Collaboration for *Poor Boy Blues* and Best Country Instrumental Performance for *So Soft, Your Goodbye* at the 33rd annual Grammy awards at Radio City Music Hall, New York.

R. FEELGOOD

e Brilleaux (vocals, guitar)
ilko Johnson (guitar)
hn B.Sparks (bass)
e Big Figure (drums)

71 Band is formed on Canvey Island, Essex, to play hard, traditional rock, R&B and electric blues, taking its name from the 1962 US hit *Doctor Feel-Good* by bluesman Piano Red (recorded under the name Dr. Feelgood & The Interns). Former Newcastle university student Johnson (b. John Wilkinson, 1947) and The Big Figure (b. John Martin, 1947) are both ex-The Roamers, and the others have played in groups in the Essex area. While establishing its own reputation, the band backs 60s star Heinz. New material, mostly by Johnson, is introduced into the stage act during 3 years of heavy club work.

74 July [8] Signed to United Artists Records, the band makes its first recording, a medley of rock oldies *Bony Moronie/Tequila*, live at Dingwall's club in London.

Aug [26] Recording sessions for first album begin with producer Vic Maile at Rockfield studios, Wales.

Nov Johnson-penned *Roxette* just fails to make UK Top 50.

75 Jan Debut album *Down By The Jetty* is released, recorded in mono to reflect the band's raw, basic, R&B sound.

May [23] A live show at City Hall, Sheffield, S.Yorks., is recorded for an album.

Oct Self-produced *Malpractice* reaches UK #17. Band tours widely in UK, finding huge support from UK's music press, which champions its hard-edged sound and dynamic live presence as a major rock trend.

Nov [24] A second gig at the Kursaal Ballroom in Southend, Essex (just 8 miles from the band's Canvey Island base) is recorded for album use.

76 Oct Live *Stupidity*, compiled from the Sheffield and Southend recordings, tops UK chart for a week.

1977 Mar Johnson leaves for a solo career, before forming Solid Senders and joining Ian Dury's band in 1980, after disagreements over the band's material. Henry McCulloch plays as temporary guitarist on a UK tour and is replaced by John "Gypie" Mayo.

June *Sneakin' Suspicion*, produced by Bert De Coteaux at Rockfield, Wales (recorded before Johnson's departure), hits UK #10. Title track, written by Johnson, is band's first hit single, reaching UK #47.

Oct *She's A Wind Up* makes UK #34. Produced by Nick Lowe, it is taken from *Be Seeing You* (the sleeve reflects a current craze within the band for Patrick McGoohan's "The Prisoner" UK TV series) and reaches UK #55.

1978 June [22] Group tops the bill of the fifth anniversary concert at Dingwall's club in London.

Oct *Down At The Doctor's* reaches UK #48. It is extracted from *Private Practice*, produced by Richard Gottehrer, which makes UK #41.

1979 Feb The Mayo/Lowe-penned *Milk And Alcohol*, also from *Private Practice*, is band's biggest-selling single, hitting UK #9. UA gimmick-releases it on white (milk) and brown (alcohol) colored vinyl.

May *As Long As The Price Is Right*, a Larry Wallis song, reaches UK #40.

June Live *As It Happens*, recorded at UK gigs at the Pavilion, Hemel Hempstead, Herts. and Crocs in Rayleigh, Essex, reaches UK #42.

Dec *Put Him Out Of Your Mind* reaches UK #73, and is their last UK hit single. It is taken from *Let It Roll*, produced by Mike Verson, which fails to chart.

1980 Sept *A Case Of The Shakes* also fails to chart, and amid some disillusionment within the band, Mayo considers leaving.

[12] Group embarks on the UK section of a world tour at the Pavilion, Hemel Hempstead.

1981 Mayo quits, to be replaced by Johnny Guitar, ex-The Count Bishops.

Aug *On The Job*, the band's third live album, recorded at Manchester University, Gtr.Manchester (and featuring Mayo), also fails to chart.

Nov Compilation *Dr. Feelgood's Casebook* is band's last release on Liberty/UA.

1982 Sparks and Figure leave. Buzz Barwell (drums, ex-Lew Lewis Band) and Pat McMullen (bass, ex-Count Bishops) replace them, leaving Brilleaux the only original member. Group tours UK and Europe despite the personnel upheavals.

Oct *Fast Women And Slow Horses* is released on independent UK label Chiswick Records.

1983 Phil Mitchell (bass) replaces McMullen and Gordon Russell replaces Guitar. Brilleaux continues to lead the band through its timeless hard R&B act. (They will work regularly in the small, noisy, club environment which suits them best.)

1989 After forming their own Grand label (on which they will release another stage set, *Live In London*, in May 1990), group resumes touring with Brilleaux, Mitchell, Kevin Morris (drums) and, from Steve Marriott's group, Steve Walwyn (guitar).

DR. HOOK

Ray Sawyer (lead vocals, guitar)
Dennis Locorriere (lead vocals, guitar)
Jance Garfat (bass, vocals)
George Cummings (steel and lead guitar)
Bill Francis (keyboards, vocals)
Rik Elswit (guitar, vocals)
John Wolters (drums, vocals)

1968 Group forms in Union City, NJ, when ex-folk singer Locorriere (b. June 13, 1949, Union City, NJ) joins Sawyer (b. Feb.1, 1937, Chickasaw, AL), Cummings (b. July 28, 1938, Meridian, MS) and Francis (b. Jan.16, 1942, Mobile, AL), who have been playing together for some years under various short-lived names. They recruit the other members, mostly from the South, and play local bars as The Chocolate Papers.

1969 Feb [18] Group has no fixed name until a club owner demands one for his advertising poster and Cummings coins Dr. Hook & The Medicine Show. (Dr. Hook becomes associated with frontman Sawyer who wears an eye patch, after losing his right eye in an auto accident, which gives him a piratical appearance.)

1970 Producer Ron Haffkine hears a Dr. Hook demo tape and asks the group to appear in, and perform *Last Morning* for, the Dustin Hoffman movie "Who Is Harry Kellerman And Why Is He Saying Those Terrible Things About Me?"

1971 June Haffkine signs the band to a recording deal before the movie opens, realizing it will be a success. A deal is completed with CBS/ Columbia and the band moves to Haffkine's home in Connecticut to spend several months in rehearsal before cutting a debut album in San Francisco, CA.

1972 June The plaintive and offbeat *Sylvia's Mother*, written by Silverstein, hits US #5, earning a gold disk for a million-plus sales. Debut album *Dr. Hook & The Medicine Show* (which includes the hit) makes US #45.
Aug *Sylvia's Mother* hits UK #2.
Sept *Carry Me, Carrie* peaks at US #71.

1973 Jan *Sloppy Seconds* makes US #41.
Mar *The Cover Of "Rolling Stone"* hits US #6 and is the group's second million-seller. In UK, the BBC refuses to play it because of the mention of the magazine, a commercial enterprise. Group records a special BBC version titled *The Cover Of "Radio Times"* (the BBC's own weekly magazine) but the single still fails to chart in UK.
[29] Group fulfils the ambition inherent in the song by appearing on the cover of **Rolling Stone** magazine.
July *Roland The Roadie And Gertrude The Groupie* climbs to US #83.
Oct *Life Ain't Easy* peaks at US #68.
Nov *Belly Up!* makes US #141.

1974 Sept Dropped by CBS and virtually bankrupt, the band shortens its name to Dr. Hook.

1975 Feb Capitol Records signs the band to a 1-year option.
July *Bankrupt* reaches US #141.
Sept *The Millionaire*, taken from the album, reaches US #95.
Nov [20] "Dr. Hook's Christmas Show" tour starts in Oxford, Oxon.

1976 Apr *Only Sixteen*, a revival of Sam Cooke's 1959 hit taken from *Bankrupt*, is halfway up the US Top 100 when Capitol's option runs out. The label continues promoting it and the band, and it climbs to hit US #6 and sells over a million copies.
Aug *A Little Bit More*, recorded in Nashville, TN, reaches US #11 and UK #2 (held from the top for 4 weeks by Elton John & Kiki Dee's *Don't Go Breaking My Heart*). The album of the same title makes US #62 and hits UK #5. The band appears on "Grand Ole Opry" and soon after relocates to Nashville.
Dec Ballad *If Not You* peaks at US #55 and hits UK #5.

1977 Jan Sawyer cuts an eponymous solo album of country songs, backed by Nashville session men.
Aug *Walk Right In*, a remake of The Rooftop Singers' 1963 smash, makes US #46. *Revisited*, compiled of material cut during the band's CBS/Columbia days, is released without charting.
Nov *Making Love And Music* reaches UK #39.

1978 Apr *More Like The Movies* reaches UK #14.

1979 Jan *Pleasure And Pain* reaches US #66. (It will be the band's only gold disk in US, selling over a half million copies.) *Sharing The Night Together*, after a 4-month chart climb, hits US #6 and earns a gold disk for a million-plus sales.
Feb *All The Time In The World* peaks at US #54.
Aug *When You're In Love With A Beautiful Woman* hits US #6 and is another US million-seller.
Nov *When You're In Love With A Beautiful Woman* tops UK chart for 3 weeks, while parent *Pleasure And Pain* reaches UK #47.

1980 Jan *Better Love Next Time* makes US #12 and UK #8.
Apr *Sexy Eyes* hits US #5 (another million-seller) and UK #4. *Sometimes You Win*, from which it is taken, makes US #71 and UK #14.
Aug *Years From Now* peaks at US #51 and UK #47.
Nov *Sharing The Night Together* reaches UK #43, almost 2 years after its US success. Capitol releases this old track after the band has left the label and signed a new deal with Casablanca Records (released through Mercury in UK).
Dec *Rising* on Casablanca/Mercury makes US #175 and UK #44. Extracted from it, *Girls Can Get It* makes US #34 and UK #40.

1981 Jan Compilation *Dr. Hook's Greatest Hits* makes US #142 and UK #2.
Apr *That Didn't Hurt Too Bad* reaches US #69.
Nov *Live Dr. Hook In London* makes UK #90.

1982 Apr *Baby Makes Her Blue Jeans Talk* reaches US #25. *Players In The Dark* reaches US #118.
July *Loveline* reaches US #60. (Band will continue to play and tour, despite lack of further recording success, into the mid-80s, eventually splitting in 1985 when both vocal frontmen Sawyer and Locorriere move to solo careers.)

1988 Sept A new version of Dr. Hook, led by Sawyer but featuring no other former members, tours UK.

DR. JOHN

1957 Dr. John (b. Malcolm John Rebennack, Nov.21, 1940, New Orleans, LA), who as a baby is featured on Ivory Soap packets, playing on countless sessions for New Orleans' Ace, Ebb and Ric R&B labels, begins to establish himself as one of a handful of white musicians working on the New Orleans R&B music scene.

Sept He records his first release *Storm Warning* for Rex, under his real name, Rebennack, .

1958 He tours with Frankie Ford and Jerry Byrne (for whom he co-writes the rock'n'roll standard *Lights Out*), and releases his first album for Ace, followed by others for Rex and the black musicians' co-operative AFO (founded by New Orleans' producer and arranger Harold Battiste).

1960 He pens Lloyd Price's US #14, *Lady Luck*.

1962 Leaving New Orleans for Los Angeles, CA, now playing piano, after his left ring finger is shot while breaking up a fight in 1961, leaving him unable to play guitar, he is an in-demand session player, working on numerous records for Sonny Bono (of Sonny & Cher), Phil Spector, H.F Barnum and Battiste (who has moved with him).

1964 Forming various bands like The Drits and Dray and Zu Zu, he develops a new identity as Dr. John Creux The Night Tripper, fusing New Orleans R&B with the emergent psychedelia of West Coast rock. He sets up Pulsar, a subsidiary of Mercury Records, recording King Floyd and Alvin Robinson.

1965 *Zu Zu Man*, for A&M, foreshadows the sound and structures of the firs Dr. John album.

1968 *Gris Gris* on Atco, includes the much-covered *Walk On Guilded Splinters*. It is highly rated by critics but does not chart.

1969 Apr *Babylon* is released.
Dec [7] Dr. John performs at the Lyceum Ballroom, London.

1970 June *Remedies* again fails to chart, despite excellent reviews.

1971 Sept Aretha Franklin's *Spanish Harlem*, featuring Dr. John on organ, hits US #2 and UK #14.
Oct Fourth Atco album *Dr. John, The Night Tripper (The Sun, Moon And Herbs)*, recorded in London and including contributions from Mick Jagger and Eric Clapton, reaches US #184.

1972 Apr [29] A revival of The Dixie Cups' *Iko Iko* is his first US chart entry peaking at US #71.
July *Dr. John's Gumbo*, produced by Jerry Wexler, reaches US #112.

1973 June Allen Toussaint-produced *In The Right Place*, his biggest-selling album, makes US #24.
[30] Extracted *Right Place Wrong Time* hits US #9, and is his only major hit single. He tours Europe, accompanied by highly-rated New Orlean band The Meters.
July *Triumvirate*, recorded with Mike Bloomfield and John Paul Hammond, reaches US #105.
Oct [27] *Such A Night* makes US #42.

1974 May [25] *(Everybody Wanna Get Rich) Rite Away* reaches US #92 and *Desitively Bonnaroo* US #105. (Increasingly beset by personal and health problems, these will be his last Atco releases and US chart entries; later albums will be mostly released via one-off label deals.)

1975 Nov *Hollywood Be Thy Name*, produced by Bob Ezrin, on United Artists, and credited to Rizzum & The Blues Revue, is released.

1976 Nov *Cut Me While I'm Hot* for DJM Records also fails.
[25] Dr. John takes part in The Band's Thanksgiving Day "The Last Waltz" farewell concert at San Francisco's Winterland Auditorium, singing *Such A Night*, performing a duet with Joni Mitchell on the latter's *Coyote*, and joining with Bobby Charles and members of The Band on *Down South In New Orleans*. His performance is recorded on both album and feature film of the event.

1977 He joins the short-lived RCO All Stars, the group formed by ex-Band drummer Levon Helm, and featuring Paul Butterfield and former MG Steve Cropper and Donald "Duck" Dunn.

1978 Solo album *City Lights* is released on A&M.

1981 Moving to New York, Dr. John, unable to secure an attractive US recording contract, concentrates on touring UK and Europe as a solo artist. He cuts 2 albums for A&M's Horizon label, before recording *Dr John Plays Mac Rebennack* for the Clean Cuts label.

1982 He releases acclaimed album, *Brightest Smile In Town* for Demon. He also records album with Chris Barber on the Black Lion label.

1984 Feb Despite his continuing health problems he still shows innovatory flair, releasing the hip-hop-infused *Jet Set*, produced by Ed "The Message" Fletcher on Arthur Baker's New York Streetwise label, whic is optioned in UK by Beggars Banquet.

1986 He co-produces Jimmy Witherspoon's *Midnight Lady Calls The Blues* with songwriting legend Doc Pomus.

1989 Jan [21] Dr. John takes part in an R&B evening at Washington Center during President Bush's inaugural celebrations with Bo Diddley, Perc Sledge, Etta James, Willie Dixon, Albert Collins and Sam Moore.
July [23] He opens 28-date, 27-city US "Tour For All Generations", as part of Ringo Starr's All-Starr Band at the Park Central Amphitheater, Dallas, TX.
Aug [5] *In A Sentimental Mood*, a tribute to Ray Charles, tops

Billboard's Traditional Jazz Albums chart for 4 weeks, having already peaked at US #142.

1990 Feb [21] *Makin' Whoopee* wins Best Jazz Vocal Performance, Duo Or Group at the 32nd annual Grammy awards at the Shrine Auditorium, Los Angeles.

1991 Jan Great Southern label releases *On A Mardi Gras Day*, a live album cut with Chris Barber at the Marquee club, London in Apr.1983, as Dr. John prepares for lengthy US tour.

Mar Dr. John, increasingly in demand writing and recording music for commercials, contributes to current Taj Mahal album sessions.

FATS DOMINO

1949 One of a family of 9, Domino (b. Antoine Domino, Feb.26, 1928, New Orleans, LA), taught to play piano in his early teens by his brother-in-law, New Orleans musician Harrison Verrett, almost lost his fingers in an accident in the bedmaking factory where he worked but regained their use and his playing ability. Having married his childhood sweetheart Rose Marie a year earlier, he is playing piano in the honky tonks in New Orleans for $3 a week when bandleader/producer Dave Bartholomew, scouting on behalf of Imperial Records, listens to him with Billy Diamond's combo at the Hideaway club, and decides to sign and record him.

Dec Bartholomew helps him rewrite *Junker's Blues* (the first song he heard Domino play) as *The Fat Man*, which is recorded in New Orleans at Domino's first session in Cosimo Matassa's J&M studio.

1950 Apr *The Fat Man*, a useful tie-in with Domino's own "Fats" nickname (and now professional name) from his 5' 5", 224lb. stature, with Herb Hardesty on sax, hits US R&B #6. (By 1953, it will have sold a million, earning Domino his first gold disk.)

Oct After 3 unsuccessful releases, *Every Night About This Time*, recorded again with Bartholomew's band, makes the R&B chart.

1951 Dec Domino forms his own band and hits US R&B #9 with *Rockin' Chair*. Bartholomew continues to help with arranging and writing (until 1955), but finds Domino's innovative playing (a "creative" approach to keeping time) difficult to work with.

1952 Apr *Goin' Home* tops US R&B chart and becomes a million-seller.

1953 June *Goin' To The River* hits US R&B #2 and is a third gold disk.

Aug *Please Don't Leave Me* hits US R&B #5.

1954 Mar *You Done Me Wrong* reaches US R&B #10. Domino fails to make the R&B chart again this year, but concentrates on touring US, with visits to New York in the spring, the West Coast and North-West in the summer, and the Mid-West and Chicago in Dec. His popularity grows steadily.

1955 Jan [28] In New York, Domino begins a 42-date US tour on the "Top Ten R&B Show", with The Clovers, Joe Turner, The Moonglows, Faye Adams and other major R&B acts.

Mar *Don't You Know* reaches US R&B #12.

May [22] A show to be headlined by Domino at the Ritz ballroom in Bridgeport, CT, is cancelled by local police, who justify the action pointing to "a recent near-riot" at New Haven Arena during a rock'n'roll dance.

June *Ain't That A Shame* tops R&B chart for 11 weeks, and is his first single to cross over and hit US #10. It is a million-seller, but is outsold by Pat Boone's version, which hits US #2 and UK #7.

Sept *All By Myself* hits US R&B #3, but fails to cross over.

Nov *Poor Me* hits US R&B at #3 but again fails to cross over.

[12] In **Billboard**'s annual US DJ poll, Domino is named the country's Favorite R&B Artist.

1956 Apr *Bo Weevil* makes US #35 (his second to cross over).

June *I'm In Love Again* hits US #3 and tops R&B chart for 7 weeks, becoming another million-seller. B-side *My Blue Heaven* reaches US #21.

Aug [28] Domino begins a co-headlining (with Frankie Lymon & The Teenagers) 10 day performance in Alan Freed's annual rock'n'roll show at the Paramount theater, Brooklyn, New York.

Sept *When My Dreamboat Comes Home* reaches US #14, with B-side *So-Long* peaking at #44. *I'm In Love Again* marks his UK chart debut, reaching UK #12.

Nov *Fats Domino – Rock And Rollin'* is his first chart album, reaching US #18.

[10] In the annual **Billboard** DJ poll, Domino is again voted Favorite R&B Artist, as well as being the ninth most-played male vocalist (Elvis Presley being the most-played).

[18] Domino appears on US TV's "Ed Sullivan Show" singing his revival of standard *Blueberry Hill*.

Dec *Blueberry Hill* hits US #3, tops US R&B chart for 8 weeks, and sells over a million. Domino's arrangement becomes the definitive one. He appears in film "Shake, Rattle And Roll", with R&B singer Joe Turner, and performs *I'm In Love Again, Honey Chile* and *Ain't That A Shame*.

1957 Jan *Ain't That A Shame* makes UK #23. Domino appears in Jayne Mansfield-starring movie "The Girl Can't Help It", singing *Blue Monday*.

Feb *Honey Chile* reaches UK #29, while *Blueberry Hill*, after a lengthy climb, hits UK #6. *Blue Monday* hits US #9 (another million-seller), and replaces *Blueberry Hill* at US R&B #1, remaining there for 8 weeks. B-side, *What's The Reason I'm Not Pleasing You* (originally a pre-war hit for Guy Lombardo) makes US #50.

[2] Domino appears on "The Perry Como Show" on US TV singing *Blueberry Hill* and *Blue Monday*.

[15] Domino begins a US tour (lasting until May 5) as part of "The Greatest Show Of 1957", a rock'n'roll caravan which also includes Chuck Berry, Clyde McPhatter, LaVern Baker and others.

Mar *This Is Fats Domino!*, which includes both *Blueberry Hill* and *Blue Monday*, reaches US #19. *Blue Monday* reaches UK #23.

Apr *Rock And Rollin' With Fats Domino* (his belatedly-charting debut album, including *Ain't That A Shame*) reaches US #17. *I'm Walkin'*, later covered by Rick Nelson, hits US #5, and spends 6 weeks at R&B #1, replacing *Blue Monday*. (By the time *I'm Walkin'* drops from R&B #1, Domino will have been at the top of the chart for 22 consecutive weeks with 3 different singles.)

May *I'm Walkin'* reaches UK #19.

July *Valley Of Tears* hits US #6 and B-side *It's You I Love* reaches US #22. In UK, *Valley Of Tears* makes #25.

Aug *When I See You* reaches US #29. B-side *What Will I Tell My Heart* makes US #64.

Oct *Wait And See* reaches US #23 and B-side *I Still Love You* US #79.

Nov [12] The rock'n'roll movie "Jamboree" (released in UK as "Disc Jockey Jamboree") premieres in Hollywood, featuring Domino singing *Wait And See* with a host of rock acts.

Dec *The Big Beat* reaches US #26. It is the title track to movie of the same name, in which Domino performs *I'm Walkin'*. B-side *I Want You To Know* makes US #48.

1958 Apr *The Big Beat* reaches UK #20.

May *Sick And Tired* reaches US #22. B-side *No No* peaks at US #55.

July *Little Mary* makes US #48, while *Sick And Tired* peaks at UK #26.

Sept *Young School Girl* peaks at US #92.

1959 Jan *Whole Lotta Loving* hits US #6 and is another million-seller.

Mar Both sides of double-A *Telling Lies/When The Saints Go Marching In* reach US #50.

June *I'm Ready* reaches US #16. B-side *Margie* makes #51 and UK #19.

Sept *I Want To Walk You Home*, another million-seller, hits US #8. B-side *I'm Gonna Be A Wheel Some Day* reaches US #17.

Oct *I Want To Walk You Home* makes UK #14.

Dec *Be My Guest* hits US #8 and is another million-seller. B-side *I've Been Around* peaks at US #33.

1960 Jan *Be My Guest*, Domino's biggest UK hit single since *Blueberry Hill*, reaches UK #11.

Mar *Country Boy* reaches US #25 and UK #19.

May *Tell Me That You Love Me/Before I Grow Too Old* makes US #51/#84.

Aug Strings-backed *Walking To New Orleans* hits US #6 and reaches UK #19, with B-side *Don't Come Knockin'* making US #21. This is Domino's last million-selling single.

Oct *Three Nights A Week* reaches US #15, its B-side *Put Your Arms Around Me Honey* peaking at US #58.

Nov *Three Nights A Week* makes US #45.

Dec *My Girl Josephine* reaches US #14, while B-side *Natural Born Lover* climbs to US #38.

1961 Jan *My Girl Josephine* makes UK #32.

Feb *What A Price* reaches US #22 and B-side *Ain't That Just Like A Woman* peaks at US #33.

Apr Both sides of *Shu Rah/Fell In Love On Monday* peak separately at US #32.

[2] Domino begins a wide-ranging tour of US and Canada as part of "The Biggest Show Of Stars 1961", with Chubby Checker, The Drifters, Bo Diddley, The Shirelles and others.

July *It Keeps Rainin'* reaches US #23 and UK #49.

[8] Domino completes a 19-day tour of South-Western US states, grossing $83,000.

Sept *Let The Four Winds Blow* reaches US #15.

Dec *What A Party* reaches US #22 and UK #43, with B-side *Rockin' Bicycle* charting briefly at US #83.

FATS DOMINO cont.

1962 Feb A revival of Hank Williams' 1952 country hit *Jambalaya (On The Bayou)* reaches US #30. B-side *I Hear You Knocking* (originally by Domino's New Orleans contemporary Smiley Lewis) makes US #67.
Mar *Jambalaya (On The Bayou)* reaches UK #41.
Apr He records what will be his last session for Imperial in New Orleans. Meanwhile, another Hank Williams revival, *You Win Again* reaches US #22 and B-side *Ida Jane* peaks at US #90.
June His last few Imperial A-sides will fail to make US Top 40 as Domino's never-changing sound begins to seem out-dated alongside the rapidly-developing R&B styles of the early 60s, and the dance disks by Chubby Checker, Dee Dee Sharp and others. *My Real Name* reaches US #59.
July *Nothing New (Same Old Thing)* and B-side *Dance With Mr. Domino* peaks at US #77/#98. Domino takes part in the Antibes Jazz Festival in Juan Les Pins, South of France.
Aug Compilation *Million Sellers By Fats* reaches US #113.
Oct *Did You Ever See A Dream Walking?*, reviving a pre-war hit by Eddy Duchin, makes US #79. This is his last hit single on Imperial.

1963 Apr [6] Domino's Imperial contract expires and he signs to ABC-Paramount Records, to record in Nashville, TN.
June *There Goes (My Heart Again)*, on ABC, an unmistakably familiar Domino sound despite the substitution of a Nashville recording session for New Orleans, reaches US #59.
Oct *Here Comes Fats Domino*, on ABC, makes US #130. Taken from it, a revival of standard *Red Sails In The Sunset*, styled towards Ray Charles' R&B/country arrangement of *I Can't Stop Loving You*, makes US #35 and UK #34.

1964 Jan *Who Cares* makes US #63. Parent album, *Fats On Fire*, fails to chart.
Mar *Lazy Lady* peaks at US #86.
Sept *Sally Was A Good Old Girl* reaches US #99.
Nov *Heartbreak Hill* is Domino's last ABC hit, also making #99.

1965 He signs a 2-year contract with Mercury Records. Few records are produced (2 singles, including a version of *I Left My Heart In San Francisco*; *Fats Domino '65*, recorded live in Las Vegas, and live *Southland USA*, which is recorded but never released).

1966 Aug Domino plays 2 4-day stints at the Village Gate in New York.
1967 Mar [27] He makes his first-ever UK visit, playing the first of 6 nights, supported by Gerry & The Pacemakers and The Bee Gees, to a rapturous nostalgic audience at London's Saville theater.
Dec The Mercury contract has expired and Domino records *The Lady In Black* and a follow-up single on his own Broadmoor label, co-owned with Dave Bartholomew. With poor distribution, they fail to chart.

1968 Sept Domino signs to Reprise Records and his last US chart single, at #100, is a cover of The Beatles' *Lady Madonna*, deliberately written in Domino style by Paul McCartney for The Beatles' original version earlier in the year. (2 similar Beatles' covers, *Lovely Rita* and *Everybody's Got Something To Hide Except Me And My Monkey*, are the follow-ups, but neither will chart.)
Oct *Fats Is Back*, on Reprise and produced by Richard Perry, makes US #189. This is Domino's final US chart album.

1970 May Compilation *Very Best Of Fats Domino* reaches UK #56 (his only UK chart album).
1973 He records a live album for Atlantic Records, in Montreux, Switzerland, and appears in the movie "Let The Good Times Roll".
1976 May *Blueberry Hill* is reissued as a UK single, and charts at #41.
1979 May Domino is now recording very rarely, but *Sleeping On The Job*, made at Sea-Saint studios in New Orleans, is released by Sonet Records. (In the 80s, Domino will spend much time living at home in New Orleans with his wife and family. He will play regularly in Las Vegas or other venues where his nostalgic style, which is still basically the same as in 1948, will bring in top money and draw an appreciative audience, but he will not undertake lengthy tours.)

1987 Feb [24] Domino is honored with the NARAS Lifetime Achievements Award at the 29th annual Grammy awards as "one of the most important links between rhythm and blues and rock and roll, a most influential performer whose style of piano-playing and 'down home' singing have led the way for generations of other performers". *Blueberry Hill* is voted into the Hall Of Fame.

1990 Domino records his first album in 5 years, a double live package recorded in New Orleans on the Tomato label and guests on The Dirty Dozen Brass Band's eponymously-titled album. His earlier work comes back into the public eye with the release of *My Blue Heaven – The Best Of Fats Domino (Volume One)* to tie in with the Steve Martin-Rick Moranis comedy movie "My Blue Heaven".

LONNIE DONEGAN

1952 Donegan (b. Anthony James Donegan, Apr.29, 1931, Glasgow, Scotland), his father a violinist with the National Scottish Orchestra, having played professionally in jazz bands since his army service in 1949 and allegedly gaining his stage name when, on the same London bill as US blues guitarist Lonnie Johnson, he is inadvertently introduced as "Lonnie" Donegan by a confused MC, joins Ken Colyer's Jazzmen as guitar and banjo player. With Colyer, where he is reunited with an army buddy, trombonist Chris Barber, Donegan's blues and folk influences earn him a solo spot in the band's act, leading a small group (Colyer on guitar, Barber on bass, and Bill Colyer on washboard) on US blues and work songs, generically dubbed "skiffle".

1953 Some Donegan "skiffle" numbers are recorded on his first studio session with Colyer's band, but the tracks are not used.

1954 Jan Barber splits from Colyer with many of his musicians, including Donegan, and forms Chris Barber's Jazz Band, signing to Decca.

1955 The band records a 10" album, *New Orleans Joy*, which contains 2 tracks, *Rock Island Line* and *John Henry*, credited to the Lonnie Donegan Skiffle Group.

1956 Feb *Rock Island Line*, learned from a Leadbelly song, is released, credited to Donegan, and is an unexpected UK hit at #8, spending 22 weeks on chart. (Donegan never receives any royalties from it, having been paid a £50 session fee when it was recorded.) He signs to Pye-Nixa in UK as a soloist.
Apr [21] *Rock Island Line* hits US #8 and takes the cumulative sales over a million.
May [19] He makes his US TV debut on "The Perry Como Show", alongside Ronald Reagan, who is appearing in some comedy sketches. Donegan, accompanied by a trio comprising stand-up bass, drums and Denny Wright on electric guitar, tours US for a month, billed as "The Irish Hillbilly".
June *Lost John*, his first Pye solo release, hits UK #2 and makes US #58. B-side *Stewball* charts briefly at UK #27.
July *Skiffle Session* hits UK #20; the first EP by a UK artist to chart.
Sept *Bring A Little Water Sylvie* and B-side *Dead Or Alive* hits UK #7. Back from the US, Donegan and group begin a lengthy UK tour, which will hardly cease over the next 2 years, prompting would-be musicians all over the UK to form easy-to-play-in skiffle groups, many of them the roots of rock'n'roll and beat careers of the late 50s and the 60s.
Dec 10" album *Lonnie Donegan Showcase* reaches UK #26 on the Singles chart. It is the first album by a UK artist to chart (UK Album charts do not exist at this time).

1957 Feb *Don't You Rock Me Daddy-O* hits UK #4, beating off a cover from The Vipers Skiffle Group which hits at #10.
Apr *Cumberland Gap* enters UK chart at #6 while *Daddy-O* is still in the Top 10 and jumps to #1, holding top position for 4 weeks. Again, it defeats a Vipers cover version which hits UK #10.
June Donegan stars in "Skiffle Sensation Of 1957" at London's Royal Albert Hall, as double A-side *Putting On The Style*/*Gamblin' Man* hits UK #1 for 2 weeks. *Putting On The Style*, recorded live, is Donegan's first excursion from folk/blues-based material into novelty/comedy.
Nov *My Dixie Darling* hits UK #10, while Donegan films appearances in a movie version of UK TV pop music show "6.5 Special".

1958 Jan *Jack O' Diamonds* reaches UK #14.
May An adaptation of Woody Guthrie's *Grand Coolie Dam* hits UK #6.
July Double A-side *Sally Don't You Grieve*/*Betty Betty Betty* hits UK #11.
Sept *Lonesome Traveller* reaches UK #28.
Nov *Lonnie's Skiffle Party* makes UK #23.
Dec Donegan covers The Kingston Trio's US #1 *Tom Dooley*, adapting the smooth original to his more frenetic style. It hits UK #3 and stays there for 6 weeks while the original climbs to #4 behind it.

1959 Feb *Does Your Chewing Gum Lose Its Flavour (On The Bedpost Overnight?)*, originally a hit in 1924 for Ernest Hare & Billy Jones, hits UK #3.
May *Fort Worth Jail* reaches UK #14.
July A cover of Johnny Horton's US chart-topper *Battle Of New Orleans* spends 4 weeks at UK #2. Donegan is forced to substitute "bloomin" for "ruddy", which is banned by BBC radio. (This is not his first brush with the BBC censor: in 1956 *Diggin' My Potatoes* was banned for "obscenity", remaining BBC-blacklisted through the 50s.)
Sept *Sal's Got A Sugar Lip* reaches UK #13.
Dec *San Miguel* peaks at UK #19.

1960 Jan He records in US with writer/producers Leiber and Stoller. (The tracks will appear in UK as EP *Yankee Doodle Donegan*.)
Mar *My Old Man's A Dustman*, recorded live on stage in Doncaster,

S.Yorks., is first single by a UK act to enter the UK chart at #1 (only Elvis Presley achieved this previously). It stays at the top for 4 weeks.

June *I Wanna Go Home*, a version of the traditional *Wreck Of The John B*, hits UK #5. (It will be revived later by The Beach Boys as *Sloop John B*.)

Sept *Lorelei* reaches UK #10.

Nov Donegan appears with Cliff Richard and Adam Faith in the pop music segment of the Royal Variety Show in London.

Dec *Lively*, a music hall-styled novelty in Donegan's *Dustman* mode, makes UK #13, while seasonal *Virgin Mary* reaches UK #27.

1961 **June** *Have A Drink On Me* hits UK #8. (Another diplomatically altered lyric: Huddie Ledbetter's original was titled *Have A Whiff On Me*.)

Sept *Michael Row The Boat*, an uptempo contrast to The Highwaymen's (US and UK #1) gentle version, backed with *Lumbered*, hits UK #6.

[25] A belated US release of *Does Your Chewing Gum Lose Its Flavor (On The Bedpost Overnight?)* is his third and last chart entry. It hits US #5, and combined UK/US sales now top a million.

1962 **Feb** *The Comancheros*, inspired by John Wayne movie, makes UK #14.

May An uncharacteristic revival of standard ballad *The Party's Over* hits UK #9. It was recorded after he sang it in a coffee bar in Timaroo, New Zealand, on an Australasian tour just before Christmas. (It was the only song that both he and the pianist knew.)

July Another ballad, self-composed *I'll Never Fall In Love Again* is only his second UK single not to chart (though it will be a million-seller for Tom Jones in the late 60s). "Putting On The Donegan" TV series airs.

Sept *Pick A Bale Of Cotton* makes UK #11 and is his last hit single. Compilation *A Golden Age Of Donegan* is his first entry in the UK Album chart, hitting UK #3 and remaining on chart for 23 weeks.

Dec [7] He releases *The Market Song* duet with Max Miller.

1963 **Feb** Compilation *A Golden Age Of Donegan Vol. 2* reaches UK #15.

1965 **Dec** Donegan records official 1966 Soccer World Cup song, *World Cup Willie*, but it fails to chart even when England wins the competition the following summer. By now, much of his live work is in cabaret and he spends half of each year in the US, much of it in Las Vegas.

1966 His publishing company Tyler Music (Tyler being his wife's maiden name), owner of the copyright of most of his hit adaptations of traditional material and well-covered songs like *I'll Never Fall In Love Again*, signs young songwriter Justin Hayward. (Hayward will later join The Moody Blues and his songs for the group, notably *Nights In White Satin*, will prove to be huge long-term earners for Tyler.)

Nov *Auntie Maggie's Remedy* is the last release on Pye. (He will release only 8 singles in 11 years. Most are his own independent Tyler Records productions, leased variously to Decca, RCA, Black Lion and Pye for UK release.) He also appears as a regular panelist on the mid-70s UK TV talent show "New Faces".

1976 Donegan suffers a heart attack and is warned to stop working. He moves to California, in semi-retirement, to recuperate.

1978 **Mar** *Putting On The Style*, produced by Adam Faith on Chrysalis, reaches UK #51, Donegan's first chart entry for 15 years. Playing on it are Ringo Starr, Elton John, Brian May of Queen, and many others who acknowledge Donegan's influence in prompting them to play music in the first place.

1979 **May** *Sundown*, again for Chrysalis, eschews the superstars and offers more country-flavored material, recorded with the help of friend and guitarist Albert Lee. He also makes a country album with fiddle player Doug Kershaw.

1981 **Nov** *Jubilee Concert* is a live set of oldies to mark his 25th anniversary. He also records a skiffle EP with Scots group The Shakin' Pyramids.

1985 Donegan undergoes surgery after recurrent heart attacks, from which he recovers sufficiently to work again at a reasonable pace.

1986 **Dec** He forms a new band, Donegan's Dancing Sunshine Band, with clarinettist Monty Sunshine, a former colleague from the Chris Barber Band 30 years earlier.

1987 Maintaining his musical popularity worldwide via live work with the new band, Donegan, still living in California but spending 3 months each year in UK, tries some straight acting and appears in BBC TV's police drama "Rockliffe's Babies".

1989 **May** Donegan performs at the Country Music Magazine festival in Lincolnshire, despite the event's very low attendance.

1990 **Sept** Among a steady stream of Donegan compilations, the latest, *Golden Hour Of Lonnie Donegan*, is issued by Knight Records on CD.

DONOVAN

1964 Donovan (b. Donovan Phillips Leitch, Feb.10, 1946, Maryhill, Glasgow, Scotland), after moving to Hatfield, Herts., at 10, having left college after a year and having made his first public appearance at the Cock in St. Albans, Herts., is living in a seaside art studio in St. Ives, Cornwall,

writing songs between waiting tables in cafes and frequently traveling around UK to play in folk clubs with kazoo player Gypsy Dave. (While in Manchester, Gtr. Manchester, he is arrested on a charge of stealing 5,000 cigarettes and some chocolates from a cinema, and spends 2 weeks on remand in Strangeways Prison.) While performing at another seaside town, Southend, he is spotted by Geoff Stephens and Peter Eden, who offer to manage him.

1965 **Jan** Demo recordings of some of his own songs, recorded at Stephens and Eden's instigation at a Denmark Street studio in London, interest both Pye Records and Bob Bickford, a production staff member of UK TV show "Ready Steady Go!".

Feb Donovan appears on "Ready Steady Go!" for 3 consecutive weeks (first act ever to have a mini-"residency" on the show), and is signed by Pye amid widespread media comments about his apparent similarity in style and appearance (denim cap, racked harmonica, guitar inscribed "this guitar kills", etc.) to folk star Bob Dylan.

Mar Donovan and Dylan meet during Dylan's UK tour (documented in D.A. Pennebaker's fly-on-the wall film "Don't Look Back"). Donovan's debut *Catch The Wind* enters the UK chart simultaneously with Dylan's first UK single *The Times They Are A-Changin'*.

Apr *Catch The Wind* hits UK #4 (Dylan's single peaks at UK #9).

[11] Donovan appears at the **New Musical Express** Poll Winners concert at Wembley Empire Pool, London, with The Beatles, The Rolling Stones, Tom Jones and others.

May Donovan and Joan Baez lead a Vietnam War protest march to Trafalgar Square in London.

June *What's Bin Did And What's Bin Hid*, including 6 of his own songs, hits UK #3.

[3] Donovan stars on the first folk and C&W series on BBC Radio, "Folk Room".

[5] He appears on UK TV's "Thank Your Lucky Stars".

July *Colours* hits UK #4.

[3] *Catch The Wind*, released in US by country/folk label Hickory Records, reaches US #23.

[7] Donovan flies to the US for a 4-day visit to promote the single, appearing on TV shows "Shindig" and "The Hollywood Palace". While there, he appears at The Newport Folk Festival, ironically on the same bill as Bob Dylan, who is booed for playing an electric set backed by The Paul Butterfield Blues Band.

Sept *Universal Soldier*, written by Buffy Saint-Marie, heads a 4-track EP of the same title devoted to anti-war protest songs (the other 3 penned by Mick Softley, Bert Jansch and Donovan). It reaches UK #13.

[6-7] Donovan films a promo clip of *Universal Soldier* for BBC TV's "Top Of The Pops" on D-Day landing beaches in Normandy, France.

[18] *Colours* peaks at US #61 and *Catch The Wind* makes US #30.

[25] Donovan begins a 28-day UK tour.

[30] Donovan's ABC TV "Shindig" debut airs.

Oct His solicitors announce that he has ended his management contract with Stephens and Eden and signed with Ashley Kozak as his business manager and his father as his personal manager, although remaining with Allen Klein in US. They also announce that the Vic Lewis Organization will act as his agents. Stephens and Eden immediately serve a High Court writ on the solicitors to prevent Donovan working with anyone else but them.

[15] He takes part in a "Ban The Bomb" concert at the Fairfield Hall, Croydon, London.

[30] *Universal Soldier* peaks at US #53. (Glen Campbell's cover makes US #45.)

Nov *Turquoise* reaches UK #30. *Fairy Tale*, mostly self-written, reaches UK #20.

[19] Donovan takes part in the Glad Rag Ball at Wembley Empire Pool, with The Hollies, The Kinks, The Who, The Merseybeats, Georgie Fame, Wilson Pickett and The Barron Knights.

Dec He records with producer Mickie Most. First result, a move away from Donovan's folk context to more experimental pop fields, is initially titled *For John And Paul*, then amended to *Sunshine Superman*. Donovan begins a 2-week Scandinavian tour at the Tivoli Gardens, Copenhagen, Denmark.

1966 **Jan** *Fairy Tale* peaks at US #85.

[19] "A Boy Called Donovan" special airs on ITV.

Feb Pye pulls *Sunshine Superman* from its release schedule while Donovan is in dispute with his original management and issues earlier recording *Josie* as a UK single, but it does not chart.

Mar [14] Donovan begins a 28-day European tour of Germany, Austria, Switzerland, France, Belgium and Holland.

July As the Donovan/Most production deal is cleared, they sign to

Epic Records for US, continuing to lease productions to Pye in UK.

Sept [3] Released first in US, *Sunshine Superman* hits #1 for a week and earns Donovan a first gold disk for a million-plus sales.

Oct *Sunshine Superman* reaches US #11 and *The Real Donovan*, a compilation of earlier tracks on Hickory, makes US #96.

Dec [10] *Mellow Yellow*, arranged by John Paul Jones and with "whispering" vocal assistance from Paul McCartney, hits US #2 and is a second million-seller, despite being banned in Boston, MA, for allegedly being about abortion. (Donovan has supplied somewhat louder than "whispering" vocal assistance on The Beatles' *Yellow Submarine*.)

1967 **Jan** *Sunshine Superman* hits UK #2. Donovan is commissioned by the National Theatre to compose incidental music for a new production of Shakespeare's "As You Like It", starring Laurence Olivier.

[15] Donovan gives a 1-man concert at London's Royal Albert Hall, including the 12-min. ballet "Golden Apples".

Feb [2-3] He takes part in the Cannes International Festival, France.

Mar *Mellow Yellow* hits UK #8.

[11] *Epistle To Dippy*, never released as a UK single, reaches US #19. *Mellow Yellow* (also not issued in UK) makes US #14.

Apr [24] He begins 6-night engagement at the Saville theater, London.

June [25] He joins an all-star chorus for live TV broadcast at EMI's London studios of the recording of The Beatles' *All You Need Is Love*.

July UK version of *Sunshine Superman* (a compilation of tracks from US albums *Sunshine Superman* and *Mellow Yellow*), reaches UK #25.

Aug [13] Donovan plays on the final day of the seventh National Blues Festival at the Royal Windsor Racecourse, Berks.

Sept [16] *There Is A Mountain*, with lyrics from a 16th-century Japanese haiku poem and featuring striking flute work by Harold McNair, reaches US #11.

Nov Budget album *Universal Soldier*, compiled from earlier EP and single tracks, hits UK #5. *There Is A Mountain* hits UK #8.

Dec [30] *Wear Your Love Like Heaven* reaches US #23.

1968 **Jan** Boxed double album *A Gift From A Flower To A Garden*, with a set of commercial material (including recent hit single) and another of children's songs, makes US #19 and earns a gold disk. The material is also released as 2 separate single albums, *Wear Your Love Like Heaven* and *For Little Ones*, which climb to US #60 and #185 respectively.

Feb [19] Donovan flies to India (in the wake of The Beatles) to attend a Transcendental Meditation course under Maharishi Mahesh Yogi and becomes his disciple for a while.

Mar *Jennifer Juniper*, written about Jenny Boyd, hits UK #5. The B-side *Poor Cow* is from the film of the same name, to which Donovan contributes several soundtrack songs.

Apr [20] *Jennifer Juniper* reaches US #26. *Like it Is, Was And Evermore Shall Be*, a compilation on Hickory, climbs to US #177.

May *A Gift From A Flower To A Garden* reaches UK #13.

June [2] Donovan plays at the "Barn Barbecue Concert & Barn Dance" at Whittlesey, near Peterborough, Northants., with John Mayall's Bluesbreakers, Fairport Convention, Blossom Toes, Fleetwood Mac, Move, James & Bobby Purify, Amen Corner and others.

July *Hurdy Gurdy Man* hits UK #4.

[7] He performs on the second day of the Woburn Music Festival in Woburn, Beds., with Fleetwood Mac, John Mayall's Bluesbreakers, Champion Jack Dupree, Tim Rose, Taste and Duster Bennett.

Aug [3] *Hurdy Gurdy Man* hits US #5.

Sept Live *Donovan In Concert*, recorded in US at the Anaheim Convention Center, CA, earlier in the year on tour, reaches US #18.

Nov [2] *Lalena*, unreleased in UK as a single, reaches US #33.

Dec *Atlantis* reaches UK #23. *The Hurdy Gurdy Man* (not released in UK) makes US #20.

1969 Donovan contributes songs to the movie "If It's Tuesday, This Must Be Belgium", starring Suzanne Pleshette and Ian McShane.

Mar [1] *To Susan On The West Coast Waiting*, again unissued in UK, makes US #35.

Apr Compilation *Donovan's Greatest Hits* hits US #4. It gains another gold disk but fails to chart in UK.

May [24] *Atlantis*, originally B-side of *To Susan On The West Coast Waiting*, out-performs its A-side and hits US #7.

Aug *Barabajagal (Love Is Hot)*, recorded with The Jeff Beck Group with Lesley Duncan and Madeleine Bell on backing vocals, reaches UK #12. It is Donovan's last UK hit single.

Sept [6] *Barabajagal (Love Is Hot)* makes US #36.

Oct *Barabajagal*, including several former hit singles, reaches US #23, but is not issued in UK.

Nov Hickory compilation *The Best Of Donovan* makes US #144.

1970 Donovan splits from Mickie Most, forming his own band Open Road, for live and studio work.

June [28] He appears at the Bath Festival Of Progressive Music with Led Zeppelin, Pink Floyd and others in Bath, Avon.

Aug [30] Donovan plays on the final day of the Isle of Wight Festival.

Sept *Open Road*, described by Donovan as an experiment in "Celtic Rock" reaches US #16 and UK #30.

[26] *Riki Tiki Tavi* peaks at US #55.

Oct Donovan marries Linda Lawrence, former girlfriend of Rolling Stone Brian Jones.

Dec Double album *Donovan P. Leitch*, a compilation of material originally released in US by Hickory, appears on Janus Records, peaking at US #128. Open Road breaks up.

1971 **Mar** *Celia Of The Seals* (on which Open Road bassist Danny Thompson has dual billing) fails to chart in UK but reaches US #84. (He spends some months writing songs and music for, and acting the title role in, David Puttnam-produced Jacques Demy film fantasy "The Pied Piper". After the filming, he moves to Ireland for an extended period, forced for tax reasons to stay outside the UK.)

July Double album *HMS Donovan*, including a selection of children's songs set to the words of Lewis Carroll, Edward Lear and W. B. Yeats, fails to chart in both US and UK, and is his last recording for Pye in UK.

Oct [21] Donovan becomes a father to daughter Astrella.

1972 He writes the score for Franco Zefferelli's film "Brother Sun, Sister Moon". While still living in Ireland, he tours with folk group Planxty.

Sept He reunites with Mickie Most and a new UK deal is signed with Epic Records. (The reunion lasts through the recording of 1 album.)

1973 **Mar** *Cosmic Wheels*, produced by Most and recorded with a star session band including Chris Spedding (guitar), Jim Horn (sax) and Cozy Powell (drums), reaches UK #15 and US #25. (It is Donovan's last album to make the UK chart.)

June [2] Extracted *I Like You* is his final US hit single, peaking at #66.

1974 **Feb** *Essence To Essence*, produced by Andrew Oldham with Carole King and Peter Frampton guesting, reaches US #174. After its release, Donovan moves to California.

Dec *7-Tease*, produced in Nashville by Norbert Putnam, is a studio concept album based on the theatrical show with the same title (with dancers, costumes, lighting and visual effects) which Donovan has staged in California during the year. It reaches US #135.

1975 He tours Australia and New Zealand, and spends much of the year resting in California with his family.

1976 **June** [19] Self-produced, US-recorded *Slow Down World* reaches US #174 and is his final US chart entry.

1977 **Oct** Another reunion with Most, and a recording move to Most's RAK label, produces *Donovan*, which does not chart.

1978 **Jan** Extracted single *Dare To Be Different* is released.

1980 **Aug** He performs at the Edinburgh Festival in Scotland and records *Neutronica* and *Love Is The Only Feeling*, released in Germany.

Dec He appears with Billy Connolly and Ralph McTell on a Christmas benefit show for children's charities at the London Palladium.

1981 **Nov** He forms a new stage band, with Danny Thompson (bass), Tony Roberts (sax, flute and woodwinds) and John Stephens (drums), who play on unsuccessful single *Lay Down Lassie* and *Love Is Only Feeling*. (His career remains quiet through the 80s, with occasional low-key tours and little in the way of recordings.)

1983 Donovan makes a recording comeback with producer Jerry Wexler, re-working earlier hits *Sunshine Superman* and *Season Of The Witch* for Allegiance label album *Lady Of The Stars*.

1989 Donovan signs to Polygram, as he takes a back seat to his successful Hollywood film acting children, Donovan Leitch and Iona Skye.

1990 **Nov** [26] Increasingly hip once more, Donovan supports The Happy Mondays at the Wembley Arena, as his new album *Rising* is released.

Dec [1] Donovan teams with UK TV comic spoof folk duo The Singing Corner to rejuvenate *Jennifer Juniper*, which peaks at UK #68.

JASON DONOVAN

1979 **Oct** Donovan (b. Jason Sean Donovan, June 1, 1968, Malvern, a suburb of Melbourne, Australia), his UK-born father Terry one of Australia's best known actors and his mother TV presenter Sue McIntosh, auditions for upcoming TV soap opera "Skyways" and gets the role, opposite actress Kylie Minogue, who is 3 days older than Donovan.

1986 After further Australian TV roles in "I Can Jump Puddles", "Home" and "Marshland", he lands the part of Scott Robinson in new daily soap opera "Neighbours" (once again playing opposite Minogue, now starring as his girlfriend Charlene – the couple will have a TV wedding, though their much rumored private union will never be confirmed), having just passed his Higher School Certificate at De La Salle College in Malvern.

987 Donovan wins the "Logie" award for Best New Talent and is awarded a commendation as Best Actor from the Australian Television Society.

988 He wins the silver "Logie" award as Most Popular Actor, and is approached by Mushroom Records to consider a career in music. Australian band Noiseworks offer him a song, and as a result he visits London to record 2 songs with Pete Hammond at PWL studios. PWL supremo Pete Waterman, who has already successfully manoeuvred Minogue's singing career, suggests that he record a Stock/Aitken/Waterman track. While still a regular on "Neighbours", he also plays "Happy" Huston in World War II TV mini-series.
Sept PWL debut *Nothing Can Divide Us* hits UK #5.

989 **Jan** [7] Duet with Kylie Minogue, *Especially For You* tops UK chart, selling more than 950,000 copies, helped by a kiss'n'cuddle performance on BBC TV's "Top Of The Pops".
Mar Donovan receives "Logie" nominations as Most Popular Personality, Most Popular Actor and Most Popular Music Video.
[11] *Too Many Broken Hearts* tops UK chart, selling over 500,000 copies, and establishes Donovan as major teen throb pin-up in UK.
Apr He embarks on Pete Waterman-hosted UK "Hit Man Roadshow" tour, singing 4 songs to backing tracks. He also films his last appearance for "Neighbours", convinced that a music career based in the UK is the best way forward.
May [20] *Ten Good Reasons* tops UK chart, will be awarded multi-platinum status, and become one of the best-sellers of the year.
June [10] *Sealed With A Kiss*, a cover of Brian Hyland's 1962 US and UK #3, tops UK chart.
Sept *Every Day (I Love You More)* hits UK #2.
Dec *When You Come Back To Me*, including seasonal Christmas lyrics, hits UK #2.

990 **Apr** [14] *Hang On To Your Love*, yet another S/A/W composition and production, hits UK #8.
June [9] *Between The Lines* debuts at UK #2, behind Soul II Soul's *Soul II Soul (1990 A New Decade)*.
July [7] *Another Night* reaches UK #18, breaking Donovan's run of 6 straight UK Top 10 hits.
Sept [8] A remake of The Cascades' 1963 US #3 *Rhythm Of The Rain* hits UK #9.
[10] Donovan begins 10-date UK tour in Southampton, Hants. Tour will end Sept.23 with the last of 3 nights at the Hammersmith Odeon, London.
Nov [10] *I'm Doing Fine*, possibly hindered by Beatles-mimicking promo video, reaches UK #22, as teen interest in Donovan wanes.

HE DOOBIE BROTHERS

atrick Simmons (guitar, vocals)
lichael McDonald (keyboards, synthesizers, vocals)
ff "Skunk" Baxter (guitars)
iran Porter (bass)
hn Hartman (drums)
eith Knudsen (drums, vocals)

970 **Mar** Group is formed in San Jose, CA, under the name Pud, playing free Sunday concerts in a local park. It comprises Johnston (b. Visalia, CA), who studied graphic design at San Jose State, and was introduced by Moby Grape's Skip Spence to Hartman (b. Mar.18, 1950, Falls Church, VA), recently arrived from West Virginia with the intention of re-forming his favorite band Moby Grape, and bassist Greg Murph, who is soon replaced by Dave Shogren (b. San Francisco, CA). They begin jamming in a house on Twelfth Street, frequented by members of San Jose's Hells Angels.
Sept Simmons (b. Jan.23, 1950, San Jose), a folk/bluegrass guitarist, joins, and the group becomes The Doobie Brothers ("Doobie" being California slang for a marijuana joint), at the suggestion of room-mate Keith Rosen. They become the house band at the Chateau Liberte, a saloon in the Santa Cruz mountains. A 6-track demo is sent by Pacific Recording studios owner Paul Curcio to Lenny Waronker at Warner Bros. Records, which signs them.

971 **Apr** *The Doobie Brothers*, produced by Ted Templeman (ex-Harper's Bizarre), fails to chart, despite the extensive Warner Bros.-sponsored "Mother Brothers" US tour to promote it.
Oct Porter, previously in a folk trio, replaces Shogren on bass, and Mike Hossack (b. Sept.18, 1950, Patterson, NJ), a second drummer/percussionist, is added to boost the live sound.

1972 **Oct** *Toulouse Street*, the group's US chart debut, reaches #21 and earns a gold disk, during a 119-week stay on the chart.
Nov [4] Johnston-penned *Listen To The Music*, taken from it, makes US #11, and will remain one of their most enduring and popular numbers.

1973 **Feb** [24] *Jesus Is Just Alright*, previously recorded by The Byrds, reaches US #35.
June *The Captain And Me* hits US #7 and is another gold disk.
[30] Extracted from it, *Long Train Runnin'* hits US #8.
Sept Hossack quits to form his own band Bonaroo, and is replaced on percussion by Knudsen (b. Oct.18, 1952, Ames, IA), ex-drummer with Lee Michaels' band.
Oct [6] *China Grove*, the third hit penned by Johnston, makes US #15.
Dec [24] Johnston is arrested in Visalia, CA, for marijuana possession.

1974 **Jan** [26] Group plays the Rainbow, London, the first of 4 UK dates on its first European tour.
Apr [6] *Listen To The Music* makes UK #29.
What Were Once Vices Are Now Habits hits US #4, earning another gold disk, and is the band's first UK chart album, at #19. It includes session guitar contributions from Baxter (b. Dec.13, 1948, Washington, DC), who is with Steely Dan, but plays live with The Doobie Brothers between Steely Dan commitments.
June [8] *Another Park, Another Sunday* reaches US #32, with the group consistently touring US.
July With the demise of Steely Dan as a live band, Baxter joins The Doobie Brothers full-time, completing their ambition to field a 3-guitar line-up on stage. They return to UK to play the Knebworth Festival.
Aug [31] *Eyes Of Silver* makes US #52.
Nov [16] *Nobody* peaks at US #58.

1975 **Jan** [12] Group opens an 18-show, 9-city tour of UK and Europe as part of Warner's "Looney Tunes" package, with Little Feat, Graham Central Station, Bonaroo, Montrose, and Tower Of Power.
Mar [15] Simmons' composition *Black Water*, originally B-side of *Another Park, Another Sunday*, hits US #1 for 1 week and is their first million-selling single.
Apr While on a 7-week US tour, Johnston becomes ill with a stomach disorder and has to drop out. Ex-Steely Dan vocalist/keyboards player McDonald (b. Dec.2, 1952, St. Louis, MO) is recruited at Baxter's suggestion; after rehearsing for 48 hours in New Orleans, LA, he joins the tour as a full-time member.
May Baxter makes a guest appearance on guitar at Elton John's London concert.
June *Stampede*, recorded prior to McDonald's arrival, hits US #4 and makes UK #14, and is the group's fourth gold album.
[21] From it, a revival of Holland/Dozier/Holland's *Take Me In Your Arms (Rock Me)* (a US hit for Kim Weston) reaches US #11 and UK #29.
[29] At a concert in Oakland, CA, Elton John joins the band to duet on *Listen To The Music*.
Aug [30] *Sweet Maxine* makes US #40.
Sept Band plays the Great American Music Fair in Syracuse, NY, an event marred by violent conflict between would-be free festival demonstrators and state troopers.
Oct Playing a concert in Nashville, TN, the band discovers that its chauffeur, provided by local Limos Unlimited, is a undercover narcotics agent. Returning to their hired plane after the concert, they find it surrounded by police. A search at 3am only reveals a bottle of vitamins.

1976 **Jan** [17] *I Cheat The Hangman* reaches US #60, as Johnston rejoins after his illness.
Apr [17] *Takin' It To The Streets* makes UK #42.
May [22] *Takin' It To The Streets* hits US #8. It is the band's first album to be certified platinum for million-plus US sales. Extracted title track, penned by McDonald, reaches US #13.
July [17] Band backs Carly Simon on her US #46 hit of McDonald composition *It Keeps You Runnin'*.
Sept [4] *Wheels Of Fortune* peaks at US #87.

1977 **Jan** [22] *Best Of The Doobies*, a compilation of hit singles, hits US #5, earning the group's second platinum album.
[29] *It Keeps You Runnin'* (included on the compilation album) makes US #37. Johnston leaves the band for a solo career.
May [7] The Doobie Brothers participate in Bill Graham's "Day On The Green #1" at Oakland Stadium, CA, in front of 57,500 fans.
July [1] Band opens a month's US tour at Rushmore Civic Plaza, Rapid City, SD.
Aug [27] A second Motown revival, of Marvin Gaye's 1966 hit *Little Darling (I Need You)*, makes US #48.
[28] Group plays the Reading Festival, Berks., as part of a short 4-date UK tour, now presenting a tighter, funkier sound (the pervasive

influence of McDonald) than their earlier guitar boogie.

Sept [17] *Livin' On The Fault Line* reaches UK #25.

[27] Band plays the "Rock'N'Bowl" at South Bay Bowl, Redondo Beach, CA, a benefit concert for US Special Olympics.

Oct [15] *Living On The Fault Line* hits US #10 (earning a gold disk).

Nov [12] *Echoes Of Love* peaks at US #66.

1978 Jan [28] Group guests on ABC TV sitcom "What's Happening!!"

July [1] The Doobie Brothers play the Catalyst, Santa Cruz, CA, in a benefit show for veteran actor Will Geer.

Aug [26] Band performs in Ontario, Canada, at the first Canada Jam festival, to 80,000 people, sharing the bill with The Commodores, Kansas, The Village People, Dave Mason, and Atlanta Rhythm Section.

1979 Mar With the band's new single and album climbing up the US chart and showing signs of being their all-time best-sellers, both Baxter and Hartman decide to leave, the former to return to session work and production, the latter to quit music and return to his horse ranch in Sonoma County.

[10] *What A Fool Believes* makes UK #31.

Apr [7] *Minute By Minute*, the result of their move into funky soul, tops US chart for 5 weeks, and is their third US million-selling album.

[14] Taken from it, *What A Fool Believes*, written by McDonald and Kenny Loggins, is the band's second US #1 (for 1 week) and second million-selling single.

May After extensive auditions, ex-Moby Grape keyboards and sax player Cornelius Bumpus (b. Jan.13, 1952), experienced session drummer Chet McCracken (b. July 17, 1952, Seattle, WA), and ex-Clover guitarist John McFee (b. Nov.18, 1953, Santa Cruz, CA), replace the departed members in time for a summer US tour.

June [23] Extracted title track *Minute By Minute* reaches US #14.

July [1] The Doobie Brothers celebrate their 10th anniversary at Los Angeles' Friars club, with Eddie Floyd, The Jacksons, Kenny Loggins and Sam And Dave joining the band in an all-star jam of *Soul Man*.

[21] *Minute By Minute* makes UK #47.

Sept [19-23] Band plays in the Musicians United For Safe Energy (MUSE) anti-nuclear concerts at New York's Madison Square Garden, alongside Bruce Springsteen, Jackson Browne, Carly Simon and others.

Oct [13] *Dependin' On You* reaches US #25.

Dec Johnston, signed to Warner Bros. as a soloist, makes US #100 with his album *Everything You've Heard Is True*.

1980 Jan [10] Johnston's *Savannah Nights* reaches US #34.

Feb [27] The Doobie Brothers win Record Of The Year and Song Of The Year for *What A Fool Believes*, Best Pop Vocal Performance By A Duo Or Group Or Chorus for *Minute By Minute* and McDonald wins Best Arrangement Accompanying Vocalist(s) for *What A Fool Believes* at the 22nd Grammy awards.

July [16] Movie "No Nukes", documenting the previous year's Madison Square Garden anti-nuclear concerts, including a set by The Doobie Brothers, premieres in New York.

Oct [25] *Real Love* hits US #5. It is taken from *One Step Closer*, which hits US #3 (their fourth and last platinum album) and UK #53.

Nov Porter quits both the group and the music scene, and session bassist Willie Weeks joins in his place for live work.

1981 Jan [10] Extracted title track *One Step Closer* reaches US #24.

Feb [7] *Wynken, Blynken And Nod* (taken from the various artists album *In Harmony* on Sesame Street Records which makes US #156 at the same time), climbs to US #76.

Mar [7] *Keep This Train A-Rollin'* peaks at US #62.

June Johnston's solo album *Still Feels Good* makes US #158.

Oct After a concert in Hawaii to complete touring for the year, the band decides to split. Simmons and McDonald are both working on solo albums, and it is felt there is too much conflict of interest within the group to continue.

Dec Compilation album *Best Of The Doobies, Volume II* reaches US #39, and earns the band's last gold disk.

1982 Feb [20] *Here To Love You* peaks at US #65.

Mar [31] The official break-up of the group is announced, with news of a forthcoming temporary re-formation for a farewell US tour.

Aug McDonald begins his successful solo career with *I Keep Forgettin'* (*Every Time You're Near*) and *If That's What It Takes*.

Sept Group plays its farewell US tour, with Warner Bros. recording performances for a final live album. (Even after the band splits, they will still reunite to play an annual benefit show for Stanford children's hospital, where they have a wing named after them.)

1983 May [7] *So Wrong*, Simmons' first solo, reaches US #30.

June Simmons' *Arcade*, on Elektra, peaks at US #52.

[2] Simmons' *Don't Make Me Do It* (written by Huey Lewis & The News) climbs to US #75.

Aug Double live *The Doobie Brothers Farewell Tour* reaches US #79.

[6] *You Belong To Me* (previously a hit for Carly Simon, and a song co-written by McDonald and Simon via mail), also peaks at US #79.

1986 Dec [17] The Doobie Brothers reunite for a benefit concert at Stanford University. This will lead to a permanent re-formation 4 months later.

1987 Jan *What A Fool Believes*, reissued as a featured track from McDonald's *Sweet Freedom: Best of Michael McDonald*, peaks at UK #57.

June [21] A new line-up of The Doobie Brothers, with Johnston back (but without McDonald), plays the last of 10 reunion concerts, at the Mountain Aire Festival, CA.

July [4] Band participates in "The July Fourth Disarmament Festival" in the Soviet Union with James Taylor, Santana, Bonnie Raitt and several Russian groups.

1988 Group, with original members Johnston, Simmons, Hartman, Porter and Hossack, returns to the studio to record a comeback album for Capitol Records.

1989 June Group embarks on major US "Cycles" tour to promote its comeback album. They are joined by Dale Ockerman (keyboards), Jimmy Fox (percussion), Richard Bryant (vocals) and Cornelius Bumpus (keyboards/saxophone) taking lead vocals on the Michael McDonald-written Doobie songs.

July [12] Caygua County Fair, Weedsport, NY, gig is cancelled when Johnston comes down with laryngitis. Further concerts will be cancelled.

[15] *The Doctor* hits US #9 as parent album *Cycles* reaches US #17.

[29] *The Doctor* peaks at UK #73.

Sept [16] *Need A Little Taste Of Love* makes US #45.

1991 Apr *Brotherhood* is released.

THE DOORS

Jim Morrison (vocals)
Ray Manzarek (keyboards)
Robbie Krieger (guitar)
John Densmore (drums)

1964 Feb Morrison (b. Dec.8, 1943, Melbourne, FL), son of a US Navy man, after dropping out of Florida State University, enrols in the Theater Arts Department of California's UCLA. 2 months after graduating, he meets Manzarek (b. Feb.12, 1935, Chicago, IL), a prodigal classical pianist who plays in blues band Rick & The Ravens, with his brothers Rick and Jim on weekends at a Santa Monica, CA, bar, and already recording for local Aura label, on a Venice, Los Angeles, CA, beach.

1965 July Morrison, who has already begun substantial abuse of drugs and alcohol experimentation which will always remain close to his image, and Manzarek decide to form a group after Morrison sings his song *Moonlight Drive* to Manzarek, who recruits Densmore (b. Dec.1, 1945, Los Angeles), a physics and psychology major, having met him in a TM course at Los Angeles' Third Street Meditation Center.

Sept Morrison, Manzarek and Densmore record a demo of Morrison's songs *Moonlight Drive*, *Summer's Almost Gone*, *Break On Through* and *End Of The Night* at World Pacific studios. They are helped by the other 2 Manzareks and a female bass player, who all leave immediately afterwards because they dislike the material. Columbia's Billy James signs the group. Former jug band/bottleneck guitarist Krieger (b. Jan.8, 1946, Los Angeles) (variously spelling his forename Robbie or Robby) who has earlier played with Densmore in The Psychedelic Rangers band, is recruited on guitar.

1966 Morrison names the group The Doors, inspired not by William Blake's "There are things that are known and things that are unknown: in between are doors" from his poem "The Doors: Open And Closed", which he reads in Aldous Huxley's document of a mescaline experience, **The Doors Of Perception**, but by another quotation within the Huxley text, "all the other chemical Doors in the Wall are labelled Dope ...." After rehearsing for 5 months, they play at the London Fog club on Sunset Boulevard, and on the last night of their tenure are seen by the booker at the Whisky A-Go-Go, who hires them to a residency as the house band. During a 6-month stint at the Whisky, they obtain a release from Columbia and are then seen by Love's Arthur Lee who recommends them to his label boss Jac Holzman, who sees them and then signs them to Elektra, before they are fired for performing Morrison's *The End*.

1967 Jan Debut album *The Doors* (on which Krieger is credited as Robby Krieger), establishes a powerful, theatrical, rock-blues style, and will hit US #2 during a 121-week stay on the chart. Extacted single *Break On Through* does not chart.

July [29] *Light My Fire*, extracted from the album in a much-abridged version (the original is, at 6 mins. 50 secs., considered too long), tops US chart for 3 weeks, sells over a million, and gives Elektra its first #1. (Band will turn down a $50,000 offer to use it in Buick car TV ad.)

Aug [16] *Light My Fire* makes UK #49.

Sept [17] Band appears on CBS TV's "Ed Sullivan Show", on which they are requested to omit the line "girl, we couldn't get much higher" from *Light My Fire*. They agree, then Morrison sings it anyway.

Oct [28] *People Are Strange*, from forthcoming album, reaches US #12.

Nov *Strange Days* hits US #3.

Dec [9] Morrison is arrested after a concert in New Haven, CT, during which he has badmouthed the police. He is charged with a breach of the peace and resisting arrest.

968 Jan [13] *Love Me Two Times*, from *Strange Days*, makes US #25.

Feb Univeral Pictures offers the band $500,000 to star in a feature film. (It is never made.)

May [4] *The Unknown Soldier* makes US #39. The band makes its own promo film for it which includes Morrison being "shot".

[10] Morrison, although not arrested, upsets law enforcers again when he incites a crowd to riot during a concert in Chicago.

[18] Band appears at Northern California Rock Festival with The Grateful Dead, The Steve Miller Band and others.

July [5-6] The Doors play at the Hollywood Bowl, Hollywood, CA, with Steppenwolf and The Chambers Brothers. The show, which is filmed, will subsequently be released on video "The Doors Live At The Hollywood Bowl".

Aug [3] *Hello I Love You*, an atypical commercial pop song, is The Doors' second US #1 (for 2 weeks) and second million-seller.

Sept [7] *Waiting For the Sun*, containing *Hello I Love You*, is the band's only US chart-topping album, spending 4 weeks at #1. (The sleeve contains the full libretto of Morrison's theatrical poem "Celebration Of The Lizard", which will not appear on record until the 1970 album *Absolutely Live*.) The Doors are filling major US rock venues but Morrison's hard-drinking, drug-infused lifestyle and overtly sexual deportment make the band a controversial success. *Hello I Love You* reaches UK #15 as the group visits UK for promotion and concerts, making its BBC TV "Top Of The Pops" debut.

Oct [6] A film documentary, "The Doors Are Open", made in London, is shown on UK TV. *Waiting For The Sun* reaches UK #16, the group's first album success in UK.

969 Feb [15] *Touch Me* hits US #3 and is another million-seller.

Mar [1] After a concert at the Dinner Key Auditorium in Miami, FL, Morrison is charged with "lewd and lascivious behavior in public by exposing his private parts and by simulating masturbation and oral copulation", in addition to profanity, drunkenness and other minor offenses. The prospect of court appearances makes tour booking impossible for the next 5 months.

Apr [3] Morrison is arrested in Los Angeles by the FBI and charged with interstate flight to avoid prosecution on his Miami charges.

[19] *Wishful Sinful* makes US #44.

June [5] Band premieres its documentary film "Feast Of Friends" at Cinemathica 16 in Los Angeles. Local politicians in St. Louis, MO, and Hawaii force cancellations of scheduled Doors appearances.

Aug [2] *Tell All The People* peaks at US #57.

Sept *Runnin' Blue* peaks at US #64 as *The Soft Parade* hits US #6.

[13] Band plays at the "Toronto Rock'N'Roll Revival Show", with John Lennon's Plastic Ono Band, Chuck Berry and others, in the Varsity Stadium at Toronto University, Canada.

Nov [11] Morrison is arrested after trying to interfere with an air hostess on a plane from Los Angeles to Phoenix, AZ. The charge is the potentially very serious one of interfering with the flight of an aircraft, as well as public drunkenness. (It will be dropped when the hostess withdraws her evidence.)

970 Jan [17-18] The Doors play 2 nights at New York's Felt Forum, recorded (as are several later concerts) for a live album.

Apr *Morrison Hotel* hits US #4 and UK #12. 1 song on it, *Queen Of The Highway*, is dedicated to Morrison's new wife, Pamela.

[10] At a Doors concert in Boston, MA, Morrison once again uncomfortable at keeping his clothes on, askes the crowd if they want to see his genitals.

May [2] *You Make Me Real/Roadhouse Blues*, taken from the album, makes US #50.

Aug [29] The Doors perform alongside Joni Mitchell, The Who, Sly & The Family Stone and others at the second day of the Isle of Wight Festival, UK.

Sept Double album *Absolutely Live*, recorded in Jan. in New York, which contains a full version of *Celebration Of The Lizard*, hits US #8 at a time when live performances by the group are sporadic.

[20] In a Miami court, Morrison is found guilty of indecent exposure and profanity, though he is acquitted on the charge of "lewd and lascivious behavior".

[26] *Absolutely Live* peaks at UK #69.

Oct [30] Morrison is sentenced for the offenses of which he was found guilty in Sept. and receives 8 months' hard labor, followed by 28 months probation, and a $500 fine by Judge Murray Goodman. He will remain free while the sentence is appealed.

Nov [8] On his 27th birthday, Morrison makes the recordings of his poetry (which will later form the basis of *An American Prayer*).

[12] The Doors play their last concert with Morrison in New Orleans, LA. (They will complete recording of another album which will be released as *L.A. Woman* 6 months later.)

1971 Jan Compilation *Doors 13* reaches US #25.

Mar Morrison moves to Paris, France to concentrate on writing poetry. His first book **The Lords And The New Creatures** goes into paperback after selling an initial 15,000 in hardback. Rest of the band continues to rehearse weekly in the hope that its focal figure will to return to music.

May [15] *Love Her Madly* is the band's biggest single for over 2 years, reaching US #11.

June *L.A. Woman*, recorded in the last sessions with Morrison with Jerry Scheff (bass) and Marc Benno (rhythm guitar) helping, hits US #9.

July [3] Morrison is found dead in a bathtub in Paris. The cause of death is given as a "heart attack induced by respiratory problems", the suddenness of the death leading to much speculation.

[9] His family having disowned him, Morrison is buried in the Père Lachaise cemetery in Paris (where his grave will become a graffiti-covered shrine). The cemetery also contains the remains of Oscar Wilde, Edith Piaf, Chopin and Balzac.

Sept [4] *Riders On The Storm* reaches US #14. It is extracted from *L.A. Woman* which climbs to UK #28, having just received a gold disk for a half-million sales in US.

Nov [25] Manzarek, Krieger and Densmore announce that they will continue as The Doors.

Dec [4] *Riders On The Storm* reaches UK #22. The remaining Doors trio releases *Other Voices*, which reaches US #31.

[25] *Tightrope Ride*, a track without Morrison, peaks at US #71.

1972 Apr Double compilation album *Weird Scenes Inside The Gold Mine* climbs to US #55 and UK #50

Sept The trio releases *Full Circle* which reaches US #68.

Oct [21] *The Mosquito* climbs to US #85.

Dec With inspiration hard to come by, and deprived of its single most important element, the band breaks up. (Manzarek will record 2 solo albums and produce many other acts. Kreiger and Densmore will form The Butts Band with Jess Roden, Phillip Chen and Roy Davies, before moving on to session and solo work. Kriger will also form Robbie Krieger & Friends and Versions in his own right.)

1973 Oct Another Doors compilation album, *Best Of The Doors*, reaches US #158, after the group has announced its break-up.

1974 Apr [25] Pamela Morrison dies from a suspected heroin overdose.

1975 Manzarek releases solo albums *The Golden Scarab* and *The Whole Thing Started With R'N'R*.

1976 Apr [10] *Riders On The Storm*, re-released in the UK, reaches #33.

1979 Jan When the 1970 tapes of Morrison reciting his poetry are unearthed, the other 3 former Doors reunite to provide a musical backing for the words and, along with snippets of original live performances, the results are released as *An American Prayer – Jim Morrison*. It makes US #54, rekindling interest in the group.

Feb [10] A picture-disk reissue of *Hello I Love You* peaks at UK #71.

Aug Morrison's most controversial song from The Doors' first album, *The End*, is prominently featured on the soundtrack of Francis Ford Coppola's film "Apocalypse Now".

1980 Manzarek will produce the first of 4 albums, over the next 3 years, for the band X.

Nov A fresh retrospective, *The Doors' Greatest Hits*, reaches US #17.

1981 July On the 10th anniversary of Morrison's death, Manzarek, Krieger and Densmore lead fans in a graveside tribute ceremony in Paris.

Sept [18] The compilation album *The Doors' Greatest Hits* is awarded a platinum disk for US sales of over a million.

1983 Nov *Alive, She Cried*, an album compiled from live tapes lost for over a decade but discovered in a Los Angeles warehouse after the former band members initiate a search for old material, reaches US #23 and UK #36.

1984 Jan [7] Extracted from the album, *Gloria* (recorded at a soundcheck in 1969) reaches US #71.

1985 June *Classics* makes US #124.

THE DOORS cont.

1987 **July** *Live At The Hollywood Bowl*, the soundtrack of a Doors gig filmed there in the late 60s (and simultaneously released on home video), reaches US #154 and UK #51. The interest generated also brings the digitally remastered compilation album *Best Of The Doors* back into the US chart to #127.

1990 Krieger, now signed to Café Records, continues to remain active having released IRS solo *No Habla* in 1989, writing the score for a Discovery TV channel documentary "Who Are They" and performing annually at the "Love Ride", benefiting Muscular Dystrophy.

1991 **Mar** [1] Public interest in Jim Morrison and the band, always at cult level since his death, is substantially revived by Oliver Stone's film "The Doors", with Val Kilmer as Morrison, Kyle MacLachlan as Manzarek, Kevin Dillon as Densmore and Frank Whalley as Krieger, which opens to generally positive reviews. Doors related books and merchandise are also launched.

Apr [13] *The Best Of The Doors*, repromoted for film tie-in, reaches US #32, while *The Doors* soundtrack album hits US #8.

LEE DORSEY

1961 **Oct** After mixed fortune in the boxing ring (as Kid Chocolate) and the US Navy, Dorsey (b. Irving Lee Dorsey, Dec.4, 1926, New Orleans, LA, although some sources claim Portland, OR), returning to his home town, records nonsensical but catchy, *Ya Ya*, supervised by studio gang boss Harold Battiste, on Bobby Robinson's Fury label. A million-seller, it hits US #7 and enables him to quit his day job in an auto wrecking yard and go on tour, playing prestigious R&B venues in California and Texas. (Among several covers of *Ya Ya* will be one by John Lennon.)

1962 **Feb** *Do Re Mi*, equally jaunty and written by local R&B hero Earl King, reaches US #27, but Fury label folds and Dorsey soon slips from public view. (Later, both Dusty Springfield and Georgie Fame cut versions of the song.)

1965 **Aug** Marshall Sehorn and Allen Toussaint team up to plan a Lee Dorsey revival. *Ride Your Pony*, written by Toussaint and released through a lease deal with Amy Records, a subsidiary of Bell, restores him to US chart, at #28. He makes a triumphant stage return at the New York Apollo, after a 3-year hiatus.

1966 **Feb** *Get Out Of My Life Woman* makes US #44 and launches him in UK, reaching #22. Like all his most notable material, it is written and produced by Toussaint.

May *Confusion* rises to UK #38 but fails to chart in US.

Sept *Working In The Coal Mine*, ostensibly a song of hapless resignation, is one of the year's hottest international soul/dance hits, making #8 in both US and UK. (It will be revived by such unlikely performers as Devo and The Judds in the 80s.) The laid-back Dorsey, described as Mr TNT by some hyperbolic promoters, tours Europe.

Nov *Holy Cow* hits UK #6, becoming his biggest UK hit but also his last. (The Band will revive the song on their 1973 *Moondog Matinee*; The Shadows and Chas & Dave will cut UK versions.)

Dec *Holy Cow* peaks at US #23. His only chart album, *The New Lee Dorsey* rises to US #129 and UK #34.

1967 **May** *My Old Car* reaches only US #97.

Oct *Go-Go Girl* makes US #62.

1969 **June** *Everything I Do Gohn Be Funky (From Now On)* proves his chart swan song at US #95.

1970 Concept album *Yes We Can* is released. (*Occapella* and *Sneaking Sally Through The Alley*, both taken from it, will subsequently be covered by Ringo Starr and Robert Palmer. Dorsey will continue to work on and off with Toussaint, but with only localized success, and will devote more time to managing his auto repair shop.)

1976 Dorsey guests on Southside Johnny's debut.

1980 **June** The Clash persuade Dorsey to come out of his semi-retirement and support them on their US tour.

1986 **Dec** [2] Dorsey dies of emphysema in New Orleans.

THE DRIFTERS

Clyde McPhatter (lead tenor)
Gerhard Thrasher (tenor)
Andrew Thrasher (baritone)
Bill Pinkney (bass)

1953 **May** Atlantic boss Ahmet Ertegun, having gone to see The Dominoes at New York's Royal Roost in Manhattan, and finding that lead singer McPhatter (b. Nov.13, 1933, Durham, NC) has been fired, locates and signs him, suggesting that he form a new group. The singer rounds up some vocalizing friends (David Baldwin, William Anderson, James Johnson and David Baughan) but the first recording session, co-produced by Ertegun and Jerry Wexler (his first time in the studio), is a disaster and the friends leave McPhatter to find a new group.

June McPhatter rehearses with other friends who form the Thrasher Wonders gospel group, then cuts the first Drifters' song *Gone* with Gerhard Thrasher, his brother Andrew and Willie Ferbee.

Aug Pinkney (b. Aug.15, 1925, Sumter, NC), from The Jerusalem Stars, replaces Ferbee on the second session and this settles down as the initial Drifters line-up. They cut *Money Honey*, written by Jesse Stone and featuring him on piano. McPhatter asks George Treadwell to manage the group.

Nov *Money Honey*, later covered by Elvis Presley and others, tops US R&B chart for 11 weeks and becomes a million-seller.

1954 **Apr** McPhatter's unorthodox, free-ranging tenor voice becomes one of the most popular sounds in US R&B: *Such A Night* (covered by Johnnie Ray in a version banned by some US radio stations and by the BBC, though it tops UK chart) hits #5 and *Lucille* hits #7. McPhatter is drafted, becoming a forces entertainer in Special Services (though he will record occasionally with the group on leave). The similar-voiced David Baughan returns to take lead vocal on stage.

Oct *Honey Love* (written by McPhatter with Atlantic's Wexler) is another US R&B #1.

Dec *Bip Bam* (also recorded by B.B. King) hits US R&B #7, while a revolutionary arrangement of *White Christmas* (later copied by Presley) hits R&B #2.

1955 **June** *Whatcha Gonna Do* hits US R&B #8. McPhatter cuts his first solo sides while on Service leave.

Aug Baughan leaves and Johnny Moore (b. 1934, Selma, AL) becomes lead singer. Andrew Thrasher is fired by Treadwell and replaced by Charlie Hughes.

Sept The Moore-fronted Drifters record in Los Angeles with producer Nesuhi Ertegun. Among the songs cut is Leiber and Stoller's *Ruby Baby* (which will make US R&B #13 and become a million-seller for Dion).

Dec The Drifters hit US pop chart for the first time as *White Christmas* reaches US #80.

1956 **Apr** [19] McPhatter is discharged from the Armed Forces. (He does not rejoin the group but begins a successful solo US chart career with *Seven Days*.)

1957 **Feb** The Drifters reach US #69 with *Fools Fall In Love*, another Leiber/Stoller song.

June After the group reaches US #79 with *Hypnotized*, Moore is drafted and Bobby Hendricks from The Flyers comes in as lead tenor. (The next 2 years will see constant short-term personnel changes.)

1958 **June** The latest Drifters line-up (Hendricks, Thrasher, Jimmy Millende and Tommy Evans) has a double-sided hit with oldie *Moonlight Bay* (US #72) and Leiber and Stoller's *Drip Drop* (US #58), but they rile manager Treadwell and he fires them.

July Treadwell, who owns The Drifters name and nominates those who trade under it, hires another vocal group, The Crowns, to become The Drifters.

1959 **June** Now freelancing for Atlantic, Leiber and Stoller supervise the new group's first session and their elaborate string-backed production transforms *There Goes My Baby* into an eerie, ethereal R&B classic. Co-written by new lead singer Ben E. King (b. Sept.28, Henderson, NC), it hits US #2 and earns the group a second gold disk.

Oct *Dance With Me* reaches US #15 and UK #17. The B-side *True Love True Love*, featuring Johnny Lee Williams on lead vocal, makes US #33.

1960 **Feb** Using their own compositions for The Coasters, Leiber and Stoller ask Brill Building tunesmiths Pomus and Shuman to write material for The Drifters. After *True Love True Love*, they create *This Magic Moment*, which makes US #16. Ben E. King is lead singer again (and will be on the group's next 3 hits).

May From the same team, *Lonely Winds* reaches US #54. Despite colossal record sales and packed houses, The Drifters receive only modest wages. King complains and, when Treadwell invites him to resign, he does.

Sept Pomus/Shuman/Leiber/Stoller writing together provide The Drifters with *Save The Last Dance For Me* which tops US chart for 3 weeks, hits UK #2 and is a million-seller.

Dec Pomus/Shuman-penned *I Count The Tears*, King's last with The Drifters, reaches US #17 and UK #28.

1961 **Mar** With Rudy Lewis (ex-Clara Ward Singers) taking lead, The Drifters cut a Goffin/King song, *Some Kind Of Wonderful*, which makes US #32.

June Co-written by Burt Bacharach, *Please Stay* reaches US #14.

Sept Pomus and Shuman's *Sweets For My Sweet* makes US #16. (The repertoire of every group on Merseyside will include Drifters' material, but only The Searchers will hit UK #1 (Aug.1963) with a revival of *Sweets For My Sweet*.)

Dec Pomus and Shuman's *Room Full Of Tears* reaches only US #72.

'62 Mar Goffin and King's *When My Little Girl Is Smiling* reaches US #28 and UK #31.

May A vocal rendering of Acker Bilk's chart topper *Stranger On The Shore* makes only US #73 and *Sometimes I Wonder* fails to chart.

Nov The Drifters hit US #5 with their fourth million-seller, *Up On The Roof*, written by Goffin and King.

'63 Mar Leiber and Stoller modify a Barry Mann and Cynthia Weil composition and allow Phil Spector to add the attractive guitar frills to *On Broadway*, which hits US #9.

June They also produce *Rat Race*, co-written with Van McCoy; it makes US #71. *Up On The Roof*, a compilation of singles, climbs to US #110.

Sept Written by Mann and Weil, *I'll Take You Home* reaches US #25 and UK #37. Leiber and Stoller withdraw from involvement with the group, to concentrate on the launch of their Red Bird label.

'64 Feb New Atlantic staff producer Bert Berns takes over and *Vaya Con Dios*, a huge seller for Les Paul and Mary Ford in 1953, reaches US #43.

May Berns' own *One Way Love* takes The Drifters to US #56 (but gives UK soul man Cliff Bennett his Top 10 breakthrough in UK).

June After Rudy Lewis dies unexpectedly, Johnny Moore returns to take over lead vocals and the group's transition from R&B to smooth soul-pop is apparent in *Under The Boardwalk* which hits US #4 and makes UK #45.

Sept A *Boardwalk* sequel, *I've Got Sand In My Shoes*, reaches US #33.

Nov Mann and Weil's *Saturday Night At The Movies* makes US #18. *Under The Boardwalk* (again, a singles compilation) makes US #40.

'65 Jan Goffin and King's *At The Club* makes US #43 and UK #35.

Feb *The Good Life* reaches only US #103.

Apr *Come On Over To My Place* peaks at US #60 and UK #40. Atlantic standard *Chains Of Love* reaches US #90.

July *Follow Me* makes US #91.

Aug Written by Jeff Barry and Ellie Greenwich, *I'll Take You Where The Music's Playing* reaches US #51.

'66 Mar A million-seller for Dean Martin in 1955, *Memories Are Made Of This* makes only US #48. The record marks the departure of producer Bert Berns, now running his own Bang And Shout Records and at legal loggerheads with Atlantic.

Dec Produced by Bob Gallo and Atlantic engineer Tom Dowd, *Baby What I Mean* peaks at US #62 and reaches UK #49.

'68 *Golden Hits* makes US #122 and UK #27.

'71 With Johnny Moore the only constant factor, The Drifters remain on the clubland circuit. Following the death of George Treadwell, his wife Faye assumes managerial control.

'72 Mar Reissued back to back *At The Club/Saturday Night At The Movies* begins climbing UK chart, eventually hitting #3.

June A reactivated *Golden Hits* reaches UK #26.

[13] Clyde McPhatter dies of heart, kidney and liver disease following serious alcohol and drug addiction.

Aug A minor hit 7 years earlier, *Come On Over To My Place*, hits UK #9.

'73 Aug Still led by Moore, The Drifters sign a deal with the UK office of Bell Records and start a run of hits – all written and produced by permutations of Roger Cook, Roger Greenaway, Geoff Stephens, Barry Mason, Les Reed and Tony Macaulay. The first of these, *Like Brother And Sister* hits UK #7.

'74 July *Kissin' In The Back Row Of The Movies* hits UK #2.

Nov *Down On The Beach Tonight* hits UK #7.

'75 Feb *Love Games* makes UK #33.

Group joins former Shirelle Shirley Alston on her version of *Save The Last Dance For Me* from her album **With A Little Help From My Friends**.

Oct The Drifters, now well-known on the UK club/cabaret/television show circuit, hit UK #3 with *There Goes My First Love*.

Dec *Can I Take You Home Little Girl* hits UK #10. Atlantic takes advantage of their renewed popularity and repackages *24 Original Hits* which hits UK #2 and remains on the Album chart for 34 weeks. Overshadowed by the reissue, the latest Bell album *Love Games* charts briefly at UK #51.

'76 *Hello Happiness* makes UK #12, *Every Nite's A Saturday Night With You* reaches US #29 and *You're More Than A Number In My Little Red Book* hits UK #5. None of the group's Bell output makes the US chart. (During the following years, The Drifters will continue to play the circuit. *Save The Last Dance For Me/When My Little Girl Is Smiling* will return to the UK chart (#69) as part of a picture disk marketing exercise

with other oldies. Johnny Moore will drop out but return, and during the mid-80s Ben E. King sings alongside him in the group – but only until the reissued *Stand By Me* returns him to the limelight. At least 40 people can legitimately claim to have been bona-fide Drifters over the group's long history and most of them have masqueraded in several bogus groups of touring "Drifters".)

1990 Nov [10] TV-advertised *The Best Of Ben E. King & The Drifters* reaches UK #15.

DURAN DURAN

Simon Le Bon (vocals)
Andy Taylor (guitar)
Nick Rhodes (keyboards)
John Taylor (bass)
Roger Taylor (drums)

1978 Band is formed in Birmingham, W.Midlands, by schoolmates club DJ Rhodes (b. Nicholas Bates, June 8, 1962, Moseley, W.Midlands) and John Taylor (b. Nigel John Taylor, June 20, 1960, Birmingham) on guitar, with bass player and clarinettist Simon Colley, vocalist Stephen Duffy and a drum machine. Group's name is taken from the character played by Milo O'Shea in Jane Fonda science fiction movie "Barbarella" and it plays many early gigs at Barbarella's club in Birmingham.

1979 Colley and Duffy leave and are replaced by vocalist Andy Wickett, ex-TV Eye, and drummer Roger Taylor (b. Apr.26, 1960, Castle Bromwich, W.Midlands), ex-local punk groups The Crucified Toads and The Scent Organs. The group cuts a demo tape with local producer Bob Lamb. John Taylor switches to playing bass, guitarist John Curtis comes and goes, and the band puts an ad in **Melody Maker** for a "live wire guitarist" and recruits Andy Taylor (b. Feb.16, 1961, Tynemouth, Tyne & Wear). Wickett leaves and the band features temporary vocalists Alan Curtis and Jeff Thomas for a while.

1980 Jan Brothers Paul and Michael Berrow, owners of Birmingham's newly-opened Rum Runner club, sign the band to a management contract and give it a residency at the club.

Apr Le Bon (b. Oct.27, 1958, Bushey, Herts.), veteran of punk band Dog Days and studying drama at Birmingham University, is recruited after 1 rehearsal, having been suggested by ex-girlfriend Fiona Kemp, who is a barmaid at the Rum Runner. (He will become the band's lyricist and lead vocalist.)

July After Le Bon finishes his term at university, he joins full-time and the group plays to great success at the Edinburgh Festival in Scotland.

Nov Duran Duran plays its first major UK tour dates, supporting Hazel O'Connor, and the Berrow brothers negotiate a worldwide recording deal with EMI Records, whose A&R director Dave Ambrose has been scouting them on the tour.

1981 Mar [28] First release *Planet Earth*, produced by Colin Thurston, reaches UK #12. The band's musical and visual style fits neatly into the "New Romantic" movement in UK rock music which is rapidly spreading as a backlash against the punk-originated new wave, with similar contemporaries like Spandau Ballet, Ultravox and Visage also hitting the chart. (Media coverage is wide and the photogenic line-up, well displayed in several promotional videos made by Australian director Russell Mulcahy, will raise Duran Duran to UK teen sensation status by the end of the year.)

Apr Group begins a world tour which will keep them on the road until Christmas.

May [23] *Careless Memories* makes UK #37.

June Band begins its first headlining UK tour at Brighton's Dome.

Aug [22] *Girls On Film*, with a risque promo video directed by Godley & Creme, banned by the BBC in UK and MTV in US, hits UK #5.

Sept [5] *Duran Duran* hits UK #3, during a 118-week chart residence.

Dec [19] *My Own Way* reaches UK #14.

1982 Apr Band starts a world tour which will last until Dec.

May [29] Synthesizer-heavy *Rio* hits UK #2 (and will stay charted for the rest of the year).

June [26] *Hungry Like The Wolf*, from the album, with a high-class promo video directed by Russell Mulcahy in Sri Lanka, hits UK #5.

July [29] Andy Taylor marries Tracie Wilson in Los Angeles, CA.

Sept [11] Radio-favorite ballad *Save A Prayer* hits UK #2.

Nov [13] *Carnival*, a US-only mini-album release, featuring earlier tracks remixed by the band and David Kershenbaum, climbs to US #98.

Dec [11] Extracted title track *Rio*, with Andy Hamilton guesting on saxophone, hits UK #9.

1983 Feb [26] Aided by US cable music station MTV's use of its promo video (along with those for most of the earlier singles), *Hungry Like The*

Wolf climbs to US #3. It hits charts in all major territories around the world and is a million-seller. *Rio*, which has been slowly climbing US chart since June 1982, hits US #6 and becomes a million-seller during a 129-week chart stay.

[19] Teen band Kajagoogoo top UK chart with Nick Rhodes/Colin Thurston-produced *Too Shy*.

Mar [26] *Is There Something I Should Know* debuts at UK #1. Band attracts 5,000 fans while making an appearance at a video shop in New York and mounted police are deployed to control the crowd. This is the first noted US manifestation of Duran-fever, though such incidents are common in UK.

May [14] Extracted title track *Rio* reaches US #14.

July [20] Band headlines a charity concert for MENCAP at the Dominion theater, London, attended by the Prince and Princess of Wales.

Aug [6] *Is There Something I Should Know* hits US #4 and is a million-seller. It is added to the US version of the band's first album *Duran Duran*, which climbs to US #10 and is also a million-seller.

Nov Band begins a 5-month, 51-concert world tour, taking in UK, Japan, Australia, Canada and US.

[5] *Union Of The Snake*, extracted from forthcoming album, hits UK #3.

Dec [3] *Seven And The Ragged Tiger*, produced by Alex Sadkin, Ian Little and the band itself, tops UK chart for 1 week.

[24] *Union Of The Snake* hits US #3.

Band's second world tour ends at Madison Square Garden, as they are voted Best Group in the **Daily Mirror**/BBC TV "Nationwide"/Radio 1 Rock & Pop Awards.

1984 **Feb** *Seven And The Ragged Tiger* hits US #8.

[11] *New Moon On Monday*, taken from the album, hits UK #9.

[28] Group wins Best Video Short Form for "Girls On Film/Hungry Like The Wolf" and Best Video Album for "Duran Duran" at the 26th annual Grammy awards.

Mar [17] *New Moon On Monday* hits US #10.

Apr Band completes its world tour, having played to over 750,000 people and having been recorded and filmed at many venues for subsequent live album and TV/video release.

May [5] *The Reflex*, remixed as a single by Nile Rodgers (ex-Chic), tops UK chart for 4 weeks.

June [23] *The Reflex* hits US #1 for 2 weeks and is another worldwide million-seller.

July [27] Roger Taylor marries Giovanna Cantonne in Naples, Italy.

Aug [18] Nick Rhodes marries American model Julie Anne in London.

Nov [17] *The Wild Boys*, produced in London by Rodgers and the band, hits UK #2, behind Chaka Khan's *I Feel For You*.

[25] Band takes part in the all-star recording session for Band Aid's *Do They Know It's Christmas?* at Sarm studios in London, with Le Bon taking one of the lead vocal lines.

Dec [15] *The Wild Boys* hits US #2 and is included on otherwise live album *Arena* (recorded on stage during the world tour) which hits UK #6 and US #4, and is the band's fourth million-selling album. Its release ties in with TV showing of "Sing Blue Silver", a documentary filmed both on stage and behind the scenes during the world tour, directed by Michael Collins and Russell Mulcahy.

1985 **Jan** While Duran Duran is temporarily inactive, Andy and John Taylor form a recording-only spare-time group with Robert Palmer, producer Bernard Edwards and fellow ex-Chic musician Tony Thompson, named Power Station after New York studio where they are recording.

Feb Power Station makes its performing debut on NBC TV's "Saturday Night Live".

[11] "Wild Boys" wins Best British Music Video at the fourth annual BRIT Awards at the Grosvenor House, London.

Mar [13] *The Reflex* wins International Hit Of The Year at the annual Ivor Novello Awards lunch in London.

[16] Duran Duran's *Save A Prayer* belatedly reaches US #16.

[30] Power Station's *Some Like It Hot*, penned by the Taylors with Robert Palmer, reaches US #14.

Apr [6] Parent album *The Power Station* debuts at UK #12.

May [11] *Some Like It Hot* hits US #6.

[25] *A View To A Kill*, the theme from the forthcoming James Bond film co-written by Duran Duran and composer John Barry, who scored the film, hits UK #2.

June [1] Power Station's revival of Marc Bolan's *Get It On*, taken from *The Power Station*, reaches US #22.

July [13] Duran Duran plays the "Live Aid" concert in Philadelphia. Power Station fails to appear as expected, since Palmer refuses to bring it out of its one-off studio-bound status as Duran Duran's *A View To A*

Kill begins a 2-week tenure at the top of US chart and is the band's sixth million-selling single. (It is the first James Bond film theme to hit #1.)

[27] *The Power Station* hits US #6.

Aug [3] Power Station's *Get It On* hits US #9, one place higher than the original 1972 T. Rex version, then titled *Bang A Gong*. Palmer is replaced in Power Station by ex-Silverhead and Chequered Past singer Michael Des Barres, since the other members are still keen to work live. New line-up makes a brief guest appearance in an episode of NBC TV "Miami Vice". Meanwhile, Le Bon, Rhodes and Roger Taylor form their own sideline recording band, Arcadia, and record an album.

[10] Le Bon is airlifted from his boat Drum after it overturns racing.

Oct [12] Power Station's *Communication* makes US #34.

Nov [9] *Communication* peaks at UK #75; Power Station then disband. Arcadia's first single *Election Day* (featuring a narration by Grace Jones) hits UK #7 and *So Red The Rose* makes UK #30.

Dec [4] Arcadia's *Election Day* hits US #6.

[27] Le Bon marries model Yasmin Parvanah.

1986 **Jan** *So Red The Rose* climbs to US #23.

Feb Arcadia's *The Promise*, extracted from the album as a second single, peaks at UK #37.

Mar [8] Arcadia's *Goodbye Is Forever* is the US follow-up from the album and reaches #33.

Apr Between Power Station winding down and Duran Duran regrouping for album recordings, John Taylor releases solo single *I Do What I Do*, the theme from movie "9½ Weeks". It makes UK #42.

[26] *I Do What I Do* reaches US #23. Roger Taylor announces he is to take a year's sabbatical from Duran Duran and retreats to his country home in Gloucestershire. (He will not return to Duran Duran.)

May Le Bon takes his yacht Drum to race in Australia.

June Beginning album sessions as a quartet, Duran Duran completes them as a trio when Andy Taylor leaves to pursue a solo career in Los Angeles, having already recorded *Take It Easy* for the soundtrack of film "American Anthem". (He moves to US, signs to MCA Records and begins work on a solo album with ex-Sex Pistols Steve Jones.)

July Arcadia's *The Flame*, remixed from the album as a third UK single, peaks at #58. Taylor rejoins Le Bon and Rhodes for a live TV appearance on a Pan-European 6-hour version of "The Tube", but this marks the end of Arcadia's activity.

Aug [2] Andy Taylor's solo single *Take It Easy* reaches US #24.

[31] Le Bon is best man at the wedding of Bob Geldof and Paula Yates.

Nov Duran Duran's *Notorious*, the title track from forthcoming album, hits UK #7.

[15] Andy Taylor's first solo release for MCA, *When The Rain Comes Down* (featured in "Miami Vice"), makes US #73.

Dec *Notorious*, co-produced by Nile Rodgers and the band, showcases the new Duran Duran trio (Andy Taylor is heard on only 4 tracks, recorded before his departure), with Warren Cuccurullo (guitar), ex-Missing Persons and Steve Ferrone (drums), ex-Average White Band and now session man. It reaches UK #16.

1987 **Jan** [10] *Notorious* hits US #2 as parent *Notorious* makes US #12.

Mar *Skin Trade*, extracted from the album, reaches UK #22.

[14] *Skin Trade* makes US #39.

Apr Duran Duran appears live at "The Secret Policeman's Third Ball" at the London Palladium, amid rumors that this might be its last concert.

May *Meet El Presidente*, a further excerpt from *Notorious*, reaches UK #24, while Andy Taylor's debut solo album *Thunder* makes UK #61 and US #46.

[16] *Meet El Presidente* peaks at US #70.

1988 **Jan** Le Bon, Rhodes and John Taylor recruit Cuccurullo as a full-time Duran Duran member plus drummer Sterling Campbell to work on a new album recorded in Paris and produced by Jonathan Elias and Daniel Abraham.

June Group signs a new management deal with Peter Rudge.

Oct *I Don't Want Your Love* reaches UK #14 as parent album *Big Thing* reaches #15.

[21] They give a free concert in the parking lot of Capitol Records on the corner of Sunset and Vine in Hollywood, drawing an estimated crowd of 5,000.

Dec [3] *I Don't Want Your Love* hits US #4 as parent album *Big Thing* makes US #24.

1989 **Jan** *All She Wants Is* hits UK #9.

Feb [18] *All She Wants Is* reaches US #22.

Apr *Do You Believe In Shame*, from *Big Thing*, reaches UK #30.

[8] *Do You Believe In Shame*, featured in Mel Gibson/Michelle Pfeiffer film "Tequila Sunrise", peaks at US #72.

Aug [25] Le Bon becomes father to daughter Amber Rose.

Nov Compilation collection of hit singles to date *Decade* hits UK #5.

Dec [16] *Burning The Ground* makes UK #31.

1990 Jan [20] *Decade* makes US #67.

Aug [11] Duran's *Violence Of Summer (Love's Taking Over)* charts in UK at #20.

Sept [1] Duran's *Liberty* immediately hits UK #8.

[15] *Liberty* makes US #46.

[29] *Violence Of Summer (Love's Taking Over)* peaks at US #64.

Oct [27] Andy Taylor's remake of The Kinks' *Lola* peaks at UK #60.

Nov [24] Duran Duran's *Serious* makes UK #48.

IAN DURY & THE BLOCKHEADS

Ian Dury (vocals)
Chaz Jankel (keyboards, guitar)
Davey Payne (saxophone)
John Turnbull (guitar)
Norman Watt-Roy (bass)
Mickey Gallagher (keyboards)
Charley Charles (drums)

1970 Nov Dury (b. May 12, 1942, Upminster, Essex), partially crippled since contracting polio at age 7, forms Kilburn & The High Roads while he is a lecturer at Canterbury College of Art, Kent. Group is initially part-time.

1971 Dec Kilburn & The High Roads play their first gigs at Croydon School of Art, London and Canterbury College.

1973 Jan Dave Robinson (later MD of Stiff Records) introduces the band to regular work on London's pub circuit, where they are spotted by writer/broadcaster Charlie Gillett, who becomes their manager, later to be replaced by Robinson.

May [3] When the band's battered transit van almost falls to pieces, 3 other pub circuit bands, Ducks Deluxe, Brinsley Schwarz and Bees Make Honey, play a benefit show at Camden Town Hall, London, to raise money for repair bills.

Oct Group tours UK as support to The Who.

1974 Jan Signed to WEA's Raft label, the band records an album produced by Tony Ashton (ex-Ashton, Gardner & Dyke) which is not issued when label closes down. WEA lets Kilburn & The High Roads go (but will release the album in UK in 1978 after Dury's subsequent fame).

July Tommy Roberts becomes group's new manager and signs to Pye Records' Dawn label.

Nov Debut release is the single *Rough Kids*, which does not sell.

1975 Feb *Crippled With Nerves* does not chart.

June *Handsome* fares no better than the singles, but will be reissued in Dury's later successful days. The disillusioned group breaks up, forcing cancellation of some projected European live dates. Dury and Rod Melvin will spend rest of year writing and planning a new Kilburns.

Nov A 6-piece group is formed, Ian Dury & The Kilburns, with Robinson as manager, organizing a regular gig at the Hope & Anchor in Islington, London.

1976 Mar Ex-Byzantium Jankel joins the band on keyboards replacing Russell Hardy, and begins to write with Dury.

June [17] Group splits after a last gig at Walthamstow Town Hall, London, mainly because Dury's doctor orders him off the road for health reasons. (Dury and Jankel stay together and spend a year writing songs for what will become the first solo Ian Dury album.)

1977 Aug Dury signs to Robinson's Stiff Records. *Sex And Drugs And Rock And Roll* is released without chart success.

Sept Ian Dury & The Blockheads is formed for the "Stiff Live Stiffs" UK promotional tour (with Elvis Costello, Nick Lowe and others). Dury and Jankel recruit several of the session men they have used in recording a new album.

Nov Dury's second solo single *Sweet Gene Vincent* is released.

1978 Feb *New Boots And Panties!* hits UK #5, staying on chart 90 weeks.

Mar Band tours US, supporting Lou Reed.

May *What A Waste* becomes Dury's first hit single at UK #9. *New Boots And Panties!* charts in US, reaching #168. Dury & The Blockheads tour UK, with comedian Max Wall as support. Wall records *England's Glory*, written for him by Dury, and released on Stiff.

June Humphrey Ocean, a former art school friend, covers Dury's *Whoops A Daisy*, also on Stiff.

Oct *Wotabunch*, the Kilburn & The High Roads' album left on the shelf at WEA in 1974, is released.

1979 Jan *Hit Me With Your Rhythm Stick* tops UK chart for a week, with over 900,000 sales over the 1978 Christmas period in UK alone.

June *Do It Yourself*, marketed in a variety of "wallpaper pattern" sleeve designs, hits UK #2.

Aug The R&B/disco-flavored *Reasons To Be Cheerful (Part 3)*, recorded in Rome, hits UK #3 and *Do It Yourself* makes US #126.

Dec Dury appears in the "People Of Kampuchea" concert at London's Hammersmith Odeon, along with Paul McCartney, The Who, Robert Plant and many others.

1980 Chaz Jankel leaves for a solo career, signing to A&M (most notably he will pen *Ai No Corrida*, a subsequent hit for Quincy Jones). Gallagher rejoins, having left to join The Clash on tour.

July [5] Wilko Johnson (ex-Dr. Feelgood and The Solid Senders) joins on guitar.

Sept *I Want To Be Straight*, Dury's first recording to feature Johnson on guitar, reaches UK #22.

Nov *Sueperman's Big Sister* (the incorrect spelling is deliberate, to avoid copyright problems) reaches UK #51.

Dec *Laughter* makes UK #48 while Dury & The Blockheads play "Soft As A Baby's Bottom" UK tour.

1981 Feb *Laughter* scores US #159.

Aug Dury signs a new worldwide deal with Polydor. He releases *Spasticus Autisticus* in time for the Year Of The Disabled, but most UK radio stations refuse to play it. It fails to chart (as will all his Polydor singles) and is deleted the following month, with a Polydor statement: "Just as nobody bans handicapped people – just makes it difficult for them to function as normal people – so *Spasticus Autisticus* was not banned, it was made impossible to function." The United Nations rejects the song as a contribution to the Year Of The Disabled.

Oct *Lord Upminster*, recorded at Compass Point studios in Nassau, Bahamas, peaks at UK #53. Sly and Robbie replace The Blockheads on all but 1 track and Jankel returns.

Nov *Juke Box Duries*, compiled from earlier Stiff singles, fails to chart.

1982 Dec Without Dury, The Blockheads release a revival of *Twist And Shout*, recorded on stage in London. It does not chart.

1983 Nov *Really Glad You Came* is released.

1984 Feb *4,000 Weeks Holiday*, credited to Ian Dury & The Music Students, reaches UK #54. Originally scheduled for the previous year, it was withheld by Polydor until *Fuck Off Noddy* and a song about holiday tycoon Billy Butlin were removed. Non-charting single *Very Personal* ends his unproductive spell with Polydor.

1985 Dury reunites with The Blockheads for live work, and acts with Bob Geldof in movie "Number One".

June Paul Hardcastle's re-mix of *Hit Me With Your Rhythm Stick*, recorded for Stiff with Dury's approval, reaches UK #55. Dury begins to be heard (if not seen) regularly on UK TV, doing voice-overs for holiday and electrical goods ads.

Nov *Profoundly In Love With Pandora*, the theme from UK TV series "The Secret Diary Of Adrian Mole, Aged 13¾", reaches UK #45.

1986 In further acting roles, Dury appears in Roman Polanski's movie "Pirates", and BBC TV series "King Of The Ghetto".

1987 Another theme for second "Adrian Mole" series is aired on UK TV. Dury appears in ill-received Bob Dylan movie "Hearts Of Fire" and scores the music for UK TV play about truckers, "Night Moves". He will successfully leave behind his flagging recording career and switch his attention to acting, writing music and his first love, painting.

1989 Nov Dury-written and conceived musical "Apples" opens at London's Royal Court theater, while its cast recording is issued on WEA Records.

1990 Sept [5] Charley Charles dies in London's Park Royal hospital from complications relating to cancer.

[25-27] One-off re-formed Blockheads play the Town & Country club, London.

BOB DYLAN

1953 Dylan (b. Robert Allan Zimmerman, May 24, 1941, Duluth, MN) begins to learn guitar, after running away to Chicago at age 10, and then travels with a Texas carnival age 13.

1954 May [22] He has his bar-mitzvah.

1959 June [5] He leaves Hibbing high school, having played regularly and formed several groups including rock'n'roll band The Golden Chords, noting in the yearbook that he is leaving "to follow Little Richard". (Though initially he starts a course at the University of Minnesota.)

1960 He leaves university to concentrate on playing and singing, and is briefly employed as pianist with Bobby Vee's backing group. Having adopted a new performing name, he travels to New York down Highway 61 to visit Woody Guthrie, chief precursor of the current folk boom (and a particular influence on Dylan), but paralyzed with a rare hereditary disease for the past 8 years.

1961 Feb [3] In New York, Dylan makes his first recordings, on some friends' home equipment, playing the standard *San Francisco Bay Blues* and similar numbers.

Apr [11] His first New York live gig is at Gerde's Folk City in Greenwich Village, opening for bluesman John Lee Hooker.

[24] Dylan earns a $50 session fee playing harmonica on recordings for Harry Belafonte's *Midnight Special*.

Sept [30] He joins folk singer Caroline Hester on an album session for CBS/Columbia, again on harmonica. He impresses producer John Hammond Sr., who noted a glowing **New York Times** review of a performance at Gerde's Folk City. Hammond offers Dylan a recording contract.

Oct [4] As a showcase, he plays New York's Carnegie Chapter Hall – to 53 people.

[20] Dylan records debut *Bob Dylan*, which includes raw, authentic versions of traditional songs.

1962 Mar The debut album is released in US. It does not chart, but causes a major stir on the folk scene. Almost rockabilly-styled *Mixed Up Confusion/Corrina Corrina* is also released, to few sales.

1963 Jan [12] On a brief visit to London, he is given a part as a folk singer in a UK BBC radio play "The Madhouse On Castle Street". In it he sings *Blowin' In The Wind* and *Swan On The River*.

Apr [12] A solo concert at New York's Town Hall draws positive reviews, and is recorded by CBS for a live album (which does not materialize).

May *The Freewheelin' Bob Dylan* is released, featuring major compositions of his own like *A Hard Rain's Gonna Fall, Blowin' In The Wind* and *Masters Of War*, it establishes him as a leader in the new folk singer-songwriter and youth protest leagues.

[12] Dylan is invited to play CBS TV's "Ed Sullivan Show". When he is forbidden to sing *Talking John Birch Society Blues*, he refuses to appear.

[17] He meets Joan Baez at the Monterey Folk Festival, Monterey, CA. (The 2 will become the stars of that year's Newport Folk Festival, at which Baez will introduce Dylan, and will develop a long-term personal and creative union.)

Aug Folk trio Peter, Paul and Mary's version of Dylan's *Blowin' In The Wind* hits US #2 and UK #13, and is a million-seller. (They will follow it with another hit cover from *The Freewheelin' Bob Dylan*, *Don't Think Twice, It's Alright*.)

Sept Following Peter, Paul and Mary's success, interest in *Blowin' In The Wind* and its writer spurs *The Freewheelin' Bob Dylan* to US #22 and a gold disk.

1964 Apr *The Times They Are A-Changin'*, much of its content on a strong protest theme, reaches US #20.

May With Dylan's name constantly promoted in UK by The Beatles and others, *The Freewheelin' Bob Dylan* makes UK #16. (It will return later in the year to top the chart.)

July *The Times They Are A-Changin'* reaches UK #20. (This will also later return with bigger sales.)

Oct *Another Side Of Bob Dylan*, less protest-oriented, makes US #43.

Dec *Another Side Of Bob Dylan* hits UK #8.

1965 Apr Dylan's UK tour, where he is received as a major celebrity, is documented on film in fly-on-the-wall fashion by D.A. Pennebaker, later released as "Don't Look Back". The movie reveals that pressure on the young star is steadily more intense as his popularity grows. *The Times They Are A-Changin'* is released as Dylan's first UK single to tie in with the tour, and hits UK #9 following sell-out London concerts. *The Times They Are A-Changin'* hits UK #4.

Apr [30] 8-date UK "Don't Look Back" tour with The Band opens at Sheffield City Hall.

May [9] Tour ends at London's Royal Albert Hall,

[15] Rock guitar-driven *Subterranean Homesick Blues* makes US #39 (his first US hit single) and hits UK #9. *The Freewheelin' Bob Dylan* finally tops the UK chart for 2 weeks after a year on sale (deposing *Beatles For Sale*). It is then swept aside by Dylan's new *Bringing It All Back Home*, which hits UK #1 for 4 weeks and US #6, earning his second gold disk. The album includes *Subterranean Homesick Blues* on a complete side of electric, rock-oriented material, backed by a group including Al Kooper and Paul Butterfield. The other side maintains his acoustic folk roots and includes *Mr. Tambourine Man*. His first *Bob Dylan* makes UK #13, giving him 4 simultaneous UK Top 20 album placings.

June The Byrds hit US #1 with their folk-rock cover of *Mr. Tambourine Man* (and will hit UK #1 a few weeks later). It is the first chart-topping Dylan composition and sparks several pop and folk-rock hit covers of his material by major acts like The Turtles (*It Ain't Me Babe*), Cher (*All I*

Really Want To Do*), Joan Baez (*It's All Over Now, Baby Blue* and *Farewell Angelina*) and Manfred Mann (*If You Gotta Go, Go Now*). *Maggie's Farm*, taken from *Bringing It All Back Home*, reaches UK #22.

[25] Dylan appears at The Newport Folk Festival and plays a full electric set backed by The Paul Butterfield Blues Band. The diehard folk "purists" in the audience try to boo him off the stage.

Aug [28] He takes part in the Forest Hills Music Festival, New York.

Sept [4] *Like A Rolling Stone*, noted for its revolutionary length (6 mins.) as well as its rock backing notably Al Kooper's rolling organ, hits US #2 and UK #4, becoming Dylan's first million-selling single.

Oct *Highway 61 Revisited*, with Dylan's individual lyrics and mainstream rock, hits US #3 and UK #4.

Nov [6] *Positively 4th Street*, in similar style to *Like A Rolling Stone*, hits US #7 and UK #8.

[22] Dylan marries Sara Lowndes.

1966 Jan [29] *Can You Please Crawl Out Your Window* peaks at US #58.

Feb [5] *Can You Please Crawl Out Your Window* reaches UK #17.

Apr *(Sooner Or Later)* One Of Us Must Know reaches UK #33.

May [5] 14-date UK tour opens at Adelphi theater, Dublin.

[21] Boisterous *Rainy Day Women #12 & 35* hits US #2, and will become Dylan's second million-selling single.

[26] Dylan plays London's Royal Albert Hall, at the end of another UK tour, this time backed by an electric band, largely consisting of The Hawks (later to become The Band). The concert is recorded for a never-released live album, though bootlegs will be prolific. Purists in the audience still consider the folk singer has "sold out" and make their feelings vocal.

June *Rainy Day Women #12 & 35* hits UK #7.

July [29] Dylan suffers injuries (never fully detailed, but apparently involving broken neck vertebrae) when he crashes his motorcycle near his home in Woodstock, NY. His recuperation, purportedly on Cape Cod, MA, leads to a period of reclusive inactivity, interpreted by many as an attempt to escape into family life from the extreme pressures of 2 years' success.

Aug Double *Blonde On Blonde*, recorded in the first 3 months of the year, hits US #9 and UK #3, and is his fourth gold album in US with sales over a half million. *I Want You*, a lightweight pop number taken from the album, reaches US #20 and UK #16.

Oct [8] *Just Like A Woman*, also from the album, reaches US #33 (but is not issued in UK, where Manfred Mann's cover hits #10). It is announced that Dylan is spending his recuperative period writing a novel. *Blonde On Blonde* hits UK #3.

1967 Feb UK compilation *Greatest Hits* hits UK #6.

June US-compiled *Greatest Hits* (different from the UK version), hits US #10 and earns another gold disk.

[3] *Leopard Skin Pillbox Hat* peaks at US #81. (During almost 18 months of "retirement", Dylan stays in Woodstock and does not appear to be active at all. Tapes later begin to circulate of sessions at Big Pink, a large old house in Woodstock, with The Band. Several acts, including Manfred Mann (*The Mighty Quinn*), Peter, Paul And Mary (*Too Much Of Nothing*) and Julie Driscoll & Brian Auger (*This Wheel's On Fire*) will have hits with songs originating from these sessions. They will form the basis of *Great White Wonder*, first big-selling bootleg rock album.)

Oct Dylan returns to the studio (without The Band) to record an album of new material.

1968 Jan [20] Dylan plays with The Band at a memorial concert for Woody Guthrie (who died, aged 55, on Sept.3, 1967) at New York's Carnegie Hall – his first public appearance since his motorcycle crash.

Feb [29] *Bob Dylan's Greatest Hits* wins Best Album Cover Photography at the 10th annual Grammy awards.

Mar *John Wesley Harding*, simpler and more country-influenced than his pre-accident output, recorded in Nashville with Charlie McCoy, Kenny Buttrey and Pete Drake, hits US #2 and tops UK chart for 10 weeks. (No Dylan single is taken from it, but Jimi Hendrix will have a hit with a hard-rock cover of *All Along The Watchtower*.)

1969 May Country-influenced *Nashville Skyline*, recorded in Nashville with assistance from Johnny Cash (they duet on *Girl From The North Country*), hits US #3 and tops the UK chart for 4 weeks. Cash and Dylan also record a TV special at the Grand Ole Opry.

June [7] *I Threw It All Away*, taken from the album, peaks at US #85 and UK #30.

Aug [31] Dylan and The Band headline UK's Isle of Wight festival, UK. Some of the set is recorded (for eventual release on *Self-Portrait*).

Sept [6] *Lay Lady Lay*, taken from *Nashville Skyline* (but originally written, by request, for film "Midnight Cowboy" and rejected), hits US #7 and UK #5. His first Top 10 single for 3 years, it will also be his last.

Nov [29] *Tonight I'll Be Staying Here With You*, also from *Nashville Skyline*, makes US #50.

1970 Mar [11] Johnny Cash's annotation for *Nashville Skyline* wins Best Album Notes of 1969 at the 12th annual Grammy awards.
June [9] Dylan is awarded an honorary Doctorate in Music from Princeton University.
July Double *Self-Portrait*, a scrapbook collection of new songs and familiar covers (including songs by Paul Simon, Gordon Lightfoot and The Everly Brothers), is pasted by critics as a waste of talent. It is Dylan's third successive UK #1 (for 1 week) and hits US #4.
Aug [15] Instrumental *Wigwam*, from *Self-Portrait*, makes US #41.
Nov [11] Dylan's long-awaited novel, the surreal **Tarantula**, is published, to wide press attention.
Dec *New Morning* hits US #7, tops the UK chart and is greeted as a return to form.
By year's end Dylan has invested in fraudulent tax-shelter Home-Stake Oil Production Company in Tulsa, OK, and is swindled out of more than $120,000.

1971 Feb Dylan documentary film "Eat The Document", mostly featuring his 1966 UK tour with The Band, is premiered at New York's Academy of Music.
Mar [16] He records *Watching The River Flow* and *When I Paint My Masterpiece* in a session with Leon Russell guesting on piano.
July [31] Dylan appears in George Harrison's "Concert For Bangla Desh" at New York's Madison Square Garden (and performs one side of the triple album of the event, which hits US #2). This is Dylan's only major live appearance of the year.
Aug [7] *Watching The River Flow* reaches US #41 and UK #24.

1972 Jan Double compilation album **Bob Dylan's Greatest Hits, Vol.II** (*More Bob Dylan Greatest Hits* in UK) reaches US #14 and UK #12, while specially-recorded protest single *George Jackson*, about the black militant shot dead in a prison fracas, makes US #33. Dylan spends the rest of the year writing the soundtrack to, and appearing as the outlaw Alias in Sam Peckinpah's movie "Pat Garrett And Billy The Kid".

1973 Sept Following the film's release, Dylan's soundtrack album, which includes 3 tracks with his vocals, is released by CBS/Columbia and reaches US #16 and UK #29. His contract with the label expires and he does not renew it.
Oct [27] The movie soundtrack's highlight, Dylan singing *Knockin' On Heaven's Door*, is released, and becomes his biggest-selling single since *Lay Lady Lay*, reaching US #12 and UK #14.
Nov It becomes clear that Dylan is not re-signing to CBS and it is announced that he will move to David Geffen's Asylum label and is recording an album with The Band. Columbia releases *Dylan*, a collection of out-takes and rejected covers from *Self-Portrait*.

1974 Jan Almost universally decried, *Dylan* reaches US #17, while extracted revival of Elvis Presley's *A Fool Such As I* makes US #55.
[3] Dylan and The Band open a 39-date US tour (the first in nearly 8 years) in Chicago, to support their first Asylum album together, cut the previous Nov. (Several dates will be recorded for a live album.) There are 5 million ticket applications.
Feb Debut Asylum *Planet Waves* is Dylan's first US chart-topper (for 4 weeks) and hits UK #7, where it is released by Island Records.
Mar [23] *On A Night Like This*, from *Planet Waves*, makes US #44.
July Double live album **Before The Flood**, a compilation of performances from the US tour produced by Phil Ramone, with The Band getting one side to itself, features reworked versions of some of Dylan's 60s hits. It hits US #3 and UK #8.
Aug [10] Dylan settles his differences with CBS chief executive Clive Davis and re-signs to the label.
[31] Live single from the album, *Most Likely You Go Your Way (And I'll Go Mine)*, peaks at US #66.
Sept Songs are recorded for a new CBS/Columbia album, **Blood On The Tracks**, but after it is scheduled for release, Dylan is dissatisfied with some of the recordings, and the album is delayed.

1975 Feb After 5 numbers have been reworked, *Blood On The Tracks* is issued. It tops the US chart for 2 weeks and hits UK #4.
Apr [5] *Tangled Up In Blue*, from the album, makes US #31.
July Dylan sanctions the official release of double *The Basement Tapes*, after years of bootlegs of these 1967 recordings with The Band. Compiled and remixed by The Band's Robbie Robertson, the album hits US #7 and UK #8.
Oct [23] Dylan previews his forthcoming "Rolling Thunder Revue" tour by playing early morning set at Folk City in Greenwich Village as a birthday surprise for the club's owner Mike Porco. Joan Baez, Ronee Blakley, Ramblin' Jack Elliott, Bob Neuwirth, Mick Ronson, Allen

Ginsberg also play.
[30] An initially low-key and spontaneous US tour, the "Rolling Thunder Revue", starts in Plymouth, MA. Musical guests joining in along the way include Joni Mitchell, Joan Baez and Roger McGuinn.
Dec [8] The "Rolling Thunder Revue" ends its first run at New York's Madison Square Garden with "Night Of The Hurricane", a benefit for boxer and convicted murderer Rubin "Hurricane" Carter. Muhammad Ali acts as compere with guest Roberta Flack.

1976 Jan *Desire*, including much of the new material sung on the tour with lyrics by Jacques Levy, vocals by Emmylou Harris and violin by Scarlet Rivera, tops the US chart for 5 weeks, earning Dylan's first US platinum disk for million-plus album sales, and hits UK #3. The track *Hurricane*, which pleads the case for Carter, is issued as a single, reaching US #33 and UK #43.
Apr [10] *Mozambique*, also from *Desire*, makes US #54, as "The Rolling Thunder Revue" begins another US tour.
[22] The show at Clearwater, FL, is taped by NBC for a projected special, but rejected.
Oct *Hard Rain*, recorded live from shows at Fort Worth, TX, and Fort Collins, CO, peaks at US #17 and hits UK #3. (The Fort Collins gig forms the basis of 60-min. TV film "Hard Rain", replacing the earlier project.)
Nov [25] Dylan joins The Band at its "The Last Waltz" farewell concert at The Winterland, San Francisco, CA, with a host of other guests. He sings *Baby Let Me Follow You Down*, *I Don't Believe You (She Acts Like We Never Have Met)*, *Forever Young* and *I Shall Be Released*, on which he is joined by an all-star cast.

1977 Mar [1] Dylan's wife Sara files for divorce. Dylan spends most of the year preoccupied with domestic matters and with completing his film "Renaldo And Clara".

1978 Feb [1] "Renaldo And Clara" is premiered in Los Angeles.
Mar [1] In the early part of a world tour, Dylan performs at Japan's Budokan concert hall. (The show is recorded for a future album.)
May [5] Dylan tracks are included on the triple album of The Band's final concert, "The Last Waltz", and he appears in Martin Scorsese's documentary film of the event.
[7] 90,000 tickets for Dylan's UK concerts at Earls Court, London, are sold out in 8 hours.
June Dylan opens his European tour at Earls Court, London.
[24] *Street Legal* hits UK #2.
July [15] Dylan plays an open-air festival at Blackbushe Aerodrome, Surrey, supported by Eric Clapton.
Aug [12] *Street Legal* makes US #11.
[19] *Baby Stop Crying*, taken from *Street Legal* and Dylan's biggest UK hit single for 5 years, interest being spurred by his Wembley concerts, reaches UK #13.
Nov [4] *Is Your Love In Vain* peaks at UK #56 (and is Dylan's last UK chart single).
Dec [16] A 3-month, 62-date, final US leg of the world tour closes in Miami, FL.

1979 Jan Dylan launches his own label, Accomplice Records, though little will come of it.
May [19] Double live *Bob Dylan At The Budokan*, recorded in Japan as part of a 10-country world tour and originally intended only for the Japanese market and released to combat the sale of bootlegs of 1978 tour recordings, hits UK #4.
June [16] *Bob Dylan At The Budokan* reaches US #13.
Aug [25] Jerry Wexler/Barry Beckett-produced *Slow Train Coming*, with its evangelistic lyrical approach confirming rumors of Dylan's conversion to Christianity, hits UK #2. Mark Knopfler of Dire Straits contributes on some tracks.
Sept [22] *Slow Train Coming* hits US #3, and is his second platinum (million-selling) album.
Nov [1] A "Slow Train Coming" US tour opens at the Fox Warfield theater, San Francisco, where the new religious material is booed.
[3] *Gotta Serve Somebody* reaches US #24.

1980 Feb [27] Dylan wins Best Rock Vocal Performance, Male for *Gotta Serve Somebody* at the 22nd annual Grammy awards.
July *Saved* continues the Christian theme, and features a sleeve painted by Dylan himself. It makes US #24 (his first since *Another Side Of Bob Dylan* not to enter US Top 20) but hits UK #3.
Nov Another US tour reintroduces earlier songs into his stage set, plus oldies unrecorded by Dylan, like *Fever* and *Abraham, Martin And John*.

1981 June A European tour to preface Dylan's forthcoming album has a repertoire which balances the newer evangelistic material with versions of familiar oldies.

Sept Religion-inspired *Shot Of Love* reaches US #33 and hits UK #6.
Oct Dylan begins a US tour to promote *Shot Of Love* at Milwaukee Auditorium.

1982 **Mar** Dylan is elected to the Songwriters Hall Of Fame.
June He joins Joan Baez at the "Peace Sunday" concert in California, duetting on *Blowin' In The Wind* and *With God On Our Side*.

1983 **Dec** Dylan, after a period when he is reported to be recording but unhappy with the results, releases *Infidels*, co-produced by Mark Knopfler of Dire Straits. This is his least overtly religious, and best-selling (gold in US) album for 4 years, reaching US #20 and hitting UK #9.

1984 **Jan** [28] *Sweetheart Like You*, taken from *Infidels*, reaches US #55 (and is Dylan's last US chart single).
Mar Dylan appears live on NBC TV's "Late Night With Letterman", playing 3 songs backed by rock band The Plugz.
Dec Live *Real Live*, recorded in London, Dublin and Newcastle while on a European tour in the summer, reaches US #115 and UK #54.

1985 **Jan** [28] Dylan takes part, with more than 30 other major US acts, in the Los Angeles session which produces USA For Africa's *We Are The World*, to benefit the starving in Africa and elsewhere. The single will top US and UK charts, selling over 7 million worldwide.
July *Empire Burlesque* reaches US #33 and UK #11. Dylan is backed on it by members of Tom Petty's band, The Heartbreakers.
[13] Dylan closes Live Aid in Philadelphia, PA, backed by The Rolling Stones' Keith Richards and Ron Wood on guitars.
Sept Backed by Tom Petty & The Heartbreakers, he performs at Farm Aid, University of Illinois, Champaign, IL.
Dec [14] Artists United Against Apartheid, comprising 49 artists including Dylan, makes US #38 and UK #21 with *Sun City*.

1986 **Jan** Retrospective 5-album box set *Biograph*, a 53-song compilaton of Dylan's recording career from 1962 to 1981, and including 18 unreleased tracks, climbs to US #33.
[20] Dylan performs at the concert, organized by Stevie Wonder, to celebrate the first Martin Luther King Day in US.
Feb He tours Australasia and Japan, backed by Tom Petty & The Heartbreakers.
Aug *Knocked Out Loaded*, produced in London by Dave Stewart of Eurythmics, reaches UK #35. Dylan returns to London to film movie "Hearts Of Fire" with Richard Marquand. In it, he plays opposite Rupert Everett and Fiona Flanagan as a jaded, middle-aged rock star.

1987 **June** Dylan tours US with The Grateful Dead, who back his set as well as playing their own (inevitably) longer one.
Oct For a European tour (which opens in Israel), he is backed by Petty's band, with ex-The Byrds Roger McGuinn supporting. George Harrison joins Dylan on stage on the final date, at Wembley, UK.
Dec Movie "Hearts Of Fire" is released in UK after an almost 6-month transatlantic delay. Critically panned, it is generally ignored by the public and considered to be one of Dylan's most ill-advised career moves.

1988 **June** *Down In The Groove*, is released. Much of the material is non-original (it was first intended to comprise only cover versions, like *Self-Portrait*, but its format is twice changed by Dylan during a 6-month delay from original release date). The list of contributing musicians includes Eric Clapton, hip-hoppers Full Force, Mark Knopfler, Ron Wood, ex-Sex Pistol Steve Jones and ex-Clash bassist Paul Simonon. Jerry Garcia, Bob Weir and Brent Mydland of The Grateful Dead also play on the album, and 2 of the new songs, *The Ugliest Girl In The World* and *Silvio*, are co-written with their lyricist Robert Hunter. The 6 covers range from Wilbert Harrison's *Let's Stick Together* to the traditional *Shenandoah*. It reaches UK #32 and US #61.
June Dylan arrives in UK for live dates in Birmingham and London.

1988 **Sept** Dylan contributes *Pretty Boy Floyd* to Woody Guthrie/Leadbelly tribute album *Folkways: A Vision Shared*.
Oct "Lucky" Dylan joins George "Nelson" Harrison, Jeff "Otis" Lynne, Roy "Lefty" Orbison and Tom "Charlie T. Jnr." Petty in The Traveling Wilburys. Their debut *Traveling Wilburys Volume One* and single *Handle With Care* are released to great success.
Nov Dylan and his brother David Zimmerman sell the Orpheum theater in Minneapolis, MN, for $1.4 million.
Dec [4] Dylan is part of the line-up (including Crosby, Stills, Nash & Young, Tracy Chapman, and The Grateful Dead) at the sell-out Oakland Coliseum Music Festival, CA.

1989 **Jan** [18] Dylan joins a superstar jam session at the finale of the Rock'N'Roll Hall Of Fame induction dinner at New York's Waldorf Astoria – and is inducted himself by Bruce Springsteen.
Feb *Dylan And The Dead* makes UK #38 and US #37. It is a live

souvenir of their 1987 double-header tour.
June Dylan plays sold-out dates in UK's Birmingham and London before returning to New Orleans to complete recording a new album with U2 producer Daniel Lanois.
July [1] US tour dates begin in Peoria, IL.
Oh Mercy, produced by Daniel Lanois with backing from the Neville Brothers' band, makes US #30 and hits UK #6.
Sept [24] Dylan participates in "L'Chai – To Life!" telethon with son-in-law Peter Himmelman (married to his daughter Maria), Harry Dean Stanton and others.

1990 **Jan** [12] Dylan opens international tour with 4-hour long warm-up concerts at Toad's Place, New Haven, CT.
[18] He opens 6-day 2-city rock festival in Sao Paulo, Brazil, on a bill with Bon Jovi, Terence Trent D'Arby, Eurythmics, Marillion and Tears For Fears.
[30] Dylan is awarded France's highest cultural honor, the Commandeur dans l'Ordre des Arts et des Lettres by Minister Jack Lang in a ceremony at the Palais Royal, Paris.
June [4] On a European tour, Dylan is joined by U2's Bono at a concert in Dublin, and will subsequently receive Van Morrison on stage in Athens and Nina Simone in Amsterdam.
Aug Gregg and Donna French buy Dylan's childhood home at 2425 W.Seventh St., Hibbing, MN, for $57,000.
Sept *Under The Red Sky*, again produced by Lanois, makes US #38 and UK #13.

1991 **Apr** *The Bootleg Series Volumes 1-3 (Rare & Unreleased) 1961-1991* is released.

THE EAGLES

Glenn Frey (guitar, vocals)
Bernie Leadon (guitar, vocals)
Randy Meisner (bass, vocals)
Don Henley (drums, vocals)

1971 **Aug** The Eagles, formed by Frey (b. Nov.6, 1948, Detroit, MI), Meisner (b. Mar.8, 1947, Scottsbluff, NB), Henley (b. July 22, 1947, Gilmer, TX) and Leadon (b. July 19, 1947, Minneapolis, MN), country-rock veteran of Los Angeles, CA, Hearts & Flowers, Dillard & Clark and The Flying Burrito Brothers, after they have all played live together backing Linda Ronstadt, are booked by Asylum Records' boss David Geffen into an Aspen, CO, club to play 4 sets a night for a month to tighten their act.

1972 **Apr** Signed to Asylum Records, group travels to UK to record first album with producer Glyn Johns at Olympic studios, Barnes, London.
July [22] *Take It Easy*, penned by Frey with friend Jackson Browne, is chart debut, reaching US #12.
Oct *The Eagles*, including the hit single, climbs to US #22.
Nov [18] *Witchy Woman*, from the album, hits US #9.
[24] The Eagles appear as part of superstar-billed, K-ROQ "Woodstock Of The West" festival. Only 32,000 show.

1973 **Mar** [10] Jack Tempchin-penned *Peaceful Easy Feeling*, also from debut album, reaches US #22.
June *Desperado*, again recorded in London with producer Johns (now at Island studios), reaches US #41. (Title track, although never a single, will be covered later by Linda Ronstadt, Bonnie Raitt, The Carpenters and others.) Movie director Sam Peckinpah plans to turn the album into a cowboy film, but plans fall through.
July [21] Extracted *Tequila Sunrise*, written by emerging songwriting tandem Henley and Frey, peaks at US #64.
Oct [27] *Outlaw Man*, also from *Desperado*, makes US #59.

1974 **Jan** Don Felder (b. Sept.21, 1947, Topanga, CA) plays slide guitar on *Good Day In Hell* for the next album sessions at The Record Plant in Los Angeles. He so impresses the band that he joins full-time. Producer Bill Szymczyk takes over from Johns in midstream, at the recommendation of Joe Walsh who toured with the band, to give the group a more rock-oriented sound.
Apr [6] The Eagles play the "California Jam" rock festival to an audience of 200,000.
[20] *On The Border* reaches UK #28.
May *On The Border* reaches US #17 (later going gold). Mostly recorded at The Record Plant, including 3 songs co-written with J.D. Souther and 1 by Tom Waits, their new producer and additional guitarist help harden the sound from country into rock.
June [29] *Already Gone* makes US #32.
Oct [12] *James Dean* stalls at US #77.

1975 **Mar** [1] Acoustic guitar-based ballad *The Best Of My Love* tops US chart for 1 week, and is their first million-selling single.

June [21] The Eagles play at Elton John's headlining concert at London's Wembley Stadium to an audience of 100,000.

[28] *Desperado* makes UK #39.

July [5] *One Of These Nights* hits UK #8.

[26] *One Of These Nights* tops US chart for 5 weeks. Helmed again by Szymczyk, all 9 tracks are penned by current band members except *I Wish You, Peace*, credited to Leadon and Patti Reagan Davis, which causes controversy when Davis says in a **Las Vegas Sun** interview she enjoys royalties received from the song. Henley writes to the paper claiming Davis' contribution is negligible.

Aug [2] *One Of These Nights* tops US chart.

Sept [6] *One Of These Nights*, their first UK chart single, reaches #23.

Nov [8] Softer follow-up *Lyin' Eyes*, written by Henley and Frey, hits US #2 for 2 weeks, behind Elton John's *Island-Girl*.

[15] *Lyin' Eyes* reaches UK #23.

Dec [20] Leadon leaves having argued over the group's musical direction. (He will re-emerge, still with Asylum Records, with The Bernie Leadon/Michael Georgiades Band in mid-1977, before playing with The Nitty Gritty Dirt Band in 80s.) Successful rock soloist and ex-James Gang member Joe Walsh (b. Nov.20, 1947, Wichita, KS) joins.

'6 Feb [28] The Eagles win Best Pop Vocal Performance By A Duo, Group Or Chorus for *Lyin' Eyes* at 18th annual Grammy awards.

Mar [6] *Their Greatest Hits, 1971-1975* hits UK #2.

[13] String-laden (arranged by Jim Ed Norman) *Take It To The Limit*, with lead vocals by co-writer Meisner, hits US #4 and UK #12, as compilation album *Their Greatest Hits, 1971-1975* tops US chart for 5 weeks, and is certified platinum. Group starts work on new album at Criteria studios in Miami, FL, (sessions will end in Oct.)

'7 Jan [15] *Hotel California* tops US chart for 1 week and is certified platinum. (It will return to US #1 for a further week in Feb., and in Mar., then 5 consecutive weeks in Apr./May, and will prove to be the group's commercial apex.)

Feb [26] Extracted *New Kid In Town*, written by Henley/Frey/Souther, hits US #1 and UK #20. It is a US million-seller.

Mar [5] *Their Greatest Hits* is voted Album Of The Year by National Association Of Record Merchandisers (NARM).

[14] Group begins a month's US tour at Civic Center, Springfield, MA.

[18] Band is joined on stage by The Rolling Stones' Ron Wood for an encore at their Madison Square Garden, New York, concert. Mick Jagger and Bill Wyman, also at the concert, remain in the audience.

Apr [25] The Eagles' European tour begins at Wembley, London. (It will end on May 18 at Scandinavium, Gothenberg, Sweden.)

[30] *Hotel California* hits UK #2.

May [7] Title track from *Hotel California*, another million-seller, tops US chart and hits UK #8.

[28-30] The Eagles join Foreigner, Heart and The Steve Miller Band, playing 2 concerts at Oakland Stadium, CA, before a crowd of 100,000.

June [18] A US summer tour begins at the Civic Center, Roanoke, VA.

[25] *Life In The Fast Lane*, written by Henley/Frey/Walsh, reaches US #11. The Leadon/Georgiades band makes US #91 with *Natural Progressions*.

Sept Following a tour of UK, Scandinavia and Europe and a summer US tour, Meisner leaves exhausted with life on the road. (He will retreat to Nebraska and pursue a solo career. (Title track of his debut album *One More Song*, with Frey and Henley on backing vocals, eulogizes his last days with The Eagles.) He is replaced by Timothy B. Schmit (b. Oct.30, 1947, Sacramento, CA), who also succeeded Meisner in Poco.

'8 Feb [23] Group wins Record Of The Year for *Hotel California* and Best Arrangement For Voices for *New Kid In Town* at 20th annual Grammy awards.

May [7] The Eagles beat **Rolling Stone** magazine 15-8 in a softball game.

Band is featured on soundtrack album to rock film "FM".

July [23] A month's Canadian tour begins in Edmonton.

Aug [5] Walsh's solo *Life's Been Good* reaches US #14.

Dec [23] A revival of Charles Brown's blues standard *Please Come Home For Christmas*, backed with their own *Funky New Year*, reaches US #18 and UK #30.

'9 Sept [3] *The Long Run* tops US chart for 8 weeks.

Oct [13] *The Long Run* hits UK #4.

Nov [10] *Heartache Tonight*, written by Frey and Henley with Bob Seger and J.D. Souther, hits US #1, selling over a million copies, but makes only UK #40.

Dec Extracted title track *The Long Run* charts briefly at UK #66 (and will be The Eagles' last UK singles chart entry).

[21] They appear with Chicago and Linda Ronstadt at a benefit show

for Presidential candidate Jerry Brown.

1980 Feb [2] *The Long Run* hits US #8.

[27] *Heartache Tonight* wins Best Rock Vocal Performance By A Duo Or Group at 22nd annual Grammy awards.

Mar [20] 28-year-old Joseph Riviera holds up Asylum Records office in New York demanding to see either Jackson Browne or The Eagles, wanting them to finance his trucking operation. He surrenders, when told that neither act is in the office as they live in California.

Apr [19] Schmit's co-written and sung ballad *I Can't Tell You Why* hits US #8.

Nov Meisner's *One More Song* makes US #50.

Dec Double album *Live* hits US #6 and UK #24. Compiled from on-stage recordings, it is released after The Eagles have been inactive throughout 1980, and have already mutually agreed to split when *The Long Run* was completed.

[6] Meisner's solo *Deep Inside My Heart* reaches US #22.

1981 Jan *Live* is certified platinum.

Feb [7] Extracted *Seven Bridges Road* reaches US #21 and is group's final US hit single. All ex-Eagles members will go on to solo careers with varying degrees of success. Henley's popularity will be the most spectacular and enduring.

Mar [14] Meisner's *Hearts On Fire* reaches US #19.

Oct [17] Felder's *Takin' A Ride*, from cartoon movie "Heavy Metal", makes US #43.

1982 Aug [7] Frey's solo *I Found Somebody* makes US #31.

[14] His debut album *No Fun Aloud*, mostly written with Jack Tempchin (co-writer of *Peaceful Easy Feeling*), reaches US #32.

Sept [18] Meisner's *Randy Meisner* makes US #94, as extracted *Never Been In Love* reaches #28. His solo career will fade despite further recordings, but he will re-emerge in 1990 with Billy Swan and Bread's James Griffin in Black Tie.

[30] Schmit peaks at US #59 with his solo revival of The Tymes' *So Much In Love*, featured in film "Fast Times At Ridgemont High".

Nov [6] Frey's *The One You Love* reaches US #15.

Dec Compilation *Eagles' Greatest Hits, Vol. 2* reaches US #52.

1983 Jan [15] Frey's *All Those Lies* makes US #41 while Felder's *Airborne* climbs to US #178, his final chart appearance.

1984 June Frey's debut album for MCA *The Allnighter* makes US #37.

Aug [18] *Sexy Girl* by Frey reaches US #20.

Oct [27] Frey's *The Allnighter* reaches US #54.

Nov Schmit's *Playin' It Cool*, released on Asylum, peaks at US #160.

1985 Mar [16] Frey hits US #2 and UK #12 with *The Heat Is On* from film "Beverly Hills Cop", while Henley's *Building The Perfect Beast* reaches UK #14.

May Compilation *The Best Of The Eagles* hits UK #8.

June [22] Frey's drug-themed *Smugglers Blues*, from NBC TV series "Miami Vice", reaches US #12 and UK #22. (Frey plays a drug smuggler in an episode of the series based around the song.)

July Frey's *The Allnighter* climbs to UK #31.

Nov [16] Frey's *You Belong To The City* hits US #2.

1987 Nov [7] Schmit's *Boys Night Out* reaches US #25.

Dec Schmit's second solo album *Timothy B.*, on MCA Records, peaks at US #106.

1988 Aug A new UK-only retrospective anthology **The Best Of The Eagles** hits #8, tying in with CD single release of *Hotel California*.

Sept Frey releases *Soul Searchin'*, which makes US #37, as *True Love* peaks at US #13.

1989 Mar [25] Frey's *Livin' Right* makes US #90.

1990 Apr Frey and Schmit join Henley on stage at Worcester, MA (the first time the 3 have sung together in a decade).

May Frey receives the Reebok From The Heart award at the T.J. Martell Foundation's Rock 'N Charity Weekend in honor of his contributions to the fight against AIDS, cancer and leukemia.

Aug *The Best Of The Eagles* returns to UK chart to peak at #57.

1991 Apr Frey's *Part Of You, Part Of Me*, from Susan Sarandon-starring movie "Thelma And Louise" is released.

STEVE EARLE

1969 Having grown up in Schertz, near San Antonio, TX, and run away from home several times, Earle (b. Jan.17, 1955, Fort Monroe, VA) drops out of high school in ninth grade and begins a 5-year period of songwriting and playing in Texas clubs, coffee houses and honky tonks, during which he will liaise with renowned songwriter Townes Van Zandt.

1975 Earle relocates to Nashville, TN, and becomes a staff writer for a succession of country and western publishers.

STEVE EARLE cont.

1982 After 7 years of writing for others, he decides to kick-start his own performing career once more, initially playing rockabilly/country mix. He signs with local Nashville label LS1, which releases his debut recordings on 4-track EP *Pink And Black*. This attracts Epic's local office, for whom he records *Cadillac*. But 2 weeks prior to scheduled release date, and with cover art work completed, Epic cans the project. (It would have included Earle-penned *My Baby Worships Me*, a later country hit for Waylon Jennings.)

1984 Following 4 unsuccessful Epic singles, *Nothing But You*, *Squeeze Me In*, *What'll You Do About Me* and *A Little Bit In Love*, label drops Earle.

1985 Through notable Nashville shaker Emory Gordy Jr., now staff producer at MCA, who has worked with him on Epic album, Earle signs to MCA.

1986 **Oct** [25] Debut MCA album, hard outlaw-country styled *Guitar Town* is released set to make US #89, and hit #1 on US Country chart during a 66-week stay. Following its success and sell-out dates throughout US, Earle will be voted Top Country Artist in **Rolling Stone** magazine and heralded as a pioneer of "new country" alongside Randy Travis and Dwight Yoakam at future country music award shows. (Epic finally releases *Cadillac* now as *Steve Earle: Early Tracks*.)

1987 **July** Now billed with his backing band as Steve Earle & The Dukes, second MCA album *Exit O* peaks at US #90 and UK #77, as further US tour dates are undertaken.

1988 **Jan** One-off country cut *Six Days On The Road*, featured in Steve Martin/John Candy-starring hit comedy "Planes, Trains And Automobiles" reaches US Country #29.
Nov [11] Moving further towards rock mainstream and signed to MCA licensee Uni Records, *Copperhead Road* makes country and rock breakthroughs, reaching US #56, and will spend 2 months on UK chart peaking at #44, accompanied by a UK concert tour. Title cut *Copperhead Road* also makes UK #45.
Dec *Johnny Come Lately* spends 1 week at UK #75.

1989 In between albums, Earle and The Dukes continue to tour, not least opening for Bob Dylan on his US summer trek.

1990 **July** [7] Co-produced by Earle and Joe Hardy, *The Hard Way* reaches UK #22, again fusing rock and country. Again, The Dukes, Zip Gibson (lead guitar), Kelly Looney (bass), Craig Wright (drums), Ken Moore (keyboards) and Bucky Baxter (steel guitar) are credited with Earle.
Aug [18] *The Hard Way* peaks at US #100.
Dec [1] Earle and The Dukes, still touring incessantly, perform in St. Louis, MO, on their latest US dates, while Earle has also found time to produce an album for The Immigrants in Los Angeles, CA.

1991 **June** Earle releases live album *Shut Up And Die Like An Aviator*.

EARTH, WIND & FIRE

Maurice White (vocals, drums, percussion, kalimba)
Verdine White (vocals, bass)
Philip Bailey (vocals, conga, percussion)
Larry Dunn (piano, synthesizers)
Al McKay (guitars)
Fred White (drums)
Ralph Johnson (drums)
Johnny Graham (guitar)
Andrew Woolfolk (tenor saxophone)

1955 Maurice White (b. Dec.19, 1944, Memphis, TN) begins playing drums with Memphis schoolfriend Booker T. Jones (later of Booker T. And The MG's).

1960 After a brief period at Roosevelt University in Chicago, IL, White attends Chicago Conservatory of Music, studying composition and percussion, with the aim of becoming a teacher.

1963 He finds work as a session drummer at Chess Records, working with Billy Stewart, Chuck Berry, Sonny Stitt, Jackie Wilson, The Impressions, The Dells and Etta James.

1966 He joins The Ramsey Lewis Trio and plays on 10 of Lewis' albums. While recording with them, he introduces the kalimba, a small finger piano from Africa.

1969 White forms The Salty Peppers, who have a local Chicago hit with *La La Time* and *Love Is Life* on Capitol Records.

1970 White changes group name to Earth, Wind & Fire. They sign to Warner Bros. Records.

1971 **Apr** Debut album *Earth, Wind And Fire*, produced by Joe Wissert and featuring initial line-up Maurice and Verdine White, Wade Flemons (vocals), Don Whitehead (piano, vocals), Sherry Scott (vocals), Michael Beal (guitar, harmonica), Yackov Ben Israel (percussion), Chet Washington (tenor sax) and Alex Thomas (trombone), reaches US #172 during a 13-week chart stay.

July [17] *Love Is Life* is first US singles chart entry at #93.

1972 **Jan** *The Need Of Love* is released, climbing to US #89.
Group leaves Warner Bros. and signs to CBS/Columbia. White dismantles the band and recruits Philip Bailey (b. May 8, 1951, Denver, CO) (vocals, percussion), Jessica Cleaves (vocals), Roland Bautista (guitar), Larry Dunn (piano, organ, clavinet), Ronnie Laws (tenor sax, flute) and Ralph Johnson (b. July 4, 1951) (drums, percussion). The only other remaining member of the original line-up is Maurice's brother Verdine (b. July 25, 1951). New group begins work on its Columbia debut with producer Wissert at Sunset Sound studios, Hollywood, CA.
Nov CBS/Columbia debut album *Last Days And Time*, including selections by Pete Seeger (*Where Have All The Flowers Gone*) and Bread (*Make It With You*), makes US #87.

1973 **June** *Head To The Sky*, again produced by Wissert, reaches US #27 (later going gold). Al McKay replaces Bautista, Andrew Woolfolk replaces Laws and Johnny Graham (b. Aug.3, 1951) is added on guitar.
Sept [15] *Evil* makes US #50.

1974 **Jan** [5] *Keep Your Head To The Sky* peaks at US #52.
Mar *Open Our Eyes* reaches US #15 and goes platinum. White produces Ramsey Lewis' *Sun Goddess* (which reaches US #12 at year end). Earth, Wind & Fire opens for Sly & The Family Stone at New York's Madison Square Garden.
May [18] *Mighty Mighty* reaches US #29.
Aug [17] *Kalimba Story* peaks at US #55.
Sept *Another Time*, a reissue of their first 2 albums, reaches US #97.
Oct [19] *Devotion* makes US #33.

1975 **Feb** [15] *Hot Dawgit*, with Ramsey Lewis, makes US #50.
Apr [19] *Sun Goddess*, also with Ramsey Lewis, makes US #44.
May *That's The Way Of The World*, billed as *Original Soundtrack From The Sig Shore Production "That's The Way Of The World"*, tops US chart for 3 weeks, eventually selling over 2 million. Earth, Wind & Fire is featured as a rock band in movie "Shining Star".
[24] Film theme, *Shining Star*, hits US #1, gaining a gold disk for a million sales. White's brother, Fred, joins on drums.
Sept [20] *That's The Way Of The World* reaches US #12. Band embarks on its first European tour, supporting Santana.

1976 **Jan** Double album *Gratitude* tops US chart for 3 weeks, and again achieves double platinum, as the group wins Favorite R&B Group at the annual American Music Awards.
Feb [7] *Sing A Song* hits US #5 and is another million-seller.
[28] Earth, Wind & Fire wins Best R&B Vocal Performance By A Duo Group Or Chorus for *Shining Star* at the 18th annual Grammy awards.
Apr *Can't Hide Love* makes US #39.
Oct [9] *Getaway* reaches US #12. *Spirit*, dedicated to White's co-producer Charles Stepney who died earlier in the year, hits US #2. Held off the top by Stevie Wonder's *Songs In The Key Of Life*, it is still double platinum-seller. Current line-up is Maurice and Verdine White, Bailey, Dunn, Johnson, now augmented by McKay (guitars, percussion), Graham (guitars), Woolfolk (saxophones, percussion) and Fred White (drums, percussion).

1977 **Jan** [29] *Saturday Nite* reaches US #21.
Mar *Saturday Nite* is UK chart debut, reaching #17.
June Backing group girl trio The Emotions, recently on tour with Earth, Wind & Fire, hits US #1 with White-written and produced *Best Of My Love*.

1978 **Jan** [7] Recorded at Hollywood Sound, Sunset Sound and Burbank studios, Los Angeles, CA, and featuring ace percussionist Paulinho DaCosta, *All'N'All* hits US #3, again reaching double platinum.
Feb [4] *All'N'All*, group's first UK album chart entry, reaches #13.
[11] *Serpentine Fire* reaches US #13.
Mar [18] *Fantasy* reaches UK #14.
Apr [22] *Fantasy* makes US #32.
May [27] *Jupiter* makes UK #41.
Aug [26] *Magic Mind* peaks at UK #54.
Sept [16] *Got To Get You Into My Life*, the Lennon/McCartney song which the band performs in film "Sergeant Pepper's Lonely Hearts Club Band", hits US #9 and is a US million-seller.
Oct [22] Earth, Wind & Fire begins a 75-date sold-out US tour in Louisville, KY.
[28] *Got To Get You Into My Life* makes UK #33.

1979 **Jan** *September* hits UK #3.
[9] The "Music For UNICEF Concert", to celebrate the International Year Of The Child, takes place in the United Nations General Assembly Hall in New York. Earth Wind & Fire sing a medley *September* and *That's The Way Of The World*, donating their royalties to UNICEF.
[10] NBC TV airs "A Gift Of Song – The Music For UNICEF Concert".

[27] Compilation *The Best Of Earth, Wind & Fire Vol.1* hits US and UK #6, the group's fourth consecutive US double platinum-seller.

Feb [10] *September* hits US #8. Maurice White establishes The American Recording Company (ARC) in Los Angeles, CA, with an artist roster including The Emotions, Deniece Williams, Weather Report and D.J. Rogers. His production skills are much in demand and he will oversee albums by other artists including Barbra Streisand, Jennifer Holliday, Ramsey Lewis and Valerie Carter.

[15] *All'N'All* wins Best R&B Vocal Performance By A Duo, Group Or Chorus and *Runnin'* wins Best R&B Instrumental Performance at the 21st annual Grammy awards.

June [23] *I Am* hits UK #5.

July [14] *Boogie Wonderland*, featuring The Emotions on guest vocals, hits UK #4 and US #6 and sells over a million while *I Am* hits US #3.

Sept [15] David Foster, Bill Champlin and Jay Graydon-penned *After The Love Has Gone* hits US #2 (another million-seller) and UK #4.

Oct [18] During another sell-out US tour, 15 youths are arrested at the group's Madison Square Garden concert, charged with mugging audience members.

Nov *Star* reaches UK #16.

[10] *In The Stone* peaks at US #58.

Dec *Can't Let Go* and *In The Stone* reach UK #46 and #53. By year's end, Earth, Wind & Fire will have toured US, Europe and Asia.

80 Jan [19] *Star* breaks their run of major US hit singles, stalling at US #64, as group prepares for a South American tour.

Feb [27] *After The Love Has Gone* wins Best R&B Vocal Performance By A Duo, Group Or Chorus and *Boogie Wonderland* wins Best R&B Instrumental Performance at the 22nd annual Grammy awards.

Oct [18] *Let Me Talk* climbs to UK #29 and US #44.

Nov Double album *Faces*, including songwriting contributions from Foster, Brenda Russell, James Newton Howard and Valerie Carter among others, is released, hitting both US and UK #10.

Dec [20] *You* makes US #48.

[27] *Back On The Road* peaks at UK #63.

81 Feb [28] *And Love Goes On* peaks at US #59, as Earth, Wind & Fire undertakes another US tour.

Nov *Raise*, with string arrangements by Foster, Billy Meyers and horn arrangements by Jerry Hey, hits US #5. Bautista rejoins, replacing McKay, who leaves to concentrate on record production.

[28] Funked-up *Let's Groove* hits UK #3.

Dec [19] *Let's Groove* hits US #3, and again goes gold. It also spends a record-breaking 11 weeks at the top of US R&B chart.

82 Jan [9] *Raise* reaches UK #14.

Feb [13] *Wanna Be With You* peaks at US #51.

[20] *I've Had Enough* reaches UK #29.

83 Feb [23] Group wins Best R&B Performance By A Duo, Group Or Chorus for *Wanna Be With You* at the 25th annual Grammy awards.

Mar [19] *Fall In Love With Me* reaches US #17 and UK #47. *Powerlight* makes US #12 and UK #22.

May [21] *Side By Side* stalls at US #76.

Sept Bailey's debut solo album *Continuation*, produced by George Duke, makes US #71.

Dec [3] *Magnetic* peaks at US #57. *Electric Universe*, repeating usual Earth, Wind & Fire formula, enters US chart, but only climbs to US #40.

84 Mar *Touch* reaches US R&B #23, but fails to cross over or sell in UK. White disbands the group, claiming he needs a long rest. (He will concentrate the next 2 years on his Kalimba production company.)

Oct Bailey records solo album *Chinese Wall* at Townhouse studios in London, with Phil Collins producing.

Nov *Easy Lover*, a duet with Phil Collins written by Bailey and Collins with Nathan East, is released as a US single and hits #2. Bailey also records spiritual solo album *The Wonders Of His Love* for US religious label Myrrh. (He has become a Christian in 1975 and will continue parallel recordings for both pop and Christian markets.) It sells a quarter million copies in US alone.

85 Feb [2] *Easy Lover* hits US #2.

Mar *Easy Lover* hits UK #1, while *Chinese Wall* reaches US #22.

Apr *Chinese Wall* reaches UK #29.

May [11] *Walking On The Chinese Wall* makes US #46. *Walking On The Chinese Wall* reaches UK #34. (Bailey will continue his solo outings but also rejoin Earth, Wind & Fire when it returns to recording during 1987.)

Oct [26] White's solo revival of *Stand By Me* makes US #50. Debut solo album *Maurice White* reaches US #61.

86 Feb [8] White's *I Need You* makes US #95.

Apr [7] *Easy Lover* is honored as Most Performed Work at the annual

Ivor Novello Awards at London's Grosvenor House.

May Third pop soul album by Bailey, *Inside Out*, peaks at US #84.

[10] Earth, Wind & Fire career retrospective *The Collection* hits UK #5.

Oct White and Bailey meet to discuss re-forming Earth, Wind & Fire.

Nov Second Bailey spiritual album, *Triumph*, finds only specialist interest.

1987 Feb [24] Bailey wins Best Gospel Performance, Male for *Triumph* at the 29th annual Grammy awards.

Nov Having achieved 6 double platinum and 2 platinum albums with numerous gold awards, Earth, Wind & Fire reunites with White, Bailey, Verdine White, Andrew Woolfolk and Sheldon Reynolds. *Touch The World*, with session musicians backing White and Bailey's vocals, fails in UK, but climbs to US #33.

Dec [12] *System Of Survival*, produced by White and Preston Glass, tops US R&B chart.

[19] *System Of Survival* makes US #60 and UK #54.

1988 June Bailey releases a further Myrrh album *Wonders Of His Love* , (followed by *Family Affair* in 1990).

Oct Following US dates, Earth, Wind & Fire visits UK as part of its "Touch The World" global tour.

1989 Mar Bailey links with Little Richard to release one-off duet *Twins*, title theme from Arnold Schwarzenegger/Danny De Vito hit movie.

1990 Mar [3] With Earth, Wind & Fire now comprising the White brothers, Bailey, Woolfolk, Johnson, Reynolds and Sonny Emory (drums), *Heritage* makes US #70, but again fails in UK. Album features current hot American acts MC Hammer, on extracted *Wanna Be The Man* and Motown teen unit The Boys, guesting on the title cut.

Sept [13] Group begins 24-date European tour at Ahoy in Rotterdam, Holland. Tour will end on Oct.17 at the Bercy, Paris, France.

1991 After nearly 2 decades with CBS, Earth, Wind & Fire signs with Warner Bros.

SHEENA EASTON

1979 June Easton (b. Sheena Orr, youngest of 6 children, Apr.27, 1959, Bellshill, Glasgow, Scotland) graduates as a teacher of speech and drama from the Royal Scottish Academy of Music and Drama, a month after successfully auditioning as a singer for EMI Records in London.

1980 Apr Debut release *Modern Girl* peaks at UK #56.

July [2] She is featured in an edition of BBC TV series "The Big Time", which allows people to sample their ambitions. Easton is seen at her audition, recording her first single, and undergoing the grooming and launch process EMI gives to a new act.

Aug Boosted by national TV exposure, well-timed second single *9 To 5* shoots to UK #3.

Sept TV has also reactivated demand for *Modern Girl*, which re-charts and hits UK #8, giving Easton the rare achievement for a British female singer of 2 simultaneous UK Top 10 hits.

Nov She appears in the Royal Variety Show, London, watched by the Queen Mother. *One Man Woman* reaches UK #14.

1981 Feb [14] Christopher Neil-produced debut album *Take My Time* reaches UK #17.

[21] Extracted title track *Take My Time* makes UK #44.

May [2] *Morning Train (9 To 5)* hits US #1 for 2 weeks, selling over a million. Title has been amended for US to avoid confusion with Dolly Parton's film theme song *9 To 5*, which hit US #1 in Mar. *Sheena Easton* reaches US #24.

[23] Ballad *When He Shines* makes UK #12.

July [18] *Modern Girl* makes US #18.

Aug [8] *For Your Eyes Only* hits UK #8. It is theme song for current James Bond movie, and Easton becomes the only Bond theme singer to be seen on screen singing the song during the credits.

Oct Easton's sell-out UK tour ends with 2 dates at the Dominion theater, London.

[10] *You Could Have Been With Me*, again produced by Neil and recorded at Caribou Ranch in Colorado, reaches UK #33.

[17] *For Your Eyes Only* hits US #4 as *Just Another Broken Heart* makes UK #33.

Nov She undertakes 12-date tour of Japan.

Dec [12] Extracted title track *You Could Have Been With Me* peaks at UK #54, as Easton is rewarded with **Daily Mirror**/"Nationwide" Rock & Pop awards Best Female Singer and **TV Times**' Readers Female Personality Of The Year award in UK.

1982 Feb [20] *You Could Have Been With Me* reaches US #15.

[24] Easton wins Best New Artist at the 24th annual Grammy awards.

Apr [3] *You Could Have Been With Me* makes US #47.

May Easton performs her first US dates.

June [5] *When He Shines* reaches US #30.

Aug She returns to US for a major 30-date tour, followed by more touring in the Far East.

[7] *Machinery* makes UK #38, and will be her last solo UK hit single for nearly 9 years.

Sept [25] *Machinery* peaks at US #57 as *Madness, Money And Music* makes UK #44.

Oct [30] *Madness, Money And Music* makes US #85.

Nov [13] *I Wouldn't Beg For Water* peaks at US #64.

1983 **Mar** [26] Easton's duet with Kenny Rogers on David Foster-produced revival of Bob Seger's *We've Got Tonight* hits US #6. It also tops US Country chart, and reaches UK #28.

Sept [25] NBC TV special "Sheena Easton ... Act 1" wins Emmy for Oustanding Directing In A Variety Or Musical Program.

Oct [29] *Telefone (Long Distance Love Affair)* hits US #9. *Best Kept Secret*, co-produced Jay Graydon and Greg Mathieson and recorded with American-only top session players, makes US #33 and UK #99.

1984 **Mar** [10] *Almost Over You* reaches US #25.

Apr [21] *Devil In A Fast Car* stalls at US #79.

Nov [24] *Strut*, pointing Easton in a new funky uptempo direction, hits US #7.

1985 **Feb** *A Private Heaven* makes US #15, becoming her most successful US album.

[26] Easton wins Best Mexican/American Performance with Luis Miguel for *Me Gustas Tal Como Eres* at the 27th annual Grammy awards.

Mar [2] *Sugar Walls*, written by Prince, hits US #9. Mildly erotic symbolism in its lyrics arouses some controversy, but does not deprive it of airplay. Easton becomes the first artist in history to achieve Top 5 hits on US pop, R&B, Country, Dance, and Adult Contemporary charts.

Apr [6] *Sweat* stalls at US #80.

Nov She sings theme *Christmas All Over The World* over the credits of Dudley Moore-starring film "Santa Claus – The Movie".

Dec [14] *Do It For Love* reaches US #29. *Do You*, produced and partly written by Nile Rodgers, makes US #40.

1986 **Mar** [1] A revival of Martha & The Vandellas' 1967 US #10 *Jimmy Mack* peaks at US #65.

July She teams with producer Narada Michael Walden for 2-song contribution to Rob Lowe movie "About Last Night".

Sept [27] *So Far So Good*, from "About Last Night", makes US #43.

1987 **Oct** [17] Easton's duet with Prince on *U Got The Look*, taken from his album *Sign O' The Times*, hits US #2, behind Lisa Lisa & Cult Jam's *Lost In Emotion*.

U Got The Look makes UK #11. Talk of romantic links is fuelled by provocative duetting on the promotional video for *U Got The Look*.

1988 **July** An interview with Esther Rantzen, hostess of original "Big Time" program that launched her career airs on BBC TV. By year's end Easton will return to the recording studio to begin work on her debut album for MCA Records.

1989 **Feb** *The Lover In Me* makes UK #15.

Mar *The Lover In Me*, completing Easton's successful transition from light pop performer to strutting dance siren, makes US #44, and is produced and co-written with current dance hit-making duo L.A. Reid and Babyface. *Days Like This* makes UK #43, as *The Lover In Me* reaches UK #30. Similar EMI career retrospectives are released, titled *For Your Eyes Only – The Best Of Sheena Easton* (UK) and *The Collection* (US). [4] *The Lover In Me* hits US #2, behind Debbie Gibson's *Lost In Your Eyes*.

July [15] *101* peaks at UK #54.

Dec [16] *The Arms Of Orion*, another Prince/Easton duet, makes US #36 on Warner Bros. and reaches UK #27.

1991 **Feb** [10] Easton joins nearly 100 celebrities in Burbank, CA, to record *Voices That Care*, a David Foster and fiancee Linda Thompson Jenner-composed and organized charity record to benefit the American Red Cross Gulf Crisis Fund.

Mar Easton's new single *What Comes Naturally* begins US chart rise.

THE EASYBEATS

"Little" Stevie Wright (vocals)
Harry Vanda (guitar)
George Young (guitar)
Dick Diamonde (bass)
Gordon "Snowy" Fleet (drums)

1963 Group forms in Sydney, Australia. 3 of its members – Wright (b. Stephen Carlton Wright, Dec.20, 1948, Leeds, W.Yorks.), Young (b. Nov.6, 1947, Glasgow, Scotland) and Fleet (b. Aug.16, 1946, Bootle,

Merseyside) – are UK-born, while Vanda (b.Harry Vandenberg, Mar.2 1947, The Hague, Holland), and Diamonde (b. Dingeman Van Der Sluys, Dec.28, 1947, Hilversum, Holland) are originally from Holland. All are in Australia due to family emigration, and meet while living at the Villawood Migrant youth hostel.

1964 Fleet coins their name, supposedly taking it from the BBC Light Programme pop show, hosted by Brian Matthew, and they become resident group at Sydney's Beatle Village club, where they meet producer Ted Albert, who gets them signed to Australian Parlophone.

1965 **Mar** After making their TV debut on "Sing Sing Sing", *For My Woman* is released.

July *She's So Fine* hits #1 in Australia, the first of 5 hits (including chart-toppers *Easy As Can Be*, *Woman* and *Come And See Her*), which rapidly establish them as a major Antipodean teen-draw.

1966 **June** Signed internationally to United Artists, they move to UK to work with producer Shel Talmy. Group's first UK single *Come And See Her* is released.

Nov [13] Group supports The Four Tops at London's Saville theater.

Dec *Friday On My Mind*, written by Vanda and Young, hits #6 in UK and #1 in Australia.

1967 **Mar** UK follow-up *Who'll Be The One?* fails to chart while the group returns to Australia to prepare for a US visit. Fleet decides against touring, and is replaced by Tony Cahill.

May [20] *Friday On My Mind* reaches US #16, boosted by the promotional trip. Album of the same name charts at US #180.

June *Heaven And Hell* does not chart.

Aug [4] Group begins US tour, with Gene Pitney, Buffalo Springfield The Buckinghams, The Happenings and The Music Explosion, in Hartford, CT.

1968 **May** Ballad *Hello, How Are You?*, reaches UK #20 – and proves to be their UK chart swan song.

Sept Final United Artists' release *Good Times* fails to chart. A new recording deal is signed with Polydor in UK and Motown subsidiary, Rare Earth in US.

1969 **Nov** [15] *St Louis* does not chart in UK, but scrapes US #100, completing their US chart career. Immediately afterwards they split.

1974 Vanda and Young, having moved back to Australia, open a studio complex in Sydney, and soon have success with John Paul Young. The will produce AC/DC in the mid-70s – Young's two brothers Angus and Malcolm are group members.

1978 **Oct** The pair will have varied success as Flash & The Pan, Paintbox and The Marcus Hook Roll Band – as Flash & The Pan they make a UI chart debut (#54) with *And The Band Played On (Down Among The Dea Men)*. (Further chart success will come with *Hey St. Peter* (US #76 in Aug.1979) and *Waiting For A Train* which hits UK #7 in June 1983.)

ECHO & THE BUNNYMEN

Ian McCulloch (vocals)
Will Sergeant (guitar)
Les Pattinson (bass)
Pete de Freitas (drums)

1977 **May** The Crucial Three is formed by McCulloch (b. May 5, 1959, Liverpool, Merseyside), Pete Wylie (b. Mar.22, 1958, Liverpool) and Julian Cope (b. Oct.21, 1957, Deri, Wales), but rehearsals in Liverpool lead to nothing.

1978 **July** McCulloch and Cope reunite briefly as members of A Shallow Madness, again with little result.

Sept McCulloch and restaurant chef Sergeant (b. Apr.12, 1958, Liverpool) record demos with the aid of a drum machine which they christen "Echo". Sergeant's previous musical experience has been in bedroom band Industrial Device with schoolfriend Paul Simpson.

Nov [11] Pattinson (b. Apr.18, 1958, Ormskirk, Merseyside), a schoolfriend of Sergeant's at Days Lane school, working at Douglas boatyard in Preston, joins on bass 4 days before the band makes its debut at Eric's club in Liverpool as Echo & The Bunnymen. Pattinson has previously adopted the character of musician Jeff Lovestone and formed group The Jeffs, in which all members are called Jeff. That evolves into psychedelic band, Love Pastels.

1979 **Mar** Trio signs to local Zoo label and releases *Pictures On My Wall*. B-side *Read It In Books* is an old Crucial Three song, written by McCulloch and Cope, who has left to join The Teardrop Explodes.

Sept With record companies clamoring, group signs to small WEA-distributed Korova label. Soon after, and like The Beatles, one drummer, Echo, is fired and replaced by another, Pete de Freitas (b. Aug.2, 1961, Port of Spain, Trinidad, West Indies).

980 May Band's second single *Rescue*, and first distributed through a major label, reaches UK #62.
July Debut album **Crocodiles** climbs to UK #17.
Sept *The Puppet* is released, but does not chart.
981 Apr [18] 5-track 12"-only EP *Shine So Hard*, with its featured track *Crocodiles*, makes UK #37.
June [6] *Heaven Up Here* hits UK #10 and peaks at US #184.
July [25] *A Promise* makes UK #49.
982 June [19] *The Back Of Love* is first major hit single, at UK #19.
983 Feb *The Cutter* is first UK Top 10 hit at #8. *Porcupine* hits UK #2 and peaks at US #137.
July Sergeant releases solo album *Themes For Grind*.
Aug *Never Stop* reaches UK #15.
Dec "Porcupine", a video collection based around the album is released by Virgin Video.
984 Feb *The Killing Moon* hits UK #9. Live mini-album *Echo & The Bunnymen*, released only in US, reaches #188.
May *Silver* reaches UK #30. It is taken from *Ocean Rain*, which hits UK #4 and makes US #87 after publicity for it describes it as the "greatest album ever made". Coinciding with the new record releases is "Echo & The Bunnymen Present A Crystal Day", an event in which the band takes its most fervent fans on a day trip around Liverpool culminating in a live show.
July *Seven Seas* reaches UK #16.
Nov McCulloch releases solo revival of Kurt Weill standard *September Song*, which makes UK #51.
985 Nov After a long spell without new material, while the group has been writing and rehearsing, *Bring On The Dancing Horses* reaches UK #21 and *Songs To Learn And Sing*, collecting most popular cuts to date, hits UK #6.
986 Jan *Songs To Learn And Sing* peaks at US #158.
Feb De Freitas leaves and is replaced by Mark Fox (b. Feb.13, 1958) ex-Haircut 100.
Sept De Freitas rejoins, ousting Fox.
Dec Retrospective Bunnymen video collection, "Picture" is issued by WEA Video.
987 June After another long musical silence, *The Game* charts at UK #28.
July *Echo & The Bunnymen*, produced by Laurie Latham, hits UK #4 and will make US #51.
Aug Rapidly-released second single from album, *Lips Like Sugar* makes UK #36.
988 Mar *People Are Strange*, from movie "The Lost Boys", is a revival of The Doors' 60s hit and is produced by ex-Doors keyboard player Ray Manzarek, who has also appeared on Echo & The Bunnymen's previous album. It climbs to UK #29. (It will also feature on WEA compilation **Under The Covers**.)
Aug Press reports state band will split, despite its denial. McCulloch quits for solo career while the others decide to continue as before.
989 June [14] De Freitas is killed when his motorbike collides with a car.
Oct [7] Now signed as a solo act to WEA, McCulloch's debut album **Candleland** peaks at UK #18, while previewing *Proud To Fall* has made UK #51 in Sept.
Nov [25] McCulloch's *Candleland* makes US #179.
990 Feb McCulloch contributes a cover of *Return To Sender* to compilation **The Last Temptation Of Elvis**, to benefit the Nordoff-Robbins Music Therapy charity.
Mar [16] McCulloch begins US tour in Dallas, TX.
Nov Still signed to Korova, remaining members of Echo & The Bunnymen fail to crack charts with either *Reverberation* or extracted *Enlighten Me*.
991 Mar [9] Reissued, following popular UK TV showing of "The Lost Boys", *People Are Strange* makes UK #36.

DUANE EDDY

958 Mar [24] Eddy (b Apr.28, 1938, Corning, NY), having moved to Tucson, AZ, then Coolidge, AZ, in his teens, is a guitarist leading a band called The Rebels when he meets DJ Lee Hazlewood and Lester Sill, who raises the finance to cut 4 sides by the band, which are leased to a new Philadelphia label, Jamie. The throbbing and reverbering *Movin' 'N' Groovin'* makes US #72 and introduces the "twangy guitar" sound of Duane Eddy.
July [28] With guitar instrumentals like Bill Justis' *Raunchy* and Link Wray's *Rumble* in the charts, Eddy concocts *Rebel Rouser*, with whooping, handclaps, tremelo effects and abundant echo. It hits US #6 after promotion on Dick Clark's "American Bandstand", where Eddy is

revealed to be young, shy and handsome. It is his first million-seller and fans are also roused in UK, where it reaches #19.
Sept [15] *Ramrod* reaches US #27. Always cut at Audio Recorders in Phoenix, using producer Hazlewood's novel drainpipe echo chamber, Eddy's hits follow the same pattern of catchy tune and rhythm, played on the bass strings of his Gretsch, and composer credits are usually shared by producer and artist.
Nov [24] With a title (like most of his hits) suggestive of its mood, *Cannonball* makes US #15 and UK #22. Eddy's studio Rebels comprise Al Casey (guitar, piano), Buddy Wheeler (bass), Donnie Owens and Corky Casey (guitar) and Mike Bermani (drums). Tracks are often taken to Gold Star studios in Hollywood, where a sax part is added by Plas Johnson or (later) Steve Douglas.
1959 Feb [16] *The Lonely One* reaches US #23. Debut album *Have Twangy Guitar Will Travel* hits US #5. (It will remain his biggest seller.)
Apr [20] *Yep!* peaks at US #30 and UK #17. B-side, Eddy's pulsating version of Henry Mancini's *Peter Gunn* (recently a US-only smash for Ray Anthony & His Orchestra), hits UK #6.
July [27] *Forty Miles Of Bad Road* hits US #9 and UK #11, with B-side *The Quiet Three* at US #46. *Have Twangy Guitar Will Travel* hits UK #6.
Aug Second album *Especially For You* reaches US #24.
Oct [19] *First Love First Tears* reaches US #59.
[26] A-side, the fast and furious *Some Kinda Earthquake* makes US #37 and UK #12.
Nov *Especially For You* hits UK #6.
1960 Jan *The Twang's The Thang* peaks at US #18. It contains none of his hits and is another mixture of new and old. The ubiquitous "rebel yells" are credited to a Ben Demotto.
[18] *Bonnie Came Back* (based on *My Bonnie Lies Over The Ocean*) makes US #26 and UK #12.
Apr In a package with Bobby Darin, Clyde McPhatter and Emile Ford, Eddy storms UK with his current Rebels, comprising Larry Knechtel (piano), Jim Horn (sax), Al Casey (bass) and Jimmy Troxel (drums). *Shazam!* (a Marvel comics exclamation) reaches US #45 and hits UK #4. *The Twang's The Thang* hits UK #2.
July [4] Title theme from film "Because They're Young", Eddy's biggest international disk, hits US #4 and UK #2 and is his second million-seller. With James Darren and Tuesday Weld, he also acts in the movie, which stars Dick Clark as a high school teacher.
Aug [29] *Kommotion* reaches US #78 and UK #13.
Nov [14] *Peter Gunn* makes a belated US chart entry, reaching #27.
Dec Folksy *Songs Of Our Heritage* makes UK #13, but fails in US.
1961 Feb A collection of hits, *A Million Dollar's Worth Of Twang*, reaches US #11. It marks the end of Eddy's relationship with the Sill/Hazlewood team.
[6] Movie theme *Pepe* reaches US #18 and hits UK #2.
Apr *A Million Dollars' Worth Of Twang* hits UK #5. Eddy makes his second movie appearance in "A Thunder Of Drums". Jamie releases 4 more Eddy hits: the familiar *Theme From Dixie* (US #39 [Apr.17], UK #7), film theme *Ring Of Fire* (US #84 [June 5], UK #17), the Knechtel/Eddy collaboration *Drivin' Home* (US #87 [July 24], UK #30) and an old album track *My Blue Heaven* (US #50 [Sept.18]).
Aug *Girls Girls Girls* reaches US #93. Eddy marries Miriam Johnson.
Oct A one-off single for Parlophone, his version of Duke Ellington's *Caravan*, makes UK #30.
1962 May [19] Eddy signs to RCA Victor. His debut single, a revival of the perennial *Deep In The Heart Of Texas*, reaches US #78 and UK #19. His first RCA album *Twistin' 'N' Twangin'* reaches US #82.
June *A Million Dollar's Worth Of Twang Vol 2* makes UK #18 but fails to chart in US.
Aug [25] Theme from Richard Boone's popular TV western series "Have Gun Will Travel", retitled *The Ballad Of Paladin*, reaches US #33 and hits UK #10. *Twistin' 'N' Twangin'* hits UK #8.
Nov *Twangy Guitar – Silky Strings* reaches US #72.
Dec [8] Reunited with Hazlewood, Eddy shuns rock'n'roll for novelty pop, complete with singalong chorus, and releases *Dance With The Guitar Man*, which makes US #12 and hits UK #4 to become his third million-seller. *Twangy Guitar – Silky Strings* reaches UK #13.
1963 Jan Third RCA album, *Dance With The Guitar Man*, reaches US #47.
Mar [9] *Boss Guitar* reaches US #27.
[16] *Boss Guitar* reaches US #28, as *Dance With The Guitar Man* reaches UK #14.
June [8] *Lonely Boy Lonely Guitar* makes only US #82 and UK #35.
Sept [14] *Your Baby's Gone Surfin'* reaches US #93 and UK #49. *My Baby Plays The Same Old Song On His Guitar All Night Long* fails to chart.
Oct *Twangin' Up A Storm* climbs to US #93.

DUANE EDDY cont.

1964 **Jan** [11] *The Son Of Rebel Rouser* makes US #97.
May *Lonely Guitar* becomes Eddy's final charting record at US #144.

1967 **Oct** [6] After appearing in the movies "The Savage Seven" and "Kona", which necessitates little on the recording scene, Eddy returns to UK to begin a tour.

1968 **May** [3] Eddy takes part in the "1968 First Rock'N'Roll Show" at the Royal, Tottenham, London.

1972 **Apr** He makes a cameo appearance on B.J. Thomas' US #15 hit *Rock And Roll Lullaby*.

1973 Eddy produces Phil Everly's solo album *Star Spangled Springer*, adding his twangy trademark to the closing moments.

1975 **Mar** *Play Me Like You Play Your Guitar*, produced by English writer/producer Tony Macaulay, returns Eddy to UK chart, hitting #9.

1978 *You Are My Sunshine*, for Elektra Records with help from Waylon Jennings and Willie Nelson, fails to chart.

1983 **May** [22] Eddy makes live comeback in US after 15 years' absence at the Baked Potato, Los Angeles, CA, with a band comprising Ry Cooder (guitar), Don Randi (keyboards), Hal Blaine (drums), Steve Douglas (sax) and John Garnache (bass). (Band will later embark on a US tour.)

1986 **Mar** The Art Of Noise enlists Eddy's aid on its revival of *Peter Gunn*. It hits UK #8 and Eddy twangs his guitar on UK TV's "Top Of The Pops" and "The Tube".
July [5] *Peter Gunn* makes US #50.

1987 **Feb** [24] *Peter Gunn* wins Best Rock Instrumental Performance (Orchestra, Group Or Soloist) at the 29th annual Grammy awards.
Sept Eddy cuts album *Duane Eddy* for Capitol Records, produced by Jeff Lynne, with help from friends Paul McCartney, George Harrison and Ry Cooder.

THE ELECTRIC LIGHT ORCHESTRA (ELO)

Roy Wood (vocals, cello)
Jeff Lynne (vocals, guitar)
Bill Hunt (keyboards)
Richard Tandy (bass)
Bev Bevan (drums)
Wilf Gibson (violin)
Hugh McDowell (cello)
Andy Craig (cello)

1967 Wood (b. Nov.8, 1946, Birmingham, W.Midlands), ex-local band Mike Sheridan & The Nightriders (now called Idle Race) is guitarist with The Move, currently Birmingham's biggest band enjoying Top 10 success.

1969 Wood offers friend Jeff Lynne (b. Dec.30, 1947, Birmingham), who joined Idle Race after Wood's departure and is leading the group, a place in The Move, but Lynne elects to stay with Idle Race.

1970 **Oct** When Move singer Carl Wayne leaves for a solo cabaret career, Lynne agrees to join, providing he can also be involved in Wood's separate group within The Move, playing "jazz and classically-influenced free-form music" with instrumentation aligned more to an orchestra than a rock band. The whole idea is financed by manager Don Arden, who secures them a contract with Harvest.

1971 Plans for the first Electric Light Orchestra (ELO) release are delayed as The Move has hits with *Tonight* and *Chinatown* and *Message From The Country*. After a US tour The Move retires from live performance (but will still nominally exist). Drummer Bevan (b. Beverley Bevan, Nov.24, 1946, Birmingham) opens a Birmingham record shop.

1972 **Apr** [16] ELO makes its live debut at the Greyhound pub in Croydon, London. Its innovative style is not well received.
May The Move's *California Man* hits UK #7.
Aug ELO's first single, Lynne's *10538 Overture*, hits UK #9. Debut album *Electric Light Orchestra*, featuring Lynne and Wood and released on Harvest, reaches UK #32. United Artists in US, having rung Arden to discover the album title and being left a message "No Answer" by a secretary who could not reach him, releases it as *No Answer*. It makes US #196.
Having planned ELO for several years, Wood surprises everyone by leaving the group to form his own more pop-oriented group Wizzard. He takes Hunt and McDowell with him while Craig leaves altogether. Lynne recruits cellists Mike Edwards and Colin Walker and bassist Mike D'Albuquerque.
[12] The new line-up debuts at Reading Festival, Berks.

1973 **Feb** First post-Wood release, a version of Chuck Berry's *Roll Over Beethoven*, with quasi-classical intro, hits UK #6.
Mar *ELO II* is released, making UK #35 and US #62.
June [2] Group begins 40-date US tour in San Diego, CA.
July [28] *Roll Over Beethoven* makes US #42.

Sept McDowell rejoins from Wizzard. Gibson and Walker leave and Mik Kaminski joins on violin.
Nov *Showdown*, later an R&B hit for Candi Staton, reaches UK #12.
Dec Lushly orchestrated concept album *On The Third Day* is released through Warner Bros. in UK but fails to chart. United Artists releases the album in US where it makes #52.

1974 **Feb** [2] *Showdown* peaks at US #53.
Apr [6] *Ma-Ma-Ma-Belle* reaches UK #22.
May [25] *Daybreaker* stalls at US #87.
Oct *Eldorado*, billed as "A Symphony By The Electric Light Orchestra" makes US #16 and earns a gold disk.
Nov Live *The Night The Light Went On In Long Beach*, is released worldwide, excluding UK and US. Harvest issues *Showdown*, a compilation of singles and tracks from the first 2 albums. Edwards and D'Albuquerque leave to be replaced by bassist Kelly Groucutt, ex-Barefoot, and cellist Melvyn Gale, ex-London Palladium orchestra.

1975 **Mar** [15] Using a 30-piece string section for the first time, ballad *Can't Get It Out Of My Head*, from *Eldorado*, becomes group's first US Top 10 hit at #9. (Band will spend most of the year touring US.)
Oct *Face The Music*, much of it recorded at Musicland studios in Munich, Germany (where the group will record most of its future work), hits US #8.

1976 **Jan** [31] *Evil Woman* hits UK #10.
Feb [14] *Evil Woman* hits US #10, as a successful US tour begins.
May [22] *Strange Magic* reaches US #14.
July *Strange Magic* makes UK #38.
Aug [28] Reissued *Showdown* peaks at US #59.
Sept ELO, signed to Arden's Jet label, releases US-only greatest hits album, *Olé ELO*, which reaches US #32.
Dec [4] *A New World Record*, written, arranged and produced by Lynne, now the main focus in the group, gains immediate radio interest and hits UK #6. It sells 5 million copies worldwide.
Livin' Thing hits UK #4.

1977 **Jan** [8] *Livin' Thing* reaches US #13, as parent album *A New World Record* hits US #5.
[17] ELO begins a major US and Canadian tour at the Veterans' Memorial Auditorium, Phoenix, AZ. (It will end 3 months later on Apr.6 at Place de Nationale, Montreal, Canada.)
Mar Dramatic *Rockaria!* hits UK #9.
Apr [2] ELO's version of The Move's only US hit, *Do Ya*, reaches US #24, after Todd Rundgren has used it in his live show. Harvest releases compilation *The Light Shines On*, as Lynne, locked away in a chalet in Bassins, Switzerland, writes songs for a new album.
June *Telephone Line*, from *A New World Record*, hits UK #8.
[11] *A New World Record* peaks at UK #6, 8 months after its release. An extensive world tour begins, which, with the year's record sales, will gross the band more than $10 million.
Sept [24] *Telephone Line* hits US #7.
Nov [12] With worldwide advance orders of 4 million, double album *Out Of The Blue*, again written and produced by Lynne, hits UK #4.
Dec [10] *Turn To Stone* reaches UK #18.

1978 **Jan** [8] *Out Of The Blue* hits US #4. (During its chart run, US distribution for Jet switches to CBS/Columbia and the band sues United Artists for allegedly allowing millions of defective copies to reach the market.)
Feb [4] *Turn To Stone* reaches US #13.
[25] *Mr. Blue Sky* hits UK #6.
Apr [29] *Sweet Talkin' Woman* reaches US #17.
June [24] *Wild West Hero* hits UK #6.
Aug [12] *Mr. Blue Sky* makes US #35. Group begins a tour featuring a elaborate set, with lasers and a huge illuminated "spaceship".
Oct [21] *Sweet Talkin' Woman* hits UK #6, becoming the fourth UK hit from *Out Of The Blue*.
Nov [18] *It's Over* peaks at US #75.
Dec [16] EP *ELO* makes US #34. (Tracks are *Can't Get It Out Of My Head*, *Strange Magic*, *Ma-Ma-Ma-Belle* and *Evil Woman*.) Lynne's first solo *Doin' That Crazy Thing* is released but, like Bevan's solo *Let There Drums*, fails to chart.

1979 **Jan** [6] Jet box set *Three Light Years*, comprising *On The Third Day*, *Eldorado* and *Face The Music*, makes UK #38. Kaminski's solo *Violinski: Clog Dance* makes UK #17.
Mar Harvest issues *The Light Shines On Vol. 2*, with little success.
May *Shine A Little Love* hits UK #6.
[4] ELO are honored with the Outstanding Contribution To British Music award at the annual Ivor Novello Awards lunch.
June [2] *Discovery* hits UK #1, group's first UK chart-topper album.

July *The Diary Of Horace Wimp* hits UK #8.

[5] *Discovery* hits US #5.

[20] ELO advertises in music press dedicating forthcoming single *Don't Bring Me Down* to "Skylab".

[21] *Shine A Little Love* hits US #8.

Sept *Don't Bring Me Down* hits UK #3.

[8] *Don't Bring Me Down* hits US #8, band's biggest US single success.

Nov *Confusion* hits UK #8.

[17] *Confusion* makes US #37.

Dec Concentrating on recording and less on live performance (band has toured every year since 1972), Lynne pares full-time band to a core of himself, Bevan, Tandy and Groucutt, calling on Gale when required.

[8] *ELO's Greatest Hits* hits UK #7.

[22] *ELO's Greatest Hits* makes US #30.

'80 Feb [2] *Last Train To London* makes US #39.

May ELO is commissioned to write songs for film "Xanadu". First release from the film, *I'm Alive*, makes UK #20.

June Title track *Xanadu* teams ELO with Olivia Newton-John and hits UK #1 (band's first UK chart-topper single!)

July Soundtrack album *Xanadu*, with one side featuring ELO and the other Olivia Newton-John, hits UK #2 and US #4. The film, however, is a box-office disaster.

[12] *I'm Alive* reaches US #16.

Aug *All Over The World*, from *Xanadu*, reaches UK #11.

Oct [4] *All Over The World* reaches US #13.

[11] *Xanadu* hits US #8.

Dec [6] *Don't Walk Away* reaches UK #21.

'81 May [19] *Xanadu* wins Best Film Song, Theme Or Score at the annual Ivor Novello Awards lunch.

Aug [29] *Time* tops UK chart and reaches US #16.

Sept [5] *Hold On Tight* hits UK #4. (It is the first disk credited to the ELO acronym. They will revert to full name in 1986, when signed to CBS/Epic.)

Oct [3] *Hold On Tight* hits US #10. Group begins a major tour, but for the first time since the early 70s plays to less than capacity audiences.

Nov [7] *Twilight*, their poorest chart showing for years, makes UK #30.

[28] *Twilight* reaches US #38.

'82 Jan [30] *Ticket To The Moon/Here Is The News* makes UK #24.

Mar For the first time since *Nightrider* 6 years earlier, an ELO single (*The Way Life's Meant To Be*) fails to chart in UK and US.

'83 Apr Dave Edmunds' *Information*, produced by Lynne, is released.

June ELO's *Rock'N'Roll Is King* makes UK #13.

July *Secret Messages* hits UK #4, but makes only #36.

Aug [20] *Rock'N'Roll Is King* reaches US #19.

Sept *Secret Messages* makes UK #48.

Oct [8] *Four Little Diamonds* stalls at US #86. (It will be the group's last hit for 2 years.) Bevan leaves to join Black Sabbath (but will rejoin in time for the next album).

'84 Sept Lynne produces 6 tracks for Dave Edmunds' *Riff Raff*.

'86 Mar Signed to CBS/Epic, ELO, now reduced to 3-piece Lynne, Bevan and Tandy, returns to US charts with *Calling America*, at UK #28.

[15] Group makes its first concert appearance in 4 years, in its home town Birmingham. George Harrison joins them on stage.

Apr [5] *Calling America* reaches US #18. Group appears at "Heartbeat '86" charity show in Birmingham (its last live appearance). *Balance Of Power* hits UK #9 and US #49, but *So Serious* and *Getting To The Point* taken from it, fail to chart.

'87 Lynne produces a track on *Duane Eddy*, Eddy's comeback album on Capitol. Long-time Beatles fan Lynne works with ex-Beatle George Harrison on his album *Cloud Nine* (featuring Lynne's US #1 and UK #2 produced *Got My Mind Set On You*).

June [5-6] Lynne takes part in the fifth annual Prince's Trust Rock Gala at London's Wembley Arena.

'88 July Lynne co-writes and co-produces *Let It Shine* with Brian Wilson for his debut solo album *Brian Wilson*.

Oct Concentrating more on production, Lynne teams with Randy Newman for tracks on *Land Of Dreams* and helps successfully relaunch Roy Orbison's recording career with what proves to be his final album *Mystery Girl*, and worldwide hit *You Got It*. Lynne also combines with Orbison as part of The Traveling Wilburys with Bob "Lucky" Dylan, George "Nelson" Harrison and Tom "Charlie T. Jnr." Petty. Debut single *Handle With Care* is released with the album from which it is taken, *Traveling Wilburys*. "Nelson" Harrison and "Otis" Lynne co-produce the project.

'89 Lynne co-writes and co-produces Tom Petty's *Full Moon Fever* and records comeback, and subsequently final, tracks for Del Shannon.

Dec [23] ELO's *The Greatest Hits*, on TV-advertised Telstar Records, reaches UK #23. (Relaunched in Oct.1990 as *The Very Best Of The Electric Light Orchestra* it makes UK #28.)

1990 May Lynne produces 2 tracks for Roy Wood for later release.

July Having successfully written and produced for a number of colleagues over the past decade, Lynne turns the spotlight on himself via solo deal with Reprise. First fruit *Every Little Thing* makes UK #59.

[21] Lynne's solo album *Armchair Theatre* makes US #92 and will reach UK #24. (ELO retrospective *Afterglow* is released.)

1991 Mar Lynne considers his legal position as Bevan gathers a number of musicians and begins a world tour under the banner ELO II.

EMERSON, LAKE AND PALMER (ELP)

Keith Emerson (keyboards)
Greg Lake (bass, vocals)
Carl Palmer (drums)

1970 Apr [11] Emerson (b. Nov.1, 1944, Todmorden, W.Yorks.), following the break-up of The Nice, teams with Lake (b. Nov.10, 1948, Bournemouth, Dorset), who has just left King Crimson. They audition drummers for a new band.

June Band forms, with Palmer (b. Mar.20, 1951, Birmingham, W.Midlands) recruited from the just-split Atomic Rooster, and formerly a member of The Crazy World Of Arthur Brown.

Aug [25] Trio makes its live debut at the Guildhall, Plymouth, Devon.

[29] It plays UK's Isle of Wight Festival on the penultimate day, alongside The Doors, The Who and Joni Mitchell.

Dec With the band signed to Island in UK and Atlantic (Cotillion label) in US, debut album *Emerson Lake & Palmer*, produced (as will all the band's subsequent albums) by Lake, hits UK #4. It sets the style for most subsequent work – flashy instrumental virtuosity and rock/classical fusions with mostly grandiose lyrical concepts. (Pete Sinfield of King Crimson becomes the trio's main lyric writer.)

1971 Mar Eponymous debut album reaches US #18.

[26] Group is recorded live at City Hall, Newcastle, playing its own arrangement of Mussorgsky's "Pictures At An Exhibition".

May [1] Not released as a UK single, *Lucky Man* (from debut album) reaches US #48.

June *Tarkus*, a concept album (though obscurely presented and understood by few: Tarkus appears to be a mechanized armadillo that engages mythical beast the Manticore in battle), hits UK #1 for a week.

Aug *Tarkus* hits US #9.

Dec Low-priced live album *Pictures At An Exhibition* hits UK #3.

1972 Feb The live album reaches US #10.

Apr Band plays at the Mar-Y-Sol festival in Puerto Rico, where its *Take A Pebble/Lucky Man* is recorded for a live album of the event.

[15] A revival of B. Bumble & The Stingers' *Nut Rocker*, originally included on *Pictures At An Exhibition*, is extracted as a US single and peaks at #70.

July Fourth album *Trilogy* hits UK #2.

Sept *Trilogy* hits US #5.

Oct [28] A US-only release, *From The Beginning*, taken from *Trilogy*, makes US #39.

1973 Feb [2] Emerson's hands are injured on stage in San Francisco, CA, during the US tour. His piano, rigged to explode as a stunt during the set, detonates prematurely.

[3] *Lucky Man*, re-promoted in US to coincide with tour, peaks at #51.

Mar The film "Pictures At An Exhibition", featuring the band in a concert performance of the title piece, premieres in Los Angeles, CA.

Dec Group's debut UK single *Jerusalem*, taken from new album *Brain Salad Surgery*, fails to chart. Both are released on band's recently formed label Manticore (named after the *Tarkus* creature). (Other early signings to Manticore will include Pete Sinfield, Little Richard and the Italian band P.F.M.)

1974 Jan *Brain Salad Surgery* hits UK #2 and US #11.

Aug Live triple album *Welcome Back My Friends To The Show That Never Ends; Ladies And Gentlemen...Emerson, Lake And Palmer* hits UK #5.

Sept The live triple set hits US #4.

Nov Manticore Records is signed to Motown for US distribution.

1975 Dec [27] Lake's solo *I Believe In Father Christmas*, a grandiose production, hits UK #2. (It will become a seasonal and occasionally re-charting standard.) In US, it makes #95 (but will become a seasonal airplay favorite).

1976 Apr Emerson's solo *Honky Tonk Train Blues*, a revival of a Meade Lux Lewis classic, reaches UK #21.

EMERSON, LAKE AND PALMER (ELP) cont.

1977 **Apr** Double album *Works* hits UK #9. It is mostly a showcase for the trio's solo works; they combine as a band only for the fourth side.
May *Works* makes US #12.
July A racing keyboards/guitar interpretation of Aaron Copland's *Fanfare For The Common Man*, extracted from *Works*, hits UK #2 behind Hot Chocolate's *So You Win Again*.
Sept [10] Lake's solo *C'est La Vie*, from *Works*, makes US #91.
Dec Compilation *Works, Volume Two*, rounding up singles (including *Honky Tonk Train Blues* and *I Believe In Father Christmas*) and previously unissued out-takes, makes UK #20 and US #37.

1978 **Dec** *Love Beach*, their final studio album, reaches UK #48 and US #55.
[30] Having played a wide-ranging farewell tour during the latter half of the year, the band announces its official break-up.

1979 **Mar** Palmer forms P.M., a quintet of himself and 4 US musicians.
Dec Live *Emerson, Lake & Palmer In Concert* is released to fulfill contractual obligations. Recorded during the band's 1978 US tour, it reaches US #73.

1980 While Emerson involves himself with film and TV soundtrack work, Lake signs to Chrysalis as a soloist.
Mar Signed to Ariola, Palmer's group P.M. issues unsuccessful *One P.M.*, while struggling to find exposure outside German TV slots.
July P.M. breaks up.
Dec Compilation *The Best Of Emerson, Lake & Palmer* makes US #108.

1981 **Jan** Palmer joins John Wetton, Steve Howe and Geoff Downes in successful rock outfit Asia.
May Emerson's soundtrack album from the movie "Nighthawks" makes US #183.
Oct Solo album *Greg Lake* makes UK and US #62.
Dec [26] Lake's solo single *Let Me Love You Once* makes US #48.

1983 **Sept** Lake reunites with Palmer when he joins Asia in place of John Wetton for a Far East tour.
Dec [6] Lake and Palmer play in Asia's major gig at the Budokan theater in Tokyo, Japan, broadcast live via satellite TV and seen by 20 million MTV viewers in US (also later as home video "Asia In Asia".)

1984 Lake leaves Asia to make way for Wetton's return, but Asia breaks up.
1985 Emerson and Lake agree to record together, aiming for a comeback like that achieved by contemporaries Yes a year earlier. The duo cannot interest Palmer in the project, so Cozy Powell (b. Dec.29, 1947) is recruited on drums instead (maintaining the ELP abbreviation).

1986 **June** Signed to Polydor, the new trio debuts with *Emerson, Lake & Powell*, which makes UK #35 and US #23.
July [19] *Touch And Go*, extracted from the album, peaks at US #60. Band tours US. (The line-up will not last long and Powell will leave to pursue other projects.)

1987 Asked again to join, Palmer agrees, and the trio spends an extended period rehearsing.
Oct After unsuccessful rehearsals, renewed ELP project is abandoned.

1988 **Feb** Emerson, Palmer and Robert Berry (b. San Jose, CA) (ex-Hush) release *To The Power Of Three*, on Geffen and credited to "3", which makes US #97.
Nov Emerson releases seasonal collection *The Christmas Album*, to little success.

ERASURE

Vince Clarke (keyboards)
Andy Bell (vocals)

1985 Clarke (b. July 3, 1960, Basildon, Essex), who has had success with Depeche Mode, Yazoo (paired with Alison Moyet) and The Assembly on Daniel Miller's independent label, Mute, and his producer Eric "E.C." Radcliffe plan to record an album with 10 different singers but it proves to be impractical and Clarke settles for one vocalist, Bell (b. Apr.25, 1964), an ex-choirboy who has been with UK Peterborough band The Void, whom he finds after auditioning 42 singers answering a "vocalist wanted" ad in UK's **Melody Maker**.
Oct Debut single *Who Needs Love Like That*, on Mute, climbs to UK #55.
Nov *Heavenly Action* makes only UK #100 and a tour is cancelled.
Dec After a short promotional visit to Germany, the duo makes its UK live debut at London's Heaven club.

1986 **Jan** Clarke calls in vocalists Jim Burkman and Derek Ian for a UK tour.
Apr *Oh L'Amour* makes UK #85. (It will achieve success for Dollar in 1988.)
June Debut album *Wonderland* reaches UK #71.
Dec *Sometimes*, an early hit throughout Europe, hits UK #2.

1987 **Mar** Similarly synthesizer-driven *It Doesn't Have To Be* reaches UK #12.
Apr Second album *The Circus* hits UK #6 as the duo takes "The

Circus" tour to Europe, Scandinavia and US.
June Erasure is the opening act on ITV's first "The Roxy" chart show, performing *Victim Of Love*, which hits UK #7, while live performance video "Erasure: Live At The Seaside" is released by Virgin Video.
July *The Circus* peaks at US #190.
Aug Erasure supports Duran Duran on US tour.
Oct *Two Ring Circus* is released, featuring 6 remixes and 3 re-recordings of original album *The Circus*, and hits UK #6.

1988 **Mar** Ballad *Ship Of Fools* hits UK #6.
Apr [14] Duo embarks on a sell-out UK tour.
[30] *The Innocents* debuts at UK #1.
May *Chains Of Love* reaches UK #11.
July [13] Erasure starts extensive US tour, *Chains Of Love* climbs towards the US Top 30 and *The Innocents* makes US Top 100.
Oct Acoustic guitar-driven *A Little Respect* hits UK #4.
[28] *Wild!* enters UK chart at #1, where it stays for 2 weeks.

1989 **Jan** [7] EP *Crackers International*, including hot airplay cuts *Stop* and *The Hardest Part*, hits UK #2.
Feb [13] Erasure wins Best British Group at the eighth annual BRIT Awards at the Royal Albert Hall, London.
Mar [4] *A Little Respect* reaches US #14, as Virgin Video's "The Innocents" package tops UK Video chart.
May *Crackers International* makes US #73.
July [18-19] Bell participates in the seventh Prince's Trust Rock Gala the NEC, Birmingham, W.Midlands, with Joan Baez, Van Morrison, Alexander O'Neal, Level 42 and others.
[22] *Stop!* makes US #97.
Oct *Drama!* hits UK #4.
Nov *Wild!* makes US #57, but no further extractions will score in US.
Dec *You Surround Me* reaches UK #15.

1990 **Apr** Extracted from *Wild!*, *Blue Savannah* hits UK #3, the duo's sevent Top 10 UK hit.
June *Star* peaks at UK #11. During the year, *Wild!*, *The Circus* and *Th Innocents* will all re-chart in their home territory. Duo will also embar on major US tour.
July BMG Video release "Wild!" becomes another best-seller in UK.
Aug [8] US tour ends at the Jones Beach theater, Wantagh, NY.
Oct Erasure contributes *Too Darn Hot* to *Red Hot + Blue*, an anthology of Cole Porter songs to benefit AIDS education.

1991 **Feb** Animal rights album, *Tame Yourself*, featuring an Erasure/Lene Lovich debut, is released.
May [2] *Blue Savannah* is named Most Performed Work Of 1990 at the annual Ivor Novello Awards lunch at the Grosvenor House, London.

DAVID ESSEX

1964 Essex (b. David Cook, July 23, 1947, Plaistow, London), having left school, is the drummer in semi-professional East London group The Everons when **Daily Express** critic Derek Bowman, his subsequent manager, sees the group play at a pub in Walthamstow, London.

1965 **Apr** First recording *And The Tears Come Tumbling Down*, on Fontana Records, fails (as will 6 Fontana singles during 1965 and 1966).

1967 He appears as a beatnik in Lynn Redgrave/Rita Tushingham film "Smashing Time".

1968 One-off singles for Uni (*Love Story*) and Pye (*Just For Tonight*) also fail.

1969 **June** He signs to Decca, but *That Takes Me Back* and follow-up *Day Th Earth Stood Still* arouse little interesst.

1971 **Oct** Essex gets the leading role as Jesus to Jeremy Irons' Judas Iscariot in Jean Michael Tebelak's religious-rock musical "Godspell" on London's West End stage, first at the Roundhouse then at Wyndhams theater. (After almost a year of success in the role, he is contacted by UK film producer David Puttnam, who is impressed with his performance and offers him a major movie role.)

1972 **Oct** [23] Essex begins a 7-week break from "Godspell" to star in film "That'll Be The Day" with Ringo Starr, Keith Moon, Billy Fury, Dave Edmunds and others on UK's Isle of Wight. He plays an aspiring rock star Jim Maclaine in Ray Connolly's drama set in the UK of the late 50

1973 **Apr** [12] "That'll Be The Day" premieres in London. Well reviewed, the movie will also become a major financial success.
May Essex receives Variety Club of Great Britain's Most Promising Newcomer Award.
Sept Signed to CBS on the strength of his stage and screen success, Essex's first single for the label, self-penned *Rock On*, which evokes the nostalgic feel of his recent movie, hits UK #3.
Dec *Lamplight* hits UK #7, and he is fast becoming a UK teen idol, while debut CBS album *Rock On*, produced by Jeff Wayne who

becomes an integral part of Essex' success, also peaks at UK #7.

1974 **Feb** [18] Essex begins filming "Stardust", the sequel to "That'll Be The Day", which shows Jim Maclaine rise to the pinnacle of his career in the 60s before excess plunges him to destruction. It co-stars Adam Faith and Larry Hagman.
Mar [9] *Rock On* hits US #5, selling over a million in US, as parent album *Rock On* makes US #22.
May [18] *America* reaches UK #18.
June [22] *Lamplight* peaks at US #71. (Essex will not reach US Singles chart again.)
Oct [24] "Stardust" premieres in London (and will be a major money-spinning movie).
Nov [16] Self-inked *Gonna Make You A Star* tops UK chart for 3 weeks. [30] *David Essex* hits UK #2.

1975 **Jan** [18] *Stardust*, the title song from the movie, hits UK #7.
July [26] *Rollin' Stone* hits UK #5.
Sept [27] *All The Fun Of The Fair* hits UK #3.
Oct [4] *Hold Me Close* tops the UK chart for 3 weeks.
As his world tour comes to a close, Essex has been a sell-out success in France, Germany, Australia, Spain, Japan and the US.

1976 **Jan** Lush ballad *If I Could* makes UK #13.
Apr Grandiose *City Lights* reaches UK #24.
June Live album *On Tour* peaks at UK #51.
Oct [23] *Out On The Street* makes UK #31. Extracted from it, *Coming Home* reaches UK #24.

1977 **Oct** *Cool Out Tonight* reaches UK #23 as *Gold And Ivory* makes #29. (These are his final recordings for CBS.)

1978 **Mar** [25] A revival of Lorraine Ellison's soul classic *Stay With Me Baby* makes UK #45.
May Essex wins Variety Club of Great Britain's Show Business Personality Of The Year.
Sept Essex plays Ché Guevara in Tim Rice and Andrew Lloyd Webber's musical "Evita" on the London West End stage. [23] His featured song, *Oh What A Circus*, and his first release for his new label Mercury, hits UK #3.
Nov [4] *Brave New World* peaks at UK #55.

1979 **Jan** CBS compilation of all his hit singles, *The David Essex Album*, makes UK #29.
Apr [7] *Imperial Wizard*, his first Mercury album (including *Oh What A Circus*), peaks at UK #12.

1980 **May** Essex stars in movie "Silver Dream Racer" with Beau Bridges. Critically panned, it is a drama of ambition and jealousy set in the dangerous world of motorbike racing, and has an Essex-penned soundtrack, from which *Silver Dream Machine*, aided by the movie's publicity, hits UK #4.
June *Hot Love* reaches UK #75. The title track peaks at UK #57.

1981 **Sept** *Be-Bop The Future* fails to chart, as do *Heart On My Sleeve* and *Be-Bop-A-Lula*.
The year's theatrical performance by Essex is playing Lord Byron in the Young Vic production of "Childe Byron".

1982 **Aug** [7] *Me And My Girl (Night Clubbing)* reaches UK #13 and *Stage-Struck* makes UK #31.

1983 **Jan** [1] TV-advertised album *The Very Best Of David Essex*, a compilation of CBS and Mercury hits, makes UK #37.
Ballad *A Winter's Tale*, co-written with Tim Rice, hits UK #2.
Oct Essex, as chief mutineer Fletcher Christian, co-stars with Frank Finlay in "Mutiny", a musical version of "Mutiny On The Bounty", written by Essex. Initially released as a studio production on record only, with backing by the Royal Philharmonic Orchestra, *Mutiny* reaches UK #39. *Tahiti*, taken from it, hits UK #8.
Dec Essex solo album, *The Whisper*, makes UK #67 and *You're In My Heart*, taken from it, peaks at UK #59.

1984 **Nov** Entirely self-penned album *This One's For You* fails to sell, as does extracted *Welcome*.

1985 **Mar** *Falling Angels Riding* reaches UK #29.
"Mutiny" is staged in London's West End, starring Essex, Finlay and new UK girl singer and current girlfriend Sinitta.

1986 **Dec** K-Tel TV-advertised album *Centre Stage*, containing Essex' versions of hit songs from stage and screen, makes UK #82.

1987 **May** *Myfanwy* reaches UK #41. It is taken from the musical "Betjeman", which consists of works by late UK Poet Laureate Sir John Betjeman, set to music by UK DJ Mike Read.

1988 **Oct** Essex stars in 6-part BBC TV sitcom "The River" as a lecherous lock-keeper.

1989 **May** Essex releases latest album *Touching The Ghost*, on his own Lamplight label, but it does not chart, neither do extracted singles.

June [3] US teen actor Michael Damian takes cover version of Essex' *Rock On* to US #1.

1990 **July** Archive specialist label Castle Communications releases *The Collection*, combining most of Essex' past hits.

1991 Essex is appointed Ambassador for charity Voluntary Service Overseas.

GLORIA ESTEFAN

1973 Emilio Estefan (b. Mar.4, 1953, Havana, Cuba), having left his native Cuba at 13 and moved to Madrid, Spain, before settling in Miami, FL, at 14, plays accordian part-time in restaurants away from his day-job in the marketing department at Bacardi. His boss there has seen him playing at an Italian eaterie on Biscayne Boulevard and asks Estefan if he could hire him to play at a private party. Estefan invites bass player Juan Avila (b. 1956, Cuba) and drummer Enrique Garcia (b. 1958, Cuba), both Miami-raised, to help him provide dance music for the engagement following which the trio begins a successful round of restaurant, wedding and party gigs as The Miami Latin Boys, later augmented by guitar, keyboards, horns and percussion.

1974 Gloria (b. Gloria Fajardo, Sept.1, 1957, Havana, Cuba), her father a Cuban soldier and bodyguard to President Fulgencio Batista, who has moved to Miami at age 2, meets Estefan when he comes to offer advice to music students at her high school. He cajoles Gloria into singing with his Miami Latin Boys at a wedding reception that she is attending with her mother. He subsequently offers Gloria a permanent slot as vocalist (insisting that there is no Miami club band currently fronted by a female singer), but she initially turns him down, being more concerned with studying for a psychology degree at the University of Miami. Her mother persuades Gloria to compromise, singing with the band at weekends and studying during the week. In addition to forming a romantic liaison, Gloria spends enough musical time with Estefan to warrant a group name-change – to Miami Sound Machine.

1976 Following the band's first single *Renacer*, local Hispanic label Audio Latino releases debut album *Renacer*, a collection of Spanish language ballads and pop dance numbers.

1978 **Sept** [1] After 2 years of romance Emilio and Gloria are married. By year's end, Gloria earns a BA in psychology from Miami University

1979 Group records its second, self-financed, album. It is eventually picked up by CBS International, which distributes it to the US Latin market.

1981 Band makes the first of 4 Spanish-language albums through to 1983 for Discos CBS International, the Miami-based Hispanic division of CBS.

1982 Line-up's current saxophonist/keyboardist Raul Murciano quits after a financial row with Estefan, and another member, Merci, will also leave.

1984 **Sept** *Dr. Beat*, the band's first single in English (and only its second track recorded in the language), is released as B-side to a Spanish-language song in US, but becomes popular in UK clubs and crosses over to hit UK #6. Group visits UK for BBC TV's "Top Of The Pops". (This success pre-dates any outside the Latin market in US.)

1985 Group appears in Japan at the 15th annual Tokyo Music Festival, where its performance wins the Grand Prize. In Miami, the city renames the street on which the Estefans live Miami Sound Machine Boulevard, in honor of the group's local success and the good PR it brings to Miami.

1986 **Feb** [8] *Conga*, based on a traditional Cuban street dance, is the group's first US chart entry, and hits #10.
Apr Sylvester Stallone asks them to write and perform the theme for a movie he is working on, and they are also requested to do a song in Tom Cruise film "Top Gun".
May [10] *Bad Boy* hits US #8.
Now a 10-piece, the group's first all-English album *Primitive Love*, which contains both *Conga* and *Bad Boy*, reaches US #23.
June *Bad Boy* reaches UK #16.
Sept [20] *Words Get In The Way*, their first ballad in English, hits US #5.
Dec *Billboard* lists the band as Top Pop Singles Act Of The Year.

1987 **Jan** [17] Last single from *Primitive Love*, *Falling In Love (Uh-Oh)* makes US #25.
Aug [1] In deference to Gloria's clear star status at the front of the group, its billing changes to Gloria Estefan & Miami Sound Machine on latin-swaying *Rhythm Is Gonna Get You*, which hits US #5, and *Let It Loose*, produced by Emilio & The Jerks (Lawrence Dermer, Joe Galdo and Rafael Vigil), which makes US #16. (Billing will be maintained on subsequent releases.)
Oct [24] Ballad *Betcha Say That* makes US #36.

1988 **Mar** [5] *Can't Stay Away From You* hits US #6.
May [14] Further love song *Anything For You*, written by Gloria, is the band's biggest hit to date, topping US chart for a week. It is taken from *Let It Loose* which re-climbs US chart, hitting #6 and earning a platinum disk.

Aug *Anything For You*, eventually recorded in English, Spanish and "Spanglish" versions, makes UK #27.

Nov *1-2-3*, taken from *Let It Loose* as a UK single, hits #9 following a promotional visit to UK, on which they perform the single on peak-time TV variety show "Live From The Palladium".

1989 Jan *Rhythm Is Gonna Get You* reaches UK #16, as Epic Records UK makes hasty effort to catch up with the band's US success, reissuing several singles throughout the year.

[30] The act wins Pop Duo Or Group category at the 16th annual American Music Awards.

Mar [3] Ballad *Here We Are* hits US #6, as *Can't Stay Away From You* will hit UK #7.

[25] UK-compiled *Anything For You* tops UK chart.

July The act's billing is shortened once more. Now hailing simply Gloria Estefan, solo star (though her professional and marital union with Emilio continues) *Cuts Both Ways* hits US #8.

Aug [5] *Cuts Both Ways* tops UK chart, as extracted *Don't Wanna Lose You* hits UK #6.

Sept [16] *Don't Wanna Lose You* tops US chart.

[20] Group files a $1 million law suit against their former manager after being dropped from the Amnesty International bill, following claims that Bruce Springsteen wanted to increase the length of his sets.

[25-27] They play 3 nights at Wembley Arena, London, during 8-date UK tour.

Oct *Oye Mi Canto (Hear My Voice)* reaches UK #16.

Nov [25] Uptempo *Get On Your Feet* reaches US #11.

Dec *Get On Your Feet* makes UK #23.

1990 Jan [22] Gloria co-hosts 17th annual American Music Awards, and also performs *There's Nothing I Can Do To Keep Me From Loving You*.

Mar [3] Ballad *Here We Are* hits US #6 and will reach UK #23.

[6] They are awarded the Crystal Globe Award at the 21 club in New York, in recognition of the fact that they have sold more than 5 million albums outside their country of origin.

[20] Group's tour bus is rammed by tractor-trailer near Tobyhanna, Scranton, PA, on a snowy highway in the Pocono Mountains on its way to a concert in Syracuse, NY. Emilio Estefan cuts his hand, their son Nayib fractures a shoulder, but Gloria suffers serious injury, fracturing and dislocating vertebrae in her spine. After treatment by Dr. William Pfeifer at nearby community medical center in Scranton, she is flown to Manhattan's Orthopedic Institute Hospital for Joint Diseases, where Dr. Michael Neuwirth carries out a 4-hour operation on Mar.22.

May Columbia Video issues Gloria Estefan-focusing "Evolution" clip collection.

[5] Uptempo *Oye Mi Canto (Hear My Voice)* makes US #48.

[20] Estefan wins Crossover Artist Of The Year in second annual Latin Music Awards.

Aug [18] Love song *Cuts Both Ways* makes US #44, having peaked at UK #49.

Oct Still the most popular Latin-American act worldwide, Spanish language versions of recent hits, mainly ballads, are successfully released as *Exitos De Gloria Estefan*.

1991 Jan [29] Estefan makes her live comeback, performing her new single *Coming Out Of The Dark*, at the American Music Awards at the Shrine Auditorium, Los Angeles.

Feb [28] Estefan is profiled on NBC TV's "First Person With Maria Shriver".

Mar [1] Estefan begins 8-month world tour at the Miami Arena, before a crowd of 12,000, set to end Oct.15.

[9] *Into The Light*, produced by Emilio with Jorge Casas and Clay Ostwald, hits US #5, having entered at UK #2 on Feb.16, behind Queen's *Innuendo*.

[30] *Coming Out Of The Dark*, a gospel-tinged ballad from *Into The Light*, whose songs partly deal with Gloria's rejuvenation and recovery from last year's accident, hits US #1, having peaked at UK #25 in Feb.

Apr Second extract *Seal Our Fate* begins US chart rise.

May [12] Estefan appears by satellite from Holland in "The Simple Truth" concert for Kurdish refugees at Wembley Arena, London.

EURYTHMICS

Annie Lennox (vocals)
Dave Stewart (keyboards and guitar)

1971 Lennox (b. Dec.25, 1954, Aberdeen, Scotland), having failed to complete a course at London's Royal Academy of Music, is working in Pippins, a restaurant in Hampstead, London, where she meets Stewart (b. David Allan Stewart, Sept.9, 1952, Sunderland, Tyne & Wear) who stowed away, at age 15, in the back of a van belonging to folk outfit Amazing Blondel after a gig in his native Newcastle. Having made his first recording with Brian Harrison as Harrison And Stewart, releasing *Dee, December* on local Multicord label in Sunderland, he joins Longdancer, helping to record 2 albums for Elton John's Rocket label in the early 70s, and develops major drug dependancy. Stewart proposes to Lennox. (They do not get married but will live together for 4 years.)

1977 Lennox and Stewart record together with his best friend Peet Coombes in trio The Catch releasing *Borderline/Black Blood*, which becomes a minor hit in Holland.

1979 June Band expands, name-changing to The Tourists, and peaks at UK #52 with their debut single *Blind Among The Flowers*.

Aug *The Loneliest Man In The World* makes UK #32.

Oct The Tourists' remake of Dusty Springfield's *I Only Want To Be With You* hits UK #4 (their biggest hit).

1980 Jan *So Good To Be Back Home* hits UK #8.

Sept Group first single for RCA, *Don't Say I Told You So*, makes UK #40. (It is The Tourists' final single. Their career also included 3 albums: *The Tourists* (UK #72), *Reality Affect* (UK #23) and *Luminous Basement* (UK #75).)

Oct While on tour in Australia, The Tourists disband.

Dec After the band splits, Stewart and Lennox go to Conny Plank's studio in Cologne, Germany, and record demos. With the help of former Can members Holger Czukay and Jaki Liebezeit and DAF members Robert Gorl and Gabi, they cut *Never Gonna Cry Again*. A week after their affair ends, Lennox and Stewart form Eurythmics. (The new name comes from a dance and mime form based on Greek format by Emil Jacques-Dalcrose in the early 1900s, to teach children music through movement.)

1981 July [4] Signed worldwide to RCA Records, their first single as Eurythmics, *Never Gonna Cry Again*, peaks at UK #63. (They will have ongoing legal problems with previous label Logo until a court case settlement in 1987.)

Aug Follow-up *Belinda* does not chart.

Oct Debut album *In The Garden* is released.

1982 Mar *This Is The House*, aided by Blondie drummer Clem Burke, is released.

June *The Walk* also fails.

Dec [4] Synthesizer-based *Love Is A Stranger*, with Kiki Dee guesting on back-up vocals, peaks at UK #54.

1983 Feb *Sweet Dreams (Are Made Of This)* hits UK #3 and makes US #15.

Mar *Sweet Dreams (Are Made Of This)* hits UK #2, behind Bonnie Tyler *Total Eclipse Of The Heart*. It is supported by an innovative video, scripted and controlled (as are all their early visuals) by the duo.

Apr *Love Is A Stranger* is re-issued, hitting UK #6.

July *Who's That Girl?* hits UK #3. The accompanying video features Bananarama (whose Siobhan Fahey will later marry Stewart).

Sept [3] *Sweet Dreams (Are Made Of This)* hits US #1 for a week and is million-seller.

Nov Bright uptempo cut *Right By Your Side* hits UK #10.

[12] *Love Is A Stranger*, belatedly released in US, makes #23.

Dec [8] Lennox flies to Vienna, Austria, to see a throat specialist about a recurring vocal problem.

1984 Jan [27] Duo begins a 175-date world tour in Australia.

Feb *Here Comes The Rain Again* hits UK #8.

[4] *Touch*, recorded at a disused church in Crouch End, London, which has become the duo's home base, tops UK chart and will hit US #7.

[21] Lennox wins Best British Female Artist at the third annual BRIT Awards at Grosvenor House, Mayfair, London.

Mar Lennox marries German Hare Krishna devotee Rahda Raman. (The marriage will last 6 months.)

[31] *Here Comes The Rain Again* hits US #4.

Apr [19] Lennox and Stewart are named Songwriters Of The Year at the annual Ivor Novello Awards luncheon at Grosvenor House.

June [23] *Who's That Girl?*, another belated US release, peaks at #21.

July Mini-album *Touch Dance*, containing 4 dance remixes from *Touch*, reaches UK #31 and US #115.

Sept [8] *Right By Your Side* makes US #29. Already used as the backing track on UK TV commercial for "Kelly Girl", it is reported that *Sweet Dreams* will be used as the theme for forthcoming US TV soap opera "Paper Dolls".

Nov *Sex Crime (1984)*, from Virgin Films' movie adaptation of George Orwell's *1984*, hits UK #4.

Dec [1] *Sex Crime (1984)* stalls at US #81.

Eurythmics' soundtrack *1984 (For The Love Of Big Brother)*, recorded at Compass Point, Nassau, reaches UK #23.

Jan Haunting ballad *Julia*, from *1984*, makes UK #44. The soundtrack album reaches US #93.

May *Would I Lie To You?* reaches UK #17.

Be Yourself Tonight hits UK #3 and US #9. The album includes a guest appearance from Elvis Costello.

July [13] *Would I Lie To You?* hits US #5. Scheduled to play Live Aid concert, Eurythmics cancel when Lennox's voice problems recur.

[27] *There Must Be An Angel*, featuring a Stevie Wonder harmonica break, tops UK chart.

Sept [21] *There Must Be An Angel* reaches US #22.

Nov *Sisters Are Doing It For Themselves*, a Lennox vocal duet with Aretha Franklin, hits UK #9.

Dec [7] *Sisters Are Doing It For Themselves* reaches US #18. Lennox makes acting debut in Hugh Hudson's film "Revolution" starring Al Pacino and Donald Sutherland.

Jan Airplay favorite *It's Alright (Baby's Coming Back)* reaches UK #12.

Feb [10] Lennox wins Best British Female Artist, for the second time, and Stewart wins Best British Producer at the fifth annual BRIT Awards at London's Grosvenor House.

Mar [8] *It's Alright (Baby's Coming Back)* stalls at US #78.

June *When Tomorrow Comes* makes UK #30.

July *Revenge* hits UK #3, and will stay charted for 52 weeks.

Sept *Thorn In My Side* hits UK #5.

Oct [11] *Missionary Man* reaches US #14, as *Revenge* makes US #12.

Dec [2] Lennox rips her bra off in front of 2,000 fans while singing *Missionary Man*.

[6] *Thorn In My Side* makes US #68. (By this time Stewart, sometimes credited as David A. Stewart to avoid confusion with a namesake, is an in-demand producer and session man working with major stars like Bob Dylan, The Ramones, Bob Geldof, Daryl Hall, Tom Petty, Mick Jagger and Feargal Sharkey.)

Ballad *The Miracle Of Love* reaches UK #25.

Mar *Missionary Man* makes UK #31.

Feb [9] Stewart wins Best British Producer, for the second year running, at the sixth annual BRIT Awards at the Grosvenor House.

[24] Eurythmics win Best Rock Performance By A Duo Or Group With Vocal for *Missionary Man* at the 29th annual Grammy awards.

Apr [15] Eurythmics are awarded Songwriters Of The Year and *It's Alright (Baby's Coming Back)* wins Best Contemporary Song at the annual Ivor Novello Awards at the Grosvenor House. Stewart and Lennox have been responsible for writing all Eurythmics hits to date.

June [4] While Eurythmics are performing in Berlin, over 1,000 East Berlin fans gather at the Berlin Wall chanting "the wall must go". Police arrive to remove the rioters.

Aug [1] Stewart marries Siobhan Fahey at Chateau Dangu, France.

Oct *Beethoven (I Love To Listen To)* reaches UK #25.

Nov *Savage* hits UK #7.

Jan *Shame* makes UK #41.

[30] *I Need A Man* makes US #46.

Feb *Savage* peaks at US #41.

Apr *I Need A Man* reaches UK #26. All 3 singles from the album have failed to make the Top 20 in both UK and US. Dave Stewart launches his own Anxious Records (his first success coming with Londonbeat's *9AM*) as Eurythmics begin work on an album of cover versions.

June *You Have Placed A Chill In My Heart* reaches UK #16.

[11] Eurythmics perform at "Nelson Mandela's 70th Birthday Party" at Wembley Stadium, London.

[24] Virgin Video releases "Savage", adding to previously best-selling Eurythmics video packages which includes "Eurythmics Live" and early clips retrospective "Sweet Dreams".

[25] *You Have Placed A Chill In My Heart* peaks at US #64.

Dec *Put A Little Love In Your Heart*, a Lennox duet with Al Green, reviving Jackie DeShannon's 1969 US #4, reaches UK #28. It is taken from the soundtrack to seasonal movie "Scrooged", starring Bill Murray. *Put A Little Love In Your Heart* hits US #8.

Jan [14] Lennox and Green's *Put A Little Love In Your Heart* hits US #9.

Feb [13] Lennox wins Best British Female Artist, for the third time, at the eighth annual BRIT Awards at the Royal Albert Hall, London.

Mar [6] She attends the launch of *Rainbow Warriors* in Moscow and films a TV clip to promote Greenpeace.

May Following his production of Russian rocker Boris Grebenshikov's new album *Radio Silence*, Stewart joins Lennox in Paris to pen songs for *We Too Are One* to be released on Arista, to which Eurythmics are newly signed.

Sept *Revival*, previewing new album, peaks at UK #26.

[23] *We Too Are One* tops UK chart.

Nov *Don't Ask Me Why* reaches UK #25.

[4] *Don't Ask Me Why* makes US #40.

Dec *We Too Are One* reaches US #34.

1990 **Feb** Lennox announces she is taking a break for 2 years to work for the homeless in UK. Stewart forms new band The Spiritual Cowboys. *King And Queen Of America* reaches UK #29.

[18] Lennox wins Best British Female Artist, for a fourth time, and Stewart wins Best British Producer, for a third time, at the ninth annual BRIT Awards at the Dominion theater, London.

Apr During a Eurythmics lay-off, Stewart, listed as David A. Stewart featuring Candy Dulfer, links with the Scandinavian saxophonist on the UK hit #6 *Lily Was Here*, the instrumental theme from film "De Kassiere", while parent album, the full soundtrack work peaks at UK #35, both released on Stewart's own Anxious label.

[16] Stewart takes part in the "Nelson Mandela – An International Tribute To A Free South Africa" concert at Wembley Stadium with Bonnie Raitt, Neil Young, Simple Minds, The Neville Brothers, Peter Gabriel, Tracy Chapman, Anita Baker and many others.

May Ballad from *We Too Are One*, *Angel*, reaches UK #23.

June [6] Stewart debuts The Spiritual Cowboys at the second International Awards in New York.

[30] Latest video selection comprising recent singles clips "We Two Are One Too" is issued by BMG Video.

July [14] Spiritual Cowboys' *Party Town*, featured in movie "Flatliners", released in US.

Sept [15] Dave Stewart & The Spiritual Cowboys eponymous debut album peaks at UK #38, while single *Jack Talking* stalls at UK #69.

Oct Lennox contributes *Ev'rytime We Say Goodbye* to *Red Hot + Blue*, an anthology of Cole Porter songs to benefit AIDS education.

[17] Spiritual Cowboys, comprising Stewart, John "Texas" Turbull (guitar), Chris James (bass), Martin Chambers (drums) and another drummer, begin US tour at the Citi, Boston, MA.

1991 **Jan** The Peace Choir, an all-star line-up of singers and musicians, including Stewart, records new version of John Lennon's peace anthem *Give Peace A Chance*, adapted by Sean Lennon and Lenny Kravitz.

Mar [16] Reissued *Love Is A Stranger* makes UK #46.

[30] Comprehensive *Eurythmics Greatest Hits* debuts at UK #1.

THE EVERLY BROTHERS
Don Everly (vocals, guitar)
Phil Everly (vocals, guitar)

1955 Don (b. Isaac Donald Everly, Feb.1, 1937, Brownie, KY) and Phil (b. Jan.19, 1939, Chicago, IL), the sons of radio performers Ike and Margaret Everly, have appeared on family shows, until their parents retired, on stations in Kentucky, IA, and in Knoxville, TN, where they now live. The brothers go to Nashville, TN, to attempt to sell some of their songs to country singers and to make a demo in the hope of picking up a recording deal. Don places *Thou Shalt Not Steal* for $600 and, after an initial lack of success, they are offered a session with CBS/Columbia Records.

Nov The Everly Brothers make their first studio recordings, 4 tracks cut in 22 mins. with country singer Carl Smith's backing band, at Nashville's Old Tulane hotel.

1956 **Feb** Columbia releases 2 original country songs, *Keep A-Lovin' Me* and *The Sun Keeps Shining* as a single. It does not sell well, and the other songs from the session, *If Her Love Isn't True* and *That's The Life I Have To Lead* are shelved. Columbia passes on its option, and the brothers again do the rounds of Nashville labels. They fail to secure a deal until their father contacts old acquaintance Chet Atkins. Via him, they are signed as songwriters by Roy Acuff and Wesley Rose's publishing company, and Rose becomes their manager.

1957 Rose persuades Archie Bleyer at New York-based Cadence Records that The Everly Brothers are the country singers he is looking for. Bleyer asks them to record a song by Felice and Boudleaux Bryant, *Bye Bye Love* (which some 30 acts have rejected). It is recorded at RCA's Nashville studio, in a session supervised by Atkins, but not in straight country fashion. The style – close harmonies over acoustic guitars and a rock'n'roll beat – becomes The Everly Brothers' trademark.

Apr They tour around Mississippi tent shows as the single is released.

May [11] They make their debut on Nashville's "Grand Ole Opry".

June [17] *Bye Bye Love* hits US #2 for 4 weeks (below Pat Boone's *Love Letters In The Sand*) and becomes a million-seller. It also hits US C&W #1 and R&B #5.

July [12] The Everly Brothers appear on DJ Alan Freed's premiere ABC TV show "The Big Beat" singing *Bye Bye Love*. Also appearing on the first show are Frankie Lymon, Buddy Knox, Connie Francis and others.

Aug *Bye Bye Love*, released in UK on London label, hits #6 during a 16-week Top 30 run.

[4] Duo guests on CBS TV's "Ed Sullivan Show" singing *Bye Bye Love* and *Wake Up Little Susie*. (By the end of the year, they will have been seen on most of US TV's top-rated variety shows, including those of Patti Page, Arthur Murray and Perry Como – the latter, also shown in UK, offers British fans their first view of The Everly Brothers.)

Oct [14] *Wake Up Little Susie*, another Bryants' song with a classic teen-calamity lyric (and, although hardly risqué, banned from airplay in Boston), tops US chart for 2 weeks and is a second million-seller. (It also hits C&W #1 and R&B #2.)

Dec *Wake Up Little Susie* hits UK #2.

1958 Feb [24] *This Little Girl Of Mine* (R&B #9 for Ray Charles in 1955) reaches US #26. Debut album *The Everly Brothers – They're Off And Running!* makes US #16.

Apr [5] They begin an 80-day tour of US and Canada at Norfolk, VA, co-starring in Irving Feld's "Greatest Show Of Stars" with Sam Cooke, Paul Anka, Frankie Avalon and others.

May [12] *All I Have To Do Is Dream*, a ballad written by the Bryants in some 15 mins., hits US #1 for 4 weeks and is another million-seller. Contrasting B-side *Claudette*, written by Roy Orbison about his wife, reaches US #30.

June *All I Have To Do Is Dream/Claudette* hits UK #1 for 8 weeks (their first UK #1).

Aug [25] Rocking *Bird Dog*, which they struggled through 15 studio takes to perfect, is a fourth million-seller and tops US chart for a week.

Sept The brothers go to the studio with bassist Floyd Chance to record country/folk songs, released as *Songs Our Daddy Taught Us*, which fails to chart.

[22] Ballad B-side *Devoted To You* hits US #10.

Nov *Bird Dog* tops UK chart for 2 weeks.

Dec [15] *Problems*, another archetypal teen-dilemma song, hits US #2 and is their fifth million-seller. B-side *Love Of My Life* peaks at US #40.

[30] The Everly Brothers headline Alan Freed's "Christmas Rock'N'Roll Spectacular" at Loew's State theater, Manhattan, New York, alongside Chuck Berry, Bo Diddley, Jackie Wilson and others.

1959 Jan [16] They make a brief UK visit (for the first time) to appear on TV show "Cool For Cats", receive a **New Musical Express** award as World #1 Vocal Group and attend a Savoy hotel reception in their honor – all within 24 hours before flying on to Europe.

Feb *Problems* hits UK #6.

May [4] *Poor Jenny* (another teen soap opera) makes US #22.

[18] A-side, the folky ballad *Take A Message To Mary* reaches US #16.

July *Poor Jenny* makes UK #14, and *Take A Message To Mary* UK #20.

Sept [21] Written by Don, *('Til) I Kissed You* hits US #4, and is another million-seller. Recorded with backing by The Crickets (Sonny Curtis playing lead guitar), it is the first Nashville-recorded rock'n'roll/country record to employ a full drumkit, with tom-toms, in the studio. (Before this, drummers use a snare drum and brushes.)

Oct *('Til) I Kissed You* hits UK #2, behind Bobby Darin's *Mack The Knife*.

[25] The Everly Brothers announce that they are considering parting from Cadence, and are talking with both RCA and newly-formed Warner Bros. Records.

Dec [15] They record their first session outside Nashville. *Let It Be Me*, an English translation of Gilbert Becaud's French *J'Appartiens* (a US hit for Jill Corey in 1957), is cut in Bell Sound studios in New York, and is their first session with an orchestral backing (8 violins and a cello, conducted by Bleyer).

1960 Feb [17] The Everly Brothers sign to Warner Bros., in a 10-year contract worth $1 million.

[22] *Let It Be Me* hits US #7.

Mar *Let It Be Me* makes UK #13. Meanwhile, the duo records 8 songs in Nashville for Warner, but none of them is felt strong enough to be a single. Don writes *Cathy's Clown* at home, it is finely tuned by Phil, and they cut it 2 days later, for rush single release.

Apr [6] They begin their first UK tour with a concert at London's New Victoria theater, backed by The Crickets.

May [23] *Cathy's Clown*, The Everly Brothers' all-time biggest seller, tops US chart for 5 weeks and UK chart for 8 (with the catalog number WB 1, it gives Warner Bros. its first UK #1 with its first release). It sells 3 million copies worldwide. B-side *Always It's You* makes US #56.

June The remaining tracks from the first Warner sessions are released on *It's Everly Time!*, which hits US #9 and UK #2 – their most successful chart album.

July [18] Cadence releases unheard Phil-penned *When Will I Be Loved*, which hits US #8 and UK #4. B-side, a revival of Gene Vincent's *Be-Bop-A-Lula* makes US #74.

Sept Cadence album *The Fabulous Style Of the Everly Brothers*, a compilation of hit singles, reaches US #23.

Oct [10] *So Sad (To Watch Good Love Go Bad)*, a country-styled ballad written by Don and extracted from the first Warner album after strong radio play, hits US #7 and UK #5. B-side revives Little Richard's *Lucille* in a new arrangement which features 8 top Nashville session guitarists strumming acoustically in unison, and it makes US #21 and UK #14.

Nov UK version of *The Fabulous Style*, a compilation with only 4 songs in common with the US version, hits UK #4.

[28] Final unheard track released on single by Cadence, Boudleaux Bryant ballad *Like Strangers*, reaches UK #22.

1961 Jan *Like Strangers* reaches UK #11, while the second Warner album *A Date With The Everly Brothers* hits US #9. The brothers move from Nashville to Hollywood and, at Rose's suggestion, take acting lessons.

Mar [27] Their most successful double A-side is *Walk Right Back* (written by Sonny Curtis of The Crickets) at UK #1 for 4 weeks and US #7 and *Ebony Eyes* (a John D. Loudermilk ballad with a poignant love and death theme) at US #8 and UK #17. *A Date With The Everly Brothers* hits UK #3.

May [19] The brothers launch their own record label, Calliope, designed as a showcase for new acts.

June [19] *Stick With Me Baby* makes US #41.

[26] A revolutionary arrangement of 1934 Bing Crosby oldie *Temptation*, making prominent use of a female chorus, reaches US #27. It was recorded against manager Rose's advice, and amid some other disagreements the brothers and he part company (the most serious effect will be the denial of Acuff/Rose-signed Bryants' songs). Jack Rael (Patti Page's manager for 15 years) is appointed new manager.

July *Temptation* hits UK #1 for 2 weeks. Amid a minor spurt of oldie-mania on US radio, original Cadence single *All I Have To Do Is Dream* re-charts at US #96. Also on US chart at #34 is the brothers' rock instrumental version of Elgar's *Pomp And Circumstance*, their only Calliope label success. Credited to "Adrian Kimberly", it is actually arranged and performed by Don with help from Neal Hefti. (Calliope label will soon become inactive.)

Oct [9] Uptempo *Muskrat* makes US #82 and UK #20.

[16] A-side *Don't Blame Me*, a ballad first recorded by Ethel Walters in 1933, reaches US #20.

Nov [25] The brothers are inducted into the US Marine Corps Reserves, initially for 6 months' active service. They report to Camp Pendleton, San Diego, CA, for duty in the 8th Battalion working as artillerymen handling 105MM howitzers.

1962 Feb Don marries Venetia Stevenson, the former wife of actor Russ Tamblyn.

[18] On weekend leave from Marine training, the brothers appear on CBS TV's "Ed Sullivan Show" to sing their new single *Crying In The Rain* – in uniform and with regulation cropped haircuts.

Mar *Crying In The Rain*, written for The Everly Brothers by Carole King and Howard Greenfield, hits #6 in both US and UK.

May [24] The brothers end their 6-month service.

June [16] *How Can I Meet Her?* peaks at US #75.

[23] A-side *That's Old Fashioned (That's The Way Love Should Be)* hits US #9 and UK #12. It is announced that The Everly Brothers' record sales top 35 million.

July *Instant Party* makes UK #20 (last UK chart album for 8 years).

Sept *The Golden Hits Of The Everly Brothers*, a compilation of singles since *Cathy's Clown*, reaches US #35, but fails in UK. (This album will still be on Warner's catalog 26 years later, when it is released on CD.)

Oct [13] Prior to the opening of a 22-date twice-nightly UK tour, Don Everly collapses on stage at London's Prince of Wales theater during rehearsal. He is hospitalized briefly, then flown back to US for medical treatment. Phil continues solo, with the Everlys' guitarist Joey Page substituting on harmony vocals. Tour, with Frank Ifield, Ketty Lester and others, will end Nov.11 at Liverpool's Empire theater, Merseyside.

Nov [3] *I'm Here To Get My Baby Out Of Jail*, from Cadence album *Songs Our Daddy Taught Us*, stalls at US #76.

[24] *Don't Ask Me To Be Friends*, on Warner, peaks at US #48. In UK, it is B-side to Gerry Goffin/Jack Keller song *No One Can Make My Sunshine Smile* which reaches UK #11.

Dec Duo's only seasonal album, *Christmas With The Everly Brothers And The Boys Town Choir*, mostly of traditional carols, is released.

1963 Jan With top Nashville session men, the brothers record *The Everly Brothers Sing Great Country Hits*, which includes versions of *I Walk*

The Line, *I'm So Lonesome I Could Cry*, *Oh Lonesome Me*, *Release Me*, and other C&W classics.

Apr *So It Always Will Be* makes UK #23. Like all the duo's releases this year, it fails to reach US Hot 100.

June *It's Been Nice* makes UK #26.

Sept [29] Duo opens a UK tour, supported by Bo Diddley and The Rolling Stones, and later joined by Little Richard.

Nov Written by Barry Mann and Cynthia Weil, *The Girl Sang The Blues* and *Love Her* (which The Walker Brothers will later revive as their first hit) climbs to UK #25.

64

July *The Ferris Wheel* reaches UK #22.

[25] *The Ferris Wheel* peaks at US #72. Also released is *The Very Best Of The Everly Brothers*, which is a compilation of new re-recordings of their biggest hits, including 6 originally on Cadence. (Warner has tried to buy The Everly Brothers' early material from Bleyer, but he has already sold it to his ex-artist Andy Williams – who wants to keep his own early tracks from being reissued outside his control.) The album does not chart (but will stay on Warner's catalog into the 80s).

Sept [16] The Everly Brothers appear on the first edition of ABC TV's "Shindig" singing *Gone Gone Gone*.

Dec [12] Co-written by The Everlys, and in a frantic Bo Diddley-like arrangement, *Gone Gone Gone* reaches US #31 and UK #36.

65

Jan *Gone Gone Gone* is released. The rift with Rose has been resolved and half the album's songs are written by the Bryants, as well as 2 by Loudermilk.

Mar *Rock'N'Soul* contains versions of 50s rock'n'roll hits, including *That'll Be The Day*, *Hound Dog* and *Kansas City*.

May A revival of Buddy Holly And The Crickets' *That'll Be the Day*, taken from the album, reaches UK #30.

June Another Everly co-written R&B/rocker, *The Price Of Love*, recorded in Nashville on Apr.4, is rush-released to tie in with a UK and European tour. It hits UK #2, but fails to chart in US.

July A West to East Coast US tour follows the European trek.

Sept Uptempo country-styled *I'll Never Get Over You* peaks at UK #35. *Beat Soul* develops the *Rock'N'Soul* theme but concentrates on R&B oldies. It shows a tougher edge to the duo than any earlier recordings, and features session players Jim Gordon and Billy Preston, and songs like *Hi-Heel Sneakers*, *People Get Ready* and *Walking The Dog*. It reaches US #141, but fails to chart in UK despite UK's current R&B fixation.

[16] The Everly Brothers appear on ABC TV's second season premiere of "Shindig", singing a revival of Mickey And Sylvia's *Love Is Strange*. (Phil is scheduled for 2 weeks' Marines service, followed by 2 more in Nov., both brothers still being US Marines Reservists.)

Oct [2] The Everlys represent the US at Holland's annual Grand Gala Du Disque at the Congresscentrum, Amsterdam.

[8] They embark on an 18-date twice-nightly UK "Star Scene '65" tour with Cilla Black, Billy J.Kramer and Paddy, Klaus & Gibson at the Granada theater, Bedford, Beds. Tour will end Oct.28 at the ABC theater, Wigan, Lancs.

Nov Boosted by appearances on ITV's "Ready Steady Go!" and BBC TV's "Top Of The Pops", *Love Is Strange* reaches UK #11.

66

Mar *In Our Image*, with their more accustomed sound, is released. It includes Don's ballad *It's All Over* (a non-selling US single which will be a UK Top 10 hit for Cliff Richard in 1967).

May They record *Two Yanks In England*, in London for the first time, which is issued 2 months later. The session musicians include guitarist Jimmy Page and bassist John Paul Jones (both later in Led Zeppelin). The Hollies also participate, with the group's Graham Nash, Tony Hicks and Allan Clarke writing 8 of the 12 songs under the pseudonym L. Ransford. The brothers also record a solo each.

June Duo returns to US following a record-breaking Far East tour.

67

Feb *The Hit Sound Of The Everly Brothers*, consisting mainly of covers and revivals like *Blueberry Hill* and *Let's Go Get Stoned*, fails to chart.

July [8] *Bowling Green*, written by Englishman Terry Slater (despite being a hymn to the Everlys' Kentucky roots), reaches US #40, after a 2-year chart absence. (Slater, the duo's bass player, has been a friend ever since his group The Flintstones opened The Everly Brothers' 1963 UK tour. He moves to Los Angeles and becomes a long-time co-writer with Phil, as the brothers' music moves to the country-rock field – even though they fail to become part of its commercial success.) *The Everly Brothers Sing*, featuring 5 Slater songs, is released.

68

May Loudermilk-penned *It's My Time* makes UK #39 (The Everly Brothers' last UK hit single for 16 years).

Nov *Roots*, with country songs and excerpts from the old Everly family radio show recorded in 1952, as well as new material including *Living Too Close To The Ground* and *Ventura Boulevard*, features a re-recording of 12-year-old *I Wonder If I Care As Much*, a Don and Phil co-composition which was B-side of *Bye Bye Love*.

1969 Despite lack of recording success they continue to tour and are a popular guest act on US network TV shows, including those of The Smothers Brothers, Johnny Cash and Glen Campbell – not only singing, but introducing comedy into their act.

Apr *I'm On My Way Home Again/The Cuckoo Bird*, recorded in Los Angeles with Clarence White and Gene Pasons of The Byrds, is issued only in US and fails to chart.

1970 **Feb** [6] The Everly Brothers record a live album at the Grand hotel, Anaheim, CA. The resulting double album *The Everly Brothers Show* is their last recording for Warner Bros. *Yves* (written by Scott McKenzie of San Francisco fame) is the Warner song single.

July [8] They host "The Everly Brothers Show" on ABC TV. It is an 11-week peak-time summer replacement for "The Johnny Cash Show", and is strongly country music-oriented, with regular comedy relief from Joe Higgins and Ruth McDevitt.

Aug US Barnaby label, owned by Andy Williams, finally makes use of the early Everly tracks purchased from Bleyer in the 60s. After years off the market, 20 are packaged on double album *The Everly Brothers' Original Greatest Hits*, with a nostalgic sleeve complete with a 50s rock'n'roll quiz. It reaches US #180.

Oct CBS issues double *Original Greatest Hits* which hits UK #7.

1971 Don Everly is the first of the duo to cut a solo (eponymous) album on Lou Adler's Ode label, which attracts little attention (the apparently brooding, angst-ridden nature of much of its material is widely thought to reflect turmoil in his personal life).

1972 **June** Signed to RCA, the brothers release *Stories We Could Tell*, recorded at Lovin' Spoonful John Sebastian's house with guest players including Ry Cooder, Delaney And Bonnie, Graham Nash and David Crosby. Songs include Rod Stewart's *Mandolin Wind*, Jesse Winchester's *The Brand New Tennessee Waltz* and the title track by Sebastian.

1973 **Feb** *Pass The Chicken And Listen*, also on RCA, marks a return to Nashville and to producer Atkins, who brings in top session men, but it fails to chart.

July [14] The personal conflict which has been building between the brothers finally comes to a head at the John Wayne theater at Knott's Berry Farm in Hollywood, CA. Entertainment manager Bill Hollinghead stops the show midway through second of 3 scheduled sets, unhappy with Don's performance, and Phil smashes his guitar and storms off. Don performs the third set solo and announces their break-up to the audience ("The Everly Brothers died 10 years ago").

Sept Phil signs a solo deal with RCA. *Star Spangled Springer*, produced by Duane Eddy and with musical assistance from Warren Zevon, Jim Horn, Earl Palmer and James Burton, was recorded just before the split. Critically acclaimed (and including the original version of *The Air That I Breathe* (later a worldwide hit for The Hollies), it fails.

1974 **June** [8] *The Very Best Of The Everly Brothers* makes UK #43.

Oct Don releases another solo album on Ode, *Sunset Towers*, backed by UK group Heads, Hands & Feet.

1975 **Jan** Phil signs to UK Pye label, releasing *There's Nothing Too Good For My Baby* (US title: *Phil's Diner*).

Nov Phil releases solo album *Mystic Line* on Pye, then requests that his contract be terminated.

Dec In UK, TV-advertised 20-track compilation album *Walk Right Back With The Everlys* sparks a major revival of interest, hitting UK #10. This inspires BBC radio to produce a multi-part "Everly Brothers Story" documentary series, which is syndicated around the world.

1977 **Feb** [10] Don starts work on solo album *Brother Juke Box*, at Acuff-Rose Sound studios, Nashville, with Rose producing. It will be released on Hickory Records in US and DJM Records in UK.

Apr *Living Legends*, a collection of Cadence material on TV-advertised label Warwick Records, reaches UK #12.

Sept Warner Bros. issues *The New Album*, which contains (with a couple of exceptions) previously unreleased Everly Brothers tracks from the 60s. It fails and Warner does not issue any more of the 60 or so unreleased songs still in its vaults.

1978 Phil appears in Clint Eastwood movie "Any Which Way But Loose", duetting on his song *Don't Say You Don't Love Me No More* with Eastwood's co-star Sondra Locke.

1979 Phil has a one-off deal with Elektra Records for Snuff Garrett-produced *Living Alone*, released only in US.

1981 Signed to Curb Records, Phil releases *Dare To Dream Again*. It collects good airplay in UK (where it is released on Epic), but fails to chart.

1982 **Nov** Now signed to Capitol, and produced in London by Shakin' Stevens' producer Stuart Colman, Phil charts at UK #47 with his debut for the label, *Louise*.

1983 Jan In UK, K-Tel's Christmas TV-advertised Everly Brothers compilation *Love Hurts* peaks at #31 and has a 22-week UK chart run.
Mar Phil's duet with Cliff Richard, *She Means Nothing To Me*, hits UK #9. Mark Knopfler of Dire Straits plays guitar on the track.
May Capitol album *Phil Everly*, produced by Stuart Colman at Eden studios, London, charts at UK #61 for a week.
June [30] After 10 years of estrangement, differences are finally settled, and The Everly Brothers announce plans for a reunion concert in Sept. Phil is quoted as saying "We settled it in a family kind of way – a big hug did it!"
Sept [23] The Everly Brothers Reunion Concert is a sell-out affair at the Royal Albert Hall, London, as the duo slips effortlessly back together to perform their repertoire in the classic style. The event is filmed (for TV and later home video release) and recorded. (More concerts will follow in US and elsewhere.)

1984 Jan Live double album *The Everly Brothers Reunion Concert*, on Impression Records, is the duo's first non-compilation album to chart in UK for 22 years, and reaches #47.
Mar Double album *Reunion Concert*, on Passport Records in US, peaks at #162, after a 14-year album chart absence.
Oct [13] Signed to Mercury, the brothers reach US #50 and hit UK #4 with *On The Wings Of A Nightingale*, written for them by Paul McCartney and produced by Dave Edmunds. It is taken from their first studio album since re-forming, Edmunds-produced *The Everly Brothers*, which reaches UK #36.
Nov The album, retitled *EB 84*, climbs to US #38, their best US album chart placing since 1962.

1986 Jan [23] Duo is inducted into the Rock'N'Roll Hall Of Fame at the first annual dinner at the Waldorf Astoria, New York.
Born Yesterday, again produced by Edmunds, makes US #83.

1987 Feb [1] Phil gives Don a custom-built guitar made from mother-of-pearl-inlaid African blackwood and a pound of gold on his 50th birthday.

1988 Aug A granite statue of The Everly Brothers is unveiled in the duo's home state, at City Hall, Everly Brothers Boulevard, Central City, KY.

1989 May *Don't Worry Baby*, featured in Mel Gibson/Michelle Pfeiffer-starring movie "Tequila Sunrise" (with The Beach Boys guesting on a revival of their 1964 hit) are released, but neither charts, and *Some Hearts* from which it is taken, are released, but neither charts.
Aug Phil duets with Nanci Griffith on *You Made This Love A Teardrop* on the latter's *Storms*, as the brothers are featured on Johnny Cash's *Ballad Of A Teenage Queen* with Rosanne Cash.

1990 Apr [27] Don's daughter Erin marries Guns N' Roses' lead singer Axl Rose at Cupid's Wedding Chapel in Las Vegas, NV.

EVERYTHING BUT THE GIRL

Tracey Thorn (vocals)
Ben Watt (guitars, keyboards, vocals)

1980 Unknown to each other at the time, Thorn (b. Sept.26, 1962) and Watt (b. Dec.6, 1962), both sign to Cherry Red Records in UK as soloists. Thorn also records as a member of The Marine Girls trio. Her solo album *A Distant Shore* costs only £120 to record, but is a UK Independent chart success and sells over 60,000.

1982 A&R man Mike Alway, a long-time friend, introduces Watt to Thorn while both are studying at Hull University, Humberside. They form a romantic and artistic union.

1983 Jan [5] Duo performs for the first time as Everything But The Girl (a name taken from a second-hand furniture store in Hull) at London's ICA theater. Paul Weller of The Style Council guests on their version of *The Girl From Ipanema*.
July *Night And Day*, a revival of the Cole Porter standard, is their only release as a duo for Cherry Red.

1984 Mar Thorn guests on The Style Council's *Café Bleu*.
May After leaving Cherry Red for new label blanco y negro (formed by Alway and Rough Trade's Geoff Travis), their first hit *Each And Everyone* reaches UK #28. Duo is unable to perform it on BBC TV's "Top Of The Pops" because both are taking their degree exams.
June [9] Working Week's *Venceremos – We Will Win*, on which Thorn is featured, peaks at UK #64.
July Debut album *Eden* reaches UK #14, while *Mine* makes UK #58.
Sept Duo embarks on a 24-date UK tour.
Oct [6] *Native Land* stalls at UK #73.

1985 May *Love Not Money*, produced by Robin Millar, hits UK #10, and gains popularity in Europe, particularly Italy and Holland.

1986 Aug Lush orchestral-arranged *Come On Home* makes UK #44.

Sept *Baby The Stars Shine Bright* reaches UK #22. It features noted UK jazz musician Peter King in the horn section, beginning a long-term liaison between him and the group.
Oct [11] *Don't Leave Me Behind* stalls at UK #72.

1987 Duo concentrates on writing new songs, and Thorn also duets with Lloyd Cole for one of his album tracks.

1988 Mar *Idlewild*, recorded at Livingston studios, London, reaches UK #13, as *These Early Days*, taken from it, spends a week at UK #75.
[10] They embark on UK tour at Loughborough University, Leics., finishing at the Brighton Dome, E.Sussex, Mar.25.
July A revival of Rod Stewart's *I Don't Want To Talk About It*, hits UK #3, their biggest hit to date.
Aug Reissued *Idlewild* reaches UK #21.
Sept Duo supports Joan Armatrading on US tour.

1990 Feb [17] *The Language Of Life*, recorded in Los Angeles, CA, with producer Tommy LiPuma and musicians Joe Sample, Michael Brecker, Jerry Hey and Stan Getz, hits UK #10.

THE FACES

Rod Stewart (vocals)
Ron Wood (guitar)
Ian McLagan (keyboards)
Ronnie Lane (bass)
Kenny Jones (drums)

1969 June Band, formed in UK from ex-members of The Small Faces and The Jeff Beck Group, signs to Warner Bros., while lead singer Stewart (b. Roderick David Stewart, Jan.10, 1945, Highgate, London) signs a separate deal for £1,000 to Mercury Records as a solo artist. Band debuts at Cambridge University, Cambs., as Quiet Melon, supplemented by Art Wood (Ron's elder brother), Long John Baldry and Jimmy Horowitz.

1970 Apr *First Step* reaches UK #45 and US #119. Group is billed in US as The Small Faces for this album, and tours to promote it, building a solid live following on both sides of the Atlantic with its "lads night out" brand of rock and shambolic stage presence. *Flying* does not chart.

1971 Mar *Long Player* reaches US #29.
May *Long Player* makes UK #31 while extracted single *Had Me A Real Good Time* fails.
Oct Stewart's solo career explodes with a worldwide chart topper *Maggie May*. Group backs him on his many TV appearances leading to a regular billing of Rod Stewart & The Faces, which causes rancor within the band.
Dec *A Nod's As Good As A Wink ... To A Blind Horse* hits UK #2 and US #6. With assistance from producer Glyn Johns, the group begins to score hit singles. A revival of The Temptations' hit, *(I Know) I'm Losing You*, more in keeping with Stewart's solo style, reaches US #24.

1972 Feb *Stay With Me* hits UK #6.
Mar *Stay With Me* reaches US #17. Group embarks on UK and US tour at large venues but Stewart's solo success overshadows the band's reputation as a unit.

1973 Mar *Cindy Incidentally* hits UK #2 and makes US #48.
Apr *Ooh La La* hits UK #1 and reaches US #21, but is publicly disowned by Stewart who has shown little interest in the project.
May Lane leaves and is replaced by Japanese bassist Tetsu Yamauchi (Lane will invest his earnings from the group into a mobile studio and form his own group, Slim Chance.)
Nov Lane adopts a gypsy lifestyle, travelling in a caravan across the UK. Slim Chance makes its debut in Romany style at Chipperfield's Circus on London's Clapham Common.

1974 Jan Double A-side *Pool Hall Richard/I Wish It Would Rain* hits UK #8.
Feb Live album *Coast To Coast Overture And Beginners*, issued on Mercury rather than Warner with the band credited as Rod Stewart & The Faces, hits UK #3 and US #63. Lane's *How Come* reaches UK #11.
June *The Poacher*, Lane's second hit, makes UK #36.
Aug Lane's *Anymore For Anymore* climbs to UK #48.
Dec *You Can Make Me Dance Sing Or Anything* reaches UK #12. Group tours US.

1975 Apr Stewart quits the UK for tax reasons.
June Wood tours US playing guitar with The Rolling Stones.
Sept Remnants of the group back Stewart on a US tour to promote his *Atlantic Crossing*, augmented by guitarist Jesse Ed Davis and a string section.
Dec Stewart announces he is quitting the group and Wood joins The Rolling Stones. Group splits while The Small Faces' *Itchycoo Park* is enjoying renewed chart success at UK #9.

76 June Jones and McLagan re-form The Small Faces unsuccessfully with Steve Marriott. (Jones will join The Who in 1979 as drummer.)

77 May *The Best Of The Faces* reaches UK #24.

June EP *The Faces*, reprising earlier hits, makes UK #41.

Oct Lane joins Pete Townshend for *Rough Mix* which makes UK #44 and US #45. (Lane will later contract Multiple Sclerosis and become involved with his rock contemporaries in raising funds for research.)

ADAM FAITH

55 July Faith (b. Terence Nelhams, June 23, 1940, Acton, London) leaves school wanting to enter the film world, which leads him to Rank Screen Services where he is employed as a messenger boy (and will eventually progress to assistant film editor).

56 When the Lonnie Donegan-led skiffle craze strikes UK, he starts to play with some fellow workers in skiffle group The Worried Men.

57 The Worried Men, still a semi-professional group, are playing a residency at the 2 I's coffee bar in Soho, London, from where an edition of BBC TV's "6.5 Special" is broadcast live. Show's director, Jack Good, notes Nelhams in the group and suggests he could succeed as a soloist, with a change of name. A more likely one is picked out of a book of boys' (Adam) and girls' (Faith) names. After a second "6.5 Special" appearance towards the end of the year, he is signed to EMI Records.

58 Jan *(Got A) Heartsick Feeling*, on EMI's HMV label, is released.

Nov Bacharach/David song *Country Music Holiday* like his debut does not chart, and HMV drops him. Faith, disillusioned, involves himself in his film editing job at Rank, temporarily abandoning his musical career.

59 Apr Recommended by John Barry (with whom he worked on "6.5 Special") for BBC TV's new "Drumbeat", Faith is offered a residency on the weekly show. (He will stay with the series through its 22-week run, performing mainly covers of US rock hits like *C'mon Everybody* and *Believe What You Say*.) *Ah! Poor Little Baby*, on Top Rank, does not chart. He gains a dynamic manager, Eve Taylor.

Oct Songwriter Johnny Worth who, while performing as a member of The Raindrops, met Faith on "Drumbeat", believes the singer to be the ideal interpreter for his song *What Do You Want*, which he and arranger Barry conceive in the mode of Buddy Holly's recent chart-topper *It Doesn't Matter Any More*. They interest EMI/Parlophone producer John Burgess, who agrees to record Faith.

Dec *What Do You Want* hits UK #1 in only its third charted week, topping the chart for 4 weeks. It is Parlophone label's first #1 hit, selling 50,000 copies a day at its peak, and a total of over 620,000 in UK alone. Establishing Faith's vocal trademarks like his hiccupping Hollyish phrasing and exaggerated pronunciation of "buy-bee" (baby), it marks the start of a long partnership between songwriter Worth (under his pen-name of Les Vandyke), Barry (whose pizzicato string arrangement is the record's other notable feature) and Faith.

60 Mar *Poor Me*, a clone of the first hit, also tops UK chart. (Faith will later borrow this title for his early autobiography.) Sell-out tours follow, teen mag coverage proliferates and Faith quickly becomes the UK's biggest teenage idol behind Cliff Richard.

Apr He appears in his first movie, the slightly controversial (and X-certificated) "Beat Girl", which also stars Shirley Ann Field in a story of teenage rebellion. Music for the movie is written by Barry, and Faith sings 3 songs.

May *Someone Else's Baby* hits UK #2, behind The Everly Brothers' *Cathy's Clown*.

June He appears in second film, "Never Let Go", a crime thriller starring Richard Todd and Peter Sellers.

July *Made You*, from "Beat Girl", hits UK #5. UK's BBC radio declines to play it because the lyric is felt to be too explicit, so B-side, a revival of traditional *When Johnny Comes Marching Home* (sung over the credits in "Never Let Go") gets airplay instead and makes UK #11.

Oct *How About That* hits UK #4.

Dec Faith appears on BBC TV's "Face To Face", a penetrating interview program featuring the incisive John Freeman, and acquits himself intelligently. Meanwhile, Faith's debut album *Adam* hits UK #6 and stays in the UK Top 20 for 36 weeks. Seasonal *Lonely Pup (In A Christmas Shop)* hits UK #4.

61 Feb *Who Am I* hits UK #5. Soundtrack album from "Beat Girl" belatedly charts in UK reaching #11.

May Lionel Bart-penned *Easy Going Me* reaches UK #12.

Aug *Don't You Know It* also makes UK #12.

Oct He stars in the film "What A Whopper!", a low-budget UK comedy concerning a Loch Ness Monster hoax.

Nov *The Time Has Come*, from "What A Whopper!", hits UK #4.

1962 Jan [28] Faith appears on BBC TV discussion program "Meeting Point" with the Archbishop of York, Dr. Donald Coggan.

Feb *Lonesome*, Faith's first slow ballad A-side, reaches UK #12.

Mar *Adam Faith* reaches UK #20.

May *As You Like It*, Faith's last single backed by Barry (now heavily committed to film work), hits UK #5.

Sept Faith stars with Anne Baxter and Donald Sinden in film "Mix Me A Person", in which he plays a man wrongly imprisoned for murder.

Oct *Don't That Beat All*, with new arranger Johnny Keating, is a notable break from the familiar sound. It hits UK #8.

Dec After 13 consecutive UK Top 20 singles, *Baby Take A Bow* makes UK #22. Faith opens in pantomime in the title role of "Aladdin" at the Pavilion, Bournemouth, Dorset.

1963 Feb *What Now* makes UK #31, as Faith, like most of his pre-Beatles contemporaries, reels under the chart onslaught of Merseybeat sounds.

July *Walkin' Tall* makes UK #23. Faith decides to recruit The Roulettes – Russ Ballard (lead guitar), Pete Salt (rhythm guitar), John Rodgers (bass) and Bob Henrit (drums) – as his backing group, adding a hard, beat group edge to his vocal sound, which becomes less mannered and more aggressive.

Oct He commissions singer/songwriter Chris Andrews to write new material and *The First Time*, with The Roulettes backing and a newly-contemporary sound, hits UK #5.

1964 Jan *We Are In Love*, from the same team, reaches UK #11. (Faith performs it on second edition of BBC TV show "Top Of The Pops".)

Apr Andrews-penned *If He Tells You* makes UK #25.

[16] Faith embarks on 3-week UK package tour, his first in 18 months, with Dave Berry, Eden Kane and others, at Colston Hall, Bristol, Avon.

June *I Love Being In Love With You* makes UK #33.

Sept Andrews' *Only One Such As You*, an unaccustomedly chest-thumping ballad, does not chart. Meanwhile, he has discovered Sandie Shaw and, impressed by her vocal talent, persuades Taylor to sign her. (Shaw covers Lou Johnson's US Bacharach/David hit *(There's) Always Something There To Remind Me* which tops UK chart.)

Dec Faith's cover of Johnson's *A Message To Martha (Kentucky Bluebird)* (also written by Bacharach and David) reaches UK #12.

[26] Faith embarks on a tour of South Africa. The Roulettes are banned from accompanying him by the Musicians' Union.

1965 Feb *Stop Feeling Sorry For Yourself* reaches UK #23. Meanwhile, the Andrews-penned, Roulettes-backed *It's Alright* (originally UK B-side of *I Love Being In Love With You*) belatedly makes US #31, a beneficiary of the "British Invasion" of US charts.

Apr *Talk About Love* reaches US #97 (his last US chart entry). In UK the reflective *Hand Me Down Things* is second chart failure on Parlophone.

June *Someone's Taken Maria Away*, a pastiche of the Bacharach/David style by Andrews and *Concrete And Clay*-influenced, makes UK #34.

Sept *Faith Alive*, recorded on stage with The Roulettes before 100 fan club members at Abbey Road studios, makes UK #19. Shortly after, he splits with The Roulettes.

1966 Feb Faith issues a writ against EMI, claiming breach of contract by not releasing a minimum of 2 records a year in Europe.

June [13] Faith makes his TV acting debut as a blackmailer on Rediffusion TV's Play Of The Week thriller "(Cat) In The Night".

Oct Following 3 more non-charting singles (including a revival of Perry Como's *Idle Gossip* and the later P.J. Proby/Tom Jones-flavored *To Make A Big Man Cry*), a cover of Bob Lind's *Cheryl's Goin' Home* makes UK #46, and will be Faith's final UK Singles chart entry.

1967 May [9] Faith guests in the first edition of new UK TV pop show "As You Like It".

Aug [19] He marries dancer Jackie Irving, a one-time girlfriend of Cliff Richard.

Nov *To Hell With Love* is Faith's final Parlophone release. (Faith has already given up cabaret appearances and will cease recording, determined to take up acting full time. Over the next 3 years, he will work from the bottom up in repertory theater around UK, progressing to the lead in a touring revival of "Billy Liar", the part of Feste in "Twelfth Night", and a role as a murderer (opposite Dame Sybil Thorndike) in Emlyn Williams' "Night Must Fall".)

1971 He takes the title role in UK ITV's drama series "Budgie", playing a constantly-stymied working-class small-timer opportunist. The series is both a critical and huge public success.

1972 Faith discovers singer/songwriter Leo Sayer, becoming his manager.

1973 Apr He produces *Daltrey*, the first solo album by The Who's Roger Daltrey, which includes several compositions by Sayer. (Shortly afterwards, he has a serious auto accident. He will later describe the near-fatal crash as a major turning point in his life.)

1974 **Feb** [18] Recovered from his accident apart from a slight limp, Faith begins filming with David Essex on "Stardust", the sequel to Essex's previous success "That'll Be The Day". He takes the rock star manager role played by Ringo Starr in the earlier movie.

July After 7 years without recording, Faith releases *I Survive*, co-produced with David Courtney, with contributions from Paul McCartney. Rated by the critics, both it and 2 extracted singles fail and Faith retires to concentrate on acting, management and production.

Oct "Stardust" premieres in London, and Faith's performance gains critical plaudits.

1976 **Mar** [4] Faith opens at London's Comedy theater in Stephen Poliakoff's play "City Sugar".

1977 **Dec** [9] *Scouse The Mouse*, an album featuring Faith, Ringo Starr, Barbara Dickson and actor Donald Pleasance, is released.

1978 **Feb** Faith produces Lonnie Donegan's *Puttin' On The Style*, a star-studded nostalgia/comeback set.

1979 He stars with Ian McShane in soccer drama movie "Yesterday's Hero", playing a soccer manager.

1980 **Apr** [30] Movie "McVicar", in which Faith stars with Roger Daltrey in the true story of prison escapee John McVicar, premieres in London.

1981 **Dec** TV-advertised compilation *20 Golden Greats* reaches UK #61.

1988 **Oct** Faith opens on the London West End stage in a musical version of "Budgie" in which he reprises his old TV role while also refurbishing his singing talent for live stage work.

1991 **Feb** [3] Faith has become an increasingly successful financial adviser and share pundit (through his own Faith Corporation), initially basing his office at the tea-room in Fortnum & Mason department store, London, when **The Sunday Times** reports that he may have to resign from the board of Savoy Management Ltd. because of his close links with the recently failed Levitt Group. His weekly investment advice column, "Faith In The City", continues to appear in the **The Mail On Sunday** UK newspaper.

FAITH NO MORE

Mike Patton (lead vocals)
Jim Martin (guitar)
Billy Gould (bass)
Roddy Bottum (keyboards)
Mike "Puffy" Bordin (drums)

1980 Gould (b. Apr.24, 1963, Los Angeles, CA) and his old school friend, classically trained pianist Bottum (b. July 1, 1963, Los Angeles) decide to form a band. They are located in the Bay Area of San Francisco, CA.

1981 Drummer Bordin (b. Nov.27, 1962, San Francisco) currently studying at Berkeley University, CA, is added to the line-up. He specializes in ferocious African drum-beat rhythms.

1982 With no permanent guitarist in sight, Bordin's friend Cliff Burton of Metallica insists that they audition his friend, Jim Martin (b. July 21, 1961, Oakland, CA), who is currently playing with Vicious Hatred. Martin eventually joins the fledgling Faith No More still based in San Francisco. (Group professes that they get their name from a greyhound on which they have placed a bet.)

1983 Unable to find a suitable singer, the band play clubs inviting an audience member to supply vocals each night. Chuck Mosely, a friend of Gould's, turns up regularly to monopolize the microphone until he eventually joins the band full time.

1984 Faith No More signs to a small San Francisco indie label, Mordam, who advance money for the recording of their eponymous debut album.

1985 Resultant album *Faith No More*, fusing funk with metal, proves popular on US college radio stations.

1986 Slash Records, a Warner Bros.-licensed label, offers the band a more substantial contract with major company backing.

1987 **Oct** Second album *Introduce Yourself* mixes rap and heavy rock styles.

1988 Despite constant US tour promotion (mainly with The Red Hot Chili Peppers) to support the album, hits are not forthcoming although the video for the extracted *We Care A Lot* is heavily rotated on US MTV.

Feb Group plays debut European performances, including a sell-out night at London's Marquee club.

May Faith No More returns for second UK visit, on which Mosely's bizarre stage performances increasingly concern the rest of the band. *Introduce Yourself* attracts little sales interest in either US or UK.

June Group fires Mosely and issue press statements which include the words "ego" and "undependable".

Nov During a search for a replacement lead singer, a demo tape from a San Francisco band Mr. Bungle arrives, featuring the vocals of Mike Patton (b. Jan.27, 1968, Eureka, CA) on the track *The Raging Wrath Of*

The Easter Bunny. He is immediately hired and invited to pen lyrics for the rhythm tracks the band has already recorded for their next album.

Dec *We Care A Lot* makes UK #53. New line-up makes its live debut in the Bay Area.

1989 **Feb** Work on their third album is completed at a studio in Sausalito, produced by Matt Wallace.

June Group plays a showcase gig at the Roxy club, Los Angeles, to preview the forthcoming album. They are joined on stage by Slash and Duff from Guns N' Roses for a version of *War Pigs*.

July *The Real Thing* is released to great critical and, ultimately, commercial success. The CD release contains 2 tracks not otherwise available.

[4] Group embarks on its third UK tour, including a slot at the Marquee club.

Oct Currently more popular in UK, they return for a full 15-date tour which fails to help chart *From Out Of Nowhere*.

Dec Band returns to US circuit, now supporting Metallica on a full arena tour.

1990 **Jan** [12] Continuing to tour in North America, band performs in Toronto, Canada with Soundgarden and Voivod.

[27] *Epic* makes UK #37, as another sell-out UK tour begins.

Feb Group receives a Grammy nomination for Best Heavy Metal/Hard Rock performance.

Apr [22] They begin UK tour at Glasgow's Barrowlands, Scotland.

[28] With new US single *Epic* receiving heavy play on MTV, UK reissued *From Out Of Nowhere* reaches UK #23, supported by further UK live dates. Previously slow-selling *The Real Thing* begins steady sales surge in both territories.

May [5] *The Real Thing* finally reaches UK #34.

July [14] *Falling To Pieces* makes UK #41.

Aug Band's faithful UK followers help just released video "Live At Brixton" reach UK Video chart.

[30] Current European tour dates include the Monsters Of Rock in Bologna, Italy.

Sept [8] *Epic* proves their major breakthrough, hitting US #9 and is reissued in UK to peak at #25. RIAA certifies *The Real Thing* a million-seller, the group's first. Peaking at US #13, it re-charts to reach UK #30, eventually spending a total of 33 weeks on the UK survey during the year. Following another Monsters Of Rock appearance in Paris, France on Sept.3, Faith No More returns to US for 37-date tour supporting Billy Idol, which will end Nov.5.

Nov [9] Group headlines bill of **Rip** magazine's fourth anniversary celebrations at the Hollywood Palladium, New York.

[10] *Falling To Pieces* stalls at US #92.

Dec [1] Group guests on NBC TV's "Saturday Night Live".

1991 **Jan** Faith No More plays at the Rock In Rio II Festival at the Maracana soccer stadium in Rio de Janiero, Brazil.

Feb [16] UK-only live album *Live At The Brixton Academy* on Slash, reaches UK #20.

Mar [2] Faith No More wins Outstanding Group, Male Vocalist, Drummer, Keyboardist/Synthesizer and *Epic* wins Outstanding Song at the 14th annual Bammy Awards at the Civic Center, San Francisco, as guitarist Jim Martin lands role as "the world's greatest guitar player" in "Bill And Ted Go To Mars", with band to be featured on original soundtrack.

MARIANNE FAITHFULL

1964 **June** Faithfull (b. Dec.29, 1946, Hampstead, London), daughter of a British university lecturer and an Austrian baroness, and an ex-pupil at St. Joseph's convent school in Reading, Berks., is taken to a party in London by boyfriend, artist John Dunbar, where she is introduced to The Rolling Stones' manager Andrew Loog Oldham. He is impressed by her looks and, learning that she has aspirations to be a folk singer, offers to sign and record her.

Sept Faithfull is signed by Oldham to Decca and records the Mick Jagger/Keith Richard ballad *As Tears Go By*, which hits UK #9.

[19] Faithfull makes live debut at the Adelphi cinema, Slough, Berks.

Oct [31] She appears on BBC TV show "Juke Box Jury", making the comment, "I'd like it at a party if I was stoned".

Nov A version of Bob Dylan's *Blowin' In The Wind*, more obviously folky than her debut, does not chart.

[4] She collapses and is confined to bed, pulling out of a scheduled 26-date UK tour, with Gerry & The Pacemakers, Gene Pitney, The Kinks and others. US singer Jackie DeShannon takes her place.

Dec [14] Faithfull flies to the US for TV and radio dates.

1965 **Jan** *As Tears Go By* reaches US #22.

Feb [16] She begins a 30-date twice-nightly UK package tour, headlined by Roy Orbison, at the Adelphi cinema, Slough. Tour will end Mar.21 at the Empire theater, Liverpool, Merseyside.

Mar *Come And Stay With Me*, written by Jackie DeShannon, is more commercial and is her biggest hit at UK #4.

Apr *Come And Stay With Me* reaches US #26.

[16] Faithfull begins a US tour with Gene Pitney (with whom she is rumored to be having a romance.)

May [6] Faithfull is married to John Dunbar at Cambridge Register Office. She parts from Oldham after disagreements and releases *This Little Bird*, which hits UK #6. A simultaneous cover (also on Decca), by Oldham-produced Nashville Teens, peaks at UK #38.

[24] She participates in one-off Brighton Song Festival at the Dome, Brighton, E.Sussex, with Lulu, Manfred Mann, Dave Berry and others, singing *Go Away From My World*.

[31] Faithfull becomes a resident guest on new look BBC2 TV series "Gadzooks! It's The In Crowd".

June *This Little Bird* makes US #32. 2 albums are issued simultaneously in UK: folk package *Come My Way*, which charts at UK #12, and *Marianne Faithfull* (including her first 2 hit singles) at UK #15.

[19] She appears at the Uxbridge Blues And Folk Festival in UK with several R&B bands, including The Who, Solomon Burke, Zoot Money and Cliff Bennett & The Rebel Rousers.

July *Marianne Faithfull* reaches US #12.

Aug *Summer Nights* hits UK #10.

[1] Faithfull collapses during a concert at Morecambe, Lancs. She cancels all future engagements, including a US tour at end Aug.

Oct *Summer Nights* reaches US #24.

Nov A cover of The Beatles' *Yesterday* loses out on UK chart to Matt Monro's version, reaching #36. Faithfull gives birth to a son, Nicholas.

Dec *Go Away From My World* (only on an EP in UK) makes US #89.

1966 Feb *Go Away From My World* reaches US #81. (Its title seems prophetic, as Faithfull and Dunbar will shortly separate. She will become Mick Jagger's constant companion and they will remain together for almost 4 years.)

Mar [24] She begins 4-week engagement at the Paris Olympia, France before going to the Golden Rose Festival in Montreux, Switzerland.

Apr Folk-flavored *North Country Maid* does not chart.

Nov *Faithfull Forever* climbs to US #147.

1967 Feb *Love In A Mist* fails to chart.

[12] She is with Jagger at Keith Richard's house in West Wittering, Sussex, when police raid the premises, but is not charged with drug possession as Jagger and Richard later are.

Mar A revival of The Ronettes' *Is This What I Get For Loving You*, with Oldham as producer, reaches UK #43.

Apr Faithfull begins an acting career, opening at London's Royal Court theater in Chekhov's "The Three Sisters".

June [25] She sings in the chorus of The Beatles' *All You Need Is Love*, recorded live during "Our World" global TV broadcast.

1968 May She co-stars with Alain Delon in film "Girl On A Motorcycle", which is savaged by the critics.

Nov [22] Faithfull miscarries the baby she is expecting by Mick Jagger.

Dec [12] She participates in filming of The Rolling Stones' "Rock And Roll Circus" musical extravaganza, meant as TV film but never shown.

1969 Feb *Something Better* is Faithfull's last single for Decca. B-side, *Sister Morphine*, a drug-weary song written with Jagger and Richard, is later regarded as one of her most notable records. This is to be her last recording for several years, as she continues her acting ambitions.

Apr Compilation *Marianne Faithfull's Greatest Hits* peaks at US #171.

May Faithfull and Jagger are arrested at their shared London home on charges of marijuana possession.

July [8] On the Australian set of film "Ned Kelly", in which she is to co-star with Mick Jagger, Faithfull is discovered in a coma, suffering from a self-inflicted overdose. She is dropped from the movie and goes to hospital for treatment of heroin addiction.

1970 Faithfull and John Dunbar are divorced after several years of separation. She stars as Ophelia with Nicol Williamson in film version of Shakespeare's "Hamlet".

1975 Nov She returns to recording after a lengthy break with a version of Waylon Jennings' *Dreaming My Dreams* for independent NEMS label. It charts in Eire but not in the UK.

1978 Mar *Faithless* is released, with backing by The Grease Band and C&W leanings in its material. It does not chart.

1979 Faithfull marries punk bass player Ben Brierly of The Vibrators.

Nov [23] She is arrested at Oslo airport, Norway, for possession of marijuana.

Dec Faithfull signs to Island Records and *Broken English* makes UK #57, despite a boycott by Island's distributor EMI over objections to its lyrical content. Extracted from the album, *The Ballad Of Lucy Jordan* is her first UK hit single for over 12 years, reaching #48.

1980 Mar *Broken English* climbs to US #82.

1981 Oct *Dangerous Acquaintances* makes UK #45 and US #104.

1983 Mar *A Child's Adventure* peaks at UK #99 and US #107.

1985 Battling a constant drug problem, she falls down a flight of stairs while stoned and breaks her jaw.

1987 July *Strange Weather* is released, featuring songs by Jagger/Richards, Dr. John and Tom Waits; despite its gloomy nature it makes UK #78.

1988 Now living in Cambridge, MA, and married to writer Giorgio Della Terza, Faithfull has a deportation order served on her by the US immigration authorities. (She will move to Eire.)

1989 Sept [2-4] She teaches "Love, Fear And The Ridiculous: Songwriting And Performing" at the Omega Institute in Rhinebeck, NY.

1990 Apr [17] *Blazing Away*, featuring live performances at New York's St. Ann's Cathedral and studio tracks, with Dr. John, Garth Hudson, Marc Ribot, Barry Reynolds and Lew Soloff guesting, is released, while Faithfull tours US, accompanied by guitarist Barry Reynolds.

GEORGIE FAME & THE BLUE FLAMES

Georgie Fame (vocals, keyboards)
Colin Green (guitar)
Peter Coe (saxes, flute)
Tony Makins (bass)
Bill Eyden (drums)
Speedy Acquaye (congas)

1959 Aug On holiday at Butlins in Pwllheli, Wales, Fame (b. Clive Powell, Sept.26, 1943, Leigh, Gtr.Manchester) stands in for injured pianist in resident group Rory Blackwell & The Blackjacks. Blackwell convinces the 16-year-old to quit his cotton factory job and move to London as a full-time Blackjack. Within a month the band folds, leaving him stranded. Rather than go home ingloriously, he lands a gig playing piano in an East End London pub.

Oct Songwriter Lionel Bart spots him and recommends an audition for top UK rock'n'roll manager Larry Parnes. With pianists at a premium, Powell is hired and given his new name. (This is a penchant of Parnes, creator of Tommy Steele, Marty Wilde, Vince Eager, Duffy Power etc.)

1960 Feb In addition to backing Parnes' stars, Fame is allowed to develop his own vocal talents by opening the second half of the Gene Vincent/Eddie Cochran show.

Apr Fame makes his disk debut playing piano on Gene Vincent's *Pistol Packin' Mama*.

1961 June Fame joins Parnes' billtopper Billy Fury's permanent backing group, The Blue Flames.

Dec Fury replaces The Blue Flames with The Tornados as his backing band. Fame & The Blue Flames secure a residency at the Flamingo, a Soho jazz cellar in London's West End. At first they play the regular "Twist Sessions" but soon amass a following for their heady jazz/rock/blues beat melange.

1962 July R&B rivals to Alexis Korner's Blues Incorporated at nearby Marquee club, The Blue Flames expand from 4 to 7, playing brassy jazz-rock.

Nov Inspired by Booker T. and Jimmy McGriff, Fame now plays a Hammond organ – one of the first in London.

1963 Aug Group begins a Friday night residency at the Scene, London.

Sept EMI's Columbia label signs The Blue Flames. Debut live album *Rhythm And Blues At The Flamingo*, cut at the Flamingo and produced by ex-Cliff Richard sidekick Ian Samwell, spreads their reputation and they play 40 gigs a month.

1964 Oct Second album *Fame At Last* reaches UK #15.

Dec For his fourth single, Fame re-works *Yeh Yeh*, an Afro-Cuban song by Lambert, Hendricks and Ross, and it hits #1 and reaches US #21, making it a million-seller.

1965 Jan With John Mayall, The Rolling Stones, The Animals and The Yardbirds, Fame leads the R&B boom. Like Mayall's Bluesbreakers, The Blue Flames is an academy for aspiring musicians. John McLaughlin, Mickey Waller and Mitch Mitchell are among those passing through.

Mar Written by jazzman Johnny Burch, *In The Meantime* takes Fame to UK #22 and US #97. Appearances on US TV shows are taped in UK because his band contains 2 blacks – a prime reason they never tour US.

[20] They begin a 21-date twice-nightly UK tour as special UK guests on the "Tamla Motown Package Show", featuring The Supremes,

Stevie Wonder, Martha & The Vandellas and others, at Finsbury Park Astoria, London, ending Apr.12 at the Guildhall, Portsmouth, Hants.

July Fame wins jazz, pop and vocal polls, but his new single *Like We Used To Do* makes only UK #33.

Aug [7] They perform at the fifth annual National Jazz & Blues Festival at the Athletic Ground, Richmond, London.

Sept [21] Group participates in the "Pop From Britain" concert at the Royal Albert Hall, London, with Cliff Bennett & The Rebel Rousers, The Fourmost and The Moody Blues.

Oct *Something* reaches UK #23.

1966 May *Sweet Things* hits UK #6.

June Fame's own composition *Get Away* tops UK chart.

July [31] Group plays at the sixth annual National Jazz & Blues Festival, at Windsor, Berks.

Sept A cover of Bobby Hebb's hit *Sunny* makes UK #13, 1 place behind the original.

[10] *Get Away* peaks at US #70.

Oct *Sound Venture* hits UK #9 but Fame disbands his Blue Flames to pursue a more flexible career. (Over the years, he will front many combos and orchestras of varying composition and size.)

[1-2] Fame plays his last gigs with The Blue Flames, representing the UK in the annual Grand Gala Du Disque in Amsterdam, Holland.

[9] He plays a jazz-oriented concert with the Harry South Orchestra at London's Royal Festival Hall.

20] With the new Georgie Fame Band, he begins a 16-date twice-nightly UK tour at Finsbury Park Astoria, London with Chris Farlowe, Eric Burdon & The Animals, and others. Tour will end Nov.6 at the Odeon cinema, Leicester, Leics.

Dec Fame reaches UK #12 with his version of Billy Stewart's *Sitting In The Park*.

[26] "Fame In 67" show opens at the Saville theater, London. It will run until Jan.17, 1967.

1967 Feb [2] Fame performs at Cannes Musical Trade Fair, Cannes, France.

Mar *Hall Of Fame* reaches UK #12, while his own composition *Because I Love You*, his debut on CBS/Columbia, makes UK #15.

May [25] Fame performs at the Royal Albert Hall, London, backed by the Count Basie Orchestra.

July *Two Faces Of Fame* reaches UK #22.

Sept *Try My World* makes UK #37.

Oct Fame takes part in the International Popular Music Festival in Rio de Janeiro, Brazil.

Dec Inspired by the movie, Mitch Murray and Peter Callender write *The Ballad Of Bonnie And Clyde*, which becomes Fame's third UK chart topper. It also hits US #7 to become his biggest (but last) US hit. Sales earn him another gold disk.

1968 Fame spends most of the year touring, but finds time to release *The Third Face Of Fame*.

1969 Jan [17] Fame performs at the Royal Albert Hall with Ten Years After and Family.

July His cover of Kenny Rankin's *Peaceful* reaches UK #16.

Dec *Seventh Son* makes UK #25 but album of same name fails to chart.

1970 Apr Fame embarks on tour of Australia.

1971 Fame teams up with ex-Animals veteran Alan Price for *Rosetta* which makes UK #11, *Fame And Price, Price And Fame Together* and a short-lived TV series. (After his heyday, Fame moves increasingly towards adult-oriented material. He plays several concerts backed by big bands or orchestras, performs a tribute to songwriter Hoagy Carmichael, appears on numerous television variety shows, makes TV commercials, fronts various bands he calls The Blue Flames and continues to record.)

1989 Fame returns to a higher profile when he is the featured keyboard player on Van Morrison's tour, also playing on his album *Avalon Sunset*.

Nov UK retrospective label Connoisseur releases authoritative collection *Georgie Fame: The First 30 Years*.

FAMILY

Roger Chapman (vocals)
Charlie Whitney (guitar)
John "Poli" Palmer (keyboards)
John Weider (bass)
Rob Townsend (drums)

1962 Band is formed by Whitney as The Farinas, while at art college in Leicester, Leics. (Chapman and Grech are in one group, Whitney and King in another. When Chapman and Grech's band folds, Grech joins

Whitney and King's band. Chapman goes to work for a building contractor, and is then asked to join up with others.)

1964 Aug The Farinas record *You'd Better Stop* without success for Fontana Records, and play widespread club and college dates.

1967 Group comes to London from Leicester, and moves into Chelsea home making contact with friend, film producer John Gilbert, who gives financial help and eventually becomes their manager. They name-change to Family, at the suggestion of US producer Kim Fowley. Line-up is Chapman (b. Apr.8, 1944, Leicester) and Whitney (b. June 4, 1944, UK), with Jim King on sax and flute, Rick Grech (b. Nov.1, 1946, Bordeaux, France) on bass and Harry Ovenall on drums.

Sept Another one-off deal, with Liberty Records, results in first Family single *The Scene Through The Eye Of A Lens*, which does not sell.

1968 July A new recording deal with Reprise Records results in *Music In A Doll's House*, featuring new drummer Rob Townsend (b. July 7, 1947, Leicester), a veteran of several Leicester bands. Produced by Traffic's Dave Mason, it makes UK #35. They make their London debut at the Royal Albert Hall, supporting US folk singer Tim Hardin.

1969 Mar *Family Entertainment* hits UK #6.

Apr John Weider (b. Apr.21, 1947, UK), formerly with Teddy & The Cannons and Eric Burdon & The Animals, joins on bass when Grech quits to join Blind Faith on the eve of Family's first US tour (cancelled after a few dates when Chapman's visa is revoked).

July [5] They support The Rolling Stones at their free concert in Hyde Park, London.

Oct Jim King leaves to join Ring Of Truth, and is replaced by ex-Eclection, Deep Feeling and Blossom Toes keyboardist John "Poli" Palmer (b. May 25, 1943).

Nov *No Mule's Fool* is their first UK hit single, reaching UK #29.

1970 Jan *A Song For Me*, the first to be produced by the band, hits UK #4.

Mar While on North American tour, Chapman's passport is stolen in New York, so rest of the band has to perform without him in Canada.

Sept EP *Strange Band*, featuring stage favorite *The Weaver's Answer*, reaches UK #11.

Nov *Anyway*, a part-live and part-studio-recorded set, hits UK #7. Jenny Fabian's cult novel **Groupie** is published, allegedly based on Family's touring exploits.

[19] Group embarks on a 10-date UK tour at Sophia Gardens, Cardiff, Wales. Tour will end Dec.1 at the De Montfort Hall, Leicester.

1971 Mar *Old Songs, New Songs* featuring up-dated versions of old Family material fails to chart.

June Weider leaves to form Stud and is replaced by John Wetton (b. July 12, 1949, Derby, Derbys.) from Mogul Thrash.

Aug *In My Own Time*, Family's most successful single, hits UK #4.

Oct *Fearless* returns them to UK Album chart at #14 – and Family's best US showing, at #177.

1972 Sept *Bandstand* yields UK #13 hit *Burlesque* and makes UK #15 itself, but Palmer and Wetton both quit, Palmer to do session work and Wetton to join King Crimson. Replacements are Tony Ashton (b.Mar.1, 1946, Blackburn, Lancs.) and Jim Cregan, ex-Stud and Blossom Toes.

1973 Sept *It's Only A Movie*, released on the band's own new Raft label, proves to be their last. It reaches UK #30.

Oct Family splits after a farewell tour. (Chapman and Whitney, the songwriters, will stay together in Streetwalkers, before Chapman pursues an active solo career; Cregan moves to Cockney Rebel, then to Rod Stewart's band; Ashton and Townsend will join Medicine Head.)

1990 Mar [17] Grech dies in Leicester General hospital of kidney and liver failure following a hemorrhage.

JOSE FELICIANO

1963 Blind since birth, Feliciano (b. Sept.10, 1945, Lares, Puerto Rico), who has lived in Harlem, New York, since age 5, mastering acoustic and 12-string guitar in his teens, leaves home to become a regular on the Greenwich Village coffee house circuit, singing with guitar in a style which encompasses Latin-American, folk and R&B influences.

1964 Signed to RCA Records, after being spotted playing at Gerde's Folk City by an A&R man visiting the club to check out another act, Feliciano releases debut single *Everybody Do The Click* and *The Voice And Guitar Of José Feliciano*. Neither charts, but the latter brings him his first airplay.

1965 He begins a series of Latin-American recordings, sung in Spanish, which are a major success in Central and South America, as well as among the US Hispanic community.

1968 Aug Feliciano's early revival of The Doors' 1967 million-seller *Light My Fire* is his first chartmaker, hitting US #3 and selling a million. Its slowed-down, sparse acoustic-with-woodwind arrangement and soul-inflected vocal defines Feliciano's style. It is taken from *Feliciano!*, on which familiar songs by Lennon/McCartney, Tom Paxton, Bacharach/David, Bobby Hebb and Gerry & The Pacemakers are similarly customized. His first chart album and also his biggest seller, it hits US #2, earns a gold disk and stays on the survey for 59 weeks.

Nov *Light My Fire* hits UK #6 (The Doors' original peaked at UK #49). *Feliciano!* also hits UK #6. US follow-up customizes Tommy Tucker's *Hi-Heel Sneakers*, which reaches UK #25 while B-side *Hitchcock Railway* makes US #77. Rush-released *The Star-Spangled Banner*, recorded live at the fifth game of the Baseball World Series (Detroit Tigers vs. St. Louis Cardinals) in Detroit, MI, makes US #50.

Dec [28] He appears at the Miami Pop Festival in Hallendale, FL, before 100,000 people, with Chuck Berry, Marvin Gaye, The Grateful Dead, Joni Mitchell and others.

9 **Jan** *Souled* reaches US #24.

Feb Taken from the album, revivals of Bruce Channel's *Hey! Baby* and The Supremes' *My World Is Empty Without You* are a minor double-sided US hit at #71/#87.

Mar [12] Feliciano wins Best Contemporary Pop Vocal Performance, Male for *Light My Fire* and Best New Artist Of 1968 at the 11th annual Grammy awards.

Apr [27] Feliciano stars in his own US TV special with guests Andy Williams, Glen Campbell, Dionne Warwick and Burt Bacharach.

May His cover of The Bee Gees' *Marley Purt Drive* peaks at US #70.

Aug *Feliciano/10 To 23* (the title arising from the inclusion of a recording taped at age 10) reaches US #16, and is his second gold disk.

Sept Self-composed *Rain* climbs to US #76.

Nov *Feliciano/10 To 23* makes UK #29. From it, *And The Sun Will Shine* (another Bee Gees cover) is his second and last UK hit single, at #25.

0 **Jan** Double *Alive Alive-O!*, recorded in concert at the London Palladium, reaches US #29, earning a third gold disk. (Feliciano had a tussle with UK authorities before performing at the Palladium, due to UK's 6-month quarantine rule for animals entering UK, which meant that his guide dog could not accompany him.)

June *Fireworks* reaches US #57.

July Double A-side *Destiny/Susie-Q* peaks at US #83.

Aug *Fireworks* makes UK #65, Feliciano's final UK chart album.

1 **May** Compilation *Encore! José Feliciano's Finest Performances* reaches US #92.

Nov *That The Spirit Needs* peaks at US #173.

3 **June** *Compartments*, recorded with Steve Cropper (ex-Booker T. And The MG's), reaches US #156.

5 **Jan** *Chico And The Man*, the theme from the Freddie Prinze/Jack Albertson TV comedy series (sung by Feliciano over the credits), stalls at US #96 while *And The Feeling's Good* makes US #136.

Sept *Just Wanna Rock 'N' Roll* reaches US #165.

6 **Sept** Leaving RCA, he records *Angela* for Private Stock label, but without chart success.

7 **Feb** *Sweet Soul Music* on Private Stock is co-produced by Jerry Wexler, and touches some of Feliciano's early R&B/soul fire, but still fails to sell.

1 He signs to Motown Latino, to concentrate on Spanish-language recordings. An album in English, *José Feliciano*, fails to chart.

3 **Apr** Motown Latino *Escenas De Amor* creates interest in the Hispanic market, but second Motown English-language album *Romance In The Night* fares no better than the first and he will not remain with the label. (Feliciano will continue regular US live and TV work in the 80s, always a popular club draw with his individualizations of familiar material, but will have no chart success.)

4 **Feb** [28] Feliciano wins Best Latin Pop Performance for *Me Enamore* at the 26th annual Grammy awards.

7 **Feb** [24] Feliciano wins Best Latin Pop Performance for *Lelolai* at the 29th annual Grammy awards.

0 **Feb** [21] Feliciano wins Best Latin Pop Performance for *Cielito Lindo* at the 32nd Grammy awards at Shrine Auditorium, Los Angeles, CA.

RYAN FERRY

4 **June** Ferry (b. Sept.26, 1945, Washington, Durham), having won tickets from Radio Luxembourg, to see Bill Haley & His Comets at the Empire theater, Sunderland, Tyne & Wear, in his teens, forms his first band, The Banshees, in Sunderland.

Sept He moves to Newcastle, Tyne & Wear, to study fine arts at university. A fan of US soul music, he becomes vocalist with The Gas Board, a soul/R&B band and works as a DJ.

1968 **July** He leaves university with a fine arts degree, moving to London to work as a van driver, antiques restorer and a ceramics teacher at a Hammersmith girls' school. He teaches himself piano and writes songs, occasionally dabbling in the visual arts.

1970 Ferry loses his teaching job when school authorities object to his turning classes into music sessions. He decides to form a band to play the songs he has been writing.

1971 **Nov** Roxy Music is formed (the name is inspired by a cinema, with Music added because there is already a US group called Roxy).

1972 The first regular line-up of Roxy Music begins playing and Ferry, the inspiration behind the band, will remain its central character throughout the group's successful career.

1973 **Oct** Ferry's first solo album *These Foolish Things*, backed by a session group which includes Roxy drummer Paul Thompson, is released by Island. It is a collection of covers of his favorite oldies. Aided by success of Roxy Music, the album hits UK #5, while extracted single, reviving Bob Dylan's *A Hard Rain's Gonna Fall*, hits UK #10.

1974 **June** [8] A revival of Dobie Gray's *The "In" Crowd* reaches UK #13.

July [27] *Another Time, Another Place* comprising, apart from Ferry-composed title track, more pop and R&B oldies by Willie Nelson, Joe South, Bob Dylan, Ike Turner and others, hits UK #4. (Like Roxy Music releases, fails to chart in US.)

Sept [28] His version of The Platters' *Smoke Gets In Your Eyes*, taken from the album, reaches UK #17.

Dec After spending most of the year on a Roxy Music world tour, Ferry plays 3 solo dates, including 1 at London's Royal Albert Hall, with backing by the group (in evening dress) and an orchestra. The dinner-jacket look has become Ferry's trademark, even though his current image with Roxy is military chic.

1975 **July** [12] *You Go To My Head* makes UK #33.

1976 **June** [26] As a Roxy Music "sabbatical" is announced, *Let's Stick Together*, a Wilbert Harrison R&B number extracted from forthcoming album *Let's Stick Together* hits UK #4.

Aug EP *Extended Play* comprises 4 assorted revivals from the recent album: *Heart On My Sleeve*, *The Price Of Love*, *Shame Shame Shame* and *It's Only Love*. The second track (originally a 1965 UK hit for The Everly Brothers) gains most airplay, and hits UK #7 – the first EP to make UK Top 10 since The Beatles' *Magical Mystery Tour* 9 years earlier. With Roxy Music drummer Paul Thompson and the group's ex-bassist John Wetton, plus session guitarist Chris Spedding, The Bryan Ferry Band is formed for live work.

Sept [25] *Let's Stick Together*, a more even mix of oldies and his own material, reaches UK #19.

Oct *Let's Stick Together* is Ferry's first US chart entry at #160.

Dec *Heart On My Sleeve*, issued as a US single on Atlantic, makes #86. Ferry is romantically linked to US model Jerry Hall (featured on the sleeve of Roxy Music's *Siren* and on the video vocals of *Let's Stick Together*) (she will later leave him for Mick Jagger).

1977 **Jan** Ferry announces the full touring line-up of his new band, which includes Roxy Music's Phil Manzanera on second guitar, Ann Odell on keyboards, a brass section and 3 backing singers.

Feb The new group tours UK as the prelude to a world tour, helping *This Is Tomorrow* to hit UK #9.

Mar As the tour moves on through Europe, *In Your Mind*, solely of Ferry compositions, hits UK #5.

Apr Ferry sings *She's Leaving Home* on the soundtrack album of Lou Reizner's film "All This And World War II".

May After a short break, the second half of the world tour begins, taking in Australia, Japan and US. *In Your Mind* reaches US #126. After the tour, the band disperses and Ferry bases himself in LA, where he writes songs for a new album.

June *Tokyo Joe*, taken from *In Your Mind*, reaches UK #15.

Dec Ferry moves to a hotel in Montreux, and over the next 3 months will record *The Bride Stripped Bare* at the Montreux Casino studio. Instrumentals are by a session crew including Waddy Wachtel and Neil Hubbard (guitars), Rick Marotta (drums) and Alan Spenner (bass).

1978 **May** [20] *What Goes On* peaks at UK #67.

Aug [26] *Sign Of The Times* makes UK #37, but a projected summer UK tour to preface the new, Montreux-recorded album, is cancelled when ticket sales are poor.

Sept [23] *The Bride Stripped Bare*, a mixture of new songs and R&B oldies like Sam And Dave's *You Don't Know Like I Know* and Al Green's *Take Me To The River*, reaches UK #13.

Nov [25] *The Bride Stripped Bare* makes US #159. Ferry reassembles Roxy Music to record *Manifesto*.

1982 **June** [26] Ferry marries Lucy Helmore at a society wedding in Sussex

BRYAN FERRY cont.

(his son will be named after Otis Redding).

1985 **June** [15] After 2 chart-topping Roxy Music albums (*Flesh And Blood* and *Avalon*) and a live mini-album (*The High Road*), Ferry re-emerges as a solo artist with *Boys And Girls*, which tops the UK chart. It features guest musicians including Mark Knopfler, David Sanborn, Nile Rodgers and David Gilmour. During its recording Ferry tells writer/producer Keith Forsey that he is too busy to record a new song *Don't You (Forget About Me)*. (It is later a US #1 for Simple Minds.) *Slave To Love* hits UK #10.

July [13] Ferry and the band play in the Live Aid concert at Wembley Stadium, London.

Aug *Boys And Girls*, released on Warner Bros., peaks at US #65.

Sept *Don't Stop The Dance* reaches UK #21.

Dec *Windswept* makes UK #46.

1986 **Apr** *Is Your Love Strong Enough?*, featured in Ridley Scott's film "Legend", reaches UK #22.

[26] TV-advertised compilation *Street Life – 20 Greatest Hits*, with both Roxy Music and Ferry solo successes, tops UK chart for 5 weeks, becoming one of the best selling albums of the year.

Ferry contributes vocals to Tangerine Dream's *Legend*, making US #96.

1987 **Oct** After another lengthy spell in the studio, Ferry's first new recording in 2 years is *The Right Stuff*, co-written with The Smiths' guitarist Johnny Marr. It reaches UK #37.

Nov Marr also features on *Bête Noire*, which hits UK #9. Released in US on Reprise, it peaks at #63.

1988 **Feb** *Kiss And Tell* reaches UK #41.

Apr Now featured in Michael J. Fox movie "Bright Lights Big City", *Kiss And Tell* moves to US #31.

Oct *Let's Stick Together* is released as a prelude to greatest hits album *The Ultimate Collection*, which will hit UK #6.

1989 **Jan** [16] Ferry plays first of 4 nights at the Wembley Arena.

Aug *Street Life – 20 Great Hits* makes US #100.

1990 **Mar** "New Town – Bryan Ferry In Europe" video is released in US.

THE 5TH DIMENSION

Marilyn McCoo (vocals)
Florence LaRue (vocals)
Lamonte McLemore (vocals)
Billy Davis, Jr. (vocals)
Ron Townson (vocals)

1966 Group forms as The Versatiles in Los Angeles, CA, with McLemore (b. Sept.17, 1939, St. Louis, MO) and McCoo (b. Sept.30, 1943, Jersey City, NJ), who has made her TV debut at 15 in "Spotlight On Young" and at 19 won Miss Bronze Grand Talent Award and Miss Congeniality, both ex-members of The Hi-Fis (along with Floyd Butler and Harry Elston, later in Friends Of Distinction), Davis (b. June 26, 1940, St. Louis), formerly of The Emeralds and The Saint Gospel Singers, before auditioning for Motown, then a member of El Toros, and Townson (b. Jan.20, 1933, St. Louis), placed third in the Metropolitan Opera auditions in St. Louis, before joining Wings Over Jordan choir and touring with Dorothy Dandridge and Nat "King" Cole and appearing in movie "Porgy And Bess", then moving to Los Angeles, CA, and forming a cappella The Celestial Choir Of Thirty Five Voices, who have known McLemore in hometown vocal groups, and LaRue (b. Feb.4, 1944, Pennsylvania) a California State University graduate and ex-teacher. They tour US with the "Ray Charles Revue" for 6 months and Marc Gordon becomes their manager. He takes them back to Los Angeles and introduces them to Johnny Rivers, who has started his own Soul City label, through Liberty Records.

1967 **Feb** Signed by Rivers, the group becomes The 5th Dimension, the name suggested by Townson and his wife Babette because Rivers says The Versatiles is dated. They cut (with Rivers producing) a cover of a Mamas And Papas' album track, *Go Where You Wanna Go*, which reaches US #16.

May *Another Day, Another Heartache*, a P.F. Sloan/Steve Barri song, makes US #45. Producer Rivers has to re-schedule sessions for a first album in order to take part in the San Remo Song Festival. During the break, rehearsal pianist Jim Webb spends a weekend at a fair, where he sees a hot air balloon in action and is inspired to write *Up, Up And Away*. Back at the studio, he plays it to the others, who insist on recording it and ask to hear other Webb songs, from which they choose 4 more to complete the album.

July *Up, Up And Away* is the group's first Top 10 hit at US #7.

Aug Debut album *Up, Up And Away* hits US #8, earning a gold disk and staying on chart for 83 weeks.

Dec *Paper Cup*, written by Webb, makes US #34.

1968 **Jan** *The Magic Garden*, produced by Bones Howe and with all but 1 song (Lennon/McCartney's *Ticket To Ride*) by Webb, is a polished, harmony-rich concept album, but with poor marketing it peaks at US #105 (though sales are consistent and it stays on chart for 31 weeks).

Feb [29] *Up, Up And Away* sweeps the 10th annual Grammy awards winning Record Of The Year, Song Of The Year, Best Performance By Vocal Group (Two To Six Persons), Best Contemporary Single, Best Contemporary Group Performance Vocal Or Instrumental. (The Johnny Mann Singers' version also wins a Grammy for Best Performance By A Chorus (Seven Or More Persons).)

Mar *Carpet Man*, from *The Magic Garden*, reaches US #29.

July A cover of Laura Nyro's laid-back summer song *Stoned Soul Picnic* hits US #3, selling over a million to become group's first gold single.

Sept *Stoned Soul Picnic* reaches US #21.

Nov *Sweet Blindness*, another Nyro song from album, makes US #13.

1969 **Feb** *California Soul* reaches US #25.

Apr *Aquarius/Let The Sunshine In* is the group's biggest hit, topping the US chart for 6 weeks and selling 2 million copies in 3 months. The medley from Broadway rock musical "Hair" was cut after the group saw Ronnie Dyson sing *Aquarius* in the show. Producer Howe linked the 2 instrumental tracks in the Los Angeles studio and the group overdubbed the final vocals in Las Vegas, NV (where they have been appearing at Caesar's Palace with Frank Sinatra).

May *Aquarius/Let The Sunshine In* reaches UK #11, the group's first UK hit. (Due to a misunderstanding, an abridged version intended for US AM radio, which omits much of *Aquarius*, is released in UK, but it does not affect sales and is not corrected.)

July *The Age Of Aquarius* hits US #2 and remains charted for 72 weeks, earning a gold disk.

Aug *Workin' On A Groovy Thing*, a Neil Sedaka co-composition taken from the album, reaches US #20.

Nov *Wedding Bell Blues*, another Nyro song also from *Aquarius*, is the group's second #1 and third million-selling single, topping US chart for 3 weeks. (Group has had its most successful year. McCoo has married Davis, and LaRue and manager Gordon have also married.)

1970 **Jan** Group leaves Soul City Records and signs to Bell label. *The Age Of Aquarius* passes a million US sales (in later years, this would qualify for a platinum disk).

Feb *Wedding Bell Blues* makes UK #16 (group's second and final UK hit), while the last extract from the album, Nyro's song *Blowing Away*, reaches US #21.

Mar First Bell single, *A Change Is Gonna Come/People Gotta Be Free*, a medley of Sam Cooke's 1965 hit and The Young Rascals' 1968 #1, reaches US #60, dually credited with B-side, *The Declaration*.

[11] *Aquarius/Let The Sunshine In* wins Record Of The Year and Best Contemporary Vocal Performance By A Group Of 1969 at the 12th annual Grammy awards.

May *The Girls' Song*, the final Soul City release, reaches US #43, while Bell single *Puppet Man* (another Sedaka song) makes US #24.

June *Portrait*, on Bell, reaches US #20, while Soul City compilation *The 5th Dimension/Greatest Hits* overtakes it to hit US #5. Both albums gain gold disks.

July *Save The Country* (again by Nyro) reaches US #27.

Sept Another Soul City compilation, *The July 5th Album*, reaches US #63, while *On The Beach (In The Summertime)*, from *Portrait*, makes US #54. (Davis sets up his own management company. His first signing is Roy Gaines.)

Oct Group represents US at Warsaw's October Festival, Poland.

Dec A Bacharach/David ballad, *One Less Bell To Answer* hits US #2 for 2 weeks (behind George Harrison's *My Sweet Lord*), and is another million-seller.

1971 **Apr** *Love's Lines, Angles And Rhymes* reaches US #17, while the title track reaches US #19.

June *Light Sings*, from Broadway musical "The Me Nobody Knows", makes US #44.

Nov Double live album *The 5th Dimension Live!!* reaches US #32, while a revival of The Association's *Never My Love*, taken from the live album, reaches US #12. Compilation *Reflections* peaks at US #112.

1972 **Jan** [28-30] Group plays its only UK career concerts, at the Royal Albert Hall, London, the Odeon cinema, Birmingham, W.Midlands, and the Empire theater, Liverpool, Merseyside.

Feb *Together Let's Find Love* makes US #37.

Apr *Individually And Collectively*, featuring group and solo performances, makes US #58.

June *Last Night I Didn't Get To Sleep At All*, penned by UK writer Tony

The Everly Brothers

The Grateful Dead

Guns N' Roses

Buddy Holly

Iron Maiden

Jimi Hendrix

George Harrison

Macaulay, is group's fifth and last million-selling single at US #8.

Nov *If I Could Reach You* hits US #10. Compilation ***Greatest Hits On Earth*** (containing the hits from both Soul City and Bell catalogs), makes US #14. (It is the group's last gold disk.) Group performs at the White House at the invitation of President Nixon.

'3 Feb *Living Together, Growing Together*, from movie "Lost Horizon", makes US #32.

Apr ***Living Together, Growing Together*** reaches US #108, while *Everything's Been Changed* peaks at US #70.

Sept *Ashes To Ashes* peaks at US #52.

'4 Jan *Flashback* climbs to US #82, and is the group's last Bell release.

'5 Sept Signed to ABC Records, the group is reunited with Jim Webb for ***Earthbound***, a concept-packaged set of his songs. It reaches US #136.

Nov McCoo and Davis leave the group for solo careers (though remain with ABC Records).

'6 Apr *Love Hangover* is last 5th Dimension hit single, at US #80 (Diana Ross' version on Motown hits #1). (Group will have no more chart hits, but retreat to the supper club circuit where it has always had a solid following.)

May McCoo and Davis peak at US #91 with their first duet *I Hope We Get To Love In Time*.

'7 Jan McCoo and Davis hit US #1 with *You Don't Have To Be A Star (To Be In My Show)*, selling over a million copies, while their ***I Hope We Get To Love In Time*** reaches US #30, and earns a gold disk.

Feb [19] *You Don't Have To Be A Star (To Be In My Show)* wins a Grammy award, as Best R&B Vocal Performance By A Duo.

Apr Duo scores its only UK success as *You Don't Have To Be A Star (To Be In My Show)* hits UK #7.

May *Your Love* by McCoo and Davis reaches US #15.

June [15] Duo co-hosts a US CBS TV summer variety series of 6 programs, "The Marilyn McCoo And Billy Davis Jr. Show".

Sept *Look What You've Done To My Heart* is McCoo and Davis' last hit, peaking at US #51. Their second (and last) ABC album ***The Two Of Us*** makes US #57.

8 Mar The 5th Dimension signs to Motown, but ***Star Dancing*** arouses little interest.

Oct McCoo and Davis sign to CBS/Columbia Records for ***Marilyn And Billy***, which peaks at US #146.

9 Apr Second 5th Dimension Motown album ***High On Sunshine*** fails to chart, and the group is dropped from the label.

0 McCoo and Davis split professionally. She moves to RCA to record solo (plus the occasional duet with Davis), but finds no chart success, and fares better on TV, hosting the show "Solid Gold". (All former members of The 5th Dimension will continue performing, in various combinations or alone, into the 80s, but the group will only be successful on the nightclub nostalgia circuit, where its hit repertoire adapts neatly to the MOR atmosphere.)

NE YOUNG CANNIBALS

land Gift (vocals)
dy Cox (guitars)
vid Steele (keyboards, bass)

4 Cox (b. Jan.25, 1960, Birmingham, W.Midlands) and Steele (b. Sept.8, 1960, Birmingham) are already rhythm veterans of hit UK act The Beat (in US, known as The English Beat), formed in 1978 with Everette Morton, Dave Wakeling and reggae toaster Ranking Roger, plying ska-influenced rock from its Birmingham base. Releasing records on the 2-Tone and subsequently their own Go-Feet labels, Top 10 hits were *Hands Off, She's Mine* (#9 Feb.1980), *Mirror In The Bathroom* (#4 May 1980), *Too Nice To Talk To* (#7 Dec.1980) and swan song *Can't Get Used To Losing You* (#3 May 1983) and chart albums ***Just Can't Stop It*** (#3 May 1980) and ***Wha'ppen*** (#3 May 1981). The Beat having split in 1983, Wakeling has gone on to form General Public with Ranking Roger, while Cox and Steele invite Gift (b. Birmingham), sax-player in ex-Hull band Acrylic Victims and actor for the Hull Community Theatre Workshop (where he has made his singing debut on an Al Jolson number), recently playing in a blues band in Finsbury Park, London, near where he is working on a Camden market stall, to form a new trio with Gift as vocalist, building on the Cox/Steele rhythm section.

Dec Calling themselves the Fine Young Cannibals, after a 1960 Natalie Wood/Robert Wagner-starring movie "All The Fine Young Cannibals", the group signs to London Records, which has spotted them performing on a home video of their song *Johnny Come Home* on Channel 4 TV's "The Tube", and begins recording debut sessions with Martin Parry on percussion aimed at a soul-dance blend which will be dominated by Gift's unique vocal sound.

1985 June Debut single *Johnny Come Home*, featuring trumpet player Graeme Hamilton, is released and, boosted by another showing of their original home video on "The Tube", will hit UK #8.

Nov Follow-up *Blue*, lyrically attacking current Conservative Party Government policies, makes UK #41.

Dec [21] Mainly self-composed ***Fine Young Cannibals*** enters UK chart, set to reach UK #11.

1986 Feb Cover version of Elvis Presley 1969 US #1 hit *Suspicious Minds*, featuring Jimmy Somerville on backing vocals, hits UK #8.

[22] On their first American visit, a concert in Boston, MA, is delayed by 2 hours due to an audience tear gas incident.

Mar [5] UK tour opens at Goldiggers in Cheltenham, Glos.

Apr Fourth extraction *Funny How Love Is* makes UK #58.

[26] *Johnny Come Home* peaks at US #76. Signed in US to IRS, parent album ***Fine Young Cannibals*** is currently on a 28-week chart ride and will reach US #49 during their first North American tour. While in US, they meet film director Barry Levinson who commissions the trio to provide 4 songs for his forthcoming Richard Dreyfus/Danny DeVito picture "Tin Men", also inviting them to feature prominently in the movie as the house band in the main restaurant scenes, where they perform their tracks, including future hit *Good Thing*.

Aug Film director Jonathan Demme asks the band to contribute a new song for his currently filming project "Something Wild".

1987 Apr Fine Young Cannibals' cover version of Buzzcocks' *Ever Fallen in Love* is chosen for the "Something Wild" soundtrack and also released, hitting UK #9, but will fail to chart in US. It will be their only release in the 3-year period between their first and second albums.

July "Tin Men", featuring the group as a 60s soul band in their movie debut, opens in US. Gift will increasingly choose a parallel acting career, appearing in major roles in the next 2 years including Stephen Frears-directed "Sammy And Rosie Get Laid" (1987), and John Hurt-starring "Scandal" (1989). These film commitments will put Fine Young Cannibals on hold for a total period of 2 years.

Oct While Gift is away, Cox and Steele contribute material to the forthcoming John Hughes movie "Planes, Trains And Automobiles" and, while experimenting in the studio, knock up an authentic-sounding house cut, *I'm Tired Of Getting Pushed Around*.

1988 Feb Having received excellent club reaction on a White label promo pressing under the deliberately non-informative act name, Two Men, A Drum Machine And A Trumpet, London Records has issued *I'm Tired Of Being Pushed Around*, which makes UK #18. Its success will encourage other UK dance acts to commission remixes and production from the duo.

June Cox/Steele-produced *Heat It Up* makes UK #21 for the Wee Papa Girl Rappers. They will also complete production of forthcoming recordings for Birmingham-based Pop Will Eat Itself, before returning to full Fine Young Cannibals sessions with Gift, which will be recorded both in London and with Prince cohort David Z at the Paisley Park studios in Minneapolis, MN.

1989 Jan [7] First fruits of new recordings, *She Drives Me Crazy*, fusing heavy rock guitar with a dance rhythm track, penned by Steele and Gift, enters UK chart set to hit #5 and begin a worldwide chart visit.

Feb [18] Second Fine Young Cannibals album ***The Raw And The Cooked***, a cunning mix of pop, dance and soul, still largely self-written and produced, tops UK chart at the start of a 66-week chart tenure.

Mar [24] Movie "Scandal" premieres in London, featuring Gift as jealous lover Johnny Edgecombe.

Apr [8] *She Drives Me Crazy* is the first song to be featured on the USA Network's TV broadcast of "American Bandstand" with new host David Hirsh.

[15] *She Drives Me Crazy* hits US #1 for 1 week, spurred by Phillipe De Couffle video, his first since New Order's "True Faith".

May *Good Thing* hits UK #7.

June [3] ***The Raw And The Cooked*** tops US chart displacing Madonna's *Like A Virgin*, and staying on top for 7 weeks.

July [8] *Good Thing* becomes Fine Young Cannibals' second #1 on US Singles chart, again topping for a week.

Aug Third extract *Don't Look Back* makes UK #34, as the band prepares for a major US tour.

Oct [7] *Don't Look Back* reaches US #11.

[14] Fine Young Cannibals play the first of 4 sell-out dates in Mountain View, CA, during US tour, with De La Soul in support.

Nov Band returns to UK to perform a short series of shows climaxing in 3 sell-out gigs at the Academy, Brixton, London.

Dec [2] *I'm Not The Man I Used To Be* peaks at US #54, having already reached UK #20. ("The Raw And The Cooked" video collection comprising 5 clips, including the promo for Two Men, A Drum Machine And A Trumpet hit, is released. Gift spends Christmas and the New Year in New Zealand, where he will buy some land.)

1990 **Feb** [18] Fine Young Cannibals win Best British Group and *The Raw And The Cooked* wins Best Album By A British Artist at the ninth annual BRIT Awards at the Dominion theater, London. They will return their awards, stating that "it is wrong and inappropriate for us to be associated with what amounts to a photo opportunity for Margaret Thatcher and the Conservative Party" and add that this action is taken "with regret".

[24] Fifth extract from the second album, *I'm Not Satisfied* stalls at UK #46, despite Cox/Steele remix.

Mar [3] *I'm Not Satisfied* stalls at US #90.

Apr [3] Returning once again to acting, Gift opens as Romeo in "Romeo And Juliet" in the Hull Truck Company Production at the Spring Street theater at the start of a UK repertory tour.

Oct [20] Cox/Steele-produced Monie Love Featuring True Image single *It's A Shame (My Sister)* reaches UK #12.

Nov [3] *Red Hot + Blue*, a various artists compilation of Cole Porter songs to benefit AIDS education and including Fine Young Cannibals' *Love For Sale* hits UK #6 on the Compilation Album chart, while Cox and Steele complete work on a remixed mini-album *The Raw And The Remixed* set for early 1991 release.

FIVE STAR

Deniece Pearson (lead vocals)
Doris Pearson (vocals)
Stedman Pearson (vocals)
Lorraine Pearson (vocals)
Delroy Pearson (vocals)

1983 Group forms first as a trio in Romford, Essex, when the 3 daughters of Buster (Stedman) and Dolores Pearson, Doris (b. June 8, 1966, Romford), Lorraine (b. Aug.10, 1967, Romford) and Deniece (b. June 13, 1968, Romford) beg their father to let them record his newly-demoed song *Problematic*. (Pearson, originally from Jamaica, is an ex-professional guitarist, who played during the 60s in tour bands behind many overseas acts working in UK, including soulsters Wilson Pickett and Lee Dorsey, and reggae singers Desmond Dekker and Jimmy Cliff. Having produced and written songs and run independent reggae label K&B, he launched Tent Records to focus on commercial dance music.) Impressed by his daughters' recording, he realizes they have potential as a professional act and records a second demo of Lorraine's song *Say Goodbye*. Dolores Pearson prompts the idea of brothers Stedman (b. June 29, 1964, Romford) and Delroy (b. Apr.11, 1970, Romford) also joining, though they are at college and school respectively. Stedman agrees readily and, through his design and choreographic skills, the group begins to fashion its own costumes, dance steps and visual image. Delroy is in line for a place in West Ham's junior soccer team when he leaves school, but lets it go to join the group. Pearson becomes their manager.

Sept Group makes its UK TV debut on BBC's "Pebble Mill At One", singing *Say Goodbye*. RCA Records is interested and Pearson begins to negotiate with them, stressing that Five Star is already contracted, but that Tent Records as a whole is a negotiable deal.

Oct *Problematic* is released by Tent, independently distributed through PRT. Club reaction is good, but sales small.

1984 **Apr** Pearson signs Tent Records to RCA. Both *Hide And Seek* and Oct.'s *Crazy* fail to chart.

1985 **June** *All Fall Down*, produced by Nick Martinelli and co-written by 70s UK hitmaker Barry Blue, reaches UK #15. It is promoted via a hectic schedule of lip-synch personal appearances in UK clubs and discos. (B-side *First Avenue*, written by Deniece, will receive a Grammy nomination as Best R&B Instrumental Of The Year.)

Aug A second Martinelli production, *Let Me Be The One*, reaches UK #18. First album *Luxury Of Life*, the work of 6 producers and 9 different studios, reaches UK #12. (It will climb further up the chart to accompany each succeeding single, eventually peaking at #12. By 1987, it will have sold over 300,000 copies in UK, earning a platinum disk.)

Oct *Love Take Over*, extracted from the album but remixed by *19* hitmaker Paul Hardcastle, makes UK #25. *All Fall Down* reaches US chart and makes R&B #10.

Nov *R.S.V.P.*, also from the album, reaches UK #45. Group visits US for the first time, on a promotional trip. The Walt Disney organization, noting Five Star's youth appeal, offers them a TV show of their own,

but Pearson declines on the grounds that the group is not yet well-enough established. *Luxury Of Life* climbs to US #57.

Dec Group appears in the "Celebration Of Youth" concert in London attended by the Queen.

1986 **Jan** They spend 6 weeks in Los Angeles, CA, recording a second album and doing club, TV and radio promotional work.

Feb *System Addict*, seventh single from the debut album, is the group's first UK Top 10 hit at #3.

Mar [1] *Let Me Be The One* peaks at US #59.

May *Can't Wait Another Minute*, recorded in Los Angeles, hits UK #7.

June Group accepts an invitation to write the theme for UK youth TV series "How Dare You", but declines George Michael's invitation to support Wham! at its farewell concert at Wembley.

Aug *Find The Time* hits UK #7.

Sept [14] "Children Of The Night" UK tour (sponsored by Crunchie Bars), with an 8-piece accompanying band, opens at Poole, Dorset.

[27] *Silk And Steel*, which includes the 2 previous hits, tops UK chart (It will be a long-term seller, eventually passing triple platinum and selling over a million in UK alone.)

Oct Extracted *Rain Or Shine*, written by Pete Sinfield and Billy Livsey proves to be Five Star's commercial peak hitting UK #2 and earning a gold disk for a half-million-plus sales.

Nov [1] *Can't Wait Another Minute* reaches US #41, and hits US R&B Top 10.

Dec *If I Say Yes*, from *Silk And Steel*, reaches UK #15, while the group makes a short US tour. *Silk And Steel* makes US #80.

1987 **Jan** The Pearson family moves from Romford to a much larger house in Sunningdale, Berks., where electronic gates and security cameras safeguard their privacy and new home recording studio.

[31] *If I Say Yes* peaks at US #67.

Feb [9] Five Star wins Best British Group at the sixth annual BRIT Awards at the Grosvenor House, Mayfair, London.

Stay Out Of My Life, the fifth single from second album and written by Deniece, hits UK #9.

May *The Slightest Touch*, last extract from *Silk And Steel*, hits UK #4.

Aug *Whenever You're Ready* reaches UK #11.

Sept *Between The Lines*, recorded in London and US, hits UK #7.

Oct *Strong As Steel*, from the album, makes UK #16.

[26-27] Major dates on the "Children Of The Night, 1987" tour (this time sponsored by Ultrabrite toothpaste), at Wembley Arena, London are filmed for UK home video release.

Dec *Somewhere, Somebody*, from the third album, makes UK #23.

1988 **June** *Another Weekend* reaches UK #18.

Aug *Rock The World*, the work of several producers including Leon Sylvers III from the US and Delroy Pearson, makes UK #17, while extracted *Rock My World* reaches UK #28.

1989 **Apr** *With Every Heartbreat* reaches UK #49.

Oct *Greatest Hits* peaks at UK #53.

1990 **May** [31] Group reportedly moves out of its Sunningdale mansion just days before the bailiffs were expected to evict them for non-payment of the mortgage.

July Epic label debut *Treat Me Like A Lady* is released in US, while *Hot Love* stalls at UK #68, marking a dramatic decline in their fortunes.

Oct [8] Stedman admits public indecency and agrees to be bound over for a year for £100 at Kingston court, after an incident at a public lavatory in New Malden, Surrey.

ROBERTA FLACK

1968 Flack (b. Feb.10, 1939, Black Mountain, near Asheville, NC), having graduated in music from Howard University in Washington, DC, then worked as a high school music teacher in North Carolina, returns to Washington to teach, and also begins singing in local clubs during the evenings. Atlantic recording artist Les McCann sees her performing and arranges an audition with label boss Ahmet Ertegun and producer Joel Dorn, which results in her signing to the label.

1970 **Jan** Debut album *First Take*, produced by Dorn, is released, initially middling US chartmaker.

Oct *Chapter Two* reaches US #33.

1971 **Aug** *You've Got A Friend*, a cover duet with Donny Hathaway of a Carole King song (simultaneously a US #1 hit for James Taylor), reaches US #29.

Nov Another duet with Hathaway, reviving *You've Lost That Lovin' Feelin'* reaches US #71.

1972 **Jan** *Quiet Fire* makes US #18.

Feb A revival of The Shirelles' 1961 hit *Will You Still Love Me Tomorrow* peaks at US #76.

Apr Through its exposure in Clint Eastwood movie *Play Misty For Me*, a track from Flack's debut album, reviving Ewan MacColl's folk ballad *The First Time Ever I Saw Your Face*, tops US chart for 6 weeks, selling 2 million copies. It is the longest running #1 hit by a solo female artist since Gogi Grant's *The Wayward Wind* in 1956. *First Take* (released in 1970) tops US chart for 5 weeks and earns a gold disk.

June Duet album *Roberta Flack And Donny Hathaway* hits #3 and is another gold disk.

July *The First Time Ever I Saw Your Face* reaches UK #14 and *First Take* makes UK #47.

Aug A third duet with Hathaway, *Where Is The Love*, hits US #5 (selling over a million), and makes UK #29.

Dec [10] Flack and 2 members of her backing group, bassist Jerry Jemmott and guitarist Cornell Dupree, are injured when Jemmott crashes their car driving into Manhattan, New York. The men both have fractured and broken bones, while Flack needs surgery on her lip.

1973 Feb *Killing Me Softly With His Song*, which Flack heard sung by Lori Lieberman (for whom it was written – about singer Don McLean) while on a TWA flight from Los Angeles, CA to New York, hits US #1 for 5 weeks and is a million-seller. (Flack has spent 3 months perfecting it in the studio prior to release.)

Mar [3] Flack wins Grammys for *The First Time Ever I Saw Your Face*, which is voted both Song Of The Year and Record Of The Year, and for *Where Is The Love*, which is named Best Pop Vocal Performance By A Duo at the 15th annual Grammy awards.
Killing Me Softly With His Song hits UK #6.

Oct *Killing Me Softly* hits US #3 (earning another gold disk) and makes UK #40, while *Jesse*, written by Janis Ian, reaches US #30.

1974 Mar [2] *Killing Me Softly With His Song* wins Record Of The Year and Song Of The Year and Flack wins Best Pop Vocal, Female at the 16th annual Grammy awards.
Dorn leaves Atlantic Records during the recording of Flack's new album *Feel Like Makin' Love*. (Flack takes over production herself but, due to her production inexperience and artistic perfectionism, it will take 8 months to complete. On release, Flack will use the production pseudonym Rubina Flake.)

Aug *Feel Like Making Love* tops US chart for a week, selling over a million, and reaches UK #34.

1975 May *Feel Like Makin' Love* makes US #24.

June *Feelin' That Glow* peaks at US #76.

Dec [8] Flack guests on Bob Dylan's "The Rolling Thunder Revue" at the end of its first run at New York's Madison Square Garden with "Night Of The Hurricane", a benefit for boxer and convicted murderer Rubin "Hurricane" Carter.

1978 Feb After a lengthy absence from the chart (during which she has cut down live performances to pursue other concerns, including her work in various educational programs for disadvantaged US youth), Flack's *Blue Lights In The Basement* hits US #8 and is another gold disk.

May Taken from the album, *The Closer I Get To You*, a ballad duet with Donny Hathaway (written by James Mtume and Reggie Lucas), hits US #2 and UK #42.

July *If Ever I See You Again*, the title song from the Joe Brooks film, reaches US #24.

Oct *Roberta Flack* reaches US #74.

1979 Jan [13] Donny Hathaway dies after falling from a New York hotel room window. (He had been working on more duet material with Flack, which will eventually emerge in 1980 in album and single form. Grieving, Flack will remain out of the public eye for much of the year.)

1980 Mar *You Are My Heaven*, duetted with Hathaway, reaches US #47.

June Uptempo *Back Together Again*, another Flack/Hathaway duet, penned by Mtume and Lucas, reaches only US #56 but hits UK #3.
Roberta Flack Featuring Donny Hathaway makes US #25 and UK #31.

Sept *Don't Make Me Wait Too Long* reaches UK #44.

1981 Jan Double live album *Live And More*, recorded with Memphis singer Peabo Bryson, reaches US #52.

July *Bustin' Loose*, the Flack-performed soundtrack from the film of the same title (released on MCA) reaches US #161. She also records a popular US TV commercial for Kentucky Fried Chicken.

1982 June The title song from Kate Jackson/Harry Hamlin film "Making Love" reaches US #13.

Aug *I'm The One* reaches US #59, with extracted title track at US #42.

1983 Jan Flack announces a tour which will take her and Bryson through Europe, the Middle East, the Far East, Australasia, South America and US. She moves from Atlantic to Capitol Records.

Sept Flack and Bryson's duet *Tonight I Celebrate My Love* reaches US #16 and hits UK #2 – Flack's biggest-selling UK single. *Born To Love*

with Bryson makes US #25 (it is Flack's last US chart album) and UK #15. She moves into a New York apartment in the Dakota building – the block in which John Lennon lived at the time of his death.

1984 Jan *You're Looking Like Love To Me*, another duet with Bryson, taken from the album, reaches US #58.

Mar Flack is honored with an hour-long musical tribute on the steps of New York's City Hall. (Washington has also given her a public honor, declaring Apr.22 Roberta Flack Day.)

Apr TV-advertised compilation album *Roberta Flack's Greatest Hits* reaches US #35.

1988 Aug [20] Flack plays a benefit concert on Nantucket Island, MA, for the island's only health care facility, the Nantucket cottage hospital.

1989 Jan [7] *Oasis* tops R&B chart in US, as parent album *Oasis*, her first in 6 years, makes US #159.

FLEETWOOD MAC

Mick Fleetwood (drums)
John McVie (bass)
Christine McVie (keyboards, vocals)
Lindsey Buckingham (guitars, vocals)
Stevie Nicks (vocals)

1967 Apr Fleetwood (b. June 24, 1942, London), ex-The Cheynes, The Bo Street Runners, Peter B's Looners and Shotgun Express (the latter with Rod Stewart) joins John Mayall's Bluesbreakers. Group comprises Mayall, Fleetwood, McVie (b. Nov.26, 1945, London) and Green (b. Peter Greenbaum, Oct.29, 1946, London), who has played with Fleetwood as a member of both the Looners and Shotgun Express and replaced Eric Clapton in The Bluesbreakers in July 1966. Fleetwood, Green and McVie form a close alliance, but within a month Fleetwood and Green are fired.

July Without Mayall, The Bluesbreakers have recently worked for Blue Horizon label owner Mike Vernon as a backing band for US bluesman Eddie Boyd. Vernon is keen to sign a domestic blues outfit for his label. After auditioning (and rejecting) Midlands-based band The Levi Set, he introduces their guitarist Jeremy Spencer (b. July 4, 1948, West Hartlepool, Lancs.) to Green and Fleetwood. Fleetwood Mac is formed comprising Green, Fleetwood, Spencer and bassist Bob Brunning.

Aug [12] They make their debut at the Windsor Jazz & Blues Festival, Berks. McVie, fired from The Bluesbreakers, joins to replace Brunning, who leaves to form The Sunflower Brunning Blues Band.

Nov [3] Group releases its debut single *I Believe My Time Ain't Long* billed as Peter Green's Fleetwood Mac. They become resident house band for the Blue Horizon label backing Otis Spann, Duster Bennett and others on a variety of albums.

1968 Mar A new blues boom hits UK and the band's debut album *Fleetwood Mac*, mixing originals with blues classics by Robert Johnson and Howlin' Wolf, hits UK #4 and makes US #198.

Apr *Black Magic Woman*, written by Green, reaches UK #37. (Santana's version will hit US #4 in Jan.1971.)

July A cover of Little Willie John's blues *Need Your Love So Bad*, highlighted by Mickey Baker's (of Mickey And Sylvia) string arrangement, reaches UK #31.

Sept *Mr. Wonderful* hits UK #10. (On it, Christine Perfect (b. July 12, 1943) (later McVie) plays piano, although still a member of the group Chicken Shack.) Green expands the group, adding a third guitarist, ex-Boilerhouse Danny Kirwan (b. Mar.13, 1950, London).

Dec [4] They begin their first US tour.
[23] Fleetwood Mac takes part in the Miami Pop Festival in Hallandale, FL, with Marvin Gaye, Steppenwolf, Three Dog Night, and The Grateful Dead among others.

1969 Jan *Albatross*, written by Green, tops the UK chart. A haunting guitar instrumental, it lifts the group out of the blues bracket and establishes its name throughout Europe.

Feb *English Rose* peaks at US #184.

May Green's *Man Of The World* hits UK #2. Group's contract with Blue Horizon ends and it signs a one-off deal with ex-Rolling Stones manager Andrew Loog Oldham's Immediate label.

Aug *Need Your Love So Bad* is reissued, this time making UK #32.

Sept *Pious Bird Of Good Omen* reaches UK #18. While the group negotiates a new contract, Blue Horizon releases a collection of old material, and re-promotes *Need Your Love So Bad*, which charts for a third time at UK #42.

Oct *Then Play On* hits UK #6 and makes US #109, marking their debut on Reprise label.

Nov *Oh Well* hits UK #2. The song's religious overtones reflect Green's renouncement of his Jewish faith and his involvement with Christianity (he begins to appear on stage in a long white robe underlining a new messianic image).

Dec *Blues Jam At Chess* is released featuring the group and a selection of Blues greats recorded in 1968.

1970 Jan Spencer releases an eponymously titled debut solo album backed by the group.

Mar *Oh Well* reaches US #55.

Apr [11] Green quits the band in Munich during a European tour, the pressures of stardom now proving intolerable. To avoid breach of contract, he agrees to finish the tour and then leave.

May [24] Green plays his last gig with the group at the Bath Festival.

June *The Green Manalishi (With The Two-Prong Crown)* hits UK #10. In his last single for the group, Green gives a heart-rending graphic description of the terrors that are haunting him.

Aug [17] McVie's wife, Christine Perfect, joins the line-up on keyboards, having been voted **Melody Maker**'s Female Vocalist Of The Year in 1969.

Oct *Kiln House* reaches UK #39 and US #69. Spencer becomes creative lead on their first album release without Green (but it will be 6 years before they have another major hit album).

Nov Green's solo album *The End Of The Game* fails to chart.

1971 Feb Spencer leaves during a US tour after telling the group at its Los Angeles hotel he is "just popping out for a bit to buy newspapers". (It is the last they see of him for 2 years. It later transpires he too has suffered the pressures that affected Green, and relinquishing his pop career, he joins the religious cult The Children Of God.) Green flies to US to help the group complete the tour but returns to his self-imposed retirement at its end. (Spencer will record an album *Jeremy Spencer And The Children Of God* in 1973 for CBS and *Flee* for Atlantic in 1979.)

Apr At the end of the tour, the group is in disarray having lost its 2 main songwriters and guitarists. Judy Wong, wife of Jethro Tull's Glenn Cornick introduces the group to Los Angeles musician Bob Welch (b. July 31, 1946, CA) who replaces Spencer. They begin recording a new album of Welch, Kirwan and Christine McVie compositions. (Welch has been playing in a soul show-band The Seven Souls in Las Vegas, NV, backing James Brown, Aretha Franklin and others, which breaks up in Hawaii in 1969, when Welch and 2 other group members head for Paris, forming R&B trio Head West. That splits, when Welch, set to take up an offer with Stax in Memphis, TN, heads back to Los Angeles.)

July *Fleetwood Mac In Chicago*, recorded in Jan.1969, makes US #190.

Oct *Black Magic Woman* makes US #143.

Nov *Future Games* peaks at US #91. They continue to tour US extensively.

1972 Feb *Greatest Hits* reaches UK #36.

May *Bare Trees* makes US #70.

Aug Kirwan leaves the band. (After refusing to appear on stage he becomes the first member of the group to be fired. In the mid 70s he will record unsuccessfully for DJM before being admitted to a psychiatric hospital.) He is replaced by Long John Baldry sideman Bob Weston, while vocalist Dave Walker also joins, recruited from Savoy Brown. Group returns to UK to record its next album.

1973 May *Penguin* reaches US #49. It features a guest appearance from Green but fails to chart in UK. The Fleetwood Mac penguin association is John McVie's idea. (He is a member of The London Zoological Society and becomes a keen student of the species.)

June Reissued *Albatross* hits UK #2. Walker's departure leaves the group as a 5-piece once more.

Dec *Mystery To Me* reaches US #67. Group begins a tour to promote the album and Weston begins an affair with Fleetwood's wife Jenny. Romantic entanglements wreck the tour and the group pulls out of all further engagements, Weston is sacked. Group's manager Clifford Davis, angered at group's decision to cut short the tour, assembles a bogus Fleetwood Mac to fulfill the dates resulting in a bitter legal battle. (The impostors later form Stretch and have a hit with *Why Did You Do It*.)

1974 Nov *Heroes Are Hard To Find* reaches US #34. As legalities are resolved, the band decides to settle permanently in California.

Dec Welch leaves. (He will form the band Paris and enjoy later solo success with albums *French Kiss*, *Three Hearts* and *Sentimental Lady*.) Fleetwood visits Sound City studios in Van Nuys, CA, to preview it as a future recording venue. As a demonstration, producer Keith Olsen plays Fleetwood a track from an album by duo Buckingham And Nicks. By chance, Lindsey Buckingham is in another part of the studio and strikes up a rapport with Fleetwood, who later meets his partner Stevie Nicks (b. May 26, 1948).

[31] Duo is invited to join Fleetwood Mac, forming the 10th line-up since 1967. (Buckingham and Nicks were members of Bay Area group Fritz. When the group split in 1971, the duo moved to Los Angeles in 1973 and recorded eponymously titled debut album on Polydor. It flopped, and in order to finance further songwriting efforts, Buckingham worked as a sessionman and toured with Don Everly, while Nicks worked as a waitress in Hollywood.)

1975 Mar *Vintage Years*, recordings 1967-69, reaches US #138.

Aug *Fleetwood Mac* enters the US chart. The songwriting talents of Christine McVie and Buckingham/Nicks begin to flower as airplay and sales increase in the next year.

Dec Reissued *Fleetwood Mac In Chicago* reaches US #118.

1976 Jan *Over My Head* reaches US #20.

June *Rhiannon (Will You Ever Win)*, also from the eponymous album, peaks at US #11.

Sept *Say You Love Me* makes US #11.

[4] 15 months after the record enters the US chart, *Fleetwood Mac* hits #1, going platinum, and will reach UK #23 on Oct.30, aided by a white vinyl format. *Say You Love Me* climbs to UK #40.

1977 Jan [26] Weeks before the group launches its new album, Peter Green attacks his accountant, who is trying to deliver a £30,000 royalty cheque, with an air rifle. Green insists that he wants no royalty and is later committed to a mental hospital. (He has been working as a gravedigger and hospital porter in recent years.)

Feb Affected by personal problems within the group (the McVies are separating, the Buckingham and Nicks relationship is unsteady and the Fleetwoods' divorce proceedings begin), *Rumours* is finally released. Creatively reflecting much of this turmoil, it will connect with radio and public alike, eventually topping both UK and US charts, with worldwide sales in excess of 15 million, spending more than 130 weeks on US chart and more than 400 weeks on UK chart.

[28] Group begins a 7 month US tour at the University of California, Berkeley, CA. (Tour will end at the Hollywood Bowl, Los Angeles, CA, on Oct.4.)

Mar *Go Your Own Way* hits US #10 and UK #38.

Apr [2] *Rumours* tops US chart.

May *Don't Stop* reaches UK #32.

Aug *Dreams* tops the US chart and makes UK #24.

Sept *Don't Stop* hits US #3.

Oct *You Make Loving Fun* peaks at UK #45.

Dec *You Make Loving Fun* hits US #9.

1978 Jan [14] *Rumours* tops UK Chart.

Feb [23] *Rumours* wins Album Of The Year at the 20th annual Grammy awards.

Mar [11] Reissued *Rhiannon* makes UK #46.

July [17] Group begins a summer US tour at Alpine Valley Music theater, Troy, WI.

Oct [30] *Fleetwood Mac* reaches UK #23, 2 years after its release.

1979 July Green's comeback, an instrumental album *In The Skies*, on Creole Records, makes UK #32.

Nov *Tusk*, recorded (and filmed) with The U.S.C. Trojan Marching Band at Los Angeles' Dodger Stadium, hits US #8 and UK #6, creating a record for the number of musicians to appear on a single.

[10] Double album *Tusk*, which the group reportedly spends $1 million on making, tops the UK chart.

[17] *Tusk* hits US #4. Its main creative force is Buckingham who has resisted record company pressure to repeat the *Rumours* formula.

[26] Group begins a lengthy US tour at the Mini-Dome, Idaho State University in Pocatello, ID.

1980 Jan Nicks-penned *Sara* reaches UK #37.

Feb *Sara* hits US #7.

May *Think About Me* makes US #20. Green releases *Little Dreamer*, on PVK Records. It peaks at UK #34 (after which Green will again fade into obscurity and live as a recluse).

June *Sisters Of The Moon* peaks at US #86.

Sept [1] Group finishes a tour at Los Angeles' Hollywood Bowl. (A long period of solo activity begins before Fleetwood Mac records together again.)

Oct [4] Buckingham, Nicks and Fleetwood present The U.S.C. Marching Band with a platinum disk for its contribution on *Tusk* at half-time during a game at Dodger Stadium.

Dec *Fleetwood Mac Live* reaches UK #31 and US #14.

1981 Feb *Fireflies* peaks at US #60.

July Mick Fleetwood's *The Visitor*, recorded at great cost in Ghana, West Africa, makes US #43. (It recoups little in sales and the losses incurred will, together with real estate ventures, contribute to Fleetwood's eventual bankruptcy.)

Aug Nicks' debut solo album *Bella Donna* tops the US chart and makes UK #11.

Sept Nicks' *Stop Draggin' My Heart Around*, with help from Tom Petty & The Heartbreakers, hits US #3 and UK #50.

Nov Buckingham's solo album *Law And Order* makes US #32.

1982
Jan Buckingham's *Trouble* hits US #9 and UK #31, while Nicks' duet with The Eagles' Don Henley, *Leather And Lace*, written for Waylon Jennings and Jessi Colter by Nicks, hits US #6.

Apr Nicks' *Edge Of Seventeen (Just Like The White Winged Dove)* climbs to US #11.

July After a 3-year studio gap, group album *Mirage* is released. It will top the US chart and hit UK #5. Nicks' solo *After The Glitter Fades* makes US #32.

[24] Fleetwood Mac's *Hold Me* hits US #4.

Sept [3-5] Group plays the US Festival, financed by Apple Computers founder Steven Wozniak, in San Bernardino, CA, to 400,000 people, along with Jackson Browne, The Cars, The Grateful Dead, Eddie Money, Police, Santana, Talking Heads and many others.

Oct *Gypsy* reaches US #12 and UK #46.

1983
Jan Fleetwood Mac's *Love In Store* reaches US #22.

Jan [29] Nicks marries Kim Anderson, former husband of her best friend Robin Anderson who had died of leukemia in 1982, outside her Los Angeles home. (The marriage will not last, and their divorce will be finalised in Apr.1984.)

Feb UK-only release, *Oh Diane*, penned by Buckingham, hits #9.

May Nicks sings backing vocals on Robbie Patton's US #52 *Smiling Islands*.

July Nicks' solo album *The Wild Heart* hits US #5 and UK #28.

Aug From it, *Stand Back*, written with Prince, hits US #5. Buckingham's solo *Holiday Road*, from the movie "National Lampoon's Vacation" peaks at US #82.

Nov Nicks' *If Anyone Falls* reaches US #14.

1984
Jan Nicks' *Nightbird* makes US #33.

Feb Christine McVie's solo album *Christine McVie* reaches US #26.

Mar Taken from her album, *Got A Hold On Me* hits US #10.

May [1] Mick Fleetwood files for bankruptcy.

June *Love Will Show Us How* climbs to US #30 for Christine McVie.

Sept *Go Insane*, a Buckingham solo, makes US #45.

Oct *Go Insane* reaches US #23.

1985
Dec Nicks' third solo album *Rock A Little* makes US #12 and UK #30.

1986
Nicks has a succession of hit singles from the album: *Talk To Me* (US #4/UK #68), *I Can't Wait* (US #16/UK #54), *Needles And Pins*, with Tom Petty & The Heartbreakers (US #37) and ballad *Has Anyone Ever Written Anything For You* (US #60). (Nicks will play 2 gigs on Tom Petty's Australian tour until immigration authorities intervene.)

Oct [18] Christine McVie marries Portuguese composer Eduardo Quintela de Mendonca in London.

1987
Apr Group reunites when Christine McVie, working on the soundtrack to Blake Edwards' film "A Fine Mess", and trying to record a version of Presley's *Can't Help Falling In Love*, enlists the help of Buckingham and John McVie. This leads to new Fleetwood Mac recordings. Having led a nomadic studio existence in the past, the new album is overdubbed and mixed in Buckingham's own studio at his Bel Air home. *Tango In The Night* is released, to become the band's biggest seller since *Rumours*.

May [30] *Big Love* hits US #5 and UK #9. B-side features part 1 of album cut *You And I Part 2*. *Tango In The Night* hits US #7.

July Buckingham, unhappy with the prospect of touring with the band to promote *Tango In The Night*, is fired.

Aug [15] *Seven Wonders* reaches US #19 and peaks at UK #56.

Sept Secret rehearsals begin in Venice, CA, with new members Billy Burnette (b. May 7, 1953) son of rockabilly star Johnny Burnette and who has released solo album *Billy Burnette* on Polydor in 1980 and Rick Vito (b. 1950), but Buckingham changes his mind, and commits himself to a final tour before embarking on a solo career.

Oct [31] *Tango In The Night* tops the UK chart.

Nov [7] *Little Lies* hits US #4 and UK #5.

1988
Jan *Family Man* peaks at UK #54.

Feb [6] *Everywhere* reaches US #14 and will hit UK #4.

Apr *Family Man* climbs to US #90.

June *Isn't It Midnight* peaks at UK #60.

Aug Group's "Shake The Cage" tour of Europe and Australia with Burnette and Vito begins.

Dec *Greatest Hits* hits UK #3.

1989
Jan [21] *As Long As You Follow* makes US #43.

May Christine McVie (and Friends) contribute *Roll With Me Henry* to Richard Perry-produced *Rock, Rhythm & Blues* compilation.

June Nicks' *The Other Side Of The Mirror* hits US #10.

July [1] Nicks' *Rooms On Fire* reaches US #16.

1990
Mar [24] Group begins "The Mask" world tour in Australia.

Apr [21] *Behind The Mask* enters UK chart at #1.

May [19] *Save Me* makes US #33 as parent album *Behind The Mask* makes US #18.

[30] Group embarks on the US leg of "The Mask" tour in Portland, OR, set to end at Jones Beach, Wantagh, NY on Aug.2.

Aug [21] European leg of "The Mask" tour begins in Ghent, Belgium.

Sept [1] Fleetwood Mac plays Wembley with Jethro Tull and Hall & Oates.

[7] Stevie Nicks and Christine McVie make their final appearance with Fleetwood Mac at the Great Western Forum, Inglewood, CA. Buckingham joins them onstage for part of the show.

1991
Feb Buckingham, Christine McVie, John Lee Hooker and others attend the opening of Mick Fleetwood's blues club, Fleetwood's, in Los Angeles.

EDDIE FLOYD

1956 Having moved to Detroit in his teens, Floyd (b. June 25, 1935, Montgomery, AL) helps to form The Falcons.

1959 **July** As a member of The Falcons, Floyd's chart debut *You're So Fine* reaches US #17.

1960 Wilson Pickett replaces Joe Stubbs as lead singer and The Falcons, originally R&B/doo-wop specialists, develop a soulful, gospel style.

1962 **May** *I Found A Love* peaks at US #75. After Pickett leaves and the group breaks up, Floyd settles in Washington, DC, where he starts Safice Records with local disk jockey Al Bell and former Moonglow Chester Simmons, but the venture is not immediately successful. He also writes songs and *Comfort Me*, penned for Carla Thomas (at university in Washington), is his introduction to the Stax label.

1965 **Oct** After Bell moves to Memphis, TN, to become national sales director for Stax, Floyd is signed as a staff songwriter. *634-5789*, a smash for ex-colleague Pickett (later covered by James Brown, Ry Cooder and Tina Turner among others) is his first collaboration with MG's guitarist Steve Cropper, followed by another Pickett hit, *Ninety Nine And A Half*, and Otis Redding classic *Don't Mess With Cupid*.

1966 **Sept** Floyd's demo of his own *Knock On Wood*, originally written with Cropper for Redding, is polished up and issued as a single. The archetypal Stax record and the acme of 60s soul, it shoots to #1 on the R&B chart, crosses to US #28 list and reaches UK #19.

1967 **Mar** *Raise Your Hand*, with Floyd formally contracted as an artist as well as writer, peaks at US #79 and UK #42. (It will become a Springsteen stage staple and be included on his 1987 boxed set. Janis Joplin and The J. Geils Band will cut interim covers.)

Apr Floyd tours Europe with the warmly-received Stax package which includes Otis Redding, Booker T. And The MG's, Sam And Dave, Arthur Conley and The Mar-Keys.

May *Knock On Wood* makes UK #36.

July *Don't Rock The Boat* is a minor US hit at #98.

Aug *Love Is A Doggone Good Thing* stalls at US #97 and *Things Get Better* becomes his final UK hit at #31.

Oct *On A Saturday Night* stalls at US #92.

1968 **Sept** *I've Never Found A Girl* makes US #40.

Dec *Bring It On Home To Me*, a Sam Cooke song and his first non-original chart entry, reaches US #17.

1969 **Aug** *Don't Tell Your Mama (Where You've Been)* peaks at US #73.

Nov *Why Is The Wine Sweeter* makes US #98.

1970 **Apr** *California Girl* makes US #45, his last chart entry. During his recording and singing career he will continue to write songs for other Stax acts, including Sam And Dave, Rufus Thomas and The Mad Lads.

1988 After 30 years on the road, Floyd's enduring popularity, especially in Europe, allows no question of retirement. His hobby is collecting cover versions of *Knock On Wood*, which has so far attracted over 60, by acts as diverse as David Bowie, Cher, Count Basie, Eric Clapton and the biggest hit version by Amii Stewart.

DAN FOGELBERG

1971 Fogelberg (b. Aug.13, 1951, Peoria, IL), a songwriter/guitarist since age 14, is studying art at Illinois University, Champaign, IL, but drops out to work the folk circuit.

1972 He tours in US as support to Van Morrison, before moving to Los Angeles, CA, to work as a session guitarist.

1973 Signed to CBS/Columbia, his debut album *Home Free*, recorded in

Nashville, TN, with producer Norbert Putnam, does not chart.

1974 He signs a management deal with Irving Azoff (whom he first met in Illinois managing R.E.O. Speedwagon) and Azoff persuades another of his acts, Joe Walsh, to produce Fogelberg's second album *Souvenirs*, for which he switches to Epic via his deal with Full Moon label, and through which all his future albums will be released. Uneasy with the Los Angeles lifestyle, he leaves, eventually settling in Boulder, CO.

1975 **Feb** *Souvenirs*, featuring Walsh, Graham Nash, Don Henley, Glenn Frey and Randy Meisner, reaches US #17.

Mar *Part Of The Plan* hits US #31 as he goes on major US tour with The Eagles. He contributes 2 songs, *Old Tennessee* and *Love Me Through And Through*, to his backing band Fools Gold's eponymous debut album.

Nov Self-produced *Captured Angel*, featuring 8 self-penned tracks, climbs to US #23.

1977 **July** [23] *Nether Lands*, co-produced by Putnam, featuring guests Henley, J.D. Souther, jazz flautist Tim Weisberg and Kenny Buttrey and recorded at the Caribou Ranch, Nederland, CO, reaches US #13 and becomes his first million-seller.

1978 **May** Fogelberg contributes *There's A Place In The World For A Gambler* to the soundtrack album *FM*.

Oct [14] *Twin Sons Of Different Mothers*, recorded with Tim Weisberg, hits US #8 and is a second million-seller.

Dec Extracted from *Twin Sons Of Different Mothers*, *The Power Of Gold* reaches US #24.

1980 **Mar** His biggest US hit successes are ballad *Longer* at US #2 and parent album *Phoenix* at US #3. Both are million-sellers. In UK, *Longer* reaches #59 while *Phoenix* makes #42. (They will be his only UK hits.)

Fogelberg donates the royalties from *Face The Fire* to the Campaign For Economic Democracy Education Fund, which promotes the use of solar energy in place of nuclear energy.

May *Heart Hotels* reaches US #21 and is featured on soundtrack to John Travolta-starring movie "Urban Cowboy".

1981 **Feb** Sentimental New Year ballad, *Same Old Lang Syne* hits US #9.

Oct *The Innocent Age*, a 17-part song cycle, featuring his previous chart single and a duet with Emmylou Harris, hits US #6 and is his fourth million-selling album. It includes *Hard To Say*, which hits US #7.

1982 **Mar** [6] *Leader Of The Band*, the third US Top 10 single from *The Innocent Age*, hits US #9.

May [29] *Run For The Roses* reaches US #18.

June [6] He appears at the anti-nuclear rally "Peace Sunday – We Have A Dream", before 85,000 people at the Rose Bowl, Pasadena, CA, with Bob Dylan, Jackson Browne, Joan Baez, Stevie Wonder and others.

Dec [4] *Missing You* reaches US #23.

[18] Compilation album *Dan Fogelberg/Greatest Hits* reaches US #15.

1983 **Mar** *Make Love Stay* reaches US #29. Fogelberg produces the debut solo album *Beauty Lies* for Michael Brewer (ex-Brewer & Shipley).

1984 **Mar** *Windows And Walls*, featuring Timothy B. Schmit, Russ Kunkel, Tom Scott and co-produced with Marty Lewis, peaks at US #15, while *The Language Of Love*, taken from it, makes #13.

May *Believe In Me*, also from the album, reaches US #48.

1985 **Apr** *Go Down Easy* reaches US #85.

June Gaining inspiration from a visit to the Telluride Bluegrass Festival, CO, in 1983, Fogelberg records a traditional country music album *High Country Snows* and enlists help from country acts including Ricky Skaggs, Charlie McCoy, Emory Gordy Jr. and The Desert Rose Band. It reaches US #30.

1987 **June** Clean shaven for the first time since *Souvenirs*, Fogelberg returns to more familiar territory with *Exiles*. Recorded in Los Angeles and co-produced with Russ Kunkel, it reaches US #48, and includes the title theme from the Warren Miller movie "Beyond The Edge".

[13] *She Don't Look Back* stalls at US #84.

1990 Inviting Schmit, David Crosby and Bruce Cockburn, who co-writes one of the tracks, to contribute, Fogelberg releases self-produced *The Wild Places*, recorded at his Mountain Bird studio in Colorado, which peaks at US #103. Extracted cover of the The Cascades 1963 US #3 *Rhythm Of The Rain* fails to score.

WAYNE FONTANA AND THE MINDBENDERS

Wayne Fontana (vocals)
Eric Stewart (guitar)
Bob Lang (bass)
Ric Rothwell (drums)

1961 While working as an apprentice telephone engineer, Fontana (b. Glyn Geoffrey Ellis, Oct.28, 1940, Manchester, Gtr.Manchester) forms The Jets, a semi-professional outfit playing the Manchester club circuit.

1963 Group gets its first break at the Oasis, with Fontana Records producer Jack Baverstock. Only Fontana and Lang (b. Jan.10, 1946) show so substitute locals, Stewart (b. Jan.20, 1945, Manchester) and Rothwell (b. Eric Rothwell, Mar.11, 1944, Stockport, Gtr.Manchester), who holds a London College of Music Diploma, are recruited at the last minute. Despite a disastrous performance, Baverstock sees enough potential to sign them. Fontana christens his new group The Mindbenders, taken from the title of a UK psychological horror film starring Dirk Bogarde, which is playing at his local cinema.

June Group debuts with revivals of Bo Diddley's *Road Runner*, which does not chart, and Fats Domino's *Hello Josephine*.

July *Hello Josephine* makes UK #46.

Oct *For You, For You*, backed with current beat favorite *Love Potion No. 9*, fails to chart.

1964 **Feb** *Little Darlin'* is released.

June Cover of Ben E. King's *Stop Look And Listen* makes UK #37.

Nov Group's cover version of Major Lance's US hit *Um Um Um Um Um Um*, written by Curtis Mayfield, is its first major UK chart success, hitting #5, as the group joins Brenda Lee's UK tour.

1965 **Feb** *The Game Of Love*, Clint Ballard Jr.'s song, brings international fame. It hits UK #2 while *Wayne Fontana And The Mindbenders* makes UK #18.

[27] Group begins a 21-date twice-nightly UK tour supporting Del Shannon, with Herman's Hermits and others, at City Hall, Sheffield, S.Yorks, ending Mar.22 at the Odeon cinema, Glasgow, Scotland.

Mar [9] Fontana is taken ill with nervous exhaustion and pulls out of the tour. The Mindbenders continue without him.

Apr US chart debut *The Game Of Love* climbs to hit #1 and is a million-seller. Group visits US for promotion, but is refused performance visas by US officials concerned about the flood of UK groups entering and working where US bands might play instead. Before being allowed in, The Mindbenders has to obtain proof from **Billboard** and **Cash Box** magazines that its single is the top-selling US record and that the visit is justifiable on popularity grounds.

May US album *The Game Of Love*, a variation on the UK release, makes US #58.

[25] Group participates in the British Song Festival at the Dome, Brighton, E.Sussex, coming third with 99 points.

July Ballard composition *Just A Little Bit Too Late* reaches UK #20 and US #45.

Oct *She Needs Love* makes UK #32, the last single released by Fontana with the group.

[2] Group represents UK in the annual Grand Gala Du Disque at the Congresscentrum, Amsterdam, Holland.

[6] An announcement is made that Fontana and The Mindbenders will split on Oct.31. The split is by mutual consent, a move prompted actively by the label, for whom both parties will continue to record.

[30] Group makes its last appearance together at the Pavilion, Buxton Gardens, Derbys.

Nov [3] Fontana begins 18-date twice-nightly tour with Herman's Hermits, The Fortunes, Billy Fury and The Gamblers, and others, at the Gaumont cinema, Wolverhampton, W.Midlands. Tour ends Nov.22 at the Odeon cinema, Manchester.

Dec Fontana's first solo success *It Was Easier To Hurt Her*, a US hit for Garnett Mimms, makes UK #36.

[11] Fontana makes his solo TV debut on "Thank Your Lucky Stars".

1966 **Jan** *Eric, Rick, Wayne And Bob*, recorded immediately prior to the split, is released.

Mar The Mindbenders rapidly outsells its former "tambourine player" (as Fontana is referred to after the split) with *A Groovy Kind Of Love*, which hits UK #2.

May *A Groovy Kind Of Love* also hits US #2, while The Mindbenders' UK follow-up *Can't Live With You, Can't Live Without You* makes #28. Fontana's *Come On Home* also charts in UK at #16.

July *The Mindbenders* reaches UK #28.

Aug The Mindbenders' US album *A Groovy Kind Of Love* peaks at US #92, while Fontana's single *Goodbye Bluebird* makes UK #49.

[12] Fontana begins Radio England's "Swingin' 66" UK tour, with The Small Faces, Crispian St. Peters, Neil Christian and Genevieve, at the Odeon cinema, Lewisham, London.

Sept The Mindbenders' *Ashes To Ashes* peaks at UK #14 and US #55, and is its final US hit.

[27] Group begins week-long UK tour at Finsbury Park Astoria, London as Dusty Springfield's guests. Tour ends Oct.3 at the Odeon cinema, Manchester.

Nov Fontana's *Pamela Pamela* reaches UK #11, his biggest solo hit, but also his last. (It is written by Graham Gouldman, who will later team up with Stewart in 10cc.)

1967 Fontana releases *24 Sycamore* (Apr.), *Impossible Years* (Sept.) and *Gina* (Nov.) but none reaches the charts.
Sept The Mindbenders appears as a beat group at a school dance in UK-made Sidney Poitier film "To Sir With Love". Band's cover of The Box Tops' *The Letter*, far outsold by the original, is its last UK chart single, reaching only #42.
Aug [5] The Mindbenders advertise in the **New Musical Express** for "top class drummer/vocalist".

1968 Lang leaves the group and is replaced for final weeks of the band's life by Graham Gouldman, a successful songwriter for artists including The Yardbirds, Herman's Hermits, Jeff Beck and The Hollies. Rothwell also departs and The Mindbenders finally dissolves. (Fontana will release 6 more singles during next 18 months before his recording career ends. Stewart will play sessions for 2 years, before joining Lol Creme and Kevin Godley in Hotlegs, to have a hit with *Neanderthal Man* at #2 in 1970, and will re-recruit Gouldman for 10cc. Lang will drop out of music, re-emerge in Racing Cars in 1976, and quit again to run a stereo equipment business. Rothwell will establish an antique business.)

1970 Fontana gives up his singing career and works for Chappell music publishers as a resident songwriter. (The "English Invasion Revival" tour of US will bring him back to the live arena in 1973, before he resumes a recording career in 1976 releasing *The Last Bus Home* for Polydor. A further rock'n'roll revival tour in 1979 encourages him to put together a new Mindbenders group to perform his old 60s hits, and fame returns when *The Game Of Love* is featured in the Robin Williams' movie "Good Morning Vietnam" and Phil Collins revives *A Groovy Kind Of Love* as a hit single from the film "Buster", both in the late 80s.)

FRANKIE FORD

1959 After forming his own band The Syncopators at high school in New Orleans, LA, and singing *Botch-A-Me*, a current Rosemary Clooney hit, on Ted Mack's "Original Amateur Hour" in 1952, Ford (b. Frank Guzzo, Aug.4, 1940, Gretna, LA), records for Johnny Vincent's Ace label, based in Jackson, MS. Vincent has already scored major US hits with New Orleans acts, notably Huey "Piano" Smith & The Clowns.
Apr Ford reaches US #14 with *Sea Cruise*, his voice having been overdubbed on Huey Smith's backing track. (The song will become a minor rock classic, with later versions including another US chart entry by Johnny Rivers in 1971.)
Aug *Alimony*, again recorded with Huey Smith & The Clowns, peaks at only US #97. Both this and *Sea Cruise* have been recorded by dubbing new vocals by Ford on to existing backing tracks by The Clowns – after erasing the original vocals by band's own singer Bobby Marchan.

1960 **Feb** *Time After Time* peaks at #75.
Oct Signing to Imperial Records, he charts in US with a cover version of fellow New Orleans artist Joe Jones' *You Talk Too Much*. But Ford's version stalls at #87, eclipsed by Jones' original which hits US #3.

1961 **Apr** His revival of the Boyd Bennett/Fontane Sisters' 1955 hit *Seventeen* reaches US #72.

1962 Ford begins a 3-year stint in US Army, which takes him to Korea, Vietnam, Guam and Thailand as part of a special entertainment unit where he writes, directs stage shows and casts musical talent.

1966 Out of the army, he has a local New Orleans hit with *I Can't Face Tomorrow*.

1971 **Jan** He buys a New Orleans club which will henceforth be the base for his activities, and starts to record again, for the Paula label in Shreveport, LA. (Ford will never again have a national hit, but continues regular performing on the New Orleans live circuit right through into the late 80s, when he appears on US and UK TV in a live Mardi Gras concert transmitted from New Orleans.)

FOREIGNER

Lou Gramm (vocals)
Mick Jones (guitar)
Rick Wills (bass)
Dennis Elliott (drums)

1976 **Feb** Band is formed by Jones (b. Dec.27, 1944, London), who has begun his career in Nero & The Gladiators and played on the same Paris Olympia bill as The Beatles in 1964 during 6 years living there working with Johnny Hallyday, also spending a short period with Spooky Tooth before emigrating to US to work with the Leslie West Band, after he

meets ex-King Crimson multi-instrumentalist Ian McDonald (b. June 25, 1946, London) in New York at a studio session for singer Ian Lloyd. He recruits Elliott (b. Aug.18, 1950, London), whom he had met at an Ian Hunter session, and 3 Americans: Ed Gagliardi (b. Feb.13, 1952, New York, NY) on bass, Al Greenwood on keyboards, and Black Sheep singer Lou Gramm (b. May 2, 1950, Rochester, NY) on lead vocals. The bi-nationality of the personnel leads to the band's name.

1977 **Feb** After a year in rehearsals, during which the group signs to Atlantic, *Foreigner* is released.
May [13] *Feels Like The First Time*, from the album, makes UK #39.
June *Feels Like The First Time* hits US #4.
Aug [26] Hard rock *Cold As Ice* reaches UK #24.
Oct *Cold As Ice* hits US #6.
[22] *Foreigner* hits US #4, but does not chart in the UK.

1978 **Feb** *Long Long Way From Home* reaches US #20.
Mar Foreigner plays at the "California Jam II" festival in Ontario, CA. Also on the bill are Aerosmith, Heart and Santana.
Aug [27] Group plays the Reading Festival, Berks., on the last day.
Sept *Hot Blooded*, from album *Double Vision* and written by Jones and Gramm, hits US #3 and is a million-seller.
[2] *Double Vision*, produced by Keith Olsen with Jones and McDonald, makes UK #32.
[9] *Double Vision* hits US #3.
Nov Title track from *Double Vision* is another million-seller, hitting US #2, but not charting in UK.
[4] *Hot Blooded* makes UK #42.

1979 **Mar** *Blue Morning, Blue Day* peaks at US #15 and UK #45.
Aug [27] Group headlines at Reading Festival, Berks. Jones replaces Gagliardi with ex-Roxy Music and Small Faces bass player Rick Wills before recording *Head Games*.
Oct *Dirty White Boy* reaches US #12.
[27] *Head Games* hits US #3.
Dec *Head Games*, the extracted title track, reaches US #14.

1980 **Jan** *Head Games* makes US #11.
Mar *Women* reaches US #41.
Sept Greenwood and McDonald leave and band stabilizes as a 4-piece.

1981 **Aug** After a lengthy gap, *4* tops US chart.
Sept *Urgent*, featuring Motown sax-man Junior Walker, hits US #4.
[5] *Urgent* peaks at UK #54.
Oct [17] *Juke Box Hero* makes UK #48.
Nov [28] Uncharacteristic ballad *Waiting For A Girl Like You*, written by Jones, becomes a US million-seller. It fails to make US #1, but spends an unprecedented 10 weeks at #2, mostly behind Olivia Newton-John's *Physical*.

1982 **Jan** [23] *Waiting For A Girl Like You*, the group's first UK Top 10 record, hits UK #8.
Feb [5] *4*, co-produced by noted rock producer Robert "Mutt" Lange, and with keyboardist Thomas Dolby, finally hits peak UK #5 and spends 62 weeks on chart.
Apr [3] *Juke Box Hero* reaches US #26.
May [5] Group begins 5-date UK tour at the Playhouse, Edinburgh, Scotland, with further dates at Birmingham NEC, W.Midlands and London's Wembley Arena.
[15] *Urgent* re-charts in UK, climbing this time to #45.
June [26] *Break It Up* reaches US #26.
Aug [14] *Luanne* peaks at US #75.
Dec Greatest hits collection *Records: The Best Of Foreigner* makes UK #58, and includes a live version of *Hot Blooded*, recorded on a US tour earlier in the year.

1983 **Feb** *Records: The Best Of Foreigner* hits US #10.
1984 **Dec** After another gap, Foreigner returns with synthesizer-dominated sound on new album, *Agent Provocateur*.
1985 **Jan** The gospel-influenced and choir-accompanied *I Want To Know What Love Is*, created by Jones, hits #1 in both US and UK and is another million-seller. It features guest contributions from The Thompson Twins' Tom Bailey, Jennifer Holliday and the New Jersey Mass Choir.
[26] *Agent Provocateur*, co-produced by Alex Sadkin and Jones, tops UK chart.
Feb *Agent Provocateur* hits US #5.
May Jones/Gramm-penned *That Was Yesterday* makes US #12, UK #28.
June A remixed version of *Cold As Ice* peaks at UK #64. *Reaction To Action* and *Down On Love* both reach US #54.

1987 **Feb** Gramm solo album *Ready Or Not* (US #27) and solo US Top 10 hit *Midnight Blue* hint at the dissolution of the band or Gramm's departure.
Apr [18] *Midnight Blue* hits US #5.
June [13] Gramm's *Ready Or Not* makes US #54.

FOREIGNER cont.

July *Say You Will* from forthcoming Foreigner album *Inside Information* peaks at UK #71.

1988 **Feb** Release of *Inside Information* confounds the break-up rumors. It reaches US #15 and UK #64.

[20] *Say You Will* hits US #6.

May *I Don't Want to Live Without You*, from the album, hits US #5. (It can only bubble under the UK Top 75, peaking at #84.)

1989 **Sept** Jones' *Mick Jones*, with songs originally written for London stage musical "Metropolis", stalls at US #184. First single from the album is *Just Wanna Hold*, co-written with Ian Hunter and Mick Jagger under the pseudonym "M. Phillips".

Nov As Gramm releases a further solo album, **Long Hard Look** (US #85), Jones concentrates more on production projects which include Billy Joel's **Stormfront** and songwriting, not least co-penning Eric Clapton's Grammy-winning *Bad Love* hit.

1990 **Jan** [27] Gramm's *Just Between You And Me* hits US #6.

Mar [31] His follow-up *True Blue Love* makes US #40.

1991 With Gramm now fully solo, Jones has recruited Johnny Edwards as Foreigner's new lead vocalist on the band's first project in 4 years, scheduled for May release.

THE FORTUNES

Glen Dale (guitar, vocals)
Barry Pritchard (guitar, vocals)
David Carr (keyboards)
Rod Allen (bass, vocals)
Andy Brown (drums)

1963 **Mar** Allen (b. Rodney Bainbridge, Mar.31, 1944, Leicester, Leics.) Pritchard (b. Apr.3, 1944, Birmingham, W.Midlands) and Dale (b. Richard Garforth, Apr.2, 1943, Deal, Kent), living in manager Reg Calvert's house (Allen and Pritchard are working as backing singers, having made their debut at age 13 on the "Carroll Levis Show" before forming a skiffle group, Dale is a solo singer in the "Danny Storm Beat Package Show"), form The Cliftones. Brown (b. Jan 7, 1946, Birmingham) and Carr (b. Aug.4, 1943, Leyton, London), recommended by Brian Poole, soon augment the trio.

Sept Renamed The Fortunes, they sign to Decca Records, becoming one of the first provincial beat groups to do so. A revival of The Jamies' *Summertime, Summertime* is issued as the group's debut.

1964 **Jan** *Caroline* does not chart but becomes a familiar radio sound in UK for some years, being adopted by UK pirate station Radio Caroline as its theme tune, and given daily plays.

1965 **Jan** [16] Group makes its UK TV debut on "Ready Steady Go!"

Aug After 2 more flops, *You've Got Your Troubles* hits UK #2.

Oct *You've Got Your Troubles* hits US #7.

Nov [3] Group begins an 18-date twice-nightly UK tour, with Herman's Hermits, Wayne Fontana, Billy Fury with The Gamblers, and others, at the Wolverhampton Gaumont, W.Midlands, ending Nov.22 at the Odeon cinema, Manchester, Gtr.Manchester.

[6] *Here It Comes Again* hits UK #4.

Dec *Here It Comes Again* reaches US #27, as *The Fortunes*, containing the hits, is released in UK.

[24] Group takes part in Murray The K's 9-day Christmas show in New York.

1966 **Feb** [4] They play the first of 6 concerts over a weekend as a rehearsal for The Who's first bill-topping UK tour starting Mar.25, with The Merseys and Screaming Lord Sutch.

Mar *This Golden Ring* reaches UK #15, but stalls at US #82 despite their recent US tour with Peter & Gordon and The Moody Blues. (It is their last hit in US or UK for more than 5 years.)

June [3] Dale leaves to go solo, replaced by Shel MacRae (b. Andrew Semple, Mar.8, 1943, Burbank, Scotland) from The Kimbos. *Is It Really Worth Your While?* is the first single released by the new line-up. Manager Reg Calvert is shot dead by business rival Major Charles Smedley. (Smedley will be cleared of all charges.)

July [9] Allen is taken to hospital after fans pull him off stage at a Starlite Rooms gig in Lincoln, Lincs.

[24] Group makes its cabaret debut with a week-long engagement at Rotherham's Greaseborough Social club, S.Yorks.

Aug Dale releases his first solo single, a cover of Lennon/McCartney's *Good Day Sunshine*.

1967 **Aug** Group moves from Decca to United Artists Records. Several UA singles between now and late 1970 are released, and the group makes considerably more money recording ad jingles (*It's The Real Thing*) for Coca Cola and playing Northern UK club dates.

1968 **Aug** Carr leaves, with the group continuing as a 4-piece.

1970 **June** A cover of Pickettywitch's (US #67) *That Same Old Feeling* is released in US on World Pacific Records in competition with the original and peaks at US #62.

1971 **May** The Fortunes sign a new deal with Capitol Records, and team with writer/producers Roger Cook and Roger Greenaway, releasing *Here Comes That Rainy Day Feeling Again*.

July *Here Comes That Rainy Day Feeling Again* fails to chart in UK, but reaches US #15.

Sept Scotsman George McAllister joins, returning band to a quintet.

Oct *Freedom Come Freedom Go* hits UK #6, and peaks at US #72.

1972 **Feb** *Storm In A Teacup* hits UK #7. (Further singles on Capitol are unsuccessful and later isolated 70s singles, on Mooncrest and Target, fare no better. Group will use their harmonic vocal strengths and back-catalog of familiar hits to continue as a supper club act in the UK, without ever finding their way back into the rock/pop mainstream.)

THE FOUR SEASONS

Frankie Valli (lead vocals)
Bob Gaudio (vocals, organ)
Nick Massi (vocals, bass)
Tommy DeVito (vocals, guitar)

1953 Valli (b. Frank Castelluccio, May 3, 1937, Newark, NJ) cuts his first record, a version of George Jessel's *My Mother's Eyes* for Mercury Records' subsidiary Corona, via a connection made by fellow Newark Central High student Paul Kapp. It is credited to Frank Valley & The Travelers, and flops (as does follow-up *Somebody Else Took Her Home*).

1954 Valli joins The Variety Trio, a vocal group comprising Hank Majewski and brothers Nick and Tommy DeVito (b. June 19, 1936, Montclair, NJ). Group changes its name to The Variatones, and works solidly on the New Jersey club circuit (including the Broadway Lounge in Passaic and Newark's Silhouette club).

1956 **June** Signed to RCA, The Variatones are renamed The Four Lovers and record Otis Blackwell's *(You're The) Apple Of My Eye*, which peaks at US #62. Despite an appearance on US TV's "Ed Sullivan Show" and several follow-ups, The Four Lovers' career goes no further.

1959 Under the name Frank Tyler, Valli releases solo *I Go Ape* (written by Bob Crewe and Frank Slay), on Okeh. Gaudio (b. Nov.17, 1942, the Bronx, New York, NY), formerly of *Short Shorts* hitmakers The Royal Teens, joins the group in place of Nick DeVito, and the name changes again, to Frank Valle & The Romans, for *Come Si Bella* on Cindy label.

1960 Massi (b. Nicholas Macioci, Sept.19, 1935, Newark), ex-local group Hugh Garrity & The Hollywood Playboys, replaces Majewski. Group teams with independent New York producer Bob Crewe, acting as his session vocal group for 2 years on productions released under such names as The Village Voices (*Redlips*) and Billy Dixon & The Topics (*I Am All Alone*) on Crewe's Topix label.

1961 Gaudio, whose developing talent as a songwriter is giving the group a solid (if as yet hit-less) repertoire of original material, records keyboard instrumental *10 Million Tears*, as Turner Di Centri. (He plays a stand-up electronic organ with the group on stage.)

1962 **Jan** Group guests on back-up vocals on Danny & The Juniors' collaboration with Freddy Cannon *Twistin' All Night Long*, which peaks at US #68.

Feb Crewe leases the group's recording of a Bell Sisters oldie, *Bermuda*, to George Goldner's Gone label, which releases it as by The Four Seasons (the name of a top New York restaurant opposite Goldner's office, and also – according to Gaudio – of a bowling alley at which the group almost got a lounge residency).

July Band spends the summer performing at Martell's Sea Breeze in Point Pleasant Beach. Crewe and arranger Charles Calello, meanwhile, analyze the gimmicks behind major recent hits and decide to incorporate as many as possible in next Four Seasons recording. Gaudio offers his recently-penned ballad *Sherry* (written in 15 mins.).

Aug Gimmick-laden *Sherry* is released, featuring prominent piercing falsetto end of Valli's 3-octave tenor range (the group is billed as The Four Seasons featuring the "sound" of Frankie Valli on most albums). Crewe almost puts disk on Perry, a label in which he has an interest, but leases it to Vee-Jay in Chicago when Randy Wood shows interest. The day after the group appears singing it on Dick Clark's "American Bandstand" on TV, Vee-Jay gets orders for 180,000 copies.

Sept *Sherry* hits US #1 in just 4 weeks, and stays on top for 5. It sells 2 million copies in US and tops R&B chart for a week.

Nov *Big Girls Don't Cry*, a similar commercial blend jointly penned by Crewe and Gaudio, also tops US chart for 5 weeks (and R&B chart for

4), and is a second million-plus seller. *Sherry*, meanwhile, hits UK #8.

Dec Debut album *Sherry And 11 Others*, including the 2 #1 singles, plus an update of The Four Lovers' *Apple Of My Eyes*, several oldies like *Peanuts*, *La Dee Dah*, *Teardrops* and *Oh Carol*, hits US #6. Seasonal collection (of carols and secular Christmas songs) *The Four Seasons Greetings* is also released, and extracted from it, a *Sherry*-styled revival of *Santa Claus Is Coming To Town*, reaches US #23.

[9] Band appears on US TV's "Ed Sullivan Show".

1963 Feb *Big Girls Don't Cry* reaches UK #13.

Mar *Walk Like A Man* tops US chart for 3 weeks, the group's third million-seller. (When this completes its #1 run, The Four Seasons have been at US #1 for 13 of the preceding 27 weeks.)

[2] Band guests in Chubby Checker's "Limbo Party" show at the Cow Palace, San Francisco, CA, with Marvin Gaye, The Crystals and others.

Apr *Walk Like A Man* reaches UK #12, while *Big Girls Don't Cry And Twelve Others*, a collection mainly of vocal group oldies like *Sincerely*, *Silhouettes* and *Goodnight My Love*, hits US #8.

May A revival of Fats Domino's *Ain't That A Shame* reaches US #22. A lot of airplay is stolen by its Crewe/Gaudio-penned ballad B-side, *Soon (I'll Be Home Again)*, which peaks at US #77.

July *Ain't That A Shame* makes UK #38, while *Sherry And 11 Others* reaches UK #20.

Aug *Ain't That A Shame And 11 Others*, a mixture of new songs and more vocal group revivals, makes US #47. Taken from it, *Candy Girl*, written by Larry Santos, hits US #3, while B-side, Gaudio's *Sherry*-like *Marlena*, makes US #36.

Oct Compilation *Golden Hits Of The Four Seasons* climbs to US #15. From previous album, Latin-styled Gaudio/Calello *New Mexican Rose* makes US #36 while B-side *That's The Only Way* peaks at US #88.

Dec Crewe and the group are at loggerheads with Vee-Jay, mainly over alleged non-payment of royalties. (Vee-Jay is a victim of its successful marketing of the group, selling millions of records with the costs this incurs, then suffering cashflow problems waiting for distributors' payments.) Group threatens to withhold future products.

1964 Feb Crewe and the group sign new deal with another Chicago-based label, Mercury, for release on Philips subsidiary. *Dawn (Go Away)*, written by Gaudio with Sandy Linzer, hits US #3 (kept from the top by The Beatles' *I Want To Hold Your Hand* and *She Loves You*) and is another million-seller.

Mar *Born To Wander*, the group's first album on Philips, is a collection of quieter, mainly folk-influenced harmonic songs (mostly Gaudio originals) following current US folk "hootenanny" craze, and makes US #84. (It includes West Coast-styled death ballad *No Surfin' Today*, which moves them into the territory of their chief US competitors The Beach Boys, and Crewe/Gaudio's *Silence Is Golden*, later a worldwide hit for The Tremeloes.)

Apr Vee-Jay, retaining rights to earlier group recordings, issues a revival of Maurice Williams & The Zodiacs' *Stay* (from *Ain't That A Shame*, and also a current UK hit for The Hollies) which makes US #16. The Four Seasons' current and former labels match each other with single and album releases. *Dawn (Go Away) And 11 Other Great Songs* reaches US #25.

May *Ronnie*, a new Crewe/Gaudio song, hits US #6.

June *Stay And Other Great Hits*, a compilation of earlier tracks on Vee-Jay, makes US #100.

July *Rag Doll*, recorded in rush Sunday session in a Broadway basement studio, the day before a US tour, tops US chart for 2 weeks and is another million-seller. On Vee-Jay, a revival of The Shepherd Sisters' oldie *Alone* (taken from *Big Girls Don't Cry*) makes US #28.

Sept *Rag Doll* hits UK #2. In US, *Rag Doll* hits #7 and Vee-Jay compilation *More Golden Hits By The Four Seasons* reaches #105.

[5] It is reported that President Lyndon Johnson has invited the group to perform at the upcoming Democratic Party national convention.

Oct *Save It For Me*, a Crewe/Gaudio song from *Rag Doll* hits US #10, while *Sincerely*, another Vee-Jay reissue, makes US #75. Vee-Jay double album *The Beatles Vs. The Four Seasons*, repackages *Introducing The Beatles* and *Golden Hits Of The 4 Seasons* and makes US #142.

Nov *Big Man In Town* reaches US #20.

1965 Feb *Bye Bye Baby (Baby Goodbye)* reaches US #12 (it will be a UK #1 in 1975 for The Bay City Rollers).

Apr *Toy Soldier* makes US #64. This is fourth Four Seasons single in a row not to be a UK hit, despite success of *Rag Doll*.

May *The 4 Seasons Entertain You*, including the recent hits, reaches US #77. Massi leaves the group, replaced temporarily by their arranger Charlie Calello, before Joe Long (b. Sept.5, 1941) joins.

Aug *Girl Come Running* reaches US #30.

Dec An adaptation of the group's sound to incorporate a brassy, Motown-like dance beat on the ultra-commercial Sandy Linzer/Denny Randell/Crewe song *Let's Hang On* hits US #3 and is group's first million-seller since *Rag Doll*. A novelty falsetto version of Bob Dylan's *Don't Think Twice, It's Alright*, credited to The Wonder Who, reaches US #12. It soon transpires that this is The Four Seasons under a pseudonym. (Valli clowned with a "Rose Murphy" voice during recordings of some Dylan songs for album use, with a result so outrageous and commercial it was felt worthy of release – though not at the expense of *Let's Hang On*, hence the pseudonym.)

1966 Jan *Let's Hang On* hits UK #4. In US, *Little Boy (In Grown Up Clothes)* peaks at #60. This unheard track is on Vee-Jay, along with *On Stage With The Four Seasons*, as part of the legal settlement between Crewe and the group and Vee-Jay, which has concluded that the former were free to continue releasing records on Philips, but owed Vee-Jay an album in lieu. (Vee-Jay will be bankrupt within months and all recorded masters will revert to producer and group.) Philips' first compilation, *The Four Seasons' Gold Vault Of Hits* hits US #10 and earns a gold disk. *Big Hits By Burt Bacharach, Hal David And Bob Dylan*, a set of mainly straight covers of familiar songs plus The Wonder Who hit *Don't Think Twice*, makes US #106.

Feb Valli's first solo *(You're Gonna) Hurt Yourself* makes US #39. When this charts, the group has 3 simultaneous hits on the US singles chart under 3 different names.

Mar *Working My Way Back To You* (later revived by The Spinners) hits US #9 and makes UK #50, while album of the same title makes US #50.

June Classical adaptation *Opus 17 (Don't You Worry 'Bout Me)* reaches US #13 and UK #20.

July The Wonder Who's double A-side gimmick *On The Good Ship Lollipop/You're Nobody Till Somebody Loves You* stalls at US #87/#96.

Oct A new arrangement of Cole Porter standard *I've Got You Under My Skin*, with inventive use of strings, hits US #9 and reaches UK #12.

Nov Valli's second solo *The Proud One* (later revived by The Osmonds) peaks at US #68.

1967 Jan Crewe and The Four Seasons acquire the early tracks from Vee-Jay, and they are repackaged into compilations *2nd Vault Of Golden Hits* (which also features the recent Philips successes) and *Lookin' Back* which reach US #22 and #107 respectively.

Feb *Tell It To The Rain*, by new Petrillo/Cifelli writing team, hits US #10 and makes UK #37.

May *Beggin'* reaches US #16. (It fails to chart in UK, but will later be a minor UK hit for Timebox.)

July Compilation *New Gold Hits* reaches US #37. Included on it is *C'mon Marianne* which hits US #9 (later revived by Donny Osmond) and The Wonder Who's *Lonesome Road* which stalls at US #89. In another triple chart representation, Valli enjoys his biggest solo hit so far, a million-seller with *Can't Take My Eyes Off You*, which hits US #2. (Andy Williams' cover will take UK honors.)

Sept Valli's *I Make A Fool Of Myself* reaches US #18.

Nov Mildly psychedelic *Watch The Flowers Grow* reaches US #30.

1968 Feb Valli's *To Give (The Reason I Live)* reaches US #29.

Mar Revival of The Shirelles' *Will You Love Me Tomorrow* makes US #24.

1969 Jan After a lengthy period with no Four Seasons disks on US chart (their *Saturday's Father* in mid-1968 having flopped), *Electric Stories* peaks at US #61.

Feb Double compilation album *Edizione D'Oro (The Four Seasons Gold Edition – 29 Gold Hits)* reaches US #37 and earns a gold disk.

Mar Group's concept album *The Genuine Imitation Life Gazette*, a lyrically serious work on sociological themes, makes US #85. Both sides of the single from it, *Something's On Her Mind/Idaho* chart briefly at US #98/#95. Gaudio pacts with CBS/Columbia Records for his own Gazette label. Its first release is Lock Stock & Barrel's *Happy People*.

July Valli's *The Girl I'll Never Know (Angels Never Fly This Low)* peaks at US #52.

Oct Group's *And That Reminds Me (My Heart Reminds Me)*, a revival of an old Della Reese number, is released on Crewe label while contract renegotiations are proceeding with Philips. It makes US #45.

1970 Apr Gaudio and Jake Holmes (who co-operated on *Imitation Life*) write and produce concept album *Watertown* for Frank Sinatra.

May *Patch Of Blue* stalls at US #94. It is the first chart single to bear the credit Frankie Valli & The Four Seasons (and will be their last to make the US chart for 5 years).

June *Half And Half*, 10 tracks split evenly between Valli solos and The Four Seasons songs, peaks at US #190. (It marks the end of the group's period with Philips.)

1971 Jan DeVito retires because of hearing difficulties, temporarily replaced by Bob Grimm. Drummer Gary Wolfe also joins. (Group has never until now used a full-time drummer on stage.) New line-up begins the group's first UK tour for 7 years.

Feb *You're Ready Now*, a 1966 track by Valli which failed, is reissued in UK after Northern dancefloor success and reaches #11.

Apr Double compilation album *Edizione D'Oro* reaches UK #11.

Sept *Whatever You Say*, a Gaudio song recorded in London in a one-off deal with UK Warner Bros., is released.

Nov UK compilation *The Big Ones* reaches UK #37. Grimm and Wolfe leave and are replaced by bassist/vocalist Demetri Callas and Paul Wilson. Keyboards player Al Ruzicka also joins.

1972 **Jan** The Four Seasons sign to Motown Records subsidiary Mowest, but only *Chameleon* and a few singles are released, none of which charts. Gaudio gives up performing to concentrate on writing and production; he is first replaced by Clay Jordan, a Motown session man, and then by Billy De Loash.

1973 Moving to Motown, The Four Seasons release 2 movie singles: *How Come* (from "Tom Sawyer") and *Scalawag Song* (from "Scalawag"). The Motown deal ends with no chart success.

1975 **Mar** Valli and Gaudio lease Valli's solo of Bob Crewe/Kenny Nolan-penned ballad *My Eyes Adore You*, which was recorded for Motown but since bought from the label, to Private Stock Records. It tops US chart for a week, becoming a million-seller, and hits UK #5.

May Motown in UK reissues *The Night*, which was unsuccessful in 1972, but has since become in demand in discos. It hits UK #7. Valli's disco-flavored *Swearin' To God* hits US #6. Gaudio recruits a new Four Seasons around Valli: John Paiva (guitar), Lee Shapiro (keyboards), ex-Critters lead singer Don Ciccone (bass) and Gerry Polci (drums and vocals), and starts writing new material with girlfriend Judy Parker. He secures a deal with Warner-Curb Records.

Oct *Who Loves You* hits UK #6.

Nov *Who Loves You* hits US #3. Valli's revival of Ruby & The Romantics' *Our Day Will Come*, produced by Hank Medress and Dave Appell, reaches US #11.

Dec *Who Loves You* reaches US #38.

1976 **Jan** Double album *The Four Seasons Story*, a best-of compilation on Private Stock, makes US #51.

Feb From *Who Loves You*, Gaudio and Parker's *December '63 (Oh, What A Night)*, (originally written about prohibition, as *December '33*), featuring Valli and Polci sharing lead vocals, tops UK chart for 2 weeks.

Mar *December '63 (Oh, What A Night)* tops US chart for 3 weeks and, after many years, is another million-seller. *Who Loves You* makes UK #12, while double compilation *The Four Seasons Story*, on Private Stock, reaches UK #20.

Apr [3] Group embarks on 11-date UK tour at the Winter Gardens, Bournemouth, Dorset, ending at Batley Variety club, W.Yorks.

May Gerry Polci-sung *Silver Star* hits UK #3 and US #38, while Valli's *Fallen Angel* makes US #36 and UK #ll.

Aug Valli's *We're All Alone* (written by Boz Scaggs) peaks at US #78.

Nov UK TV-advertised compilation *Greatest Hits*, on K-Tel, hits UK #4.

Dec *We Can Work It Out*, from Lou Reizner's *All This And World War II* album (and film documentary), makes UK #34.

1977 **May** *Helicon* peaks at US #168.

June *Rhapsody* makes UK #37.

Aug *Down The Hall* peaks at US #65 and UK #34.

Sept Valli announces he is leaving The Four Seasons to pursue a wholly MOR-oriented career. (During their years together, The Four Seasons have sold more than 85 million records and had more chart disks than any other US group.)

1978 **Aug** Valli tops US chart for 2 weeks with Barry Gibb's title song from the movie "Grease". It is his all-time biggest solo, earning a platinum disk for 2 million US sales. It hits UK #3.

1979 **Feb** Valli's *Fancy Dancer*, produced by Gaudio, stalls at US #77.

1980 Valli has 3 ear operations to cure a problem brought on by otosclerosis, a rare disease which had rendered him deaf.

Aug Valli's Where Did We Do Wrong, a duet with Chris Forde, peaks at US #90.

Dec The Four Seasons' Spend The Night In Love stalls at US #91.

1984 Valli and The Four Seasons team with The Beach Boys on the appropriately titled single East Meets West for FBI Records.

1985 **Sept** Valli and The Four Seasons are reunited on Curb/MCA album Streetfighter, which involves many old collaborators including Calello, Linzer and Gaudio (who produces).

1988 May The Collection makes UK #38.

Oct After a successful summer US tour, Valli and The Four Seasons return to UK charts with a Ben Leibrand re-mix of *December '63 (Oh,*

What A Night) and *Big Girls Don't Cry* featured on the soundtrack of "Dirty Dancing II". (Valli will continue to tour US with a variety of Four Seasons backing him, and also pursue a movie career, appearing in "Eternity" and "Modern Love".)

THE FOUR TOPS

Levi Stubbs (lead vocals)
Renaldo "Obie" Benson (vocals)
Abdul "Duke" Fakir (vocals)
Lawrence Payton (vocals)

1953 Benson (b. Detroit, MI), Fakir (b. Dec.26, 1935, Detroit), Payton (b. Detroit) and Stubbs (b. Levi Stubbles, Detroit) are asked to sing together at a friend's birthday party in Detroit. The combination works so well that they meet to repeat it at Fakir's house the next day and form The Four Aims. They begin singing at high school graduation parties, church and school functions, and local one-nighters.

1954 After several auditions they are accepted by a talent agency which books them first into small clubs in Detroit, then further afield, beginning with a week at the Ebony Lounge, Cleveland, OH, which earns $300, having made their first public appearance in Flint, MI.

1956 As The Four Aims, the group sings back-up or opens for such acts as Brook Benton, Count Basie, Della Reese and Billy Eckstine. The name is changed to The Four Tops (at the suggestion of their musical conductor) to avoid confusion with The Ames Brothers. Stubbles has also shortened his name to Stubbs.

May They record *Kiss Me Baby/Could It Be You*, for Chess in Chicago, but it fails to attract attention so they decide to concentrate on their club act, polishing dance routines and vocal arrangements.

1958 They begin tour through US with the Larry Stelle Revue, through 1959. Another one-off record for the Red Top label also fails.

1960 **Sept** Signed by John Hammond to Columbia, the group stays only long enough to release *Ain't That Love*, another poor seller.

1962 Group tours with Billy Eckstine's revue, frequently working in Las Vegas. They release a version of the standard *Where Are You?*, which is also a current hit for Dinah Washington, on Riverside label.

1963 **Mar** Group meets Berry Gordy Jr., head of fast-growing Motown Records in Detroit, and signs to his label for an advance of $400. The first recordings are jazz-oriented and Gordy plans to put the group on the specialist Workshop label. They spend the rest of the year singing back-up on other Motown artists' records, including The Supremes' first Top 30 hit *When The Lovelight Starts Shining Through His Eyes*.

1964 The Four Tops are singing at Detroit's 20 Grand club when Motown producers Holland, Dozier and Holland, call them to the studio after their performance. Eddie Holland sings them a song he thinks will suit them, and through the small hours they record *Baby I Need Your Loving*

Oct *Baby I Need Your Loving* hits US #11. (Mersey group The Fourmost make UK #24 with their cover.)

Dec *Without The One You Love* peaks at US #43.

1965 **Feb** Ballad *Ask The Lonely* reaches US #24.

Apr Debut album *Four Tops* climbs to US #63.

May [21] During a UK promotion trip, band appears on "Ready Steady Goes Live!".

June Holland/Dozier/Holland's *I Can't Help Myself* tops US chart for weeks, and R&B chart for 9 (deposing on both another Motown/H/D/H production, The Supremes' *Back In My Arms Again*) and is the group's first million-seller.

July *I Can't Help Myself* is the first UK Four Tops hit (reaching #23), and the group begins a sell-out club tour of UK and Europe, with the UK leg arranged by The Beatles manager, Brian Epstein.

Aug Speedy Motown follow-up *It's The Same Old Song* is recorded on Thursday, in shops by the next Monday, and hits US #5. Columbia reissues *Ain't The Love*, which peaks at US #93.

Sept *It's The Same Old Song* reaches UK #34.

Dec *The Four Tops' Second Album* climbs to US #20, while *Something About You* reaches US #19.

1966 **Apr** *Shake Me, Wake Me (When It's Over)* makes US #18.

June Slower-paced *Loving You Is Sweeter Than Ever* peaks at US #45.

Sept *Four Tops On Top* reaches US #32, while in UK *Loving You Is Sweeter Than Ever* makes #21.

Oct Revolutionary *Reach Out I'll Be There*, with an unorthodox instrumental blend of flutes, oboes and arab drums, tops US chart for 2 weeks and is the group's second million-seller. Within 2 weeks, it is also at UK #1 (for 3 weeks) and seals the group's worldwide success.

Nov [13] Group plays only UK appearance of the year at the Saville theater, London.

Dec *Four Tops On Top* is their first UK album success, hitting #9.

1967
Jan Live album *Four Tops Live!*, recorded at The Roosertail in Detroit, and containing versions of songs like *If I Had A Hammer* and *Climb Every Mountain*, displays the group's more MOR side. It reaches US #17, while *Standing In The Shadows Of Love*, a highly-commercial near-clone of *Reach Out*, hits #6 in both US and UK.
[28] Group embarks on 9-date twice-nightly UK tour, with The Merseys, The Dakotas, Madeleine Bell, The Remo Four and The Johnny Watson Band, at London's Royal Albert Hall. The tour will end Feb.5 at the De Montfort Hall, Leicester, after which the band will visit Italy, France, Germany and Spain for TV appearances.
Mar *Four Tops Live!* hits UK #4 (and will be a consistent seller, remaining on chart for 72 weeks).
[9] A Four Tops TV spectacular airs on BBC2.
Apr *Bernadette* hits US #4 and UK #8, becoming another million-seller.
May Another cabaret-styled album, *Four Tops On Broadway*, containing mainly show tunes, reaches US #79.
June *Seven Rooms Of Gloom* reaches US #14 and UK #12, while B-side *I'll Turn To Stone* makes US #76.
Sept *Four Tops Reach Out* makes US #11.
Oct *You Keep Running Away* reaches US #19 and UK #26. (Holland, Dozier and Holland leave Motown over royalty disputes and the group will be supervised by other Motown house producers like Frank Wilson, Smokey Robinson, Ivy Hunter and Johnny Bristol.)
Nov *The Four Tops Greatest Hits*, a compilation of singles, hits US #4.

1968
Jan A revival of The Left Banke's 1966 hit *Walk Away Renée*, taken from *The Four Tops Reach Out*, hits UK #3. The album hits UK #4.
Feb [10] Compilation album *Greatest Hits* tops UK chart for a week. The Tops are the first black act to achieve this distinction (stablemates The Supremes' repeat it a week later).
Mar Following its UK success, *Walk Away Renée* is extracted as a US single and reaches #14.
Apr Another album extract, the group's version of Tim Hardin's *If I Were A Carpenter* (a 1966 hit for Bobby Darin), hits UK #7.
June *If I Were A Carpenter* makes US #20.
Sept *Yesterday's Dreams* climbs to US #49 and UK #23.
Oct *Yesterday's Dreams* reaches US #93, while *I'm In A Different World* (a belatedly-released Holland/Dozier/Holland song/production) makes US #51.
Dec *I'm In A Different World* climbs to UK #27.

1969
Feb *Yesterday's Dreams* reaches US #37.
June *What Is A Man* makes US #53 and UK #16.
July *Four Tops Now!* climbs to US #74.
Oct Jim Webb-penned *Do What You Gotta Do* reaches UK #11.
Dec *Don't Let Him Take Your Love From Me* makes US #54, while *Soul Spin* reaches US #163.

1970
Apr *I Can't Help Myself* is reissued in UK and hits #10.
May [24] Currently on UK tour, during which Stubbs stands trial for a drugs offense, they perform at the Fairfield Hall, Croydon, London.
June A revival of much-recorded *It's All In The Game* makes US #24 and hits UK #5. *Still Waters Run Deep* reaches US #21 and UK #29.
Oct Taken from the album, mellow-grooving *Still Water (Love)*, produced by Frank Wilson, reaches US #11 and hits UK #10.
Nov *Changing Times* makes US #109. The Four Tops team with The Supremes for *The Magnificent 7*, which makes US #113.

1971
Jan The Four Tops and The Supremes' duetted version of *River Deep, Mountain High* peaks at US #14.
Feb *Just Seven Numbers (Can Straighten Out My Life)* makes US #40.
Apr Benson's collaboration with Al Cleveland and Marvin Gaye, *What's Going On*, hits US #2, for Gaye.
May *Just Seven Numbers* makes UK #36.
[29] *The Magnificent 7* enters UK chart, set to hit UK #6.
June Another teaming with The Supremes on *You Gotta Have Love In Your Heart* makes US #55. *River Deep, Mountain High* reaches UK #11.
July *In These Changing Times* peaks at US #70, and a further collaboration with The Supremes on *The Return Of The Magnificent Seven* reaches US #154.
Oct Group's revival of Webb's *MacArthur Park* makes US #38.
[22] Band embarks on UK tour at Regal theater, Edmonton, London, to include a week-long residency at the Fiesta club, Sheffield, S.Yorks.
Nov The Four Tops record a dynamic version of a Moody Blues' B-side *A Simple Game*, with The Moody Blues' producer Tony Clarke, who interested the group in the song when he gave them a demo during a UK tour. Among the backing musicians on the track (and another Moody Blues song *So Deep Within You* cut at the same time), are uncredited Moody Blues members. It is the biggest UK Four Tops hit

(at #3) since *Walk Away Renée*. Compilation album *Greatest Hits Vol. 2* reaches US #106 and UK #25. From it, the duet with The Supremes, *You Gotta Have Love In Your Heart*, reaches UK #25.

1972
Jan Third Four Tops/Supremes collaboration album, *Dynamite*, climbs to US #160.
Feb *A Simple Game* makes only US #90.
Apr UK reissue, *Bernadette* reaches US #23.
June *Nature Planned* makes US #50. Gordy moves Motown's base from Detroit to Hollywood. The Four Tops decide not to move with the company. They are negotiating with Dunhill when the label's writer/producers Dennis Lambert and Brian Potter walk in with demos of 2 songs composed with The Four Tops in mind, *Keeper Of The Castle* and *Ain't No Woman*. The quality of these prompts the group to sign to Dunhill.
July *In These Changing Times* peaks at US #70.
Aug *Walk With Me Talk With Me Darling* makes UK #32.
Oct *(It's The Way) Nature Planned It* reaches US #53.
Dec Debut Dunhill label album *Keeper Of The Castle* climbs to US #33.

1973
Jan *Keeper Of The Castle*, the group's first single for Dunhill, hits US #10 and makes UK #18 (on Probe).
Apr *Ain't No Woman (Like The One I've Got)* hits US #4 and earns a gold disk for millon-plus sales.
May Motown album *The Best Of The Four Tops* peaks at US #103.
Aug *Are You Man Enough*, taken from the soundtrack of film "Shaft In Africa", hits US #15.
Oct Second Dunhill album *Main Street People* makes US #66.
Nov *Sweet Understanding Love* peaks at US #33 and UK #29. Motown's UK double compilation album *The Four Tops Story, 1964-72*, makes UK #35 (the last UK chart entry in the 70s).

1974
Feb *I Just Can't Get You Out Of My Mind* reaches US #62.
May *Meeting Of The Minds* peaks at US #118.
June *One Chain Don't Make No Prison* reaches US #41.
Sept *Midnight Flower* climbs to US #55.
Nov Live album *Live And In Concert* peaks at US #92.

1975
May *Seven Lonely Nights*, the first release on ABC (which absorbed its Dunhill subsidiary) peaks at US #71.
June *Night Lights Harmony* peaks at US #148.
Dec *We All Gotta Stick Together* charts at US #97 for 1 week.

1976
Nov *Catfish* peaks at US #71 (the group's last hit with ABC/Dunhill). The album of same title reaches US #124.

1978
Apr The Four Tops perform Stevie Wonder's *Isn't She Lovely* at Aretha Franklin's wedding.

1981
Nov Group stages a comeback on a new label, disco-oriented Casablanca Records.
[7] First single for the label, *When She Was My Girl*, reaches US #11.
[14] *When She Was My Girl* hits UK #3.
Dec *Tonight!*, on Casablanca, reaches US #37.

1982
Jan [30] *Don't Walk Away*, taken from the album, reaches UK #16.
Mar [13] Ballad *Tonight I'm Gonna Love You All Over*, third single from *Tonight!*, reaches UK #43.
[27] UK TV-advertised K-Tel compilation album *The Best Of The Four Tops* reaches UK #13.
June [5] *Back To School Again*, from the soundtrack of movie "Grease 2", peaks at US #71.
[26] *Back To School Again* makes UK #62.
Aug *One More Mountain*, on Casablanca, is released to coincide with the group's first UK tour for some time but fails and they leave label.
Sept [4] *Sad Hearts*, the final release on Casablanca, peaks at US #84.

1983 The Four Tops return to Motown for the company's 25th anniversary NBC TV special, re-signing with Berry Gordy shortly after. The "Battle Of The Bands" with The Temptations during the special leads the 2 groups to tour together, initially in US and then internationally.
Nov *I Just Can't Walk Away*, on Motown, reaches US #71. *Back Where I Belong* is not a strong seller.

1985 **July** *Magic*, on Motown, reaches US #140.
1986 Stubbs provides the voice for the man-eating plant Audrey II in the film version of musical "The Little Shop Of Horrors".
July Stubbs is immortalized by UK singer Billy Bragg in *Levi Stubbs' Tears*, which makes UK #29.
Oct *Hot Nights* is the group's last of its second spell with Motown.

1987 **July** [29] Michigan State Governor, James Blanchard, declares an annual state-wide "Four Tops Day", honoring the group for its contribution to American music and its civic activities in Detroit.

1988 **Sept** The Four Tops sign to Arista Records, releasing *Indestructible* which makes US #149. It includes contributions from Phil Collins, Aretha Franklin, Kenny G, Huey Lewis and Narada Michael Walden.

THE FOUR TOPS cont.

Title track *Indestructible* makes US #35 and UK #55. Band contributes *Loco In Acapulco* to the soundtrack of Phil Collins movie "Buster".

1989 Jan *Loco In Acapulco* hits UK #7.

Feb [10] Group plays warm-up gig at London's Town & Country club before embarking on 12-date UK tour at Manchester's Apollo theater, set to end Feb.25 at the Colston Hall, Bristol, Avon.

Mar [3] The Four Tops return to US to perform at the 24th Rock & Roll Revival Spectacular with Sha Na Na, Jay Black & The Americans, and Tommy James & The Shondells at Madison Square Garden, New York.

May Band guests on labelmate Aretha Franklin's *Through The Storm*. Reissued *Indestructible* now peaks at UK #30.

1990 Jan [12-14] Group begins US tour with 3 dates in Atlantic City, NJ.

[17] Stevie Wonder inducts The Four Tops into the Rock'N'Roll Hall Of Fame at the fifth annual dinner at the Waldorf Astoria, New York. At the traditional after-dinner jam, the group sings *I Can't Help Myself*.

1991 Jan [12] *Their Greatest Hits*, a UK only Telstar TV-advertised collection, peaks at UK #47.

THE FOURMOST

Brian O'Hara (guitar, vocals)
Mike Millward (guitar, vocals)
Billy Hatton (bass)
Dave Lovelady (drums)

1958 O'Hara (b. Mar.12, 1942, Liverpool, Merseyside) and Hatton (b. June 9, 1941, Liverpool) are in a group with 2 friends while still at Bluecoat Grammar school, Liverpool. For 3 years, the quartet plays gigs on a part-time basis around Liverpool, as The Four Jays.

1961 Mar [1] The Four Jays, still amateurs, make their debut at Liverpool's Cavern club, 3 weeks before The Beatles' first performance there.

Nov Millward (b. May 9, 1942, Bromborough, Cheshire), an old friend of O'Hara and Hatton, moves to Liverpool to join the group when a guitar slot falls vacant.

1962 Sept Lovelady (b. Oct.16, 1942, Liverpool) replaces an earlier drummer, joining from another semi-professional band in Crosby, Liverpool. All 4 still have day jobs: O'Hara is an accountant's clerk, Millward, a solicitor's clerk, Hatton, an apprentice engineer and Lovelady, a student architect.

Nov Deciding to turn professional, and now with a stable line-up, the group changes its name to The Four Mosts.

1963 June Brian Epstein takes over the band's management, amends the name to The Fourmost, and signs it to EMI's Parlophone label.

July [3] Debut single *Hello Little Girl* is recorded at Abbey Road studios. It is an early Lennon/McCartney song which The Beatles have chosen not to record commercially. As in his launch of Billy J. Kramer, Epstein encourages full exploitation of this Beatles connection.

Oct [19] *Hello Little Girl* hits UK #9.

Dec [24] The Fourmost take part in "The Beatles Christmas Show", with Rolf Harris, The Barron Knights, Tommy Quickly, Billy J. Kramer & The Dakotas and Cilla Black, mixing music and pantomime, which opens at London's Finsbury Park Astoria. It runs until Jan.11.

1964 Jan [25] A second Lennon/McCartney song, the soft-rock ballad *I'm In Love*, reaches UK #17.

Apr [26] Group plays at the **New Musical Express** Poll Winners Concert at the Empire Pool, Wembley, London, with The Beatles, The Hollies, The Rolling Stones and a host of other major names.

May Band starts an 8-month residency, with stablemate Cilla Black and Frankie Vaughan and Tommy Cooper, in the "Startime Variety Show" at the London Palladium. (Their career will suffer by being locked into this contract, unable to tour UK.)

[23] *A Little Loving*, written by Russ Alquist, hits UK #6.

[24] A Pathé Pictorial film, in which they are featured singing *A Little Lovin'* in Dougie Millings' Soho tailor shop, goes on general release.

Aug [15] *How Can I Tell Her*, an upbeat Carter/Lewis song in unusual march time, makes UK #33.

Dec [12] "Startime Variety Show", at the London Palladium, ends.

1965 Jan [23] *Baby I Need Your Lovin'*, a cover of The Four Tops' first US hit, reaches UK #24 (causing some dissension between US Motown and EMI, since it inadvertantly breaks an agreement that EMI, as UK Motown distributor, will not release cover versions of the latter's singles). Group makes a cameo appearance in Gerry & The Pacemakers' film "Ferry Cross The Mersey", performing *I Love You Too*.

[29] Band begins 22-date twice-nightly UK tour, with Cilla Black, P.J. Proby, Tommy Roe, Tommy Quickly and Sounds Incorporated, at the ABC cinema, Croydon, London, ending Feb.21 at the Liverpool Empire.

Mar [1] Group begins 15-date twice-nightly UK tour of independent

theaters in "The P.J. Proby Show", with Proby and Brian Poole & The Tremeloes, at Finsbury Park Astoria, London. Tour ends Mar.16 at the Usher Hall, Edinburgh, Scotland.

July *Everything In The Garden* fails to chart, as the commercial appeal of the Merseybeat sound rapidly fades.

Sept Group's only album, *First And Fourmost*, with 14 tracks which are mostly covers of US rock and pop originals, is released.

[21] The Fourmost participate in the "Pop From Britain" concert at the Royal Albert Hall, London, with Cliff Bennett & The Rebel Rousers, Georgie Fame & The Blue Flames and The Moody Blues.

Dec *Girls Girls Girls*, a Leiber/Stoller song previously recorded by The Coasters and Elvis Presley, makes UK #33 – their final chart success. Millward is admitted to Clatterbridge hospital, Babbington, Cheshire, suffering from leukemia.

[13] Freddie Self, who has deputized before, fills in for Millward at a gig at the Savoy hotel, London.

[27] George Peckham becomes Millward's permanent replacement. (Bill Parkinson (b. Morecambe, Lancs.), will take his place for a time, before Peckham rejoins full-time.)

1966 Mar [7] Millward dies, aged 23, in Bromborough hospital, Cheshire.

May [1] Group plays on a bill topped by The Beatles and The Rolling Stones at the **New Musical Express** Poll Winners Concert at the Empire Pool, Wembley, London.

Aug *Here, There And Everywhere*, a cover of a track from The Beatles' album, *Revolver*, is released.

Nov Group's last Parlophone single is a revival of George Formby's *Auntie Maggie's Remedy*.

1967 July Now signed to CBS Records, The Fourmost release a cover of Jay & The Techniques' US hit *Apples, Peaches, Pumpkin Pie*. (2 further CBS singles, including *Rosetta*, produced by Paul McCartney, will follow. Group will move into musical/comedy cabaret in UK Northern clubs during the remainder of the 60s, before eventually disbanding.)

PETER FRAMPTON

1972 May Frampton (b. Apr.22, 1950, Beckenham, Kent), after leaving Humble Pie in Oct.1971, signs to A&M Records as a soloist and releases *Wind Of Change*, which features Ringo Starr, Billy Preston and other star session men.

Sept [16] Frampton makes his first stage performance in New York, supporting The J. Geils Band, with his own new band, Frampton's Camel: Mike Kellie (ex-Spooky Tooth) on drums, Mickey Gallagher (ex-Bell & Arc) on keyboards and Rick Wills (ex-Cochise) on bass, all 3 having just left Parrish & Gurvitz.

Oct *Wind Of Change* reaches US #177.

1973 May *Frampton's Camel* sees Kellie replaced by US drummer John Siomos, formerly with Mitch Ryder. The album does not chart in UK, and reaches only #110 in US.

1974 June After another UK non-chart album, but US #25, *Somethin's Happening* (on which "Camel" appendix is dropped), Gallagher leaves to join Glencoe and is replaced by former Herd member Andy Bown, who also doubles on bass when Wills leaves to play with Roxy Music.

1975 May *Frampton*, recorded with Siomos and Bown, sells well in US, reaching #32.

1976 Apr *Frampton Comes Alive!*, a double set recorded on stage at Winterland, San Francisco, CA, is released. With blanket US rock radio support it will become the most successful live album in rock history, eventually selling over 10 million copies. It initially tops US chart for a week and will return to US #1 in July (1 week), Aug. (3 weeks) and Sept./Oct. (5 weeks).

May *Show Me The Way*, taken from the album, hits US #6. It features a Frampton trademark sound: the "voicebox" guitar technique of forming words by channelling the sound through a mouthpiece.

June *Show Me The Way* hits UK #10.

[12] *Frampton Comes Alive!* hits UK #6.

Aug *Baby, I Love Your Way*, also from the live album, reaches US #12.

Sept *Baby, I Love Your Way* makes UK #43.

[8] Frampton spends the day at the White House at the invitation of President Ford, passing the time watching TV with Stephen Ford.

Nov *Do You Feel Like We Do* hits US #10 and makes UK #39.

1977 July A new studio recording, grandiose ballad *I'm In You*, and Frampton's biggest US hit single, hits US #2 for 3 weeks and makes UK #41 where it is his final chart single.

[16] *I'm In You* hits US #2 and reaches UK #19.

Oct A revival of Stevie Wonder's *Signed, Sealed, Delivered (I'm Yours)*, with Wonder guesting on harmonica, reaches US #18.

78 **Jan** *Tried To Love* makes US #41.
Apr [1] The Philadelphia Furies, a soccer team co-owned by Frampton, Mick Jagger, Paul Simon and Rick Wakeman, loses its first match of the North America Soccer League 3-0 to The Washington Diplomats.
June [29] Frampton suffers a broken arm and cracked ribs in a car crash in the Bahamas, which will put him out of action for months.
July Robert Stigwood's film "Sergeant Pepper's Lonely Hearts Club Band" is released, co-starring Frampton (as Billy Shears) and The Bee Gees. The film is a failure both critically and commercially.
Aug Soundtrack album from "Sergeant Pepper's Lonely Hearts Club Band" hits US #5 and UK #38.
79 **July** [21] *Where I Should Be* reaches US #19.
Extracted *I Can't Stand It No More* makes US #14, and is Frampton's last US hit single.
81 **July** The sleeve of *Breaking All The Rules* features new short-haired image, which fails to help him regain former glory, as the album reaches US #47.
82 **Sept** [18] *The Art Of Control* peaks at only US #174, and its poor sales prompt A&M and Frampton to split after more than a decade.
85 After a period of inactivity, Frampton signs to Virgin Records.
86 Synthesizer-laden *Premonition* is released on Virgin (UK)/Atlantic (US), and makes US #80.
Mar [1] *Lying* peaks at US #74.
87 He joins one-time schoolfriend David Bowie as guitarist for Bowie's world-wide "Glass Spider" tour.
88 **July** Increasingly inclined to session work, Frampton features on new Karla Bonoff album *New World*.
Dec [3] *Will To Power* tops US chart, reviving Frampton's *Baby I Love Your Way* and Lynyrd Skynyrd's *Freebird*, in a medley.
89 **Oct** *When All The Pieces Fit* makes US #152, after which Frampton will once again return to a period of inactivity.

CONNIE FRANCIS

55 Connie Francis (b. Concetta Rosa Maria Franconero, Dec.12, 1938, Newark, NJ), a child accordianist and a star turn at family gatherings and neighborhood shows, graduating to local television at age 10, having appeared on Arthur Godfrey's networked talent show (he suggests the name-change), divides her time between schooling and singing (4 years as a regular on NBC TV's "Star Time"). She signs at age 16 to MGM Records and makes demos singing soundalikes of Kay Starr and Jo Stafford while singing voice for Tuesday Weld in Alan Freed's film "Rock Rock Rock". Her first 9 singles fail to chart and she is about to enrol at New York University when her fortunes change.
57 **Nov** She makes her chart debut supporting country singer Marvin Rainwater on *The Majesty Of Love* – a 1 week hit at US #93 which becomes an accredited million-seller.
58 **Mar** To please her father, she uses the last 20 mins. of a session to record one of his favorite songs, *Who's Sorry Now*. Featured on the first broadcast of Dick Clark's "American Bandstand" and plugged on the program, it hits US #4, becoming a million-seller. In UK it hits #1 for 6 weeks, displacing Rainwater's *Whole Lotta Woman*.
June 1918 oldie, *I'm Sorry I Made You Cry*, makes US #36 and UK #11.
July *Heartaches/I Miss You So* misses the Hot 100. (No other Connie Francis single will miss US Top 50 until 1965.)
Sept *Stupid Cupid*, by Neil Sedaka (before his own hits) and Howard Greenfield, reaches US #17. Coupled with the 30-year-old Guy Lombardo standard *Carolina Moon*, it hits UK #1 for 6 weeks.
Nov Another Sedaka/Greenfield composition, *Fallin'* reaches US #30 and UK #20. The oldie B-side *I'll Get By* reaches US #19.
59 **Jan** A 1933 weeper, *My Happiness* hits US #2 and UK #4 to become another million-seller. Unreleased in US, *You Always Hurt The One You Love* (a 1944 smash for the Mills Brothers) hits UK #13.
Apr *If I Didn't Care*, a Jack Lawrence 30s standard, reaches US #22.
May Francis asks Sedaka and Greenfield to write a song called *Bobby* to celebrate her romance with Bobby Darin. Instead they give her a paean to Frankie Avalon, *Frankie*, which hits US #9. B-side *Lipstick On Your Collar* becomes one of her most memorable hits at US #5 and UK #3, and her third gold disk.
Sept *You're Gonna Miss Me* makes US #34, paired with her own composition *Plenty Good Lovin'*, which makes US #69 and UK #18.
Dec Francis personalizes a gloomy 1927 ballad, *Among My Souvenirs*. It makes US #7 and UK #11. Patriotic B-side, *God Bless America*, stirs only American hearts, reaches US #36 and is another million-seller.
60 **Mar** *Rock'N'Roll Million Sellers* makes UK #12 and *Valentino*,

unreleased in US, reaches UK #27.
Apr [2] Francis wins Best Selling Female Artist at first annual NARM awards. (She also wins the award in 1961 and 1962.)
Recorded in UK, *Mama*, a sentimental ballad learned from her grandmother and sung in Italian, hits US #8 and UK #2 to become her fifth gold disk. It features on her first US chart album, *Italian Favorites*, which hits #4, while *Connie's Greatest Hits* makes US #17. *Mama*'s B-side, *Teddy*, written by Paul Anka, reaches US #17.
May Written by Greenfield and his new partner Jack Keller, the countryish *Everybody's Somebody's Fool* hits US #1 and UK #5.
June B-side, another Italian song, *Jealous Of You*, hits US #19, becoming gold disk number 6. *Mama/Robot Man*, a UK-only release, hits #2.
Sept Same duo provides *My Heart Has A Mind Of Its Own*, which hits US #1, displacing Chubby Checker. (Francis becomes the first female singer ever to have consecutive #1s.) It hits UK #3 and earns another gold disk. The B-side *Malaguina* reaches US #42.
Dec Hitting US #7 and UK #12, Winfield Scott's bouncy *Many Tears Ago* brings her fourth million-seller of the year. B-side *Senza Mamma (With No One)* charts for 1 week at US #87. *More Italian Favorites* reaches US #9.
1961 **Feb** *Connie's Greatest Hits* climbs to UK #16. (It will be her last UK chart album for 16 years.)
Mar Francis hits US #4 and UK #5 with another Sedaka/Greenfield-penned million-seller, *Where The Boys Are*, also the title of her first MGM movie starring George Hamilton. B-side *No-One* reaches US #34.
May Greenfield/Keller's country-flavored *Breakin' In A Brand New Broken Heart* hits US #7 and UK #12. Live album *Connie At The Copa* reaches US #65. *Jewish Favorites* makes US #69 for the convent educated girl.
Aug Reverting to oldies, she releases a 1928 song, *Together*. It hits #6 in US and UK and is gold disk number 10. B-side, *Too Many Rules*, also charts at US #72. *More Greatest Hits* climbs to US #39.
Oct Double-sided *(He's My) Dreamboat/Hollywood* reaches US #14/#42 but fails in UK. *Never On Sunday*, a collection of movie themes, her fourth hit album of the year, reaches US #11.
Dec Double-sided *When The Boy In Your Arms (Is The Boy In Your Heart)/Baby's First Christmas* hits US #10/#26. Only *Baby's First Christmas* charts in UK at #30. (Cliff Richard has already hit UK #3 with a male version of the A-side.)
1962 **Feb** *Don't Break The Heart That Loves You* is her third US #1 but reaches only UK #39.
Apr *Do The Twist* reaches US #47.
June *Second Hand Love* (co-written by Phil Spector) hits US #7 but fails in UK.
[30] She records 4 tracks for movie "Follow The Boys" in London with Norman Newell, Geoff Love and Ron Goodwin.
Aug Containing 5 of her recent Top 10 hits, *Connie Francis Sings* reaches only US #111.
Sept Co-written by Francis, *Vacation* hits US #9 and UK #10. (It will be her last significant UK hit.) Francis' book *For Every Young Heart* is published in US by Prentice Hall.
Oct *I Was Such A Fool (To Fall In Love With You)/He Still Thinks I Care* reaches US #24/#57. B-side, taken from her US #22 album *Country Music Connie Style*, was originally a George Jones C&W item.
1963 **Jan** *I'm Gonna Be Warm This Winter* reaches US #18 but only UK #48. B-side, *Al Di La*, reaches US #90.
Francis maintains her US popularity, reaching the Top 50 with 5 singles: *Follow The Boys* (the title song from her second movie – #17), *If My Pillow Could Talk* (#23), *Drownin' My Sorrows* (#36), *Your Other Love* (#28) and the President Kennedy tribute *In The Summer Of His Years* (#46). Chart albums include: *Modern Italian Hits* (#103), *Follow The Boys* (#66), *Award Winning Motion Picture Hits* (#108), *Great American Waltzes* (#94), *Big Hits From Italy* (#70) and *The Very Best Of Connie Francis* (#68).
1964 Francis places 4 hit singles: *Blue Winter* (#24), *Be Anything (But Be Mine)* (#25), *Looking For Love* (the theme song from her third movie – #45) and *Don't Ever Leave* (#42). Albums are: *In The Summer Of His Years* (#126), *Looking For Love* (#122) and *A New Kind Of Connie* (#149).
Apr Francis begins a round-the-world tour in Hawaii.
1965 **May** She makes her 25th appearance on CBS TV's "Ed Sullivan Show", believed to be a record.
[20] She arrives in UK for TV and radio dates, including "Ready Steady Goes Live!", "The Eamonn Andrews Show" and "Thank Your Lucky Stars".
[21] Francis begins work on new album at Pye's London studios with

musical director Johnny Gregory and recording manager MGM's A&R chief Danny Davis.

June *My Child* reaches UK #26.

6 singles miss US Top 40 but all make Top 80. *Connie Francis Sings For Mama* reaches US #78.

1966 **Jan** *Jealous Heart* reaches UK #44. *When The Boy Meets The Girls* makes US #61 and is also the title of her fourth and last movie in which she co-stars with Harve Presnell.

1969 *The Wedding Cake* becomes her US chart swan song at #91, but Francis continues to headline on the night club/cabaret circuit, taking time out for charity shows and entertaining troops in Vietnam.

1972 **Sept** She sings for President Lyndon Johnson at the White House.

1974 **Nov** [8] After an appearance at the Westbury Music Fair in New York, Francis is attacked at knifepoint and raped in a second floor room at Howard Johnson's Motel. Emotionally shattered, she retreats from public view. (She will be awarded $3 million in damages.)

1977 **June** *20 All Time Greats* hits UK #1 and earns a platinum disk.

1978 **Sept** Francis appears on Dick Clark's "Live Wednesday" TV show singing a medley of her hits.

1981 **Nov** Only recently recovered from her brother's gangland-style death, Francis returns to the concert stage for the first time in 7 years.

1984 **Sept** After some 70 singles and 60 albums, Francis titles her autobiography **Who's Sorry Now**, after her first hit.

1988 Recently released from a mental home, Francis performs in Hollywood, CA and Las Vegas, NV.

1989 In an unlikely collusion, Francis records *Something Stupid* with Boy George.

FRANKIE GOES TO HOLLYWOOD

"Holly" Johnson (vocals)
Paul Rutherford (vocals)
Brian "Nasher" Nash (guitar)
Peter "Ged" Gill (drums)
Mark O'Toole (bass)

1980 **Aug** The 5 members of the band come together and play their first gig, as support to Hambi & The Dance. Johnson (b. William Johnson, Feb.19, 1960, Khartoum, Sudan) has been with Big In Japan, appearing on their eponymous single and their EP *From Y To Z And Never Again*, leaving to go solo and releasing singles *Yankee Rose* on Eric's Records and *Hobo Joe* before forming band Hollycaust. Rutherford (b. Dec.8, 1959, Liverpool, Merseyside) has been with The Spitfire Boys, singing on their only single *Mein Kampf* and briefly with The Opium Eaters, before moving to live temporarily in US. O'Toole (b. Jan.6, 1964, Liverpool) has been playing in local groups, while his cousin Nash (b. May 20, 1963, Liverpool) has played with Dancing Girl and then Sons Of Egypt with Gill (b. Mar.8, 1964, Liverpool).

Sept Band changes name to Frankie Goes To Hollywood taking inspiration from a headline about Frank Sinatra's move into films.

1982 **Nov** They make their national debut on UK radio with a live session for DJ David "Kid" Jensen. Their TV first is an appearance on Channel 4's "The Tube", including a rough video version of their track *Relax*. Their performance attracts record company interest, particularly from "The Tube" theme composer and noted producer Trevor Horn.

1983 **Nov** *Relax* is released as the first single on the Zang Tumb Tumm label, produced by company co-owner Horn. The B-side is a cover of fellow Merseyside act Gerry & The Pacemakers' *Ferry Cross The Mersey*. "Relax" and "Frankie Says ..." T-shirts, the idea of journalist Paul Morley, start to appear. The initial video is banned by UK TV and a second version is filmed.

1984 **Jan** [13] Radio 1 announces a ban on *Relax*, after a one-man campaign against the record by DJ Mike Read, who calls it "obscene", as the rest of the BBC, both radio and TV, follow.

[28] *Relax* tops UK chart, after a 10-week climb. BBC's "Top Of The Pops" is unable to feature the disk while it is still banned.

Mar Sales of *Relax* reach 1 million, spurred by the ban and the myriad releases and 7 remixes of the single on 7", 12", picture disk and "cassingle". It hits US #10 (and will be featured in US movie "Police Academy").

June With much media and public anticipation, the Horn-produced follow-up, *Two Tribes*, enters at UK #1. It goes silver in 2 days and gold in 7. Frankie Goes To Hollywood becomes the first band to achieve this with its second release. BBC Radio 1 receives the airplay premiere. The record intros includes an impersonation of Ronald Reagan by UK mimic Chris Barrie. A video directed by Godley & Creme features Reagan and Chernenko lookalikes wrestling and keeps sales alive. The record stays at #1 for 9 weeks, and sells 1 million in UK. (Group is the only act to have platinum singles with first 2 releases.)

Relax returns to the chart where it eventually re-hits at UK #2, with *Two Tribes* still at UK #1.

Nov [10] Double album **Welcome To The Pleasure Dome** enters UK chart at #1, with the UK's biggest album ship-out to date. (It will be their only album produced by Horn.)

Dec [8] Festive ballad *The Power Of Love* hits UK #1, with the help of Godley & Creme nativity video, and Frankie Goes To Hollywood becomes the first band since Gerry & The Pacemakers to have a UK #1 with its first 3 singles. In typical ZTT promotion, the pre-release poster for the single have proclaimed: "*The Power Of Love* – Frankie Goes To Hollywood's third number one."

Welcome To The Pleasure Dome reaches US #33.

1985 **Feb** *Welcome To The Pleasure Dome* hits UK #2.

[11] Group wins Best British Newcomer, *Relax* wins Best British Single and Trevor Horn wins Best British Producer at the fourth annual BRIT Awards at the Grosvenor House, London.

Mar [12] Band begins a 3-week tour, opening at RDS Simmons Court Dublin, and covering UK.

[13] *Two Tribes* wins Best Contemporary Song at the annual Ivor Novello Awards at London's Grosvenor House.

Apr [9] A major tour of Europe opens in Copenhagen, Denmark, and the group has to spend the rest of 1985 exiled from UK for tax reasons.

Nov Recording begins in Amsterdam for a new album.

1986 **May** Band appears at Montreux Rock Festival and destroys its equipment in front of a later TV audience of 20 million.

Aug *Rage Hard*, from the forthcoming album, hits UK #4.

Nov *Liverpool*, costing over twice as much to record as double album *Welcome To The Pleasure Dome*, hits UK #5. *Liverpool* makes US #88.

Dec *Warriors Of The Wasteland* reaches UK #19.

1987 **Jan** [11] Group begins what will be a final tour at Manchester's Grand Metropolitan center.

Mar *Watching The Wildlife* reaches UK #28. Condoms are given away free as a promotional gimmick. Group's last public appearance is on Channel TV's "Saturday Live", after which a split is announced, and then denied.

Apr Johnson appears solo at an AIDS benefit concert in London. Band's break-up is finally made official.

July Johnson signs a solo deal with MCA in UK, which supports him during forthcoming litigation.

Aug ZTT serves an injunction against Johnson. Johnson counters. The rest of Frankie Goes To Hollywood form a new outfit called The Lads (who fail to release any material).

Oct *The Power Of Love* is used as a backing track to first UK TV condom commercial.

1988 **Jan** The ZTT and Perfect Songs case against "Holly" Johnson in London's High Court attracts much media attention.

Feb In its outcome Johnson wins an important test case for British recording artists relating to contracts and royalty payments, winning substantial costs.

Aug Rutherford signs a solo deal with the 4th & Broadway label. Newspaper reports state that the remainder of the band (with new lead singer Dee Harris), desperate to make a comeback, indulge in an orgy of alcohol, drugs and vandalism during recording sessions at the Music Works studio, Highbury, North London.

Oct Rutherford's debut "house" single *Get Real* makes UK #47.

1989 **Feb** Holly Johnson's self-penned debut solo *Love Train* hits UK #4.

May Johnson's *Americanos* also hits UK #4, as parent album **Blast** debuts at UK #1.

July Third extraction *Atomic City* reaches UK #18.

[8] *Love Train* peaks at US #65.

Sept While Rutherford's single *Oh World* has recently made UK #61, Johnson's *Heaven's Here* stalls at UK #62.

1990 **Feb** Johnson contributes a cover of *Love Me Tender* to the compilation album **The Last Temptation Of Elvis**, to benefit the Nordoff-Robbins Music Therapy charity.

Dec Previewing second solo project Johnson's *Where Has Love Gone* peaks at UK #73.

1991 While Rutherford forms Pressure Zone with Tommy Payne, Marco Perry and Dave Clayton, Johnson's self-penned *Across The Universe* fails to chart as will parent second solo album.

ARETHA FRANKLIN

1950 Franklin (b. Mar.25, 1942, Memphis, TN), the fourth of 6 children raised by her father after her mother left (and later died), begins to learn piano by listening to Eddie Heywood records, but rejects the offer of professional lessons from her father, Rev. C.L. Franklin, pastor of the

4,500-member New Bethel church, Detroit, MI, and the most famous gospel preacher of the 50s – commanding $4,000 a sermon, and dubbed the "Million Dollar Voice". Franklin has been taught to sing by family friends Mahalia Jackson and The Ward Sisters, Frances Steadman and Marion Williams.

'52 Gospel star James Cleveland comes to live with the Franklin family and encourages her musical ambitions, but her biggest influence is her father's friend, hymn writer and gospel singer Clara Ward. Having heard Ward sing *Peace In The Valley* at a relative's funeral, she resolves on a singing career.

'56 Franklin's first recordings, for Checker label, are live versions of Ward hymns, recorded at her father's church.

'60 After dropping out of school, Franklin tours as a gospel vocalist. Then, encouraged by Sam Cooke, she tailors her style to the secular field. Leaving the family home in Detroit, she moves to New York, taking dance and vocal lessons, and gets a manager, Joe King.
Aug [1] She makes her first secular recordings in a New York demo studio, cutting 4 tracks: *Right Now, Over The Rainbow, Love Is the Only Thing* and *Today I Sing The Blues*. The latter comes to the attention of CBS/Columbia Records veteran A&R man John Hammond, who signs her following an audition arranged by Major "Mule" Holly, bassist with jazz pianist Teddy Wilson.
Oct Her first Columbia album, *The Great Aretha Franklin*, is released. Produced by Hammond, it is a mixture of jazz, R&B and standards. *Today I Sing The Blues* is issued as a single and hits US R&B #10.
Dec [11] Franklin makes her New York stage debut at the Village Vanguard, with a program of standards.

'61 **Mar** Her US chart debut, at #76, is *Won't Be Long*, recorded with The Ray Bryant Trio.
Nov A revival of *Rock-A-Bye Your Baby With A Dixie Melody* reaches US #37 (and will be Franklin's only sizeable US hit on Columbia).

'62 **Feb** *I Surrender, Dear* reaches US #87 and B-side *Rough Lover* makes US #94. Meanwhile album *The Electrifying Aretha Franklin* is released and she marries Ted White, now her manager.
July *Don't Cry, Baby* peaks at US #92.
Sept *Try A Little Tenderness* reaches US #100.
Dec *The Tender, The Moving, The Swinging Aretha Franklin* climbs to US #69.

'63 **Jan** *Trouble In Mind* peaks at US #86 and *Laughing* is released.

'64 **Oct** *Runnin' Out Of Fools* reaches US #57 and *Unforgettable: A Tribute To Dinah Washington* is released.

'65 **Jan** *Can't You Just See Me* peaks at US #96, while *Runnin' Out Of Fools* reaches US #84.
July *Yeah!!!* makes US #101.

'66 **Aug** *Soul Sister*, her last album for Columbia, climbs to US #132.
Sept Dissatisfied with the artistic direction and lack of commercial success (which has made a $90,000 loss over 6 years), Franklin is unwilling to re-sign to Columbia. Atlantic Records outbids CBS for her, producer Jerry Wexler believing her Mitch Miller-guided recording path has been wrong and that she needs a tough R&B frame to recapture her gospel vocal fire. (This leads to a long and fruitful working relationship between Franklin and Wexler, later assisted by Arif Mardin and Tom Dowd.)

'67 **Jan** For her first Atlantic sessions, Wexler takes Franklin to Rick Hall's Florence Alabama Music Emporium (FAME) studios in Muscle Shoals, Alabama, using the rhythm section that paired her with Wilson Pickett. A week's sessions to cut an album are planned; but after 1 day's recording which produces just *I Never Loved A Man (The Way I Love You)* (a song Franklin has discovered herself and told Wexler she wanted to record) and a backing track for *Do Right Woman – Do Right Man*, a heated exchange between her husband and one of the horn players results in a quick return to New York.
Feb [8] With Wexler-distributed acetates of *I Never Loved A Man* already getting airplay on top US R&B stations Franklin, with the help of sisters Erma and Carolyn, completes *Do Right Woman, Do Right Man* in New York, so that the single has a B-side and can be released.
May *I Never Loved A Man (The Way I Loved You)* tops US R&B chart for 9 weeks, crossing over to hit US #9. It earns Franklin's first gold disk for million-plus sales. The album of same title hits US #2 (also earning a gold-disk), and the media and music business dub her "Lady Soul".
June New arrangement of Otis Redding's R&B hit *Respect* tops US chart for 4 weeks and R&B chart for 8 weeks, her second million-seller.
July *Respect* hits UK #10. In US, Columbia releases compilation album of earlier material, *Aretha Franklin's Greatest Hits*, which makes US #94.
Aug [12] *I Never Loved A Man* reaches UK #36, as she headlines New York's first Jazz Festival at the Downing Stadium.
Sept *Baby I Love You* is Franklin's third million-selling single, hitting US #4 (and topping R&B chart for 6 weeks). It climbs to UK #39.
Oct *Aretha Arrives*, recorded in New York in June, hits US #5, while another Columbia compilation album, *Take A Look*, peaks at US #173 and its title track makes US #56.
Nov *(You Make Me Feel Like A) Natural Woman*, written by Carole King, hits US #8.
Dec 2 more Columbia singles chart briefly in US: *Mockingbird* (#94) and *Soulville* (#83). Franklin is named **Billboard** magazine's Top Female Vocalist Of The Year.

1968 **Feb** *Chain Of Fools*, a revival of an R&B hit by Don Covay, hits US #2 and earns another gold disk. Paired with her revival of The Rolling Stones' *(I Can't Get No) Satisfaction*, it makes UK #43. *Aretha: Lady Soul*, mostly recorded just before Christmas, also hits US #2. (Eric Clapton guests on track *Good To Me As I Am To You*.)
[29] Franklin wins her first Grammy awards as *Respect* wins Best R&B Recording and Best R&B Solo Vocal Performance, Female Of 1967 at the 10th annual Grammy awards.
Apr *(Sweet Sweet Baby) Since You've Been Gone* hits US #5 (and is another million-seller), while B-side *Ain't No Way* reaches #16. The A-side also makes UK #47, while *Lady Soul* reaches UK #25.
May [7] On her first tour of Europe, Franklin performs at the Olympia theater, Paris, France; her concert is recorded for future album release.
July *Think* hits US #7 (Franklin's first self-penned million-seller) and makes UK #26. B-side, reviving Sam Cooke's *You Send Me*, reaches US #56. Franklin opens the Democratic Party's national convention in Chicago, IL, singing *The Star Spangled Banner*.
Aug *Aretha Now* hits US #3, as *Lady Soul* is certified gold.
Sept While Franklin spends time in the studio working on her next album, her revival of Dionne Warwick's *I Say A Little Prayer* hits UK #4. In US, where it is a double A-side with *The House That Jack Built*, it hits #10 and #6 respectively, another million-seller. *Aretha Now* hits UK #6.
Nov *Aretha In Paris*, recorded at May's concert, reaches US #13.
Dec Another Covay revival, *See Saw*, peaks at US #14 and B-side *My Song* reaches US #31. This is another US million-seller.

1969 **Feb** [15] Vickie Jones is arrested for fraud for impersonating Franklin on concert at Fort Meyers, FL. No-one in the audience asks for their money back.
Mar *Soul '69*, from the Sept. sessions, including some pop-jazz fusions, makes US #15. She tours US, but some performances are described as patchy (attributed to a collapsing marriage heading for divorce).
[12] Franklin wins Best R&B Vocal Performance, Female for *Chain Of Fools* at the 11th annual Grammy awards.
Apr A revival of The Band's *The Weight* reaches US #19 and B-side, reviving The Miracles' *Tracks Of My Tears*, reaches #71.
May She works on another album in the studio, with slide guitarist Duane Allman (later of The Allman Brothers Band) joining the regular session musicians for some tracks.
June *I Can't See Myself Leaving You* reaches US #28. B-side, John Hartford's much-covered *Gentle On My Mind*, makes US #76.
[13] She headlines a major R&B music spectacular, "Soul Bowl '69", at Houston Astrodome, TX, with Ray Charles, The Staple Singers, Sam And Dave, Percy Sledge, Jimmy Witherspoon, Johnny "Guitar" Watson, Clara Ward and many others – including Franklin's old friend, gospel singer James Cleveland.
July [22] Franklin is arrested for causing a disturbance in a Detroit parking lot, a symptom of the personal difficulties she is facing as her 7-year marriage to White fragments.
Aug Compilation album *Aretha's Gold* reaches US #18.
Oct *Share Your Love With Me* reaches US #13, while Franklin records for the first time at Criteria studios in Miami, FL, cutting 9 tracks (again with Allman in attendance) including a revival of The Beatles' *Eleanor Rigby* and her own composition *Call Me*.
Dec *Eleanor Rigby* reaches US #17.

1970 **Mar** *This Girl's In Love With You*, a mixture of the year's New York and Miami recordings, reaches US #17. It includes a version of The Beatles' *Let It Be*, recorded in Dec.1969 before the release of The Beatles' own version. Franklin returns to Miami for further sessions at Criteria, mostly to cut strong R&B and gospel oldies with The Dixie Flyers.
[11] Franklin wins Best R&B Vocal Performance, Female for *Share Your Love With Me* at the 12th annual Grammy awards.
May *Call Me*, coupled with a revival of Dusty Springfield's *Son Of A Preacher Man*, also recorded in Miami, makes US #13.
July *Spirit In The Dark* reaches US #23.
Aug Returning to New York to record, she cuts a version of *Bridge Over Troubled Water*, with Billy Preston among the session musicians. (It will be released in 1971.)

Sept A revival of Ben E. King's *Don't Play That Song* reaches US #11 and UK #13, and is her first million-selling single since *See Saw* in 1968. Remarried, and with a new backing band led by saxman King Curtis (comprising Cornell Dupree on guitar, Richard Tee on piano, Jerry Jemmott on bass and Bernard Purdie on drums), Franklin begins a series of well-received US concerts.

Oct *Spirit In The Dark* reaches US #25.

Dec A cover of Elton John's *Border Song (Holy Moses)* reaches US #37.

1971

Mar [5-7] Franklin plays 3 nights at the Fillmore West in San Francisco, with Ray Charles (they do an encore duet on the third night), King Curtis and Tower Of Power.

[16] Franklin wins Best R&B Vocal Performance, Female for *Don't Play That Song* at the 13th annual Grammy awards.

Apr A revival of Marvin Gaye and Tammi Terrell's *You're All I Need To Get By* reaches US #19.

June Franklin's version of Paul Simon's *Bridge Over Troubled Water* (he had already claimed to have had her in mind when writing the song, prior to Simon & Garfunkel's own version in 1970) hits US #6. Coupled with *A Brand New Me*, it is another million-seller.

July *Aretha Live At Fillmore West*, recorded in Mar., hits US #7.

Aug [17] Franklin sings at the funeral of King Curtis (fatally stabbed on a street 4 days earlier) in New York, with Stevie Wonder, Cissy Houston and others, as the Rev. Jesse Jackson preaches the sermon.

Oct *Aretha's Greatest Hits* reaches US #19. Her revival of Ben E. King's *Spanish Harlem* hits US #2 and UK #14, another million-seller.

Dec *Rock Steady*, a further million-seller, hits US #9.

1972

Feb [1] Franklin sings *Take My Hand, Precious Lord* at the funeral of her old friend and one-time mentor Mahalia Jackson, in Chicago.

Mar *Young, Gifted And Black* reaches US #11, and is a gold disk.

[14] Franklin wins Best R&B Vocal Performance, Female for *Bridge Over Troubled Water* at the 14th annual Grammy awards.

June *Day Dreaming*, her fourth consecutive million-seller, hits US #5.

July Double gospel album *Amazing Grace*, made with James Cleveland and the Southern California Community Choir, and recorded at a church in Watts, LA, in Jan. hits US #7. Her last Wexler-produced album, it earns a gold disk for a half-million sales. Columbia compilation album *In The Beginning/The World Of Aretha Franklin 1960-1967* reaches US #160.

Aug *All The King's Horses* makes US #26.

Sept *Wholy Holy*, with James Cleveland, peaks at US #81.

1973

Mar *Master Of Eyes (The Deepness Of Your Eyes)* makes US #33.

[3] Franklin wins Best R&B Vocal Performance, Female for *Young, Gifted And Black* and Best Soul Gospel Performance for *Amazing Grace* at the 15th annual Grammy awards.

Apr Franklin begins a major US stadium tour.

Aug Jazz-tinged album *Hey Now Hey (The Other Side Of The Sky)*, recorded in Los Angeles with producer Quincy Jones, makes US #30.

Sept A revival of Jimi Hendrix' *Angel* reaches US #20 and UK #37.

1974

Mar A revival of Stevie Wonder's *Until You Come Back To Me (That's What I'm Gonna Do)* makes US #3 (selling over a million) and UK #26.

[2] Franklin wins Best R&B Vocal Performance, Female for *Master Of Eyes (The Deepness Of Your Eyes)* at the 16th annual Grammy awards.

Apr With Wexler, Mardin and Dowd producing again, *Let Me In Your Life* reaches US #14. Franklin is made an Honorary Doctor of Law at Bethune-Cookman college, OH.

June *I'm In Love* makes US #19.

Sept *Ain't Nothing Like The Real Thing*, another Gaye/Terrell revival, climbs to US #47.

Dec *Without Love* reaches US #45.

1975

Jan *With Everything I Feel In Me* peaks at US #57.

Mar [1] Franklin wins her 10th Grammy for Best R&B Vocal Performance, Female for *Ain't Nothing Like The Real Thing* at the 17th annual Grammy awards, her eighth successive win in the category.

Oct *Mr. D.J. (5 For The D.J.)* reaches US #53.

Dec *You* peaks at US #83.

1976

July Franklin and Curtis Mayfield co-produce the soundtrack album for blaxploitation movie "Sparkle", which makes US #18.

Aug *Something He Can Feel* (from *Sparkle*) makes US #28.

Oct *Jump*, also from the film soundtrack, peaks at US #72.

1977

Jan [19] Franklin performs an a cappella *God Bless America* at Jimmy Carter's Inaugural Eve Gala in Washington, DC. Compilation album *Ten Years Of Gold* reaches US #135.

Feb *Look Into Your Heart* makes US #82.

June *Break It To Me Gently* makes US #85, but hits US R&B #1 for 1 week.

July Lamont Dozier-produced album *Sweet Passion* reaches US #49.

1978

Apr Franklin marries actor Glynn Turman. At the ceremony, conducted by her father, The Four Tops sing *Isn't She Lovely*.

June *Almighty Fire* makes US #63.

[21] She begins a 5-date appearance at Las Vegas, her first engagement there in 8 years.

July [9] Franklin disappoints the audience at the Rev. Gibson's 18th annual "Youth On Parade Program" at Los Angeles' Good Shepherd Baptist church with a lackluster performance.

1979

Feb [13] She opens a cabaret season at Harrah's restaurant in Lake Tahoe, NV.

Nov [10] *La Diva* reaches US #146.

1980

June [20] "The Blues Brothers", featuring Franklin as a waitress, singing *Think*, opens throughout US. Shortly afterwards, she ends her 15-year association with Atlantic and signs to Arista, under the executive production of Clive Davis.

Nov *Aretha*, produced by Mardin, is her Arista debut, making US #47.

Dec [13] A cover of The Doobie Brothers' *What A Fool Believes* makes UK #46.

1981

Jan *United Together* makes US #56.

June *Come To Me* peaks at US #84.

Sept *Love All The Hurt Away*, duet with George Benson, makes US #46.

[26] *Love All The Hurt Away* makes UK #49. The album, of which the duet is the title track, climbs to US #36.

1982

Feb [24] Franklin wins Best R&B Vocal Performance, Female for *Hold On, I'm Comin'* at the 24th annual Grammy awards.

Sept [25] *Jump To It* makes UK #42.

Oct [9] Luther Vandross-produced third Arista album *Jump To It* reaches US #23 and earns a gold disk.

Title track *Jump To It* makes US #24, tops R&B chart for 4 weeks and reaches UK #42.

Nov [25] She performs at the Jamaica World Music Festival, to an audience of 45,000 at the Bob Marley Performing Center in Montego Bay, with The Clash, The Grateful Dead, Gladys Knight and others.

1983

July *Get It Right* peaks at US #61 and UK #74.

Aug *Get It Right*, again produced by Vandross, reaches US #36.

1984

Franklin wins US *Ebony* magazine's annual award for American Black Achievement, but her year is marred when she is succesfully sued for breach of contract when she is unable, mainly through her continuing fear of flying, to open in the Broadway musical "Sing, Mahalia, Sing". Producer Ashton Springer is awarded $234, 364.

1985

May Franklin's voice is proclaimed "one of Michigan's natural resources" by the State Government.

July *Who's Zoomin' Who?*, produced by Narada Michael Walden, is issued: it will make US #13, becoming her first certified million-selling album, gaining a platinum disk. The Rev. C.L. Franklin is shot during civil rights campaign. (He survives, but goes into a coma.)

Oct *Freeway Of Love* hits US #3 but makes only UK #68.

Nov Further uptempo dance smash *Who's Zoomin' Who* hits US #7 and reaches UK #11.

Dec Franklin duets with Annie Lennox of Eurythmics on *Sisters Are Doin' It For Themselves*, which makes US #18 and hits UK #9.

1986

Jan *Who's Zoomin' Who* reaches UK #49.

Feb [25] Franklin wins Best R&B Vocal Performance, Female for *Freeway Of Love* at the 28th annual Grammy awards.

Mar *Another Night* reaches US #22 and makes UK #54.

May A reissue of *Freeway Of Love* peaks at UK #51.

[24] TV-advertised compilation *The First Lady Of Soul* makes UK #89.

Nov [11] Title song from Whoopi Goldberg movie "Jumpin' Jack Flash", produced by its co-writer Keith Richard, reaches US #21 and UK #58.

1987

Jan [21] Keith Richards inducts Franklin into the Rock'N'Roll Hall Of Fame at the second annual dinner at the Waldorf Astoria, New York.

Feb [7] Duet with George Michael, *I Knew You Were Waiting (For Me)*, written by Climie Fisher and Dennis Morgan, tops UK chart, as *Jimmy Lee* reaches US #28.

Mar *Aretha*, produced by Walden, makes US #32 and UK #51.

Apr [18] *I New You Were Waiting (For Me)* tops US chart.

July [4] *Rock-A-Lott* stalls at US #82.

[27] Over a 3-day period, Franklin records gospel songs at the New Bethel Baptist church on C.L. Franklin Boulevard, Detroit, with guests the Rev. Jesse Jackson, The Franklin Sisters and Mavis Staples. Meanwhile, her father has died, having never come out of his coma.

1988

Feb Double album *One Lord, One Faith, One Baptism* from the sessions commemorating Rev. Franklin, makes US #106.

Mar [2] Franklin wins Best R&B Vocal Performance, Female for *Aretha* and Best R&B Performance By A Duo Or Group With Vocal with George Michael for *I Knew You Were Waiting (For Me)* at the 30th annual Grammy awards.

Aug [22] PBS TV airs "Aretha Franklin: The Queen Of Soul", a 1-hour documentary with contributions from Ray Charles, Eric Clapton, Whitney Houston and Smokey Robinson.

Sept Franklin joins George Michael on stage in Detroit and sings duet *I Knew You Were Waiting (For Me)*.

89 Feb [22] Franklin wins Best Soul Gospel Performance, Female for *One Lord, One Faith, One Baptism* at the 31st annual Grammy awards.

May [27] *Through The Storm*, a duet with Elton John, reaches US #16 and makes UK #41.

June [3] Star-heavy album *Through The Storm* makes UK #46. It includes duets with labelmates The Four Tops and Whitney Houston and James Brown, recorded just prior to his recent incarceration, and peaks at US #16 and UK #41.

July [29] *It Isn't, It Wasn't, It Ain't Never Gonna Be*, with Whitney Houston, makes US #41.

Gimme Your Love, with James Brown, makes #41 on US R&B chart as *Through The Storm* makes US #55.

Sept *It Isn't It Wasn't, It Ain't Never Gonna Be* reaches UK #29.

91 Mar [23] Franklin sings at the funeral of Army Specialist Anthony Riggs at the Little Rock Baptist church, Detroit. Riggs had been back in the US for a day, after returning from the Gulf War where he was part of a Patriot missile battery group. At first, he was thought to be the victim of a random act of violence, but his wife and brother-in-law will be arrested for his murder.

FREDDIE & THE DREAMERS
Freddie Garrity (vocals)
Derek Quinn (lead guitar)
Roy Crewsdon (rhythm guitar)
Pete Birrell (bass)
Bernie Dwyer (drums)

61 Group is formed by Garrity (b. Nov.14, 1940, Manchester, Gtr.Manchester), a former milkman, who has previously sung in local skiffle group Red Sox, making his first public appearance at the British Legion Hall in Chorlton, Lancs., followed by the John Norman Four and then The Kingfishers, in which Crewsdon (b. May 29, 1941, Manchester) also played. Quinn (b. May 24, 1942, Manchester), Birrell (b. May 9, 1941, Manchester) and Dwyer (b. Sept.11, 1940) all join as new group evolves from The Kingfishers.

Oct They make their first UK TV and radio appearances, on BBC's "Let's Go" and "Beat Show" respectively.

63 Mar After a year of growing popularity in Northern England, followed by seaside dates at Dreamland, Margate, Kent, and then a stint in Hamburg, Germany (at the Top Ten club), they are signed to EMI's Columbia label after intense talent scouting by the company in Manchester/Liverpool following the rapid success of The Beatles.

May [31] Group plays at the Royal Albert Hall, London, on a bill with Billy Fury, Mark Wynter, The Tornados, Shane Fenton & The Fentones, Heinz and others.

June Debut recording, reviving James Ray's *If You Gotta Make A Fool Of Somebody*, hits UK #2. They quickly become popular UK TV favorites, thanks to a zany, low-comedy stage act focused on Garrity's kicks, jumps and giggles while performing.

Aug A Mitch Murray (writer of the first 2 Gerry & The Pacemakers chart-toppers) song *I'm Telling You Now* also hits UK #2.

Dec *You Were Made For Me*, another Murray composition, makes a UK hit hat-trick at #3, while debut album *Freddie And The Dreamers* hits UK #5. Group makes film debut in "What A Crazy World", starring Joe Brown, Marty Wilde and Susan Maughan and pantomime debut in "Cinderella" at the Royalty theater, Chester, Cheshire.

64 Feb *Over You* hits UK #10.

Mar [22] Group plays on "Sunday Night At The London Palladium".

Apr [18] They embark on UK tour, with Roy Orbison, at Slough Adelphi, Berks., ending May 16 at Newcastle City Hall, Tyne & Wear.

May A revival of Paul Anka's *I Love You Baby* reaches UK #19.

July *Just For You* makes UK #41.

Nov A revival of The G-Clefs' 1961 hit *I Understand* returns them to UK Top 10, hitting #6.

[26] Group appears in low-budget UK musical film "Every Day's A Holiday" (US title: *Seaside Swingers*) as a bunch of singing holiday camp chefs with fellow singers Mike Sarne and John Leyton which premieres at the Warner cinema in London's Leicester Square.

Dec [26] Group opens in "The Beatles Christmas Show" at the Hammersmith Odeon, London.

1965 Feb During a world tour, a timely US visit places them on national TV shows "Shindig" and "Hullaballoo", where their stage antics and catchy songs are an immediate success, prompting Tower Records to reissue *I'm Telling You Now*, and Mercury Records (to which their latest material is signed) to release *I Understand*.

Mar [8] Group embarks on tour of Australia and New Zealand.

Apr A US bubblegum manufacturer distributes gum with Freddie & The Dreamers cards. A full set of 66 makes a 3' square group picture. [10] *I'm Telling You Now* tops US chart for 2 weeks, taking its total sales over a million, while *I Understand* makes US #36.

May *A Little You* climbs to UK #26, while album *Freddie And The Dreamers* reaches US #19.

June [5] Band begins 18-week season at Queen's theater, Blackpool, Lancs., with comedians Tommy Cooper and Jewel & Warriss. *Do The Freddie* and *You Were Made For Me*, released on Mercury and Tower respectively, are simultaneous US hits. The former is recorded specifically for US market, creating a teen dance based on Garrity's stage movements, and reaches #18, while the latter reissue makes #21.

July *Do The Freddie* climbs to US #85.

Aug *A Little You* is their final US hit, at #48.

Oct Group begins US tour of concert and college dates.

Nov Final UK hit revives Dick & Deedee's *Thou Shalt Not Steal*, and peaks at #44. (They will then move into club and cabaret work, including regular winter pantomime and summer seaside residency, where a family audience will replace the pop fans.)

Dec [16] They open in "Aladdin And His Magic Lamp" pantomime at the Palace theater, Manchester.

1966 Apr [11] Group begins a 4-week variety tour at the Hippodrome, Bristol, Avon.

July [7] They begin another US tour.

1967 Feb [12] Group plays an 8-day tour of Germany, appearing on TV show "Beat Beat Beat", and playing 6 concerts at US bases.

June [16] Summer season begins at the Windmill theater, Great Yarmouth, Norfolk.

1968 Oct Group splits, with Garrity and Birrell moving on to UK children's TV in weekly show "Little Big Time".

1970 Children's album *Oliver In The Overworld* is final group release after 4 years of unsuccessful singles and albums.

1976 Garrity re-forms the group with new personnel, to play UK 60s revival concerts. They also join oldies tours in US and Australia.

1988 Garrity debuts as a serious stage actor in a UK production of "The Tempest", while continuing a lucrative cabaret career.

FREE
Paul Rodgers (vocals)
Paul Kossoff (guitar)
Andy Fraser (bass)
Simon Kirke (drums)

1968 May Group is formed in London, by 2 ex-members of R&B band Black Cat Bones: Kossoff (b. Sept.14, 1950, London), son of actor David Kossoff, and Kirke (b. July 28, 1949, Shrewsbury, Shrops.). They recruit Rodgers (b. Dec 12, 1949, Middlesbrough, Cleveland), ex-Roadrunners and Brown Sugar, after hearing him at the Fickle Pickle, an R&B club in Finsbury Park, London. Fraser (b. Aug.7, 1952, London) joins after being fired by John Mayall's Bluesbreakers. Alexis Korner watches their first gig and names them Free, after his own 60s trio Free At Last.

Nov Signed to Island Records, who want the group to be called The Heavy Metal Kids, it releases *Tons Of Sobs*, which does not chart in UK (but makes US #197 almost a year on).

1969 July Debut single *Broad Daylight* also fails but the group builds a huge live reputation through constant UK touring.

Sept Band tours US, supporting Blind Faith.

Nov *Free* is UK chart debut at #22, but *I'll Be Creepin'* fails to chart.

1970 May [24] Group takes part in the Hollywood Music Festival near Newcastle-under-Lyme, Staffs.

July *All Right Now*, a highly commercial riff-based rocker, hits UK #2 for 3 weeks, unable to dislodge Mungo Jerry's *In The Summertime*, and establishes Free as a major act.

Aug *Fire And Water*, including the hit, climbs to UK #2, after group makes a major impact at the UK's Isle of Wight Festival.

Oct *All Right Now* hits US #4 and *Fire And Water* makes US #17.

1971 Jan Follow-up single *Stealer* climbs to US #49 after failing in UK.

Feb *Highway* reaches UK #41 but only US #190.

May [9] At the end of a Pacific tour, group splits to pursue individual projects, frustrated by intra-group frictions and disappointed by lack of sales consistency.

June *My Brother Jake*, released 2 weeks before the split, hits UK #4.

July *Free Live!*, released as a souvenir of the band, also hits UK #4.

Oct *Free Live!* climbs to US #89.

Nov Kossoff and Kirke release *Kossoff, Kirke, Tetsu And Rabbit*, with bassist Tetsu Yamauchi (b. Oct.21, 1947, Fukuoka, Japan) and keyboardist John "Rabbit" Bundrick. Rodgers forms Peace with Stewart McDonald (bass) and Mick Underwood (drums), which tours UK supporting Mott The Hoople. Andy Fraser forms an unsuccessful trio, Toby (with Adrian Fisher on guitar and Stan Speake on drums).

1972 Jan Free re-forms after Rodgers and Fraser's projects (Peace and Toby) fail. Band tours UK and recommences recording.

June *Free At Last* hits UK #9 and US #69. *Little Bit Of Love* makes UK #13. Group tours US but Kossoff suffers drug abuse-associated health problems which cause him to miss several dates.

July [22] Fraser leaves to form Sharks, on the eve of Free's tour of Japan. Kossoff's drug problems render him unavailable, so Tetsu and Rabbit are recruited for the trip, on which Rodgers plays guitar.

Oct Kossoff, fit again, rejoins for UK tour and to record an album, but leaves Free officially to make his own album, *Back Street Crawler*. (He will form a band of that name in 1974, signing to Atlantic Records and releasing *The Band Plays On* and *Second Avenue*.)

1973 Jan Wendell Richardson of Osibisa is temporary guitar for UK tour.

Feb *Wishing Well* hits UK #7; *Heartbreaker* makes UK #9 and US #47.

July Free announces its final split. Rodgers, after turning down an offer to join Deep Purple, stays with Kirke to form Bad Company, while Tetsu replaces Ronnie Lane in The Faces. (Rabbit will join The Who as sideman.)

Aug *All Right Now* is reissued in UK and re-charts, reaching #15.

1974 Mar Compilation *The Free Story* hits UK #2.

1975 May *The Best Of Free* is released in US only. It reaches #120.

1976 Mar [19] Kossoff dies of heart failure on a flight to New York after a history of drug abuse.

1978 Mar *The Free EP*, compiling *All Right Now*, *My Brother Jake* and *Wishing Well*, reaches UK #11. (This will remain a steady seller in Island Records' UK catalog and will re-chart, reaching #57, in Oct. 1982.)

1982 Mar Fraser has a minor US hit with *Do You Love Me*, reaching #82, having worked with Robert Palmer on *Clues* and Eno on *Before And After Science*. (Rodgers joins Jimmy Page in The Firm, before forming The Law with Kenney Jones.)

1991 Feb Timely UK reissue of *All Right Now* coincides with its use for a Wrigleys Chewing Gum ad, and becomes a hit for the third time.

Mar [2] *All Right Now* makes UK #8.

[9] *The Best Of Free – All Right Now* makes UK #9.

BOBBY FREEMAN

1955 Freeman (b. June 13, 1940, San Francisco, CA) is at high school in San Francisco when, as a singer and pianist, he has first taste of recording with vocal group The Romancers, who record briefly and unsuccessfully for Dootone Records.

1958 Apr Still at high school, he is spotted playing in a club and signed to Josie Records, recording his own composition *Do You Wanna Dance*.

June *Do You Wanna Dance* hits US #5, and becomes a much-revived rock standard: there will be later hit versions in US or UK by Cliff Richard (1962), Del Shannon (1964), The Beach Boys (1965), The Mamas And The Papas (1968), Bette Midler (1973) and The Ramones (1978).

Aug *Betty Lou Got A New Pair Of Shoes* makes US #37.

Dec *Need Your Love* peaks at US #54.

1959 Feb Freeman graduates from high school, turning professional with 3 US hits already under his belt, but 2 Josie singles during this year will be less successful: *Mary Ann Thomas* making US #90 in June and *Ebb Tide* #93 in Dec.

1960 Oct He resurges with dance-craze song *(I Do The) Shimmy Shimmy* on the King label, which makes US #37 and stays on chart for 3 months.

1964 Jan After a long recording silence, and while resident at a club in North Beach, San Francisco, Freeman becomes the first act to work with local DJs Tom Donahue and Bob Mitchell when they set up Autumn Records. He cuts Autumn's debut single *Let's Surf Again*.

Aug Freeman's *C'mon And Swim* is Autumn's second release, and hits US #5, equalling *Do You Wanna Dance*. The single is produced by another local DJ, Sylvester Stewart (later to find fame as Sly Stone of Sly & The Family Stone).

Nov *S-W-I-M*, another Stewart production, is less successful, peaking at US #56, and becoming Freeman's last US chart hit. (He continues

working, still mainly around the San Francisco area. In the later 60s and early 70s he will record intermittently in a less rock-oriented soul style, for labels such as Double Shot and Touch.)

THE BOBBY FULLER FOUR

Bobby Fuller (vocals, guitar)
Randy Fuller (bass)
Jim Reese (rhythm guitar)
Dwayne Quirico (drums)

1960 Fuller (b. Oct.22, 1942, Goose Creek, TX) builds a studio in his parents' home in El Paso, TX, and begins recording a number of tracks and placing them with local labels like Yucca and Todd. He also runs a local teen nightclub, the Rendezvous, and plays there with a group called The Embers, who will later become The Fanatics, and eventually (after many personnel changes) The Bobby Fuller Four.

1964 He closes the Rendezvous in the summer, forms his own label, Exeter Records, and releases a new single on it every few weeks, including surf music and an early version of *I Fought The Law* by Bobby Fuller & The Fanatics.

Nov Group leaves Texas for Hollywood, CA, and hoped-for stardom, taking tapes of Fuller's songs. The name is changed to Bobby Fuller & The Cavemen for a gig at La Cave Pigalle, then to The Bobby Fuller Four when they acquire a residency at PJ's, breaking all attendance records at their first gig.

Dec They sign with Bob Keene, owner of a group of small Los Angeles, CA, record labels, who decides to try them in different guises on several of his outlets. First release is *Those Memories Of You*, as Bobby Fuller & The Fanatics, on Donna Records.

1965 Feb *Take My Word*, with the group as The Bobby Fuller Four, is released on another of Keene's labels, Mustang Records.

Mar They sign to appear as a surf band in the movie "Ghost In The Invisible Bikini". Producer Phil Spector sits in with the group on piano at gigs and attempts, unsuccessfully, to sign them to his Philles label.

July They have a Los Angeles area hit with *Let Her Dance*, (its riff a re-working of *La Bamba*), leased to Liberty Records for national distribution, though it fails to sell outside California, and appear on several US TV shows like "Shindig", "Shebang" and "Hollywood A Go-Go". Debut album *KRLA King Of Wheels* is released, in co-operation with a Los Angeles radio station.

Sept *Never To Be Forgotten* also sells well in Los Angeles but fails to chart nationally.

Oct Fuller revamps *I Fought The Law*, a revival of a Crickets' song which he has attempted before. This time it is a powerful guitar-driven version which will prove his breakthrough success.

1966 Mar *I Fought The Law* hits US #9.

Apr *I Fought The Law* makes UK #33, while second album *The Bobby Fuller Four: I Fought The Law* climbs to US #144.

May Another revived Crickets' song in similar style, *Love's Made A Fool Of You*, reaches US #26 as band embarks on its first national tour.

June As *The Magic Touch* is issued, Fuller falls out with Keene over the choice of A-side, plus Keene's decisions not to record a live album at PJ's (a project close to Fuller's heart), and to cancel projected UK visit. He decides to quit the tour and go solo, while the single flops.

July [18] Fuller is found dead in his car outside the apartment he shares with his mother at 1776 Sycamore, West Hollywood, Los Angeles, his body badly beaten and reeking of gasoline. The circumstances of his death are never uncovered, and Keene releases a statement dismissing police reports which call it accidental death or suicide. The question of foul play never arises, despite the odd mode of death. (The group continues for a while under Bobby's brother as The Randy Fuller Four, but with no chart success will split in 1968.)

BILLY FURY

1958 Oct Former St. Silas Church of England, Dingle, Liverpool-schoolmate of Beatle Ringo Starr, Ronald Wycherley (b. Apr.17, 1941, Liverpool, Merseyside), following a childhood fraught with illness (including rheumatic fever which has left him with a weak heart), is a deckhand on River Mersey tug boats and writing songs with his guitar as a hobby, when Larry Parnes' "Rock Extravaganza", headlined by Marty Wilde, comes to Birkenhead Essoldo, across the Mersey from his home. Wycherley talks his way into Wilde's dressing room hoping to interest him in some songs. Parnes, impressed by the teenager's obvious vocal talent and the strength of his on-the-spot demos, offers to sign him if

Wycherley will go on stage and sing a couple of his songs as a "local addition" to the bill. Although petrified, Wycherley complies, and the audience reaction makes Parnes realize his hunch is right. He signs the singer to a management contract, and re-christens him Billy Fury, quickly getting him on tour and on UK TV in Jack Good's "Oh Boy!"

Nov [26] Fury is signed by Parnes to Decca Records, and records his first session at the company's studio in West Hampstead, London.

1959 Feb Self-penned *Maybe Tomorrow* charts in UK, reaching #18, aided by Fury's success in nationwide tour exposure.

June *Margo Don't Go* reaches UK #28.

Oct The curtain is dropped during Fury's act at Dublin's Theatre Royal: his wild, Presley-like stage movements are deemed "offensive" by the management.

1960 Apr *Colette*, dual-tracked in an Everly Brothers' style untypical of Fury, is nevertheless his first UK Top 10, hitting #9.

June *That's Love*, another Fury original, reaches UK #19. By now, he is also a huge TV success in UK, starring weekly on the rock music shows "Boy Meets Girls" (with Marty Wilde) and "Wham!" (which he headlines). 10" album **The Sound Of Fury** reaches UK #18. It features self-penned (under the name Wilbur Wilberforce) Elvis-style rockabilly tracks produced by Jack Good, and backed by Joe Brown and other top session players. It will later be regarded by critics as the great early UK rockabilly album, but Decca does not see Fury's recording career in this direction, sensing the commercial potential of strong rock ballads and carefully-chosen US cover versions.

Oct *Wondrous Place* reaches UK #25.

1961 Feb *A Thousand Stars*, a cover of US hit by Kathy Young & The Innocents, reaches UK #14.

Apr A cover of Marty Robbins' *Don't Worry* makes UK #40.

Aug A cover of Goffin/King ballad *Halfway To Paradise* (a US hit for Tony Orlando), is Fury's biggest UK disk yet, hitting #3 and staying on chart for over 5 months. With big orchestral backing, this confirms him as a teen heart-throb rather than rockabilly hero.

Oct Dramatically-backed revival of the oldie *Jealousy* also hits UK #3. *Halfway To Paradise* hits UK #5.

1962 Jan *I'd Never Find Another You* (another Goffin/King/Tony Orlando cover) hits UK #2, also winning a Carl-Alan award in UK as Favorite Dancefloor Record.

Mar Eager to record some R&B Fury covers Gladys Knight & The Pips' *Letter Full Of Tears*. It reaches UK #17. Fury collapses during UK tour.

June Big production ballad *Last Night Was Made For Love* hits UK #5.

July Promised an Elvis-like career in films, Fury stars in Michael Winner's "Play It Cool", essentially playing himself. The movie is lightweight but popular. *Once Upon A Dream*, from the film, hits UK #7, while the other movie songs are gathered on EP *Play It Cool*, which sits at #2 on UK EP chart for many weeks.

Sept Just before embarking on 50-date UK tour, Fury comes down with suspected measles and misses the first 11 dates.

Nov *Because Of Love*, also sung by Elvis Presley in movie "Girls! Girls! Girls!", reaches UK #18.

1963 Mar *Like I've Never Been Gone* takes him back into the UK Top 5, at #3.

May [31] Fury stars at the Royal Albert Hall, London, topping a bill featuring Mark Wynter, The Tornados, Freddie & The Dreamers, Shane Fenton & The Fentones, Heinz and others.

June *When Will You Say I Love You* hits UK #3. By now Fury is flanked in UK Top 10 by a whole new wave of UK hitmakers from his native Liverpool – Billy J. Kramer (at #1), The Beatles (#2), and Gerry & The Pacemakers (#6). *Billy* hits UK #6.

Aug Untypically lightweight *In Summer* is last of a trio of consecutive UK Top 5 hits, at #5. With the beat boom on the ascendant, Fury is now associated with the old school of balladeers (even though he performs much rock in similar style to most beat groups on stage, backed by The Tornados), and will henceforth have a tougher time commercially. (He survives, however, as a major chart name longer than any of his pre-beat contemporaries, apart from Cliff Richard.)

[9] He tops the bill on first edition of UK TV's major pop show "Ready Steady Go!".

Oct *Somebody Else's Girl* reaches UK #20.

[3] Fury embarks on UK tour with Joe Brown and Karl Denver.

Nov Live album **We Want Billy** reaches UK #14.

Dec [7] The Beatles, appearing on BBC TV show "Juke Box Jury", vote Fury's new single *Do You Really Love Me Too* a hit.

1964 Jan Uptempo *Do You Really Love Me Too (Fool's Errand)* makes UK #13.

[3] The Tornados undertake their final engagement with Fury in Amsterdam, Holland.

Mar [21] Fury makes his radio debut with new backing band The

Gamblers on "Saturday Club".

May Ballad *I Will*, a cover of a US hit by Vic Dana, reaches UK #13.

Aug Fury revives Conway Twitty's former #1 *It's Only Make Believe*, hitting UK #10.

Nov [4] "The Billy Fury Show" debuts on UK TV.

Dec [31] Fury enters the London Clinic with a mystery illness. Taken ill over Christmas, he is expected to stay in the clinic for 2 weeks.

1965 Jan [6] He leaves the clinic after tests prove negative. *I'm Lost Without You*, a Teddy Randazzo ballad which is the most startlingly melodramatic of all Fury's recordings, reaches UK #16.

Mar [1] Fury makes his US TV debut on "Shindig".

Apr [18] Film "I Gotta Horse", starring Fury and his racehorse Anselmo, opens in London's West End. (Anselmo had finished fifth in the 1964 Derby.)

May [22] Fury makes a rare TV appearance, topping the bill of "Thank Your Lucky Stars".

July [17] He guests on 200th edition of "Thank Your Lucky Stars".

Aug *In Thoughts Of You* hits UK #9, and is his final UK Top 10 hit.

Oct *Run To My Lovin' Arms*, covered from Jay & The Americans, reaches UK #25.

Nov [3] Fury and The Gamblers embark on an 18-date twice-nightly UK tour with Herman's Hermits, Wayne Fontana, The Fortunes and others, at the Gaumont cinema, Wolverhampton, W.Midlands. Tour ends Nov.22 at the Odeon, Manchester, Gtr. Manchester.

1966 Feb *I'll Never Quite Get Over You* reaches UK #35, Fury's poorest UK chart performance for 5 years. (He records title song *How's The World Treating You?* from play at the Wyndhams theater, where it features each night.)

Aug Revival of Tennessee Ernie Ford's *Give Me Your Word* reaches UK #27, bringing to an end Fury's hit run and also his contract with Decca. His remarkable total of 20 UK Top 20 entries is surpassed in the 60s only by The Beatles, Elvis Presley and Cliff Richard.

1967 Jan He signs a new recording contract with EMI's Parlophone label, which will produce 11 singles before the end of 1970, but no hits at all. Fury, wary of his recurring heart problems which have occasionally hospitalized him and caused tour date cancellations, takes a back seat from most live performance and spends much time on his farm, devoting efforts to horse breeding and pursuing his animal conservation interests.

1972 May He releases a one-off single, *Will The Real Man Please Stand Up*, on his own label, Fury Records, but it is not a hit.

1973 Apr [12] Movie "That'll Be The Day" starring David Essex premieres in London's West End. Fury has a cameo role as Stormy Tempest, a clone of his younger self, and sings several songs including *Long Live Rock*, written for him by Pete Townshend of The Who.

1981 Oct After many years in retirement, much of it brought on by his poor health, Fury decides to regenerate his recording career, signing to Polydor Records and working with Shakin' Stevens' producer Stuart Colman. First release is *Be Mine Tonight*.

1982 Sept *Love Or Money* returns him to UK Singles chart after 16-year gap, though it peaks at only #57.

Nov A revival of Bobby Vee's *Devil Or Angel* is another minor UK chart entry, at #58.

1983 Jan [28] Fury dies from heart failure, which has dogged him all his adult life. (His *I'm Lost Without You* is played at his funeral.)

Feb Compilation **The Billy Fury Hit Parade** makes UK #44.

Mar *The One And Only*, completed with Stuart Colman only shortly before Fury's death, peaks at UK #54.

June *Forget Him* provides an inappropriately-titled posthumous UK chart swan song, climbing to #59.

PETER GABRIEL

1975 May Gabriel (b. May 13, 1950, Cobham, Surrey) leaves Genesis after a final concert as lead vocalist at St. Etienne, France. He remains with Charisma Records as a solo artist, though will not release any records or perform live for almost 2 years.

Aug [16] He makes a belated press announcement concerning his departure from Genesis for personal reasons.

Nov He sings a cover version of *Strawberry Fields Forever* on compilation album **All This And World War II**, which makes UK #23.

1976 July He begins recordings for a solo album at Nimbus studios, Toronto, Canada.

1977 Mar *Peter Gabriel*, produced by Bob Ezrin and the first of 4 eponymously-titled albums, hits UK #7. Gabriel begins his first solo tour in US and Canada.

Apr *Solsbury Hill* reaches UK #13. He makes his London solo stage debut backed by, among others, Robert Fripp of King Crimson on guitar. A short European tour follows.

May *Peter Gabriel* reaches US #38.

[21] *Solsbury Hill* peaks at US #68.

July *Modern Love* is released in UK but fails to chart.

1978 **May** *DIY* is issued in UK, again without charting.

June Second album titled *Peter Gabriel*, produced by Robert Fripp, hits UK #10.

Aug *Peter Gabriel* reaches US #45.

Sept A remix of *DIY*, issued as a UK single, again fails to chart. He appears at Knebworth, Herts., with Frank Zappa.

1979 Gabriel spends part of the year working with writer Atejanmdo Jodorowsky on the screenplay for a movie version of Genesis' concept album/stage show "The Lamb Lies Down On Broadway", due to be financed by Charisma, but the movie never materializes.

Mar The Tom Robinson Band's *Bully For You*, co-written by Gabriel, reaches UK #68.

May [12] Gabriel joins Kate Bush and Steve Harley in a benefit concert at London's Hammersmith Odeon, for the family of Bush's lighting engineer Billy Duffy, who died in an accident. He also sings guest vocals on Robert Fripp's album *Exposure*.

1980 **Mar** *Games Without Frontiers* is his first solo Top 10 single, hitting UK #4. Kate Bush guests on back-up vocals, with whistling provided by Steve Lillywhite, Hugh Padgham, and Gabriel.

May *No Self Control* makes US #33.

June [14] Third album *Peter Gabriel*, produced by Steve Lillywhite and including guest appearances by Phil Collins, Robert Fripp, Paul Weller of The Jam, and Kate Bush, tops UK chart for 2 weeks. Charisma has leased it to US Mercury after Atlantic, US licensee of the 2 previous *Peter Gabriel* albums, turned it down. Noting UK chart success of (the included) *Games Without Frontiers*, Atlantic tries to buy the album back, but to no avail. (On a special release of the album in Germany, Gabriel sings in German.)

July Jimmy Pursey (ex-Sham 69) releases *Animals Have More Fun* in UK, co-written and co-produced by Gabriel.

Aug Third album *Peter Gabriel* peaks at US #22. *Biko*, a protest song concerning the death in South Africa of black activist Steve Biko, reaches UK #38.

Sept [20] *Games Without Frontiers* in US release by Mercury makes #48.

1982 **July** Gabriel inaugurates the "World Of Music Arts And Dance" (WOMAD) Festival at Shepton Mallet, Somerset. Becoming a regular event for many years, it brings together artists from around the world, predating later "World Music" trend. He loses money on the venture.

Sept Fourth album *Peter Gabriel*, produced by Gabriel and David Lord and the last to use this title, hits UK #6. The German market receives a German-language version.

Oct [2] A one-off reunion with Genesis at Milton Keynes Bowl, Bucks., for a WOMAD benefit concert, helps offset some of the losses of the Shepton Mallet Festival.

Shock The Monkey, taken from the new album, makes UK #58.

Nov The fourth eponymous album *Peter Gabriel* reaches US #28. Geffen, his new label in the US, stickers the sleeve with the word "Security" to give it a separate identity from the earlier 3.

Dec *I Have The Touch* is released from the album as a UK single, without charting.

1983 **Jan** [29] *Shock The Monkey* reaches US #29 and is his first single to perform better in US than UK.

May [5] Gabriel and Genesis win the award for Outstanding Contribution To British Music at the annual Ivor Novello Awards lunch at the Grosvenor House, Mayfair, London.

June Double album *Peter Gabriel Plays Live*, instigated by US Geffen, to satisfy fans in the absence of new studio material (though in fact Gabriel adds new studio overdubbing on the tracks), hits UK #8.

July *I Don't Remember*, taken from the live album, reaches UK #62.

Aug Double album *Peter Gabriel Plays Live* peaks at US #44.

Sept [10] A live version of the early hit *Solsbury Hill*, taken from it, makes US #84.

Nov Tom Robinson reaches UK #39 with *Listen To The Radio: Atmospherics*, co-written with Gabriel.

1984 **June** *Walk Through The Fire*, taken from film soundtrack of "Against All Odds" (but actually an unheard out-take from the third album), makes UK #69.

1985 **Apr** Soundtrack album from film "Birdy", composed and performed by Gabriel and co-produced with Daniel Lanois, reaches UK #51.

Dec [14] Artists United Against Apartheid, comprising 49 artists

including Gabriel, featured on the track *No More Apartheid*, makes US #38 and UK #21 with extracted single *Sun City*.

1986 **May** *Sledgehammer*, accompanied by an acclaimed "claymation" promo video by Steve Johnson, using stop-motion techniques with revolutionary flair, hits UK #4.

[31] *So*, co-produced by Gabriel and Lanois, enters UK chart at #1.

June [4] Amnesty International's "A Conspiracy Of Hope" 2-week US tour begins, featuring Gabriel, U2, Sting, Bryan Adams and Lou Reed at Cow Palace, San Francisco, CA.

[28] Gabriel takes part in anti-apartheid concert on Clapham Common, London, with Elvis Costello, Boy George, Sade, Sting, Billy Bragg and Hugh Masekela among others, before an estimated half-million crowd.

July [26] *Sledgehammer* tops US chart for a week, becoming a million-seller internationally and *So* hits US #2.

Oct [25] *In Your Eyes*, taken from the album and with backing vocals by Youssou N'Dour, reaches US #26.

Nov Gabriel's ballad duet with Kate Bush on *Don't Give Up*, taken from *So*, hits UK #9 and is promoted by 2 different videos. *Biko* is included on all-star compilation album *Conspiracy Of Hope*, released in aid of Amnesty International.

1987 **Feb** [9] Gabriel is voted Best British Male Artist and Best British Music Video, for "Sledgehammer" at the sixth annual BRIT Awards at the Grosvenor House, London.

Mar *Big Time* reaches UK #13 and hits US #8, accompanied by another eye-catching video and featuring Stewart Copeland on drums. He performs live in Japan for the "Hurricane Irene" benefit.

Apr [15] *Don't Give Up* is named Best Song Musically And Lyrically at the annual Ivor Novello Awards at the Grosvenor House, London.

[25] *Don't Give Up* peaks at US #72.

July Third extract from *So*, *Red Rain* makes UK #46.

Nov A new live version of *Biko*, taken from the soundtrack album of film "Cry Freedom", makes UK #49. Gabriel contributes to ex-Band member Robbie Robertson's eponymous first album, notably on the cut *Fallen Angel*.

1988 Gabriel's impressive collection of video hits, released as "CV", tops UK Music Video charts.

June [5-6] He participates in the sixth annual Prince's Trust Rock Gala at the Royal Albert Hall, London.

[11] Gabriel appears at "Nelson Mandela's 70th Birthday Party" at Wembley Stadium, London, playing his anti-apartheid anthem *Biko*.

July It is announced that he will participate with other major acts (including Sting, Bruce Springsteen and Tracy Chapman) in the Amnesty International world tour.

Aug The Martin Scorsese-directed film "The Last Temptation Of Christ", with a Gabriel score, opens in US and UK to much controversy.

1989 **Mar** [6] Gabriel attends launch of the *Greenpeace – Rainbow Warriors* album (which is released on the Melodiya label), in Moscow, Soviet Union, with Annie Lennox, The Thompson Twins and U2.

June Following their Amnesty performances together, Gabriel contributes to Youssou N'Dour album *Set* and extracted duet UK #61 single *Shaking The Tree*, which will later provide the title for a Gabriel greatest hits compilation.

[17] *Passion* reaches UK #29 and US #60.

July [8] *In Your Eyes* makes US #41.

1990 **Feb** [21] Gabriel wins Best New Age Performance for *Passion – Music For The Last Temptation Of Christ* at the 32nd annual Grammy awards at the Shrine Auditorium, Los Angeles, CA.

Apr [16] Gabriel participates in "Nelson Mandela – An International Tribute To A Free South Africa" concert at Wembley Stadium, London, with Bonnie Raitt, Neil Young, Simple Minds, The Neville Brothers, Aswad and Tracy Chapman among others.

Dec [1] Gabriel hit collection, *Shaking The Tree: Sixteen Golden Greats* enters UK chart, set to reach UK #11. Album sleeve photo of Gabriel has been shot by controversial photographer Robert Mapplethorpe.

1991 **Feb** [9] *Shaking The Tree: Sixteen Golden Greats* reaches US #48.

May [12] Gabriel appears by satellite from Holland in "The Simple Truth" concert for Kurdish refugees at Wembley Arena, London.

ART GARFUNKEL

1970 Garfunkel (b. Nov.5, 1941, New York, NY) and long-time musical partner Paul Simon, whom he met at school in Queens, New York, at age 11, have established the most successful duo since The Everly Brothers. They split for professional reasons but remain firm friends. Garfunkel's first solo project is playing the character of Negley in Mike Nichols' black comedy war drama movie "Catch 22", which has filmed in Italy in May 1969.

1971 He appears opposite Ann-Margret and Candice Bergen with Jack Nicholson in film "Carnal Knowledge".

1973 **Oct** Having spent a characteristically long period of time crafting his music, Garfunkel emerges with debut solo single, the Jimmy Webb-penned ballad *All I Know* and *Angel Clare*, co-produced with ex-Simon & Garfunkel producer Roy Halee, which hits US #5 and reaches UK #14.
Nov [10] *All I Know* hits US #9.

1974 **Feb** [9] *I Shall Sing* makes US #38.
Oct [26] Garfunkel's version of Tim Moore's lost love-themed *Second Avenue* makes US #34.

1975 **Oct** [19] Garfunkel reunites with Simon for the first time on NBC TV's "Saturday Night Live."
[25] A revival of The Flamingos' 1959 hit *I Only Have Eyes For You* tops UK chart.
Nov *Breakaway*, produced by Richard Perry, climbs to hit #7 in both US and UK.
[29] *I Only Have Eyes For You* reaches US #18.
Dec Reunion cut with, and written by, Simon, and included on *Breakaway*, *My Little Town* hits US #9.

1976 **Jan** [31] Third single and title cut, *Breakaway*, written by Gallagher & Lyle, makes US #39.

1977 **Aug** From forthcoming album project recorded mostly at Muscle Shoals studio, *Crying In My Sleep* falls short of both charts.

1978 **Feb** *Watermark* is released, making US #19 and UK #25.
Mar [18] Extracted cover of Sam Cooke classic *Wonderful World*, recorded as a trio with James Taylor and Paul Simon, reaches US #17. (CBS/Columbia insist on the extra song to boost the commerciality of the album.) 1 other cut is recorded with Irish folk band The Chieftains, while the remaining 10 compositions are all penned by songwriter Jimmy Webb with whom Garfunkel is developing a lasting professional relationship.
[24] During a 50-city US tour, his first since Simon & Garfunkel days, he performs the first of 2 sell-out dates at Carnegie Hall, New York, 1 performed with Webb.

1979 **Feb** Garfunkel hosts popular US TV show, NBC's "Saturday Night Live" in which Paul Simon also appears.
Apr During a busy period, fourth album *Fate For Breakfast* reaches US #67 and hits UK #2, aided considerably by a surprise UK #1 single, *Bright Eyes*. Written by UK composer Mike Batt, it is heavily featured in cartoon film of Richard Adams' **Watership Down**. Enjoying a 19-week stay on UK chart, it becomes a rare UK million-seller. In US it disappears without trace.
July A cover of The Skyliners' 1959 hit *Since I Don't Have You* reaches US #53 and UK #38.
Sept His acting career flourishes with a lead role in Nicholas Roeg-directed "Bad Timing". While he is filming it in Europe, his girlfriend commits suicide in New York. He also makes the more modest film "Illusions".

1981 **Sept** *Scissors Cut* reunites him with Roy Halee. It reaches US #113 and UK #51.
[19] *A Heart In New York* peaks at US #66, but the album fails to produce any hit singles, despite songwriting contributions from Gallagher & Lyle, Jules Shear, Clifford T. Ward and Jimmy Webb.
Oct Simon & Garfunkel unite for a concert in New York's Central Park. Following its success (documented on film, TV and video), the duo continues around the world for a 12-month tour. Press reports indicate growing personality friction as tour progresses.

1982 **Apr** [19] Simon & Garfunkel announce a reunion (though it will be mainly for nostalgic live concerts).

1984 **Nov** A UK compilation, *The Art Garfunkel Album*, with the help of a TV campaign, climbs to UK #12. It is not released in US.

1986 **July** Garfunkel is featured in the role of a teacher in a "go-go rap" movie "Good To Go".
Dec Having performed a Jimmy Webb seasonal work, "The Animals Christmas", in London and New York, Garfunkel releases a non-charting album of it with gospel singer Amy Grant also featured.

1988 *So In Love*, a reworking of The Tymes' 1963 hit, is released from forthcoming album. While promoting it in UK, Garfunkel is visibly upset by the interviewer's probing emotional questioning on BBC TV show "Wogan" and refuses to perform the song. It fails to chart.
Mar *Lefty* peaks at US #134 but fails in UK.
May A cover version of Percy Sledge classic *When A Man Loves A Woman* fails to score.
Sept Plans are announced by manager Ken Greengrass for Garfunkel

to return to live European work including a scheduled appearance at the Prince's Trust charity concert in London with James Taylor.

1989 **July** [12] Disney announces its forthcoming TV channel's Shelley Duvall-produced "Mother Goose Rock'N'Rhyme", with a host of music celebrities, including Art Garfunkel as the Rhymeland bartender.

1990 **Jan** [17] Garfunkel sings *Bridge Over Troubled Water* and *The Boxer* with Paul Simon at the musical jam after the fifth annual Rock'N'Roll Hall Of Fame dinner, at which Simon and Garfunkel are inducted, at the Waldorf Astoria, New York.
June Garfunkel performs in Sofia, Bulgaria, at the request of US State Department at an outdoor rally for democracy attended by an audience estimated at 1.4 million.
Dec [15] Wife Kathryn Cermak gives birth to their son.

MARVIN GAYE

1957 Gaye (b. Marvin Pentz Gaye Jr., Apr.2, 1939, Washington, DC), the son of an apostolic minister, returns to Washington with an honorable discharge from the US Navy and joins doo-wop group The Marquees who record, via an introduction from friend and adviser Bo Diddley, *Hey Little School Girl* (produced by Diddley) and *Baby You're My Only Love* for Okeh.

1958 The Marquees are recruited by Harvey Fuqua, who is re-forming his seminal doo-wop group The Moonglows in Washington.

1959 Moving to Chicago, IL, the group, as Harvey & The Moonglows, records *Almost Grown* for Chess Records.

1960 Fuqua and Gaye leave The Moonglows and move to Detroit, where Fuqua sets up Tri-Phi and Harvey labels. He signs as an artist to Gwen Gordy's Anna label, a subsidiary of her brother Berry Gordy's Motown Records, into which his own labels are then absorbed. Through this connection, Gaye finds work as a session drummer (for The Miracles) and back-up vocalist (for The Marvelettes) at Anna and Motown.

1961 Gaye signs to Motown as a solo artist and marries Berry Gordy's younger sister Anna.
May He records his first solo, *Let Your Conscience Be Your Guide*, and *The Soulful Moods Of Marvin Gaye*, a collection of ballads and only the second album released by Motown. Neither chart.

1962 **Oct** With "The Motown Revue" (including The Miracles, The Contours, Mary Wells, The Supremes and Little Stevie Wonder), Gaye begins a 2-month US tour.
Dec In a change of pace with new producer William "Mickey" Stevenson, *Stubborn Kind Of Fellow*, with backing vocals by Martha & The Vandellas, is Gaye's US chart debut at #46. It also makes R&B Top 10. An album of the same title follows.
[19] Gaye begins a 10-day run at the Apollo theater in Harlem, New York, with "The Motown Revue".

1963 **Mar** *Hitch Hike* (covered 2 years later by The Rolling Stones) reaches US #30.
July *Pride And Joy* hits US #10. *Live On Stage* is released.
Dec *Can I Get A Witness* (again covered by The Rolling Stones) makes US #22, and B-side *I'm Crazy 'Bout My Baby* climbs to US #77.

1964 **Apr** Under Gordy's direction, Gaye is teamed with Mary Wells to record *Together*.
May *You're A Wonderful One* reaches US #15.
June *Once Upon A Time*, a duet with Wells, makes US #19. It is taken from *Together*, which reaches US #42.
July *Once Upon A Time* is Gaye's UK chart debut, at #50 for 1 week. In US, B-side *What's The Matter With You Baby* makes US #17. *Greatest Hits*, a compilation of Gaye's singles to date, reaches US #72.
Sept *Try It Baby* peaks at US #15. Gaye performs on Murray The K's "Rock'N'Roll Extravaganza" at the Brooklyn Fox theater, with label mates The Temptations, The Supremes, The Miracles, The Contours and Martha & The Vandellas, plus UK group The Searchers and others.
Oct *Baby Don't You Do It* (later revived by The Who) climbs to US #27.
[28] Gaye participates in US TV's "TAMI Show" with The Beach Boys, The Rolling Stones, Chuck Berry and others.
Nov Motown pairs Gaye with another girl singer, Kim Weston, on *What Good Am I Without You*, which makes US #61.
[17] Gaye arrives in UK for TV appearances, meeting up with Dionne Warwick that night after hearing about her car crash. He appears in "Scene at 6.30" (Nov.18), "Ready Steady Go!" (Nov.20), "Thank Your Lucky Stars" (Nov.28) and "Saturday Club" (Dec.5).
Dec *How Sweet It Is (To Be Loved By You)* is Gaye's first solo UK success, reaching #49.

1965 **Jan** *How Sweet It Is (To Be Loved By You)* hits US #6.
Mar *How Sweet It Is To Be Loved By You* makes US #128.

May *I'll Be Doggone* hits US #8, becoming Gaye's first US R&B #1 and million-seller.

Aug *Pretty Little Baby* reaches US #25.

Nov *Ain't That Peculiar* hits US #8 and R&B #1, and is another million-seller. Gaye releases 2 albums which reveal different sides of his style: *A Tribute To The Great Nat "King" Cole* and *Hello Broadway* (a collection of show tunes).

1966 Mar Gaye reportedly screen tests for title role in film "The Nat King Cole Story". *One More Heartache* peaks at US #29.

July *Take This Heart Of Mine* reaches US #44.

Aug *Moods Of Marvin Gaye*, mostly a singles compilation, climbs to US #118.

Sept *Little Darlin' (I Need You)* makes US #47 and UK #50.

Oct Another compilation album, *Marvin Gaye Greatest Hits, Vol.2*, peaks at US #178.

1967 Mar Gaye and Weston duet on *Take Two*, from which *It Takes Two* makes US #14 and UK #16.

July Gaye duets with Philadelphia singer Tammi Terrell on *Ain't No Mountain High Enough*, which reaches US #19. (This will be Gaye's most enduring collaboration; he and Terrell will record together until her tragic death.)

Aug *Your Unchanging Love* makes US #33.

Nov Gaye and Terrell's *Your Precious Love* hits US #5, while duet album *United* reaches US #69.

1968 Jan Duo enjoys its second US Top 10 success with *If I Could Build My Whole World Around You* which hits US #10 and makes UK #41. B-side *If This World Were Mine* reaches US #68.

Feb Gaye's solo *You* makes US #34.

Mar *Greatest Hits* makes UK #40.

May Another Gaye/Terrell duet, *Ain't Nothing Like The Real Thing*, hits US #8 and UK #34.

Sept *You're All I Need To Get By*, with Terrell, hits US #7.

Oct Terrell collapses on stage in Gaye's arms during a concert at Hampton-Sydney college in Virginia. Doctors diagnose a brain tumor. Meanwhile, the duo's *You're All I Need* reaches US #60.

Nov Gaye's solo *Chained* makes US #32, while *You're All I Need To Get By* climbs to UK #19. Another duet with Terrell, *Keep On Lovin' Me Honey*, makes US #24.

Dec Gaye's first US #1 (for 7 weeks), and also Motown's longest-running #1, is *I Heard It Through The Grapevine*, a Norman Whitfield/Barrett Strong song (a million-seller for Gladys Knight & The Pips on Motown in 1967). After lying unused for some months after he recorded it, Gaye's dramatically different version becomes the biggest-selling single of Motown's first 20 years of operations. It is taken from *In The Groove*, which reaches US #63.

[28] Gaye performs at the Miami Pop Festival in Hallendale, FL, with Chuck Berry, Junior Walker, Fleetwood Mac and others.

1969 Feb *You Ain't Livin' Till You're Lovin'*, a Terrell duet, climbs to UK #21.

Mar *I Heard It Through The Grapevine* hits UK #1 for 3 weeks and is a worldwide hit. Gaye and Terrell's duet *Good Lovin' Ain't Easy To Come By* makes US #30.

June *Too Busy Thinking About My Baby* hits US #4 and is another million-seller. (B-side *Wherever I Lay My Hat* will be a UK #1 in 1983 for Paul Young.)

July *Good Lovin' Ain't Easy To Come By* reaches UK #26. *M.P.G.* is Gaye's first US album Top 50 placing at #33. At the same time, compilation *Marvin Gaye And His Girls*, featuring duets with Terrell, Wells and Weston, peaks at US #183.

Sept *Too Busy Thinking About My Baby* hits UK #5.

Oct Duet *Easy* with Terrell makes US #184, while solo *That's The Way Love Is* hits US #7, but fails to chart in UK. The album of the same title reaches US #189.

Dec *What You Gave Me*, with Terrell, reaches US #49. Another Terrell duet, *The Onion Song* hits UK #9 (the last hit for the duo). (It will reach US #50 5 months later.)

1970 Feb *How Can I Forget* reaches US #41.

Mar [16] Terrell dies, aged 24, in Graduate hospital, Philadelphia, PA. She has had 6 brain operations in 18 months. Grief-stricken, Gaye retires from the public eye.

[21] *Gonna Give Her All The Love I've Got* peaks at US #67.

June *Abraham, Martin And John*, written by Dick Holler (a US hit for Dion and on Motown for The Miracles), hits UK #9. *Marvin Gaye And Tammi Terrell's Greatest Hits* reaches US #171 and UK #60.

July *The End Of Our Road* makes US #40.

Dec Compilation *Marvin Gaye Super Hits* climbs to US #117.

1971 Jan [17] Gaye sings the American national anthem before Super Bowl V between the Baltimore Colts and the Miami Dolphins at the Orange Bowl, Miami, FL.

Apr Gaye returns to the spotlight with a creative tour-de-force in a new, subtler style (the result of his own writing and production), voicing concern about poverty, pollution and the Vietnam War. *What's Going On* hits US #2 for 3 weeks (behind Three Dog Night's *Joy To The World*) and is a million-seller.

July *What's Going On* hits US #6.

Aug *Mercy Mercy Mercy (The Ecology)*, from the album, hits US #4 and is another million-seller.

Nov Third US single from *Inner City Blues (Make Me Wanna Holler)*, hits US #9. In UK, where the new style has not met the same reaction, both album and single of *What's Going On* fail to chart, although both will historically be viewed as classics by critics. *Save The Children* is extracted from the album and reaches UK #41.

1972 June *You're The Man* hits US #50.

1973 Feb Following the success of Isaac Hayes and Curtis Mayfield in similar ventures, Gaye writes and performs soundtrack for a detective movie, "Trouble Man". Title track hits US #7, while soundtrack album (with 3 vocals and 10 instrumental tracks) reaches US #14.

Sept *Let's Get It On*, again self-produced (with Ed Townsend), but this time in an earthier R&B style than the ethereal *What's Going On*, tops US chart for 2 weeks, is another million-seller and makes UK #31.

Oct *Let's Get It On*, a celebration of sexuality, performed in appropriate muscular, steamy style, hits US #2.

Nov *Let's Get It On* makes UK #39.

Dec Motown teams Gaye with his fourth female singing partner, Diana Ross, and they record *Diana And Marvin*, which climbs to US #26. The duet single *You're A Special Part Of Me* reaches US #12, while Gaye's solo *Come To Get This*, from *Let's Get It On*, makes US #21.

1974 Feb *You Sure Love To Ball*, also from the album, reaches US #50.

Apr *You Are Everything*, a Gaye/Ross revival of The Stylistics' US hit, hits UK #5.

May Another Ross/Gaye duet, *My Mistake (Was To Love You)*, reaches US #19. Triple compilation *Marvin Gaye Anthology*, containing most of his hit singles to date, reaches US #61.

Aug Gaye/Ross duet *Don't Knock My Love* reaches US #46, while *Marvin Gaye Live!*, recorded in concert at Oakland, CA, (a return to live stage after a 6-year absence) hits US #8.

Nov Gaye's solo *Distant Lover* (later a favorite stage performance) reaches US #28.

1976 June *I Want You* hits US #4 and makes UK #22, while extracted title track reaches US #15.

Aug *After The Dance*, also from the album, reaches US #74.

Sept Gaye plays sold-out, rave-reviewed concerts in London at the Royal Albert Hall and Palladium, the latter recorded for album release.

Nov Compilation *Marvin Gaye's Greatest Hits* reaches US #44. It is retitled *The Best Of Marvin Gaye* in UK, where it reaches #56.

1977 Apr Though they have not lived together for years, Gaye and Anna Gordy are only now divorced. Gaye marries Janis Hunter.

June Dance-oriented *Got To Give It Up*, another million-seller, tops US chart and hits UK #7. Double live *Marvin Gaye Live At The London Palladium*, which includes *Got To Give It Up* as its only studio track, hits US #3.

1978 Oct It is reported that Gaye is in a state of financial collapse, with unsecured debts of $7 million.

Nov Janis Hunter files for divorce.

1979 Feb Double *Here, My Dear*, a tortured reflection on the break-up of Gaye's marriage to Anna Gordy, reaches US #26. Gaye teams with Stevie Wonder, Diana Ross and Smokey Robinson for *Pops We Love You* a tribute to Berry Gordy's father's 90th birthday. It reaches US #59. Gaye, beset by problems, including hard drugs (especially free-base cocaine), and pursued by US Internal Revenue Service (IRS) with an unpaid tax bill over $2 million, moves to self-imposed exile and seclusion in Hawaii (where he reportedly tries to commit suicide with a cocaine overdose) and lives in a trailer.

1980 July [4] He plays Independence Day celebrations at London's Venue.

1981 Mar *In Our Lifetime*, Gaye's last new album for Motown, issued without his approval, reaches US #32 and UK #48. Now increasingly erratic as a performer and suffering from paranoid delusions brought on by years of drug abuse, Gaye divides his time between London and Ostend, Belgium. He severs his contract with Motown. CBS pays Motown $1.5 million to buy his contract.

1982 Nov Signed, after lengthy negotiations (involving the IRS, which is due most of Gaye's royalties), to CBS/Columbia, Gaye's *(Sexual) Healing*, a sensual progression from *Let's Get It On*, hits UK #4.

Dec *Midnight Love*, recorded at Studio Katy in Ohaine near Brussels in Belgium, with old friend Fuqua and brother-in-law Gordon Banks, hits US #7 and UK #10, achieving million-plus sales. *(Sexual) Healing* tops US R&B chart for 10 weeks, the first disk to do so since Ray Charles' *I Can't Stop Loving You* in 1962. Gaye returns to US, living in Hollywood and then Palm Springs.

983 **Jan** *(Sexual) Healing* hits US #3 (also selling a million), while *My Love Is Waiting* reaches UK #34.

Feb Gaye sings *The Star Spangled Banner* at the NBA (National Basketball Association) All-Star Game.

[25] Gaye wins his first Grammy award for *(Sexual) Healing* named Best Male Vocal Performance Of The Year.

June A US tour to promote the new material is not a financial success, and the pressure again pushes Gaye into a drug retreat.

Sept Gaye's version of *I Heard It Through The Grapevine* is used over the credits of movie "The Big Chill".

Nov *Every Great Motown Hit Of Marvin Gaye* reaches US #80. Gaye moves into his parents' house (purchased by him for them in the 60s) in Crenshaw, Los Angeles, CA.

Dec TV-advertised compilation *Greatest Hits* reaches UK #13.

984 **Mar** Gaye announces more than once to relatives that he intends to take his own life – once having a gun forcibly removed from his grasp.

Apr [1] Gaye, still living at his parents' home at 2101 South Grammercy in Los Angeles, and with family and friends concerned over his mental state, is shot dead by his father, Marvin Gaye Sr., during a violent argument.

[5] Gaye is buried at Forest Lawn Cemetery in Los Angeles. The funeral service is attended by Smokey Robinson, Stevie Wonder, Motown's Berry Gordy, Harvey Fuqua, Quincy Jones, Ray Parker Jr., producers Norman Whitfield and Eddie and Brian Holland. Robinson reads the 23rd Psalm, and Wonder sings *Lighting Up The Candle*.

Nov Gaye's father gets 5 years for voluntary manslaughter.

985 **Jan** [1] "The Star Spangled Banner" is first video to air on VH1.

Apr Lionel Richie writes Gaye-tribute *Missing You*, a US #10 for Diana Ross.

May *Sanctified Lady* reaches UK #51.

June *Dream Of A Lifetime*, a compilation of tracks recorded shortly before his death and unreleased material from Gaye's time at Motown, reaches UK #46.

Dec *Romantically Yours*, drawn from unissued 1979 jazz-oriented big band sessions, is released, without charting.

986 **May** *Motown Remembers Marvin Gaye*, a compilation of previously unreleased 1963-72 material, peaks at US #193. *I Heard It Through The Grapevine* is reissued in UK after being used on a TV ad for Levi's jeans, and hits UK #8.

988 **Nov** As Gaye's back-catalog continues to be re-promoted, *Love Songs*, combining individual ballad hits of Gaye and Smokey Robinson, a UK-only release, peaks at #69.

990 **Sept** [27] Gaye receives a star on the Hollywood Walk Of Fame at 1500 Vine Street.

Nov UK TV-advertised *Love Songs* peaks at #39.

THE J. GEILS BAND

Peter Wolf (vocals)
J. Geils (guitar)
Danny Klein (bass)
Seth Justman (keyboards and vocals)
Magic Dick (harmonica)
Stephen Jo Bladd (drums and vocals)

967 Geils (b. Jerome Geils, Feb.20, 1946, New York, NY), and Klein (b. May 13, 1946, New York), having performed in a jug band in Worcester Tech, MA, and dropped out of college to go professional, moving to Boston and switching from jug band music to blues and playing in local band The Hallucinations, with Dick (b. Richard Salwitz, May 13, 1945, New London, CT), Wolf (b. Peter Blankfield, Mar.7, 1946, New York), an ex-DJ on Boston's WBCN with an encyclopedic knowledge of R&B music, and Bladd (b. July 13, 1942, Boston, MA). The J. Geils Blues Band is formed and Geils, Dick, Klein, Wolf and Bladd will provide the band's nucleus for 16 years.

969 Justman (b. Jan.27, 1951, Washington, DC) joins and "Blues" is dropped from the name. The group's reputation builds, performing at local club the Catacombs, followed by much success at the Boston Tea Party. Atlantic promotion man Mario Medious sees the band in Boston, on a bill with Dr. John.

Aug They are asked to take part in the Woodstock Festival, but turn it

down, Geils explaining "3 days in the mud – who needs it?"

1971 **Jan** Group cuts eponymous first R&B album (including covers of John Lee Hooker and Otis Rush songs) for Atlantic, which wins it the Most Promising New Band award from **Rolling Stone** magazine. Critics praise the band as the best white blues/R&B act since Paul Butterfield. Album reaches only US #195.

June [27] Band plays the final night of the Fillmore East with The Beach Boys, The Allman Brothers and Mountain.

Dec Follow-up album *The Morning After* reaches US #64.

1972 **Jan** [15] A cover of Bobby Womack's *Looking For A Love*, the group's first Singles chart entry, makes US #39.

Apr [1] 4 people die, including a 16-year-old hacked to death in his sleeping bag, during the Mar Y Sol Festival, Puerto Rico, at which The J. Geils Band is performing.

Nov *Live – Full House* makes US #54.

1973 **Apr** Band appears on ABC TV's "In Concert" but is censored due to the offensive lyrics of a song.

May *Bloodshot* hits US #10.

June [23] *Give It To Me* reaches US #30 and pushes sales of *Bloodshot* to gold status.

Sept [8] *Make Up Your Mind* makes only US #98.

1974 **Jan** *Ladies Invited* makes US #51 and *Nightmares ... And Other Tales From The Vinyl Jungle* reaches US #26. They represent a departure from the band's traditional R&B base.

Aug [7] Wolf marries actress Faye Dunaway in Beverly Hills, Los Angeles. (The marriage will end in divorce.)

1975 **Jan** [4] *Must Of Got Lost* reaches US #12.

Oct *Hotline* makes US #36.

Nov Band records gigs in Boston and at Detroit's Cobo Arena for the next album.

1976 **May** [1] *Where Did Our Love Go* peaks at US #68.

June Double live *Blow Your Face Out* climbs to US #40.

1977 **July** The J. Geils Band changes name to Geils for self-produced *Monkey Island*, which is its final Atlantic album and reaches US #51.

Aug [20] *You're The Only One* climbs to US #83.

1979 **Feb** Group leaves Atlantic for EMI America. *Sanctuary* reaches US #49 and earns another gold disk.

[3] Extracted *One Last Kiss* makes US #35.

Apr [7] *Take It Back* peaks at US #67.

June *One Last Kiss* makes UK #74.

July Atlantic issues *Best Of The J. Geils Band*, which peaks at US #129.

1980 **Feb** *Love Stinks* makes US #18 and earns a gold disk.

Mar [22] Extracted *Come Back* makes US #32.

May [31] Title cut *Love Stinks* makes US #38.

June [1] Band performs at the Lyceum Ballroom, London, as part of an extensive European tour.

Wolf is injured in pub fight in London after being attacked by 6 thugs. 6 stitches are required for facial cuts. 5 days later the band plays Pink Pop Festival in Holland and Wolf appears on crutches.

July [19] *Just Can't Wait* reaches US #78.

1981 **Dec** [25] Group plays at the Norfolk Prison, Boston.

1982 **Feb** [6] Jaunty pop-rock hit *Centerfold* and parent album *Freeze Frame* both top US charts.

Apr [10] Title track *Freeze Frame* hits US #4, while *Centerfold* becomes the group's biggest UK hit at #3. *Freeze Frame* reaches UK #12.

May *Freeze-Frame* makes UK #27.

July [3] *Angel In Blue*, the third single from *Freeze Frame*, makes US #40 and UK #55. Band tours UK supporting The Rolling Stones.

1983 **Jan** Live *Showtime!* reaches US #23.

[8] *I Do* climbs to US #24. Wolf leaves for a solo career as the press reports suggest he has been sacked, though his departure will end all commercial success for the band.

Mar [19] *Land Of A Thousand Dances* reaches US #60.

1984 **Aug** Wolf's solo *Lights Out*, co-written and co-produced by Michael Jonzun, reaches US #24.

Sept [8] Title track *Lights Out* reaches US #12.

Nov [24] Wolf's *I Need You Tonight* makes US #36.

Dec [1] Group's *Concealed Weapons* peaks at US #63. Its first post-Wolf album *You're Getting Even While I'm Getting Odd* reaches US #80. (As Wolf prepares for first solo tour, EMI-America announces a major corporate re-organization. Support for him is withdrawn and the tour is cancelled. Wolf leaves the label.)

1985 **May** [18] *Oo-Ee-Diddley-Bop!* makes US #61.

July Wolf duets with Aretha Franklin on the latter's *Push* from *Who's Zoomin Who*.

Aug [17] *Fright Night* from the film of the same name, reaches US #91.

THE J. GEILS BAND cont.

Dec Wolf is featured on *Let Me See Your I.D.* track from the Artists United Against Apartheid album.

1986 **Nov** Justman guests on Deborah Harry solo album *Rockbird*.

1987 **Apr** [25] *Come As You Are*, recorded at the Synchro Sound studio, Boston, reaches US #15.
May Wolf's *Come As You Are* peaks at US #53.
June EMI America issues J.Geils Band retrospective *Flashback*.
[6] *Can't Get Started* peaks at US #75.

1989 Wolf moves to Nashville, TN, where he lives for 6 months working with songwriters Taylor Rhodes and Robert White Johnson for new album *Up To No Good*, while Justman and Dick form a new band.

GENESIS

Tony Banks (keyboards)
Mike Rutherford (guitars)
Phil Collins (drums, vocals)

1965 **May** 2 groups are formed at public school Charterhouse in Godalming, Surrey: Peter Gabriel (b. May 13, 1950, London) and Banks (b. Mar.27, 1951, East Heathly, Sussex) are in The Garden Wall, with Chris Stewart (drums); Rutherford (b. Oct.2, 1950, Guildford, Surrey) and Anthony Phillips are members of The Anon with Rivers Job (bass), Richard MacPhail (vocals) and Rob Tyrell (drums).

1966 **Sept** Joining forces as The (New) Anon after some pupils have left the school, Phillips, Rutherford, Gabriel, Banks and Stewart make a 6-track demo tape of mostly Phillips/Rutherford songs.

1967 **Jan** They send the tape to ex-Charterhouse pupil Jonathan King at Decca Records, who is impressed, finances more demos and renames the group Genesis.
Dec Still at school, the group signs a 1-year contract to Decca and King produces its first session at Regent Sound studio in London.

1968 **Feb** Debut single *The Silent Sun* is released, but does not chart.
May Stewart departs and John Silver joins on drums. *A Winter's Tale* is released by Decca but fails to chart.
Aug King books studio time in the school summer holidays to produce and record a Genesis album.

1969 **Mar** *From Genesis To Revelation* is released, an orchestra having been added after the sessions to make them sound like The Moody Blues. (The album allegedly sells just 650 copies.)
June *Where The Sour Turns To Sweet*, the last Decca release, fails to sell.
July With all members now finished at school (though Banks has begun a physics course at Essex University), the group decides to go professional. Silver leaves and is replaced on drums by John Mayhew, recruited through a **Melody Maker** classified ad.
Sept After Aug. rehearsals, Genesis plays its first paid gig (at a private party; fee £25), moving on to a series of youth club, social club and college bookings (Twickenham technical college pays a princely £50).
Oct For 5 months the group lives together in a cottage near Dorking, Surrey, practising and rehearsing its stage act and writing songs for the second album.

1970 **Mar** Charisma Records owner Tony Stratton-Smith sees Genesis live, signs them to his label and becomes their manager.
July After completing the new album, Phillips and Mayhew leave. (Phillips will record several guitar-based solo albums in the late 70s.)
Aug Collins (b. Jan.31, 1951, Chiswick, London), in Flaming Youth band, joins on drums after auditioning with 14 others in reply to **Melody Maker** ad looking for drummer "sensitive to acoustic music".
Oct *Trespass* is released in UK but fails to chart.
Dec Mick Barnard, a temporary replacement for Phillips, is in turn replaced by ex-Quiet World member Steve Hackett (b. Feb.12, 1950, London) on guitar.

1971 **Jan** 2-part single *The Knife*, taken from *Trespass*, does not sell. Band begins to gig constantly in UK, building a solid live following.
June Gabriel breaks his ankle, which halts touring for a while, and the group works in the studio on a new album.
Nov *Nursery Cryme*, on which Collins sings his first lead vocal on 1 track, does not chart. In live shows Gabriel's props and masks attract the attention of the music press, though these and his between-songs stories are initially there to cover up the band's tuning and to settle Gabriel's own nerves.

1972 **Jan** First live gig outside UK is in Brussels, Belgium.
May *Happy The Man* is released but does not chart.
Oct *Foxtrot* reaches UK #12. Its 24-min. track *Supper's Ready* becomes an early live anthem for the band.
Dec [11] Band plays its debut US gig, at Brandeis University near Boston, MA.

1973 **Jan** First headlining tour of major UK venues is undertaken.
Mar Band begins its first full US tour.
Aug *Genesis Live*, recorded live in Leicester, Leics. and Manchester, Gtr.Manchester, originally taped for a US radio broadcast, hits UK #9.
Oct *Selling England By The Pound*, co-produced by Genesis and John Burns, and again featuring a Collins lead vocal track, hits UK #3. Promoter Tony Smith takes over from Tony Stratton-Smith (no relation) as manager.
Nov Another major UK tour is followed by a second extensive US trek.

1974 **Jan** Genesis performs 5 sell-out nights at London's Drury Lane theater.
Feb *Selling England By The Pound*, is their first US chart entry, at #70.
Apr *I Know What I Like (In Your Wardrobe)*, an edited version of a track from recent album *Selling England By The Pound* is Genesis' first hit single, at UK #21.
May [11] 18-month-old *Nursery Cryme* makes a belated UK chart showing at #39.
June *Genesis Live* reaches US #105.
Oct London Records in US releases the 1969 *From Genesis To Revelation*, which crawls to US #170.
Nov *Counting Out Time* does not chart. Group begins a world tour, with a show based around new double album, *The Lamb Lies Down On Broadway*, which it will perform 102 times.
Dec Double *The Lamb Lies Down On Broadway*, recorded on the Island studios mobile, hits UK #10.

1975 **Jan** *The Lamb Lies Down On Broadway* reaches US #41.
Apr *The Carpet Crawlers* does not chart.
May At the end of the highly theatrical "Lamb Lies Down" world tour in St. Etienne, France, Gabriel plays his last show with the band before departing for unrevealed personal reasons (eventually to embark on a successful solo career).
Nov Hackett releases *Voyage Of The Acolyte* which peaks at UK #26.

1976 **Mar** *A Trick Of The Tail*, produced by David Hentschel, hits UK #3 with Collins on lead vocals as well as drums since the search for a new singer to replace Gabriel has proved unsuccessful. Title track fails to chart as a single.
[28] Ex-Yes and King Crimson drummer Bill Bruford joins for a US tour, freeing Collins for vocal duties.
Apr *A Trick Of The Tail* makes US #31. Group has decided on individual writing credits for this album.
Dec After a series of UK gigs, Bruford returns to session work and is replaced by American session drummer Chester Thompson. On a further UK tour, Genesis is the first band to play the re-opened Rainbow theater, Finsbury Park, London.

1977 **Jan** *Wind And Wuthering*, produced by Hentschel and Genesis and recorded in Holland the previous Nov. hits UK #7.
Feb [1] The film "Genesis In Concert" is premiered in London, with Princess Anne in attendance.
Band begins a 3-month, 45-city North American tour.
Mar Ballad *Your Own Special Way* makes UK #43.
Apr [2] *Your Own Special Way* is also their first US hit single, at #62. *Wind And Wuthering* makes US #26.
June 3-track EP *Spot The Pigeon* reaches UK #14. Genesis plays 3 sold-out nights at Earls Court, London. Hackett leaves (he will have 6 hit solo albums in the UK and US in 6 years). Band is honored with the Silver Clef Award from the Nordoff-Robbins Music Therapy Centre.
Nov Double live *Seconds Out* (with Hackett) hits UK #4. The remaining members work on a new album as a trio, recording in Holland with Hentschel.

1978 **Jan** *Seconds Out* reaches US #47.
Feb American guitarist Daryl Steurmer replaces Hackett as a guest for stage work only.
Mar [29] Band arrives in US for a 20-date tour, the first leg of "World Tour 78", which will keep them on the road for most of the year.
Apr First trio release, *Follow You, Follow Me*, hits UK #7. *And Then There Were Three*, referencing new line-up total, hits UK #3.
May *And Then There Were Three* earns the band its first gold disk, reaching US #14.
[15] Group begins European leg of its world tour.
June [24] Band shares top billing with Jefferson Starship at the Knebworth Festival, Herts., as *Follow You, Follow Me* makes US #23.
July *Many Too Many* peaks at UK #43.

1979 After months of arduous live work, Genesis is put on hold as Banks and Rutherford record solo albums and Collins tries to resolve marital difficulties.
Nov Banks' *A Curious Feeling*, featuring Chester Thompson and singer Kim Beacon, charts at UK #21 and US #171.

'80 Mar [29] Band begins a 7-month world tour in Vancouver, Canada. Rutherford's solo *Smallcreep's Day* reaches UK #13 and US #163.
Apr [5] *Duke*, recorded at Abba's Polar studios in Stockholm, Sweden, is their first UK #1, for 2 weeks. *Turn It On Again* hits UK #8.
May [24] Collins, Banks and Rutherford amuse Los Angeles fans by turning up at the Roxy club box office to sell tickets personally for their performance.
June *Duchess* climbs to UK #46. *Duke* reaches US #11 and will earn the band's second US gold disk.
Aug [16] Taken from the album, *Misunderstanding* reaches US #14.
Sept *Misunderstanding* makes UK #42.
Oct [4] *Turn It On Again* peaks at US #58.

'81 Feb With Collins' parallel solo career now underway, Genesis launches its own Duke Records label, distributed by Atlantic in the US. John Martyn, Leo Kosmin and the band Nine Ways To Win are all signed, but the project is short-lived.
Sept [26] *Abacab*, featuring the horn section from Earth, Wind & Fire, and generally a far cry from *Trespass/Nursery Cryme* days, is the group's second UK #1 (for 2 weeks), while the title track hits UK #9.
Nov *Abacab* hits US #7. Their first US Top 10 success, it earns the group a platinum disk. *Keep It Dark* makes UK #33.
[28] *No Reply At All* reaches US #29.

'82 Feb [20] Title track *Abacab* reaches US #26.
Mar *Man On The Corner* makes UK #41.
May [8] *Man On The Corner* makes US #40.
June 3-track EP *3 x 3*, featuring *Paperlate*, hits UK #10. Double *Three Sides Live* (fourth side has unreleased studio cuts 1979-81), hits UK #2.
July [7] *Paperlate* makes US #32 as double album *Three Sides Live* hits US #10, earning a gold disk.
Oct [2] The "Six Of The Best" concert at Milton Keynes Bowl, Bucks., sees the present Genesis line-up reunited as a one-off with Gabriel, while Hackett also joins for the encore *I Know What I Like*. Rutherford's second solo album *Acting Very Strange* climbs to UK #23 and US #145.

'83 June Banks releases 2 albums, his soundtrack for Michael Winner film "The Wicked Lady" (on Atlantic) and his own *The Fugitive*, which reaches UK #50.
Oct Drum-heavy opus *Mama* hits UK #4.
[15] *Genesis*, co-produced with Hugh Padgham, tops UK chart.
[29] *Mama* peaks at US #73.
Nov *Genesis* hits US #9 and is the group's second US million-seller.
Dec *That's All!* reaches UK #16.

'84 Feb *Illegal Alien* makes UK #46.
[11] *That's All!* hits US #6.
Mar Albums *Nursery Cryme* and *Trespass* are reissued in UK, and will chart briefly at #68 (Mar.31) and #98 (Apr.21) respectively.
Apr [21] *Illegal Alien* makes US #44.
July [28] *Taking It All Too Hard* reaches US #50.

'86 Feb Rutherford's extra-curricular band Mike & The Mechanics, featuring Paul Carrack (ex-Ace, Squeeze, Nick Lowe among others), Paul Young (ex-Sad Café), Petre Van Hooke and Adrian Lee, hits US #6 and UK #21 with *Silent Running*, the theme from film "On Dangerous Ground".
Mar *Mike & The Mechanics* reaches UK #78.
June [7] A second Mike & The Mechanics single and airplay favorite, *All I Need Is A Miracle*, hits US #5 but stalls at UK #53.
[21] Genesis' *Invisible Touch* tops UK chart, while the title track *Invisible* reaches UK #15.
[28] With solo group projects littering US chart, ex-Genesis or Genesis related singles currently account for 7 positions on this week's Hot 100.
July [12] GTR, a 5-piece UK rock band with Steve Hackett, ex-Yes and Asia, Steve Howe and Max Bacon, reaches US #14 with *When The Heart Rules The Mind*. *GTR* reaches US #11.
[19] *Invisible Touch* tops US chart, becoming their first #1 single on both sides of the Atlantic, while the album hits US #3.
Aug [9] Third Mike & The Mechanics single, *Taken In*, reaches US #32.
Sept [6] GTR's *The Hunter* makes US #85.
Oct Ballad *In Too Deep*, from movie "Mona Lisa", reaches UK #19.
[11] *Throwing It All Away*, taken from *Invisible Touch*, hits US #4.
Nov Collection of recent video promos released as "Visible Touch" tops UK Music Video chart.

'87 Jan [31] *Land Of Confusion* benefits from a popular video, created by UK TV puppet masters Fluck and Law from the "Spitting Image" series, and hits US #4 and peaks at UK #14.
Feb *Tonight, Tonight, Tonight* reaches UK #18.
Apr [4] *Tonight, Tonight, Tonight*, through its exposure as a TV beer commercial, hits US #3.

June [27] *In Too Deep* hits US #3 as the group completes a lengthy world tour.
Throwing It All Away reaches UK #22.

1988 Mar [2] Genesis wins Best Concept Music Video for "Land Of Confusion" at the 30th annual Grammy awards.
Nov Mike & The Mechanics' *The Living Years* hits UK #2.
Dec Virgin Video releases comprehensive Genesis clips set "Genesis 1" and "Genesis 2", also twinned as a box-set.

1989 Jan [28] Mike & The Mechanics' *The Living Years*, with a poignant father/son relationship lyric co-written by Rutherford and B.A. Robertson, hits UK #2 and will top US chart.
Feb *Nobody's Perfect* is heavily used as theme for UK beer commercial.
May Virgin Video releases last tour-chronicling "Invisible Touch Tour" performance video.
July [18-19] Mike & The Mechanics take part in the seventh annual Prince's Trust Rock Gala at the NEC, Birmingham, W.Midlands.
[28] Mike & The Mechanics' US tour begins at Lake Compounce, Bristol, CT, set to end Aug.27 at Pacific Amphitheater, Costa Mesa, CA.

1990 June [30] Phil Collins and Genesis join with Pink Floyd, Robert Plant, Paul McCartney, Cliff Richard And The Shadows, Status Quo, Eric Clapton, Elton John, Mark Knopfler and Tears For Fears, all previous Silver Clef winners, at Knebworth Park, Herts., in aid of the Nordoff-Robbins Music Therapy Centre.

1991 Mar Third Mike & The Mechanics album *Word Of Mouth*, and extracted title track, emerge. Genesis commences its first recordings in 5 years.

GERRY & THE PACEMAKERS

Gerry Marsden (vocals, lead guitar)
Les Chadwick (bass)
Les Maguire (piano, saxophone)
Freddie Marsden (drums)

1959 Group is formed by Gerry Marsden (b. Gerard Marsden, Sept.24, 1942, Liverpool, Merseyside), his brother Freddie Marsden (b. Oct.23, 1940, Liverpool) and Chadwick (b. John Leslie Chadwick, May 11, 1943, Liverpool), with pianist Arthur Mack, initially as a part-time skiffle and rock outfit. The original name is The Mars Bars (a naive ploy to seek sponsorship from the confectionary maker – instead, the company insists it is changed). The Pacemakers is agreed as an alternative. Group makes its first public appearance at Holyoak Hall, Liverpool.

1960 June [6] They play with The (Silver) Beatles on the first of many occasions, at the Grosvenor Ballroom, Liscard, Merseyside.
Dec Mack leaves and Chadwick switches from lead to bass guitar. Group is offered a 4-month contract to play in Hamburg, Germany. They give up their day jobs (Gerry is a tea-chest maker) to turn professional.

1961 May Maguire (b. Dec.27, 1941, Wallasey, Merseyside), ex-The Undertakers, joins on piano and occasional saxophone, rounding off the group's sound, which (with a repertoire of 300 songs acquired prior to and during the German trip) is now wholly rock/R&B based.
Oct [19] Group makes a one-off tie-up with The Beatles, playing at Litherland Town Hall, Merseyside, as "The Beatmakers". (The 2 groups will constantly play alongside each other on engagements at the Cavern club and other Liverpool venues throughout 1961 and 1962.)

1962 June Brian Epstein, already managing The Beatles, signs the group to a management contract.
Nov EMI's George Martin sees the group playing at a Birkenhead, Merseyside, ballroom and signs it to the Columbia label.

1963 Jan [22] The first recording session in London produces Gerry's own *Away From You*, the standard *Pretend* (saved for an album), and Mitch Murray's *How Do You Do It* (a song Martin had wanted The Beatles to cut, but which they rejected and wrote *Please Please Me* to replace).
Mar [7] Group participates in the "Mersey Beat Showcase" concert with The Beatles, Billy J. Kramer & The Dakotas and The Big Three.
[14] Gerry is fined £60 at Uxbridge Magistrates Court for attempting to evade customs duty on a guitar bought in Hamburg when arriving at Heathrow airport Dec.1, 1962.
Apr *How Do You Do It* hits UK #1 for 3 weeks, selling a half million copies, with Gerry & The Pacemakers becoming the first Liverpool group to top the charts.
June *I Like It*, this time custom-written for the group by Murray, tops the UK chart for 4 weeks.
Oct An anthemic revival of Rodgers and Hammerstein's *You'll Never Walk Alone* (from the musical "Carousel") tops UK chart for 4 weeks

and is their biggest UK seller (776,000 copies). It also gives them the distinction of having hit UK #1 with their first 3 singles. (This record will stand for 21 years until equalled in 1984 by another Liverpool group, Frankie Goes To Hollywood. The B-side of Frankie's first chart-topper *Relax* will be a revival of Gerry's *Ferry Cross The Mersey*.)
[30] They make their first TV appearance on "They've Sold A Million".
Nov *How Do You Like It?*, featuring *You'll Never Walk Alone* hits UK #2.
Dec [13] Group tops the bill on UK TV's "Sunday Night At The London Palladium" (but this particular show comes from the Prince Of Wales theater).
[23] Group opens in "Babes In The Wood" pantomime at the Gaumont cinema, Hanley, Staffs.

1964 Feb Written by Gerry, *I'm The One* hits UK #2 for 2 weeks, held from the top by The Searchers' *Needles And Pins*.
[8] Group begins a 21-date twice-nightly package tour, with The Fourmost, Ben E. King, Jimmy Tarbuck, Tommy Quickly and others, at the Odeon cinema, Nottingham, Notts., ending Mar.1 at the De Montfort Hall, Leicester, Leics.
Mar [7] First issue of the **Gerry & The Pacemakers Monthly**, published from the source of the **Beatles Monthly**, goes on sale.
Apr [4] Group begins a tour of Australia and New Zealand, with Brian Poole & The Tremeloes.
May [3] Their US TV debut, singing *Don't Let The Sun Catch You Crying*, is on the "Ed Sullivan Show". The song, a ballad written by Gerry, hits UK #6, the group's first single not to make UK Top 5.
[6] They make their North American live debut at the Eaton Auditorium, Toronto, Canada.
June [2] Group starts work on its own feature film with Gerry writing a batch of new songs for the soundtrack.
July *Don't Let The Sun Catch You Crying* hits US #4, their first and biggest US hit. *I'm The One*, having failed in US earlier, makes US #82.
Aug *How Do You Do It*, issued in US to follow up the Top 10 success, hits US #9. US *Don't Let The Sun Catch You Crying* (compiled from UK singles and album tracks) reaches US #29.
Sept *It's Gonna Be Alright*, an uptempo taster of music from their movie, makes only UK #24 – a chart disaster by the group's previous standards, but also a sign that pop music in UK is rapidly developing away from the Pacemakers' pure Merseybeat style.
Nov [7] *I Like It*, a late issue in US, reaches #17, as the group embarks on a 26-date twice-nightly UK tour, with Gene Pitney, The Kinks, Marianne Faithfull and others, at the Granada cinema, Walthamstow, London. The tour ends Dec.6 at the Scarborough Futurist, N.Yorks.
Dec [6] "Ferry Cross The Mersey", written by Tony Warren, creator of UK TV's "Coronation Street", premieres at the New Victoria cinema, London. The movie stars Gerry & The Pacemakers as a facsimile of themselves, rising to success in a beat contest. Cilla Black, The Fourmost and some lesser-known Liverpool acts make cameo appearances in the largely location-shot movie.
[26] Group opens in Brian Epstein's presentation "Gerry's Christmas Cracker" at the Odeon cinema, Liverpool, with The Hollies, Tommy Quickly, The Fourmost and Cliff Bennett & The Rebel Rousers.
US *Gerry And The Pacemakers' Second Album*, another compilation from UK singles and album tracks, peaks at US #129.

1965 Jan [24] "Ferry Cross The Mersey" is shown at the Liverpool Odeon in aid of the Variety Club Of Great Britain. The ballad title song, written by Gerry, returns the group to UK Top 10 at #8. In US a revival of Bobby Darin ballad *I'll Be There* is released and reaches US #14.
Feb Soundtrack album *Ferry Cross The Mersey* makes UK #19.
Mar As the movie is released in US, *Ferry Cross The Mersey* gives the group its last US Top 10 success (as it already has in UK), hitting #6. The soundtrack album reaches US #13, while simultaneously-released US *I'll Be There* (pairing the ballad hit with revived 50s rock numbers) makes US #120.
Apr [17] Group begins a 10-day stint in Murray The K's show at the Brooklyn Fox theater, New York, at the start of a major US tour.
May *It's Gonna Be Alright* reaches US #23.
June *You'll Never Walk Alone* is finally promoted as a US single and reaches #48.
July Compilation *Gerry And The Pacemakers' Greatest Hits*, not released in UK, makes US #44.
Sept *Give All Your Love To Me*, a ballad not released in UK, reaches US #68.
[21] Group participates in the "Pop From Britain" concert at London's Royal Festival Hall.
Oct [11] Gerry marries former fan club secretary Pauline Behan at St. Mary's Church, Woolton.
Dec A revival of 50s ballad *Walk Hand In Hand*, an attempt to recapture

the *You'll Never Walk Alone* spirit, climbs to UK #29. (It is the group's final UK chart entry.)
[3] Group plays 3 days at the Star-Club, Hamburg, Germany, their firs appearance there since 1961.

1966 Feb *La La La*, an *I Like It*-styled beater, and now unfashionable, is the group's first single to miss UK chart.
Apr *La La La* makes US #90.
June [10] Group opens in "The Big Star Show Of 1966" summer seaso at the Royal Aquarium, Great Yarmouth, Norfolk.
Aug [7] TAMI show movie "Gather No Moss", in which the group features, has its UK premiere at Birmingham's Futurist cinema.
Oct *Girl On A Swing*, reaches US #28.

1967 Mar [27] Group is the guest attraction on a bill with Fats Domino on his UK debut and The Bee Gees for a week at London's Saville theater.
May [8] Group announces it intends to split in the next few months, recognizing it can no longer keep pace with the rapidly changing UK rock scene. Gerry announces he will continue as a solo vocalist.
June [2] Marsden's first solo single *Please Let Them Be* is released on CBS, but does not chart. (A fate which will be shared by 6 more solo releases on CBS, NEMS, Decca, Phoenix and DJM over the next 10 years, despite success in other showbiz areas.)
July [7-13] Marsden heads UK team, also featuring Dodie West, Roge Whittaker, Lois Lane and Oscar, at the annual Knokke-Le-Zoute song contest in Belgium. They beat Holland to win for the second year running.

1968 Jan Gerry takes over the leading role from Joe Brown in the musical "Charlie Girl" on London's West End stage. (He will stay with the show for 2 years.)

1970 Gerry gains a regular slot on UK children's TV on the "Sooty And Sweep Show".

1973 June [28] Gerry puts a new Pacemakers line-up together for the "British Re-Invasion Show" at Madison Square Garden, New York, playing with The Searchers, Herman's Hermits and Wayne Fontana And The Mindbenders.

1975 Nov With new Pacemakers, Gerry plays a successful 8-week nostalgia tour of Australia. (He will subsequently divide his time between solo live and TV work, and nostalgia tours and hit re-recordings with new Pacemakers groups. *20 Year Anniversary* containing new versions of old group favorites will appear in UK in 1983.)

1985 June With *You'll Never Walk Alone* having been adopted as a crowd anthem by Gerry's own favorite soccer team, Liverpool FC, soon after his 1963 hit, he has been asked to perform the song on several special occasions such as the memorial service in Liverpool Cathedral following the death of Bill Shankly, Liverpool's former manager. Whe a fire at the ground of Bradford City football club, W.Yorks., kills over 50 spectators, a multi-artist recording of the song, credited as The Crowd, is arranged by 10cc's Graham Gouldman, money from its sale contributing to a fund for the victims' families. Gerry takes the lead vocal in the hymnal style of his original recording and the record tops UK chart – making him the first-ever act to hit #1 with 2 different versions of the same song.

1989 May [20] A collaboration teaming Marsden, Paul McCartney, The Christians, Holly Johnson and Stock Aitken & Waterman enters UK chart at #1 with *Ferry 'Cross The Mersey*, to raise funds for the Hillsborough football ground disaster fund, after 95 fans die at the sta of a Liverpool semi-final cup game.

1990 July [13] UK retrospective specialist label Connoisseur issues comprehensive archive album *The Collection*.
Dec "Gerry's Christmas Cracker" tour begins a seasonal UK trek.

ANDY GIBB

1973 Gibb (b. Mar.5, 1958, Manchester, Gtr.Manchester), after moving to Australia aged 6 months with his family and returning to London 9 years later, following his brothers' success as The Bee Gees in the 60s, moves with his parents to Ibiza, Spain, and plays in local clubs before moving to Isle of Man, UK.

1975 He returns to Australia and has a huge hit with *Words And Music* on th ATA label. He supports The Bay City Rollers on tour and opens for Th Sweet in Sydney.

1976 He marries Kim Reeder. (The marriage will last only 2 years.)

1977 Gibb signs to Robert Stigwood's RSO label (to whom his brothers, The Bee Gees, are also signed).
July *I Just Want To Be Your Everything*, written by brother Barry durin an intensive 2-day session at Stigwood's Bermuda estate, tops US cha after a 14-week climb. It makes UK #26. *Flowing Rivers* makes US #1

8 **Mar** *(Love Is) Thicker Than Water*, co-written with Barry and featuring Joe Walsh on guitar, replaces The Bee Gees' *Stayin' Alive* at US #1, but is itself replaced a week later by The Bee Gees' *Night Fever*.

June Gibb becomes the first artist to hit US #1 with his first 3 releases when *Shadow Dancing*, penned by all 4 Gibbs, tops the chart. It reaches UK #42. *Shadow Dancing*, recorded at The Bee Gees' creative center, Criteria studios, Miami, FL, hits US #7 and UK #15.

July Gibb is joined on stage by The Bee Gees at a concert in Miami. It is the first time all 4 brothers have appeared live together.

Sept *An Everlasting Love* hits UK #10 and US #5.

Dec Ballad *(Our Love) Don't Throw It All Away* hits US #9.

'9 **Feb** *(Our Love) Don't Throw It All Away* reaches UK #32.

0 **Mar** *Desire* hits US #4. Barry Gibb-produced and co-written album, *After Dark*, reaches US #21.

May *I Can't Help It*, a duet with Olivia Newton-John, reaches US #12.

Dec *Andy Gibb's Greatest Hits* reaches US #46.

1 **Feb** *Time Is Time* makes US #15.

Apr *Me (Without You)* reaches US #40.

June [10] Gibb opens as Frederic in Gilbert and Sullivan's "The Pirates Of Penzance" at Los Angeles, CA's Ahmanson theater.

Sept *All I Have To Do Is Dream*, a duet with current flame "Dallas" TV star Victoria Principal, makes US #51.

2 Gibb is fired as TV host on US show "Solid Gold" for missing several tapings. (He will be replaced by Rex Smith, who originally played the role of Frederic in the New York production of "The Pirates Of Penzance".) He is also dismissed from the Broadway production (he had already starred in Los Angeles and Canadian productions) of "Joseph And The Amazing Technicolor Dreamcoat", for missing 12 performances in a month.

5 Gibb is treated for drug dependency at the Betty Ford Clinic in California, following a well-publicized addiction to cocaine, which he blames on the break-up of his affair with Ms. Principal.

7 He files for bankruptcy in Miami claiming less than $50,000 in assets and debts of more than $1 million.

8 **Jan** Gibb signs to Island Records to record a new album in UK.

Mar [7] While working on the album, Gibb is admitted to the John Radcliffe Hospital, Oxford, Oxon., with severe stomach pains.

[10] Gibb dies of unspecified causes.

EBBIE GIBSON

3 Gibson (b. Aug.31, 1970, Long Island, NY) has been writing songs since childhood (including *Make Sure You Know Your Classroom* at age 6) and learning piano (with Morton Estrin, who has also taught Billy Joel) from age 5. Her parents, recognizing her skills (she has already won $1,000 in a songwriting contest with *I Come From America* at age 12) and her perfect pitch singing voice, invite Doug Breithart to become her manager. Under his guidance she learns to play, write, arrange, engineer and produce songs, and will demo-record over 100 of her own in a multi-track home studio.

5 Gibson is offered lead role in US production of "Les Miserables" but is turned down when producers discover she is only 15. (She has been an extra in movies "Ghostbusters" and "Sweet Liberty".)

6 **Sept** [2] Still at school, she signs worldwide to Atlantic and begins recording album *Out Of The Blue* with producer Fred Zarr.

7 **Sept** [5] Self-penned chart debut, *Only In My Dreams*, hits US #4.

Oct *Only In My Dreams* peaks in UK at #54.

Dec [19] *Shake Your Love* hits US #4.

8 **Feb** *Shake Your Love* hits UK #7, while debut album *Out Of The Blue*, featuring 10 songs written by Gibson and 4 tracks produced by her, hits US #7. US critics hail her as the most versatile and talented of a sudden crop of successful teenage female singers.

Mar *Only In My Dreams* is reissued in UK to tie in with Gibson's short promotional and mini-concert tour. It reaches UK #11.

Apr Title track from *Out Of The Blue* hits US #3.

May *Out Of The Blue*, an early UK 3" CD single, reaches UK #19, while album *Out Of The Blue* peaks at #28.

June [25] *Foolish Beat* is her first #1, topping US chart for a week. Gibson becomes the youngest artist ever to write, produce and perform a US #1 single.

[26] Gibson graduates, with honors, from Calhoun high school, Merrick, NY.

July *Foolish Beat* hits UK #9.

[1] She begins her first headlining major US concert tour, supported by labelmates, Times Two, in Boston, MA.

Sept [16] A concert in Pittsburgh, PA, is filmed for future video release "Live In Concert – The Out Of The Blue Tour".

[24] *Staying Together* reaches US #22.

Oct [8] "Out Of The Blue" video makes #29 on US Video chart.

[15] *Staying Together* peaks at UK #53.

[31] Gibson holds a seance at a Halloween party, in an attempt to contact Liberace and Sid Vicious.

Dec *Out Of The Blue* is awarded multi-platinum for 3 million sales.

1989 **Feb** Ballad *Lost In Your Eyes* makes UK #34, as parent album *Electric Youth* hits UK #8.

Mar [4] *Lost In Your Eyes* tops US chart.

[11] *Electric Youth*, again co-produced with Zarr and recorded at the Z studio in Brooklyn, New York, tops US chart for 5 weeks.

Apr [19] Gibson participates in a Prince's Trust Rock Gala at the London Palladium with Paula Abdul, Erasure, T'Pau, Wet Wet Wet and others.

May [13] *Electric Youth* reaches US #11 and UK #14.

June [25] Gibson deputizes for Shadoe Stevens on US syndicated radio show "American Top 40".

Aug [12] *No More Rhyme* reaches US #17, as *We Could Be Together* reaches UK #22.

Sept [30] *We Could Be Together* peaks at US #71.

1990 **Dec** [15] Gibson's third album, *Anything Is Possible*, peaks at US #41. Looking beyond her usual studio band, Gibson has completed the 16-track album with assistance from Jocelyn Brown, Lamont Dozier, Paul Buckmaster, Jerry and Freddie Jackson among others, much of its early preparation being done in Gibson's home recording studio.

1991 **Jan** Extracted title cut co-written and co-produced with Dozier fails.

Feb Chris Cuevas, managed by Gibson's mother, releases debut single *Hip Hop*, co-written with Gibson.

[10] Gibson joins nearly 100 celebrities in Burbank, CA, to record *Voices That Care*, a David Foster and fiancee Linda Thompson Jenner-composed and organized charity record to benefit the American Red Cross Gulf Crisis Fund.

[14] Gibson makes a cameo guest appearance on Fox TV's "Beverly Hills 90210". Her clothing boutique in the Harajunkin district of Tokyo, Japan, continues to trade.

Mar [9] *Anything Is Possible* makes UK #51; parent album fails in UK.

GARY GLITTER

1958 Taking his stepfather's surname to front Paul Russell & His Rebels, Glitter (b. Paul Gadd, May 8, 1940, Banbury, Oxon.) and his group secure a residency at the Safari club in Trafalgar Square, London, where he meets film producer Robert Hartford Davis, who becomes his manager and arranges a contract with Decca Records.

1960 **Jan** Ballad *Alone In The Night* is released on Decca under the name Paul Raven. It fails to sell, despite an airing on UK TV's "Cool For Cats".

Feb He tours at the bottom of a bill including Anthony Newley, Mike Preston and Mike & Bernie Winters. The Rebels accompany him but quit when the manager suggests they go professional.

1961 Glitter (as Raven) has a small part in Davis' film "Stranger In The City", and tours Scandinavia.

Aug Second single, *Walk On Boy* is released on Parlophone, but is only successful in the Middle East.

Nov *Tower Of Strength* is a version of a Bacharach/Hilliard song but Frankie Vaughan hits UK #1 with it, and Parlophone drops Raven. He shelves a recording career, becoming a warm-up man for UK TV's "Ready Steady Go!" Linking with the Mike Leander Orchestra, he makes a short tour as vocalist before it splits. He forms Paul Raven & Boston International, later The Bostons. (Group becomes a popular live act in Germany where it will spend much of the next 5 years.)

1968 Leander is made UK head of MCA Records, and signs him to the label.

June Written by Leander, *Musical Man* is released under the name Paul Monday but it flops.

Aug Reverting to Paul Raven, his next single, *Soul Thing*, also flops.

1969 **Oct** Released under the name Rubber Bucket, *We Are All Living In One Place* features a chanting chorus of 3,000 people assembled in front of the MCA offices to watch police evict squatters next door. Despite heavy publicity, it does not chart. A version of George Harrison's *Here Comes The Sun* (released as Paul Monday) also flops.

1970 **July** A version of Sly Stone's *Stand*, as Paul Raven, is his last MCA single.

Oct He appears on the soundtrack album *Jesus Christ Superstar*.

1971 With a switch of image and musical direction he records a 15-min. dance stomp, *Rock'N'Roll*, under the new name Gary Glitter (chosen after considering Terry Tinsel, Stanley Sparkle and Vicky Vomit).

1972 **Mar** Bell UK releases *Rock'N'Roll*, split between both sides of a single (with *Rock'N'Roll Part 2* as the featured side). Initially it looks like being yet another flop, but UK discos, then Radio Luxembourg, and finally Radio 1, pick up on it.

June *Rock'N'Roll* hits UK #2, where it stays for 3 weeks.

Sept *Rock'N'Roll* hits US #7.

Oct Second Gary Glitter single, *I Didn't Know I Loved You (Till I Saw You Rock'N' Roll)* hits UK #4.

Nov First album, *Glitter*, hits UK #8, but makes only US #186.

Dec *I Didn't Know I Loved You (Till I Saw You Rock'N'Roll)* reaches US #35. (Bell will release 5 more Glitter singles in US but this will prove his US swan song.)

1973 Jan Glitter buries his Paul Raven persona when he ceremoniously places old records and photos of his former self in a coffin which he sinks in the river Thames.

Feb *Do You Wanna Touch Me (Oh Yeah)*, with the established Glitter style, hits UK #2.

Apr *Hello Hello I'm Back Again* also hits UK #2.

July *I'm The Leader Of The Gang (I Am)* hits UK #1 for 4 weeks. Second album, *Touch Me*, hits UK #2.

Nov *I Love You Love Me Love* enters UK chart at #1 where it will stay for 4 weeks, eventually selling more than a million copies in UK alone. Glitter's shows at London's Rainbow theater are filmed for documentary "Remember Me This Way".

1974 Mar Glitter's backing band begins a separate career as The Glitter Band and debut *Angel Eyes* hits UK #4. (They will score several more hits in their own right in 18 months.) As well as touring and recording on their own, they continue to work with Glitter, whose *Remember Me This Way* hits UK #3.

June *Always Yours* hits UK #1.

July *Remember Me This Way* hits UK #5.

Dec *Oh Yes! You're Beautiful* hits UK #2.

1975 May *Love Like You And Me* hits UK #10.

June *Doin' Alright With The Boys* hits UK #6.

Nov Remake of The Rivingtons' *Papa Oom Mow Mow* scrapes UK #38.

1976 Jan Glitter bows out of live performance with a televised "farewell" show. (For the next few years his concert appearances will be sporadic.)

Mar *You Belong To Me* reaches UK #40. Compilation *Greatest Hits* makes UK #33.

[7-14] He plays the Liverpool Empire, Merseyside, followed by 5 dates at the London Victoria.

1977 Feb *It Takes All Night Long* reaches UK #25.

May The Glitter Band splits.

July *A Little Boogie Woogie In The Back Of My Mind* reaches UK #31. (Glitter will spend much of the next few years touring outside UK on the strength of his 70s fame. He has a stint as a very portly Frank-N-Furter in Antipodean production of "The Rocky Horror Show" and, unable to trim his spending, he will be declared bankrupt, with substantial tax debts.)

1980 Sept GTO releases 4-track EP *Gary Glitter*, which makes UK #57.

Nov [13] Glitter launches a comeback tour at Cromwell's club, Norwich, Norfolk. He releases *What Your Momma Don't See (Your Momma Don't Know)*.

1981 Oct A Bell track, *And Then She Kissed Me*, reaches UK #39. With a reunited Glitter Band he completes a UK tour which is not a financial success. He signs to Arista.

Dec *All That Glitters*, a segued mix of his biggest hits, makes UK #39.

1982 Apr Glitter contributes *Suspicious Minds* to Heaven 17's ambitious British Electric Foundation project *Music Of Quality And Distinction*.

July Joan Jett & The Blackhearts' version of *Do You Wanna Touch Me* reaches UK #20. In UK, Glitter is increasingly regarded as a fatherly figure who, by his own admission, will never go away.

1984 July *Dance Me Up*, an updated version of his 70s style, reaches UK #25 and Glitter appears on BBC TV's "Top Of The Pops".

Dec *Another Rock'N'Roll Christmas* hits UK #7.

1986 Mar [1] Glitter is admitted to hospital suffering from an accidental overdose of sleeping pills.

1987 Nov Hits compilation *C'mon C'mon The Gary Glitter Party* is released on Telstar.

1988 June The Timelords' *Doctorin' The Tardis* which borrows from Glitter's *Rock'N'Roll*, hits UK #1 and Glitter teams with the group to record a remix. He appears on the cover of UK music paper **New Musical Express** and has his own chat segment on UK ITV's late-night show "Night Network". Always larger-than-life, he continues to provide popular cult entertainment, increasingly for UK's advertising industry.

1989 Sept He participates in "A Slice Of Saturday Night" pop concert.

1990 Dec Now an annual event, his still popular Christmas tour "The Gary Glitter Gang Show" keeps Glitter in the UK public eye.

GODLEY & CREME

Kevin Godley (vocals, drums)
Lol Creme (vocals, guitar)

1969 Both Godley (b. Oct.7, 1945, Manchester, Gtr.Manchester) and Creme (b. Sept.19, 1947, Manchester), while attending art school in Manchester, ha been in local band The Sabres, when The Whirlwinds, featuring Graham Gouldman, releases a single with Creme-penned B-side *Baby Not Like M* Gouldman's next band, The Mockingbirds, featuring Godley as drumme releases *That's The Way It's Gonna Stay*, the first of many over the next 2 years on EMI/Columbia, Decca and Immediate labels. Gouldman, by no a successful songwriter (*For Your Love*, *Bus Stop* and *No Milk Today*) listen to demos made by Godley & Creme and invites them to join him on a project to be financed by Giorgio Gomelsky's Marmalade Records in London. 4 songs are recorded and released, including 2 on a single credited to Frabjoy & Runcible Spoon. They are signed as writers by the London office of the Kasenatz-Katz production house.

1970 Aug They team with Gouldman and ex-Mindbender Eric Stewart to form Hotlegs, and release *Neanderthal Man*, which hits UK #2.

1971 Godley & Creme become staff producers and writers at the Stewart part-owned Strawberry studios in Stockport, Gtr.Manchester.

1972 After recording a demo of *Donna* for Apple, the quartet signs to Jonathan King's UK Records. He christens them 10cc and they have 8 Top 10 UK hits in 4 years.

1976 Nov Godley & Creme split from 10cc and begin work on a 3-min. tra which will eventually evolve into a 3 album set. (Gouldman and Stewart stay together and continue as 10cc.)

1977 Nov Triple box set *Consequences*, (featuring Sarah Vaughan and Pet Cook) reaches UK #52. *Five O'Clock In The Morning*, taken from the album, flops. Their guitar attachment the "Gizmo", featured on the album, also fails to take off, despite promotion as a major new music innovation. (An excerpt from *Consequences* will later be used in a UK cinema cigarette ad.)

1978 Sept *L*, with assistance from Andy Mackay on saxes and US DJ Paul Gambaccini playing the role of "The Bad Samaritan" on the track *The Sporting Life*, reaches UK #47.

1979 Jan *Sandwiches Of You* is released, but fails to chart.

Feb *Music From Consequences* is released, featuring selected songs from the triple set.

Oct The duo, signed to Polydor, releases *An Englishman In New York*, but despite radio play it fails to chart.

Nov Paul McCartney guests on *Freeze Frame*, but this also fails.

1981 2 further unsuccessful singles are followed by production work on Mickey Jupp's *Long Distant Romancer*.

Oct Reverting to the commercial direction of 10cc, *Under Your Thum* hits UK #3.

Nov *Ismism* reaches UK #29.

Dec *Wedding Bells* hits UK #7. Concurrently running an increasingly successful career as video directors/producers, their work includes clips for Visage, Duran Duran and Toyah.

1982 They direct a TV ad for a UK jeans company.

Sept A video for *Save A Mountain For Me* is shot on Alcatraz Island, San Francisco, CA, but fails to help sales.

1983 Apr *Birds Of Prey* and single *Samson* are released to indifferent reaction. They direct 3 videos from Police's *Synchronicity* project (including award-winning *Every Breath You Take*), moving on to Herb Hancock's *Rockit* and a brief reunion with Gouldman and Stewart directing 10cc's *Feel The Love* promo clip.

Nov Video for *Rockit* wins awards for Most Innovative Video and Be Art Direction at *Billboard* magazine's Video Music Awards ceremor in Pasadena, CA, the latest in a long series of video trophies.

1984 Much of the year is spent directing videos for hot new UK act, Frank Goes To Hollywood. They also complete the "Rebellious Jukebox" series for US MTV and release *Golden Boy*, which fails to score.

1985 Apr *Cry*, produced by Trevor Horn, makes UK #19 and US #16, aide by their own highly acclaimed, and later copied, video, featuring continuous 3-second face changes. (The song will rechart the followir year at UK #66 after being featured in an edition of US TV show "Miami Vice".) Horn remixes 10cc and Godley & Creme material for *The History Mix Volume I*. A video of *History Mix* compiled from promo clips and others they have directed is issued in US.

1986 *Mondo Video*, an experimental project, is made and set to be released their Videola label in 1988.

1987 They direct a **NYNEX Yellow Pages** TV ad for the US market.

Sept Compilation *The Changing Faces Of 10CC And Godley And Creme* hits UK #4, and achieves gold status.

88 Feb *Goodbye Blue Sky*, featuring songs using harmonicas of all shapes and sizes, is released to critical acclaim, as is *A Little Bit Of Heaven*; both flop. They begin work on debut feature film "Howling At The Moon".

90 Feb [28] Godley begins work on "One World, One Voice" TV special week-long series of programs about the environment, with contributions from Sting, Peter Gabriel, Lou Reed, Chrissie Hynde, Stewart Copeland, Joe Strummer, Wayne Shorter, Afrika Bambaataa, Laurie Anderson, Johnny Clegg, Dave Stewart, Robbie Robertson and others. Godley is co-founder of UK environmental organization ARK.
June Resultant *One World One Voice* album, overseen by Godley and Rupert Hine, peaks at UK #27 following TV broadcast specials.

ESLEY GORE

52 While still studying at the Dwight preparatory school for girls, Englewood, NJ, Gore (b. May 2, 1946, New York, NY) sings with a 7-piece jazz group at the Prince George hotel, Manhattan, New York. Group sends demos via its booking agent Joe Glaser to Mercury's Irving Green. Unimpressed by the group, he sees soloist potential in Gore, and agrees to a contract guaranteeing the release of some singles.

53 Feb Armed with more than 250 demos, Mercury staff producer Quincy Jones visits Gore at her home in Tenafly, NJ to choose material for her first single.
June [1] Released 3 days after Gore's 17th birthday, *It's My Party* tops US chart and is a million-seller. (The song will receive a Grammy nomination for Best Rock'N'Roll Record the following year.)
July *It's My Party* hits UK #9.
Aug Follow-up *Judy's Turn To Cry*, continuing the storyline of the first single, hits US #5. *I'll Cry If I Want To* reaches US #24.
Oct [19] Gore begins "Greatest Record Show Of 1963" UK tour with Dion, Brook Benton, Trini Lopez and Timi Yuro at Finsbury Park Astoria, London.
Dec *She's A Fool* hits US #5. Gore undertakes a pre-Christmas UK tour. She receives several awards: The National Association Of Record Merchants (NARM) votes her the Most Promising Female Vocalist Of 1963; she wins the Most Promising Female Vocalist Popularity Poll Of 1963 by the American Disk Jockeys; and **16** magazine votes her Best Female Vocalist at their Third Annual Gee-Gee Awards.

54 Feb *You Don't Own Me*, Gore's second million-seller, hits US #2, held off the top spot for 3 weeks by The Beatles' *I Want To Hold Your Hand*. *Lesley Gore Sings Of Mixed-Up Hearts* peaks at US #125.
Apr *That's The Way The Boys Are* reaches US #12.
June *I Don't Wanna Be A Loser* makes US #37. Gore graduates from high school.
Aug *Boys, Boys, Boys* reaches US #127. Gore flies to California to appear in first annual "TAMI Show" (Teenage Awards Music International) at the Santa Monica Civic Auditorium. She makes a cameo appearance in film "Girls On The Beach".
Sept Gore enrolls at Sarah Lawrence college. Jeff Barry and Ellie Greenwich-penned *Maybe I Know* reaches US #14.
Oct *Maybe I Know* makes UK #20.
Nov *Hey Now* reaches US #76. B-side *Sometimes I Wish I Were A Boy* reaches only US #86.
Dec *Girl Talk* reaches US #146. US trade magazines **Cashbox**, **Music Business** and **Record World** name her the year's Best Female Vocalist.

5 Feb *Look Of Love* makes US #27.
Apr *All Of My Life* makes US #71.
Aug *Sunshine, Lollipops And Rainbows*, penned by Marvin Hamlisch, from Frankie Avalon movie "Ski Party" in which Gore has a cameo role, makes US #13. *The Golden Hits Of Lesley Gore* reaches US #95.
[7] TAMI show movie "Gather No Moss", in which she features, has its UK premiere at Birmingham's Futurist cinema.
Oct *My Town, My Guy And Me* makes US #32.
Dec *My Town, My Guy And Me* reaches US #120. Gore's self-penned, with brother Michael, *I Won't Love You Anymore (Sorry)* reaches US #80.

6 Feb *We Know We're In Love* peaks at US #76.
July During her summer vacation, Gore makes her TV acting debut in "The Donna Reed Show".
Aug [29] Gore appears on the final broadcast of US NBC TV's "Hullabaloo" with Paul Anka, The Cyrkle and Peter And Gordon. *Young Love* makes US #50.

7 Jan [19] Gore appears on "Batman" as Catwoman's assistant Pussycat, singing *California Nights*.
Mar *California Nights* reaches US #16.
May *California Nights* makes US #169.
June Gore makes her theatrical stage debut in "Half A Sixpence".

July *Summer And Sandy* peaks at US #65.
Oct *Brink Of Disaster* stalls at US #82.

1968 May Gore receives a B.A. degree in English and American literature.
1969 Having recorded Laura Nyro's *Wedding Bell Blues*, Gore leaves the Mercury label.
1970 Gore signs to ex-Four Seasons producer Bob Crewe's label, cutting 4 singles, none of which charts, and recording a duet with Oliver under the name Billy & Sue.
1972 She signs to Mowest Records cutting *Someplace Else Now*, but returns to the nightclub circuit, where she has made her living over the past few years. She also returns to stage work, appearing in summer stock productions of "Finian's Rainbow" and "Funny Girl".
1975 Gore appears on the bill of "Richard Nader's Rock'N'Roll Revival" at New York's Madison Square Garden. She reunites with Quincy Jones who signs her to A&M to record *Love Me By Name*. Produced by Jones, musical assistance comes from The Brothers Johnson, Dave Grusin, Herbie Hancock, Tom Scott and Toots Thielemans.
1980 Nov She contributes lyrics (*Out Here On My Own*, a US #19 for Irene Cara), to brother Michael's Academy Award-winning score for "Fame".
1981 Oct Dave Stewart and Barbara Gaskin's cover of *It's My Party* hits UK #1. (During the 80s Gore will, on occasion, embark on oldies package tours in the US during the summer months.)

GRAND FUNK RAILROAD

Mark Farner (vocals, guitar)
Craig Frost (keyboards)
Mel Schacher (bass)
Donald Brewer (drums)

1967 Brewer (b. Sept.3, 1948, Flint, MI), ex-leader of The Jazz Masters, and Farner (b. Sept.29, 1948, Flint) join Terry Knight & The Pack and *I (Who Have Nothing)*, on local Flint label Lucky Eleven, makes US #46.
1968 They are joined by bassist Schacher (b. Apr.3, 1951, Owosso, MI), ex-? & the Mysterians. Knight becomes manager and changes the group's name, inspired by The Grand Trunk Railroad.
1969 July Capitol Records signs the band after seeing it play the Atlanta Pop Festival in front of 125,000 people.
Aug Group participates in the 3-day Texas International Pop Festival at Dallas, TX. A reported 120,000 see Grand Funk perform with Chicago, Led Zeppelin, Janis Joplin and many others.
Oct *Time Machine* makes US #48.
Nov *On Time* climbs to US #27.
Dec *Limousine Driver* makes US #97.
1970 Feb *Heartbreaker* stalls at US #72. *Grand Funk* reaches US #11.
June Band spends $100,000 on a block-long billboard in New York's Times Square to promote new *Closer To Home*.
Aug *Closer To Home* hits US #6.
Sept *Closer To Home* makes US #22.
1971 Jan *Mean Mistreater* reaches US #47. *Live Album* hits US #5.
Feb *Inside Looking Out* makes UK #40. (It will be the group's only UK chart single.)
May [3] 150 reporters are invited to New York's Gotham Hotel to meet the band; only 6 show. *Feelin' Alright* makes US #54.
June [5] Breaking The Beatles' box-office record, Grand Funk sells out an appearance at New York's Shea Stadium in 72 hours. *Survival* hits US #6.
Sept *Gimme Shelter* reaches US #61.
1972 Jan *E Pluribus Funk* hits US #5.
Mar *Footstompin' Music* reaches US #29.
[27] Group fires manager Knight, setting off a series of multi-million dollar lawsuits between the 2 parties. John Eastman, Paul McCartney's brother-in-law, takes over.
Apr *Upsetter* peaks at US #73.
June Compilation *Mark, Don & Mel 1969-71* climbs to US #17.
Nov *Rock'N'Roll Soul* reaches US #29. *Phoenix* hits US #7. Band drops "Railroad" from its name. *Mark, Don And Terry 1966-67* charts briefly at US #192.
Dec [23] Knight turns up at a charity concert with 2 deputy sheriffs and a court order giving him the right to seize $1 million in money or assets pending the settlement of several outstanding lawsuits.
1973 Keyboardist Frost (b. Apr.20, 1948, Flint, MI) joins the group.
Sept *We're An American Band*, produced by Todd Rundgren, is the group's first as Grand Funk and hits US #2. *We're An American Band* hits US #1.
1974 Jan *Walk Like A Man* reaches US #19.
May A cover of Little Eva's *The Locomotion* hits US #1 in 8 weeks. For

GRAND FUNK RAILROAD cont.

only the second time in rock history a cover version tops the chart after the original has hit #1. (The first was *Go Away Little Girl*. A third time will occur when The Carpenters hit US #1 with *Please Mr. Postman* after The Marvelettes have done the same.) *Shinin' On* hits US #5.

Sept *Shinin' On* reaches US #11.

1975 Jan *All The Girls In The World Beware!!!* hits US #10. Jimmy Ienner takes over as producer. *Some Kind Of Wonderful* hits US #3 and *Bad Time* hits US #4.

Oct Group reverts to its original name Grand Funk Railroad, but *Caught In The Act* makes only US #21. *Born To Die*, intended to be the group's last, reaches US #47.

1976 Feb *Take Me* reaches US #53.

Apr *Sally* reaches US #69.

Sept Frank Zappa offers to produce the band and it stays together to record *Good Singin' Good Playin'*, signing to MCA. It reaches US #52. *Can You Do It* makes US #45.

Nov Capitol issues *Grand Funk Hits* which reaches US #126.

1977 Group splits when Farner goes solo, cutting one album for Atco. The rest form Flint with guitarist Billy Elworthy.

1981 Jan Grand Funk re-forms with Farner, Brewer and bassist Dennis Bellinger (Frost is with Bob Seger). They cut *Grand Funk Lives* for Full Moon label. It reaches US #149. (Farner opens Singing Spruce Enterprises, a store selling health foods. He becomes a Christian after his wife and 2 children leave him. They later reconcile, and a third child is born in 1988.)

1983 *What's Funk?* is released. It is the second and last album from the re-formed group who appeared on "Heavy Metal" film soundtrack. Band finally splits, having sold in excess of 20 million records. Brewer joins Frost in Bob Seger's Silver Bullet Band.

1988 Farner records *Just Another Injustice* for Christian label Frontline and it is only sold in Bible bookstores. He hits US #2 on Inspirational chart with *Isn't It Amazing*, and is subsequently nominated as New Artist Of The Year at the 21st Dove Awards.

GRANDMASTER FLASH, MELLE MEL & THE FURIOUS FIVE

Joseph Saddler (Grandmaster Flash)
Melvin Glover (Melle Mel)

1977 Flash (b. Joseph Saddler, Jan.1, 1958, New York, NY), having worked as a mobile DJ in the Bronx, New York, begins developing the scratch mixing technique originated by Bronx DJ Jamaican Kool Herc. Adding rappers Cowboy, Kid Creole and Melle Mel to his road show, he forms Grandmaster Flash & The 3 MCs. He adds 2 more rappers, Duke Bootee (b. Ed Fletcher) and Kurtis Blow, later replaced by Raheim, and the group becomes Grandmaster Flash & The Furious Five.

1979 Following the success of The Sugarhill Gang's *Rapper's Delight*, New York labels sign other rap outfits, and Flash makes his recording debut on Enjoy label with *Superrappin'*, whose rapid fire rap exchanges by The Furious Five galvanize the street scene. Disappointed by lack of chart success, Flash seeks an alternative label deal, releasing *We Rap More Mellow* for Brass label (as The Younger Generation) and *Flash To The Beat* for Bozo Meko (as Flash & The Five) before signing to Sylvia Robinson's Sugarhill label.

1980 Their debut on Sugarhill, *Freedom*, despite not making the Hot 100, is awarded a gold disk and is popular in their native New York.

1981 They follow up with *The Adventures Of Grandmaster Flash On The Wheels Of Steel* which also goes gold. It is hailed as a definitive disk in rap history, featuring serious sampling for the first time. Follow-up *Flash To The Beat* fails to attract the same attention.

1982 May Robinson asks the group to record *The Message*, written by her and Bootee.

Aug New York club interest spreads to UK where *The Message* hits #8.

Nov *The Message*, having gone gold in 25 days, climbs only to US #62, failing to cross over completely from its specialist market. *The Message* makes US #53 and UK #77.

1983 June Discord within the group affects recording. Melle Mel, the dominant voice in The Furious Five, begins to emerge in his own right and records *The Message II (Survival)* with Bootee but it fails to chart.

Nov Earlier recorded *White Lines (Don't Don't Do It)*, a combination of Grandmaster Flash and Melle Mel, is an anti-cocaine rap anthem. It becomes a US dance hit but fails to chart. Flash leaves the group and begins a lengthy $5 million court case against Sugarhill to use the full group name (which he will lose). Mel, still on Sugarhill, is with rapping buddies, Scorpio and Cowboy but Raheim and Kid side with Flash.

1984 Feb *White Lines (Don't Don't Do It)* re-enters UK chart to hit #7.

June Sugarhill compilation *Greatest Messages* climbs to UK #41. Now established as Grandmaster Melle Mel & The Furious Five, their contribution to the breakdance movie "Beat Street" titled *Beat Street Breakdown Part 1*, on Atlantic, peaks at UK #42.

Aug *Beat Street Breakdown Part 1* reaches only US #86.

Sept Mel's *We Don't Work For Free* reaches UK #45.

Oct Mel is featured as intro rapper on worldwide Chaka Khan smash *Feel For You* which hits US #3 and UK #1. Sugarhill *Work Party*, released only as Grandmaster Melle Mel, climbs to UK #45.

1985 Jan Mel hits UK #8 with *Step Off (Part 1)*. Grandmaster Flash signs a worldwide solo contract with Elektra.

Feb Grandmaster Flash solo release *Sign Of The Times* charts briefly at UK #72, as debut solo *They Said It Couldn't Be Done* makes a 1-week appearance at UK #95.

Mar Grandmaster Melle Mel's *Pump Me Up* makes UK #45.

1986 May Flash's *The Source* makes US #145.

1987 Apr [25] *Ba Dop Boom Bang* peaks at US #197, while single *U Know What Time It Is?* makes #57 on US R&B chart.

A lack of commercial success encourages all parties involved to reunite as Grandmaster Flash, Melle Mel & The Furious Five at a charity concert hosted by Paul Simon at New York's Madison Square Garden.

1988 Feb Still contracted as a solo artist to Elektra, Grandmaster Flash releases *On The Strength*. (*White Lines (Don't Don't Do It)* will continue to be reissued and remixed, not least by mixmaster Ben Liebrand in 1990.)

EDDY GRANT

1960 Grant (b. Edmond Montague Grant, Mar.5, 1948, Plaisance, Guyana) moves with his parents to London, where his first musical experience as a trumpeter in the Camden Schools' Orchestra. He later takes up piano and guitar.

1965 He forms a group with 2 friends from Acland Burghley school in Hornsey Rise, London: Pat Lloyd (b. Mar.17, 1948, Holloway, London) and John Hall (b. Oct.25, 1947, Holloway). Joined by twin brothers Derv and Lincoln Gordon (b. June 29, 1948, Jamaica), they rehearse for almost a year, since Grant is the only one who plays any instrument.

1966 Group emerges as The Equals (Derv Gordon on lead vocals, Grant on lead guitar, Lincoln Gordon on rhythm guitar, Lloyd on bass and Hall on drums), with a repertoire of ska-influenced R&B songs mostly written by Grant. UK independent label President Records hears some demos and signs the group. Debut single *I Won't Be There* gets UK pirate radio airplay, but does not sell. As a sideline from the group, Grant makes one of the first English ska albums, *Club Ska*, under a string of pseudonyms to give the impression of a compilation album.

Dec *Hold Me Closer* again fails to chart. Several DJs pick up instead on the riff-driven Grant-penned B-side, *Baby Come Back*.

1967 The Equals spend 6 months working in Europe, particularly Holland and Germany. Ariola Records in Germany releases *Baby Come Back*. It becomes a major hit, bringing the group extensive TV work, and *Baby Come Back* hits #1 in Holland and Belgium.

Dec Low-price *Equals Explosion*, promoted on pirate station Radio Caroline as an ideal party album, hits UK #10 and puts the group in the unusual position of having a UK chart album before a single.

1968 Feb Supported by pirate stations (Caroline in UK and Radio Veronica from Holland, much heard in UK), *I Get So Excited* makes UK #44.

Mar *Equals Explosion* reaches UK #32. (It includes Grant's *Police On My Back*, which will be revived by The Clash on their 1980 *Sandinista*.)

July *Baby Come Back*, reissued in UK as an A-side, tops UK chart for 3 weeks (deposing The Rolling Stones' *Jumpin' Jack Flash*). UK sales top 250,000 and The Equals receive a gold disk for total European/UK sales of over a million.

Sept *Laurel And Hardy* makes UK #35. It will also be the group's only US hit on Oct.26 at #32. (Further Equals UK hits will follow: *Softly Softly* (#48, Dec.1968), *Michael And The Slipper Tree* (#24, Apr.1969), *Viva Bobby Joe* (which will be taken up by soccer crowds who sing the adaptation *Viva Bobby Moore* at appearances by the England captain) (#6, Aug.1969), *Rub-A-Dub-Dub* (#34, Jan.1970) and *Black Skin Blue Eyed Boys* (#9, Jan.1971).

Dec *Softly Softly* makes UK #48.

1969 Sept [22] During a visit to Germany, Grant's car veers off an autobahn and he is hospitalized.

1972 Following an illness which keeps him off the road, Grant leaves The Equals to set up his own production company, the first step towards his own complete recording operation. (He will continue for a while to produce The Equals, in which he is replaced by Jimmy Haynes. Hayns will leave in mid-1973, to be replaced by Dave Martin, while Hall will quit early in 1975 and Neil McBain will take over on drums. The Equals will never again have any commercial impact on record, but will remain a popular UK and Continental live attraction until the mid-70s.)

1973 For the next 3 years, Grant will work as a producer (for The Pioneers and others), using the songwriting and performing royalties from his Equals days to set up his own label Ice Records (initially in Guyana) and The Coach House recording studio in London.

1977 Grant's debut solo album is *Message Man*, on which he studio-overdubs every voice and instrument himself (setting a pattern for later recordings).

1979 July His solo career is launched via a deal between Ice and UK label Ensign. Self-performed *Walking On Sunshine* is released, and from it, *Living On The Front Line*, a hard-edged reggae/funk blend is a major disco hit and reaches UK #11.
Nov *Walking On Sunshine*, does not chart in UK as a single, but is Grant's debut US R&B at #86.

1980 Dec *Do You Feel My Love*, taken from *Love In Exile*, hits UK #8.

1981 May *Can't Get Enough Of You*, his first single with an Ice/Ensign label co-credit, reaches UK #13.
June *Can't Get Enough*, featuring its near-namesake hit, is his first UK chart album, at #39.
Aug *I Love You, Yes I Love You* makes UK #37.

1982 Grant relocates his home and Ice recording studio to the Caribbean at St. Phillip, Barbados.
Sept Title track of Grant's *Walking On Sunshine*, revived by US group Rocker's Revenge, hits UK #4.
Nov With Ice Records signed in a new marketing and distribution deal to RCA, *I Don't Wanna Dance* tops UK chart for 3 weeks, becoming one of the UK's biggest-selling singles of 1982.

1983 Feb *Killer On The Rampage* is Grant's biggest-selling UK album, hitting #7. Taken from it, *Electric Avenue* hits UK #2.
Mar Double A-side reissue, *Living On The Frontline/Do You Feel My Love* on Mercury (which still holds the rights originally leased to Ensign), reaches UK #47.
Apr *War Party* peaks at UK #42.
July [2] Via a deal with Portrait Records, *Electric Avenue* hits US #2 and earns a gold disk for over a US million sales. *Killer On The Rampage* hits US #10 and is another gold disk.
Sept [17] *I Don't Wanna Dance* peaks at US #53.
Nov *Till I Can't Take Love No More* makes UK #42.

1984 May *Romancing The Stone*, written by Grant for the Michael Douglas/Kathleen Turner film "Romancing The Stone" (though not used in it) peaks at UK #52.
July [21] *Romancing The Stone* reaches US #26 as *Going For Broke*, not a UK chart success, makes US #64.
Nov TV-advertised compilation *All The Hits: The Killer At His Best* reaches UK #23.

1988 Mar His Ice label is licensed in UK through PRT Records and Grant returns to UK chart after a 4-year absence with *Gimme Hope Jo'anna*, an anti-apartheid song, dressed as reggae-funk, aimed at South Africa. It hits UK #7.
Apr Parlophone Records releases *File Under Rock*.
Oct Grant appears alongside U2, Aztec Camera, Joan Armatrading and others in the televised "Smile Jamaica" benefit concert at London's Dominion theater, to raise money to aid Jamaica's recovery after Hurricane Gilbert. *Put A Hold On It* is released.

1989 May [27] Reissued *Walking On Sunshine* peaks at UK #63.
July Further compilation *Walking On Sunshine (The Best Of Eddy Grant)* reaches UK #20.

1990 Oct Parlophone *Restless World* fails to return Grant to UK or US charts.

THE GRASS ROOTS

Warren Entner (vocals, guitar)
Creed Bratton (guitar)
Rob Grill (bass, vocals)
Ricky Coonce (drums)

1966 Songwriters/producers P.F. Sloan and Steve Barri initiate The Grass Roots name as a label of convenience for a studio project as a Byrds/Turtles-type folk-rock duo, when working for Lou Adler's Dunhill label. Their first release is a cover of Bob Dylan's *Mr. Jones (Ballad Of A Thin Man)*, which does not sell.
July Sloan and Barri's own song *Where Were You When I Needed You*, in a strident folk-rock arrangement, gives The Grass Roots a US chart debut, reaching #28. Album of the same title, played, sung and mostly

written by the duo, is released, without charting.
Sept *Only When You're Lonely*, again performed by Sloan and Barri as The Grass Roots, reaches US #96.

1967 Sloan and Barri recruit Entner (b. July 7, 1944, Boston, MA), Bratton (b. Feb.8, 1943, Sacramento, CA), Grill (b. Nov.30, 1944, Los Angeles, CA) and Coonce (b. Aug.1, 1947, Los Angeles), already playing together as Los Angeles bar band, The Thirteenth Floor, to become The Grass Roots. Duo continues to produce and write for the group.
July *Let's Live For Today*, a cover of an Italian hit by Italy-based UK group The Rokes, hits US #8.
Sept *Let's Live For Today*, with Sloan and Barri singing and playing alongside the new members (and featuring 7 of their songs), peaks at US #75. Extracted from it, *Things I Should Have Said* reaches US #23. Sloan severs his ties with the group but Barri continues as producer.
Nov *Wake Up, Wake Up* reaches US #68.
Dec *Feelings* fails to chart.

1968 Nov *Midnight Confessions*, a minor hit in the North-West for The Evergreen Blues Band and written by their manager Lou Josie, hits US #5 and earns a gold disk for million-plus US sales. (Like their entire output, it fails completely in UK.)
Dec Compilation *Golden Grass* reaches US #25, earning a gold disk for a half million US sales.

1969 Jan *Bella Linda* makes US #28.
Mar A cover of Marmalade's 1968 UK hit *Lovin' Things* reaches US #49.
Apr *Lovin' Things* climbs to US #73. Bratton leaves and is replaced on guitar and vocals by Denny Provisor, who has recorded as a soloist for Valiant Records.
May *The River Is Wide*, a revival of The Forum's US #45 hit of almost 2 years earlier, reaches US #31.
Sept *I'd Wait A Million Years* makes US #15.
Dec *Heaven Knows* reaches US #24.

1970 Jan *Leaving It All Behind* peaks at US #36.
Mar *Walking Through The Country* reaches US #44.
June *Baby Hold On* makes US #35.
Oct *Come On And Say It* reaches US #61.
Dec Second album *More Golden Grass*, a compilation of hit singles since the original volume, peaks at US #152.

1971 Mar *Temptation Eyes* reaches US #15.
July *Sooner Or Later* hits US #9.
Nov Compilation *Their 16 Greatest Hits* reaches US #58 and earns a gold disk for a half million US sales.
Dec *Two Divided By Love* reaches US #16.

1972 Mar *Glory Bound* reaches US #34. Extensive personnel changes lead to a new 5-piece line-up for the next album. Entner and Grill remain, but Coonce and Provisor depart, and are replaced by Reed Kailing and Virgil Webber (guitars) and Joel Larson (drums).
July *The Runway* makes US #39, while *Move Along* peaks at US #86.

1973 Mar *Love Is What You Make It* reaches US #55 (the group's last single for Dunhill).

1975 Sept Now signed to Haven label, *Mamacita* reaches US #71 (their final hit single). Also on Haven, *Grass Roots* fails to chart. (Group fades from the chart, but continues to work regularly on the live circuit.) Grill quits the band.

1980 Grill solo album *Uprooted*, with Mick Fleetwood and Lindsey Buckingham guesting, is released.

1982 Grill assembles a new Grass Roots.

1983 Apr [5] US Interior Secretary James Watt announces that The Beach Boys and The Grass Roots are being banned from performing at the annual Fourth of July celebration in Washington, DC, citing that the acts attract "the wrong element of people."

1987 June VH1 presents "Classic Superfest" reunion concerts with The Grass Roots, Herman's Hermits, The Byrds, Paul Revere & The Raiders and The Turtles. (The group continues to play the oldies circuit throughout the US.)

THE GRATEFUL DEAD

Jerry Garcia (lead guitar)
Bob Weir (rhythm guitar)
Ron "Pigpen" McKernan (organ, harmonica)
Phil Lesh (bass)
Bill Kreutzmann (drums)

1963 Garcia (b. Jerome John Garcia, Aug.1, 1942, San Francisco, CA), previously a founder member of Bay Area bohemian troupe The Thunder Mountain Tub Thumpers and half of Jerry & Sarah Garcia duo, who record 2 demos which will miraculously appear on a 1982

Italina bootleg *California Easter*, McKernan (b. Sept.8, 1945, San Bruno, CA), who has recently been in a short-lived group with Garcia, named The Zodiacs which has also included future Dead drummer Kreutzmann, Weir (b. Robert Hall, Oct.6, 1947, San Francisco), Tom Stone, Robert Hunter, Marshall Leicester, David Parker and Bob Matthews, all veterans of varied Northern California folk, bluegrass and blues outfits, including The Wildwood Boys, The Black Mountain Boys and The Hart Valley Drifters, come together in Palo Alto, CA, as Mother McCree's Uptown Jug Champions. (Matthews and Parker will remain part of the later Grateful Dead "family", as soundman and accountant respectively.)

1965 **Apr** As the jug band formula hardens into a rock/R&B mix, the personnel fluctuates until the group re-emerges as The Warlocks (its name taken from an Egyptian prayer that Garcia discovers in a dictionary), with Garcia, McKernan and Weir, joined by Kreutzmann (b. Apr.7, 1946, Palo Alto), Lesh (b. Philip Chapman, Mar.15, 1940, Berkeley, CA) and bassist Dan Morgan, playing Rolling Stones and Chess Records R&B numbers around the Bay Area bars.

May [3] The Warlocks record mainly instrumental demos at a Los Angeles, CA, studio, later to emerge, like so much Dead material, as a bootleg.

July The Warlocks become involved with Ken Kesey's (author of **One Flew Over The Cuckoo's Nest**) Merry Pranksters commune in La Honda and, as the regular band, accompany Kesey's "Acid Tests", a series of public experimentations with still-legal hallucinogenic LSD. The LSD experience changes The Warlocks' music profoundly, moving it towards high amplification and intensity, and also their audience, from R&B fans to members of the new drug culture. Group is renamed The Grateful Dead, having considered the tag The Emergency Crew, after Garcia finds the name in the Oxford Dictionary while at a pot party at Lesh's house. They also acquire a financial benefactor in chemist Owsley Stanley, wholesale manufacturer of LSD, who designs them a customized hi-tech PA system. Designer Rick Griffin also links up with the band, which continues to develop an original and highly improvisatory style.

Nov [6] Alongside Jefferson Airplane, The Grateful Dead play the opening night at Bill Graham's Fillmore Auditorium in San Francisco.

1966 **June** Group moves to the Haight-Ashbury neighborhood of San Francisco, center of the new hippy culture, to live communally at 710, Ashbury Street. It becomes the base for an exhaustive series of free concerts, played in addition to their paid performances. A one-off debut single, *Don't Ease Me In*, backed with *Stealin'*, is recorded for Scorpio label, a subsidiary of Berkeley-based Fantasy Records.

Oct Band plays at the "LSD Made Illegal" meeting in San Francisco. (By year's end, the group will also have performed at the Avalon Ballroom, San Francisco, with Jefferson Airplane, Quicksilver Messenger Service and others, though plans to release a 10-album set from the live sessions are shelved.)

1967 **Jan** [14] They play at the first "Human Be-In", at Golden Gate Park, San Francisco, along with Jefferson Airplane, Dizzy Gillespie's band, and Quicksilver Messenger Service.

The Grateful Dead are signed to Warner Bros.

May *Grateful Dead* is recorded in 3 days. Gaining muted critical response, since it clearly does not capture the group's live essence in the studio, it reaches US #73. (It will sell consistently over some years and eventually earn a gold disk.)

June [16] Band plays Monterey Pop Festival (though disagreements with music industry executives will mean they are left out of the film documentary of the event, despite being one of its main attractions).

Oct [2] All members of the band are charged with possession of cannabis, following a police raid on the Ashbury Street house.

1968 **Feb** Recordings begin for a second album, which in sharp contrast to the debut, will take 6 months to complete. During this time the Haight-Ashbury scene begins to dissolve, while the band acquires a second drummer, Mickey Hart (a fan who became friendly with Kreutzman, jammed with the group and was recruited), and a keyboardist, Tom Constanten, Lesh's room-mate, whose use of prepared tapes arouses the band's interest. Hart's father Lenny becomes their manager.

May [18] Band appears at Northern California Rock Festival with The Doors, The Steve Miller Band and others.

Aug [4] Group plays the Newport Pop Festival in Costa Mesa, CA, alongside The Byrds, Steppenwolf, Sonny and Cher, Canned Heat, Jefferson Airplane and many more.

Sept *Anthem Of The Sun*, featuring 8 live and 4 studio recordings, and also heralding the return to the Dead fold of Hunter as lyricist, sells

fairly well, reaching US #87, but not well enough to cover the considerable recording costs (halfway through, they fired producer Dave Hassinger and took over the recording themselves), which will leave the band in debt to Warner until the early 70s.

[2] Group appears at 3-day Sky River Rock Festival and Lighter-Than-Air Fair, in Sultan, WA, with Santana, Muddy Waters, Country Joe & The Fish, The Youngbloods and others.

Dec [28] Band plays the Miami Pop Festival in Hallandale, FL, with acts including Chuck Berry, Joni Mitchell, The Box Tops, Fleetwood Mac, Marvin Gaye, Steppenwolf and Country Joe & The Fish.

1969 Continuing financial problems lead The Grateful Dead to accept Bill Graham's long-standing offer to handle their bookings. They still play free gigs but Graham books them into packed clubs around the nation.

Aug *Aoxomoxa* reaches US #73, but they still owe Warner $100,000 and 1 more album.

[15] The Grateful Dead play the Woodstock Festival, to more than 400,000 people.

[31] They perform at the New Orleans Pop Festival in Prairieville, LA, with Country Joe & The Fish and Jefferson Airplane.

Dec [6] They play at the ill-fated Rolling Stones concert at Altamont Speedway, Livermere, CA, where a murder occurs during the Stones' act. (The event is later recalled by the group in *New Speedway Boogie* on *Workingman's Dead*.)

1970 **Feb** Band at last releases a full live recording, double *Live/Dead* (recorded "live" in the studio before an audience of friends), which reaches US #64. It includes a 4-page lyric booklet and a 25-min. version of stage favorite *Dark Star*. Constanten leaves to concentrate on Scientology studies.

May [23] Band plays its first gig outside the US, a 4-hour set at the Hollywood Rock Music festival in Newcastle-under-Lyme, Staffs.

Aug On *Workingman's Dead*, the complexity of earlier albums is dropped in favor of Garcia's country-rock roots and harmony vocals, though a psychedelic sensibility remains. The album includes contributions from 2 new members of Dead's constantly expanding "family", John Dawson and David Nelson. It reaches US #27 (earning a gold disk) and UK #69, and extracted *Uncle John's Band* makes US #69.

Nov On Sunflower label, *Vintage Dead*, with live recordings from the Avalon Ballroom, San Francisco, in 1966, reaches US #127.

Dec In a similar vein to *Workingman's Dead*, *American Beauty* reaches US #30 and earns another gold disk. The album's guests include The New Riders Of The Purple Sage, which in reality is a Garcia-led spinoff country outfit, featuring him on pedal steel, Dawson, Nelson, Hart and Dave Torbert. Band will become a permanent aggregation, opening for The Grateful Dead, and even signing to CBS in 1971. Unable to cope with his dual role, Garcia will however, quit the New Riders after its debut album release.

1971 **May** [31] 36 fans are treated after unknowingly drinking LSD-laced cider at a Grateful Dead Winterland Ballroom concert.

July *Historic Dead*, a compilation of early 1966 recordings on Sunflower, reaches US #154. Garcia cuts his debut solo album *Hooteroll*, released on the Douglas label.

Sept Lenny Hart is arrested and charged with embezzlement of $70,000 dollars from the group. He is fired, while his son feels obligated to leave, though will later rejoin.

Dec Double live *Grateful Dead* reaches US #25.

[25] Extracted *Truckin'* peaks at US #64.

1972 Members begin to splinter off into other projects, Garcia in particular playing on several other projects. His second solo album is *Garcia*, with a cover shot showing his missing third finger on his right hand, the result of a childhood accident.

Apr [22] Extracted *Sugaree* peaks at US #94. Weir cuts *Ace* (the track *One More Saturday Night* will become a staple of The Grateful Dead's concerts) and Hart's album is *Rolling Thunder*. Meanwhile, McKernan has sustained serious liver damage and is forced to rest and stop drinking, to be temporarily replaced by Merle Saunders. They tour Europe for 2 months, including their first full UK concerts.

1973 **Jan** Triple live album *Europe '72*, a celebration of the group's European trek, reaches US #24, and introduces latest group annex, husband/wife Keith (b. July 19, 1948) and Donna Godchaux on keyboards and vocals.

Feb [10] *Sugar Magnolia* peaks at US #91.

Mar [8] McKernan dies from a stomach hemorrhage in a friend's back yard.

With the Warner Bros. contract fulfilled, the group sets up Grateful Dead Records for the band's work, and Round Records for more esoteric releases from members of the "family". In the next 2 years, it will issue further Garcia solo album *Reflections*, a Lesh/Ned Lagin set

Seastones, a Weir/Torbert offshoot *Kingfish*, and solo albums by chief lyricist Hunter. (These will lead eventually to the band's own studio, publishing company, booking agency and travel agency, but the labels will fail.)

July [28] With The Band and The Allman Brothers Band, the group co-headline the Watkins Glen Festival, which draws the all-time high festival audience of 600,000 people.

Aug [1] On his 31st birthday, Garcia is greeted by a naked dancer bursting out of a gigantic birthday cake during a Dead concert.

Sept Live *History Of The Grateful Dead Volume 1 (Bear's Choice)*, recorded at the Fillmore East, New York, in Feb.1970, reaches US #60.

Dec *Wake Of The Flood*, first album on The Grateful Dead's own label, indicates attempts to place their improvization in more of a jazz context. It reaches US #18.

74 Apr Compilation *The Best Of/Skeletons From The Closet*, on Warner, makes US #75.

July [20] *Grateful Dead From The Mars Hotel* makes UK #47.

Aug *Grateful Dead From The Mars Hotel* reaches US #16. They decide to cut down on touring.

75 Sept [28] Group plays a free concert in Lindley Park, San Francisco, to end a year's lay-off from live work.

Oct *Blues For Allah*, marking a new licensing deal with United Artists, reaches US #12.

[18] *Blues For Allah* makes UK #45. Hart returns to the band.

Nov [15] *The Music Never Stopped* makes US #81.

76 Aug [7] Group plays Wembley Stadium, London, with Santana and The New Riders Of The Purple Sage.

Sept Double live *Steal Your Face*, recorded at Winterland, San Francisco in Sept.1974, reaches US #56 and UK #42. It is released chiefly to recoup losses made on a disastrous group film project.

77 June Documentary film "The Grateful Dead" premieres.

July The record label experiment fails, and the band signs direct to Arista (who will also issue Dead solo material including Garcia's current *Cats Under The Stars* album, his 1982 *Run For The Roses* and Weir's 1977 *Heaven Help The Fool* and 1981 *Bobby And The Midnights*.) First release is Keith Olsen-produced *Terrapin Station*, which reaches US #28 and UK #30.

Sept Group headlines an 11-hour concert at Old Bridge, NJ, with New Riders Of The Purple Sage and The Marshall Tucker Band.

Dec Warner double retrospective *What A Long Strange Trip It's Been: The Best Of The Grateful Dead* reaches US #121. (The title will be borrowed 9 years later by **Rolling Stone** magazine, for a book of its own finest moments.)

78 Sept [14-16] Band performs 3 dates at the Sound & Light Amphitheater in the shadow of the Great Pyramid in Cairo, Egypt, the last of which is timed to coincide with a lunar eclipse. The proceeds from the concerts going to the Egyptian Department of Antiquities and Faith & Hope Society For The Handicapped.

Dec [31] The Grateful Dead play their 48th, and last, gig at the Winterland Ballroom, San Francisco, before Bill Graham closes it.

79 Jan *Shakedown Street*, produced by Lowell George of Little Feat, reaches US #41. Weir's second solo album, *Heaven Help The Fool*, is also released by Arista.

Apr The Godchauxs are asked to leave the band because of musical differences. Band is rumored to be booked for 2 large UK festivals but fails to confirm for either. Brent Mydland (b. Oct.21, 1952, Munich, Germany), ex-Silver and now with Weir's side band Bobby & The Midnights, joins on keyboards and vocals. As The Rhythm Devils, Kreutzmann, Hart and Lesh contribute the percussion soundtrack to Francis Ford Coppola's Vietnam epic "Apocalypse Now".

80 Jan [13] The Grateful Dead co-headline a benefit concert for the people of Kampuchea with The Beach Boys and Jefferson Starship, at Alameda Coliseum, Oakland, CA.

June *Go To Heaven*, notable in being the first album cover to feature a group photo, reaches US #23 and *Alabama Getaway* makes US #68.

[5] Band celebrates its 15th Anniversary with a commemorative concert at Compton Terrace in Phoenix, AZ.

July [2] Weir, Hart and manager Danny Rifkin are arrested on suspicion of inciting a riot, after they intervene in an attempted drug arrest during a Grateful Dead concert at San Diego Sports Arena.

[21] Former keyboardist Keith Godchaux is seriously injured when his car is in collision with a flat-bed truck near Marin County, CA. He dies 2 days later.

81 Mar Group plays its first UK gig for 5 years, at London's Rainbow theater.

May Double live *Reckoning*, recorded in New York in 1980, and featuring a totally acoustic set, reaches US #43.

Oct Further double live *Dead Set*, from a San Francisco concert, makes US #29.

1982 Group abandons recording and tours periodically. The treks are by now communal experiences for "Deadheads" (the fans who follow their heroes around US – the fan tours are arranged by the "family" business), who are encouraged by the band to plug home tape recorders into the mixing desk at concerts to make instant bootlegs, a unique and popular advantage of attending a Grateful Dead gig. Fans also begin to write to the group expressing concern at Garcia. He has become addicted to heroin, and both his health and standard of contribution to the band deteriorate.

May [28] Group plays at a benefit concert for the Vietnam Veterans Project at San Francisco's Moscone Center. Country Joe & The Fish and Jefferson Starship also take part.

Sept [3-5] Group performs at the US Festival, financed by Apple Computers founder Steven Wozniak, in San Bernardino, CA, to 400,000 people, along with Jackson Browne, The Cars, Fleetwood Mac, Eddie Money, Police, Santana, Talking Heads and many others.

Nov [25] Band plays the Jamaica World Music Festival at The Bob Marley Performing Center near Montego Bay.

1985 Jan Garcia's drug problem comes to a head: the others tell him the band cannot continue if he stays addicted. He agrees to take treatment, but several days later is busted in his car and is put into a drug diversion program.

1986 July With Garcia seemingly fit, the band resumes full-time touring, including summer dates with Tom Petty & The Heartbreakers, but it proves too much for the still-fragile guitarist.

[10] Garcia lapses into a 5-day diabetic coma. (He recovers and begins to play with R&B keyboardist Merle Saunders.)

1987 The Grateful Dead complete a video and record a long-overdue studio album. The initial plan is to record old songs, but Hunter becomes involved and the album takes on a theme of ageing and redirection.

June The Grateful Dead tour again, supporting Bob Dylan. At his insistence, the traditional encouragement of tape-recording by the audience is suspended.

Aug Comeback project *In The Dark* hits US #6.

[23] An escapee from a drug treatment center shoots a policeman and is then shot dead himself at a Grateful Dead "Summer Of Love" 20th anniversary celebration concert.

Sept [15] The Grateful Dead receive a platinum disk – their first – for US sales of *In The Dark*, as it also makes UK #57.

[26] *Touch Of Grey* hits US #9 (the band's first major hit single).

1988 June Garcia, Weir and Mydland guest on Dylan's new album *Down In The Groove*. *The Ugliest Girl In The World* and *Silvio*, are co-written by Dylan and Robert Hunter.

Sept [24] Group closes a 9-concert series at New York's Madison Square Garden with an extra benefit show for Cultural Survival, Greenpeace and Rainforest Action Network. They are joined on stage by Bruce Hornsby & The Range, Daryl Hall and John Oates, Suzanne Vega, former Rolling Stone Mick Taylor and ex-Hot Tuna Jack Casady. The 10 concerts gross $3,768,244.

Dec [4] Group plays the sell-out Oakland Coliseum Music Festival, with Crosby, Stills, Nash & Young, Tracy Chapman, and Dylan.

1989 Feb Live album, from the 1987 Bob Dylan/Grateful Dead tour, *Dylan And Dead*, released by CBS, peaks at US #37 and UK #38.

Apr Solo album *Music To Be Born* by Mickey Hart, uses a recording from the womb of his son Taro's heartbeat.

May [18] The Grateful Dead plays an AIDS benefit in Oakland with Tracy Chapman, Huey Lewis & The News, John Fogerty among others. (Garcia also jams with Elvis Costello and James Burton at the Sweetwater club in San Francisco to celebrate the 21st anniversary of the Village Music record store in Mill Valley.)

July [12] Garcia, Weir and Hart appear before Congressional caucus to draw attention to destruction of Malaysian rain forests. Rhode Island's Republican Representative Claudine Schneider urges band to encourage Dead Heads to vote.

Nov *Built To Last* peaks at US #27.

Dec [10] Patrick Shanahan dies after a Grateful Dead Los Angeles gig after being taken into police custody and having chokehold used on him to restrain him.

In the year's- end Forbes' annual list of the 40 highest paid entertainers in the world, The Grateful Dead is ranked 29th with an estimated annual income of $12.5 million.

1990 Feb [25-27] Band begins another major US tour with dates in Oakland.

June [7] Band celebrates 25 years together.

July [26] Mydland dies from overdose of morphine and cocaine outside his Lafayette, CA, home.

Aug Oakland police issue arrest warrant for Randall Delpiano, who has been jailed in the past for impersonating Weir. He violates his parole on a 15 month jail sentence on fraud and theft charges. Weir takes part in 200 mile cycle trip across Montana's Flathead National Forest to draw attention to clear-cuttings threatening forests.

[16] RCA Records announces that Bruce Hornsby "has responded affirmatively to a request from his longtime friends (The Grateful Dead) to help them through this difficult period", with reference to Hornsby playing dates with them after the death of their keyboard player Brent Mydland. (He will perform with the band at Madison Square Garden Sept.15-20 and other various dates. Garcia is featured on *Across The River*, the first single from Hornsby's new album.)

Sept Hart signs deal with Harper & Row Books to write 2 non-fiction works, the first to be called **Drumming At The Edge Of Magic** with the proviso that 2 trees must be planted for every tree cut down to produce his books. He also releases solo album on Rykodisc, *At The Edge*.

[7] Ex-Tubes keyboardist Vince Welnick is recruited as permanent replacement for Mydland and makes his Dead debut at Richfield, Coliseum, OH.

Oct [20] First official live album in 9 years, **Without A Net**, makes US #43, as incessant touring around the world, always accompanied by the Dead Head family, continues unabated.

1991   **Apr** [3-5] 57 people are arrested during a 3 day set of Grateful Dead concerts in Atlanta, GA. The total drug haul from the arrests is 4,856 "tabs" of LSD, 29 bags of mushrooms, 24 "lids" of marijuana, 1 vial of crack cocaine and 18 cylinders of nitrous oxide.

[23] **Deadicated**, a collection of Grateful Dead songs recorded by various artists, is released. Featured are Burning Spear (*Estimated Prophet*), Elvis Costello (*Ship Of Fools*), Cowboy Junkies (*To Lay Me Down*), Dr. John (*Deal*), The Harshed Mellows (*U.S.Blues*), Bruce Hornsby & The Range (*Jack Straw*), Indigo Girls (*Uncle John's Band*), Jane's Addiction (*Ripple*), Los Lobos (*Bertha*), Lyle Lovett (*Friend Of The Devil*), Midnight Oil (*Wharf Rat*), Suzanne Vega (*China Doll*), Dwight Yoakam (*Truckin'*) and Warren Zevon and David Lindley (*Casey Jones*), with a portion of the proceeds sales going to the Rainforest Action network and Cultural Survival.

AL GREEN

1959   Having moved to Grand Rapids, MI at age 9, Green (b. Al Greene, Apr.13, 1946, Forrest City, AR), having formed gospel quartet with brothers Walter, William and Robert, gradually moves to secular pop. (Sam Cooke is also making a similar gospel to pop transition.) His father reportedly fires him from the quartet after catching him listening to the "profane" music of Jackie Wilson.

1964   He moves with his family to Michigan where, with high school friends Palmer James, Curtis Rogers and Gene Mason, he forms The Creations, playing the "chitlin' circuit" and enjoying local success with recordings on Zodiac label.

1967   As Al Greene & The Soul Mates, they form their own record company, Hot Line Music Journal, to release their debut single, *Back Up Train*.

1968   **Feb** *Back Up Train* climbs to US #41 and wins the group a spot at the prestigious Apollo theater in New York. Follow-up *Don't Hurt Me No More* fails to chart and, unable to keep up their momentum, they break up and Green goes solo, dropping the last letter of his surname to become Al Green, and returning to club singing.

1969   In Midland, TX, Green meets bandleader Willie Mitchell, also chief producer and vice president of Hi Records in Memphis, TN who, after hearing Green sing, signs him to the label. He takes him to Memphis to record with the Hi label house band, comprising Al Jackson (drums), Leroy Hodges (bass), Mabon Hodges (guitar), Charles Hodges (organ), Wayne Jackson (trumpet), James Mitchell (baritone sax), Andrew Love (tenor sax), Ed Logan (tenor sax) and Jack Hale (trombone). (With minor variations, they play on all Al Green records until 1978.) The first 2 releases are a version of The Beatles' *I Want To Hold Your Hand*, which flops, and *You Say It* which is a minor R&B hit.

1971   **Jan** Green's slowed-down version of The Temptations' hit *Can't Get Next To You* makes US #60.

Nov *Tired Of Being Alone* reaches US #11 and hits UK #4. *Al Green Gets Next To You* makes US #58.

Dec [3] Green begins a short UK tour at the New Century Hall, Manchester, Gtr.Manchester.

1972   **Feb** *Let's Stay Together* enters US chart, hitting #8, and goes gold. It also tops R&B chart for 10 weeks.

[12] *Let's Stay Together* tops US chart at the beginning of a 9-week stay and hits UK #7. (Tina Turner will revive it in 1983.)

May *Look What You Done For Me* hits US #4 and will reach UK #44. *Let's Stay Together* hits US #8 and is another gold disk.

Sept *I'm Still In Love With You* hits US #3, Green's third consecutive U million-seller, and reaches UK #35. *Al Green*, recorded during his Soul Mates days, reaches US #162 on Bell label.

Nov *Guilty* peaks at US #69.

Dec *You Ought To Be With Me* hits US #3 and is a fourth million-seller *I'm Still In Love With You* hits US #4 during a 67-week chart stay.

1973   **Feb** *Hot Wire*, another Soul Mates track, makes US #71. *Green Is Blues* reaches US #19.

Apr *Call Me (Come Back Home)* hits US #10.

July *Call Me* also hits US #10.

Oct *Here I Am (Come And Take Me)* hits US #10 again.

1974   **Feb** *Livin' For You* makes US #19. Album of same title peaks at US #24

May *Let's Get Married* reaches US #32.

Oct [25] While Green is taking a shower at his Memphis home, ex-girlfriend Mary Woodson bursts in and pours boiling hot grits over him and then shoots herself fatally with his gun. Green is hospitalized with second-degree burns. (Rumors persist that the incident prompts Green to become a born-again Christian, but Green claims his spiritua rebirth had already taken place in 1973. His Christianity becomes mor evident from this point.)

Dec *Sha-La-La (Make Me Happy)* hits US #7 and UK #20.

1975   **Jan** *Al Green Explores Your Mind* reaches US #15, becoming his 12th gold disk. (Included is *Take Me To the River*, which will become Talkin Heads' first hit in 1978.)

Apr *L-O-V-E (Love)* reaches US #13 and UK #24. *Al Green's Greatest Hits* makes US #17 and UK #18, Green's first UK chart entry.

July *Oh Me, Oh My (Dreams In My Arms)* climbs to US #48.

Oct *Al Green Is Love* reaches US #28.

Dec *Full Of Fire* makes US #28.

1976   **Apr** *Full Of Fire* peaks at US #59. Green buys a church building in Memphis and becomes its minister, having been ordained a pastor of the Full Gospel Tabernacle. (He will continue his pop career and preac at the church when he is not away on tour.)

Dec *Have A Good Time* climbs to US #93.

1977   **Jan** *Keep Me Cryin'* reaches US #37 (his final collaboration with producer Mitchell).

July *Al Green's Greatest Hits, Volume II* reaches US #134. Green breaks from Mitchell and forms a band to record at his own American Music studio in Memphis. It comprises Reuben Fairfax (bass), James Bass (guitar), Johnny Toney (drums), Buddy Jarrett (alto sax), Fred Jordan (trumpet) and Ron Echols (tenor and alto sax).

1978   **Jan** Following non-charting *Truth 'N' Time*, **The Belle Album** reaches US #103. *Belle* peaks at US #83. The lyric confirms Green's inner confli between the sexual and the spiritual life.

Feb [13] Los Angeles, CA, declares the day "Al Green Day" as Green performs at the Dorothy Chandler Pavilion.

June [17] Green wins the Grand Prize, and $14,000, for his performance of *Belle* at the seventh Tokyo Music Festival in Japan.

1979   After a bad fall from a stage in Cincinnati, OH, Green decides to make a full commitment to his church.

1980   He releases **Cream Of Al Green**. *The Lord Will Make A Way* is Green's first of a string of pure gospel releases, which only find success in the specialist area.

1982   **Feb** **Higher Plane**, including versions of *Amazing Grace* and *Battle Hymn Of The Republic*, is released.

Sept [9] Green opens on Broadway with Patti LaBelle in a productior of Vinnette Carroll's gospel musical "Your Arms Too Short To Box With God". (The show will run until Nov.)

Nov *Precious Lord*, a mix of standard hymns and songs written by Green with Moses Dillard, begins a new series of gospel albums.

1987   **May** Spiritual *Soul Survivor* makes US #131, released on A&M.

1988   **June** [11] Green appears at "Nelson Mandela's 70th Birthday Party" concert and reaches new fans.

Oct Following a biographical interview on UK TV show "Wired", Green, making a commercial comeback, links with Eurythmics' Annie Lennox for duet *Put A Little Love In Your Heart* (which will make UK #28 and, Jan.14 1989, hit US #9) from Bill Murray movie "Scrooged". Meanwhile, UK compilation *Hi-Life – The Best Of Al Green*, is still climbing at UK #34, and old hit *Let's Stay Together*, used on a UK TV aftershave ad, is reissued.

1989   **Oct** Arthur Baker & The Backbeat Disciples' *The Message Is Love*, with Green the featured vocalist, makes UK #38.

Green christens 4-month old Walker Louis Baron, son of A&M's West Coast publicity director Diana Baron. Green also sings *You Are My Everything* at the ceremony.

1990 **Feb** [21] *As Long As We're Together* wins Soul Gospel, Female Or Male Grammy at 32nd awards at the Shrine Auditorium, Los Angeles, CA.

GUESS WHO

Burton Cummings (vocals, keyboards)
Randy Bachman (guitar)
Jim Kale (bass)
Garry Peterson (drums)

1962 Group forms in Winnipeg, Canada, as Chad Allan & The Reflections, from members of 2 local teenage bands with Allan Kobel (guitar, vocals), Bob Ashley (piano) and Kale, all ex-Allan & The Silvertones, and Bachman and Peterson, ex-The Velvetones. Kobel changes his name to Chad Allan. Group's first release is a cover of Mike Berry's UK hit *Tribute To Buddy Holly*, recorded in Minneapolis for Canadian-American Records. Much of the group's early repertoire is Cliff Richard songs and Shadows instrumentals, learned from imported UK singles, and this material makes them unique in southern Canada.

1963 **Mar** *Tribute To Buddy Holly* makes Winnipeg radio station CKY's Top 10 and attracts the attention of Canada's largest label, Quality, which signs the group.
Dec *Shy Guy*, on Quality, is another local CKY hit at #20.

1964 **Jan** Through Allan's UK friends, the group has obtained and learned The Beatles' first UK album, and moved into the Merseybeat style. Allan and Bachman trade in their old Gretsch and Jazzmaster guitars for more appropriate Rickenbackers.
May When Detroit group The Reflections has a US and Canadian Top 10 hit with *(Just Like) Romeo And Juliet*, the band changes its name to Chad Allan & The Original Reflections, releasing *A Shot Of Rhythm And Blues* in an arrangement similar to Gerry & The Pacemakers' version. To avoid confusion as both Reflections groups are on Quality, the name is finalized as Chad Allan & The Expressions.

1965 **May** Group's revival of Johnny Kidd's *Shakin' All Over* (learned from an old UK single) becomes Canadian #1. With the "British Invasion" in full swing, and the group's style a close approximation to the UK sound, Quality credits *Shakin' All Over* to "Guess Who?" and the publicity hints at a major UK group moonlighting. US licensee Scepter Records follows suit, and this ploy seems to work.
June *Shakin' All Over* reaches US #22 and the band tours US with The Turtles and The Crystals. The pressure of constantly appearing on stage causes Ashley to suffer increasing nervous problems. One night, when The Crystals mischievously pull him on stage during their act, he cracks and quits the group. Cummings (b. Dec.31, 1947, Winnipeg), ex-Winnipeg group The Deverons, replaces Ashley and becomes joint lead vocalist with Allan. *Tossin' And Turnin'*, under the group's real name, becomes Canadian #1.
July *Shakin' All Over* has a sleeve credit to "Guess Who? – Chad Allan & The Expressions". The name sticks because the group has had a hit single and is adopted, at the request of Scepter Records, which takes them to New York to cut follow-up material for US market. *Hey Ho, What You Do To Me* fails, as does ballad *Hurting Each Other* (later revived by The Carpenters), and the group fades from US view.

1966 Allan leaves, after suffering voice problems which are aggravated whenever he forces his vocals during live gigs. He is briefly replaced by Bruce Dekker, an ex-Deverons colleague of Cummings. Group reduces to a quartet, with Cummings handling all vocals.

1967 **Feb** After wide pirate radio airplay, *His Girl*, leased from Quality by independent UK King label, enters UK chart at #45. Group visits UK for promotion but falls out with King label, which wants a direct UK signing before organizing a tour. Band refuses and returns to Canada, $25,000 in debt. One recording session is held in UK, with the group cutting some songs by UK writers Jimmy Stewart and Jerry Langley.

1968 The Quality contract has lapsed and the group takes a regular TV slot on CBC show "Where It's At" (with Allan rejoining). Through this, they meet producer Jack Richardson, who is working for an ad agency. Impressed by the band, he has them record a promotional album for Coca-Cola, then mortgages his house to pay for the recording of an album (which will become **Wheatfield Soul**) and sets up the Nimbus 9 label to release it.

1969 **Jan** Third Guess Who single on Nimbus 9, Cummings/Bachman composition *These Eyes*, is a hit in Canada and gains the group and the label a US deal with RCA.
May Having topped the Canadian chart, *These Eyes* hits US #6.

June **Wheatfield Soul** makes US #45. Band is urged to move to Los Angeles, CA (but will remain based in Winnipeg and provide an example to Canadian rock talent which has always felt the need to move to US to succeed).
[25] *These Eyes* wins a gold disk for a million-plus US sales.
Aug *Laughing*, another Cummings/Bachman ballad, reaches US #10 and is a second million-seller.
Nov **Canned Wheat Packed By The Guess Who** reaches US #91. *Undun*, B-side of *Laughing*, climbs to US #22.

1970 **Feb** *No Time* hits US #5, the third consecutive million-seller.
Apr [16] Group flies to UK to appear on "Top Of The Pops", staying in the country for 1 day.
May Double A-side *American Woman/No Sugar Tonight* tops US chart for 3 weeks – the fourth gold disk and the band's biggest US seller. (Because the song's lyric is a put-down of less desirable US attitudes, from a Canadian point of view, when the group is invited to play at the White House, it is specifically asked not to play *American Woman*.) The album of the same title, also a gold disk winner, hits US #9.
July *American Woman* reaches UK #19, Guess Who's second and final UK chart single. Bachman leaves, his Mormon religion proving impossible to reconcile with the high-living band style which arrives with success. (He will team again with Allan, plus 2 other Bachman brothers, to form Brave Belt, emerging later – minus Allan – as Bachman-Turner Overdrive.) A new Guess Who album featuring Bachman is shelved. Cummings takes control of the band and recruits 2 guitarists – Kurt Winter (ex-Brother, another Nimbus 9 act) and Greg Leskiw (ex-Wild Rice).
Sept *Hand Me Down World* reaches US #17.
Dec *Share The Land* hits US #10, while album of the same title reaches US #14 (earning another gold disk).

1971 **Feb** *Hang On To Your Life* peaks at US #43.
June Compilation **The Best Of The Guess Who** reaches US #12. Double A-side *Albert Flasher/Broken* makes US #29.
Sept *So Long, Bannatyne*, lacking Cummings' lyrics and Bachman's music, reaches US #52.
Oct *Rain Dance*, from the album, reaches US #19.
Dec *Sour Suite* makes US #50.

1972 **Apr** *Heartbroken Bopper* makes US #47. *Rockin'* reaches US #79. Leskiw leaves the group (to form Mood Jga Jga and record for Warner Bros.) and is replaced on guitar by Don McDougall.
June *Guns, Guns, Guns* makes US #70.
Oct *Runnin' Back To Saskatoon* reaches US #96. **Live At The Paramount**, recorded at a Seattle, WA, concert, reaches US #39. Bassist and founder member Kale leaves (to record with Scrubaloe Caine and later front his own Jim Kale Band in Winnipeg). He is replaced by Bill Wallace, an ex-colleague of Winter's in Brother.

1973 **Feb** *Artificial Paradise* reaches only US #112.
Mar *Follow Your Daughter Home*, from the album, makes US #61.
Aug **#10** reaches US #155. (The title is not strictly accurate: this is the 10th album since **Wheatfield Soul**.)

1974 **Jan** **The Best Of The Guess Who, Volume II** makes US #186.
Apr *Star Baby* reaches US #39. Winter and McDougall are fired by Cummings. They are replaced by Toronto, Canada-born Domenic Troiano, who has been playing guitar with the James Gang. He is the first (and last) member of Guess Who not to hail from Winnipeg.
June **Road Food**, recorded before Winter and McDougal's departure, reaches US #60.
Sept *Clap For The Wolfman*, from **Road Food**, including snatches of dialogue from renowned US radio DJ Wolfman Jack, hits US #6.
Dec *Dancin' Fool* reaches US #28 (and will be their final US hit single).

1975 **Feb** **Flavors** makes US #48.
Aug **Power In The Music** makes US #87.
Cummings disbands the group, signs to Portrait as a soloist and moves to Los Angeles. Troiano returns to Toronto and forms his own band. Peterson forms the unsuccessful Delphia and Wallace plays with various groups around Winnipeg.
Dec Cummings' self-penned first solo on Portrait, *Stand Tall*, hits US #10 and is a million-seller. His first solo album **Burton Cummings**, produced by Richard Perry, makes US #30. (He will have 3 minor hits, all failing to reach US Top 60, during 1977 and 1978. Second solo album **My Own Way To Rock** will reach US #51. *You Saved My Soul*, on Alfa, will make US #37 in 1981.)

1977 **May** Compilation **The Greatest Of The Guess Who** reaches US #173.

1979 Kale and McDougall, along with Allan McDougall (vocals), David Inglis (guitar), Vince Masters (drums) and David Parasz (horns), regroup as Guess Who, recording **All This For A Song**. The album, single *Sweet Young Thing* and a reunion all fail (and other attempted regroupings will also prove fruitless).

1980 Cummings releases solo *Woman Love* on Epic in Canada only.

1985 **Apr** Cummings is featured with fellow Canadians Neil Young, Bryan Adams, Joni Mitchell, Anne Murray, Gordon Lightfoot and others on *Tears Are Not Enough*, the charity record made by Canadian artists under the name Northern Lights, in aid of African famine relief.

1989 **May** [12] Guess Who embarks on a Dick Clark's "American Bandstand" tour at the RPI Fieldhouse, Troy, NY, with current line-up Kale, Ken Carter (vocals), Dale Russell (vocals, guitar), Peterson and Mike Hanford (keyboards).

GUNS N' ROSES

W Axl Rose (lead vocals)
Slash (guitar)
Izzy Stradlin (guitar)
Duff Rose McKagan (bass)
Steven Adler (drums)

1985 Rose (b. William Bailey, 1962 – to discover his real surname is Rose when he is 17, his real father having left home when he was a baby and his mother, Sharon, having remarried to L. Stephen Bailey) from Lafayette, IN, calling himself Axl after one of the local bands he has played with in Indiana, his first musical experience singing in a church choir at age 5, hitch-hikes to Los Angeles, CA, to meet up with old friend Stradlin (b. Jeffrey Isbell), who has been playing for years on Los Angeles club circuit without success, and hook up with guitarist Tracii Guns to form Rose, then Hollywood Rose, then LA Guns. Adler (b. OH) and Slash (b. Saul Hudson, Stoke-on-Trent, Staffs.) (his father, Anthony, designed album covers, including Joni Mitchell's *Court And Spark*, while his clothes designing mother Ola seamed David Bowie's suits for the film "The Man Who Fell To Earth"), schoolfriends from Bancroft junior high, are playing in Road Crew, when Slash sees Rose and Stradlin at Los Angeles club Gazzari's. (Adler has already lost out to C.C. DeVille to play in Poison.) McKagan (b. Michael McKagan) playing in Seattle bands is the last to join, after he replies to a classified ad for a bassist for Road Crew. The members are united by a desire to play earthy, gutsy rock'n'roll and settle on the band name after rejecting Heads Of Amazon and AIDS. 2 people show up for their first official Los Angeles gig. They become local cult favorites matching their vision of punk nihilism with traditional heavy metal.
June The group begins US "The Hell Tour '85".

1986 **May** Guns n' Roses release 10,000 copies of 4-track EP *Live ?!*@ Like A Suicide* on Uzi/Suicide label.
July Following intensive live work in California and record label competition, the band is signed worldwide to Geffen Records by A&R heads Tom Zutaut and Teresa Ensenat. Prior to signing, Rose has his birth-name legally changed to W. Axl Rose. They sign to management team Alan Niven and Doug Goldstein of Satrvinsky Brothers Management, after Aerosmith's manager Tim Collins turns the band down, and they have fired early manager Vicky Hamilton.
Aug Group begins recording at Rumbo studios in Canoga Park, Los Angeles, with producer Mike Clink.

1987 **Jan** Geffen releases Uzi/Suicide EP *Live ?!*@ Like A Suicide*.
Apr Group supports Iron Maiden's US tour, but pulls out half way through when Rose loses his voice. At the same time, Slash is sent to Hawaii to recuperate from ongoing chemical abuse. Most band members openly acknowledge drug and drink problems.
June On a first UK visit, Guns N' Roses play the Marquee, London.
July They begin a US tour, this time behind Motley Crue.
Aug Debut album *Appetite For Destruction*, recorded at Daryl Dragon's Rumbo Recorders studio, is released. Produced by Mike Clink, it is written, arranged and performed by Guns N' Roses. It begins a slow rise up both the US and UK surveys.
Oct [3] *Welcome To The Jungle* peaks at UK #67.
Nov Guns N' Roses visit UK for their first major venue tour inviting heavy metal group Faster Pussycat to support. The dates include a sell-out performance at London's Hammersmith Odeon. Adler breaks his hand in a bar room brawl and is replaced on tour by Cinderella drummer Fred Coury.

1988 **May** In the middle of an unbroken 14-month touring period, Guns N' Roses begin a major venue US tour behind Aerosmith, but soon become the main attraction. A rider in their contract insists that Guns N' Roses confine chemical abuse to the dressing room, so as not to tempt Aerosmith members.
[28] McKagan gets married, finding a 1-day replacement for a gig with Aerosmith.

Aug [6] Their debut album finally hits US #1 after 57 weeks on chart, having sold more than 5 million copies. It will also hit UK #5 over 1 year later.
[20] The band interrupts a US tour to play the ninth annual "Monsters Of Rock" Festival at Castle Donington, Leics., before an estimated crowd of 92,000. Their third major festival appearance is marred as "slam dancing" crowd antics result in 2 deaths during their performance of *It's So Easy*. Not knowing this until after their set has finished, Rose allegedly tells the crowd upon leaving the stage: "Have a good fuckin' day, and don't kill yourselves". The group had already stopped playing 3 times in an attempt to calm the situation. Band joins Iron Maiden's "Summer '88" tour, but have to cancel some California dates when Rose loses his voice.
Sept [10] *Sweet Child O' Mine*, written about Axl's girlfriend, tops US chart, despite Axl's anger that Geffen edited the track from 6 to 4 mins. and reaches UK #24.
Oct *Welcome To The Jungle*, used in latest Clint Eastwood Dirty Harry movie "Dead Pool", in which the group has a cameo spot (also used by the Cincinnati Bengals football team as its theme), enters US chart at #57 and UK at #31, where it is released as double A-side with *Night Train*. Rose guests at recordings of Don Henley's third solo album.
Nov Finishing a US tour with Aerosmith, on which Rose was arrested in Atlanta, GA, Chicago, IL, and Philadelphia, PA, the band cancels plans for a follow-on UK visit with Metallica in favor of a long rest. Reissued *Welcome To The Jungle*, doubled with *Nightrain*, now reaches UK #24.
Dec 8-track mini-album *G N' R Lies*, featuring 4 tracks from earlier EP *Live – Like A Suicide* added to 4 new cuts, is released as the group visits Japan for live dates. *Appetite For Destruction* earns multi-platinum status for 6 million sales.
[24] *Welcome To The Jungle* hits US #7.

1989 *G N' R Lies* hits US #2, and will peak at UK #22 during a 39-week chart tenure.
Jan [30] *Sweet Child O' Mine* wins Favorite Pop Single at American Music Awards. Don Henley fills in on drums for the performance of *Patience* as Adler is absent with flu.
Feb [11] With *Appetite For Destruction* (#2) and *G N' R Lies* (#5), both in US Top 5 Album survey, the group becomes the first to achieve this chart feat in 15 years.
Mar [11] *Paradise City* hits US #5, and will hit UK #6, as Guns N' Roses are pulled from AIDS benefit "Rock And A Hard Place" at Radio City Music Hall, after gay activists object to homophobic lyrics of album track *One In A Million*, which has already been accused of being racist by the Simon Wiesenthal Center. (The benefit will never take place.)
June [3] *Patience* hits US #4. (Band makes a failed attempt to begin pre-production work on new album in Chicago, IL.)
Sweet Child O' Mine, remixed and reissued hits UK #6.
July *Patience* hits UK #10.
Aug [5] *Nightrain* stalls at US #93.
[30] Stradlin is arrested for making a public disturbance (he urinated on the floor, verbally abused a stewardess, and smoked in the non-smoking section) on a US Air flight.
Sept [6] Group wins Heavy Metal award for *Sweet Child O' Mine*, at the sixth annual MTV Music Video Awards at Universal Amphitheater Los Angeles, at which Rose sings *Free Fallin'* with Tom Petty.
Nightrain, now reissued for the third time in UK, reaches UK #17.
Oct Stradlin pleads guilty to his public disturbance charge. A Phoenix court orders him to pay a $2,000 fine, $1,000 for cleaning costs and a 6-month probation during which he must get counseling.
[18] At Los Angeles Coliseum gig opening for The Rolling Stones, for whom the Roses are opening on a limited number of US dates, Rose accuses Slash of "dancing with Mr. Brownstone", a veiled drug reference, and then says that this might be "his last gig" with the band.
[19] Rose, back on stage, delivers a 5-min. anti-drug oration and apologizes for saying he would quit.
Dec [23] Group wins Top Pop Album Artists and Top Pop Album Artists – Duos/Groups in *Billboard*'s The Year In Music.

1990 **Jan** [22] Slash and McKagan, obviously inebriated, utter obscenities on live TV during the 17th American Music Awards. Band wins Favorite Heavy Metal Artist and Favorite Metal Album for *Appetite For Destruction*.
Mar [8] Rose is voted Worst Male Singer and Worst Dressed Male Rock Artist in **Rolling Stone** magazine's 1989 awards, though the group is voted Best Heavy Metal Band.
Apr [7] Band performs *Civil War* and *Down On The Farm*, a UK Subs cut, at Farm Aid IV at the Hoosier Dome, Indianapolis, IN. (They will

contribute *Civil War* to the Romanian Angel Appeal charity album *Nobody's Child*.)

[28] Rose marries Erin Invicta Everly, daughter of singer Don Everly, at Cupid's Wedding Chapel in Las Vegas, NV.

May [24] Rose files for divorce citing irreconcilable differences in Los Angeles. (They will subsequently reconcile and then split again.)

June Guns N' Roses version of Bob Dylan's *Knockin' On Heaven's Door* is featured in Tom Cruise vehicle "Days Of Thunder", and will become a heavily rotated live video clip on MTV.

July [31] 13 deputies arrive at Rose's West Hollywood apartment with batons drawn. He files a complaint against the Sheriff's department.

Oct Adler leaves band. Following try-outs by former Pretender Martin Chambers and Sea Hag's Adam Maples, Cult's Matt Sorum replaces him, after Slash has been impressed by his performance at a Cult gig at the Universal Amphitheater, Universal City, CA. Guns N' Roses sue K-Mart chain for $2 million for allegedly using their name and picture in ads for a toy drum kit. The suit claims that the group has "suffered damage to their reputation, loss of goodwill and mental anguish".

[30] Rose is released on $5,000 bail, having been arrested for allegedly hitting a neighbor, Gabriela Kantor, over the head with a bottle after she has rung the police complaining about loud music.

Nov [19] Rose files documents prohibiting Kantor from having any further contact with him or his wife.

Dec Band continues recording 35 songs, for a double album *Use Your Illusion I And II* scheduled for release in June 1991. Set for inclusion, covers of Paul McCartney's *Live And Let Die* and The Damned's *New Rose*, with guests Alice Cooper and Dizzy Reed, who becomes the band's regular keyboardist.

91 Jan Rose is granted an annulment after 9 months of marriage.

[20] Group performs in front of a 120,000 audience at the "Rock In Rio II" festival at the Maracana soccer stadium in Rio de Janeiro, Brasil.

Apr Manager Alan Niven announces that at all future interviews given by the band, journalists must sign a restrictive contract giving the band's management final approval on all material.

AIRCUT 100

ck Heyward (guitar, vocals)
aham Jones (guitar)
s Nemes (bass)
il Smith (saxophone)
ark Fox (percussion, congas)
air Cunningham (drums)

80 Heyward (b. May 20, 1961), Nemes (b. Dec.5, 1960) and Jones (b. July 8, 1961), form the group in Beckenham, Kent.

81 Jan They play local gigs around South London, with friend Patrick Hunt on drums.

Mar They recruit session drummer Cunningham (b. Oct.11, 1957, Memphis, TN) as a permanent member to replace Hunt, and to help record a studio demo tape with engineer Karl Adams, who will shortly become their manager. Smith (b. May 1, 1959) is also asked to join, after helping out on the demo as a session player.

May Adams hawks the demo around UK record companies in search of a deal, finding increasing interest as the group plays higher-profile gigs and begins to attract music press attention with their perky, clean-cut pop sound and similarly ingenuous visual image. Some UK media are hailing them as the new Monkees before they have played more than half a dozen fully-fledged shows.

Sept They sign to Arista Records, linking with producer Bob Sargeant.

Nov Debut single *Favourite Shirts (Boy Meets Girl)* hits UK #4.

Dec Fox (b. Feb.13, 1958), after sitting in on studio rehearsals, becomes a full member.

82 Mar *Love Plus One* rises to hit UK #3. Album debut *Pelican West* confirms them as UK teen idols of the moment, hitting #2 and selling over 300,000 in its first week. It will remain on chart for 34 weeks.

May *Fantastic Day* hits UK #9.

Aug *Pelican West* reaches US #31 while *Love Plus One* makes US #37, though it is to be their only US hit single.

Sept *Nobody's Fool* hits UK #9.

Nov Second album release is postponed, as Heyward leaves amid general acrimony, and Fox (who had left because of a personality clash with singer/songwriter Heyward) returns to take up lead vocals.

83 Jan Heyward is retained as a solo act by Arista, which lets Haircut 100 move to Polydor Records. Polydor aims the group at an older market, with a college tour and less emphasis on a wide-eyed youthful image.

Apr Heyward has first UK solo hit with *Whistle Down The Wind*, at #13.

July *Take That Situation*, written originally by Heyward for second Haircut 100 album, becomes his second UK solo hit, peaking at #11.

Aug Haircut 100's *Prime Time*, without Heyward, makes UK #46, but subsequent singles such as *Two Up Two Down*, fail to sell.

Oct Heyward's solo *Blue Hat For A Blue Day* reaches UK #14. His solo *North Of A Miracle*, using noted session players like Steve Nieve (from Elvis Costello's Attractions) and Tim Renwick (Quiver), is acclaimed for its maturity of performance and songwriting, and hits UK #10.

Dec *On A Sunday*, taken from the album, performs disappointingly, reaching only UK #52.

1984 Jan *North Of A Miracle* stalls at US #178.

June *Love All Day* reaches UK #31 for Heyward.

July Haircut 100 album *Paint On Paint*, long delayed in hope of a boost from a hit single, is released but flops, and the group splits.

Nov Heyward's *Warning Sign*, a notable musical shift from schoolboy-type pop into funk, reaches UK #25.

1985 June *Laura* climbs to UK #45.

1986 May *Over The Weekend* is Heyward's second in a row to miss UK Top 40, stalling at #43. (The track does receive exposure in US through its inclusion in Tom Hanks/Jackie Gleason film "Nothing In Common".)

Oct Second Heyward solo album *Postcards From Home* aims its style and appeal at an older age group than former teenage fans, but flops.

1988 Sept Heyward's *You're My World* peaks at UK #67.

1989 Feb Heyward's debut album for Warner Bros. *I Love You Avenue* continues pop-aimed style but fails to score.

Dec BMG issues *Best Of Nick Heyward And Haircut 100* compilation from Arista days.

BILL HALEY & HIS COMETS

Bill Haley (vocals, guitar)
Frannie Beecher (lead guitar)
Al Pompilli (bass)
Rudy Pompilli (saxophone)
Ralph Jones (drums)

1942 After leaving school in Booth-Win, PA, Haley (b. William John Clifton Haley, July 6, 1925, Highland Park, Detroit, MI), who has shown musical aptitude since his early youth, and has played guitar and yodelled, Jimmie Rodgers-style, with his own C&W band in school (playing at dances, fairs and local clubs) hits the road as a musician. He works first as a yodeler with a traveling show, then with country bands, including The Down Homers and The Range Drifters.

1948 Forming The Four Aces Of Western Swing, Haley makes his first record, *Too Many Parties, Too Many Pals*, for small Cowboy label in Philadelphia, PA.

1949 He joins radio station W-PWA in Chester (near Booth-Win) as a DJ, also playing on air with The Four Aces.

1950 He disbands The Four Aces and recruits guitarist Billy Williamson and pianist Johnny Grande to form The Saddlemen. They record for country labels Keystone and Centre and cut a single for Atlantic Records, backing singer Lou Graham.

1951 Haley is asked by Essex Records boss Dave Miller to record *Rocket 88*, an R&B hit for Jackie Brenston on Chess. Haley's version, released on Essex subsidiary label Holiday, sells about 10,000 copies. Similar *Green Tree Boogie*, a Haley original, fares no better.

1952 Haley moves to Essex, and C&W *Icy Heart*, coupled with *Rock The Joint*, another R&B cover of a 1949 Jimmy Preston record, sells 75,000 copies.

1953 Haley drops the cowboy label and renames his group Bill Haley & His Comets, bringing in a new drummer, Dick Richards. First release under new name is Haley's own *Crazy Man Crazy*. The song is promptly covered by Ralph Marterie and receives considerable airplay, but Haley's version benefits in sales. It becomes the first rock'n'roll disk to enter *Billboard*'s pop chart, reaching #15.

1954 Apr [12] Now signed to Decca Records following a split with Miller, Haley's first session at Pythian Temple studios, New York, produces *Thirteen Women* backed with *Rock Around The Clock*. The A-side attracts little attention. *Shake, Rattle And Roll*, Haley's second Decca single, reaches US #12.

Dec Released on Brunswick in UK, *Shake, Rattle And Roll* hits #4, while *Rock Around The Clock* charts briefly at UK #17.

1955 Jan *Dim, Dim The Lights (I Want Some Atmosphere)* makes US #11.

Mar *Mambo Rock* reaches US #17 and *Birth Of The Boogie* makes US #26.

Apr *Mambo Rock* peaks at UK #14.

May *(We're Gonna) Rock Around The Clock*, featured in film "The Blackboard Jungle" starring Glenn Ford, enters US chart.

July [9] *Rock Around The Clock* begins the first of 8 weeks at US #1. It will become one of the biggest-selling singles in chart history. It spends 24 weeks in US Top 40 – 19 in Top 10. Many will regard its success as marking the birth of the rock era.

Sept *Razzle Dazzle/Two Hound Dogs* reaches US #15/#9.

Oct *Rock Around The Clock* re-enters UK chart, to spend 5 weeks at #1 in 2 separate spells. Film "The Blackboard Jungle" is on UK release and youths rip up cinema seats and dance in the aisles, in the country's first experience of post-war hooliganism.

Nov *Burn That Candle* makes US #16. B-side *Rock-A-Beatin' Boogie* peaks at US #41.

1956 Jan *Rock-A-Beatin' Boogie* hits UK #4.

Feb *See You Later, Alligator* hits US #6. A million-seller, it will be Haley's last US Top 10 hit.

Mar *See You Later, Alligator* hits UK #7.

Apr *R-O-C-K*, which makes US #29, features in the first rock'n'roll exploitation movie, "Rock Around The Clock", which has Haley starring with Alan Freed and Little Richard. The film and hasty follow-up "Don't Knock The Rock" are hugely popular worldwide (although some countries ban them), causing unprecedented scenes in theaters. They are a major boost to Haley's stardom, but also serve to undermine it – revealing a chubby family man sharing the screen with outrageously-imaged Little Richard. *The Saints Rock'N'Roll*, a rock version of traditional *When The Saints Go Marching In*, reaches US #18.

May *The Saints Rock'N'Roll* hits UK #5.

June *Hot Dog Buddy Buddy* peaks at US #60. B-side *Rockin' Through The Rye* update of Scottish folk tune *Comin' Through The Rye* makes US #78.

Aug *Rockin' Through The Rye*, Haley's fifth consecutive UK Top 10, hits #3. His version of Little Richard's *Rip It Up* peaks at US #25, while B-side *Teenager's Mother (Are You Right?)* makes US #68.

Sept *Razzle Dazzle* reaches UK #13. Given impetus by Haley's movie appearances, *Rock Around The Clock* (#5) and *See You Later, Alligator* (#12) re-enter UK chart.

Oct *Rock'N'Roll Stage Show* reaches UK #18.

Nov *Rip It Up* hits UK #4. In same week *Rock'N'Roll Stage Show* makes UK #30 (there will be no separate album chart until 1958). *Rudy's Rock* makes US #34 and UK #30.

Dec Title track from *Don't Knock The Rock/Choo Choo Ch'Boogie* reaches US #45. *Rudy's Rock* (at #26) and *Rock Around The Clock* (at #24) both re-enter UK chart.

1957 Jan Both *Rockin' Through The Rye* and *Rock Around The Clock* re-enter UK chart at #19 and #25 respectively, the latter dropping for a week before making its fifth and final re-entry on Brunswick at #22.

Feb [5] Haley arrives by liner at Southampton, Hants, for his long-awaited UK concert debut. The first US rock artist to tour UK, he is mobbed for 20 mins. by fans when his train reaches London.

[6] UK tour opens at Dominion theater, London, where fan mania is again rife. 1952-recorded *Rock The Joint* is issued and peaks at UK #20. Title track from *Don't Knock The Rock* hits UK #7.

Apr *Forty Cups Of Coffee/Hook, Line And Sinker* peaks at US #70.

June *(You Hit The Wrong Note) Billy Goat* makes US #60.

1958 May *Skinny Minnie* reaches US #22.

Aug *Lean Jean* peaks at US #67.

1959 Oct *Joey's Song* makes US #46.

1960 *Skokiaan (South African Song)* is Haley's last US hit for Decca, at #70. He signs to new Warner Bros. label, and releases a re-recording of his 1948 *Candy Kisses*. (But it and subsequent singles for label fail to chart, despite heavy promotion. After Warner drops him he will record for a series of small labels.)

1964 Haley briefly returns to Decca, recording *Green Door/Yeah, She's Evil*, which again fails. (He is successful with some Latin dance hits in South America, records for Mexican Orfeon label and tours Europe regularly.)

1968 Apr MCA reissues *Rock Around The Clock* and it makes UK #20. With a UK rock'n'roll revival, Haley tours the country, including appearing at London's Royal Albert Hall. (He will continue his career on the increasingly successful rock'n'roll revival circuits in US and UK.)

May *Rock Around The Clock*, on Ace of Hearts label, reaches UK #34.

1969 Haley is given an 8-min. ovation at Richard Nader's "Rock'N'Roll Revival" show in New York's Madison Square Garden (but in years to come it will be UK and German fans who will remain most faithful).

1973 Haley stars in "Let The Good Times Roll", a film compiled from Nader's concerts of the past 4 years.

1974 Apr *Rock Around The Clock* re-enters UK chart, reaching #12, coinciding with a visit by Haley. It also re-enters US chart, peaking at #39.

1976 Feb [5] Former Comets sax player Rudy Pompilli dies.

1979 Nov Despite having been ill for much of the decade, Haley gives a spirited performance in his last UK appearance, on the Royal Variety

Show at the London Palladium.

1980 UK tour is cancelled as he is reported seriously ill with a brain tumor.

1981 Feb [9] Haley dies of a heart attack in Harlingen, TX. (He has sold an estimated 60 million records in his seminal rock'n'roll career.)

Apr *Haley's Golden Medley* makes UK #50.

1984 Sept Among several career compilations issued posthumously, most complete is *Rock Rollin' Bill Haley*, a 5-album box set on MCA.

DARYL HALL & JOHN OATES

Daryl Hall (vocals, guitar)
John Oates (vocals, guitar)

1967 Students at Temple University, Hall (b. Daryl Franklin Hohl, Oct.11, 1949, Pottstown, PA) and Oates (b. Apr.7, 1949, New York, NY) first meet while fleeing in the same freight elevator from a gang fight at a dance in Philadelphia, PA's, Adelphi Ballroom, where Hall has been leading his own band, The Temptones, and Oates his band, The Masters. (Hall has had piano and vocal training as a child, while Oates has been playing guitar since age 8, and begun his music career with a Motown covers band in the sixth grade. Both have been raised in the suburbs of Philadelphia, but have frequented the ghetto areas, absorbing music influences and later joining R&B/doo-wop groups. Hall has recorded a single as part of Kenny Gamble & The Romeos (with Gamble, Leon Huff and Thom Bell, who will all become major soul producers) and done regular session work for Gamble and Huff at Sigma Sound studios.) Discovering shared interests, they team to sing in various R&B and doo-wop outfits, before going their separate ways, Oates to a new college, and Hall to his first serious band, Gulliver.

1969 Oates also joins Gulliver (which has recorded an album for Elektra), just before it disbands. He makes a trip to Europe, while Hall finds studio work in Philadelphia, singing back-up for The Stylistics, The Delfonics, The Intruders and others.

1972 They sign to Atlantic as a duo, but debut album, *Whole Oats*, produced by Arif Mardin, fails. Gigging around Philadelphia builds a solid live following.

1974 Jan Having moved to Greenwich Village, New York, R&B-styled *Abandoned Luncheonette*, also produced by Mardin (since described by Hall as "our first real album") is released.

Feb The album reaches US #33 and extracted *She's Gone* makes US #60 unaided by their first video, produced by John's sister Diane. (The song will be a US R&B #1 6 months later for Tavares.)

June Duo begins work on a new album, with Todd Rundgren producing, at Secret Sound studios, New York.

Nov *War Babies* climbs to US #86. Overtly rock-oriented, it is a departure from previous work: Atlantic terminates the duo's contract citing stylistic inconsistency.

1975 Sept Duo signs to RCA, where *Daryl Hall And John Oates* (generally known as the *Silver Album* because of the silver make-up sleeve shot of the duo, created by Mick Jagger's make-up man Pierre LaRoche) is a slow US chart mover until extracted *Sara Smile* (written by Hall for girlfriend Sara Allen) takes off.

1976 May [19] Duo embarks on 8-date UK tour at the Colston Hall, Bristol, Avon, set to end May 28 at the Town Hall, Leeds, W.Yorks.

June *Sara Smile* hits US #4 after 5 months on the chart and is a million-seller, while *Daryl Hall And John Oates* reaches US #17, earning a gold disk for a half million sales.

July [3] *Daryl Hall And John Oates* spends a week at UK #56.

Oct *She's Gone*, reissued by Atlantic, hits US #7 and reaches UK #42.

Nov *Bigger Than Both Of Us*, recorded at Cherokee studios and Sound Labs in Los Angeles with producer Chris Bond, peaks at US #13 (Hall & Oates' first platinum album) and UK #25.

Dec Extracted *Do What You Want, Be What You Are* makes US #39.

1977 Mar *Rich Girl* (written about a friend of Sara Allen's whose father is a fast-food king) is the third single from *Bigger Than Both Of Us*, and becomes the duo's first #1 hit, topping US chart for 2 weeks. (The notorious serial killer David Berkowitz, known as "Son of Sam", will later claim the song as a motivation for his murders.)

Apr *No Goodbyes*, collected early Atlantic tracks, peaks at US #92.

June *Back Together Again* reaches US #28.

Aug *It's Uncanny*, on Atlantic, reaches US #80. Hall records tracks for solo album with Robert Fripp producing (not released until 1980).

Oct *Beauty On A Back Street* (which Oates will later claim as the duo's only recording he hates) peaks at US #30 and UK #40.

Nov *Why Do Lovers (Break Each Other's Heart?)* reaches US #73.

1978 June *Livetime*, recorded on the road with the duo's regular band – Caleb Quaye (lead guitar), Kenny Passarelli (bass), Roger Pope (drums), David Kent (keyboards, backing vocals) and Charles DeChant (sax, keyboards, percussion) – makes US #42. They spend much of year playing live, including a tour, sponsored by Care-Free chewing gum, of high schools which have sent Care-Free the most gum wrappers.

Sept *Along The Red Ledge* reaches US #27. (Hall will later comment that producer David Foster "tried to make us sound like Earth, Wind & Fire".)

Oct *It's A Laugh*, taken from the album, reaches US #20.

1979
Jan *I Don't Wanna Lose You* makes US #42.

Nov *X-Static* reaches US #33. Duo has spent much of the year touring, concentrating on club dates. Oates writes soundtrack for Peter Fonda/Susan Saint James film "Outlaw Blues".

1980
Jan Extracted *Wait For Me* reaches US #18.

Mar Hall & Oates hire Studio C at New York's Electric Lady studios and start producing themselves, using their road band for back-up – G.E. Smith (lead guitar), Tom "T-Bone" Wolk (bass, synthesizers, guitar), Mickey Curry (drums) and Charles DeChant (sax).

May Hall's solo album *Sacred Songs*, recorded in 1977 with Robert Fripp, reaches US #58.

June *Running From Paradise* (from *X-Static*, and not released as a US single) makes UK #41 (the duo's first UK hit single for almost 4 years).

Sept Self-produced *Voices*, from the New York sessions, reaches US #17 in a 100-week chart run during which it will go platinum. It includes *Every Time You Go Away*, which Paul Young will revive as a hit in 1985, and *Diddy Doo Wop (I Hear The Voices)*, which is Hall's reaction to the "Son of Sam" revelations. The first single extracted, *How Does It Feel To Be Back* peaks at US #30, while a revival of The Righteous Brothers' *You've Lost That Lovin' Feelin'* makes UK #55.

[11] 11-date UK tour begins at the Hippodrome, Bristol, set to end Sept.24 at the Odeon theater, Birmingham, W.Midlands.

Nov On US release, *You've Lost That Lovin' Feelin'* reaches #12.

Dec *Kiss On My List*, also from *Voices*, climbs to UK #33.

1981
Apr *Kiss On My List* (written by Hall with Sara Allen's younger sister Janna, who reputedly has never written a song before), tops US chart for 3 weeks, selling over a million.

July *You Make My Dreams* hits US #5.

Sept *Private Eyes*, self-produced in 4 more months of sessions at Electric Lady studios, is Hall and Oates' first US Top 10 album, hitting #5 and earning a platinum disk. Title track tops US chart for 2 weeks, and is another million-seller.

1982
Jan *I Can't Go For That (No Can Do)* also tops US chart, deposing Olivia Newton John's *Physical* (which had toppled *Private Eyes* 10 weeks earlier). Their third million-seller in 4 releases, it also spends a week at US R&B #1 (extremely rare for a white act – only the fourth instance since 1965). In addition, they are listed under "Black Music" in **World Book Encyclopedia**.

Feb *I Can't Go For That (No Can Do)* (written by the duo with Sara Allen in the studio, and recorded on the spot) is its biggest UK Singles chart success to date, hitting #8, as parent album *Private Eyes* hits UK #8.

Apr *Private Eyes*, reissued as UK follow-up, makes #32.

May *Did It In A Minute* is the third Top 10 US single from album *Private Eyes*, hitting #9.

Aug *Your Imagination* reaches US #33, as the duo works on a new album at Electric Lady studios (being filmed by MTV for a documentary, during the final recording work).

Dec *Maneater*, the duo's fifth (and sixth million-seller) tops the chart for 4 weeks, while in UK it hits #6 – their highest UK chart placing. It is taken from their 10th album *H2O*, which hits US #3 (also a million-seller) and reaches UK #24.

1983
Jan Also from *H2O*, ballad *One On One* reaches UK #63.

Apr *One On One* hits US #7.

May *Family Man*, the fourth single from the album, and a cover of a 1982 UK hit by Mike Oldfield, makes UK #15.

June *Family Man* hits US #6.

Nov *Say It Isn't So* peaks at UK #69. Duo releases album *Rock 'N' Soul (Part 1)*, a compilation of 11 US Top 10 hits (including the current single and forthcoming release *Adult Education*), which hits US #7 and UK #16 and will become another platinum disk.

Dec *Say It Isn't So* hits US #2, where it spends 4 weeks behind Paul McCartney and Michael Jackson's *Say Say Say*.

1984
Mar *Adult Education* reaches UK #63.

Apr With *Adult Education* at its US chart peak of #8, the Recording Industry Association Of America (RIAA) confirms suggestions in **Billboard** and **Newsweek** that Hall & Oates are now the most successful duo in US recording history, amassing a total 19 US gold and platinum awards. Duo, meanwhile, takes a rest from the road prior

to the next round of recording, with Hall collaborating with other acts, and Oates honing his skiing and race driving skills.

Aug Hall duets on Elvis Costello's second US chart success, *The Only Flame In Town*, which peaks at #56.

Oct Hall writes and produces *Swept Away* for Diana Ross, which peaks at US #19. *Big Bam Boom* is released, their first new album in 2 years. After self-producing for some time, they bring in New York electro producer Arthur Baker to help with mixing and production on the album, which is recorded at the Electric Lady studios in New York.

Nov *Out Of Touch* tops US chart for 2 weeks (the duo's sixth US #1 single) and makes UK #48. *Big Bam Boom* hits US #5 (their fifth consecutive platinum album) and reaches UK #28.

1985
Jan [28] Hall takes part in the all-star session in Los Angeles to produce USA For Africa charity single *We Are The World*.

Feb *Method Of Modern Love* hits US #5 and reaches UK #21.

May Hall & Oates pay tribute to the soul music that inspired them in their teen years when the legendary Apollo theater in Harlem is re-opened and they conceive a show featuring David Ruffin and Eddie Kendricks of The Temptations, to benefit the United Negro College Fund. Meanwhile, *Some Things Are Better Left Unsaid*, third single from the album, reaches US #18.

June UK RCA releases a remixed version of *Out Of Touch*, which peaks at UK #62.

July *Possession Obsession*, also from *Big Bam Boom*, reaches US #30.
[13] Mick Jagger performs at Live Aid at the JFK Stadium, Philadelphia, PA, backed by Hall & Oates.

Sept Live single, *A Night At The Apollo Live!*, a medley of 2 of The Temptations' 60s hits *The Way You Do The Things You Do* and *My Girl*, taken from the Apollo benefit concert, reaches US #20.

Oct *A Night At The Apollo Live!* makes UK #58, while the live album of the May concert, *Live At The Apollo With David Ruffin And Eddie Kendricks*, reaches US #21 and UK #32.

Dec [14] Artists United Against Apartheid, comprising 49 artists including Hall & Oates, makes US #38 and UK #21 with *Sun City*.

1986
Aug Hall teams with Jagger and Eurythmics' Dave Stewart to write US #51 *Ruthless People*, which Jagger performs for the Bette Midler/Danny DeVito-starring movie "Ruthless People".

Sept Rumors of a split seem confirmed as Hall releases his second solo album, *Three Hearts In The Happy Ending Machine*, produced by Dave Stewart, which reaches US #29 and UK #26. His solo single *Dreamtime* reaches UK #28. Oates produces an album for The Parachute Club and co-writes *Electric Blue* (which will be a major US hit for Australian band Icehouse).

Oct [4] *Dreamtime* hits US #5.

Dec [12] Hall's solo *Foolish Pride* makes US #33.

1987
Jan [21] Hall & Oates induct Smokey Robinson into the Rock'N'Roll Hall Of Fame at its second annual dinner at the Waldorf Astoria, New York.

Feb [21] Hall's *Someone Like You* peaks at US #57.

1988
June Reunited and signed to Clive Davis' Arista Records, duo releases *Ooh Yeah!*, co-producing it with T-Bone Wolk, the only remaining member of the previous backing band. It will reach US #24 and UK #52. Extracted Hall-penned *Everything Your Heart Desires* hits US #3.

Aug Also from the album, *Missed Opportunity* reaches US #29.

Sept [24] Hall & Oates, together with Suzanne Vega and Bruce Hornsby & The Range, join The Grateful Dead for the end of their series of 9 concerts at New York's Madison Square Garden, in a benefit show to help save the world's tropical rain forests. Duo performs *Every Time You Go Away*, a song now also featured in the closing scenes of John Hughes' hit movie "Planes, Trains And Automobiles" and Marvin Gaye's *What's Going On* with The Grateful Dead, plus the finale, *Good Lovin'*, with the whole assembled company.

1989
Jan [18] Hall & Oates induct The Temptations into the Rock'N'Roll Hall Of Fame at the fourth annual dinner at the Waldorf Astoria.

Nov Hall guests on Eric Clapton's *Journeyman*.

1990
Feb Duo contributes a cover of *Can't Help Falling In Love* to the compilation album *The Last Temptation Of Elvis*, to benefit the Nordoff-Robbins Music Therapy charity.

Mar [17] Hall & Oates join their labelmates to celebrate Arista Records 15th anniversary "That's What Friends Are For" concert at Radio City Music Hall, raising more than $2 million, the proceeds going to Gay Men's Health Crisis and other AIDS organizations. The show airs on CBS TV Apr.17.

Apr [22] Duo participates in "Earth Day" festivities in Central Park, New York with The B52's and others.

Aug Oates takes part in 200-mile cycle trip across Montana's Flathead

National Forest to draw attention to clear-cuttings threatening US forests.

Dec [1] Ballad *So Close* makes US #11, having stalled at UK #69.

[15] Second Arista album *Change Of Season* peaks at US #60, marking a return to a basic musical style.

1991 Feb [10] Duo begins "Change Of Season" tour, an all-acoustic affair, including 2 classic instrumentalists Eileen Ivers and Lisa Haney, which has already premiered in Europe at smaller than usual venues including London's Town & Country club, at the Mid-Hudson Civic Center, Poughkeepsie, NY.

[16] *Don't Hold Back Your Love* makes US #41.

Mar [5] Tour date is cancelled after Hall is taken ill.

May [3] Duo plays USA Harvest National Hunger Relief "food-raising" concert at Louisville Gardens, KY, during Kentucky Derby Festival Week.

[12] Hall & Oates appear by satellite from US in "The Simple Truth" concert for Kurdish refugees at Wembley Arena, London.

MC HAMMER

1987 MC Hammer (b. Stanley Kirk Burrell, Mar.30, 1962, Oakland, CA), begins career in music with a $40,000 investment from Oakland A's baseball players Mike Davis and Dwayne Murphy. Born the youngest son of 7 siblings and a poker club-managing father, he was nicknamed "Little Hammer" when working as a batboy for the Oakland A's, allegedly due to his likeness to home-run king Henry "Hammerin' Hank" Aaron. After high school Hammer pursued a college degree in communications and a career as a professional baseball player, but failed on both counts. He then joined the Navy and was stationed in California for most of his 3-year service as well as spending 6 months in Japan. On leaving the service he became a regular churchgoer and avid Bible reader, forming a religious rap duo The Holy Ghost Boys. He now forms Bustin' Records, selling his debut single *Ring 'Em* from the trunk of his car. (He agrees to give the investing baseball stars 10% of all his earnings.) Hammer forms a group with 2 DJs and backing group Oaktown's 3-5-7, with Tabatha "Terrible T." King, Djuana "Sweet L.D." Johnican and Phyllis "Little P" Charles, and cuts *Feel My Power* with producer Felton Pilate, once of Con Funk Shun. It sells 60,000 copies.

1988 May Capitol Records A&R executive Joy Bailey sees Hammer at Oakland's Oak Tree cabaret. He secures a multi-album deal and a $750,000 advance. Label reissues *Feel My Power* as *Let's Get It Started* adding 4 new songs, going on to sell more than 1.5 million copies.

1989 Apr [8] *Let's Get It Started* tops US R&B chart, and will go on to reach US #30.

1990 Feb Hammer guests on Earth, Wind & Fire's *Heritage*, on the cut *Wanna Be The Man*. 2 of Hammer's growing entourage, Kent Wilson (Lone Mixer) and Kevin Wilson (2 Bigg), leave.

Mar [10] Second album *Please Hammer Don't Hurt 'Em*, released on Capitol, enters US Album chart at #69.

June Hammer contributes to a West Coast Rap All-Stars single *We're All The Same*, which is featured on the eponymously titled various artists rap collection on Warner Bros., also including Tonë Loc and Young MC. Increasingly in demand for commercial opportunities, Hammer signs a 1-year sponsorship deal with British Knights athletic footwear which will include "U Can't Touch This" video-style ads. He will also parade for Pepsi-Cola in a multi-package tour/commercials/sponsorship agreement into 1991.

[9] *Let's Get Started* leaves US Top 200 Album chart after an 80-week residence and will not be available until a Capitol re-promotion in both US and UK in 6 months time. In the same week, *Please Hammer Don't Hurt 'Em* hits US #1 at the start of a debut record 21 chart-topping weeks. By Dec., the rap album recorded for $10,000, will have logged the longest uninterrupted residence in either the #1 or #2 positions since separate mono/stereo albums listings began in 1963.

[15] 60-city "Please Hammer Don't Hurt 'Em" US tour begins in Louisville, KY.

[16] *U Can't Touch This* hits US #8, sampling Rick James' *Super Freak*, for which James will ultimately be remunerated. The dance smash will become Hammer's signature tune, while its accompanying video, featuring hot dance routines in ultra baggy bright trousers will become the most heavily rotated video on MTV during the year.

July Hammer's Bustin' Records and Capitol enter into agreement to provide albums by new acts like Oaktown's 3-5-7, One Cause One Effect and Special Generation.

[28] US success begins translating on a worldwide basis as *Please*

Hammer Don't Hurt 'Em enters UK chart, set to hit #8, while *U Can't Touch This* hits UK #3 during an unusual 4-month chart stay.

Sept [15] Follow-up single, now recalling The Chi-Lites 1973 US and UK #3 hit *Have You Seen Her?* hits US #4, and become his first RIAA gold certified single.

Oct *Have You Seen Her?* hits UK #8.

Nov Still a hot seller at US #2 behind white rapper Vanilla Ice's #1 *To The Extreme*, with whom Hammer is conducting a mutually promotion-seeking ongoing rap duel, the RIAA confirms 7 million unit sales of *Please Hammer Don't Hurt 'Em*.

[2] Criticism that Hammer is incapable of creating his own material fails to impress consumers as *Pray*, heavily sampling Prince's *When Doves Cry* hits US #2.

Dec [7] Los Angeles enjoys "MC Hammer Day".

[29] *Pray* hits UK #9.

1991 Jan [22] Fremont, CA, declares "MC Hammer Day" to honor Hammer's contributions as a role model and for his charity work, as settlement between Hammer and Murphy and Davis over monies due to them for their original investment is reached.

[28] Hammer wins 5 awards: Soul/Rhythm & Blues Album and Rap Album for *Please Hammer Don't Hurt 'Em*, Soul/Rhythm & Blues Single for *U Can't Touch This*, Soul/Rhythm & Blues and Rap Male Artist, at the 18th annual American Music Awards at the Shrine Auditorium, Los Angeles.

Feb [9] In a dramatic and unexpected fall from favor, *Here Comes The Hammer* stalls at US #54, despite a $1 million promotional mini-film video clip, and even the current availability of a Mattel doll of Hammer Man. It is the first chart single Hammer has penned alone and features no sampling. It is also featured in the movie "Rocky V".

[10] Hammer wins Best International Newcomer at the 10th annual BRIT Awards at the Dominion theater London.

[20] He wins Best R&B Song and Best Rap Solo Performance for *U Can't Touch This* and Best Music Video, Longform for "Please Don't Hurt 'Em The Movie" at the 33rd annual Grammy awards at Radio City Music Hall, New York.

[23] Hammer guests on NBC TV comedy show "Amen" playing a dual role as himself and The Reverend Pressure.

Mar [2] Hammer wins Musician Of The Year and *Please Hammer Don't Hurt 'Em* wins Outstanding Album at the 14th Bammy awards at the Brooks Hall Civic Auditorium, San Francisco, as *Here Comes The Hammer* reaches UK #15.

[3] *Please Hammer Don't Hurt 'Em* wins International Album Of The Year at the 20th annual Juno Awards at the Queen Elizabeth theater, Vancouver, Canada.

[7] Hammer is named Best Male Rapper, Best Dressed Male Artist and Worst Male Singer in the annual **Rolling Stone** Readers' Picks.

[9] Hammer-produced single, also from "Rocky V", *Go For It! (Heart And Fire)*, by Joey B. Ellis and Tynetta Hare, reaches UK #20. (It has already made US #70 in Dec.1990.)

[12] Hammer wins Best Rap Album with *Please Hammer Don't Hurt 'Em*, Best R&B/Urban Contemporary Song Of The Year with *U Can't Touch This* and the Sammy Davis Jr. Award to recognize outstanding achievements in music and entertainment in 1990 at the fifth annual Soul Train Awards at the Shrine Auditorium, Los Angeles.

[18] Hammer and Pepsi-Cola, the sponsor of his world tour, donate $7,700 to the Open Family Foundation in Melbourne, Australia, a charity which helps homeless youngsters.

[26-27] Hammer's world trek hits the Dome, Tokyo, Japan, for 2 sell-out performances.

May [12] Hammer appears live at "The Simple Truth" concert for Kurdish refugees at Wembley Arena, London.

HAPPY MONDAYS

Shaun Ryder (vocals)
Mark "Cow" Day (guitar)
Paul Davis (keyboards)
Paul Ryder (bass)
Gary "Gaz" Whelan (drums)
Mark "Bez" Berry (percussion)

1980 Hailing from Salford, near Manchester, Gtr.Manchester, Shaun Ryder (b. Aug.23, 1962, Little Hulton, Gtr.Manchester), brother Paul (b. Apr.24, 1964, Manchester), Whelan (b. Feb.12, 1966, Manchester) and Day (b. Dec.29, 1961, Manchester) form loose outfit based around music and alcohol, and begin practicing in a local school room in Swinton, Gtr.Manchester. Ryder has left home at 14, spent time in youth custody for theft and worked for the Post Office for 3 years before being fired.

1981 Davis (b. Mar.7, 1966, Manchester) is recruited to perform on keyboards. Un-named band play mainly cover versions at local Manchester youth clubs.

1983 Day, inspired by New Order hit *Blue Monday*, coins band name, Happy Mondays.

1984 Group is beaten into last place at a "Battle Of The Bands" contest in Blackpool, Lancs.

1985 **Feb** Clubbing at the Factory Records Hacienda club, Manchester, Davis and the Ryder brothers meet clothes shop owner Phil Sachs, who is impressed by their demo tape and offers to manage the band, securing them a spot on a Hacienda "Opportunity Knocks" talent night and subsequent one-off support dates for New Order.
Oct Debut single *Delightful*, a 3-track EP produced by Mike Pickering, is released on Factory.
Nov Berry (b. Apr.18, 1964, Manchester) completes the line-up, recruited as a percussionist and dancer.

1986 **Aug** New Order's Barney Sumner produces second single, *Freaky Dancin'*.
Dec Factory boss Tony Wilson links Happy Mondays with former Velvet Underground member John Cale for a 10-day recording session.

1987 **Mar** *Tart Tart* makes impression on UK Independent chart and spawns UK tour.
May Succinctly titled debut album, the Cale-produced *Squirrel & G-Man Twenty Four Hour Party People Plastic Face Carnt Smile (White Out)*, again makes Independent chart dent, but bleak industrial North-West song themes find few commercial friends.
June Group supports New Order at major London dates, followed by live appearances at the New Music Seminar in New York.
Nov *Twenty Four Hour Party People* is released, again to indie favor.

1988 During a year of extensive gigging, Happy Mondays recruit Nathan McGough as their manager.
June Factory labelmeister Tony Wilson decides to launch the band in US via a series of showcase performances.
Sept Group enters a Yorkshire recording studio to work on new songs.
Nov Second album *Bummed*, produced by Factory's Martin Hannett, is applauded by UK music press. Its hallucinatory dance rhythms beckon the growing UK dance craze of Acid House, for which Happy Mondays will be much revered. The album's inner sleeve depicting a naked woman results in some retail resistance.

1989 **Jan** Group headlines Panic Station's birthday celebration at the Kilburn National Ballroom, London, but ends the month with 2 drug busts. Berry is fined £700 for possession of cannabis while Ryder is detained in Jersey with cocaine in his pockets.
Feb They record a session for BBC Radio 1's "John Peel Show" and head for New York for a second promotional visit.
Mar Group embarks on sell-out nationwide UK tour.
May Shaun Ryder teams with 60s singer Karl Denver to re-record the vocals on the Happy Mondays album cut *Lazyitis (One Armed Boxer)*. An additional hot UK mix-master Paul Oakenfold remix adds samples from David Essex' *Rock On* and Sly & The Family Stone's *Family Affair*.
June Group begins first full-length US tour including sell-out dates in Los Angeles attended by The Beastie Boys, Guns N' Roses and David Bowie.
Sept *W.F.L.* becomes their chart debut, peaking at UK #68. It is a remix, by Erasure's Vince Clarke of their fourth single *Wrote For Luck*. Happy Mondays are now inextricably associated with the current Manchester dance craze sweeping the UK's acid house raves.
Nov [30] Band makes its BBC TV "Top Of The Pops" debut, on the same show as fellow Mancunian new-wavers, also debuting, The Stone Roses with Kirsty MacColl as guest vocalist.
Dec Group enjoys first major UK hit as *Madchester Race On EP* peaks at UK #19. Recorded at Richard Branson's Oxfordshire studios, it features *Hallelujah*, *Holy Ghost* and *Clap Your Hands*. Promotion for the single includes a sell-out major venue UK tour.

1990 **Jan** Band tops several UK music magazines "Best Newcomer" polls and sets off for European tour, together with an army of fanatical Happy Mondays followers. Meanwhile, *Bummed* finally charts, peaking at UK #59.
Feb They attend a "house" weekend organized by London's Brain club in Iceland.
Mar Group appears alongside Karl Denver in a Bailey Brothers' movie "Mad Fuckers".
[24-25] Band performs 2 sell-out dates at Manchester's G-Mex Centre.
Apr Their cover version of John Kongos' 1971 UK #4 hit *He's Gonna Step On You Again*, simply issued as *Step On*, hits UK #5 and reactivates

Bummed to UK #60. The single has been recorded at the instigation of the band's US label Elektra, who have requested cover versions by a number of their acts for their 40th anniversary *Rubáiyát*. (The track which will appear on the album will however be a cover of Kongos' other hit *Tokoloshe Man*.)
[7] They sell-out the Wembley Arena, London, for a one-off concert which continues well beyond the venue's 11 o'clock curfew time.
May Happy Mondays are featured in ITV documentary about the rise of the Manchester music scene, "Madchester: Sound Of The North". Strange Fruit Records issue "The Peel Sessions" featuring 3 tracks from those recordings.
June While the re-issued *Lazyitis (One Armed Boxer)* makes UK #46, the group begins 6-city US tour under the banner "Hacienda Trance American Tour". A second New York Seminar appearance becomes the hottest ticket at this year's event.
[22-24] Group participates in the Glastonbury Festival of Contemporary Performing Arts, Somerset.
July Happy Mondays begin recording their new album in Los Angeles. During the sessions, Shaun Ryder cuts a version of Donovan's *Colours* (with the help of fellow Mancunians, Barney Sumner and Johnny Marr) for future solo release. Live footage video is released titled "Party G-Mex" adding to 1989 release of "Rave On – The Video".
Nov [3] *Rubáiyát*, Elektra's 40th anniversary compilation, including the *Tokoloshe Man* track, makes US #140.
Major UK tour begins in support of their third album, Oakenfold co-produced *Pills 'N' Thrills And Bellyaches*, which immediately hits UK #4. Band-penned *Kinky Afro* hits UK #5, as UK press stories circulate claiming that notorious substance abuser Ryder has checked into a rehab facility.
Dec [6] **The Sun** newspaper confirms Ryder has booked himself into the Priory Clinic rehabilitation detox facility in Hale, Gtr.Manchester.

1991 **Jan** Ryder and Berry appear in nude spread with similarly unclothed models, posing in the Jan. UK issue of **Penthouse**.
Feb [16] Ryder and girlfriend Trish's baby is born.
Mar [23] *Loose Fit* reaches UK #17.
Apr [6] Elektra-released *Pills 'N' Thrills And Bellyaches* enters US Top 100 Album chart as *Step On* begins Hot 100 chart rise.

STEVE HARLEY & COCKNEY REBEL

Steve Harley (vocals)
Duncan Mackay (keyboards)
Jim Cregan (guitar)
George Ford (bass)
Stuart Elliott (drums)

1973 **Jan** Harley (b. Steven Nice, Feb.27, 1951, London), an ex-local newspaper journalist (for the Colchester Gazette) and folk singer, advertises in the music press for musicians to form a band, and selects Milton Reame James (keyboards), Jean Paul Crocker (electric violin, guitars), Paul Jeffreys (bass) and Elliott (drums). With Harley on lead vocals, they become Cockney Rebel, and debut at Beckenham Arts Lab, Kent, before working on the London club circuit.
June Group signs to EMI Records.
Aug Harley-penned *Sebastian* is the debut single, but does not chart.
Nov Debut album **Human Menagerie** is released.

1974 **June** *Judy Teen*, again written by Harley, is the group's breakthrough single, hitting UK #5.
July *The Psychomodo* hits UK #8.
Aug By the time *Mr. Soft* hits UK #8, the group has been broken up, following internal friction (partly over Harley's obsession with self-promotion and his provocative stance against UK music press).
Oct For a concert at the Rainbow theater, London, and an earlier performance at the Reading Festival, Berks., Harley assembles a new group: Elliott from the original Cockney Rebel plus Cregan (guitar), MacKay (keyboards) and Ford (bass).
Nov The new line-up begins work on an album at EMI's Abbey Road studios and AIR studios in London.

1975 **Feb** With the new label credit of Steve Harley & Cockney Rebel, *Make Me Smile (Come Up And See Me)* is Harley's biggest UK seller, topping the chart for 2 weeks.
Mar *Make Me Smile (Come Up And See Me)* is the band's only US hit, reaching #96. They tour US to promote it.
Apr Harley co-produces *The Best Years Of Our Lives* with Alan Parsons, and it hits UK #4. Band plays London's Hammersmith Odeon.
June *Mr. Raffles (Man It Was Mean)* reaches UK #13.
Oct *Black Or White* fails to chart, giving UK's music press the chance to

predict Harley's commercial eclipse.

Dec Group supports The Kinks on US tour.

1976 **Feb** *Timeless Flight* reaches UK #18 as the band tours UK to promote it. Extracted *White White Dove*, however, does not chart.

[9] Group embarks on 10-date UK tour at the Apollo Centre, Glasgow, Scotland. Tour will end Feb.22 at Colston Hall, Bristol, Avon.

Aug A revival of George Harrison's *Here Comes The Sun*, credited just to Harley, hits UK #10.

Nov *Love's A Prima Donna* makes UK #41.

Dec *Love's A Prima Donna* reaches UK #28. Harley breaks up the band again, and moves to live in US, continuing to record for EMI.

1977 **Aug** Live album by the mark 2 Cockney Rebel, *Face To Face – A Live Recording*, reaches UK #40.

1978 **Aug** *Hobo With A Grin*, recorded in US, is released.

1979 **Oct** Having released 3 more unsuccessful singles, Harley returns to UK. His solo *Freedom's Prisoner* reaches UK #58. Steve Harley/Jimmy Horowitz-produced *The Candidate* does not chart and EMI drops him.

1980 EMI releases compilation *The Best Of Steve Harley & Cockney Rebel*.

1981 **Mar** A one-off on Chrysalis Records, *I Can't Even Touch You*, featuring Midge Ure, fails to chart.

1983 **Aug** Comeback single *Ballerina (Prima Donna)*, on Stiletto label, makes UK #51.

1986 **Feb** After a period of apparent inactivity, Harley teams with Sarah Brightman on a specially-recorded duet of the title song from Andrew Lloyd Webber's forthcoming musical "The Phantom Of The Opera". It hits UK #7. Harley is subsequently astonished to be overlooked by the show's producers in favor of Michael Crawford for the lead role.

Apr Harley signs to RAK as a solo artist, releasing *Heartbeat Like Thunder* and *Irresistible* without success.

Oct Video "Live From London", featuring many of Cockney Rebel's hits from a 1984 performance, is released.

1988 **Mar** Use of *Mr. Soft* in a UK TV ad leads to its reissue by EMI and a second compilation, *Greatest Hits*.

Nov [18] Harley contributes to UK TV telethon charity single *Whatever You Believe*, credited to Jon Anderson, Steve Harley and Mike Batt.

Dec [21] Early band member Jeffreys is killed on Pan Am flight 103 over Lockerbie, Scotland.

1989 Harley embarks on "All Is Forgiven" reunion tour, with original member Elliott in the line-up, and Harley's younger brother Ian Nice on keyboards as new single *When I'm With You* is released on the Vital Vinyl label.

Dec [22] Harley plays London's Hammersmith Odeon at the end of a 10-month UK tour.

1990 **Apr** Raffles United, comprising Harley and several Cockney Rebel members, plays 4 consecutive Sunday gigs as a house band in Sudbury, Suffolk.

GEORGE HARRISON

1968 **Nov** Harrison (b. Feb.25, 1943, Wavertree, Liverpool, Merseyside) becomes the first Beatle to issue material independently of the group with album soundtrack of film "Wonderwall", which reaches US #49.

1969 **Mar** [12] Harrison and his wife Patti are arrested and charged with possession of 120 joints of marijuana, as Paul McCartney marries. *Electronic Sound*, which makes US #191, consists of Harrison experimenting with new acquisition, a moog synthesizer.

Oct He produces various Apple artists, including Radha Krishna Temple on *Hare Krishna Mantra*, which reaches UK #12.

Nov Having become the second writing force behind Lennon and McCartney within The Beatles, the first single he has penned is released by the group, *Something* which hits UK #4 and US #1. (It will become a show biz standard with hundreds of cover versions recorded in the coming years.)

Dec Harrison plays a number of concerts with Delaney & Bonnie.

1970 **Mar** [12] Harrison moves to Friar Park, Henley-upon-Thames, Berks.

May [26] He begins recording *All Things Must Pass*.

Dec *All Things Must Pass* is released and hits UK #4 and US #1. After The Beatles split, Harrison is the first to secure a chart-topping album. Released to tie in with the first non-Beatle Christmas since 1962, it achieves worldwide sales of 3 million copies. The triple album box set is a showcase of his talent and will never be equalled by future releases. Co-produced by Phil Spector, Harrison is backed by an all-star band, including Ringo Starr, Ginger Baker, Billy Preston, Badfinger and debut of Derek & The Dominoes, featuring Eric Clapton. Bob Dylan contributes 2 songs: *I'd Have You Anytime*, co-written with Harrison, and *If Not For You*, later covered by Olivia Newton-John (1971 UK #7,

US #25). Third record in the set is a loose session entitled *Apple Jam*. At one point, the musicians break into Cliff Richard's 1968 chart-topper *Congratulations* and UK songwriters, Bill Martin and Phil Coulter, successfully claim a royalty entitlement from Harrison.

[26] *My Sweet Lord* hits US #1, giving Harrison a second accolade as the first ex-Beatle with a chart-topping single. Originally given away by Harrison to Billy Preston for his Apple album *Encouraging Word* and even scheduled as a Preston single release, it becomes a worldwide #1, selling over 5 million copies.

1971 **Jan** [30] *My Sweet Lord* tops UK chart.

Feb [23] Harrison is fined and banned from driving for a year.

Mar Bright Tunes, which owns copyright of the late Ronnie Mack's song *He's So Fine*, a hit for The Chiffons (1963 UK #16, US #5), makes a legal claim that *My Sweet Lord* plagiarizes its former client's hit, and all royalty payments are frozen. Harrison claims that his song is inspired by The Edwin Hawkins Singers' hit *Oh Happy Day* (1969 UK #2, US #4). (On Sept.7, 1976 in US, District Court Judge, Richard Owens, will rule in favor of the plaintiff, but will allow that Harrison perhaps subconsciously adapted the song. Bright Tunes is paid $587,000 and is taken over by ex-Beatles' manager, Allen Klein, who continues a damage suit.) The Chiffons releases a cover version of *My Sweet Lord*.

[27] *What Is Life* hits US #10.

Aug [1] After a personal plea for help from friend Ravi Shankar, Harrison organizes 2 "Concerts For Bangladesh" to aid victims of famine and war in Bangladesh. Held at New York's Madison Square Garden, the line-up of artists includes Bob Dylan, Eric Clapton, Ringo Starr, Leon Russell and Ravi Shankar. Due to legal problems, proceeds are frozen and Harrison writes his own check to maintain the fund.

Sept [11] *Bangla Desh* hits UK #10 and makes US #23.

Dec [4] Bangladesh concert airs on CBS TV.

1972 **Jan** *The Concert For Bangla Desh*, another triple box-set, tops UK chart and hits US #2.

Feb [28] The Harrisons are involved in a minor car crash.

Mar [23] "The Concert For Bangladesh" film premieres in New York.

June [5] Harrison and Shankar are honored with the "Child Is Father To The Man" award by UNICEF, because of their efforts to aid famine relief in Bangladesh.

1973 **Mar** [3] *The Concert For Bangla Desh* wins Album Of The Year at the 15th annual Grammy awards.

Apr [26] Harrison forms The Material World Charitable Foundation Trust.

June *Living In The Material World* hits UK #2 and tops US chart.

[30] *Give Me Love (Give Me Peace On Earth)* hits UK #8 and tops US chart. Harrison returns to his own career, having recently appeared on albums for Nilsson and Ringo Starr.

July [25] Making known his displeasure, Harrison pays £1,000,000 in taxes, due from monies collected from the "Concerts For Bangladesh", to the Inland Revenue.

1974 **May** [23] Harrison announces the formation of his own record label, Dark Horse. Its first signing is Ravi Shankar but Splinter is the only success for the label, other than Harrison himself, with *Costafine Town* which will reach UK #17 and US #77 in Nov.

July Harrison announces a US tour supported by Ravi Shankar and Billy Preston. It is pounded by critics as audiences expect some sprinkling of Beatle-magic, but instead are treated to a handful of Fab Four songs with changed lyrics.

Nov [2] Harrison begins a 30-date North American tour at the Pacific Coliseum, Vancouver, Canada, set to end Dec.20 at Madison Square Garden, New York.

Dec *Dark Horse* hits US #4, but fails to chart in the UK. An introspective set, it includes a version of The Everly Brothers' *Bye Bye Love*, a farewell to his former wife, Patti Boyd, who has recently left him for Eric Clapton. (Patti provides backing vocals on the track.)

[13] While in Washington, DC, for a concert, Harrison visits President Gerald Ford at the White House.

1975 **Jan** *Ding Dong* makes UK #38. The B-side *I Don't Care Anymore* reflects his mood of the time.

[11] *Dark Horse* reaches US #15.

Feb [8] *Ding Dong* makes US #36.

Oct *Extra Texture (Read All About It)* peaks at UK #16 and hits US #8. It proves to be his last Apple album and the label features a partly eaten apple core.

Nov [1] *You* makes UK #38 and US #20.

Dec [26] Harrison guests on BBC TV's "Rutland Weekend Television".

1976 **Apr** [20] He joins the chorus of "The Lumberjack Song" at a Monty Python's Flying Circus performance at the City Center, New York.

Sept [28] A&M sues Harrison for $6 million over non-delivery of an album.

Nov [20] Harrison guests on NBC TV's "Saturday Night Live", turning down producer Lorne Michaels' offer of the union minimum payment for The Beatles to reunite on the show. Ironically McCartney is staying with Lennon in New York, and both see the show.
[30] Back in the UK, he appears on BBC TV's "Old Grey Whistle Test".
Dec [4] *Thirty-Three And A Third* climbs to UK #35.
[25] EMI/Capitol album *The Best Of George Harrison* makes US #31.

'77 Jan [8] *This Song* makes US #25. Commenting wryly on the *My Sweet Lord* court case, it refers in its lyrics to the publishers of *He's So Fine*.
[15] *Thirty-Three And A Third* reaches US #11.
Mar [26] *Crackerbox Palace* makes US #19.
June [9] George and Patti Harrison are divorced.
Dec [17] Harrison plays an unannounced live set at his local pub in Henley-upon-Thames.

'78 Jan [25] Harrison offers his congratulations to ITV's "This Is Your Life" subject, bike-racing driver Barry Sheene.
Mar [27] Eric Idle's pastiche of The Beatles, "All You Need Is Cash", in which Harrison cameos, airs on BBC TV.
Apr [26] Harrison guests on Ringo's US TV special "Ringo".
Aug [1] Harrison and his girlfriend Olivia Arias have a son, Dhani, at Princess Christian Nursing Home, Windsor, Berks.
Sept [2] Harrison and Arias marry at Henley Register Office.

'79 Mar *George Harrison* peaks at UK #39 and US #14. His major new interest in Formula One motor racing is highlighted by the track *Faster*, inspired by racing driver Jackie Stewart's book of the same name and Niki Lauda's fight to overcome his crash injuries.
May [5] *Blow Away* reaches UK #51 and US #16. Harrison's film company, Handmade Films, launched with US businessman, Denis O'Brien, scores an unexpected hit during the year: EMI drops out of backing Monty Python film "The Life Of Brian". Harrison, friendly with the Pythons after appearing on US TV's "Saturday Night Live" with Eric Idle in 1977, raises money with his partner to continue the project and it becomes one of the biggest grossers in the US that year. Harrison appears in the film in a very brief cameo role. EMI also lands Handmade another success when they sell on the rights to "The Long Good Friday" which is deemed too violent. (Films in the 80s will include "The Time Bandits", "The Missionary", "Mona Lisa" and "A Private Function", among many hits.)
[19] Harrison, McCartney and Starr play an impromptu set after the wedding of ex-wife Patti to Eric Clapton in Clapton's house in Ewhurst, Surrey.
Aug [22] Harrison's autobiography **I Me Mine** is published in a limited edition of 2,000 copies at £148 each.

'81 June *Somewhere In England* reaches UK #13 and US #11.
July [4] *All Those Years Ago* reaches UK #13 and hits US #2, and Harrison returns to single success with his tribute to John Lennon, which features the 2 other remaining Beatles.

'82 Nov *Gone Troppo* makes US #108. Harrison shows no interest in promoting this album and his label, Warner Bros., lets it slip with similar lack of interest.
Dec [4] *Wake Up My Love* peaks at US #53.

'84 Dec [14] Harrison, now spending much of his time at his Australian home, joins Deep Purple on stage in Sydney, Australia.

'85 Jan [18] Handmade Films' "Water", in which Harrison appears with Clapton and Starr in a scene set at the United Nations in New York, premieres in London.
July He performs an unreleased Bob Dylan song *I Don't Want To Do It* on the soundtrack of film "Porky's Revenge".
Oct [21] Harrison takes part in the Carl Perkins' Channel 4 TV special "Blue Suede Shoes", with Eric Clapton, Dave Edmunds, Ringo Starr and others, recorded at Limehouse studios in London. (The program is shown at Christmas and subsequently released on video.)

'86 Mar [15] He performs at the "Heartbeat 86" charity concert at the NEC Birmingham, W.Midlands, sharing vocals on *Johnny B. Goode* with Robert Plant and Denny Laine.
Sept Harrison contributes on 2 tracks for Duane Eddy comeback album *Duane Eddy*. Handmade Films' "Shanghai Surprise" flops. Harrison had publicly attempted to appease its 2 stars Madonna and Sean Penn.

'87 Jan [5] Harrison begins recording his first album in 5 years at his home studio.
Feb [19] He joins a jam session at Hollywood's Palamino club with Bob Dylan, Taj Mahal, and John Fogerty.
June [5-6] Harrison participates in the fifth annual Prince's Trust Rock

Gala at Wembley Arena, London, with Elton John, Bryan Adams, Dave Edmunds, Alison Moyet and Ringo Starr, with whom he performs *While My Guitar Gently Weeps* and *Here Comes The Sun*.
Oct [17] Harrison joins Dylan on stage at the latter's Wembley Arena concert, guesting on *Rainy Day Women #12 & 35*.
Nov *Cloud Nine* hits UK #10. Harrison collaborates with The Beatles' afficionado, ELO's Jeff Lynne, and together they create a highly commercial confection of songs far removed from Harrison's 70s persona. He wins over a whole new generation of fans, many of whom were born after The Beatles split. *Got My Mind Set On You*, reviving James Ray's 1962 original, hits UK #2.

1988 Jan [16] In one of the greatest comebacks in rock history, Harrison tops US chart with *Got My Mind Set On You*. It is nearly 24 years since he first topped the chart with The Beatles and *I Want To Hold Your Hand*. *Cloud Nine* hits US #8.
[18] He attends the third annual Rock'N'Roll Hall Of Fame induction dinner at the Waldorf Astoria, New York, with Ringo Starr and Yoko Ono to receive entry as a member of The Beatles. In his speech Harrison claims: "I don't have much to say 'cause I'm the quiet Beatle."
Feb *When We Was Fab* reaches UK #25 and US #23. Harrison gives a tongue-in-cheek nod to The Beatles sound with a Godley & Creme produced video that includes Ringo Starr.
Mar [5] Harrison and Starr guest on ITV's "Aspel & Co" talk show.
June [7] He makes an after dinner speech at Eric Clapton's 25th anniversary dinner at the Savoy hotel, London.
Aug Reports emanate from US that Harrison, Starr and Lynne plan an album and may tour. **USA Today** reports that a mystery group, The Traveling Wilburys, will release its debut album in Oct. and that the group comprises Harrison with Roy Orbison, Tom Petty, Bob Dylan and Jeff Lynne.
Nov *Traveling Wilburys: Volume One* featuring Harrison as "Nelson" is released to worldwide success. It includes hit singles *Handle With Care* and *End Of The Line*.

1989 Jan [8] "The Movie Life Of George" airs on ITV.
Mar He attends the annual Grammy awards at Los Angeles' Shrine Auditorium with fellow Wilburys Petty and Lynne.
Harrison guests on Petty's *Full Moon Fever* and Clapton's *Journeyman*, and contributes *Cheer Down* from "Lethal Weapon 2".
Nov *Best Of Dark Horse 1976-1989* makes US #132.

1990 Apr [20] Harrison appears on Simon Bates' BBC Radio 1 program backing his wife's "Romania Aid" charity Angel. Harrison contributes a Traveling Wilburys track and a duet with Paul Simon from NBC TV's "Saturday Night Live" to the *Nobody's Child* charity album.

DONNY HATHAWAY

1964 Hathaway (b. Oct.1, 1945, Chicago, IL), having been raised in St. Louis, MO, and been a gospel singer throughout his childhood and teens, majors in music theory at Howard University, Washington, DC, where he meets singer Roberta Flack, while playing keyboards with the Ric Powell Jazz Trio in Washington clubs.

1968 Back in Chicago, he meets Curtis Mayfield, who invites him to produce for fledgling Curtom label, where he works with singer June Conquest and records some duets with her. He moves on to work at Chess Records with Woody Herman, and then freelances on production work for Stax with Carla Thomas and The Staple Singers.

1969 He becomes friendly with session saxophonist King Curtis, who recommends him to Atlantic, to whom Hathaway signs as a producer, writer and recording artist.

1970 Feb *The Ghetto (Part 1)* makes US #87. Hathaway records his debut album, *Everything Is Everything*, which initially does not chart.

1971 June *Donny Hathaway* reaches US #89 and is followed by *Everything Is Everything*, which peaks at US #73.
Aug His duet with Flack on a cover of Carole King's *You've Got A Friend* reaches US #29. (James Taylor is currently at US #1 with it.)
Nov Also duetted with Flack, a revival of The Righteous Brothers' 1965 #1 *You've Lost That Lovin' Feelin'* peaks at US #71.

1972 May Live album *Donny Hathaway Live* is his first Top 20 entry, peaking at US #18. It earns a gold disk for a half million US sales.
June *Giving Up* peaks at US #81, while his duet with June Conquest, on Curtom, a revival of Sam And Dave's *I Thank You*, makes US #94.
Aug *Where Is The Love*, a duet with Flack, hits US #5 and sells over a million, earning a gold disk. It also reaches UK #29 – Hathaway's first UK hit. Their joint album *Roberta Flack And Donny Hathaway* hits US #3 and also goes gold.
Sept Hathaway composes and performs the music for Godfrey

DONNY HATHAWAY cont.

Cambridge film "Come Back Charleston Blue". The soundtrack album makes US #198.

[2] He sings the theme song for CBS TV comedy series "Maude" (a spin-off from "All In The Family", which will run until 1978).

Nov *I Love You More Than You'll Ever Know* peaks at US #60.

1973 **Mar** [3] Hathaway and Flack win Best Pop Vocal Performance By A Duo, Group Or Chorus for *Where Is The Love* at the 15th annual Grammy awards.

Aug *Love, Love, Love* makes US #44 and *Extension Of A Man* US #69.

1974 He forms his own freelance production company, and work in the control booth (for Aretha Franklin, Jerry Butler and others) will keep him out of the studio as an artist for some time (as will recurrent personal problems).

1978 **May** After 6 years, he duets with Flack again, on *The Closer I Get You*, a James Mtume/Reggie Lucas song from her album *Blue Lights In The Basement*. It hits US #2 (a million-seller) and UK #42.

Sept Hathaway's solo *You Were Meant For Me* reaches US R&B #17 but does not cross over. (It will be his last hit during his lifetime.)

1979 **Jan** [13] Hathaway dies, aged 33, after falling from the 15th floor of the Essex House hotel, New York. The death is officially registered as suicide, though some close friends are sceptical.

1980 **Apr** His duet with Flack, *You Are My Heaven*, makes US #47.

May *Roberta Flack Featuring Donny Hathaway*, on which Hathaway was completing work at the time of his death, climbs to US #25 and earns a gold disk.

June Uptempo *Back Together Again*, taken from the album with Flack, reaches US #56 and hits UK #3. Boosted by it, *Roberta Flack Featuring Donny Hathaway* reaches UK #31, his final chart monument.

1990 **Oct** [20] Daughter Lalah's self-titled debut album makes US #191.

RICHIE HAVENS

1962 Havens (b. Jan.21, 1941, Brooklyn, New York, NY), a former street corner singer and teenage member of the McCrea Gospel Singers, starts to sing and play guitar on the burgeoning Greenwich Village folk scene, having first come to the area as a painter. His unique guitar style uses open E-chord tuning and a rapid strumming style which uses the instrument as percussion.

1965 He signs to small label Douglas Records, releasing debut album *A Richie Havens Record*, which sells only to his Greenwich Village underground following.

1966 *Electric Havens* is also only a cult favorite, but his reputation as an individual club and cafe entertainer leads him, and several contemporaries from the same Village scene, to a contract with MGM's new progressive Verve Forecast label.

1967 Debut Verve Forecast album *Mixed Bag* sets the pattern for almost all subsequent releases; open strumming style and intense vocals in a personalized selection of traditional songs and covers like *Just Like A Woman* (Bob Dylan) and *Eleanor Rigby* (Lennon/McCartney). It does not chart initially, but gains wide notice.

1968 **Jan** [20] Havens appears with Dylan, Judy Collins, Arlo Guthrie, Pete Seeger and others in a tribute concert to Woody Guthrie at New York's Carnegie Hall.

Mar *Something Else Again* is his US chart debut, peaking at #184.

July *Mixed Bag* reaches US #182.

Dec Revived by his growing popularity, the second Douglas album *Electric Havens* also finally charts, making US #192.

[28] He plays the Miami Pop Festival at the Gulfstream Racing Park, Hallandale, FL, to 100,000 people, along with Chuck Berry, Three Dog Night, Fleetwood Mac, Marvin Gaye and many others.

1969 **Feb** Double album *Richard P. Havens, 1983*, highlighted by Beatles and Dylan adaptations, reaches US #80.

Aug [16] Havens appears at the Woodstock Festival, NY, where his late-night impassioned set is rapturously received. His song *Freedom* becomes one of the anthems of the festival and is included in the movie "Woodstock".

[31] Havens plays the Isle of Wight Festival with Dylan, The Band, The Who, The Moody Blues, The Nice, Joe Cocker and others.

1970 **Jan** [28] He takes part in a 7-hour benefit concert at New York's Madison Square Garden, with Jimi Hendrix, Judy Collins, The Young Rascals and others, to raise funds for Vietnam Moratorium Committee.

Feb Havens forms his own Stormy Forest label. First release is *Stonehenge*, which includes an offbeat version of The Bee Gees' *I Started A Joke*. It reaches US #155.

Aug [30] He appears at UK's Isle of Wight Pop Festival with Free, Donovan, Jethro Tull, Joan Baez, Hendrix and others.

Nov An MGM reissue of *Mixed Bag* puts it back on US chart at #190.

1971 **Feb** *Alarm Clock*, his most successful chart album, climbs to US #29.

May Taken from it, a revival of George Harrison's *Here Comes The Sun* (original is on The Beatles' *Abbey Road*) is his only single to gain widespread US airplay and only US Top 20 entry, making US #16.

Oct [19] On a UK visit, Havens is recorded live at BBC TV Theatre, London, for a special on his music (also to be released on his live album in 1972).

Dec *The Great Blind Degree* peaks at US #126.

1972 **Oct** Double live album *Richie Havens On Stage* is his second biggest seller, reaching US #55. It includes 3 stage performances from London BBC TV Theatre, Santa Monica Civic Center, CA, and The Westbury Music Fair, NY. This reprises mainly material from earlier albums, including his Woodstock highlight *Freedom*.

Dec [9] Havens takes part in debut of Pete Townshend's rock opera "Tommy" at London's Rainbow theater, with Steve Winwood, Merry Clayton, Keith Moon, Rod Stewart, Peter Sellers and Roger Daltry.

1973 **June** *Portfolio* reaches US #182.

1974 Havens appears as Othello in Patrick McGoohan-directed movie of Jack Good's musical "Catch My Soul", based on Shakespeare's "Othello". He co-stars with Tony Joe White, Lance LeGault and Delaney & Bonnie, and sings 6 songs.

1975 **Oct** *Mixed Bag II* peaks at US #186.

1976 **Oct** After a year's hiatus, Havens signs to A&M Records for *The End Of The Beginning*, which reaches US #157, his last US chart album.

1977 **Apr** [5] Havens appears with Jackson Browne, John Sebastian, Country Joe McDonald and others in a 3-day rally in Los Angeles, CA, which raises $150,000 to help preserve whales and dolphins from the international fishing industry.

Second A&M album *Mirage* fails to sell, and the label drops him. Havens writes and performs music for, and appears in, Richard Pryor-starring movie "Greased Lightning".

1980 Havens is signed to Elektra for *Connections*, which fails to chart. (During the 80s, little will be seen or heard of him in the music field, though he will occasionally appear in films, including Dylan's 1987 movie "Hearts Of Fire".)

1987 **Oct** Now signed to RBI Records, Havens returns to US chart with *Simple Things* which peaks at #173.

1989 Havens is featured on children's album *American Children* with Rick Danko, Maria Muldaur and Dave Van Ronk on Vermont label Alacazam.

1990 **Aug** [29] Havens, after forming Natural Guard environmental group, plants tree seeds in Angeles National Forest in Southern California.

HAWKWIND

Dave Brock (guitar, vocals)
Nick Turner (sax, flute, vocals)
Mick Slattery (guitar)
John Harrison (bass)
Terry Ollis (drums)
Dik Mik (electronics)

1969 **July** Brock and Slattery are in Famous Cure and Turner is in Mobile Freakout when, having met by chance on tour in Holland, they meet again after their return to UK. They debut as Group X (but change name to Hawkwind Zoo) at a 10-min. gig at All Saint's Hall, Notting Hill, London.

Oct Manager Doug Smith secures the band, now shortened to Hawkwind, a deal with Liberty. Huw Lloyd Langton replaces Slattery. Occasional drummer Viv Prince (ex-Pretty Things) attracts extra police attention through his membership of Hell's Angels.

1970 Dick Taylor (also ex-Pretty Things), is brought in to produce the group and ends up playing on the sessions.

July Hawkwind's first release is *Hurry On Sundown/Mirror Of Illusion*. Harrison leaves and is replaced on bass by Thomas Crimble.

Aug Debut album *Hawkwind* is released. True to their "people's band" tag, they play at Canvas City, a series of free gigs performed on the perimeter of UK's Isle of Wight Festival.

Sept Langton leaves (he will return 9 years later), as does Crimble.

1971 **May** Dave Anderson (ex-Amon Duul) is recruited. Soundman Del Dettmar plays synthesizer, replacing Dik Mik (who will rejoin 3 months later).

June Group plays Glastonbury Fayre, Somerset, with dancer Stacia appearing for the first time and poet Robert Calvert as vocalist.

Aug Lemmy (b. Ian Kilmister) joins on bass after Anderson leaves. (Initially on 6-months' trial, he stays nearly 4 years.)

Oct *In Search Of Space* reaches UK #18. Its "space-rock" image is partially inspired by Calvert.

'72 Jan Simon King replaces Ollis on drums.

Feb Group plays the "Greasy Truckers Party" at London's Roundhouse. The performance is recorded and excerpts appear on albums *Greasy Truckers Party* and *Glastonbury Fayre*. Calvert joins the band full-time and sings many of the lead vocals.

Aug One of Calvert's songs, *Silver Machine*, taken from the "Greasy Truckers" recordings, remixed with Calvert's original vocal re-recorded by Lemmy, begins UK chart rise, eventually hitting UK #3.

Dec Third album *Doremi Fasol Latido* reaches UK #14. The success of *Silver Machine* enables Hawkwind to create a lavish 30-date touring show entitled "The Space Ritual".

'73 June Double *Space Ritual Alive*, based on the live show, hits UK #9.

Aug Dik Mik quits. *Urban Guerilla* makes UK #39 but is withdrawn because they are worried about association with current IRA activity.

Nov Group makes its US debut at Howard Stein's Academy of Music in New York.

Dec *Space Ritual Live* makes US #179 during the band's first US tour. [15] On its return, Hawkwind begins 7-date UK tour at Bracknell sports center, Berks., set to end on Dec.22 at the Empire theater, Edinburgh, Scotland.

74 Feb Hawkwind begins second US tour and plays a benefit for acid guru Timothy Leary, back in jail after escaping and being recaptured in Switzerland.

Apr Simon House, who played on recent US tour, joins on keyboards, synthesizer and violin. Dettmar leaves the stage line-up to operate his synthesizer from the mixing desk.

May Calvert's solo album, *Captain Lockheed & The Starfighters*, is released on United Artists.

June Dettmar leaves the group and emigrates to Canada.

July Simon King breaks ribs playing soccer and Alan Powell (ex-Chicken Shack, Stackridge, Vinegar Joe) is brought in temporarily. (He will stay when King recovers, giving the group 2 drummers.)

Sept Fifth album, *Hall Of The Mountain Grill* reaches UK #16 and US #110. Band plays Harrow Free Festival, London, and begins a US tour, which is halted in Indiana when state police impound their gear under a new tax law. They return home.

Oct Group returns to US to play 21 re-scheduled dates.

Dec A UK tour commences which will run until Feb.

75 June *Warrior On The Edge Of Time* reaches UK #13 and US #150. Group tours US again and includes dates in Canada. At the border, Canadian customs mistakenly identify amphetamine pills Lemmy has in his luggage for cocaine. The offense is elevated to a felony from a misdemeanor and he spends 5 days in a police cell and, on release, finds band has sacked him. Paul Rudolph (ex-Deviants, Pink Fairies, Uncle Dog) is flown out to complete the tour (and will join full-time). Back in UK, Lemmy announces plans for his new group, Motorhead. Hawkwind tours France.

Aug Group tops the bill at Reading Festival, Berks. Calvert re-joins for a one-off appearance and decides to stay. His second solo album, *Lucky Leif And The Longships*, produced by Brian Eno, fails to chart. Stacia leaves to get married. (Band enters a period of stability and ends the year with a UK tour.)

76 Jan Hawkwind signs to Charisma Records.

Apr Compilation album *Road Hawks* makes UK #34.

June *The Time Of The Hawklords*, a sci-fi novel by Michael Butterworth with the band as fantasy heroes, is published.

July *Kerb Crawler/Honky Dorky*, on Charisma, fails to chart. [24] Group plays at Cardiff Castle, Wales, on a bill with Status Quo, The Strawbs, Curved Air and Budgie.

Sept *Astounding Sounds, Amazing Music* makes UK #33.

77 Jan Turner, encouraged by Rudolph and Powell, leaves the band and forms Sphynx.

Feb Rudolph and Powell are themselves purged by Calvert and Brock and a new Hawkwind line-up (with Adrian Shaw on bass) debuts at the Roundhouse, London, and begins to record a new album. United Artists release another compilation album, *Masters Of The Universe*.

July *Quark Strangeness And Charm* makes UK #30 as group tours UK.

Oct House leaves to join David Bowie's world tour and is replaced by Paul Hayles.

78 Feb Hawkwind is on an unhappy US tour. Calvert sells his guitar minsutes after the final concert finishes. They return home and Shaw forms a group with House.

June Calvert forms The Hawklords (the name changed for legal reasons) with Smith returning as manager. Shelving *PXR-5*, the new

group records *25 Years On*. Line-up is Calvert, Brock, Martin Griffiths (drums), Steve Swindell (ex-Pilot and String Driven Thing, keyboards) and Harvey Bainbridge (bass).

Oct *25 Years On* makes UK #48. The group tours UK. United Artists re-releases *Silver Machine* which makes UK #34.

Dec Griffiths quits the band.

1979 Jan Calvert leaves to go solo. King rejoins on drums and the 4-piece band reassumes the name Hawkwind and rehearses and records in Wales. Swindell leaves soon after.

May *PXR-5*, released by Charisma, makes UK #59. Tim Blake (ex-Gong) replaces Swindell and Langton rejoins. Group plays UK's Leeds Science Fiction Festival.

1980 July *Shot Down In The Night* reaches UK #59.

Aug Smith arranges a deal which includes Hawkwind, Motorhead and Girlschool, with Bronze Records. *Live 1979*, recorded in St. Albans in Nov., makes UK #15. Group begins a tour of UK and Europe (which will last the rest of the year).

Sept Ginger Baker (ex-Cream and Blind Faith) joins, replacing King, who has been fired in July.

Oct [10] A 22-date UK tour begins at the Apollo theater, Manchester, Gtr.Manchester, set to end Nov.5 at the City Hall, St. Albans, Herts.

Nov *Levitation* reaches UK #21.

1981 Mar Baker is sacked before a scheduled Italian tour, which is cancelled. Griffiths rejoins and the group plays UK's Stonehenge and Glastonbury Festivals.

(During the next 7 years, the band will continue to tour mainly in Europe, with modifying line-ups, and release albums with decreasing success (*Sonic Attack* UK #19, 1981; *Church Of Hawkwind* UK #26, 1982; *Choose Your Masques* UK #29, 1982; *Zones*, released via new deal with Flicknife, UK #57, 1983; EMI's re-issued *Hawkwind* UK #75, 1984 and *Chronicle Of The Black Sword* UK #65, 1985) while the much revered rock classic *Silver Machine* will make a third UK chart appearance at UK #67 in Jan.1983.)

1982 Aug [21] Group takes part in the third annual "Monsters Of Rock" Festival at Castle Donington, Leics.

1988 Apr In support of a forthcoming album celebrating a new label deal with the GWR label, Hawkwind begins an extensive UK tour with a new line-up: Brock, Langton, Bainbridge (now on keyboards), Allan Davis (bass) and Danny Thompson (drums).

May [14] *The Xenon Codex* makes UK #79.

Aug [14] Calvert dies after a heart attack at his home in Kent. He had recently played with his new band, The Starfighers.

1990 Sept Refusing to quit, Hawkwind releases *Space Bandits*, still on GWR Records.

ISAAC HAYES

1958 Hayes (b. Aug.20, 1942, Covington, TN) moves from rural Tennessee, where he has been brought up by his sharecropper grandparents and sung in church for many years, to Memphis, TN. He plays in his high school band, and on saxophone and keyboards with various local amateur groups including The Teen Tones and The Swing Cats.

1964 Some gigs in Memphis with Gene "Bowlegs" Miller and a meeting with musicians from Stax Records group The Mar-Keys lead to an invitation from Stax president Jim Stewart for session work at the label's studios.

1965 Now a regular member of the Stax house band, but holding down a day job in a Memphis meat-packing plant, Hayes meets David Porter, an insurance salesman with songwriting aspirations. They form a partnership which produces successful material for Stax.

1966 Hayes plays on many of the label's most successful mid-60s releases, including Otis Redding, Carla Thomas, William Bell and Eddie Floyd hits. Hayes and Porter will also co-write and produce a string of Sam And Dave hits, including *You Don't Know Like I Know*, *Hold On I'm Coming*, *Soul Man* and *When Something Is Wrong With My Baby*.

1968 Debut album *Presenting Isaac Hayes* is the result of a post-party late-night session by Hayes with MG's bassist "Duck" Dunn and drummer Al Jackson, Jr. Sales are unspectacular.

1969 Oct Stax simultaneously releases 27 albums to tie in with a publicity campaign following its new link with Paramount and Gulf & Western. It introduces subsidiary Enterprise label, on which *Hot Buttered Soul* is initially marketed as a makeweight alongside more obviously commercial items by Booker T. & The MG's, Eddie Floyd, Johnnie Taylor and others. DJs are hooked by the unique formula which Hayes introduces on the 4-song album – familiar songs in extended, personalized versions, an intimate "rap" monologue, and arrangements with wah-wah guitars and muscular funk rhythm sections in symphonic layers of strings. The album is by far the biggest success of the 27, hitting US #8 and earning a gold disk. Double-sided *Walk On By/By The Time I Get To Phoenix*, in sharply edited form, also makes US #30/#37.

1970 **May** *The Isaac Hayes Movement*, in similar style to the first (with which Hayes, with refinements and some exceptions, will stick throughout his recording career), also hits US #8. Its sleeve promotes Hayes' striking visual image: shaven headed, shaded and bearded, stripped to the waist and garlanded with gold chains. He maintains this appearance on his tours (undertaken with a 40-piece orchestra).
Sept From *Movement*, a reworking of Jerry Butler's *I Stand Accused* climbs to US #42.

1971 **Jan** *To Be Continued* makes US #11.
Mar Revival of *The Look Of Love*, from the third album, makes US #79.
June A personalized cover of The Jackson 5's *Never Can Say Goodbye* reaches US #22 only weeks after the original hit #2.
Sept MGM's film "Shaft", starring Richard Roundtree as a black New York private eye, opens in US, with a soundtrack composed and performed by Hayes.
Nov *Theme From Shaft* tops US chart for 2 weeks, becoming Hayes' only million-selling single. Double soundtrack album also hits US #1 and earns a gold disk.

1972 **Jan** Double album *Black Moses* is packaged in a sleeve which folds out to form a large cross and illustrates a biblically-attired Hayes by a riverbank. It hits US #10 and earns another gold disk. *Theme From Shaft* hits UK #4, while soundtrack album makes UK #17. The music from the film is the chief factor in spreading the commercial success of Hayes' music outside US.
[15] Hayes plays the first of 5 German dates during a European tour which will be highlighted by his being banned from playing a scheduled date at the Royal Albert Hall, London, Jan.24.
Feb [12] *Black Moses* makes UK #38.
Mar [14] *Theme From Shaft* wins Best Instrumental Arrangement and Best Engineered Recording and *Shaft* wins Best Original Score Written For A Motion Picture at the 14th annual Grammy awards. The theme also wins an Oscar for Best Film Song, and a similar honor at the Golden Globe Awards. Meanwhile, his 1968 debut album, reissued by Atlantic Records as *In The Beginning*, makes US #102.
Apr *Do Your Thing*, an edited version from *Shaft*, climbs to US #30. Hayes' sax-playing instrumental cover of Al Green's *Let's Stay Together* reaches US #48.
May Hayes and Porter duet on soul ballad *Ain't That Loving You (For More Reasons Than One)*, which makes only US #86.
Aug Hayes plays at "Wattstax '72" in Los Angeles, a benefit concert by Stax artists (others include The Staple Singers, Carla Thomas, Luther Ingram and Albert King) for the seventh annual Watts Festival.
Dec *Theme From The Men*, written by Hayes for US ABC TV anthology series of spy and police thrillers "The Men", reaches US #38.

1973 **Jan** Hayes makes his first live UK appearance.
Mar [3] *Black Moses* wins Best Pop Instrumental Performance By An Arranger, Composer, Orchestra And/Or Choral Leader at the 15th annual Grammy awards.
July Double live *Live At The Sahara Tahoe*, which features his full, orchestra-backed cabaret act, makes US #14, earning another gold disk.
Dec *Joy* reaches US #16.

1974 **Jan** Hayes completes work on 2 movie soundtrack projects for release later in the year, while *Joy, Part 1* makes US #30.
June *Wonderful* peaks at US #71, while Hayes' soundtrack album from film "Tough Guys" makes US #146.
Aug Double soundtrack album from movie "Truck Turner", in which Hayes also has a star acting role, peaks at US #156.

1975 After an altercation with Stax over royalty payments, Hayes moves from Enterprise to set up his own Hot Buttered Soul label through ABC Records. (He will tailor his output more closely to prevailing disco styles.)
Aug *Chocolate Chip* reaches US #18 (and earns a further gold disk), though the extracted title track peaks at US #92. Enterprise releases compilation album *The Best Of Isaac Hayes*, which makes US #165.

1976 **Jan** [25] Hayes plays alongside Stevie Wonder and Bob Dylan's "The Rolling Thunder Revue" at "Night Of The Hurricane 2" in front of 40,000 people at Houston Astrodome, TX. The concert is a benefit show for imprisoned boxer "Hurricane" Carter.
Feb *Disco Connection*, billed as by The Isaac Hayes Movement, reaches US #85.
Mar *Groove-A-Thon* peaks at US #45.
May The instrumental title track from *Disco Connection* hits UK #10

(Hayes' only UK hit single in addition to *Shaft*).
Aug *Juicy Fruit (Disco Freak)* reaches US #124.
Dec [22] Hayes files for bankruptcy.

1977 **Mar** Double album *A Man And A Woman*, recorded live with Dionne Warwick, makes US #49, his last release on Hot Buttered Soul, and the end of Hayes' association with ABC. He and Warwick also make a join guest appearance on an episode of TV's "The Rockford Files".
June Declared a bankrupt with $6 million debts, Hayes moves from Memphis to Atlanta (where he will work regularly at Master Sounds studios) and signs a new deal with Polydor.

1978 **Jan** His first Polydor album *New Horizon* makes US #78.
Dec *For The Sake Of Love* reaches US #75. From it, *Zeke The Freak* is a big disco success but fails to chart.

1979 **Nov** *Don't Let Go* reaches US #39 and stays on chart for 30 weeks (it will be his final gold disk for a half million US sales).
Dec Hayes duets with Millie Jackson on *Royal Rappin's*, which makes US #80.

1980 **Jan** The title track *Don't Let Go*, an updated hustling disco-style reviva of Jesse Stone's R&B standard peaks at US #18.
June *And Once Again* reaches US #59.

1981 **Apr** Hayes appears as the villain in John Carpenter's film "Escape From New York", and will become an increasingly active actor during the decade.

1985 **Feb** 2 dancefloor-aimed revivals of *Theme From Shaft*, by Eddy & The Soul Band and Van Twist, return the Hayes composition to the UK chart, reaching #13 and #57 respectively.

1986 Hayes has TV cameo acting roles in "The A-Team" and "Hunter" (in his archetypal black tough guy role), and co-stars with Paul Sorvino and Barry Bostwick in TV movie "Betrayed By Innocence".
Dec Hayes, signed to CBS/Columbia, releases a revival of Freddie Scott's 1963 hit *Hey Girl* which incorporates a topically-relevant anti-crack rap, with *Ike's Rap* on the flip. It hits US R&B #9, while parent album *U-Turn* makes US R&B #37.

1987 **Feb** Hayes begins a US promotional tour for *U-Turn*, co-produced wit the members of Surface. Hayes plays all instruments, replacing the symphony orchestras with synth-created "orchestral" arrangements.
Mar *Thing For You* makes #43 on US R&B chart.
He appears in movie "Counter Force" with George Kennedy and Andrew Stevens, and also completes "Dead Aim" with Corbin Bernser and Ed Marinaro. Meanwhile, US R&B group The Fabulous Thunderbirds revive Hayes' early composition *Wrap It Up*.

1989 **Feb** [23] Hayes is jailed by Atlanta judge for owing $346,300 in child support and alimony, and is subsequently unable to promote his recen Columbia release *Love Attack*.

HEART

Ann Wilson (lead vocals)
Nancy Wilson (guitar, vocals)
Roger Fisher (guitar)
Howard Leese (keyboards, guitar)
Steve Fossen (bass)
Michael Derosier (drums)

1970 Ann Wilson (b. June 19, 1951, San Diego, CA), living in Seattle, WA, and ex-local bands Ann Wilson & The Daybreaks and Bordersong (with sister Nancy (b. Mar.16, 1954, San Francisco, CA), joins Seattle-based group The Army, formed by Fossen and brothers Mike and Roger Fisher in 1963, who play local bar circuit. She takes over lea vocals, but their music mix remains hard-rock covers of material by Led Zeppelin and others. Wilson and Roger Fisher also strike up a romantic relationship.

1972 The Army renames itself White Heart and continues touring on the club circuit in the Pacific North-West.

1974 After college and a spell as a solo folk singer, Nancy Wilson also joins the band, which abbreviates its name to Heart. She replaces Mike Fisher in the playing line-up, as he becomes sound engineer and manager, and her boyfriend.

1975 Group relocates to Vancouver, Canada, primarily to avoid Mike Fisher being drafted. After establishing a renewed live reputation in Canada, Heart signs to Shelly Siegal's Vancouver-based independent Mushroom label, which records *Dreamboat Annie*, a mixture of folky ballads and hard rock. It sells 30,000 copies in Canada.

1976 **June** With independent distribution, Mushroom releases *Dreamboat Annie* in US, with extracted *Crazy On You*, which is the group's US chart debut at #35.
Oct *Magic Man* hits US #9, and after a slow chart climb, *Dreamboat*

Annie hits US #7 (eventually spending 100 weeks on chart and selling over 2 million).

Dec Group returns to Seattle, signing a new US deal with CBS/Portrait Records. Mushroom sues for breach of contract, and the group countersues to prevent the release of a second Mushroom album made up of allegedly unfinished demos.

1977 Jan The title song from *Dreamboat Annie* reaches US #42.

Feb *Dreamboat Annie* is released by Arista in UK and makes #36.

May [28, 30] Heart plays 2 concerts at Oakland Stadium, CA, in front of 100,000, on a bill featuring The Eagles, Foreigner and Steve Miller.

July Debut Portrait album *Little Queen* hits US #9 (a second million-seller) and climbs to UK #34.

Aug *Barracuda*, taken from the album, reaches US #11.

Oct The title track from *Little Queen* makes US #62.

Dec *Kick It Out* reaches US #79.

1978 Feb Reissued Mushroom single *Crazy On You* peaks at US #62.

Mar [18] Band plays the California Jam 2 festival in Ontario, CA, to 250,000 people, with Aerosmith, Santana, Ted Nugent and others.

June *Magazine*, the second Mushroom album, reaches US #17. It has finally been issued after a Seattle judge decides that Mushroom may release the album, but that Heart first had the right to remix and re-record the material. The sleeve bears a disclaimer. Despite the group's reluctance to acknowledge it, it becomes a million-selling platinum album. From it, *Heartless* reaches US #24.

Nov *Straight On* reaches US #15. It is taken from second Portrait album *Dog And Butterfly*, which reaches US #17, their fourth million-seller.

1979 Mar Title track from *Dog And Butterfly* makes US #34.

1980 Jan While the band is completing the recording of its next album, the Wilson sisters/Fisher brothers relationships sour. Roger Fisher leaves, later to form his own band in Seattle.

Apr Portrait is absorbed into Epic label for album *Bebe Le Strange*, which hits US #5 as they play a 77-date US tour, with Leese and Nancy Wilson jointly covering Fisher's guitar role. The album is another million-seller and extracted *Even It Up* makes US #34.

Dec Double *Greatest Hits/Live*, a compilation of hit singles with 6 tracks recorded live on the tour earlier in the year, reaches US #13.

1981 Jan *Tell It Like It Is*, a revival of Aaron Neville's 1967 million-seller, hits US #8 – Heart's first US Top 10 hit since *Magic Man* in 1976.

Apr Heart's *Unchained Melody* becomes the eighth version of the song to make the US Hot 100, at US #83.

May Group begins an extensive 6-month US tour. (At the end of it, Fossen and Derosier will leave and the Wilson sisters will take a sabbatical before recruiting new musicians and planning next album.)

Oct [2] Ann and Nancy Wilson perform, alongside Paul Simon, Joan Baez and others in the Bread & Roses festival at the Greek theater, Berkeley, CA, to benefit a prisoners' aid group operated by Baez' sister Mimi Farina.

1982 June Nancy Wilson appears in film "Fast Times At Ridgemount High" (and will also act in later movie "The Wild Life").

July *Private Audition* reaches US #25 and UK #77. Group line-up is now the Wilson sisters and Leese, plus newcomers Mark Andes (b. Feb.19, 1948) (ex-Spirit, Jo Jo Gunne, and Firefall) on bass, and Denny Carmassi (ex-Montrose and Gemma) on drums. *This Man Is Mine*, taken from the album, reaches US #33. (By year's end, Heart will have toured UK, opening for Queen.)

1983 Sept *How Can I Refuse*, from the forthcoming album, reaches US #44.

Oct *Passionworks*, their last for Epic, reaches US #39.

Nov Final Epic single *Allies* peaks at US #83.

1984 July Ann Wilson duets with Loverboy's Mike Reno on *Almost Paradise*, love theme from movie "Footloose", which hits US #7. (Reno replaces the film's producers' original male choice, Foreigner's Lou Gramm, who rejects the project.)

1985 Jan Now signed to Capitol Records, band starts work on a new album.

Aug First Capitol single *What About Love?* hits US #10.

Nov [11] Group opens a UK tour at the Apollo, Manchester, Gtr. Machester, supporting Tears For Fears.

Dec Ron Nevison-produced *Heart*, their first for Capitol, is released, set to top US chart and reach UK #19. Extracted *Never* hits US #4.

1986 Mar [22] Ballad *These Dreams*, written by Martin Page and Bernie Taupin, and dedicated to 21-year-old cancer victim Sharon Hess, who has spent 2 weeks with the band before dying, tops US chart for a week, displacing Starship's *Sara*.

Apr *These Dreams* reaches UK #62, Heart's first UK chart single, as parent *Heart* hits US #1, the group's first US chart-topping album, earning a platinum disk.

June [21] *Nothin' At All* hits US #10.

Aug [9] *If Looks Could Kill* reaches US #54.

1987 Jan [24] Ann Wilson's solo *The Best Man In The World*, featured in Eddie Murphy movie "The Golden Child", makes US #61.

July [11] Power ballad *Alone* becomes the group's biggest hit single, topping US chart for 3 weeks. Written by hit-writers Billy Steinberg and Tom Kelly, it gives the songwriting duo a third US #1 (the previous 2 being Madonna's *Like A Virgin* and Cyndi Lauper's *True Colors*).

Aug *Alone* hits UK #3, their first UK Top 10 single, and prompts UK visit for promotion and major tour dates. UK press becomes obsessed with Ann's weight problems. Nevison-produced *Bad Animals*, which includes *Alone*, hits US #2 (another platinum disk) and UK #7.

Oct [3] *Who Will You Run To*, also taken from the album, hits US #7 and reaches UK #30.

Dec *There's The Girl* makes UK #34.

1988 Jan [23] *There's The Girl* reaches US #12.

Mar *These Dreams/Never* hits UK #8, a double A-side reissue of 2 tracks from 1985 album *Heart*, which also charts at UK #19. *I Want You So Bad* reaches US #49. Heart video compilation "If Looks Could Kill", heavily featuring the Wilson sisters, is released.

June Still using the back catalog, *What About Love* climbs to UK #14.

Oct Reissued *Nothin' At All* makes UK #38.

Nov Capitol releases UK only Heart collection, *With Love From Heart*.

1989 Mar [11] Ann Wilson teams with Cheap Trick's Robin Zander for *Surrender To Me*, from Mel Gibson/Kurt Russell film "Tequila Sunrise". It hits US #6.

1990 Apr [14] Richard Zito-produced *Brigade* hits UK #3.

May [19] *Brigade* hits US #3, on its way to RIAA double platinum certification. [26] Robert John "Mutt" Lange-written *All I Wanna Do Is Make Love To You* hits US #2, having already hit UK #8.

June Heart undertakes extensive 6-month North American tour to promote recently released *Brigade* project.

July [28] *I Didn't Want To Need You* makes UK #47.

Aug [18] *I Didn't Want To Need You* reaches US #23.

Oct Early members Fossen, Derosier and Roger Fisher re-emerge in new hard rock act Alias, linking with ex-members of Sheriff.

Dec [1] Third *Brigade* extract, *Stranded* reaches US #13, having peaked at UK #60 on Nov.17.

1991 Feb Ann Wilson adopts Marie Lamoureaux Wilson, born Feb.3.

Mar [2] *Secret* peaks at US #64.

HEAVEN 17

Glenn Gregory (vocals)
Ian Craig Marsh (synthesizer)
Martyn Ware (synthesizer)

1980 Oct One-time computer operators, Marsh (b. Nov.11, 1956, Sheffield, S.Yorks.) and Ware (b. May 19, 1956, Sheffield), quit The Human League and establish British Electric Foundation (soon abbreviated to B.E.F.), a production umbrella for several projects. The first to get underway is Heaven 17 (named after a group in Anthony Burgess' book *A Clockwork Orange*), an electronic dance-styled outfit, with ex-photographer Gregory (b. May 16, 1958, Sheffield), whom they met at Sheffield's Meatwhistle drama center, recruited as vocalist.

1981 Apr *Music For Stowaways*, an entirely instrumental limited edition cassette, is the first B.E.F. UK release, on Virgin. Heaven 17 debuts on the same label with *(We Don't Need This) Fascist Groove Thang*, which overcomes a BBC radio ban (because of the title) and climbs to UK #45. Follow-up *I'm Your Money* does not chart.

Oct *Penthouse And Pavement* climbs to UK #14, and *Play To Win* makes UK #46. (*Let's All Make A Bomb* was rejected as a third single as the title was open to misinterpretation and another possible ban.) B.E.F.'s *Music For Listening To* is released, to moderate sales.

Nov Title track from *Penthouse And Pavement*, with Josie Jones as guest vocalist, peaks at UK #57. John Wilson joins the group on bass.

Dec Ware and Marsh produce, and write several songs for, Hot Gossip's *Geisha Boys And Temple Girls*.

1982 Feb *Height Of The Fighting (He-La-Ho)*, a re-recording (from *Penthouse And Pavement*) with jazz-funk band Beggar & Co.'s horn section, fails.

Apr B.E.F.'s *Music Of Quality And Distinction, Vol.1*, with guest singers (including Billy Mackenzie, Paul Jones, Tina Turner, Sandie Shaw and Gary Glitter) of mainly classic pop oldies, makes UK #25, but the expensive project loses £10,000. Gregory sings on 2 tracks: *Perfect Day* and a revival of Glen Campbell's *Wichita Lineman*. It is B.E.F.'s last project, and Marsh and Ware concentrate their energies on Heaven 17.

Nov *Let Me Go* makes UK #41.

HEAVEN 17 cont.

1983   **Mar** *Let Me Go*, released in US by Arista, peaks at #74 and *Heaven 17* reaches US #68.
  May *Temptation*, on which Gregory duets lead vocals with Carol Kenyon, is their biggest UK hit at #2. *The Luxury Gap* hits UK #4.
  July *Come Live With Me* hits UK #5, as *The Luxury Gap* makes US #72.
  Sept *Crushed By The Wheels Of Industry* reaches UK #17.
  Dec Tina Turner's first solo hit *Let's Stay Together* is co-produced by Ware, with Gregory on backing vocals. It hits UK #6 and will peak 3 months later at US #26.

1984   **Sept** *Sunset Now* reaches UK #24.
  Oct *How Men Are* reaches UK #12.
  Nov *This Is Mine* reaches UK #23.
  [25] Gregory takes part in the all-star recording for Band Aid's *Do They Know It's Christmas?*

1985   **Jan** *...(And That's No Lie)* peaks at UK #52.
1986   **Apr** *The Foolish Thing To Do* does not chart. The group is now hardly seen or heard. Marsh and Ware traditionally shunned the spotlight and Gregory's TV guest slots and magazine profiles are also less frequent.
  July *Endless*, a compilation of hit singles and earlier album tracks, is released only on cassette and CD. It is a minor UK success, at #70.
  Nov *Pleasure One*, the group's first new recording for 2 years, makes a brief UK chart showing at #78.

1987   **Jan** *Trouble*, taken from *Pleasure One*, peaks at UK #51.
  Apr *Pleasure One* peaks at US #177.
  Aug Ware co-produces *Introducing The Hardline According To Terence Trent D'Arby*, which tops UK chart.

1988   **Aug** After a year off the recording scene, Heaven 17 releases *The Ballad Of Go Go Brown*.
  Sept Final Virgin album, *Teddy Bear, Duke & Psycho* is released but flops. Ware and Gregory will now re-focus on production projects.

1990   With the UK proliferation of hit cover versions, Ware and Marsh resurrect the B.E.F. project, which in many ways foreshadowed the current trend. Working on a second volume, they approach a number of artists requesting versions of their favorite songs.

JIMI HENDRIX

1954   Hendrix (b. James Marshall, Nov.27, 1942, Seattle, WA), his mother Lucille a full-blooded Cherokee Indian, is given an acoustic guitar at age 12, which his father James Allen Hendrix, a landscape gardener, has got in a trade-in for his own saxophone. Being left-handed, he turns his guitar upside down and teaches himself to play it by listening to the records of bluesmen Muddy Waters, Elmore James and B.B. King and rockers Chuck Berry and Eddie Cochran, devoting more attention to this than his school studies.

1959   Hendrix enlists for 26 months as a paratrooper in the 101st Airborne Division, to avoid being drafted into the army.

1960   **Feb** [20] Hendrix plays his first gig in high school in Seattle.
He plays with Isleys, then a tour comes through town with B.B. King, Sam Cooke, Chuck Jackson, Solomon Burke, Jackie Wilson and Hank Ballard for which Hendrix gets a job. He auditions for Little Richard in Atlanta and gets a gig, which gets him to Los Angeles, CA, where he plays with Ike & Tina Turner.

1961   He is discharged after back injuries suffered during his 26th parachute jump. He had already played in high school groups before enlisting and decides to use his obvious talent for the guitar. Adopting the stage name Jimmy James, he starts with an obscure R&B group, touring the South on the "chitlin' circuit", but will eventually move to more prestigious work behind Sam Cooke, Little Richard (with whom Hendrix will perform his Veejay sessions in June 1964), Ike & Tina Turner, Wilson Pickett and Jackie Wilson.

1964   Hendrix relocates to New York, where he plays the club circuit with The Isley Brothers (also playing guitar on all their 1964 recordings), King Curtis and John Paul Hammond. He strikes up a relationship with soul singer Curtis Knight and they write and record together. (One of the songs they will record is the prophetic *Ballad Of Jimi*, written by Knight in 1965 after Hendrix tells him he will die in exactly 5 years time.)

1965   Hendrix forms his own group, Jimmy James & The Blue Flames, who play a mix of R&B standards and original material. They will eventually head to Greenwich Village in New York.
  Oct [15] Hendrix signs a recording contract with Ed Chalpin, head of PPX Productions. He receives $1 and a guarantee of 1% royalty on records he is currently recording with Curtis Knight. (Chalpin will enforce this agreement on post-fame Hendrix collaborations with Knight recorded in 1967, and will also cause continued litigation problems for Hendrix and major record labels for many years.)

1966   Hendrix's reputation begins to spread in New York and his band is recommended by Keith Richard's girlfriend, Linda Keith, to The Animals' Chas Chandler, now turned to management. After seeing Hendrix play at the Café Wha?, Chandler persuades him to go to London with him to form a new band.
  Sept [21] Hendrix and Chandler arrive in London (legend has it that on the flight Hendrix decides to change his name from Jimmy to Jimi) and recruit drummer Mitch Mitchell (b. John Mitchell, June 9, 1947, Ealing, London), who has been playing in ITV's "Ready Steady Go!" session band and with Georgie Fame's Blue Flames, and Noel Redding (b. David Redding, Dec.25, 1945, Folkestone, Kent) to form the 3-piece Jimi Hendrix Experience. (Mitchell has a background in the arts, having worked as a child actor in TV commercials, appearing in BBC TV series "Jennings At School" and "Whacko" and ITV series "Emergency Ward 10" and "Redcap" and compering ITV's "In Search Of Adventure", before moving on to music in his teens.) Redding, having been to art school and played with The Modern Jazz Group and Loving Kind, joins on bass, despite having been auditioned for The Animals on guitar.
  Oct [18] The Jimi Hendrix Experience's first gig is as support for French pop star Johnny Hallyday at the Paris Olympia. Chandler spends much of his own money publicizing the new group.
  Nov Hendrix begins recording tracks for his debut album at the Kingsway studios, London.
  Dec The first Jimi Hendrix Experience single, a cover of The Leaves hit (although Hendrix prefers Tim Rose's version), *Hey Joe*, is released on Polydor after being rejected by Decca.

1967   **Jan** [11] Chandler's high-profile press reception at the Bag O' Nails club coincides with *Hey Joe*'s entry into the UK chart.
  Feb It hits UK #6 and Hendrix's "wild man" image is promulgated in the press. The group supports The Who at the Saville theater, its first non-club outing, while album recordings are completed, now at the Olympic studios, London.
  Mar *Purple Haze* is released on new Track label after a deal with Kit Lambert. Amid allusions to mind-expanding drugs, it is taken up as an anthem for the new "love generation".
  [31] Group begins its first UK tour, a 24-date package with Cat Stevens, The Walker Brothers and Englebert Humperdinck, at the Astoria theater, Finsbury Park, London, set to end Apr.30 at the Granada theater, Tooting, London. (In addition to his guitar distortion and feed-back stage devices, Hendrix will make a nightly habit of setting fire to his guitar at the end of the group's set and playing the instrument with his teeth. Rank theaters warn Hendrix to tone down his act during the tour.)
  Apr During an appearance on BBC TV's "Top Of The Pops", a technician inadvertently puts on the backing track of Alan Price's *Simon Smith And His Amazing Dancing Bear* instead of *Watchtower*, to which Hendrix responds "I don't know the words to that one, man."
  [4] Hendrix guests on the first broadcast of BBC TV's "Dee Time".
  May [29] The Jimi Hendrix Experience tops the bill at "Barbecue '67" at Tulip Bulb Auction Hall, Spalding, Lincs., with The Move, Cream, Geno Washington, Zoot Money and, bottom of the bill, Pink Floyd. *Purple Haze* hits UK #3. Debut album *Are You Experienced?* is released, with Hendrix using a Stratocaster guitar. It hits UK #2 during a 33-week chart stay, held off the top by The Beatles' *Sgt. Pepper*. By this time the group's month-long European tour is breaking attendance records at many venues.
  June Plans for a live EP are shelved in favor of ballad *The Wind Cries Mary*, which hits UK #6, Hendrix's third successive Top 10 hit.
  [4] Band plays at the Saville theater, London, with Procol Harum, The Chiffons, Denny Laine & His Electric String Band.
The Jimi Hendrix Experience makes its US debut at the Monterey Pop Festival in Monterey, CA, having been booked at the urging of Paul McCartney. They only play 4 original songs, but Hendrix's versions of *Wild Thing* and *Like A Rolling Stone* get a tumultuous reception, especially when he sets fire to, and smashes, his guitar for the familiar finale (but at their next performance on a bill with The Mamas And The Papas at the Hollywood Bowl, CA, they are booed).
  July [7] US tour with The Monkees opens at the Braves Stadium in Atlanta, GA. As in UK, Hendrix quickly gains fame (and notoriety) through the media. The group's music and Hendrix's outrageous showmanship are entirely inappropriate for The Monkees' teenybop audience and they are pulled off after only 7 gigs. (Chandler claims that protests from the right-wing Daughters of the American Revolution have brought this about, but in reality Chandler planned the support spot as a publicity stunt knowing the outrage Hendrix's act will cause.)
  [20] Group records *Burning Of The Midnight Lamp* in New York, which

features Hendrix on harpsichord and Aretha Franklin's backing group, The Sweet Inspirations, on backing vocals.

Sept *Burning Of The Midnight Lamp* reaches UK #18.

[25] Hendrix performs at a Guitar-In at London's Royal Festival Hall.

Oct Hendrix achieves first US chart entries, on Reprise, when *Purple Haze* peaks at #65 and *Are You Experienced?* hits #5 in a 101-week run.

Nov [14] Group begins 15-date twice-nightly UK package tour, with The Move, Pink Floyd, Amen Corner, The Nice and others, which opens at the Royal Albert Hall, London, set to end Dec.5 at Green's Playhouse, Glasgow, Scotland. The Experience will have played a total of 180 dates in 1967 alone.

Dec Second album, *Axis: Bold As Love*, is issued in UK and enters the chart to hit #5. The trio tours UK, including the "Christmas On Earth" concert with The Who, The Move and Pink Floyd. Capitol Records releases *Get That Feeling*, a UK #39 and US #75, featuring Hendrix with Curtis Knight, recorded in the summer in US to appease ex-manager Ed Chalpin, who claims Hendrix has broken his contract.

1968 Jan Group plays European dates, but tensions develop, both within the group and with the management. Hendrix is incarcerated overnight in a Swedish jail after wrecking a hotel room during an argument with Redding. *Foxy Lady* peaks at US #67.

Feb *Axis: Bold As Love* hits US #3 during a year-long chart stay.

[1] Group begins a 3-month US tour, during which they gross $75,000 per gig. Hendrix cuts out his stage antics and concentrates on the music during the tour.

Mar *Up From The Skies* peaks at US #82.

Apr Prematurely titled *Smash Hits*, comprising both sides of the first 4 singles and 4 tracks from the first album, hits UK #4 and, with a different US track listing including *All Along The Watchtower*, US #6.

May [20] Hendrix formally signs to US Reprise.

June After finishing the tour, the trio begins sessions for a new album that will stretch to 6 months. Hendrix brings in other musicians, and Steve Winwood (keyboards) and Jefferson Airplane's Jack Casady play on *Voodoo Chile*.

July [6] Band performs at the Woburn Music Festival, Beds., and will then go on to play at opening of their manager's Sergeant Pepper club in Majorca.

Sept A revival of Dylan's *All Along The Watchtower* hits UK #5 and is Hendrix's first US Top 20 success, at #20.

Oct Double album *Electric Ladyland*, with a controversial sleeve picturing Hendrix surrounded by naked women, is released. Some shops refuse to display it, but despite this it hits UK #6 and tops US chart. It includes guest performances by Al Kooper, Buddy Miles and Steve Winwood among others.

[10-12] The Jimi Hendrix Experience plays 3 concerts at San Francisco's Winterland Arena, at the beginning of a full US tour.

Dec *Crosstown Traffic* peaks at US #52. Pressures on Hendrix increase, with disagreements between his management team, Chandler and more commercially-minded Mike Jeffrey, resulting in Chandler selling his share in the band to Jeffrey. The group temporarily splits and Mitchell and Redding return to UK without Hendrix.

1969 Jan Hendrix performs on BBC TV show "Lulu" and plays an unrehearsed *Sunshine Of Your Love* as a tribute to recently-split Cream, to the annoyance of the progam's producers.

Feb [24] Jeffrey reverses the apparent split by convincing the group to play the Royal Albert Hall, London, followed by European dates and a spring US tour.

Apr *Crosstown Traffic* makes UK #37.

May Hendrix is arrested arriving at Toronto International Airport, Canada, charged with possession of heroin. He is released on $10,000 bail, denying hard drug use (but a cloud will hang over him until his acquittal in Dec.).

[24] The Jimi Hendrix Experience performs at the International Sports Arena, San Diego, CA.

June [29] Band plays its final concert on the last date of the 3-day Denver Pop Festival, CO. Redding, fearing being fired, elects to quit, having already formed his own band Fat Mattress, which has opened for The Experience during the recent tour. (Hendrix will spend the summer recording in New York, with Electric Flag drummer/vocalist Buddy Miles and bassist Billy Cox, a friend from his army days.)

July [2] Mitchell and Redding announce their split from Hendrix is permanent (but Mitchell is back with him the same month for a performance at the Newport Jazz Festival, RI).

Aug [17-18] Hendrix plays the Woodstock Festival, backed by the Electric Sky Church, drawn from musicians he has played with during the year, including Mitchell, Cox, Larry Leeds (rhythm guitar), Juma

Lewis and Jerry Velez (both percussion). The set is highlighted by *The Star Spangled Banner* and his performance is captured on the "Woodstock" film and album. He is paid the highest fee of any attending performer, $125,000. (His second set ends the Festival.)

Dec Ed Chalpin wins suit against Hendrix, in ongoing litigation over their 1965 agreement, and Hendrix will have to hand over a new album of live material for release by Chalpin.

[8] The Toronto Supreme Court finds Hendrix not guilty on charges of possession of heroin and marijuana. Hendrix testifies at his trial that he has experimented with drugs but has since "outgrown" the experience. After 8 hours of deliberation the jury finds him not guilty.

[31] Hendrix' Band Of Gypsys, comprising Hendrix, Miles and Cox, debuts at the Fillmore East, New York, the concert will be recorded for the live album *Band Of Gypsys*.

1970 Jan [1] Their second performance, in front of 19,000 people at a peace rally in New York's Madison Square Garden, ends abruptly when Hendrix says, "I'm sorry we just can't get it together" and walks off stage in the middle of the second number. Group splits.

Mar [30] The new Jimi Hendrix Experience, with Cox replacing Redding, plays 2 concerts at the Community Center in Berkeley, CA.

Apr [26] Illegal recordings of this gig at the Forum, Los Angeles, appear as the first Hendrix bootleg *Enjoy*, on Rubber Dubber label, though a plethora of earlier recordings will also emerge.

May *Band Of Gypsys* hits US #5, during a 61-week chart stay, given to Capitol in a one-off deal to compensate ex-manager Chalpin, who also receives $1 million payment and percentage on future Hendrix earnings.

July [1] Hendrix records his first session at Electric Ladyland studios in New York. (A great deal of money and effort has been spent in creating a state-of-the-art "dream" studio.)

[3-5] Hendrix plays at the 3-day Atlanta Pop Festival at the Middle Georgia Raceway in Byron, GA, to 200,000 people, with Jethro Tull, B.B. King, Johnny Winter and others.

[28] He plays his last gig in his hometown Seattle at Sick's Stadium, during which he abuses the audience. While there, he is awarded an honorarium by Garfield high school, the school which he attended but never graduated from. Following this, the band goes to Hawaii to take part in the Rainbow Bridge Vibratory Color-Sound Experiment occult organization to perform at the Magical Garden as part of a film project, recordings of which will emerge on 6 subsequent bootlegs.

Aug [17] Hendrix takes part in the Randall Island Rock Festival with Grand Funk Railroad, Jethro Tull, Little Richard and Steppenwolf.

[25] A party is held to celebrate the official opening of Electric Ladyland studios.

[30] He comes on stage at 3am to play what will be his last UK performance at the Isle of Wight Festival, UK, as *Band Of Gypsys* hits UK #6. It is only his second UK performance in 3 years.

Sept [6] Hendrix makes his final formal concert appearance at the Isle of Fehmarn, Germany.

[14] After bad experiences in Denmark (he leaves stage with the words "I've been dead for a long time") and Germany (the audience boo his late appearance), the European tour formally comes to end when gig in Rotterdam, Holland, is cancelled, after Cox is flown back to the US suffering a bad drug experience and the group returns to London, Hendrix going to stay with current belle Monika Danneman.

[16] Hendrix joins Eric Burdon and War on stage at Ronnie Scott's in London, his final public appearance.

[18] After leaving the tragic message "I need help bad, man" on Chandler's answering machine, Hendrix is pronounced dead on arrival at St. Mary Abbot's hospital, London, at 11.45am.

[21] Eric Burdon appears on TV talking of a suicide note.

[23] An inquest is adjourned by Dr. Gavin Thurston awaiting the pathologist's report.

[28] Pathologist Professor Donald Teale reports death is due to inhalation of vomit due to barbiturate intoxication. An open verdict is recorded. (A shared album with Otis Redding, a side each, from Monterey Pop Festival has already entered US chart and reaches #16, but will not be released in UK.)

Oct [1] Hendrix is buried in the Greenwood cemetery at the Dunlap Baptist church, where his aunt played organ during his childhood, in his hometown of Seattle, with fellow musicians Eric Clapton, Bobby Whitlock, Carl Radle, Miles Davis, Johnny Winter, Jim Gordon, Eric Burdon and Buddy Miles in attendance.

Reprise label issued *Monterey Pop* reaches US #16.

Nov *Voodoo Chile* tops UK chart, as film documentary "Experience" shows at the ICA, The Mall, London.

1971 Mar *The Cry Of Love*, the last album sanctioned and recorded by Hendrix, is released and hits US #3 and UK #2. It contains songs he had been working on for his planned concept album, *The First Rays Of The Rising Sun*. The US chart also sees the first cash-in album, *Two Great Experiences Together!* on Maple Records, featuring Hendrix and sax player Lonnie Youngblood. It peaks at #127. (Due to Hendrix's complicated contractual affairs the market will be flooded throughout the early 70s by albums bearing his name; the majority are jam sessions never intended for release.)

May *Freedom* peaks at US #59.

Sept Ember label album *Experience*, drawn from Royal Albert Hall performances in Feb.1969, hits UK #9.

Oct *Rainbow Bridge*, not containing any recordings made during his visit to Hawaii in July 1970, but rather a random collection of 1968-70 performances, reaches US #15. Extracted *Dolly Dagger* makes US #74.

Nov *Gypsy Eyes/Remember* makes UK #35. *Jimi Hendrix At The Isle Of Wight* reaches UK #17.

Dec *Rainbow Bridge* reaches UK #16.

1972 Feb *Hendrix In The West*, a collection of live performances, recorded at the Berkeley Community Center, San Diego Sports Arena and the Isle of Wight Festival, highlighted by a version of Chuck Berry's *Johnny B. Goode* which makes UK #35, hits UK #7 and US #12. It is assembled by producer Alan Douglas.

Dec *War Heroes*, a curious mixture of unfinished studio material including a version of Henry Mancini's *Peter Gunn Theme*, makes UK #23 and US #48.

1973 Mar [5] Former manager Jeffrey is killed in a plane crash over France.

July *Soundtrack Recordings From The Film Jimi Hendrix*, a documentary of Hendrix's life, makes UK #37 and US #89.

1974 Jazz arranger Gil Evans, with whom Hendrix was due to record the week he died, releases *The Gil Evans Orchestra Plays The Music Of Jimi Hendrix*.

1975 Mar *Jimi Hendrix* makes UK #35.

Aug *Crash Landing* is the first of 3 posthumous albums produced by Alan Douglas, who had been given stewardship of the 600 hours of tapes that were part of Hendrix's estate. (On some cuts Douglas has used session musicians to overdub existing parts so only the original guitar and vocal remain.) The album hits US #5 and UK #35.

Nov The second Douglas release, *Midnight Lightning*, makes US #43 and UK #46.

Dec Redding releases his first album in 5 years, *Clonakilty Cowboys*.

1978 Aug *The Essential Jimi Hendrix* makes US #114.

1979 Aug *The Essential Jimi Hendrix Volume 2* peaks at US #156. Both volumes will be issued by Reprise as a 32-track twin CD set in 1989, again under the supervision of Douglas.

1980 Apr The final Douglas release, *Nine To The Universe*, featuring Hendrix's jamming on sessions during recording of his final album in 1969, climbs to US #127.

May [22] 4 Hendrix gold albums are stolen from the Electric Ladyland studios.

1982 Aug *The Jimi Hendrix Concerts*, another selection of live recordings 1968-70, makes US #79 and UK #16.

1983 Feb *The Singles Album* peaks at UK #77.

1984 Nov *Kiss The Sky*, compiling further miscellaneous recordings 1967-69, makes US #148.

1986 Mar *Jimi Plays Monterey* stalls at US #192.

1988 Oct U2's album of their 1987 US tour *Rattle And Hum* highlights Hendrix's version of *The Star Spangled Banner* from "Woodstock" as the intro to *Bullet The Blue Sky*.

(The fortunes of ex-Hendrix sidemen vary: Redding is now living in Eire, playing in the Secret Freaks band, Mitchell sells Hendrix's white Fender Stratocaster for $340,000 at a Sothebys auction, while Buddy Miles is most prominently featured as one of the voices of the California Raisins TV advertising raisin combo.)

1989 Mar Previously unavailable BBC recorded radio sessions are issued by Castle Collectors in UK, titled *Radio One*, which makes UK #30.

1990 Apr [21] Neatly combining promotion efforts to prepare consumers for "Hendrix Year" releases and the current use of the song for a Wrangler Jeans TV commercial, *Crosstown Traffic* peaks at UK #61. (Respected UK journalist Charles Shaar Murray authors a universally well-reviewed Hendrix appraisal *Crosstown Traffic*.)

Aug *If 6 Was 9 – A Tribute To Jimi Hendrix* is released, featuring cover versions of Hendrix material by acts including Thin White Rope, Monks Of Doom, Thee Hypnotics, Giant Sand and an alleged pseudonymous XTC.

Sept [18] During the 20th anniversary reminders of Hendrix' death, "Live At The Isle Of Wight" video is released. Redding, being interviewed on BBC Radio 1, claims that he has been defrauded of £8 million in royalties since Hendrix's death.

Oct [20] EP *All Along The Watchtower* peaks at UK #52.

Nov [3] Having generally repromoted Hendrix products all year long in a 20th death anniversary jamboree, Polydor hits UK #5 with *Cornerstones 1967-1970*, another Hendrix retrospective collection. (During his lifetime, Hendrix only released 5 albums. In the 20 years since his death over 300 different titles have emerged, not including bootlegs.)

DON HENLEY

1980 Following the release of their final US #1 studio album *The Long Run*, The Eagles, which Henley (b. July 22, 1947, Gilmer, TX) has formed with Glenn Frey in 1971, both having served apprenticeships in a number of West Coast combos including Linda Ronstadt's backing band, Henley continues with a solo recording contract with Asylum, which has issued all Eagles material.

Nov [21] Henley is arrested when a naked 16-year-old girl is found in his Los Angeles, CA, home suffering from a drug overdose. He will be fined $2,000, given 2 years probation and ordered to attend a drug counselling scheme.

1981 As tail-end Eagles' releases wind up an enormously successful group career dominated by Henley/Frey compositions and vocals, Henley enters the Record One studio in Sherman Oaks, CA, with co-producers Danny Kortchmar and Greg Ladanyi to record his debut album.

1982 Jan Henley duets with Fleetwood Mac's Stevie Nicks on her *Leather And Lace* ballad, which peaks at US #6.

Oct [2] Henley's first single, the illiteracy-themed *Johnny Can't Read* makes US #42 as parent album *I Can't Stand Still* will reach US #24. Guests on the album include Bob Seger, J.D. Souther, ex-Eagles' Timothy B. Schmit and Joe Walsh, Toto's Steve Lukather and Jeff Porcaro, Andrew Gold, Russ Kunkel, Louise Goffin, Max Gronenthal and Warren Zevon.

1983 Jan [8] Gutter press-attacking *Dirty Laundry* hits US #3, becoming a million-seller, and peaks at UK #59.

Feb [26] Title cut *I Can't Stand Still* makes US #48.

1984 Dec Now signed by former Asylum chief David Geffen to his new Geffen Records, second album *Build The Perfect Beast* is released set to make US #13. With the same production team, it features contributions from Lindsey Buckingham, Sam Moore, J.D. Souther, Randy Newman, David Paich and others.

1985 Feb [9] Premier cut, aided by an award-winning black and white video, *The Boys Of Summer* hits US #5 and reaches UK #12.

Mar *Building The Perfect Beast* reaches UK #14.

May [4] *All She Wants To Do Is Dance* hits US #9.

July [27] *Not Enough Love In The World* makes US #34.

Oct [19] *Sunset Grill*, the fourth cut from the album, reaches US #22.

Dec [31] At Henley's New Year's Eve party at his ranch in Aspen, CO, guests Gary Hart and Donna Rice meet each other.

1986 Feb [25] Henley wins Best Rock Vocal Performance, Male for *The Boys Of Summer* at the 28th annual Grammy awards.

1989 Jan [30] Henley drums with Guns N' Roses at the American Music Awards.

Aug Title track from forthcoming album *The End Of The Innocence*, with Henley's lyrics added to a Bruce Hornsby melody, who also plays distinctive piano accompaniment, hits US #8 and UK #48. [8] Major US tour begins in St.Louis, MO.

Oct *The End Of Innocence*, featuring Axl Rose, Bruce Hornsby, Edie Brickell, J.D. Souther and co-produced with Danny Kortchmar, begins rise to hit US #8.

Dec [9] Extracted ballad *The Last Worthless Evening* reaches US #21.

1990 Feb [12] Henley jams with Sting, Bruce Springsteen and Paul Simon a benefit for the Rainforest Foundation at the China club, Hollywood, raising $1 million. [21] Henley wins Best Rock Vocal Performance, Male for *The End Of The Innocence* at 32nd annual Grammy awards at the Shrine Auditorium, Los Angeles.

Apr [5] Further ballad *The Heart Of The Matter* reaches US #21. [24-25] During major US tour, Henley plays benefit concerts to preserve the historic Walden Woods at the Centrum, Worcester, MA. He is joined over the 2 nights by Glenn Frey, Jimmy Buffett, Bonnie Raitt, Timothy B. Schmit and actors Ed Begley Jr., Carrie Fisher, Don Johnson and Dana Delany. (Henley's tour band comprises Scott Plunkett (synthesizer), John Corey (guitar, synthesizer), Timothy Drury (piano, synthesizer), Frank Simes (guitar), Jennifer Condos (bass) and Ian Wallace (drums).

Aug [13] Henley, Bonnie Raitt, Arlo Guthrie, Aimee Mann and members of the group Boston, announce they have purchased of 25 acres of Walden.

[25] *How Bad Do You Want It?* makes US #48, as Henley and Kortchmar produce title track of Timothy B. Schmit's new *Tell Me The Truth*.

Dec [22] Final cut from third album, *New York Minute* makes US #48.

1991 Feb [9] Henley joins Arlo Guthrie at daylong environmental benefit Indian River Festival, near Vero Beach, FL.

HERMAN'S HERMITS

Peter Noone (vocals)
Derek "Lek" Leckenby (lead guitar)
Keith Hopwood (rhythm guitar)
Karl Green (bass)
Barry "Bean" Whitwam (drums)

1961 Noone (b. Nov.5, 1947, Davyhulme, Manchester, Gtr.Manchester), having studied at the Manchester School of Music and Drama and appeared in UK TV soap "Coronation Street", is offered a part in a film starring Judy Garland, but his parents veto it. (While still at school, Noone will sell programs at Manchester United soccer matches.)

1963 Noone, already in a group with Green (b. July 31, 1947, Salford, Gtr.Manchester) and Hopwood (b. Oct.26, 1946, Manchester) meets Leckenby (b. May 14, 1946, Leeds, W.Yorks.) in the Cavern, Manchester, who is playing in The Wailers with Whitwam (b. July 21, 1946, Manchester). They team up as The Heartbeats with Noone using the name Peter Novak. They work in youth clubs and teen dancehalls and are signed by managers Harvey Lisberg and Charlie Silverman. Group's name changes after Green notes a likeness between Noone and the character Sherman in TV cartoon "The Rocky And Bullwinkle Show". "Sherman" becomes "Herman" and the group name develops to Herman & His Hermits, later shortened to Herman's Hermits.

1964 Lisberg and Silverman send producer Mickie Most a plane ticket and book him into Manchester's Midland hotel before taking him to see the group on stage in Bolton, Gtr.Manchester. Most sees a facial likeness between Noone and a young John F. Kennedy and decides that the singer's "little boy lost" look would make him the ideal frontman for a pop act to be aimed as much at mums and dads as teenagers.

Sept Signed to Most, and via him to EMI's Columbia label, the group tops UK chart for 2 weeks with debut single *I'm Into Something Good*, a cover of Earl-Jean's US #38 hit. (Like most of the records which follow, it includes little of The Hermits themselves; Noone's vocals are backed by sessionmen such as guitarists Jimmy Page and Big Jim Sullivan, with John Paul Jones (later to form Led Zeppelin with Page) taking care of the bass and most of the arrangements.)

Dec *Show Me Girl*, submitted by *Something Good* writers Goffin and King who are impressed by the Hermits' cover version, reaches UK #19. *I'm Into Something Good* climbs to US #13. A million-seller, it earns the group's first gold disk.

1965 Jan On first US visit, the group makes a cameo appearance in teen movie "When The Boys Meet The Girls", starring Connie Francis and Harve Presnell.

Feb [27] Group begins a 21-date twice-nightly UK package tour headed by Del Shannon, at the City Hall, Sheffield, S.Yorks. Tour ends Mar. 22 at the Odeon cinema, Glasgow, Scotland.

Mar A revival of The Rays' 1957 million-seller *Silhouettes* hits UK #3. The John Carter/Ken Lewis (Ivy League) *Can't You Hear My Heartbeat* hits US #2 and is the group's second million-seller.

Apr [11] Band appears at the **New Musical Express** Poll Winners Concert at the Empire Pool, Wembley, London, with The Beatles, The Rolling Stones, The Kinks and many others.

[30] Group begins its first full US tour, a 34-day trek on Dick Clark's "Caravan Of Stars". Tour will end June 2.

May *Mrs Brown You've Got A Lovely Daughter* tops US chart for 3 weeks, having entered at #12, the highest first-week placing for a single in 7 years, due to unprecedented airplay. It is extracted from US album *Introducing Herman's Hermits* which hits US #2. *Mrs Brown You've Got A Lovely Daughter* earns a gold disk on a million-plus US sales but is not released as a single in UK; the group is not enamored of it and thinks the arrangement too corny for the UK market. *Silhouettes* hits US #5 and is a million-seller on combined US/UK sales. An update of Sam Cooke's *Wonderful World* hits UK #7.

June [6] Group appears on US TV's "Ed Sullivan Show".

July Noone is voted one of the 10 best-dressed men in UK. The group's

second US album *Herman's Hermits On Tour* hits US #2 while the first is still in the Top 10. *Wonderful World* hits US #4.

[14] Group plays a dance for Doncaster Rovers football club at the Doncaster Top Rank Ballroom before leaving for US tour.

[22] Dick Clark package tour begins in US. (After Bridgeport, CT, concert, local police chief states "I can assure any organization planning to sponsor entertainment of this type in the future that no permit will be issued by the police department", citing unruly behavior by teenagers.) Tour will close Aug.8.

Aug *I'm Henry VIII, I Am*, a revival of 1911 music hall song, extracted as a US-only single from *Herman's Hermits On Tour*, again after strong pre-release airplay, hits #1. It is another US million-seller. On holiday in Hawaii, Noone meets (and "interviews", for **New Musical Express**) Elvis Presley, who is on location for film "Paradise, Hawaiian Style".

Sept *Just A Little Bit Better* reaches UK #15. *Herman's Hermits*, a belatedly-released UK compilation of 2 US albums, makes #16.

Oct *Just A Little Bit Better* hits US #7.

Nov [3] Group begins an 18-date twice-nightly UK tour, with Billy Fury, Wayne Fontana, The Fortunes and others, at the Gaumont cinema, Wolverhampton, W.Midlands, ending Nov.22 at the Odeon cinema, Manchester.

Dec Compilation *The Best Of Herman's Hermits* hits US #5.

1966 Jan *A Must To Avoid*, often referred to by Noone as *Muscular Boy*, a dig at his own indistinct phrasing of the lyrics, hits UK #6 and US #8, and is another million-seller.

[21] Group begins its first tour of Australasia.

Mar US-only *Listen People*, the group's first A-side slow ballad, hits US #3 and earns another gold disk.

Apr UK-only *You Won't Be Leaving*, with *Listen People* on the B-side, reaches UK #20. Group sings 11 songs in teen movie "Hold On!" Soundtrack album *Hold On!* reaches US #14.

[7] Group begins a 12-date twice-nightly UK tour with Dave Berry, The Mindbenders, David and Jonathan and Pinkerton's Assorted Colours, at the ABC cinema, Dover, Kent, ending Apr.20 at the ABC cinema, Edinburgh, Scotland.

[21] Movie "Hold On!" opens in Los Angeles, CA.

May [1] They play at their second annual **New Musical Express** Poll Winners Concert at the Empire Pool, Wembley, London, on a bill topped by The Beatles and The Rolling Stones.

Extracted from *Hold On!*, *Leaning On A Lamp Post*, a revival of George Formby oldie, hits US #9.

June [25] Group guests on the last edition of UK TV show "Thank Your Lucky Stars".

July [1] They begin another US tour with The Animals, Jerry Lee Lewis and Lou Christie in Honolulu, HI. Tour ends Aug.10.
This Door Swings Both Ways reaches US #18.

Aug *This Door Swings Both Ways* reaches US #12.

Sept *Both Sides Of Herman's Hermits* peaks at US #48.

Nov *No Milk Today*, written by Graham Gouldman later of 10cc, hits UK #7. *Dandy*, written by Ray Davies of The Kinks, hits US #5.

[2] "The Canterville Ghost", with Noone, Sir Michael Redgrave and Douglas Fairbanks Jr., airs on US TV.

Dec *East West*, also by Gouldman, reaches UK #37 and US #27.

1967 Jan *The Best Of Herman's Hermits, Volume II* peaks at US #20.

Mar *There's A Kind Of Hush (All Over The World)* hits UK #7 and US #4, and is a US million-seller. US B-side is former UK hit *No Milk Today*, which makes #35.

May *There's A Kind Of Hush All Over The World* reaches US #13.

July [13] Band opens North American tour with The Who (on their first US tour) as support act and The Blues Magoos in Calgary, Canada. Tour will end Sept.9 in Honolulu, HI.
Don't Go Out Into The Rain (You're Going To Melt) reaches US #18 but is not released as a UK single.

Sept *Museum*, written and also recorded by Donovan (Mickie Most later admits he used the same backing track for both versions) reaches US #39. It is released in UK but is the group's first chart failure.

Oct *Blaze* reaches US #75 but is not released in UK.

1968 Jan *The Best Of Herman's Hermits, Volume III* reaches US #102.

Feb *I Can Take Or Leave Your Loving* climbs to UK #11 and US #22.

May [10] Band begins a 10-date twice-nightly UK tour, with Amen Corner, Dave Berry, The Paper Dolls, John Rowles and The Echoes, at the Town Hall, Birmingham, W.Midlands, ending May 19 at the Theatre Royal, Nottingham, Notts.

June *Sleepy Joe* reaches UK #12 but only US #61 as a new generation of US bands has eclipsed Herman's Hermits, though they have lasted longer than most of their contemporaries.

Aug *Sunshine Girl* hits UK #8.

Sept Group, with Noone as romantic lead opposite Sheila White, stars in film "Mrs. Brown You've Got A Lovely Daughter", inspired by the hit single. Soundtrack album makes US #182.

Nov [5] Noone marries French girl, Mireille Strasser in London on his 21st birthday.

He enters into business partnership with Graham Gouldman, which includes studio production work and the opening of a New York boutique named Zoo.

Dec [25] "Pinocchio", with Herman in the title role and Burl Ives as Gepetta, airs on US TV.

1969 Jan *Something's Happening*, a rewrite of a continental song, hits UK #6.

May *My Sentimental Friend* hits UK #2 and is the group's second-biggest UK success.

Nov *Here Comes The Star*, a cover of an Australian hit noted during a tour there, peaks at UK #33.

1970 Mar *Years May Come, Years May Go* hits UK #7 and is the group's last release on UK Columbia.

June *Bet Yer Life I Do*, on Most's newly-formed RAK label and written by members of Hot Chocolate, makes UK #22.

Dec *Lady Barbara*, another Hot Chocolate song, which reaches UK #13, is the group's final UK hit single. It is credited to Peter Noone & Herman's Hermits, leading to speculation of a split, which occurs once the record is a hit. The Hermits base themselves in US to work the nostalgia circuit; Noone stays in UK, recording on Most's RAK label.

1971 June Noone's only hit, at UK #12, is David Bowie's *Oh You Pretty Thing*, featuring Bowie playing piano. (The follow-up, another Bowie song, *Right On Mother*, will fail to chart as will later 70s solos on RAK, Philips, Casablanca and Bus Stop.)

Oct Compilation *The Most Of Herman's Hermits* reaches UK #14. The Hermits without Noone sign to RCA Records and release *She's A Lady*. (Occasional later UK singles without Noone will also flop, though the group will continue to play as a live act for several years.)

1973 June [28] Noone briefly reunites with The Hermits to top the bill of the "British Invasion" nostalgia concert at New York's Madison Square Garden, to 13,000 people. Also playing are The Searchers, Gerry & The Pacemakers and Wayne Fontana And The Mindbenders. (Noone and the group will permanently part company later in the year, with Noone continuing in cabaret and on theatrical stage.)

1975 The Hermits assist former Shirelle Shirley Alston on her version of *Silhouettes* from her album *With A Little Help From My Friends*.

1977 Oct TV-advertised compilation album *Greatest Hits* makes UK #37.

1980 Living in Los Angeles, Noone forms The Tremblers, with Gregg Inhofer and Gee Connor on guitars, Mark Browne on bass and Robert Williams on drums, and records album *Twice Nightly* and single *Steady Eddy*, but without chart success.

1983 Noone has his biggest stage success with starring role (as Frederic) in a London version of Gilbert and Sullivan's "The Pirates Of Penzance", having taken over the role from Rex Smith on Broadway in 1982.

1989 Noone re-records *I'm Into Something Good* to be featured in movie "The Naked Gun". (Noone will become a veejay on US cable TV channel VH1 and interviewer for the station's music magazine "My Generation", while the Hermits, currently Leckenby, Whitwam, Geoff Foote and Rod Gerrard, continue to tour regularly.)

1990 Apr Archive label See For Miles issues retrospective *E.P. Collection*.

THE HOLLIES

Allan Clarke (vocals)
Graham Nash (guitar)
Tony Hicks (guitar)
Eric Haydock (bass)
Bobby Elliott (drums)

1961 Group is formed in Manchester, Gtr.Manchester, by former schoolfriends Clarke (b. Harold Allan Clarke, Apr.5, 1942, Salford, Gtr.Manchester) and Nash (b. Feb.2, 1942, Blackpool, Lancs.), who were The Two Teens duo, joined by Haydock (b. Feb.3, 1943, Stockport, Gtr.Manchester) and Don Rathbone (drums), becoming The Fourtones, then The Deltas, and with another guitarist, becoming The Hollies.

1963 Jan EMI producer Ron Richards, checking out the UK beat scene in the wake of The Beatles' initial success, sees the group perform at the Cavern club in Liverpool, and invites them for an EMI audition in London. The second guitarist does not want to turn professional, so group manager Allan Cheetham invites Hicks (b. Dec.16, 1943, Nelson, Lancs.), from local group The Dolphins, to audition instead. When EMI signs the band, Hicks joins full-time.

Apr [4] The first Hollies recording session produces the debut single, a revival of The Coasters' *(Ain't That) Just Like Me*.

June *(Ain't That) Just Like Me* reaches UK #25.

July Rathbone moves from drums to the group's management, and is replaced by Elliott (b. Dec.8, 1942, Burnley, Lancs.), an ex-colleague of Hicks in The Dolphins who has been playing with Shane Fenton & The Fentones. The new line-up tours widely in UK.

Sept [13] Nash, driving down from Scotland in the group's van, checks to see if the door is locked. It isn't, and he falls out as it travels at 40mph. Band continues on to London to deputize for Gene Vincent on "Go Man Go".

Oct *Searchin'*, a revival of another Coasters oldie, reaches UK #12 (despite a unanimous thumbs-down review from BBC TV's "Juke Box Jury", on which panellist Pat Boone advises viewers to go out and buy the original version).

[29] Group begins sessions for its first album, and by year's end will have made its UK TV debut on "Scene At 6.30".

1964 Jan [1] The Hollies sing *Stay* on the first edition of long-running BBC TV show "Top Of The Pops".

Third single, a revival of Maurice Williams & The Zodiacs' *Stay*, a copy of which Elliott and Hicks had found in a junk shop in the middle of a tour of Scotland, is the group's first UK Top 10 entry, hitting #8.

Feb [29] The Hollies are featured on ITV's "Thank Your Lucky Stars".

Mar Debut album *Stay With The Hollies* hits UK #2.

Apr A revival of Doris Troy's *Just One Look* hits UK #2, as the group begins recording its second album.

[26] Group takes part in the annual **New Musical Express** Pollwinners Concert at the Empire Pool, Wembley, London, with The Beatles, The Dave Clark Five, Gerry & The Pacemakers and many others.

May *Just One Look* is the group's first US chart entry, at #98.

June *Here I Go Again* hits UK #4.

Oct *We're Through*, The Hollies' first self-penned A-side (by Clarke, Hicks and Nash under the name L. Ransford), hits UK #7.

[24] Clarke has his tonsils removed in Manchester hospital, and all tour dates are cancelled until Nov.15.

Nov *In The Hollies Style* is released in UK, but does not chart.

Dec [26] Group open as guests on Brian Epstein presentation "Gerry's Christmas Cracker", headlined by Gerry & The Pacemakers with Cliff Bennett & The Rebel Rousers and Tommy Quickly, at the Liverpool Odeon, Merseyside.

1965 Mar The Gerry Goffin/Russ Titelman song *Yes I Will* (later recorded by The Monkees as *I'll Be True To You*) hits UK #9.

[5] Group begins a 14-date twice-nightly UK package tour headlined by The Rolling Stones with Dave Berry & The Cruisers, Goldie & The Gingerbreads, The Checkmates and others, at the Regal theater, Edmonton, London. Tour will end Mar.18 at the ABC theater, Romford, Essex.

Apr [16-23] Group makes its first visit to the US, playing a week-long engagement at the Paramount theater, Brooklyn, New York, with Little Richard and others. They also record an appearance on "Hullabaloo".

May [5] On return from US, the group records *I'm Alive* at Abbey Road studios.

June Nash, Clarke and Hicks form Gralto Music publishing company.

July *I'm Alive*, written by Clint Ballard Jr., tops UK chart for 3 weeks, deposing Elvis Presley's *Crying In The Chapel* and yielding to The Byrds' *Mr. Tambourine Man*.

Sept [18] Group begins US tour at McCormack's Place, Chicago, IL, alongside The Yardbirds.

Oct Graham Gouldman's song *Look Through Any Window* hits UK #4, while *The Hollies* hits UK #8.

Nov [19] The Hollies take part in the Glad Rag Ball at the Empire Pool, Wembley, London, with Donovan, The Kinks, The Who, The Merseybeats, Georgie Fame, Wilson Pickett and The Barron Knights.

1966 Jan At George Martin's suggestion, the group covers George Harrison's *If I Needed Someone* (from The Beatles' *Rubber Soul* album). Harrison publicly denounces their interpretation as "soul-less", and it halts at UK #20. Meanwhile, *Look Through Any Window* reaches US #32.

Feb *Hear! Here!* makes US #145.

Mar *I Can't Let Go*, a Chip Taylor composition selected by Hicks from 2 demos at Dick James Music (the other is John Phillips' *California Dreamin'*) hits UK #2.

[8] Group begins a 12-day tour of Poland with Lulu in Warsaw.

Apr After missing several gigs, Haydock is asked to leave.

May *I Can't Let Go* reaches US #42.

[10] Group records the theme for Peter Sellers film "After The Fox" at Abbey Road studios, with Sellers doing a spoken part. Between bass

players, they hire Jack Bruce for the session, while the track's composer Burt Bacharach plays piano.

[18] Bernie Calvert (b. Sept.16, 1942, Brierfield, Lancs.), previously with Hicks in The Dolphins, joins the group on bass, playing on another Gouldman song, *Bus Stop*, on his first day.

June Clarke, Hicks and Nash are invited by The Everly Brothers to submit songs for an album to be recorded in UK. After a day sifting material at the London Mayfair hotel, The Hollies join The Everlys in the studio for recording, along with sessioneers Jimmy Page and John Paul Jones (later both of Led Zeppelin).

July *Bus Stop* hits UK #5, while *Would You Believe* reaches UK #16.

Sept [2] Calvert makes TV debut with group on "Five O'Clock Club".

[17] *Bus Stop*, the group's US breakthrough, hits US #5.

Oct [15] Band begins a 20-date twice-nightly UK tour, with The Small Faces, Paul Jones, Paul & Barry Ryan and others, at the ABC cinema, Aldershot, Hants, ending Nov.6 at City Hall, Newcastle, Tyne & Wear.

Nov *Stop Stop Stop*, written by the group, and powered by an unusual 6-string banjo riff, hits UK #2.

Dec *For Certain Because* reaches UK #23.

1967 Jan [11] Group begins sessions for a new album at Abbey Road, while *Bus Stop* reaches US #75.

Feb [9] They begin a short tour of Germany and Yugoslavia. While in Hamburg, Elliott is taken to hospital where it is reported that he is "very ill with an inflamed appendix, but responding to treatment." He is hospitalized for several weeks, and when the group returns to London to complete the album, session drummers Clem Cattini and Dougie Wright deputize.

Mar [11] They begin a 21-date twice-nightly UK tour with The Spencer Davis Group, The Tremeloes, Paul Jones and others, at the Granada theater, Mansfield, Notts. (Former Sounds Incorporated drummer Tony Newman deputizes for Elliott.) Elliott will defy doctors' orders and join the tour Mar.25. Tour will end Apr.2 at the Empire theater, Liverpool. *On A Carousel*, taken from the album sessions, hits UK #4, as *Stop! Stop! Stop!* (US equivalent of *For Certain Because*) reaches US #91.

May *On A Carousel* reaches US #11.

June *Carrie-Anne*, another Clarke/Hicks/Nash song, almost 2 years in the writing (and finished during rehearsals at a TV studio), hits UK #3.

[13] Hicks enters St. George's Hospital, London, for a minor operation to cure a sinus condition.

[25] Nash joins an invited-only select few to sing on The Beatles' live TV recording of *All You Need Is Love*.

July *Evolution* reaches UK #13 and US #43. US distribution switches from Imperial Records to Epic. As Imperial exercises its sell-off period (with additional releases), product from the 2 labels overlaps. *Pay You Back With Interest*, on Imperial, reaches US #28, while *Carrie-Anne*, on Epic, hits US #9. Imperial compilation album *The Hollies' Greatest Hits* reaches US #11.

Aug [28] Group begins a 3-week US tour with The Turtles.

Sept They begin recording *Butterfly*, an admittedly Sergeant Pepper-influenced set, influenced by the prevailing "Summer Of Love" psychedelic aura of mid-1967.

Oct *King Midas In Reverse*, chiefly written by Nash, and released as a single against the advice of producer Richards (who feels its more experimental structure and lyric will alienate traditional Hollies fans), reaches UK #18 and US #51.

Nov Imperial reissues *Just One Look* in US, which makes #44.

Dec *Dear Eloise*, released as a US-only single to tie in with the group's US tour, reaches #50. In Los Angeles, Nash meets David Crosby, ex-The Byrds, while attending a recording session by The Mamas And The Papas.

1968 Jan Group records Clarke/Nash song *Wings* for inclusion on World Wildlife Fund charity album *No One's Gonna Change My World*.

Mar Work starts in the studio on a new album, but most of the material is not used or left unfinished (including Nash's *Marrakesh Express*, later a hit for Crosby, Stills & Nash).

Apr *Jennifer Eccles*, written by Clarke and Nash as a deliberate contrast to the complexity of *King Midas* (Jennifer is Clarke's wife's forename and Eccles is Nash's wife's maiden name), hits UK #7.

May [17] Group begins the 12-date twice-nightly "Spring Tour '68", with The Scaffold, Paul Jones and The Mike Vickers Orchestra, at the Granada theater, Shrewsbury, Shrops. Tour will end May 29 at the Odeon theater, Derby, Derbys. The Lewisham Odeon concert is recorded by EMI for a live album (but never used).

[18] *Jennifer Eccles* makes US #40.

July The Hollies' management announces that Nash and Bernie Calvert are both planning solo albums. Nash has grown unhappy with

the group's musical direction since *King Midas*, and speculation is already rife that he will leave.

Aug Group plays a UK cabaret season, wearing matching suits and widening the stage repertoire to include songs like *Puff (The Magic Dragon)* and Roger Miller's *Dang Me*.

Sept *Do The Best You Can* stalls at US #93.

Oct In disagreement with a Hicks-proposed plan to record an album entirely of Bob Dylan songs, Nash announces that he will leave in Dec. Meanwhile, compilation album *The Hollies' Greatest* tops UK chart for 7 weeks and *Listen To Me* makes UK #11.

Dec [8] Nash leaves at the end of a charity concert at the London Palladium (and goes into rehearsal in London with David Crosby and Stephen Stills for their new trio project).

1969 Jan The group auditions for a new singer/guitarist, and Terry Sylvester (b. Jan.8, 1947), ex-The Escorts and The Swingin' Blue Jeans, is recruited, and will make his live debut with them at Cardiff University.

Feb Sylvester's first studio session with the group is for *Sorry Suzanne*, after which the group proceeds with *Hollies Sing Dylan*.

[24] Sylvester makes his Hollies TV debut on BBC TV's "Dee Time".

Apr *Sorry Suzanne*, penned by Tony Macaulay and Geoff Stephens, hits UK #3 but stalls at US #56.

June *Hollies Sing Dylan* hits UK #3.

[25] Group records *He Ain't Heavy, He's My Brother*, with Elton John playing piano. Sessions continue for *Hollies Sing Hollies*, a set entirely of compositions by group members.

Oct Group appears on "The Bobbie Gentry Show" on UK TV, singing several unaccustomed country-style songs.

Nov *He Ain't Heavy, He's My Brother* hits UK #3, while *Hollies Sing Hollies* is released without charting.

1970 Mar *He Ain't Heavy, He's My Brother* hits US #7, and total world sales top a million.

[10] Elton John joins them again at Abbey Road, playing piano on *I Can't Tell The Bottom From The Top*.

May *I Can't Tell The Bottom From The Top* hits UK #7.

"Oh Flux", a musical co-written by Clarke with his brother-in-law, opens at the Gulbenkian theater, Canterbury, Kent.

June *He Ain't Heavy, He's My Brother* reaches US #32, while *I Can't Tell The Bottom From The Top* peaks at US #82.

Oct *Gasoline Alley Bred*, penned by Tony Macaulay with Roger Greenaway and Roger Cook, reaches UK #14.

Dec *Confessions Of The Mind* makes UK #30.

1971 Feb *Moving Finger* (US equivalent of *Confessions Of The Mind*) reaches US #183, while the group plays a Far East tour.

Mar [16] The Hollies' first session at AIR studios in London produces *Hey Willy*.

June *Hey Willy* reaches UK #22, while *Distant Light* is released without charting in UK.

Oct [25] Manager Robin Britten announces Clarke is leaving band. He will sign to RCA and record *My Real Name Is 'Arold*. Swedish singer Mikael Rickfors, ex-Bamboo (who have recently toured with The Hollies), is recruited on lead vocals.

Dec [13] A week-long stint at Batley Variety club, Batley, W.Yorks., will seemingly be Clarke's last Hollies dates.

1972 Mar *The Baby*, written by Chip Taylor, is the first with Rickfors' lead vocal, and the only hit, reaching UK #26. It is also the group's first release on new UK label, Polydor.

Sept *Distant Light* makes US #21. Extracted *Long Cool Woman In A Black Dress*, a Creedence Clearwater Revival-styled near-solo track penned by Clarke, belatedly hits US #2, earning the group a gold disk for million-plus sales, and, re-promoted by EMI, also reaches UK #32.

Nov *Magic Woman Touch* is the first Hollies UK single not to chart.

Dec Also from *Distant Light*, *Long Dark Road* reaches US #26.

1973 Mar *Magic Woman Touch* reaches US #60 and *Romany* makes US #84.

July Clarke is invited back into the group, having cut 2 solo albums with little success, and Rickfors returns to Sweden. Clarke's new agreement with the others will allow him to make solo albums alongside the group's work.

Oct Clarke's song *The Day That Curly Billy Shot Crazy Sam McGhee*, in similar style to *Long Cool Woman* reaches UK #24.

Nov [15] Group records *The Air That I Breathe* after being introduced to Phil Everly's version of the song. Meanwhile, compilation album *The Hollies' Greatest Hits* reaches US #157.

1974 Mar *The Air That I Breathe* hits UK #2 and *Hollies* reaches UK #38.

May *Son Of A Rotten Gambler* fails to chart in UK (as does *I'm Down*, 6 months later).

June *Hollies* makes US #28.

THE HOLLIES cont.

Aug *The Air That I Breathe* hits US #6 and is a million-seller, collecting another gold disk.

1975 **Apr** *Sandy*, a Bruce Springsteen song discovered by Clarke (who is an early champion of the US artist in UK, recording several of his songs on later solo albums), stalls at US #85. (Months later when the band are playing the Bottom Line in New York, Springsteen comes backstage to voice his approval of their version.) *Another Night* climbs to US #123. Neither charts in UK.
July Title track *Another Night* makes US #71.

1976 **Mar** [5] Group embarks on a 14-date UK tour at the Royal Albert Hall, London, promoting *Boulder To Birmingham*. Tour will end Mar.28 at Norwich theater, Norfolk.
Write On and *Russian Roulette*, and 4 singles from them, all fail to chart. Group splits from producer Richards.

1977 **Apr** Live album *The Hollies Live Hits*, recorded on stage in Christchurch, New Zealand, in Feb.1976, hits UK #4.

1978 **Mar** *A Crazy Steal* fails to chart, and Clarke leaves the group again to concentrate on his solo career.
July TV-advertised compilation *20 Golden Greats*, on EMI, hits UK #2.
Aug Clarke rejoins, and the group begins its first studio sessions for over a year.

1979 **Mar** Group is reunited with Richards for *Five Three One – Double Seven O Four* (the title comes from its Polydor catalog number). It fails to chart.

1980 **June** Band links with writer/producer Mike Batt for *Soldier's Song*, recorded with the London Symphony Orchestra. It is the group's first UK chart single since *The Air That I Breathe*, but stalls at #58.
Oct *Buddy Holly*, a return to the *Hollies Sing Dylan*-concept, this time featuring entirely Buddy Holly songs, is advertised on UK TV by Polydor but fails to chart.

1981 **May** Sylvester leaves after an acrimonious argument. Within days, Calvert follows him, leaving Clarke, Hicks and Elliott as a trio.
June Attempts to work with other musicians and vocalists include never-released *I Don't Understand You*, with Labi Siffre, and *Carrie*, with its writer John Miles. (*Carrie* will be released in 1988 as B-side of hit reissue *He Ain't Heavy, He's My Brother*.)
July [30] At EMI's invitation, Hicks and Elliott put together the segued tracks *Holliedaze* and *Holliepops*, a variation on the currently huge "Stars On 45" craze.
Sept *Holliedaze (A Medley)* reaches UK #28. Hicks, Clarke and Elliott reunite with Graham Nash (who flies to UK from Hawaii) and Eric Haydock to perform it on BBC TV's "Top Of The Pops".

1982 Nash decides he would like to record with the group again, and he and Clarke make a deal with WEA Records in US, for a Nash-Hollies reunion album. Instrumental parts for the tracks are recorded in London and Los Angeles in Mar., May and June.

1983 **Feb** Nash, Clarke, Hicks and Elliott record the vocals and final tracks for *What Goes Around* at Nash's Rudy Records studios in Los Angeles.
July A revival of The Supremes' *Stop! In The Name Of Love* reaches US #29. It is taken from *What Goes Around* which makes US #90. Both fail to chart in UK. A US tour follows, featuring Hollies classics with later Nash material, before the reunion ends as Nash returns to his solo career and work with David Crosby.

1984 **Nov** The Hollies re-sign to EMI, this time to appear on the Columbia label. The line-up comprises the Clarke/Hicks/Elliott core, plus keyboards player Denis Haines, Alan Coates on harmony vocals, and Ray Stiles (a member of Mud during the 70s) on bass.

1985 **May** *Too Many Hearts Get Broken* is released without charting.
1987 **Jan** Further Columbia singles *This Is It* and *Reunion Of The Heart* fail to chart.
Oct On tour in Germany, the group is approached to record *Stand By Me* (not the Ben E. King song), which makes the German chart on release, but is not issued in UK.

1988 **Sept** *He Ain't Heavy, He's My Brother*, reissued following exposure in a UK Miller Lite Beer TV ad, tops UK chart, finally giving the group its second UK #1 single. It holds off a challenge from Bill Medley's version, from the film "Rambo III". Group begins major UK tour, and *All The Hits And More – The Definitive Collection*, an EMI released double-album rounding up all Hollies hit singles and live favorites, makes UK #51. Re-promoted *20 Golden Greats* also climbs to UK #64.
Dec Reissued *The Air That I Breathe* makes UK #60.

BUDDY HOLLY AND THE CRICKETS

Buddy Holly (vocals, guitar)
Sonny Curtis (guitar)
Joe B. Mauldin (bass)
Jerry Allison (drums)

1949 **Sept** Holly (b. Charles Hardin Holley, Sept.7, 1936, Lubbock, TX) enters Hutchinson junior high school, where he meets Bob Montgomery and they form a duo, Buddy & Bob, playing mainly country and bluegrass, but also influenced by major R&B/doo-wop vocal groups. They become a popular attraction around Lubbock.

1953 **Sept** Buddy & Bob perform on radio for the first time, on local country station K-DAV. Adding Larry Welborn on bass, the group earns a regular Saturday afternoon slot "The Buddy And Bob Show".

1954 At K-DAV, they record several demos (which will eventually appear as *Holly In The Hills* after Holly's death).

1955 Growth of rockabilly in the wake of tumultuously-received tours by Elvis Presley, encourages Holly to move his music from its pure country base. Drummer Allison (b. Aug.31, 1939, Hillsboro, TX) joins.
Oct [14] Buddy & Bob appear supporting Bill Haley & His Comets on a show booked by K-DAV, where the group is spotted by Nashville, TN-based agent Eddie Crandall.
[15] Buddy & Bob open for Elvis Presley at Lubbock's Cotton club.
Dec Crandall wires K-DAV's Dave Stone from Nashville, asking if Holly can cut some demos and send them to him.

1956 **Jan** Via talent scout Jim Denny, Crandall interests Decca Records in Nashville in recording Holly but not Montgomery. The trio splits, with Montgomery insisting that Holly grab the opportunity. (Montgomery will stay in music on the production and publishing side, and will still have a thriving career in the 80s.) Holly recruits Curtis (b. May 9, 1937, Meadow, TX) (guitar) and Don Guess (bass) for a session in Nashville.
[23] Holly & The Two Tunes begin 14-date US tour, bottom of the bill on a Hank Thompson tour, in Little Rock, AR.
[26] At Bradley's Barn studio, Nashville, the group records as Buddy Holly & The Three Tunes.
Apr [16] Holly's first single, *Blue Days, Black Nights* is released.
May Group (still Holly, Allison, Curtis and Guess) tours the South-Eastern states.
July [22] They cut a second Nashville session. (Decca will sit on these recordings and release them after Holly's success with The Crickets, as *That'll Be The Day*, credited to Buddy Holly & The Three Tunes.)
Sept Holly leaves Decca, following mutual dissatisfaction. He and Allison drive to New Mexico to see independent producer Norman Petty, who has a studio in Clovis.

1957 **Feb** Holly forms a new band with Allison, Niki Sullivan (rhythm guitar) and Mauldin (bass). They tape several demos for Petty, naming themselves The Crickets in the process.
[25] The Crickets record a new, tighter version of Holly's composition *That'll Be The Day* at Petty's Clovis studio.
May [27] *That'll Be The Day* is released by Brunswick Records (an associate company of Decca).
July Petty becomes the group's manager, and it begins a wide-ranging tour to promote the new single, including a date at the Apollo in Harlem, New York (which has booked them unseen as a black R&B act on the strength of *That'll Be The Day*).
Aug [2] The Crickets open a month's US tour with Clyde McPhatter, The Cadillacs, Otis Rush and others at the Washington DC's Howard theater, ending Aug.30 at the Brooklyn Paramount theater, New York.
Sept [1] "The Biggest Show Of Stars For 1957" package tour with Buddy Holly And The Crickets, Chuck Berry, Paul Anka, The Drifters, Frankie Lymon & The Teenagers, The Everly Brothers, Clyde McPhatter and others, opens at the Brooklyn Paramount. The show will end Nov.24 at the Mosque, Richmond, VA. (The white artists on the bill are unable to play on several dates because of segregation laws which forbid black and white acts to perform on the same stage.)
[23] *That'll Be The Day* tops US chart for a week, selling over a million. At the end of the month, a second single is released on Brunswick's sister label Coral, and credited just to Buddy Holly (a dual release ploy which will continue for the next year). The song is *Peggy Sue*, originally written by Holly as *Cindy Lou*, then renamed after Allison's girlfriend.
Nov *That'll Be The Day* tops UK chart for 3 weeks. *The Chirping Crickets* is released in US.
Dec [1] Band appears on US TV's "Ed Sullivan Show", performing *That'll Be The Day* and *Peggy Sue*, and Sullivan interviews Holly.
[30] *Peggy Sue* hits US #3 and is a million-seller.

1958 **Jan** [20] Follow-up *Oh Boy!* hits US #10, while *Peggy Sue* hits UK #6.

[26] Group makes a second appearance on US TV's "Ed Sullivan Show" performing *Oh Boy*, and follows it with a 6-day tour of Australia, playing in Melbourne, Sydney and Brisbane, with Jerry Lee Lewis and Paul Anka.

Feb *Oh Boy!* hits UK #3.

Mar [1] Band begins its only UK tour, a 25-date twice-nightly package with Gary Miller, The Tanner Sisters, Des O'Connor and Ronnie Keene & His Orchestra, at the Trocadero, Elephant & Castle, London. Tour will end Mar.25 at the Gaumont theater, Hammersmith, London.

[2] Holly & The Crickets appear on peak-time UK TV in the live variety show "Sunday Night At The London Palladium". (During the tour, they will also be seen on TV in Jack Payne's "Off The Record" show, while *Listen To Me* reaches UK #16, giving them 4 UK Top 20 hits in the same week.)

[28] Back in US, the group begins 61-date "Alan Freed's Big Beat Show" package tour with Jerry Lee Lewis, Chuck Berry, Frankie Lymon, The Diamonds, Danny & The Juniors and others, at the Paramount theater, Brooklyn, New York. Tour ends May 9 at the Arena, Hershey, PA.

Apr [7] *Maybe Baby* reaches US #17 and will hit UK #4. Holly solo ***Buddy Holly*** is issued in US.

June Holly records his first sessions without The Crickets, covering 2 Bobby Darin songs, *Early In The Morning* and *Now We're One* in New York, backed by a small group (including saxophonist Sam "The Man" Taylor) organized by Coral A&R man Dick Jacobs. While in New York, Holly meets Maria Elena Santiago when visiting a music publisher, and they form a romantic attachment.

[9] *Rave On* makes US #37 and will hit UK #5. Holly fails a medical which might have led to military call-up, because of a stomach ulcer.

July [4] Group starts an 11-date "Summer Dance Party" tour with Tommy Allsup's Western Swing Band in Angola, IN.

Aug [4] *Think It Over/Fool's Paradise* reaches US #27/#58.

[15] Holly and Santiago marry at Holly's parents' home in Lubbock.

[25] Holly solo *Early In The Morning* reaches US #32 and UK #17. In Clovis, while recording more solo material, Holly produces the first single by his friend Waylon Jennings, *Jolé Blon*.

Oct Following a decision by Holly to end his association with Norman Petty (with whom relations have soured), and also to set up a base in New York with his wife, Holly And The Crickets separate. Allison (also recently married, to Peggy Sue) and Mauldin return to Texas, and Holly gives them full rights to The Crickets' name so they can continue recording. Earl Sinks replaces Holly on vocals and Tommy Allsup joins on guitar, replacing the already departed Sullivan. (Sinks and Allsup will both leave shortly, leaving The Crickets as a duo, before Curtis returns.) Allison, meanwhile, has a solo US hit (#68) under the pseudonym Ivan (his middle name), with a song picked up on the Australian tour, Johnny O'Keefe's *Real Wild Child*.

[3] Group begins 19-date "The Biggest Show Of Stars For 1958 – Autumn Edition" tour with Frankie Avalon, Bobby Darin, Dion & The Belmonts, Bobby Freeman, Clyde McPhatter, The Coasters and others, at the Auditorium, Worcester, MA. Tour ends Oct.19 at the Mosque, Richmond, VA.

[21] In a New York studio session, Holly records for the first time accompanied by a string section, the Dick Jacobs Orchestra.

Nov *It's So Easy* (one of the last recordings made by the team, with the addition of Tommy Allsup on guitar) reaches UK #19, having failed to chart in US.

1959

Jan [19] *Heartbeat*, a Holly solo (with the original version of the much-revived *Well All Right* on B-side) reaches US #82 and UK #30.

[23] Holly begins 24-date "Winter Dance Party" tour, with back-up band comprising Tommy Allsup (guitar) Carl Bunch (drums) and Waylon Jennings (bass), and The Big Bopper, Ritchie Valens, Frankie Sardo and Dion & The Belmonts, at George Devine's Million Dollar Ballroom, Milwaukee, WI. The tour is scheduled to end Feb.15 at the Illinois State Armoury, Springfield, IL.

Feb [2] After the 11th date of the tour, at the Surf Ballroom in Clear Lake, IO, Holly, Valens and The Big Bopper, tired of bus travel (the day before a concert in Appleton, WI, has been cancelled as a result of bad weather and a bus breakdown) hire a Beechcraft Bonanza plane to take them to the next date at Moorhead, MN, to give them time to rest. In bad weather, the plane crashes in a field only minutes after take-off near Mason City, IO. Holly, Valens, The Big Bopper and pilot Roger Peterson are killed.

[3] Bobby Vee, a local singer with a style closely modelled on Holly's, fills in on the tour at Moorhead; Jimmy Clanton and Frankie Avalon also join to make up the decimated troupe.

[7] Holly's funeral is held at the Tabernacle Baptist church in Lubbock, with over 1,000 people attending. The pallbearers are Montgomery, Allison, Mauldin, Sullivan, Curtis and Phil Everly. He is buried in Lubbock city cemetery.

Mar [30] The ironically-titled *It Doesn't Matter Anymore*, a song written for Holly by Paul Anka, and recorded at his final New York sessions, with an innovatory pizzicato string arrangement, reaches US #13.

Apr [6] B-side *Raining In My Heart* makes US #88. In UK, *It Doesn't Matter Anymore* tops chart for 3 weeks, while The Crickets, on their first without Holly, make US #26 with *Love's Made A Fool Of You* (a Holly composition, first cut by him as a demo for The Everly Brothers).

May A memorial album, ***The Buddy Holly Story***, compiling most of his hits both solo and with The Crickets, reaches US #11 and hits UK #2. (It will stay charted in both countries for over 3 years, and become Coral's biggest-seller ever.)

Aug Holly will have no more hit singles in US, but a long series of posthumous UK chart successes with either reissued or discovered material begins with *Midnight Shift*, which reaches UK #26.

Oct *Peggy Sue Got Married*, a lyrical sequel to his first solo hit, and taken from one of Holly's demos (with extra over-dubbing by The Jack Hansen Combo), makes UK #13.

1960 **Jan** The (post-Holly) Crickets, rejoined by Sonny Curtis, reach UK #27 with *When You Ask About Love*.

May *Heartbeat*, promoted in competition with new cover version, re-enters UK chart, at #30. The Crickets' *Baby My Heart* makes UK #33.

June *True Love Ways*, one of Holly's final New York studio recordings (and later one of his most-covered ballads) peaks at UK #25.

Oct *Learning The Game*, another overdubbed home demo, reaches UK #36, while compilation ***The Buddy Holly Story Vol.2*** hits UK #7.

1961 **Feb** *What To Do* makes UK #34.

Apr *In Style With The Crickets* reaches UK #13.

Aug A cover of Elvis Presley's *Baby I Don't Care*, originally on Holly's 1958 solo album, is issued as a UK single, and peaks at #12.

Nov *That'll Be The Day* (a compilation of 1956 Decca recordings, reissued at low price) hits UK #5.

1962 Norman Petty, after agreements between himself, Coral Records, and Holly's parents, acquires control of Holly's released and unreleased recordings. Taking the large number of solo home demos, he works in the studio with The Fireballs (already hitmakers with instrumentals *Torquay* and *Bulldog*, and later to be bigger still with *Sugar Shack* and *Bottle Of Wine*), replacing the early over-dubbings with backing more sympathetic to Holly's style and intentions.

Mar *Listen To Me* re-enters UK chart at #48.

Aug The Crickets, now comprising Allison, Curtis, pianist Glen D. Hardin (b. May 18, 1939, Wellington, TX), and new vocalist Jerry Naylor (b. Mar.6, 1939, Chalk Mountain near Stephenville, TX), have their biggest post-Holly hit with the Goffin/King song *Don't Ever Change*, which hits UK #5 but fails in US.

Oct *Reminiscing*, an unreleased track made with sax star King Curtis in Holly's final sessions, reaches UK #17.

Nov [2] The Crickets embark on a 21-day UK tour, their first since 1958, with Bobby Vee.

1963 **Feb** *Reminiscing*, compiled by Petty from unissued material with Fireballs backing tracks, is released after long rumors of its coming and several apparent delays. Reviews, 4 years after Holly's death, are excellent. The Crickets reach UK #17 with the Holly-like Sonny Curtis song *My Little Girl*, featured by them in UK pop movie "Just For Fun".

Apr A racing version of Chuck Berry's *Brown-Eyed Handsome Man* hits UK #3. It is taken from *Reminiscing*, which reaches US #40 and hits UK #2 (behind The Beatles *Please Please Me*).

July *Bo Diddley*, another rocking cover from the album, hits UK #4.

Sept *Wishing*, a newly-dubbed version of another demo cut by Holly for The Everly Brothers, hits UK #10.

1964 **Jan** *What To Do* re-enters UK chart, making #27.

May *You've Got Love* makes UK #40.

June ***Buddy Holly Showcase*** hits UK #3, while The Crickets' country-styled *Don't Try To Change Me* reaches UK #37.

Aug The Crickets' final hit single, at UK #21, is a re-write of Ritchie Valens' *La Bamba*, titled *(They Call Her) La Bamba*. (The Crickets will continue to re-form through the late 80s. Line-up changes are extensive and continuous, but always revolving around Jerry Allison, who owns the name, and usually Sonny Curtis.)

Sept *Love's Made A Fool Of You*, Holly's original demo for The Everly Brothers, reaches UK #39.

1965 **Mar** The Crickets disband, although Allison, who retains the name, says a band may well re-form at some point in the future.

July *Holly In The Hills*, compiling the early Holly and Montgomery radio station recordings, reaches UK #13.

1967 July Compilation *Buddy Holly's Greatest Hits* hits UK #9.

1968 Apr In the middle of a general rock'n'roll revival, a reissue of *Peggy Sue/Rave On* reaches UK #32.

1969 Apr [12] *Giant*, made up of Holly's home recordings, reaches UK #13.
Dec *The Buddy Holly Story* is finally certified gold for a half million US sales.

1971 Aug Reissued *Buddy Holly's Greatest Hits* reaches UK #32.

1975 July *Buddy Holly's Greatest Hits* is reissued again, making UK #42.

1976 Sept [7] Paul McCartney commemorates Holly's 40th birthday with the inauguration of "Buddy Holly Week" in UK. (McCartney, a long-time Holly fan, has purchased the publishing rights to his song catalog.) At the same time, The Buddy Holly Memorial Society is formed in US.

1977 Sept Allison, Mauldin and Curtis perform at the second "Buddy Holly Week" celebration.

1978 Mar [25] *20 Golden Greats* tops UK chart, and reaches US #55.
May [18] The biopic "The Buddy Holly Story", with Holly played by Gary Busey, has its world premiere in Dallas, TX.

1979 Feb [3] A concert, hosted by Wolfman Jack, at the Surf Ballroom in Clear Lake commemorates the final performances of Buddy Holly, The Big Bopper and Ritchie Valens exactly 20 years previously. Acts appearing include Jimmy Clanton, Del Shannon and The Drifters.
Mar A 6-album box set *The Complete Buddy Holly*, containing every one of Holly's recordings, is released in UK.

1980 Feb [27] Jerry Allen, Sheriff of Mason City, unearths manila envelope marked "Charles Hardin Holley" containing Holly's glasses, The Big Bopper's watch and several other items.
Mar A statue of Holly is erected in front of Lubbock civic center.

1983 *For The First Time Anywhere*, containing original recordings without dubbing or the later backing tracks, is released.

1984 Sept [8] *Greatest Hits* makes UK #100.

1988 Apr The Crickets release *Three Piece* on Allison's Rollercoaster label, their first album in over a decade.
Sept The Crickets sign to CBS and are to record *Got The T-Shirt*, winner of the 1987 Buddy Holly Week Song Contest.
[7] McCartney joins The Crickets on stage at the Buddy Holly Week festival in London.
Dec MCA re-releases *True Love Ways* after exposure on TV ad for Terry's All Gold chocolate. It reaches UK #65.

1989 Feb UK TV-advertised compilation *True Love Ways* hits UK #8, giving Holly a Top 10 album in each decade since the 50s.

1990 Gary Busey pays $242,000 for an acoustic guitar owned by Holly at auction.

JOHN LEE HOOKER

1943 Hooker (b. Aug.22, 1917, Clarksdale, MS), having learned guitar as a teenager from his musician stepfather Will Moore, joined the army at age 14 and been booted out 3 months later, has drifted through Memphis, TN, and Cincinnati, OH, during the 30s, as a gospel singer, playing the blues (sitting in with local musicians like Robert Nighthawk) now moves to Detroit, MI. He works as a janitor at the Chrysler car plant by day and plays at night in clubs like the Forest Inn and Club Basin, having actually made his first public appearance at the City Auditorium, Atlanta, GA, with a 3 or 4-piece blues band (typically, Bob Thurman on piano, Otis Finch on sax, and Tom Whitehead on drums), making a name as a popular blues act.

1948 Oct Modern Records talent scout Lee Sensation hears Hooker play in Detroit bar the Monte Carlo and signs him.
Nov [3] A debut recording session is held in a local studio with just Hooker and guitar. Self-penned *Boogie Chillun* sets the pattern for his primitive, intense blues style and is a huge US hit nationally in the burgeoning "race" (later R&B) market (and over the next 5 years will sell a million copies).
Dec His second session is for independent producer Joe Von Battle, who circumvents the Modern contract by selling *Black Man Blues* to King Records for release as by "Texas Slim". (Hooker will record for anyone who shows interest, avoiding contractual complications by using a new name. Between 1949 and 1954 he will issue about 70 singles on 21 different labels, under 10 different pseudonyms, including Delta John, Johnny Lee, Johnny Williams and John Lee Booker.)

1949 *Crawlin' King Snake*, on Modern, sells strongly and will be much covered by late-60s electric blues bands.

1951 *I'm In The Mood* is his second major R&B hit, another estimated million-seller over a period of some years, and will appear on the movie soundtrack "The Hot Spot" in 1990.

1952 He makes his debut as a radio DJ in Detroit.

1955 Oct He signs to Vee-Jay Records in Chicago, IL, which recognizes his potentially wider appeal and molds him into a tighter, more commercial performer on disk, backing him with disciplined R&B session men like guitarist Eddie Taylor.

1956 Mar [27] He records *Dimples*. (It will be a UK hit 8 years later.)

1960 June [24] He is one of the few purely blues artists at the second annual Newport Folk Festival. The performance is recorded by Vee-Jay, for later release as *Concert At Newport*.

1961 Apr [11] Bob Dylan makes his first New York appearance opening for Hooker at Gerde's Folk City in New York.

1962 Hooker tours Europe and UK with the "American Blues Folk Festival 1962" concert package.
July Self-composed *Boom Boom* is his only crossover success, reaching US #60. (It will be a hit cover by The Animals in 1964.)

1964 June [1] Hooker arrives for 28-day UK tour.
July With the UK R&B boom in full swing, and many of Hooker's songs revived by UK bands, familiar oldies by his contemporaries like Howlin' Wolf and Jimmy Reed are making UK Singles chart. Hooker's *Dimples* (also covered by The Animals) climbs to UK #23. He visits UK and plays it on ITV's "Ready Steady Go!".

1965 May [10] Hooker embarks on his fourth UK tour.

1966 He signs to ABC Records, recording albums for its Impulse (jazz) and Bluesway (blues) subsidiary labels as well as ABC itself, over the next 8 years. One of the first releases is an album recorded in concert, *Live At The Café Au Go-Go*.

1967 Feb *House Of The Blues*, a budget-price reissue of tracks recorded for Chess in the early 50s, is a rare Hooker UK chart album, reaching #34.
June [8] He returns to tour UK until July 2.

1970 Aug [11] He headlines the Ann Arbor Blues & Jazz Festival, MI, with Buddy Guy, Johnny Winter and others.

1971 Apr Double album *Hooker'N'Heat*, recorded with Canned Heat for Liberty, reaches US #73 (his first US chart album).
May *Endless Boogie*, on ABC, makes US #126.

1972 Apr *Never Get Out Of These Blues Alive* reaches US #130.

1974 He signs to Atlantic Records, cutting albums *Detroit Special* and *Don't Turn Me From Your Door*.

1978 Double album *The Cream*, a selection of classic songs recorded live at the Keynote club in Palo Alto, CA, is recorded for US independent blues label Tomato Records.

1979 Apr Hooker, with Lightnin' Hopkins, Big Mama Thornton and others, appears at "The Boogie'N'Blues Concert" at New York's Carnegie Hall.

1980 June Like several other blues and R&B performers (including Ray Charles, James Brown and Aretha Franklin), Hooker has a cameo role in movie "The Blues Brothers". (Hooker will carry on touring both solo and as part of package blues bills.)

1986 His music is featured in Steven Spielberg's movie "The Color Purple".

1988 At age 71, Hooker continues to tour US and overseas. His style, and some of his repertoire, is virtually unchanged over more than 30 years; the stark, fierce vocal/guitar combination still making him unique, as well as a rare survivor among his late 40s blues contemporaries. In mid-year, he records a new album with a cast of long-time admirers, including Robert Cray, Carlos Santana, Bonnie Raitt, Los Lobos, George Thorogood and others.

1989 July Chameleon Records releases the album, *The Healer*, in US. It will peak at US #62 and spend 38 weeks on the Album survey.
[30] Hooker performs at 30th Newport Folk Festival, Fort Adams State Park, Newport, RI, with Emmylou Harris, Pete Seeger, John Prine, Leon Redbone, The Clancy Brothers and Theodore Bikel.
Aug [22] Hooker celebrates his 72nd birthday at the Bay Area club, Sweetwater, with Albert Collins, Robert Cray, Ry Cooder and Carlos Santana.
Sept He features on Pete Townshend's concept album *The Iron Man*.

1990 Feb [21] *I'm In The Mood*, a duet with Bonnie Raitt, wins Best Traditional Blues Recording at the 32nd annual Grammy awards at the Shrine Auditorium, Los Angeles.
Mar Having briefly entered UK chart in 1989, *The Healer* now peaks at UK #63, released on the Silvertone label.
July [7] During a UK visit, Hooker performs at the Hammersmith Odeon, London.
Oct [16] "A Tribute To John Lee Hooker" at Madison Square Garden, New York, is part of the Benson & Hedges Blues '90 season with guests Gregg Allman, Joe Cocker, Albert Collins, Ry Cooder, James Cotton, Bo

Diddley, Willie Dixon, Mick Fleetwood, John Hammond, Al Kooper, Huey Lewis, Charlie Musselwhite, Johnny Winter and members of Little Feat.

1991 Jan [17] Hooker is inducted into the Rock'N'Roll Hall Of Fame at the sixth annual dinner at the Waldorf Astoria in New York, as yet another generation of reviewers and audiences become hooked on him.'

MARY HOPKIN

1967 After singing in her local Congregational Tabernacle choir since age 4, then moving to folk club performances and regular spots on Welsh TV, Hopkin (b. May 3, 1950, Pontardawe, Wales), makes her first recording, *Llais Swynol Mary Hopkin*, a Welsh language EP on Cambrian label.

1968 May She wins UK TV talent show "Opportunity Knocks", where she is spotted by model Twiggy who recommends her to Paul McCartney, and signs to The Beatles' new Apple label.
Aug [27] *Those Were The Days*, produced by McCartney and written by Gene Raskin, based on the melody of traditional Russian folk song *Darogoi Dlimmoyo*, launches Apple in UK alongside The Beatles' own *Hey Jude*.
Sept *Those Were The Days* replaces *Hey Jude* at UK #1, topping chart for 6 weeks and selling over 750,000 copies. (Hopkin is the first female to top UK charts in 1968.)
Oct Hopkin appears on the "Ed Sullivan Show" in US, singing *Those Were The Days*.
Nov [2] *Those Were The Days* hits US #2 for 3 weeks, behind The Beatles' *Hey Jude*, and is a million-seller. (She also records it in Spanish, French, German, Italian and Hebrew and by early 1969 the cumulative worldwide sales will be over 8 million.)

1969 Mar *Post Card*, produced by McCartney and including covers of songs by Harry Nilsson and Donovan, hits UK #3.
[21] Hopkin begins her first UK tour with headliner Engelbert Humperdinck at the Gaumont cinema, Worcester, Hereford & Worcs. It will end at the Odeon cinema, Manchester, Gtr.Manchester, Apr.12.
Apr *Goodbye*, written and produced by McCartney, hits UK #2. Hopkin meets her future husband, record producer Tony Visconti, while recording more foreign language versions of her songs. She sings the theme to movie "Where's Jack?" for Paramount Pictures.
May *Goodbye* makes US #13, while *Post Card* makes US #28.
Dec Hopkin stars in "Dick Whittington" pantomime at the London Palladium with Tommy Steele.

1970 Feb *Temma Harbour*, produced by Mickie Most, hits UK #6. Hopkin appears on Cilla Black's UK BBC TV show, singing 6 songs from which UK's entry for the 1970 Eurovision Song Contest will be selected.
Mar *Temma Harbour* makes US #39.
Apr *Knock Knock Who's There*, having been selected as the UK Eurovision entry, hits UK #2. (The contest is won by Eire's entry, Dana's *All Kinds Of Everything*.)
July A McCartney-produced revival of Doris Day's *Que Sera, Sera (Whatever Will Be, Will Be)* climbs to US #77.
Nov *Think About Your Children*, written by Hot Chocolate's Errol Brown, reaches UK #19 and US #87.

1971 July *Let My Name Be Sorrow* makes UK #46.
Oct Hopkin's own favorite recording, *Earth Song – Ocean Song*, produced by Tony Visconti and including contributions from Ralph McTell and Dave Cousins of The Strawbs, is released.
Dec *Water, Paper And Clay* is her last release on Apple and fails to chart. Hopkin marries Tony Visconti, and will work with him through the 70s, often singing back-up vocals on his productions for David Bowie and others.

1972 Aug A UK single made for Bell with Visconti, under the name Hobby Horse, reviving The Jamies' 1958 US hit *Summertime·Summertime*, is released.
Nov Compilation *Those Were The Days*, collating the Apple singles, is released but fails to chart in UK or US.
Dec The seasonal *Mary Had A Baby* is released in UK on Regal Zonophone. (Mary is pregnant in real life at.this time, and son Morgan is born shortly afterwards.) In US Apple issues *Knock Knock Who's There*, which makes #92.

1976 Mar *If You Love Me*, recorded for Visconti's Good Earth label, makes UK #32.

1977 May *Wrap Me In Your Arms*, also on Good Earth, is released. Hopkin features with various artists on Chrysalis fantasy concept album *The King Of Elfland's Daughter* and takes lead vocal on extracted single *Lirazell*. Neither charts.
Dec *Beyond The Fields We Know*, another single from the concept album,

with Hopkin's vocals, is released.
1980 After devoting time to her children, Hopkin teams with Mike Hurst (ex-Springfields) and Mike D'Albuquerque (ex-ELO) as Sundance, a harmony trio which signs to Bronze Records.
1981 Oct *What's Love* is released. The group plays support to Dr. Hook on a UK tour, after which Hopkin leaves, unwilling to move into the MOR cabaret circuit. Her marriage to Visconti ends and a relationship with Dr. Hook vocalist Dennis Locorriere develops.
1984 May She returns to UK chart as lead vocalist with Oasis, a group which includes Peter Skellern on piano and vocals and Julian Lloyd Webber on cello. *Hold Me* does not chart but *Oasis* reaches UK #23. The group does not continue on a permanent basis because Hopkin becomes ill and leaves in advance of a planned tour.
1988 She participates with other artists in EMI recording of Dylan Thomas' *Under Milk Wood*, produced by George Martin.

BRUCE HORNSBY & THE RANGE
Bruce Hornsby (vocals, keyboards, accordion)
David Mansfield (violin, mandolin, guitar)
George Marinelli (guitar, vocals)
Joe Puerta (bass, vocals)
John Molo (drums)

1978 Having excelled at basketball and piano in high school, practiced at home on the family's Steinway grand, and studied music at Miami University and the Berklee School of Music, Boston, MA, Hornsby (b. Nov.23, 1954, Williamsburg, VA), whose father played saxophone in his uncle's band Sherwood Hornsby & The Rhythm Boys, forms a home town group The Bruce Hornsby Band with his older brother Bobby and a drummer friend John Molo, and begins playing endless bars and lounges on the road around the Southern states. He also begins a 7-year habit of recording demo tapes of his newly-written material, sending them regularly to record companies.
1980 At the invitation of Michael McDonald, who has been impressed by a performance he has seen at a Steak & Ale Bar, Hornsby moves to Los Angeles, CA, with his brother John, where both work for 3 years at 20th Century Fox Publishing, writing production-line pop songs. They have been directed there with the help of McDonald and his fellow Doobie Brother Jeff Baxter, who was able to arrange a showcase for the Hornsby siblings attended by 20th Century Fox executive Ronnie Vance.
1982 In Hollywood, Hornsby has met Huey Lewis who is impressed by his writing and playing abilities, and made demos with producer David Foster. He becomes friends with Lewis but, hoping his own success will come shortly, Hornsby turns down Lewis' request to include Hornsby song *Let The Girls Rock* on his forthcoming album *Sports*.
1983 Hornsby, recommended as a keyboardist by friend and bass player Joe Puerta, is invited to join the backing band being formed for a lengthy US tour by Sheena Easton.
1985 Years of writing, recording and submitting dozens of demo tapes to over 70 record companies finally pay off when Hornsby and his newly-formed band, The Range, are signed worldwide to RCA, having recently turned down an offer from new-age label Windham Hill.
1986 Aug [23] Chart debut *Every Little Kiss* peaks at US #72.
Group starts first full US tour and dates sell out when *The Way It Is* is released. Title track receives heavy airplay and is issued as a single.
Sept *The Way It Is* also receives immediate heavy UK radio attention and reaches UK #15. *The Way It Is* (which includes 3 tracks produced by Lewis) climbs to UK #16.
Oct Hornsby & The Range tour UK as support to Huey Lewis & The News, making a strong BBC TV impact on primetime show "Wogan".
Dec [13] *The Way It Is*, after a steady climb on US chart since Sept., hits #1 for a week and will remain charted for 22.
1987 Feb [24] Hornsby & The Range win Best New Artist at the 29th annual Grammy awards.
Mar [14] Huey Lewis & The News top US chart with tele-evangelist-criticizing *Jacob's Ladder*, written by Bruce and John Hornsby in the summer of 1985. Track is relegated to a B-side in UK.
[21] *Mandolin Rain* hits US #4, while *The Way It Is*, after a 6-month US chart climb, hits #3.
Apr *The Way It Is* receives ASCAP Award as the Most Played Song Of The Year. Meanwhile, *Mandolin Rain* charts briefly at UK #70.
July [11] A remixed *Every Little Kiss* reaches US #14. (His distinctive keyboard style increasingly in demand, Hornsby guests on Clannad's *Sirius*, and on album by Tom Wopat (former "Dukes Of Hazzard" star turned country singer)). *The Way It Is* sales top 2 million.
Oct Band begins work on second album, with Neil Dorfsman sharing

production credits with Hornsby. Peter Harris replaces Mansfield in The Range.

1988 **June** *Scenes From The Southside*, a musical biography of the Hornsby brothers' adolescence in America's South, includes their own version of *Jacob's Ladder*. It hits US #5, as does the simultaneously-extracted *The Valley Road*.
July [2] In UK, the album reaches #18, and the single #44. Hornsby also plays accordion on albums by Patti Austin (*The Real Me*), Kim Carnes (*View From The House*) and Huey Lewis (*Small World*).
Sept [3] *Look Out Any Window*, extracted from *Scenes From The Southside*, reaches US #35.

1989 **Aug** [26] *The End Of The Innocence*, a collaborative songwriting and production effort by Hornsby for Don Henley, hits US #8.
Dec Hornsby guests on new Columbia signing Shawn Colvin's debut album *Steady On* (US #112). She will return the favor for Hornsby's third album.

1990 **Feb** [21] *The Valley Road*, a collaboration with The Nitty Gritty Dirt Band on the latter's *Will The Circle Be Unbroken, Vol.2*, wins Best Bluegrass Recording at the 32nd annual Grammy awards at the Shrine Auditorium, Los Angeles.
[23] Herbie Hancock recruits Bruce Hornsby and others for a taping of Showtime-TV's "Coast To Coast" show at Los Angeles' China club.
Apr Band performs at an "Earth Day" eve concert at the Merriweather Post Pavilion, Columbia, MD, with Indigo Girls, Stipe & Buck, 10,000 Maniacs, Billy Bragg and others.
July Group embarks on major US tour, supported by Cowboy Junkies.
[28] *A Night On The Town* reaches US #20, having already made UK #27. It showcases harder Hornsby style relying less on his distinctive piano treats.
Aug [16] RCA announces that Hornsby "has responded affirmatively to a request from his longtime friends (The Grateful Dead) to help them through this difficult period", with reference to Hornsby playing dates with them after the death of their keyboard player Brent Mydland. He will perform with the band at Madison Square Garden Sept.15-20 and other dates.
[18] First single from current album, *Across The River*, featuring the Grateful Dead's Jerry Garcia, reaches US #18.
Sept Hornsby guests on current Cowboy Junkies 45 *Rock And Bird*.
Nov [3] Bruce Hornsby & The Range with Shawn Colvin ballad *Lost Soul* stalls at US #84.

1991 **Feb** [10] Hornsby performs an instrumental rendition of the American national anthem with Branford Marsalis at the NBC All-Star game in Charlotte, NC.
Apr [20] Hornsby takes part in the "Earth Day 1991 Concert" at Foxboro Stadium, Foxboro, MA, with Billy Bragg, Jackson Browne, Rosanne Cash, Bruce Cockburn, Indigo Girls, Queen Latifah, Ziggy Marley, Willie Nelson and 10,000 Maniacs, as he nears completion as producer of hero Leon Russell's comeback album.

HOT CHOCOLATE

Errol Brown (vocals)
Tony Wilson (bass, vocals)
Harvey Hinsley (guitar)
Larry Ferguson (keyboards)
Patrick Olive (percussion)
Tony Connor (drums)

1969 Group is formed in Brixton, London, by Olive (b. Mar.22, 1947, Grenada) with drummer Ian King and guitarist Franklyn De Allie. Songwriters Brown (b. Nov.12, 1948, Kingston, Jamaica) and Wilson (b. Oct.8, 1947, Trinidad) join shortly afterwards, followed by Ferguson (b. Apr.14, 1948, Nassau, Bahamas). De Allie departs.
Oct Group's reggae-styled adaptation (with his agreement) of John Lennon's *Give Peace A Chance* is a one-off on Apple but fails to chart. Mavis Smith of Apple names them The Hot Chocolate Band.

1970 The band signs to Mickie Most's RAK Records after Brown and Wilson approach Most with 3 of their songs. Most agrees that *Bet Yer Life I Do* is ideal for Herman's Hermits and takes *Think About Your Children* for Mary Hopkin. He suggests that Hot Chocolate (to which the name is now shortened) should record *Love Is Life*.
Aug Hot Chocolate debuts at the Nevada Ballroom, Bolton, Gtr.Manchester.
Sept *Love Is Life* hits UK #6, introducing a trademark sound characterized by Brown's distinctive pop/soul voice and a percussive, commercial instrumental backing. Brown's shaved head becomes a visual focus.

Oct Hinsley (b. Jan.19, 1948, Northampton, Northants.), ex-Cliff Bennett's Rebel Rousers, joins on guitar.

1971 **Apr** *You Could Have Been a Lady* reaches UK #22.
Sept *I Believe (In Love)* hits UK #8.
Nov *You'll Always Be A Friend* reaches UK #23.

1973 **Mar** Connor (b. Apr.6, 1947, Romford, Essex), ex-Audience and Jackson Heights, replaces King on drums.
May *Brother Louie*, lyrically themed on inter-racial love and racism, hits UK #7.
Aug *Rumours* makes UK #44, while Stories' cover version of *Brother Louie* tops US chart. Group signs to the MAM agency for live work (and will play a UK tour approximately every 18 months).

1974 **Apr** *Emma* hits UK #3.
June Group's debut album *Cicero Park* is released.
Dec *Cheri Babe* makes UK #31.

1975 **Apr** Released in US by Big Tree Records, *Emma* hits US #8 and spurs *Cicero Park* to make US #55.
June *Disco Queen* reaches UK #11 and US #28.
Sept *A Child's Prayer* hits UK #7.
Nov Wilson leaves to sign a solo deal with Bearsville Records. Percussionist Olive takes over on bass. *Hot Chocolate* becomes their first UK chart album, making #34.
Dec *You Sexy Thing*, a harder dance number, hits UK #2.

1976 **Feb** *You Sexy Thing* hits US #3. (It is the group's biggest US hit, selling over a million.) *Hot Chocolate* makes US #41.
Apr *Don't Stop It Now* reaches UK #11 and US #42.
July *Man To Man* makes UK #14.
Aug *Man To Man* makes UK #32.
Sept *Heaven Is The Back Seat Of My Cadillac* reaches UK #25.
Oct *Man To Man* peaks at US #172.
Dec Compilation *Hot Chocolate 14 Greatest Hits* hits UK #6, selling 500,000 copies in UK alone.

1977 **July** *So You Win Again*, a rare outside composition for the group written by ex-Argent singer Russ Ballard, is its biggest UK hit, topping the chart for a week.
Sept *So You Win Again* makes US #31.
Dec *Put Your Love In Me* hits UK #10.

1978 **Apr** *Every 1's A Winner* reaches UK #12 and album of the same title climbs to #30.
Dec Ballad *I'll Put You Together Again*, from the musical "Dear Anyone", reaches UK #13.

1979 **Feb** *Every 1's A Winner*, released via a new deal with Infinity Records in US, hits #6 and earns the group's second gold disk for a million-plus sales. Album of the same title reaches US #31.
June *Mindless Boogie*, the group's first UK 12" single, makes UK #46.
July Group plays its first headlining US tour of 12 auditorium dates, followed by a 45-date UK trek.
Aug *Going Through The Motions* peaks at UK and US #53. Album of the same title makes US #112. Group follows its UK tour with a long tour of Europe, especially Germany, where its popularity is enormous.
Dec TV-advertised compilation *20 Hottest Hits* hits UK #3 and is another half-million seller.

1980 **June** *No Doubt About It*, written for the group by Steve Glen, Mike Burns and Mickie Most's brother Dave, about a real-life UFO sighting by Glen and Burns, hits UK #2.
Aug *Are You Getting Enough Of What Makes You Happy* reaches UK #17.
Dec *Love Me To Sleep* peaks at UK #50. *Class* does not chart.

1981 **June** *You'll Never Be So Wrong* peaks at UK #52.

1982 **May** *Girl Crazy* hits UK #7.
Aug *It Started With A Kiss* hits UK #5.
Oct *Chances* makes UK #32 as parent album *Mystery* reaches UK #24.

1983 **Jan** *Are You Getting Enough Happiness*, released in US after the group signs to EMI America, peaks at US #65, but is its last US chart hit.
June *What Kinda Boy You Looking For (Girl)* hits UK #10.
Oct *Tears On The Telephone* makes UK #37.

1984 **Mar** *I Gave You My Heart (Didn't I)* reaches UK #13, and is the last new recording by Hot Chocolate to chart.

1987 **Feb** Dutch disco DJ Ben Liebrand creates a new dance remix of the group's *You Sexy Thing*, adding 80s percussion and rhythm tracks to the original recording. Released as a single, it hits UK #10.
Mar 16-track TV-advertised compilation *The Very Best Of Hot Chocolate* tops UK chart with sales of a half million. It continues the tradition that the group's only substantial selling albums are collection of its hit singles.
Apr A "Groove Mix" of *Every 1's A Winner*, created by Liebrand in similar fashion to *You Sexy Thing*, peaks at UK #69.

May After a long musical silence (apart from reissues), it is confirmed that Hot Chocolate has split when Brown signs to WEA Records as a soloist and records with producers Tony Swain and Steve Jolley.
Aug Brown's solo *Personal Touch* reaches UK #25.
Dec Brown's *Body Rockin'*, produced by Richard James Burgess, peaks at UK #51.

88 Sept Following a rest in the Caribbean, Brown returns with new single *Maya*.

89 Feb Brown's debut solo album *That's How Love Is*, released on WEA, fails to score.

90 Dec Tipped by producer Pete Waterman as a UK Christmas chart-topper, Brown's *Send A Prayer*, produced by Stock/Aitken/Waterman, marks the beginning of a new solo recording contract for Brown with S/A/W label, PWL.

HE HOUSEMARTINS

orman **Cook** (vocals)
aul **Heaton** (vocals, guitar)
an **Cullimore** (bass)
ugh **Whitaker** (drums)

84 Band forms in Hull, Humberside, around Heaton (b. May 9, 1962, Birkenhead, Merseyside), who arrives in the town after a year traveling around Europe. He posts a postcard in his front-room window, requesting young musicians to get in touch with him. Cullimore (b. Apr.6, 1962), who lives in the same street, responds, while Whitaker and Ted Key are recruited from Hull band The Gargoyles. The group gains local live experience, then tours widely for 7 months playing small gigs throughout the UK, many of which support left-wing political causes including miners' support groups and CND, eventually coming to the attention of record labels.

85 Oct The Housemartins sign to Andy McDonald's Go! Discs Records in London, who are impressed with demo tape songs *Flag Day* and *Sitting On The Fence* and are promoted as "the fourth best band in Hull". Debut single *Flag Day* does not chart.
Nov Cook (b. Quentin Cook, July 31, 1963), an ex-club DJ from Brighton, E.Sussex, replaces Key who departs to open a vegetarian restaurant in Hull.

86 Feb During early touring on "The Twisted Roadshow", the band, claiming poverty, help pay for National Travel bus passes by collecting Mars bar chocolate wrappers with promotion coupons, and introduce "Adopt-A-Housemartin": wherever the band is playing, they ask members of the audience to invite band members to stay at their home for the night, thus saving their hotel bills.
Mar *Sheep* receives substantial airplay in UK, and is the band's chart debut, reaching UK #54.
June *Happy Hour*, helped by strong airplay and an inventive semi-animated promotional video showing the band in similar light to early Madness promos, hits UK #3.
[20-22] The Housemartins appear at the annual Glastonbury Festival, Somerset, alongside The Cure, The Pogues, Lloyd Cole and others.
July Debut album *London 0 Hull 4* (a title play on the band's continual promotion of its home town and provincial working-class pride) hits UK #3. (The album will climb to US #124 in a year's time.)
Sept [30] Group begins a UK tour in Birmingham, W.Midlands.
Nov Ballad *Think For A Minute* reaches UK #18.
Dec With 2 well-timed UK TV specials heavily plugging new single, group tops UK chart at Christmas with its biggest seller, an a cappella version of Isley Jasper Isley's *Caravan Of Love*. The original reached US #51 and UK #52 the previous Dec. An a cappella vocal set supporting The Housemartins' on their UK tour is merely the band's alter ego unit.
[27] Box set *The Housemartins' Christmas Singles Box* spends 1 week on the UK Album survey at #84.

87 Feb [9] Group wins Best British Newcomer at the sixth annual BRIT Awards at the Grosvenor House, Mayfair, London.
Mar The popular UK tabloid press reveals that some members of the band are gay and not the cheeky, affable, working-class lads from Hull they pertain to be, and that Cook's real forename is Quentin and his background is from relatively wealthy South of England instead of his poor Northern Housemartin image.
June *Five Get Over Excited*, reaching UK #11, is the first release with drummer Dave Hemmingway, from local Hull band The Velvetones, replacing Whitaker who quit due to ideological differences with rest of the group. They appear in "Red Wedge" concerts, encouraging the young left-wing vote, in the run-up to the UK General Election.
Aug *Me And The Farmer* reaches UK #15.

Oct *The People Who Grinned Themselves To Death* hits UK #9.
Dec *Build* reaches UK #15.

1988 Feb Band announces that it is to split, claiming The Housemartins was only planned as a 3-year project. Cook is already finding parallel success as a dance record remixer, using his club DJ background to remix tracks by James Brown, Nitro Deluxe and Eric B. & Rakim among others, and will eventually go on to form flexible dance troup Beats International.
May *There Is Always Something There To Remind Me* (not Sandie Shaw's 1964 hit but a new song by Heaton and Cullimore, taken from a BBC Radio 1 session) is their swan song single, reaching UK #35. Double album *Now That's What I Call Quite Good*, a compilation of hits, rarities and out-takes, is the band's farewell hit at UK #8.

1989 May Heaton launches his new outfit, equally sarcastically named The Beautiful South with fellow ex-Housemartin Hemmingway, bassist Sean Welch, singer and co-writer David Rotheray, female vocalist Briana Corrigan, ex-Anthill Runaways and drummer, former Housemartin roadie, David Stead.
June Debut single, ballad *Song For Whoever* is released by Go! Discs, set to hit UK #2, while the band finishes recording debut album in Milan.
July Cook's collaborative effort with labelmate Billy Bragg, as Beats International, *Won't Talk About It/Blame It On The Bassline* reaches UK #29, released on Go! Discs dance offshoot Go! Beat.
Nov Cook's Lester-issued *For Spacious Lies* makes UK #48, while Housemartins' acoustic ditty *You Keep It All In* hits UK #8.
[4] *Welcome To The Beautiful South* hits UK #2. Its initial album cover, featuring a suicidal girl with the barrel of a gun in her mouth, is replaced by more consumer friendly cuddly teddy bear photo set.

1990 Jan Beautiful South ballad *I'll Sail This Ship Alone* makes UK #31.
Mar Cook, now fully helming Beats International, releases cover version of S.O.S. Band's *Just Be Good To Me*, now as *Dub Be Good To Me*, featuring Lindy Layton. It hits UK #1.
June Beats International re-releases *Won't Talk About It*, which hits UK #9, while debut album *Let Them Eat Bingo* has reached UK #17.
Sept Beats International's *Burundi Blues* peaks at UK #51.
Oct [27] Heaton/Rotheray marital angst ballad *A Little Time* hits UK #1 for a week, aided by popular knife-featuring domestic scene mini-drama video.
Nov [3] *Rubáiyát*, Elektra's 40th anniversary compilation, to which Beautiful South contributes a cover of *Love Wars*, makes US #140.
[10] Following experimental dates in US, where their brand of barbed lyricism and off-beat UK council house leatherette sofa humor is lost in translation, second Beautiful South album *Choke* is immediate UK #2.

1991 Feb [10] "A Little Time" wins Best Music Video at the 10th annual BRIT Awards at the Dominion theater, London. In typical fashion, Heaton's full acceptance speech is "Nice one".

WHITNEY HOUSTON

1983 Clive Davis, head of Arista Records, sees and hears potential in Houston (b. Aug.9, 1963, New Jersey) at a showcase arranged by Arista A&R executive Gerry Griffith, and signs her to a worldwide contract. She has already signed a management deal with Seymour Flics and Gene Harvey in 1981. (Houston, like her singing mother Cissy and cousin Dionne Warwick, has begun her vocals career, at age 8, singing *Guide Me, O Thou Great Jehovah* in a gospel setting – The New Hope Baptist Junior Choir.) Within 4 years she is sought for backing vocals for such recording artists as Chaka Khan and Lou Rawls. In the meantime, Houston sings with her mother at nightclub and concert engagements, develops her own solo numbers and sings lead vocals on Michael Zager Band's second album title cut *Life's A Party*. Zager offers to sign Houston to a recording contract, but her mother declines on her behalf. She also pursues a career as a model, featured in US magazine **Glamor** and on the front cover of **Seventeen**, and as an actress, appearing in TV shows including "Silver Spoons" and "Gimme A Break".

1984 June Although an early commercial glimpse of her is witnessed on a duet with Teddy Pendergrass (*Hold Me* makes US #46), Davis continues to protect, teach and nurture his prodigy in a quest to record the perfect debut album. He enlists the help of many significant songwriters (Michael Masser, Peter McCann, Linda Creed and Gerry Goffin) and producers (Narada Michael Walden, Michael Masser and Kashif).

1985 Mar *Whitney Houston* is finally released in US. Its early progress is quiet (it will take 9 months to top the US chart).
July Debut single *You Give Good Love*, produced by Kashif, slowly climbs to hit US #3. Its release in UK sparks some club/dance interest but fails to make the chart.

Oct [26] Released in Aug., Masser-produced ballad *Saving All My Love For You*, a cover of a 1978 Marilyn McCoo & Billy Davis Jr. album cut, hits US #1.

Dec *Saving All My Love For You* becomes an international smash and hits US #1. Debut album *Whitney Houston*, although destined to spend over 100 consecutive weeks on the UK chart, peaks at #2.

1986 **Feb** [15] Uptempo Walden-produced *How Will I Know* tops US Pop and R&B charts and hits UK #5.

[25] Houston wins Best Pop Vocal Performance, Female for *Saving All My Love For You* at the 28th annual Grammy awards.

Mar Having collected 5 US music awards, Houston's next single *The Greatest Love Of All* (originally B-side of *You Give Good Love*) is a cover version of the 1977 hit by George Benson. It is her third consecutive US #1 and hits UK #8.

[8] *Whitney Houston* tops US chart.

May [17] *Greatest Love Of All* tops US chart.

Aug She wins a US Emmy award for Outstanding Individual Performance In A Variety Program On US TV and announces her first major live US dates. She celebrates her 23rd birthday.

Nov Houston arrives in UK for her first European live dates, which are all sell-outs.

1987 **Jan** With Davis again in role of Executive Producer, a similar grouping of writers and producers is recruited to attempt to repeat the formula.

Apr She completes early promotion work for new single with a live appearance at the Montreux Rock Festival, Switzerland.

June [6] George Merrill/Shannon Rubicam, later of Boy Meets Girls duo, penned, Walden-produced *I Wanna Dance With Somebody (Who Loves Me)* tops UK chart.

[13] Her second album *Whitney* enters UK chart at #1.

[27] *I Wanna Dance With Somebody (Who Loves Me)* tops US chart. *Whitney* becomes the first album by a female singer to debut at #1 on the **Billboard** chart. It continues a familiar mix of sassy dance pop numbers and ballads (including a duet version, with mother Cissy, of the "Chess" musical standard *I Know Him So Well*). It remains at #1 for 11 weeks.

Sept [26] Ballad *Didn't We Almost Have It All*, co-written by producer Michael Masser and Will Jennings, continues the US run as another #1, and reaches UK #14. A world tour in support of the second album is announced.

Dec Tom Kelly/Billy Steinberg-penned *So Emotional* hits UK #5.

1988 **Jan** [9] *So Emotional* tops US chart, her sixth consecutive US #1.

Mar [2] Houston wins her second Best Pop Vocal Performance, Female for *I Wanna Dance With Somebody (Who Loves Me)* at the 30th annual Grammy awards.

Apr [23] *I Wanna Dance With Somebody (Who Loves Me)* hits US #1, as Houston breaks a chart record: *Where Do Broken Hearts Go* climbs to US #1, pipping Billy Ocean's *Get Outta My Dreams (Get Into My Car)*, to become her seventh consecutive US chart-topper, overtaking the previous record of 6 achieved by The Beatles and The Bee Gees. In UK, it makes only #14.

June [11] Already in the middle of a sell-out world tour, Houston headlines "Nelson Mandela's 70th Birthday Party" celebration at Wembley Stadium, London. Fifth single from *Whitney*, *Love Will Save The Day*, is released to tie-in with UK visit and hits UK #10.

Sept *Love Will Save The Day* breaks the chart-topping run at US #9.

Oct On the way down the chart, it passes her newly-recorded and climbing *One Moment In Time*, a ballad headlining Davis' current project – a special 1988 Olympics various-artists musical tribute *One Moment In Time*, which eventually hits US #5 and UK #1.

1989 **Jan** [30] Houston wins Pop Female Vocal and Soul/R&B Female Vocal at the American Music Awards.

Aug Houston duets on labelmate and longtime friend Aretha Franklin's *It Isn't, It Wasn't, It Ain't Ever Gonna Be*, which makes US #41, set to make UK #29. While Houston prepares her third album with new producers, she is increasingly showered with Hollywood scripts and is alternately most rumored to be considering movies starring opposite Robert De Niro and friend Eddie Murphy.

1990 **May** [30] Houston receives the 1990 Hitmaker Award at the Songwriters Hall Of Fame 21st annual induction dinner at the Hilton Hotel, New York.

Oct [3] Houston attends a celebration at the White House, Washington, DC, for National Children's Day.

[20] First single from third album, dance swinging *I'm Your Baby Tonight*, begins world chart rise, first hitting UK #5.

Dec [1] *I'm Your Baby Tonight* hits US #1.

[8] Blocked out by rappers Vanilla Ice and MC Hammer albums, *I'm*

Your Baby Tonight can only hit US #3. It is mostly co-written and produced by R&B hit making production duo L.A. Reid and Babyface.

1991 **Jan** [12] Houston receives an award for Distinguished Achievement by the American Cinema Award Foundation in Los Angeles, in a ceremony which also recognizes James Stewart and Lauren Bacall.

[19] Houston achieves her ninth US #1 in just over 5 years as *All The Man That I Need*, a 1982 Sister Sledge US R&B #45, hits US #1 for the first of 2 weeks, as *I'm Your Baby Tonight* approaches triple platinum US sales.

[27] Houston captures America's heart performing *The Star Spangled Banner* at Super Bowl XXV at Joe Robbie Stadium, Miami, FL. Even though her vocal segment was pre-recorded, she synthesizes current American patriotism, related to the Gulf War crisis. Demand for the performance results in a single and video release.

Feb [23] Houston appears as the musical guest on NBC TV's "Saturday Night Live".

Mar *The Star Spangled Banner* reaches US #20.

[31] HBO TV airs live Houston concert from the Norfolk Naval Air Station, at which she welcomes home US troops from the Persian Gulf and repeats *The Star Spangled Banner*.

Apr Third cut from recent album, *Miracle*, begins US chart climb.

May [12] Houston appears by satellite from US in "The Simple Truth" concert for Kurdish refugees at Wembley Arena, London.

HOWLIN' WOLF

1948 Following some years of farm labor and then US Army service, Wolf (Chester Arthur Burnett, June 10, 1910, West Point, MS), moves to West Memphis, AR, to try to earn a living as a musician, forming The House Rockers, who build a local reputation as a hot electric blues band.

1949 Wolf and the band secure a daily half-hour live music spot on local West Memphis radio station KWEM. (By now he is known as Howlin' Wolf. The "Howlin'" refers to his early singing style, a personal adaptation of Jimmie Rodgers' "blue yodel" and legend suggests he was called "The Wolf" by his family, from **Little Red Riding Hood**, when he misbehaved as a child.)

1951 Via his radio slot, Wolf comes to the attention of Ike Turner, working the area as field A&R man for Los Angeles, CA-based Modern Records, and Memphis, TN-based producer Sam Phillips, a regular supplier of local recordings to Modern and to Chess Records in Chicago, IL.

May [14] Phillips records Wolf at his Sun studio, leasing the results to Chess. This angers Modern, who claims rights to Wolf and arranges for Turner to record him independently at KWEM.

Nov Different recordings of the same Wolf composition, *Moanin' At Midnight*, are released both on Modern's subsidiary RPM, and on Chess. The song is incorrectly labelled *Mornin' At Midnight* on RPM, while Chess avoids split sales by promoting the other side, *How Many More Years*. The RPM release reaches US R&B Top 20 first, to be quickly replaced by the Chess single.

1952 **Feb** Modern relinquishes its claims to Wolf when Phillips produces a contract signed the previous Aug. – but 2 more Turner-produced records appear on RPM anyway.

July [10] Phillips records the last of 5 Howlin' Wolf sessions. Wolf signs directly to Chess, persuaded by a cash advance, and takes his guitarists Hubert Sumlin and Willie Johnson with him.

1953 In Chicago, he secures his first club dates with the help of Muddy Waters, and starts to record at Chess studios, with house musicians Willie Dixon (bass), Otis Spann (piano) and Earl Phillips (drums) augmenting the band. (Over the next 10 years he will record most of his classic repertoire for the label, including his own compositions *Smokestack Lightnin'*, *No Place To Go*, *Sitting On Top Of The World*, *Evil*, *Killin' Floor*, *I Ain't Superstitious* and *Who's Been Talking*, and Willie Dixon's *Spoonful*, *Down In The Bottom*, *Back Door Man*, *The Red Rooster* and *Wang Dang Doodle*.)

1961 **Nov** [24] He arrives in UK for his first tour. *Little Baby* is released by Pye Records as his first UK single, but does not sell.

1962 Secretary of State Dean Rusk, in his capacity as co-chairman of the Washington Jazz Festival, asks Chess if Wolf is available to appear.

1963 **July** Wolf is recorded live with Spann, Buddy Guy and Muddy Waters, at Chicago's Copa Cabana club. (The recordings will appear in 1964 as *Folk Festival Of The Blues*.)

1964 **June** His first (and only) pop hit is *Smokestack Lightnin'*; it belatedly reaches UK #42 (it was recorded in 1956). (Wolf's songs are now staple repertoire for new UK R&B groups. Among them, *Smokestack Lightnin'* will be covered by The Yardbirds and Manfred Mann; *Spoonful* by Cream and Ten Years After; *The Red Rooster* (as *Little Red Rooster*) by

The Rolling Stones, and *I Ain't Superstitious* by Jeff Beck, Rod Stewart and Savoy Brown. In US, *Back Door Man* is revived by The Doors, *Killin' Floor* by Electric Flag and *How Many More Years* by Little Feat.)

Oct [19] Wolf begins 5-date American Negro Blues Festival, with Willie Dixon, Lightnin' Hopkins, Sonny Boy Williamson and others, at Fairfield Hall, Croydon, London.

Nov [26] UK club tour kicks off at the Marquee, London.

65 May [26] At the group's invitation, he appears with The Rolling Stones on a US TV "Shindig" slot.

67 Sept With Bo Diddley and Muddy Waters, Wolf records *The Super Super Blues Band*, including new versions of several familiar songs.

69 Apr Envious of the success of Waters' "psychedelic" *Electric Mud*, Wolf records similarly-conceived *The Howlin' Wolf Album* (which in private he calls "birdshit").

71 Sept Wolf travels to London with Sumlin to record with a UK superstar line-up including Eric Clapton, Ringo Starr, Steve Winwood, and Bill Wyman and Charlie Watts of The Rolling Stones. *The London Howlin' Wolf Sessions*, compiled from the UK recordings, is his only US chart hit, making #79.

72 Sept [8] Wolf appears at Ann Arbor Jazz & Blues Festival, MI (organized in memory of blues pianist Otis Spann), with Muddy Waters, Dr. John, Bobby Bland and many others.

73 Shortly after suffering 2 heart attacks, Wolf is badly injured in a car crash and is hospitalized for weeks with kidney damage. He continues to gig and record sporadically, and releases *The Back Door Wolf*.

75 Nov He performs live at the Chicago Amphitheater, with B.B. King, Bobby "Blue" Bland and Little Milton, but he returns to hospital with kidney complications.

76 Jan [10] He dies in hospital in Hines, IL, following brain surgery.

91 Jan [16] Howlin' Wolf is inducted into the Rock'N'Roll Hall Of Fame at the sixth annual ceremonies at the Waldorf Astoria in New York.

THE HUMAN LEAGUE

Philip Oakey (vocals)
Martin Ware (synthesizer)
Ian Craig Marsh (synthesizer)
Adrian Wright (on stage slides, films)

77 Ware (b. May 19, 1956, Sheffield, S.Yorks.) and Marsh (b. Nov.11, 1956, Sheffield), both computer operators, form dual synthesizer band The Dead Daughters in Sheffield, the name coming from a sci-fi game, Star Force. Their synthesizer and tape-oriented approach is out of step with the Punk times.

June Addy Newton joins and the band becomes The Future, recruiting Oakey (b. Oct.2, 1955, Sheffield), a hospital porter and friend of Ware's.

Sept They re-name the group The Human League (a name taken from a computer game). Newton leaves to join Clock DVA and Wright (b. June 30, 1956, Sheffield) joins to handle "stage visuals".

78 Jan A demo of *Being Boiled*, *Circus Of Death* and *Toyota City* is recorded in Sheffield and sent to independent UK labels.

Mar On the strength of the demo, group signs to Edinburgh-based Fast Product Records, and label owner Bob Last acts as their manager.

June Debut on Fast is *Being Boiled*, Oakey's first composition. Ex-Sex Pistol Johnny Rotten hears it and dubs them "trendy hippies".

79 Mar Group tours UK as support to Siouxsie & The Banshees.

Apr Virgin Records negotiates with Fast, and announces a long-term deal with The League. Instrumental EP *Dignity Of Labour* is released on Fast.

May Band supports Iggy Pop on a European tour.

July First Virgin single, 12" *I Don't Depend On You*, is credited to The Men.

Oct Debut album *Reproduction* (containing a new recording of original demo *Circus Of Death*) and *Empire State Human* are released. The League sets up its own Monumental Pictures recording studios in Sheffield.

Dec Group is dropped from the supporting slot on a Talking Heads UK tour because its "remote-controlled entertainment" concept seems unpopular with audiences.

80 May 2-single package *Holiday '80*, with a new recording of *Being Boiled*, peaks at UK #56, as they lead the way for UK synthesizer-based acts. *Travelogue* reaches UK #16.

[15] Group begins a 12-date UK tour at the Mayfair, Newcastle, Tyne & Wear. It will end May 29 at Unity Hall, Wakefield, W.Yorks.

June *Empire State Human* is reissued, peaking at UK #62. Wright, previously their slide projectionist and lightshow operator, appears on stage as a full band member. The band appears in the new wave rock showcase movie "Urgh! A Music War".

Oct After internal disagreements, Ware and Marsh leave to form British Electric Foundation (and later Heaven 17). Oakey and Wright are left with the rights to the band's name. Bassist Ian Burden (b. Dec.24, 1957, Sheffield) is recruited from local band Graf, and Oakey brings in 2 teenage girl dancers, Joanne Catherall (b. Sept.18, 1962, Sheffield) and Suzanne Sulley (b. Mar.22, 1963, Sheffield), whom he spotted dancing in a Sheffield club where they are working as cocktail waitresses. The new group sets off for a month-long tour of Europe.

1981 Mar The new line-up introduces a more mainstream commercial sound with producer Martin Rushent. *Boys & Girls*, featuring the new girls' vocals, peaks at UK #48.

May *The Sound Of The Crowd* reaches UK #12. Jo Callis (b. May 2, 1955, Glasgow, Scotland), ex-guitarist for Scottish pop-punk band The Rezillos, is added to the line-up on synthesizer.

July Synth-dominated *Love Action (I Believe In Love)* (credited to Human League Red) hits UK #3.

Aug Debut album *Reproduction* finally charts in UK (and will climb to #49 in an almost 6-month chart stay).

Oct Group announces its biggest UK tour from the end of Nov. *Open Your Heart* (credited to Human League Blue) hits UK #6.

[31] Parent project *Dare* tops the UK chart and will remain charted for 71 weeks. (Containing the recent and future singles, this album will sell over 5 million copies worldwide.)

Dec *Don't You Want Me*, taken from the album, and featuring traded vocals between Oakey and Catherall, hits UK #1 for 5 weeks, aided by film-within-a-film video clip. It is the biggest-selling UK single of 1981, topping a million, and is also Virgin's first UK #1 single.

1982 Jan Capitalizing on the group's success, the original *Being Boiled* is reissued through EMI. Despite its dissimilarity to current League material, it hits UK #6.

Feb *Holiday '80* double-pack is reissued in UK and makes #46.

[24] Group wins Best British Newcomer at the first annual BRIT Awards at the Grosvenor House, Mayfair, London.

July *Don't You Want Me* hits US #1 for 3 weeks, and is a million-plus seller. *Dare*, on US chart since Feb., hits #3. UK mini-album *Love And Dancing* of dance-oriented re-mixes from *Dare* hits UK #3.

Sept *Love And Dancing* makes US #135.

Nov *Mirror Man* hits UK #2.

1983 May *(Keep Feeling) Fascination* also hits UK #2. (It will be the group's last recording for a year as it spends much studio time working on a new album, during which disputes with Rushent will result in his quitting the project.)

Aug *(Keep Feeling) Fascination* hits UK #8. Mini-album *Fascination!*, only released in US, reaches #22.

Nov *Mirror Man*, belatedly released in US, reaches #30.

1984 May *The Lebanon* reaches UK #11. It is a departure for the group in its highlighting of Callis' guitar and for its lyric. *Hysteria* hits UK #3 but stays charted for just 18 weeks, partly because the group refuses to tour or do any promotion for it (but later admits this was a mistake: "We thought we were so popular we didn't have to").

June *The Lebanon* peaks at US #64.

July Ballad *Life On Your Own* reaches UK #16.

Aug *Hysteria* makes US #62.

Oct Oakey teams with disco producer Giorgio Moroder for *Together In Electric Dreams*, the theme from movie "Electric Dreams", which hits UK #3 and features a Peter Frampton guitar solo.

Dec *Louise* reaches UK #13, followed by a period of public silence.

1985 Group retires to Oakey's 24-track home studio and begins recording with Colin Thurston, producer of their first album (and Magazine, Duran Duran and Kajagoogoo). Callis departs to work with Feargal Sharkey and the sessions are joined by Associates drummer Jim Russell and members of Comsat Angels.

July A second Oakey/Moroder collaboration, *Goodbye Bad Times*, makes UK #44.

Aug *Philip Oakey And Giorgio Moroder* peaks at UK #52.

Sept On the assigned released date, the new Human League album does not appear (the sessions with Thurston have been ditched).

1986 Group, now with bassist Ian Burden, travels to Minneapolis, MN, to work with Jimmy Jam and Terry Lewis, the men behind Janet Jackson's multi-platinum album *Control*, and the hottest producers of the moment. 4 months are spent in recording a new album.

Sept *Human*, the first release from the Jam/Lewis sessions, hits UK #8. *Crash* hits UK #7. It emerges that Jam and Lewis have brought in session singers and players as seen fit during the recordings. Oakey admits that the sessions had ended in acrimony, but the album re-establishes the group in the international marketplace.

THE HUMAN LEAGUE cont.

Nov [22] Ballad *Human* tops US chart, while *Crash* reaches US #24. Following re-establishment of its public profile, group plans first live performances in 4 years. *I Need Your Loving* spends a week at UK #72.

1987 **Jan** [24] *I Need Your Loving* makes US #44.

1988 **Oct** *Love Is All That Matters*, remixed from 2-year-old album *Crash*, makes UK #41.

Nov *Human League's Greatest Hits* hits UK #3, helped by a seasonal TV advertising campaign.

1990 **Sept** *Heart Like A Wheel*, previewing new album, reaches UK #29.

[23] Reuniting the band, now comprising Oakley, Sulley and Catherall with Russell Dennett (guitar) and Neil Sutton (keyboards), with producer Rushent, and after a traditionally lengthy period, Human League's sixth album *Romantic?* immediately reaches UK #24, but disappears from the survey after only 2 weeks.

Nov [10] *Heart Like A Wheel* makes US #32.

JANIS IAN

1963 Ian (b. Janis Eddy Fink, Apr.7, 1951, New York, NY), already a competent guitarist and pianist, begins her folk-styled, observational songwriting while still in junior high school, and her song *Hair Of Spun Gold* is published in the folk music magazine **Broadside**, to which she has regularly been sending her work.

1965 **July** Ian begins regular live work at New York folk haunts like the Village Gate (where she is spotted by Elektra Records, which wants to sign her as a songwriter, but passes on her as a singer) and the Gaslight club. She writes *Society's Child (Baby I've Been Thinking)*, a song dealing with older-generation hypocrisy and discrimination when faced with teenage inter-racial love and meets with producer Shadow Morton, who cuts the track. Atlantic pays for the session, but refuses to release it. 22 companies then turn it down.

1966 Jerry Schoenbaum signs her to Verve Folkways Records, which releases *Society's Child* as her debut single. Initial progress is slow, with many US radio stations banning it because of its words.

1967 **Apr** Leonard Bernstein features *Society's Child* in a TV special, which results in renewed airplay and US Singles chart debut. (**New York Times** critic Robert Shelton had given Bernstein's TV producer a copy.)

July [15] *Society's Child (Baby I've Been Thinking)* reaches US #14, and debut album *Janis Ian* makes US #29.

1968 **Jan** *For All The Seasons Of The Mind*, released on progressive Verve Forecast label, climbs to US #179.

The Secret Life Of J. Eddy Fink is released (with Richie Havens playing drums), but does not chart. Extensive US club and college touring and the demands of the pop marketplace leave her disillusioned, so she retires to live in Philadelphia, PA, where she marries.

1971 Ian returns to live appearances, and signs to Capitol Records. *Present Company* is released, but fails to sell.

1973 **Oct** Ian's ballad *Jesse*, recorded by Roberta Flack, reaches US #30.

1974 **Jan** Ian signs to CBS/Columbia, where her work will develop an introspective, sensitive style incorporating her folk roots with acquired jazz and blues influences.

July First CBS/Columbia album *Stars*, which includes her own version of *Jesse*, makes US #83. (Its title track will be covered by Cher and Glen Campbell, among others.)

1975 **Sept** [13] *At Seventeen* hits US #3, her first million-seller.

Between The Lines, which includes the hit single, tops US chart for a week, earning a gold disk for a half million sales.

1976 **Feb** [28] Ian wins Best Pop Vocal Performance, Female at the 18th annual Grammy awards. *Between The Lines* wins a grammy for Best Engineered Recording (Non-Classical) as *Aftertones* makes US #12.

1977 **Feb** [14] Ian receives 461 Valentine Day cards, after indicating that she had never received any in the lyrics of *At Seventeen*.

Mar *Miracle Row*, self-produced with Ron Frangipane, makes US #45.

1978 **Oct** Joe Wissert-produced album *Janis Ian* peaks at US #120.

1979 **Dec** *Fly Too High*, which makes UK #44 is her first UK success. It was written and recorded by Ian and producer Giorgio Moroder for movie "Foxes", starring Jodie Foster, with rhythm section Keith Forsey and Harold Faltermeyer. It is taken from *Night Rains* which fails to chart in US and UK, despite Chick Corea, Ron Carter and Bruce Springsteen's E Street Band saxophonist Clarence Clemons guesting.

1980 **July** *The Other Side Of The Sun*, also from *Night Rains* makes UK #44.

1981 **July** [18] *Under The Covers* peaks at US #71, while *Restless Eyes*, recorded in Los Angeles, CA, with producer Gary Klein, climbs to US #156. (This is Ian's final chart appearance, though she will remain a popular live performer in the singer-songwriter ranks through the 80s, before moving to Nashville, TN, at the end of the decade.)

ICEHOUSE

Iva Davies (guitar, vocals)
Guy Pratt (bass)
Andy Qunta (keyboards)
Michael Hoste (keyboards)
Bob Kretschmer (guitar)
John Lloyd (drums)

1980 **Jan** Band, formed by Davies (b. May 22, 1955), ex-teenage member of the ABC National Training Orchestra in Sydney, Australia, (with Lloyd on drums, Keith Welsh, bass and Anthony Smith, keyboards) under its original name Flowers, signs to Australian indie label, Regular Records.

May Debut single *Can't Help Myself* written by Davies, and follow-up *We Can Get Together* are Australian Top 10 hits.

Oct *Icehouse*, produced by Davies and Cameron Allan, hits AUS #4 will be one of the year's biggest sellers there and in New Zealand.

1981 **Feb** Band signs worldwide to Chrysalis Records, changing its name to Icehouse (after the album) to avoid conflict with Scots group The Flowers, and embarks on a short UK tour followed by a longer one in US and Canada.

July Icehouse returns to UK again, supporting Simple Minds.

Aug [22] *We Can Get Together* peaks at US #62.

Sept *Icehouse* makes US #82.

Nov Simple Minds supports Icehouse on Australian tour. *Love In Motion*, recorded solo by Davies, but credited to the band, hits Australian Top 10.

1982 **Jan** The original line-up splits, and Davies continues on under the Icehouse name.

May Davies records *Primitive Man* on his own, working in Sydney and Los Angeles with co-producer Keith Forsey.

Aug Needing a band to tour in support of album *Primitive Man* (which hits Australian Top 10 along with *Great Southern Land*), Davies recruits Pratt (ex-Killing Joke) and Qunta in London, and Kretschmer in Australia. Drummer Lloyd and keyboardist Hoste (who played in the early Flowers before leaving to complete his studies) rejoin.

Oct *Primitive Man* makes US #129.

Dec *Hey Little Girl* taken from the album becomes another local Top 10 hit as the band plays an extensive Australian tour.

1983 **Mar** A remix of *Hey Little Girl* reaches UK #17 and the band appears on BBC TV's "Top Of The Pops". *Primitive Man* is reissued in UK as *Love In Motion* to include the new version of the hit and makes UK #64.

May *Street Café* peaks at UK #62.

June Icehouse supports David Bowie on a major tour in UK, followed by dates in Holland.

Dec Davies completes work on soundtrack music for video director Russell Mulcahy's first feature film "Razorback", made in Australia.

1984 **June** *Sidewalk* is released, as the group embarks on tours of Europe and Australia.

1985 **Dec** "Boxes", a ballet written by Davies and Kretschmer, opens at Sydney Opera House.

1986 **May** *No Promises* peaks at UK #72, extracted from *Measure For Measure*, which reaches US #55.

Aug [9] *No Promises* stalls at US #79.

1988 **Jan** [23] Band's US chart debut, *Crazy*, reaching #14, is extracted from *Man Of Colours*, which will make US #43 during a 44-week chart stay. It has also topped Australian chart while the single hits #4.

Mar Reissued *Crazy* makes US #38.

Apr [2] *Man Of Colours* makes UK #93.

May *Electric Blue*, co-written with John Oates, also from the album *Man Of Colours*, finally gives the band a US Top 10 hit, hitting #7, but reaches only UK #53.

July [16] Follow-up *My Obsession* makes US #88.

1989 **Oct** [21] From forthcoming album, *Touch The Fire*, stalls at US #84.

1990 **Feb** *Great Southern Land* fails to score in either UK or US, though its title cut will be used extensively as the theme to Australian Tourist Board commercials worldwide.

BILLY IDOL

1976 **Aug** Already seen on UK television as a Sex Pistols fan follower on the group's notorious Bill Grundy hosted "Today" TV shocker and a member of the band's dedicated Bromley contingent fan annex, Idol (b. William Broad, Nov.30, 1955, Stanmore, London.) meets bassist Tony James, ex London S.S. and future Sigue Sigue Sputnik, equally keen on the burgeoning UK punk movement. Within 2 weeks of meeting, they join Gene October's Chelsea, with Idol playing guitar.

Oct [18] Idol makes his first formal live appearance with Chelsea at the ICA, London. Within 2 months, however, both he and James will quit the band taking drummer John Towe with them.

Dec [10] Also recruiting guitarist Bob Andrews, allowing Idol to assume full lead vocal role, new punk combo Generation X makes its live debut at the Central College of Art and Design, London.

[21] Generation X baptises the Roxy Club, Covent Garden, London.

77 July Having grabbed attention via a 4-song "John Peel Show" Radio 1 session, the band signs to Chrysalis.

Sept First release *Your Generation*, a sound of the times, makes UK #36. (Before the end of the decade, Generation X, billed as Gen X from late 1979, will have 4 more UK chart singles: *Ready Steady Go* (#47, Mar.1978), *King Rocker* (#11, Jan.1979), *Valley Of The Dolls* (#23, Apr.1979) and *Friday's Angels* (#62, June 1979) and the albums *Generation X* (#29, Apr.1978) and *Valley Of The Dolls* (#51, Feb.1979). John Towe will leave in Dec.1977 to join The Adverts and be replaced by Mark Laff.)

80 Oct *Dancing With Myself*, a masturbation-themed Idol-penned single, which he will retain in his solo repertoire, stalls at UK #62 for Gen X.

Nov Andrews and Laff quit, but Idol and James are determined to continue and recruit ex-Clash drummer Terry Chimes and Chelsea's James Stephenson on guitar.

81 Final Gen X album *Kiss Me Deadly* fails to score and reissued *Dancing With Myself* stalls at UK #60. Idol, additionally dissatisfied and the lack of creative control he has with the label, quits the band and heads for New York, where he links with Kiss manager Bill Aucoin and producer Keith Forsey, both of whom will help steer his solo career. Idol forms a new band around himself, with New York guitarist Steve Stevens a key element. Aucoin secures Idol an ongoing solo Chrysalis contract with a $250-a-week retainer.

Nov Debut solo album *Don't Stop*, produced by Forsey and already directing Idol away from the rawness of punk toward more mainstream new wave rock, reaches US #71, and includes a solo version of *Dancing With Myself*. It will remain charted for over a year but will fail in his native UK, where his solo records will always prove significantly less popular.

82 Sept Hot summer rock anthem, *Hot In The City* makes US radio breakthrough to reach US #23 (and UK #58) and spurs parent second album *Billy Idol*, again Forsey-helmed, to US #45 during a 2-year residence.

83 July [2] Demonic rock-driven *White Wedding* makes US #36.

Dec *Rebel Yell* is released set to hit US #6. His most accessible rock outing to date, it will eventually earn double platinum.

84 Mar [24] *Rebel Yell* makes US #46 and UK #62.

July Idol finally has a major UK hit when melodic *Eyes Without A Face* reaches #18. It also becomes his biggest US single, hitting US #4.

Sept Always eager to explore sexual themes, *Flesh For Fantasy* is a disappointing UK #54, but US #29.

Dec [8] *Catch My Fall* makes US #50.

85 Jan Idol is controversially featured on the cover of the Jan.31 issue of **Rolling Stone** magazine, wearing even less of his rock bondage gear than usual and showing a considerable area of buttock.

June Chrysalis UK releases compilation album *Vital Idol*. It initially spends 6 months on chart, hitting UK #7.

July *White Wedding* is re-released in UK, for the third time, and hits #6.

Sept Reissued *Rebel Yell* hits #6, while its parent album *Rebel Yell* makes UK #36 3 years after its original US success.

86 Oct *To Be A Lover* reaches UK #22.

Nov Fourth solo album *Whiplash Smile* hits UK #8.

Dec [20] *To Be A Lover* hits US #6, as parent album *Whiplash Smile* hits US #6.

87 Mar [7] *Don't Need A Gun* reaches UK #26 and US #37.

June [27] Idol-penned acoustic guitar-led ballad *Sweet Sixteen* reaches US #20.

July *Sweet Sixteen* climbs to UK #17.

Oct Revived Tommy James & The Shondells' *Mony Mony* hits UK #7.

Nov [21] *Mony Mony "Live"* tops US chart, as *Vital Idol* hits US #10.

88 Jan The "exterminator" mix of *Hot In The City* returns it to the UK chart at #13.

[23] *Hot In The City* also re-charts in US at #48.

June Idol and girlfriend Perri Lister have a son, Willem Wolf Broad.

July A second compilation album *Idol Songs – 11 Of The Best* hits UK #2, as Idol takes a lengthy recording hiatus.

Aug A belated release of *Catch My Fall* makes UK #63.

89 Aug [24] Idol takes part in a benefit production of Pete Townshend's "Tommy" at Universal Amphitheater, Universal City, CA, playing the role of Kevin, with Elton John as The Pinball Wizard, Steve Winwood as The Hawker, Patti LaBelle as The Acid Queen) and Phil Collins as Uncle Ernie.

1990 Feb [6] Idol is hospitalized at Cedars-Sinai Medical Center, Los Angeles, after fracturing his right leg and left wrist in a motorcycle accident after apparently running a stop sign and smashing into a car.

June [23] With Stevens departed to solo projects, *Charmed Life*, showing Idol's sneer to be intact despite his accident, featuring new axeman TX guitarist Mark Younger-Smith, reaches US #11 and UK #15.

July Idol performs impromptu duets at Los Angeles' nightclub Spice with Tom Jones, singing *Got To Be Your Lover*, *Great Balls Of Fire* and *Babaloo*.

Aug [4] *Cradle Of Love*, aided by teen-babe MTV award-winning video clip, hits US #2, but has stalled at UK #34. (It will also be featured in Andrew Dice Clay movie "The Adventures Of Ford Fairlane".)

[25] "Charmed Life" tour begins in Montreal, Canada, with Idol happily brandishing his walking stick.

Oct [6] Revival of The Doors' *L.A. Woman* makes US #52 and UK #70.

Nov At the end of the month, Idol has to cancel 4 European dates on his "Charmed Life" tour after his corneas are lacerated by grit following an outdoor gig in Norway.

1991 Jan [20] Idol performs at "Rock In Rio II" festival at the Maracana soccer stadium in Rio de Janeiro, Brazil.

THE IMPRESSIONS

Jerry Butler (vocals)
Curtis Mayfield (vocals)
Arthur Brooks (vocals)
Richard Brooks (vocals)
Sam Gooden (vocals)

1957 3 members of a Tennessee vocal quintet, The Roosters, Brooks brothers Arthur (b. Chattanooga, TN) and Richard (b. Chattanooga) with Gooden (b. Sept.2, 1939, Chattanooga), relocate to Chicago, IL, leaving behind Fred Cash (b. Oct.8, 1940, Chattanooga,) and Emanuel Thomas. Songwriter/producer Butler (b. Dec.8, 1939, Sunflower, MS) joins as a temporary replacement and recruits his friend Curtis Mayfield (b. June 3, 1942, Chicago) to make the line-up a quintet. Their releases on small Chicago labels, Bandera *Listen To Me* and Swirl *Don't Leave Me*, fail.

1958 Group demos *Pretty Baby* and *My Baby Loves Me* for Vee-Jay label. Vi Muszynski, having heard the group, decides to make them the first act on her label, which she is trying to link up with Vee-Jay, but negotiations break down and the group signs directly to Vee-Jay.

Apr Under the supervision of Vee-Jay A&R man Calvin Carter, and rechristened The Impressions, the group records 4 songs, 2 written by Butler and the Brooks brothers.

May One of these, *For Your Precious Love*, is the group's first single, credited to Jerry Butler & The Impressions.

Aug *For Your Precious Love* peaks at US #11. Its success prompts Butler to go solo and he is replaced by original Rooster Cash. But, without Butler's name, the group fades into obscurity and 2 further Vee-Jay singles fail. The Impressions temporarily split and Mayfield earns a living playing guitar on Butler's records and writing songs for him, including hits *Let It Be Me* and *He Will Break Your Heart*.

1959 Mayfield re-forms the group, now clearly the leader and songwriter, and it moves to New York.

1960 He secures The Impressions a contract with ABC/Paramount.

1961 Dec More than a year after signing with the label, *Gypsy Woman* reaches US #20.

1962 Feb *Grow Closer Together* spends a week at US #99.

July *Little Young Lover* reaches US #96.

1963 Feb *I'm The One Who Loves You* peaks at US #73. Mayfield returns to Chicago, taking Cash and Gooden with him. The Brooks brothers stay in New York.

May The first single as a trio, *Sad, Sad Girl And Boy*, peaks at US #84.

Sept Debut album *The Impressions*, featuring Johnny Pate's arrangement of a strong horn section and gospel-style vocal interplay, reaches US #43.

Nov The Impressions' biggest success is *It's All Right*, which hits US #4. As they begin to influence other acts, Major Lance and Gene Chandler make Mayfield's songs (chiefly through his role as staff producer at Okeh Records), as do UK R&B groups.

1964 Feb *Talking About My Baby* reaches US #12.

May *I'm So Proud* makes US #14, while *The Never-Ending Impressions* climbs to US #52.

July Gospel-flavored *Keep On Pushing* hits US #10.

THE IMPRESSIONS cont.

Oct *You Must Believe Me* reaches US #15, while the group's biggest-selling album, **Keep On Pushing**, hits US #8.

1965 **Jan** Taken from the album, Mayfield-penned gospel song *Amen* hits US #7 and is featured in film "Lilies Of The Field".

Mar *People Get Ready*, reflecting Mayfield's increasing social awareness, makes US #14. (It will be a hit for Aretha Franklin and covered by dozens of artists.)

Apr *People Get Ready* makes US #23 and **The Impressions' Greatest Hits** reaches US #83.

May Upbeat R&B *Woman's Got Soul* reaches US #29.

June *Meeting Over Yonder* makes US #48.

Sept *I Need You* peaks at US #64.

Oct *Just One Kiss From You* falters at US #76 while **One By One** makes US #104.

1966 **Jan** *You've Been Cheatin'* makes US #33. Mayfield sets up his own record label, Windy C. (He signs The Five Stairsteps and June Conquest, but after only 7 releases, the label folds.)

Feb *Since I Lost The One I Love* peaks at US #90.

Mar *Ridin' High* reaches US #79.

Apr *Too Slow* peaks at US #91.

Sept *Can't Satisfy* makes US #65.

1967 **Mar** *You Always Hurt Me* reaches US #96.

July **The Fabulous Impressions** makes US #184.

Sept *I Can't Stay Away From You* peaks at US #80.

Dec With *We're A Winner*, Mayfield explicitly confronts black politics and the disk is partly banned by US radio.

1968 **Feb** Despite radio censorship, *We're A Winner* reaches US #14. It is the group's last single for ABC. When the contract expires Mayfield and Thomas establish their Curtom label.

Apr ABC continues to release existing Impressions material. **We're A Winner** makes US #35, the group's best placing in 3 years.

May *We're Rolling On (Part 1)* reaches US #59.

Aug *I Loved And I Lost* climbs to US #61.

Oct *Fool For You*, the first Curtom single, reaches US #22. ABC compilation album **The Best Of The Impressions** peaks at US #172.

Dec On Curtom, *This Is My Country* reaches US #25, while on ABC *Don't Cry My Love* makes US #71.

1969 **May** *Seven Years* climbs to US #84.

June **The Young Mods' Forgotten Story** reaches US #104.

Aug *Choice Of Colors*, from the album, makes US #21.

Nov Also from the album, *Say You Love Me* reaches US #58.

1970 Mayfield quits The Impressions to go solo but continues to oversee all aspects of their career, writing and producing some of their Curtom releases and recruiting his replacement, Leroy Hutson.

June *Check Out Your Mind* reaches US #28.

Sept *(Baby) Turn On To Me* peaks at US #56.

1971 **Mar** *Ain't Got Time* makes US #53. ABC compilation album **16 Greatest Hits** peaks at US #180.

Aug *Love Me* is the last Mayfield-penned Impressions song to chart, reaching US #94.

1972 **Apr** *Times Have Changed* spends 2 weeks at US #192.

1973 **Mar** **Curtis Mayfield/His Early Years With The Impressions** charts at US #180.

Hutson leaves for a solo career. Cash and Gooden recruit Reggie Torian and Ralph Johnson and this line-up records the soundtrack for movie "Three The Hard Way". Chicago TV station WTTW reassembles most of the original Impressions, the 60s line-up and the current group for TV special "Curtis". (Most of the sound recordings will later be released on **Curtis In Chicago**.)

1974 **July** Still with Curtom, The Impressions reach US #17 with *Finally Got Myself Together*, written and produced by Ed Townsend. **Finally Got Myself Together** makes US #176.

1975 **July** *Sooner Or Later* peaks at US #68.

Aug **First Impressions** makes US #115.

Nov *Same Thing* peaks at US #75.

Dec The title track from **First Impressions** becomes the group's only UK chart entry – reaching #16.

1976 Johnson leaves to form his own group, Mystique. He is replaced by Nate Evans.

Mar *Loving Power* makes US #195.

1977 **Feb** **The Vintage Years**, featuring 13 hits by The Impressions and 13 by Jerry Butler solo, reaches US #199.

1981 **Sept** *Fan The Fire* and album of the same title, released through 20th Century, fail to sell. (Mayfield is now working for Neil Bogart's Boardwalk label.)

1982 **In The Heat Of The Night** is released on MCA.

1983 Butler and Mayfield briefly rejoin the group for a reunion tour.

1991 **Jan** [16] The Impressions are inducted into the Rock'N'Roll Hall Of Fame at the sixth annual ceremonies at New York's Waldorf Astoria.

JAMES INGRAM

1973 Ingram moves to Los Angeles, CA, from Akron, OH, with band Revelation Funk. He will spend 2 years touring with Ray Charles, playing piano and singing background vocals, before becoming Leon Haywood's musical director, playing on his hit single *Don't Push It Don't Force It*. He will also play keyboards for The Coasters on Dick Clark's oldies package tours, and begin working for publishing company ATV, singing on demos.

1980 Russ Titelman sends Quincy Jones a demo of Barry Mann and Cynthia Weil's *Just Once* with Ingram the vocalist. Jones invites Ingram to be one of the featured vocalists on his album **The Dude**.

Aug Ingram sings backing vocals on Carl Carlton's US #22 hit *She's A Bad Mama Jama*.

Nov Soul ballad *Just Once*, from **The Dude**, credited to Quincy Jones, but sung by Ingram, reaches US #17.

1981 **Feb** [25] Ingram performs *Just Once* at the 23rd annual Grammy awards. He is nominated in 3 categories: Best New Artist, Best Pop Male Vocal and Best R&B Vocal.

Jones invites him to tour Japan, where he performs in front of 20,000 people backed by Jones' 50-piece orchestra.

1982 **Feb** Ingram song *Hold On* is covered by sax man Ernie Watts on his album **Chariots Of Fire**.

[24] Ingram wins Best R&B Vocal Performance, Male for *One Hundred Ways* at the 24th annual Grammy awards, the only artist to do so without having released an album.

Mar *One Hundred Ways*, from Jones' **The Dude**, reaches US #14.

May *Baby Come To Me*, a duet with Qwest labelmate Patti Austin, peaks at US #73.

Dec Ingram joins a star cast of singers to back Donna Summer on *State Of Independence*.

1983 **Feb** *Baby Come To Me*, used and revived as the love theme for ABC TV soap "General Hospital", tops US chart for 2 weeks, prior to Michael Jackson's *Billie Jean*.

Apr Ingram joins Austin on stage at the 1982 Academy Awards to sing *How Do You Keep The Music Playing?*. Producer Quincy Jones assembles an all-star cast of musicians and writers for Ingram's debut album including Larry Carlton (guitar), David Paich, Michael McDonald, David Foster, Greg Phillinganes, Jimmy Smith (keyboards, synthesizers), Louis Johnson and Nathan East (bass), Harvey Mason (drums) and Watts and Tom Scott (reeds). Work starts on the album at Westlake Audio studios, Los Angeles, CA.

Aug *How Do You Keep The Music Playing?*, the theme to Goldie Hawn/Burt Reynolds movie "Best Friends", makes US #45.

Nov Debut album **It's Your Night** is released, and goes gold despite peaking at only US #46.

Dec Michael Jackson's *P.Y.T. (Pretty Young Thing)*, written by Ingram, hits US #10.

1984 **Jan** Ingram guests on a 2-hour Quincy Jones US TV special.

Mar *Yah Mo B There*, an inspirational duet with Michael McDonald, reaches US #19.

Apr Barry Mann-penned *There's No Easy Way* peaks at US #58. **It's Your Night** reaches UK #25. Michael Jackson's *P.Y.T. (Pretty Young Thing)* reaches UK #11.

Dec *What About Me?*, sung with Kenny Rogers and Kim Carnes, and produced by David Foster, reaches US #15.

1985 **Feb** A remixed *Yah Mo B There* reaches UK #12, after 2 false starts the previous year (#44 Feb. and #69 Apr.).

[26] Ingram and McDonald win Best R&B Performance By A Duo Or Group With Vocal for *Yah Mo Be There* at the 27th annual Grammy awards.

1986 **Aug** Second album **Never Felt So Good** is released. Produced by Keith Diamond, it makes US #123 and UK #72, but sees no UK or US chart singles action.

1987 **Mar** [14] Ballad *Somewhere Out There*, with Linda Ronstadt, from Spielberg-produced animated movie "An American Tail", hits US #2.

July *Better Way*, featured in film "Beverly Hills Cop II", peaks at #66 on US R&B chart.

Aug *Somewhere Out There* hits UK #8.

1988 **Mar** [2] *Somewhere Out There* wins a Grammy for Song Of The Year at 30th annual Grammy awards.

July Ingram guests on Patti Austin's **The Real Me**.

Oct [20] *I Don't Have The Heart*, co-produced with Thom Bell, tops US chart. (After 7 previous Top 40 hits, either uncredited or a part of a duo, this is Ingram's first solo hit.)
Nov [10] *It's Real*, originally released in 1989, climbs to US #117.

INXS

Michael Hutchence (vocals)
Tim Farriss (guitar)
Kirk Pengilly (guitar, saxophone, vocals)
Andrew Farriss (keyboards)
Garry Beers (bass, vocals)
Jon Farriss (drums, vocals)

'79 Sept [1] Having originally formed as The Farris Brothers in Sydney, Australia in 1977, to play their debut at member Tim Farriss' 20th birthday party and spent 1978 writing and performing in Perth, Australia, newly named INXS (with its original 6-member line-up of Hutchence, the Farriss brothers, Pengilly and Beers, remaining unchanged throughout its history, is back in its native Sydney and performs its first concert under its new name at the Oceanview Hotel, Toukley. Band will spend the next 4 years playing over 200 pub and club gigs a year and build up a dedicated and large Australian rock fan following.

'80 May Debut single *Simple Simon/We Are The Vegetables* is released in Australia on Deluxe label.
Oct Debut album *INXS* is issued and the group has its first Australian hit with *Just Keep Walking*.

'81 INXS plays 300 dates in Australia during the "Fear And Loathing Tour", "The Campus Tour", "Stay Young Tour" and "The Tour With No Name".
Mar *The Loved One* (which will be re-recorded in 1987 for album *Kick*) is released.
Oct Group signs to RCA, releasing its second Australia-only album *Underneath The Colours*, which includes native hits *Stay Young* and *Loved One*, while lead singer Hutchence also appears on 2 songs with Cold Chisel on the Australian movie "Freedom" soundtrack (*Speed Kills* and *Forest Theme*).

'82 Jan Group tours New Zealand, and on its return records *The One Thing*.
Apr Hutchence, Pengilly and Andrew Farriss travel to UK and US to consider the next stage in INXS' career.
July WEA signs the group for Australasia, releasing its third album *Shabooh Shoobah*.

'83 Jan INXS signs to Atlantic in US and embarks on a tour as guests of The Kinks and Adam & The Ants.
Mar Group makes its US debut with *The One Thing* which, with a heavy rotation promo video on MTV, reaches #30. *Shabooh Shoobah* makes US #46, while *Don't Change* is the group's first (unsuccessful) UK release.
May Band's first New York headlining date is at The Ritz.
July *Don't Change* reaches US #80.
Sept *Original Sin* is recorded at New York's Power Station studio, with Nile Rodgers producing and Daryl Hall and Dave Stewart guesting on vocals.
Oct Mini-album *Dekadence*, with remixes of 4 tracks from *Shabooh Shoobah*, reaches US #148.

'84 Jan Group plays a sell-out Australian tour as *Original Sin* tops the local chart.
May INXS' UK live debut is at the Astoria theater, London, at the beginning of a determined effort to introduce the band to a worldwide audience. *Original Sin* reaches US #58.
June *The Swing* makes US #52.
July The first 2 albums, *INXS* and *Underneath The Colours*, are belatedly released in US.
Aug *I Send A Message* peaks at US #77 and *INXS* reaches US #164.
Sept Group sets out on a 3-month US tour concluding with a sell-out show at the Hollywood Palladium. A video collection, "The Swing And Other Stories", documenting the band's Australian history, is heavily featured on MTV and is vital in breaking them in the US.
Nov Returning home, INXS stops off at Guam in the Pacific, becoming the first international group to play there.

'85 Mar INXS starts work on fifth album *Listen Like Thieves* at Sydney's Rhinoceros studios, with Chris Thomas producing. *The Swing* achieves double-platinum status in Australia.
July [13] Group appears at the Australian venue of the Live Aid concert, beamed worldwide by satellite.

Aug Work finishes at London's AIR studios on *Listen Like Thieves*.
[28] "The 1985 INXS World Tour" commences in Australia.
Nov In mid-tour, the group briefly returns home to perform at the "Rockin' The Royals" charity concert in the presence of the Prince and Princess of Wales.
Dec *This Time* reaches US #81. Video *The Swing And Other Stories* is issued in US by Atlantic Video, and in UK by Channel 5. By year's end INXS will have collected 7 trophies at Australian Countdown Awards.

1986 Feb Signed to Mercury in UK, *Listen Like Thieves* makes UK #48.
Apr [12] *What You Need* hits US #5, and will peak at UK #51. Hutchence makes his acting debut in movie "Dogs In Space", and has a solo Top 10 hit in Australia with *Rooms For The Memory*, from the film.
May Group embarks on "If You Got It, Shake It!" world tour, highlighted by 2 sell-out shows supporting Queen at London's Wembley Stadium.
June [14] *Listen Like Thieves* peaks at US #54, and will make UK #46.
Listen Like Thieves reaches US #11.
Sept *Kiss The Dirt (Falling Down The Mountain)* makes UK #54. Group returns home for "Si Lo Tienes Muevelo" tour.
Oct Video "What You Need" is released.

1987 Jan Group heads a major Australian tour with 8 other bands under the banner "Australian Made".
Aug [1] *Good Times*, from the movie "The Lost Boys" and teaming the group with singing compatriot Jimmy Barnes, makes US #47.
Oct *Need You Tonight* reaches UK #58.
[16] INXS' 1987-88 world tour opens in East Lansing, MI.
Dec [2-14] Group tours UK.

1988 Jan [30] Guitar-stuttered *Need You Tonight* becomes its first US #1 hit, aided not least by round-the-clock MTV video exposure.
Kick hits US #3 and UK #9. *New Sensation* makes UK #25.
Mar *Devil Inside* reaches US #47, hitting US #2 4 weeks later.
June [24] INXS sells out Wembley Arena, London, during its European tour. (Jon Farriss is injured in a skateboard fall, causing the rest of the tour to be cancelled.)
July *Never Tear Us Apart* reaches UK #24 and hits US #7.
Aug Video compilation "Kick Flicks" is released, while *New Sensation*, the fourth single from *Kick*, which is on its way to 4 RIAA certified platinum disks, heads toward US #3.
Dec Reissued *Need You Tonight* hits UK #2.

1989 Hutchence forms Max Q with Ollie Olsen of Australian band No.
Apr Further *Kick* extract, *Mystify*, reaches UK #14.
Nov Max Q debut album *Max Q*, also on UK Mercury, makes UK #65 and US #182 (on Atlantic), both INXS respective territory labels.

1990 Feb Max Q's dance remixed *Sometimes* makes UK #53.
May [4] Roger Corman's "Frankenstein Unbound", in which Hutchence plays Percy Shelley, opens in cinemas across the US.
Sept From forthcoming album, *Suicide Blonde* reaches UK #11.
Oct [20] *X*, recorded in Rhinoceros Studio 2, Sydney, and their third consecutive album produced by Chris Thomas, and featuring harmonica great Charlie Musselthwaite, hits US #5, having already hit UK #2.
[27] *Suicide Blonde* hits US #9.
Nov [25-26] During "X" world tour, band performs sell-out UK dates at the London Arena, Docklands, 2 of 11 UK concerts.
Dec [15] *Disappear* reaches UK #24.

1991 Jan [19] Band performs at "Rock In Rio II" on the festival's second day at the Maracana soccer stadium in Rio de Janiero, Brazil, before an estimated 100,000 fans.
Feb [3] INXS appears on NBC TV's "Saturday Night Live", while they are in US for major concert appearances.
[10] INXS wins Best International Group and Hutchence wins Best International Artist, Male at the 10th annual BRIT Awards at the Dominion theater, London.
[16] *Disappear* hits US #8.
Mar 24-video clip collection, including 5 MTV Award winners, "INXS Video – Greatest Hits 1980-1990" is released.
Apr [6] *By My Side* makes UK #42.
May [4] *Bitter Tears* climbs to US #47, and continues to rise.
[12] INXS appear by satellite from Australia in "The Simple Truth" concert for Kurdish refugees at Wembley Arena, London.

IRON BUTTERFLY

Doug Ingle (vocals, keyboards)
Erik Braunn (guitar, vocals)
Lee Dorman (bass)
Ronald Bushy (drums)

1966 Formed in San Diego, CA, by Ingle (b. Sept.9, 1946, Omaha, NB), the son of a church organist, Bushy (b. Sept.23, 1945, Washington, DC), bassist Jerry Penrod (b. San Diego), guitarist Danny Weis (b. San Diego) and vocalist Darryl DeLoach (b. San Diego), Iron Butterfly relocates to Los Angeles, CA.

1967 Group works at Bido Lito's, the Galaxy and the Whisky A-Go-Go and signs to Atlantic Records' subsidiary Atco.

1968 **Mar** *Heavy* climbs to US #78 during a 49-week stay on the chart, sustained by touring as the opening act for The Doors and Jefferson Airplane. DeLoach quits and Penrod and Weis leave to form Rhinoceros. Dorman (b. Sept.19, 1945, St. Louis, MO) and Braunn (b. Aug.11, 1950, Boston, MA) replace them.
May Iron Butterfly's *Possession* and *Unconscious Power* are featured with material from Cream in film "Savage Seven".
July *In-A-Gadda-Da-Vida* enters US chart and will hit #4.
Aug Iron Butterfly plays at Newport Pop Festival at Costa Mesa, CA.
Oct [26] *In-A-Gadda-Da-Vida*, edited from the 17-min. album version, reaches US #30.
Dec Group joins a star bill for the 3-day Miami Pop Festival at Hallendale, FL.

1969 **Feb** *Ball* enters US chart and will hit #3.
Mar [15] *Soul Experience* peaks at US #75.
June Group joins Joe Cocker, Creedence Clearwater Revival, Jimi Hendrix and many others on the bill of the Denver Pop Festival held at the Mile High Stadium, Denver, CO.
July [4-5] Group plays New York's Fillmore East, with Blues Image.
[19] *In The Time Of Our Lives* makes US #96.
Aug Iron Butterfly performs at the 3-day Atlantic City Pop Festival in New Jersey.
Sept Braunn quits, later forming Flintwhistle with DeLoach and Penrod. Guitarists Larry Reinhardt and ex-Blues Image Mike Pinera replace him.

1970 **May** *Iron Butterfly Live* reaches US #20.
Aug *Metamorphosis*, with new members Pinera and Reinhardt, makes US #16. Pinera proclaims: "You gotta change, you better get hip."
Nov [21] *Easy Rider (Let The Wind Pay The Way)*, from cult movie success "Easy Rider", on which Iron Butterfly sings the title track, peaks at US #66.

1971 **Apr** *In-A-Gadda-Da-Vida* drops off US chart after 140 weeks, selling over 3 million copies and is Atlantic Records' biggest album success. (It will remain so until the advent of Led Zeppelin.)
May [23] Group splits after its farewell live appearance.

1972 **Jan** *The Best Of Iron Butterfly/Evolution* makes US #137.
1973 Compilation album *Star Collection* is released.
1975 **Feb** Braunn and Bushy regroup with Phil Kramer (b. July 12, 1952, Youngtown, OH) and Howard Reitzes (b. Mar.22, 1951, Southgate, CA) to sign with MCA Records, releasing albums *Scorching Beauty* (US #138) and *Sun And Steel* before splitting again.

IRON MAIDEN

Bruce Dickinson (vocals)
Dave Murray (lead, rhythm guitar)
Adrian Smith (guitar)
Dennis Stratton (guitar)
Steve Harris (bass)
Nicko McBrain (drums)
Eddie

1976 **May** Harris (b. Mar.12, 1957, Leytonstone, London), after earlier ambitions to be a professional soccer player, having formed pub band Smiler, meets Murray (b. Dec.23, 1958, London) and forms new group Iron Maiden (named after the medieval instrument of torture from **The Man In The Iron Mask**), determined to keep heavy metal alive in face of the new punk wave. Band features Harris (the only original member to remain in future line-ups), Murray (b. Dec.23, 1958), vocalist Paul Di'anno (b. May 17, 1959, Chingford, London) and drummer Doug Sampson. Iron Maiden's live debut is at the Cart & Horses pub, Stratford, in London's East End.

1977 The new band bases itself in Leytonstone, London, and plays local live gigs in the summer.

1978 Group powers through regular stints at London pubs the Bridgehouse, Canning Town, and Ruskin Arms, East Ham. Despite constant gigging it is unable to interest any A&R men. Cult following develops and Iron Maiden releases an EP of demos, recorded on Dec.30, featuring *Iron Maiden*, *Prowler* and *Strange World* on its own label. DJ Neal Kay of the Bandwaggon Soundhouse in London is sent a copy and the tape becomes a massive heavy metal club hit. Iron Maiden will appear regularly at the Soundhouse over the next 12 months.

1979 **Feb** Band has £12,000 worth of equipment stolen from its van. (Ilkay Bayram from London is later convicted of theft, and most of the equipment is returned.)
May DJ Kay organizes his "Heavy Metal Crusade" at London's Music Machine. Iron Maiden appears in what is remembered as the first concert of the "New Wave Of British Heavy Metal" (NWBHM), a phrase coined by **Sounds** journalist Geoff Barton.
June Roderick Smallwood from the MAM Agency hears the demo and invites the band to play at the Windsor Castle and the Swan pubs, subsequently finding them nationwide UK gigs. Di'anno is arrested for carrying a knife.
Oct A showcase at London's Marquee is ignored by every major label.
Nov EP *The Soundhouse Tapes* is released through mail-order, having been recorded a year earlier in Cambridge. New guitarist Tony Parsons joins and they record 2 tracks for compilation album *Metal For Muthas*, released through EMI.
[28] Group signs with EMI Records.

1980 **Jan** Parsons is replaced by Stratton (b. Nov.9, 1954, London), ex-Remus Down Boulevard. Sampson leaves for health reasons and is replaced by Clive Burr.
Feb Debut single *Running Free* reaches UK #34. Band refuses to mime on BBC TV's "Top Of The Pops", becoming the first act to play live on the show since The Who in 1973.
Apr Debut album *Iron Maiden* hits UK #4, helped by a UK tour with Judas Priest.
June *Sanctuary* reaches UK #29. On its sleeve, Derek Riggs, the group's artistic designer, depicts Iron Maiden's mechanical psycho-killing mascot Eddie knife-slashing PM Margaret Thatcher. After legal threats her eyes are blacked out. EMI holds a special Iron Maiden party at Madame Tussaud's Chamber of Horrors.
[20] Band plays at the Rainbow theater, London.
Aug Iron Maiden is featured on ITV show "20th Century Box" special on NWBHM, as it begins a European tour backing Kiss.
[23] They play at the Reading Festival, Berks.
Oct Stratton is fired, replaced by ex-Urchin guitarist Smith (b. Feb.27, 1957, London).
Nov *Woman In Uniform*, with picture sleeve featuring PM Thatcher waiting for revenge on Eddie holding a machine gun, climbs to UK #35. Eddie is introduced as part of the live act (and will grow in physical and popular stature over the coming years).

1981 **Feb** Half live, half studio album *Killers*, containing 4 new tracks, reaches UK #12 and US #78.
Mar *Twilight Zone/Wrath Child* makes UK #31.
May Iron Maiden begins a sold-out Japanese tour, as part of its "The Killer World Tour" set to play in 15 countries, and during which it will make its US debut again opening for Judas Priest.
June *Purgatory* makes UK #52.
Sept At the end of the tour, Di'anno leaves. He will continue to record with Lone Wolf and Battlezone.
Oct He is replaced by ex-Samson vocalist and private school educated Dickinson (b. Paul Bruce Dickinson, Aug.7, 1958, Worksop, Notts., but raised from age 4 in Sheffield, S.Yorks.), who has spent a short time in the Infantry before going to Queen Mary College, London University to study history. After playing with the group Speed, he then joins Shots with Tony Lee and Doug and Tony Siviter, and is seen by 2 members of Samson singing in the Prince of Wales pub in Gravesend, Kent. He is invited to join, and after finishing his history degree examinations in the summer of 1979, becomes the group's lead singer. Live EP *Maiden Japan* peaks at UK #43 and US #89.
Nov [15] Dickinson makes his live debut with Iron Maiden.
Dec Group plays a pub gig as Genghis Khan.

1982 **Feb** [25] "Beast On The Road" tour begins in Dunstable, Beds., set to end 11 months later in Niggata, Japan. During the 179-date, 16-country sojourn, they will play to over a million people.
Mar *Run To The Hills* hits UK #7. It is also their first video to be shown on US MTV.
Apr [10] Iron Maiden knocks Barbra Streisand off the top spot as *The Number Of The Beast*, produced by Martin Birch, hits UK #1. It reaches

US #33 (where it will have a 65-week chart run and earn a gold disk). Group relocates to the Bahamas for tax purposes.

May *The Number Of The Beast* reaches UK #18.

[11] Group begins a 6-month US leg of "Beast On The Road" tour in Flint, MI, set to end on Oct.23 in Rochester, NY, including a sold-out date at the Palladium, New York on June 29, where a larger (12') than life Eddie holds aloft a "bitten-off" head of Ozzy Osbourne. (Dickinson will wear a surgical collar for some of the gigs, a result of too much head-banging.)

July A soccer match with The Scorpions ends in 0-0 tie.

Aug Band flies from El Paso, TX, to London, to make a one-off performance at the annual Reading Rock Festival, Berks. After their appearance, they will fly to Los Angeles to continue the tour.

'83 Jan Drummer Burr quits the line-up amicably, to be replaced by McBrain (b. June 5, 1954), ex-Trust, a French band which had supported on Iron Maiden's 1981 UK tour, and Streetwalkers.

May *Flight Of Icarus* peaks at UK #11. *Piece Of Mind*, recorded in Nassau, hits UK #3 and US #14 (where it will become platinum).

[2] 4-month "World Piece" universal tour, including their first headlining US dates, begins at the City Hall, Hull, Humberside.

July *The Trooper* reaches UK #12.

Dec Readers of UK heavy metal magazine *Kerrang* vote *Piece Of Mind* and *The Number Of The Beast* the top 2 heavy metal albums of all time. Iron Maiden wins a soccer match against Def Leppard in Germany 4–2.

'84 Aug *2 Minutes To Midnight* reaches UK #11. The "World Slavery" tour begins in Poland (running through to July 1985 ending in Southern California after 200 shows).

Sept [11] UK leg of the "World Slavery" tour begins at the Apollo theater, Glasgow, Scotland.

Oct [8] Group plays first of 4 sell-out dates at the Hammersmith Odeon, London, at the end of the 24-date UK leg.

Nov *Aces High* reaches UK #20. *Powerslave*, recorded at Le Chalet, France, hits UK #2 and reaches US #21.

'85 Mar [14-17] Iron Maiden plays sell-out dates at the Long Beach Arena, CA, during US tour.

Apr The "World Slavery" tour continues through South-East Asia.

June *Iron Maiden* is reissued, reaching UK #71.

July [5] "World Slavery" tour ends in California with a "British Independence Day Celebration" concert.

Oct *Live Running Free* makes UK #19. Their recent 11-month, 26-country tour is documented by double album *Live After Death*, which will hit UK #2 and US #19.

Dec Live *Run To The Hills* makes UK #26. Group plays a gig at the Marquee in London as *The Entire Population Of Hackney*.

'86 Sept *Wasted Years* peaks at UK #18. *Somewhere In Time* hits UK #3 and US #11, and marks the beginning of yet another tour.

Nov *Stranger In A Strange Land* reaches UK #22. Band plays a charity gig at London's Hammersmith Odeon with special guests, the heavy metal pastiche combo Bad News.

'87 Jan Dickinson is arrested in Lubbock, TX, for allegedly hitting someone with a microphone and then strangling him with the cord back in Mar.1985.

May Iron Maiden finishes a 7-month world tour and begins work on a new studio project.

'88 Apr [23] *Seventh Son Of A Seventh Son* enters UK chart at #1 and peaks at US #12. *Can I Play With Madness* hits UK #3. Both confirm Iron Maiden's position as UK's top metal act.

Aug *Evil That Men Do* hits UK #5.

[20] Band, in the midst of its "Seventh Tour Of A Seventh Tour" world trek, makes its only UK appearance of the year at Monsters Of Rock festival at Castle Donington, Leics.

Oct A tape by Iron Maiden wakes fan Gary Dobson from a coma 8 weeks after he was crushed at Donington.

Nov [19] *The Clairvoyant* hits UK #6.

'89 A keen fencer and swordsman, Dickinson is ranked seventh in Great Britain in the domestic rankings for Men's Foil. His club the Hemel Hempstead fencing club are national champions and go to Paris to represent Great Britain in the European Cup.

Dickinson's song *Bring Your Daughter To The Slaughter*, featured in the film "A Nightmare On Elm Street 5: The Dream Child" receives a Golden Raspberry award for Worst Original Song.

Nov [18] *Infinite Dreams* hits UK #6.

Dec Dickinson collaborates with Ian Gillan, Brian May and Robert Plant as Rock Aid Armenia for a remake of *Smoke On The Water*, which makes UK #39, with all profits from the record going to the victims of the recent Armenian earthquake disaster.

1990 Feb [12] EMI releases 2 12" singles, as a double-package mini-album, the first of a limited edition collection of 10 such releases, to celebrate 10 years of Iron Maiden's recording career with the label. The mini-albums will be released consecutively every week for 10 weeks and will chart on the UK Album survey in the following chronological order: Feb.: *Running Free/Sanctuary* #1; Mar.: *Women In Uniform/Twilight Zone* #10, *Purgatory/Maiden Japan* #5, *Run To The Hills/The Number Of The Beast* #3, *Flight Of Icarus/The Trooper* #7, *2 Minutes To Midnight/Aces High* #11; Apr.: *Running Free (Live)/Run To The Hills (Live)* #9, *Wasted Years/Stranger In A Strange Land* #9, *Can I Play With Madness/Evil That Men Do* #10 and *The Clairvoyant/Infinite Dreams (Live)* #11.

Apr [28] Dickinson's debut solo *Tattooed Millionaire* reaches UK #18.

May [8] Dickinson solo album *Tattooed Millionaire* is released. Tracks are written with new Iron Maiden recruit, ex-White Spirit guitarist, Janick Gers. He replaces Adrian Smith, who leaves to form A.S.A.P, with Zak Starkey (drums), Dave Colwell and Andy Barnett (guitars), Robin Clayton (bass) and Richard Young (keyboards). Jagged Edge drummer Fabio Del Rio also plays on the album.

[17] Sidgwick & Jackson publish Dickinson's first novel **The Adventures Of Lord Iffy Boatrace**.

[19] Dickinson's *Tattooed Millionaire* reaches UK #14.

June [19] Dickinson's 7-date UK solo tour begins at the Mayfair, Newcastle, Tyne & Wear, ending at London's Astoria theater, May 28.

[23] Dickinson's cover version of Mott The Hoople's *All The Young Dudes* reaches UK #23.

July [7] *Tattooed Millionaire* climbs to US #100.

[15] Dickinson begins the US leg of his tour in Norfolk, VA. The 25-date trek is set to end on Aug.15 at the Whiskey in Los Angeles.

Aug [25] *Dive! Dive! Dive!*, recorded at the first Astoria gig on June 27, makes UK #45.

Sept [20] Iron Maiden embark on first leg of their latest world tour at the Mayflower, Southampton, Hants. The 21-date trek is set to end on Oct.18 at the Hammersmith Odeon, London.

[22] *Holy Smoke* from forthcoming studio album hits UK #3.

Oct [13] New album *No Prayer For The Dying* hits UK #2 in debut release week.

[21] 55-date "No Prayer On The Road" tour begins in Barcelona, Spain.

Nov [3] *No Prayer For The Dying* reaches US #17.

Dec [17-18] Iron Maiden plays at the Wembley Arena, during its brief "No Prayer For Christmas Tour".

1991 Jan [5] *Bring Your Daughter To The Slaughter* hits UK #1, Iron Maiden's first single chart-topper. EMI are criticized by the media for cynical marketing of several formats of the release which they know die-hard Maiden fans will immediately buy in quantity, thus boosting the sales performance of the release during a weak sales period.

[26] Group begins 33-date US leg of "No Prayer On The Road" in New Haven, CT, set to end on Mar.14 in San Francisco, CA.

CHRIS ISAAK

1984 Isaak (b. June 26, 1956, Stockton, CA), youngest of 3 sons of his forklift driver father and housewife mother Dorothy, both of whom are enthusiastic rockabilly and country music lovers, has been musically inspired by Dean Martin, Bing Crosby and band leader Louis Prima, but most particularly by a reissue of the "Sun Sessions" collection of Elvis Presley recordings 1954-55, which he hears for the first time while studying in Japan, participating in the University of The Pacific exchange program, where he also practices amateur boxing and acts as a tour guide for a film studio. He has returned to Stockton, where he graduates with a degree in English and Communication Arts, and with the help of his first manager Mark Plummer, now forms a rockabilly trio called Silvertone, consisting of guitarist James Calvin Wilsey, bassist Rowland Salley and drummer Kenney Dale Johnson (who will all remain his permanent backing band), which Isaak fronts, performing on the San Francisco, CA, club circuit, most regularly at the Mabuhay Gardens new wave venue.

1985 Spotted by subsequent manager Erik Jacobsen, who had produced a number of fine late 60s folk/pop acts, Isaak and the band sign to Warner Bros. Records and tour extensively along the US West Coast to promote their Jacobsen-produced debut disk *Silvertone*. Highlighted by Isaak's stark countrybilly songs and Roy Orbison-influenced vocal style, the album fails to rise above critical acclaim.

1987 Apr [11] Following extensive US and European touring, his second album *Chris Isaak*, again produced by Jacobsen and backed by Silvertone, peaks at US #194.

Oct Isaak appears on Channel 4 TV's Jonathan Ross-hosted "The Last Resort", performing *Blue Hotel*, which fails to score anywhere, except France where it is a major hit.

Dec *Chris Isaak* is included in **USA Today** newspaper's Top 10 albums of the year.

1988 US and European touring is interrupted only by Isaak's acting debut in the Jonathan Demme-directed movie "Married To The Mob".

1989 **Aug** Third album *Heart Shaped World* reaches US #149, but is largely unpromoted by Warner Bros., which considers the self-penned dark, brooding 50s style country love song set to be uncommercial, following its initial playback to company executives in San Francisco. One cut, however, *Wicked Game*, interests movie maker David Lynch, who has already used Isaak material for "Blue Velvet", who requires an instrumental version of the song for his forthcoming Nicolas Cage-starring "Wild At Heart". (Isaak's music is increasingly in demand for visual projects, including US soap "Days Of Our Lives", Sunday Night movie "The Preppie Murder" and "Private Eyes" series.)

1990 **Oct** Lee Chestnut, music director at Power 99, an Atlanta, GA, rock station, having seen "Wild At Heart" 3 times, tracks down the Isaak instrumental and starts playing the vocal version from the 1989 album. Other rock and Top 40 stations follow as listener response explodes.

Dec [15] *Wicked Game*, prominent through the more successful European release of "Wild At Heart", hits UK #10. Becoming an overnight media hit after 5 years, hip good looks have also propelled Isaak to fashion spreads in **Esquire** and **Elle** magazines, and caused **People** magazine to list Isaak as one of the most beautiful people in the world. He will also shortly be seen in the Jodie Foster/Anthony Hopkins movie "The Silence Of The Lambs" playing a S.W.A.T. leader.

1991 **Feb** [16] Repackaged *Heart Shaped World* as *Wicked Game* for UK market, hits UK #3.

[23] During a hectic UK promo visit, during which affable and witty Isaak endears himself to audiences and interviewers alike, 1987 track *Blue Hotel* reaches UK #17.

Mar [2] Aided by a second promo video lensed by Herb Ritts in Hawaii, and after 14 weeks of climbing, *Wicked Game* finally hits US #6 as hastily rediscovered and repromoted parent album *Heart Shaped World* begins US chart rise into the Top 10.

Apr [6] *Heart Shaped World* hits US #7, having topped 1 million world sales (and counting).

[24] Isaak sings the national anthem before the Minnesota Twins-Oakland Athletics baseball game at the Metrodome, Minneapolis, MN. He also joins the commentators in their broadcast booth for a couple of innings.

THE ISLEY BROTHERS

Ronald Isley (lead vocals)
Rudolph Isley (vocals)
O'Kelly Isley (vocals)

1955 4 Isley brothers, Rudolph (b. Apr.1, 1939, Cincinnati, OH), Ronald (b. May 21, 1941, Cincinnati), O'Kelly (b. Dec.25, 1937, Cincinnati) and Vernon leave the church choir in their native Cincinnati to form a vocal quartet. They begin church touring but quit when Vernon is killed in a bicycle accident. After a year's break, their parents, Kelly and Sallye Bernice Isley, persuade the 3 brothers to re-form.

1957 The Isley Brothers travel to New York looking for a record deal. Their first single, doo-wop *The Cow Jumped Over The Moon* is released on Teenage label, but fails to chart, as do subsequent releases on Mark-X, Gone and Cindy labels.

1958 Although they have yet to succeed as recording artists, their polished live work secures a contract with the influential General Artists' Corporation management agency.

1959 During a summer appearance at the Howard theater in Washington, DC, they are seen by RCA's Howard Bloom, who signs them. Bloom brings in production duo Hugo and Luigi to supervise The Isley Brothers' recording. First effort *Turn To Me* fails.

July [29] The Isleys record their second RCA single, *Shout*. An adaptation of stage favorite *Lonely Teardrops*, with the intro line "you know you make me want to shout", it features their church organist Professor Herman Stephens.

Sept *Shout* makes only US #47 but is a huge R&B hit. (It will become a standard and a million-seller.) Its success allows the brothers to move the rest of the family from Cincinnati to New Jersey.

Oct *Shout* is released, but sells poorly, as does extracted *Respectable*.

1960 The Isleys leave RCA for Atlantic, where they are teamed up with writer/producers Jerry Leiber and Mike Stoller (fresh from their

successes with The Coasters), but Leiber and Stoller are unable to work The Isleys' gospel energy into a commercial package and their 4 single all fail to sell.

1962 The Brothers move to Wand Records, where they team with producer Bert Berns. Blues ballad *Right Now* is another flop but, for the follow-up, Berns presents his own song *Twist And Shout*, originally recorded by The Top Notes in 1961.

July *Twist And Shout* tops R&B chart and peaks at US #17, becoming a classic reaching a wider audience through The Beatles' version.

Oct With the current Twist dance craze, Wand has the Isleys record *Twistin' With Linda*; it makes US #54. *Twist And Shout* makes US #61.

1963 After the release of *Hold On Baby*, essentially a rewrite of *Twist And Shout*, The Isleys leave Wand for United Artists, continuing to work with Berns. UA debut *Tango* flops and the label instructs the group to record *Surf And Shout*.

July *Twist And Shout* reaches UK #42.

1964 Hardened by record company demands, the brothers set up their own label, T-Neck (named after Teaneck, NJ, where the family now lives). First release, *Testify*, fails to chart. (The record features Jimi Hendrix, a member of the Isleys' touring band, on guitar.) The group re-signs to Atlantic. Group makes its first UK tour, supporting Dionne Warwick. On their return they embark on US tour headlined by Frankie Avalon, with UK singer Cliff Richard making his first American visit.

1965 **Sept** After further unsuccessful singles, Atlantic drops the group.

Dec The Isleys are signed by Berry Gordy's Tamla-Motown which teams them with writers and producers Holland, Dozier and Holland.

1966 **Apr** Group's first Tamla single, *This Old Heart Of Mine*, makes US #12 and UK #47.

June *Take Some Time Out For Love* reaches US #66. *This Old Heart Of Mine* peaks at US #140.

Aug *I Guess I'll Always Love You* makes US #61 and UK #45.

1967 **May** *Got To Have You Back*, their last US pop hit on Tamla, spends 2 weeks at #93.

1968 Parting with Motown in US, the Isleys visit UK.

Nov *This Old Heart Of Mine* is reissued and hits UK #3.

Dec *This Old Heart Of Mine* makes UK #23.

1969 **Jan** Encouraged by their UK success, the brothers return to US and revive T-Neck, with Ronald as president, Rudolph vice-president and O'Kelly secretary/treasurer. They begin writing and producing their own material (and will produce other artists on the label, including The Brothers Three, Dave Cortez, Privilege and Judy White).

Feb *I Guess I'll Always Love You* reaches UK #11.

Apr *Behind A Painted Smile*, another old Tamla cut, hits UK #5.

June First single on T-Neck label, *It's Your Thing* hits US #2 (held off # by The Beatles' *Get Back*) and makes UK #30.

July *It's Our Thing* enters US chart to peak at #22. Despite not making US Top 20, it will sell over 2 million copies.

Aug *I Turned You On* makes US #23 and *It's Your Thing* UK #30.

Sept *Black Berries* peaks at US #79. From Tamla back catalog, *Put Yourse In My Place* reaches UK #13. Ronnie, Rudolph and Kelly (he has dropped the "O") invite brothers Ernie (b. Mar.7, 1952) (guitar, drums) and Marvin (bass, percussion) and cousin Chris Jasper (keyboards) to form an extended Isley Brothers, continuing to use brass sections live and in the studio. They later recruit (non-related) drummer Everett Collins.

Oct *Was It Good To You* peaks at US #83. *The Brothers: Isley* reaches U #180. Group is featured on one side of double album *Live At Yankee Stadium* (US #169), with The Edwin Hawkins Singers and Brooklyn Bridge on the other.

1970 **Mar** [11] *It's Your Thing* wins Best R&B Vocal Performance By A Group Or Duo Of 1969 at the 12th annual Grammy awards.

Oct *Get Into Something* peaks at US #89, after 2 previous singles *Keep On Doin'* (Feb.) and *Girls Will Be Girls, Boys Will Be Boys* (Aug.) climb n higher than US #75.

1971 **Feb** *Freedom* peaks at US #72.

Aug The Isleys' cover of Stephen Stills' *Love The One You're With* is their biggest hit in 2 years, reaching US #18.

Oct *Spill The Wine* climbs to US #49. *Givin' It Back*, comprising only cover versions, including James Taylor's *Fire And Rain*, 2 Stephen Stills songs, and a medley of Neil Young's *Ohio* and Jimi Hendrix's *Machine Gun*, makes US #67.

1972 **Jan** A cover of Dylan's *Lay Lady Lay* peaks at US #71.

Apr *Lay-Away* climbs to US #54.

Aug *Brother, Brother, Brother* begins a 33-week US chart run, peaking at #29.

Sept *Pop That Thang* reaches US #24.

Nov *Work To Do* makes US #51.

73 Apr *The Isleys Live* climbs to US #139.

July *That Lady*, with T-Neck switching distribution from Buddah to CBS, begins a 20-week chart run, hitting US #6 and selling over 2 million copies.

Sept *That Lady* makes UK #14. Rock-tinged *3+3*, recorded at Record Plant West, Hollywood, enters US chart to hit #8, but fails in UK.

Dec *The Isleys' Greatest Hits* makes US #195.

74 Jan *What It Comes Down To* reaches US #55.

Feb *Highway Of My Life* makes UK #25.

Apr A revival of Seals & Crofts' smash *Summer Breeze* peaks at US #60.

June *Summer Breeze* makes UK #16.

Sept *Live It Up* reaches US #52, as live album *Live It Up* makes US #14 and goes platinum.

75 Jan *Midnight Sky* peaks at US #73.

June *The Heat Is On* begins a 40-week US chart run, during which it will top US chart, giving the group its second platinum album.

July *Fight The Power* hits US #4. The Isleys play the Bay area Kool Jazz Festival, CA.

76 Jan Ballad *For The Love Of You (Part 1 & 2)* reaches US #22.

May *Harvest For The World* sells a half million copies in its first 3 days of US release. It hits US #9 and makes UK #50, The Isleys Brothers' third consecutive platinum album.

June *Who Loves You Better* reaches US #47.

July Title track from *Harvest For The World*, an anti-hunger peace song, makes US #63 but hits UK #10.

77 Apr *Go For Your Guns* begins a 34-week US chart run. It hits #6 and earns another platinum disk.

May *The Pride* makes US #63, as *Go For Your Guns* reaches UK #46.

June *Livin' In The Life* climbs to US #40.

Sept Second T-Neck compilation, *Forever Gold*, reaches US #58.

78 Apr *Showdown* is released. It will hit US #4 and be the group's fifth consecutive platinum album.

May Disco single *Take Me To The Next Phase* peaks at UK #50.

June [10] *Showdown* makes UK #50.

79 June *Winner Takes All*, recorded at Bearsville studio, New York, enters US chart to peak at #14.

Dec Hard-funk *It's A Disco Night (Rock Don't Stop)*, stalls at US #90 but makes UK #14.

80 Apr *Go All The Way* hits US #8 and goes platinum. *Don't Say Goodnight (It's Time For Love)* makes US #39.

81 Mar *Grand Slam* peaks at US #28.

May *Hurry Up And Wait* reaches US #58.

Oct The Isleys' second album of the year, *Inside You*, peaks at US #45, the first to fail after 9 successive gold or platinum albums.

82 Aug *The Real Deal* stalls at US #87.

83 June *Between The Sheets* returns them to gold status, reaching US #19.

July Title track *Between The Sheets* makes UK #52.

84 After 15 years together, the 2 younger Isley brothers and Chris Jasper split from the group to form Isley, Jasper, Isley, and negotiate a separate deal with CBS/Epic. (The split is apparently acrimonious and the 2 groups will have little to do with each other.)

85 Feb Isley, Jasper, Isley's *Broadway's Closer To Sunset Boulevard* reaches US #135, while *Kiss And Tell* peaks at US #63. They almost exclusively reflect the rock side of The Isley Brothers and soul fans reject the album.

Nov Isley, Jasper, Isley's gospel-styled *Caravan Of Love* makes UK #52. The album of the same title peaks at US #77 with Isley, Jasper, Isley having returned to soul. In their promotion they claim they were responsible for all The Isley Brothers' hits of the past 10 years.

Dec *Masterpiece*, with The Isley Brothers signed to Warner Bros., peaks at US #140, but *Colder Are My Nights* fails to chart.

86 Jan [25] *Caravan Of Love* makes US #51.

Mar [31] O'Kelly Isley dies of a heart attack, aged 48.

Dec UK group The Housemartins top UK chart with an a cappella version of *Caravan Of Love*.

87 June Third Isley, Jasper, Isley album *Different Drummer* fails to chart.

July The Isley Brothers *Smooth Sailin'* makes US #64. It is written and produced by US soul singer Angela Winbush.

88 Feb Chris Jasper solo album *Superbad* peaks at US #182.

Mar The Isley Brothers *Greatest Hits*, including cuts by Isley, Jasper, Isley, is a UK-only compilation and makes #41.

Sept The Christians' revival of *Harvest For The World* hits UK #8, taken from summer Olympics album *One Moment In Time*.

89 Sept Now listed as The Isley Brothers featuring Ronald Isley, the group makes US #89 with *Spend The Night*, while extracted title cut *Spend The Night* hits US R&B #3.

1990 Apr [14] Released on Elektra, Ernie Isley solo album *High Wire* peaks at US #174.

May [26] Rod Stewart's second revival of *This Old Heart of Mine*, now featuring Ronald Isley, hits US #10, produced by Bernard Edwards and Trevor Horn.

Nov [3] *Rubáiyát*, Elektra's 40th anniversary compilation, to which Ernie Isley contributes a cover of *Let's Go*, makes US #140.

FREDDIE JACKSON

1983 Jackson (b. Oct.2, 1956), the third of 5 children raised by his mother in Harlem, having sung in his local White Rock Baptist church, where he met Ashford & Simpson, and earned dollar bills given by old ladies who thought he was cute, after leaving high school and working in a bank as a computer operator until he has saved enough to pursue an artistic career, teamed up with Paul Laurence and formed a band called LJE, playing Top 40 covers in New York night clubs. Jackson moves to the West Coast, where he joins Mystic Merlin.

1984 On his return to New York, Jackson begins vocal backing on tours for Evelyn King, Lillo Thomas, Angela Bofill and others including Harry Belafonte and Melba Moore. She signs him to her Hush Productions management company and secures a worldwide deal with Capitol.

Oct [2] Jackson starts recording his debut album.

1985 May Soul-filled debut *Rock Me Tonight* is released. It will hit US #10, and top the US R&B Album chart for 16 consecutive weeks, and reach UK #27. Jackson sets out on an 89-date US tour with Melba Moore.

Aug Deceptively-titled soul ballad *Rock Me Tonight (For Old Times Sake)* reaches US #18 and tops the US R&B chart for 6 weeks.

Nov *You Are My Lady* reaches US #12 and UK #49, while parent album goes platinum.

1986 Feb [22] *He'll Never Love You (Like I Do)* peaks at US #25.

Mar *Rock Me Tonight (For Old Times Sake)* reaches UK #18.

Sept Jackson and Joe Cocker guest on syndicated TV "Melba And Friends" 1-hour special.

[23] Jackson, James Brown and Moore headline an anti-crack rally at New York's Plaza hotel.

Oct *Tasty Love* peaks at UK #73.

[30] Jackson begins a 55-city tour at the Civic Center, Saginaw, MI, as US leg of worldwide "Tasty" tour, with Levert and Meli'sa Morgan.

Nov [8] Jackson and Moore top US R&B chart with *A Little Bit More*. The following week Jackson replaces himself at #1 with *Tasty Love*. He becomes the first artist to achieve this feat since Dinah Washington's *This Bitter Earth* replaced her Brook Benton-duet, *A Rockin' Good Way*.

Dec [6] *Just Like The First Time* tops US R&B chart for 26 weeks.

[20] *Tasty Love* makes US #41, as second album *Just Like The First Time* reaches US #23 and UK #30.

[31] Jackson joins Air Supply, Gladys Knight & The Pips and Melba Moore for CBS TV's "Happy New Year America".

1987 Feb *Just Like The First Time* spends 26 weeks at the top of the R&B chart, crosses over to make US #23 and is certified platinum (Jackson's second).

[21] *Have You Ever Loved Somebody* tops US R&B chart.

Mar [14] *Have You Ever Loved Somebody* makes US #69.

Aug [15] *Jam Tonight* tops US R&B chart and he becomes the only artist in the 80s to have 6 R&B #1s.

[29] *Jam Tonight* makes US #32.

Nov *Look Around* makes US R&B #69.

1988 July *Nice'N'Slow*, featuring Naje on sax, makes UK #56.

Aug *Don't Let Love Slip Away*, produced by Paul Laurence, reaches US #48 and UK #24. Jackson begins a world "Up Close And Personal" tour in US as part of the Budweiser Music Festival, including brief stint at the Lunt Fontanne theater, Broadway, New York.

Sept Jackson visits UK to play 4 sell-out concerts at the Hammersmith Odeon, London, before embarking on a tour of Japan. *Crazy (For Me)* is extracted from *Don't Let Love Slip Away* as a UK single, and makes #41. *Nice'N'Slow* reaches US #61.

[27] *Nice'N'Slow* tops US R&B chart.

Oct [15] *Don't Let Love Slip Away* tops US R&B chart.

Dec [2] *Hey Lover* tops US R&B chart.

1989 Jan [30] Jackson wins Favorite Soul/R&B Single for *Nice'N'Slow* at the annual American Music Awards. His only released recording for the remainder of the year will be *All Over You*, featured in the movie "Def By Temptation", in which Jackson will also make a cameo appearance.

Nov [17] Following a 2-year hiatus, Jackson releases *Do Me Again*. Co-produced and co-written with Barry Eastmond and Paul Laurence, it immediately makes UK #48.

Dec [8] Fourth album *Do Me Again* peaks at US #59, and his string of US R&B chart-toppers continues.

1991 **Apr** [12] Jackson embarks on 35-date US tour with En Vogue at the Music Hall, Cincinnati, OH.

[27-28] Jackson studies with jazz vocal teacher, as he makes plans for a jazz album with Anita Baker.

JANET JACKSON

1973 Jackson (b. May 16, 1966, Gary, IN), the youngest in a family of 9 and sister of The Jackson 5, appears in her brothers' stage show for the first time at age 7, at MGM Grand hotel, Las Vegas, NV.

1977 **Sept** She appears as Penny Gordon Woods on CBS TV's sitcom "Good Times". This leads to further acting roles in "Different Strokes", "Fame" and "A New Kind Of Family".

1982 **Nov** Signed to A&M Records, she promotes her debut album *Janet Jackson* by touring high schools and encouraging kids to stay in school. The album reaches US #63. By year's end, Jackson will have attended a concert in Chicago, IL, with her mother. They go to see R&B outfit The Time, whose line-up includes Jimmy Jam and Terry Lewis.

1983 **Jan** *Young Love*, taken from the album, peaks at US #64.
Mar *Come Give Your Love To Me* makes US #58.

1984 **Aug** She elopes with James DeBarge to Michigan Falls, MI.
Sept [7] Jackson announces that she and DeBarge have wed. (The marriage will be annulled 7 months later and she will return to the Jackson family home, shared with Michael, Tito, and mother Katherine, in Encino, CA.)
Nov *Dream Street* climbs to US #147, with help from Jesse Johnson, Giorgio Moroder and a duet with Cliff Richard, which fails to score.

1986 **Jan** *Control*, produced and co-written by Jimmy Jam and Terry Lewis after A&M's urban music director John McClain has teamed them, is released. It will transform both Jackson's image and celebrity status.
Mar Jackson begins a 13-city US promo tour.
[22] Crisp funk dance number *What Have You Done For Me Lately* tops US R&B chart.
Apr [5] *Control* enters UK chart, to hit #8 during a 72-week chart tenure.
[19] *Control* tops US R&B chart for 8 weeks.
May [17] *What Have You Done For Me Lately* hits US #4.
What Have You Done For Me Lately hits UK #3.
June [14] *Nasty* tops US R&B chart and climbs to UK #19.
July [5] *Control* tops the US chart, achieving platinum status. Jackson, just turned 20, becomes the youngest artist, since 13-year-old Little Stevie Wonder, to top the album chart.
[19] *Nasty* hits US #3.
Sept *When I Think Of You* hits UK #10.
Oct [11] *When I Think Of You* tops the US chart for 2 weeks. 14 years since brother Michael Jackson topped the charts with *Ben*, they become the first siblings in the rock era to have solo #1s.
Nov *Control* peaks at UK #42. "Control – The Videos", featuring Paula Abdul-choreographed set dance pieces which have dominated MTV all year, is released.
Dec Jackson begins a US tour. She tops **Billboard**'s year end survey in 6 categories: Top R&B Artist, Top Pop Singles Artist, Top Pop Singles Artist Female, Top Dance Sales Artist, Top Dance Club Play Artist and Top R&B Singles Artist.

1987 **Jan** [10] *Control* tops US R&B chart.
[24] *Control* hits US #5.
[26] Jackson is nominated in 9 categories at the 14th annual American Music Awards at Shrine Auditorium, Los Angeles. She wins 2: Best R&B Single (*Nasty*) and Best Female R&B Video Artist.
Feb [1] Jackson guests on the first "Hitline USA" TV show.
[24] Jackson makes an impressive live appearance at the 29th annual Grammy awards singing *What Have You Done For Me Lately* with help from producers Jam and Lewis, but fails to win any awards.
[14] Ballad *Let's Wait Awhile* tops US R&B chart.
[21] *Let's Wait Awhile* hits US #2, making Jackson the first artist to have 5 Top 10 hits from one album, all in different positions in the Top 5.
Apr A remix of *Let's Wait Awhile* launches A&M's dance-oriented Breakout label in UK, and hits #3.
June Jackson guest-vocals on A&M co-owner Herb Alpert's Jam and Lewis-produced *Diamonds*. It hits US #5 and tops the R&B chart.
Pleasure Principle reaches UK #24.
Aug [8] A remix of sixth extract *The Pleasure Principle* reaches US #14 and tops US R&B chart.
"Control – The Videos Part II" is released.

Sept [11] "Nasty" video wins an award for its choreographer Paula Abdul at MTV Video Music awards at the Universal Amphitheater, Universal City, CA.
Nov An 8-track remixes collection of 5 hits, *Control, What Have You Done For Me Lately, Nasty, Let's Wait Awhile* and *When I Think Of You* released as *Control – The Remixes* reaches UK #20.

1988 **June** Jackson spends the latter part of the year re-teamed with Jam and Lewis at their Flyte Time Production studios in Minneapolis, MN, dedicated to repeating the groundbreaking success of *Control*.

1989 **Oct** [7] First fruits of their second collaboration, the Jam and Lewis-penned and produced *Miss You Much* hits US #1, having already made UK #25.
[28] In its fourth week of release, *Janet Jackson's Rhythm Nation 1814* (the 1814 refers to the year that the US national anthem was composed by Francis Scott Key) hits US #1 for the first of 4 weeks. (It will remain on the chart well into 1991 on its way to at least 6 RIAA platinum sales awards. Its UK performance will be less dramatic – it has already peaked at UK #4 in its release week (Sept.30) and will leave the survey after only 12 weeks, returning regularly, however, during 1990 for a further 29 weeks.) The album is once again produced by Jam and Lewis, except *Black Cat*, while they also write or co-write all of the songs, again except Jackson-penned *Black Cat*.
Nov UK follow-up *Rhythm Nation* reaches UK #23.

1990 **Jan** [6] Title cut *Rhythm Nation* hits US #2, behind Phil Collins' Christmas chart-topper *Another Day In Paradise*. Its video clip once again features Jackson's dance army, mostly clad in black, performing synchronized set pieces to great effect for MTV and VH1 audiences.
[22] Jacksons wins Favorite Dance Single and Favorite Soul/R&B Single for *Miss You Much* at the 17th American Music Awards.
Feb Ballad *Come Back To Me* reaches UK #20.
[21] "Rhythm Nation 1814" wins Best Music Video, Long Form, at the 32nd annual Grammy awards at the Shrine Auditorium, Los Angeles, though none of the hit singles or the albums or Jackson herself will win any Grammys for the current project.
Mar [1] "The Rhythm Nation World Tour 1990", her first ever, begins in Miami Arena. Opening act Chuckii Booker acts as musical director.
[3] *Escape* hits US #1 for first of 3 weeks, peaking at UK #17 in Apr.
[14] Jackson wins R&B/Urban Contemporary Album Of The Year, Female for *Rhythm Nation 1814*, Best R&B/Urban Contemporary Single, Female for *Miss You Much* and Best R&B/Urban Contemporary Music Video for "Rhythm Nation" at the fourth annual Soul Train Awards at the Shrine Auditorium.
Apr She meets President George Bush at the Ritz Carlton in Dearborn, MI. (She is in town for a concert, he is at a fundraiser in the hotel.)
[20] Jackson is bestowed a star on the Hollywood Walk Of Fame, at the start of "Janet Jackson Week" in Los Angeles, CA.
May [16] Jackson celebrates her 24th birthday at Tokyo's Disneyland, while on Japan for 5-date tour. (She has already made a TV commercial for Japan Airlines to tie in with this leg of the tour.)
Aug [4-5] Jackson cancels both dates in St. Louis, MO, because of an inner ear infection. She is treated in St. Louis hospital. Subsequent dates in Auburn Hills, MI, are also cancelled.
[18] *Come Back To Me* hits US #2.
Sept [15-16] Jackson ends the North American leg of her tour in New York. After the final date, she hands over a check for $450,000 to the United Negro College Fund at New York's 21 club.
Oct [21] Jackson plays first of a number of sell-out concerts at Wembley Arena, London, during her European tour.
[27] Fifth extract, Jackson and Jellybean Johnson-produced rocking *Black Cat* hits US #1, having just made UK #15.
Nov *Love Will Never Do (Without You)* makes UK #34.
[26] Jackson wins Hot 100 Singles Artist, Top Pop Album, Hot R&B Singles Artist, Top R&B Albums Artist, Top R&B Album, Top R&B Artist, Top Dance Club Play Artist and Top Dance 12" Singles Sales Artist at the 1990 **Billboard** Music Awards Show in Santa Monica, CA. (The show will air on Fox TV on Dec.10.)

1991 **Jan** [12] *Love Will Never Do (Without You)* climbs to US #4, making Jackson the first artist to achieve 7 Top 5 hits from the same album.
[19] Jam and Lewis-penned *Love Will Never Do (Without You)* gives Jackson her fifth US #1.
[28] Jackson wins Favorite Pop/Rock Female Artist, Soul/Rhythm & Blues Female Artist and Dance/Music Artist at the 18th annual American Music Awards at the Shrine Auditorium.
Feb [9] In its 72nd week on the chart, *Janet Jackson's Rhythm Nation 1814* is still in Top 20 at US #12.
Mar [11] Jackson signs the most lucrative contract in recording history

(her brother Michael is simultaneously negotiating an even higher remunerative package with Sony, which he will ink, thus superceding Janet within a week) worth $50 million with Virgin Records. Virgin supremo Richard Branson says "A Rembrandt rarely becomes available. When it does, there are many people determined to get it. I was determined." Details concerning any involvement of Jam and Lewis within the deal for future recordings are undisclosed.

JOE JACKSON

1973 Jackson (b. Aug.11, 1954, Burton-upon-Trent, Staffs.), having grown up in Portsmouth, Hants., since age 1, learns music at an early age, going to violin school classes and then taking up piano to write classical pieces. Leaving school with an "S-Level" examination pass in music, he has already played pub gigs next to a glue factory, when he enrols at the Royal College of Music, London. While studying on a 3-year scholarship for composition, orchestration, piano and percussion, he has also played in a jazz big band led by Johnny Dankworth and in the National Youth Jazz Orchestra. Leaving the college, he now joins pub band Arms & Legs playing covers, eventually recording 6 unsuccessful singles for UK MAM, all penned by him. (Mark Andrews is lead singer, later to emerge on A&M as Mark Andrews & The Gents.)

1977 Jackson leaves Arms & Legs to go to Portsmouth, and becomes a featured performer at the local Playboy club, and then musical director for TV show "Opportunity Knocks" winners, Coffee & Cream, who are popular on the cabaret circuit.

1978 Moving to London, he records a demo album of his own songs. Through these sessions he nearly signs to United Artists, but the album is passed to Albion Music. David Kershenbaum of A&M hears it and signs him, after Virgin and Stiff Records have both passed.
Oct Aggressive ballad *Is She Really Going Out With Him?* is released. Jackson forms a regular band; himself on vocals and keyboards, Gary Sandford on guitar, Graham Maby ex-Arms & Legs on bass and Dave Houghton on drums.

1979 **Jan** *Look Sharp!*, produced by Kershenbaum, reaches UK #40 and US #20. *Sunday Papers* and *One More Time* are both extracted releases.
May Jackson tours US where *Is She Really Going Out With Him?* reaches US #21. Reissued in UK, it climbs to #13.
Oct *I'm The Man*, Kershenbaum-produced, makes UK #12 and US #22.

1980 **Feb** *It's Different For Girls* hits UK #5.
Mar Follow-ups *Kinda Kute* and *The Harder They Come* both fail.
June [7] Jackson takes part in "The Summer Of '80 Garden Party" at the Concert Bowl, Crystal Palace, London, on a bill with Average White Band, Q-Tips and headlined by Bob Marley.
July Jackson produces UK reggae act The Rasses' album *Natural Wild*.
Oct [5] Jackson begins 18-date UK tour at the Top Rank Ballroom, Cardiff, Wales. Tour will end at King George's Hall, Blackburn, Lancs., on Nov.5.
Now showing a jazz swing bent, *Beat Crazy*, credited to The Joe Jackson Band, reaches UK #42 and US #41. It is the last album with his regular rock line-up, as all extracted singles fail to score.
Dec Initial Joe Jackson Band splits.

1981 **June** *Joe Jackson's Jumpin' Jive* featuring 40s and 50s bop and jive music, makes UK #14 and US #42. Title track reaches UK #43. Jackson tours with the band featured on the album, which includes an extensive horn section. He also produces an album by Portsmouth-based band The Keys.

1982 After the break-up of his marriage, he moves to New York.
June Returning to a more mainstream sound, his most radio friendly album to date *Night And Day* becomes his biggest UK hit at #3, after beginning as a poor seller, and hits US #4.
Oct *Steppin' Out* hits UK #6.

1983 **Jan** Again following US success, *Steppin' Out* finally hits UK #6.
Feb Ballad *Breaking Us In Two* reaches UK #59 and US #18.
Sept Soundtrack album *Mike's Murder* reaches US #64. It is his first attempt at movie scoring. He was originally commissioned to write 1 song but completed the entire project (though much of the music is excised from the film itself). Extracted *Memphis* reaches US #85.

1984 **Mar** *Body And Soul*, another Jackson and Kershenbaum production, the last to feature Graham Maby on bass, peaks at UK #14 and US #20.
Apr *Happy Ending*, with vocals from Elaine Caswell, makes UK #58.
June Ballad *Be My Number Two* reaches UK #70 and *You Can't Get What You Want* climbs to US #15.
Aug *Happy Ending* peaks at US #57.

1985 **Jan** [23] Jackson begins first of 5 live recording sessions/concerts at the Roundabout theater in New York.

Jackson composes 20-min. music score for Japanese movie "Shijin No Ie (House Of The Poet)", recorded with Tokyo Symphony Orchestra..

1986 **Apr** 3-sided live album *Big World*, recorded direct to 2-track in New York, is released to limited appeal and reaches US #34 and UK #41.

1987 **Apr** Never one to repeat a particular style, Jackson's latest project *Will Power*, mainly instrumental with orchestra and jazz session players including Ed Roynesdal, Gary Burke, Vinnie Zumo and Tony Aiello, peaks at US #131.

1988 **May** Double album *Live 1980/86*, featuring 22 live songs from 4 world tours and 4 differing line-ups, reaches UK #66 and US #91. He produces album for reggae outfit The Toasters.
Jackson completes a Grammy nominated movie score for Jeff Bridges-starring Francis Ford Coppola vehicle "Tucker", and oversees and performs its recording.
Nov Jackson begins recording forthcoming *Blaze Of Glory* recorded at Bearsville studios, New York.

1989 **Apr** His 10th and last album for A&M, *Blaze Of Glory* makes UK #36.
May *Blaze Of Glory* begins 21-week chart rise to US #61, though extracted *Nineteen Forever* fails to score, despite typically innovative ageing-themed video, a necessity Jackson publically despises.
Aug [8-9] Current US dates include 2 nights at the Beacon theater, New York.

1990 **Apr** Jackson releases his debut for Virgin, *Laughter And Lust*, with heavy metal pastiche video for first single *Obvious Song*.

1991 **May** [22] 6-date UK mini-tour starts at the Nottingham Royal Concert Hall, Nottingham, Notts., set to climax May 28 at the Hammersmith Odeon, London.

MICHAEL JACKSON

1963 Jackson (b. Aug.29, 1958, Gary, IN) is seen by his mother Katharine practising dance steps in front of the mirror. She and husband, Joe, are keen to nurture and promote their 9 offsprings' musical ability. Michael, age 5, also performs *Climb Every Mountain* to his kindergarten class. (With Joe as manager, Michael will join 4 of his brothers, Jackie, Tito, Jermaine and Marlon to form The Jackson 5.)

1969 As Berry Gordy has signed the group to his Motown label, the Jackson family moves to Los Angeles, CA, the label's new headquarters. At a Sammy Davis Jr. showbiz gathering, Quincy Jones meets 10-year-old Jackson for the first time (although Jackson will not recall the event).

1970 The Jackson family settles in Encino, CA.

1971 **Dec** 2 years after the first Jackson 5 hit, Jackson, signed as a soloist to Tamla Motown, hits US #4 with ballad *Got To Be There*. He also appears on labelmate (and life-time friend) Diana Ross' US TV special "Diana".

1972 **Mar** *Got To Be There* hits UK #5, while the album of the same name peaks at US #14. Jackson spends much time with Ross on the set of her current movie, "Lady Sings The Blues".
May *Rockin' Robin*, reviving Bobby Day's 1958 US #2, also hits US #2, kept off the top by Roberta Flack's *The First Time Ever I Saw Your Face*.
June With parallel group and solo careers in full swing, Jackson's *Rockin' Robin* hits UK #3, as UK release of *Got To Be There* makes #37.
July *I Wanna Be Where You Are* reaches US #16.
Sept With the Bill Withers original a flop in UK, Motown releases Jackson's version of *Ain't No Sunshine* in UK only. It hits #8. Meanwhile, his second solo album *Ben* hits US #5.
Oct [14] Extracted title track *Ben* hits US #1. Penned by American composer Walter Scharf and UK lyricist Don Black, the ballad was written for movie "Ben" (a follow-up to "Willard"), and originally intended for Donny Osmond. Black is responsible for suggesting that Jackson vocalizes the song.
Dec *Ben* hits UK #7, as parent album reaches UK #17.

1973 **May** Tamla releases *Music And Me*, which peaks at US #92, while *With A Child's Heart* makes US #50.

1975 **Mar** *We're Almost There*, written by Brian and Eddie Holland, peaks at US #54, but Jackson's final official solo Motown album release, *Forever, Michael*, makes only US #101. (He will not release another solo album for 4 years.)
May Although brother Jermaine will stay at the label, the remaining group quits Motown and re-starts as The Jacksons on Epic. Still in the family line-up, Michael also signs a solo deal with Epic which allows creative freedom and a considerable rise in The Jackson 5 2.7% Motown royalty.
July Tamla single, *Just A Little Bit Of You*, reaches US #23.
Oct The first of many Motown Jackson compilation albums, *The Best Of Michael Jackson*, climbs to US #156.

1977 **July** Rehearsals begin in New York for a movie version of musical

MICHAEL JACKSON cont.

"The Wiz", already a stage success adapted from "The Wizard Of Oz". Jackson is chosen to play the Scarecrow opposite Diana Ross' Dorothy and Richard Pryor's Wiz. While filming, Jackson stays at sister LaToya's Manhattan apartment. The project links Michael professionally with producer Quincy Jones, responsible for its soundtrack.

1978 Oct Soundtrack album *The Wiz* is released through MCA, on which Ross and Jackson duet on *Ease On Down The Road*, which makes US #41 and UK #45. Jackson spends 6 months recording his debut solo album for Epic.

1979 Mar [3] First single for Epic, *You Can't Win*, climbs to US #81, during a 3-week stay on the Hot 100.

Oct Released on July 28, Jackson-penned hot dance number, *Don't Stop 'Til You Get Enough*, originally demoed at Jackson's 24-track home studio with brother Randy, hits US #1, his first for 7 years. It also hits UK #3 and propels parent album, *Off The Wall* (released in Aug. and produced by Jones) to hit US #3 and UK #5. (It will sell over 10 million copies worldwide.)

Dec *Off The Wall* title track hits UK #7.

1980 Jan [19] Dreamy *Rock With You*, the first of many ex-Heatwave member Rod Temperton songs which will be recorded by Jackson (including 3 on the current album), also hits US #1, nudging KC & The Sunshine Band's *Please Don't Go*.

Feb [27] Jackson wins Best R&B Vocal Performance, Male for *Don't Stop 'Til You Get Enough* at the 22nd annual Grammy awards.

Mar *Rock With You* hits UK #7.

Apr Title cut from *Off The Wall* hits US #10.

May Ballad *She's Out Of My Life*, featuring an emotionally cracked Jackson vocal, hits UK #3 and peaks at US #10 within a month. Jackson becomes the first solo artist to enjoy 4 hits from 1 album (a record he himself will break).

Aug *Girlfriend*, penned by Paul McCartney, reaches UK #41, as he rejoins The Jacksons to promote new album *Triumph*.

1981 May Motown issues unreleased tracks compilation album *One Day In Your Life*. It peaks at US #144. During The Jacksons' "Triumph" tour, he collapses from exhaustion in New Orleans, LA.

June [27] Becoming an instant middle-of-the-road airplay favorite, Motown-released *One Day In Your Life* tops the UK chart and becomes Jackson's first UK #1.

Aug [1] Repromoted album *Best Of Michael Jackson* reaches UK #11 as *One Day In Your Life* makes UK #29.

[8] Motown follow-up *We're Almost There* makes UK #46, 6 years after charting in the US.

Dec [25] Jackson calls McCartney and suggests they write and record together, so McCartney flies to Los Angeles to cut *The Girl Is Mine*.

1982 June Jackson and Jones work on a story-telling record book of Steven Spielberg's hit movie "E.T."

Aug Jackson and Jones begin work on a new album, to be called *Thriller* at Westlake studios, Los Angeles. In addition to a formidable session musician line-up, Jones again invites song contributions from, amongst others, Rod Temperton, who offers the title track.

Oct Recorded earlier in the year, Diana Ross releases Jackson-written *Muscles*, which will hit US #10 and UK #15. (The title is also the name of Jackson's pet snake, one of an increasing number of unusual animal companions Jackson will choose to share his Encino mansion.)

Nov [6] Donna Summer's *State Of Independence*, on which Jackson joins Quincy Jones-created all-star chorus, makes US #41.

[20] First extract from forthcoming album, the McCartney duet, *The Girl Is Mine* hits UK #8.

Dec [1] *Thriller* is released. (With demos originally recorded at Jackson's 24-track Encino home, some with Temperton present, the album, produced by Jones and engineered by Bruce Swedien, will break all sales records and become the most celebrated and chart successful album of all time. It will sell over 40 million copies worldwide and hit #1 in every Western country including UK and US, where it will spend a record 37 weeks at #1. From it will come an unprecedented 7 Top 10 US hit singles. It will sell over 1 million copies in Los Angeles alone and receive a record 12 Grammy nominations.)

1983 Jan Playfully feuding Jackson/McCartney duet *The Girl Is Mine* hits US #2. Jackson makes a quick visit to London to link with McCartney to complete further songs for release on his new album.

Feb *E.T. – The Extra-Terrestrial*, released on MCA, peaks at UK #82. It includes a previously unreleased Jackson track and a souvenir booklet featuring pictures of Jackson cuddling E.T.

Mar [5] Jackson-penned *Billie Jean* hits US #1. (It stays there for 7 weeks and coincides for 1 week with its UK #1 position. Having

entered the US chart in Jan., it transforms the fortunes of *Thriller*, Jackson's career, the financial status of Epic Records and the fabric of modern music itself. Only when it hits US #1, does MTV, previously reluctant to air "black videos", begin showing the *Billie Jean* clip. Featuring self-choreographed dancesteps, the visuals combine with audio innovation to provide what many critics regard as the perfect modern single project. In contrast to future recording, Jackson's vocals for *Billie Jean* were made in one take.)

Apr [23] *Beat It* hits UK #3, behind David Bowie's *Let's Dance* and Culture Club's *Church Of The Poison Mind*. The song features Jones-invited Eddie Van Halen on lead guitar, which Van Halen offers free of charge. The accompanying video, directed by Bob Giraldi at a cost of $160,000, boosts the disk's success. It features group dance routines led by Jackson, co-created with "Dreamgirls" choreographer Michael Peters.

[30] In an unprecedented chart feat, and separated only by Dexy's Midnight Runners' *Come On Eileen*, Jackson hits US #1 with *Beat It*, failing to replace himself at the top spot by only 1 week, the shortest gap registered since The Beatles in 1964.

May [16] Jackson links with his brothers to perform both group and solo spots for "25 Years Of Motown" on US NBC TV. It includes a specially-choreographed performance of *Billie Jean* which is nominated for an Emmy TV award, and features his celebrated "Moonwalking" dance style.

June [25] Feet-aimed *Wanna Be Startin' Somethin'* hits UK #8.

July [16] *Wanna Be Startin' Somethin'* hits US #5.

[30] Motown tries to cash in with *Happy*, the love theme from "Lady Sings The Blues", which peaks at UK #52.

Sept Ballad *Human Nature*, penned by lyricist John Bettis and Toto's Steve Porcaro and also from *Thriller*, hits US #7. Meanwhile, opportunist female singer Lydia Murdock records "answer" disk to accusatory *Billie Jean: Superstar* fails in US but makes UK #14, borrowing heavily from the *Billie Jean* riff.

Nov [19] *Say Say Say*, another McCartney duet, but for the ex-Beatle's current album, hits UK #2 for 2 weeks, behind Billy Joel's *Uptown Girl*. (Jackson also sings on *The Man* from McCartney's *Pipes Of Peace*.)

[26] Title track, *Thriller*, featuring a ghostly rap from horror movie veteran Vincent Price (who will not appear in the Jon Landis directed mini-epic video, the peak of Jackson's current video triumphs), hits UK #10, 6 months ahead of its US release. Meanwhile, *P.Y.T. (Pretty Young Thing)*, written by Jones and James Ingram, hits US #10.

Dec [2] US MTV airs the full-length "Thriller" video for first time.

[10] *Say Say Say* tops the US chart for 5 weeks, knocking Lionel Richie's *All Night Long (All Night)* off the summit.

[24] Jackson wins Top Dance Artist and Top Audience Response Singles/Albums in **Billboard**'s Year In Music.

At the end of his most successful year to date, Jackson announces a $5 million sponsorship deal with Pepsi Cola. A rider in the contract ensures that Jackson will not have to hold or drink a can of Pepsi in any promotion. A UK-only released *Michael Jackson 9 Single Pack* makes UK #66.

1984 Jan [26] Jackson is hospitalized with scalp burns following an accidental flare explosion on the set filming a Pepsi commercial. A spark ignites his hair on the sixth take of the Giraldi-directed ad. Marlon Brando's son Miko, working as a bodyguard for The Jacksons, is the first to dowse the flames.

Doubleday Publishers announce that they will be producing a Jacqueline Onassis-edited Jackson autobiography. It will be written with the help of author Stephen Davis.

Feb Jackson features strongly on Berry Gordy Jr.'s son Kennedy's (aka Rockwell) hit single *Somebody's Watching Me* (US #2 and UK #6).

[21] Jackson is unable to attend the third annual BRIT Awards at the Grosvenor House, Mayfair, London, to collect trophies for Best British Album (*Thriller*) and Best International Solo Artist.

[27] The Pepsi ad premieres on MTV.

[28] Jackson wins Record Of The Year and Best Rock Vocal Performance, Male for *Beat It*, Album Of The Year and Best Pop Vocal Performance, Male for *Thriller*, Best R&B Vocal Performance, Male and Best New R&B Song for *Billie Jean*, Best Recording For Children for *E.T. The Extra-Terrestrial* and Producer Of The Year (Non-Classical), shared with Quincy Jones, at the 26th annual Grammy awards.

Mar [3] *Thriller*, seventh and final single from the album, hits US #4.

Apr [5] Jackson wins the latest in a string of Best Video awards at the second annual American Video Awards. Appropriately, video "The Making Of Michael Jackson's Thriller" is released in UK and US and becomes the best-selling music video to date. In addition to featuring

Janis Joplin

Janet Jackson

Paul McCartney & Michael Jackson

The Jackson Five

John Lennon

Led Zeppelin

Jerry Lee Lewis

the full length Landis-directed "Thriller" film, it also includes *Beat It*, *Billie Jean* and previously unseen rehearsal clips.

[7] *P.Y.T.* reaches UK #11.

[14] Song parody specialist "Weird Al" Yankovic reaches US #12 with novelty *Eat It*, with Rick Derringer assuming Eddie Van Halen's solo.

[27] Philadelphia radio station W-WSH broadcasts a "No Michael Jackson" weekend in protest to his airwave saturation of the past year. Jackson returns to hospital for further scalp and facial laser surgery.

May During a New York stay, Jackson expresses interest in a jacket worn by elevator operator, Hector Cormana, who gives him a spare.

[5] Yankovic's *Eat It* makes UK #36.

June Jackson dons Cormana's jacket on a visit to the White House to receive a Presidential Award from President and Mrs. Reagan.

[30] Motown vault issues *Farewell My Summer Love* which reaches US #38 and UK #7. Album of same name makes US #46 and hits UK #9. Compilation *Michael Jackson & The Jackson 5 – 14 Greatest Hits* reaches US #168 from Motown. Jackson, meanwhile, rejoins The Jacksons for newly-announced album, *Victory* and subsequent tour. (Completed by Jackson as a favor to his brothers, the tour will be dogged by financial and organizational problems from the moment boxing promoter Don King offers $3 million upfront advances. Michael's dissatisfaction with the reunion and the subsequent money squabbles leads him to donate his portion to children's charities.) Jackson duets with Mick Jagger on the album's lead-off single *State Of Shock* (US #3 and UK #14).

July The official Michael Jackson doll, complete with white glove, is launched.

Aug Jackson receives death threats during the "Victory" tour and his personal security is doubled.

Sept [8] *Girl You're So Together* reaches UK #33 on Motown. He appears as duet vocalist on brother Jermaine's new album, on track *Tell Me I'm Not Dreaming*.

Nov Jackson unveils his Hollywood Star on the Walk Of Fame, 6856, Hollywood, Los Angeles.

1985 Jan Following UK success of Band Aid's single, Jackson co-writes US version, *We Are The World* for star group USA For Africa, with Lionel Richie, in 2 hours.

Feb [26] "Making Michael Jackson's Thriller" wins Best Video Album at the 27th annual Grammy awards. (To emphasis Jackson's influence on the current scene, Weird Al Yankovic wins Best Comedy Recording for *Eat It*, his spoof of *Beat It*.)

Mar [3] Jackson visits UK to attend Madame Tussaud's Waxworks in London, which is inaugurating his waxwork lookalike. Traffic comes to a standstill as Jackson jumps on to his car to wave to crowds. He also visits legendary Abbey Road recording studios.

May Jackson receives $58 million in royalties from Epic Records.

July During a year which will see no new singles or album releases, Jackson's 15-min. 3D space fantasy film, produced with George Lucas, begins shooting in California. "Captain Eo", starring Jackson and featuring new material will take over a year to premiere, during which time exclusive distributor Disneyland/World will build a movie theater on both sites specifically to show the project.

Aug [14] Competing with both Paul McCartney and Yoko Ono, Jackson outbids everyone to secure the ATV music publishing catalog. At $47.5 million, he gains rights to more than 250 songs written by Lennon/McCartney. Reports indicate that it severely and irreparably sours relationships between McCartney and Jackson. Jackson has also bought rights to all Sly Stone songs.

1986 Feb 14-year-old heart transplant patient Donna Ashlock, a devoted Jackson fan, receives a surprise phone call from the star, who invites her to his home for lunch and movies the following month.

[25] *We Are The World* wins Song Of The Year at the 28th annual Grammy awards.

Mar Jackson's manager Frank DiLeo, business affairs adviser John Branca and Pepsi president Roger Enrico complete Jackson's second contract for the soft drinks giant. This time for $15 million, it will include 2 further commercials and sponsorship of a world solo tour.

Aug [4] Jackson and co-producer Jones move into studio D at Westlake studios to record a follow-up to *Thriller*. Jackson has already written 62 songs for consideration and Jones invites outsiders to offer more. (The Beatles' *Come Together* is recorded, but rejected.) Jackson insists that his 300-lb. snake, Crusher, and constant chimp companion, Bubbles, are present at recording sessions. (Bubbles will enjoy studio rides on back of engineer Bruce Swedien's Great Dane.)

Sept As increasingly health-conscious Jackson buys an oxygen chamber to prolong his lifespan, a Jackson-written and produced track

is released as title cut for new Diana Ross album *Eaten Alive*.

[18] After more than a year's preparation, Jackson's "Captain Eo", produced by sci-fi film maker George Lucas, premieres at Disneyland in Anaheim, CA. It includes never-released dance number *We Are Just Here To Save The World*, written and performed by Jackson.

Nov Shooting begins in New York on video for the title cut from new album *Bad*. A 17-min. mini-film, directed by Martin Scorsese, its locations include the Bronx subway and the Dobbs Ferry school.

1987 Feb As recording of *Bad* enters the final stage, Jackson tapes video clips for 2 planned singles, *The Way You Make Me Feel* and *Smooth Criminal* (at a reported cost of over $5 million).

Mar During the US televised Grammy awards, Pepsi airs the new Michael Jackson teaser commercial: "This Spring ... The Magic Returns".

May [29] Jackson offers $50,000 to buy the remains of the "Elephant Man", John Merrick. Eventually doubling his offer, it is rejected by the London Hospital.

June [6] Jackson severs ties with Jehovah's Witnesses, for whom he has been a long-term supporter.

Cabaret artist Valentino Johnson spends $40,000 in plastic surgery to look like Jackson and subsequently mimics his act. DiLeo considers legal action.

July [13] 50 of America's biggest record retail heads are invited to Jackson's Encino home to preview *Bad*. Hosted mainly by LaToya and Joe Jackson, dinner and a tour of the mansion are included with Michael appearing only briefly to pose for photos.

Aug [8] First single from the album, a ballad duet with Siedah Garrett, *I Just Can't Stop Loving You* debuts on US and UK charts. It will top both surveys in the coming weeks, initally hitting UK #1 in its second week of release. (The duet was initially rejected by Whitney Houston and Barbra Streisand. A Spanish language version of the hit *Todo Mi Amor Eres Tu*, translated and co-produced by Ruben Blades, will be released.)

[27] Jackson's *Bad* is previewed 4 days ahead of release on a Los Angeles radio station.

[31] On a CBS TV special, "Michael Jackson – The Magic Returns", the 17-min. "Bad" video is aired for the first time. It is clear that, with tour and promotion efforts surrounding *Bad*, Jackson intends to outsell *Thriller*, aiming for the first 50-million-selling album. *Bad* is released and is the biggest-shipped album ever worldwide. It enters US and UK charts at #1. Extensive sleeve notes include thanks to Cary Grant and Marlon Brando.

Sept [12] As *Bad* debuts at UK #1, Jackson, having promised a solo world tour to both Pepsi and his fans, chooses 38,000-capacity Korakuen stadium, Toyko, Japan, to begin dates that will take over 1 year to complete. (The biggest grossing tour of all, it will take in Japan, Australia, where some concerts will be cancelled through poor ticket sales, US, Canada, UK and Europe. Jackson's personal entourage will be more than 250-strong including a chef, hairdresser and manager DiLeo, who will handle all interviews. Also included are 2 recent business managers, Jimmy Osmond and Marlon Brando's son, Miko.)

[19] *I Just Can't Stop Loving You* tops US Hot 100 and R&B chart.

[26] *Bad* tops US chart, staying at #1 for 6 weeks.

Oct [3] *Bad* begins an 18-week stay at the top of US R&B chart.

[17] *Bad* tops US R&B chart.

[24] Title cut *Bad*, written and co-produced by Jackson, hits US #1 and UK #3, boosted by Scorsese-lensed gang-dancing video clip which extends Jackson's current "Bad" image of belts, buckles, straps and custom-designed black streetwear. UK TV compilation, credited to Michael Jackson and Diana Ross, *Love Songs*, climbs to UK #15.

Dec Dance-chugging *The Way You Make Me Feel* hits UK #3. Another UK-only mix album of old Jackson and Jackson 5 hits, *The Michael Jackson Mix*, is released. It will peak at UK #27.

[26] *The Way You Make Me Feel* tops US R&B chart.

1988 Jan [23] *The Way You Make Me Feel* tops US chart. It gives producer Jones the unique achievement of the longest span between chart-topping single productions in US chart history, his first US #1 being Lesley Gore's *It's My Party* in June 1963.

Feb Siedah Garrett/Glen Ballard-penned social conscience song, *Man In The Mirror*, with backing vocals by The Winans, The Andrae Crouch Choir and Garrett herself, reaches UK #21.

[8] Jackson does not attend the seventh annual BRIT Awards at the Royal Albert Hall, London, to collect his Best International Solo Artist award.

Mar [26] *Man In The Mirror* tops US Hot 100 and R&B #1.

Apr A UK-remix by Stock/Aitken/Waterman studio PWL of Motown hit *I Want You Back '88* hits UK #8 for a surprised Michael Jackson & The Jackson 5.

May From recent Stevie Wonder album *Characters*, Jackson duet *Get It* reaches US #80 and UK #37.

[5] Jackson becomes the first non-Soviet to be featured advertising a product on Russian television.

June Video compilation "The Legend Continues" immediately becomes the best-selling UK music video of all time, out-shipping "The Making Of Michael Jackson's Thriller". As all Jackson's Epic albums re-enter the UK chart, old Motown compilation *18 Greatest Hits* peaks at UK #85. With press silence still maintained, the much-anticipated autobiography, **Moonwalk**, is published but fails to satisfy public thirst for Jackson trivia. An immediate best-seller, he makes the point that he believes he is one of the loneliest people in the world.

July The world tour arrives in London for a series of dates, including a record 7 sell-out Wembley Stadium (72,000-capacity) performances. (At one of them, he will present audience members the Prince and Princess of Wales with a 6-figure check for the Prince's Trust Charity.) Chimp Bubbles is refused entry to UK under strict quarantine laws, but tour companion US TV actor Jimmy Safechuck is allowed in. He has appeared with Jackson in a recent Pepsi commercial and will also perform on stage. During the trip, Jackson visits London toy store, Hamleys (where he buys a doll of himself), and record store HMV, when both agree to open for him after hours. Meanwhile a limited UK-only 5-singles souvenir pack, *Bad*, enters the UK Album chart for 1 week at #91, and *Dirty Diana* hits UK #4.

[2] *Dirty Diana*, featuring Billy Idol's guitarist Steve Stevens, hits US #1. (Jackson becomes the only artist ever to pull 5 chart-topping singles off one album.)

Sept Jackson returns to UK for more dates, including a concert at Liverpool's Aintree racecourse, Merseyside. UK press over-reacts to serious crowd problems caused by the number of fans. *Another Part Of Me* reaches US #11 and UK #15.

[17] *Another Part Of Me* tops US R&B chart.

Oct [23] Jackson joins Berry Gordy Jr. to tour the house where Gordy launched Motown Records in 1959. Jackson donates $125,000 to the Motown Museum as he prepares for 2 Detroit concerts in Nov.

Nov *Smooth Criminal*, seventh single from *Bad*, hits US #7 and UK #8.

[13] Los Angeles' Mayor Tom Bradley proclaims "Michael Jackson Month" as the singer performs at the Sports Arena.

Dec "Moonwalker", starring Jackson and featuring Sean Lennon among others, opens in movie theaters throughout US and UK.

1989 Jan [14] Jackson wins Best Male Artist and Best Album Of The Year, for *Bad*, at the NAACP 21st Image Awards, broadcast on NBC.

Feb Jackson picks up statuettes at the American Music Awards, presented to him by Eddie Murphy, a noted Jackson mimic.

[1] Lavon A. Muhammad is sentenced to a maximum of 2½ years for violating a court order to stay away from Jackson. The 41-year-old former legal secretary, also claims that Jackson is the father of her 6-year-old twins. She loses a £100 million paternity suit.

[7] Jackson visits Cleveland school, Stockton, CA, the scene of Jan.17 schoolyard massacre in which 5 children were fatally shot.

[13] Jackson fires manager Frank DiLeo, who reportedly seeks a $60 million settlement to prevent him revealing Jackson's lifestyle secrets to the media. Jackson also sends taped message in receiving Best Music Video, ("Smooth Criminal"), Best International Solo Artist and Best International Artist, Male at the eighth annual BRIT Awards held at the Royal Albert Hall, London.

[18] "Moonwalker" replaces "E.T." at top of **Billboard**'s Video Sales chart.

Mar *Leave Me Alone*, originally only available as a bonus track on CD version of *Bad* (which has now hit #1 in 24 countries), hits UK #2 but remains unreleased as a single in US. Its video is extracted from movie "Moonwalker", which has proved more popular in UK than US.

Apr [12] Jackson receives third annual Heritage Award and first Sammy Davis Jr. award for outstanding stage performance.

May Jackson moves to a custom-designed 2,700-acre ranch in Santa Barbara, CA.

[2] Jackson in wig, fake moustache and false teeth, enters Zales jewellers in Simi Valley, CA. Shopping center security guard H.N. Edwards thinking him to be a robber alerts police, who quickly arrive with 3 squad cars and make Jackson strip off his disguise.

[16] Sister Janet, on the VIP tour at Universal studios, is hounded by fans mistaking her for her more famous brother. Michael meanwhile takes the tour in disguise (and peace and quiet).

June He begins shooting video of ballad *Liberian Girl*, an unprecedented eighth UK-only single release from *Bad*.

July *Liberian Girl* reaches UK #13.

LaToya Jackson's manager Jack Gordon alleges Jackson has offered LaToya $5 million to stop publication of her autobiography **La Toya: Growing Up In The Jackson Family**.

Sept [13] Jackson signs a $28 million deal with LA Gear Sportswear to be its spokesperson. The campaign will be unsuccessful and will be dropped after 1 commercial.

[18] California Raisins commercial featuring a claymation version of Jackson airs on US TV. Jackson donates his $25,000 royalty to charity.

1990 Jan [27] The American Cinema Foundation crowns Jackson Entertainer Of The Decade. Sophia Loren presents his award.

Feb [21] "Leave Me Alone" wins Best Music Video – Short Form at the 32nd annual Grammy awards at the Shrine Auditorium, Los Angeles.

Mar [14] Jackson wins the the Silver Award as 1980s Artist Of The Decade at the fourth annual Soul Train Music Awards at the Shrine Auditorium.

Apr [5] Jackson is invited to the White House by President Bush.

May [8] To celebrate its 50th anniversary, BMI presents its first Michael Jackson award to the singer himself at the Regent Beverly Wilshire hotel, Beverly Hills, CA. Attendees at the luncheon include Little Richard, Brian Wilson, Herbie Hancock, Gerry Goffin, Jeff Barry and Holland, Dozier and Holland.

June [3] Jackson is admitted to St. John's hospital & health center, Santa Monica, CA, to undergo tests after experiencing chest pains. He is diagnosed as having costochondritis – the cartilage at the front of his rib cage was inflamed.

Lawyer Thomas Wampold files a class-action lawsuit alleging Jackson was not sick, as he said, when he cancels 3 Tacoma, WA, concerts, therefore committing a breach of contract for 72,000 fans.

Aug [18] Jackson invites 130 YMCA children to his ranch to visit his zoo, video arcade and movie theater.

[21] An announcement is made confirming Sandy Gallin as Jackson's new manager.

1991 Mar A week after Janet Jackson has announced the most lucrative record deal in pop history, Michael's new contract with Sony makes his sister's agreement look trivial: with an $18 million cash advance for his forthcoming *Dangerous* album release alone, Jackson is made CEO of his own newly formed Nation Records, itself a subsidiary of the Jackson Entertainment Complex which will also include TV, video and film divisions. His record royalty rate is negotiated at an unprecedented $2 and 8 cents per unit album with guarantees for post *Dangerous* album advances of $5 million per project. Heralded as the first billion dollar entertainer contract, it is also announced that movie directors David Lynch, Tim Burton, Christopher Columbus and Sir Richard Attenborough are already lined-up to lense forthcoming promo film clips to accompany the *Dangerous* singles.

THE JACKSONS

Jackie Jackson (vocals)
Tito Jackson (vocals)
Jermaine Jackson (vocals)
Marlon Jackson (vocals)
Michael Jackson (vocals)

1963 Group is first formed as a trio in Gary, IN, by Jackie (b. Sigmund Jackson, May 4, 1951, Gary), Tito (b. Toriano Jackson, Oct.15, 1953, Gary) and Jermaine (b. Dec.11, 1954, Gary), the 3 eldest sons of steelworks crane driver Joe Jackson (an ex-guitarist for The Falcons) and wife Kathy. Initially known as The Jackson Family, the trio recruits cousins Johnny Jackson and Ronnie Rancifer as drummer and pianist, and eventually begins to play dates around Gary.

1964 Younger brothers Marlon (b. Mar.12, 1957, Gary) and Michael (b. Aug.29, 1958, Gary) join in place of the cousins (who nevertheless stay around as backing musicians), and they become The Jackson 5.

1965 They enter and win a local talent contest at Roosevelt high school in Gary, performing The Temptations' *My Girl*.

1966 After making their debut at Mr.Lucky's, a nightclub in Gary, The Jacksons begins to play further afield, with father as manager, driving them to other cities (most frequently Chicago, IL) in a Volkswagen van On a trip to New York, they compete in another talent contest at the Apollo theater, Harlem, New York, and win.

1967 They support Gladys Knight & The Pips at an Indiana gig, and Knight, recently signed to Motown herself, notes to label boss Berry Gordy Jr. that the act is worth considering.

1968 *Big Boy*, produced by Gordon Keith, is recorded for Ben Brown's Gary-based Steeltown label, without success. The group is again noted by a Motown act, Bobby Taylor & The Vancouvers, which also recommends that the label should check it out.

1969 After seeing the brothers perform, while attending a campaign benefit concert for Gary's Mayor Richard Hatcher with Diana Ross, Berry Gordy Jr. signs them and moves them to Hollywood, CA, for grooming and rehearsals. The Jackson family moves to California.

Aug [11] Ross introduces the group to 350 invited guests at Daisy club, Beverly Hills, CA.

Oct [18] The Jackson 5's first live performance as a Motown act is at the Hollywood Palace, with Diana Ross And The Supremes and others. Their first Motown recording is a song written by Freddie Perren, Fonce Mizell and Deke Richards, (collectively, with Gordy, The Corporation), originally intended for Gladys Knight & The Pips. Gordy suggests it should be re-written with the new, young group in mind.

1970 **Jan** *I Want You Back*, with Michael on lead vocal, tops US chart for 4 weeks and is a million-seller.

Feb Debut *Diana Ross Presents The Jackson 5*, a Berry Gordy PR exercise giving the impression that it is Ross who has discovered the brothers, hits US #5, as *I Want You Back* hits UK #2.

Apr *ABC*, written by the same team in a similar style to *I Want You Back*, affirms the popularity of the group's sound, unlike anything else heard on Motown, and is a second million-seller. It tops US chart for 2 weeks, deposing The Beatles' *Let It Be*. The debut album, meanwhile, reaches US #16.

June Group becomes the first act to top Hot 100 with its first 3 chart entries, as *The Love You Save*, a third million-seller, hits #1 for 2 weeks. Meanwhile, *ABC* hits UK #8.

Aug *The Love You Save* hits UK #7, The brothers' second album, *ABC*, hits US #4 and UK #22.

Sept [26] Motown announces that The Jackson 5 have sold a million disks in 9 months.

Oct *Mama's Pearl*, written by The Corporation in a similar uptempo style to the 3 previous chart-toppers, intended as the fourth single, is passed over by Gordy in favor of a complete contrast, the ballad *I'll Be There*, co-written by the group's producer Hal Davis. It tops US chart for 5 weeks, and is Motown's biggest-selling single to date, in excess of 4 million copies. *Third Album*, which includes the single, hits US #4.

Dec *The Jackson 5 Christmas Album*, combining traditional and contemporary seasonal songs, is 1970's top-selling Christmas disk. (#1 on **Billboard**'s annual Christmas albums chart, it will re-chart during the festive seasons of the next 3 years.)

1971 **Jan** *I'll Be There* hits UK #4.

Mar *Mama's Pearl* is issued as follow-up and hits US #2, held from #1 by The Osmonds' *One Bad Apple*, an imitation of The Jackson 5 sound by a group which had earlier specialized in country-styled harmony singing. *Mama's Pearl* is a further million-seller, also reaching UK #25.

June *Never Can Say Goodbye*, another slower-paced song written by Clifton Davis, is the brothers' sixth consecutive million-seller, hitting US #2, behind Three Dog Night's *Joy To The World*, and making UK #33. Their third album, *Maybe Tomorrow*, reaches US #11.

Aug Title track *Maybe Tomorrow* reaches US #20.

Sept [11] An animated "Jackson 5" series premieres on ABC TV.

Nov *Goin' Back To Indiana* reaches US #16. It is the soundtrack of a US Jackson 5 TV special.

1972 **Feb** *Sugar Daddy* hits US #10, but fails to chart in UK. Meanwhile, *Jackson 5 Greatest Hits*, a compilation of the singles to date, reaches US #12.

May A revival of Thurston Harris' *Little Bitty Pretty One* (a close musical relative of Michael's solo US #13 revival of *Rockin' Robin*) reaches US #13.

Aug *Lookin' Through The Windows* hits US #7. Title track *Lookin' Through The Windows* reaches US #16.

Oct Compilation *Jackson 5 Greatest Hits* reaches UK #26.

Nov Following Michael's solo successes for Motown, the label releases Jermaine's first solo single *That's How Love Goes*, which reaches US #46 with *Jermaine* peaking at US #27.

Dec *Corner Of The Sky*, from Broadway musical "Pippin", reaches US #18. In UK, *Lookin' Through The Window* reaches #16 and extracted title track hits #9, their first UK hit single for almost 18 months. At the same time, the brothers' version of the seasonal *Santa Claus Is Coming To Town* is released in UK, and makes #43.

1973 **Mar** Group's version of Jackson Browne's *Doctor My Eyes*, recorded as an album track, is released as a UK single after the writer's own US hit version has failed in UK, and hits #9. In US, Jermaine follows his hit debut with a revival of Shep & The Limelites' 1961 doo-wop ballad *Daddy's Home*, taken from his debut album after strong radio play. It hits US #9, and earns him a solo gold disk.

May *Skywriter* makes US #44, while *Hallelujah Day*, taken from it, reaches US #28.

July The Jacksons are the first major US black group ever to tour Australia. Meanwhile, *Hallelujah Day* reaches UK #20, and Jermaine's solo album *Come Into My Life* makes US #152.

Sept Title track *Skywriter*, not released as US single, reaches UK #25.

Oct *Get It Together*, the title track from the brothers' forthcoming album, reaches US #28.

Nov *Get It Together* climbs to US #100, while Jermaine's single *You're In Good Hands* peaks at US #79. (It will be his last solo success for 3 years.) Motown tries out another brother, Jackie, as a soloist, but his album *Jackie Jackson* fails and the experiment is not repeated.

Dec [15] Jermaine marries Berry Gordy's daughter Hazel, at the Beverly Hills hotel in Los Angeles. (This will have important ramifications when the group eventually decides to leave Motown.)

1974 **Feb** A tour of Africa is cut short after only 1 week, when the brothers are unable to adjust to the food and water.

Apr Group plays at the Grand hotel, Las Vegas, NV.

May *Dancing Machine*, taken from *Get It Together*, hits US #2 behind Ray Stevens' *The Streak*, and is the group's biggest-selling US single since *Never Can Say Goodbye*.

[13] 43 arrests are made at a concert by the group at RFK Stadium, Washington, DC, after bottles are hurled by youths outside the venue, injuring over 50 people.

Nov *Dancing Machine* (the second consecutive Jackson 5 album to contain the title track) reaches US #16. Meanwhile, the group sings backing vocals on Stevie Wonder's *You Haven't Done Nothin'*, which tops US chart.

Dec Taken from the album, *Whatever You Got, I Want* makes US #38.

1975 **Jan** Michael Jackson and Donny Osmond co-present the first American Music Awards.

Mar A 2-part single, *I Am Love* (7 mins. 56 secs. in total), makes US #15.

May The Jackson 5 leave Motown to sign to Epic Records in a deal which will allow more recording freedom. (Michael will also sign a solo deal with the label.) It is revealed that they were receiving only 2.7% royalties on Motown sales and were not allowed to write their own material. Motown files a $20 million suit for breach of contract (the case will finally be settled in 1980). Jermaine, married into the Gordy family, remains at Motown as a soloist and leaves the group. Younger brother Randy (b. Oct.29, 1962, Gary) replaces him and sisters LaToya (b. May 29, 1956, Gary) and Rebbie (b. Maureen Jackson, May 29, 1950, Gary) join the line-up temporarily.

July *Moving Violation*, the group's last Motown recording, makes US #36, while *Forever Came Today*, reviving former Motown stablemates The Supremes' 1968 hit, peaks at US #60.

1976 **June** [16] "The Jacksons", a 4-week summer variety show, airs for the first time on CBS TV. The shows feature the group plus sisters LaToya, Rebbie and Janet, plus guests and a regular comedy sketch team.

Aug A Motown triple compilation album *Jackson Five Anthology* (which also includes Michael's and Jermaine's solo hits on the label) reaches US #84.

Nov Jermaine's solo album *My Name Is Jermaine*, on Motown, makes US #164, and extracted *Let's Be Young Tonight*, peaks at US #55.

1977 **Jan** CBS TV series "The Jacksons" has a second and longer run (through Mar.).

Feb *Enjoy Yourself*, the group's first Epic single (as The Jacksons, since Motown owns The Jackson 5 name) is their biggest-seller since *Dancing Machine* 3 years earlier, hitting US #6 and earning a gold disk. Debut Epic album *The Jacksons* makes US #36.

Apr *Enjoy Yourself* peaks at UK #42.

May On tour in UK for the first time in 5 years, The Jacksons participate in the celebrations for Queen Elizabeth II's Silver Jubilee at the King's theater, Glasgow, Scotland. Meanwhile, written by and recorded with producers Kenny Gamble and Leon Huff at Philadelphia International Records, *Show You The Way To Go* reaches US #28.

June Boosted by the group's just-completed UK concert tour, *Show You The Way To Go* tops the UK chart for a week, their first and only UK #1 hit.

July *The Jacksons* makes UK #54.

Sept *Dreamer*, taken from the album, makes UK #22, while Jermaine's solo album *Feel The Fire* peaks at US #174.

Nov *Goin' Places*, the title track from the group's forthcoming album, makes US #52 and UK #26.

Dec *Goin' Places* makes US #63 and UK #45.

1978 **Feb** *Even Though You've Gone* reaches UK #31.

Mar [1-3] Jackie Jackson wins 4 trophies at the first annual "Rock'N'Roll Sports Classic", a charity event to be televised in May, pitting celebrities against each other in sporting contests.

Nov *Blame It On The Boogie* reaches US #54 and hits UK #8, outselling a competing version on Atco by its writer Mick Jackson (no relation).

1979 **Feb** *Destiny*, the first self-produced brothers album, reaches US #11 and is a million-seller. Title track *Destiny* makes UK #39.
May *Shake Your Body (Down To The Ground)*, taken from *Destiny*, hits US #7 and sells over 2 million copies in the US, earning a platinum disk. It also hits UK #4, while *Destiny* reaches UK #33.

1980 The 1975 Motown suit is finally settled, with The Jacksons making a payment of $600,000 (Motown having claimed $20 million), and the label retaining all rights to the use of the name The Jackson 5.
July Jermaine returns after a 3-year chart absence, with Stevie Wonder-written and produced *Let's Get Serious*, which hits US #9. It is his first solo UK success, hitting #8. Simultaneously, *Let's Get Serious* hits US #6, earning a gold disk, and reaches UK #22.
Aug *Burnin' Hot*, extracted from Jermaine's solo album as a UK-only single, makes UK #32.
Sept In US, *You're Supposed To Keep Your Love For Me*, also Wonder-penned, is Jermaine's solo follow-up and makes US #34.
Oct The Jacksons' self-produced *Triumph* reaches UK #13.
Nov *Lovely One* makes US #12 and UK #29, taken from *Triumph*, which hits US #10 and is their second consecutive platinum album.
Dec LaToya Jackson, the fifth oldest in the family (and the second daughter), signed as a solo artist to Polydor, reaches US #116 with debut album *LaToya Jackson*.

1981 **Jan** Group's *Heartbreak Hotel*, also from *Triumph*, reaches US #22 and UK #44. Meanwhile, Jermaine's solo album *Jermaine*, his second for Motown by this title, makes US #44.
Apr Group's *Can You Feel It* hits UK #6 but stalls at US #77.
May Jermaine's *You Like Me, Don't You?*, makes US #50 and UK #41.
July The Jacksons begin a 36-city US tour, during which live recordings are made for *Jacksons Live*. (It will be released at the end of the year and the tour will gross $5.5 million, $100,000 being donated to Atlanta Children's Foundation after a gig at the Omni in Atlanta, GA.)
Aug *Walk Right Now* makes only US #73, but is a second consecutive UK Top 10 hit at #7.
Sept LaToya Jackson's *My Special Love* peaks at US #175.
Nov Jermaine's solo album *I Like Your Style* makes US #86, while extracted *I'm Just Too Shy* peaks at US #60.

1982 **Jan** Double live album *Jacksons Live* makes US #30.
Sept Jermaine's *Let Me Tickle Your Fancy*, with backing vocals by Devo, reaches US #18, while album of the same title (his last for Motown) makes US #46.

1983 **May** [16] Michael and Jermaine reunite with the brothers to perform on Motown's televised 25th anniversary spectacular, on NBC TV.
Aug UK TV-advertised compilation album *18 Greatest Hits*, on the Telstar label, tops UK chart for 3 weeks.
Nov [21] A press conference called by promoter Don King, at the Tavern On The Green in New York, announces an 18-city, 40-date US tour by The Jacksons (6-strong, with Jermaine rejoining his brothers after leaving Motown), to commence the following summer.

1984 **Feb** Jermaine signs a solo deal with Arista Records.
[27] The Jacksons' Pepsi ad premieres on US MTV.
May Following a promotional UK visit, during which Jermaine performs tracks from his forthcoming Arista debut to delegates at the World DJ Convention in London, his UK-only single release, *Sweetest, Sweetest* makes #52.
June *Jermaine Jackson*, Jermaine's Arista debut, reaches US #19 (and UK #57, where it is retitled *Dynamite*), while sister LaToya signs to Private I label. Her only solo hit single is *Heart Don't Lie* at US #56 as her album of the same name climbs to US #149.
[13] *State Of Shock*, taken from the group's new album, and featuring Mick Jagger duetting on lead vocals with Michael, is released. Los Angeles radio station K-IQQ plays it for 22 hours continuously.
July [6] The 40-date "Victory" tour opens in Kansas City, MO (and will gross $5.5 million). It marks the first time in 8 years that all 6 Jackson brothers have performed together on the live stage. Meanwhile, Motown capitalizes on the renewed interest and releases compilation album *Michael Jackson & The Jackson 5 – 14 Greatest Hits* (on a picture disk), which makes US #168.
Aug *State Of Shock* hits US #3, earning a gold disk, and reaches UK #14. It is taken from *Victory*, which hits UK #3.
Sept *Torture*, also from the album, reaches US #17 and UK #26. *Victory* hit US #4, and earns the group's third album platinum disk. Meanwhile, Jermaine's first US single for Arista, *Dynamite*, reaches US #15, as Marlon launches a solo career.
Nov *Body*, a third single from the album, makes US #47.
Dec Michael writes and produces *Centipede*, the only hit single for

older sister Rebbie, who is signed to CBS/Columbia. It reaches US #24 and the album of the same title makes US #63.
[9] The Jacksons play their last show together at Dodger Stadium, Los Angeles.

1985 **Jan** Jermaine's *Do What You Do* reaches US #13.
[28] Michael, Jackie, Marlon, Randy, Tito and LaToya Jackson all participate in the recording of USA For Africa's *We Are The World*, in aid of African famine relief, which will be a worldwide #1 and multi-million seller.
Mar Jermaine duets with actress/singer Pia Zadora on *When The Rain Begins To Fall*, taken from film "Voyage Of The Rock Aliens". It makes US #54 and UK #68, while *Do What You Do* is Jermaine's biggest-selling UK single, hitting #6.
July Jermaine's *(Closest Thing To) Perfect*, from Jamie Lee Curtis movie "Perfect", peaks at US #67.

1986 **Mar** [8] *Whitney Houston*, with 3 Jermaine-produced tracks, tops US chart.
Apr [26] *I Think It's Love* by Jermaine is his biggest solo seller for 2 years, peaking at US #16.
July [19] Jermaine's solo *Do You Remember Me?* makes US #71. Parent album *Precious Moments* reaches US #46.

1987 **Oct** Marlon releases debut album, *Baby Tonight*, which makes US #188. Singles *Don't Go* and *Baby Tonight* both have success on the R&B chart, but fail to cross over.
Rebbie teams with Cheap Trick's Robin Zander, making #50 on US R&B chart with *You Send The Rain Away*, as The Jacksons' *Time Out For The Burglar*, from movie "Burglar", makes US R&B #88.

1988 **Apr** Motown reissue *I Want You Back* hits UK #8.
1989 **July** The Jacksons' (now comprising Jackie, Jermaine, Tito and Randy) *2300 Jackson Street* is the group's first album without Michael (although he sings briefly on the title track, which is sung by the entire clan, including Marlon, Janet, Rebbie, LaToya and 16 nieces and nephews). Produced by LA & Babyface and Michael Omartian, its title referring to the street in Gary where they lived, the album makes US #59 and UK #39. Extracted *Nothin (That Compares 2 U)* peaks at US #77 and UK #33.
Sept [20] Los Angeles Superior Court Judge Francis Rothchild award Alejandra Oaiza $3,000 a month child support, after Randy Jackson fails to show up for a case which seeks to prove him the father of the child Oaiza is due to give birth to in Nov.
Oct [21] Jermaine's *Don't Take It So Personal* peaks at UK #69.

1991 As siblings Michael and Janet sign the 2 biggest contracts in recording history, the next generation of Jacksons (Tito's 3 children and 2 of Jermaine's 5) looks set to emerge.

THE JAM

Paul Weller (vocals, bass)
Bruce Foxton (guitar)
Rick Buckler (drums)

1975 Weller (b. May 25, 1958) meets Buckler (b. Paul Richard Buckler, Dec.6 1955) at school in Woking, Surrey, where they jam together during lunch hour in the music room. Using the session as group name inspiration, they link with Foxton (b. Sept.1, 1955) and Steve Brookes to play local social and working men's clubs. Brookes leaves, Foxton moves to bass, with Weller now on lead guitar and vocals. (The Jam will remain a trio for the rest of its career.)

1976 Concentrating on live work in London, The Jam plays gigs at the Marquee, 100 Club and regular jaunts at the Red Cow pub, where the group is viewed and dismissed by EMI Records.

1977 **Feb** [25] Following a month's Red Cow residence and a frenzied gig at the Marquee, The Jam, managed by Weller's father, John, signs to Polydor Records for £6,000 advance offered by A&R man Chris Parry. (A 4-year deal, it will be re-negotiated after 90 days.) UK music press links the band with the burgeoning punk movement but The Jam moves to its own niche and a later spotlight in a UK mod revival. They currently sport mohair suits and Rickenbacker guitars.
May Debut single *In The City*, produced by Parry, makes UK #40.
June With all songs penned by the group's leader, 19-year-old Weller *In The City* reaches UK #20. It has taken 11 days to record. The Jam begins a 42-date UK debut tour in the group car, a red Ford Cortina.
Aug Aided by a first appearance on UK TV's "Top Of The Pops", *All Around The World* reaches UK #13.
Nov *The Modern World* makes UK #36. Group visits US for a 16-date club tour, which is not successful.
Dec Parent album *This Is The Modern World* reaches UK #22 and is

criticized by UK press. A major UK tour starts, highlighted by a brawl between the band and rugby players at a hotel in Leeds, W.Yorks. Leeds Crown Court subsequently acquits Weller, who moves to London with his first love, Gill.

1978 **Mar** While the band supports Blue Öyster Cult on an ill-billed US tour, *News Of The World* makes UK #27.
Aug *David Watts*, a cover of a Kinks' track, backed with *"A"Bomb In Wardour Street* peaks at UK #25.
[25] The Jam plays Reading Festival, Berks., as the punk "small venue" ideal fades.
Oct *Down In The Tube Station At Midnight* climbs to UK #15.
Nov *All Mod Cons*, produced by Vic Coppersmith-Heaven and featuring 11 Weller compositions, hits UK #6. It coincides with the start of a European tour.

1979 **Mar** *Strange Town* peaks at UK #15. The Jam begins its first world tour, visiting US, Canada and Europe.
Sept *When You're Young* makes UK #17.
Nov With The Jam firmly established as a "quick" singles band, *The Eton Rifles* hits UK #3 and parent album, *Setting Sons*, hits UK #4.

1980 **Mar** Their first US chart appearance, *Setting Sons* peaks at US #137 (major US success will always elude this particularly British band). Meanwhile *Going Underground/The Dreams Of Children* becomes the first UK single of the 80s to debut at #1. The band is in Los Angeles, CA, when the news breaks.
Aug *Start* tops UK chart.
Dec *Sound Affects* hits UK #2. Band begins major UK tour ending in sell-out dates at favored venue, London's Rainbow theater. (Weller is using his royalties to set up a publishing company, Riot Stories, for political works.)

1981 **Jan** UK magazine **Melody Maker** arranges for Weller to meet former hero The Who's Pete Townshend. During the interview, both artists confirm that they do not like the other's band.
Feb German import single, *That's Entertainment*, reaches UK #21. *Sound Affects* reaches US #72, as The Jam sets off on another world tour incorporating Japan.
June *Funeral Pyre* hits UK #4.
Aug Weller makes a program on class awareness for UK BBC TV series "Something Else".
Oct *Absolute Beginners* hits UK #4 as Weller finances 2 new enterprises: **Jamming** magazine, to be run by Jam devotee Tony Fletcher, and his own Respond record label.
Dec The Jam sweeps **New Musical Express** Readers' Poll, as it plays 4 standing-room-only Christmas dates in London.

1982 **Jan** Album *The Jam*, a mini-collection of 5 UK hits, reaches US #176. During new recording, Weller has a breakdown and quits drinking.
Feb *Town Called Malice/Precious*, released as a 12" single, hits UK #1. The Jam becomes first band since The Beatles to play 2 numbers on the same edition of BBC TV's "Top Of The Pops" when it plays both sides.
Mar *The Gift*, featuring a new soul slant, tops UK chart and reaches US #82. As the group sets off on another UK, Europe, Canada, US and Japanese 4-month tour called "Trans Global Unity Express", an early gig at Bingley Hall, Stafford, Staffs. is filmed for video release.
July Import single, *Just Who Is The Five O'Clock Hero*, hits UK #8. Weller takes 2 weeks' vacation in Italy with Gill. Disillusioned with The Jam formula and keen to seek new soul direction, he decides to disband The Jam.
Sept With the public still unaware, and the group recently committed to CND anti-nuclear cause, The Jam's *The Bitterest Pill (I Ever Had To Swallow)*, featuring Belle Star Jenny McKeowen duetting with Weller, hits UK #2.
Oct [28] The Jam announces its split, but will honor a last UK tour.
Dec *Beat Surrender* enters at UK #1, as the band plays farewell dates. Censored by US radio, it fails, as with every Jam single release, to make the Hot 100. *Dig The New Breed*, a 14-track live compilation 1977-82, hits UK #2, while UK hits compilation album, released in US only, *The Bitterest Pill (I Ever Had To Swallow)* reaches US #135.

1983 **Jan** Polydor re-issues all of The Jam's 16 singles, which establishes the precedent of all re-charting simultaneously in UK. Weller folds **Jamming** magazine.
Feb *Dig The New Breed* peaks at US #131.
Apr US-only EP, *Beat Surrender* reaches US #171.
Aug [27] Reissued *In The City* makes UK #100.
Oct While Weller has formed The Style Council with ex-Merton Parka Mick Talbot, his Respond label signs Questions and Tracie. Buckler joins new group Time UK and Foxton releases solo album *Touch Sensitive* on Arista. The Jam's double hits album *Snap!* hits UK #2. A

similar video tops UK music video chart. (Weller, always politically active, will join the Labour Party-promoting "The Red Wedge Tour" in time for next UK General Election.)

RICK JAMES

1967 James (b. James Johnson, Feb.1, 1952, Buffalo, NY) goes AWOL from US Navy, settles in Toronto, Canada, and forms rock/soul band, The Mynah Birds, with his room mate, local singer Neil Young.

1968 Group goes to Detroit, MI. It signs to Motown, but no material is released. James completes production work for Bobby Taylor, The Spinners and The Marvelettes.

1970 He moves to London, and forms blues band, The Main Line. (For the next 7 years he will commute between London, Canada and US. Rumors persist that he spends time in a US prison for desertion from the Navy.)

1977 James returns to US where he forms The Stone City Band. Inspired by George Clinton he develops a rock/funk-style he dubs "funk'n'roll". Impressed by his demo tapes, Motown signs him to a worldwide deal.

1978 **July** *You And I* reaches UK #46, while debut album *Come Get It!* eventually climbs to US #13.
Sept *You And I* reaches US #13, and is awarded a gold disk.
Oct *Mary Jane*, a barely disguised hymn to marijuana, hits US R&B #3 but initially fails to cross over. Second album *Bustin' Out Of L Seven* is released. James, with The Stone City Band and vocal trio, The Mary Jane Girls, embarks on his first US tour. His wildly extrovert show attracts wide media attention and enthusiastic audiences.
Nov He is out of action for several months with hepatitis. Official sources give "exhaustion" as the cause of the illness. (There are also rumors of drug-related causes.)

1979 **Jan** *Mary Jane* finally reaches US #41.
Mar *Bustin' Out Of L Seven* makes US #16.
Apr *High On Your Love Suite* stalls at US #72.
May *Bustin' Out* falters at US #71.
July James produces new Motown artist Teena Marie's debut album *Wild And Peaceful* and single *I'm A Sucker For Your Love*, with James featured as co-vocalist, which makes US #43. (James and Marie will continue to contribute to each other's recordings.)
Dec Third album *Fire It Up* reaches US #34.

1980 **Apr** James-produced debut album by The Stone City Band, *In 'N' Out*, reaches US #122.
Sept *Big Time* peaks at UK #41. Fourth album *Garden Of Love* is released. An uncharacteristic ballad set, it reaches only US #83.

1981 **Apr** James-produced second Stone City Band album, *The Boys Are Back*, is released.
June Fifth album *Street Songs* is released. An extrovert return to funk'n'roll, it hits US #3 and achieves double platinum status. (It will stay in the Top 100 Album chart for 54 weeks, and hit US R&B #1, staying on top for 20 weeks.)
July *Give It To Me Baby*, taken from *Street Songs*, tops US R&B chart for 5 weeks and makes US #40 and UK #47.
Sept *Super Freak (Pt 1)*, also from the album, reaches US #16. James embarks on a successful US tour with Teena Marie, Cameo and The Sugarhill Gang.

1982 **June** James guests on The Temptations' *Standing On The Top* which climbs to US #53. Sixth album *Throwin' Down* is released.
July *Dance Wit' Me* reaches US #64 and UK #53. *Throwin' Down* reaches US #13 and UK #93.
Nov [25-27] James joins Aretha Franklin, Gladys Knight, The Clash and others performing to 45,000 at the Jamaica World Music Festival.
Dec James visits UK for promotion-only work.

1983 **June** James-produced Mary Jane Girls album *Mary Jane Girls* is released.
Aug *Cold Blooded*, on Motown, hits US R&B #1 but, like all James singles, it is cold-shouldered by MTV and stalls at US #40.
Sept *Cold Blooded* hits US R&B #1. James-produced Stone City Band album *Out From The Shadow* is released.
Oct *Cold Blooded* reaches US #16.

1984 **Jan** *Ebony Eyes*, sweet-soul duet with Smokey Robinson makes US #43.
Aug *17* reaches US #36.
Oct *Reflections*, a retrospective compilation with 3 new recordings added, reaches US #41.

1985 **Apr** *Can't Stop* makes US #50.
June [8] James-penned and produced *In My House* for Mary Jane Girls hits US #7.
Sept James' contract with Motown ends in acrimony and he retreats to

work in his Le Joint recording studios at home in Buffalo.
Dec His first project is to write, arrange and produce US comedian Eddie Murphy's debut album. *Party All The Time* hits US #2 while Murphy's *How Could It Be* will reach US #26.

1986 **July** *The Flag*, released on Motown's Gordy offshoot, and his last for the label, makes US #95.

1987 James signs to Reprise Records.

1988 **Aug** [20] First release featuring rap lady Roxanne Shante, *Loosey's Rap*, tops US R&B chart, but fails to cross over, as parent album *Wonderful*, featuring traditional sexual over- and undertones, peaks at US #148.

1989 **May** *This Magic Moment/Dance With Me*, a medley of Drifters hits from Warner Bros.' Richard Perry-produced *Rock, Rhythm & Blues* project, peaks at #74 on US R&B chart.

1990 **June** [16] MC Hammer's *U Can't Touch This*, using *Super Freak* as its rhythm track, hits US #8. James will successfully negotiate appropriate royalties from the Hammer camp, as the central riff becomes a Hammer "trademark" throughout the year.

TOMMY JAMES & THE SHONDELLS

Tommy James (vocals)
Eddie Gray (guitar)
Mike Vale (bass)
Peter Lucia (drums)
Ronnie Rosman (organ)

1960 At age 12, James (b. Thomas Gregory Jackson, Apr.29, 1947, Dayton, OH) forms a group at school in Niles, MI.

1962 Group cuts *Long Pony Tail* for a local label.

1963 Some months after the disk first appears, DJ Jack Douglas on station W-NIL hears it, contacts James, and asks if he has any other material. James has heard *Hanky Panky* performed in a night club in South Bend, IN. (It is the B-side of a single by The Raindrops, who are actually its writers, Jeff Barry and Ellie Greenwich.) When he records the song for Douglas' Snap label, with producer Bob Mack, James ad-libs most of the lyrics. It sells well in Michigan, Illinois and Indiana.

1965 **Dec** Out of work following high school graduation, James receives a phone call from a DJ in Pittsburgh, PA, who has been playing the 2-year-old *Hanky Panky*. James flies there to appear on local TV and radio. He forms a new Shondells, after the original group refuses to move from Indiana, by hiring local band The Raconteurs. The line-up is Rosman (b. Feb.28, 1945), Vale (b. July 17, 1949), Vince Pietropaoli, drums, and George Magura, sax. The latter 2 soon leave, to be replaced by Gray (b. Feb.27, 1948) and Lucia (b. Feb.2, 1947).

1966 **July** Picked up for national release by Roulette Records in New York, *Hanky Panky* hits US #1, sells a million, and makes UK #38. James signs to Roulette.
Sept *Hanky Panky* reaches US #46. R&B-style *Say I Am (What I Am)* reaches US #21. The label teams the group with songwriter/producers Bo Gentry and Richie Cordell, in a partnership which will produce a melodic, exhilarating and commercial style.
Dec *It's Only Love* makes US #31.

1967 **Apr** *I Think We're Alone Now*, a distinctive bubbling arrangement, hits US #4.
June *Mirage* hits US #10 and *I Think We're Alone Now* makes US #74.
July *I Like The Way* reaches US #25.
Sept *Gettin' Together* makes US #18.
Nov *Out Of The Blue* reaches US #43.

1968 **Feb** *Get Out Now* makes US #48, marking the end of the group's lightweight pop period.
Mar Compilation album *Something Special! The Best Of Tommy James And The Shondells* reaches US #174.
June *Mony Mony*, written by Gentry and Cordell with Bobby Bloom (later of *Montego Bay* fame) and James himself, with the group's sound hardened into a rock-solid dance beat, hits US #3. (The writers get the title of the song from a Mutual Of New York sign outside James' apartment in New York.)
July *Mony Mony* makes US #193.
Aug Lack of UK chart success ends as *Mony Mony* hits #1 for 4 weeks, becoming country's most popular dancefloor disk of the summer. US follow-up *Somebody Cares* peaks at #53 but is not used as UK follow-up.
Nov *Mony Mony*-like *Do Something To Me* makes US #38. Issued as the UK follow-up, it does not chart. The group has developed strong ideas of what its new work should be sounding like, and persuades Roulette to let it self-produce the next album.

1969 **Feb** *Crimson and Clover*, a shortened version of the 5-min. album title track, launches the new self-produced Shondells sound: a complex weave of vocal and instrumental sounds with an ethereal, layered melody, hints of psychedelia and a solid commercial hook. It tops US chart and wins a gold disk, becoming the group's biggest US seller.
May *Sweet Cherry Wine*, a similar production with innovative tempo and rhythm changes, hits US #7. *Crimson And Clover* hits US #8.
July [26] *Crystal Blue Persuasion*, a laid-back summer sound which is James' favorite of his own recordings, hits US #2, behind Zager & Evans' *In The Year 2525*, and is another million-seller.
Nov *Ball Of Fire* makes US #19. *Cellophane Symphony* makes US #141.

1970 **Jan** *She* reaches US #23.
Feb Compilation album *The Best Of Tommy James And The Shondells* peaks at US #21.
Mar *Gotta Get Back To You*, a shift back to R&B style, makes US #45.
May *Travelin'* reaches US #91.
June *Come To Me* makes US #47. James collapses on stage in Alabama. The Shondells quit to become the (unsuccessful) Hog Heaven, while James recuperates on his farm in upstate New York.
Aug James produces US #7 hit *Tighter And Tighter* for Brooklyn group Alive & Kicking (a song he intended to cut as his first solo, but did not complete due to remaining nervousness about his vocal performance).
Sept Encouraged by the group's success, James records solo *Ball And Chain*, which peaks at US #57.

1971 **Jan** *Church Street Soul Revival* makes US #62.
Mar *Adrienne* climbs to US #93.
Aug James' biggest solo success, *Draggin' The Line*, hits US #4 and is another million-seller.
Sept *Christian Of The World* reaches US #131.
Oct *I'm Comin' Home* makes US #40.
Dec *Nothing To Hide* reaches US #41.

1972 **Feb** *Tell 'Em Willie Boy's A'Comin'* peaks at US #89.
June *Cat's Eye In The Window* climbs to US #90.
Sept *Love Song* makes US #67.
Nov *Celebration* reaches US #95.

1973 **Mar** *Boo, Boo, Don't 'Cha Be Blue* makes US #70 and James turns to the club circuit after 18 months of minor US chart placings.

1977 James signs to Fantasy Records and releases Jeff Barry-produced album *Midnight Rider*. He covers several UK hits by Gary Glitter, who briefly serves as an influence.

1980 **Mar** James, signed to Millennium Records, makes US #19 with *Three Times In Love*, after a 7-year chart absence.
Apr *Three Times In Love* reaches US #134.

1981 **May** *You're So Easy To Love* peaks at US #58.

1982 **May** Joan Jett's version of *Crimson And Clover* hits US #7, beginning an era in which many old James hits will be rediscovered by several acts.

1987 **Nov** Billy Idol's cover of *Mony Mony* knocks Tiffany's cover of *I Think We're Alone Now* off the top of US chart. (Tiffany will hit UK #1, while Idol will hit UK #7.)

1989 **July** James signs with Aegis Records, releasing his first album in some years.

JAN AND DEAN

Jan Berry (vocals)
Dean Torrence (vocals)

1957 Berry (b. Apr.3, 1941, Los Angeles, CA) and Torrence (b. Mar.10, 1940, Los Angeles) meet while members of Los Angeles' Emerson junior high school football team where, discovering that the showers are a great place to sing, they form a vocal group named The Barons with 4 friends. When this also moves outside school, neighbors Bruce Johnston and Sandy Nelson join on piano and drums.

1958 Group splits, leaving only Berry, Torrence and Arnie Ginsburg. Ginsburg becomes infatuated with a stripper at nearby Follies Burlesque and the trio, with Torrence on lead vocals, records *Jennie Lee*, inspired by her, in Berry's garage. While Torrence is away for 6 months following call-up to Army Reserves, this tape comes to the attention of Joe Lubin at Arwin Records (a small Los Angeles label owned by Doris Day's husband Marty Melcher), who offers to release it. Berry and Ginsburg sign and the disk is issued credited to Jan & Arnie.
Aug *Jennie Lee* hits US #8.
Oct Torrence returns from service shortly after Jan & Arnie's follow-up *Gas Money* peaks at US #81. Arwin releases 1 more Jan & Arnie single, *I Love Linda*, but it flops, and Ginsberg drops out. Remaining duo starts recording again in Berry's garage.

1959 They meet Lou Adler and Herb Alpert, 2 youth veterans of Los Angeles music business who work frequently with Sam Cooke, and also manage small Dore label, which has just had a million-seller with *To*

Know Him Is To Love Him by The Teddy Bears. Adler and Alpert become Jan And Dean's managers and work with them on recordings, taking the basic garage-cut tracks and overdubbing fuller arrangements (written by Alpert) in a professional 2-track studio.

Sept [7] Duo performs, with Frankie Avalon, Duane Eddy, The Coasters and many others, in Dick Clark's stage show at the Michigan State Fair, to an audience of 15,000 over 4 performances.

Oct *Baby Talk*, a cover of obscure Californian group original and first under new work arrangement with Alpert and Adler, hits US #10. Early copies are marketed as by Jan & Arnie, to capitalize on earlier success; once it sells, credit becomes Jan And Dean. Duo appears on Dick Clark's "American Bandstand" on US TV for the first time.

Nov Alpert and Adler write follow-up *There's A Girl*, reaching US #97.

Mar A revival of traditional *Clementine* (credited as a Berry/Torrence composition) peaks at US #65, losing out to Bobby Darin's coincidental swing-style revival which reaches US #21.

Sept After *White Tennis Sneakers* has failed, a revival of The Moonglows' oldie *We Go Together* makes US #53.

Dec Another revival, The Crows' *Gee*, falters at US #81. (2 further Dore singles over next 7 months, *Baggy Pants* and *Let's Fly Away*, plus an album which includes 12 singles tracks, will all fail.)

May Determined to sign to a major label and benefit from fuller promotion, duo cuts a revival of Hoagy Carmichael and Frank Loesser's *Heart And Soul* in gimmicky uptempo vocal treatment. With Adler, they try to gain a deal with Liberty Records. (Alpert despises the track, and drops out of the team and business partnership with Adler to develop his ideas for instrumental music with his trumpet – he will co-found A&M Records in 1962.) Liberty is interested in Jan And Dean, but agrees with Alpert about *Heart And Soul*. Adler and duo sign an interim 2-record deal with independent Challenge label, owned by Gene Autry.

July *Heart And Soul*, released on Challenge, hits US #25, their biggest success for 2 years.

Sept *Heart And Soul* is first of only 2 UK Jan And Dean hits, at #24. In US, quick follow-up *Wanted One Girl* fails, and duo signs to Liberty.

Jan Liberty debut, a revival of *A Sunday Kind Of Love*, peaks at US #95.

May Staff producer Snuff Garrett is brought in to work on *Tennessee*, written by Leon Russell and Buzz Cason, and it makes US #69.

Aug Duo meets The Beach Boys for the first time, when both groups play a teen hop. (The Beach Boys will occasionally back Jan And Dean live during fall 1962, and each group becomes familiar with the other's repertoire.)

Feb *Linda*, a revival of Jack Lawrence's 1944 song about his lawyer's daughter Linda Eastman (later to become Mrs. Paul McCartney), borrows some of the beat and falsetto vocalizing of the recent Four Seasons hits, and reaches US #28. Adler recommends that the duo should get involved in the burgeoning California surf music scene (until now mainly instrumental) since both are keen surfers. For *Jan And Dean Take Linda Surfin'*, mainly of cover versions, they record 2 surfing songs they know from singing them live – Brian Wilson's *Surfin'* and *Surfin' Safari*, enlisting the help of Wilson and the other Beach Boys to back them in the studio.

July Constant musical and social fraternization with Brian Wilson and The Beach Boys leads to Wilson giving the duo *Surf City* to complete and record. With The Beach Boys' voices as back-up, it tops US chart for 2 weeks (a year before The Beach Boys' own first #1 with *I Get Around*), and sells over a million, the duo's biggest-selling single. *Jan And Dean Take Linda Surfin'* reaches US #71.

Sept *Surf City* is the second and last Jan And Dean UK hit, at #26.

Oct *Honolulu Lulu*, written by Berry with Los Angeles DJ Roger Christian, reaches US #11, while *Surf City And Other Swingin' Cities* reaches US #32. Featuring mostly Jan And Dean versions of oldies with US city names in their titles, the album is (like *Honolulu Lulu*) arranged and produced by Berry, and features what will become the duo's staple studio backing crew: the Phil Spector school of with-session musicians like drummer Hal Blaine, guitarists Tommy Tedesco, Glen Campbell and Billy Strange, keyboardists Leon Russell and Larry Knechtel, and sax player Steve Douglas.

Jan Like The Beach Boys, Jan And Dean expand their lyrical concerns to include cars and the hot rod craze: Berry/Wilson/Christian-penned *Drag City* hits US #10.

Mar *Drag City*, featuring mostly original material, plus The Routers' *Sting Ray* and The Beach Boys' *Little Deuce Coupe*, reaches US #22.

May *Dead Man's Curve*, a car race melodrama in pounding arrangement with car horns and crash effects, hits US #8. B-side *The New Girl In School*, originally a Brian Wilson song titled *Gonna Hustle You*, with new lyrics by Berry, reaches US #37.

June *Dead Man's Curve/The New Girl In School* peaks at US #80. It eschews surfing concerns in favor of car and girl songs, and has P.F. Sloan and Steve Barri (AKA The Fantastic Baggys) as back-up vocalists, together with Berry's girlfriend Jill Gibson (who will later replace Michelle Phillips in The Mamas And The Papas).

Aug *The Little Old Lady (From Pasadena)* hits US #3. It is penned by Roger Christian with Don Altfield, a student with Berry at California College of Medicine (both Berry and Torrence continue their education throughout these hitmaking years; the latter initially in medicine, then switching to architecture and graphic design at USC).

Sept [4] Duo appears with The Animals, Chuck Berry and Del Shannon in a 10-day stand at Paramount theater, Brooklyn, New York.

Oct Theme from Fabian movie, "Ride The Wild Surf", another Berry/Christian/Wilson collaboration, reaches US #16. B-side is near-nonsensical *The Anaheim, Azusa And Cucamonga Sewing Circle, Book Review And Timing Association*, which climbs to US #77.

Nov *The Little Old Lady From Pasadena* and movie soundtrack album *Ride The Wild Surf* are released within a week of each other, and peak at US #40 and #66 respectively. Both feature Sloan and Barri as backing vocalists and as writers. Both contain *Sidewalk Surfin'*, also extracted as a single. A reworking of The Beach Boys' *Catch A Wave* with new lyrics about skateboarding, makes US #25 (and promotes sales of the Jan And Dean "Little Old Lady" skateboard, merchandised at the same time).

1965

Mar *(Here They Come) From All Over The World*, a Sloan/Barri song, reaches US #56. It is theme from "The TAMI Show", a videotaped TV spectacular (later released as movie "Gather No Moss" in UK) hosted by the duo, and including performances from The Rolling Stones, Chuck Berry, The Beach Boys, Marvin Gaye, James Brown and many others. Jan And Dean's own slot on the show is captured on *Command Performance/Live In Person*, which makes US #33.

July Ballad *You Really Know How To Hurt A Guy*, written by Berry and Christian with Jill Gibson, reaches US #27. Torrence hates the song, and Berry ejects him during recording, so he is not heard on it.

Oct At another Jan And Dean session, brought to a halt by a technical hitch, Torrence relieves his boredom by walking to a nearby studio where The Beach Boys are holding "live-in-studio" sessions with friends for an off-the-cuff style album, *Beach Boys Party*. Asked if he wants to sing something, he suggests old Regents hit *Barbara Ann*. After a few minutes' rehearsal, the song is recorded with Torrence on lead vocal. (The track appears on the album, and will also be the next Beach Boys hit at US #2 and UK #3, but for contractual and inter-label political reasons, Torrence is not credited on it.)

Nov *I Found A Girl*, a near-psychedelic arrangement of a Sloan/Barri song, reaches US #30, as *Jan And Dean Golden Hits, Volume 2* compilation of singles from *Linda* onward, peaks at US #107.

Dec *The Universal Coward*, a patriotic and apparently right-wing song borrowed from Buffy Saint-Marie's *The Universal Soldier*, is released as a Jan Berry solo after Torrence disowns it. It fails to chart, as does Jan And Dean's opportunistic *Folk City* which follows close behind.

1966

Jan *Folk'N'Roll*, including the recently unsuccessful singles, several covers of hits, and some Sloan/Barri items including *Eve Of Destruction*, makes US #145.

Feb Familiar in concert, and partially present on most albums, Jan And Dean's surreal comedy bent is given full rein on *Jan And Dean Meet Batman*, a cash-in on the new cult-appeal TV series. The album fails to chart, but extracted *Batman* makes US #66.

Mar Duo prepares to film "Easy Come, Easy Go" with Elvis Presley, and signs to do a weekly ABC TV show. The contract with Liberty expires, and although label wants it to re-sign, duo plans its own Jan & Dean Records as a subsidiary of Lou Adler's Dunhill label.

Apr [12] Berry, preoccupied with his just-received draft notice and with an imminent medical school exam, crashes his Corvette into a parked truck on Whittier Boulevard in Los Angeles, and is almost killed. (He will be initally in a coma and then totally paralyzed for several months, suffering partial paralysis for long after. He will also suffer brain damage which will necessitate re-learning processes. Recovery will be slow over many years.)

June *Filet Of Soul*, consisting of out-takes from duo's TAMI Show performance and unused studio rejects, is released to Torrence's displeasure, and reaches US #127. Unhappy with Liberty's plunder-the-vaults policy, but with Berry out of action for the forseeable future (if not for good), Torrence decides to keep the duo's name active on his own terms, while also helping pay Berry's hospital bills. Setting up independent J&D Records and Magic Lamp

JAN AND DEAN cont.

Productions, he puts a new lyric over *The Little Old Lady*'s instrumental track, titling it *Tijuana*, but it fails to chart.

July *Popsicle*, originally on *Drag City*, reaches US #21. An album of the same title, compiled entirely from old tracks, fails to sell.

Aug Second J&D release, a revival of The Jamies' oldie *Summertime, Summertime*, coupled with *California Lullaby*, produced by Torrence, with poor promotion fails to sell.

Sept Unissued *Fiddle Around*, released by Liberty, reaches US #93, and is Jan And Dean's last chart entry.

1967 Mar Torrence concludes 1-year deal with CBS/Columbia to take Jan And Dean releases from Magic Lamp Productions. *Yellow Balloon* is released, but is defeated by duo's original version, also called *Yellow Balloon*.

Apr Torrence cuts *Save For A Rainy Day* with Jan And Dean's old studio session musicians. A collection of new and old songs around a general theme of rain, it is released in Los Angeles on J&D, and scheduled for national distribution by Columbia. Berry, who is slowly recovering, refuses to be a sleeping party to it, and CBS cancels, not being interested in only half of Jan And Dean to promote it.

June Torrence puts his graphic design degree to use, and launches Kittyhawk Graphics, getting an assignment from White Whale Records to design The Turtles' *Golden Hits* sleeve, and later White Whale's display advertising and other corporate artwork.

Oct After collaborating with Brian Wilson on some tracks for The Beach Boys' *Smiley Smile*, Torrence is given the song *Vegetables* and records a version of it with help of session men Joe Osborn and Larry Knechtel. White Whale releases it under the name The Laughing Gravy, but it does not chart.

Nov Berry signs a deal with Warner Bros., supposedly as a therapeutic measure after pressure from his father and doctors. Torrence declines to take part, feeling Berry is ill-served by not having full-time professional help, but does not object to use of his name. (Label releases 3 unsuccessful singles as by Jan And Dean. Berry later states that vocals on them were actually by session singers, mainly Ron Hicklin.)

1971 Aug With United Artists Records (inheritors of Liberty) as a client of Kittyhawk Graphics, Torrence works closely with the company on double *Jan & Dean Anthology Album*, which includes all the hits and a live performance side, from *Jennie Lee* in 1958 to The Laughing Gravy's *Vegetables* in 1967.

1972 Jan Berry signs a solo deal with Lou Adler's Ode label, releasing self-penned *Mother Earth*.

Mar In a short-term deal with United Artists, Torrence forms The Legendary Masked Surfers with Bruce Johnston and Terry Melcher (once both The Rip Chords and Bruce & Terry, as well as their Beach Boys connections), using old Jan And Dean backing tracks for *Gonna Hustle You* (*The New Girl In School*) with the original, raunchier lyrics.

May Berry revives Huey "Piano" Smith & The Clowns' *Don't You Just Know It* on Ode.

July Second Legendary Masked Surfers release updates Bruce & Terry's 1964 hit *Summer Means Fun*, written by Sloan and Barri. (After this, the group becomes California, and later California Music, involving varied personnel including Curt Becher, Gloria Grinel, Kenny Hinkle and Chad Stuart. Torrence's involvement ends here.)

1973 Jan And Dean re-form for a California Surfer's Stomp Festival and a projected US tour, miming to backing tracks because of Berry's uncertainty about performing, but it turns out to be a disaster.

1974 July Berry releases solo *Tinsel Town*, co-written with Roger Christian and Joan Jacobs.

1975 June Duo performs on stage again at a rock revival show put together by DJ Jim Pewter, this time with no embarrassing disasters.

Aug Jan And Dean reunite on Ode to record *Fun City*, written by Berry with Alan Wolfson and Jim Pewter.

1978 Feb [3] ABC TV's "Dead Man's Curve" biopic, starring Bruce Davison and Richard Hatch as Jan And Dean, airs in US. Interest in the duo rekindles, and, with Berry's health improved, they embark on a lengthy coast-to-coast US tour.

1980 July *The Jan And Dean Story* reaches UK #67.

Torrence joins The Beach Boys' Mike Love to record several tracks for a cassette-only release of 60s hits.

1982 Rhino Records releases live Jan And Dean album *One Summer Night – Live*. (The duo will continue to make increased live performances throughout the 80s.)

JAPAN

David Sylvian (vocals, guitar)
Rob Dean (guitar)
Richard Barbieri (keyboards)
Steve Jansen (drums)
Mick Karn (saxophone)

1977 Band having formed in Lewisham, London, with Sylvian (b. David Batt, Feb.23, 1958, Lewisham), his brother Jansen (b. Steve Batt), and school friends Barbieri and Karn (b. Anthony Michaelides, July 24, 1958, London), and played Roxy Music-influenced music at local gigs recruits Dean from an ad for a second guitarist. Band wins a talent contest sponsored by German record company Ariola-Hansa (which has just opened London offices), and is signed to the label. The Batt brothers and Michaelides adopt their stage names.

1978 Mar Debut UK release *Don't Rain On My Parade* (an oldie from musical "Funny Girl") fails to chart.

Apr *Adolescent Sex* is issued. To promote it, the band tours UK as support to Blue Öyster Cult, but sales are few. (2 further singles, *The Unconventional* and *Sometimes I Feel So Low*, and second album, *Obscure Alternatives* are released in UK to little success.)

1979 May *Life In Tokyo*, produced by Giorgio Moroder, fails to chart in UK (but the band has some chart success in Japan).

1980 Feb *Quiet Life* is UK chart debut, reaching #53.

Mar A cover of Smokey Robinson's *I Second That Emotion* is the band's last recording on Ariola-Hansa.

July Band signs to Virgin Records, and begins work with producer John Punter.

Oct Virgin debut *Gentlemen Take Polaroids* makes UK #60. The growing popularity of the fashion and music of the New Romantic movement, which Japan's style has anticipated, is a key element in Japan's increased UK airplay, press coverage and consequent chart success.

Dec *Gentlemen Take Polaroids* reaches UK #45.

1981 May Dean leaves, moving to Los Angeles, CA. *The Art Of Parties*, makes UK #48.

Sept Karn exhibits his sculpture work in Japan.

Oct Title track from *Quiet Life*, released on Hansa after the group's departure, reaches UK #19. A compilation of early material, *Assemblage*, reaches UK #26.

Nov Newly-recorded on Virgin, *Visions Of China* makes UK #32 and *Tin Drum* UK #12. Both reveal oriental influences.

1982 Feb Hansa reissue of *European Son* (B-side of *Life In Tokyo*) climbs to UK #31.

Apr Ballad *Ghosts* gains widespread UK airplay and hits UK #5.

June *Cantonese Boy* makes UK #24, amid reports of constant disagreements between Sylvian and Karn, and rumors concerning the band's break-up. These are further fuelled by news of solo projects. Karn is first to release a solo for Virgin, *Sensitive*, which does not chart.

July Hansa reissue of *I Second That Emotion* hits UK #9.

Aug Karn and Jansen play on an album by Japanese act Akiko Yano, and Barbieri produces Swedish band Lustans Lakejer. Sylvian teams with Japanese musician Ryuichi Sakamoto of The Yellow Magic Orchestra, on *Bamboo Houses*. Released under the name Sylvian Sakamoto, it reaches UK #30.

Oct *Life In Tokyo*, reissued by Hansa, makes UK #28 as Japan tours UK.

Nov [22] Japan officially announces its break-up, following a final UK concert at London's Hammersmith Odeon. Karn's solo *Titles* charts in the same week, making UK #74.

Dec *Night Porter*, a late Virgin release, reaches UK #29.

1983 Mar Hansa's final Japan release, reviving The Velvet Underground's *All Tomorrow's Parties* (originally on *Quiet Life*), reaches UK #38.

May A live version of *Canton* is Japan's final UK Singles hit, at #42.

June Double live album *Oil On Canvas*, recorded during the group's final tour, hits UK #5.

July Sylvian and Ryuichi Sakamoto collaborate on *Forbidden Colours*, the theme to David Bowie/Tom Conti movie "Merry Christmas Mr. Lawrence" (in which Sakamoto also stars). It climbs to UK #16.

1984 Jan Sylvian solo *Red Guitar* reaches UK #17.

June Sylvian exhibits his Polaroid photo montages at London's Hamilton's Gallery.

July His solo album *Brilliant Trees* hits UK #4.

Aug Sylvian's *The Ink In The Well* makes UK #36.

Nov His *Pulling Punches* reaches UK #56. Karn teams with former Bauhaus lead singer Peter Murphy as Dali's Car. Signed to Paradox Records, their debut is *The Judgement Is The Mirror*, peaking at UK #66.

Dec Double album *Exorcising Ghosts*, a compilation of Japan's Virgin material, peaks at UK #45. Dali's Car *The Waking Hour* makes UK #84.

1985 **Dec** Sylvian solo *Words With The Shaman* makes UK #72. His *Alchemy – An Index Of Possibilities*, released only as a cassette, fails to chart.

1986 **Aug** Sylvian's *Taking The Veil* reaches UK #53.
Sept Sylvian double album *Gone To Earth* makes UK #24.

1987 **Jan** Karn's *Buoy*, featuring Sylvian on guest vocals, reaches UK #63.
Feb Karn solo *Dreams Of Reason Produce Monsters* charts at UK #89.
Oct Sylvian's *Let The Happiness In* reaches UK #66.
Nov Sylvian's third album *Secrets Of The Beehive* makes UK #37.

1988 **Apr** Sylvian teams with Holger Czukay for *Plight And Premonition*, which makes UK #71, as his solo *Orpheus* fails to chart.

1989 **Sept** The original band returns to the studio to record as Japan.
Dec Virgin presses 30,000 CDs only of all Sylvian's solo work as *The Weather Box* compilation.

1990 The re-formed Japan spends most of the year recording new material for Virgin.

AL JARREAU

1968 Jarreau (b. Mar.12, 1940, Milwaukee, WI) having sung since age 4, influenced by his older brothers' interest in jazz and singing, begins improvizing vocals, singing along to radio songs. Choosing music over a career in sports (he is a gifted basketball/baseball player), he works with guitarist Julio Martinez in a Sausalito, CA, club. (He will spend the next 4 years developing his improvizing vocal style in Los Angeles, CA, clubs including Dino's, the Troubadour and the Bitter End.)

1972 He plays concerts at the Improvization in New York, where he meets other artists, including Quincy Jones, Bette Midler and comedian Richard Pryor.

1973 Jarreau plays a residence (lasting into 1974) at Los Angeles coffee house, the Bla Bla Café, where he develops his writing and performs his own material.

1975 Spotted by Warner Bros. playing at the Troubadour, he is signed up and releases critically-acclaimed debut album *We Got By*.
Dec During a European promotional tour, he wins a German Grammy award for Best International Soloist (reflecting his early popularity in Europe).

1976 **Sept** *Glow* reaches US #132.

1977 **Jan** He begins his first world tour.
Aug Double live album *Look To The Rainbow/Live In Europe*, recorded on his world tour, makes UK #49.

1978 **Feb** [23] Jarreau wins Best Jazz Vocal Performance for *Look To The Rainbow* at the 20th annual Grammy awards.
Nov *All Fly Home* peaks at US #78.

1979 **Feb** [15] Jarreau wins his second Best Jazz Vocal Performance for *All Fly Home* at the 21st annual Grammy awards.

1980 **Mar** Jarreau wins the Silver Award at the Tokyo Music Festival.
Aug *This Time* reaches US #27.

1981 **Feb** [24] Jarreau wins Best Pop Vocal Performance, Male for *Breakin' Away* and Best Jazz Vocal Performance, Male for *Blue Rondo A La Turk* at the 24th annual Grammy awards.
Mar Jarreau begins another world tour including Brazil, The Philippines and Japan.
Sept *We're In This Love Together* reaches US #15. *Breakin Away'* hits US #9 and UK #60.
Oct *We're In This Love Together* peaks at UK #55.

1982 **Jan** *Breakin' Away'* makes US #43. He plays standing-room-only dates in UK and Scandinavia.
Feb [24] Jarreau wins Best Pop Vocalist, Male at the 24th annual Grammy awards.
Apr *Teach Me Tonight* peaks at US #70.

1983 **May** *Mornin'*, written with David Foster and Jay Graydon, reaches US #21. *Jarreau* reaches US #13 and UK #39.
June *Mornin'* reaches UK #28.
July *Boogie Down* peaks at US #77. *Trouble In Paradise* makes UK #36.
Oct *Boogie Down* peaks at UK #63.
Nov *Trouble In Paradise* peaks at US #63.

1984 **Nov** *After All* peaks at US #69. *High Crime* makes US #49 and UK #81, as Jarreau plays sold-out US and UK dates.

1985 **Oct** *Al Jarreau In London*, recorded on his 1984 visit, makes US #125.

1986 **Apr** Jarreau teams with Melissa Manchester to sing *The Music Of Goodbye*, the love theme from the movie "Out Of Africa".
June Guesting on Bob James and David Sanborn's *Double Vision*, Jarreau revives Lenny Welch's 1963 hit *Since I Fell For You*. Featured in ABC TV series "Moonlighting", it will be included on the soundtrack album. Video "Live In London", filmed on his 1984 tour, is released.

Sept *L Is For Lover*, his 10th album for Warner Bros., makes US #81 and UK #45.

1987 **Mar** Jarreau's title theme from "Moonlighting" hits UK #8.
July [18] *Moonlighting* reaches US #23.
TV soundtrack *Moonlighting*, featuring Jarreau on 2 tracks, is released.

1988 **Feb** UK only issue by K-Tel, *Soul Men*, a separate collection of songs by Jarreau and Lou Rawls, fails to chart.
Sept *So Good*, produced by George Duke from forthcoming *Heart's Horizon*, is released.

1989 **Jan** [21] *Heart's Horizon* tops US Contemporary Jazz chart and makes US #75 on pop Album chart.
Apr Jarreau contributes vocals to Joe Sample's *Spellbound*.

1991 **Feb** [10] Jarreau joins with nearly 100 celebrities in Burbank, CA, to record *Voices That Care*, a David Foster and fiancee Linda Thompson Jenner-composed and organized charity record to benefit the American Red Cross Gulf Crisis Fund.

JEFFERSON AIRPLANE/STARSHIP

Grace Slick (vocals)
Marty Balin (vocals)
Paul Kantner (guitar)
Jorma Kaukonen (guitar)
Jack Casady (bass guitar)
Spencer Dryden (drums)

1965 **July** [6] Jefferson Airplane is formed in San Francisco, CA, by Balin (b. Jan.30, 1942, Cincinnati, OH), who has previously cut solo singles *Nobody But You* and *I Specialize In Love* for Challenge label and spent some time in Los Angeles, CA, folk group The Town Criers. First recruit is guitarist Kantner (b. Mar.12, 1942, San Francisco), whom Balin meets at local club the Drinking Gourd. Upright bass player Bob Harvey, singer Signe Toly Anderson, guitar/vocalist Kaukonen (b. Dec.23, 1940, Washington, DC) and drummer Jerry Peloquin also join. Peloquin is soon replaced by Skip Spence. (Jefferson Airplane is a paper match split at one end to act as a "roach clip" for a marijuana cigarette.)
Aug [13] Group debuts at the first night of the Matrix club, which is co-owned by Balin, on Fillmore Street, San Francisco.
Oct [16] Jefferson Airplane plays on the same bill as another local group, The Great Society, at the first Family Dog commune "A Tribute To Dr. Strange" dance at Longshoreman's Hall. Kantner is much taken with the other band's singer, Slick (b. Grace Wing, Oct.30, 1939, Chicago, IL) and follows the band just to hear her sing.
Nov Harvey is replaced by Kaukonen's friend, Casady (b. Apr.13, 1944, Washington, DC), with whom he had played in The Triumphs. Band signs to RCA Records, for a reported $25,000. (The Great Society signs to CBS/Columbia for an even larger sum.)

1966 **Feb** Jefferson Airplane's debut single, *It's No Secret*, is released.
Oct Spence leaves to form Moby Grape, and is replaced by jazz-schooled drummer Dryden (b. Apr.7, 1938, New York, NY) from The Peanut Butter Conspiracy.
Nov Debut album *Jefferson Airplane Takes Off*, recorded in Dec.1965, is released in US by RCA, and makes US #128 (it will not be released in UK until 1971). Anderson leaves to have a baby and Slick joins, bringing with her 2 songs she has performed with The Great Society – *White Rabbit* and *Somebody To Love*. (The Great Society have recorded 2 live albums but Columbia will not release them until Slick finds fame with Jefferson Airplane.)

1967 **Jan** [14] They play at the first Human Be-In, in Golden Gate Park, San Francisco, before embarking on their first East Coast tour.
June *Surrealistic Pillow*, the first to feature Slick's vocal, is produced by Rick Jarrard, with The Grateful Dead's Jerry Garcia as musical adviser. It hits US #3, earning a gold disk, while *Somebody To Love* (written by Darby Slick, Grace's brother-in-law) hits US #5 and is a million-seller.
[16] Group takes part in the Monterey International Pop Festival, CA.
Aug *White Rabbit*, written by Slick, and a surreal interpretation of **Alice In Wonderland**, hits US #8, also a million-seller.
Sept *Surrealistic Pillow* is released in UK, in an edited form which excludes major tracks like *White Rabbit* and *Plastic Fantastic Lover*, and substitutes tracks from the unissued-in-UK first album.
Oct *Ballad Of You And Me And Pooneil* makes US #42.
Dec *Watch Her Ride* reaches US #61.

1968 **Feb** *After Bathing At Baxter's*, the beginning of a working relationship with producer Pat Ieraci, reaches US #17. Casady plays on Jimi Hendrix's album *Electric Ladyland* and Country Joe & The Fish's album *Together*.
Apr *Greasy Heart* makes US #38.

July Group buys a house at 2400 Fulton in San Francisco, which will become its headquarters.

Aug [4-5] Band performs at the Newport Pop Festival in Costa Mesa, CA, alongside The Byrds, Canned Heat, The Grateful Dead, Sonny & Cher, Steppenwolf and others.

[29] Jefferson Airplane makes its first UK live appearance at a party at the Revolution club in London, at the start of its first European tour, which includes a well-received appearance at UK's Isle of Wight festival and a free gig at Parliament Hill Fields in London.

Sept [6-7] Group plays 2 nights at the Roundhouse, London, with The Doors.

Nov *Crown Of Creation* hits US #6, and the extracted title track makes US #64. French movie director Jean-Luc Godard films the band playing on a rooftop, for his projected "An American Movie" film. After Godard drops his plans, the footage is picked up by documentary film-maker D.A. Pennebaker and used in "One P.M.." Kaukonen and Casady form a splinter group, at first called Hot Shit, then renamed Hot Tuna.

1969 Jan Slick is hospitalized with a suspected throat growth.

Apr Live album *Bless Its Pointed Little Head* makes US #17.

June *Bless Its Pointed Little Head* becomes the group's first UK chart entry, spending a week at #38.

Aug [15] Jefferson Airplane plays an early morning set at the Woodstock Festival, Bethel, NY.

Dec *Volunteers*, the band's most overtly political work, reaches US #13, while its title track makes US #65.

[6] Band takes part in The Rolling Stones' ill-fated concert at Altamont Speedway, CA. Balin is attacked halfway through a song by one of the Hells Angels handling security.

1970 Feb *Volunteers* reaches UK #34. After an argument with Balin, Dryden leaves to join New Riders Of The Purple Sage. He is replaced by Joey Covington, who has been drumming with Hot Tuna.

[27] Group is fined $1,000 for obscenity in Oklahoma City, OK.

May [16] Balin is arrested for drug possession.

Oct Slick, now pregnant by Kantner, is unable to make live appearances. Casady and Kaukonen, who have for some time been playing occasional support gigs to Jefferson Airplane as Hot Tuna, either with other musicians or as an acoustic duo, formalize the offshoot group. They recruit violinist Papa John Creach (b. May 28, 1917, Beaver Falls, PA), who also becomes a member of Jefferson Airplane. Kaukonen switches to electric guitar and Covington plays drums. A Hot Tuna gig at the New Orleans House, Berkeley, is recorded and given a low-key album release.

Nov Kantner and Slick invite Jerry Garcia, David Crosby and Graham Nash to contribute to *Blows Against The Empire*, billed as by Paul Kantner and Jefferson Starship (the first use of this name). The album reaches US #20 and is the first to be nominated for the sci-fi writers' Hugo Awards.

1971 Jan [25] Slick and Kantner's daughter China is born.

Feb Compilation*The Worst Of Jefferson Airplane* reaches US #12.

Apr Balin leaves the group. He retires from music, apart from producing the band Grootna for Columbia.

May [13] Slick crashes her Mercedes in San Francisco. Her injuries are slight, but cause Jefferson Airplane recording sessions to be cancelled.

July Hot Tuna's second album *First Pull Up Then Pull Down* makes US #43.

Aug Band launches its own RCA-distributed label, Grunt Records.

Oct The first Grunt release, Jefferson Airplane album *Bark*, climbs to US #11 (earning a gold disk) and UK #42.

Nov *Pretty As You Feel*, an edit from a 30-min. studio jam featuring Jerry Garcia, Carlos Santana and Creach, is taken from *Grunt* and makes US #60.

1972 Jan Slick and Kantner's *Sunfighter*, which features baby China on the cover, makes US #89. Creach also releases his first solo album on Grunt, featuring guest spots from Airplane members, while Hot Tuna appears on David Crosby's *If Only I Could Remember My Name*.

Apr The Jefferson Airplane members regroup for *Long John Silver*. During the sessions, Covington leaves, and is replaced by ex-Turtles drummer John Barbata.

May Hot Tuna's *Burgers* makes US #68.

Aug [21] Slick is maced and Kantner slightly injured when a scuffle ensues after the group's equipment manager calls police "pigs".

Sept *Long John Silver* reaches US #20 and UK #30.

Oct Group begins a US tour, with guitarist David Frieberg added. On the last date of the tour Balin takes the stage for 3 songs. The Hot Tuna members make a final break and resist any attempts to woo them back.

(Band will make 6 more albums before breaking up in 1978.)

1973 Apr *30 Seconds Over Winterland*, a live album recorded during the last US tour, is released.

July Kantner, Slick and Frieberg's *Baron Von Tollbooth And The Chrome Nun* reaches US #52.

1974 Feb Slick's debut solo album, *Manhole*, makes US #127, while Hot Tuna's *The Phosphorescent Rat* reaches US #148. Slick, Kantner, Creach, Barbata, 19-year-old guitarist Craig Chaquico (b. Sept.26, 1954) (ex-Steelwind and the Kantner-Slick solo efforts) and Kaukonen's bass-playing younger brother Peter (under the name Peter Kangaroo) begin rehearsing under the name Jefferson Starship.

Mar [19] Jefferson Airplane officially becomes Jefferson Starship.

Apr Jefferson Starship begins its first US tour. Peter Kaukonen will leave, at its conclusion to be replaced by UK session player Pete Sears, who had worked on *Manhole*.

June *Early Flight*, an album of unreleased and rare Jefferson Airplane material, peaks at US #110.

July The new group goes into the studio for the first time.

Nov *Ride The Tiger* peaks at US #84.

[21] Balin, having vowed he would never perform with them again, joins the band on stage in San Francisco.

Dec *Dragonfly* reaches US #11, and earns a gold disk.

1975 Jan With earlier differences now resolved, Balin rejoins permanently.

May Hot Tuna's *America's Choice* reaches US #75.

Aug Creach leaves to settle in Los Angeles and front his own band.

Sept *Red Octopus* tops the US chart for 4 weeks, and will sell over 2 million copies.

[30] Jefferson Starship joins The Grateful Dead for a free concert at San Francisco's Lindley Park.

Oct Balin's song *Miracles* hits US #3, and is a million-seller.

Dec *Play On Love* reaches US #49. Hot Tuna's *Yellow Fever* makes US #97.

[29] Slick and Kantner break up after living together for 7 years. (She will marry the group's 24-year-old lighting engineer, Skip Johnson.)

1976 July *Spitfire* reaches UK #30.

Sept *With Your Love* makes US #12. It is taken from *Spitfire* which hits US #3, achieving platinum status.

Nov Slick and Johnson are married.

Dec *St. Charles* peaks at US #64. Hot Tuna's *Hoppkorv* makes US #116.

1977 Mar *Flight Log (1966-1976)*, an anthology of Airplane, Starship, Hot Tuna, Slick and Kantner material, reaches US #37.

1978 Apr Hot Tuna's *Double Dose* reaches US #92.

May *Count On Me* hits US #8 as its parent album *Earth* hits US #5.

June [17] Slick's alcohol problem prevents her from taking the stage at the Lorelei Festival in Hamburg, Germany. As a result, fans riot, stealing or destroying much of the band's equipment.

[24] Group appears at the Knebworth Festival, Herts., without Slick (who has effectively quit the band).

July *Runaway* reaches US #12.

Sept *Crazy Feelin'* makes US #54. Balin leaves the band, leaving Kantner as the only original member.

1979 Apr [12] The vocal gap is filled by Mickey Thomas (who sang lead vocal on Elvin Bishop's *Fooled Around And Fell In Love*). Barbata leaves and is replaced by Aynsley Dunbar (b. 1946, Liverpool, Merseyside). Second hits album collection *Jefferson Starship Gold* reaches US #20.

May [12] The new line-up debuts live at a free concert in Golden Gate Park, San Francisco.

Nov *Jane* reaches US #14.

[12] Balin presents a rock opera, *Rock Justice*, in a 4-day run at the Old Waldorf club, San Francisco.

Dec [31] Jefferson Starship's New Year's Eve concert at X6s club, San Francisco, is widely broadcast live on US radio.

1980 Jan Group plays a benefit concert at Almeda Coliseum, Oakland, CA, in aid of the people of Kampuchea, with The Grateful Dead and The Beach Boys.

Feb *Girl With The Hungry Eyes* makes US #55. Parent album *Freedom At Point Zero* hits US #10 and UK #22. *Jane* reaches UK #21.

May Slick releases solo album *Dreams*, making US #32 and UK #28.

Oct [25] Kantner suffers a stroke. (He will recover fully.)

1981 Mar Slick rejoins Jefferson Starship, just as her solo album *Welcome To The Wreckers' Ball* peaks at US #48.

Apr Group's *Find Your Way Back* reaches US #29.

May Balin's ballad *Hearts* hits US #8.

June Group album *Modern Times* reaches US #26. Balin's first solo album, *Balin*, peaks at US #35.

Aug Group's *Stranger* reaches US #48.

Sept The second single from Balin's album, *Atlanta Lady (Something About Your Love)* enters the US chart, reaching #27.

'82 May [28] Group takes part in a benefit concert for the Vietnam Veterans' Project, at Moscone Center in San Francisco, with Boz Scaggs, Country Joe McDonald and The Grateful Dead.
Aug [8] Mickey Thomas marries Sara Kendrick, in San Francisco.
Oct Drummer Don Baldwin (ex-Elvin Bishop Band) joins, Dunbar having left after album sessions have been completed. *Be My Lady* reaches US #28.

'83 Jan *Winds Of Change* makes US #26, and the extracted title track makes US #38.
Feb Balin single, *What Love Is*, reaches US #63.
Mar His second solo album, *Lucky*, makes US #165.
Aug Kantner releases solo album, **The Planet Earth Rock And Roll Orchestra**, in US only.

'84 Jefferson Starship begins an extensive US tour.
May Power ballad *No Way Out* reaches US #23.
June Group begins a US tour to promote **Nuclear Furniture**, which enters the US chart, reaching #28.
Sept *Layin' It On The Line* peaks at US #66.
Oct Kantner appears on stage with Balin's band at Golden Gate Park to perform old Jefferson Airplane song *It's No Secret*.

'85 After much legal wrangling, Kantner departs from the band with a lump sum of $250,000 and the provision that Jefferson is dropped from the band's name. Frieberg follows him. Thomas goes on MTV to state that the 2 have been sacked. Group initially plays as Starship Jefferson but soon settles on just Starship.
Mar The Kantner, Balin and Casaday Band debuts at the eighth Annual Bay Area Music Awards. After club appearances and a free gig in Golden Gate Park, Balin leaves his own band to join the KBC Band full time.
Nov [16] First Starship single, *We Built This City* tops the US chart for 2 weeks and reaches UK #12. It is written by Martin Page, Bernie Taupin, Dennis Lambert and Peter Wolf and achieves a chart peak not attained by either Jefferson Airplane or Jefferson Starship. With Freiberg departing during its recording, parent album **Knee Deep In The Hoopla** hits US #7, but fails to chart in UK.
Dec The KBC Band makes its official debut at the re-opening of the Fillmore. Signe Anderson takes the stage for *It's No Secret*.

'86 Feb *Sara* peaks at UK #66.
Mar [15] *Sara* tops the US chart for a week. (Though written by co-producer Peter Wolf with his wife Ina, Starship's Mickey Thomas' wife is named Sara.)
Apr [23] Starship cancels a tour of Europe.
May [24] *Tomorrow Doesn't Matter Tonight* reaches US #26.
July China Kantner makes a guest appearance on US MTV. Band becomes the first national spokesgroup for the National Network Of Runaway Youth Services.
[26] Starship's *Before I Go* peaks at US #68.
Dec [13] The KBC Band, comprising Kantner, Balin and Casady, makes US #89 with *It's Not You, It's Not Me*, while parent debut album **KBC Band** makes US #75.

'87 Apr [4] Power ballad *Nothing's Gonna Stop Us Now*, used as the theme for film "Mannequin", tops US chart for 2 weeks.
May [9] Starship's first UK chart-topper finally comes more than 2 decades after the original formation of Jefferson Airplane: *Nothing's Gonna Stop Us Now* hits UK #1 for 4 weeks, and is the second-biggest selling single of the year in UK. Meanwhile, in US double compilation album **2400 Fulton Street**, credited to Jefferson Airplane, and including re-mastered versions of songs from the group's first 6 studio albums, reaches US #138.
June [20] Starship participates in the 20th anniversary "Summer Of Love" concert in San Francisco.
July *No Protection* reaches UK #26.
Aug [29] *It's Not Over ('Til It's Over)* hits US #9.
Sept *No Protection*, including both recent Top 10 hits, reaches US #12.
Nov [7] *Beat Patrol*, taken from the album, reaches US #46.

'88 Nov Slick, Kantner, Kaukonen and Casady begin writing and rehearsing for a forthcoming album and tour.
Dec [17] Donny Baldwin marries Lisa Avila.

'89 Jan [14] Starship's contribution to Tom Cruise-starring movie "Cocktail", *Wild Again* stalls at US #73.
June [22] Slick, commenting about Jefferson Airplane's forthcoming reunion album (which will reunite her with Kantner, Kaukonen, Casaday and Balin for a permanent new Jefferson Airplane), "We're your parents' worst nightmare because now you are your parents."

Aug Starship's **Love Among The Cannibals**, recorded by remaining band with new members Brett Bloomfield (bass) and Mark Morgan (keyboards) makes US #64.
[29] During US tour, Jefferson Airplane, augmented by Kenny Aronoff (drums), Peter Kaukonen (guitar), Zebra's Randy Jackson (guitar) and Tim Gorman (keyboards), plays the New York State Fair, Syracuse, NY.
Sept [23] Jefferson Airplane's comeback album **Jefferson Airplane**, released on Epic Records, and featuring current line-up of Balin, Slick, Kantner, Kaukonen and Casady now joined by Kenny Aronoff, who has effectively replaced Dryden, enters US chart, set to make #85.
Oct [7] Jefferson Airplane gives a free concert in Golden Gate Park for 65,000 crowd. Each fan is asked to bring of can of food to donate to the San Francisco Food Bank, as Starship's *It's Not Enough* reaches US #12.
Nov Starship, now comprising Mickey Thomas (vocals), Donny Baldwin (drums), Craig Chaquico (guitar), Morgan (keyboards) and Bloomfield (bass), have to postpone a planned tour after Thomas suffers facial injuries in a bar-room brawl. He is hospitalized with a broken cheekbone, which requires reconstructive plastic surgery.
Dec [16] Starship's *I Didn't Mean To Stay All Night* peaks at US #75.

1990 Mar [8] Jefferson Airplane is awarded Most Unwelcome Comeback in **Rolling Stone** magazine's 1989 Critics Award.

THE JESUS & MARY CHAIN
William Reid (guitar, vocals)
Jim Reid (guitar, vocals)
Douglas Hart (bass)
Bobby Gillespie (drums)

1983 William Reid (b. 1958, East Kilbride, Scotland) and his younger brother Jim (b. 1961, East Kilbride) decide to form a band with Hart and Gillespie, after writing and recording songs at home on a portastudio, bought by their father with his severance pay. William has already worked at a cheese-packing plant at age 16, while Jim, also leaving school at 16 has been employed by Rolls-Royce Aerospace.

1984 May Having recruited Murray Daglish (drums) to play their first gig at Glasgow's Nightmovers club, the Reid brothers and Hart move to London where they meet Alan McGee, owner of small independent Creation label, who signs them and becomes their manager.
June [9] Having moved into a bedsit in Fulham in May, they play at McGee's the Living Room club above the Roebuck pub in Tottenham Court Road, London.
Nov *Upside Down*, produced by McGee's friend "Slaughter" Joe Foster, is released with little initial success. Recorded at a cost of £174, it will eventually sell over 35,000 copies. (The B-side revives Syd Barrett's *Vegetable Man*). McGee's expert promotion of the band brings media attention. As the band plays live sets sometimes consisting of only 2 songs, UK music press becomes increasingly interested.
Dec Group is arrested in Germany and charged with possession of amphetamine sulphate after playing at the UK ICA Rock Week.

1985 Feb *Upside Down* tops UK Independent chart for 2 weeks. McGee signs the band to WEA-marketed label blanco y negro.
Mar *Never Understand*, produced by the Reid brothers, spends 4 weeks on UK chart, peaking at #47. A riot follows a particularly short, and over-booked, gig at North London polytechnic, increasing their notoriety, during a much cancelled UK tour.
May WEA's record plant staff refuse to press the group's third single as they feel proposed B-side *Jesus Sucks* is obscene and blasphemous.
June *You Trip Me Up* peaks at UK #55.
Oct Atypical ballad *Just Like Honey* makes UK #45.
Nov Debut album **Psychocandy**, heralded as a post-punk masterpiece by UK music press, makes UK #31.

1986 Jan Group takes a 6-month lay-off and Gillespie leaves to form his own band Primal Scream.
Feb *Psychocandy* makes US #188.
Aug *Some Candy Talking* reaches UK #13, helped by a ban by BBC Radio 1 DJ Mike Smith, who refuses to play it because of apparent references to drugs. Live UK performances follow with John Moore joining on drums.

1987 May Follow-up *April Skies* hits UK #8.
Aug *Happy When It Rains* peaks at UK #25.
Sept *Darklands* features William Reid writing and singing lead vocal for the first time and hits UK #5. The album only features the Reid brothers with no guest musicians. The group, now split from McGee, tours without a drummer, employing a roadie to play a drum tracks cassette through the PA. The gigs are poorly received.
Oct *Darklands* peaks at US #161, as sometime band member John

Moore quits the group permanently to set up John Moore's Expressway.

Nov US and Canada tour is dogged by gig violence, including an incident at the RPM club in Toronto, Canada, when Reid is arrested after allegedly hitting troublesome fans with a mike stand. Charged with assault, he is later acquitted. Extracted *Darklands* reaches UK #33.

Dec Group is banned from appearing on the US TV version of "Top Of The Pops" because its name is considered blasphemous.

1988 Apr Jim Reid is given an absolute discharge after agreeing to pay £500 to the Salvation Army, the judge's nominated charity, for the Nov.1987 Toronto offense.

Aug *Sidewalking* peaks at UK #30, as new drummer Richard Thomas joins ex-Dif Juz. Meanwhile, *Barbed Wire Kisses*, a compilation of B-sides, out-takes and unreleased material, is issued in the absence of a newly-recorded album, and hits UK #9 and US #192.

1989 Sept *Blues From A Gun*, written and produced by the Reids, charts at UK #32.

Oct Fourth album, again self-produced *Automatic* reaches UK #11 and will climb to US #105. Band recruits guitarist Ben Laurie on UK tour to promote the release.

Nov Second extract, *Head On*, peaks at UK #57.

1990 Jan [28] Group begins major US tour in Portland, OR, set to end on Mar.25 in Pittsburgh, PA.

Feb Group contributes a cover of *Guitar Man* to the compilation album *The Last Temptation Of Elvis*, to benefit the Nordoff-Robbins Music Therapy charity.

Sept [8] 6-date UK mini-tour begins at the Town & Country club, London, as 4-track *Rollercoaster* EP makes UK #46.

JETHRO TULL

Ian Anderson (vocals, flute)
Mick Abrahams (guitar)
Glenn Cornick (bass)
Clive Bunker (drums)

1963 Anderson (b. Aug.10, 1947, Edinburgh, Scotland) forms The Blades (named after James Bond's club) in Blackpool, Lancs., with fellow blues-minded school friends, Jeffrey Hammond-Hammond (b. July 30, 1946) on bass and John Evans (a.k.a. Evan, b. Mar.28, 1948) on drums. Their first gig at a youth club nets £2.

1965 They play jazz-blues and danceable soul music for Northern club audiences and name-change first to The John Evan Band and then John Evan's Smash (apparently to please Evans' mother, who paid for the group's van).

1967 Cornick (b. Apr.24, 1947, Barrow-in-Furness, Cumbria) replaces Hammond-Hammond on bass.

Nov Group travels to London, hoping to succeed at the heart of the UK blues boom. Within days the road-weary crew has left but Anderson and Cornick stay in London.

Dec Duo forms a new band with guitarist Abrahams (b. Apr.7, 1943, Luton, Beds.) and drummer Bunker (b. Dec.12, 1946), and signs to Terry Ellis and Chris Wright's booking agency, playing 2 gigs a week under a variety of names like Navy Blue and Bag Of Blues. Jethro Tull, after the 18th-century agriculturalist, receives most audience enthusiasm, and sticks.

1968 Feb MGM releases Abrahams' *Sunshine Day*, taken from a Derek Lawrence-produced demo, with an earlier Lawrence recording of The John Evan Band on the B-side. The first pressing mistakenly credits the band as Jethro Toe, but it fails to chart.

June Band gains a residency at London's Marquee club. Ellis and Wright suggest that Anderson should abandon his flute, giving the focus to lead guitarist Abrahams, but this is resisted.

[29] Band supports Pink Floyd at the first free rock festival in London's Hyde Park.

Aug Jethro Tull becomes the sensation of the Sunbury Jazz & Blues Festival, gaining rapturous music press notices. On the strength of this, Island Records offers a recording contract.

Nov Debut album *This Was* hits UK #10, but *A Song For Jeffrey* (dedicated to ex-member Hammond-Hammond) fails to chart.

Dec A personality clash develops between Anderson and Abrahams, who leaves to form Blodwyn Pig.

[12] Band takes part in The Rolling Stones' "Rock'N'Roll Circus" (filmed as a TV spectacular but never screened).

1969 Jan *Love Story*, the last featuring Abrahams, reaches UK #29. Tony Iommi (later of Black Sabbath) and Davy O'List of The Nice are interim members, before Martin Barre (b. Nov.17, 1946) joins permanently.

[24] Jethro Tull makes its US debut sharing the bill with Blood, Sweat & Tears at the Fillmore East, New York, at the start of a 2-month tour.

Apr Reprise issues *This Was* in US. It reaches #62.

May *Living In The Past*, the first featuring Barre, hits UK #3. Group appears on BBC TV's "Top Of The Pops" for the first time.

[6] Jethro Tull embarks on a 6-date UK tour with Ten Years After and Clouds at the Free Trade Hall, Manchester, Gtr.Manchester, set to end May 15 at the Town Hall, Birmingham, W.Midlands.

June [20-22] Jethro Tull participates in the '69 Pop Festival at Northridge, CA.

July Band performs at the Newport Jazz Festival, Newport, RI.

Aug [9] *Stand Up*, in a gatefold sleeve from which card figures of the band actually "stand up" when opened, tops UK chart. All songs are written by Anderson, apart from his arrangement of Bach's *Bouree*.

Nov *Stand Up* climbs to US #20, while *Sweet Dream* hits UK #7. It is the band's first release on Ellis and Wright's formative Chrysalis label (Island will still handle the next 2 albums).

1970 Jan Double A-side *The Witch's Promise/Teacher* hits UK #4.

Apr *Benefit* has John Evan guesting. (Joining initially on a temporary basis, he will stay for 10 years.)

May *Benefit* hits UK #3 and US #11, and features the line-up Anderson, Barre, Bunker, Cornick and newly-joined Evan.

July [3-5] Group plays at the 3-day Atlanta Pop Festival at the Middle Georgia Raceway in Byron, GA, to 200,000 people, with Jimi Hendrix, B.B. King, Johnny Winter and others.

Oct Band returns to US for a 31-date tour, including Hammond-Hammond and drummer Barrie Barlow.

Nov [4] In the midst of the tour, the band plays a benefit concert at Carnegie Hall in New York, in the presence of the Duke and Duchess of Bedford at which $10,000 is raised to benefit the Phoenix House Drug Rehabilitation Center.

Dec Cornick leaves to form his own band, Wild Turkey, and Hammond-Hammond rejoins.

1971 Apr Fourth album *Aqualung* hits UK #4.

May [10] Band plays in a cloud of tear gas at the Red Rock Amphitheater, Denver, CO, after police fire canisters into the audience. On return to UK, Bunker leaves to get married (going on to form Jude with Robin Trower, Frankie Miller and Jim Dewar), and is replaced by Barriemore Barlow (b. Sept.10, 1949).

June *Aqualung* hits US #7, the group's first US Top 10 success.

Aug From *Aqualung*, *Hymn 43* is the group's first US chart single at #91. It receives heavy FM airplay, as do the album cuts *Locomotive Breath* and *Crosseyed Mary*.

Sept A 5-song EP headed by *Life Is A Long Song* reaches UK #11.

Oct [18] Jethro Tull makes its Madison Square Garden, New York, debut during a US tour.

1972 Apr *Thick As A Brick* hits UK #5.

June *Thick As A Brick* hits US #1 for 2 weeks.

July Double compilation album *Living In The Past*, featuring mostly unreleased or singles-only material, plus a live side recorded at New York's Carnegie Hall, hits UK #8.

Nov *Living In The Past* hits US #3, and will subsequently be critically regarded as a career peak.

1973 Jan *Living In The Past*, extracted for first time as US single, makes #11.

June [22-23] Band previews material from its forthcoming album *A Passion Play* at concerts in Wembley, London.

July *A Passion Play* is poorly received by many critics. Anderson announces that the group will cease playing live. Album still makes UK #1 and hits US #1 (a single edit of title track having already peaked at US #80).

1974 Nov Largely orchestral (but song-based) album *War Child* reaches UK #14 and hits US #2. (The album had been developed in conjunction with a planned film which never surfaces.) The long world tour to promote the album includes a string quartet augmenting the band.

1975 Jan Extracted *Bungle In The Jungle* makes US #11.

Sept Recorded in the band's new mobile studio, *Minstrel In The Gallery* reaches UK #20 and US #7.

Oct The album title track reaches US #79.

Dec Hammond-Hammond leaves to concentrate on art, and is replaced by John Glascock (b. 1953, London).

1976 Jan *M.U. – The Best Of Jethro Tull Vol. 1* contains a previously unreleased track, *Rainbow Blues*. It reaches US #13 and UK #44.

Mar *Locomotive Breath*, issued as a US single, reaches #62.

May *Too Old To Rock'N'Roll, Too Young To Die* makes UK #25 and US #14. It contains material taken from a play planned by Anderson and David Palmer and never staged, but forms the basis of the band's ITV special.

Dec Seasonal EP *Ring Out Solstice Bells* reaches UK #28. Jethro Tull appears again on BBC TV's "Top Of The Pops" (as a last-minute replacement for Rod Stewart).

977 Feb Group's first UK tour in 3 years introduces *Songs From The Wood* which reaches UK #13 and will hit US #8. The album explores Anderson's interest in folk music (he has recently produced an album for Steeleye Span).
May *The Whistler* peaks at US #59. Keyboards player David Palmer joins the band.
Oct *Repeat: The Best Of Jethro Tull Vol. 2* is released. With only 1 new track, it stalls at US #94 and fails to make UK Top 50.

978 Apr *Heavy Horses* reaches UK #20 and US #19. Group promotes the album with an extensive UK tour.
Oct *Live: Bursting Out* reaches UK #17 and US #21. Band's US tour is highlighted by a concert at New York's Madison Square Garden, broadcast live to several countries.

979 Oct *Stormwatch* reaches UK #27 and US #22. Glascock, who has never played live with the band, has become too ill to record, leaving Anderson to play the bass.
[12] Anderson is pierced in the eye by a thorn thrown by an over-zealous fan at a concert in New York's Madison Square Garden.
Nov [17] Glascock dies after open heart surgery, aged 26. Dave Pegg (ex-Fairport Convention) joins the band.

980 June Anderson records a solo album. As well as Barre and Pegg from Jethro Tull, he brings in Eddie Jobson (ex-Roxy Music) on keyboards and violin and Mark Craney on drums. Bowing to company pressure, Anderson releases it as a Jethro Tull album, but discards Barlow, Evan and Palmer in favor of the new line-up.
Sept The resultant album, *A*, with Jobson's influence evident, reaches UK #25 and US #30. Jobson stays only for the subsequent tour before leaving to go solo. (He will feature on the 1981 full-length video *Slipstream*.)

982 Apr *Broadsword And The Beast*, with new drummer Gerry Conway and keyboard player Peter-John Vettesse, reaches UK #27, after the band tours UK to promote it.
May *Broadsword And The Beast* makes US #19.

983 Nov Anderson's solo debut, the synthesizer-oriented *Walk Into Light*, with help only from Vettesse, is released but reaches only UK #78.

984 Sept *Under Wraps* makes UK #18 and US #76. It features new drummer Doane Perry with Vettesse making another important contribution. Band tours UK and Europe, but during a US tour Anderson develops a throat infection serious enough to postpone dates. *Lap Of Luxury* reaches UK #70.

985 Group performs a special for German TV, with Jobson (temporarily) back on keyboards, and features in a London Symphony Orchestra presentation of Jethro Tull's music, which plays in Europe and US.
Oct *Original Masters*, a compilation of the band's best work up to 1977, is released with limited UK TV campaign, but makes only UK #63.

986 Jan *Said She Was A Dancer* peaks at UK #55.
A Classic Case – The London Symphony Orchestra Plays The Music Of Jethro Tull, from the earlier German TV special, makes US #93.

987 Sept *Crest Of A Knave* makes UK #19 and US #32.

988 June Group, now comprising Anderson, Barre, Pegg, Perry and Martin Allcock (keyboards), embarks on 4-week US tour as part of its 20th anniversary celebration.
July Chrysalis releases *20 Years Of Jethro Tull* 65-track collection documenting the band's history, available in 5-album, 3-cassette, or 3-CD format. It makes UK #78 and US #97. Band plays a major anniversary concert at London's Wembley Arena.

989 Feb [22] Group wins Best Hard Rock/Metal Performance for *Crest Of A Knave* at the 31st annual Grammy awards, the first time the award has been presented.
Sept *Rock Island* reaches UK #18 and will make US #56.
Oct [23] Group embarks on the "Rock Island Tour" at RPI Fieldhouse, Troy, NY, set to end Dec.10 at the Civic Center, San Francisco, CA.

990 Apr [5] Jethro Tull undertakes 24-date UK tour.

BILLY JOEL

964 Feb Joel (b. William Martin Joel, May 9, 1949, The Bronx, New York, NY), whose major preoccupations while growing up in Hicksville, Long Island, NY, have been studying the piano and boxing (he has broken his nose as a local young welterweight champ) is inspired by seeing The Beatles on US TV's "Ed Sullivan Show", and looks for a band to join, finding The Echoes, who become a popular local live attraction with a repertoire built around UK group hits.

1965 He finds work playing piano on sessions at a studio at Levittown, notably for Artie Ripp's Kama Sutra Productions, and producer George "Shadow" Morton. He also continues to play with The Echoes, who become The Emeralds, and then The Lost Souls.

1967 He joins Long Island group The Hassles as keyboard player. Signed to United Artists, their first single is a cover of Sam And Dave's *You Got Me Hummin'* (their only UK release, which Joel will still perform live during the 80s). The Hassles release 4 singles and 2 albums, *The Hassles* and *Hour Of The Wolf*, over an 18-month period.

1969 When The Hassles split, keyboard player Joel and drummer Jon Small form an organ/drums hard rock duo called Attila. Joel also briefly becomes a rock critic for arts magazine **Changes** and plays on sessions for TV ads, including Chubby Checker ad for Bachman Pretzels.

1970 *Attila* is released by Epic in US, with Joel and Small dressed as barbarians for the sleeve picture. It bombs and the band splits immediately. Joel enters a period of acute depression (aggravated by the ending of a serious romance), checking himself into Meadowbrook hospital, where he is placed under psychiatric observation.

1971 Joel signs as a soloist to Family Productions, owned by Ripp. The deal involves a lifetime agreement (Ripp will still receive royalties from Joel's hit career in the 80s).
Nov *Cold Spring Harbor*, recorded in California, is released on Family Productions, through Paramount. Due to mixing/mastering incompetence the album is pressed sounding too fast (an error not corrected until it is re-mixed in 1984). Joel puts together a band to begin a promotional tour.

1972 Embarrassed by the album, despite good live reviews, he leaves for Los Angeles, CA, with girlfriend Elizabeth Weber (ex-wife of Jon Small), where he spends 6 months at the Executive Room on Wilshire Boulevard playing bar piano in a lounge, using the name Bill Martin (the experience produces his song *Piano Man*).
Apr [1] Still an unknown, he plays the Mar Y Sol Festival in Vega Baja, Puerto Rico, where he comes to the interest of CBS/Columbia records.

1973 Joel and Weber marry, and she attends UCLA's Graduate School of Management. He is sought by several major labels after *Captain Jack* is played constantly on station WMMR-FM (having been taken from a Philadelphia show broadcast live over the station in 1972).
CBS/Columbia's chief executive Clive Davis goes to see Joel in the piano bar in Los Angeles. Label signs him, but to pacify Ripp has to retain Family Products Romulus and Remus logo on future Joel releases (for which Ripp will receive 25 cents from each album sold).

1974 Apr Debut Columbia album *Piano Man* makes US #27 (earning a gold disk for a half million sales 2 years later), as title track makes US #25.
July *Worse Comes To Worst*, also from the album, makes US #80.
Aug *Travelin' Prayer* peaks at US #77. Joel puts together a stage band comprising guitarist Don Evans, bass player Pat McDonald, steel guitar and banjo player Tom Whitehorse and drummer Rhys Clark, and plays dates supporting The Beach Boys, The J. Geils Band and The Doobie Brothers. First major live success is in Philadelphia where he headlines.

1975 Jan *The Entertainer* makes US #34 as *Streetlife Serenade* makes US #35. Joel joins James William Guercio and Larry Fitzgerald's Caribou management company. He and his wife move back from California to New York, where Joel finds renewed songwriting creativity (he claims to have written *New York State Of Mind* within 20 mins. of entering his New York home).

1976 July *Turnstiles* peaks at US #122. It includes *Say Goodbye To Hollywood*, a celebration of the Joels' move and a Phil Spector tribute, which will later be covered by Ronnie Spector, as well as the E Street Band. Produced by Joel and recorded in New York with Elton John's sidemen Nigel, Olsson and Dee Murray, the sessions have not, in Joel's opinion, been entirely successful. Having fired producer Guercio early in the recording, Joel also leaves Guercio's Caribou management, appointing his wife Elizabeth as manager. She renegotiates his contract with Columbia, fixing new and more favorable royalty rate of $1 an album.

1977 Sept He appears on NBC TV's "Saturday Night Live", playing new song *Just The Way You Are* to a viewing audience of 20 million.
Dec Also recorded in New York, *The Stranger* hits US #2 and earns a platinum disk. (It will become Columbia Records' second biggest selling album of all time after Simon & Garfunkel's *Bridge Over Troubled Water*.)

1978 Feb *Just The Way You Are*, from the album, hits US #3 (selling over a million) and makes Joel's UK chart debut at #19. (The ballad will attract over 200 cover versions, including another million-selling version by Barry White.)
May *Movin' Out (Anthony's Song)*, also taken from *The Stranger*, makes US #17 (and UK #35 a month later). *The Stranger* reaches UK #25.

July *Only The Good Die Young* makes US #24. The song causes Joel to be banned by Catholic radio stations in US, due to its apparent anti-Catholic views – which he denies.

Oct *She's Always A Woman*, fourth from *The Stranger*, reaches US #17.

1979 Jan *My Life*, Joel's second million-selling single, hits US #3 and UK #12. It is taken from *52nd Street*, which tops US chart for 8 weeks, selling over 2 million copies in first month of release, and hits UK #10.

Feb [15] Joel wins Record Of The Year and Song Of The Year for *Just The Way You Are* at the 21st annual Grammy awards.

Mar *Big Shot*, also from *52nd Street*, reaches US #14.

May *Until The Night*, a track from *52nd Street* arranged as a tribute to The Righteous Brothers, is issued as a UK single and makes #50. Meanwhile, *Honesty* reaches US #24.

1980 Feb [27] Joel wins Best Pop Vocal Performance, Male and Album Of The Year for *52nd Street* at the 22nd annual Grammy awards.

May *You May Be Right* hits US #7, while *All For Leyna* makes UK #40.

June *Glass Houses* tops US chart for 6 weeks, (another platinum disk) and hits UK #9.

July *It's Still Rock'N'Roll To Me* tops US chart for 2 weeks, selling over a million.

Sept *It's Still Rock'N'Roll To Me* makes UK #14, while *Don't Ask Me Why*, also from the album, reaches US #19.

Nov *Sometimes A Fantasy*, last cut from *Glass Houses* makes US #36.

1981 Feb [25] Joel wins Best Rock Vocal Performance, Male for *Glass Houses* at the 23rd annual Grammy awards.

Nov Live album *Songs In The Attic*, consisting mostly of earlier, pre-*Stranger* songs, hits US #8 and UK #57. It is the first digitally-recorded live album. Extracted from it, a new version of *Say Goodbye To Hollywood* hits US #17.

1982 Jan *She's Got A Way* reaches US #23.

Apr [15] Joel breaks his left wrist when a car hits his motorcycle, in Long Island, NY. (He will remain in hospital more than a month for surgery on his hand.)

July Joel and his wife Elizabeth are divorced.

Nov *The Nylon Curtain* hits US #7 (a further million-seller) and makes UK #27. Taken from it, *Pressure* makes US #20. Meanwhile, on vacation in St. Barthlemy in the Caribbean, Joel, playing piano in the bar of a hotel, meets model Christie Brinkley. *Allentown* enters US chart.

Dec [27] Joel plays a benefit concert in Allentown, PA.

[29] Another benefit concert, at Nassau Coliseum in Uniondale, NY, raises $125,000 for Joel's own Charity Begins At Home organization, which will distribute the sum between over 60 different causes.

1983 Feb *Allentown* reaches US #17.

Apr *Goodnight Saigon* makes US #56.

Sept *Tell Her About It*, from his new album, tops US chart for a week, another million-seller.

Oct *An Innocent Man*, with tracks as individual tributes to musical styles and stars which influenced Joel's formative years, hits US #4 (selling over 2 million copies) and UK #2.

Nov *Uptown Girl*, a track from *An Innocent Man* in the mold of the early Four Seasons hits, sells a million and hits US #3. In UK, it tops chart for 5 weeks, and is by far his biggest seller with sales topping 900,000. Promo video features Christie Brinkley, now Joel's fiancee.

1984 Feb Title track *An Innocent Man* hits US #10 and UK #8. *Cold Spring Harbor* is reissued in remixed form by Columbia, and reaches US #158 and UK #95.

May Fourth single from *An Innocent Man*, *The Longest Time*, reaches US #14 and UK #25.

Aug *Leave A Tender Moment Alone*, featuring a Toots Thielemans harmonica solo, reaches US #27 and UK #29. As Joel arrives in UK for a concert tour, he has 5 albums in UK Top 100.

1985 Jan [28] Joel takes part in the recording of USA For Africa's *We Are The World* in Los Angeles. All proceeds go to African famine relief. (The single will be a multi-million seller and worldwide chart-topper.)

Mar *Keeping The Faith* reaches US #18.

[23] Joel marries Christie Brinkley.

Aug *You're Only Human (Second Wind)* hits US #9. It is one of 2 new recordings included on double compilation album *Greatest Hits Volumes 1 & 2*, which hits US #6 and UK #7.

Nov *The Night Is Still Young* makes US #34.

1986 Feb Double A-side reissue of *She's Always A Woman/Just The Way You Are* reaches UK #53.

July [26] *Modern Woman*, taken from the soundtrack of film "Ruthless People", hits US #10.

Aug *The Bridge*, with *Nylon Curtain*-style songs, includes a guest appearance by Ray Charles on *Baby Grand*. It hits US #7 and UK #38.

Sept [29] "The Bridge" tour starts at Civic Center, Glens Fall, NY.

Oct [18] *A Matter Of Trust* hits US #10 and makes UK #52.

1987 Jan [31] *This Is The Time* reaches US #18.

From *The Bridge*, *Big Man On Mulberry Street*, later becomes the central theme of an episode of NBC TV series "Moonlighting".

Apr [25] *Baby Grand*, the duet with Ray Charles, makes US #75. He plays a series of concerts in USSR, including a date at Leningrad which is recorded for album release.

Nov Live double album *Kohyept*, taken from his Leningrad show, reaches US #38 and UK #92.

1988 May [1] Nevada judge clears Joel of defamation charges after he had called musician John Powers a "creep" in **Playboy** interview.

Nov Joel is featured on various artists' album *Oliver And Company*, singing *Why Should I Worry?* from the forthcoming Disney movie of the same name.

1989 Jan [22] Joel sings the American national anthem at Super Bowl XXIII between the San Francisco 49ers and the Cincinnati Bengals at Joe Robbie Stadium, Miami, FL.

Aug [30] Joel fires his manager, and former brother-in-law, Frank Weber, after an audit reveals discrepancies. Joel will subsequently sue him for $90 million.

Sept [24] Joel is taken sick at New York's Kennedy airport on his way to London and is hospitalized with severe abdominal pain from kidney stones.

[25] Joel files suit in New York charging Weber with fraud and breach of fiduciary duty.

[26] Joel has operation to remove kidney stone at New York university medical center.

Oct *We Didn't Start The Fire* hits UK #7.

Nov Joel begins month-long rehearsal at Suffolk County Police Academy, West Hampton, Long Island, NY, for his upcoming tour. His new band comprises Liberty DeVitto (drums), David Brown (guitar), Mark Rivera (sax), Crystal Taliefero (vocals/percussion), Mindy Jostyn (rhythm guitar/violin/harp), Jeff Jacobs (synthesizers) and Schuyler Deale (bass). *Stormfront* hits UK #5.

Dec *Leningrad* peaks at UK #53.

[6] US tour opens at the Centrum, Worcester, MA.

[9] *We Didn't Start The Fire* hits US #1.

[16] Parent album *Stormfront*, produced by Foreigner's Mick Jones, also hits US #1.

1990 Jan [26] CBS Records issues cassettes of *We Didn't Start The Fire* with a 10-min. talk by Joel with the **Junior Scholastic** magazines and **Update** magazine for 40,000 students, after the fifth grade class at the Banta elementary school in Menasha, WI, had used the song's lyrics to select topics for history reports.

[22] New York supreme court judge awards Joel $2 million in a partial summary judgement against Frank Weber.

Mar *I Go To Extremes* peaks at UK #70.

[17] *I Go To Extremes* hits US #6.

Apr [11] Richmond, VA, judge dismisses $30 million countersuit filed by Frank Weber.

May [21] Joel plays Wembley Arena, London, during European tour.

June [2] *The Downeaster Alexa* peaks at US #57. (Joel donates part of the royalties to the Coast Alliance and the East Hampton Baymen's Association charities.)

[22-23] Joel plays 2 sell-out dates at Yankee Stadium, The Bronx, New York, during his current world tour.

Aug [18] *That's Not Her Style* stalls at US #77.

[30] Joel sings *Sea Cruise* with Paul Simon, at Simon's benefit concert a Deep Hollow Ranch, Montauk, for the preservation of Montauk Point Lighthouse, near his Long Island home. (A week later, Joel and Simon will reprise their performance at Joel's benefit for the East Hampton Baymen's Association.)

Dec [1] *And So It Goes* makes US #37.

[5] Joel is honored by NARAS as a Grammy Living Legend, with Johnny Cash, Aretha Franklin and Quincy Jones.

1991 Jan [22] Joel begins an Australian tour with 7 shows at the Entertainment Centre, Sydney, followed by shows in Melbourne, Brisbane, Adelaide and Perth.

Mar [7] Joel is named Best Keyboard Player in the annual **Rolling Stone** Readers' Picks music awards.

Joel is presented with a crystal award by Sony Music Australia, for being the biggest selling artist in the company's history.

May [19] Joel receives an honorary doctorate of humane letters from Fairfield university, Fairfield, CT.

ELTON JOHN

'61 John (b. Reginald Kenneth Dwight, Mar.25, 1947, Pinner, London), son of an ex-Royal Air Force trumpeter, Stanley and his wife, Sheila Dwight, having started piano lessons at age 4 and played at a local music festival at age 12 (his early piano idols are Winifred Atwell and Charlie Kunz), has already attended the Royal Academy of Music, London, to which he won a part-time scholarship in 1958, when he joins locally performing R&B outfit Bluesology (its name taken from a Django Reinhardt disk), playing piano with existing members Stuart Brown (guitar), Rex Bishop (bass) and Mike Inkpen (drums). Their first paying gig is at the Northwood Hills hotel, Northwood, London.

'63 Still a teenager, he attends Pinner County Grammar school, but quits 3 weeks before his exams. Through his cousin Roy (a professional soccer player, who has scored a goal and broken his leg in the 1959 FA Cup Final between Nottingham Forest and Luton Town) he hears of a job as a "junior" at London's Mills Music Publishers. He will earn £4 10s a week.

'65 Bluesology turns professional, with the help of talent agent Roy Tempest and for 18 months will back major US R&B artists playing UK club dates, including Major Lance, who recommends it to other US acts, including Patti LaBelle & The Blue Belles, The Inkspots, Doris Troy and Billy Stewart among others, for tours throughout Europe.
July He writes Bluesology's first release *Come Back Baby*, produced by Jack Baverstock and released on Fontana.

'66 **Dec** Long John Baldry becomes front man for Bluesology. He expands the group into a 9-piece, adding American guitarist Caleb Quaye and Elton Dean on sax, plus Pete Gavin, Mark Charig and Neil Hubbard. It becomes known as The John Baldry Show, and moves to the cabaret circuit.

'67 **June** Disillusioned with the music he is playing for Baldry, Dwight auditions for Liberty Records (currently establishing an independent London office, and advertising in music paper **New Musical Express** for artists and writers) at Regent Sound studios in London where he sings Jim Reeves' songs *I Love You Because* and *He'll Have To Go* among others, too nervous to perform his own. He fails, but Liberty's Ray Williams gives him lyrics sent to the label by Lincolnshire writer Bernie Taupin (b. May 22, 1950, Lincolnshire), whose mother has rescued his letter, intended for Liberty but discarded, in a waste-paper basket. They begin to write by correspondence (and do not meet until about 20 songs have been completed), meeting in the reception area of Dick James House, when Dwight calls out "Is there a lyricist here?", and sign to Gralto, The Hollies publishing company.
Oct Baldry's *Let The Heartaches Begin* is released and hits UK #1. B-side *Lord You Made Me Love You Too Long*, written by John and Taupin, is the first disk to bear that credit. (He has changed his name from Dwight, borrowing Elton Dean and John Baldry's forenames.)

'68 Baldry Show member Quaye finds work as an engineer at Dick James Music's newly-opened 2-track studio in London's West End. John and Taupin sign to Dick James Music Publishing (DJM) for £10 a week each as staff writers. (They will write together, with 1 break, for over 20 years.)
Mar [1] The first Elton John solo single, *I've Been Loving You Too Long* is produced by Quaye and released on Philips, but fails to chart. Meanwhile Roger Cook records John and Taupin's *Skyline Pigeon* for his first solo single, on UK Columbia.

'69 **Jan** *Lady Samantha*, John's second and final Philips release (produced by EMI plugger Steve Brown), like everything out now, does not chart (selling close to 10,000 copies), but finds significant UK airplay, and will be included on the next album by top US act Three Dog Night. Meanwhile, John auditions for lead singer with Robert Fripp's new group King Crimson, but is turned down.
Feb Lulu performs John and Taupin's *I Can't Go On Living Without You* on her BBC TV show, as one of the final 6 British entries for the Eurovision song contest. (Peter Warne and Alan Moorhouse's *Boom Bang A Bang* is the chosen song.)
May *It's Me That You Need* is John's first release on DJM Records.
June DJM debut album *Empty Sky* is released, containing all John and Taupin songs.
[25] John plays piano on The Hollies' session for *He Ain't Heavy He's My Brother*, at Abbey Road studios, London.
He contributes *From Denver To L.A.* to movie "The Games". (It will be released as a US single on Viking in 1970.) He begins to do work on sessions for budget cover version UK labels including Music For Pleasure and Pickwick, as well as playing on other artists' demos and sessions.

1970 **Mar** *Border Song*, featuring the Barbara Moore Choir, receives UK airplay, but fails to reach UK Top 50.
May [9] He again plays piano on an Abbey Road studio session for The Hollies, on *I Can't Tell The Bottom From The Top* (and is guest organist on their *Perfect Lady Housewife* for inclusion on **Confessions Of The Mind**).
Aug [22] At the invitation of label boss Russ Regan, John signs to MCA Records' Uni subsidiary in US, and *Border Song*, from *Elton John*, marks his US singles chart debut at #92.
[25] John makes his live debut in US, performing at the 20th anniversary celebrations for Doug Weston's Troubadour in Los Angeles, CA, opening for singer/songwriter David Ackles, followed by a 17-day tour.
Oct *Elton John* enters US chart, and will hit #4. It is produced by Gus Dudgeon, and features the first Elton John Band, with John on vocals and keyboards, Quaye on guitar, Dee Murray (b. David Murray Oates, Apr.3, 1946, Southgate, London) on bass and Nigel Olsson (b. Feb.10, 1949, Wallasey, Merseyside) on drums.
Nov [17] A concert in New York forms a live radio broadcast for station W-PLJ FM (and is recorded for album release in 1971).
[20-21] John plays at the Fillmore East, New York, with Leon Russell.

1971 **Jan** *Elton John* reaches UK #11.
[23] Ballad *Your Song* hits UK #7 and US #8.
Feb *Tumbleweed Connection*, featuring Dusty Springfield as a backing vocalist, hits UK #6 and US #5. Dick James enlists Motown label manager John Reid as John's personal manager. He will remain with the singer for over 20 years.
Apr [24] John's title song from film "Friends" makes US #34, as he embarks a major US tour, set to end in June.
May Soundtrack album *Friends* reaches US #36, while *17-11-70* (US title: *11-17-70*), from the Nov. concert, reaches UK #20 and US #11.
Nov John embarks on a major UK tour, and by year's end, he will have changed his name by deed poll to Elton Hercules John.

1972 **Feb** Ex-Magna Carta guitarist, Davey Johnstone (b. May 6, 1951, Edinburgh, Scotland) joins John's band.
[5] *Levon* reaches US #24.
Apr Arriving at Los Angeles airport for the start of a US tour, his stage boots, with 8" lifts, are checked for drugs.
[8] Ballad *Tiny Dancer* makes US #41.
May *Rocket Man* hits UK #2. *Madman Across The Water* makes UK #41 but hits US #8.
June *Honky Chateau*, a reference to its recording location (Strawberry studios in Chateau d'Herouville, 30 miles from Paris, France), hits UK #2. It is his sixth consecutive album produced by Gus Dudgeon.
July [15] *Rocket Man* hits US #6 as *Honky Chateau* begins a 5-week run at US #1.
Sept Uptempo honky-tonk *Honky Cat* makes UK #31.
[23] *Honky Cat* hits US #8 as he begins a US tour.
Oct He makes a guest appearance in Marc Bolan's movie "Born To Boogie".
[30] John appears in the Royal Variety Show in London.
Nov Full throttle pop'n'roll *Crocodile Rock* hits UK #5.

1973 **Feb** [3] *Crocodile Rock* tops US chart for 3 weeks, earning a gold disk, while *Daniel* hits UK #4.
[10] Parent album *Don't Shoot Me, I'm Only The Piano Player* tops UK chart for 6 weeks.
Mar [3] *Don't Shoot Me, I'm Only The Piano Player* tops US chart for 2 weeks.
May John launches Rocket Records at a village railway station in the English countryside.
June [2] Plane-leaving ballad *Daniel* hits US #2, and is another gold single.
July Aggressive rocker *Saturday Night's Alright For Fighting* hits UK #7.
Aug [15] US tour begins, set to end Oct.21.
Sept [7] John plays before a crowd of 25,000 at Los Angeles' Hollywood Bowl, where porn movie star Linda Lovelace acts as hostess for the evening.
[15] *Saturday Night's Alright For Fighting* reaches US #12.
Oct *Goodbye Yellow Brick Road* hits UK #6.
Nov John becomes Vice President of Watford Football Club.
[8] Double album *Goodbye Yellow Brick Road* hits US #1 for 8 weeks and earns a US gold disk.
Dec [4] "Elton John And Bernie Taupin Say Goodbye Norma Jean And Other Things" airs on UK TV. (ABC TV will show an extended version in the US in 1974.)
[8] Title track hits US #2 for 3 weeks, again going gold. Seasonal *Step Into Christmas* makes UK #24.

[22] *Goodbye Yellow Brick Road* tops UK chart (his second successive #1) for 2 weeks.

1974 Mar A Taupin ode to Marilyn Monroe, *Candle In The Wind*, peaks at UK #11.

Apr [13] UK B-side to *Candle In The Wind*, *Bennie & The Jets* is issued as US A-side and hits #1, again a million-seller. It also becomes his first US R&B chart hit, at #15.

May John cancels a 17-date UK tour, suffering from exhaustion. He will perform 2 charity events however, for Watford Football Club and the Invalid Children's Society.

June *Don't Let The Sun Go Down On Me* reaches UK #16 and hits US #2 (another million-seller).

July [13] *Caribou* recorded at James William Guercio's studio, the Caribou Ranch, with help from The Beach Boys, tops both UK and US charts. John re-signs with MCA in US for an $8 million, 5-album deal, the highest in recording history.

Aug He forms his own publishing company, Big Pig Music.

[5] His overwhelming popularity in US is reaffirmed as tickets for 3 Oct. concerts in Los Angeles sell out in minutes, causing a fourth show to be added.

Sept *The Bitch Is Back* reaches UK #15. John duets with John Lennon on the former Beatle's *Whatever Gets You Through The Night* (which climbs to UK #36 and hits US #1).

Oct John embarks on 44-date North American tour, which will be seen by approximately 750,000 people.

Nov [2] *The Bitch Is Back* hits US #4.

[23] Compilation album *Elton John's Greatest Hits* hits UK #1.

[28] John and Lennon sing *I Saw Her Standing There* at a Thanksgiving concert at New York's Madison Square Garden.

[30] *Elton John's Greatest Hits* hits US #1 (for 10 weeks).

Dec A revival of The Beatles *Lucy In The Sky With Diamonds*, with a guest appearance by Lennon, hits UK #10.

1975 Jan [4] *Lucy In The Sky With Diamonds* tops US chart, becoming another million-seller.

Feb [2] Neil Sedaka's *Laughter In The Rain*, released on John's Rocket Records in US, tops US chart.

Apr *Philadelphia Freedom* penned for John's friend Billie Jean King (after her Philadelphia-based tennis team The Freedoms), credited to The Elton John Band with an arrangement by Thom Bell, makes UK #12.

[12] *Philadelphia Freedom* tops US chart for 2 weeks (also becoming his second R&B hit at #32) as Ringo Starr hits US #3 with double A-side singles, including John/Taupin's *Snookeroo*. John's first album *Empty Sky* is reissued in US and hits #6. He appears in Ken Russell's movie version of The Who's "Tommy".

[19] John fires band members Murray and Olsson on the eve of the release of autobiographical album *Captain Fantastic And The Brown Dirt Cowboy*.

May [3] John makes his debut on US TV show "Soul Train".

June [7] *Captain Fantastic And The Brown Dirt Cowboy* hits UK #2, held off the top by *The Best Of The Stylistics*, and becomes the first album ever to go straight to US #1, where it stays for 7 weeks. (The songs were written on a cruise liner.)

[21] John tops the bill at a sell-out open-air concert at Wembley Stadium, London.

[29] At an Oakland Coliseum concert by The Doobie Brothers and The Eagles, John jams on stage with both bands on *Listen To The Music* and Chuck Berry's *Carol*.

July Ballad *Someone Saved My Life Tonight*, a partly autobiographical account of John's recent suicide attempt, reaches UK #22.

Aug [16] *Someone Saved My Life Tonight* hits US #4.

[25] He plays 2 benefit shows at Los Angeles' Troubadour, scene of his US live debut 5 years earlier, for UCLA's Jules Stein Eye Institute, raising over $150,000.

Nov Caribbean-tinged *Island Girl* reaches UK #14.

[1] *Island Girl* hits US #1 for 3 weeks, selling a million (and deposing Neil Sedaka's Rocket single *Bad Blood*, with John on backing vocals). *Rock Of The Westies* hits UK #5 and US #1.

[8] John becomes godfather to John and Yoko Lennon's son Sean.

[21] John receives a star on Hollywood's Walk Of Fame as Los Angeles declares it "Elton John Day".

[26] He concludes US "West Of The Rockies" tour at Los Angeles' Dodger Stadium (the first artist to play there since The Beatles in 1966), dressed in a sequined Dodgers uniform.

1976 Feb [28] Double A-side *Grow Some Funk Of Your Own/I Feel Like A Bullet (In The Gun Of Robert Ford)* reaches US #14, but fails in UK.

Mar [7] John is immortalized in wax at Madame Tussaud's in London

(the first rock star since The Beatles to be so honored).

Apr [3] *Pinball Wizard*, from film "Tommy", released in re-recorded form, hits UK #7.

[29] John begins 29-date UK tour at the Grand theater, Leeds, W.Yorks., set to end at the Capitol theater, Cardiff, Wales, on June 4.

[22] *Here And There*, recorded live in London and New York, become his final DJM album and hits UK #6.

June [12] *Here And There* hits US #4.

July [24] John's first UK Singles chart-topper (a duet with Kiki Dee, recorded in Toronto, Canada) is *Don't Go Breaking My Heart*, which stays at #1 for 6 weeks.

Aug [7] Pseudonymously credited to Ann Orson and Carte Blanche, also tops US chart for 4 weeks, and earns a gold disk. (He will perform the song on ITV's "The Muppet Show" with Miss Piggy.)

[10] John begins a 7-date series of sell-out shows at New York's Madison Square Garden (taking $1.25 million in ticket receipts and breaking the house record set a year earlier by The Rolling Stones).

Oct [9] *Bennie And The Jets*, reissued on DJM as a UK A-side, makes UK #37.

Nov [13] Double album *Blue Moves*, with backing vocal assistance from David Crosby, Bruce Johnston, Toni Tennille and Graham Nash, hits both UK and US #3. (It will be the last album for the time being produced by Dudgeon and written totally with Taupin.)

Dec [4] Ballad cut *Sorry Seems To Be The Hardest Word* reaches UK #1

[25] *Sorry Seems To Be The Hardest Word* hits US #6.

1977 Mar [5] *Bite Your Lip (Get Up And Dance)* reaches US #28.

[19] *Crazy Water*, recorded with help from The Captain & Tennille, reaches UK #27.

June [25] *Bite Your Lip (Get Up And Dance)*, backed with *Chicago* (another duet with Kiki Dee) reaches UK #28. John achieves a lifetime ambition when he becomes chairman of Watford Football Club.

Oct [1] He becomes the first rock artist to be honored in Madison Square Garden's Hall Of Fame in New York.

Nov [3] Having recently collapsed during 2 concert performances, John announces his retirement from live work, during a concert at Empire Pool, Wembley, London.

Dec [3] Compilation album *Elton John's Greatest Hits Volume Two* reaches US #21. He records several tracks with US producer Thom Be at Kay Smith studio in Seattle, WA, and Sigma and Sound studios, Philadelphia, PA.

1978 Jan [21] *Elton John's Greatest Hits Volume Two* hits UK #6.

Apr [15] Rock-pomped *Ego*, his last collaboration with Taupin for 3 years, makes UK #34.

May [6] *Ego* makes US #34.

Dec [9] First album without Taupin lyrics, *A Single Man*, produced John with Clive Franks, reaches US #15. (The album is dedicated to Watford's manager Graham Taylor and 2 tracks feature the soccer tea as backing vocalists.)

[16] Extracted *Part Time Love* reaches UK #15 and US #22.

1979 Jan [13] *Song For Guy*, an instrumental dedicated to Guy Burchett, Rocket's motorcycle messenger boy who died in an accident at age 17 hits UK #4.

[20] Parent album *A Single Man* hits UK #8.

Feb [3] He makes his first live appearance since "retiring", in Swede

Mar John begins his comeback tour, his first since 1976, of 30 dates around UK, accompanied only by percussionist Ray Cooper.

May The Thom Bell sessions are released as EP *Are You Ready For Lo* reaching UK #42. In US, treated as a mini-album, it will make #51 on the Album chart (Sept.1). John plays concerts in Israel, the first Weste rock star to do so, as part of the country's independence celebrations.

[21] John plays the first of 8 unique concerts in Leningrad. He is the first Western solo pop star to tour USSR. (The trip is filmed for documentary "To Russia With Elton".)

Aug [25] *Mama Can't Buy You Love*, from the mini-album, hits US #9

Sept [27] He collapses on stage at Hollywood's Universal Amphitheater, suffering from exhaustion due to a bout of 'flu. After recovering and resting for 10 mins., he resumes for a 3-hour show.

Oct Dance-oriented *Victim Of Love*, produced by Pete Bellotte and with vocal support from The Doobie Brothers, Michael McDonald an Patrick Simmons, peaks at UK #41 and will make US #35 (Nov.24).

Nov [17] Title track makes US #31 (the only single from the album to cha

1980 Mar [8] Compilation album *Lady Samantha*, containing DJM label rarities, peaks at UK #56.

June [7] *Little Jeannie* makes UK #33 and hits US #3.

[14] *21 At 33*, referring to his 21st album in his 33rd year, reaches UK #12. Co-writers include Judie Tzuke, Tom Robinson, Gary Osbourne

and Taupin, with backing vocals from Bruce Johnston, Toni Tennille, Glenn Frey, Timothy Schmit and Peter Noone.

July [19] *Little Jeannie* hits US #3 as parent *21 At 33* makes US #13.

Sept [6] *(Sartorial Eloquence) Don't You Wanna Play This Game No More* makes UK #44.

[21] John signs to Geffen Records in US.

[27] *(Sartorial Eloquence) Don't You Wanna Play This Game* makes US #39. John co-writes Tom Robinson's *Never Gonna Fall In Love Again*, while John's *Dear God* fails to chart.

Nov [8] K-Tel TV-advertised *The Very Best Of Elton John* reaches #24 on UK chart.

1981 Mar *I Saw Her Standing There Live*, a live track recorded with John Lennon in 1974, released as a tribute, makes UK #40.

June [6] *Nobody Wins*, a re-write of a French song, makes UK #42 as parent album *The Fox*, produced by Chris Thomas, reaches UK #12.

[20] *Nobody Wins* reaches US #21.

[27] *The Fox* reaches US #21. (*Just Like Belgium*, the UK follow-up single, will fail to chart).

Sept [19] *Chloe* makes US #34.

1982 Mar [8] John's first tour for 2 years opens in New Zealand.

Apr [24] *Blue Eyes* hit UK #8.

[30] 25-date European tour opens in Stockholm, Sweden, set to end May 30 in Lille, France.

May [1] *Jump Up!* reaches UK #13.

[29] *Empty Garden (Hey Hey Johnny)*, a tribute to John Lennon, reaches US #13.

June [12] *Jump Up!* reaches US #17.

[26] *Empty Garden (Hey Hey Johnny)* peaks at UK #51.

Oct [2] *Blue Eyes* reaches UK #12.

Nov [2] 42-date UK tour begins at the City Hall, Newcastle, Tyne & Wear, set to end on Christmas Eve at the Hammersmith Odeon, London, the last of 14 consecutive shows at the venue.

[13] Compilation album *Love Songs* climbs to UK #39. *Princess* and *All Quiet On The Western Front* both fail to chart.

1983 May *I Guess That's Why They Call It The Blues* hits UK #5.

June *Too Low For Zero*, his first album written entirely with Taupin since *Blue Moves* in 1976, hits UK #7 and US #25.

July [9] *I'm Still Standing*, helped by innovative video, reaches US #12.

Aug *I'm Still Standing* hits UK #4.

Oct *Kiss The Bride* reaches UK #20 and US #25.

Dec Seasonal *Cold As Christmas* makes UK #33.

1984 Jan [28] *I Guess That's Why They Call It The Blues* hits US #4.

Feb [14] John marries studio engineer, Renate Blauer, in Darling Point, Sydney, Australia.

Apr [17] He begins a 44-date European tour in Sarajevo, Yugoslavia, set to end at Wembley Stadium, London, on June 30.

May John flies from Copenhagen, Denmark to see Watford Football Club play in their first ever FA Cup Final at Wembley. They lose to Liverpool, 2-0.

June *Sad Songs (Say So Much)* hits UK #7. *Breaking Hearts* hits UK #2 and makes US #20.

Aug [11] *Sad Songs (Say So Much)* hits US #5.

Sept Anti-apartheid themed *Passengers*, his 50th UK single, hits UK #5.

Nov *Who Wears These Shoes* makes UK #50 and US #16.

1985 Jan [12] *In Neon* makes US #38.

Feb *Breaking Hearts (Ain't What It Used To Be)* released for Valentine's Day and John's own first wedding anniversary, reaches UK #59.

Mar [13] John presents George Michael with the Best Songwriter award at the annual Ivor Novello ceremony at London's Grosvenor House, proclaiming Michael to be a "major songwriter in the tradition of Paul McCartney and Barry Gibb".

June A duet with Millie Jackson, *Act Of War*, makes UK #32. (Tina Turner has been offered the song but turned it down.)

[28] John duets with Michael on *Candle In The Wind* in Wham!'s farewell concert at London's Wembley Stadium.

July [13] John participates in Live Aid, with Michael, duetting on *Don't Let The Sun Go Down On Me*.

Nov Ballad *Nikita*, with vocal help from Michael, hits UK #3. *Ice On Fire* hits UK #3 and US #48.

[15] 5-month non-stop European tour begins in Dublin, Eire, set to end Apr.26, 1986 in Brussels, Belgium.

Dec *Wrap Her Up*, again featuring Michael on vocals (and in the video), reaches UK #12 and US #20.

1986 Jan John joins Gladys Knight and Stevie Wonder on Dionne Warwick & Friends' AIDS fund-raising single *That's What Friends Are For*, which hits US #1 and makes UK #16.

[29] John and Taupin are awarded £5 million in back royalties from Dick James Music, after a lengthy and bitter court case.

Feb [10] John is honored for his Outstanding Contribution To British Music at the fifth annual BRIT Awards at the Grosvenor House, London.

Mar [22] *Nikita* hits US #7, as *Cry To Heaven* makes UK #47.

June [20] John participates in the first Prince's Trust concert in London, with Bryan Adams, Eric Clapton and Tina Turner.

Aug [15] He begins a US tour in Detroit, MI.

Oct *Heartache All Over The World* makes UK #45 as parent album *Leather Jackets* makes UK #24 and US #91.

Nov [22] *Heartache All Over The World* makes US #55.

Dec [9] John collapses on stage during a concert in Sydney, Australia.

[14] A further Sydney concert is recorded for future release. John duets with Cliff Richard on *Slow Rivers* which makes UK #44.

1987 Jan [5] John enters a Sydney hospital for throat surgery, planning to cancel all concerts for the coming year.

Feb [24] John wins Best Pop Performance By A Duo Or Group With Vocal with Dionne Warwick, Gladys Knight and Stevie Wonder for *That's What Friends Are For* at the 29th annual Grammy awards.

Mar John and his wife Renate announce they have split up. He re-signs with MCA in US.

Apr John appears at an AIDS benefit show in London, his first live show since his throat operation.

July [11] He duets with Jennifer Rush on *Flames Of Paradise*, which makes US #36.

Sept Boxed double album *Live In Australia*, chronicling his 1986 tour, makes UK #70 and US #24. *Greatest Hits Volume Three*, on Geffen, reaches US #84.

Dec John tries, unsuccessfully, to sell his soccer club, Watford.

1988 Jan [23] Live *Candle In The Wind*, recorded with the Melbourne Symphony Orchestra, hits US #6.

Feb *Candle In The Wind* hits UK #5, confirming the song's enduring popularity.

Mar Re-promoted double album *Live In Australia* (without its original boxed packaging) peaks at UK #43.

June *I Don't Want To Go On With You Like That* makes UK #30.

July *Reg Strikes Back* reaches UK #18 and US #16. *Town Of Plenty* peaks at UK #74.

Aug [27] Uptempo *I Don't Want To Go On With You Like That* hits US #2, behind George Michael's *Monkey*.

Sept [6-9] 2,000 items of John's personal memorabilia are auctioned at Sotheby's in London. His giant "Pinball Wizard" boots from film "Tommy" sell for $11,000, as dozens of other items, from gold disks to personalized spectacles, contribute to a 7-figure sale.

[9] US tour begins at the Miami Arena, Miami, FL.

[23] John concludes 5 sell-out performances, supported by Wet Wet Wet, at New York's Madison Square Garden. (His final concert breaks The Grateful Dead's career record of 25 sell-out Madison Square Garden concerts.)

Oct The Sun newspaper settles a libel action out of court with John for £1 million and prints an apology admitting that their recent rent-boy sex scandal story was false. John produces and writes for Olivia Newton-John's *The Rumour*.

Nov [12] *A Word In Spanish* reaches US #19, as Elton and Renate John announce an "amicable" divorce.

1989 Mar [20] John embarks on a 50-date European trek with Nik Kershaw as a support act, in Lyons, France, which will end June 2 in Edinburgh, Scotland. (He celebrates his 42nd birthday with a party in Paris.)

May [11] John performs at the Songwriters Hall Of Fame 20th anniversary dinner and wins National Academy of Popular Music's Hitmaker Award at Radio City Music Hall, New York.

[27] John begins UK leg of the tour with sold-out dates, while *Through The Storm* duet with Aretha Franklin makes US #16 and UK #41. He also contributes *I'm Ready* to Richard Perry-produced *Rock, Rhythm & Blues* compilation.

June [3] He takes part in "Our Common Future", a 5-hour ecological awareness world telecast concert.

Aug Ballad *Healing Hands* makes UK #45.

[24] John recreates his role as The Pinball Wizard at a benefit performance of "Tommy" at the Universal Amphitheater, Los Angeles, with Steve Winwood as The Hawker, Patti LaBelle as The Acid Queen, Phil Collins as Uncle Ernie and Billy Idol as Cousin Kevin.

Sept *Sleeping With The Past* initially hits UK #6 and US #23.

[6] John plays the first of 8 concerts at Madison Square Garden, New York, during a 3-month US tour.

Oct [20] *Healing Hands* reaches US #13.

Nov Taupin/John-penned single *Sacrifice* initially peaks at UK #55.
Dec No longer with a financial interest in the club, John is given the honorary position of Life President of Watford Football Club.

1990 **Mar** [31] *Sacrifice* reaches US #18.
Apr [7] John makes a surprise appearance at Farm Aid IV in the Hoosier Dome, Indianapolis, IN. (He dedicates *Candle In The Wind* to AIDS victim Ryan White, for whom John has been maintaining a bedside vigil. White will die hours later.)
[11] John sings *Skyline Pigeon* and acts as pall bearer at White's funeral in the Second Presbyterian church in Indianapolis.
May [18-19] He plays inaugural concert at the Trump Taj Mahal Casino Resort, Atlantic City, NJ.
June Revived *Sleeping With The Past* hits UK #1.
[23] Reissued after continuous airplay, *Sacrifice* (now a double A-side with also reissued *Healing Hands*) hits UK #1, his first ever solo UK chart-topper and 66th single release. John announces on BBC TV chat show "Wogan" that the royalties from this and all his future singles will go to various AIDS charities.
July [7] *Club At The End Of The Street* reaches US #28.
Aug *Club At The End Of The Street/Whispers* makes UK #47.
Oct [27] Ballad *You Gotta Love Someone* makes UK #33.
Nov [10] Double album *The Very Best Of Elton John*, his latest collection, hits UK #1.
Dec [15] Box-set CD compilation *To Be Continued...* chronicling John's career to date, makes US #82.

1991 **Jan** [5] *You Gotta Love Someone* makes US #43.
Feb [10] John wins Best British Male Artist at the 10th annual BRIT Awards at the Dominion theater, London.
Mar [10] John performs at a Rainforest Foundation benefit show held at Carnegie Hall, New York, singing *Come Down In Time* with Sting. John crashes Rod Stewart's Wembley concert, dressed to look like Stewart's new bride, Rachel Hunter. (The new Mrs. Stewart helps John with his make-up.)

GRACE JONES

1976 Jones (b. May 19, 1952, Spanishtown, Jamaica, West Indies), having spent her teenage years in Syracuse, NY, has been a fashion model in Paris (appearing on the covers of **Vogue**, **Elle** and **Stern**) after being discovered by French artist/photographer Jean-Paul Goude, whom she subsequently marries, and studied acting and had a part in movie "Gordon's War", when she turns to singing as the disco music boom hits Europe. Recording in France, her early releases are licensed to Beam Junction Records in US and Polydor in UK.

1977 **Feb** Debut Double A-side *Sorry/That's The Trouble* reaches US #71.
May *I Need A Man* makes US #83. Both this and its predecessor are huge hits on the New York club/disco circuit, where she concentrates her early outrageous live performances, cultivating a decadent androgynous image, mostly carefully designed by Goude.
Oct She signs to Island Records and cuts the first of 3 disco albums, *Portfolio*, which makes US #109.

1978 **Aug** *Fame* reaches US #97. She becomes the first artist to perform a live set at New York's most exclusive disco, Studio 54.

1979 **Sept** *Muse* features the club hits *What I Did For Love* and *I Need A Man*, and peaks at US #156.

1980 **Aug** *Warm Leatherette* marks a transition in sound from glossy disco to a sparse, relaxed reggae-funk. Produced by Island's owner Chris Blackwell at Compass Point studios in Nassau, Bahamas, it features top Jamaican reggae sessioneers Sly & Robbie on instrumentation, and includes a cover of a Motown oldie (The Marvelettes' *The Hunter Gets Captured By The Game*), plus new wave material by The Normal (the title track) and The Pretenders (*Private Life*). It makes UK #45 and US #132, while extracted *Private Life* becomes her first UK hit single, at #17.
Oct Jones takes umbrage with BBC TV chat show host Russell Harty while being interviewed on his program, and physically attacks him before a prime-time audience.

1981 **June** *Nightclubbing* repeats previous team and formula and introduces Jones as writer, as well as including songs by David Bowie/Iggy Pop and Vanda and Young. It reaches US #32 and UK #35. *Pull Up To The Bumper*, taken from the album, makes UK #53 and hits US R&B chart.

1982 **Nov** Double A-side *The Apple Stretching/Nipple To The Bottle* charts in UK at #50.
Dec *Living My Life* features more of Jones' own lyrics, and makes US #86 and UK #15.

1983 **Apr** *My Jamaican Guy* peaks at UK #56.

1984 **June** Jones stars with Arnold Schwarzenegger in the fantasy action movie "Conan The Destroyer", in the role of Zula.

1985 **May** She appears as May Day, a sophisticated martial arts villainess, opposite Roger Moore, in James Bond film "A View To A Kill".
Nov Trevor Horn-written and produced *Slave To The Rhythm* is released in UK on ZTT/Island, and is Jones' biggest hit single, peaking at UK #12. The album of the same title also makes UK #12, while in US it marks the beginning of a deal with EMI Manhattan and reaches #73.

1986 **Feb** Compilation *Island Life* hits UK #4, her most successful UK album, and US #161. *Pull Up To The Bumper* (backed with *La Vie En Rose*), is reissued and reaches UK #12.
Mar A revival of Roxy Music's *Love Is The Drug*, also from *Island Life*, makes UK #35.
Nov Jones signs to EMI Manhattan for UK as well as US. *I'm Not Perfect (But I'm Perfect For You)* peaks at UK #56. Nile Rodgers-produced *Inside Story*, from which the single is taken, makes UK #61.
Dec "One Man Show" live video footage is released.

1987 **Jan** [10] *I'm Not Perfect (But I'm Perfect For You)* peaks at US #69.
Mar *Inside Story* makes US #81 while *Party Girl*, issued as a UK single, fails to chart. An extended period of recording inactivity follows.

1988 **Aug** Jones claims that police drag her and her 2 children off an American Airlines jet in Kingston, Jamaica, after her boyfriend, Chris Stanley, demands an apology from the pilot for the delay of the flight.

1989 **Oct** [11] Jones' trial in Kingston, Jamaica, on charges of possessing cocaine is postponed for the fifth time until Oct.26.
Spectrum Video issues live performance "A One Woman Show".

1990 **Feb** Jones features on benefit album *Requiem For The Americas* for the Save The Children Fund.
Mar Jones begins major UK tour to support her latest EMI Manhattan release *Bullet Proof Heart*. At a Brixton Academy, London gig, she keeps the audience waiting for 4½ hours, allegedly a new house record.
Aug Jones makes a rare live appearance, performing at the New York Palladium in aid of ACT-UP, raising funds to fight AIDS.

HOWARD JONES

1970 Jones (b. Feb.23, 1955, Southampton, Hants), already an accomplished pianist, begins to write songs and joins his first group while living temporarily with his parents in Canada, where his father's lecturing job keeps the family on the move.

1973 He starts music college in Manchester, Gtr.Manchester, but will leave to work in a factory and later become a full-time piano teacher (one of his pupils is his future wife Jan) and play in amateur bands.

1979 He buys a synthesizer which damages received after a road accident and begins to sing, with his own synth accompaniment, in pubs and clubs around his home in High Wycombe, Bucks., and meets Jed Hoile, a mime artist who will later become his partner on stage.

1983 As the result of a 24-track demo tape of *New Song* and *What Is Love*, Jones signs to WEA Records in UK and Elektra in US.
Oct Debut *New Song*, produced by Colin Thurston, hits UK #3. He makes his UK TV debut with pre-programmed synthesizer backing.

1984 **Jan** *What Is Love* hits UK #2.
Mar *Hide And Seek* reaches UK #12 and debut album *Human's Lib*, produced by Rupert Hine and featuring Hine's own drummer Trevor Morais and Jones' brother Martin playing bass, enters UK chart at #1, selling 100,000 copies in its first week. *New Song* charts in US, at #27.
June *Pearl In The Shell* hits UK #7. *What Is Love* makes US #33 and *Human's Lib* US #59.
July He tours US with Eurythmics.
Aug *Like To Get To Know You Well*, issued also as title track of a long-form performance video, hits UK #4.
Dec Low-priced *The Twelve Inch Album* makes UK #15, a compilation mini-album of re-mixes and extended versions of earlier singles, with 2 previously unreleased tracks. Jones tours UK, supported by Strawberry Switchblade, culminating in major London shows on Christmas Eve.

1985 **Feb** *Things Can Only Get Better*, with the help of The TKO Horns and Afrodiziak, hits UK #6. Jones appears on UK TV for the first time with a group calling itself The Howard Jones Big Band.
Mar *Dream Into Action*, produced by Hine, hits UK #2.
Apr [16] He plays major London concert at Wembley Arena.
May *Look Mama* hits UK #10.
June *Things Can Only Get Better* hits US #5; *Dream Into Action* US #10.
July *Life In One Day* hits UK #14.
[13] He participates in Live Aid concert at Wembley Stadium, London.
Sept *Life In One Day* reaches US #19.
Nov Belatedly released in US, *Like To Get To Know You Well* makes #49.

'86 **Mar** Re-recorded version of ballad *No One Is To Blame* (of original on *Dream Into Action*), produced by Phil Collins, reaches UK #16.
July [5] Revamped *No One Is To Blame* proves a bigger success in US, where it hits #4, his highest-placed US record, as 6-track mini-album *Action Replay*, including *No One Is To Blame*, climbs to US #34.
Oct *All I Want* reaches UK #35. *One To One*, made with US producer Arif Mardin, hits UK #10.
Nov He contributes *Little Bit Of Snow* to Anti-Heroin Project charity album *Live-In World*. Proceeds go to Phoenix House rehabilitation center for drug and alcohol addicts. *One To One* peaks at US #56. "Last World Dream" and "Howard Jones Live" are released on video.
Dec *You Know I Love You ... Don't You?* makes UK #43 and US #17.
'87 **Feb** [14] *All I Want* stalls at US #76.
Mar *A Little Bit Of Snow* peaks at UK #70. Jones, a lacto-vegetarian, eating dairy products but no fish or meat, opens a vegetarian restaurant in New York, which burns down within 12 months. (He will continue to support various causes with performances during 1987, including more anti-drug projects and the Hurricane Irene concerts but will not record. His future in the restaurant business is uncertain.)
'89 **Mar** *Everlasting Love* peaks at UK #62.
Apr *Cross That Line* makes UK #64 and US #65.
June [3] *Everlasting Love* reaches US #12, as he embarks on a US tour.
Aug [26] *The Prisoner* reaches US #30.
'90 **Nov** [3] *Rubáiyát*, Elektra's 40th anniversary compilation, to which Jones contributes a cover of David Ackles 1968 original *Road To Cairo*, makes US #140.

ICKIE LEE JONES

'61 One of 4 children, Jones (b. Nov.8, 1954, Chicago, IL), at age 7 writes her first song, *I Wish*.
'65 She breaks a tooth riding a mare in an amateur rodeo.
'69 Jones runs away from home for the first time, fleeing with a girlfriend from Phoenix, AZ, to San Diego, CA. They steal a car, but the adventure only lasts 3 days.
'70 Having moved to Olympia, WA, she is asked to leave 3 schools in succession, including Timberline high school in Olympia where she is removed for insubordination.
'73 Jones arrives in Los Angeles, CA, and begins waitressing in an Echo Park area Italian restaurant. She starts playing her own songs, some in spoken word monologues, at clubs includiing the Troubadour.
'76 Jones writes *Easy Money* while working (and part-time singing) at Venice coffee house, Suzanne's.
'77 **Aug** She composes *The Last Chance Texaco* and *Chuck E.'s In Love*, the latter about fabled Los Angeles figure Chuck E. Weiss, whom Jones has met in the kitchen at the Tropicana motel, Los Angeles. They then meet Tom Waits, a Tropicana resident who becomes Jones' sometime beau.
'78 Linking with manager Nick Mathe, they send Warner Bros. label a 4-song EP, *Company, Young Blood, The Last Chance Texaco* and *Easy Money*, recorded as a demo originally for A&M. Warner's A&R producer Lenny Waronker also sees Jones at a Troubadour showcase. Little Feat's Lowell George tips the scales when he chooses to record *Easy Money* on his solo album *Thanks, I'll Eat Here*, having heard it sung down the phone. Warner Bros. signs Jones to a worldwide contract, on her stipulation that Waronker co-produce her debut.
Nov She appears as the blond on cover of Tom Waits' *Blue Valentine*.
'79 **Apr** Debut album *Rickie Lee Jones* is released simultaneously with single *Chuck E.'s In Love*. (The single will hit US #4 and UK #18 in July.) The album hits US #3, earning a platinum disk, and makes UK #18.
May Following a limited showcase US tour of small clubs, Jones appears on NBC TV's "Saturday Night Live", despite arguing with producers over her choice of song. She wins out performing *Coolsville*.
June Jones takes part in a 3-hour jam with Bruce Springsteen and Boz Scaggs at Los Angeles' Whisky A Go-Go club.
Aug As follow-up *Young Blood* makes US #40, Jones begins her first major tour, including sell-out dates at New York's Carnegie Hall.
'80 **Feb** [27] Jones wins Best New Artist Of 1979 at the 22nd annual Grammy awards.
'81 **Aug** After a 2-year hiatus, Jones returns with her second album *Pirates*. It will hit US #5, achieving gold status, but make only UK #37.
Oct *A Lucky Guy* peaks at US #64.
'82 Jones moves from Los Angeles to New York, then to Paris, France, in an attempt to cope with pressures of fame.
'83 **July** After another 2-year retreat, 10" 7-track mini-album *Girl At Her Volcano* is released, making US #39 and UK #51. With 2 live cuts, it features revivals of *On Broadway* and *Walk Away Renée* and a new Tom

Waits number *Angel Wings*. Another Jones-performed Waits ballad will also feature in Martin Scorsese's movie "King Of Comedy".
1984 **Feb** Jones returns to live in Los Angeles with a new boyfriend and cat.
Oct New single *The Real End* peaks at US #83 while parent album *The Magazine* is released. Co-produced by James Newton Howard, it only makes US #44 and UK #40 and features musical assistance from Toto band members.
Nov "The Magazine" tour begins in US Mid-West.
1985 **Jan** Jones plays her first Australian dates, followed by a European visit including sell-out UK concerts and Eastern bloc gigs, after which she goes to Tahiti where she meets husband-to-be French musician Pascal Nebet-Meyer. They live in France for a year before moving to Ojai, CA.
1988 **Oct** Pregnant with her first child, Jones records her bi-annual album, produced by Walter Becker.
1989 **Apr** She gives birth to daughter Charlotte.
Aug Jones is a featured artist on Rob Wasserman's *Duets* album.
Oct *Flying Cowboys*, Becker-produced, makes US #39 and UK #50.
1990 **Feb** [21] *Makin' Whoopee* wins Best Jazz Vocal Performance, Duo Or Group at the 32nd annual Grammy awards at the Shrine Auditorium, Los Angeles.
Mar 2 week "Flying Cowboys Saloon Tour" plays such places as Toads and Slim's in San Francisco, CA.
May [30] Jones begins major US tour with Lyle Lovett in Atlanta, GA.

TOM JONES

1963 Jones (b. Thomas Jones Woodward, June 7, 1940, Pontypridd, Wales), having made his TV debut on "Donald Peers Presents", forms his first band, Tommy Scott & The Senators, who record some tracks for EMI with producer Joe Meek.
1964 He is spotted supporting Mandy Rice-Davies at Pontypridd, by Gordon Mills, an ex-member of UK vocal group The Viscounts, who becomes his manager and changes his name to Tom Jones, after the film of the same name.
Aug Jones is signed to Decca Records, where his first release revives Ronnie Love's 1961 US hit *Chills And Fever*, which fails to chart.
Dec [3] Jones makes his radio debut on the BBC Radio's "Top Gear".
1965 **Mar** Second single *It's Not Unusual*, written by Mills and Les Reed (originally with Sandie Shaw in mind) tops the UK chart for a week, instantly establishing Jones as a leading male solo vocalist in a scene dominated by groups.
[13] He makes his first major UK TV appearance on BBC TV's "Billy Cotton Band Show".
Apr [11] Jones appears at the annual **New Musical Express** Poll Winners concert at the Empire Pool, Wembley, London, backed by new stage group The Squires (who will play with him live throughout the mid-60s) on a bill which includes The Beatles, The Rolling Stones, The Animals and many others. Later in the day he makes his debut on ITV's "Sunday Night At The London Palladium"
[26] He records *What's New Pussycat* in London with Burt Bacharach.
May *Once Upon A Time* makes UK #32, while *It's Not Unusual* hits US #10. (It also makes the R&B chart, many programmers on black radio stations hearing it "blind" assume Jones is American and black.)
[2] Jones makes his US TV debut on CBS TV's "Ed Sullivan Show", on a bill also featuring The Rolling Stones.
[10] Jones is part of a 4-week UK variety tour which opens at the New theater, Cardiff, Wales, followed by further weeks at the Theatre Royal, Nottingham, Notts., Hippodrome theater, Birmingham, W.Midlands and Hippodrome theater, Bristol, Avon.
June Debut album *Along Came Jones* reaches UK #11. *Little Lonely One*, a pre-Decca track recorded with Meek, is released in US by Tower Records (a subsidiary of Capitol/EMI), to cash in on the success of *It's Not Unusual*. It makes US #42.
[13] Jones makes his second appearance on the "Ed Sullivan Show".
[18] He begins a 1-week stint at New York's Paramount theater.
July A revival of Billy Eckstine's *With These Hands* reaches UK #13.
[14] Jones heads the bill on a week-long Murray The K's Brooklyn Fox stage show, with Ben E. King, Gary Lewis & The Playboys and others.
Aug *What's New Pussycat*, a Bacharach/David song which is the theme to movie of the same name, reaches UK #11 and US #3. US album *It's Not Unusual* (a re-titling of *Along Came Jones*) reaches US #54.
[1] He embarks on a coast to coast US Dick Clark package tour with The Drifters. The tour will end on Sept.6.
Sept *With These Hands* reaches US #27. Jones says in an interview that, having spent most of the year in US, he faces the prospect that "my long-term career will be in Britain".

Oct *What's New Pussycat?*, compiled specifically for the US market, makes US #114.

Jones records Burt Bacharach's *Promise Her Anything* from Leslie Caron film of same name. He duets with Joan Baez on *If You Need Me* on her US TV special.

Nov [17] Jones stars in his first TV special "Call In On Tom" on ITV.

Dec [2] He takes part in a charity show at Carnegie Hall, New York, with Sammy Davis Jr. and Louis Armstrong.

[29] Jones attends premiere of "Thunderball" at the London Pavilion.

1966 Jan *Thunderball*, Jones-sung theme from the fourth James Bond film and written in similar style to highly successful *Goldfinger* from the previous Bond movie, reaches UK #35 and US #25.

Mar *Promise Her Anything*, another movie theme, reaches US #74.

[15] Jones wins Best New Artist of 1965 at the 8th annual Grammy awards.

[18] He embarks on Australian tour with Herman's Hermits.

Apr [12] Jones goes into hospital, ostensibly to have his tonsils removed, although there is speculation that his real intention is to have cosmetic surgery to diminish the size of his nose.

May [6] Jones makes his first TV appearance since leaving hospital, on ITV's "Ready Steady Go!".

June *Not Responsible*, in Jones' *It's Not Unusual* style, reaches UK #18.

[21] Jones receives 14 stitches in his forehead after his Jaguar car crashes into a barrier at Marble Arch, London.

July *Not Responsible* makes US #58.

Aug *This And That* peaks at UK #44.

[14] Jones guests in the premiere of ITV's "Bruce Forsyth Show".

Oct *From The Heart* reaches UK #23.

Dec Sentimental ballad *Green Green Grass Of Home*, based on Jerry Lee Lewis' version, becomes Jones' all-time biggest-selling single. It tops the UK chart for 7 weeks, and sells over 1,220,000 copies in UK, giving Decca its first UK million-selling single by a UK artist.

1967 Jan [7] Jones guests on the first edition of ITV's "Doddy's Music Box".

[23] He leaves for a 6-day tour of South America, which will include 4 TV shows in Venezuela.

Feb *Green Green Grass Of Home* reaches US #11.

[12] He headlines ITV's "Sunday Night At The London Palladium".

Mar Jones stays with country music on a revival of Bobby Bare's *Detroit City*, which hits UK #8 and reaches US #27.

[1] He begins a month long stand at the Talk Of The Town, London.

[18] Jones opens a youth club in Harpenden, Herts.

Apr *Green Green Grass Of Home* hits UK #3 and reaches US #65.

May *Funny Familiar Forgotten Feelings* hits UK #8 and makes US #49.

July Live album *Live At The Talk Of The Town*, recorded at the London supper club, hits UK #6.

[4] Jones appears on the first telecast of CBS TV show "Spotlight", recorded in London as a summer replacement for "The Red Skelton Show". (He will star regularly on the show during its 2-month run.)

Aug Jones revives a ballad written and originally recorded by Lonnie Donegan, though never a hit: *I'll Never Fall In Love Again*. It hits UK #2.

A rock revival of Tennessee Ernie Ford's *Sixteen Tons* makes US #68.

Oct *I'll Never Fall In Love Again* reaches US #49.

Nov [2] Jones begins his first UK tour in almost 3 years at the Astoria, theater, Finsbury Park, London. It will end Nov.26 at Coventry theater, W.Midlands.

Dec *I'm Coming Home* hits UK #2.

1968 Jan *13 Smash Hits* (not a compilation, but a selection of covers of familar songs by other artists, plus *I'll Never Fall In Love Again*, hits UK #5. *I'm Coming Home* reaches US #57.

Mar *Delilah*, a dramatic song of passion and revenge (which becomes the archetypical spoof number for Jones impressionists) hits UK #2.

Apr [17] Jones performs at the Hollywood Bowl during a US tour.

May *Delilah* reaches US #15.

July *The Tom Jones Fever Zone* makes US #14.

Aug *Help Yourself* hits UK #5.

Sept *Help Yourself* makes US #35.

[21] *Delilah* tops the UK chart.

Oct [10] Jones begins 19-date UK tour at the New Victoria theater, London. The tour will end on Dec.3 at the Odeon theater, Birmingham, W.Midlands.

Dec *A Minute Of Your Time* reaches UK #14.

1969 Jan *Help Yourself* hits UK #4 and US #5. *A Minute Of Your Time* reaches US #48.

Feb [7] The weekly musical variety show "This Is Tom Jones" airs for the first time on ABC TV. (Originated variously in London and Hollywood, and with guest stars who normally duet with Jones on at

least 1 song, the series, at Friday evening peak time, will bring in high ratings and cement Jones' stature as an "all-round entertainer" in US. This in turn will lead him to settle in US and play in Las Vegas during the 70s and much of the 80s. The TV show will run for 2 years.)

May *Love Me Tonight* hits UK #9. *Tom Jones Live!* reaches US #13.

June Jones is invited to sing at the investiture of the Prince of Wales.

July *Love Me Tonight* makes US #13. *This Is Tom Jones* hits UK #2 and US #4.

Sept Following a good response to *I'll Never Fall In Love Again* on the TV show, it is reissued in US and hits #6, earning a gold disk.

[22] Jones appears with The Beatles, James Brown, Crosby, Stills, Nash & Young, Three Dog Night and others on the first telecast of ABC TV's "The Music Scene".

Nov Live album *Tom Jones Live In Las Vegas* hits both UK and US #3.

1970 Jan A revival of Clyde McPhatter oldie *Without Love (There Is Nothing)* hits UK #10.

Feb *Without Love (There Is Nothing)* hits US #5.

Mar [17] Jones begins the first of 4 shows at the Hammersmith Odeon London.

May *Daughter Of Darkness* hits UK #5 and US #13. *Tom* hits UK #4 and US #6.

June [12-13] Jones breaks the Madison Square Garden, New York, box-office record with takings of $364,743.

July He then breaks the box-office record at Holmdel, NJ, taking $250,000 for 6 nights.

Sept A revival of Ben E. King/Shirley Bassey oldie *I (Who Have Nothing)* reaches UK #16 and US #14.

Nov *I (Who Have Nothing)* hits UK #10 and reaches US #23.

Dec *Can't Stop Loving You*, never released in UK, reaches US #25.

1971 Jan [15] Weekly TV series "This Is Tom Jones" airs for the last time.

Feb *She's A Lady* reaches UK #13.

Apr *She's A Lady* hits US #2 and is a US million-seller.

June *Puppet Man*, written by Neil Sedaka, reaches UK #49 and US #26. *She's A Lady* hits UK #9 and US #17.

Nov *'Til*, a 1962 Top 20 hit for The Angels, hits UK #2 and US #41.

Dec Live album *Live At Caesar's Palace*, recorded in Las Vegas, reaches UK #27 and US #43.

1972 May *The Young New Mexican Puppeteer* hits UK #6 and reaches US #80.

June *Close Up* reaches UK #17 and US #64.

1973 May *Letter To Lucille* makes UK #31 and US #60.

June *The Body And Soul Of Tom Jones* reaches UK #31 and US #93.

1974 Jan Compilation album *Greatest Hits* peaks at UK #15 and US #185.

Sept *Something 'Bout You Baby I Like* reaches UK #36.

1975 Mar Double album *20 Greatest Hits* tops the UK chart for 4 weeks.

1977 Apr *Say You'll Stay Until Tomorrow* makes UK #40 and US #15, while album of the same title reaches US #76. *Tom Jones Greatest Hits* climbs to US #191.

1978 Oct *I'm Coming Home* reaches UK #12.

1981 May *Darlin'* peaks at US #179.

1983 With his style out of vogue on the pop charts, Jones concentrates on recording country music, signing a new deal with Mercury Records in Nashville. *Touch Me (I'll Be Your Fool Once More)* hits US Country #4. (For the next 3 years, Jones' US success will be on US Country chart: Sept.1983 – *It'll Be Me* (#34), Feb.1984 – *I've Been Rained On Too* (#13), June 1984 – *This Time* (#30), Jan.1985 – *I'm An Old Rock'N'Roller (Dancin' To A Different Beat)* (#67) and 1986's *It's Four In The Morning* (#36), while albums *Don't Let Our Dreams Die Young* makes US #9 (Dec.1983), *Love Is On The Radio* makes US #40 (1984) and *Tender Loving Care* makes US #54 (1986).)

1987 Apr Jones returns to UK for the first extended period since settling in US in the early 70s. The main reason is to promote his role in the album version of the new musical by Mike Leander, "Matador", released by Epic. Based on the true story of a star of the Spanish bullring who rose from poverty in Andalucia, the work is mooted for a London stage production, and Jones is keen to take the lead role should it materialize.

May *A Boy From Nowhere*, a ballad in traditional powerful Jones' style from "Matador", hits UK #2, his first UK Top 10 for 15 years, held off by Starship's *Nothing's Gonna Stop Us Now*.

June To capitalize on Jones' chart success, Decca reissues his original chart-topper *It's Not Unusual* (which is already getting plays in some UK discos because its distinctive rhythm matches a current Euro-beat dance trend), and it re-charts at UK #17. Also cashing in on the revival of Jones' interest is TV-promoted compilation album *Tom Jones – The Greatest Hits* on Telstar Records, which also makes UK #16.

Meanwhile, studio cast-recorded album *Matador* makes UK #26.

1988 Jan Second cut from *Matador*, *I Was Born To Be Me*, makes UK #61.

Oct Following a performance by Jones of Prince's number *Kiss* on Jonathan Ross' late-night C4 TV show "The Last Resort", he is contacted by Anne Dudley of UK instrumental group The Art Of Noise, suggesting that he record the song as guest vocalist on a version by the group. Vocal and instrumental tracks are eventually recorded on opposite sides of the Atlantic, and then meshed into the finished production by Dudley. (She and the rest of the group do not actually meet Jones until the disk is in the shops.) Released on China Records (to which The Art Of Noise is contracted), it is an instant UK smash, hitting #5, promoted by an appearance on UK TV variety show "Live From The London Palladium".

Nov Jones appears with other Welsh entertainers on George Martin-produced music version of Dylan Thomas' **Under Milk Wood**, which is released on album by EMI. Meanwhile, as a soloist, Jones signs a new recording contract with Jive Records.

1989 Jan [14] *Kiss* reaches US #31.

May *At This Moment* makes UK #34, as extracted cover of Phyllis Nelson's hit *Move Closer* makes UK #49.

June [3] Jones takes part in "Our Common Future" satellite broadcast seen in over 100 countries, featuring live performances by Sting in Rio de Janeiro, Brazil, Stevie Wonder in Warsaw, Poland, and others, with Jones singing from Oslo, Norway.

[27] Jones receives a star on the Hollywood Walk Of Fame.

July *After Dark*, recorded for Stylus, climbs to UK #46.

[16] 27-year-old Katherine Berkery files a paternity suit against Jones. Manhattan Family Court Judge Judith B. Sheindlin finds in her favor and orders Jones to pay $200 a week.

Sept [22] Jones and Berkery agree terms for her child's support.

1991 Jan [26] After a 1-year hiatus, during which Jones and his wife have spent time at their 2-knocked-into-1 council house in Wales, and he has signed a new recording deal with Chrysalis subsidiary Dover Records in UK, he makes UK #51 with a ballad penned by Diane Warren/Albert Hammond, *Couldn't Say Goodbye*.

Mar Jones beats Theophilus P. Wildebeest, portrayed by comedian Lenny Henry, in a TV vote for sexiest hunk in a live and overtly sexual writhe-act as part of UK Comic Relief telethon.

[21] Jones kicks off a major 25-date UK tour at the Apollo theater, Oxford, Oxon, set to end on Apr.20 at the Hammersmith Odeon, London.

[23] Van Morrison-penned and produced *Carrying A Torch* peaks at UK #57. It is one of 4 tracks on which the Irish and Welsh icons have collaborated live for Jones' forthcoming album, also titled *Carrying A Torch*, recorded at the Townhouse studios, London.

Apr [5] *Carrying A Torch* debuts at UK #44.

May Jones appears live at "The Simple Truth" concert for Kurdish refugees at Wembley Arena, London.

JANIS JOPLIN

1960 Saving money to make a trip to California, Joplin (b. Jan.19, 1943, Port Arthur, TX) earns a living singing in clubs in Austin, TX, and Houston, TX, and becomes part of The Waller Creek Boys trio, together with R. Powell St. John (later a member of Mother Earth), a songwriter for the 13th Floor Elevators.

1963 Jan Joplin hitch-hikes to San Francisco, CA, where she sings in North Beach clubs, either solo or with Jorma Kaukonen (later of Jefferson Airplane) or Roger Perkins. Her 3-octave vocal range impresses those close to her, but she does not progress beyond sporadic singing jobs.

1966 Joplin returns to Texas to straighten out from her increasingly hippy, druggy, California lifestyle. She enrolls at college, makes marriage plans and gives up singing.

June With marriage plans abandoned, she is about to join the 13th Floor Elevators but returns to San Francisco as lead singer with Big Brother & The Holding Company, house band at the Avalon Ballroom.

Aug During a visit to Chicago, IL, Big Brother signs to Mainstream Records.

1967 June Group plays a show-stopping performance at the Monterey Pop Festival, CA. As lead singer, Joplin is clearly the star and Bob Dylan's manager Albert Grossman signs the group.

Aug Mainstream releases band's debut album, which reaches US #60.

1968 Feb Big Brother & The Holding Company, now a major draw on the West Coast, makes its New York debut at the Anderson theater on Second Ave.

Mar [8] Big Brother plays on the opening night of the Fillmore East, a converted movie theater on New York's Second Ave. and Sixth Str. CBS/Columbia Records buys the group's Mainstream contract and

books it into Studio E in New York to record its label debut.

Aug Producer John Simon, unhappy with the quality of the recordings, is over-ruled by CBS/Columbia, which releases **Cheap Thrills** (the title shortened, at the label's insistence, from *Dope, Sex And Cheap Thrills*).

Sept Grossman announces Joplin is to split from the group at the end of the year.

Oct *Cheap Thrills*, after 7 weeks on chart, hits US #1, where it will stay for 8 weeks. Mainstream releases *Down On Me*, from the album, which makes US #43.

Nov *Piece Of My Heart* reaches US #12. Also on Mainstream, *Coo Coo* climbs to US #84.

Dec [1] Joplin makes her last official appearance with Big Brother & The Holding Company and group disbands.

[21] Joplin, backed by The Kozmic Blues Band, appears at the "Stax-Volt Yuletide Thing" for the record company's annual convention in Memphis, TN.

1969 Feb [11-14] Joplin plays 4 nights at New York's Fillmore East. Ex-Big Brother guitarist Sam Andrews (b. Dec.18, 1941, Taft, CA) joins Joplin's new group, initially called Janis & The Joplinaires. Other members include Brad Campbell (bass), Terry Clements (sax) and Marcus Doubleday (trumpet). Line-up changes throughout the year, and Andrews leaves. Joplin continues to develop alcohol and drug dependence.

Apr [21] Joplin and The Kozmic Blues Band perform in UK at London's Royal Albert Hall.

June Joplin performs at the Newport 69 Pop Festival, with Joe Cocker, Jimi Hendrix, Buddy Miles, Edwin Hawkins.

Aug Having recently sung at the Texas International Festival and the Atlanta Pop Festival, Joplin plays the 2-day New Orleans Pop Festival in Prairieville, LA.

Oct *I Got Dem Ol' Kozmic Blues Again Mama!* hits US #5.

Nov [15] Joplin is arrested at a gig in Tampa, FL, after allegedly badmouthing a policeman. Charges are eventually dropped.

Dec The soul-based Kozmic Blues Band has been unsuccessful with live appearances since *I Got Dem Ol' Kozmic Blues Again Mama!* and disbands. *Kozmic Blues* makes US #41.

1970 Bassist Peter Albin (b. June 6, 1944, San Francisco, CA) and drummer David Getz (b. Brooklyn, New York, NY), who played with Country Joe & The Fish, recruit guitarist James Gurley (b. Detroit, MI), Andrews and guitarist Dave Shallock to re-form Big Brother & The Holding Company.

Apr Joplin appears with Big Brother at the Fillmore West, California, and the Winterland.

May Joplin's new group, The Full-Tilt Boogie Band, makes its debut at a Hells Angels benefit in San Rafael, CA. Line-up is Campbell, John Till (guitar), Richard Bell (piano), Ken Pearson (organ) and Clark Pearson (drums). They will tour constantly in the coming months.

Aug [6] Joplin participates in a 12-hour antiwar rock festival at New York's Shea Stadium on the 25th anniversary of the dropping of the first atom bomb on Hiroshima.

[8] Joplin buys a headstone for the grave of her greatest influence Bessie Smith at the Mount Lawn cemetery in Philadelphia, PA. (Smith died in 1937 after being refused admission to a whites-only hospital.)

Sept Joplin begins recording a new album (which is not finished) at Columbia's West Coast studios in Hollywood.

Oct [4] After partying at Barney's Beanery at 8447 Santa Monica Blvd., Joplin is found dead at the Landmark hotel, 7047 Franklin Ave., Hollywood, with fresh needle marks in her arm. An inquest rules that death is due to an accidental heroin overdose. (She had been scheduled to record the vocal for *Buried Alive In The Blues* the following day.)

Nov Big Brother & The Holding Company's *Be A Brother*, featuring uncredited contributions from Joplin, reaches US #134.

1971 Feb *Pearl*, drawn from the unfinished sessions, hits US #1 for 9 weeks.

Mar Joplin's much-praised version of Kris Kristofferson's *Me And Bobby McGee* tops US chart.

Apr *Pearl* makes UK #50.

June *Cry Baby* (one of several Jerry Ragavoy songs on *Pearl*) reaches UK #42. B-side is her better-known *Mercedes Benz*. The re-packaged CBS/Columbia debut album, peaks at US #185.

Sept *Get It While You Can*, by Ragavoy, climbs to US #78. Big Brother album *How Hard It Is*, featuring occasional vocals from new singer Kathi McDonald, makes US #157.

1972 May *Janis Joplin In Concert* hits US #4.

July *Janis Joplin In Concert* reaches UK #30. Taken from it, *Down On Me* makes UK #91.

1973 Aug *Janis Joplin's Greatest Hits* reaches US #37.

1975 **May** *Janis*, the soundtrack from Joplin documentary of the same name featuring early recordings 1963-65, makes US #54. It contains live and TV recordings with her 2 post-Big Brother bands and folk-blues material recorded in Texas before she joined Big Brother.

1979 **Oct** [10] "The Rose", starring Bette Midler, supposedly based on Joplin's life, premieres in Los Angeles.

1982 **Feb** *Farewell Song* reaches US #104. It contains a song with The Kozmic Blues Band, one with Full-Tilt, one recorded live in Los Angeles with The Paul Butterfield Blues Band and 6 from Big Brother & The Holding Company. The Big Brother tracks feature added instrumentation from 80s session musicians.

1988 **Jan** [19] A memorial in Joplin's honor at the Southeast Texas Musical Heritage Exhibit in Port Arthur is unveiled.

JOURNEY

Steve Perry (vocals)
Neal Schon (guitar)
Ross Valory (bass)
Jonathan Cain (keyboards)
Steve Smith (drums)

1973 **Feb** Band is formed in San Francisco, CA, at the suggestion of Santana's ex-production manager Walter Herbert, by ex-Santana guitarist Schon (b. Feb.27, 1954, San Mateo, CA), who recruits ex-Fruminous Bandersnatch and Steve Miller Band member Valory (b. Feb.2, 1949, San Francisco), Tubes drummer Prairie Prince (b. May 7, 1950, Charlotte, NC) and George Tickner on guitar. Originally The Golden Gate Rhythm Section, a San Francisco radio station holds a competition to find the band a new name, and Journey is chosen. Herbert becomes the band's manager.
June Keyboards player and vocalist Gregg Rolie (b. 1948), also ex-Santana, joins the line-up as the band begins to play large venue support to bigger groups, as well as local club work.
Sept Prince leaves to join The Tubes.

1974 **Feb** After 30 drummers have been tried, ex-Jeff Beck, Frank Zappa and John Mayall sideman Aynsley Dunbar (b. 1946, Liverpool, Merseyside), is persuaded to join.
Nov Band signs to CBS/Columbia Records.

1975 **Apr** Tickner leaves for medical school after completion of first album. He is not replaced and the band continues with a single guitarist.
May Debut album *Journey* reaches US #138.

1976 **Apr** *Look Into The Future* makes US #100.
Nov Band plays a UK tour, supporting Santana.

1977 **Mar** *Next* peaks at US #85. Band feels it is failing to develop commercially because of lack of a strong front-focus vocalist (Rolie handles most vocals from behind his keyboards), and a search begins.
June Robert Fleischmann is recruited as frontman and plays a summer US tour with Journey, but he proves incompatible and is asked to leave.
Oct [10] Fleischmann is replaced by Perry (b. Jan.22, 1953, Hanford, CA), ex-Tim Bogert's band Alien Project, who has sent an audition tape to manager Herbert.

1978 **Apr** *Infinity*, with Perry on lead vocals and Roy Thomas Baker producing, reaches US #21, and will stay charted for 123 weeks, earning a platinum disk for a million-plus sales.
May From the album, *Wheel In The Sky* is the band's first US chart single, reaching #57.
July *Anytime*, also from *Infinity*, makes US #83.
Sept Third single from the album, *Lights*, reaches US #68.
Nov Dunbar leaves to join Jefferson Starship, and is replaced on drums by Smith (b. Aug.21, 1954, Los Angeles, CA), from Ronnie Montrose's group.

1979 **Feb** Journey signs an advertising deal with Budweiser beer.
Mar Band plays 7 dates in UK, where it has made no chart progress.
May *Evolution* reaches US #20 and is a second million-seller. Extracted from it, *Just The Same Way*, peaks at US #58.
July [28] Journey takes part in the "World Series Of Rock" at Cleveland Stadium, Cleveland, OH. Also on the bill are Aerosmith, Ted Nugent and Thin Lizzy.
Oct First Top 20 hit single is *Lovin', Touchin', Squeezin'*, making US #16.

1980 **Jan** *Too Late* reaches US #70, while a retrospective album of tracks from the first 3 albums *In The Beginning* peaks at US #152.
Apr *Any Way You Want It* reaches US #23, while *Departure* hits US #8, the third million-seller.
July *Walks Like A Lady* makes US #32.
Sept Double A-side *Good Morning Girl/Stay Awhile* stalls at US #55.
[22] Band plays a one-off UK concert at the Rainbow theater, London.

1981 **Mar** Live double album *Captured* hits US #9, and earns the band's fourth platinum disk.
Apr *The Party's Over (Hopelessly In Love)* from *Captured* makes US #34. Rolie, tired of touring, leaves the band and is replaced on keyboards by Cain (b. Feb.26, 1950, Chicago, IL), ex-The Babys.
Sept *Escape*, the most successful to date, hits US #1, staying charted for a total of 146 weeks (and for more than a year in Top 20), and selling over 2 million copies. Taken from it, *Who's Crying Now*, is the band's biggest-selling single, hitting US #4.
Nov Schon releases *Untold Passion* in collaboration with keyboards player Jan Hammer. It peaks at US #115.
Dec *Don't Stop Believin'*, from *Escape*, hits US #9.

1982 **Feb** *Open Arms* hits US #2 for 6 weeks, behind Joan Jett's *I Love Rock'N'Roll*, and is the band's first million-selling single.
Mar A minor UK breakthrough comes when *Don't Stop Believin'* peaks at UK #62, and *Escape* makes a belated first entry into UK chart.
July *Still They Ride* reaches US #19.
Sept *Escape* makes UK #32, and reissued *Who's Crying Now* UK #46.
Oct Perry duets with Kenny Loggins on his single *Don't Fight It*, reaching US #17.

1983 **Feb** Second Schon/Hammer collaboration, *Here To Stay*, climbs to reach US #122.
Mar *Separate Ways (Worlds Apart)* hits US #8. It is taken from *Frontiers*, which hits US #2 for 9 weeks (behind Michael Jackson's *Thriller*), and is a further platinum disk, spending 85 weeks on chart. It also hits UK #6; the band's most successful album in UK. Meanwhile, a video game is marketed in US, inspired by Journey's *Escape*.
June *Faithfully*, from *Frontiers*, reaches US #12.
Aug *After The Fall* reaches US #23, while in UK the 1979 album *Evolution* charts briefly at #100.
Nov *Send Her My Love* reaches US #23.

1984 **Apr** Schon's live *Through The Fire*, in collaboration with Sammy Hagar, Kenny Aaronson, and Santana's Mike Shrieve, makes US #42.
June Perry records a solo album, *Street Talk*, which reaches US #12 and UK #59. *Oh Sherrie*, extracted from it, hits US #3.
Aug His second solo single *She's Mine* reaches US #21.
Oct Perry's solo *Strung Out* makes US #40.

1985 **Jan** [28] Perry joins a host of major US rock acts in Los Angeles at the recording session for USA For Africa's *We Are The World*, on which he contributes a line of the lead vocal.
Feb Last single from Perry's solo album, *Foolish Heart*, reaches US #18.
Mar *Only The Young*, from the soundtrack of movie "Vision Quest", hits US #9. This is the first Journey release for 2 years, the band having relaxed its earlier formidable touring and recording schedule for an extended rest while members have pursued solo projects.

1986 **May** Regrouped as just a 3-man core of Perry, Schon and Cain, with musical help from Randy Jackson on bass and Larrie Londin on drums Journey releases concept album *Raised On Radio*, produced by Perry, which hits US #4 and also reaches UK #22.
[31] *Be Good To Yourself*, taken from the album, hits US #9.
Aug [16] *Suzanne*, also from the album, reaches US #17. Mike Baird and Randy Jackson are added to the line-up.
Nov [1] Third album extract *Girl Can't Help It* also reaches US #17.

1987 **Feb** [28] A fourth single from the album, *I'll Be Alright Without You* reaches US #14. (After this, the group members will pursue solo career and the break-up appears to be permanent. Perry will spend much of 1988 working on a second solo album.)
May [23] *Why Can't This Night Go On Forever* peaks at US #60.

1989 **Jan** *Greatest Hits* (issued in UK as *The Best Of Journey*) hits US #10.

JOY DIVISION

Ian Curtis (vocals)
Bernard Albrecht (guitar)
Peter Hook (bass)
Steven Morris (drums)

1977 **May** [29] Having come together in Manchester, Gtr.Manchester, as The Stiff Kittens some 6 months earlier, but without any live exposure, the band renames itself Warsaw (from a track on David Bowie's *Low*) for a live debut at Manchester's Electric Circus, bottom of the bill to Th Buzzcocks and Penetration.
July [18] Warsaw records a demo of 4 songs (*Inside The Line, Gutz, At A Later Date* and *The Kill*) at Pennine Sound studios.
Dec Band becomes Joy Division (name taken from Nazi concentration camp novel **House Of Dolls**) to avoid confusion with London punk band Warsaw Pakt, which has just released its first album.

1978 Apr [14] Band plays the Stiff Test/Chiswick Challenge, an audition night organized by the 2 UK independent labels at Manchester's Rafters club. It performs last, at 2am, but impresses the club DJ, and future manager, Rob Gretton. Journalist Tony Wilson, boss of the new Factory Records label (known for his Manchester-based TV music show "What Goes On") also sees the band's performance.

May [27] Group records Radio Manchester interview "An Ideal For Living And Chat".

June The 1977 demos are released as EP *An Ideal For Living* on the band's own Enigma label (the fold-out sleeve is inscribed "this is not a record – it is an enigma").

July [27] Virgin Records issues a 10" various artists album *Cross Circuit: Live At The Electric Circus* which features Joy Division's *At A Later Date*.

Dec [24] Joy Division's *Digital* and *Glass*, both produced by Martin "Zero" Hannett, appear on Factory Records double compilation EP *A Factory Sample*, with Cabaret Voltaire, John Dowie and Durutti Column.

1979 Jan [31] Group records *Exercise One, Insight, Transmission* and *She's Lost Control* for BBC Radio 1's "John Peel Show".

May Gretton and Joy Division, with an offer to release first album *Unknown Pleasures* on Radar, through major label WEA, choose instead to sign with Factory.

June Joy Division contributes *From Safety To Where* and *Autosuggestion* to the Fast Product compilation EP *Earcom 2: Contradiction*.

July Debut album *Unknown Pleasures* is released after Wilson uses his life savings of £8,500 to press 10,000 copies. Live performances are increased, putting inevitable pressure on Curtis, an epilepsy sufferer.

Aug Joy Division plays all-day open air concert in Leigh, Gtr.Manchester, with A Certain Ratio, Echo & The Bunnymen, OMD and Teardrop Explodes. An estimated 300 people witness the event.

Sept [15] Group is interviewed and performs on BBC TV's "Something Else".

Oct *Atmosphere/Dead Souls*, under the title *Licht Und Blindheit*, and *Transmission/Novelty* are released.

Nov [26] Group records second "John Peel Show" session for BBC Radio 1.

1980 Apr *Love Will Tear Us Apart* is released, to overwhelming critical praise, but initially it reaches only UK Independent chart. Factory takes the innovatory step of providing record shops with a flexi-disc containing the tracks *Komakino, Incubation* and *As You Said*; not to be sold, but to be given away to fans. Group completes a new album with Hannett and plays a series of impromptu live UK dates, several of which have to be cancelled as Curtis falls ill.

May [18] In the early hours of the morning, with Iggy Pop's *The Idiot* on his turntable and Werner Herzog's "Strojek" on video, Curtis hangs himself, 4 days before the group is due to fly to US. Tour is cancelled immediately. (Joy Division's greatest success will come after the singer's death).

July *Love Will Tear Us Apart* reaches UK #13 and second album *Closer* hits UK #6. *Unknown Pleasures* spends 1 week at UK #71.

1981 Jan Joy Division re-emerges as New Order, with Albrecht, now calling himself Barney Sumner, on vocals.

Oct Joy Division's double album *Still*, a collection of live and studio material, hits UK #5.

1982 Aug Factory's video division Ikon issues "Here Are The Young Men", a 60-min. live Joy Division video.

1983 Nov *Love Will Tear Us Apart* re-enters UK chart, peaking at #19.

1988 July A reissue of Joy Division's *Atmosphere* reaches UK #34 but is a top independent seller. (New York group The Swans release a version of *Love Will Tear Us Apart*; it has also been covered by Paul Young and P.J. Proby, with assistance from Hook.) Factory issues Joy Division double compilation *1977-1980 Substance*, which hits UK #7.

JUDAS PRIEST

Rob Halford (vocals)
K.K. Downing (guitar)
Glenn Tipton (guitar)
Ian Hill (bass)
Dave Holland (drums)

1969 The original Judas Priest (the name is taken from Bob Dylan's *The Ballad Of Frankie Lee And Judas Priest* on his album *John Wesley Harding*) is formed in Birmingham, W.Midlands, as a pop/rock covers band playing around the Midlands clubs. (Only Downing and Hill will survive from the initial line-up to the band's recording days.)

1971 Band gains a strong vocalist and frontman in ex-theatrical lighting engineer Halford (b. Aug.25, 1951, Birmingham) the brother of Hill's girlfriend. Drummer John Hinch also joins, and the quartet's music hardens into the rock mode currently successful for Deep Purple and fellow Birmingham group Black Sabbath.

1974 Tipton joins as second guitarist. After more than 4 years of playing clubs, the band signs to Gull Records. Debut album, produced by Rodger Bain, *Rocka Rolla*, with the title track also released as a single, fails to chart. Hinch is replaced on drums by Alan Moore.

1976 Mar *The Ripper* is released, trailering the band's second Gull album.

Apr *Sad Wings Of Destiny* sells only marginally better than its precedecessor, but marks the band's US debut release, via Janus Records.

[6] Group begins 11-date UK tour at the Plaza, Truro, Cornwall, set to end Apr.17 at the City Hall, St. Albans, Herts.

Aug Judas Priest makes its first appearance at Reading Festival, Berks.

1977 Jan With the aid of Halford's flamboyant stage act the band is developing a strong grass-roots following with consistent UK touring, and gains a new, major contract with CBS/Columbia (as well as a new drummer, ex-sessionman Simon Phillips.)

May *Sin After Sin*, the first for CBS, is produced by ex-Deep Purple bassist Roger Glover, and provides the group's first chart entry, at UK #23. From the album, their rock version of Joan Baez's *Diamonds And Rust* is released as a single, but fails to chart. Tours of UK and Europe follow, in support of the album, and new drummer Les Binks joins in place of Phillips.

July [23] On a first US tour, Judas Priest supports Led Zeppelin at Oakland Coliseum, CA.

1978 Jan A revival of Spooky Tooth's *Better By You, Better By Me*, from the next album, fails to chart.

Mar *Stained Class*, produced by Dennis Mackay, reaches UK #27. Gull, meanwhile, compiles *Best Of Judas Priest* from its 2 earlier albums, but this fails to chart.

Apr *Stained Class* makes US #173, the band's US chart debut.

Nov *Killing Machine*, produced by James Guthrie, reaches UK #32, as the band plays 2 sell-out dates at the Hammersmith Odeon, London, during a nationwide UK tour.

1979 Feb Judas Priest's first hit single is *Take On The World*, extracted from *Killing Machine*, which reaches UK #14.

Apr The album is retitled *Hell Bent For Leather* (a deliberate play on the group's leather-clad image) in US, and includes an additional track, reviving Fleetwood Mac's *The Green Manalishi (With The Two-Prong Crown)*. It makes US #128.

May *Evening Star* peaks at UK #53. The band tours abroad again, finding huge success in the Far East.

Sept Group also supports Kiss on major US tour.

Oct Live album *Unleashed In The East*, recorded at the Koseinenkin and Nakano Sunplaza Halls in Tokyo, Japan, proves to be a chart breakthrough, hitting UK #10 and reaching US #70. It is produced by Tom Allom – a partnership which will become lasting. Drummer Binks has left, physically and mentally exhausted by the band's gruelling tour schedule. His place is taken by Dave Holland.

1980 Mar [9] Band starts 17-date UK tour at the Colston Hall, Bristol, Avon.

Apr *Living After Midnight* makes UK #12. It is taken from *British Steel* (the first to feature Holland on drums), which is the group's biggest UK success, hitting #4 (and will reach US #34).

June *Breaking The Law*, also from *British Steel*, peaks at UK #12.

July *British Steel* reaches UK #34, earning the band a US gold disk for a half million sales.

Aug [16] Judas Priest appears at the first Monsters Of Rock festival at Castle Donington, Leics., second on the bill to Rainbow, which also includes Scorpions, April Wine, Saxon and Riot.

Sept *United*, the third single from *British Steel*, makes UK #26.

1981 Feb *Don't Go*, from the next album, peaks at UK #51.

Mar Tom Allom-produced *Point Of Entry* reaches UK #14.

May *Hot Rockin'* peaks at UK #60, while *Point Of Entry* makes US #30.

1982 July *Screaming For Vengeance* reaches UK #11.

Aug Extracted *You've Got Another Thing Comin'* peaks at UK #66.

Oct *Screamin' For Vengeance* makes US #17 for several weeks and is a million-seller, earning the group's first platinum album. The 9-year-old album *Rocka Rolla* also finally gets a US release on the Visa label. Group continues to tour intensively, the live show often highlighted by Halford roaring across the stage on a Harley Davidson motorbike.

Nov *You've Got Another Thing Comin'* is the group's only US Singles chart entry, at #67. (Huge demand for Judas Priest in US in the wake of this single, and the album from which it is taken, will involve the group in touring there for much of 1983.)

1983 **May** [29] Judas Priest performs on the Heavy Metal Sunday during the second US Festival, alongside Triumph, Scorpions, Van Halen and others in San Bernardino, CA.

1984 **Feb** *Defenders Of The Faith*, recorded in Ibiza and mixed by Allom in Miami, peaks at UK #19, as extracted *Freewheel Burnin'* makes UK #42.

Apr *Defenders Of The Faith*, another US gold album, peaks at #18. After some live dates to promote it, the band members take a break for much of this year and next, settling in their new home in Phoenix, AZ.

1985 **July** [13] Judas Priest emerges from its lengthy lay-off to play the Live Aid concert in Philadelphia, PA.

Dec [23] Teenage Reno, NV, Judas Priest fans Raymond Belknap and James Vance shoot themselves, reportedly after listening to *Stained Class*. Vance survives, but Belknap who holds a sawn-off shotgun to his chin and fires, dies.

1986 **Apr** Group returns to record *Turbo*, with the sound broadened with synth guitars and electronic effects. It makes UK #33 and US #17.

May Halford takes part in the Hear'N'Aid heavy metal charity single *Stars* to benefit famine relief in Ethiopia, which reaches UK #26. Band begins a world tour in US, moving on to Japan and Europe before playing their first UK live dates at the end of the year.

Dec [3] James Vance and the family of Raymond Belknap sue Judas Priest and CBS Records, contending that they were responsible for the teenagers forming a suicide pact and shooting themselves in the head after listening to the band's records for 6 hours.

1987 **June** Recordings made on the 1986 tour are released as *Priest Live*, which reaches UK #47 and US #38.

1988 **Apr** Band's revival of Chuck Berry's *Johnny B. Goode*, from the Anthony Michael Hall film of the same title, reaches UK #64.

June *Ram It Down*, first studio set in 2 years, makes UK #24 and #31.

Nov [29] Vance, now aged 20, having lived 3 more years after shooting himself and having gone into a methadone overdose-induced coma on Thanksgiving Day, dies.

1990 **July** [16] The Vance/Belknap $6.2 million suit against Judas Priest and CBS Records begins in Reno, NV, before Washoe County district judge Jerry Whitehead.

Aug [24] Whitehead rejects the suit, but does however award $40,000 sanctions against CBS Records on the grounds it attempted to withhold original master recordings for the album *Stained Class*, after much of the prosecution's case was based on supposed subliminal messages contained in the record. Downing says, "It will be another ten years before I can even spell subliminal".

Sept [15] *Painkiller* stalls at UK #74.

[22] Parent album *Painkiller* reaches UK #24.

Oct [21] Group embarks on major North American tour, with new drummer Scott Travis, ex-Racer X, in Montreal, Canada, the first leg set to end Dec.23 in Orlando, FL.

Nov UK tour begins, supported by Annihilator.

[3] Band donates the proceeds from Lawlor Events Center, Reno, NV, gig to the Community Runaway Youth Services organization, in the same week that *Painkiller* peaks at US #26.

1991 **Mar** [23] *A Touch Of Evil* spends 1 week on UK chart at #58.

KANSAS

Steve Walsh (vocals, keyboards)
Kerry Livgren (guitar)
Rich Williams (guitar)
Dave Hope (bass)
Phil Ehart (drums)
Robby Steinhardt (violin)

1970 Livgren (b. Sept.18, 1949, Kansas), Hope (b. Oct.7, 1949, Kansas) and Ehart (b. 1951, Kansas), all friends from West Topeka high school, KS, form a Frank Zappa-inspired band with other local musicians. They play mainly dances and club dates locally, but with frequent personnel changes, the original trio remains the only constant.

1971 The trio recruits classically-trained violinist Steinhardt (b. 1951, Mississippi) (son of a senior Kansas university music lecturer), and relaunches as White Clover, playing around Kansas until the end of the year when Ehart leaves and the band splits.

1972 Ehart goes to UK in search of musical inspiration but returns home 4 months later. Back in Topeka, he re-forms White Clover, with Hope, Walsh (b. 1951, St.Joseph, MO), Williams (b. 1951, Kansas) and Steinhardt, and they recruit guitarist Williams. Livgren rejoins shortly afterwards, and the name is changed to Kansas. Band begins live work, developing a style which blends UK progressive influences with a refined form of early US heavy metal.

1973 Group records a $300 demo in a Liberal, KS, studio, and Ehart mails a copy to an East Coast friend with record industry contacts. Months later, while the band is gigging in Dodge City, Kirshner Records' Wally Gold calls from New York, saying he wants to see them play live.

1974 **July** Signed to Kirshner, the group releases debut album *Kansas*; it makes US #174 and with constant touring eventually sells 100,000.

1975 **May** *Songs For America* reaches US #57, earning a gold disk for a half million sales. The band continues to tour constantly all over US.

1976 **Feb** *Masque* reaches US #70, earning another gold disk in a 20-week chart run.

1977 **Apr** *Leftoverture*, produced by Jeff Glixman, is the band's commercial breakthrough. It hits US #5 and is a million-seller, going platinum. Extracted *Carry On Wayward Son*, penned by Livgren (now their chief songwriter), is Kansas' US Singles chart debut at #11.

1978 **Jan** *Point Of Know Return* hits US #4, and is a second platinum seller, while the title track reaches US #28.

Mar *Dust In The Wind*, also from *Point Of Know Return*, hits US #6. Kansas' only Top 10 single, it earns a gold disk for million-plus sales, and will become the group's most revered recording.

May Walsh is guest vocalist on ex-Genesis guitarist Steve Hackett's second solo album *Please Don't Touch*.

June [27] In a ceremony at New York's Madison Square Garden, Kansas is the first group to be chosen by UNICEF as its Deputy Ambassadors of Goodwill.

July *Carry On Wayward Son* reaches UK #51, more than a year after its US success. (It will be the band's only UK hit. No Kansas albums will make the UK chart.) Meanwhile, *Portrait (He Knew)* peaks at US #64.

Aug [26] Band plays the first Canada Jam festival in Ontario, to 80,000 people, with The Commodores, Earth, Wind & Fire, The Village People, Dave Mason and Atlanta Rhythm Section.

1979 **Jan** Double live album *Two For The Show*, recorded on tour, makes US #32 and is the group's third consecutive platinum album.

Feb *Lonely Wind* peaks at US #60.

July *Monolith*, the first album self-produced by the band, hits US #10 and goes gold. Kansas plays an 80-city US tour to support the album, opening at Von Braun civic center, Huntsville, AL.

Aug *People Of The South Wind* reaches US #23.

Oct *Reason To Be* peaks at US #52.

1980 **Mar** Walsh's solo *Schemer Dreamer*, on which other band members also play, reaches US #124. Livgren becomes a born-again Christian as, shortly afterwards, does Hope. Livgren expresses his new-found faith through solo album *Seeds Of Change* which does not chart.

Oct *Hold On*, from the forthcoming Kansas album, peaks at US #40.

Nov *Audio-Visions* reaches US #26.

1981 **Jan** Another track from the album, *Got To Rock On*, peaks at US #76. Walsh leaves, and is replaced by John Elefante (b. Levittown, NY).

1982 **July** *Vinyl Confessions*, with Elefante on lead vocals, makes US #16, while extracted *Play The Game Tonight* reaches US #17.

Sept Second single from the album, *Right Away*, peaks at US #73.

1983 **Sept** Group moves from Kirshner to CBS Associated label, and *Drastic Measures* makes US #41. (The lower chart placing is a reflection of the year's tour results: like most US stadium-filling bands of the previous 2 or 3 years, Kansas has experienced a sharp downturn in audience attendance which is leaving venues unfilled.)

Oct *Fight Fire With Fire*, taken from the album, peaks at US #58. Group comes off the road and, for a while, calls it a day.

1984 **Sept** Compilation album *The Best Of Kansas* makes US #154.

1986 **Oct** Walsh, Ehart and Williams reunite to resurrect Kansas. New recruits are Steve Morse (ex-Dixie Dregs) on guitar and Billy Greer on bass. Band signs to MCA and records a comeback album.

1987 **Jan** Kansas' reunion album *Power* reaches US #35.

[17] *All I Wanted*, extracted from *Power*, reaches US #19.

Feb [28] *Power* climbs to US #84.

1988 **Nov** *In The Spirit Of Things* climbs to US #114, but fails to produce a hit single.

1990 Ehart and Walsh produce tracks for new group The Blondz.

KC & THE SUNSHINE BAND

Harry Wayne Casey (vocals, keyboards)
Richard Finch (bass)
Jerome Smith (guitar)
Robert Johnson (drums)
Fermin Goytisolo (congas, percussion)

1973 Casey (b. Harold Wayne Casey, Jan.31, 1951, Hialeah, FL) working as a record store assistant, collects records as part of his job from Tone

Distributors. He works part-time in their studios for free, and begins to learn production skills, also meeting bass player and TK Records' engineer, Finch (b. Jan.25, 1954, Indianapolis, IN). Together they form KC (from Casey's nickname) & The Sunshine Junkanoo Band ("junkanoo" being a style of local dance music). Band plays locally with a line-up varying between 9 and 11.

'74 They sign to Henry Stone's Miami-based TK label, and release debut single *Blow Your Whistle* (recorded by Casey, Finch and session musicians, and inspired by the whistle flute sound which the duo first heard at a wedding reception for local R&B artist Clarence Reid), which sells locally and becomes a club hit in Europe.
July For TK, Casey and Finch write and produce George McCrae's million-seller *Rock Your Baby*, which tops both US and UK charts.
Sept Band makes its UK chart debut with *Queen Of Clubs* (released earlier in US to no reaction), which hits UK #7, licensed from TK by President Records and released on disco-oriented Jay Boy label.
Dec *Sound Your Funky Horn* reaches UK #17, while Casey and Finch write and produce McCrae's second UK hit *You Can Have It All*, which peaks at #23.

'75 **Apr** *Get Down Tonight*, recorded by a now-permanent group line-up which goes on tour (and includes female back-up singers Beverley Champion and Jeanette Williams), reaches UK #21.
Aug *Get Down Tonight* is band's US chart debut. After climbing for several weeks while they are on a European tour, it hits #1 for a week as they return home. Simultaneously, Casey/Finch-written and produced *That's The Way (I Like It)* hits US #4. (As resident house band at TK studios, they also back Betty Wright on her UK #25 hit *Where Is The Love* and George McCrae on his UK #23 *It's Been So Long*.)
Sept Debut album *KC And The Sunshine Band* reaches UK #26, while instrumental single *Shotgun Shuffle*, credited only to The Sunshine Band, charts briefly at US #88.
Nov *That's The Way (I Like It)* (according to Casey, a toned-down re-cut of an original more lascivious version on which the repeated "a-has" were sensual moans), tops US chart for 2 weeks, and is a million-seller. Meanwhile, *I'm So Crazy* reaches UK #34. Group becomes a major live touring attraction, pulling critical praise for its melding of R&B and gospel with a white rock sound.
Dec *KC And The Sunshine Band* hits US #4, while instrumental *The Sound Of Sunshine*, credited to The Sunshine Band, makes US #131.

'76 **Apr** *Queen Of Clubs* is re-promoted in US, and this time charts at #66.
Aug After an 8-month hiatus between UK releases, *(Shake Shake Shake) Shake Your Booty* reaches UK #22.
Sept In US, *(Shake Shake Shake) Shake Your Booty* tops chart for a week (deposing The Bee Gees' *You Should Be Dancing*); another million-seller.
Dec *Part 3* peaks at US #13.

'77 **Jan** *Keep It Comin' Love* reaches UK #31, while in US *I Like To Do It* makes #37.
May Taken from *Part 3*, *I'm Your Boogie Man* makes UK #41.
June *I'm Your Boogie Man* tops US chart for a week, making The Sunshine Band only the second group after The Jackson 5 to achieve 4 US #1 singles in the 70s.
Sept Released months after its UK chart run, *Keep It Comin' Love* (also from *Part 3*, on which it was segued with *I'm Your Boogie Man*) hits US #2 and tops R&B chart.

'78 **Jan** *Wrap Your Arms Around Me*, B-side of 6-month-old *I'm Your Boogie Man*, picks up US airplay, and is elevated to A-side, making US #48.
Mar *Boogie Shoes*, originally released as B-side of *Shake Your Booty*, is reissued as an A-side and makes US #35. The track is included on soundtrack album of movie "Saturday Night Fever", which spends 25 consecutive weeks at US #1 between Jan. and July, and 18 weeks at UK #1. With total sales of *Saturday Night Fever* exceeding 25 million copies, it means *Boogie Shoes* sells to more people than the combined total of everything else released by KC & The Sunshine Band.
May *Boogie Shoes* makes US #34.
June A revival of The Four Tops' *It's The Same Old Song* makes US #35.
Aug *It's The Same Old Song* climbs to UK #49.
Sept *Who Do Ya (Love)* reaches US #36.
Oct *Do You Feel All Right* peaks at US #63.

'79 **Jan** *Who Do Ya love*, title track from recent album, stalls at US #68.
July *Do You Wanna Go Party*, a deliberate effort to move back from the prevailing disco sound to a more basic funk mixture, peaks at US #50, followed by an album of the same title which also climbs to US #50.

'80 **Jan** Untypical ballad *Please Don't Go*, a Casey/Finch song written in the studio during recordings for the previous album, on which it was included, is extracted to provide the group with its final US chart-topper and million-seller. It is the first US #1 of the 80s (for 1

week, after 19 weeks' climbing the Hot 100), and hits UK #3.
Feb Casey duets with Casablanca Records' girl singer Teri DeSario, on a revival of Barbara Mason's 1965 hit *Yes, I'm Ready*. Credited to Teri DeSario with KC, it hits US #2 only weeks after *Please Don't Go* has left the top, and earns the duo a gold disk for a million-plus sales.
Mar Compilation *Greatest Hits* reaches US #132. An album of the same title, though with a different track listing, hits UK #10.
July Second DeSario/KC duet, *Dancin' In The Streets*, peaks at US #66.

1981 TK Records goes bankrupt and the group disbands. Casey signs to Epic, where he records *The Painter* (under the group name) and *Space Cadet* (as a solo), but without much promotion both fail to chart.

1982 **Jan** [15] Casey is seriously injured in a head-on collision near his home in Hialeah. (He loses all feeling on the right side of his body as the result of injury to a nerve, and is confined to a wheelchair, before spending most of the year recuperating while learning to walk again. When he is fit enough to re-enter the studio, he cuts *All In A Night's Work*, for Epic, but it does not chart.

1983 **Aug** *Give It Up* is extracted from *All In A Night's Work* by Epic in UK, and becomes KC's first hit in over 3 years and biggest-ever in UK. After 10 years of UK chart entries, it is his first UK #1 (for a week). US Epic declines to issue the single, leading Casey to negotiate his release from the label along with the rights to the track. He launches his own independent US label, Meca Records (Musical Enterprise Corporation Of America), and releases *Give It Up*.
Sept *All In A Night's Work* reaches UK #46.
Oct Extracted *(You Said) You'd Gimme Some More* makes UK #41.

1984 **Mar** *Give It Up* reaches US #18, while *KC Ten*, also on Meca, peaks at US #93. (Despite having no further chart entries, KC will continue to tour US playing the party-type R&B music in which The Sunshine Band specialized.)

CHAKA KHAN

1969 Khan (b. Yvette Marie Stevens, Mar.23, 1953, Great Lakes, IL), having performed since age 12 when she and some girlfriends from school entered local talent shows as The Crystalettes, and later been a member of the Afro-Arts theater in Chicago, adopting her new name while working for the Black Panther movement's Breakfast Program ("Chaka" meaning fire), joins the group Shades Of Black.

1970 She marries at 17, and sings in the group Lock & Chain, before joining soul/dance band Lyfe.

1971 Khan meets Chicago-based funk/jazz group Ask Rufus, formed out of the remnants of pop band The American Breed, former million-sellers with *Bend Me, Shape Me*.

1972 When lead singer Paulette McWilliams leaves Ask Rufus, Khan is invited to replace her.

1973 **Aug** Signed to ABC Records, the group shortens its name to Rufus. The other members with Khan are Tony Maiden (guitar), Kevin Murphy (keyboards), Nate Morgan (keyboards), Bobby Watson (bass) and Andre Fischer (drums). Debut album *Rufus* makes US #175.

1974 **Aug** Rufus' Singles chart debut is a Stevie Wonder song, *Tell Me Something Good*, which hits US #3 and earns a gold disk for a million sales. *Rags To Rufus* hits US #4, and also goes gold.
Dec *You Got The Love* reaches US #11.

1975 **Apr** *Once You Get Started* hits US #10, and the album from which it is taken, *Rufusized*, hits US #7, the band's second gold album. It also makes UK #48, Rufus' first UK chart entry.
May [22] Band joins Joe Cocker, Pure Prairie League and Earl Scruggs in the "Music – You're My Mother" concert at Fort Campbell, KY, to 17,000 US Army troops and their families.
June *Please Pardon Me (You Remind Me Of A Friend)* makes US #48.
[21] On tour in UK, Rufus supports Elton John at Wembley, London, along with The Beach Boys, The Eagles and Joe Walsh.
Dec Curtis Mayfield, who claims she is signed to his Curtom label, by way of her ex-membership of The Babysitters, sues Khan for $800,000.

1976 **Apr** Rufus' second million-seller is *Sweet Thing*, which hits US #5. It is extracted from *Rufus Featuring Chaka Khan*, which hits US #7, and is a third gold disk.
June *Dance With Me* makes US #39.

1977 **Apr** *At Midnight (My Love Will Lift You Up)* reaches US #30. *Ask Rufus* is the band's biggest-selling album to date, reaching US #12 and topping a million sales, to earn a platinum disk.
June *Hollywood* makes US #32.
Sept [27] Khan participates in the Rock'N'Bowl benefit for US Special Olympics at South Bay Bowl, Redondo Beach, CA.

1978 **Jan** Khan duets with Joni Mitchell on the latter's *Don Juan's Restless Daughter*.

CHAKA KHAN cont.

Apr *Street Player* reaches US #14, and earns another gold disk.

June Group billing changes to Rufus & Chaka Khan, beginning with *Stay*, which makes US #38.

July Khan sings lead vocals on Quincy Jones' hit single *Stuff Like That*.

Dec Amid some bad feeling between herself and the rest of Rufus, Khan signs a solo deal with Warner Bros. Her first solo album *Chaka* reaches US #12, earning a gold disk for a half million sales. Produced by Arif Mardin, it features instrumental help from Average White Band, George Benson and Rufus.

1979 Jan Taken from the album, *I'm Every Woman*, written by Ashford and Simpson, reaches US #21 (having already topped R&B chart for 3 weeks) and UK #11.

Mar Rufus' *Numbers* makes only US #81.

[22] A day before her 26th birthday, Khan has a son, Damien Holland.

Aug Now split from Rufus (though she is contracted to make 2 further albums for ABC with the group), Khan guests on Ry Cooder's *Bop Till You Drop*. Rufus, meanwhile, recruits David Wolinski for lead vocals, alongside existing member Tony Maiden.

1980 Feb Fulfilling her contract, Khan cuts *Do You Love What You Feel* with Rufus, which reaches US #30. Rufus album *Masterjam* reaches US #14, and earns another gold disk.

Aug Solo album *Naughty* makes US #43.

1981 May Rufus' *Party 'Til You're Broke* peaks at US #73.

June Khan's solo album *What Cha' Gonna Do For Me*, including an up-date of Dizzy Gillespie's *Night In Tunisia* featuring Herbie Hancock, David Foster and Gillespie himself, reaches US #17 and earns a gold disk, while the title track peaks at US #53.

Dec A Rufus & Chaka Khan single, *Sharing The Love*, climbs to US #91. It is taken from *Camouflage*, which makes US #98.

1982 Feb With their differences behind them, Chaka Khan and Rufus perform together at New York's Savoy theater, the show being recorded for a live album. Meanwhile, Khan contributes vocals to Lenny White's *Echoes Of An Era*. Along with Chick Corea, Stanley Clarke and Freddie Hubbard, she records new versions of jazz classics.

1983 Feb A revival of Michael Jackson's hit *Got To Be There* peaks at US #67. It is taken from *Chaka Khan*, which makes US #52.

Nov Double album *Live – Stompin' At The Savoy*, a recording of the Feb.1982 Khan/Rufus reunion concert, is released by Khan's label Warner Bros., and makes US #50.

Dec *Ain't Nobody*, taken from the live album, reaches US #22.

1984 Feb [28] Khan wins Best R&B Vocal Performance, Female, for *Chaka Khan*, Best R&B Performance By A Duo Or Group With Vocal with Rufus for *Ain't Nobody* and Best Vocal Arrangement For Two Or More Voices with Arif Mardin for *Be Bop Medley* at the 26th annual Grammy awards.

May *Ain't Nobody* hits UK #8 (Rufus' only UK hit single), while *Live – Stompin' At The Savoy* makes UK #64.

Nov Khan's revival of *I Feel For You*, written by Prince and originally on his second album *Prince* in 1979, features a rap intro by Grandmaster Melle Mel and harmonica fills by Stevie Wonder. It tops UK chart for 3 weeks, and hits US #3, selling over a million to earn a gold disk. Mardin-produced album of the same title reaches US #14 and UK #15, and is a US million-seller, earning a platinum disk.

1985 Feb *This Is My Night*, exemplifying the electro-funk feel of the album, reaches UK #14, but peaks at US #60. Khan's UK tour which follows is plagued by her throat problems.

[26] Khan wins Best R&B Vocal Performance, Female, for *I Feel For You* at the 27th annual Grammy awards. (The song wins Prince a Grammy as Best New R&B Song.)

May *Eye To Eye* makes UK #14, as ballad *Through The Fire* makes US #60.

Oct Khan's *Can't Stop The Street* is featured in the break dance/rap movie "Krush Groove".

1986 Jan [25] *Own The Night*, featured in an episode of NBC TV's "Miami Vice", peaks at US #57.

May Khan arranges vocals for Robert Palmer's US #1 *Addicted To Love*.

July Written and produced by Scritti Politti, *Love Of A Lifetime* peaks at UK #52. Khan duets with David Bowie on *Underground*, from the soundtrack of "Labyrinth".

Aug [9] *Love Of A Lifetime* peaks at US #53. Parent album *Destiny* makes US #67 and UK #77. Producer Mardin is assisted on it by son Joe, and it includes a song written by Genesis' Mike Rutherford. Khan contributes vocals to Steve Winwood's US #1 *Higher Love*.

1988 Nov [5] Khan begins a month's tour of Europe in Hamburg, Germany, as new single *It's My Party*, written by Cecil and Linda Womack and produced by Russ Titelman, is released.

1989 Jan *It's My Party* reaches UK #71 as parent album *C.K.* makes US #125.

May Remixed issue of 1979's *I'm Every Woman* hits UK #8. Khan contributes *Fever* to Warner Bros. Richard Perry-produced *Rock Rhythm & Blues* compilation.

June *Life Is A Dance – The Remix Project*, a UK only cash-in of remixed Khan/Rufus hits, reaches UK #14.

Oct Extracted remixed version of *I Feel For You* makes UK #45.

1990 Jan [27] Quincy Jones' *I'll Be Good To You*, with Khan and Ray Charles the featured vocalists, reaches US #18.

JOHNNY KIDD AND THE PIRATES

Johnny Kidd (vocals)
Alan Caddy (guitar)
Brian Gregg (bass)
Clem Cattini (drums)

1959 Jan Group is formed in London by Kidd (b. Frederick Heath, Dec.23, 1939, Willesden, London), former leader of skiffle group The Five Nutters. Caddy (b. Feb.2, 1940, London) is also an ex-Nutter. The rest of the early line-up is variable, with session men playing on first 3 singles.

June A booking on BBC radio's "Saturday Club" show leads to a contract with EMI's HMV label and debut single *Please Don't Touch* (written by Kidd and manager Guy Robinson), which reaches UK #25.

Dec A revival of music hall standard *If You Were The Only Girl In The World* flops.

1960 Jan Gregg and Cattini, former session men in the Larry Parnes' tour back-up band The Beat Boys, join to complete a powerful live group: all in pirate gear playing in front of a galleon backdrop, and Kidd in an eye-patch which he later admits temporarily upsets his eyesight after every show.

Feb A cover of Marv Johnson's US hit *You Got What It Takes* reaches UK #25.

Aug *Shakin' All Over*, almost issued as a B-side, hits UK #2 behind Cliff Richard and The Shadows' *Please Don't Tease*. Driven by a powerful guitar riff from session player Joe Moretti, it becomes a UK standard.

Oct *Restless*, in similar style to *Shakin'*, reaches UK #19.

1961 Apr A cover of Ray Sharpe's US hit *Linda Lu* makes UK #47.

July The Pirates leave Kidd to back Tommy Steele's brother Colin Hicks as The Cabin Boys, before becoming the basis of producer Joe Meek's studio house band The Tornados. They are replaced by Frank Farley (drums), Johnny Spence (bass) and Johnny Patto (guitar), previously Cuddly Dudley's backing group The Redcaps.

1962 Mar Guitarist Mick Green, also formerly with The Redcaps (whose ability to play simultaneous lead and rhythm mark him as UK's answer to James Burton), replaces Patto.

July Group begins 3 weeks at Hamburg's Star-Club, Germany.

1963 Jan A cover of Arthur Alexander's *A Shot Of Rhythm And Blues*, firmly in an R&B mold, creeps into UK chart at #48 after 2 flop singles.

Sept Merseybeat-flavored *I'll Never Get Over You* is Kidd's second-biggest UK single, hitting #4.

Dec *Hungry For Love*, a stage favorite with many UK beat groups, reaches UK #20.

1964 Jan The Pirates, minus Kidd, release an R&B single with Spence vocalizing, a revival of Little Walter's *My Babe*, which is not a hit. Group guests on a handful of dates on The Rolling Stones' "Group Scene 64" package tour.

Apr Kidd adds Vic Cooper on organ to the group. *Always And Ever*, an unlikely rock adaptation of Latin standard *La Paloma*, is Kidd's last UK chart entry, making #46.

July Green leaves to join Billy J. Kramer & The Dakotas. He is replaced by John Weider.

Oct A revival of Marvin Rainwater's *Whole Lotta Woman* fails to sell, as will all later Kidd records.

Nov [30] Group joins the Brenda Lee tour at the Town Hall, Birmingham, W.Midlands.

1966 Apr Acknowledging his depression about declining interest in his music, seen as outdated, Kidd splits from The Pirates. Spence and Farley keep the name, and with guitarist Jon Morshead, record *Casting My Spell* for Polydor before disbanding.

May Kidd recruits The Regents, former backing group of Buddy Britten, as The New Pirates. They play UK one-nighters continuously.

Oct [7] While on tour, Kidd dies in a car crash in Radcliffe, near Manchester, Gtr.Manchester. (Nick Simper, a member of The New Pirates, survives the crash and later will be a founding member of Deep Purple.) Group carries on for a while as The Pirates, but bookings dry up without Kidd's name (and they will split in May 1967).

1976 **Dec** Former Kidd sidemen Mick Green, Johnny Spence and Frank Farley re-form as The Pirates, and become one of the most highly-rated UK live acts of the late 70s in pubs, clubs and larger venues. Debut album *Out Of Their Skulls* charts in UK at #57 (but 3 later albums and a plethora of singles will sell less well despite continuing onstage success, and the lack of record sales will again lead to a split in 1982).

B.B. KING

1949 King (b. Riley King, Sept.16, 1925, Itta Bena, MS), cousin of bluesman Bukka White, has been playing blues guitar professionally since his US Army service. While leading a trio in Memphis, TN, his local popularity is noted by radio station W-DIA, and he secures his own regular show. The station's publicity man dubs King "The Beale Street Blues Boy", which is shortened to Blues Boy and eventually B.B. Towards the end of the year, King signs to Bullet label, debuting with *Miss Martha King*.

1950 King is signed to the Kent/Modern/RPM group of labels by talent scout Ike Turner. (He will remain with the company until 1962.)

1951 King hits US R&B #1 with *Three O'Clock Blues*, his eighth single. Ike Turner is featured on piano, Willie Mitchell on trumpet and Hank Crawford on alto sax.

1952 *You Didn't Want Me* is another R&B chart-topper. (King will continue to enjoy regular R&B chart success for the next 5 years.)

1954 **Aug** [19] King and his band play at the Savoy Ballroom in Hollywood, CA, with Johnny Otis and The Platters, to a packed audience of 2,400.

1955 He is now averaging 300 gigs a year (a rate he will maintain until the late 70s).

1957 **May** [29] King plays with Ray Charles, The Drifters, Ruth Brown, Jimmy Reed and others at an outdoor R&B festival at Herndon Stadium in Atlanta, GA.
July *Be Careful With A Fool* is King's first crossover success at US #95.
Nov *I Need You So Bad* makes US #85.

1960 **Feb** *Sweet Sixteen* hits US R&B #2 but does not cross over.

1962 King moves from Kent to larger ABC label (with which he will stay until it is absorbed into MCA in 1979).

1964 **Mar** *How Blue Can You Get It*, his first ABC success, peaks at US #97.
May *Rock Me Baby*, recorded for Kent before the label move, is King's first sizeable pop hit, reaching US #34. (It will be much covered and adapted by the UK R&B fraternity.)
June *Help The Poor*, on ABC, climbs to US #98.
Nov *Beautician Blues* peaks at US #82 as *Never Trust A Woman* makes US #90.
[21] King plays a concert at the Regal theater, Chicago, IL (which will be released as *Live At The Regal* in 1965).

1965 **July** *Blue Shadows* peaks at US #97.

1966 **Oct** *Don't Answer The Door* makes US #72.

1967 **Apr** *The Jungle*, another stockpiled oldie from Kent, reaches US #94.

1968 **Apr** *Paying The Cost To Be The Boss*, on ABC's Bluesway label, is his second US Top 40 hit, at #39. King is in dispute with his manager Lou Zito over financial affairs. It is mediated by King's accountant Sidney Seidenberg, who is appointed as new manager.
[4] On the night after Martin Luther King is shot, King, Buddy Guy and Jimi Hendrix gather in a club to play an all-night blues session and pass a hat around to collect money for King's Southern Christian Leadership.
July *I'm Gonna Do What They Do To Me* climbs to US #74.
Aug *The Woman I Love* stalls at US #94.
Oct Double A-side *The B.B. Jones/Put It On Me*, featured on the soundtrack to movie "For The Love Of Ivy", makes US #98/#82. King's first album chart success is with *Lucille*, on Bluesway, which makes US #192. (Lucille is the name King gives to his customized Gibson guitar.)

1969 **Apr** [29] King plays at the Free Trade Hall, Manchester, Gtr.Manchester, during a short UK visit.
May *Why I Sing The Blues* makes US #61.
July *Live And Well*, produced by Bill Szymczyck, with one studio side and the other recorded at New York's Village Gate club, makes US #56. King plays at the Newport Jazz Festival, Newport, RI, jamming with Johnny Winter.
Aug [1] King performs at the Atlantic City Pop Festival, to 110,000 people, alongside Creedence Clearwater Revival, Jefferson Airplane, The Byrds and others.
Get Off My Back Woman peaks at US #74.
[30] He plays the International Pop Festival at Dallas Speedway in Lewisville, TX, along with Janis Joplin, Canned Heat, Santana, Led Zeppelin and many more.

Oct *Just A Little Love* peaks at US #76. Under Seidenberg's encouragement, King starts to widen his following from the traditional (and declining) black audience towards a young, international white one, booking rock-oriented venues like the Fillmores East and West, and audiences already weaned on blues-derived rock bands.
Dec *The Thrill Is Gone*, using an imaginative string arrangement, is King's biggest hit single, making US #15.

1970 **Feb** *Completely Well*, which includes *The Thrill Is Gone*, makes US #38.
Apr *So Excited* peaks at US #54. *The Incredible Soul Of B.B. King* peaks at US #193. King begins work on a new album, and in an attempt to repeat the pop chart success of *Completely Well*, features leading white rock musicians, including Carole King, Leon Russell and Joe Walsh.
July *Hummingbird* makes US #48.
[3-5] He plays at the 3-day Atlanta Pop Festival at the Middle Georgia Raceway in Byron, GA, to 200,000 people, with Jimi Hendrix, Jethro Tull, Johnny Winter and others.
Nov *Indianola Mississippi Seeds*, recorded with King's star sidemen, reaches US #26. *Chains And Things* climbs to US #45.

1971 **Feb** *Ask Me No Questions* peaks at US #40.
Mar [16] King wins Best R&B Vocal Performance, Male for *The Thrill Is Gone* at the 13th annual Grammy awards.
Apr *Live In Cook County Jail* reaches US #25. King is taking an active interest in prisoner welfare (and will become co-chairman of FAIRR – Foundation For The Advancement Of Inmate Rehabilitation And Recreation). *That Evil Child* peaks at US #97.
June *Help The Poor*, an instrumental version of the 1964 release, makes US #90.
Sept *Ghetto Woman* climbs to US #68.
Oct *Live At The Regal*, reissued from 1965, reaches US #78.
Nov *B.B. King In London*, featuring sidemen Peter Green, Alexis Korner, Steve Marriott and Ringo Starr, reaches US #57, as *Ain't Nobody Home* makes US #46.
[19] King marks his 25th anniversary in the music business by opening a European tour in London.

1972 **Mar** *L.A. Midnight* reaches US #53. From it, a new version of *Sweet Sixteen* makes US #93.
Apr [1] King plays at the Mar Y Sol Festival in Vega Baja, Puerto Rica, with Black Sabbath, The Allman Brothers Band, Emerson, Lake And Palmer and many more.
May *I Got Some Help I Don't Need It* peaks at US #92.
Aug *Guess Who* reaches US #65. From it, *Guess Who* makes US #62.

1973 **Mar** Compilation album *The Best Of B.B. King* makes US #101.
Aug *To Know You Is To Love You* peaks at US #38 as album of the same title climbs to US #71.
Dec *I Like To Live The Love* reaches US #28.

1974 **June** *Who Are You* peaks at US #78.
Aug *Friends* makes US #153.
Nov *Philadelphia* peaks at US #64.
Dec *Together For The First Time ... Live*, a collaboration with King's old friend and associate Bobby Bland, reaches US #43.

1975 **Nov** *Lucille Talks Back* climbs to US #140.

1976 **Aug** Again with Bland, *Together Again ... Live*, reaches US #73.

1977 **Feb** *King Size* makes US #154.
Oct [9] During another UK visit, King plays at the Hammersmith Odeon, London.

1978 **Apr** King joins top defense lawyer F. Lee Bailey, his fellow co-chairman of FAIRR, for a joint rap session and concert for the inmates of Norfolk prison in Boston, MA, sections of which are filmed by ABC TV for showing on "Good Morning America".
May *Midnight Believer* peaks at US #124. King switches labels as ABC is absorbed into parent company MCA.

1979 **Apr** King plays a month-long, 30-date USSR tour.
Aug *Take It Home* makes US #112, and gives King his first UK album chart success at #60.
[24] King celebrates his 30th anniversary making music by performing at Los Angeles' Roxy.

1980 **May** Live album *Now Appearing At Ole Miss* climbs to US #162.

1981 **Mar** *There Must Be A Better World Somewhere* peaks at US #131.

1982 **Jan** [21] King donates his entire record collection (20,000, including 7,000 rare blues 78s) to Mississippi University's Center for the Study of Southern Culture.
Feb [24] King wins Best Ethnic Or Traditional Recording for *There Must Be A Better World Somewhere* at the 24th annual Grammy awards.
May *Love Me Tender* makes US #179.
Sept [16] He records *Blues 'N' Jazz* on his 57th birthday.

B.B. KING cont.

1983 **June** [23] King plays at the Kool Jazz Festival in New York, alongside Ray Charles, Miles Davis and others.
July *Blues 'N' Jazz* reaches US #172.

1984 **Feb** [28] King wins Best Traditional Blues Recording for *Blues 'N Jazz* at the 26th annual Grammy awards.

1985 **Feb** King makes a cameo appearance in John Landis' movie "Into The Night", playing himself (with his guitar).

1986 **Feb** [25] King wins Best Traditional Blues Recording for *My Guitar Sings The Blues* from *Six Silver Strings* at the 28th annual Grammy awards.
Nov [16] King co-hosts America's seventh National Blues Awards with Carl Perkins.

1987 **Jan** [21] King is inducted into the Rock'N'Roll Hall Of Fame at the second annual induction dinner at the Waldorf Astoria, New York.

1988 **Mar** [2] King is honored by the NARAS at the 30th annual Grammy awards with a Lifetime Achievement Award, noting that he is "one of the most original and soulful of all blues guitarists and singers, whose compelling style and devotion to musical truth have inspired so many budding performers, both here and abroad, to celebrate the blues".

1989 **Apr** [29] He is a prominent guest on U2's *When Love Comes To Town*, which peaks at US #68, but hits UK #6.
June [21-25] King performs at the Benson & Hedges Blues Festival in Dallas, TX, the proceeds going to the National Coalition For The Homeless and the Dallas-based homeless group, Common Ground.
[29] He plays at the 30th Newport Folk Festival at Fort Adams State Park, Newport, RI, with Randy Newman, John Hiatt, Buckwheat Zydeco and others.
Sept [6] King and U2 win Best Video From Film award at the 6th annual MTV Music Video Awards ceremony at the Universal Amphitheater, Universal City, CA, for *When Love Comes To Town*, from U2's movie "Rattle And Hum".
Dec [23] King is featured on the *Happy Anniversary, Charlie Brown!* homage (US #65), commemorating the 40th year of the "Peanuts" comic strip.

1990 **Jan** [1] King travels on the Mississippi Tournament Of Roses Association float at the 1990 Rosebowl Parade in Pasadena, CA.
[23] Herbie Hancock recruits King and others, including Rickie Lee Jones, Lou Reed, Bonnie Raitt, Bruce Hornsby and Sting for a taping of Showtime TV's "Coast To Coast" from China club in Los Angeles.
Feb [24] King participates in the Roy Orbison All-Star Benefit Tribute held at the Universal Amphitheater, Universal City, CA. The event raises $500,000 for the Shelter Partnership and The National Coalition For The Homeless.
Apr [27] King is hospitalized in Las Vegas, NV, after cancelling 2 dates at the New Orleans Jazz & Heritage Festival because of health problems related to his diabetes.
May [30] King receives a Lifetime Achievement award at the Songwriters Hall Of Fame 21st annual induction dinner at the Hilton hotel, New York.
Aug [17] He takes part in the annual JVC Jazz Festival at Fort Adams State Park, Newport, RI, with Miles Davis, George Benson and others.
Sept *Live At San Quentin*, recorded 20 years eailrer, is released. He also duets with Randy Travis on *Waiting On The Light To Change*, from Travis' album *Heroes And Friends*.
[7] King becomes the 1,917th star to have a number on the Hollywood Walk Of Fame.
[29] King begins World tour with Ray Charles in Taipei, Taiwan.

1991 **Jan** [17] Bonnie Raitt inducts King into the Rock'N'Roll Hall Of Fame at the sixth annual dinner at the Waldorf Astoria in New York.
Feb King leads the Zulu Social Aid & Pleasure Club float during the Mardi Gras parade in New Orleans.
[19] The Gibson guitar company honor King ("Lucille" is a Gibson) with a Lifetime Achievement award at New York's Hard Rock Café.
[20] King wins Best Traditional Blues Recording for *Live At San Quentin* at the 33rd Grammy awards at Radio City Music Hall, New York.
Mar [14] King appears on NBC TV's "Tonight" show.
May [2] King opens his own 350-seater restaurant and nightclub, B.B. King's Memphis Blues Club, on Beale Street, Memphis.
[3-4] He takes part in the annual "Memphis In May Beale Street Music Festival".
[14] GRP Records releases *Am I Cool, Or What?* a homage to cartoon feline Garfield, featuring King's *Monday Morning Blues*.

BEN E. KING

1957 King (b. Benjamin Earl Nelson, Sept.23, 1938, Henderson, NC), after moving to Harlem as a boy, graduates from church choir to street corner doo-wop, singing with The Four Bs and The Moonglows before joining The Crowns. *Kiss And Make Up* is issued to minor R&B success.

1958 **May** This band shares New York Apollo theater bill with The Drifters.
June The Drifters' manager George Treadwell fires its members.
July Owning the trademark, Treadwell hires The Crowns to become The Drifters.

1959 King is featured vocalist on *There Goes My Baby, Dance With Me, This Magic Moment, Save The Last Dance For Me* and *I Count The Tears* – smash hits which make The Drifters the hottest vocal group of the era.

1960 **May** Treadwell fires King after he complains about low wages.
Oct [27] Signing a solo deal with Atlantic subsidiary Atco, King, with producers Leiber and Stoller, cuts 4 sides in 3 hours. (*Spanish Harlem, First Taste Of Love, Young Boy Blues* and *Stand By Me*, which will become the basis of a lifelong career.)

1961 **Mar** King's double-sided *Spanish Harlem*, a rare collaboration between Jerry Leiber and his apprentice Phil Spector, hits UK #10. *First Taste Of Love*, written by Spector and Doc Pomus, reaches US #53 but its B-side reaches UK #27. (Aretha Franklin's revival of *Spanish Harlem* will hit US #2 10 years later.)
June *Stand By Me*, polished up by Leiber and Stoller in The Drifters' Latin style, hits US #4 and UK #27, but will become an enduring soul standard. (John Lennon will revive it for a US Top 20 hit in 1975.)
Aug *Spanish Harlem* climbs to US #57.
Sept King's version of the standard *Amor* makes US #18 and UK #38 (it will be his last UK chart appearance for 25 years).
Oct Pomus/Spector-written *Young Boy Blues* is finally released, rising to US #66. B-side *Here Comes The Night* charts at US #81. (In 1984, Robert Plant will revive *Young Boy Blues* on his album *Honeydrippers*.)

1962 **Mar** Another Pomus/Spector composition, *Ecstasy*, peaks at US #56.
June Co-written by King (under his wife's name) and Atlantic boss Ahmet Ertegun, *Don't Play That Song* climbs to US #11. (Aretha Franklin's version will be a million-seller in 1970.)
Aug *Too Bad* charts for only 2 weeks, at US #88.

1963 **Apr** *How Can I Forget*, a King original, reaches US #85.
Aug King's version of Leiber and Stoller's (later much-recorded) *I (Who Have Nothing)* reaches US #29 (and will be his last Top 40 hit for 12 years).
Nov From musical "My Fair Lady", *I Could Have Danced All Night* reaches US #72.

1964 **Feb** [3] King arrives in UK for his first visit, having just taken part in the San Remo Song Festival in Italy.
[7] He makes his UK TV debut on "Ready Steady Go!"
As soul becomes more synonymous with the modern sounds of Motown and Stax, King's pioneering brand loses impetus; he only has modest US chart hits: *That's When It Hurts* (#63) and *It's All Over* (#72).

1965 **Jan** *Seven Letters* makes US #45.
Apr *The Record (Baby I Love You)* peaks at US #84.
July King takes part in Murray The K's stage show at the Brooklyn Fox, with Tom Jones, Gary Lewis & The Playboys, and others.

1967 **Sept** [29] King embarks on a UK tour. 3 minor hits conclude his 7-year solo run on Atco: *Goodnight My Love* (US #91), *So Much Love* (#96) and *Tears Tears Tears* (#93), while *Spanish Harlem* spends 3 weeks on the UK chart, climbing to #30.

1968 King will work cabaret, club and supper circuits – mixing his own hits with those of current stars – during the next 5 years.

1974 **Dec** King makes a cameo appearance on Genesis album *The Lamb Lies Down On Broadway* – singing the phrase "on Broadway" (even though his was not the voice on The Drifters' recording!)

1975 **Apr** Ahmet Ertegun, seeing King perform in a Miami nightclub, convinces him to re-sign with Atlantic rather than Atco. Produced by Bert DeCoteaux, *Supernatural Thing* hits US #5.
June *Supernatural* makes US #39.

1977 **July** King joins Average White Band for *Benny And Us*, which makes #33 on US chart.

1978 Between now and 1986, King will experience more lean years as his popularity dwindles. After an unsuccessful union with Don Covay, Joe Tex, Wilson Pickett and Solomon Burke as The Soul Clan, King will rejoin The Drifters for European tours. He will release 1 album, *Street Tough*, for Atlantic, in May 1981.

1986 **Dec** [20] Featured as the title of a film based on a Stephen King novella, *Stand By Me* hits US #9 after a 27-year gap. Its undated sound and production values testify to Leiber and Stoller's studio innovation and King's vocal prowess. (King will donate the sheet music of *Stand By Me* to the Hard Rock Café.)

1987 Jan [21] King inducts Clyde McPhatter into the Rock'N'Roll Hall Of Fame at the second annual dinner at the Waldorf Astoria in New York.
Feb Before "Stand By Me" premieres in UK, an advertising agency uses part of the song in a TV commercial promoting Levi 501 jeans. Its nightly exposure in UK takes *Stand By Me* to UK #1. Percy Sledge's *When A Man Loves A Woman*, featured in the same ads, hits UK #2.
Mar *Stand By Me (The Ultimate Collection)*, featuring both King solos and Drifters tracks, including *Spanish Harlem*, makes UK #14.
June EMI releases *Dancing In The Night* through its dance label Syncopate.
July On the strength of revived fortunes, EMI Manhattan Records sign King and release an updated version of *Save The Last Dance For Me*, which reaches UK #69.
[5-6] King takes part in the fifth annual Prince's Trust Rock Gala at the Wembley Arena, London, on a bill with Elton John, George Harrison, Ringo Starr and Alison Moyet.
1988 Feb King joins stars including Billy Joel, Joe Walsh, Duane Eddy, Warren Zevon, Robert Cray, Roberta Flack, Cyndi Lauper, Carole King and Ashford And Simpson for NBC TV's "David Letterman's Sixth Anniversary Special" at Radio City Music Hall, New York.
Apr EMI Manhattan releases all new Ben E. King album *Save The Last Dance For Me*, recorded with guests producers Mick Jones, John Paul Jones, Preston Glass and Lamont Dozier and featuring Mark Knopfler on guitar.
1989 Aug King guest vocals with Wilson Pickett, Bobby Womack, Don Covay, Darlene Love, Marvis Staples and Ellie Greenwich on *What Is Soul?* from Paul Shaffer's *Coast To Coast*, as he records new album for Atlantic with producer Bert D'Coteaux.
1990 Jan [17] King inducts songwriters Gerry Goffin and Carole King into the Rock'N'Roll Hall Of Fame at the fifth annual dinner at the Waldorf Astoria, New York. At the perfunctory after-dinner jam, he joins with them on a rendition of *Will You Love Me Tomorrow*.
1991 Jan King combines with Bo Diddley and Doug Lazy to remake The Monotones' *Book of Love* on Atlantic, featured in the movie "The Book Of Love".

CAROLE KING

1958 While at Queen's College, New York, King (b. Carole Klein, Feb.9, 1940, Brooklyn, New York, NY), having received singing and piano lessons from her mother at age 6 and formed a high school vocal quartet The Co-Sines, meets Paul Simon, and begins writing songs professionally. She also meets lyricist Gerry Goffin, who is working in a pharmacy, and the 2 write together for Don Kirshner and Al Nevin's Aldon Music based in New York's Brill Building.
1959 Mar King releases debut single *Baby Sittin'*, on ABC/Paramount, followed by *Short-Mort* on RCA-Victor and *Oh! Neil* (her response to Neil Sedaka's *Oh! Carol*), on Alpine.
1961 Jan [30] Goffin and King-penned *Will You Love Me Tomorrow* by The Shirelles tops US chart. (During the next 6 years, Goffin and King will write dozens of US Hot 100 hits.)
Sept [18] Goffin/King-penned *Take Good Care Of My Baby* by Bobby Vee hits US #1.
1962 Aug Kirshner hears a demo of *It Might As Well Rain Until September* King has made for Bobby Vee and persuades her to release her own version. After an initial pressing on Companion Records, Aldon Music establishes its own Dimension label, specifically to release Goffin/King compositions and issues the track. Meanwhile, Goffin and King's *The Locomotion* tops US chart, sung by their babysitter, Little Eva.
Oct King-sung *It Might As Well Rain Until September* reaches US #22 and hits UK #3.
1967 Jan [12] Still accumulating many songwriting hits with Goffin, their *Go Away Little Girl* hits US #1 for Steve Lawrence.
Goffin and King separate (and will later divorce). King forms Tomorrow Records with journalist Al Aronowitz. She releases her own version of *Some Of Your Lovin'* (previously a hit for Dusty Springfield) and an album by The Myddle Class, which includes bass player Charles Larkey (who will become King's second husband).
1968 King forms new band The City with Larkey and guitarist Danny "Kootch" Kortchmar. Their album *Now That Everything's Been Said* is released on Lou Adler's Ode label. Due to King's nerves, the band does not tour (and will soon break up).
1969 Now based in California, King plays piano on James Taylor's album *Sweet Baby James*.
1970 Mar King records debut album *Writer: Carole King* at Crystal Sound

studio in Los Angeles, where she now lives, which fails to sell.
Oct King records *Tapestry* with Larkey, Kortchmar and drummer Russ Kunkel, who will become her regular band, with James Taylor playing guitar and singing backing vocals.
1971 May Double A-sided *It's Too Late/I Feel The Earth* hits US #1.
June *Tapestry* tops US chart. It will stay at #1 for 15 weeks and on chart for 302 weeks, selling over 15 million worldwide. Re-promoted *Writer: Carole King* reaches US #84. James Taylor's version of King's *You've Got A Friend* tops US chart.
July *Tapestry* enters UK chart as it goes gold in US. It will hit UK #4. King is the first artiste to perform at New York's Philharmonic Hall at Lincoln Center, traditionally a classical venue.
Aug *So Far Away/Smackwater Jack* makes US #14.
Sept *It's Too Late* hits UK #6.
1972 Jan *Sweet Seasons* hits US #9, as *Music*, with lyrics by Toni Stern, tops US chart and reaches UK #18. Overcoming her fear of playing live, King tours US and UK.
Mar [9] King performs with James Taylor and Barbra Streisand at a benefit for Presidential candidate George McGovern at the Forum, Los Angeles.
[14] King wins Record Of The Year for *It's Too Late*, Album Of The Year and Best Pop Vocal Performance, Female for *Tapestry* and Song Of The Year for *You've Got A Friend* at the 14th annual Grammy awards.
Nov *Been To Canaan* reaches US #24. *It Might As Well Rain Until September* is reissued and makes UK #43.
Dec *Rhymes And Reasons* hits US #2 and climbs to UK #40.
1973 May [25] King performs a free concert in New York's Central Park to an audience of 100,000. Soundman Chip Monck ensures that everyone can hear the performance.
July *Believe In Humanity/You Light Up My Life*, from the forthcoming album, reaches US #28.
Aug *Fantasy* hits US #6.
Oct *Corazon* peaks at US #37.
1974 Feb [14] King joins Dylan at the last gig of his 39-date US tour in Los Angeles.
Apr [29] King gives birth to her fourth child, Levi.
Aug *Jazzman*, with Tom Scott guesting on sax, hits US #2.
Nov *Wrap Around Joy*, with lyrics by David Palmer, tops US chart.
1975 Jan *Nightingale* hits US #9.
Apr Original TV soundtrack album *Really Rosie*, which includes background vocal contributions from King's daughters Sherry and Louise Goffin, reaches US #20.
1976 Feb *Only Love Is Real* makes US #28.
Mar King teams with ex-husband Goffin to work on songs for *Thoroughbred*, which has vocal support from David Crosby, Graham Nash, James Taylor and J.D. Souther. The album hits US #3.
1977 Apr King, newly-signed to Capitol Records, where she forms her own Avatar label, starts work on *Simple Things* in Los Angeles. Self-produced with Norm Kinney, King uses recently Capitol-signed band Navarro, which includes Rick Evers (who becomes her third husband), to back her.
July *Hard Rock Café* makes US #30.
Sept *Simple Things* reaches US #17.
1978 Jan Again using Navarro, King records *Welcome Home* at Sound Labs, Hollywood.
Mar Evers dies from an apparent drug overdose.
Apr *Her Greatest Hits* reaches US #47.
June *Welcome Home* reaches US #104.
1979 Mar King records *Touch The Sky* at Pecan Street studios, Austin, TX, with a group of musicians she heard on Jerry Jeff Walker's *Jerry Jeff*.
July *Touch The Sky* peaks at US #104.
1980 Jan King records 10 of her most famous early songs for *Pearls – Songs Of Goffin And King*, using the studios at Pecan Street, Austin. Ex-husband Larkey plays bass, and recent Warner Bros. signing Christopher Cross plays rhythm guitar on *The Locomotion, Chains* and *Hi De Ho*.
July *Pearls – Songs Of Goffin And King* reaches US #44.
1982 Apr Now signed to Atlantic Records, King releases *One To One*, which reaches US #119. Despite brief promotional visit, it fails to chart in UK.
1983 *Speeding Time* reunites King with producer Adler, musicians Kortchmar and Kunkel and lyricist Goffin. King records, for the first time, her own version of The Everly Brothers 1961 hit *Crying In The Rain*, which she wrote with Howard Greenfield, with a sax solo from Plas Johnson.
1985 Mar "The Care Bears" movie, with songs by King and John Sebastian, premieres.

CAROLE KING cont.

1987 **Mar** [9] Goffin and King are inducted into the 18th annual Songwriters Hall Of Fame awards at New York's Plaza Hotel.

Apr [23] King sues Lou Adler for breach of contract. She claims that over $400,000 in royalties is owed to her, and requests the rights to all of her old recordings.

1988 **Feb** In a rare live appearance, King joins a star group of musicians, including Billy Joel, Joe Walsh, Duane Eddy, Warren Zevon, Robert Cray, Roberta Flack, Cyndi Lauper, Ben E. King and Ashford And Simpson, to make up the house band for NBC TV's "David Letterman's Sixth Anniversary Special" at Radio City Music Hall, New York.

July A celebration of King's music, "Tapestry", opens a 2-month run at the Cincinnati Playhouse, OH.

Dec [3] Goffin and King receive the National Academy Of Songwriters Lifetime Achievment award.

1989 **May** King releases her first album in 6 years, *City Streets* on Capitol. Guest performers include Eric Clapton, Michael Brecker, Branford Marsalis and Sherry Goffin and it is produced by King with Rudy Guess. It makes US #111.

1990 **Jan** [17] Goffin and King are inducted into the Rock'N'Roll Hall Of Fame at the fifth annual dinner at the Waldorf Astoria in New York.

1991 **Mar** [21] King is featured on ABC TV's "Afterschool Special – It's Only Rock'N'Roll".

KING CRIMSON

Robert Fripp (guitar)
Greg Lake (bass, vocals)
Ian McDonald (saxophone)
Mike Giles (drums)
Pete Sinfield (lyricist)

1967 **Aug** Giles, Giles & Fripp is formed in Bournemouth, Dorset, by Giles brothers Pete (bass) and Mike (b. 1942, Bournemouth) (drum, vocals) with guitarist Robert Fripp (b. 1946, Wimborne, Dorset).

Sept Trio moves to London but finds gigs hard to obtain.

1968 **June** McDonald (b. June 25, 1946, London) joins with ex-Fairport Convention singer Judy Dyble, and the group signs to Deram Records. Sinfield arrives as lyricist a few weeks later and Dyble departs.

Sept *The Cheerful Insanity Of Giles, Giles And Fripp* is released by Deram. Sales are supposedly less than 600 copies and the band splits.

1969 **Jan** [13] Disillusioned, Pete Giles leaves and the group changes its name to King Crimson, recruiting Lake (b. Nov.10, 1948, Bournemouth) from The Gods, and signing for management to new E.G. company.

Apr [9] After a week's limber-up in Newcastle, Tyne & Wear, (still as Giles, Giles & Fripp), the first King Crimson gig is at the Speakeasy in London, followed by a lengthy residency at the Marquee club.

July [5] Band supports The Rolling Stones at London's Hyde Park concert in front of 650,000 people.

Nov Self-produced debut album *In The Court Of The Crimson King*, on Island, hits UK #5. Band plays 18-date US tour, opening at Goddard College, Plainfield, VT, to support album's US Atlantic release.

Dec Group returns to UK and McDonald and Giles leave. (They will record *McDonald And Giles* in 1970 and McDonald will help form Foreigner in 1978.)

1970 **Feb** *In The Court Of The Crimson King* reaches US #28. The extracted title track makes US #80.

Mar Lake leaves to form Emerson, Lake and Palmer (ELP). Left as a duo, Fripp and Sinfield recruit assorted friends to record a second album. Meanwhile *Cat Food*, made with help from Giles brothers and jazzman Keith Tippett, is released. It fails to chart but secures the temporary line-up an appearance on UK TV's "Top Of The Pops". Fripp is invited to join Yes after Emerson turns him down for ELP but decides to re-form King Crimson instead.

May Following album sessions, Fripp and Sinfield keep vocalist/bassist Gordon Haskell (ex-Fleur De Lys) and saxophonist Mel Collins (ex-Circus) in the band. *In The Wake Of Poseidon* hits UK #4.

Aug Andy McCullough joins as drummer.

Oct Haskell and McCullough leave after recording the third album while *In The Wake Of Poseidon* climbs to US #31.

Nov Ian Wallace joins on drums and Boz Burrell is recruited as a singer and bassist, having been tutored accordingly by Fripp.

1971 **Jan** *Lizard* reaches UK #30. Tippett guests again and Jon Anderson of Yes sings guest vocals on 1 track.

Apr *Lizard* peaks at US #113. Band plays 4 dates in Germany.

May Band begins live performing in UK (continuing until Oct.).

Dec After second US tour Fripp asks Sinfield to leave. (He will produce the first Roxy Music album, write for ELP and go on to concentrate on songwriting success.)

1972 **Jan** *Islands* reaches UK #30.

Feb Group returns to tour US and *Islands* makes US #76.

Apr Back in UK, all the band except Fripp depart, having failed to agree with him over the structure of King Crimson's stage act. (Burrell will later co-found Bad Company.)

June Live album *Earthbound* recorded in US in Mar. fails to chart in UK and US Atlantic refuses to release it.

July Fripp puts together a new band with Bill Bruford (b. May 17, 1948, London) (ex-Yes) (drums), John Wetton (b. July 12, 1949, Derby, Derbys.) (ex-Family) (bass, vocals), Jamie Muir (percussion) and David Cross (b. Plymouth, Devon) (flute, violin).

Oct [13] New line-up makes its live debut in Germany, playing there and in UK for 3 months.

1973 **Feb** Muir leaves, supposedly to enter a Tibetan monastery, and is not replaced.

Apr *Larks' Tongues In Aspic* reaches UK #20. It is generally hailed as the group's best effort for years, with strong lyrics written by Richard Palmer-James.

June With the band midway through a 5-month US tour, *Larks' Tongues In Aspic* makes US #61.

[24] Sinfield makes his solo debut at the Sadlers Wells theater, London, backed by King Crimson.

Oct A short UK tour ends in Bristol, Avon, which is the last King Crimson UK gig for 8 years.

Nov Fripp releases *No Pussyfootin'*, a collaboration with Brian Eno (ex-Roxy Music), which does not chart.

1974 **Apr** *Starless And Bible Black* makes UK #28.

June Band is again on a lengthy (38-date) US tour when *Starless And Bible Black* peaks at US #64.

May [1] The current line-up plays live for the last time, in New York's Central Park. Cross leaves the band.

Sept [25] After completing album sessions with help from ex-members Collins, Cross and McDonald, they decide not to play together again. (Wetton moves to join Uriah Heep; he will later form UK with Bruford and eventually join Asia.)

Oct [18] Fripp announces that King Crimson has disbanded for good. *Red* charts briefly in UK the following week at #45.

1975 **June** Live album *USA*, recorded on 1974 US tour, fails to chart in UK but reaches US #125.

Nov Fripp and Eno collaborate on second album, *Evening Star*, which does not chart.

1976 **Feb** Fripp compiles a retrospective of the band's career, double *A Young Person's Guide To King Crimson*, issued with a companion booklet and including 2 previously unreleased tracks.

May Fripp solo album *Exposure* charts at UK #71 and US #79.

1980 **May** Fripp's *God Save The Queen/Heavy Manners* makes US #110, having failed to chart in UK. The set is entirely instrumental, featuring an electronic style dubbed "Frippertronics".

Nov Fripp forms one-off band, The League Of Gentlemen, with Barry Andrews (keyboards), Sarah Lee (bass) and Johnny Toobad (drums). *Heptaparaparshinokh* does not chart, but is notable for its B-side solo by Fripp, *Marriagemuzic*, playing at 33rpm and 11 mins. 45 secs. long.

1981 **Apr** The League Of Gentlemen's all instrumental eponymous album does not chart in UK but reaches US #90.

May Fripp reunites with Bruford to form Discipline, with top New York session man Tony Levin (who has played on John Lennon's *Double Fantasy* and Peter Gabriel's solo albums) on bass and Adrian Belew (who has worked with Frank Zappa and Talking Heads) on vocals and guitar. Band plays 2 months' live UK and European dates, combining traditional Crimson repertoire with new material.

Oct By the time its first album is released, Discipline's name has changed to King Crimson and the album title becomes *Discipline*. It charts in UK at #41.

Nov *Matte Kudasai* is released as UK single, as album makes US #45.

1982 **July** *Beat*, which includes song lyrics by Belew based on US beat poet Jack Kerouac's work, reaches UK #39 and US #52. Its recording marks a widening rift between Fripp and the others which will lead to another split. Meanwhile the band embarks on a lengthy tour which takes in most of the UK. A gig at the Hammersmith Odeon, London, marks its final UK appearance (but further European dates will follow into 1983).

Dec Fripp records instrumental *I Advance Masked* with Andy Summers of The Police. It does not chart in UK but makes US #60.

1984 **Mar** *Sleepless*, extracted from the forthcoming album and remixed into a 7-min.-plus 12" dance version just fails to crack UK Top 75.

Apr Final King Crimson album *Three Of A Perfect Pair* reaches UK #30 and US #58. The band is inactive after its release and has effectively broken up after completing the recording. (Fripp will continue a production relationship with The Roches, 3 sisters recording for Warner Bros. Belew will record 2 solo albums for Island and form The Bears on IRS. Bruford will record solo, with Patrick Moraz of The Moody Blues and with the band Earthworks, while Levin will concentrate on session work.)

Nov Second album collaboration between Fripp and Summers, *Bewitched*, reaches US #155 but fails to chart in UK. (Fripp will go on to make *God Save The King* with The League Of Gentlemen in 1985, an eponymous album as The League Of Crafty Guitarists in 1986, and *The Lady Or The Tiger* in 1987 in collaboration with Toyah.)

1989 Dec E.G. releases *Box Set*, a CD collection comprising the more popular albums from the King Crimson archive.

THE KINGSMEN

Lynn Easton (saxophone, vocals)
Jack Ely (guitar, vocals)
Mike Mitchell (lead guitar)
Bob Nordby (bass)
Don Gallucci (organ)
Gary Abbott (drums)

1958 Easton and Ely meet as teenagers when playing in school group at the David Douglas school in Portland, OR. Ely joins Easton's band, The Journal Juniors, when their guitarist fails to show for a gig. The 2 eventually form a duo to play locally, then add Mitchell on guitar.
Sept Nordby joins. Another local band breaks up and Easton's parents arrange for the acquisition of their name, The Kingsmen.

1962 Having built a live reputation playing R&B songs and rock instrumentals, and now joined from a rival group by Don Gallucci on keyboards, they are firmly part of the US North-West touring scene which also includes Paul Revere & The Raiders. A revival of Richard Berry's 1956 R&B song *Louie Louie*, learned from a popular local version by Seattle group, The Wailers, is added to their repertoire and becomes their most in-demand live item, sometimes leading to outrageous 45-min. stage versions.

1963 May *Louie Louie* is recorded for $50 in a small Portland studio, with Ely on lead vocals. The following day, Paul Revere & The Raiders record their version in the same studio. The Kingsmen version is placed with local label Jerden, while Revere's is picked up (from Jerden) by major label CBS/Columbia Records, along with group's recording contract.
Aug Friction occurs in the band when Easton announces that he owns the name (because his parents had arranged the paperwork that way), and wants to assume frontman vocal duties, moving Ely to drums. Instead, Ely and Nordby leave, to be replaced by Gary Abbott (drums) and Norm Sundholm (bass). At the same time The Kingsmen's version of *Louie Louie* becomes a big hit in Boston, prompting Wand Records to acquire it from Jerden for national distribution.
Dec *Louie Louie* hits US #2, selling over a million copies. Group appears on TV with Easton miming to Ely's vocals.

1964 Feb [1] Widespread controversy over whether Ely's indistinct vocal on *Louie Louie* is masking off-color lyrics comes to a head when Matthew Welsh, Governor of Indiana, delares the song "pornographic", and asks the State's radio stations to ban it. Berry and Ely are called in to confirm what they wrote and sung respectively. An FCC investigation concludes "the record to be unintelligible at any speed we played it". *Louie Louie* reaches UK #26, and is their sole UK hit. It is a huge underground success with London's mod dancers, whose reaction to it in clubs spurs most UK sales, since BBC radio shuns the record.
Mar *Louie Louie: The Kingsmen In Person*, recorded (apart from the hit single) live at a Portland club, reaches US #20. It will stay on chart for 131 weeks.
May A revival of Barrett Strong's *Money* reaches US #16.
Aug *Little Latin Lupe Lu*, a revival of The Righteous Brothers' US hit of 14 months previously, makes US #46.
Oct *Death Of An Angel* makes US #42.
Nov *The Kingsmen – Vol.2* reaches US #15. It repeats first album's formula of familiar cover versions.

1965 Mar *The Jolly Green Giant*, based on TV canned produce ad, hits US #4.
Apr *The Kingsmen – Vol.3* reaches US #22.
May *The Climb* (about a dance), peaks at US #65.
Sept *Annie Fannie*, celebrating a **Playboy** magazine cartoon character, makes US #47.
Dec Live album *The Kingsmen On Campus* peaks at US #68.

1966 Apr *Killer Joe*, reviving a 1963 US Rocky Fellers hit, makes US #77.
May A continuing seller since 1963 because it has been US radio's most-played "oldie", *Louie Louie* briefly re-enters US chart, at #97.
Sept *15 Great Hits* reaches US #87 in US, and is their final chart entry.
1967 Easton leaves The Kingsmen, which has been through numerous other personnel changes. Band splits permanently 6 months later.
1989 July [14] 432 guitarists break the Guinness world record for most guitarists playing in unison for the longest period of time at the Peach Festival, Gaffney, SC, when they play *Louie Louie* for 30 mins.

THE KINKS

Ray Davies (vocals, guitar)
Dave Davies (vocals, guitar)
Pete Quaife (bass)
Mick Avory (drums)

1958 Ray Davies (b. Raymond Douglas Davies, June 21, 1944, Muswell Hill, London) persuades his parents to buy a guitar for younger brother Dave (b. Feb.3, 1947, Muswell Hill). The brothers play together at a variety of gigs, including a local pub.

1963 Ray meets Alexis Korner after a gig and through his contacts becomes part of London's growing R&B scene led by The Rolling Stones. (Interest in Muddy Waters and Chuck Berry will be a major influence in early Kinks' hits.) Ray splits his time between gigging with blues combo, The Dave Hunt Band, and brother Dave's R&B outfit, The Ravens, which includes Quaife (b. Dec.31, 1943, Tavistock, Devon).
Sept Ray quits The Ravens, who attract the interest of businessmen Robert Wace and Grenville Collins. They become their managers, booking them at society gatherings and country parties. Wace also arranges a meeting with pop impresario Larry Page.
Nov Group records a 5-track demo. Page places 1 song but fails to interest record companies. The demo comes to the attention of American producer Shel Talmy, who has a contract with Pye. Page provides the band's new name, The Kinks and Avory (b. Feb.15, 1944, Hampton Court, London) is added as drummer.
Dec [31] They make their first appearance at the Lotus House restaurant, London.

1964 Jan Contractual problems arise. Kinks management now includes Wace, Collins, Page, tour promoter Arthur Howes and Talmy.
[23] The Kinks signs to Pye and record 4 songs within a week.
Feb First single *Long Tall Sally* is released, without charting.
[7] Intense hype earns the band an appearance on ITV's "Ready Steady Go!" and much press coverage.
Apr Follow-up single *You Still Want Me* also fails to chart.
Aug [2] The Kinks supports The Beatles at the Gaumont cinema, Bournemouth, Hants.
Sept Group's third single *You Really Got Me* rockets to hit UK #1 and US #7. Its insistent riff lays the base for all Kinks' singles in this period.
Oct Debut album *Kinks*, comprising R&B covers and Ray Davies compositions, hits UK #3.
[9] They join the Billy J. Kramer tour.
[19] A 6-date tour of Scotland begins at Glasgow Barrowland.
Nov *All Day And All Of The Night* hits UK #2.
Dec *You Really Got Me* reaches US #29.
[6] The Kinks embarks on a 1-week tour at the New Theatre, Oxford, Oxon., with Gene Pitney.
[11] They come second in **New Musical Express** Pollwinners' Best New Group section and sixth in the British Vocal Group section.
[12] Ray marries 17-year-old Kinks fan, Lithuanian art student Rasa Dicpetri in Bradford, Yorks., with brother Dave as best man.

1965 Jan [1] Group guests on BBC TV's "Beat In The New Year".
[12] They fly to Paris, France, to appear in marathon 3-day TV and radio show "Musicorama".
Ray Davies and manager Larry Page pen *Revenge*, the new "Ready Steady Go!" theme.
Feb *Tired Of Waiting For You* is band's second UK #1. The Kinks appear on ABC TV's "Shindig", as *All Day And All Of The Night* hits US #7.
[23] They perform at the Olympia theater, Paris, France.
Mar *Kinda Kinks* hits UK #3.
[22] Quaife collapses in a cinema in Muswell Hill, and is taken to hospital where he has stitches to a head wound. 4 dates are cancelled.
Apr *Tired Of Waiting For You* hits US #6 as *Kinks-Size* makes US #13.
[11] Band takes part in the annual **New Musical Express** Pollwinners Concert at the Empire Pool, London. *Everybody's Gonna Be Happy* peaks at UK #17. It sees a change of style, influenced by Earl Van Dyke, who has recently toured with The Kinks.

[30] Group embarks on a 21-date twice-nightly UK package tour, with The Yardbirds, Goldie & The Gingerbreads and others, at the Adelphi theater, Slough, Bucks.

May [23] Ray Davies becomes a father.

[25] They pull out of the tour after Dave Davies receives 10 stitches to head injuries after being hit by an errant Mick Avory cymbal during a concert at Cardiff, Wales. The Walker Brothers take their place.

[31] Band continues engagements with a TV show in Paris.

June *Set Me Free*, written for Cilla Black, hits UK #9 and US #23.

[5] They make their first stage show since Davies' injury at the Astoria theater, Rawtenstall, Lancs.

[19] The Kinks makes its US debut, with The Moody Blues, at the Academy of Music in New York, but the rest of the tour is unsuccessful, and is cancelled after 5 dates. (They fail to perform at 1 gig, and will be blacklisted from playing in US for 4 years).

July [18] They begin a tour of Australia.

Aug *Kinda Kinks* makes US #60.

Sept *See My Friend* hits UK #10. *Who'll Be The Next In Line* reaches US #34. The Kinks split from their management, setting up their own company. (This leads to court cases which will not be resolved until 1970.)

[2] Group embarks on 10-day tour of Denmark, Finland and Sweden.

Nov [10] Larry Page issues statement that he has served a writ against managers Wace and Collins over alleged breach of contract and to enforce his claim to part-management of group.

Dec *Kinks Kontroversy* hits UK #9 as *Kinks Kinkdom* makes US #13.

[23] The Kinks appear in the Christmas pantomime version of "Ready Steady Go!"

1966 Jan *Till The End Of The Day* hits UK #8. The Kinks appear on the last broadcast of ABC TV's "Shindig!"

Feb *A Well Respected Man* reaches US #13.

Mar [11-21] Group embarks on a tour of Belgium with Mick Grace of The Cockneys deputizing for Ray Davies, who is suffering from flu and overstrain.

[31] Davies rejoins the band for the BBC TV's "Top Of The Pops", but all other UK dates are cancelled.

Apr With a softer songwriting style, *Dedicated Follower Of Fashion* hits UK #4. Group makes a promo film to support it in the clothes shops of London's Carnaby Street. *Kinks Kontroversy* makes US #95.

[28] Avory falls ill with tonsilitis. Session drummer, and former Tornado, Clem Cattini deputizes at a gig at the Mecca Ballroom, Nottingham, Notts.

May *Till The End Of The Day* peaks at US #50.

June *Dedicated Follower Of Fashion* makes US #36.

[4] Quaife breaks his right foot in a car crash. John Dalton, from The Mark Four, fills in as his replacement for 6 weeks.

[9] Dalton makes his BBC "Top Of The Pops" debut with the band.

[12] Group embarks on a extensive European tour in Madrid, but are refused permission to work as Quaife's name, not Dalton's, is on the work permit.

July Group signs a business management deal with Allen Klein.

[9] *Sunny Afternoon* hits UK #1, deposing The Beatles' *Paperback Writer*.

Aug *The Kinks Greatest Hits!* hits US #9.

Sept Budget compilation album *Well Respected Kinks* hits UK #5. Quaife leaves the band temporarily, his absence covered by John Dalton.

[3] Group embarks on tour of Holland, Italy, Germany, Norway, Denmark and Finland, set to end on Sept.25.

[16] Quaife leaves the band for good, with Dalton staying on as permanent replacement.

Oct *Sunny Afternoon* reaches US #14.

Nov *Face To Face* peaks at UK #12.

Dec *Dead End Street* hits UK #5, but falters at US #73. BBC TV bans the promo film, which features the group leaping in and out of coffins.

[3] Quaife rejoins after a change of heart.

1967 Feb *Face To Face* peaks at US #135.

Apr Group records UK concerts for a future live album.

May *Waterloo Sunset* hits UK #2.

[13] Ray Davies announces he is leaving the band to concentrate on writing and producing. Manager Wace issues a denial.

[16] Davies changes his mind.

July *Mr. Pleasant* peaks at US #80. (It will be their last US chart appearance for 3 years.)

Aug Dave Davies, in brother Ray's shadow for so long, hits UK #3 with solo *Death Of A Clown*. It is, however, written by Ray.

Sept *The Live Kinks* climbs to US #162.

Oct *Something Else* makes UK #35. (It will be the group's last original album to chart in UK.)

Nov *Autumn Almanac* hits UK #3.

Dec Dave Davies' *Susannah's Still Alive* makes UK #20. *Sunny Afternoon*, a budget compilation hits UK #9.

1968 Jan *Live At Kelvin Hall* reflects the rawness of The Kinks' live performance, but sells poorly.

Feb [23] The Kinks plays the Granby Halls, Leics., with Traffic and The Bonzo Dog Doo Dah Band.

Mar *Something Else By The Kinks* makes US #153.

Apr *Wonderboy* reaches UK #36.

[6] Group begins a 20-date twice-nightly UK tour, with The Herd, The Tremeloes, Gary Walker & The Rain and others, at the Granada theater, Mansfield, Notts., set to end Apr. 28 at Coventry theater, W.Midlands.

Aug *Days* makes UK #12.

Oct [20] Group begins a week long cabaret engagement at the Fiesta, Stockton-on-Tees, Cleveland, regarded as a "cabaret circuit graveyard".

Nov *(The Kinks Are) The Village Green Preservation Society* is released. Ray's homage to England, it sells poorly.

1969 Apr *Plastic Man* makes UK #31, partly due to a BBC ban for inclusion of the word "bum" in the lyric. Quaife leaves the band permanently, and is again replaced by Dalton. Ray produces *Turtle Soup* for The Turtles, writes a song a week to feature in BBC TV series "Where Was Spring?" starring Eleanor Bron, and co-writes the theme for the film version of "Till Death Us Do Part".

Oct *Arthur (Or The Decline And Fall Of The British Empire)* is released. Commissioned as a ITV play but never produced, its subject is an ordinary man reflecting on his life. It fails to chart in UK, but makes US #105. Group begins its first US tour in 4 years as support to Spirit after resolving problems with the American Federation of Musicians for The Kinks' "unprofessional conduct".

1970 Jan *Victoria* makes US #33.

Mar *Victoria* peaks at US #62.

June Ray flies from New York to London and back during The Kinks' US tour to re-record lyric in *Lola*, changing "Coca-Cola" to "cherry cola" to appease the BBC and copyright holders.

July Ray announces he is quitting the band again, but changes his mind.

Aug The Kinks' *Lola* hits UK #2 and matches *All Day And All Of The Night*'s 14-week stay.

Oct [15] Ray Davies stars in BBC TV's Play For Today "The Long Distance Piano Player".

Dec *Lola Vs. Powerman And The Moneygoround, Part One* reaches US #35

1971 Jan *Apeman* also spends 14 weeks on chart, hitting UK #5 and climbing to US #45. Again Ray has to re-record a lyric.

Mar Soundtrack album for film "Percy", about a penis transplant, is released.

Apr John Gosling joins the band on keyboards.

Oct *Golden Hour Of The Kinks* reaches UK #21.

Nov Group signs to RCA Records.

1972 Jan *Muswell Hillbillies*, eulogizing Ray's North London childhood, reaches US #100. Group is now re-gaining a large US following, already nostalgic for the 60s. For touring it expands the live line-up, adding a horn section and female backing vocalists.

Apr *The Kinks Kronikles* reaches US #94, a greatest hits package reflecting the group's revived interest in US.

June *Supersonic Rocket Ship* reaches UK #16.

Aug *Everybody's In Showbiz, Everybody's A Star*, a double set with a live album showcasing their US oldies act and a studio album augmented by The Mike Cotton Sound brass ensemble, reaches US #70

Oct Group previews new work as a West End stage show "The Kinks Are The Village Green Preservation Society", and plays London's Rainbow theater at end of a short UK tour.

1973 Mar *The Great Lost Kinks Album* reaches US #145.

May Group opens its own Konk studios in Hornsey, London.

July Ray Davies walks out on his wife and children. After 2 drug overdoses, he announces at a rainy pop festival at London's White City stadium, that he is retiring. He returns within a week. Brother Dave does leave the group, however, returning in 1975.

Dec *Preservation Act I* reaches US #177. The album is an extension of the themes first introduced in "Village Green".

1974 July *Preservation Act II* makes US #114.

Oct The Kinks launch their own short-lived label, Konk, with Claire Hammill's *Stage Door Johnnies*.

1975 June *Soap Opera*, based on TV musical "Starmaker" which Ray had written last year, peaks at US #51.

Dec *Schoolboys In Disgrace* reaches US #45, the group's last for RCA.

1976 June *The Kinks Greatest – Celluloid Heroes* climbs to US #144. The group relocates to US, and signs a deal with Arista.

Nov Dalton leaves, and is temporarily replaced by Andy Pyle.

Dec Press reports a fight between Ray and a Konk act, Café Society's Tom Robinson.

1977 Mar Arista debut *Sleepwalker* reaches US #21.

May *Sleepwalker* makes US #48.

July Ray Davies announces yet again that he is quitting.

Nov *Father Christmas* is released.

Dec Group plays a Christmas show at London's Rainbow theater.

1978 Apr Pyle leaves. (He will form the group United with Gosling.)

May Group begins a 1-month tour to tie in with release of *Misfits*.

June *Misfits* makes US #40. Having recently rejoined, Dalton now leaves permanently. Gosling also quits. They are replaced by Gordon Edwards (keyboards) and Jim Rodford (b. July 7, 1945) (bass).

Sept The Kinks have their first US Top 40 chart success in 8 years with *Rock'N'Roll Fantasy*, which reaches US #30.

Oct *20 Golden Greats* makes UK #19.

1979 Feb The Pretenders have a debut hit with *Stop Your Sobbing*, originally a Kinks album track. (They will also chart with *I Go To Sleep*, another Kinks album track.)

June *(I Wish I Could Fly Like) Superman* reaches US #41. Group begins its first major tour for 3 years.

July Ian Gibbons joins on keyboards.

Sept *Low Budget* makes US #11, and is certified gold.

1980 June *One For The Road* reaches US #14.

July Dave releases first solo album *PL 13603* (UK title: *AFL1-3603* both titled after the disk's catalog number).

Sept *Second Time Around* peaks at US #177.

Dec The Kinks, now comprising the Davies brothers, Avory, Rodford and Gibbons, begin a short UK tour.

1981 July Dave releases second solo album *Glamour*. It makes US #152, as The Kinks' single *Better Things* reaches US #46.

Sept Ray is divorced from his second wife, Yvonne.

Oct Band plays New York's Madison Square Garden for the first time. The public learns of Ray's romance with The Pretenders' Chrissie Hynde.

Nov *Give The People What They Want* reaches US #15. *Destroyer* peaks at US #85.

1982 Jan Ray begins work on project "Return To Waterloo" which will be shown on C4 TV, and be subsequently released on video and album.

Sept The Kinks participate in the 3-day US Festival at San Bernardino.

1983 Feb Hynde's (and Ray's) daughter Natalie is born.

May *Come Dancing* hits US #6, aided by exposure on MTV.

Aug *State Of Confusion* reaches US #12.

Sept *Come Dancing* reaches UK #12, the group's first UK single success in 11 years.

Oct Old *You Really Got Me*, at UK #47, wins out over new *Don't Forget To Dance*, which makes UK #58 (but also US #29).

Nov *Kinks Greatest Hits – Dead End Street* peaks at UK #96. Dave releases third solo album *Chosen People*.

1984 May Hynde leaves Ray for Simple Minds' Jim Kerr. An unofficial biography of The Kinks by Johnny Rogan is published. *Word Of Mouth* is released.

Nov An official biography of The Kinks by Jon Savage is published.

1986 Ray appears in film "Absolute Beginners" as Patsy Kensit's father. Band signs a deal with London Records, releasing *Think Visual*.

July *Come Dancing With The Kinks – The Best Of The Kinks 1977-1986* makes US #159.

1987 Jan *Think Visual* makes US #81, as the band embarks on US tour. Virgin Video releases a compilation of Kinks promotional videos. PRT releases all of the Kinks' Pye albums on CD.

1988 Mar MCA US-released *Live – The Road*, recorded during their US summer tour of 1987, makes US #110.

1989 The Kinks begin a US tour with new additions, keyboardist Mark Haley and and drummer Bob Henrit (b. May 2, 1945).

Aug *Shangri-La*, a various artists compilation of Kinks songs featuring The Cardiacs, The Fleshtones, Cud and The Patch-Up Boys (a pseudonym for The Go-Betweens), is released.

Sept *The Ultimate Collection* makes UK #35.

Nov *UK Jive* climbs to US #122.

1990 Jan [17] The Kinks are inducted into the Rock'N'Roll Hall Of Fame at the fifth annual dinner at the Waldorf Astoria in New York. (The original line-up are all present, including Quaife now an airbrush artist living in Ontario, Canada.)

Apr Ray Davies and The Kinks are bestowed with the Special Contribution to British Music honor at the annual Ivor Novello Awards at the Grosvenor House, London.

KISS

Gene Simmons (bass, vocals)
Paul Stanley (guitar, vocals)
Ace Frehley (guitar, vocals)
Peter Criss (drums, vocals)

1972 Band is formed part-time in New York by Simmons (b. Chaim Witz, Aug.25, 1950, Haifa, Israel), a teacher, and Stanley (b. Paul Eisen, Jan.20, 1950, Queens, New York), acquaintances from an earlier part-time group. Criss (b. Peter Crisscoula, Dec.27, 1947, Brooklyn, New York) is discovered through his own ad in **Rolling Stone**, and they rehearse as a trio while continuing day jobs. Frehley (b. Paul Frehley, Apr.22, 1951, Bronx, New York) is recruited as guitarist from an ad in **Village Voice**.

1973 Jan [30] Band plays its first gig, at the Coventry club in Queens. Deliberately, its immediate impact is visual and theatrical.

Dec [31] They make their Academy of Music, New York, debut with Blue Öyster Cult, Iggy Pop and Teenage Lust.

1974 Jan [8] Casablanca Records signs the band.

Feb Debut album, *Kiss*, is launched with nationwide promotion – including marathon kissing competitions. It climbs to US #87, staying on the chart for 23 weeks.

June *Kissin' Time* makes US #83.

Nov Sophomore album *Hotter Than Hell* peaks at US #100.

1975 Apr Through constant touring, Kiss builds a strong following. *Dressed To Kill* climbs to US #32.

May *Rock'N'Roll All Nite* peaks at US #68.

Nov *Alive!*, recorded on tour, hits US #9. Extracted from it, *Rock'N'Roll All Nite* reaches US #12.

1976 Feb [20] 4 sets of Kiss footprints are placed on the sidewalk outside Grauman's Chinese theater in Hollywood, CA.

Apr *Destroyer* reaches US #11 and is the group's first platinum selling disk. *Shout It Out Loud* climbs to US #31.

May [15-16] Group plays at the Hammersmith Odeon, London, during a brief 4-date UK visit.

June *Flaming Youth* stalls at US #74 as *Destroyer* makes UK #22 and *Alive!* reaches UK #49.

Aug *The Originals*, a repackaging of the first 3 albums and containing a comic book history of Kiss, peaks at US #36.

Nov Atypical ballad, written and sung by Criss, *Beth*, with B-side *Detroit Rock City*, hits US #7. Group plays UK again but interest is limited and its image is taken less seriously as the band only conducts interviews in full make-up. *Rock And Roll Over* enters US chart. It will make #11, go platinum, and have a 45-week stay on the chart.

Dec [11] Frehley receives an electric shock during a concert at Lakeland, FL. He is not seriously hurt.

1977 Feb *Hard Luck Woman* makes US #15.

May *Calling Dr. Love* reaches US #16.

June Marvel Comics publishes **The Kiss Comic Book** based on the masked men.

July *Christine Sixteen* makes US #25.

Aug [25-27] Kiss plays 3 shows at Los Angeles' Forum, which are recorded for forthcoming *Kiss Alive II*.

Sept *Love Gun* hits US #4, but the title track falters at #61.

Nov *Alive II* hits US #7 and becomes the group's fourth platinum disk. It charts for 1 week in UK, at #60.

1978 Jan A live version of 1976 hit *Shout It Out Loud* peaks at US #54.

Apr *Rocket Ride* makes US #39.

May *Double Platinum*, a 2-record set of Kiss "classics", makes US #24.

Oct The 4 members simultaneously issue solo albums which are launched in a high profile campaign, with each cover featuring a matching portrait of the artist in full make-up. Each album is shipped platinum, but sales fail to match expected demand. Simmons' effort fares best, reaching US #22, followed by Frehley (#26), Stanley (#40) and Criss (#43).

[30] NBC TV airs the animated cartoon "Kiss Meets The Phantom Of The Park", in which the heroes foil a mad scientist gone beserk in an amusement park.

1979 May Kiss returns with *I Was Made For Lovin' You* which makes US #11 and is the group's UK Singles chart debut at #50.

June *Dynasty* hits US #9 and reaches UK #50.

Sept *Sure Know Something* makes US #47.

1980 May [17] Criss leaves the group to pursue a solo career.

June *Kiss Unmasked*, the first to miss the US Top 30, peaks at #35 and makes UK #48. *Shandi*, from the album, reaches US #47.

July [25] Band plays New York's Palladium, with new drummer Eric Carr (b. July 12, 1950).

Aug Kiss embarks on a European tour.

1981 Jan [12] The RIAA donates some 800 rock albums to the Library of Congress. Included is Kiss' *Alive!*.

Casablanca releases *Best Of The Solo Albums*.

Dec *Music From The Elder*, a concept album unlike much of the band's previous material, reaches US #75 and fails to go gold. It makes UK #51. Taken from it, *A World Without Heroes* reaches US #56 and UK #55.

1982 Frehley leaves the group and is replaced by Vinnie Vincent. (Frehley will resurface with his own group, Frehley's Comet.)

June *Killers* makes UK #42.

Nov *Creatures Of The Night* makes US #45 and UK #22. It is dedicated by band to Casablanca label boss Neil Bogart, who died from cancer.

1983 Apr *Creatures Of The Night* makes UK #34.

Aug Kiss cancels 3-day tour of Argentina when the extremist Free Fatherland Nationalist Commando movement threatens to stop tour even if it "goes so far as to cost the very lives of that unfortunate band".

Sept [18] Kiss reveals all when members appear on MTV without make-up.

Oct *Lick It Up* begins a new phase in the band's career. Now signed to the Mercury label, the album cover features the group without make-up. It achieves gold at US #24, and hits UK #7.

Nov *Lick It Up* makes US #66 and UK #31.

1984 Mark St. John replaces Vincent (who will later form Vinnie Vincent's Invasion).

Oct *Animalize*, returns the group to platinum status, making US #19 and UK #11. *Heaven's On Fire* reaches US #49 and UK #43.

Dec Simmons stars as the villain opposite Tom Selleck's hero in film "Runaway".

1985 St. John leaves, and is replaced by Bruce Kulick.

Oct *Asylum* makes US #20 and UK #12. *Tears Are Falling* reaches US #51 and UK #57.

1986 May Kiss contributes *Runaway* on the various artists album *Hear 'N' Aid*, for heavy metal music's fund-raising activities for famine relief.

June Simmons stars in film "Never Too Young To Die", with Robert Englund and George Lazenby. (He also stars with Ozzy Osbourne in "Trick Or Treat" and Rutger Hauer in "Wanted Dead Or Alive".)

1987 June Ace Frehley's *Frehley's Comet* makes US #43.

Oct *Crazy Crazy Nights* peaks at US #65.

Nov *Crazy Nights* is Kiss' biggest UK hit, peaking at #4, but stalls at US #65. *Crazy Nights* reaches US #18 and hits UK #4.

1988 Jan [30] Ballad *Reason To Live* makes US #68 and UK #33.

July [8] Group embarks on summer tour of North America with Cheap Trick, at the Forum, Halifax, Canada.

Aug Simmons starts the Simmons record label.

[28] 29-date North American tour ends at the Forum, Los Angeles, CA.

Sept *Turn On The Night* makes UK #41. Kiss plays the opening night of the newly relocated Marquee in London's Charing Cross Road.

Dec Greatest hits collection *Smashes, Thrashes And Hits* reaches US #21 and UK #62.

1989 Jan [14] *Let's Put The X In Sex* makes US #97.

Mar Frehley's Comet's *Live Plus One*, a live album released on Megaforce, makes US #84.

June New Frehley's Comet's studio set *Second Sighting* makes US #81.

Nov *Hide Your Heart* peaks at UK #59 as new studio album *Hot In The Shade* reaches US #29 and UK #35. Frehley's Comet's *Trouble Walkin'* makes US #102.

1990 Jan *Hide Your Heart* single, originally recorded by Bonnie Tyler and then Motley Crue and Robin Beck, reaches US #22.

Mar [31] Ballad *Forever*, written by Stanley with Michael Bolton, makes UK #65.

Apr [21] *Forever* hits US #8, the group's first Top 10 hit in 14 years.

May [4] Group begins 6-month North American tour in Lubbock, TX.

June [30] *Rise To It* stalls at US #81.

THE KNACK

Doug Fieger (vocals, guitar)
Berton Averre (guitar)
Prescott Niles (bass)
Bruce Gary (drums)

1978 May Group forms in Los Angeles, CA, with the intention of presenting a tight update of the mid-60s beat group style – a sound which comes to be dubbed "power pop". Fieger (b. Detroit, MI) is former bassist of Detroit group Sky, and Gary (b. Apr.7, 1952, Burbank, CA) is ex-Jack Bruce Band. Niles (b. May 2, New York, NY) and Averre (b. Dec.13, Van Nuys, CA) are fellow veterans of Los Angeles session work.

1979 Feb Huge live success on Southern California club scene has 13 record

labels bidding to sign them, with Capitol succeeding. They are teamed with Blondie's producer Mike Chapman, with whom they produce an album's-worth of songs, with little overdubbing (early mid-60s style) in only 11 days, and for $18,000.

Aug Debut *My Sharona* is an instant US smash, topping the chart for 6 weeks. It sells over a million inside 2 weeks, adding a second million in less than a month in US. In UK it hits #6. *Get The Knack* performs similarly, topping US chart for 5 weeks. It will sell over 5 million copies worldwide by the end of 1979. In UK, it stalls at #65.

Nov *Good Girls Don't*, also from debut album, reaches US #11, but stalls at UK #66.

1980 Mar Constant Beatles comparisons and associations contribute to an early critical backlash against the group, which in turn hits their record sales: *But The Little Girls Understand* reaches US #15, and sales of 600,000 are only a fraction of first album's total. *Baby Talks Dirty* is extracted, and makes US #38.

Apr Hasty follow-up *Can't Put A Price On Love* peaks at US #62.

1981 Nov *Pay The Devil (Ooo Baby Ooo)* reaches US #67. Taken from *Round Trip*, it fizzles out at US #97, convincing the group members that they have lost the knack. They play a final US tour, then disband. Fieger forms Taking Chances, and the others stay together as The Game, but these ventures will not renew commercial success.

1983 Aug Fellow Detroiters Was (Not Was) employ Fieger as a guest vocalist on their album *Born To Laugh At Tornados*.

1991 Feb Re-formed Knack, with Fieger, Averre, Niles and new drummer Billy Ward, debut with *Serious Fun* on Charisma, produced by Don Was, but it fails to chart.

GLADYS KNIGHT & THE PIPS

Gladys Knight (vocals)
Merald "Bubba" Knight (vocals)
William Guest (vocals)
Edward Patten (vocals)

1951 Knight (b. May 28, 1944, Atlanta, GA), whose parents are singers in Wings Over Jordan Gospel choir, wins $2,000 for singing *Too Young* on US TV's "Ted Mack's Original Amateur Hour". She has already sung gospel widely around the South with The Morris Brown choir.

1952 Sept [4] After an impromptu performance together at a 10th birthday party for brother Merald (b. Sept.4, 1942, Atlanta), Gladys, Merald and sister Brenda form a vocal group with cousins William (b. June 2, 1941, Atlanta) and Elenor Guest, singing gospel and ballads at family and church functions (at the Mount Mariah Baptist church in Atlanta).

1957 Having been persuaded by another cousin, James "Pips" Woods (whose nickname they purloin and who becomes their manager), to turn professional, the quintet cuts its first (unsuccessful) disk, *Whistle My Love*, for Brunswick. The Pips also tour with Sam Cooke, B.B. King and Jackie Wilson.

1959 Brenda Knight and Elenor Guest both leave the group to get married, and are replaced by 2 male vocalists: a further cousin, Edward Patten (b. Aug.2, 1939, Atlanta) and Langston George.

1960 Group records a 1952 Johnny Otis song, *Every Beat Of My Heart*, for Atlanta-based Huntom label, initially with little success, but eventually with enough sales interest for Huntom to sell the master to larger R&B independent Vee-Jay in Chicago.

1961 May Group is signed by Bobby Robinson's New York-based Fury label, and re-records *Every Beat Of My Heart*.

June Both versions of *Every Beat Of My Heart* chart at the same time. The newer recording on Fury peaks at US #45, but the Vee-Jay original, credited to The Pips, is still climbing.

July *Every Beat Of My Heart* on Vee-Jay hits US #6 and tops R&B chart for a week. The group is in huge demand for tour and club dates.

1962 Feb *Letter Full Of Tears*, on Fury, reaches US #19. UK singer Billy Fury's cover will make UK Top 20 a few weeks later.

Apr *Operator* peaks at US #97, and shortly afterwards George quits, leaving the group as a quartet. (It will subsequently remain a quartet. Knight herself will depart for some 2 years to marry and have a baby. The Pips will work as back-up session singers.)

1964 June Knight returns and the group signs to another independent R&B label, Maxx Records. *Giving Up*, written by Van McCoy, makes US #38.

Sept *Lovers Always Forgive* makes US #89, following which the label goes bankrupt and leaves the group without an outlet.

1966 Still busy on the live circuit, with a tight, sharply choreographed act behind Knight's gospel-influenced soul leads, Gladys Knight & The Pips are booked as special guests on a Motown touring package, and on the strength of audience reception, offered a recording contract by label boss Berry Gordy Jr. They sign to Motown Records, which places them on Soul label, alongside Jimmy Ruffin and Junior Walker & The All-Stars. First release *Just Walk In My Shoes*, produced by Harvey Fuqua and Johnny Bristol, fails.

1967
May Group switches to producer Norman Whitfield for *Take Me In Your Arms And Love Me*, which makes US #98.
July Their UK chart debut is *Take Me In Your Arms And Love Me* which, aided by massive airplay on UK pirate radio stations, reaches #13.
Aug *Everybody Needs Love* makes US #39.
Dec Gladys Knight & The Pips' major chart breakthrough comes with their original version of Whitfield and Barrett Strong's *I Heard It Through The Grapevine* (later one of the most successful and re-recorded songs in the Motown catalog). It hits US #2 and sells over 1 million copies, held from the top by The Beatles' *Hello Goodbye*. It also tops US R&B chart for 6 weeks, but makes only UK #47. Group also has its first US hit album, *Everybody Needs Love*, including *Grapevine* , at #60.
[3] Group plays at the Saville theater, London, supporting Joe Tex.

1968
Mar Another Whitfield/Strong song, *The End Of Our Road* (like *Grapevine* later also revived by Marvin Gaye) reaches US #15.
July *It Should Have Been Me* peaks at US #40, while *Feelin' Bluesy* reaches US #158.
Sept *I Wish It Would Rain*, released only 7 months after The Temptations' US #4 version, climbs to US #41.

1969
Feb *Silk'N'Soul* makes US #136.
Mar [7] Band performs at the Grand Gala Du Disque, Amsterdam, on a bill including The Moody Blues.
Apr Ashford & Simpson-penned and produced *Didn't You Know (You'd Have To Cry Sometime)* makes US #63.
Sept Group's unexpected, gospel-tinged revival of Shirley Ellis' 1964 dance hit, *The Nitty Gritty*, makes US #19.
Dec Another gospel-based song, Whitfield/Strong's *Freedom Train*, reaches US #17. Both it and the previous hit are included on **Nitty Gritty**, which climbs to US #81.

1970
Apr *You Need Love Like I Do (Don't You)*, again penned by Whitfield and Strong, makes US #25.
May Compilation album *Gladys Knight & The Pips' Greatest Hits* reaches US #55.

1971
Feb After a gap between releases, during which the group has ceased working with Whitfield (producer of 9 of their last 10 hits), it is teamed with producer Clay McMurray for *If I Were Your Woman*, written by McMurray with Pam Sawyer and Leon Ware. It hits US #9 and becomes the group's second US million-seller.
June [6] They guest on final edition of CBS TV's "Ed Sullivan Show".
July *I Don't Want To Do Wrong*, the first single A-side to be part-written by group members (with producer Bristol and Catherine Schaffner), reaches US #17. It is taken from *If I Were Your Woman*, which reaches US #35 – their highest-placed album to date.

1972
Jan McMurray-penned and produced *Make Me The Woman That You Go Home To* climbs to US #27.
Feb *Standing Ovation* reaches US #60.
Apr *Help Me Make It Through The Night*, the group's revival of Kris Kristofferson's ballad (a million-seller for Sammi Smith in 1971), reaches US #33.
July First Motown single *Just Walk In My Shoes* is reissued in UK, and reaches US #35 – the group's first UK chart entry in 4 years.
Dec *Help Me Make It Through The Night* hits UK #11 (their biggest UK hit to date).

1973
Jan Having nursed a growing feeling that they have not been getting the support and career-development from Motown which has been accorded to its other leading acts, despite a string of hits, they decide to leave when their contract expires. They are quickly signed by New York-based Buddah Records.
Mar A 1968 album track, Bacharach/David ballad *The Look Of Love*, is picked by UK Motown as follow-up to *Help Me Make It Through The Night*, and reaches UK #21.
Apr A number by Mississippi songwriter Jim Weatherly, *Neither One Of Us (Wants To Be The First To Say Goodbye)*, produced by Joe Porter, is released as the group leaves Motown. It is their second-biggest success on the label, and third million-seller, hitting US #2 (behind Vicki Lawrence's *The Night The Lights Went Out In Georgia*).
May *Neither One Of Us* is their first Top 10 album, hitting US #9.
June From the album, *Daddy Could Swear, I Declare*, co-written by Gladys and Bubba Knight with producer Bristol, reaches US #19, while *Neither One Of Us (Wants To Be The First To Say Goodbye)* makes UK #31.
July Buddah label debut is Weatherly's *Where Peaceful Waters Flow*, which reaches US #28.

Sept Another album on Soul, *All I Need Is Time*, featuring tracks cut shortly before the group's Motown exit, reaches US #70. Title track, produced by Porter, reaches US #61.
Oct *Midnight Train To Georgia*, another Weatherly-written song (originally *Midnight Plane To Houston*, in which form he has cut it himself), tops US chart for 2 weeks, and spends 4 weeks at R&B #1. A soul classic, it is another million-seller, and the first of 4 consecutive gold singles on Buddah.

1974
Jan *I've Got To Use My Imagination*, a million-seller, hits US #4. It is taken from the group's debut Buddah album **Imagination**, which hits US #9, and also includes *Midnight Train To Georgia*. The album earns a gold disk for a half million sales, and is the first to feature the group as co-producers (with Tony Camillo, Kenny Kerner and Richie Wise).
Mar [2] Group wins Best Pop Vocal Performance By A Duo, Group Or Chorus for *Neither One Of Us (Wants To Be The First To Say Goodbye)* and Best R&B Vocal Performance By A Duo, Group Or Chorus for *Midnight Train To Georgia* at the 16th annual Grammy awards.
[28] They embark on a European tour.
Apr Similarly styled ballad *Best Thing That Ever Happened To Me*, another Weatherly song from **Imagination**, hits US #3 and is a further million-seller. Double compilation album **Anthology**, on Motown, reaches US #77, while Soul issues **Knight Time**, containing unissued material by the group. It makes US #139.
May Group's soundtrack album from film "Claudine", featuring songs written and produced by Curtis Mayfield, reaches US #35 and earns another gold disk.
July *On And On*, taken from **Claudine**, hits US #5 to become the group's fourth consecutive gold single.
Aug *Between Her Goodbye And My Hello* is a final single on Soul, and climbs to US #57.
Dec *I Feel A Song (In My Heart)* reaches US #21, and is taken from **I Feel A Song**, which peaks at US #17 and earns a gold disk.

1975
Apr *Love Finds Its Own Way* makes US #47. Knight gets married, for the second time, to ex-social worker Barry Hankerson, and moves her family home to Detroit.
May Final Soul album, *A Little Knight Music*, stalls at US #164.
June A medley of *The Way We Were/Try To Remember*, from the long-running off-Broadway musical "The Fantasticks!", recorded live at a club in Detroit, and prefaced by a spoken passage from Knight, hits UK #4 and reaches US #11. *I Feel A Song* becomes the group's first UK chart album, reaching UK #20.
July [10] Group begins a 4-week run of "The Gladys Knight And The Pips Show" on NBC TV in a summer replacement slot. The 1-hour shows mix music with comedy and guest stars.
Aug After UK Top 10 hit *The Way We Were* (which sets the standard of sophisticated supper club soul on which the group will concentrate for the rest of its Buddah career), the label's UK licensee tries the UK market with earlier US Buddah hits which originally failed in UK. First of these is *Best Thing That Ever Happened To Me*, which now hits UK #7.
Oct *Money* makes US #50.
Dec David Gates-penned *Part Time Love* reaches US #22 and UK #30, while **2nd Anniversary** (a reference to completing 2 successful years with Buddah) reaches US #24.

1976
Mar *The Best Of Gladys Knight And The Pips*, a compilation of Buddah singles, hits US #6 and reaches UK #36.
June *Midnight Train To Georgia* belatedly hits UK #10 after being extracted from the compilation album – the second Buddah single UK hit long after its original US success.
Aug *Make Yours A Happy Home* reaches UK #35.
Oct Knight makes her movie acting debut in "Pipe Dreams", a romantic drama set in the Alaskan oilfields, produced by and co-starring husband Hankerson. The Pips do not feature in acting roles, but join her in singing 8 songs on the soundtrack.
Nov *So Sad The Song*, from *Pipe Dreams*, makes US #47 and UK #20.
Dec Soundtrack album *Pipe Dreams* peaks at US #94.

1977
Jan *Nobody But You*, another song from *Pipe Dreams*, reaches UK #34.
June [10-11] They play the third Kool Jazz Festival in San Diego, CA.
July *Still Together* reaches US #51 and UK #42. The title is ironic since throughout 1977-79 Gladys Knight & The Pips will be unable to record together, even though they continue to perform live as a team. The forced separation on disk is due to complex legal problems involving several record labels (the group is trying to move to CBS, and still has a $1.7 million suit hanging over it from the end of the Motown days, as well as a dispute over royalties with Motown). Previously recorded material is released and the untypical and uptempo *Baby Don't Change Your Mind* (the group's last US hit single on Buddah), a blend of

traditional Motown with a hint of the new disco style, reaches US #52 and hits UK #4, their biggest UK release.

Oct *Home Is Where The Heart Is* reaches UK #35.

Nov TV-advertised double album *30 Greatest*, on K-Tel, hits UK #3.

1978 **Apr** *The One And Only*, theme song from the Henry Winkler film of the same title, reaches UK #32.

July *Come Back And Finish What You Started*, in the uptempo mode of *Baby Don't Change Your Mind*, reaches UK #15.

Sept *The One And Only* peaks at US #145.

Oct *It's A Better Than Good Time* reaches UK #59.

1979 Knight records an enforced solo album, *Miss Gladys Knight* for Buddah, The Pips secure a deal with Casablanca Records and release 2 albums, *At Last ... The Pips* and *Callin'*, without her. All fail to chart.

1980 **July** Complex legalities finally solved, Gladys Knight & The Pips reunite for recording and sign a new deal with CBS/Columbia. *Landlord*, 1 of only 2 Columbia US singles successes, peaks at US #46 and hits R&B #3. Ashford & Simpson-produced Columbia album *About Love* reaches US #48.

Sept Uptempo disco-aimed *Taste Of Bitter Love* makes UK #35.

Oct *A Touch Of Love*, another UK TV-advertised compilation on K-Tel, this time of the group's ballads, reaches UK #16.

Dec Dance-oriented track *Bourgie Bourgie* reaches UK #32, after finding major success in UK discos, but fails in US.

1981 **Oct** *Touch* reaches US #109.

1982 **Nov** [25] Knight appears at the World Music Festival in Jamaica at the Bob Marley Performing Center near Montego Bay. Also on the bill are Aretha Franklin, The Clash, Squeeze, The Grateful Dead and others.

1983 **May** Leon Sylvers III-produced *Save The Overtime (For Me)* hits US R&B #1 for a week. It makes US #66 but fails in UK.

July *Visions* is the group's biggest-selling album in US for 8 years, reaching US #34 and earning a gold disk.

1984 **Feb** A third UK TV-advertised compilation album, *The Collection – 20 Greatest Hits*, on Starblend Records, reaches UK #43.

1985 **Apr** *Life* reaches US #126.

Knight stars with Flip Wilson in US TV sitcom "Charlie And Company". The group leaves CBS and signs to MCA Records.

1986 **Jan** Knight, along with Stevie Wonder and Elton John, is one of the "friends" to contribute to Dionne Warwick's *That's What Friends Are For*, which tops US chart for 4 weeks, becomes the best-selling single of the year, with sales over a million, and reaches UK #16.

June Knight teams with Bill Medley to sing *Loving On Borrowed Time*, the love theme from Sylvester Stallone movie "Cobra", whose soundtrack makes US #100.

Dec [31] Knight & The Pips join Air Supply, Freddie Jackson and Melba Moore for CBS TV's "Happy New Year America".

1987 **Feb** [24] Knight wins Best Pop Performance By A Duo Or Group With Vocal with Dionne Warwick, Elton John and Stevie Wonder for *That's What Friends Are For* at the 29th annual Grammy awards.

Sept [28] Knight joins Smokey Robinson to guest for a week on US TV show "$10,000 Pyramid" (known in UK as "The Pyramid Game").

1988 **Feb** [27] *All Our Love* tops US R&B chart and makes US #39 as parent album *All Our Love* makes UK #80.

Mar With *Love Overboard* reaching US #13, having topped R&B chart Jan.23, Gladys Knight & The Pips celebrate 30 years of recording.

1989 **Jan** [14] They win Best Vocal Group category at the NAACP 21st Image Awards.

[30] Group wins Favorite Soul/R&B Duo Or Group category at the 16th annual American Music Awards.

Feb [22] Group wins Best R&B Performance By A Duo Or Group With Vocal for *Love Overboard* at the 31st annual Grammy awards. (This will be the group's swan song as Knight splits from The Pips. Patten and Guest will work in the ice cream business, while brother Merald will continue to tour with Gladys.)

Mar [30] Knight makes her solo debut at Bally's in Las Vegas, NV.

July Now signed as a solo artiste to MCA, Knight's Narada Michael Walden-produced title theme to the latest James Bond movie "Licence To Kill" hits UK #6, though it will not chart in US.

Oct TV-advertised *The Singles Album* reaches UK #13.

BUDDY KNOX

1955 Knox (b. Wayne Knox, Apr.14, 1933, Happy, TX), Jimmy Bowen (b. Nov.30, 1937, Santa Rita, NM) and Don Lanier, all students on athletics scholarships at West Texas university, form The Rhythm Orchids to play college dances and parties, with Knox and Lanier on guitars and Bowen stand-up bass.

1956 In a 3-day session at Norman Petty's recording studio in Clovis, NM, where they meet and recruit drummer Dave Alldred, the trio records 3 of its own songs. Local Dumas, TX, businessman Chester Oliver presses 1,500 copies of a single, coupling *Party Doll*, sung by Knox (and written by him at age 15) and *I'm Sticking With You*, sung by Bowen. The record sells out around Dumas and Amarillo (helped by Amarillo DJ Dean Kelly playing *Party Doll*), and the trio decides to form its own label, Triple-D after KDDD in Dumas where Bowen has been a DJ, to fill continuing local demand for it.

1957 **Jan** Lanier's sister in New York sends a copy of the single to Phil Kahl at Roulette Records, which signs the group and flies it to New York to record additional tracks. Roulette markets both sides of the original separately with new B-sides, so *Party Doll* is released, credited to Buddy Knox & The Rhythm Orchids, while *I'm Sticking With You* credits Jimmy Bowen & The Rhythm Orchids.

Mar *Party Doll*, the first self-penned rock'n'roll record, tops US chart, selling over a million. It is joined on the survey by 3 hasty cover versions by Steve Lawrence (#10), Wingy Manone (#56), and Roy Brown (#89). *I'm Sticking With You* reaches US #14.

Apr [12] Group stars in Alan Freed's "Rock'N'Roll Easter Jubilee" show at New York's Brooklyn Paramount.

[18] Knox joins the Tank Corps for 6 months' active duty as a US Army Reserve lieutenant. (Roulette organized a 20-song session in New York with him and the group, to avoid a future shortage of tracks.)

May *Party Doll* reaches UK #29.

June With Knox in the Army, the follow-up is credited to "Lieutenant Buddy Knox". Another group original, *Rock Your Little Baby To Sleep*, reaches US #23.

Oct The Hawaiian-flavored *Hula Love*, written by Knox as a teenager and closely based on the 1911 song *My Hula, Hula Love*, makes US #12.

Nov Knox and The Rhythm Orchids perform *Hula Love* in rock movie "Jamboree".

Dec Alldred leaves the group to become "Dicky Doo" in Dicky Doo & The Don'ts and is replaced by Chico Hayak.

1958 **Mar** *Swingin' Daddy* climbs to US #80.

Aug *Somebody Touched Me*, a revival of 1954 Ruth Brown R&B hit, reaches US #22. It is the last single to credit The Rhythm Orchids. (Bowen will move to record production, initially with Chancellor. In the mid-60s, he will become an MOR producer working with Bing Crosby, Frank Sinatra, Dean Martin, Kenny Rogers and others, later running his own Amos label and by the 80s becoming Nashville president of MCA Records.)

1959 **Jan** Double-sided *That's Why I Cry/Teasable Pleasable You*, with Bobby Darin guesting on piano, climbs to US #88/#85.

May *I Think I'm Gonna Kill Myself* peaks at US #55, his last hit for Roulette. A Knox original, it will be covered by Waylon Jennings.

1961 **Jan** After 2 flops, Knox moves to Liberty, where Snuff Garrett produces a remake of the 6-year-old Clovers R&B hit *Lovey Dovey*, which reaches US #25.

Mar Knox unearths *Ling Ting Tong*, a 1955 Charms/Five Keys R&B novelty, which peaks at US #65 and is his last US chart appearance.

1962 **Aug** Knox makes a surprise return to UK chart with *She's Gone* (#45).

1968 **May** After unsuccessful recording on Ruff and Reprise labels, Knox signs to United Artists with his style more firmly aimed at the C&W market. *Gypsy Man* is a US country hit, without crossing to the pop chart, and a fair-selling album of the same title follows.

1972 He appears in country music movie "Traveling Light", with Waylon Jennings, Bobby Bare and Jerry Allison of The Crickets, with whom he co-writes the soundtrack.

1974 Knox becomes a Canadian citizen and settles on a farm near Winnipeg, but spends much of the year touring the country and rock'n'roll nostalgia circuits. He becomes an active businessman, co-owning a club in Vancouver, Canada, and having real estate in Seattle, WA.

1977 **Apr** He tours UK with contemporaries Jack Scott, Warren Smith and Charlie Feathers and is recorded live with them at London's Rainbow theater by EMI, for *Four Rock'N'Roll Legends*. (He will later record for Redwood Records and his own Sunnyhill label but releases will be sporadic. In the 80s he will work regularly and successfully as a live act in Canada, Europe and US.)

1989 The Rhythm Orchids reunite for a concert in Canyon, TX.

KOOL & THE GANG

James "J.T." Taylor (lead vocals)
Robert "Kool" Bell (bass)
Ronald Bell (saxophones)
Claydes Smith (guitar)
George Brown (drums)
Dennis "Dee Tee" Thomas (sax)
Robert "Spike" Mickens (trumpet)

1964 Group is formed by Bell (b. Oct.8, 1950, Youngstown, OH), whose father has played with jazz pianist Thelonious Monk, with fellow students at Lincoln high school, Jersey City, NJ, as jazz combo The Jazziacs. Original line-up features Bell, his brother Ronald (b. Nov.1, 1951, Youngstown, OH), Brown (b. Jan.5, 1949, Jersey City), Mickens (b. Jersey City), Thomas (b. Feb.9, 1951, Jersey City), with Woody Sparrow (guitar) and Rick Westfield (keyboards).

1967 Sparrow leaves, and is replaced on guitar by Smith (b. Sept.6, 1948, Jersey City). Finding little earning power in jazz, the band moves toward R&B, and a local Jersey City promoter finds it regular gigs backing soul acts, under the name The Soul Music Review. Band still plays jazz in its spare time in churches and coffee bars, frequently jamming with jazzmen Leon Thomas and Pharoah Saunders.

1968 Group becomes an R&B attraction first as The New Dimensions, then The New Flames, known colloquially on the local scene as Kool & The Flames. To avoid confusion with James Brown's Famous Flames, a switch is made to Kool & The Gang.

1969 While playing New York club dates, the band meets writer/producer Gene Redd, who is setting up his own label, De-Lite Records. Impressed with the group's tightness as a live unit, and its original material, Redd offers a recording deal.
Oct With the youngest members just graduated from high school, the band debuts for De-Lite with self-penned funk instrumental *Kool And The Gang*, which makes US #59 (and R&B #19).

1970 **Jan** Another instrumental, *The Gang's Back Again*, peaks at US #85. Debut album *Kool And The Gang* is released.
July *Let The Music Take Your Mind* reaches US #78.
Oct *Funky Man* makes US #87 (and R&B #16).

1971 **Apr** Live album *Live At The Sex Machine* is the band's first charted album, at US #122. It includes group compositions and versions of Dionne Warwick's *Walk On By* and Jim Webb song *Wichita Lineman*.
Oct *The Best Of Kool And The Gang*, an optimistic early compilation of singles to date, peaks at US #157.

1972 **Jan** Wholly instrumental *Live At P.J.'s*, reaches US #171.

1973 **Apr** *Good Times* makes US #142.
Oct *Funky Stuff*, the band's first major commercial breakthrough, makes US #29 (and R&B #5).
Dec *Wild And Peaceful*, including *Funky Stuff*, is entirely written, produced and arranged by the band, and reaches US #33, earning a gold disk for a half million sales, during a 60-week chart stay.

1974 **Jan** Instrumental album *Kool Jazz*, gathering up the most jazz-oriented tracks from 3 previous albums, reaches US #187.
Mar From album *Wild And Peaceful*, the band's first million-selling single is *Jungle Boogie*, which hits US #4.
June *Hollywood Swinging* hits US #6, and is a second million-seller.
Oct *Higher Plane*, from the band's next album, peaks at US #37.
Dec *Light Of Worlds* reaches US #63, earning the band's second gold album in a 34-week chart run.

1975 **Jan** Band visits Europe for the first time, playing at the MIDEM music industry festival in Cannes, France, followed by a UK tour. Tracks from their Rainbow theater gig, London, are recorded for future album use.
Feb *Rhyme Time People*, co-written by the band with their early live collaborators Thomas and Saunders, and taken from *Light Of Worlds*, peaks at US #63.
May Compilation *Kool And The Gang Greatest Hits!* reaches US #81.
July *Spirit Of The Boogie*, the title track from forthcoming album, reaches US #35. B-side *Summer Madness*, from *Light Of Worlds*, collects airplay in its own right (and is featured in movie "Rocky"), and is later chart-listed as a double A-side.
Oct *Spirit Of The Boogie*, again written and produced by the band, reaches US #48.
Dec Extracted *Caribbean Festival* makes US #55.

1976 **May** *Love And Understanding*, which couples 5 new tracks with live versions of *Hollywood Swinging*, *Summer Madness* and *Universal Sound* from the early 1975 London Rainbow concert, reaches US #68. Title track *Love And Understanding* makes US #77. Otha Nash (trombone) and Larry Gittens (trumpet) join the band temporarily.

1977 **Jan** *Open Sesame* peaks at US #110, while the title track makes #55. (It is the group's last US hit single for 3 years – a symptom of their early sound now being eclipsed by the exploding disco genre.)
July [2-4] Group performs the Brute Music Festival, Callaway, MD, in front of 100,000 fans.

1978 **Jan** Band's *Open Sesame* is included on the soundtrack album of movie "Saturday Night Fever", which hits US #1 for 25 weeks and UK #1 for 18 (eventually selling over 25 million copies).
Feb *The Force* reaches US #142, the band's lowest chart ebb. Westfield leaves. As they search for a fresh dance direction, Bell meets soul vocalist James Taylor (b. Aug.16, 1953, South Carolina), and invites him to join the line-up. A chance meeting in the studio with jazz-funk keyboardist and producer Eumir Deodato (1973 hitmaker with *Also Sprach Zarathustra*), results in him becoming the group's new producer (a role he will hold through to 1982). Earl Toon, Jr. also joins the band on keyboards in Westfield's place (but will not remain a permanent member). These various changes will result in a simpler more commercial sound, including ballads.

1979 **Feb** [15] *Saturday Night Fever* wins Album Of The Year at the 21st annual Grammy awards.
Dec The first Deodato-produced, Taylor-fronted Kool & The Gang album, *Ladies Night*, reaches US #13 and is the group's first million-selling platinum album. Title track hits US #8, selling over a million to earn a gold disk, and hits UK #9.

1980 **Mar** *Too Hot*, also from the album, hits US #5 and reaches UK #23.
July A third single from *Ladies Night*, *Hangin' Out* makes UK #52.
Dec Ronald Bell/Kool & The Gang-penned *Celebration* hits UK #7.

1981 **Feb** *Celebration* hits US #1 for 2 weeks and is the band's biggest-selling single, earning a platinum disk for over 2 million US sales. (The song has been used as the welcoming-home anthem for the American hostages returned from captivity in Iran on Jan.26, and the theme song of the 1981 US Superbowl, later becoming the theme for the Oakland A's baseball team.) *Celebrate*, from which it is taken, hits US #10 and is also a platinum-seller.
Mar Divorce-themed swayer *Jones Vs. Jones*, also from *Celebrate*, reaches UK #17.
June *Take It To The Top*, a third single from from the million-selling album, reaches UK #15, while *Jones Vs. Jones* makes US #39.
Dec *Steppin' Out* reaches UK #12, while *Take My Heart (You Can Have It If You Want It)* climbs to US #17.

1982 **Jan** Uptempo *Get Down On It* hits UK #3, their first UK Top 5 success. *Something Special*, which includes both this and the 2 Dec. US/UK hit singles, reaches US #12 (the band's third consecutive platinum album), and hits UK #10 – their first UK chart album.
Feb *Steppin' Out* peaks at US #89.
Mar *Take My Heart (You Can Have It If You Want It)* reaches UK #29.
May *Get Down On It* hits US #10.
Aug Bell/Taylor/Gang-composed *Big Fun* reaches UK #14.
Oct *Big Fun* makes US #21.
[15-18] Band plays 4 nights at London's Apollo Victoria theater, followed by live UK dates in Manchester and Birmingham.
Nov *As One*, their last Deodato-produced album, makes US #29 (a gold album) and UK #49, as *Ooh La La La (Let's Go Dancin')* hits UK #6.

1983 **Jan** *Hi De Hi, Hi De Ho* reaches US #29, as *Ooh La La La (Let's Go Dancin')* makes US #30.
June UK-only compilation *Twice As Kool*, of the group's hit singles to date, hits UK #4.

1984 **Jan** *Straight Ahead* reaches UK #15, and is taken from *In The Heart*, produced by the group itself, which makes US #29 (another gold disk) and UK #18.
Feb *Joanna*, a Taylor/Smith ballad from *In The Heart*, hits US #2 (behind Culture Club's *Karma Chameleon*) and is a million-seller, becoming the band's biggest US Singles chart success after *Celebration*.
Mar *Joanna/Tonight* is released as a UK double A-side from the album, and hits #2, the group's highest-placed UK single.
May *Tonight*, released independently of *Joanna*, climbs to US #13, while the album's title song *(When You Say You Love Somebody) From The Heart* hits UK #7.
Nov While the band is on tour in UK, Bell and Taylor take part in the recording of Band Aid's *Do They Know It's Christmas?*, in aid of African famine relief. (This will top UK chart over Christmas and become the biggest-selling single of all time in UK – over 3 million copies.)
Dec Jim Bonneford-produced light dance pop chugging *Fresh* reaches UK #11.

1985 **Jan** *Emergency* reaches US #28 and UK #47.
Mar *Misled* hits US #10 and reaches UK #28.

June *Fresh*, belatedly issued as a US single, hits #4.
Sept Bell/Taylor ballad *Cherish* hits US #2 for 3 weeks, despite beach located video promo clip, behind Dire Straits' *Money For Nothing*. It is another million-seller and hits UK #4.
Nov Extracted title track from *Emergency* reaches US #18 and UK #50.
Dec Band tours UK, with major dates at Birmingham's National Exhibition Centre, the Brighton Centre and London's Wembley Arena.

1987 Jan [24] Taylor/Bell/Gang-written *Victory* hits US #10, having reached UK #30. It is taken from *Forever*, which reaches US #25. Both are produced by Khalis Bayyan (who is actually Ronald Bell, having adopted a Moslem name in accordance with his faith. Brother Robert becomes Amir Bayyan). Curtis "Fitz" Williams is now on keyboards, with Clifford Adams and Michael Ray as trombonist and second trumpeter respectively. The album sleeve also notes the death of ex-member Rick Westfield.
Feb The group begins a US tour.
Mar *Stone Love* reaches UK #45.
May [2] *Stone Love* hits US #10.
July [25] *Holiday* peaks at US #66.
Oct [31] *Special Way* peaks at US #72.

1988 Feb Taylor leaves the band to pursue a solo career. He is replaced by a trio of new lead singers – Gary Brown, Skip Martin (ex-Dazz Band) and Dean Mays.
Aug Compilation album *Greatest Hits* is released, including 3 new tracks, one of which is the band's new single *Rags To Riches*.
Nov UK-only *The Singles Collection* reaches UK #28.

1989 Mar Building his solo career as James "J.T." Taylor, he hits US R&B #2 with soulstress Regina Belle duet ballad *All I Want Is Forever*, also included on the soundtrack to current "Spinal Tap" movie.
Apr [3] Kool & The Gang begins a short UK tour at the Edinburgh Playhouse, Scotland, ending Apr.8 at London's Hammersmith Odeon.
July Now signed to Mercury Records, Taylor-less Kool & The Gang struggle commercially as album *Sweat* fails to cross over.
Dec Taylor's debut album for MCA, *Master Of The Game* is released and is also found on the current *Ghostbusters II* soundtrack album.

1990 Sept [1-3] Group takes part in "Rock'N'Roll's Main Event" at Glen Helen Regional Park in San Bernardino, CA, with Jerry Lee Lewis, The Commodores, Fats Domino, Don McLean, Johnny Rivers, Rick Derringer and Edgar Winter and others.
Oct [27] Among 4 Kool & The Gang retrospectives issued during the year, *Kool Love*, released by UK TV-advertising label Telstar, peaks at UK #50.

KRAFTWERK

Ralf Hutter (keyboards, drums, vocals, woodwind, strings)
Florian Schneider-Esleben (keyboards, drums, vocals, woodwind, strings)
Wolfgang Flur (electronic drums)
Klaus Roeder (violin, guitar)

1970 Hutter (b. 1946, Krefeld, Germany) and Schneider-Esleben (b. 1947, Dusseldorf, Germany), having met while at Dusseldorf Conservatory, join Organisation, influenced by the new wave of German keyboard groups. Debut album *Tone Float*, produced by Conny Plank and recorded at a studio inside a Dusseldorf oil refinery, is released through RCA. Hutter and Schneider-Esleben leave to form their own band, Kraftwerk (German for "powerplant") with Klaus Dinger and Thomas Homann.

1971 Band's debut album *Highrail*, on German Philips label, attracts critical attention, but few sales, and Dinger and Homann leave to form Neu.

1972 *Var* is released in Germany. UK Vertigo releases *Kraftwerk*, a compilation of material from the group's first 2 albums.

1973 Nov *Ralf And Florian* is released. Self-produced, with help from Plank, it contains a mix of experimental synthesizer music with traditional string and woodwind parts.

1974 Hutter and Schneider add Flur and Roeder to create a 4-piece band.
Nov *Autobahn* is released. Its centerpiece is the 22min. 30sec. title track about a journey on the German highway system.

1975 May Receiving unexpected airplay in both UK and US, an edited version of *Autobahn* reaches UK #11 and US #25. The album hits UK #4 and US #5. (Its rhythmic synthesized style will open the door for many futurist and Eurodisco acts in the next 10 years.)
Oct Reissued *Ralf And Florian* makes US #160. Roeder is replaced by Karl Bartos. Band leaves Philips/Vertigo to form its own Dusseldorf-based Kling Klang label licensed through EMI.
Nov *Radio Aktivitaet* is released in Germany.

1976 Jan Its English language equivalent album *Radio-Activity*, released by

Capitol, reaches US #140. Vertigo issues compilation album *Exceller 8*.

1977 May *Trans-Europe Express*, recorded at their own Kling Klang studio, peaks at US #119.
Band tours UK, appearing on stage in robotic style, wearing mannequin outfits.

1978 May *The Man-Machine* (German title: *Mensch Maschine*) hits UK #9, selling over 100,000 copies, but makes only US #130.
June *Trans Europe Express* makes a belated US #67.
Nov *Neon Lights* peaks at UK #53.

1981 May After a 2-year UK chart absence, *Pocket Calculator* makes UK #39.
Computer World reaches UK #15 and US #72 (it will later influence Neil Young's *Trans*), as the band embarks on a world tour with a transportable stage version of their Kling Klang studio.
July Double A-side *Computer Love/The Model* makes UK #36.

1982 Jan Re-issued, and by now both a dancefloor and airplay favorite, *Computer Love/The Model* tops UK chart.
Feb *Trans-Europe Express* makes UK #49.
Mar *Showroom Dummies* reaches UK #25 as the group begins UK tour.

1983 With the boom in rhythm boxes and portable tape machines, many electro pop bands emulate Kraftwerk's rhythm patterns. (One of the more successful is Afrika Bambaataa's *Planet Rock*, which borrows the *Trans Europe Express* riff.)
Apr *Techno Pop* is scheduled for release (catalogue number: EMC 3407), but cancelled without official reason. Group also cancels a UK tour in its traditional inexplicable style.
Aug *Tour De France*, commissioned by the organizers of the European bicycle race as the official theme, is released from 4-song album *Set* and reaches UK #22.

1984 Sept Following its exposure in movie "Breakdance", *Tour De France* is remixed, peaking now at UK #24.

1985 June *Autobahn*, reissued by Parlophone, makes UK #61.

1986 Nov First EMI album *Electric Café* climbs to UK #58. Released in US through Warner Bros., it peaks at #156. Its sleeve features computer graphics from the New York Institute who subsequently produce an entirely computer-generated video for the title cut.

1987 Jan Kraftwerk performs well-received UK live dates as second single *Telephone Call* joins unsuccessful *Musique Non-Stop*.

1990 Feb After another traditionally lengthy activity gap, Kraftwerk re-emerges to perform 4 dates in Genoa, Italy.
Nov Another planned album release date comes and goes, as the band continues recording, Fritz Hijbert having replaced Wolfgang Flur.

BILLY J. KRAMER AND THE DAKOTAS

Billy J. Kramer (vocals)
Mike Maxfield (lead guitar)
Robin MacDonald (rhythm guitar)
Ray Jones (bass)
Tony Mansfield (drums)

1962 Dec Kramer (b. William Howard Ashton, Aug.19, 1943, Bootle, Merseyside), a British Rail apprentice fitter during the day, is spotted singing at Liverpool's Cavern club with The Coasters, who have just been voted #3 favorite group in local **Mersey Beat** magazine poll, by Brian Epstein, who buys Kramer's contract from manager/promoter Ted Knibbs, for £50.

1963 Jan [6] Kramer signs to 6-year management deal with Epstein's NEMS company. The Coasters, who want to keep their day jobs, leave to team up with local singer Chick Graham. Failing to obtain the services of Liverpool's Remo 4 as a backing group, Epstein teams Kramer with Manchester group The Dakotas. Maxfield (b. Feb.23, 1944, Manchester, Gtr.Manchester), MacDonald (b. July 18, 1943, Nairn, Scotland), Jones (b. Oct.22, 1939, Oldham, Gtr.Manchester) and Mansfield (b. Anthony Bookbinder, May 28, 1943, Salford, Gtr.Manchester) have been playing professionally since Feb.1962.
Feb After rapid rehearsals and a show at the Cavern, Kramer And The Dakotas leave for a 3-week season at the Star-Club in Hamburg, Germany. They hone their stage act before returning to UK.
Mar Group is signed to Parlophone by EMI's George Martin. Liverpool songwriter Ralph Bowdler offers *She's My Girl* to record, but because of the Epstein connection, the group has access to John Lennon and Paul McCartney's songs and chooses *I'll Be On My Way*, on which The Beatles have passed, and *Do You Want To Know A Secret*, just recorded by The Beatles for their first album.
[7] Group participates in the "Mersey Beat Showcase" concert with The Beatles, Gerry & The Pacemakers and The Big Three.
June Debut single *Do You Want To Know A Secret?* hits UK #2 behind

The Beatles' own *From Me To You*. On the single, the "J." is inserted into Kramer's name for the first time to distinguish him from other singers named Billy. (This idea is credited to John Lennon.)

Group embarks on UK tour supporting The Beatles.

Bad To Me, written by Lennon specifically for Kramer, tops UK chart for 2 weeks but is dethroned by The Beatles' *She Loves You*. The Dakotas hit UK #18 with instrumental *The Cruel Sea*, written 18 months earlier by Maxfield who chose the title at random when he spotted Nicholas Monserrat's novel on a bookshelf.

[10] Group appears on the 100th edition of UK TV show "Thank Your Lucky Stars" with Cliff Richard, The Shadows, The Searchers, Brian Poole & The Tremeloes and Alma Cogan.

Sept Kramer wins **Melody Maker** poll award as UK's Best Newcomer Of The Year.

Oct [27] Group appears on UK TV's variety show, "Sunday Night At The London Palladium", 2 weeks after The Beatles own debut.

Nov [5] Kramer visits New York on a promotional visit with Epstein. *I'll Keep You Satisfied*, group's third Lennon/McCartney-penned single, hits UK #4, promoted by a 20-date UK tour titled "The Billy J. Kramer Pop Parade", with The Fourmost and Johnny Kidd & The Pirates.

Dec *Listen To Billy J. Kramer* reaches UK #11.

[24] "The Beatles Christmas Show", with Billy J. Kramer & The Dakotas, Rolf Harris, The Barron Knights, Tommy Quickly, The Fourmost and Cilla Black, mixing music and pantomime, opens at London's Finsbury Park Astoria. It runs until Jan.11.

1964 Feb [29] Group begins a 20-date twice-nightly UK package tour with Gene Pitney and Cilla Black at the Odeon cinema, Nottingham, Notts.

Mar Released on single against Epstein's advice but at Kramer's insistence, US song by Mort Shuman and John McFarland, *Little Children*, gives the group its biggest UK seller so far, topping UK chart after selling 78,000 copies in a day. It dethrones another of Epstein's acts, Cilla Black, but is displaced by The Beatles' *Can't Buy Me Love*.

Apr [26] Band plays the annual **New Musical Express** Poll Winners Concert at the Empire Pool, Wembley, London, with The Beatles, Cliff Richard And The Shadows, The Rolling Stones, and other UK names.

June *Little Children* hits US #7 and is a worldwide million-seller, as the group tours US and appears on US TV's "Ed Sullivan Show".

July *Bad To Me*, having originally flopped in US, is reissued as B-side to *Little Children*. It picks up airplay in its own right and replaces its A-side in US Top 10, at #9. Jones leaves The Dakotas, MacDonald switches to bass and Mick Green, ex-Johnny Kidd & The Pirates, joins on rhythm guitar.

[9] Group plays before the Queen Mother at the Royal Agricultural Hall, Stoneleigh Abbey, Kenilworth, Warwicks.

Aug *From A Window*, a new Lennon/McCartney song, hits UK #10. *I'll Keep You Satisfied* reaches US #30 and *Little Children* makes US #48.

Oct *From A Window* makes US #23.

Dec [16] "The Music Of Lennon-McCartney", a 50-min. tribute featuring Billy J. Kramer, Peter Sellers, Marianne Faithfull, Cilla Black, Peter And Gordon, Lulu, Esther Phillips and Richard Anthony, airs on UK commercial TV in London. (The rest of the UK sees the program the following night.)

1965 Jan *It's Gotta Last Forever* proves an ironic title when it is unexpectedly a UK chart failure.

Feb *Billy J. Plays The States*, a 4-track live EP recorded on stage at Long Beach, CA, is released in UK, to moderate sales. *It's Gotta Last Forever* reaches US #67.

May [25] Group participates in the British Song Festival at the Dome, Brighton, E.Sussex.

June Group's last hit is Burt Bacharach's *Trains And Boats And Planes* which makes UK #12 losing to Bacharach's own version, which hits UK #4 but is not released as a single in US, where Kramer's makes #47.

Aug [22] Maxfield leaves The Dakotas to concentrate on songwriting activities, and signs with Brian Epstein. The Dakotas decide to remain a trio after his departure.

Oct [8] Group embarks on 18-date twice-nightly "Star Scene 65" UK tour, with bill-toppers The Everly Brothers, Cilla Black and others at Bedford Granada, Beds. It will end Oct.28 at the ABC cinema, Wigan, Gtr.Manchester.

Nov *Neon City* fails to chart. Relying on outside songwriters for its material and closely associated with the now-lapsed Mersey boom, the group is failing to develop with the rapid changes on the pop scene and among its audience.

1966 May [30] They begin a 2-week tour of Poland.

Aug [7] "Gather No Moss", filmed before a live audience in Santa Monica, CA, premieres in UK at the Futurist cinema, Birmingham,

W.Midlands. Group finds more live work on Northern UK club and cabaret circuit where recent nostalgia proves a strong popularity factor. Mansfield leaves and Frank Farley (ex-Johnny Kidd sideman) joins. *You Make Me Feel Like Someone* is the last release credited to the group.

1967 Jan *Sorry*, a solo by Kramer although he still plays live with The Dakotas, does not chart and his contract is not renewed by EMI.

[28] The Dakotas embark on 9-date twice-nightly UK tour, with the headlining The Four Tops, The Merseys, Madeline Bell, The Remo Four and The Johnny Watson Band, at the Royal Albert Hall, London, ending Feb.5 at the De Montfort Hall, Leicester, Leics.

Apr Kramer covers The Bee Gees *The Town Of Tuxley Toy Maker* on a one-off release for Reaction Records.

1968 Mar The Dakotas split and Kramer continues his cabaret career as a soloist. He marries shortly afterwards and releases a cover of Nilsson's *1941* on NEMS Records, which gains much UK airplay but no chart place. (He will also revive Lennon and McCartney's *A World Without Love* on NEMS later in the year, before moving to MGM Records for another unsuccessful one-off, *The Colour Of My Love*).

1971 June Cover of Neil Diamond's *And The Grass Won't Pay No Mind*, is a Polydor release under Kramer's real name, William Howard Ashton.

1973 Kramer tours US with a new group of Dakotas as part of Richard Nader's "British Re-Invasion Show". (Maintaining his performing career in clubs in UK and Europe, and joining the occasional major nostalgia concert, Kramer remains an active performer. Despite lack of chart success, he continues to record: 11 singles appear on 7 different UK labels, including 2 in a brief return to EMI, between 1973 and 1983.)

L.L. COOL J.

1981 Having started rapping at age 9 when his grandfather buys him some DJ equipment, Cool J. (b. James Todd Smith, 1968, St. Albans, Queens, New York, NY), is a mature 13-year-old when he starts sending out demos taped in his home basement.

1984 Nov Impressed by the demos, Rick Rubin, a senior at New York University in the process of setting up his own Def Jam record label, signs Cool J. and releases *I Need A Beat*, the label's first 12" single.

1985 Having established his personality name (standing for Ladies Love Cool James), he performs first on film, when *I Can't Live Without My Radio* is featured in first rap movie "Krush Groove". This leads to a 50-city tour with New York City Fresh Festival, also featuring Run D.M.C., The Fat Boys, Whodini and Grandmaster Flash.

Nov A distribution deal with CBS/Columbia Records, sees international release of debut album *Radio*. Cool J. also contributes his song *Can You Rock It Like This* to Run D.M.C.'s *King Of Rock*.

Dec [23] A fight breaks out at a Baltimore, MD., roller-rink during a Cool J. show: 1 person is trampled underfoot, 3 are shot.

1986 Feb On his first UK visit he is spotlighted as a new rap hero by the music press and media. *I Can't Live Without My Radio* fails to chart, but *Radio* makes US #46.

[15] *Radio* peaks at UK #71.

Apr Cool J. supports Run D.M.C. on their "Raising Hell" tour.

1987 June He headlines the "Def Jam '87" tour of US and UK with Public Enemy, Eric B., Doug E. Fresh and Whodini. A near-riot occurs at sell-out London Hammersmith Odeon gigs, creating media interest.

July [4] *I'm Bad* peaks at UK #71.

[11] *Bigger And Deffer* tops US R&B chart for 11 weeks.

[18] *I'm Bad* peaks at UK #84.

Aug *Bigger And Deffer* hits US #3 and UK #54. It includes the first-ever rap ballad, *I Need Love*, recorded with West Coast US rap group Los Angeles Posse.

Sept [12] *I Need Love*, from the album, becomes his first major hit single, reaching US #14, and topping US R&B chart 2 weeks later.

Oct *I Need Love* hits UK #8, confirming Cool J. as one of the leading voices in the progressive rap movement.

Nov [21] *Go Cut Creator Go* peaks at UK #66.

1988 Feb Double A-side *Going Back To Cali/Jack The Ripper* reaches US #31 and UK #37, as Cool J. continues to tour.

Nov [30] Cool J. plays the first rap concert in Côte d'Ivoire, Africa. Halfway through the concert people faint, fights break out, and the stage is stormed and the show is ended.

1989 June *I'm That Type Of Guy* makes UK #43.

July *Walking With A Panther* makes UK #43.

[15] *I'm That Type Of Guy* tops US Rap chart.

[22] *Walking With A Panther* tops US R&B chart.

Aug [9] He begins 21-date US tour at Bloomington, MN, set to end in Miami, FL, on Sept.10.

11] Singer David Parker, band technician Gary Saunders, bodyguard Christopher Tsipouras, all members of Cool J.'s retinue, are charged with first-degree criminal sexual conduct after allegedly raping a 15-year-old girl who attends an after-concert party after going backstage on a pass won in a Minneapolis radio concert.

1990 **Apr** [7] Cool J. takes part in Farm Aid IV at the Hoosier Dome, Indianapolis, IN.

June *To Da Break Of Dawn*, from rap-themed "House Party" movie, is released.

Oct [13] *Mama Said Knock You Out* debuts at peak UK #49.

Nov [3] *Mama Said Knock You Out* reaches US #16.

Dec [1] *Around The Way Girl/Mama Said Knock You Out* makes UK #41.

[11] Cool J. kicks off national "The Cool School Video Program", which encourages children to stay in school by taking part in a make-your-own-video contest, at Martin Luther King middle school in Dorchester, MA.

1991 **Jan** He participates in The Peace Choir, an all-star remake of John Lennon's *Give Peace A Chance*.

Mar [2] *Around The Way Girl* hits US #9.

Michael J. Fox/James Woods movie "The Hard Way", in which Cool J. plays a cop, opens throughout US.

[16] Reissued *Around The Way Girl* now makes UK #36.

PATTI LaBELLE

1961 LaBelle (b. Patricia Holt, May 24, 1944, Philadelphia, PA), forms girl vocal group The Blue Belles in Philadelphia, with Nona Hendryx, Sarah Dash and Cindy Birdsong. (Holt and Birdsong have been members of The Ordettes, from high school, and Dash and Hendryx of The Del Capris). Together, they perform at local gigs organized by promoter Bernard Montague, which leads to them meeting producer Bobby Martin and signing via him to new label Newtown Records.

1962 **May** *I Sold My Heart To The Junkman*, first recorded unsuccessfully by The Four Sportsmen for Newtown, whose vocal track Martin wipes from the original, adding new vocals by the girls, climbs to US #15.

1963 **Nov** Holt is on lead vocals so Martin boosts her billing in the group, and she becomes Patti LaBelle. After some unsuccessful singles, ballad *Down The Aisle (The Wedding Song)*, credited to Patti LaBelle & The Blue Belles, makes US #37.

1964 **Feb** Parkway Records, part of Cameo, Philadelphia's leading independent label, signs the group. Their version of standard ballad *You'll Never Walk Alone*, from musical "Carousel" (a UK chart-topper by Gerry & The Pacemakers only 3 months earlier), climbs to US #34.

Dec Another standard ballad, Irish *Danny Boy (Londonderry Air)*, makes US #76.

1965 **Dec** After a year of non-action, the group signs to Atlantic and records new material. *All Or Nothing* climbs to US #68.

1966 **Jan** [11] Band begins a short UK tour at the Cromwellian club in London. (It also appears on ITV's "Ready Steady Go!" Jan.14 and "Thank Your Lucky Stars" Jan.22.)

June [24] 46-date US tour of one-nighters opens in Greensboro, NC, with Otis Redding, Sam And Dave, Percy Sledge, and others.

Dec *Take Me For A Little While* reaches US #89. (It will be covered by several UK groups, including The Koobas, who just miss the UK Top 50 with it, and will also be revived by another Atlantic act, Vanilla Fudge.)

1967 **Dec** Birdsong leaves the group to join The Supremes in place of Florence Ballard. The Blue Belles continue as a trio, but leave Atlantic when no more hits are forthcoming.

1970 With the trio's career at a low ebb, Vicki Wickham, a UK expatriate who first met the girls as a UK TV "Ready Steady Go!" executive when they guested on the show during a 1966 promotional visit, becomes their manager. She abbreviates the group name to LaBelle and updates its image and material.

1971 **Oct** In a new deal with Warner Bros., the trio cuts *LaBelle*, which gains good reviews but does not chart, despite a US tour supporting The Who. More successful is the album on which they sing back-ups to Laura Nyro on a collection of group oldies, *Gonna Take A Miracle*, which reaches US #46.

1972 On second Warner album *Moonshadow*, 6 of the songs are written by Hendryx, and the group's sound has developed into a sleek rock/funk hybrid. It still fails to chart.

1973 Group unveils a new visual image while headlining at New York's Bottom Line club: tight, shiny lam "space" suits, reminiscent of the glitter-pop costumes sported by many groups currently on UK chart.

1974 **July** They sign to Epic and record *Nightbirds* with producer Allen Toussaint in New Orleans, backed by The Meters.

Dec *Nightbirds* is released in US, with single *Lady Marmalade*, which becomes a big club and disco hit.

1975 **Mar** *Lady Marmalade*, with its distinctive French-language chorus line "voulez-vous coucher avec moi ce soir?" tops US chart for a week and is a million-seller. It is written by Bob Crewe and Kenny Nolan (who, almost uniquely, have also penned the song it has deposed at US #1, Frankie Valli's *My Eyes Adored You*). *Nightbirds* hits US #7 and earns the group a gold disk.

Apr *Lady Marmalade* is the group's only UK hit, peaking at #17.

June *What Can I Do For You?* reaches US #48.

Oct *Phoenix* peaks at US #44.

1976 **Oct** *Chameleon* makes US #94, after which the trio splits, with LaBelle and Hendryx following diametrically opposed musical directions. (All 3 will have subsequent solo careers; Dash finding least success.)

1977 **Nov** Remaining signed to Epic, Patti LaBelle's solo album *Patti LaBelle* reaches US #62.

1978 **July** *Tasty* peaks at US #129.

1979 **May** *It's Alright With Me* creeps to US #145.

1980 **May** Her last Epic album, *Released*, makes US #114.

1981 **Oct** She signs to Gamble and Huff's Philadelphia International label, but despite hometown support (LaBelle still lives in Philadelphia with her husband and 3 children), *The Spirit's In It* only climbs to US #156.

1982 **Sept** [9] She opens on Broadway, co-starring with Al Green in Vinnette Carroll's gospel musical "Your Arm's Too Short To Box With God", at the Alvin theater. (The scheduled limited engagement of 30 shows will be extended to 80 after rave reviews.)

1984 **Mar** After a long quiet period, but still signed to Philadelphia International, LaBelle's *If You Only Knew* reaches US #46. Its parent album *I'm In Love Again* makes US #40, and in a 35-week chart stay sells over a half million copies in US, earning a gold disk.

Apr LaBelle guest duets with Bobby Womack on *Love Has Finally Come At Last*, extracted from his album *The Poet II* on Beverly Glen label. It reaches US #88.

Sept LaBelle plays Big Mary in film "A Soldier's Story".

1985 **May** She signs to MCA Records, and records 2 tracks for soundtrack of film "Beverly Hills Cop", starring Eddie Murphy. From the soundtrack album, *New Attitude* is released as a single, and reaches US #17.

July [13] She performs prominently at the Live Aid spectacular in her hometown of Philadelphia.

Aug Her second "Beverly Hills" Cop track, *Stir It Up*, makes US #41.

1986 **May** [17] *On My Own* tops US R&B chart.

June [14] *On My Own*, a Burt Bacharach/Carole Bayer Sager ballad duetted with Michael McDonald (in separate studios on separate coasts – they do not meet until performing the song together on Johnny Carson's "Tonight Show" on US TV), tops US chart for 3 weeks. *Winner In You* tops US R&B chart for 8 weeks. The record hits UK #2, behind Spitting Image's novelty *The Chicken Song*, though it will hit #1 on airplay-integrated Network chart.

July [19] *Winner In You*, her first album for MCA, including the duet, also tops US chart for a week, turning platinum, and makes UK #30.

Aug *Oh, People*, with video shot by Godley & Creme, reaches UK #26.

Sept [26] *Oh People* makes US #29.

Oct LaBelle stars in NBC TV movie "Unnatural Causes".

Dec [1] She receives an Award of Merit from the Philadelphia Art Alliance.

On My Own is named Top R&B Single on **Billboard** magazine's year end survey.

1987 **Feb** *Something Special (Is Gonna Happen Tonight)*, from Bette Midler/Shelley Long-starring film "Outrageous Fortune", makes #50 on US R&B chart.

Aug *Just The Facts*, written and produced by Jimmy Jam and Terry Lewis for Dan Aykroyd/Tom Hanks film "Dragnet", is another US R&B hit at #33.

1989 **Aug** [24] LaBelle plays the Acid Queen in an all-star performance of The Who's "Tommy" at the Universal Amphitheater, Universal City, CA, with Elton John, Steve Winwood, Phil Collins and Billy Idol.

Oct [21] LaBelle sung love theme *If You Asked Me To* from soundtrack to current James Bond movie "Licence To Kill" makes US #79.

Nov [15] LaBelle undertakes an extensive US tour in Minneapolis, MN, set to end Mar.11, 1990 in New York, in support of her recent MCA release.

1990 **Jan** [15] LaBelle is honored with a Lifetime Achievement Award at the 6th annual CORE (Congress Of Racial Equality) awards dinner at the Sheraton Center, New York.

[18-19] During current tour, LaBelle performs at the Fox theater, Atlanta, GA, with James Ingram.

Feb Motown releases *Forgotten Eyes*, a charity single featuring 100 artists including Labelle. (All proceeds from the record will go to benefit Retinitis Pigmentosa International.)
Dec [4] LaBelle is inducted into Philadelphia's Music Foundation Hall Of Fame. She is honored with a bronze plaque on Broad Street.

'91 Mar LaBelle duets with country star Ronnie Milsap for the track *Love Certified* on his latest album *Back To The Grindstone*.
[12] She co-hosts the fifth annual Soul Train Awards at the Shrine Auditorium, Los Angeles with Dionne Warwick and Luther Vandross.
Apr [6] LaBelle takes part in NBC TV's "Bob Hope's Yellow Ribbon Party" to celebrate the homecoming of American troops from the Gulf.
May [16] GRP Records releases *Am I Cool, Or What?*, a homage to cartoon feline Garfield, featuring LaBelle's *I Love It When I'm Naughty*.

YNDI LAUPER

'68 Lauper (b. June 20, 1953, New York, NY) moves from Williamsburg suburb to Queens with her mother, brother and sister, after her parents divorce.
'70 She leaves home to hitch-hike through Canada with her dog Sparkle.
'71 She spends a year at Vermont College studying art.
'74 Back in New York, Lauper joins Long Island band, Doc West, as lead singer, then covers band Flyer, where she will spend the next 3 years.
'77 Lauper loses her voice after intense vocal performing. Doctors say she will never sing again, but she regains her voice through vocal training with Katie Ayresta.
'78 She meets sax/keyboards player John Turi and they form Blue Angel.
'79 Blue Angel signs to Polydor.
'80 *Blue Angel* fails to chart. Band splits after management and label squabbles. Lauper finds work in clothes store, Screaming Mimi's.
'81 Lauper meets David Wolff, her future manager and beau, while working at Miho's bar in New York, singing current Top 40 songs.
'82 She is declared bankrupt in court case relating to her Blue Angel days.
'83 Wolff secures Lauper a deal with CBS subsidiary, Portrait, and she begins work on her debut album, with help from Eric Bazilian and Rob Hyman of Philadelphia, PA, band The Hooters.
Dec Debut album *She's So Unusual* is released.
'84 Mar *Girls Just Want To Have Fun*, penned by Robert Hazard, hits US #2, held off #1 by Van Halen's *Jump*, and UK #2, where it is beaten by Frankie Goes To Hollywood's *Relax*.
Apr [5] Lauper's video "Girls Just Want To Have Fun" wins Best Female Video at the second annual American Video Awards.
June Ballad *Time After Time*, written by Lauper and Hyman, hits US #1 and UK #3, held off #1 by Frankie Goes To Hollywood's *Two Tribes* and *Relax*. Its video features her mother Catrine, boyfriend Wolff and mentor, wrestling administrator, Lou Albano. (Her first 2 singles will both be used in UK TV ads.) Parent album *She's So Unusual* hits US #4 and UK #16 (and will sell over 4 million copies).
Sept *She Bop* hits US #3, but makes UK #46.
Dec A cover of Jules Shear's *All Through The Night* hits US #5, but peaks at UK #64. It is her fourth consecutive Top 5 US hit in a year.
'85 Jan [28] Following the American Music Awards celebrations, Lauper joins 45 other artists as USA For Africa at the A&M studios, Hollywood, CA, to record *We Are The World*.
Feb *Money Changes Everything*, the fifth single from *She's So Unusual*, reaches US #27.
[26] Lauper wins Best New Artist at the 27th annual Grammy awards.
May Shear's *Steady*, written by Shear and Lauper when she was with Blue Angel, reaches US #57.
July *The Goonies 'R' Good Enough*, from film "The Goonies" hits US #10.
'86 Aug Ballad *True Colors*, penned by Tom Kelly and Billy Steinberg and first extracted single from forthcoming *True Colors*, reaches UK #12.
Sept *True Colors* hits US #4 and UK #25. It includes Lauper co-written originals and covers of *What's Goin' On* and *Iko Iko*. Lauper begins a tour of Australia and Japan.
Oct [25] *True Colors* tops US chart for 2 weeks.
'87 Jan [10] *Change Of Heart*, written with Essra Mohawk, and with The Bangles on vocals, peaks at UK #67.
Feb [14] *Change Of Heart* hits US #3.
Mar *What's Going On* peaks at UK #57.
May [9] *What's Going On* reaches US #12.
June [20] *Boy Blue* peaks at US #71.
Aug Video "Cyndi Lauper In Paris", filmed at Le Zenith concert hall, Paris, France, is released.
Lauper becomes a born-again Christian, having spent 2 years heavily involved in the promotion of professional US wrestling.

1988 She begins work on her motion picture debut.
July [39] *Hole In My Heart (All The Way To China)*, from the film "Vibes", peaks at US #54.
Oct Lauper joins several US writers and performers at the "Music Speaks Louder Than Words" summit in USSR.
1989 June *I Drove All Night* hits UK #7, her first Top 10 single for 5 years.
July *A Night To Remember* reaches US #37 and UK #9.
[8] *I Drove All Night* hits US #6.
Aug *My First Night Without You* peaks at US #62 and UK #53. (The accompanying video is closed-captioned for the hearing impaired.)
Dec [30] *Heading West* peaks at US #68.
1990 Now pursuing an acting career – she plays Mary in Disney Channel's Shelley Duvall-produced "Mother Goose Rock'N'Rhyme" and a mermaid in the movie "Paradise Paved" – Lauper returns to Richmond Hill school in Queens to collect her high school diploma.
July *Music Speaks Louder Than Words* compilation, with Lauper's *Cold Sky*, recorded at the 1988 Moscow summit, is released.
[21] Lauper takes part in Roger Waters' performance of "The Wall" at the site of the Berlin Wall in Potzdamer Platz, Berlin, Germany. The event is broadcast live throughout the world, and raises money for the Memorial Fund For Disaster Relief.

LED ZEPPELIN
Robert Plant (vocals)
Jimmy Page (guitar)
John Paul Jones (bass)
John Bonham (drums)

1968 Mar The Yardbirds, on their final US tour, perform *I'm Confused* (later titled *Dazed And Confused*) and *White Summer* (both become part of Led Zeppelin's repertoire).
July The Yardbirds split after a gig at Luton, Beds. Page (b. Jan.9, 1944, Heston, London) and bassist Chris Dreja decide to form The New Yardbirds and are booked for a 10-day tour of Scandinavia, but Page decides to launch the group with a new line-up and Dreja quits to become a photographer. Jones (b. John Baldwin, June 3, 1946, Sidcup, Kent), an ex-session man and arranger like Page, joins on bass. Terry Reid and B.J. Wilson of Procol Harum reject the group, but Reid recommends 19-year-old Midlands R&B vocalist Plant (b. Aug.20, 1948, West Bromwich, W.Midlands). Page and group manager Peter Grant see Plant perform with a band called Hobbstweedle in Birmingham. Plant is invited to join and leaves the Midlands with only his rail fare in his pocket. Plant suggests Bonham (b. May 31, 1948, Bromwich), who is backing acts likes Joe Cocker, Chris Farlowe and Tim Rose on the club circuit, and he joins, leaving his own group Band Of Joy.
Sept The New Yardbirds tour Scandinavia, having recorded their debut album in 2 weeks.
Oct [15] They make their live debut at Surrey University as Led Zeppelin. (The Who's drummer Keith Moon had often used the phrase "going down like a lead Zeppelin" to describe disastrous gigs, Page likes the phrase, drops the "a" and the group is renamed Led Zeppelin, after a short spell as The New Yardbirds featuring Led Zeppelin.)
[18] Band makes its Marquee club, London debut, and will shortly appear on BBC TV's "How It Is".
Dec [26] Group begins its first US tour in Boston, MA, backing Vanilla Fudge and The MC5, and is an immediate success.
1969 Jan [31] They open for Iron Butterfly, who are so unsettled by their reception, that they refuse to go on.
Feb *Led Zeppelin* begins climb to hit US #10. It includes several numbers already popular at their live gigs, including versions of Willie Dixon's *You Shook Me* and Otis Rush's *Can't Quit You*.
Apr *Led Zeppelin* hits UK #6. A decision not to release singles in UK (at Grant's insistence) leads to lack of airplay on UK radio and only rare TV appearances. Group begins its second US tour, this time as bill-toppers. *Good Times Bad Times* makes US #80.
[24-27] 5-week US tour, the group's second, begins with 3 nights at Fillmore West.
June [13] 5-date UK tour starts at the Town Hall, Birmingham, W.Midlands.
[27] Group performs at the Playhouse theater, London for BBC Radio's "In Concert".
[28] They play Bath Festival Of Blues And Progressive Music, Avon.
[29] Led Zeppelin tops the bill at the Pop Proms at the Royal Albert Hall, London.
July They participate in the Newport Jazz And Blues Festival, Newport, RI, despite promoter George Wein announcing the group

will not be appearing because of illness. (The authorities had demanded the cancellation after trouble 2 nights earlier.) They go on anyway at 1am Monday morning.

Oct Band appears at a "Sunday Lyceum" concert promoted by Tony Stratton-Smith, and receives the highest fee ever paid to a UK band for a one-off concert.

[17] Led Zeppelin plays Carnegie Hall, New York, at the start of a 3½-week US tour. It is the first rock concert held there since 1965, when The Rolling Stones caused a ban.

Nov *Led Zeppelin 2* hits #1 in UK and US, and stays charted for 138 weeks and 98 weeks respectively. Recorded and written in hotel rooms and during rehearsals on tour, it features *Whole Lotta Love*, which will become a group anthem, though only released as a single cover version by Alexis Korner's C.C.S.

Dec The **Financial Times** announces the group has made $5 million in US sales, and comments that, unlike The Beatles, they have not been awarded MBEs for their export achievements. Band is awarded 2 platinum disks and a gold disk at London's Savoy hotel by Mrs. Gwyneth Dunwoody, Parliamentary Secretary to UK Board of Trade.

1970 Jan *Whole Lotta Love* hits US #4, as the group begins a UK tour.
[31] Plant discharges himself from Kidderminster General hospital, Hereford & Worcs., after facial injuries received in a car crash.

Feb [28] Following a threat by Eva von Zeppelin, relative of airship designer Ferdinand von Zeppelin, to sue if her family name is used in Denmark, Led Zeppelin play a gig in Copenhagen as The Nobs.

Mar Led Zeppelin performs at the Montreux Jazz Festival.

Apr [6] During a US tour, the group is given the keys to the city of Memphis, TN, before a concert.
Group returns home after almost a year and a half of touring and recording. *Living Loving Maid (She's Just A Woman)*, B-side of *Whole Lotta Love*, stalls at US #65.

June They tour Iceland and turn down $200,000 to play 2 US concerts, so they can play the Bath Festival for a second time.

Aug The group embarks on another US tour.

Sept Their appearances in New York's Madison Square Garden gross over $100,000 per performance. Band is voted Top Group in UK music weekly **Melody Maker** poll after years of Beatles' domination. With The Rolling Stones in tax exile and The Beatles split, Led Zeppelin is currently #1 group in the world.

Oct *Led Zeppelin 3*, with a change of style and a more acoustic feel, hits #1 in both UK and US.

1971 Jan *Immigrant Song* reaches US #16.
[9] Group plays at London's Royal Albert Hall during a short UK tour.

Mar [5] Led Zeppelin begins a "thank you" tour for its UK fans in the clubs and ballrooms they played in their early days in 1968. They agree to play for their original 1968 fee if the promoter charges the 1968 admission fee.

Sept A concert in Milan, Italy, ends in a riot, with police tear-gassing the crowd.

Nov Fourth album is released untitled and hits UK #1 and US #2. It becomes known as **Led Zeppelin 4** or **Four Symbols** after the runic images on its inner sleeve. The group's selling power is underlined by the lack of any title or name on the album cover. The album contains *Stairway To Heaven*, which becomes the group's new anthem and will later be regarded as a landmark in rock history.
[20-21] They play Wembley Arena, London, with circus and novelty acts, during an 11-date UK tour.

1972 Feb *Black Dog* makes US #15.

Apr *Rock And Roll* climbs to US #47. Robert and Maureen Plant have a son, Karac.

July Manager Grant tries to organize a Led Zeppelin concert at London's Waterloo train station, but fails.

Dec Group plays 2 concerts at London's Alexandra Palace.

1973 Apr *Houses Of The Holy* hits UK and US #1. The sleeve again shows no official title or name.

May The **Financial Times** quotes Grant as saying that Led Zeppelin will earn $30 million in US in the coming year. The group's concert, before 56,800 people, at Tampa Stadium, FL, grosses $309,000, breaking the US attendance and box office record held by The Beatles (for their 1965 Shea Stadium performance).

July [30] A Madison Square Garden concert is filmed for inclusion in movie "The Song Remains The Same". The band is robbed of $180,000 from New York's Drake hotel deposit box; it is never recovered. *Over The Hills And Far Away* reaches US #51.

Oct Group works on fantasy film sequences for a forthcoming movie. Page appears on Maggie Bell's album *Suicide Sal* and Jones writes,

produces and plays on Madeleine Bell's album *Comin' Atcha*.
Dec *D'yer Mak'er* makes US #20.

1974 Jan The formation of Led Zeppelin's own label, SwanSong, named after an unreleased Page instrumental, is announced.

May SwanSong is launched with parties in US and London. As well releasing all further Led Zeppelin product, SwanSong will sign Bad Company, The Pretty Things and Dave Edmunds among others.

1975 Jan [8] 60,000 tickets for 3 Led Zeppelin concerts at New York's Madison Square Garden sell out in 4 hours.

Mar First SwanSong album, double *Physical Graffiti* is released, featuring Page on frantic sitar on *Kashmir*, topping UK and US charts.

Apr 51,000 tickets for 3 UK concerts at Earls Court, London, sell out 2 hours.

May US President Gerald Ford's daughters tell Dick Cavett on his ta[l] show that Led Zeppelin is their favorite group. *Trampled Underfoot* reaches US #38. Band plays 5 4-hour shows at Earls Court, London.

June Band members go into tax exile in Switzerland.

Aug [5] Plant and his wife are badly injured in a car crash on holida[y] in Rhodes, Greece. He is flown to UK for treatment in plaster casts, b[ut] is flown out again on a stretcher to Jersey to recuperate when the time limit on his UK visit, before paying full income tax for the year, is abo[ut] to expire.

1976 Apr *Presence* hits US and UK #1.

Oct [20] Led Zeppelin's film "The Song Remains The Same" premiere[s] at the Cinema One in New York, raising $25,000 for the Save The Children Fund, and the soundtrack double album hits both US and U[K] #1. Group makes its first US TV appearance playing *Black Dog*, a form[er] US release, on "Don Kirshner's Rock Concert".

1977 Feb [1] They postpone US tour when Robert Plant contracts tonsiliti[s].

May [6] They play before a crowd of 76,000 in Michigan, breaking their own attendance record.
[12] Group receives a Special Award for their contribution to British music at the annual Ivor Novello Awards.

July [23] On US tour, Bonham, manager Peter Grant, and a bodygua[rd] are arrested and charged with assault on a security employee of promoter Bill Graham.
[27] Plant's son dies after falling ill with a stomach infection. US tour cancelled, as Plant flies home. Rumors spread that the group, appalle[d] by its bad luck, is to split up.

1978 July After a quiet year with his family, Plant re-emerges to play with local musicians, and Led Zeppelin regroups to prepare a new album.

Dec They record at Abba's Polar studios, Stockholm, Sweden, durin[g] their tax exile.

1979 June Group embarks on tour of Switzerland, Belgium, Austria, Holland and Germany, for what will be its last tour.

Aug Zeppelin tops the bill for 2 dates at Knebworth Fair, Knebworth Herts., a major UK outdoor festival.

Sept *In Through The Out Door* is released worldwide in 6 different sleeves and tops UK and US charts, selling over 4 million copies in U[S].

Dec Plant, Jones and Bonham join the all-star line-up of UNICEF "Rock For Kampuchea" concert at the Hammersmith Odeon, London[.] Robert and Maureen Plant have a second son, Logan Romero.

1980 Feb *Fool In The Rain* reaches US #21.

May Band announces its first full-scale European tour for 7 years.

July [7] Led Zeppelin plays its final concert, at the Eissporthalle, We[st] Berlin, Germany at the end of their European tour, on the 12th anniversary of the Yardbirds break-up which gave birth to the group[.]

Sept They meet at Page's Windsor, Berks., house to rehearse for US tour.
[25] Bonham is found dead in bed, having choked in his sleep after a[n] heavy drinking bout.

Oct [10] Bonham's funeral takes place at his local Rushnock parish church, Hereford & Worcs.

Dec [4] A statement is released announcing the group's decision no[t to] continue after "the loss of our dear friend".

1982 Feb Page-composed soundtrack album for Michael Winner's movie "Death Wish II" reaches UK #40 and US #50.

Dec *Coda*, compiled by Page from unissued band material, hits UK [...]

1983 Jan *Coda* hits US #6.

Sept Page appears at ARMS concert in aid of Multiple Sclerosis victi[ms] at London's Royal Albert Hall with Eric Clapton, Steve Winwood an[d] Jeff Beck, and performs *Stairway To Heaven*.

1984 July Page appears with Roy Harper at the Cambridge Folk Festival, Cambridge, Cambs.

1985 Mar Page joins Harper for *Whatever Happened To Jugula?* which makes UK #44. Page, having formed a new combo, The Firm, with Ba[...]

Company's vocalist Paul Rodgers, bassist Tony Franklin and drummer Chris Slade, releases *The Firm*. It makes UK #15 and US #17.

Apr The Firm's *Radioactive* reaches US #28.

May The Firm's *Satisfaction Guaranteed* stalls at US #73.

July [13] Zeppelin re-forms (with Phil Collins on drums) for Live Aid extravaganza at JFK Stadium, Philadelphia, PA.

Nov Multi-national group The Far Corporation takes *Stairway To Heaven* into UK chart for the first time, hitting #8.

1986 Jan The group rehearses for a week with Chic's Tony Thompson on drums, but decides not to re-form.

Mar [22] The Firm's *All The Kings Horses*, a trailer for its new album, peaks at US #61.

Apr The Firm's *Mean Business* peaks at US #22 and UK #46.

Oct [18] The Far Corporation's version of *Stairway To Heaven* makes US #89.

1987 A belated plagiarism accusation filed by Willie Dixon, who claims similarities between his *You Need Love* and Zeppelin's *Whole Lotta Love* is settled out of court.

1988 May [14] Zeppelin regroups, with Jason Bonham filling his father's role, and performs, reluctantly on Plant's part, *Stairway To Heaven* and *Whole Lotta Love* at New York's Madison Square Garden as part of Atlantic Records' 40-year celebration concert.

June Plant's solo career continues, and Page releases first solo album *Outrider*, which makes UK #27 and US #26.

Sept As Plant's summer tour closes, Page launches American dates (now employing Jason Bonham and John Miles (vocals) and Durban Laverde (bass)) to promote recent Geffen-released album *Outrider*, which reaches US #26 and UK #27.

1989 Feb Los Angeles rock station K-LOS begins playing an hour of Led Zeppelin music every night of the year.

Apr New band, Dread Zeppelin starts playing reggae versions of Led Zeppelin classics throughout California.

May Long-time manager Peter Grant states that the band will never re-form for touring or any future recording work.

June [9] Page plays with Les Paul at his 72nd birthday party at New York's Hard Rock Café.

1990 Jan [1] WKRL radio station in St. Petersburg, FL, plays *Stairway To Heaven* for 24 hours as a prelude to all-Led Zeppelin format.

[12] The station begins alternating with Pink Floyd.

May [5] Plant, Page and Jones join Jason Bonham, who is continuing his own career fronting Bonham, for a 5-song set at the reception at the Heath hotel, Bewdley near Kidderminster, after Bonham's wedding to childhood sweetheart Jan Charteris.

Aug [18] Page joins Aerosmith on stage at the Monsters Of Rock festival at Castle Donington, Leics., before a crowd of 72,500 playing *Train Kept A-Rollin'*.

[20] Page joins them on stage again at their Marquee club, London gig, playing a blues jam which ends with *Immigrant Song*.

BRENDA LEE

1956 Mar Lee (b. Brenda Mae Tarpley, Dec.11, 1944, Lithonia, GA), after many local talent contests, makes her debut at age 11 on "Ozark Jubilee" TV show, hosted by country singer Red Foley, and also tours with Foley's road show, before making national TV appearances on the "Perry Como Show" and the "Ed Sullivan Show".

July She signs to Decca Records, which promotes her as "Little Miss Brenda Lee" highlighting her young age and diminutive stature.

1957 Mar After some country success with *Jambalaya* and *I'm Gonna Lassoo Santa Claus*, her chart debut is *One Step At A Time*, backed by The Anita Kerr Singers, which makes US #43.

Aug *Dynamite* makes US #72 and leads to her revamped billing as "Little Miss Dynamite" – a reference to her dynamic stage presence – which will stay with her until the mid-60s.

1959 Mar She is booked to play the Olympia in Paris, France (partly to help drum up publicity in US). The original show is cancelled when the promoter discovers her age, but her manager leaks a story to the local press that she is a 32-year-old midget, and then gains publicity denying it. Held over at the Olympia for 5 weeks, Lee becomes an in-demand name in Europe, doing shows in Germany, Italy and UK.

1960 Apr After 2 years without hits, Lee records Ronnie Self's rock ballad *Sweet Nothin's* which hits US #4 and is a million-seller.

May *Sweet Nothin's* hits UK #4. Also written by Self, country-styled *I'm Sorry* tops US chart for 3 weeks and is another million-seller. B-side *That's All You Gotta Do* hits US #6.

July *I'm Sorry* reaches UK #12.

Sept Lee embarks on "The Fall Edition Of The Biggest Show Of Stars For 1960" US tour with Chubby Checker, Bobby Vinton, Fabian and Jimmy Clanton.

Oct Italian-originated ballad *I Want To Be Wanted* tops US chart for a week and is her third consecutive million-seller. B-side *Just A Little* makes US #40. Debut album *Brenda Lee*, which includes the hit singles, hits US #5 (and will spend 13 months on chart).

Nov *I Want To Be Wanted* makes UK #31.

Dec *Rockin' Around The Christmas Tree* reaches US #14 (and will becomes a Christmas standard).

1961 Jan *This Is ... Brenda* hits US #4.

Feb Ballad *Emotions* hits US #7 while B-side *I'm Learning About Love* peaks at US #33.

Mar An early rocker, *Let's Jump The Broomstick* is reissued in UK and makes UK #12.

Apr *Emotions* reaches UK #45, reflecting a decreasing interest in UK of her ballad style despite US Top 10 consistency.

May *You Can Depend On Me* hits US #6.

June *Emotions* reaches US #24.

[25] Lee performs in Alan Freed's show at the Hollywood Bowl, Los Angeles, CA, with Bobby Vee, Jerry Lee Lewis, The Shirelles and others.

Aug A return to uptempo material with Jackie DeShannon-penned gimmick-rocker *Dum Dum* hits US #4 and makes UK #22. Ballad B-side *Eventually* reaches US #56.

Oct *All The Way*, including *Dum Dum* reaches US #17.

Nov Country ballad *Fool #1* hits US #3 (another gold disk) and makes UK #38. Uptempo B-side *Anybody But Me* climbs to US #31.

Dec *Rockin' Around The Christmas Tree* , re-promoted in US, makes US #50.

1962 Mar Ballad *Break It To Me Gently* hits US #4 and UK #46. Uptempo B-side *So Deep* makes US #52.

Apr *Sincerely* reaches US #29.

May Not released in US, uptempo *Speak To Me Pretty* is Lee's biggest UK hit at #3. It is taken from children's movie "Two Little Bears" in which Lee has a cameo role. Meanwhile, ballad *Everybody Loves Me But You* hits US #6 and rock B-side *Here Comes That Feeling* peaks at US #89.

Aug Uptempo *Here Comes That Feeling* is chosen instead of the A-side by Decca as UK follow-up to *Speak To Me Pretty* and hits UK #5. In US, slow DeShannon song *Heart In Hand* reaches US #15 and uptempo B-side *It Started All Over Again* reaches US #29. Lee performs in a production of the musical "Bye Bye Birdie" in Kansas City, MO.

Oct Uptempo *It Started All Over Again* is again picked as UK A-side and reaches #15.

Nov *All Alone Am I* hits US #3 and is another million-seller. B-side *Save All Your Lovin' For Me* makes US #53. *All The Way* belatedly reaches UK #20.

Dec *Rockin' Around The Christmas Tree* is released in UK for the first time and hits UK #6. On its third US release, it makes #59. *Brenda, That's All* reaches US #20.

[30] Lee is slightly hurt as fire guts her Nashville, TN, home and she tries to rescue her poodle Cee Cee, who dies of smoke inhalation.

1963 Feb *All Alone Am I* breaks Lee's UK "ballad jinx" hitting #7. In US, double A-side *You Used To Be/She'll Never Know* makes #32/#47. *Brenda, That's All* reaches UK #13.

Apr *All Alone Am I* makes US #25.

[24] Lee is married to considerably taller Ronnie Shacklett in Nashville.

May *Losing You* hits US #6 and UK #10 and *All Alone Am I* hits UK #8.

[3] After 8 days' honeymoon, Lee opens at the Copacabana, New York.

July She signs a 20-year contract with Decca, guaranteeing her $35,000 a year. It also includes a 2-film deal with Universal Pictures.

Aug Double A-side *My Whole World Is Falling Down/I Wonder* reaches US #24/#25. This time UK issues ballad *I Wonder* as A-side and it makes UK #14.

Nov *The Grass Is Greener* reaches US #17 and uptempo B-side *Sweet Impossible You* climbs to US #70 and UK #28.

1964 Jan *Let Me Sing*, which includes *Break It To Me Gently* and *Losing You*, reaches US #39. New ballad *As Usual* reaches US #12.

Feb *As Usual* hits UK #5.

Apr *Think* reaches US #25 and UK #26 (the first indication that Lee's chart consistency is being affected by the rise of Merseybeat and group-oriented music which has swept many contemporaries from the chart.)

May [1] Daughter Julie LeAnn is born.

July *Alone With You* makes US #48 as *By Request* climbs to US #90.

Sept *When You Loved Me* makes US #47.

Oct Lee records in UK with The Animals' and Herman's Hermits' producer Mickie Most in an effort to meet the new musical trends head-on. *Is It True*, penned by UK writers John Carter and Ken Lewis, is rush released in UK and reaches US #17.

Nov *Is It True* also makes US #17.

[2] Lee takes part in the "Royal Command Performance" at the London Palladium.

[14] She begins a 17-date twice-nightly UK tour, with Manfred Mann, Marty Wilde, Johnny Kidd & The Pirates, Bern Elliott, Heinz, Wayne Fontana & The Mindbenders and The John Barry Seven, at Finsbury Park Astoria, London, ending Dec.12 at Blackpool's Opera House.

Dec Extracted from *Merry Christmas*, *Christmas Will Be Just Another Day* reaches UK #29.

[7] Lee performs in "Pop Beat" at the Royal Albert Hall, London with Dave Berry & The Cruisers, Brian Poole & The Tremeloes, The Nashville Teens, The Miracles, Wayne Fontana & The Mindbenders and The Yardbirds.

1965 **Feb** Second Most production, *Thanks A Lot* makes US #45 and UK #41. B-side, a cover of Dave Berry's 1964 UK hit *The Crying Game*, climbs to US #87.

May *Truly, Truly, True* peaks at US #54.

July A return to country ballad-style, *Too Many Rivers* makes US #13, her biggest hit single for over 2 years.

Aug *Too Many Rivers* makes UK #22 (her final UK Singles chart entry).

Oct *Too Many Rivers* reaches US #36.

Nov *Rusty Bells* makes US #33.

1966 **May** Lee plays a 2-week stint at the Cocoanut Grove in Hollywood.

July *Bye Bye Blues* makes US #94 and UK #21, while *Ain't Gonna Cry No More* peaks at US #77.

Aug Compilation *10 Golden Years*, featuring a hit from each year 1956-65, reaches US #70.

Dec Now uncharacteristic rock *Coming On Strong* makes US #11.

1967 **Feb** *Coming On Strong* reaches US #94 and, taken from it, *Ride, Ride, Ride* makes US #37.

June *For The First Time*, with jazzman Pete Fountain, reaches US #187.

1969 **Apr** *Johnny One Time* makes US #41, after a 2-year chart absence. In her country ballad-style, it has much in common with mainstream late 60s country music, into which Lee is inevitably drawn.

May *You Don't Need Me For Anything Anymore* makes US #84.

June *Johnny One Time* reaches US #98.

1973 **Apr** Kris Kristofferson-penned *Nobody Wins* is her last US Hot 100 entry at US #70. It tops US Country chart (and Lee will work in this field from now on).

1977 **July** Released from Decca before official contract expiry, Lee moves to Elektra (her only recording for the label is a country single).

1979 Lee re-signs to MCA Records (Decca's successor) in Nashville.

1980 TV-promoted compilation *Little Miss Dynamite*, on Warwick Records, makes UK #15.

1981 **Mar** Lee appears in Burt Reynolds/Jackie Gleason film "Smokey And The Bandit II" as the Nice Lady.

1984 **Jan** Double compilation *25th Anniversary* peaks at UK #65.

1985 **Apr** Another TV-promoted compilation album *The Very Best Of Brenda Lee* reaches UK #16.

1989 **Aug** [25] Lee and MCA reach settlement on $20 million suit she brought against the label for allegedly cheating her of royalties owed 1962-77 while with Decca, which MCA buys.

1990 **Jan** Still performing regularly in the country field, Lee is featured on soundtrack of "Dick Tracy" movie.

THE LEFT BANKE

Michael Brown (keyboards)
Steve Martin (vocals)
Jeff Winfield (guitar)
Tom Finn (bass)
George Cameron (drums)

1964 Working in New York as an assistant at his father's World United recording studio and playing piano for Reparata & The Delrons, classically-trained musician Brown (b. Michael Lookofsky, Apr.25, 1949, New York, NY) first meets Martin, Cameron and Finn (the latter a member of The Magic Planets).

1965 Brown and friends form The Left Banke while experimenting in World United studio with a sound blending classical influences with "British invasion"-style pop-rock. Brown's father Harry Lookofsky grooms their talent for harmony singing and unusual arrangements, and builds their tracks to professional production standards.

1966 **Mar** They record *Walk Away Renée*, a baroque-styled arrangement of a ballad written by Brown, which will prove sufficiently offbeat to be turned down by several labels before it is released by Mercury's subsidiary label, Smash Records, in July.

Oct *Walk Away Renée* hits #6 in US.

1967 **Feb** *Pretty Ballerina* climbs to US #15. Like *Walk Away Renée* it fails to chart in UK. Rick Brand replaces Winfield on guitar while they are recording tracks for debut album.

May *Walk Away Renée/Pretty Ballerina* peaks at US #67, by which time there has been a rift in the group, and as owner of the name Left Banke, Brown retires to the studio to record *Ivy Ivy* alone. This fails to chart while Smash declines to promote it while the 2 group factions are at loggerheads. By the time they reconcile, both *Ivy Ivy* and rapidly-issued follow-up *She May Call You Up Tonight* are lost causes.

Oct *Desire* creeps to US #98 and is their last chart entry. Brown leaves for good, followed by Brand.

1968 The Left Banke name this time is left with Finn, Martin and Cameron, who record 4 more unsuccessful singles, and *Left Banke, Too* (released in 1969) as a trio.

Jan A cover version of *Walk Away Renée* by The Four Tops hits UK #3, then US #14, 2 months later.

Aug A more unexpected cover version of *And Suddenly* (the B-side of ill-fated *Ivy Ivy*) by Cherry People reaches US #45.

1969 Brown joins forces with a group named Montage, producing, playing keyboards, vocally arranging and writing most of, their one album *Montage* for Laurie Records.

1971 Martin releases *Two By Two/Love Songs In The Night*, both written by Brown, but it is a one-off reunion. Brown and vocalist Ian Lloyd then form Stories, with Steve Love (guitar) and Brian Madey (drums), and they sign to Kama Sutra Records.

1972 **Aug** Stories' *I'm Coming Home* makes US #42, while debut album *Stories* peaks at #182.

1973 **Aug** Stories enjoy their biggest hit with a cover of Hot Chocolate's *Brother Louie*, which tops US chart and sells over a million. Brown leaves the group during the recording sessions for this and *Stories About Us*, which reaches US #29.

1976 Brown forms The Beckies, who release 1 (unsuccessful) album on Sire Records, with Mayo James McAllister and Gary Hodgden, from Kansas City band Chesmann Square, and Scott Trusty. Tom Finn provides harmony vocals for 1 song on the album.

1978 **Feb** Martin, Finn and Cameron attempt to re-form The Left Banke. They record an album's worth of material which will remain unreleased until 1986, and *And One Day*, a single issued in US during the autumn by Camerica Records. (In the mid-80s, US and UK archive labels Rhino and Bam Caruso will reissue all Left Banke material, including originally unreleased tracks and obscurities.)

JOHN LENNON

1967 **Oct** Still a member of The Beatles, Lennon (b. Oct 9, 1940, Liverpool) makes his first and only solo appearance (as Private Gripweed) in a feature film, "How I Won The War", directed by Richard Lester.

1968 **Nov** *Unfinished Music No 1 - Two Virgins* is released. A melange of sound effects and disjointed music, it is made famous by its cover of Lennon and girlfriend Yoko Ono (b. Feb.18, 1933, Tokyo, Japan) in a naked, full-frontal pose. Lennon takes the photo himself on a delayed shutter release, reportedly too embarrassed to employ a professional photographer. EMI refuses to distribute the album and it is handled by Track which wraps it in brown paper bags for retail.

Dec [10] Lennon makes his first solo TV performance, at the filming of "The Rolling Stones' Rock 'N' Roll Circus", singing 'Yer Blues'.

1969 **Feb** *Unfinished Music No 1 - Two Virgins* makes US #124.

Mar [2] John and Yoko play "natural music" concert at Lady Mitchell Hall, Cambridge, Cambs.

[20] Lennon marries Ono in the British Consulate office in Gibraltar.

Apr [22] Lennon changes his middle name from Winston to Ono by deed poll on the roof of the Apple building in Savile Row, London.

May *Unfinished Music No 2 - Life With The Lions* makes US #174. A continuation of the first album, it has a free-form live concert on one side while the other is recorded on a cassette player at Queen Charlotte hospital, Hammersmith, London, during Ono's pregnancy (which ends in miscarriage).

[26] The Lennons begin an 8-day bed-in for peace in Room 1742 of Hotel La Reine Elizabeth, Montreal, Canada.

July *Give Peace A Chance* hits UK #2, and becomes the definitive peace anthem for pacifists worldwide. It is recorded during a "bed-in", a

form of protest invented by Lennon and Ono in which they stayed in bed to protest for world peace and asked the media to film and interview them in the hotel. The disk is credited to The Plastic Ono Band (a name Lennon will use for the musicians he is recording with over the next few years). Appearing on it are Lennon, Tommy Smothers, Petula Clark, Timothy Leary and Allen Ginsberg.
Sept *Give Peace A Chance* reaches US #14.
[13] The Plastic Ono Band, with a line-up of Eric Clapton, Klaus Voorman and Alan White, appears in a hastily-arranged slot at the "Toronto Rock'N'Revival Show" at the Varsity Stadium, Toronto university, Canada. Group rehearses on the flight to Toronto and performs a shaky set of rock'n'roll classics and Lennon originals.
Nov *Cold Turkey*, on the agonies of drug withdrawal, makes UK #14.
[25] Lennon returns his MBE to Buckingham Palace with a note: "Your Majesty, I am returning this MBE in protest against Britain's involvement in the Nigeria-Biafra thing, against our support of America in Vietnam, and against *Cold Turkey* slipping down the charts. With love, John Lennon of Bag." This action alienates him from the British Establishment and prompts his emigration to America.
Dec *The Wedding Album*, an avant-garde recording which includes souvenirs of the event, makes US #178. **Melody Maker**'s Richard Williams reviews a pre-release copy of the album, pressed on 2 disks, each with a blank B-side, and notes that these B-sides contain single tones maintained throughout, reproduced electronically and altering by a microtone or semitone to produce an uneven beat. (They are in fact an engineer's test signal.) Lennon and Ono send him a telegram saying: "We both feel that this is the first time a critic topped the artist."
[15] Lennon makes his last live appearance in UK at a UNICEF "Peace For Christmas" benefit at the Lyceum Ballroom, London.
70 Jan *Cold Turkey* peaks at US #30 as *The Plastic Ono Band – Live Peace In Toronto 1969* hits US #10.
Feb *Instant Karma*, recorded in a day and produced by Phil Spector, hits UK #5 and US #3. George Harrison plays guitar and Allen Klein and assorted club-goers from London's Hatchetts club provide chorus.
Mar Lennon and Ono begin an intensive 6-month course of primal scream therapy conducted by its originator, Dr. Arthur Janov. During this, Lennon writes most of the material for his first solo album, with The Beatles now defunct.
71 Jan *John Lennon And The Plastic Ono Band* traces themes from Lennon's troubled adolescence and topics brought to the surface during his primal therapy treatment. It makes UK #11 and hits US #6 (acclaimed in later years a creative pinnacle). *Mother* climbs to US #43.
Apr Anthemic *Power To The People* hits UK #7 and US #11.
June [6] The Lennons join Frank Zappa onstage at the Fillmore East, New York.
Sept [3] John Lennon flies from Heathrow Airport to New York. (He will never set foot on British soil again.)
Oct *Imagine*, commercially his most successful album, features a melodic pop sound and is acclaimed as his best solo work. The album, containing 2 thinly-veiled attacks on Paul McCartney in *Crippled Inside* and *How Do You Sleep?*, tops both UK and US charts.
Nov Peace-themed *Imagine* hits US #3; Lennon resists its UK release.
Dec *Happy Xmas (War Is Over)* is released in US only and fails to chart (which it will continue to do on subsequent re-releases).
[17] The Lennons appear onstage at the Apollo theater, Harlem, New York, at a benefit concert for the wives of the victims of the Sept. Attica State prison riot.
72 Feb [15-18] Lennon and Ono co-host US TV's "The Mike Douglas Show" for 4 days and Lennon jams with his rock'n'roll hero Chuck Berry.
Mar [16] The Lennons lodge an appeal with the US Immigration & Naturalization Office in New York, after they are served with deportation orders, arising from his 1968 cannabis possession conviction.
June *Woman Is The Nigger Of The World* peaks at US #57.
July For double *Some Time In New York City*, Lennon teams for one disk with group Elephant's Memory (who contributed to the soundtrack of *Midnight Cowboy*) to record overtly political comment on causes ranging from N.Ireland to the imprisonment of radicals, Angela Davis and John Sinclair. The other disk is concert recordings with The Mothers Of Invention. Album makes US #48. The Beatles' song publishing arm, Northern Songs, refuses to recognize some of Yoko Ono's composer credits with Lennon, and release of the album is delayed in UK.
Aug [30] Lennon makes his only major appearance at a concert in New York's Madison Square Garden for the One To One charity.

Critics regard it as his first solo performance. He is joined on stage by Stevie Wonder and Roberta Flack for *Give Peace A Chance* finale.
Oct *Sometime In New York City* reaches UK #11.
Dec *Happy Xmas (War Is Over)* hits UK #4, and makes the first of many chart visits having been held up from UK release due to the Ono song-credit dispute.
1973 Mar [23] Lennon is ordered to leave the US within 60 days by Immigration Authorities and begins his long fight to gain the necessary green card to enable him to remain in the country.
Oct [24] Lennon sues the US Government, accusing it of tapping his telephone.
Nov *Mind Games* climbs to UK #26 and US #18. *Mind Games*, a return to the commercial texture of *Imagine*, makes UK #13 and hits US #9.
1974 Jan Lennon asks the Queen for a Royal Pardon in connection with his 5-year-old UK drug conviction to enable him to go to and from US.
Mar Lennon enters a dark period of his life, embarking on a drunken Los Angeles lifestyle after a temporary split from Ono. He is seen in the company of his former personal assistant, May Pang, and at an infamous incident at Los Angeles' Troubadour club, he throws insults at The Smothers Brothers and punches their manager and a cocktail waitress before being forcibly removed from the premises. The episode makes headlines worldwide.
Aug He produces Harry Nilsson's *Pussycats*, a mixture of cover versions, to little acclaim.
Oct *Walls And Bridges* hits UK #6 and tops US chart.
Nov [16] *Whatever Gets You Through The Night* hits US #1, and makes UK #36. He becomes the last of the 4 ex-Beatles to hit US #1. Elton John plays on the session for the single and, recognizing the song's potential, makes a bargain with Lennon that if the disk got to #1, Lennon would have to appear in concert with him. Lennon accepts, confident of the record's non-#1 status.
[28] On Thanksgiving Night, Lennon makes what will be his final concert appearance at New York's Madison Square Garden joining Elton John for 3 songs: *Whatever Gets You Through The Night, Lucy In The Sky With Diamonds* and *I Saw Her Standing There* (released as an EP in UK in Mar.1981, it makes UK #40).
1975 Jan *Happy Xmas (War Is Over)* belatedly makes UK #48, as Lennon returns to live with Yoko.
Feb *#9 Dream* reaches UK #23 and hits US #9.
Mar For *Rock'N'Roll*, Lennon finally achieves his aim to record an album of his favorite rock'n'roll songs. (The project was begun in 1973 with Phil Spector producing. After disagreements between the 2 , Spector disappeared with the master tapes and Lennon, unhappy with the production work, re-recorded the set.) It is reported that Lennon has struck up an agreement with Morris Levy, Chuck Berry's publisher, that he would cover certain Berry songs for a new album as Levy threatened a lawsuit against Lennon for using Berry's song *You Can't Catch Me* in the shape of *Come Together* on **Abbey Road**. Lennon subsequently gives Levy some master tapes of songs which, without Lennon's authorization, he releases as TV-advertised mail order *Roots – John Lennon Sings The Great Rock & Roll Hits* on Adam VIII label. Apple promptly releases *Rock'N'Roll* to kill off the disk and Lennon successfully sues Levy, winning compensation of $45,000. The album hits both UK and US #6. Lennon co-writes *Fame* with Carlos Alomar and David Bowie (which reaches UK #17 and tops US chart), for Bowie's **Young Americans**. On this album, he also plays guitar with Bowie on The Beatles' song *Across The Universe*.
Apr Lennon's remake of Ben E. King's *Stand By Me* makes UK #30 and US #20.
June [13] He makes his last TV appearance on "Salute To Sir Lew Grade", performing *Slippin' And Slidin'* and *Imagine*.
Oct [7] The New York State Supreme Court votes by a 2 to 1 majority to reverse Lennon's deportation order.
[9] Sean Taro Ono Lennon is born. The birth of his only child by Ono has a profound effect on Lennon. (He retires for 5 years to become a househusband in his Manhattan apartment building, the Dakota, while Ono runs his business empire.)
Nov [22] Greatest hits compilation *Shaved Fish* hits UK #8. Released as a UK single for first time, *Imagine* hits #6.
Dec [13] *Shaved Fish* reaches US #12.
1976 July [27] Judge Ira Fieldsteel approves Lennon's application for his Green Card (no: A17-597-321) allowing permanent residence in the US. Gloria Swanson and Norman Mailer appear at the hearing as character witnesses.
1977 Jan [20] The Lennons attend President Jimmy Carter's inaugural gala in Washington, DC.

1980 **Aug** After his hiatus, Lennon begins songwriting again on a holiday in Bermuda and records sessions at the Hit Factory in New York, for forthcoming *Double Fantasy* (named after a flower Lennon saw in a botanical garden in Bermuda). Lennon is not signed to any label, but David Geffen offers to release the album without hearing any of the material.

Nov *Double Fantasy* is released and will top both UK and US charts. It receives positive reviews as Lennon returns to the limelight.

Dec [8] Lennon and Ono return home from the recording studio at 10:50 EST. As they enter the courtyard of the Dakota building, Lennon turns around when he hears a voice say "Mr. Lennon?" He is shot 5 times by Mark Chapman and dies of blood loss shortly after at the Roosevelt hospital.

Record sales soar immediately. *(Just Like) Starting Over* hits #1 in UK and US. EMI in UK receives orders from record shops for over 300,000 copies of *Imagine*.

[14] Ono calls for 10-min. silent vigil around the world at 2pm EST.

1981 **Jan** [10] *Imagine* tops UK chart, with *Happy Xmas (War Is Over)* at #2. *Give Peace A Chance* reaches UK #33.

[22] A picture of Lennon naked next to a fully-clothed Ono appears in an obituary issue of **Rolling Stone** magazine.

Feb *Woman* completes a hat trick of UK #1s in a 9-week period. Roxy Music's tribute version of *Jealous Guy* hits UK #1.

Mar *Woman* hits US #2.

May *Watching The Wheels* reaches UK #30 and US #10.

Dec *Happy Xmas (War Is Over)* makes UK #28.

1982 **Feb** [24] Lennon is honored at the first annual BRIT Awards, held at the Grosvenor House, Mayfair, London, for his Outstanding Contribution To British music.

Nov Compilation *The John Lennon Collection* hits UK #1 and US #33. *Love* climbs to UK #41.

Dec *Happy Xmas (War Is Over)* makes UK #56.

1984 **Jan** *Nobody Told Me* hits UK #6. *Heart Play – Unfinished Dialogue*, featuring excerpts from a **Playboy** magazine interview given shortly before his death, reaches US #94.

Feb *Milk And Honey*, featuring 6 of Lennon's songs recorded just before his death in 1980, hits UK #3 and US #11.

Mar *Nobody Told Me* hits US #5.

Apr *Borrowed Time* makes UK #32 as *I'm Stepping Out* peaks at US #55.

Nov Son Julian, from Lennon's marriage to Cynthia Twist, has his first hit with *Too Late For Goodbyes*, at UK #6 and *Valotte*, which reaches UK #20 and US #17. Many critics note a similar vocal style to his father's. Lennon's *Jealous Guy* peaks at UK #65.

1986 **Mar** *Live In New York City* makes UK #55 and US #41. His Aug.1972 US concert is released on video.

Dec *Menlove Avenue*, of studio sessions from the *Rock'N'Roll* and *Walls And Bridges* period, makes US #127.

1988 **Sept** Ono produces a syndicated series for radio on Lennon's life which features many unheard songs and interviews. A biography by Albert Goldman, who has previously written a book on Elvis Presley, outrages fans with its claims and is denounced by Yoko.

Oct A movie and soundtrack, under the generic title "Imagine" and produced by Ono, are simultaneously released. They include out-takes, videos, home movies and previously unheard material.

Nov *Imagine: Music From The Motion Picture* stalls at UK #64 and US #31. Lennon is given a star on Hollywood's Walk Of Fame.

Dec [3] 3-track single *Imagine/Happy Xmas (War Is Over)/Jealous Guy* is issued in UK and peaks at #45.

1989 **Jan** [18] As a Beatle, Lennon is inducted into the Rock'N'Roll Hall Of Fame at New York's Waldorf Astoria. Sean and Yoko attend.

Apr Cynthia Lennon opens Lennon's Restaurant in London. Dishes include Sgt. Pepper Steak and Penny Lane Pate. As Yoko embarks on a movie career, Sean spends time with David Bowie during the Tin Machine recording sessions in New York.

May "Imagine John Lennon" (the 1988 movie) and old live footage compiled as "Sweet Toronto" are released as video cassettes.

Aug At Julian Lennon concert at the Beacon theater, New York, half-brother Sean comes onstage to sing *Stand By Me* with Julian.

1990 **May** [5] The "John Lennon Tribute Concert" is held at the Pier Head Arena in Merseyside to celebrate the songs of Lennon. Artists taking part, either live or on video, include Al Green (*All You Need Is Love* and *Power To The People*), The Christians (*Revolution*), Joe Cocker (*Come Together* and *Isolation*), Lenny Kravitz (*Cold Turkey*), Kylie Minogue (*Help*), Natalie Cole (*Lucy In The Sky With Diamonds* and *Ticket To Ride*), Wet Wet Wet (*I Feel Fine*), Ringo Starr with Jim Keltner, Jeff Lynne, Tom Petty and Joe Walsh (*I Call Your Name*), The Moody Blues (*Across*

The Universe), Lou Reed (*Jealous Guy* and *Mother*), Terence Trent D'Arby (*You've Got To Hide Your Love Away*), Randy Travis (*Nowhere Man*), Cyndi Lauper (*Working Class Hero* and *Hey Bulldog*), Deacon Blue (*A Hard Day's Night*), Lou Gramm (*You Can't Do That*), Dave Stewart (*Instant Karma*), Ray Charles (*Let It Be*), Dave Edmunds (*A Day In The Life, Strawberry Fields Forever* and *Working Class Hero*), Hall & Oates (*Don't Let Me Down* and *Julia*) and Roberta Flack (*In My Life*). Proceeds from the event go to the John and Yoko-established Spirit Foundation.

June [9] An international music festival "Muzeco '90" in Donetsk, Russia, is dedicated to the 50th anniversary of Lennon's birth.

Oct [9] *Imagine* is played simultaneously in 130 countries to commemorate what would have been Lennon's 50th birthday. A live worldwide broadcast is beamed from the United Nations consisting of a short introduction by Marcela Pérez de Cuéllar, wife of the UN Secretary-General, a taped message of Lennon and then *Imagine* .

[10] George Martin presents the John Lennon songwriting awards to 3 students at Salford College of Technology.

Dec [21-22] 2 Lennon tribute concerts take place at the Tokyo Dome, Tokyo, Japan, with Miles Davies (performing *Strawberry Fields Forever*) Natalie Cole & Toshinobu Kubota (*Ticket To Ride*), Linda Ronstadt (*Good Night*), Daryl Hall & John Oates (*Julia* and *Don't Let Me Down*) and Sean Lennon (*You've Got To Hide Your Love Away*).

LEVEL 42

Mark King (vocals, bass)
Mike Lindup (keyboards, vocals)
Boon Gould (guitar)
Phil Gould (drums)

1980 Band forms in London, though 3 of its members are from the Isle of Wight, UK, where King has been a drummer with various holiday camp groups, before switching to bass and moving to the UK capital. Band's name is taken from Douglas Adams' book **The Hitch-Hiker's Guide To The Galaxy**, in which "42" is the answer to question "What is the meaning of life?" First London club gigs are played as a purely instrumental jazz-funk outfit.

May Debut single *Love Meeting Love*, featuring a vocal by King (urged by producer/label owner Andy Sojka as a vital selling-point) is recorded for Sojka's UK dance-oriented independent label, Elite Records. It receives strong UK disco play and makes the Dance chart, attracting interest from larger record companies in the group.

Aug Band signs to Polydor, which reissues its first single (the Elite pressing having sold out).

Sept *Love Meeting Love* makes UK #61.

Nov *(Flying On The) Wings Of Love* is released. It again makes the UK Dance chart but fails to cross over.

1981 **May** *Love Games* from the band's debut album, reaches UK #38.

Aug *Turn It On* reaches UK #57, as debut album *Level 42*, produced by Mike Vernon, peaks at UK #20.

Nov *Starchild*, also from the album, makes UK #47. Band tours Germany supporting Police.

Dec Elite releases a limited-edition album, *Strategy*, containing the rest of the material recorded prior to the band's Polydor signing.

1982 **Apr** *The Early Tapes, July-August 1980*, a reissue by Polydor of the Elite limited-edition album, makes UK #46.

May *Are You Hearing (What I Hear?)* reaches UK #49.

Oct *Weave Your Spell* peaks at UK #43. It is taken from **The Pursuit Of Accidents**, which makes UK #17. Band follows with a "Pursuit Of Accidents" tour of UK and Europe, which brings it in contact with Larry Dunn and Verdine White of Earth, Wind & Fire, who offer to produce the next album.

1983 **Feb** *The Chinese Way* is their first UK Top 30 single, reaching UK #24.

Apr *Out Of Sight, Out Of Mind*, written by all 4 band members, makes UK #41.

Aug Light funk *The Sun Goes Down (Living It Up)* hits UK #10.

Sept *Standing In The Light*, produced in Los Angeles by Dunn and White, hits UK #9. Band follows with a 6-week US tour.

Oct *Micro Kids*, taken from the album, reaches UK #37. Following the band's return from US, it plays another UK tour into the New Year.

1984 **July** King releases solo album *Influences* which makes UK #77. He also releases *Freedom*, with Lindup but credited to Thunderthumbs and the Toetsenman (their nicknames).

Oct *Hot Water* becomes a live highlight and reaches UK #18. It is taken from **True Colours**, which makes UK #14.

Nov *The Chant Has Just Begun*, also from **True Colours**, makes UK #41

1985 **July** Double live album *A Physical Presence*, mostly recorded at small

UK club tour venues, climbs to UK #28.

Oct *Something About You* hits UK #6, their best-selling UK single so far.

Nov *World Machine*, produced by Wally Badarou, widens the group's sound into more commercial pop and hits UK #3, during a 72-week chart stay.

Dec Ballad *Leaving Me Now*, from *World Machine*, reaches UK #15. It prominently features Lindup's vocals alongside King's, a trend which will continue on most single releases.

86 May [31] *Something About You* is the group's US chart debut, hitting #7, as parent album *World Machine* reaches US #18.

June *Lessons In Love*, with Gary Barnacle on saxophone (and coupled with a live version of stage favorite *Hot Water*), hits UK #3. (It is the group's highest chart placing and will be the second biggest-selling single of the year in Europe, reaching #1 in 8 countries.) It is followed by a successful long-running world tour.

[20] Group takes part in the fourth Prince's Trust Rock Gala at Wembley Arena, London, with Eric Clapton, Phil Collins, Elton John, Paul McCartney and others.

Aug [2] *Hot Water* is the band's second US chart entry, at #87. Group tours US supporting Steve Winwood.

87 Jan King is voted Best Bass Player in **Making Music** magazine's poll.

Feb Uptempo *Running In The Family* hits UK #6. Group tours UK and Europe promoting it.

Apr Ballad *To Be With You Again* hits UK #10.

June [5-6] King and Lindup perform at the fifth annual Prince's Trust Rock Gala, for the second successive year, at the Wembley Arena.

[27] *Lessons In Love* reaches US #12, while *Running In The Family*, including the 2 previous singles, and again produced by Badarou, hits UK #2 and US #23. In support, the band plays a UK tour, which includes 2 dates at Birmingham NEC and 8 at Wembley Arena, and follows with a tour of Europe and US.

Aug [22] *Running In The Family* stalls at US #83.

Sept *It's Over*, another ballad, hits UK #10. As well as the usual 7" and 12" singles formats, it is released experimentally as one of UK's first CD video disks and sells out its pressing despite the fact that CD video players are not available on the UK market.

Dec Both Gould brothers leave the group, Boon suffering from an ulcer and Phil from nervous exhaustion. (Boon Gould will later release a solo album.) Neil Conti from Prefab Sprout joins temporarily on drums. *Children Say*, another track from the album (promoted by a video which features just King and Lindup), reaches UK #22. Proceeds are donated to London's Great Ormond Street children's hospital appeal fund.

88 Sept *Heaven In My Hands* reaches UK #12.

Oct *Staring At The Sun* hits UK #2, and will make US #128, while extracted *Take A Look* makes UK #32.

[29] Level 42 begins a European tour in Hamburg, Germany. (The 10-date tour will end Nov.12 in Barcelona.)

89 Feb *Tracie* reaches UK #25.

July [18-19] King, Lindup and Husband take part in the seventh annual Prince's Trust Rock Gala.

Nov Career hits retrospective *Level Best* hits UK #5, and includes current UK #39 *Take Care Of Yourself*.

90 June Lindup releases solo album *Changes*.

Pia King sues for divorce after her husband runs off with their children's nanny (and her best friend) Ria van de Brom.

Dec [10] They play first of 9 nights at London's Hammersmith Odeon.

Nov [19] Pia King is granted an uncontested "quickie" divorce.

91 Mar Level 42 and Polydor part company. The label, unhappy with direction of the band's new album, releases the group, to let them sign with RCA.

ARY LEWIS AND THE PLAYBOYS

ary Lewis (vocals, drums)
Ramsey (guitar)
an West (guitar)
avid Costell (bass)
avid Walker (keyboards)

54 Aug Lewis (b. Gary Levitch, July 31, 1946, New York, NY), the son of movie comedian Jerry Lewis, having played drums since age 14, forms a band in Hollywood, CA, with neighbors Ramsey (b. July 27, 1943, New Jersey), West (b. July 31, 1939, Uhrichsville, OH), Costell (b. Mar.15, 1944, Pittsburgh, PA) and Walker (b. May 12, 1943, Montgomeryville, AL). Initially together to play just local parties, they audition at Disneyland, and are hired for a summer season at the park.

They also have a cameo musical role in the Raquel Welch movie "A Swingin' Summer".

1965 Feb Signed to Liberty Records by producer Snuff Garrett, the group's debut is Leon Russell-arranged *This Diamond Ring*, co-written by Al Kooper and previously turned down by Bobby Vee. An instant hit, it tops US chart for 2 weeks and is a million-seller. Group performs on US TV's "Ed Sullivan Show".

May *Count Me In*, written by Glen D. Hardin of The Crickets, hits US #2 behind Herman's Hermits' *Mrs. Brown You've Got A Lovely Daughter*, in a chart dominated by UK acts. Lewis is the only American artist on the survey. Debut album *This Diamond Ring* reaches US #26.

Aug The sing-a-long *Save Your Heart For Me* (on which Lewis whistles as well as singing), hits US #2 behind Sonny & Cher's *I Got You Babe*.

Oct *Everybody Loves A Clown*, a joint composition by Lewis, Garrett and Russell, hits US #4. *A Session With Gary Lewis & The Playboys*, which includes the previous 2 hit singles, reaches US #18.

Dec *Everybody Loves A Clown* makes US #44.

1966 Jan The Beach Boys-like *She's Just My Style*, again jointly penned by singer, producer and arranger, hits US #3. Group appears in the pop/espionage B-movie "Out Of Sight", with The Turtles, The Knickerbockers, and Freddie & The Dreamers.

Apr *Sure Gonna Miss Her* hits US #9, while *She's Just My Style* reaches #71. Lewis joins the US Air Force Reserve.

June *Green Grass*, a UK song by Roger Cook and Roger Greenaway, hits US #8 (the last of Lewis's 7 consecutive US Top 10 hits).

July *Gary Lewis Hits Again!* makes US #47.

Aug *My Heart's Symphony*, another Hardin song, reaches US #13.

Oct Lewis plays lead role in the musical "Bye Bye Birdie" in Kansas City, MO.

Nov *(You Don't Have To) Paint Me A Picture* reaches US #15.

Dec Compilation *Golden Greats*, containing all the group's Top 10 singles, hits US #10. It is Lewis' most successful album, earning a gold disk for a half million sales, and staying on chart for 46 weeks. The group appears in Lewis' father Jerry's film "Way Way Out".

1967 Jan [1] Lewis is drafted into the US Army, and the band is forced to split. (Bitter at the interruption to his career, he will refuse to form a Special Services band to entertain troops, and instead spends his time as a clerk/typist in Korea.) *Where Will The Words Come From*, released just before his call-up, reaches US #21.

Apr Liberty continues to issue earlier-recorded Lewis disks, but with the band off the road and unavailable for TV promotion, *The Loser (With A Broken Heart)* reaches only US #43, while *You Don't Have To Paint Me A Picture* peaks at US #79.

June *Girls In Love* makes US #39.

July *New Directions* climbs to US #185.

Sept [16] *Jill* peaks at UK #52.

1968 Aug Out of the army, and with a new group of Playboys, Lewis' revival of Bryan Hyland's *Sealed With A Kiss* reaches US #19.

Sept Newly-recorded *Gary Lewis Now!* sells moderately, reaching US #150, but will be Lewis' last successful album.

1969 June Lewis tries another revival, of The Cascades' *Rhythm Of The Rain*, but it halts at #63 (although it charts for 12 weeks). It will be his final US Singles chart entry.

Sept *Rhythm Of The Rain* does not chart. (Lewis tries to escape the teenybop appeal of his earlier hits by evolving a more serious singer/songwriter style, but makes little headway. With the advent of 60s nostalgia shows and tours in US, Lewis re-forms The Playboys in the 70s to concentrate on playing his early hits on the oldies circuit, and finds regular touring work.)

1975 Feb In an unexpected postscript, *My Heart's Symphony* is reissued in UK, where Lewis and The Playboys made no impression during the 60s, after dancefloor success (as a "rare oldie") on the Northern soul scene, and it makes UK #36.

HUEY LEWIS & THE NEWS

Huey Lewis (vocals)
Sean Hopper (keyboards)
Chris Hayes (lead guitar)
Johnny Colla (saxophone, guitar)
Mario Cipollina (bass)
Bill Gibson (drums)

1976 Nov Lewis (b. Hugh Anthony Cregg III, July 5, 1950, New York, NY), a latecomer member (on harmonica and occasional vocals) to San Francisco band Clover when it signs to Vertigo Records in UK, sings lead vocal on its debut single *Chicken Funk*, produced by Nick Lowe.

HUEY LEWIS & THE NEWS cont.

1977 **Feb** Clover issues first of 4 singles and 2 albums (*Unavailable* and *Love On The Wire*), none chart successes. Band backs Elvis Costello on *My Aim Is True*, and tours supporting Thin Lizzy and others.

1979 **May** After leader John McFee leaves to join The Doobie Brothers, Clover breaks up. Lewis plays briefly in London on sessions for Nick Lowe and Dave Edmunds (albums *Labour Of Lust* and *Repeat When Necessary*), then returns to Mill Valley, CA, involving himself in a yoghurt business by day, and joining regular Monday night jam sessions at Uncle Charlie's club in Marin County with a group of musicians (who will form the core of his next band). They record a disco version of the *Exodus* theme, titled *Exodisco*, which is picked up by Mercury Records, and issued under the name American Express.

1980 **May** After playing informally together for some months, The News is formed permanently when Chrysalis signs the group on the strength of demos recorded by the Monday night jammers at Different Fur studio in Marin County. Lewis and Sean Hopper (b. Mar.31, 1953, California) are both ex-Clover, Hayes (b. Nov.24, 1957, California) has been with California jazz bands, and Colla (b. July 2, 1952, California), Gibson (b. Nov.13, 1951, California), and Cipollina (b. Nov.10, 1954, California) are all ex-members of Soundhole, which backed Van Morrison.
July *Huey Lewis And The News*, produced by Bill Schnee and of almost all self-penned material, fails to sell.

1982 **Apr** *Do You Believe In Love*, written by Clover's producer Robert John Lange, is the band's debut US hit, climbing to #7, but fails in UK.
June *Picture This* makes US #13 and again fails in UK. It has more non-Lewis compositions than the first album and covers of songs by Wet Willie, Phil Lynott, and The Hollywood Flames (their 1957 hit *Buzz Buzz Buzz*). The song from Wet Willie's Michael Duke, *Hope You Love Me Like You Say You Do*, is extracted and makes US #36. Lynott's song *Tattoo (Giving It All Up For Love)* is issued in UK, but fails to chart.
Sept *Workin' For A Livin'*, also from the second album, peaks at US #41.

1983 **Sept** *Sports* is released and initially hits US #6. (It is destined to be a long-term US seller, topping 7 million.)
Nov *Heart And Soul*, a Chinn/Chapman song earlier recorded by Exile, hits US #8 (the first US hit from *Sports*).

1984 **Mar** *I Want A New Drug (Called Love)* hits US #6. (Lewis later sues Ray Parker Jr., writer of the similarly-styled "Ghostbusters" theme, for alleged plagiarism of this song; the case will be settled out of court to Lewis' satisfaction.)
June *Sports* hits US #1 for a week, having been on chart for 8 months. Third extract, *The Heart Of Rock And Roll*, hits US #6 for 4 weeks.
July [24] Group performs at the North Dakota State Fair, before a crowd of over 18,000.
Sept *If This Is It*, also from *Sports*, peaks at US #6. It finally gives Lewis a UK chart debut, reaching #39.
Dec Final *Sports* extract, *Walking On A Thin Line*, reaches US #18.

1985 **Jan** [28] Lewis and the band participate in the recording of USA For Africa's *We Are The World*, in Los Angeles. Lewis takes a solo vocal line on the single.
July Lewis opts out of playing at Live Aid, resenting the over-publicity involved in the event.
Aug *The Power Of Love*, written for movie "Back To The Future" (in which Lewis has a cameo acting role as a music teacher) tops US chart for 2 weeks, becoming a million-seller.
Sept *Sports* finally charts in UK, reaching #23, while *The Power Of Love* is the band's first UK Top 20 hit, climbing to #11.
Dec EP *Heart And Soul*, a compilation of US Top 10 hits *The Heart Of Rock And Roll* and the title track, plus *Hope You Love Me Like You Say You Do* and *Buzz Buzz Buzz* from *Picture This*, reaches UK #61.

1986 **Feb** [10] Band wins Best International Group at the fifth annual BRIT awards at the Grosvenor House, Mayfair, London, and also performs live at the ceremony.
[25] "Huey Lewis & The News: The Heart Of Rock'N'Roll" wins Best Music Video, Long Form at the 28th annual Grammy Awards.
Mar Following the release in UK of film "Back To The Future", *The Power Of Love* is reactivated (as a double A-side with a reissue of the band's first US hit *Do You Believe In Love*), and hits UK #9.
May *The Heart Of Rock And Roll*, released for the third time in UK, finally makes #49.
Sept [20] *Stuck With You*, aided by desert island video clip, tops US chart for 3 weeks, and reaches UK #12.
Oct [18] *Fore!*, which includes *Stuck With You* and *The Power Of Love*, hits US #1 and UK #8.
Dec [6] *Hip To Be Square* hits US #3 and makes UK #41.
[7] Lewis & The News sing the US national anthem a cappella before the San Francisco 49ers vs. New York Jets football game at Candlestick

Park, San Francisco.

1987 **Mar** [14] *Jacob's Ladder*, the fourth single from *Fore!*, hits US #1. Written by Bruce and John Hornsby (whose first album Lewis has partly produced, and whose group has supported The News on tour), the song is a swipe at US TV evangelists.
Apr *Simple As That*, released in UK instead of *Jacob's Ladder*, makes #
May [30] *I Know What I Like* hits US #9.
Sept [19] *Doing It All (For My Baby)* hits US #6; the album *Fore!* has generated 6 US Top 10 hits.

1988 **Aug** *Small World* is released, set to reach US #11 and UK #12.
Sept Extracted *Perfect World* hits US #3, but only makes UK #48, the band's last 80s charting single.
Nov [26] Title cut *Small World* reaches US #25.

1989 **Feb** [11] Final album extract *Give Me The Keys (And I'll Drive You Crazy)* makes US #47.
May [18] Group takes part in AIDS benefit concert with Tracy Chapman, The Grateful Dead, Los Lobos and Linda Ronstadt at the Coliseum, Oakland, CA.
Sept [8-9] Group plays under the name The Sports Section at the Clu Casino, Hampton, NJ, to try out new songs.

1991 **May** Now signed to EMI, Lewis & The News release *Hard At Play* with first extract *Couple Days Off*. The project is produced by the grou with Bill Schnee.

JERRY LEE LEWIS

1949 Lewis (b. Sept.29, 1935, Ferriday, LA) shows an early talent for music, so his parents mortgage their house to buy him a piano, which he teaches himself to play in 2 weeks. He is exposed to a rich mix of musical cultures – jazz (through his parents), hillbilly (and its more commercial offspring, country and western), gospel and cajun. He makes his first public performance at an auto show featuring the year new model Fords in Natchez, LA. When he earns $9 singing *Hadacol Boogie* with a local C&W band, his father encourages his musical care loading the piano on the family truck and driving him to shows.

1950 Lewis attends the fundamentalist Assembly of God Institute Bible school in Waxahachie, TX, where he studies music and theology. (He later expelled.)

1952 **Feb** Lewis, at age 16, marries preacher's daughter Dorothy Barton (whom he soon abandons in favor of club life).

1953 **Sept** Lewis gets married, bigamously, to Jane Mitcham at a shotgun wedding, encouraged by her brothers.
Oct Lewis finally divorces Barton.
Jane gives birth to Jerry Lee Lewis Jr.

1956 Lewis and his father sell 33 dozen eggs to finance a trip to Memphis, TN, hoping to audition for Sun Records. They arrive to find label hea Sam Phillips has just left for Nashville, TN. Lewis threatens to sit on doorstep until he is allowed in to perform. Eventually Jack Clement in him in to cut a tape and tells him to return in a month. When he does so, Phillips invites him to record *Whole Lotta Shakin' Goin' On* and Cra Arms for a Sun single. Released near the end of the year, it is promptl banned by most of the country's radio stations because of its vulgarit
Dec [4] Lewis joins Elvis Presley and Carl Perkins in an impromptu recording session at Sun studios in Memphis. (These recordings will become known as "The Million Dollar Quartet". Johnny Cash leaves the session just before its start, at the insistence of his wife, who want to go shopping.)

1957 Lewis, on extensive tour, meets Sam Phillips' brother Judd at a show Alabama. He offers Lewis national TV exposure and takes him to New York, securing a contract for 2 appearances on the "Steve Allen Show"
Mar [31] He begins a major tour of Southern states with Perkins and Cash at Little Rock, AR.
July [28] Lewis makes his US TV debut on the "Steve Allen Show". (His second appearance is the only time Allen's show is ever to top E Sullivan's in the national ratings. Before it *Whole Lotta Shakin' Goin' O* had sold about 30,000 copies, mainly in the South. Afterwards, it sells more than 6 million nationally, not hitting its #3 chart peak until Sept when Sun is shipping 50-60,000 copies a day. It tops C&W and R&B charts simultaneously.)
Oct *Whole Lotta Shakin'*, released on London label, hits UK #8.
Nov [12] Movie "Jamboree" (UK title: "Disc Jockey Jamboree") with Lewis, Fats Domino, Carl Perkins and many others, premieres in US.
Dec [11] Still married to Jane Mitcham, Lewis secretly marries his 13-year-old second cousin Myra Gale Brown, daughter of his bass player Jay, in Hernando, MS. (Lewis' other cousins include country singer Mickey Gilley and TV evangelist Jimmy Swaggart.)

958 Jan *Great Balls Of Fire* hits US #2 for a month, kept from the top by Danny & The Juniors' *At The Hop*. It sells a million copies in its first 10 days of release (and will sell over 5 million in US). It tops UK chart.
Feb Hank Williams' *You Win Again* (a 1952 US #13 for Tommy Edwards), B-side of *Great Balls Of Fire*, makes US #95.
Apr *Breathless* hits both US and UK #7, as Lewis is legally divorced from Jane Mitcham.
May [22] Lewis' unorthodox marriage has earned condemnation from the church in US but the real storm hits when he arrives for his first UK tour. Waiting reporters ask who his young companion is and he tells them she is his wife and cousin and that he has been married twice before. Newspapers seize on the story. The resulting hysteria leads to his being booed off stage and forced to cancel 34 of the scheduled 37 concerts. On his return he finds that Sun, panicked by the scandal, has not serviced his new record, *High School Confidential*, to DJs.
June [9] Lewis takes out a 5-page trade ad to explain his recent divorce. He writes, "I hope that if I'm washed up as a performer, it won't be because of this bad publicity." He also re-weds Myra in a ceremony of impeccable legality. *High School Confidential*, from the film of the same name in which Lewis appears, makes US #21, selling a half million copies. (Sales of Lewis' subsequent Sun releases will be limited by lack of radio play and the label's hesitancy in promoting its artist.)
Sept *Break Up* makes US #52 as B-side *I'll Make It All Up To You* peaks at US #85. (Both songs are written by Charlie Rich.)
959 Jan *I'll Sail My Ship Alone* stalls at US #93.
Feb *High School Confidential* makes UK #12. Myra gives birth to Lewis' second son, Steve Allen.
May *Lovin' Up A Storm* reaches UK #28.
960 Constantly touring, Lewis develops a serious problem with alcohol and pep pills.
June *Baby Baby Bye Bye* climbs to UK #47.
961 May *What'd I Say* makes US #30 and UK #10.
962 Apr [24] Lewis' son Steve Allen drowns in their home swimming pool, as Myra fixes Easter dinner.
[29] Lewis returns to UK for the first time in 4 years amid favorable public response at the City Hall, Newcastle, Tyne & Wear.
June *Jerry Lee Lewis Vol. 2* reaches UK #14.
Sept Lewis' version of Chuck Berry's *Sweet Little Sixteen* stalls at US #95, but makes UK #38.
963 Mar His cover of Little Richard's *Good Golly Miss Molly* makes UK #31.
Sept [6] Lewis leaves Sun and signs to Mercury subsidiary Smash.
Sept His daughter Phoebe Allen is born.
964 Mar *The Golden Hits Of Jerry Lee Lewis*, a re-recording of his Sun hits for Smash, becomes Lewis' first US chart album, reaching #116 during an 8-week chart stay.
Apr Lewis' first single for Smash, *I'm On Fire* stalls at US #98.
Nov Live *High Heel Sneakers* peaks at US #91.
[22] Lewis begins UK tour with The Yardbirds, Twinkle, The Quiet Five and others, at the Hippodrome, Brighton, E.Sussex. Tour ends Dec.7 at the Town Hall, Birmingham, W.Midlands.
Dec *The Greatest Live Show On Earth*, recorded in Birmingham, AL, July 1, 1964, makes US #71.
965 Mar [31] Lewis begins a European tour in Germany.
Apr [18] He appears in film "Be My Guest", which goes on general release as a B feature to Morecambe & Wise film "The Intelligence Men" in UK.
June *The Return Of Rock* makes US #121.
966 May *Memphis Beat* makes US #145.
July [1] Lewis begins a US tour with Herman's Hermits, The Animals and Lou Christie in Honolulu, HI.
Aug [21] Lewis is signed to play Iago in Jack Good's London stage production of "Catch My Soul", his rock opera adaptation of Shakespeare's "Othello".
Oct [17] Lewis embarks on first UK tour in 2 years in Bradford, W.Yorks., with 2 cabaret gigs at the Guiseley Paradise and the Lyceum Rainbow.
968 Mar Lewis switches to recording country music, and *Another Place, Another Time* peaks at US #97 but hits US C&W #1.
July *What Made Milwaukee Famous (Has Made A Loser Out Of Me)* stalls at US #94, but is another big country hit (one of more than 30 by Lewis in the next 10 years). *Another Place, Another Time* peaks at US #160, during a 12-week stay.
Aug Lewis takes part in the 8th National Jazz & Blues Festival in Richmond, London.
Nov *To Make Love Sweeter For You* tops US Country chart.
969 Feb *She Still Comes Around (To Love What's Left Of Me)* makes US #149.

May 2 Smash albums, *Jerry Lewis Sings The Country Music Hall Of Fame, Volume 1* and *Volume 2*, reach US #127 and US #124.
Sept 2 Sun compilation albums simultaneously make the US chart. *Original Golden Hits Vol.1* (including the first 3 singles) reaches #119 and *Vol.2* makes #122.
Sept [13] Lewis takes part in "The Rock'N'Revival Concert" in Toronto, Canada, with fellow rockers Chuck Berry, Gene Vincent, Bo Diddley, Little Richard and (making their live debut) John Lennon's Plastic Ono Band.
1970 Feb *She Even Woke Me Up To Say Goodbye* spends 2 weeks in US chart, making #186.
May *The Best Of Jerry Lee Lewis*, a collection of his country hits, peaks at US #114.
Oct *Live At The International, Las Vegas*, his first album for main label Mercury, reaches US #149. Myra, Lewis' wife, files for divorce. She will later claim that she only spent 3 nights alone with Lewis in 13 years of marriage. He is shocked into embracing the church and shunning alcohol, cigars and the pursuit of young women. (This abstinence will last 2 months.)
1971 Jan *There Must Be More To Love Than This* makes US #190. The title track tops US Country chart.
Aug *Touching Home* climbs to US #152.
Dec *Would You Take Another Chance On Me* makes US #115. The title track tops US Country chart.
[18] Lewis and wife Myra Brown divorce, as he prepares to marry Memphis divorcee, 29-year-old Jaren Elizabeth Gunn Pate.
1972 Jan Lewis' version of Kris Kristofferson's *Me And Bobby McGee* becomes his biggest pop hit in more than 13 years, climbing to US #40.
Apr Lewis returns to rock'n'roll covering The Big Bopper's *Chantilly Lace*, which reaches US #43. It also tops US Country chart. *The "Killer" Rocks On* begins a 12-week US chart run, peaking at #105.
May *Chantilly Lace* makes UK #33 (his first UK hit in 9 years and his last to date).
July *Turn On Your Love Light* stalls at US #95.
1973 Mar *The Session* enters US chart and at #37 is his best album chart result. It is a collection of oldies recorded in London with the help of Peter Frampton, Rory Gallagher, Albert Lee, Alvin Lee and others.
May Extracted from the album, *Drinkin' Wine Spo-Dee O'Dee*, a cover of 1949 R&B #2 for Stick McGhee and one of the first songs Lewis ever performed, reaches US #41 (and will be his last US pop hit).
Nov [13] Lewis' 19-year-old son Jerry Lewis Jr., the drummer in his band, is killed in an auto accident in DeSoto county. He has recently been in mental hospitals and suffered from drug abuse.
1976 Sept [29] Lewis accidentally shoots his bass player Norman Owens in the chest, while blasting holes in his own office door. Owens survives but sues his boss.
Nov [22] Lewis drives his Rolls Royce into a ditch and is arrested for drunk driving.
[23] 10 hours later, he is arrested for brandishing a Derringer pistol outside Elvis Presley's Gracelands home in Memphis, demanding to see the "King".
1977 Lewis hits US C&W #4 with aptly-titled *Middle Age Crazy*.
1978 Lewis signs to Elektra Records. *Rockin' My Life Away* receives some FM radio play but the relationship between artist and company is soon strained and ends in mutual lawsuits.
1979 May Elektra album *Jerry Lee Lewis* makes US #186.
1980 June Lewis is featured on "Roadie" film soundtrack.
1981 Apr [23] A concert for German TV in Stuttgart reunites the 3 surviving members of Sun's 1956 "Million Dollar Quartet": Lewis, Carl Perkins and Johnny Cash, who this time is not whisked away by his wife to shop. (Recordings from the show will be released in 1982 on CBS album *The Survivors*.)
June [30] Lewis is hospitalized in Memphis Methodist hospital with a hemorrhaging stomach ulcer. From his bed, he countersues Elektra Records for $5 million as label dispute ends his contract. (After 2 serious operations doctors estimate his chances of survival at 50:50. He is back on the road within 4 months and recording for new label MCA.)
1982 Lewis appears on the year's Grammy awards telecast with cousin Mickey Gilley, as ex-wife Myra's book **Great Balls Of Fire** is published. (Myra Williams, now remarried, is an Atlanta real estate broker.)
June [8] Lewis' estranged fourth wife drowns in a swimming pool.
1983 Feb *My Fingers Do The Talkin'* makes US C&W #62. (2 singles also make C&W chart later in the year: *Come As You Were* (US #66) and *Why You Been Gone So Long* (US #69).)
June [7] Lewis marries his fifth wife and companion of 2 years, 25-year old Shawn Michelle Stevens.

Aug [24] Shawn is found dead at Lewis' Mississippi home. An autopsy finds the cause of death to be a methadone overdose and a grand jury finds no reason to suspect foul play, despite widespread media interest.

1984 **Feb** [16] Lewis surrenders himself to federal authorities in Memphis for arraignment and to plead not guilty to charges of evading federal income taxes 1975-80.

Apr [24] Lewis marries wife number 6, 22-year-old Kerrie McCarver.

Oct After a long battle with the Internal Revenue Service, a Federal Court jury acquits Lewis of tax evasion. A **Rolling Stone** article by Pulitzer Prize winner Richard Ben Cramer points to disturbing circumstantial evidence surrounding Shawn's death – broken glass on the floor, a sack of bloodstained clothes in the room where she died and blood and bruises on her body. Her mother claims Shawn had called her the day before her death and said she was going to leave Lewis after they had had physical fights. "The Killer" survives the scandal.

1985 Lewis recovers from another spell on the critical list, with 2 bleeding ulcers. Rhino Records releases **Milestones**, a collection of Lewis' work 1956-77. He begins recording an album with Gilley.

1986 **Feb** Lewis is inducted into the Rock'N'Roll Hall Of Fame.

June [5] Lewis joins Ray Charles as Fats Domino's guests at the Storyville Jazz Hall, New Orleans, LA, recording a US HBO TV special "Fats Domino And Friends". Ron Wood plays guitar for Lewis.

Dec [2] Lewis checks into the Betty Ford Clinic to overcome a painkiller addiction.

1987 **Jan** [28] Kerrie gives birth to Jerry Lee Lewis III – Lewis' only surviving son – in Memphis.

1988 Production begins on filming of Lewis' life in movie "Great Balls Of Fire" starring Dennis Quaid, who receives piano lessons from Lewis. Lewis takes part in the Barcelona Olympic Ceremony.

Dec Lewis, still under investigation by the IRS, appears in Memphis Federal Bankruptcy court filing for protection, saying he owes over $3 million to some 22 creditors, including $2 million in back taxes.

1989 **July** Biopic "Great Balls Of Fire" opens in US theaters, dramatizing the early years of "The Killer's" career. Both Quaid and Lewis have already quibbled over who will sing the vocals on the film's songs. The result is a 50:50 arrangement with Lewis performing new versions of his old hits on the soundtrack album.

1990 **Apr** A tour of Europe is cancelled when Lewis fails to turn up for 6 shows. Promoter Mervyn Conn threatens suit.

[15] Conn persuades Lewis' wife to fly to UK in the hope that Lewis will follow her and thereby honor his agreement.

GORDON LIGHTFOOT

1958 Lightfoot (b. Nov.17, 1938, Orillia, Canada), having shown musical talent since age 8 and later learned the piano, moves from his home town on the shore of Lake Simcoe to study orchestration and harmony at Westlake College, Los Angeles, CA, but becomes homesick after 14 months and returns to Canada. While turning out piano pieces for a living, he starts to take a deep interest in folk and country music.

1960 He begins to play guitar, inspired by listening to Pete Seeger and Bob Gibson. He teams with Terry Whelan as The Two Tones and has a local hit with Nashville-cut *Remember Me, I'm The One*, on Chateau Records.

1961 Lightfoot makes his US debut at La Cave in Cleveland, OH, sharing a bill with José Feliciano.

1963 Having spent a year working in UK, Lightfoot performs folk-styled material around Toronto clubs with his guitar and, hearing Bob Dylan for the first time on disk, begins to absorb his influence.

1964 Singing at Steel's Tavern in Toronto, he meets Ian & Sylvia Tyson, a leading Canadian folk duo, who decide to record his *For Lovin' Me* and *Early Morning Rain*. (The 2 songs are passed on for consideration by Peter, Paul And Mary, who also record them and have US hits with both during 1965.) Lightfoot is signed by Albert Grossman, manager of both the Tysons and Peter, Paul And Mary (as well as Dylan).

1965 He recruits 2 back-up musicians, Red Shea (guitar) and John Stockfish (bass) for his live gigs, and signs to United Artists Records. (He will record 5 albums in 4 years for the label, starting with **Lightfoot**, but none will chart.) Country singer Marty Robbins hits US C&W #1 with his *Ribbon Of Darkness*. Lightfoot receives the first of many Juno awards, the Canadian music industry's Grammy equivalent.

1966 **Feb** [16] Lightfoot begins a 9-date UK tour with the Ian Campbell Folk Group, Ian & Sylvia and The Settlers at the De Montfort Hall, Leicester, Leics., ending Feb.25 at Fairfield Hall, Croydon, London.

1967 He makes his debut at New York's Town Hall, as his growing popularity takes his touring further afield.

1969 **June** [2] Lightfoot makes a one-off London appearance at the Royal Festival Hall.

Dec His last album for UA is **Sunday Concert**, recorded live at Massey Hall, Toronto, Canada.

1970 **Jan** He signs to the Warner Bros. subsidiary label Reprise, working with producer Lenny Waronker.

1971 **Feb** Lightfoot's singles chart debut *If You Could Read My Mind* hits US #5, while the album of the same title (originally called **Sit Down Young Stranger** and retitled after the single's success) reaches US #12, selling over a half million copies to earn a gold disk.

July *If You Could Read My Mind* reaches UK #30. Follow-up *Talking In Your Sleep* peaks at US #64, while **Summer Side Of Life** makes US #38. United Artists compilation album **Classic Lightfoot (The Best Of Gordon Lightfoot, Vol.2)** makes US #178.

Sept *Summer Side Of Life* peaks at US #98.

1972 **May** **Don Quixote** reaches US #42 and UK #44.

July *Beautiful*, taken from **Don Quixote**, peaks at US #58.

Dec **Old Dan's Records** makes US #95.

1974 **June** *Sundown* tops US chart, going gold with million-plus sales, as does the album of the same title, which hits US #1 for 2 weeks.

Aug *Sundown* makes UK #33, while album of the same title reaches UK #45. In US, United Artists compilation **The Very Best Of Gordon Lightfoot** makes US #155.

Nov *Carefree Highway*, taken from **Sundown**, hits US #10.

1975 **Apr** **Cold On The Shoulder** hits US #10.

May Extracted cut, *Rainy Day People* reaches US #26.

1976 **Jan** Double compilation **Gord's Gold** (the first component album which has new re-recordings of songs from his United Artists days) makes US #34, and earns a gold disk. By now, Lightfoot is playing some 70 concerts a year in US and Canada, backed by a stage band consisting of Red Shea and Terry Clements (guitars), Pee Wee Charles (steel guitar) and Rick Haynes (bass). (There is no drummer on live shows, though Jim Gordon plays drums on recording sessions.)

Nov *The Wreck Of The Edmund Fitzgerald*, the true account of the sinking of an ore vessel on Lake Superior on Nov.11, 1975 with the loss of all 29 crew members, hits US #2 for 2 weeks (behind Rod Stewart's *Tonight's The Night*), and is Lightfoot's second gold single.

Dec **Summertime Dream**, which includes *The Wreck Of The Edmund Fitzgerald*, hits US #12 and is a million-seller, earning a platinum disk. He appears on stage with Dylan's "Rolling Thunder Revue".

1977 **Jan** *The Wreck Of The Edmund Fitzgerald* makes UK #40.

Mar *Race Among The Ruins* peaks at US #65.

1978 **Mar** He moves to Warner Bros. for **Endless Wire**, which climbs to US #20, earning another gold disk.

Apr *The Circle Is Small (I Can See It In Your Eyes)*, taken from **Endless Wire**, makes US #33.

Oct *Daylight Katy*, not issued as a US single, makes UK #41.

1980 **May** **Dream Street Rose** reaches US #60.

1982 **Mar** **Shadows** peaks at US #87.

May *Baby Step Back*, taken from **Shadows**, makes US #50, and is Lightfoot's final US Hot 100 chart entry.

1983 **Jan** Lightfoot presents 5 songs to Kenny Rogers. He turns them down, but Lightfoot will re-work them to record on a future album.

1985 **Apr** He sings on *Tears Are Not Enough* by Northern Lights, the Canadian multi-artist recording in aid of the USA For Africa trust, sharing vocals with fellow Canadians like Neil Young, Joni Mitchell, Bryan Adams, Baron Longfellow and many others.

Aug *Salute* peaks at US #175.

1986 **Sept** **East Of Midnight**, produced with help from compatriot David Foster, climbs to US #165. Extracted first single *Anything For Love* makes #71 on US C&W chart.

1987 **Nov** Lightfoot ends his North American tour in Atlantic City, NJ.

1988 **Apr** Lightfoot & The Lightfoot Band, now comprising Terry Clements, Rick Haynes and recent additions Barry Keane on drums and Mike Heffernan on keyboards, begin re-recording 13 Lightfoot songs at Eastern Sound studios, Toronto, Canada. The songs, plus previously unrecorded *If It Should Please You*, will be released as **Gord's Gold Volume II** at the end of the year.

1989 **Oct** [3] Lightfoot plays at the Westbury Music Fair, Westbury, NY, during an extended North American tour.

ITTLE FEAT

owell George (vocals, guitar)
aul Barrere (lead guitar)
ill Payne (keyboards)
red Tackett (guitar)
enny Gradney (bass)
ichie Hayward (drums)
am Clayton (percussion)

970
Mar Guitarist George (b. Apr.13, 1945, Hollywood, CA), ex-Factory, The Standells and The Seeds, having briefly joined Frank Zappa's Mothers Of Invention to replace Ray Collins (his rhythm guitar and vocals preserved on Zappa track *Didja Get Any Onya* from *Weasels Ripped My Flesh*), is encouraged by Zappa to form his own band after Zappa hears George's song *Willing*. George takes Zappa's advice and his bass player, Roy Estrada (b. Santa Ana, CA). They link with Payne (b. Mar.12, 1949, Waco, TX) and Hayward (b. Ames, IA), ex-The Fraternity Of Man. (Jimmy Carl Black of The Mothers Of Invention provides the band's name when laughing at George's small shoe size.)
May Little Feat signs to Warner Bros. and *Strawberry Flats/Hamburger Midnight* is released to critical acclaim.

971
Debut album *Little Feat*, completed for a while, is released, produced by Russ Titelman with guests Ry Cooder and Sneaky Pete Kleinow.

972
Second album *Sailin' Shoes* is released. Estrada leaves to join Captain Beefheart's Magic Band.

973
Third album *Dixie Chicken* includes Gradney (b. New Orleans, LA) on bass and percussionist Clayton (b. New Orleans), both ex-Delaney & Bonnie. Ex-Lead Enema Barrere (b. July 3, 1948, Burbank, CA) also joins and the new line-up plays its first gig at the Easter Festival, Hawaii, HI. The cycle of touring and destructive personal habits becomes too much and the band breaks up. Payne joins The Doobie Brothers but quits mid-tour to join Bonnie Raitt's band. The rest of the band signs to Zappa's Discreet label to provide backing for unknown Los Angeles, CA singer Kathy Dalton. Freddie White joins from Donny Hathaway's band on drums. There are rumors that ex-Vinegar Joe singer Robert Palmer will be asked to replace the increasingly erratic George, who in turn is rumored to be forming a band with John Sebastian and Phil Everly.

974
Nov Warner Bros. offers the band money to re-form and it re-enters its Blue Seas studio in Hunts Valley, MD, to cut *Feats Don't Fail Me Now*. Bonnie Raitt, Emmylou Harris and Van Dyke Parks guest on the album, which reaches US #36, the band's first gold disk.

975
Jan [12] Group begins a 9-city, 18-show European tour under the banner "The Warner Brothers Music Show". The other bands on tour, The Doobie Brothers, Tower of Power, Bonaroo, Montrose and Graham Central Station are upstaged by Little Feat which gets the rave reviews. As they record *The Last Record Album*, George contracts hepatitis.
Dec *The Last Record Album* reaches US and UK #36.

976
June [13] On a return UK visit, the band plays at the Odeon theater, Birmingham, W.Midlands.

977
June *Time Loves A Hero* is released with George only contributing 1 song. The album reaches US #34 and hits UK #8.

978
Mar Live shows around double album *Waiting For Columbus* are considered lackluster, but it reaches US #18 and UK #43, becoming the band's second gold disk.

979
Apr As George mixes Little Feat's album, Payne and Barrere tour with Nicolette Larson. It is well-received, Warners signs the backing band and Payne announces Little Feat is disbanded. George sets out on tour with solo album *Thanks, I'll Eat It Here*, which makes US and UK #71.
June [29] 2 months after Little Feat's break up and the day after a sell-out solo performance in Washington, DC, George, aged 34, is found dead from a heart attack brought on by drug abuse in a motel in Arlington, VA.
Aug [4] The surviving members of Little Feat are joined by Jackson Browne, Emmylou Harris, Nicolette Larson, Michael McDonald, Bonnie Raitt and Linda Ronstadt in a benefit concert at Los Angeles' Forum. The 20,000 crowd raises over $230,000 for George's widow.
Dec Little Feat album *Down On the Farm* (originally titled *Duck Lips*) reaches US #29 and UK #46.

981
Aug Compilation album *Hoy-Hoy!* makes UK #76.
Sept *Hoy-Hoy!* reaches US #39.

983
Barrere cuts solo album *On My Own Two Feet*, on Mirage.

988
Apr Original line-up, with Craig Fuller assuming George's position, re-signs with Warner Bros., and the group records a new album.

Aug *Let It Roll* is released, but meets with scant interest.

1989
Sept [12] Group ends US tour at the Greek theater, Los Angeles, CA.

1990
May [19] *Representing The Mambo* reaches US #45.
June [29] Now managed by Peter Asher (of Peter And Gordon) Little Feat plays the Hammersmith Odeon, London.
July [13] Band begins 2-month US tour in Columbus, OH. The tour will end Sept.18 in Los Angeles, CA.

LITTLE RICHARD

1950
Little Richard (b. Richard Wayne Penniman, Dec.5, 1935, Macon, GA) having grown up with 11 brothers and sisters, the children of Charles and Leva Mae, and the Seventh Day Adventist faith (his father and grandfather are preachers), and sung in church, with the Penniman Singers, developing strong gospel links, as The Tiny Tots Quartet, after running off with Dr. Hudson's Medicine Show, selling snake oil at fairs and carnivals, he then sings with Sugarfoot Sam's Minstrel Show. Adopted by the white family of Ann and Johnny Johnson, who run Ann's Tick Tock club in Macon, he begins performing R&B numbers, having learned to play gospel piano from a character named Esquerita. He also picks up a job washing dishes in a bus station and sings with the B. Brown Orchestra.

1951
Oct [16] Richard makes his first recordings in Atlanta, GA, for RCA Camden, arranged after singer Billy Wright has introduced him to a Georgia DJ with RCA connections, who had entered him in a radio audition contest at Atlanta's Eighty One theater. Wright, with his heavy make-up and gelled hair, is to be a major visual influence on Richard. (Tracks from this session and another in Jan.1952, including *Every Hour* and *Get Rich Quick*, are released in 1952 on 4 US singles and on album in US and UK in 1959 and 1970.)

1953
Richard moves to Houston to record 8 tracks for Don Robey's Peacock label, initially credited to sessions vocal group, The Tempo-Toppers, but after 1955 the billing is changed to feature Little Richard.

1954
Richard meets Lloyd Price, who suggests sending blues demos recorded at Macon radio station W-BML, to Art Rupe at Speciality Records in Los Angeles.

1955
Feb Richard auditions for Specialty. Tracks recorded include the a cappella gospel piece *He's My Star* and piano boogie *Chicken Shack Baby*. He fronts the Johnny Otis Orchestra for 2 singles and tours small black nightclubs, where he mainly sings the blues.
Sept [14] Specialty contacts Richard, while he is working in Fayetteville, TN, and he enters the studio for a 48-hour session in New Orleans with the Crescent City rhythm section (who feature on many of Fats Domino's disks) and producer Robert "Bumps" Blackwell, who is also Richard's manager. Richard plays piano and sings. After recording blues numbers *Kansas City* and *Directly From My Heart*, he records a version of a live number he has written – *Tutti Frutti*. (The lyrics are cleaned up by local songwriter Dorothy La Bostrie.) The histrionic vocal and bashing piano style sets the mold for Little Richard's image as Blackwell insists on a live feel to studio recordings. Richard signs to Specialty (the deal gives him half a cent for every record sold).

1956
Feb *Tutti Frutti*, its publishing rights sold to Specialty for $50, reaches US #17. It stays on chart for 12 weeks but will sell over 3 million copies.
Mar Richard enters the recording studio again. (He will record 6 more sessions between now and Feb.1957, using a band based around Earl Palmer (drums), Red Tyler and Lee Allen (saxes), Frank Fields (bass), Ernest McLean and Justin Adams (guitars) and supplementary pianists Huey Smith, Edward Frank, Little Booker and Salvador Doucette.) Pat Boone's version of *Tutti Frutti* reaches US #12.
May *Long Tall Sally* makes US #13. Originally titled *The Thing*, then *Bald Headed Sally*, the song was sanitized for Boone to record his own version (US #8).
June B-side *Slippin' And Slidin'*, based on the ribald New Orleans blues number *I Got The Blues For You*, reaches US #33.
Aug *Rip It Up* reaches US #17. B-side *Ready Teddy* peaks at US #44.
Dec *Rip It Up*, released on London label, is his UK chart debut at #30.

1957
Feb Richard heads for Los Angeles with his own band, the Upsetters, beginning an intensive schedule of touring and film work (including movie "Mr. Rock'N'Roll").
Mar *The Girl Can't Help It*, from Jayne Mansfield-starring film of the same name, peaks at US #49. (Richard appears in the film, and also appeared in Bill Haley movie "Don't Knock The Rock" the previous year.) *Long Tall Sally* hits UK #3 during a 16-week stay. B-side *Tutti Frutti* spends a week at UK #29.
Apr *Lucille*, penned by Richard, peaks at US #27. B-side *Send Me Some Lovin'* climbs to US #54. *She's Got It* reaches UK #15.

May *The Girl Can't Help It* hits UK #9, as its A-side *She's Got It* re-enters UK chart for 2 weeks, reaching #28.

July *Jenny, Jenny* makes US #14, as B-side *Miss Ann* peaks at US #56.

Aug *Lucille* hits UK #10. Richard's only US chart album in the 50s, *Here's Little Richard*, enters the chart to peak at #13 during a 5-week run. (He will never have a UK chart album.)

Sept *Jenny, Jenny* reaches UK #11.

Oct *Keep A Knockin'*, from film "Mr. Rock'N'Roll", hits US #8.

[12] After a year of whirlwind success, Little Richard, on the fifth date of a 2-week Australian tour in Sydney, publicly renounces rock'n'roll and embraces God. (He will later tell the story of dreaming of his own damnation, and praying to God after one of the engines in a plane he is in catches fire.)

[13] On his return to US, Specialty arranges a final 8-song session before he enters theological college. Specialty tries to keep his conversion quiet. (Label artist Joe Lutcher has been warning Richard for some time that pop music is "evil". Richard and Lutcher will tour US as the "Little Richard Evangelistic Team".)

Dec *Keep A Knockin'* reaches UK #21.

1958 Jan [27] Richard enters Oakwood theological college in Huntsville, AL (where he will receive a BA and become ordained as a Seventh Day Adventist minister).

Mar *Good Golly, Miss Molly*, from the final Specialty session, hits US #10 and UK #8. (B-side *Hey Hey Hey Hey* will be revived in 1964 by The Beatles on *Beatles For Sale*, in a medley with *Kansas City* which fails to credit Richard's song. Several years later, after strong approaches by the song's publisher, it is fully credited on the album and back royalties are paid by EMI.)

June *Ooh! My Soul* makes US #35.

July B-side *True Fine Mama* climbs to US #68.

Aug *Ooh! My Soul* reaches UK #22.

Oct Richard's version of *Baby Face*, written in 1926, peaks at US #41.

1959 Jan *Baby Face* hits UK #2, behind Elvis Presley's *I Got Stung/One Night*.

Apr His version of *By The Light Of The Silvery Moon* makes US #17.

May *Kansas City*, his last US chart hit for 5 years, reaches US #95, eclipsed by Wilbert Harrison's #1 version of it.

June *Kansas City* makes UK #26. During the summer Richard returns to the studio to record gospel tracks for Gone/End Records. (The basic vocal/piano/organ tracks are overdubbed with a choir and have extra instrumentation added when they are re-released on Coral and Guest Star labels in the 60s.)

1960 Having sold an estimated 18 million singles during the 50s, Richard will spend the next 2 years recording 20 gospel songs with Quincy Jones producing, for release on albums on Mercury label. 7 more gospel tracks, including *Crying In The Chapel*, are cut for Atlantic, with Jerry Wexler producing.

1962 Late in the year, the Rev. Little Richard returns to rock'n'roll with a UK comeback tour promoted by Don Arden. Paul McCartney asks Richard to teach him his singing style. Brian Epstein books Richard into the Cavern, Liverpool, and he headlines a concert with The Swinging Blue Jeans, Cilla Black and Gerry & The Pacemakers.

Oct On Mercury, *He Got What He Wanted* makes UK #38.

[7] Richard makes his UK debut on ITV's "Thank Your Lucky Stars".

[8] He embarks on his first UK package tour. During the 20-date tour, 2 people are treated in hospital after a Bristol show, an attendant is injured when crowd tries to storm stage in Slough and police with dogs go onstage after a show in Walthamstow to clear the audience.

1963 Richard tours Europe with The Beatles (with whom firm mutually respecting relationships have been formed), The Rolling Stones and others. He later notes that the young groups know his records better than he does.

Oct [5] Little Richard joins The Everly Brothers' UK tour, ostensibly to boost poor ticket sales.

1964 Mar He records first of 7 sessions for Vee-Jay. Early tapings produce versions of *Whole Lotta Shakin' Goin' On* and *Good Lawdy Miss Clawdy*.

May [8] Richard appears on ITV's "Ready Steady Go!" with Brian Poole, The Swinging Blue Jeans and Carl Perkins, on a short UK visit.

June On his second UK tour, *Bama Lama Bama Loo* reaches UK #20, his last UK hit for 13 years.

Aug *Bama Lama Bama Loo* peaks at US #82.

Oct [3] Richard fails to appear at the beginning of a UK tour at the Cellar Hall, Kingston, Surrey.

Dec Richard re-records his greatest hits for Vee-Jay. (In UK, various combinations of the tracks appear on Stateside, Fontana, Sue, President and Joy labels over the next 4 years.)

1965 Vee-Jay issues albums *Little Richard Is Back* and *Little Richard's*

Greatest Hits, released in UK on Fontana.

Nov *I Don't Know What You've Got But It's Got Me* is the only Vee-Jay single to chart, spending a week at US #92.

Dec Richard records 7 studio tracks for Modern Records, including *Holy Mackerel*, *Don't You Want A Man Like Me* and *Baby What You Want Me To Do*.

1966 Jan He records Modern label album *Little Richard Sings His Greatest Hits – Recorded Live*. Songs from it are combined with studio tracks and released, with overdubbed applause, in UK on Polydor and Contour labels.

Richard begins recording 5 sessions for soul label Okeh.

Dec [11] He makes a sole London appearance at the Saville theater.

1967 As a rock'n'roll revival in Europe gains momentum, Richard revisits for successful tours. He becomes increasingly involved in drug abuse (which will dog his career into the 70s).

Aug Another live compilation, *Little Richard's Greatest Hits*, on Okeh, peaks at US #184, and is his first chart album in 10 years.

1968 Richard records 6 tracks for Brunswick, which are released as US singles. The first 2, *Try Some Of Mine* and *She's Together* (produced by Don Covay) are also issued by MCA in UK.

1969 Apr [14] The Monkees' NBC TV special "33⅓ Revolutions Per Monkee", featuring Little Richard and others including Jerry Lee Lewis, Fats Domino, Clara Ward Singers, Brian Auger, Buddy Miles and Julie Driscoll, airs.

Sept [13] Little Richard takes part in the "Rock'N'Revival Concert" in Toronto, Canada, with Jerry Lee Lewis, Gene Vincent, Bo Diddley and John Lennon's newly-formed Plastic Ono Band.

Now living in Riverside, CA, he signs to Warner/Reprise Records.

1970 July Reprise *Freedom Blues*, recorded at Muscle Shoals, makes US #47.

[18] Richard takes part in the Randall Island Rock Festival with Jimi Hendrix, Jethro Tull, Grand Funk Railroad, Steppenwolf and others.

Sept *Greenwood Mississippi* stalls at US #85. He appears at Toronto Pop Festival, documented in D.A. Pennebaker's film "Keep On Rockin'".

1971 Nov *The King Of Rock'N'Roll* makes US #184.

1972 Apr Richard sings on Canned Heat's *Rockin' With The King*, which makes US #88. He contributes 2 tracks to the soundtrack of Warren Beatty/Goldie Hawn-starring movie "$" (UK title: "The Heist") and reunites with Blackwell, Earl Palmer and Lee Allen to record *The Second Coming*.

June [2] Richard takes part in the 29th Rock & Roll Spectacular with Lloyd Price, Shirley & Lee, Danny & The Juniors, The Cleftones, The Exciters, Dion & The Belmonts (who re-form specially for the date) at Madison Square Garden, New York. (He has been, and will be, a regular performer on this bill over the years.)

Aug [5] Little Richard takes part in an ill-conceived "Rock'N'Revival" concert in London.

1973 After leaving Reprise (and an unissued country album *Southern Child*) he records for ALA with Blackwell (his last work with the producer).

June [20] He rises from his sickbed to make an appearance on Dick Clark's retrospective 20th anniversary "Bandstand" show on ABC TV.

1975 Richard records a one-off single, *Call My Name*, for Emerson, Lake & Palmer's Manticore label.

1976 He re-records 20 of his greatest hits in London for SJ Records. After the death of his brother Tony, Richard is reborn to Christianity for the second time and works temporarily for Memorial Bibles International.

1977 July Creole's release of SJ recordings of *Good Golly Miss Molly/Rip It Up* makes UK #37.

1979 Richard becomes a fully-fledged evangelist, preaching the story of his salvation throughout US, stating that "if God can save an old homosexual like me, he can save anybody". (He will relate the experience of his redemption in lengthy *Little Richard's Testimony*, included on his gospel album *God's Beautiful City*.)

1985 Charles White publishes book **The Life And Times Of Little Richard.**

1986 Jan [23] Little Richard is inducted into the Rock'N'Roll Hall Of Fame at the first annual induction dinner at the Waldorf Astoria, New York.

Apr [12] *Great Gosh A'Mighty (It's A Matter Of Time)*, from forthcoming Richard Dreyfuss/Bette Midler-starring movie, "Down And Out In Beverly Hills", in which he also appears, makes US #42.

June *Great Gosh A'Mighty (It's A Matter Of Time)* peaks at UK #62.

Oct He signs to WEA Records, which releases **Lifetime Friend.** Extracted *Operator* makes UK #67. Vigorous media promotion mixes gospel attitude with legendary Little Richard style.

Dec He teams with The Beach Boys for *Happy Endings* from film "The Telephone".

1987 Feb Richard guests on New Edition's *Tears On My Pillow*, which makes #41 on US R&B chart.

988 **Sept** He contributes to Woody Guthrie/Leadbelly tribute album *Folkways: A Vision Shared*.

Nov Now seen as a media evangelist, Richard duets with Phillip Bailey on the title track for Arnold Schwarzenegger/Danny DeVito film "Twins" on new CBS subsidiary WTG Records.

989 **Jan** [18] Richard inducts the late Otis Redding into the Rock'N'Roll Hall Of Fame at the fourth annual dinner at the Waldorf Astoria in New York. He and Mick Jagger sing *I Can't Turn You Loose* at the after-dinner musical bash.

Feb [7] Georgia State Representative Billy Randall introduces bill to make *Tutti Frutti* the state's official rock song.

July [12] Press conference is held to announce Disney Channel's Shelley Duvall-produced Mother Goose Rock'N'Rhyme. Among those taking part are Little Richard as Old King Cole.

990 **June** [21] Richard is bestowed with a star on the Hollywood Walk Of Fame on "Little Richard Day" in Los Angeles.

Sept Richard performs a guest rap on *Elvis Is Dead* from Living Colour's new album, *Time's Up*.

[23] Richard plays at the City Auditorium, Macon – his first hometown concert in 35 years.

991 **Feb** [10] Little Richard joins with nearly 100 celebrities in Burbank, CA, to record *Voices That Care*, a David Foster and fiancee Linda Thompson Jenner-composed and organized charity record to benefit the American Red Cross Gulf Crisis Fund.

Mar Disney releases *For Our Children*, a benefit album for the Pediatric AIDS Foundation, which features Richard on *Itsy Bitsy Spider*.

THE LITTLE RIVER BAND

Glenn Shorrock (vocals)
David Briggs (guitar)
Beeb Birtles (guitar)
Graham Goble (guitar)
George McArdle (bass)
Derek Pellicci (drums)

974 When London-based Australian band Mississippi breaks up after 2 years, 3 of its members, Goble (b. May 15, 1947, Adelaide, Australia), Birtles (b. Gerard Birtlekamp, Nov.28, 1948, Amsterdam, Netherlands) and Pellicci meet Shorrock (b. June 30, 1944, Rochester, Kent, raised in Elizabeth, Australia), late of Esperanto, and fellow Australian Glenn Wheatley, working in management in London. The 5 decide to meet in Australia in the New Year.

975 **Mar** Back in Australia, they re-form as Mississippi, with Wheatley as manager. Criticized for having an American name, they become The Little River Band, chosen at random from a small community 30 miles outside Melbourne, Australia.

May Adding guitarist Rick Formosa and bassist Roger McLachlan, they cut debut album *Little River Band*. (Released in Australia, it will be voted Album Of The Year.)

976 **Apr** They sign to EMI's Harvest label, which releases *Little River Band* worldwide. Group begins a tour of Europe, Canada and US, without Formosa and McLachlan, who have left to be replaced by Briggs (b. Jan.26, 1951, Melbourne) and McArdle (b. Nov.30, 1954, Melbourne).

Dec *It's A Long Way There* is the group's first US hit single, reaching #28. *Little River Band* makes US #80.

977 **Mar** *I'll Always Call Your Name* peaks at US #62. *Diamantina Cocktail*, a compilation of 2 previous Australian albums (*After Hours* and *Diamantina Cocktail*), reaches US #49, and is the first US gold album by an Australian group.

Nov *Help Is On Its Way*, taken from *Diamantina Cocktail* and produced by American John Boylan, reaches US #14.

978 **Mar** *Happy Anniversary* reaches US #16.

Oct *Reminiscing* hits US #3, earning a gold disk, while *Sleeper Catcher* reaches US #16 (and will earn a platinum disk). Band returns home from its second world tour, to find it has swept the first Australian Rock Awards, and Wheatley has been named Manager Of The Year.

979 **Jan** Group tours US again. Afterwards, McArdle leaves, giving away all his money and retreating to the Blue Mountains to undertake a 3-year Bible study course. He is replaced on bass by Barry Sullivan, and New Zealander Mal Logan joins on keyboards.

Apr *Lady* hits US #10.

Sept *Lonesome Loser*, marking a change of label from Harvest to Capitol, hits US #6.

Oct *First Under The Wire*, on Capitol and including *Lonesome Loser*, hits US #10, and also achieves platinum status.

980 **Jan** *Cool Change*, taken from *First Under The Wire*, hits US #10.

Apr Briggs is replaced by Wayne Nelson (b. Chicago, IL), and guitarist Stephen Housden also joins.

May *It's Not A Wonder* peaks at US #51.

June Double live album *Backstage Pass* makes US #44.

[6] Group plays one-off UK concert at the Rainbow theater, London, supporting Kevin Ayers.

1981 **Nov** *The Night Owls* hits US #6. It is taken from *Time Exposure*, produced by George Martin, which makes US #21, earning a gold disk.

1982 **Mar** *Take It Easy On Me*, also from *Time Exposure*, hits US #10.

May Third extract *Man On Your Mind* reaches US #14.

1983 **Feb** *The Other Guy* reaches US #11, while compilation album *Little River Band/Greatest Hits* makes US #33.

June *We Two* reaches US #22. Shorrock leaves to go solo, to be replaced by John Farnham (b. Adelaide, Australia).

Aug *The Net*, which includes *We Two*, peaks at US #61.

Sept *You're Driving Me Out Of My Mind*, also taken from *The Net*, makes US #35.

Oct Shorrock's solo single *Don't Girls Get Lonely* peaks at US #69, but his solo album does not chart.

1985 **Mar** After more personnel changes, Goble is left as the only original member and the band's credit changes to LRB on *Playing To Win*, which makes US #75. The title track peaks at US #60.

1987 **Mar** Farnham leaves to go solo (and will have a major international hit with *You're The Voice*, which tops the Australian chart and hits UK #6).

1988 After a 2-year recording hiatus, Little River Band signs to MCA, its renewed activity due largely to Shorrock rejoining. New line-up appears on a TV concert from the World Expo in Brisbane, Australia.

Apr Band plays a concert in Melbourne to launch new album *Monsoon* and single *Love Is A Bridge*.

Aug Glenn Frey joins the band on stage at the Sydney Entertainment Centre, Australia. The reunited LRB joins Frey on The Eagles hits *Desperado*, *Lyin' Eyes* and *Take It Easy* as well as their own hits *Cool Change* and *Night Owls*.

1990 **Mar** Dennis Lambert-produced comeback album, *Get Lucky*, with Shorrock back as lead vocalist after a 7-year lapse, is released on Curb.

May [18] North American tour begins in Vancouver, Canada.

LIVING COLOUR

Corey Glover (vocals)
Vernon Reid (guitar)
Muzz Skillings (bass)
Will Calhoun (drums)

1984 Reid (b. England, to West Indian parents, raised in Brooklyn from age 2), son of Post Office worker James and supermarket worker Mary, received his first guitar at age 15, from a cousin. Having gained informal instruction from Melvin the barber and subsequently Ted Dunbar and Rodney Jones, he has studied performing arts for 2 years at the Manhattan community college before earning his musical spurs with electric jazz outfit Defunk and subsequently graduates from Ronald Shannon Jackson's avant-garde jazz-fusion collective Decoding Society. Based in New York, he now forms power trio Living Colour, taking their name from pioneering NBC TV announcement "the following program is brought to you in living color", with drummer William Calhoun, a 1986 graduate of the Berklee School of Music, where he has won the Buddy Rich Award for percussion excellence and toured with Harry Belafonte, and bassist Muzz Skillings, graduate of City College. Intent on fusing dance, soul and jazz elements with hard rock and heavy metal, an innovative idea for an all-black group, they are joined by Corey Glover (having just completed work on Oliver Stone's movie "Platoon"), whom Reid has heard singing "Happy Birthday" at a mutual friend's party 18 months before.

1985 Reid forms the Black Rock Coalition pressure movement with journalist Greg Tate.

1986 Having seen the band performing at CBGB's in New York, Mick Jagger invites them to play on his forthcoming solo album *Primitive Cool*. (He will subsequently produce 2 demos for the group which will help them secure a recording deal with Epic Records, *Glamour Boys* and *Which Way To America*. Jagger will continue to champion the band.)

1988 **Sept** Debut album, with Jagger-produced tracks, *Vivid* emerges set to hit US #6 and stay on the survey for over a year. Constant touring to promote the project includes support slots for Cheap Trick, Robert Palmer, Anthrax and Billy Bragg.

Oct Reid features on Keith Richard debut solo album *Talk Is Cheap*, a popular session choice. He will guest on Bernie Worrell's *Funk Of Ages*.

1989 **Apr** Living Colour are musical guests on NBC TV's "Saturday Night Live".

May [6] Hard funk rock driven *Cult Of Personality*, sampling part of a President John F. Kennedy speech, reaches US #13.

[31] Group performs live at the first International Rock Awards held in Lexington Avenue Armory, New York. They win an Elvis Award as Best New Band.

July Reid co-hosts a benefit concert with Nona Hendryx at the Music Machine, Los Angeles, CA, for local branch of the Black Rock Coalition.

[22] Follow-up *Open Letter (To A Landlord)* stalls at US #82.

Aug Group headlines Beacon theater, New York, concert to benefit the New York-based Partnership For The Homeless, raising $50,000. John Mellencamp joins them onstage for an electric version of Pink Houses.

[31] Living Colour embarks on the Rolling Stones' "Steel Wheels North American Tour 1989" at Veterans Stadium, Philadelphia, PA, on Labor Day, before a sell-out crowd of 55,000.

Sept [6] Mick Jagger presents group with Best New Artist, Best Group Video and Best Stage Performance awards at the sixth annual MTV Music Video Awards ceremony backstage at the Three Rivers Stadium, Pittsburgh. Group supports "Stones On Steel Wheels" tour.

Oct [21] Jagger-helmed *Glamour Boys* makes US #31.

1990 **Feb** [21] Living Colour wins Best Hard Rock Performance for *Cult Of Personality* at the 32nd annual Grammy awards at the Shrine Auditorium, Los Angeles.

Mar [8] Group wins Best New American Band in **Rolling Stone** magazine's Readers Picks and Reid wins Best Guitarist in the magazine's Critics Picks. (Glover is also named Best New Drummer by **Modern Drummer**.)

Sept Reid writes and produces 4 tracks for a forthcoming album by B.B. King, on sessions which include Paul Griffin, Wilbur Bascomb and Living Colour's Calhoun.

Oct [6] Despite no Hot 100 extractions, second album *Time's Up* reaches US #13, having already made UK #21 in Sept. Produced by Ed Stasium, the album features Little Richard rapping on *Elvis Is Dead*, Carlos Santana, rapper Queen Latifah and, of course, Jagger.

[27] *Type* anchors at UK #75.

Nov [3] "The Miracle Biscuit Tour" begins in Albany, NY.

1991 **Jan** Skillings and Glover are invited to be guest professors at the PS20 elementary school, Brooklyn, New York.

Feb [20] Living Colour wins Best Hard Rock Performance, Vocal Or Instrumental, for *Time's Up* at the 33rd annual Grammy Awards at Radio City Music Hall, New York.

Mar [7] Group wins Best Band category in the annual **Rolling Stone** Critics' Picks 1990 music awards.

[16] Remixed by Soulshock and Cutfather from *Time's Up*, *Love Rears Its Ugly Head* reaches UK #12, spurring album to re-peak at UK #20.

[29] Band begins a headlining UK tour.

LOS LOBOS

Cesar Rosas (guitar, vocals)
Conrad Lozano (bass)
David Hidalgo (guitar, accordian, vocals)
Steve Berlin (saxophone)
Luis Perez (drums)

1974 Hidalgo and Perez, friends from an art class in Garfield high school in East Los Angeles, CA, Rosas and Lozano, all Spanish-Americans living in Los Angeles' Chicano community and refugees from Top 40 cover bands (Lozano has been in future hitmaking group Tierra), decide to form an acoustic group to rediscover and revitalize traditional Chicano folk music. They name the quartet Los Lobos (Spanish for The Wolves). (They will spend 2 years researching and rehearsing before making their debut at a Veteran of Foreign Wars Hall in Los Angeles suburb Compton, then performing regularly at Chicano weddings, bars and benefits in the Los Angeles area. An immediate success with the older generation of Chicanos, Los Lobos are also popluar among members of their own generation anxious to retain elements of Mexican culture.)

1978 Group records (and finances, with help from friends) its debut album *Just Another Band From L.A.*, selling the record at gigs.

1980 Los Lobos supports Public Image Ltd at a concert in Los Angeles. Its acoustic set receives a hostile reception from the hardcore punk audience (they are pelted with bottles, and give up after about 10 mins.), but the band comes to the attention of the local Anglo-American music industry. Los Lobos begins to integrate an electric sound into the previously acoustic-only Spanish and American tunes.

1983 Signing to Los Angeles independent label Slash, Los Lobos records EP *And A Time To Dance*, which labelmate Blasters' saxist Steve Berlin plays on and co-produces with T-Bone Burnett. (Berlin (b. Philadelphia,

PA), who has moved west with The Soul Survivors, before they become The Beckmeier Brothers, cutting an album for Casablanca, then joined Top Jimmy & The Rhythm Pigs and The Plugz before becoming a Blaster, has liked the band's work ever since they supported The Blasters at the Whiskey in Los Angeles and will join the band full time soon after. He has already played with the band at manager Gary Ibanez's Pico Rivera garage, which doubles as a rehearsal studio.) The EP will sell 50,000 copies and allow them to buy a second-hand Dodge van in which to tour US.

1984 **Feb** [28] Los Lobos win Best Mexican/American Performance for *Anselma* at the 26th annual Grammy awards.

Dec *How Will The Wolf Survive?* enters US chart; it will climb to #47.

1985 **Mar** *Will The Wolf Survive?* reaches US #78.

Apr Released in UK via London Records, double A-side *Don't Worry Baby/Will The Wolf Survive?* makes UK #57. *How Will The Wolf Survive?* climbs to UK #77.

1986 Los Lobos receives increasing media attention in US and UK, cited as a leading roots band. Group excels on stage, and develops substantial following, but the year passes without US or UK chart entries.

1987 **Mar** *By The Light Of The Moon* makes US #47 and UK #77.

Band contributes 8 tracks to soundtrack (and later album) of movie "La Bamba", based on the life of 50s Chicano pop star Ritchie Valens. It includes versions of Valens' compositions *Come On Let's Go, Ooh! My Head, Donna* and his 1959 hit *La Bamba* (a traditional Mexican song).

Aug [1] Los Lobos' version of *La Bamba* (English translation: *Wedding Song*) hits UK #1 for 2 weeks, becoming the first all-Spanish sung record to do so. Valens' original version charts briefly at UK #49.

[29] *La Bamba* tops US chart for the first of 3 weeks.

Sept [12] Soundtrack album *La Bamba* hits US #1 and makes UK #24.

Oct Extracted *C'mon On, Let's Go* makes UK #18.

Nov [7] *C'mon On, Let's Go* reaches US #21.

1988 **Oct** *La Pistola Y El Corazon* (English translation: *The Pistol And The Heart*) is released. Containing traditional Mexican/American folk songs, it avoids deliberate commercial exploitation of *La Bamba* success.

1989 **May** [18] They take part in AIDS benefit concert with Tracy Chapman, The Grateful Dead, Huey Lewis & The News and others at the Coliseum, Oakland, CA.

1990 **Feb** [21] Los Lobos wins Best Mexican/American Performance for *La Pistola Y El Corazon* at the 32nd annual Grammy awards at the Shrine Auditorium, Los Angeles.

June Hidalgo produces Buckwheat Zydeco's *Where There's Smoke There's Fire*.

Sept [11] Group plays at the Town & Country club, London during a short UK visit.

[29] *The Neighborhood*, mainly English tracks, peaks at US #103.

Oct [23] Back in the US, Los Lobos begin US dates at the Marlboro club, Atlanta, GA.

NILS LOFGREN

1969 Lofgren (b. June 21, 1951, Chicago, IL), of Italian and Swedish parents, having been a classical music student for 10 years, and played in Beatles/Kinks-influenced high school bands like The Waifs and The Grass, in Maryland, DC, before running away from home (or, more specifically, from school) with $100 in his pocket and sleeping for 2 weeks in doorways in Greenwich Village, New York, after returning home forms the band Paul Dowell & The Dolphin, which successfully auditions for Sire Records and releases 2 singles, but splits after both fail and the group is beset by management and contract problems. New group Grin is formed, with Lofgren on vocals, keyboards and guitar, Bob Berberich (b. 1949, Maryland), ex-Reekers, on drums, and Bob Gordon (b. 1951, Oklahoma), ex-Paul Dowell & The Dolphin, on bass.

1970 **Feb** Having seen him playing with Grin at the Cellar Door club in Washington, DC, in 1969, Neil Young invites Lofgren to play piano (and uncredited guitar) on his album *After The Goldrush*. He plays frequently with Young and his band Crazy Horse after the album, but does not join the group full-time, being keen to make a success of Grin.

1971 **Feb** He plays on and writes songs for the eponymous debut album by Crazy Horse.

Aug Grin signs to Spindizzy/Columbia, and debut album *Grin* reaches US #192. Group tours supporting Edgar Winter.

1972 **Feb** Second Grin album *1+1* climbs to US #180, and extracted *White Lies* is Grin's only US chart single, peaking at #75.

1973 **Mar** Lofgren's younger brother Tom is recruited on second guitar for Grin's third album *All Out*, which makes US #186.

Nov Signing a new deal with A&M, the band records *Gone Crazy*; it does not chart. Disillusioned, Grin splits. After playing briefly with The Dubonettes and producing their debut A&M album (released under a new name, Charlie & The Pep Boys), Lofgren accepts another invitation to join Crazy Horse for Neil Young's "Tonight's The Night" tour.

1974 **Mar** He leaves Crazy Horse to go solo again, and the press speculates that The Rolling Stones will recruit Lofgren as lead guitarist in place of departed Mick Taylor.

1975 **Apr** He re-signs to A&M as a soloist, and *Nils Lofgren*, including a homage to Keith Richards in *Keith Don't Go (Ode To The Glimmer Twin)*, reaches US #141. He follows it by extensive touring (including a UK visit), with a band including Tom Lofgren (guitar), Scotty Ball (bass) and Mike Zack (drums).
Nov [4] Lofgren appears on BBC TV's "The Old Grey Whistle Test".
[5] He begins a short UK tour, supporting Joan Armatrading, at Leeds University, Leeds, W.Yorks.

1976 **Jan** The "official bootleg" album *Back It Up*, a recording of a live show broadcast on radio station K-SAN in San Francisco, CA, is acclaimed by the press, despite limited availability.
Mar He starts US club and concert tour introducing new studio album.
May *Cry Tough*, part produced by Al Kooper, and part by David Briggs, reaches US #32 and hits UK #8. It includes a revival of The Yardbirds' *For Your Love*.
[5] Lofgren begins 9-date UK tour to promote *Cry Tough* at Colston Hall, Bristol, Avon. It will end May 15 at Leeds University.

1977 **Apr** *I Came To Dance* reaches US #36 and UK #30. On it, Wornell Jones and Andy Newmark are his new bass player and drummer, while Newmark also co-produces with Lofgren. Patrick Henderson joins the live band on keyboards.
Nov Double live album *Night After Night*, recorded on tour earlier in the year, makes US #44 and UK #38.

1979 **Aug** *Nils*, featuring 3 songs with lyrics by Lou Reed, and also Randy Newman's *Baltimore*, makes US #54.
[19] Along with The Stranglers and AC/DC, he supports The Who in a concert at Wembley Stadium, London.

1981 **Oct** He signs to new MCA-distributed Backstreet label for *Night Fades Away*, which makes US #99 and UK #50.

1982 **May** Compilation *A Rhythm Romance* (on A&M) reaches UK #100.

1983 **Feb** He tours again with Neil Young and plays on Young's controversial synthesizer-based *Trans*.
Aug *Wonderland* is released and sells poorly, after which Lofgren loses his MCA/Backstreet recording contract.

1984 He joins Bruce Springsteen's E Street Band as guitarist, replacing Steve Van Zandt, and tours with Springsteen (whom he first met during a Fillmore East audition night in 1972) into 1985.

1985 **June** Lofgren is signed as a soloist by UK independent label Towerbell and *Flip*, recorded at Philadelphia, PA's Warehouse studios with producer Lance Quinn, reaches UK #36. Taken from it, *Secrets In The Street* is his only UK solo chart single at UK #53.

1986 **Apr** Following the release of his third live set, double album *Code Of The Road* (which makes UK #86), Towerbell label hits financial problems and folds, and Lofgren puts his solo career on ice in favor of a supporting role to Springsteen.

1987 **Nov** He appears on only 2 tracks of Springsteen's *Tunnel Of Love* (but remains a full stage member of The E Street Band and plays on early 1988 "Tunnel Of Love Express" US and European tour).

1988 **Sept** He plays the "Human Rights Now!" Amnesty International tour with Springsteen.

1989 **July** [23] Lofgren joins Ringo Starr & His All-Starr Band on a 28-date, 27-city US tour, opening at the Park Central Amphitheater, Dallas, TX. Billed as the "Tour For All Generations", it is the first tour by a Beatle in 13 years. Also in the band are Dr. John, Billy Preston, Joe Walsh, Rick Danko, Levon Helm, Jim Kettner and Clarence Clemons.

KENNY LOGGINS & JIM MESSINA

1967 Messina (b. Dec.5, 1947, Maywood, CA), having formed a high school surf instrumental group, Jim Messina & The Jesters, which becomes popular on the California "Battle Of The Bands" circuit and records 2 albums, *Jim Messina And The Jesters* for Thimble Records and hot rod-oriented *The Dragsters* for Audio Fidelity, with *Drag Bike Pookie* being a hit in parts of California only, moves to studio work in Los Angeles, CA, as a guitarist and as an engineer and producer, when the surf craze evaporates.
Sept From being the group's studio engineer, Messina joins Buffalo Springfield on bass, in place of Bruce Palmer.

1968 Loggins (b. Jan.7, 1948, Everett, WA), having moved to California with his family as a child, and majored in music at Pasadena city college, CA, leaves to join studio group Gator Creek, which records for Mercury, and then joins Second Helping.
Aug Messina and fellow ex-Buffalo Springfield member Richie Furay form Poco, with George Grantham, Rusty Young and Randy Meisner. Messina assembles *Last Time Around* from latter-day studio tapes after Buffalo Springfield has split.

1969 After joining (for 1 tour) ex-hitmakers The Electric Prunes, Loggins becomes a full-time songwriter (on $100 a week) at Wingate Music, a division of ABC Records.

1970 **Nov** Messina leaves Poco to concentrate on production work at Columbia Records.

1971 **June** Loggins' first hit composition is *House At Pooh Corner* for The Nitty Gritty Dirt Band, which peaks at US #53. It is one of 4 Loggins songs cut by the band on its album *Uncle Charlie And His Dog Teddy*.
Sept At the instigation of friend and A&R man Don Ellis, Loggins signs to CBS/Columbia as a soloist. He meets Messina, now a staff producer, who works with him to prepare a debut solo album. Their collaboration is such that *Kenny Loggins With Jim Messina Sittin' In* is released as a joint effort and they decide to continue to work together, making a live debut at the Troubadour billed as The Kenny Loggins Band With Jim Messina.

1972 **May** The debut album reaches US #70 (and in a 113-week chart stay will earn a gold disk), while extracted *Vahevala* climbs to US #84.
June *Nobody But You*, written by Messina, makes US #86. Both this and the previous single are credited to Kenny Loggins With Jim Messina.

1973 **Jan** *Your Mama Don't Dance* hits US #4 and is a million-seller, earning the duo's only gold single. (The song will be covered by Elvis Presley, among others.) It is included on *Loggins And Messina* (also produced by Messina), which reaches US #16, and also earns a gold disk.
Apr Anne Murray's version of *Danny's Song* (written by Loggins for his brother Dan's son) hits US #7.
May *Thinking Of You* reaches US #18 and is credited to Loggins & Messina, as are subsequent duo releases.
Dec *Full Sail* hits US #10, as *My Music*, taken from it, reaches US #16.

1974 **Mar** *Watching The River Run*, a joint composition, peaks at US #71.
July Double live album *On Stage* hits US #5, and is another gold disk.
Dec *Mother Lode* hits US #8 and ranks another gold disk.

1975 **Feb** *Changes*, taken from *Mother Lode*, makes US #84.
May *Growin'* peaks at US #52.
Sept A revival of Chris Kenner/Dave Clark Five hit *I Like It Like That* climbs to US #84. It is extracted from *So Fine*, a nostalgic set of R&B oldies from the 50s and early 60s, which reaches US #21.
Oct Also from the oldies album, a revival of Clyde McPhatter's *A Lover's Question* makes US #89, the final Loggins & Messina hit single.

1976 **Jan** Loggins turns down an offer to co-star with Barbra Streisand in film "A Star Is Born". Shortly after, he cuts his hand with a craft knife while practising his wood-carving hobby at home – a serious injury which requires surgery.
Mar *Native Sons* reaches US #16 and earns a gold disk. A lengthy tour begins, with a new back-up band. Loggins has a cast on his injured hand and is unable to play guitar.
Nov Duo splits following a final concert in Hawaii (both are, in any case, signed individually to Columbia, the hitmaking liaison having always been on an informal basis). Loggins marries Eva Ein, a long-time friend of Messina's wife Jenny.

1977 **Jan** *The Best Of Friends*, compiled duo hit singles, makes US #61.
July *Celebrate Me Home*, Loggins' first solo album, reaches US #27. (In a 33-week chart stay, it will sell over a million to earn a platinum disk.) He tours US for the first time as a soloist, backed by a new band (Mike Hamilton on guitar, Brian Mann on keyboards, Vince Denham on saxes, Jon Clarke on woodwinds, George Hawkins on bass and Tris Imboden on drums), supporting Fleetwood Mac.
Sept Loggins' first solo hit single, *I Believe In Love*, peaks at US #66.

1978 **Jan** A second double live album by Loggins & Messina, *Finale*, assembled after the duo's break-up, makes US #83.
Sept *Nightwatch*, produced by jazzman Bob James, hits US #7 and is Loggins' second consecutive platinum album. It includes a revival of Billy Joe Royal's 1965 hit *Down In The Boondocks*, and also Loggins/Michael McDonald-penned *What A Fool Believes* (which will be a US #1 hit for McDonald's band The Doobie Brothers in 1979).
Oct From the album, *Whenever I Call You Friend*, with Stevie Nicks of Fleetwood Mac guest-duetting (and co-written by Loggins with singer Melissa Manchester), hits US #5.

1979 **Jan** *Easy Driver* peaks at US #60.
Nov Messina's solo *Oasis* makes US #58.

1980 **Feb** Loggins' *Keep The Fire*, with new producer Tom Dowd, reaches US #16, earning a gold disk. It includes songs co-written with Michael McDonald, Stephen Bishop and Loggins' wife Eva, and has guest appearances by McDonald and Michael Jackson.
[27] Loggins and McDonald win Song Of The Year for *What A Fool Believes* at the 22nd annual Grammy awards.
Oct *I'm Alright*, the theme from movie "Caddyshack", hits US #7. Loggins also performs half the film's soundtrack album, which makes US #78.
Nov Double live album *Kenny Loggins: Alive* reaches US #11 and earns a further gold disk.

1981 **Feb** [25] Loggins wins Best Pop Vocal Performance, Male, for *This Is It* at the 23rd annual Grammy awards.
July Messina moves to Warner Bros. for his second solo hit album *Messina*, which peaks at US #95. (Messina will take a break from performing, investing his money into his own Gateway studios in Carpinteria, CA.)

1982 **Oct** Loggins' *High Adventure* reaches US #13, and earns a gold disk, as *Don't Fight It*, a duet with Steve Perry from Journey, makes US #17.

1983 **Jan** *Heart To Heart* reaches US #15.
May *Welcome To Heartlight*, a song inspired by writings of children from Heartlight school, reaches US #24.

1984 **Mar** *Footloose*, the Loggins/Dean Pitchford-penned theme from the film of the same title, tops US chart for 3 weeks, and is a million-seller. (The song has been written in a hotel room in Lake Tahoe, NV, where Loggins has been performing – despite broken ribs still mending after a fall off stage at a concert in Provo, UT.)
Apr Soundtrack album *Footloose*, which Loggins shares with Deniece Williams, Bonnie Tyler and others, tops US chart for 10 weeks and is a million-seller.
May *Footloose* hits UK #6, Loggins' first UK chart success. The film soundtrack album hits UK #7.
July Also taken from the movie, *I'm Free (Heaven Helps The Man)* reaches US #22.

1985 **Jan** [28] Following the American Music Awards celebrations, Loggins joins 45 other artists as USA For Africa at the A&M studios, Hollywood, CA, to record *We Are The World*.
May *Vox Humana*, partly produced by David Foster, makes US #41, while the title track reaches US #29.
July *Forever* makes US #40.
Oct *I'll Be There* climbs to US #88.

1986 **July** [26] *Danger Zone*, theme from the Tom Cruise movie "Top Gun", hits US #2 as soundtrack album tops US chart for 5 weeks.
Sept [13] *Playing With The Boys*, also from "Top Gun", peaks at US #60.
Nov Soundtrack album *Top Gun* hits UK #4.
Dec *Danger Zone* makes UK #45.

1987 **June** [13] Loggins' ballad *Meet Me Half Way* from Sylvester Stallone's "Over The Top", reaches US #11.

1988 **Sept** *Back To Avalon* peaks at US #69, while extracted *Nobody's Fool* (the theme from film "Caddyshack 2") hits US #8.
Nov [26] *I'm Gonna Miss You* climbs to US #82.

1989 **Feb** [25] *Tell Her* peaks at US #76. (As Loggins rests from his recording career, he announces that he and his wife Eva intend to divorce.)
Apr Messina rejoins Poco for its comeback *Legacy*.
[15] Heavy metal outfit Poison update Loggins and Messina's 1973 US #4 hit *Your Mama Don't Dance* to hit US #10 (and UK #13).

LOVE

Arthur Lee (guitar, vocals)
Bryan MacLean (guitar, vocals)
John Echols (lead guitar)
Ken Forssi (bass)
Alban "Snoopy" Pfisterer (drums, keyboards)

1965 The group, originally formed in Los Angeles, CA, as The Grass Roots, comprising Lee (b. 1945, Memphis, TN), ex-Byrds roadie MacLean (b. 1947, Los Angeles, CA), Echols (b. 1945, Memphis), Johnny Fleckenstein and Don Conka, changes name to Love (The Grass Roots being taken up by another Los Angeles band, who become major US hitmakers), and original members Conka and Fleckenstein are replaced by Forssi (b. 1943, Cleveland, OH) and Pfisterer (b. 1947, Switzerland).
Apr Love makes its live debut in Los Angeles and builds a strong reputation playing clubs on Sunset Strip.

1966 Having established itself with the West Coast underground, Love takes up a residency at Bido Lito's club in Hollywood. It becomes the first rock group to sign to Elektra Records.

May Debut album *Love* makes US #57.
June *My Little Red Book*, a Bacharach/David song originally cut by Manfred Mann for film "What's New Pussycat?", peaks at US #52.
Sept *7 And 7 Is* makes US #33.

1967 **Mar** *Da Capo*, recorded with the addition of Tjay Cantrelli on flute and saxophone and Michael Stuart on drums, makes US #80. Pfisterer and Cantrelli depart, leaving the band with Lee, Forssi, MacLean, Echols and Stuart.
Nov *Forever Changes* is regarded as the group's (and Lee's) masterwork. It reaches UK #24 but only US #152.

1968 **Jan** *Alone Again Or*, taken from the album, makes US #99.
Aug Lee emerges with a restructured band, bringing in Frank Fayad (bass), George Suranovich (drums) and Jay Donnellan (lead guitar).

1969 **Sept** *Four Sail*, the band's last for Elektra, makes US #102.
Dec Love moves to Blue Thumb Records and uses material remaining from *Four Sail* sessions for double album *Out Here* which reaches US #176. Suranovich is fired and replaced by Drachen Theaker, ex-Crazy World Of Arthur Brown, who leaves shortly thereafter.

1970 **May** *Out Here* reaches UK #29.
Sept Compilation album *Love Revisited* on Elektra, containing tracks mostly from the first 3 albums, peaks at US #142.
Dec Lee re-forms the band again, with Fayad, Suranovich, Gary Rowles and Nooney Rickett on guitars, for *False Start*. Jimi Hendrix guests on 1 track. Soon after the album's release, Lee dismisses the rest of the group.

1972 **Aug** Lee releases solo *Vindicator* for A&M.

1973 Compilation *Love Masters* is released. Lee records solo *Black Beauty* which is never issued.

1974 **Dec** Lee forms yet another version of Love, which includes Melvan Whittington (guitar), John Sterling (guitar) and Joe Blocker (drums), with Sherwood Akuna and Robert Rozelle sharing bass duties. It records soul-influenced *Reel To Reel* for RSO Records. Lee returns to playing occasional one-off dates.

1977 Sterling convinces Lee to re-form Love and attempt to recapture the spirit of earlier times. The band's line-up is Lee, MacLean, Sterling, Kim Kesteron (bass) and George Suranovich (drums), with The Knack's drummer Bruce Gary also playing at one point, but it never releases any recordings.

1979 Various late 70s/early 80s Love reunions include one with Lee and MacLean on a Southern California tour.

1980 Rhino Records re-releases *Best Of Love* to cater for ongoing cult demand.

1981 **July** Rhino and Beggars Banquet in UK release *Arthur Lee*, a solo effort compiled from earlier left-over tracks.

1982 2 Love albums are released: Rhino's *Love Live*, a compilation of onstage recordings, and MCA's *Love*.

1986 The Damned revives Love's 1968 single *Alone Again Or* which reaches UK #27.

1989 **Jan** [27] Arthur Lee & Love play on "The Psychedelic Summer Of Love" bill at the Universal Amphitheater, Los Angeles.

THE LOVIN' SPOONFUL

John Sebastian (vocals, guitar, harmonica, autoharp)
Zal Yanovsky (guitar, vocals)
Steve Boone (bass, vocals)
Joe Butler (drums, vocals)

1964 **Feb** Among friends invited to Cass Elliot's house to watch The Beatles' US TV debut on the "Ed Sullivan Show" are Sebastian (b. John Benson Sebastian, Mar.17, 1944, New York, NY) and Yanovsky (b. Zalman Yanovsky, Dec.19, 1944, Toronto, Canada). They discuss the possibility of forming a rock group and play guitars until dawn. Sebastian, whose father recorded harmonica singles for Archie Bleyer's Cadence label in the 50s, is a college drop-out Greenwich Village folkie who backed local heroes Fred Neil and Tom Rush, and made sporadic appearances (including on their Elektra album) as a member of the Even Dozen Jug Band. Yanovsky is guitarist with The Halifax Three, a sharp-suited folk group from Nova Scotia.
June In the height of Beatlemania The Halifax Three folds. Yanovsky and founder member Denny Doherty join Elliot and James Hendricks – ex-The Big Three (completed by Tim Rose). As The Mugwumps, they become prototypical electric folkies. Gigs are disastrous and recordings so inept that Warners releases their album only after they become famous elsewhere. Between studio gigs backing Judy Collins, Jesse Colin Young and Tim Hardin, Sebastian becomes a Mugwump, but the group disbands.

Dec Doherty, having joined The Journeymen for 7 months before they split, goes with Elliott to the Virgin Islands, where they join The Mamas And The Papas. Their song *Creeque Alley* chronicles the comings and goings of the clique.

1965
Jan With producer Erik Jacobsen, Sebastian and Yanovsky plan a group – to be called The Lovin' Spoonful (after a phrase from Mississippi John Hurt's *Coffee Blues*). They find Boone (b, Sept.23, 1943, North Carolina) and Butler (b, Sept.16, 1943, Glen Cove, Long Island, NY) and rehearse in the basement of the rundown Albert hotel. Early attempts at gigging and recording are unsuccessful.

June After a residency at the Night Owl in Greenwich Village, they work on Sebastian's innovative compositions. Jacobsen secures a deal with the recently formed Kama Sutra label.

Oct A celebration of rock'n'roll, *Do You Believe In Magic* hits US #9.

Dec Debut album *Do You Believe In Magic* makes US #32. They evolve their own style – a light, lyrical synthesis they call "good time music". Others call it "folk rock". With their striped jerseys and mischievous image, they become America's mop tops from Manhattan.

1966
Jan *You Didn't Have To Be So Nice* hits US #10.

Apr *Daydream* hits US #2 and is a million-seller. *Daydream* hits US #10 and UK #8. Compilation *What's Shakin'*, on Elektra, includes 4 Spoonful tracks – given to them in early 1965 in return for musical equipment. One track *Good Time Music* defines the group's raison d'être.

[13] Group appears on UK TV show "Ready Steady Go!" at the start of its first UK tour.

June [25] Group plays on "The Beach Boys Summer Spectacular", with Chad & Jeremy, Percy Sledge and The Byrds, in Anaheim, CA.

July Written in a taxi en route to the studio, *Did You Ever Have To Make Up Your Mind* hits US #2.

Aug Featuring atmospheric street noise and engineer Roy Halee's booming drum experiments (which he continues on Simon & Garfunkel's *Bookends*), *Summer In The City* becomes their biggest hit, tops US chart for 3 weeks and hits UK #8. They are awarded their second gold disk. Group embarks on State Fairs tour in the New York area as "What's Up Tiger Lily?", starring Woody Allen and featuring the band, opens throughout US cinemas.

Oct Soundtrack album for movie "What's Up Tiger Lily?" reaches only US #126 but the film, a Japanese thriller on to which Woody Allen and Louise Lasser dub unrelated American dialogue, remains a cult item.

Nov *Rain On The Roof* hits US #10.

[4] Group embarks on 6-week US tour.

Dec Their third album of the year, *Hums Of The Lovin' Spoonful* makes US #14.

1967
Jan *Nashville Cats* becomes their sixth consecutive Top 10 success, hitting US #8, and making UK #26. B-side *Full Measure* makes US #87.

Mar With full orchestral backing, *Darling Be Home Soon* reaches US #15 and UK #44 (their last UK hit). *The Best Of The Lovin' Spoonful* is the first of many compilations. It hits US #3 and spends a year on chart.

May Their second soundtrack album, for Francis Ford Coppola's "You're A Big Boy Now", reaches US #118.

June Joe Wissert become their producer and *Six O'Clock* makes US #18.

[24] Yanovsky quits after a performance at the Forest Hills Music Festival, New York, following media indignation over a marijuana bust where he allegedly incriminated others to avoid prosecution. His replacement is Jerry Yester, ex-The Modern Folk Quartet.

Sept Yanovsky debuts with his solo disk *As Long As You're Here*.

Nov *She's Still A Mystery* reaches US #27.

1968
Feb *Money* peaks at US #48. *Everything Playing* reaches only US #118.

Apr *The Best Of The Lovin' Spoonful Vol 2* makes US #156.

Aug *Never Going Back* reaches US #73. (It is written by John Stewart and produced by Chip Douglas fresh from their success with The Monkees' *Daydream Believer*.)

Oct After "2 glorious years and a tedious one", Sebastian leaves the group, which soon crumbles. Subsequent individual output confirms that, to all intents and purposes, he was The Lovin' Spoonful. Sebastian's first solo venture is writing songs for "Jimmy Shine", a Broadway musical starring Dustin Hoffman but his score is rejected, the show fails and he moves to California.

Nov A final album, *Revelation Revolution 69* mentions only Joe Butler. Any Spoonful ingenuity is absent.

1969
Jan *She's A Lady*, Sebastian's solo debut, reaches US #84.

Feb The Lovin' Spoonful's *Me About You* reaches US #91. It is a lackluster swan song for one of the era's top US pop groups.

Aug Clad in the tie-dyes which will become his trademark, Sebastian appears at the Woodstock Festival. He performs Spoonful song *Younger*

Generation, which becomes a highlight of the movie, and *I Had A Dream*, the opening track on *Woodstock*.

1970
Mar While MGM and Warner/Reprise argue about who owns his contract, Sebastian's first album, Paul Rotchild-produced *John B. Sebastian* (issued on both labels!) rises to US #20.

Sept At UK's Isle of Wight Festival Sebastian reunites with Yanovsky (there as part of Kris Kristofferson's band). (Yanovsky's solo *Alive And Well In Argentina* (co-produced with Jerry Yester) finds only cult acceptance. He returns to Ontario, Canada to open his Chez Piggy's restaurant. Yester cuts albums with his wife Judy Henske, and the group Rosebud, and joins his brother Jim in The Association for a brief spell. He will re-form The Modern Folk Quartet in the 80s, but wins more acclaim as a producer (Aztec Two Step and Tom Waits) and as a string arranger in Los Angeles. Butler appears on Broadway in "Hair" and Boone moves to Baltimore, MD where he works as a musician.)

Oct Loser in the contract battle, MGM issues unauthorized live album *John Sebastian Live*, recorded during Lovin' Spoonful days. It peaks at US #129.

1971
Apr Reprise retaliates with a bona fide live album *Cheapo Cheapo Productions Presents ...* It reaches US #75.

Sept Sebastian's *The Four Of Us*, inspired by a cross-country vacation, reaches US #93. (Sebastian will spend time touring as a one-man show and between times play harmonica on albums by Stephen Stills, Ohio Knox, Rita Coolidge and The Everly Brothers.)

1974
Sept Sebastian's first album in 3 years, *The Tarzana Kid* does not chart but marks a reunion with Spoonful producer Erik Jacobsen.

1976
May After 5 singles fail, Reprise are on the point of dropping Sebastian when his song for John Travolta's TV series "Welcome Back Kotter", *Welcome Back* hits US #1. Double *The Best Of The Lovin' Spoonful* reaches US #183. Sebastian's *Welcome Back* makes US #79.

Aug Sebastian's *Hideaway* makes only US #95.

1980
Oct 15 years after The Lovin' Spoonful's inception, the 4 original members reunite for a cameo appearance in Paul Simon's movie "One Trick Pony". (Sebastian will continue to tour, with friends and solo; write for TV and films ("The Care Bears", "Strawberry Shortcake" and NBC TV's "The Jerk II"), and in 1991 present the Arts & Entertainment US TV cable channel's "The Golden Age Of Rock'N'Roll" series).

LULU

1963 Lulu (b. Marie McDonald Lawrie, Nov.3, 1948, Lennox Castle, near Glasgow, Scotland) joins Glasgow group The Gleneagles, which begins to play regularly at Lindella and Le Phonographe clubs. The latter's owner Tony Gordon, impressed by audience reactions, introduces the group to his sister Marion Massey, who is in showbiz management in London. Massey becomes the group's manager and changes the name to Lulu & The Luvvers. The line-up is Lulu (vocals), Ross Nelson (lead guitar), Jim Dewar (rhythm guitar), Alec Bell (keyboards), Jimmy Smith (saxophone), Tony Tierney (bass) and David Miller (drums).

1964
May [16] Group debuts on UK TV's "Thank Your Lucky Stars".

June Massey negotiates a contract with Decca, and the group's first disk is a revival of The Isley Brothers' *Shout*, which hits UK #7. (Similar follow-up *Satisfied* will fail to chart.)

Aug *Shout* makes a minor US chart showing at #94.

Nov *Here Comes The Night* (a UK Top 5 hit for Them, also on Decca, a few months later) charts briefly at UK #50.

Dec [26] Lulu opens in role of Witch Hazel in pantomime "Once Upon A Fairytale" at the Gaumont theater, Doncaster, S.Yorks.

1965 Partly thanks to her adaptability to musical styles and her easy TV demeanor, Lulu begins to be booked as a solo act (while still performing regular club and package show gigs with The Luvvers) and also records solo. (The Luvvers do not appear on disk after the first unsuccessful singles.)

May [25] Lulu performs *Leave A Little Love* as a soloist at the televised Brighton Song Festival at the Dome, Brighton, E.Sussex. The Les Reed-penned song is placed second (behind Kenny Lynch's *I'll Stay By You*) and is her biggest hit since *Shout*, at UK #8.

Sept *Try To Understand* reaches UK #25.

Oct [4] Lulu heads the cast of new BBC TV 13-part series "Stramash" (a Scottish word meaning riot or disturbance).

[22] Group embarks on 28-date twice-nightly UK package tour with Gene Pitney, Peter And Gordon, The Rockin' Berries and others, at Finsbury Park Astoria, London. Tour will end Nov.21 at the Odeon cinema, Leeds, W.Yorks.

1966
Jan [5] Group appears in the first broadcast of BBC TV "The Whole Scene Going" teenage magazine series.

317

Mar [8] Lulu becomes first UK girl singer to appear behind the Iron Curtain when she begins a Polish tour with The Hollies in Warsaw. [19] She returns from tour, at which point Lulu and The Luvvers split. [25] Lulu embarks on her first solo tour, a 31-date twice-nightly UK package tour with Roy Orbison, The Walker Brothers and others at Finsbury Park Astoria, London. Tour will close May 1 at the Coventry theater, W.Midlands.

May [31] Lulu begins filming "To Sir With Love" on location and at Pinewood Studios, with Sidney Poitier.

Dec [24] Lulu opens in "Babes In The Wood" pantomime at the Wimbledon theater, Wimbledon, London.

1967 Feb Lulu signs 5-year recording deal with producer Mickie Most.

Apr [23] The first of 6 30-min. BBC2 TV shows titled "Three Of A Kind" airs.

May Moving from Decca to Columbia with Most, their first collaboration, on a cover of a Neil Diamond B-side is *The Boat That I Row*, which hits UK #6. She tours UK supporting The Beach Boys.

June [4] Lulu attends the world premiere of "To Sir With Love" in New York.

July *Let's Pretend* reaches UK #11. B-side is the Don Black/Mark London song *To Sir With Love*. The song is not promoted in UK, despite good box office for the film.

Oct *To Sir With Love*, issued as US A-side to coincide with release of the movie in US, tops chart for 5 weeks, and becomes her only million-selling single.

Nov *Love Loves To Love Love* makes UK #32. A reissue of *Shout* (due to popularity of *To Sir With Love*) makes US #96. [13] Lulu participates in the "Royal Variety Show" at the London Palladium.

Dec *To Sir With Love* peaks at US #24.

1968 Feb *Best Of Both Worlds* makes US #32.

Mar *Me The Peaceful Heart* hits UK #9.

June *Boy* reaches UK #15. [17] While on tour in North America, Lulu appears at Vancouver, Canada's Issy's club wearing an eye patch, after receiving a black eye while traveling on a boat that morning.

July [5] Lulu begins a week-long engagement at Disneyland in Anaheim, CA.

Sept A cover of Tim Rose's *Morning Dew* makes US #52.

Nov *I'm A Tiger* hits UK #9.

Dec [27] She hosts her own musical variety show on UK TV, with special guests The Jimi Hendrix Experience. Hendrix causes production consternation when he switches in mid-act to an unscheduled number, Cream's *Sunshine Of Your Love*.

1969 Feb [18] Lulu marries Maurice Gibb of The Bee Gees, at Gerrards Cross, Bucks., with Bee Gee Robin Gibb as best man.

Apr She represents UK in the Eurovision Song Contest with *Boom-Bang-A-Bang*. In the most bizarre result in the history of the contest, it ties for first place with the entries from France, Spain and Holland. *Boom-Bang-A-Bang* hits UK #2.

Nov Lulu leaves Mickie Most and Columbia, and signs to Atlantic subsidiary Atco Records, debuting with *Oh Me Oh My (I'm A Fool For You Baby)*, penned by Glaswegian Jim Doris, and recorded in Muscle Shoals, AL, with production by Jerry Wexler, Tom Dowd and Arif Mardin. It makes UK #47.

1970 Feb *Oh Me Oh My (I'm A Fool For You Baby)* climbs to US #22.

Mar *New Routes* on Atco makes US #88.

May Lulu teams with The Dixie Flyers on *Hum A Song (From Your Heart)*, which reaches US #54.

June [20] NBC TV show "Andy Williams Presents Ray Stevens" with Lulu and Mama Cass as regular guests, premieres on US TV.

1971 Aug [28-29] She takes part in the "Berlin Disc Gala" with Ray Charles, Nancy Wilson, Henry Mancini and Gilbert Becaud in Germany.

Oct Compilation *The Most Of Lulu* reaches UK #15.

1973 Lulu and Maurice Gibb separate (and will later divorce).

1974 Feb Now signed to Polydor, she revives David Bowie's *The Man Who Sold The World*, with Bowie producing and featuring on saxophone and back-up vocals. It hits UK #3.

1975 Apr *Take Your Mama For A Ride*, on Wes Farrell's Chelsea label, makes UK #37.

1976 Lulu marries hairdresser John Frieda.

1977 June [18] Lulu gives birth to a son.

1981 Oct She signs to Alfa Records (marketed by CBS), and releases *I Could Never Miss You (More Than I Do)*, which reaches US #18. *Lulu* peaks at US #126.

Dec *I Could Never Miss You (More Than I Do)* makes UK #62.

1982 Jan *If I Were You* makes US #44.

1985 Dec Lulu takes part in Carol Aid, an all-star Christmas carol concert to raise money for the Band Aid Trust, at London's Heaven nightclub. Others singing include Chris De Burgh, Sandie Shaw and Cliff Richard.

1986 Aug She signs to Jive records and re-records *Shout*, in a similar but updated arrangement to the original, which hits UK #8. The original version is later reissued by Decca, and the sales of this are added to those of the new recording for UK chart purposes. (Although her recording career will cease, Lulu will still occasionally play in cabaret and take intermittent acting roles.)

FRANKIE LYMON & THE TEENAGERS

Frankie Lymon (lead vocals)
Sherman Garnes (vocals)
Joe Negroni (vocals)
Herman Santiago (vocals)
Jimmy Merchant (vocals)

1955 Lymon (b. Sept.30, 1942, Washington Heights, NY), a fellow student at Edward W Stitt junior high in the Bronx, New York, joins The Premiers, a quartet formed at the school, consisting of 2 blacks, tenor Merchant (b. Feb.10, 1940) and bass man Garnes (b. June 8, 1940) and 2 Puerto Ricans, lead singer Santiago (b. Feb.18, 1941) and baritone Negroni (b. Sept.9, 1940).

Nov The Premiers impress Richard Barrett, leader of The Valentines, who use the same school for rehearsal, and talent scout/A&R man for George Goldner.

Dec Goldner, a dance instructor and multiple label owner, signs the group to Gee, named after his recent Crows' smash. The soprano-voiced Lymon assumes lead role and the group records *Why Do Fools Fall In Love*, a Lymon composition. At the suggestion of a session saxophonist the name is changed to The Teenagers.

1956 Feb Credited to The Teenagers featuring Frankie Lymon, *Why Do Fools Fall In Love* reaches the top of the R&B chart and crosses into the pop list, hitting US #7, with sales exceeding a million.

Apr Sidelining academic pursuits, the group embarks on a hectic non-stop touring schedule. A second single, *I Want You To Be My Girl*, giving Lymon billing over the group, reaches US #17.

July *I Promise To Remember* peaks at US #57 but *Why Do Fools Fall In Love* hits UK #1. 13-year-old Lymon becomes an unlikely teen heart-throb.

Oct *The ABCs Of Love*, the group's fourth release, climbs to US #77.

1957 Mar Designed as a riposte to the growing body of rock'n'roll detractors, *I'm Not A Juvenile Delinquent* fails in US despite promotion in Alan Freed movie "Rock Rock Rock" but it reaches UK #12. Group UK tour includes 2 weeks topping the bill at the London Palladium. At 14, Lymon is the youngest ever headliner, having already been the youngest chart topper at 13.

Apr *Baby Baby*, the flip of *I'm Not A Juvenile Delinquent*, also in the Freed film, attracts UK airplay in the wake of The Teenagers' tour and outsells the A-side, hitting UK #4.

July Lymon is encouraged to break from The Teenagers but his first solo effort, *Goody Goody*, recorded in England, reaches only US #22 and #24 in UK, where it is his last hit.

1960 Aug After 3 years in the doldrums, during which time Roulette absorbs the bankrupt Goldner's labels, *Little Bitty Pretty One*, originally recorded for a 1958 album, returns Lymon to US chart at #58. The comeback is short-lived as his broken voice has robbed him of his major asset.

1961 On the advice of distraught friends, Lymon submits to a drug rehabilitation program.

1964 Following his failure as a restyled night club act, Lymon is arrested and found guilty of narcotics offenses.

1968 Feb [28] Lymon's body is discovered in the 165th Street house in which he grew up. A nearby syringe figures in every news report. A star at 13, all but spent at 14, he is dead at 25.

1981 Oct Diana Ross revives *Why Do Fools Fall In Love* for a Top 10 hit and dedicates her album to Lymon's memory. (The original endures as one of rock's most popular oldies and a reconstituted group of The Teenagers, led by Santiago and Merchant (both Negroni and Garnes died in the late 70s), with Pearl McKinnon duplicating Lymon's soprano, continues to gather momentum on the rock revival and lounge circuits.)

YNYRD SKYNYRD

onnie Van Zant (vocals)
ary Rossington (guitar)
llen Collins (guitar)
lly Powell (keyboards)
eon Wilkeson (bass)
ob Burns (drums)

65 Group is formed in high school in Jacksonville, FL, under the name My Backyard, later changed to immortalize school gym teacher Leonard Skinner, a legendary antagonist of long-haired students.

68 Debut single *Need All My Friends* is released on Jacksonville-based Shade Tree label.

71 After some years of touring in the South, the group releases second single *I've Been Your Fool*.

72 Al Kooper (ex-Blood, Sweat & Tears) is touring with Badfinger and looking for suitable talent for his new label Sounds Of The South, marketed by MCA, when he spots the group playing at Funocchio's bar in Atlanta, GA. Kooper is impressed by Skynyrd's "Dixie rock" style, and signs the band.

73 **Nov** Debut album *Pronounced Leh-Nerd Skin-Nerd* is produced by Kooper and features a new third guitarist, Ed King (ex-Strawberry Alarm Clock, and more recently a session man), whose joining gives the group a near-unique 3-guitar stage line-up. The album reaches US #27 and earns a gold disk; its big airplay track is *Free Bird*, a tribute to the late Duane Allman of The Allman Brothers Band.
Dec Skynyrd tours North America as support on The Who's "Quadrophenia" tour.

74 **Oct** *Sweet Home Alabama* is the group's first US chart single, hitting #8. (The song is seen as a Southerners' answer to Neil Young's 1971 *Southern Man*.) It is taken from *Second Helping*, again produced by Kooper, which reaches US #12 and earns a second gold disk.
Dec Burns leaves, and is replaced on drums by Artimus Pyle (b. Spartanburg, SC).

75 **Jan** *Free Bird*, belatedly issued as a single (soon to become the band's anthem and a perennial on FM radio), reaches US #19. King leaves after playing in sessions for the next album.
May *Nuthin' Fancy* hits US #9, earning another gold disk, and reaches UK #43, following the group's UK live debut as support to Dutch group Golden Earring.
July *Saturday Night Special* reaches US #27.

76 **Feb** [10] Group begins a 5-date UK tour at Colston Hall, Bristol, Avon.
Mar *Double Trouble* makes US #80, while *Gimme Back My Bullets*, produced by Tom Dowd, reaches US #20 (the fourth gold disk) and UK #34. Band gains an English manager, Peter Rudge. Van Zant is being arrested continually for brawling – usually in bars – as they begin to develop a reputation for in-fighting and general physical aggravation.
Aug [21] Group appears at Knebworth Festival, Knebworth, Herts., alongside The Rolling Stones, Todd Rundgren and 10cc.
Sept 3-track EP comprising *Free Bird*, *Sweet Home Alabama* and *Double Trouble* reaches UK #31.
[5] Rossington is injured in a car crash in Jacksonville.
Nov New third guitarist Steve Gaines (b. Seneca, MO) joins and a female back-up trio is added for Skynyrd's double live *One More For The Road*, recorded in Atlanta. It hits US #9 and UK #17 and is the group's biggest seller, earning a platinum disk for a million US sales.
Dec A live version of *Free Bird*, from the double album, makes US #38.

77 **Apr** [15] Van Zant and Collins present the gold disk awarded them for *One More For The Road* to Maynard Jackson, mayor of Atlanta, in appreciation of the band's Atlanta fans. Another gold disk goes to Fox theater, Atlanta, where the album was recorded. Several group members, plus James Brown and other celebrity Georgians are honored at a ceremony in the Atlanta Braves' baseball stadium, prior to the team's opening home game.
Oct [20] Van Zant, Steve Gaines, his sister Cassie Gaines (one of the 3 female back-up singers) and personal manager Dean Kilpatrick are killed when Skynyrd's rented single-engined Convair 240 plane, short of fuel, crashes into a swamp in Gillsburg, MS, while en route from Greenville, SC, to Baton Rouge, LA, to play at Louisiana university, on a 50-city tour. Rossington, Collins, Powell and Wilkeson are all seriously injured (but will eventually recover). MCA withdraws the sleeve of just-released *Street Survivors*, which pictures the group standing amid flames.
Nov *Street Survivors*, a second platinum disk, hits US #5 and UK #13.

78 **Mar** *What's Your Name*, taken from *Street Survivors*, reaches US #13.
Apr Group's last US hit single is *You Got That Right*, which makes #69.

Nov *Skynyrd's First And Last*, containing unreleased 1970-72 recordings, reaches US #15 and UK #50, and becomes another platinum album.

1979 **Oct** With the exception of Pyle, the surviving Lynyrd Skynyrd members form a new group, The Rossington-Collins Band, with female lead vocalist, Dale Krantz, who has earlier been a back-up singer for .38 Special, the band fronted by Van Zant's brother Donnie. Guitarist Barry Harwood (to give a 3-guitar line-up again) and drummer Derek Hess also join. Group remains signed to MCA.

1980 **Jan** EP *Free Bird* re-charts in UK, reaching #43.
Feb Double compilation *Gold And Platinum* reaches US #12 and UK #49, earning a final platinum disk.
Aug The first Rossington-Collins Band album *Anytime, Anyplace, Anywhere* reaches US #13, and earns a gold disk, while extracted *Don't Misunderstand Me* is the band's only hit single, peaking at US #55. On stage, the group plays an instrumental version of *Free Bird* to close its act, the tune now being a dedication to Ronnie Van Zant.

1981 **Nov** *This Is The Way* by The Rossington-Collins Band makes US #24. It is dedicated to Collins' wife Katy, who died a year earlier. Shortly after, the band breaks up.

1982 **Feb** [13] The inscribed 300lb. marble slab is stolen from the grave of Ronnie Van Zant in a cemetery at Orange Park, FL. (Police will find it 2 weeks later in a partially dried-up river bed.)
Mar Pyle forms a new quintet, The Artimus Pyle Band, which begins touring US.
June EP *Free Bird* charts for the third time in UK, this time hitting its highest position of #21.
Dec *Best Of The Rest*, a compilation of Skynyrd rare tracks and out-takes, reaches US #171.

1986 Powell joins a Christian band, Vision, after being released from 30 days in jail. Collins' car runs off the road, crashing into a culvert, paralyzing him from the waist down and killing his girlfriend Debra Jean Watts.

1987 Vision join ex-Grand Funk Railroad singer Mark Farner on a club tour. They perform Lynyrd Skynyrd material, and the audience response convinces them that Skynyrd should re-form.
Sept A new Lynyrd Skynyrd is formed, comprising Rossington, Powell, Pyle, Wilkeson, King, Johnny Van Zant (vocals) and Randall Hall (guitar), with Dale Krantz Rossington and Carol Bristow (The Honkettes) on backing vocals. The group plays Charlie Daniels' 13th Volunteer Jam Reunion in Georgia, and a 32-date reunion tour, marking the 10th anniversary of the fatal plane crash.
Nov Compilation *Legend* by original Lynyrd Skynyrd is released by MCA, containing previous B-sides, unreleased and uncompleted songs. Produced by Dowd with the surviving members, it makes US #41.

1988 **Sept** The new Lynyrd Skynyrd's double live album *For The Glory Of The South* is released on MCA, consisting of tracks recorded on the Sept.1987 reunion tour.
Dec [3] *Will To Power* tops US chart, reviving Peter Frampton's *Baby I Love Your Way* and Lynyrd Skynyrd's *Freebird*, in a medley.

1990 **Jan** [23] Hospitalized since Sept., Collins dies of pneumonia at Memorial medical center, Jacksonville, FL.

MADNESS

Graham "Suggs" McPherson (vocals)
Mike Barson (keyboards)
Chris "Chrissie Boy" Foreman (guitar)
Mark "Bedders" Bedford (bass)
Lee "Kix" Thompson (saxophone, vocals)
Dan "Woody" Woodgate (drums)
Carl "Chas Smash" Smyth (horns)

1976 Barson (b. May 21, 1958), Thompson (b. Oct.5, 1957, London) and Foreman (b. Aug.8, 1958), all from Gospel Oak school in Camden and living in Kentish Town, London, form bluebeat-based The Invaders.

1977 **June** [30] Band makes its first public appearance with John Hasler on drums and Smyth (b. Cathal Smyth, Jan.14, 1959) on bass, and adopts its "nutty sound".

1978 **Feb** Temporary vocalist Dikron is replaced by McPherson (b. Jan.13, 1961, Hastings, E.Sussex).
Sept The constantly changing line-up settles around original trio with McPherson, Bedford (b. Aug.24, 1961, London) and Woodgate (b. Oct.19, 1960, London).

1979 **Jan** [1] The Invaders play their last gig at the London Film-makers Co-op, after which they change their name to Madness.
Mar McPherson strikes a friendship with The Specials AKA after seeing them perform at the Hope & Anchor pub, Islington, London,

and Madness signs to Specials' leader Jerry Dammers' 2-Tone label.

Oct Debut disk *The Prince*, tribute to ska hero Prince Buster written by Thompson, makes UK #16, 2-Tone's second release. Band signs to Dave Robinson's Stiff Records in UK (after a wedding party) and Sire in US.

Nov *One Step Beyond*, produced by Clive Langer and Alan Winstanley (who will produce most of the band's records), hits UK #2 during a 78-week chart stay. Meanwhile, the band completes 3-week US tour of New York, California and Texas.

Dec *One Step Beyond* hits UK #7.

[30] Madness headlines a concert at the London Lyceum.

1980 **Jan** *My Girl* hits UK #3. (It is later covered by another Stiff artist Tracey Ullman as *My Guy*.)

Feb Madness returns from a European tour and plays a Saturday morning gig at London's Hammersmith Odeon for "under 16s".

Mar Group's progress is marred by unwanted attentions of National Front extremists while on tour with The Specials. *One Step Beyond* reaches US #128, released on Sire Records.

Apr EP *The Work Rest And Play* hits UK #6, with *Night Train To Cairo* as the lead track and a cut rebutting the National Front.

July Group begins a 30-date tour of Europe.

Oct *Baggy Trousers* hits UK #3 (helped by a Dave Robinson-produced video featuring "flying" sax player Thompson), as parent album *Absolutely* hits UK #2, during a 46-week chart stay.

[8] A UK tour begins in Blackpool, Lancs.

Nov *Absolutely* makes US #146. (Group is subsequently released from Sire, under an agreement which stated that if the second album did not sell a certain amount, Madness could leave the label.) They begin a "Twelve Days Of Madness" tour. Each date includes an "under 16s" matinee, where all tickets sell for £1, in addition to an evening show. (Tour ends in 5 sell-out gigs at London's Hammersmith Odeon, among them a Christmas Eve charity show.)

Dec *Embarrassment* hits UK #4, as Madness are voted Singles Artists Of The Year by **New Musical Express**, having spent 46 weeks on chart during 1980.

1981 **Feb** Instrumental *Return Of The Los Palmas Seven* hits UK #7. Group appears in 2-Tone movie "Dance Craze".

Mar Madness begin work on full-length feature movie "Take It Or Leave It", directed by Stiff Records' boss Dave Robinson. They embark on the "Absolutely Madness One Step Beyond Far East Tour" of Australasia, Japan and US.

May *Grey Day* hits UK #4.

Oct *Shut Up* hits UK #7, as parent album *Seven*, recorded at Compass Point studios in Nassau, Bahamas, hits UK #5. "Take It Or Leave It" movie premieres to poor reviews. Group sets out on a 36-date UK tour.

1982 **Jan** Group's revival of Labi Siffre's 1972 hit *It Must Be Love* hits UK #4. (Siffre makes a cameo appearance on the video and children are warned on UK TV not to copy the band who jump into a swimming pool clutching electric guitars.) Suggs marries singer Bette Bright.

Mar *Cardiac Arrest* makes UK #14, their first single since *The Prince* to miss the Top 10. There is resistance from radio on grounds of bad taste.

May *House Of Fun* hits UK #1, with another original video filmed at a fun fair, toppling Eurovision winner Nicole's *A Little Peace*. Compilation album of hits *Complete Madness* also hits UK #1, while a video collection of the same title becomes a best-seller.

July *Driving In My Car* hits UK #4.

Nov *The Rise And Fall* hits UK #10.

Dec *Our House* hits UK #5.

1983 **Feb** **[21]** Madness begins its annual UK tour.

Mar *Tomorrow's (Just Another Day)* hits UK #8.

Apr Group, now with Geffen Records for US, enjoys its biggest US Album chart success with *Madness*. It reaches US #41.

July *Our House* becomes the group's biggest US hit at #7.

Sept *Wings Of A Dove* hits UK #2, held off #1 by UB40's *Red Red Wine*.

Oct *It Must Be Love* makes US #33.

Nov *The Sun And The Rain* hits UK #5.

Dec **[21]** Founding member and writer Barson announces his intention to leave and settle in Holland with his Dutch wife, Sandra.

1984 **Feb** *Michael Caine*, with guest appearance by Caine, reaches UK #11.

Mar Parent album *Keep Moving* hits UK #6. *The Sun And The Rain* stalls at US #72.

Apr *Keep Moving* peaks at US #109, and is their US chart swan song.

June *One Better Day* makes UK #17, and is the group's last release for Stiff, on which they hit Top 20 with every UK release.

Oct Group forms its own label, Zarjazz (derived from its favorite comic **2000 AD**), through Virgin. First release is Feargal Sharkey's *Listen To Your Father*, written by Madness and originally intended as a

group release. It makes UK #23.

1985 **Feb** Smyth and McPherson as The Fink Brothers (characters in **2000 AD**), peak at UK #50 with *Mutants In Mega City*.

Mar Madness, with UB40, The Specials, General Public and others, assemble as Starvation to record *Starvation Tam-Tam Pour L'Ethiope*, to raise funds for the starving in Ethiopia, Eritrea and the Sudan. The single makes UK #33.

Sept Madness' *Yesterday's Men*, their first on Zarjazz, reaches UK #18.

Oct *Mad Not Mad* makes UK #16.

Nov *Uncle Sam*, with a return to "nutty sound" video style, makes UK #21 – the first to fail to make Top 20 in 21 attempts.

Dec **[21]** Madness participates in Greater London Council Christmas party for the unemployed with Marc Almond, Ian Dury and others.

1986 **Feb** *Sweetest Girl*, a revival of Scritti Politti's hit, makes UK #35.

Sept **[1]** Group officially announces that it will split.

Nov *Waiting For The Ghost Train* makes UK #18.

Dec A second hits album **Utter Madness** is released, making UK #29.

1987 **Mar** *The Voice Of The Beehive's Just A City* features Bedders and Woody. (Bedders will later begin work on film scores.)

1988 **Feb** Madness, re-formed as 4-piece The Madness, signs to Virgin.

Mar Sitar-fused *I Pronounce You* stalls at UK #44.

May *The Madness* makes US #65.

June *What's That* is the first Madness disk to fail to chart in UK. (Suggs will become a regular comedy host at the Mean Fiddler club in North London.)

1990 Having produced their first single in 1985, Suggs is now full-time manager for UK hit combo The Farm.

MADONNA

1977 After a year at the University of Michigan, to which she wins a scholarship, Madonna (b. Madonna Louise Ciccone, Aug.16, 1958, named after her mother who died when Madonna was 6, Rochester, Detroit, MI) heads for New York, at the urging of her ballet teacher. Subsequently moving to university in North Carolina, she is awarded another scholarship (having completed a 6-week dance workshop) to work with choreographer Pearl Lang. While in New York, she will also take a number of jobs, including modelling and working in a doughnut shop in Times Square. (She has initially studied piano before switching to ballet, but finds theater her forte when studying at Rochester Adams high school and playing lead roles in school productions.)

1979 She lands a place in the "Patrick Hernandez Revue", working in Paris, France. Hernandez is a disco star looking to capitalize on his worldwide hit, *Born To Be Alive*. She leaves the revue to form a band with her boyfriend Dan Gilroy. Calling the band The Breakfast Club, they play local venues, with Madonna starting behind the drum kit, but soon stepping out front to sing.

1980 Madonna leaves the band and starts her own group Emmenon, shortened later to Emmy. When the first drummer leaves, an old boyfriend from Detroit, former waiter Steve Bray, joins and she leaves the dance company and begins working with him on demo tapes at his home studio. She also lands a part in Stephen Jon Lewicki's low-budget 60-min. movie thriller "A Certain Sacrifice". Late in the year she signs to rock manager Adam Alter's Gotham Productions.

1982 She splits from Gotham having spent a wasted year, recording in studios and waiting for a record deal. (Gotham will later sue her and receive an insubstantial settlement.) Madonna's break comes when she gives DJ/producer Mark Kamins at Danceteria club a tape of the dance material she has made with Bray. Kamins introduces her to Sire Records' executive Michael Rosenblatt, who hears the cassette and agrees to sign her – subject to label boss Seymour Stein's approval. Stein, hospitalized, agrees and the deal is signed. Kamins produces *Ain't No Big Deal*, intended as the first single but dropped in favor of *Everybody*, which breaks on dance radio stations and climbs the dance chart. Lip-synching, she debuts at the Danceteria.

Dec *Everybody* is released in UK, but fails to chart.

1983 *Physical Attraction*, penned by Reggie Lucas, is another big club hit.

June Dance happy *Holiday*, written by current flame and producer John "Jellybean" Benitez, is released. During a UK promo trip, Madonna lip-synchs at London's Music Machine.

Sept *Madonna*, produced by Lucas, enters the US chart to eventually hit #8. *Lucky Star* is released in UK.

Oct *Holiday* peaks at US #16.

1984 **Feb** *Holiday* hits UK #6. Madonna performs on BBC TV's "Top Of The Pops". *Madonna* hits UK #6.

Apr Re-released *Lucky Star* makes UK #14.

June *Borderline* hits US #6, but stalls at UK #56.

Oct *Lucky Star* hits US #4, giving a boost to the album and pushing its sales over a million. Madonna begins work on her first major film role, in Susan Seidelman's "Desperately Seeking Susan", alongside Rosanna Arquette.

Nov Dance-dominated *Like A Virgin*, which includes a cover version of Rose Royce hit ballad *Love Don't Live Here Anymore*, produced by Nile Rodgers and featuring Chic's rhythm section, enters the UK chart.

Dec *Like A Virgin*, written by Tom Kelly and Billy Steinberg, and suggested to Madonna by Warner Bros. A&R head Mo Ostin, tops the US chart for 6 weeks.

1985

Jan *Like A Virgin* hits UK #3.

Feb *Like A Virgin* tops the US chart.

[13] Madonna and actor Sean Penn have their first date at the Private Eyes club in New York.

Mar *Material Girl* hits US #2 and UK #3, aided not least by a Marilyn Monroe pastiche video, an image Madonna will persist with through the decade.

Apr Madonna begins her first tour. Titled "The Virgin Tour", it plays to 355,000 fans in 27 cities. Up and coming rap act The Beastie Boys support her. On the final tour date, she is carried off stage by her father, Tony.

May Jon Lind/John Bettis-penned ballad *Crazy For You* from Matthew Modine-starring film "Vision Quest", tops the US chart. Madonna is syndicated worldwide clothed in beachwear for fashion magazines.

June *Angel* hits US #5 as *Crazy For You* hits UK #2.

July "Desperately Seeking Susan" is premiered, while movie release of earlier Madonna featuring soft-porn "A Certain Sacrifice" is planned.

Aug [3] From "Desperately Seeking Susan" movie and co-written by Madonna and Bray, uptempo dance smash *Into The Groove* is Madonna's first UK chart-topper. (In US, it will only appear on the B-side of 12" *Angel* so will never make **Billboard** Hot 100.) Sire later adds the song to *Like A Virgin* and also repackages *Madonna* as *The First Album*. *Holiday* re-enters the UK chart, this time hitting #2 – kept out by *Into The Groove* (only The Beatles, John Lennon and Frankie Goes To Hollywood have also filled the top 2 places simultaneously).

[13] Madonna performs solo and with The Thompson Twins in the Philadelphia leg of Live Aid. She is introduced by Bette Midler who claims that Madonna is "a woman who pulled herself up by her bra-straps".

[16] Madonna marries actor Sean Penn on her 26th birthday. As the cliffside coastal wedding takes place, news crews buzz overhead in a fleet of helicopters.

[17] *Dress You Up* enters the US chart to hit #5. After her honeymoon, she begins working on a new album which she will dedicate to her husband, "the coolest guy in the universe".

Sept After nearly a year on chart, *Like A Virgin* hits UK #1. Meanwhile *Angel* hits UK #5. **Penthouse** and **Playboy** magazines publish nude spreads she sat for while penniless in New York in 1977.

Oct *Dress You Up* hits US #5 as *Gambler* hits UK #4.

Dec *Dress You Up* hits UK #3 and becomes Madonna's eighth Top 10 hit of the year. (She becomes the only woman to have 3 disks in UK Top 15 for nearly 30 years, joining Ruby Murray.)

1986

Jan *Borderline* and *Gambler* both re-enter the UK chart, hitting #2 and #61 respectively. Madonna and Penn travel to China to film scenes for a new movie. She wins Best Selling Video award in UK for "Like A Virgin The Video EP".

Mar While filming "Shanghai Surprise", press harassment causes much publicized Mr. and Mrs. Penn reaction. **The Sun**'s photographer Dave Hogan is knocked down by the Penns' car. UK tabloid press picks up on the incident and on rumblings of discontent on film set. Producer George Harrison calls a press conference to defuse the situation.

Apr Due to recording commitments Madonna is unable to appear opposite Bruce Willis in scheduled movie "Blind Date". "Like A Virgin – Live" video documentary is released.

June [7] Cementing their songwriting and production partnership which will steer Madonna's career to the end of the decade, Patrick Leonard/Madonna-written *Live To Tell*, a ballad from film "At Close Range", starring Sean Penn, hits US #1, having already hit UK #2.

July Produced by Madonna, with Stephen Bray and Leonard, *True Blue* enters the UK chart at #1 and will also climb to US #1.

[12] Father/daughter-focusing *Papa Don't Preach* tops UK chart.

Aug She shoots a video in Los Angeles' Echo Park district featuring UK youngster Felix Howard.

[16] *Papa Don't Preach* and *True Blue* top the US chart.

Oct *True Blue* tops the UK chart, tying Sandie Shaw's record of most UK number #1s (3) by a female act.

Nov [15] *True Blue* hits US #3. "Shanghai Surprise" premieres to savage reviews.

Dec Co-written by Madonna, Gardner Cole and Peter Rafelson, *Open Your Heart* hits UK #4.

1987

Feb [7] *Open Your Heart* becomes Madonna's fifth US chart-topper, and her third from *True Blue*.

Mar Madonna receives the dubious distinction of being voted "Favorite Artist Of Record Pirates" by a special **Billboard** panel, a measure of her worldwide popularity.

Apr Madonna becomes the only female artist to have 4 UK #1s when *La Isla Bonita* tops the chart.

May [2] *La Isla Bonita* hits US #4.

June [14] A record-breaking Japanese tour begins in Osaka.

July *Who's That Girl*, also the title of the new movie in which she stars with Griffin Dunne and Sir John Mills, hits both UK and US #1. Again critically mauled, the film fails to match the single's success. Madonna tours UK for the first time, playing 1 show in Leeds and 3 at London's Wembley Stadium under the banner "Who's That Girl Tour".

Aug [22] *Who's That Girl* tops US chart.

Sept *Who's That Girl* hits US #7 and UK #4.

Oct [24] *Causin' A Commotion* hits US #2 and UK #4.

Dec *The Look Of Love* hits UK #9. Album of dance remixes, *You Can Dance*, hits UK #5. Madonna guests on A&M's *A Very Special Christmas*, reviving Eartha Kitt's *Santa Baby*.

[4] Madonna files for divorce from Sean Penn in Malibu, CA, but will change her mind a week later.

1988

Jan *You Can Dance* reaches US #14.

[5] Madonna serves divorce papers on Sean Penn.

Mar [29] Madonna opens on Broadway in "Speed The Plow" with Joe Mantegna and Ron Silver.

Sept Against her wishes, a video of film "A Certain Sacrifice" becomes publicly available as a new Patrick Leonard produced-album is recorded in Los Angeles.

Oct Press reports state that Meryl Streep wins the title role in the film version of "Evita", after Madonna is turned down, for demanding a $5-million fee and refusing to do a screen test. (The on-off project will return to Madonna's camp in 1991.)

Dec [12] Madonna signs a 2-year, 5-film deal with Columbia Pictures.

1989

Jan [25] Madonna files for divorce for the second time from Penn at Los Angeles County Superior Court. Assault charges against Penn filed by Madonna at Malibu Sheriff's office on Dec.28 are dropped. She moves into a new 3 bedroom house in the Hollywood Hills, CA.

Feb She appears unannounced at the AIDS Dance-a-thon at the Shrine Auditorium, Los Angeles.

Mar [2] Madonna begins a $5 million sponsorship deal with Pepsi-Cola. For the first time, a major star uses a song for a TV commercial ahead of its retail release. *Like A Prayer* airs during NBC TV's "The Cosby Show".

[3] Italian TV refuses to air the clip on the grounds that it's blasphemous. Pepsi begins reassessing its deal with Madonna. *Like A Prayer* tops UK and US charts. Its promo video causes a worldwide media and religious storm, and is banned by the Vatican. Because of its strong religious imagery, Pepsi drops its commercial and withdraws Madonna's sponsorship claiming consumer confusion between the commercial and the video. Her proposed 1989 tour is cancelled.

Apr Parent album *Like A Prayer*, co-produced with Patrick Leonard and including *Love Song*, a duet with Prince, hits US #1 and UK #1.

May Madonna takes part in the ecological awareness benefit "Don't Bungle The Jungle" at the Brooklyn Academy of Music, New York, duetting with girlfriend Sandra Bernhard on *I Got You Babe*.

July [15] *Express Yourself*, supported by steamy video directed by David Fincher, hits US #2. (Madonna overtakes The Beatles on the list of all-time consecutive Top 5 hits. Her total of 16 is now only surpassed by Elvis Presley's 24.)

Sept [6] "Like A Prayer" wins Best Viewer's Choice Video at the sixth annual MTV Music Video Awards ceremony at the Universal Amphitheater, Universal City, CA.

Oct [7] *Cherish* hits US #2.

Dec [23] Dreamy child-themed *Dear Jessie* hits UK #5 as Madonna wins Top Adult Contemporary Artist in **Billboard**'s Year In Music annual survey. (By year's end, Madonna will also have completed filming of "Bloodhounds On Broadway".)

1990

Jan [6] *Oh Father* reaches US #20.

Mar [8] Madonna wins Worst Female Singer and Worst Video ("Like A Prayer") in **Rolling Stone**'s Readers Poll and Best Video ("Like A Prayer") in the magazine's Critics Awards.

[31] *Keep it Together* hits US #8.

Apr [13] 54-date worldwide "Blond Ambition" tour opens at the Chiba Marine Stadium in Tokyo, Japan, featuring expected revealing costumes designed by Jean Paul Gaultier.

[14] From forthcoming album, *Vogue* hits UK #1 and will earn a gold disk.

May [4-5] US leg of the "Blond Ambition" tour opens in Houston, TX. (She will cancel a concert at the Rosemont Horizon, Rosemont, IL, suffering from infected vocal chords. Subsequent concerts will also have to be called off.)

[12] *Vogue*, which via accompanying video, begins a mini-fad for dance stance "vogueing", hits US #1 for 3 weeks.

[26] As *Vogue* holds at #1, the US Top 5 are all female artists, the first time since June 1979 when Anita Ward was at the top.

June [2] Marketed in line with her current role as Breathless Mahoney, *I'm Breathless* hits UK #2.

[23] *I'm Breathless* hits UK #2, unable to dislodge MC Hammer. 13-year-old Keith Sorrentino files $500,000 lawsuit against Madonna, claiming he suffers nightmares and bed-wetting problems from an incident that occurred in May 1988 outside Madonna's Central Park West apartment in New York. The complaint charges that Madonna grabbed his camera, flung him to the ground and choked him after he asked to take her photo. Madonna, in response, files a third-party countersuit against Sorrentino's older sister, Darlene, claiming her to be an obsessive fan who has subjected Madonna to "threatening, abusive, vexatious and obscene statements" over the years.

July [6] Generally praised for her teasing role as Breathless Mahoney in current beau Warren Beatty's "Dick Tracy" movie, the film makes its European premiere in Leicester Square, London.

[11] Madonna's second scheduled show at the Flaminio Stadium, Rome, Italy, is cancelled, reportedly due to poor ticket sales and a general laborers' strike.

[18] Dogged by UK gutter press, Madonna goes jogging in Hyde Park, causing criticism in the press, which states she had agreed to help launch charity record *Nobody's Child* to benefit Romanian orphans.

[20-22] Madonna performs at Wembley Stadium, at the start of UK leg of world tour.

[28] Extracted *Hanky Panky* hits US #10 and UK #2.

Aug [5] "Madonna – Live! Blond Ambition World Tour '90" concert airs on HBO, and becomes the most watched show in the station's 18-year history.

Sept Following a regal Victorian costumed perfection-timed dance troupe performance of *Vogue* at the MTV Awards, Madonna sings *Vogue* at a benefit for AIDS Project Los Angeles at the Wiltern theater, Los Angeles.

Nov [2] Greatest hits collection *The Immaculate Collection*, concurrently released with a similar video package, but not including the album's *Justify My Love*, immediately hits UK #1, where it will stay for 9 weeks on its way to 5 platinum UK sales disks.

[27] MTV announces a ban on the video, filmed at the Royal Monceau Hotel in Paris, France, of newly released *Justify My Love*, which as a result will be lucratively released as a video sales cassette.

Dec [3] ABC TV airs the video in full on "Nightline". Anchorman Forrest Sawyer quizzes Madonna on its subject matter.

[15] New single *Justify My Love* hits UK #2.

[22] *The Immaculate Collection* hits US #3, with domestic sales approaching 2 million.

1991 **Jan** Rabbi Abraham Cooper of the Simon Wiesenthal Center in Los Angeles wants copies of *The Immaculate Collection* removed from record stores, because one of the tracks has lyrics of biblical reference which the Center believes could incite antisemitism.

[5] Co-written by Madonna and Lenny Kravitz and produced by Kravitz, partly spoken *Justify My Love* hits familiar US #1, boosted by the banning of accompanying steamy hotel bedroom-shot black and white video co-starring current beau Tony Ward.

[28] Madonna wins Favorite Dance/Music single for *Vogue* at the 18th annual American Music Awards at the Shrine Auditorium.

Mar [2] *Rescue Me* enters US Hot 100 at #15, the highest-debuting single by a female artist in rock history. The previous record was held by Joy Layne, whose *Your Wild Heart* entered at #30 in 1957. The single will, however, only hit US #9.

[3] *Vogue* wins International Single Of The Year at the 20th annual Juno Awards at the Queen Elizabeth theater, Vancouver, Canada.

[7] *Vogue* is named Best Single and Best Video in the annual **Rolling Stone** Readers' Picks music awards. Madonna's "Blond Ambition Tour" is named Best Tour and she wins Best Dressed Female Artist and Sexiest Female Singer categories. "Justify My Love" wins Best Video and Hype Of The Year in the Critics' Picks.

[25] She sings Stephen Sondheim's "Dick Tracy"-featured *Sooner Or Later (I Always Get My Man)* at the 63rd annual Academy Awards ceremony at the Shrine Auditorium, Los Angeles. The song will win the Oscar for Best Song. (Her escort for the evening's festivities is Michael Jackson.)

May [10] "Truth Or Dare: On The Band Behind The Scenes, And In Bed With Madonna", a Madonna-commissioned warts-and-all roving bio-documentary, premieres.

THE MAMAS AND THE PAPAS

John Phillips (vocals)
Denny Doherty (vocals)
Cass Elliot (vocals)
Michelle Gilliam (vocals)

1964 Group comes together as trio The New Journeymen in St. Thomas in the Virgin Islands, when Doherty teams with the 2 remaining Journeymen, Phillips and Gilliam. Phillips (b. Aug.30, 1935, Parris Island, SC) as a member of folk trio The Journeymen (with Scott McKenzie and Dick Weissman), released 3 albums on Capitol, Gilliam (b. Holly Michelle Gilliam, June 4, 1945, Long Beach, CA), married Phillips after meeting at San Francisco's Hungry I club in 1962 and joined The Journeymen, and Doherty (b. Nov.29, 1941, Halifax, Canada), has sung with similar group The Halifax Three, recording for Epic, before joining Elliot (b. Ellen Naomi Cohen, Sept.19, 1941, Baltimore, MD), ex-lead singer of The Big Three, in The Mugwumps (with Zalman Yanovsky and John Sebastian who form The Lovin' Spoonful). The Mugwumps release *I Don't Wanna Know*, on Warner Bros., cut some more material not issued at the time and, after working on "Freak Out" movie soundtrack, split. The New Journeymen rehearse to fulfill contractual obligations.

1965 **Jan** Elliot has become a waitress, but joins them briefly in the Virgin Islands, and then full time when the group relocates to California. Here they meet up with an old friend, ex-New Christy Minstrel Barry McGuire, who introduces them to his producer, and owner of the new Dunhill label, Lou Adler.

Oct Adler hires them to sing back-ups on sessions for McGuire's *This Precious Time* and uses Phillips' song *California Dreamin'* for McGuire. The New Journeymen sign to Dunhill in their own right; after toying with name The Magic Circle, they become The Mamas And The Papas.

Dec *Go Where You Wanna Go* is recorded as debut single, but Adler releases the group's own version of *California Dreamin'* instead (it uses the same backing track as McGuire's album version).

1966 **Mar** *California Dreamin'* hits US #4 and earns a gold disk for a million-plus US sales.

May *Monday Monday*, another Phillips song (which everyone apart from him in the group dislikes), is the follow-up. It tops US chart for 3 weeks, and is another million-seller. Meanwhile *California Dreamin'* reaches UK #23 and *If You Can Believe Your Eyes And Ears*, which contains both songs, tops US chart for a week, selling over a million copies in its 105-week chart stay.

June *Monday Monday* hits UK #3.

July *I Saw Her Again* hits US #5, while the album (retitled *The Mamas And The Papas* in UK) hits UK #3.

[8] Gilliam is fired from the group, and is replaced temporarily by Jill Gibson, long-time girlfriend of Jan Berry from Jan And Dean.

Aug Phillips and Gilliam reconcile, and she returns to the group, replacing Gibson.

Sept *I Saw Her Again* reaches UK #11.

Oct [14] Group plays at Carnegie Hall, New York.

Nov *Look Through My Window* reaches US #24 (but fails to chart in UK) while the group's second album *The Mamas And The Papas* hits US #4 and earns another gold disk. They make a US TV special.

1967 **Jan** *Words Of Love*, a lead vocal showcase for Elliot, hits US #5 and is a third million-selling single. The B-side, a revival of Martha & The Vandellas' *Dancing In The Street* peaks at US #73.

Feb The second album (retitled *Cass, John, Michelle And Denny* in UK) reaches UK #24. *Words Of Love* makes UK #47.

Mar [2] *Monday Monday* wins Best Contemporary (Rock'N'Roll) Group Performance Vocal Or Instrumental Of 1966 at the 9th annual Grammy awards.

Apr Revival of The Shirelles' *Dedicated To The One I Love* hits US #2 for 3 weeks (behind The Turtles' *Happy Together*), and is the group's fourth million-selling single. It is taken from *The Mamas And The Papas Deliver*, which spends 7 weeks at US #2 and is another million-seller.
[26] Mama Cass gives birth to a daughter, Owen Vanessa, in a Los Angeles, CA, hospital.

May *Dedicated To The One I Love* also hits UK #2, while uptempo *Creeque Alley*, the story-song of the group's history up to its first successes, hits US #5.

June [16] With Adler, the group are prime movers in the organization of the Monterey International Pop Festival, in Monterey, CA. The Mamas And The Papas appear on the bill alongside The Who, Jimi Hendrix, Simon & Garfunkel, Otis Redding, The Grateful Dead and many more. The event is filmed by D.A. Pennebaker for movie "Monterey Pop".

July *The Mamas And The Papas Deliver* hits UK #4. Meanwhile, Phillips' composition *San Francisco (Be Sure To Wear Some Flowers In Your Hair)*, recorded by ex-Journeyman Scott McKenzie, hits US #4.

Aug *Creeque Alley* hits UK #9 (and is the group's last UK hit single), while McKenzie's *San Francisco* tops UK chart for 4 weeks.

Sept *Twelve Thirty (Young Girls Are Coming To The Canyon)* makes US chart, at #20.

Oct [7] Elliot spends a night in jail in London, accused of stealing from a hotel. Plans for UK concert and TV group appearances are cancelled.

Nov *Glad To Be Unhappy*, originally recorded by the group for a Rodgers And Hart TV tribute show, makes US #26.

Dec Compilation *Farewell To The First Golden Era* hits US #5, and is the group's last gold album, while *Dancing Bear* is their first disk not to enter the US Top 50, peaking at #51.

68 Mar [8] Group is included for the first time in the new publication of **Who's Who In America**.

June *Safe In My Garden* peaks at US #53.
[28] Phillips, Doherty and Elliot write to Gilliam informing that she is fired from the group.

July *The Papas And The Mamas* makes US #15. Group then breaks up, while Phillips and Gilliam also head for a personal split.

Aug A live track with Elliot taking a solo vocal, *Dream A Little Dream Of Me*, and credited to Mama Cass, reaches US #12 and UK #11.

Sept The theme from film "For The Love Of Ivy" peaks at US #81.

Oct Dunhill Records sues Phillips, Doherty and Gilliam, charging that they have not met their contractual obligations to the label since disbanding the group.
[8] Elliot opens as a soloist at Caesar's Palace in Las Vegas, NV, but suffering from tonsilitis and hampered by an under-rehearsed band, she cancels the 2-week engagement after the opening night.

Nov Second compilation album, *Golden Era, Vol.2*, makes US #53, while first Mama Cass solo album *Dream A Little Dream* makes US #87, and her second solo single *California Earthquake* peaks at US #67.

Dec A revival of Bobby Freeman's *Do You Wanna Dance* makes US #76.

69 Cass records with the group Electric Flag, but the results of the sessions are never released.

Apr UK compilation *Hits Of Gold* hits UK #7. Mama Cass' *Move In A Little Closer, Baby* peaks at US #58.

June Mama Cass' *Bubblegum, Lemonade, And ... Something For Mama* peaks at US #91.

Aug Mama Cass' *It's Getting Better* reaches US #30 and hits UK #8 (her last UK hit).

Nov US compilation *16 Of Their Greatest Hits* makes US #61, while Mama Cass' *Make Your Own Kind Of Music* reaches US #36. On it (and subsequent singles) she is billed as Mama Cass Elliot.

Dec Mama Cass' *Make Your Own Kind Of Music*, a reissue of her previous solo set plus the hit title track, reaches US #169.

70 Feb Mama Cass' *New World Coming* makes US #42.

May Phillips solo album *John Phillips (John The Wolfking Of L.A.)* makes US #181.

July *Mississippi*, from Phillips' album, climbs to US #32 (his only solo hit single). Phillips also co-produces, with Lou Adler, Robert Altman's film "Brewster McCloud".

Aug Mama Cass' *A Song That Never Comes* peaks at US #99 (her last US solo hit).

Oct [31] After Gilliam and Phillips have divorced, she marries actor Dennis Hopper. (The marriage will last 8 days.)

71 Mar Mama Cass' compilation *Mama's Big Ones* peaks at US #194.

Apr *Dave Mason And Mama Cass*, duetted by Elliot with the ex-member of Traffic, makes US #49. Doherty's solo *Whatcha Gonna Do?* does not chart.

Nov Group attempts a reunion with *People Like Us*, but it peaks at US #84 after lukewarm reviews, and they decide to split again.

1972 Feb *Step Out*, taken from the reunion album, makes US #81.

1973 Mar Double compilation *20 Golden Hits* reaches US #186.

July [30] At a press conference organized by New York Senator James Buckley, the former group members announce a $9 million suit against ABC-Dunhill Records. Phillips claims in a press statement that the label has been guilty of "systematic, cold-blooded theft of perhaps up to $60 million, stolen from each and every artist who recorded for it during a 7-year period". The label says the charges are "without foundation".

1974 July [29] Elliot dies while staying in London, aged 32, from a heart attack while choking on food and inhaling vomit.

1977 Michelle Phillips (she has kept her original married surname as her professional name) becomes a successful actress and appears in cinema and TV movies such as "Dillinger" and "Valentino". She also records a solo album, *Victim Of Romance* for A&M, which does not chart.

July TV-promoted compilation *The Best Of The Mamas And The Papas* hits UK #6.

1980 July [30] Phillips is arrested in Los Angeles by federal narcotics agents for possession of cocaine.

1981 Apr [20] Phillips is jailed for 5 years after pleading guilty in a Los Angeles court to drug possession charges. (The sentence will be suspended after 30 days, in exchange for 250 hours of community service by Phillips. He will tour US, lecturing against drugs.)

1982 Mar [3] Phillips and Doherty re-form the group for a reunion tour which opens at New York's Other End club. The female group members are both new: Phillips' daughter MacKenzie (b. Nov.10, 1959) (who has starred in film "American Graffiti") and Spanky McFarlane (ex-lead singer of Spanky & Our Gang). This new line-up releases nothing new on disk but remains on the oldies touring circuit in the US.

1986 July The re-formed Mamas And The Papas are hired by the Florida Panhandle real estate company to play a beach gig at Destin, FL, in order to attract prospective condominium buyers.

1988 Nov Phillips co-writes The Beach Boys' US #1 *Kokomo*.

1989 The group, now comprising John and MacKenzie Phillips, Spanky McFarlane and Scott McKenzie embark on "An Evening Of California Dreamin' – The Tour" with Brewer & Shipley, Maria Muldaur, Canned Heat and New Riders Of The Purple Sage, throughout US.

MANFRED MANN

Paul Jones (vocals, harmonica)
Manfred Mann (keyboards)
Mike Vickers (guitar)
Tom McGuinness (bass)
Mike Hugg (drums)

1962 Dec Group is formed in London as The Mann-Hugg Blues Brothers, after Mann (b. Michael Lubowitz, Oct.21, 1940, Johannesburg, South Africa) and Hugg (b. Aug.11, 1942, Andover, Hants), have met in the summer while playing piano and vibes respectively at a Butlin's holiday camp. They recruit Jones (b. Paul Pond, Feb.24, 1942, Portsmouth, Hants), Vickers (b. Apr.18, 1941, Southampton, Hants), and Dave Richmond on bass, with an occasional horn section comprising Ian Fenby (trumpet), Tony Roberts (tenor sax) and Don Fay (baritone sax).

1963 Mar [11] Group's Marquee club debut in London is one of a series of notable engagements which attracts record companies' attention.

May With a change of name to Manfred Mann, group signs to EMI's HMV label.

July Debut single, jazz/R&B instrumental *Why Should We Not?* fails.

Oct *Cock-A-Hoop* is an uptempo R&B vocal, and again does not chart.

1964 Jan Richmond leaves for session work, and is replaced by McGuinness (b. Dec.2, 1941, Wimbledon, London), who has played with Eric Clapton in The Roosters and then Casey Jones & The Engineers, but at the time of joining is lugging furniture for Bentalls department store. (Jones and McGuinness have played 1 gig in a band in summer 1964, before splitting up.) Group is asked to write a new theme tune for UK TV pop show "Ready Steady Go!", and comes up with *5-4-3-2-1*.

Feb With promotion of TV show (on which the group frequently also guests), *5-4-3-2-1* hits UK #5. (Its lyric reverses several thousand years of Greek mythology – in this song, Trojans wait at the gates of Troy, and Greeks are inside!)

May Uptempo R&B style *Hubble Bubble Toil And Trouble* makes UK #11.

Aug Group covers *Do Wah Diddy Diddy*, an obscure Jeff Barry/Ellie Greenwich song originally cut without success by The Exciters. It deposes The Beatles' *A Hard Day's Night* to top UK chart for 2 weeks, and sells 650,000 copies in UK.

Oct Debut album *The Five Faces Of Manfred Mann*, a collection mainly of R&B covers with a few originals, hits UK #3. Meanwhile, *Do Wah Diddy Diddy* is US chart debut, hitting #1 for 2 weeks.

Nov A revival of The Shirelles' *Sha La La* hits UK #3.

Dec US compilation *The Manfred Mann Album* reaches US #35.

1965 Jan *Sha La La* makes US #12.

Feb Group's first down-tempo A-side, *Come Tomorrow*, hits UK #4.

Mar *Come Tomorrow* reaches US #50, while *The Five Faces Of Manfred Mann* peaks at US #141.

May *Oh No Not My Baby*, a revival of Maxine Brown's US hit, reaches UK #11.

June Group appears in televised Brighton Song Festival in UK, performing autobiographical *The One In The Middle*. It also performs Bacharach/David's *My Little Red Book* on soundtrack of movie "What's New, Pussycat?"; released as a US single, it fails to chart.

July *The One In The Middle* is title song of a 4-track EP, which sells as strongly as a single in UK, and hits #6. (Main selling point is inclusion of a version of Bob Dylan's *With God On Our Side*, which receives wide airplay.)

Oct Another Dylan song, *If You Gotta Go, Go Now*, hits UK #2 behind Ken Dodd's *Tears*.

Nov *Mann Made*, again a mix of covers and originals, hits UK #7. Vickers leaves to concentrate on arranging and studio work, and McGuinness switches to guitar. Group recruits new bassist Jack Bruce (b. May 14, 1943, Glasgow, Scotland), but he has to work out a month's notice with John Mayall, so Pete Burford and David Hyde each fill in on bass for 2 weeks. Group also experiments with a 2-piece horn section of Henry Lowther on trumpet and Lyn Dobson on sax to augment its sound.

1966 Jan [26] The Animals' Eric Burdon sings lead vocals for Manfred Mann at a London gig, while Paul Jones is recovering from a minor car crash.

May *Pretty Flamingo* tops UK chart for 3 weeks.

July *You Gave Me Somebody To Love* peaks at UK #36.

[31] Jones leaves the group, having given a year's notice of his intention. Bruce departs at the same time, to form Cream with Eric Clapton and Ginger Baker.

Aug After group has considered Rod Stewart, Long John Baldry and Wayne Fontana, Jones is replaced by Mike D'Abo (b. Mar.1, 1944, UK), ex-A Band Of Angels, and Bruce by Klaus Voorman (b. Apr.29, 1942, West Berlin, Germany) from Paddy, Klaus & Gibson. *Pretty Flamingo* peaks at US #29. Meanwhile, group changes record labels in UK from HMV to Fontana, and links with producer Shel Talmy.

Sept A cover of Bob Dylan's *Just Like A Woman*, from his album *Blonde On Blonde*, is group's first Fontana single (and first with D'Abo on lead vocals). It hits UK #10 but is not released in US where Dylan has the hit single, and Dylan's version is not on a UK single.

Oct Compilation *Mann Made Hits* on HMV reaches UK #11.

Nov *Semi-Detached Suburban Mr. James* hits UK #2. (The title originally used more common name Jones; but was changed while recording in case it should be interpreted as a reference to Paul Jones.) Meanwhile, Jones, who has remained contracted to HMV as a soloist, releases his first single *High Time*, which hits UK #4. Manfred Mann's first Fontana album *As Is* reaches UK #22.

1967 Jan *Soul Of Mann*, a compilation on HMV of the group's instrumental tracks, makes UK #40.

Feb Jones' solo *I've Been A Bad Bad Boy* hits UK #5.

Apr Group's *Ha! Ha! Said The Clown* hits UK #4.

May Jones stars in Peter Watkins' film "Privilege", with model Jean Shrimpton. An EP of songs from the movie tops the UK EP chart, but does not make singles chart.

June Manfred Mann's instrumental revival of Tommy Roe's *Sweet Pea* makes UK #36.

Sept Jones' *Thinkin' Ain't For Me* reaches UK #32, while group's version of Randy Newman's *So Long Dad* fails to chart.

1968 Jan UK movie "Up The Junction" has songs and music written and performed by the group. The soundtrack album fails to chart.

Feb Group covers another Dylan song (as yet unrecorded by him), *The Mighty Quinn (Quinn The Eskimo)*, which tops UK chart for 2 weeks.

Apr *The Mighty Quinn* hits US #10.

June *The Mighty Quinn* makes US #176; in UK titled *Mighty Garvey*, it fails to chart.

July A cover of John Simon's *My Name Is Jack*, which the group has seen featured in film "You Are What You Eat", hits UK #8.

1969 Jan *Fox On The Run* peaks at US #97.

Feb *Fox On The Run* hits UK #5, while Jones' final UK solo chart success, at UK #45, is *Aquarius* (from musical "Hair"). (He drops out of music to concentrate on theater work for the next 10 years, including appearances in "Conduct Unbecoming" (a 2-year stint), "Hamlet" and "Joseph And The Amazing Technicolor Dream Coat".)

May Manfred Mann's *Ragamuffin Man* hits UK #8.

June Group splits after a series of farewell gigs. Mann forms a jazz group named Emanon ("no name" backwards), but this soon disbands. He and Hugg work together on advertising jingles and similar projects working for Michelin, Ski Yogurt, and other commercial products.

Oct McGuinness forms McGuinness Flint, with Hughie Flint (drums), Benny Gallagher (guitar, vocals), Graham Lyle (guitar, vocals) and Dennis Coulson (keyboards, vocals).

Nov Mann and Hugg re-group with session musicians as Manfred Mann Chapter Three, issuing an eponymous album on Philips' "progressive" label Vertigo. It fails to sell.

1970 Oct *Manfred Mann Chapter Three, Volume Two* also fails, after which group splits.

Dec McGuinness Flint's *When I'm Dead And Gone* hits UK #2, but the band is mainly studio-bound and rarely plays live gigs.

1971 Feb *McGuinness Flint* hits UK #9 and US #155, while *When I'm Dead And Gone* reaches US #47.

May *Malt And Barley Blues* by McGuinness Flint hits UK #5.

Sept McGuinness Flint *Happy Birthday, Ruthy Baby* makes US #198.

1972 Mar Mann forms Manfred Mann's Earth Band in a more progressive rock style, with Mick Rogers (vocals, guitar), Colin Pattenden (bass) and Chris Slade (drums). New group's debut album *Manfred Mann's Earth Band* makes US #138.

Apr Earth Band's *Living Without You* climbs to US #69.

1973 June Earth Band's *Get Your Rocks Off* peaks at US #196.

Oct Group hits UK #9 with *Joybringer*, based instrumentally on *Jupiter*, from Holst's "The Planets".

1974 Apr Group signs a new recording deal with Bronze Records and *Solar Fire* reaches US #96.

Dec *The Good Earth* makes US #157.

1975 Feb McGuinness Flint splits after 2 further unsuccessful albums. McGuinness and keyboards player Lou Stonebridge (latter-day replacement for Coulson) continue as Stonebridge McGuinness, but will have no chart success.

Oct Earth Band album *Nightingales And Bombers* reaches US #120.

1976 Apr Band's version of Bruce Springsteen's *Spirit In The Night* reaches US #97.

Sept Another Springsteen cover, *Blinded By The Light* hits UK #6.

Oct First Earth Band album to chart in UK is *The Roaring Silence* (including *Blinded By The Light*), which hits UK #10. Chris Thompson replaces Mick Rogers as lead vocalist.

1977 Feb *Blinded By The Light* tops US chart for a week and is a million-seller.

Mar *The Roaring Silence* hits US #10, the band's only gold album.

June *Spirit In The Night* is reissued in a remixed version and climbs to US #40.

1978 Apr *Watch* reaches US #83.

June *Davy's On The Road Again* hits UK #6, as *Watch* makes UK #33.

1979 Feb Jones and McGuinness reunite to form The Blues Band, initially only part-time, with Dave Kelly on guitar and vocals, Gary Fletcher on bass and Hughie Flint on drums. (Rob Townsend will replace Flint midway through the band's existence.)

Mar Earth Band's version of Dylan's *You Angel You* peaks at UK #54, and its parent album *Angel Station* reaches UK #30.

Apr The Blues Band makes its live debut at The Bridge House, Canning Town, London.

June Earth Band's *You Angel You* makes US #58, while *Angel Station* peaks at US #144.

July *Don't Kill It Carol*, also from *Angel Station*, peaks at UK #45.

Oct TV-advertised *Semi-Detached Suburban*, a compilation of Manfred Mann's 60s hits, demonstrates their enduring appeal by hitting UK #9.

1980 Mar The Blues Band's *Official Bootleg Album* makes UK #40.

July The Blues Band's eponymous EP (featuring *Maggie's Farm*, *Ain't It Tuff*, *Diddy Wah Diddy* and *Back Door Man*) peaks at UK #68.

Nov *Ready* by The Blues Band makes UK #36.

1981 Mar Earth Band's *Chance* climbs to US #87.

Oct The Blues Band's *Itchy Feet* makes UK #60.

1982 Apr Jones contributes *There's A Ghost In My House* to Heaven 17's British Electric Foundation project *Music Of Quality And Distinction*.

Dec After 4 years of over 600 gigs in UK, Canada and Europe, The

Blues Band splits following farewell concerts at The Venue in London. (Jones will return to stage work, appearing in "Cats" in 1982, followed by long residencies in "Guys And Dolls" and "The Beggar's Opera".)

1983 **Feb** Earth Band's *Somewhere In Africa*, a concept album about Mann's homeland of South Africa, makes UK #87.
Apr [30] The original Manfred Mann reunites for the 25th anniversary of London's Marquee club.

1984 **Mar** *Runner* reaches US #22, while a new, amended version of *Somewhere In Africa* (on band's new US label Arista) peaks at US #40.

1986 **July** With Bronze Records having gone into liquidation 2 years earlier, band re-emerges after a lengthy silence on 10 Records with *Criminal Tango*, consisting of revivals of other's oldies. It does not chart.

1987 **Nov** Second 10 album *Masque* offers a new sound without vocalist Thompson, but also fails to chart.

1990 **Nov** Released on UK independent label Cohesion, *20 Years Of Manfred Mann's Earth Band 1971-1991* is the latest of many archive collections.

THE MARCELS

Cornelius "Nini" Harp (lead vocals, guitar)
Ronald "Bingo" Mundy (first tenor vocal)
Gene Bricker (second tenor vocal)
Dick Knauss (baritone vocal)
Fred Johnson (bass vocal)

1960 The multi-racial vocal quintet (3 black vocalists and 2 whites, with a name taken from a hairstyle) is based in Pittsburgh, PA, where its club act consists mainly of versions of R&B and doo-wop group oldies. It disbands and re-forms more than once before manager Julius Kruspir sends a sampler tape of group's vocal efforts to producer Stu Phillips at New York-based Colpix Records.

1961 **Feb** Phillips calls group in for an after-hours recording session. After cutting 3 tracks, they experiment with the Rodgers and Hart oldie *Blue Moon*, turning in an outrageous version which kicks tempo high and buries original melody under bass singer Johnson performing an exaggerated parody of the traditional bass doo-wop role. This proves to be the gimmick which hooks first radio DJs and then record buyers. Murray The K at station W-INS in New York plays a borrowed advance tape 26 times in one show, creating a demand in the city overnight.
Apr *Blue Moon* tops US chart for 3 weeks (displacing Elvis Presley's *Surrender*), and is a US million-seller. (It also hits R&B #1 for 2 weeks.)
May Licensed by Pye International Records, *Blue Moon* also tops UK chart for 2 weeks, despite criticism from panelists on UK BBC TV's "Juke Box Jury" and in most of the press.
June A straighter, gimmick-free revival of George Gershwin's *Summertime* makes US #78 and UK #46. Group's 2 white vocalists Bricker and Knauss leave, and are replaced by Walt Maddox and Fred Johnson's brother Allen. Next single, a revamp of another oldie, *You Are My Sunshine*, fails to chart.
Dec A revival of Ted Weems' 1947 million-seller *Heartaches*, given the *Blue Moon* treatment, hits US #7 but fails in UK. Group appears alongside Chubby Checker and Dion in low-budget twist craze exploitation movie "Twist Around The Clock", singing *Merry Twistmas*.

1962 **Feb** *My Melancholy Baby* (on which group parodies itself, starting with *Blue Moon* bass man intro, halting proceedings with a hammy "oh no, not that ole thing again – sing *Melancholy Baby*", and then doing just that, but in *Blue Moon* style), makes US #58. The gimmick approach is wearing thin, and it will be the group's last hit. Mundy leaves, followed by Harp, as group encounters managerial problems. Final Colpix single, *I Wanna Be The Leader* has the once-again highlighted bass vocalist bewailing his restriction to singing "ba-ba-ba's" – he wants to be lead vocalist and handle real lyrics.
Group cuts its final single, *How Deep Is The Ocean*, for Kyra label, and disbands afterwards.

1963 **Apr** Johnny Cymbal pays tribute to The Marcels' sound on his *Mr. Bass Man*, which reaches US #16 and UK #24. (The 5 original Marcels reunite on several occasions in the 70s for Ralph Nader's "Rock'N'Roll Revival" shows and *Blue Moon* remains a perennial favorite oldie, being used, for example, over closing credits of John Landis' 1980 movie "An American Werewolf In London".)

MARILLION

Fish (vocals)
Steve Rothery (guitar)
Mark Kelly (keyboards)
Peter Trewavas (bass)
Ian Mosley (drums)

1978 **Dec** Silmarillion, named after the novel by J.R.R. Tolkien, is formed in Aylesbury, Bucks., by Doug Irvine (bass) and Mick Pointer (b. July 22, 1956) (drums) as an instrumental group, playing a 1-hour set at the Hanborough tavern in Southall, London.

1979 **Aug** Rothery (b. Nov.25, 1959, Brampton, S.Yorks.), answering a music paper ad, is chosen from 30 applicants and joins the band on guitar.
Oct Brian Jelliman is added on keyboards, and the group shortens its name to Marillion.

1980 **Nov** Irvine leaves. While the group advertises for a bassist/vocalist, it records instrumental *The Web* at Leyland studio in Buckingham, Bucks., and sends the tape to 2 musicians from Scotland, who had been in touch with them.

1981 **Jan** [2] Fish (b. Derek William Dick, Apr.25, 1958, Dalkeith, near Edinburgh, Scotland) and Diz Minnitt, both members of Nottingham band The Stone Dome, arrive, with lyrics to *The Web*, to audition. (Fish, the son of a garage proprietor, having left school to do a 4-year degree course with the Forestry Commission in Cumbria, has sung with small bands in Scotland. His nickname has stuck when a landlady accuses him of wallowing in the bath like a fish.)
Mar [14] New line-up debuts at Red Lion pub, Bicester, Oxon.
July Marillion records a 3-track demo, comprising *Garden Party*, *He Knows You Know* and *Charting The Single* at Roxon studio, Oxon., which is later sold at gigs.
Aug Band supports Spirit at local venue, the Friars, Aylesbury.
Nov Kelly (b. Apr.9, 1961, Dublin, Eire), playing with Romford, Essex-band Chemical Alice, replaces Jelliman.

1982 **Jan** [25] Band plays its first headlining gig at London's Marquee.
Feb The group records a session for BBC Radio's Tommy Vance's "The Friday Rock Show". A Marillion fan club called "The Web" is established.
Mar Minnitt quits and is replaced by Trewavas (b. Jan.15, 1959, Middlesborough, Cleveland) from local group The Metros.
May Marillion begins 25-date 6-week tour of Scotland.
July It headlines the Friars, Aylesbury, first unsigned band to do so.
Aug Band takes part in the Theakston and Reading festivals.
Sept Marillion signs a worldwide contract with EMI Records.
Nov Debut *Market Square Heroes* peaks at UK #60, as group tours UK.
Dec Marillion plays 3 sell-out dates at London's Marquee.

1983 **Feb** *He Knows You Know* reaches UK #35. The readers of UK music paper **Sounds** vote Marillion Best New Band Of 1982.
Mar *Script For A Jester's Tear*, recorded at London's Marquee studios in Dec. with producer Nick Tauber, hits UK #7. Lyrics are all penned by Fish, who has now adopted a central live role.
[15] Marillion begins a 29-date UK tour, supported by Peter Hammill, at Norwich University, Norfolk, set to end on Apr.18 with a sell-out date at Hammersmith Odeon, London.
Apr *Market Square Heroes* re-enters at UK #53. Group sacks Pointer replacing him with ex-Camel drummer Andy Ward.
May [20] Group makes its BBC TV debut on "The Old Grey Whistle Test".
June *Garden Party* reaches UK #16. Marillion makes its first appearance on BBC TV's "Top Of The Pops".
[17] Group headlines the Glastonbury Festival, Somerset.
July Marillion embarks on a 5-week tour of North America, during which *Script For A Jester's Tear*, released through Capitol, makes US #175. The tour is curtailed when Ward leaves the band.
Aug Band plays the Reading Festival for the second year, with John Marter temporarily on drums.
Sept Marillion supports Rush for 5 nights at New York's Radio City Music Hall.
Oct Video "Recital Of The Script", filmed at Apr.18 Hammersmith Odeon concert, is released. Jonathan Mover is recruited as drummer, but leaves almost immediately.
Nov Group starts work on its new album at Manor studios, Oxon., with drummer Mosley (b. June 16, 1953, Paddington, London), who has been a student at Guildhall School of Music, before playing with Curved Air, The Gordon Giltrap Band and Steve Hackett and as a member of the orchestras for both "Hair" and "Jesus Christ Superstar" in London's West End.

Dec Taking a break from recording, Marillion plays a 5-date "Farewell To 83" tour and invites Mosley to join the band full-time.

1984 Feb *Punch And Judy* reaches UK #29.

Mar *Fugazi*, again produced by Tauber, hits UK #5. Video "Grendel And The Web" is released.

Apr Group begins 24-date sell-out tour of UK, before touring Europe and North America.

May *Assassing* reaches UK #22.

July [21] Marillion plays Milton Keynes Bowl, Bucks., on a bill with Status Quo, Nazareth and Jason & The Scorchers.

Aug Group tours Europe, playing a series of festivals in Germany, returning to UK to headline the final of the Nostell Priory Festival.

Nov Budget-priced live album *Real To Reel*, recorded in Leicester, Leics., and Montreal, Canada, is released to counter the many bootlegs available and in response to requests from Marillion's fan club "The Web". It hits UK #8.

[3] Marillion plays the Royal Court theater, Liverpool, Merseyside, at the start of 14-date UK "Real To Reel" tour, set to end on Dec.22 at the Friars, Aylesbury.

1985 Mar Group starts work on new album at Hansa studios in Berlin, Germany, with producer Chris Kimsey.

May [25] Marillion starts a European tour.

June Ballad *Kayleigh* hits UK #2, behind The Crowd's charity chart-topper *You'll Never Walk Alone* as parent album *Misplaced Childhood*, last of a trilogy of concept albums, enters UK chart at #1.

Aug [17] Group plays the Z.Z.Top-headlined Monsters Of Rock Festival at Castle Donington, Leics.

Sept *Lavender* hits UK #5 as Fish loses his voice, causing cancellation of a 23-date UK tour.

Oct *Kayleigh* makes US #74.

Nov *Heart Of Lothian* reaches UK #29, as group postpones its US tour after Fish is advised to rest his throat, while *Misplaced Childhood* makes US #47.

1986 Jan [8-10] Band plays 3 nights at Hammersmith Odeon, London, at the start of a month-long UK tour, before beginning a 3-month tour of North America, releasing *Brief Encounter*, a mini-album of live tracks and B-sides, which makes US #67.

Feb [9] Marillion takes part in the "Colombian Volcano Appeal Concert" at London's Royal Albert Hall, with Annie Lennox, Chrissie Hynde, David Gilmour, Pete Townshend, The Communards and Working Week.

June Video "1982-1986 The Videos", featuring 7 of the band's hits and B-side *Lady Nina*, is released.

[28] Marillion plays the "Welcome To The Garden Party" at Milton Keynes Bowl, Bucks.

Oct Fish and Tony Banks, from Genesis, team for *Shortcut To Somewhere* which makes UK #75.

Dec Band ends year with a short series of sell-out Christmas shows.

1987 May *Incommunicado* hits UK #6.

June Parent album *Clutching At Straws* hits UK #2, as band sets off on a 9-month world tour.

July *Sugar Mice* makes UK #22. *Clutching At Straws* peaks at US #103.

Sept [18] Marillion begins a US tour.

Nov *Warm Wet Circles* reaches UK #22, while video "Live At Loreley" is released.

1988 July *B-Sides Themselves*, a CD-only collection of non-album material, makes UK #64, while the band meets in Scotland to discuss Fish's increasing disagreement over Marillion's musical direction.

Sept Band and Fish announce they are to split.

Nov *Freaks (Live)* reaches UK #24.

Dec *The Thieving Magpie*, recorded during the 1984 "Fugazi" and 1987 "Clutching At Straws" tours and named after Rossini's "La Gaza Ladra", with which they open their live shows, reaches UK #25.

1989 Jan With Marillion's new album half finished and several auditioned singers proving unsuitable, the band's management receives a tape sent by Steve Hogarth's publishers.

Apr [1] Hogarth, ex-The Europeans, officially replaces Fish as Marillion's lead singer.

Sept *Hooks In You*, Hogarth's debut, makes UK #30.

Oct *Season's End*, with lyrics mostly written by Hogarth and John Helmer, hits UK #7 as Marillion embarks on a tour of Europe. Fish's debut solo single *State Of Mind* makes UK #32.

Dec Extracted *Uninvited Guest* peaks at UK #53.

[3] Marillion begins 12-date UK tour at City Hall, Newcastle, Tyne & Wear, set to end on Dec.18 at the Hammersmith Odeon, London.

1990 Jan Fish's *Big Wedge* reaches UK #23.

Feb [10] His debut album *Vigil In A Wilderness Of Mirrors* hits UK #5, his first and only solo album for EMI.

Mar Fish ballad *A Gentleman's Excuse Me* makes UK #30.

Apr [14] Marillion's *Easter* makes UK #34.

May Fish embarks on tour of Europe.

July [12] Marillion plays at Wembley Arena, London.

Dec [18] Marillion begins short 5-date Christmas tour at Rock City, Nottingham, Notts., ending Dec.22 at London's Town & Country club.

1991 Apr EMI allows Fish to buy himself out of his current contract, as the ex-lead singer signs new solo deal with Polydor.

BOB MARLEY & THE WAILERS

Bob Marley (vocals, guitar)
Peter Tosh (vocals, guitar)
Bunny Wailer (vocals, percussion)
Carlton Barrett (drums)
Aston "Family Man" Barrett (bass)

1961 Marley (b. Robert Nesta Marley, Feb.6, (Passport date: Apr.6), 1945, Nine Miles, Rhoden Hall, St. Ann's, Jamaica), the son of English army captain Norval Sinclair Marley from Liverpool, Merseyside, (a superintendent for the Crown lands) and Jamaican Cedella Booker, comes to the attention of Kingston, Jamaica, label owner and producer Leslie Kong and records original pop song *Judge Not (Unless You Judge Yourself)* for Kong's Beverley label, credited to Bob Morley.

1962 Marley cuts a second single for Kong, *One Cup Of Coffee*.

1964 Marley forms The Wailin' Wailers with childhood friends from the Trenchtown ghetto of West Kingston, Tosh (b. Winston Hubert McIntosh, Oct.19, 1944, Church Lincoln, Westmoreland, Jamaica), Livingston (soon known as Bunny Wailer, b. Neville O'Riley, Apr.10, 1947, Kingston), Junior Braithwaite and Beverley Kelso, and begins a prolific 4-year recording relationship with top Kingston producer Clement Seymour (Sir Coxsone) Dodd, owner of Studio One label.

1965 **Feb** The Wailin' Wailers' first Studio One single, *Simmer Down*, is a big Jamaican hit (said to have sold 80,000 copies on the island). (Recording as The Wailin' Wailers and The Wailin' Rudeboys, group will cut some 80 sides for Studio One between now and 1966 – notably *Put It On*, *The Ten Commandments Of Love* and *Love And Affection*.)

1966 **Feb** [10] Marley marries Alpharita Constantia Anderson.
[11] He leaves Kingston for US to visit his mother in Wilmington, DE. He finds work as a waiter, lab assistant for DuPont, forklift driver on a nightshift in a warehouse, and assembly line worker in the Chrysler plant, using the name Donald Marley.

1967 He returns to Kingston with $700 savings with which he sets up his own Wailin' Soul label, and signs a deal with Johnny Nash, releasing *Reggae On Broadway*. (Nash will later have hits with *Stir It Up* and *Guava Jelly*, both written by Marley.) He reunites with Tosh and Wailer (and will record 11 singles for Kong's Beverley label from late 1967 to early 1968). Wailer serves 14 months in jail after being convicted of marijuana possession.

1969 The Wailers become committed Rastafarians and leave Kong to work with similarly-inclined producer Lee "Scratch" Perry on their newly-formed Tuff Gong label. (With Perry, The Wailers will record successful singles, some will become reggae standards – *Soul Rebel*, *Duppy Conqueror*, *400 Years* and *Small Axe*.)

1972 Island Records head Chris Blackwell signs the group, aiming to break it in the international market. With the rhythm section of the Barrett brothers, Aston "Family Man" (b. Nov.22, 1946, Kingston) and Carlton (b. Dec.17, 1950, Kingston) (who have been working with the group since the Perry sessions), The Wailers release *Catch A Fire* which, with unprecedented promotional support, establishes them as strong contenders for mainstream pop stardom – a promise fulfilled later in the year with second Island album *Burnin'*.

1973 Marley is fired from the Sly & The Family Stone US tour for overshadowing them.

1974 Despite growing international recognition, Tosh and Wailer leave The Wailers, unhappy with the Island-generated public perception of Bob Marley & The Wailers. Female vocal trio The I-Threes (Judy Mowatt, Marcia Griffiths and Marley's wife, Rita), Bernard "Touter" Harvey and Earl "Wire" Lindo (keyboards) and Al Anderson (guitar) join.

Sept Eric Clapton tops US chart with Marley's *I Shot The Sheriff*. (Marley's own version is included on *Burnin'*.)

1975 **May** A US breakthrough comes with the group's third Island album, *Natty Dread* which makes US #92.

Aug Bob Marley & The Wailers begin a UK tour with a new line-up of Tyrone Downie (keyboards), Alvin "Seeco" Patterson (percussion) and

Madonna

Bob Marley

The Mamas And The Papas

Roy Orbison

Mike Oldfield

New Kids On The Block

Julian "Junior" Murvin (guitar), who replace Harvey and Lindo.
Oct *No Woman No Cry*, extracted from forthcoming *Live!*, reaches UK #22. *Natty Dread* makes UK #43 while *Burnin'* makes US #151.
Nov *Catch A Fire* peaks at US #171.
Dec *Live!*, recorded at the Lyceum Ballroom, London, on July 18, makes UK #38.

1976 **May** *Rastaman Vibrations* reaches UK #15.
July *Roots Rock Reggae*, written by Vincent Ford, makes US #51. *Rastaman Vibrations* hits US #8, during a 22-week stay on chart.
Dec [3] An attempt is made on Marley's life when 7 gunmen burst into his Kingston home, and injure Marley, his wife and his manager Don Taylor. (Believing it to be politically motivated, Marley will leave Jamaica for an 18-month exile in Miami, FL, where *Exodus* will be partly recorded.)
[5] Marley participates in the Smile Jamaica Concert.
Live! makes US #90.

1977 Marley has an operation at Cedars of Lebanon hospital, Miami, to remove a toe after a cancerous growth is found. Media is informed that he has received a foot injury while playing his favorite game, soccer.
June *Exodus* hits UK #8.
July *Exodus* reaches UK #14.
Aug *Exodus* makes US #20.
Oct *Waiting In Vain* reaches UK #27, as the group plays a week at the Rainbow theater, Finsbury Park, London.

1978 **Feb** Double A-side *Jamming/Punky Reggae Party* hits UK #9.
Apr *Is This Love* hits UK #9. *Kaya*, with Lindo rejoining, hits UK #4.
[22] Returning to Jamaica, the group headlines "One Love Peace Concert" in Kingston, where Marley unites Prime Minister Michael Manley and his opponent Edward Seaga on stage in avowals of unity and common purpose.
May *Kaya* makes US #50.
July *Satisfy My Soul* reaches UK #21.
Dec Live double album *Babylon By Bus*, recorded during 1980 world tour, makes UK #40.

1979 **Feb** *Babylon By Bus* makes US #102. Group headlines at New York's Apollo theater in Harlem, the first reggae band to do so.
Oct *Survival* reaches UK #20.
Nov *So Much Trouble In The World* makes UK #56.
Dec *Survival* makes US #70.

1980 **Apr** [17] Marley performs at the Independence Day celebrations in Salisbury, Zimbabwe, in front of Prince Charles and President Mugabe, 2 years after his first trip to Africa, visiting Kenya and Ethiopia. Group begins a major European tour, including a 100,000 sell-out show in Milan, Italy.
June [7] Marley headlines the "Summer Of 80 Garden Party" at the Crystal Palace Concert Bowl, London, with Average White Band, Q-Tips and Joe Jackson.
July *Could You Be Loved* hits UK #5 as parent album *Uprising* hits UK #6.
[10] Marley opens a European tour in Dublin, Eire, which will encompass Germany, France, Norway, Sweden, Denmark, Belgium, Holland, Italy, Spain and Ireland.
[13] Tour ends at Bingley Hall, Stafford, Staffs.
Aug *Uprisin'* reaches US #45.
Sept [20-21] Marley & The Wailers play New York's Madison Square Garden with The Commodores.
Oct *Three Little Birds* reaches UK #17.
[8] Marley, preparing for a major US tour with Stevie Wonder, collapses in New York. (Cancer is diagnosed and Marley attends Sloan-Kettering hospital in New York as an out-patient. The tour is cancelled.)
Dec Marley flies to Dr. Josef Issels Clinic in Bavaria, Germany, for treatment. Stevie Wonder hits US #5 with his tribute to Marley, *Master Blaster (Jammin')*.

1981 **Apr** Marley is awarded Jamaica's Order Of Merit. In his absence, his son Ziggy accepts the honor.
May [11] Marley dies of lung cancer and a brain tumor, age 36, at the Cedars of Lebanon hospital, Miami, having flown to his mother's home in Miami.
[20-21] His body lies in state at the National Arena in Kingston.
[21] A Jamaican legend, Marley is buried with full state honors in St. Ann's, after an Ethiopian Orthodox Festival is held in Kingston, attended by thousands.
July *No Woman No Cry* hits UK #8. *Live*, re-titled *Live At The Lyceum*, re-enters UK chart at #68.
Aug [6] The Fourth International Reggae Sunsplash Festival in Jarrett

Park, Montego Bay, Jamaica, billed as a tribute to Marley, is attended by 20,000 people. 4 of Marley's children appear as The Melody Makers.
Nov *Chances Are*, on Cotillion, recorded between 1968 and 1972, makes US #117.

1982 **Dec** [29] Jamaica issues a Bob Marley commemorative stamp.
1983 **June** *Buffalo Soldier* hits UK #4 and *Confrontation* hits UK #5.
July *Confrontation* reaches US #55.
1984 **May** Island releases compilation album and video *Legend* to commemorate the third anniversary of Marley's death. The album hits UK #1 in its week of entry. It will stay there for 12 weeks and on chart for 2 years. Double A-side *One Love/People Get Ready* hits UK #5.
July Third single from the album, *Waiting In Vain* reaches UK #31.
Oct *Legend* reaches US #54.
Dec *Could You Be Loved* makes UK #71.
1986 **July** *Rebel Music* makes UK #54.
1987 **Apr** [17] Carlton Barrett is shot dead outside his home in Kingston.
May [19] The Wailers, having ousted Rita Marley as executor of Marley's will, call for an investigation of his estate.
Sept [11] Tosh is murdered by burglars.
1989 Following further legal wrangles, Island Records boss Chris Blackwell wrests total control of the Marley copyright on songs.
Mar New label Slam Records announces plan to issue previously unreleased 1967-72 Marley material originally recorded for Tuff Gong label. His son, Ziggy, increasingly assuming the Marley mantle, returns to the studio to record a follow-up to his successful *Conscious Party*.
1990 **Feb** [6] To commemorate the birth of Bob Marley, it is proclaimed a national holiday in Jamaica.
June Chris Blackwell inaugurates the Bob Marley Memorial Fund in New York by presenting a check for $75,000 to Amnesty International. (The donation will be given annually for 10 years at the Penta hotel in New York.)
Sept [1] Re-promoted and issued on CD, *Legend* peaks at US #72.
1991 **Feb** [6] Tuff Gong commemorates Marley's birthdate by releasing *Talkin' Blues*, a compilation of unreleased material and interviews conducted in 1975.
Mar [9] *Talkin' Blues* makes US #104.

MARTHA & THE VANDELLAS
Martha Reeves (lead vocals)
Annette Sterling (vocals)
Rosalind Ashford (vocals)

1960 Reeves (b. July 18, 1941, Alabama), having moved to Detroit, MI, in her teens, does some solo club singing as Martha LaVelle, and performs with ex-high school friends Sterling and Ashford (b. Sept.2, 1943, Detroit) as vocal trio The Del-Phis. They record an unsuccessful single for Checkmate label. Reeves then joins Tamla Motown Records as a secretary in the A&R department. Among other tasks and since she is known to have a good voice, one of her jobs is to sing new song lyrics on to tapes for artists (normally back-up singers) who need to learn the words prior to recording sessions.
1961 When a backing singer is absent from a recording session through illness, the producer, familiar with Reeves' voice from demo tapes, suggests she fills the role. This is the first of many such appearances.
1962 **July** Getting regular studio opportunities, Reeves mentions her 2 former partners, and Motown tries out all 3 as an integrated back-up trio. First session on which they sing is for Marvin Gaye's *Stubborn Kind Of Fellow*, which also becomes his first single, reaching US #46.
Sept After also backing Gaye on *Hitch Hike* (which will make US #30 in Mar.1963), the trio is signed as an act in its own right, to Motown's Gordy label, and renamed Martha & The Vandellas (partly inspired by Reeves' favorite singer, Della Reese). Debut single *I'll Have To Let Him Go* fails to chart.
1963 **June** Second single, mid-tempo beat-ballad *Come And Get These Memories*, climbs to US #29. Debut album, titled after the hit, fails.
Sept Bounding dance number *Heat Wave*, written by Holland/Dozier/Holland, hits US #4 and tops R&B chart for 5 weeks (replacing fellow new Motown star Stevie Wonder's *Fingertips*), to sell over a million.
Dec Same writing team's *Quicksand*, in similar dance-oriented style, hits US #8. First chart album is *Heat Wave* which makes US #125. In spite of their new-found success, Sterling leaves to get married, and is replaced by Betty Kelly (b. Sept.16, 1944, Detroit).
1964 **Mar** *Live Wire* reaches US #42.
May *In My Lonely Room* makes US #44.
Sept The group plays 10 days at the Fox theater in Brooklyn, New

York, in Murray The K's rock'n'roll extravaganza, along with Marvin Gaye, The Supremes, The Searchers, The Shangri-Las and many others.

Oct The group's version *Dancing In The Street*, co-written by Marvin Gaye and turned down by Mary Wells, becomes one of the most consistently-played dance records of all time. Their second million-seller, it hits US #2 for 2 weeks, behind Manfred Mann's *Do Wah Diddy Diddy*.

Nov *Dancing In The Street* is UK chart debut, reaching #28, helped by a promotional visit which sees the trio on "Ready Steady Go!" and "Thank Your Lucky Stars".

1965 Jan *Wild One* makes US #34.

Mar [20] The trio begins 21-date twice-nightly UK Tamla Motown package tour at Finsbury Park Astoria, London, with labelmates The Supremes, The Miracles, Stevie Wonder, The Temptations and special guests Georgie Fame & The Blue Flames.

Apr [12] Tour ends at Guildhall, Portsmouth, Hants.

The trio returns to US Top 10 with *Nowhere To Run* which hits US #8. It also reaches UK #25 (one of the first batch of 3 singles released in UK launch of Tamla Motown label).

June *Dance Party* (including *Dancing In The Street* and *Nowhere To Run*) makes US #139.

Sept *You've Been In Love Too Long* reaches US #36.

Dec After many DJs have turned A-side *You've Been In Love* over, B-side Holland/Dozier/Holland's ballad *Love (Makes Me Do Foolish Things)* reaches US #70.

1966 Mar *My Baby Loves Me* climbs to US #22.

[29] The group begins a UK tour.

June *What Am I Gonna Do Without Your Love?* makes US #71.

July *Greatest Hits*, a compilation of singles to date, reaches US #50.

Dec *I'm Ready For Love*, written by Holland/Dozier/Holland for The Supremes but turned down, hits US #9 and reaches UK #29.

1967 Feb *Watchout!*, including *I'm Ready For Love*, peaks at US #116.

Apr *Jimmy Mack*, extracted from *Watchout!*, hits US #10, and tops R&B chart for a week, becoming another million-seller. It reaches only UK #21 (but will be a consistent seller in UK because of its universal danceability and equal popularity of B-side *Third Finger, Left Hand*, for the next 15 or so years).

Sept *Love Bug Leave My Heart Alone* reaches US #25.

Oct Live *Martha And The Vandellas Live!* peaks at US #140.

Dec The group's name is amended to Martha Reeves & The Vandellas on *Honey Chile*, which climbs to US #11.

1968 Jan Kelly leaves and is replaced by Reeves' younger sister Lois, previously with The Orlons.

Feb *Honey Chile* reaches UK #30.

May Double A-side *I Promise To Wait, My Love/Forget Me Not* makes US #62 and #93 respectively.

June *Ridin' High* peaks at US #167.

Sept *I Can't Dance To That Music You're Playin'* reaches US #42.

[15] Trio appears on the first edition of US NBC TV's black audience-targetted music show "Soul", alongside Lou Rawls and comedian Red Foxx.

Nov *Sweet Darlin'* stalls at US #80.

1969 Feb *Dancing In The Street* is reissued in UK and, with particular support of Alan Freeman's major national radio show "Pick Of The Pops", is a bigger UK success than first time around, hitting #4.

Apr *Nowhere To Run*, reissued as UK follow-up, reaches #42.

May *(We've Got) Honey Love* makes US #56. Reeves has a breakdown, which puts group off the road and out of the studio for a time.

1970 Sept *Jimmy Mack* re-charts in UK at #21.

Nov *I've Gotta Let You Go* reaches US #93.

1971 With Reeves recovered, they regroup, but without Ashford, who has left to be replaced by Sandra Tilley, ex-Motown group The Velvelettes.

Mar *Forget Me Not*, a minor 1968 US hit, is released in UK and climbs to #11.

May Group plays a comeback show at P.J.'s club in Los Angeles, CA.

Nov *Bless You* reaches US #53, and is the group's last US chart single.

1972 Jan *Bless You* is also final UK chart entry, making #33.

Apr *Black Magic* is group's final US chart album, at #146.

Dec [1] The group gives its farewell performance in Detroit. Reeves begins a solo career, and sister Lois joins Quiet Elegance, recording for Hi in Memphis, TN.

1973 Signed as a soloist to MCA, Reeves works with J.J. Johnson on the music for black action movie "Willie Dynamite". On the soundtrack, she sings 3 songs, *Willie D*, *King Midas* and *Keep On Movin' On*, backed by The Sweet Things.

1974 Apr Reeves' only solo hit single is *Power Of Love*, on MCA, which

makes US #76. It is taken from *Martha Reeves*, produced by Richard Perry, which does not chart, despite musicianship of Billy Preston, Joe Sample, Nicky Hopkins and Ralph McDonald.

1976 She moves to Arista Records, but solo *The Rest Of My Life* fails.

1978 Reeves releases disco-oriented *We Meet Again* on Fantasy Records, reuniting her with Motown producer Henry Cosby. It fails to chart.

July [1] Martha & The Vandellas re-form for the first time in 10 years in a benefit for actor Will Geer at the Santa Cruz Catalyst, CA.

1989 Oct [21] The trio begins a UK tour at the Talk Of The Town, Manchester. (They will subsequently tour US, brought out of retirement by Reeves, but keeping their day jobs – Sterling working in a hospital and Ashford working for a phone company.)

RICHARD MARX

1982 At age 18, Marx (b. 1964, Chicago, IL), having been brought into music from an early age by his father (Richard Sr., a jazz pianist and top jingle writer) and sung on TV commercials since his pre-teens, receives a call from Lionel Richie. Richie has heard a demo tape of 4 Marx songs, and invites him to sing some album backing vocals, including cuts *All Night Long*, *You Are* and *Running With The Night*. (Richie will also introduce him to many industry figures and contacts.)

1984 With Canadian producer David Foster and Kenny Rogers, he co-writes *What About Me?* a US #15 by Rogers with Kim Carnes and James Ingram, and Rogers' *Crazy*, which makes US #79. (From this highly successful springboard, Marx will collaborate with many artists over the next 2 years, writing for Chicago (*We Are The World* album track *Good For Nothing*), Philip Bailey (*The Goonies* album track *Love Is Alive*) and others.)

1986 Friend Bobby Colomby (ex-Blood, Sweat & Tears, now an A&R executive) introduces Marx to the president of EMI Manhattan who sees solo artist potential in his songs and signs Marx to the label worldwide. Colomby also teams him with producer David Cole, who will co-produce his debut album.

1987 Aug Marx begins a lengthy US tour supporting R.E.O. Speedwagon.

[29] *Don't Mean Nothing*, with Joe Walsh guesting, is his US chart debut, hitting #3.

Dec [12] *Should've Known Better* hits US #3.

1988 Mar Marx is nominated for (though does not win) a Grammy award for Best Rock Vocal Performance. Meanwhile, *Should've Known Better* makes US #50, while *Endless Summer Nights* hits US #2.

Apr *Richard Marx* peaks at UK #68, and reaches US #19 during an 86-week chart lease.

May *Endless Summer Nights* equals his previous UK peak, making #50.

July [23] Rock ballad *Hold On To The Nights* tops the US chart and Marx becomes the first male singer to notch 4 Top 3 hits from a debut album. His solo career hits a new peak, and Marx continues to pursue writing for and producing projects with other artists, including Randy Meisner (Ex-Eagles), Fee Waybill (ex-Tubes), and new all-girl rock group Vixen.

1989 Jan [8] Marx marries actress/singer Cynthia Rhodes.

June [24] First single from recently released second album *Repeat Offender*, *Satisfied* hits US #1 and makes UK #52.

Aug [12] Piano-led ballad, self-penned and co-produced with David Cole, *Right Here Waiting* also tops US chart and will hit UK #2.

Sept [2] *Repeat Offender* tops US chart, having already hits UK #8. It will sell over 3 million in US and 6 million copies worldwide.

Dec [2] Further ballad *Angelia* hits US #4.

1990 Jan [24] Marx begins 1990 on the road in Pittsburgh, PA.

Mar [3] *Too Late To Say Goodbye*, written with former Tubes lead singer Fee Waybill, reaches US #12 and UK #38.

[8] Marx wins Worst Male Singer category in **Rolling Stone**'s 1989 Critics' Award.

May [10] Marx donates $52,000 to the Children Of The Night organization to help teenage runaways and under-age prostitutes at the site of a planned children's shelter in Los Angeles. (Marx has now donated $100,000 royalties from current single *Children Of The Night*.)

June [23] Fifth extract *Children Of The Night* reaches US #13.

July [7] *Children Of The Night* peaks at UK #54.

Aug Further Marx-produced tracks appear on Vixen album *Rev it Up*. Other current production and songwriting credits include projects by Animotion, Poco (*Nothin' To Hide*) and Kevin Cronin.

[31] North American tour ends in Honolulu, HI.

Sept [1] Ambitious EMI issue of twinned *Endless Summer Nights* and *Hold On To The Night* stalls at UK #60.

[11] Son Brandon is born in Los Angeles.

1991 **Mar** Marx teams with David Crosby, Bill Champlin and Kevin Cronin to record Gulf War-related *Hard To Believe*.

Apr Marx, and 4 other acts, are released by EMI, following a dispute with his Left Bank Management company. EMI President Sal Licata is quoted as saying: "The reasons behind my decision are multi-fold, but were based on business logic."

[15] President/CEO of Capitol Industries, Joe Smith, announces that Marx will be switched from EMI to Capitol.

MATTHEWS SOUTHERN COMFORT

Ian Matthews (vocals, guitar)
Mark Griffiths (guitar)
Carl Barnwell (guitar)
Gordon Huntley (pedal steel)
Andy Leigh (bass)
Raymond Duffy (drums)

1966 Matthews (b. Ian Matthew McDonald, 1946, Lincs.) joins London-based harmony vocal group Pyramid, having turned down a career as a professional soccer player.

1967 **Jan** Pyramid's only single *Summer Of Last Year* is released by Deram, without success.

Nov Matthews leaves Pyramid to join Fairport Convention as joint lead vocalist.

1969 **Jan** He leaves Fairport Convention after recording 2 albums with them to form Matthews Southern Comfort. He recruits Griffiths, Barnwell, Huntley, Leigh and Duffy. They sign to EMI Records.

1970 **Jan** Debut album *Matthews Southern Comfort* is released and shows Matthews veering away from his previous folk-rock sound toward a country style.

July *Second Spring* makes UK #52.

Oct A smooth, steel guitar-backed country style version of Joni Mitchell's *Woodstock* tops UK chart for 3 weeks. (It has already been a US Top 20 hit in the spring for Crosby, Stills, Nash & Young.)

Nov Marshall Chess, head of administration for The Rolling Stones' proposed new label, is keen to sign the band, but Jagger turns them down, reportedly on the grounds that the band "is not funky enough".

Dec Matthews leaves the group, after failing to turn up for a gig, just before the last Matthews Southern Comfort album *Later That Same Year* is released.

1971 **Jan** Matthews signs a solo deal with Vertigo, releasing *If You Saw Thru' My Eyes*.

Mar *Woodstock* reaches US #23.

Apr Band becomes Southern Comfort following Matthews' departure, signing to Harvest Records for eponymous album *Southern Comfort*. Meanwhile, *Later That Same Year* makes US #72.

July *Frog City* by Southern Comfort is released and makes US #196. The group's *Mare, Take Me Home* peaks at US #96.

Oct *Tell Me Why* by Southern Comfort reaches US #98.

1972 **Feb** Matthews' *Tigers Will Survive* climbs to US #196, while his a cappella revival of The Crystals' *Da Doo Ron Ron* makes US #96. He forms Plainsong, with singer/guitarist Andy Roberts, keyboards player Dave Richards and bassist Bobby Ronga.

Sept Plainsong's *In Search Of Amelia Earhart* is issued on Elektra, but does not chart. Meanwhile, Southern Comfort's *Stir Don't Shake* is its last album, after which the group disbands.

Dec Ronga leaves Plainsong as the group records a second album for Elektra (which is never released, although 5 tracks will be heard on Matthews' solo albums). Plainsong splits after the sessions and Matthews moves (at the suggestion of Elektra boss Jac Holzman) to Los Angeles, CA, to work with Michael Nesmith.

1973 **Sept** His first solo Elektra album *Valley Hi*, produced by Nesmith at his Countryside studios, reaches US #181. Matthews tours US, supporting America, with his own band comprising ex-Nazz drummer Tom Mooney and the Curtis brothers from Crazy Horse.

1974 Matthews tours US under the name Ian Matthews & Another Fine Mess, with a band comprising Tommy Nunes (guitar), Joel Tepp (harmonica), Don Whaley (bass) and John Ware (drums).

June *Some Days You Eat The Bear ... Some Days The Bear Eats You* is his last album for Elektra.

Aug *Journey From Gospel Oak*, a compilation of unreleased 1971-72 material recorded in Nov.1972 and scheduled for release by Vertigo, is issued by Mooncrest in UK, with Matthews unaware of its release.

Oct *The Best Of Matthews Southern Comfort* is released, again without Matthews' knowledge.

1975 Matthews draws up a contract with Arista Records, but does not sign.

Aug Matthews' contract with Elektra expires.

1976 **May** *Go For Broke*, Matthews' first for CBS/Columbia, is produced by Norbert Putnam.

Oct *Distilled* by Southern Comfort is a compilation released on UK Harvest.

1977 **May** *Hit And Run*, Matthews' second and final album for CBS/Columbia, includes a remake of *Tigers Will Survive*.

1978 **Oct** *Stealin' Home*, issued by Mushroom Records, reaches US #80. Folk label Rockburgh, owned by Sandy Roberton, releases it in UK. *Shake It* gets airplay in US and reaches #13, his first hit for 8 years.

1979 **Mar** *Give Me An Inch* (later a hit for Robert Palmer) peaks at US #67.

Aug *Siamese Friends* does not chart.

1980 **Mar** *Discreet Repeat*, a double compilation of solo material, is his last for Mushroom and Rockburgh.

June On RSO, *A Spot Of Interference* is released and again fails to sell.

1981 Matthews, living in Seattle, WA, is involved in a legal dispute with Mushroom, which he claims owes him more than $500,000 in royalties. He then releases 2 albums *Moods For Mallard* and *Shook*.

1983 Abandoning his own recording career, Matthews moves to Los Angeles and takes up a post as A&R man for Island Records.

1987 He moves to an A&R post at new age pioneering label, Windham Hill. *Meet Southern Comfort* and *Fairport Convention's Heydays*, an album of UK BBC radio broadcasts from 1968-69, both featuring Matthews' work, are released in UK.

Aug Matthews participates in Fairport Convention's 20th anniversary celebrations by appearing live with the band.

He leaves his A&R post at Windham Hill to begin recording a new album for the same label – some view this as perfect A&R.

1988 **Apr** *Walking A Changing Line – The Songs Of Jules Shear* is released on Windham Hill. This is the label's first all-vocal set and receives significant critical acclaim.

1990 Matthews, now signed to Gold Castle, releases *Pure And Crooked*, reverting to the original Gaelic spelling of his first name, Iain. It is released in UK via a label license with Virgin.

JOHN MAYALL

1962 Mayall (b. Nov.29, 1933, Macclesfield, Cheshire), having studied at Manchester Art College, done National Service in the British Army (including some time in Korea), and then worked in a Manchester, Gtr. Manchester art studio attached to an advertising agency, forms his first group, The Blues Syndicate. Gigging mostly at Manchester's Twisted Wheel club, the group (a quintet featuring guitar, piano, trumpet, alto sax, and Hughie Flint on drums) plays raw R&B, inspired by Alexis Korner's London-based Blues Incorporated.

1963 **Jan** Encouraged by Korner, Mayall moves to London, where he gets a job as a draughtsman, and tries to form a new R&B band.

July After trying out many musicians, Mayall debuts The Bluesbreakers with himself on vocals, keyboards and harmonica, Bernie Watson on guitar, John McVie on bass and Peter Ward on drums (to be replaced once full-time gigging starts by Martin Hart).

Aug The Bluesbreakers begin a Thursday night residency at The Scene, Great Windmill Street, London.

1964 **Apr** Mayall signs a short-term deal with Decca, and records single *Crawling Up A Hill*. Almost immediately after it, the band's personnel changes, reducing to a quartet comprising Mayall, McVie, Roger Dean on guitar and a returning Flint.

May [8] *Crawling Up A Hill* is released.

1965 **Mar** [26] Debut album is *John Mayall Plays John Mayall*, recorded live at Klook's Kleek R&B club on Dec.7, 1964, in West Hampstead, London. Second single *Crocodile Walk* is also released, after which the Decca deal expires and is not renewed.

Apr Hearing that Eric Clapton has left The Yardbirds, Mayall invites him to join The Bluesbreakers. Clapton, keen to play blues (the reason why he split from The Yardbirds), agrees. He is hired in place of Dean, who is dismissed in a fashion which will become a Mayall trademark. Clapton's presence in the group is sufficient to boost the audiences at Mayall's gigs enormously.

[23] Group appears on ITV's "Ready Steady Goes Live!".

June [19] The Bluesbreakers play the Uxbridge Blues And Folk Festival, alongside The Who, Long John Baldry, The Spencer Davis Group, and others.

Aug Clapton, tired of 1-night gigs and wanting some sunshine, departs without notice, with a car full of friends, for 3 months to Greece. Mayall muddles through with temporary replacement guitarists, but audience attendances begin to wane as word spreads of Clapton's exit.

Oct McVie is fired by Mayall for being drunk once too often, and Jack Bruce, ex-The Graham Bond Organization, replaces him on bass.

Nov Mayall finds Peter Green, a guitarist good enough to step into Clapton's shoes, when Clapton himself returns with a tan and slips back into his job. Green is forced out after only 3 days as a Bluesbreaker. Shortly after Clapton's return, Bruce leaves because Mayall is unable to pay him enough. McVie rejoins the line-up. With Clapton, The Bluesbreakers record *I'm Your Witchdoctor* in a 1-off deal with Immediate Records.

1966 Mar Producer Mike Vernon convinces Decca that Mayall should be re-signed, and the group cuts its first studio album *Blues Breakers* (having also made another 1-off single, *Lonely Years* for small Purdah label between contracts).

July *Blues Breakers*, credited to John Mayall with Eric Clapton for maximum commercial appeal, becomes Mayall's first major success, hitting UK #6. While the album is in the Top 10, Clapton leaves for the second and final time, to join Jack Bruce and Ginger Baker in Cream.

[17] Mayall persuades an initially-uncertain Peter Green to replace Clapton, this time on a firm basis.

Sept [18] Flint leaves, and is replaced on drums by Aynsley Dunbar, ex-The Mojos.

Oct 2 singles on Decca, *Parchman Farm* and *Looking Back* (the first featuring Clapton, the second Green) are issued in rapid succession, neither charting.

1967 Mar *A Hard Road*, the only studio album featuring Green, with a sleeve painting by Mayall, hits UK #10.

Apr Dunbar leaves to join Jeff Beck's group, and is replaced first by Mickey Waller, then by ex-Shotgun Express drummer Mick Fleetwood.

June [15] Fleetwood is fired by Mayall for excessive drinking, and Green follows him (they will form Fleetwood Mac). Mayall, left with just himself and McVie (who has already been approached re Fleetwood Mac, but refused) hires several new musicians: Mick Taylor (ex-Gods) on guitar, Chris Mercer on sax, Keef Hartley (ex-Artwoods) on drums and second sax player Rip Kant (who vanishes after 2 months). This line-up is the first to tour US.

Aug [13] Mayall plays on the final day of the seventh National Blues Festival at Balloon Meadow on the Royal Windsor Racecourse, Berks.

Sept *Crusade* hits UK #8. McVie is tempted away to Fleetwood Mac and is followed in The Bluesbreakers by a succession of short-lived bassists lasting 8 months between them: Paul Williams, Keith Tillman and Andy Fraser. At the same time, the brass section of the band is enlarged, as Henry Lowther on trumpet and Dick Heckstall-Smith on sax join existing sax player Mercer.

Dec *The Blues Alone*, a solo by Mayall (with Hartley playing drums on some tracks), makes UK #24.

1968 Jan Band begins a US tour at the Cafe Au-Go-Go club in New York.

Mar *Diary Of A Band Vol.1*, recorded live on the road during 1967, reaches UK #27. Its companion volume, *Diary Of A Band Vol.2* makes UK #28. Meanwhile, Mayall has his first US chart album with *Crusade*, which makes #136.

Apr Hartley leaves to form his own band. Mayall asks an initially sceptical Jon Hiseman (ex-Graham Bond Organization) to replace him on drums for an extended US tour. Tony Reeves from The New Jazz Orchestra joins on bass, after Fraser leaves going on to form Free.

June Solo album *The Blues Alone* makes US #128.

Aug *Bare Wires*, recorded by the extended, brass-featuring band line-up, hits UK #3.

[11] They take part in the eighth National Jazz & Blues Festival, before embarking on a lengthy US tour, at the end of which Mayall breaks up the band and settles in Los Angeles, retaining Taylor on guitar, and recruiting bassist Steve Thompson and drummer Colin Allen to return to his old quartet format.

Oct *Bare Wires* reaches US #59.

1969 Jan *Blues From Laurel Canyon*, recorded in Los Angeles by the quartet, makes UK #33.

Apr *Blues From Laurel Canyon* reaches US #68.

[6] Mayall's band plays the Palm Springs Pop Festival in CA., where a riot breaks out when police helicopters try to disperse an audience too large for the festival site.

[8] They open at The Whiskey A-Go-Go in Los Angeles.

May Taylor leaves to join The Rolling Stones, and Allen departs to Stone The Crows.

June Mayall forms a new band (dropping the Bluesbreakers tag), featuring a revolutionary line-up without drums. Thompson remains

on bass, while Marianne Faithfull's former stage guitarist Jon Mark is recruited, with Duster Bennett (guitar) and Johnny Almond (sax).

July [7] The new line-up plays at the Woburn Music Festival, after appearing at the Bath Festival in June.

[11-12] They play the Fillmore East in New York, with Spooky Tooth.

Aug Compilation album *Looking Back*, with tracks recorded between 1964 and 1967 (including some with Clapton), reaches UK #14.

Oct *Don't Waste My Time* makes US #81, Mayall's only US hit single, taken from *The Turning Point*, recorded at the Fillmore East.

Nov *The Turning Point*, recorded by the drumless line-up, and the first result of a new recording deal with Polydor, peaks at UK #11 and US #32. In a 55-week stay on US chart, it becomes Mayall's only gold disk. Mayall announces the launch of his own Crusade label.

[10] He embarks on an 8-date UK tour at the Free Trade Hall, Manchester. The tour will end Nov.29 at the Granada theater, Walthamstow, London.

1970 Apr *Empty Rooms* hits UK #9, while *Diary Of A Band* (the same as UK *Diary Of A Band, Vol.1*) makes US #93.

May *Empty Rooms* reaches US #33.

June Band splits, with Mark and Almond forming the duo Mark-Almond, and the others moving to sessions or solo work.

Nov [20] A UK tour opens the Fairfield Hall, Croydon, London.

Dec *U.S.A. Union*, on which Mayall collaborates with an entirely US-originated group (Harvey Mandel on guitar, Larry Taylor on bass and Don "Sugarcane" Harris on violin) for the first time, reaches UK #50 and US #22.

1971 May *John Mayall – Live In Europe* (equivalent to UK *Diary Of A Band, Vol.2*) creeps to US #146.

June Double album *Back To The Roots*, a reunion with previous Bluesbreakers Clapton, Taylor and Hartley, alongside Mayall's current US players, makes UK #31 and US #52. This is Mayall's last album to chart in UK.

Dec Double compilation album *Thru The Years*, containing mostly unreleased 60s Bluesbreakers material, makes US #164. New album *Memories*, cut by a trio comprising Mayall, Larry Taylor on bass and ex-Ventures lead guitarist Jerry McGee on guitar, climbs to US #179.

1972 July Live album *Jazz Blues Fusion*, recorded in New York and Boston with guitarist Freddie Robinson, trumpeter Blue Mitchell and standup bassist Victor Gaskin, reaches US #64.

Nov *Moving On*, with Robinson and Mitchell, makes US #116.

1973 Mar Double album *Down The Line*, combining an album of mid-60s studio cuts with the original *John Mayall Plays John Mayall* live album, peaks at US #158.

Oct Double album *Ten Years Are Gone* makes US #157.

1974 Mar Mayall cuts *The Latest Edition* with Hightide Harris and Randy Resnick (lead guitar), Red Holloway (saxes/flute), Soko Richardson (drums).

Apr [14] Mayall, with a band comprising Jesse Ed Davis, Larry Taylor (bass), Red Holloway (sax) and Soko Richardson (drums), begins UK tour at the Town Hall, Birmingham, W.Midlands.

1975 Mar Mayall signs to ABC/Blue Thumb Records for *New Year, New Band, New Company*, which makes US #140, and is his final US chart entry. The new band of the title includes earlier cohorts Taylor and Don Harris, plus Rick Vito (guitar), Jay Spell (keyboards), Soko Richardson (drums), and for the first time, a female vocalist, Dee McKinnie.

1979 May After several further album releases, Mayall signs to DJM Records, issuing *Bottom Line*, to minimal sales.

Dec Second DJM album *No More Interviews* is again a minor seller.

1980 Third DJM album *Road Show Blues* is released.

1982 Mayall reunites with Mick Taylor and John McVie for US and Australian tours.

1984 He puts together a new Bluesbreakers with Coco Montaya, Walter Trout (guitars), Bobby Haynes (bass), Joe Yuele (drums). They will release *Behind The Iron Curtain* on GNP Crescendo in 1986.

1987 Mayall signs to German label Entente for live *The Power Of The Blues*.

1988 Polygram issues vintage Mayall from the 60s as album *Archives To Eighties: Featuring Eric Clapton And Mick Taylor*.

Dec Mayall signs to Island, releasing *Chicago Line*.

1990 June *A Sense Of Place* is released on Island, as Mayall, still a California resident, embarks on major US tour.

Sept [22] Mayall returns to US chart for first time in over 15 years as *A Sense Of Place* makes US #170.

1991 Feb [8] Mayall appears on NBC TV's "Tonight" show, as he continues to tour the US, playing his own special brand of blues.

Apr Mayall joins Z.Z.Top's US tour, replacing just-fired Black Crowes.

CURTIS MAYFIELD

'70 **Oct** [1] Mayfield (b. June 3, 1942, Chicago, IL), after 13 years as a member of The Impressions (11 years as leader, chief songwriter and producer), leaves for a solo career – after finding his own replacement, Leroy Hutson. (The Impressions remain on his Curtom label and he will continue to direct their career.)
Dec Debut solo album *Curtis* reaches US #19. It includes 2 lengthy funk pieces, *Move On Up* and *(Don't Worry) If There's A Hell Down Below, We're All Going To Go*. The latter, edited as a US single, reaches US #29.

'71 **July** Double live album *Curtis/Live!*, with a mixture of new and recent songs and Impressions oldies, recorded at the Bitter End in New York, reaches US #21. (In contrast to his rich studio productions, Mayfield's 70s live band will be his own guitar and vocals, plus drummer, percussionist and bass player, and occasionally a second guitarist.)
Aug *Move On Up*, from the first album, becomes a UK dancefloor hit, and UK chart debut, reaching #12. (Neither album charts in UK.)
Dec *Roots* peaks at US #40. It contains anti-war song *We Got To Have Peace*, but is mostly concerned with romantic themes. Extracted *Get Down* makes US #69. Mayfield devotes the next few months to work on his first film soundtrack.

'72 **Oct** His soundtrack album from film "Superfly" (one of the rash of "blaxploitation" movies which appear in the wake of 1971's highly successful "Shaft" with its innovative Isaac Hayes score) tops US chart for 4 weeks, and earns a gold disk. Much of the music is downbeat, despairing at the violence and drug culture in the film rather than glorifying it. Cautionary tale *Freddie's Dead* is extracted and hits US #4, his first solo million-seller.

'73 **Jan** Title track from "Superfly" hits US #8, a second million-seller.
Mar Soundtrack *Superfly* reaches UK #26, his only UK chart album.
Aug *Back To The World*, featuring mainly social consciousness songs, with rich, layered production, makes US #16, and is his third and final gold album. Taken from it, *Future Shock* makes US #39.
Oct Chicago's WTTW-TV produces a musical special based around Mayfield, titled "Curtis In Chicago". It features both original and current Impressions line-ups, plus Jerry Butler, Gene Chandler, and other artists with whom Mayfield has been involved, and following various solo and group spots, the show ends with an ensemble rendition of The Impressions' *Amen*.
Nov *If I Were Only A Child Again*, from the TV show, reaches US #71.
Dec *Curtis In Chicago*, soundtrack of the TV show, makes US #135.

'74 **Jan** *Can't Say Nothin'* peaks at US #88.
May Mayfield produces and plays on Gladys Knight & The Pips' soundtrack album from film "Claudine", which reaches US #35.
Aug *Sweet Exorcist* makes US #39. It contains a collaboration with Donny Hathaway on *Suffer*, while extracted *Kung Fu* reflects current media craze and peaks at US #40.
Dec *Got To Find A Way* reaches US #76.

'75 **July** *There's No Place Like America Today*, a downbeat set dealing with racial prejudice, violence and deprivation, peaks at US #120.
Oct From it, uniquely upbeat ballad *So In Love* peaks at US #67 – his last US hit single.
Dec Mayfield works with The Staple Singers on their soundtrack album from film "Let's Do It Again", which reaches US #20.

'76 **July** Disco aimed *Give, Get, Take And Have* peaks at US #171, and reveals no hit singles.
Aug He produces Aretha Franklin's *Sparkle*, which reaches US #18.

'77 **Apr** *Never Say You Can't Survive* (featuring his own version of *Sparkle*) creeps to US #173.
Oct Soundtrack album *Short Eyes*, from low-budget prison movie featuring both Mayfield and Tex-Mex country singer Freddy Fender, follows the *Superfly* mold, but with no commercial success.

'78 **June** He produces Aretha Franklin again, on *Almighty Fire*, which makes US #63, but marks the final collaboration between them.
Oct *Do It All Night*, entirely disco-styled, fails to chart in US and is not given UK release.
Dec *No Goodbyes*, a lengthy disco track which is Mayfield's first UK single for 3 years, is issued only on 12" and peaks at UK #65.

'79 Curtom label hits financial difficulties and Mayfield sells out to RSO, which insists he find an outside producer for his next disk. He chooses Philadelphia team Norman Harris, Ronald Tyson and Bunny Sigler.
Sept *Heartbeat*, part-produced by the trio, and partly (3 tracks) by Mayfield, makes US #42. It includes *Between You Baby And Me*, a duet with his recent discovery Linda Clifford.

'80 **July** *The Right Combination*, again with Clifford, stalls at US #180.

Aug Mayfield's solo *Something To Believe In* charts for 10 weeks in US, reaching #128. It is his last album with RSO, and his final US chart entry.

1981 Mayfield transfers to Neil Bogart's Boardwalk label. Disco producer Dino Fekaris produces *Love Is The Place*, which does not chart and is not issued in UK. (Mayfield's prospects seem even gloomier when Bogart dies shortly after, and label affairs are plunged into confusion.)

1982 **Oct** *Honesty*, also on Boardwalk, is released in US. Self-produced, it has some political comment amid romantic material.

1983 **Mar** *Honesty* is released on Epic in UK, where reviews are good, and he tours twice in quick succession – his concerts featuring no material recorded after *Superfly*. (Later in the year, both Mayfield and Jerry Butler rejoin The Impressions for a brief US tour. A studio album from the reunion is rumored, but none emerges.)

1985 **Sept** With Curtom defunct, Mayfield forms new label CRC. It releases US-only album *We Come In Peace With A Message Of Love*.

1986 **Nov** *Baby It's You* is released in both US and UK (on 98.6 label); an album is announced, but does not appear.

1987 **May** Still without a recording contract, Mayfield makes a short UK tour when he is invited to record with The Blow Monkeys, one of the young UK groups who regard his early 70s work as inspirational.
June The Blow Monkeys' *Celebrate (The Day After You)*, featuring Mayfield, is released. (As an apparent pre-election attack on UK's Prime Minister, it is banned by the BBC as possibly prejudicial, until after the event, and stalls at UK #52.)

1988 **June** Mayfield tours UK, Switzerland, Austria, Germany, Holland and France, as Curtom label is revived internationally by independent soul label Ichiban Records. Soundtrack album *Superfly* is reissued in UK.
July *Move On Up*, always Mayfield's most popular recording in UK (and subsequently repromoted by Mayfield fan Paul Weller, who revived it with The Jam), is reissued as a UK 12" single, and charts briefly at #87.

1990 **Aug** [13] Mayfield is paralyzed when a strong gust of wind blows a lighting rig on him during a rainstorm at an outdoor concert at Wingate Field in Brooklyn, New York.
[24] Paralyzed from the neck down, Mayfield is transferred from King's County hospital to Shepherd Spinal Center near his Atlanta, GA, home. (Doctors fear he will remain paralyzed.)
Sept Recorded before his accident, a fashionably updated version of *Superfly*, namely *Superfly 1990*, featuring rap insertions by co-credited hip-hop star Ice-T makes UK #48.

PAUL McCARTNEY

1969 **Mar** [12] Famed Beatle McCartney (b. June 18, 1942, Liverpool, Merseyside) marries Linda Eastman (b. Sept.24, 1942, Scarsdale, New York, NY) at Marylebone Register Office, London.

1970 **Apr** [11] McCartney announces that he will not record with John Lennon again, as The Beatles split officially.
May Home-recorded album *McCartney* hits UK #2 and tops US chart. His solo debut adds to tension between members of The Beatles as it is released almost simultaneously with the group's *Let It Be*.

1971 **Apr** [17] Debut solo single *Another Day* hits UK #2 and US #5.
June *Ram* hits UK #1 and US #2. While his former writing partner Lennon bases his early solo career on songs of personal angst and political commentary, McCartney settles into a simpler pop groove which will remain a constant for most of his recording career.
Sept [4] *Back Seat Of My Car* makes UK #39, as US-only release *Uncle Albert/Admiral Halsey* tops US chart.
Nov As a member of The Beatles, McCartney was reluctant to stop live performance and so sets up a group to perform under the name Wings, comprising Paul and Linda McCartney, Denny Laine on guitars and vocals and Denny Seiwell on drums.
[8] He launches album *Wings Wildlife* at the Empire Ballroom, Leicester Square, London, with Ray McVay & His Band Of The Day and The Frank & Peggy Spencer Formation Team.
Dec *Wings Wildlife* reaches UK #11 and US #10. His second album in 6 months, it is savaged by the critics.

1972 **Feb** Group, augmented by Henry McCullough on guitar and vocals, tours UK, arriving at colleges unannounced and asking social secretaries if they would like Wings to perform in their hall that evening.
Apr [8] *Give Ireland Back To The Irish* reaches UK #16 and US #21. Written after the "Bloody Sunday Massacre" in N.Ireland in Jan., it is banned by the BBC and the IBA.
June Embittered by the ban on his single, McCartney puts music to

nursery rhyme *Mary Had A Little Lamb*. It hits UK #9.
July [9] Wings makes its formal concert debut at Chateauvillon, France.
[22] *Mary Had A Little Lamb* reaches US #28.
The McCartneys are arrested for possession of drugs in Sweden during a Wings European tour.
Sept They are arrested again for drug possession at their Scottish farmhouse.

1973 **Jan** *Hi Hi Hi* is banned by the BBC, claiming that the record endorses drug use. It is later promoted with B-side *C Moon*, and hits UK #5.
Feb [3] *Hi Hi Hi* hits US #10.
Mar [8] McCartney is arrested again for growing marijuana on his farm in Scotland.
Apr Ballad *My Love* hits UK #9 as McCartney hints at a possible Beatles reunion.
May *Red Rose Speedway*, credited to Paul McCartney & Wings, hits UK #5 and tops US chart. Wings begins a UK tour.
[10] "James Paul McCartney" special airs on UK TV. A musical extravaganza, it features McCartney in a crowded Liverpool pub for a singalong, performing a Fred Astaire-style dance routine and ending with a solo performance of *Yesterday*.
June [2] *My Love* hits US #1, and is later deposed by George Harrison's *Give Me Love (Give Me Peace On Earth)*. *Live And Let Die*, the theme to forthcoming James Bond film, hits UK #9. Music producer George Martin has played the song in its finished form to the film's producer Harry Saltzmann, who assumes it is a demo and suggests that Thelma Houston should cut the song. Martin reassures Saltzmann that this is a finished item by an ex-Beatle. (The song stands but Brenda Arnau will cover it on the film's soundtrack album.)
Aug [11] *Live And Let Die* hits US #2, kept off the top by Diana Ross' *Touch Me In The Morning* and then by Stories' *Brother Louie*.
McCullough and Seiwell quit the group. The remaining 3 fly to Ginger Baker's ARC studios in Lagos, Nigeria, to record *Band On The Run*.
Dec *Helen Wheels*, a song written about McCartney's Landrover jeep (known affectionately as "Hell On Wheels"), reaches UK #12.

1974 **Jan** [12] *Helen Wheels* hits US #10.
Mar [30] *Jet*, inspired by McCartney's pet labrador puppy, hits both UK and US #7.
Apr [13] *Band On The Run* tops US chart, after receiving rave reviews. (It will sell 6,000,000 copies worldwide and spend over 2 years on both UK and US charts. The cover features personalities Michael Parkinson, James Coburn, Kenny Lynch, Clement Freud, Christopher Lee and John Conteh posing with the group as escaped convicts caught in a searchlight. McCartney had invited them to lunch, and then asked them to pose for the photo.) After many refusals, due to drug convictions, McCartney finally gets a US visa.
May Group becomes a 5-piece again. Jimmy McCulloch (b. June 4, 1953) (ex-Thunderclap Newman and Stone The Crows) joins on guitar and vocals and former UK karate champion Geoff Britton on drums.
June McCartney produces UK #7 hit *Liverpool Lou* for brother Mike McGear's group Scaffold.
[8] *Band On The Run* tops US chart. Group travels to Nashville, TN, to record, and for McCartney to produce Peggy Lee's *Let's Love*.
July [13] *Band On The Run* tops UK chart.
Aug *Band On The Run* hits UK #3, backed with the theme to UK TV series "The Zoo Gang".
Oct Wings release *Walking In The Park With Eloise*, written by McCartney's father James, under the pseudonym The Country Hams. (When McCartney appears on BBC radio program "Desert Island Discs", he chooses it as one of his favorite records.)
Dec *Junior's Farm*, written during McCartney's stay in Nashville at Junior Putnam's farm, reaches UK #16.

1975 **Jan** [11] *Junior's Farm* hits US #3.
Feb Joe English (b. Rochester, NY) replaces Britton on drums.
[22] *Sally G* makes US #39.
June *Listen To What The Man Said* hits UK #6.
[14] *Venus And Mars*, containing a version of the theme to popular UK TV soap opera "Crossroads" (later adopted by TV show for a period), tops UK chart.
July [19] *Listen To What The Man Said* and *Venus And Mars* top US charts.
Sept [9] Wings begins 13-month tour of 10 countries at the Gaumont theater, Southampton, Hants. They will play to over 2 million people.
Oct [25] *Letting Go* makes UK #41 and US #39.
Dec [13] *Venus And Mars Rock Show* reaches US #12, but fails in UK, his first chart miss in 13 years.

1976 **Apr** [3] *Wings At The Speed Of Sound* hits UK #2, behind the soundtrack to UK TV show "Rock Follies". McCartney's democratic approach to Wings affords each member a lead vocal cut.
[24] *Wings At The Speed Of Sound* tops US chart.
May [3] The Wings world tour arrives in US as "Wings Over America", and McCartney makes his first US stage appearance in 10 years at Tarrant County Convention Center, Fort Worth, TX.
[22] *Silly Love Songs* tops US chart.
June [12] *Silly Love Songs* hits UK #2, but is kept from the top by labelmates The Wurzels with the novelty *Combine Harvester*.
July McCartney buys Edwin H. Morris Music, which includes the entire Buddy Holly catalog.
Aug [14] *Let 'Em In* hits US #3.
[28] *Let 'Em In* hits UK #2.
Sept [7] After buying Holly's song catalog, McCartney commemorat Holly's 40th birthday by instituting an annual "Buddy Holly Week".
[25] Wings play a Unesco concert in St. Mark's Square, Venice, Italy, draw attention to the decay and neglect in the historic city. The conce is a success but the weight of equipment used by the group causes areas of subsidence damage in the square.
Dec [21] World tour ends with 3 standing-room-only nights at the Empire Pool, Wembley, London.

1977 **Jan** *Wings Over America*, a 30-track documentary of the group's US tour – including 5 Beatles songs, hits UK #8 and US #1.
Mar [5] *Maybe I'm Amazed*, a live version of a song from McCartney's debut solo album, reaches UK #28.
Apr [2] *Maybe I'm Amazed* hits US #10.
Thrillington, an orchestral interpretation of McCartney's *Ram*, is released, featuring orchestra leader Percy "Thrills" Thrillington, a pseudonym for McCartney.
Nov McCulloch leaves to join the re-formed Small Faces, while Engli joins Sea Level, reducing Wings to a trio again.
Dec *Waltz Mull Of Kintyre* tops UK chart for 9 weeks. It is co-written by Laine about the southern tip of the Kintyre peninsula, 11 miles fro McCartney's farmhouse in Campbelltown, Scotland. (Laine later sells McCartney his rights to the song after being declared bankrupt.)
[17] Mr. David Ackroyd purchases the 1-millionth copy of *Mull Of Kintyre* in UK and becomes the first record buyer in the world to receive a gold disk for his purchase. (It will be the biggest-selling UK single of all time at 2.5 million, replacing The Beatles *She Loves You*, until Band Aid's 1984 *Do They Know It's Christmas?*).

1978 **Jan** [14] *Mull Of Kintyre* fails in US, where B-side *Girls School* is promoted and makes US #33.
Apr *With A Little Luck* hits UK #5, as parent album *London Town*, recorded in London and on the yacht "Fair Carol", in the Virgin Islands, hits UK #4 and US #2. It features *Girlfriend*, later covered by Michael Jackson on *Off The Wall*.
May [20] *With A Little Luck* tops US chart.
July *I've Had Enough* makes UK #42. Wings becomes a 5-piece, joined by Laurence Juber on guitar and vocals and ex-sessionman Steve Hol on drums.
Aug [5] *I've Had Enough* reaches US #25.
Sept *London Town* peaks at UK #60.
Oct [14] *London Town* makes US #39.
Dec *Wings Greatest Hits* hits UK #5 and US #29.

1979 **Mar** [16] "Wings Over The World" airs on US TV.
May [19] *Goodnight Tonight* hits UK and US #5, where it is released c Columbia label, with which McCartney signs a multi-million dollar deal.
June *Old Siam Sir* makes UK #35 as parent album *Back To The Egg* h UK #6 and US #8.
July [28] *Getting Closer* reaches US #20.
Aug *Haven't I Met Somewhere Before?*, written by McCartney for film "Heaven Can Wait" but rejected, is featured as opening song in film "Rock'N'Roll High School", performed by The Ramones. Linda McCartney releases *Seaside Woman*, under the name Suzy & The Red Stripes. Despite McCartney's production, the single does not chart.
Sept *Getting Closer/Baby's Request* makes UK #60. Wings appear on stage at London's Hammersmith Odeon with The Crickets.
Oct [13] *Arrow Through Me* reaches US #29.
[24] McCartney receives a medallion cast in rhodium from the UK an minister after being declared the most successful composer of all time From 1962-78, he has written or co-written 43 songs that have sold ov a million copies each. He has sold 100 million singles and 100 million albums.
Dec [29] Wings play the last night of the "Concerts For The People

332

Kampuchea" at London's Hammersmith Odeon, with *Rockestra Theme* revived with an all-star band, most of whom featured on the disk.

1980 Jan Festive *Wonderful Christmastime*, McCartney's first solo single since 1971, hits UK #6.
[16] McCartney is jailed in Tokyo for marijuana possession. (Laine later sympathetically relates McCartney's experience in *Japanese Tears*.)
[25] He is released and extradited from Japan. He is not keen to return.
May *Coming Up* hits UK #2.
June [28] B-side *Coming Up* features a live version, recorded at Glasgow Apollo in Dec.1979, which becomes popular on US radio and tops US chart, so different forms of the song chart in US and UK. In the video promoting it, McCartney takes on role of 5 stars, which include Frank Zappa, Ron Mael, Buddy Holly, Andy Mackay and himself as a Beatle with collarless suit, in a group dubbed The Plastic Macs. Like his solo debut, *McCartney II* is recorded at home, using microphones plugged directly into the tape machines. It hits UK #1 and US #3.
July Ballad *Waterfalls* hits UK #9.
Sept *Temporary Secretary*, released as a limited edition 12" single, fails.
Nov [26] Film "Rockshow", a Wings concert from their 1976 US tour, premieres at New York's Ziegfeld theater.

1981 Feb *McCartney Interview*, originally a promotional record for US radio stations, is released due to public demand and makes US #158. It is deleted on the day of release in UK, but still reaches #34.
Mar [3] McCartney guests on UK radio show "Desert Island Discs".
Apr [21] He attends the wedding of Ringo Starr and Barbara Bach.

1982 Apr [24] *Ebony And Ivory*, calling for racial harmony and written by McCartney as a duet with Stevie Wonder, tops UK chart. McCartney becomes first of The Beatles to gain an entry in **Who's Who**.
May [15] *Ebony And Ivory* tops US chart.
Tug Of War, recorded with help from Stevie Wonder, Eric Stewart, Ringo Starr and Carl Perkins, hits both UK and US #1.
Aug [21] *Take It Away* reaches UK #15 and US #10.
Oct [23] *Tug Of War* makes both UK and US #53.
Nov *The Girl Is Mine*, a duet with Michael Jackson on his album *Thriller*, hits UK #8.

1983 Jan [8] *The Girl Is Mine* hits US #2.
Feb [8] McCartney wins Best British Male Artist and the Sony Trophy For Technical Excellence at the second annual BRIT Awards at the Grosvenor House, London.
Oct McCartney makes a cameo appearance in Tracey Ullman's video "They Don't Know".
Nov *Say Say Say*, another duet with Jackson promoted by a $500,000 video, hits UK #2, as parent album *Pipes Of Peace* hits UK #4 and US #15. McCartney writes theme to Richard Gere film "The Honorary Consul".
Dec [10] *Say Say Say* tops US chart.

1984 Jan Another costly video recreating the famous Christmas Day truce during the Great War in 1914, helps *Pipes Of Peace* top UK chart.
Feb [11] *So Bad*, with *Pipes Of Peace* on the B-side, makes US #23.
Oct *No More Lonely Nights*, trailering McCartney's first feature film, hits UK #2. A-side features a ballad version with an uptempo re-recording of it on the flip.
Nov *Give My Regards To Broad Street* forms the soundtrack to film starring McCartney, based on his script and described as a "musical fantasy drama". Album comprises re-recordings of Beatles tracks and McCartney hits and is overseen by ex-Beatle producer George Martin. The film is a critical and box-office failure, but the album hits UK #1 and US #21. McCartney is awarded the Freedom of Liverpool in a ceremony at Liverpool's Picton Library.
Dec [8] *No More Lonely Nights* hits US #6. McCartney, who now owns rights to Rupert Bear cartoon stories, which have appeared in UK's **Daily Express** newspaper for over 50 years, makes a short pilot film featuring song *We All Stand Together*, credited to Paul McCartney & The Frog Chorus. It hits UK #3, and will become an annual Christmas favorite. The video will also become a UK best-seller.

1985 July [13] McCartney sings *Let It Be* as climax to Live Aid spectacular at Wembley Stadium, London.
Dec *Spies Like Us*, theme to Dan Aykroyd/Chevy Chase film, hits UK #13. *We All Stand Together*, repromoted at Christmas, reaches UK #37.

1986 Feb [8] *Spies Like Us* hits US #7.
Aug *Press* reaches UK #25.
Sept [13] *Press* reaches US #21.
Press To Play hits UK #8 and US #30.
Nov [29] *Stranglehold* stalls at US #81.
Dec [17] The McCartneys escape injury when their car bursts into

flames on the way to a recording of UK TV show "The Tube" in Newcastle, Tyne & Wear.
Only Love Remains reaches UK #34.

1987 Nov Greatest hits album *All The Best!* hits UK #2.
Dec *Once Upon A Long Ago* hits UK #10. (CD version of single harks back to McCartney's first love with versions of *Don't Get Around Much Anymore* and *Kansas City*.) B-side *Back On My Feet* is co-written with Elvis Costello.

1988 Jan *All The Best!* makes US #62 (with different track listing).
[20] Claiming he still has business differences with the rest of the group, McCartney does not attend the induction of The Beatles into the Rock'N'Roll Hall Of Fame at New York's Waldorf Astoria.
June It is reported that McCartney has been asked to record an album of his rock'n'roll favorites for exclusive release in USSR on the state Melodiya label.
July [12] McCartney receives a honorary doctorate from Sussex University.
Aug Moscow News reports that plans are being laid for McCartney to play 8 concerts in Moscow in 1989, as work continues on new album.
Sept [7] McCartney joins The Crickets on stage at the "Buddy Holly Week" festival in London.
Nov McCartney produces *Let The Children Play* (profits of which will go to the annual Children In Need fund-raising event).

1989 Feb USSR's Melodiya label presses 40,000 copies *Back In The USSR*, featuring McCartney's interpretations of several classic rock'n'roll hits, including *Kansas City*, *Lawdy Miss Clawdy*, *Lucille*, *That's All Right Mama*, and *Ain't That A Shame*.
Mar *Veronica* cements co-writing relationship with Elvis Costello. (Forthcoming albums from both artists will feature co-written songs and McCartney claims in interviews that the collaboration reminds him of working with Lennon.)
Apr [4] McCartney receives a standing ovation when collecting the Outstanding Services To British Music award at the annual Ivor Novello lunch at the Grosvenor House, London. Accepting the statuette, he performs an impromptu rap in front of many peers.
May He teams with fellow Liverpudlians Gerry Marsden, Holly Johnson and The Christians to record *Ferry 'Cross The Mersey* in aid of the Hillsborough Disaster Fund (UK #1). McCartney embarks on major promotion in support of *My Brave Face*, which reaches UK #18, and forthcoming album, including appearances on BBC TV's "Wogan" chat show, a **Rolling Stone** magazine front cover, and an 8-part BBC Radio 1 series "Paul McCartney Story".
June *Flowers In The Dirt* is released. Containing Costello collaborations (including a vocal duet), its producers include Trevor Horn, Neil Dorfsman, Chris Hughes and David Foster with musical assistance from Nicky Hopkins and David Gilmour. It hits UK #1 (aided by a BBC 1 TV special) and begins a US rise to #21. Plans are announced for a 6-month world tour, starting in Scandinavia in Sept. The backing band will be Hamish Stuart (ex-Average White Band), Robbie McIntosh, Chris Whitten, Paul Wickens and Linda McCartney. Press reports that McCartney and Sting will lead a UK BBC radio campaign to raise listeners' awareness of environmental issues.
July [8] *My Brave Face* reaches US #25.
[27] McCartney announces world tour at press conference and treats 400 fan club members to 90-min. set previewing live show.
Aug He rehearses for a week at the Lyceum theater, New York.
Sept [16] *This One* stalls at US #94, having reached US #18 in Aug.
[21] McCartney performs at Studio 6, Goldcrest studios, Elstree, Herts., for winners of a BBC Radio 1 concert.
[26] His world tour opens at Drammenshallen, Oslo, Norway.
Nov [23-24, 27, 29] North American leg of the tour begins at the Great Western Forum, Inglewood, Los Angeles, CA. (During the third show, Wonder joins McCartney on stage to sing *Ebony And Ivory*.)
Figure Of Eight makes UK #43.
Dec McCartney is honored by the PRS for his "unique achievment in popular music" at a luncheon at Claridge's, London.
[15] McCartney donates $100,000 to Friends Of The Earth.

1990 Jan [2] He begins UK leg of his world tour at NEC in Birmingham, W.Midlands. (It is his first UK concert appearance in a decade.)
[5] At a further concert at the NEC, a man turns up backstage claiming to be Father McKenzie (McCartney's fictional character in *Eleanor Rigby*). McCartney is heard to respond "Where's Mr.Kite and Billy Shears? Are they here too?"
[11] McCartney plays the first of 11 concerts at the Wembley Arena, London, before crowds totalling 137,000.
[13] *Figure Of Eight* stalls at US #92.

[16] McCartney meets 21-year-old Polish teacher Agnieska Czarniecka, who for 4 years has run the Paul McCartney Kindergarten in Cracow, where 200 children are taught English through McCartney's songs.

Feb McCartney contributes a cover of *It's Now Or Never* to the compilation album *The Last Temptation Of Elvis*, to benefit the Nordoff-Robbins Music Therapy charity.

[17] *Put It There* makes UK #32.

[21] McCartney is presented with NARAS Lifetime Achievement Award at the 32nd annual Grammy awards by Meryl Streep, noting that McCartney "as a member of The Beatles, had an impact not only on rock'n'roll but also on Western culture, and, as a solo performer and songwriter, continues to develop and grow after 3 decades".

Mar [9] McCartney donates $250,000 to the Sloan-Kettering Cancer Centre and Friends Of The Earth during an 11-date stint at the Dome, Tokyo, Japan.

Apr [21] McCartney gains a place in the **Guinness Book Of World Records** when he plays before the largest paid attendance of a 184,000 people at a public event at the Maracana Stadium, Rio de Janeiro, Brazil. It breaks the record of 175,000 set by Frank Sinatra at the same venue on Jan.26, 1980.

July [29] McCartney's world tour ends at Chicago's Soldier Field in front of 53,000 fans. (The tour has lasted 45 weeks, during which he has played 102 concerts in 46 cities.)

Oct *Birthday* reaches UK #29.

Nov *Tripping The Live Fantastic* reaches UK #17.

[18] McCartney's birth certificate is sold for $18,000 in Houston, TX, despite allegations of auction-rigging to get an inflated price for the document.

Dec [1] *Tripping The Live Fantastic* reaches US #26.

[15] *Tripping The Live Fantastic,* a special limited edition version of the album, climbs to US #157.

1991 **Jan** [25] McCartney records an acoustic set before a small audience for US MTV program "Unplugged". (Show will premiere in US on Apr.3.)

Mar [7] McCartney is named Best Bassist in the annual **Rolling Stone** Readers' Picks music awards.

May [13] *I Lost My Little Girl* is scheduled for release.

June McCartney's semi-autobiographical "Liverpool Oratorio" is performed by the Royal Liverpool Philharmonic Orchestra in Liverpool Cathedral.

THE McCOYS

Rick Zehringer (lead guitar, vocals)
Bobby Peterson (organ)
Randy Hobbs (bass)
Randy Zehringer (drums)

1962 Group is formed in Union City, IN, by brothers Rick (b. May 8, 1947, Fort Recovery, OH) and Randy Zehringer, with friends Dennis Kelly (bass) and Ronnie Brandon (keyboards), while at high school. They name themselves after The Ventures' 1960 rock instrumental *The McCoy*, B-side of US #2 hit *Walk Don't Run*.

1965 After name changes from Rick & The Raiders to The Rick Z Combo, under which they release *You Know That I Love You* during early post-high school gigs, they revert to being The McCoys, with Hobbs and Peterson replacing college-bound Kelly and Brandon.

June The McCoys sign to producer/songwriter Bert Berns' new New York label Bang Records, after opening for Bang artists The Strangeloves (aka producers Feldman/Goldstein/Gottehrer) at a gig in Dayton, OH. The Strangeloves put The McCoys into the studio to record one of Berns' own songs, *Hang On Sloopy*, a 1964 US hit for The Vibrations as *My Girl Sloopy*.

Oct *Hang On Sloopy* tops US chart, selling over a million copies, and hits UK #5 and is first release on independent label Immediate Records, owned by The Rolling Stones' manager Andrew Loog Oldham.

Dec A revival of Peggy Lee's 1958 hit *Fever* in a *Hang On Sloopy*-based arrangement hits US #7 and reaches UK #44. (B-side *Sorrow* will be revived in UK a few months later by The Merseys and hit UK #4. David Bowie will revive it again in 1973.) *Hang On Sloopy* climbs to US #44.

[9] While on tour in UK, Rick Zehringer is admitted to the National Temperance hospital suffering from a severe reaction to smallpox inoculation.

1966 **Feb** *Up And Down* reaches only US #46 and fails in UK.

Mar A revival of Ritchie Valens' *Come On Let's Go* reaches US #22, the group's last US Top 30 hit.

Aug Second album *(You Make Me Feel) So Good* fails to chart, but the title track climbs to US #53.

Oct Eschewing previous R&B-based style, The McCoys record psychedelic *Don't Worry Mother, Your Son's Heart Is Pure* in an attempt to expand their image but highest US placing is #67.

1967 **Jan** *I Got To Go Back* recalls *Sloopy*-R&B style but makes only US #69.

May *Beat The Clock* reaches US #92, after which the group splits from Bang Records.

1968 **Oct** Signed to Mercury Records in search of wider artistic freedom, group issues **Infinite McCoys**. Fashionably psychedelic, it features Blood, Sweat & Tears' brass section and is produced by Rick Zehringer but fails to chart. *Jesse Brady*, which makes a brief showing at US #98, the last McCoys chart entry. Mercury album **Human Ball** fails to chart.

1969 After the group has become a regular feature at Steve Paul's Scene club in New York, Paul takes over The McCoys' management and links them (minus Peterson, who leaves) with albino blues guitarist Johnny Winter, whom he also manages.

1970 **Oct** Rick Zehringer changes surname to Derringer to produce *Johnny Winter And ...*, which reaches US #154 but makes UK #29. Rick, Randy and Hobbs are the backing group on it (and on Winter's follow-up album *Live – Johnny Winter And ...*, also produced by Derringer, which will climb to US #40 and UK #20 in 1971).

1971 **Oct** Rumors abound of group rehearsing in Laurel Canyon, Los Angeles, CA, with Rick Derringer, Danny Whitten, "Whitey" Glan (drummer from Bush) and Nick St. Nicholas, ex-Steppenwolf, but nothing comes of the liaision.

1972 **May** When Winter stops touring to cure a drug habit, Derringer joins brother Edgar Winter's band White Trash on the road and performs on *Roadworks* which makes US #23.

1973 **May** Derringer produces Edgar Winter's group's *Frankenstein*, which tops US chart and makes UK #18, and *They Only Come Out At Night*, which hits US #3.

Dec Signed to Steve Paul's Blue Sky label as a soloist, Derringer releases *All American Boy*, which reaches US #25.

1974 **Mar** *Rock And Roll Hoochie Koo*, from solo album, peaks at US #23 and is Derringer's only major solo hit single. While recording solo, he continues to play with and produce albums for both Winter brothers.

1975 **May** Solo *Spring Fever* reaches only US #141.

1976 **Aug** Derringer forms hard rock quartet, Derringer, with Danny Johnson (guitar), Kenny Aaronson (bass) and Vinnie Appice (drums), but *Derringer* makes only US #154. (Later albums *Sweet Evil*, *Live* (both 1977) and *If I Weren't So Romantic, I'd Shoot You* (1978) will fail to make US Top 100, though the group will constantly tour US.)

1979 Derringer returns to solo recording with moderately-selling *Guitars And Women* and *Face To Face* and turns to smaller club venues. (He will continue to get credits as a well-respected session musician, appearing on albums by Steely Dan (who write their 1979 hit *Rikki Don't Lose That Number* about Derringer), Donald Fagen, Todd Rundgren, Bette Midler and others.)

1984 **Apr** He produces Weird Al Yankovic's *In 3-D*, a selection of hit parody/pastiches, which reaches US #17. Taken from it, *Eat It*, a parody of Michael Jackson's *Beat It*, hits US #12 and UK #36. (Derringer produces 5 albums for Yankovic.)

1986 Derringer returns to the live stage as guitarist for Cyndi Lauper.

1988 **Aug** For Weird Al Yankovic, Derringer produces *Fat*, a parody of Michael Jackson's *Bad*, timed to coincide with Jackson's world tour. It charts briefly at UK #91. (Derringer will continue to be in demand, embarking on a major US tour with Edgar Winter and writing *Real American*, subsequently used as World Wrestling Federation Champion Hulk Hogan's theme song.)

MICHAEL McDONALD

1964 McDonald (b. Dec.2, 1952, St. Louis, MO), son of a St. Louis bus driver while at high school forms his first band, Mike & The Majestics, which proves popular at local fraternity parties and is the first of a string of bands McDonald will play with including Jerry Jay & The Sheratons, The Del Rays and Blue.

1972 McDonald signs his first recording deal with RCA Records. Self-penned *God Knows I Love My Baby* fails and RCA passes on the option to release an album. His session work includes songs and vocals for acts including David Cassidy and Jack Jones.

1973 Signed to Bell Records, McDonald releases some unsuccessful singles, all produced by Rick Jarrard, including *Dear Me* and *When I'm Home*.

1974 Without a solo contract again, McDonald joins Steely Dan on live keyboards and vocals.

1975 He auditions for The Doobie Brothers in New Orleans, LA, and is chosen to replace exiting Tom Johnston. McDonald is required to learn and rehearse the live Doobies repertoire for a solid 48 hours prior to an immediate band tour. McDonald enjoys his first #1 as a songwriter, with Kenny Loggins, as *What A Fool Believes* hits #1 for the group, and wins 2 Grammies at the annual award ceremonies. His lead vocal work, songwriting and keyboard playing dominates The Doobie Brothers' output for his 7-year stay, and he will be largely credited with reviving the act's fortunes.

78 **June** Always looking to collaborate his songwriting skills (including efforts with Kenny Loggins, Michael Johnson, Brenda Russell and others), McDonald co-writes, via the US mail service, *You Belong To Me* with and for Carly Simon, which will hit US #6.

79 **Aug** He provides vocal assistance on Christopher Cross' successful debut album, particularly prominent on hit *Ride Like The Wind*.
[4] McDonald joins Jackson Browne, Emmylou Harris, Nicolette Larson, Bonnie Raitt, Linda Ronstadt and members of Little Feat in a benefit concert in aid of Lowell George's widow at the Forum, Los Angeles. The 20,000 crowd raises over $230,000.

80 **Jan** His first non-band success is a duet with Nicolette Larson on his *Let Me Go Love*. It reaches US #35.
He cuts original track *If You Remember Me* for Jon Voight/Faye Dunaway-starring movie *The Champ*, which will later be a hit for Chris Thompson.
Oct McDonald co-produces, with Patrick Henderson, debut album for his wife, Amy Holland.

82 **Mar** Arista album *That Was Then – The Early Recordings Of Michael McDonald* is released. Collecting material from his days at Bell, it features 7 previously released cuts and rough versions of 4 unreleased tracks including a cover of The Allman Brothers *Midnight Rider*.
[31] The Doobie Brothers announce they are splitting. (McDonald will immediately sign a deal with Warner Bros. and resume his solo career.)
Aug *I Keep Forgettin' (Every Time You're Near)* is released as first Warner single. It will hit US #4 and remain his biggest solo success. (He will later be sued by Leiber and Stoller for "using" their Chuck Jackson hit *I Keep Forgettin'* – he loses the case and future royalties will be split as Leiber/Stoller/McDonald/Sanford.) Debut album *If That's What It Takes* is released simultaneously. It begins a 32-week chart stay and will hit US #6. Produced by Ted Templeman and Lenny Waronker, it features many guest session players including members of Toto and Steve Gadd, Greg Phillinganes, Willie Weeks, Kenny Loggins and Lenny Castro.
Nov McDonald joins an all-star chorus on Quincy Jones-created Donna Summer hit *State Of Independence*.
Dec From his album, *I Gotta Try* makes US #44. This year's Kenny Loggins album *High Adventure* features strong songwriting and vocal contributions from McDonald, particularly the hit *Heart To Heart*.

83 Spending much of the year composing and collaborating, McDonald writes and produces a second Amy Holland album, *On Your Every Word*, for Capitol.
May McDonald joins Chris Thompson to help ex-Doobie Brother Patrick Simmons revive The Chi-Lites' *Have You Seen Her* on his solo debut album *Arcade*.

84 **Feb** A duet with James Ingram for his debut album is the inspirational *Yah Mo B There* which peaks at US #19 and makes UK #44 (it re-enters in Apr. at UK #69).

85 **Jan** "Jellybean" Benitez' remix of *Yah Mo B There* makes UK #12.
Feb [26] McDonald and Ingram win Best R&B Performance By A Duo Or Group With Vocal for *Yah Mo Be There* at the 27th annual Grammy awards.
July *No Lookin' Back* is released and will make US #34.
Sept Parent album *No Lookin' Back* begins a 4-month US chart stay where it peaks at #45 (but will fail in UK). Produced by McDonald and Templeman, it features a similar session line-up to first Warner album. *Our Love*, featured in Richard Gere/Kim Basinger movie *No Mercy*, is released as a single.

86 **June** [14] His duet with Patti LaBelle, Bacharach/Sager-penned ballad *On My Own* hits US #1. It is included on LaBelle's *The Winner In You*, for which she cut her vocal track in Philadelphia, PA, and sent the tape to McDonald to add vocals in Los Angeles. They have yet to meet and even tape the promotional video on opposite coasts. It also hits UK #2, though UK #1 on the airplay integrated Network Chart survey.
July UK re-issue *I Keep Forgettin'* climbs to UK #43.
Aug [30] Released on MCA for film soundtrack *Running Scared*, starring Billy Crystal and Gregory Hines, *Sweet Freedom*, penned by Rod Temperton, hits US #7.
Sept *Sweet Freedom* peaks at UK #12, prompting a UK promotional visit including a BBC TV "Top Of The Pops" appearance. McDonald

also links with James Ingram again as they join ex-Ambrosia front man David Pack on his *I Can't Let Go* for Pack's Warner album *Anywhere You Go*.
Nov McDonald sings on Toto's US #11 hit *I'll Be Over You*.
Dec UK-only compilation album *Sweet Freedom* hits UK #6, staying on chart for over 6 months. A premature greatest hits package, it features The Doobie Brothers' *What A Fool Believes*, plus specially licensed *On My Own* and *Sweet Freedom*, from MCA, and *Yah Mo B There*, from Qwest.

1987 McDonald shares lead vocals on gospel group The Winans' *Decisions* album cut *Love Has No Color*.
Apr McDonald visits UK for sell-out dates, including 2 nights at London's Hammersmith Odean, where he is joined by UK singer Jaki Graham for *On My Own* (prompting McDonald to provide her with a song for her next album) and encores with soul classic *When A Man Loves A Woman*.
[15] *Sweet freedom* wins Best Film Theme Or Song at the annual Ivor Novello Awards lunch.
Dec [29] McDonald becomes father to son Dylan Michael.

1988 **Aug** McDonald appears again on a Christopher Cross album *Back Of My Mind*.
Nov [12-13] McDonald returns to UK for 2 live concerts in preparation for a third Warner album and major touring activity in 1989.

1989 **May** McDonald contributes *For Your Precious Love* to Richard Perry-produced *Rock, Rhythm & Blues* compilation.

1990 **Feb** [24] McDonald participates in the "Roy Orbison All-Star Benefit Tribute" at the Universal Amphitheater, Universal City, CA, alongside Bonnie Raitt, Bob Dylan and many others, raising $500,000 for the Shelter Partnership and The National Coalition For The Homeless.
May [26] *Take It To Heart*, featuring David Lasley, Don Was, Jeff Porcaro and Abraham Laboriel among others, reaches UK #35, though all extracted singles fail to make UK survey.
June [9] *Take It To Heart*, the title cut from new album, co-written with Diane Warren, stalls at US #98.
[21] McDonald undertakes a world tour which begins in North America. His live band includes Bernie Chiaravalle (lead guitar, vocals), Charles Frichter (bass, vocals) Chuck Sabatino (keyboards, vocals), Tim Heintz (keyboards), George Perilli (drums) and Vince Denham (saxophone).
July [11] Tour reaches UK, including some dates as special guest on Tina Turner's farewell trek.
[14] *Take It To Heart* peaks at US #110.
Aug [4] Tour returns to US until month's end.
Sept [23] McDonald begins a week of concerts in Japan.

1991 **Mar** [1-2] McDonald performs at the second "Rock'N'Soul Revue" at The Beacon theater, New York, alongside organizer Donald Fagen, Boz Scaggs, Patti Austin and others.
[9] The Peace Choir's *Give Peace A Chance*, to which McDonald contributes vocal support, makes US #54.

DON McLEAN

1961 McLean (b. Oct.2, 1945, New Rochelle, NY), an asthmatic child who has been interested in music from an early age, decides to pursue a career in music after the death of his father.

1963 Having performed at concerts while at high school and as a student at Villanova university (where he has played with Jim Croce), he starts performing in clubs around New York, Baltimore, MD, Philadelphia, PA, and Canada, and meets and works with Lee Hays, Brownie McGhee and Josh White.

1968 McLean makes Saratoga Springs, NY's Café Lena his base, and through the club's owner, Lena Spencer, he is appointed "The Hudson River Troubadour" by the New York State Council on the Arts. He plays in 50 river communities, 3 times a day for a month, earning $200 a week.

1969 Having heard about McLean hitch-hiking from Mount Marcy in the Adirionacks to Riverside Park on 125th St., New York, giving impromptu concerts on the way, Pete Seeger invites him to join an expedition to sail the Hudson River, to tell people living on the waterway about the dangers of industrial pollution. The sloop, Clearwater, with McLean as a crew member and part of The Sloop Singers, sails from South Bristol, ME, to New York in 6 weeks, singing 25 concerts. A TV special, "The Sloop At Nyack", chronicling the trip, airs on US NET's "Sounds Of Summer" series.

1970 McLean spends 6 weeks singing in elementary schools in Massachusetts. While staying at Mrs. Sedgewich's lodging house, McLean reads a book about painter Vincent Van Gogh and, inspired by the subject, writes *Vincent*, 1 of only 6 songs penned during the year. Debut album *Tapestry*, rejected by 34 labels, is released on Mediarts label. Produced by The Youngbloods' Jerry Corbitt, and dedicated to The Weavers, it does not chart.

1971 United Artists releases title track from forthcoming *American Pie*, an 8-min. 36-sec. track divided into 2 parts. The single, against all conventions, picks up airplay across US. (At the end of the year, radio station W-ABC in New York names it the most-played record of 1971.)

1972 **Jan** *American Pie* tops US chart, as album of same title, dedicated to Buddy Holly, hits US #1 for 7 weeks.
Mar *Vincent*, coupled with *Castles In The Air*, reaches US #12 and McLean's first album *Tapestry* belatedly makes US #111. *American Pie* hits UK #2, kept from the top by Chicory Tip's *Son Of My Father*. *American Pie* hits UK #3.
June *Vincent*, played daily at the Van Gogh Museum in Amsterdam, Holland, tops UK chart for 2 weeks. Performing at the Troubadour in Los Angeles, McLean is seen by singer Lori Lieberman. Inspired by his performance, she asks her writers/producers Charles Fox and Norman Gimbel to write a song about him. They write *Killing Me Softly With His Song*, which she records for her debut album *Lori Lieberman*. (It is later a big hit for Roberta Flack.)
July *Tapestry* reaches UK #16 as McLean begins a UK tour.

1973 **Feb** *Dreidel* makes US #21 as parent *Don McLean* reaches US #23.
Apr A revival of Buddy Holly's *Everyday*, from forthcoming *Playin' Favorites*, makes UK #38.
May *If We Try*, from *Don McLean*, stalls at US #58.
June Perry Como makes US #29 with McLean ballad *And I Love You So*, having hit UK #3 in May.
Nov *Playin' Favorites*, a collection of non-originals fails to chart in US but makes UK #42. From it, *Mountains O' Mourne* tops chart in Eire.

1974 **Dec** *Homeless Brother*, produced by Joel Dorn with top New York session musicians, Richard Tee, Hugh McCracken, David Spinozza and Willie Weeks, makes US #120. McLean covers George Harrison's *Sunshine Life For Me (Sail Away Raymond)* and *Crying In The Chapel*, a US #3 in 1965 for Elvis Presley, with vocals from The Persuasions.

1975 **June** *Wonderful Baby*, later recorded by Fred Astaire, makes US #93.

1976 **Sept** *Solo*, a live double album recorded on his earlier UK tour, including a free concert in London's Hyde Park attended by 85,000 people, is released.

1977 **Apr** *The Pattern Is Broken*, from new album *Prime Time*, is featured in film "Fraternity Row".

1978 **June** [26] Signed to Millennium Records, McLean begins work on new album at the Jack Clement recording studio, Nashville, TN.

1980 **June** *Crying*, reviving Roy Orbison's 1961 US #2, tops UK chart for 3 weeks. Parent album *Chain Lightning* makes UK #19. Both disks are on EMI International in UK.
Sept *The Very Best Of Don McLean* hits UK #4, as McLean tours extensively in UK.

1981 **Mar** *Crying* hits US #5. *Chain Lightning* reaches US #28.
May *Since I Don't Have You*, reviving The Skyliners' 1959 US #12, reaches US #23.
Aug *It's Just The Sun* stalls at US #83.
Dec *Castles In The Air*, a new recording of his 1972 hit, makes US #36.

1982 **Jan** *Believers*, dedicated to The Weavers' Lee Hays, who died in Aug.1981 after a long battle with diabetes, peaks at US #156.
May *Castles In The Air* makes UK #47.

1984 **Jan** Video "The Music Of Don McLean", featuring McLean in concert and being interviewed by DJ Paul Gambaccini, is released.
Apr [18] McLean begins a UK tour in Cardiff, Wales. (It will end at the Royal Festival Hall in London on May 12.)

1987 **Apr** EMI America releases *Don McLean's Greatest Hits – Then And Now*, coupling 5 McLean hits with 5 new tracks recorded in New York and Berkeley, CA, with producer Dave Burgess (ex-member of The Champs), who is now acting as McLean's manager. Extracted *He's Got You* makes #73 on US Country chart.
Nov McLean concludes another sell-out UK tour at London's Royal Festival Hall. (McLean will have toured UK almost every other year since his first visit in 1972.)
Dec *You Can't Blame The Train*, from forthcoming *Love Tracks*, reaches US C&W #49.

1988 Now firmly settled in the country field, McLean, signed to Capitol Records, releases *Love Tracks*, recorded at Nightingale studios, Nashville, TN, which unusually for the artist features new songs by outside writers.

1990 Now signed to Gold Castle, and having released *For The Memories Volumes 1 & 2* which features standards from the 30s, 40s and 50s,

McLean's *Greatest Hits Live!*, recorded at London's Dominion theater during his autumn 1980 UK tour, is released. (Although McLean no longer remains a big album-seller, he remains a major attraction on the live circuit.)

MEAT LOAF

1961 Born to a gospel-singing family, Marvin Lee Aday (b. Sept.27, 1948, Dallas, TX) steps on the foot of his high school football coach, who gives him the nickname Meat Loaf.

1967 Having left his home in Dallas for Los Angeles, CA, Meat Loaf builds reputation with Los Angeles band Meat Loaf Soul, now Popcorn Blizzard, which stays together for 3 years, opening for acts including The Who, Ted Nugent, Iggy Pop and Johnny & Edgar Winter.

1969 Living in a communal home in Echo Park, Los Angeles, he applies for job as a parking-lot attendant at the Aquarius theater, when he meets an actor appearing in musical "Hair". Auditioning at the actor's suggestion, he is cast as Ulysses S. Grant in Los Angeles production.

1970 **June** Production opens at the Vest Pocket theater, Detroit, MI. Playing Sheila in the show is female singer Stoney, with whom Meat Loaf will record 1 album for Rare Earth, and tour with Alice Cooper and labelmates Rare Earth. The duo splits shortly after (Stoney later joins Bob Seger's band as backing singer).

1971 **Mar** Meat Loaf rejoins the road tour of "Hair" at the Hanna theater, Cleveland, OH.
June While still with the show, Meat Loaf makes his US chart debut (with Stoney) as *What You See Is What You Get* reaches US #71.
Sept He has moved to New York with "Hair", when the show closes.

1972 **Dec** Meat Loaf is cast as Buddha in musical "Rainbow".

1974 **Jan** "More Than You Deserve", a musical written by Jim Steinman, opens off Broadway, with Meat Loaf in the roles of Perrine and Rabbit (Steinman, a New Yorker raised in California, is in high school band, Clitoris That Thought It Was A Puppy, when he writes play "Dream Engine" which impresses New York producer Joseph Papp. Steinman relocates to New York to work frequently with Papp.)

1975 **Mar** Meat Loaf opens at Belasco theater on Broadway in Richard O'Brien's "The Rocky Horror Show" as Eddie and Dr. Scott. (He will recreate the role for film "The Rocky Horror Picture Show".) Meat Loaf and Steinman tour US with the "National Lampoon Road Show".

1976 **Feb** Meat Loaf plays the priest in "Rockabye Hamlet", a musical version of "Hamlet", at New York's Minskoff theater.
Aug He sings on Ted Nugent's *Free For All*.

1977 **Jan** Steinman and Meat Loaf start rehearsing at the Ansonia hotel, New York, on songs Steinman has written for musical "Neverland", a futuristic version of "Peter Pan", which has recently been presented at Washington's Kennedy Center.
After extensive rehearsal, they sign a deal with RCA Records, but pull out when label refuses to include producer Todd Rundgren as part of the package. Bearsville Records funds the project for a period, as does Rundgren, before Warner Bros. steps in and agrees to release the album, but with limited promotion. Meat Loaf, Steinman and Rundgren reject the offer. In desperation, manager David Sonenberg plays the tapes to fledgling Cleveland International company, which persuades Epic to release the project. Meat Loaf performs at the CBS Records convention in New Orleans, LA. (His appearance will result in CBS commissioning promo films for tracks *Bat Out Of Hell*, *Paradise By The Dashboard Lights* and *You Took The Words Right Out Of My Mouth*.)
Oct *Bat Out Of Hell* is released in US and makes #14 during an 88-week chart stay.

1978 **Jan** *Bat Out Of Hell* is released in UK. Sales soar after a promo video clip of title track is shown on BBC TV's "The Old Grey Whistle Test". The album will hit UK #9, selling over 2 million copies during a record 395 weeks on chart.
June *You Took The Words Right Out Of My Mouth* makes UK #33.
July Meat Loaf tours Australia, where *Bat Out Of Hell* knocks *Saturday Night Fever* off the top of the chart. *Two Out Of Three Ain't Bad* reaches US #11.
Aug *Two Out Of Three Ain't Bad* makes UK #32.
Sept *Paradise By The Dashboard Lights*, with Ellen Foley on female vocals and Phil Rizzuto as the baseball announcer, peaks at US #39.
Oct Meat Loaf ends his North American tour in Cleveland, OH, his 170th date in under a year as the album goes platinum. (In Toronto, an over-exuberant Meat Loaf falls off stage and tears ligaments in his leg, leaving him in a wheelchair for a month.)

1979 **Jan** *You Took The Words Right Out Of My Mouth* makes US #39.
Feb *Bat Out Of Hell* reaches UK #15.

June [13] Film "Roadie", in which Meat Loaf stars with Blondie's Debbie Harry, premieres in US.

Aug [15] Meat Loaf's second film of the year, "Americathon", premieres in Los Angeles.

1 **May** Intended as follow-up to *Bat Out Of Hell*, Steinman releases solo album *Bad For Good*, having tired of waiting for Meat Loaf, who has had vocal chord problems brought about through too much touring, to lay down vocal tracks. It reaches US #63 and hits UK #7.

Sept Meat Loaf's second album *Deadringer*, with all songs written by Steinman, enters UK chart and spends 2 weeks at #1. It reaches US #45. Extracted *I'm Gonna Love Her For Both Of Us* makes US #84 and UK #62.

2 **Feb** *Dead Ringer For Love*, a duet with Cher, hits UK #5, helped by a duo video. Meat Loaf begins a major tour.

3 **Mar** Now pursued by other acts, Steinman writes and produces Bonnie Tyler's UK #1 *Total Eclipse Of The Heart*.

May Meat Loaf's *Midnight At The Lost And Found*, produced by Tom Dowd without Steinman, hits UK #7, as extracted *If You Really Want To* peaks at UK #59.

Oct *Midnight At The Lost And Found* reaches UK #17. *Total Eclipse Of The Heart* hits US #1.

4 **Jan** *Razor's Edge* makes UK #41.

Meat Loaf appears on TV's "Rebellious Jukebox" with Jools Holland.

Oct *Modern Girl*, Meat Loaf's first for new label Arista, reaches UK #17.

Nov *Bad Attitude*, with Roger Daltrey guesting, hits UK #8, as Meat Loaf begins a tour.

5 **Jan** *Nowhere Fast* peaks at UK #67. Epic's compilation *Hits Out Of Hell* hits UK #2, as a simultaneous video package also sells.

Apr *Piece Of The Action* peaks at UK #47.

6 **July** Meat Loaf appears as Gil in film "Out Of Bounds".

Sept *Rock'N'Roll Mercenaries*, a duet with John Parr, reaches UK #31.

Oct *Blind Before I Stop*, recorded in Rosbach, Germany, with producer Frank Farian, reaches UK #28.

7 **June** Increasingly a UK TV media favorite, Meat Loaf plays for the Duchess of York's team in the fund-raising "The Grand Knockout Tournament" at Alton Towers, Alton, Staffs.

Nov *Live At Wembley* makes UK #60, as his Arista contract expires.

0 **Jan** Meat Loaf begins public Ultra Slim-Fast diet.

OHN COUGAR MELLENCAMP

2 Mellencamp (b. Oct.7, 1951, Seymour, IN), second of 5 children of an electrical engineer and a Miss Indiana runner-up, born with a tumor in his neck which doctors remove with 2 vertebrae (resulting in a 4-F draft deferment), joins his first band in fifth grade, miming to current hits.

5 He links with his first live band, Crepe Soul, and performs with them for 18 months.

6 He joins Snakepit Banana Barn, playing fraternities for $30 a weekend.

7 He is sacked by the band because they claim he cannot sing, and he buys his first acoustic guitar.

0 Having graduated from Seymour high school, Mellencamp leaves the family home, moving to an apartment in the small town of Valonia. He marries and becomes a father, finds work as a carpenter's helper, while his wife Priscilla works as a telephone operator.

1 He forms glitter-rock group Trash, with guitarist friend Larry Crane, covering mainly 60s hits.

5 After graduating from Vincennes University, Mellencamp (now separated from his wife and child) works for a telephone company, before being laid off. With a year's severance pay, he sets out for New York with a demo he has made of Paul Revere & The Raiders' *Kicks*. An admirer of David Bowie, Mellencamp calls his management company, MainMan. He meets Tony De Fries, who offers to record him and arranges a deal with MCA Records.

6 Mellencamp records his first album *Chestnut Street Incident*, mainly comprising cover versions. When it is released, still in demo form, Mellencamp discovers that De Fries has re-named him Johnny Cougar, and he has to participate in De Fries-inspired "Johnny Cougar Day", driving through hometown Seymour, in an open-top car motorcade.

7 Parting company with MainMan, he moves to Bloomington, IN, where he rehearses self-written material with his newly-formed band, The Zone, records demos for Gulcher label and cuts a second album, *The Kid Inside*. He meets Billy Gaff, president of Riva Records and manager of Rod Stewart, who signs him to the label.

8 **Mar** *A Biography*, not released in US, is issued in UK, as Mellencamp begins a UK tour, heralded by Gaff as the next Springsteen. Despite a massive publicity campaign (posters spring up bearing the legend "Cougar" and little else), the disk and promotion fail.

1979 **Aug** *John Cougar* featuring some material from *A Biography*, makes US #64.

Dec *I Need A Lover* reaches US #28.

1980 **Feb** *Small Paradise* stalls at US #87. After nearly 3 years on the road, Mellencamp returns to the studio to cut a new album.

Oct *Nothing' Matters And What If It Did*, produced by Steve Cropper, reaches US #37.

Dec *This Time* makes US #27.

1981 **May** *Ain't Even Done With The Night* reaches US #17.

1982 Mellencamp, now divorced, remarries. He begins a major US tour with his own band, comprising Larry Crane, Mike Wanchic (guitar), Toby Meyers (bass) and Kenny Aronoff (drums), supporting Heart before headlining later in the year.

July [3] He gives a free concert for 20,000 high school students in Fort Wayne, IN, who had sandbagged for 8 days in Mar.1982, during the state's worst flood crisis.

Aug *Hurts So Good* hits US #2 for 4 weeks and is a million-seller, kept off the top by Human League's *Don't You Want Me*.

Sept [11] As *American Fool* tops US chart, *Jack And Diane* moves up to US #4 and *Hurts So Good* falls to US #8, Mellencamp becomes the only male artist to have 2 US Top 10 hits and a #1 album simultaneously. *American Fool* stays at US #1 for 9 weeks, achieving platinum sales.

Oct Mellencamp-penned *Jack And Diane* hits US #1 for 4 weeks.

Nov *Jack And Diane* reaches UK #25, while *American Fool* makes UK #37. (It becomes the biggest-selling album of the year in US, selling over 3 million copies.)

1983 **Jan** *Hand To Hold On To* hits US #9. Mellencamp cancels an appearance at the US Festival, after promoters insist on all video rights to his performance.

Oct *Crumblin' Down* hits US #9 as he changes his name to John Cougar Mellencamp. *Uh-huh* hits US #9 and is his second platinum-seller.

1984 **Feb** *Pink Houses* hits US #8.

Mar *Uh-huh* peaks at US #92.

May *Authority Song* reaches US #15.

July Susan Miles wins MTV "Party House With Mellencamp" competition. She paints her house pink. He writes screenplay "Ridin' The Cage" in which Warner Bros. shows interest. He also produces Mitch Ryder's comeback album *Never Kick A Sleeping Dog*.

1985 **Mar** Mellencamp produces *Colored Lights* for The Blasters' *Hard Line*.

July [13] Mellencamp turns down the opportunity to participate in Live Aid, stating "concerts that just raise money aren't a good idea".

Sept [22] He organizes Farm Aid with Willie Nelson and Neil Young, held in Champaign, IL. (During the show he asks the audience to write to their congressmen demanding action to help American farmers.)

Oct *Lonely Ol' Night* hits US #6.

Nov Recorded in his newly-built studio, *Scarecrow*, dedicated to his grandfather Speck, hits US #2.

Dec Home-themed *Small Town* hits US #6.

[6] At a concert in New York's Madison Square Garden, the sound system breaks down twice. Mellencamp waits patiently for the problem to be resolved. When he returns to the stage, he plays for 2 hours and tells the audience that anyone with a ticket stub can get their money back if they so wish.

1986 **Feb** *Small Town* makes UK #53.

Apr [5] *R.O.C.K. In The USA* hits US #2.

May *R.O.C.K. In The USA* peaks at UK #67.

June [14] *Rain On The Scarecrow* makes US #21.

July [14] Mellencamp participates in Farm Aid II at Manor Downs, Austin, TX.

Aug [16] *Rumbleseat* makes US #28.

Sept Mellencamp and his band start work with producer Don Gehman on a new album at Belmont Hall studio, IN.

1987 **Sept** [19] Mellencamp participates in Farm Aid III at University of Nebraska's Memorial Stadium with Neil Young, Joe Walsh, Lou Reed and others.

Oct [3] *Paper In Fire*, his first release on Mercury and in part inspired by the film "Hud", as are other songs of his, hits US #9 as parent album *The Lonesome Jubilee* hits US #6 and UK #31.

[30] Mellencamp begins a 6-week US tour in Terre Haute, IN, set to end on Dec.15.

Dec He contributes *Run Rudolph Run* to the Various Artists' *Special Olympics* charity album *A Very Special Christmas*.

[16] Mellencamp performs 2 free concerts for the people of Chilicothe, OH, after local radio station WFBC has initiated a petition.

1988 **Jan** [9] *Cherry Bomb* hits US #8.

[25-26] Mellencamp returns to UK to play 2 concerts at London's Hammersmith Odeon.

Apr *Check It Out* reaches US #14.

May [26] He opens a US tour at Irvine Meadows, Los Angeles, CA, set to end July in Milwaukee, WI.

June *Rooty Toot Toot* peaks at US #61.

Aug [13] Mellencamp appears with Paul Simon on NBC TV's "Coca Cola Presents Live: The Hard Rock".

[14] Mellencamp becomes a grandfather at 37 when his 18-year-old daughter from his marriage to Priscilla, Michelle gives birth to Elexis Suzanne Peach.

[18] Wife Victoria files for divorce in Monroe Superior Court after 8 years of marriage and seeks custody of their 2 children.

Sept Mellencamp contributes *Do Re Mi* to Woody Guthrie/Leadbelly tribute album *Folkways: A Vision Shared*.

Mellencamp produces *Too Long In The Wasteland* the debut album from James McMurtry (son of **The Last Picture Show** author Larry McMurtry).

Nov He directs video for Dylan's *Political World* in Bloomington, IN.

1989 **May** *Big Daddy* reaches US #25.

June [17] Anti-fame single *Pop Singer* reaches US #15, aided by appropriately disdainful video clip.

July *Big Daddy* hits US #7.

Aug [12] *Jackie Brown* makes US #48.

1990 **July** Mellencamp begins filming for his screen debut as a singer returning home to celebrate his grandfather's 84th birthday in rural Indianapolis in "Souvenirs". He records the soundtrack album with John Prine, Dwight Yoakam, Joe Ely and James McMurtry.

1991 **Mar** After a 2-year recording hiatus, Mellencamp returns to the studio with his current band Toby Myers, John Kascella, David Griffom, Mike Wanchic and Kenny Aronoff, having completed the movie project "Falling From Grace".

MEN AT WORK

Colin Hay (vocals)
Ron Strykert (guitar)
Greg Ham (sax, keyboards, flute)
John Rees (bass)
Jerry Speiser (drums)

1979 Band forms in Melbourne, Australia, after Hay (b. June 29, 1953, Scotland, but emigrated at age 14 with his parents to Australia) and Strykert (b. Aug.18, 1957, Australia), who have met while performing in musical "Heroes" in Sydney, decide to form an acoustic duo. They are joined first by Rees and then by Hay's old friends from Melbourne's La Troube university, Speiser and Ham (b. Sept.27, 1953, Australia).

1980 They work regularly as the house band at the Cricketer's Arms, a Richmond, Melbourne pub, where they are noted by customer Peter Karpin, who works for CBS Records' Australian office. Through his persistence, CBS signs them.

1982 Debut single *Who Can It Be Now?* (written by Hay, as will be all the subsequent hit singles) and *Business As Usual* are produced by Peter Mclan, an American. Both top the Australian charts (the album for 10 weeks, beating a record established by Split Enz' *True Colours*) and Men At Work becomes the highest-paid band in Australia.

Oct Following a US tour supporting Fleetwood Mac, *Who Can It Be Now?*, with its promo video getting saturation MTV play, tops US chart for a week and is a million-seller.

Nov *Business As Usual* also tops US chart, and sells over 4 million copies in US to rank quadruple platinum. It holds #1 for 15 weeks (beating the record of 12 weeks for a debut album, established by The Monkees in 1967), before surrendering to Michael Jackson's *Thriller*. Group begins a 50-date headlining US tour, supported by fellow Australians Mental As Anything. Meanwhile UK debut is *Who Can It Be Now?* which makes UK #45.

1983 **Jan** *Business As Usual* hits UK #1 for 6 weeks. Extracted *Down Under* (another Australian #1 during 1982) tops both US and UK charts, for 4 and 3 weeks respectively. For 2 weeks, the group has both best-selling single and album in US and UK simultaneously - a feat previously achieved by only a few, including The Beatles, Rod Stewart and Simon & Garfunkel. *Down Under* is a second US million-selling single.

Feb [23] Men At Work wins Best New Artist at the 25th annual Grammy awards.

May *Cargo*, originally cut the previous summer but held over because of the success of its predecessor, hits US #3 (a second platinum album) and UK #8, while *Overkill*, taken from it, makes UK #21.

[28] Group appears on first day of the 3-day "US '83 Festival" in San Bernardino, CA. They co-headline the day's bill with The Clash and The Stray Cats.

June *Overkill* hits US #3.

July Also extracted from the second album, anti-war themed *It's A Mistake* makes UK #33.

Aug *It's A Mistake* is their fourth consecutive US Top 10 hit at #6.

Oct *Dr. Heckyll And Mr. Jive*, third single from *Cargo*, reaches US #28 and UK #31 (and is the group's last UK chart entry).

1984 Rees and Speiser leave the group and are not replaced; session men take the bass and drum roles for the band's third album.

1985 **June** After a lengthy period with no releases, the group makes US #4 with Hay's *Everything I Need*.

July *Two Hearts*, containing the hit single, earns a US gold disk, reaching US #50.

Nov Group, with Hay (the only original member remaining), James Black, ex-Mondo Rock, Colin Bayley, ex-Mi-Sex, Jeremy Alsop and Chad Whackerman, tours Japan and also performs 3 concerts in China. Soon after, Men At Work will split.

1987 **Mar** Recorded in London with producer Robin Millar, Hay's solo album *Looking For Jack*, released under the name Colin James Hay, reaches US #126.

[7] Extracted *Hold Me* reaches US #99.

1990 **Feb** Hay returns with the Colin Hay Band and album *Wayfaring Son* on MCA.

METALLICA

James Hetfield (vocals, guitar)
Kirk Hammett (guitar)
Jason Newsted (bass)
Lars Ulrich (drums)

1981 **July** Having left his family in Los Angeles, CA, where they have emigrated in Aug.1980 from Denmark and encouraged him to become a professional tennis player, Ulrich goes to London and tours UK with New Wave British Heavy Metal outfit Diamond Head (Ulrich has already been instrumental in compiling the various artists album *The New Wave Of British Heavy Metal* with **Kerrang!** magazine editor Geoff Barton in 1979, a movement which will influence a whole generation of hard rockers.

Oct Ulrich returns to US and determines to form a band to record a track offered him by Metal Blade label owner Brian Slagel on a forthcoming compilation *Metal Massacre*. From a Los Angeles magazine ad, Ulrich recruits Hetfield (ex-Obsession and Leather Charm) and records *Hit The Lights* with lead guitarist Lloyd grant. They will re-record the same cut for a Canadian release of the album with Dave Mustaine on lead and Ron McGovney on bass.

1982 Following the recording of a 7-track demo *No Life Till Leather*, McGovney quits and is replaced by Cliff Burton, who Ulrich spends 4 months trying to persuade to leave his existing band, Trauma, who are based in San Francisco, CA, to where Metallica now relocates.

1983 **Mar** At the instigation of Megaforce label boss John Zazula, who offers the group a management and record deal, Metallica, now moves to New Jersey, living in Jamaica Queens, New York.

Apr Mustaine leaves the band (and will cut debut solo album *Killing Is My Business ... And Business Is Good*) and is replaced by Hammett (ex-Exodus), who has played with mentor Joe Satriani.

May Group begins recording debut album *Kill 'Em All* (working title *Metal Up Your Ass*), which is licensed, with great cult interest in UK, to fledgling independent heavy metal label, Music For Nations. It is produced by Paul Curcio at Music America studios, and supported by a short UK tour with Raven.

1984 **Aug** Second album *Ride The Lightning* is released on Megaforce in US but picked up by Elektra 3 months later, a result of moves by the major label's A&R man Michael Alago. Its reviews, particularly in UK, confirm Metallica as the pioneering force in the "thrash/speed" metal movement. Group signs with Peter Mensch and Cliff Burnstein of management team Q-Prime, which handles Def Leppard. The album sells a half million copies before the end of the year and reaches US #100. Still on Music For Nations in Europe, it reaches UK #87.

1985 **Aug** [17] Metallica performs at the annual Monsters Of Rock heavy metal festival at Castle Donington, Leics.

1986 **Mar** *Master Of Puppets* is released and climbs to US #29 and UK #41, despite no hit singles, while the group spends 6 months as guests on Ozzy Osbourne's US tour. Unusually for a metal band in the age of MTV, they achieve all this without the aid of a promo video. The tour only hitch comes when Hetfield breaks his wrist skateboarding (a favored band activity). Roadie James Marshall deputizes.

Apr With touring reviving sales interest in the earlier albums, *Kill 'Em All* makes US #155.

Sept Metallica begins a European tour with successful UK dates. [27] Between Scandinavian dates, the tour bus leaves the road, killing Burton instantly. No one else is seriously injured. (Band returns to California and attends Burton's funeral in San Francisco.)

Nov Group tours Japan and US, with new bass player Jason Newsted (b. Battle Creek, MI), from Phoenix-based Flotsam And Jetsam.

87 **Jan** Metallica returns to Europe to complete the postponed tour.

Feb [13] "Master Of Puppets" world tour finally ends in Gothenburg, Sweden.

Mar Group enters an expensive Marin County, CA, rehearsal studio to demo material for a new album. Unaccustomed to the plush environment, the band elects to play outside the studio, instead of inside, and Hetfield breaks his arm, again skateboarding in an empty pool. Group leaves the studio and decides to soundproof Ulrich's home garage in San Francisco. When Hetfield is fit to play, rather than writing songs, they work on covers of their favorite UK metal bands.

July Band moves into Ulrich's garage and cut 5 tracks in 6 days, covering band favorites Budgie, Diamondhead, Killing Joke and The Misfits. Released as *The $5.98 EP – Garage Days Revisited*, it reaches UK #27, on the singles chart, the first fruit of the band's new UK deal with rock-oriented Vertigo label.

Aug [22] Metallica returns to perform at the Monsters Of Rock festival at Castle Donington. After 2 more Monsters Of Rock dates at German festivals it returns to Ulrich's garage to work on a new album.

Oct *The $5.98 EP – Garage Days Revisited* makes US #28 on album chart.

88 **May** Metallica joins Van Halen, The Scorpions and others as part of a further Monsters Of Rock package tour in US and Europe. (They also play 2 warm-up gigs at the Troubadour club, Los Angeles, under the pseudonym Frayed Ends.)

Sept [3] *Harvester Of Sorrow* enters the UK chart at #20, but drops 12 places the following week.

[17] *... And Justice For All* released simultaneously in US and UK precedes a headlining US tour scheduled to begin mid-Nov. The album hits UK #4 immediately, but will rise to hit US #6 in a 1-year chart residence.

89 **Feb** [22] Metallica performs *One* at the 31st annual Grammy awards at the Shrine Auditorium, Los Angeles, though Jethro Tull will win the Best Hard Rock/Heavy Metal category.

Apr *One* debuts at UK #13 peak, and will make US #35. Band embarks on major "Damaged Justice Tour" of North America.

90 **Feb** [21] Metallica wins Best Metal Performance for *One* at the 32nd annual Grammy awards at the Shrine Auditorium.

May [19] Vertigo releases 6 12" singles of early Metallica material under the collective album title *The Good, The Band And The Live*, which peaks at UK #56.

Nov [3] *Rubáiyát*, Elektra's 40th anniversary compilation, to which Metallica contributes a cover of *Stone Cold Crazy*, makes US #140.

91 **Feb** [20] Metallica wins Best Metal Performance (Vocal Or Instrumental) for *Stone Cold Crazy* from *Rubáiyát* at the 33rd annual Grammy awards at Radio City Music Hall, New York.

June Metallica's fifth album, produced by Bob Rock, is scheduled for release.

EORGE MICHAEL

75 Michael (b. Georgios Kyriacou Panayiotou, June 25, 1963, Finchley, London) meets Andrew Ridgeley at Bushey Meads comprehensive school, Herts.

79 Michael and Ridgeley form their first band, The Executive, with other friends.

81 Michael begins serious songwriting and co-pens, with Ridgeley, future hits including *Careless Whisper*. Supporting themselves with casual jobs, they form Wham! (which will become the most successful UK pop band of the 80s).

82 Michael, set to become the only songwriting force in the band in the next 4 years, signs a publishing contract with Morrison Leahy.

83 **Aug** As Wham!-mania grips Europe, Michael travels to Muscle Shoals studios in Alabama to record a solo version of *Careless Whisper* with Jerry Wexler producing. Sessions are instructive but unsuccessful and Michael returns to London to re-record it for later release.

84 **June** He flies to Miami, FL, to cut his first solo video for *Careless Whisper*.

July He produces and co-writes a single for friend David Austin, *Turn To Gold* which makes UK #68.

Aug *Careless Whisper* is released in UK as Michael's debut solo while Wham!'s popularity continues to rise. Ridgeley and Michael feel the ballad, strikingly opposed to Wham!'s fun uptempo style, will benefit as a solo release. It hits UK #1, selling over a million copies, and will become a worldwide radio favorite. Michael dedicates the song to his parents, to whom he will remain very close: "5 minutes in return for 21 years."

Dec Invited by Bob Geldof to sing on Band Aid's *Do They Know It's Christmas?*, Michael performs a lead vocal section.

1985 **Feb** [16] With Wham! at the peak of its success, the duo elects to release *Careless Whisper* in US credited to "Wham! featuring George Michael". It hits US #1 for 3 weeks.

Mar [13] Michael is named Songwriter Of The Year at the annual Ivor Novello awards at the Grosvenor House, Mayfair, London. Presented with the award by Elton John, which he accepts with great emotion, Michael becomes its youngest ever recipient.

May Increasingly independent musically from Ridgeley, Michael sings 2 duets with Smokey Robinson and Stevie Wonder at a Motown celebration in New York.

July [13] Michael sings lead vocals to Elton John's performance of *Don't Let The Sun Go Down On Me* at the Live Aid spectacular at Wembley Stadium, London.

Nov Continuing the association, Michael completes falsetto backing on John's hit *Nikita* and duets on *Wrap Her Up*, both for John's album *Ice On Fire*.

Dec Michael and Ridgeley decide to split Wham! in 1986, leaving both free to pursue solo directions.

[28] Michael features on 4 Top 20 records in UK Christmas chart: Wham!'s *I'm Your Man*, Wham!'s re-entered *Last Christmas*, Band Aid's re-entered *Do They Know It's Christmas?* and as backing vocalist on Elton John's still charting *Nikita*.

1986 **Feb** [28] Michael announces that Wham! will split in the summer.

Apr Second Michael solo single and another ballad, *A Different Corner*, chronicling Michael's current fragile emotional state, tops UK chart.

June [14] *A Different Corner* hits US #7.

[20] Michael performs at the fourth annual "Prince's Trust Rock Gala" at the Wembey Arena, London.

[28] Wham! plays "The Final" date at Wembley Stadium. (Following a rest, Michael will begin work on his debut solo album, recording in SARM studios, Notting Hill, London, and PUK studios, Denmark, and will sign with management team Michael Lippman and Rob Kahane.)

Sept Michael flies to US to record a duet with Aretha Franklin and film the accompanying video. The song will only appear on her new album.

1987 **Feb** Michael/Franklin *I Knew You Were Waiting (For Me)*, written by Simon Climie and Dennis Morgan and produced by Narada Michael Walden, appears on Arista (Franklin's label) in US and Epic (Michael's label) in UK. It hits both UK and US #1 [Apr 18].

June First post-Wham! Michael solo single, *I Want Your Sex*, is released ahead of debut album. Featured on soundtrack album *Beverly Hills Cop II* starring Eddie Murphy, the song causes protest particularly in UK where reactionary radio prohibits airplay in the AIDS era. US MTV re-edits the video 3 times before it is acceptable. Michael insists that the lyrics promote monogamous relationships and spells this out on the accompanying video which stars his current girlfriend, US make-up artist Kathy Jueng. Despite the radio ban, it hits UK #3.

July Speculation in UK will remain unconfirmed that Michael is at least a backing vocalist on a version, reportedly recorded by his cousin, of The Bee Gees *Jive Talkin'* released under the name Boogie Box High. It hits UK #7.

Aug [8] *I Want Your Sex*, with all instruments and vocals completed by Michael, hits US #2.

Oct The title cut from forthcoming album *Faith* hits UK #2.

Nov Debut solo album *Faith* is released. It is written, arranged and produced by Michael and features him on most instruments, though Wham! bassist Deon Estus remains as a Michael regular. It hits US #1 and UK #1 and will stay on US chart for over a year.

Dec [12] Benefitting from heavy US MTV rotation of the video, *Faith* hits US #1 for 4 weeks.

1988 **Jan** *Father Figure* hits UK #11 as Michael prepares for forthcoming live work. On discovering that his accountants are investing in US arms company, he instructs all stock to be sold.

[16] *Faith* tops US chart for 12 weeks.

Feb [8] Michael wins Best British Male Artist at the seventh annual BRIT Awards at the Royal Albert Hall, London.

[19] Michael opens a world "Faith" tour at Budokan, Tokyo, Japan, to a wildly enthusiastic reception.

[27] In only its seventh week on chart *Father Figure* hits US #1 as *Faith* holds for its fifth consecutive week on US Album list. Including Wham! hits, *Father Figure* becomes Michael's sixth US #1.

Mar During Australian dates, Michael unveils a giant white stage cage which opens and closes the show in dramatic fashion. He can only use the device at appropriate venues, including all US gigs (which are divided between spring and fall).

[2] Michael wins Best R&B Performance By A Duo Or Group With Vocal with Aretha Franklin for *I Knew You Were Waiting (For Me)* at the 30th annual Grammy awards.

May Ballad *One More Try* hits UK #8.

[28] *One More Try* becomes third US chart-topper from his debut album, which has also returned to pole position, now quadruple platinum in 6 months.

June As the tour reaches Europe, some dates are cancelled and postponed when Michael is admitted for a minor throat operation in London.

[11] Having resumed the tour at Earls Court in London, Michael plays an early slot for "Nelson Mandela's 70th Birthday Party" concert at Wembley. He performs only cover versions by black artists including Marvin Gaye's *Sexual Healing*. 6 hours later, Michael is performing at another sold-out Earls Court solo date.

[18] *One More Try* tops US R&B chart.

July Fifth extracted single, *Monkey*, remixed by producers Jimmy Jam and Terry Lewis, is his least successful authorized UK single (including Wham! releases) at #13.

Aug [27] *Monkey* tops the US chart and is his eighth US #1 of the 80s, a record beaten only by Michael Jackson with 9.

Second section of US tour begins with sold-out dates and more rave reviews. Michael announces that he will donate proceeds of his forthcoming single *If You Were My Woman*, a remake of Gladys Knight's *If I Were Your Woman*, to anti-apartheid groups. (The record will, however, not be released.)

Oct [31] The "Faith" tour ends at Pensacola, FL.

Dec Another ballad from his album, *Kissing A Fool*, reaches UK #18 and hits US #5. "Faith", a collection of video clips, becomes an instant best-seller, rounding off one of the most successful debut album promotions in pop history.

1989 Jan [30] Michael is voted Male Vocalist (Pop And Soul/R&B) and Soul/R&B Album for *Faith* at American Music Awards.

Feb [2] Michael wins Album Of The Year for *Faith* at the 31st annual Grammy awards.

Michael accepts undisclosed damages in excess of £100,000 from **The Sun** newspaper in the High Court in a libel action over articles printed on Oct.13 and 15, 1986, which stated that he gatecrashed a party being given by Andrew Lloyd Webber and was drunk and abusive.

Apr [4] *Faith* is named International Hit Of The Year while Michael is elected Songwriter Of The Year for the second time at the annual Ivor Novello Awards lunch at the Grosvenor House, London.

May Long-time Michael cohort, Estus, benefits from Michael-produced and co-written *Heaven Help Me*, which makes UK #41, but hits US #5. (He is also featured on Jody Watley's current album *Larger Than Life*.)

Sept [6] Madonna presents Video Vanguard Award to Michael at the sixth annual MTV Music Awards ceremony at the Universal Amphitheater, Los Angeles.

1990 Sept Michael is the subject of an introspective documentary on Melvyn Bragg's ITV "The South Bank Show", which will be subsequently be edited for video release.

[1] Previewing his second solo album, social awareness ballad *Praying For Time* hits UK #6.

[15] *Listen Without Prejudice, Vol. 1*, again written, arranged and produced by Michael, (a second volume is reportedly already in the can), immediately hits UK #1 and begins a mulit-platinum stay on both UK and US charts. With its launch, and that of his auotbiography **Bare**, Michael announces that he is rejecting much of the traditional rock star lifestyle, not least appearing in videos and performing world tours, and intends to concentrate more on songwriting than success.

Oct [13] *Praying For Time*, boosted as it connects with many military personnel leaving the US for Gulf duty, hits US #1, ousting Maxi Priest's *Close To You*.

[20] *Listen Without Prejudice, Vol. 1* hits US #2, held off pole position by MC Hammer's *Please Hammer Don't Hurt 'Em*.

Nov [10] *Waiting For That Day* reaches UK #23.

Dec [22] *Freedom!* hits US #8, and will peak at UK #30 a week later. (Also known as *Freedom! 90* to distinguish it from Wham!'s 1985 hit

Freedom, it benefits from super-model (Christy Turlington, Linda Evangelista, Naomi, Cindy Crawford and Tatiana) starring video in which Michael's biker jacket, synonymous with his "Faith" period image is symbolically burnt.

1991 Jan [15] Michael performs the first of 2 nights at the NEC, Birmingham, W.Midlands, on the beginning of his "Cover To Cover" tour. Playing mini-tours in selected territories over the next few months, the majority of his set is devoted to his interpretations of som of his favorite songs, which include many Stevie Wonder and Elton John hits, and even Adamski's *Killer*.

[25] Michael makes his first live appearance since 1988 on the seventh day of the Rock In Rio II festival at the Maracana soccer stadium in Ri de Janeiro, Brazil.

[28] Michael reunites with Ridgeley to close Rock In Rio II festival.

Feb [10] *Listen Without Prejudice, Vol.1* wins Best British Album at the 10th annual BRIT Awards at the Dominion theater, London. Collecting the award, Michael dedicates the trophy to Epic Records marketing manager Ronnie Fischer, who died, age 34, in Nov.1990.

[23] *Heal The Pain*, an early-Beatlesque acoustic cut, makes UK #31, becoming Michael's first UK solo single not to make the Top 30.

Mar [2] *Waiting For That Day* reaches US #27. Following its release, t B-side ballad *Mother's Pride*, rapidly makes airplay gains and becomes the second Michael cut to become an unwitting Gulf War favorite and in a rare 90s Hot 100 practice, charts separately from its A-side, peakin in the same week at US #46.

[7] Michael is named Best Male Singer and Sexiest Male Artist in the annual **Rolling Stone** Readers' Picks music awards.

[22-23] "Cover To Cover" tour returns to the UK for sold-out concerts at Wembley Arena.

MIDNIGHT OIL

Peter Garrett (vocals)
Jim Moginie (guitar)
Martin Rotsey (guitar)
Dwayne "Bones" Hillman (bass)
Rob Hirst (drums)

1976 Sydney schoolboy friends Moginie, Hirst and Rotsey playing on low budget tours in the group Farm, place newspaper ad for a lead singer Garrett, on sabbatical from his law studies at Australian National University in Canberra, and a member of local band Rock Island Line, is the only reply and is recruited.

1977 Hillman, New Zealand-born, ex-The Swingers, joins on bass and Midnight Oil's name is chosen by a keyboard player briefly in line-up In the summer, Garrett receives his law degree from the University of New South Wales.

1978 Now playing clubs and pubs 5 nights a week, the group establishes it own Powderworks label, having been rejected by every major record company in Australia. They are becoming one of the hottest and most articulate acts and begin to forge links with a number of ecological an charitable causes including Greenpeace, the Movement Against Uranium and the Tibet Council.

1979 As one of Australia's most popular live acts, Midnight Oil, angered by the monopoly of booking agencies and promoters, establishes its own agency and blacklists 22 Australian venues which refuse to exert reasonable limitations on door prices. By year end, the band's debut album **Head Injuries** earns a gold disk in Australia.

1980 Further establishing themselves as a pioneering spirit in environment health with Garrett taking an increasingly political stance, Midnight Oil's follow-up Australia-only released album **Bird Noises** again achieves gold status. Hirst wins the first of 8 consecutive Best Drummer Awards in the annual **Ram** magazine readers' poll.

1981 Third Powderworks album **Place Without A Postcard**, recorded in Sussex, UK, with producer Glyn Johns, achieves Australian platinum success, and will result in the group signing a worldwide contract wit CBS/Columbia.

1982 Band undertakes first major US dates, in support of **Red Sails In The Sunset**, produced by Nick Lounay, and also performs in Japan, during which time Garrett visits Hiroshima.

1983 June Countdown-to-destruction-titled **10, 9, 8, 7, 6, 5, 4, 3, 2, 1** is released, again to great domestic success backed by live touring.

1984 Feb [4] **10, 9, 8, 7, 6, 5, 4, 3, 2, 1** makes international breakthrough charting in US and set to reach US #178. More politically prominent than ever, Garrett is asked to run for 6-year senate seat in the Australian Senate for the newly-formed Nuclear Disarmament Party. He receives 200,000 votes.

1985 **Jan** [1] Midnight Oil kicks off the New Year with a live simulcast on the Australian Broadcasting System and FM radio with a performance from an island near Sydney Harbor, Australia.
Aug *Red Sails In The Sunset* makes US #177.
Dec Garrett contributes to the Artists United Against Apartheid album, which spawns hit single *Sun City*.

1986 *Diesel And Dust* goes Australian gold in 17 hours, platinum in 3 days and is confirmed as the largest ship-out in Australian record history.

1987 Garrett is made president of the Australian Conservation Foundation.

1988 **Feb** [13] *Diesel And Dust* is finally released worldwide and enters US survey, set to make US #21 during a 21-week chart stay.
July [2] Extracted *Beds Are Burning* reaches US #17, having already made UK debut at #48.
The Dead Heart, extracted from *Diesel And Dust*, stalls at UK #68. It has been written for the Australian movie "Uluru – An Anangu Story".
Sept [17] *The Dead Heart* peaks at US #53.

1989 **Apr** Reissued *Beds Are Burning* hits UK #6.
July Re-released *The Dead Heart* makes UK #62. Midnight Oil spends much of the year recording its next album, and only perform 2 gigs, for the Aboriginal Rights Association and the Tibet Council.

1990 **Feb** [10] *Blue Sky Mine*, trailering forthcoming album project, and focusing on the plight of postwar immigrants to Western Australia who became victims of blue asbestos cancer (8,000 still suffering) working as miners, peaks at UK #66.
[18] Band participates in an 8-hour benefit concert for victims of the Dec.28, 1989 New South Wales earthquake alongside Crowded House and others at the International Sports Center, Newcastle, Australia.
Mar [10] Parent album *Blue Sky Mining*, including some of the band's most politically scathing work to date, reaches UK #28.
[24] *Blue Sky Mine* makes US #47.
Apr [14] *Blue Sky Mining* reaches US #20, achieving RIAA gold certification. Its US issue by Columbia uses recycled paper for the controversial "long box" CD display pack. Follow-up single *Forgotten Years*, theming on the wastes of war and promoted via a video lensed at a cemetery in Verdun, France, where 700,000 perished during World War I, is released.
May [15] "The Blue Sky Mining" North American tour begins in Charlotte, NC, set to end June 26 at Thunderbird Stadium, Vancouver, Canada.
[30] In New York to perform at Radio City Music Hall gigs, Midnight Oil plays a noontime concert in front of the Exxon Building on 6th Avenue in Manhattan to protest at their global polluting activities, not least the Exxon Valdez oil spill in Alaska. 10,000 attend the free agit-pop event which features a large back-drop reading "Midnight Oil Makes You Dance ... Exxon Oil Makes Us Sick".

1991 **Apr** [23] *Deadicated*, a collection of Grateful Dead songs recorded by various artists, to which Midnight Oil contributes *Wharf Rat*, is released, with a portion of the proceeds from the sale of the album going to the Rainforest Action network & Cultural Survival.

ROGER MILLER

1956 Miller (b. Jan.2, 1936, Fort Worth, TX), after 3 years in the US Army in Korea, in which he has been assigned to Special Services and played in a country band, settles in Nashville, TN, attempting to become a successful songwriter while working at various day jobs.

1957 In Nashville, he begins recording for RCA without success, but finds better luck via his songs, writing *Invitation To The Blues* for Ray Price (US #92 in 1958) and *(In The Summertime) You Don't Want My Love* for Andy Williams (US #64 in 1960), among others.

1962 He joins Faron Young's band as drummer and back-up vocalist and writes *Swiss Maid* for Del Shannon, which hits UK #2.

1964 **Mar** He is taking acting lessons and preparing to move to Los Angeles, CA, in an attempt to break into films when he signs to Mercury Records' Smash label, and debut release, self-penned novelty *Dang Me*, starts to accumulate airplay and sales.
July *Dang Me*, produced in Nashville by Jerry Kennedy, hits US #7 and becomes a million-seller.
Aug *Roger And Out* makes US #37. It will stay on chart for 46 weeks, earning a gold disk for a half million US sales.
Oct Taken from it, novelty country rocker *Chug-A-Lug* hits US #9.
Dec *(And You Had A) Do-Wacka-Do* makes US #31.

1965 **Mar** *King Of The Road*, in a more restrained, jazzy style, sells 550,000 copies in its first 18 days on release. It hits US #4 and is his second million-seller.
Apr [13] Miller wins Best C&W Song, Best C&W Single and Best C&W Vocal Performance, Male for *Dang Me*, Best C&W Album for *Dang Me/Chug-A-Lug* and Best New C&W Artist Of 1964 at the 7th annual Grammy awards.
May *King Of The Road* tops UK chart for a week. (Miller will later open a hotel in Nashville, named "The King of the Road"). *The Return Of Roger Miller* hits US #4.
June *Engine Engine No.9*, a close melodic relative of The Everly Brothers' *Walk Right Back*, hits US #7 and makes UK #33.
Aug *One Dyin' And A Buryin'* makes US #34, while *The 3rd Time Around* reaches US #13.
Oct Bittersweet *Kansas City Star* reaches US #31 and UK #48.
Dec *England Swings*, naively-written but catchily commercial, about London trendiness, hits US #8. *Golden Hits*, a compilation of his singles to date, hits US #6, and is his third gold album, remaining on chart for 13 months.

1966 **Jan** Despite UK reviews dismissing it as "pure corn", *England Swings* makes UK #13.
Mar Introspective *Husbands And Wives* makes US #26.
[15] Miller wins Best Contemporary (Rock'N'Roll) Single, Best Contemporary (Rock'N'Roll) Vocal Performance, Male, Best C&W Single, Best C&W Song and Best C&W Vocal Performance, Male Of 1965 for *King Of The Road* and Best C&W Album Of 1965 for *The Return Of Roger Miller* at the 8th annual Grammy awards.
July Nonsense song *You Can't Roller Skate In A Buffalo Herd* climbs to US #40.
Sept [12] "The Roger Miller Show", a musical variety half-hour on US NBC TV, starts a weekly run on Monday evenings.
Oct Another novelty, *My Uncle Used To Love Me But She Died*, reaches US #58.
Nov A revival of Elvis Presley's *Heartbreak Hotel* (Miller's first hit single not written by him) peaks at UK #84.
Dec [26] Miller's US TV show ends its run after moderate success, while *Words And Music* peaks at US #108.

1967 **Apr** *Walkin' In The Sunshine* reaches US #37.
July *Walkin' In The Sunshine* makes US #118, as Miller's record sales enter a steep decline from his 1964/65 peak.

1968 **Apr** Reflectively sentimental *Little Green Apples*, written by Bobby Russell, reaches US #39. (It will win 2 Grammy awards as Best Song and Best Country Song Of 1968.)
May *Little Green Apples* makes UK #19, after a 2-year UK chart absence, (but will be his last UK hit).
Sept *A Tender Look At Love* stalls at US #173.
Dec *Vance* peaks at US #80, and will be Miller's last US Top 100 entry (although he will continue to make the C&W chart).

1969 **May** *Little Green Apples* re-enters UK chart and reaches #39.
Sept *Roger Miller* makes US #163.

1970 **Feb** *Roger Miller 1970* reaches US #200 for 2 weeks. (It will be his last US chart album but he will be an active songwriter and live performer in US throughout the 70s and 80s, despite a lack of hits).

1985 **Apr** [25] "Big River", a musical written by Miller, based on Mark Twain's **Huckleberry Finn**, opens at the Eugene O'Neill theater on Broadway, New York, and will win a Tony theater award as Best Musical Of The Year, as Miller continues to have recording success in the country field. (Among cover versions of Miller hits, Scottish twin-set, The Proclaimers' recording of *King Of The Road* will prove a big UK Christmas hit in 1990.)

THE STEVE MILLER BAND

Steve Miller (vocals, guitar)
James "Curley" Cooke (guitar, vocals)
Lonnie Turner (bass, vocals)
Tim Davis (drums, vocals)

1948 Miller (b. Oct.5, 1943, Milwaukee, WI), son of a pathologist raised in Dallas, TX, receives his first guitar lesson from family friend Les Paul.
1955 While at Woodrow Wilson high school, he forms his first band The Marksmen Combo, with schoolfriend Boz Scaggs, playing around Texas, Louisiana and Oklahoma.
1957 Aged 14, he backs blues legend Jimmy Reed in a Dallas bar.
1961 Miller and Scaggs attend Wisconsin University, Madison, WI, where they play in R&B/Motown covers band, The Ardells, which becomes The Fabulous Night Train with Ben Sidran.
1963 Miller leaves college, returning to Texas to write songs, which will provide much of the material for **Children Of The Future**, before studying at Copenhagen University, Denmark.
1964 He returns to US and moves to Chicago, IL, where he works with

THE STEVE MILLER BAND cont.

Muddy Waters, James Cotton, Howlin' Wolf and The Butterfield Blues Band, among others.

1965 He joins Barry Goldberg to form The World War Three Band, which becomes The Goldberg Miller Blues Band, releasing a single for Epic Records, *The Mother Song*.

1966 **Nov** Miller moves to San Francisco, CA, forming The Miller Band, with Cooke, Turner (b. Feb.24, 1947, Berkeley, CA) and Davis. Band starts gigging, making its live debut at the Matrix in San Francisco.

1967 **Apr** Band participates in the San Francisco Stage College Folk Festival. Jim Peterman joins on organ and vocals.
June Group performs at the Monterey International Pop Festival, CA.
Sept Scaggs returns and joins the band, which backs Chuck Berry on his live album *Live At The Fillmore*. Cooke leaves to form Curley Cooke's Hurdy Gurdy Band.
Oct Band signs to Capitol Records, before starting a major US tour.

1968 **Jan** The Steve Miller Band arrives in UK to record its debut album with producer Glyn Johns at Olympic studios in Barnes, London.
Feb 3 Steve Miller Band tracks are featured on the soundtrack to movie "Revolution" on United Artists.
May [18] Band appears at Northern California Rock Festival with The Doors, The Grateful Dead and others.
June *Children Of The Future* makes US #134.
Aug Scaggs leaves shortly after completion of the group's new album *Sailor*, as does Peterman. Group continues as a trio. (Ben Sidran will join briefly on keyboards.)
Nov *Living In The USA* makes US #94 as parent *Sailor* reaches US #24.

1969 **Mar** Nicky Hopkins, ex-Jeff Beck's group, joins on keyboards.
June *Brave New World*, like the previous 2 recorded in UK with Glyn Johns, reaches US #22. (Track *My Dark Hour* features Paul McCartney on bass using the pseudonym Paul Ramon.)
Nov *Your Saving Grace* peaks at US #38. Turner and Hopkins both leave; Hopkins to join Quicksilver Messenger Service. Bob Winkelman joins on bass and vocals.

1970 **July** *Number Five*, recorded in Nashville, TN, and produced by the band, reaches US #23. Davis leaves for a solo career, cutting 2 albums for Metromedia.
Aug Miller recruits Ross Valory on bass and vocals and Jack King on drums and vocals.
Sept *Going To The Country* peaks at US #69.

1971 **Oct** *Rock Love* makes US #82.
Dec Valory quits. (He will later join San Francisco rock band Journey.)

1972 **Jan** After the poor showing of *Rock Love*, Miller augments the band with keyboardist Dicky Thompson, bassist Gerald Johnson and second drummer Roger Alan Clark.
Feb Band makes its UK debut at London's Rainbow theater, where it previews its forthcoming album.
Mar Clark and King both leave, the latter being replaced by namesake John King.
Apr *Recall The Beginning ... A Journey From Eden* peaks at US #109. After its release, Miller contracts hepatitis, forcing a 6-month layoff.
Oct The Steve Miller Band begins a 50-city US tour, for which Turner returns, replacing Johnson, who leaves to join Boz Scaggs' band. (Cooke joins for some gigs at the latter end of the tour.)
Dec Capitol releases double album *Anthology* which climbs to US #56, the band's first gold disk.

1973 **Apr** The band returns to London to play at the Rainbow theater.
Oct *The Joker* hits US #2.

1974 **Jan** *The Joker*, featuring an innovative acoustic guitar track is a radio hit, and climbs to US #1, displacing Jim Croce's *Time In A Bottle*.
Apr *Your Cash Ain't Nothing But Trash* peaks at US #51.
May Thompson and King depart.
June Reissued *Living In The USA* makes US #49. (Miller takes a sabbatical, buying a 312-acre farm in Medford, OR, and installing a 24-track studio.)

1975 **July** [5] Miller, making his first appearance in 14 months, assembles a new Steve Miller Band, comprising Turner, Les Dudek on guitar and vocals and Doug Clifford on drums, for the Knebworth Festival, Herts., where Pink Floyd tops the bill.
Oct Band reverts to a trio with Miller and Turner, with new drummer Gary Mallaber (b. Oct.11, 1946, Buffalo, NY).

1976 After returning from a break, Miller forms his own Sailor Records, licensed to Capitol in US and Mercury in UK and Europe.
May *Fly Like An Eagle*, his first album in 2 years, hits US #3, going platinum during a 97-week chart stay.
June *Fly Like An Eagle* reaches UK #11, his first UK album success.
July *Take The Money And Run* reaches US #11.

Oct Miller assembles yet another Steve Miller Band comprising Turner, Mallaber, David Denny (b. Feb.5, 1948, Berkeley, CA) (guitar), Norton Buffalo (harmonica, vocals), Greg Douglas (b. Oct.11, 1949, Concord, CA) (guitar, vocals) and Byron Allred (b. Oct.27, 1948, Logan, UT) (keyboards).
Nov *Rock 'N' Me* is his second US #1 and reaches UK #11.

1977 **Mar** *Fly Like An Eagle* hits US #2, kept off the top by Barbra Streisand's *Evergreen*. (**Rolling Stone** magazine will vote *Fly Like An Eagle* Best Album Of The Year.)
May *Book Of Dreams*, recorded at the same sessions as *Fly Like An Eagle* hits US #2, his second platinum album.
June *Fly Like An Eagle* reaches UK #12.
July *Jet Airliner* hits US #8.
[24] Miller begins US tour at the Omni, San Francisco, ending Aug.18.
Oct *Jungle Love* reaches US #27.
Dec *Swingtown* reaches US #17.

1978 **Dec** *Greatest Hits 1974-1978* is released and will climb to US #18 and go platinum.

1981 **Nov** *Circle Of Love* is released. Despite a 4-year layoff, it will reach US #26 and earn a gold disk.
Dec *Heart Like A Wheel* reaches US #24.

1982 **Feb** *Circle Of Love* peaks at US #55.
June *Abracadabra*, produced by Miller and Mallaber, hits US #3 (earning a platinum disk) and UK #10 (and is a worldwide hit).
[19] Miller begins an extensive US tour with new guitarists Kenny Lewis and John Massaro.
Aug *Abracadabra* hits UK #2, held off by Captain Sensible's *Happy Talk*.
Sept *Abracadabra* becomes Miller's third US chart-topper, in an edited form, while *Keeps Me Wondering Why* peaks at UK #52.
Nov *Cool Magic* climbs to US #57.

1983 **Jan** *Give It Up* peaks at US #60.
May *The Steve Miller Band Live!*, recorded on UK tour in 1982, stalls at US #125 and UK #79. A live video is simultaneously issued.

1984 **Oct** *Shangri-La* peaks at US #57.
Nov *Italian X-Rays* reaches US #101 but does not chart in UK, where it will be his last release for Mercury.

1985 **Feb** *Bongo Bongo* climbs to US #84.

1986 **Nov** [22] *I Want To Turn The World Around*, from the forthcoming album, makes US #97.
Dec *Living In The 20th Century* is released, climbing to US #65. It is dedicated to Jimmy Reed with whom Miller had played as a teenager. His first for Capitol in UK under a new Sailor deal, it includes familiar Miller associates, among them Mallaber, Buffalo and guitarist Les Dudek, and one side is devoted to covers of blues classics.

1988 **Oct** *Born 2 B Blue* reaches US #108. It celebrates his 20th year at Capitol with a set of blues and jazz standards, with musical help from Phil Woods on sax and Milt Jackson on vibes, and includes a jazz version of *Zip-A-Dee-Doo-Dah* and a cover of Lee Dorsey's *Ya Ya*.
Nov [10] Miller begins his first tour in 6 years in Burlington, VT.

1990 **June** [1] Miller embarks on a major US tour in Bloomington, MN. The tour will end Sept.12 at the Coliseum, Seattle, WA.
Sept [15] *The Joker* tops UK chart during its use on a Levi jeans ad. In the first publically admitted case in UK chart history, chart compilers Gallup confirm that 2 singles tied for this week's #1, achieving identical panel sales tallies: Deee-Lite's *Groove Is In The Heart* is pipped by Miller's oldie by the subsequently much criticized ruling that *The Joker's* panel sales increase over its previous week's performance was greater than Deee-Lite's.
Oct [6] *The Best Of Steve Miller 1968-1973* makes UK #34.

KYLIE MINOGUE

1979 **Mar** Minogue (b. May 28, 1968, Melbourne, Australia), daughter of Australian accountant Ron and Welsh mother Carol, gets first acting role, as a Dutch girl in Australian TV soap opera, "The Sullivans".
Oct Supported by her parents, Minogue is offered the character of Robin in another soap, "Skyways", which also features future colleague and Stock/Aitken/Waterman protege, Jason Donovan.

1984 Having successfully completed her High School Certificate, Minogue joins another soap, "The Hendersons", as Charlotte Kernow.

1985 2 further TV shows, "Fame And Misfortune" and "The Zoo Family" feature Minogue.

1986 She quits school and accepts the role of Charlene Robinson in new soap "Neighbours", again linking with Donovan.

1987 **Apr** Minogue wins Australian TV Logie award as "Neighbours" tops the nation's ratings.

July At an Australian Rules Football game in Sydney, Minogue is invited to sing. She performs Little Eva's hit *The Locomotion*. It attracts the attention of Australian label Mushroom, which signs her to record the song.

Aug *The Locomotion* hits #1 in Australia for 7 weeks before being deposed by Los Lobos' *La Bamba*.

Sept Spotted by UK producer Pete Waterman, Minogue is invited to record at S/A/W's London studios during a 10-day visit and cuts *I Should Be So Lucky*. Meanwhile, UK ratings of "Neighbours" approach 14 million viewers per episode.

Nov *The Locomotion* is certified Australia's biggest-selling single of the 80s and is a hit in New Zealand and the Far East.

1988 Jan Light pop dance ditty *I Should Be So Lucky*, written and produced by S/A/W, is released on its own independent PWL label, after all major record companies have turned it down.

Feb [20] *I Should Be So Lucky* hits UK #1 on its way to becoming the UK's first gold single of the year. It also hits #1 in Australia. Minogue is awarded 4 further TV Logie awards.

May As *I Should Be So Lucky* tops charts in 12 other territories, follow-up *Got To Be Certain* hits UK #2, held off the top by Wet Wet Wet's *With A Little Help From My Friends*.

July Debut album *Kylie*, written and produced by S/A/W, enters at UK #1, on its way to platinum sales. Signed to Geffen in US, *I Should Be So Lucky* peaks at US #28.

Aug Remixed by S/A/W for UK and US release, *The Locomotion* hits UK #2 in its first week of release.

Sept Minogue begins a US promotional visit.

Oct Fourth single from debut album, *Je Ne Sais Pas Pourquoi* hits UK #2 (confirming Minogue as the most successful debut solo female singer).

Nov [12] *The Locomotion* hits US #3, as *Kylie* makes US #53 and first video hits collection "Kylie: The Videos" tops UK music sales chart.

Dec Minogue is only the third woman to achieve the best selling album of the year in the UK. Barbra Streisand (*Love Songs*) and Madonna (*True Blue*) are the other 2.

1989 Jan [7] *Especially For You*, duet with Jason Donovan, tops UK chart.

Feb [11] *It's No Secret* makes US #37.

May [13] Another typically commercial uptempo S/A/W pop dance confection *Hand On Your Heart* hits UK #1.

Aug [5] *Wouldn't Change A Thing* hits UK #2, her seventh straight #1 or #2 UK smash.

Oct [21] Second album completely created at PWL studio by S/A/W team debuts at UK #1 on its way to multi-platinum UK awards.

Nov [4] Extracted *Never Too Late* hits UK #4, breaking Top 2 run. (None of the 1989 UK releases have charted in the US.) Right on cue, "Kylie: The Videos 2" again tops UK music video sales chart.

Dec [23] Peter Waterman-instigated Band Aid II's re-recording of *Do They Know It's Christmas?*, including vocal support from Minogue and Donovan, hits UK #1. Minogue appears in Australian-lensed movie "The Delinquents".

1990 Jan [27] Remake of Little Anthony & The Imperials 1958 US #4 *Tears On My Pillow* hits UK #1, her fourth chart-topper.

Apr Video "Live In Japan" is released by Video Collection.

May [19] Returning to uptempo S/A/W dance material *Better The Devil You Know*, featured in movie "If Looks Could Kill", hits UK #2.

June [18] During UK tour, Minogue performs at the Wembley Arena, London.

Oct [10] 70s soul retrospective *Step Back In Time*, aided by similar era styled video, hits UK #4.

Nov [24] As rumors circulate that Minogue has left the S/A/W stable, a decision influenced not least by her close liaison with current beau fellow Australian and INXS lead singer Michael Hutchence, S/A/W dominated third album *Rhythm Of Love*, marking a deliberate attempt to harden her previously candy coated image to a sexier adult projection, hits UK #9, but US success remains elusive.

1991 May Further extract, *Shocked*, is released.

THE MISSION

Wayne Hussey (guitar, vocals)
Simon Hinkler (guitar)
Craig Adams (bass)
Mick Brown (drums)

1985 Dec Hussey (b. May 26, 1959) and Adams, after the break-up of The Sisters Of Mercy plan a follow-on band named The Sisterhood, but legalities prevent use of this name. Hinkler (ex-Artery) and Brown (ex-Red Lorry Yellow Lorry) are recruited, and the quartet becomes The Mission.

1986 Jan Band plays its first live dates (still billed as The Sisterhood), supporting The Cult on a European tour.

Feb First radio sessions are broadcast on BBC Radio 1's "Janice Long Show".

May Signed to independent label Chapter 22, based in Solihull, W.Midlands, the band begins its first headlining UK tour "Expedition 1 – Keeping The Faith", supported by Pauline Murray and The Storm.

June Debut single *Serpents Kiss* tops the UK Independent chart, and climbs to UK #70.

July Several major UK labels are interested and their contract is bought from Chapter 22 by Phonogram as they tour Italy and Germany.

Aug Double A-side *Garden Of Delight* and a revival of Neil Young's *Like A Hurricane*, released on Chapter 22 prior to the new deal, tops the Independent chart and makes UK #50. Band plays a mini-tour of Holland and Belgium, and UK's Reading Festival, Berks.

Oct *Stay With Me*, the group's debut on Phonogram's Mercury label, reaches UK #30.

Nov The Mission plays a UK tour to launch *God's Own Medicine*, which reaches UK #14.

1987 Jan *Wasteland*, edited from its album version, reaches UK #11, as the band plays overseas dates titled "The World Crusade".

Mar *Severina*, also from the album, peaks at UK #25. Group returns to tour UK.

Apr Band makes its live US debut on a 2-month coast-to-coast tour, billed as Mission UK to avoid a name-clash with an existing US band as *God's Own Medicine* makes US #108. (Adams will be sent home early during the tour suffering from physical and mental exhaustion.)

July Band tours Europe briefly between 2 major UK dates supporting U2 in Leeds, W.Yorks., and Edinburgh, Scotland. Compilation album *The First Chapter*, rounding up 9 tracks recorded for Chapter 22 (including the first 2 hit singles), makes UK #35.

Sept Band plays at the Reading Festival, this time as headliners, then begins recording a new album at Richard Branson's Manor studios near Oxford, Oxon., with ex-Led Zeppelin John Paul Jones producing.

1988 Feb *Tower Of Strength* reaches UK #12.

Mar *Children* hits UK #2, supported by a UK tour.

Apr The Mission begins a 10-month headlining world tour, while *Beyond The Pale*, taken from the album, reaches UK #32.

May *Children* peaks at US #126.

Oct Goth-heavy video collection "From Dusk To Dawn" is released in UK by Channel 5.

Dec At the end of its world trek, Mission plays sell-out dates at the Wembley Arena, London, and the NEC, Birmingham, W.Midlands.

1989 May Devoting much of the year to recording its new album, the group participates in 2 benefit concerts, 1 for the Lockerbie Air Disaster Fund, the other for the relatives of the Hillsborough soccer tragedy.

1990 Jan [20] Ballad *Butterfly On A Wheel* reaches UK #12.

Feb [17] Tim Palmer-produced *Carved In Sand* hits UK #7, as concurrent video collection "Waves Upon The Sand" is released.

Mar [10] *Deliverance* reaches UK #27, as Mission embarks on 1-month major venue UK tour.

Apr [16] 24-date US tour opens in Port Chester, NY, set to end in New York City on May 25.

[28] *Carved In Sand* peaks at US #101, though major breakthrough US hit single is still elusive.

June [2] *Into The Blue* makes UK #32.

Nov [2] Out-takes and remixes associated with the last album project, collected as *Grains Of Sand* reaches UK #28.

[17] Extracted *Hands Across The Ocean* also reaches UK #28.

JONI MITCHELL

1962 Mitchell (b. Roberta Joan Anderson, Nov.7, 1943, Fort McLeod, Alberta, Canada) enters Alberta College of Art, Calgary, having shown an early aptitude for visual arts, aiming for a career as a commercial artist. She also sings and plays the ukelele, which she has learnt from a Pete Seeger teach-yourself record. Gradually, music becomes more important than her art studies, and at a friend's suggestion she sings at the local Depression coffee house with Peter Albling.

1964 On her way to perform at the Mariposa Folk Festival in Ontario she writes her first song, blues number *Day After Day*. After the festival she does not go back to school, but enters Toronto's Yorktown folk scene and starts playing in local coffee bars.

1965 June She marries fellow folk singer Chuck Mitchell and they begin working as a duo on the Northeastern US circuit.

1966 The Mitchells move to Detroit, MI, but their marriage dissolves soon after. Keeping her married name, she relocates to New York. Tom Rush, having met Mitchell in Detroit, records her *Urge For Going*, after failing to persuade Judy Collins to do so.

1967 Mitchell bases herself in New York, looking after her own bookings and finances until she meets Elliot Roberts, who sees her opening for Richie Havens at the Café Au Go Go in Greenwich Village. He becomes her manager and secures a deal with Reprise Records. After a period in London, Mitchell moves to Los Angeles to record an album produced by David Crosby, who had "discovered" her singing in a club in Coconut Grove, FL. Judy Collins records Mitchell's *Both Sides Now* and *Michael From Mountains* on her album *Wildflowers*.

1968 **June** Mitchell's debut album *Joni Mitchell* (sometimes known as *Song For A Seagull*), produced by Crosby and featuring Mitchell on piano and guitar with Stephen Stills on bass, makes US #189.
Dec [28] She participates in the Miami Pop Festival, in Hallandale, FL., with Fleetwood Mac, Marvin Gaye, Three Dog Night and Canned Heat. It is the start of a 40-week spell on the road, playing festivals in Atlanta, Newport, Big Sur, New York and Monterey and opening for Crosby, Stills & Nash.

1969 **Feb** [1] Mitchell makes her debut at New York's Carnegie Hall.
Aug [18] Scheduled to take part in the Woodstock festival in Bethel, NY., Mitchell pulls out on the advice on David Geffen because of a commitment to appear on Dick Cavett's TV talk show. Instead of appearing at the momentous event, Mitchell writes *Woodstock*.
Oct Second album *Clouds*, featuring Mitchell's own versions of *Both Sides Now* and *Chelsea Morning*, reaches US #31, aided by her appearances on Johnny Cash's TV show, where she meets Bob Dylan for the first time.

1970 **Feb** [17] Mitchell announces that she is quitting live performance during a concert at London's Royal Albert Hall.
Mar [11] Mitchell wins Best Folk Performance for *Clouds* at the 12th annual Grammy awards in New York.
May *Ladies Of The Canyon*, recorded while she is living with Graham Nash in Laurel Canyon, reaches US #27 and is her first gold album. Crosby, Stills, Nash & Young make US #11 with her *Woodstock*.
July *Big Yellow Taxi* reaches UK #11 as parent album *Ladies Of The Canyon* hits UK #8.
Aug *Big Yellow Taxi* makes US #67.
[29] Mitchell plays on the fourth day of the Isle of Wight Festival.
Oct Matthews Southern Comfort tops the UK chart with Mitchell-penned festival-chronicling *Woodstock*.
Nov [21] Mitchell plays at the Royal Festival Hall, London.

1971 **July** Mitchell tours US and Europe with Jackson Browne, and sings backing vocals on James Taylor's US #1 *You've Got A Friend*.
Aug *Blue*, recorded at A&M studios Los Angeles with Stephen Stills (bass), James Taylor (guitar), Russ Kunkel (drums) and "Sneaky" Pete Kleinow (pedal steel), reaches US #15 and hits UK #3.
Sept *Carey*, from *Blue*, spends 1 week on US Hot 100, at #93.

1972 **Dec** After a sabbatical, spent in the woods of Canada where she writes material for her new album, she releases *For The Roses*, her first for David Geffen's Asylum Records.

1973 **Jan** *You Turn Me On, I'm A Radio*, from *For The Roses*, makes US #25.
Feb *For The Roses* reaches US #11.
Nov Nazareth's version of her *This Flight Tonight* reaches UK #11.

1974 **Jan** *Raised On Robbery* stalls at US #65.
Mar *Court And Spark* is Mitchell's first fully-electric album, with help from Larry Carlton, Joe Sample, Wilton Felder, Robbie Robertson and L.A. Express. It reaches UK #14.
May *Help Me* hits US #7. Parent album *Court And Spark* hits US #2 for 4 weeks.
Sept *Free Man In Paris*, with José Feliciano guesting on guitar, reaches US #22.
[11] Mitchell performs at London's Wembley Stadium, on a bill with Crosby, Stills, Nash & Young and The Band.
Dec [24] Mitchell joins Linda Ronstadt, Carly Simon and James Taylor singing christmas carols on the streets of Los Angeles.

1975 **Feb** A live version of *Big Yellow Taxi* makes US #24. Double album *Miles Of Aisles*, from a concert with L.A. Express – Tom Scott (woodwinds/reeds), Robben Ford (guitar), Larry Nash (piano), Max Bennett (bass) and John Guerin (drums) – hits US #2 and makes UK #34. (The concert comprises familiar Mitchell material with only 2 new songs, *Love Or Money* and *Jericho*.)
Mar [1] Mitchell and Tom Scott win Best Arrangement Accompanying Vocalists for *Down To You* from *Court And Spark* at the 17th annual Grammy awards.
She joins Bob Dylan's "Rolling Thunder Revue", initially as a spectator,

but then taking part at certain gigs.

1976 **Jan** *The Hissing Of Summer Lawns*, again using L.A. Express, hits US #4 and reaches UK #14.
Feb Extracted *In France They Kiss On Main Street* peaks at US #66.
Nov *Hejira*, mostly written in her car while driving through US and strongly jazz-oriented, is released.
[20] Mitchell, with John Sebastian, Country Joe McDonald and Fred Neil, takes part in "California Celebrates The Whales Day" at the Memorial Auditorium, Sacramento, CA.
[25] She participates in The Band's farewell concert "The Last Waltz" at the Winterland, San Francisco, singing *Helpless* with Neil Young, performing *Coyote* with Dr. John and joining an all-star cast on *I Shall Be Released*.
Dec *Hejira* reaches UK #11.

1977 **Jan** *Hejira* reaches US #13.

1978 **Feb** *Don Juan's Reckless Daughter*, with guests Chaka Khan, Wayne Shorter, Jaco Pastorius, Glenn Frey and J.D. Souther, reaches US #25, earning her eighth and final gold disk, and makes UK #20.
Apr Jazz giant Charles Mingus, fighting Lou Gehrig's disease, contacts Mitchell to ask whether she would assist him on T.S. Eliot's *Four Quartets*. It comes to nothing, but Mitchell agrees to write and sing lyrics to 6 melodies he has written, and begins work in her Regency Hotel apartment in New York.

1979 **Jan** [5] Charles Mingus dies, age 56, in Cuernavaca, Mexico.
July *Mingus*, using jazz musicians Gerry Mulligan, John McLaughlin, Jan Hammer and Stanley Clarke, is released. (Mitchell is quoted as saying "Mingus wanted his stock to go up before he died, there was an element of choosing me to write his epitaph, help ensure he got a bigger funeral.") It makes US #17 and UK #24.
Sept A concert at Santa Barbara County Bowl is recorded for forthcoming album *Shadows And Light*. Mitchell's band for the show Pat Metheny (lead guitar), Jaco Pastorius (bass), Don Alias (drums), Lyle Mays (keyboards), Michael Brecker (sax) and The Persuasions (vocals).

1980 **Oct** Double live album *Shadows And Light* makes US #38 and UK #63.
Dec [2] "Shadows And Light" concert special airs on the Showtime-TV channel.

1981 **Feb** [5] Canadian Prime Minister Pierre Trudeau inducts Mitchell into Canada's Juno Hall Of Fame.

1982 Now signed to David Geffen's Geffen label, during recording of her new album *Wild Things Run Fast* she parts company with Roberts, her manager for 17 years. After a few weeks' handling her own affairs, she teams with Peter Asher.
Nov [21] Mitchell marries her bassist Larry Klein in Malibu, CA.
Dec *(You're So Square) Baby, I Don't Care*, originally sung by Elvis Presley in 1957 film "Jailhouse Rock", makes US #47. Parent album *Wild Things Run Fast*, with guest vocalists Lionel Richie and James Taylor, makes US #25 and UK #32.

1983 Mitchell undertakes a US tour, her last of the decade.

1985 She changes direction yet again for *Dog Eat Dog*, using UK synthesizer-directed Thomas Dolby as co-producer. (Rod Steiger is featured as an evangelist on track *Tax Free*.)
Nov *Dog Eat Dog* peaks at UK #57.
Dec *Dog Eat Dog* makes US #63.

1986 **Jan** [11] *Good Friends*, with guest vocalist Michael McDonald, stalls at US #85.

1988 **Apr** *Chalk Mark In A Rainstorm*, self-produced with Klein and recorded in US and UK, features guests Peter Gabriel, Don Henley, Thomas Dolby, Tom Petty, Willie Nelson, Wendy & Lisa and Billy Idol. It makes US #45 and UK #26.

1990 **July** [21] Mitchell takes part in Roger Waters' performance of "The Wall" at the site of the Berlin Wall in Potzdamer Platz, Berlin, Germany. The event is broadcast live throughout the world, and raises money for the Memorial Fund For Disaster Relief.
Sept [10-21] Mitchell's paintings, now her main interest, form a major part of "Canada In The City", an exhibition of Canadian art, music and culture at the Broadgate center in London.

1991 **Mar** [9] Mitchell and Klein-produced *Night Ride Home* debuts at UK peak #25 and begins US rise into the Top 50.

MOBY GRAPE

Alexander "Skip" Spence (guitar, lead vocals)
Peter Lewis (guitar, vocals)
Jerry Miller (guitar)
Bob Mosley (bass)
Don Stevenson (drums)

1966
Sept Band is formed in San Francisco, CA, by Lewis (b. July 15, 1945, Los Angeles, CA) and Mosley (b. Dec.4, 1942, Paradise Valley, CA), as Peter & The Wolves, originally with Joel Scott Hill (guitar) and Kent Dunbar (drums) but Hill and Dunbar drop out and Spence (b. Apr.18, 1946, Windsor, Canada), ex-Jefferson Airplane and Quicksilver Messenger Service, Stevenson (b. Oct.15, 1942, Seattle, WA), and Miller (b. July 10, 1943, Tacoma, WA), both ex-The Frantics, join.
Nov [25-27] After 2 months rehearsing in Sausalito, CA, and developing a local reputation, the group plays at the Fillmore, San Francisco, where 14 record labels express interest. David Rubinson of CBS/Columbia signs it.

1967
Mar Debut album *Moby Grape* is accompanied by a publicity hype involving the simultaneous release of 5 singles. The band tours with record label backing and the album reaches US #24.
May *Omaha*, one of the 5 singles, charts briefly at US #88.
Nov After disastrous Los Angeles sessions for a follow-up album, the band is sent to record *Wow* in New York, where Columbia insists on discipline.

1968
June *Wow*, with a track playing at 78rpm, plus the bonus live album *Grape Jam*, and guests Al Kooper and Mike Bloomfield, reaches US #20. Shortly after its release, Spence leaves with drug problems and checks into hospital for 6 months. (He will re-emerge with solo *Oar* in Oct.1969.)
July Band almost splits but re-groups to record third album as quartet.

1969
Feb 4-piece group undertakes a short UK and European tour.
Mar Mosley leaves, dropping out to become a school janitor. *Moby Grape '69* reaches US #113.
Apr Remaining trio records a contractual obligation-filling album in Nashville, TN, with session man Bob Moore playing bass. Trio splits and Miller and Stevenson join Bill Champlin's Rhythm Dukes. (Champlin will later join Chicago.)
Oct *Truly Fine Citizen*, from the Apr. recordings, scrapes US #157.

1970
Jan Mosley enlists in the US Marines. (He will last 9 months before being discharged for fighting an officer.)
Dec A fake Moby Grape, put on the road by manager Matthew Katz, who owns the name, plays some dates including a gig outside the gates of The Rolling Stones/Jefferson Airplane concert at Altamont, CA.

1971
Apr The original quintet reunites, adding Gordon Stephens (viola, mandolin) and signs to Reprise Records.
Aug The band splits again without playing any live gigs.
Oct *20 Granite Creek*, titled after the house where it was recorded, is released 6 weeks after the band's final split, making US #177.

1972
Mar Bob Mosley releases eponymous solo album, which fails to chart.

1973
Oct Lewis, Mosley and Miller team again, with drummer John Craviotta and guitarist Jeff Blackburn, who have both been with Miller for 2 years in Silver Wings, based in Santa Cruz, CA. Since Katz still owns the Moby Grape name, the band calls itself The (Original) Grape.

1974
Group plays small-time live dates but is unable to attract a record deal, meanwhile *Great Grape* is issued by a fake Katz-backed aggregation.

1975
May Group splits again and Mosley, Miller and Craviotta form Fine Wine with ex-H.P. Lovecraft guitarist Michael Been. *Fine Wine* is released in Germany only.

1977
May Mosley, Craviotta and Blackburn link as Ducks and are joined briefly by Neil Young, gaining live prestige in Santa Cruz but not recording.
July Spurred by Ducks' growing reputation, Lewis and Miller form yet another Grape, joined by long-absent Spence, plus drummer Jon Oxendine, who played with Miller in The Rhythm Dukes in 1969, Christian Powell on bass, and Cornelius Bumpus (who will join The Doobie Brothers late on in their career) on sax.

1978
Feb Mosley rejoins after Ducks folds.
Apr *Live Grape* is released by the new group in US on Escape label but it finds little success. (Lewis and Spence will leave during the year but with now ever-fluctuating personnel, Grape continues into 80s obscurity in minor Southern California live circuits.)

1989
Original Moby Grape, minus Spence, reunites as The Melvilles. (Legal reasons prevent them using their name. They choose The Melvilles as a subtle link by way of **Moby Dick**.) Meanwhile tribute band, Grape Escape with Craig Juan (bass), Mark Lashlly and Lynn Giles (guitars),

George Hastings (drums) and Grant Ewald (keyboards), releases *Paint The White House Black* with Jerry Miller guesting on lead guitar.
1990 The Melvilles recruit Don Abernethy and rename as Legendary Grape.

EDDIE MONEY

1977
Money (b. Edward Mahoney, Mar.2, 1949, Brooklyn, New York, NY), the son of a New York policeman, attending the NYPD police academy, also fronts a Long Island, NY, rock band by night under the pseudonym of Eddie Money. Faced with a choice of careers, he quits the force and moves to Berkeley, CA, where he becomes a regular vocalist on the San Francisco Bay bar circuit. Concert promoter Bill Graham spots his potential and becomes his manager, negotiating a recording deal with CBS/Columbia.

1978
May Debut album *Eddie Money* reaches US #37 (it will sell over a million copies to earn a platinum disk in almost a year on chart), boosted by *Baby Hold On*, which is extracted and reaches US #11. (Following this success, Money begins to tour US as support to The Rolling Stones, Ted Nugent, and Cheap Trick, and then headlining.)
Sept *Two Tickets To Paradise*, also from the album, reaches US #22.

1979
Jan A revival of The Miracles' *You've Really Got A Hold On Me* peaks at US #72.
Mar *Maybe I'm A Fool* reaches US #22. It is extracted from his second album *Life For The Taking*, which climbs to US #17 and earns a gold disk for a half million sales.
June *Can't Keep A Good Man Down*, also from *Life For The Taking*, peaks at US #63.
Sept Money sings *Get A Move On* on the soundtrack of film "Americathon"; as a single it makes US #46.

1980
Sept *Runnin' Back* climbs to US #78. It is taken from his third album *Playing For Keeps*, which makes US #35.
Nov A duet with Valerie Carter, *Let's Be Lovers Again* peaks at US #65.

1982
Sept Money returns to US chart after a 2-year absence with *Think I'm In Love*, which reaches #16, trailing his fourth album.
[3-5] Money plays the US Festival, financed by Apple Computers founder Steven Wozniak, in San Bernardino, CA, to 400,000 people, along with Jackson Browne, The Cars, Fleetwood Mac, The Grateful Dead, Police, Santana, Talking Heads and many others.
Oct *No Control*, produced by Tom Dowd, reaches US #20 and earns a gold disk.
Nov Taken from the album, *Shakin'* peaks at US #63.

1983
Dec *Where's The Party?* makes US #67, his lowest-selling album so far.

1984
Jan *The Big Crash*, taken from the album, peaks at US #54.
Mar Also from *Where's The Party?*, *Club Michelle* peaks at US #66.

1986
Nov [15] Following a gap between recordings of almost 3 years, during which he battles to overcome a drug problem, Money returns with his biggest-selling single, as *Take Me Home Tonight* hits US #4. It features guest vocalist Ronnie Spector, singing the opening line of *Be My Baby*, her 1963 million-seller with The Ronettes.
Dec *Can't Hold Back*, including the Top 5 single, reaches US #20, earning a gold disk.

1987
Mar [14] *I Wanna Go Back*, taken from *Can't Hold Back*, makes US #14.
June [27] *Endless Nights* reaches US #21.
Sept [26] *We Should Be Sleeping* stalls at US #90.

1988
Dec [24] *Walk On Water* hits US #9, to bring Money his second biggest hit, from new album *Nothing To Lose*, which makes US #49.

1989
Mar [18] *The Love In Your Eyes* reaches US #24.
May [13] *Let Me In* peaks at US #60.
Dec *Sound Of Money Greatest Hits* makes US #53.

1990
Feb [10] *Peace In Our Time* reaches US #11.

THE MONKEES

Davy Jones (vocals, guitar)
Mike Nesmith (vocals, guitar)
Peter Tork (vocals, keyboards, bass, guitar)
Mickey Dolenz (vocals, drums)

1965
Writer/director/producer Bob Rafelson teams with Bert Schneider to form Raybeat company in US to produce, for Screen Gems, a pilot episode of a sitcom based around a Beatles-type group using Richard Lester's film "A Hard Day's Night" as its framework.
Sept [8] An ad appears in Los Angeles's **Daily Variety**: "Madness!! Running parts for 4 insane boys, aged 17 to 21. Wanted spirited Ben Franks'-type." 437 hopefuls are auditioned including Stephen Stills, who is allegedly turned down because of bad teeth, Paul Williams,

Charles Manson and future leader of Three Dog Night, Danny Hutton, who makes the last 8.

Oct The 4 signed are Jones, Nesmith, Dolenz and Tork. Jones (b. Dec.30, 1945, Manchester, Gtr.Manchester), ex-apprentice jockey and actor, has made his TV debut in BBC play "June Evening", starred as Ena Sharples' grandson Colin Lomax in ITV show "Coronation Street" in 1961; in the first episode of "Z-Cars" in 1962; in both London and New York productions of "Oliver" as The Artful Dodger and "Pickwick" and had TV roles in "Ben Casey" and "Farmer's Daughter". He has also appeared on CBS TV's "Ed Sullivan Show" as part of the "Oliver" cast with The Beatles on their US TV debut. He is already a minor teen sensation in US, where he has made an album and hit US #93 with *What Are We Going To Do?* Nesmith (b. Robert Michael Nesmith, Dec.30, 1942, Dallas, TX.), a member of Los Angeles' folk circuit, has released singles for the Colpix label under the name Michael Blessing. Dolenz (b. George Michael Dolenz Jr. Mar.8, 1945, Tarzana, Los Angeles, CA), son of Hollywood character actor George Dolenz, and child star of US TV show "Circus Boy", under the name Mickey Braddock playing the lead role Corky and acted in "Peyton Place", "Route 66" and "Mr.Novak", has been a member of The Missing Links and made an unsuccessful single. Tork (b.Peter Halsten Thorkelson, Feb.13, 1944, Washington, DC), recommended to the producers by his friend Stephen Stills, has also drifted around Los Angeles's folk circuit playing in the Au Go Go Singers with Ritchie Furay.

Nov The pilot episode, in its mixture of silent comedy and slow and fast motion film technique, is a big success with a test audience of teenagers and the show is placed with NBC for its 1966 fall schedule.

1966 Mar Acting and grooming lessons begin. Group members are encouraged to record and write themselves, but their efforts are found wanting. Songwriters Tommy Boyce and Bobby Hart, who have already written *Last Train To Clarksville* and *The Monkees Theme*, are overlooked as musical producers for the show. Mickie Most passes and a combination of Leon Russell and Snuff Garrett is a failure.

Apr [3] Tork makes his solo debut at Hollywood's Troubadour, on a bill headed by Muddy Waters.

July With the show due to start in Sept., Screen Gems music chief Don Kirshner takes over and appoints Boyce and Hart as producers, and with Lester Sill is responsible for molding The Monkees' sound and musical persona. Gerry Goffin and Carole King, Neil Diamond, Barry Mann and Cynthia Weil and Neil Sedaka, all signed to Kirshner's Aldon Music company, are brought in to write songs.

Sept [12] "The Monkees" TV show premieres on US NBC TV.

Nov Debut album *The Monkees*, released on Colgems, tops the US chart for 13 weeks and earns a gold disk, selling 3,200,000 copies in 3 months.

[5] Despite a hesitant start for the TV show, debut single *Last Train To Clarksville* hits US #1, providing the perfect counterpoint to The Beatles' "yeah yeah yeah" with "no no no", and earns a gold disk.

[26] *I'm A Believer*, written by Neil Diamond, is released with advance orders of 1,051,280.

Dec Band hits US #1 with *I'm A Believer*. try-out concerts in Hawaii erupt in fan riots, confirming Beatlemania-like success.

[31] "The Monkees" TV show premieres on BBC TV.

1967 Jan [20] *I'm A Believer* tops the UK chart for 4 weeks, selling over 750,000 copies.

Feb *More Of The Monkees*, released with advance orders of over 1.5 million, tops the US chart for 18 weeks. *The Monkees* hits UK #1. *Last Train To Clarksville* belatedly charts in UK, reaching #23.

A successful US concert tour gives the group more confidence as musicians in a real band. Nesmith insists that The Monkees should be allowed to play on their own records with more of their own songs (at this point, James Burton, Glen Campbell, Leon Russell, David Gates and Hal Blaine are regular session players on their disks) and insists that either he or Don Kirshner goes. Schneider gives him backing and Kirshner resigns as chief executive of Screen Gems Music. UK magazine **Monkees Monthly** is launched.

[11] During a UK promotional visit, the group announces that in future they will play on their own records and not use session men.

Mar Another Neil Diamond composition, *A Little Bit Me, A Little Bit You* hits US #2 (a third million-selling single) and UK #3. Jones forms short-lived record company, Davy Jones Presents.

Apr Group starts a brief tour of Canada.

[17] Tork plays short acoustic set on Hootenanny Night at the Troubadour.

May *More Of The Monkees* tops the UK chart, unseating *The Sound Of*

Music (which had dethroned *The Monkees*).

[16] *Headquarters*, their third consecutive album to sell over a million copies, is released. Nesmith brings in producer Chip Douglas. Group plays on the album supplemented by only 3 outsiders.

June *Headquarters* hits US #1 for 1 week, before being displaced by The Beatles' *Sgt. Pepper*.

[4] "The Monkees" wins an Emmy award for Outstanding Comedy Series 1966-67.

[9-10] Group plays The Hollywood Bowl, Los Angeles.

[30] They play the first of 3 sold-out concerts at The Empire Pool, Wembley, London.

July *Alternate Title* hits UK #2. (Its original title *Randy Scouse Git* had been heard by Dolenz on UK TV show "Till Death Us Do Part".) *Headquarters* hits UK #2, kept from the top by *Sgt.Pepper*.

[7] The Monkees begin 31-date US tour at the Braves Stadium, Atlanta GA, with Jimi Hendrix as opening act. (He quits the tour within 2 weeks.)

Aug Sunny *Pleasant Valley Sunday* hits US #3 and UK #11. B-side *Wore* reaches US #11.

Nov Nesmith gathers together 54 of Los Angeles's top session men to give his songs a big band treatment and self-finances *The Wichita Train Whistle Sings*, on Dot.

[17] Jones opens a boutique, Zilch I, in Greenwich Village, New York.

Dec *Pisces, Aquarius, Capricorn & Jones Ltd.* tops the US chart for 5 weeks. *Daydream Believer*, written by ex-Kingston Trio member John Stewart, tops the US chart for 4 weeks and hits UK #5. (Jones had trouble interpreting the lyrics, so the engineer used a code to number different takes. Jones asks at the beginning of the record "what number is this?" To which everyone in the studio replies "7a".) Band complete filming of a second TV series. Tim Buckley and Frank Zappa make guest appearances.

1968 Jan *Pisces, Aquarius, Capricorn & Jones Ltd.* hits UK #5.

Feb [15] Shooting begins for feature film "Head", directed by Bob Rafelson.

Mar *Valleri* becomes the band's sixth million-selling single, hitting US #3 and UK #12. The Monkees collect their 10th gold disk in 18 months

[25] The 58th (final) episode of the TV series is broadcast.

May *The Birds, The Bees And The Monkees*, on which each group member contributes individual tracks, hits US #3. Band performs a free concert in Salt Lake City, UT., to be filmed for live segments of "Head"

June The TV series (along with "Batman") is axed.

July The Monkees' revival of The Coasters' *D.W. Washburn* reaches US #19 and UK #17.

[12] Dolenz and Samantha Juste marry at their Laurel Canyon home.

Oct *Porpoise Song* peaks at US #62.

Nov [20] "Head" premieres in Los Angeles. Given a budget of $750,000 by Columbia Pictures, Rafelson, expected to deliver a standard teen flick, has instead, with Jack Nicholson (who has become part of the Monkees' clique), created a film about the manipulation of The Monkees, mixed in with a tribute to classic Hollywood movies. The resultant bizarre pot-pourri features a variety of guest appearances, from boxer Sonny Liston to Victor Mature as The Big Victor representing capitalism. It includes scenes of The Monkees committing suicide by jumping from a bridge, and a concert intercut with Vietnam war atrocities. (It is a box-office disaster and will not be shown in UK until Mar.1977.)

Dec Soundtrack album *Head* makes US #45.

[30] Tork quits, buying out his contract for $160,000, and after years of conspicuous living is left completely broke. The remaining members are also keen to call it a day, but are scared off by Tork's highly-priced contract buy-out. He forms new group Release with Ripley Wildflower (bass and vocals) and girlfriend Reine Stewart (drums).

1969 Feb *Tear Drop City* reaches US #56 and UK #46.

Mar *Instant Replay* makes US #32.

Apr [14] NBC TV special "33⅓ Revolutions Per Monkee", recorded in 1968, with Little Richard, Jerry Lee Lewis, Fats Domino, Clara Ward Singers, Brian Auger, Buddy Miles and Julie Driscoll, airs.

June *Listen To The Band*, written by Nesmith, and using musicians who will become Area Code 615, climbs to US #63. *Someday Man* peaks at UK #47. *The Monkees Greatest Hits* makes US #93, as the group tours US as a trio.

Oct *Good Clean Fun* falters at US #82.

Nov *The Monkees Present* makes US #100.

1970 Jan [3] Davy Jones announces that he is to leave the Monkees.

Mar [1] Nesmith, his contractual obligations complete, quits The Monkees to form his own group, The First National Band. He signs a solo deal with RCA, receiving a $20,000 advance. Dolenz and Jones carry on recording *Changes*, but it fails to sell. (The industry joke is that the next album will be by The Monkee.)

June *Oh My My* peaks at US #98 and Dolenz and Jones decide to end The Monkees.

Oct Nesmith's solo *Joanne* makes US #21 and his album *Magnetic South* reaches US #143.

1971 Jan Nesmith's *Silver Moon* makes US #42, while parent album *Loose Salute* peaks at US #159.

May *Nevada Fighter*, also by Nesmith, reaches US #70.

July Jones makes US #52 with *Daisy Jane*.

1975 Group meets to discuss re-forming. McDonald's have offered a TV commercial, but Tork declines as he is a vegetarian. Nesmith is only interested if a feature film is part of the package. Dolenz and Jones re-form the band with writers Tommy Boyce and Bobby Hart, and begin a 2-year tour, "The Golden Great Hits Of The Monkees Show – The Guys Who Wrote 'Em And The Guys Who Sang 'Em". They sign a deal with Capitol, which issues *Dolenz, Jones, Boyce And Hart*.

1976 Aug Compilation album *The Monkees Greatest Hits* capitalizes on the group's reactivity, reaching US #58.

1977 Mar Nesmith's first UK success is with *Rio* at #28, in part due to the creation of his Pacific Arts Corporation, a video company which films a promo for the single. (He will subsequently produce films including "Elephant Parts", "Time Rider" and "Repo Man". The National Film Theatre in UK imports a copy of "Head" to meet cult demand. It runs for a season at the Electric Cinema in Notting Hill, London.)

1978 Dec Dolenz and Jones star in Harry Nilsson's "The Point" at London's Mermaid theater.

1979 Dolenz stays in UK, to work as a freelance director in TV ("Metal Mickey") and stage ("Bugsy Malone"). (Nesmith's mother Bette sells her patent for Liquid Paper to the Gillette Corporation for $47 million. She will die in 1980, leaving Nesmith as her sole beneficiary.) Nesmith's album *Infinite Rider On The Big Dogma* makes US #151.

1980 Jones tours Japan after *Daydream Believer* is used in a Kodak commercial, and Monkeemania breaks loose once again in Japan.

Mar 4-track EP *The Monkees*, containing *I'm A Believer*, *Daydream Believer*, *Last Train To Clarksville* and *A Little Bit Me, A Little Bit You*, reaches UK #33.

1981 Tork tours Japan with his group The New Monks, after working as a waiter and telling **National Enquirer** that he is a "professional has-been".

Nov Retrospective *The Monkees* makes UK #99.

1986 Feb [22-23] To celebrate the 20th anniversary of the group, MTV airs "Pleasant Valley Sunday", a 22-hour broadcast of every "Monkees" TV episode.

Rhino inadvertently creates the foundation for a Monkees revival with the release of the first in a series of albums. The label reissues all the band's albums along with much previously unavailable material.

May *Then And Now ... The Best Of The Monkees* continues the revival and is on its way to US #21. Comprising all Monkees hits, it also includes 3 new songs by Tork and Dolenz. Dolenz, Jones and Tork re-form the group to begin a US summer tour, as *The Monkees Greatest Hits* recharts to make US #69.

June [22-23] MTV repeats "Pleasant Valley Sunday".

Aug Mini-Monkeemania explodes in US again with the group occupying 7 positions on US Album chart: *Then And Now ... The Best Of The Monkees* (#21), a best of with 3 new tracks by Dolenz and Tork, *The Monkees* (#92), *More Of The Monkees* (#96), *Headquarters* (#121), *Pisces, Aquarius, Capricorn & Jones Ltd.* (#124), *The Birds, The Bees And The Monkees* (#145) and *Changes* (#152), featuring only Dolenz and Jones.

[1-3] "The Monkees Convention" is held in Philadelphia, PA., while the group headlines "The Monkees 20th Anniversary World Tour", with Gary Puckett & The Union Gap, Herman's Hermits and The Grass Roots.

[12] Auditions are held for The New Monkees. Jason Nesmith and Bobby Darin's son Dodd both fail to make the final four.

[30] *That Was Then This Is Now* single makes US #20 and UK #68.

Oct [18] As the group plays Atlanta, the mayor Andrew Young declares it "Monkees Day".

Nov [8] *Daydream Believer* peaks at US #79.

1987 Rhino releases 2 further albums of rare material, *Missing Links* and *Live 1967*.

Sept Newly-recorded album *Pool It!*, produced by Roger Bechirian, makes US #72.

Oct [10] *Heart And Soul* peaks at US #87.

1988 Dec VH1 airs a "Monkees Week Marathon", broadcasting all "The Monkees" TV episodes.

1989 Apr EP *The Monkees*, issued by Arista, peaks at UK #62, while K-Tel compilation *Hey Hey It's The Monkees – Greatest Hits* reaches UK #12.

May [4] Columbia Pictures serves a court order on Jones, Dolenz and Tork to stop using the name The Monkees.

July [9] During The Monkees summer tour, Nesmith joins them on stage – the first time all 4 have appeared together on stage in 20 years.

[10] Group receives a star on the Hollywood Walk Of Fame in Hollywood, CA, as they enjoy the most lucrative period of their careers.

THE MOODY BLUES

Denny Laine (vocals, guitar)
Mike Pinder (keyboards)
Ray Thomas (flute, harmonica, vocals)
Clint Warwick (bass)
Graeme Edge (drums)

1964 May [4] Laine (b. Brian Hines, Oct.29, 1944, off the Jersey coast in a boat) disbands Denny Laine & The Diplomats and forms a new group in Birmingham, W.Midlands, comprising Thomas (b. Dec.29, 1942, Stourport-on-Severn, Hereford & Worcs.) and Pinder (b. Dec.27, 1941, Birmingham, W.Midlands), who have been playing at the Top Ten club in Hamburg, Germany, for nearly a year with The Crewcats, and now both from local rock group El Riot & The Rebels, and Edge (b. Mar.30, 1942, Rochester, Staffs.), from Gerry Levene & The Avengers and Warwick (b. Clinton Eccles, June 25, 1940, Birmingham), from The Rainbows. They secure a residency at the Carlton Ballroom in Birmingham. The club owners get £2,000 from brewers Mitchell & Butlers for publicity purposes, so the band, in deference to the brewers, adopts the name The MB Five. They soon decide that the M should stand for Moody and the B for Blues, becoming The Moody Blues Five. They sign with London manager Tony Secunda, who secures them a contract with Decca Records.

Aug Group performs its debut single *Lose Your Money* on ITV's "Ready Steady Go!".

1965 Jan [8] Group begins a 24-date twice-nightly UK tour, with Chuck Berry, at the Odeon theater, London, which will end Jan.31 at the Regal theater, Edmonton, London.

[28] *Go Now*, a cover of Bessie Banks' US R&B hit, tops the UK chart. (New York DJ B. Mitchell Reed had given the group a copy of the record on a visit to London.)

Mar *I Don't Want To Go On Without You*, a revival of a Dritfers' B-side, makes UK #33.

[5] Group makes its first live broadcast on the BBC Radio's "Joe Loss Pop Show".

Apr *Go Now* holds down anchor position in a unique US Top 10 in which 9 of the singles are from the UK.

[11] The Moody Blues take part in the annual **New Musical Express** Pollwinners Concert at the Empire Pool, London, with The Beatles, The Rolling Stones, The Kinks, The Animals and many others.

May [24] Group takes part in the British Song Festival at the Dome, Brighton, E.Sussex.

June [5] They guest on ITV's "Thank Your Lucky Stars".

[19] The Moody Blues make their US debut, with The Kinks, at the Academy of Music in New York.

July *From The Bottom Of My Heart* reaches UK #22 and US #93, while *The Magnificent Moodies*, produced by Denny Cordell, does not chart.

Aug [6] They play on opening day of the fifth annual National Jazz & Blues Festival at the Richmond Athletic Ground, Richmond, Surrey.

Sept [6] They sign a management contract with NEMS.

[21] Group participates in "Pop From Britain" concert at the Royal Albert Hall, London, with Cliff Bennett & The Rebel Rousers, Georgie Fame & The Blue Flames & The Fourmost.

Nov *Everyday* makes UK #44.

Dec [19] Band appear on CBS TV's "Ed Sullivan Show".

1966 Apr *Stop!* spends a week on US Hot 100, at #98.

June Warwick leaves the group. He will quit the music business.

July [14] His replacement, Rod Clarke, from Les Garcons, plays his first date with the group at the Locarno, Coventry, W.Midlands.

Aug [6] Group begins a 9-day tour of Denmark.

Oct [12] Band splits, after its only release of the year *Boulevard De La Madelaine* flops and Laine leaves to sign a solo deal with Deram, before joining ex-Move member Trevor Burton in the band Balls and Paul McCartney's Wings in 1973.

Nov After the quickest reunion in rock'n'roll history, Pinder, Thomas and Edge recruit 2 new members. John Lodge (b. July 20, 1945, Birmingham), has been in El Riot & The Rebels with Thomas and Pinder, before playing with The Carpetbaggers, The John Bull Breed and The Falcons. Justin Hayward (b. David Justin Hayward, Oct.14, 1946, Swindon, Wilts.), who after leaving school spends 6 months as a trainee salesman with a building firm, before working in a theatrical repertory company, joining The Offbeats theater ensemble in Jersey. He then joins Marty Wilde's Wildcats for 2 days, before forming trio with Marty and his wife. They work in cabaret before Hayward goes solo, signing with Pye A&R chief Alan Freeman and manager Lonnie Donegan. Hayward, with releases on Parlophone and Decca as well, writes to Eric Burdon who is forming the New Animals. Burdon, already with his band signed up, passes his name on to the Moodies. New line-up moves to Belgium, to avoid UK taxman.

1967 Apr [14] Laine releases his first solo single *Say You Don't Mind* which fails (but is later a hit for Colin Blunstone).

Sept Group begins a 3-month US tour. During the tour the band performs *Days Of Future Passed* with Stan Kenton Orchestra, at his request, at the Hollywood Bowl, Hollywood, CA.

1968 Jan Hayward-penned *Nights In White Satin* reaches UK #19. It is taken from their first album *Days Of Future Passed*, a concept album based around a theme of different times of the day and night, which makes UK #27. The London Festival Orchestra, a group of session musicians conducted by Peter Knight also plays a major part, though its orchestrated passages are edited between and around The Moody Blues tracks so the orchestra does not actually accompany the group. (The original idea, abandoned early on, was for band and orchestra to record Dvorak's "New World Symphony" together as a stereo sampler.) The album is also the start of a long-term relationship between The Moody Blues and producer Tony Clarke.

May [4] *Days Of Future Passed* enters US chart to hit #3, earning the group its first gold disk, during a chart run of 102 weeks.

June [29] Band makes a rare concert appearance in London at the Queen Elizabeth Hall.

Aug *Voices In The Sky* makes UK #27, as parent album *In Search Of The Lost Chord*, another concept album, hits UK #5.

Sept *Tuesday Afternoon*, taken from *Days Of Future Passed*, makes US #24. *In Search Of The Lost Chord* makes US #23 and earns a second gold disk.

Nov *Ride My See Saw*, extracted from *In Search Of The Lost Chord*, peaks at US #61.

Dec *Ride My See Saw* makes UK #42. Its B-side is little heard *A Simple Game* (later a UK #3 for The Four Tops with Clarke producing).

1969 Mar [7] Band performs at the Grand Gala Du Disque, Amsterdam, Holland, on a bill including Gladys Knight & The Pips.

May *On The Threshold Of A Dream* tops the UK chart for 2 weeks and reaches US #20 during a 136-week chart run, their third gold disk.

July *Never Comes The Day* stalls at US #91.

Aug [30] Group plays the opening day of Isle of Wight Festival, UK.

Oct *Watching And Waiting* is the first single release on the band's own Threshold label.

Dec *To Our Children's Children* hits UK #2. Band moves to Cobham, Surrey and opens a chain of Threshold record stores.

[12] Group performs at the Royal Albert Hall, London, during a UK tour. The concert is recorded (and released as part of *Caught Live Plus Five* in June 1977).

1970 Jan *To Our Children's Children* makes US #14 and is the group's fourth gold album.

May Hayward's dramatic *Question*, the group's first release on its own Threshold label, hits UK #2, kept off the top by the England World Cup Squad's *Back Home*.

June *Question* reaches US #21.

Aug *A Question Of Balance*, written and recorded in 5 weeks, hits UK #1 for 3 weeks.

[30] Band plays on the final day of the Isle of Wight Festival.

Sept *A Question Of Balance* hits US #3, the group's fifth gold disk.

Oct [30] The Moody Blues play London's Royal Festival Hall.

Dec [3] Group embarks on US tour, making its Carnegie Hall, New York debut on Dec.14.

1971 Aug *Every Good Boy Deserves Favour*, the acronym for the notes on a treble stave, tops the UK chart.

Sept *The Story In Your Eyes* reaches US #23. (The UK equivalent is withdrawn, at the band's request.) Parent album *Every Good Boy Deserves Favour* hits US #2.

Oct During a US visit, the band is presented with a gold disk (their

sixth) for *Every Good Boy Deserves Favour*. Given the choice by the record company to select the presenter of the award, they decide on actor Jay Silverheels (Tonto in "The Lone Ranger" TV series).

1972 June Lodge-penned dreamy ballad *Isn't Life Strange* reaches UK #13 and US #29.

Nov Re-issued *Nights In White Satin* hits US #2, passing a million sales, as parent album *Days Of Future Passed* hits US #3 while the group tours US. *Seventh Sojourn* hits UK #5.

Dec *Seventh Sojourn* tops the US chart for 5 weeks and earns a further gold disk.

1973 Jan *Nights In White Satin* hits UK #9, 10 places higher than its previous appearance 5 years earlier.

Feb *I'm Just A Singer (In A Rock'N'Roll Band)* makes UK #36. (This will be their last new release until 1978.)

Mar *I'm Just A Singer (In A Rock'N'Roll Band)* reaches US #12.

1974 Feb Group ends a 9-month world tour in US, and decides to split for the time being to concentrate on solo projects.

June Hayward and Lodge start recording at The Moody Blues' new, as yet unopened, studio backed by 3-piece Idaho group Providence.

July [17] The Moody Blues open their own studio (the first quadrophonic in the world) in West Hampstead, London.

Nov Double compilation album *This Is The Moody Blues* reaches UK #14 and US #11, earning a gold disk.

1975 Mar [10] Hayward and Lodge's *Blue Jays* is launched in US at a listening party in New York's Carnegie Hall. It hits UK #4.

Aug Thomas' solo album *From Mighty Oaks* makes US #68.

Oct Hayward and Lodge's *Blue Guitar*, co-produced by 10cc, hits UK #8. The Graeme Edge Band featuring Adrian Gurvitz makes US #107 with *Kick Off Your Muddy Boots*.

1976 Aug Thomas' second solo album *Hope Wishes And Dreams* makes US #147.

1977 Feb Lodge's solo album *Natural Avenue* reaches UK #38.

Mar Hayward's solo album *Songwriter* makes UK #28 and US #37.

May Lodge's album *Natural Avenue* reaches US #121.

June Double album *Caught Live + 5*, featuring 3 sides of the Dec.1969 Royal Albert Hall concert and a fourth side of unreleased studio recordings from the late 60s, makes US #26, and is the group's first album not to be certified gold.

July Second Graeme Edge Band album *Paradise Ballroom* makes US #164.

1978 June The Moody Blues re-unite for new album *Octave*, their first disk for 6 years, which they record at the Record Plant, Los Angeles. Midway through the recording producer Clarke leaves, having been effectively the sixth Moody Blue for over a decade, and closely identified with the development of their symphonic sound of the 70s.

July *Octave* hits UK #6 and reaches US #13, and becomes the group's first platinum disk. Pinder quits the band and the music business, and is replaced by Patrick Moraz (b. Switzerland), ex-Refugee and Yes. Hayward's solo *Forever Autumn*, extracted from Jeff Wayne's concept album *War Of The Worlds*, hits UK #5.

Aug *Steppin' In A Slide Zone*, written by Lodge, makes US #39.

Oct Group begins its first live appearances in 4 years, for a sell-out world tour. *Driftwood* peaks at US #59.

1979 Dec *Nights In White Satin* is re-issued a second time, making UK #14. TV-promoted K-Tel compilation *Out Of This World* reaches UK #15.

1980 July Hayward's second solo album *Night Flight*, produced by Jeff Wayne, reaches UK #41 and US #166.

1981 May *Long Distance Voyager*, on Threshold, hits UK #7.

July *Long Distance Voyager* tops the US chart for 3 weeks, turning platinum.

Aug *Gemini Dream*, from *Long Distance Voyager*, reaches US #12.

Oct *The Voice* makes US #15.

Dec *Talking Out Of Turn* stalls at US #65. By year's end the band's 11-date sixth US tour will have grossed $571,000.

1983 Sept *Blue World* makes UK #35 as parent album *The Present* reaches UK #15 and US #26.

Oct *Sitting At The Wheel* makes US #27.

Dec *Blue World* peaks at US #62.

1985 Mar [13] The Moody Blues are presented with the Award For Outstanding Contribution To British Music at the annual Ivor Novello Awards lunch at the Grosvenor House, Mayfair, London.

Apr Retrospective album *Voices In The Sky/The Best Of The Moody Blues*, including the group's hits from 1967-83, reaches US #132.

Oct Hayward's third solo album *Moving Mountains*, on Towerbell Records, reaches UK #78.

1986 May Band switches to Polydor for *The Other Side Of Life*, which makes UK #24 and hits US #9.

June [19] The Moody Blues open a major US tour in Chastain Park, Atlanta, GA. The tour will end on Oct.7.

July [12] *Your Wildest Dreams* hits US #9.

Sept [2] Hayward is hospitalized having collapsed from exhaustion after a concert in Los Angeles.

[20] *The Other Side Of Life* makes US #58.

1987 **July** Hayward's *It Won't Be Easy* theme to the BBC TV series "Starcops" is released, but does not chart.

1988 **July** *Sur La Mer* reaches US #38, having made UK #21.

Aug *I Know You're Out There Somewhere* makes US #30 and UK #52.

1989 **Oct** Hayward links with producer/arranger Mike Batt to record UK #47 album *Classic Blue* with the London Philharmonic Orchestra, released by UK-only Trax Records.

Dec Threshold retrospective *Greatest Hits* makes US #113.

1990 **July** [21] The Moody Blues close the Goodwill Games in Seattle, WA, at the end of a 33-city US tour, where they remain highly popular.

1991 **June** After a long lay-off, the group releases new album *Keys Of The Kingdom*.

VAN MORRISON

1960 Morrison (b. George Ivan, Aug.31, 1945, Belfast, N.Ireland), having left school to concentrate on a career in music, and influenced not least by the music of Hank Williams and Leadbelly, encouraged from an early age by his parents to have an interest in blues and jazz, plays guitar and soprano sax with local rock'n'roll and jazz groups, including the country-rock group Deanie Sands & The Javelins.

1961 He tours UK and Europe playing sax with local R&B group The Monarchs, who will cut an instrumental single in Germany in 1963, *Twingy Baby*, and then forms Them, from members of The Monarchs, including guitarist Billy Harrison and some old schoolfriends.

1964 After a popular stint at the Maritime hotel, Belfast, Them is signed to Decca. They begin a UK tour, where they attract the attention of American producer Bert Berns, writer of *Twist And Shout*, *Shout* and *Hang On Sloopy*.

July Berns produces *Don't Start Crying Now/One Two Brown Eyes* for Them, and their successful career, fronted by Morrison begins.

1966 **Aug** Morrison retires to Belfast to rest and write songs and consider his future, after a gruelling US group tour.

1967 **Mar** He disrupts Them by signing a solo contract with Berns, traveling to New York to record for his Bang label. Group continues without Morrison, replacing him with vocalist Ken McDowell.

June *Brown Eyed Girl*, the first of 4 Berns-Morrison singles, hits US #10, and marks the beginning of Morrison's solo career.

Oct Berns issues an album of Morrison's recordings, *Blowin' Your Mind* without the singer's knowledge. It reaches US #182.

Dec Berns dies of a heart attack. Morrison, now living in Cambridge, MA, and playing in a bass, flute, guitar jazz-blues trio, negotiates with other companies and signs a solo contract with US Warner Bros., after the label's vice-president Joe Smith has extracted Morrison from his contract with Bang.

1968 **July** With producer Lewis Merenstein, he records *Astral Weeks* in 48 hours in New York. (Without a hit single, the album will take time to generate sales, but will move into the US charts by the end of the year, and become regarded as a seminal 60s album.)

1970 **Apr** Critically acclaimed *Moondance*, including popluar track *Into The Mystic*, never to be released as a single, peaks at US #29 and UK #32, aided in US by *Come Running* which makes #39. The album features steady band members John Platania (guitar), Jeff Labes (keyboards) and Jack Shroer (drums).

Sept *His Band And The Street Choir* is released to poor reviews (and will climb to US #32 in 1971).

Dec From the album, *Domino* hits US #9, as Morrison moves to live in California.

1971 **Feb** *Blue Money* makes US #23. Morrison becomes a much-respected live act in US, assembling an 11-piece Caledonia Soul Orchestra, including string players and guitarist John Platania, a mainstay of his studio work.

June *Call Me Up In Dreamland* makes US #95.

Oct *Wild Night* reaches US #28. Ted Templeman-produced *Tupelo Honey* is released, featuring John McFee and Ronnie Montrose guesting on guitars, making US #27. It is conceived as a suite of love songs to Morrison's wife, Janet Planet. During its recording, Morrison jams for 2 days with John Lee Hooker, results of which will only appear on 2 Hooker tracks, featured on albums *Never Get Out Of These Blues Alive* and 1973's *Born In Mississippi, Raised In Tennessee*.

Dec Morrison cuts sessions with The Band to be issued on their *Cahooots* album.

1972 **Jan** *Tupelo Honey* title track peaks at US #47.

June Morrison performs several dates in California, including cover versions of Bob Dylan's *Just Like A Woman* and Doris Day's *Que Sera Sera* in the repertoire.

Aug *Jackie Wilson Said (I'm In Heaven When You Smile)* makes US #61. Critically revered as another milestone work, and including original of future Dexy's Midnight Runners' hit *Jackie Wilson Said (I'm In Heaven When You Sing)* *St. Dominic's Preview* enters the US chart, staying 6 months there and peaking at #15.

Oct *Redwood Tree* reaches US #98.

1973 **July** [23-24] Morrison plays 2 nights at the Rainbow theater, Finsbury Park, London.

Aug Prior sessions producing Jackie De Shannon are followed by the release of *Hard Nose The Highway*, including 10-min. *Autumn Song*, making UK #22 and US #27. Morrison's personal life, always kept from public view, hits trouble and he is divorced. Following a popular European tour with the Caledonia Soul Orchestra, he returns to Ireland to write songs.

1974 **Jan** *T.B. Sheets*, of tracks from the *Blowin' Your Mind* sessions, is released but reaches only US #181.

Mar Double live album *It's Too Late To Stop Now*, documenting his much celebrated live work, with Morrison and the Caledonian Soul Orchestra, makes only US #53. Morrison disbands the orchestra and tours Europe with a 5-piece band, playing sax and harmonica himself.

June Morrison records 2 tracks in Holland, a cover of Fleecie Moore's *Caledonia*, to be released as an unsuccessful single with B-side *What's Up Crazy Pup*.

Nov *Verdon Fleece*, an intensely personal record of songs written in Ireland in 1973, makes only US #53 and UK #41, and marks the beginning of a 3-year reclusive period of reflection away from touring or record releasing though he will spend much in the studio.

1976 **Mar** Morrison guests on harmonica and guitar for Bill Wyman's album *Stone Alone*. He will also contribute a song for Sammy Hagar album *Nine On A Scale of Ten*.

Nov [25] Morrison is one of many special guests at The Band's farewell concert "The Last Waltz", singing *Tura Lura Lural* and *Caravan* and joining an all-star cast on *I Shall Be Released*.

1977 **May** After scrapping a tentatively titled album *Mechanical Bliss*, and experimental sessions with Joe Sample, Morrison's "comeback" album, *A Period Of Transition*, makes UK #23 and US #43. It features co-producer Dr. John on piano.

Nov *Moondance* is re-released and briefly makes US #92.

1978 **Oct** Self-produced *Wavelength* is released, making US #28 and UK #27, and including a Jackie DeShannon co-penned number *Santa Fe*. The title track peaks at US #42. *Bright Side Of The Road*, Morrison's only UK chart single, reaches #63.

1979 **Sept** *Into The Music* makes UK #21 and US #43. His records are now distributed by Warners in US and by PolyGram elsewhere.

1980 **Sept** *Common One*, with Morrison edging further towards renewed spiritualism and Celtic musical traditions, reaches UK #53 and US #73.

1982 **Feb** After another break of more than a year, *Beautiful Vision*, with Morrison again the soul mystic and heavily themed on his Belfast memories, reaches UK #31 and US #44.

1983 **Mar** *Inarticulate Speech Of The Heart* is released. Striking a chord with fans of his earlier solo recordings, and aided by instrumental *Celtic Swing* (for which Morrison makes a promo video), it makes UK #14 and US #116.

1984 **Mar** *Live At The Grand Opera House*, recorded in Belfast, reaches UK #44, further evidence of his still sell-out live status.

July He receives a big reception when he joins Bob Dylan at Wembley Stadium, London, in front of 72,000 people. They perform Dylan's *It's All Over Now, Baby Blue*, a song Morrison recorded in the early 60s.

Nov Morrison leaves his base in Marin County, CA., to begin nomadic traveling between Dublin, Belfast and London.

1985 **Feb** *A Sense Of Wonder*, returning further to the realms of poetry and spirituality, including a musical backdrop for the William Blake poem **Let The Slave (Price Of Experience)**, reaches UK #25 and US #61. (The credits include a thank you to Scientology founder L. Ron Hubbard.)

1986 **May** [17] He joins U2, Elvis Costello and The Pogues for Dublin's Self-Aid concert, a post Live Aid effort at raising funds for the unemployed in Eire.

July *No Guru, No Method, No Teacher* (the title Morrison's rebuttal of press attempts to characterize his spirituality and cast him as a devotee of scientology) peaks at UK #27 and US #70.

1987 Sept *Poetic Champions Compose* reaches UK #26 and US #90.

1988 July *Irish Heartbeat*, an exploration of his Celtic musical roots recorded with The Chieftains, Ireland's top traditional music group, makes UK #18 and US #102. Morrison is in his most cheerful form and is even seen to smile in concert, during regular tour outings.

1989 June Now signed to Polygram's Polydor in UK and Mercury in US, *Avalon Sunset*, featuring Georgie Fame on keyboards (now a regular member of his musical troupe) and guest Cliff Richard, reaches UK #13 and US #91.

July [1] Extracted ballad *Have I Told You Lately* makes UK #74.

[18-19] Morrison takes part in the seventh annual Prince's Trust Rock Gala at the NEC, Birmingham, W.Midlands.

Nov He is joined on stage by John Lee Hooker at the Beacon theater, New York, performing *Boom Boom* and *It Serves Me Right To Suffer*.

Dec Spiritual brothers Van Morrison and Cliff Richard duet on *Whenever God Shines His Light*, released for the festive season to good effect at UK #20.

1990 Apr [7] *The Best Of Van Morrison*, an incomprehensive Polydor anthology, hits UK #4 and US #50.

June [3] Morrison participates in the Fleadh 1990 Festival in Finsbury Park, London with a host of Irish acts.

July [21] Morrison takes part in Roger Waters' performance of "The Wall" at the site of the Berlin Wall in Potzdamer Platz, Berlin, Germany. The event is broadcast live throughout the world, and raises money for the Memorial Fund For Disaster Relief.

Oct [20] Increasingly popular once more, traditionally self-composed and produced *Enlightenment* hits UK #5 and will climb to US #62 in Feb.1991. It includes the unsuccessful single *In The Days Before Rock'N'Roll*, a notable ode to radio somehow including a reference not only to music legends of the past but also race jockey Lester Piggott.

1991 Mar [16] BBC TV's "Arena" program broadcasts "One Irish Rover" documentary.

[23] Van Morrison-penned and produced Tom Jones single *Carrying A Torch* peaks at UK #57. It is 1 of 4 tracks on which they have collaborated live for Jones' forthcoming album, also titled *Carrying A Torch*, recorded at the Townhouse studios, London.

Apr [5] *Carrying A Torch* debuts at UK #44.

THE MOTELS

Martha Davis (vocals)
Jeff Jourard (guitar)
Marty Jourard (keyboards, sax)
Michael Goodroe (bass)
Brian Glascock (drums)

1978 July Group is formed in Los Angeles, CA, by Davis (b. Jan.15, 1951, Berkeley, CA) (married at age 15 and the mother of 2 daughters), who has led a 3-piece version for some 5 years (initially as The Warfield Foxes and The Angels Of Mercy in Berkeley, and then as The Motels in Los Angeles) and Jeff Jourard (though other early members including Dean Chamberlain (later of Code Blue) and Richard Andrea (later of The Know) will come and go). They recruit the latter's brother, ex-classical guitarist-turned-jazz/rock bassist Goodroe and (after rejecting dozens of other drummers) UK expatriate Glascock, once in Toe Fat with Cliff Bennett, and since a session man for Joan Armatrading, The Bee Gees and others.

1979 Jan Regular work at the Whiskey A-Go-Go, and as house band at Madame Wong's, in Hollywood, CA, and dates around other Los Angeles clubs, attract a strong live following, and also initiate record company interest.

Mar Capitol Records signs the group on Mother's Day.

Sept Debut album *Motels*, produced by John Carter, at first flops.

Oct Group begins extensive tour in support of the album, playing Canada, Australia (where they will always achieve popular success, returning for 4 more tours before 1985), UK and US.

Dec The album belatedly reaches US #175 following the tour exposure. Jeff Jourard leaves after disagreements with Davis, replaced on lead guitar by Tim McGovern from The Pop.

1980 Sept Second album *Careful*, dedicated to Glascock's brother John, Jethro Tull's bassist, who has died aged 26 on Nov.17, 1979, after open heart surgery, reaches US #45.

Oct *Whose Problem?*, taken from *Careful*, peaks at UK #42 following a successful US tour and strong radio play, though album fails in UK.

1981 Jan *Days Are O.K.*, also from the album and written by McGovern, makes UK #41 (completing the band's UK Singles chart career before its US equivalent has even begun).

Mar [31] Group begins recording new album *Apocalypso*, but Capitol rejects it and tells them to return to the studio to record it again.

1982 Mar [7] New album, now retitled *All Four One*, is completed. Producer Val Garay has recruited Kim Carnes' backing band to play on the album and, during the sessions, McGovern has left to be replaced by ex-Elephant's Memory guitarist Guy Perry.

July *All Four One* reaches US #16, earning a gold disk for a half million sales in a 41-week chart run. Extracted *Only The Lonely* is US Singles chart debut, hitting #9.

Oct *Take The L (Out Of Lover)*, second single from *All Four One*, peaks at US #52.

Dec *Forever Mine* peaks at US #60.

1983 Jan [?] Group, with additional guitarist and keyboard player Scott Thurston, begins recording new album at Record One studios in Los Angeles, once again with Garay.

Nov *Suddenly Last Summer* hits US #9, helping parent album *Little Robbers*, also produced by Garay, to US #22 (and a second gold disk).

1984 Jan *Remember The Nights*, extracted from *Little Robbers*, makes US #36.

Apr [4] Tina Turner's version of The Motels' *Total Control* is included on USA For Africa's fund-raising *We Are The World* album.

1985 Sept *Shame* reaches US #21. It is taken from the band's fifth album *Shock*, which climbs to US #36.

Nov Extracted title track from *Shock* climbs to US #84.

1987 Dec [12] Having overcome cancer, which had contributed to the break-up of The Motels, Davis, still signed to Capitol, returns with *Don't Tell Me The Time* which makes US #80 and is taken from *Policy* (many tracks of which were originally recorded at Motels' sessions), which reaches US #127.

1990 *No Vacancy – The Best Of The Motels*, a 19-track retrospective, is issued by Capitol.

MOTLEY CRUE

Vince Neil (vocals)
Mick Mars (guitar)
Nikki Sixx (bass)
Tommy Lee (drums)

1981 Jan Frank Carlton Serafino Ferrano (b. Dec.11, 1958, Seattle, WA) who, on Jan.17 decides to begin calling himself Nikki Sixx leaves US group London, to start new band Christmas and recruits Lee (b. Thomas Lee Bass, Oct.3, 1962, Athens, Greece, to a Greek mother and US military father) from local Los Angeles, CA, band, Suite 19. They link with guitarist Bob Deal (b. Apr.4, 1955, Terre Haute, IN), whom they meet after he has placed an ad in a Los Angeles newspaper – "loud, rude, aggressive guitarist available". He changes his name to Mick Mars. Firing an early vocalist, Neil (b. Vincent Neil Wharton, Feb.8, 1961, Hollywood, CA), a former schoolmate of Neil's at Southern California's Royal Oak high school, is recruited from Cheap Trick covers group, Rock Candy, and Motley Crue is born.

1982 They begin playing increasingly outrageous gigs in the Los Angeles area, including dates at the Starwood club, where they chainsaw mannequins and set their trousers on fire. Signed to their own independent Leathur label, they release first album *Too Fast For Love*, recorded for under $20,000, and single *Toast Of The Town*, but the label soon goes out of business.

Mar They play Santa Monica Civic Auditorium, CA, and come close to selling out the 3,500-seat venue.

Oct Group headlines Halloween Special in Los Angeles with Y&T and Randy Hansen.

1983 May Impressed by their live performances, Elektra signs Motley Crue and puts them into the studio to record songs penned mainly by Sixx, having re-released the Leathur album minus 1 track.

Nov Second album *Shout At The Devil*, produced by veteran rock producer Tom Werman, is released. Accompanied by nationwide US tour supporting Kiss, it eventually peaks at US #17.

[11] Group embarks on 78-date North American headlining tour in San Bernardino, CA, set to end in Phoenix, AZ, on Apr.1, 1984.

Dec Debut album *Too Fast For Love*, now licensed to Elektra, climbs to US #77.

1984 Jan [12] Group plays New York's Madison Square Garden, supporting Ozzy Osbourne.

Feb *Looks That Kill* makes US #54.

June *Too Young To Fall* peaks at US #90.

Aug [18] Group makes its UK debut at the Monsters Of Rock festival at Castle Donington, Leics.

Dec [8] Vocalist Neil, while driving a Pantera sports car, is involved in a serious accident in Redondo Beach, CA, which kills Hanoi Rocks member Nick "Razzle" Dingley and injures 2 others. (Neil is charged with vehicular manslaughter and released on $2,500 bail. He will serve 20 days in jail, pay $2.6 million compensation to the injured parties, serve 200 hours of community service and begin school and college lectures on the dangers of drugs and alcohol.)

Hit Parader magazine readers' poll votes Motley Crue #1 Rock Act Of 1984.

985 Feb *Shout At The Devil* is voted #1 album by readers of **Circus** magazine.

June Third album *Theatre Of Pain*, with the group reunited, ships gold in US, eventually hits US #6 and makes UK #36 (their UK chart debut). (The album's liner notes convey the message: "To all Crue fans – if, and or when, you drink, don't take the wheel. Live and learn so we can all rock our asses off together for a long time to come. The Crue. We love you!")

July A revival of Brownsville Station's *Smokin' In The Boys Room* is Motley Crue's biggest single to date, making US #16 and UK #71. Much of its success is due to heavy rotation of video on MTV. Neil and Mars participate in heavy metal charity single *Stars*, to raise money for Ethiopian famine relief.

Sept Motley Crue begins world "Theatre Of Pain" tour, and drops *Kill 'Em Dead Kid* from its live act. (At the conclusion of the tour, Sixx undergoes drug and alcohol rehabilitation.)

Nov Japanese dates sell out as *Home Sweet Home* peaks at US #89.

986 Feb [6] Group begins 9-date UK tour at the Apollo theater, Manchester, with special guests Cheap Trick, set to end Feb.14/15 with dates at Hammersmith Odeon, London.

Mar *Home Sweet Home* is double A-side in UK with reissued *Smokin' In The Boys Room* and makes UK #51. The band finishes its world tour with sell-out US dates.

May [10] Tommy Lee marries Heather Locklear from ABC TV show "Dynasty" and has "Heather" tattooed on his left forearm. (He first met her at an REO Speedwagon concert.)

987 May Epitomizing the group's musical and personal attitude, *Girls Girls Girls* is released and will hit US #2 and UK #14. Its title track reaches US #12 and UK #26.

June Embarking on a world "Girls Girls Girls" tour, they use their own Lear jet for US dates. The 100-show tour grosses $21,100,000, but is truncated and finally scrapped after Sixx's reported drug overdose. This dramatic event prompts each member to enter drug and alcohol abuse rehabilitation programs in the coming months, after which members will report for work as "clean".

July Sixx announces plans to marry ex-Prince girlfriend Vanity in Dec.

Dec [12] *You're All I Need* stalls at US #83.

988 Jan Matthew John Trippe sues the group's management, claiming he was asked to masquerade as Sixx after the latter was injured in a serious car accident in 1983. Trippe claims he wrote and performed as Sixx for 2 years before Sixx rejoined the group in summer 1985 and demands royalty payments for songs he has written under Sixx's name. *You're All I Need/Wild Side* reaches UK #23.

[19] Manager Doc McGhee pleads guilty to importing more than 40,000 lb of marijuana. (His other act, Bon Jovi, was one of the first to do Rock Against Drugs commercials.)

Feb [17] A 12-year-old fan sets legs on fire while trying to imitate a stunt shown in group's "Live Wire" video.

June [16] Neil marries mud wrestler Sharisse Rudell at a Bel Air hotel in Los Angeles. Lee is the couple's best man.

989 May Lee goes to see Barry Manilow concert in New York.

Aug [12-13] Motley Crue participates in Moscow Music Peace Festival at Lenin Stadium with Bon Jovi, Ozzy Osbourne, The Scorpions, Cinderella, Skid Row and from USSR Gorky Park, Nuance, CCCP and Brigada S. All proceeds go to programs that fight drug and alcohol abuse in US and USSR.

Sept *Dr. Feelgood* hits UK #4.

[6] Group presents the Heavy Metal category at the MTV Video Music Awards. Neil and Guns N'Roses' Izzy Stradlin get into fight backstage.

Oct [5] Band plays a warm up tour date at the Whiskey, Los Angeles as The Foreskins.

[28] *Dr. Feelgood* hits US #6, while parent album *Dr. Feelgood* tops US chart, the group's first #1 album.

Nov *Dr. Feelgood* makes UK #50.

990 Jan [27] *Kickstart My Heart* reaches US #27.

[28] Band walks off stage for 20 mins. at Rushmore Plaza Civic Center, Rapid City, SD, concert after Neil is hit in the face by a cup of ice.

Mar [25] Lee is arrested in Augusta, GA, for baring his bottom to the audience during the Augusta-Richmond County Civic Center concert.

He is charged with indecent exposure and performing a sexually implicit act. Detective D.N. Bourbo makes the arrest.

Apr [7] Lee is injured during New Haven Coliseum, CT, concert, receiving mild concussion after falling during stunt that goes wrong. He spends the night in Yale-New Haven hospital.

[28] *Without You* hits US #8.

May Only remaining bachelor Sixx marries onetime **Playboy** playmate Brandi Brandt in Hawaii. *Without You* makes UK #39.

July [21] *Don't Go Away Mad (Just Go Away)* reaches US #19.

Sept [29] *Same Old Situation (S.O.S.)* stalls at US #78.

1991 Jan [25] Nikki and Brandi Sixx become parents to 8lb son Gunner Nicholas in Tarzana, CA.

[28] Motley Crue wins Heavy metal/Hard Rock Album for *Dr. Feelgood* at the 18th annual American Music Awards at the Shrine Auditorium, Los Angeles.

Mar [7] Group is named Best Heavy Metal Band in the annual **Rolling Stone** Readers' Picks music awards.

MOTORHEAD

Lemmy (bass, vocals)
Eddie Clarke (guitar)
Phil Taylor (drums)

1964 Lemmy (b. Ian Kilmister, Dec.24, 1945, Stoke-on-Trent, Staffs.), a vicar's son who has abandoned a career in horsebreaking, having heard a Little Richard record and begun his musical career in Blackpool, Lancs., as a member of soul bands The Rainmakers and The Motown Sect, and subsequently The Rockin' Vickers (wearing dog collars and Finnish national costume), moves to London, initially staying at Ron Wood's mother's house, playing in bands Sam Gopal's Dream and Opal Butterfly, and is a roadie for Jimi Hendrix.

1971 Aug He joins Hawkwind after bassist Dave Anderson leaves, initially for 6 months but stays for nearly 4 years. He does not even own a bass guitar, but will sing on their biggest hit *Silver Machine*.

1975 May Lemmy is dismissed from Hawkwind after spending 5 days in a Canadian jail for drug possession.

June On return to UK, Lemmy announces plans for a new band. Initially the name is to be Bastard, but is changed to Motorhead (the title of the last song he wrote for Hawkwind). The song itself becomes the group's anthem. Other members are Larry Wallis (still with The Pink Fairies) on guitar and Lucas Fox on drums. Lemmy's description of his musical approach is: "We're the kind of band that if we moved in next to you, your lawn would die."

July Motorhead debuts at London's Roundhouse, supporting Greenslade.

Sept Band conflicts with producer Dave Edmunds in studio sessions for debut album on United Artists, and Fritz Fryer takes over.

Oct They support Blue Öyster Cult at London's Hammersmith Odeon.

Dec Fox is replaced by Lemmy's friend Philthy Animal (b. Philip Taylor, Sept.21, 1954, Chesterfield, Derbys.), who has not played professionally before.

1976 Jan United Artists rejects Motorhead's debut album. (The tapes will be released in 1979 as *On Parole*.)

Feb "Fast" Eddie Clarke joins as second guitarist, and after 1 rehearsal as a 4-piece Wallis walks out. (The remaining trio, generally regarded as the definitive Motorhead line-up, will stay together for 6 years.) For 7 months, group has no manager, no recording contract and no income.

Dec 2 tracks, *White Line Fever* and *Leavin' Here*, are recorded for Stiff Records (Stiff will release the tracks 2 years later in a singles box set, and on compilations *A Bunch Of Stiffs* and *Hits Greatest Stiffs*.)

1977 Apr Band records a gig at the Marquee club, London. There is a recording hitch rendering the tapes unusable. Chiswick Records boss Ted Carroll offers them 2 days in the studio as consolation. They record 11 songs and Chiswick puts up money to finish an album.

June Motorhead supports Hawkwind on tour. Taylor breaks bones in his hand punching someone in a fight after the third gig, but carries on. Chiswick releases *Motorhead/City Kids* and then *Motorhead*, which makes UK #43.

Aug On a headlining UK tour, Taylor breaks bones again when he hits the tour manager's face. Remaining dates are cancelled.

1978 Taylor, Clarke, Speedy Keen and Billy Rath gig as The Muggers.

July Motorhead signs to Bronze Records, as part of a deal which includes Hawkwind and Girlschool.

Sept First Bronze single, a cover of *Louie Louie*, makes UK #68.

1979 Mar *Overkill* reaches UK #24 and the title track peaks at UK #39.

July *No Class* makes UK #61.

MOTORHEAD cont.

Oct *Bomber* reaches UK #12, while the title track climbs to UK #34.
Dec Liberty/UA releases the rejected 1976 album *On Parole*. It makes UK #65.

1980 **May** EP *The Golden Years* hits UK #8.
July [26] Motorhead headlines the "Heavy Metal Barn Dance" at Bingley Hall, Stafford, Staffs.
Oct Uncomprising fast hard-rock guitar-driven (as is all Motorhead material) *Ace Of Spades* reaches UK #15 and album of the same name hits UK #4 as the group tours constantly.
[22] Group begins 33-date UK tour at the Gaumont theater, Ipswich, Suffolk. The tour will end on Nov.29 with the last of 4 dates at the Hammersmith Odeon, London.
Dec Chiswick releases EP of old material, *Beer Drinkers And Hell Raisers* which makes UK #43.
[20] Taylor accidentally breaks a bone in his neck while partying after a show in Belfast. (By year's end Lemmy will have to fly to UK in mid-tour after infection in bone at back of hand sets in when a coin is thrown at him during gig in Ljubljana, Yugoslavia. He will spend 6 days in hospital.)

1981 **Feb** Motorhead unites with its feminine counterpart Girlschool as Headgirl and cover each other's songs (*Bomber* and *Emergency*) and Johnny Kidd & The Pirates' *Please Don't Touch* on EP *St. Valentine's Day Massacre* which hits UK #5. Lemmy collaborates with The Nolan Sisters, Cozy Powell and others on *Don't Do That*.
Apr Group begins its first US tour.
June *No Sleep Till Hammersmith*, a live album recorded at the Hammersmith Odeon in 1980, becomes possibly the noisiest UK #1 album ever, and proves a career peak.
July Live single *Motorhead/Over The Top* hits UK #6. Motorhead has become the clear ascendant of New Wave of British Heavy Metal (NWBHM), a movement which will inspire US bands like Metallica.

1982 **Mar** *Iron Fist* reaches UK #29.
Apr *Iron Fist* hits UK #6.
May Motorhead begins a major US tour. Lemmy's plan to record a version of Tammy Wynette's *Stand By Your Man* with The Plasmatics' Wendy O. Williams is the final straw for Clarke, who quits the tour. (He will later form Fastway.) Brian Robertson (ex-Thin Lizzy) is brought in as replacement.
June *Iron Fist* makes US #174.

1983 **Feb** Big Beat releases *What's Words Worth*, recorded live at London's Roundhouse early in the band's career. It reaches UK #71.
May *I Got Mine* makes UK #46.
June *Another Perfect Day* peaks at UK #20.
July *Shine* makes UK #59.
Aug *Another Perfect Day* reaches US #153. Robertson and Taylor both leave. Lemmy auditions guitarists, and Phil Campbell and Wurzel (b. Oct.23, 1949) join. Ex-Saxon drummer Pete Gill also joins the new 4-piece Motorhead.

1984 **May** The new Motorhead debuts at the Hammersmith Odeon.
Sept *Killed By Death* reaches UK #51 and double album compilation of mainly old material *No Remorse* makes UK #14. Group leaves Bronze. (The label serves an injunction on them and the band will be unable to record for nearly 2 years.)
Oct The new line-up tours UK – to rave reviews. A lack of funds means the band has to stop touring. They move into a house in suburban London (next door to a clergyman).

1985 **June** Lemmy records a single with 19-year-old UK model Samantha Fox (her first) but an injunction means the record is never released.

1986 **May** Motorhead contributes to a post-Live Aid heavy metal fund-raising *Hear N' Aid*, which makes UK #50 and US #80. Single *Stars* reaches UK #26.
June *Deaf Forever* reaches UK #67. It is the first collaboration with Bill Laswell and new label GWR, which also re-releases the Motorhead back catalog.
July *Orgasmatron*, written in 2 days and recorded in 3 weeks, reaches UK #21.
Aug [16] Motorhead takes part in the seventh annual Monsters Of Rock festival at Castle Donington, Leics.
Dec *Orgasmatron* peaks at US #157.

1987 **Apr** Lemmy contributes to Ferry Aid's *Let It Be*, released to benefit those bereaved by the Zeebrugge ferry disaster. The record sells over a half million copies, topping the charts for 3 weeks.
Sept Lemmy plays in comic strip movie "Eat The Rich". His performance wins no awards but the Motorhead theme tune for the film appears on Motorhead album *Rock'N'Roll* which makes UK #34 and US #150.

1988 **Oct** [15] Second live album, *No Sleep At All*, stalls at UK #79.
1990 **Feb** Lemmy & The Upsetters with Mick Green contributes a cover of *Blue Suede Shoes* to the compilation album *The Last Temptation Of Elvis*, to benefit the Nordoff-Robbins Music Therapy charity.
Group signs to WTG Records, and makes new album with Ed Stasium and Dave Edmunds (neither of whom last the distance) in Los Angeles, CA, where Lemmy is now fully resident though the state's health and fitness lifestyle makes little impression on the hardened non-stop drinking party machine.
1991 **Jan** With a current line-up of Wurzel, Campbell, re-joined Taylor and Lemmy, and licensed to Epic Records, Motorhead's uncomprising consistency continues to be rewarded as *The One To Sing The Blues* peaks at UK #45, while parent album *1916*, including a rare cello backed ballad, produced by Peter Solley, reaches UK #24. On the group's 16th anniversary, Lemmy is quoted as saying: "We've been going 4 years longer than the Third Reich."
Apr [20] *1916* makes initial US peak at #151.

MOTT THE HOOPLE

Ian Hunter (vocals, guitar)
Mick Ralphs (guitar)
Verden Allen (keyboards)
Overend Watts (bass)
Dale "Buffin" Griffin (drums)

1968 Watts (b. Peter Watts, May 13, 1949, Birmingham, W.Midlands), Griffin (b. Oct.24, 1948, Ross-on-Wye, Hereford & Worcs.), Allen (b. May 26, 1944, Hereford, Hereford & Worcs.) and Ralphs (b. May 31, 1944, Hereford) come together as The Shakedown Sound after meeting as members of The Doc Thomas Group. They switch names to Silence (previously used by Watts and Griffin for a post-school band), and vocalist Stan Tippins joins.

1969 Ralphs sends a demo tape to Guy Stevens at Island Records, and he becomes their manager and producer. Tippins is sacked and Stevens places an ad in UK music paper **Melody Maker** for a new singer/keyboards player. Hunter (b. June 3, 1946, Shrewsbury, Shrops) replies and wins the audition. He is a veteran of clubs in Hamburg, Germany, and has played on singles by the 1958 Rock'N'Roll Show and Charlie Wolfe in 1968.
June Stevens renames the group Mott The Hoople (after a 1967 novel by Willard Manus).
Oct First single on Island is *Rock'N'Roll Queen* which fails to chart.
Nov Debut album *Mott The Hoople* (originally to have been titled *Talking Bear Mountain Picnic Massacre Disaster Dylan Blues* but overruled by Island) includes covers of The Kinks, Sonny Bono and Doug Sahm (Sir Douglas Quintet) material, and highlights Hunter's distinctive vocals. (In 1970, it will make UK #66 and US #185.)

1970 **Oct** *Mad Shadows* makes UK #48. Band tours widely in UK, becoming a major live attraction to a degree not reflected by record sales. Rather more chaotic US visits help promote the group in the US.
1971 **Apr** *Wild Life* climbs to US #44. It includes a live version of Little Richard oldie *Keep A Knockin'*.
July [8] They play London's Royal Albert Hall and cause a minor riot leading to a temporary ban on rock gigs at the venue. The group is also ordered to pay a "damages to property" bill of £1,467.
Aug *Brain Capers*, the band's last album for Island, fails to chart.
Oct *Midnight Lady*, produced by George "Shadow" Morton, is final Island single but fails to chart.
1972 **Mar** [26] After a show in Zurich, Switzerland, they decide to split. Long-time Mott fan David Bowie, hearing of the decision, offers them one of his new songs to continue recording. After turning down *Suffragette City*, they choose *All The Young Dudes*.
July Extracting itself from the Island contract, the band signs a new deal with CBS.
Sept *All The Young Dudes*, produced by Bowie, hits UK #3, causing a minor controversy over the line "stealing clothes from Marks and Sparks" (later changed to "unmarked cars").
Oct *All The Young Dudes* reaches UK #21. It includes contributions from both Bowie and his guitarist Mick Ronson. Island issues *Rock'N'Roll Queen*, a compilation of earlier tracks.
Nov As *All The Young Dudes* makes US #37 and the album reaches US #89, the group begins its first major US tour (which Hunter chronicles in a diary).
[25] Band plays the Woodstock Of The West Festival in Los Angeles, CA, with Stevie Wonder, The Eagles and The Bee Gees among others.
Dec On return from US, Allen quits to pursue solo projects. He is not

1973

Jan *One Of The Boys*, taken from the album, makes US #96. The band plays its first UK gigs as a 4-piece.

July *Honaloochie Boogie*, their first release with new members Morgan Fisher (ex-Love Affair) (piano) and Mick Bolton (organ) makes UK #12.

Aug Band headlines a highly successful US tour, including a sell-out week at Broadway's Uris theater, New York. *Mott* hits UK #7 and reaches US #35. Ralphs leaves to form new band Bad Company, and is replaced by Luther Grosvenor from Spooky Tooth, now calling himself Ariel Bender.

Sept *All The Way From Memphis* hits UK #10.

Dec *Roll Away The Stone* hits UK #8.

[14] Group ends 22-date UK tour at the Hammersmith Odeon, London.

1974

Apr *The Golden Age Of Rock And Roll* reaches UK #16 and *The Hoople* makes UK #11.

June *The Hoople* reaches US #28, while *The Golden Age Of Rock And Roll* peaks at US #96 (the band's last US hit single). Hunter's book, the revealing **Diary Of A Rock'N'Roll Star** (based on the band's touring exploits), is published.

July *Foxy Foxy* peaks at UK #33. Bolton leaves, apparently on religious grounds, and is replaced by ex-Amen Corner keyboardist Blue Weaver. Meanwhile, early compilation *Rock'N'Roll Queen*, issued in US on Atlantic, makes US #112.

Sept [21] Bender quits, to be replaced on guitar by Mick Ronson.

Oct Hunter collapses from exhaustion in US, prior to planned UK and European dates.

Nov *Saturday Gigs* reaches UK #41, while live album *Mott The Hoople- Live*, recorded in Nov.1973 at London's Hammersmith Odeon and in New York in May 1974, makes UK #32 and US #23.

Dec [16] With Hunter not fully recovered, and problems looming over rescheduling of gigs, the band decides to split.

1975

Jan Hunter and Ronson form The Hunter-Ronson Band, designed to tour to promote the solo albums on which both are working.

Mar Ronson's solo *Play, Don't Worry* reaches UK #29 and US #103.

May Buffin, Watts and Fisher regroup under the truncated name Mott, adding new members Ray Major (guitar) and Nigel Benjamin (vocals), while Hunter's solo *Ian Hunter* reaches UK #21 and US #50. The Hunter-Ronson Band plays a sell-out UK tour, and then makes a short visit to US, before splitting.

June Hunter's solo single *Once Bitten, Twice Shy* reaches UK #14.

Oct Mott's *Drive On* reaches UK #54 and US #160, and will be the group's last chart success.

1976

June Hunter's *All American Alien Boy* makes UK #29 and US #177, while Mott's *Shouting And Pointing* fails to chart.

Nov Benjamin leaves Mott and the band splits.

1977

May Mott regroups again, adding John Fiddler from Medicine Head, as British Lions. (They will last some 2 years, after which Fisher will form his own Pipe label, and Buffin and Watts their own Grimstone Productions, producing Slaughter & The Dogs and Department S, among others. Buffin will revert to his real name and occasionally produce live sessions for BBC's Radio 1. Allen and Grosvenor will release material through Jet and Spinet Records over the next 5 years.) After 2 years' living and working in US (re-publishing an updated version of his book, as **Reflections Of A Rock'N'Roll Star**), Hunter returns to UK with a new 4-piece backing band named Overnight Angels (after his new album). Band plays 10 well-received dates in UK, but the album fails to chart there and is not issued in US. (Hunter will follow it with 18 months' resting in New York, though he will produce Generation X's *Valley Of The Dolls* during 1978.)

1979

May Hunter's *You're Never Alone With A Schizophrenic*, his first for new label Chrysalis, reaches UK #49 and US #35.

June [28] Hunter appears at New York's Palladium theater with Mick Ronson and Ellen Foley.

Sept Hunter's *Just Another Night* reaches US #68.

1980

Apr Hunter's double live album *Ian Hunter Live: Welcome To The Club*, recorded during a record-breaking 7-night sell-out at Los Angeles's The Roxy, reaches UK #61 and US #69.

1981

Sept Hunter's *Short Back And Sides*, with help from Todd Rundgren and 2 members of The Clash, reaches UK #79 and US #62.

1983

Aug Hunter switches back to CBS/Columbia for *All Of The Good Ones Are Taken*, which fails to chart in UK but makes US #125.

1989

After a long period out of the public eye, Hunter returns as co-writer of Mick Jagger's *Just Wanna Hold* and The Hunter-Ronson Band re-forms, with new Bernard Edwards-produced *Y U I ORTA*, making US #157.

1990

Feb *Y U I ORTA*, released in UK on Mercury Records, is supported with a few sell-out UK dates.

THE MOVE

Carl Wayne (vocals)
Roy Wood (vocals, guitar)
Trevor Burton (lead guitar)
Ace Kefford (bass)
Bev Bevan (drums)

1966

Feb Group is formed in Birmingham, W.Midlands, by members of 3 of the city's best existing beat groups: Wood (b. Ulysses Adrian Wood, Nov.8, 1946, Birmingham) ex-Mike Sheridan & The Nightriders; Wayne (b. Aug.18, 1944, Moseley, W.Midlands), Kefford (b. Christopher Kefford, Dec.10, 1946, Moseley), Bevan (b. Nov.24, 1944, Birmingham) ex-Carl Wayne & The Vikings and Burton (b. Mar.9, 1944, Aston, W.Midlands) ex-Danny King & The Mayfair Set. Stabilizing as a quintet after initial jams at Birmingham's Cedar club, group builds strong local reputation, links with manager Tony Secunda and moves to London.

July [30] Group performs at the 6th annual National Jazz & Blues Festival, Windsor, Berks. (They set off distress flares during their act.)

Dec With a cult following gained by several Secunda-initiated PR stunts and from regular outrageous behavior during a residency at London's Marquee club (taken over from The Who), the group signs with producer Denny Cordell and, via him, to Deram Records.

1967

Jan *Night Of Fear*, a Roy Wood song with a riff based on the 1812 Overture, hits UK #2.

Apr Band offers a £200 reward for information leading to the recovery of tapes stolen from their agent's car in London's Tin Pan Alley. (The tapes will subsequently be found on a building site in North London. The laborer who finds them receives the £200 reward.)

[29] Group plays on a 14-hour "Technicolour Dream" concert in the Great Hall of the Alexandra Palace, London, with Pink Floyd, Tomorrow and John's Children (featuring Marc Bolan).

May *I Can Hear The Grass Grow*, developing Wood's flirtation with psychedelia, hits UK #5. Group begins to gain a reputation for Who-type destruction (usually smashing TV sets or obliterating effigies of people like Adolf Hitler) on its stage act and on TV appearances.

Sept [30] BBC Radio 1 is launched in UK, with The Move's *Flowers In The Rain* as the first disk played.

Oct *Flowers In The Rain* hits UK #2. Group has switched, with other Cordell-produced acts, to Regal Zonophone Records (a label previously reserved for Salvation Army music).

Nov The Move is successfully sued by UK Prime Minister Harold Wilson over a nude caricature of him on promotional postcard for *Flowers In The Rain*. All the royalties earned by the record go to charity as part of the settlement. *Cherry Blossom Clinic*, scheduled as the next single, is dropped since its lyric (concerning a mental asylum) is considered likely to create more unfavorable publicity. (The track will appear on the group's first album.)

1968

Mar *Fire Brigade* climbs to UK #3.

Apr Debut album *Move* makes UK #15. Kefford leaves group due to illness. He does not return and will subsequently pursue a solo career. (He will record a single as The Ace Kefford Stand for Atlantic, reviving The Yardbirds' *For Your Love*.) Burton switches to bass and the group continues as a quartet. Richard Tandy (who will later play with Burton in Balls and with Wood and Bevan in ELO) occasionally joins on keyboards and bass.

July *Wild Tiger Woman* does not chart.

Sept Live *Something Else* is released. It is an unusual 5-track 33rpm 7" EP, later to become an expensive collector's item, but it fails to chart.

1969

Feb *Blackberry Way* tops UK chart for a week, The Move's only #1 hit. Burton, tired of the group's commercial material, quits on the eve of a US tour, which has to be cancelled. (Burton will join The Uglys and then form Balls with ex-Moody Blues' vocalist Denny Laine.)

Mar Jeff Lynne (b. Dec.30, 1947, Birmingham, W.Midlands) of The Idle Race and Rick Price (b. June 10, 1944, Birmingham) of Sight And Sound are invited to join The Move. Lynne decides against it but Price comes in as bassist.

Aug *Curly* reaches UK #12.

Oct The Move's only US tour is unsuccessful and the Northern UK cabaret gigs which follow cause a rift between Wayne and the others.

1970

Jan Wayne leaves for a solo cabaret and TV career which will see moderate success (but not on disk) during the 70s. Lynne agrees to join in his place, admitting to being more interested in the "Electric Light Orchestra" project currently being mooted by Wood.

Feb *Shazam* fails to chart but Wood's track *Hello Susie* is covered by Amen Corner and hits UK #4.

May *Brontosaurus*, an uncharacteristically heavy rocker, hits UK #6.

June [1] Rick Price signs solo and production deal with President Records.

Oct *Looking On* fails to chart, as does *When Alice Comes Back To The Farm*, taken from it.

1971 **July** The band moves to EMI's Harvest label, with Wood and Lynne jointly producing. *Tonight* reaches UK #11 but *Message From The Country* fails to chart.

Oct The Move makes its final live appearances, after which Price leaves. (He will form Sheridan/Price and then Mongrel, but will later rejoin Wood in Wizzard. The only Move performances will be on UK TV, promoting its final 2 singles.)

Nov *Chinatown* peaks at UK #23. Plans are made for transforming The Move into The Electric Light Orchestra (later known as ELO), with the recruitment of 5 (mostly strings) players, including ex-Move part-timer Richard Tandy.

1972 **Feb** Wood releases solo *When Grandma Plays The Banjo*; it fails to chart. (Later sideline solo efforts in Wizzard will net him 4 UK Top 20 hits.)

Apr [16] First live appearance of ELO, in Croydon, London, signifies the end of The Move.

June Final Move single *California Man* hits UK #7.

Aug Wood leaves ELO to form Wizzard.

Nov *Do Ya*, by Lynne on UK B-side of *California Man*, is issued as an A-side in US and gives The Move its only US chart entry, reaching #93. (The song will later be a bigger US hit for ELO.)

ALISON MOYET

1982 **Jan** Moyet (b. Genevieve Alison Moyet, June 18, 1961, Essex), nicknamed "Alf" from childhood by her French father, having sung with Southend R&B groups The Vicars and The Screaming Abdabs, joins ex-Depeche Mode keyboardist and songwriter Vince Clarke to form Yazoo. The unlikely combination of Moyet's bluesy vocals and Clarke's synthesizers is successful and provides 18 months of UK hit singles and albums.

1983 **July** Yazoo splits after completing its second album. Clarke remains with Yazoo's label Mute but Moyet signs as soloist to CBS, using the name Alison Moyet rather than the "Alf" she has been through Yazoo's career. Recording is delayed until contractual difficulties are sorted out with US Sire, to which Moyet is still tied via Yazoo's US deal.

1984 Moyet marries long-time boyfriend Malcolm Lee and moves from Essex to Hertfordshire.

Aug CBS debut *Love Resurrection*, with a lusher sound than the sparse electronics of Yazoo, hits UK #10.

Nov Traditional soul-styled *All Cried Out* reaches UK #8. *Alf*, produced and written by Tony Swain and Steve Jolley, with 1 song, *Invisible*, by Lamont Dozier, hits UK #1 and will stay on chart for a year. Moyet begins a major UK tour to promote the album.

Dec *Invisible* reaches UK #21.

1985 **Feb** [10] She heads the bill of a benefit concert at the London Palladium for National Jazz Centre, on a varied line-up which includes Jools Holland from Squeeze and The Humphrey Lyttleton Band.

[11] Moyet wins Best British Fenale Artist at the fourth annual BRIT Awards at the Grosvenor House, London.

Apr In a change of style to acknowledge her original musical preferences, Moyet revives Billie Holiday's jazz standard *That Ole Devil Called Love* and has her biggest UK hit at #2. She gives birth to her first child (but her marriage will fail within the year).

June She follows her Billie Holiday revival with a UK tour accompanied by a jazz band, but receives much criticism for over-reaching herself, and does not commit the stage set to record.

July [13] She appears in Live Aid at Wembley, London, duetting with Paul Young on *That's The Way Love Is*.

1987 **Jan** After a long silence, *Is This Love* reaches UK #3.

Apr *Raindancing* hits UK #2; *Weak In The Presence Of Beauty* UK #6.

June *Ordinary Girl* proves a disappointing UK seller, peaking at #43.

July *Raindancing* makes US #94.

Dec A revival of Ketty Lester oldie *Love Letters*, remaining true to Lester's hit arrangement, hits UK #4, aided by a popular domestic scene video co-starring UK comediennes French & Saunders.

1988 **Feb** [8] Moyet wins Best British Female Artist at the seventh annual BRIT Awards at London's Royal Albert Hall.

1989 **May** [19] Moyet is granted an uncontested divorce from hairdresser husband Malcolm Lee after 5-year marriage, on the grounds they had lived apart for more than 2 years.

1990 Moyet spends much of the year recording her third solo album which will be released by (newly-named) Columbia/Sony in Apr.1991.

May [12] Moyet appears live at "The Simple Truth" concert for Kurdish refugees at Wembley Arena, London.

MUD

Les Gray (vocals)
Rob Davis (lead guitar, vocals)
Ray Stiles (bass, vocals)
Dave Mount (drums, vocals)

1966 **Feb** Gray (b. Apr.9, 1946, Carshalton, Surrey), a veteran of skiffle and trad jazz bands, and Mount (b. Mar.3, 1947, Carshalton), both from different local groups, team to form Mud. They recruit local musicians, Davis (b. Oct.1, 1947, Carshalton) and Stiles (b. Nov.20, 1946, Carshalton), ex-Trolls and Remainder.

Apr They make their first live appearance at Streatham Ice Rink, South London, and release one-off debut single *Flower Power*, for CBS.

Oct The band makes its radio debut on UK BBC's "Monday Monday".

1967 **Apr** Pye signs group after it wins national "Search For Sound" contest.

1968 **Apr** After 2 years' gigging as a semi-professional band, Mud turns professional and re-signs with CBS, releasing *Up The Airy Mountain*.

1969 **May** Group makes its UK TV debut on BBC's "The Basil Brush Show", as Philips Records releases the band's third single *Shangri-La*.

1970 **June** *Jumping Jehosaphat*, also on Philips, like the first 3 singles, fails.

1973 **Feb** Mud begins a UK tour as support to US singer Jack Jones.

Apr *Crazy* reaches UK #12.

July *Hypnosis* makes UK #16.

Dec *Dyna-Mite*, produced and written, like many of Mud's early hits, by song-writing team Nicky Chinn and Mike Chapman, hits UK #4.

1974 **Feb** *Tiger Feet* tops UK chart for 4 weeks, and starts a short-lived UK dance craze. (Labelmate Suzi Quatro will knock them from the top with *Devil Gate Drive*.)

Mar [15] Group begins a 30-date UK tour at Coventry College of Education, W.Midlands.

May *The Cat Crept In* hits UK #2.

Aug *Rocket* hits UK #6.

Sept *Mud Rock* hits UK #8. Mud signs to Private Stock Records. (First single for the label will not be released until Oct.1975.)

Dec *Lonely This Christmas*, on which Gray indulges his passion for Elvis Presley vocal inflections, tops UK chart over Christmas period.

1975 **Mar** *The Secrets That You Keep* (another Presley pastiche), released on St. Valentine's Day, hits UK #3.

May *Oh Boy*, a revival of The Crickets 1957 UK #3, tops UK chart, deposing The Bay City Rollers' *Bye Bye Baby*.

July *Moonshine Sally* hits UK #10 while *Mud Rock Vol.2* hits UK #6.

Aug *One Night* makes UK #32.

Oct *L-L-Lucy*, the group's first release on Private Stock, hits UK #10.

Nov *Mud's Greatest Hits* reaches UK #25.

Dec Ballad *Show Me You're A Woman* hits UK #8 and *Use Your Imagination* makes UK #33.

1976 **June** *Shake It Down* reaches UK #12.

Dec *Lean On Me*, a 1972 UK #18 for its writer Bill Withers, hits UK #7. (This will end Mud's chart-making career, but the group will subsequently record for RCA.)

1977 **Mar** Gray, signed to Warner Bros. as a solo artist, reaches UK #32 with a revival of The Mindbenders 1966 UK #2 *A Groovy Kind Of Love*.

1985 **Dec** Re-issued *Lonely This Christmas* peaks at UK #61, as Mud continues its UK cabaret circuit.

1988 **Sept** Stiles makes his first "Top Of The Pops" appearance in almost 12 years as a member of The Hollies, performing *He Ain't Heavy, He's My Brother*.

RICKY NELSON

1957 **Apr** [10] Nelson (b. Eric Hilliard Nelson, May 8, 1940, Teaneck, NJ), second son of US showbiz couple Ozzie and Harriet Nelson (formerly a bandleader and band vocalist), has played "himself" in family radio show "The Adventures Of Ozzie And Harriet" since Mar.1949, and since its switch to ABC TV in Oct.1952. He sings Fats Domino's *I'm Walking* for the first time on the show, eliciting a huge teenage response. In real life, Nelson has told a girlfriend he intends to record a single, as a defensive reaction to her adulation of Elvis Presley. Ozzie Nelson arranges through contacts at Verve Records to have the song recut in a studio session (arranged by guitarist Barney Kessel), along with 2 other tracks.

May Verve releases single *A Teenager's Romance* coupled with *I'm Walking* and, with instant TV exposure, it sells 60,000 copies in 3 days.

June *A Teenager's Romance* hits US #8 and *I'm Walking* makes US #17, with total sales topping a million.

Sept Third track from debut session, *You're My One And Only Love*, is issued coupled with Kessel's instrumental *Honey Bop* and makes US #14. No contract has been signed with Verve and, when it becomes clear that the label is withholding royalties, Ozzie Nelson initiates legal proceedings, and agrees to Lou Chudd of Imperial Records (which had Fats Domino's original *I'm Walking*) signing Ricky. Additionally, 1 of his songs is included in each subsequent episode of "The Adventures Of Ozzie And Harriet" (which will guarantee maximum exposure through to 1966, when the series ends).

Oct *Be-Bop Baby*, his Imperial debut (a self-confessed try at a Carl Perkins-type rockabilly track), hits US #5 and is a second million-seller. B-side cover of Elvis Presley's recent version of *Have I Told You Lately That I Love You* reaches US #29.

1958 Jan Uptempo *Stood Up* hits US #5 (earning another gold disk) and B-side *Waiting In School*, written by Johnny and Dorsey Burnette, makes US #18. Debut album *Ricky*, a mixture of familiar rock songs and ballads, tops US chart for 2 weeks.

Feb Nelson forms his own full-time band for live work and for recording sessions as well as "Ozzie And Harriet" TV slots. He recruits James Burton (guitar) and James Kirkland (bass) after hearing them play in the studio with Bob Luman, plus Gene Garf (piano) and Richie Frost (drums). (Kirkland will later be replaced by Joe Osborn.) Meanwhile, *Stood Up* is his UK chart debut, at #27.

Apr *Believe What You Say*, another Johnny and Dorsey Burnette composition, hits US #8, and is coupled with country-flavored *My Bucket's Got A Hole In It*, which makes US #18.

Aug *Poor Little Fool*, written by Sharon Sheeley, becomes Nelson's first #1 single, topping US chart for 2 weeks, and selling well over a million.

Sept Second album *Ricky Nelson*, including *Poor Little Fool*, hits US #7.

Oct *Poor Little Fool* hits UK #4.

Nov Introspective ballad *Lonesome Town*, the first song submitted to Nelson by songwriter Baker Knight, hits US #7, while B-side *I Got A Feeling*, also penned by Knight, hits US #10, combining to make a further million-seller.

Dec UK follow-up to *Poor Little Fool* is familiar oldie *Someday (You'll Want Me To Want You)*, which competes with a UK chart version by Jodi Sands. It hits UK #9, while B-side *I Got A Feeling* makes UK #27.

1959 Jan He co-stars in western "Rio Bravo", directed by Howard Hawks, with John Wayne and Dean Martin.

Mar *Ricky Sings Again*, another compendium of rockers and country-style ballads, reaches US #14.

Apr 2 tracks taken from the album form the next million-selling double A-side single: Knight's ballad *Never Be Anyone Else But You* hits US #6, while rocking Dorsey Burnette composition *It's Late* hits US #9.

May *It's Late* hits UK #3.

June *Never Be Anyone Else But You* reaches UK #14.

Aug Another double A-side US Top 10 has both *Sweeter Than You* (a Knight ballad) and *Just A Little Too Much* (a Burnette rocker) independently hitting US #9.

Sept *Sweeter Than You* makes UK #19 and *Just A Little Too Much* reaches UK #11.

Nov *Songs By Ricky*, including both sides of last hit, reaches US #22.

Dec Offbeat and laid-back *I Wanna Be Loved* reaches US #20 and B-side *Mighty Good* makes US #38.

1960 Jan *I Wanna Be Loved* reaches UK #30.

May *Young Emotions* makes US #12, with B-side *Right By My Side* peaking at US #59.

July *Young Emotions* stalls at UK #48.

Sept *I'm Not Afraid* peaks at US #27 and B-side revival of *Yes Sir, That's My Baby* at US #34.

Oct *More Songs By Ricky* makes US #18. He appears in comedy film "The Wackiest Ship In The Army", with Jack Lemmon.

1961 Jan *You Are The Only One* reaches US #25. B-side is *Milk Cow Blues* (one of the earliest songs recorded by Elvis Presley), which peaks at US #79.

May Jerry Fuller-penned *Travelin' Man* (originally offered to Sam Cooke, but rejected) tops the US chart for 2 weeks, giving Nelson another million-seller after a long run of smaller successes. B-side *Hello Mary Lou*, a Gene Pitney composition, hits US #9.

[8] On his 21st birthday, Nelson officially changes his performing name from Ricky to Rick.

July *Rick Is 21*, containing both sides of the recent single, hits US #8, while *Hello Mary Lou* gets A-side promotion in UK and hits #2.

Nov *A Wonder Like You* makes US #11. B-side *Everlovin'* makes US #16.

Dec *Everlovin'* is UK A-side and reaches US #23.

1962 Apr *Young World*, written by Fuller, hits US #5; B-side revival of Gershwin's *Summertime* reaches US #89.

May *Young World* makes UK #19.

June *Album Seven By Rick* reaches US #27.

Sept *Teenage Idol*, a pseudo-autobiographical lament on the isolation of fame, hits US #5 and climbs to UK #39.

1963 Feb Nelson's last new single for Imperial, *It's Up To You*, another Fuller song, hits US #6 and makes US #22. Nelson signs new $1 million contract with Decca Records, to last 20 years.

Mar Compilation *Best Sellers By Rick* makes US #112.

Apr Both sides of Decca debut single *You Don't Love Me Anymore /I Got A Woman* chart at US #47 and #49, while Imperial's *That's All/I'm In Love Again* makes US #48 and #67. Nelson has time to promote neither: he marries Kristin Harmon, daughter of American football star Tom Harmon, and she joins him (also playing his wife) in the cast of "Ozzie And Harriet".

June *String Along*, previously recorded by Fabian, and given the same guitar riff by Burton as *Poor Little Fool*, reaches US #25.

July *For Your Sweet Love* makes US #20.

Oct First major Decca hit is Latin-rhythm revival of Glenn Miller's *Fools Rush In*, which makes both US and UK #12.

1964 Jan Imperial releases an old album track, Gene Pitney song *Today's Teardrops*, which reaches US #54.

Feb Another revival on Decca, 1930 song *For You*, repeating the Latin arrangement, hits US #6 and UK #14. It is his last US Top 10 disk, and last UK chart entry, for 8 years. *Rick Nelson Sings For You* makes US #14, and will be his last album chart entry until 1970.

May Another Latin revival, *The Very Thought Of You*, reaches US #26.

Sept *There's Nothing I Can Say* peaks at US #47.

Nov He features in movie "Love And Kisses" (adapted from a Broadway play), co-starring with wife Kristin, but it arouses little attention in an entertainment world where The Beatles and the "British invasion" have swept aside much that was previously established.

Dec *A Happy Guy* makes US #82.

1965 Mar Billy Vera composition, *Mean Old World*, peaks at US #96, and will be his last US single chart entry for almost 5 years.

1966 May He enters the country music phase of his career with critically acclaimed *Bright Lights And Country Music* but it fails to chart.

Sept [3] "The Adventures Of Ozzie And Harriet" finally ends on US TV after 14 years.

1967 Apr Second country album *Country Fever* again reaps critical plaudits but small sales.

1968 Nov *Another Side Of Rick*, with folkier country material and including a trio of Tim Hardin compositions, is released.

1969 May Nelson forms a new road and recording band, with Allen Kemp (guitar), Tom Brumley (steel guitar), ex-Poco member Randy Meisner (bass) and Pat Shanahan (drums). (This will become The Stone Canyon Band.)

1970 Jan *Rick Nelson In Concert* features the still-unnamed Stone Canyon Band. Recorded at the Troubadour in Los Angeles, CA, it inlcudes 3 Bob Dylan songs, plus Nelson's own oldies *I'm Walking* and *Hello Mary Lou*. Dylan's *She Belongs To Me*, is also released in a studio-recorded version, and puts Nelson back on US Singles chart, at #33.

Apr Nelson's own composition *Easy To Be Free* makes US #48.

Nov *Rick Sings Nelson* peaks at US #196.

1971 June *Rudy The Fifth* fails to chart but is regarded as one of his best, highlighted by The Rolling Stones song *Honky Tonk Women* (a Nelson concert favorite around this time) and *Gypsy Pilot*, which is also issued (unsuccessfully) as a single. Meisner leaves The Stone Canyon Band after the recording, to co-found The Eagles.

Oct [15] Booed at the seventh annual Rock'N'Roll Revival concert at Madison Square Garden, New York, on a bill with Gary U.S. Bonds, The Coasters, The Shirelles, Bobby Rydell, Bo Diddley and Chuck Berry, when he plays new material alongside his early hits, Nelson pens *Garden Party* as a response.

1972 Oct *Garden Party* hits US #6 (in a Top 10 which includes Elvis Presley and Chuck Berry) and is Nelson's first million-seller since 1961.

Nov *Garden Party* makes UK #41 – his first UK hit single for 8 years, but also his last. He makes his first visit to UK, playing mainly at US bases with The Stone Canyon Band.

1973 Jan *Garden Party* reaches US #32.

Feb *Palace Guard*, taken from the album, peaks at US #65. This is his first release on MCA, as US Decca Records is renamed.

1974 Mar *Windfall*, the last with The Stone Canyon Band, makes US #190. Following this, the MCA contract (officially with 9 years to run) is terminated.

1977 Sept Nelson signs to Epic, releasing self-produced *Intakes*, which does not chart. (His short period with Epic is unsuccessful but he experiments with material from a wide range of sources including John Fogerty and UK's Gallagher & Lyle. His wife Kristin divorces him.)

1981 **Feb** He signs a new deal with Capitol and releases *Playing To Win* (produced by Jack Nitszche), which is his last US chart entry, at #153. (He will continue to gig widely, both in US and overseas, during the early to mid-80s, mixing new material with old in audience-pleasing fashion. He also has guest acting roles on TV drama series like "McCloud" and "Petrocelli".)

1983 He features in US NBC TV movie "High School USA", playing a school principal, with his mother Harriet portraying his secretary.

1985 **Aug** [22] Nelson co-stars with Fats Domino in a live spectacular at Universal Amphitheater in Los Angeles, CA. (The show is taped as a TV special for syndicated US airing in Jan.1986. Following his death, it will be re-edited as a tribute show. A subsequent show, also recorded, features Nelson singing John Fogerty's *Big Train (From Memphis)* with Johnny Cash, Jerry Lee Lewis, Roy Orbison and Carl Perkins.)
Nov He tours UK on a well-received nostalgia package which co-stars Bobby Vee, Bo Diddley and Del Shannon.
Dec [31] Nelson dies, along with his fiancee Helen Blair, his sound engineer Clark Russell and back-up band members Bobby Neal, Patrick Woodward, Rick Intveld and Andy Chapin, when a chartered DC3 carrying them between concert dates in Guntersville, AL, and Dallas, TX, catches fire and crashes near De Kalb, TX. (Rumors ensue that the fire was caused by the plane's occupants freebasing cocaine.)

1986 **Jan** [6] A memorial service for Nelson is held in the Church Of The Hills at Forest Lawn Memorial Park, Hollywood, CA.
A posthumous album, *All The Best*, is released, consisting of recent re-recordings of his hits.

1990 After several attempts, Nelson's twin sons, Matthew and Gunnar, find commercial success as lite-metal duo, Nelson.

SANDY NELSON

1958 Nelson (b. Sander Nelson, Dec.1, 1938, Santa Monica, CA), inspired at age 7 to play drums after seeing Gene Krupa live, is a neighbor of Dean Torrence (later of Jan And Dean), and in a high school-based group with both Jan And Dean and future Beach Boys member Bruce Johnston, though he leaves before the recording of Jan & Arnie-credited hit *Jennie Lee*. With Johnston, he joins local club/dance band Kip Tyler & The Flips as their drummer, and plays on some singles recorded for Ebb and Challenge labels. He begins regular session work on small-label productions around Los Angeles, CA (notably those involving the Kim Fowley/Bruce Johnston/Gary "Skip" Paxton "brat pack"), and makes his first major hit appearance drumming on Phil Spector's first disk, The Teddy Bears' *To Know Him Is To Love Him.*

1959 **July** Nelson finances the recording of his own drums-highlighting instrumental, *Teen Beat* (with Johnston playing piano), at DJ Art Laboe's Original Sound studio in Hollywood, CA. Laboe, who has just launched Original Sound Records (and has a current US #14 hit with its fourth release, Preston Epps' *Bongo Rock*), hears commercial potential and decides to release *Teen Beat* as a one-off.
Aug [3-6] As part of a session band including Jackie Kelso (sax) and Red Callender (bass), Nelson backs Gene Vincent on tracks for his *Crazy Times* in Capitol Tower studios, Hollywood.
Oct *Teen Beat* hits US #4 and is a million-seller, interesting other labels in Nelson (who has no contract with Laboe) and he signs to Imperial.
Nov Imperial debut *Drum Party* fails to chart (as will 3 singles which follow it in 1960-61).
Dec *Teen Beat* hits UK #7.

1960 **Jan** Gene Vincent's *Wild Cat*, with Nelson on drums, reaches UK #21. Meanwhile, Nelson's first album *Teen Beat* features a re-recording of the title track (Original Sound holds on to the hit version, and will continue to profit from it on reissues and compilation albums for the next 2 decades), plus a mixture of Nelson originals and cover versions, but does not chart.
July Nelson drums and sings (screams) back-up vocals on The Hollywood Argyles' *Alley-Oop*; it tops US chart and is a million-seller.

1961 **Dec** *Let There Be Drums*, featuring Richie Allen (Richard Podolor) on guitar, hits US #7 and is Nelson's second million-seller.

1962 **Jan** *Let There Be Drums* hits UK #2, behind Cliff Richard's *The Young Ones.*
Mar *Drums Are My Beat* reaches US #29, while B-side *The Birth Of The Beat*, at US #75, is edited from its 10-min. version on Nelson's *Let There Be Drums*, which is his best-selling album, hitting US #6 and remaining on chart for 46 weeks.
Apr *Drums Are My Beat* climbs to UK #30.

May *Drummin' Up A Storm* makes US #67 and B-side *Drum Stomp* peaks at US #86. *Drums Are My Beat* reaches US #29.
July *All Night Long* makes US #75 and *Drummin' Up A Storm* UK #39.
Aug Both feature on *Drummin' Up A Storm*, which peaks at US #55.
Oct *And Then There Were Drums* reaches US #65.
Nov *Compelling Percussion*, including *And Then There Were Drums* and offbeat *Drums – For Strippers Only*, climbs to US #141.
Dec *Golden Hits*, not a compilation of his own successes but a collection of instrumental versions of oldies like *Splish Splash*, *Kansas City* and *What'd I Say*, makes US #106.

1963 Following a motorcycle accident, Nelson has his right foot and part of his leg amputated. After recuperation, he returns to drumming despite this disability. (His 1963 album *Beat That Drum*, released by Imperial during his absence, reissues earlier tracks under new titles to give the false impression of being new material.)

1964 **Oct** *Teen Beat '65*, an update of his original hit, with a dubbed-on audience to give it a live feel, makes US #44.
Dec *Live! In Las Vegas* (in fact dubbed in Los Angeles) makes US #122

1965 **Mar** *Teen Beat '65* makes US #135.
July Another "live" album, *Drum Discotheque*, including the updated *Let There Be Drums '66*, peaks at US #120.
Oct *Drums A-Go-Go* (the title track has hovered just below US Hot 100 with original version by The Hollywood Persuaders) reaches US #118.

1966 **Jan** *Boss Beat*, mainly covers of recent pop hits, reaches US #126.
Apr Nelson's final US chart entry is *"In" Beat*, another set of pop covers, which makes #148. (He will remain with Imperial until the early 70s, releasing 2 or 3 albums per year of either current cover versions, or on stylistic themes like jazz or country, or reviving the big band sound – like *Manhattan Spiritual* in 1969.)

1972 **June** Nelson visits UK with producer Nik Venet. Some recordings are made in London, and he gives a detailed radio interview to DJ Charlie Gillett about his career, on BBC Radio London's show "Honky Tonk".

1982 After a decade of playing regularly around Los Angeles, usually with a small jazz group, in which he is able to improvise on drums more freely than within earlier rock/pop constraints, Nelson returns to recording via his own label, Veebltronics. *A Drum Is A Woman* become a cult favorite in rock instrumental circles (notably in UK, where it is imported), but runs foul of a feminist organization in Los Angeles. Nelson, taken aback ("I only meant a drum is sensual and sexy"), reissues it under the non-controversial title *Drum Tunnel*. (His small group work will continue through the 80s, with occasional releases for devotees on his own label.)

1988 **Nov** UK combo Boss Beat releases *Let There Be Drums* in a typical contemporary vein.

WILLIE NELSON

1939 Nelson (b. Apr.30, 1933, Abbott, TX) is bought a Stella guitar by his mother and at age 6 is surrounded by music. His grandparents are learning music through mail-order courses and passing their knowledge on to Willie (they help raise him following the divorce of his parents Ira and Myrle) and his older sister Bobbie Lee. Willie will begin writing songs at age 7 and spend much time listening to the radio, favoring the Grand Ole Opry concerts and Texas western swing (particularly Bob Wills), while his family's dedication to the church and gospel music will also make a profound impression.

1943 At age 10, Nelson joins John Paycheck's Bohemian Polka Band on a part-time basis.

1946 His sister Bobbie marries fiddle player Bud Fletcher, and both she and Willie play for Fletcher's friend Bud Wills.

1952 Nelson joins the airforce, serving in Korea for a short period, but has to leave the same year with a bad back, shortly thereafter studying agriculture and business at Baylor University.

1953 He marries Martha Matthews and they have first daughter Lana. Still writing songs, he starts playing small clubs and bars in Fort Worth, TX

1955 He begins broadcasting a radio show in Washington state which features a half-hour live set by his own band.

1956 Second daughter, Susie, is born. With composing skills maturing, he finances his own recording of *No Place For Me*, which he sells to his radio listeners (2,000 copies) in Vancouver, WA, where he is currently a successful DJ.

1958 After 3 years away from Texas trying various jobs ranging from encyclopedia selling, DJ and vacuum cleaner salesman, Nelson returns to Houston where he works as a DJ and also performs at the Esquire nightclub. His songwriting has become prolific, but his dire financial position forces him to sell songs cheaply, including future country standard *Family Bible* for $50 and *Night Life* (later a hit for Ray Price) for $150. His son Billy is born.

1960 The Nelsons move to Nashville, where he meets other struggling musicians including Mel Tillis, Roger Miller and Kris Kristofferson, who hang out in Tootsie's Orchid Lounge.

1961 With the help of Hank Cochran, Nelson signs a publishing contract with Pamper Music. His song *Crazy* is picked up by Patsy Cline and hits #1 on the Country chart and later hits US #9, her first Top 10. He also pens *Hello Walls*, a US #2 for Faron Young, the biggest hit of his career. With his songwriting a success, Nelson, again aided by Cochran, secures a recording deal with Liberty.

1962 Debut album *...And Then I Wrote* is released. Nelson has success on the Country chart with Shirley Collie on *Willingly* and solo *Touch Me*. As other artists including Perry Como, Eydie Gorme and Jimmy Elledge enjoy hits with Nelson material, crossover success will elude him. He replaces Danny Young in Ray Price's Cherokee Cowboys as a working musician, but the strains of touring result in divorce for Willie and Martha.

1963 Jan Second album *Here's Willie Nelson* is released featuring Leon Russell on piano. It achieves little in sales, and Nelson moves to Monument, while Liberty closes down its country operations.
Dec Nelson's *Pretty Paper* is a big Christmas hit for Roy Orbison, peaking at US #15 (and UK #6 a year later).

1964 Nov [28] Nelson achieves a childhood ambition and makes his debut at Nashville's Grand Ole Opry, performing initially as an opening act for Roger Miller and later forming a band with Wade Ray.
Dec Nelson signs to RCA Records, which insists that he conforms to its traditional country requirements. First album *Country Willie - His Own Songs* fails to chart.

1965 Nelson marries Shirley Collie and they settle in Ridgetop, TN, taking up hog-farming. (Ray Price asks Nelson to raise one of his fighting roosters. Nelson shoots it when it kills 2 of his hens and Price refuses to record any Nelson song ever again.) RCA album *Country Favorites Willie Nelson Style* collects few sales.

1966 A performance at Panther Hall, Fort Worth is recorded for release as *Country Music Concert*.

1967 Nelson divorces Collie, who has recently become a martial arts expert.

1968 Nelson marries glass factory worker Connie Koepke, whom he has met at a concert in Cut'N'Shoot, TX.

1969 Daughter Paula is born.

1970 Through showbusiness lawyer, Neil Rushen, Nelson signs to Atlantic Records, which allows him the creative freedom that had frustrated him at RCA. Atlantic debut is gospel-tinged *The Troublemaker* (later issued by CBS/Columbia in 1976).
Dec [23] The Nelsons' house in Ridgetop, on the outskirts of Nashville, TN, burns to the ground. (Nelson will move his family back to Texas and will live there (and in Colorado) for the next 20 years.)

1971 Atlantic album *Shotgun Willie* becomes his best-selling vocal project to date (it includes a version of Leon Russell's *A Song For You*) and Nelson begins his biggest tour with a major date in every state.

1972 July [4] Nelson inaugurates his annual "Fourth Of July Picnic" (to be held every year until 1980 at different Texas locations) at Dripping Springs, TX.

1973 Daughter Amy Lee is born. Still without a solo hit single or album, Nelson is inducted into the Nashville Songwriters Hall Of Fame.

1974 *Phases And Stages*, recorded at Muscle Shoals studio and produced by Jerry Wexler, is released but fails to sell beyond the country market.

1975 After 14 unsuccessful years, CBS/Columbia Records signs Nelson to a worldwide deal.
July First CBS/Columbia album *Red Headed Stranger* climbs to top Country chart as *Blue Eyes Crying In The Rain* crosses over to peak at US #21. Its success will help the album climb to US #28. As Nelson's pioneering and innovative "outlaw" country style becomes more popular, *Red Headed Stranger* begins a run of US album success which will see at least 1 Nelson project chart every year for 14 years. The album's simple instrumentation and sparse production is against current Nashville style and will spend 43 weeks on the pop chart.
Nov RCA begins extensive re-releasing and repackaging of old Nelson material: *What Can You Do To Me Now* reaches US #196. *Wanted: The Outlaws*, recorded with Waylon Jennings, Tompall Glaser and Jessi Colter, is the first country album to be a million-seller. It tops the Country chart, but fails to cross over.

1976 Jan *Remember Me* makes US #67.
Feb [28] Nelson wins Best Country Vocal Performance, Male for *Blue Eyes Crying In The Rain* at the 18th annual Grammy awards, as Columbia album *The Sound In Your Mind* is released, making US #48.

Meanwhile, RCA single *Good Hearted Woman*, recorded with Waylon Jennings, climbs to US #25.
May [8] Nelson performs at Bob Dylan's second benefit gig for convicted boxer Rubin "Hurricane" Carter. Following the Houston gig, Nelson is served with a subpoena for grand jury investigation into drug offenses.
RCA album *Willie Nelson Live* (originally *Country Music Concert*) peaks at US #149.
June Atlantic reissues *Phases And Stages*, which reaches US #187.
Oct Fourth chart album of the year, newly-licensed *The Troublemaker* climbs to US #60.

1977 May *Before His Time*, released by RCA, is a compilation of earlier recordings remixed by Waylon Jennings, and peaks at US #78.
July A tribute to Lefty Frizzell, who died in 1975, Columbia album *To Lefty From Willie* peaks at US #91.

1978 Feb Nelson teams with Jennings for *Waylon And Willie*. Released through Jennings' RCA contract (Columbia will be flexible with Nelson's contract for many years), it benefits from US #42 single *Mamas Don't Let Your Babies Grow Up To Be Cowboys*, making US #12. Nelson sets up his own short-lived label Lone Star, to record other artists.
May Columbia album *Stardust*, featuring US #84 version of Hoagy Carmichael's *Georgia On My Mind*, is released. An album of pop standards 1926-55 produced by Booker T. Jones, it begins a 2-year chart stay and will peak at US #30. It stays on Country chart over 500 weeks.
Dec Recorded live at Harrah's, Lake Tahoe, NV, double album *Willie And Family Live* begins a rise to US #32 and a 1-year chart stay.

1979 Feb [15] Nelson wins Best Country Vocal Performance, Male for *Georgia On My Mind* and Best Duo Or Group Vocal Performance for *Mamas Don't Let Your Babies* at the 21st annual Grammy awards. He also wins CMA Entertainer Of The Year award. RCA album *Sweet Memories* peaks at US #154.
June New studio album *One For The Road* is released by Nelson and Leon Russell and peaks at US #25.
Nov Columbia album *Willie Nelson Sings Kristofferson* unites him with another old friend and makes US #42.
Dec Seasonal album *Pretty Paper* hits **Billboard** Top 10 Christmas chart and US #73.

1980 Jan Nelson makes his movie debut, alongside Robert Redford and Jane Fonda in "Electric Horseman". The soundtrack album, featuring a side of Nelson songs and another of instrumental themes by Dave Grusin, makes US #52.
Feb A single from the film, digging at his 1978 hit, *My Heroes Have Always Been Cowboys* reaches US #44.
Mar Finding ever-inventive ways of using old material, RCA invites Danny Davis to score orchestral backing for earlier Nelson recordings. Subsequent album *Danny Davis And Willie Nelson With The Nashville Brass* peaks at US #150.
June Nelson and Ray Price finally settle their 15-year feud, recording *San Antonio Rose* together. It begins a 25-week run peaking at US #70.
Sept Nelson appears in a second movie, country-dominated "Honeysuckle Rose". As single *On The Road Again*, from the film, climbs to US #20, the soundtrack album featuring a Nelson duet with Emmylou Harris will make US #11.

1981 Feb [25] Nelson wins Best Country Song for *On The Road Again* at the 23rd annual Grammy awards. Studio album *Somewhere Over The Rainbow* is released, rising to US #31.
June Nelson is taken sick in Hawaii with a collapsed lung. He spends his hospital stay writing songs.
July [4] The "Fourth Of July Picnic" is held at Caesar's Palace, Las Vegas, NV.
Aug RCA issues *The Minstrel Man* which stalls at US #148.
Sept *Willie Nelson's Greatest Hits (And Some That Will Be)* is released by Columbia. In a 93-week chart stay, it will make US #27.

1982 Mar *Always On My Mind* is released. The title track, a version of Presley's live favorite, becomes the biggest success of Nelson's career, hitting US #5, and propelling sales of parent album to hit US #2 for 4 weeks during a 99-week chart stay.
June Nelson appears with Gary Busey in movie "Barbarosa" and in TV movie "In The Jailhouse Now" with John Savage. 2 albums released for the country market, *Old Friend* with Roger Miller and the *In The Jailhouse Now* soundtrack recorded with Webb Pierce, fail to chart.
July His only solo UK chart single is *Always On My Mind* which makes UK #49 during a 3-week stay. (No album will chart in UK.)
Aug *Let It Be Me* makes US #40. Nelson is now performing as many as 250 concerts per year including dates with Frank Sinatra, Waylon Jennings, The Stray Cats, Z.Z. Top, Neil Young, Dolly Parton and Linda

Ronstadt, with live success in all territories including New Zealand, Australia, Europe, Canada and Japan.

Oct Jennings and Nelson re-appear on RCA for *WWII* which makes US #57 and includes *Just To Satisfy You* (US #52 in Mar.).

Dec Nelson wins Top Artists Country, Top Country Album (*Always On My Mind*) and Top Country Singles (*Always On My Mind*) categories in *Billboard*'s Year In Music survey. (Nelson will also be voted ACM Entertainer Of The Year.)

1983 Jan Nelson contributes to Kris Kristofferson's duets album *The Winning Hand*.

Feb *Poncho And Lefty*, on Epic Records through Merle Haggard's new contract, is credited to Haggard/Nelson. It tops Country chart and makes US #37.

[23] Nelson wins Best Country Vocal Performance, Male for *Always On My Mind* at the 25th annual Grammy awards. (It will also win an award as CMA's Single Of The Year.) Meanwhile, new solo studio album *Tougher Than Leather* is released, set to make US #39.

Mar [7] Nelson receives a Lifetime Achievement award from the Songwriters' Hall Of Fame.

Apr Third album with Waylon Jennings, *Take It To The Limit*, their first for Columbia, makes US #60.

May Nelson becomes the first country artist to receive the National Academy Of Popular Music's Lifetime Achievement award.

July [4] After a 3-year gap, Nelson reinstates his annual "Fourth Of July Picnic", but will extend it to a 3-day event held in different US locations, including Syracuse, NY, and Atlanta, GA.

Nov *Without A Song* reaches US #54. It features Nelson's first duet with Julio Iglesias on their version of *As Time Goes By*.

Dec More RCA songs reappear on *My Own Way*, peaking at US #182.

1984 May Another duet with Iglesias, ballad *To All The Girls I've Loved Before* hits US #5 and UK #17.

June *Angel Eyes*, featuring guitarist Jackie King, is released stalling at US #116.

Aug *City Of New Orleans* starts 6-month US chart stay, to peak at #69.

Oct [7] "Songwriter", starring Nelson and Kristofferson, has its Nashville premiere, while album soundtrack *Music From Songwriter*, released by both artists, climbs to US #152.

1985 Jan [28] Nelson joins 44 other artists at A&M studios, Hollywood, to record *We Are The World*, to raise funds to help feed the starving in Africa and US.

Mar *Me And Paul*, referring to his long serving drummer Paul English, peaks at US #152. The year's collaboration album *Funny How Time Slips Away* with Faron Young only makes the Country chart.

Apr Nelson and Iglesias win CMA Vocal Duo Of The Year award for *To All The Girls I've Loved Before*.

Sept Inspired by Band Aid's idea, Nelson becomes a main organizer and president of Farm Aid, aimed to raise funds and help the plight of US farmers. Farm Aid I is held amid massive US media interest and the concerts will pool over $10 million in donations. *Highwayman*, a collaboration between Nelson, Johnny Cash, Waylon Jennings and Kristofferson, tops Country chart and climbs to US #92. (*Highwayman* is voted ACM Single Of The Year.)

Oct *Half-Nelson*, comprising only duets, peaks at US 178.

Nov His *Time Of The Preacher* is used in BBC TV nuclear-thriller "Edge Of Darkness" and he writes *They're All The Same* for Johnny Cash, having been told by Cash that he dreamt Nelson has written a song with that title.

1986 May *The Promiseland* fails to chart but hits C&W #1, joining 5 albums already on the Country chart.

June He begins sold-out UK dates, including a performance attended by Prince Charles.

July [4] His annual "Fourth Of July Picnic" turns into a Farm Aid II benefit concert in Austin, TX.

Sept Nelson receives Roy Acuff Community Service Award from the Country Music Federation.

Nov [7] Nelson appears as a corrupt lawman in US TV "Miami Vice".

1987 Feb He appears in a film based on his early Columbia concert album *Red Headed Stranger*.

July [4] The "Fourth Of July Picnic" is held at Carl's Corner, TX. His live band is still Bobbie Nelson (piano), Jody Payne (guitar), Grady Martin (guitar), Mickey Raphael (harmonica), Bee Spears (bass) and Paul English (drums). *Island In The Sea* only makes US C&W #14.

Sept Nashville's Country Hall Of Fame opens a multi-media exhibition of the life and career of Willie Nelson.

1988 Sept Nelson contributes *Philadelphia Lawyer* to Woody Guthrie/Leadbelly tribute album *Folkways: A Vision Shared*.

Oct *What A Wonderful World*, of oldie cover versions, is released, set to hit US Country #6, as extracted duet with Iglesias *Spanish Eyes* will hit US Country #8. It is his 30th album for Columbia in 13 years, of which 15 have earned gold disks and 8 have earned plantinum ones.

1989 Jan [30] Nelson is presented with a Special Merit Award for his contribution to the music industry at the American Music Awards.

July [25] Nelson heads a fundraiser at the Bellevue hotel, Washington, DC, for the family of Dixon Terry, president of the Family Farm Coalition, killed by lightning while baling hay on his farm in Greenfield, IA, Memorial Day weekend, leaving his wife and 2 children and a $300,000 debt over his farm.

Aug This year's country album is *A Horse Called Music*, which hits US #2 on Country chart, spawning US Country #1 smash *Nothing I Can Do About it Now*.

Sept Aptly titled latest Columbia album *Born For Trouble* begins US Country chart rise.

Before year's end, Nelson will receive the Governor's Award from the Nashville chapter of NARAS, and will host a 24-hour wild west show on the Cowboy Television Network, a cable channel Nelson has been instrumental in establishing.

1990 Feb Nelson embarks on "Highwaymen 2" tour with Waylon Jennings, Johnny Cash and Kris Kristofferson to support the same titled second album by the quartet, which will make US #79.

May Group is allowed to continue using the Highwaymen name, after 60s group The Highwaymen has sought to block the name's use. The original group's lead guitarist and singer is now Federal Appeals Court Judge Stephen Trott. (Nelson contributes *Birth Of The Blues* to Randy Travis' album of duets *Heroes & Friends*.)

Apr [1] Nelson's tour bus crashes into a car in Riverdale, Canada, on the way to Newfoundland for concerts. The car driver dies.

May *Always On My Mind* is voted Country Single Of The Decade by *Billboard*.

Nov [9] The Internal Revenue Service seizes Nelson's bank accounts and real estate holdings to satisfy a $16.7 million tax debt.

1991 Jan [4] The Revenue auctions Nelson's 3-bedroomed house, valued at $72,000, in Yakima, WA for $50,500. (Nelson had never lived in it.)

[29] Nelson's 44-acre Dripping Springs ranch and house in San Marco, TX, are sold for the minimum required bid of $203,840.

Mar [5] Former Texas university football coach Darrell Royal pays $117,375 for Nelson's 76-acre spread, comprising a golf course, country club and Nelson's Pedernales recording studio. (Personal items from the property raise a further $68,000.)

Apr [9] Nelson stars with Kris Kristofferson in CBS TV's "Another Pair Of Aces: Three Of A Kind".

[18] The Revenue sells Nelson's 22-acre fishing camp, on a 668-acre spread which also includes a Wild West movie set, to George and Mary Larson for $86,100.

[20] Nelson takes part in the "Earth Day 1991 Concert" at Foxboro Stadium, Foxboro, MA, with Billy Bragg, Jackson Browne, Rosanne Cash, Bruce Cockburn, Bruce Hornsby & The Range, Indigo Girls, Queen Latifah, Ziggy Marley, and 10,000 Maniacs.

THE NEVILLE BROTHERS

Art Neville (vocals, piano)
Aaron Neville (vocals)
Charles Neville (sax)
Cyril Neville (vocals, percussion)

1955 Eldest brother Art (b. Dec.17, 1937, New Orleans, LA) records *Mardi Gras Mambo*, as vocalist and pianist with 7-piece New Orleans R&B band The Hawketts, which becomes a local standard, reissued annually by Chess for the Mardi Gras celebrations. Shortly afterwards, younger brother Aaron (b. 1941, New Orleans) joins vocal group The Avalons.

1957 Still performing with The Hawketts, Art signs solo deal with Specialty Records and releases several singles (including *Zing Zing* and *Cha Dooky-Doo*) popular in the R&B market. Third brother Charles, who left home at age 14 to get married, joins the house band at New Orleans' Dew Drop Inn club, touring the South with various blues players.

1958 Art joins the US Navy and Aaron fills his place in The Hawketts. Aaron's adventures outside the band will include getting married and serving 6 months in prison for car theft.

1960 Out of prison, Aaron records *Over You* with Allen Toussaint for Minit, beginning a long working relationship. It reaches US R&B #21.

1962 Jan Back with The Hawketts after military service, Art has a regional hit with *All These Things*. (He will follow Aaron to Toussaint as a solois but neither will have any major chart success with Minit.) Charles leaves New Orleans to play in New York with Joey Dee & The Starliters, while baby brother Cyril starts showing an interest in music. (He will shortly join Art and Aaron in an 8-piece New Orleans gig circuit band named The Neville Sounds.)

'66 Aaron records blues ballad *Tell It Like It Is* for New Orleans label, Parlo. Written by Lee Diamond and ex-Hawketts member George Davis, it reputedly sells 40,000 copies in New Orleans in its first week of release. (It will later be adapted as anthem of the US Black Power movement.)

'67 **Jan** Soul classic *Tell It Like It Is* hits US #2 and is a million-seller. It tops R&B chart for 4 weeks.
Feb On the strength of his hit, Aaron begins several months of live work around the US, including an appearance at the prestigious Apollo theater in Harlem, New York. His backing band for the tour is The Neville Sounds with Art on keyboards.
Apr Aaron's follow-up *She Took You For A Ride* reaches US #92.

'68 The Neville Sounds splits, with Aaron and Cyril branching off as The Soul Machine, and Art keeping the rhythm section ("Ziggy" Modeliste on drums, George Porter on bass, Leo Nocentelli on guitar, and himself on keyboards) to form The Meters, who rapidly become New Orleans' equivalent of Memphis' Booker T. & The MG's, playing as house band behind many Allen Toussaint and Marshall Sehorn productions.

'69 **Mar** Toussaint and Sehorn decide to emulate Booker T. by recording The Meters as an R&B instrumental group in its own right and leasing it to New York's Josie Records. Debut *Sophisticated Cissy* makes US #34.
June The Meters' *Cissy Strut* reaches US #23.
July *The Meters*, a wholly instrumental collection, peaks at US #108.
Aug The Meters' *Ease Back* reaches US #61.

'70 **Jan** The Meters' *Look-Ka Py Py* climbs to US #56 but album of the same title makes only US #198.
May The Meters' *Chicken Strut* reaches US #50.
July The Meters' *Hand Clapping Song*, the last Sehorn and Toussaint single, reaches US #89. *Struttin'* makes only US #200.

'72 Group signs to Reprise, releasing *Cabbage Alley* which fails. (The Meters' own hit career will now fade, but its session work will include major acts like Dr. John on *In The Right Place*, *Desitively Bonaroo* and his 1973 US Top 10 hit *Right Place, Wrong Time*, and Robert Palmer on his first solo album *Sneakin' Sally Through The Alley*.)

'74 *Rejuvenation* includes slide guitar from Lowell George of Little Feat.

'75 **Sept** Cyril joins The Meters as percussionist/vocalist and the band tours Europe as support for The Rolling Stones. *Fire On The Bayou* reaches US #179.

'76 Art brings in the 2 remaining brothers and the group performs and releases, on Island, an eponymous album as The Wild Tchoupitoulas (the name is from the Mardi Gras tribe of their Indian uncle), with their uncle George Landry. It also records *Trick Bag* as The Meters.

'77 **Oct** Final Meters album *New Direction* is released. It does not chart but extracted *Be My Lady* reaches US #78. The band changes its name to The Neville Brothers. Charles leaves again, but only temporarily.

'78 **Mar** *The Neville Brothers* is released by Capitol.

'81 **Sept** *Fiyo On The Bayou*, a play on an earlier Meters title, on A&M, reaches US #166. They are increasingly popular with their musical peers and Bette Midler has lobbied A&M to sign the band.

'84 **June** *Neville-ization*, recorded live in 1982 at New Orleans' Tipitina's, is released but fails to chart.
Linda Ronstadt meets Aaron during the World's Fair in New Orleans. She has finished performing with Nelson Riddle, and goes to Pete Fountain's club to see The Neville Brothers perform.

'87 **Apr** *Treacherous: A History Of The Neville Brothers 1955-1985*, a 30-year retrospective double album of the brothers' career released by Rhino, peaks at US #178.
May *Uptown*, featuring a more mainstream soul music production than previous releases with guests Jerry Garcia, Keith Richards, Carlos Santana and others, makes US #155.

'88 **Aug** Aaron Neville sings *Stardust* on Rob Wasserman's *Duets*.
Dec [10] Aaron's son Ivan, learning his musical skills playing in Keith Richards' band, makes US #26 with *Not Just Another Girl* from his debut album *If My Ancestors Could See Me Now* (US #107).

'89 **Apr** As the band is increasingly "discovered" by a young rock soul audience, *Yellow Moon* enters US survey on a 24-week ride during which it makes #66, but it fails in UK despite a tour visit.
July [15] Group embarks on major US dates, supporting Jimmy Buffett on his "Off To See The Lizard Tour '89".
Oct [7] Aaron Neville enjoys his biggest hit in 23 years, duetting on Linda Ronstadt's *Don't Know Much*, produced by Peter Asher for her

current album *Cry Like A Rainstorm – Howl Like The Wind*, which heavily features Neville on 3 further duet cuts.
[27] Aaron sings *Amazing Grace* and *How Great Thou Art* at the wedding of actor John Goodman to fine arts student Annabeth Hartzog at the St. Charles Avenue Presbyterian church, New Orleans.
Dec Extracted group ballad from *Yellow Moon*, *With God On Our Side*, makes UK #47, while *Don't Know Much* hits UK #2.

1990 **Jan** [28] Aaron sings the national anthem at Superbowl XXIV between the San Francisco 49ers and the Denver Broncos at the Superdome, New Orleans, LA.
Feb Aaron contributes a cover of *Young And Beautiful* to the compilation album *The Last Temptation Of Elvis*, to benefit the Nordoff-Robbins Music Therapy charity.
[21] Group wins Best Pop Instrumental Performance for *Healing Chant* and Aaron, with Linda Ronstadt, wins Best Pop Performance By A Duo Or Group With Vocal for *Don't Know Much* at the 32nd annual Grammy awards at the Shrine Auditorium, Los Angeles.
Mar Aaron's "Tell It Like It Is" video, with guests Bonnie Raitt, Gregg Allman, John Hiatt, Buckwheat Zydeco and Dennis Quaid, is released in US. (Aaron has appeared as a heavy in Quaid's film "Everybody's All-American".)
[8] Aaron is voted Best Male Singer and The Neville Brothers Best Band in **Rolling Stone** magazine's 1989 Critics' awards.
Apr [16] Group participates in the "Nelson Mandela – An International Tribute To A Free South Africa" concert at Wembley Stadium, London.
June [22-24] They participate in the Glastonbury Festival of Contemporary Performing Arts, Somerset.
July [7] *Bird On The Wire*, featured in Mel Gibson/Goldie Hawn movie of the same name, peaks at UK #72.
Aug Celebrating 10 years with A&M, latest Neville Brothers' album, co-produced by Dave Stewart, *Brother's Keeper* makes UK #35.
[9] US tour begins in Austin, TX, set to end Sept.30 in Santa Barbara, CA, as special guests of Linda Ronstadt.
Sept [8] *Brother's Keeper* peaks at US #60.
Oct Group contributes *In The Still Of The Night* to *Red Hot + Blue*, an anthology of Cole Porter songs to benefit AIDS education.

1991 **Feb** [20] Neville and Ronstadt win Best Pop Performance By A Duo Or Group With Vocal for Karla Bonoff-composed *All My Life* for a second consecutive year at the 33rd annual Grammy awards at Radio City Music Hall, New York.
Mar [3] Aaron Neville sings *Bird On A Wire* at the induction of Leonard Cohen into the Juno Hall Of Fame at the 20th annual Juno Awards at the Queen Elizabeth theater, Vancouver, Canada.
[7] Aaron wins Best Male Singer in the **Rolling Stone** Critics' Picks 1990 music awards.
May [5] Band performs at the New Orleans Fair, as part of its 24-date US tour, as Aaron nears completion of Ronstadt-produced solo project and guests on son Ivan's forthcoming second album *Sound Of Love*.

NEW EDITION

Bobby Brown (vocals)
Ricky Bell (vocals)
Ralph Tresvant (vocals)
Michael Bivins (vocals)
Ronald DeVoe (vocals)

1983 **Feb** [5] Having established itself over 2 years as Boston, MA, talent show champs and with several lip-synching gigs in the Northeastern states, 5-member R&B teen unit New Edition (all are aged between 13 and 15): Bell (b. Sept.18, 1967), Tresvant (b. May 16, 1968, Boston), Bivins (b. Aug.10, 1968), DeVoe (b. Nov.17, 1967) and Brown (b. Robert Baresford Brown, Feb.5, 1969, Roxbury, MA) makes its residency debut at New York's Copacabana club, under the wing of pop entrepreneur, manager, producer Maurice Starr, who has already secured a recording deal with local independent Streetwise label.
May [28] Molded by Starr as an 80s version of The Jackson 5, New Edition hits UK #1, via a Streetwise license to London Records, and makes US #46 with sugar coated pop/R&B confection *Candy Girl*.
Aug UK follow-up *Popcorn Love* makes UK #45.
Oct *Is This The End* peaks at US #85, while parent album *Candy Girl* climbs to US #90 (the group will never score a UK chart album).

1984 Band splits acrimoniously from Starr and signs to MCA Records as a 5-year legal wrangle begins over the rights to use the New Edition title.
Nov Breakthrough US MCA hit, *Cool It Now*, hits US #4, as second

album *New Edition* begins US rise to hit #6.

1985 **Feb** Extracted *Mr. Telephone Man* reaches US #12 and UK #19 (the group's last UK chart entry). A further single from their album, *Lost In Love*, will also make US #35.

Dec *Count Me Out* peaks at US #51 as second MCA outing *All For Love* begins climb to US #32.

1986 **Apr** *A Little Bit Of Love (Is All It Takes)* makes US #38.

July *With You All The Way* peaks at US #51.

Oct Revival of The Crewcuts 1955 US #3 *Earth Angel* reaches US #21, aided by its inclusion on the "Karate Kid II" movie soundtrack.

Dec New Edition releases its final album with Brown in the line-up: *Under The Blue Moon*, including the recent *Earth Angel*, is a collection of updated 50s and 60s pop/R&B standards and will make US #43.

1987 Brown signs a solo deal, also with MCA, which will supersede New Edition's achievements towards the end of the decade. Meantime, the band recruits former gospel singer and Stacy Lattisaw session vocalist Johnny Gill (b. 1965, Washington, DC) who, at 22, is the oldest member. Only chart action of the year sees *Helpless In Love*, included in the Dan Aykroyd/Tom Hanks movie "Dragnet" at US R&B #20.

1988 **Sept** [17] New Edition makes an impressive return to chart form as *If It Isn't Love* hits US #7. It is taken from US #12 album *Heart Break*, which is mostly written and produced by smash R&B duo Jimmy Jam and Terry Lewis (2 cuts will be co-written and co-produced with New Edition and Tresvant). Album marks a deliberate effort to shed their teeny-bop image and head for the adult market. Group begins US tour supporting Brown, who also appears for 10 mins. with his old line-up as part of a contractual obligation (all members are still friendly).

Nov [19] *You're Not My Kind Of Girl* stalls at US #95.

Dec Ballad *Can You Stand The Rain* hits US R&B #1 for 2 weeks.

1989 While Bobby Brown's solo career goes multi-platinum, New Edition members elect to divide, amicably, and on the provision that the central team will continue to operate, with additionally recruited members if necessary, whenever it needs to, into a new R&B/hip trio Bell Biv DeVoe (clearly combining Bell, Bivins and DeVoe), and 2 solo careers for Tresvant and Gill, who is already featured vocalist on the George Howard single (US R&B #77, Jan.) *One Love*.

Mar [11] New Edition's *Can You Stand The Rain* makes US #44.

July [9] Still touring as New Edition, the group's production manager Ronald Byrd, 30, is charged with criminal homicide after allegedly chasing support group Guy's security chief Anthony Bee from the Civic Arena to the Hyatt hotel in Pittsburgh, PA, and shooting him prior to the 2 groups' appearances that night (subsequently postponed) at the Budweiser Summerfest concert series. Recent New Edition recruit Michael Clark is also listed in critical condition at Pittsburgh Allegheny hospital with facial injuries suffered from a beating from 4 Guy stagehands with baseball bats. (The dispute had begun in Greensboro, NC, on July 8 when Guy played over its time limit.)

1990 **Jan** Reuniting with Lattisaw, Gill duet *Where Do We Go From Here* hits US R&B #1.

June [9] During a year in which all 3 New Edition splinter acts will dominate US R&B and pop charts, Bell Biv DeVoe are first, hitting US #3 with Dr. Freeze-produced *Poison* R&B/hip-hop concoction, while parent album *Poison* holds at peak US #5.

Aug [4] Gill, signed to Motown, the only New Edition-related act (including Brown) not to remain with MCA, hits US #3 with *Rub You The Right Way*, while his debut album *Johnny Gill*, including guest producers Jam and Lewis and L.A. Reid & Babyface, sticks at US #8. Meanwhile, Bell Biv DeVoe's *Poison* reaches UK #19 (the album will also make UK #35 in Sept.).

Sept [8] Bell Biv DeVoe follow-up *Do Me!* hits US #3 and is their second US R&B chart-topper (it will also make UK #56).

[29] Gill's *My, My, My* hit US #10, while *Poison* is certified RIAA double platinum for 2 million US sales.

Nov [24] Bell Biv DeVoe's *B.B.D. (I Thought It Was Me)* reaches US #26.

[26] Bell Biv DeVoe wins Top New Pop Artist at the 1990 **Billboard** Music Awards held in Santa Monica, CA.

Dec [15] L.A.Reid & Babyface-produced *Fairweather Friend* reaches US #28 for Gill.

1991 **Jan** [8] Bell Biv DeVoe and Johnny Gill embark on major US tour with Keith Sweat and Monie Love in Savannah, GA.

[26] Tresvant solo career kick-starts with soulful *Sensitivity* finally hitting US #4.

[28] With all 3 acts swarming the US surveys, New Edition reunites with all original members (including Brown) to perform at the 17th annual American Music Awards, where Bell Biv DeVoe also wins Best New Artist.

Feb [2] MCA issued, produced by Jam and Lewis, Tresvant solo debut album *Ralph Tresvant* peaks at US #17 while platinum Gill is still at #67 and Bell Biv DeVoe at #22 in the same week. *Sensitivity* also reaches UK #18.

[16] Bell Biv DeVoe's *When Will I See You Smile Again?* peaks at US #6.

[23] Gill's *Wrap My Body Tight* makes UK #57 as album *Ralph Tresvant* debuts at UK peak #37.

Mar [30] *Wrap My Body Tight*, remixed by Vaughn Halyard, stalls at US #84.

Apr [13] Tresvant's *Stone Cold Gentleman* makes US #34. With third Bobby Brown solo album due in the summer, New Edition is responsible for 5 US Top 10 acts in 8 years.

NEW KIDS ON THE BLOCK

Donnie Wahlberg (vocals)
Danny Wood (vocals)
Jordan Knight (vocals)
Jonathan Knight (vocals)
Joey McIntyre (vocals)

1984 Music veteran and entrepreneur Maurice Starr (b. Larry Johnson), ex-The Johnson Brothers with his brother Michael Jonzun, has also cut 2 solo albums for RCA, *Flaming Starr* and *Spicey Lady*, already responsible for finding and promoting teen unit New Edition in 1981, is keen to find a "white New Edition" and enlists the help of old friend talent agent Mary Alford, also a personnel officer at the Massachusetts Department of Education. (During the search, Starr receives a call from the FBI inquiring why he had given his phone number to a young boy in a flower shop.) Alford discovers Wahlberg (b. Aug.17, 1970, Dorchester, MA) at local Dorchester Copley Square high school, one of 9 children of a divorced working mother and a bus driver. Wahlberg, in turn, suggests auditioning former classmates from William M. Trotter elementary school in nearby Roxbury, where he, Wood (b. Daniel William Wood, May 14, 1971, Boston, MA), Jordan (b. May 17, 1971, Boston) and Knight (b. Nov.29, 1969, Boston) were all bussed to school. Starr molds and trains the group, initially known as Nynuk, over a year during which early member Jamie Kelley will drop out to be replaced by McIntyre (b. Joseph Mulrey McIntyre, Dec.31, 1973, Needham, MA). Donnie's elder brother Mark and friend Pete Fitzgerald will also drop out of the original line-up.

1985 **Mar** Nynuk performs its first gig at the Joseph Lee school, Dorchester, where they lip-synch to early demo tapes.

1986 **Jan** They sign to CBS Records Black division, who are interested in the idea of commercial rap dance pop mix, as shown in their 4-song demo tape, and persuade Starr to use new name, New Kids On The Block.

Apr Debut release *Be My Girl* fails to interest.

July [4] New Kids perform at City Kids Speak On Liberty program at Battery Park, New York. They will subsequently support The Four Tops at the Dorchester Kite Festival and open for Lisa Lisa & Cult Jam at the 9 Lansdowne club, Boston.

1987 Debut album *New Kids On The Block* is released, selling 5,000 copies.

1988 **Mar** Following a year of intermittent, but largely unnoticed club and PA engagements, program director Randy Kabrich of WRBQ, Tampa, FL-radio station begins playing New Kids' fourth single *Please Don't Go Girl*, originally recorded by Starr-created threesome Irving & The Twins. It is added by many other pop stations as the ball begins rolling.

June New Kids start 6-week US tour supporting Tiffany, followed by a month-long headliner of their own.

Nov [21] Returning from a Japanese trip, during which they film TV commercials, the band plays a benefit for the Police Athletic League in Boston, on a bill with Jeffrey Osborne and The Pointer Sisters.

1989 **Jan** [4-5] The New Kids take part in the annual United Cerebral Palsy telethon for the third year running.

Feb Band undertakes a 4-month return tour of US with equally popular teen-queen Tiffany.

Mar [11] During a half-year chart residence pop rap *You Got It (The Right Stuff)* hits US #3 as the New Kids teen-throb bubble bursts all over North America. Parent album *Hangin' Tough*, helmed by Starr, also hits US #4, and will remain charted for over 2 years, accumulating 8 RIAA platinum disks, launching the hottest teen-idol group phenomenon of the decade.

Apr [24] Massachusetts Governor Michael Dukakis designates today "New Kids On The Block Day" (the Kids will also perform at a Dukakis-formed Alliance Against Drugs benefit later in the year), 1 day ahead of the Boston Music Awards at which the beantown boys win Outstanding R&B Single, Outstanding Music Video and Starr wins Producer Of The Year.

June [17] During summer engagements at Disneyland, CA, and Disneyworld, FL, ballad *I'll Be Loving You (Forever)* hits US #1.

Aug Revived and re-promoted debut *New Kids On The Block* peaks at US #25.

Sept [9] *Hangin' Tough* album and its title song hit US #1 simultaneously, aided by a now familiar teen-screaming promo clip featuring band's synchronized dance troupe style and white rap antics.

[23] UK campaign begins with *Hangin' Tough* making #52, while the band visits for 4-day promotional tour, including an appearance on **Smash Hits**' TV awards show.

Nov [4] *Cover Girl* hits US #2.

[11] B-side of *Hangin' Tough*, a cover of The Delfonics' *Didn't I (Blow Your Mind)*, hits UK #8.

Dec While US-only issued seasonal *Merry, Merry Christmas* hits US #9, *You Got It (The Right Stuff)* hits UK #1 and *Hangin' Tough* begins lengthy UK chart service, hitting #2. Group ends the year having completed 250 nights on the road and with 3 albums in the US Top 30, and as victors in **Billboard**'s Year In Music survey for Top Pop Singles Artists and Duos/Groups.

[27] New Kids present Boston Against Drugs group with a $25,000 check at the World Trade Center, Boston. (A further $25,000 is earmarked for the Governor's Alliance Against Drugs.)

Jan [6] Starr-penned and produced lush sentimental ballad *This One's For The Children* hits US #7, with all profits set to go to the United Cerebral Palsy charity.

[13] *Hangin' Tough* hits UK #1.

Feb [5] During another major US tour, Hasbro, a Rhode Island-based toy manufacturer, unveils its New Kids dolls at a press conference at the Hard Rock Café, New York. (When they hit the stores in Dec., over 1 million will be sold.)

[6] Disney Channel airs New Kids' "Hangin' Tough In Concert" TV special.

Mar [8] **Rolling Stone** magazine's Readers' Picks vote New Kids the Worst Band, the Worst Tour and *Hangin' Tough* the Worst Single and Worst Album in its annual poll.

Apr [26] During band's first European tour, Wood injures his ankle in Manchester, Gtr.Manchester, when he trips over a stuffed toy animal thrown on stage by a fan. He flies back to Boston to receive treatment from Boston Celtics' trainer Ed Lacerte.

May [12] *Cover Girl* hits UK #4.

June [16] *Step By Step* hits UK #2.

[24] During the band's "Magic Summer '90" US tour, sponsored by McDonald's, Wahlberg falls through an unlocked trapdoor mid-concert at the Saratoga Raceway, Saratoga Springs, NY. Tour is set to close Sept.15 at Dodger Stadium, Los Angeles, CA.

[30] *Step By Step* debuts at UK #1, and hits US #1 in its second week of release, as title cut *Step By Step*, originally recorded by another Starr group The Superiors, tops US chart.

July [13] The world's first heart/liver recipient, 13-year-old Stormie Jones meets band backstage after their Hanover Township, TX, show.

[21] Wahlberg's duet with Japanese singing starlet Seiko, *The Right Combination*, makes US #54. (Jordan will also duet during the year with teen star Ana for *Angel Of Love*.)

Aug [4] During gig at the Olympic Stadium, Montreal, Canada, 3 armed robbers steal souvenir sales proceeds valued at $260,000.

[8] Jordan Knight is involved in an incident in Atlanta, GA, bar after his bodyguard Steven Chandler allegedly assaults 2 people.

[18] Harmonious and melodic *Tonight* hits UK #3.

Sept [2] Wahlberg allegedly assaults 20-year-old **Harvard Crimson** editor Benjamin Dattner aboard a Delta Airlines flight from Salt Lake City, UT, to Atlanta. (Dattner is treated for a scratched cornea and head injuries at Fulton County hospital.)

[8] *Tonight* hits US #7, the same day ABC TV airs the first New Kids cartoon series.

[15] New Kids' business manager James Rossi has his briefcase, containing $100,000 in cash, stolen as he checks out of the Bel Air hotel, Hollywood.

Oct [12] Band performs at the Amnesty International benefit concert at the National Stadium, Santiago, Chile, alongside Sting, Sinead O'Connor and Peter Gabriel among others.

[13] *Let's Try It Again/Didn't I (Blow Your Mind)* hit UK #8.

Nov [3] Belated UK issue of debut *New Kids On The Block* album, marking a considerable change of image from current projection of mature earnest urban streetwise dudes of current product, nevertheless hits UK #6. *Let's Try It Again* hints at a burst bubble, stalling at US #53.

[7] The Knight brothers appear on NBC TV's "Unsolved Mysteries", urging fans to help find missing Ausable Forks, NY, teenager Cari

Lynn Nixon. (Someone watching the New Kids video "Hangin' Tough Live" thinks she has seen Nixon in the audience on the video.)

Dec [7] US cable subscribers are offered pay-per-view broadcast of "Live No More Games" concert.

[15] *This One's For The Children* hits UK #9, while now issued *Merry, Merry Christmas* reaches UK #13. By the end of the year one of the most successful marketing stories of pop history will be complete: in addition to the record sales (all 5 of their albums are still charted on the **Billboard** Top 200 Album chart), New Kids will have notched up the 3 best-selling music video collections of all time in US ("Hangin' Tough" 1.2 million, "Step By Step" 1 million and "Hangin' Tough Live" 1.25 million), launched best-selling dolls, Simon & Schuster books, comics, Saturday morning TV cartoon show, tour merchandise and a 1-900-9095 KIDS recorded telephone message line, which at its peak attracted 100,000 calls a week. A conservative estimate of their income for the year is reported at $861 million.

1991 Jan [5] *No More Games/Remix Album* reaches US #19.

Band performs at the Rock In Rio II festival at the Marcana Stadium, Rio de Janeiro, Brazil.

[31] Group performs at the Tokyo Dome, Tokyo, Japan.

Feb [16] *Games* reaches UK #14.

Mar [2] *No More Games/Remix Album* reaches UK #15.

[7] New Kids are voted Worst Band, *Step By Step* is voted Worst Single and *Step By Step* Worst Album in the annual **Rolling Stone** Readers' Picks music awards.

[27] Wahlberg is arrested after allegedly setting fire to the carpet outside Rooms 942 and 944 in the Seelbach hotel, Louisville, KY. (He will plead guilty to a charge of criminal mischief.)

May [12] Group appears by satellite from Holland in "The Simple Truth" concert for Kurdish refugees at Wembley Arena, London.

[14-16] New Kids perform the first 3 of 8 nights at Wembley Arena.

NEW ORDER

Barney Sumner (guitar, vocals)
Peter Hook (bass)
Stephen Morris (drums)
Gillian Gilbert (keyboards)

1980 May [18] Joy Division comes to a sudden end with the suicide of lead singer Ian Curtis.

June Remaining group members, Sumner (b. Bernard Dicken, Jan.4, 1956, Salford, Gtr.Manchester, known as Bernard Albrecht in Joy Division), Hook (b. Feb.13, 1956, Salford) and Morris (b. Oct.28, 1957, Macclesfield, Cheshire) resolve to continue recording under a new name. While previously completed and scheduled Joy Division recordings, *Love Will Tear Us Apart* and *Closer* are released, they decide on New Order as new band name, despite claims of Nazi connotations by some UK music press.

July [29] Trio plays debut gig at the Beach club in home base of Manchester, Gtr.Manchester.

Sept [20] New Order plays first of 4 US East Coast dates, which Joy Division had been booked to play in May, at Maxwell's, Hoboken, NJ.

Oct Gilbert (b. Jan.27, 1961, Manchester), ex-all-girl punk band The Inadequates and long-time friend of Morris, joins New Order on keyboards and occasional guitar. She has recently studied at Stockport technical college, Gtr.Manchester.

[25] Band plays its first gig as a quartet at the Squat club, Manchester.

Dec They enter Strawberry studios, Stockport, to record debut material.

1981 Jan New Order begins series of UK dates between recording sessions.

[25] Hook records 5 min. interview for UK BBC Radio 1's "Walters Weekly".

Feb [9] First London date is supposedly secret gig at the Heaven club. 1,000 tickets sell out immediately. Supporting acts include Section 25 and The Stockholm Monsters.

[16] Debut UK radio session is broadcast on "The John Peel Show" on BBC Radio 1.

Mar *Ceremony*, released by Factory Records (for whom Joy Division had recorded) reaches UK #34.

Apr [24] Group begins 2 weeks' recording at Strawberry studios with producer Martin Hannett, for its first album, and films TV special for Granada TV for whom Factory supremo Tony Wilson moonlights.

May A short European tour takes in France, Belgium, Germany, Denmark, Sweden and Norway.

June [18] New Order documentary "Celebration" broadcast on Granada TV.

[20] Group plays Glastonbury Fayre, benefiting the Campaign For Nuclear Disarmament.

Oct Double A-side *Procession/Everything's Gone Green* peaks at UK #38.

Dec Debut album *Movement* reaches UK #30. Another Granada TV performance sees band members dressed in Santa Claus outfits.

1982 Jan [4] They appear on UK TV on BBC 2's "Riverside", playing *Temptation* and *Death Rattle*.

Mar [6] Group is interviewed on Irish radio RTE2.

Apr [8] On European mini-tour, riot occurs at New Order gig in Rotterdam, Holland. Hook is knocked unconscious.

June *Temptation*, released as a 33rpm 12"-only single, reaches UK #29.

[1] Session by the band on BBC Radio 1's "John Peel Show" includes unrecorded *Turn The Heater On*, penned by reggae artist Keith Hudson.

[16-22] Group plays mini-tour of Italy.

[26] The Hacienda club in Manchester, owned by Factory Records, and in which New Order has a financial interest, opens with a free members' evening highlighted by a performance by the group.

Sept [11] Group headlines first day of fourth Futurama Festival in Leeds, W.Yorks.

[19] Group plays in a basketball stadium in Athens, Greece, as part of the first Festival Of Independent Rock'N'Roll.

Oct [22] Recordings begin for second album at Britannia Row studios, London.

Nov 6-track mini-album *New Order, 1981-1982*, compiling tracks from UK and Belgian singles, is released in US and Canada.

[25] Group begins a 10-date tour of Australia and New Zealand, opening at Palais theater, Melbourne, Australia.

1983 Feb Group records for 2 weeks in New York with US dance producer and mix-master Arthur Baker.

Apr *Blue Monday*, released only as 12" single, climbs to UK #12.

May *Power, Corruption And Lies*, produced by the group, hits UK #4.

Sept 12"-only single, *Confusion*, produced and co-written by Baker, reaches UK #12. Group is now increasingly successful on US new rock/dance market, aided by release of *Blue Monday*, on Baker's dance oriented Streetwise label.

Oct Having remained on UK Top 100 since its release, *Blue Monday* now hits UK #9. (By 1987, UK 12"-only release will have sold over 600,000 copies to become the biggest-selling 12" single and with worldwide totals of over 3 million.)

1984 Apr Group makes its first visit to Japan playing sell-out shows in Tokyo and Osaka. A brief recording session in Tokyo produces *State Of The Nation* for future release.

May *Thieves Like Us* reaches UK #18, again produced and co-written with Baker. Factory's European off-shoot label, Factory Benelux releases rare single: New Order's *Murder*, for Belgium market.

1985 Feb New Order is signed to Quincy Jones' Qwest Records in US.

May Group embarks on Far East tour.

[25] *The Perfect Kiss* (which will reach UK #46) is simultaneously released with parent album *Low Life* which immediately hits UK #7.

July *Low Life* marks US chart debut at #94.

Aug Currently touring US where *Perfect Kiss* is Top 5 on **Billboard** Dance chart, group is featured on UK BBC TV's marathon music video show "Rock Around The Clock".

Sept Factory draws up its first contracts. New Order's stipulates that the band only has to give 6 months' notice if it wishes to leave the label.

Nov *Sub-Culture* stalls at UK #63.

1986 Apr *Shellshock* (with *Shellcock* on B-side), featured as 1 of 3 New Order tracks on new John Hughes movie "Pretty In Pink", reaches UK #28. Factory's Ikon video label releases long-form home video controversially titled "Pumped Full Of Drugs".

Sept While current Factory release, *State Of The Nation* peaks at UK #30, a June 1982 "John Peel Show" radio session, released on a 12" EP as part of an archive series by Strange Fruit Records, makes UK #54.

Oct *Brotherhood*, recorded in London, Dublin and Liverpool, hits UK chart at #9.

Nov *Bizarre Love Triangle* makes UK #56 during 2-week chart stay, despite Shep Pettibone remix, as *Brotherhood* makes US #117.

1987 Apr In between tours of US and South-East Asia, New Order records tracks for movie soundtrack "Salvation" which is to be released later in the year on Les Disques De Crépuscule, a Belgian indie label.

Aug *True Faith*, released to worldwide critical and commercial enthusiasm, hits UK #4. Produced by Stephen Hague, it is a major international breakthrough, aided by innovative accompanying video.

[29] *Substance*, recalling all 1980-87 UK 12" singles, hits UK #3 on release. (It will eventually sell over 400,000 copies in UK alone, though only a few of these will be on the DAT (digital audio tape) format for

which *Substance* is one of the earliest releases.)

Nov *Substance* climbs to US #36. A second Strange Fruit 12" EP *Peel Sessions Volume II* is released. Sumner announces intention to work as soloist during 1988.

Dec [26] *True Faith* becomes US Singles chart debut, reaching #32, while *Touched By The Hand Of God* peaks at UK #20. European dates include sell-out shows in London, Dusseldorf and Paris.

1988 Feb [8] "True Faith" is named Best British Music Video at the seventh annual BRIT Awards at London's Royal Albert Hall.

Group appears at San Remo Festival in Italy where they "mime" for the first time.

Mar New Order performs before the Duke and Duchess of York at the Stock Exchange nightclub in Los Angeles, CA, during UKLA Week (a festival aimed at strengthening UK/US business ties).

May Perennial *Blue Monday* is reissued, remixed by John Potoker and overseen by Quincy Jones, and retitled *Blue Monday 1988*. It hits UK #3 but only makes US #68.

June Group begins 3 months of recording in Ibiza and Bath, Avon.

Nov Film producer Chris Bernard commissions New Order to record the soundtrack for a forthcoming BBC TV series "Making Out".

Dec *Fine Time*, first single from forthcoming album, peaks at UK #11, much to the disappointment of their manager Rob Grettons who had bet each member of the band £250 that it would hit Top 10. Group sets off on tour of South America, following their only UK concert of the year at the G-Mex Centre, Manchester, where they are supported by labelmates Happy Mondays.

1989 Jan [20] Group plays first of 2 dates in Southern France.

Feb [11] Sixth album *Technique*, co-produced with Stephen Hague, debuts at UK #1 and will peak at US #32.

[21] Group appears live on UK TV Channel 4's "Big World Café".

Mar *Round And Round* reaches UK #21, aided by rare live performance on UK BBC TV's "Top Of The Pops". (Wilson resigns as Factory chairman over bet with manager Gretton that it would make Top 5.) B-side features their theme tune to current UK ITV soccer series "Best And Marsh". They also perform 2 concerts in Glasgow, Scotland, and Birmingham, W.Midlands.

Apr [8] Group kicks off first stage of North American tour at San Juan, Puerto Rico.

June Group returns to Europe to attend the Hacienda's seventh birthday party held at the Roxy club, Amsterdam, Holland.

[14] 21-date "Monsters Of Art Tour", with Public Image Ltd and The Sugarcubes, restarts at Shoreline Amphitheater, Mountain View, CA.

Sept *Run 2* from *Technique* makes UK #49.

Dec Sumner releases first fruits of work away from New Order, linking with The Pet Shop Boys' Neil Tennant and The Smiths' Johnny Marr in ad-hoc outfit Electronic. Resulting *Getting Away With It*, released on Factory, reaches UK #12.

1990 May While Morris and Gilbert have recently continued soundtrack work, Hook forms Revenge with Dave Hicks and Chris Jones, releasing Factory in UK and Capitol in US debut album *One True Passion*.

[19] *Getting Away With It* makes US #38.

June [9] Under one-off band name, England New Order, the group combines with the England World Cup Football Squad to hit UK #1 with *World In Motion ...*, the team's officially commissioned World Cup theme. Song, and accompanying soccer-based video, includes rap by UK soccer hero John Barnes. The hit is written by New Order and UK comedian Keith Allen.

Aug Sumner joins Marr and both Pet Shop Boys for Electronic's first live performance at Los Angeles' Dodgers Stadium. They support Depeche Mode in a slot originally booked for The Jesus & Mary Chain who have withdrawn.

RANDY NEWMAN

1961 Newman (b. Randolph Newman, Nov.28, 1943, New Orleans, LA), nephew of Alfred and Lionel Newman (heads of music at 20th Century-Fox Pictures) and a graduate in music composition at UCLA, releases US debut *Golden Gridiron Boy* on Dot, produced by Pat Boone.

1962 He joins the staff at Metric Music, Liberty Records' music publishing division, writing songs full-time for $50 a week.

Nov The Fleetwoods record *They Tell Me It's Summer* as B-side of US #36 hit *Lovers By Night, Strangers By Day*; Newman's first to be covered.

Dec Another composition, *Somebody's Waiting*, is B-side of Gene McDaniels' *Spanish Lace*, which makes US #31.

1964 July Newman's first song to reach US chart in its own right is Jerry Butler's version of *I Don't Want To Hear It Anymore*, at US #95.

1965 **May** His first composition to chart in UK is Cilla Black's recording of *I've Been Wrong Before*, which reaches UK #17. (Over the next 2 years, he establishes himself as a major popular writer, with hit covers of his songs by Alan Price (*Simon Smith And His Amazing Dancing Bear*) and Gene Pitney (*Nobody Needs Your Love* and *Just One Smile*), as well as recordings by Judy Collins, Manfred Mann, Frankie Laine, Jackie DeShannon, The Walker Brothers, The Nashville Teens, Harpers Bizarre, and many more.)

1966 He releases instrumental album *The Randy Newman Orchestra Plays Music From The Hit Television Series "Peyton Place"*, on US Epic, with help from his uncles at 20th Century-Fox.

1967 He becomes a staff arranger-producer at Warner Bros., working with The Beau Brummels, Van Dyke Parks and Harpers Bizarre.

1968 **June** Debut vocal album *Randy Newman* is released on Warner's Reprise label, along with single *Bee Hive State*. It includes already-covered songs like *Love Story* and *So Long Dad*, plus *Cowboy* (which Newman has submitted unsuccessfully after being invited to write a theme song for film "Midnight Cowboy"). Many copies of the album are allegedly given away as a loss-leader publicity stunt by Warner, and the album does not chart.

1969 **Nov** He arranges Peggy Lee's Leiber/Stoller-penned *Is That All There Is?*, which hits US #10.

1970 **Mar** Harry Nilsson releases *Nilsson Sings Newman*, with covers of 10 Newman songs, including some not yet recorded by Newman but he guests on vocals on 2 tracks.
Apr *Twelve Songs* features guest musicians Ry Cooder, Clarence White and Gene Parsons of The Byrds, and includes *Mama Told Me (Not To Come)*, left off the previous album because Newman has not rated it that highly.
July His first #1 song is Three Dog Night's version of *Mama Told Me (Not To Come)*, which tops US chart for 2 weeks. Meanwhile, Newman contributes to music of film "Performance", starring Mick Jagger (on soundtrack of which he sings *Gone Dead Train*) as to Dick Van Dyke/Bob Newhart comedy "Cold Turkey" (for which he writes score).

1971 **Oct** Live album *Randy Newman Live*, recorded at the Bitter End club, is his US chart debut, at #191.

1972 **July** *Sail Away*, with a much-covered title track, peaks at US #163, selling 100,000 copies in an 18-week chart stay.

1974 **Oct** [5] Newman plays the Atlanta Symphony Hall accompanied by an 87-piece orchestra conducted by another uncle, Emil Newman.
Dec *Good Old Boys*, with guest backing vocals by Glenn Frey and Don Henley of The Eagles, reaches US #36, his biggest-selling album to date, which stays on chart for 5 months. He promotes it with a 20-city US tour, accompanied by the Atlanta Symphony Orchestra.

1978 **Jan** *Short People*, his Singles chart performance debut, hits US #2 behind medium-height band The Bee Gees at #1 with *Stayin' Alive*, and is a million-seller. A parody on bigotry (a familiar Newman theme), it makes him a target for hatred by short people throughout US for a while, though he (measuring 5' 11") is publicly unrepentant. The song comes from *Little Criminals*, his first to hit US Top 10, at #9, earning a gold disk for a half million sales. Album back-up band includes members of The Eagles. (Neither the album nor single charts in UK, but Newman makes a UK tour during the year, and his live set is taped for a BBC TV show.)

1979 **Sept** *Born Again*, one of the first digitally-recorded albums (and for which he has commuted to Los Angeles and written the songs in an office, 9 to 5 fashion), peaks at US #41. It features guest harmony vocals by Stephen Bishop, and includes the (non-chart) single *Story Of A Rock'N'Roll Band*, a send-up of the Electric Light Orchestra story, in theatrical Jeff Lynne-style.

1980 **July** UB40 revives Newman's haunting *I Think It's Going To Rain Today*, from his first album. A double A-side single (with the group's own *My Way Of Thinking*), it hits UK #6.

1982 **Feb** His soundtrack to Milos Forman movie "Ragtime", starring James Cagney, is released on Elektra, and peaks at US #134. (*One More Hour* is nominated for an Oscar as Best Original Song.)

1983 **Feb** A duet with Paul Simon, *The Blues*, is Newman's second US Singles chart entry, reaching #51.
Mar *Trouble In Paradise* reaches US #64. As well as the duet with Simon, it has guest appearances by Bob Seger, Rickie Lee Jones, Linda Ronstadt, Jennifer Warnes, Don Henley, and Lindsay Buckingham and Christine McVie from Fleetwood Mac.

1984 **Aug** His song *I Love L.A.*, from *Trouble In Paradise*, is used for US TV ads promoting the Los Angeles Olympics.
Oct He writes and performs the soundtrack to Robert Redford movie "The Natural", released as a non-charting album on Warner Bros.

1985 **Sept** Newman participates in the Farm Aid benefit.

1986 **Nov** He writes and records the soundtrack music for Steve Martin/Chevy Chase comedy film "The Three Amigos" (which also has his first screeplay work, in collaboration with Martin).

1987 **May** Compilation album *Lonely At The Top*, surveying a variety of his work, is released in Europe to promote a tour.

1988 **Oct** *Land Of Dreams*, Newman's first album in 5 years, part-produced by Jeff Lynne and Mark Knopfler, is released, set to make US #80, while cynical and humorous extract *It's Money That Matters* peaks at US #60.

1990 **June** [9-10] Newman, with Paula Abdul, B.B. King, Alice Cooper, Kenny Loggins and Quincy Jones, film video at A&M studios promoting recycling based on *Yakety Yak*. Sponsored by the Take It Back Foundation, "Yakety Yak, Take It Back!", also features Bugs Bunny, and will be released in Apr.1991.
Having contributed *Falling In Love* to Tom Selleck movie "Her Alibi" and *Burn On* to "Major League", Newman scores soundtrack to Robin Williams/Robert De Niro hit movie "Awakenings".

1991 **May** [7] Newman begins a short US tour, playing the first of 2 nights with the Boston Pops Orchestra, of selections from his film music.

OLIVIA NEWTON-JOHN

1964 Newton-John (b. Sept.26, 1948, Cambridge, Cambs.), having moved to Melbourne, Australia, with her family at age 5, and sung in a folk vocal group in her early teens, becoming a frequent performer on local TV with singing partner Pat Carroll, wins a Johnny O'Keefe national talent contest, for which the prize is a trip to UK.

1965 Having postponed the prize trip for a year to complete school, she travels to UK with Carroll, to perform as a duo in pubs and clubs.

1966 **May** After Carroll's visa has expired and she has returned to Australia, Newton-John remains in UK performing solo, and makes an unsuccessful one-off single for Decca, recording Jackie DeShannon's *Till You Say You'll Be Mine*.
Sept Meeting Bruce Welch of The Shadows at a concert in Bournemouth, she is offered the chance to star in the Cliff Richard And The Shadows London Palladium pantomime "Cinderella", but declines to return to Australia for Christmas.

1967 Back in UK, she sets up home with Bruce Welch in West London.

1968 **June** She is cited in Bruce Welch's divorce proceedings.

1970 Newton-John is recruited by producer Don Kirshner to join the group Toomorrow, with Ben Thomas, Karl Chambers and Vic Cooper and Chris Slade, formed to star in a movie of the same title.
Aug 2 Toomorrow singles are issued simultaneously in UK, on different labels (Decca and RCA); neither sells.
[27] "Toomorrow" (a science fiction musical comedy) opens in cinemas throughout the UK, and RCA releases a soundtrack album by the group. Both fail, and after spending time on promotional work for the film, the quartet disbands.

1971 **Jan** Newton-John duets with Cliff Richard on *Don't Move Away*, B-side of his UK hit *Sunny Honey Girl*, after which she joins Richard's tour of Holland, Belgium, Germany and Switzerland.
Apr Her belated second solo single, made for UK Pye International via a deal signed with Festival Records in Australia, covers Bob Dylan's *If Not For You*, and hits UK #7. It is produced by John Farrar, now married to her ex-partner Pat Carroll, and also a member of Marvin, Welch & Farrar with Bruce Welch, to whom she is engaged.
Aug [30] She appears on BBC TV guesting in Cliff Richard's holiday special "Getaway With Cliff".
Sept *If Not For You* is her US debut at #25.
Oct [25] She begins a season at the London Palladium on a bill topped by Cliff Richard.
Dec Her revival of folk standard *Banks Of The Ohio*, produced by Welch and Farrar, hits UK #6, and creeps to US #94. *If Not For You* makes US #158.

1972 **Jan** She begins a 13-week guest residency on Cliff Richard's BBC TV series "It's Cliff Richard".
Apr A cover of George Harrison's *What Is Life* reaches UK #16. Shortly after, Newton-John and Welch break up.
Aug *Just A Little Too Much* does not chart.

1973 **Feb** Another cover, of John Denver's *Take Me Home, Country Roads*, makes UK #15.
June *Let Me Be There*, written by ex-Shadows member John Rostill, fails to chart in UK.
Aug She plays a recorder solo on Marvin, Welch & Farrar's *Music Makes My Day*.

1974 **Feb** *Let Me Be There* hits US #6 (after topping Country chart), her first major US success, and the first of 5 consecutive US million-seller singles. The album of the same title makes US #54.

Mar Her third album, *Music Makes My Day*, is the first to chart in UK, reaching #37.

[2] She wins Best Country Vocal Performance, Female for *Let Me Be There* at the 16th annual Grammy awards.

Apr She represents UK in the Eurovision Song Contest, held in Brighton, E.Sussex, with *Long Live Love*. The song fails in the competition (won by Abba with *Waterloo*), but reaches UK #11.

June *Long Live Love* marks a move to EMI Records in UK, and peaks at UK #40. *If You Love Me (Let Me Know)* fails to chart in UK, but after the US success of *Let Me Be There* it hits US #5, earning a gold disk.

Oct Ballad *I Honestly Love You* reaches UK #22, while in US it is her first chart-topper, holding #1 for 2 weeks and selling over a million. Her US album *If You Love Me, Let Me Know* also tops US chart for a week, earning a gold disk.

1975 Newton-John, new boyfriend Lee Kramer (who becomes her manager in US, at the suggestion of original manager Peter Gormley) and her writer/producer Farrar move from UK to US, to capitalize on her huge 1974 US success. (She will take up residence in Malibu, CA.)

Mar [1] *I Honestly Love You* wins Record Of The Year and Newton-John wins Best Pop Vocal Performance, Female at the 17th annual Grammy awards. (She is also voted Female Vocalist Of The Year by the Country Music Association, the first UK performer to be so honored. The choice angers many prominent CMA members, who leave to form the Association of Country Entertainers. She surmounts the criticism by heavily playing the country music circuit, and recording in Nashville.)

[8] *Have You Never Been Mellow*, written and produced by Farrar, US chart for a week, and is another million-seller. The album of the same title also hits US #1 for a week, and earns a further gold disk.

Apr *Have You Never Been Mellow* makes UK #37.

Aug *Please Mr. Please* (written by Welch and originally his only solo single in 1974) hits US #3, her fifth million-selling single in a row.

Nov *Clearly Love* reaches US #12 and earns another gold disk. From it, *Something Better To Do* makes US #13.

1976 **Jan** *Let It Shine/He Ain't Heavy ... He's My Brother* climbs to US #30. She duets with John Denver on *Fly Away*, which reaches US #13.

May *Come On Over* makes US #13 and UK #49. Title track reaches US #23. Kramer resigns as her manager, and the couple's personal relationship also breaks up.

Sept *Don't Stop Believin'* makes US #33.

Nov [17] Her first US TV special is aired on ABC TV, with guests including Elliot Gould and Lynda Carter.

Dec *Don't Stop Believin'* reaches US #30. Taken from it, *Every Face Tells A Story* climbs to US #55.

1977 **Apr** *Sam*, taken from *Don't Stop Believin'*, reaches US #20.

[14] Newton-John begins a US tour.

May [8] She makes New York live debut, at the Metropolitan Opera House, and is approached to play the lead role of Sandy in a movie adaptation of the Broadway hit musical of 50s nostalgia, "Grease".

[28] As part of the Queen's Silver Jubilee celebrations, she stars in "The Big Top Show" at Windsor Castle, Berks., with Elton John and Leo Sayer.

June *Making A Good Thing Better* stalls at US #87.

July *Sam* hits UK #6.

Aug *Making A Good Thing Better* peaks at US #34 and UK #60.

Oct Newton-John and Kramer are reunited both professionally and personally.

Dec A reissue of *I Honestly Love You* peaks at US #48.

1978 **Jan** Compilation album *Olivia Newton-John's Greatest Hits* makes US #13 and UK #19, selling over a million in US.

May TV special "Olivia" airs on ABC TV. She sues her US label, MCA Records, for $10 million, alleging "failure to adequately promote and advertise" her records.

June [10] Written and produced by John Farrar, *You're The One That I Want*, a duet with co-star John Travolta from movie "Grease", tops US chart for a week, selling over 2 million to earn a platinum disk. It will also hit UK #1 for 9 weeks, where it sells over 1,870,000 copies, making it the third best-selling single in UK pop history to date.

[16] Movie "Grease" opens across US.

July Soundtrack album *Grease* tops US chart for 12 weeks, and is a multi-million seller.

Sept *Summer Nights*, a second *Grease* duet with Travolta, hits US #5, topping a million sales. It tops UK chart for 7 weeks, selling over 1,500,000 copies in UK, and giving the duo a second entry among UK's

10 best-selling singles of all time. Her solo from *Grease*, ballad *Hopelessly Devoted To You*, hits US #3, and is a further million-seller.

Dec *Hopelessly Devoted To You* hits UK #2.

1979 **Jan** *A Little More Love* hits US #3 and UK #4, while parent album *Totally Hot* hits US #7 and is another million-seller. It makes UK #30.

[9] The "Music For UNICEF" concert, to celebrate the International Year Of The Child, takes place in the General Assembly Hall of the United Nations in New York. Newton-John sings *Rest Your Love On Me* with Andy Gibb and *The Key*, donating the royalties from the songs to UNICEF.

[10] NBC TV airs "A Gift Of Song – The Music For UNICEF Concert".

June *Deeper Than The Night* makes US #11 and UK #64.

Aug *Totally Hot*, the title track from the last album, makes US #52. B-side *Dancin' Round And Round* reaches US #82.

1980 **May** She duets with Andy Gibb on *I Can't Help It*, which makes US #12. (She also appears on Gibb's *After Dark*.)

July Newton-John stars with Gene Kelly in fantasy musical movie "Xanadu", which is slaughtered by the critics and a box office failure, but spins off a highly successful music soundtrack. The title track *Xanadu*, with The Electric Light Orchestra, tops UK chart for 3 weeks, and the movie's soundtrack album is UK #1 for 2 weeks.

Aug [2] Her solo *Magic*, from *Xanadu*, tops US chart for 4 weeks.

Sept Soundtrack album *Xanadu*, shared between Newton-John and ELO, hits US #4, while *Magic* peaks at UK #32.

Nov *Suddenly*, a ballad duet with Cliff Richard from *Xanadu*, reaches UK #15.

1981 **Jan** *Suddenly* reaches US #20.

Aug [5] Newton-John receives a star on the Hollywood Walk Of Fame in Hollywood, CA.

Nov [21] *Physical*, banned by some radio stations for supposed sexual innuendo, hits US #1 for 10 weeks, the equal second longest holding chart-topper in pop history behind Elvis Presley's 11-week *Hound Dog*, selling over 2 million copies. It will also hit UK #7, and become one of the first and most identifiable aerobic themes.

Dec *Physical*, promoted by a US TV special based around the songs of the album (her fourth such TV vehicle), hits US #6, and is another million-seller, also making UK #11.

1982 **Feb** *Landslide* reaches UK #18.

Apr *Make A Move On Me* hits US #5 and peaks at UK #43.

July *Landslide* makes US #52. She makes a rare US tour, partly filmed for video release.

Nov *Heart Attack* hits US #3 and makes UK #46. TV-promoted compilation *20 Greatest Hits* hits UK #8. A different compilation, *Olivia's Greatest Hits, Vol.2* reaches US #16.

1983 **Jan** Reissued *I Honestly Love You*, from the compilation, makes UK #52.

Feb *Tied Up* peaks at US #38.

[23] "Physical" wins Best Video at the 25th annual Grammy awards.

Nov *Twist Of Fate*, from film "Two Of A Kind", in which she stars again with John Travolta, reaches UK #57.

1984 **Jan** Soundtrack album *Two Of A Kind*, containing 4 Newton-John songs, peaks at US #26, while *Twist Of Fate* hits US #5.

Mar Also from the movie, *Livin' In Desperate Times* peaks at US #31.

Aug She hosts a reception in Los Angeles for the Australian 1984 Olympic team.

1985 Newton-John marries actor/dancer Matt Lattanzi, whom she first met while working on "Xanadu".

Nov *Soul Kiss* reaches US #20, while the album of the same title peaks at US #29.

1986 **Jan** [17] Daughter Chloe is born.

Mar *Soul Kiss* makes UK #66, her final 80s UK chart appearance.

July [5] She sings guest vocal on David Foster's *The Best Of Me*, which makes US #80.

1988 **Sept** *The Rumour*, co-produced by Elton John, makes US #67. Title track, written by Elton John and Bernie Taupin, reaches US #62.

1989 Newton-John is appointed Goodwill Ambassador for the United Nations Environment Programme.

Dec Newton-John is warned to increase security after Ralph Nau, having haunted her since 1981, seeks release from Elgin Mental Health Center, IL.

1990 **Jan** [6] Still running her own Koala Blue Australian-style clothing business, started in 1984 with Farrar's wife Pat, and now signed to Geffen Records, Newton-John releases a collection of favorite nursery rhymes, lullabies and standards she sings to daughter Chloe as the album *Warm And Tender*, which makes US #124.

967 **Nov** Nilsson (b. Harry Nelson, June 15, 1941, Brooklyn, New York, NY) having lived in California since childhood, is (as Harry Nelson) a computer specialist at the Security First National Bank in Van Nuys, and has been for many years (as Nilsson) a part-time songwriter (with some unsuccessful early 60s singles on Mercury and Capitol) and half of a bogus Jan And Dean, when The Monkees record his song *Cuddly Toy* on their *Pisces, Aquarius, Capricorn & Jones Ltd.* With interest in his material running high, RCA signs him as a singer/songwriter.

968 **Mar** Debut album *Pandemonium Shadow Show*, produced by Rick Jarrard, has 6 Nilsson originals (including *Cuddly Toy*), plus covers including The Beatles' *You Can't Do That* and *She's Leaving Home*, and a carbon-copy of Phil Spector's arrangement of Ike & Tina Turner's *River Deep, Mountain High*. The album does not chart, but gets wide airplay: John Lennon hears it and names Nilsson his favorite US singer. 3 of the new songs are quickly covered: *1941* (Tom Northcott and Billy J. Kramer), *Without Her* (Jack Jones) and *It's Been So Long* (Kenny Everett).
Sept *Aerial Ballet* contains all Nilsson originals apart from Fred Neil's *Everybody's Talkin'*, which is issued as a single without success. The album does not chart, but the single, plus *Together* (covered by Sandie Shaw) and *One* gain extensive radio play.

969 **Jan** He writes the score for Otto Preminger's film "Skidoo", including a vocal version of the movie's credits. He has a small role in the movie (starring Jackie Gleason and Carol Channing), as a security guard.
June Three Dog Night's revival of *One*, a Nilsson composition from *Aerial Ballet*, hits US #5, becoming his first million-selling song.
July He writes and plays piano on The Turtles' *The Story Of Rock And Roll*, which reaches US #48.
Sept *Harry* is his first to chart, making US #120. Mainly self-produced, it contains *The Puppy Song* (later a hit for David Cassidy) and his first Randy Newman cover, *Simon Smith And The Amazing Dancing Bear*. He writes *Best Friend*, the theme for new TV comedy series "The Courtship Of Eddie's Father" and also composes incidental music for the show.
Oct Nilsson's version of Fred Neil's *Everybody's Talkin'*, from *Aerial Ballet*, is chosen as the theme tune to film *Midnight Cowboy*, despite prospective songs having been commissioned from several writers, including Bob Dylan's *Lay Lady Lay* and Nilsson's own *I Guess The Lord Must Be In New York City* (included on *Harry*). The resulting exposure belatedly turns it into his first US chart single, hitting #6.
Nov *Everybody's Talkin'* makes UK #23. Follow-up *I Guess The Lord Must Be In New York City* peaks at US #34.

970 **Mar** He releases *Nilsson Sings Newman*, a collection of 10 songs written by Randy Newman (who also plays piano). It does not chart.
[11] *Everybody's Talkin'* wins Best Contemporary Vocal Performance, Male Of 1969 at the 12th annual Grammy awards.

971 **Apr** Nilsson writes, narrates and sings the songs in "The Point", an animated children's fantasy produced by Murakami-Wolf Films for US TV. The soundtrack reaches US #25, his biggest-selling album to date.
May *Me And My Arrow*, from *The Point*, reaches US #34.
July *Aerial Pandemonium Ballet*, a compilation of tracks from the first 2 albums, makes US #149.

972 **Jan** *The Point* makes UK #46.
Feb Recording in UK with producer Richard Perry, Nilsson hears Badfinger's *Without You*, written by the group's Pete Ham and Tom Evans, and determines to record it. Released as a single, it tops US chart for 4 weeks, and is his only million-seller. Its Perry-produced parent album *Nilsson Schmilsson* hits US #3, and collects a gold disk for a half million sales.
Mar *Without You* tops UK chart for 5 weeks, selling almost 800,000 copies in UK, while *Nilsson Schmilsson* hits UK #4.
Apr *Jump Into The Fire*, also from the album, makes US #27.
June *Coconut*, a third single from *Nilsson Schmilsson* peaks at UK #42.
Aug *Son Of Schmilsson*, a second gold album, makes US #12 and UK #41, while *Coconut* hits US #8.
Nov Self-penned *Spaceman*, from *Son Of Schmilsson*, makes US #23.

973 **Jan** *Remember (Christmas)*, also self-written, reaches US #53.
Mar Nilsson wins a Grammy award for *Without You*, named Best Male Pop Vocal Performance Of 1972.
Aug *A Little Touch Of Schmilsson In The Night*, a set of standard ballad revivals with an orchestra conducted by Gordon Jenkins, reaches US #46 and UK #20 (his last UK chart album).
Sept From the album, a revival of *As Time Goes By* peaks at US #86.

74 **Mar** [12] Nilsson and John Lennon are thrown out of Los Angeles' Troubadour club after heckling comedian Tommy Smothers' act.
May Self-penned *Daybreak* reaches US #39, his last US hit single. It is

taken from film "Son Of Dracula", a horror-spoof-musical directed by Freddie Francis in which Nilsson and Ringo Starr appear. The soundtrack album, containing Nilsson's songs and Paul Buckmaster's incidental music, makes US #160.
Oct *Pussy Cats*, produced by Lennon, reaches US #60. It includes offbeat revivals of rock standards like *Rock Around The Clock* and Dylan's *Subterranean Homesick Blues*.

1975 **Apr** *Duit On Mon Dei* makes US #141.
1976 Adapted for the stage, "The Point" runs successfully at London's Mermaid Theatre.
Feb *Sandman* peaks at US #111.
Aug *Nilsson ... That's The Way It Is* stalls at US #158.
Nov *Without You* is reissued in UK and climbs to #22.

1977 **Aug** *All I Think About Is You* makes UK #43, and is Nilsson's last UK chart entry. It is taken from *Knnillssonn*, which makes US #108, and is his last new album for RCA.

1978 **July** Compilation *Greatest Hits*, his final US chart album, makes #140.
1980 **Sept** He signs a new deal with Mercury Records, releasing (for the first time credited to his full name Harry Nilsson) *Flash Harry*, produced by Steve Cropper. It has song collaborations with John Lennon, Ringo Starr and Van Dyke Parks, among others, plus 2 items by new Nilsson acquaintance Eric Idle. 1 track, *Harry*, is a tribute to Nilsson, sung by Idle and Charlie Dore. A commercial flop, the album is not followed.

1981 **Apr** [27] He attends the wedding of Ringo Starr and Barbara Bach. (Otherwise, his activities during the 80s are low-key to the apparent point of retirement).

1988 **Dec** With the majority of back catalog now available on CD, *A Touch More Schmilsson* is issued, featuring previously unreleased out-takes from the original Schmilsson sessions.

1990 **Oct** An up-dated collection of past glories, *Without Her – Without You* is released by BMG Enterprises.

TED NUGENT

1966 Nugent (b. Dec.13, 1948, Detroit, MI), having played guitar since age 9, and led local bands The Royal High Boys and The Lourdes in his early and mid-teens, forms heavy garage band The Amboy Dukes in Detroit, with himself and Steve Farmer on guitars, John Drake on vocals, Rick Lober on keyboards, Bill White on bass and Dave Palmer on drums (although the personnel will change frequently throughout the group's existence as vehemently anti-drugs Nugent will summarily dismiss any group member he suspects of indulging).

1967 The Amboy Dukes sign to Mainstream Records, and find local success with their first single, a revival of Them's *Baby Please Don't Go*.

1968 **Feb** The group's first album *The Amboy Dukes* is also a US chart debut, reaching #183.
Aug *Journey To The Center Of The Mind* is the group's only US hit single, reaching #16, while album of the same title makes US #74. (A third album for Mainstream, *Migration*, will fail to chart.) The band tours almost continuously, with some 150 dates a year, mostly in the North-West and in the South (and a stage act which starts out as quasi-psychedelic punk rock will become ever more dominated by Nugent's flashy Jimi Hendrix-inspired guitar fireworks).

1970 **Mar** Group signs to Polydor, and *Marriage On The Rocks/Rock Bottom* creeps to US #191.

1971 **Mar** Second Polydor album, live *Survival Of The Fittest*, recorded at the Eastown theater in Detroit, reaches US #129. On it, the name of the band changes to Ted Nugent & The Amboy Dukes.

1973 In an ongoing campaign of self-publicity while touring between record deals, Nugent stages live "guitar battles" with other heavy feedback merchants like Iron Butterfly's Mike Pinera (currently with the New Cactus Band), The MC5's Wayne Kramere, and Frank Marino of Mahogany Rush.

1974 With another label change to Frank Zappa's Discreet label, and credited as Ted Nugent's Amboy Dukes, 2 albums *Call Of The Wild* and *Tooth, Fang And Claw* fail to chart. (Both titles are indicative of Nugent's highly-publicized passion for blood-sports and hunting. He is adept with firearms and bow and arrow, and an active supporter of the National Rifle Association. From his Michigan farm he frequently hunts wild game which becomes food for the Nugent household.)
Oct Nugent wins the US National Squirrel-Shooting Archery Contest, downing a squirrel at 150 yards. Over the 3-day event, he also shoots over 2 dozen other live moving targets.

1975 The Amboy Dukes split, and Nugent is signed to a solo deal by Epic, teaming with producer Tom Werman, retaining bass player Rob Grange from the final Dukes line-up, and adding Derek St. Holmes from Detroit band Scott on rhythm guitar and vocals and Cliff Davies on drums, to make up his new backing band. He is also taken over by Aerosmith's managers, Leber-Krebs, who organize his blitzkrieg live tours into commercially successful operations.

Dec [28] He is threatened on stage in Spokane, WA, by a member of the audience, David Gelfer, who aims a .44 Magnum at him before being taken away to be charged with "intimidating with a weapon".

1976 **Apr** Nugent's first solo hit single is *Hey Baby*, which peaks at US #72. It is taken from his debut Epic album *Ted Nugent*, which provides his first US Top 30 album, peaking at #28, and collecting a gold disk during its 62 weeks on chart.

Sept *Ted Nugent* makes UK #56, his UK chart debut.

Nov *Free For All*, with guest vocals by Meat Loaf, reaches US #24 and UK #33, and becomes Nugent's first million-seller, earning a platinum disk. *Dog Eat Dog*, taken from the album, makes US #91.

1977 **July** *Cat Scratch Fever* peaks at US #17 (his second platinum album) and UK #28.

Sept Title track from *Cat Scratch Fever* is Nugent's biggest-selling solo single, reaching US #30.

1978 **Jan** Nugent causes controversy when he signs his autograph on a fan's arm with the tip of a Bowie knife.

Feb Instrumental single *Home Bound* reaches US #70.

Mar Double live album *Double Live Gonzo!* makes US #13 (his third in a row to go platinum) and UK #47.

[18] He plays at the California Jam II festival in Ontario, CA, to an audience of 250,000, alongside Heart, Santana, Aerosmith, Dave Mason and others.

Apr *Yank Me, Crank Me*, from the live album, climbs to US #58.

Dec *Weekend Warriors* is Nugent's fourth consecutive (and last) platinum album, reaching US #24. It fails to chart in UK, where Nugent is regarded as anachronistic in post-punk New Wave atmosphere.

1979 **Jan** *Need You Bad*, taken from *Weekend Warriors*, peaks at US #84.

Apr [7] Nugent plays the California Music Festival, at the Memorial Coliseum, Los Angeles, to 110,000 people, sharing the bill with Van Halen, Cheap Trick, Aerosmith and The Boomtown Rats.

June *State Of Shock* peaks at US #18 and earns a gold disk.

July [28] Nugent appears at the "World Series Of Rock" concert at Cleveland Stadium, OH, with Aerosmith, Journey and Thin Lizzy.

1980 **June** *Scream Dream* reaches US #13 (his last gold album) and UK #37.

July [6] More than 30 people at a Nugent concert in Hollywood are arrested in the audience, for violence and drug offenses.

Aug *Wango Tango*, extracted from *Scream Dream*, makes US #86, and is Nugent's final hit single.

1981 **Apr** Live album *Intensities In 10 Cities* peaks at US #36 and UK #75.

1982 **Jan** Compilation album *Great Gonzos! The Best Of Ted Nugent* makes US #140. It is Nugent's final release on Epic, as he signs a new deal with Atlantic Records. He also revamps his band, bringing in one-time Vanilla Fudge drummer Carmine Appice and recruiting previous accompanists Derek St. Holmes (vocals) and Dave Kiswiney (bass).

Aug Debut Atlantic album *Nugent* makes US #51.

1984 **Apr** *Penetrator*, on Atlantic, peaks at US #56.

1985 **Jan** [10] Nugent appears in NBC TV series "Miami Vice".

1986 **Apr** He plays on *Stars*, the single made to profit the USA For Africa Foundation by heavy metal star aggregation Hear 'N' Aid, as *Little Miss Dangerous* makes US #76.

[20] Nugent strips a 19-year-old fan down to her underwear, but is not arrested by police. He later states, "I did such a good job, they didn't have the heart to arrest me."

May [13] Nugent, appearing on sex therapist Dr. Ruth Westheimer's TV show, says, "life is one big female safari and Dr. Ruth is my guide".

1988 Nugent sings *Love Is Like A Chain Saw* in horror film "State Park".

Mar Final solo album for Atlantic, *If You Can't Lick 'Em ... Lick 'Em* makes US #112.

Dec [31] Nugent participates in third annual Whiplash Bash at Cobo Arena, Detroit, MI.

1989 Nugent forms new heavy metal battalion Damn Yankees with ex-Styx Tommy Shaw, ex-Night Ranger Jack Blades and drummer Michael Cartellone, signing to Warner Bros.

1990 **Mar** [3] A Lansing, MI, benefit for Nugent's various hunting projects features an acoustic set from Nugent. (He has started monthly hunting magazine, **Ted Nugent's World Bowhunters**. Nugent sells 20,000 copies of *Fred Bear – American Hunter's Theme Song* through his mail-order business.)

May [19] Damn Yankees' *Coming Of Age* peaks at US #60.

[26] Ron Nevison-produced *Damn Yankees* initially makes US #30.

1991 **Jan** [12] *High Enough* hits US #3, with songwriting credited to Tom, Jack and Ted.

Feb [9] In its 46th charted week, *Damn Yankees* re-peaks at US #13, a they play in Birmingham, AL, during US tour with Bad Company.

Apr [20] Damn Yankees headline a welcome home concert for returning Gulf War troops at the Norfolk Naval Air Station in Norfolk VA, during their now-dubbed "Operation Rock'N'Roll Storm Tour" as third extract from album, *Come Again* enters US Hot 100 at #81.

GARY NUMAN

1977 Numan (b. Gary Webb, Mar.8, 1958, Hammersmith, London), the son of a British Airways bus driver, whose former groups have included Meanstreet (who appeared on punk compilation album *Live At The Vortex*), assumes the group name Tubeway Army, calling himself "Valerium", drafting in Paul Gardiner aka "Scarlett" (bass) and Numan's uncle, Gerald Lidyard, aka "Rael" (drums) for live appearances. As he discovers synthesizers, his sound moves from guitars towards electronic rock.

1978 **Feb** Numan quits his job at W.H. Smith on the day the first Tubeway Army single *That's Too Bad* (funded by his father Tony) is released on Beggars Banquet.

Aug Second single *Bombers* fails to chart. Numan sings a TV commercial for Lee Cooper jeans.

1979 **Apr** *Down In The Park* also flops.

May Numan makes his BBC TV "Top Of The Pops" debut, singing synthesizer-dominated *Are Friends Electric?*

June *Are Friends Electric?*, from Tubeway Army's *Replicas*, tops UK chart, boosted by first pressing of 20,000 picture disks. Numan assembles a touring band: Paul Gardiner (bass), Russell Bell (guitar, synthesizer), Chris Payne (synthesizer), Cedric Sharpley (drums) and Ultravox moonlighter Billy Currie (keyboards, synthesizer).

Sept The Tubeway Army name is dropped, and *Cars* is released credited to Gary Numan, topping UK chart. *The Pleasure Principle* enters UK chart at #1, a week after *Tubeway Army*, Numan's 1978 debut album, reaches UK #14.

[20] Numan begins a 13-date UK tour at the Apollo theater, Glasgow, Scotland. As with all future tours, Numan and accompanists are all dressed in modernist boiler suit uniforms and remain static througho the robotic performance. After selling out London's Hammersmith Odeon he announces a second show there, with proceeds going to the Save The Whales Fund.

Oct *Replicas*, released on Atco Records, makes US #124.

Dec *Complex* hits UK #6.

1980 Numan's world tour continues through Europe, US, Japan, Australia and New Zealand.

May *We Are Glass* hits UK #5. Video "The Touring Principle", filmed Numan's Hammersmith Odeon concert Sept.28, 1979, is released. *The Pleasure Principle* reaches US #16.

June *Cars*, Numan's only US chart success, hits US #9.

Sept *I Die: You Die*, premiered on BBC TV's "Kenny Everett Video Show", hits UK #6, as parent album *Telekon* enters UK chart at #1. Numan is featured on Robert Palmer UK #31 album *Clues*, notably on the hit *Johnny And Mary* (UK #44).

[4] Numan embarks on his second UK tour, a 17-date trek titled "The Gary Numan Teletour 80", at the Odeon, Birmingham, W.Midlands, through to Sept.29 at the City Hall, Newcastle, Tyne & Wear.

Nov *Telekon* makes US #64.

1981 **Jan** *This Wreckage* reaches UK #20.

Apr [26-28] He plays 3 sell-out shows at the Wembley Arena, Londo and on the final night announces his retirement from live work.

May Boxed album *Living Ornaments 1979-1980* hits UK #2, while *19* makes UK #47 and *1980* reaches UK #39.

July Numan vocalizes on Paul Gardiner's UK #49 *Stormtrooper In Dr*

Sept *She's Got Claws* hits UK #6. *Dance*, written about the aftermath of his first real love, hits UK #3, with guests Mick Karn of Japan and Roger Taylor from Queen.

[18] Numan embarks on a round-the-world trip in his single-engine Cessna plane. The attempt ends in India, when he is forced to make a unscheduled landing, which leads to him and his co-pilot being place under house arrest, finally arriving back in UK on Christmas Eve.

Nov *Dance* makes US #167.

Dec Numan sings vocals on touring backing band Dramatis' *Love Needs No Disguise*, which makes UK #33.

1982 **Jan** [29] Returning from a meeting in Cannes, France, Numan's plan crash-lands near Southampton. The ever imaginative UK press claims that he has landed on the A3057 between Southampton and Andover after running low on fuel.

Mar *Music For Chameleons*, with Dollar's Therese Bazar guesting, reaches UK #19.

[9] Numan appears at Uxbridge Magistrates Court, London, charged with carrying an offensive weapon, a baseball bat. The charges will be dropped.

June *We Take Mystery (To Bed)* hits UK #9.

Aug *White Boys And Heroes* makes UK #20.

Sept *I, Assassin* hits UK #8.

Oct [8] Numan returns to the live arena, opening an 18-date US tour at Perkins Palace in Pasadena, CA, set to end Nov.8 in Chicago, IL.

Nov Dramatis makes UK #57 with *I Can See Her Now*.

Dec Compilation album *New Man Numan – The Best Of Gary Numan* peaks at UK #45.

33 Sept *Warriors* makes UK #20 as album of the same title, produced by Bill Nelson, reaches UK #12, aided by a 40-date UK tour.

Oct *Sister Surprise*, last release for Beggars Banquet, makes UK #32.

84 Numan forms his own label, Numa Records, signing Hohokam, Steve Braun, John Webb (Numan's brother) and model Caroline Munro. *Venus In Furs*, by Paul Gardiner, who has recently died from a drug overdose, is the label's first release.

Oct *The Plan*, credited to Tubeway Army & Gary Numan, charts in UK at #29.

Nov First Numan release on his own label, *Beserker* reaches UK #32, as album of the same title climbs to UK #45.

Dec *My Dying Machine* peaks at UK #66.

85 Mar Numan teams with Shakatak's Bill Sharpe for *Change Your Mind*, from Sharpe's forthcoming Polydor album *Famous People*, which makes UK #17.

Apr *White Noise Live* peaks at UK #29.

May EP *The Live* reaches UK #27.

Aug *Your Fascination* makes UK #46.

Sept *Call Out The Dogs* climbs to UK #49. *The Fury* reaches UK #24, as Numan plays 17-date "The Fury" tour.

Oct Sharpe and Numan's *New Thing From London Town* makes UK #52.

Nov *Miracles* makes UK #49.

36 Apr *This Is Love* reaches UK #28.

June *I Can't Stop* makes UK #27.

Nov *Strange Charm* peaks at UK #59.

Dec *I Still Remember*, with all proceeds going to the Royal Society For The Prevention Of Cruelty To Animals (RSPCA), falters at UK #74.

37 Apr Group Radio Heart, with Numan, reach UK #35 with *Radio Heart*.

June Second Radio Heart single, *London Times*, makes UK #48.

Sept *Cars (E Reg Mix)*, a remix of Numan's 1979 #1, reaches UK #16.

Oct Double album *Exhibition*, a Beggars Banquet compilation of hits, makes UK #43, as early Numan albums are released on CD.

38 Oct With his own label defunct, Numan signs to Miles Copeland's Illegal label, and makes UK #48 with *Metal Rhythm*, while extract *New Anger* makes UK #46, as Numan embarks on 19-date UK tour.

Nov Single *America* peaks at UK #49.

39 Oct Numan plays 14-date "The Skin Mechanic" tour as IRS-released *Skin Mechanic* makes UK #55.

91 Mar [16] Still with IRS, *Heart* enters at peak UK #43.

[30] Self-produced *Outland*, still perpetuating robotic synthesizer heavy direction makes UK #39, as he finishes a 12-date UK tour, with a freshly boiler-suited ex-Kajagoogoo member Nick Beggs, now in Numan's touring troupe.

ILLY OCEAN

74 Ocean (b. Leslie Sebastian Charles, Jan.21, 1950, Trinidad, West Indies), having become interested in music at age 4 when he is given a toy ukelele, has moved with his family (including 5 brothers and sisters) to London. On leaving Stepney Green school, he became an apprentice tailor's cutter, and his boss, Benjamin Sollinger, lent him £30 to buy a piano. Ocean has sung with local London East End band Shades Of Midnight at a pub in Petticoat Lane, and with groups The Go and Dry Ice, and as a solo act in his own right using pseudonyms including Joshua and Sam Spade. Working at a Savile Row tailors in London, he releases first single under pseudonym Scorched Earth. It flops. He goes to work at Ford Motors in Dagenham, Essex, where he works by night so he can write and record during the day.

75 Dec He quits and signs to Dick Leahy's GTO label. Teaming with producer Ben Findon, his first single *Whose Little Girl Are You* fails.

1976 Apr Disco-soul *Love Really Hurts Without You* hits UK #2 and reaches US #22.

Aug *L.O.D. (Love On Delivery)* makes UK #19.

Dec *Stop Me (If You've Heard It All Before)* peaks at UK #12.

1977 Apr He meets Laurie Jay, who becomes his manager. GTO rejects his latest song *Who's Gonna Rock You*. (It will become a 1980 UK #12 for The Nolan Sisters.) *Red Light Spells Danger*, his second UK Top 10 success, hits #2.

1979 Sept *American Hearts* peaks at UK #54.

1980 Feb *Are You Ready* makes UK #42.

Oct La Toya Jackson's debut album includes 2 Ocean-penned songs, *Are You Ready* and *Stay The Night*.

1981 May He self-finances GTO-rejected *Nights (Feel Like Getting Down)* which makes US R&B Top 5. (It will later appear without permission on Jane Fonda's first "workout" album, and Ocean will be awarded substantial royalties.)

July *Nights (I Feel Like Getting Down)* fails in UK but climbs to US #152, his previous 2 having failed to chart in either territory.

1982 GTO is sold to CBS/Epic as *Inner Feeling* fails to chart.

1984 After 2 years of inactivity, Ocean signs to Jive in UK, where he is teamed with producer, and fellow Trinidadian, Keith Diamond.

May First Ocean/Diamond collaboration, *European Queen (No More Love On The Run)*, flops.

Nov [3] *European Queen*, retitled, at his manager's suggestion, and reissued as *Caribbean Queen (No More Love On The Run)* hits US #1, US R&B #1 and #1 on the Dance chart. (It will also receive a third title and version as *African Queen* in the relevant territories.) Parent album *Suddenly* hits US #9, earning a US platinum disk. *Caribbean Queen (No More Love On The Run)* hits UK #6 and *Suddenly* hits UK #9.

1985 Feb *Loverboy*, penned by Ocean with producer Robert "Mutt" Lange, hits US #2, held off #1 by Foreigner's *I Want To Know What Love Is*. Ocean begins a 2-month US tour, playing his first live dates with a band in 10 years. *Loverboy* makes UK #13.

Mar Ocean wins Best R&B Vocal Performance at the 27th annual Grammy awards.

May Ocean begins his first major tour, "Ocean Across America", including a performance at Live Aid, Philadelphia, PA.

June Ballad title track from *Suddenly* hits #4 in both UK and US.

July *Mystery Lady* peaks at US #24.

Aug *Mystery Lady* stalls at UK #49.

1986 Feb [15] Pop-dance *When The Going Gets Tough, The Tough Get Going*, featured on the soundtrack for Michael Douglas/Kathleen Turner movie "The Jewel Of The Nile", hits US #2.

Mar *When The Going Gets Tough, The Tough Get Going* gives Ocean his first UK #1, despite a UK video ban for featuring US non-Musicians Union members Douglas, Kathleen Turner and Danny De Vito.

May Ballad *There'll Be Sad Songs (To Make You Cry)* reaches UK #12. *Love Zone* hits UK #2.

June [28] *There'll Be Sad Songs (To Make You Cry)* tops US R&B chart.

July [5] Written by Wayne Braithwaite with Ocean and Diamond, who have contributed 9 of the 10 songs on the parent album, *There'll Be Sad Songs (To Make You Cry)* is Ocean's second US #1.

Aug *Love Zone* peaks at UK #49 while *Love Zone* hits US #6.

Sept [27] *Love Zone* hits US #10.

Oct *Bittersweet* stalls at UK #44. Ocean begins a sell-out UK tour. Having received 2 American Music Awards, *Sad Songs* is nominated for a Grammy.

Dec [27] *Love Is Forever* reaches US #16.

1987 Jan *Love Is Forever* makes UK #34.

He spends the year creating third Jive-released album with writers and producers Lange, Keith Diamond and Wayne Braithwaite.

1988 Mar Co-penned with Lange, *Get Outta My Dreams (Get Into My Car)* hits UK #3 and *Tear Down These Walls* also hits UK #3.

Apr [9] Ocean's third US chart-topper *Get Outta My Dreams* deposes Michael Jackson's *Man In The Mirror*.

[16] *Get Outta My Dreams* tops US R&B chart.

May *Tear Down These Walls* makes US #18. He starts UK tour, going on to world venues until the fall as *Calypso Crazy* climbs to UK #35.

June *The Colour Of Love* hits US #17, but stalls at UK #65, as the tour reaches US and Canada.

Oct *Stand And Deliver* fails to chart in UK.

1989 Nov [18] *Licence To Chill*, unrelated to current James Bond movie, peaks at US #32, as retrospective *Greatest Hits*, from the period 1984 to 1989, makes US #77, already hitting UK #4.

1990 Jan Hip-hop extraction *Greatest Hits* package, *I Sleep Much Better (In Someone Else's Bed)*, featuring The Fresh Prince and Mimi, fails to score.

SINEAD O'CONNOR

1982 O'Connor (b. Dec 12, 1966, Glenageary, Eire), having grown up, the third of 4 children, in suburban Dublin, and been placed in a Dominican nun-run residential center for girls with behavioral problems after shoplifting (her parents having split up when she was 8, her mother subsequently dying in a car crash in 1985), has been asked, at age 14, by a teacher at Mayfield College, Drumcondra to sing at her wedding. Her performance of *Evergreen* is heard by the bride's brother Paul Byrne, drummer with Irish band In Tua Nua for whom O'Connor will later co-write their first single *Take My Hand*.

1985 O'Connor having taken further education at a Waterford boarding school before running away to Dublin where she attends the Dublin College of Music and gets part-time jobs including being a kiss-o-gram French maid, begins performing gigs, mainly of Bob Dylan covers, in Dublin pubs at night. She then joins local band Ton Ton Macoute and links with future manager and boyfriend Fachtna O'Ceallaigh who has persuaded U2 guitarist The Edge to feature her vocals on the soundtrack album he is working on for film "Captive".

1986 While perfoming with Ton Ton Macoute, she is spotted by Ensign Records executives Nigel Grainge and Chris Hill. She tells Grainge she is leaving the band and he invites her to London with a complimentary plane ticket to begin a contract with Ensign, contrary to the advice of U2's Bono. The agreement allows for her to serve an apprenticeship at the label's office prior to beginning her recording career.
Sept Virgin Records release *Heroine* as the main theme single from "The Captive "soundtrack, featuring O'Connor on vocals.

1987 **Apr** O'Connor, who is currently featured on labelmate World Party's debut album *Private Revolution*, begins work on her own project, self-producing following unsuccessful sessions with producer Mick Glossop.
June O'Connor and boyfriend John Reynolds, who is drumming on the current recordings, have a son, Jake.
Oct Ensign releases O'Connor's first single, the unsuccessful *Troy*.

1988 **Jan** Breakthrough single, *Mandinka*, launches O'Connor's career, set to make UK #17. Her striking closely shaved head and stridently voiced opinions immediately attract media interest – visual and mental projections she will persist with for some years. Debut album *The Lion And The Cobra*, including guests Enya and ex-Ant Marco Pirroni, is also released, set to make UK #27 and US #36, where the album will be popular on college and alternative radio, during a 28-week residence. O'Connor spends much of year touring UK, US and Europe in support of the album, issued on Chrysalis Records outside the UK.
June [3] During her current UK tour, a gig at the Dominion theater, London is filmed for subsequent TV and video release.
Sept *Jump In The River*, released in 2 versions (one a duet with Karen Finley), fails to score in UK as has *I Want Your Hands On Me* (in Apr.), which features rapper MC Lyte. *Jump In The River*, featured in the Jonathan Demme-directed movie "Married To The Mob "reaches #17 on **Billboard**'s Modern chart, but she has yet to secure a Hot 100 hit.

1989 **Mar** O'Connor and Reynolds are married. O'Connor performs *Mandinka* at the 31st annual Grammy awards ceremony at the Shrine Auditorium, Los Angeles, and has been nominated for Best Female Vocalist category.
Apr John Maybury-directed screening of last year's Dominion theater performance is released on video as "The Value Of Ignorance".
May O'Connor duets with Matt Johnson on his UK #4 The The album *Mind Bomb*, on the track *Kingdom Of Rain*.
Dec O'Connor splits with ex-boyfriend and manager O'Ceallaigh, 2 days prior to the filming of a video for her forthcoming single, which she will later claim made her feel sad and tearful during its filming.

1990 **Jan** [20] Previewing her second album, *Nothing Compares 2 U*, is released. It is a cover version of a Prince song featured on a 1985 self-titled album by Paisley Park act Family. With an arrangement by Soul II Soul's Jazzie B and Nellee Hooper, and produced by O'Connor and Hooper, the melancholy lost-love ballad becomes one of the fastest selling singles in chart history worldwide.
Feb [3] *Nothing Compares 2 U* hits UK #1, for the first of 5 weeks.
[21] O'Connor makes acting debut in the, subsequently Channel 4 TV screened, film "Hush-A-Bye-Baby", playing a 15-year-old schoolgirl, also called Sinead, which premieres at the Dublin Film Festival.
Mar [24] Second album *I Do Not Want What I Haven't Got* immediately hits UK #1. Including performances from husband Reynolds, ex-Smith Andy Rourke and Jah Wobble, it is produced by O'Connor and Hooper and will remain charted for the rest of the year as it begins to hit #1 in 13 worldwide territories.

Apr [14] A world tour kicks off in Cornwall, under the banner "Year Of The Horse Tour".
[21] On its way to #1 in 18 territories, *Nothing Compares 2 U* tops US chart for 1 month. Its sales are boosted by innovative John Murphy-directed video, during which O'Connor cries to great dramatic effect i a continuous face on camera shot, intercut with somber walking scene It becomes MTV's most requested video of the year, and together with the single, will win a clutch of awards in the next 12 months.
[28] *I Do Not Want What I Haven't Got* begins a 6-week sit-in at the top of US album chart on its way to triple platinum sales.
May US leg of world tour starts in Atlanta, GA.
[12] With ever increasing media notoriety, O'Connor refuses to appe on NBC TV's "Saturday Night Live" show in protest at the inclusion c guest host, the equally controversial comedian, Andrew "Dice" Clay.
June [23] During 3-day Glastonbury Festival of Contemporary Performing Arts on Michael Eavis' Farm in Pilton, near Glastonbury, Somerset, O'Connor and band perform on a bill featuring Happy Mondays, De La Soul, The Cure, Jesus Jones, Del Amitri and labelmat World Party.
[26] O'Connor returns to Eire to perform at the Dublin Point.
July [21] O'Connor participates in Roger Waters' performance of "T Wall" at the site of the Berlin Wall, Potzdamer Platz, Berlin, Germany The event, also released as an album and video, is broadcast live worldwide, raising money for the Memorial Fund For Disaster Relief.
[28] Uptempo *The Emperor's New Clothes* stalls at US #60 and UK #31.
Aug [1] US tour resumes in St. Paul, MN.
[24] O'Connor refuses to perform her scheduled gig at New Jersey's Garden State Arts Center in Holmdel, NJ, if the American national anthem is played, initially in protest at the idea of US patriotism and subsequently in protest at the current wave of music censorship prevailing in the US. The incident becomes a major international new story, also amid rumors that she has left her husband and is involved with her support act, UK soul singer Hugh Harris.
[29] While some US radio stations ban O'Connor records, a bewigged and made-up O'Connor joins an anti-O'Connor patriotic demonstrati being staged outside her own concert prior to her evening performanc in Saratoga Springs, NY.
Sept [7] O'Connor wins 3 Silver Astronauts for Best Video Of The Year, Best Female Video and Best Post Modern Video categories at th annual MTV Awards. At the backstage party, she is reported to have asked Living Colour's Vernon Reid, "Will you marry me and have my love child?", to which he replied: "Mmm ... OK."
Oct [2] Mike Reichtien, working in the meat section of Mrs. Gooch's Natural Food store in Beverly Hills, CA, sings the American national anthem to O'Connor while she is in the store, and is subsequently fire
[12-13] O'Connor performs at the Amnesty International benefit "Fro Chile ... An Embrace of Hope", alongside Sting, New Kids On The Block, Crosby Stills & Nash, Ruben Blades, Wynton Marsalis, Jackson Browne and others, duetting not least the Kate Bush vocals with Pete Gabriel for *Don't Give Up*.
[27] Third album extract, ballad *Three Babies*, promoted by sleeping horse video clip, makes UK #42.
Nov [3] O'Connor contributes a version of *You Do Something To Me* t *Red Hot + Blue*, an anthology of Cole Porter songs to benefit AIDS education. She will also perform live at the album's press launch.
[6] O'Connor performs at the Royal Albert Hall, London.
[26] During World AIDS week, O'Connor presents a series of 5 min. TV shorts entitled "AIDS Up-dates".

1991 **Jan** [9] O'Connor, now living in a rented Hollywood Hills, CA, hous with her son Jake and long-time friend and assistant Ciara O'Flanaga tops the annual list of US fashion doyen Mr. Blackwell's worst-dresse women of the year, calling her the "bald-headed banshee of MTV".
Feb [1] Having also announced that she is pulling out of the forthcoming annual BRIT Awards in London, O'Connor says she will not attend the Grammy awards in a letter sent to the National Academy of Recording Arts & Sciences (NARAS), saying that she doe not like the music industry's values and that, "I signed my record dea when I was 17 and it has taken me this time to gather enough information and mull it over and reach a conclusion. We are allowing ourselves to be portrayed as being in some way more important, more special than the very people we are supposed to be helping – by the way we dress, by the cars we travel in, by the "otherworldliness" of o shows and by a lot of what we say in our music". (NARAS' Michael Greene will respond caustically in future interviews, questioning O'Connor's motives, noting that she did not have any problem with attending both the MTV and the American Music Awards.)

[10] O'Connor wins Best International Artist, Female at the 10th annual BRIT Awards at the Dominion theater, London. In her absence to collect the award, and as a tribute to her, organizer Jonathan King plays a video clip from another nominee in the category, Whitney Houston singing her current single *The Star Spangled Banner*.

[20] Expected to win a brace of awards, O'Connor wins Best Alternative Music Performance, Vocal Or Instrumental for *I Do Not Want What I Haven't Got* at the 33rd annual Grammy awards at Radio City Music Hall, New York.

Mar [7] O'Connor is named Artist Of The Year and Best and Worst Female Singer in the annual **Rolling Stone** Readers' Picks. *I Do Not Want What I Haven't Got* wins Best Album. She also wins Artist Of The Year, Best Female Singer, Best Single and Best Album categories in the Critics' Picks.

May [12] O'Connor appears by satellite from Holland at "The Simple Truth" concert for Kurdish refugees at Wembley Arena, London.

THE O'JAYS

Eddie Levert (vocals)
Walter Williams (vocals)
William Powell (vocals)

1958 The Mascots form as an R&B/doo-wop group at McKinley high school, Canton, OH, with Levert (b. June 16, 1942, Canton), Williams and Powell, plus Bobby Massey and Bill Isles.

1961 They record for the first time, cutting *Miracles* for Wayco label, and come under the wing of Cleveland, OH, DJ Eddie O'Jay, who hones their stage act to professionalism, and gives career guidance. As a return gesture, they rename themselves The O'Jays. Further singles follow on King, but fail to chart.

1963 **Sept** Group signs to Imperial Records, and US chart debut, at #97, is *Lonely Drifter*, produced by label owner H.B. Barnum.

1965 **June** A revival of Benny Spellman's 1962 hit *Lipstick Traces (On A Cigarette)* reaches US #48.
Aug *I've Cried My Last Tear* makes US #94.
Nov Debut album *Comin' Through*, on Imperial, fails to chart.

1966 **Aug** Isles leaves to work as a songwriter, but maintains links with the group, which still performs as a quartet, moving back to Cleveland.
Oct *Stand-In For Love* peaks at US #95. Group leaves Imperial, moving to associated Minit label.

1967 **May** Second album *Soul Sounds*, released on Minit, again fails and has no spin-off hit singles.

1968 **Jan** Signed to New York-based Bell Records, *I'll Be Sweeter Tomorrow (Than I Was Today)* climbs to US #66.
July *Look Over Your Shoulder* makes US #89.
Sept Last success on Bell is *The Choice*, which creeps to US #94.

1969 Group plays the Apollo theater in Harlem, New York, with The Intruders, who are working with Kenny Gamble and Leon Huff, and recommend their producers to check out The O'Jays.
Sept Group links with Gamble and Huff's independent production company, with releases appearing on Philadelphia-based Neptune label. The first of these, *One Night Affair*, reaches US #68.

1970 **May** *Deeper (In Love With You)* makes US #64.
Sept *Looky Looky (Look At Me Girl)* stalls at US #98, and is their last Neptune release.

1971 Massey leaves to go into record production, and they continue as a trio. (Massey will find success as a producer with Cleveland group The Ponderosa Twins.) Revival of Sam Cooke's *You Send Me* makes US #78.

1972 Gamble and Huff form their own label, Philadelphia International Records, and suggest to Levert that he might like to sign to it as a soloist. Levert is only interested in working as part of the group, so The O'Jays are signed as a unit (having also been approached by Motown and Invictus Records).
Oct *Backstabbers*, a departure for the group into a hard-hitting, socially aware lyric (penned by Gamble and Huff), hits US #3, becoming the group's first million-seller, and reaches UK #14. Album of the same title hits US #10, and is both The O'Jays' and Philadelphia International's first gold album.
Dec Taken from the album, *992 Arguments* makes US #57.

1973 **Mar** [24] Group tops US chart for a week with its second million-selling single, *Love Train*, again written and produced by Gamble and Huff, and also from album *Backstabbers*.
Apr *Love Train* hits UK #9.
May *The O'Jays In Philadelphia*, rounding up Neptune recordings, makes US #156.
July *Time To Get Down* makes US #33.

1974 **Jan** *Ship Ahoy*, written and produced by Gamble and Huff, reaches US #11, and earns another gold disk.
Mar *Put Your Hands Together*, taken from *Ship Ahoy*, hits US #10.
June Group's third million-seller, also from *Ship Ahoy*, is *For The Love Of Money*, which hits US #9.
Aug Live album *The O'Jays Live In London*, recorded on first UK and European tour, makes US #17, becoming the group's third gold album.

1975 **Jan** *Sunshine* peaks at US #48.
June *Give The People What They Want* makes US #45. It is taken from *Survival*, which reaches US #11 and earns another gold disk.
Aug *Let Me Make Love To You* peaks at US #75.

1976 **Jan** Group's fourth million-selling single, *I Love Music*, hits US #5. It is taken from *Family Reunion*, which hits US #7 and is a million-seller.
Feb *I Love Music* reaches UK #13. Prior to the group's biggest US tour, Powell leaves. (He has had cancer diagnosed, and his health has deteriorated so he has no strength to face the rigors of the road.) Replacement is Sammy Strain, who has previously sung for 12 years with Little Anthony & The Imperials. Group also forms its own Shaker Records in Cleveland, designed as a "community-style" label to help nurture new talent in its home region.
Apr *Livin' For The Weekend* makes US #20.
Oct *Message In Our Music* peaks at US #49, while parent album *Message In The Music* reaches US #20.

1977 **Feb** *Darlin' Darlin' Baby (Sweet Tender Love)* makes US #72 and UK #24.
May [26] Powell dies of cancer, at home in Canton.
July *Travelin' At The Speed Of Thought* reaches US #27.

1978 **Jan** Double compilation album *The O'Jays: Collectors' Items* peaks at US #132.
Apr A remixed reissue of *I Love Music*, released to capitalize on a new lease of UK disco success by the song, makes UK #36.
June *So Full Of Love* hits US #6, earning another platinum disk, and marks a return from social consciousness and rock crossover fusions to the romantic R&B of The O'Jays' roots.
July *Used Ta Be My Girl*, taken from the album, hits US #4, and is The O'Jays' fifth and last million-selling single. In UK, it reaches #12.
[12] Group celebrates its 20th anniversary at the Greek theater, Los Angeles, CA.
Oct Ballad *Brandy* makes US #79 and UK #21.

1979 **Oct** *Sing A Happy Song* makes UK #39, while parent album *Identify Yourself* is another platinum disk-earner, reaching US #16.

1980 **Feb** *Forever Mine* makes US #28 – the group's first US Top 30 entry in almost 4 years.
Oct Group switches from Philadelphia International to associated TSOP label for *Girl, Don't Let It Get You Down*, its last US Singles chart entry, at #55. On the same label, *The Year 2000* makes US #36.

1982 **July** *My Favorite Person* climbs to US #49.

1983 Group celebrates its 25th anniversary playing a 75-city US tour on a bill with Rufus and Johnny "Guitar" Watson.
Aug *Put Our Heads Together* reaches UK #45, while *When Will I See You Again* makes US #142.

1986 **Sept** [13] *(Pop, Pop, Pop, Pop) Goes My Mind* by Levert, a group comprising Eddie Levert's sons Gerald and Sean and friend Marc Gordon, tops US R&B chart.

1987 **Nov** Group makes its first UK visit in 15 years, playing 3 nights at the Hammersmith Odeon, London.
[7] The O'Jays return to top US R&B chart with *Lovin' You*.
Dec Band returns to the recording scene via a new deal with EMI Manhattan Records and *Let Me Touch You* climbs to US #66.

1989 **June** *Serious* climbs to US #114, featuring US R&B #1 *Have You Had Your Love Today*, which features a rap solo by Jaz.

1990 **Jan** [22] Group wins Favorite Soul/R&B category at the 17th American Music Awards.

1991 **Apr** [13] EMI-released *Emotionally Yours*, its title track penned by Bob Dylan, peaks at US #89, while related Levert unit's latest album *Rope A Dope Style* stands at US #161.

MIKE OLDFIELD

1968 **Nov** Oldfield (b. May 15, 1953, Reading, Berks.) releases *Children Of The Sun* as Sallyangie, with his sister Sally, on UK Transatlantic label.

1969 **Sept** After *Two Ships* fails, Sallyangie splits and Oldfield forms short-lived band Barefeet, which does not record.

1970 **Mar** Oldfield joins Kevin Ayers' backing band, The Whole Wide World, as bass player.
Oct He plays on Ayers' Harvest label *Shooting At The Moon*.

1971 **Aug** He goes solo when The Whole Wide World breaks up (Harvest releases another album, *Whatevershebringswesing*, after the split.)

1972 With financial backing from Virgin record shops' owner Richard Branson, who is planning to launch his own Virgin label, Oldfield begins work at Abbey Road studios in London on a 50-min. instrumental composition. Virgin signs him and gives studio time at the newly-opened Manor complex.

1973 **May** Virgin label launches with Oldfield's lengthy *Tubular Bells*, which enters UK chart a few weeks later. Not entirely solo (it has contributions from Jon Field on flute, Steve Broughton on drums and ex-Bonzo Dog Doo-Dah Band vocalist Viv Stanshall as occasional narrator, among others), the album features hundreds of studio overdubs by Oldfield playing different parts.

1974 **Apr** *Tubular Bells* hits US #3 and earns a gold disk (eventually selling 3 million copies).
May A segment from side 1 of *Tubular Bells* is used as main theme to movie "The Exorcist" and, extracted as a US single, hits US #7 (Oldfield's only US single success).
July Bowing to public request, Virgin issues *Mike Oldfield's Single*, containing an edit from *Tubular Bells* similar to the US release. It reaches UK #31. Meanwhile, the album, after a year on UK chart, much of it in the Top 10, reaches its highest placing to date – #2 behind Paul McCartney & Wings' *Band On The Run*.
Sept Oldfield's second album, similarly-constructed *Hergest Ridge*, enters UK chart at #1. After 3 weeks, it is deposed by *Tubular Bells*, finally peaking at #1 after 16 months on sale. (It will spend a total of 264 weeks on UK chart.)
Oct *Hergest Ridge* reaches US #87.
Nov Oldfield guests on guitar on friend David Bedford's *Stars End*, played by the Royal Philharmonic Orchestra.

1975 **Feb** *The Orchestral Tubular Bells*, arranged by Bedford and performed by the Royal Philharmonic Orchestra, with Oldfield on guitar, makes UK #17. Second Oldfield single *Don Alfonso* fails to chart.
Mar [1] Oldfield wins a Grammy award for *Tubular Bells*, named Best Instrumental Composition Of 1974.
Nov *Ommadawn*, incorporating wider influences (Celtic and African) than the 2 previous works, hits UK #4.

1976 **Jan** Seasonal double A-side, combining traditional *In Dulce Jubilo* with (vocal) *On Horseback*, hits UK #4, while *Ommadawn* peaks at US #146.
Dec *Boxed*, a 4-album box-set containing remixed versions of his first 3 albums and a compilation of singles and guest appearances, reaches UK #22.

1977 **Jan** *Portsmouth*, a traditional tune arranged by Oldfield, hits UK #3.
Feb Oldfield's arrangement of *William Tell Overture* fails to chart (as will its follow-up *The Cuckoo Song*).

1978 **Dec** Double album *Incantations*, 3 years in the writing and making, reaches UK #14. For the first time, Oldfield is willing to give interviews and spend time promoting an album, after receiving a course of Exegesis training in self-assertiveness.

1979 **Jan** 4-track *Take Four*, reprising *Portsmouth*, *In Dulce Jubilo* and 2 traditional re-arrangements, makes UK #72.
May *Guilty*, made with a New York rhythm section, surprises many with its disco leanings, but reaches UK #22. Its release is followed by Oldfield's first tour, with a 50-piece accompaniment which includes string players and a choir. The shows are audio-visual events, incorporating films by Ian Eames.
Aug Double live album *Exposed*, recorded on tour, reaches UK #16.
Dec *Platinum*, a less serious and more varied collection than its predecessors, peaks at UK #24.

1980 **Jan** Oldfield's version of the theme from UK BBC TV children's show "Blue Peter" makes UK #19.
July Live group Oldfield Music is formed for a UK and European tour to promote *Platinum*.
Sept Oldfield's version of Abba's *Arrival*, with a parody of Abba's "helicopter" album sleeve, fails to chart.
Nov *QE2* reaches UK #27, but his revival of The Shadows' *Wonderful Land* fails.

1981 **July** *QE2*, on Epic in US, makes #174. Virgin announces that worldwide sales of *Tubular Bells* have passed 10 million. (Oldfield will subsequently sue Richard Branson over royalty payments throughout his time with Virgin. They settle their differences out of court.) Oldfield is entered in the UK edition of **Who's Who** – the only rock musician included apart from Paul McCartney.
[28] Oldfield plays a free concert in London on the eve of Prince Charles and Lady Diana Spencer's wedding, composing new music for the occasion. (This helps him gain the award of the Freedom of the City of London in 1982 in recognition both of his charity works and his export contribution from overseas sales and earnings.)

1982 **Mar** The Mike Oldfield Group is formed for live work, with Maggie Reilly (vocals), Tim Cross (keyboards), Maurice Pert (percussion, keyboards), Rick Fenn (bass) and Pierre Moelen (drums).
Apr *Five Miles Out*, partly inspired by his experiences as a private pilot, hits UK #7. The title track climbs to UK #43.
May Oldfield's last US chart entry, at #164, is *Five Miles Out*.
June *Family Man*, from *Five Miles Out*, reaches UK #45. (The song will be revived as a US Top 10 hit in 1983 by Daryl Hall & John Oates.)

1983 **June** *Crises* hits UK #6.
July *Moonlight Shadow*, taken from *Crises*, and with a vocal by Maggie Reilly, hits UK #4. Re-promoted *Tubular Bells* recharts at UK #28.
Sept *Shadow On The Wall*, also from *Crises*, with a guest vocal by ex-Family singer Roger Chapman, fails to chart.

1984 **Jan** *Crime Of Passion* peaks at UK #61.
July *Discovery* reaches UK #15, while *To France*, taken from it, makes UK #48.
Dec Oldfield's soundtrack album of his music from movie "The Killing Fields" makes UK #97.

1985 **Dec** *Pictures In The Dark*, featuring Aled Jones, makes UK #50, as compilation *The Complete Mike Oldfield* reaches UK #36.

1986 **Apr** *Shine*, with Yes singer Jon Anderson on guest vocals, fails to chart (Oldfield will spend the rest of the year producing a video album, which will eventually appear in 1988 as *Wind Chimes*.)

1987 **Oct** *Islands* reaches UK #29. The title track (also issued as a UK single) features vocals by Bonnie Tyler.

1988 **Mar** *Islands* makes US #138.

1989 **July** *Earth Moving* reaches UK #30.

1990 **June** With no pre-release hit singles, *Amorok* stalls at UK #49 and will prove Oldfield's least successful album to date with only a 2-week chart stay.
Dec *Etude* fails to chart in UK despite its extensive use as advertising theme for Nurofen painkillers.

ALEXANDER O'NEAL

1972 Raised and based in Minneapolis, MN, ex-North Natchez high school footballer and active civil rights supporter, O'Neal (b. Nov.14, 1953) settles on a musical direction, starting out on the local club scene.

1978 He links up with the burgeoning black Minneapolis music elite to form Flyte Time. Co-members include future production force Jimmy Jam and Terry Lewis. Prince, already leading the local music scene, invites them to become his full time backing band. Apparently due to his arrogance and unwillingness to conform, O'Neal is fired and sets up a temporary and unsuccessful rival band.

1984 Maintaining an association with Jam and Lewis, O'Neal, now solo, accepts their offer to write and produce a debut album to be released on Jam/Lewis controlled label Tabu (licensed through CBS/Columbia). The producers invite other stable, and ex-Time, member Monte Moir to oversee 3 cuts. Moir, Jam and Lewis also form O'Neal's backing band, The Secret, for the album.

1985 **Apr** Debut album *Alexander O'Neal*, recorded at Creation Audio, Minneapolis, is released, peaking at US #91. It features 3 US Hot R&B Singles chart hits (*Innocent*, a duet with Tabu artiste Cherrelle, *A Broken Heart Can Mend* and *If You Were Here Tonight*), but none crosses over.
June The debut album climbs to UK #19 after strong import demand.
Dec His duet with labelmate soulstress Cherrelle on her *Saturday Love* hits UK #6, but fails again to lift O'Neal out of US specialist charts.

1986 **Feb** *If You Were Here Tonight*, written and produced by Monte Moir, reaches UK #13.
Apr *A Broken Heart Can Mend* peaks at UK #53.
[19] *Saturday Love* makes US #26.
July Suffering from severe cocaine and alcohol addiction, O'Neal enters Minnesota's Hazelden Clinic. During his treatment, Jam and Lewis promise they will produce a follow-up album after his rehabilitation and also contribute half the cost of O'Neal's hospital bill.

1987 **Aug** Having recovered and married for a second time (O'Neal already has 3 children), he releases second album, *Hearsay*. All tracks bar one are written and produced by Jam and Lewis after their recent success with Janet Jackson. It will hit UK #4 and US #29, earning a platinum disk in both territories. First cut from the album, the crisply funked *Fake* makes US #25, having already topped US R&B chart, and made UK #33, helped by an energetic black and white video.
Sept [16] O'Neal begins a co-headlining US tour with Force MD's.
[26] *Fake* reaches US #25.

Oct Co-written by O'Neal and Jellybean Johnson, *Criticize* peaks at US #70, but hits UK #4.

Dec O'Neal performs sold-out dates in London.

[19] *Criticize* peaks at US #70.

88 Feb From *Hearsay*, a duet with Cherrelle, *Never Knew Love Like This* climbs to UK #26 and US #28, while "The Voice On Video" hits #3 on the UK Music Video chart.

May Ballad *The Lovers* reaches UK #28.

July *What Can I Say To Make You Love Me*, released to coincide with standing-room-only UK dates, makes UK #27. One of his Wembley performances is filmed for later TV showing.

Oct With parent album *Hearsay* now on US and UK charts for over a year, UK-only reissue (and remix) of *Fake*, titled *Fake '88*, peaks at UK #16. BBC TV airs the full Wembley Arena concert recorded in July.

Nov Seasonal album *My Gift To You*, featuring traditional Christmas songs and Jam/Lewis originals, is released, set to make US #149 and UK #53. O'Neal guests on Cherrelle's new album *Affair*, on tracks *Keep It Inside* and *Everything I Miss At Home*. UK-only *Hearsay All Mixed Up*, featuring remixed tracks from the second album *Hearsay* is released, to boost Christmas sales.

Dec *Christmas Song/Thank You For A Good Year* reaches UK #30.

89 Feb From the UK remix project, *Hearsay '89* peaks at UK #56.

July [18-19] O'Neal takes part in the seventh annual Prince's Trust Rock Gala at the NEC, Birmingham, W.Midlands.

Sept *Sunshine*, released 2 years after the issue of its parent album, stalls at UK #72. The *Hearsay All Mixed Up* combination has remained on the UK survey for over 2 years.

Dec Not satisfied with releasing remixed versions, those remixes are now segued into *Hitmix (Official Bootleg Mega-Mix)*, making UK #19.

91 Jan [19] New material emerges, his first in 3 years, in the shape of *All True Man*, which reaches UK #18 and will make US #43.

Feb [1] O'Neal embarks on major UK tour dates, supported by UK soul troupe, The Pasadenas.

[2] Parent album *All True Man*, again mostly written and produced by Jam and Lewis, hit UK #2 in its first release week.

Mar [2] *All True Man* makes US #52.

May [12] O'Neal appears live at "The Simple Truth" concert for Kurdish refugees at Wembley Arena, London.

OY ORBISON

54 Orbison (b. Apr.23, 1936, Vernon, TX) brought up in Wink, TX (after spending the war in Fort Worth, TX), having a Saturday afternoon radio show on K-ERB in Kermit, TX, with Charline Arthur, and in his teens performed with local hillbilly group The Wink Westerners, winning a talent contest organized by the Pioneer Furniture Company in Midland, TX, which leads to appearance on K-MID TV show, goes to North Texas State University in Denton, TX, studying geology (while there, classmate Pat Boone has his first hit *Two Hearts*).

55 Singing with The Teen Kings, he records at Norman Petty's studio in Clovis, NM. *Trying To Get To You* is released on Jewel Records, but does not sell.

56 July Having auditioned in Memphis, TN, for Sam Phillips at Sun Records, his first Sun single, uptempo rockabilly *Ooby Dooby*, written by 2 college mates, Wade Moore and Dick Penner, at North Texas State, makes US #59.

57 3 further unsuccessful singles are released on Sun, all in rockabilly mode, which is not the best forte for Orbison's high, expressive voice. Orbison moves to Nashville, TN, to concentrate on his songwriting.

58 May Writing songs for Acuff-Rose Music, he places *Claudette*, written for his wife (which he has recorded as a demo at Sun, but will be released 2 decades later), with The Everly Brothers. Released as B-side of *All I Have To Do Is Dream*, it reaches US #30 and shares in worldwide sales of several million.

59 Jan In Nashville, he signs to RCA, but *Seems To Me* and *Almost 18* fail and, guided by manager Wesley Rose, he parts from the label to sign to newer, smaller outfit: Monument Records, owned by Fred Foster.

60 Feb Orbison's second Monument single *Up Town*, with an Anita Kerr string arrangement, charts at US #72.

July Self-penned *Only The Lonely*, written for Elvis Presley and also offered to The Everly Brothers, is his breakthrough, hitting US #2 and selling over a million. Its wordless vocal accompaniment becomes a much-covered gimmick.

Oct *Only The Lonely*, his UK chart debut, tops UK chart for 2 weeks, dethroned by the year's biggest-seller, Elvis Presley's *It's Now Or Never*.

Nov *Blue Angel*, similarly styled to *Only The Lonely*, hits US #9.

Dec *Blue Angel* reaches UK #11.

1961 Jan *I'm Hurtin'* makes US #27.

Apr Orbison is treated for a duodenal ulcer.

June [5] Starkly melodramatic *Running Scared* is another million-seller, topping US chart for a week, and will hit UK #9.

Oct *Cryin'*, his third million-seller, hits US #2 and makes UK #25. B-side *Candy Man*, written by Fred Neil, makes US #25. (Both titles will be much revived by other acts.)

1962 Mar Orbison's fourth million-seller is uptempo (and also frequently revived) *Dream Baby*, which hits US #4.

[8] The Beatles make their radio debut on BBC program "Teenager's Turn" singing Orbison's *Dream Baby*.

Apr *Dream Baby* hits UK #2, below The Shadows' *Wonderful Land*.

June *Crying* is his first album to chart, reaching US #21.

July Less commercial *The Crowd* makes US #26 and UK #40.

Nov Double A-side ballad/beat combination *Leah/Working For The Man* reaches US #25 and #33. In UK, only *Working For The Man* is promoted and peaks at UK #50. Meanwhile, compilation album *Roy Orbison's Greatest Hits* reaches US #14.

1963 Mar Self-penned ballad *In Dreams* (which will become one of Orbison's most enduring songs) hits US #7.

Apr *In Dreams* hits UK #6.

May Orbison, who needs always to wear glasses to see properly, leaves his only regular pair on a plane while flying to Alabama to perform and has to wear his dark-tinted sunglasses. Due to fly to UK for a tour immediately, he has to keep on wearing these and they become such a trademark during his widely-photographed and reported trek with The Beatles that Orbison accepts them as his new image (which he will keep).

[18] He begins a UK tour with The Beatles and Gerry & The Pacemakers, opening at the Granada, Slough, Bucks.

June After the UK tour, *Lonely And Blue* reaches UK #15, while *Crying* makes UK #17.

July *Falling* reaches US #22 and hits UK #9, entering Top 20 while *In Dreams* is also still present. (B-side *Distant Drums* is covered by, and will be a posthumous hit for, Jim Reeves.)

Sept [11] Orbison embarks on 23-date UK package tour with Brian Poole & The Tremeloes, The Searchers and Freddie & The Dreamers, set to end on Oct.6 at King George's Hall, Blackburn, Lancs.

Oct Another double A-side couples Elvis Presley oldie *Mean Woman Blues*, which hits US #5, with Orbison/Joe Melson ballad *Blue Bayou*, which reaches US #29. Meanwhile, *In Dreams* peaks at US #35, as Orbison tours Canada.

Nov *Blue Bayou* hits UK #3, while the rock side peaks at UK #19. *In Dreams* hits UK #6.

Dec Seasonal ballad *Pretty Paper* makes US #15. (It is not released in UK at this time, due to the continuing success of *Blue Bayou*.)

1964 Jan Orbison embarks on tour of Australia with The Beach Boys, Paul & Paula, The Surfaris and The Joy Boys.

Mar *Borne On The Wind*, issued only in UK as a single, reaches #15.

Apr [18] Orbison embarks on a UK tour with Freddie & The Dreamers at the Adelphi theater, Slough, Bucks., set to end on May 16 at the City Hall, Newcastle, Tyne & Wear.

[26] He celebrates his 28th birthday with a party attended by The Beatles.

May [23] *It's Over*, another enduring ballad, hits US #9.

June *It's Over* tops UK chart for 2 weeks – the first time a US act has had a UK #1 since the beginning of Aug.1963, when Elvis Presley topped with *(You're The) Devil In Disguise*.

July *Exciting Sounds Of Roy Orbison*, a compilation of his early Sun tracks on Ember Records, reaches UK #17.

Sept [26] Distinctive uptempo arrangement of *Oh, Pretty Woman*, written by Orbison and Bill Dees, tops US chart for 3 weeks and will sell 7 million copies worldwide.

Oct [8] *Oh, Pretty Woman* tops UK chart for 3 weeks, while still at #1 in US. (Between Aug.8, 1963 and this week, no American artist tops the UK chart, except Orbison.)

Nov Orbison divorces Claudette on the grounds of her cruelty. She had been having an affair with their builder Braxton Dixon.

Compilation album *More Of Roy Orbison's Greatest Hits* reaches US #19, while *Early Orbison*, compiling tracks from his first 2 (non-charting) Monument albums, peaks at US #101.

Dec *Pretty Paper*, released a year late in UK, hits #6. *Oh Pretty Woman*, a compilation of singles released only in UK, hits UK #4.

1965 Jan Orbison tours Australia with The Rolling Stones.

Feb [16] He begins a 30 date twice-nightly package tour with

Marianne Faithfull, The Rockin' Berries, Cliff Bennett & The Rebel Rousers and others, at the Adelphi theater, Slough, set to end on Mar.21 at the Empire theater, Liverpool, Merseyside.

Mar *Goodnight* reaches US #21 and UK #14.

July [17] 18-date Irish tour begins in Bray, ending in Waterford on Aug.1.

Aug Orbison and Claudine remarry in Nashville.

Latin-styled *(Say) You're My Girl* makes US #39 and UK #23. Meanwhile, Orbison's contract with Monument expires. He signs a new deal for US with MGM Records, which offers movie as well as recording opportunities. He is satisfied with the way London Records has marketed its Monument repertoire in UK and many other territories around the world and signs a new direct international deal with London, which automatically gives it the product recorded for MGM. *Ride Away* is first single under the new arrangement: it peaks at US #25 and UK #34. *There Is Only One Roy Orbison*, also his first recorded for MGM, reaches US #55 and hits UK #10.

Nov A revival of R&B standard *Let The Good Times Roll*, released by Monument in competition with newer releases, makes US #81.

Dec Ballad *Crawling Back* reaches US #46 and UK #19. Monument compilation *Orbisongs* makes US #136.

1966 Feb Uptempo *Breakin' Up Is Breakin' My Heart* peaks at US #31 and UK #22. *The Orbison Way* reaches US #128 and UK #11.

Mar [20] Orbison tops the bill at ITV's "Sunday Night At The London Palladium".

[25] He begins a 31-date twice-nightly UK tour with The Walker Brothers, Lulu and others, at the Astoria theater, Finsbury Park, London, set to end on May 1 at Coventry theater, W.Midlands.

[27] Orbison falls off his motorcycle while scrambling at Hawkstone Park, Birmingham, W.Midlands. He fractures his foot and is taken to Thorpe Coombe General hospital, London, and will continue the tour sitting on a stool on stage, on crutches.

Apr *Twinkle Toes*, another uptempo rocker, makes US #39 and UK #29.

[24] He takes part in the London to Brighton vintage car rally.

May [1] Orbison performs at the **New Musical Express** Poll Winners Concert at the Empire Pool, Wembley, London, with an all-star cast.

June [6] Tragedy strikes when the Orbisons are returning from the National Drag Races meeting near Bristol, TN. A truck pulls out from a side road near Gallatin, TX and hits Claudette on her motorcycle. She dies, age 25, an hour later at Sumner Memorial hospital.

July *Lana*, previously an album track, now issued as a UK single, reaches #15.

Aug *Too Soon To Know*, a highly personalized ballad widely recognized as referring to the loss of his wife, hits UK #3 but stalls at US #68. *The Classic Roy Orbison* reaches UK #12.

[7] Orbison begins pre-recording of "The Fastest Guitar Alive" soundtrack in Nashville.

Sept Compilation album *The Very Best Of Roy Orbison* makes US #94, and is Orbison's final US chart album.

[7] He begins filming "The Fastest Guitar Alive" at MGM'S Hollywood studios, in a role originally intended for Elvis Presley.

1967 Jan *There Won't Be Many Coming Home*, from the film, makes UK #18. Meanwhile, in US *Communication Breakdown* reaches #60.

[22] A tour of Australia and Far East with The Walker Brothers and The Yardbirds, begins at Sydney Stadium, Australia.

Mar *So Good* makes UK #32.

[3] Orbison embarks on 32-date twice-nightly UK tour with The Small Faces, Paul & Barry Ryan, Jeff Beck and others at Finsbury Park Astoria, London, set to end on Apr.9 at ABC theater, Romford, Essex.

July *Orbisongs* peaks at UK #40.

Aug *Cry Softly Lonely One*, which sees a reconciliation with Joe Melson, reaches US #52, and will be Orbison's final US solo hit single.

Sept Compilation *Roy Orbison's Greatest Hits* climbs to UK #40.

1968 Aug *Walk On*, a dramatic ballad, makes UK #39.

[5] Orbison opens a 1-month season at the Talk Of The Town, London.

Sept [14] While Orbison is on tour in UK, performing in Birmingham, his home in Nashville catches fire, and the 2 eldest of his 3 sons, Roy Jr. and Tony, die in the blaze.

Oct *Heartache* makes UK #44.

1969 Mar [25] Orbison marries German-born Barbara Wellhonen, whom he met in a club in Leeds, W.Yorks.

May *My Friend* climbs to UK #35.

Oct Gimmicky uptempo *Penny Arcade* reaches UK #27.

1970 Apr The Orbisons move to Bielefeld near Dusseldorf, Barbara's birthplace.

Oct [18] Son Roy Kelton is born.

1971 *So Young*, the love theme from the movie "Zabriskie Point", is released

1973 Jan Compilation album *All-Time Greatest Hits* makes UK #39. Orbison leaves MGM to sign a 1-year deal with Mercury. (He will then return to Monument.)

1976 Jan TV-promoted compilation *The Best Of Roy Orbison* tops UK cha for a week.

Apr [23] At the nadir of his career, Orbison plays the Van-A-Rama auto show in Cincinnati Gardens, OH, before a crowd of less than 100

1977 Mar [14] Orbison opens for The Eagles, who are currently #1 with *Hotel California*.

1978 Jan [18] Orbison undergoes coronary by-pass surgery at St. Thomas' hospital in Nashville.

1980 July He returns to US Singles chart for the first time in 13 years, duetting with Emmylou Harris on *That Lovin' You Feelin' Again*, from the soundtrack of film "Roadie", in which he also makes a cameo appearance.

Sept [5] Orbison plays the second annual Buddy Holly Memorial Concert at the Civic Center, Lubbock, TX.

A projected movie biography "The Living Legend", with Martin Shee as the Big O, is scrapped after Orbison withdraws his support it.

1981 Feb [25] *That Lovin' You Feelin' Again* wins Best Country Performance By A Duo Or Group With Vocal at the 23rd annual Grammy awards.

July [18] *Golden Days* makes UK #63.

[19] Odessa, TX, announces "Roy Orbison Day". He plays there for th first time in 15 years, and is given the keys to the city.

1982 Sept Orbison sues Rose for $50 million, claiming mismangement and under-accounting of royalties.

1986 Sept Now living in Malibu, CA, (where his home will be featured on TV program "Lifestyles Of The Rich And Famous" in 1987), Orbison experiences a major career resurgence when film director David Lync uses *In Dreams* during an integral part of his movie "Blue Velvet". Orbison is opposed to its use in the film, but Lynch uses it anyway.

1987 Jan [21] Orbison is inducted into the Rock'N'Roll Hall Of Fame at the second annual dinner at New York's Waldorf Astoria. He is joined by Bruce Springsteen, who inducts him, singing *Oh, Pretty Woman*.

Apr [23] Orbison re-records some of his greatest hits with producer T-Bone Burnett at Oceanways studios in Los Angeles, CA.

May [22] He guests on NBC-TV's "Saturday Night Live" with host Dennis Hopper.

July Orbison signs to Virgin Records in UK, releasing re-recorded T-Bone Burnett sessions as *In Dreams: The Greatest Hits*, which make UK #86.

Aug [14] Orbison embarks on US tour at the Paul Masson Winery, Saratoga, CA, set to end on Sept.4 at the Hilton Ballroom, Eugene, OR

Sept [30] "A Black And White Night", a club concert at which Orbis is backed by a cast of star admirers, including Bruce Springsteen, Elvi Costello, Bonnie Raitt, k.d. lang, Jackson Browne, J.D. Souther, Jennife Warnes and Tom Waits, takes place at the Coconut Grove, Ambassad hotel in Los Angeles. Musical content mostly features his familiar hits of the 60s.

1988 Jan Orbison's duet with k.d. lang of *Crying* is featured in film "Hidin Out", and makes #42 on US Country chart.

Apr [23] Orbison celebrates his 52nd birthday at a Bruce Springsteer concert. The audience sings *Happy Birthday*.

Nov Orbison participates in George Harrison's all-star recording ensemble The Traveling Wilburys, which also features Bob Dylan, To Petty and Jeff Lynne of ELO. The group's eponymous album, with major contributions from Orbison, races up both US and UK charts, a does extracted single *Handle With Care*.

[19] He makes his last TV appearance at the Diamond Awards Festiv in Antwerp, Belgium.

Dec [4] Orbison makes what will be his last performance at the Fron Row theater, Highland Heights, near Cleveland, OH.

[6] Orbison is rushed to Hendersonville hospital (after suffering a heart attack at 11.00pm in his mother's bathroom), where he dies within minutes of admittance, at 11.54pm.

[9] Wink mayor Maxie Watts declares Roy Orbison Memorial Day.

[13] "Celebration Of Life" tribute to Orbison, with Bonnie Raitt, J.D. Souther, The Stray Cats and others, takes place at the Wiltern theater, Los Angeles.

1989 Jan *You Got It*, co-penned with fellow Wilburys Lynne and Petty, hits UK #3 as Rhino anthology *For The Lonely: An Anthology, 1956-1965* climbs to US #110 and *In Dreams: The Greatest Hits* makes US #95.

[21] Telstar TV-advertised compilation *The Legendary Roy Orbison* tops UK chart.

Mar *Mystery Girl* hits US #5 and US #2.

Apr *You Got It* hits US #9 as *She's A Mystery To Me*, written by U2's Bono and The Edge, reaches UK #27.
[23] Roy Orbison Day is declared in Texas.
May [11] Orbison is inducted into the Songwriters' Hall Of Fame at its 20th anniversary ceremonies.
Nov *A Black And White Night* makes UK #51, and will make US #123. Wink's mayor Maxie Watts launches The Roy Orbison Memorial Monument Fund to erect a monument to the singer.
By year's end, Acuff-Rose Music sues Orbison's estate over ownership of songs including *Mystery Girl* and *Travelling Wilburys*. Suit alleges Barbara Orbison persuaded Orbison to break 1985 5-year contract to write songs for the firm annually.

1990 Feb [24] The Roy Orbison Concert Tribute to benefit the homeless, with host Whoopi Goldberg and Dwight Yoakam, k.d. lang, Bruce Hornsby, Gary Busey, Dean Stockwell, Roger McGuinn, David Crosby, Chris Hillman, Bob Dylan, Bonnie Raitt, Was (Not Was) and B.B. King among others, takes place at the Universal Amphitheater, Universal City, CA.

1991 Feb [20] Orbison wins Best Pop Vocal Performance, Male for *Oh, Pretty Woman*, from *A Black And White Night Live*, at the 33rd annual Grammy awards at Radio City Music Hall, New York.

ORCHESTRAL MANOEUVRES IN THE DARK (OMD)

Andy McCluskey (vocals)
Paul Humphreys (synthesizers)

1977 Sept Liverpool, Merseyside schoolfriends McCluskey (b. June 24, 1959, Wirral, Merseyside) and Humphreys (b. Feb.27, 1960, London) having played together and separately in various short-lived school bands (for one of these, Equinox, McCluskey has written *Orchestral Manoeuvres In The Dark*), jointly form The Id, with Gary Hodgson (guitar), Steve Hollis (bass) and Malcolm Holmes (drums). Group performs several songs which will later be part of the OMD repertoire and also has 8 transient members during its year of existence. One Id track, *Julia's Song* (words by ex-member Julia Kneale) is recorded for inclusion on Open Eye label compilation album *Street To Street – A Liverpool Album* (which will be released in July 1979).

1978 Aug The Id splits, and McCluskey joins local experimental band Dalek I Love You as vocalist, but will stay for only a month before becoming disillusioned by the band's chaotic approach and leaving to work in the Customs and Excise office at Liverpool docks. Following this, he and Humphreys decide to start a new group, initially named VCL XI.
Oct [12] First gig – regarded by the duo as a self-indulgent experiment in non-group music – is at Liverpool club Eric's. They perform, with the help of backing tracks provided by their tape recorder "Winston", and rename themselves for the evening Orchestral Manoeuvres In The Dark (after McCluskey's old song) because it is the most self-indulgent name they can think of. To their surprise, their performance is a success with Eric's audience, and they realize that the group has a viable future.

1979 June OMD's *Electricity* is released on Manchester-based independent Factory label, in a 5,000 pressing which quickly sells out. OMD signs to DinDisc, a label set up by Richard Branson to have an all-female staff. DinDisc reissues *Electricity*, but it fails to chart.
Aug OMD plays at all-day open air concert in Leigh, with A Certain Ratio, Echo & The Bunnymen, Joy Division and Teardrop Explodes. An estimated 300 people witness the event.
Sept [20] Group begins a 13-date UK tour supporting Gary Numan at Glasgow's Apollo theater.
Dec [7-8] They support Talking Heads at London's Electric Ballroom.

1980 Feb OMD's second single, *Red Frame White Light* debuts at UK #67.
[15] Group's first headlining tour opens at Eric's, Liverpool.
Mar Debut album *Orchestral Manoeuvres In The Dark*, recorded in their own Liverpool studio, peaks at UK #27.
May *Messages* reaches UK #13.
[9] Group begins a 10-date UK tour at Manchester's Russell club, ending at the Cedar Ballroom, Edinburgh, Scotland May 23.
Oct *Enola Gay*, titled after the plane which dropped the atomic bomb on Hiroshima, hits UK #8.
Nov Second album *Organisation* hits UK #6. Augmented by Dave Hughes on synthesizer and Malcolm Holmes on drums, OMD tours UK, Europe and US (through early 1981, during which Hughes leaves and is replaced by Martin Cooper).

1981 Oct After almost a year's chart absence, band hits UK #3 with *Souvenir*.

Nov *Architecture And Morality* also hits UK #3, during 39-week run.
Dec Anthemic synthesizer-heavy *Joan Of Arc* hits UK #5.

1982 Feb *Maid Of Orleans*, a sequel to *Joan Of Arc*, hits UK #4. *Architecture And Morality* peaks at US #144. (McCluskey and Humphreys will spend most of the year in their studio, working on a fourth album.)

1983 Mar *Genetic Engineering* makes UK #20 as *Dazzle Ships* hits UK #5. (DinDisc is now absorbed by Virgin which releases OMD's product.)
Apr *Telegraph* makes UK #42.
May *Dazzle Ships* climbs to US #162.

1984 May *Locomotion* hits UK #5. *Junk Culture* begins UK chart run of 27 weeks, during which it hits #9.
July *Talking Loud And Clear* reaches UK #11.
Sept *Tesla Girls* makes UK #21. (Nikolai Tesla is one of the pioneers of electrical technology.)
Nov *Never Turn Away* peaks at UK #70. *Junk Culture*, through A&M, makes US #182.
Dec After touring Europe, US, Japan and Australia in the past 2 years, Humphreys decides the pressure is too great and that he will quit and settle down with his American wife. A week and a half later he has changed his mind and is back in OMD.

1985 June Ballad *So In Love* reaches UK #27. *Crush* makes UK #13.
July [7] OMD, with Aswad and Working Week, plays a free concert in London's Battersea Park, as part of Greater London Council's "Jobs For A Change" scheme.
Aug *Secret* makes UK #34. Group becomes more popular in US, partly as a result of support tours for acts including The Thompson Twins and Power Station.
Oct *So In Love* is OMD's first US singles success, peaking at #26. Group begins a series of anti-racism concerts with other artists in Europe.
Dec *La Femme Accident* makes UK #42.

1986 Feb [1] *Secrets* peaks at US #63, as *Crush* makes US #38.
[2] 17-date UK tour begins at the Empire theater, Liverpool, set to end Feb. 24-25 with dates at the Hammersmith Odeon, London.
May *If You Leave* makes UK #48. McCluskey says in an interview, "America is the only place where we're still hip."
[31] *If You Leave*, featured on the soundtrack of John Hughes' film "Pretty In Pink", hits US #4.
Oct *(Forever) Live And Die* makes UK #11. *The Pacific Age* reaches UK #15 and US #47.
Nov *We Love You* peaks at UK #54.
Dec [6] *(Forever) Live And Die* reaches US #19.

1987 May *Shame* peaks at UK #52.

1988 Feb *Dreaming* makes UK #50, and UK #60 when reissued 6 months later. Virgin Video releases "The Best Of OMD" video clips package.
Mar *In The Dark – The Best Of OMD* begins 30-week UK chart run, hitting #2, and makes US #46.
May [21] *Dreaming* reaches US #16.

1989 Sept McCluskey guests on producer Arthur Baker's album *The Message Of Love*.

1991 Apr [2] New album *Sugar Tax*, and extracted single *Sailing On The Seven Seas*, are released. (Humphreys has now formed own band The Listening Pool, leaving McCluskey as the sole Orchestral Manoeuvre.)

TONY ORLANDO & DAWN

Tony Orlando (vocals)
Joyce Vincent Wilson (vocals)
Telma Hopkins (vocals)

1957 Orlando (b. Michael Anthony Orlando Cassivitis, Apr.3, 1944, Manhattan, New York, NY), of Greek/Puerto Rican heritage, has been singing with local doo-wop group The Five Gents, and is currently cutting demos for a music publisher.

1960 Having met Don Kirshner at Aldon Music, Orlando is teamed with young writer Carole King to sing demos of her compositions. An early King song, written with Gerry Goffin, *Halfway To Paradise* is sold to Epic Records.

1961 June Epic releases Orlando's demo of *Halfway To Paradise* and it makes US #39. (In UK Billy Fury will hit #3 with it.)
Oct Barry Mann/Cynthia Weil-penned *Bless You* reaches US #15.
Nov *Bless You* hits UK #5.
Dec *Happy Times (Are Here To Stay)*, Orlando's last for Epic, reaches only US #82.

1962 Feb [9] Orlando begins a 15-date twice-nightly UK tour with Bobby Vee, Clarence "Frogman" Henry, The Springfields and others, at the Gaumont cinema, Doncaster, S.Yorks.
[25] Tour ends at the Winter Gardens, Bournemouth, Dorset.

1963 Having had little further success, Orlando goes to work at music publishers Robbins, Feist and Miller and also gets married.

1968 Completing 5 years in music publishing, Orlando is working for Clive Davis at April-Blackwood publishers involved with writers James Taylor and Laura Nyro.

1970 Bell Records, interested in releasing *Candida*, produced by Hank Medress and Dave Appell with unknown trio Dawn (named after Bell boss Wes Farrell's daughter), are unhappy with the lead singer. They keep backing vocal track by session singers Hopkins (b. Oct.28, 1948, Louisville, KY) and ex-Debonaires Wilson (b. Dec.14, 1946, Detroit, MI). Medress and Appell ask Orlando to record the lead vocal. He hears the results 2 months later on New York radio as the disk is taking off.
Oct *Candida* hits US #3.
Dec Parent album *Candida* reaches US #35.

1971 **Jan** Follow-up *Knock Three Times* hits US #1. It features Orlando on lead vocals and is released under the group name Dawn, but Orlando has still not met Hopkins and Wilson, who recorded the backing vocals in California. Orlando finally meets the girls through producer Tony Camillo and insists on forming a full-time unit to promote and tour.
Feb *Candida* hits UK #9.
Apr *I Play And Sing* reaches US #25.
May *Knock Three Times* tops UK chart during a 27-week chart stay.
July *Summer Sand* makes US #33.
Aug *What Are You Doing Sunday* hits UK #3.
Sept [20] The trio makes its UK cabaret debut with a week-long stint at the Talk Of The Town, Manchester.
Nov *What Are You Doing Sunday* makes US #39.
Dec *Dawn Featuring Tony Orlando* stalls at US #178.

1972 **Feb** *Runaway/Happy Together* makes US #79.
July *Vaya Con Dios* reaches US #95.

1973 **Jan** *You're A Lady* peaks at US #70, beaten by Peter Skellern's original version at US #50.
Mar *Tuneweaving* reaches US #30 and is the group's first gold album.
Apr Dawn records *Tie A Yellow Ribbon Round The Old Oak Tree*, based on a true tale of a convict returning home to White Oak, GA, hoping to see a sign that his wife still loves him. The song begins a 4-week stay on top of US chart. (It is the year's best-selling single, sells over 6 million internationally and will have over 1,000 cover versions.)
[21] *Tie A Yellow Ribbon Round The Old Oak Tree* begins similar 4-week stay at UK #1 during a 39-week residence.
Sept *Say, Has Anybody Seen My Sweet Gypsy Rose* hits US #3 and makes UK #12.
Oct *Dawn's New Ragtime Follies* is released, making US #43.

1974 **Feb** Head of programming for CBS TV, Fred Silverman, sees Dawn perform *Tie A Yellow Ribbon* at the 16th annual Grammy awards and gives the trio a 4-week summer tryout variety series. ("Tony Orlando And Dawn" will air for 2 seasons.)
Mar Now credited as Tony Orlando & Dawn, *Who's In The Strawberry Patch With Sally* makes UK #37.
Apr *It Only Hurts When I Try To Smile* climbs to US #81.
May *Golden Ribbons* makes UK #46.
Oct *Steppin' Out (Gonna Boogie Tonight)* hits US #7.
Dec *Who's In The Strawberry Patch With Sally* makes US #27 and *Prime Time* US #16, taking the band's worldwide sales to over 25 million.

1975 **Jan** The trio's first and second albums are reissued, *Candida & Knock Three Times*, making US #170, and *Tony Orlando & Dawn II* US #165.
Feb *Look In My Eyes Pretty Woman* reaches US #11.
May Dawn moves with Bell promotion man and friend Steve Wax from Bell to Elektra. Group's cover of Jerry Butler's 1960 US Top 10 smash *He Don't Love You (Like I Love You)* tops US chart for 3 weeks. Parent album *He Don't Love You (Like I Love You)* is released, reaching US #20.
June *Tony Orlando And Dawn's Greatest Hits* reaches US #16 on its way to gold status.
Aug *Mornin' Beautiful* makes US #14.
Sept *You're All I Need To Get By*, a 1968 US #7 for Marvin Gaye and Tammi Terrell, reaches US #34.
Nov *Skybird* peaks at US #93, as extracted title track makes US #49.

1976 **Mar** A cover of Sam Cooke's 1961 US #7, *Cupid*, reaches US #22.
Apr *To Be With You* makes US #94.

1977 **Apr** *Sing* peaks at US #58.
July [22] During a show at "The Music Show" in Cohasset, MA, Orlando stuns Hopkins and Wilson announcing to the audience that "this is my last day as a performer". (He recently suffered when close friend comedian Freddie Prinze committed suicide and his 21-year-old sister Rhonda died.)

Nov No longer with Dawn, Orlando returns to playing the Las Vegas, NV, circuit.

1979 **Aug** Orlando, signed to Casablanca, makes US #54 with *Sweets For My Sweet*.
Sept Hopkins begins a TV acting career in ABC TV's "A New Kind Of Family". (She will appear regularly in "Gimme A Break" and "Bosom Buddies"). Orlando begins an acting career in TV movie "Three Hundred Miles For Stephanie" and guests on "The Cosby Show".

1981 **Jan** When American hostages are returned from 444 days in captivity in Iran, US revives Dawn's lasting image of yellow ribbons.
Orlando takes over the leading role in "Barnum" on Broadway, while Jim Dale is on vacation.
Nov [15] Orlando joins a star cast in "Hey, Look Me Over!", a one-off benefit for the American Musical and Dramatic Academy at the Avery Fisher Hall, New York.

1988 **Aug** Orlando, Hopkins and Wilson re-form to perform at Trumps in Atlantic City, NJ. (Hopkins will continue her acting career, starring in ABC TV series "Family Matters".)

JEFFREY OSBORNE

1970 Osborne (b. Mar.9, 1948, Providence, RI), having been a regular at the Ebony Lounge, New London, CT, nightspot and taught himself to play drums at age 15, then sung and drummed with local bands, is offered the chance to join L.T.D. (the name stands for Love, Togetherness and Devotion), a 10-man funk group from Greensboro, NC, after he sits in with the group on a tour date in Providence, their drummer having been hauled off to jail for fighting. Despite being married with 2 small daughters, he follows his mother's advice to grab the opportunity, and becomes L.T.D.'s lead singer.

1973 Before finding any commercial success, L.T.D. has toured R&B circuit just to make a living, Osborne supplementing his income by doing session work (drums, back-up vocals) for acts like The Sylvers and Smokey Robinson. The road work and consequent absence from home takes its toll on his marriage, which ends in divorce.

1974 L.T.D., having inked a production deal with Jerry Butler's Foundation Records, signs to A&M Records, but debut album *Love, Togetherness And Devotion* fails. (Follow-up *Gettin' Down* will fare similarly.)

1976 **Nov** Group's breakthrough is *Love Ballad*, written by Skip Scarborough, which makes US #20 and tops R&B chart for 2 weeks.
Dec *Love To The World* reaches US #52.

1977 **Feb** Extracted title track *Love To The World* peaks at US #91.
Nov *(Every Time I Turn Around) Back In Love Again* dethrones Barry White on US R&B chart for 2 weeks, a month later crossing over to hit US #4. Their biggest hit single, it earns gold disk for million-plus sales.

1978 **Jan** *Something To Love* reaches US #21 and turns gold, with sales of a half million.
Apr *Never Get Enough Of Your Love* peaks at US #56.
Sept Group has its third US R&B #1 for 2 weeks with *Holding On (When Love Is Gone)*, which also crosses over to US #49 and makes UK #70 (the group's only UK chart entry). The track is taken from *Togetherness*, which is their biggest-selling album yet, reaching US #18 and going platinum with sales of over a million.

1979 **Aug** *Devotion* climbs to US #29, and earns another gold disk.

1980 **Oct** *Shine On* reaches US #28.

1981 **Jan** Extracted title track soul ballad *Shine On*, on which Osborne's vocals gleam, makes US #40, the group's last chart single.

1982 **Jan** *Love Magic* makes US #83, following which Osborne leaves and the group splits. He remains with A&M as a soloist.
Aug Osborne's debut solo album *Jeffrey Osborne*, produced by George Duke, reaches US #49. *I Really Don't Need No Light*, taken from it, makes US #39.
Dec Another extract from the album, soaring ballad *On The Wings Of Love*, reaches US #29.

1983 **Apr** *Eenie Meenie* makes US #76.
Sept *Don't You Get So Mad* from Osborne's second album, reaches US #25 and UK #54, his first solo UK chart entry.

1984 **Jan** Funky *Stay With Me Tonight*, the title song from the second album, reaches US #30.
Mar *Stay With Me Tonight* peaks at US #25 after more than 6 months on chart. It becomes Osborne's first solo gold album.
Apr *We're Going All The Way*, taken from the album, makes US #48.
May *Stay With Me Tonight* climbs to UK #18, while album of the same title makes UK #56.
July *On The Wings Of Love* reaches UK #11.
Oct Osborne duets with Joyce Kennedy on *The Last Time I Made Love*,

which makes US #40. (Kennedy is ex-soul group Mother's Finest, whose first solo album *Lookin' For Trouble* is Osborne's first venture into production. The album peaks at US #79, and will earn him a producer's Grammy nomination.) *Don't Stop* peaks at UK #61, and album of the same title at UK #59.

Dec *Don't Stop* and extracted *Don't Stop* peak at US #39 and #44.

1985 **Mar** A second cut from the album, *The Borderlines*, reaches US #38.

1986 **Aug** [23] *You Should Be Mine (The Woo Woo Song)* reaches US #13. *Soweto* makes UK #44. Both tracks are from *Emotional*, on which Osborne has worked with producers Richard Perry, Michael Masser and Rod Temperton, in addition to long-time collaborator George Duke. 3 of the tracks are also self-produced, as Osborne builds on the studio experience gained from working with Kennedy. The album peaks at US #26, but does not chart in UK.

1987 **Feb** Osborne sings spine-tingling a cappella *The Star-Spangled Banner* prior to the NBA All-Star game in Seattle, WA.

Aug [29] *Love Power*, duet with Dionne Warwick, reaches US #12.

1988 **Aug** After a 2-year recording hiatus, during which Osborne has spent more time with second wife Sheri and daughter Tiffany, he returns with *One Love – One Dream*, again with a variety of co-producers, including Bruce Roberts (who also co-writes with Osborne), Andy Goldmark, Ross Vanelli, and David "Hawk" Wolinski.

Sept [24] Dance-tempo *She's On The Left* is extracted as a single, and tops US R&B chart, while album peaks at US #86.

1989 **Sept** Osborn is featured on soundtrack album *Rooftops*.

Nov Now signed to Clive Davis' Arista Records, Osborne is initiated via a duet with labelmate Dionne Warwick on the ballad *Take Good Care Of You And Me*, which will only make US R&B #46.

1990 **Feb** [14] "In Performance At The White House" in the East Room at President's Day celebration, featuring Osborne and others, airs on US public television.

[16] Debut Arista solo album *Only Human* peaks at US #95. Produced and arranged by Barry Eastmond, it includes guest appearances from Joey Diggs, Vincent Henry and Grover Washington Jr.

Mar [17] Osborne and a host of labelmates take part in Arista Records 15th anniversary at Radio City Music Hall, "That's What Friends Are For" concert, raising over $2 million for Gay Men's Health Crisis and other AIDS organizations. Show airs on CBS TV Apr.17.

1991 **Feb** [10] Osborne joins with nearly 100 celebrities in Burbank, CA, to record *Voices That Care*, a David Foster and fiancee Linda Thompson Jenner-composed and organized charity record to benefit the American Red Cross Gulf Crisis Fund.

Apr [9] Osborne sings the American National Anthem on the opening day of the Oakland A's 1991 baseball season, against the Minnesota Twins, at the Oakland Coliseum.

OZZY OSBOURNE

1967 Osbourne (b. John Michael Osbourne, Dec.3, 1948, Aston, Birmingham, W.Midlands), whose early career as a burglar is halted by 2 months served in Winson Green Prison following conviction, on release takes a job in a slaughterhouse, but soon becomes unemployed. With 3 other Birmingham youths, he forms Polka Tulk, which takes the name of one of their early songs and becomes Black Sabbath.

1970 After the release of their eponymous debut album, Black Sabbath will become hugely successful and help create a new genre – heavy metal. The group and Osbourne in particular also set standards for hard rock musicians in their consumption of alcohol and drugs.

1978 Osbourne leaves Black Sabbath after 7 albums, following a major row with group member Tony Iommi. He is replaced by ex-Savoy Brown vocalist Dave Walker before returning briefly later in the year after plans to form a band with guitarist Gary Moore and ex-Deep Purple bassist Glenn Hughes fail.

1980 **July** Osbourne signs a solo deal with Jet Records, with an album already recorded with his new band, The Blizzard Of Ozz, comprising ex-Quiet Riot Randy Rhoads, ex-Rainbow bassist Bob Daisley and ex-Uriah Heep drummer Lee Kerslake. Jet is owned by Don Arden, who has recently ceased to handle Black Sabbath.

Aug [14] Group begins a UK mini-tour at the Nite club during Edinburgh Rock Festival.

Sept *Crazy Train* makes UK #49 as parent album *Ozzy Osbourne's Blizzard Of Ozz* hits UK #7. Group begins its first UK tour.

Nov *Mr. Crowley*, written about occultist Aleister Crowley, reaches UK #46, the group having played warm-up gigs under the name Law.

1981 **Apr** *Blizzard Of Ozz* enters US chart, where it will stay for 2 years and peak at #21, also going platinum.

May Osbourne begins US tour with a new Blizzard of Ozz. Kerslake and Daisley leave to join Uriah Heep, and are replaced by Tommy Aldridge, Tennessee-born, Florida-raised, ex-Black Oak Arkansas, Pat Travers Band and Gary Moore's band on drums and Rudy Sarzo (b. Havana, Cuba) ex-Quiet Riot and Angel on bass. (In a notorious incident Osbourne bites the head off a live dove before assembled CBS/Columbia executives at a meeting in Los Angeles.)

Aug Group returns to UK to headline the "Heavy Metal Holocaust" at Stoke-On-Trent – following Black Sabbath's withdrawal.

Nov Osbourne's second album *Diary Of A Madman* (title taken from Crowley's autobiography) reaches UK #14 and US #16, earning a second US platinum disk.

1982 **Jan** Daisley returns, replacing Aldridge, and Don Airey (ex-Rainbow) is added on keyboards.

[20] At the beginning of a US tour, Osbourne bites the head off a bat during a show in Des Moines, IA – the bat bites back and Osbourne reportedly has to undergo rabies injection as a precaution.

Mar [19] During high jinks near Orlando, FL, the party's tour plane is buzzing their bus, making mock dive-bomb runs. On the last run the wing of the plane clips the bus and it is thrown out of control and crashes into a house, killing 25-year-old Randy Rhoads, Osbourne's hairdresser Rachel Youngblood and pilot Andrew Aycock. (Osbourne decides to complete the tour, bringing in ex-Gillan guitarist Bernie Torme as a temporary replacement for Rhoads.)

May *Mr. Crowley*, a live picture disk EP, enters US Album chart, reaching #120 during an 18-week stay. Black Sabbath is preparing to release *Live At Last*, which features performances of old songs with Dio on vocals, who claims the songs are his own. Osbourne books 2 nights at the New York Ritz and, with Aldridge, Sarzo and Brad Gillis (guitar) records a double album's worth of old Sabbath numbers, which will be released as *Talk Of The Devil*.

June Jake E. Lee, ex-Los Angeles band Rough Cutt joins on guitar.

July [4] Osbourne marries Don Arden's daughter Sharon, his personal manager (having left his wife Thelma in 1981) in Maui, HI. Aldridge is best man.

Nov *Talk Of The Devil* enters UK chart, peaking at #21.

Dec [10] 7-date "Talk Of The Devil" tour starts at St. Austell Coliseum, ending Dec.20 at the Royal Court theater, Liverpool, Merseyside.

1983 **Jan** *Talk Of The Devil* reaches US #14.

May The Ozzy Osbourne Band plays the US festival in California. Following a tour and new recording sessions, Aldridge leaves again. He is replaced by Carmine Appice, ex-Vanilla Fudge, as Sharon and Don Arden quarrel. She assumes full management control of Osbourne's affairs, taking him to sign with CBS in US and Epic in UK. Family relations will remain difficult.

Dec *Bark At The Moon* enters UK chart at the end of the month, to peak at #21, aided by a werewolf transformation video, a device which also becomes popular on stage. Parent album *Bark At The Moon* reaches US #19 and UK #24.

1984 Splintered glass from a broken mirror used in the filming of the video for single *So Tired* lodges in Osbourne's throat, but there are no permanent ill effects.

Mar Appice leaves and Aldridge returns for another extensive tour.

June Ballad *So Tired* makes UK #20 as Osbourne is urged by his wife to enter the Betty Ford Clinic for treatment of drug/alcohol dependency.

1985 **Jan** Osbourne and The Blizzard Of Ozz play Rock In Rio festival. Airey is no longer with the group and after the festival Aldridge quits, never to return. Daisley follows, but will continue to help in studio recordings. Osbourne recruits drummer Randy Castillo, from Lita Ford's band, and bassist Phil Soussan, with recent recruit San Diegan Don Costa (bass).

July [13] Osbourne, Tony Iommi, Geezer Butler and Bill Ward re-form for a day as Black Sabbath to play Live Aid in Philadelphia. (The day before the concert Osbourne was served with a writ from Don Arden, charging that he is trying to re-form Sabbath as a performing unit and claiming $1.5m in damages. Band plays on and Arden loses the suit.)

1986 **Jan** Ozzy Osbourne biography **Diary Of A Madman** is published.

Feb *Shot In The Dark* reaches US #20 as parent album *The Ultimate Sin* hits UK #8.

[12] Osbourne begins his first full UK tour in 3 years at City Hall, Newcastle, Tyne & Wear, set to end 15 dates later on Mar.4 at St. George's Hall, Bradford, W.Yorks.

Apr [26] *Shot In The Dark* peaks at US #68.

May Osbourne embarks on tours of US and Japan.

June *The Ultimate Sin* hits US #6.

Aug Title track *The Ultimate Sin/Lightning Strikes* spends a week at UK

#72. Osbourne takes a break from his US tour to play the Monsters Of Rock heavy metal festival at Castle Donington, Leics.

Dec [19] A California Superior Court judge denies a motion to reinstate the lawsuit served on Jan.13 against Osbourne and CBS Inc. which had sought to implicate Osbourne in the suicide of Californian teenager John McCollum, who it was claimed had been influenced by the lyrics of Osbourne's *Suicide Solution*. Judge John L. Cole states that the case involved areas "clearly protected by the First Amendment".

1987 In a parody of the attention he has received from fundamentalist US Christian groups, Osbourne plays a Bible-bashing preacher in heavy metal film "Trick Or Treat".

May Double album *Tribute*, dedicated to Randy Rhoads and consisting of live recordings from 1981 featuring Rhoads' guitar playing, reaches UK #13.

June *Tribute* hits US #6.

July [17] Osbourne begins a 16-week tour of prisons, highlighted by a heavy metal version of *Jailhouse Rock*.

1988 **Feb** Osbourne recruits a new guitarist, 21-year-old Zakk Wylde (b. Jan.14, 1967, New Jersey), who has been teaching guitar in New Jersey. During preparations for a new album Soussan quits, leaving Castillo on drums, John Sinclair on keyboards and Daisley as studio-only bassist.

Apr [10] Osbourne announces he would like to tour the world's insane asylums.

July [18] A California appeals court upholds a decision to dismiss a wrongful death suit brought against the singer by parents of a suicide victim.

Oct *No Rest For The Wicked*, produced by Roy Thomas Baker, is released, to peak at UK #23 and US #13. Osbourne embarks on a 2-month US tour, opening in Omaha, NE (and ending in Long Beach, CA) after which he will return to domestic security with his wife and 3 children at their 18th-century Buckinghamshire home.

Dec Osbourne once again undertakes major US tour with current band line-up Zakk Wylde, Geezer Butler and Randy Castillo. *No Rest For The Wicked* is awarded gold status for million sales.

1989 **June** [4] Osbourne donates $15,000 to AIDS research after a concert in Philadelphia.

[17] Heavy metal ballad duet with peroxide axeist Lita Ford *Close My Eyes Forever* hits US #8, having spent 1 week at UK #75 last Dec.

Aug [12-13] Osbourne participates in the Moscow Music Peace Festival at Lenin Stadium with Bon Jovi, Motley Crue, The Scorpions, Cinderella, Skid Row and from USSR Gorky Park, Nuance, CCCP and Brigada S. All proceeds go to programs that fight drug and alcohol abuse in US and USSR.

Sept [2] He is charged with threatening to kill his wife but released on condition he immediately go into detox and keeps away from her. The case is dropped when the couple decide to reconcile.

1990 **Mar** Osbourne guests stars in Sam Kinison's "Under My Thumb" video as the Judge. (Paul Williams acts as defense attorney.)

[17] Live *Just Say Ozzy*, recorded at Brixton Academy, London, makes UK #69, the same week it peaks at US #58.

Aug [18] Priority label-issued old material, released as *Ten Commandments*, stalls at US #163.

Oct Geezer Butler leaves Osbourne's band.

[4-5] 2 cases are filed in Macon, GA, against Osbourne and CBS by the parents of teenagers Michael Waller and Harold Hamilton who shot themselves in the head, Waller in May 1986 and Hamilton in Mar.1988.

Nov [14] A motion is filed to dismiss the suit.

Dec Speaking at the Foundation Forum's censorship panel, Osbourne says, "if I wrote music for people who shot themselves after listening to my music, I wouldn't have much of a following."

THE OSMONDS

Alan Osmond (vocals)
Wayne Osmond (vocals)
Merrill Osmond (vocals)
Jay Osmond (vocals)
Donny Osmond (vocals)

1959 Group is formed as a barber shop-style harmony quartet by 4 of the sons of George and Olive Osmond, Alan (b. June 22, 1949, Ogden, UT), Wayne (b. Aug.28, 1951, Ogden), Merrill (b. Apr.30, 1953, Ogden) and Jay (b. Mar.2, 1955, Ogden) in their hometown, Ogden, where they sing at their Mormon church's Family Nights.

1962 On a visit to Los Angeles, the group meets a professional barber shop quartet in Disneyland and, after performing impromptu harmonies with them, is introduced to the park's talent booker, who signs it for the "Disneyland After Dark" show.

Dec [20] As The Osmond Brothers, the group appears for the first time on new weekly "Andy Williams Show" on NBC TV, harmonizing on *I'm A Ding Dong Daddy From Dumas* and *Side By Side*. (They will remain regulars on the show throughout its first 5-year run.)

1963 **Dec** 6-year-old Donny (b. Donald Clark Osmond, Dec.9, 1957, Ogden) joins the group, singing with his brothers on their numbers and soloing on *You Are My Sunshine* on the "Andy Williams Show".

1967 **May** The weekly "Andy Williams Show" comes to an end.

Sept Group begins regular guest appearances on ABC TV's "The Jerry Lewis Show" (which will last until mid-1969).

1968 **July** The Osmonds are the first signing to singer Andy Williams' Barnaby label, before moving to Uni Records.

1971 **Feb** [13] Now known as The Osmonds, they have debuted on the US chart after being signed to MGM Records by Mike Curb, who sees their potential as an answer to The Jackson 5. Curb has sent them to Fame studios in Muscle Shoals, AL, where producer Rick Hall records them on the Jacksons-cloning *One Bad Apple* (written by George Jackson – no relation). It tops US chart for 5 weeks and is a million-seller. *Osmonds*, which includes the hit, makes US #14 and earns a gold disk.

Mar *I Can't Stop*, reissue from their previous label Uni, makes US #96.

June Aware of the teen idol appeal of his youthful good looks (he has had the major share of US teen magazine coverage since the success of *One Bad Apple*), MGM records Donny as a solo act, beginning with *Sweet And Innocent*, which hits US #7, and is the first solo million-seller by a member of the family.

July *Double Lovin'* makes US #14.

Aug *Home-Made* reaches US #22, and earns a gold disk, while Donny's first solo album *The Donny Osmond Album*, which includes *Sweet And Innocent*, makes US #13 and earns a gold disk.

Sept [11] A revival of Goffin and King-penned Steve Lawrence/Mark Wynter 1963 hit *Go Away Little Girl*, recorded solo by Donny, tops US chart for 3 weeks – his second million-seller in 2 solo releases.

Oct *Yo-Yo*, written by Joe South, hits US #3, the group's second million-selling single.

Dec Donny's album *To You With Love, Donny* reaches US #12 and earns a gold disk.

1972 **Jan** Donny's revival of Freddie Scott's *Hey Girl*, released as a double A-side with a new version of Billy Joe Royal's *I Knew You When*, hits US #9 and is another million-seller.

Mar *Down By The Lazy River*, written by Merrill and Alan, hits US #4 and is another million-seller. Group's album *Phase Three*, including both this hit single and *Yo-Yo*, hits US #10 and is a million-seller.

Apr *Down By The Lazy River* is the group's UK chart debut, reaching #40, while in US, Donny's revival of Paul Anka's 1960 million-seller *Puppy Love* hits #3, and is Donny's fourth gold disk out of 4 singles.

May *Portrait Of Donny* is released, set to hit US #6 and become his third gold album.

June Little Jimmy Osmond (b. Apr.16, 1963, Canoga Park, CA), the youngest of the family (and notably overweight though he will lose the surplus pounds in his teenage years), makes his recording debut on a solo novelty, *Long-Haired Lover From Liverpool*, which climbs to US #38, but will score its biggest sales in UK at the end of the year. (Interviewed, the 9-year-old admits that he has no idea where Liverpool actually is.)

July Donny's *Puppy Love* is his UK chart debut. It tops chart in its second week, holding #1 for 5 weeks, and is the start of Osmond fan mania in UK, which will outstrip its US counterpart and give the group and solo members huge UK live, TV and record success over the next 5 years. Donny's revival of Nat "King" Cole's *Too Young* reaches US #13, while parent *Too Young* enters US chart to rise to #11.

Aug Group's *Hold Her Tight* makes US #14, while live album *The Osmonds Live* reaches US #13 and earns a gold disk.

Sept Donny's album *Portrait Of Donny* hits UK #5.

[16] The Osmonds cartoon TV series starts on ITV.

Oct Donny's *Too Young* hits UK #5, while his double A-side *Why/Lonely Boy* (revivals of Frankie Avalon and Paul Anka hits respectively) hits US #13.

Nov Live album *Osmonds Live* reaches UK #13, while the group sings guest vocals (and is duly credited) on Steve Lawrence and Eydie Gormé's *We Can Make It Together*, which reaches US #68.

Dec Little Jimmy tops UK chart for 5 weeks with *Long-Haired Lover From Liverpool*, which becomes the year's biggest UK seller, shifting over 985,000 copies. He is the youngest individual (age 9) ever to hit UK #1. Group's rock original *Crazy Horses* lines up at UK #2 behind it, while it peaks at US #14. Donny's *Why* hits UK #3, while the group's album *Crazy Horses* makes US #14 (their fifth and last gold album) and hits UK #9. Donny's solo album *Too Young* hits UK #7, as his album *My Best To You* begins a climb to US #29.

1973
Feb Little Jimmy's *Killer Joe* makes UK #20 and peaks at US #105, while his revived LaVern Baker 50s hit *Tweedle Dee* makes US #59.
Apr Donny's revival of Johnny Mathis/Cliff Richard hit *The Twelfth Of Never* hits US #8, selling over a million, and tops UK chart, while Little Jimmy's *Tweedle Dee* hits UK #4.
May Donny's *Alone Together* makes US #26 and hits UK #6.
July Group's rocker *Goin' Home* reaches US #36.
Aug *Going Home* hits UK #4, while the group's concept album *The Plan*, an expression of their Mormon faith, hits US #58 and UK #6.
Sept Donny's revival of Tab Hunter's *Young Love* tops UK chart for 4 weeks, having peaked at US #23, released as a double A-side with a revival of Jimmy Charles' *A Million To One*.
Oct Group's harmony ballad *Let Me In* reaches US #36.
Nov Marie Osmond, the group's younger sister (b. Oct.13, 1959, Ogden, UT), who has recently begun singing in concert with her brothers, debuts on US chart with a country-style ballad (produced by country star Sonny James), reviving Anita Bryant's 1960 million-seller *Paper Roses*. It hits US #5 and is a million-seller as parent album *Paper Roses* makes US #59.
Dec *Let Me In* hits UK #2 (behind Gary Glitter's *I Love You Love Me Love*). Marie's *Paper Roses* hits UK #2 for Christmas (behind *Merry Christmas Everybody* by Slade). Donny's *When I Fall In Love* hits UK #4, and his solo *A Time For Us* also hits UK #4, while heading for US #58.

1974
Jan Donny's double A-side revival of Elvis Presley's *Are You Lonesome Tonight?* and Nat "King" Cole's *When I Fall In Love* reaches US #14.
Feb Marie's *Paper Roses* peaks at UK #46.
Apr Little Jimmy revives Eddie Hodges' 1961 hit *I'm Gonna Knock On Your Door*, reaching UK #11.
May Group's *I Can't Stop* climbs to UK #12.
July Marie's *In My Little Corner Of The World* enters US chart, set to make #164. Alan marries Suzanne Pinegar.
Aug Osmonds' *Our Best To You* hits UK #5.
[12] Group begins 6 evenings of live BBC TV shows, aired at peak time.
Sept Group's *Love Me For A Reason*, a ballad penned by Johnny Bristol, tops UK chart for 3 weeks. Donny & Marie begin a series of duets with a revival of Dale & Grace's *I'm Leaving It (All) Up To You*, which hits US #4 (selling over a million) and UK #2. Donny & Marie's *I'm Leaving It All Up To You* enters charts, set to reach US #35 and UK #13.
Oct *Love Me For A Reason* hits UK #10.
Dec Donny's *Where Did All The Good Times Go* makes UK #18, while *Love Me For A Reason* makes US #47 and UK #13. *Donny* enters US chart, reaching #57. Wayne marries beauty queen Cathy White, who relinquishes her Miss Utah title.

1975
Jan Group embarks on tour of Australia. Donny & Marie's *Morning Side Of The Mountain*, a revival of Tommy Edwards' 1959 success, hits US #8 and UK #5.
Feb Donny's *Donny* makes UK #16.
Mar Group's *Having A Party*, not released as a US single, makes UK #28, while Donny's solo *I Have A Dream* reaches US #50.
Apr Marie's solo revival of Connie Francis' *Who's Sorry Now* reaches US #40 as same titled album makes US #152.
June *I'm Still Gonna Need You* makes UK #19.
July A revival of Frankie Valli's *The Proud One* hits UK #5. Donny & Marie's revival of Eddy Arnold's country ballad *Make The World Go Away* makes US #44 and UK #18, and the duo's album of the same title makes US #133 and UK #30.
Sept *The Proud One* reaches US #22, while the group's album of the same title reaches US #160.
Dec *I'm Still Gonna Need You* makes UK #32.

1976
Jan *Around The World – Live In Concert* makes US #148 and UK #41.
[16] "Donny & Marie", a 1-hour musical/comedy/variety show, heavily featuring all the Osmond family, debuts on ABC TV.
Feb Donny & Marie's revival of Nino Tempo & April Stevens' *Deep Purple* reaches US #14 and UK #25.
May *Donny & Marie – Featuring Songs From Their Television Show* peaks at US #60.
June Donny & Marie's *Deep Purple* makes UK #48. Group has a short BBC TV series (through July).
July Donny revives The Four Seasons' *C'mon Marianne*, which makes US #38.
Oct Donny's *Discotrain* makes US #145 and UK #59, while the group has another short UK BBC TV series (through Dec.).
Nov Group's *I Can't Live A Dream* reaches US #46 and UK #37, and is The Osmonds' last Singles chart entry. *Brainstorm* makes US #145.

1977
Jan *Donny & Marie – A New Season* makes US #85 while festive album *The Osmonds Christmas Album* peaks at US #127.
Feb Donny & Marie revive Marvin Gaye/Tammi Terrell's duet *Ain't Nothing Like The Real Thing*, reaching US #21.
May *This Is The Way That I Feel*, by Marie, makes US #152.
June Marie's *This Is The Way That I Feel* reaches US #39, and is her last solo US hit single.
[6] A US tour begins in Tucson, AZ.
Oct Aimed at older market, *Donald Clark Osmond* stalls at US #169.
Dec The "Donny & Marie" TV show, previously made in Hollywood, originates (in a Christmas Special edition) from the family's present home town of Orem, UT, where the Osmonds have built their own $2 million studio facility to house all their subsequent film, TV and video projects. This show features 28 Osmond family members, and has the Mormon Tabernacle choir guesting.

1978
Jan Donny & Marie revive The Righteous Brothers' *(You're My) Soul And Inspiration*, reaching US #38. *The Osmonds Greatest Hits* reaches US #192.
Mar *Winning Combination*, by Donny & Marie, makes US #99.
Nov Donny & Marie's *On The Shelf* is their final duetted chart entry, reaching US #38.
Dec Soundtrack *Goin' Coconuts*, from feature film starring Donny & Marie, climbs to US #98.

1980
Feb Group has its final BBC TV series (through Mar.).
Aug Group breaks up.
Dec [12] Marie begins her own NBC TV series "Marie", produced by Osmond Productions. (The music/comedy hour will run for 2 months, and will briefly return to the screen the following Sept., but will not find the success of the "Donny & Marie" show.)

1982 The 4 older Osmonds re-form, without Donny, to concentrate on country music, and sign to Mercury Records.
Mar [21] Donny takes title role in Broadway revival of musical "Little Johnny Jones" at the Alvin theater. (It closes after only 1 performance.)

1983 The Osmond family's film and video studio center in Utah is sold to a Texan banker. (It will be repurchased 5 years later by Jimmy Osmond, from profits of his many successful businesses – including promoting Prince's Far East tour.)

1984
Apr The Osmonds, their repertoire now wholly country music (and signed to Warner Bros.), visit UK to play at Mervyn Conn's annual Country Music Festival at Wembley, London.

1985
Apr Group returns to play Wembley festival for second year running.
1986
Oct [28] Marie marries her engineer/producer Brian Blosil.
1987
May Merrill teams with Jessica Boucher for *You're Here To Remember*, which peaks at #62 on US Country chart.
Sept Donny, having not recorded for a decade, signs a new recording deal, only for UK release, with Virgin Records. (He has married Debra Glenn and the couple have 3 children in Provo, UT, and has spent the past few years as a TV producer, fronting his own production company Night Star, and director and satellite TV entrepreneur, while Jimmy has become a rock impresario (not least assisting Michael Jackson on his forthcoming "Bad" world tour), restauranteur, and owner of the Oz-Art advertising and design company.) Having auditioned to be lead singer of David Foster's group Airplay and appeared in a Jeff Beck video for his single *Ambitious*, Donny has a chance meeting at a UNICEF function with Peter Gabriel which has led to him recording at Gabriel's Bath studios, with George Acogny, a Sengal-born jazz guitarist living in Queens, New York, producing. His first single *I'm In It For Love* peaks at UK #70. Marie, now signed to Capitol Records, makes the Country chart with *Everybody's Crazy 'Bout My Baby* (#24) and *Cry Just A Little* (#50), from *I Only Wanted You*, and is becoming a major country artiste.

1988
Feb [22] Donny begins his comeback tour, with band comprising Rory Kaplan, Jeffrey Suttles, Jenny Douglas, Oneida James, Ron Reinhardt and Jon Clarke, at the Crazy Horse Saloon in Los Angeles.
Sept With a new image aimed squarely at the George Michael market, Donny's *Soldier Of Love* reaches UK #29 – the first Top 30 pop hit by any of The Osmonds in the 80s.
Nov Donny's *If It's Love That You Want* reaches UK #70.
Dec Marie wins the 1988 Roy Acuff Community Service Award.

1989
June [3] Hailed by the US media as one of the most surprising comebacks in pop history, Donny's *Soldier Of Love* hits US #2, kept off the top by Michael Damian's *Rock On*. Osmond has been signed for US release by Capitol, the same label as Marie.
Aug [3] Federal Deposit Insurance Corporation (FDIC) files suit against the Osmond brothers, alleging they owe $150,000 on a 1980 loan from the now-closed Utah First Bank.

[26] No-fluke follow-up *Sacred Emotion* reaches US #13, while parent album *Donny Osmond* enjoys 33-week ride to US #54.

1990 **Mar** [8] Donny is voted Most Unwelcome Comeback in **Rolling Stone** magazine's 1989 Music awards.

Apr Looking to a new generation to assume the famous Osmond mantle, 4 of Alan Osmond's 8 offspring are launched as The Osmond Boys and release remake of *Hey Girl*, produced by Alan Osmond, on ARO label in US.

July The Osmond Boys, Michael, Nathan, Douglas and David, debut with album *Osmond Boys* on Reprise.

Aug [29] Marie collapses during county fair in Canton, OH, and requires hospital treatment for a stomach virus.

Nov [17] Donny's *Eyes Don't Lie* climbs to US #177.

Dec [8] Donny's *My Love Is A Fire* reaches US #28.

1991 **Feb** [10] Donny joins with nearly 100 celebrities in Burbank, CA, to record *Voices That Care*, a David Foster and fiancee Linda Thompson Jenner-composed and organized charity record to benefit the American Red Cross Gulf Crisis Fund.

Mar [13] Marie appears on CBS TV's "48 Hours".

Apr [6] She guests on NBC TV's "Bob Hope's Yellow Ribbon Party", as Donny forms an unlikely duet with Dweezil Zappa on the latter's remake of The Bee Gees' *Stayin' Alive*.

GILBERT O'SULLIVAN

1968 **Apr** O'Sullivan (b. Raymond Edward O'Sullivan, Dec.1, 1946, Waterford, Eire), having moved to Swindon, Wilts., with his family at age 13, where he has played in bands The Doodles and Rick's Blues while at Swindon Art College studying graphic design, and had his songs *You* and *Come On Home* covered by The Tremeloes on their album *Here Comes The Tremeloes*, releases his first single, *What Can I Do*, for CBS.

1970 After a second one-off single, *Mr. Moody's Garden* on Major Minor, has also failed, O'Sullivan sends a demo tape and a photo of himself looking unusual enough to be sure to attract attention, to Gordon Mills, manager of Tom Jones and Engelbert Humperdinck. Mills is impressed, signs him to his newly-formed MAM record label, changes Ray's name to Gilbert and becomes his producer on disk.

Dec Debut MAM single, with his surname added, self-penned (as will be all his subsequent hits) social-awareness ballad *Nothing Rhymed* hits UK #8. O'Sullivan makes TV and personal appearances with strikingly obtuse visual image: short trousers, sleeveless sweater, flat cap and pudding basin haircut (the image in the photo which had caught Mills' attention, but will be retained only for the first couple of releases).

1971 **Apr** *Underneath The Blanket Go* makes UK #40. EMI's Columbia label reissues Major Minor single as by Gilbert O'Sullivan, but flipped over to feature *I Wish I Could Cry*. It gains some airplay, but fails to chart.

Sept *We Will* reaches UK #16. (American singer Andy Williams will subsequently ask O'Sullivan if he can record the song, but wants to change the lyrics of colloquial line "I bagsy be in goal", which he does not understand.)

[29] O'Sullivan makes his live debut in concert in aid of the World Wildlife Fund at London's Royal Albert Hall, with Dave Edmunds' Rockpile, The Sweet and Ashton Gardner & Dyke.

Oct *Gilbert O'Sullivan – Himself* hits UK #5, and will stay on UK chart for 82 weeks.

Dec *No Matter How I Try* hits UK #5.

1972 **Apr** Ballad *Alone Again (Naturally)*, chronicling the death of his parents, hits UK #3.

July Uptempo *Ooh-Wakka-Doo-Wakka-Day* hits UK #8.

[29] *Alone Again (Naturally)*, his US debut (complete with new, longer-haired, college sweater image), tops chart for 6 weeks, selling over a million copies.

Sept *Gilbert O'Sullivan – Himself* (amended to include *Alone Again (Naturally)*, not on the UK version a year earlier) hits US #9.

Nov *Clair* tops UK chart for 2 weeks. The song is written about Mills' daughter (for whom O'Sullivan used to babysit).

Dec *Clair* hits US #2, held off the top by Billy Paul's *Me And Mrs. Jones*, then by Carly Simon's *You're So Vain*. *Clair* is his second gold disk.

1973 **Jan** *Back To Front* hits UK #1 for a week, and stays on chart for 64 weeks. O'Sullivan hosts his own BBC TV special in UK, to coincide with its release.

Feb *Back To Front* reaches US #48.

Apr He switches from acoustic to electric piano on *Get Down*, which tops UK chart for 2 weeks. ("Get down" is an admonition to his dog with regard to furniture, not an instruction for dancers.)

May *Out Of The Question*, not released as a UK single, and taken from *Back To Front*, makes US #17.

[25] O'Sullivan embarks on 18-date tour at the Royal Festival Hall, London. The tour will end June 19 at the Carlton, Dublin, Eire.

Aug *Get Down* hits US #7, and is O'Sullivan's third US gold disk.

Sept *Ooh Baby* reaches UK #18.

Oct *I'm A Writer Not A Fighter* hits UK #2.

Nov *Ooh Baby* makes US #25, while the album creeps to US #101, and is O'Sullivan's final US chart album.

Dec Heart-broken ballad *Why Oh Why Oh Why* hits UK #6.

1974 **Mar** *Happiness Is Me And You* climbs to UK #19.

Apr *Happiness Is Me And You* peaks at US #62, and is O'Sullivan's final US chart single.

Aug O'Sullivan incurs the wrath of the feminist movement with *A Woman's Place*, which makes UK #42.

Nov *Stranger In My Own Back Yard* hits UK #9.

Dec Seasonal *A Christmas Song* reaches UK #12.

1975 **July** *I Don't Love You But I Think I Like You* peaks at UK #14.

1976 **Dec** Compilation album *Greatest Hits* reaches UK #13.

1977 **Nov** *Southpaw* fails to chart.

1979 **June** [8] O'Sullivan begins legal proceedings against MAM and Mills for unpaid royalties, despite continuing to record for the label.

1980 **Oct** Debut CBS release, *What's In A Kiss?* reaches UK #19. *Off Centre* is released, to poor sales. O'Sullivan by now has become a resident of Jersey in the Channel Islands.

1981 **Sept** Compilation album *20 Golden Greats*, a TV-promoted release on K-Tel, makes UK #98.

1982 **May** At the case of O'Sullivan versus MAM/Mills, the judge rules in favor of the plaintiff, agreeing that his original contract with Mills had been unreasonable, and that he had not received his due share of the revenue created by his songs and records. The court awards him payment of substantial back royalties. (Mills will die in 1986.)

Oct *Life And Rhymes*, produced by Graham Gouldman, is released on CBS, without charting.

1988 After a long absence from record and retirement from live performances, *Frobisher Drive*, named after his old address in Swindon, is released in Germany, with a UK release and tour planned.

1989 **Nov** Now signed to Chrysalis, *In The Key of G*, depicting O'Sullivan carrying on upright piano up a street on the front cover, is released, still in his understated melodic style.

1990 **Feb** [24] In an unlikely UK #72 chart entry, Chrysalis remixes extract *So What*, pre-release promoting it as a rare Italian house dance cut, thereby exciting moderate sales interest.

June [18] Extracted *At The Very Mention Of Your Name*, re-recorded and mixed by David Foster is released.

July [7] O'Sullivan makes a rare TV appearance on ITV's "Cannon And Ball" show.

1991 **Mar** O'Sullivan undertakes a poorly attended UK tour with his piano, a string section and a small troupe of actors. During the concerts the actors dramatize scenes from O'Sullivan's life, intercut with performances of his most memorable songs.

JOHNNY OTIS

1948 Berkeley, CA-raised Otis (b. John Veliotes, Dec.28, 1921, Vallejo, CA) has been a musician since his teens, playing drums in Count Otis Matthews' West Oakland House Rockers, in West Oakland, CA. He has drummed and played piano and vibes with several bands in Denver, CO, Kansas City, MO and Los Angeles, CA, before forming his own band in 1945 (featuring later successful solo talent like Bill Doggett, Jimmy Rushing and Big Jay McNeely), and having a US hit with *Harlem Nocturne*. Sensing musical changes, he pioneers the development of R&B on US West Coast when he opens the Barrelhouse club in Los Angeles. It is LA's first major venue to feature exclusively R&B music, mostly local acts whom Otis – with an unerring ear for talent – has discovered. These include the teenage Little Esther (Phillips) and The Robins (later to become The Coasters).

1950 He tours with The Johnny Otis Show, an R&B revue featuring the pick of talent from the Barrelhouse. Several R&B-oriented record companies have noted Otis' ear for finding strong performers, and he becomes a traveling talent scout while on the road with his show. (Legend has him note and recommend to King Records 3 future major acts in 1 night, while visiting Detroit, MI: Jackie Wilson, Little Willie John and The Royals, later to become Hank Ballard & The Midnighters.)

1952 Through the next 3 years Otis discovers and works with (among others) Big Mama Thornton (producing her original version of *Hound*

Dog), Bobby Bland, Little Richard and Johnny Ace (producing *Pledging My Love*).

957 Otis signs to Capitol, to record as The Johnny Otis Show, with various featured singers taking the vocals.

958 **Jan** *Ma! He's Making Eyes At Me*, with Marie Adams on lead vocal, hits UK #2.
Feb *Bye Bye Baby* reaches UK #20.
Aug *Willie And The Hand Jive* hits US #9. (It will be covered in 1960 by Cliff Richard And The Shadows, and be a UK and international hit.)
Nov *Crazy Country Hop* peaks at US #87.

959 **May** *Castin' My Spell*, with Marci Lee on lead vocal, reaches US #52.

960 **Feb** *Mumblin' Mosie* makes US #80. The run of Capitol hits ceases. (Otis will move to King Records, but will not chart again in the 60s.)

969 Blues-based album *Cold Shot*, recorded for Kent Records and highlighting Otis' son Shuggie (a talented slide guitarist) and blues vocalists Gene Connors and Delmar "Mighty Mouth" Evans, gains positive reviews and good sales, and includes R&B hit *Country Girl*. The same team, thinly anonymous, concocts a pornographic blues album, *Snatch And The Poontangs*.

970 **Mar** *Here Comes Shuggie Otis* reaches US #199.
The Otis band plays the Monterey Jazz Festival, which is recorded for a live album by Epic Records.

974 Otis launches his own Blues Spectrum label, concentrating on R&B recordings, including Charles Brown and Joe Turner, backed by the Otis band.

975 **Mar** *Inspiration Information* by Shuggie Otis makes US #181.

982 After a lengthy absence from disk, Otis signs to US independent Alligator label with a new version of The Johnny Otis Show. New line-up includes Shuggie and Delmar Evans, drummer Nicky Otis, 2 new vocalists, Barbara Morrison and Charles Williams, and guest players like Plas Johnson on sax. The revue tours and records ensemble-fashion much as it did in the 50s.

ROBERT PALMER

969 After a Services' childhood based mostly in Malta, and a post-schooldays' "apprenticeship" in semi-pro Scarborough, N.Yorks, rock'n'roll band Mandrake Paddle Steamer, Palmer (b. Alan Palmer, Jan.19, 1949, Batley, W.Yorks.) moves to London to join The Alan Bown Set as vocalist, replacing Jess Roden.
Nov He sings on Bown's Deram label single *Gypsy Girl*, and also records new vocals to replace Roden originals on *The Alan Bown!* (though US release on Music Factory retains Roden's vocals).

970 He joins avant garde jazz rockers Dada in place of Paul Korda, who has sung (with Elkie Brooks) on their album *Dada* for Atco Records. They splinter before recording again.

971 Palmer sticks with ex-Dada musicians who form Vinegar Joe, aiming in a more blues-rock direction. He shares vocals with Elkie Brooks, and other members are Pete Gage (guitar), Mike Deacon (keyboards), Steve York (bass) and Pete Gavin (drums).

972 **Apr** Signed to Island Records, they release *Vinegar Joe*, but like all their records, it fails to chart in UK or US.

974 **Mar** [9] After much live acclaim, particularly in Europe, but poor sales for 2 albums *Rock'N'Roll Gypsies* and *Six-Star General*, Vinegar Joe plays it last UK gig at St.Paul's College, Cheltenham, Glos., followed by a 2-week tour of Yugoslavia.
Sept Retained by Island as a soloist, Palmer records *Sneakin' Sally Through The Alley* in New Orleans, with assistance from The Meters and Little Feat's Lowell George. It fails to chart in UK, but receives much US airplay, and eventually makes US #107 in July 1975.

975 Palmer and his wife leave London to live in New York.
Dec *Pressure Drop*, released after he has toured in US as support and back-up singer with Little Feat, features the group and a Motown rhythm section, with string settings by Barry White's arranger Gene Page. It reaches US #136, but does not chart in UK.

976 Palmer moves from New York to Nassau, Bahamas, where he will be based until 1987.
Nov *Some People Can Do What They Like* peaks at US #68, and is a UK chart debut at #46.

977 **Jan** First hit single is album extract *Man Smart, Woman Smarter*, which reaches US #63.

978 **Apr** *Double Fun* makes US #45 but fails to chart in UK.
June *Every Kinda People*, extracted from *Double Fun*, is Palmer's breakthrough single: it reaches US #16, and gives him a UK Singles chart debut at #53.

979 **July** *Secrets* reaches UK #54, while *Bad Case Of Loving You (Doctor Doctor)*, from the album, makes #61.
Sept He continues to sell better in US, as *Secrets* reaches #19, and *Bad Case Of Loving You (Doctor Doctor)* hits #14.

1980 **Feb** Revival of Todd Rundgren's *Can We Still Be Friends* makes US #52.
Sept *Clues*, which includes collaborations with Gary Numan, reaches UK #31, his highest album chart placing yet in UK, while the extracted *Johnny And Mary* makes UK #44.
Nov *Clues* reaches US #59. A concert at the Dominion theater in London, UK, is recorded for live album project.
Dec *Looking For Clues*, from *Clues*, climbs to UK #33.

1982 **Apr** Combined concert (from the Nov.1980 recording) and studio-recorded *Maybe It's Live* reaches UK #32. One of the non-live tracks revives The Persuaders' 1973 US hit *Some Guys Have All The Luck*, which reaches #16.
May *Maybe It's Live* sells poorly in US, reaching only #148.

1983 **Apr** *Pride* reaches UK #37 and US #112, and contains minor UK hit single *You Are In My System*, a cover of a US dance hit by The System. The original makes US #64 while Palmer is hitting US #53.
June *You Can Have It (Take My Heart)* reaches UK #66.
July After a long absence, he returns to US Singles chart with *You Are In My System*, which makes #78.

1985 **Jan** He joins Duran Duran's John and Andy Taylor and Chic's drummer Tony Thompson providing vocals, on a temporary basis in Power Station, designed as a one-album studio project.
Apr Power Station's *The Power Station* reaches UK #12 and goes on to hit US #6, spawning hit singles: *Some Like It Hot* (US #6, UK #14), *Get It On* (US #9, UK #22) and *Communication* (US #34, UK #75).
July He leaves Power Station after dispute with other members, who want to continue the project, particularly for touring not least to play at Live Aid. Michael Des Barres replaces him.
Nov *Discipline Of Love (Why Did You Do It)* makes US #82, but fails in UK on first release, while *Riptide* makes a poor initial UK showing, reaching #69 before dropping.

1986 **May** [3] *Addicted To Love*, from *Riptide*, hits US #1, and is Palmer's first worldwide million-selling single, aided by a striking black mini-skirted models strumming instruments video shown widely on TV. *Riptide* boosted by *Addicted To Love*'s presence, hits US #8.
June *Addicted To Love* hits UK #5.
July [19] *Hyperactive* reaches UK #33.
Aug Jimmy Jam/Terry Lewis-produced *I Didn't Mean To Turn You On*, originally US #79 in 1984 for Cherrelle, hits UK #9, once again aided by his girl-model video backing band, while *Riptide*, boosted back into UK chart by the singles' success, finally hits #5.
Sept [5] Palmer wins Best Male Video category at the annual MTV awards.
Nov [8] *I Didn't Mean To Turn You On* hits US #2. *Discipline Of Love (Why Did You Do It)*, reissued in UK, now charts briefly at #68.

1987 Palmer and his family move to Lugano, Switzerland, where he works on music for the soundtrack of film "Sweet Lies".
Feb [24] Palmer wins Best Rock Vocal performance, Male for *Addicted To Love* at the 29th annual Grammy awards at the Shrine Auditorium, Los Angeles.
Sept He begins commuting from Lugano to Milan, Italy, to work at Logic studios on tracks for next album.

1988 **Apr** It is announced that he will sign to EMI/Manhattan Records, while Island releases *Sweet Lies* in UK. It is a minor hit, reaching #58, having already stalled in US at #94.
July EMI debut *Heavy Nova* enters at its peak of UK #17, and climbs to US #25, while *Simply Irresistible* reaches UK #44.
Sept [10] *Simply Irresistible* hits US #2.
Nov Ballad *She Makes My Day* hits UK #6.
Dec [17] Faithful update of Gap Band's 1982 US #24 *Early In The Morning* reaches US #19.

1989 **Feb** [22] Palmer wins (his second) Best Rock Vocal Performance, Male for *Simply Irresistible* at the 31st annual Grammy awards.
June *Change His Ways* reaches US #28.
Aug [5] From forthcoming album, *Tell Me I'm Not Dreaming*, featuring female vocalist B.J. Nelson, peaks at US #60, while *It Could Happen To You* stalls at UK #71 3 weeks later.
Nov *Addictions: Volume 1*, a greatest hits retrospective of his Island days, emerges set to hit UK #7 and US #79.

1990 **Mar** [8] Palmer wins Best Dressed Male Rock Artist in **Rolling Stone** magazine's 1989 Music Awards.
Apr Richard Gere/Julia Roberts hit movie soundtrack album *Pretty Woman* begins multi-platinum success, featuring Palmer's *Life In Detail*.

Nov [17] Cover version with UB40 of Dylan's *I'll Be Your Baby Tonight* hits UK #6, as second EMI album *Don't Explain* reaches UK #25.

Dec [22] *Don't Explain* stalls at US #88.

1991 Jan [19] Self-produced and co-written *You're Amazing* reaches US #28.

[26] A medley of Marvin Gaye's *Mercy Mercy Me* and *I Want You* hits UK #9.

Mar [1] Palmer embarks on a UK tour.

[19] Palmer guests on Fox TV's "Arsenio Hall" show.

GRAHAM PARKER & THE RUMOUR

Graham Parker (vocals)
Brinsley Schwarz (guitar)
Bob Andrews (keyboards)
Andrew Bodnar (bass)
Steve Goulding (drums)

1975 Having returned to UK from a tomato-picking and drug-abusing stay in Guernsey, Channel Islands, Parker (b. Nov.18, 1950) is introduced to his eventual backing band, The Rumour (comprising members from UK roots band Ducks DeLuxe, Brinsley Schwarz and Bontemps Roulez) through future Stiff Records boss, Dave Robinson. Parker has sent a demo tape of original R&B cuts to Hope & Anchor pub above which Robinson runs a small studio.

1976 Jan [9] Parker signs to Phonogram Records, after A&R chief Nigel Grainge has heard *Between You And Me* on Charlie Gillett's "Honky Tonk" radio show.

Mar [26] His debut single *Silly Thing* is released as Parker begins UK tour with Thin Lizzy.

Apr Debut album *Howlin' Wind*, produced by Nick Lowe, is released to much critical acclaim and accompanied by a well-received sell-out club tour, spurring 30,000 sales.

Sept Official bootleg album *Live At Marble Arch* secures a US deal with Mercury. With only 1,000 pressed, it is itself much bootlegged.

Oct Third album of the year, *Heat Treatment*, produced by Robert "Mutt" Lange, featuring a semi-permanent brass section, sells 60,000.

1977 Jan *Heat Treatment* makes US #169.

Mar EP *The Pink Parker* is his first UK Singles hit at #24. Lead track is a cover of The Trammps' disco classic *Hold Back The Night*, featuring guest guitarist Thin Lizzy's Brian Robertson.

Apr *Hold Back The Night* peaks at US #58.

May Lowe-produced *Stick To Me*, featuring 9 Parker written songs, peaks at US #125.

July The Rumour releases first Parker-less album *Max*.

Oct *Stick To Me* makes UK #19.

1978 May *Don't Ask Me Questions* makes UK #32 as live double parent *The Parkerilla*, actually 3 sides of live studio material with a 12" single fourth side, reaches UK #14.

July *The Parkerilla* makes US #149.

[15] Parker & The Rumour support Bob Dylan at Blackbushe Aerodrome, Surrey, open-air concert.

1979 Feb The Rumour releases a cover of Duke Ellington's *Do Nothing Till You Hear From Me*. They sign to Stiff, while Parker remains at Vertigo and releases *Frozen Years*.

Mar *Squeezing Out Sparks*, a 10-track Parker-written album, produced by Jack Nitzsche, the band's most accomplished studio recording to date, makes UK #18 and, through new deal with Arista, US #40, with the aid of promo album *Live Sparks*, a concert version of the studio disk. Graham Parker & The Rumour begin a major US tour suppporting Cheap Trick, including a sell-out date at New York's Palladium. During the tour, Parker dedicates anti-Mercury Records song *Mercury Poisoning* to his new record boss, Arista's Clive Davis. Rumour releases its second album without Parker on Stiff, *Frogs, Sprouts, Clogs And Krauts*.

May *Emotional Traffic*, pressed in red, amber and green vinyls, is later flipped but *Hard Enough To Show* also fails to chart.

Nov *Issues*, under the pseudonym The Duplicates is released on Stiff.

1980 Apr Parker signs to Stiff and releases *Stupefaction* and Jimmy Iovine-produced *The Up Escalator*, which includes Bruce Springsteen on backing vocals on the cut *Endless Night*. The album reaches UK #11 – Parker's biggest UK success, and begins rise to US #40.

Aug *Purity Of Essence*, Rumour's third and last album, is released, along with single *My Little Red Book*.

With Andrews already gone, the group splits from Parker and disbands after backing US singer/songwriter Garland Jeffreys on his album *Escape Artist*. Parker publishes sci-fi book **The Great Trouser Mystery**.

1982 Mar Self-penned ballad *Temporary Beauty* makes UK #50 as his RCA debut *Another Grey Area*, produced by Jack Douglas, reaches UK #40.

1983 Sept *The Real Macaw*, produced by David Kershenbaum and featuring Schwarz, Graham Small (keyboards), Kevin Jenkins (bass) and Gilson Lavis (drums), makes US #59. Extracted *Life Gets Better* stalls at US #94.

1985 Apr Parker signs to Elektra and releases *Steady Nerves* with backing band The Shot (including Schwarz).

June [22] *Wake Up (Next To You)* makes US #39, Parker's only US Top 40 single.

1986 June He begins a European tour, backed by Schwarz and Bodnar.

1988 May At Atlantic's 40th anniversary concert at New York's Madison Square Garden, Bob Geldof performs Parker's abortion-themed song, *You Can't Be Too Strong* from *Squeezing Out Sparks*.

July *The Mona Lisa's Sister*, with help form Schwarz, Bodnar and drummer Pete Thomas, appears on Demon (RCA in US), having been rejected by A&R-confused Atlantic. It costs $60,000 to record, less than his last video with Elektra, and makes US #77.

Sept [24] Parker begins a solo acoustic US tour at Rhode Island University.

1989 May *Human Soul* is released to little commercial success.

1991 Feb RCA album *Struck By Lightning*, featuring John Sebastian on harmonica and Garth Hudson on organ and accordian, is released, having already failed to score in UK.

Apr [10] Parker guests on NBC TV's "Late Night With Letterman".

RAY PARKER JR.

1970 Parker (b.May 1, 1954, Detroit, MI), having played the guitar since age 12, and toured supporting The Spinners with his post-high school group Jeep Smith & The Troubadours, becomes a guitarist in the house band at Detroit's biggest club, the Twenty Grand, which leads to studio sessions for Motown and for Holland/Dozier/Holland's Invictus and Hot Wax labels.

1972 May After working with Parker in the studio (on sessions for album *Talking Book*), Stevie Wonder invites him to join the road band for his North American tour with The Rolling Stones.

1973 After playing on Stevie Wonder's *Innervisions*, Parker moves to Los Angeles, CA, where he begins songwriting in earnest (inspired by working with Wonder), and becomes a regular session guitarist, playing with Barry White (and White's various groups), Boz Scaggs and LaBelle, among others.

1974 Dec Parker's first hit composition is *You Got The Love*, recorded by Rufus, which reaches US #11. He also has a bit part in movie "Uptown Saturday Night".

1976 Apr Barry White's *You See The Trouble With Me*, which Parker co-write and plays on, hits UK #2.

1977 Parker opens his own Ameraycan recording studio in Los Angeles. A demo tape impresses Arista Records chief Clive Davis and he is signed to the label. He forms the band Raydio, with himself on vocals and guitar, Arnell Carmichael on synthesizer, Charles Fearing on guitar, Vincent Bonham on keyboards, Jerry Knight on bass and Larry Tolbert on drums – all ex-studio cohorts from early 70s in Detroit.

1978 Apr Raydio's debut single *Jack And Jill*, written and produced by Parker, hits US #8 and is a million-seller, while *Raydio* makes US #27 and earns a gold disk for a half million sales. Bonham leaves the group which tours US with Bootsy Collins.

May *Jack And Jill* reaches UK #11.

Aug *Is This A Love Thing*, also from the album, makes UK #27.

1979 Aug Raydio's second album *Rock On* peaks at US #45 (also a gold disk), while extracted *You Can't Change That* hits US #9.

1980 June Group changes name to Ray Parker Jr. & Raydio for its third album *Two Places At The Same Time*, which makes US #33 and is Parker's third gold album. The title track peaks at US #30.

1981 June *A Woman Needs Love*, fourth consecutive gold disk, reaches US #13. From it, *A Woman Needs Love (Just Like You Do)* hits US #4, the highest-placed single yet.

Sept *That Old Song*, also from the fourth album, reaches US #21. Parke produces soul songstress Cheryl Lynn's *Shake It Up Tonight*, which reaches US #70, and parent album *In The Night*, which makes US #104.

1982 June Parker disbands the group to record as a soloist, and his *The Other Woman* reaches US #11 (again earning a gold disk). The title track (inspired, according to Parker, by listening to Rick Springfield's *Jessie's Girl*), hits US #4.

Aug *Let Me Go*, also from the album, peaks at US #38.

1983 Jan Third single from *The Other Woman*, *Bad Boy* peaks at US #35.

Compilation *Greatest Hits*, covering both Parker's Raydio and solo career to date, makes US #51.

984
Jan *I Still Can't Get Over Loving You* reaches US #12. It is taken from *Woman Out Of Control*, which peaks at US #30.
Aug Parker's theme for Bill Murray/Dan Aykroyd film "Ghostbusters", written and recorded within 2 days, tops US chart for 3 weeks and is Parker's second US million-selling single. Its promo video is directed by Ivan Reitman and includes Murray and Aykroyd, plus guest cameos by Danny De Vito, Peter Falk and others. (The song will earn Parker an Academy Award nomination but he will be successfully sued by Huey Lewis for plagiarizing Lewis' *I Want A New Drug*.)
Sept *Ghostbusters* hits UK #2 for 3 weeks behind Stevie Wonder's million-selling *I Just Called To Say I Love You*.

985
Jan *Jamie* reaches US #14. It is taken from Parker's *Ghostbusters*, which makes US #60 (but is overshadowed by movie soundtrack album, which as well as the theme song has tracks by Elmer Bernstein, The Thompson Twins, Air Supply and others, and hits US #6 and UK #24).
Dec *Girls Are More Fun* makes US #34, and *Sex And The Single Man* reaches US #65.

986
Jan As the film opens in UK to repeat its US box office success, *Ghostbusters* re-charts in UK, at #6. (Total UK sales will top 800,000.)
Feb Parker's duet with UK singer Helen Terry on *One Sunny Day/Dueling Bikes*, from soundtrack of film "Quicksilver", is released on Atlantic and peaks at US #96. *Girls Are More Fun* makes UK #46.

987
Sept [19] Parker signs a new deal with Geffen Records, his debut single *I Don't Think That Man Should Sleep Alone* peaking at US #68.
Oct Geffen album *After Dark* reaches US #86 and UK #40.
Nov *I Don't Think That Man Should Sleep Alone*, from *After Dark*, climbs to UK #13.

988
Jan *Over You*, a duet with Natalie Cole, makes UK #65.

990
Sept Parker emerges once more in a cameo vocal role, this time on Glen Medeiros' *All I'm Missing Is You*.

DOLLY PARTON

946
Jan [19] Dolly Rebecca Parton, the fourth of Robert and Avie Lee Parton's 12 children is delivered by Dr. Robert F. Thomas (whom she later immortalizes in song) in Locust Ridge, Sevier County, TN. The family is so poor, they pay the doctor with a sack of corn meal.

957
Having already appeared on Cass Walker's Knoxville, TN, radio show, Parton takes a Greyhound bus to Lake Charles, LA, to record her first single *Puppy Love*, penned with her uncle, for local Gold Band label.

958
Drumming with the Sevier County high school marching band, Parton makes her debut at "The Grand Ole Opry".

962
She records *It's Sure Gonna Hurt* for Mercury, credited to Dolly Parton with The Merry Melody Singers, which includes 3 members of The Jordanaires.

964
June [1] Parton relocates to Nashville, TN, the day following her high school graduation, staying with relatives. She then signs with Monument Records, which, with Ray Stevens producing, initially aims her at the pop market, but her first success is as a songwriter – Bill Phillips' US Country Top 10 hit with *Put It Off Until Tomorrow*.

966
May [30] Parton weds Carl Dean (whom she met in the Wishy Washy laundromat on her first day in Nashville), in Catoosa County, GA.

967
Oct [7] "Dolly Parton Day" is celebrated in Sevier County. 7,000 locals attend her concert at the courthouse to celebrate her signing to RCA and replacing Norma Jean (to whom she had earlier sent some songs) on "The Porter Wagoner Show" TV program. (Parton's RCA debut *Just Because I'm A Woman* makes US Country #19.)

968
Parton becomes a regular on "The Grand Ole Opry" show. She and Wagoner are named Best Duet Of The Year by the Country Music Association (CMA). They receive the first of 3 Grammy nominations.

969
Jan [4] Parton is welcomed into the Grand Ole Opry.
Mar *Just The Two Of Us*, with Porter Wagoner, makes US #184. (The partnership will produce 18 country hits – the first a cover of Tom Paxton's *The Last Thing On My Mind*.)
Aug Parton/Wagoner album *Always, Always* peaks at US #162.
Nov Solo album *My Blue Ridge Mountain Boy* climbs to US #194.

970
Apr Parton/Wagoner album *Porter Wayne And Dolly Rebecca* climbs to US #137.
Aug *A Real Live Dolly*, recorded at her high school, makes US #154.
Oct *Once More*, again with Wagoner, makes US #191.

971
Mar *Two Of A Kind*, Parton's last chart album with Wagoner, climbs to US #142.
June Solo *Joshua* creeps to US #198. (The title track gave Parton her first US Country #1 in 1970.)

1974
Mar Jealous girlfriend-themed *Jolene* makes US #60 and tops US Country chart – the second of 4 consecutive Country #1s.
Apr [21] Parton and Wagoner perform their last live show together in Salinas, KS.
Parton forms The Traveling Family Band, which includes 4 siblings and 2 cousins.

1975
Apr Parton takes part in annual Country Festival at Wembley, London.
Oct Parton, having been nominated on 5 previous occasions, is voted Female Vocalist Of The Year by the CMA.

1976
Feb Syndicated TV series "Dolly", recorded in Nashville and featuring country stars, airs in US.
June *Jolene* hits UK #7.
Vocal problems will result in her cancelling 65 dates in the latter part of the year. Parton is named CMA Female Vocalist Of The Year for a second successive year.

1977
She signs to West Coast management team Ray Katz and Sandy Gallin.
May Parton participates in a concert in Scotland at Glasgow's King theater to celebrate Queen Elizabeth's Silver Jubilee. She is introduced to Prince Philip, Duke of Edinburgh, backstage.
[6] She makes her New York debut at the Bottom Line club.
July *Light Of A Clear Blue Morning* stalls at US #87, while parent album *New Harvest ... First Gathering*, which features a shift away from country, makes US #71.

1978
Jan Mainstream pop song, *Here You Come Again*, written by Barry Mann and Cynthia Weil, hits US #3. **Here You Come Again** reaches US #20, and is Parton's first platinum album.
May *Two Doors Down* reaches US #19.
Sept *Heartbreaker* makes US #37.
Oct Parton appears on the front cover of **Playboy** magazine, in bunny costume. She is named Entertainer Of The Year by the CMA as *Heartbreaker* makes US #27.
Dec Compilation album *Both Sides* makes UK #45.

1979
Feb Parton becomes the first country artist to have a disco hit, with *Baby I'm Burnin'*, which also makes US #25 and tops Country chart.
[15] Parton wins Best Country Female Vocal Performance at the 21st annual Grammy ceremonies.
July *You're The Only One* peaks at US #59 as parent album *Great Balls Of Fire* makes US #40.
Oct *Sweet Summer Lovin'* stalls at US #77.

1980
May *Starting Over Again* makes US #36, while parent album *Dolly Dolly Dolly* makes US #71.
Dec [19] "Nine To Five", in which Parton makes her movie debut, as a secretary, with Jane Fonda and Lily Tomlin, premieres in US.

1981
Feb [21] Self-penned *9 To 5*, written for the movie, tops US chart, but stalls at UK #47.
Mar *9 To 5 And Odd Jobs* reaches US #11.
May *But You Know I Love You* makes US #41.
Sept *The House Of The Rising Sun* peaks at US #77.
Dec *9 To 5* is Top Country Album in **Billboard**'s Year In Music survey.

1982
Feb [24] Parton wins Best Country Vocal Performance, for the second time, for *9 To 5* at the 24th annual Grammy awards.
Mar [25] TV version of "9 To 5" airs, with Parton's sister Rachel Dennison reprising her role.
May *Heartbreak Express* makes US #106.
July Parton stars with Burt Reynolds in movie "The Best Little Whorehouse In Texas", as a madam.
Sept Ballad *I Will Always Love You*, from "The Best Little Whorehouse In Texas" and a remake of Parton's 1974 Country chart-topper, makes US #53 and is her 15th Country #1 as **The Best Little Whorehouse** soundtrack album climbs to US #63. (Parton duets with Burt Reynolds on *Sneakin' Around* cut.)
Dec *Greatest Hits* climbs to US #77.

1983
June *Burlap And Satin* makes US #127.
Oct [29] *Islands In The Stream*, a duet with Kenny Rogers, written by The Bee Gees and co-produced by Barry Gibb, tops US chart, the only platinum selling single in the year. (It will go on win a cluster of awards, including the AMA's Best Country Single and the ACM's Single Record Of The Year.)

1984
Jan *Save The Last Dance For Me* makes US #45 as parent album *The Great Pretender*, reprising hits of the 50s and 60s, reaches US #73.
Apr *Downtown* reaches US #80, as *Here You Come Again* makes UK #75.
June [18] Sylvester Stallone/Dolly Parton-starring picture "Rhinestone", based on Larry Weiss' song *Rhinestone Cowboy*, opens in US. (The project is Parton's first since major stomach surgery.) Soundtrack album *Rhinestone*, featuring Parton songs, makes US #135.
Dec Festive album, produced by David Foster, *Once Upon A*

DOLLY PARTON cont.

Christmas, with Kenny Rogers, is released, set to make US #31.

1985 **Jan** *The Greatest Gift Of All*, from Parton and Kenny Rogers' Christmas TV special, makes US #81, as she prepares for a US tour with Rogers.
June *Real Love*, another duet with Rogers, peaks at US #91. Construction begins on Dollywood, an 87-acre theme park near her birthplace in the Smoky Mountains.
Aug Further Rogers duet, *Real Love*, stalls at US #91.
Sept *Greatest Hits* makes UK #74.
Dec ABC TV airs "A Smoky Mountain Christmas". It becomes the network's highest-rated Sunday night program in over 2 years.

1986 **Jan** [19] Parton begins work on often-postponed album project with Emmylou Harris and Linda Ronstadt, as her country smash *Think About Love* hits US Country #1.

1987 **Mar** Parton's collaboration with Emmylou Harris and Linda Ronstadt, *Trio*, makes UK #60.
May *Trio* tops US Country chart for 5 weeks, and is set to hit US #6. (Extracted *To Know Him Is To Love Him* tops Country chart.)
Sept [27] ABC TV premieres "Dolly", a variety show scheduled as the network's prime-time Sunday evening show. (Despite attempts to re-vamp the program, it fails to achieve ratings, and ABC will pull it.)
Dec *Rainbow*, a mainstream pop album and Parton's first for CBS/Columbia, stalls at US #153 and US Country #18.

1988 **Feb** [20] Parton and Porter Wagoner perform on "Dolly", together for the first time since their 1974 break-up.
Mar Parton visits UK to promote *Rainbow* and appears on ITV show "Aspel & Co."
[2] *Trio* wins Parton, Ronstadt and Harris a Grammy for Country Vocal, Duo Or Group at the 30th annual Grammy awards. It is Parton's fourth.
May Parton duets with Smokey Robinson for ballad, *I Know You By Heart*, which fails to chart.
By year's end, Parton will have lensed "Steel Magnolias" with fellow actresses Sally Field, Shirley MacLaine, Julia Roberts, Daryl Hannah and Olympia Dukakis and established the Dollywood Foundation program that promises a college scholarship to every student who graduates from any of the 3 high schools in Parton's home county in Tennessee.

1989 **June** Returning to country flavors, *White Limozeen* hits US Country #3 and spawns 2 US Country #1 singles, *Why'd You Come In Here Lookin' Like That* and *Yellow Roses*.
July [13] During a Los Angeles concert, Parton is surprised when her back-up singer on *Islands In The Stream* turns out to be Kenny Rogers.

1990 **Jan** [8] Parton visits Carl Perkins at his house in Jackson, TN, and co-writes 4 songs.
Mar She buys W-SEV, (pending FCC approval) hometown station in Sevierville, TN, the first staion she ever sang on, with the intention of moving the station to Dollywood and make it an attraction at the Pigeon Forge, TN, theme park. (When she was 9, Parton and Uncle Bill Owens went to W-SEV to tape songs, including *Puppy Love* and *Girl Left Alone*, subsequently first release on Gold Band Records.)
Sept Parton is fined $20,000 by the US Department of Labor for making her teenage staff put in longer to 9 to 5 hours at Dollywood, Pigeon Forge, TN.
Parton guests on *Do I Ever Cross Your Mind* from Randy Travis' duets album *Heroes & Friends*.

1991 **Apr** *Eagle When She Flies* returns Parton to pop Albums Hot 100 as it begins to climb.

TEDDY PENDERGRASS

1969 Pendergrass (b. Mar.26, 1950, Philadelphia, PA), whose mother was a Philadelphia nightclub performer, has taught himself the drums in his early teens after a childhood steeped in gospel music, and is drumming with local group The Cadillacs when they are invited to become the instrumental back-up team for Harold Melvin & The Blue Notes, a Philadelphia R&B group with a 13-year history and its roots in doo-wop, and a minor hit single, *My Hero* (US #78 in 1960).

1970 On a French West Indies tour, The Blue Notes lead singer John Atkins leaves and Pendergrass replaces him as front man.

1971 Group signs to Kenny Gamble and Leon Huff's Philadephia International label, based in its own home town.

1972 **Aug** Group's first hit is *I Miss You*, which reaches US #58.
Dec *If You Don't Know Me By Now*, a ballad written and produced by Gamble and Huff, hits US #3 and sells over a million, establishing band firmly in the pop field as well as R&B, where it has previously been known. First album *Harold Melvin And The Blue Notes* makes US #53.

1973 **Feb** *If You Don't Know Me By Now* hits UK #9.
Mar *Yesterday I Had The Blues* peaks at US #63.
Dec *The Love I Lost*, again a Gamble/Huff composition, hits US #7, and is the group's second million-seller. Second album *Black And Blue* peaks at US #57.

1974 **Feb** *The Love I Lost* makes UK #21.
May *Satisfaction Guaranteed (Or Take Your Love Back)* makes US #58 and UK #32.
Nov Penned by Gene McFadden and John Whitehead, *Where Are All My Friends* reaches US #80.

1975 **May** *To Be True* makes US #26, earning a gold disk for a half million sales during its 32-week chart run.
June *Bad Luck*, also by McFadden and Whitehead, makes US #15, while UK-only reissued oldie on Route label, *Get Out*, makes UK #35.
Aug *Hope That We Can Be Together Soon*, featuring guest vocalist Sharon Paige duetting on lead with Pendergrass, reaches US #42.

1976 **Feb** Group's last major US hit single is social awareness themed ballad *Wake Up Everybody* (penned by McFadden and Whitehead), which reaches US #12. The album of the same title hits US #9 earning a second gold disk.
Mar *Wake Up Everybody* reaches UK #23.
Apr *Tell All The World How I Feel About 'Cha Baby* stalls at US #94. It is the group's last single for Philadelphia International and also last with Pendergrass' lead vocal. He leaves for a solo career, staying with Gamble and Huff's label, while Harold Melvin & The Blue Notes move to ABC Records, with new lead singer David Ebo.
Aug Group compilation album *All Their Greatest Hits* reaches US #51.

1977 **Mar** To compete with Thelma Houston's revival, Harold Melvin & The Blue Notes' version of Gamble/Huff/Gilbert song *Don't Leave Me This Way*, previously an album track, is issued as a UK single, and outsells Houston's, hitting UK #5.
July Pendergrass' first solo hit single is Gamble and Huff's *I Don't Love You Anymore*, which makes US #41. It is taken from his debut solo album *Teddy Pendergrass*, which peaks at US #17 and spends 35 weeks on chart, selling over a million copies to earn a platinum disk. A different single, *The Whole Town's Laughing At Me*, is extracted in UK and reaches #44. Having taken a year's absence from live performance after splitting with Melvin, he begins to tour with the 15-piece Teddy Bear Orchestra (the name taken from Pendergrass' nickname). His sultry ballads, addressed directly to the females in the audience, quickly bring him a reputation as a ladies' man entertainer.
Aug Pendergrass joins Lou Rawls, Billy Paul, Archie Bell and others on The Philadelphia All-Stars' *Let's Clean Up The Ghetto* (all profits will go to a 5-year charity product in areas of urban decay). It reaches US #91 and UK #34.
[22-27] Pendergrass participates in "Let's Clean Up The Ghetto Week" in Los Angeles, CA, at the instigation of Mayor Tom Bradley.

1978 **Sept** Second solo album *Life Is A Song Worth Singing* and extracted *Close The Door* are both US million-sellers, reaching US #11 and #25.
[2] Pendergrass performs a "For Women Only" midnight concert at Avery Fisher Hall, New York, NY. The audience are handed white chocolate teddy bear-shaped lollipops. (Further "ladies only" concerts (invariably standing-room-only) follow: a PR exercise by manager Shep Gordon to capitalize on the perception of Pendergrass as aural seducer.
Nov In UK, *Close The Door* is double A-side with *Only You* making #41.

1979 **Aug** *Teddy* hits US #5 and earns another platinum disk. *Turn Off The Lights*, taken from it, peaks at US #48.

1980 **Feb** Double live album *Teddy Live! Coast To Coast*, with 3 sides recorded in concert and a fourth containing interviews and new studio tracks, makes US #33, reaching gold status. A UK tour is cancelled, partly because of Pendergrass' liaison with the wife of Marvin Gaye – who is touring UK for the same promoter at the same time.
Sept *T.P.* reaches US #14, and is Pendergrass' fourth album to turn platinum with US sales over a million. It includes a duet with Stephanie Mills on *Feel The Fire*.
Oct *Can't We Try*, taken from *T.P.*, climbs to US #52.

1981 **Jan** Another extract from the album, *Love T.K.O.*, reaches US #44.
Apr He tours UK for the first time as a soloist and, as in US, his shows are hugely successful with female audiences in particular.
July Pendergrass duets again with Stephanie Mills on her single *Two Hearts* on 20th Century. It peaks at US #40 and UK #49.
Oct *It's Time For Love* reaches US #19, earning another gold disk. The first single from it, *I Can't Live Without Your Love*, just fails to chart.

1982 **Feb** *You're My Latest, My Greatest Inspiration* makes US #43. He makes his movie debut in "Soup For One" and sings *Dream Girl* on the soundtrack, produced by Nile Rodgers and Bernard Edwards of Chic.

He also makes a second successful UK visit.

Mar On the way home from a basketball game, Pendergrass crashes his Rolls Royce into a barrier after skidding off the road in Philadelphia. He is pulled from the wreck with a severely injured spinal chord, and hospitalized in a critical condition. (He is paralyzed from the neck down for some time and gradually recovers only partial movement, but it will keep him from recording and performing for over 2 years.)

Oct *This One's For You*, consisting of material recorded before the accident, makes US #59.

1984 Jan *Heaven Only Knows*, his last for Philadelphia International, stalls at US #123.

July Pendergrass, confined to a wheelchair, returns to recording and signs to Asylum Records, where his debut is *Love Language*, at US #38.

Aug From the album, *Hold Me* reaches US #44. The single is a duet with Whitney Houston (her first chart entry).

1985 July [13] Pendergrass makes his comeback to the live arena, performing at Live Aid in Philadelphia, PA.

1986 Jan *Workin' It Back* makes US #96.

Feb *Hold Me*, having failed in 1984, is reissued in UK after Whitney Houston tops chart with *Saving All My Love For You*, and this time climbs to UK #44.

1988 June Now signed to Elektra, new album *Joy* reaches UK #45.

[25] *Joy* tops US R&B chart.

July Single and album *Joy* make US #77 and US #54 respectively.

1990 June [30] Pendergrass duets with Lisa Fisher on *Glad To Be Alive* featured in Andrew Dice Clay movie "The Adventures Of Ford Fairlane".

Nov [3] *Rubáiyát*, Elektra's 40th anniversary compilation, to which Pendergrass contributes a cover of *Make It With You*, makes US #140.

1991 Mar [13] Pendergrass appears on Fox TV's "Arsenio Hall" show, promoting current album *Truly Blessed*.

Apr [6] *Truly Blessed* peaks at US #55, his 12th solo album.

CARL PERKINS

1950 Perkins (b. Carl Lee Perkings, Apr.9, 1932, Ridgely, near Tiptonville, TN), from a poor sharecropping family, whose father Buck is an invalid with a lung disorder, begins to play bars and honky tonks around Tennessee, with brothers Jay and Clayton as The Perkins Brothers Band, to earn extra money.

1953 Jan [24] He marries Valda Crider in Corinth, MS, who encourages him to make a career in music. (During their first year together, he picks cotton and she takes in laundry to make ends meet.)

1954 Perkins begins to play professionally, still on the honky tonk circuit, singing and playing electric guitar. His brothers back him on acoustic guitar and double bass. They mix country and hillbilly music with the occasional blues and uptempo R&B number, and earn around $30 a month. Perkins relocates to Jackson, MS, where he and his wife move into a government housing project.

Aug He hears Elvis Presley's first single *Blue Moon Of Kentucky* on the radio, and recognizes a similar blend of styles to those he is playing himself. After watching Presley at a high school dance in Betthel Springs, MS, The Perkins Brothers Band travels to Memphis, TN, to audition for Presley's record company, Sun.

Oct The 3 brothers, with new drummer W.S. Holland, impress Sam Phillips at Sun, particularly with Perkins' original material. Phillips offers Perkins a contract if he can come up with more new songs.

1955 Jan [22] The first Sun recording session produces *Movie Magg* and *Turn Around*, which are issued as a single on Phillips' new label Flip Records, to little success.

Feb Perkins supports Elvis Presley on a tour of the South.

July [11] Uptempo rockabilly *Gone Gone Gone* is recorded for Perkins' second single, on Sun label itself.

Nov When Presley's contract is sold to RCA, Phillips decides to mold Perkins into a suitable replacement, and encourages him to play up the emerging rock'n'roll elements in his writing and recording. The band is signed to Phillips' Stars Inc. promotional agency.

Dec [19] Perkins and the band record his own composition *Blue Suede Shoes* (based on a true incident spotted in a gig audience). Sensing its commercial potential, Phillips rush-releases it with heavy promotion.

1956 Mar [3] *Blue Suede Shoes* enters US Top 100 simultaneously with Presley's first national hit *Heartbreak Hotel*.

[17] Perkins makes his first TV appearance, on Red Foley's country show "Ozark Jubilee".

[22] Perkins brothers are driving to New York for an appearance on "The Perry Como Show" on NBC TV when their car hits a pick-up truck near Dover, DE. Perkins and brother Jay are both hospitalized with their injuries, and media promotion made possible by *Blue Suede Shoes'* success slips away while they are recovering.

Apr *Blue Suede Shoes* hits US #3, and sells over a million. Presley's cover is released as lead song on an EP after he, rather than Perkins, sings it on national TV, and it reaches US #24.

[10] When Perkins leaves hospital and returns to Memphis, he is presented with a new 1956 Cadillac Fleetwood by Sam Phillips, in celebration of *Blue Suede Shoes'* million sales.

June *Blue Suede Shoes* hits UK #10 (his only UK chart single), but Presley's cover hits UK #9.

July Perkins' follow-up *Boppin' The Blues* stalls at US #70.

Dec [4] While Perkins and the band are in Sun studios in Memphis recording *Matchbox* (with label newcomer Jerry Lee Lewis playing piano on the session), they are visited by Johnny Cash (on the way downtown to shop for Christmas with his wife), and then by Presley, who has just returned to Memphis for Christmas. After Cash leaves, the other 3 settle down to a studio jam session on familiar gospel, country and R&B numbers, while Phillips leaves the tape running. (These impromptu recordings become legendary as "The Million Dollar Quartet" tapes and segments will be released in the late 70s and mid-80s, after Presley's death.)

1957 Mar *Your True Love* peaks at US #67, and is Perkins' last hit for Sun.

[31] Perkins opens a tour of US South, co-headlining with Johnny Cash (and supported by Jerry Lee Lewis, among others), in Little Rock, AR.

Nov [12] Rock'n'roll movie "Jamboree" (released as "Disc Jockey Jamboree" in UK) premieres in Hollywood and features Perkins performing *Glad All Over*.

1958 Feb [19] Perkins leaves Sun to sign a new recording deal with CBS/Columbia. (Johnny Cash will follow within months.)

May *Pink Pedal Pushers* reaches US #91.

Oct Jay Perkins, never fully recovered from the car crash 2 years before, and since diagnosed as having cancer, dies.

1959 June *Pointed Toe Shoes* peaks at US #92, and will be Carl Perkins' last US pop chart entry.

1963 He leaves Columbia for US Decca (but will have no successful recordings on the label). He tours Europe for the first time, playing US bases in France, Italy and Germany.

1964 May [9] He opens his first major UK tour, co-headlining with Chuck Berry, at Finsbury Park Astoria, London. Also on the bill are The Animals and The Nashville Teens. (His arrival at London airport has been greeted by fans holding a banner proclaiming "Welcome Carl 'Beatle Crusher' Perkins". In fact, The Beatles are ardent fans and play a jam session with him the first time their touring paths cross, which inspires the group to cut 3 Perkins compositions (of the many they have traditionally played on stage) before the end of the year.

Perkins records *Big Bad Blues* with backing by The Nashville Teens, in London. It does not chart, despite his touring success.

Oct [18] Perkins begins 28-date twice-nightly UK tour, with The Animals, Gene Vincent, The Nashville Teens and others, at the Odeon cinema, Liverpool, Merseyside.

Nov [15] Tour ends at the Winter Gardens, Bournemouth, Dorset. The Beatles' revival of Perkins' *Matchbox* reaches US #17. (Perkins is present at the recording of the track.)

Dec The Beatles revive 2 more Perkins songs – *Honey Don't* (original B-side of *Blue Suede Shoes*) and *Everybody's Trying To Be My Baby* – on their chart-topping *Beatles For Sale* (*Beatles '65* in US). These covers earn Perkins more in songwriter royalties than he has earned from all his own post-*Blue Suede Shoes* recordings.

1966 Perkins signs to country label Dollie Records, where he will cut a series of highly-rated, but non-charting, singles like *County Boy's Dream* and *Lake County Cotton Country*.

1967 He joins Johnny Cash's touring revue (and will spend several years playing back-up guitar for Cash and performing in his own right in the shows). He is featured in Cash's weekly TV show, and in his documentary movie and million-selling album recorded at San Quentin prison, among other notable appearances. Both Cash and Perkins forswear alcohol and pills which have been threatening to blight their lives and support each other with a joint "dry" pact. They also become born-again Christians.

1969 Feb *Daddy Sang Bass*, a Perkins song recorded by Cash, reaches US #42.

1970 Jan Back with CBS, he works on *Boppin' The Blues* with rock revival band NRBQ which backs him on several remakes of his early hits.

1971 He writes songs for the soundtrack of Robert Redford movie "Little Fauss And Big Halsy".

1974 Perkins signs to Mercury Records' country label, cutting *My Kind Of Country*, and singles which include a revival of Kenny Rogers' *Ruby (Don't Take Your Love To Town)*.

Dec His brother Clayton, troubled with a severe drink problem, takes his own life (shortly before Perkins' father dies of cancer).

1976 He launches his own production company and label, Suede Records, in US. He also leaves the Johnny Cash troupe after 9 years on the road, and launches his own new road band which includes his 2 sons.

1977 **Oct** Following Elvis Presley's death, he releases tribute single *The EP Express*, largely made up from titles of Presley hits.

1978 **Apr** In a brief deal with UK Jet label, Perkins records *Ol' Blue Suedes Is Back*, containing remakes of his early material, which is given TV promotion (and also supported by a tour), and reaches UK #38 – the only hit album of his career.

1981 **Apr** [23] Perkins, Johnny Cash and Jerry Lee Lewis record a joint session in Stuttgart, Germany, which will result in *The Survivors* (a reference to the Dec.1956 "Million Dollar Quartet" session).
Paul McCartney invites Perkins to the sessions for his *Tug Of War*, writing one song, *Get It*, as a duet for the pair.

1985 **Feb** Perkins appears as Mr. Williams, a nightclub bouncer, in John Landis' film "Into The Night".

Mar He cuts a new version of *Blue Suede Shoes* for the soundtrack of film "Porky's Revenge", backed by Lee Rocker and Slim Jim Phantom of The Stray Cats.

Oct [21] At Limehouse studios, London, a TV special is taped to mark the 30th anniversary of *Blue Suede Shoes*. It consists of a performance by "Carl Perkins And Friends", the latter including George Harrison, Ringo Starr, Eric Clapton, Dave Edmunds (who co-ordinates the band and music), and The Stray Cats' Rocker and Phantom.

1986 **Jan** [1] "Blue Suede Shoes" TV special has its first showing, on UK Channel 4 TV. (It will also be released as a home video.)

Dec [1] A Coca-Cola commemorative bottle goes on sale in Perkins' hometown of Jackson, MS, at $10 apiece. Proceeds go to the Carl Perkins Child Abuse Center, founded in 1982.

1987 **Jan** [21] Perkins is inducted into the Rock'N'Roll Hall Of Fame at the annual ceremonies at the Waldorf Astoria, New York.

1989 **Aug** [10] TBS TV airs "Coming Home – A Rockin' Reunion" filmed in 1985 as the class of 55 reunion with Roy Orbison, Jerry Lee Lewis and Johnny Cash. (Perkins continues to tour regularly with his sons Greg and Stan in his backing band.)

THE PET SHOP BOYS

Neil Tennant (vocals)
Chris Lowe (keyboards)

1981 **Aug** Tennant (b. Neil Francis Tennant, July 10, 1954, Gosforth, Tyne & Wear), who has already been in Newcastle-based folk outfit Dust and has a degree in history, is assistant editor of UK pop magazine **Smash Hits**, having already worked as editor for hero comic publishers Marvel when, in a hi-fi shop in London's King's Road, he meets Lowe (b. Christopher Sean Lowe, Oct.4, 1959, Blackpool, Lancs.), son of a jazz trombonist, who has been in 7-piece band One Under The Eight, where he learned keyboards, but is studying architecture at Liverpool University. They write songs and record demos for 2 years, naming themselves The Pet Shop Boys after friends who worked in an Ealing pet shop.

1983 **Aug** On assignment to interview Sting for **Smash Hits** in New York, Tennant meets long-time hero, disco producer Bobby "O" Orlando, who offers to produce them.

1984 **June** Orlando-produced debut *West End Girls* becomes a cult success in France and Belgium but its UK release on Epic goes unnoticed and the duo is dropped.

Nov They sign with manager Tom Watkins.

1985 **Feb** After competitive bidding over new demos, EMI signs the duo to its Parlophone label.

July *Opportunities (Let's Make Lots Of Money)* fails to chart despite strong airplay.

Aug Duo makes its first live appearance at the ICA, London, being interviewed by Max Headroom.

Oct Re-recorded version of *West End Girls*, now produced by Stephen Hague, is released and takes 3 months to make Top 10 breakthrough.

1986 **Jan** [11] *West End Girls* tops UK chart for 2 weeks, knocking Shakin' Stevens' *Merry Christmas Everyone* from the top, selling 700,000 copies in the UK.

Apr Debut album synthesizer-dominated *Please*, produced by Hague, hits UK #3 while *Love Comes Quickly* makes UK #19.

May Remixed *Opportunities (Let's Make Lots Of Money)* is re-released and reaches UK #11.

[10] *West End Girls* soars to US #1 and is a #1 hit in 8 countries.

Aug Despite pressure from the public, press and record company, the group refuses to tour anywhere, a policy it will maintain for 3 years.

[2] *Opportunities (Let's Make Lots Of Money)* hits US #10, as *Please* hits US #7.

Sept Extracted from it, fourth single *Suburbia* hits UK #8.

Oct [4] *Love Comes Quickly* stalls at US #62.

Nov 6 special 12"-mixes of hits from *Please* are repackaged as UK mini-album *Disco*, which reaches UK #15.

1987 **Jan** A video collection of promo clips, "Television", tops UK Music Video chart. *Disco* makes US #95.

[24] *Suburbia* makes US #70.

Feb [9] *West End Girls* is voted Best Single Of The Year at the sixth annual BRIT Awards at the Grosvenor House, Mayfair, London. Tennant receives their award from Boy George, while traditionally shy-boy Lowe watches the show from home on TV.

Apr [15] *West End Girls* is named International Hit Of The Year at the annual Ivor Novello Awards at London's Grosvenor House, Mayfair.

June After 6 months' writing and recording an album, the duo release synth-swept melodramatic hi-nrg-tinged *It's A Sin* which tops UK chart and will go on to similar success worldwide.

Aug [14] Duo performs a cover version of *Always On My Mind* on ITV special "Love Me Tender", marking the 10th anniversary of Elvis Presley's death.

A collaboration with Dusty Springfield on 3-year old Tennant/Lowe composition *What Have I Done To Deserve This?*, produced by Hague, hits UK #2.

Sept *Actually* hits UK #2, at the beginning of a 59-week multi-platinum chart tenure.

Oct *Rent*, The Pet Shop Boys' fifth UK Top 10, hits #8 while they spend 2 weeks promoting it in Japan.

Nov [14] *It's A Sin* hits US #9 as *Actually* climbs to US #25.

Dec *Always On My Mind* is finally released as a single. It is the duo's first non-original single and becomes UK Christmas #1.

1988 **Jan** Duo writes and produces Eighth Wonder's debut single *I'm Not Scared*. Led by vocalist Patsy Kensit, it will hit UK #7 in Feb.

Feb [8] The Pet Shop Boys win Best British Group at the seventh annual BRIT Awards at the Grosvenor House. Dusty Springfield joins them to sing *What Have I Done To Deserve This?* live at the ceremony.

[20] *What Have I Done To Deserve This?* hits US #2.

It's A Sin is named International Hit Of The Year at the annual Ivor Novello Awards lunch at the Grosvenor House.

Apr *Heart* tops UK chart.

May *Always On My Mind* hits US #4. Repackaged US version of *Actually* is issued in UK, with previously omitted *Always On My Mind*.

June They appear live in a benefit concert at the Piccadilly theater, London, after being persuaded by actor Ian McKellen.

July A Pet Shop Boys feature film, "It Couldn't Happen Here", co-starring Joss Ackland, Neil Dickson, Barbara Windsor and Gareth Hunt, is released in UK, but interest is short-lived.

Sept *Domino Dancing* hits UK #7, and is followed by 6-track album *Introspective* containing their own version of *I'm Not Scared*, a Frankie Knuckles house mix of *I Want A Dog*, a new version of *Always On My Mind* and 2 tracks produced by Trevor Horn.

Oct Duo appears on TV's "Wogan" to promote *Domino Dancing*.

[22] *Introspective* hits UK #2 at beginning of 39-week chart stay.

Nov Horn-charged *Left To My Own Devices* hits UK #4, as recent promo clips video collection "Showbusiness" hits best seller video lists.

1989 **Feb** A second collaboration with Dusty Springfield produces *Nothing Has Been Proved*. Used over the end titles of the film "Scandal", it reaches UK #16 for the 60s star.

[4] *Left To My Own Devices* stalls at US #84.

June [29] The Pet Shop Boys embark on their first tour, taking in Hong Kong, Japan and UK. Admittedly nervous about the venture, their performances, prominently featuring a number of visual art enhancements, are well achieved.

July The duo's *It's Alright* hits UK #5.

Aug They produce Liza Minnelli's *Losing My Mind*, which gives her a UK chart debut, hitting #6. (2 minor hits will follow from this liaison, *Don't Drop Bombs* and *So Sorry I Said*, and *Results*, which hits UK #6.)

Dec Tennant teams up with New Order's Bernard Sumner and ex-Smiths guitarist Johnny Marr to form Electronic. The combo's debut *Getting Away With It* reaches UK #12.

1990 **May** [19] *Getting Away With It* makes US #38.

July [7] Dusty Springfield's *Reputation*, which features *Nothing Has Been Proved* and 4 other tracks produced by The Pet Shop Boys and Julian Mendelsohn, reaches UK #18.

Aug Tennant and Lowe make their US debut guesting on 2 songs during an Electronic concert at Dodgers stadium, Los Angeles, CA, supporting Depeche Mode.

Oct [6] *So Hard*, from forthcoming *Behavior*, hits UK #4 in its first week on the chart.

Nov [3] *Behavior*, co-produced with Harold Faltermeyer, hits UK #2, unable to dislodge Paul Simon's *The Rhythm Of The Saints*.
The Pet Shop Boys play their first ever US gig at the Mayan club, Los Angeles, CA.
[24] *So Hard* stalls at US #62, in the same week that parent album *Behavior* reaches its US peak #45.

Dec [1] *Being Boring* reaches UK #20, despite highly physical semi-naked model-starring black and white video.

1991 Feb [23] *How Can You Expect To Be Taken Seriously?* stalls at US #93.

Mar [19] 17-date North American tour opens at the James L. Knight Center in Miami, FL, set to end Apr.14 in Massey Hall, Toronto, Canada.
[30] *Where The Streets Have No Name/Can't Take My Eyes Off You*, an uptempo Euro-disco coupling of the U2 song with the Frankie Valli 1967 US #2, hits UK #4, issued as a double A-side with *How Can You Expect To Be Taken Seriously?*

June [8-9] The Pet Shop Boys close short UK tour with 2 nights at the Wembley Arena, London.

PETER AND GORDON

Peter Asher (vocals)
Gordon Waller (vocals)

1959 Asher (b. June 22, 1944, London) and Waller (b. June 4, 1945, Braemar, Scotland), boths sons of doctors, meet at Westminster boys' school and are part of a quasi-Shadows trio, playing school events and coffee bars.

1964 Jan EMI's A&R chief Norman Newell hears them during a 2-week booking at London's Pickwick club. They are summoned to EMI to record one of their own compositions, *If I Were You*.
[21] Inviting Paul McCartney, then Asher's sister Jane's boyfriend, to help finish a song he had started, the duo rushes to record it at EMI.

Mar *A World Without Love* enters UK chart and gives the duo a #1 debut with 2 weeks in the top slot.

May *A World Without Love* hits US #1 and tops charts in 9 other countries.

June *Nobody I Know*, written by McCartney, hits UK #10 and US #12. *A World Without Love* reaches US #21.
[19] The duo begins US tour at New York's World Fair.

July [5] Tour ends in Honolulu, HI.

Aug *Peter And Gordon* makes UK #18. EP *Just For You* makes UK #20.

Sept Second EP *Nobody I Know* is released.

Oct *I Don't Want To See You Again* reaches US #16. Also a McCartney composition, it fails to make UK Top 50.

Nov Peter And Gordon appear on "The Ed Sullivan Show".

Dec *In Touch With Peter And Gordon* is released in UK. *I Don't Want To See You Again* makes US #95.

1965 Jan [7] The duo flies to South Africa for tour amidst harsh criticism from the Musicians' Union.

Feb *I Go To Pieces*, given to them by Del Shannon while on tour together in Australia, hits US #9 but has no UK success.

Apr *True Love Ways* hits UK #2 but only US #14. *I Go To Pieces* is released in US and climbs to #51.

July *To Know You Is To Love You* hits UK #5 and peaks at US #24. *True Love Ways*, released in US only, makes #49.
[2] They headline Dick Clark's "Caravan Of Stars" tour throughout the US. (Tour will end Sept.6.)

Oct *Hurtin' 'N' Lovin'* is released.
[22] The duo embarks on 28-date twice-nightly UK package tour, with headliner Gene Pitney, Lulu & The Luvvers, The Rockin' Berries and others, at Finsbury Park Astoria, London. (The tour will end Nov.21 at the Odeon cinema, Leeds, W.Yorks.)

Nov Van McCoy song *Baby I'm Yours* reaches UK #19. A Barbara Lewis #11 hit 3 months earlier in US, it is flipside of *Don't Pity Me*, which stalls at UK #83.

Dec [15] They fly to Nashville, TN, to cut a country and western album, before flying to New York to begin tour with Murray The K.
[24] Murray The K's "Christmas Show" opens at New York's Brooklyn Fox theater.

1966 Feb US-only *Peter And Gordon Sing And Play The Hits Of Nashville* is released.

Mar The duo releases *Woman*. Paul McCartney, growing tired of people assuming his songs are only hits because he has written them, pens the song as Parisian student Bernard Webb. It reaches UK #28. In US, McCartney adds co-writing credit of A. Smith. It reaches US #14. *Woman*, released in US only, peaks at #60.

Apr The duo appears on final episode of NBC TV's "Hullaballoo". *There's No Living Without Your Love* charts only in US, at #40.

June *Don't Pity Me* is released in UK without success. *Peter And Gordon* is released.

July *The Best Of Peter And Gordon* is released in US making #72, while *To Show I Love You* reaches US #98.

Oct *Lady Godiva* reaches UK #16, despite being banned in Lady Godiva's hometown of Coventry, W.Midlands, and being branded obscene by the city's mayor.

Nov *Lady Godiva* climbs to US #6. Its sales will total a million by 1967, the duo's fourth million-seller.

Dec *Somewhere ...* is released.

1967 Jan *Knight In Rusty Armour* reaches US #15, as *Lady Godiva* makes US #80.
[7] Duo guests on first edition of ABC TV's "Doddy's Music Box".

Feb Peter And Gordon announce that they are splitting as a full-time act, although they will continue to record together from time to time.

Mar *Knight In Rusty Armour* is released in US.

Apr *Sunday For Tea* makes US #31 and *The Jokers* makes US #97. They are the duo's final US chart entries and neither charts in UK.

May [15] Waller plays a disk-jockey in BBC2 TV play "The Fantastist".

June *In London For Tea* is released in US. Waller releases a US solo single *Speak For Me*.

1968 Jan Waller releases a solo cover of Jim Webb's *Rosecrans Boulevard*.

June Waller's *Every Day* will be followed at Christmas by *Weeping Analeah*, but both fail to chart.

Aug *You've Had Better Times*, released in UK in July, is the duo's last US single release. *Hot, Cold And Custard* is released in US.

Sept The duo splits finally. Asher becomes A&R manager at The Beatles' Apple Records; Waller pursues a solo career.

Dec James Taylor's eponymous debut album is released, produced by Asher. Asher leaves Apple to develop his career as producer and manager (starting with James Taylor in the 60s, through a host of artists in the 70s, most notably Linda Ronstadt, and is still producing and managing acts in the 80s, including 10,000 Maniacs and Randy Newman). Waller releases a second US solo single *Every Day*.

1969 Apr Waller signs to Bell, releasing *I Was A Boy When You Needed A Man*. Like its 3 predecessors on Columbia, it fails to chart.

May *I Can Remember (Not Too Long Ago)* is the duo's final UK release.

1970 May Waller's *You're Only Gonna Hurt Yourself* is his final single release.

1972 Apr Waller's only solo album *Gordon* is released. (It will be prefixed *... And Gordon* when released in US in May.)

1973 May Waller is cast as Pharaoh in the London production of Tim Rice and Andrew Lloyd Webber's musical "Joseph And His Amazing Technicolor Dreamcoat".

1978 Feb [23] Asher wins Producer Of The Year at the 20th annual Grammy awards.

1990 Feb [21] Asher wins his second Producer Of The Year award at the 32nd Grammy awards at the Shrine Auditorium, Los Angeles.

TOM PETTY & THE HEARTBREAKERS

Tom Petty (vocals, guitar)
Mike Campbell (guitar)
Howard Epstein (bass)
Benmont Tench (keyboards)
Stan Lynch (drums)

1968 Petty (b. Oct.20, 1953, Gainesville, FL) inspired by Elvis Presley whom he saw filming "Follow That Dream" on location in Ocala, FL, near his Gainesville home at age 7, having formed his first band The Sundowners (name-changing to The Epics), with 3 schoolfriends, graduates from Gainesville high school.

1971 Now calling themselves Mudcrutch, the band, comprising Petty (bass, guitar), Tommy Leadon, brother of Eagle Bernie Leadon (lead guitar), Campbell (b. Feb.1, 1954, Panama City, FL) (guitar) and Randall Marsh (drums), makes its first recordings, financed by Gerald Maddox (a bell pepper farmer from Bushnell, FL), at Criteria studios, Miami, FL, with producer Ron Albert.

1973 Petty takes a Mudcrutch demo tape to Los Angeles, CA, and finds interest from 7 record labels, including Denny Cordell's Shelter Records, which signs the band.

1975 The only Mudcrutch single, *Depot Street*, is released but after moving to Los Angeles and recording an album for Shelter, the band breaks up. (The album is not released.) Cordell retains Petty on Shelter and suggests working solo, but he forms new back-up band The Heartbreakers, with ex-Mudcrutch members Campbell and Tench (b. Sept.7, 1954, Gainesville) and recruiting Ron Blair (b. Sept.16, 1952, Macon, GA) and Jeff Jourard, both playing in Gainesville band RGF and Lynch (b. May 21, 1955, Gainesville), drummer with another Gainesville band, Road Turkey. (With a surfeit of guitarists, Jourard will soon leave and form The Motels with brother Marty.)

1976 **Nov** Debut album *Tom Petty And The Heartbreakers* is released, but initially sells poorly (only 6,500 after 3 months).

1977 **May** Petty's song *American Girl* is recorded by ex-Byrds member Roger McGuinn (another of Petty's early influences). The group works hard on the road to promote itself and the debut album (playing over 200 dates around US, Europe and UK). First notable sales are in UK.
June *Tom Petty And The Heartbreakers* reaches UK #24.
July *Anything That's Rock'N'Roll*, from the album, makes UK #36.
Aug *American Girl*, also from the album, makes UK #40.

1978 **Feb** A further album extract, *Breakdown*, is the group's US chart debut at #40, while debut album *Tom Petty And The Heartbreakers*, having entered the chart in Sept., makes US #55.
May Group appears in movie "FM", about a California radio station. Petty track *Breakdown* is included on the soundtrack album, which hits US #5 and makes UK #37.
July Second album, *You're Gonna Get It!* reaches UK #34.
Aug *You're Gonna Get It!* makes US #23 and earns Petty's first gold disk. Extracted *I Need To Know* peaks at US #41.
Oct *Listen To Her Heart* reaches US #59.

1979 **May** [23] Petty files for Chapter 11 Bankruptcy (the right to work out a reorganization of his debts). (This has partly arisen out of a record company dispute: Shelter has been sold to ABC, which has now been bought by MCA Records, and Petty is said to owe MCA $575,000, which will only be automatically repaid if he remains one of its acts and cuts 6 further albums. MCA sues for breach of contract but the bankruptcy declaration, revealing assets of only $56,000 causes the suit to be withdrawn as pointless. A solution is reached via establishment of new MCA-controlled label, Backstreet Records, to be run by Danny Bramson and devoted wholly to Petty & The Heartbreakers.)
Sept Petty hands over the tapes for a new album and tours US under the banner "Why MCA?"
[19-23] Band plays the Musicians United For Safe Energy (MUSE) anti-nuclear concerts at New York's Madison Square Garden alongside Bruce Springsteen, Jackson Browne, Carly Simon, The Doobie Brothers and others.
Nov *Damn The Torpedoes* peaks at UK #57.

1980 **Feb** *Don't Do Me Like That* hits US #10, while parent album *Damn The Torpedoes* hits US #2 for 7 weeks (behind Pink Floyd's *The Wall*), earning Petty his first platinum disk.
Mar *Refugee*, from the album, reaches US #15.
May Third extract, *Here Comes My Girl*, peaks at US #59.

1981 **May** *Hard Promises* makes UK #32. Petty has initially withheld the tapes for this, until MCA agrees not to implement a proposed $1 price rise to $9.98 on the US release. Petty, whose sales have accounted for almost 25% of MCA's 1980 profits, has accused the label of greed, and it backs down.
June *The Waiting* reaches US #19 as parent album *Hard Promises* hits US #5, Petty' second platinum disk.
Aug *A Woman In Love (It's Not Me)* peaks at US #79.
Sept Stevie Nicks' *Stop Draggin' My Heart Around* with Petty & The Heartbreakers backing her, hits US #3 and makes UK #50.

1982 Blair, tired of touring, leaves, to be replaced by Howard Epstein, who has played in John Hiatt's band and toured with Del Shannon.
June [6] Petty plays "Peace Sunday: We Have A Dream", an anti-nuclear concert to launch Peace week, at the Rose Bowl, Pasadena, CA. Also on the bill are Bob Dylan, Jackson Browne, Stevie Wonder and many more.
Sept [1] Epstein makes his live debut with The Heartbreakers at the Santa Cruz Auditorium, CA.
[5] Petty plays the US Festival in San Bernadino, CA, alongside Fleetwood Mac, The Police, Talking Heads and a host of others.
Nov *Long After Dark* makes UK #45.

1983 **Jan** *Long After Dark* hits US #9 (earning a gold disk), while extracted *You Got Lucky* reaches US #20.

Apr *Change Of Heart*, also from *Long After Dark*, makes US #21.
May Del Shannon releases *Drop Down And Get Me*, produced by Petty and backed by The Heartbreakers.

1985 **Apr** *Southern Accents*, co-produced by Petty, Jimmy Iovine and Dave Stewart of Eurythmics, reaches UK #23. *Don't Come Around Here No More*, taken from it and written with Stewart, makes UK #50.
May *Southern Accents* hits US #7, earning another gold disk, while *Don't Come Around Here No More* reaches US #13.
July [6] *Make It Better (Forget About Me)* peaks at US #54.
[13] Petty & The Heartbreakers play Live Aid in Philadelphia, PA.
Sept [7] *Rebels* peaks at US #74.
[22] Petty plays Farm Aid in US.

1986 **Feb** Group tours Australia, New Zealand and Japan, backing Dylan, as double live album *Pack Up The Plantation* reaches US #22.
Mar [1] *Needles And Pins*, with Stevie Nicks, makes US #37. Meanwhile, Dylan, with Petty & The Heartbreakers backing, releases *Band Of The Hand* (theme song to movie of the same title) on MCA.
June Petty begins 40-date US "True Confessions" tour with Dylan, preceded by a major concert for Amnesty International.

1987 **Mar** [4] Petty obtains a restraining order against the B.F.Goodrich Tire Company from using a song similar to Petty's *Mary's New Car*.
May [17] Fire destroys Petty's house in Los Angeles (damage is estimated at $800,000).
Let Me Up (I've Had Enough) peaks at UK #59.
June [20] *Jammin' Me* reaches US #18.
July *Let Me Up (I've Had Enough)* reaches US #20.
Oct Petty & The Heartbreakers open a tour with Dylan in Israel, moving to Europe and UK.

1988 **Nov** Petty joins George Harrison, Bob Dylan, Roy Orbison and Jeff Lynne of ELO as The Traveling Wilburys. Their eponymous album climbs the charts in both US and UK, as does extracted *Handle With Care*. Lynne co-produces new Petty album *Songs From The Garage*, with contributions from Harrison and Orbison.
Dec [12] Petty attends a memorial for Roy Orbison, with Don Henley, Graham Nash, Bonnie Raitt and others.

1989 **May** *I Won't Back Down*, first single from forthcoming album *Full Moon Fever*, reaches UK #28.
July *Full Moon Fever*, credited as a Petty solo album, although The Heartbreakers play on most tracks, hits UK #8 while *I Won't Back Down* reaches US #12.
[5] Petty begins 44-date US tour at Miami Arena, FL.
[6] On second night of the tour at Bayfront Center, St. Petersburg, FL, Petty is joined on stage by Roger McGuinn for 4 Byrds's numbers.
Aug *Runnin' Down A Dream* peaks at UK #55.
Sept [23] *Runnin' Down A Dream* reaches US #23.
Nov *Free Fallin'* peaks at UK #64.

1990 **Jan** [27] *Free Fallin'* hits US #7.
Mar [1] During a concert at Great Western Forum in Ingelwood, CA, Pety is joined on stage by Dylan and Springsteen, singing Creedence Clearwater Revival's *Travelin' Band* and The Animals' *I'm Crying*.
[24] *A Face In The Crowd* makes US #46.

1991 **Feb** Petty contributes to The Peace Choir's *Give Peace A Chance*.

WILSON PICKETT

1961 Pickett (b. Mar.18, 1941, Prattville, AL), having moved to Detroit as a teenager in 1955, has sung in gospel groups, before joining R&B band The Falcons (veterans of 1959 US #17 hit *You're So Fine*) after he is heard singing and playing his guitar on the front porch of his home.

1962 **May** The Falcons' *I Found A Love*, with Pickett on lead vocal, reaches US #75.

1963 **May** Falcons producer Robert Bateman suggests that Pickett should go solo and arranges an audition with singer Lloyd Price, owner of Double L label. Price signs him, and *If You Need Me*, a Bateman/Pickett composition, peaks at US #64 (a cover by better-known Solomon Burke makes US #37).
Sept *It's Too Late*, his second on Double L, makes US #49.
Nov *I'm Down To My Last Heartbreak*, also on Double L, makes US #96.

1965 **May** Atlantic Records buys Pickett's contract and after 2 unsuccessful releases (*I'm Gonna Cry* and *Come Home Baby*), producer Jerry Wexler records him at Stax studio, Memphis, TN, with Booker T. & The MG's.
Sept *In The Midnight Hour*, co-written by Pickett with MG's guitarist Steve Cropper, reaches US #21. It becomes a much-covered soul classic and Pickett gains the nickname "The Wicked Pickett" at Atlantic (often used in his publicity) – supposedly because of his interest in the ladies at the record company.

Oct *In The Midnight Hour* is his UK chart debut, at #12.

Nov [9] Pickett makes his live debut in UK at Scotch of St. James club in London. (3 members of The Animals back him.) He then embarks on a 17-date UK tour.

Dec *Don't Fight It* makes US #53 and UK #29, while *In The Midnight Hour* climbs to US #107.

966 Jan *634-5789* reaches US #13 and UK #36, and is Pickett's first US R&B #1 (for 7 weeks).

Mar Pickett begins his second UK tour, causing a sensation among the burgeoning UK mod and R&B audience.

July Staying with numbers for titles, *Ninety Nine And A Half (Won't Do)* makes US #53.

Sept Recorded at Muscle Shoals studios, AL, Pickett's revival of Chris Kenner's *Land Of 1,000 Dances* (also a 1965 US Top 20 for Cannibal & The Headhunters) is the only Top 10 hit of this much-covered song, at US #6. It climbs to UK #22.

Oct *The Exciting Wilson Pickett* reaches US #21.

Dec *Mustang Sally*, written by Mack Rice (ex-The Falcons) peaks at US #23 and UK #28.

967 Mar *The Wicked Pickett* makes US #42, while his revival of Solomon Burke's *Everybody Needs Somebody To Love* reaches US #29.

[28] Pickett participates in Murray the K's Easter Show "Music In The 5th Dimension" at Manhattan RKO Theater, New York (ending Apr.2).

Apr Pickett records a solo version of his Falcons success *I Found A Love*, which makes US #32.

July US radio airplay is divided on double-sided *Soul Dance Number Three/You Can't Stand Alone* which peaks at US #55/#70.

Sept Pickett's cover of Dyke & The Blazers' *Funky Broadway* (a minor hit in the spring) hits US #8 and R&B #1 (for 1 week). *The Sound Of Wilson Pickett*, containing the hit, reaches US #54.

Oct *Funky Broadway* makes UK #43.

Nov A revival of former mentor Price's million-seller *Stag-O-Lee* reaches US #22, but is replaced by radio DJs playing B-side *I'm In Love*, which climbs to US #45. These are among several tracks cut at renewed sessions in Memphis, in partnership with Bobby Womack.

Dec *The Best Of Wilson Pickett*, a compilation of hit singles to date, peaks at US #35 (in a year-long chart run).

968 Mar *Jealous Love* makes US #50, while *I'm In Love* reaches US #70.

May *She's Lookin' Good* reaches US #15.

July *I'm A Midnight Mover*, in *Midnight Hour* style, makes US #24.

Aug *The Midnight Mover* peaks at US #91.

Oct *I Found A True Love* (not to be confused with *I Found A Love*) makes US #42, while *I'm A Midnight Mover* makes UK #38 (after a year's absence on UK chart).

Dec *A Man And A Half* makes US #42.

969 Jan Recording at Muscle Shoals again, Pickett covers The Beatles' *Hey Jude* (at the suggestion of Duane Allman of The Allman Brothers, who plays guitar on it), and it reaches US #23 while the original version is still on chart. It climbs to UK #16 (and is Pickett's final UK chart entry).

Apr *Hey Jude* peaks at US #97 and *Minnie Skirt Minnie* makes US #50.

970 May Pickett's rock cover (again with Duane Allman) of Steppenwolf's *Born To Be Wild* peaks at US #64.

June A cover of The Archies' *Sugar Sugar*, double A-side with tribute song *Cole, Cooke And Redding*, reaches US #25.

Aug A further rock cover, *Hey Joe*, peaks at US #59, but follow-up, a revival of *You Keep Me Hanging On*, makes only US #92.

Nov Recorded in Philadelphia, PA, with producers Kenny Gamble and Leon Huff and with a sharp new Pickett sound on original material, *(Get Me Back On Time) Engine Number 9* reaches US #14 (and R&B #3). From these sessions, *Wilson Pickett In Philadelphia*, makes US #64.

971 Mar Another Philadelphia production, *Don't Let The Green Grass Fool You*, reaches US #17 (and R&B #2), and is his first certified million-selling single.

Apr Pickett headlines with other artists on a tour of Ghana, Africa, to celebrate the country's independence. (He features prominently in the movie and album of the event, *Soul To Soul*.)

June *Don't Knock My Love, Pt 1*, recorded with Brad Shapiro and Dave Crawford in Miami, FL, reaches US #13, and is Pickett's second million-seller.

July Compilation *The Best Of Wilson Pickett, Vol.II* reaches US #73.

Sept *Call My Name, I'll Be There* peaks at US #52.

972 Feb A cover of UK band Free's *Fire And Water* reaches US #24, while *Don't Knock My Love* makes #132.

July *Funk Factory* peaks at US #58.

Nov Pickett's revival of Randy Newman song (and Three Dog Night million-seller) *Mama Told Me Not To Come*, charts briefly at US #99, after

which Pickett and Atlantic Records part company.

1973 Apr Pickett signs to RCA, with *Mr. Magic Man* managing a week at US #98, while album of the same title makes US #187.

Oct *Take A Closer Look At The Woman You're With* makes US #90 (Pickett's last US Top 100 entry). (3 albums and many singles follow on RCA in the next 3 years, none of them successful - but *Pickett In The Pocket*, another Pickett/Shapiro Miami production, is critically rated.)

1974 Nov [21] Pickett is arrested in Andes, New York, for possession of a dangerous weapon, after he pulls a gun during an argument. Frequently temperamental, especially when indulging his appetite for alcohol, Pickett has an offstage reputation to match his fiery passion while performing.

1978 Pickett makes widely vocal his contempt for the disco explosion, for its emasculation of the traditional soul style. He attempts to blend artistic preference with commercial necessity on *A Funky Situation*, produced by Rick Hall in Muscle Shoals, but it finds few sales.

1979 Pickett signs to EMI America (which will release 2 unsuccessful disco-influenced albums, *I Want You* and *The Right Track*). He is more successful on US live circuit, reverting to his best-known material, and often touring with "The Soul Clan", an aggregation of his 60s contemporaries like Eddie Floyd, Don Covay and Joe Tex.

1988 Oct Pickett signs to Motown, cutting a new version of *In The Midnight Hour*, which reaches UK #62, and *American Soul Man*.

1991 Jan [16] Pickett is inducted into the Rock'N'Roll Hall Of Fame at the annual ceremonies held at the Waldorf Astoria in New York.

PINK FLOYD

Roger Waters (vocals, bass)
Rick Wright (keyboards)
David Gilmour (vocals, guitar)
Nick Mason (drums)

1965 Waters (b. Sept.9, 1944, Great Bookham, Cambs.), Wright (b. July 28, 1945, London) and Mason (b. Jan.27, 1945, Birmingham, W.Midlands) meet as students at Regent Street polytechnic in London. They are members of various college bands. Waters invites friend Syd Barrett (b. Roger Barrett, Jan.6, 1946, Cambridge, Cambs.) to join the trio in a new band, which Barrett names Pink Floyd after Georgia bluesmen Pink Anderson and Floyd Council. Late in the year the group plays its first gig, a mix of R&B and 12-bar blues, at the Countdown club in London.

1966 Mar London's Marquee club begins the "Spontaneous Underground", a Sunday afternoon psychedelic groove with Pink Floyd as regulars. Group drops its blues sound and begins playing extended musical numbers with Barrett writing the material. It quickly becomes the hippest band among London's early psychedelic set and experiments with feedback and electronic sound with back-projected film shows and lights.

Dec Group's reputation for experimentation and innovation continues with the establishment of the UFO club which becomes the focal point of British psychedelia. Despite the name, the club is an Irish dance hall on other nights, called the Blarney club, in a basement on London's Tottenham Court Road. Here the group verifies its future recorded sound with songs like *Interstellar Overdrive* and *Astronomie Domine*.

1967 Feb Pink Floyd records its first single *Arnold Layne*, but still has no record contract.

Mar EMI signs the group and purchases *Arnold Layne*. (Legend has it that when introduced to label executives, one asked "Which of you is "Pink?" – referred to on later album *Wish You Were Here*.)

[5] Group supports Lee Dorsey at London's Saville theater.

Apr *Arnold Layne* reaches UK #20. Surprisingly, despite the transvestite subject matter, BBC radio continues to play the record while pirate station, Radio London, bans it.

[29] Group takes part with other acts in 14-hour all-night "Technicolor Dream" concert in the Great Hall of Alexandra Palace, London.

May [29] Pink Floyd plays at "Barbeque '67" at the Tulip Bulb Auction Hall, Spalding, Lincs., with Jimi Hendrix, Cream, The Move, Geno Washington and Zoot Money.

July *See Emily Play* hits UK #6. British DJ Pete Murray describes the group as a "con" on BBC TV's "Juke Box Jury". They will not have another hit single for 12 years.

[29-30] They take part in an all-night "International Love-In" at Alexandra Palace, London with The Animals and others.

Aug Debut album *The Piper At The Gates Of Dawn* hits UK #6.

Nov Group visits US for first time. Barrett is developing LSD drug dependency. Interviewed on "The Pat Boone Show", he responds to questions with a blank stare. *Apples And Oranges* fails to chart.

1968 **Jan** Barrett's behavior causes concern, and Waters invites friend Dave Gilmour (b. Mar.6, 1947, Cambridge, Cambs.) to join the group, excusing Barrett from live appearances to concentrate on songwriting. Gilmour has been a member of local band Jokers Wild, who once appeared with The Pink Floyd Sound and Paul Simon.

Apr Barrett is asked to leave and group reverts to a 4-piece minus its main songwriter. (Barrett goes into immediate seclusion in Cambridge.) *It Would Be So Nice* is released.

June *A Saucerful Of Secrets* hits UK #9. Group plays the first-ever free concert in London's Hyde Park with Jethro Tull and Roy Harper.

Nov [14] Pink Floyd begins a 15-date twice-nightly UK package tour, with The Jimi Hendrix Experience, The Move, Amen Corner and The Nice among others, at the Royal Albert Hall, London, set to end Dec.5 at Green's Playhouse, Glasgow, Scotland.

Dec *Point Me At The Sky* is released.

1969 **July** Soundtrack of Barbet Schroeder's film "More" makes UK #9.

Aug [8] Group takes part in the 9th National Jazz, Pop, Ballads & Blues Festival at Plumpton Racecourse near Lewes, E.Sussex.

Oct Double-set *Ummagumma*, consisting of 1 record of live performances and the other contributions from each member of the group, hits UK #5.

Dec [6] Group plays at the Indoor Sports Centre, Port Talbot, Wales, with Fairport Convention, East Of Eden and Sam Apple Pie. Barrett is retained as a solo act by EMI's Harvest label, and *Octopus* is released as a first sample of his new material, but it is unsuccessful.

1970 **Jan** Barrett releases debut album *The Madcap Laughs*, with help from Gilmour and Waters. It reaches UK #40. *Ummagumma* makes US #74.

Feb [7] Group performs at the Royal Albert Hall, London, during a short UK tour.

Mar They contribute 3 songs on the soundtrack of Michaelangelo Antonioni's film "Zabriskie Point".

July [18] Pink Floyd gives a free concert in Hyde Park, London, with Edgar Broughton, Deep Purple, Third Ear and Formerly Fat Harry.

Oct *Atom Heart Mother* defines the sound which will elevate Pink Floyd to worldwide superstar status in the next decade. It becomes the group's first UK chart-topper but reaches only US #55. Waters' *Music From The Body*, created with his golfing partner Ron Geesin for a Roy Battersby documentary film "The Body", is released on Harvest.

Nov Barrett releases *Barrett*, but does no promotion for the album, staying in seclusion except when in the recording studio. It proves to be his swan song and he returns to his hometown of Cambridge to become a recluse, resisting all efforts by Pink Floyd members and others to step back into the limelight.

1971 **Aug** EMI releases budget-priced compilation album *Relics*. It contains first 2 singles which had been deleted and makes UK #32 and US #152.

Nov *Meddle* is released. Side 2 is taken up by *Echoes* which becomes a live favorite. The album hits UK #3, climbing to US #70. In a **Melody Maker** poll, the group is voted second in Best Group category. The winners are Emerson, Lake And Palmer.

1972 **Jan** 14-date "Tour '72" begins at the Dome, Brighton, E.Sussex, set to end with 3 nights at the Rainbow theater, Finsbury Park, London on Feb.17-19, premiering *Dark Side Of The Moon*.

Feb Barrett makes a brief reappearance in Stars, a Cambridge-based trio featuring Jack Monk (bass) and Twink (drums), but after 3 local appearances they split without recording, and Barrett becomes a recluse again. Renewed critical interest in him prompts EMI to reissue Barrett's 2 earlier albums as a double pack.

June Another soundtrack for Barbet Schroeder's film "Obscured By Clouds" hits UK #6 and becomes Pink Floyd's highest-charting album in US at #46.

Sept Film (made for European TV) "Pink Floyd Live At Pompeii" receives its premiere at the Edinburgh theater. (It is released in 1974 in the cinema.)

1973 **Mar** *Dark Side Of The Moon* is released, a concept project dealing with madness which has taken most of the previous year to record. Sound effects and music are molded into Pink Floyd's most commercial outing. It sells more than 13 million copies worldwide and is the group's first US #1 (and still on the **Billboard** chart in 1988, 736 weeks later). It reaches only UK #2 despite a 294-week chart run. (In the 80s CD boom, it is reported that there is a pressing plant in Germany that only produces *Dark Side Of The Moon* and no other CDs.) Group spends the rest of the year touring to perform the album in its entirety with an appropriately grandiose stage production.

July Extracted track *Money* is released in US (but not UK), making #13.

1974 **Jan** *A Nice Pair*, a re-package of their first 2 albums, makes UK #21 and US #36.

1975 **July** Group plays Knebworth Festival, Herts., and performs one of its most celebrated shows including real spitfire planes and quadrophonic sound.

Sept *Wish You Were Here* tops both UK and US charts. It contains a tribute to Syd Barrett, *Shine On You Crazy Diamond*, which is sung by Roy Harper. (Barrett visits the band in the studio while the album is made, but he is never again tempted from his self-induced seclusion into any active part in music.) Violinist Stephane Grappelli makes an uncredited contribution on the album.

1976 **Dec** Group makes headlines when film shoot for sleeve of *Animals* goes disastrously wrong. A 40' tall inflatable pig is moored above Battersea Power Station but breaks loose from its mooring. The Civil Aviation Authority issues a warning to all pilots in London airspace that a pig is on the loose. It is last sighted at 18,000' over Chatham, Kent, but is never seen again.

1977 **Feb** *Animals* hits UK #2 and US #3. Group spends the rest of the year touring with the "Animals" stage show.

1978 Group members concentrate on solo projects. Mason produces British punk band The Damned's second album *Music For Pleasure* and Steve Hillage's *Green*.

May Solo album *David Gilmour*, recorded with friends Willie Wilson and future Foreigner bassist Rick Wills, reaches UK #17 and subsequently US #29.

Nov Rick Wright debut solo, *Wet Dream* is released on Harvest.

Dec [9] Gilmour performs a solo set, although he names his studio trio as Bullit, on BBC TV's "The Old Grey Whistle Test".

1979 Despite enormous earnings, the group is in perilous financial state due to the collapse of investment company, Norton Warburg, which has handled its business affairs. Waters comes to the forefront as a writer, composing almost all of the group's forthcoming album *The Wall*.

Dec *The Wall* hits UK #3 and tops US chart for 15 weeks. Taken from it, *Another Brick In The Wall (Part II)* is UK Christmas #1, and will top the US chart in Jan.

1980 Group tours with a "Wall" show which explores the theme of the group's alienation from its audience. One of the most celebrated stage spectaculars in rock history, a 160' long, 30' high wall is built between group and audience and then ceremonially destroyed after the intermission. Due to its enormous financial outlay, the show is only performed 29 times and is a loss. Wright leaves the band after the tour due to personal differences with Waters.

Feb [7] US leg of "The Wall" tour begins.

May *Run Like Hell* makes US #53.

Aug Group plays 5 nights at Earls Court, London.

1981 **May** Mason's *Nick Mason's Fictitious Sport* collaboration with jazz singer Carla Bley featuring Robert Wyatt on vocals, makes US #170.

Dec Greatest hits collection *A Collection Of Great Dance Songs* makes UK #37 and US #31.

1982 Movie version of "The Wall", directed by Alan Parker and starring Bob Geldof, premieres.

Aug *When The Tigers Break Free* makes UK #39.

1983 **Apr** *The Final Cut* is released, giving the group its third UK #1 and hitting US #6. The album, co-produced with Michael Kamen, has an anti-war theme and is almost entirely the work of Waters.

May *Not Now John* makes UK #30. In a career spanning 16 years, it is only Pink Floyd's fifth UK hit. The division between Waters and the other 2 members proves divisive and they split acrimoniously.

1984 **Mar** Gilmour releases second solo album *About Face*, including lyrical contributions from Pete Townshend, making UK #21 and US #32.

[30] Gilmour makes a promotional appearance on Channel 4 TV's "The Tube", as a prelude to a solo world tour. He will include the popular Floyd classic *Money* in his repertoire.

Apr Recording with ex-Fashion frontman Dee Harris under collective name Zee, Wright releases *Identity*, on the day that Waters releases his first solo single *5.01 A.M. (The Pros And Cons Of Hitch-Hiking)*.

May Waters releases solo opus *The Pros And Cons Of Hitch Hiking*, featuring guests Eric Clapton, Ray Cooper, Michael Kamen and David Sanborn, which makes UK #13 and US #31. During the remainder of the year, Waters will tour extensively throughout the world playing 1 set of self-penned Floyd standards and a second half of solo material. With sets designed by Gerald Scarfe, visuals by film director Nicholas Roeg and a large backing band, including Clapton, and lacking Pink Floyd brand name, it proves a great personal financial strain.

Gilmour plays a variety of sessions including Bryan Ferry's *Bete Noire* Grace Jones' *Slave To The Rhythm* and Arcadia's *So Red The Rose*.

1985 **Sept** Second Mason album *Profiles* emerges, released simultaneously with a 30-min. autobiographical film "Life Could Be A Dream", an account of his double career as a drummer and a racing driver.

1986 **Feb** [6] Gilmour, fresh from a stint in Pete Townshend's solo project band Deep End, forms David Gilmour & Friends, with several Deep End members including Kamen, Simon Phillips and Bad Company's Mick Ralphs.
[9] They perform at the "Colombian Volcano Appeal" concert at the Royal Albert Hall, London, with Annie Lennox, Chrissie Hynde, Pete Townshend, Marillion, The Communards and Working Week.
Oct Increasingly isolated from the band, Waters releases *When The Wind Blows*, the soundtrack from Raymond Briggs/Jimmy Mukarami's movie length cartoon of the same name. The project, which mainly consists of performances by his current group, The Bleeding Heart Band, also includes David Bowie and other various artist tracks.
[31] Waters brings suit in the Chancery Division of the High Court in London, asking the court to dissolve the partnership and, as band leader and creator of the most successful Pink Floyd recordings, to block Gilmour and Mason from using the band name for future recording and touring.

1987 Gilmour and Mason reunite to record again. They decide their project should be under the Pink Floyd banner, but Waters claims in court they have no right to use the name. Wright returns to the band on a salary and band wins temporary rights against Waters to continue with name.
May [30] Waters' *Radio Waves* spends a week on UK chart at #74.
June *Radio K.A.O.S.* reaches UK #25 and US #50. During the subsequent world tour, with his Bleeding Heart Band, Waters installs temporary phone booths throughout concert halls enabling fans to call him on stage and make song requests. Each concert, often playing in direct competition to Gilmour's Pink Floyd sojourn, is previewed by a video film of Pink Floyd's 1967 standard, *Arnold Layne*.
Sept Group releases *A Momentary Lapse Of Reason* which hits UK and US #3. Extracted *Only Learning To Fly* is released on CD only in UK, but fails to chart.
[7] Despite threats to promoters from Waters that he will stop any shows given by Pink Floyd, "The Momentary Lapse Of Reason" world tour starts in Ottawa, Canada. (The 60-date tour will make $27,700,000.)
Oct [31] *Learning To Fly* peaks at US #70.
Nov [7] Waters' performance in Quebec, Canada, is recorded by Westwood One for later broadcast throughout North America.
[21] Waters' live concert at the Wembley Arena, London, is recorded for broadcast by Capital Radio next Apr.
Dec *On The Turning Away*, extracted from *A Momentary Lapse Of Reason*, peaks at UK #55.

1988 **Jan** Waters makes UK #54 with *The Tide Is Turning (After Live Aid)*.
May 20-min. Waters' video "Radio K.A.O.S." is released. (Waters is rumored to have recorded an anti-Pink Floyd song *Amused To Death*, but elects not to issue it.)
June *1 Slip*, from *A Momentary Lapse Of Reason*, makes UK #50.
Aug "The Momentary Lapse Of Reason" tour visits UK with sold-out dates at Wembley Stadium, London. At Manchester City Football Club's Maine Road ground concert, video cameras spy on the crowd to spot drug use. 9 arrests are made.
Sept Tour concludes at Nassau Coliseum, Uniondale, NY. In the 12 months on the road, the band has been seen by more than 10 million people at 155 concerts in 15 different countries, as a new generation of Pink Floyd fans tunes in to its music.
Dec *The Delicated Sound Of Thunder* reaches UK and US #11.

1989 **July** [22] Band plays a concert which is televised worldwide, on a giant barge moored off St. Mark's Basilica, Venice, Italy.

1990 **June** [30] Pink Floyd takes part in the Silver Clef award winners show at Knebworth Park, Herts., with Phil Collins, Paul McCartney, Status Quo, Tears For Fears and others.
July [21] An estimated 200,000 people attend Waters' most ambitious solo project to date, a complete performance of "The Wall" at the site of the Berlin Wall in Potzdamer Platz, Berlin, Germany. Highlighted by the destruction of an artificial wall during the concert, featured performers include Bryan Adams, The Band, James Galway, The Hooters, Cyndi Lauper, Ute Lemper, Joni Mitchell, Van Morrison, Sinead O'Connor, The Scorpions, Marianne Faithfull, actors Tim Curry and Albert Finney and long-time Floyd collaborator and ex-Thin Lizzy guitarist Snowy White. The event is broadcast live throughout the world, and raises money for the Leonard Cheshire-established Memorial Fund For Disaster Relief.
Aug *The Wall*, the original Floyd double set, re-enters UK survey, making #52 and US #120.
Sept Waters's *The Wall – Live In Berlin* reaches UK #27 and US #56. Recorded using state-of-the art technology, it is issued simultaneously with a same titled video.

GENE PITNEY

1959 Pitney (b. Gene Francis Pitney, Feb.17, 1941, Hartford, CT), having grown up in Rockville, CT, where he started writing songs while still at Rockville high school, makes his first single, self-penned *Classical Rock And Roll*, as half of duo Jamie & Jane, with Ginny Mazarro, on Decca.

1960 Regularly making demos of his songs and sending them to a New York music publisher, Pitney has his first cover, when The Kalin Twins (of *When* fame) record *Loneliness*.
Nov Pitney's *Today's Teardrops* is recorded by Roy Orbison as B-side of *Blue Angel*, which hits US #9.

1961 **Jan** His first Top 10 success as a writer is with *Rubber Ball*, recorded by Bobby Vee. The song is credited to "Orlowski" (his mother's maiden name) because of publishing complications.
Feb He quits Connecticut University, where he has been studying electronics, to concentrate on music. *(I Wanna) Love My Life Away*, recorded as a demo on 4-track equipment, with Pitney singing all parts and playing most of the instruments (and costing $30 – the session fee to the bass player), is placed with Musicor Records, distributed through United Artists. It is Pitney's US chart debut, reaching #39 after heavy promotion touring around radio and TV stations.
Apr *I Wanna Love My Life Away* reaches UK #26.
May Ricky Nelson has a US and UK Top 10 hit with Pitney's song *Hello Mary Lou*. (It will become one of his most revived songs.)
Sept Goffin/King song *Every Breath I Take*, co-produced at Bell Sound studios in New York by Phil Spector (part of a fully orchestral 4-song session costing an astronomical $13,000), makes US #42, and will be best remembered by its extended falsetto ending – a product of Pitney's heavy cold during the session.

1962 **Jan** *Town Without Pity*, the Ned Washington/Dmitri Tiomkin-penned theme from Kirk Douglas film of the same name, reaches US #13.
Feb [4] Pitney appears on UK TV show "Thank Your Lucky Stars", at the start of his first UK visit.
Mar *Town Without Pity* makes UK #32.
June *(The Man Who Shot) Liberty Valance*, written by Bacharach and David as theme to John Wayne/James Stewart western (but not used on soundtrack because film is released early without it), hits US #4.
Nov Another Bacharach/David song, *Only Love Can Break A Heart*, hits US #2, and is Pitney's first million-seller. It is kept from the top by his own composition *He's A Rebel*, given to Phil Spector for The Crystals. *Only Love*'s B-side, *If I Didn't Have A Dime (To Play The Jukebox)*, peaks at US #58.

1963 **Feb** *Only Love Can Break A Heart* reaches US #48, while *Half Heaven – Half Heartache*, co-written by Pitney's publisher Aaron Schroeder, reaches US #12.
May *Mecca* makes US #12, while *Gene Pitney Sings Just For You* peaks at US #85.
Aug *True Love Never Runs Smooth*, another Bacharach/David ballad, reaches US #21, while *World Wide Winners* climbs to US #41.
Dec *24 Hours From Tulsa* reaches US #17, as *Blue Gene* makes US #105.

1964 **Jan** Boosted by a UK promotional visit, in which Pitney appears widely on TV, Bacharach/David's *24 Hours From Tulsa* becomes his first major UK success, hitting UK #5. After returning to US because of illness, he visits UK again after the single is established on chart for a full UK tour.
Feb *That Girl Belongs To Yesterday*, written by The Rolling Stones' Keith Richard and Mick Jagger, makes US #49. (Pitney has met The Rolling Stones via their manager Andrew Oldham, who is also his UK publicist, and has been present at sessions for their first album and played piano on *Little By Little*.)
[29] Pitney embarks on 20-date twice-nightly UK tour, with Cilla Black, Billy J.Kramer & The Dakotas, The Swinging Blue Jeans and others, at Odeon cinema, Nottingham, Notts.
Mar [21] Tour ends at the Odeon cinema, Guildford, Surrey.
Apr *That Girl Belongs To Yesterday* hits UK #7, as does *Blue Gene*. Compilation *Gene Pitney's Big Sixteen* makes US #87.
May *Yesterday's Hero* peaks at US #64, and is not released in UK. (Its substitute *I'm Gonna Find Myself A Girl* fails to chart in UK.)
Oct *It Hurts To Be In Love* hits US #7 and makes UK #36.
Nov *It Hurts To Be In Love* climbs to US #42.
[7] Pitney begins a 26-date twice-nightly UK tour, with Gerry & The Pacemakers, The Kinks, Marianne Faithfull and others, at Granada cinema, Walthamstow, London (ending Dec.6 at the Futurist, Scarborough, N.Yorks.). During a concert in Birmingham, W.Midlands, his head is cut open by some castanets thrown by member of audience.
Dec *I'm Gonna Be Strong*, written by Barry Mann and Cynthia Weil,

hits US #9 and UK #2, held off the top by The Rolling Stones' *Little Red Rooster* and then The Beatles' *I Feel Fine*. It becomes one of his most celebrated records because of its falsetto final notes (which Pitney will always reproduce on stage).

1965 Feb Compilation *Gene Pitney's Big 16* reaches UK #12.
[5] Pitney arrives in UK for 3-day promotional visit, during which he appears on "Ready Steady Go!", "Top Of The Pops" "Juke Box Jury" and "Thank Your Lucky Stars".
Mar *I Must Be Seeing Things* makes US #31 and hits UK #6. *I'm Gonna Be Strong* reaches UK #15, while Nashville-recorded album of country songs duetted with George Jones, *George Jones And Gene Pitney*, makes US #141.
[8] Pitney begins a tour of Australia and New Zealand with Freddie & The Dreamers, ending Mar.25.
Apr *I've Got Five Dollars And It's Saturday Night*, a duet with Jones from the album, stalls at US #99.
June *Last Chance To Turn Around* reaches US #13.
July Another Mann/Weil song, *Looking Through The Eyes Of Love* (with B-side *Last Chance To Turn Around*) hits US #3. *I Must Be Seeing Things* makes US #112.
Aug *Looking Through The Eyes Of Love* makes US #28.
Sept *Looking Through The Eyes Of Love* climbs to US #43 and heads for UK #15.
Oct [17] Pitney appears on UK TV show "Sunday Night At The London Palladium".
[22] He begins a 28-date twice-nightly UK package tour, with Lulu & The Luvvers, Peter And Gordon, The Rockin' Berries and others at London's Finsbury Park Astoria, ending at Odeon cinema, Leeds, W.Yorks., on Nov.21.
Dec *Princess In Rags* makes US #37 and hits UK #9.
1966 Jan Pitney comes second in the San Remo Song Contest in Italy, with *Nessuno Mi Puo Guidicare*.
Feb [12] Pitney begins 14-date twice-nightly UK tour with Dave Dee, Dozy, Beaky, Mick and Tich, Len Barry and others, at Gaumont cinema, Ipswich, Suffolk (ending Feb.27 at ABC cinema, Southampton, Hants).
Mar *Backstage* hits UK #4, as compilation *Big Sixteen, Volume 3* climbs to US #123.
May *Backstage* reaches US #25. A film role is mooted for Pitney in movie "Sweet Wind Of Spring", but Italian-based production does not materialize.
July Having failed to chart in US, *Nobody Needs Your Love*, written by Randy Newman, hits UK #2, behind The Kinks' *Sunny Afternoon*.
Oct *Nobody Needs Your Love* reaches UK #13.
Nov [14] Pitney appears in the Royal Variety Show at the London Palladium.
Dec A second Newman composition, *Just One Smile*, hits UK #8, while new compilation *Greatest Hits Of All Times* climbs to US #61.
1967 Jan *Just One Smile* stalls at US #64. Meanwhile, Pitney marries childhood sweetheart Lynn Gayton in the Roman Catholic church at Ospedaletti near San Remo, Italy, where he is representing US in the Song Festival. (They will have 2 sons, Christopher and Todd.)
Feb [17] Pitney embarks on 28-date twice-nightly UK tour, with The Troggs, David Garrick, Sounds Incorporated, The Loot and Normie Rowe & The Playboys, at London's Finsbury Park Astoria, ending Mar.19 at Coventry theater, W.Midlands.
Mar *Young, Warm And Wonderful* climbs to UK #39.
Apr Compilation *Gene Pitney's Big Sixteen* peaks at UK #40.
Aug [4] Pitney begins US tour with Buffalo Springfield, The Easybeats, The Buckinghams, The Happenings and The Music Explosion, in Hartford, CT.
Nov *(In The) Cold Light Of Day* makes UK #38.
Dec *Something's Gotten Hold Of My Heart*, a British song by Roger Cook and Roger Greenaway, hits UK #5.
1968 Apr *Somewhere In The Country* makes UK #19.
[5] Pitney begins a 28-date twice-nightly UK tour with Amen Corner, Status Quo, Don Partridge, Simon Dupree & The Big Sound and others, at Odeon cinema, Lewisham, London (ending May 7 at Granada cinema, Walthamstow, London).
July *She's A Heartbreaker*, an R&B performance of a song written by Charlie Foxx and Jerry Williams ("Swamp Dog"), reaches US #16.
Sept *She's A Heartbreaker* climbs to US #193.
Nov *Billy You're My Friend* stalls at US #92, while *Yours Until Tomorrow*, a Goffin/King song, makes UK #34.
1969 Feb [7] Pitney begins a 27-date twice-nightly UK tour (his sixth), with The Marmalade, Joe Cocker, The Iveys and others, at Odeon cinema, Birmingham (ending Mar.9 at ABC cinema, Blackpool, Lancs.).

Mar UK-composed (by Tony Hazzard) *Maria Elena* reaches UK #25.
Oct Compilation *Best Of Gene Pitney* hits UK #8.
1970 Jan *She Lets Her Hair Down (Early In The Morning)*, an adaptation of Silvikrin shampoo TV ad, stalls at US #89.
Mar *A Street Called Hope*, another Cook/Greenaway song, makes UK #37, as Pitney begins another UK tour, with Badfinger and Clodagh Rodgers.
Oct *Shady Lady* reaches UK #29.
1973 May *24 Sycamore*, written by Les Reed and Barry Mason, and previously recorded by UK singer Wayne Fontana, makes UK #34.
1974 May Pitney signs a new worldwide recording deal with UK label Bronze Records.
Aug First Bronze release, *Blue Angel*, peaks at UK #39. After voice strain and some bouts of ill-health, he cuts down on his previously almost continuous worldwide touring to 6 months in each year, to spend the other half at home with his family.
1975 Apr [10] The Gene Pitney Appreciation Society presents him with a plaque in honor of his regular twice-annual UK tours. The presentation is made during a tour, on stage at the Fiesta club, Sheffield, S.Yorks.
Oct Alan O'Day-penned *Train Of Thought* on Bronze collects good UK airplay, but fails to chart, as does Bronze album *Pitney '75*.
Nov He opens a UK concert tour to promote both records, at Batley Variety club, Yorks.
1976 Oct TV-promoted compilation *His 20 Greatest Hits* hits UK #6.
1977 Jan He signs to Epic Records, but 3 singles during the year all fail, and the deal is not extended.
1978 Dec Still a twice-annual UK visitor, he plays the London Palladium supported by Co-Co, the group which has performed UK's entry in the 1978 Eurovision Song Contest.
1989 Jan [28] After many years away from recording (though still touring all over the world for 6-8 months each year), Pitney adds guest vocals to a new version of his hit *Something's Gotten Hold Of My Heart*, by UK singer Marc Almond, formerly of Soft Cell, which hits UK #1.
July [10] Pitney, B.J. Thomas and The Shirelles appear in Nashville, TN, Federal court as trial begins in lawsuit against Gusto Records and GML over alleged improper payment of royalties of re-released hits.
1990 May [2] Pitney is awarded $187,762 by US District Court Judge Thomas Higgins in case against Gusto Records.
Oct [27] Pitney, always more popular in UK than US, returns to UK chart with *Backstage – The Greatest Hits And More*, a collection of his hits and 8 new tracks produced by David Courtney. It reaches UK #17.

THE PIXIES

Black Francis (vocals, guitar)
Kim Deal (bass, vocals)
David Lovering (drums, vocals)
Joey Santiago (lead guitar)

1986 Francis (b. Charles Michael Kitridge Thompson IV), aka Black Francis, an anthropology major at University of Massachusetts, Amherst, MA, studying Spanish on an exchange program in Puerto Rico, drops out with the intention of forming a band. He persuades college room-mate Santiago to quit as well and relocate with him to Boston, MA. Placing an ad for a bassist "into Husker Du and Peter, Paul and Mary", they hire the only respondent, Deal, aka Mrs. John Murphy, a former high-school cheerleader in Ohio. At her suggestion they recruit Lovering, and begin performing a mostly experimental chaotic set around the Boston club scene, most often at Green Street Station, the Rat and T.T. The Bear's, calling themselves The Pixies chosen by Santiago flicking through a dictionary.

1987 Oct Having sent a demo tape to London-based independent label 4AD head Ivo Watts, via Throwing Muses' manager Ken Goes, the company releases it as 8-track mini-album *Come On Pilgrim*, which receives European critical raves and tops UK Independent Album chart.

1988 Mar Second album for 4AD, Steve Albini-produced *Surfer Rosa* is hailed as an underground classic and again tops UK Independent Album survey. (Its CD release includes the *Come On Pilgrim* set.) Band makes UK debut supporting Throwing Muses at the Mean Fiddler, London.
Apr [8] The Pixies sell out the Mean Fiddler, the first date of a European tour, while US labels jostle to sign them.
Aug 4-track EP *Gigantic*, again a UK indie item, is released to coincide with the group's first full UK tour.

1989 Apr [1] Trailering forthcoming album, *Monkey Gone To Heaven* peaks at UK #54.
[29] Gil Norton-produced, and subsequently more commercially

framed third project, *Doolittle*, marks The Pixies debut for US Elektra, while 4AD is rewarded in UK as album immediately hits UK #8. During a 6-month US chart residence, it will reach #98, while extracts, the recent and forthcoming UK chosen singles, will also prove popular US modern and college tracks. Pixies begin 50-date "Sex And Death" European leg of a 150-date world tour. (During a Manchester gig, Francis will slice his finger.)

July [1] *Here Comes Your Man* peaks at UK #54.

Aug Pixies contribute their version of *Winterlong* for the compilation album *The Bridge: A Tribute To Neil Young*, as US leg of tour begins.

Oct [31] US "Doolittle" tour begins in Eugene, OR.

1990 Mar [8] Pixies are named Best New American Band in **Rolling Stone**'s 1989 Critics Award.

Apr [19] Further honors are collected at their homebase SKC Boston Music Awards, held at the Wang Center, as the band wins Outstanding Debut Pop/Rock Album, for *Doolittle*, their first US release.

June [9] Deal, still very much a Pixie, launches off-shoot unit The Breeders with Throwing Muses' Tanya Donnelly (guitar), ex-Perfect Disaster Josephine Wiggs (bass) and only male member, drummer Shannon Doughton. Their debut album *Pod* immediately reaches UK #22, released by 4AD, and recorded in Edinburgh, Scotland, with Albini producing.

July [28] Pixies' *Velouria* reaches UK #28 and becomes another hot US alternative radio add-on.

Aug [25] With its lead-off track *Cecilia Ann*, an unusual cover of an early 60s Surftones disk, fourth Pixies album *Bossanova* hits UK #3, as band plays Reading Festival at Little John's Farm, Reading, Berks.

Sept [5] Extensive European tour continues with first German date in Linz.

[15] Again produced by Gil Norton, *Bossanova*, peaks at US #70.

Nov [3] *Rubáiyát*, Elektra's 40th anniversary compilation, to which group contributes a cover of *Born In Chicago*, makes US #140.

[10] Second *Bossanova* extract *Dig For Fire* stalls at UK #62.

1991 June [22] The Pixies play a one-off UK date at the G-Mex Centre, Manchester, Gtr.Manchester.

ROBERT PLANT

1966 Nov Plant (b. Aug.20, 1948, West Bromwich, W.Midlands), after abandoning a chartered accountancy course 2 years earlier, while living in Walsall, W.Midlands has sung with several local R&B and blues groups including Black Snake Moan, The Banned and The Crawling King Snakes, makes his recording debut as a member of Birmingham, W.Midlands-based band Listen, on *You Better Run* for CBS Records.

1967 He cuts 2 solo singles for CBS, but neither *Our Song* nor *Long Time Coming* sells. He also sings on The Exceptions' *The Eagle Flies On Friday*, another chart failure. He joins Birmingham group Band Of Joy, along with John Bonham, which releases no records (an album of its archive material will be issued by Polydor in 1978).

1968 Aug While debating whether to join Alexis Korner's new band as singer, he is asked by Jimmy Page to join The New Yardbirds (who become Led Zeppelin). Plant will remain lead singer with Led Zeppelin who will enjoy phenomenal international success for the next 12 years (until splitting after the death of drummer John Bonham in Dec.1980).

Nov [9] Plant marries long-time girlfriend Maureen.

1979 Dec [29] He sings with Dave Edmunds' band Rockpile in third "Concert For The People Of Kampuchea" at London's Hammersmith Odeon.

1981 Apr Plant begins a solo career, playing live with his part-time band, The Honeydrippers. Group will make occasional appearances in London and Birmingham, playing R&B and blues covers, and he will also work with The Big Town Playboys.

Sept Plant begins recording at Rockfield studios.

1982 July Plant's first solo album *Pictures At Eleven*, released on Led Zeppelin's SwanSong label, hits UK #2 and US #5.

Oct Extracted *Burning Down One Side* makes UK #73 and US #64.

Nov *Pledge Pin* peaks at UK #74.

By year's end, Plant returns to Rockfield for further recordings now with Phil Collins, Robbie Blunt (guitar), Jezz Woodroffe (keyboards), Paul Martinez (bass) and Barriemore Barlow (drums).

1983 June Due to have his live set shown on Channel 4 TV show "The Tube", Plant, dissatisfied with his performance, vetoes its transmission.

July *Big Log* reaches UK #11 and US #20 and he appears on BBC TV's "Top Of The Pops" (which Led Zeppelin had never done) to sing it. *The Principle Of Moments* hits UK #7 and US #8.

1984 Jan *In The Mood* reaches US #39.

Nov After Plant tours with The Honeydrippers, mini-album *The Honeydrippers, Vol.1* hits US #4 and UK #56. Project lines up as Plant, Jimmy Page, Jeff Beck and Chic's Nile Rodgers, who also produces.

1985 Jan The Honeydrippers' revival of Phil Phillips' *Sea Of Love*, from the mini-album, hits US #3 and makes UK #56.

Feb The Honeydrippers' *Rockin' At Midnight* reaches US #25.

June *Shaken 'N' Stirred* makes UK #19 and US #20.

July *Little By Little*, taken from the album, reaches US #36.

[13] Plant plays Live Aid in Philadelphia, PA, in a one-off Led Zeppelin reunion (with Phil Collins on drums).

1986 Jan Plant, Page, bassist Charlie Jones and drummer Tony Thompson rehearse in a small hall near Bath, Avon, with the idea of reviving Led Zeppelin, but after a few days the idea is abandoned.

Mar With several other Birmingham-based acts, he participates in the "Heartbeat 86" benefit show for a children's hospital.

1988 Feb Plant plays live in Folkestone, Kent, with his new band, credited as The Band Of Joy (for 1 night only). Line-up is Plant, Doug Boyle (guitar), Phil Johnstone (keyboards) and Chris Blackwell (drums). All are young Led Zeppelin fans who have sent Plant a demo tape which impressed him. (Johnstone is also the writer of the group's material and he and Plant collaborate on *Heaven Knows* and *Tall Cool One* for Plant's new album.) *Heaven Knows* reaches UK #33.

Apr *Now And Zen*, with a guest appearance from Jimmy Page and sampled Led Zeppelin tracks, hits UK #10 and US #6.

May Plant plays with Led Zeppelin on another one-off reunion at Atlantic Records' 40th anniversary concert at New York's Madison Square Garden (with John Bonham's son Jason on drums).

July Plant guests on Page's *Outrider*. Plant's *Tall Cool One*, featuring a Page guitar solo and used in US TV ads for Coca-Cola, reaches US #25.

Sept [3] Ballad *Ship Of Fools* makes US #84.

1989 Dec Plant collaborates with Ian Gillan, Brian May and Bruce Dickinson in one-off benefit group Rock Aid Armenia with a remake of *Smoke On The Water*, which makes UK #39, with all profits from the record going to the victims of the Armenian earthquake disaster.

1990 Feb Plant contributes a cover of *Let's Have A Party* to the compilation album *The Last Temptation Of Elvis*, to benefit the Nordoff-Robbins Music Therapy charity.

Mar [31] Co-self-produced *Manic Nirvana* reaches UK #15.

Apr *Hurting Kind (I've Got My Eyes On You)* makes UK #45, US #46.

[28] *Manic Nirvana* reaches US #130.

July [5] "Manic Nirvana" tour begins in Albany, NY, set to end Nov.26 in Muskogee, OK, and features his now regular backing band of Chris Blackwell, Doug Boyle, Phil Johnstone and Charlie Jones.

THE PLATTERS

Tony Williams (lead vocals)
David Lynch (vocals)
Paul Robi (vocals)
Herb Reed (vocals)
Zola Taylor (vocals)

1953 Group is formed as a doo-wop quartet in Los Angeles, CA, by lead singer Williams (b. Apr.5, 1928, Elizabeth, NJ), Lynch, Reed and Alex Hodge, and while performing in Los Angeles clubs they meet manager/producer Buck Ram.

1954 Feb [15] Ram signs The Platters to a management agreement.

May At Ram's instigation, female singer Taylor from The Teen Queens joins the group to widen and sweeten the vocal blend.

July Hodge has a run-in with the law and leaves. Ram recruits Robi, completing the line-up of The Platters, which will become the most successful black group of the 50s. The group signs to Federal Records, an R&B subsidiary of King, but debut release *Only You (And You Alone)* does not chart. Ram provides the group with excellent live bookings, and their financial success persuades another Los Angeles vocal group, The Penguins, to sign to Ram.

1955 After The Penguins score a million-seller on independent Dootone label with *Earth Angel*, Mercury Records approaches Ram to sign them. He agrees provided Mercury signs The Platters too.

Nov Group debuts on Mercury with a new version of *Only You (And You Alone)*, which hits US #5, pushed by DJ Hunter Hancock. Label now agrees with Ram that The Platters should be considered a popular ballad, rather than R&B, group.

1956 Feb *The Great Pretender* tops US chart for 2 weeks, selling over a million, and B-side *I'm Just A Dancing Partner* makes US #87. (Ram has told Mercury that *The Great Pretender* will be the next hit before he has even written a song to go with the title.)

May *(You've Got) The Magic Touch* hits US #4 and is a second million-seller. B-side *Winner Take All* makes US #50.

July Group's debut album *The Platters* hits US #7.

Aug *My Prayer* (offered by its English lyricist Jimmy Kennedy to Ram after he has heard *The Great Pretender*) tops US chart for 5 weeks, earning another gold disk, while B-side *Heaven On Earth* makes US #39.

Sept *The Great Pretender* coupled with *Only You* is the group's UK debut at #5.

Nov *You'll Never Never Know* reaches US #11, while B-side *It Isn't Right* makes US #23. Meanwhile, *My Prayer* hits UK #4.

1957 Jan *On My Word Of Honor* makes US #20 and B-side *One In A Million* makes US #31. Double A-side *You'll Never Never Know/It Isn't Right* peaks at UK #23.

Feb *The Platters, Volume Two* reaches US #12.

Apr *I'm Sorry* reaches US #19 and B-side *He's Mine* makes US #23.

June *I'm Sorry* reaches UK #18.

July *My Dream* makes US #24.

Nov *Only Because*, peaking at US #65, is the group's first US Top 50 failure since signing to Mercury.

1958 Mar *Helpless* peaks at US #56.

Apr *Twilight Time*, co-written by Ram with The Three Suns (who had a major hit with it in 1944), and originally issued as B-side of *Out Of My Mind*, is premiered on "Dick Clark's Saturday Night TV Show". It tops US chart for a week and becomes another million-seller. Mercury also produces a film clip, which it promotes to US TV shows – an early ancestor of the music video.

July B-side *You're Making A Mistake* makes US #50. *Twilight Time* hits UK #3.

Oct Group plays an extended European tour and records *Smoke Gets In Your Eyes* while performing in Paris, France. Meanwhile, *I Wish* makes US #42 and B-side *It's Raining Outside* creeps to US #93.

1959 Jan *Smoke Gets In Your Eyes*, originally a 1934 hit for Paul Whiteman (and a Jerome Kern/Otto Harbach song from 1933 musical "Roberta"), is another million-seller, topping US chart for 3 weeks.

Feb *Smoke Gets In Your Eyes* topples Elvis Presley's *I Got Stung/One Night* from UK #1, where it stays for 5 weeks.

Apr *Remember When?* reaches US #15.

May *Enchanted* peaks at US #12.

July The title song from *Remember When* makes US #41.

Aug *Remember When* reaches UK #25.

[10] The 4 male members of the group are arrested in Cincinnati, OH, having been found in flagrante delicto with 4 19-year-old women (3 of them white). Wide coverage of the arrest results in radio stations across US removing The Platters records from playlists.

Oct *Where*, an adaptation of Tchaikovsky's "Symphonie Pathétique", makes US #44. B-side *Wish It Were Me*, from film "Girls' Town", peaks at US #61.

Dec [10] The male group members are acquitted of charges of lewdness, assignation, and aiding and abetting prostitution, arising from their Aug. arrest. Judge Gilbert Bettman lectures them in court about responsibility to their public.

1960 Feb Another oldie, *Harbor Lights*, hits US #8 and UK #11. B-side *Sleepy Lagoon* peaks at US #65. Compilation *Encore Of Golden Hits* enters US chart, to hit #6 during a 174-week stay in which it is certified gold.

May *Ebb Tide*, credited as by "The Platters featuring Tony Williams", makes US #56.

Aug *Red Sails In The Sunset* reaches US #36.

Nov *To Each His Own* makes US #21.

Dec Compilation *More Encores Of Golden Hits* reaches US #20.

1961 Williams leaves the group (and will sign as soloist to Frank Sinatra's Reprise label later in the year). Sonny Turner (b. Charles Edward Turner) replaces him as lead vocalist.

Feb *If I Didn't Care* makes US #30.

[14] Ram and the group sue Mercury Records for refusing to accept recordings without Williams' lead vocal. Ram states that the contract does not stipulate who should sing lead, and that other members have previously done so on some 25 Platters tracks.

Apr *Trees* peaks at US #62.

Sept *I'll Never Smile Again* makes US #25.

1962 Feb *It's Magic* at US #91 is the group's last Top 100 for Mercury and last chart entry for over 4 years. Taylor and Robi leave to go solo and are replaced by Sandra Dawn and Nate Nelson (ex-The Flamingos). The Platters tour Poland (the first US group to appear there without a Government subsidy). They also announce they will not play in Atlanta, GA, again if audiences are segregated.

1966 June Now signed to Musicor Records, and with traditional ballad style

modified to more contemporary soul, The Platters make US #31 with *I Love You 1,000 Times* (also an R&B success).

July Musicor album *I Love You 1,000 Times* climbs to US #100.

Dec *I'll Be Home*, a revival of 1956 Moonglows/Pat Boone hit, peaks at US #97.

1967 Apr Motown-influenced *With This Ring* is the biggest chart success for the new-style Platters, reaching US #14.

Aug Also uptempo, *Washed Ashore (On A Lonely Island In The Sea)* makes US #56.

Oct [18] Group appears on Richard Nader's first Rock'N'Roll Revival Concert at Madison Square Garden, New York, alongside Chuck Berry, Bill Haley & His Comets, and others.

Nov *Sweet, Sweet Lovin'* peaks at US #70, and is the final Platters US chart entry. (The group will continue as a worldwide live nightclub attraction through the next 2 decades, still with Ram until Jean Bennett takes over in mid-80s.)

1978 Apr Compilation *20 Classic Hits*, featuring 50s Mercury repertoire, and promoted via a nostalgic TV campaign, hits UK #8.

1990 Jan [17] The Platters are inducted into the Rock'N'Roll Hall Of Fame with The Four Seasons, The Who, Bobby Darin, The Kinks, Simon & Garfunkel, The Four Tops and Hank Ballard at the Waldorf Astoria, New York. (The current line-up of Tony Williams, Martha Robi, Zola Taylor, Herb Reed and Rosalyn Atkins still performs throughout US, mainly in cabaret.)

POCO

Richie Furay (guitar, vocals)
Jim Messina (guitar, vocals)
Rusty Young (pedal steel)
Randy Meisner (bass, vocals)
George Grantham (drums, vocals)

1968 Aug After the break-up of Buffalo Springfield, band forms as Pogo, a Los Angeles, CA, country-rock outfit, around ex-members Furay (b. May 9, 1944, Yellow Springs, OH) and Messina (b. Dec.5, 1947, Maywood, CA) who join Young (b. Feb.23, 1946, Long Beach, CA), Grantham (b. Nov.20, 1947, Cordell, OK), both ex-Colorado band Boenzee Cryque, and Meisner (b. Mar.8, 1946, Scottsbluff, NB) ex-Poor. Young rejects an offer from Gram Parsons to join his new Flying Burrito Brothers outfit, preferring instead to join the ex-Springfield members, who were his favorite band of the time.

Nov The group makes its debut at the Troubadour, Los Angeles, CA.

1969 Jan [15] Pogo signs to Epic after Atlantic agrees "to assign to CBS all right, title, etc., to the exclusive services of Richard Furay" in exchange for acquiring the rights to Graham Nash, who is still signed to Epic through The Hollies. (This releases Furay to record for Epic as part of Pogo.)

Mar Because of threatened court action by **Pogo** comic strip creator Watt Kelly, they change name to Poco.

Apr During debut recording sessions, Meisner quits after a personality clash, and will return home to Scottsbluff and work at John Deere tractor factory, before joining Rick Nelson's Stone Canyon Band. Timothy Schmit (b. Oct.30, 1947, Sacramento, CA) is invited to replace him, but turns the offer down to stay in college and avoid the draft. Poco continues as a 4-piece.

June Debut album *Pickin' Up The Pieces* enters US chart and reaches #63, and will sell over 100,000 copies.

1970 Feb Invited a second time, Schmit joins. (He has been in Sacramento folk trio, Tim, Tom & Ron in 1962, becoming surf band The Contenders in 1963, before joining New Breed and then Glad, who name-change to Redwing.)

July Furay-produced second album *Poco*, dedicated to David Geffen, though they will shortly sign a management deal with Shiffman & Larson, reaches US #58.

Nov *You Better Think Twice* makes US #72. Messina leaves for a solo career, replaced by Paul Cotton, (b. Feb.26, 1943, Los Angeles) who joins from Illinois Speed Press, recommended by Chicago's Peter Cetera.

1971 Feb Live album *Deliverin'*, produced by Messina and recorded at the Boston Music Hall and New York Forum, reaches US #26.

May *C'mon* peaks at US #69.

Dec Furay-helmed *From The Inside*, the group's first with Cotton, makes US #52.

1972 Feb Poco makes its live UK debut at the Rainbow theater, Finsbury Park, London.

Nov The band appears on debut program of ABC TV's "In Concert".

1973
Jan *Good Feelin' To Know* reaches US #69.

Feb Recording begins on Poco's next album, whose title track *Crazy Eyes* is a song Furay has written about Gram Parsons 4 years previously, and will include a Parsons' cut, *Brass Buttons*.

Sept Furay leaves to join Souther-Hillman-Furay Band.

Nov *Crazy Eyes* reaches US #38.

1974
June Produced by Jack Richardson, *Seven*, with the band now reduced to a 4-piece, makes US #68.

Nov [9] During current US tour, band performs at Yale University, New Haven, CT.

Dec Band-written and produced *Cantamos*, recorded at the Record Plant, Los Angeles, and the last for Epic, peaks at US #76.

1975
July The group signs to ABC and releases *Head Over Heels*, produced by Poco with Mark Harmon, which reaches US #43.

Aug Epic releases double album *The Very Best Of Poco*, which climbs to US #90.

Nov ABC-issued *Keep On Tryin'* makes US #50, and is their first chart single in 4 years.

1976
Apr Also on Epic, *Poco Live*, recorded during their 1974 winter tour, peaks at US #169.

May *Rose Of Cimarron* makes US #89. Group begins a major US tour, supporting the Stills-Young band. When Rusty Young causes the tour to close and new member Al Garth quits, Poco comes close to disbanding once again.

Aug Title track *Rose Of Cimarron* stalls at US #94, but will become an airplay favorite in future years.

Dec Group starts recording at Scoring Two studios, but leaves 3 weeks later to assess its future.

1977
May *Indian Summer*, with Poco's country roots replaced by the synthesizer playing of Steely Dan's Donald Fagen, reaches US #57.

Sept Schmit leaves to join The Eagles (to once again replace Meisner), as *Indian Summer* makes US #50.

1978
Jan Grantham also leaves, to join Secrets. (He will then move to Nashville, TN, working as Ricky Skaggs' drummer for some years, and then with Steve Wariner.)

Mar After exhaustive auditions, Britons Charlie Harrison and Steve Chapman are chosen.

Dec Kim Bullard (b. Atlanta, GA), ex-Crosby, Stills & Nash's US tour, joins on keyboards.

1979
Jan Produced by Richard Sanford Orshoff, *Legend* earns the group its first gold disk, reaching US #14, while CBS issues retrospective *Poco: The Songs Of Richie Furay*.

Mar Extracted acoustic guitar-led ballad *Crazy Love*, penned by Young, is the band's biggest hit at US #17.

July *Heart Of The Night* makes US #20.

1980
July Band, now on MCA Records which has absorbed the ABC label, releases *Under The Gun*, produced by Mike Flicker. It reaches US #46.

Aug *Under The Gun*, helped by Michael Nesmith video, makes US #48.

Oct Cotton-penned *Midnight Rain* peaks at US #74.

1981
July *Blue And Gray* makes US #76.

1982
Mar *Cowboys And Englishmen* climbs to US #131.

Dec Poco moves to Atlantic Records for *Ghost Town*, which makes US #195. Recorded in Silverlake, CA, it is co-produced by the band with John Mills.

1983
Feb Young ballad *Shoot For The Moon* reaches US #50.

1984
June Furay reunites the early line-up for *Inamorata*, which makes US #167, as *Days Gone By* peaks at US #80. (The group will shortly break up once again.)

1989
Apr Original group re-forms with Furay, who is now a minister in a Boulder, CO, church, Young, Messina, Grantham and Meisner, and signs to RCA.

Nov [4] Young-written *Call It Love* reaches US #18, Poco's biggest hit in 10 years. *Legacy*, mainly produced by David Cole, rises to US #40, their biggest success in over 10 years.

1990
Jan *Nothin' To Hide*, co-penned and produced by Richard Marx, makes US #39, as the group embarks on major US tour with Marx. Paul Cotton solo album *Changing Horses* is released on Sisapa label, while early Poco retrospective double CD *Poco: The Forgotten Trail (1969-74)* is released on CBS Legacy series.

THE POGUES

Shane MacGowan (guitar, vocals)
Jem Finer (banjo)
James Fearnley (accordian)
Spider Stacy (tin whistle)
Caitlin O'Riordan (bass)
Andrew Ranken (drums)

1983 Band is formed in London by MacGowan (b. Dec.25, 1957, Kent, but growing up in Tipperary), ex-punk band The Nipple Erectors (later The Nips) before going on to join Stacy in The Chainsaws, then linking with Finer to play punk/folk mix in the Cabaret Futura club, London, originally under the name Pogue Mo Chone ("kiss my arse" in Gaelic). Adding 2 drinking partners from King's Cross pubs, Ranken and Feanrley, the band plays a mixture of country, rockabilly and assorted Scots and Irish folk. O'Riordan is recruited as the group's early gigs include playing at the Irish Centre, Camden, London, and supporting psychobilly act King Kurt.

1984 **May** Forming its own Pogue Mahone label, with independent distribution by Rough Trade, band releases debut single *The Dark Streets Of London*, which is banned from daytime BBC radio play when the meaning of the group's name becomes apparent.

June Stiff Records picks up the single and signs the band, reputedly for half a crate of Guinness beer, but persuades the group to abridge the name to The Pogues.

Nov Debut album *Red Roses For Me*, produced by Stan Brennan, mixes group originals with traditional folk songs, and charts briefly at UK #83. Extracted *Boys From The County Hell* fails, despite the band's growing reputation as a live act, not least, recently supporting Costello on a UK trek.

1985 **Apr** *A Pair Of Brown Eyes*, produced by Elvis Costello, reaches UK #72. The promo video is filmed by Alex Cox (with whom the band will make a feature film).

June *Sally Maclennane* peaks at UK #51, aided by a special limited pressing in the shape of a shamrock.

Aug Following a successful Cambridge Folk Festival appearance and a headlining slot at a benefit concert for Nicaragua in Brixton, London, Costello-produced *Rum, Sodomy And The Lash* (a title reportedly taken from Winston Churchill's description of life in the Royal Navy) reaches UK #13.

Sept *Dirty Old Town*, a revival of Ewan MacColl's folk song, makes UK #62. It is produced by Philip Chevron (ex-Radiators From Space), who joins The Pogues as guitarist, after subbing during Finer's paternity leave.

1986 **Jan** Band makes its US live debut with a short tour – during which O'Riordan briefly walks out between New York shows, leaving Pogues roadie Darryl Hunt to deputize on bass.

Mar A plan to revive The Lovin' Spoonful's *Do You Believe In Magic?* is shelved, and the band releases 4-track EP *Poguetry In Motion*, which climbs to UK #29.

Apr MacGowan is hit by a London taxicab as he leaves a restaurant and suffers a fractured arm and torn ligaments, though his already inconsistent front row of teeth, for which he has become notoroious, is thankfully unharmed.

May [16] O'Riordan marries Elvis Costello in Dublin, Eire.

[17] Band appears in Dublin at the Self Aid concert (raising funds to help young Irish unemployed to set up in business), with U2, Van Morrison, Elvis Costello, Chris De Burgh and others.

June [20] Band plays the Glastonbury Fayre, Somerset, with The Cure, Level 42, The Housemartins and many other acts.

Sept *Haunted*, written by O'Riordan and originally used on soundtrack of Cox-directed film "Sid And Nancy", peaks at UK #42 while most of the band are in Spain's Sierra Nevada with Cox, filming surreal western "Straight To Hell" (they play the homicidal McMahon gang).

Nov O'Riordan leaves the group and Hunt takes over on bass.

1987 **Mar** [6] The band appears on Irish TV, with U2 and other guests, in a 25th anniversary celebration of Irish folk group The Dubliners.

Apr *The Irish Rover*, teaming them with The Dubliners, hits UK #8.

June The band has 4 songs on the soundtrack album from "Straight To Hell". The movie is released to mixed reviews. *The Good, The Bad And The Ugly* (from the film) is scheduled as a single, but then cancelled. Pogues manager Frank Murray persuades a close friend, veteran Irish musician Terry Woods, who has retired from the music business and is working in a plastics factory, to join the band on concertina.

Nov After the collapse of Stiff, and its absorption by Trevor Horn's ZTT Records, the band's Pogue Mahone label is revived within the new set-up to release its records.

Dec *A Fairytale Of New York*, with seasonal lyrics (and some ripe language), intended as a MacGowan/O'Riordan duet 2 years earlier, features Kirsty MacColl guesting in the female vocals. It hits UK #2 during Christmas week, kept off the top by The Pet Shop Boys' *Always On My Mind*.

1988 **Jan** *If I Should Fall From Grace With God*, produced by Steve Lillywhite (MacColl's husband), hits UK #3. The band is on a 3-week US tour on which Joe Strummer, ex-The Clash (and co-star of "Straight To Hell") joins as a temporary member – adding The Clash hits *London Calling* and *I Fought The Law* to The Pogues' on stage repertoire.
Mar Title track *If I Should Fall From Grace With God* peaks at UK #58.
Apr *If I Should Fall From Grace With God* reaches US #88.
July *Fiesta* makes UK #24.
MacGowan collapses at Heathrow en route for San Francisco, CA, to support Bob Dylan. He misses 10 days of concerts and the band plays on without him.
Dec *Yeah Yeah Yeah Yeah Yeah* makes UK #43.

1989 **July** *Misty Morning, Albert Bridge* makes UK #41, while parent album *Peace And Love* hits UK #5 and makes US #118.
[10] "Slaughtered Lambs Of New Wave Tour" with Violent Femmes begins at Poplar Creek Music theater, Hoffman Estates, IL.
Oct [7] James Fearnley marries actress Danielle Von Zerneck.

1990 **Feb** Group contributes a cover of *Got A Lot O' Livin' To Do* to the compilation album *The Last Temptation Of Elvis*, to benefit the Nordoff-Robbins Music Therapy charity.
June Once again featuring The Dubliners, double A-side *Jack's Heroes*, the unofficial theme for the Irish World Cup soccer team, and *Whiskey In The Jar* peaks at UK #63.
Sept *Summer In Siam* climbs to UK #64.
Oct The Pogues and Kirsty MacColl contribute *Miss Otis Regrets/Just One Of Those Things* to *Red Hot + Blue*, an anthology of Cole Porter songs to benefit AIDS education.
[13] *Hell's Ditch* reaches UK #12.
Dec *Hell's Ditch* climbs to US #187.

POISON

Bret Michaels (vocals)
C.C. DeVille (guitar)
Bobby Dall (bass)
Rikki Rockett (drums)

1984 Michaels (b. Mar.15, Pittsburgh, PA) and Rockett (b. Mechanicsburg, PA) have already formed The Spectres in hometown Pittsburgh and gone on to join up with licensed cosmetologist Dall (b. FL, but settled in Mechanicsburg at age 8) and Matt Smith to form Paris, playing mostly rock covers in local bars, when they decide to relocate to Hollywood, CA, in a $700 ambulance Michaels has bought, in an effort to succeed as a heavy metal band.

1985 Guitarist Smith is replaced by DeVille (b. Cecil DeVille, Brooklyn, New York, NY), a clinical psychology major at NYC and veteran of many rock outfits, including Lace, The Broken Toys, The Shears, Screaming Mimi & Saint James, Van Gogh's Ear and Roxx Regime, the forerunner of Stryper. His experience enables the quartet to hone its hard rocking glam heavy metal style as the band prominently gigs around the Los Angeles, CA, club circuit in search of a record deal.

1986 **Aug** Having secured a contract with Enigma Records, licensed to Capitol, Poison's debut album *Look What The Cat Dragged In* begins the first of 101 weeks on US Album chart during which it will hit #3. Band embarks on a US tour opening for Ratt and Cinderella.

1987 **May** [16] As word spreads and gig venues get bigger, *Talk Dirty To Me*, aided by what will become typically Poison-featuring peroxide-drenched babe-heavy promo video clip, popular with MTV US viewers, hits US #9 and UK #67.
July [25] Follow-up *I Want Action* makes US #50.
Nov [21] Third extract *I Won't Forget You* reaches US #13. By year's end, Poison is voted Best New Artist Of Group in specialist US rock magazine *Circus*' Readers Poll.

1988 **May** [21] Second album, produced by Tom Werman, *Open Up And Say ... Aah!* begins multi-platinum rise to hit US #2 and UK #18, while Poison supports David Lee Roth on his US trek, until Aug. In their concert contract, the band demands and receives, ample dressing room supplies at each venue of Kentucky Fried Chicken, Reese's Peanut Butter Cups, shrimp cocktails, Domino's pepperoni pizza and a tour total of 876 boxes of Trojan condoms.
July [9] *Nothin' But A Good Time*, having already made UK #35 in May, hits US #6.

Aug Poison makes its UK debut on the "Monsters Of Rock" Festival bill at Castle Donington, Leics.
Oct [8] *Fallen Angel* reaches US #12 and UK #59.
Dec [24] As Poison is inducted into *Circus* magazine's Hall Of Fame, ballad *Every Rose Has Its Thorn* tops US chart for the first of 3 weeks. Written by the 4 group members, it will earn an RIAA gold disk and become the second biggest-selling single of the year, behind Steve Winwood's *Roll With It*.

1989 **Feb** *Every Rose Has Its Thorn* is UK breakthrough, reaching #13.
[28] Poison wins Most Underrated Group category in *Circus*' Readers Poll.
Apr [15] Still from *Open Up* album, update of Loggins & Messina's *Your Mama Don't Dance* hits US #10 and will reach UK #13.
Sept UK reissued *Nothin' But A Good Time* makes UK #48, as band prepares its third album.

1990 **Aug** [18] Within only 4 weeks of release, Bruce Fairbairn and Mike Fraser-produced *Flesh And Blood* hits US #2, behind MC Hammer, and has already hit UK #3.
Sept [1] Lead-off single *Unskinny Bop* hits US #3, having already reached UK #15, and will be gold certified.
[19] Headlining "Flesh And Blood" US tour opens at the Brown County Arena, Green Bay, WI, set to extend until the end of the year, while *Flesh And Blood* has already earned Poison its third platinum selling album.
Oct [27] *Something To Believe In* makes UK #35.
Nov [3] While Michaels has recently co-written and produced much of Giant Records signing Susie Hatten's debut album, DeVille's axework can currently be heard on Warrant's US #10 smash *Cherry Pie*.
Dec [1] DeVille spends 6 hours in a Louisville, KY, jail, following a public drunkenness and criminal mischief arrest.
[8] Ballad *Something To Believe In*, written about the death of the group's security guard, Kimo, hits US #4.

1991 **Mar** [23] *Ride The Wind* makes US #38.
May [4] *Life Goes On* enters US Hot 100 at #95.

THE POLICE

Sting (vocals, bass)
Andy Summers (guitar, vocals)
Stewart Copeland (drums, percussion, vocals)

1977 **Jan** [9] Copeland (b. July 16, 1952, Alexandria, Egypt), a US citizen drumming with progressive rockers Curved Air, (who are managed by Copeland's brother Miles) and bassist/vocalist Sting (b. Gordon Sumner, Oct.2, 1951, Wallsend, Tyne & Wear), an ex-primary school teacher, from jazz combo Last Exit, meet in London.
[12] They begin rehearsing with guitarist Henri Padovani (b. Corsica) at Copeland's studio in his Mayfair apartment.
Feb [12] The Police records its first single, *Fall Out*, at Pathway studios. (The 2 sides cost £150 to record.)
[21] Band begins rehearsals with New York singer Cherry Vanilla, to back her on a UK tour.
Mar [3] Cherry Vanilla, Johnny Thunders & The Heartbreakers and The Police tour starts at London's Roxy club in Covent Garden.
[19] The Police begins a tour of Holland, supporting Wayne County & The Electric Chairs.
May *Fall Out* is released on Copeland's Illegal label, selling out its initial pressing of 2,000 copies immediately and entering UK Independent chart.
[28] After Gong reunites to play at the Circus Hippodrome in Paris, France, ex-Gong member Mike Howlett invites Copeland and Sting to join guitarist Summers (b. Andrew Somers, Dec.31, 1942, Poulton Le Fylde, Lancs.) to play as Strontium 90. (Summers is ex-New Animals, Soft Machine and Kevin Ayers, and has contributed to Neil Young's *Everybody Knows This Is Nowhere*.) Summers adds an echo unit which, combined with Copeland's inverted reggae drum style, provides rhythm back-drop to forthcoming Sting lyrics.
June The Police plays London's Marquee, after which Summers is formally added to the line-up.
Aug [10] The Police records a session with producer John Cale.
[12] Padovani quits the band.
[18] Band plays first gig as trio at Rebecca's, Birmingham, W.Midlands.
Oct [22] The Police travels to Munich, Germany, to record and play with Eberhard Schoener, for his EMI album *Video Flashback*.

1978 **Jan** [13] Band begins recording its first album at Surrey Sound studio with Nigel and Chris Gray engineering.
Feb [22] The Police appears in a Wrigley's Chewing Gum ad for US TV, having to dye their hair blond for it. (Mistakenly associated as part

of UK's punk movement, the blond visual image will give the group a strong identity for the next 2 years.)

Mar [10] The Police supports US group Spirit at the start of a UK tour promoted by Miles Copeland.

[22] Miles Copeland secures an option deal with A&M Records to release *Roxanne*.

Apr *Roxanne* is released in UK but fails as the band, currently working with Schoener's Laser theater in Germany, is unable to promote it.

July Copeland releases *Don't Care* under the name of Klark Kent. An eponymous 10" album, on green vinyl, also fails.

Oct Group's second for A&M, *Can't Stand Losing You*, makes UK #42.

[16] The Police appears on BBC Radio 1's "Kid Jensen Show" before setting off on its first US tour.

[20] Group makes its US debut at New York's CBGB's, at the start of a 23-date North American tour.

Nov First album *Outlandos D'Amour* is released, with single *So Lonely*. The album hits UK #6.

Dec A&M America does not release debut A&M single *Roxanne*; it is available only as UK import. It and other tracks from *Outlandos D'Amour* (recorded for only £3,000) become popular with college radio. Band begins a UK tour, supporting Alberto Y Los Trios Paranoias.

'79 Feb [13] Group starts work on second album at Surrey Sound studios.

Mar [1] They embark on 29-date US tour at the Whiskey, Los Angeles.

Apr [25] The Police makes its debut on BBC TV's "Top Of The Pops" as re-released *Roxanne* climbs UK chart. Band heads back to US for its third tour, where the single reaches #32.

May *Roxanne* makes UK #12 as parent album *Outlandos D'Amour* hits UK #6 and US #23.

June The Police begins its first headlining UK tour.

July [24] Band headlines the Reading Rock Festival, Reading, Berks.

Aug Re-released *Can't Stand Losing You* hits UK #2, behind The Boomtown Rats' *I Don't Like Mondays*.

[11] Sting appears on BBC TVs "Juke Box Jury".

[16] "Quadrophenia" premieres, as Sting rejects numerous film offers, including the villain in Bond film "For Your Eyes Only". (He will, however, frequently appear in other films.)

Sept [10] *Message In A Bottle* is released as the group begins an 11-date UK tour, at the Assembly Rooms, Derby, Derbys. (ending at London's Hammersmith Odeon). It tops UK chart after 2 weeks of release.

[27] The Police plays New York's Diplomat hotel at the start of a 2-month US tour (which will include a visit to Kennedy Space Center in Houston to film a video for forthcoming single *Walking On The Moon*).

Oct Second album *Reggatta De Blanc*, co-produced by the group with Nigel Gray, hits UK #1 for 4 weeks. It will also reach US #25, where it will be issued as a double 10" album.

Nov *Fall Out*, originally released through Illegal label in 1977, makes UK #47.

Dec *Walking On The Moon* hits UK #1. Like every Police single released on A&M, it is written by Sting who now visually and musically dominates the line-up. *Message In A Bottle* stalls at US #74.

[18] In the middle of a German and UK tour, The Police plays London's Hammersmith's Palais and Odeon on the same night. (Group makes the short journey between venues in an army personnel carrier, with 40 police officers on standby to maintain order.)

'80 Jan [20] Group plays the State University of New York, Buffalo, NY, at the start of its first world tour (which takes in 37 cities in 19 countries, ending in Sting's home town Newcastle, where it plays 2 charity concerts for the Northumberland Association of Boys' Clubs. Group sets up its own charity called the Outlandos Trust, headed by Conservative Member of Parliament Anthony Steen.)

Mar Re-issued *So Lonely*, the group's fourth UK Top 10, hits #6.

[25] The Police is first Western group to perform in Bombay, India.

June *Six Pack*, a collection of first Police singles, now on blue vinyl, makes UK #17, as Sting and Summers exit to Eire for tax purposes.

July [7] The Police begins work on its third album at Wisseloord studio in Hilversum, Holland.

[26] Group headlines the "Reggatta De Bowl" charity gig at Milton Keynes, Bucks.

[28] They play the Dalymount Festival in Dublin, Eire, with U2 and Squeeze.

Aug [8] Band begins a month's tour of Europe at Wechter Festival in Belgium.

Sept [27] *Don't Stand So Close To Me* hits UK #1 for 4 weeks.

Oct [3] BBC TV airs "Police In The East" documentary.

[11] *Zenyatta Mondatta*, produced by Police and Nigel Gray, hits UK #1 for 4 weeks.

[21] The Police begins a 33-date North American tour at the Winnipeg Arena, Canada.

Dec *De Do Do Do, De Da Da Da* hits UK #5.

[14-16] The Police plays 3 concerts at Buenos Aires and Mar Del Plata in Argentina.

1981 Jan *De Do Do Do, De Da Da Da* hits US #10. *Zenyatta Mondatta* is the group's first US Top 10, at #5. Band begins a 2-month tour of North America, Japan, Australia and New Zealand in Montreal, Canada.

Feb [25] *Reggatta De Blanc* wins Best Rock Instrumental Performance at the 23rd annual Grammy awards.

Mar [1] Sting begins work on BBC TV play "Artemis 81".

Apr *Don't Stand So Close To Me* hits US #10.

June [15] The Police begins recording its fourth album at AIR studios in Montserrat in the Caribbean, with Hugh Padgham co-producing. The project is again filmed by BBC TV. (Hosted by Squeeze member and TV presenter Jools Holland, it will air in UK at Christmas.)

Oct *Invisible Sun*, inspired by the troubles in N.Ireland, hits UK #2, kept off the top by Adam And The Ants' *Prince Charming*. Parent album *Ghost In The Machine*, co-produced by Padgham, hits UK #1 at the start of a 3-week run.

Nov *Every Little Thing She Does Is Magic* tops the UK chart, the only cut from the album recorded at Le Studio, Quebec, Canada.

Dec *Every Little Thing She Does Is Magic* hits US #3. *Spirits In The Material World* reaches UK #12.

1982 Jan *Ghost In The Machine* hits US #2 for 6 weeks.

Feb [24] The Police wins Best British Group at the first annual BRIT Awards at the Grosvenor House, Mayfair, London, and hours later wins Best Rock Vocal Performance By A Duo Or Group for *Don't Stand So Close To Me* and Best Rock Instrumental Performance for *Behind My Camel* at the 24th Grammy awards.

Mar *Spirits In The Material World* reaches US #11.

May *Secret Journey* makes US #46.

July Copeland scores Francis Ford Coppola's movie "Rumble Fish".

Sept Sting's first solo single, a revival of *Spread A Little Happiness* from soundtrack of "Brimstone & Treacle", makes UK #16. It will be the start of an increasingly successful solo career.

[3-5] The Police plays the US Festival, financed by Apple Computers founder Steven Wozniak, in San Bernardino, CA, to 400,000 people, along with Jackson Browne, The Cars, Fleetwood Mac, The Grateful Dead, Eddie Money, Santana, Talking Heads and many others.

Oct Summers releases solo instrumental album *I Advance Masked* with King Crimson's Robert Fripp as Copeland writes ballet score for the San Francisco Ballet's production of "King Lear".

1983 June *Every Breath You Take*, a Sting song about obsessive love, hits UK #1 for 4 weeks as parent *Synchronicity* (Swiss psychologist Carl Jung's theories of the collective unconsciousness and mystical coincidence, most of which Sting wrote at Ian Fleming's former Jamaican home and again recorded in Montserrat and Le Studio, Quebec, enters UK chart at #1, where it will stay for 2 weeks. Sting bases its lyrical direction strongly on written works by Arthur Koestler.

July [9] *Every Breath You Take* hits US #1 for 8 weeks, helped by a Godley & Creme-shot video on heavy US MTV rotation. *Synchronicity* hits US #1 for 17 weeks, achieving multi-platinum status.

Aug *Wrapped Around Your Finger* hits UK #7 and US #8.

Nov *Synchronicity II* reaches UK #17. *King Of Pain* hits US #3.

Dec *Synchronicity II* makes US #16. *Every Breath You Take* is named Top Single in **Billboard**'s Year In Music survey.

1984 Jan *King Of Pain* peaks at UK #17.

Feb [28] *Every Breath You Take* is named Song Of The Year and Best Pop Performance By A Duo Or Group With Vocal and *Synchronicity* is named Best Rock Performance By A Duo Or Group With Vocal at the 26th annual Grammy awards.

Mar *Wrapped Around Your Finger* hits US #8.

Apr [5] *Every Breath You Take* is awarded Best Group Video at the second annual American Video Awards.

Sept Summers and Fripp release *Bewitched*.

1985 Feb [11] The Police wins the Outstanding Contribution To British Music at fourth annual BRIT Awards at London's Grosvenor House.

May Copeland cuts African-influenced album *The Rhythmatist*.

June Sting releases first solo album *Dream Of The Blue Turtles*.

1986 June [11] The Police reunites at an Amnesty International concert in Atlanta, GA, performing 5 songs.

July [21] Group begins recording for the follow-up to *Synchronicity*, but abandons the sessions soon after, as Sting insists on pursuing solo musical and acting interests.

Oct A revised edition of earlier hit *Don't Stand So Close To Me '86* makes UK #24, as a prelude to a greatest hits package.

Nov *Every Breath You Take – The Singles*, reprising the group's career, is its fifth successive UK #1, and hits US #7.

[29] *Don't Stand So Close To Me '86* makes US #46.

1987 **July** Summers' *XYZ* is released, the first to feature his vocals.

1988 **Jan** Copeland releases instrumental album *The Equalizer And Other Cliff Hangers*, which includes US TV's "The Equalizer" theme, as a prelude to future new age albums on brother Miles' newly-established specialist label, No Speak. He will continue to be successful as a composer, writing the scores for films "Wall Street", "First Power" and others, and composing the opera "Holy Blood And Crescent Moon" for the Cleveland Opera, before forming Animal Logic with Deborah Holland and Stanley Clarke.

1989 **Dec** *Animal Logic* makes US #106.

Sept Sting, with many acting roles and TV commercials behind him, begins filming "Quadrophenia", based on The Who's album. He plays the character Ace.

BRIAN POOLE AND THE TREMELOES

Brian Poole (vocals)
Rick West (lead guitar)
Alan Blakley (rhythm guitar)
Alan Howard (bass)
Dave Munden (drums)

1959 The group is formed in Dagenham, Essex, by ex-schoolfriends Poole (b. Nov.2, 1941, Barking, Essex), on vocals and guitar, Blakley (b. Apr.1, 1942, Bromley, Kent) on drums and Howard (b. Oct.17, 1941, Dagenham) on saxophone and Brian Scott on lead guitar, before Munden (b. Dec.12, 1943, Dagenham) joins on drums, allowing Blakley to switch to rhythm guitar and Poole to sing. Howard changes from sax to bass guitar, and the group begins as a dancehall band playing cover versions, including impersonations of Buddy Holly And The Crickets (Poole wears Holly-type horn-rimmed glasses). First public appearance at Ilford Palais, Essex.

1961 **July** After 2 years of solid gigging, during which West (b. Richard Westwood, May 7, 1943, Dagenham) has joined as lead guitarist making it a quintet, UK BBC radio producer Jimmy Grant spots the group playing in Southend, Essex, and books it for featured spots on Light Progamme's popular "Saturday Club" show. The group also plays a summer season as a successful rock ballroom band at Butlin's holiday camp at Ayr, Scotland, billed as Brian Poole & The Tremilos.

Dec Group turns professional after an audition for Decca Records.

1962 **Jan** Group is signed to Decca, after being selected in preference to The Beatles, both groups auditioning on New Year's Day, but local availability swings it for producer Mike Smith when he has to choose.

Mar Debut single *Twist Little Sister* does not chart, but picks up UK airplay and earns them a spot on TV's "Thank Your Lucky Stars".

Sept An album of cover versions, *Big Hits Of '62*, is released on Decca's low-price Ace of Clubs label. The group backs The Vernons Girls on their cover of Little Eva's *The Loco-Motion*. (The Tremeloes also back Mike Sarne on *Come Outside* and John Leyton on *Wild Wind*.)

1963 **Mar** With advent of the Merseybeat boom, they adapt a harder rocking stance. Poole abandons his Holly specs for contact lenses, and through energetic marketing by Decca, they become part of new R&B/beat movement, but *Keep On Dancing* (featured in UK pop movie "Just For Fun") fails.

Aug Group hits UK #5 with its cover of *Twist And Shout*, hugely popular on The Beatles debut album but not available as a Beatles single. Further progress is halted by The Beatles' EP *Twist And Shout*, which is a bigger-seller.

Sept [11] Group embarks on 23-date UK package tour with Roy Orbison, The Searchers and Freddie & The Dreamers.

Oct Group's revival of The Contours' *Do You Love Me?* tops UK chart for 3 weeks, fighting off The Dave Clark Five version. A major UK tour supporting Roy Orbison follows.

Nov [8] They begin a UK tour, with The Searchers, Freddie & The Dreamers, Dusty Springfield and Dave Berry, in Halifax, W.Yorks.

Dec *I Can Dance*, almost a clone of *Do You Love Me?* peaks at UK #31.

1964 **Mar** Fast-rocking revival of Roy Orbison B-side *Candy Man* hits UK #6.

Apr [4] They begin a tour of Australia and New Zealand with Gerry & The Pacemakers.

[26] The band appears at the **New Musical Express** Poll Winners Concert at Empire Pool, Wembley, London, with The Beatles, Cliff Richard and many others.

June First ballad hit, a revival of a Crickets B-side, *Someone Someone*,

hits UK #2. Group spends time in Ireland filming a spot in movie "A Touch Of Blarney".

Sept Return to the beat *Twelve Steps To Love* makes UK #32. *Someone Someone* reaches US #97 – the group's only US chart entry with Poole.

1965 **Feb** Another ballad, reviving The Browns' *The Three Bells*, featuring Norman Petty on piano, reaches UK #17.

Mar [1] Group embarks on 15-date twice-nightly UK tour of independent theaters known as "The P.J. Show", with P.J. Proby and The Fourmost, at London's Finsbury Park Astoria.

[16] Tour ends at Usher Hall, Edinburgh, Scotland.

Aug A cover of The Strangeloves' US hit *I Want Candy* makes UK #25 and will be the group's last hit in its present form.

Nov *Good Lovin'* (later a US #1 for The Young Rascals) does not chart.

1966 **Jan** Poole and Howard return to UK after being arrested in Finland over a disputed £200 Helsinki hotel bill.

[28] Poole and The Tremeloes announce they are splitting.

May Mickie Clark, from Dagenham, replaces Alan Howard who leaves the music business to establish a dry-cleaning business. Poole releases solo *Hey Girl* which fails to chart.

June [6] Poole begins solo tour of Denmark, Sweden and Norway.

[10] The Tremeloes' solo career also starts unremarkably, as a Poole-less cover of Paul Simon's *Blessed* fails to chart.

July Group moves to CBS but cover of The Beatles' *Good Day Sunshine* from *Revolver* fails. New front man Len "Chip" Hawkes (b. Nov.11, 1946, London), replacing Clark on bass, helps develop a strong harmony vocal blend which will highlight subsequent records.

1967 **Mar** A "good-time" cover of Cat Stevens' *Here Comes My Baby* begins group's second and stronger lease of chart life, hitting UK #4.

[11] Group begins 21-date UK tour with The Spencer Davis Group, The Hollies and Paul Jones at Granada cinema, Mansfield, Notts.

[23] Poole releases his solo debut on CBS, a David & Jonathan song *That Reminds Me Baby*.

Apr [2] The Tremeloes' tour ends at Liverpool Empire, Merseyside.

May A revival of a Four Seasons B-side, *Silence Is Golden*, showcasing the group's perfected harmony vocals, is its biggest-seller, topping UK chart for 3 weeks. Meanwhile, *Here Comes My Baby* reaches US #13.

June [30] The Tremeloes embark on debut US tour in Ohio. (On their arrival at Kennedy airport, New York, their plane lands with full emergency. During the tour, they are made freemen of Jersey Shore, PA, and receive golden keys from the mayor.)

July *Here Come The Tremeloes* (re-titled **Here Comes My Baby** in US) makes UK #15 and US #119 (the group's only album success).

Aug Uptempo *Even The Bad Times Are Good* hits UK #4, as *Silence Is Golden* makes US #11 and is a million-seller.

Oct *Even The Bad Times Are Good* makes US #36.

Nov Although the group is now a familiar sight on UK TV and live circuit, record success varies, its material aligning it away from the progressing rock scene. More subtle and less commercial ballad *Be Mine* makes only UK #39.

1968 **Feb** *Suddenly You Love Me* identifies group's pop market by blending strongly commercial ingredients. It hits UK #6.

Mar *Suddenly You Love Me* reaches US #44, the group's final US chart entry. The Tremeloes tour South America, playing 14 shows in Argentina and 6 in Uruguay.

Apr They begin UK package tour with The Kinks, The Herd and others. (Munden misses the start because of chickenpox.)

May Latin-tinged uptempo *Helule Helule* reaches UK #14.

Oct *My Little Lady*, another exuberant harmony rocker, hits UK #6.

Dec Band changes pace with a more serious cover of Bob Dylan's *I Shall Be Released*, reaching UK #29.

Nov [28] The Tremeloes N.American tour begins in Toronto, Canada.

1969 **Mar** Poole bows with new backing group The Seychelles on President label with *Send Her To Me*. (His solo career fails to take off, and he returns to the family's butchery business in Dagenham.)

Apr *Hello World* reaches UK #14.

May [11] The Tremeloes play the 17th **New Musical Express** Poll Winners Concert.

Oct West misses Hawkes wedding to Carol Dilworth after he's kidnapped by students.

Nov *(Call Me) Number One* hits UK #2 and is one of the group's biggest UK sellers.

1970 **Apr** *By The Way* makes UK #35.

Oct *Me And My Life* hits UK #4, the group's final Top 10 entry.

1971 **July** *Hello Buddy* makes UK #32 and is the group's last hit single, as it becomes eclipsed by newcomers in UK teen market, like T.Rex, Sweet and Slade. With almost a decade's worth of familiar hits to draw upon,

The Tremeloes join the cabaret and northern UK club circuit, where the nostalgia factor ensures a consistently lucrative living.

'74 **Nov** Hawkes leaves for a solo vocal career, concentrating on country music (but will find no greater success).

'75 **Jan** Blakley leaves the group.

'88 The Tremeloes, having made a brief recording comeback covering F.R. David's hit *Words*, are still on the cabaret circuit and 60s nostalgia tours around UK, sometimes with original leader as Brian Poole And The Tremeloes, performing early beat-era material, and sometimes as The Tremeloes, playing later hits.

'89 **June** Poole joins The Troggs' Reg Presley, The Searchers' Mike Pender, Clem Curtis from The Foundations and The Merseybeats' Tony Crane to temporarily form The Corporation (aka The Travelling Wrinklies). They perform hit medleys from the 60s on a UK summer tour and release a version of *Ain't Nothing But A House Party* on their own label. Ultimately all return to their day jobs.

IGGY POP

'64 Pop (b. James Jewel Osterburg, Apr.21, 1947, Muskegan, Ann Arbor, MI) joins The Iguanas as drummer and singer, and has one-off jobs drumming for Junior Wells, Buddy Guy, The Shangri-Las and others.

'65 The Iguanas release a cover of Bo Diddley's *Mona*, of which 1,000 copies are made and sold at gigs. He meets Ron Asheton and James Williamson, and leaves The Iguanas to join The Prime Movers with Asheton on bass (who is sacked after 2 weeks and later joins The Chosen Few). He adopts the name Iggy Pop: Iggy after The Iguanas, Pop after local junkie Jim Popp.

'66 Pop moves to Chicago, IL, with friend Sam Lay, drummer with The Butterfield Blues Band.

'67 He returns to Michigan and forms The Psychedelic Stooges with Asheton and his brother Scott on drums.
Oct [31] Iggy & The Stooges make their live debut at an Ann Arbor, MI, Halloween party.
Dec Dave Alexander joins on bass. Pop appears in an obscure art movie with Nico.

'68 Band continues to play live, mostly around Michigan, supporting Blood, Sweat & Tears at 1 gig. Pop is also busted for indecent exposure.

'69 Elektra A&R employee Danny Fields, in Detroit, MI, to sign The MC5, sees the group, now abbreviated to The Stooges, and signs it. The Stooges are advanced $25,000 to record a debut album.
Aug *The Stooges* reaches US #106. It is produced by John Cale and recorded in 4 days.

'70 Band adds Steve Mackay on sax and ex-roadie Bill Cheatham on guitar.
July *Fun House* is released, produced by Don Gallucci (who produced The Kingsmen's *Louie Louie*). James Williamson joins on guitar.
Aug Alexander and Cheatham quit, while Zeke Zettner, another ex-roadie, joins.

'71 **Aug** Band splits due to drug related problems and Pop moves to Florida to improve his golf, and cuts lawns for a living.

'72 He turns down an offer to return to Elektra Records. He meets admirer David Bowie and his then manager Tony DeFries in New York. They persuade Pop to sign with MainMan Management and he re-forms The Stooges.
July Iggy & The Stooges, featuring Pop, the Asheton brothers and Williamson, play UK debut at a King's Cross cinema, London. They begin sessions for a new album.

'73 **Apr** *Raw Power* is released, the first of a 2-album deal with CBS, and reaches US #182. A new album is planned, but disagreements between band and management prevent its release. (Out-takes and sessions from it are later issued by US Bomp and French Siamese Records in the late 70s.) DeFries sacks Williamson over drug problems and Scott Thurston joins on keyboards.
Oct Band moves back to US for a tour which ends in violence at 2 gigs in Detroit. One of the shows, recorded on a cassette machine, is issued as *Metallic K.O.*

'74 The Stooges split from MainMan, and then disband.

'75 Williamson becomes a recording engineer in Los Angeles, CA, while Asheton forms new short-lived US band The New Order, and later Destroy All Monsters with ex-MC5 members.
May New sessions for Pop are sponsored by rock journalist Bob Edmonds and songwriter Jimmy Webb. Pop, Williamson and Thurston begin to record 9 tracks, which remain incomplete as Pop disappears. (He has checked himself into a Los Angeles psychiatric institute for drug rehabilitation. Reportedly David Bowie is his only visitor.)

'76 **Mar** [21] Pop and Bowie are involved in a drug bust in their hotel room in Rochester, NY.

1977 **Jan** Pop appears on Bowie's *Low*.
Apr Pop's first solo album *The Idiot* is released by Bowie's current label RCA and is "recorded" by Bowie, rather than produced. It reaches US #72 and UK #30, and includes the first version of future Bowie hit *China Girl* co-written by the pair. Pop tours (with Bowie playing keyboards) and support band Blondie. Throughout the summer, old Stooges numbers become regular features of punk live sets including those by The Sex Pistols, The Damned and others.
June *Raw Power* is re-issued and reaches UK #44. (The track *Hard To Beat* is re-titled *Your Pretty Face Has Gone To Hell*.)
Sept *Lust For Life* reaches US #120 and UK #28, produced by Bowie. It was recorded and mixed in 13 days in Berlin and includes *The Passenger*, inspired by a Jim Morrison poem.

1978 *Skydog In France* and *Kill City* from the May 1975 sessions are released on Bomp in USA and Radar in UK. Live album, taken from the 2 most recent tours, is issued as *TV Eye (1977 Live)* on RCA, produced by Bowie.
June He plays shows at London's Music Machine.

1979 Pop signs to Arista Records and begins work on a new album.
Mar He forms a new touring band, including ex-Sex Pistols Glen Matlock, ex-Ike & Tina Turner band leader Jackie Clark and regular Pop keyboardist Scott Thurston.
Apr Tour strikes problems because of associations with Matlock's former band and several gigs are cancelled by authorities.
May *New Values* and single *I'm Bored* are released.
June *Five Foot One* is released.
Oct *New Values* reaches US #180 and UK #60. It is produced by Williamson and reunites Pop with Thurston, Scott Asheton, Williamson and MC5's guitarist Fred "Sonic" Smith. They tour UK with guest Matlock on bass. The inclusion of an ex-Sex Pistol leads to a ban by Dunstable Council which has still not lifted its ban on The Sex Pistols.

1980 **Mar** *Soldier* peaks at US #125 and UK #62. XTC's Barry Andrews replaces Thurston, who leaves to join The Motels. Other guests include Simple Minds, Bowie, Ivan Kral of The Patti Smith Group and Glen Matlock.
May [30-31] Pop plays at the Music Machine in London, following a German tour.
Aug *No Fun*, a Stooges compilation on Elektra, is released.

1981 **Sept** *Party*, his last for Arista, makes US #166, and track *Bang Bang* becomes a popular US dance hit.

1982 Pop publishes a book of anecdotes, **I Need More**, and moves to Brooklyn, New York.
Sept *Zombie Birdhouse* is issued on Blondie Chris Stein's Animal label. It fails to chart. Pop and Stein work on the soundtrack to movie "Rock'N'Rule".

1984 Pop sings title song on the soundtrack to Alex Cox movie "Repo Man".
1985 He appears in another Cox movie "Sid And Nancy".
1986 Pop signs to A&M worldwide.
Oct Debut single for the label is *Cry For Love* co-written by Steve Jones. *Blah Blah Blah*, produced by Dave Richards and Bowie, reaches US #75 and UK #43.

1987 **Jan** A cover of 1957 Johnny O'Keefe song *Real Wild Child* is Pop's first major single success, hitting UK #10. He also makes a cameo appearance in Paul Newman film "The Color Of Money".

1988 He appears on soundtrack of Australian movie "Dogs In Space".
June *Instinct*, produced by Bill Laswell and featuring ex-Sex Pistol Steve Jones on guitar (who also co-writes 4 songs), reaches US #110 and UK #61, while single *Cold Metal* fails to chart.

1990 **Feb** *Livin' On The Edge* makes UK #51.
Apr [6] John Waters movie "Cry Baby", in which Pop stars, opens in cinemas throughout US.
[16] He guests in NBC TV premiere "Shannon's Deal", having appeared in "Tales From The Crypt" and "Miami Vice".
July [21] *Brick By Brick*, produced by Don Was, reaches UK #50. (The track *My Baby Wants To Rock'N'Roll* is penned with Guns N' Roses' Slash, who plays on 4 tracks on the album, with Gunner Duff.)
Aug [18] *Brick By Brick* makes US #90.
Oct Pop and Debbie Harry contributes *Well Did You Evah* to **Red Hot + Blue**, an anthology of Cole Porter songs to benefit AIDS education.
[6] Pop participates in "A Gathering Of Tribes" festival held at the Shoreline Amphitheater, San Francisco, CA.
[13] Duet with The B52's Kate Pierson, *Candy*, peaks at UK #67.

1991 **Jan** Pop and Harry duet *Well Did You Evah* makes UK #42.
Feb *Candy* reaches US #28.
Mar Pop takes the role of famed Los Angeles District Attorney Vincent Bugliosi in John Moran's opera "The Manson Family".

PREFAB SPROUT

Paddy McAloon (guitar, vocals)
Martin McAloon (bass)
Wendy Smith (vocals, guitar)

1982 Prefab Sprout forms as a trio in Consett, Durham, based around Newcastle University English student Paddy McAloon (who has wanted to use the band name since he first thought of it in 1973). The early line-up, performing only McAloon songs, includes his brother Martin, Smith and drummer Mick Salmon, and plays local pub gigs in the Durham area.

Aug Rejected by all major labels, Prefab Sprout releases 1,000 copies of *Lions In My Own Garden* on its own Candle label. It impresses Newcastle record store owner and label head Keith Armstrong.

1983 **Mar** Armstrong signs Prefab Sprout to his Kitchenware label.
Oct *The Devil Has All The Best Tunes*, on Kitchenware, becomes a UK Independent hit.

1984 **Jan** *Don't Sing*, with Kitchenware signing the band to a distribution deal with CBS/Epic, peaks at UK #62.
Mar Debut album *Swoon* is released. Produced by Prefab Sprout and David Brewis, it reaches UK #22. Graham Lant has replaced Salmon. From it, *Couldn't Bear To Be Special* fails to chart.
Nov Ballad *When Love Breaks Down* also fails, but features another new drummer, Neil Conti.

1985 **Mar** *When Love Breaks Down* re-mix is released again, but fails.
June Critically revered *Steve McQueen*, produced by Thomas Dolby, makes UK #21. It is re-titled *Two Wheels Good* in US, after objections to original title from Steve McQueen's daughter and features extra cuts.
July From the album, *Faron Young* makes UK #74.
Sept *Appetite* fails to chart.
Nov *When Love Breaks Down* reaches UK #25 at the third attempt.

1986 **Feb** *Johnny Johnny* peaks at UK #64. Group plays a one-off gig at London's Hammersmith Odeon, before beginning a tour of Japan.

1987 Prefab Sprout retreats to create a new album around Paddy McAloon's compositions.

1988 **Feb** *Cars And Girls*, a McAloon commentary on Bruce Springsteen songs, makes UK #44.
Mar *From Langley Park To Memphis* hits UK #5. Produced by Paddy McAloon with Jon Kelly, Andy Richards and Thomas Dolby (who was scheduled to produce the whole album but could not because of illness), it features Stevie Wonder, Pete Townshend and The Andrae Crouch Gospel Singers. The album sells a half million copies in Europe in its first 10 weeks of release.
Apr *The King Of Rock'N'Roll* hits UK #7, but band is unwilling to tour.
June McAloon, still living in his parents' home in Consett, begins work on the soundtrack to an unwritten movie, "Zorro The Fox".
July *Hey Manhattan!* peaks at UK #72.
Nov Ballad *Nightingales*, featuring Stevie Wonder on harmonica, is released in UK.

1989 **July** *Protest Songs* reaches UK #18.

1990 **Aug** *Jordan: The Comeback*, again produced by Thomas Dolby, and featuring percussionist Luis Jardim, harmonica by Judd Lander and voices from actress Jenny Agutter, is released.
Aug [25] *Looking For Atlantis* peaks at UK #51.
Sept [8] *Jordan: The Comeback* hits UK #7.
Oct [27] *We Let The Stars Go* makes UK #50 (but will become one of the final nominations for the 1990 Ivor Novello Awards in the Best Song Musically & Lyrically category).

1991 **Jan** [12] *Carnival 2000*, promoted by unlikely appearance on UK TV kids' show "Going Live" makes UK #35, as 1 track on *Jordan: The E.P.*

ELVIS PRESLEY

1948 **Sept** [12] Presley (b. Jan.8, 1935, Tupelo, MS), one of twin sons (brother Jesse being stillborn), moves with his parents to Memphis, TN, where father Vernon finds a job at a paint company and mother Gladys works at a hospital as a nurse's aide. He goes to L.C. Humes high school by day, mowing lawns or cinema ushering in the evening to help make ends meet.

1949 **Aug** After a year in a cramped 1-room apartment, the family qualifies for federal housing. Presley, naturally shy, makes few friends at school and does not shine academically.

1953 **June** [14] Having become noted in his final year as a performer in the Christmas 1952 school show, and as an eye-catching dresser, Presley gains his high school diploma and leaves.

July [18] Employed by Crown Electric Co. as a truck driver, he calls one Saturday afternoon at Memphis Recording Service at 706, Union Ave., paying $4 to make a private recording. Marion Keisker, office manager for Sam Phillips, who owns the company and associated Sun Records label, finds his voice interesting, and keeps a tape of *My Happiness*, a reworking of a minor 1949 Ella Fitzgerald hit, and *That's When Your Heartaches Begin* to play for Phillips.

1954 **Jan** [4] Presley returns to cut a second private record, singing *Casual Love Affair* and *I'll Never Stand In Your Way*. This time, Phillips asks for Presley's address and a phone number, promising to contact him to do something in the studio.
Apr Looking for a vocalist to record *Without You*, a song he has received on an anonymous Nashville, TN, demo, Phillips agrees to Keisker's suggestion of Presley. He has several attempts but finds no empathy with the song, so Phillips lets Presley try out his gospel, country, R&B and Dean Martin material, and suggests some rehearsal sessions with other musicians. He calls guitarist Scotty Moore who runs local club band The Starlight Wranglers and, with the band's bass player Bill Black, they begin practice sessions.
July [5] Phillips tries a formal recording session with Presley, Moore and Black on country ballad *I Love You Because*. During a break, Presley fools with an uptempo romp through Arthur Crudup's blues number *That's All Right Mama*, and is joined by the other 2 in an impromptu jam session. Phillips, hearing the individual "something" for which he has been trying in vain with Presley, has them repeat it with tapes running and after a handful of run-throughs, a satisfactory master is made.
[6] Similar experimentation marks the next day's song – Bill Monroe's bluegrass *Blue Moon Of Kentucky*, which is accelerated to a racing tempo. Moore suggests the strange hybrid of (black) blues and (white) country will offend the Southern radio and musical community, but Phillips hears commercial potential, and couples *That's All Right Mama* with *Blue Moon Of Kentucky* as a Sun single.
[10] Phillips takes acetates of the recorded tracks to DJ Dewey Phillips (unrelated) at Memphis radio station WHBQ. The DJ rates *That's All Right Mama* and plays it on his R&B show "Red Hot And Blue" at 9.30pm. The switchboard immediately lights up with requests for repeat spins. Phillips phones Presley's home to ask him to come to the studio for an interview but Presley, forewarned by Sam Phillips of the single's likely airing, is at a movie, unable to face the embarrassment of hearing his voice on the radio. His parents seek him out and take him to WHBQ, where Phillips puts him at his ease, and Memphis learns that this hot new R&B singer is a local white 19-year-old.
[12] Presley signs a recording contract with Sun and a management deal with Scotty Moore, and gives notice to quit Crown Electric.
[19] With over 5,000 orders from the Memphis area, the single is released as Presley's Sun debut. (It will top the local chart by the end of the month, with action on both sides: Dewey Phillips plays *That's All Right Mama*, while Sleepy Eye John on WHEM and most other Memphis DJs play *Blue Moon Of Kentucky*.)
[20] The trio's first public performance is playing on a flatbed truck outside a new drugstore on Lamar Ave., Memphis, to mark its opening to a swelling and increasingly excited crowd. (Local engagements at the Eagle's Nest and Bel Air clubs follow, and Moore and Black leave The Starlight Wranglers to work with Presley full-time.)
Aug [10] Local agent Bob Neal books Presley low on the bill of a 2-performance show at Overton Park Shell auditorium in Memphis, headlined by Slim Whitman. After a polite reception to 2 country ballads during the afternoon show, he is advised by Dewey Phillips to perform uptempo material in the evening. He sings *Good Rockin' Tonight* and *That's All Right Mama*, with leg and body movements. The sensual performance drives the audience wild; Presley exits the stage bewildered by screams and shouts which all but drown the music and is pushed back by Phillips to encore, to a similar reception. Established country artist Webb Pierce, waiting to follow him, stands stunned and uncomprehending.
Sept [9] *Good Rockin' Tonight* (with *I Don't Care If The Sun Don't Shine*) is recorded as follow-up single.
[25] Sam Phillips gains a booking for Presley on Nashville's "Grand Ole Opry", aired live from Ryman Auditorium. He is introduced by Hank Snow and sings *Blue Moon Of Kentucky*, but fails to impress the staid audience, or the talent booker Jim Denny, who suggests he take up truck driving again.
Oct [16] He gets a better reception on country music radio show "The Louisiana Hayride", on KWKH in Shreveport, LA. After he sings *That's All Right Mama* to an enthusiastic live audience, station director Horace Logan signs Presley to a year's contract, for $18 per weekly slot. He is

Prince

Elvis Presley

Pink Floyd

also contracted to sing a radio commercial for one of the show's sponsors, a doughnut manufacturer.

Nov Neal (with Moore's agreement) takes over management and books the trio (billed as Elvis Presley, The Hillbilly Cat, And His Blue Moon Boys), initially at Nashville's annual Country Convention and then into 1-night dates all over the South.

Dec [18] Third single *Milk Cow Blues Boogie/You're A Heartbreaker* is recorded at Sun, with several versions of *I'm Left, You're Right, She's Gone.*

Jan Oscar Davis, right-hand man to talent entrepreneur Col. Tom Parker (manager of Eddy Arnold and Hank Snow), is impressed by Presley's power over an audience when he sees him at Memphis Airport Inn while visiting Neal. He reports the local phenomenon back to Parker, who negotiates with Neal to have Presley on his "Hank Snow Jamboree" package shows of country acts playing the Southern states. Parker views Presley performing in Texarkana, AR, then sets up a meeting in Memphis with Neal and Presley, where he offers guidance and suggests that Presley should be recording elsewhere than at Sun – a notion rejected both by Neal and Presley. *Milk Cow Blues Boogie* is released, but proves a poor seller.

Feb [5] Presley records a cover of Arthur Gunter's *Baby Let's Play House,* for which he invents a hiccuping rockabilly vocal style which will characterize many later impersonations of his singing. It is his first recording with drums, played by Johnny Bonnero from local Dean Beard Band.

Mar [5] Presley has his first TV exposure when the weekend edition of "The Louisiana Hayride" is televised locally. (Neal also gains the group an audition on Arthur Godfrey's "Talent Scouts" show in New York. Having to fly to the audition unnerves Presley and tryout performance of *Good Rockin' Tonight* is not his best. Godfrey's producers turn him down (and will pick up instead on his biggest 50s rival in popularity, Pat Boone).)

Apr *Baby Let's Play House/I'm Left, You're Right, She's Gone* is released by Sun, to better sales than its predecessor.
[5] Parker pays for Presley's parents to travel to see him on a "Hank Snow Jamboree" in Chattanooga, TN, and suggests that their son is being overworked (having previously ascertained Gladys Presley's fears on this) and that he needs more professional management. Gladys is cautious, mentioning Presley's obligations to Neal, Sun and "The Louisiana Hayride" (a contract now extended to 18 months), but Parker finds an ally in Vernon Presley (who will later give him signed permission to negotiate a new recording deal on his son's behalf).

May [13] Presley's stage act causes an audience riot for the first time, in Jacksonville, FL. He has much of his clothing ripped off, but escapes uninjured.

July *Baby Let's Play House* is Presley's first national chart entry, hitting #10 on **Billboard**'s Country chart, and Presley buys his first Cadillac. Parker begins to promote Presley outside the South, impressing New York music publisher Arnold Shaw with Presley's records and reputation, and via Shaw, top Cleveland, OH, DJ Bill Randle, who gives him heavy airplay which slowly spreads to New York.

Aug *Mystery Train/I Forgot To Remember To Forget,* Presley's final Sun single, is released. Parker spreads word that his contract with Sun may be for sale. Decca Records bids $5,000 and is turned down by Phillips, as is Dot Records' offer of $7,500. Parker hears that Mercury Records is considering a $10,000 bid, and makes it known to CBS/Columbia's Mitch Miller, who says he will up it to $15,000. Parker hints that RCA is considering $20,000, and Miller intimates that "no singer is worth that much". Ahmet Ertegun of Atlantic disagrees, and is willing to risk $25,000, but Parker insists that nearly twice as much is "more realistic".

Oct [15] Presley plays Lubbock, TX, where the opening act is local hillbilly duo Buddy (Holly) And Bob.

Nov With Neal's management contract about to expire, Parker takes up the negotiating power granted him by Presley's parents and works out a deal in New York with RCA Records and Aberbach publishing, which will pay Sun $35,000 for the Presley contract and all previously-recorded material, and Presley himself $5,000 as a past royalty settlement. (The publisher pays $10,000 of the sum for Presley's future song publishing on its Hill And Range subsidiary.)
[12] Presley is voted Most Promising Country And Western Artist in the annual US DJ poll, and Parker has him in prominent attendance at the Country Music DJ's Convention in Nashville.
[22] Neal's contract with Presley expires, and RCA/Aberbach/Parker's offer to Sam Phillips becomes official. In need of expansion capital (and with only a year of Presley's contract still to run), Phillips accepts. (Phillips begins investing in the fledgling Holiday Inn hotel chain,

which will make him a bigger fortune than the record industry.) RCA reissues all 5 Presley singles on its own label, though Sun still has a sell-off period for existing stock.

1956

Jan [10-11] Presley records his first RCA sessions, in Nashville. First cut is a cover of Ray Charles' *I Got A Woman,* and second is new song, *Heartbreak Hotel.* The session uses more musicians than the Sun recordings, including Dominic ("D.J.") Fontana on drums, ex-housedrummer with "The Louisiana Hayride", who has also been touring regularly with Presley.
[27] *Heartbreak Hotel* is issued to tie in with his US network TV debut.
[28] The William Morris agency books Presley into the first of 6 weekly guest slots (for $1,250 each) on Tommy and Jimmy Dorsey-hosted "Stage Show", aired live from New York on CBS. He performs *Heartbreak Hotel* and a cover of Carl Perkins' *Blue Suede Shoes.*
[30] In RCA's New York studios, Presley begins recording his own version of *Blue Suede Shoes,* plus 7 more tracks for his debut album. (Session will end Feb.1.)

Feb [4] On his second "Stage Show" appearance he sings *I Was The One* (B-side of *Heartbreak Hotel*) and Little Richard's *Tutti Frutti.*
[11] On "Stage Show" he performs *I Got A Woman* and a medley of *Shake, Rattle & Roll/Flip, Flop And Fly* and is introduced by Bill Randle, the first DJ to have played his records on the East Coast.
[18] Another "Stage Show" slot features *Baby Let's Play House* and a repeat of *Tutti Frutti.*

Mar *Heartbreak Hotel* debuts on US chart.
[17] Presley returns to "Stage Show", singing *Blue Suede Shoes* and *Heartbreak Hotel.*
[24] His final "Stage Show" appearance features *Money Honey* and *Heartbreak Hotel.*

Apr *Heartbreak Hotel* tops US chart for 8 weeks, becoming Presley's first million-seller (it also hits C&W #1 and R&B #5). B-side *I Was The One* makes US #23. *Blue Suede Shoes,* released as lead track on an EP, makes US #20 (Carl Perkins' original hits #2, behind *Heartbreak Hotel*).
[1] A screen test at Paramount studios in Hollywood, CA, for producer Hal Wallis results in a 3-film contract guaranteeing $450,000.
[3] Presley returns to US TV on NBC's "Milton Berle Show", aired live from aircraft carrier USS Hancock, moored at San Diego, CA. 25,000 people apply for tickets, and an estimated 40 million (a quarter of the US population) watch him sing *Heartbreak Hotel, Money Honey* and *Blue Suede Shoes.* He earns $5,000 from the show.
[10] Presley buys his parents a new $40,000 home in Audubon Park, Memphis, TN.
[11] Presley is flying to Nashville for a recording session when his plane develops engine trouble and has to make an emergency landing. Shaken, he records *I Want You, I Need You, I Love You* later in the day, but the incident creates an aversion to flying which lasts for years.
[23] Parker books Presley into an unsuitable Las Vegas, NV, residency – 2 weeks at the Venus Room of the Frontier hotel, paying $8,500 a week. Middle-aged audiences are cool (and Presley will not return to Vegas for 13 years). However, he appropriates an uptempo arrangement of R&B oldie *Hound Dog* from the hotel's lounge group, Freddie Bell & The Bell Boys.

May Debut album **Elvis Presley** tops US chart for 10 weeks (with advance orders of 362,000, making it RCA's biggest-selling album to date before it is even issued). Meanwhile, a cover of The Drifters' *Money Honey,* lead track on Presley's second EP, reaches US #76.

June *Heartbreak Hotel* is UK chart debut, hitting #2 (behind Pat Boone's *I'll Be Home*), while *Blue Suede Shoes* hits UK #9.
[5] On a second "Milton Berle Show", Presley does a comedy routine with Berle, singing *I Want You, I Need You, I Love You* and *Hound Dog,* in a hip-shaking performance which invites a storm of protest.

July [1] Presley returns to US NBC TV on "The Steve Allen Show" in New York, where the producers attempt to quieten the criticism by involving him in more comedy, and insisting on more sedate performances of *I Want You, I Need You, I Love You* and *Hound Dog* (the latter sung in white tie and tails to an actual (unmoved) Bassett hound).
[2] Presley records *Hound Dog* at RCA's New York studio, finally satisfied after 31 takes. He also cuts quicker final versions of *Don't Be Cruel* and *Any Way You Want Me ,* with The Jordanaires (Gordon Stoker, Ben Speer and Brock Speer) who have started out as gospel group in Springfield, MO, supplying backing vocals for the first time.
[4] He returns to Memphis (by train) to play a charity concert at the 14,000-seater Russwood Auditorium.
[28] *I Want You, I Need You, I Love You* tops US chart for a week and is his second million-selling single. B-side *My Baby Left Me* (like *That's All Right Mama* an Arthur Crudup song), reaches US #31.

Aug Presley's most successful single is released, coupling *Don't Be Cruel* (which hits US #1 for 7 weeks) and *Hound Dog* (which lines up behind it at #2). US sales top 5 million.

[22] Filming begins in Hollywood on "The Reno Brothers", for which Hal Wallis "loans" his new movie property to 20th Century Fox. A Civil War western starring Richard Egan and Debra Paget, it is adapted to feature Presley and to include 4 songs, all period-style written by Ken Darby (whose trio backs Presley on them). Ballad *Love Me Tender* (based on traditional *Aura Lee*), is sufficiently strong and the producers re-title the movie after it.

Sept *I Want You, I Need You, I Love You* makes UK #14 (in the same week *Heartbreak Hotel* drops out of UK Top 10, having already spent 18 weeks in Top 30).

[1-3] At Radio Recorders studios in Hollywood, with his usual musicians, Presley records 13 songs for his second album. In Hollywood, he also buys his mother a pink Cadillac.

[9] A Presley segment aired from Hollywood is slotted into the New York-transmitted "Toast Of The Town" show hosted by Ed Sullivan on CBS. (Sullivan is originally on record as saying he would never have Presley on his show, but Steve Allen's success in direct competition has changed his mind, and Parker negotiates $50,000 for 3 slots.) It is watched by an estimated 54 million people (a third of the US population), and features *Don't Be Cruel*, *Love Me Tender*, *Ready Teddy* and *Hound Dog*. Sullivan himself is ill, and the show is hosted by Charles Laughton.

[10] On Monday after the show, record stores are deluged with requests for *Love Me Tender*, not scheduled for release for many weeks.

[26] He returns to Tupelo, MS, to perform at the annual Mississippi-Alabama Fair And Dairy Show. Tupelo declares it "Elvis Presley Day" in his honor, and he plays afternoon and evening open-air shows, donating his $10,000 fee to the town.

Oct *Blue Moon*, one of 6 simultaneously-released singles comprising the whole debut album in 45rpm form, reaches US #55 while Sun track *I Don't Care If The Sun Don't Shine*, released by RCA on an EP, makes US #74. RCA, unable to resist huge advance orders (856,237 by the end of Sept.), releases *Love Me Tender* before the movie premiere. It tops the US chart in its second week and holds #1 for 5 weeks, selling over 2 million. In UK, *Hound Dog* hits #2.

[16] "Love Me Tender" premieres at New York's Paramount theater. Critics slay it but it recoups its $1-million budget in little more than a week and 20th Century Fox releases a record 550 prints around US.

[28] He appears on Ed Sullivan's "Toast Of The Town" show again, performing *Don't Be Cruel*, *Love Me Tender*, *Hound Dog* and *Love Me* .

Nov *Any Way You Want Me*, B-side of *Love Me Tender*, reaches US #27.

[10] **Billboard**'s national DJ poll reveals that Presley is the most-played male artist and country artist of 1956.

Dec Second album *Elvis* tops US chart for 5 weeks, while *Love Me*, lead track on EP *Elvis, Vol.1* (extracts from the album) hits US #6. Also from the EP, *When My Blue Moon Turns To Gold Again* and *Paralyzed* make US #27 and #59 respectively. From a similar EP of extracts, *Elvis, Vol.2*, sentimental ballad *Old Shep* reaches US #47. *Don't Be Cruel* peaks at UK #17, *Blue Moon* hits UK #9 and B-side *I Don't Care If The Sun Don't Shine* makes UK #23.

[4] At home in Memphis for Christmas, Presley wanders into Sun studios in afternoon where Carl Perkins and his group are recording a session, with Jerry Lee Lewis guesting on piano. Johnny Cash is also present but his wife draws him away to go shopping. The others settle down to a jam session, mostly on gospel songs and recent hits. Phillips tapes these and they become the legendary "Million Dollar Quartet Session" (issued on disk after Presley's death). The "Million Dollar Quartet" phrase is coined by **Memphis Press Scimitar** entertainment editor Bob Johnson.

[13] Movie "Love Me Tender" premieres in London.

1957 Jan In Hollywood, he films his first contracted movie for Hal Wallis, "Loving You" (originally titled "Lonesome Cowboy"), co-starring with Lizabeth Scott and Wendel Corey. Presley's parents stay with him at Hollywood's Knickerbocker hotel during filming. Meanwhile, *Poor Boy*, from the EP of songs from *Love Me Tender*, reaches US #35 and *Love Me Tender* hits UK #10.

[4] Presley has a medical check-up at Kennedy Veterans hospital. It is a preliminary to his call-up by the US Army.

[6] His last appearance on network TV for some years is the third contracted Ed Sullivan slot in New York. During uptempo numbers, he is shown on screen only from waist up.

[12-13 and 19] 3 sessions at Radio Recorders produce 12 new tracks, including *Peace In The Valley* and *All Shook Up*.

Feb *Too Much*, introduced on his last Ed Sullivan appearance, tops US chart for 3 weeks and is another million-seller. B-side *Playing For Keeps* makes US #34.

Mar Sun single *Mystery Train* is released for the first time in UK and peaks at #23 while *Rip It Up*, from *Elvis*, is also extracted as a UK single, and makes #27.

[19] He buys Graceland, a large house in 13 acres of ground in Memphis suburb Whitehaven.

Apr *All Shook Up*, written by Otis Blackwell (who also penned *Don't Be Cruel*), tops US chart for 8 weeks, selling 2 million copies. B-side ballad *That's When Your Heartaches Begin* (which includes a short spoken recitation) reaches US #58.

[30] The songs for forthcoming "Jailhouse Rock" are cut at Radio Recorders studios, with songwriters Jerry Leiber and Mike Stoller.

May In Hollywood, he films "Jailhouse Rock" for MGM, co-starring Judy Tyler and Mickey Shaughnessy. Meanwhile, *Peace In The Valley*, now on an EP of 4 religious songs, reaches US #25 (and #3 on US Album chart).

June *Too Much* hits UK #6.

July *(Let Me Be Your) Teddy Bear*, from film "Loving You", tops US chart for 7 weeks, and is another 2-million-plus seller. The film's ballad title song is B-side and reaches US #28. *Loving You*, which has the soundtrack recordings on one side and a second side of new non-movie songs (including a cover of Bing Crosby/Grace Kelly hit ballad *True Love*), hits US #1 for 10 weeks, earning a gold disk for half million sales. Meanwhile, *All Shook Up* is released in UK, and becomes Presley's first UK #1, topping the chart for 7 weeks and selling over a half million copies.

[9] Movie "Loving You" is released in US.

Aug The UK outlet for Presley's recordings changes, as RCA's own label is launched through Decca. EMI, which has previously issued RCA product on the HMV label, has a lengthy sell-off period for recordings already licensed, and for several months the UK chart is flooded by competing Presley singles on 2 labels. One of the first US RCA singles released is *(Let Me Be Your) Teddy Bear*, which hits UK #2 for 2 weeks (behind *All Shook Up*, which is on HMV).

[2] The Official UK Elvis Presley Fan Club is launched. (In US, there are already thousands of Presley fan clubs.)

[23] Film "Loving You" opens in London.

[31] He plays his first Canadian live date, at the Empire Stadium in Vancouver, where fans rush the stage during the show. Presley and his band have to flee to avoid being trampled.

Sept EP *Loving You, Vol.1*, a 4-song extract from the soundtrack, reaches US Album chart #18, while EP *Just For You*, which has 4 songs from the album's non-film side, makes US #16 on the Album chart. In UK, HMV (in its sell-off period) releases *Paralyzed*, from *Elvis*, and it hits UK #8, giving Presley 3 simultaneous UK Top 20 entries.

Oct *Jailhouse Rock*, Leiber/Stoller-written title song from the film, tops US chart for 7 weeks, selling over 2 million. Also from the movie, B-side *Treat Me Nice* makes US #27.

[21] Film "Jailhouse Rock" opens in US.

Nov With the movie not yet scheduled for UK release, RCA holds *Jailhouse Rock* back until the New Year in UK, and releases *(Let's Have A) Party*, another rocker from *Loving You*. It hits UK #2. B-side *Got A Lot O' Livin' To Do* makes UK #18. At the same time, *Loving You*, B-side of *Teddy Bear*, reaches UK #24, while HMV pushes out yet another single, coupling *Lawdy Miss Clawdy* and *Trying To Get You*. Both sides chart, at UK #15 and #16 respectively. In the week ending Nov.2, Presley has 8 titles in UK Top 20 (at 3, 11, 17, 19, 21, 24, 26 and 30).

Dec *Elvis' Christmas Album* tops US chart for 4 weeks. Initially packaged as a deluxe gift item, with a sleeve incorporating 10 pages of photos, it has a side of secular Christmas material (including *Blue Christmas* and an appropriation of Clyde McPhatter and The Drifters' arrangement of *White Christmas*) and a side of carols and hymns which incorporates 4 songs from EP *Peace In The Valley*. It earns a gold disk (and over 2 decades of repeat Christmas sales will sell well over a million copies). In UK, where album sales are still minimal, RCA extracts *Santa Bring My Baby Back (To Me)* and it hits UK #7.

[20] Against nationwide teenage protest, Presley's draft notice for the US Army is served to him (at home at Graceland, where he has returned for Christmas with his parents) by Milton Bowers, Chairman of the Memphis Draft Board.

[21] Paramount Pictures petitions the Army to defer Presley's induction date, so that movie "King Creole" can be completed. The draft board agrees to a 2-month delay, which incurs a barrage of public comment alleging "special treatment".

Jan Presley travels from Memphis to Hollywood by train, to film "King Creole", co-starring Walter Matthau and Carolyn Jones. He records the songs for the film soundtrack at Radio Recorders, with his usual Nashville musicians.

[10] *Jailhouse Rock*, due for release as a UK single on this day, is put back for a week because Decca's pressing plant is unable to have enough copies ready to meet advance orders of 250,000.

[16] Film *Jailhouse Rock* premieres in London.

[17] *Jailhouse Rock*, released in UK, sells 500,000 copies in first 3 days.

[25] *Jailhouse Rock* enters UK chart at #1 (the first time this feat has been achieved), and stays at the top for 3 weeks, selling 750,000 copies. Meanwhile, last UK HMV single, old Sun track *I'm Left, You're Right, She's Gone*, peaks at UK #18.

Feb *Don't*, Presley's first slow ballad A-side since *Love Me Tender*, tops US chart for 5 weeks, topping 2 million sales – aided by B-side *I Beg Of You*, which hits US #8. In UK, the 5-song EP from "Jailhouse Rock" joins the single on chart, reaching #15.

[1] His last recording session prior to Army induction produces 4 songs, including *Your Cheating Heart* (not issued until 1965) and *Wear My Ring Around Your Neck* (his next single).

[17] Movie "Jailhouse Rock" goes on general UK release, while in US production of "King Creole" moves to New Orleans, LA, for location filming. Presley takes over a floor of the Roosevelt hotel with his entourage. The city declares it "Elvis Presley Day" as he arrives, and the streets are so choked with people that filming is initially impossible.

Mar *Don't* hits UK #2 for 3 weeks, held from the top by Perry Como's *Magic Moments*.

[24] Presley is sworn in as US private 53310761 at 5pm at the Memphis draft office, then leaves by bus for Fort Chaffee, AR, for full induction. He earns $83 a month as a private.

Apr *Wear My Ring Around Your Neck* peaks at US #2, behind David Seville's *Witch Doctor*. US sales are over a million, and B-side *Doncha' Think It's Time* makes US #21.

May *Elvis' Golden Records*, a compilation of singles from *Heartbreak Hotel* to *Jailhouse Rock*, hits US #3, earning a gold disk, and staying in US Top 25 for 74 weeks. Meanwhile, *Wear My Ring Around Your Neck* hits UK #2 for 2 weeks, behind Connie Francis' *Who's Sorry Now?*

June [4] Film "King Creole" is on US.

[10-11] On his first weekend's leave from US Army, Presley records 2 sessions in Nashville (which will provide his hit singles of late 1958 and 1959). New guitarist Hank Garland plays in place of Moore, who is busy with other recording projects since Presley's draft has ended his live work. Bass is played by Bob Moore. (Black is working in Memphis on his own projects since finishing work with Presley in Feb. and will have success with his instrumental Bill Black Combo.)

[25] Presley's parents celebrate their 25th wedding anniversary while living in a house he has rented for them, close to Fort Hood, TX, where he is undergoing basic training.

July *Hard-Headed Woman*, from the soundtrack of "King Creole", tops US chart for 2 weeks, selling over a million. In keeping with the movie's setting, its arrangement incorporates elements of Dixieland jazz in rock backing. B-side *Don't Ask Me Why*, also from the film, reaches US #28.

Aug *Hard-Headed Woman* hits UK #2 for 2 weeks, held from #1 by The Everly Brothers' *All I Have To Do Is Dream/Claudette*.

Gladys Presley falls ill, and is returned to Memphis and admitted to the Methodist hospital where the family doctor and 4 specialists diagnose acute hepatitis. After 3 days, her condition worsens and the hospital advises Presley to return home. After initial reluctance (the Army fearing press allegations of "preferential treatment"), he is granted compassionate leave. Against Gladys' wishes, he flies from Texas.

[12] He visits his mother in hospital, staying the night and much of the following day.

[14] He has returned home to rest when Gladys dies of heart failure at 3.15am, with Vernon Presley at her bedside.

[15] Her funeral is held at the National Funeral Home in Forest Hill, Memphis. Presley is so overcome with grief that he is unable to stand for much of the proceedings and has to be supported. 500 policeman keep a gigantic crowd at bay.

[28] Film "King Creole" opens in London.

Sept Its sell-off period expired, EMI deletes all Presley and other RCA product from its HMV catalog.

[22] After giving a press conference at Brooklyn Army Terminal, New York (by special dispensation of the military), Presley sets sail for a tour of duty in Germany, on troopship USS Randall.

Oct [1] Presley arrives in Germany at Bremerhaven and is transported to the US Army base at Friedburg, near Frankfurt, where he joins his unit – Company D, 1st Battalion, 3rd Armor Corps. (He will buy a house in nearby Bad Neuheim, taking advantage of a military rule which allows him to live off camp if he has family to support. He will move his father, grandmother, some friends and staff into it. On the base, he will be a Specialist Fourth Class (Corporal) driving a jeep for his platoon sergeant, Billy Wilson.)

Soundtrack album from "King Creole" hits US #2, behind Frank Sinatra's *Only The Lonely*. In UK, the title song is extracted and hits #2, again behind Connie Francis with *Stupid Cupid/Carolina Moon*. (Moving it aside from #2 the following week is newcomer Cliff Richard with *Move It*, which is also held at #2 by Francis.)

Nov The introduction of a UK Album chart sees *Elvis' Golden Records* and *King Creole* hit UK #3 and #4 respectively.

Dec *One Night*, a heavy blues-rock treatment of a 1956 Smiley Lewis R&B hit (with lyrics altered from the suggestive originals to ensure radio play), hits US #4, as double A-side frantic rocker *I Got Stung* hits US #8. US sales again top a million.

1959 Jan *I Got Stung/One Night*, combined for chart purposes in UK, enters UK chart at #1, and holds for 5 weeks.

Mar RCA releases the pre-Germany press conference and interviews as a spoken-word EP, *Elvis Sails*.

Apr Compilation *For LP Fans Only*, rounding up singles B-sides and EP tracks, including some Sun recordings, reaches US #19. UK equivalent (with extra tracks) is titled *Elvis*, and hits #4.

May Another double A-side release, *A Fool Such As I* (revival of 1953 country hit by Hank Snow) hits US #2 and wild rocker *I Need Your Love Tonight* hits US #4, selling over 2 million in US. In UK, the sides are combined, like the previous single, for 1 chart listing. It tops UK chart for 6 weeks (dethroning Buddy Holly's *It Doesn't Matter Anymore*).

June Presley develops an abscessed tonsil. After treatment, he travels to Paris, France, where he will give an impromptu performance for the staff of the Lido night club.

Aug *A Big Hunk O' Love*, one of Presley's fastest-paced rockers, tops US chart for 2 weeks, selling over a million, while B-side ballad *My Wish Came True* peaks at US #12. In UK, *A Big Hunk O' Love* hits #3. These are the last of the June 1958 recordings to be issued on single. (A dearth of new Presley records will follow until after his 1960 Army release – with the approval of Parker, who wants fans sufficiently starved of product to prepare for the post-Army releases.)

Sept In Bad Neuheim, he is introduced to a young American girl, 14-year-old Priscilla Beaulieu, stepdaughter of a US Air Force captain, who lives nearby.

Oct Compilation *A Date With Elvis*, another gathering of singles and EP tracks, makes US #32 and hits UK #4 (the UK version has an amended and expanded track listing). Its sleeve includes a calendar for counting down the days to Presley's US Army release.

1960 Jan [20] Presley is promoted to Sergeant.

Feb 4-song EP *Strictly Elvis*, featuring sentimental *Old Shep* (unavailable in UK since 1958), reaches UK #26.

Mar Compilation *50 Million Elvis Fans Can't Be Wrong – Elvis Gold Records, Vol.2* makes US #31, earning a gold disk.

[1] The US Army hosts a "Farewell Elvis" press conference at Friedburg base in Germany.

[2] He flies home for demobilization from Frankfurt. The plane makes a refuelling stop at Prestwick Airport, Scotland, and while it is on the ground, Presley talks to fans through an airport fence. This is the only occasion on which he sets foot on UK soil.

[3] At 7.42am, he lands in a snowstorm at McGuire Air Force Base, US.

[5] Presley is demobbed from the US Army at Fort Dix, NJ.

[7] He arrives home in Memphis, having come from Fort Dix by train.

[20-21] His first post-Army recording session takes place in Nashville, with Moore back in the band (Black will never play again with Presley). His regular studio pianist is now Floyd Cramer (who will become a hitmaker in his own right). 6 tracks are recorded, including *Stuck On You* and *Fame And Fortune*, which are rush-scheduled by RCA.

[23] He travels by train from Nashville to Miami, FL, to tape a TV show slot with Frank Sinatra.

[26] The Timex-sponsored Sinatra show is recorded at Fontainebleu hotel, Miami Beach. Presley guests with Sammy Davis Jr. and Sinatra's daughter Nancy. He sings *Fame And Fortune* and *Stuck On You* in a solo slot, and duets with Sinatra on a traded duet of *Love Me Tender* and *Witchcraft*. Parker has negotiated $125,000 for the appearance. (He also sings *It's Nice To Go Traveling* in army uniform with the rest of the cast.)

Apr [3-4] A longer Nashville session is later rated one of Presley's most artistically successful, producing material for *Elvis Is Back*, and 2

million-selling singles, *It's Now Or Never* and *Are You Lonesome Tonight*.
[18] He travels with his father from Memphis to Hollywood on
Missouri Pacific Railroad's Texas Eagle Express, to begin filming "G.I.
Blues."
[25] *Stuck On You*, released with advance US orders of 1,275,077, tops
US chart for 4 weeks. B-side *Fame And Fortune* makes US #17. *Stuck On
You* hits UK #2 (behind Lonnie Donegan's *My Old Man's A Dustman*).
[26] Filming begins for Wallis and Paramount on "G.I. Blues", which
co-stars Juliet Prowse, and typecasts Presley as a young US soldier in
Germany (though in an entertainment unit, from which the Army had
withheld Presley for fear of more "special treatment" accusations).
May [6] The songs for "G.I. Blues" soundtrack are recorded in
Hollywood.
[12] "Frank Sinatra – Timex Show" is aired on US ABC TV.
June Presley has his tonsils removed in hospital in Memphis.
Meanwhile, *Elvis Is Back*, with tracks from the Apr. Nashville session,
hits US #2 (behind The Kingston Trio's *Sold Out*) and earns a gold disk.
In UK, it hits #1 as compilation *Elvis' Gold Records, Vol.2* hits UK #4.
July [3] Vernon Presley marries divorcee Dee Stanley, whom he has
met while living in Germany (her ex-husband having been a master
sergeant in US Army).
[25] Filming of "Flaming Star" (originally titled "Flaming Lance")
begins at 20th Century Fox studios in Hollywood. Co-starring Steve
Forrest and Barbara Eden, it is a western directed by Don Siegel, with
Presley in a troubled role as a half-breed.
Aug *It's Now Or Never*, recorded at the Apr.3 session but not used on
the album, tops US chart for 5 weeks. It is an adaptation of 1901 Italian
song *O Sole Mio* and, with its semi-operatic Latin sound, stands apart
from anything Presley has recorded before. (Worldwide, it will become
his biggest-selling single, with total sales over 20 million.) B-side, the
contrasting *A Mess Of Blues* reaches US #32. In UK, a copyright wrangle
over *It's Now Or Never* temporarily prevents its release, so RCA
promotes *A Mess Of Blues* and pairs it with *The Girl Of My Best Friend*
from *Elvis Is Back*. Both sides chart, and for the first time both sides of
a Presley single obtain UK Top 10 positions, with *A Mess Of Blues*
hitting #3 and *The Girl Of My Best Friend* hitting #5.
[8-12] 4 songs intended for film "Flaming Star" are recorded at 20th
Century Fox studios, Hollywood. (Only the title song and 1 other will
be used in the movie.)
Presley is named Public Enemy #1 by the East German communist
newspaper **Young World**, following a riot for which he is blamed. 6
Elvis fans are jailed for between 1 and 2 years for forming an Elvis fan
club and singing rock'n'roll songs in the street.
Oct [20] Film "G.I. Blues" opens in US.
[28] Copyright problems resolved, *It's Now Or Never* is released in UK,
having built up advance orders of 500,000, the largest known in UK.
[30-31] In Nashville, Presley records his first lengthy gospel music
session. (It will form much of his 1961 inspirational *His Hand In Mine*.)
Nov *It's Now Or Never* enters UK chart at #1, holding for 9 weeks. *Are
You Lonesome Tonight*, a ballad originally popular in the mid-20s via Al
Jolson, hits US #1 for 6 weeks, selling 2 million copies. In it, Presley
updates the midsong narration technique originally employed on *That's
When Your Heartaches Begin* in 1957, which splits listeners into
love-or-hate camps. B-side *I Gotta Know* makes US #20.
[7] Songs for film "Wild In The Country" are recorded in Hollywood.
[10] "G.I. Blues" premieres in London.
Dec With her parents' permission, Priscilla Beaulieu flies to Memphis
to spend Christmas with Presley and his family at Graceland.
Meanwhile, the soundtrack album from "G.I. Blues" tops US chart for
10 weeks, earning a gold disk, and tops UK chart for 25 weeks (well
into mid-1961).
[13] *It's Now Or Never* passes the million sales mark in UK in 6 weeks:
the one-millionth copy leaves Decca's pressing plant at 3.30pm. This is
a new record time for a disk achieving this total in UK – the previous
holder, Harry Belafonte's *Mary's Boy Child* in 1957, took 8 weeks.
[20] Film "Flaming Star" opens in US, to disappointing box office
returns compared with "G.I. Blues."
1961 Jan *Are You Lonesome Tonight?* tops UK chart for 4 weeks, having
entered at #2.
[13] Film "Flaming Star" opens in London.
[25] Presley performs at a benefit concert on "Elvis Presley Day" at
Ellis Auditorium in Memphis in aid of local charities including the
Elvis Presley Youth Center in Tupelo, raising $51,000. During the show,
he is presented with a plaque by RCA to mark record sales of 76
million worldwide.
Feb *His Hand In Mine*, his first wholly religious album (made up of

most of the gospel songs recorded at the end of Oct.), reaches US #13
and will earn a gold disk for a half million sales.
Mar The only secular recording at the Oct.1960 gospel session,
Surrender, another dramatic adaptation of old Italian ballad *Come Back
To Sorrento*, hits US #1 for 2 weeks, and is a million-seller. B-side is
Lonely Man, written for "Wild In The Country" but cut from the
completed film. In UK, *Wooden Heart* from **G.I. Blues** is released as a
single (in common with most of the world, but not US). It tops UK
chart for 4 weeks, staying in UK Top 50 for 27 weeks. Some location
filming is done for movie "Blue Hawaii".
[25] Presley plays another benefit show, at Bloch Arena in Pearl
Harbor, HI, raising $53,000 for USS Arizona Memorial Fund. (His
17-song set will be his last stage appearance for nearly 8 years.)
May EP *Elvis By Request*, an experimental 4-track release at 33rpm,
headed by the title song from "Flaming Star", reaches US #14. In UK,
Surrender enters the chart at #1 and holds for 4 weeks.
June Gospel *His Hand In Mine* hits UK #3. Presley turns to R&B for
revival of Chuck Willis' *I Feel So Bad*, which hits US #5. B-side is balla
title song from "Wild In The Country", which makes US #26.
[15] Film "Wild In The Country", a drama co-starring Presley with
Tuesday Weld and Hope Lange, opens in US. Like "Flaming Star", it
has few songs and is serious in intent. (It is also not a huge
money-maker, inevitably leading Col. Parker back to lighter, more
lucrative "G.I. Blues"-type films.)
Aug *Something For Everybody*, divided into ballad and beat sides, a
recorded with *I Feel So Bad* in Nashville on Mar.12/13, tops US chart
3 weeks, earning a gold disk. At the last minute, *I Slipped, I Stumbled,
Fell*, aggressive rocker recorded for "Wild In The Country", is added
Sept The popularity of *Wild In The Country* and *I Feel So Bad* is revers
in UK, as the former hits #2 and the latter reaches #20.
Oct The coupling of classic-style rockers, *(Marie's The Name) His Late
Flame* and *Little Sister*, proves to be Presley's most potent double A-si
since *A Fool Such As I/I Need Your Love Tonight*, hitting US #4 and #5
respectively, and topping a million sales.
Nov *(Marie's The Name) His Latest Flame* tops UK chart for 3 weeks,
while *Little Sister* reaches UK #20. **Something For Everybody** hits UK
(behind **Another Black And White Minstrel Show** by The George
Mitchell Minstrels).
[14] Film "Blue Hawaii", a romantic musical with 14 songs and
co-starring Presley with Joan Blackman and Angela Lansbury, is
released in US. (It will be a huge box office success, setting the seal o
money-making Presley movie formula.)
Dec Soundtrack album from "Blue Hawaii" tops the US chart for 20
weeks, and is Presley's biggest-selling album to date, topping 2 milli
sales. In UK, it holds at #1 for 18 weeks (and will remain in UK Top 2
for 65 weeks). Meanwhile at Christmas, *Elvis' Christmas Album*
re-charts at US #120.
1962 Jan *Can't Help Falling In Love*, from **Blue Hawaii**, hits US #2 (behind
Chubby Checker's *The Twist*), and is another million-seller. (This will
become one of Presley's most enduring and much-covered ballads, a
during the 70s will be the song with which he will invariably close h
live appearances.) B-side *Rock-A-Hula Baby*, also from the movie, pea
at US #23.
Feb *Rock-A-Hula Baby*, initially promoted as UK A-side, hits #3.
Mar *Can't Help Falling In Love*, having overtaken *Rock-A-Hula Baby* o
UK chart, hits #1 for a week (dethroning Cliff Richard's *The Young O
after 8 weeks at the top). This makes the single Presley's all-time mos
successful double-sided hit in UK.
[29] Film "Follow That Dream", a romantic comedy partly filmed on
location in the rural deep South, opens in US, again to good box offic
receipts. It co-stars Presley with Anne Helm and Arthur O'Connell, a
features only 5 songs.
Apr Loping rockaballad *Good Luck Charm* tops US chart for 2 weeks
(and will be Presley's last US #1 single for 9 years). Its sales top a
million. B-side ballad *Anything That's Part Of You* makes US #31.
May *Good Luck Charm* tops UK chart for 5 weeks.
June The EP of 4 songs from "Follow That Dream", led by the title
track, reaches US #15. (25 years later, *Follow That Dream* will often be
revived in concert by Bruce Springsteen. Presley will never sing it
during his live touring.)
July *Pot Luck* hits US #4, and tops UK chart for 10 weeks. EP *Follow
That Dream* makes UK #12, Presley's highest-charting EP in UK.
[25] Film "Kid Galahad", a remake of 1937 Humphrey Bogart/Edwa
G. Robinson movie, and starring Presley as a potential boxing
champion (featuring Gig Young and Charles Bronson), opens in US.
Sept *She's Not You* hits US #5, another million-seller, and tops UK

chart for 3 weeks. B-side *Just Tell Her Jim Said Hello* reaches US #55.

Oct 6-song soundtrack EP from "Kid Galahad", led by rocker *King Of The Whole Wide World*, makes US #30.

Nov *Return To Sender*, a traditionally-styled (Otis Blackwell co-penned) medium-pace Presley rocker from movie "Girls! Girls! Girls!", hits US #2 for 5 weeks (held off #1 by The Four Seasons' *Big Girls Don't Cry*), its sales topping 2 million. B-side ballad *Where Do You Come From?*, also from the movie, peaks at US #99. In UK, EP *Kid Galahad* reaches #16.

[2] "Girls! Girls! Girls!", a romantic musical co-starring Presley with Stella Stevens and Laurel Goodwin, opens in US.

Dec *Return To Sender* tops UK chart for 3 weeks, selling 700,000 copies. *Elvis' Christmas Album* re-charts in US at #59 while in UK, Presley's second album *Elvis* (subtitled in UK *Rock'N'Roll No.2*) is reissued after some years' unavailability since deletion by HMV, hitting UK #3.

1963

Jan The soundtrack album from "Girls! Girls! Girls!" hits US #3 and earns a gold disk. Priscilla Beaulieu returns to Memphis to stay at Graceland with Vernon and Dee Presley. Presley has arranged with her parents that she should complete her education in Memphis. She attends the Immaculate Conception high school, joining in Presley's social life when he is at home during breaks between filming.

Feb Soundtrack album *Girls! Girls! Girls!* hits UK #2, behind Cliff Richard's soundtrack album *Summer Holiday*.

Mar Blackwell/Scott co-penned short uptempo *One Broken Heart For Sale*, from film "It Happened At The World's Fair", sets a precedent for a new Presley single by not entering the US Top 10 – it peaks at #11, while hitting UK #8. Also from the film, ballad B-side *They Remind Me Too Much Of You* peaks at US #53.

Apr **[3]** Film "It Happened At The World's Fair", featuring Presley with Joan O'Brien and Gary Lockwood in another romantic musical, partly filmed on location at the Seattle World Fair, WA, opens in US.

May Soundtrack album *It Happened At The World's Fair* hits both US and UK #4.

Aug *(You're The) Devil In Disguise* hits US #3 and is a million-seller. In UK, it hits #1 for a week. (It will be Presley's last UK chart-topper until mid-1965 and last single by any US act to reach UK #1 until Roy Orbison's *It's Over* in 1964.)

Oct *Elvis' Gold Records, Volume 3*, a compilation of most hit singles from *Stuck On You* to *She's Not You*, hits US #3 and earns a gold disk.

Nov Leiber/Stoller's *Bossa Nova Baby*, taken from film "Fun In Acapulco", hits US #8 and tops a million sales. R&B-rocker *Witchcraft* (a revival of little-known 1956 R&B hit by The Spiders) makes US #32. In UK, *Bossa Nova Baby* reaches #11.

[21] Movie "Fun In Acapulco" opens in US, co-starring Presley with Ursula Andress, known for her role in James Bond film "Dr. No".

1964

Jan Soundtrack album *Fun In Acapulco*, almost entirely Latin-influenced, hits US #3 and UK #9, earning another gold disk. *Kiss Me Quick*, from *Pot Luck*, belatedly issued as a single after being a major hit in Eire and several European countries, reaches UK #11.

Mar *Kissin' Cousins*, title song from the film, reaches US #12. B-side soul-style ballad (later regarded a Presley classic), *It Hurts Me* makes US #29. It is 1 of just 3 cut recently in a now-rare Nashville studio session, on Jan.12.

[6] Movie "Kissin' Cousins", a hillbilly comedy in which Presley plays dual roles as an Air Force officer and his mountain boy cousin (the latter in a blonde wig), opens in US. In UK, location-filmed "Viva Las Vegas", which has also been completed for the same company (MGM) is released instead, with the title amended to "Love In Las Vegas". (A musical titled "Viva Las Vegas" has been released in UK in the early 50s by MGM.) Presley's "Las Vegas" co-star is Ann-Margret, better-known than most of his leading ladies. (Off-screen, a romance between them is rumored, which comes to nothing, though both will remain close friends. Ann-Margret will attend his funeral.)

Apr *Viva Las Vegas* reaches UK #17, while compilation *Elvis' Gold Records, Volume 3*, released belatedly in UK, hits UK #6.

[20] Movie "Viva Las Vegas" is released in US (both it and "Kissin' Cousins" will show in the Top 20 US box office takers of 1964).

May *Kiss Me Quick*, released in US as special double "Gold Standard Series" coupling with *Suspicion* (to catch spin-off sales from Terry Stafford's US #3 hit revival of the latter), makes US #34. Soundtrack album *Kissin' Cousins* hits US #6.

June A revival of Ray Charles' *What'd I Say*, cut in gospel-rock style with The Carol Lombard Quartet on back-up vocals, makes US #21. It is taken from "Viva Las Vegas" and the film's title song is on the B-side, reaching US #29.

July 4-track soundtrack EP from "Viva Las Vegas" (not including the 2 songs already on a single) charts briefly at US #92, while *Kissin' Cousins*

hits UK #12, and the soundtrack album hits UK #5.

Aug *Such A Night*, a revival of 1954 Johnnie Ray hit which Presley had recorded in Apr.1960 (and originally issued on *Elvis Is Back*) is released and makes US #16.

Sept *Such A Night* reaches UK #13.

Nov For the first time since 1961, both sides of a Presley single reach US Top 20. First is rocker *Ain't That Loving You Baby*, which is released for the first time (but was recorded during Presley's Army leave weekend session in June 1958, along with *I Got Stung*, *A Fool Such As I* and others). It reaches US #16, but is overtaken by organ-backed ballad *Ask Me*, an Italian-originated song recorded in Jan. this year at the same time as *It Hurts Me*. This makes US #12, and combined sales give Presley another million-seller. In UK, *Ain't That Loving You Baby* reaches #15, while *Ask Me* gets no UK exposure.

[12] Film "Roustabout", a romantic drama teaming Presley with established actress Barbara Stanwyck, opens in US and at London's Columbia theater. Much of it features him riding a motorcycle and a minor accident has to be written in to the script to accommodate a facial cut.

Dec *Blue Christmas*, extracted from the 1957 Christmas album as a UK seasonal single, climbs to UK #11.

1965

Jan Soundtrack album from "Roustabout" (which does not spin off a single release) tops US chart for 1 week (dethroned by *Beatles '65*), earning another gold disk. In UK, it reaches #12.

[22] Movie "Girl Happy", co-starring Presley with actress/singer Shelley Fabares (whose *Johnny Angel* his *Good Luck Charm* replaced at US #1 in 1962), opens in US.

Mar Presley and Parker note the 10th anniversary of their partnership, with the announcement that they have made $150 million from sales of 100 million records, and a further $135 million from Presley's first 17 movies.

Apr *Do The Clam*, a dance number from "Girl Happy", makes US #21 and UK #19.

May Soundtrack album *Girl Happy* hits both US and UK #8.

June Originally released to coincide with Easter, Presley's revival of gospel ballad *Crying In The Chapel* (recorded in 1960 with the tracks which formed *His Hand In Mine*, but held for release until now) becomes his first US Top 10 hit since *Bossa Nova Baby*, hitting #3 and selling a million. It also tops UK chart for 3 weeks.

[15] Film "Tickle Me", co-starring UK actress Jocelyn Lane, opens in US. None of its 9 songs are purpose-written: it uses tracks from earlier Presley albums, back to his first post-army days.

July Presley travels to Hawaii to film "Paradise, Hawaiian Style", staying at Ilikai hotel, Waikiki. Meanwhile, *(Such An) Easy Question*, originally from *Pot Luck* and now included in "Tickle Me", makes US #11, but is not released in UK. B-side *It Feels So Right*, US #55, is also from the movie, though originally a 1960 cut from *Elvis Is Back*. At the same time, an EP of 5 further "Tickle Me" songs, all from earlier Presley albums, climbs to US #70 (his last EP to make the US chart – the format is all but dormant in US by now).

Aug **[27]** Presley plays host to The Beatles, who are on a break in Los Angeles from a US tour, at his house in Perugia Way, Bel Air. They talk and play together for hours late into the night, jamming along to records, while managers Tom Parker and Brian Epstein play pool.

Sept *Elvis For Everyone*, a collection of unissued studio and film recordings cut between Presley's Sun days and 1964, and released to mark his 10th anniversary with RCA, hits US #10.

Oct *I'm Yours*, from *Pot Luck* but also revived for "Tickle Me", makes US #11, with a narration on the original cut removed. This again is not issued in UK, but *Flaming Star And Summer Kisses*, a UK compilation made up of tracks from deleted *Loving You* and unissued-in-UK EP *Elvis By Request*, reaches UK #11.

[22] Bill Black dies in Memphis at the Baptist hospital, having not recovered from surgery on a brain tumor.

Dec *Puppet On A String*, a light ballad from film "Girl Happy", which has sustained airplay ever since the movie soundtrack's release, is finally issued as a US single for the Christmas market, and reaches #14. In UK, *Tell Me Why*, an unreleased song recorded in 1957 (at the same session as *All Shook Up*) is released with *Puppet On A String* as its B-side, and makes UK #15. Meanwhile, soundtrack album *Harem Scarum* hits US #8 and *Elvis For Everyone* hits UK #8.

[15] Movie "Harem Scarum", which co-stars Presley and Mary Ann Mobley in an unlikely "Desert Song"-type setting, is released in US. In UK, it is retitled "Harem Holiday". It is ill-received even by fans and UK publication **Elvis Monthly** advises Presley followers to complain to producer Sam Katzman about the poor quality of the production.

1966 Jan *Tell Me Why* makes US #33, while B-side *Blue River* makes US #95. In UK, soundtrack album *Harem Holiday* reaches #11. Having left Graceland to live with her parents after graduating from high school, Priscilla Beaulieu returns, to live again with Presley's grandmother. Rumors of a secret engagement ensue when she is seen regularly with Presley on his between-films breaks throughout the year.

Mar *Blue River* is UK A-side and peaks at #22.

Apr Presley's revival of standard *Frankie And Johnny*, also the title song from his next film, reaches US #25 and UK #21, though much US airplay goes to ballad B-side *Please Don't Stop Loving Me* (also from the movie), which climbs to US #45.

[20] Movie "Frankie And Johnny", a romantic musical/comedy based on the traditional song, opens in US. It co-stars Presley with Donna Douglas from TV's "The Beverly Hillbillies".

May Soundtrack *Frankie And Johnny* makes US #20 and UK #11.

[25] At a 4-day recording session in Nashville, Presley works with producer Felton Jarvis for the first time.

June [8] "Paradise, Hawaiian Style", a largely location-shot romantic musical designed to re-create the magic (and money-making power) of "Blue Hawaii", opens in US, featuring Presley with UK actress Suzannah Leigh. With inferior songs and dulled charisma, movie does only a fraction of earlier Hawaiian picture's box office.

July *Love Letters*, one of 18 tracks cut in a productive return to the Nashville studios at the end of May, is rush-released, reaching US #19 and hitting UK #6. It is an exact revival of Ketty Lester's 1962 distinctive voice/piano arrangement.

Aug Soundtrack album *Paradise, Hawaiian Style*, reaches US #15 and hits UK #7.

Nov *Spinout*, the movie title song, peaks at US #40, while its double A-side coupling *All That I Am*, also from the film, makes US #41 and, as the only promoted side in UK, reaches UK #18. (It is the first Presley recording to feature strings in the accompaniment.)

Dec *If Every Day Was Like Christmas*, a new seasonal song recorded in Nashville on June 10, reaches US #13. (It does not chart in US because of a policy of restricting Christmas records to a special Christmas chart at this time.) Meanwhile, soundtrack album *Spinout* makes US #18, and (as *California Holiday*) UK #17. It includes 3 non-movie bonus tracks: a revival of The Clovers' R&B rocker *Down In The Alley*, Hawaiian ballad *I'll Remember You* and a lengthy version of Bob Dylan's *Tomorrow Is A Long Time* (which Dylan will, 3 years later, quote as being his favorite cover version of one of his songs).

[14] Musical comedy film "Spinout", co-starring Shelley Fabares again, opens in US. In UK, it is re-titled "California Holiday".

1967 Feb *Indescribably Blue*, recorded at the same June session as *If Every Day Was Like Christmas*, reaches US #33 and UK #21.

May Presley's second religious album *How Great Thou Art*, including *Crying In The Chapel*, and recorded in Nashville alongside *Love Letters*, reaches US #18, earning a gold disk, and UK #11. (It will also win Presley's first Grammy award, for Best Religious Recording Of 1967.) In UK, double A-side *You Gotta Stop/The Love Machine* , taken from film "Easy Come, Easy Go", makes UK #38.

[1] Presley marries Priscilla Beaulieu at Aladdin hotel, Las Vegas, at 9.41am, before 100 invited guests, in a civil ceremony conducted by Nevada Supreme Court Justice David Zenoff. Presley's assistant Joe Esposito is best man, and bride's sister Michelle is maid of honor. After a reception in the hotel, they fly to Palm Springs to begin a honeymoon.

[4] After a day in Hollywood where Presley puts finishing touches to movie "Clambake", they fly home to Memphis to complete their honeymoon.

[14] Film "Easy Come, Easy Go" opens in US, featuring a cameo role from veteran actress Elsa Lanchester.

[29] A second wedding reception is held at Graceland, for 125 friends and relatives unable to attend in Las Vegas.

June *Long Legged Girl (With The Short Dress On)*, a novelty rocker from *Double Trouble*, peaks at US #63. Its B-side *That's Someone You Never Forget*, a revival of a *Pot Luck* track, makes US #92.

July Soundtrack album *Double Trouble* reaches US #47.

[24] Movie "Double Trouble", a comedy thriller, is released in US. Much of it is set in UK and Europe (though all shot in Hollywood), and features some UK supporting actors like Norman Rossington and leading lady Annette Day.

Aug *Long Legged Girl (With The Short Dress On)* makes UK #49.

Sept 2 tracks taken from 1961 album *Something For Everybody*, *There's Always Me* and *Judy*, peak at US #56 and #78 respectively. They fail to chart in UK, but soundtrack album *Double Trouble* peaks at UK #34.

Nov Cut at a rare Nashville studio session of R&B and country

numbers on Sept.10/11, Presley's revival of bluesman Jimmy Reed's *Big Boss Man*, with Charlie McCoy playing harmonica, reaches US #38. From the same session, B-side *You Don't Know Me* (a 1962 hit for Ray Charles) reaches US #44, but fails in UK.

Dec [4] Film "Clambake" opens in US, co-starring Presley for the third time with Shelley Fabares plus TV actors Will Hutchins and Bill Bixby.

1968 Jan Parker announces that Singer Sewing Machine Company is to sponsor Presley's first TV spectacular, to be made by NBC TV for year-end telecast.

Feb *Guitar Man*, written by country-rock singer-guitarist Jerry Reed (and featuring him on guest guitar), reaches US #43. Soundtrack album *Clambake* (which also includes a side of non-movie bonus songs, including *Guitar Man*, *You Don't Know Me* and *Big Boss Man*) reaches US #40.

[1] Daughter Lisa Marie is born at 5.01pm at the Baptist Memorial hospital, Memphis.

[29] *How Great Thou Art* wins Best Sacred Performance Of 1967 at the 10th annual Grammy awards.

Mar *Guitar Man* makes UK #19.

[11] Presley records 4 songs for film "Live A Little, Love A Little" at MGM Sound studios in Hollywood. (One of the songs, *Wonderful World*, by UK songwriting team Fletcher and Flett, has also just been recorded by Cliff Richard with slightly different lyrics as one of UK's 6 shortlisted songs for the Eurovision Song Contest.)

[14] Film "Stay Away Joe", a comedy western made on location in Arizona, and starring Presley as an American Indian, opens in US.

Apr Released as a special single for Easter, Presley's revival of inspirational *You'll Never Walk Alone* (originally from musical "Carousel", but best known via Gerry & The Pacemakers' interpretation) makes US #92. Compilation *Elvis' Gold Records, Volume 4*, anthologizing mostly post-1962 hit singles, reaches US #33, while soundtrack album *Clambake* makes UK #39.

May *U.S. Male*, another Reed song in similar style to *Guitar Man* (and again with him playing guitar), reaches US #28 and UK #15. Its B-side is *Stay Away*, taken from film "Stay Away Joe", and sung to the traditional tune of *Greensleeves*.

June Movie "Speedway" opens in US, co-starring Presley with Nancy Sinatra (as a tax inspector, out to get him). They duet on 1 song on the soundtrack. Presley donates a Rolls Royce to auction for SHARE, a Hollywood women's charity, with the proceeds going to retarded children.

[27] Work begins on the Singer/NBC TV special, produced and directed by Steve Binder (whose previous credits include the all-star T.A.M.I. show in 1964). Binder has won a lengthy battle with Parker over the format of the show, which he sees as an opportunity to relaunch the magnetism of Presley as a live performer. (Parker had wanted Presley to sing 20 Christmas songs and say goodnight.)

[28] Taping continues for the special at NBC's studios in Burbank, where for 2 extended sessions, Presley, Scotty Moore, Charlie Hodge and D.J. Fontana play in the round with an audience gathered about them, jamming in familiar material. These sessions continue the next day, interspersed with choreographed set pieces involving such Presley songs as *Trouble*, *Guitar Man*, *It Hurts Me*, *Little Egypt* and a gospel medley. A new song, *If I Can Dream*, is specially written for the show's finale by Earl Brown. (By June 30, Binder and NBC have hours of tape to edit into a 1-hour program.)

July The coupling of *Let Yourself Go/Your Time Hasn't Come Yet, Baby* from "Speedway", peaks at US #71/#72. It fails in UK, but *You'll Never Walk Alone*, appearing some months after its US release, makes UK #44

[7] Presley cuts the title song from "Charro", with a backing track by the Hugo Montenegro Orchestra, in Hollywood. (It will be released in 1969 as B-side to *Memories*.)

Aug Soundtrack album *Speedway* makes US #82. This is unique in being the only Presley album on which a track is sung entirely by somebody else – in this case, co-star Nancy Sinatra's *Your Groovy Self*. It fails to chart in UK but *Your Time Hasn't Come Yet, Baby* reaches US #22.

Oct The coupling of *A Little Less Conversation/Almost In Love*, both from "Live A Little, Love A Little", makes US #69/#95.

[9] Film "Live A Little, Love A Little" opens in US, a slightly more adult comedy than usual, co-starring Presley (as a photographer) with Michele Carey.

Dec [3] The Singer TV special "Elvis" airs on US NBC. It draws rave critical reactions, and also the year's largest viewing figures for a musical special.

1969 Jan The critically-rated closing number from the TV special, *If I Can Dream*, restores Presley to the US Top 20, reaching #12.

[13] He begins lengthy recording sessions at Chips Moman's American recording studios in Memphis, the first time he has recorded in his home town since working with Sam Phillips. Between Jan.16-17 and Jan.20-23, he will record 20 songs which will form the basis of a highly-rated series of singles and an album.

[25] Recording complete, Presley flies to Aspen, CO, with his wife and entourage, for a skiing vacation.

Feb *Elvis*, the soundtrack from the NBC TV special, hits US #8, his highest-placed album in US since 1965, and the first since *How Great Thou Art* to pass half-million sales and earn a gold disk.

[17-22] More recording sessions at American studios produce a further 14 new tracks, including revivals of many favorites from other artists' repertoires.

Mar *If I Can Dream* reaches UK #11.

Apr *Memories*, an orchestrally-backed ballad extracted from the TV show, makes US #35.

May *Elvis Sings Flaming Star*, a collection of tracks either unissued or (like the title track) not previously on album, is released at low price and reaches US #96. (This is actually a reissue by RCA of an album titled *Singer Presents Elvis*, pressed up for sale only through Singer Sewing Machine shops at the time of the TV special, as a promotional tie-in. Copies of the original album will become high-priced collectors' items, because of scarce availability.) In UK, the NBC TV show album *Elvis* hits #2. After completing work on film "Change Of Habit" in Hollywood, Presley and Priscilla vacation for 2 weeks in Honolulu, HI.

June Mac Davis' song *In The Ghetto*, with a stark socially-conscious lyric and subtle, arresting arrangement, is the first release from the Memphis sessions and hits US #3 (his first Top 10 in 4 years), selling over a million (his first since *Crying In The Chapel*, 4 years earlier).

[10] Presley flies to Las Vegas to discuss arrangements for what is to be his comeback to the live stage after 8 years.

July *From Elvis In Memphis*, a varied collection from the Jan. session, receives the best reviews of a Presley album since *Elvis Is Back* and reaches US #13, earning another gold disk. In UK, *Elvis Sings Flaming Star* tops the chart for 2 weeks, while *In The Ghetto* hits #1 for a week before giving way to The Rolling Stones' *Honky Tonk Women*.

[5] Presley flies to Las Vegas to begin rehearsals for his comeback show.

[26] Presley opens at the Showroom of the International hotel, Las Vegas, the beginning of a 4-week engagement which nets him $1 million. (The concerts are universally acclaimed a triumph, with the magnetic Presley stage presence of old still intact and doing justice to both 50s material and new songs.) His new live back-up band includes Rick Nelson's ex-guitarist James Burton, bassist Jerry Scheff, guitarists John Wilkinson and Charlie Hodge, keyboards player Larry Muhoberac (who will be replaced on future engagements by ex-Crickets Glen D. Hardin) and drummer Ronnie Tutt. Back-up vocal groups are The Imperials (The Jordanaires having turned down the gig because of Nashville commitments) and The Sweet Inspirations.

Aug *Clean Up Your Own Back Yard*, taken from film "The Trouble With Girls", reaches US #35.

[17] The TV special is re-shown on US NBC, with *Blue Christmas* edited out and replaced by *Tiger Man*, in deference to the midsummer season.

[28] After 57 shows at the International, Presley's season closes. He and Priscilla fly to Palm Springs for a 3-week vacation.

Sept *From Elvis In Memphis* tops the UK chart for a week, while *Clean Up Your Own Back Yard* reaches UK #21.

[3] Movie "Charro", a spaghetti-type western in which Presley plays a drifter with a constant 4-day stubble growth, opens in US, largely to indifference.

Nov For the first time in 7 years, Presley tops US Singles chart, with Mark James' *Suspicious Minds*, another recording from the Jan. Memphis session. It holds #1 for a week, and sells almost 2 million copies (but will be his last US chart-topper).

Dec *Suspicious Minds* hits UK #2 (behind Rolf Harris' *Two Little Boys*).

[10] Film "The Trouble With Girls (And How To Get Into It)" opens in US, featuring cameo appearances by John Carradine and Vincent Price. Again, it has little action at the box office, and the low-budget Presley movie era is over.

1970 Jan *Don't Cry Daddy* hits US #6 and is another million-seller. B-side *Rubbernecking*, taken from film "Change Of Habit", reaches US #69. Double album *From Memphis To Vegas/From Vegas To Memphis*, featuring 2 sides of live performance and 2 from the Memphis sessions, reaches US #12 and earns a gold disk.

[21] Film "Change Of Habit", in which Presley co-stars as a ghetto doctor with Mary Tyler Moore as a nun, opens in US.

[26] Presley returns to the International hotel for a second season, earning $1 million for a month's shows.

Feb [27] He begins 6 days of performances at the Astrodome, Houston, TX, to a total of 200,000 people.

Mar *Kentucky Rain* reaches US #16, as *Don't Cry Daddy* hits UK #8.

Apr *From Memphis To Vegas/From Vegas To Memphis* hits UK #3.

May Budget album *Let's Be Friends* makes US #105.

June *The Wonder Of You*, a live revival of old Ray Peterson hit, recorded in Las Vegas, hits US #9, and earns a gold disk for a million US sales. Meanwhile, *Kentucky Rain* reaches UK #21.

July Live album *On Stage - February 1970*, recorded at the second International hotel season, reaches US #13, earning a gold disk, and hits UK #2.

Aug *The Wonder Of You* tops UK chart for 6 weeks, selling over 700,000 copies in UK, while double A-side *I've Lost You/The Next Step Is Love* makes US #32.

[22] It is announced that Presley will play his first US live tour since the mid-50s (6 dates opening in Phoenix, AZ).

Sept 4-album boxed compilation set *Worldwide 50 Gold Award Hits, Vol.1*, containing most of his major hits, reaches US #45 and UK #49, earning a gold disk.

Nov A live-recorded revival of Dusty Springfield's *You Don't Have To Say You Love Me* makes US #11, while B-side fast country-rocker *Patch It Up* reaches UK #90.

Dec *I've Lost You* hits UK #9. Budget album *Almost In Love*, mostly collating film songs from earlier EPs, reaches US #65, while *Elvis' Golden Records, Vol.1* is reissued in UK, and makes #21.

[15] Movie "Elvis – That's The Way It Is", a documentary of his summer 1970 Las Vegas shows, is released in UK.

1971 Jan *You Don't Have To Say You Love Me* hits UK #9, as soundtrack album *Elvis: That's The Way It Is* reaches US #21 and UK #12, and earns another gold disk. Meanwhile, from forthcoming *Elvis Country*, a revival of *I Really Don't Want To Know* reaches UK #21.

[9] Presley receives the Jaycee's Award as one of the Ten Outstanding Young Men Of The Year. (The other winners are all from outside the entertainment field and include President Richard Nixon's press secretary, Ronald Ziegler.)

Mar *Elvis Country (I'm 10,000 Years Old)*, recorded during a lengthy Nashville session in June 1970, reaches US #12, earning a further gold disk, and hits UK #6.

Apr *Where Did They Go, Lord?* makes US #33, while B-side *Rags To Riches* (originally 1953 R&B hit for Jackie Wilson & The Dominoes, and a pop #1 for Tony Bennett) reaches US #45, while religious compilation *You'll Never Walk Alone*, released for Easter, makes US #69. In UK, a revival of Engelbert Humperdinck's *There Goes My Everything* (B-side of *I Really Don't Want To Know* in US) hits UK #6.

June *Rags To Riches* hits UK #9, while *Life* climbs to US #53 and B-side *Only Believe* makes US #95.

[1] The 2-room shack in Tupelo, Presley's birthplace, is opened as a tourist attraction.

Aug Unusual folk-styled *I'm Leaving* peaks at US #36, while *Love Letters From Elvis*, recorded at the same sessions as *Elvis Country*, reaches US #33 and UK #7. Budget album *C'mon Everybody*, with more tracks from earlier film EPs, makes US #70 and hits UK #5. In UK, *You'll Never Walk Alone* reaches UK #20, while *Heartbreak Hotel* is reissued on a maxi-single (coupled with *Hound Dog* and *Don't Be Cruel*) and hits UK #10.

Sept [8] Presley receives the Bing Crosby Award, from US National Academy of Recording Arts and Sciences, given to people who "during their lifetimes, have made creative contributions of outstanding artistic or scientific significance to the field of phonograph records". (He is the sixth recipient, predecessors being Bing Crosby, Frank Sinatra, Duke Ellington, Ella Fitzgerald and Irving Berlin.)

Oct *It's Only Love* reaches US #51, but is not released in UK at this time. 4-album boxed compilation *Worldwide Gold Award Hits, Vol.2* (each copy contains a small rectangle cut from an item of Presley's clothing) makes US #120. *I'm Leaving* reaches UK #23.

Dec Budget album *I Got Lucky*, with another set of film EP tracks, reaches US #104 and UK #26, while *Elvis' Christmas Album* is reissued in UK at budget price and hits UK #7.

1972 Jan A revival of B.J. Thomas' *I Just Can't Help Believing*, taken from the soundtrack of "Elvis: That's The Way It Is" hits UK #6, while UK maxi-single reissue *Jailhouse Rock*, in the wake of *Heartbreak Hotel*'s success, makes UK #42.

Feb [23] Presley and Priscilla are legally separated.

Mar A revival of Buffy Saint-Marie's ballad *Until It's Time For You To*

Go reaches US #40 and hits UK #5. It is taken from *Elvis Now*, which peaks at US #43 and UK #12.

May Live-recorded revival of Mickey Newbury's *An American Trilogy* (combining traditional *Dixie*, *All My Trials* and *Battle Hymn Of The Republic*) reaches US #66, while third gospel album, **He Touched Me**, climbs to US #79 and UK #38.

June [9-11] He plays his first concerts in New York: 4 shows at Madison Square Garden to a total of 80,000 people, earning $730,000.

July *An American Trilogy* hits UK #8.

Aug Live *Elvis As Recorded At Madison Square Garden* reaches US #11, earning a gold disk, and hits UK #3, while compilation *Elvis Sings Hits From His Movies, Vol.1* peaks at US #87. Divorce proceedings begin between Presley and Priscilla.

Oct Presley has his first US Top 10 and first million-selling single since *The Wonder Of You* in 1970, with Dennis Linde's R&B rocker *Burning Love* (originally recorded by Arthur Alexander). It hits US #2, behind Chuck Berry's *My Ding-A-Ling*, and UK #7.

Dec *Burning Love And Hits From His Movies, Vol.2*, combining the recent hit with earlier film songs, reaches US #22.

1973 Jan [14] "Aloha From Hawaii" TV show is aired live via satellite from Honolulu International Center, to Japan and the Far East. (US and Europe see a taped version, but UK declines to take it. Its total worldwide audience is estimated as 1 billion – the largest ever for any TV show.) The concert is a benefit for Kuiokalakani Lee Cancer Fund and raises $75,000; Presley sings Lee's best-known song *I'll Remember You* during the telecast.

Ballad *Separate Ways*, from film "Elvis On Tour" (and widely interpreted as having been recorded because of his recent separation from Priscilla), reaches US #20. In UK, it is flipped to make *Always On My Mind* A-side which hits UK #9.

Feb Budget *Separate Ways*, again compiling the recent hit with earlier material, makes US #46.

Mar [3] *He Touched Me* wins Presley his second Grammy award (and second for a religious album), as Best Inspirational Performance Of 1972.

May Double album *Aloha From Hawaii Via Satellite*, a recording of the Jan. telecast, tops US chart for a week, earning another gold disk. (It is Presley's first #1 album in 9 years – and his last.) In UK, it makes #11.

June A live version of James Taylor's *Steamroller Blues*, from "Aloha From Hawaii" show, reaches US #17, while his live revival of Tony Joe White's *Polk Salad Annie* (an on-stage favorite) reaches UK #23 as a UK-only single.

[6] Movie "Elvis On Tour", filmed on the road the previous year, opens in US. (It will win a Golden Globe award as Best Documentary Of The Year.)

Aug *Elvis*, with recently-recorded material, makes US #52, UK #16.

Sept *Fool* (US B-side of *Steamroller Blues*) makes UK #15.

Oct Double A-side *Raised On Rock/For Ol' Times Sake* reaches US #41.

[9] Presley and Priscilla are divorced at a courthouse in Santa Monica, CA. (The tension between them will evaporate and they will remain close friends.)

Dec *Raised On Rock* makes UK #36.

1974 Jan *Raised On Rock/For Ol' Times Sake*, combining recently-cut rock and country material, makes US #50.

Mar A revival of Billy Lee Riley's *I've Got A Thing About You, Baby* peaks at US #39 and UK #33.

Apr *Elvis – A Legendary Performer, Vol.1*, compiled as a historical overview and combining notable hits with unreleased material and interviews, makes US #43, earning a gold disk, and UK #20.

May *Good Times* makes US #90 and UK #42.

Aug *If You Talk In Your Sleep* reaches US #17 and UK #40. 2 of his Las Vegas Hilton (as the International hotel has now been re-named) shows are cancelled due to Presley having 'flu. During the month, he also receives his 8th Degree Black Belt in Karate.

Sept Live album *Elvis Recorded Live On Stage In Memphis* reaches US #33 and UK #44.

Nov *Having Fun With Elvis On Stage*, containing clips of Presley's between-songs stage patter and jokes, makes US #130. (It had originally been sold by Parker as a souvenir item at concerts.)

Dec A hard-rocking revival of Chuck Berry's *Promised Land* reaches US #14, while a revival of ballad *My Boy*, originally recorded by Richard Harris, hits UK #5.

1975 Jan Presley is hospitalized in Memphis. A stomach complaint is diagnosed. He is ordered a special diet and a treatment of cortisone, which has the side-effect of causing notable weight gain. (He will fight to maintain a balance between his health and weight for the rest of his

life, with prescription drugs in often grossly over-prescribed amounts.)

Feb *Promised Land* hits UK #9.

Mar [1] Presley wins his third Grammy award, as his 1974 live version of *How Great Thou Art* is named Best Inspirational Performance. *My Boy* reaches US #20, as *Promised Land* reaches US #47 and UK #21.

June *T-R-O-U-B-L-E* makes US #35 and UK #31. It is taken from *Today*, which climbs to US #57 and UK #48.

July TV-advertised double album *40 Greatest Hits*, marketed in UK by Arcade Records, tops UK chart.

Sept *The Elvis Presley Sun Collection* (the first time the early tracks have all been released on one album) makes UK #16.

Nov *Bringing It Back* peaks at US #65.

Dec *Green, Green Grass Of Home*, a revival of Tom Jones's hit, is issued as a UK-only single, and makes #29.

1976 Mar *Elvis – A Legendary Performer, Vol.2*, another historical overview, reaches US #46 and earns a gold disk.

Apr [29] Bruce Springsteen, on tour in Memphis, attempts to see Presley by climbing the fence at Graceland. He is escorted off the premises by security guards while still trying to explain who he is. Presley is not disturbed.

May A revival of Timi Yuro's 1961 hit *Hurt* reaches US #28 and UK #37, while compilation *The Sun Sessions* makes US #76.

July *From Elvis Presley Boulevard, Memphis, Tennessee* (recorded in Feb. at his new studio at Graceland) reaches US #41 and earns a gold disk. In UK, it makes #29.

Oct 1960 hit *The Girl Of My Best Friend* is reissued in UK and hits #9.

Nov Jerry Lee Lewis is arrested outside Graceland when he appears, drunk and with a .38 Derringer pistol, demanding to see Presley.

1977 Feb *Elvis In Demand*, a UK fan club-compiled set of hard-to-find tracks, reaches UK #12. On it is 1962 track *Suspicion*, which is also issued as a UK single, and hits #9.

Mar *Moody Blue* reaches US #31 and hits UK #6, while B-side ballad *She Thinks I Still Care* (a revival of a George Jones song) is a Top 10 Country hit.

Apr He makes his final recordings, in a session following a concert at the Civic Center, Saginaw, MI.

May Compilation *Welcome To My World*, mixing live and studio country songs, makes US #44 but hits UK #7. (It will earn a platinum disk for million-plus sales, after his death.)

June [26] Presley's final concert is at the Market Square Arena in Indianapolis, IN.

Aug [1] Book **Elvis: What Happened?**, written by former Presley payroll members Red and Sonny West and Dave Hebler, exposing the apparent darker side of Presley's private personality, is published.

[16] Presley is discovered lying on the floor in a bathroom at Graceland by girlfriend Ginger Alden. He fails to respond to resuscitation attempts by aide Joe Esposito and is rushed to hospital, but pronounced dead at 3.30pm. His death of heart failure at age 42 makes major headlines throughout the world.

[17] Thousands of fans from all over US and even overseas arrive in Memphis to pay their respects (25,000 file past his coffin at Graceland during the afternoon). In Washington, DC, President Jimmy Carter issues a tribute statement: "Elvis Presley's death deprives our country of a part of itself. He was unique and irreplaceable." Carter notes how Presley's unique meld of styles "changed the face of American popular culture ... he was a symbol to people the world over, of the vitality, rebelliousness and good humor of this country".

[18] Presley's funeral service is held at Graceland, with 150 people attending, and 75,000 more outside the gates. His body is moved by hearse in a 19-Cadillac cortege to Memphis' Forest Hill cemetery, for entombment at 4.30pm in a mausoleum alongside his mother.

Sept *Way Down* reaches US #18, and sells over a million in US, topping UK chart for 5 weeks and selling more than 600,000. *Moody Blue*, containing his final recordings (including *Way Down*), is also a million-seller, hitting both US and UK #3. (The UK chart is flooded by Presley back-catalog albums, resulting in Top 30 positions for *G.I. Blues*, *Blue Hawaii*, *Hits Of The 70s*, *Loving You* and *Elvis' Golden Records, Vol.2*, and by old singles, of which *It's Now Or Never*, *Jailhouse Rock*, *All Shook Up*, *Crying In The Chapel*, *Are You Lonesome Tonight*, *The Wonder Of You*, *Wooden Heart* and *Return To Sender* all make the Top 50. Double album *40 Greatest Hits* tops the UK chart again.)

Oct The bodies of Presley and his mother are removed from Forest Hill cemetery and re-buried side-by-side in the Meditation Garden at the rear of Graceland, because of an attempt to steal his body from the public cemetery. US CBS TV shows "Elvis In Concert", a special filmed during his final tour in June in Omaha and Rapid City.

Nov Double album *Elvis In Concert*, combining the soundtrack from the TV show with June 1977 tour recordings, hits US #5 and reaches UK #13, and is another platinum disk.

Dec *My Way*, a 1977 live recording of Frank Sinatra standard, reaches US #22 and hits UK #9, and is Presley's final million-selling single.

78 June Gospel compilation *He Walks Beside Me* reaches US #113 and UK #37, while UK compilation of early tracks *The '56 Sessions, Vol.1* makes UK #47.

July *Don't Be Cruel* is reissued as a UK single to tie in with the album, and reaches #24.

Nov *Elvis – A Canadian Tribute* includes all his recordings by Canadian writers and makes UK #86.

79 Jan *Elvis – A Legendary Performer, Vol.3* makes US #113 and UK #43 (and will earn a gold disk).

Apr *Our Memories Of Elvis*, on which producer Felton Jarvis re-edits tapes to remove horns and strings and highlight Presley's voice against small-group accompaniment, makes US #132 and reaches UK #72.

June [26] Vernon Presley dies in Tupelo of a heart attack, aged 63. (He will be buried beside his wife and son at Graceland.)

Dec TV-promoted double compilation *Love Songs* hits UK #4, while seasonal *It Won't Seem Like Christmas (Without You)* reaches UK #13.

80 Mar At a Sotheby's auction in London, a paper napkin from Las Vegas Riviera hotel with Presley's authenticated signature on it, sells for $500.

May [16] Dr. George Nichopoulous is indicted in Memphis on 14 counts of overprescription of drugs, notably to Presley, Jerry Lee Lewis, and 9 other patients.

July Compilation *Elvis Presley Sings Leiber And Stoller* charts in UK at #32.

Sept 8-album boxed set *Elvis Aron Presley* reaches US #27 and UK #21. It consists largely of unheard material, including Presley's Apr.1956 Las Vegas appearance and the 1961 charity concert in Hawaii. Only 250,000 copies are produced worldwide.

Oct *It's Only Love*, released on single for the first time in UK after inclusion on the boxed set, is his final UK Top 10 hit, at #3.

Dec TV-promoted gospel compilation *Inspirations* hits UK #6, while seasonal *Santa Claus Is Back In Town* (from the 1957 Christmas album) makes UK #41.

81 Mar *Guitar Man*, in a version with updated accompaniment added by Jarvis, peaks higher than its first appearance in 1968, at US #28. In UK, it reaches #43. The album of the same title, also with updated accompaniment, reaches US #49 and UK #33.

Apr Warner Bros. film "This Is Elvis", a documentary of his life using original concert and movie footage, plus specially-filmed linking material using actors, opens in US.

May Double soundtrack album *This Is Elvis* makes US #115 and UK #47, while *Loving Arms* (from *Guitar Man*) reaches UK #47.

82 Feb Compilation *The Sound Of Your Cry*, rounding up rare tracks, makes UK #31.

Mar A live version of *Are You Lonesome Tonight* on which Presley breaks up laughing in mid-song is issued as a UK single, reaching #25.

June The title track from *The Sound Of Your Cry* makes UK #59.

Dec Presley's final US hit single is *The Elvis Medley*, assembled from clips taken from *Jailhouse Rock, Teddy Bear, Hound Dog, Don't Be Cruel, Burning Love* and *Suspicious Minds*. It makes US #71. An album of the same title, coupling the medley with 9 hits, reaches US #133.

83 Feb A further UK reissue of *Jailhouse Rock* on its 25th anniversary re-charts at UK #27.

Apr *Jailhouse Rock/Love In Las Vegas*, compiling songs from both films, reaches UK #40. Taken from it, *Baby I Don't Care*, makes UK #61.

June *I Was The One*, with additional modern accompaniment to several 50s hits, makes US #103 and UK #83.

84 Jan Presley's version of Billy Swan hit *I Can Help* is released as a single for the first time, and reaches UK #30.

Mar *Elvis – The First Live Recordings* gathers extremely early tapes of Presley performing on "The Louisiana Hayride" and makes US #163 and UK #69.

Nov His version of Roger Whittaker's ballad *The Last Farewell* makes UK #48.

Dec To mark the 50th anniversary of Presley's birth, 6-album boxed set *Elvis – A Golden Celebration* is issued and climbs to US #80. It concentrates on 1956-57 unreleased live and TV show material, together with posthumously-discovered tapes of Presley singing at home with friends.

85 Priscilla Beaulieu, now a successful actress (and a star of TV show "Dallas") publishes **Elvis And Me**, her account of love and life with Presley.

Feb *A Valentine Gift For You*, compiling Presley love songs, makes US #154. *The Elvis Medley* finally appears as a UK single, and reaches #51.

May *Reconsider Baby*, a collection of Presley's notable blues recordings, makes UK #92.

Aug A little-heard version of *Always On My Mind*, from the soundtrack of *This Is Elvis*, reaches UK #59.

1987 Apr *Bossa Nova Baby* is reissued in UK to tie in with a Latin music fad in dance clubs, and makes UK #47. A new extended mix of it is produced by UK DJ/producer Simon Harris.

Sept To mark the 10th anniversary of Presley's death, double album *Presley – The All-Time Greatest Hits*, compiling 45 hit tracks, hits UK #4. (Parallel US double album *The Top 10 Hits* reaches #117.) *Love Me Tender/If I Can Dream* is extracted as double A-side and makes UK #56.

1988 Jan Following its use on a TV ad for glue, Presley's *Stuck On You* is reissued and charts at UK #58.

Oct Presley's only child, daughter Lisa Marie, marries musician Danny Keough.

1989 Jan Retired airline pilot Ed Leek is offered over $1 million for the acetate of Presley's 1953 recording of *That's When The Heartaches Begin*. *Stereo '57 (Essential Elvis Volume 2)* makes UK #60. Liverpool solicitor David Deacon's company Park McMaddy signs with Presley estate to build Elvis Presley Centre at Blackpool's Golden Mile, Lancs.

Feb At the height of "I've seen Elvis" rumor spread by the world's tabloid press, UK newspaper **The Sun** offers £1 million to anyone who can bring a live Presley to its offices.

Apr Sun Records signs deal with Ed Leek, owner of the purported first Elvis acetate, to release it as a single.

May [29] Lisa Marie gives birth to 7lb. 2oz. girl Danielle Riley at St. John's Hospital, Santa Monica, CA.

June Priscilla, as chief executive of his increasingly valuable estate, commissions a new US TV program concentrating on Elvis' early rock'n'roll years. (The weekly series on ABC, although receiving overwhelmingly positive reviews from the critics will fail to find an audience and is taken off the air within a matter of weeks.)

July Officials at Graceland deny a request from the Mississippi Tournament Of Roses Association to use a giant likeness of Presley's head spinning on a record on the float for the 1990 Rosebowl Parade.

[15] White suit and cape worn during "Aloha From Hawaii" 1973 concert is stolen from Los Gatos, CA, home of Presley impersonator Charlie Stickerod. (The thief leaves behind 24 carat gold Elvis disks and other memorabilia.)

[27] Destitute Louisiana woman Rhonda Boler, 20, auctions gold necklace give to her by Elvis during 1974 comeback concert in Monroe, LA, on US TV show "A Current Affair".

Aug [10] Colorized version of "Jailhouse Rock" airs for first time on US TV station TBS.

1990 July *Hits Like Never Before* makes UK #71.

Sept *The Great Performances* makes UK #62. It includes *My Happiness*, the first ever issue of his debut recording from 1953. Buena Vista Video releases 2 Presley videos, "Vol.1 – Center Stage" and "Vol.2 – The Man and His Music" which both include never before seen footage. Both earn triple platinum award status by year-end.

Dec While the trustees of Presley's estate continue to manage and market a multitude of Presley promotions, the latest "Elvis – the Cologne" is launched with the ad-line "America has had 41 Presidents ... but only one King."

THE PRETENDERS

Chrissie Hynde (vocals, guitar)
Pete Farndon (bass)
James Honeyman-Scott (guitar)
Martin Chambers (drums)

1965 Hynde (b. Sept.7, 1951, Akron, OH), heavily influenced by current US soul stars and also practising on a baritone ukelele, attends a Mitch Ryder & The Detroit Wheels concert at a local amusement park.

1967 She begins playing guitar and joins band Saturday Sunday Matinee which includes future Devo keyboardist Mark Mothersbaugh.

1973 Having spent 3 years at Kent State University, studying art, Hynde leaves for London. She sells leather handbags in Oxford Street and models at St. Martin's School of Art. She also meets **New Musical Express** magazine journalist Nick Kent, who invites her to become a contributing writer. (Her first review is of a Neil Diamond album.)

1974 Hynde works part-time at future punk guru Malcolm McLaren's clothes shop Sex. She then relocates to Paris, France, to join The

Frenchies, and meets session guitarist Chris Spedding.

Nov [1] The Frenchies perform their first gig with Hynde on vocals, supporting The Flaming Groovies at L'Olympia, Paris.

1975 Hynde returns to Cleveland, OH, and joins R&B group Jack Rabbit.

1976 She returns to UK and forms short-lived band, Berk Brothers, but is deposed by Johnny Moped as lead singer.

1977 **Feb** Hynde sings backing vocals on Spedding's *Hurt*, produced by Chris Thomas.

Aug She cuts a demo tape of *The Phone Call* and links with Anchor Records' Dave Hill, who is forming new Real Records and invites her to join on an ad-hoc basis and helps fund further demo sessions.

1978 **Mar** Hynde puts together a band with Hereford-based musicians Farndon on bass, drummer Gerry Mackleduff (who will be replaced by Chambers (b. Hereford, Hereford & Worcs.) following the recording of the first single) and Honeyman-Scott (b. 1957, Hereford) on guitar. The group, still nameless, records Ray Davies' *Stop Your Sobbing*, with producer Nick Lowe for the Real label. Hynde settles on The Pretenders, inspired by The Platters hit *The Great Pretender*.

1979 **Feb** *Stop Your Sobbing* is UK chart debut at #34. Group begins club touring, including dates at London's Marquee club and the Moonlight.

July Produced by Thomas, follow-up *Kid* climbs to UK #33 as the group begins a month's UK tour, including a headline concert at London's Lyceum.

Oct [22] The Pretenders begin 4 consecutive Monday night gigs at the Marquee club, as Hynde/Honeyman-Scott-penned *Brass In Pocket* begins a climb to hit UK #1.

Dec Christmas is celebrated with 2 festive dates at favored Marquee. Band also performs in the "Concert For Kampuchea" at London's Hammersmith Odeon.

1980 **Jan** Hill leaves Real to become The Pretenders' full-time manager (the label is bought by US company Sire, which retains the band). As the group begins a 30-date UK tour, debut album *Pretenders* enters the UK chart at #1 and begins a US climb to #9.

Apr *Talk Of The Town* hits UK #8 as The Pretenders visit US for the first time and Hynde meets former hero Ray Davies at a New York club (they begin a 3-year relationship). The album has already sold over a half million and *Brass In Pocket (I'm Special)* reaches US #14. The band plays 3,500-seater Santa Monica, CA, Civic Auditorium, sold out in 2 hours, and a benefit gig for the United Indian Development Association in Hollywood.

May Towards the end of a US mini-tour, Hynde is involved in a fight with a Memphis bouncer and spends a night in jail.

June *Stop Your Sobbing* peaks at US #65.

July Grace Jones covers Hynde's *Private Life*.

Aug A North American tour includes a performance before 50,000 at the New Wave Festival in Toronto, Canada.

Oct [6] A 15-date UK tour begins in Newcastle, Tyne & Wear.

1981 **Feb** *Message Of Love* reaches UK #11.

Apr US EP *Extended Play*, featuring *Message Of Love*, *Talk Of The Town*, *Porcelain*, *Cuban Slide* and *Slide*, reaches #27 on the Album survey but remains unreleased in UK.

[10] Honeyman-Scott marries US model Peggy Sue Fender, in London.

May [16] Chambers marries Tracey Atkinson.

Aug *Pretenders II* is released, set to hit US #10 and UK #7. Group begins a 3-month US tour, during which Chambers smashes a lamp in his hotel room and injures his fist. The rest of the tour is cancelled.

Sept *Day After Day* makes UK #45.

Nov *I Go To Sleep* hits UK #7.

Dec Shortly before planned UK Christmas dates, Chambers damages his other hand and more concerts are postponed.

1982 **Jan** The Pretenders resume US dates, followed by concerts in Japan, Hong Kong and Australia.

Mar Farndon and Honeyman-Scott return to Japan to meet respective model girlfriend and wife.

Apr On their planned wedding day, Davies and Hynde are refused marriage by a registrar concerned that they are rowing too much.

May Honeyman-Scott plays for The Beach Boys on a US tour.

June [14] Farndon is fired – he is viewed as incompatible with the other members.

[16] Honeyman-Scott dies following a period of cocaine and heroin addiction.

July Hynde flies to US to be with Ray Davies on The Kinks' US tour.

Sept Tony Butler fills in on bass temporarily (he will rejoin Big Country), while Billy Bremner (ex-Rockpile) joins on lead guitar.

1983 **Jan** *Back On The Chain Gang* hits US #5 (where it is used in DeNiro film "King Of Comedy") and makes UK #17.

Feb Hynde gives birth to her and Davies' daughter, Natalie. Mick Green of Johnny Kidd & The Pirates helps audition new guitarists and Robbie McIntosh (ex-Manfred Mann's Earth Band and Night) become new lead guitar while he recommends Malcolm Foster, who is hired a bassist.

Apr [14] Farndon, who had been in the process of forming a group with Rob Stoner and ex-Clash Topper Headon, dies of a drug overdos in the bathtub.

May [28-30] The Pretenders participate in the 3-day US Festival at Sa Bernardino, CA.

Nov Festive *2000 Miles* reaches UK #15.

1984 **Jan** *Learning To Crawl* makes UK #11 and is set to hit US #5. Band begins "The Pretenders World Tour". Natalie joins her mother on the trek but Davies' Kinks commitments keep the family apart.

Feb *Middle Of The Road* reaches US #19.

May [5] *Show Me* reaches US #28 as, following a whirlwind romance Hynde marries Simple Minds vocalist Jim Kerr.

July *Thin Line Between Love And Hate*, reviving The Persuaders 1971 h now with Paul Carrack on keyboards, stalls at US #83 and UK #49.

1985 **July** [13] The Pretenders perform at Live Aid spectacular in Philadelphia, PA, following Simple Minds.

Sept UB40 invites Hynde to guest on a revival of Sonny & Cher hit *I Got You Babe*. It tops UK chart and reaches US #28.

1986 **Nov** Following a lengthy recording session featuring a variety of musicians, based around Hynde, new album *Get Close* produced by Jimmy Iovine, is released, set to hit UK #6 and US #25.

Dec Extracted *Don't Get Me Wrong*, aided by UK TV show "Avengers style black and white video, hits UK #10.

[27] *Don't Get Me Wrong* hits US #10.

1987 **Jan** *Hymn To Her* hits UK #10.

[14] The Pretenders begin an 8-month world tour in Plattsburgh, NY. The line-up Hynde assembles comprises Robbie McIntosh (guitar), T.M. Stevens (bass), Bernie Worrell (keyboards) and Blair Cunningha ex-Haircut 100, (drums).

Mar [7] *My Baby* (following an addition to the Kerr family) peaks at US #64.

Sept *If There Was A Man*, recorded for soundtrack album for James Bond movie "The Living Daylights", under the name Pretenders For 007, makes UK #49.

Nov Compilation *The Singles* hits UK #6 and US #69, as re-mixed version of *Kid* fails to chart.

1988 **July** A second collaboration between UB40 and Hynde, after performing together in June at "Nelson Mandela's 70th Birthday Part concert in Wembley, London, *Breakfast In Bed*, hits UK #6.

1989 **June** [8] At a Greenpeace Rainbow Warriors press conference in London, noted vegetarian Hynde says she once firebombed McDonalds.

[9] McDonalds in Milton Keynes, Bucks., is firebombed. McDonalds threatens legal action against Hynde and asks her to sign written statement agreeing not to repeat her statements. She signs.

1990 **Apr** [7] Chambers, now an in-demand player, drums with Guns N' Roses at Farm Aid IV, amid rumors that he is joining the band.

May [26] *Packed!* reaches UK #19, while extracted singles *Never Do That* and *Sense Of Purpose* fail to chart, despite a video appearance for the latter by Hynde's current beau, UK boxer Gary Stretch.

June [16] *Packed!* makes US #48.

THE PRETTY THINGS

Phil May (vocals)
Dick Taylor (lead guitar)
Brian Pendleton (rhythm guitar)
John Stax (bass)
Viv Prince (drums)

1962 Taylor (b. Jan.28, 1943, Dartford, Kent), a student at Sidcup Art Colleg Kent, with Keith Richard, is a member of Little Boy Blue & The Blue Boys (an embryonic Rolling Stones) but quits when group changes name to Rollin' Stones and is about to turn professional, to begin a course at the Royal College of Art.

1963 Taylor forms a group with fellow R&B fan May (b. Nov.9, 1944, Dartford) taking the name from Bo Diddley's *Pretty Thing*.

Dec The line-up, comprising Taylor, May, Prince (b. Aug.9, 1944, Loughborough, Leics.), Pendleton (b. Apr.13, 1944, Wolverhampton, W.Midlands) and Stax (b. John Fullegar, Apr.6, 1944, Crayford, London), is signed to Fontana after a gig at London's Central School Art, and in the next few months will appear on UK TV's "Ready Stea

Go" and feature in **The Sunday Times** color supplement.

1964 June Group creates media interest with its no-holds-barred style of R&B, long-haired, unkempt image which takes The Rolling Stones persona one step further. May holds claim to having the longest hair on a man in UK. Bryan Morrison and James Duncan take over the group's management and Duncan writes debut hit *Rosalyn* (based on Benny Spellman's *Fortune Teller*), which makes UK #41.

Nov *Don't Bring Me Down* hits UK #10 as the group's image reaches its peak of notoriety when attempts are made to evict the members from their communal home in Belgravia. Newspapers print tales of their exploits on the road and moral outrage is voiced by the establishment.

1965 Mar *The Pretty Things* hits UK #6, as extracted *Honey I Need* reaches UK #13.

Apr [24] Group embarks on second half of the Billy Fury tour at ABC cinema, Gloucester, Glos., with Brian Poole & The Tremeloes, Dave Berry and The Zephyrs.

May [9] Tour ends at Colston Hall, Bristol, Avon.

July *Cry To Me*, written by Bert Berns, reaches UK #28.

Sept The Pretty Things appear on US TV show "Shindig!" alongside The Yardbirds, Jerry Lee Lewis and Raquel Welch.

Nov Skip Alan (b. Alan Skipper, June 11, 1948, London), formerly with Them, replaces Prince. Prince claims he is asked to leave because he has been involved in bad publicity.

Dec *Get The Picture* fails to chart as the group's popularity begins to wane together with the R&B boom.

1966 Jan *Midnight To Six Man* makes UK #46.

[6] Group begins location filming on 15-min. feature "A Day In The Life Of The Pretty Things".

May *Come See Me* peaks at UK #43.

July Group makes its final UK chart entry at #50 with Ray Davies-penned *A House In The Country*.

Dec Pendleton collapses and the band continues as a 4-piece.

1967 Apr [29] Group takes part in 14-hour all-night "Technicolor Dream" concert in the Great Hall of Alexandra Palace, London.

May *Emotions* completes contract with Fontana, with basic tracks smothered with strings against the group's wishes. Group signs to EMI, releasing 3 singles without success. Stax leaves and is replaced by 2 former members of Bern Elliott's Fenmen, organist/pianist Jon Povey (b. Aug.20, 1944, London) and bassist Wally Allen, and group reverts to original 5-piece.

1968 Mar John "Twink" Alder replaces Alan.

Dec Rock opera *SF Sorrow* is released. The group is now involved in London's flourishing psychedelic underground scene, far removed from its R&B origins. Despite critical acclaim, the album is not a hit.

1969 Jan The Pretty Things perform "SF Sorrow" in its entirety at London's Camden Roundhouse.

Group makes a cameo appearance in Norman Wisdom film "What's Good For The Goose".

Nov Taylor quits to become a producer with drummer Alder. (They will later work together when Alder becomes a member of The Pink Fairies.) Alan returns and Vic Unitt, from The Edgar Broughton Band, replaces Taylor.

1970 June *Parachute* is a critical success, but only makes UK #43. **Rolling Stone** magazine will vote it Album Of The Year.

1971 June The group splits.

Nov The Pretty Things are prompted to re-form by manager Bill Shepherd and sign to Warner Bros. May, Povey and Alan are joined by Peter Tolson (b. Sept.10, 1951, Bishops Stortford, Herts.) on guitar, Stuart Brooks on bass and Gordon Edwards (b. Dec.26, 1946, Southport, Merseyside) on keyboards.

1973 Group tours US for first time.

Nov David Bowie pays homage to the group on his album of cover versions *Pin Ups*, which includes *Rosalyn* and *Don't Bring Me Down*.

1974 Oct Group signs to Led Zeppelin's SwanSong label, and makes US #104 with *Torpedo*.

Dec Jack Green (b. Mar.12, 1951, Glasgow, Scotland) replaces Brooks and the group undertakes a long US tour.

1976 May *Savage Eye* makes US #163.

June The Pretty Things disband for a second time, when May, the only surviving original member, quits. They play a few final gigs supporting Uriah Heep and Bad Company at the Empire Pool, Wembley, London.

July May forms Phil May & The Fallen Angels which includes Bill Lovelady and ex-T. Rex bongo player Mickey Finn with ex-Pretty Thing Wally Allen. The group releases an album in Holland only, where The Pretty Things still enjoy cult status.

1977 The remaining members continue under the name Metropolis (until

1980 quitting at the end of the year).

Aug Group re-forms to work part-time, playing clubs and pubs and releases *Cross Talk*.

They appear performing the title theme in Vincent Price horror movie "The Monster Squad".

1984 Members of the group provide music for an episode of UK TV series "Minder" under the name Zac Zolan & Electric Banana.

Aug The band also begins a residency at a club in London's Little Venice and records "live" album *Live At Heartbreak Hotel*, in front of an invited audience.

1987 The group records new album *Out Of The Island* in Germany.

LLOYD PRICE

1950 Pianist, composer and vocalist Price (b. Mar.9, 1933, Kenner, LA) begins leading an R&B quintet in New Orleans, LA, and writing and performing jingles and songs for local radio station W-BOK. One of these, *Lawdy Miss Clawdy*, results in Price signing to Specialty Records. (He had been rejected by Imperial label in favor of Fats Domino.)

1952 *Lawdy Miss Clawdy* (with Domino on piano) hits US R&B #1 (and will have numerous cover versions, including one by Elvis Presley).

1953 Price advises fellow singer Little Richard to send tapes to his producer Art Rupe. *Ain't It A Shame* is another Top 10 R&B success. Drafted into US Army, Price forms a band which entertains troops in Japan, Korea and the Far East.

1956 Discharged from the Army, Price moves to Washington, DC, where he sets up his own Kent Record Company.

1957 Apr He leases *Just Because* to ABC-Paramount and it reaches US #29. (Like every further chart success, except *Never Let Me Go* and *Misty*, *Just Because* is an original Price composition.)

Sept *Lonely Chair*, on KRC, climbs to US #88.

1959 Feb On ABC-Paramount, Price's *Stagger Lee*, his R&B rewrite of folk tune *The Ballad Of Stack-O-Lee*, hits US #1 for 4 weeks.

Mar *Stagger Lee* hits UK #7. With Bo Diddley, The Coasters, Clyde McPhatter and Little Anthony & The Imperials, Price begins a 7-week "Biggest Show Of Stars" package tour in Richmond, VA. *Where Were You (On Our Wedding Day)* reaches US #23.

Apr *Personality* hits US #2 for 3 weeks, held from the top by Johnny Horton's *The Battle Of New Orleans*.

May *Where Were You* reaches UK #15.

June Price's first UK Top 10 is *Personality* at #9.

Aug *Personality* re-enters UK chart and climbs to #25.

Sept *I'm Gonna Get Married* hits US #3 and makes UK #23.

Nov *Won't'cha Come Home* reaches US #43.

Dec Its A-side, *Come Into My Heart*, makes US #20, as Price completes the year on US R&B package tours and TV appearances.

1960 Mar *Lady Luck* makes US #14, while B-side *Never Let Me Go* peaks at US #82.

May *No Ifs No Ands* climbs to US #40 as *Lady Luck* makes UK #45.

Aug *Question* reaches US #19.

Sept *Just Call Me (And I'll Understand)* climbs to US #79.

Dec *(You Better) Know What You're Doin'* makes only US #90.

1963 Nov A cover of Errol Garner's standard *Misty* is Price's first US Hot 100 single in almost 3 years at #21. It is released on his own Double-L label, which issues the first solo recording by Falcons' lead vocalist Wilson Pickett.

1964 Jan *Billie Baby*, also on Double-L, reaches US #84. (Price concentrates on other music business interests and investments and establishes a fund, providing black students with scholarships to attend college.)

1967 Dec Wilson Pickett's remake of *Stag-O-Lee* reaches US #22.

1969 Price, based in New York, establishes a new label, Turntable, and opens a club of the same name, at former jazz venue Billboard. (This follows the murder of his Double-L partner Harold Lugan at their New York office; his body is found while record player spins a Lloyd Price disk.)

1971 Oct *Stagger Lee* reaches US chart (#25) for a third time with Tommy Roe's cover.

1972 Price releases *The Roots And Back* on GSF label.

1974 Sept With boxing promoter Don King, Price co-promotes the 3-day "Zaire 74" music festival in Zaire, Africa.

1976 Price and King form LPG label in New York, having unsuccessfully dabbled in Muscle Shoals soul (on Scepter) and versions of Broadway hits (on Ludix label).

PRINCE

1968 Prince (b. Prince Rogers Nelson, June 7, 1958, Minneapolis, MN), named after The Prince Roger Trio, which is led by his jazz-pianist father John Nelson (and occasionally featuring his mother Mattie as a vocalist), has already begun teaching himeslf the piano and performed in school talent shows, is taken by his stepfather, Hayward Baker, to whom his mother has recently married, to see James Brown in concert, a seminal musical experience which will permeate into Prince's own recordings and live performances as an adult artist.

1970 At age 12, Prince (experiencing problems with his stepfather) runs away from home and drifts, sometimes staying with his father (who buys him a guitar which he teaches himself to play). He is eventually adopted by the Anderson family, whose son Andre (later Andre Cymone) becomes a close friend and future musical collaborator. Prince begins writing songs and starts to play saxophone, drums and bass guitar. (He will master over 2 dozen instruments.)

1972 Drummer Charles Smith, a cousin, invites Prince to play guitar (with Cymone on bass) in his junior high school-based band, Grand Central, which also has Cymone's sister Linda on keyboards. Their repertoire is mainly current hit covers, which Prince arranges.

1973 Prince goes to Minneapolis Central high school, where fellow students include Mark Brown (later bassist Brown Mark) and Terry Lewis (later of Time). Grand Central becomes Champagne, Morris Day replaces Smith on drums, and Prince becomes band leader, although most of his own songs fall flat with audiences. His writing influences include, alongside several major R&B names, folk singer Joni Mitchell.

1974 Even before he leaves school at 16, Prince and his cohorts have developed their own Minneapolis musical scene and sound, known to its young adherents as "Uptown", around Prince's outfit Flyte Tyme, which includes drummer Jellybean Johnson, bassist Terry Lewis and singer Alexander O'Neal. (The influential "Minneapolis Sound" of the 80s is rooted here.)

1976 Prince is invited to play guitar on sessions at Sound 80 studios in Minneapolis by Brooklyn artist Pepe Willie, produced by Motown's Hank Cosby, and also featuring Colonel Abrams. (This is the source of instrumental out-takes album *The Minneapolis Genius: 94 East*, released in 1986 by Willie on Hot Pink label.) Meanwhile, a demo tape is produced by English sound engineer Chris Moon, who recognizes Prince's talent and teaches him studio technique in return for half the proceeds from items on which they collaborate (mainly lengthy funk workouts on sexual themes).
June While Prince heads for New York to seek a recording deal, Moon demo attracts attention of Minneapolis businessman Owen Husney.
Sept Prince returns to Minneapolis, and Husney forms management company American Artists with attorney Gary Levinson. Convincing Prince to mold his songs into more accessible form, he puts up money for the recording of high-quality demos.

1977 **Mar** Record company negotiations start from the premise that Prince will produce himself. After a studio audition, Warner Bros. agrees to the terms and offers a long-term contract.

1978 **Nov** Debut album *For You*, which has taken 5 months to produce (and used double the money advanced by Warner for 3 albums), is almost entirely played by Prince, on synthesizers, and makes US #163. Extracted, *Soft & Wet* (a title of which many radio stations are wary), reaches US #92 and R&B #12, selling almost 350,000 copies, mainly in the R&B market. (Follow-up *Just As Long As We're Together*, from the album, fails to chart.)

1979 **Jan** At Minneapolis' Capri theater (and chiefly to assembled Warner executives), Prince debuts the band he has formed after completing the first album (with Cymone on bass, keyboard player Gayle Chapman and drummer Bobby Z, plus rock guitarist Dez Dickerson and keyboardist Matt Fink, the result fusing rock and funk styles.)
Feb Prince leaves Husney and American Artists, turning variously and unsatisfactorily for management to Hollywood-based Perry Jones and Bob Marley's ex-manager Don Taylor, before his Warner-appointed agent Steve Fargnoli introduces him to Cavallo & Ruffalo (managers of Earth, Wind & Fire and Ray Parker Jr.).
June Recording begins for a new album (which this time will be completed in 6 weeks.)
Oct *Prince* peaks at US #22, initially selling a half million copies (it will sell double, going platinum). From it comes another R&B (but not crossover) hit (#13), *Why You Wanna Treat Me So Bad?* It also contains *I Feel For You* (which Chaka Khan will revive for a #1 hit in 1984).
Nov Extracted *I Wanna Be Your Lover* tops R&B chart for 2 weeks and makes US #11, his first major hit single.

1980 **Jan** Prince tangles with Motown funk artist Rick James while supporting him on a US tour. Meanwhile, *I Wanna Be Your Lover* is his UK chart debut at #41.
Feb Chapman leaves and is replaced by Lisa Coleman (daughter of Los Angeles session veteran Gary Coleman), who has auditioned via a demo (and will stay with Prince for 6 years).
[9] Prince performs a showcase in Minneapolis, but the venue is far from full and reactions to his overtly sexual stage antics are mixed.
Mar Always a prolific songwriter, often creating tracks on his Fender Telecaster guitar, Prince begins recording another album; a rough-edged, mostly solo affair cut on his own 16-track equipment, which emerges as *Dirty Mind*.
Dec After being remixed in Los Angeles, *Dirty Mind* makes US #45 and earns a gold disk. It breaks Prince to a wider audience but is criticized by some as too sexual, particularly on cuts like *Head* and *Sister*. From it, *Uptown* makes US R&B #5, but fails to cross over.

1981 **Jan** Prince and his band (soon to be known as The Revolution) begin to tour widely in US.
June [2] Prince makes his UK debut at the Lyceum Ballroom, London. The attendance is poor and the rest of the tour is cancelled. (He will not play UK again for 5 years.)
On returning to US, Cymone quits the band for solo projects. (He signs with American Artists and will release 2 albums, before concentrating on production.)
July Warner Bros. release an eponymous album by Minneapolis group Time, with all songs credited to Jamie Starr (an early Prince pseudonym). The album had originated when Prince invited Morris Day to sing over 6 tracks he had already completed. The band has been formed only after the album was completed and includes former Flyte Tyme members Lewis and Johnson, plus keyboardists Jimmy Jam and Monte Moir. (The members will later pay tribute to Prince's role as motivator in shaping the group.)
Dec Prince's fourth album *Controversy* reaches US #21, while extracted title track peaks at US #70. (Another cut, *Let's Work* hits R&B #9, but does not cross over.) This album will also turn platinum, spending 63 weeks on US chart. Time backs Prince on his US tour.

1982 **Mar** He buys a mansion in suburban Minneapolis, where he will permanently reside.
Oct A 6-month tour begins in support of new album *1999*. It is a Minneapolis revue, with Prince & The Revolution following Time and Prince's new all-girl group Vanity 6 (blonde Bostonian Brenda Bennett, Canadian Dee Dee Winters aka Vanity, and 16-year-old Minneapolis native Susan Moonsie).
Dec Title track *1999* makes US #44. The double album begins slow US chart rise (but will be a major seller during 1983). Although Prince has played and produced most of its tracks, album credits Prince & The Revolution for the first time.

1983 **Jan** Prince is added to white act-dominated MTV playlist with his video for *Little Red Corvette*, from *1999*. Always uneasy with interviews, he begins almost blanket press silence, which he will always maintain.
Feb *1999* finally picks up momentum, aided by wide exposure for *Little Red Corvette*, now issued as a single, while *1999* makes UK #25. However, the tour does not go well. Time, despite a successful second album *What Time Is It?* (which has reached US #26), is relegated to backing Vanity 6 from behind a curtain, while Jam and Lewis are fired by Prince after missing a show (through being stranded by snow in Atlanta, where they were producing The SOS Band).
Apr Tour finishes and Prince begins work on a film with Hollywood scriptwriter William Blinn, while UCLA film graduate Albert Magnoli is brought to Minneapolis to discuss directing the project. Dickerson leaves The Revolution, and is replaced by Wendy Melvoin (daughter of session keyboardist Mike Melvoin), who will appear in the film.
May *Little Red Corvette* hits US #6 and makes UK #54, while *1999* finally hits US #9, earning a platinum disk for million-plus sales, staying on chart for more than 2 years.
July Title song *1999* re-charts at US #12.
Aug Prince premieres some of his forthcoming project *Purple Rain* material at First Avenue club in Minneapolis.
Oct *Delirious*, third single from the album, hits US #8.
Nov Filming of "Purple Rain" begins (and will take 7 weeks, at a cost of $7 million). Wendy and Lisa begin contributing as a songwriting team as part of the project. *Purple Rain, Baby I'm A Star* and *I Would Die 4 U* are recorded live at Minneapolis' First Avenue club, where the movie's performance scenes are filmed.
Dec *Little Red Corvette* is reissued in UK, but stalls at #66.

1984 **Jan** Double A-side *Let's Pretend We're Married/Irresistible Bitch* peaks at US #52.

July [7] Recorded at Sunset Sound studio, Los Angeles, self-penned, self-produced *When Doves Cry*, taken from the forthcoming movie and album *Purple Rain*, gives Prince his first chart-topper, hitting US #1 for 5 weeks, and selling over 2 million copies to earn a rare single platinum disk (it will be the biggest-selling single of 1984). In UK, it is also his biggest success to date, hitting #4.
[27] "Purple Rain" opens nationwide in US (and in UK 4 days later), its plot taking romantic liberties with Prince's past, his relationship with his parents and his rise through the Minneapolis scene. It is well received despite its cast of non-actors, and takes $60 million in 2 months at the US box office.
Aug Soundtrack album *Purple Rain* sells over a million in its first week in US (eventually selling 9 million in US). It stays at US #1 for 24 weeks and hits UK #7.
Sept [29] *Let's Go Crazy* also from *Purple Rain*, tops US chart for 2 weeks, selling a million (but is not issued in UK at this time).
Oct Title song, anthemic ballad *Purple Rain* hits US #2 (another million-seller) and UK #8.
Nov 100-date US tour gets underway. (By the time it ends in Apr.1985 over 1,692,000 tickets will have been sold. Throughout the schedule Prince plays unpublicized free concerts for handicapped children.) The 2-hour show features his latest protegee, percussionist/singer Sheila E. (daughter of Santana percussionist Pete Escovedo, and introduced to Prince by Carlos Santana), with whom he has already recorded *The Glamorous Life* in June 1984.
85 Jan *I Would Die 4 U*, also from movie, hits US #8 and makes UK #58.
[28] Although expected to join the all-star session for USA For Africa's *We Are The World*, he declines on the grounds that he does not record with other acts – but offers to donate an exclusive track (*4 The Tears In Your Eyes*) to the follow-up benefit album.
Feb Double A-side *1999/Little Red Corvette* becomes Prince's most successful UK single, hitting #2 (behind Elaine Paige and Barbara Dickson's *I Know Him So Well*), while *1999* makes UK #30.
[11] Prince wins Best International Solo Artist and *Purple Rain* wins Best Film Soundtrack at the fourth annual BRIT Awards at the Grosvenor House, London.
Mar *Take Me With You*, duetted with another female protegee, Apollonia (who replaces Vanity, to lead Apollonia 6), is the only single from *Purple Rain* not to hit US Top 10, peaking at #25. It is bettered by Scottish singer Sheena Easton's *Sugar Walls*, which Prince has written for her under the pseudonym Alexander Nevermind, and which hits US #9. In UK, *Take Me With You* is issued as double A-side with *Let's Go Crazy* and hits UK #7.
[2] Prince wins Best Group Rock Vocal Performance for *Purple Rain* and R&B Song Of The Year for *I Feel For You* at the 27th annual Grammy awards.
[25] Prince wins the Best Original Score Oscar for "Purple Rain" at the Academy awards.
May *Around The World In A Day* tops US chart for 3 weeks and hits UK #5. The album has evolved from rehearsals for Prince's next tour, and has been recorded at the newly-built Paisley Park studios at his Minneapolis HQ, the Warehouse. In contrast to its predecessor, it is released with minimal promotion, and Prince reportedly has to be persuaded by Warner Bros. into releasing singles from it. Tracks include the spiritual *The Ladder* (co-written with his father) and *Temptation*, which purportedly features a conversation with God. Prince instructs Fargnoli to announce that he is retiring from live performance. Paisley Park (the studio and now the label) will become the center of Prince-orchestrated projects and acts, including The Family (featuring his regular sax player Eric Leeds and Susannah Melvoin) and Madhouse (a jazzy project, also featuring Leeds), in addition to independent protegees like Sheila E. and Jill Jones.
June Prince visits Paris, France, to plan and write songs for a new movie, after which he and Fargnoli travel to South of France to schedule shooting for his next film"Under The Cherry Moon". When work starts, Prince relegates director Mary Lambert to an advisory role, and takes full control. Meanwhile, *Paisley Park* reaches UK #18.
July The first US extract from *Around The World In A Day*, Raspberry Beret, hits US #2. It is also the first single released on his own Paisley Park label.
Aug *Raspberry Beret* makes UK #25.
Sept *Pop Life*, from *Around The World In A Day*, hits US #7. Prince breaks his press silence to talk to Neal Karlen for **Rolling Stone**. The interview, vetted by Prince and his management, is unrevealing.
Oct *Pop Life* peaks at UK #60.
Nov *America*, a further single from the album, peaks at US #46.

1986 Apr [5] *Kiss* tops US R&B chart.
[19] *Kiss*, taken from the forthcoming movie and soundtrack album *Parade*, tops US chart for 2 weeks, selling over a million. Behind it at #2 is *Magic Monday* by The Bangles, written by Prince under the pseudonym Christopher. In UK, *Kiss* hits #6.
May *Parade – Music From Under The Cherry Moon* hits US #3 and UK #4, earning a platinum disk. Prince decides to return to live work and the "Parade" tour is launched, with a big band, dazzling choreography replacing technoflash and greater R&B emphasis. Reviews are ecstatic.
June Lisa Barber, a Sheridan, WY, motel chambermaid, is the 10,000th caller to win an MTV contest number. She wins a date with Prince to attend the premiere of "Under The Cherry Moon" in her hometown.
[7] Prince's birthday show in Detroit is filmed.
July [1] "Under The Cherry Moon" film premieres in Sheridan, WY. Barber tells Prince she enjoys the movie. After the showing, at the party at the Holiday Inn, Prince plays an impromptu 45-min. set.
[2] "Under The Cherry Moon" opens nationwide at 941 US theaters.
[5] *Mountains*, written by Wendy and Lisa and taken from *Parade*, reaches US #23 and makes UK #45.
Aug Prince submits a song to one of his long-time favorite artists, Joni Mitchell, but she finds it unsuitable and declines to record it.
[9] *Anotherloverholenyohead*, from *Parade*, peaks at US #63.
[12-14] Prince plays 3 sell-out nights at Wembley Arena, London, his first UK dates in 5 years. (These are among his final live appearances with The Revolution, which he will disband before the end of the year.)
Sept *Girls And Boys*, released only as a UK single, reaches #11.
Nov *Anotherloverholenyohead* peaks at UK #36.
1987 Mar Prince prepares a new stage show, recruiting musicians and dancers. He retains Fink, Leeds, Greg Brooks and Wally Safford from The Revolution, recalls Sheila E. and adds guitarist Mico Weaver, keyboardist Boni Boyer, bassist Seacer and dancer/singer Cat Glover.
Apr [11] Stark urban-themed *Sign O' The Times* tops US R&B chart.
[25] *Sign O' The Times*, title song from the forthcoming album, hits US #3 and UK #10, as rehearsals for a European tour take place at the NEC, Birmingham, W.Midlands.
May Double album *Sign O' The Times* hits US #6 and UK #4, earning a platinum disk.
June [20] *If I Was Your Girlfriend* (on which Prince's alter-ego "Camille" is credited with lead vocal), makes US #67 and UK #20, as the European tour begins.
July Prince's 2 Wembley Stadium dates are cancelled. The official reason given is poor weather (and hoped-for alternative dates at the indoor Earl's Court arena cannot be arranged in time), but rumors cite inter-promoter politics as a factor. No attempt is made to stage the "Sign O' The Times" tour in US (because, it is assumed, of the large costs involved), but a movie of the same title, largely consisting of the tour show as filmed in Rotterdam, Holland, serves as a substitute for both US and UK audiences. (It will also be issued as a home video.)
Oct [17] *U Got The Look*, a duet from *Sign O' The Times* with Sheena Easton and aided by steamy performance video clip (rumors of a romantic liaison between them persist), hits US #2 and reaches UK #11.
Dec *I Could Never Take The Place Of Your Man*, another track from *Sign O' The Times*, hits US #10 and makes UK #29. Meanwhile, the music press runs stories concerning a mysterious Prince album, featuring back-to-his-roots raw sex and funk tracks, which he is apparently asking Warner to rush out on their carefully-planned Christmas release schedules. Label staff admit to knowing less about the project than the press, but rumors persist that Prince wants the album released in plain black sleeves with no recording credits.
1988 Jan [1] Prince performs an after-midnight concert to benefit Minnesota Coalition for the homeless. He is joined on stage by Miles Davis. Wendy and Lisa's *Sideshow* is released by Virgin Records. The *Black Album*, as it will become known, fails to officially materialize. Several thousand are pressed in Europe and, when the recall notice comes, 100 copies slip out of WEA Records' German pressing plant. These (directly or via a German radio broadcast) and advance promo cassettes, are the sources for a flood of *Black Album* bootlegs. The album is a series of hardcore erotic funk out-takes; track listing is: *Le Grind, Cindy C, Dead On It, When 2 R In Love, Bob George, Supercalifragisexi, 2 Nigs United 4 West Compton* and *Hard Rock In A Funky Place*.
Feb [6] *I Could Never Take The Place Of Your Man* hits US #10, as B-Side *Hot Thing* makes US #63.
May *Alphabet St.*, from the forthcoming album (which is announced as definitely not being the *Black Album*), hits UK #8 and UK #9.
June *Lovesexy*, an unlikely blend of sexy R&B and spiritual concerns, reaches US #11 and gives Prince his first UK #1 album. It also concerns

itself with the "battle" between Camille (the good or positive side of Prince's personality) and Spooky Electric (the bad). A Prince-penned Warner press release suggests that the *Black Album* was Spooky Electric's idea, but that Camille won over and stopped the "evil" record. (Some critics suggest that the whole business of the mystery album was merely an elaborate pre-release scam for *Lovesexy*.) Meanwhile, Prince's sister Tyka Nelson signs to Chrysalis Records, and releases an album, to little sales interest.

July The "Lovesexy" tour begins in Paris, France, and includes 7 nights at London's Wembley Arena. In a return to a flashier stage style, Prince enters the circular stage on an outsize pink Cadillac. Latest Prince female cohort Cat disrobes him on a neon bed and then ties him to a chair. (After some of the gigs, Prince adjourns to small clubs, where he performs an additional late-night 3-hour set for invited guests.)

Aug *Glam Slam*, from *Lovesexy*, reaches UK #29.

Sept [14] A 20-date US tour, Prince's first in 4 years, starts at the Met Center, Bloomington, MN., set to end in Worcester, MA, on Oct.22. Prince plays a benefit concert in Boston, MA, to establish a scholarship in the name of 17-year-old Frederick Weber, who was killed when hit by an automobile while waiting in line for Prince concert tickets outside Boston's Tower Records store.

Nov *I Wish U Heaven*, from *Lovesexy*, reaches UK #24. Prince ends the year collaborating with other artists, working with Sheena Easton, duetting with Madonna on her forthcoming album and signing George Clinton to Paisley Park (having helped pay off the latter's tax bill).

1989 Jan [23] Dave Hill's book **Prince: A Pop Life** is published in UK.

Apr Prince's half-sister Lorna Nelson loses court battle insisting that he stole her lyrics for use in *U Got The Look*.

Aug [5] *Batdance,* first cut from Prince-composed and produced soundtrack which forms part of the massive multi-entertainment Warner Bros. project based around the summer's hot movie "Batman", hits US #1. A stuttered and sampled house/dance cut, it includes dialog snippets from the film's stars Michael Keaton and Jack Nicholson and is third Prince US #1 as a performer (it also hits UK #2). Parent album *Batman* is also in its third of 6 weeks at US #1, having already hit UK #1 on July 1.

Sept [24] Prince opens the 15th anniversary NBC TV "Saturday Night Live" special.
Follow-up *Partyman* reaches UK #14 and US #18.

Dec [16] Further *Batman* extract, *The Arms Of Orion*, a duet with Easton, makes US #36 (having already made UK #27 in Nov.).
By year's end, Prince will have begun work on his next film project "Graffiti Bridge", written and produced an album, released on Paisley Park, for Mavis Staples and completed further production work for Morris Day, Jerome Benton and even short-term belle, "Batman" actress Kim Basinger.

1990 Feb [18] *Batman* wins Best Soundtrack at the 9th annual BRIT Awards at the Dominion theater, London.

Apr [30] He previews his forthcoming "Nude Tour" at 650 ticket Rupert's Nightclub in Golden Valley, Minneapolis. The $100-a-ticket benefit going to the family of his former bodyguard, Charles "Big Chick" Huntsberry, who died on Apr.2 of heart failure age 49.

June [19] 17-date UK leg of "Nude Tour" tour opens at London's Wembley Arena, set to end on Aug.24.

Aug [30] Japanese leg of his world tour begins, set to end on Sept.10.

Sept *Graffiti Bridge* tops UK chart and will hit US #6.

[22] *Thieves In The Temple* hits US #6

Oct [6] Minneapolis Mayor Don Fraser declares the day Prince Day, though the star is reported to be in Los Angeles.

Nov [17] *New Power Generation* peaks at US #64.

1991 Jan [6] Prince premieres his latest backing band, The New Power Generation: Tony M (raps), Rosie Gaines (6 octave range singer), Michael Bland (drums), Levi Seacer Jr. (guitar), Kirk Johnson (guitar), Damon Dickson (dancer), Sonny T (bass) and Tommy Barbarella (keyboards) at Glam Slam club in Minneapolis.

[18] Prince performs at the opening night of the "Rock In Rio II" festival at the Maracana soccer stadium in Rio de Janeiro, Brazil, before an estimated crowd of 60,000.

Feb Having been fired in 1988, Prince's ex-managers Joseph Ruffalo, Robert Cavallo and Steve Fargnoli, bring a $600,000 lawsuit against their former boss, suing for severance pay and punitive damages.

Mar [7] Prince is named Best Songwriter in the annual **Rolling Stone** Readers' Picks music awards.

Apr [13] From "Graffiti Bridge", teen star Tevin Campbell reaches US #12 with Prince-penned and produced *Round And Round*.

Aug Prince is scheduled to release his fifth album in 5 years,

Diamonds And Pearls, backed by the New Power Generation, and prepares for a concurrent US arena tour, while Spike Lee has been booked to film the video for extracted *Willing And Able.*

P.J. PROBY

1957 Proby (b. James Marcus Smith, Nov.6, 1938, Houston, TX), after an education at military school, moves to Los Angeles, CA, with ambition to become a star. Taking the name Jett Powers, he has singing and acting lessons and picks up bit parts in B-movies and on TV.

1958 As Powers, he records 2 solo singles (*Go Girl Go* and *Loud Perfume*) for small Los Angeles labels, without success. He also forms The Moondogs with Marshall Leib (later one of Phil Spector's Teddy Bears), Larry Taylor (later of Canned Heat) and Elliott Ingber (later in Frank Zappa's Mothers Of Invention); despite its later credentials, this quartet achieves little.

1959 Working as a demo singer, he signs to Liberty Records as a songwriter (his *Clown Shoes* will be Johnny Burnette's last UK hit in 1962).

1961 He begins recording for Liberty, both as Jett Powers and as Orville Wood, but a series of singles fails to make any impression.

1963 Fellow songwriter Jackie DeShannon introduces him to UK TV producer Jack Good (of "Oh Boy!" fame), currently working in Hollywood. Good earmarks him for the role of Iago in a rock version of "Othello" which he is hoping to stage with Cassius Clay as Othello, but the project founders.

1964 Apr Good is commissioned by Brian Epstein to produce a Beatles TV special in London for BBC TV, and invites Powers – now using the name P.J. Proby, which meets with Good's approval – to UK as a guest act for the show. Good, who engineered Gene Vincent's moody black leather image for UK TV 5 years earlier, molds a startling visual appearance for Proby, with tight trousers, loose smock top, and 18th-century-type ponytailed hairstyle.

May [6] The show "Around The Beatles" is screened in UK and Proby's rocking guest slot arouses great interest. In anticipation, Good produces *Hold Me*, a 1939 ballad revived as a raucous rave-up, with Proby self-duetting in abandoned style. He sells it to Decca for release.

July *Hold Me* hits UK #3, rocketing Proby to stardom in UK, where he settles to take advantage of a flood of TV and live work.

Sept Marketed in US as part of the "British Invasion", *Hold Me* peaks at US #70.

Oct *Together*, a 1961 Top 20 hit for Connie Francis, is rocked up in similar style to *Hold Me* (with Jimmy Page, later of Led Zeppelin, on guitar), and hits UK #8. Liberty Records, to which Proby is still contracted in US, enforces its contract and wins a court action to prevent Decca releasing further Proby material. He transfers to Liberty in UK. (The label has already released *Try To Forget Her*, from his Jett Powers days, in competition with *Together*. Despite a reported large advance order figure, it failed to chart in UK.)

1965 Jan His first new Liberty recording, *Somewhere*, from "West Side Story", is a melodramatic arrangement with Proby in quivering, over-the-top ballad vocal form. It hits UK #6.

[29] Proby begins a 22-date twice-nightly package tour with Cilla Black, The Fourmost, Tommy Roe & The Roemans, Tommy Quickly and Sounds Incorporated at the ABC cinema, Croydon, London.

Feb [1] After Proby performs his first number during which his pants split, the manager of the ABC Luton draws the curtain and hands back audience's money. Concerts at Croydon and Walthamstow also end in controversy. Near blanket ban of UK concert halls is imposed on Proby.

[8] ABC TV follows its theater chain namesake with a ban on Proby screen appearances, because of the trouser-splitting.

[24] BBC TV bans Proby from appearance on any shows.
Somewhere peaks at US #91.

Mar A revival of Billy Eckstine's *I Apologise*, with another exaggeratedly dramatic vocal performance, reaches UK #11. *I Am P.J. Proby* climbs to UK #16 (his only chart album).

[1] 15-date twice-nightly UK tour of independent theaters, where he is not banned, known as "The P.J. Show", with The Fourmost and Brian Poole & The Tremeloes, opens at Finsbury Park Astoria, London.

[9] Proby is taken ill in Manchester. Tom Jones deputizes following 2 nights and, when Proby fails to resume the tour, it is cancelled.

June Affected by the bans, Proby begins to lose his performing reliability and becomes eccentric off stage, with a penchant for outrageous pronouncements to the media (he informs a **Sunday Time** interviewer that he aims to star in a movie "about a pop star who goes off his head and believes he's Jesus Christ").

July *Let The Water Run Down*, in rocking R&B style, reaches UK #19.

[23] Proby announces he will not appear on "Ready Steady Go!" again after he is faded out in the middle of his second number on the show.

Oct A Lennon/McCartney ballad not recorded by The Beatles, *That Means A Lot*, reaches UK #30.

Nov [6] Proby splits with his manager of a year, John Heyman.

[10] He signs a management deal with Bertie Green and Mel Collins. (It will be ended by mutual agreement within a week.)

[29] Tito Burns becomes Proby's agent.

Dec Proby's straight and sensitive version of *Maria*, from "West Side Story", hits UK #8.

[4] Proby's work permit expires, and shortly afterwards he is told to leave his Chelsea house, when his lease runs out, after complaints from neighbors.

66 **Feb** *You've Come Back* makes UK #25.

Mar Proby refuses to enter recording studio until a dispute he has with Liberty over royalties is settled.

[12] He begins 6-date twice-nightly farewell UK tour with The Searchers and others, at the Town Hall, Birmingham, W.Midlands. Tour ends Mar.27 at the Empire theater, Liverpool, Merseyside.

[29] Proby leaves UK when his permit expires.

Apr [18] He begins US tour with Gene Pitney.

May Manager Terence Hillman returns to London after terminating his contract by mutual agreement.

June *To Make A Big Man Cry*, having failed as a single for Adam Faith, makes UK #34.

Nov *I Can't Make It Alone*, a Goffin/King ballad with Spectoresque production by Jack Nitzsche, makes UK #37.

67 **Feb** Proby files for bankruptcy in Los Angeles, listing debts of £180,000.

[13] Proby is granted 2-week work permit to perform in UK.

Mar *Niki Hoeky*, an R&B-rocker written by Pat and Lolly Vegas (later to find fame as Redbone with *Witch Queen Of New Orleans*), reaches US #23. It is Proby's biggest US hit (it fails to chart in UK).

68 **Mar** MOR/country ballad *It's Your Day Today* makes UK #32; Proby's final UK hit single. Shortly afterwards, he is declared a bankrupt, with debts of £60,000, and returns to US, reputedly to Texas to breed horses, which also fails. (He will continue recording for Liberty, much of it country-styled material, with the occasional oddity like 7-min. *Mery Hopkins Never Had Days Like These*, but no disk will chart.)

70 **Aug** *It's Goodbye* is, appropriately, Proby's last Liberty release.

Oct Proby returns to UK at Jack Good's request to play Cassio in Good's rock musical version of "Othello", titled "Catch My Soul" in the '69 Theatre Company production at the University theater, Manchester, Gtr.Manchester. The show transfers to the West End of London, where it has a successful run.

72 **Mar** A one-off single for EMI's Columbia label coupling the standard *We'll Meet Again* with his own song *Clown Shoes* makes no impact. (Similar one-offs for a variety of labels like Ember, Seven Sun and Rooster will characterize his sparse recorded output through the next decade. Live work will mainly be in UK cabaret, playing a nostalgic show to appeal to those with memories of the mid-60s. In contrast to his earlier public eccentricities, he will be reclusive off stage.)

77 Proby is signed, again by Jack Good, to portray the 70s Elvis Presley in stage musical "Elvis" in London's West End. (Presley at younger periods of his life is played by other singers, including Shakin' Stevens. The musical will run successfully for 19 months and pick up a theater award as Best Musical Of The Year. Proby's performance will deteriorate after excellent initial reviews, and he will be sacked.)

85 **Sept** After living in UK in comparative obscurity for several years (though regularly playing small club and cabaret dates), Proby signs to Manchester independent label Savoy Records, releasing a revival of Soft Cell's *Tainted Love* on a 12"-only single, which generates music press interest, but is not a hit.

Nov A rapid follow-up on Savoy, a revival of Joy Division's *Love Will Tear Us Apart*, has more positive reviews than sales. (Further, often eccentric, releases on the label – including a recitation from T.S. Eliot's poem "The Waste Land" – will also only remain cult items, despite the fact that in the late 80s Proby is recording more regularly than at any time since his chart heyday.)

PROCOL HARUM
Gary Brooker (vocals, piano)
Matthew Fisher (keyboards)
Robin Trower (guitar)
Dave Knights (bass)
Barry J. Wilson (drums)

1959 While Brooker (b. May 29, 1945, Southend, Essex), Trower (b. Mar.9, 1945, Southend) and bass player Chris Copping (b. Aug.29, 1945, Southend) are still at secondary school in Southend, they team with singer Bob Scott and drummer Mick Brownlee to form The Paramounts. The group becomes popular locally, playing covers of rock hits in local youth clubs, and when Scott drops out, pianist Brooker takes over vocals.

1962 After the group leaves school and gains a manager, Peter Martin, its gigs (still semi-professional) expand, as does the repertoire, which includes covers of US R&B singles by Ray Charles, James Brown, Bobby Bland and others. The group becomes resident band at Southend's Shades club.

1963 **Jan** Brownlee, the only one who does not wish to turn professional, leaves, and is replaced by Wilson (b. Mar.18, 1947, Southend) on drums, recruited through a small ad in **Melody Maker**.

Sept Copping leaves to go to Leicester University, and is replaced on bass by Diz Derrick.

Oct A demo coupling covers of The Coasters' *Poison Ivy* and Bobby Bland's *Further On Up The Road* gains the group an EMI audition, and it signs to Parlophone label, working with The Hollies' producer, Ron Richards.

1964 **Jan** *Poison Ivy* is released as first single, and hits UK #35. It receives a boost from The Rolling Stones, who name The Paramounts their favorite UK R&B group after the 2 bands have worked together on TV's "Thank Your Lucky Stars" pop show.

Mar A revival of Thurston Harris' *Little Bitty Pretty One* is plugged via a "Ready Steady Go!" TV appearance, but fails to chart (as will 3 more singles released to the end of 1965).

1966 **Sept** Group splits after its live gigs have reduced in quality (i.e. backing Sandie Shaw and Chris Andrews on tours of Europe). Derrick leaves the music business, Trower and Wilson play with other R&B circuit bands, and Brooker decides to concentrate on songwriting, teaming with lyricist Keith Reid, whom he has met via a mutual acquaintance, R&B producer Guy Stevens.

1967 **Apr** With a batch of material in need of a band to play it, Brooker and Reid advertise for musicians in **Melody Maker**, and the first version of Procol Harum (after the Latin (procul) for "far from these things") is formed calling themselves The Pinewoods, with Brooker on piano and vocals, Fisher (b. Mar.7, 1946, Croydon, London) on organ, Ray Royer (b. Oct.8, 1945) on guitar, Knights (b. June 28, 1945, Islington, London) on bass and Bobby Harrison (b. June 28, 1943, East Ham, London) on drums. Producer Denny Cordell, a long-time acquaintance of Brooker, produces the first recording: Reid's surreal poem *A Whiter Shade Of Pale*, set by Brooker to music adapted from one of the movements of Bach's "Suite No.3 in D Major (Air On The G String)".

May Band performs *A Whiter Shade Of Pale* at London's Speakeasy club, and Cordell places the record with Decca's Deram label, also sending a demo to pirate radio ship Radio London to see how it sounds on the radio.

[12] Rave listener reaction to the first few exclusive plays of it on "Big L" prompt Deram to rush-release it in UK.

June *A Whiter Shade Of Pale* tops UK chart for 6 weeks, selling 606,000 copies, dethroned by The Beatles' *All You Need Is Love*. (Procol Harum becomes only the sixth act to top UK chart with a debut release.)

[4] Group makes its London concert debut supporting Jimi Hendrix at the Saville theater, London.

July *A Whiter Shade Of Pale* hits US #5, taking its sales over a million (eventual worldwide sales will top 6 million). Meanwhile, after dissension within the group (plus panic that there is no act and no other repertoire with which to tour on the back of the hit), Royer and Harrison are asked to leave (they form their own band, Freedom), and Brooker recruits his old Paramounts cohorts Trower and Wilson to take over on guitar and drums.

Oct Cordell's production company moves its outlet from Deram to EMI's Regal Zonophone label (Brooker's father Harry once recorded for the label when a member of Felix Mendelsohn's Hawaiian Serenaders), and *Homburg*, in similar style to the first single, hits UK #6. Meanwhile, *Procol Harum*, not a chart item in UK, reaches US #47. US pressing includes *A Whiter Shade Of Pale* among the tracks, unlike the

UK version, and all but one of the other tracks are Brooker/Reid collaborations.

Nov *Homburg* peaks at US #34.

1968 **Apr** *Quite Rightly So* makes UK #50.

Nov Group is signed to A&M Records in US for second album, *Shine On Brightly*, which reaches US #24 but on Regal Zonophone in UK it fails to chart.

Dec [28] On tour in US, the group plays Miami Pop Festival, in Hallendale, FL, to 100,000 people, along with Chuck Berry, Fleetwood Mac, The Turtles, Canned Heat, and many more.

1969 **Mar** Knights and Fisher both leave, to take up management and production respectively. Copping, his university studies at Leicester complete, rejoins his former Paramounts co-members, on both bass and organ. Line-up of early 1969 Procol Harum is now the same as early 1963 Paramounts.

Apr [6] Group plays with Ike & Tina Turner, John Mayall and others at Palm Springs Pop Festival, CA, where an audience too large for the drive-in car park venue riots when police helicopters try to disperse it.

June *A Salty Dog* (recorded before the departure of Fisher and Knights, and produced by the former) makes US #32, while the title track reaches UK #44.

[22] Group plays Toronto Rock Festival, Canada, to 50,000 people, alongside The Band, Chuck Berry, Steppenwolf and Blood, Sweat & Tears.

July *A Salty Dog* is first Procol Harum album to chart in UK, at #27.

Aug [1] Group plays Atlantic City Pop Festival, NJ, with Creedence Clearwater Revival, Janis Joplin, B.B. King, The Byrds and others, to 110,000 people.

1970 **June** *Home*, on which Chris Thomas takes over as producer (also for the next few albums), makes UK #49.

July Band plays the 3-day Atlanta Pop Festival, in Byron, GA, to 200,000 people, along with Jimi Hendrix, Captain Beefheart, Jethro Tull, The Allman Brothers Band and others.

Aug *Home* makes US #34.

[28] Procol Harum plays on the second day of UK's Isle of Wight Festival.

1971 **July** Group signs a new contract with Chrysalis Records in UK, for release (via Island) of *Broken Barricades*. It makes UK #41 and US #32.

[16] Trower leaves for a solo career. (He will become successful as a guitarist heading his own group through the 70s, with big album sales in US.) Dave Ball (b. Mar.30, 1950) joins on guitar, while Alan Cartwright (b. Oct.10, 1945) comes in on bass to allow Copping to concentrate on keyboards.

Aug [6] Group plays a concert with the Edmonton Symphony Orchestra and the Da Camera Singers, in Edmonton, Alberta, Canada. Mostly consisting of newly-arranged versions of earlier album tracks, the show is recorded for live album release.

1972 **May** Live *Procol Harum In Concert With The Edmonton Symphony Orchestra*, from the Canadian concert, makes UK #48. A double-pack reissue combining *A Whiter Shade Of Pale* (the debut album with the title track added) and *A Salty Dog* reaches UK #26.

June *A Whiter Shade Of Pale* is reissued in UK as lead track on a maxi-single (with *Homburg* and *A Salty Dog*), and climbs to UK #13.

July The live album is more successful in US, where it is Procol Harum's best-selling album, hitting US #5 and earning a gold disk for a half million-plus sales. Taken from it, a new orchestra-backed version of *Conquistador* (originally a track on the debut album) makes US #16.

Aug Live *Conquistador* reaches UK #22.

Sept Ball leaves to work with Long John Baldry and is replaced by ex-Plastic Penny and Cochise member Mick Grabham.

1973 **May** *Grand Hotel*, featuring guest vocal back-up by The Swingle Singers, reaches US #21.

Nov US compilation *The Best Of Procol Harum*, on A&M, creeps to US #131.

1974 **May** *Exotic Birds And Fruit* (its title a reference to the sleeve painting by Jakob Bogdani) fails to chart in UK but makes US #86.

1975 **Mar** [16] Along with Kevin Coyne and John Martyn, Procol Harum headlines "Over The Rainbow" closing-down concert at London's Rainbow theater in Finsbury Park.

Sept *Procol's Ninth* reaches UK #41 and US #52. It is produced, at Brooker's request, by Jerry Leiber and Mike Stoller, and includes their song *I Keep Forgettin'* (formerly a hit for Chuck Jackson), as well as a revival of The Beatles' *Eight Days A Week*. Extracted from it, *Pandora's Box* makes UK #16, but (with the album) will be the group's last UK chart records.

1976 **July** Cartwright leaves, and Copping moves back to bass, as Pete Solley joins on keyboards.

1977 **Apr** *Something Magic* peaks at US #147 (failing to chart in UK), and is final Procol Harum album. Group decides to split, considering that its particular strand of music has been fully explored, and recognizing a less favorable musical climate as punk rock catches hold in UK. A round of live dates supporting the last album becomes a farewell tour.

Oct [18] *A Whiter Shade Of Pale* is named joint winner (with Queen's *Bohemian Rhapsody*) as Best British Pop Single 1952-1977 at the British Record Industry Britannia Awards, to mark the Queen's Silver Jubilee held at Wembley Conference Centre, London (shown on UK TV 2 day later). Procol Harum re-forms for the occasion to perform the song live.

1979 Brooker releases George Martin-produced solo *No Fear Of Flying* on Chrysalis, which fails to chart.

1982 Moving to Mercury, Brooker releases second unsuccessful solo *Lead Me To The Water*, despite musical contributions from Phil Collins, Eri Clapton and George Harrison. (He will be less visible on disk through the rest of the 80s.)

PUBLIC ENEMY

Chuck D
Flavor Flav
Terminator X
Professor Griff

1982 **Nov** Future Public Enemy managers and producers Hank Shocklee and Bill Stephney are classmates at the Adelphi University, Long Island, New York, NY, where Chuck D (b. 1960, Carlton Ridenhour) is studying graphic design. As college radio station WBAU program director, Stephney invites Chuck D and Shocklee to mix a show.

1983 **Jan** Stephney gives the duo their own program, "The Super Spectrum Mix Show".

1984 Shocklee and Chuck D record their own basement tapes for broadcast on WBAU, including the track *Public Enemy Number 1*, from which the will name their group.

1986 The steady diet of early hip-hop rap mixed with their own aggressive DJ style becomes a cult success attracting, not least, Def Jam record label entrepreneur Rick Rubin, while Public Enemy recruits flexible group members, including Flavor Flav (b. William Drayton), who use to work with Chuck D for D's father's V-Haul company, DJ Terminato X (b. Norman Rogers) and Professor Griff, Minister of Information (b. Richard Griffin) and others, S1WS Roderick Chillous, James Allen and James Norman. Chuck D and Shocklee also run a mobile deejay and concert promotion company called Spectrum City and manage Long Island's first hip-hop venue, the Entourage in Bayshore, NY.

1987 **May** Signed to Def Jam by Rubin, Public Enemy's innovative aggressive urban rap (they are described by Stephney as "the black panthers of rap") is trademarked with the release of debut album *You Bum Rush The Show*, which makes US R&B #28. Title cut is a reworking of the demo track *Public Enemy No.1*.

Nov Debut UK single *Rebel Without A Pause* makes UK #37 as the group's live performance attracts headlines and tight police security.

1988 **Feb** Following a UK re-entry #71 of *Rebel Without A Pause*, *Bring The Noise* makes UK #32 and debut album climbs to US #125.

July *Don't Believe The Hype* makes US R&B #18 and UK #18, where repeated short live visits prop genuine urban sympathy and sales for their social/political based rap anthems. Second album *It Takes A Nation Of Millions To Hold Us Back* immediately hits UK #8 and begins US chart rise to #42.

Sept [24] *It Takes A Nation Of Millions To Hold Us Back* hits US R&B #1.

Oct Extracted *Night Of The Living Baseheads* stalls at UK #63 and US R&B #62, where a mainstream Hot 100 showing is prevented due to poor airplay ratings beyond the specialist hip-hop outlets.

1899 **May** *Black Steel In The Hour Of Chaos* stalls at US R&B #86.

June [21] Chuck D announces the dismissal from the group of Professor Griff after a May 22 interview with **Washington Times** reporter David Mills, in which he allegedly made anti-Semitic statements including, "Jews are responsible for the majority of wickedness that goes on across the globe".

[22] Chuck D again prematurely announces break-up of Public Enem on New York radio station WLIB. In a subsequent MTV interview, he guardedly retracts the statement.

[24] Featured as the repetitive central theme to Spike Lee's hit urban jungle movie "Do The Right Thing", *Fight The Power* reaches UK #29. Released from the hip-hop Motown soundtrack album, it will also reach US R&B #20, aided by a video partly filmed in New York's notorious Riker's Island jail.

1990 Jan [20] *Welcome To The Terrordome* reaches UK #18.

Mar [21] 8-day visit to UK for selected live dates begins, supported by labelmate hip-hoppers 3rd Bass, including 2 dates at the Brixton Academy, London.

Apr [7] Emergency/Police emergency line call-up criticizing *911 Is A Joke* makes UK #41, while Griff, now signed to Skywalker Records, releases debut album, hard-core rapping *Pawns In The Game*.

[28] Third Public Enemy album *Fear Of A Black Planet* instantly hits UK #4, and begins climb to US Top 10.

May [26] *Fear Of A Black Planet* hits US #10, a major sales breakthrough, though consistent lack of mainstream radio support means that all single extracts will fail to crack the Hot 100.

June [23] *Brothers Gonna Work It Out* makes UK #46.

[27] US leg of "Tour Of A Black Planet" opens at the Coliseum, Richmond, VA, their first US trek in 2 years.

Aug [25] Mid-tour, their concert at the Shoreline Amphitheater, Mountain View, CA, erupts into an open audience brawl.

Nov [3] *Can't Do Nuttin' For Ya Man* makes UK #53, as Terminator X begins solo career with unsuccessful Def Jam single *Want To Be Dancin'*.

1991 Feb [10] Flavor Flav is arrested at his Long Island home on charges of assaulting his live-in girlfriend, and mother of his 3 children, Karen Ross. (He will plead guilty to third degree assault. Nassau District Court Judge Richard LaPera sentences him to serve 30 days, orders him to pay $334 for medical expenses and grants Ross a permanent order of protection against Flav.)

Mar [7] Group is named Best Rap Group in the annual **Rolling Stone** Readers' Picks music awards.

Apr Public Enemy's future is once again cast in doubt as Stephney and Shocklee split over business differences. Chuck D also announces that there will not be any group live dates in the near future.

PUBLIC IMAGE LTD.

John Lydon (vocals)
Keith Levene (guitar)
Jah Wobble (bass)
Jim Walker (drums)

1978 Apr After The Sex Pistols split at the end of their Dec.1977 US tour, lead singer Johnny Rotten reverts to his real name John Lydon (b. Jan.31, 1956, Finsbury Park, London) and, having taken a short holiday in Jamaica, returns to UK to form a new band with ex-Clash member Levene, novice bass player Wobble (b. John Wardle) and Canadian Walker, who has played drums with The Furys, and is recruited through an ad and auditions. The quartet's name is chosen as a sanitized anti rock'n'roll statement. Public Image Ltd. signs to Virgin (The Sex Pistols' label).

July [25] The formation of the group is officially announced by Lydon.

Nov Debut single *Public Image*, released in a mock-newspaper sleeve, hits UK #9. Group is billed on this as Public Image Ltd. (but most subsequent singles will simply credit PiL).

Dec *Public Image Ltd.* reaches UK #22.

[25] First live gig is a Christmas Day showcase at London's Rainbow theater. (Scattered live dates will follow in early 1979, but PiL will not mount a full tour until the late 80s. Walker will leave, to be replaced on drums by Richard Dudanski and then by Martin Atkins.)

1979 June [30] Lydon guests on BBC1 TV's "Juke Box Jury", along with Joan Collins.

July *Death Disco* reaches UK #20.

Oct *Memories* peaks at UK #60.

Dec *Metal Box* reaches UK #18, so titled because the original release is packaged in a round 12" metal container with the album inside in the form of 3 12" singles.

1980 Feb [13] Lydon's London house is raided by the police, who smash open the front door to find him waving a ceremonial sword at them from the top of the stairs. The only illegal item found on the premises is a canister of tear gas, claimed to be for defense against intruders.

Mar *Metal Box* is reissued in conventional form as double album *Second Edition* and reaches UK #46. Band plays some European dates, including a Paris, France, concert which is recorded for a live album.

May Double album *Second Edition* makes US #171.

June Returning from a short US tour which has had a mixed reception, the band announces that it will not play live again, and Atkins leaves to join Brian Brain.

Aug Wobble departs for a solo career (and will later form Human Condition.)

Oct [6] Lydon is arrested for assault, after a pub brawl in Dublin, Eire.

(Sentenced to 3 months in jail for disorderly conduct, he will be acquitted on appeal.)

Nov Live album *Paris Au Printemps (Paris In The Spring)*, from the concert earlier in the year (and released mainly to counter bootleg albums of PiL's live show), makes UK #61. Jeanette Lee joins the group for "visual assistance" – she organizes its video projections.

1981 Mar From new recordings by Lydon, Levene and Lee, *Flowers Of Romance* makes UK #24.

Apr *The Flowers Of Romance*, with Atkins drumming on 3 tracks, reaches UK #11.

May [15] PiL plays a show at New York's Ritz club (deputizing for Bow Wow Wow) posing behind a video screen while the music is played from tapes. They are showered with missiles and booed off stage by the 1,500 audience, whom Lydon insults in return. (The band considers the show successful, having videoed the debacle for movie use.) A second show the following night is cancelled.

June *The Flowers Of Romance* makes US #114.

1982 Lydon sets up permanent home in New York, and Lee quits the group.

1983 July Levene departs, leaving Lydon as PiL's only full-time member.

Oct *This Is Not A Love Song* hits UK #5, the group's biggest hit single, while double album *Live In Tokyo*, its second live set, makes UK #28. Lydon appears in movie "Cop Killer" with Harvey Keitel.

1984 May Lydon assembles a new band for *Bad Life* which peaks at UK #71.

July *This Is What You Want ... This Is What You Get* makes UK #56.

1985 Feb Lydon teams with New York hip-hop artist Afrika Bambaataa under the name Time Zone, on *World Destruction*, making UK #44.

1986 Feb *Rise*, on which Ginger Baker plays drums, reaches UK #11. It is taken from *Album* (the cassette release is titled *Cassette* and the CD *Compact Disc*), produced by Material member Bill Laswell (and also featuring Baker on drums and percussion), which makes UK #14 and US #115. PiL tours to promote the release.

May *Home*, also from *Album*, peaks at UK #75.

Dec Virgin Video releases "Public Image Ltd.: The Videos" , comprising promotion clips to date.

1987 Sept *Seattle* reaches UK #47 as parent album *Happy?* makes UK #40 and US #169.

1988 Aug PiL, comprising Lydon with John McGeogh (guitar), Lu Edmonds (keyboards, guitar), Alan Dias (bass) and Bruce Smith (drums), embarks on tour supporting Big Country.

Sept 500 fans storm the stage in Athens, Greece, during a PiL set, destroying equipment and setting fire to trees in the park. Greek anarchists join in throwing rocks and petrol bombs. A reported £1 million-worth of damage is caused.

1989 May PiL's *Disappointed* charts at UK #38.

June Stephen Hague-produced *Nine* (PiL's ninth release) makes UK #36 and US #106, as Lydon embarks on another round of provocative promotion. Group embarks on US tour with New Order.

1990 Nov [10] *Greatest Hits ... So Far* reaches UK #20, while *Don't Ask Me* makes UK #22.

SUZI QUATRO

1958 Quatro (b. Suzi Quatrocchio, June 3, 1950, Detroit, MI) having been taught to play drums and piano by her father, who makes sure his 4 daughters and 1 son get a good grounding in music, and played bongos in her father's semi-professional Art Quatro Trio at age 8, forms her own group at school.

1964 Determined to make a career in music, she leaves school and forms The Pleasure Seekers with her sisters, Arlene, Patti and Nancy, appearing on local TV as Suzi Soul. They become regulars at Detroit's Hideout club, the main venue for new young rock talent.

1965 The Pleasure Seekers' *Never Thought You'd Leave Me* is released on Dave Leone and Punch Andrews' (later Bob Seger's manager) Hideout label, but not distributed outside Michigan.

1966 Mar *Light Of Life*, on Mercury, is second (and last) on Pleasure Seekers.

1967 Suzi and her sisters travel to Vietnam to tour casualty wards.

1968 Suzi and Nancy form Cradle, playing hard-edged progressive rock.

1969 UK producer Mickie Most, in Detroit to work with Jeff Beck at Motown studios, sees Cradle at a club and, impressed by Suzi, invites her to come to UK and record for his RAK label.

1970 Cradle splits, and Suzi takes up Most's offer to move to UK. She arrives with Arlene, who is acting as her manager but returns to Detroit, after Most signs her.

1972 July After 18 months of writing and rehearsing, Quatro's *Rolling Stone* is released.

1973 June Quatro's second single, *Can The Can*, written for her by RAK's newly-signed writing team, Nicky Chinn and Mike Chapman, hits UK #1 for a week. She tours UK, supporting Slade. A touring band is assembled comprising Len Tuckey (guitar), Dave Neal (drums) and Alastair McKenzie (keyboards), who is soon replaced by Mike Deacon from Vinegar Joe.

Aug *48 Crash* hits UK #3.

Oct Debut album, *Suzi Quatro,* makes UK #32, as her leather cat-suit clad image becomes familiar to fans.

Nov *Daytona Demon* reaches UK #14.

Dec Quatro is named Best-selling Female Artist Of The Year in UK.

1974 **Feb** *Devil Gate Drive* is her second UK #1, for 2 weeks, dethroning labelmate Mud's *Tiger Feet.*

Apr *Suzi Quatro* makes US #142.

July *Too Big* reaches UK #14.

Sept *All Shook Up,* on Bell, peaks at US #85. (She receives a message from Elvis Presley complimenting her on her version of it and inviting her to Graceland – an offer she does not have the nerve to take up.) [30] She begins a tour of Germany, supported by The Arrows.

Oct *Quatro* climbs to US #126.

Nov *The Wild One* hits UK #7.

1975 **Feb** *Your Mama Won't Like Me* makes UK #31.

Apr After 7 consecutive chart singles, *I Bit Off More Than I Could Chew* fails.

May *Your Mama Won't Like Me* reaches US #146. Quatro undertakes a 3-month US tour, supporting Alice Cooper.

1976 **Mar** Nearly 3 years after its UK release, *Can The Can,* on Big Tree, climbs to US #56.

1977 **Mar** Quatro's first release since Aug.1975, *Tear Me Apart* makes UK #27. The producers of US TV series "Happy Days", having spotted Quatro on the cover of **Rolling Stone**, cast her as female rocker Leather Tuscadero. She is written into further episodes, but declines the offer to star in a spin-off series and settles in UK with her husband, Len Tuckey.

1978 **Apr** After another non-chart single, Quatro hits UK #4 with *If You Can't Give Me Love.*

July *The Race Is On* reaches UK #43.

Nov *Stumblin' In,* a duet with Smokie's lead singer Chris Norman, makes UK #41.

1979 **May** *Stumblin' In,* on RSO, hits US #4.

June *If You Knew Suzi,* the Chapman-produced album which contains *Stumblin' In,* reaches US #37. *If You Can't Give Me Love* makes US #45.

Oct *I've Never Been In Love* peaks at UK #44. *Suzi ... And Other Four Letter Words* climbs to US #117.

Nov *She's In Love With You* is Suzi's only UK hit for the year, reaching UK #11. *She's In Love With You* makes US #41.

1980 **Jan** *Mama's Boy* reaches UK #34.

Apr TV-advertised *Suzi Quatro's Greatest Hits,* hits UK #4. *I've Never Been In Love* makes US #56.

Oct After leaving RAK and signing to Chinn and Chapman's new Dreamland label, *Rock Hard,* on Dreamland, peaks at UK #68. It is featured in movie "Times Square".

Nov *The Rock Hard* reaches US #165.

1981 **Feb** *Lipstick* makes US #51.

1982 Quatro quits touring and daughter, Laura, is born.

Nov Signed to Polydor following the demise of Dreamland, *Heart Of Stone* peaks at UK #60 but parent album *Main Attraction* fails to chart.

1983 Quatro re-signs to RAK (but future chart action will not be forthcoming). She will be seen on television, hosting a UK daytime program "Gas".

1990 **May** EMI issues career retrospective collection *Wild One: The Greatest Hits.*

1991 **Feb** [14] Now involving herself mostly in the visual arts, Quatro, who has spent the last 3 years working on ITV, begins a 4-week stint playing scandalous actress Tallulah Bankhead in the new musical she has co-penned with Willy Russell, "Tallulah Who?", which opens in Hornchurch, Essex. This follows her 9-month run in London's West End in "Annie Get Your Gun". (Quatro, whose sister Arlene has recently succeeded in the part of Sherilyn Fenn's mother on TV's "Twin Peaks", continues to live in ex-Prime Minister Ramsay MacDonald's Elizabethan house in Essex with husband Lenny and children Laura (8) and Richard (6).)

QUEEN

Freddie Mercury (vocals)
Brian May (guitar)
John Deacon (bass)
Roger Taylor (drums)

1963 **May** (b. July 19, 1947, Twickenham, London) and his father make a guitar, hand-carved from a 19th-century fireplace. Using a moving pick-up arrangement, a wide number of tones and echoes are created, with May using a coin as a pick (the genesis of the future distinctive Queen guitar sound). He leaves school, with 10 "O-level" and 3 "A-level" examination passes, to study at Imperial college, London to become an infra red astronomer. (He has been in teenage band The Others, releasing *Oh Yeah* in both UK and US on Fontana.)

1966 He is invited by Sir Bernard Lovell to work at Jodrell Bank, but chooses a music career instead.

1967 May forms band Smile with Taylor (b. Roger Meddows-Taylor, July 26, 1949, King's Lynn, Norfolk) and Tim Staffell, whom he met at Imperial college, on bass.

1969 Smile's only single is US-only *Earth,* on Mercury.

1970 During the summer Staffell leaves to join ex-Bee Gee Colin Petersen's group Humpy Bong but persuades flatmate Mercury (b. Frederick Bulsara, Sept.5, 1946, Zanzibar, Tanzania) to join May and Taylor. (Mercury has moved to England in 1959 with his family, living less than 100 yards from May's home in Feltham, London, although they do not meet until 1970, and has sung for unrecorded group, Wreckage.) Queen is formed but the group still seeks a regular bass player.

1971 **Feb** Science graduate Deacon (b. Aug.19, 1951, Leicester, Leics.) joins on bass. They begin playing clubs and colleges (their debut gig is at the College of Estate Management, London) but continue to pursue their own ambitions. May is working towards a doctorate, Taylor is reading for a biology degree, Deacon is teaching and Mercury is studying design and running a clothes stall at Kensington Market, London.

1972 Queen is invited to showcase new recording hardware at De Lane Lea studios. Present while they record a demo tape are engineers Roy Thomas Baker and John Anthony (who had worked on the Smile single). They are impressed with the group and suggest to their employers, Trident Audio Productions, that Queen should be signed.

Nov After Trident executives have attended a Queen concert, the company signs the band to a production, publishing and management deal. While Baker and Anthony start work on a debut at Trident's studios, recording in vacant studio time, the company employs US A&R man Jack Nelson to negotiate a record deal. He hawks a 24-track demo and EMI signs the group.

1973 **Apr** [9] EMI launches Queen with a gig at London's Marquee.

June While Queen awaits launch of its first album, Mercury, as Larry Lurex, releases a revival of *I Can Hear Music.*

July EMI releases Queen's debut single *Keep Yourself Alive* and eponymous album. (The single will fail to chart.) Band supports Sparks at London's Marquee.

Nov [12] Queen begins a UK tour as support to Mott The Hoople at Leeds Town Hall, W.Yorks.

1974 **Mar** [1] Group begins its first headlining UK tour at Blackpool's Winter Gardens (ending in a gig at London's Rainbow). (The flamboyant Mercury is becoming the central character in the line-up.)

Apr [6] *Queen 2* hits UK #5 during a 29-week chart stay. (Group utilizes state of the art studio technology during its recording.) [12] Queen begins a US tour, again supporting Mott The Hoople, in Denver, CO, as debut album, released on Elektra in the US, makes #83. Second single *Seven Seas Of Rhye,* a reworking of a track from the first album, hits UK #10. (Queen makes its BBC1 TV "Top Of The Pops" debut when a David Bowie promo film is unavailable and the group is slotted into the show, making a major impact.)

May A US tour is abandoned when May contracts hepatitis followed by a duodenal ulcer. *Queen 2* makes US #49.

Nov [30] With May fully recovered, *Sheer Heart Attack* hits UK #2, and charts for 42 weeks. Extracted *Killer Queen* also hits UK #2. Group begins another UK tour, at Manchester's Palace theater (ending with a performance at London's Rainbow theater).

1975 **Feb** [5] Queen begins a US tour in Columbus, OH. *Now I'm Here* peaks at UK #11 as Queen is voted "Band Of The Year" in UK music paper **Melody Maker.**

May *Killer Queen* is Queen's first US hit, reaching #12, as does parent album *Sheer Heart Attack.* After touring US and Far East (a territory to which Queen will pay much attention), the group begins recording a new album, with Baker producing, using 6 different studios.

Sept [19] Group splits acrimoniously with Trident, and signs with Elton John's manager John Reid.

Nov First product of new sessions is classical pastiche *Bohemian Rhapsody*, the pinnacle of Baker's lavish production and Mercury's rock operatic writing style. EMI is reluctant to release the 7-min. single, but a copy is leaked to DJ Kenny Everett at London's Capital Radio, which creates a sales demand through heavy airplay.

Dec *Bohemian Rhapsody*, now edited to 5 mins. 52 secs., tops UK chart for 9 weeks, the longest run at #1 since Paul Anka's *Diana* in 1957. Bruce Gowers' promotional film helps make it a hit in other territories. (Although the promo costs only £5,000, it begins a new trend in the music industry to produce videos to promote records.)

[14] A UK tour begins at the Empire theater, Liverpool, Merseyside.

[24] Group's most successful year ends with a live simultaneous broadcast on BBC1 TV and Radio 1 of its London's Hammersmith Odeon show.

[27] *A Night At The Opera* hits UK #1 in a chart run of nearly a year and hits US #4.

'76 Jan [27] Queen begins a 4-month tour of US, Japan and Australia at the Palace theater, Waterbury, CT.

Feb [7] Queen's debut album *Queen* reaches UK #24, more than 2 years after its release.

Apr *Bohemian Rhapsody* hits US #9. "Queen At The Rainbow" film is released in UK, supporting Burt Reynolds' "Hustle".

July Second single from the album, *You're My Best Friend*, reaches US #16 and hits UK #7. Recording for a new album begins. Band breaks from sessions to play a free concert in London's Hyde Park, plus dates in Edinburgh and Cardiff.

Dec [1] Queen, scheduled to appear on UK TV show "Today", pulls out at the last minute. EMI replaces it with recent signing The Sex Pistols, who cause a furore with their behavior.

Somebody To Love hits UK #2. (Group members have moved into other activities during the year: Mercury producing Eddie Howell's *Man From Manhattan* (on which he and May also play) and all members, bar Deacon, playing on Ian Hunter's *All American Alien*.)

'77 Jan [8] *A Day At The Races* tops UK chart and eventually hits US #5 as Queen begins a tour of US and Canada, in an outrageous visual style led by Mercury's stage costumes. *Somebody To Love* reaches US #13.

Mar *Tie Your Mother Down* makes UK #31.

Apr *Tie Your Mother Down* peaks at US #49.

May As the group tours UK and Europe, EP *Queen's First EP*, with lead track *Good Old Fashioned Lover Boy*, reaches UK #17.

July Recording for a new album begins. Taylor, the first group member to cut a solo, releases *I Wanna Testify*.

Oct With album completed, Queen begins a US tour that will end at Christmas.

[18] *Bohemian Rhapsody* ties with Procol Harum's *A Whiter Shade Of Pale* as Best British Pop Single, 1952-1977 at the British Record Industry Britannia Awards, honoring the Queen's Silver Jubilee and the centenary of recorded sound at Wembley Conference Centre, London.

Nov Anthemic *We Are The Champions* hits UK #2. It is released as a double A-side with *We Will Rock You*. Parent album *News Of The World* hits UK #4, and starts a climb to US #3.

'78 Feb *Spread Your Wings* reaches UK #34. *We Are The Champions* hits US #4, and goes platinum. Meanwhile, Queen completes a tour of Europe, including only 2 large UK dates. May contributes guitar to one-time skiffle king Lonnie Donegan's comeback album, *Puttin' On The Style*.

May *It's Late* peaks at US #74.

July Band begins a 3-month stay at Montreux, Switzerland, recording a new album at its own studio.

Nov Double A-side *Bicycle Race/Fat Bottomed Girls* reaches UK #11. Queen starts a 6-month tour of US, Japan and Europe. *Jazz* hits UK #2 and eventually US #6.

[16] The audience at New York's Madison Square Garden is treated to the sight of semi-nude female cyclists during Queen's performance of *Fat Bottomed Girls* (a visual device also used in the video).

'79 Mar *Don't Stop Me Now* hits UK #9, but climbs to US #86.

June *Bicycle Race/Fat Bottomed Girls* reaches US #24, as the group begins a UK tour.

July *Live Killers*, recorded in UK on tour, is released, with extracted *Love Of My Life*. They hit UK #3 and #63 respectively.

Aug *Live Killers* reaches US #16.

Nov Light-hearted rockabilly *Crazy Little Thing Called Love* hits UK #2. It represents a diversion for Queen, including Mercury's debut as a rhythm guitarist, and was recorded in Munich, Germany, with a producer known only as Mack, the first outside producer other than

Baker to work with Queen. The group makes a full UK tour.

Dec US Elektra finally releases *Crazy Little Thing Called Love* after US stations begin playing imported copies.

1980 Feb *Save Me* enters UK chart, reaching #11. It is not released in US. *Crazy Little Thing Called Love* tops US chart.

July *Play The Game* reaches UK #14 and US #42. Parent album *The Game* tops UK chart. Queen begins a US tour that will last until Sept.

Sept Third single from *The Game*, Deacon's *Another One Bites The Dust*, with its distinctive Chic-style disco bass line, hits UK #7. *The Game* is the group's first US #1, where it will stay for 5 weeks.

Oct *Another One Bites The Dust* tops US chart. Unexpected support for the single has come from black radio stations and it hits US R&B #2.

Nov *Need Your Loving Tonight* makes US #44 as group tours UK and Europe.

Dec Queen's soundtrack for film "Flash Gordon" hits UK #10 and makes US #23.

1981 Jan Extracted *Flash* hits UK #10.

Feb Queen plays Japan again, before setting off on a groundbreaking South American tour, taking in Argentina and Brazil, under the banner "Gluttons For Punishment Tour". (Their South American popularity will soar throughout the decade. A concert in São Paulo is performed before a world record paying audience of 231,000.)

[14] *Flash* makes US #42.

Apr Taylor's second solo *Future Management* peaks at UK #49, as parent album *Fun In Space* reaches UK #18 and US #121.

June Taylor's *Man On Fire* is released.

Nov *Greatest Hits* tops UK chart, beginning a 312-week chart run, and reaches US #14. Queen collaborates with David Bowie for *Under Pressure*, which hits UK #1 (the group's first UK chart-topper since *Bohemian Rhapsody*).

1982 Jan *Under Pressure* reaches US #29.

June Queen's *Body Language* reaches UK #25 and US #11. Dance-based *Hot Space* hits UK #4 and US #22. The group, in the middle of a European tour, plays a concert at Milton Keynes Bowl, Bucks., which is filmed by Channel 4 TV. (The tour will continue to North America, followed by Japan in the fall.)

July *Las Palabras De Amor* reaches UK #17.

Aug Elektra releases *Calling All Girls* as the US single but it stalls at #60. *Back Chat* makes UK #40.

1983 Queen begins a year-long group sabbatical.

Apr [21-22] May gathers a group of friends for a session at Record Plant studios in Los Angeles, CA, including Eddie Van Halen (guitar), Fred Mandel (keyboards), Phil Chen (bass) and REO Speedwagon drummer Alan Gratzer.

Nov First product of May's star-session is *Star Fleet*, based on a Japanese children's puppet sci-fi series theme, which reaches UK #65. Mini-album *Star Fleet Project* reaches UK #35 and US #125. (During the year a change of US distribution to EMI-owned Capitol Records is negotiated.)

1984 Feb Queen's *Radio Ga Ga* enters UK chart at #4 and climbs to #2, held off the top by Frankie Goes To Hollywood's *Relax*, which is boosted by a further 12" remix to increase its sales for the week. The single is an apparent criticism of contemporary radio programming. Its video effectively integrates a backdrop of scenes from film "Metropolis". Composed by Taylor, this hit completes a unique chart feat as all 4 group members have now individually penned a Top 10 hit.

Mar *The Works* hits UK #2 and US #23. It stays on UK chart for 93 weeks and is the group's second largest-selling UK album, after *Greatest Hits*.

Apr *I Want To Break Free* hits UK #3, as *Radio Ga Ga* reaches US #16.

May *I Want To Break Free* makes US #45.

July *It's A Hard Life* hits UK #6, but stalls at US #72. Taylor's second solo album, *Strange Frontier*, reaches UK #30.

Aug After a month of rehearsals, Queen begins a European tour which will include 4 nights at Wembley Arena. The European dates are followed by a controversial 8-show visit to Sun City in South Africa, putting them on the United Nations cultural blacklist.

Oct *Hammer To Fall*, fourth single from *The Works*, reaches UK #13. Mercury's first solo *Love Kills*, taken from new soundtrack by Giorgio Moroder to Fritz Lang's classic 1926 film "Metropolis", hits UK #10.

Dec Queen's seasonal *Thank God It's Christmas* reaches UK #21.

1985 Jan Queen plays the "Rock In Rio" festival in Rio de Janeiro, Brazil.

May Mercury's second solo *I Was Born To Love You* reaches UK #11 and US #76. (While the other band members' solos have been with EMI, he has signed to CBS.) His solo *Mr. Bad Guy*, also self-produced and all songs self-written, including *Foolin' Around*, from soundtrack to movie "Teachers", hits UK #10. Taylor produces actor Jimmy Nail's UK #3 *Love Don't Live Here Anymore*, a revival of Rose Royce's 1978 hit.

July [13] Queen performs at Live Aid at Wembley Stadium, London. Mercury's second single from *Mr. Bad Guy*, *Made In Heaven*, stalls at UK #57. Taylor co-produces Feargal Sharkey's UK #26 *Loving You*.

Sept Mercury's *Living On My Own* makes UK #50.

Nov Queen's *One Vision*, from the soundtrack of film "Iron Eagle", hits UK #7. May and Deacon guest on Elton John's *Ice On Fire*.

Dec *The Complete Works*, a 14-album boxed set, containing all the group's albums except *Greatest Hits*, plus a bonus disk of previous single-only tracks, is released.

1986 **Jan** [11] *One Vision* stalls at US #61.

Mar *A Kind Of Magic* hits UK #3. (The song and its flipside, *A Dozen Red Roses For My Darling*, are written for film "Highlander".)

Apr Mercury contributes 3 tracks to the cast recording of Dave Clark's stage musical "Time".

May Deacon temporarily forms The Immortals, to provide *No Turning Back* for film "Biggles".

June Mercury's *Time*, from the album, makes UK #32. *A Kind Of Magic* enters UK chart at #1 and makes US #46.

July Extracted *Friends Will Be Friends* reaches UK #14. A Wembley Stadium concert is taped for simultaneous broadcast on UK independent TV and radio. Mercury releases a video EP of his 4 singles. [27] Queen plays Budapest's Nepstadion in Hungary in front of 80,000 fans during a European tour. The concert, filmed as "Magic In Budapest", is the first by a Western act since Louis Armstrong in 1964, and the first concert to be filmed in Eastern Europe.

Aug [9] Queen returns to UK to play Knebworth Festival, Herts., as *A Kind Of Magic* makes US #42.

Oct *Who Wants To Live Forever* reaches UK #24.

Dec *Live Magic* hits UK #3.

1987 **May** Mercury's version of The Platters' *The Great Pretender* hits UK #5.

Oct Taylor, playing guitar rather than drums, forms The Cross, which signs to Virgin, and *Cowboys And Indians* makes UK #75.

Nov Increasingly operatic over the years, Mercury duets with Spanish opera singer Monserrat Caballé on *Barcelona*, which hits UK #8.

Dec A 3-volume video compilation, "The Magic Years", chronicles Queen's extensive recording and visual career, superseding previous Queen video collections, all of which have been worldwide best-sellers.

1988 **Feb** The Cross album *Shove It!* peaks at UK #58 as the group begins a mini-tour. May produces *Bohemian Rhapsody* by The Young Ones comic troupe heavy metal alter egos Bad News. (He will also produce singles for current flame, actress Anita Dobson.)

Oct Mercury and Caballé highlight a star-studded show to launch Barcelona's successful bid for the 1992 Olympic Games at the Avinguda De Maria Cristina stadium. The pair's album, also titled *Barcelona*, reaches UK #25.

1989 **May** *I Want It All* heralds Queen's collective return, hitting UK #3 and beginning a US climb.

June Parent album *The Miracle* recalls an earlier Queen sound and hits UK #1. Co-produced with Dave Richards, it also includes follow-up UK hit *Breakthru'*.

[17] *I Want It All* makes US #50 as *The Miracle* goes on to US #24.

July *Breakthru'* hits UK #7.

Aug *The Invisible Man* reaches UK #12.

Oct *Scandal* reaches UK #25.

Dec *The Miracle* reaches UK #21. May collaborates with Ian Gillan, Robert Plant and Bruce Dickinson as Rock Aid Armenia with a remake of *Smoke On The Water*, which makes UK #39, with all profits from the record going to the victims of the Armenian earthquake disaster. [16] *At The Beeb* peaks at UK #67.

1990 **Nov** May composes the score for a London production of "Macbeth".

1991 **Jan** *Innuendo* tops UK chart in its week of release. (At 6 mins. 32 secs., it is the third longest UK #1 of all time, behind The Beatles' *Hey Jude* and Simple Minds' *Belfast Child*.) *Headlong* is the first release on new US label, Hollywood Records, which has signed Queen in North America for an 8-figure advance which the label hopes to recoup not least by long-awaited US CD release of Queen's back catalog.

Feb [16] *Innuendo* enters UK chart at #1. Produced by the band with David Richards, it also begins rapid US chart rise.

Mar Brian May co-produces, co-writes and performs on UK Comic Relief 1991 charity single *The Stonk*, recorded by Hale & Pace And The Stonkers.

QUICKSILVER MESSENGER SERVICE

Gary Duncan (guitar)
John Cipollina (guitar)
Greg Elmore (drums)
David Freiberg (bass)

1964 **Dec** Group forms in San Francisco, CA, with Murray on vocals and harmonica, Cipollina (b. Aug.24, 1943, Berkeley, CA) on guitar, Freiberg (b. Aug.24, 1938, Boston, MA) on bass and Casey Sonoban on drums. Skip Spence is briefly involved during early rehearsals at the Matrix club, while Dino Valenti is lead vocalist, but a drugbust and imprisonment quickly put him out of the picture.

1965 **June** Elmore (b. Sept.4, 1946, San Diego, CA) and Duncan (b. Gary Grubb, Sept.4, 1946, San Diego), both ex-Brogues, join in a new version of the group.

Dec Group gives its first public performance, after several months of rehearsal in a North Beach basement.

1967 **Jan** [14] Group performs at first "Human Be-In" at the Polo Fields, Golden Gate Park, San Francisco, alongside Jefferson Airplane and Big Brother & The Holding Company.

June Band plays Monterey International Pop Festival, Monterey, CA.

July Having become a huge live attraction around San Francisco (75 gigs at the Avalon ballroom), group makes a cameo appearance, performing 2 songs, in hippie exploitation movie "Revolution".

Oct Murray leaves and the group signs to Capitol. It is one of the last current Bay Area bands to sign a recording contract, having held out until Capitol has agreed to all its conditions.

1968 **Aug** Eponymous debut album, strong on instrumental passages due to lack of a notable lead vocalist, makes US #63. Group appears at the 2-day Newport Festival in Costa Mesa, CA.

1969 **Jan** Duncan leaves to form a band with Valenti.

May *Happy Trails*, including live performances from the Fillmores East and West, with Cipollina and Duncan guitar-led improvisations on Bo Diddley's *Who Do You Love* and *Mona*, makes US #27.

Aug Nicky Hopkins on piano (ex-Steve Miller band and Rolling Stone sideman) joins just in time to prevent the remaining 3-piece band from splitting. *Who Do You Love* is extracted in shortened form from the previous album and makes US #91.

Dec With Hopkins, band records *Shady Grove*, which makes US #25.

1970 **Jan** [1] Valenti rejoins permanently and Duncan returns, after playing a New Year's Eve reunion gig.

July Hopkins leaves, and is replaced on keyboards by Mark Naftalin, ex-Paul Butterfield.

Oct *Just For Love*, recorded in Hawaii, displays a new more vocal style. It reaches US #27, as Cipollina, disillusioned by the new Valenti-dominated direction, leaves to produce a Jim Murray solo album, the sessions for which result in the band Copperhead.

Nov *Fresh Air*, taken from the album, is the group's biggest US hit single, making #49.

1971 **Mar** *What About Me* reaches US #26 and extracted title track (later covered by Moving Hearts) peaks at US #100.

July Freiberg is arrested for drug possession, fined $5,000 and jailed for 2 months. He is replaced on bass by Mark Ryan. (Freiberg will join Jefferson Airplane in Aug.1972.)

Oct Naftalin leaves and is replaced by Chuck Steaks.

Dec *Quicksilver* peaks at US #114.

1972 **May** *Comin' Thru* makes US #134.

Aug Group is scheduled again to play a UK tour but for the third time it is cancelled, as the members consider splitting up after playing a week-long "closing down celebration" concert series in San Francisco. Triple set *Last Days Of The Fillmore* includes 3 Quicksilver tracks and reaches US #40.

1973 **June** Group does not split but virtually ceases activity, while compilation *Anthology*, reaches US #108. Ryan leaves and John Nicholas (ex-It's A Beautiful Day) joins on bass.

1974 A 7-man version of the group maintains low live profile and does not record. New members are Harold Aceves (drums), Bob Hogan (keyboards) and Bob Flurie (bass), with Duncan, Elmore and Valenti remaining.

1975 **Dec** In another line-up change, Valenti/Duncan/Elmore reunite, now with Skip Olsen on bass and Michael Lewis on keyboards and record *Solid Silver*, which makes US #89. After this, they finally disband.

1987 Gary Duncan exhumes the Quicksilver Messenger Service name for *Peace by Piece*.

1989 **May** [29] Cipollina dies from emphysema.

June [16] Freiberg, Duncan, Elmore, Peter Albin, Spencer Dryden,

Robert Hunter, Pete Sears, Mickey Hart, Bob Weir and Huey Lewis & The News' Gibson, Hayes and Cipollina, participate in a tribute concert at the Fillmore West, San Francisco.

GERRY RAFFERTY

1968 Rafferty (b. Apr.16, 1947, Paisley, Scotland) quits the last of a series of Scottish-based rock cover groups and joins The Humblebums, a folk-based group featuring singer/comedian Billy Connolly and Tam Harvey, which signs to Transatlantic Records.

1970 The Humblebums split after 2 poorly-received albums, *Humblebums* (1969) and *Open Up The Door* (1970).

1971 Rafferty records his first solo album, *Can I Have My Money Back?*, also for Transatlantic, but it makes little commercial impact.

1972 In London, he forms Stealers Wheel, conceived as "a Scots version of Crosby, Stills, Nash & Young", with Joe Egan, a colleague from Paisley, Rab Noakes (guitar), Ian Campbell (bass) and Roger Brown (drums, vocals). By the time the group is signed to A&M, this line-up has already splintered, and the eponymous debut album, produced by Jerry Leiber and Mike Stoller, has Rafferty and Egan as joint lead vocalists, playing guitar and keyboards respectively, Rod Coombes (drums), Tony Williams (bass) and ex-Big Three guitarist Paul Pilnick. Rafferty leaves the group shortly after the album is recorded and, dissatisfied with the music business, returns to Scotland with his wife and baby. He is replaced by Luther Grosvenor, ex-Spooky Tooth, and Delisle Harper replaces Williams.

1973 **May** *Stuck In The Middle With You* hits US #6. It is taken from the debut album, which makes US #50.
June *Stuck In The Middle With You* hits UK #8 and Rafferty is persuaded to rejoin the group.
Sept *Everyone's Agreed That Everything'll Turn Out Fine* reaches US #49 and UK #33. It proves inappropriate, as Pilnick, Coombes and Williams all leave the band. Rafferty and Egan record a second album as a duo, with session help from Joe Jammer (guitar), Gary Taylor (bass) and Andrew Steele (drums).

1974 **Feb** *Star*, from the forthcoming album, reaches UK #25 and US #29.
Apr *Ferguslie Park*, named after a district of Paisley, fails to chart in UK but makes US #181.

1975 **Mar** *Right Or Wrong*, recorded by Rafferty and Egan with Bernie Holland (guitar) and Dave Wintour (bass), and produced by Mentor Williams, fails to chart. Rafferty and Egan split.

1978 **Feb** Rafferty resurfaces after an enforced absence through management and label problems. Signed to United Artists as a soloist, he releases *City To City*.
Apr The album title track is issued as a single and fails to sell, but self-penned *Baker Street*, driven by an arresting sax riff from session player Raphael Ravenscroft, is released. With saturation UK airplay, it hits #3 behind Kate Bush's *Wuthering Heights* and Blondie's *Denis (Denee)* respectively, and the album hits UK #6. (Its total worldwide sales will be 4 million copies.)
June *Baker Street* hits US #2 for 6 weeks behind Andy Gibb's *Shadow Dancing*, and earns a gold disk for million-plus US sales. In UK, ballad *Whatever's Written In Your Heart* is follow-up but fails to chart despite strong airplay (as does a competing reissue of old Transatlantic track *Mary Skeffington*).
July *City To City* tops US chart, displacing *Saturday Night Fever* soundtrack (which has held #1 for almost 6 months). The album earns a platinum disk for a million US sales. He makes a US promotional visit, but declines (and will continue to refuse) to tour US.
Oct *Right Down The Line*, is US follow-up, reaching US #12.

1979 **Jan** *Home And Dry*, third US single from *City To City*, makes #28.
June Rafferty's second United Artists album, *Night Owl*, hits UK #9.
July *Night Owl* peaks at US #29, earning a gold disk for a half million US sales. The title track is extracted as a UK single, hitting #5, while in US, *Days Gone Down (Still Got The Light In Your Eyes)* is taken from the album, reaching US #17.
Sept *Get It Right Next Time*, also from *Night Owl*, reaches UK #30 and US #21.

1980 **Apr** *Bring It All Home*, from Rafferty's next album, peaks at US #54.
May *Snakes And Ladders* reaches UK #15.
June *The Royal Mile (Sweet Darlin')*, taken from *Snakes And Ladders*, peaks at UK #67 (his last UK hit single).
July *Snakes And Ladders* makes US #61.
Aug *The Royal Mile (Sweet Darlin')* peaks at US #54 (his last US hit).

1982 **Oct** *Sleepwalking* reaches UK #39.
1983 **Feb** He contributes to Mark Knopfler's soundtrack of movie "Local Hero".

1987 **Nov** Rafferty produces Scottish twins The Proclaimers' *Letter From America*, which hits UK #3.

1988 **May** He signs a new recording deal with London Records, releasing *North And South*, which makes UK #43. It is recorded with long-term friend and producer Hugh Murphy and reveals unsuccessful single, *Shipyard Town*.

1990 **Mar** [24] A remixed version of *Baker Street* peaks at UK #53, taken from *Right Down The Line – The Best Of Gerry Rafferty*, issued simultaneously by EMI.

RAINBOW

Ritchie Blackmore (lead guitar)
Ronnie James Dio (vocals)
Tony Carey (keyboards)
Jimmy Bain (bass)
Cozy Powell (drums)

1975 **Apr** [7] Blackmore (b. Apr.14, 1945, Weston-super-Mare, Avon) leaves Deep Purple after a show in Paris, France. (He has become disillusioned by the band's direction, despising just-completed *Stormbringer*, and has recorded *Black Sheep Of The Family*, rejected by Deep Purple, with American band Elf, which has toured as Deep Purple's support band and recorded its second album *Carolina County Ball* for Purple records.)
May After Elf has recorded final album *Trying To Burn The Sun*, in London with producers Roger Glover and Martin Birch, the group (minus its guitarist Steve Edwards, who departs to Florida) with Dio on vocals, Mickey Lee Soule on keyboards, Craig Gruber on bass and Gary Driscoll on drums, teams with Blackmore as Ritchie Blackmore's Rainbow. He takes the band to Musicland studios, Munich, Germany, to record *Ritchie Blackmore's Rainbow*.
July Gruber leaves as soon as the album sessions are complete, and is replaced on bass by Bain, ex-Harlot.
Sept *Ritchie Blackmore's Rainbow* is released on Purple's offshoot Oyster label and reaches UK #11 and US #30. As it charts, Soule and Driscoll leave the band, and Blackmore recruits Powell (ex-Bedlam and solo success with *Dance With The Devil*, but more recently driving racing cars for Hitachi) and Carey (from Los Angeles, CA, country group Blessings) to join himself, Dio and Bain.

1976 **July** *Rainbow Rising*, recorded by the new line-up, reaches UK #11 (on Polydor) and US #48.
Aug [31] Group makes its UK stage debut to promote the album (and will tour US, Canada, Europe and Far East for remainder of the year).

1977 **Jan** Bain is fired by Blackmore for being out of step, musically, with the band (or at least with its leader). His replacement on bass is Mark Clarke, ex-Uriah Heep among other groups.
May Group records a new album at Le Chateau studio in Paris, France. During the sessions, Blackmore becomes disenchanted with both Carey and Clarke, and elbows both from the band. Studio recordings are halted and Blackmore decides to assemble a live album instead.
July David Stone, keyboards player with Canadian band Symphonic Slam, joins after auditioning in Los Angeles for Blackmore, while Australian bassist Bob Daisley, ex-Steve Ellis' band Widowmaker, is also recruited.
Aug Double live album *On Stage*, recorded by the band's second line-up during its late 1976 tours, with the billing shortened to Rainbow, hits UK #7 and makes US #65.
Sept *Kill The King* is Rainbow's first chart single, making UK #44. A UK tour is postponed while the new players are being broken in, and rescheduled for Nov.
Dec Band returns to the Paris studios to complete third studio album.

1978 **Jan** Rainbow tours Japan (then around US for much of the year).
Apr *Long Live Rock'N'Roll*, trailering the new album, climbs to UK #33.
May Produced by Martin Birch, *Long Live Rock'N'Roll* hits UK #7 and reaches US #89.
Oct Extracted from the album and pressed on red vinyl, *L.A. Connection* reaches UK #40.
Nov After a lengthy period on the road, perfectionist Blackmore has become more disillusioned with most of his band. At the end of a US tour, he unloads everybody but Powell (Dio will re-emerge as vocalist with Black Sabbath). He settles to rest in his US home in Connecticut before attempting more recruitment.
Dec Blackmore plays at London's Marquee club with ex-Deep Purple colleague Ian Gillan's band over Christmas. He fails to persuade Gillan to become Rainbow's vocalist, but recruits Don Airey, ex-Colosseum, on keyboards.

1979 **Apr** Blackmore recruits vocalist Graham Bonnet, one-time hitmaker as half of The Marbles but later less successful as a solo singer, and Roger Glover, ex-Deep Purple with Blackmore and now mainly producing, joins on bass.

Sept *Down To Earth*, recorded by the new line-up and produced by Glover, hits UK #6 and reaches US #66.

Oct Extracted *Since You Been Gone*, written by ex-Argent singer/writer Russ Ballard (and a 1978 US chartmaker for Head East), hits UK #6.

Dec *Since You Been Gone* peaks at US #57.

1980 **Mar** *All Night Long*, a Blackmore/Glover composition, also from *Down To Earth*, hits UK #5.

Aug [16] Powell quits the band following its headlining appearance at the first Monsters Of Rock festival in Castle Donington, Leics.

Oct [1] Bonnet also leaves, to pursue a solo career signed to Vertigo records. Joe Lynn Turner, ex-US group Fandango, joins as lead singer, while Bobby Rondinelli is recruited on drums.

1981 **Feb** *I Surrender*, another Russ Ballard song, gives Rainbow its highest singles hit at UK #3. It is taken from *Difficult To Cure*, produced by Glover, which also hits UK #3.

Apr *Difficult To Cure* makes US #50, while the band tours US to promote it.

July *Can't Happen Here*, a remixed version of a Blackmore/Glover song from *Difficult To Cure*, reaches UK #20.

Aug Polydor in UK reissues both the band's first hit single *Kill The King* and its original album *Ritchie Blackmore's Rainbow* and they re-chart at UK #41 and #91 respectively.

Nov Airey leaves (later to join Ozzy Osbourne's group), and is replaced on keyboards by Dave Rosenthal in time for a UK tour.

Dec Compilation album *The Best Of Rainbow* reaches UK #14, while 4-track 12" EP *Jealous Lover* (the title track having been UK B-side of *Can't Happen Here*, recorded at a leisurely tour break session in a church hall) peaks at US #147.

1982 **Apr** *Stone Cold* climbs to UK #34. It is taken from *Straight Between The Eyes*, which hits UK #5.

June *Stone Cold* makes US #40 and *Straight Between The Eyes* US #30. The band plays a world (excluding UK) tour to promote the album.

1983 **Sept** Rondinelli is replaced by former Brand X drummer Chuck Burgi for *Bent Out Of Shape*, which reaches UK #11. Taken from it, *Street Of Dreams* peaks at UK #52. (MTV in US bans its promo video, since it visually demonstrates hypnosis.)

Oct Band plays its first UK tour since 1981, playing a set mainly from the recent album.

Nov *Can't Let You Go*, also from *Bent Out Of Shape*, reaches UK #43, while the album makes US #34.

Dec *Street Of Dreams* peaks at US #60.

1984 **Mar** Blackmore decides to fold the band when both he and Glover are invited to join the most successful line-up of Deep Purple (with Jon Lord, Ian Gillan and Ian Paice); Rainbow plays its final tour in Japan. [14] In Rainbow's final live show, in Japan, it is accompanied by a Japanese symphony orchestra, and the set includes Blackmore's adaptation of Beethoven's "Ninth Symphony".

Apr Deep Purple officially re-forms, with Blackmore and Glover as members, and Rainbow splits.

1986 **Mar** Double compilation *Finyl Vinyl*, remixed for release by Glover, and containing many unheard live items by Rainbow, plus scarce tracks previously only on singles B-sides, reaches UK #31 and US #87, a successful coda to the band's career.

BONNIE RAITT

1967 Raitt (b. Bonnie Lynn Raitt, Nov.8, 1949, Burbank, CA) daughter of Broadway musical star ("Oklahoma", "Carousel" and "Kiss Me Kate") John Raitt, has grown up in Los Angeles, CA, since 1957 with her Quaker family, who also take a liberal and pacifist political stance, which will influence much of her benefit and charity work in the future. She has taken up guitar at age 8 when she received a $25 Stella instrument as a Christmas gift, and has been encouraged by her father, and is a proficient blues and folk guitarist by the time she relocates to Radcliffe College.

1969 Raitt leaves Radcliffe College, MA, where she has been reading African studies, to begin playing blues guitar at small coffee houses, like Club 47, in the Boston, MA, area, after boyfriend, musician Dick Waterman has introduced her to Otis Rush, Fred McDowell and Son House, and promoted her early shows.

1970 Raitt enjoys increasing cult success on the burgeoning East Coast folk and blues scene, regularly playing at such venues as The Gaslite, New York, and Main Point, Philadelphia, PA. Influenced not least by the recordings of Joan Baez, Bob Dylan, Muddy Waters and John Hammond, Raitt performs with her regular sideman, bassist Freebo.

1971 **Nov** Signed to Warner Bros., Raitt's debut *Bonnie Raitt* showcases her musical range with blues material from Robert Johnson and Sippie Wallace, sitting alongside early R&B and country.

1972 **Dec** Follow-up album *Give It Up*, produced by Michael Cuscuna and including 3 self-penned songs and contributions from Jackson Browne and Eric Kaz, makes US chart debut, peaking at #138.

1973 **Dec** Having moved back to Los Angeles, *Takin' My Time* reaches US #87, aided by constant US touring. Produced by John Hall (of Orleans), it features Lowell George, Bill Payne, Jim Keltner and Taj Mahal among many session luminaries. It also includes an early recording of Eric Kaz-penned *Cry Like A Rainstorm* (to become the title album cut for Linda Ronstadt's platinum album of 1989.) and *Guilty*, inked by Randy Newman.

1974 **Dec** Now firmly set in the alternate pattern of touring and recording, Raitt's latest album has been taped at the Hit Factory in New York, with the help of the best New York session players. the resultant *Streetlights* peaks at US #80.

1975 **Dec** Fifth album *Home Plate*, produced in Los Angeles by Paul Rothchild and featuring her growing family of guest musicians and friends (not least Freebo), including John Hall, J.D. Souther, Bill Payne, Tom Waits and Jacksone Browne, reaches US #43, prompting her first appearance on the cover of **Rolling Stone** magazine.

1976 **May** Now performing up to 100 concerts per year, Raitt embarks on a US tour supporting Little Feat.

1977 **July** Her most successful Warner Bros. album *Sweet Forgiveness* reaches US #25. With her regular touring band of Will McFarlane (guitar), Jef Labes (keyboards), Dennis Whitted (drums) and Freebo (bass), and additional vocalists Michael McDonald and J.D. Souther, the Rothchild-produced set includes a revival of Del Shannon's *Runaway* which gives Raitt her first chart single at US #57.

1979 **Aug** [4] Raitt joins Jackson Browne, Emmylou Harris, Nicolette Larson, Michael McDonald, Linda Ronstadt and members of Little Feat in a benefit concert in aid of Lowell George's widow at the Great Western Forum, Inglewood, CA. The 25,000 crowd raises $230,000.

Sept [19-23] Raitt plays at the Musicians United For Safe Energy (MUSE) anti-nuclear concerts at New York's Madison Square Garden, alongside Bruce Springsteen, Jackson Browne, Carly Simon, The Doobie Brothers and others.

Oct [13] Following a 1-year recording hiatus, *The Glow* is released, set to make US #30. Co-produced by Val Garay and Peter Asher, it again showcases the depth and variety of Raitt's musical style and highlights both her electric and slide steel guitar experience and expertise.

1980 **Jan** Extracted Robert Palmer-penned *You're Gonna Get What's Coming* climbs to US #73.

1982 **Mar** [6] *Green Light* is released, featuring a new backing group The Bump Band, including keyboardist Ian McLagan (ex-Small Faces), drummer Ricky Fataar (ex-Beach Boys), bassist Ray Ohara and guitarist Johnny Lee Schell. Marking a move towards a rockier, more pop-oriented sound, the album will reach US #38.

1985 **Dec** [14] Following a period of semi-retirement (during which Raitt has continued her battle with alcohol and drug abuse), Artists Against Apartheid, comprising 49 acts including Raitt, makes US #38 and UK #21 with *Sun City*.

1986 **Sept** *Nine Lives*, Raitt's ninth (and last) album for Warner Bros., reaches US #115. Produced by Billy Payne and George Massenburg, it includes songs from Karla Bonoff, Tom Snow, Bryan Adams, Will Jennings, Richard Kerr and, as on each of her albums to date, Eric Kaz. It also features her old friend and blues mentor Sippie Wallace singing on her revival of Toots & The Maytals' *True Love Is Hard To Find*.

Dec Still consistently touring, Raitt performs at the Beverly theater, Los Angeles.

1987 **Apr** Having recently joined a program for recovering alcoholics, Raitt spends 2 days in recording sessions in Minneapolis, MN, with Prince, who had seen her perform in Dec.1986.

July [4] Raitt participates in "The July Fourth Disarmament Festival" in the Soviet Union with James Taylor, Santana, The Doobie Brothers and several Russian groups.

Dec By year's end, her increasing involvement in charity, political and benefit causes will see her organize the "Stop Contra Aid" concert featuring herself along with Don Henley, Herbie Hancock and others, participate in Amnesty International and Farm Aid annual gatherings and film a homeless awareness video "Wake Up America" with Bonnie Bramlett and Rita Coolidge.

1988 During a year in which she signs a new recording contract with Capitol, and begins taping her label debut, Raitt also contributes her version of the Dumbo classic *Baby Mine* to Hal Wilner's A&M compilation of Disney standards, *Stay Awake* and another song to the Marlo Thomas organized project for children album *Free To Be A Family*. Both tracks are produced by Don Was (of Was (Not Was)), who will be recruited to oversee production of her forthcoming album.
Dec [12] Raitt attends a memorial tribute to Roy Orbison with Tom Petty, Graham Nash, and Don Henley among others.

1989 **Apr** [15] Raitt's tenth album, *Nick Of Time*, produced by Was, enters US Album chart. It will be regarded as her most consistent work to date, eventually selling over 2 million US copies and will stay charted for exactly 2 years. It includes guest contributors Was (Not Was) vocalists Sweet Pea Atkinson and Sir Harry Bowens, Crosby & Nash, Kim Wilson, Herbie Hancock, David Lasley and regulars Fataar and Schell.
Oct While album cuts *Thing Called Love* and *Love Letter* prove popular on US radio, Raitt is featured on John Lee Hooker's *The Healer*. A long-standing and popular recording guest, Raitt's other recent contributions include projects by David Crosby, Colin James, Emmylou Harris, B.B. King, Ivan Neville, Little Feat and Jackson Browne.
Nov Raitt performs a week-long series of concerts benefitting the National Sanctuary Defense Fund, an organization aiding Central American refugees.

1990 **Feb** [21] At her career peak, Raitt sweeps the 32nd annual Grammy awards, held at the Shrine Auditorium, Los Angeles, winning Album Of The Year (*Nick of Time*), Best Pop Vocal Performance, Female (*Nick Of Time*), Best Rock Vocal Performance, Female (*Nick Of Time*) and Best Traditional Blues Recording (*I'm In The Mood* from John Lee Hooker's *The Healer*).
[24] Raitt takes part in the "Roy Orbison Concert Tribute To Benefit The Homeless", with host Whoopi Goldberg and Dwight Yoakam, k.d. lang, Bruce Hornsby, Gary Busey, Dean Stockwell, Roger McGuinn, David Crosby, Chris Hillman, Bob Dylan, Was (Not Was) and B.B. King among others, at the Universal Amphitheater, Universal City, CA.
Mar [8] Raitt wins Best Female Singer category in **Rolling Stone** magazine's Critics Awards.
Apr [7] In its 52nd chart week, *Nick Of Time*, finally hits US #1 though extracted *Have A Heart*, featured in Bob Hoskins/Denzil Washington movie "Heart Condition", stalls at US #49 (proving Raitt to be a firmly albums based artist). The album also gives Raitt her UK chart debut at #51. Raitt takes part in Farm Aid IV at the Hoosier Dome, Indianapolis, IN.
[16] Raitt participates in the "Nelson Mandela – An International Tribute To A Free South Africa" concert at Wembley Stadium, London.
[24-25] Raitt joins a host of celebrities at Don Henley's benefit concerts to preserve historic Walden Woods, at the Centrum, Worcester, MA.
May [26] *Nick Of Time* stalls at US #92.
July [25] Sell-out US tour begins at Poughkeepsie, NY, where Raitt had attended summer camp as a child, supported by blues guitarist Jeff Healey and R&B piano legend Charles Brown.
Aug [25] Warner Bros.-issued retrospective *The Bonnie Raitt Collection*, compiled by Raitt herself, peaks at US #61, and includes previously unavailable live duet with Sippie Wallace of her *Women To Be Wise*.
[31] Raitt sings *Amazing Grace* with Jackson Browne and Stevie Wonder at the memorial service for Stevie Ray Vaughan at the Laurel Land Memorial Park, Oak Cliff, Dallas, TX.
Oct [4] Raitt joins Rickie Lee Jones, Melissa Etheridge and Dianne Reeves at a "Vote Choice" concert to benefit the pro-choice activism of the Hollywood Women's Political Committee at the Wadsworth theater, Los Angeles.
Nov [16-17] Raitt joins Bruce Springsteen and Jackson Browne in 2 all-acoustic benefit concerts at the Shrine Auditorium, Los Angeles, the proceeds of which will go to the Christic Institute to finance a lawsuit claiming that the US government sanctioned illegal arms sales and drugs trafficking to finance covert operations in the Iran-contra affair.
Dec [16] Raitt and Jackson Browne perform at a concert in Sioux Falls, ND, to commemorate the 100th anniversary of the massacre of Sitting Bull at Wounded Knee.
[25] Raitt and actor Michael O'Keefe announce their engagement.

1991 **Apr** [28] Raitt and O'Keefe marry at the Union Church, Tarrytown, NY. The bride is given away by her father.
June Raitt's second outing for Capitol, *Luck Of The Draw*, with guests Richard Thompson, Bruce Hornsby and John Hiatt among others, is released.

THE RAMONES
Joey Ramone (vocals)
Johnny Ramone (guitar)
Dee Dee Ramone (bass)
Tommy Ramone (drums)

1974 **Aug** [16] After a first gig at a private party, The Ramones, having formed in Forest Hills, NY, begin a residency at New York's CBGB's club. The original line-up is Johnny Ramone (b. John Cummings, Oct.8, 1948, Long Island, NY), Ritchie Ramone, soon to be replaced by Dee Dee Ramone (b. Douglas Colvin, Sept.18, 1952, Fort Lee, VA) and Joey Ramone (b. Jeffrey Hyman, May 19, 1952, Forest Hills). Tommy Ramone (b. Thomas Erdelyi, Jan.29, 1949, Budapest, Hungary) takes over on drums to let Joey sing. They all adopt the working surname Ramone.

1975 **June** Band auditions for Rick Derringer and Blue Sky Records by opening for Johnny Winter at Waterbury, CT, in front of a 20,000 audience. The label does not sign them.
Nov Danny Fields becomes the band's manager, and negotiates a recording contract with Sire Records.

1976 **Feb** Group records its debut album on a $6,400 budget.
May *Blitzkrieg Bop*, the debut single, fails to chart. *The Ramones* makes US #111.
July [4] Group celebrates the US bicentennial by making its debut at London's Roundhouse with fellow patriots The Flamin' Groovies. They appear in the punk film "Blank Generation".

1977 **Mar** *Leave Home* reaches US #148.
May *Leave Home* makes UK #45 while the group begins its first UK tour, popularizing its no-frills "1-2-3-4" intros to every song, and the "Gabba gabba hey!" catchphrase.
June *Sheena Is A Punk Rocker* reaches UK #22.
July The Heartbreakers release *Chinese Rocks*, co-written by Dee Dee Ramone. The band is invited to Phil Spector's home, as its winter UK tour is cancelled.
Aug *Swallow My Pride* makes UK #36.
Sept *Sheena Is A Punk Rocker* climbs to US #81.
Dec *Rocket To Russia* reaches US #49 and UK #60.

1978 **Jan** *Rockaway Beach* peaks at US #66.
May Tommy Ramone leaves the band (but remains producer, credited as T. Erdelyi). He is replaced by Marc Bell from Richard Hell's Voidoids, who takes the name Marky Ramone. *Do You Wanna Dance* peaks at US #86.
Oct *Don't Come Close* makes UK #39. *Road To Ruin*, on which the group makes an effort to write songs lasting more than their usual 2 mins., reaches US #103 and UK #32.

1979 **Apr** [25] Roger Corman's film "Rock'N'Roll High School" premieres in Los Angeles, CA. Band is featured in the film, performing the title track and a new Paul McCartney song *Did We Meet Somewhere Before*.
June Live album *It's Alive*, recorded at London's Rainbow theater, reaches UK #27.
Aug Soundtrack album *Rock'N'Roll High School*, with The Ramones tracks re-mixed by Phil Spector, is released.
Sept *Rock'N'Roll High School* peaks at UK #67. (Spector has reportedly listened to the opening chord for 10 hours.)

1980 **Jan** *End Of The Century*, produced by Spector, makes US #44 and UK #14. (Recorded in 5 different studios, the band will later denounce *Century* as their worst album).
Feb *Baby I Love You*, a cover of the Spector-produced Ronettes hit from 1964, hits UK #8.
Apr *Do You Remember Rock'N'Roll Radio* peaks at UK #54.
Aug [18] Group begins a 6-week European tour at the Derby Assembly Rooms, Derbys. (They will play the Hammersmith Odeon, London, the following night and the Edinburgh Playhouse Aug.24 during Edinburgh Rock Festival week.)

1981 **Aug** *Pleasant Dreams*, produced by Graham Gouldman in New York and England, makes US #58.
Sept [3-5] The Ramones perform in front of almost 500,000 at the US Festival in San Bernardino, CA.

1983 **Apr** *Subterranean Jungle*, produced by Beserkley Records' Ritchie Cordell and Glen Kolotkin, makes US #83. Marky Ramone leaves the group and is replaced by Richard Beau from The Velveteens, who becomes the second Ritchie Ramone.
Aug [15] Joey Ramone is rushed to St. Vincent's hospital, New York, where he undergoes emergency brain surgery. (He was in a fight with fellow musician Seth Macklin over his girlfriend Cynthia Whitney.)

1984 **Nov** *Too Tough To Die*, with contributions from Talking Heads' Jerry

Harrison and Tom Petty & The Heartbreakers' Benmont Tench, makes US #171.

1985 Jan Signed to Beggars Banquet in UK, The Ramones' *Too Tough To Die* reaches UK #63.

Feb *Howling At The Moon*, co-produced by Eurythmics' Dave Stewart, makes UK #85.

June *Bonzo Goes To Bitburg*, a reference to a controversial visit by President Ronald Reagan to a Nazi war grave, is released.

[22] The Ramones perform at Milton Keynes Bowl, Bucks., supporting bill-toppers U2.

Dec [14] Artists United Against Apartheid, comprising 49 artists including Joey Ramone, makes US #38 and UK #21 with *Sun City*.

1986 May *Somebody Put Something In My Drink/Something To Believe In* peaks at UK #69. *Animal Boy* reaches US #143 and UK #38.

1987 Oct *Halfway To Sanity* makes US #172 and UK #78.

1988 June Retrospective album *Ramones Mania* makes US #168.

Aug Johnny Ramone joins Debbie Harry for duet *Go Lil' Camaro Go*.

1989 June *Brain Drain* makes US #122.

Aug Dee Dee leaves group to become rap performer Dee Dee King. His replacement is C.J. Ramone (b. 1965). Meanwhile Joey appears as himself in film "Roadkill".

[19] *Brain Drain* peaks at UK #75.

Group contributes music to the film of Stephen King's "Pet Semetary", with help from Debbie Harry and Chris Stein.

1990 Jan Joey tears ligaments in ankle at New York's Ritz club, causing cancellation of Feb. dates.

June [12] A best of CD *The Ramones ... All The Stuff Plus More* is released on Sire.

[28] "The Escape From New York" world tour with Jerry Harrison, Deborah Harry and Tom Tom Club begins in Columbia, MD.

Sept [27] Dee Dee is arrested on a marijuana possesssion misdemeanor charge in a drug sweep of Greenwich Village's Washington Square Park area in New York.

CHRIS REA

1970 Rea (b. Mar.4, 1951, Middlesbrough, Cleveland), while working in his family's ice cream parlor in Middlesbrough, and doing part-time laboring, buys his first guitar after being inspired by Joe Walsh and Ry Cooder albums.

1973 He becomes a proficient enough guitarist to join local professional band, Magdelene (whose singer David Coverdale has just left to join Deep Purple), and begins to develop his songwriting skills.

1974 May Rea cuts *So Much Love*, a Magnet Records one-off, to little notice.

1975 Magdelene changes its name to The Beautiful Losers, and wins **Melody Maker**'s Best Newcomers Of 1975 award, but little comes of this.

1977 Rea splits from the group to sign to Magnet as a soloist, and works with producer Gus Dudgeon on a debut album. The Beautiful Losers splits. (Rea will later estimate that by the end of the band's time, around 30 members have passed through its ranks.)

Nov He is one of many guitarists guesting on *The Hank Marvin Guitar Syndicate*, a solo instrumental project by The Shadows' lead guitarist.

1978 Apr *Fool (If You Think It's Over)* is released and initially fails.

June Dudgeon-produced album, *Whatever Happened To Benny Santini?*, with session contributions from Pete Wingfield, Rod Argent and others, is released. (The title refers to Magnet having considered at one time re-christening Rea Benny Santini.) Rea claims the album sounds "too American", and that Dudgeon has smoothed away all the rough edges of his style.

Sept In the less new wave-obsessed US market, *Fool (If You Think It's Over)*, released on United Artists, gains airplay and climbs to US #12, pulling *Whatever Happened To Benny Santini?* to US #49 and a gold disk for a half million sales. Rea is offered a major US tour, but turns it down to concentrate on further recording in UK.

Oct The single's US success prompts Magnet to repromote it in UK, and this time *Fool (If You Think It's Over)* makes UK #30. (Elkie Brooks' 1982 revival of it will make UK #17.)

Nov The title track from *Whatever Happened To Benny Santini?* reaches US #71.

1979 Feb *Fool (If You Think It's Over)* is nominated for (but does not win) a Grammy at the 1978 awards in US.

Apr *Diamonds*, a track taken from Rea's second album *Deltics*, makes both UK and US #44.

May *Deltics*, produced by Dudgeon, is Rea's UK Album chart debut at #54, but fails in US.

1980 Apr Rea's first self-produced album, *Tennis*, reaches UK #60. (2

singles, *Tennis* and *Dancing Girls* are extracted from it, but neither charts.) (He spends most of the next 2 years on the road in UK, continuing to write songs, but eschewing recording in favor of stage work. He also marries long-time girlfriend Joan.)

1982 Mar *Chris Rea* makes UK #52. In US, it marks a new deal with CBS/Columbia, but fails to chart.

Apr *Loving You*, the opening track from *Chris Rea*, is his first chart single in 3 years, reaching UK #65 and US #88.

1983 June *Water Sign* makes UK #64.

Oct *I Can Hear Your Heartbeat*, taken from *Water Sign*, climbs to UK #60, but is a bigger hit in Eire and Europe, hitting Top 20 in several countries, as does the album. This helps build his European reputation to a level far exceeding his still cult-sized UK following. He undertakes a successful tour of Europe, and Germany, particularly, affords him near superstar status.

1984 Mar *I Don't Know What It Is But I Love It*, a taster from his next album, climbs to UK #65.

May *Wired To The Moon* peaks at UK #35, but *Bombollini*, the second single taken from it, fails.

1985 May *Stainsby Girls*, following strong UK airplay, reaches UK #27.

June *Shamrock Diaries*, which includes *Stainsby Girls*, is Rea's first UK Top 20 album, reaching #15.

July *Josephine*, second single from the album, peaks at UK #67.

1986 Mar *It's All Gone* reaches UK #69.

May *On The Beach* is Rea's best-seller in UK, making #11 with a 24-week chart run.

June A remixed version of *On The Beach*, title song from the album, reaches UK #57.

1987 July Rea's self-penned *Let's Dance* (the third different UK hit single by this title, following Chris Montez's 1962 #2 and David Bowie's 1983 #1) reaches UK #12, to become his biggest-selling UK single. *On The Beach* also re-charts in UK, reaching #75, its sales revitalized by the success of *Let's Dance*.

Aug *Loving You Again* climbs to UK #47.

Sept Self-produced *Dancing With Strangers* (which includes *Let's Dance*) hits UK #2, behind Michael Jackson's *Bad*, earning a gold disk in its first week of release, and confirming Rea's star status in UK, comparable to that which he enjoys in Europe.

[5] In US, *Let's Dance*, Rea's first release via a new deal with Motown, makes US #81, but parent album, on the same label, fails to chart. Meanwhile, he makes his first concert tour of Australia, followed by another European trek, supported by a now-regular road band: Robert Ahwaii (guitar), Max Middleton (keyboards), Kevin Leach (keyboards), Dave Kemp (saxophone), Eogham O'Neil (bass), Dave Mattacks (drums) and Rea's brother Kevin (percussion and vocals).

Dec Seasonal *Joys Of Christmas* is released, but does not chart.

1988 Feb *Que Sera* peaks at UK #73.

Aug *On The Beach Summer '88*, a re-mixed version of the earlier hit, is Rea's first single for WEA, which has acquired Magnet, and reaches UK #12. WEA repromotes *On The Beach* which makes UK #37.

Oct *I Can Hear Your Heartbeat* peaks at UK #74.

Nov Compilation album *The Best Of Chris Rea – New Light From Old Windows* hits UK #5, becoming a chart mainstay.

Dec *Driving Home For Christmas* peaks at UK #53.

1989 Feb *Working On It* peaks at UK #53.

Mar *New Light Through Old Windows*, released through Geffen, makes US #92.

Apr [15] *Working On It* peaks at US #73.

Oct *The Road To Hell (Part 2)* (concerning itself with Greater London ringroad, the M25) hits UK #10.

Nov *The Road To Hell* enters UK chart at #1, where it stays 3 weeks.

1990 Feb [24] Child-abuse themed *Tell Me There's A Heaven* reaches UK #24.

May [5] *Texas* peaks at UK #69.

1991 Mar [2] Previewing forthcoming album, *Auberge* peaks at UK #16.

[9] With all 11 tracks written by Rea and produced by Jon Kelly, *Auberge* enters UK chart at #1. Rea announces plans for 11-date UK tour starting at Manchester's G-Mex Centre Nov.23, set to finish at London's Wembley Arena Dec.15.

OTIS REDDING

1957 Redding (b. Sept.9, 1941, Dawson, GA) leaves school in Macon, GA, to take a variety of day jobs, and sing in talent shows at every opportunity, frequently finding success with his Little Richard imitation.

59 He begins to gig regularly in clubs with R&B band Johnny Jenkins & The Pinetoppers, and makes his first recording locally with the group backing him. *She's Alright*, a Little Richard pastiche, remains initially unreleased.

Dec During a talent contest at Macon's Douglas theater, he meets his future wife Zelda.

60 **Sept** After 6 months in Los Angeles, CA, looking for a break in music (but finding only a car wash job), Redding returns to Macon and records *Shout Bamalama* (again in Little Richard style) for Confederate label, distributed by King Records. It is released, but does not sell well.

61 Redding gains a residency at Macon's Grand Dukes club, and cuts another single, *Gettin' Hip*, for Alshire Records. Phil Walden, The Pinetoppers' manager, takes over Redding's management.

Aug Redding marries Zelda and they set up home in Macon.

62 **Feb** Still associated with The Pinetoppers (he regularly chauffeurs the group to gigs and is given vocal spots in its act), Redding accompanies Jenkins and the group on a college tour of Tennessee and Alabama. In Atlanta, GA, they record *Love Twist* for local Gerald label, which is picked up by Atlantic and sells well in Southern states.

Oct At the suggestion of Atlantic's Joe Galkin, Jenkins & The Pinetoppers (with Redding again driving) travel to Memphis, TN, to record a session at Atlantic-distributed Stax Records. At the end of the (unproductive) Jenkins session, with studio time in hand, Redding persuades Stax's owner Jim Stewart to let him record 2 of his own songs: Little Richard-styled *Hey Hey Baby* and slow, pleading *These Arms Of Mine*, in which Stewart hears commercial potential. Atlantic (which has paid for the session, and technically has Redding contracted) allows Stax to issue it as a single on new Volt label.

63 **Mar** Following local Memphis success, *These Arms Of Mine* reaches #20 on US R&B chart.

June *These Arms Of Mine* debuts Redding on US Hot 100, reaching #85. [24] With his debut finally peaking, Redding's second recording session is held at Stax. He is now officially an Atco (Atlantic subsidiary) artist, but by special arrangement records as part of the Stax set-up and continues to have feature releases issued on Volt.

Oct *That's What My Heart Needs*, cut in June, makes US R&B #27 but does not cross over.

Nov On the strength of 2 hits and the fast-climbing third release *Pain In My Heart*, Redding is invited to play (for $400) a week at New York's Apollo theater in Harlem (his performance being recorded for Atco's live compilation *Saturday Night At The Apollo*, released in 1964).

64 **Feb** *Pain In My Heart*, an adapted cover of Irma Thomas' current Southern R&B hit *Ruler Of My Heart*, makes US #61, and is his biggest seller to date.

Apr Redding/Walden song *Come To Me*, recorded with Booker T. & The MG's (as will be virtually every Redding track) but with Jenkins playing additional guitar, peaks at US #69.

May Debut album *Pain In My Heart* makes US #103 while extracted *Security* stalls at US #97 (though is much-covered by UK R&B groups).

Nov Self-penned *Chained And Bound* peaks at US #70.

65 **Mar** *Mr. Pitiful* makes US #41 as B-side *That's How Strong My Love Is* climbs to US #74.

Apr *The Great Otis Redding Sings Soul Ballads* makes US #147.

June Deep soul ballad *I've Been Loving You Too Long (To Stop Now)* becomes his breakthrough release on the US pop chart, reaching US #21 (and R&B #2).

July [3] Though Redding has not yet had a UK hit, when UK R&B chart is launched he has 2 Top 20 placings, with *Mr. Pitiful* (#6) and *Pain In My Heart* (#16).

Oct Uptempo *Respect*, penned by Redding, makes US #35 (and R&B #4). (2 years later, the song will be revived in a still more commercial arrangement by Aretha Franklin and become a million-selling US chart-topper.)

Nov *Otis Blue/Otis Redding Sings Soul* (often cited by later critics as one of the all-time great soul albums) makes US #75.

Dec *Just One More Day* stalls at US #85.

66 **Jan** UK Atlantic's Tony Hall selects Redding's version of Smokey Robinson-penned *My Girl* (a US #1 for The Temptations in 1965, but not a big UK seller) as a UK single from *Otis Blue*. It gets strong airplay and is his UK chart debut, reaching #11.

Mar *Otis Blue/Otis Redding Sings Soul* gives him his first UK chart album, hitting UK #6, and staying in the Top 30 for 21 weeks.

Apr *The Great Otis Redding Sings Soul Ballads* finds belated UK sales, peaking at #30. Meanwhile, Redding's version of The Rolling Stones' *(I Can't Get No) Satisfaction* reaches US #31 (R&B #4) and UK #33. (Redding will tour UK and Europe to great success later in the

year, and in UK will record "Ready Steady Otis!", an entire edition of UK TV pop show "Ready Steady Go!")

June *My Lover's Prayer* peaks at US #61 (and R&B #10) while *The Soul Album*, from which it is taken, makes US #54.

[24] Redding begins a 46-date US tour of one-nighters, with Sam And Dave, Patti LaBelle & The Bluebelles, Percy Sledge, Garnett Mimms and others, in Greensboro, NC.

Aug *The Soul Album* makes UK #22 and *My Lover's Prayer* climbs to UK #37. Redding launches his own label, Jotis Records. Among its acts is Arthur Conley, for whom Redding writes and produces *Sweet Soul Music* (a reworking of Sam Cooke's *Yeah Man* which will hit US #2 and UK #7 in 1967).

Sept R&B dance track *I Can't Turn You Loose* makes UK #29 (having hit US R&B #11).

Nov *Fa-Fa-Fa-Fa-Fa (Sad Song)* reaches US #29 and UK #23.

1967 **Jan** *Complete And Unbelievable ... The Otis Redding Dictionary Of Soul* makes US #73 and UK #23 while, taken from it, a revival of standard ballad *Try A Little Tenderness* is his second-biggest US hit single to date, reaching #25.

Feb A UK reissue of *Otis Blue* (following a change of Atlantic's UK licensee), after an extended absence from the shops, hits UK #7, while *Try A Little Tenderness* makes UK #46.

Mar [17] Redding begins 13-date UK "Soul Concert Sensation '67" tour with Sam And Dave, Eddie Floyd, Arthur Conley, Carla Thomas, The Markeys and Booker T. And The MG's, at Finsbury Park Astoria, London. The tour will end Apr.8 at the Hammersmith Odeon, London.

Apr *I Love You More Than Words Can Say* peaks at US #78, while his revival of The Beatles' *Day Tripper* reaches UK #43. Redding's live performance at Los Angeles' Whiskey A-Go-Go club is recorded by Atlantic (and will be released after his death).

May Redding's debut album *Pain In My Heart* is belatedly released for the first time in UK and reaches #28, while *Let Me Come On Home* peaks at UK #48.

June Redding duets with Stax artist (and daughter of Rufus *Walking The Dog* Thomas) Carla Thomas on an adaptation of Lowell Fulson's *Tramp*, which reaches US #26, while his solo revival of Sam Cooke's *Shake!* makes US #47. Redding's duet album with Thomas, *King And Queen*, reaches US #36.

[16] Redding participates in the Monterey Pop Festival – seen as a deliberate move to capture the attention of the young, white rock audience. Redding's biggest asset is the passionate strength of his live performance, and he gets a rapturous reception from the largely hippy audience. (Part of his set will be included in D.A. Pennebaker's film "Monterey Pop".)

July *Shake* reaches UK #28.

Aug *Glory Of Love* peaks at US #60, while *King And Queen* with Carla Thomas reaches UK #18 and their duetted single *Tramp* makes UK #18.

Sept Live *Otis Redding Live In Europe*, recorded on the Stax/Volt tour, reaches US #32. Meanwhile, Redding's second duet single with Thomas, a version of Eddie Floyd's much-covered *Knock On Wood*, reaches US #30.

Oct *Knock On Wood* makes UK #35.

[14] Second UK tour of the year, the "Soul Explosion" with Sam And Dave, Percy Sledge, Arthur Conley, Eddie Floyd, Carla Thomas, Booker T. And The MG's, opens at London's Finsbury Park Astoria. The tour ends Nov.6 at the Fairfield Halls, Croydon, London.

Dec [7] Redding goes to the studio to record a song he has written with Stax guitarist Steve Cropper, *(Sittin' On) The Dock Of The Bay*. (A relaxed soul ballad, it will become his biggest hit, but Redding will not live to see its release.)

[10] En route to a concert in the Mid-West, the twin-engined chartered plane carrying Redding and his road band, The Bar-Kays, goes down in the icy waters of Lake Monoma, near Madison, WI. The only survivor is Memphis-born Ben Cauley – at 20, the oldest of The Bar-Kays. (At Redding's funeral, the pall-bearers are fellow soul singers Joe Tex, Joe Simon, Johnnie Taylor, Solomon Burke, Percy Sledge, Don Covay and Sam Moore, of Sam and Dave.)

1968 **Jan** Compilation *History Of Otis Redding* hits US #9, a bigger seller than any album during his lifetime.

Mar Posthumously-released *(Sittin' On) The Dock Of The Bay* tops US chart for 4 weeks, selling over a million, and hits UK #3. Meanwhile, another Otis and Carla Thomas single, *Lovey Dovey* makes US #60, and a UK reissue of *My Girl* reaches #36.

Apr *History Of Otis Redding* hits UK #2 (behind Bob Dylan's *John Wesley Harding*), while live *Otis Redding In Europe* reaches UK #14.

May *Dock Of The Bay*, a collection of tracks from his final sessions in late 1967, hits US #4 while, taken from it, *The Happy Song (Dum Dum)* reaches US #25.

June *Dock Of The Bay* tops UK chart for a week, while *The Happy Song (Dum Dum)* reaches UK #24.

July Also taken from the album, a revival of The Impressions' *Amen* makes US #36 and B-side *Hard To Handle* peaks at US #51. This, like subsequent posthumous singles, is released on Atco rather than Volt.

Aug *Hard To Handle*, elevated to A-side in UK, makes US #15, while *The Immortal Otis Redding*, assembling more of his last recordings, reaches US #58.

Nov Ballad *I've Got Dreams To Remember* makes US #41, while parent album *The Immortal Otis Redding* reaches UK #19.

Dec *Otis Redding In Person At The Whiskey A-Go-Go*, recorded in Apr.1967, reaches US #82, while a revival of James Brown's *Papa's Got A Brand New Bag* makes US #21 – his biggest US hit since *(Sittin' On) The Dock Of The Bay*.

1969 **Mar** A revival of Clyde McPhatter's 50s hit *A Lover's Question* climbs to US #48.

[12] *(Sittin' On) The Dock Of The Bay* wins Best R&B Vocal Performance, Male, and Best R&B Song Of 1968 at the 11th annual Grammy awards.

June *Love Man* peaks at US #72.

July *Love Man* makes UK #43 (Redding's final UK chart single), while the album of the same title makes US #46.

1970 **Aug** *Tell The Truth*, containing Redding's last unissued recordings from 1967, creeps to US #200.

Nov Reprise Records issues live *Monterey International Pop Festival*, on which one side each is devoted to the acts of Redding and Jimi Hendrix at the June 1967 festival. It climbs to US #16.

1972 **Oct** Double anthology *The Best Of Otis Redding* peaks at US #76 and is his final US chart entry.

1973 **Nov** Redding's 12-year-old son Dexter releases *God Bless*, on Phil Walden's Capricorn label.

1980 **Dec** Brothers Dexter (vocals, bass) and Otis Redding III (guitar) and their cousin Mark Locket (vocals, drums, keyboards), now a trio named The Reddings and signed to Believe label, have their first chart entry with *Remote Control*, which makes US #89.

1981 **Jan** The Reddings' *The Awakening* makes US #174.

Aug Second Reddings' album *Class* reaches US #106.

1982 **July** The Reddings' version of *(Sittin' On) The Dock Of The Bay* makes US #55 (and R&B #21), and is taken from their third album *Steamin' Hot*, which reaches US #153.

1989 **Jan** [18] Little Richard inducts Redding posthumously into the Rock'N'Roll Hall Of Fame at the fourth annual dinner at the Waldorf Astoria in New York.

JIMMY REED

1955 **Feb** Having moved to Chicago, IL, where his laid-back, boogie-influenced style makes him a popular figure on the Southside club and bar scene, Reed (b. Mathis James Reed Leland, Sept.6, 1925, Dunleith, MS), one of 10 children, signs to newly formed label, Vee-Jay, and *You Don't Have To Go Boogie In The Park* hits US R&B #9.

1956 *Ain't That Loving You Baby* is another R&B success.

1957 **July** Reed's first Hot 100 pop hit is *The Sun Is Shining* at US #65.

Nov *Honest I Do* makes US #32. Reed is now the biggest draw on the Southside club scene (eclipsing even Muddy Waters).

1958 **Apr** [5] Irvin Feld's "Greatest Show Of Stars" opens its 80-date US tour in Norfolk, VA. Reed stars with Sam Cooke, The Everly Brothers, Clyde McPhatter and many others.

Aug *Down In Virginia* charts briefly at US #93.

1959 **May** [29] Reed performs in pouring rain at an outdoor festival in the Herndon Stadium, Atlanta, GA. Other artists on the bill include Ray Charles, The Drifters and B.B. King.

1960 **Mar** *Baby What You Want Me To Do* makes US #37.

May *Found Love* peaks at US #88.

Oct *Hush-Hush* reaches US #75.

1961 During the year, *Big Boss Man* (the description by which Reed will become known) reaches US #78 and *Bright Lights Big City* makes US #58 (both are big R&B hits). The blues declines in popularity in favor of R&B/soul, and the UK R&B/beat boom emerges. Double album *Jimmy Reed At Carnegie Hall*, comprising a studio re-creation of Reed's Carnegie Hall concert and a "best of" selection, makes US #46.

1962 *Aw Shucks, Hush Your Mouth* reaches US #93 and *Good Lover* makes US #77. Both are big R&B hits. *Just Jimmy Reed* reaches US #103.

1963 **Apr** *Shame Shame Shame* makes US #52.

1964 **Sept** *Shame Shame Shame* climbs to UK #45.

Oct Reed begins an extensive UK club and concert tour. The Rolling Stones cover his *Honest I Do* on their first album. Other UK groups to cover Reed tracks include The Pretty Things, The Animals (both record *Big Boss Man*) and Them (*Bright Lights Big City*). Reed is unable to capitalize on this due to increasing ill-health (epilepsy and alcoholism) (He remains inactive for most of the late 60s and early 70s.)

1976 **Aug** [29] Reed dies in San Francisco, CA, from an epileptic seizure after completing a 3-night engagement at the Bay Area's Savoy club.

LOU REED

1965 Reed (b. Louis Firbank, Mar.2, 1942, Freeport, Long Island, NY), after playing in local teenage bands like The Shades, attending Syracuse University, and working for Pickwick Records as a writer and recorder of low-budget cash-in records for supermarket racks (and getting a near-hit single in New York with *The Ostrich* by The Primitives), becomes a founder member of The Velvet Underground with John Cale and Sterling Morrison. (During his time with the band he will be its lead singer and most prominent songwriter.)

1970 **Sept** Following a Velvet Underground residency at Max's Kansas City club, New York, Reed leaves the group and returns to his parents' home in Long Island, partly to recuperate from the excesses of the group's finale.

1971 Having spent the early part of the year working as an office typist, Reed continues to write poetry and songs and is persuaded to sign a solo contract with RCA.

1972 **June** Helmed by Flamin' Groovies' producer Richard Robinson, debut solo album *Lou Reed*, recorded in London with Yes members Steve Howe and Rick Wakeman (among others), reaches US #189, and includes old Velvet Underground material. He tours UK with a backing band named The Tots.

1973 **Jan** [9] Reed marries a cocktail waitress, Betty, in New York.

Mar [24] Reed is bitten on the posterior by a fan who leaps on stage at a concert in Buffalo, NY. The man is seized and ejected from the theater, leaving Reed to end the show and contemplate a sore bum.

Apr *Transformer*, produced in London by labelmate, and erstwhile Reed fan, David Bowie and Mick Ronson, reaches US #29. Extracted *Walk On The Wild Side* reaches US #16, and is Reed's only solo US chart single.

June *Walk On The Wild Side* hits UK #10, and does not draw a half-anticipated BBC radio ban over its lyrics, because the producers fail to understand street idioms like "giving head" used by Reed. As in US, it is his only UK chart single. (It will become regarded as a rock classic and will be much covered, even as a dance/hip-hop version by Tabu artist Jamie J. Morgan in 1990.) *Transformer* makes UK #13, and stays on UK chart for 6 months.

Sept [22] Reed headlines the annual Crystal Palace Garden Party in London, during a world tour.

Nov *Berlin*, the third in a row to be recorded in London, produced this time by Bob Ezrin, and featuring Steve Winwood and Jack Bruce among others, makes UK #7.

1974 **Apr** Live album *Rock'N'Roll Animal*, recorded at New York's Academy of Music, with a line-up of Reed (guitar, vocals), Dick Wagner (guitar), Steve Hunter (guitar), Prakash John (bass), Josef Chirowsky (keyboards) and Whitney Glen (drums), climbs to US #45 and UK #26, and with consistent sales earns Reed his first gold disk.

Nov *Sally Can't Dance* hits US #10; his only US Top 20 effort.

1975 **Apr** Further performance set *Lou Reed Live* contains another section of the previous year's Academy of Music concert, and is a companion to live album *Rock'N'Roll Animal* from the same occasion.

July Double album *Metal Machine Music* is the most controversial of Reed's career, and the least accessible, having 4 sides of white noise, whines, whistles, feedback and screams. The sleeve implies that it is a live set. Originally to have been released by Red Seal (RCA's classical music division) as an experimental piece of music, the set fails to sell after poor (and bewildered) reviews, and is withdrawn by RCA within a few months.

1976 **Mar** *Coney Island Baby*, in Reed's normal style, peaks at US #41 and UK #52, his last for RCA.

Nov Reed signs a new deal with Arista Records, producing *Rock And Roll Heart*, which makes US #64, and includes 11-min. saga *Street Hassle*.

1977 **May** Compilation album *Walk On The Wild Side: The Best Of Lou Reed*, on RCA, halts at US #156.

1978 **May** *Street Hassle* makes US #89.

[17] Reed begins a week of concerts at New York's Bottom Line club,

which are recorded for planned live album *Take No Prisoners*.

979 Mar Double live *Take No Prisoners*, including his persistent berating of the audience, due to a contractual wrangle, is released by Arista in US and by RCA elsewhere. It fails to chart.

June Arista album *The Bells* has a brief 4-week US chart run, peaking at #130, but is critically panned as being his strangest effort since *Metal Machine Music*.

980 Feb [14] On St. Valentine's Day, Reed marries Sylvia Morales, in a ceremony at his apartment on Christopher Street, Greenwich Village, New York. (His previous marriage had foundered early on.)

May *Growing Up In Public*, his second album release inside 12 months, stalls at US #158.

Oct Reed has a cameo role as a record producer in Paul Simon's film "One Trick Pony".

Dec Last Arista album is *Rock And Roll Diary, 1967-80*, a history of Reed's earlier career, with most tracks by The Velvet Underground. It creeps to US #178.

982 Mar He returns to RCA with *The Blue Mask*, which makes US #169, and features guitarist Robert Quine. It is dedicated to long-time Reed inspiration, the poet Delmore Schwartz.

July *Transformer* is reissued in UK at mid-price, and re-charts at #91.

983 Apr *Legendary Hearts* peaks at US #159, featuring popular alternative radio cuts *New Sensation* and *I Love You Suzanne* (which is accompanied by a comic promo video).

984 Aug *New Sensations* makes US #56 and UK #92.

985 Oct Reed's version of *September Song* is released on A&M, taken from compilation *Lost In The Stars*, as a tribute to Kurt Weil.

Dec He appears with 48 other acts on the Artists United Against Apartheid single *Sun City* on Manhattan Records, which reaches US #38 and UK #21.

986 May Straight rock-aimed *Mistrial*, featuring the cut *The Original Wrapper*, makes US #47 and UK #69.

987 Feb Sam Moore and Reed duet on a re-working of Sam And Dave's million-seller *Soul Man*, now used as the theme to the movie of the same name. It reaches UK #30.

988 Aug Reed appears on Rob Wasserman's *Duets* album. (He also co-writes 3 tracks with Rubén Blades on the latter's album *Nothing But The Truth*.)

989 Jan [7-8] He works with John Cale for 2 shows at St. Ann's Church, New York, as a tribute to Andy Warhol.

[28] Back-to-the-basics set *New York*, with Reed and Mike Rathke (guitars), Rob Wasserman (bass), Fred Maher (drums) and Maureen Tucker on 2 tracks, is critically applauded, making UK #14 and US #40.

Mar Reed plays 6 nights at the St. James theater, Broadway, New York.

Aug [19] During a major US tour, Reed breaks his ankle after a sound check in Cleveland, OH, and has to cancel the remainder of the dates.

Oct Anthology *Retro* reaches UK #29.

Nov [29] *Songs For 'Drella: A Fiction*, a 50-min. suite written with John Cale as a tribute to Andy Warhol, is performed at Brooklyn Academy of Music.

990 Apr [16] Reed participates in the "Nelson Mandela – An International Tribute To A Free South Africa" concert at Wembley Stadium, London.

May Reed/Cale album *Songs For 'Drella* reaches UK #22 and US #103.

[5] Reed sings *Jealous Guy* and *Mother* at the "John Lennon Tribute Concert", held at the Pier Head Arena in Merseyside to celebrate the songs of Lennon.

Dec During the bitter **New York Daily News** workers' strike, Reed performs at a $55,000-raising benefit "News Aid" with Pete Seeger, The Roches and others.

R.E.M.

Michael Stipe (vocals)
Peter Buck (guitar)
Mike Mills (bass)
Bill Berry (drums)

978 Stipe (b. Decatur, GA), who has already sung in a garage band in Illinois, a student of painting and photography at University of Georgia, meets Buck in their native Athens, GA, record store Wuxtry Records, where Buck works, and keeps a guitar behind the counter eagerly learning licks in between serving customers. Both share an interest in the UK new wave music.

980 Feb They meet Berry (b. Hibbing, MN) and Mills at a party and R.E.M. is formed soon after (the letters mean Rapid Eye Movement – a physiological term for the sleep cycle stage in which dreaming occurs).

Apr [5] R.E.M. makes its concert debut in an old converted

1981 Episcopalian church in Athens.

Jefferson Holt becomes their manager and invites ex-Sneaker Mitch Easter to produce recordings. 1,000 copies of first single *Radio Free Europe* are released on the local Hib-Tone label. It is picked up by US college radio network and becomes an airplay favorite. **Village Voice** magazine votes it Best Independent Single Of The Year. Easter also records their second track *Sitting Still*.

1982 Impressed by *Radio Free Europe*, R.E.M. is signed by Miles Copeland's I.R.S. label. 5-track mini-album Easter-produced *Chronic Town* is released and is heavily praised by rock critics. Dense layers of guitars add to Stipe's often inaudible lyrics, adding an air of mystique to the band which is developing cult status.

1983 May Debut album the dreamlike *Murmur*, co-produced by Easter and Don Dixon, is released on I.R.S. It peaks at US #36 during a 30-week chart stay, as the band becomes a popular college radio item. Live performances now mix original material with covers of songs including *Born To Run*, *In The Year 2525* and *Paint It Black*.

July A re-recorded version of *Radio Free Europe* is US chart single debut, at #73, but fails in UK.

Band plays a series of 7 stadium dates opening for The Police.

1984 May *Reckoning*, featuring a more straightforward (Byrds-style) guitar jangling , more accessible for US radio play, will spend over 1 year on US chart, peaking at #27 and is UK debut at #91. As with all their 80s releases, R.E.M. embarks on extensive touring to support the album.

June From it, *S. Central Rain (I'm Sorry)* peaks at US #85. Follow-up *(Don't Go Back To) Rockville* gets airplay in US and UK but fails to chart.

Dec *Reckoning* extract *Windout* is incongruously included in the "Bachelor Party" movie soundtrack.

1985 Jan R.E.M. travels to UK for live dates and to record a new album with veteran folk-rock producer Joe Boyd. Stipe suffers mental and physical breakdown during the sessions.

June *Fables Of The Reconstruction* enters the US chart, selling over 300,000 copies in 3 months and reaching US #28. All attempts at hit singles fail (though extracted *It's The End Of The World As We Know It* will become a popular live staple), but with a growing fan following (with worship by a group of "Distiples" who believe that Stipe is a guru) and critical enthusiasm, it makes UK #35.

1986 Sept Rock-based *Life's Rich Pageant*, produced by John Cougar Mellencamp's collaborator Don Gehman, reaches US #21 and UK #43.

Oct [11] *Fall On Me* makes US #94.

1987 Jan R.E.M. begins a successful US tour.

Feb *Life's Rich Pageant* is certified gold.

May A collection of out-takes and B-side material is released as *Dead Letter Office*. (Its CD version will include the *Chronic Town* mini-album tracks.)

June *Dead Letter Office* reaches US #52, selling over 250,000 copies, and makes UK #60 for 2 weeks. In its sleeve notes, Buck writes "listening to this album should be like browsing through a junkshop". (All band members, except Stipe, back Warren Zevon on *Sentimental Hygiene*.)

Sept Fifth album *Document*, recorded in Nashville, TN, and the last of new material for I.R.S., is released. It hits US #10 and UK #28, on MCA. A collection of plot-free videos, "Succumbs", tops **Billboard**'s video chart.

Oct R.E.M. plays its first UK concerts in 2 years, while 2 R.E.M. recordings, *Swan Swan H* and a cover of The Everly Brothers' classic *All I Have To Do Is Dream* are included on I.R.S. released compilation, *Athens GA: Inside Out*.

Dec [5] Folk/rock melody *The One I Love*, from *Document*, hits US #9 and makes UK #51.

1988 Jan UK magazine **New Musical Express** readers vote 4 R.E.M. albums into the all-time Top 100. **Rolling Stone** magazine devotes its front cover to R.E.M. with the heading "America's Best Rock'N'Roll Band".

Feb [20] Belatedly released *It's The End Of The World As We Know It* peaks at US #69.

Apr *Finest Worksong* makes UK #50.

June Following 7 I.R.S. album releases, R.E.M. signs worldwide to Warner Bros. for a reported 7 figure sum.

Oct Stipe, with 10,000 Maniacs' singer Natalie Merchant and The Roches, contributes *Little April Shower* to various artists Walt Disney compilation *Stay Awake*. I.R.S. releases greatest hits retrospective *Eponymous* (including the rare and original version of their debut single *Radio Free Europe*), which makes US #44 and UK #69.

Nov Warner debut *Green* reaches US #12 and UK #27.

1989 Feb Extracted *Stand* falls at UK #51.

Mar [1] "Green World Tour", the group's first arena trek, opens at the

Louisville Gardens, KY. (Group guests on support act Indigo Girls album debut.)

Apr [8] *Stand* hits US #6, and will subsequently be featured as the theme to Fox TV's Chris Elliott-starring comedy "Get A Life".

Berry collapses in Munich from bronchial infection. Band cancels rest of German tour.

June *Orange Crush* reaches UK #28.

[24] *Pop Song '89* climbs to US #86.

Aug *Stand* re-peaks at higher UK #48.

During an R.E.M. recording hiatus, Mills scores music for movie by friend Howard Libov, Buck tours with friend Kevin Kenney (with local band Drivin'N'Cryin') and teams with Robyn Hitchcock as The Crosses to cut a track for The Byrds tribute album *Time Inbetween*, while Stipe produces local band The Chickasaw Muddpuppies' debut album *White Dirt*, duets with Syd Straw on *Future 40's* from Straw's debut album *Surprise* and forms his own film and video company C-OO, which films and releases "R.E.M.: Tourfilm" and opens his own vegetarian restaurant in Athens, called The Grit.

1990 Stipe conceives a series of public service commercials on AIDS, abortion, the environment and racism. Natalie Merchant and Rapper KRS-One are among artists who contribute.

Dec [8] Having formed an ad-hoc offshoot in 1986 known as The Hindu Love Gods, which released the singles *Narrator* and *Good Time Tonight*, Buck, Mills and Berry, now teamed with Warren Zevon, for whom they have played on 2 of his last 3 albums, release loose collection of blues covers *Hindu Love Gods* under the same band name. It peaks at US #168.

By year's end, the band has received many honors, including Earth Day 1990 Award For Environmentally Responsible Business and the Athens-Clarke Heritage Foundation Inc. Award for support of Historic Preservation In Athens, their attorney Bertis Downs is president of the local Historic Society. Stipe has produced all-girl outfit Swell, Opal Fox Society, The Beggarweeds and Hetchy Hetchy. Still firmly based at the R.E.M./Athens Ltd. headquarters in Georgia, where they work in management and rehearsal rooms, they have also recently completed their second album for Warner Bros.

1991 **Mar** [16] *Losing My Religion*, first from new album, makes UK #19.

[23] Parent album, the baroque-tinged, love-themed *Out Of Time*, which includes guest Rapper KRS-One, with whom Stipe has recently made a Public Service Announcement video about world peace and recorded hip-hop single *The Greenhouse Effect*, and B52 bomber Kate Pierson, enters UK chart at #1.

Apr [13] R.E.M., with Pierson as added vocalist, appears as the musical guest on NBC TV's "Saturday Night Live".

[28] R.E.M. plays its only concert of 1991 in Charlotte, WV.

May [18] *Out Of Time* tops US chart as *Losing My Religion*, now at US #21, continues to climb Hot 100. Unlike previous releases, R.E.M. elects not to tour in support of the project.

REO SPEEDWAGON

Kevin Cronin (vocals)
Gary Richrath (guitar)
Neal Doughty (keyboards)
Bruce Hall (bass)
Alan Gratzer (drums)

1968 Group is formed in Champaign, IL (named after a make of antique fire engine), with local Illinois university students Gratzer (b. Nov.9, 1948, Syracuse, New York, NY) and Doughty (b. July 29, 1946, Evanston, IL), who recruit the band's chief songwriter Richrath (b. Oct.18, 1949, Peoria, IL), vocalist Terry Luttrell and bass player Craig Philbin. REO Speedwagon becomes the town's most popular live band.

1972 **Feb** Irving Azoff becomes the group's manager (he will later also manage The Eagles) and Cronin (b. Oct.6, 1951, Evanston, IL), whom Richrath has discovered via a "Musicians' Referral Service" in Chicago, IL, replaces Luttrell on lead vocals as the band signs to Epic, recording debut album *REO Speedwagon*, which fails to chart. Band begins to tour extensively (as it will throughout the 70s, often sharing major treks with fellow Mid-Western acts like Bob Seger's Band and Kansas).

Dec On *R.E.O. T.W.O.*, Mike Murphy takes over on lead vocals, Cronin having left to become a solo singer/songwriter after differences with Richrath.

1974 **Feb** *Ridin' The Storm Out* is their first to chart in US, making #171.

Dec *Lost In A Dream* reaches US #98.

1975 **Aug** *This Time We Mean It*, the last to feature Murphy as lead vocalist, makes US #74. The band splits from manager Azoff.

1976 **July** Hall (b. May 3, 1953, Champaign, IL) replaces Philbin on bass and Cronin rejoins on lead vocals for *R.E.O.*, which makes US #159. Cronin and Richrath will co-produce the group from here on, and jointly provide most of its songs.

1977 **Apr** Live double *You Get What You Play For* reaches US #72. Staying on chart for 2 weeks short of a year, it earns the band's first platinum album for a million-plus sales. The heavy touring schedule continues.

June First US chart single is a live version of *Ridin' The Storm Out*, taken from the double album, which creeps to US #94.

1978 **May** Group makes a cameo appearance in movie "FM", performing *Ridin' The Storm Out*.

June *You Can Tune A Piano, But You Can't Tuna Fish*, makes US #79 and is a second platinum album, spending 11 months on chart.

Extracted *Roll With The Changes* climbs to US #58.

Aug *Time For Me To Fly* peaks at US #56.

1979 **Sept** *Nine Lives* (also the band's ninth album) makes US #33, earning a gold disk.

1980 **June** Double compilation *A Decade Of Rock'N'Roll, 1970 To 1980*, rounding up tracks from the group's first 10 years, makes US #55, and also goes gold. A reissue of *Time For Me To Fly* (also on the compilation) from 2 years earlier, peaks at US #77.

1981 **Feb** *Hi Infidelity* finally achieves the band's major chart breakthrough, toppling John Lennon's *Double Fantasy* from US #1 and holding #1 for a total of 15 weeks to the end of June (in 3 separate runs). It sells 7 million copies and earns another platinum disk.

Mar Cronin's song *Keep On Loving You*, the first single from *Hi Infidelity*, also tops US chart (for a week) and is another million-seller. After a decade as one of the busiest and most continually-mobile tour support bands in US, REO Speedwagon becomes one of the biggest stadium-fillers.

May *Take It On The Run*, also from *Hi Infidelity*, hits US #5, while *Keep On Loving You* is UK chart debut, hitting #7.

July Third single from the album, *Don't Let Him Go*, makes US #24.

Aug [8] US MTV features REO Speedwagon live from Denver, CO, for its first stereo concert broadcast.

Take It On The Run is a second UK hit single, reaching #19, while *Hi Infidelity* hits UK #6 during a 29-week chart run.

Oct *In Your Letter* reaches US #20.

1982 **Aug** *Good Trouble* hits US #7 (the group's fourth platinum album) and reaches UK #29. Taken from it, *Keep The Fire Burnin'* also hits US #7.

Oct Also from the album, *Sweet Time* reaches US #26.

1984 **Dec** After more than 2 years since the band's last single, *I Do Wanna Know* reaches US #29.

1985 **Jan** *Wheels Are Turnin'* hits US #7 and earns a platinum disk.

Mar *Can't Fight This Feeling*, written by Cronin on Hawaiian island Molokai, and taken from *Wheels Are Turnin'*, hits US #1 for 3 weeks, and is the band's second million-selling single.

Apr *Can't Fight This Feeling* reaches UK #16.

June Another track from the album, *One Lonely Night*, reaches US #19.

Aug *Live Every Moment* makes US #34.

Nov UK-only compilation album *Best Foot Forward* is released, but fails to chart.

1987 **Feb** First new album in nearly 2 years, *Life As We Know It* enters US chart. It will reach US #28 during a 48-week chart stay.

Apr [4] *That Ain't Love* reaches US #16.

June [6] *Variety Tonight* peaks at US #60.

Oct [24] *In My Dreams* reaches US #19.

1988 **Aug** Compilation retrospective *The Hits* peaks at US #61.

1990 **Sept** [15] *The Earth, A Small Man, His Dog And A Chicken*, with Dave Amato (ex-Ted Nugent band), Bryan Hitt (ex-Wang Chung) and Jesse Harms, climbs to US #129.

Nov [3] *Love Is A Rock* peaks at US #65.

PAUL REVERE & THE RAIDERS

Paul Revere (keyboards)
Mark Lindsay (vocals, saxophone)
Drake "Kid" Levin (guitar)
Philip "Fang" Volk (bass)
Mike "Smitty" Smith (drums)

1959 Lindsay (b. Mar.9, 1942, Eugene, OR), working in a bakery by day, and singing with his own high school band by night, is watching a band at a local Elks Hall gig, when he plucks up courage to ask them whether he can sing with them. They accept and he performs Jerry Lee Lewis' *Crazy Arms*. Group leader, Revere (b. Jan.7, 1938, Harvard, NB), an ex-hairdresser raised in Boise, ID, now running the Reed'N'Bell drive-in restaurant in Caldwell, ID, invites Lindsay to replace lead vocalist Red Hughes, as they name-change to The Downbeats.

'60 They cut half a dozen instrumentals at IMM Productions studios in Boise. Revere takes the tapes from the sessions to Los Angeles, CA, where he meets John Guss at the Gardena pressing plant. Guss cuts a record from tape, renaming the band Paul Revere & The Raiders, and releasing debut single *Beatnik Sticks*.

'61 **Apr** Group's local hit *Like, Long Hair* (another instrumental) makes US #38. Shortly after, Revere will be drafted and the group disbands. An album and 4 follow-up singles, on Gardena, fail through lack of live promotion.

'63 Revere and Lindsay regroup in Portland, OR, where Smith (playing at teen club Headless Horseman, Volk and Levin join the re-vamped line up. Group becomes part of the buoyant Portland/Seattle live scene, alongside groups like The Wailers, The Sonics and The Kingsmen. It signs to leading North-Western label Jerden and the resulting single *So Fine* fails to sell, but brings the group to the notice of CBS/Columbia, which buys its contract.

June The first Columbia single is a version of the staple of every North-Western band's live act, Richard Berry's *Louie Louie*, with a vocal by Lindsay. (The Kingsmen's version is released nationally by Wand Records almost simultaneously and, despite Columbia's promotion, The Kingsmen's will hit US #2 and sell over a million.)

'64 Lindsay leaves, while follow-up *Louie – Go Home* also fails to chart.

'65 **Apr** The Raiders move to Los Angeles and Lindsay rejoins. A revival of *Ooh Poo Pah Doo* also fails.

June Impressed by their showmanship and teen appeal (and their startling Revolutionary War stage outfits, a band trademark), "American Bandstand" presenter Dick Clark adopts the group as house band for his new ABC TV show "Where The Action Is", which launches on June 27. (This constant national exposure turns them into teen idols, and guarantees excellent promotion for subsequent records. Photogenic Lindsay becomes a pin-up heart-throb in US.)

Oct Columbia pairs the group with producer Terry Melcher, and *Steppin' Out* reaches US #46. **Here They Come**, featuring mostly familiar rock standards and released to coincide with the TV show launch, peaks at #71 – the group's first chart album.

'66 **Jan** [18] The Kinks-influenced *Just Like Me* (a cover of a local record by Rick Dey & The Wild Knights) reaches US #11.

Apr Levin is drafted, and is replaced on guitar by Jim Valley, ex-Viceroys and Don & The Goodtimes.

May [10] Propelled by an arresting guitar riff, *Kicks*, an anti-drug song penned by Barry Mann and Cynthia Weil for UK group The Animals, hits US #4, and **Just Like Us!** hits US #5. (It will stay charted for 43 weeks, earn a gold disk, and become the first Columbia album by a rock group to sell a million.)

July [26] *Hungry*, another Mann/Weil song in hard rock style, hits US #6, while mostly group-written album **Midnight Ride**, its second gold disk, hits US #9.

Oct [25] The first group-penned hit single is *The Great Airplane Strike*, by Lindsay and producer Melcher. It makes US #20.

'67 **Jan** [10] Lindsay and Melcher's good *Good Thing* hits US #4.

Feb **The Spirit Of '67**, which includes *Hungry* and *Good Thing*, hits US #9 (third consecutive Top 10 album) and again goes gold.

Mar [14] *Ups And Downs* makes US #22. Meanwhile, Volk and Smith leave to join Levin (now out of the service) and form Brotherhood, while Valley departs to work as a soloist.

Apr [30] Freddy Weller (b. Sept.9, 1947, GA), whom Revere had spotted in Ohio while working for Billy Joe Royal, joins for the band's CBS TV "Ed Sullivan Show", to promote *Him Or Me – What's It Gonna Be?* Then bassist Charlie Coe (b. Nov.19, 1944), had been in the original line-up in Boise, but left to continue education majoring in music at Boise College, and drummer Joe Correro (b. Nov.19, 1946, Greenwood, MS), who had played at high school with Bobbie Gentry and in Memphis-based Flash & The Board of Directors, who had done a 2-week tour with The Raiders, both join.

June [6] *Him Or Me – What's It Gonna Be?* hits US #5. With influences from The Monkees and The Rolling Stones clearly showing, this is later selected by many critics as the group's finest.

July Compilation album **Greatest Hits** reaches US #15, and is the group's last gold album.

Sept [19] *I Had A Dream*, a heavy rocker with a hint of psychedelia, makes US #17.

Oct **Revolution!**, highlighted by *Him Or Me – What's It Gonna Be?* and featuring session musicians Ry Cooder, Van Dyke Parks, Hal Blaine

and Glen Campbell among others, reaches US #25.

Dec *Peace Of Mind* peaks at US #42. It is the group's last single produced by Melcher.

1968 **Jan** Group has its own Saturday morning Dick Clark-produced ABC TV show, "Happening '68", which will run until Sept.1969. Its still-strong teen appeal makes it more unfashionable with rock fans drifting in the direction of West Coast, psychedelic and progressive sounds, but the music is much less out on a limb, credibility-wise, than the group's image and presentation.

Mar [12] Lindsay produces The Rolling Stones-influenced *Too Much Talk*, which reaches US #19. (Lindsay will continue to be the group's producer until the end of its chart days, but will also have a parallel solo vocal career.)

Apr *Goin' To Memphis*, recorded with producer Chips Moman, reaches US #61.

July [23] *Don't Take It So Hard* climbs to US #27.

Aug Coe leaves and is replaced by "Where The Action Is" regular Keith Allison.

Oct *Cinderella Sunshine* peaks at US #58, while **Something Happening** climbs to US #122.

1969 **Apr** *Mr. Sun, Mr. Moon* reaches US #18.

May *Hard'N'Heavy (With Marshmallow)* makes US #51. Lindsay announces his solo career.

July *Let Me* reaches US #20.

Aug Lindsay's first solo single *First Hymn From Grand Terrace*, part of Jimmy Webb's epic *Hymn From Grand Terrace* featured on Richard Harris' **The Yard Went On Forever**, is a minor US success at #81.

Oct *Alias Pink Puzz*, named after they use the pseudonym The Pink Puzz so radio stations, turned off by the Paul Revere name, will play their records, reaches US #48, while from it, Weller-penned *We Gotta All Get Together* makes US #50. These are the last disks credited to Paul Revere & The Raiders.

1970 **Feb** *Just Seventeen*, credited to The Raiders, peaks at US #82. Lindsay's biggest solo success is *Arizona*, a song recorded by Steve Rowland's UK group Family Dogg as follow-up to 1969 hit *Way Of Life*. Lindsay's revival hits US #9, and earns a gold disk for million-plus sales. (It is also a typical example of Lindsay's solo output, which tends to be tuneful ballads in Glen Campbell mold, which would not fit into the invariably uptempo and rocking Raiders group style.)

Apr Lindsay's first solo album **Arizona** makes US #36.

May **Collage**, the first album credited just to The Raiders, peaks at US #154. Lindsay's solo *Miss America*, from *Arizona*, reaches US #44.

July Lindsay has another hit with *Silver Bird*, which makes US #25.

Oct Lindsay's solo album **Silver Bird** climbs to US #82.

Nov Lindsay's version of Neil Diamond's *And The Grass Won't Pay No Mind* reaches US #44.

1971 **Jan** *Problem Child*, another Lindsay solo, halts at US #80.

Feb Lindsay embarks on a solo tour of US, supporting The Carpenters.

June Lindsay's cover of Bread's *Been Too Long On The Road* scrapes the US Hot 100 at #98.

July A revival of John D. Loudermilk's *Indian Reservation (The Lament Of The Cherokee Reservation Indian)*, previously a US and UK Top 20 hit for Don Fardon (and recommended to the group by Columbia A&R man Jack Gold), hits US #1 for a week, The Raiders' only US chart-topper. Freddy Weller sings lead vocal (he will later have a successful career as a solo country singer) and Lindsay still produces. (Group has now split as a live unit and has session men playing most of the instrumental parts on the current recordings.)

[20] Musical variety show "Make Your Own Kind Of Music", headlined by The Carpenters with Lindsay a regular feature, airs on NBC TV, set to end on Sept.7.

Aug **Indian Reservation** reaches US #19. Correro leaves the band, and Smith returns in his place. Omar Martinez and Robert Woolley are added to the line-up.

Oct Group's version of Joe South's *Birds Of A Feather* makes US #23, while Lindsay's solo **You've Got A Friend** stalls at US #180 and single *Are You Old Enough* falters at US #87.

1972 **Feb** The Raiders' *Country Wine* peaks at US #51.

June *Powder Blue Mercedes Queen* makes US #54.

Aug Double compilation album **All-Time Greatest Hits**, rounding up the chart singles, makes US #143.

Nov *Song Seller* creeps to US #96.

Dec Smith quits the band again.

1973 **Feb** The last Raiders chart single is *Love Music*, which peaks at US #97.

May Weller leaves, and Revere recruits Doug Heath, from Merrilee Rush's band.

June [20] Group appears on the 20th anniversary special edition of Dick Clark's "American Bandstand", alongside Little Richard, Three Dog Night and others.

1975 Jan Lindsay quits the band. Revere promotes drummer Omar Martinez to lead vocalist.

Apr Allison leaves the band, and is replaced by Ron Foos.

1976 June [26] *Ain't Nothin' Wrong*, written by KC and Richard Finch, is released on Drive/TK.

July *The British Are Coming* is released on 20th Century during USA's bicentennial celebrations. Revere and Lindsay take full advantage of the promotion the bicentennial is giving to the group, touring through the summer, but Revere will disband the group by year's end.

1978 Revere reassembles The Raiders, now comprising Martinez, Foos, Woolley and led by Heath.

Dec [31] Revere re-joins the band, as they embark on a 250 to 300 dates a year schedule, with this line-up still together in 1991.

1983 Edsel in UK releases compilation album *Kicks*. With Revere and Lindsay having enjoyed many successful years singing TV and radio jingles and now touring regularly on the rock'n'roll/oldies circuit, *Paul Revere Rides Again* is released in US on Hitbound.

1985 July [17] "Rock'N'Roll Summer Action", with Paul Revere & The Raiders as regulars, airs for the first time on ABC TV, set to end on Aug.28.

CLIFF RICHARD

1948 Sept Richard (b. Harry Rodger Webb, Oct.14, 1940, Lucknow, India) arrives in England on the wartime troopship SS Ranghi to live in Carshalton, Surrey, with his parents, Rodger and Dorothy, and sisters, Donella and Jacqueline.

1952 His family moves to Enfield, London. He attends Cheshunt Secondary Modern school, where he forms 5-piece vocal group, The Quintones, which splits when the 3 girl members go to secretarial college.

1957 Aug After leaving school with an "O-level" pass in English, he finds work as a credit control clerk at Atlas Lamps factory in Enfield. He also joins The Dick Teague Skiffle Group, playing pubs in Ware, Cheshunt and Hoddesdon.

1958 He and the group's drummer Terry Smart leave to form a rock'n'roll band with Norman Mitham on guitar, calling themselves Harry Webb & The Drifters. Teddy Boy John Foster, employed at the local sewage works, sees the band at the Five Horseshoes pub in Hoddesdon and offers to manage them. Foster persuades his parents to finance the recording of a demo. For £10, they cut *Breathless* and *Lawdy Miss Clawdy* at HMV Records store in London's Oxford Street. They play a week's engagement at the 2 I's coffee bar in London's Soho district. After a gig they are approached by Ian Samwell, wishing to join the group as its lead guitarist. He is accepted, and proves also to have songwriting talent. Promoter Bob Greatorex books the group for a 1-night stand at a dance hall in Ripley, Derbys., but is unhappy with the lead singer's name. After a discussion at the Swiss pub near the 2 I's, they settle upon Cliff Richard & The Drifters. (Samwell suggests leaving the "s" off Richards, the initial suggestion, pointing out that when Richard corrects people who get it wrong, they will keep his name in mind.)

July Foster arranges for Richard & The Drifters to take part in a talent contest at the Gaumont cinema on Shepherd's Bush Green in London. He persuades variety agent George Ganjou to see the band and Ganjou takes Richard's demo tape to Norrie Paramor, head of A&R at EMI Records' Columbia label, who invites the group to audition for him.

[24] *Move It* and *Schoolboy Crush* are recorded in number 2 studio at Abbey Road.

Aug [9] Richard signs to EMI and leaves his job at Atlas. With The Drifters, he begins a 4-week residency at Butlins holiday camp in Clacton-on-Sea, Essex. Mitham quits the band, Samwell switches to bass and Ken Pavey, a professional player working at the holiday camp, fills in the guitar slot.

[29] Debut single *Schoolboy Crush* (a cover of a US release by Bobby Helms) backed with *Move It* (a rock number written by Samwell and completed on a bus on the way to the studio) is released. 2 session players, guitarist Ernie Shears and bassist Frank Clarke, are on the tracks at Paramor's insistence, to ensure a strong sound.

Sept Group is signed to appear on a UK package tour headed by *When* hitmakers The Kalin Twins. Minus a lead guitarist since Mitham's departure, Foster visits the 2 I's to recruit singer/guitarist Tony Sheridan, but cannot find him. Instead, he spots Hank Marvin, a regular at the club and known to be an excellent player. Marvin agrees to join Richard on tour provided his rhythm guitar-playing partner

Bruce Welch is taken on too.

[13] Richard makes his UK TV debut in Jack Good's "Oh Boy" (where he will become a program resident). Good has heard the single, disregarded *Schoolboy Crush*, but raved over *Move It*. He orders Richard to sing without his customary guitar and minus his sideburns. (He also encourages a sexy stage act which will have newspapers complaining about TV depravity and the corruption of the young.) At the same time *Move It*, now promoted to A-side after most radio DJ's have shared Good's judgement of it, makes its debut on the UK chart.

Oct [5] Richard & The Drifters, comprising Marvin (lead guitar), Welch (rhythm guitar), Samwell (bass) and Smart (drums), make their concert debut at the Victoria Hall, Hanley, Stoke-on-Trent, at the start of The Kalin Twins' UK tour, which also features trumpeter Eddie Calvert and The Most Brothers. (Teen reaction to Richard will be such that, almost from the outset, The Kalin Twins will find it hard to follow his act.)

[25] Richard makes his UK radio debut, on BBC Light Programme's "Saturday Club".

Nov *Move It* hits UK #2, behind Connie Francis' *Stupid Cupid*. By the end of the tour, Samwell has been eased to a songwriting/ management role to make way for a stronger bass player – Jet Harris, who was touring with The Most Brothers but has been helping The Drifters on most dates. Smart leaves, feeling he is not up to the standard of the more recent recruits, and announces his intention to join the Merchant Navy. He is replaced by Harris' drummer friend, Tony Meehan.

[17] Richard & The Drifters open variety season at the Metropolitan theater in the Edgware Road, London. (They follow with 2 weeks at London's Chiswick Empire and Finsbury Park Empire.)

Dec Follow-up *High Class Baby*, another Samwell composition, hits UK #7, though Richard hates the song (and will never perform it again). On a tour of 1-nighters, Richard loses his voice and so as not to disappoint fans at a concert in Hull, he mimes while Wee Willie Harris stands in the wings, providing an impersonation of Richard.

1959 Jan [24] Richard, with the new line-up, begins his first headlining UK tour at York's Rialto theater, N.Yorks., on a bill with Wee Willie Harris and Tony Crombie & His Rockets.

Feb *Livin' Lovin' Doll* reaches UK #20, as Richard wins the Best New Singer award in the annual **New Musical Express** poll.

May *Mean Streak* hits UK #10 while B-side *Never Mind* reaches UK #21 (both are written by Samwell). Debut album *Cliff* hits UK #4.

[14] Film "Serious Charge", starring Anthony Quayle, premieres in London. Richard features as a young semi-delinquent trying to make it as a rock singer, and sings 3 songs.

[30] Richard & The Drifters top the bill on the last-ever broadcast of "Oh Boy".

July [31] *Living Doll*, written by Lionel Bart for "Serious Charge", but revamped for single release as a mid-tempo, slightly country song, tops the UK chart for 5 weeks, selling over 500,000 copies. The song wins an Ivor Novello award, and the single, on international sales, earns his first gold disk.

Oct [30] *Travellin' Light*, in similar style to *Living Doll*, tops the UK chart for 5 weeks, while rocking B-side, Samwell's *Dynamite*, reaches UK #16 (and will be a popular concert item throughout Richard's career and be re-recorded more than once).

Nov Second album *Cliff Sings* hits UK #2.

[23] *Living Doll*, issued in US on ABC Records, reaches US #30.

[27] Film "Expresso Bongo" premieres in London. Based on Wolf Mankowitz' stage play, it stars Laurence Harvey, with Richard as the manipulated teenage rock star Bongo Herbert.

Dec Richard & The Shadows (to which The Drifters have changed their name to avoid confusion with the US Drifters), open at Stockton Globe theater, in pantomime "Babes In The Wood".

1960 Jan Richard & The Shadows begin a 5-week US package tour with Freddy Cannon, Bobby Rydell, Clyde McPhatter and bill-topper Frankie Avalon.

[21] Richard guests on ABC TV's "The Pat Boone Show", singing 5 songs including *Living Doll*.

Feb *A Voice In The Wilderness*, a ballad from "Expresso Bongo", hits UK #2 for 3 weeks (held from the top by Anthony Newley's *Why*), while the EP of 4 songs from the film reaches UK #14 (representing uncommonly large sales for the time by an EP).

[21] Richard wins Top British Male Singer award in the **New Musical Express** poll, and takes a 2-day break from the US tour to attend the presentation in London.

Apr *Fall In Love With You* hits UK #2. Meanwhile, Richard and his family move into their first owned home in Percy Road, Winchmore Hill, London.

May [16] Richard participates in the Royal Variety Performance at London's Victoria Palace, in the presence of the Queen, appearing in a "youth" segment alongside Adam Faith and Lonnie Donegan.

June Richard & The Shadows open a 6-month season at the London Palladium, in "Stars In Your Eyes".

July [28] *Please Don't Tease*, written by Welch of The Shadows with Pete Chester (son of comedian Charlie), is chosen by members of Richard's fan club, invited to a preview hearing of recently-recorded tracks, as the best bet for a hit single. It tops the UK chart for 4 weeks but is deposed by The Shadows' first instrumental hit, *Apache*.

Oct Fast rocker *Nine Times Out Of Ten* (the fans' third choice) is released as follow-up and hits UK #3.

[14] Richard receives more than 5,000 cards on his 20th birthday.

Nov *Me And My Shadows* hits UK #2, behind soundtrack album *South Pacific*.

Dec [29] *I Love You* tops UK chart for 2 weeks.

'61 Feb [4] It is announced that Richard and his manager Tito Burns are parting, amicably. (The following month, Australian Peter Gormley, who is already handling The Shadows, becomes Richard's manager.)

Mar *Theme For A Dream* hits UK #3.

Apr [8] Richard sits on the panel of BBC TV's "Juke Box Jury".

May *Gee Whiz It's You* (from *Me And My Shadows*), pressed as a single for export, begins to sell in UK and is made generally available. Making the Top 20 while *Theme For A Dream* is still in the Top 5, it hits UK #4. Meanwhile, **Listen To Cliff** hits UK #2.

[15] Richard's father dies in hospital, aged 56.

[20] Richard makes his debut on ITV's "Thank Your Lucky Stars", singing *A Girl Like You*.

June *A Girl Like You* hits UK #3.

Aug [17] Richard & The Shadows open a European tour at the Tivoli Gardens, Copenhagen, Denmark.

[28] Richard opens a 6-week summer season at the Opera House, Blackpool, Lancs.

Oct *When The Girl In Your Arms Is The Girl In Your Heart*, a ballad from forthcoming film "The Young Ones", hits UK #3.

Nov [4] *21 Today* tops the UK chart for a week.

Dec [10] "The Young Ones" premieres in London.

'62 Jan [11] As the movie opens throughout the UK (it will be the second-biggest box office grosser of the year, after "The Guns Of Navarone"), the title song from "The Young Ones" enters the UK chart at #1, where it stays for 8 weeks, selling more than a million copies.

[15] Soundtrack album **The Young Ones** knocks Elvis Presley's **Blue Hawaii** from UK #1, and tops the chart for 6 weeks before surrendering again to the Presley soundtrack. Press reports that Richard is to marry 17-year-old Valerie Stratford are quickly dismissed.

[28] UK package tour opens at the Gaumont cinema, Derby, Derbys.

Feb Richard wins **New Musical Express**'s Top British Male Singer award for the second consecutive year.

Mar [13] Richard receives an award as Show Business Personality Of The Year from the Variety Club of Great Britain.

May *I'm Looking Out The Window*, a revival of a Peggy Lee ballad, backed with a revival of Bobby Freeman's *Do You Wanna Dance?*, hits UK #2 (behind Elvis Presley's *Good Luck Charm*).

[5] Richard is awarded a gold disk for UK million sales of *The Young Ones*.

Sept A revival of Jerry Lee Lewis' rocker *It'll Be Me* hits UK #2, behind Elvis Presley's *She's Not You*.

[21] Richard pays a brief visit to US to appear on CBS TV's "Ed Sullivan Show".

[28] Richard appears on BBC TV's "The Billy Cotton Band Show", singing *It'll Be Me*.

Oct Richard begins a week of concerts at the London Palladium, while *32 Minutes And 17 Seconds With Cliff Richard* hits UK #3.

Nov [30] Richard & The Shadows begins a UK tour at the Gaumont cinema, Doncaster, Yorks.

Dec On ITV's "Sunday Night At The London Palladium", Richard premieres both sides of *The Next Time/Bachelor Boy* (the latter Richard's first co-writing credit, and both taken from forthcoming film "Summer Holiday").

'63 Jan [5] *The Next Time* tops the UK chart for a week (before being deposed by The Shadows' *Dance On*), while *Bachelor Boy* hits UK #3. Total UK sales approach 950,000.

[10] "Summer Holiday", filmed largely on European locations in summer 1962, premieres in London.

[21] Radio Luxembourg devotes its entire "ABC Of The Stars" program to Richard.

Feb Soundtrack album *Summer Holiday* tops UK chart for 14 weeks.

[11] Richard appears at a charity concert in Nairobi, Kenya, Africa.

Mar [14] Title song *Summer Holiday* tops the UK chart for 2 weeks, replacing The Beatles' *Please Please Me*.

Apr [14] Richard & The Shadows appear on CBS TV's "Ed Sullivan Show", singing *Summer Holiday*.

May A revival of Ruth Brown's *Lucky Lips* hits UK #4.

June Richard & The Shadows star in "Holiday Carnival", a summer variety show at Blackpool (set to end Sept.).

July *Cliff's Hit Album*, a compilation of singles from *Move It* to *Do You Want To Dance?*, hits UK #2.

Aug US teen magazine **16** votes Richard Most Promising Singer in its annual poll.

[10] Richard & The Shadows appear on the 100th edition of ITV show "Thank Your Lucky Stars" with Alma Cogan, Billy J. Kramer, Brian Poole & The Tremeloes and The Searchers.

Sept A revival of Tommy Edwards' *It's All In The Game* hits UK #2, behind The Beatles' *She Loves You* while in US (where he is now signed to Epic) *Lucky Lips* becomes Richard's first US chart single since *Living Doll*, and peaks at #62.

Oct *When In Spain*, recorded in Barcelona in Spanish, hits UK #8.

[20] Richard appears again on CBS TV's "Ed Sullivan Show", singing *It's All In The Game*.

Nov [3] Richard & The Shadows appear on ITV's "Sunday Night At The London Palladium", singing *Don't Talk To Him*.

Nov *Don't Talk To Him* hits UK #2, held from the top by The Beatles' *She Loves You* (enjoying its second run at #1).

Dec [2] Richard & The Shadows begin filming "Wonderful Life" in the Canaries.

1964 Feb *I'm The Lonely One* hits UK #8, while *It's All In The Game* reaches US #25 – his biggest US hit to date.

Mar [28] Richard & The Shadows begin a 22-date twice-nightly UK tour at the ABC cinema, Southampton, Hants, ending at the Odeon cinema, Leeds, W.Yorks., on Apr.19.

Apr *I'm The Lonely One* stalls at US #92.

[2] Richard & The Shadows open a UK tour at Kingston-upon-Thames, Surrey.

May *Constantly*, an English-lyric version of an Italian ballad, hits UK #4, while US-compiled *It's All In The Game* makes US #115. Richard & The Shadows begin a European tour with a week of concerts at the Olympia, Paris, France.

[26] Richard & The Shadows perform at the annual **New Musical Express** Poll Winners Concert at the Empire Pool, Wembley, London.

June *On The Beach*, from film "Wonderful Life", hits UK #7.

July [2] Richard attends the world premiere of his new film "Wonderful Life" at the Empire, Leicester Square in London. Soundtrack album *Wonderful Life* hits UK #2, behind The Beatles' *A Hard Day's Night*.

Aug *Bachelor Boy* spends a week at US #99.

[10] Richard receives a gold disk for a million sales of *Bachelor Boy/The Next Time* on ITV show "Thank Your Lucky Stars".

[19-21] At the invitation of Epic Records, Richard records in Nashville, TN, with producer Billy Sherrill and vocal backing from The Jordanaires.

Oct A revival of Johnny Mathis' *The Twelfth Of Never* hits UK #8.

[25] Richard & The Shadows take part in "The Greatest Pop Concert Of 1964" at the Empire Pool, Wembley, with The Dave Clark Five, The Seekers and others with comperes DJ Pete Murray and actor Roger Moore.

Nov Richard & The Shadows perform at the Royal Variety Show in London.

Dec *I Could Easily Fall (In Love With You)* hits UK #9. It is taken from the London Palladium pantomine "Aladdin And His Wonderful Lamp", which stars Richard & The Shadows with Arthur Askey and Una Stubbs.

1965 Jan *Aladdin And His Wonderful Lamp* reaches UK #13.

Feb Richard denies rumors that he is quitting show business.

Apr *The Minute You're Gone*, cut in Nashville, tops the UK chart for a week. (B-side *Just Another Guy* is one of the first covers of a song by Neil Diamond.) Meanwhile, *Cliff Richard* hits UK #9.

June [8-14] Richard & The Shadows play a week of concerts in Birmingham, W.Midlands.

July *On My Word* reaches UK #12.

[9] Richard & The Shadows begin 8-date Scandinavian tour in

Copenhagen, ending July 20 in Gothenburg, Sweden.

Aug Compilation album *More Hits By Cliff* reaches UK #20.

Sept *The Time In Between* reaches UK #22, while *When In Rome*, sung in Italian, does not chart.

Oct [3] Richard & The Shadows open a UK tour in Derby.

[9] Richard comperes ITV's "Sunday Night At The London Palladium".

Nov Richard & The Shadows participate in the annual Royal Variety Show.

Dec *Wind Me Up (Let Me Go)*, another ballad from the Nashville sessions, hits UK #2 for 3 weeks, behind The Beatles' *We Can Work It Out/Day Tripper*.

[7] Richard appears on ITV show "Cinema", discussing his films.

1966 Jan *Love Is Forever*, a collection of romantic ballads, reaches UK #19.

Feb [21] Richard & The Shadows make their cabaret debut at London's Talk Of The Town.

Apr *Blue Turns To Grey*, written by Mick Jagger and Keith Richards of The Rolling Stones, reaches UK #15.

[3] Richard & The Shadows take part in the "Stars' Organization For Spastics"concert at the Empire Pool, Wembley, London.

May [1] Richard & The Shadows participate in the annual **New Musical Express** Poll Winners Concert at the Empire Pool, on a bill with The Beatles, The Rolling Stones, Roy Orbison, Dusty Springfield, The Yardbirds, The Spencer Davis Group and many others.

June *Kinda Latin* hits UK #9.

[16] Richard joins evangelist Billy Graham on stage at Earls Court, London, and talks of his discovery of the Christian faith, before singing *It Is No Secret*.

Aug Ballad *Visions* (later used as the closing theme for his TV series) hits UK #7.

Oct *Time Drags By*, from forthcoming movie "Finders Keepers", hits UK #10.

[8] Richard attends the premiere of film "Finders Keepers" in London.

Dec [10] Richard opens in the London Palladium pantomime "Cinderella", with music entirely written by The Shadows.

[12] Richard & The Shadows attend the premiere of film "Thunderbirds Are Go!" in which their puppet likenesses appear, singing *Shooting Star*.

1967 Jan *In The Country*, taken from "Cinderella", hits UK #6, while soundtrack album *Finders Keepers* hits UK #6 and *Cinderella* reaches UK #30. Richard states in a **New Musical Express** article that he intends to give up showbiz and teach religious instruction in school.

Apr *It's All Over*, previously cut by The Everly Brothers, hits UK #9.

May *Don't Stop Me Now* reaches UK #23.

[7] Richard participates in the annual **New Musical Express** Poll Winners Concert at the Empire Pool, on a bill with The Beach Boys, Stevie Winwood, Georgie Fame, Lulu and Dusty Springfield.

June *I'll Come Running*, penned by Neil Diamond (as is B-side *I Got The Feeling*), reaches UK #26.

Sept *The Day I Met Marie*, written by Hank Marvin, hits UK #10. (For many years, Richard will cite this as his favorite of his own recordings.)

[23] Richard is voted Top Male Singer by readers of **Melody Maker**.

Nov Gospel *Good News*, his first religious release, makes UK #37.

Dec Ballad *All My Love* hits UK #6.

[6] He is confirmed into membership of the Church of England by Graham Leonard, Bishop of Willesden, at St. Paul's church, Finchley, London.

1968 Feb Richard fills in on drums for The Shadows at the Talk Of The Town, London, when Brian Bennett falls sick.

Apr *Congratulations*, Bill Martin/Phil Coulter's song chosen to represent UK in the Eurovision Song Contest, tops the UK chart for 2 weeks – his first #1 hit in 3 years (and last until 1979). It will be a worldwide million-seller, partly thanks to multi-lingual versions.

[6] Richard sings *Congratulations* in the Contest held at London's Royal Albert Hall. He comes second to Spain's Massiel, with *La La La*. Richard appears in UK TV drama "A Matter Of Diamonds".

May Richard & The Shadows participate in the annual **New Musical Express** Poll Winners Concert at Wembley's Empire Pool, on a bill with Lulu, The Rolling Stones, Dusty Springfield, Scott Walker and others.

June Live album *Cliff In Japan*, recorded at Sankei Hall, Tokyo, reaches UK #29. *Congratulations* spends 3 weeks on US Singles chart, peaking at #99.

[28] He appears in a TV concert special on ITV, "Talk Of The Town", taped at the London venue of the same name.

July *I'll Love You Forever Today*, co-written by Richard for his forthcoming film "Two A Penny", reaches UK #27.

[11] UK TV airs a "Cliff Richard & The Shadows" special to celebrate their 10 years together.

Aug *Two A Penny* does not chart. It is partly the soundtrack of the film, a morality drama, which Richard has made, without a fee, for th Billy Graham organization.

Oct *Marianne*, written by actor Bill Owen (of UK TV's"Last Of The Summer Wine" fame) reaches UK #22.

[11] Richard & The Shadows begin a season at the London Palladium

Nov *Established 1958*, half Cliff Richard and half Shadows tracks, celebrating their 10th anniversary in show business, reaches UK #30.

Dec *Don't Forget To Catch Me*, from the 10th anniversary album, reaches UK #21.

1969 Mar *Good Times (Better Times)* reaches UK #12.

May [12] Richard guests on UK children's TV "Sooty" show.

June *Big Ship*, written by Raymond Froggatt, hits UK #8.

Aug Compilation album *The Best Of Cliff* hits UK #5.

Oct *Throw Down A Line*, a duet with Hank Marvin, hits UK #7, while *Sincerely* reaches UK #24.

[7] Richard & The Shadows begin a Japanese tour at the Alaska, Toky

Nov [7] Richard & The Shadows commence a UK tour in Finsbury Park, London.

Dec *With The Eyes Of A Child* reaches UK #20.

[10] Richard participates in a special gala midnight performance at th London Palladium in aid of the Royal Society for the Prevention of Cruelty to Animals (RSPCA).

1970 Jan [3] Richard's own UK TV series starts on BBC 1.

Mar A second duet with Marvin, *The Joy Of Living* (also the theme of the TV series) reaches UK #25.

May [11] Richard makes his straight stage acting debut in Peter Shaffer's "Five Finger Exercise" at the New Theatre, Bromley, Kent.

July *Goodbye Sam, Hello Samantha*, widely promoted as his 50th single, hits UK #6 while live-recorded album *Cliff Live At The Talk Of The Town* does not chart.

Aug [31] BBC TV airs a Cliff Richard special with guest Aretha Franklin.

Sept *I Ain't Got Time Anymore* reaches UK #21.

Oct Religious album *About That Man* does not chart.

[21] Richard & The Shadows begin a UK tour in Golders Green, London.

Dec *Tracks'N'Grooves* makes UK #37.

1971 Jan [2] BBC TV airs the first of a 13-week series "It's Cliff Richard", with resident guests Hank Marvin and Una Stubbs.

Feb *Sunny Honey Girl* reaches UK #19.

Apr Marvin-penned, ecological-themed *Silvery Rain* reaches UK #27.

May [17] Richard opens at the Sadlers Wells theater in London in pl "The Potting Shed". (The show had been scheduled to open a week earlier at Bromley, but the New Theatre was gutted by fire before the opening night.)

June [13] Richard & The Shadows take part in "A Night With The Stars", a tribute to recently deceased UK singer Dickie Valentine, at th London Palladium. (Richard joins Petula Clark in a duet of *I Want To Hold Your Hand*.)

July [5] Richard receives an Ivor Novello award for outstanding service to UK music, at the Rose D'Or Festival in Juan Les Pins, in which he performs with Olivia Newton-John.

Aug *Flying Machine* makes UK #37.

Oct [25] Richard & The Shadows start a season at the London Palladium.

Dec *Sing A Song Of Freedom* reaches UK #13.

1972 Jan BBC TV airs the first of 13-week series "It's Cliff Richard", with resident guests Olivia Newton-John and The Flirtations.

Mar *Jesus* makes UK #35.

Apr [14] Richard is voted the Top Male Pop Personality by **The Sun** newspaper for the third year running.

Sept *Living In Harmony* reaches UK #12.

[2] UK TV airs "The Case", a musical comedy-thriller starring Richar Newton-John and comedian Tim Brooke-Taylor.

Nov [17] Richard begins a UK tour, at Fairfield Hall, Croydon, London. He is joined on stage by Olivia Newton-John.

Dec *The Best Of Cliff, Volume Two* makes UK #49, while *A Brand Ne Song* becomes his first single not to make the UK Top 50.

1973 Jan [10] Richard appears on BBC TV's "Cilla Black Show", singing 6 entries chosen to represent UK in the Eurovision Song Contest. *Power To All Our Friends* is chosen as the UK entry by TV viewers.

Apr [7] *Power To All Our Friends* comes third in the Contest, before going on to hit UK #4.

May *Help It Along*, a 4-track EP containing the Eurovision entry songs, reaches UK #29.

Dec *Take Me High* reaches UK #27. It is the theme from Richard's movie of the same title, co-starring Debbie Watling and George Cole, filmed on location in Birmingham, W.Midlands.

1974 Jan Soundtrack album *Take Me High* makes UK #41.

Mar Richard is awarded the Silver Clef for outstanding services to the music industry by the Nordoff-Robbins Music Therapy charity.

Apr [3-11] Richard plays the London Palladium. He falls ill, and Rolf Harris deputizes for 3 performances.

June *(You Keep Me) Hangin' On* reaches UK #13. Meanwhile, live album *Help It Along* is released with all profits going to TEAR Fund (an international Christian aid organization), but does not chart.

July [3] Richard plays Bottom in a production of "A Midsummer Night's Dream" with past and present members of his old school at Cheshunt.

[9] The International Cliff Richard Movement meets for the first time at the United Reform Church in Crouch End, London.

Oct [27] Richard & The Shadows play together for the first time in 6 years in a charity concert at the London Palladium.

Nov *The 31st Of February Street*, produced by Dave Mackay, fails.

1975 Mar *It's Only Me You've Left Behind* does not chart.

June [5] Richard participates in a charity concert in Manchester's Free Trade Hall for the families of 2 policemen who died in the course of duty.

July [9] BBC TV airs "Jim'll Fix It", in which fan Helen Moon from Cromer, Norfolk, meets Richard.

Sept [6] BBC TV series "It's Cliff And Friends" debuts.

Oct *(There's A) Honky Tonk Angel (Who Will Take Me Back In)* does not chart, after Richard belatedly becomes aware of the implications of the song's lyric and refuses to promote it.

1976 Feb Bruce Welch of The Shadows takes over as Richard's producer, and *Miss You Nights* restores him to UK Singles chart after a 20-month absence, reaching #15. EMI Records releases *I'm Nearly Famous* and *The Best Of Cliff Richard* in USSR. He becomes the third UK artist to achieve such an honor.

May *Devil Woman* hits UK #9.

June Welch-produced *I'm Nearly Famous*, including the 2 recent Top 20 singles, hits UK #5.

Sept Also from the album, *I Can't Ask For Anything More Than You, Babe* reaches UK #17.

[16] Richard begins a USSR tour with a concert at the Hall Of The October Revolution, Leningrad, to a rapturous audience.

[25] Richard is invited to a reception at the British Embassy in Moscow, as *Devil Woman* becomes his first US Top 10, hitting #6 (higher than it attained in UK). It earns a US gold disk for a million-plus sales.

Oct *I'm Nearly Famous* makes US #76.

Dec *Hey, Mr. Dream Maker* makes UK #31, while *I Can't Ask For Anymore Than You, Babe* stalls at US #80. Richard travels to his birthplace, India, where he meets Mother Teresa.

[7-8] He appears in concert at the Kalamandir Auditorium, New Delhi, India.

1977 Mar *My Kinda Life* reaches UK #15.

Apr *Every Face Tells A Story* hits UK #8.

July *When Two Worlds Drift Apart* makes UK #46.

[2] *Don't Turn The Light Out* peaks at US #57.

Sept [5] Richard's book **Which One's Cliff?**, written with Bill Latham, is published.

Oct [18] The British Phonographic Institute (BPI) awards Richard the Britannia Award as Best British Male Solo Artist Of The Last 25 Years, to coincide with the Queen's Silver Jubilee celebrations.

[28] Richard receives the Gold Badge Award from the Songwriters' Guild of Great Britain.

Nov TV-advertised double compilation album **40 Golden Greats** tops the UK chart for a week – his first #1 album since **Summer Holiday**.

1978 Feb [27] Richard & The Shadows begin 2 weeks of reunion concerts at the London Palladium.

Mar Gospel album **Small Corners** makes UK #33, but *Yes! He Lives*, taken from it, does not chart.

June [29] Richard & The Shadows are awarded the Silver Clef Award for outstanding services to British music at the annual Nordoff-Robbins Music Therapy charity lunch.

Aug *Please Remember Me*, coupled with a new version of the former #1 hit *Please Don't Tease*, does not chart.

Oct *Green Light* reaches UK #25.

Nov Extracted *Can't Take The Hurt Anymore* misses UK Top 50.

1979 Feb [1] EMI Records organizes a special lunch at Claridge's, London, to celebrate its 21-year relationship with Richard.

[13] Richard & The Shadows receive a special award at the annual **Music Week** awards, celebrating 21 years as hitmaking artists.

Mar TV-promoted live album **Thank You Very Much**, featuring highlights of the previous year's Palladium concerts with The Shadows, hits UK #5.

Apr The title song from **Green Light** peaks at UK #57.

July [5] Richard is guest of honor at the Variety Club of Great Britain lunch at the Dorchester, London.

Aug [25] *We Don't Talk Anymore*, an Alan Tarney song produced by Welch, tops the UK chart for 4 weeks, his first UK #1 after more than 11 years. It will become his biggest-selling single worldwide, with total sales of over 5 million.

Sept *Rock'N'Roll Juvenile* hits UK #3. Norrie Paramor, Richard's original producer, dies.

[22] Richard participates in "Hosannah '79", an anti-racist festival in Birmingham.

Oct [4] Richard and Kate Bush perform with the London Symphony Orchestra at London's Royal Albert Hall, as part of the Hall's 75th birthday appeal.

Nov *Hot Shot*, from *Rock'N'Roll Juvenile*, makes UK #46.

Dec [2] Richard participates in a carol concert in Camberley, Surrey, in aid of the International Year Of The Child.

[16] Richard leads an estimated 30,000 people in carol singing outside Buckingham Palace, as part of the International Year Of The Child activities.

1980 Jan [1] Richard is included in the Queen's New Year Honours List, being awarded an OBE (Order of the British Empire).
We Don't Talk Anymore hits US #7, while the album of the same title (a revised version of *Rock'N'Roll Juvenile*) makes US #93.

Feb *Carrie*, from the album, hits UK #4.

Apr [16] Mother-of-2 Kim Kayne pays £1,400 for the privilege of having lunch with Richard as part of the fund raising activities of London's Capital Radio "Help A London Child" charity.

[19] *Carrie* makes US #34.

July [23] Richard receives his OBE from the Queen at Buckingham Palace.

Aug *Dreaming* hits UK #8.

Sept *I'm No Hero* hits UK #4.

Oct Richard plays 5 nights at London's Apollo theater.

Nov *Suddenly*, a duet with Olivia Newton-John from the soundtrack of film "Xanadu", reaches UK #15.

[22] *Dreaming* hits US #10.

1981 Jan [17] *Suddenly* makes US #20.

Feb *A Little In Love* reaches UK #15, while *I'm No Hero* makes US #80.

[24] Richard receives **The Daily Mirror** newspaper's readers' award as Outstanding Music Personality Of The Year at London's Café Royal.

Mar [3] Richard begins a 7-week 35-date North American tour, opening in Seattle, WA.

[14] *A Little In Love* reaches US #17.

[16] Richard appears on US TV show "Solid Gold".

[20] While he is away, "Cliff In London" airs on BBC TV. Richard's first home video, "The Young Ones", is released by Thorn EMI Video.

Apr [18] Richard ends his US tour in Los Angeles, CA.

May The "Cliff Richard Rock Special" takes place at London's Hammersmith Odeon – all audience members dress in 50s clothes.

June [6] *Give A Little Bit More* makes US #41.

July [11] Compilation album **Love Songs**, featuring familiar ballads, tops UK chart for 5 weeks.

Sept *Wired For Sound* hits UK #4.

Oct *Wired For Sound* hits UK #4 and US #132.

[24] *Wired For Sound* peaks at US #71.

Dec *Daddy's Home*, a revival of Shep & The Limelites' 1961 US smash recorded live in concert, hits UK #2, behind The Human League's *Don't You Want Me*.

1982 Feb [24] Richard wins Best British Male Artist at the first annual BRIT Awards at the Grosvenor House, London.

Mar [20] *Daddy's Home* reaches US #23.

Aug *The Only Way Out* hits UK #10.

Sept *Now You See Me ... Now You Don't*, including his previous and next singles, hits UK #4.

Oct *Where Do We Go From Here?* peaks at UK #60.

[23] *The Only Way Out* makes US #64.

Dec Seasonal *Little Town*, a new uptempo arrangement of Christmas carol "O Little Town Of Bethlehem", reaches UK #11.

1983 Mar Richard duets with Phil Everly on the Stuart Colman-produced rocker *She Means Nothing To Me*, which hits UK #9.

May A revival of Buddy Holly's *True Love Ways*, recorded live with the London Philharmonic Orchestra, hits UK #8. It is taken from live album *Dressed For The Occasion*, which hits UK #7.

June [4] *Drifting*, a ballad duetted with Christian singer Sheila Walsh, peaks at UK #64.

Sept Dance-oriented *Never Say Die (Give A Little Bit More)* reaches UK #15. This is the first Richard single to have an extended 12" dance version.

Oct *Silver*, marking 25 years as a recording artist, hits UK #7. It is briefly available as a boxed set which includes a second album, *Rock'N'Roll Silver*, with versions of several 50s oldies.

Nov [12] *Never Say Die (Give A Little Bit More)* peaks at US #73.

Dec *Please Don't Fall In Love*, taken from *Silver*, hits UK #7.

1984 Apr *Baby You're Dynamite*, a rocker from the album, reaches UK #27.

May [19] After heavy radio play of B-side ballad *Ocean Deep*, it charts at UK #72 in place of the A-side.

July *20 Original Greats*, with Richard & The Shadows, makes UK #43.

Sept *Two To The Power*, a duet with Janet Jackson on her label A&M, does not chart.

Nov *Shooting From The Heart* peaks at UK #51.

Dec *The Rock Connection* (including several rock tracks first heard on *Rock'N'Roll Silver*, plus *She Means Nothing To Me*), makes UK #43. (This compilation is released because his lapsed EMI contract will take time to renegotiate; meanwhile, he is not available for recording.)

1985 Feb *Heart User* makes UK #46.

Oct It is announced that Richard is to star in London's West End in 1986 in the first stage production of Dave Clark's musical "Time". The first recording of a song from the show is *She's So Beautiful*, produced by Stevie Wonder and featuring him on all instruments, with Richard handling the vocals. It reaches UK #17.

Dec *It's In Every One Of Us*, penned by US writer David Pomeranz several years earlier but from "Time", makes UK #45.

[19] Richard joins Chris De Burgh, Lulu, Sandie Shaw and others for Carol Aid, a carol-singing event at London's Heaven club to raise funds for the Band Aid appeal.

1986 Mar Richard returns to UK #1 with a revival of his own former chart-topper *Living Doll*, recorded with alternative TV comedy team The Young Ones, with all proceeds going to the Comic Relief charity. With Hank Marvin guesting on guitar, it tops the UK chart for 3 weeks and sells over 500,000 copies.

Apr [6] Richard opens at London's Dominion theater as lead in Dave Clark's musical "Time" (which also features an electronic/holographic "cameo" by Lord Olivier). (The show and star are well reviewed and initially draw capacity audiences; Richard will stay in it for a year, after which David Cassidy will take over.)

May *Born To Rock'N'Roll*, taken from "Time", does not chart, while the original all-star album of the show, featuring Richard and other guest performers including Freddie Mercury, Dionne Warwick and Julian Lennon, reaches UK #21.

Sept *All I Ask Of You*, from rival West End musical (Andrew Lloyd Webber's "The Phantom Of The Opera"), Richard's duet with the show's female lead Sarah Brightman, hits UK #3.

Dec *Slow Rivers*, a duet with Elton John, makes UK #44.

1987 July Richard re-signs to EMI and records a new album with writer/producer Alan Tarney. From it, *My Pretty One* hits UK #6.

Sept *Some People* hits UK #3, while parent album *Always Guaranteed* hits UK #5 – eventually outselling all previous Richard albums to turn platinum.

Oct A 50-date European tour is followed by 6 sell-out nights at the NEC, Birmingham, W.Midlands.

Nov *Remember Me*, also from *Always Guaranteed*, makes UK #35.

Dec He hosts a Pro-Celebrity charity tennis tournament.

1988 Feb *Two Hearts*, a final extract from the album, makes UK #34.

Sept The 30th anniversary of his first hit with *Move It* is noted by tributes in a variety of media, and a 30th anniversary 47-date UK tour begins at the end of Sept. ending mid-Dec. Every ticket sells out within 3 days, giving a combined tour audience of over 200,000.

Dec [10] Richard's 99th single, seasonal *Mistletoe And Wine*, tops the UK chart for 4 weeks, to become the biggest-selling UK single of 1988.

[24] *Private Collection*, a double compilation album rounding up a decade of hits from *We Don't Talk Anymore* to new *Mistletoe And Wine* (and including most of Richard's duets with other artists), tops the UK

chart and turns quadruple platinum, with sales of over a million.

1989 Feb Richard is honored for his Outstanding Contribution To British Music at eighth annual BRIT Awards at London's Royal Albert Hall.

Apr He receives a special Ivor Novello award for services to British music, an extraordinary award for a non-songwriter. Following the success of his greatest hits video package, "Private Collection", video "Guaranteed Live '88" is released.

May His 100th hit single, *The Best Of Me*, written by David Foster, Richard Marx and Jeremy Lubbock is released and hits UK #2, held off by Jason Donovan's *Sealed With A Kiss*.

June [16-17] "Cliff Richard – The Event" takes place before 2 capacity crowds of 72,000 at Wembley Stadium, London. Support acts are all chosen by Richard and include Aswad (with whom he duets *Share A Dream With Me*), Gerry & The Pacemakers, The Searchers, The Kalin Twins (with whom he toured in 1958) and The Shadows. Richard also performs a forthcoming Stock/Aitken/Waterman single *I Just Don't Have The Heart*.

Nov *Stronger* hits UK #7.

Dec Richard's duet with Van Morrison, *Whenever God Shines His Light*, reaches UK #20.

1990 Mar *Stronger Than That* reaches UK #14.

June [30] Richard appears with The Shadows at the Nordoff Robbins Music Therapy Silver Clef charity concert at Knebworth, Herts.

Sept *Silhouettes* hits UK #10.

Oct Richard's cover of Julie Gold standard, *From A Distance*, reaches UK #11.

Nov [1] Richard begins 38-date UK tour with 12 shows at the NEC, Birmingham, ending at the Wembley Arena, on Jan.3.

Dec [29] *Saviours Day* tops UK chart as *From A Distance ... The Event* hits UK #3.

LIONEL RICHIE

1967 Richie (b. Lionel Brockman Richie Jr., June 20, 1949, Tuskegee, AL), the son of a retired army captain and a teacher, having been raised in a religious environment and been singing in the Episcopal Church choir, is encouraged to seek a career in the ministry, but his Uncle Bertram buys him a saxophone and his grandmother encourages him to practise the piano. Now studying economics at predominantly black Tuskegee Institute (where he was born – his grandfather having worked on campus), he meets other ambitious musicians including Thomas McClary and William King to form The Commodores. He also meets his future wife, Brenda Harvey.

1974 Delayed by touring and disk success of The Commodores, he finally graduates in economics.

1978 Aug Richie has become the dominant creative and vocal force within The Commodores, and writes and sings lead on their first US #1, *Three Times A Lady*.

1979 Oct The Commodores' ballad *Still*, written and sung by Richie, hits US #1. Relying increasingly on his ballad-writing skills, The Commodores will enjoy 8 Richie-penned Top 10 hits prior to his departure.

1980 Nov [15] Richie's first composition outside The Commodores, *Lady*, sung by Kenny Rogers, reaches UK #12 and hits US #1 for 6 weeks. Richie also produces the song, which is recorded in only 4 hours, and he meets Rogers' manager, Ken Kragen.

1981 Mar Still with The Commodores, but increasingly in demand as a solo, Richie enters the studio with Rogers to produce *Share Your Love* (US #6), which spawns US #3 hit *I Don't Need You*.

Apr While working on Rogers' project and a new Commodores album, Richie is contacted by film producer, Franco Zeffirelli, who needs a song for his forthcoming Brooke Shields movie "Endless Love". He offers Diana Ross as a possible co-vocalist. Richie accepts and flies to Reno, NV, for a 3am recording session with Ms. Ross.

July He appears on his final Commodores studio album **In The Pocket**. From it, Richie-penned and performed ballad *Oh No* hits US #4 and makes UK #44.

Aug [15] Richie/Ross duet *Endless Love* hits US #1 for 9 weeks, and UK #7. (The song becomes the most successful Motown single and soundtrack single. Its achievements coincide with Richie signing a solo management deal with Kragen, although he is still officially with The Commodores.)

1982 Mar Richie begins work in Los Angeles, CA, on his debut solo album with Commodores' producer James Carmichael who enlists top session musicians including Greg Phillinganes, Paulinho DaCosta and Michael Boddicker. Joe Walsh, Kenny Rogers and even tennis star Jimmy Connors also guest. On many tracks Richie plays on the same studio piano used by Carole King on her album *Tapestry*.

[29] Richie performs *Endless Love* at the annual Academy Awards ceremony in Los Angeles.

Aug With his debut album completed, Richie and The Commodores, still theoretically together, are shocked by the death of their manager Benny Ashburn at age 54.

Oct Richie formally announces his split from the band. First solo single is *Truly*, a ballad from Motown-issued *Lionel Richie*. The album will hit US #3 and UK #9 and is dedicated to Ashburn.

Nov *Truly* hits US #1 and UK #6.

1983 Feb *You Are* makes UK #43 as Richie appears on the "Motown 25th Anniversary" TV celebration.

Mar *You Are* hits US #4 as Richie, with 17 previous nominations for a Grammy, finally wins one for *Truly*. Album sales now exceed 3 million.

May Ballad *My Love* hits US #5 and makes UK #70. Richie is already recording a follow-up album and planning a first solo tour.

Sept He begins a 48-date world tour, including 3 weeks in the Far East, opening at Lake Tahoe, NV. Supported by The Pointer Sisters, his backing band includes Prince percussionist Sheila E. For *Endless Love*, Richie uses a life-like Diana Ross laser projection.

Oct [29] The Mayor of Tuskegee, AL proclaims it "Lionel Richie Day".

Nov [12] Uptempo dance cut *All Night Long (All Night)* hits US #1 during a 5-month chart stay (4 weeks at #1) and UK #2. It outsells *Endless Love* to become Motown's biggest single worldwide to date and is helped by promo video produced by ex-Monkee Mike Nesmith. *Can't Slow Down* is released, set to hit both US and UK #1, and beginning chart stays of nearly 3 years. It features co-written tracks with Cynthia Weil and David Foster, and includes session help from Toto's Steve Lukather and Jeff Porcaro.

[22] Los Angeles' Mayor Bradley pronounces it "Lionel Richie Day".

Dec Richie and his wife move house from Kenny Rogers' estate to a Bel Air, Los Angeles, mansion. During tour dates, Richie's plane crashlands in Phoenix, AZ, but no one is hurt.

1984 Jan *Running With The Night*, spurred by Bob Giraldi-directed video, hits US #7 and UK #9.

Feb Richie hosts US TV American Music Awards, winning 2 himself.

Mar Pepsi-Cola announces an $8.5 million sponsorship deal with Richie, for which he will record a series of song-associated TV commercials; they will fund 2 tours in 2 years.

Apr *Hello* hits UK #1 (his first solo UK chart-topper).

May [12] With a second major tour underway (with opening act Tina Turner), *Hello* hits US #1. (Originally slated for inclusion on the debut album, the typical Richie ballad is supported by emotive video using the dramatic effect of a blind girl, directed by Giraldi. Richie plays the part of Mr. Reynolds, a teacher.)

Aug [4] Album extract *Stuck On You* hits US #3 and UK #12.

[12] Richie is asked by Los Angeles Olympic Games producer David Wolper to perform the final song at the closing ceremony. In a larger than life extravaganza, Richie performs *All Night Long*, featuring an occasion-written extra verse. Helped by 200 dancers, Richie is seen by an estimated worldwide TV audience of 2.6 billion.

Nov From *Can't Slow Down*, *Penny Lover*, co-written with his wife Brenda, hits US #8 and UK #18.

Dec Diana Ross hits US #10 with Richie-written and produced *Missing You*, a tribute to the late Marvin Gaye.

1985 Jan Encouraged by Kragen, Richie is asked by Quincy Jones to co-write a song with Michael Jackson for USA For Africa supergroup effort to raise money for famine relief. Prepared over a 3-day period, they take only 2 hours to write *We Are The World* – a worldwide #1 which also features Richie's vocal contributions.

Mar Richie receives Album Of The Year for *Can't Slow Down*, now selling over 10 million copies worldwide, at the Grammy awards.

Dec [21] Hitting UK #8, *Say You Say Me* hits US #1 for Christmas period. Although not written specifically for the movie, it features as the theme to Gregory Hines/Mikhail Baryshnikov film "White Nights". Motown does not allow the song to appear on the Atlantic movie soundtrack album. The US chart-topper sets a new record as Richie becomes the only songwriter in history to achieve 9 #1s in 9 consecutive years.

1986 Jan Richie returns to the studio to cut his long-awaited third album.

Mar [24] *Say You, Say Me* wins an Oscar for Best Original Song at the Academy Awards ceremony.

May Richie is named ASCAP's Writer Of The Year.

Aug *Dancing On The Ceiling* is released, with its title cut already heading to hit UK #7. Repeating his proven formula, Richie adds the talents of Eric Clapton, Alabama and others. "Dancing On The Ceiling"

video, featuring gravity-defying Richie dancing round all 4 sides of a room, is directed by Stanley Donen.

Sept [13] *Dancing On The Ceiling* hits US #2 behind Berlin's *You Take My Breath Away*.

[27] ***Dancing On The Ceiling*** tops US chart.

Nov [29] *Love Will Conquer All* hits US #9.

Love Will Conquer All makes UK #45.

Dec Ballad *Ballerina Girl* reaches UK #17.

1987 Jan [26] Richie wins Favorite Male Vocalist (Pop), Favorite Male Vocalist (R&B) and Favorite Pop Video Single categories at the 14th annual American Music Awards.

Feb Richie ends a 3-month US tour, seen by over 1 million people.

[14] Unusual for the 80s, B-side of *Ballerina Girl*, country-flavored *Deep River Woman* peaks at US #71 as it is flipped by radio. The song features Alabama on backing vocals. It also hits #10 on US Country chart.

[21] *Ballerina Girl* hits US #7.

May [16] Final extract from *Ceiling* project, *Sela* reaches US #20 and UK #43. Richie's world tour hits UK with standing-room-only dates in major cities.

1988 June Richie's wife Brenda is arrested for "investigation of corporal injury to a spouse, resisting arrest, trespassing, vandalism, battery and disturbing the peace". Ms. Richie is apparently upset when she discovers her husband with model-actress Diane Alexander in the latter's apartment.

1989 May [11] Richie performs at the Songwriters' Hall Of Fame 20th Anniversary, before retreating once again to work on new album.

THE RIGHTEOUS BROTHERS

Bill Medley (vocals)
Bobby Hatfield (vocals)

1962 Medley (b. Sept.19, 1940, Santa Ana, CA), having been a member of The Paramours and recorded *There She Goes* on Moonglow, meets Hatfield (b. Aug.10, 1940, Beaver Dam, WI), who had been with The Variations and released a solo, *Hot Tamales*, also on Moonglow, and they form a duo. They debut at a high school prom in Anaheim, CA. (They are dubbed The Righteous Brothers by black marines who see them perform at the Black Derby in Santa Ana – the name sticks.)

1963 June Moonglow releases *Little Latin Lupe Lu*, a Medley-penned R&B/dance number, which makes US #49, after being used as an ad by Los Angeles, CA, radio station K-RLA. 2 further Moonglow singles, *Koko Joe* and *My Babe* are released, the latter reaching US #75.

1964 Phil Spector expresses an interest in producing them, after seeing their performance on a package bill at the Cow Palace, San Francisco, CA, but they are still contracted to Moonglow. Spector makes a deal whereby they appear on his own Philles label in US and London in UK while other territories receive their masters through Moonglow. They become Philles' first white act. Spector commissions husband and wife team Barry Mann and Cynthia Weil to write a song for the brothers.

Aug [19] The Righteous Brothers support The Beatles as they begin their US tour at the Cow Palace, San Francisco.

Sept [16] They are featured with real-life brothers, Don and Phil Everly, and Sam Cooke on the premiere of ABC TV show "Shindig!"

Dec Their first Philles single, *You've Lost That Lovin' Feelin'*, will top both US and UK charts. (Earning the description "classic" over a period of time, the pop record will later be a hit in US or UK for Dionne Warwick, Daryl Hall & John Oates and actor Telly Savalas. Many critics feel it is the definitive Spector "Wall Of Sound" disk.)

1965 Jan *You've Lost That Lovin' Feelin'* is featured on BBC TV's "Juke Box Jury". The 4 panelists dismiss it, one questioning whether it has been played at the right speed, and vote it a "miss". A UK cover by Cilla Black charts the following week, but producer Andrew Loog Oldham places a self-paid ad in the UK music press extolling the virtues of the original over the cover. It works. The Righteous Brothers leap-frog Black's version and hit UK #1, halting Black's cover at #2.

[11] The duo arrives in UK for a promotional visit, performing on TV shows "Scene At 6.30", "Ready Steady Go!" and "Discs A Go-Go". *You've Lost That Lovin' Feelin'* hits US #4. Moonglow releases their early material on *Right Now!*, which reaches US #11, and extracted *Bring Your Love To Me*, which reaches US #83. (Moonglow follows with albums *Some Blue-Eyed Soul* (US #14) and *This Is New!* (US #39).)

Feb [13] Medley is operated on for an injured spleen at the Martin Luther hospital in Anaheim, CA.

May The duo's legitimate follow up to *Lovin' Feelin'*, *Just Once In My Life*, penned by husband and wife team Gerry Goffin and Carole King, hits US #9. (2 further Moonglow singles chart – *You Can Have Her* (US

#67) and *Justine* from the film "A Swingin' Summer" (US #85).)
June *Just Once In My Life* hits US #9.
Aug Another Goffin/King song, *Hung On You*, is the follow-up and makes US #47, but DJs prefer its B-side, the 50s smash *Unchained Melody*, which hits US #4 and UK #14.
Dec MGM Records offers $1 million for The Righteous Brothers' contract. Spector, now interested in Ike & Tina Turner, sells.

1966 Jan Spector chooses another oldie for follow-up: *Ebb Tide* hits US #5, but makes only UK #48. *Back To Back* reaches US #16. (Moonglow has its final success with the duo, as *Georgia On My Mind* peaks at US #62.)
Apr MGM debut, on subsidiary Verve, is *(You're My) Soul And Inspiration*, which Mann and Weil had intended as a follow-up to *You've Lost That Lovin' Feelin'*. It hits US #1 and makes UK #15. Medley's production, to some, differs little from Spector's work. *Soul And Inspiration* hits US #7.
June Moonglow releases *The Best Of The Righteous Brothers*, compiled from 4 albums recorded 1962-63. It makes US #130.
July *He* reaches US #18. B-side *He Will Break Your Heart* makes US #91.
[5] Medley has an operation to remove nodes from his vocal chords in Los Angeles hospital.
Sept *Go Ahead And Cry* reaches US #30. *Go Ahead And Cry* climbs to US #32.
Nov *White Cliffs Of Dover*, a reissue of a Philles album track, makes UK #21. *On This Side Of Goodbye* reaches US #47. *Soul And Inspiration* is certified gold.
Dec *Island In The Sun* climbs to UK #36.

1967 Apr *Sayin' Somethin'* stalls at US #155.
May *Melancholy Music Man* reaches US #43.
June *Stranded In The Middle Of No Place*, their last single for Verve, makes only US #72.
Oct *Greatest Hits* reaches US #21, while *Souled Out* spends 2 weeks at US #198.
Nov Medley leaves to pursue a solo career (on MGM/Verve until 1969, but will have no notable success). Hatfield re-forms the duo with Jimmy Walker, ex-Knickerbockers. For legal reasons, new duo is not allowed to use the name The Righteous Brothers on record for 1 year.

1968 Verve issues 2 albums by The Righteous Brothers featuring unreleased titles and singles. Hatfield records solo singles while he waits out the legal delay. Medley releases debut album *100%* on MGM, which makes US #188, having already had 3 minor solo hits with *I Can't Make It Alone* (US #95), *Brown Eyed Woman* (US #43) and *Peace Brother Peace* (US #48).
Dec Live album *One For The Road* reaches US #187.

1969 Jan *You've Lost That Lovin' Feelin'* is reissued in UK and hits US #10. Medley releases 2 further albums. Hatfield and Walker, now recording as The Righteous Brothers, release *Re-Birth*.
Mar Hatfield's solo *Nothing Is Too Good For You* makes US #84.
Apr *Greatest Hits, Vol.2* reaches US #126. Medley's solo album *Soft And Soulful* peaks at US #152.

1971 Medley releases the Herb Alpert-produced, Michel Colombier-arranged *A Song For You* for A&M, which despite impressive title track, *The Long And Winding Road* and a new version of *You've Lost That Lovin' Feelin'*, fails to chart.

1974 July With the production team of Lambert and Potter, Medley and Hatfield re-form to hit US #3 with Alan O'Day-penned *Rock'N'Roll Heaven* on Capitol's Haven subsidiary. The song is a tribute to dead rock'n'roll stars.
Aug *Give It To The People* reaches US #27.
Sept Extracted title track, *Give It To The People*, reaches US #20.
Dec *Dream On* peaks at US #32.

1975 Feb [23] The Righteous Brothers make a sole UK appearance at the New Victoria theater, London.

1977 Nov *You've Lost That Lovin' Feelin'*, reissued again, makes UK #42.

1981 Medley resumes his solo recording career after a 5-year absence (following the murder of his wife Karen in 1976) and records *Sweet Thunder* in Berry Hill, TN, with producers Michael Lloyd, Brent Maher and Randy Goodrum. He signs with top management team Kragen & Company. *Don't Know Much* makes US #88. (The song will win Linda Ronstadt & Aaron Neville a Grammy in 1990.)

1982 Medley releases *Right Here And Now*, produced by Richard Perry on his Planet label. The title track makes US #58. He opens Medleys club in Los Angeles. He and Hatfield re-form again for a US TV special celebrating the 30th anniversary of "American Bandstand". They sing an updated version of *Rock'N'Roll Heaven*.

1986 *You've Lost That Lovin' Feelin'* reaches a new audience through its exposure in Tom Cruise film "Top Gun". It is B-side of the main hit,

Berlin's *Take My Breath Away*.

1987 Sept *(I've Had) The Time Of My Life* hits UK #6.
Nov [28] Medley duets with Jennifer Warnes on *(I've Had) The Time O[f] My Life*. Taken from the **Dirty Dancing** film soundtrack, it tops US chart as the film's popularity spreads. The album is the most successful soundtrack album since **Saturday Night Fever**, selling more than 14 million copies worldwide.

1988 Mar [2] Medley wins Best Pop Performance By A Duo Or Group Wit[h] Vocal with Jennifer Warnes for *(I've Had) The Time Of My Life* at the 30th annual Grammy awards.
Aug Medley records *He Ain't Heavy He's My Brother* for the soundtrac[k] to Sylvester Stallone's "Rambo III". (He has already recorded a duet with Gladys Knight for a previous Stallone movie "Cobra".) It reaches UK #25, but The Hollies' reissue tops UK chart.

1990 Jan [25] Medley makes the first of 2 appearances, as himself, on NBC TV's "Cheers".
Oct [20] *Unchained Melody*, spurred by its inclusion in hit movie "Ghost", reaches US #13, as a different and newly recorded Medley-produced version on Curb also enters Top 30, becoming the first time that 2 versions of the same song by the same artist have charted since Bobbie Gentry's *Ode To Billie Joe* in 1967. **The Righteous Brothers Greatest Hits** makes US #31.
[27] Rhino compilation **Anthology (1962-1974)** peaks at US #178.
Nov [3] As "Ghost" becomes the biggest-grossing movie of the year i[n] UK, *Unchained Melody* tops UK chart for 4 weeks, as the re-recorded Curb version peaks at US #19.
[24] **The Best Of The Righteous Brothers**, on Curb, climbs to US #161.
Dec [1] **The Very Best Of The Righteous Brothers** reaches UK #11.
[22] *You've Lost That Lovin' Feelin'* hits UK #3.

1991 Jan [26] Medley's duet with Jennifer Warnes of *(I've Had) The Time Of[?] My Life* hits UK #8, due to the movie's recent UK TV exposure.
[31] Hatfield also makes an appearance on "Cheers" singing *Unchaine[d] Melody*, much to the chagrin of Frazier Crane.
Feb [28] 4-date UK tour opens in Manchester. The tour will end Mar.[?] at B.I.C., Bournemouth, Dorset.

JOHNNY RIVERS

1960 Rivers (b. John Ramistella, Nov.7, 1942, New York, NY), having grow[n] up in Baton Rouge, LA, where he formed his first rock'n'roll groups i[n] high school, then commuted in his later teens between New York and Nashville, TN, trying to gain an entry into the music business, has me[t] DJ Alan Freed, who has been impressed by his songs and helped him get a one-off deal with Gone Records, also suggesting the new name Rivers from the river bayou country of his upbringing. After playing i[n] Las Vegas, NV, and Lake Tahoe, NV, with Louie Prima's band, he moves to Los Angeles, CA, where he has had *I'll Make Believe* recorded by Ricky Nelson in 1958.

1961 A revival of *Blue Skies* for Chancellor label gains some airplay, but fails to chart.

1963 He gets a live residency at Los Angeles' Gazzari's club, which first gains him notice as a performer.

1964 Rivers moves to newly-opened Whiskey A Go-Go club, where his live rock oldie sets intersperse record sessions, all the music being aimed primarily at the dancefloor. He becomes a success with regular patron[s] and the buzz reaches Imperial Records, which signs him to a recording contract and tapes his live stage act.
June Live debut album *Johnny Rivers At The Whiskey A Go Go* reaches US #12.
July Extracted revival of Chuck Berry's *Memphis* (also a major hit in instrumental form for Lonnie Mack a year previously) hits US #2, behind The Four Seasons' *Rag Doll*.
Sept Another Berry live revival, *Maybelline*, reaches US #12.
Oct *Here We A Go Go Again!*, another set of mainly oldies from his club act, makes US #38.
Nov [12] Rivers arrives in London for short promo visit.
Dec Rivers' revival of Harold Dorman's R&B oldie *Mountain Of Love* hits US #9.

1965 Feb *Johnny Rivers In Action!* peaks at US #42.
Mar *Midnight Special*, a rocked-up version of Paul Evans' 1960 US hit, reaches US #20 (and in 1973 will be used as the theme to US NBC TV's music series of the same title), while B-side revival of Sam Cooke's *Cupid* peaks at US #76.
May Rivers debuts at New York's Copacabana nightclub.
June *Meanwhile Back At The Whiskey A Go Go* reaches US #21.
July *Seventh Son* is his third US Top 10 hit, at US #7.

Sept *Johnny Rivers Rocks The Folk* makes US #91.

Nov Taken from the folk/rock album, a revival of The Kingston Trio's *Where Have All The Flowers Gone?* makes US #26.

1966 Jan *Under Your Spell Again* reaches US #35.

Apr Rivers records *Secret Agent Man*, the theme from Patrick McGoohan TV spy series "Secret Agent" (a re-titling of UK series "Danger Man"), which hits US #3. . . . *And I Know You Wanna Dance* peaks at US #52.

July A revival of *(I Washed My Hands In) Muddy Water* (cut by Charlie Rich as B-side to his 1965 hit *Mohair Sam*) makes US #19.

Sept *Johnny Rivers' Golden Hits*, a compilation of his hit singles to date, reaches US #29.

Nov *Poor Side Of Town*, an original ballad written by Rivers and producer Lou Adler, is his all-time biggest-selling single, topping the US chart for a week, and selling over a million.

Dec *Changes*, featuring *Poor Side Of Town* and other material with a similar, more contemporary sound, makes US #33. Rivers sets up his own music publishing company Rivers Music (signing Jim Webb, among others), and while in renegotiation of his recording contract with Imperial, launches his own Liberty/Imperial-distributed label, Soul City Records (which will be a production base for Rivers' scouting for new talent, including The 5th Dimension in 1967). He puts together a regular studio band of acclaimed sessioneers Hal Blaine (drums), Joe Osborn (bass – an old friend from Baton Rouge) and Larry Knechtel (keyboards).

1967 Jan Rivers participates in San Remo Song Festival.

Mar Passing over Webb's song *By The Time I Get To Phoenix* as a single (which he suggests instead for Glen Campbell), Rivers cuts a lush revival of The Four Tops' *Baby I Need Your Lovin'*, and hits US #3.

June *Rewind* reaches US #14.

[16] Rivers is a co-organizer, with Lou Adler and The Mamas And The Papas, of the Monterey International Pop Festival, CA.

July A second Motown revival, The Miracles' *The Tracks Of My Tears*, hits US #10.

1968 Jan *Summer Rain*, with hints of flower power in arrangement and lyric (which refers to The Beatles' *Sergeant Pepper's Lonely Hearts Club Band*), reaches US #14.

Feb [29] He wins a Grammy award as co-producer of The 5th Dimension's *Up, Up And Away*, which is named Record Of The Year For 1967.

May *Look To Your Soul* makes US #49.

June *Realization* hits US #5.

Dec *Right Relations*, with a socially-conscious lyric, peaks at US #61.

1969 Rivers retires almost completely from live concert appearances to spend more time at his retreat in Carmel, CA.

Mar A cover of Joe South's *These Are Not My People* makes US #55.

June *A Touch Of Gold* peaks at US #26.

Aug *Muddy River* reaches US #41.

Nov *One Woman*, an excursion into soul music, stalls at US #89. Rivers sells Soul City Records for $2 million. (Now a rare performer, he will spend much time traveling in India and Japan, investigating disciplines such as yoga, transcendental meditation and vegetarianism.)

1970 June A cover of Van Morrison's *Into The Mystic* makes US #51.

Aug *Slim Slo Slider*, featuring songs by Gram Parsons, Van Morrison and John Fogerty, reaches US #100.

Sept *Fire And Rain*, a cover of James Taylor's ballad, stalls at US #94.

1971 May A revival of Frankie Ford's *Sea Cruise*, back in his original straightforward rock style, makes US #84. This is Rivers' first release on United Artists, which has absorbed Imperial and Liberty Records.

Sept *Think His Name*, an inspirational number backed by The Guru Ram Das Ashram Singers, peaks at US #65, while *Home Grown* makes US #148.

Dec He sells his Rivers Music publishing house, with a stock of valuable copyrights, for over $1 million.

1972 Nov *L.A. Reggae*, on which he is backed by members of The Crickets and other guests, and which showcases mainly rock and R&B covers, peaks at US #78.

1973 Jan From the album, a revival of Huey "Piano" Smith's *Rockin' Pneumonia And The Boogie Woogie Flu* hits US #6, and sells over a million to earn a gold disk.

May In similar style, a revival of Carl Perkins' *Blue Suede Shoes* makes US #38 (though the album of the same title, a mixture of new and old songs, fails to chart).

1975 Aug Rivers leaves UA (disagreements with the label over contracts disincline him from re-signing), to record on a one-off (and unsuccessful) basis for Atlantic, and then to sign to Epic Records for

Help Me Rhonda (a revival of The Beach Boys' 1965 US #1, on which Brian Wilson assists with back-up vocals). It reaches US #22 and *New Lovers And Old Friends* makes US #147.

1977 Feb *Ashes And Sand*, issued on his own revived Soul City label (to which he has re-acquired the title rights), stalls at US #96.

[4] Rivers takes part in the all-star celebrity band (with Chuck Berry, Gregg Allman and others) on the 25th anniversary special of Dick Clark's "American Bandstand" on US ABC TV.

Oct A cover of Jack Tempchin & The Funky Kings' *Swayin' To The Music (Slow Dancin')*, recorded for Big Tree label, hits US #10, and is his final million-selling single.

1978 Jan *Outside Help* on Big Tree reaches US #142.

Feb Rivers' final US chart entry is a revival of a Major Lance hit, *Curious Mind (Um, Um, Um, Um, Um, Um)*, which makes US #41. (Following this, he will take little active part in music making, except for a religious album in the mid-80s, content in retirement against a background of having sold some 30 million records over 15 years – though he leaves a whole generation of successful songwriters and acts for whom he was original sponsor and champion.)

SMOKEY ROBINSON

1954 Robinson (b. William Robinson, Feb.19, 1940, Detroit, MI) puts together The Matadors vocal group from friends at Northern high school: Ronnie White (b. Apr. 5, 1939, Detroit), Bobby Rogers (b. Feb.19, 1940, Detroit) and Pete Moore (b. Nov.19, 1939, Detroit), plus guitarist Marv Tarplin.

1957 Having become established on the Detroit club scene, changing their name to The Miracles when Rogers' sister Claudette (b. 1942) joins, replacing another brother, Emerson, who goes into the US Army (she will marry Robinson in 1963), they audition for Jackie Wilson's manager (who turns them down). They are heard by Berry Gordy Jr., who has just written *Reet Petite* for Wilson, but is still working at Ford Motors while trying to break into the music business full-time. He sees potential in the young group and helps it secure a deal with End Records.

1958 Feb [19] End releases The Miracles' first single, *Got A Job*, a Robinson/Gordy/Tyrone Carlo-penned "answer" to The Silhouettes' hit *Get A Job*.

1959 Oct Gordy, now closely involved with the group, leases Robinson-penned ballad *Bad Girl* to Chess Records. It is The Miracles' US pop chart debut, at #93.

Nov [7] Robinson marries Claudette. (They will have 2 children, Berry and Tamla.)

1960 Using royalties from work with Jackie Wilson and Marv Johnson, and a loan of $800, Gordy forms his own company, Motown Records, and sets up the Tamla label to feature The Miracles. First Tamla release is The Miracles' dance tune *Way Over There*, which does not chart.

1961 Feb *Shop Around*, an early model of the ultra-commercial dance sound (and later much-covered), hits US #2, and is the group's and Motown's first million-seller, as The Miracles become the first Motown act to appear on ABC TV's "American Bandstand".

Apr Follow-up *Ain't It Baby* makes US #49.

Aug *Mighty Good Lovin'* peaks at US #51.

Nov *Everybody Gotta Pay Some Dues* peaks at US #52 (and like all immediate post-*Shop Around* releases, is a bigger hit on local R&B charts). Robinson is by now becoming an increasingly important part of the growing Motown operation, both arranging and writing for young artists on the label, and Gordy makes him company vice-president.

1962 Feb *What's So Good About Goodbye* makes US #35.

June *I'll Try Something New* reaches US #39.

Sept A reissue of *Way Over There* this time peaks at US #94.

1963 Feb *You've Really Got A Hold On Me* is the group's second US Top 10 hit, at #8. (It will be covered by The Beatles on their second album and become a staple of UK beat groups' repertoires.)

May *A Love She Can Count On* makes US #31.

June *The Fabulous Miracles* peaks at US #118.

Sept Robinson-penned dance number *Mickey's Monkey* is The Miracles' second US Top 10 of the year, hitting #8. (Reportedly, it is also the first disk Michael Jackson buys.)

Oct Live album *The Miracles On Stage* reaches US #139.

1964 Jan *I Gotta Dance To Keep From Crying* makes US #35, while *Doin' Mickey's Monkey* climbs to US #113. Claudette Robinson retires from performance with the group, to look after home and family (though will later guest with it on occasion). She will continue to sing on records however.

Apr Now adept at writing songs for other Motown acts, Robinson pens The Temptations' first major hit, *The Way You Do The Things You Do*, which reaches US #11. At the same time, The Miracles' *(You Can't Let The Boy Overpower) The Man In You* peaks at US #59.

May Robinson has his first #1 as a writer, when Mary Wells' version of his and Ronnie White's *My Guy* tops US chart.

Aug *I Like It Like That* reaches US #27.

Oct *That's What Love Is Made Of* makes US #35.

Dec [1] The Miracles arrive in UK for short promotional tour, which will include appearances on TV shows "Ready Steady Go!", "Thank Your Lucky Stars" and BBC radio's "Saturday Club".

1965 Jan *Come On Do The Jerk* reaches US #50.

Mar Another Temptations' release of Robinson/White song, *My Girl*, tops US chart and is a million-seller. (On various songs, both for The Miracles and other acts, Robinson collaborates with group members: Moore, White or Tarplin. Like all label's chief writers, he also oversees production and arrangement, using the Hitsville USA house band.)

[20] Group begins a 21-date twice-nightly UK tour at Finsbury Park Astoria, London, to launch Tamla Motown's own identity in UK, with labelmates The Supremes, Martha & The Vandellas, Stevie Wonder, The Temptations and special guests Georgie Fame & The Blue Flames. The tour will end Apr.12 at the Guildhall, Portsmouth, Hants.

Apr [17] Tamla Motown spectacular airs on UK TV.

May Ballad *Ooh Baby Baby* reaches US #16.

June Double compilation album *Greatest Hits From The Beginning* is the group's first big album seller, reaching US #21.

Sept Another Robinson ballad, *The Tracks Of My Tears*, reaches US #16 (and will later be much covered).

Nov *My Girl Has Gone* makes US #14.

1966 Feb A return to the dance idiom, *Going To A Go-Go* reaches US #11 and is the group's UK chart debut, making #44. The album of the same title hits US #8. Robinson begins to produce Marvin Gaye, renewing Gaye's US Top 10 status with *Ain't That Peculiar*.

July Another dance number, *Whole Lot Of Shakin' In My Heart (Since I Met You)* makes US #46.

Dec *(Come Round Here) I'm The One You Need* makes US #17, UK #45.

1967 Jan *Away We A Go-Go* makes US #41.

[13] The Miracles play at the re-opening of the Whisky A Go-Go in Hollywood, CA.

Mar [28] They play in Murray The K's week-long Easter show "Music In The 5th Dimension" at the Manhattan RKO theater, New York.

Apr Robinson's status within the group is recognized by Motown when, with *The Love I Saw In You Was Just A Mirage* (which makes US #20), the billing becomes Smokey Robinson & The Miracles.

July *More Love* (later revived by Kim Carnes) reaches US #23.

Nov *Make It Happen* makes US #28.

Dec *I Second That Emotion*, later also much covered, is the group's first US Top 10 hit in 4 years, at #4.

1968 Jan *I Second That Emotion* is their first Top 30 UK hit, reaching #27.

Apr *If You Can Want* reaches US #11 and UK #50. (Robinson's golden songwriting period of the 60s is now drawing to a close, as his Motown corporate duties draw him away from composition. The group's later albums will contain many songs from outside sources.)

July *Yester Love* makes US #31.

Sept *Special Occasion* reaches US #26.

Nov *Special Occasion* makes US #42.

1969 Mar *Baby, Baby Don't Cry* hits US #8, while *Live!* makes US #71.

June *The Tracks Of My Tears*, is reissued not a hit first time in UK, and becomes the group's biggest UK success to date, hitting #9.

July *Doggone Right* makes US #33 while the group's rush-released version of Dion hit *Abraham, Martin And John*, originally an album track, also makes US #33 (in competition with a simultaneous US #35 version by black comedienne Moms Mabley).

Sept *Time Out For Smokey Robinson And The Miracles* makes US #25.

Oct *Here I Go Again*, B-side of *Doggone Right*, reaches US #37.

1970 Jan *Point It Out* also makes US #37, while *Four In Blue* reaches US #78.

Feb Group records "This Is Tom Jones" TV special in London.

June *Who's Gonna Take The Blame* makes US #46, while *What Love Has Joined Together* climbs to US #97.

Sept *The Tears Of A Clown*, originally recorded in 1967 and released on *Make It Happen*, is released in UK and tops chart for a week, selling almost 900,000 copies.

Nov *A Pocketful Of Miracles* peaks at US #56.

Dec Motown releases *The Tears Of A Clown* in US on the strength of its UK success. It tops US chart for 2 weeks (their first US #1) and sells well over a million, becoming the group's most successful single ever.

1971 Feb Another former UK non-hit, *(Come 'Round Here) I'm The One You Need*, is reissued as follow-up to *The Tears Of A Clown*, making UK #13.

May New recording *I Don't Blame You At All* charts in US at #18 and UK at #11.

July Dance song *Crazy About The La La La* peaks at US #56.

Oct *One Dozen Roses* climbs to US #92.

1972 Jan *Satisfaction* makes US #49.

July [16] At the end of a 6-month farewell US tour, Robinson, who has wanted to leave the group to pursue his own projects since 1970, makes his last appearance with The Miracles in Washington, DC, prior to launching his solo career via Motown. (William Griffin replaces him.)

Aug *We've Come Too Far To End It Now* makes US #46, while *Flying High Together* reaches US #46.

1973 Jan *I Can't Stand To See You Cry*, the last single released by Robinson with The Miracles, makes US #45. Double compilation album *1957-1972* reaches US #75.

Sept The Miracles' *Don't Let It End ('Til You Let It Begin)* peaks at US #56 (the first of only 4 hit singles the group will have without Robinson). Robinson's first solo album *Smokey* peaks at US #70 (critics feel it lacks the assurance of his best work with The Miracles). Extracted *Sweet Harmony* makes US #48.

1974 Feb *Baby Come Close* is his first solo Top 30 hit, reaching US #27, while *Just My Soul Responding* is released as a UK single and makes #35.

June *Pure Smokey*, an overtly romantic set, reaches US #99, while extracted *It's Her Turn To Live* climbs to US #82.

Oct The Miracles' *Do It Baby* makes US #13.

Nov *Virgin Man* peaks at US #56.

1975 Jan The Miracles' *Don't Cha Love It* peaks at US #78, while Robinson's *I Am I Am* climbs to US #56.

June *Baby That's Backatcha* reaches US #26 and tops R&B chart for a week, as parent album *A Quiet Storm* makes US #36.

Nov Also from the album, *The Agony And The Ecstasy* makes US #36.

1976 Feb The title song from *A Quiet Storm* peaks at US #61.

Mar *Love Machine* by The Miracles tops US chart, selling over a million, and hits UK #3 (but is the group's final hit).

Apr *Smokey's Family Robinson* makes US #57.

[4] Robinson begins 14-date UK tour at the Locarno, Portsmouth, Hants. It will end Apr.18 at the Top Rank Suite, Reading, Berks.

July *Open* peaks at US #81.

Oct A reissue of *The Tears Of A Clown* makes UK #34.

1977 Apr *Deep In My Soul* peaks at US #47, while extracted *There Will Come A Day (I'm Gonna Happen To You)* makes US #42.

Aug Robinson is executive producer of, and writes and produces the music for, movie "Big Time".

1978 May *Love Breeze* makes US #75.

July *Daylight And Darkness* peaks at US #75.

1979 Feb Double live album *Smokin'* makes US #165, while Robinson teams with Diana Ross, Marvin Gaye and Stevie Wonder on *Pops We Love You*, a tribute for Berry Gordy's father's 90th birthday. It peaks at US #59 and UK #66.

Oct *Where There's Smoke* reaches US #17.

1980 Feb Extracted *Cruisin'* is Robinson's first Top 10 solo hit, at US #4.

May *Warm Thoughts* reaches US #14 while, taken from it, *Let Me Be The Clock* makes US #31.

1981 May *Being With You*, produced by George Tobin (to whom Robinson has originally submitted it for Kim Carnes after she revived *More Love* successfully) hits US #2 and earns a gold disk for million-plus sales. The album of the same title hits US #10 and also earns a gold disk.

June *Being With You* tops UK chart for 2 weeks, while the album makes UK #17 – his only UK chart album.

July *You Are Forever* peaks at US #59.

Dec [12] ABC TV's "American Bandstand" airs "Smokey Robinson 25th Anniversary Special".

1982 Mar *Yes It's You Lady* reaches US #33, as does extracted *Tell Me Tomorrow* (which also peaks at UK #51).

May *Old Fashioned Love* makes US #60.

1983 Mar *Touch The Sky* makes US #50.

May [16] Robinson is reunited with The Miracles on the "Motown 25th Anniversary" NBC TV special.

Aug *Blame It On Love*, a duet with Barbara Mitchell of High Inergy, makes US #48.

Sept Compilation album *Blame It On Love And All The Great Hits* climbs to US #124.

1984 Jan Robinson duets with fellow Motown hitmaker Rick James on *Ebony Eyes*, which makes US #43.

July *Essar* peaks at US #141.

985 Jan [28] Robinson takes part in the recording of USA For Africa's single *We Are The World*.

986 Mar *Smoke Signals* peaks at US #104.

987 Jan [21] Robinson is inducted into the Rock'N'Roll Hall Of Fame at the annual Waldorf Astoria hotel dinner in New York.

Apr *Just To See Her* makes UK #32, following Robinson's performance of it at TV-aired Montreux Rock Festival from Switzerland.

July [4] *Just To See Her* hits US #8, Robinson's first Top 10 single in 6 years, while *One Heartbeat* reaches US #26 and tops US R&B chart.

Sept [28] Robinson and Gladys Knight guest on US TV show "$10,000 Pyramid" for a week.

Oct [3] The title song from *One Heartbeat* hits US #10.

Dec [12] *What's Too Much* stalls at US #79.

988 Mar [2] Robinson wins Best R&B Vocal Performance, Male, for *Just To See Her* at the 30th annual Grammy awards – his first Grammy award. *Love Don't Give No Reason* makes US R&B #35, while Robinson features in a duet with Dolly Parton on *I Know You By Heart*.

Aug Robinson guests as Chicago commodities trader Link Greer on daytime TV soap "Generations".

Nov *Love Songs*, combining individual Robinson and Marvin Gaye ballads, makes UK #69.

989 Mar [4] *We've Saved The Best For Last* with Kenny G makes US #47.

Nov NARAS honors Robinson as Grammy Living Legend.

990 Mar [24] *Love, Smokey* makes US #138.

May [30] Robinson is inducted into the Songwriters Hall Of Fame by Whitney Houston at its 21st annual induction dinner at the Hilton hotel, New York.

991 Mar [12] Robinson receives the Heritage Award for outstanding career achievments at the 5th annual Soul Train awards at the Shrine Auditorium, Los Angeles, CA.

TOMMY ROE

958 Roe (b. May 9, 1943, Atlanta, GA) forms rock group Tommy Roe & The Satins, while still at Brown high school, Atlanta. Heavily influenced by Buddy Holly And The Crickets, they play school hops and fraternity parties at Georgia University.

960 Offered a recording deal by local Judd Records (run by Judd Phillips, brother of Sun Records' Sam Phillips), the band records *Sheila*, written by Roe at age 14. It gains local sales but is not promoted nationally.

961 Roe graduates from school and works as a technician for General Electric company, still performing evenings and weekends. Atlanta DJ Paul Drew (with whom The Satins have played many live gigs) recommends him to Felton Jarvis, a producer at ABC/Paramount Records (and later to produce Elvis Presley), who likes his style and self-penned material, and signs him.

962 June *Sheila* is re-recorded for ABC (originally as a B-side) in an arrangement similar to Holly's *Peggy Sue*, in line with Roe's Holly-like vocal treatment. When it picks up major airplay in US, the label advances him $5,000 to quit his GE job and tour to promote it.

Sept *Sheila* tops US chart for 2 weeks and is Roe's first million-seller.

Oct *Sheila* hits UK #2 (behind The Tornados' *Telstar*), having aroused interest in UK before Top 30 simultaneously with Buddy Holly's posthumous *Reminiscing*.

Nov A revival of Robin Luke's *Susie Darlin'* reaches US #35, while *Sheila* makes US #110.

Dec *Susie Darlin'* makes UK #37.

963 Mar [9] Roe begins a month-long UK tour at East Ham Granada, London, co-headlining with *Let's Dance* hitmaker Chris Montez. The Beatles are the main support act.

Apr Rush-released in UK because of the tour, Merle Kilgore's slow ballad *The Folk Singer* hits UK #4.

May *The Folk Singer* makes US #84. (His next 2 singles, including a revival of Russ Hamilton's 1957 hit *Rainbow*, will fail to chart.)

Oct *Everybody*, a gospelly rocker written by Roe on his UK tour, is also released first in UK, where it hits #9.

Nov [9] Roe begins a UK tour with Freddie & The Dreamers, The Searchers and Brian Poole And The Tremeloes at the Odeon cinema, Bolton, Merseyside.

Dec *Everybody* hits US #3, and is his second million-seller.

964 Feb *Come On*, in similar style to *Everybody*, reaches US #36.

May *Carol* makes US #61.

Dec *Party Girl* also peaks at US #61.

965 Jan [29] After a 2-year spell in the Army reserves, Roe embarks on a 22-date twice-nightly package tour with Cilla Black, The Fourmost,

P.J. Proby, Tommy Quickly and Sounds Incorporated at the ABC Cinema, Croydon, London. The tour will end Feb.21 at the Empire theater, Liverpool, Merseyside.

1966 July He writes and records *Sweet Pea* in a chunky pop style (presaging the "bubblegum" pop phase 2 years later). It hits US #8 and is Roe's third million-seller.

Nov *Hooray For Hazel*, in similar style, hits US #6.

Dec Compilation *Sweet Pea*, rounding up the year's 2 hits and earlier singles back to *Everybody*, makes US #94.

1967 Feb *It's Now Winter's Day* reaches US #23.

Apr *Sing Along With Me* charts for a week at US #91.

June *Little Miss Sunshine* also charts for only a week at US #99. *It's Now Winter's Day* peaks at US #159.

1968 With no recording in the year, Roe tours in Dick Clark's "Caravan Of Stars".

1969 Mar Steve Barri becomes Roe's producer, with the intention of resurrecting his "Buddy Holly" sound, but instead the 2 concoct *Dizzy*, co-written by Roe with hometown friend Freddy Weller (a member of Paul Revere & The Raiders) while they were on tour together in 1968. Driven by a sledgehammer Hal Blaine drum track and an off-beat sawing violin arrangement by Jimmy Haskell, the song is a very sophisticated bubblegum blend which tops US chart for 4 weeks. It is Roe's biggest seller, topping 2 million copies in US, with similar sales worldwide.

May *Heather Honey* makes US #29 and *Dizzy* reaches US #25.

June *Dizzy* tops UK chart for a week, deposing The Beatles' *Get Back* and being replaced by The Beatles' *The Ballad Of John And Yoko*.

Aug *Heather Honey* makes UK #24 (his last UK hit).

Oct *Jack And Jill* peaks at US #53.

Dec *Jam Up Jelly Tight* hits US #8, and is Roe's fifth and last million-seller.

1970 Feb Compilation *12 In A Roe: A Collection Of Tommy Roe's Greatest Hits*, peaks at US #21.

Mar *Stir It Up And Serve It* reaches US #50.

July *Pearl* also peaks at US #50.

Oct *We Can Make Music* makes US #49, while album of the same title climbs to US #134.

1971 Oct Following a summer US tour with long-time friends Joe South and Billy Joe Royal, Roe has his last hit for ABC and his last US Top 30 entry with a revival of Lloyd Price's *Stagger Lee*, which makes US #25.

1972 Sept Dissatisfied with West Coast life, and no longer with ABC Records, Roe returns to Georgia, where he signs with Atlanta-based MGM South, and reaches US #92 with *Mean Little Woman, Rosalie*.

1973 May *Working Class Hero*, also on MGM South, makes US #97, and is Roe's final hit single.

1976 Returning to Los Angeles, CA, after 4 years in Atlanta, Roe records 2 albums for Monument Records, *Energy* and *Full Bloom*, but neither is successful. (He will drift out of the public eye in later 70s and the 80s, although he will have success in US Country charts in 1986 and 1987.)

KENNY ROGERS

1944 Rogers (b. Kenneth Donald Rogers, Aug.21, 1938, Houston, TX) earns his first dollars as a 6-year-old, singing *You Are My Sunshine* for the residents of a nursing home near his home in Houston.

1955 While at Jefferson Davis high school, Rogers forms doo-wop combo The Scholars, who record *Poor Little Doggie* and *Spin The Wheel* for Jimmy Duncan's local Cue label and *Kangewah*, written by Hollywood gossip columnist Louella Parsons, for Imperial Records.

1958 Through his brother Lelan, a promoter for Decca Records, Rogers meets Ray Doggett (who has recently had success writing *On My Mind Again* for Gale Storm) and records Doggett's *That Crazy Feeling* at ACA Recording studio in Houston. Originally released on local Lynn label, Carlton Records picks it up and has Rogers (credited on it as Kenneth Rogers The First) make a major promotional tour, which includes an appearance on Dick Clark's ABC TV show "American Bandstand".

May [15] 19-year-old Rogers marries for the first time.

1959 He cuts further Carlton singles concurrently with releases on Ken-Lee, a label set up with brother Lelan.

Sept Rogers joins jazz-styled Bobby Doyle Trio (its front man is a blind pianist) as a stand-up bassist and singer.

[15] Rogers' wife Janice gives birth to a daughter, Carole Lynne.

1960 Jan [26] Janice files for divorce.

Oct 22-year-old Rogers marries a second time, to Jean Laverne Massey.

1961 The Bobby Doyle Trio tours US extensively, frequently as support to The Kirby Stone Four.

1962 **Mar** Trio starts work in New York on first album for CBS/Columbia. **July** *In A Most Unusual Way* is released.

1963 **Oct** [22] 24-year-old Rogers marries for the third time, to Margo Gladys Anderson.

1964 **May** [24] Rogers becomes a father for a second time when son Kenneth Ray Rogers II is born.

1965 **June** Rogers cuts solo single *Take Life In Stride* for Mercury. [24] Rogers with fellow Bobby Doyle member, Don Russell and Anthony Navarro open the Act Three club on Main Street in Houston, where the trio will play regularly.
Dec Rogers and Russell decide not to renew their license for the club.

1966 Having spent a short period with 4-part harmony group The Lively Ones (Rogers, Russell, Paula Chase and Paul Mussarra) and working at the Houstonaire supper club, Rogers joins The New Christy Minstrels, earning $750 a week. He records 1 album with the group, *New Kick!* (*The New Christy Minstrels Sing The Hits Of Today And Tomorrow*).

1967 **July** Ken Kragen, co-manager of The Smothers Brothers and co-producer of their CBS TV show "The Smothers Brothers' Comedy Hour", sees the group at Ledbetter's in Los Angeles, CA, and signs them to a management deal.
[10] The contracts of Rogers and fellow Minstrels Mike Settle, Terry Williams (his father was Tommy Dorsey's first-chair trombonist and vocalist) and Thelma Camacho expire.
[11] Rogers, Settle, Williams and Camacho start recording a debut album as The First Edition, for Reprise Records, having auditioned for producer Jimmy Bowen during their time with The Minstrels.
Dec *The First Edition* is released.

1968 **Jan** The First Edition makes its TV debut on "The Smothers Brothers' Comedy Hour".
Mar *Just Dropped In (To See What Condition My Condition Was In)*, with a heavy rock arrangement and mock-"psychedelic" lyric, written by Mickey Newbury (and rejected by Jerry Lee Lewis), hits US #5. Debut album *The First Edition* reaches US #118.

1969 Mary Arnold replaces Camacho in The First Edition. (Karen Carpenter also auditioned for the slot.)
Mar *But You Know I Love You*, written by Settle in a more country music direction, reaches US #19.
Apr *The First Edition '69* makes US #164.
Aug *Ruby, Don't Take Your Love To Town*, concerning a crippled Korean War veteran, written several years earlier by country singer Mel Tillis, hits US #6. Highlighting Rogers' solo vocal, it credits the group for the first time as Kenny Rogers & The First Edition.
Nov *Ruben James*, in similar style to *Ruby*, makes US #26.
Dec *Ruby, Don't Take Your Love To Town* hits UK #2 for 5 weeks, behind Rolf Harris' *Two Little Boys*. Meanwhile, the album of the same name (and first album credited to the extended group name) reaches US #48.

1970 Settle leaves the band, to be replaced by Kin Vassy.
Feb *Something's Burning*, penned by Mac Davis, reaches US #11 and hits UK #8.
June *Something's Burning* makes US #26.
Aug *Tell It All Brother* reaches US #17.
Nov *Heed The Call* makes US #33.
Dec Featuring both the previous hit singles, *Tell It All Brother* peaks at US #61.

1971 **Apr** *Someone Who Cares*, from James Caan/Katharine Ross film "Fools", peaks at US #51. Group's compilation album *Greatest Hits* makes US #57.
July *Take My Hand* – gospel-flavored, Rogers-penned – stalls at US #91.
Sept Canadian-produced syndicated TV program "Rollin' On The River", starring The First Edition, airs on US TV. Filmed in a riverboat setting, it features music guests, including Kris Kristofferson, Mac Davis and B.J. Thomas.
Oct *Transition* reaches US #155.

1972 **Apr** *School Teacher*, with Vassy on lead vocal, stalls at US #91. It is taken from double album *The Ballad Of Calico*, a concept album about the 1889 mining town of Calico, CA, which makes US #118.

1973 **May** [27] Compilation album *Greatest Hits* is certified gold after more than 2 years on sale.

1974 The First Edition splits, leaving Rogers $65,000 in debt.

1975 He signs to United Artists Records as a solo artist.
Mar His first UA single, *Love Lifted Me*, stalls at US #97.

1977 **June** *Lucille* hits US #5, selling a million, and tops UK chart.
July Debut solo album *Kenny Rogers* reaches US #30 and UK #14.
Aug *Daytime Friends* reaches US #28.
Oct *Daytime Friends* makes UK #39, while the album of the same title peaks at US #39. Rogers gets married for the fourth time, to Marianne

Gordon, an actress on US TV show "Hee Haw". He also has his first book **Making It With Music**, written with Len Epand, published.
Nov Rogers begins UK concert tour with UA label-mate Crystal Gayle.

1978 **Jan** *Sweet Music Man* peaks at US #44. *Lucille* is named Country Single Of 1977 at the American Music Awards in Santa Monica, CA.
Feb [23] Rogers wins Best Country Vocal Performance, Male, for *Lucille* at the 20th annual Grammy awards. It is his first Grammy.
Apr *Ten Years Of Gold*, 1 side featuring re-recorded solo versions of The First Edition hits, reaches US #33. (In 103 weeks on US chart, it will sell over a million copies, earning Rogers' first platinum disk.)
July *Love Or Something Like It* reaches US #32.
Sept *Love Or Something Like It* makes US #53, and earns a gold disk.

1979 **Mar** *The Gambler* reaches US #16, while the album of the same title peaks at US #12, and becomes Rogers' second platinum album.
June *Classics*, an album of duets between Rogers and country singer Dottie West, makes US #86.
July Steve Gibb-penned *She Believes In Me*, taken from *The Gambler*, hits US #5 and peaks at UK #42.
Aug [16] Rogers performs at the Ohio State Fair to 80,000 fans.
Sept [14] "Kenny Rogers' Day" is proclaimed in Los Angeles, as Rogers receives a star on the Hollywood Walk Of Fame.
Nov *You Decorated My Life* hits US #7, while parent album *Kenny* hits US #3 and is another million-seller. Rogers' footprints are immortalized in cement at the Country Palace in Toledo, OH.
[12] Rogers begins filming "The Gambler", a TV movie based on the song of the same title, which marks his acting debut.
Dec UK compilation *The Kenny Rogers Singles Album* makes #12. CBS TV airs the documentary "Kenny Rogers And The American Cowboy".

1980 **Jan** *Every Time Two Fools Collide*, another duetted set with West, climbs to US #186.
Feb *Coward Of The County*, taken from *Kenny*, hits US #3, earning a gold disk, and tops UK chart for 2 weeks.
[27] Rogers wins his second Best Country Vocal Performance, Male, for *The Gambler* at the 22nd annual Grammy awards.
Apr TV movie "The Gambler" airs on CBS TV.
May *Don't Fall In Love With A Dreamer*, a duet with Kim Carnes, hits US #4. It is taken from *Gideon*, which reaches US #12, earning another platinum disk. Meanwhile, *Kenny* hits UK #7.
Aug *Love The World Away* reaches US #14.
Nov *Lady*, penned by Lionel Richie, tops US chart for 6 weeks, selling over a million, and hitting #1 on US R&B, C&W and Adult Contemporary charts. It will also reach UK #12, and is Rogers' first release on Liberty label (as United Artists Records is renamed).
Dec Rogers shares the Top Male Vocalist Of 1980 award with Michael Jackson in *Record World* magazine. His compilation album *Kenny Rogers' Greatest Hits*, of hit singles up to *Lady*, tops US chart for 2 weeks, and is his fifth platinum album, staying charted 181 weeks.

1981 **Feb** UK-compiled album *Lady* makes UK #40.
June *What Are We Doin' In Love*, a duet with West, reaches US #14.
Aug *I Don't Need You* hits US #3. It is taken from *Share Your Love*, produced by Richie, which hits US #3 and earns another platinum disk. Rogers also stars in TV movie "Coward Of The County", in which he plays a Southern preacher.
[17] Rogers headlines Nassau Coliseum, Uniondale, NY, benefit concert for singer Harry Chapin, killed a month earlier in a car crash.
Oct *Share Your Love With Me*, from album of same title, reaches US #14.
Dec *Blaze Of Glory*, again from the album, peaks at US #66, while seasonal *Christmas* makes US #34.
[4] Kenny and Marianne Rogers have a son, Christopher Cody.

1982 **Mar** *Through The Years*, from *Share Your Love*, peaks at US #13.
Aug Film "Six Pack", starring Rogers, opens in US. From the movie, *Love Will Turn You Around* reaches US #13, while album of the same title peaks at US #34 and earns a gold disk.
Nov *A Love Song* peaks at US #47.
[23] Rogers and his wife Marianne present the first World Hunger Media Awards at the UN in New York.
Dec *Christmas* re-charts at US #149, passing the platinum sales mark.

1983 **Mar** Rogers duets with Sheena Easton on a revival of Bob Seger's *We've Got Tonight*, which hits US #6 and UK #28.
Apr *We've Got Tonight* reaches US #27, earning a gold disk. This is his last new album for Liberty, as he signs to RCA Records in a deal worth more than $20 million.
June *All My Life*, from *We've Got Tonight*, makes US #37.
Aug *Scarlet Fever*, also from the album, and Rogers' last Liberty single, stalls at US #94.
Sept [18] Kenny Rogers' special airs on HBO TV.

Oct *Islands In The Stream*, a duet with Dolly Parton written by The Bee Gees, tops US chart and becomes the only platinum (US million-selling) single of 1983. It is also awarded an American Music Award (AMA) as Best Country Single (Rogers' 15th), and named Vocal Duet Of The Year and Single Record Of The Year by the Academy Of Country Music. The single is taken from his debut RCA album *Eyes That See In The Dark*, co-produced by Barry Gibb, which hits US #6 and earns a platinum disk as he and Parton host the annual CMA Awards. Meanwhile, *Eyes That See In The Dark* makes UK #53 and extracted title track UK #61.
Nov *Islands In The Stream* hits UK #7. TV movie "The Gambler II", starring Rogers, Bruce Boxleitner and Linda Evans, airs on US TV.

1984
Jan Liberty compilation album *Twenty Greatest Hits* makes US #22, and is another platinum album.
Mar *This Woman*, from *Eyes That See In The Dark*, reaches US #23.
May The title track from *Eyes That See In The Dark* stalls at US #79.
June Liberty album *Duets*, compiling Rogers' hits with Sheena Easton and Kim Carnes with 8 cuts duetted with Dottie West, makes US #85.
Oct *What About Me?* charts at US #31 (a further platinum seller) and makes UK #97.
Nov *What About Me?*, sung with Carnes and James Ingram, reaches US #15, as parent album *The Heart Of The Matter* makes US #51.
Dec [2] Rogers and Dolly Parton's "A Christmas To Remember" special airs on US TV. Duo's album of seasonal duets, *Once Upon A Christmas*, produced by David Foster, reaches US #31, selling over a million, while extracted *The Greatest Gift Of All*, makes US #81.

1985
Jan [28] Rogers takes part in recording USA For Africa's *We Are The World* in Los Angeles, the session having been largely co-ordinated by his manager Ken Kragen, after initial approaches by Harry Belafonte. The disk will top US and UK charts, selling several million worldwide.
Feb *Crazy* makes US #79, as Rogers and Parton begin a joint US tour.
May *Love Is What We Make It*, a Liberty compilation of previously released material, makes US #145.
June Rogers duets on *Real Love*, the title cut from Parton's new album, which peaks at US #91.
Aug TV-promoted compilation album *The Kenny Rogers Story*, on Liberty, hits UK #4.
Oct *I Prefer The Moonlight* stalls at US #163, but reaches US C&W #18.
Nov Title cut from *I Prefer The Moonlight* hits US C&W #2 for 2 weeks.
Dec *Morning Desire*, from *I Prefer The Moonlight*, peaks at US #72.

1987
Jan *They Don't Make Them Like They Used To* makes US #137.
Sept *Make No Mistake, She's Mine*, a duet with country singer Ronnie Milsap, tops US Country chart for a week but fails to cross over.

1988
Mar [2] Rogers wins Best Country Vocal Performance, Duet, for *Make No Mistake, She's Mine*, with Ronnie Milsap at the 30th annual Grammy awards.

1989
June Rogers makes US #141 with his Reprise label debut, *Something Inside So Strong*. (Duet with Dolly Parton of Mickey & Sylvia's *Love Is Strange* is released as single.)
Sept [10] NBC TV broadcasts first annual International Very Special Arts Festival from the lawn of the White House. Festival celebrates accomplishments of physically and mentally handicapped artists from around the world. Other performers include U2, Mikhail Baryshnikov, Lauren Bacall and Michael Douglas.
Dec *Christmas In America* makes US #119.

1991
Feb [10] Rogers joins with nearly 100 celebrities in Burbank, CA, to record *Voices That Care*, a David Foster and fiancee Linda Thompson Jenner-composed and organized charity record to benefit the American Red Cross Gulf Crisis Fund.

THE ROLLING STONES

Mick Jagger (vocals, harmonica)
Keith Richard (rhythm guitar)
Brian Jones (lead guitar)
Bill Wyman (bass)
Charlie Watts (drums)

1951
Feb Jagger (b. Michael Philip Jagger, July 26, 1943, Dartford, Kent) and Richard (b. Keith Richards, Dec.18, 1943, Dartford) become friends while at Wentworth Junior County Primary school, but lose contact.

1960
Jagger is a student at the London School of Economics and Richard, who has been part of a choir that sings Handel's "Messiah" at Westminster Abbey, in the presence of the Queen, is attending Sidcup Art School when they meet again on a train. Friendship is rekindled when they discover a joint love of R&B and a passion for records on Chess label, particularly Chuck Berry. Richard subsequently joins R&B group, Little Boy Blue & The Blue Boys, with Dick Taylor, Bob

Beckwith, Allen Etherington and vocalist Jagger.

1962
Jones (b. Lewis Brian Hopkin-Jones, Feb.28, 1942, Cheltenham, Gloucs.), after a brief spell in hometown band The Ramrods, moves to London where he finds a job in a department store, and under the alias of Elmo Lewis, advertises in **Jazz News** for R&B musicians to form a band. An all-round musician, he frequently guests with Alexis Korner's Blues Incorporated which has a Saturday residency at the Ealing Blues club. (He has met Korner at a concert in Cheltenham.) Pianist Ian Stewart answers the ad and begins to rehearse with Jones. Through Stewart, Jones meets singer Andy Wren and guitarist Geoff Bradford. Jagger and Richard become friendly with Jones after visiting the club and the nucleus of a group is formed comprising Jagger, Richard, Jones, Stewart, Geoff Bradford and Dick Taylor, with a variety of drummers sitting in. Jagger also becomes vocalist with Blues Incorporated and plays with the group on his nights off from Alexis Korner's band.
Mar [17] Blues Incorporated, featuring Korner on guitar, Dave Stevens on piano, Andy Hoogenboom on bass, Cyril Davies on harmonica, Dick Heckstall-Smith on tenor sax and Charlie Watts on drums, begins a regular Saturday night gig at the Ealing Jazz club.
Apr [7] Jagger, Richards and Taylor bump into Jones, now playing in a band with Ian Stewart, Geoff Bradford and singer P.P. Bond (later to find success with Manfred Mann as Paul Jones), at the Ealing Jazz club.
June Tony Chapman, drummer with The Cliftons, auditions for The Rollin' Stones.
July Blues Incorporated is booked to appear on BBC Radio's "Jazz Club", broadcast live on Thursday evenings, but the BBC deems Jagger not suitable as a vocalist and Long John Baldry takes his place. Blues Incorporated, however, needs a group to sub for its Thursday night Marquee club sessions and Jagger and cohorts eagerly accept the gig.
[12] The Rollin' Stones, comprising Jagger, Richard, Jones, Taylor, Stewart and future Kink Mick Avory on drums, make their debut at the Marquee Jazz club, taking their name from a Muddy Waters song.
Oct [27] Group, comprising Jagger, Richard, Jones, Stewart and Tony Chapman, makes its first studio recordings at Curly Clayton studios in Highbury, London. Musical covers of Muddy Waters' *Soon Forgotten*, Jimmy Reed's *Close Together* and Bo Diddley's *You Can't Judge A Book (By Looking At The Cover)*, which are submitted to record companies with little success.
Dec [7] Wyman (b. William Perks, Oct.24, 1936, Lewisham, London), a former Royal Air Force AC1 Air Craftsman First Class and in The Cliftons with Chapman, auditions for the Stones at the Wetherby Arms at World's End in Chelsea, London.
[15] Wyman makes his debut with the group at the youth club, Church Hall, Putney, London.

1963
Jan [14] Jagger, Richard, Jones, Wyman, Stewart and new recruit Watts (b. Charles Robert Watts, June 2, 1941, Islington, London), a designer with a Regent Street ad agency, who has been a regular drummer with Blues Incorporated and approached several times to join the fledgling Stones, but resisting for financial security, and now replacing Chapman, play together for the first time at the Flamingo Jazz club in Soho, London.
[28] The Stones record 5 tracks at IBC studios with engineer Glyn Johns.
Feb [24] They begin a Sunday residency at the Station hotel, Richmond, Surrey, earning £24 and attracting an audience of 66.
Mar [3] They begin a weekly daytime residency at Studio 51, Ken Colyer club, London, which will continue until Sept.23, 1963.
Apr [13] Group begins to attract large audiences at the Crawdaddy and receives its first press write-up in **The Richmond & Twickenham Times** by Barry May.
[23] Group, without Wyman and Watts, auditions for BBC Radio program "Jazz Club".
[28] Andrew Oldham, age 19, an ex-PR man for The Beatles, travels to Richmond with business associate Eric Easton to see the band, on the recommendation of **Record Mirror** journalist Peter Jones.
May [1] Oldham and Easton sign a management contract with the group to their newly formed Impact Sound company, effective May 6. Group becomes The Rolling Stones (adding the "g") at Oldham's insistence. (Stewart, pushed to a backseat role of roadie and backing musician in the studio, with his straight image seen by Oldham at odds with the style he intends to create for the group, becomes an integral part of the group, unseen by the public, and is known as the sixth Stone until his death in 1985.)
[4] They play at a **News of the World** charity gala in Battersea Park, London.

[9] They sign a 3-year recording contract with Impact, who sign a tape/lease agreement with Decca Records, which has recently rejected The Beatles.

[10] Group enters Olympic Sound studio to record an obscure Chuck Berry song, *Come On*. Decca rejects the recording as "dreadful".

[11] **New Record Mirror** writer, and R&B fan, Norman Jopling writes a piece entitled "The Rolling Stones – Genuine R&B".

June [7] Group's first single, the re-recorded *Come On*, is released in UK. The line "Some stupid jerk" is altered to "Some stupid guy" to ensure radio play.

[20] Group begins a 4-week Thursday residence at the Scene club, London.

July [7] Group makes its TV debut on ITV's "Thank Your Lucky Stars", coerced into wearing matching check velvet collared jackets with matching ties and trousers, performing *Come On*.

[19] A performance at the coming out party of Lord and Lady Killernan's daughter Roxanna in Hastings, Sussex, is cancelled when Jones falls ill on the way to the booking.

[20] Group makes its ballroom debut at the Corn Exchange, Wisbech, Cambs.

Aug [11] Group plays at the third National Jazz & Blues Festival at the Athletic Grounds, Richmond, Surrey.

[28] They make their debut on ITV's "Ready Steady Go!"

Sept [7] *Come On* reaches UK #21.

[10] With The Rolling Stones unable to decide on a second single, a chance meeting between Oldham and his former employers The Beatles' John Lennon and Paul McCartney, who have just left the Variety club lunch, leads to their visiting the Studio 51 jazz club, where the Stones are rehearsing. The duo play part of a new song they have written, *I Wanna Be Your Man*, and within minutes complete the rest of the number, putting the Stones in the rare and privileged position of recording an unreleased Lennon/McCartney composition.

[15] Group plays at the "Great Pop Prom" at the Royal Albert Hall, London.

[20] *Poison Ivy*, scheduled follow-up to *Come On* and allocated catalog number F11742, is withdrawn.

[29] Group starts its first UK tour, a 32-date package supporting The Everly Brothers and Bo Diddley at London's New Victoria theater. The tour, with Little Richard midway through, will end on Nov.3 at the Hammersmith Odeon, London.

Oct [5] BBC Radio's "Saturday Club", on which Jones, Wyman and Watts back Bo Diddley, airs.

Nov [17] Jagger/Richard meet Gene Pitney at the recording of ITV's "Thank Your Lucky Stars" and present him with *That Girl Belongs To Yesterday*, which hits US and UK charts, beginning a songwriting partnership which will provide other artists with songs, but it will be almost a year before they write an original for a Stones' single.

Dec [20] The group is voted Sixth Best British Vocal Group in **New Musical Express** annual readers' poll.

[28] *I Wanna Be Your Man* (now also on **With The Beatles** sung by Ringo), reaches UK #12. The Stones make the song a hard-driving R&B number, with whining steel guitar.

1964 Jan [2] The Stones sing *I Wanna Be Your Man* on the first edition of BBC TV's "Top Of The Pops".

[6] Group begins its second UK tour, its first as bill-toppers, a 14-date "Group Scene 1964" package supported by The Ronettes, Marty Wilde, The Swinging Blue Jeans, Dave Berry & The Cruisers, The Cheynes and compere Al Paige, at the Granada theater, Harrow-on-the-Hill, London. **New Musical Express** describes the group as a "caveman-like quintet". The Stones are now attracting a major following with screaming fans and press reports of their wild concerts. The image of long-haired tearaways becomes compounded as an antidote to The Beatles clean showbiz image. Tour ends on Jan.27 at Colston Hall, Bristol, Avon.

Feb [1] Group plays the "Valentine Charity Pop Show" at the Royal Albert Hall, on a bill with Dusty Springfield, The Swinging Blue Jeans and Brian Poole & The Tremeloes.

[8] They begin another UK tour, a 28-date package with John Leyton, Mike Berry, Jet Harris, Billie Davis, The Innocents, Don Spencer, The LeRoys and Billy Boyle, at the Regal theater, Edmonton, London, set to end on Mar.7 at the Winter Gardens, Morecambe, Lancs.

Mar [21] Group remodels Buddy Holly's *Not Fade Away* in Bo Diddley style, with Phil Spector lending a hand on maracas and co-writing B-side *Little By Little* with Jagger, and it hits UK #3.

Apr [8] They cause a minor riot at the "Ready Steady Go! Mad Mod Ball" before an audience of 8,000 at the Empire Pool, London.

[22] The **Daily Mirror** reports that the president of The National Federation Of Hairdressers is offering a free haircut to the next group to reach #1, claiming The Rolling Stones are the worst of the lot – "one of them looks as if he's got a feather duster on his head".

[26] The Rolling Stones take part in the **New Musical Express** annual Poll Winner's concert at the Empire Pool, Wembley, with The Beatles and others.

May [2] Released with 100,000 advance orders, debut album *The Rolling Stones* tops the UK chart, replacing **With The Beatles**. Oldham makes the first of many marketing ploys by leaving the group's name off the album's front cover, unheard of in the history of record releases (It is the first time in just under a year that The Beatles are not at #1.) Group makes first appearance on US chart at #98 with *Not Fade Away*.

[11] In the midst of another UK tour, the group is refused lunch at The Grand Hotel, Bristol, Avon, where they are staying because they are not wearing jackets and ties.

[27] 11 boys are suspended at a school in Coventry, W.Midlands., for having Mick Jagger haircuts.

[31] Group takes part in the "Pop Hit Parade" concert at London's Empire Pool, Wembley.

June [1] The Stones arrive at Kennedy airport, New York, on BA flight 505, for their debut US tour.

[2] They make their US TV debut on "The Les Crane Show".

[5] 9-date US tour opens at the Swing Auditorium in San Bernardino, CA, their first concert outside the UK. The tour will end on June 20 at Carnegie Hall, New York.

[10-11] The Stones record at Chess studios in Chicago, IL, where they meet Chuck Berry, Muddy Waters and Willie Dixon.

[13] Group appears on ABC TV's "The Hollywood Palace", following Bertha The Elephant and her daughter Tina, and is subsequently subjected to quips from host Dean Martin. After comic acrobat Larry Griswold's act, Martin tells the audience: "That's the father of The Rolling Stones; he's been trying to kill himself ever since.'"

[22] On the day they return from the US tour, they play at a Commemoration Ball at Magdalen College, Oxford, Oxon, fulfilling an engagement booked a year earlier.

July [4] The Stones appear on BBC TV's "Juke Box Jury" (the only time the show has 5 panelists rather than 4), and cause controversy over their languid comments and hair.

[18] A cover of The Valentinos' *It's All Over Now*, recorded at Chess studios, tops the UK chart. With assistance from engineer Ron Malo, The Rolling Stones begin to define a harder rock sound which will become their trademark. *Not Fade Away* reaches US #48.

[24] They cause a riot at Blackpool's Empress Ballroom, during a series of UK dates. 30 fans and 2 policemen are treated in hospital. 4 fans appear in court the following day, charged with assault and carrying offensive weapons.

Aug [8] *Tell Me (You're Coming Back)* reaches US #24.

[10] Jagger is fined £32 in Liverpool, Merseyside, for driving without insurance and breaking the speed limit. His solicitor explains "Mr. Jagger was on an errand of mercy visiting 2 fans injured in a car crash".

[22] US only-released *England's Newest Hit Makers – The Rolling Stones*, UK album with added single *Not Fade Away*, reaches US #11.

Sept [5] Group begins 31-date twice-nightly UK tour with Inez & Charlie Foxx, The Mojos, Mike Berry, Billie Davis and Simon Scott, at the Astoria, Finsbury Park, London. The tour will end on Oct.11 at the Hippodrome, Brighton, E.Sussex.

[11] 16-year-old Laurie Yarham wins Mick Jagger impersonation concert at the Town Hall, Greenwich, only to reveal his true identity – Jagger's younger brother Chris.

[19] Jagger's girlfriend Marianne Faithfull hits UK #9 with Jagger/Richard's *As Tears Go By*, as *It's All Over Now* reaches US #26.

Oct [9] The Stones announce the cancellation of their South African tour, complying with the wishes of the Musicians' Union and its opposition to apartheid.

[14] Watts and Shirley Ann Shepherd are married by Registrar Mr. J. H. Hinkins in Bradford.

[20] They play at the Olympia theater, Paris, France, as 150 are arrested for damage caused both inside and outside the theater.

[24] The Stones begin their second US tour with 2 shows at New York's Academy of Music. The 12-date tour will end on Nov.15 at the Arie Crown theater, McCormick Place, Chicago, IL.

[25] Group makes its debut on CBS TV's "Ed Sullivan Show". After riotous scenes in the audience, Sullivan announces "I promise you they'll never be back on our show. It took me 17 years to build this show; I'm not going to have it destroyed in a matter of weeks."

[28-29] The Stones record the "TAMI Show" (Teen Age Music

Slade

Simon & Garfunkel

Soul II Soul

Diana Ross & The Supremes

Otis Redding

The Rolling Stones

Cliff Richard

Lou Reed

International Show) at the Civic Auditorium in Santa Monica, CA, with The Barbarians, Chuck Berry, The Beach Boys, James Brown, Marvin Gaye, Gerry & The Pacemakers, Jan And Dean, Billy J. Kramer & The Dakotas, Smokey Robinson & The Miracles and The Supremes. (The show will open in the UK at the Futurist, Birmingham, W.Midlands as "Gather No Moss" on Aug.7, 1966.)

Nov [3] A 17-year-old falls from balcony during Stones' concert at the Public Hall, Cleveland, OH. Mayor Ralph Locker says, in banning them, "such groups do not add to the community's culture or entertainment".

[13] Group's official biography **Our Own Story** is published.

[15] Jones is admitted to Passavant hospital in Chicago with a 105°F temperature, after missing the group's last 4 concerts.

[20] On their return to the UK, the group plays at the "Glad Rag Ball", with Long John Baldry, The Animals, The Pretty Things, Gene Vincent and Cliff Bennett, at the Empire Pool, Wembley.

[27] In Jagger defense for further driving offenses in Tettenshall, Staffs., Dale Parkinson, his solicitor, tells the court not to be prejudiced by his client's long hair, advising them "The Duke of Marlborough had much longer hair than my client and he won some famous battles. He powdered his too, because of the fleas. My client has no fleas. The Emperor Caesar Augustus also had rather long hair. He won many great victories. Barristers, too, wear long hair in the shape of wigs with curled-up ends. A lost license will seriously affect Jagger's mobility and that of The Rolling Stones group. Britain needs every dollar she can earn, and The Rolling Stones earn more dollars than many professional exporters. Put out of your minds the nonsense talked about these young men, The Rolling Stones. They are not long-haired idiots, but highly intelligent university men." Jagger is fined £16.

Dec [5] Group's revival of Willie Dixon's *Little Red Rooster*, despite critics' scepticism that a purist blues record will be a hit, tops UK chart, as a cover of Irma Thomas' *Time Is On My Side* hits US #6.

[6] The Stones are voted #1 UK R&B group and Best New Group in **New Musical Express** annual readers' poll. Jagger is voted Best New Disc Or TV Singer.

[12] *12 x 5* hits US #3.

[26] In a **New Musical Express** ad, the group wishes starving hairdressers and their families a Happy Christmas.

1965 Jan Group appears on the season-opener of ABC TV's "Shindig".

[9] Marianne Faithfull reaches US #22 with *As Tears Go By*.

[15] Watts' book **Ode To A High Flying Bird**, tribute to jazz giant Charlie Parker, is published.

[21] 3,000 fans greet the Stones as they arrive at Sydney airport, Australia.

[22] Group begins a 16-date tour of Australia, New Zealand and the Far East, with Roy Orbison, Rolf Harris and Dionne Warwick, at the Manufacturers' Auditorium, Agricultural Hall, Sydney, Australia. The tour, covering 36 shows in 16 days, will end on Feb.16 at Badminton Stadium, Singapore.

Feb [6] *The Rolling Stones No. 2*, again with no title or artist name on the sleeve, hits UK #1, replacing *Beatles For Sale*. It includes covers of US R&B hits including Otis Redding's *Pain In My Heart* and Solomon Burke's *Everybody Needs Somebody To Love*, but also a greater number of Jagger/Richard compositions than their debut set. Jack Nitzsche contributes keyboards with the ever present Stewart.

[20] *Heart Of Stone* reaches US #19.

Mar [5] Group begins a 14-date twice-nightly UK tour, with Dave Berry & The Cruisers, Goldie & The Gingerbreads, The Konrads, The Checkmates and special guests The Hollies, at the Regal theater, Edmonton, London, set to end Mar.18 at ABC theater, Romford, Essex.

[7] Teenage girl falls from dress circle at the Palace theater, Manchester, Gtr.Manchester, onto some people below, breaking only a few teeth.

[11] Portuguese pianist Sergio Varella-Cid vents his anger to the press after his recital is drowned out by The Stones playing in another part of the City Hall, Sheffield, S.Yorks.

[19] **The Tailor And Cutter** magazine carries a plea to The Rolling Stones to wear ties to save tie-makers from financial disaster. (Years later the magazine will name Jagger one of the Hot Hundred Best Dressed Men.)

[20] *The Last Time*, recorded at RCA's Hollywood studios with engineer Dave Hassinger (and with Phil Spector and Jack Nitzsche providing production assistance), tops the UK chart.

[26] On the opening night of a 7-date Scandinavian tour at the Fyns Forum in Odense, Denmark, Wyman is knocked unconscious by a 220 volt shock on stage.

Apr [9] Band makes its live debut on ITV's "Ready Steady Goes Live!"

[10] A schoolteacher in Wrexham attacks parents who allow their children to wear Rolling Stones' "corduroy" trousers.

[11] The Stones make their second appearance at the **New Musical Express** annual Poll Winners concert at the Empire Pool, Wembley.

[16-18] They play 3 dates at the Olympia theater, Paris.

[23] Group begins 21-date tour of North America at the Maurice Richard Arena, Montreal, Canada. Tour will end May 29 at the Academy of Music, New York.

[24] US only-released *The Rolling Stones, Now!* hits US #5.

[26] During a concert at the Treasure Island Gardens in London, Canada, the chief of police unplugs mikes and amps to stop the show.

May [1] *The Last Time* hits US #9.

[2] Despite its host's previous comments, the Stones appear on CBS TV's "Ed Sullivan Show", on a bill with Tom Jones, Dusty Springfield and Morecambe & Wise, performing *The Last Time*, *Little Red Rooster*, *Everybody Needs Somebody*, and *2120 South Michigan Avenue*.

[22] *The Last Time* B-side, *Play With Fire*, makes US #96.

June [24] 4-date Scandinavian tour begins in Oslo, Norway.

July [10] *(I Can't Get No) Satisfaction*, held back in UK because of the EP's success, tops the US chart for 4 weeks, the group's first US #1. Based around a definitive riff which entered Richard's head after waking up in the middle of the night in a hotel room, it is notable for its use of a fuzz box distorting the sound, and its risque lyrics about female monthly cycles. (Richard will later claim this famous riff is based on Martha & The Vandellas' *Dancing In The Street*.)

[22] Jagger, Wyman and Jones are fined £5 each with joint costs of 15 guineas at East Ham Magistrates' Court, London, after being found guilty of insulting behavior on Mar.18 when, denied use of the private toilet at the Francis Service Station on the Romford Road in East Ham by mechanic, Charles Keely, they urinated against the garage wall and drove off "making a well-known gesture".

[28] Watts buys 16th-century timbered mansion in Sussex from Lord Shawcross. Watts' father comments "We can't understand why he prefers an old place like this to something modern."

[29] Group re-signs with Decca in the UK. (Group does not however sign with London in US.)

Aug [1] Band makes its London Palladium debut, playing 2 shows supported by The Walker Brothers, The Moody Blues, The Fourmost, Steam Packet, The Quiet Five and Julie Grant.

[21] *Out Of Our Heads*, first Stones album to be recorded in stereo, hits US #1 for 3 weeks.

[28] Allen Klein becomes co-manager of the group with Oldham, as the group signs a £1.7 million contract with Decca to make 5 movies.

Sept [5] Group flies directly from a concert at ABC theater in Belfast, N.Ireland to Los Angeles to record *Get Off Of My Cloud*, returning for a concert at the Palace Ballroom, Douglas, Isle of Man concert where they have to climb in through a toilet window to avoid fans.

[10] ITV's "Ready Steady Go!", devoted entirely to The Stones, who act as interviewers and hosts, with their guests Manfred Mann, Goldie & The Gingerbreads and The Preachers, who play their current single, the Wyman-produced, *Hole In My Soul*, airs.

[11] *(I Can't Get No) Satisfaction* tops UK chart.

[18] Wyman's wife Diane (whom he married in Penge, Kent, in 1959) writes "My Life As A Stone's Wife" in UK music paper **Disc**.

[24] They begin their sixth UK tour, a 24-date twice-nightly package with The Spencer Davis Group, Unit 4+2, Mike Sarne, The Checkmates, Charles Dickens, The Habits, The End and Ray Cameron, at the Astoria theater, Finsbury Park, London. Tour will end Oct.17 at the Granada theater, Tooting, London. (Group's scheduled Oct.16 date at the Odeon theater, Southend, Essex, is cancelled, after local authorities state that the police will be too busy controlling the crowds at the town's illuminations to concentrate on The Stones.)

Oct [16] *Out Of Our Heads*, the first album recorded entirely in US and featuring covers of soul classics rather than R&B and 4 Jagger/Richard originals, hits UK #2, held off the top by **The Sound Of Music** soundtrack.

[29] Group's North American tour begins at the Forum, Montreal, Canada. The 37-date tour will end Dec.5 at the Sports Arena, Los Angeles.

Nov [1] A concert at the Memorial Auditorium, Rochester, NY, is stopped by police after 7 mins., when 3,000 fans try to storm the stage.

[6] *Get Off Of My Cloud* tops UK and US charts.

[29] Colorado's Governor John A. Love declares "Rolling Stones Day" throughout the state, as the group plays a sell-out concert at the Coliseum in Denver that evening.

Dec [3] Richard is knocked unconscious by an electric shock on stage at the Memorial Hall in Sacramento, CA, when his guitar makes contact with his microphone during *The Last Time*.

[10] *Satisfaction* is voted Best Record Of The Year in the annual **New Musical Express** readers' poll.

1966
Jan [8] US only *December's Children (And Everybody's)* hits US #4.
[29] From the US album, the group's version of *As Tears Go By* hits US #6. It is intended as lead track on the next UK EP, but is withdrawn.
Feb [1] An announcement is made that the Stones will begin shooting their first feature film "Back Behind And In Front" on Apr.10.
[19] After 3 successive #1s, *19th Nervous Breakdown* hits UK #2 for 3 weeks, behind Nancy Sinatra's *These Boots Are Made For Walkin'*.
[18] Group begins 11-date tour of Australia and New Zealand in Sydney. The 20-show tour will end Mar.2 at the Capitol theater, Perth.
Mar [10] Decca vetoes release of projected album *Could You Walk On The Water*. The original track line-up is also abandoned, and the project develops into *Aftermath* (hence its title).
[19] *19th Nervous Breakdown* hits US #2, held off the top for 3 weeks by S/Sgt. Barry Sadler's *The Ballad Of The Green Berets*.
[26] Group begins 7-date European tour in The Hague, Holland. The 11-show tour will end Apr.5 in Copenhagen, Denmark.
[21] They win Most Outstanding Group Of 1965 at the annual Carl-Alan Awards in London.
Apr [30] *Aftermath*, the first Stones album composed entirely of Jagger/Richard songs, tops the UK chart for 8 weeks. Notable is the track *Going Home* which lasts 11 mins. 35 secs. (the final 7 mins. studio-improvized while the tapes still rolled). Produced by Oldham, Jones begins to add sitar and dulcimer on some tracks.
[30] Otis Redding names The Stones his favorite group (he covers *Satisfaction*).
May [1] Band makes its third consecutive appearance at the **New Musical Express** Poll Winners Concert at the Empire Pool, Wembley.
[14] *Big Hits (High Tide And Green Grass)* hits US #3.
[28] *Paint It Black* hits UK #1.
June [11] *Paint It Black* hits US #1.
[21] The Stones sue 14 New York hotels for a total of £1,750,000 over an alleged booking ban injurious to the group's reputation, and discriminatory in violation of New York's Civil Rights law.
[24] Group begins a North American tour, with The Chiffons, Bobby Goldsboro, Bobby Vee and Bobby Comstock, at the Manning Bowl in Lynn, MA. (The crowd is subdued with tear gas. It will be the last rock concert at the venue until 1985, when Aerosmith and Motley Crue perform.) The 31-date tour will end July 28 at the International Sports Center, Honolulu, HI.
July [23] *Sittin' On The Fence* by Twice As Much, written by Jagger/Richard, released on Immediate, reaches UK #25.
[29] Jagger/Richard's *Out Of Time* hits UK #1 for Chris Farlowe.
Aug [13] US-only release *Mother's Little Helper* hits US #8. B-side ballad *Lady Jane* makes US #24, as *Aftermath* hits US #2 for 2 weeks behind the Beatles' *Yesterday And Today*.
Sept [23] 12-date twice-nightly "Rolling Stones '66" tour with Ike & Tina Turner, The Yardbirds, Peter Jay & The Jaywalkers, The Kings Of Rhythm Orchestra, The Ikettes, Jimmy Thomas, Bobby John and Long John Baldry, opens at the Royal Albert Hall, London, amidst scenes which see hundreds of screaming teenagers rushing on to the stage at the start of the group's performance. Band leaves the stage and an announcement is made that unless everyone returns to their seats, the show will be cancelled. Order is restored and the group plays its set. The tour will end Oct.9 at the Gaumont theater, Southampton, Hants.
Oct [7] Group makes its last appearance on ITV's "Ready Steady Go!"
[15] *Have You Seen Your Mother, Baby, Standing In The Shadow?*, suffering from bad studio mix due to Decca's haste to release it, hits UK #5. (The Stones appear in drag at a photo call to promote the single on New York's Park Avenue.)
[29] *Have You Seen Your Mother, Baby, Standing In The Shadow?* hits US chart at #9.
Nov First Decca compilation, 14-track album *Big Hits (High Tide And Green Grass)*, hits UK #4.
Dec [23] Jagger appears on final edition of ITV's "Ready Steady Go!"
1967
Jan [15] The Stones appear on the "Ed Sullivan Show" and are forced to change the lyrics of *Let's Spend The Night Together* to "Let's Spend Some Time Together".
[21] Live album *got LIVE if you want it!*, recorded at the Royal Albert Hall, London, on Sept. 23 during recent UK tour, hits US #6.
[22] They make their first and last appearance on ITV's "Sunday Night At The London Palladium", singing *Let's Spend The Night Together*, *Ruby*

Tuesday, *It's All Over Now* and *Connection*. Showbiz tradition in UK dictates that artists wave to the audience on a revolving stage during the program's fade out. The Stones refuse and incur the wrath of press and public.
[29] Comedians Peter Cook and Dudley Moore, at the close of "Sunday Night At The London Palladium", wave to the audience with paper dummies of the group.
Feb [4] *Between The Buttons* hits UK #3. Featuring Watts' cartoon drawings on its back cover, it is the last to be produced by Oldham and points towards a greater self-sufficiency.
[5] Sunday newspaper **News Of The World** names Mick Jagger in an article about drug-taking pop stars. Jagger, appearing on ITV's "Eamonn Andrews Show", announces a writ for libel is served.
[11] *Let's Spend The Night Together* backed by *Ruby Tuesday* hits UK #3.
[12] Richard's Sussex home "Redlands" is raided by 15 policemen with a warrant under the Dangerous Drugs Act. (Charges are made against Richard and Jagger.)
Mar [4] *Ruby Tuesday* tops the US chart, as B-side *Let's Spend The Night Together* makes US #55.
[11] *Between The Buttons* hits US #2 for 4 weeks, behind The Monkees' *More Of The Monkees*.
[25] Group begins 16-date European tour in Malmo, Sweden, set to end Apr.17 in Athens, Greece.
Apr [13] The Stones play their first gig behind the Iron Curtain at the Palace of Culture, Warsaw, Poland. Police break up a crowd of 3,000, using batons and tear gas.
May [10] Jagger and Richard appear in Chichester Crown Court, Sussex, charged with being in possession of drugs. They elect to go to trial, pleading not guilty and being granted £1,000 bail each. Jones is arrested in his London flat, charged with unlawful possession of drugs and released on £250 bail.
[16] Group enters Olympic studios to start 4-day recording session.
June [8] Jones plays alto sax on The Beatles' *You Know My Name (Look Up The Number)* at Abbey Road studios.
[25] Jagger and Richard are among a group of friends who take part in the live recording of The Beatles' *All You Need Is Love* for TV show "Our World", broadcast from EMI's Abbey Road studios to an estimated 400 million people across 5 continents.
[27] Jagger is tried at West Sussex Quarter Sessions in Chichester, on a charge of unlawfully possessing 4 benzedrine tablets containing amphetamine sulphate and methyl amphetamine hydrochloride, which he had bought legally in Italy. The jury finds him guilty after a 6 min. deliberation, once the judge has ruled that his defense is not admissible. He is remanded in Lewes Jail overnight.
[29] Richard is tried on a charge of allowing his house to be used for the illegal smoking of cannabis. He too is found guilty. Judge Leslie Block sentences Richard to 1 year in jail and a £500 fine and Jagger to 3 months in jail and £100 costs. Jagger goes to Brixton jail, London, Richards to Wormwood Scrubs, London.
[30] Jagger and Richard are released by the High Court on bail of £7,000 each, and given leave to appeal their sentences.
July [1] **The Times** newspaper prints an editorial by William Rees-Mogg headlined "Who breaks a butterfly on a wheel?", protesting against the punishment meted out to the 2 group members.
[6] Jones collapses, waiting for his trial to start, and is admitted to hospital for nervous strain.
[31] Richard's conviction is quashed after some of the evidence against him had been deemed inadmissible. Jagger's sentence is reduced to a conditional discharge.
Aug [12] *Flowers*, compiled singles and studio out-takes, hits US #3.
[26] Jagger and girlfriend Marianne Faithfull visit the Maharishi Mahesh Yogi with The Beatles.
Sept [9] *We Love You*, the group's thank you to fans after events of the last few months, backed with *Dandelion*, hits UK #8. It opens with the sound of footsteps and cell doors being slammed and features backing vocals from Lennon and McCartney. They make a promotional film for it based on "The Trials Of Oscar Wilde", but it is banned by the BBC.
[29] It is announced that Oldham and The Stones are parting company
Oct [7] *We Love You* makes US #50.
[14] A-side *Dandelion* reaches US #14.
[30] Jones is found guilty of drug possession and allowing his flat to be used for drug-taking at the Inner London Sessions and sentenced to 9 months in jail.
[31] Pending an appeal against his sentence, Jones is released from Wormwood Scrubs, on £750 bail.
Dec [12] Jones' sentence is quashed, in favor of a £1,000 fine and 3

years probation, after 3 psychiatrists concur he is in a poor mental state and has suicidal tendencies.

[14] Jones collapses and is rushed to St. George's hospital, though he discharges himself shortly thereafter.

[16] **New Musical Express** reports that Marianne Faithfull is the first signing to The Stones' new Mother Earth label.

68 Jan [6] Now split from Oldham, self-produced hallucinatory influenced album *Their Satanic Majesties Request* hits UK #3. (This contribution to psychedelia is delivered months after the "Summer Of Love" and suffers from comparison with The Beatles' *Sgt. Pepper*.) The album's complex 3-D sleeve photo is designed to outdo the recent Beatles effort. It also hits US #2 for 6 weeks, behind The Beatles' *Magical Mystery Tour*, as Wyman makes US #87 with *In Another Land*, also from the album.

[27] *She's A Rainbow*, with a John Paul Jones string arrangement, reaches US #25.

May [12] Group makes its first live appearance in more than a year at the annual **New Musical Express** Poll Winners Concert at the Empire Pool, Wembley.

[21] Jones appears at Great Marlborough Street Magistrates Court on a charge of possession of marijuana, and is released on £200 bail.

June [11] Jones is committed for trial at the Inner London Sesssions.

[22] *Jumping Jack Flash* tops UK chart, their first #1 in 2 years. The Stones team with Traffic producer Jimmy Miller and return to R&B/rock-based recordings.

July [6] *Jumping Jack Flash* hits US #1.

[26] Decca withdraws *Beggars Banquet* from its scheduled release, objecting to the sleeve which depicts a graffiti-covered toilet. (Jagger is incensed by the company's double standard, citing the earlier release of Tom Jones *A-tom-ic Jones*, which features the singer standing in front of a nuclear explosion.)

Sept [26] Jones is found guilty of possession of cannabis and fined £50 with 100 guineas costs.

Oct [5] *Street Fighting Man*, banned by many US radio stations fearing that the lyrics may incite civil disorder, makes US #48.

Nov [13] Jones buys Cotchford Farm in Hartfield, Sussex, former home of **Winnie The Pooh** author A.A. Milne.

Dec [11-12] TV show "Rock And Roll Circus", created by the group, is filmed in a London studio by director Michael Lindsay-Hogg, with performances from artists including The Who, Jethro Tull, Eric Clapton and John Lennon. (The show is never transmitted.)

[28] *Beggars Banquet*, released in a plain white sleeve depicting an invitation, hits UK #3. (The press launch for the album at the Queensgate hotel, London, is an actual banquet, which degenerates into a custard-pie fight between those present, which does not include a sick Richard who is deputized by Lord Harlech.) Produced by Miller and engineered by Glyn Johns, with mainly acoustic overtones, the album will be regarded by many as their finest achievement and includes particular critics favorite *Sympathy For The Devil*. Jones is gradually being excised from the group's activities, drug abuse and life in the fast lane having taken their toll on him. Since the sleeve dispute, the group's relationship with Decca has also worsened (when the album is re-promoted in the 80s by Decca, it will only be available in the toilet sleeve).

969 Jan [11] *Beggars Banquet* hits US #5.

May [28] Jagger and Faithfull are arrested at their London home, charged with possession of cannabis and released on £50 bail each.

June [8] Jones, in poor mental and physical shape, quits. He is quoted as saying "I no longer see eye to eye with the disks we are cutting" at a time when the group is recording some of its purest blues sounds (Jones' first love).

[9] The Rolling Stones announce Jones will be replaced by Mick Taylor (b. Michael Taylor, Jan.17, 1948, Welwyn Garden City, Herts.), guitarist with The John Mayall Band.

July [3] Jones is found dead in his swimming pool at Hartfield by girlfriend Anna Wohlin after taking a midnight swim. (The coroner records a verdict of misadventure "drowning while under the influence of alcohol and drugs.")

[5] The Rolling Stones, with Taylor making his debut, play a free concert in Hyde Park, London, attended by 250,000 fans. Jagger pays tribute to Jones by reciting Shelley's **Adonais**, and 3,000 butterflies are released. The event is filmed by ITV as "The Stones In The Park" and broadcast on Sept.2, 1969.

[6] Jagger flies to Australia with Marianne Faithfull to begin work on film "Ned Kelly".

[8] Faithfull attempts suicide after Jagger says their relationship is over, and lies in a coma for 8 days.

[10] Jones is buried in Cheltenham. The other Stones, excluding Jagger, are present. Canon Hugh Evan Hopkins reads Jones' own epitaph: "Please don't judge me too harshly."

[26] *Honky Tonk Women* tops the UK chart for 5 weeks.

Aug [10] Richard's girlfriend Anita Pallenberg gives birth to a son, Marlon. (Richard and Pallenberg will be seen starring with David Warner in film "Michael Kohlhaas", which will be withdrawn shortly after release.)

[23] *Honky Tonk Women* tops the US chart for 4 weeks.

Sept *Through The Past Darkly (Big Hits Volume 2)*, a second greatest hits set, dedicated to the memory of Brian Jones, hits UK #2. Jean Luc Godard's impressionistic film of the group at work, "Sympathy For The Devil" premieres at the Edinburgh Festival.

Oct [11] *Through The Past Darkly (Big Hits Volume 2)* hits US #2, behind Creedence Clearwater Revival's *Green River*.

Nov [7] The Stones begin their sixth US tour at the State University, Fort Collins, CO. The 17-date tour will end Nov.29 at Boston Garden, Boston, MA. Writer (and later rock biographer) Albert Goldman compares Jagger to Adolf Hitler in **The New York Times**.

[30] Group plays at a festival at the International Raceway, West Palm Beach, FL.

Dec [6] Aiming to repeat their successful Hyde Park concert, The Stones close their US tour with a free concert at Altamont Speedway, Livermore, CA. Having employed UK Hells Angels to act as security men in London, the group hire their San Francisco counterparts, who prove to be less placid and, due to a mixture of drink and drugs, provoke angry scenes. In a confused atmosphere, 18-year-old black youth Meredith Hunter is stabbed to death by bikers when he pulls a gun at the front of the stage midway through the Stones' set. Group rushes through its numbers before escaping in a helicopter. The disastrous concert is seen by many as an epitaph to the good times of the 60s and the closing of an era.

[19] Jagger and Faithfull appear at Great Marlborough Street Magistrates Court. Jagger is found guilty and fined £200 with 50 guineas costs. Faithfull is acquitted.

[20] *Let It Bleed* enters UK chart at #1, knocking off The Beatles' *Abbey Road*, which returns to the top the following week. It includes guest artists ranging from Ry Cooder to Merry Clayton, and is highlighted by *Midnight Rambler*, with Jagger portrayed in the role of the Boston Strangler Albert de Salvo, and closes with The London Bach Choir singing the introduction to *You Can't Always Get What You Want*. It also includes the original conception of *Honky Tonk Women*, recorded as *Country Honk*.

[25] Group makes its 50th appearance on BBC's "Top Of The Pops".

[27] *Let It Bleed* hits US #3, behind *Led Zeppelin II* and *Abbey Road*.

1970 Feb [19] Residents and landowners of Altamont file a £375,000 suit claiming damage to their land.

Mar [11] "One Plus One" opens in US.

July [28] "Ned Kelly" film premieres in Australia.

[31] The Stones' contract with Decca ends. (Still to deliver a single to complete the deal, they provide unreleasable *Cocksucker Blues*.)

Aug [1] Film "Performance" premieres, having been delayed for 2 years because of worries over its excessive violence. Jagger receives critical accolades for his performance as retired rock star Turner.

Sept [3] Jagger is cited in the divorce proceedings between Marianne Faithfull and her husband John Dunbar.

[19] Live album *Get Yer Ya-Ya's Out!*, recorded at New York's Madison Square Garden on Nov.27 and 28, 1969, hits UK #1 for 2 weeks, fulfilling the band's final contractual obligation to Decca.

[23] Jagger meets Bianca Rose Perez Moreno de Macias after a concert at Paris Olympia.

Oct [1] A riot breaks out outside the Palazzo Del Sport, Milan, Italy. Police, using batons and tear gas, arrest 63 people.

[7] "Ned Kelly" premieres in UK.

[24] *Get Yer Ya-Ya's Out!* hits US #6.

[26] Meredith Hunter's mother files a £28,000 suit against the Stones and others.

[30] Jagger is ordered to pay £200 costs as Dunbar is granted a divorce from Faithfull.

Nov [28] Jagger's solo *Memo From Turner*, taken from *Performance* soundtrack, reaches UK #32.

Dec [6] "Gimme Shelter" concert film opens in New York. (It documents their 1969 US tour ending with the events at Altamont.)

1971 Mar [4] Group begins a UK tour at the City Hall, Newcastle, Tyne & Wear, and announces decision to live in South of France as tax exiles.

[18] Ticket touts charge up to £10 for tickets at their farewell concert at the Roundhouse, London.

[26] They play at the Marquee for a US TV special.

Apr [3] *Stone Age* hits UK #4 as Decca begins re-packaging Stones' material. (This will extend into the mid-70s and cause anger from the group who publicly decry the process.)

[6] Band forms its own label Rolling Stones Records to be distributed worldwide by the Kinney group, now owners of Warner Bros. Marshall Chess is chosen to run the label, while Andy Warhol designs its logo.

May [8] *Sticky Fingers*, with a Warhol-designed sleeve of a male torso from the waist down clad in jeans, complete with a real zip fastener, using a horn section to fill out their sound with heavy brass inflections, tops UK chart. Again produced by Miller, it includes guests Billy Preston, Jim Price, Bobby Keyes, Ry Cooder, Nitzsche and Stewart.

[12] Jagger and Bianca marry at St. Tropez Town Hall, France.

[15] *Brown Sugar*, the first release on Rolling Stones label and in UK backed with *Bitch* and *Let It Rock*, hits UK #2, held off the top by Dawn's *Knock Three Times*. (It is the group's first hit in 2 years, and will be considered another classic.)

[22] *Sticky Fingers* tops US chart for 4 weeks.

[29] Extracted *Brown Sugar* tops US chart.

July [23] Group, and Brian Jones' father, file a multi-million lawsuit against Klein, alleging "mismanagement of funds".

[24] Acoustic guitar-led *Wild Horses* reaches US #28.

[31] Decca-released *Street Fighting Man* reaches UK #21.

Aug [31] The Stones and Jones file a High Court writ against Andrew Oldham and Eric Easton for "royalty deprivation".

Sept [25] *Gimme Shelter*, a Decca best of, released against the group's wishes, but to tie in with the film premiere of the same name and featuring one side of a live Albert Hall performance, reaches UK #19.

Oct [21] Jade, a daughter to Mick and Bianca Jagger, is born in Paris.

1972 **Feb** [12] Double retrospective album *Hot Rocks 1964-1971*, compiled by Klein, hits US #4.

[16] Shirley Watts is arrested at Nice airport, for hitting and swearing at French Customs officials. (She will receive a suspended sentence.)

[16] A Hell's Angel is acquitted for the murder of Meredith Hunter, and immediately sues The Stones for £20,000 for invasion of privacy.

Mar [18] *Milestones* reaches US #14.

Apr [17] Richard's and Pallenberg's daughter Dandelion is born.

May [13] *Tumbling Dice*, from a forthcoming album, hits UK #5.

[10] A press release is issued stating that the group and Klein have settled their differences, and will co-operate with each other in their claim against Easton.

[27] *Tumbling Dice* hits US #7.

June [3] Group begins North American tour with Stevie Wonder and Martha Reeves in Vancouver, Canada. 30 police are injured by gatecrashers.

[10] *Exile On Main Street*, the group's only double studio set, and recorded mainly in The Stones' mobile studio unit in France, under Richard's creative guidance, tops UK chart. Clean-up TV campaigner Mary Whitehouse claims BBC radio should not air the album due to its obscene nature. Chairman Lord Hill listens to the disk and claims to hear nothing wrong, although it is littered with swear words.

[17] *Exile On Main Street* tops US chart for 4 weeks.

July [17] A bomb explodes, believed to be the work of French separatists, under the group's equipment van before a concert in Montreal, Canada.

[18] Jagger is arrested in Warwick, RI, on his way to a concert at the Boston Garden, after an altercation with a photographer. Boston Mayor Kevin White bails him out so they can play their scheduled concert.

Aug [19] *Happy* reaches US #22.

Oct [10] The lawsuits between The Rolling Stones, ABKCO, Decca, Eric Easton and Andrew Oldham are all settled.

Nov [6] Wyman appears at Chelmsford Magistrates Court and is fined £20 and loses his license for speeding on the A12 in his Mercedes.

[11] Decca compilation album *Rock'N'Rolling Stones* makes UK #41.

Dec [4] The Stones, with the exception of Jagger, appear in court in Nice, France, charged with use of heroin and hashish at Richard's villa near Villefranche-sur-Mer. The case is dismissed when 5 prosecution witnesses testify that the police intimidated them to make false statements.

[26] The Jaggers fly to Nicaragua to search for Bianca's relatives, missing after the earthquake.

1973 **Jan** [4] An entry ban is placed on an unnamed Stone by the Immigration Ministry in Australia, where the group is to tour shortly. 5 days later the ban will be lifted, without the Stone in question being named.

[6] Carly Simon's *You're So Vain*, on which Jagger adds a notable back-up vocal, tops US chart.

[18] Group plays a benefit concert at Los Angeles' Forum in aid of victims of the Nicaraguan earthquake disaster. It raises over $400,000.

Feb [13] Another Klein double compilation album *More Hot Rocks (big hits & fazed cookies)* hits US #9.

Apr [7] Warwick, RI, judge refuses motion to dismiss the charges arising from the July 18, 1972 incident, announcing that Jagger and Richard would stand trial the next time they set foot on US soil.

May [8] The Jaggers are honored in Washington, DC, with A Golden Key for the efforts toward Nicaraguan Earthquake Relief.

June [9] *You Can't Always Get What You Want* (the B-side of 1969 #1 *Honky Tonk Women*) makes US #42.

[18] Marsha Hunt files an affiliation order at Marylebone Court, alleging that Jagger is the father of her 2-year-old daughter.

[26] Richard and Pallenberg are arrested at their Cheyne Walk house on charges of possession of cannabis and a Smith & Wesson revolver.

[27] They appear at Marylebone Court and are freed on £1,000 bail.

July [31] Richard's house "Redlands" is razed to the ground.

Aug Richard falls asleep in his room at the Londonderry House hotel in Hyde Park, London, and accidentally sets fire to himself. All group members are subsequently banned from staying there.

Sept [11] Group begins a UK tour.

[15] *Angie*, an acoustic love song, hits UK #5, amid great press interest in its alleged subject, David Bowie's wife Angie.

[22] *Goat's Head Soup*, recorded at Byron Lee's Dynamic Sound studios, Kingston, Jamaica, tops UK charts. It marks the last Jimmy Miller-produced Stones album.

Oct [10] Jagger and Taylor perform with Billy Preston & The God Squad at the Rainbow, Finsbury Park, London.

[13] *Goat's Head Soup* tops US chart for 4 weeks.

[15] Richard is found guilty of use, supply and trafficking of cannabis in a Nice court. He receives a 1-year suspended sentence and a 5,000 franc fine for similar charges involving heroin, and is banned from entering France for 2 years.

[20] *Angie* hits US #1 for a week.

[24] Richard appears in Great Marlborough Street Magistrates Court and is given a conditional discharge and a £205 fine for possession of cannabis, Mandrax tablets, Chinese heroin, firearms and ammunition at his Cheyne Walk home.

1974 **Feb** [23] *Doo Doo Doo Doo Doo (Heartbreaker)*, also from *Goat's Head Soup*, reaches US #15.

Mar [27] Group turns down a $100,000 request to play a week at the Tropicana hotel in Las Vegas, NV.

June [8] Wyman, the first Stone to release a solo album, makes UK #3 with album *Monkey Grip*. It peaks at US #99.

July [13-14] Richard joins Faces's guitarist Ron Wood's band at the Kilburn State theater, London.

Aug [17] *It's Only Rock'N'Roll* hits UK #10. Its release is heralded by an outbreak of graffiti across London bearing the title, and marks the debut of production credits to "The Glimmer Twins" – a pseudonym for Jagger/Richard.

Sept [21] *It's Only Rock'N'Roll* reaches US #16.

Oct [26] Glimmer Twins-produced *It's Only Rock'N'Roll* hits UK #2, held off the top by The Bay City Rollers' *Rollin'*. Recorded in Munich, Germany, its guest musicians include Nicky Hopkins, percussionist Ray Cooper, Willie Weeks and Kenney Jones.

Nov [23] *It's Only Rock'N'Roll* tops US chart.

Dec After over 5 years with the group, Taylor quits, suffering from the pressure of being a member of the world's most popular group, as The Stones prepare to start work on their new album in Munich, Germany. "The last 5½ years with the Stones have been very exciting and proved to be a most inspiring period. And as far as my attitude to the other 4 members concerned, it is one of respect for them, both as musicians and people. I have nothing but admiration for the group, but I feel now is the time to move on and do something new." Jagger states "After 5½ years, Mick wishes a change of scene and wants the opportunity to try out new ventures, new endeavors. While we are all most sorry that he is going, we wish him great success and much happiness." Taylor will join The Jack Bruce Band with Carla Bley and Max Middleton.

[14] A revival of The Temptations' *Ain't Too Proud To Beg*, from *It's Only Rock'N'Roll*, reaches US #17.

[31] Ron Wood (b. Ronald Wood, June 1, 1947, Hillingdon, London) of The Faces denies rumors that he is joining the group, stating The Faces are more important to him. Jagger says "No doubt we can find a brilliant 6' 3" blond guitarist who can do his own make up."

1975 Apr [14] Wood is confirmed as Taylor's replacement for touring purposes only.

May [31] During a press conference at the Fifth Avenue hotel in New York to announce a Stones US tour, the group comes into view performing live on a flat-bed truck, to the surprise of journalists.

June [3] A US tour begins, with Wood guesting.

[14] Decca-released *Metamorphosis*, mainly a collection of Jagger/Richard songs demoed for other artists during the 60s (though it includes a rare Wyman-penned cut *Downtown Suzie*) makes UK #45.

[28] First Rolling Stones Records issued compilation album *Made In The Shade* reaches UK #14.

July [6] Richard is charged with reckless driving and carrying a offensive weapon, a 7" hunting knife in Fordyce, AR, and released on $162 bail. Richard, who is accompanied by Ronnie Wood, states that he "bent down to change the waveband on the radio, and the car swerved slightly. A police patrol vehicle then pulled out from a lay-by and stopped us. I was also questioned about having a concealed weapon, which turned out to be a penknife complete with tin-opener and a device for removing stones from horse's hooves." (He will subsequently be cleared.)

[12] A version of Stevie Wonder's *I Don't Know Why*, from *Metamorphosis* peaks at US #42, as the album (with slightly fewer tracks than the UK version) hits US #8.

[19] *Made In The Shade* hits US #6.

Sept [6] *Out Of Time*, also from the album, featuring a Jagger solo over the backing track to his 1966 production for Chris Farlowe, climbs to US #81.

[20] *Out Of Time* makes UK #45.

Nov [22] Decca double compilation album *Rolled Gold – The Very Best Of The Rolling Stones* debuts at UK #7.

Dec [6] A preacher in Tallahassee, FL, pronounces The Stones records "sinful", after concluding a survey of 1,000 unmarried mothers and discovering that 984 of them had conceived to the sound of rock music, although not necessarily The Stones. His congregation has a bonfire of Rolling Stones and Elton John records.

1976 Mar [26] Tara, a son to Keith Richard and Anita Pallenberg, is born.

Apr [17] Wyman's *Stone Alone* makes US #166.

[24] *Black And Blue*, more dance-slanted than usual, hits UK #2.

May [10-12] Group begins 13-date UK tour with 3 performances at the Apollo Centre, Glasgow, Scotland, set to end May 27 with 6 nights at Earl's Court, London, for which promoters have received 1 million postal applications.

[15] *Black And Blue* tops US chart for 4 weeks.

[19] Richard falls asleep at the wheel of his car and crashes on the M1 near Newport Pagnell. Cocaine and marijuana are found in the vehicle (and he will later be fined).

June [4] Richard's 10-week-old son Tara dies from pneumonia in Geneva, Switzerland.

[5] Extracted ballad *Fool To Cry* hits UK #6 and US #10.

July [17] US B-side *Hot Stuff* makes US #49.

Aug [21] The Stones headline Knebworth Festival, Herts., in front of 200,000 fans, and perform a retrospective set tracing their roots back to their debut album in 1964.

Nov [25] Wood joins an all-star cast on *I Shall Be Released* at The Band's "The Last Waltz" Farewell Concert at San Francisco's Winterland.

1977 Jan [10] Richard appears at Aylesbury Crown Court, Bucks., charged with cocaine and LSD possession. He is found guilty of possessing cocaine and fined £750 with £250 costs, but acquitted on the charge of LSD possession.

Feb [16] It is announced that The Rolling Stones have signed a distribution deal with EMI for the group's next 6 albums.

[24] Richard and girlfriend Anita Pallenberg are stopped at customs when they arrive in Toronto, Canada.

[27] Richard is arrested by the Royal Canadian Mounted Police at Toronto's Harbour Castle hotel for possession of 22 gms of heroin and 5 gms of cocaine. (A charge of trafficking in heroin will hang over him for 18 months.) Bail will be set at $25,000.

Mar [4-5] Group performs 2 gigs at 300-capacity El Mocambo night club in Toronto. (The second set is recorded and later appears as *Love You Live*.)

[14] Richard makes his second court appearance and is remanded on bail until June 27.

[18] Wood, in the audience with Jagger and Wyman, joins The Eagles on stage for an encore at the band's Madison Square Garden, New York concert.

Apr [1] The Stones re-sign with Atlantic for North American

distribution of Rolling Stones Records in a deal reportedly worth $21 million for 6 albums.

June [27] Richard fails to show up for his Toronto court appearance.

Sept [20] BBC TV's "The Old Grey Whistle Test" airs an hour-long film of 1976 Paris concert.

[23] "Ladies And Gentlemen, The Rolling Stones" movie premieres at the Rainbow, London.

[24] Performance album *Love You Live* hits UK #3.

Oct [29] *Love You Live* hits US #5.

Dec [2] Richard appears in Toronto court, and is remanded again.

[17] Quickly deleted UK-only issued TV advertised anthology, *Get Stoned* hits UK #8.

1978 Jan [26] Wood signs a solo deal with CBS Records at MIDEM in Cannes, France.

Apr [1] The Philadelphia Furies, a soccer team co-owned by Jagger, Peter Frampton, Paul Simon and Rick Wakeman, loses its first match of the North America Soccer League 3-0 to the Washington Diplomats.

June [10] The Stones open a 25-date tour of North America, their ninth, at the Civic Center, Lakeland, FL, set to end at the Oakland Coliseum July 26.

[15] Glimmer Twins-produced *Some Girls*, causing some controversy for its attitude towards women and use of photos of Lucille Ball, Raquel Welch and Farrah Fawcett-Majors in a mock wig ad on the sleeve and changed after litigation threats, tops the US chart.

[17] *Miss You*, influenced by the current disco trend and the group's first 12" single and backed with jangling country ballad *Far Away Eyes*, hits UK #3 as parent album *Some Girls* hits UK #2.

[29] A fan is shot and 17 are arrested at the group's Rupp Arena, Lexington, KY, concert.

July [9] The Stones, minus Wyman, jam with Muddy Waters on stage at the Chicago nightlcub the Quiet Knight.

[10] Wyman is knocked unconscious when he falls off stage at a concert at the Coliseum, St. Paul, MN .

Aug [5] *Miss You* tops US chart.

Oct [7] The Stones guest on NBC TV's "Saturday Night Live".

[24] Richards (having reverted to his given name) pleads guilty to possession of heroin. Judge Lloyd Graburn imposes a 1-year suspended sentence and orders him to continue his addiction treatment and to play a special concert at the Canadian National Institute for the Blind within the next 6 months.

[28] Rolling Stones Records roster reggae artist Peter Tosh's *(You Got To Walk And) Don't Look Back*, a duet with Jagger, makes UK #43.

Nov [4] *Respectable* reaches UK #23.

[11] *Beast Of Burden* hits US #8.

[25] *(You Got To Walk And) Don't Look Back* makes US #81.

1979 Feb [3] *Shattered* makes US #31. Richards releases solo single, a revival of Chuck Berry's *Run Rudolph Run*.

Apr [22] The Stones and The New Barbarians, a group assembled by Richards for the occasion with Ron Wood (guitar), Ian McLagan (keyboards), Stanley Clarke (bass), Ziggy Modeliste (drums) and Bobby Keyes (sax), perform at the Civic Auditorium, Oshawa, Ontario, for the Canadian National Institute for the Blind.

[24] The New Barbarians begin an 18-date US tour in Ann Arbor, MI. Tour ends May 21 at the Forum, Los Angeles.

Aug [11] The New Barbarians play at the Knebworth Festival.

Sept [2] Wyman joins Kiki Dee, Dave Mason, Todd Rundgren and Ringo Starr in a band raising funds for the Jerry Lewis Muscular Dystrophy Telethon, broadcast from Las Vegas, NV.

1980 Jan [13] Fans riot in Milwaukee, WI, when The New Barbarians play a concert, without Richards.

Feb [18] In an interview in the **Daily Express**, Wyman says that he intends to leave The Stones in 1982, on the group's 20th anniversary.

[22] Wood and girlfriend Jo Howard are arrested for cocaine possession on St. Martin in the Dutch Antilles, and spend 5 days in jail.

July [3] Richards and Pallenberg separate. (He begins a new relationship with Patti Hansen.)

[5] *Emotional Rescue*, continuing the band's dance-oriented feel, tops UK chart.

[26] *Emotional Rescue* tops US chart for 7 weeks, as extracted title track *Emotional Rescue* hits UK #9.

Sept [6] Jagger falsetto-sung *Emotional Rescue* hits US #3.

Oct [3] Wyman begins work on the soundtrack to the Ryan O'Neal/Omar Sharif movie "Green Ice".

[18] *She's So Cold* makes UK #33.

Nov [5] The Jaggers are divorced.

[8] *She's So Cold* reaches US #26.

1981 **Feb** Jagger walks out of the filming of Werner Herzog's "Fitzcarraldo" in Peru, after 5 members of the crew are killed.

Apr [18] Compilation album *Sucking In The Seventies* reaches US #15.

June Richard sees Chuck Berry's set at the Ritz in New York, after which Berry punches him in the eye.

Aug [22] Wyman's *(Si Si) Je Suis Un Rock Star* reaches UK #14. (It will be revived in the 80s as a TV ad jingle.)

[14] The Stones begin rehearsals at Long View Farm, Brookfield, MA, for an, as yet unannounced, American tour.

Sept [12] *Tattoo You*, comprising unreleased songs dating back to 1972 from the *Goat's Head Soup* sessions, hits UK #2 as extracted *Start Me Up* hits UK #7.

[14] Group plays a warm-up gig as Blue Monday & The Cockroaches, at the 350-capacity Sir Morgan's Cave, Worcester, MA. Word of the show leaks out, and more than 4,000 fans turn up, resulting in 11 arrests.

[19] *Tattoo You* tops US chart for 9 weeks.

[25] Group begins its 10th US tour at JFK Stadium, Philadelphia, PA, before a crowd of 90,000. The 50-date tour, attended by more than 2 million people and grossing over $50 million, will end Dec.19 at the Hampton Coliseum, Hampton Roads, VA.

Oct [28] 22-year-old Wesley Shelton is murdered by a 16-year-old outside the Astrodome, Houston, TX, where the Stones are playing.

[31] *Start Me Up* hits US #2 for 3 weeks, held off the top by Christopher Cross' *Arthur's Theme (Best That You Can Do)* and then Daryl Hall & John Oates' *Private Eyes*.

Nov [9] 12 people are hurt and 56 arrested at a Civic Center, Hartford, CT, concert.

[22] Jagger, Richards and Wood jam with Buddy Guy and Muddy Waters at the Checker Board Lounge, Chicago.

Dec [14] Mick Taylor joins the band for its Kemper Arena, Kansas City, MO, concert.

[19] Easy flowing ballad *Waiting On A Friend* makes UK #50.

1982 **Feb** [6] *Waiting On A Friend* reaches US #13.

Mar [27] Wyman's *A New Fashion* makes UK #37.

Apr [10] Third solo album *Bill Wyman* peaks at UK #55.

May [8] *Hang Fire* makes US #20.

[26] The Stones begin a European tour at the Capitol theater, Aberdeen, Scotland, supported by The J. Geils Band. Tour will end July 25 at Roundhay Park, Leeds, W.Yorks.

[31] Group gigs at the 100 club in London's Oxford Street, before a crowd of 400.

June [19] *Still Life (American Concert 1981)*, a record of the 1981 US tour, hits UK #4.

[25] The Stones receive the Silver Clef Award for outstanding achievement to British music from the Nordoff-Robbins Music Therapy charity in London. Wyman accepts the award on the group's behalf. Group plays Wembley Stadium in the evening.

[26] *Going To A Go-Go*, a revival of The Miracles hit, reaches UK #26.

July [10] *Still Life* hits US #5.

[17] *Going To A Go-Go* reaches US #25.

Aug [7] Import album *In Concert* makes UK #94.

Oct [9] *Time On My Side*, from the live album, peaks at UK #62.

Dec [25] TV-promoted compilation album *Story Of The Stones* makes UK #24.

1983 **Jan** [14] Jagger films his part of the Chinese Emperor in "The Nightingale" as part of Showtime TV's "Faerie Tale Theatre" series.

Feb [11] "Let's Spend The Night Together", the Hal Ashby-directed documentary of the group's 1981 tour, premieres at the Loew theater in New York.

Mar [24] "Let's Spend The Night Together" is released in UK.

Aug [20] Wood becomes a father to Tyrone.

[25] Jagger and Richards reach agreement with CBS head Walter Yetnikoff to sign with the label at 3am in the Ritz hotel, Paris. Reportedly worth $28 million, the deal calls for 4 band albums.

Sept [20-21] Wyman and Watts join Jeff Beck, Eric Clapton, Jimmy Page, Steve Winwood, Joe Cocker, Paul Rodgers, Kenney Jones, Andy Fairweather Low, Ray Cooper and Ronnie Lane (himself a sufferer) in a benefit concert at the Royal Albert Hall, London, in aid of ARMS (Action For Research Into Multiple Sclerosis). The second show will be performed in the presence of the Prince and Princess of Wales.

Oct [28] Jagger guests on the first edition of C4 TV's "The Tube".

Nov [19] *Undercover Of The Night*, despite a Julien Temple-lensed gun-toting video ban by BBC TV's "Top Of The Pops", reaches UK #11, as parent album *Undercover* hits UK #3.

[28] Wyman and Watts begin 9-date, 4-city US tour, in aid of the ARMS charity, at the Reunion Arena, Dallas, TX, with Ron Wood joining the same group of musicians featured at the Royal Albert Hall on Sept.20.

Dec [10] *Undercover* hits US #4.

[18] Richards marries long-time belle Patti Hansen at Cabo San Lucas, Mexico on his 40th birthday.

[23] Jagger guests in Bette Midler's video for her forthcoming single, a cover of *Beast Of Burden*.

[24] *Undercover Of The Night* hits US #9.

1984 **Jan** [20] Press reports state that Jagger has donated £32,000 to Great Britain's gymnastic hopefuls for the forthcoming Olympic Games in Los Angeles.

Feb [25] *She Was Hot* makes UK #42.

Mar [2] Jerry Hall gives birth to Elizabeth Scarlett Jagger.

[3] *She Was Hot* makes US #44.

May [6-10] Jagger records *State Of Shock* with The Jacksons at New York's A&R studio.

June [14] The Rolling Stones become the first act to be inaugurated into the Madison Square Garden Hall Of Fame.

July [21] The Jacksons' *State Of Shock*, with Jagger trading lead vocals with Michael Jackson, reaches UK #14. Another Stones retrospective *Rewind 1971-1984 (The Best Of The Rolling Stones)* reaches UK #23.

[28] Extracted re-issue *Brown Sugar* peaks at UK #58.

Aug [4] *State Of Shock* hits US #4.

[18] *Rewind* makes US #86.

Nov [13] Stones' compilation video "Rewind" is released and becomes the first music video in UK to receive 18 certificate.

1985 **Mar** Wyman begins *Willie & The Poor Boys* album and video project to benefit ARMS. Andy Fairweather Low, Kenney Jones, Jimmy Page, Chris Rea, Paul Rodgers, Ringo Starr, Charlie Watts and Terry Williams also contribute.

[9] Jagger launches a long-awaited solo career with *Just Another Night*, which reaches UK #32.

[16] Jagger's solo album *She's The Boss*, produced with Bill Laswell and Nile Rodgers and recorded at Compass Point studios, Nassau, Bahamas, debuts at its UK peak position of #6.

[30] *Just Another Night* reaches US #12.

Apr [20] *She's The Boss* reaches US #13.

June [1] *Lucky In Love*, Jagger's second solo single, makes US #38.

July [13] Jagger performs at Live Aid at the JFK stadium, Philadelphia, PA, backed by Daryl Hall & John Oates, and is joined by Tina Turner on a medley of *State Of Shock* and *It's Only Rock'N'Roll*. Wood and Richards join Bob Dylan for his set at the conclusion of the event. Earlier in the day, a video of Jagger and Bowie's duet *Dancing In The Street*, recorded on June 29, is premiered.

Aug [28] James Jagger is born.

Sept [7] *Dancing In The Street* enters the UK chart at #1, going gold in a week and becoming the fastest-selling single of the year.

Oct [12] *Dancing In The Streeet* hits US #7.

Nov [18] Charlie Watts & His Big Band begins a week of performances at Ronnie Scott's jazz club, London.

Dec [12] Stewart dies of a heart attack in his doctor's Harley Street, London, reception room, while waiting to see him.

1986 **Jan** [23] Richards inducts Chuck Berry at the first annual Rock'N'Roll Hall Of Fame ceremonies at the Waldorf Astoria in New York. Richards says "I lifted every lick he ever played."

Feb [23] The Stones play at the small 100 club in Oxford Street, London, in memory of Ian Stewart.

[25] The Rolling Stones are honored by NARAS at the 29th annual Grammy awards with a Lifetime Achievement Award citing the band "who poured the foundation for modern pop and rock performers and writers to build their careers upon; who through their abilities to grow and to change with society's dynamics both musically and lyrically awakened the senses and consciousness of America and the world."

Mar [22] *Harlem Shuffle*, a remake of Bob & Earl's 1964 US #44, reaches UK #13.

[23] The Charlie Watts Orchestra makes its debut at the Town Hall, Fulham, London. (During April, the orchestra plays a 1-week stint at Ronnie Scott's Jazz club.)

Apr [5] *Dirty Work*, dedicated to the memory of Ian Stewart, and the group's first for CBS though still via their own Rolling Stones Records, hits UK #4.

May [3] *Dirty Work*, co-produced by the Glimmer Twins and Steve Lillywhite, hits US #4 and extracted *Harlem Shuffle* hits US #5.

June [6] Richards joins Chuck Berry on stage at the third annual Chicago Blues Festival in Grant Park, Chicago.

[20] Jagger and David Bowie perform *Dancing In The Street* at the Prince's Trust charity concert at the Empire Pool, Wembley.
[28] *One Hit (To The Body)*, accompanied by a Russell Mulcahy-directed video, makes US #28 but is the group's first UK chart miss.
July [5] Wood and Wyman join Rod Stewart on stage at the end of Stewart's Wembley Stadium concert.
[7] Richards produces Aretha Franklin's version of *Jumpin' Jack Flash* at Detroit's Tamla Motown United Sound studio. Wood plays guitar on the session.
Aug [3] The **News Of The World** prints an exclusive interview with 16-year-old model Mandy Smith, who reveals she has been having an affair with Bill Wyman for 2½ years.
[30] Jagger's solo *Ruthless People*, from the film of the same name and written with Dave Stewart and Daryl Hall, peaks at US #51.
Sept [16] Jagger punches a photographer while dining at a Los Angeles restaurant with Dave Stewart.
Oct [16] After a week of rehearsals at Chuck Berry's farm in Wentzville, MO, Richards joins Eric Clapton, Julian Lennon, Linda Ronstadt, Etta James and Chuck Berry on stage at the Fox theater, St. Louis, MO, for a concert being filmed for Taylor Hackford's Berry documentary "Hail! Hail! Rock'N'Roll."
Nov [15] Jagger begins recording new album at Wisseloord studio, Hilversum, Holland.
[23] Richards joins Eric Clapton on stage at the Ritz in New York, for *Cocaine* and *Layla*.
[29] The Charlie Watts Orchestra begins a 5-date US tour at the West Hartford Music Hall, Hartford, CT.

1987 **Apr** [13] Wyman launches his AIMS Project (Ambition, Ideas, Motivation, Success) at a press conference at the Champagne Exchange, London. The plan is to travel the UK with The Stones' mobile studio and record unknown bands.
Sept [26] Jagger's second solo album, *Primitive Cool*, featuring Vernon Reid from Living Colour whom Jagger promotes and produces over the next 2 years, reaches UK #26.
Oct [17] *Primitive Cool* makes US #41.
[24] Extracted *Let's Work*, written and produced with Eurythmics' Dave Stewart, makes UK #31 and US #39.
Nov [4] Wood and Bo Diddley, collectively known as The Gunslingers, open a North American tour at the Newport Music Hall, Columbus, OH. Tour will end Nov.25 at the Ritz, New York.
Dec [19] Jagger's *Throwaway* peaks at US #67.

1988 **Jan** [20] Jagger inducts The Beatles at the third annual Rock'N'Roll Hall Of Fame dinner at the Waldorf Astoria in New York, before taking part in a jam session with Bob Dylan, George Harrison, Elton John and Bruce Springsteen.
Feb [20] Wyman and Wood join Phil Collins, Elvis Costello, Ian Dury, Chris Rea, Eddy Grant, Terence Trent D'Arby and Kenney Jones at a benefit concert, organised by Wyman, at London's Royal Albert Hall, to raise money for the Great Ormond Street Hospital for Sick Children's "Wishing Well Appeal."
Mar [2] Wood begins a 2-week tour of Japan with Bo Diddley, as The Gunslingers.
[15] Jagger plays his first-ever Japanese concert at the Castle Hall, Osaka, in front of 11,000 people at the start of his solo tour.
[23] Tina Turner joins Jagger on stage at the Kerakuen Dome in Tokyo, Japan, duetting with him on *Brown Sugar* and *It's Only Rock'N'Roll*.
Apr [18-26] Jagger attends a lawsuit in White Plains Court in New York, brought by reggae musician Patrick Alley, who claims Jagger has plagiarized the song *Just Another Night*. Jagger will win the case.
May [18] All 5 group members meet for the first time in 2 years at the Savoy hotel, London.
June [28] The Gunslingers play the Hammersmith Odeon, before embarking on month-long tour of Germany, Italy and Spain.
Sept *(I Can't Get No) Satisfaction* is voted #1 by **Rolling Stone** magazine on its Top 100 Singles Of All Time list.
[17] Jagger plays a warm-up gig at the 400 capacity Kardomah Cafe in Sydney, Australia.
[22] Jagger begins his Australasian tour at the Boondall Entertainment Centre, Brisbane. Tour will end Nov.5 at the Western Spring Stadium, Auckland, New Zealand.
Oct [15] Richards debut solo album *Talk Is Cheap* makes UK #37.
[16] Richards, his own Jamaican home damaged by the recent hurricane, takes part in the "Smile Jamaica" benefit, to aid its victims, at the Dominion theater, London.
Nov [9] Wood jams with Jerry Lee Lewis at his recently opened Woody's On The Beach club in Miami, FL.

[19] *Talk Is Cheap* reaches US #24.
[24] Richards embarks on 15-date US tour at the Fox theater, Atlanta, GA, through to Dec.17. His back-up band, called The X-Pensive Winos, comprises Ivan Neville, Bobby Keys, Sarah Dash, Steve Jordan, Charley Drayton and Waddy Wachtel.

1989 **Jan** [13] Jagger and Richard meet in Barbados to start writing material for new album.
[18] Group is inducted into the Rock'N'Roll Hall Of Fame at the fourth annual induction dinner at the Waldorf Astoria in New York. At the perfunctory after-ceremony jam, Jagger joins Stevie Wonder on a medley of *Uptight* and *Satisfaction*, and Tina Turner on a duet of *Honky Tonk Women*. Little Richard joins Richards, Wood and Mick Taylor on *Can't Turn You Loose* and *Bony Maronie*, and then Jagger, Richards, Wood and Taylor perform *Start Me Up*.
[21] Wood jams with Bo Diddley, Willie Dixon, Percy Sledge, Koko Taylor and Republican Party Chairman Lee Atwater at one of President-Elect George Bush's inauguration parties at the Convention Center in Washington, DC.
Mar [9] Wyman and Wood arrive in Barbados to join the other Stones as they start work on new album at Eddy Grant's Barbados studio.
[15] The Stones sign a $70 million contract, the largest in rock history, with Michael Cohl, of Canadian-based Concert Promotions International, to play 50 North American dates. (MTV will sponsor the American dates, while Labatt will sponsor the Canadian leg.)
Apr [29] The Stones finish recording at AIR studios in Montserrat.
May [17] Wyman's Sticky Fingers restaurant opens in Kensington, London.
[31] Richards is inducted as a Living Legend, receiving his Elvis statuette from Eric Clapton at the first International Rock Awards at the Armory in New York.
June [2] 52-year-old Wyman, who married for the first, and only previous, time in 1959, secretly marries Mandy Smith, now 19, in Bury St. Edmunds, Suffolk, 3 days ahead of the press-reported date. His 28-year-old son Stephen is best man. The couple appear on BBC TV chat show "Wogan" that evening.
[5] The couple's marriage is blessed at St. John the Evangelist, Hyde Park Crescent, London, followed by a reception at the Grosvenor House hotel, attended by all The Stones and their wives. Wyman makes full use of a walking frame given to him as a wedding present by comedian Spike Milligan.
July Group arrives in Washington, CT, to commence rehearsals for upcoming US tour, their first in 8 years, at Wykeham Rise school, a former girls' boarding school.
[11] A press conference is held off Track 42 in New York's Grand Central Station. The Stones step off a Metro North train boarded at 125th Street to announce full details of the tour and album release. Jagger previews *Steel Wheels* on boombox in front of 500 assembled journalists.
[19] Residents in Washington, form a "Roll The Stones Out Of Town" action committee, citing the band has "ruined their tranquility".
Aug [12] As a warm-up to the tour, the group plays Toad's Place, New Haven, CT, a club with a 700 capacity and $3 admission. Their set, lasting 56 mins., features 11 songs.
[31] The "Steel Wheels North American Tour 1989" opens at Veterans Stadium, Philadelphia, PA, on Labor Day, before a sell-out crowd of 55,000. Tour line-up includes Bobby Keys (sax), Chuck Leavell and Matt Clifford (keyboards), Cindy Mizelle, Bernard Fowler and Lisa Fischer (backing vocals), with US band Living Colour the support act.
Sept [6] During the concert at Three Rivers Stadium in Pittsburgh, PA, The Stones, linked by satellite to MTV's studios in New York, perform *Mixed Emotions* at the MTV Awards ceremony.
[16] *Mixed Emotions* makes UK #36.
[23] Recorded at AIR studios in Montserrat, *Steel Wheels* hits UK #2.
[30] CD/Cassette box-set retrospective of earlier hits, *Singles Collection: The London Years* makes US #91.
Oct [7] *Steel Wheels* hits US #3.
[14] *Mixed Emotions* hits US #5.
[28] Eric Clapton joins the band on stage at Shea Stadium, playing lead guitar on *Little Red Rooster*.
Nov [4] Jagger spends an hour in 30,000-populated Watsonville, CA, with victims of the earthquake prior to the group's concert at Alameda County Stadium, Oakland, CA. Band donates $500,000 to the Red Cross Disaster Relief Fund.
[19] The "Steel Wheels" tour ends with a Pay-Per-View performance at Convention Center, Atlantic City, NJ.
Dec [2] *Rock And A Hard Place* peaks at UK #63.

[23] *Rock And A Hard Place* reaches US #23.

1990 **Feb** [14] Band plays first of 10 sell-out dates at Tokyo Dome.

Mar [8] Group wins Artist Of The Year, Best Band Of 1989, Best Tour, Worst Album Cover (*Steel Wheels*), Comeback Of The Year in the annual **Rolling Stone** magazine Music Awards of 1989. They also win Artist Of The Year, Best Tour and Best Drummer (Charlie Watts) in the Critics Award category.

[10] Ballad extract *Almost Hear You Sigh* makes US #50.

May [18] 22-date "Urban Jungle Europe 1990" tour opens in Rotterdam.

June [18] Wyman video "Digital Dream" released.

[30] *Paint It Black* peaks at UK #61.

July [7] Richards cuts his finger, which is subsequently diagnosed as being septic, causing the cancellation of concerts at Cardiff and Wembley.

[7] *Almost Hear You Sigh* makes UK #31.

Aug Covers album *Stoned Again – A Tribute To The Stones*, featuring The Shop Assistants, Dave Kusworth, Death Of Samantha, The Henry Kaiser Band and others, is released.

[18] Group ends its "Urban Jungle Europe 1990" in Prague, Czechoslavakia, at the invitation of Vlacek Havel. (Their only other Eastern European appearance was in Poland in 1964.)

Nov [12] Wood breaks both his legs trying to wave traffic away from his broken down car on the M4 motorway near Marlborough, Wilts.

[21] After a lengthy and exhaustive courtship, Mick Jagger and Jerry Hall finally marry in Bali, while on vacation.

[22] Wyman's lawyer Wright Webb Syrett announces the end of his 17-month marriage to Mandy Smith.

1991 **Feb** Klein, president of ABKCO publishing, accepts offer from "Snickers" candy bar makers to use *Satisfaction* as its theme tune for advertising purposes, after refusing their bids for years. He finally gives way when the company offers $4 million. Jagger and Richards' reported share is $2.8 million. The commercial will not, however, be permitted to use the original recording.

[30] *Highwire* makes UK #29 and US #57.

Apr [20] Live album, recorded during the 1990 world tour, *Flashpoint*, debuts at UK peak #6 and enters US chart at #29, beginning chart rise. (Jagger begins filming "Free Jack" in Atlanta with Emilio Estevez, Anthony Hopkins and David Johansen, as Richards plays on albums by John Lee Hooker and Johnnie Johnson.)

THE RONETTES

Veronica Bennett (lead vocals)
Estelle Bennett (vocals)
Nedra Talley (vocals)

1961 Bennett sisters Veronica (b. Aug.10, 1943, New York, NY) and Estelle (b. July 22, 1944, New York) with cousin Talley (b. Jan.27, 1946, New York) become resident dancers at Peppermint Lounge, the focus of the Twist craze in New York. Earning $10 a night, they tour with Joey Dee, dancing on DJ Clay Cole's "Twist Package", as The Dolly Sisters (and appear in Cole-featuring dance exploitation movie "Twist Around The Clock").

June After appearing with DJ Murray The K as dance regulars in his Brooklyn Fox stage shows, the trio is signed by Colpix Records.

Aug *I Want A Boy*, released on Colpix, with the group credited as Ronnie & The Relatives, fails to chart.

1962 **Apr** They become The Ronettes on their second single *Silhouettes*, which is issued on subsidiary May label, and again does not sell. (2 further unsuccessful releases, *I'm On The Wagon* and *Good Girls*, will follow during the next 12 months.)

1963 Georgia Winters of **16** magazine has Phil Spector meet the trio when he is talent-scouting in New York, and Spector is particularly impressed by Veronica's (generally known as Ronnie) voice. Via a subterfuge involving a professed desire to return to school and complete their education, the girls obtain a release from the Colpix contract.

Aug Spector signs the trio to his Philles label, and spends a month working on *Be My Baby* and *Baby I Love You*.

Oct The group's debut, *Be My Baby*, with archetypal Spector "Wall Of Sound" production, hits US #2 (behind Jimmy Gilmer & The Fireballs' *Sugar Shack*), and sells over a millon.

Nov *Be My Baby* hits UK #4.

[13] The Ronettes open in Teaneck, NJ, as part of Dick Clark's "Caravan Of Stars" tour.

Dec Group appears on Spector's various artists seasonal compilation *A Christmas Gift For You*, singing *Frosty The Snowman*, *Sleigh Ride* and *I Saw Mommy Kissing Santa Claus*, tracks which will be airplayed as a Christmas radio tradition every subsequent Yuletide.

1964 **Jan** *Baby I Love You* reaches US #24. The group begins UK "Group Scene 1964" tour, supporting The Rolling Stones.

Feb *Baby I Love You* reaches UK #11.

[8] Returned to New York, The Ronettes greet The Beatles on their first arrival in US, and ask them questions in a radio interview.

Apr Ronnie Bennett cuts solo *So Young*, which Spector places on his new subsidiary label Phil Spector Records, but does no more than test-market it on a limited basis.

May *(The Best Part Of) Breaking Up*, written by Spector with Pete Anders and Vinnie Poncia, makes US #39.

Aug Pounding *Do I Love You?*, from the same songwriting team, reaches US #34, while *(The Best Part Of) Breaking Up* makes UK #43.

Oct *Do I Love You?* reaches UK #35 (the trio's final UK hit).

Dec *Walking In The Rain*, a dramatic Spector/Mann/Weil-penned ballad with heavy Spector dressing, climbs to US #23. (In UK it is released as *In The Rain* to avoid a copyright wrangle, but fails to chart. The record will earn a Grammy award for its special sound effects.

1965 **Jan** *Presenting The Fabulous Ronettes, Featuring Veronica* reaches #9 on the US chart.

Feb *Born To Be Together* peaks at US #52.

June *Is This What I Get For Loving You?* (later revived by Marianne Faithfull) reaches US #75.

Aug The Ronettes tour US, supporting The Beatles – though without Ronnie, who has left the group to be with Spector (whom she shortly marries). Cousin Elaine joins in her place.

1966 **Oct** After a lengthy silence, the group returns with Jeff Barry-produced *I Can Hear Music* (revived by The Beach Boys and others), but it makes only US #100 and is The Ronettes' last US chart entry. Group disbands almost immediately after this; both Estelle and Talley leave the music business (and will marry and settle into family life).

1969 **Mar** With Spector recording again via a production deal with A&M Records (which brings him 3 hits by Sonny Charles & Checkmates Ltd.), he cuts a single by Ronnie Spector: *You Came, You Saw, You Conquered*, released credited to "The Ronettes, featuring the voice of Veronica". It does not chart.

1971 **Mar** Ronnie records tracks for her first solo album, at Abbey Road studios, London, with her husband producing, and George Harrison (who has invited her on to Apple label) contributing and writing songs.

May *Try Some, Buy Some* by Ronnie Spector (a Harrison song) is released on Apple Records. It is not a hit and the projected album does not appear.

1973 Ronnie appears at a Richard Nader Rock'N'Roll Revival show at New York's Madison Square Garden, performing with new back-up singers Denise Edwards and Chip Fields as Ronnie & The Ronettes.

Nov Signed to Buddah Records by producer Stan Vincent, Ronnie & The Ronettes release unsuccessful *Lover, Lover*, produced by Vincent.

1974 **Apr** Second Buddah release is a Vincent-produced version of *I Wish I Never Saw The Sunshine*, originally recorded by Spector with The Ronettes in 1965, but not released. This, too, fails to chart. By now she is divorced from Spector (whose first alimony payment to her of $1,300 is allegedly delivered in nickels).

1976 **Nov** Ronnie provides back-up vocals for Bruce Springsteen, when he and the E Street Band play 6 nights at the Palladium in New York.

1981 **Jan** She finally records a solo album, *Siren*, released on independent labels Polish in US and Red Shadow in UK.

1986 **Nov** She sings the line *Be My Baby* on Eddie Money's US #4 *Take Me Home Tonight*.

1987 **July** Signed to CBS Records, Ronnie releases solo album *Unfinished Business*, signalling a determined return to recording and performance.

1990 Ronnie's autobiography (written with Vince Waldron) *Be My Baby* is published revealing, amongst other notable events, that as a 12-year-old she had to fend off the advances of a 13-year-old Frankie Lymon.

LINDA RONSTADT

1964 Ronstadt (b. July 15, 1946, Tucson, AZ) the daughter of Mexican/German parents, whose hardware store owner father sings and plays Mexican songs in his spare time, leaves the University of Arizona, after 1 semester, to join guitarist Bob Kimmel (with whom she has performed, with her older brother and sister, in local clubs) in Los Angeles, CA, where they form folk trio The Stone Poneys, with second guitarist Kenny Edwards.

1965 Group performs regularly at Los Angeles' Troubadour club. Promoter

Herb Cohen, keen to manage Ronstadt as a solo act, is persuaded by her to take on the trio. Mercury Records offers a deal if the group will switch to a surf repertoire, but it declines.

1966 Cohen gains them a recording contract with Capitol, but debut album *The Stone Poneys* fails to sell.

1968 **Jan** *Different Drum*, written by Mike Nesmith of The Monkees and extracted from The Stone Poneys' *Evergreen, Volume 2*, reaches US #13. On it Ronstadt is featured singing solo, with session men backing her. The album makes US #100 and the group tours, but Edwards leaves soon after.
Mar *Up To My Neck In High Muddy Water*, credited to Linda Ronstadt and The Stone Poneys, stalls at US #93.

1969 **Apr** Ronstadt is left solo with an album obligation to Capitol. She records *Hand Sown, Home Grown*, which does not sell.

1970 **Oct** *Silk Purse* peaks at US #103, while extracted *Long Long Time* makes US #25 and is nominated for a Grammy award.

1971 **Feb** *(She's A) Very Lovely Woman/The Long Way Around* peaks at US #70.
Apr She recruits a group of musicians from Los Angeles' Troubadour club as a tour band, including Bernie Leadon (guitar), Glenn Frey (guitar), Randy Meisner (bass) and Don Henley (drums) (who will become The Eagles).

1972 **Mar** *Linda Ronstadt*, with backing by the road band, reaches US #163, while extracted *Rock Me On The Water* makes US #85.
Dec She works on *Don't Cry Now* with producer John Boylan for Asylum Records, but the project founders, with Ronstadt heavily in debt, and Capitol also demanding a further contracted album.

1973 Peter Asher, ex-Peter & Gordon, takes over Ronstadt's management and production after seeing her perform at New York's Bitter End club, and steers *Don't Cry Now* to completion, after it has taken a year of sessions, 3 producers, and $150,000.
Dec *Don't Cry Now* reaches US #45 (remaining on chart for 56 weeks and earning a gold disk).

1974 **Jan** *Love Has No Pride*, from *Don't Cry Now*, reaches US #51.
Mar *Different Drum* on Capitol (a compilation of Stone Poneys and early solo tracks) makes US #92.
May From the Asylum album, *Silver Threads And Golden Needles* (a 1962 hit by The Springfields) peaks at US #67.
Dec [24] Ronstadt, Joni Mitchell, Carly Simon and James Taylor are sighted singing Christmas carols together in Los Angeles.

1975 **Feb** With Asher producing, she records her contractual obligation album for Capitol, *Heart Like A Wheel*. Establishing what will be a familiar Ronstadt pattern of mixing carefully chosen oldie revivals with new songs, it tops the US chart for a week, earning a gold disk while, taken from it, a revival of Betty Everett's *You're No Good* (with Andrew Gold playing most of the instruments) also tops the US chart for a week and earns a gold disk.
June *When Will I Be Loved*, a revival of The Everly Brothers' 1960 smash, also taken from *Heart Like A Wheel*, hits US #2. Its B-side, reviving Buddy Holly's *It Doesn't Matter Anymore*, makes US #47. Meanwhile, Capitol issues another compilation of early material, *The Stone Poneys Featuring Linda Ronstadt*, which creeps to US #172.
Nov Recording for Asylum again, with Asher (who will remain her producer hereafter), Ronstadt releases *Prisoner In Disguise*, which hits US #4 and earns another gold disk. Extracted *Heat Wave/Love Is A Rose*, coupling an early Motown (Martha & The Vandellas) hit and a folky ballad, hits US #5.

1976 **Feb** Also from *Prisoner In Disguise*, her revival of The Miracles' 1965 hit *The Tracks Of My Tears* makes US #25.
Mar Ronstadt wins Best Female Country Vocal Performance for *I Can't Help It (If I'm Still In Love With You)* at the 18th annual Grammy awards.
May *The Tracks Of My Tears* is her UK chart debut at #42.
Sept *Hasten Down The Wind* makes UK #32.
Oct Another Buddy Holly revival, *That'll Be The Day*, reaches US #11. It is taken from *Hasten Down The Wind*, which hits US #3 and is her first million-selling album, earning a platinum disk.

1977 **Jan** Extracted Karla Bonoff-penned *Someone To Lay Down Beside Me* peaks at US #42, while compilation album *Greatest Hits*, which includes hit singles from both Capitol and Asylum, hits US #6, and is a second platinum album.
[19] Ronstadt participates in the Inaugural Eve Gala Performance for President Elect Jimmy Carter.
Feb [19] Ronstadt wins Best Female Pop Vocal Performance for *Hasten Down The Wind* at the 19th annual Grammy awards.
Mar [5] *Hasten Down The Wind* wins NARM's awards for Best Album By A Female Artist and Best Album By A Female Country Artist.

June *Lose Again* stalls at US #76, while double compilation album *A Retrospective* on Capitol reaches US #46, earning a gold disk.
July [21] Ronstadt duets with Mick Jagger on *Tumbling Dice* at a Rolling Stones concert at the Community Center, Tucson, AZ.
Dec A revival of Roy Orbison's *Blue Bayou* hits US #3 and is a million-seller. An almost simultaneous release is another Buddy Holly oldie, *It's So Easy*, which hits US #5. *Simple Dreams*, from which both are taken, tops the US chart for 5 weeks, earning another platinum disk, and reaches UK #15.

1978 **Jan** *Poor, Poor Pitiful Me*, also from *Simple Dreams*, makes US #31, while *Blue Bayou* peaks at UK #35.
Apr [3] Film "FM", in which Ronstadt is featured singing *Love Me Tender*, premieres in Los Angeles. (Continuing a current trend, a DJ will take Ronstadt's version of the song and splice it with Elvis Presley's version to create a "duet".)
May A revival of The Rolling Stones' *Tumbling Dice* reaches US #32.
Oct *Back In The USA*, a revival of a Chuck Berry song included on her new album, peaks at US #16.
Nov *Living In The USA* tops the US chart for a week, becoming another million-seller, and makes UK #39.

1979 **Jan** A revival of Smokey Robinson's *Ooh Baby Baby*, taken from *Living In The USA*, hits US #7.
[17] Ronstadt, Dolly Parton and Emmylou Harris announce plans to record an album together. (The project will take some years to complete.)
Mar A revival of Doris Troy's *Just One Look* makes US #44.
May She covers Elvis Costello's *Alison*, which is issued as a UK single, and makes #66.
Aug [4] Ronstadt joins Jackson Browne, Emmylou Harris, Nicolette Larson, Michael McDonald, Bonnie Raitt and members of Little Feat in a benefit concert in aid of Lowell George's widow at the Forum, Los Angeles. The 20,000 crowd raises over $230,000.
Dec [21-22] Ronstadt is joined by Chicago and The Eagles to play 2 benefit concerts in San Diego and Las Vegas, raising $150,000 for Presidential candidate Jerry Brown (whose constant companion she becomes).

1980 **Mar** *How Do I Make You* hits US #10.
Apr *Mad Love*, with backing from Los Angeles group The Cretones, and including *How Do I Make You*, hits US #3, another million-seller, and makes UK #65.
May A revival of Little Anthony & The Imperials' *Hurt So Bad*, taken from *Mad Love*, hits US #8.
July [15] Ronstadt makes her acting debut in "The Pirates Of Penzance" at the Delacorte theater in New York's Central Park.
Aug *I Can't Let Go*, a third single from *Mad Love*, peaks at US #31.

1981 **Jan** [8] "The Pirates Of Penzance" moves to Broadway, opening at the Uris theater. (It will win a Tony award.)
Dec Compilation album *Greatest Hits, Volume 2* reaches US #26, earning a gold disk.

1982 **June** [12] Ronstadt joins Jackson Browne, Bruce Springsteen and others to perform at the Peace Rally in New York's Central Park.
Nov *Get Closer* makes US #31, earning a gold disk, while the title track reaches US #29.

1983 **Feb** A revival of Billy Joe Royal's *I Knew You When*, taken from *Get Closer*, makes US #37. Meanwhile , the movie version of Ronstadt-starring "The Pirates Of Penzance" opens in US.
May *Easy For You To Say*, written by Jimmy Webb and also from *Get Closer*, peaks at US #54.
[16] She appears as a special guest on Motown's 25th Anniversary special on NBC TV, duetting with Smokey Robinson on *The Tracks Of My Tears* and *Ooh Baby Baby*.
Dec *What's New*, of standards arranged by Nelson Riddle and recorded with his orchestra, hits US #3 and earns a platinum disk, while the extracted title track reaches US #53.

1984 **Feb** *What's New* makes UK #31.
Oct [30] Ronstadt makes her operatic debut in "La Boheme", opening in New York.

1985 **Jan** *Lush Life*, also with the Nelson Riddle Orchestra, makes UK #100.

1986 **Apr** Ronstadt contributes vocals on 2 tracks from Philip Glass' *Songs From Liquid Days*, with songwriting contributions from Paul Simon, David Byrne, Suzanne Vega and Laurie Anderson. It makes US #91.
Nov *For Sentimental Reasons* reaches US #46 as *'Round Midnight*, comprising *What's New*, *Lush Life* and *For Sentimental Reasons*, makes US #129.

1987 **Mar** [14] *Somewhere Out There*, a duet with James Ingram from Spielberg-produced animated feature "An American Tail", hits US #2.

May *Trio*, duetted with Dolly Parton and Emmylou Harris, hits US #6, earning a platinum disk, and peaks at UK #60. From it, a revival of The Teddy Bears' *To Know Him Is To Love Him* hits US C&W #1 but does not cross over (2 more tracks from the album, *Telling Me Lies* and *Those Memories Of You*, will also be Top 5 country hits).

Aug *Somewhere Out There* hits UK #8.

1988 Feb *Canciones De Mi Padre (My Father's Songs)*, an entirely Spanish-sung collection of 13 traditional Mexican songs which Ronstadt learned as a child from her father, reaches US #42. (She will follow it with a major international tour including only Spanish-language repertoire.)

Mar [2] Ronstadt wins her third Grammy, for Best Country Vocal – Duo/Group, for her work with Dolly Parton and Emmylou Harris on *Trio*, at the 30th annual Grammy awards.

1989 May [6] Ronstadt performs at UCLA's Mexican Arts Series benefit.

Aug [3] She is nominated for Emmy in Individual Performance In A Variety Or Musical Program for PBS TV's "Great Performances : Canciones De Mi Padre".

Nov *Cry Like A Rainstorm – Howl Like the Wind* hits US #7 and reaches UK #43.

Dec [23] *Don't Know Much*, previously a 1981 US #88 for Bill Medley, hits US #2, having also missed UK #1 by 1 place in Nov.

1990 Feb [21] *Don't Know Much* wins Best Pop Performance By A Duo Or Group With Vocal at 32nd Grammy awards at the Shrine Auditorium, Los Angeles. *Cry Like A Rainstorm – Howl Like The Wind* wins Best Engineered Recording for George Massenburg.

Mar [31] *All My Life*, a further duet with Neville, reaches US #11.

June [2] Again with Neville, *When Something Is Wrong With My Baby*, reviving Sam And Dave's 1967 US #42, stalls at US #78.

[8] Ronstadt performs at the T.J. Martell Foundation For Leukemia Cancer & AIDS Research 1990 Humanitarian Award concert at Avery Fisher Hall, Lincoln Center, New York City.

Aug [9] Ronstadt begins a major US tour, with The Neville Brothers as support, in Austin, TX, set to end Sept.30 in Santa Barbara, CA.

Nov [3] *Rubáiyát*, Elektra's 40th anniversary compilation, to which Ronstadt contributes a cover of *The Blacksmith*, makes US #140.

Dec [21-22] Ronstadt takes part in 2 John Lennon tribute concerts at the Tokyo Dome, Japan, with Miles Davies, Natalie Cole, Daryl Hall & John Oates and Sean Lennon. She performs *Good Night*.

1991 Feb [20] Ronstadt and Neville win Best Pop Performance By A Duo Or Group With Vocal for *All My Life* for a second consecutive year at the 33rd annual Grammy awards at Radio City Music Hall, New York.

DIANA ROSS

1970 Mar [8] 7 weeks after leaving The Supremes, Ross (b. Mar.26, 1944, Detroit, US) makes her solo stage debut, in Framingham, MA. Motown invests $100,000 in her new act.

June Debut solo single *Reach Out And Touch (Somebody's Hand)*, written and produced by Ashford And Simpson, reaches US #20.

Aug *Reach Out And Touch (Somebody's Hand)* makes UK #33.

Sept Ashford And Simpson-produced and penned *Ain't No Mountain High Enough* is Ross' first solo US chart-topper, holding #1 for 3 weeks and selling a million. It also hits UK #6. (It had originally been a hit duet for Marvin Gaye and Tammi Terrell in 1967, but Ross' version is a complete re-arrangement, making notable use of spoken passages.) It and the previous single are included on *Diana Ross*, which climbs to US #19.

Nov *Diana Ross* makes UK #14.

1971 Jan Second solo album *Everything Is Everything* reaches US #42.

Feb Taken from the album, *Remember Me* reaches US #16.

Apr *Remember Me* hits UK #7.

May A revival of The Four Tops' *Reach Out I'll Be There* makes US #29 while the soundtrack album from TV special "Diana" (which also includes Bill Cosby, Danny Thomas and The Jackson 5) makes US #46.

June *Everything Is Everything* reaches UK #31.

Aug Released as a UK single from the album at the urging of BBC Radio 1 breakfast show DJ Tony Blackburn, who plugs it incessantly, *I'm Still Waiting*, by Deke Richards, tops the UK chart for 4 weeks.

Sept *Surrender* peaks at US #56, as extracted title song makes US #38.

Oct TV soundtrack album *Diana!* makes UK #43.

Nov *Surrender* hits UK #10, as does *I'm Still Waiting* (which is US album *Surrender* with the UK #1 added). Meanwhile, *I'm Still Waiting*, released as a US single on the strength of UK success, peaks at US #63.

1972 June *Doobedood'ndoobe Doobedood'ndoobe* reaches UK #12.

Nov UK Compilation album *Greatest Hits* makes UK #34.

Dec Ross makes her major movie acting debut opposite Billy Dee

Williams in the role of Billie Holiday, in Motown co-production "Lady Sings The Blues", a dramatization of Holiday's life. She is nominated for (though does not win) an Oscar for her performance.

1973 Mar *Good Morning Heartache*, from "Lady Sings The Blues", makes US #34.

Apr Soundtrack double album *Lady Sings The Blues* tops the US chart for 2 weeks, earning a gold disk.

Aug *Touch Me In The Morning*, the first song written for her by Michael Masser (with Ron Miller), tops the US chart for a week and is a million-seller. In UK, it hits #9.

Sept *Touch Me In The Morning* hits US #5 and UK #7.

Oct *Lady Sings The Blues* makes UK #50, following a moderate reception for the movie's UK release.

Nov *You're A Special Part Of Me*, duetted with Marvin Gaye, reaches US #12.

Dec Duet album *Diana And Marvin* reaches US #26.

1974 Feb *Last Time I Saw Him* reaches US #14, while *All Of My Life* hits UK #9. Both are taken from *Last Time I Saw Him*, which makes US #52 and UK #41. Meanwhile, *Diana And Marvin* hits UK #6.

Apr Revived Stylistics' *You Are Everything*, with Gaye, hits UK #5.

May From the album with Gaye, *My Mistake (Was To Love You)*, makes US #19, while belatedly released *Last Time I Saw Him* reaches UK #35.

June *Sleepin'* stalls at US #70.

July Live album *Diana Ross Live At Caesar's Palace*, a recording of her club act from Las Vegas, makes US #64 and UK #21.

Aug *Don't Knock My Love*, with Marvin Gaye, peaks at US #46 while another Stylistics revival with Gaye, *Stop, Look, Listen (To Your Heart)* makes UK #25.

Oct *Love Me* reaches UK #38.

1975 Apr *Sorry Doesn't Always Make It Right* makes UK #23.

Dec Her second feature film "Mahogany", directed by Berry Gordy Jr. and with music by Michael Masser, again co-stars Billy Dee Williams. It does not match either the critical or commercial success of "Lady Sings the Blues". The soundtrack album, with Ross singing the title song, plus incidental music, reaches US #19.

1976 Jan *Theme From Mahogany (Do You Know Where You're Going To)*, written by Masser and Gerry Goffin, tops the US chart for a week, selling over a million. It is nominated for (but fails to win) a Best Song Oscar at the Academy Awards.

Apr *I Thought It Took A Little Time (But Today I Fell In Love)* peaks at US #47, while *Theme From Mahogany (Do You Know Where You're Going To)* hits UK #5. *Diana Ross*, containing the 2 previous hit singles, hits US #5 and UK #4.

May *Love Hangover*, a long disco-flavored track from *Diana Ross*, gains wide airplay and is covered on single by The 5th Dimension, so Motown rushes it out on the slow-moving heels of *I Thought It Took A Little Time*. It tops the US chart for 2 weeks and is another million-seller.

June Ross stars in her own Broadway show, "An Evening With Diana Ross". (Following its New York run, it will tour US for the rest of the year. While touring, she will also be divorced from rock manager Robert Silverstein, whom she married in 1971.)

July *I Thought It Took A Little Time* makes UK #32.

Oct *One Love In My Lifetime* makes US #25, while *Diana Ross' Greatest Hits* reaches US #13 and hits UK #2.

Nov A UK reissue of former #1 hit *I'm Still Waiting* peaks at UK #41.

1977 Mar [6] "An Evening With Diana Ross", a 90-min. spectacular incorporating much of the stage show, airs on US TV.

Apr Double live album *An Evening With Diana Ross*, recorded in 1976 at Ahmanson theater, Los Angeles, makes US #29 and UK #52.

Oct She stars as Dorothy in film "The Wiz", directed by Sidney Lumet. It is a black version of "The Wizard Of Oz" adapted from the successful Broadway stage musical. (Michael Jackson features as The Scarecrow.) Director John Badham reportedly quits the project rather than accept Ross in the role of Dorothy.

Nov *Baby It's Me* reaches US #18.

Dec Taken from it, *Gettin' Ready For Love* reaches US #27 and UK #23.

1978 Apr *Your Love Is So Good For Me*, also from the album, makes US #49.

Aug *You Got It* peaks at US #49, while *Lovin' Livin' And Givin'* makes UK #54.

Oct *Ease On Down The Road*, a duet with Michael Jackson from the soundtrack of "The Wiz", released by MCA, reaches UK #41.

Nov *Ease On Down The Road* makes US #45, *Ross* reaches US #49.

1979 Feb *Pops, We Love You (A Tribute To Father)*, sung with Marvin Gaye, Smokey Robinson and Stevie Wonder, in honor of Berry Gordy's father's 90th birthday, peaks at US #59 and UK #66.

Aug *The Boss* reaches US #14 and UK #52, while the extracted title

song makes US #19 and UK #40.
Oct *No One Gets The Prize*, from *The Boss*, peaks at UK #59.
Dec *It's My House*, also from the album, makes UK #32, while TV-advertised UK compilation album *20 Golden Greats*, including all her UK chart singles, hits UK #2.

1980 **July** *Diana*, produced by Nile Rodgers and Bernard Edwards of Chic (though heavily remixed by Ross herself – to the producers' initial dismay – to emphasize the vocals more strongly), hits US #2, selling over a million, and UK #12.
Sept Taken from *Diana*, Edwards/Rodgers-penned *Upside Down* tops the US chart for 4 weeks, also selling over a million, and hits UK #2.
Oct Also from the album, *My Old Piano* hits UK #5.
Nov *I'm Coming Out*, again from *Diana*, hits US #5 and UK #13.

1981 **Jan** *It's My Turn*, the theme from Michael Douglas/Jill Clayburgh movie of the same title, hits US #9 and UK #16.
Feb [19] Price Waterhouse CPA, Glenn Kannry, pleads guilty to siphoning cash from Ross' bank account.
Apr *One More Chance* peaks at UK #49 and US #79. It is taken from *To Love Again*, which makes US #32 and UK #26.
June *Cryin' My Heart Out For You* peaks at UK #58.
Aug *Endless Love*, duetted with the song's writer/producer Lionel Richie, tops the US chart for 9 weeks, selling over 2 million copies. It is the theme from the film of the same name, featuring Brooke Shields, and was recorded in a rapid early-morning session in Reno, NV, the 2 vocalists meeting briefly amid heavy schedules elsewhere. The single is released on Motown. (Ross has just left the label after 2 decades, signing a new North American deal with RCA and an international one with EMI/Capitol but both new labels allow the duet on the basis of her guesting with Richie, who is contracted to Motown as one of The Commodores.)
Oct *Endless Love* hits UK #7.
Dec First RCA/Capitol single is self-produced revival of Frankie Lymon & The Teenagers' 1956 million-seller *Why Do Fools Fall In Love*, which hits US #7 and UK #4. It is taken from the album of the same title, which makes US #15 and UK #17, and earns a US platinum disk. Meanwhile, double compilation album *All The Greatest Hits*, on Motown, makes US #37 and UK #21; with singles up to *Endless Love*.

1982 **Jan** *Tenderness*, on Motown, makes UK #73.
Feb *Mirror, Mirror*, taken from the RCA/Capitol album, hits US #8 and makes UK #36.
May Aerobic *Work That Body* makes US #44 while, in UK, it is extremely popular in discos and hits UK #7 a few weeks later.
July [4] Ross opens a world tour at Meadowlands, East Rutherford, NJ. Miles Davis plays support.
Aug *It's Never Too Late* peaks at UK #41.
Nov *Muscles*, written and produced by Michael Jackson, hits US #10 and makes UK #15. It is taken from *Silk Electric*, which peaks at US #27 (earning a gold disk) and UK #33.
Dec TV-promoted compilation album *Love Songs*, put together by K-Tel in UK from Motown recordings, hits UK #5.

1983 **Feb** *So Close* peaks at US #40 and UK #43.
May [16] Ross reunites with Mary Wilson and Cindy Birdsong as The Supremes, during the "Motown 25" US NBC TV spectacular to celebrate the label's 25th birthday.
July [22] Ross gives a free concert in New York's Central Park, abandoned the previous night after only 3 songs, due to a torrential downpour and strong winds.
Aug *Ross* makes US #32 and UK #44 while, from it, *Pieces Of Ice* peaks at US #31 and UK #46. Double compilation *Diana Ross Anthology*, on Motown, reaches US #63.

1984 **Jan** TV-advertised compilation *Portrait* hits UK #8, while *Let's Go Up* peaks at US #77.
Sept *All Of You*, a ballad duetted with Julio Iglesias, reaches US #19, while *Touch By Touch* peaks at UK #47.
Oct *Swept Away*, written and produced by Daryl Hall of Hall And Oates, makes US #19. It is taken from the album of the same title, which reaches US #26 and UK #40.

1985 **Jan** [28] She participates in USA For Africa's *We Are The World*.
Apr Ballad *Missing You*, taken from *Swept Away*, hits US #10. The song, dedicated to the memory of Marvin Gaye, is written and produced by Lionel Richie.
Oct *Eaten Alive*, featuring Michael Jackson on back-up vocals, makes US #77 and UK #71.
Nov *Eaten Alive*, produced by Barry Gibb of The Bee Gees, reaches US #45 and UK #11.
Dec *Chain Reaction*, written by The Bee Gees, stalls at US #95.

1986 **Feb** [1] Ross marries Norwegian shipping magnate Arne Naess, in Geneva, Switzerland, before a gathering of 240 people with the Norwegian Silver Boys Choir singing. Stevie Wonder performs at the reception.
Mar *Chain Reaction*, Ross' biggest UK single since *I'm Still Waiting*, tops UK chart for 3 weeks, helped by black and white video including mock 60s footage.
May *Experience*, also from *Eaten Alive*, makes UK #47.
[24] A new mix of *Chain Reaction* peaks at US #66.
Nov Compilation album *Diana Ross And Others: Their Very Best Back To Back* makes UK #21.

1987 **Jan** [26] Ross hosts the American Music Awards in Los Angeles.
June *Red Hot Rhythm'N'Blues*, containing versions of R&B oldies, makes US #73 and UK #47. Taken from it, *Dirty Looks* makes US R&B #12, failing to cross over, but reaches UK #49.
Oct Ross gives birth to her fourth child, Ross Arne.

1988 **Aug** [26] Ross gives birth to her fifth child, a boy.
Oct Ross' revival of The Bobettes' 50s hit *Mr. Lee*, taken from *Red Hot Rhythm'N'Blues*, makes UK #58.
Nov With Peter Asher producing, Ross sings *If We Hold On Together*, the theme from Steven Spielberg-produced cartoon film "The Land Before Time". UK remix of *Love Hangover* anchors at UK #75.

1989 **Feb** 1989 issue of *Stop! In The Name Of Love* makes UK #62 as UK TV compilation *Love Supreme* by Diana Ross & The Supremes hits UK #10.
Apr [20] Ross warms up for her UK tour, lipsynching at the Brixton Academy on an Aswad bill.
[23] She begins the UK leg of her European tour, set to include dates at the Scottish Exhibition and Conference Centre, Glasgow, Scotland, the NEC, Birmingham, W.Midlands and Wembley Arena, London.
May *Workin' Overtime*, produced by Nile Rodgers and released on newly-formed Ross label, peaks at US #116 and UK #23. The US release is delayed to gauge reaction to the first single on the label, the title track, which makes UK #32.
June [23] Ross participates in a worldwide ecological awareness broadcast "Our Common Future".
[24] Ross begins a 2-month North American tour as *Workin' Overtime* fails to make the Hot 100 but is a success on R&B and Dance charts.
July Extracted *Paradise* peaks at UK #61.
Nov *Greatest Hits Live*, on EMI UK, makes UK #34.

1990 **July** Curious updated remix of classic *I'm Still Waiting*, by Phil Chill, reaches UK #21.

1991 **Apr** Ross appears in Herb Ritts-lensed GAP commercials with daughter Tracee, who is launching a solo music career.

ROXETTE

Per Gessle (guitar, vocals)
Marie Fredriksson (vocals)

1986 Both friends since 1979 and veterans of the Swedish music scene, Gessle, who had already fronted successful rock group Gyllene Tider until its split in 1984, going on to concentrate on a solo career and songwriting (including a song *Threnody* on Abba's Frida Lyngstad's debut album *Something's Going On*) links with Fredriksson, who is established as one of Sweden's top songwriters with over 300,000 copies already sold of her 3 solo albums, to form straight rock duo Roxette. They release *Pearls Of Passion*, on Swedish-only record label.

1987 **June** As Roxette undertakes its debut tour of Sweden, *Pearls Of Passion* earns a native platinum (100,000) disk and has spun-off 2 gold (25,000) singles.

1988 **Oct** Second album *Look Sharp!*, co-produced by permanent Roxette collaborator Clarence Ofwerman, is released in Sweden, hitting #1 for an initial 3-month run, selling close to 500,000 copies and becoming the second best-selling album in Sweden, behind Abba's *The Album*. While on holiday in Scandinavia, a US college student on an exchange visit, hooked on the Roxette tracks he has heard on Swedish radio, takes a copy of the CD back home to Minneapolis, MN, and suggests to his local station that they play extract *The Look*. After overwhelming listener response, the track, copied on cassette and distributed to other US stations, becomes a much requested airplay favorite.

1989 **Feb** [11] Still without an official US record deal, saturation airplay alone brings *The Look* onto the Singles chart. It is subsequently snapped up by EMI USA and begins a steady rise to hit US #1, eventually becoming the eighth most successful single of the year in US.
Apr [8] *The Look* tops US chart.
[22] Parent album *Look Sharp!* enters US chart set to make #23, and initially UK #45, during a 71-week chart stay.

May *The Look* hits UK #7, as the band continues on a non-stop worldwide promotion trip.

July [29] Punchy rock follow-up *Dressed For Success* reaches US #14, having made UK #38.

Nov [4] Power ballad *Listen To Your Heart*, again written by the duo, hits US #1, the first chart-topper available in cassette form only, though it stalls at UK #62.

Dec Roxette ends the year with a 3-week European tour, their first live dates performed outside Sweden.

1990 Mar [3] Fourth extract from *Look Sharp!*, *Dangerous* rises to hit US #2 for 2 weeks, behind Janet Jackson's *Escapade*.

June [16] While Fredriksson and Gessle begin recording follow-up to multi-platinum *Look Sharp!* at EMI's Stockholm studios, ballad *It Must Have Been Love*, prominently featured in Richard Gere/Julia Roberts hit movie "Pretty Woman" tops US chart. It also hits US #3 spurring revived interest in the *Look Sharp!* album which now hits UK #4.

Oct Reissued *Listen To Your Heart* twinned with *Dangerous* hits UK #6.

Nov UK re-released *Dressed For Success* reaches #18.

1991 Mar [23] Inspired by the Paul McCartney quote: "... writing songs with John Lennon was like being on a joyride", Beatles fan Gessle has written *Joyride*, which hits UK #4. It will also hit #1 in most European territories, including Sweden, Germany, Netherlands and hit AUS #1 and CAN #2. It is the title track from the duo's third album set for April release and featuring production and programming by Ofwerman and guest guitar work from Jonas Isacsson.

May [11] *Joyride* hits US #1.

June Roxette are scheduled to begin maiden world tour in Canada.

ROXY MUSIC

Bryan Ferry (vocals)
Andy Mackay (sax, woodwinds)
Phil Manzanera (guitar)
Brian Eno (keyboards)
Rik Kenton (bass)
Paul Thompson (drums)

1970 Nov Ferry (b. Sept.26, 1945, Washington, Tyne & Wear), a fine arts graduate, former R&B vocalist and spare-time songwriter, and ex-university colleague (and bass player) Graham Simpson decide to form a band to play the songs Ferry has been writing.

1971 Jan Mackay (b. July 23, 1946, London), introduced to Ferry by a mutual friend, joins and brings with him electronics expert and synthesizer player Eno (b. May 15, 1948, Woodbridge, Suffolk), an acquaintance from Reading University.

June Following ads in UK music paper **Melody Maker**, Roger Bunn joins on guitar and American classically-trained tympanist Dexter Lloyd on drums. Band plays no live dates but records demos of Ferry's material, which he hawks, initially without success, around London record companies.

July Bunn and Lloyd leave. Ferry recruits a guitarist he has long admired, Davy O'List (formerly with Keith Emerson in The Nice), while another **Melody Maker** ad brings in drummer Thompson (b. May 13, 1951, Jarrow, Tyne & Wear), who has backed Billy Fury.

Dec Following positive press coverage from **Melody Maker**'s Richard Williams on the strength of the early demos, Roxy Music plays 2 try-out live gigs, at the Friends of the Tate Gallery Christmas show and the Union Ball at Reading University.

1972 Jan [21] Band plays in session on BBC Radio 1's "Sounds Of The Seventies", the early demo tape having impressed presenter John Peel.

Feb O'List leaves. Manzanera (b. Philip Targett-Adams Manzanera, Jan.31, 1951, London), who has been doing the group's sound mixing but was previously guitarist with experimental band Quiet Sun, joins in his place. EG Management signs the band to a contract which includes recording and leasing product to a record company.

Mar Debut album is recorded for £5,000 at Command studios, London, with ex-King Crimson lyricist Pete Sinfield producing.

May Simpson is dismissed from the project and Kenton, a bass-playing friend of Sinfield, replaces him.

[30] With Kenton, the band plays its first major gig, at the Great Western Express Festival in Lincolnshire.

June Roxy Music's first tour is as support to Rory Gallagher around the North of England.

[20] Group's TV debut is on BBC2's "The Old Grey Whistle Test".

July Band supports Alice Cooper at the Empire Pool, Wembley, London. Press reviews applaud Roxy Music's act at Cooper's expense.

Aug Following a release deal signed by EG with Island Records, debut

album *Roxy Music*, following ecstatic reviews, hits UK #10.

Sept Ferry-penned *Virginia Plain* (not on the album) hits UK #4.

Oct During Roxy Music's first headlining UK tour, Ferry's voice begins to suffer (he has a history of tonsilitis) and a break in the tour follows while he is hospitalized to have his tonsils removed.

Dec Band plays its first US tour, opening for Jethro Tull, Humble Pie, The Allman Brothers Band, and others.

1973 Jan Kenton is fired and not replaced. During recordings for the second album, session man John Porter plays bass.

Apr *Pyjamarama* hits UK #10, though the band claims it as a hasty release pressured by Island. It is not included on *For Your Pleasure*, which hits UK #10, promoted by a sell-out UK tour.

July Eno quits the band after personality clashes with Ferry, who recruits Curved Air's violinist Eddie Jobson (b. Apr.28, 1955, Billingham, Cleveland) as a replacement (initially a controversial move as he does not consult the rest of the band).

Aug *For Your Pleasure* is the band's US chart debut, at #193.

Oct Ferry releases his first solo album *These Foolish Things* (for some time, his solo projects will continue in tandem with Roxy Music).

Nov Band tours UK, with Jobson handling all keyboards (Ferry and Eno had previously shared them), and Ferry moves to center stage as vocalist without an instrument.

Dec *Street Life* hits UK #9. It is taken from Chris Thomas-produced *Stranded*, which tops UK chart for a week – the band's first #1 hit. For the first time, 2 tracks are co-written (by Manzanera and Mackay). Bass player on the album is John Gustafson, ex-The Big Three and The Merseys, while the sleeve model is **Playboy**'s Playmate Of The Year Marilyn Cole. A successful European tour follows.

1974 May Mackay releases solo, largely instrumental, album *In Search Of Eddie Riff*, which does not chart.

June Band plays another US tour, where its appeal is still cult-fashionable rather than commercial. *Stranded* creeps to US #186.

Oct *All I Want Is You*, heralding a new album (recorded in Aug. with John Porter, who had produced Ferry's solo albums), reaches UK #12 as the band plays another sold-out UK tour, with John Wetton joining temporarily on bass. Ferry introduces new stage images, appearing in gaucho attire and US military-style uniform.

Dec *Country Life*, again with Ferry co-writing material with other members of the band, hits UK #3. (Its sleeve, showing 2 scantily-clad models, causes controversy, notably in US where it has to be sold in opaque green shrinkwrap.)

1975 Feb Band begins tour of US, Japan, Australia and New Zealand, still retaining Wetton on bass. While the band is on the road in US, *Country Life* becomes its first major US seller, reaching #37.

Oct A UK tour is mounted to promote the next album, this time without Wetton (who has joined Uriah Heep). Gustafson plays bass (he will stay in the group on a semi-permanent basis for several months).

Nov *Siren*, produced again by Thomas and with co-writing credits for Mackay, Jobson and Manzanera, hits UK #6. The sleeve photo is of Texan fashion model Jerry Hall (with whom Ferry will later become romantically linked). Extracted *Love Is The Drug*, an R&B-based dance number, hits UK #2 – the band's biggest hit single to date.

Dec Band tours US again, as *Siren* climbs to US #50.

1976 Jan *Both Ends Burning*, also from *Siren*, makes UK #25.

Mar *Love Is The Drug*, the band's first US hit single, reaches US #30 as Roxy Music tours US again.

May On return to UK, Mackay follows a solo project with music for ITV series "Rock Follies", Manzanera works with new outfit 801, Ferry completes more solo work and Jobson returns to US to play with Frank Zappa. It is decided to rest Roxy Music indefinitely.

June [26] After frequent press rumors, the band finally announces: "We have all decided to go our separate ways, for the rest of the year at least, to have a rest from Roxy Music for a while."

Aug With the band still inactive, live album *Viva! Roxy Music*, assembled from concert recordings made 1972-75, is released, hitting UK #6 and making US #81.

1977 Nov EG transfers the Roxy Music catalog from Island to Polydor Records in UK. Earlier material is repromoted and *Virginia Plain*, reissued as a single (coupled with *Pyjamarama*), reaches UK #11.

Dec Compilation album *Greatest Hits* reaches UK #20.

1978 Nov After an 18-month hiatus (the recent months having seen Ferry's solo chart success dwindle), Ferry, Mackay, Manzanera and Thompson regroup to cut a new Roxy Music album at Basing Street studios, London. Keyboards player Paul Carrack (ex-Ace) and bassist Gary Tibbs (ex-new wave band The Vibrators) are recruited.

1979 Mar *Trash*, heralding the new album, makes UK #40.

Apr *Manifesto*, produced by the band, hits UK #7. Band supports it with a reunion tour of UK and Europe (with Tibbs on bass and David Skinner on keyboards), then moves on to play US and Japan.

May *Manifesto* reaches US #23.

June From the album, *Dance Away* hits UK #2 and makes US #44.

Sept *Angel Eyes*, a disco-flavored excerpt from *Manifesto* (and also available in a dance-floor-aimed extended 12" version) hits UK #4. (It is on UK chart simultaneously with same-titled but different song *Angeleyes* by Abba.)

30 A new album is recorded in London by Ferry, Mackay and Manzanera, who co-produce with Rhett Davies, with other players (including Tibbs, Carrack, guitarist Neil Hubbard, and drummers Andy Newmark and Allan Schwartzberg) being hired for work on specific tracks. 2 oldies, Wilson Pickett's *In The Midnight Hour* and The Byrds' *Eight Miles High*, are included among the new Ferry and Ferry/Manzanera songs.

May *Over You* hits UK #5 as *Flesh And Blood* tops UK chart for 1 week.

June Group begins 60-date European tour. Andy Newmark deputizes for Paul Thompson, who breaks his hand in a motorcycle accident on eve of tour. The live band retains Carrack, Hubbard and Tibbs.

July [14] Ferry collapses in his hotel room at Port Barcares in Southwest France. He is flown by charter plane to London hospital the following day with a kidney infection.

[23] Band resumes its tour in UK at the Conference Centre, Brighton, E.Sussex. Tour will close Aug.2 at Wembley Arena, London.

Aug *Oh Yeah (On The Radio)* hits UK #5. It is from *Flesh And Blood* which returns to UK #1 for 3 weeks and makes US #35, while *Over You* makes US #80, the band's third and final US Singles chart entry.

Nov *The Same Old Scene*, third single from the album, reaches UK #12.

Dec Manzanera and Mackay, credited as The Players, release *Christmas* on US indie label Rykodisc.

31 Mar A specially-recorded version of John Lennon's *Jealous Guy*, cut as a tribute following Lennon's murder, tops UK chart for 2 weeks – Roxy Music's only #1 single.

32 Apr After a lengthy recording hiatus, *More Than This* hits UK #6, heralding what will be the band's last studio album, again recorded by Ferry/Mackay/Manzanera with session musicians. Mackay publishes a book, *Electronic Music*, written while the band was inactive.

June *Avalon*, produced by Davies, tops UK chart for 3 weeks. The sleeve features Lucy Helmore, whom Ferry marries on June 26.

July Extracted title song from *Avalon* makes UK #13.

Aug *Avalon* reaches US #53.

Oct *Take A Chance With Me*, also from the album, reaches UK #26.

33 Mar Mini-album *Musique/The High Road*, recorded live at Glasgow's Apollo theater (and the soundtrack to a live home video of the same title featuring the band), reaches UK #26.

May Mini-album *Musique/The High Road* makes US #67 as the band tours US for the last time, in an 8-piece line-up. (This effectively ends all Roxy Music activities, as the 3 remaining core members turn to solo projects again.)

Nov Compilation album *The Atlantic Years 1973-1980* (US-originated by the band's US label Atlantic) reaches UK #23.

34 June Mackay and Manzanera re-emerge in The Explorers, with Ferry-like vocalist James Wraith, but debut single on Virgin Records, *Lorelei*, does not chart.

35 June Eponymous debut album by The Explorers is released, again without chart success. At the same time, Ferry re-launches his solo career with *Boys And Girls*, which tops UK chart.

36 Apr TV-promoted double compilation album *Street Life – 20 Great Hits*, containing both Roxy Music and Ferry solo singles, tops UK chart for 5 weeks, earning a platinum disk.

38 Nov TV-promoted compilation album *The Ultimate Collection*, again mixing Roxy Music and Ferry solo material, hits UK #6.

90 Sept [24] Live *Love Is The Drug*, from forthcoming concert set *Heart Still Beating*, recorded in Frejus, South of France, in 1982, is released.

Nov *Manzanera & Mackay* is released on Manzanera's recently formed Expression label. (The label also releases Manzanera's *Southern Cross* and Mackay's *Resolving Contradictions* on CD for the first time.)

UN DMC

son Mizell, Jam Master Jay (DJ)

eph "Run" Simmons (voice)

C Darryl "D" McDaniels (voice)

82 Having all grown up in New York suburb Hollis, Simmons (b. 1964, New York, NY), McDaniels (b. 1964, New York) and Mizell (b. 1965, New York) start rap trio Run DMC after graduating from St. Pascal's

Catholic school, New York.

1983 Managed by Simmons' brother Russell, who has set up Rush Productions, Run DMC signs a recording deal with Profile Records in New York for $2,500, after rejections by all major labels.

June Spurred by early specialist interest in first rap singles, debut *Run – D.M.C.* is released. It will peak at US #53, spend over 1 year on chart and become the first US gold rap album.

July Run DMC begins a rap package tour which includes L.L. Cool J.

1985 Feb Still without crossover singles, follow-up album *King Of Rock* is released, set to peak at US #52.

May Run DMC appears in first rap movie "Krush Groove". It is based on the life-story of Russell Simmons who has now also become co-chairman of Run DMC producer Rick Rubin's new label, Def Jam.

Nov Run DMC contributes to Artists Against Apartheid protest song and video *Sun City* which makes US #38 and UK #21.

1986 Jan Run DMC team with El DeBarge, Whitney Houston, Stacy Lattisaw, Lisa & Full Force, Teena Marie, Menundo, Stephanie Mills, New Edition, James "J.T." Taylor, Kurtis Blow, The Fat Boys, Grandmaster Melle Mel and Whodini as The King Dream Chorus & Holiday Crew for *King Holiday*, a tribute to Martin Luther King Jr., with all proceeds benefiting the Martin Luther King Jr. Center for Non-Violent Social Change. The record reaches #30 on US R&B chart.

July Run DMC, having become closely allied to a training shoe manufacturer, debuts on UK chart at #62 with new single *My Adidas/Peter Piper*. It ties in with release of third album *Raising Hell* which also benefits. (It will hit US #3 in Sept., with sales over 2 million, and UK #41. It also becomes rap's first platinum album.)

Aug At the end of a mini promotion summer European visit, Run DMC signs a 6-figure sponsorship update deal with Adidas in Munich, Germany.

[16] *Raising Hell* tops US R&B chart for 7 weeks.

[17] Following 5 1986 US gigs where crowd trouble has been prevalent (Pittsburgh, Cleveland, Atlanta, Cincinnati and New York), a riot between rival gangs erupts at a Long Beach, Los Angeles, concert; 42 of the 14,500 audience are seriously injured. The incident sparks outbursts and future bans from many other US venues.

Sept Still promoting recent album, the group appears on NBC TV's "Saturday Night Live" and co-raps with the hostess on "The Late Show Starring Joan Rivers". The City of Los Angeles rescinds an invitation for Run DMC to take part in the Los Angeles Street Scene Festival because of recent troubles at the rap trio's gigs.

[27] An update of heavy metal outfit Aerosmith's *Walk This Way* a mix of Run DMC rap and heavy metal as provided by the original band's vocalist Steve Tyler and guitarist Joe Perry, attracts heavy MTV rotation and hits US #4.

Oct *Walk This Way* hits UK #8, as mini-tour dates sell-out in UK.

Nov Run DMC accepts an invitation from Michael Jackson to have dinner at Jackson's studio to discuss possible collaboration on his forthcoming album, but plans will fizzle. Run DMC contribute with fellow rappers to *Rap's Greatest Hits* album, which makes US #114.

Dec Strengthening group resolve to make teenagers more aware of gang and drug-related problems, Run DMC travels to Los Angeles to hold street seminars, some of which are co-hosted by band hero Barry White.

[20] *You Be Illin'* reaches US #29.

1987 Jan Run DMC begins writing and producing its own feature length movie, "Tougher Than Leather", planned as a rapping adventure thriller, in which they appear as rappers hunting down a drug-dealing record producer who has shot their roadie, and will also finance the project at an unexpected $10 million.

Apr As a prelude to a UK tour with similar Rubin-produced Beastie Boys, both bands appear at Montreux Pop Festival, Switzerland.

[11] *It's Tricky* peaks at US #57.

May *You Be Illin'* reaches UK #16.

Dec Run DMC contributes nativity rap song *Christmas In Hollis* to Jimmy Iovine seasonal compilation album *A Special Christmas*. It stalls at UK #56.

1988 Jan Release of (12 months in the making) movie and album is delayed as a legal dispute opens between the band and its label, Profile.

Feb [11] Group performs at Eastside high school, Paterson, NJ in honor of principal Joe Clark.

May *Run's House* is released and makes UK #37, but fails in US.

June With the dispute settled (Run DMC have to pay legal costs, but are now tied to a 10-album deal with Profile), *Tougher Than Leather* is finally released to lukewarm response. It reaches UK #13 (but only spends 5 weeks on chart) and hits US #9, also falling off quickly.

July Run DMC headlines "Run's House" US tour with DJ Jazzy Jeff and Fresh Prince, Public Enemy and others. At a Los Angeles gig, Run DMC are joined on stage by The Beastie Boys.

[17] They receive the keys to Kansas City and Independence, MO, in honor of their support of the Work Works Campaign.

Aug *Mary Mary*, a cover of the Mike Nesmith-penned Monkees song, makes US #75 but fails in UK.

1989 **Sept** Run DMC sings *Ghostbusters* on soundtrack album, as *Pause* stalls at UK #65.

1990 **Dec** [1] *What's It All About* makes UK #48.

1991 **Mar** [15] The rap trio appears on Fox TV's "Arsenio Hall" show.

Apr [17] Run DMC embarks on US tour, supported by EPMD, in Richmond, VA.

THE RUNAWAYS

Cherrie Currie (vocals)
Lita Ford (lead guitar)
Joan Jett (rhythm guitar)
Jackie Fox (bass)
Sandy West (drums)

1976 After a gig on the roof of an Los Angeles, CA, apartment block, all-girl teen rock'n'roll group The Runaways signs to Mercury Records. Group was formed when record producer and entrepreneur Kim Fowley, looking for a female Ramones, introduced Jett (b. Sept.22, 1960, Philadelphia, PA) to West (b. 1960). Line-up includes Currie (b. 1960, Los Angeles), Fox (b. 1960) and Ford (b. Sept.23, 1959, London).

Aug Debut album *The Runaways*, produced and co-written by Fowley, reaches US #194.

Sept Group makes its New York debut at CBGB's with Television and Talking Heads.

1977 **Feb** Fowley/Earle Mankey-produced *Queens Of Noise* makes US #172.

June Group tours Japan (which will produce *Live In Japan*). Jett assumes lead vocals when Currie leaves.

July [1] Fox, suffering from exhaustion (she has recently attempted suicide) leaves and is replaced by Vickie Blue.

Dec *Waitin' For The Night*, again produced by Fowley, fails to chart.

1978 Currie releases solo album *Beauty Is Only Skin Deep*. (She will later form a duo with sister Marie and record for Capitol, achieving some success in Japan. After the sisters split, she will pursue an acting career.) Laurie McAlister joins the band.

Dec [31] Band plays a concert in San Francisco (it will be its last one).

1979 **Apr** They have no funds and no recording deal. Jett wants to keep the band strictly rock'n'roll, while Ford favors a move towards heavy metal. Band is due to appear in movie "We're All Crazy" but splits prior to the commitment. Jett moves to London, where she cuts tracks with ex-Sex Pistols Paul Cook and Steve Jones.

July *And Now ... The Runaways* issued on Cherry Red Records in UK.

1980 **Feb** Currie appears with Jodie Foster in the film "Foxes". Cherry Red releases Runaways *Flaming Schoolgirls* a half live/half studio set from the original line-up.

July [15-16] Jett performs at the 2-day new wave festival "Urgh!" in Santa Monica, CA. Her performance is filmed for movie "Urgh! A Music War".

Aug Jett, having been in hospital suffering from a heart-valve infection and pneumonia, forms her own backing band The Blackhearts with Ricky Byrd (guitar), Gary Ryan (bass) and Lee Crystal (drums). She records *Joan Jett* with producers Kenny Laguna and Ritchie Cordell. With no record company interest, Laguna releases the album himself.

1981 **Jan** Joan Jett & The Blackhearts sign to Boardwalk Records.

Feb Jett opens at New York's Peppermint Lounge as a prelude to a US tour to promote her forthcoming album.

Apr Jett's group's debut album *Bad Reputation* reaches US #51.

Dec Jett releases a hard rock version of *Little Drummer Boy*.

1982 **Mar** Jett releases a cover of The Arrows' *I Love Rock'N'Roll*, which she had seen them perform on UK TV during a UK tour, but had failed to convince The Runaways of its potential. It tops the US chart and album of the same name will hit US #2. Currie stars in horror film "Parasite".

May *I Love Rock 'N' Roll* hits UK #4 as parent *I Love Rock 'N' Roll* reaches UK #25.

June For a follow-up, Jett covers Tommy James & The Shondells' 1969 chart topper *Crimson And Clover*. It hits US #7 but makes only UK #60.

Sept A cover of Gary Glitter's *Do You Wanna Touch Me (Oh Yeah)* is Jett's third US hit at #20. *I Love Rock 'N' Roll* is certified US platinum.

1983 **Aug** Jett's *Fake Friends* reaches US #35. *Album* makes US #20.

Oct Jett cuts Sly & The Family Stone's 1969 US #1 *Everyday People*, which peaks at US #37.

1984 **Aug** Ford's solo album *Dancin' On The Edge* makes US #66 and UK #96, having been at UK #66 for 1 week.

Nov Jett's *Glorious Results Of A Misspent Youth* reaches US #67.

1986 **Oct** [25] Jett's *Good Music*, with backing vocals from The Beach Boys, makes US #83 as parent album *Good Music* climbs to US #105.

1987 Jett stars with Michael J. Fox in movie "Light And Day", as leader of rock band, The Barbusters.

Apr [4] *Light Of Day*, written by Bruce Springsteen and featured in th movie, makes US #33.

1988 **June** [18] Ford, having recorded hard rock-oriented albums for Mercury and Vertigo, reaches US #12 on RCA with solo *Kiss Me Deadl* Her album *Lita* peaks at US #29.

July Jett solo album *Up Your Alley* reaches US #19.

Oct [1] Jett's *I Hate Myself For Loving You* hits US #8 and UK #46.

Dec [17] Hard-rocking *Kiss Me Deadly* makes UK #75.

1989 **Jan** [21] *Little Liar* reaches US #19 for Jett.

Feb Jett plays 5 sell-out concerts at Lunt-Fontanne theater, New York

May Duet with Ozzy Osbourne *Close My Eyes Forever* makes UK #47.

June [17] *Close My Eyes Forever* hits US #8.

[26] Ford marries W.A.S.P. guitarist Chris Holmes at Lake Tahoe, CA Cherie Currie signs a record deal with SBK Records and appears in movie "Rich Girl".

Sept [28] Jett abruptly ends gig after she is hit in the face by a bracele thrown from the crowd.

1990 **Feb** Cherie Currie, now in hard rock band Redd Kross, begins filming "Natural Born Killers", as she prepares her autobiography **Neon Angel: The Cherie Currie Story**.

[24] Jett's *The Hit List*, an album of cover versions including *Dirty Deeds, Tush, Have You Seen The Rain, Love Me Two Times* and *Time Has Come Today*, among others, makes US #36.

[28] Ford is inducted into *Circus* magazine's Hall Of Fame.

Mar [10] Jetts *Dirty Deeds* makes US #36.

July [27] Ford's *Stiletto* reaches US #52 and UK #66 .

RUSH

Alex Lifeson (guitar)
Geddy Lee (vocals, bass)
Neil Peart (drums)

1969 Lifeson (b. Aug.27, 1953, Fernie, Canada) and Lee (b. July 29, 1953, Willowdale, Toronto, Canada) meet in the Toronto suburb of Sarnia while at high school, and team with drummer John Rutsey to form a band playing Cream, Hendrix and Led Zeppelin-influenced music. They begin performing the bar and club circuit when the legal drinkin age is reduced from 21 to 18.

1973 Band supports The New York Dolls in Toronto. They recruit produce Terry Brown (who has worked with Procol Harum and fellow Canadians April Wine), and at Toronto's Sound studios cut an album for $9,000. Unable to interest record labels, they set up their own Moo label to release debut album *Rush*. A copy of it is sent to Cleveland, OH, radio station W-MMS DJ Donna Halper, who brings the band to the attention of Mercury Records. Group signs to Mercury with a 2-album deal worth $200,000.

1974 **July** *Rush* is released. Rutsey quits and Peart (b. Sept.12, 1952, Hamilton, Canada) auditions and takes his place.

Aug [19] Rush embarks on its debut US tour, playing support dates until Christmas.

Oct *Rush* reaches US #105.

1975 **Jan** Group starts work on its second album at Toronto Sound.

Feb Rush wins Most Promising Group at the annual Juno awards (Canada's equivalent of the Grammys).

Mar *Fly By Night* makes US #113, as the group begins a US tour supporting Aerosmith and Kiss.

Nov *Caress Of Steel* peaks at US #148.

1976 **May** Fourth album in 2 years, *2112* reaches US #61.

June [11-13] Rush plays 3 sell-out nights at Toronto's 4,000-seater Massey Hall.

Sept Group begins a tour of Canada.

Nov Double album *All The World's A Stage*, recorded live in Toronto makes US #40.

Dec Band plays selected US dates in New York, Chicago, Indianapol and Boston.

1977 **Jan** *Fly By Night/In The Mood* charts briefly at US #88.

Apr Determined to break nationwide, the band begins a US tour of th

Northeast and Mid-West.
June [2] Band opens its first UK tour at the Manchester Free Trade Hall. The first 7 dates are sold-out.
July Work commences on a new album at Rockfield studios, Wales.
Oct *A Farewell To Kings* reaches US #33 and marks the group's UK debut at #22.
Nov Albums *2112*, *All The World's A Stage* and *A Farewell To Kings* are all certified gold.
Dec *Closer To The Heart* climbs to US #77.
978 Jan Group's first UK chart single, *Closer To The Heart*, makes UK #36.
Feb Rush wins Best Group at the annual Juno awards.
[12] Rush opens its second sell-out UK tour at the Odeon cinema, Birmingham, W.Midlands.
Apr *Archives*, a triple set reissue of the group's first 3 albums, makes US #121.
Oct Rush embarks on the "Hemispheres" tour covering Canada, US, UK and Europe. (It will last until June and include 113 dates.)
Dec *Hemispheres* reaches US #47 and UK #14.
979 Jan [8] Canadian Government names Rush official Ambassadors Of Music.
Feb Rush wins consecutive Best Group Juno awards.
Apr Band embarks on a 3-month tour of UK and Europe.
980 Jan Rush sets out on 5-month "Permanent Waves" tour of US.
Feb *Permanent Waves* hits US #4 and UK #3.
Mar *Spirit Of The Radio* peaks at US #51 and UK #13.
June Rush visits UK for another sell-out tour, including 5 nights at London's Hammersmith Odeon.
981 Feb Band starts "Moving Pictures" US tour to promote new album.
Mar *Moving Pictures* hits both US and UK #3.
Apr *Limelight* reaches US #55. *Vital Signs/A Passage To Bangkok* makes UK #41.
Aug *Tom Sawyer* climbs to US #44.
Nov *Tom Sawyer* reaches UK #25. *Exit ... Stage Left*, a second live double, hits US #10 and UK #6.
982 Jan A live version of *Closer To The Heart* makes US #69.
Mar Lee guests on vocals for fellow Canadians Dave Thomas and Rick Moranis (Bob and Doug McKenzie from Canadian TV comedy show "SCTV") on *Take Off* which reaches US #16. *Great White North* hits US #8 and earns a gold disk.
Oct *New World Man* reaches US #21 and UK #42. *Signals* hits US #10 and UK #3.
Nov *Subdivisions* peaks at UK #53.
983 May *Countdown*, with a live version of *New World Man* on the flipside, makes UK #36.
984 May *The Body Electric* peaks at UK #56. *Grace Under Pressure* hits US #10 and UK #5.
985 Oct *The Big Money* makes UK #46.
Nov *Power Windows*, produced by the band and Peter Collins, hits US #10 and UK #9.
986 Jan [11] *The Big Money* makes US #45.
987 Oct *Time Stand Still*, with guest vocal by Til Tuesday's Aimee Mann, makes UK #42, but fails to crack US Hot 100. *Hold Your Fire*, recorded in England, Montserrat, Toronto and Paris with Collins again producing with the band, hits US #13 and UK #10.
988 Apr *Prime Mover* makes UK #43.
989 Jan *A Show Of Hands* reaches US #21 and UK #12.
Dec *Presto* reaches US #16 and UK #27.
990 May [16-17] Rush performs 2 shows in Toronto, during a 6-month North American tour.
Oct [13] Retrospective collection *Chronicles* makes UK #42.

EON RUSSELL

958 Russell (b. Hank Wilson, Apr.2, 1941, Lawton, OK), a child piano prodigy who has learned to play the trumpet and formed his own band in his mid-teens (lying about his age to get a job in a Tulsa, OK, nightclub and playing with visiting Ronnie Hawkins and Jerry Lee Lewis), moves to Los Angeles, CA. Still lying about his age, he starts a career as a sessionman, learning guitar from James Burton and playing in studios alongside Glen Campbell, Dorsey Burnette and others.
962 He becomes a regular member of Phil Spector's "Wall Of Sound" session crew, playing on hits by The Crystals, Bob B. Soxx & The Blue Jeans and others, sometimes using the pseudonym Russell Bridges. He also plays on Herb Alpert's *A Taste Of Honey* and The Byrds' *Mr. Tambourine Man*.
965 At Liberty Records, he begins arranging for Gary Lewis & The

Playboys and is rewarded with a gold disk for Lewis' first single, *This Diamond Ring*.
1966 Russell's own recording career gets off to a false start with a one-off single for A&M, which quickly disappears.
1967 He builds a recording studio, and his session work includes playing on ex-Byrd Gene Clark's solo album, and arranging *Feelin' Groovy* for Harper's Bizarre.
1968 Russell teams with guitarist Marc Benno for *Asylum Choir*. Released on Mercury subsidiary Smash, it is critically rated, but does not sell. He joins "Delaney & Bonnie And Friends" tour and comes to the attention of Joe Cocker's manager Denny Cordell, following which Cocker's second album is recorded at Russell's studio; it includes *Delta Lady* (originally written by Russell for Rita Coolidge).
1969 Apr A second Asylum Choir album is recorded, but Smash declines to release it. Cordell suggests that Russell records with him in UK. The sessions go well, and they return to California to apply finishing touches to the album, and set up their own label, Shelter Records.
1970 June Russell organizes the band for Cocker's "Mad Dogs And Englishmen" US tour. His high profile in these live shows establishes a personal following, which benefits *Leon Russell*, Shelter's first release: it reaches US #60. (He also plays with Bob Dylan, The Rolling Stones and Eric Clapton during the year). His own show airs on National Educational TV in US – a relaxed affair filmed in his recording studio and featuring a variety of friends, musicians, girlfriends and children.
1971 Jan [22] Movie "Mad Dogs And Englishmen", documenting tour of the same name, with Russell in a prominent role, premieres in London.
July *Leon Russell And The Shelter People*, recorded throughout 1970, climbs to US #17, earning a gold disk, and also reaches UK #29 – his only UK chart entry.
Aug [1] He plays in George Harrison's "Concert For Bangla Desh" at New York's Madison Square Garden.
1972 Jan Russell buys the tapes of *Asylum Choir II* from Smash. Released on Shelter, it reaches US #70.
Sept *Carney* is Russell's most successful album, hitting US #2 (for 4 weeks) and going gold, with a 35-week chart stay.
Oct *Tight Rope*, taken from *Carney*, reaches US #11.
1973 Sept Triple live album *Leon Live*, recorded at Long Beach Arena, CA, in front of 70,000 people, hits US #9 and earns another gold disk. *Queen Of The Roller Derby*, from the live album, reaches US #89.
Oct Double A-side Hank Wilson single *Roll In My Sweet Baby's Arms/I'm So Lonesome I Could Cry* makes US #78. Both come from Russell's "pseudonymous" (it uses his real name) country *Hank Wilson's Back*, which climbs to US #28. (His future wife Mary McCreary's *Butterflies In Heaven* is also released on Shelter.)
1974 May Russell's revival of Tim Hardin's *If I Were A Carpenter* charts at US #73.
Aug *Stop All That Jazz* peaks at US #34.
1975 July *Will O' The Wisp* makes US #30, and is Russell's fourth gold disk.
Nov *Lady Blue*, extracted from *Will O' The Wisp*, reaches US #14.
1976 Jan *Back To The Island* makes US #53. Russell marries Mary McCreary (vocalist with the Sly & The Family Stone spin-off group Little Sister). He also cuts his ties with Shelter Records and establishes new label Paradise Records.
July *The Wedding Album*, recorded with his wife, climbs to US #34.
Sept *Rainbow In Your Eyes* by Leon and Mary Russell, released on Paradise, peaks at US #52. (This will be Russell's last chart single.)
Dec Shelter compilation *Best Of Leon* makes US #40 and is another gold disk.
1977 Feb [19] Russell's song *This Masquerade* wins a Grammy in the hit version by George Benson, named Record Of The Year For 1976.
July Another duetted album with Mary Russell, *Make Love To The Music*, peaks at US #142.
1978 Sept Solo *Americana* makes US #115.
1979 Aug Russell moves closer to his country-blues roots on double album *Willie And Leon*, recorded with Willie Nelson for his label, Columbia. It reaches US #25 and earns another gold disk.
1981 Apr *The Live Album*, recorded by Russell with bluegrass band The New Grass Revival, creeps to US #187, and is his last chart album.
1990 After a decade during which little has been heard of Russell, he begins work on new project with Bruce Hornsby producing.

MITCH RYDER & THE DETROIT WHEELS

Mitch Ryder (vocals)
Jim McCarty (guitar)
Joe Kubert (guitar)
Jim McCallister (bass)
John Badanjek (drums)

1963 Having left R&B vocal group The Peps, Ryder (b. William Levise Jr., Feb.26, 1945, Detroit, MI) forms Billy Lee & The Rivieras, with Badanjek, McCarty, Kubert, and Earl Elliott on bass, in Detroit. They headline regularly at the Village club and record *Fool For You* on local gospel-oriented Carrie label.

1964 With Ryder having built a reputation as a white soul singer, the group becomes the house band at Detroit's Walled Lake Casino, attracting audiences of 3,000, and records a version of *Do You Want To Dance* for local label Hyland Records.

1965 Following a recommendation by local DJ Dave Prince, producer Bob Crewe signs The Rivieras to his New Voice label, taking them to New York for 6 months to rehearse and adapt live repertoire for recording.
July The name Mitch Ryder is picked out of a phone book and the group becomes The Detroit Wheels in order to to sound more "contemporary". *I Need Help* is released but does not chart.

1966 **Jan** *Jenny Take A Ride*, a medley of 2 rock oldies, *See See Rider* and Little Richard's *Jenny Jenny*, hits US #10.
Mar *Jenny Take A Ride* makes UK #27, while *Take A Ride* makes US #78. Kubeck and Elliot are drafted into the US Army. Mark Manko and Jim McCallister replace them.
Apr A revival of The Righteous Brothers' *Little Latin Lupe Lu* reaches US #17 and UK #48.
June *Break Out* peaks at US #62. (It will become a cult favorite on Northern UK dancefloors in the mid-70s but will never chart in UK.)
July *Takin' All I Can Get* reaches only US #100.
Sept *Breakout...!!!* hits US #3. (Ryder is sidelined by a bout of mono-nucleosis brought about through overwork.)
Nov *Devil With A Blue Dress On/Good Golly Miss Molly*, another medley taken from *Breakout...!!!*, is the band's biggest hit at US #4 and a million-seller. Crewe decides that Ryder's future is as a solo artist and he splits singer and band after the sessions which produce the next album and 2 hit singles.

1967 **Mar** *Sock It To Me – Baby!* hits US #6.
[28] Ryder participates in Murray The K's Easter "Music In The 5th Dimension" show at the Manhattan RKO theater, New York.
May *Sock It To Me!* climbs to US #36, while medley single *Too Many Fish In The Sea/Three Little Fishes* makes US #24. Crewe puts Ryder on the road solo in extravagant costumes, with a 40-piece orchestra, grooming him for the Las Vegas circuit. (The Detroit Wheels, without Ryder, will release 3 further singles before disbanding.)
July First solo *Joy*, a more subdued production than the exuberant group efforts, peaks at US #41.
Oct Solo revival of *What Now My Love* reaches US #30.
Nov Another revival, *You Are My Sunshine*, peaks at US #88 but solo *What Now My Love* fails to chart.
Dec *All Mitch Ryder Hits!*, rounding up both group and solo singles, climbs to US #37.

1968 **Feb** Ryder returns to the medley formula with 2 1959 revivals, *(You've Got) Personality/Chantilly Lace*. It is his last Crewe-produced solo and falters at US #87. Ryder splits from Crewe and signs to Dot Records.

1969 *The Detroit-Memphis Experiment*, produced by Steve Cropper of Booker T. And The MG's, has good reviews but it and *Sugar Bee* flop.

1970 Reunited with Detroit Wheels drummer Badanjek, Ryder forms the 7-man hard rock band Detroit, signing to Dot associate label Paramount Records.

1972 **Feb** *Detroit*, the band's only album release, makes US #176.

1978 With a new 8-piece backing band, Ryder releases critically acclaimed but non-charting *How I Spent My Vacation*, for US independent label Seeds & Stems and German reissue specialists Line Records.

1979 Live EP *Rock'N'Roll Live* is issued in Germany by Line.

1980 Line/Seeds & Stems release another album, *Naked But Not Dead*, while an EP *We're Gonna Win* is released in Germany.

1981 Ryder, now a cult figure in Germany, has the double album set *Live Talkies*, which includes a bonus maxi-single, issued on Line.

1982 **Sept** Ryder solo album *Smart Ass* is released by Line and in UK by Safari but fails to chart.

1983 After more than 15 years, Ryder returns to US chart at #120 with solo *Never Kick A Sleeping Dog*, produced by John Cougar Mellencamp for Riva Records. Extracted *When You Were Mine*, written by Prince, climbs to US #87.

1988 *Detroit* is reissued in CD form, with previously unreleased material included, as Ryder remains a cult favorite.

SADE

Sade Adu (vocals)
Stewart Matthewman (sax)
Paul Denman (bass)
Andrew Hale (keyboards)
Paul Cook (drums)

1980 Adu (b. Helen Folasade Adu, Jan.16, 1959, Ibadan, Nigeria), brought with her family by her English mother to Clacton, Essex, in 1963, where she has been raised, and working part-time at London rock venue, the Rainbow, now attending St. Martin's School of Art, joins her first group, Arriva, having written songs for some years (her first is *Kisses From The Karma Sutra*), and Arriva's most popular live number will be *Smooth Operator*, penned by Adu and guitarist Ray St. John.

1981 She joins 8-piece North London funk band Pride, where she links with manager Lee Barrett and future Sade band members Denman, Hale and Matthewman.

1983 With little record company interest, she quits Pride and forms her own band, Sade, inviting Cook to join the other 3. Barrett invests £8,000 in the project and secures enthusiasm from several labels, particularly Virgin, helped by several gigs at Ronnie Scott's club, Soho, London, a venue well suited to the band's smokey jazz-tinged soul material.

1984 **Jan** She signs to CBS/Epic as a solo artist for an advance of £60,000 and 14¾% of album sales. The Sade band members in turn sign to her.
Feb Sade's debut single *Your Love Is King* is released and hits UK #6, helped by the first BBC1 TV "Top Of The Pops" appearance.
Mar Band begins recording debut album with producer Robin Millar as Adu moves into a converted fire station in North London with current beau, journalist Robert Elms.
May Follow-up *When Am I Gonna Make A Living* makes UK #36.
July First album *Diamond Life* is released in UK and hits #2, confirming her as a predominently album-selling artiste. It spends 98 weeks on chart and will sell over 6 million copies worldwide.
Aug Starting with selected UK dates, the band begins a hectic promotional tour of Europe, taking in Switzerland, Germany and Italy. Sade donates money to striking UK coal miners' families.
Sept As *Smooth Operator* reaches UK #19 and becomes a big European hit, the band performs 5 shows in Tokyo, Japan. During her stay, Sade experiences an earthquake in bed. The earth moves, but she is unhurt.
Nov She sings and chats on BBC1 TV show "Wogan". She also moves apartment to Camden, London.
Dec She returns to Nigeria for Christmas to see her 82-year-old grandmother.

1985 **Feb** A US campaign is launched by her US label, CBS subsidiary Portrait, as *Diamond Life* enters the chart. It will peak at US #5 with platinum sales.
[11] *Diamond Life* wins Best British Album at the fourth annual BRIT Awards at the Grosvenor House, London.
Apr Band rejects an offer to perform at the annual Montreux Pop Festival to concentrate instead on recording follow-up album.
May *Smooth Operator* finally hits US #5 after months of airplay.
July [13] Sade performs at the Live Aid spectacular at Wembley Stadium, London, as *Your Love Is King* stalls at US #54.
Sept "Diamond Life" video is released in US.
Nov With recording over, the band begins a UK tour, followed by selected gigs at small US venues. First single from the new album, *Sweetest Taboo*, makes UK #31.
[16] Second album, *Promise*, again featuring group originals, tops UK chart, and wins a multi-platinum award.

1986 **Jan** Band begins a lengthy world tour to support the album. (It will include major US dates in May.)
Feb *Is It A Crime* makes UK #49.
[15] *Promise* tops US chart for 2 weeks. (It also spends 11 weeks at #1 on the US R&B chart.)
[25] Sade wins Best New Artist at the 28th annual Grammy awards in Los Angeles, CA.
Mar [1] *The Sweetest Taboo* hits US #5.
Apr She joins a select number of performers who have featured on the front cover of US magazine *Time*. As elsewhere, it is assumed that Sade is not a band but only a solo performer.
May [17] *Never As Good As The First Time* reaches US #20.

1987 **Apr** She appears in cult film "Absolute Beginners" as torch singer Athene Duncannon and contributes *Killer Blow* to the soundtrack.

She relocates to Spain and will subsequently begin work with the band members on third album.

88 **Apr** Sade re-emerges with *Love Is Stronger Than Pride*, making UK #44.
May Third album, *Stronger Than Pride*, hits UK #3.
June *Paradise* reaches UK #29.
July Sade begins a 40-date US tour, joined by vocalist Leroy Osbourne. *Paradise* makes US #16 as parent album *Stronger Than Pride* hits US #7.
[9] *Paradise* tops US R&B chart.
Nov [21-22] Sade plays sold-out dates at London's Wembley Arena as part of the European leg of a world tour.

89 **Feb** [11] Now based in Spain, Sade marries Spanish music video producer Carlos Scola in Vinuelas Castle, outside Madrid.

91 **Jan** Sade continues to write and record for her fourth album.

AM AND DAVE

m Moore (vocals)
ave Prater (vocals)

61 Moore (b. Oct.12, 1935, Miami, FL), son of a Baptist deacon and ex-member of gospel group The Melonaires, now a secular soloist, is joined spontaneously on stage at the King of Hearts club in Miami by Prater (b. May 9, 1937, Ocilla, GA), a jobbing vocalist working at the club as a chef. Audience reaction is favorable so they form a duo.

62 Signed by Morris Levy of Roulette Records in New York, the duo records gospel-flavored R&B for 4 years without much success. (An eponymous album will be compiled from these Roulette singles after Sam And Dave have become successful.)

65 They leave Roulette to sign with Atlantic, where Jerry Wexler arranges recording sessions in Memphis, TN, at Stax Records. The deal with Stax owner Jim Stewart is that their records are released on his label. The duo is teamed with songwriters Isaac Hayes and David Porter, with backing provided by The Memphis Horns.

66 **Jan** *You Don't Know Like I Know* reaches US #90 and R&B #7.
June *Hold On, I'm Comin'* makes US #21, topping R&B chart 1 week.
[24] Duo begins a 46-date US tour, with Otis Redding, Patti LaBelle & The Bluebelles, Percy Sledge, Garnett Mimms and others, in Greensboro, NC.
Sept *Hold On, I'm Comin'* reaches US #45.
Oct *Said I Wasn't Gonna Tell Nobody* peaks at US #64.
Dec *You Got Me Hummin'* makes US #77.

67 **Feb** *Double Dynamite* reaches US #118.
Mar The success of UK dates puts *Hold On, I'm Comin'* on UK chart at #37. *When Something Is Wrong With My Baby*, an intense soul ballad, in contrast to previous uptempo funk hits, reaches US #42.
[17] Now signed to Otis Redding's manager Phil Walden, Sam And Dave embark on the 13-date Stax/Volt UK "Soul Concert Sensation '67" tour, with Otis Redding, Eddie Floyd, Arthur Conley, Carla Thomas, The Markeys and Booker T. And The MG's, at Finsbury Park Astoria, London, ending Apr.8 at Hammersmith Odeon, London.
Apr A revival of Sam Cooke's *Soothe Me* is the duo's first UK chart single at #35.
May *Double Dynamite* reaches UK #28.
July *Soothe Me* peaks at US #56.
Oct *Soul Man* hits US #2 and tops R&B chart for 7 weeks. It sells over a million and earns a gold disk.
Dec *Soul Man* reaches UK #24.

68 **Jan** *Soul Men* makes US #62.
Feb [29] *Soul Man* wins Best R&B Group Performance Vocal Or Instrumental (Two Or More) Of 1967 at 10th annual Grammy awards.
Mar *I Thank You* hits US #9 and is another international million-seller. In UK it peaks at #34 while *Soul Men* makes UK #32.
May Stax splits from Atlantic after its distribution deal expires and the duo's recordings revert to Atlantic label, with its recording sessions relocating to Miami, FL. Prater shoots his wife during a domestic argument but, because of the circumstances of the incident, he avoids prosecution or imprisonment.
June *You Don't Know What You Mean To Me* makes US #48. *I Thank You* is released in US but does not chart.
Aug *Can't You Find Another Way (Of Doing It)* peaks at US #54.
Nov *Everybody Got To Believe In Somebody* peaks at US #73.

69 **Jan** *Soul Sister, Brown Sugar* makes US #41.
Mar *Born Again* makes only US #92 and is Sam And Dave's last US chart single (though Atlantic will release a further 8, after the duo itself splits, up to June 1971). Compilation *The Best Of Sam And Dave* winds up their US chart career, reaching #87. *Soul Sister, Brown Sugar* is their last but biggest UK hit at #15.

June Sam And Dave appear at the Soul Bowl '69 Festival at the Astrodome, Houston, TX, alongside Aretha Franklin, The Staple Singers, Ray Charles and other major R&B names.

1970 **Jan** [22] The duo opens in the "Soul Together" UK package tour with Joe Tex, Arthur Conley and Clarence Carter at the Royal Albert Hall, London. The tour will end Feb.11 at Finsbury Park Astoria, London. Now on notoriously bad terms with each other, Sam And Dave split up for solo careers. Moore stays with Atlantic and releases 3 solo singles, none of them hits. Prater signs to Alston.

1971 With no solo success, they reunite, signing to United Artists.

1975 *Back Atcha'* is released without chart success. Duo drifts apart again.

1979 **Feb** With popularity renewed because of The Blues Brothers' revival of *Soul Man* (which reaches US #14), the duo is reactivated again.
Sept Sam And Dave tour US incongrously supporting The Clash. *Sweet And Funky Gold*, consisting of re-recordings of their (and others') hits, is released on US Gusto label.

1980 **Oct** Duo appears as Sam And Dave in Paul Simon's semi-autobiographical movie "One Trick Pony".

1981 Duo finally splits for good after a decade of its on-off relationship.

1982 Prater tours with singer Sam Daniels as Sam And Dave.

1987 **Feb** Moore re-records *Soul Man* with Lou Reed as the title theme to a teen comedy film. Released as a single, it reaches UK #30.
June Prater is arrested for selling crack to an undercover cop. He is sentenced to 3 years probation, a $2,500 fine and 150 hours of community service.

1988 **Apr** [9] Prater is killed when his car leaves the road and hits a tree near Syracuse, GA.
May [14] Moore appears at Atlantic Records' 40th anniversary show at Madison Square Garden, New York, with "Blues Brother" Dan Aykroyd duetting.

1989 **Jan** [21] Moore participates in celebration for "Young Americans For President Bush" at the Presidential inauguration at the Convention Center, Washington, DC.

SANTANA

Carlos Santana (guitar, vocals)
Tom Frazer (guitar)
Gregg Rolie (keyboards)
David Brown (bass)
Rod Harper (drums)

1966 **Oct** Santana (b. July 20, 1947, Autlan de Navarro, Mexico), having grown up in Tijuana, Mexico, and then San Francisco, CA, (where he first discovers R&B and the blues) meets keyboards player Rolie after leaving high school, and with him forms The Santana Blues Band, which includes Brown (bass), Frazer (guitar) and Harper (drums). They play extensively at San Francisco club and park gigs.

1968 Band debuts at the Fillmore West in San Francisco, shortens its name to Santana, and undergoes personnel shifting, as its sound begins to encompass the Latin music of Santana's own background into its blues-based approach. Percussionists Mike Carabello and José Chepito Areas are added to the line-up. Frazer and Harper leave, and Michael Shrieve joins on drums.
Sept [2] Group appears at 3-day Sky River Rock Festival and Lighter-Than-Air Fair, in Sultan, WA, with The Grateful Dead, Muddy Waters, Country Joe & The Fish, The Youngbloods and others.

1969 **Feb** Carlos Santana plays on *The Live Adventures Of Al Kooper And Mike Bloomfield*.
Aug [1] Band takes part in the Atlantic City Pop Festival in New Jersey alongside Jefferson Airplane, B.B. King, Creedence Clearwater Revival and others.
[15] Now signed to CBS/Columbia, the band appears at the Woodstock Festival, which brings it national notice. (*Soul Sacrifice*, from the festival, is included in *Woodstock* triple album and movie.)
[30] Band plays a third major festival in a month, the Texas International Pop Festival, at Dallas International Motor Speedway, Lewisville, TX.
Nov Debut album *Santana*, boosted by the Woodstock appearance and positive critical response, hits US #4. (It will spend over 2 years on US chart and earn a gold disk.)
Dec *Jingo*, a percussive highlight from the album, peaks at US #56.
[6] Santana play on the bill of The Rolling Stones' concert at Altamont Speedway, Livermore, CA, where a murder is committed during The Stones' act.

1970 **Mar** *Evil Ways*, also from the debut album, hits US #9.
Apr [18] Santana plays at the Royal Albert Hall, London, with It's A

SANTANA cont.

Beautiful Day and Taj Mahal.

May *Santana* reaches UK #26.

Oct Second album *Abraxas* tops US chart for 6 weeks, selling over a million copies.

Dec *Abraxas* hits UK #7 (and will spend a year on UK chart).

1971 Jan A cover of Fleetwood Mac's *Black Magic Woman*, from *Abraxas*, hits US #4, and is the band's biggest hit single. Neal Schon joins on guitar and vocals.

Apr *Oye Como Va*, also from *Abraxas*, and a Latin-rock adaptation of a salsa number by Tito Puente, reaches US #13.

Oct Brown and Carabello leave the band, joining forces with ex-Santana members Areas, Escovedo and Reyes. Santana, Rolie, Schon and Shrieve remain.

Nov *Santana III* tops US chart for 5 weeks, earning another gold disk, and hits UK #6.

Dec Band breaks up as a live unit and, although it will regroup for recording, founder member Rolie and Schon leave. (After an 18-month rest, Rolie will join Schon in Journey.) Meanwhile, *Everybody's Everything*, taken from *Santana III*, reaches US #12.

1972 Mar *No One To Depend On*, also from the third album, makes US #36.

Sept Carlos Santana cuts a live album at Hawaii's Diamond Head volcano with drummer Buddy Miles, from which double A-side *Evil Ways/Them Changes* makes US #84. *Carlos Santana And Buddy Miles, Live!* hits US #8 and reaches UK #29.

Dec *Caravanserai*, moving the band's music into freer, jazzier forms, hits US #8 (another gold disk) and UK #6.

1973 Feb Group plays with The Rolling Stones at the latter's Los Angeles, CA, benefit concert for victims of the Nicaraguan earthquake, to 19,000.

Apr Carlos Santana marries Urmila, a Sri Chinmoy adherent.

Aug *Love Devotion Surrender*, a duetted instrumental between Carlos Santana and guitarist Mahavishnu John McLaughlin, reaches US #14 and hits UK #7. (Like his wife and McLaughlin, Santana has now become a devotee of Sri Chinmoy, and taken the additional religious name Devadip – which means "The light of the lamp of the Supreme".)

Dec *Welcome* reaches US #25, earning another gold disk, and hits UK #8. The band's personnel is changing extensively with every new album, but its music continues in a more jazzy direction.

1974 Sept Compilation album *Santana's Greatest Hits* reaches US #17 and UK #14.

Oct *Samba Pa Ti*, an instrumental from *Abraxas*, is issued as a UK single, and reaches UK #27.

Nov Carlos Santana teams with Alice Coltrane (another disciple of Sri Chinmoy) for instrumental album *Illuminations*, which makes UK #40.

Dec *Borboletta*, with guest appearances from Stanley Clarke and Brazilian musicians Airto Moriera and Flora Purim, reaches US #20 and UK #18.

1975 June Bill Graham, first to book the band in the 60s, becomes manager.

Dec Triple live album *Lotus*, a deluxe package recorded and originally only released in Japan, appears belatedly in US and UK, but its expensive nature prevents it from charting.

1976 Jan [25] Carlos Santana guests with Bob Dylan's "Rolling Thunder Revue" at the "Night Of The Hurricane II" concert at the Houston Astrodome, TX, a benefit show for Ruben "Hurricane" Carter. He duels on guitar with fellow guest Stephen Stills on *Black Queen*.

May *Amigos* hits US #10, earning a gold disk, and reaches UK #21. Taken from the album, *Let It Shine* makes US #77.

Aug Group plays Wembley, London, with The Grateful Dead and The New Riders Of The Purple Sage.

Dec They perform at the Royal Albert Hall, London, the concert broadcast simultaneously by BBC TV and stereo radio.

1977 Feb *Festival* reaches both US and UK #27, and is another US gold disk.

Apr Band plays with Joan Baez and others, at a free concert for the inmates of Soledad prison in California, organized by the Bread & Roses charitable foundation.

Nov A revival of The Zombies' 1964 hit *She's Not There* becomes the group's biggest UK hit at #11.

Dec *She's Not There* reaches US #27. Double live *Moonflower* hits US #10 (a further gold disk) and UK #7.

1978 Mar Band plays at California Jam II in Ontario, CA, to 250,000 people, alongside Ted Nugent, Aerosmith, Heart, and others.

Oct After a summer US tour, the band begins a European tour.

Dec *Inner Secrets* reaches US #27 (another gold disk) and UK #17. Taken from it, a revival of Buddy Holly's *Well All Right* peaks at US #69 and UK #53.

1979 Feb Also from *Inner Secrets*, a revival of The Classics IV's *Stormy* makes US #32.

Apr Carlos Santana's instrumental solo *Oneness/Silver Dreams – Golden Reality*, half studio cuts and half live recording from Osaka, Japan, peaks at UK #55.

May *One Chain (Don't Make No Prison)*, extracted from *Inner Secrets* (and a 1974 middling US hit for The Four Tops), peaks at US #59.

Nov *Marathon* reaches US #25 and UK #28.

1980 Feb *You Know That I Love You*, taken from *Marathon*, makes US #35.

Mar *All I Ever Wanted*, also from the album, peaks at US #57.

Sept Another Carlos Santana instrumental solo double album, *The Swing Of Delight* (with guest appearances by jazzmen Herbie Hancock, Wayne Shorter and Ron Carter), makes US #74.

1981 Apr *Zebop!* reaches UK #33.

June *Zebop!* hits US #9 and earns the band a gold disk.

July *Winning*, a Russ Ballard song from *Zebop!*, reaches US #17.

Aug Also from the album, *The Sensitive Kind* peaks at UK #56.

1982 Sept [3-5] Band plays the US Festival, financed by Apple Computers founder Steven Wozniak, in San Bernardino, CA, to 400,000 people, along with Jackson Browne, The Cars, Fleetwood Mac, The Grateful Dead, Eddie Money, Police, Talking Heads and many others.

Oct *Hold On* reaches US #15. It is taken from *Shango*, which reaches US #22 and UK #35.

Dec *Nowhere To Run*, also from *Shango*, peaks at US #66.

1983 Apr *Havana Moon*, a Carlos Santana solo with guest support from Willie Nelson, Booker T. Jones and The Fabulous Thunderbirds, make[s] UK #84.

July Group tours Europe and UK, supporting Bob Dylan.

1985 Apr *Beyond Appearances* makes US #50 and UK #58 while, taken fro[m] it, *Say It Again* makes US #46.

July [13] Band plays at Live Aid in Philadelphia, PA.

1986 July [20] Santana celebrates its 20th anniversary with a concert in Sa[n] Francisco. All previous group members come on stage to make a 17-piece band.

Nov UK-compiled TV-promoted *Viva! Santana – The Very Best* mak[es] UK #50. (Carlos Santana produces the music for Ritchie Valens biopi[c] "La Bamba".)

1987 Apr *Freedom* peaks at US #95. Band plays a lengthy "Freedom Worl[d] Tour", with founder member Rolie rejoining the current line-up of Carlos Santana (guitar), Chester Thompson (keyboards), Alfonso Johnson (bass), Tom Coster (synthesizers), Graham Lear (drums), Armando Peraza, Raul Rekow and Orestes Vilato (all percussion) an[d] Buddy Miles (vocals).

Nov [7] Carlos Santana's instrumental solo *Blues For Salvador* make[s] US #195.

1988 July Santana plays a 1988 summer tour with jazz saxophonist Wayne Shorter as a guest player.

Nov *Viva Santana*, a live compilation of material recorded between 1969 and 1987, makes US #142.

1989 Feb [22] Carlos Santana wins Best Rock Instrumental Performance, Orchestra, Group Or Soloist, for *Blues For Salvador* at the 31st annua[l] Grammy awards.

Carlos Santana guests on John Lee Hooker's *The Healer*.

Aug Carlos Santana launches his own Guts & Grace records.

Nov [4] Carlos Santana joins Living Colour on stage during their set [in] Oakland, CA.

1990 May [30] Santana performs the first of 3 nights at the Hammersmith Odeon, London.

July [14] *Spirits Dancing In The Flesh*, with current band Chester Thompson (keyboards), Armando Peraza (percussion), Alex Ligertwood (guitar, vocals), Benny Rietveld (bass) and Walfredo Rey[es] (drums), peaks at UK #68.

Aug [1] *Spirits Dancing In The Flesh* makes US #85. (Extracted first single is cover of Curtis Mayfield's *Gypsy Woman*.)

1991 Jan [20] Santana appears at mega-fest "Rock In Rio II", Brazil.

LEO SAYER

1968 Sayer (b. Gerard Hugh Sayer, May 21, 1948, Shoreham-by-Sea, Sussex[)], having studied at Worthing Art College, W.Sussex, and worked in London as a magazine illustrator, playing harmonica in folk clubs by night, returns to Sussex after a nervous breakdown, and works in a factory while starting to write songs.

1972 Having been a member of The Terrorplane Blues Band, he forms his own group Jester, and then Patches. David Courtney, an ex-drummer for Adam Faith, places an ad in the **Brighton Evening Argus** auditioning singers, bands and comedians at the Pavilion theater, Brighton, E.Sussex. 50 groups turn up, with Patches the last to auditio[n]

Courtney signs the band and becomes Sayer's co-writer. Patches record one-off single *Living In America*, but it is never released. Courtney and Sayer take their songs and the group to Faith, who signs them to a management contract and, when Patches splits, takes over Sayer as a soloist. Gerard becomes Leo from a nickname given him by Faith's wife Jackie; with his wide mane of thick curly hair, she calls him the "little (he is only 5'4" tall) lion".

73 **Mar** Faith and Courtney record Sayer at a studio owned by The Who's Roger Daltrey. Daltrey's own debut album, ***Daltrey***, is almost entirely written by Sayer (lyrics) and Courtney (music). (It gives Daltrey his biggest solo hit, at UK #5, with extracted *Giving It All Away*.)
Aug Faith has Sayer signed to a solo deal with Chrysalis, which releases his debut single *Why Is Everybody Going Home*, but it fails to chart. Sayer marries a librarian, Janice.

74 **Jan** Second single *The Show Must Go On* hits UK #2 (Three Dog Night's cover will hit US #4 in May), and is extensively promoted by Sayer on TV and live appearances (with Roxy Music), on which he wears pierrot costume and make-up designed by Kursty Clino.
Feb Debut album *Silver Bird* hits UK #2. He makes a promotional US tour, after which the pierrot costume is abandoned because of negative US reaction.
July *One Man Band* is belated follow-up and hits UK #6.
Oct *Long Tall Glasses* (originally written as *I Can Dance*, but amended in the studio after he has forgotten some of the original lyrics) hits UK #4. Second album *Just A Boy* (the title comes from a line in *Giving It All Away*) hits UK #4.

75 **Feb** He begins a 2-month US tour, where he is signed to Warner Bros., which releases ***Just A Boy***.
May Sayer's US chart debut is *Just A Boy*, which reaches US #16, and *Long Tall Glasses (I Can Dance)* which hits US #9.
June *One Man Band* creeps to US #96.
Sept *Moonlighting* hits UK #2, behind Rod Stewart's *Sailing*.
Oct Third album ***Another Year***, featuring Sayer's by-now regular band of Chris Stainton (keyboards) and Grahame Jarvis (drums), hits UK #8. Courtney leaves as Sayer's producer and co-writer to work solo. He is replaced by ex-Supertramp bassist Frank Farrell.
Nov *Another Year* stalls at US #125. Sayer has to cancel a follow-up US tour when he is hospitalized for a wisdom tooth operation.

76 **Apr** [8] Sayer embarks on 9-date UK tour at the Gaumont cinema, Ipswich, Suffolk. It will end at the Opera House, Blackpool, Lancs.
May [1] 9-date UK tour begins at Glasgow Apollo, Scotland. Tour will end May 10 at the ABC cinema, Peterborough, Cambs.
Nov *You Make Me Feel Like Dancing*, an R&B-styled song written by Sayer with Vini Poncia, and recorded in Los Angeles, CA, with new producer Richard Perry, hits UK #2. Sayer promotes it and his forthcoming album with a tour of UK and Australia.

77 **Jan** *You Make Me Feel Like Dancing* tops US chart for a week, selling over a million copies.
Feb *When I Need You*, written by Albert Hammond and Carole Bayer Sager, tops UK chart, while parent album *Endless Flight* hits UK #4.
Apr Sayer contributes *I Am The Walrus* to the all-star *All This And World War II* album/movie project, which features cover versions of Beatles songs.
May *When I Need You* tops US chart for a week, while *How Much Love* hits UK #10. Sayer plays a 56-city US tour, which grosses $2 million.
June *Endless Flight* hits US #10, selling over a million copies to earn Sayer a platinum disk.
Aug *How Much Love* reaches US #17.
Oct *Thunder In My Heart* makes UK #22, while parent album of the same title hits UK #8.
Nov *Thunder In My Heart* makes US #38, as the album makes US #37.

78 **Jan** *Easy To Love* makes US #36.
Feb [23] *You Make Me Feel Like Dancing* wins Best Rhythm & Blues Song Of 1977 at the 20th annual Grammy awards.
July Sayer hosts NBC TV's "Midnight Special".
Sept *Leo Sayer* reaches UK #15, but stalls at US #101. He begins a weekly TV series "Leo" on BBC1 TV.
Oct *I Can't Stop Lovin' You (Though I Try)* hits UK #6.
Nov A revival of Buddy Holly's *Raining In My Heart* makes UK #47.
Dec *Raining In My Heart* reaches UK #21.
[14] Sayer guests on the "Perry Como Christmas Show" on US TV.

79 **Apr** Compilation *The Very Best Of Leo Sayer* tops UK chart for 3 weeks.
Oct *Here* makes UK #44.

80 **Aug** A revival of Bobby Vee's 1961 UK #4 *More Than I Can Say*, produced by Alan Tarney, hits UK #2.
Sept *Living In A Fantasy* reaches UK #15.

Dec *More Than I Can Say* hits US #2.
1981 **Mar** *Living In A Fantasy* reaches US #23, while album of the same title makes US #36.
1982 **Apr** *Have You Ever Been In Love* hits UK #10.
July Bee Gee's penned *Heart (Stop Beating In Time)* reaches UK #22.
Aug *World Record* reaches UK #30.
1983 **Jan** Sayer begins another BBC1 TV series, "Leo Sayer".
Apr *Orchard Road* reaches UK #16.
Oct *Till You Come Back To Me* peaks at UK #51.
Nov *Have You Ever Been In Love*, promoted by a TV campaign, reaches UK #15.
1984 **May** Sayer embarks on a 50-date 2-month UK tour.
1986 **Feb** A revival of *Unchained Melody*, included on the soundtrack of film "Car Trouble", peaks at UK #54.
1988 **July** He plays a self-financed UK tour with no recording contract.
Nov His former manager Faith pays Sayer a reported £650,000. Details are not revealed, but the payment appears to be in settlement of owed earnings and record royalties.
1990 **July** Sayer returns with his first album in 7 years, ***Cool Touch***, on EMI, produced by Alan Tarney. Title track is released as single, but both fail to score despite much promotion.

BOZ SCAGGS

1959 Scaggs (b. William Royce Scaggs, June 8, 1944, Ohio), having grown up in Texas, meets Steve Miller at school in Dallas, TX, and joins his band The Marksmen on vocals and tambourine. Miller teaches him guitar.
1961 Scaggs and Miller are together at Wisconsin University, Madison, WI, where they play in R&B/Motown covers group The Ardells, which becomes The Fabulous Night Train.
1963 He returns to Texas and forms R&B band The Wigs with John "Toad" Andrew on guitar, Bob Arthur on bass and George Rains on drums.
1964 Band quits college and travels to UK to find work, but fails to make an impression. As The Wigs split, Scaggs moves to Europe.
1965 He arrives in Stockholm, Sweden, where he records debut album *Boz* for Polydor, released only in Sweden. Scaggs continues his world tour which reaches India before returning to US.
1967 **Sept** [1] On arrival back in San Francisco, CA, he rejoins The Steve Miller Band, replacing singer/guitarist James Cooke.
1968 Scaggs is featured on The Steve Miller Band's 2 US chart albums *Children Of The Future* (#134) and *Sailor* (#24), both recorded in UK with producer Glyn Johns. Following the sessions, he leaves the band due to musical differences with Miller.
1969 With the help of **Rolling Stone** editor Jann Wenner, Scaggs gains a solo deal with Atlantic, and records at Muscle Shoals studios in Alabama with top session players, including Duane Allman.
Aug *Boz Scaggs*, produced by Wenner, is released to critical acclaim, but few sales. He is dropped by Atlantic.
1970 After several months in the Southern states, Scaggs moves back to the West Coast and forms The Boz Scaggs Band, which signs to CBS/Columbia at the end of the year.
1971 **May** Debut Columbia album *Moments* reaches US #124, while extracted *We Were Always Sweethearts* makes US #61.
July *Near You*, also from the album, stalls at US #96.
Dec *Boz Scaggs And Band*, recorded in London, falters at US #198.
1972 **Oct** *Dinah Flo* peaks at US #86, while parent album *My Time* reaches US #138. Scaggs tours US with guest band members Steve Miller and George Rains.
Dec He forms a new band, with Les Dudek (guitar), Tom Rutley (bass), Jimmy Young (keyboards), Rick Schlosser (drums) and Jack Schroer (sax).
1974 **Apr** [27] Scaggs plays the Cherry Blossom Music Festival in Richmond, VA, alongside The Steve Miller Band.
May *Slow Dancer* reaches US #81.
July Capitalizing on Scaggs' recent success, Atlantic reissues his only album for the label, *Boz Scaggs*. It reaches US #171.
1976 **Apr** [16] When he attempts to see Bobby Bland backstage after a show at Antone's club in Austin, TX, Scaggs is thrown out by bouncers.
May *It's Over*, from his next album, makes US #38.
Sept *Silk Degrees*, produced by Joe Wissert and arranged by David Paich, is Scaggs' most successful album. It hits US #2, spends 115 weeks on chart and sells over a million copies in US, to earn a platinum disk. Back-up session players include future members of Toto.
Oct *Lowdown*, from the album, hits US #3 and is a million-seller.
Nov *Lowdown* is Scaggs' UK chart debut, at #28. Third album extract *What Can I Say?* reaches US #42.

1977 **Feb** [19] *Lowdown* wins Best Rhythm & Blues Song Of 1976 at the 19th annual Grammy awards.
Mar *What Can I Say?* hits UK #10.
May Fourth single from the album, *Lido Shuffle*, reaches US #11 and UK #13.
July *Silk Degrees*, more than a year after its release, reaches UK #20.
[13] A Scaggs concert at New York's Avery Fisher Hall is ended midway by a power cut in the city.
Aug Rita Coolidge's cover of *We're All Alone*, a Scaggs ballad from *Silk Degrees*, hits US #7 and UK #6, her biggest solo single.
Nov *Hard Times* peaks at US #58.
Dec *Down Two Then Left* reaches US #11 (his second platinum album) and UK #55. (Its title was originally announced as *Still Falling For You*.)
1978 **Jan** *Hollywood* makes US #49 and UK #33, and is his last UK hit single.
1979 **June** [3] Scaggs and Rickie Lee Jones join Bruce Springsteen and The E Street Band for a jam session on stage at the Whiskey A-Go-Go in Los Angeles, CA, at the wedding reception of Springsteen's lighting man Mark Brickman.
1980 **May** *Breakdown Dead Ahead* reaches US #15.
June *Middle Man* hits US #8 (his third consecutive platinum album) and makes UK #52.
Aug *Jo Jo*, taken from *Middle Man*, reaches US #17.
Oct *Look What You've Done To Me* makes US #14.
1981 **Feb** Compilation album *Hits*, dominated by tracks from *Silk Degrees*, reaches US #24. Scaggs' last US chart single is *Miss Sun*, a duet with Lisa Dal Bello, which reaches US #14.
1982 **May** [28] Scaggs plays a benefit concert for the Vietnam Veterans Project at Moscone Center, San Francisco, CA, with Jefferson Starship and The Grateful Dead.
1983 Scaggs retires from the music scene. He opens his own Southern-style restaurant in San Francisco.
1988 He is persuaded by CBS/Columbia to return to the studio to record a new album.
Apr Scaggs appears at the Montreux Pop Festival in Switzerland.
July *Other Roads* is released. The set includes 3 songs co-written with singer/poet Jim Carroll and features assistance from members of Toto. It climbs to US #47, but does not chart in UK. From it, *Heart Of Mine* makes US #35. Scaggs announces plans to open a jazz/blues club in San Francisco.
1990 Again quiet on the recording scene, Scaggs produces San Francisco's Smoking Section debut for RCA.

SCRITTI POLITTI
Green Gartside (vocals)
Nial Jinks (bass)
Tom Morley (linn drums)

1977 Group is formed by Gartside (b. Green Strohmeyer-Gartside, June 22, 1956, Cardiff, Wales), an ex-schoolmate of Soft Cell's Marc Almond, Jinks and Morley, all friends at Leeds Art School, after Green is inspired by a Sex Pistols' concert in Leeds, W.Yorks.
1978 Scritti Politti, with temporary members including Matthew Kay, moves to London and begins low-key gigging at mainly punk venues.
1979 Band supports Joy Division and Gang Of Four on tour, but suffers a setback when Green collapses with a heart complaint.
Oct EP *Four 'A' Sides* is released on Scritti Politti's own St. Pancras label and features a photocopied sleeve, but goes unnoticed.
Nov Further EP *John Peel Session* is released.
1980 Green spends the year convalescing at home with his parents and begins writing new songs, now heavily influenced by R&B music. Meanwhile Jinks leaves the band.
1981 Group's first new track, *The Sweetest Girl*, appears on **New Musical Express** music newspaper cassette.
Nov Leading UK independent label Rough Trade releases it and it peaks at UK #64. Jinks rejoins shortly afterwards.
1982 **May** *Faithless* makes UK #56 and tops UK Independent chart.
Aug Double A-side *Asylums In Jerusalem/Jacques Derrida*, with guest Robert Wyatt on keyboards, is the group's first UK Top 50 entry at #43.
Sept Debut album *Songs To Remember*, produced by Adam Kidron, reaches UK #12, and again tops UK Independent chart.
Nov Morley quits.
1983 Green signs to Virgin Records and moves to New York to work on an album with new members David Gamson (keyboards) and Fred Maher (drums) and producer Arif Mardin.
1984 **Apr** *Wood Beez (Pray Like Aretha Franklin)* hits UK #10.
July *Absolute* reaches UK #17.

Nov *Hypnotise* peaks at UK #68.
1985 **May** *The Word Girl* hits UK #6.
June Mardin-produced *Cupid And Psyche '85*, containing the first 5 Virgin singles, hits UK #5 and makes US #50. It is described by Green as: "very super, hyper, syncopated, ping-ponged bif pow zip thing".
Sept *The Perfect Way* is the group's first US hit at #11. (Miles Davis w. later cover it.)
1986 **Feb** Madness' version of *The Sweetest Girl* makes UK #35.
[10] *Wood Beez (Pray Like Aretha Franklin)* climbs to US #91.
Aug Chaka Khan makes US #53 and UK #52 with Green-penned *Lov Of A Lifetime*.
Sept Green and Gamson write the title cut for Al Jarreau's *L Is For Lover*.
Dec Self-titled video collection is released by Virgin.
1987 **Aug** Scritti Politti contributes a song for Madonna's "Who's That Gir soundtrack.
1988 **Mar** Group takes part in the annual Montreux Pop Festival in Switzerland.
May *Oh Patti (Don't Feel Sorry For Loverboy)*, with Miles Davis guesti on trumpet, reaches UK #13.
June *Provision*, recorded in New York, hits UK #8 and US #113. It h taken 3 years to complete, delayed by Green's need always to use the latest state of the art studio technology.
July *First Boy In This Town (Lovesick)* peaks at UK #63.
Aug *Boom! There She Was* peaks at US #53.
Oct Maher produces Information Society's US #3 *What's On Your Mi (Pure Energy)*, having also produced Marlon Jackson's debut album.
Nov *Boom! There She Was* peaks at UK #55.
1989 Green retreats to his Welsh hideaway for 2 years to work on new material and experiment with the latest technology.
1991 **Mar** Scritti Politti releases cover version of Lennon/McCartney's *She A Woman* with toasting assistance from ragga-reggae star Shabba Ranks. It is the first of 3 ragga cover singles, the second is scheduled be the Gladys Knight hit *Take Me In Your Arms And Love Me* with Sweetie Irie.

SEALS & CROFTS
Jim Seals (vocals, guitar, saxophone, violin)
Dash Crofts (vocals, guitar, mandolin)

1958 Seals (b. Oct.17, 1941, Sidney, TX) and Crofts (b. Aug.14, 1940, Cisco, TX) are playing guitar and drums respectively in the backing group rock singer/pianist Dean Beard (and have cut some unsuccessful singles with him for Edmoral and Atlantic), when Beard is invited to join The Champs (who have had a million-selling rock instrumental with *Tequila* earlier in the year) and they join with him, relocating fro Texas to Los Angeles, CA.
1965 They both leave the fragmenting Champs; Seals stays in California to write songs and play sessions and Crofts returns to Texas.
1966 Seals teams with guitarist Louie Shelton, bassist Joseph Bogan and, i need of a drummer, persuades Crofts back to Los Angeles. This quar becomes The Dawnbreakers, which is augmented by the 3 Day sister as vocalists. (Crofts marries 1 of them, Billie Lee Day.)
1969 Following the example of group manager Marcia Day, The Dawnbreakers are converted to the Baha'i faith (founded by Persian prophet Baha'u'llah in the 19th Century). Seals marries Ruby Anderson, a member of the community living with the group at its manager's Los Angeles home.
1970 The Dawnbeakers split, with Shelton turning to production and Boga to studio engineering. With their help, Seals and Crofts remain togeth as a duo, and record an eponymous debut album for Talent Associat label. It does not chart, but their extensive live work gains a followin
Nov *Down Home*, their second and last on Talent Associates, makes US #122, and attracts Warner Bros., which signs them.
1972 **Jan** Warner debut, *Year Of Sunday*, produced by Shelton, and augmenting the duo's harmony vocal blend with horn and string accompaniment, reaches US #133.
Nov *Summer Breeze* (later revived by The Isley Brothers) is their first Singles chart entry, hitting US #6. It is taken from the album of the same title, which hits US #7 and earns a gold disk. Crofts and his wif have a daughter.
Dec Seals and his wife have a son.
1973 **Mar** *Hummingbird*, with lyrics strongly influenced by Baha'i, reaches US #20.
June *Diamond Girl* hits US #4, earning a second gold disk.
July Extracted title cut *Diamond Girl* (jointly written in tribute to thei

wives, both new mothers) hits US #6.

Nov *We May Never Pass This Way (Again)* makes US #21.

'74 Apr *Unborn Child* makes US #14, while the title track peaks at US #66.

June *King Of Nothing*, from *Unborn Child* makes US #60. The duo tours constantly, punctuating its middle of the road harmony material on stage with mandolin features by Crofts, and sax pieces and dance reels on the violin by Seals.

Sept Warner acquires release rights to the duo's first 2 albums from Talent Associates, and reissues them as double album *Seals And Crofts I And II*, which peaks at US #86.

'75 May *I'll Play For You* makes US #30, earning their fourth gold disk.

June Extracted title track *I'll Play For You* reaches US #18.

Dec *Seals And Crofts' Greatest Hits*, a compilation of hit singles to date, reaches US #11 and earns another gold disk.

'76 July *Get Closer*, featuring Carolyn Willis (from hitmaking group The Honey Cone), hits US #6.

Sept *Get Closer* makes US #37, earning another gold disk.

Dec *Baby, I'll Give It To You*, from *Get Closer*, makes US #58.

'77 Jan *Sudan Village* peaks at US #73.

Feb [9] Seals & Crofts take part in US ABC TV's "American Bandstand's 25th Anniversary Special".

Nov *My Fair Share*, from film "One On One", makes US #28, while Seals/Crofts-composed and performed soundtrack album from the movie peaks at US #118.

'78 32-track Dawnbreaker studios is financed by Seals & Crofts' earnings, and is built to the duo's specifications at the HQ of manager Marcia Day's management company Day Five Productions, in San Fernando Valley, CA. (The Baha'i religious community is also based there.)

June *Takin' It Easy*, the first recorded at Dawnbreaker studios, makes US #78 and is the duo's last album to chart, while *You're The Love*, taken from it, reaches US #18.

Sept Title song from *Takin' It Easy* stalls at US #79 (and is the duo's last chart entry).

[9] Drama series "The Paper Chase", a spin-off from the film of the same title, first airs on US CBS TV, with Seals & Crofts performing theme song *The First Years*. (Seals & Crofts will quit the music business to devote their full-time efforts to the Baha'i community, although rumors will, from time to time, suggest a reunion.)

THE SEARCHERS

Mike Pender (vocals, lead guitar)
Tony Jackson (vocals, bass)
John McNally (vocals, rhythm guitar)
Chris Curtis (vocals, drums)

'61 McNally (b. Aug.30, 1941, Liverpool, Merseyside) and Pender (b. Michael Prendergast, Mar.3, 1942, Liverpool) form an instrumental duo and perform at their local pub in Kirkdale, Liverpool, naming themselves The Searchers after a John Wayne movie. They meet Jackson (b. July 16, 1940, Liverpool) and drummer Norman McGarry, and the group begins regular work backing singer Johnny Sandon.

'62 Mar Sandon leaves to front The Remo Four, and they continue as a quartet, perfecting their harmony vocal style. Regularly playing clubs like the Cavern, the Casbah, and the Hot Spot, they build a reputation at the Iron Door, whose owner becomes their manager.

Sept McGarry leaves to replace Ringo Starr in Rory Storm & The Hurricanes, and Curtis (b. Chris Crummy, Aug.26, 1941, Oldham, Gtr.Manchester) joins on drums. While playing clubs in Hamburg, Germany, several tracks are recorded live at the Star-Club by Philips Records.

'63 May Having heard a demo by the group, Pye Records A&R man Tony Hatch views them in action at the Iron Door and signs them to Pye.

Aug Debut single, reviving The Drifters' *Sweets For My Sweet*, tops UK chart for 3 weeks, deposing Elvis Presley's *Devil In Disguise*.

[10] Group appears on the 100th edition of commercial TV show "Thank Your Lucky Stars" with Cliff Richard & The Shadows, Billy J. Kramer, Brian Poole and Alma Cogan.

[31] Band appears at B-Day, a 13-hour outdoor rock festival in Liverpool, with The Hollies, Billy J. Kramer & The Dakotas and more than 20 other bands.

Sept *Meet The Searchers* hits UK #2.

[11] Group begins a 23-date UK package tour with Roy Orbison, Brian Poole & The Tremeloes, Freddie & The Dreamers and others. The tour will finale on Oct.6 at King George's Hall, Blackburn, Lancs.

Oct *Ain't Gonna Kiss Ya*, a 4-track EP from which the title song receives wide UK airplay, reaches UK #12. *Sugar And Spice* hits UK #3, while

Sweet Nothin's, from the live Hamburg recordings released on Philips, makes UK #48.

Nov *Sugar And Spice* hits UK #5.

[8] Group begins another UK tour, with Dusty Springfield, Freddie & The Dreamers, Brian Poole & The Tremeloes and Dave Berry in Halifax, W.Yorks.

1964 Jan [24] Group starts its own 15-min. weekly show on Radio Luxembourg.

Feb *Needles And Pins*, a cover of Jackie DeShannon's minor US hit, written by Jack Nitzsche and Sonny Bono, tops UK chart for 3 weeks. It is the group's biggest hit, with total UK sales of over 850,000.

[11] McNally is taken ill with a septic throat.

[29] Band begins a 29-date twice nightly UK package tour with Dusty Springfield, Bobby Vee and Big Dee Irwin at the Adelphi cinema, Slough, Bucks. Tour will end Mar.29 at the Liverpool Empire.

Apr *Needles And Pins* reaches US #13 (taking sales over a million), and The Searchers guest on US TV's "Ed Sullivan Show".

[26] Group appears in the **New Musical Express** Poll Winners Concert at the Empire Pool, Wembley, London.

May *Don't Throw Your Love Away*, a revival of a Shirelles song, is the group's third UK #1. *(Ain't That) Just Like Me* reaches US #61 and *Meet The Searchers - Needles And Pins* is first US album chartmaker at #22.

[24] Group makes its debut on commercial TV's "Sunday Night At The London Palladium".

[28] They begin a 2-week US tour at the World's Fair in New York.

June *It's The Searchers* hits UK #4.

July *Don't Throw Your Love Away* reaches US #16. Live *Hear! Hear!*, a compilation of early tracks recorded in Hamburg, makes US #120.

Aug *Some Day We're Gonna Love Again*, a cover of a Barbara Lewis track, reaches UK #11. Jackson departs for a solo career, signing to CBS, and is replaced by Frank Allen (b. Francis McNeice, Dec.14, 1943, Hayes, London), ex-Cliff Bennett's Rebel Rousers.

Sept *Some Day We're Gonna Love Again* makes US #34.

Oct *When You Walk In The Room*, another Jackie DeShannon cover, hits UK #3, while *This Is Us* reaches US #97.

Nov *When You Walk In The Room* reaches US #35.

Dec *What Have They Done To The Rain?*, an anti-nuclear protest song written by Malvina Reynolds, highlights the group's softer, folk-influenced side, normally restricted to album tracks (and influential on many mid-60s folk-rock groups). It reaches UK #13.

1965 Jan A revival of the Clovers' *Love Potion #9*, only available in UK as an album track, hits US #3 and is a million-seller.

Feb *What Have They Done To The Rain?* reaches US #29.

Mar *Goodbye My Love* hits UK #4.

[25] 12-date twice-nightly UK package tour, with Dusty Springfield, Heinz, The Zombies, special guest star Bobby Vee and others, opens at the Odeon cinema, Stockton, Cleveland. The tour will close Apr.10 at the Sophia Gardens, Cardiff, Wales.

Apr *Bumble Bee*, a revival of a LaVern Baker hit, is a US-only release (though it finds UK success as leading track on an EP), making US #21. Band plays **New Musical Express** Poll Winners Concert at the Empire Pool, Wembley. *Sounds Like The Searchers* hits UK #8 (and is the group's last UK chart album). *The New Searchers LP* makes US #112.

[14] Group appears on Granada TV's "The Bacharach Sound" with Dionne Warwick, Dusty Springfield and others.

May *Goodbye My Lover Goodbye* (a US re-titling, for copyright reasons, of *Goodbye My Love*) peaks at US #52.

July *He's Got No Love* reaches UK #12.

[14] The group leaves for 4-5 week US tour.

Aug *He's Got No Love* stalls at US #79.

Oct *When I Get Home* makes UK #35. In US *The Searchers No.4* charts at #149.

Dec A harder folk-rock style on P.F. Sloan's *Take Me For What I'm Worth* reaches UK #20.

1966 Jan [26] Group starts tour of Far East, Australia and US in Hong Kong.

Mar *Take Me For What I'm Worth* stalls at US #76.

[12] A 6-date twice-nightly UK tour with bill-topper P.J. Proby and others, begins at the Town Hall, Birmingham, W.Midlands. The tour will end Mar.27 at the Empire theater, Liverpool. John Blunt (b.Mar.28, 1947, Croydon, London) fills in for Chris Curtis, who is suffering from nervous exhaustion. (Curtis does not rejoin the band, becoming a producer at Pye. Blunt stays with the band.)

May A cover of The Rolling Stones' *Take It Or Leave It* makes UK #31.

Oct *Have You Ever Loved Somebody?* makes UK #48 (while Paul And Barry Ryan's version makes #49). (It will be the group's last UK chart single.)

THE SEARCHERS cont.

Dec *Have You Ever Loved Somebody?* peaks at US #94.

1968 Group leaves Pye for Liberty for 2 singles, then joins RCA.
Dec Blunt is replaced on drums by Billy Adamson.

1971 **Sept** *Desdemona* reaches US #94.

1972 *Second Take* is released on RCA.

1973 **June** Group tours US in the "British Re-Invasion Show", with Wayne Fontana, Herman's Hermits and Gerry & The Pacemakers.

1979 Band signs to Sire Records and, given a free recording hand, uses material from a variety of songwriters such as Tom Petty.

1980 **Mar** *The Searchers* on Sire reaches US #191.

1981 *Play For Today* (US title: *Love's Melodies*) is released, but fails to chart.
Nov [23] Group performs at the Royal Variety Show with Adam And The Ants, Lonnie Donegan and Cliff Richard reunited with The Shadows.

1985 **Dec** [23] Pender plays his last gig with the group, before leaving to form his own touring band, Mike Pender's Searchers. He is replaced by Spencer James.

1987 **May** Group begins a successful UK "Solid 60s Silver" tour with Gerry & The Pacemakers and Peter Sarstedt. (It will run until June.) PRT reissues all the Pye material on album and CD in UK.

1988 **June** The Searchers take action against Mike Pender's use of The Searchers' name.

NEIL SEDAKA

1952 Sedaka (b. Mar.13, 1939, Brooklyn, NY), a piano student since age 9, begins to write songs with his 16-year-old lyricist neighbor and Lincoln high school colleague Howard Greenfield, their first composition being *My Life's Devotion*. While at high school, Sedaka will be chosen as New York City's outstanding classical pianist by Arthur Rubinstein.

1955 Impressed by The Penguins' hit *Earth Angel*, Sedaka and Greenfield write their first semi-rock'n'roll song, doo-wop ballad *Mr. Moon*, which Sedaka performs with great success at a school talent show. He joins high school vocal group, The Tokens, with Hank Medress (who will later co-found another group of that name and have several hits in the 60s). Also a school colleague and romantic attachment at this time is Carole Klein, who later becomes hit singer/songwriter Carole King.

1957 Sedaka wins a piano scholarship to New York's Juilliard School of Music (with the recommendation of Arthur Rubinstein). Studying serious music does not affect his pop interests and he and Greenfield continue to write regularly, while Sedaka records one-off single *Fly, Don't Fly On Me* for Philadelphia-based Legion label, which flops.

1958 Songwriters Doc Pomus and Mort Shuman put Sedaka and Greenfield in contact with Don Kirshner and Al Nevins, publishers at Aldon Music in Broadway's Brill Building in New York, who sign them to an exclusive contract and start placing their songs with recording acts. The first to be recorded is *Passing Time*, cut by Atlantic all-girl group The Cookies.
Feb Sedaka releases his own second single *Laura Lee* on Decca, but still with no success.
Sept Connie Francis records Sedaka/Greenfield composition *Stupid Cupid* (originally written for The Shepherd Sisters), reaching US #14 and topping UK chart.
Dec [1] After Nevins has played Sedaka's demo of *The Diary* to Steve Scholes of RCA, he signs Sedaka to RCA as a recording artist.

1959 **Feb** *The Diary*, Sedaka's first RCA single, reaches US #14.
May Follow-up *I Go Ape*, a wild rocker, is his UK chart debut, hitting #9. It makes US #42 following a ban by several US radio stations. Sedaka tours US for the first time, to promote the single.
June Busy with session work, as well as writing and recording (and studying at Juilliard), Sedaka plays piano on Bobby Darin's US and UK chart-topper *Dream Lover*. His own *Crying My Heart Out For You* flops.
Dec *Oh! Carol*, a public display of affection for Carole Klein (to which she responds with little-heard *Oh! Neil*), hits US #9 and UK #3. His debut album *Rock With Sedaka* is released, but does not chart.

1960 **May** *Stairway To Heaven* hits US #9 and UK #8.
Sept Ballad *You Mean Everything To Me* reaches US #17 and UK #45, while uptempo B-side *Run Samson Run* makes US #28.

1961 **Feb** *Calendar Girl* hits US #4 and UK #8.
June *Little Devil* reaches US #11 and hits UK #9.
Oct *Sweet Little You* peaks at US #59.
Dec *Happy Birthday, Sweet Sixteen*, one of Sedaka and Greenfield's most enduring songs, hits US #6.

1962 **Feb** *Happy Birthday, Sweet Sixteen* hits UK #3.
May March-tempo *King Of Clowns*, which will become the official theme of the Ringling Brothers' Barnum & Bailey circus, makes US #45 and UK #23.

Aug Sedaka has his first US chart-topper and first million-seller with *Breaking Up Is Hard To Do*, which holds US #1 for 2 weeks, and hits UK #7. The distinctive gibberish chorus line was conceived after the rest of the song, coming in a flash of inspiration during a sleepless night. Sedaka is touring UK while the single is on the charts.
Nov *Next Door To An Angel*, almost a clone of *Breaking Up*, hits US #5 and reaches UK #29, where soundalike follow-ups are generally ill-regarded.

1963 **Jan** Compilation *Neil Sedaka Sings His Greatest Hits*, rounding up major singles from *Oh! Carol* to *Next Door To An Angel*, makes US #55.
Mar *Alice In Wonderland* reaches US #17, but fails in UK (where the Merseybeat boom is just stirring on chart and the subsequent "British invasion" will be instrumental in Sedaka's decision to retire from recording during the second half of the 60s).
May *Let's Go Steady Again* reaches US #26 and UK #42.
Aug *The Dreamer* peaks at US #47.
Nov Skeeter Davis, a million-seller earlier in the year with *The End Of The World*, hits US #7 with Sedaka's *I Can't Stay Mad At You*.
Dec *Bad Girl* makes US #33.

1964 **Aug** *Sunny* stalls at US #86.

1965 **Oct** *The World Through A Tear* makes US #76.

1966 **Feb** *The Answer To My Prayer* proves anything but, ending Sedaka's run of hits on RCA. Aware that he is now out of fashion with pop mainstream, Sedaka gives up recording and live performances at around the same time. He and Greenfield are contracted as staff writers, via Kirshner, for Screen Gems Music.

1968 **Sept** He signs to Screen Gems' label SGC Records in US, releasing 2 unsuccessful singles. Meanwhile, his song *Workin' On A Groovy Thing* takes Patti Drew to US #62.

1969 **Aug** The 5th Dimension's revival of *Workin' On A Groovy Thing* reaches US #20.

1970 **May** The 5th Dimension's version of Sedaka/Greenfield's *Puppet Man* makes US #24.

1971 **June** Tom Jones revives *Puppet Man*, taking it to US #26 and UK #50. Sedaka visits UK for the first time in several years, for a 4-month tour, mostly of Northern clubs, where his act proves immensely popular.

1972 **Jan** Tony Christie's version of Sedaka/Greenfield's *Is This The Way To Amarillo* reaches UK #18. Sedaka signs to Kirshner's new eponymous label and, inspired by the success of friend Carole King's *Tapestry*, records *Emergence*, credited simply as Sedaka. *I'm A Song (Sing Me)* and *Superbird* from the album are given strong airplay in UK and a lengthy tour follows, including a major date at London's Royal Albert Hall. Sedaka moves his wife Leba and children Dara and Marc to London, and sets up a new working base from a flat in Mayfair. This move splits him from Greenfield and he begins to write with new lyricist, Phil Cody.
June He records self-produced *Solitaire* for Kirshner Records at Strawberry studios, Stockport, Gtr.Manchester, with the 4 musicians who will shortly be known as 10cc. Eric Stewart engineers the sessions while Lol Creme, Kevin Godley and Graham Gouldman back Sedaka.
Nov *Beautiful You* makes UK #43, but *Solitaire*, from which it is taken, does not chart. Sedaka appears on BBC1 TV's "Top Of The Pops".
Dec A UK reissue of *Oh! Carol* (on a maxi-single with *Breaking Up Is Hard To Do* and *Little Devil*) makes UK #19.

1973 **Mar** *That's When The Music Takes Me*, from *Solitaire*, makes UK #18.
June *Standing On The Inside*, his first release under a new UK and European recording deal with MGM Records, reaches UK #26.
Sept It is taken from *The Tra-La Days Are Over*, on MGM, again recorded at Strawberry studios with 10cc. Also extracted as a UK single is *Our Last Song Together*, written as a swan song with Greenfield, which makes UK #31.

1974 **Feb** *A Little Loving*, released on Polydor (which has now absorbed subsidiary MGM label), reaches UK #34. Meanwhile, Andy Williams' cover of *Solitaire* hits UK #4.
July Sedaka/Cody composition *Laughter In The Rain* reaches UK #15, while album of the same title (this time recorded in Los Angeles, CA, with producer Robert Appere and sessioneers including David Foster, Danny Korthchmar and Russ Kunkel) reaches UK #17.
Aug At a party in the Sedakas' London flat to celebrate the UK success of *Laughter In The Rain*, Sedaka discusses with guest Elton John his current lack of a US recording contract. (His recent UK successes have not been released in US.) John, a long-time fan, offers a deal to issue the Polydor recordings in North America on his own Rocket label.
Nov Live album *Live At The Royal Festival Hall*, recorded with the Royal Philharmonic Orchestra, makes UK #48.

1975 **Feb** Released on Rocket, *Laughter In The Rain* tops US chart for a week, and gives Sedaka his second million-selling single, more than 12 years after the first. It is also included on US album *Sedaka's Back*, a compilation from the last 3 UK albums, which makes US #23 and earns a gold disk for a half million US sales.

Mar *Overnight Success* reaches UK #31, while *Neil Sedaka Sings His Greatest Hits*, a reissue of the 1963 compilation, makes US #161. Sedaka plays Las Vegas, opening for The Carpenters at the Riviera hotel, but is asked to leave the show halfway through the 2-week engagement when his act starts getting a better response. (The Riviera will invite him back as a headliner.)

Apr *The Queen Of 1964*, from *Overnight Success*, makes UK #35, and is Sedaka's final UK hit single.

May *The Immigrant*, from *Laughter In The Rain* which is dedicated to John Lennon (currently fighting US authorities to stay in the country), reaches US #22.

June The Captain & Tennille's cover of *Love Will Keep Us Together*, originally from *The Tra-La Days Are Over*, tops US chart for 4 weeks and reaches UK #32.

Aug A belated US release of *That's When The Music Takes Me* climbs to US #27.

Sept Uptempo *Bad Blood*, on which Sedaka is joined by Elton John on backing vocals, tops US chart for 3 weeks, and is his biggest-selling single, topping 1.4 million in US. (It is deposed by John's *Island Girl*.)

Nov *The Hungry Years*, a revised version of *Overnight Success*, and including *Bad Blood*, reaches US #16 and earns a second gold album.

Dec A re-recording of *Breaking Up Is Hard To Do*, in a slow ballad format, hits US #8 (the only former US #1 to return to the Top 10 in a different version by the same artist).

'76 **May** *Love In The Shadows* makes US #16.

[2] Sedaka begins short UK tour at the Hammersmith Odeon, London.

June *Steppin' Out* reaches US #26.

July 18-track compilation *Laughter And Tears: The Best Of Neil Sedaka Today*, promoted on TV, hits UK #2. (It will be his last UK chart album.) Meanwhile, the title song from *Steppin' Out* (with Elton John on backing vocals) makes US #36.

Oct His last hit single on Rocket is *You Gotta Make Your Own Sunshine*, which peaks at US #53 as a reissue on RCA of Kirshner album *Solitaire* makes US #159.

'77 **June** Sedaka signs a new recording deal with Elektra, debuting with a new version of *(Is This The Way To) Amarillo*, which makes US #44. Debut Elektra album *A Song* reaches US #59.

Nov On Rocket, compilation album *Neil Sedaka's Greatest Hits*, anthologizing the 70s material, peaks at US #143.

'80 **June** A duet with his daughter Dara, *Should've Never Let You Go*, reaches US #19, and is his last US Singles chart entry. It is taken from *In The Pocket*, which peaks at US #135.

'84 He signs a new deal with MCA/Curb Records, and releases *Come See About Me*, which does not chart.

'87 Sedaka's autobiography, **Laughter In The Rain** is published.

'90 **Apr** [3] Sedaka is admitted to Danbury hospital, CT, for treatment of diverticulitis.

OB SEGER

'64 Seger (b. May 6, 1945, Dearborn, MI), the son of clarinet-playing leader of 13-piece Stewart Seger Orchestra, a postwar attraction at nearby Walled Lake casino resort, has cut an acetate of self-penned *The Lonely One*, recorded in Max Crook's (the musitron player on Del Shannon's *Runaway*) basement, which a kindly DJ at Ann Arbor, MI's W-PAG plays one night in 1961, and has led his own rock trio, The Decibels, with Eddie "Punch" Andrews and Dave Leone, in high school, then played full-time in Ann Arbor, with The Town Criers, when he joins Doug Brown & The Omens (the city's leading group) on keyboards. He begins to write songs with vocalist Brown, and they record several demos, paid for by local-based hitmaker Del Shannon, who becomes their publisher. (One of his songs, *Such A Lovely Child*, is recorded by local band The Mushrooms, with lead singer Glenn Frey.)

'66 **Mar** The Omens, under the pseudonym of The Beach Bums, record *The Ballad Of The Yellow Beret* (a parody of Barry Sadler's US chart-topper *Ballad Of The Green Berets*) on Are You Kidding Me? label. The gimmick is a favorite with local college students, but is withdrawn when Sadler sends a telegram threatening a lawsuit.

May The result of a $1,200 recording session is *East Side Story*, Seger's first release under his own name, billed as Bob Seger & The Last Heard (the band being the remnants of The Omens). It is a sizeable hit in Detroit on Hideout Records (selling 50,000 copies), and is picked up for

national distribution by Cameo – as is follow-up *Persecution Smith*.

Dec Cameo buys out his contract and issues seasonal rocker *Sock It To Me, Santa*.

1967 Seger & The Last Heard continue to record for Cameo, cutting *Vagrant Winter* and *Heavy Music Parts 1 & 2*, the latter being a major hit in Detroit but prevented from nationwide success by the sudden demise of Cameo. Brown splits from Seger to pursue his own music; Punch Andrews, who has produced *Heavy Music*, becomes Seger's manager.

1968 **Jan** Seger re-forms his band as The Bob Seger System and signs to Capitol Records, despite a bigger offer from Motown. First Capitol single, *2 + 2 = ?*, an anti-war heavy rocker, only sells in Michigan.

1969 **Feb** *Ramblin' Gamblin' Man* becomes Seger's US chart success, reaching #17, while debut album, titled after the single, makes US #62.

May *Ivory* peaks at US #97.

1970 **Apr** After completing work on second album, *Noah*, Seger breaks up The System (which has been increasingly prone to internal strife), and announces that he is quitting music for a year to return to college. (He will enroll, but not stay.) The album does not chart but, from it, *Lucifer* peaks at US #84.

Nov *Mongrel*, recorded after a short layoff, with new musicians, climbs to US #171.

1971 Without a band, Seger records solo, acoustic, singer/songwriter-style *Brand New Morning*, which fails to sell. He experiments with a new band named STK, including Oklahoma duo Dave Teegarden and Skip "Van Winkle" Knape. (STK is not successful, but its members will form the core of Seger's next stage group.)

Nov *Looking Back* makes US #96, after which Seger leaves Capitol. He and Andrews form Palladium Records, which is signed to Warner/Reprise.

1972 **Aug** A cover version of Tim Hardin's *If I Were A Carpenter* makes US #76. It is taken from first Palladium album *Smokin' O.P.'s* ("O.P.'s" refers to smoking other people's cigarettes), which makes US #180 and includes a remake of *Heavy Music*.

1973 **Mar** *Back In '72*, part-recorded at Muscle Shoals studios, AL, with guests including J.J. Cale, stalls at US #188.

1974 **Aug** *Get Out Of Denver* reaches US #80. Later revived by UK acts Dave Edmunds and Eddie & The Hot Rods, it is taken from *Seven/Contrasts*, which fails to chart.

1975 **May** Seger re-signs to Capitol after Warner/Reprise turns down *Beautiful Loser*. On Capitol, it reaches US #131.

Oct *Katmandu*, from *Beautiful Loser*, makes US #43 (and is a Top 10 hit in Detroit). Seger tours US with newly-formed backing group, The Silver Bullet Band, featuring Drew Abbott (guitar), Robyn Robbins (keyboards), Alto Reed (saxophones), Chris Campbell (bass) and Charlie Allen Martin (drums). (Band membership will change often over subsequent years, with bassist Campbell the only enduring member. First to go will be drummer Martin, after being injured in a car accident, replaced by Teegarden, who played in STK with Seger.)

1976 **Apr** First album to credit The Silver Bullet Band is double live *Live Bullet* recorded on stage at Cobo Hall, Detroit, during the previous year's tour. It reaches US #34, and will sell over a million copies in a 140-week chart stay.

June *Nutbush City Limits*, a live cover of Ike & Tina Turner's hit, taken from the double album, reaches US #69.

1977 **Jan** [23] Seger plays in Tampa, FL, supported by The Patti Smith Group, but loses his support star for the remainder of the tour when Smith falls off stage and is badly injured.

Mar *Night Moves*, featuring The Silver Bullet Band on one side and The Muscle Shoals Rhythm Section on the flip, hits US #8, earning Seger's second consecutive platinum disk. The title track is extracted and gives Seger his first Top 10 single, hitting US #4.

May *Mainstreet*, also from *Night Moves*, reaches US #24.

Aug Another track from the album, *Rock 'N' Roll Never Forgets* climbs to US #41.

1978 **June** A year in the making, *Stranger In Town* is released, hitting US #4, and is his third million-selling album, staying on US chart for over 2 years. It also marks Seger's UK chart debut at #31. The album uses both The Silver Bullet Band and The Muscle Shoals Rhythm Section, and has guest appearances by The Eagles' vocalist Glenn Frey (whom Seger has known since youth in Detroit) and Bill Payne of Little Feat.

July *Still The Same*, first single from the album, hits US #4.

Oct *Hollywood Nights*, also from *Stranger In Town*, reaches US #12, and is his first UK chart single, peaking at #42.

1979 **Jan** From the album, ballad *We've Got Tonight* is third extracted single, reaching US #13.

Feb *We've Got Tonight* peaks at UK #41.

BOB SEGER cont.

1980
May Final single from the album, *Old Time Rock'N'Roll*, makes US #28.
Mar [19] A US tour to promote forthcoming *Against The Wind* opens in Fayetteville, NC.
May *Against The Wind*, produced by Bill Szymczyk, is the product of almost 2 years' work. Another million-seller, it tops US chart for 6 weeks during a 110-week chart stay. In UK, it makes #26. *Fire Lake*, the first extracted single, hits US #6.
June The title song from the album, *Against The Wind*, hits US #5.
Oct Third single from the album, *You'll Accomp'ny Me* reaches US #14.
[3] During a concert by Bruce Springsteen in Ann Arbor, Seger joins him on stage for a duet on *Thunder Road*.
Dec *The Horizontal Bop*, final extract from *Against The Wind*, climbs to US #42.

1981
Feb [25] Seger wins Best Rock Performance By A Duo Or Group With Vocal for *Against The Wind* at the 23rd annual Grammy awards.
Oct A second double live album, *Nine Tonight*, recorded in Boston, MA, and Detroit, hits US #3 and UK #24. From it, a live version of *Hollywood Nights* makes US #49.
Nov Also from the live album, *Tryin' To Live My Life Without You* hits US #5.

1982
Feb *Feel Like A Number* climbs to US #48, while a live version of *We've Got Tonite*, from *Nine Tonight*, reaches UK #60.

1983
Feb *Shame On The Moon*, written by country star Rodney Crowell, is Seger's biggest-selling single, hitting US #2. It is taken from *The Distance*, produced by Seger and Jimmy Iovine over 14 months (and originally intended as a double album), which hits US #5 (his sixth consecutive platinum album) and reaches UK #45. On the album, Seger uses new musicians: Russ Kunkel (drums), Waddy Wachtel (guitar) and Roy Bittan from Bruce Springsteen's E Street Band (piano), alongside bassist Chris Campbell, keyboardist Craig Frost and saxophonist Alto Reed from the current Silver Bullet Band. This angers the band's regular guitarist, Drew Abbott, who leaves the line-up.
Mar Kenny Rogers and Sheena Easton's cover of *We've Got Tonite* hits US #6 and UK #28, bettering Seger's original in both territories.
May *Even Now*, also from the album, climbs to US #12 and UK #73.
June *Roll Me Away* reaches US #27.
Nov *Old Time Rock'N'Roll* is reissued as a single due to its inclusion in Tom Cruise movie "Risky Business", and this time peaks at US #48.

1985
Jan *Understanding*, taken from the soundtrack of movie "Teachers", reaches US #11.

1986
May [3] *American Storm* reaches US #13. It is taken from *Like A Rock*, again a platinum-seller, which hits US #3 and UK #35. For the first time, Seger has a co-writer, Craig Frost, on his songs.
June *Live Bullet*, originally US #34 in 1976, re-charts to US #135.
July [12] Extracted title song from *Like A Rock* reaches US #12.
Sept [20] *It's You*, also from *Like A Rock*, peaks at US #52.
Nov [29] Last single from the album, *Miami*, peaks at US #70. (It will later be used in NBC TV series "Miami Vice".)

1987
Aug [1] *Shakedown*, recorded for movie "Beverly Hills Cop II" (and originally intended for Michigan buddy, ex-The Eagles' Glenn Frey, prevented by laryngitis from recording it) gives Seger his first US chart-topper. It is not released on Capitol, but MCA, which holds the soundtrack rights. Seger rewrites some of Keith Forsey's original lyrics before recording it.
Dec Seger is one of the artists on the Special Olympics benefit album *A Very Special Christmas*, with his version of *The Little Drummer Boy*.

1988
Aug He makes a guest appearance on Little Feat's comeback album *Let It Roll*, and files for divorce after a brief marriage.

THE SEX PISTOLS

Johnny Rotten (vocals)
Steve Jones (guitar)
Sid Vicious (bass)
Paul Cook (drums)

1971
London schoolfriends Cook (b. July 20, 1956, London) and Jones (b. Sept.3, 1955, London), meet Fine Arts graduate Malcolm McLaren who is opening a shop called "Let It Rock" in King's Road, Chelsea, London.

1972
Cook, Jones and friend Wally Nightingale decide to form a band. Cook scrapes together money for a drumkit and Jones and Nightingale steal equipment for the latter to use, with Jones taking vocals.

1973
McLaren renames his shop "Too Fast To Live, Too Young To Die". He takes an interest in the band and Glen Matlock, an assistant at the store, hearing of an opening for a bassist, joins the band.

1974
They rehearse throughout the year as The Swankers, learning a variety of 60s covers, and also begin to write their own material.

1975
The Swankers makes its only public performance, singing 3 songs at a party above Tom Salter's Café in the King's Road.
May McLaren returns from 6 months in US, working with The New York Dolls, and decides that Nightingale will not fit into his scheme for the group. Jones moves to guitar, leaving the band looking for a singer.
June McLaren suggests ex-Television Richard Hell (who has already invented a punk look for himself), but the band wants an unknown London vocalist.
Aug John Lydon (b. Jan.31, 1956) meets the group at McLaren's shop, now renamed "Sex", and is asked to join as singer. His audition is to stand by the shop's juke box and sing along to Alice Cooper's *School's Out*. Group becomes The Sex Pistols, and Jones christens Lydon "John Rotten", after his catchphrase, "You're rotten, you are."
Nov [6] The Sex Pistols play their first gig at St. Martin's School of Art in London, following with a series of small gigs, mainly at art schools.

1976
Apr The Sex Pistols support Joe Strummer's band The 101ers at the Nashville Rooms. Group spends the summer building a cult reputation in London, playing in a variety of venues.
Aug The Sex Pistols are banned from the European Punk Rock Festival in Mont de Marsan, France, by organizers who dislike their image. (They have already been banned from several London venues, including Dingwalls and the Rock Garden.)
[29] Group plays the Screen On The Green, Islington, London, supported by The Buzzcocks and The Clash.
Sept [3] Band plays the Club de Chalet du Lac in Paris. Devoted follower of the band, Billy Idol drives to France in his ex-Post Office van with Siouxsie and Steve Severin of The Banshees to see the gig.
[17] They play a concert for inmates at Chelmsford prison, Essex.
[20] Band headlines the 100 club punk rock festival which sees the debuts of Subway Sect and Siouxsie & The Banshees, featuring Sid Vicious (b. John Simon Ritchie, May 10, 1957, London) on drums. The Sex Pistols make their first UK TV appearance singing *Anarchy In The UK* on "So It Goes".
Oct [8] A week after Rotten appears on the cover of music paper New Musical Express, The Sex Pistols are signed to EMI for a £40,000 advance. (Chrysalis, RAK and Polydor have all made bids.) They record *Anarchy In The UK* with producer Chris Thomas.
Nov [26] *Anarchy In The UK* is released.
[28] The Sex Pistols appear on BBC TV's "Nationwide" and ITV's "London Weekend Show".
Dec [1] Group appears on ITV's early evening magazine program "Today". Taunted by interviewer Bill Grundy, they respond with verbal abuse and make the cover of every newspaper the next day, establishing the group's name across the country.
[5] The "Anarchy In The UK Tour" (also featuring The Clash, The Damned and The Heartbreakers) is due to start, but many dates are cancelled. (Only 3 out of 19 gigs go ahead.)
[7] The Sex Pistols are discussed at EMI's AGM. Chairman Sir John Read apologizes for the group's behavior.
[18] *Anarchy In The UK* makes UK #38.

1977
Jan [6] EMI issues a statement saying it feels unable to promote The Sex Pistols' records in view of the adverse publicity generated over the last 2 months, but that press reports of their behavior seem to have been exaggerated. (EMI honors their contract, promising the £40,000 advance; *Anarchy In The UK* sells 55,000 copies before it is withdrawn.)
Feb Vicious, a member of Flowers Of Romance, auditioned as bass player to replace Matlock, joins despite his rudimentary playing skills.
Mar Matlock forms band The Rich Kids, with Steve New (guitar) and Rusty Egan (drums).
[10] The Sex Pistols sign to A&M Records in a ceremony outside Buckingham Palace.
[16] Due to pressure from other A&M artists and the Los Angeles head office, A&M fires the band, having pressed 25,000 copies of *God Save The Queen*. Group has earned £75,000 for its 6 days with the label.
May Group signs to Virgin for £15,000. Virgin strikes problems pressing the group's new single *God Save The Queen* at the CBS plant when workers threaten to walk out, but problems are smoothed over. Jamie Reid's sleeve depiction of the Queen with a safety pin through her mouth causes a furore in the press.
[27] *God Save The Queen* is released, and reportedly sells 150,000 copies in 5 days, despite being banned from daytime play by UK BBC Radio 1 and leading chainstores.
June [7] Virgin Records hires a boat called "Queen Elizabeth" for a party on the River Thames. The Sex Pistols perform *Anarchy In The UK* outside the Houses of Parliament and members of the party are arrested when the boat docks.

[11] *God Save The Queen* hits UK #2. Claims are made that the record is outselling Rod Stewart's #1 *I Don't Want To Talk About It*. Virgin Records, trying to buy airtime during "Today" commercial breaks to advertise the record, are turned down.

[18] Rotten, producer Thomas and engineer Bill Price are attacked with razors as they leave a public house in North London on their way back to nearby Wessex studio.

[19] Cook is attacked by 5 men wielding knives and an iron bar outside Shepherds Bush underground station.

July [30] *Pretty Vacant* hits UK #6, while the group tours Scandinavia. McLaren meets film director Russ Meyer to discuss making a Sex Pistols film. (Meyer will pull out of the project.)

Aug Group undertakes an "undercover" UK tour as Spots (an acronym for Sex Pistols On Tour Secretly), and also plays as The Tax Exiles, Special Guest, The Hampsters and Acne Rabble.

Oct [29] *Holidays In The Sun* hits UK #8. The Belgian Travel Service issues a summons claiming the sleeve infringes copyright of one its brochures. (The sleeve is withdrawn from sale.)

Nov [12] *Never Mind The Bollocks – Here's The Sex Pistols* enters UK chart at #1, displacing Cliff Richard's *40 Golden Greats*. It stays on top for 2 weeks, before being dethroned by Bread's *The Sound Of Bread*. A policewoman sees the album sleeve in a shop window and informs the retailer he is contravening the 1889 Indecent Advertsing Act because of the word "bollocks" on the sleeve. (Magistrates "reluctantly" declare 2 weeks later that it is not an offense to display the record.) The Sex Pistols sign to Warner Bros. for US.

Dec Vicious and his US girlfriend Nancy Spungen are arrested on suspicion of possessing illegal substances, but are released without charge. The Sex Pistols return from a tour of Holland, to play UK dates. (Their last UK gig is in Huddersfield, W.Yorks., on Christmas Day at Ivanhoe's club, in front of local children in aid of charity.) Listeners to Israeli Radio vote *God Save The Queen* the worst single of the year.

'78 Jan [5] The Sex Pistols begin a US tour at the Great Southeast Music Hall, Atlanta, GA.

[10] Band makes its US TV debut on "Variety".

[14] After gigs in Memphis, Baton Rouge, Dallas and Tulsa, the group plays what will be its last live show, at the San Francisco Winterland Ballroom. Rotten quits the tour and heads for New York.

[16] Vicious overdoses and goes into hospital. McLaren returns to London, while Cook and Jones use plane tickets to Rio de Janeiro, Brazil, previously purchased for a planned one-off concert. Virgin declares there will be "no more Sex Pistols releases".

Never Mind The Bollocks makes US #106.

Feb Cook and Jones stay in Rio as guests of "great train robber" Ronald Biggs.

[23] Vicious and Spungen are arrested for possession of drugs.

Apr Cook and Jones play dates with Johnny Thunders at London's Speakeasy club. Vicious also performs as a vocalist with Thunders. After The Sex Pistols split Rotten reverts to his real name John Lydon and, having taken a short holiday in Jamaica, returns to UK and forms new band with ex-Clash member Keith Levene (guitar), novice bass player Jah Wobble (b. John Wardle) and Canadian Jim Walker (drums), who has played with The Furys and is recruited through auditions and an ad. Quartet's name, Public Image Ltd. (PiL), is chosen as a sanitized anti-rock'n'roll statement. PiL signs to Virgin (The Sex Pistols' label).

July Virgin refuses to release the single Cook and Jones recorded with Biggs under the title *Cosh The Driver*. Instead it is released as *No One Is Innocent (A Punk Prayer By Ronnie Biggs)*, as a double A-side with Vicious' version of *My Way*. Vicious plays a farewell gig at the Electric Ballroom, London, under the banner "Sid Sods Off" with The Vicious White Kids – Rat Scabies, Glen Matlock and Steve New.

[25] Formation of Public Image Ltd. is officially announced by Lydon.

Oct [11] Vicious, living at the Chelsea hotel in New York with Spungen, calls police to say someone has stabbed her. He is arrested, charged with murder and placed in the detox unit of a New York prison. (McLaren eventually bails him out with money from Virgin.)

'79 Feb [2] Vicious dies at a New York party from an accumulation of fluid on the lungs caused by a heroin overdose.

The Sex Pistols, McLaren and Virgin go to court in an attempt to resolve the group's financial affairs. The High Court judge appoints a receiver to sort out finances, including money tied up in the movie and album *The Great Rock'N'Roll Swindle*, currently in production. He tells those concerned to sort out who owns the name The Sex Pistols and whether Lydon is still under contract to McLaren. (In the course of the week Cook and Jones change sides, joining Lydon/Virgin against McLaren.)

Mar The Sex Pistols' revival of Eddie Cochran's *Something Else*, coupled with *Friggin' In The Riggin'*, hits UK #3. **Great Rock'N'Roll Swindle**, a double set of out-takes and jokey songs, hits UK #7. (It is later re-released as a single album.)

Apr *Silly Thing*, double A-side with Tenpole Tudor's *Who Killed Bambi*, hits UK #6.

July *C'mon Everybody* hits UK #3.

Aug *Some Product – Carri On Sex Pistols*, containing interviews, commercials and the "Today" interview, but no music, hits UK #6.

Oct "The Great Rock'N'Roll Swindle" movie premieres. Julien Temple's film is a collection of early Pistols footage and comic situations, with McLaren tongue-in-cheek claiming the whole phenomenon was no more than his inspired hype. Rotten is largely absent from the movie. *The Great Rock'N'Roll Swindle*, double A-side with Tenpole Tudor's *Rock Around The Clock*, reaches UK #21. Cook and Jones' band The Professionals make UK #43 with *1-2-3*.

Dec *Sid Sings* makes UK #30.

1980 **Feb** Last Virgin album, *Flogging A Dead Horse*, reaches UK #23.

July *(I'm Not Your) Stepping Stone*, reviving The Monkees' hit, makes UK #21.

1986 **Jan** [13] Lydon, Jones, Cook and Vicious' mother sue McLaren for £1 million. (They will settle out of court.) The official receiver awards the 3 remaining band members and Vicious' mother £1 million. (Lydon is a member of Public Image Ltd, living in Los Angeles, works as a session guitarist, while Cook has disappeared from view.)

July [20] Film "Sid And Nancy", directed by Alex Cox with Gary Oldman as Sid and Chloe Webb as Nancy, premieres in London.

1988 A video documentary of Sex Pistols' TV footage appears as "Buried Alive" video cassette.

THE SHADOWS

Hank Marvin (lead guitar)
Bruce Welch (rhythm guitar)
Brian Bennett (drums)

1958 **Apr** [6] Marvin (b. Brian Rankin, Oct.28, 1941, Newcastle, Tyne & Wear) and Welch (b. Bruce Cripps, Nov.2, 1941, Bognor Regis, Sussex), having left school in Newcastle, travel to London with their part-time skiffle quintet The Railroaders, to enter a national talent contest; they come third.

May The Railroaders split after the contest. Welch and Marvin remain in London and form The Five Chesternuts with comedian Charlie Chester's drummer son Pete, a vocalist and a bass player. (One of the group's first appearances is backing comedian Benny Hill on *Gather In The Mushrooms* at a charity concert at the Town Hall in Stoke Newington, London.

Aug Group records a one-off single for EMI's Columbia label, *Teenage Love*, which leads to an appearance on BBC TV's "6.5 Special", but no further success. Welch and Marvin take jobs at the 2 I's coffee bar in Soho, London, where they play guitar in the basement club as "The Geordie Boys", and operate the orange juice and coke machines.

Sept Marvin, having played a 2-week UK tour as temporary guitarist with The Vipers, is seen by Cliff Richard's manager John Foster playing at the 2 I's. Richard has been offered a UK tour supporting The Kalin Twins, but his group The Drifters has just lost guitarist Ken Pavey and needs a replacement. Foster intended to offer Tony Sheridan the job, but he cannot be found. Marvin is asked to join instead and insists that Welch joins too. Foster agrees after they play for him at home.

Oct [5] Richard goes on tour backed by a Drifters line-up of Marvin (lead guitar), Welch (rhythm guitar), Ian Samwell (bass) and Terry Smart (drums). Marvin is recruited by The Kalin Twins to play guitar for them too.

[19] As the tour ends, Samwell leaves The Drifters. Fellow 2 I's regular Jet Harris (b. Terence Harris, July 6, 1939, Kingsbury, London), on the tour backing The Most Brothers and asked by The Drifters to play along behind the curtain to boost Samwell's hesitant bass playing, is asked by Richard to replace Samwell.

Nov [14] The Drifters take part in their first studio session at Abbey Road, backing Cliff Richard on *Livin' Lovin' Doll* and *Mean Streak*.

[17] Richard & The Drifters open variety season at the Metropolitan theater in the Edgware Road, London. (They follow with a further 2 weeks at the Chiswick Empire and the Finsbury Park Empire.)

Dec Smart leaves The Drifters to join the Merchant Navy. Harris suggests Tony Meehan (b. Daniel Meehan, Mar.2, 1943, London), ex-Vipers drummer, with whom he, Marvin and Welch have all played at the 2 I's, as replacement.

1959 **Jan** New quartet plays together on record for first time on Richard's *Livin' Lovin' Doll* and backs him at Manchester Free Trade Hall.
[9] The Drifters audition for EMI at Abbey Road. *Feelin' Fine*, the first track recorded at the session, becomes the group's debut single.
Feb Offered a recording deal in their own right by Columbia's Norrie Paramor, on the strength of their playing with Richard, The Drifters release *Feelin' Fine*, a vocal written by ex-member Samwell (who becomes their manager for ventures independent of Richard). B-side *Don't Be A Fool (With Love)*, written by Marvin and Welch's ex-Chesternuts colleague Chester is performed by the group on ITV's "Oh Boy!", but is a flop.
[5] The Drifters sign a contract with EMI to record 4 sides in the first year with no guarantee of release. If any material is released, the group will earn a royalty rate of a penny per record, split 4 ways.
May Group records its first instrumental, *Chinchilla*, for the soundtrack of Richard's film "Serious Charge".
June Harris marries Carol DaCosta.
July *Jet Black*, an instrumental written by Harris, is the second Drifters single but does not chart. It is released in US as by The Four Jets, since *Feelin' Fine* had to be withdrawn from the US market when Atlantic group The Drifters issued an injunction to prevent duplication of their name. Band decides a permanent change is necessary: Harris suggests The Shadows while drinking at the Six Bells pub in Ruislip, London.
Aug [29] Welch marries Anne Findley. Cliff Richard is best man.
Dec *Saturday Dance*, another vocal written by Marvin and Chester, is the first single credited to The Shadows, but another flop. Group appears with Richard in pantomime "Babes In The Wood" in Stockton-on-Tees, Cleveland. During the run, Harris is involved in a car crash, injuring himself and Marvin slightly. Harris is fined £35 and 15 shillings for dangerous driving, failing to display L plates and driving unaccompanied by a qualified driver.

1960 **Jan** They tour US with Cliff Richard on 38-date "The Biggest Show Of Stars" package including Frankie Avalon, Bobby Rydell and Freddy Cannon. (On tour they make their CBS TV "Ed Sullivan Show" debut.)
Apr On a UK tour, the group meets singer/songwriter Jerry Lordan, who demonstrates his composition *Apache* on the ukelele. They record it with Richard sitting on bongoes.
June Peter Gormley becomes their full-time manager.
[17] *Apache* is recorded at Abbey Road.
Aug *Apache* hits UK #1 for 6 weeks, deposing Richard's *Please Don't Tease*. (Danish guitarist Jorgen Ingmann's cover, recorded without hearing The Shadows' version, steals US chart honors.)
Sept [25] Group plays first solo concert at Colston Hall, Bristol, Avon.
Dec *Man Of Mystery*, a version of the theme from the Edgar Wallace movie series, hits UK #6. B-side *The Stranger* climbs to UK #11. Marvin marries long-time girlfriend Billie, with Welch as best man. *Apache* is voted Record Of The Year in **New Musical Express**.

1961 **Feb** *FBI*, credited to manager Gormley because of a publishing wrangle, but a Marvin/Welch/Harris composition, hits UK #4.
Mar Group tours southern Africa, Australasia and the Far East with Richard and first live recording is a 4-track EP cut at the Colosseum, Johannesburg.
June Film theme *The Frightened City* hits UK #3. Group films movie "The Young Ones" with Richard at UK's Elstree studios.
Sept Debut album *The Shadows*, featuring new instrumentals and vocals, hits UK #1 for 6 weeks.
Oct *Kon-Tiki* hits UK #1. The Shadows hold UK #1 in the first week of the month with their album, single, and EP (*The Shadows To The Fore* (which includes *Apache*). Meehan leaves during a 6-week residency with Richard at Blackpool, Lancs. He wants to move into production and starts work for Decca as an A&R man. Bennett (b. Feb.9, 1940, London) an acquaintance from the 2 I's and ex-Marty Wilde's Wildcats and instrumental group The Krew Kats drummer, is backing Tommy Steele when Welch phones him. He joins The Shadows in time to tour Australia with Richard.
Nov *The Savage*, written by producer Norrie Paramor and taken from film "The Young Ones", hits UK #10.

1962 **Mar** *Wonderful Land*, a Jerry Lordan composition and the first Shadows track with orchestral backing, tops UK chart for 8 weeks, but is toppled by another instrumental, *Nut Rocker* by B. Bumble & The Stingers.
Apr Differences between Welch and Harris come to a head, and Harris walks out to pursue a solo career. Brian "Liquorice" Locking, another acquaintance who played with Bennett in The Krew Kats groups backing Vince Taylor and Marty Wilde, joins on bass.
[13] Group is presented belatedly with a gold disk for worldwide million-plus sales of *Apache*.

[15] Harris makes his final appearance with The Shadows at the **New Musical Express** Poll Winners Concert.
[23] Welch collapses on stage at the Queen's theater, Blackpool. Pete Carter from The Checkmates steps in.
[27] Harris signs to Decca as a solo singer/guitarist, and Jack Good becomes his manager and producer.
May [6] Locking makes his first West End appearance with the group at the "Our Friends The Stars" charity concert.
Group travels to Greece to film "Summer Holiday" with Cliff Richard. Welch and Bennett write the title song.
June Harris's 6-string bass guitar solo version of *Besame Mucho* (with Meehan on drums) reaches UK #22.
Aug *Guitar Tango*, the first Shadows single to feature acoustic guitars, hits UK #4.
[19] Harris makes his live debut at the Princess theater, Torquay, Devon, with his backing group The Jetblacks, on a bill with Craig Douglas and Mark Wynter.
Sept Harris' second solo single, a revival of *Main Title Theme*, from 50s Frank Sinatra film "Man With The Golden Arm", reaches UK #12.
Oct *Out Of The Shadows*, featuring tracks with Harris, hits UK #1 for 3 weeks (it will have further runs at the top in Nov., Dec. and Jan.1964)
Nov EP *The Boys*, featuring music by the group from UK movie of the same title, tops UK EP chart. They appear with Richard at the Royal Variety Show in London.

1963 **Jan** The Shadows' *Dance On*, written by vocal group The Avons, hits UK #1 for 2 weeks. It is replaced by *Diamonds*, a Lordan composition co-credited to Jet Harris & Tony Meehan (on top for 3 weeks).
Mar *Foot Tapper*, from "Summer Holiday", tops UK chart for 1 week, deposing Richard's title song. (It will be group's final UK #1 single.)
May *The Shadows' Greatest Hits*, compiled singles to date, hits UK #: behind The Beatles' *Please Please Me*, and will stay in UK Top 20 for 4 weeks. Harris and Meehan's second duet *Scarlet O'Hara* hits UK #2.
June *Atlantis*, a ballad instrumental with strings, peaks at UK #2 for 2 weeks behind Gerry & The Pacemakers' *I Like It*. Group plays 16-week summer season, "Holiday Carnival", in Blackpool with Richard.
July Harris is slightly injured in a car crash.
Aug Pressures of work begin to fray Welch's nerves and he announces that he will leave the group for a desk job in The Shadows' organization after a tour of Israel and France in Oct.
[10] Group appears on 100th edition of ITV's "Thank Your Lucky Stars" with Cliff Richard, The Searchers, Billy J.Kramer, Brian Poole and Alma Cogan.
Sept Harris and Meehan's *Applejack* hits UK #4, but their joint career stops when Harris and girlfriend, singer Billie Davis, are injured in an accident involving their car and a bus. Harris is left in poor physical and mental shape. He leaves Meehan 3 weeks later on an ITV "Ready Steady Go" show, goes home and smashes all his guitars.
Oct *Shindig* hits UK #6. EP *Los Shadows*, with 4 Spanish tunes recorded in Barcelona during the summer, makes UK #42. (EPs by The Beatles and The Searchers are in UK Singles chart at the same time.) Locking, who has become committed to his Jehovah's Witness faith, announces that he is to leave. Marvin and Welch consider recruiting John Paul Jones, bassist with Harris and Meehan's backing group (and later with Led Zeppelin), but settle on ex-Interns bass player John Rostill (b. June 16, 1942, Birmingham, W.Midlands). Welch has overcome his nervous problems with medical help, and decides not to leave.
Dec Group films "Wonderful Life" in the Canary Islands with Cliff Richard, while *Geronimo* reaches UK #11 (their first to miss UK Top 10)

1964 **Jan** With Harris out of action, Meehan records *Song Of Mexico* as The Tony Meehan Combo. It reaches UK #39 (but will be Meehan's last hit)
Mar Rostill plays on stage with The Shadows for the first time on a UK tour with Richard.
Apr *Theme For Young Lovers*, from **Wonderful Life** soundtrack, reaches UK #12. Marvin's 18-month-old twin sons almost drown in the backyard pond, but he saves them with the "kiss of life" and the rescue is widely publicized.
May Group tours Europe while *Dance With The Shadows* hits UK #2
June *The Rise And Fall Of Flingel Bunt*, The Shadows' hardest-rocking single since *The Savage*, hits UK #5. Harris is divorced by wife Carol.
Aug Group makes its own 25-min. musical comedy film, "Rhythm And Greens", a series of short historical sketches in costume. It is shown in UK as support to Dirk Bogarde's "King And Country".
Sept Title track *Rhythm And Greens* peaks at UK #22.
Nov Group plays 3 numbers in the Royal Variety Show, as well as backing Richard.
[22] The Shadows write the score for, and have acting and musical

roles in, the Richard-starring pantomime "Aladdin And His Wonderful Lamp" at the London Palladium, with Arthur Askey and Una Stubbs, which runs for 15 weeks.

1965 Jan *Genie With The Light Brown Lamp*, from pantomime, makes UK #17.
Mar Ballad *Mary Anne*, written by Lordan and the first vocal Shadows single since *Saturday Dance*, climbs to UK #17.
June More familiar sounding instrumental *Stingray* peaks at UK #19. The Shadows support Richard on another European tour.
July *The Sound Of The Shadows* hits UK #4.
Sept Vocal *Don't Make My Baby Blue* (previously recorded by Frankie Laine), hits UK #10 (it will be the last Shadows Top 10 single for almost 13 years).
Dec *The War Lord* theme from a Charlton Heston movie makes UK #18.
[21] Group writes (but does not perform) the music for Frank Ifield's pantomime "Babes In The Wood" at the London Palladium. *More Hits!* a compilation of further hit singles, is the group's first album not to chart in UK.

1966 Apr Vocal *I Met A Girl* reaches UK #22.
May [1] Group takes part in an all-star cast at the annual **New Musical Express** Poll Winners Concert at the Empire Pool, Wembley, London.
Group begins filming "Finders Keepers".
June *Shadow Music* hits UK #5.
July *A Place In The Sun*, an instrumental in the *Wonderful Land* mode (and written by Lordan's wife Petrina) peaks at UK #24, while the group is filming "Finders Keepers" with Richard.
Nov Marvin-penned vocal *The Dreams I Dream* makes UK #42.
Dec [20] The Shadows write the music for, and feature as the Brokers Men in Cliff Richard's pantomime "Cinderella", with Terry Scott and Hugh Lloyd as the Ugly Sisters, which opens at the London Palladium. (The show closes Apr.1.) Puppet likenesses of Richard and The Shadows appear in Gerry Anderson's movie "Thunderbirds Are Go!", in a nightclub scene as "Cliff Richard Jr. And The Sons Of The Shadows". Group writes and performs 4 tracks on film soundtrack, released as an EP.

1967 May *Maroc 7*, theme from a Gene Barry movie, peaks at UK #24. Welch parts from his wife and moves in with Australian singer Olivia Newton-John.
July *Jigsaw* hits UK #8.
Aug The Shadows win the Split Song Festival, in Yugoslavia, with *I Can't Forget*. They tour Australia and Spain (without Richard).
Sept *Tomorrow's Cancelled* is the first Shadows single since before *Apache* not to chart in UK.
Oct Bennett releases *Change Of Direction*, with a 6-piece group which includes Rostill.
Dec *From Hank, Bruce, Brian And John*, released, by Shadows standards, very hastily after its predecessor (5 months) fails to chart.
[25] The Shadows appear in UK TV's production of pantomime "Aladdin".

1968 Jan [1] Group begins a 3-week cabaret at the Talk Of The Town club, its first in London without Richard. (After a week, Rostill suffers a minor nervous breakdown and is ordered to rest, while Bennett is ill with appendicitis. Ex-members Locking and Meehan fill in.)
Marvin releases first solo single, *London's Not Too Far*, without success.
Mar With the current line-up back together, the group tours Japan, while in UK *Dear Old Mrs. Bell* fails to chart.
May They play short season at the London Palladium with Tom Jones.
Oct Cliff Richard & The Shadows celebrate their 10th anniversary in the music business with *Established 1958*, which contains equal shares of Shadows-backed Richard vocals and group instrumentals. Welch and his wife are divorced, and he is engaged to Olivia Newton-John. It is reported that Welch and Bennett plan to leave group at end of year.
Dec [14] Welch plays his final date with The Shadows at the end of their London Palladium season. Marvin presents him with an engraved clock.
[19] Following bad feeling and arguments within the group, it is admitted between the quartet that tiredness, disenchantment, and a loss of creativity have set in, and that a split is necessary. They play their last (10th anniversary) show with Richard, at the London Palladium.

1969 Mar Marvin releases solo *Goodnight Dick*, which fails to chart. Bennett plays for 7 days in Washington, DC, as Tom Jones' drummer.
Sept Marvin duets with Richard on *Throw Down A Line*, which hits UK #7. Bennett releases *The Illustrated London Noise*, which fails.
Oct With no plans to re-form the group, but attracted by the offer, Marvin, Rostill and Bennett play a short tour of Japan as The Shadows,

with keyboards player Alan Hawkshaw, an old friend of Bennett's. A live album is recorded by Japanese EMI/Odeon at Sankei Hall, Tokyo. In UK, a lengthy version of Richard Rodgers' *Slaughter On 10th Avenue*, recorded earlier without Welch, is released coupled with Marvin's solo version of *Midnight Cowboy* theme, but does not chart.
Nov Marvin's first solo album, *Hank Marvin*, reaches UK #14.

1970 Mar Second "Cliff and Hank" duet, *Joy Of Living*, peaks at UK #25. It is the theme for a weekly Cliff Richard TV series, on which Marvin is a resident guest, featuring in comedy sketches as well as playing and singing. He declines an invitation by Roy Wood to join The Move.
May [3] Group plays at the annual **New Musical Express** Poll Winners Concert.
Aug Marvin and Welch (back in action after 18 months) consider setting up as a vocal duo, and invite Australian singer/guitarist/ songwriter John Farrar, whom they met on their 1967 tour of Australia, to join them for experimental rehearsals.
Oct *Shades Of Rock*, a collection of hard-rock oldies (recorded earlier in the year by Marvin, Bennett, Hawkshaw and several different bassists), is released as by The Shadows. It reaches UK #30.

1971 Jan Having settled as a harmony vocal trio, Marvin, Welch and Farrar debut on Cliff Richard's UK TV show, appearing 5 times in the series. Marvin gets married again (to Carole).
Mar Trio, backed by Bennett on drums and Dave Richmond on bass, tours Germany, Switzerland and the Benelux countries and includes several Shadows tracks in its act due to audience demand.
Apr *Marvin, Welch And Farrar* reaches UK #30, but *Faithful* flops. Welch and Farrar begin producing Olivia Newton-John; her *If Not For You* hits UK #7.
Nov Marvin, Welch and Farrar album *Second Opinion* fails to chart.
Dec Trio, with Bennett, supports Cliff Richard on a UK tour.

1972 Mar Newton-John breaks off her engagement to Welch, which shatters him and he attempts suicide.
Sept Marvin and Farrar, continuing as a duo and backed by Hawkshaw (keyboards), Rostill and Bennett, tour the Far East with Newton-John and Richard.

1973 Apr Marvin and his wife Carole become Jehovah's Witnesses.
Aug *Hank Marvin And John Farrar* fails to chart.
Nov Marvin, Welch, Farrar and Bennett record *Turn Around And Touch Me* as The Shadows, but it does not chart. The recording session is Welch's return to working life. (He and Newton-John had reconciled in Apr., then parted again in June, by mutual consent.)
[26] Rostill, who played in Las Vegas, NV with Tom Jones, but returned to UK to work, dies from accidental electrocution while playing guitar in his home studio. Welch, who has been writing songs with him, discovers his body when he arrives for a demo session.

1974 Apr *Rockin' With Curly Leads*, is recorded by Marvin, Welch, Farrar and Bennett, with Alan Tarney playing bass, as The Shadows. It reaches UK #45. Welch releases solo *Please Mr. Please*, written by himself and Rostill, but it fails to sell.
May Group's 11-year-old compilation album *The Shadows' Greatest Hits* is reissued in stereo and re-charts at UK #48.
Aug Bennett joins Georgie Fame's band The Blue Flames on drums for a UK tour.
Oct At a charity concert at the London Palladium, The Shadows' appearance (meant as a one-off) prompts BBC TV boss Bill Cotton Jr. to ask them to represent UK in the 1975 Eurovision Song Contest. The group plays some UK concerts to regain the feel of live performance together. Brian Goode from Peter Gormley's office becomes their manager.

1975 Apr The Shadows perform *Let Me Be The One* in the Eurovision Song Contest in Stockholm, Sweden, to a TV audience of 300 million. It is beaten into second place by Dutch group Teach-In with *Ding-A-Dong*, but The Shadows peak at UK #12 with it (1 place above Teach-In).
Specs Appeal, containing the 6 Eurovision songs from which UK's entry was selected on BBC TV and other new material, reaches UK #30. A demand for more of The Shadows, following all the TV publicity, prompts the recording of a live album at the Olympia theater in Paris (intended as this line-up's final concert).
Nov *Live At The Paris Olympia* is released without charting.

1976 May *It'll Be Me Babe* fails to chart. Farrar moves to US to write for and produce Olivia Newton-John, while Welch produces Cliff Richard on *Miss You Nights* and *Devil Woman*.
Aug Bennett travels to Russia as Richard's drummer on a pioneering tour of USSR by a major Western rock act.

1977 Feb Compilation album *20 Golden Greats*, promoted via an acclaimed TV ad involving young lads doing The Shadows' high kicks with

THE SHADOWS cont.

cricket bat "guitars", is the group's first UK Top 10 album for 9 years. It hits UK #1 for 6 weeks and is the group's biggest seller – over a million copies in UK.

Mar Signed as a soloist to DJM Records (owned by publisher Dick James), Bennett releases concept album *Rock Dreams*, on which Cliff Richard sings some guest vocals. It fails to chart.

May Group plays a rapturously-received "20 Golden Dates" UK tour to follow up the hits album, with Alan Jones on bass and Francis Monkman on keyboards

Aug Marvin wins the CBS Arbiter award for services to British music, with fellow guitarists Joe Brown and Bert Weedon.

Sept *Tasty*, of new Shadows material, fails to sell.

Nov Recruiting several noted guitarists, Marvin issues *The Hank Marvin Guitar Syndicate*, which fails to chart.

1978 Feb Cliff Richard & The Shadows reunite for a series of London Palladium concerts to mark their 20th anniversary. Films and recordings are made of these, for the TV special and live album *Thank You Very Much*.

Apr Bennett releases his second DJM album *Voyage*, subtitled "A Journey Into Discoid Funk", again without success.

Aug *Love Deluxe* receives good airplay in UK but fails to chart.

Sept Group plays a UK tour, with Jones again on bass, and ex-Cliff Richard band member Cliff Hall on keyboards.

1979 Jan *Don't Cry For Me Argentina*, an instrumental version of Julie Covington's #1 hit from Rice/Lloyd Webber musical "Evita", is The Shadows' first Top 10 single since 1965, hitting UK #5.

June *Theme From The Deer Hunter (Cavatina)*, in competition with John Williams' solo guitar version (which makes #13), hits UK #9.

Aug [1] Welch marries again; his new wife Lynne has been a close friend for some years.

1980 Mar *String Of Hits*, after several months on chart, hits UK #1 for 3 weeks following a TV ad campaign, while *Riders In The Sky*, a disco-flavored revival of The Ramrods' 1961 hit, makes UK #12. Group's recording contract with EMI expires, and is not renewed when the company fails to agree to The Shadows recording independently and leasing the results. Polydor signs a 3-year contract with the group's newly-formed production company Rollover Records, to take 3 albums.

Aug Compilation album *Another String Of Hot Hits* makes UK #16, while the group's first Polydor release, a cover of Jean-Michel Jarre's *Equinoxe, Part 5*, reaches UK #50.

Sept *Change Of Address* reaches UK #17.

1981 May A revival of Anton Karas' theme from film "The Third Man" peaks at UK #44, and is the last Shadows hit single.

Sept Group tours UK to promote *Hits Right Up Your Street*.

Oct The album reaches UK #15.

1982 Mar Marvin's solo album *Words And Music* makes UK #66, while extracted *Don't Talk* peaks at UK #49 (his only solo single success).

Oct Double album (2 for the price of 1) *Life In The Jungle/Live At Abbey Road*, on which the second disk features a session cut before a live studio audience, peaks at UK #24.

1983 May Group wins an Ivor Novello award from the British Academy of Songwriters, Composers and Authors, to mark 25 years of outstanding contribution to British music.

Oct *XXV*, celebrating the group's 25th anniversary, makes UK #34.

1984 Nov *Guardian Angel* makes UK #98 for a week.

1986 Mar Marvin reprises his guitar solo on Richard's 1959 chart-topper *Living Doll*, on new charity version by Richard and comedy team The Young Ones, in aid of Comic Relief. It tops UK chart for 3 weeks.

May *Moonlight Shadows* hits UK #6.

1987 Nov *Simply Shadows* makes UK #11.

1988 Oct Marvin, who is living in Australia, flies to London to play at Jean-Michel Jarre's London's Docklands open-air concert, a journey which costs Jarre a reported £20,000.

1989 Jan Marvin guests on Jarre's UK #52 *London Kid*.

May *Steppin' To The Shadows* reaches UK #11.

Dec *At Their Very Best* reaches UK #12.

1990 Oct Issued on their own Rollover Record label, *Reflections*, hits UK #6.

SHALAMAR

Howard Hewett (vocals)
Jody Watley (vocals)
Jeffrey Daniel (vocals)

1977 May Group name is created by producers Dick Griffey and Simon Soussan to give an identity to *Uptown Festival*, a disco medley incorporating 5 classic Motown hits, made by session singers and

musicians in Los Angeles, CA. It reaches US #25 and UK #30, released on Soul Train label, since Griffey is talent booker for the TV show of the same name, produced by his partner Don Cornelius.

July *Uptown Festival*, also cut by sessioneers, hits US #8.

1978 Nov Having formed his own record label, Solar (Sound Of Los Angeles Records), Griffey assembles a group to continue as Shalamar. He recruits "Soul Train" dancers Watley (b. Jan.30, 1959, Chicago, IL), whose godfather is Jackie Wilson and Daniel (b. Aug.24, 1955, Los Angeles, CA) and lead singer Gerald Brown, pairing them with label producer Leon Sylvers III to record dance-oriented *Disco Gardens*, which stalls at US #171.

1979 Jan Co-penned by Sylvers, extracted *Take That To The Bank* reaches US #79 (and R&B #11) and UK #20. Brown leaves and is replaced by Hewett (b. Oct.1, 1955, Akron, OH), as lead singer.

Nov *The Second Time Around*, from the second Sylvers-produced album *Big Fun*, makes UK #45.

1980 Feb *Right In The Socket*, also from the album (which does not chart in UK) peaks at UK #44.

Mar *The Second Time Around* becomes the trio's biggest US success, hitting #9 and selling over a million (also topping R&B chart, dethroning Michael Jackson's *Rock With You*). *Big Fun* makes US #23 and earns a gold disk, Solar's first. Daniel marries soul vocalist and Broadway star of "The Wiz", Stephanie Mills. (They will divorce in less than a year.)

Oct *I Owe You One* reaches UK #13.

1981 Feb *Full Of Fire* makes US #55.

Apr *Make That Move* peaks at UK #30.

May Once again helmed by Sylvers III (who is by now creating a Solar sound for other label acts including The Whispers and Dynasty) *Three For Love* makes US #40, and is the group's second gold album. Watley co-writes 2 tracks and claims on the sleeve notes to "love ... cooking, going to the movies and Michael Jackson". Taken from it, *Make That Move* reaches US #55.

Nov *Go For It* peaks at US #115. In addition to 4 Daniel-penned cuts, includes a Hewett and James Ingram track, also produced by the pair, *You've Got Me Running*, and features Mills singing on *The Final Analysis*

1982 May *Friends* climbs to US #35, and is Shalamar's third and last US gold album. Extracted from it, *A Night To Remember* makes US #44, while *I Can Make You Feel Good*, the UK extract co-written by Hewett, hits UK #7, and is the group's first of 3 consecutive UK Top 10 hits with songs from *Friends*. The group begins "Friends World Tour".

July Co-written and produced by Sylvers, *A Night To Remember* hits UK #5, and is the second dance smash in a run of highly commercial crossover successes.

Sept Compilation album *Greatest Hits* reaches UK #71.

Oct *There It Is* hits UK #5.

Dec Title track *Friends* reaches UK #12.

1983 Jan [8] Daniel appears on BBC TV show "Jim'll Fix It" demonstrating the street dance art of body popping.

Friends peaks at UK #6 (having been on chart for over 40 weeks), while the trio is touring UK.

July *Dead Giveaway* hits UK #8. It is from *The Look* which hits UK #7. (Title cut is written by Hewett with Stanley Clarke.)

Sept *Dead Giveaway* makes US #22, while parent album *The Look* reaches US #38.

Nov *Over And Over*, also from *The Look*, makes UK #23.

1984 Daniel leaves the group, moving to UK to become host of newly-launched Channel 4 TV version of "Soul Train" and star in the West End in Andrew Lloyd Webber musical "Starlight Express". Watley also leaves for a solo vocal career (and will begin success fully in 1987). Group continues, with Hewett now joined by Delisa Davis and Micki Free.

Apr Taken from the soundtrack of film "Footloose" and released on CBS/Columbia, *Dancing In The Sheets* climbs to US #17, their most successful US single for over 4 years, and UK #41, in simultaneous competition with *Deadline USA* (from another movie "Street Fleet") which makes UK #52.

Nov [25] Watley takes part in the recording of Band Aid's *Do They Know It's Christmas?* (UK's all-time best-selling single) in London.

Dec *Amnesia* is the trio's last US chart single, making #73. In UK, it reaches #61. Shalamar's *Don't Get Stopped In Beverly Hills* is featured in Eddie Murphy's film "Beverly Hills Cop".

1985 Jan *Heart Break* makes US #90, the trio's last album to chart in US.

Feb *My Girl Loves Me*, from *Heart Break*, peaks at US #45.

[14] Group begins a short UK tour at the Dominion theater, London, set to end at the Colston Hall, Bristol, Avon on Feb.5.

986 Feb Shalamar's *Razzle Dazzle* is featured in Goldie Hawn movie "Wildcats". Hewett is arrested outside a Miami shopping center by FBI agents and charged with 4 counts of conspiracy to possess cocaine. (He is later acquitted.)

[25] Hewett contributes to *Beverly Hills Cop*, which wins Best Album Of Original Score Written For A Motion Picture Or Television Special at the 28th annual Grammy awards.

May TV-promoted compilation album *The Greatest Hits*, surveying the group's entire chart career, hits UK #5. Meanwhile, a remixed version of their biggest UK hit *A Night To Remember* climbs to UK #52, closing the group's UK chart career. Hewett leaves for a solo career. Sidney Justin, an ex-Los Angeles Rams football player replaces him.

Nov [8] Hewett, signed to Elektra, has a minor US hit with *I'm For Real*, on which he is backed by George Duke, Stanley Clarke and Wilton Felder, from his debut solo album *I Commit To Love*, making US #159.

987 **May** [2] Signed to MCA as a soloist, Watley hits US #2 for 4 weeks (behind Cutting Crew's (*I Just*) *Died In Your Arms* and U2's *With Or Without You*) with *Looking For A New Love*, which also reaches UK #13 as *Jody Watley* hits US #10, and includes a duet with George Michael.

July [11] Watley's *Still A Thrill* makes US #56.

Shalamar make US R&B chart with *Circumstantial Evidence* (#30) and *Games* (#11).

Sept [5] *Jody Watley* peaks at UK #62.

Oct Watley peaks at UK #55 with *Don't You Want Me*.

Dec [19] *Don't You Want Me* hits US #6.

988 **Mar** [2] Now a major US dance/soul star in her own right, Watley wins Best New Artist at the 30th annual Grammy awards, as Hewett's duet with Dionne Warwick, *Another Chance To Love*, makes #42 on US R&B chart.

Apr [16] Watley's *Some Kind Of Lover* hits US #10.

May Hewett's second solo effort, the soul-filled *Forever And Ever*, peaks at US #110.

June [4] Watley's *Most Of All* peaks at US #60.

989 **May** Hewett contributes *The Ten Commandments Of Love* to Richard Perry-produced *Rock, Rhythm & Blues* compilation.

[20] Watley hits US #2 with *Real Love* (which has already made UK #31), as her André Cymone-produced album *Larger Than Life* reaches US #16 and will make UK #39.

June [28] Watley embarks on US tour in Charleston, NC, set to end on July 27 in Denver, CO.

Aug [26] Watley with rap assistance from Eric B & Rakim hits US #9 with *Friends* and reaches UK #21.

990 **Jan** [6] *You Wanna Dance With Me?*, a compilation of previously unreleased remixed versions of Watley's hits, makes US #86.

[20] Watley's ballad cut *Everything* hits US #4, but will stall at UK #74.

Apr Daniel, now signed to Epic, releases *She's The Girl* as "Jody Watley: Dance To Fitness" video is released.

June [9] Hewett finally breaks through as third solo album *Howard Hewett*, featuring 3 tracks co-written and produced by ex-Shalamar producer Sylvers, peaks at UK #54. It also includes assistance from multi-instrumentalist Scritti Politti member Dave Gamson.

Oct Watley contributes *After You Who* to *Red Hot + Blue*, an anthology of Cole Porter songs to benefit AIDS education.

Nov [3] *Rubáiyát*, Elektra's 40th anniversary compilation, to which Hewett contributes a cover of *I Can't Tell You Why*, makes US #140. By year's end, Shalamar, still comprising Free, Davis and Justin, return to the recording scene with *Wake Up*, released on Solar through Epic.

991 **Jan** Hewett's *I Can't Tell You Why*, from Elektra's 40th anniversary compilation *Rubáiyát*, is released.

THE SHANGRI-LAS

Mary Weiss (lead vocals)
Betty Weiss (vocals)
Marge Ganser (vocals)
Mary Ann Ganser (vocals)

964 When discovered singing at part-time gigs (while still attending St. Michael's Catholic school in Queens, New York, NY) by George "Shadow" Morton, sisters Betty (b. Elizabeth) and Mary Weiss and twins Marge and Mary Ann Ganser have previously worked briefly with Artie Ripp's Kama Sutra Productions and recorded *Wishing Well* for the small Spokane label under the name The Bon Bons, but without success. Morton, who has gained the attention of songwriter/producers Jeff Barry and Ellie Greenwich and promised to deliver them a hit record, writes *Remember (Walking In The Sand)* for the group, records it as a demo in a Long Island basement studio and suitably

impresses Barry and Greenwich with the result. Duo organizes the signing of both Morton (as a writer and producer) and the newly-renamed Shangri-Las to Leiber and Stoller's Red Bird label.

Aug After coming to an arrangement with Kama Sutra Productions, which still has the girls under contract, Red Bird releases *Remember (Walkin' In The Sand)*.

Sept Instantly a huge US airplay hit with its offbeat, atmospheric production (including the sounds of ocean and seagulls), *Remember (Walkin' In The Sand)* rockets to US #5, as the group is rushed into a round of TV and live performances for which the older 3 immediately leave school, leaving Mary Weiss, the youngest, still studying. They also join the bill of a live package at the Brooklyn Fox, New York, with Marvin Gaye, The Searchers and Martha & The Vandellas.

Oct [22] The 3-piece group arrives in London for UK promotional trip, as the single climbs to UK #14. (TV shows "Thank Your Lucky Stars", "Ready Steady Go!" and "The Eamonn Andrews Show" ban the group from singing their new single *Leader Of The Pack*.) On the girls' return to the US, Betty Weiss leaves, and sister Mary leaves school to replace her, taking the lead vocal slot. (During the 2 years of regular road work which follow the initial success, the girls will regularly permutate 3 out of 4, leaving and returning to replace each other, and rarely appearing as more than a trio.)

Nov *Leader Of The Pack*, written by Morton, Barry and Greenwich, tops US chart for a week, becoming a million-seller and definitive "teen death" record (storyline: girl meets boy, parents disapprove, boy dies on motorbike). This time the sound effects are of a revving motorbike, brought into the studio by its owner, recording engineer Joey Veneri.

Dec The Shangri-Las take part in Murray The K's "Big Holiday Show" in New York.

1965 **Jan** Ron Dante, under the name The Detergents, hits with a parody of *Pack* titled *Leader Of The Laundromat*, which reaches US #19, as The Shangri-Las' own follow-up, *Give Him A Great Big Kiss*, reaches US #18, and the girls' simultaneously-issued revival of The Chantels' *Maybe* makes US #91.

Feb Despite a BBC radio ban because of the nature of its lyric, *Leader Of The Pack* makes UK #11.

Mar *Leader Of The Pack* (with dubbed audience noise on side 2 to sound like a live concert by the group) climbs to US #109.

Apr The group tours US on Dick Clark's "Caravan Of Stars", with Del Shannon, Tommy Roe, The Zombies and others.

May *Out In The Streets* peaks at US #53.

July *Give Us Your Blessings*, a return to the story-song formula (this time with boy and girl both dying), reaches US #29.

Oct *Right Now And Not Later*, an uncharacteristic Motown pastiche, makes only US #99. Second album, *Shangri-Las '65* is released but fails.

Dec *I Can Never Go Home Anymore*, a return to the group's expected melodrama (this time a mother dies after a daughter's indifference), hits US #6. The second album is reissued with this as the title.

1966 **Mar** *Long Live Our Love*, makes US #33.

May *He Cried*, a gender-switched revival of Jay & The Americans' 1961 hit *She Cried*, returns to melodrama, but peaks at US #65.

July *Past, Present And Future*, a spoken narration by Mary Weiss accompanied by Beethoven's "Moonlight Sonata", peaks at US #59 and will be the group's last US hit. (The Red Bird label folds a few weeks later and the group will move to Mercury, which will also lease the back-catalog to compile a *Greatest Hits* collection. Further singles, including *The Sweet Sounds Of Summer*, will appear on Mercury, but without success. The girls will continue to tour, but for a while are denied The Shangri-Las name because of legal wrangles over its ownership.)

1971 The trio line-up, after a hiatus, begins to play oldies tours of US.

1972 **Nov** *Leader Of The Pack* is reissued in UK by Kama Sutra, which still owns half rights to it. Despite being slightly edited from the original, it hits UK #3, this time unhindered by radio.

1976 **July** *Leader Of The Pack* is reissued in UK yet again, simultaneously on the Charly and Contempo labels, due to a non-exclusive licensing situation. Combined sales of both releases take it to hit UK #7.

1984 **Jan** A musical, "Leader Of The Pack", based around the songs of Ellie Greenwich, opens at the Bottom Line in Greenwich Village, New York.

1989 **June** [3] Group, comprising Mary Weiss Stokes, Betty Weiss Nelson and Mary Ann Ganser Droste, (Marge Ganser has died of an accidental drug overdose in 1976) reunites for Cousin Brucie's "First Palisades Amusement Park Reunion" at the Meadowlands, East Rutherford, NJ. Also on the bill are Little Anthony, Lesley Gore, Freddy Cannon, The Tokens and Bobby Rydell.

DEL SHANNON

1960 Shannon (b. Charles Weeden Westover, Dec.30, 1934, Coopersville, MI) having begun singing and playing guitar in high school, then entertained several months in "Get Up And Go" forces radio show in Germany) when drafted into the military, becomes resident guitarist and vocalist in the band of the Hi-Lo club in Battle Creek, MI, by night, working as a carpet salesman by day. He collaborates on songs with the band's keyboards player, Max Crook, and their promising sound and original material catches the ear of DJ Ollie McLaughlin on radio station W-GRV in nearby Ann Arbor, MI. He introduces Shannon and Crook to Detroit entrepreneurs Harry Balk and Irving Micahnik, who sign Shannon to their Embee Productions, and arrange recording sessions in New York via a deal with Big Top Records. After an unexciting first session, Shannon and Crook write *Runaway*, which is considered by Big Top as commercial enough to be issued as the first single.

1961 **Apr** *Runaway* tops US chart for 4 weeks, selling over a million to earn Shannon his only gold disk. Crook plays the song's instrumental break on a patent high-pitched electronic keyboard called a musitron, and this arresting sound is a major factor in the record's success (which will be repeated worldwide).
June *Runaway* also tops UK chart for 4 weeks, selling a half million copies.
Aug *Hats Off To Larry*, another self-composed song in *Runaway* style and arrangement (with a second hook-laden musitron solo by Crook), hits US #5.
Sept *Hats Off To Larry* hits UK #6.
Oct *So Long Baby*, an uptempo rocker with the musitron replaced by a kazoo solo, peaks at US #28.
Dec *Hey! Little Girl* makes US #38.

1962 **Jan** *So Long Baby* hits UK #10.
May *Hey! Little Girl* hits UK #2. UK B-side is *You Never Talked About Me*, which Shannon sings in a cameo slot in UK pop/jazz movie "It's Trad, Dad".
June *Cry Myself To Sleep*, his first recording in Nashville, TN, with vocal backing by The Jordanaires, peaks at US #99.
Sept *Cry Myself To Sleep* hits UK #29.
[16] Shannon begins his first UK tour, with Dion.
Oct Another Nashville recording, *The Swiss Maid*, written by Roger Miller, features Shannon yodelling and makes US #64.
Dec *The Swiss Maid* hits UK #2 (behind Frank Ifield's *Lovesick Blues*).

1963 **Feb** *Little Town Flirt* hits US #12 and UK #4.
May *Two Kinds Of Teardrops* reaches US #50 and hits UK #5. *Hats Off To Del Shannon* (a UK compilation of singles A and B-sides) hits UK #9. He tours UK with Johnny Tillotson, and enthuses to UK press about the new musical boom sweeping UK, and particularly about The Beatles, whose material he (as a songwriter) rates highly.
[9] Shannon plays a concert at London's Royal Albert Hall with The Beatles, and suggests covering one of Lennon and McCartney's hits to help give them more exposure in US.
July Returning home, Shannon records his own version of The Beatles' recent UK chart-topper *From Me To You*. It makes US #77 – the first Lennon/McCartney song to chart in US – while *Little Town Flirt* reaches US #12.
Sept *Two Silhouettes*, US B-side of *From Me To You*, is UK A-side and peaks at #23.
Oct **[4]** Shannon begins UK tour with Gerry & The Pacemakers and Jet Harris & Tony Meehan at the Odeon cinema, Lewisham, London. Tour will end Nov.4.
Nov Attempting to sever ties with Balk and Micahnik after disagreements over royalties and other business practices, Shannon forms his own label, Berlee Records, and issues The Four Seasons-influenced *Sue's Gotta Be Mine* which reaches US #71 and UK #21. *Little Town Flirt*, belatedly released in UK, makes #15.

1964 **Mar** *Mary Jane* fails to chart in US, but peaks at UK #35.
Aug Shannon moves to New York-based Amy Records for a high-tempo revival of Jimmy Jones' 1960 million-seller *Handy Man*, which makes US #22 and UK #36.
Sept He plays on an all-star bill supporting current US chart-toppers The Animals at the Paramount theater, Brooklyn, New York. Other performers include Jan And Dean and Chuck Berry.
Oct *Do You Want To Dance?*, revived in identical style to *Handy Man*, peaks at US #43.

1965 **Jan** Shannon hits US #9 after a 3-year Top 10 absence with *Keep Searchin' (We'll Follow The Sun)*.

Feb *Keep Searchin' (We'll Follow The Sun)* hits UK #3. Peter And Gordon's cover of his *I Go To Pieces* hits US #9.
[27] Shannon begins a 21-date twice-nightly UK package tour, with Wayne Fontana And The Mindbenders, Herman's Hermits and others, at the City Hall, Sheffield, S.Yorks. Tour will close Mar.22 at the Odeon cinema, Glasgow, Scotland.
Mar *Stranger In Town* reaches US #30 and UK #40, and is his last UK chart single.
May *Break Up* stalls at US #95.
June Shannon turns down a request from songwriter Tommy Boyce to record *Action*, the theme song to new Dick Clark US TV series "Where The Action Is". (Freddy Cannon makes US #13 with it in Sept.)

1966 Shannon moves from Michigan to Los Angeles, CA, and signs a new deal with Liberty Records.
May A revival of Toni Fisher's *The Big Hurt* is Shannon's only hit on Liberty, reaching US #94.

1967 Shannon records extensively for Liberty in UK, with Andrew Oldham producing. Intended as an album, the completed tracks mostly sit on the shelf for more than a decade.

1969 **Oct** Leaving Liberty, Shannon produces other acts rather than seeking a new deal for himself. His first production success is with the group Smith, whose Shannon-arranged revival of The Shirelles' *Baby It's You* hits US #5. He records himself for Dunhill, the label on which he has worked with Smith, but only 2 unsuccessful singles result.

1970 **Nov** Shannon produces Brian Hyland, a long-time friend, on a revival of The Impressions' *Gypsy Woman*, which hits US #3 and is a million-seller.

1973 **June** *Live In England*, on United Artists, is a recording of a concert in Manchester from his UK tour the previous year.

1974 **Oct** Dave Edmunds produces *And The Music Plays On*, recorded in UK (but not a hit).

1975 **May** He signs to US Island Records, debuting with a revival of The Zombies' *Tell Her No* which gains excellent reviews, but lacks the promotion to sell.
Aug Second Island single is *Cry Baby Cry*, recorded in collaboration with Jeff Lynne of Electric Light Orchestra. Again, it is insufficiently exposed to succeed, and Shannon leaves Island after its release.

1978 **Mar** *And The Music Plays On* combines Edmunds-produced title track from 1974 with unreleased tracks cut with Oldham in 1967.

1979 **Feb** **[3]** He plays a nostalgia show at the Surf Ballroom, Clear Lake, IA, to mark the 20th anniversary of the final performances by Buddy Holly, Ritchie Valens and The Big Bopper (before their deaths in a plane crash). Also playing are The Drifters and Jimmy Clanton (who was on the "Winter Dance Party" tour of 1959).

1982 **Jan** *Drop Down And Get Me*, produced by Tom Petty on Elektra, reaches US #123, and will be his last album.
Feb Petty-produced revival of Phil Phillips' *Sea Of Love* is Shannon's first US Singles chart entry for 15 years, and peaks at US #33.

1984 He signs to Warner Bros., and records new material in Nashville.
1986 **Oct** Luis Cardenas, ex-LA band Renegade, revives *Runaway* and takes it to US #83. Shannon (with Donny Osmond) has a cameo role in Cardenas' promotional video.

1988 **May** Shannon tours UK on a nostalgic package with his contemporaries Bobby Vee and Brian Hyland.

1990 **Feb** **[3]** He performs at the annual Buddy Holly memorial concert in Fargo, ND.
[8] Shannon dies from a self-inflicted gunshot wound at his Santa Clarita Valley, CA, home.

1991 **Mar** *Rock On!* emerges on UK Silvertone Records, the fruits of his second collaboration with Jeff Lynne (and Tom Petty) recorded shortly before his death. It includes the single *Walk Away*, written by all 3 and featuring their noted combined efforts at "slapping thighs".

HELEN SHAPIRO

1961 **Jan** Shapiro (b. Sept.28, 1946, Bethnal Green, London) is still at school and taking weekly vocal classes at the Maurice Berman singing academy in Baker Street, London, when EMI producer John Schroeder hears her and is impressed by her deep, mature voice and phrasing. He arranges a demo session and EMI's Columbia label A&R head Norrie Paramor (who initially refuses to believe he is listening to a 14-year-old girl on the demo) signs her to a recording contract.
May Schroeder writes *Don't Treat Me Like A Child* for her debut and, aided by radio and TV slots (including Saturday prime time "Thank Your Lucky Stars"), it hits UK #3.
Aug *You Don't Know*, a mid-tempo Schroeder/Mike Hawker ballad, in

contrast to its bouncy teenbeat predecessor, tops UK chart for 2 weeks, shifting 40,000 copies in a day at its peak. (It also becomes a major hit in many other territories and worldwide sales will top a million by the end of the year.)

Sept [28] She celebrates her birthday establishing a UK performing record: the first female to make over a dozen radio and TV appearances before the age of 15. This also marks the end of school for her and the beginning of a schedule of live appearances which takes in a short London Palladium season and several European tours.

Oct From the same writing team, teen rocker *Walkin' Back To Happiness*, released with advance orders of 300,000, hits UK Top 10 while *You Don't Know* is still in it, and tops the chart for 4 weeks before surrendering to Elvis Presley's *His Latest Flame*.

Dec *Walkin' Back To Happiness* spends a week at #100 on the US chart, regarded as a major achievement for a UK girl singer at this time. Worldwide sales again top a million. Shapiro is voted Top UK Female Singer in the annual **New Musical Express** poll. This success gives her some leeway to follow her own inclinations over material, and she releases 4-track EP of standards, from which *Goody Goody* gains considerable airplay and tops UK EP chart.

1962
Jan [15] UK tour begins at the Granada cinema, East Ham, London.
Mar Shapiro just fails to achieve 3 consecutive UK #1 singles – a feat never achieved by a female performer or a UK act – as *Tell Me What He Said*, a US song written by Jeff Barry, peaks at UK #2, held off by The Shadows' *Wonderful Land*.
Apr Debut album *Tops With Me*, a collection of personal favorite oldies like *Lipstick On Your Collar* and *Will You Love Me Tomorrow?*, hits UK #2. She has a lead role, opposite Craig Douglas, in UK pop/jazz movie "It's Trad, Dad", (US title : "Ring-A-Ding Rhythm") which is a UK box office success.
May Soundtrack *It's Trad, Dad*, on which she sings *Let's Talk About Love* and *Sometime Yesterday*, hits UK #3. *Let's Talk About Love* is also released as a single and peaks at UK #23.
Aug *Little Miss Lonely*, her first slow ballad on single (and a return to Schroeder/Hawker material) hits UK #8, but will be her last major hit single. Meanwhile, she makes a cameo appearance in Billy Fury film "Play It Cool", singing *Cry My Heart Out* and *But I Don't Care*.
Nov *Keep Away From Other Girls*, a Bacharach/Hilliard song originally cut in US by Babs Tino, stalls at UK #40.
[9] Shapiro begins a UK tour with Eden Kane and The Vernons Girls, at the Ritz cinema, Belfast, N.Ireland. Tour will end Dec.16 at the Odeon cinema, Colchester, Essex.

1963
Feb She begins UK tour, opening at Bradford Gaumont, W.Yorks. The Beatles are among the supporting acts, and Lennon and McCartney tell her that their song *Misery* was written for her, but rejected by Paramor. *Queen For Tonight* makes UK #33.
Apr *Helen's Sixteen* (referring both to her age and its number of tracks) fails to chart.
May *Woe Is Me*, recorded at her first US sessions, in Nashville the previous month, reaches UK #35. (She also cuts the original version of *It's My Party*, but the planned release is cancelled when Lesley Gore's version appears.)
July *Not Responsible*, another Nashville recording, is her first single not to chart in UK.
Oct *Look Who It Is* makes UK #47, while *Helen In Nashville*, from the sessions earlier in the year, fails to chart.

1964
Feb A revival of Peggy Lee's *Fever* reaches UK #38, her final hit single. She is one of the large generation of immediately pre-beat boom stars whose styles are now out of public fashion.
Mar [7] Shapiro begins a 5-week Far East tour of Japan, Malaysia and the Philippines in Hong Kong.
Nov Doctors advise Shapiro not to sing for a month.

1965
Feb [10] She embarks on a 9-day tour of Poland.
May [24] After 4 unsuccessful singles, Shapiro sings *Here In My Arms* in the British Song Festival at the Dome, Brighton, E.Sussex, but even TV coverage fails to help it chart.
July [17] Shapiro guests at the 200th edition of commercial TV's "Thank Your Lucky Stars" with The Searchers, Dusty Springfield and others.

1967
May [2] She begins an 8-date twice-nightly UK/Irish tour, headlined by The Beach Boys with Simon Dupree & The Big Sound, Terry Reid with Peter Jay's Jaywalkers, The Nite People and The Marionettes, at the Adelphi cinema, Dublin, Eire. (The tour will end May 10, at the Edinburgh ABC, Scotland.)
July [24] She makes her straight-acting theater debut in the farce "I'll Get My Man" at the Ashton Pavilion, St. Anne's, Lancs.

1968 With UK hits long gone, but still finding plenty of live work,

particularly overseas, she switches labels from Columbia to Pye (rejoining John Schroeder, who has made the same move), and has a near-chartmaker with *Today Has Been Cancelled*.

1970 Shapiro begins a successful career in cabaret work and on the London West End stage in musicals like "The French Have A Word For It" and, in 1979, a new production of "Oliver". She cuts one-off singles for Phoenix, DJM, Magnet and Arista, including Russ Ballard's *Can't Break The Habit*.

1978 Shapiro's second marriage, to childhood friend Morris Gundlash, ends in divorce.

1983 Signing to Oval Records, a label with a reputation for artistic freedom, she records her first album in almost 2 decades, *Straighten Up And Fly Right*, with mature versions of standards and personal favorites. UK music paper **New Musical Express** gives a rave review to her *Cry Me A River* and UK BBC Radio 2 plays the album extensively. She showcases the material on stage in a series of dates at Fairfield Hall, Croydon, London.

1985 She begins to work with jazzman Humphrey Lyttleton and his band, jointly recording *Echoes Of The Duke*, a tribute to Duke Ellington.

1986 20-track compilation *Helen Shapiro 25th Anniversary Album*, on EMI, celebrates her quarter-century of recording, as she continues a busy career in cabaret and stage musicals.

1989 Shapiro weds for the third time – to actor (and subsequently her manager) John Judd.

1990 She devotes part of the year to a series of gospel concerts.

1991 **Mar** [30] Shapiro teams with Cliff Richard for a gospel music event at London's Royal Albert Hall.

SANDIE SHAW

1964
Apr Shaw (b. Sandra Goodrich, Feb.26, 1947, Dagenham, Essex) is working as an IBM machine operator and singing in her spare time when she talks her way backstage at an Adam Faith And The Roulettes one-nighter, impressing them with an impromptu vocal demonstration. Their manager Eve Taylor is only marginally impressed, but sees potential in her style, and signs her to a management contract, renaming her Sandie Shaw.
July After recording demos with producer Tony Hatch, Shaw is signed to Pye Records, and debuts with *As Long As You're Happy*.
Oct [24] A cover of Lou Johnson's US hit *(There's) Always Something There To Remind Me*, written by Bacharach and David, tops UK chart for 3 weeks, deposing Roy Orbison's *Oh, Pretty Woman*. Shaw is immediately seen on several UK TV spots and gains as much notoriety from the fact that she always sings barefoot as from her hit single. (The bare feet are a gimmick dreamed up by Taylor, who predicts that this will be a source of interest for the press. Shaw continues to sing barefoot on stage for several years.)
Dec *(There's) Always Something There To Remind Me*, released in US on Reprise, peaks at US #52 (Johnson's version had peaked at #49 Oct.3.)

1965
Jan Third single is *I'd Be Far Better Off Without You*, written by Chris Andrews, but several reviewers and DJs note that B-side *Girl Don't Come* is the stronger song. Pye switches promotion to it and *Girl Don't Come* hits UK #3.
Feb [21] She makes her concert debut, supporting Faith at De Montfort Hall, Leicester, Leics., at the start of a UK tour.
Mar *I'll Stop At Nothing*, written by Andrews for Faith, is given to Shaw instead and hits UK #4. Debut album *Sandie* hits UK #3, and will be her only UK chart album.
Apr *Girl Don't Come* makes US #42, her biggest US chart success. She attempts to visit US to promote it, but is refused a performing visa by US immigration authorities because of the deluge of UK acts hitting success in US; she is deemed "not of sufficiently distinguished ability", and a projected season at New York's Paramount theater is cancelled. Instead, Shaw makes a short promotional visit to Canada.
May [29] Another Andrews composition, *Long Live Love* (rhythmically reminiscent of Tom Jones' *It's Not Unusual*, a UK chart-topper 2 months earlier and which Shaw had turned down) is her second UK #1, for 3 weeks.
June She is finally allowed into US and appears on CBS TV's "Ed Sullivan Show", singing *Long Live Love* (which stalls at US #97 2 weeks later and is her final US chart entry). *Sandie Shaw* peaks at US #100.
Oct *Message Understood*, also Andrews-penned, hits UK #6.
[6-26] Shaw plays a 3-week season at the Paris Olympia, France, with Richard Anthony.
Nov *Me* is released, but does not chart. She makes her cabaret debut at London's Savoy hotel, backed by The Paramounts, faring moderately

well through a 3-week stint after a disastrous opening night.
Dec *How Can You Tell* peaks at UK #21.

1966 **Feb** *Tomorrow* hits UK #9. She is given the chance to record the theme song to forthcoming Michael Caine film "Alfie" as the follow-up, but Taylor rejects it. (The song will be a hit for Cilla Black in UK and Cher in US.)
[18] Shaw begins a European tour in Bordeaux, France.
Apr Low-priced compilation *The Golden Hits Of Sandie Shaw* anthologizes her hit singles to date.
June *Nothing Comes Easy* reaches UK #14.
July She performs in the Venice Song Festival in Italy.
Sept *Run* peaks at UK #32, during a year when Shaw is concentrating her efforts abroad in Europe.
Dec *Think Sometimes About Me* also reaches UK #32.

1967 **Jan** *I Don't Need Anything* charts for only 1 week at UK #50.
[21] Shaw sings the first of the "A Song For Europe" entries for the upcoming Eurovision Song Contest on "The Rolf Harris Show".
Mar She is named as the "other woman" in a widely publicized divorce case, with the judge delivering her a public reprimand.
Apr [8] Shaw represents UK in the Eurovision Song Contest in Vienna, Austria, with Bill Martin and Phil Coulter's *Puppet On A String*. The song wins, with 47 votes, more than twice as many as the second placed act, Sean Dunphy's *If I Could Choose*, representing Eire. It is UK's first win after coming in second 5 times.
[29] *Puppet On A String* tops the UK chart for 3 weeks, selling over 500,000 copies. It also becomes her biggest international success, with sales in Germany exceeding 750,000, and worldwide total estimated at 4 million. The success brings a flood of work offers from all over Europe and elsewhere.
June [14-17] Shaw represents Britain in the second Bratislava International Festival Of Pop Music in Czechoslovakia.
July Martin and Coulter also pen her follow-up, *Tonight In Tokyo*, which reaches UK #21.
Nov *You've Not Changed*, written by Andrews, reaches UK #18. Shaw appears in the Royal Variety Show in London.
Dec Despite the year's singles successes, album *Love Me, Please Love Me* fails.

1968 **Feb** *Today* reaches UK #27.
[28] Shaw celebrates her 21st birthday with a party in the Chamber Of Horrors in Madame Tussaud's, London.
Mar [6] She marries fashion designer Jeff Banks, in London.
Apr *Don't Run Away* is Shaw's first since her debut single not to make UK Top 50. (*Show Me* in June and a cover of Nilsson's *Together* in Aug. will fare equally poorly.)
Sept She covers Mary Hopkin's debut *Those Were The Days* and sings it on BBC TV's "Top Of The Pops". The Hopkin version, gaining radio play and promotion, shared with The Beatles' *Hey Jude* and the launch of Apple Records, hits UK #1 and Shaw's flops.
Nov BBC musical series "The Sandie Shaw Supplement" proves popular, but album of the same title with music from the show fails.

1969 **Apr** *Monsieur Dupont* is a notable, if short-lived, UK singles chart comeback, hitting #6.
May *Think It All Over* makes UK #42 (and will be Shaw's last hit single for 15 years).

1970 **Feb** [23] Shaw attends Prime Minister Harold Wilson's reception for Germany's Chancellor Willy Brandt at 10 Downing Street, London.

1971 **Feb** She covers Lynn Anderson's *Rose Garden*, but Anderson's version has the chart success.
Aug After several more flop singles, the last a cover of Cat Stevens' *Father And Son*, her contract with Pye lapses and is not renewed.

1977 **June** After 5 years with no records, concentrating on cabaret and overseas work, plus straight theater roles (in Shaw's "St. Joan" and Shakespeare's "Hamlet"), she signs to CBS. *One More Night* fails to chart, however, and follow-up *Your Mama Wouldn't Like It* also flops. (No album is recorded before this deal lapses and she will disappear from the recording scene for 5 years.)

1982 **Apr** Shaw contributes *Anyone Who Had A Heart* to Heaven 17's ambitious British Electric Foundation cover versions project *Music Of Quality And Distinction*.

1983 *Choose Life*, released on Palace Records in association with the World Peace Exposition, is a Buddhist-inspired set of songs written by Shaw herself. (Shaw is now married to Nik Powell, boss of the Palace record, film and video company and the Video Palace shops.) Extracted *Wish I Was* is also released.

1984 **May** A revival of The Smiths' first single, *Hand In Glove*, recorded with the group and released on Rough Trade (to which they are contracted),

charts at UK #27. (Smiths' lead singer Morrissey is a long-time Sandie Shaw fan, and has satisfied a personal ambition by working with her and having her record one of his compositions.)

1985 **Dec** [19] She takes part in Carol Aid, an all-star Christmas carol service held at London's Heaven club, to raise money for Band Aid, along with Cliff Richard, Lulu and Chris De Burgh.

1986 **June** Having made a conscious decision to resume her performing career with a higher profile, after several years of mainly domestic life, Shaw signs to Polydor. A revival of Lloyd Cole & The Commotions' *Are You Ready To Be Heartbroken?* is a minor UK chart entry, at #68, as she makes a successful university tour.

1988 **Sept** Shaw signs to Rough Trade for album *Hello Angel*. With musical assistance of George Michael's bassist Deon Estus, The Communards' Richard Coles and The Pretenders' Chrissie Hynde (who plays harmonica on *Nothing Less Than Brilliant*), it features songs written by The Jesus & Mary Chain, Fairground Attraction's Mark Nevin, Clive Langer and Morrissey with new collaborator Stephen Street. Morrissey and producer Street's song *Please Help The Cause Against Loneliness* trailers the album.

1991 **Apr** She publishes **The World At My Feet**.

THE SHIRELLES
Shirley Owens (lead vocals)
Addi "Micki" Harris (vocals)
Doris Coley (vocals)
Beverly Lee (vocals)

1957 Group is formed as The Poquellos, at high school in Passaic, NJ, by classmates Owens (b. June 10, 1941, Passaic), Harris (b. Jan.22, 1940, Passaic), Coley (b. Aug.2, 1941, Passaic) and Lee (b. Aug.3, 1941, Passaic), initially to sing at school parties and dances, where their speciality piece is group-composed *I Met Him On A Sunday*. Another schoolfriend, Mary Jane Greenberg, persuades them to audition this for her mother Florence Greenberg, who owns small local Tiara Records.

1958 **Jan** Greenberg records *I Met Him On A Sunday* with the group, but insists on a more commercial-sounding name to put on the release; The Shirelles is the girls' own choice.
Apr The single starts to sell well, and Tiara, without resources to promote a national success, leases it to Decca.
May *I Met Him On A Sunday* makes US #50. (It will be followed by 2 more Tiara recordings leased to Decca, *My Love Is A Charm* and *I Got The Message*, but neither will chart.)

1959 **May** Greenberg forms Scepter Records with writer/producer Luther Dixon, and The Shirelles are signed. Dixon becomes their producer and Greenberg their manager.
July A revival of The Five Royales' ballad *Dedicated To The One I Love* is a moderate success at US #83; follow-up *A Teardrop And A Lollipop* fails.

1960 **Oct** After another failure with *Please Be My Boyfriend*, Owens and Dixon co-write *Tonight's The Night*, which makes US #39.
Dec The group appears in a Christmas all-star show at Brooklyn's Paramount theater, New York, alongside Ray Charles, Dion, Chubby Checker, The Coasters, Neil Sedaka, and many others.

1961 **Feb** Owing songwriters Goffin and King a favor, Dixon produces an uptempo string-backed arrangement of their ballad *Will You Love Me Tomorrow* (with King herself helping with the arrangement and playing drums), which tops US chart for 2 weeks and is a million-seller. It is the first recording by an all-girl group to hit US #1.
Mar *Dedicated To The One I Love* is reissued as follow-up and this time is a smash, hitting US #3 and becoming the group's second million-seller. Meanwhile, *Will You Love Me Tomorrow* is their UK chart debut, hitting #4.
Apr [2] Group begins a major US tour in Irving Feld's "Biggest Show Of Stars, 1961", debuting in Philadelphia, PA. Also on the bill are Chubby Checker, Fats Domino, The Drifters, Bo Diddley, and others.
June *Mama Said* hits US #4.
[25] Group appears at the Hollywood Bowl, in an Alan Freed outdoor spectacular also starring Brenda Lee, Bobby Vee, Jerry Lee Lewis, and others.
Aug *A Thing Of The Past* halts at US #41, much of its airplay is being stolen by B-side Goffin and King's *What A Sweet Thing That Was*, which climbs to US #54.
Nov *Big John* makes UK #21, at the same time as Jimmy Dean's *Big Bad John* (a different song) is at US #1. **The Shirelles Sing To Trumpet And Strings** is released without charting.

1962 **Feb** A Bacharach/David song, *Baby It's You* (molded for the group at Dixon's urging from its original form as *I'll Cherish You*), hits US #8. (A year later, The Beatles will revive it on their debut album, along with a version of *Boys*, B-side of *Will You Love Me Tomorrow*.)

May *Soldier Boy*, in simple, uptempo C&W style with a widely applicable lyric, written by Dixon and Greenberg in a few minutes and recorded as rapidly at the end of a session, becomes the group's third million-seller, topping US chart for 3 weeks.

June *Baby It's You* reaches US #59, while *Soldier Boy* makes UK 23.

July *Welcome Home Baby* peaks at US #22. Greenberg turns down Gene Pitney's song *He's A Rebel* as follow-up, when offered it for The Shirelles by publisher Aaron Schroeder. (She is afraid the title will prove controversial in the South, but Phil Spector will record it with The Crystals and take it to US #1.)

Oct *Stop The Music* reaches US #36. (B-side *It's Love That Really Counts* will later be a UK hit for The Merseybeats.)

1963
Jan A revival of Doris Day's 1958 hit *Everybody Loves A Lover* makes US #19. After this, they record without Dixon, who leaves Scepter to work at Capitol Records.

Mar Compilation *The Shirelles' Greatest Hits* reaches US #19. Their best-selling album, it stays charted for 49 weeks.

May *Foolish Little Girl* hits US #4, the group's last Top 10 success. By now, the girl-group sound, of which The Shirelles have been the hitmaking pioneers, has taken a major hold on US charts, and competition from groups like The Angels, The Chiffons and Phil Spector's The Crystals, for both songs and chart placings, is intense.

June *Foolish Little Girl* reaches UK #38; their third and final UK hit.

July *Don't Say Goodnight And Mean Goodbye* reaches US #26, while *Foolish Little Girl* makes US #68.

Sept *What Does A Girl Do?* peaks at US #53.

Oct The group sings the theme song to film *It's a Mad, Mad, Mad, Mad World*, but it makes only US #92.

Nov [9] The Shirelles begin their first UK tour, with Little Richard and Duane Eddy, at the Regal cinema, Edmonton, London. Owens and Coley have both married by this time, and are now Shirley Alston and Doris Kenner respectively. (Dionne Warwick, also with Scepter Records, often fills in on stage for one or the other of them during 1963 when family commitments call.)

1964
Jan *Tonight You're Gonna Fall In Love With Me* reaches US #57. The group is no longer recording for Scepter, having fallen out with Greenberg and the label after discovering that trust fund money from their hit earnings, supposedly theirs at age 21, does not exist. The group attempts to leave but is prevented from signing elsewhere because of extended legal proceedings. (Meanwhile, Scepter will continue to release Shirelles singles regularly, from already-cut material, until the end of the year – though without any great promotion. Dionne Warwick has just broken with *Anyone Who Had A Heart* and is now the label's priority act.)

Apr *Sha-La-La* (revived as a bigger hit by Manfred Mann a few months later) makes US #69.

Aug *Thank You Baby* reaches US #63.

Nov *Maybe Tonight* stalls at US #88.

1965
Jan *Are You Still My Baby?* makes US #91, and is the last Shirelles chart entry for 2 years.

1967
Aug *Last Minute Miracle* is recorded after legal and other difficulties between the group and Scepter are finally solved. It stalls at US #99 and the group signs to Mercury, where *I'll Stay By Your Side* and *There's A Storm Going On In My Heart* both fail to sell.

1968 Kenner leaves group because of family commitments (she has married again, and is now Mrs. Doris Jackson). The others continue as a trio.

1969
Feb They sign to Bell Records as Shirley And The Shirelles. *Look What You've Done To My Heart* gains some UK airplay (and later some specialist sales as a Northern dancefloor favorite), but fails to chart in either US or UK.

Oct Group appears in Richard Nader's first "Rock'N'Roll Revival Concert" at New York's Felt Forum, alongside Bill Haley & His Comets, Chuck Berry, The Platters, The Coasters, and others.

1972 Trio is signed to RCA, recording *Happy In Love* and *The Shirelles*. Both contain strong songs (by Bill Withers, Carole King, Marvin Gaye and others) but fail to sell.

1973 Group sings *Soldier Boy* and *Everybody Loves A Lover* in "Let The Good Times Roll", a documentary of a New York Madison Square Garden rock revival show interspersed with vintage performance clips.

1975 Doris Jackson returns to the group to replace Alston, who leaves for a solo career but is prevented by the other 3 from billing herself as "Shirley Of The Shirelles". She signs to Prodigal Records and records *With A Little Help From My Friends*, a collection of oldies on which she is joined on individual tracks by artists originally associated with

the songs, such as The Drifters (*Save The Last Dance For Me*, The Five Satins (*In The Still Of The Night*), Herman's Hermits (*Silhouettes*) and The Flamingos (*I Only Have Eyes For You*). The album attracts critical interest, but does not sell.

1976
Jan *Let's Give Each Other Love*, on RCA, is the group's last album.

1977 Alston records 2 further solo albums, *Lady Rose* and *Sings The Shirelles' Biggest Hits*, for US Strawberry label, without success.

1982 Though now without recording contracts, both Alston and the 3-piece Shirelles continue performing careers, the latter still popular on nostalgia dates and tours.

June [10] After a live show in Atlanta, Harris collapses and dies of a heart attack. (Memorial service is held in group's home town Passaic.)

1983
Oct Dionne Warwick invites The Shirelles to sing *Will You Love Me Tomorrow* for her new album *How Many Times Can We Say Goodbye*.

1989
Sept [14] Shirley Alston Reeves joins forces with members of The Belmonts, The Five Satins, The Jive Five, The Falcons and The Silhouettes outside the Berklee Performance Center in Boston, MA, in an impromptu doo-wop session to announce the introduction of the Doo-Wop Hall Of Fame Of America.

SIMON & GARFUNKEL

Paul Simon (vocals, guitar)
Art Garfunkel (vocals)

1953 Simon (b. Oct.13, 1941, Newark, NJ), the son of Louis Simon, a bass-playing veteran of CBS TV shows "Arthur Godfrey And His Friends", "The Garry Moore Show" and "The Jackie Gleason Show" and New York session musician, and Garfunkel (b. Arthur Garfunkel, Nov.5, 1941, Queens, New York, NY) meet at Forest Hills high school in New York and, while in sixth grade, play The White Rabbit and The Cheshire Cat respectively in a production of "Alice In Wonderland".

1955 After singing *Sh-Boom* at assembly at Parsons high school, they start writing songs together, registering their copyright of *The Girl For Me* at the Library of Congress for $4.

1957 They tape a demo of Simon's song *Hey Schoolgirl*, at Sande's recording studio in New York and are heard by Sid Prosen, who secures them a deal with Big Records for the track.

Nov They adopt the name Tom & Jerry (Garfunkel is Tom Graph and Simon Jerry Landis), and *Hey Schoolgirl* is released on Big Records. Duo appears on Dick Clark's TV show "American Bandstand", performing *Hey Schoolgirl* directly after Jerry Lee Lewis sings *Great Balls Of Fire*.

1958
Jan *Hey Schoolgirl* makes US #49, selling 120,000 copies, but will be Tom & Jerry's only chart success, despite further singles on Big, including *Don't Say Goodbye* and *Our Song*. Most of the tracks are variations of The Everly Brothers' style and sound. Simon releases unsuccessful solo *True Or False*, as Tru Taylor.

1959 After high school, Tom & Jerry drift apart. Garfunkel goes to Columbia University to study mathematics and architecture, while Simon goes to Queens College to study English. He starts making demo tapes for other singers and cutting further solo singles as Jerry Landis, including *Anna Belle* on MGM, which is another failure. He makes money cutting demos, having been introduced to music publishers by fellow demo-maker Carole Klein (later Carole King).

1960 Between now and 1963, Simon records several singles for Warwick Records, including *I Want To Be The Lipstick On Your Collar* and *Play Me A Sad Song*, which fail to sell, before he moves (still making more money from demos than his own releases) to Madison Records where he records as Tico and Tico & The Triumphs (*Motorcycle* reaches US #99 in Jan.1962. As Jerry Landis, Simon's *The Lone Teen Ranger* on Amy, which has bought Madison, reaches US #97 in Jan.1963.) He also writes and produces for others, including Ritchie Cordell, The Fashions and Dotty Daniels, and begins to play Greenwich Village clubs like Gerde's Folk City at night and plug songs to publishers by day. Garfunkel releases 2 singles under the name Artie Garr on Octavia and Warwick labels. While at law school, Simon teams up again with Garfunkel (completing a Mathematics degree) and they perform folk-style material for the first time as Simon & Garfunkel.

1964 Dropping out of law school, Simon travels to UK (joined during summer vacation by Garfunkel), where he plays the folk circuit, and is befriended by London social worker Judith Piepe, with whom he lodges. As Jerry Landis he records *He Was My Brother*, written about a friend killed during the US civil rights disturbances, for UK independent label Oriole Records. (In US, it is credited to Paul Kane and issued by Tribute Records.) Simon & Garfunkel reunite and are signed by Tom Wilson at CBS/Columbia Records.

Oct Debut album *Wednesday Morning, 3:AM*, combining Simon's songs with folk standards like *Go Tell It On The Mountain* and Bob Dylan's *The Times They Are A-Changin'*, is released without success.

1965 Jan Simon returns to UK, where he contributes songs to a series of Piepe's commentaries on daily BBC radio religious series "Five To 10". He also plays the UK folk circuit, with fellow Americans Tom Paxton, Carolyn Hester and Buffy St. Marie.

May Thanks to his US Columbia contract, Simon records solo album *The Paul Simon Songbook* for UK CBS. (Not a big seller, it contains solo acoustic versions of several songs which will reappear on the next duo album.)

Sept Simon writes *Homeward Bound*, dedicated to his girlfriend Kathy Chitty, on the platform of the railway station in Widnes, Cheshire, after playing at the Howff folk club. He makes his debut on commercial TV's "Ready Steady Go!"

Oct Without informing Simon or Garfunkel, Wilson takes *The Sound Of Silence*, an acoustic track from the debut album, and re-mixes it, adding drums, percussion and stinging electric guitar. The resulting commercial blend is issued as a single. (A similar episode will be recounted in Simon's 1980 movie "One-Trick Pony".)

Nov The disk has hit #1 in Boston when Simon, living at Al Stewart's house in UK, is informed by Columbia of the duo's success. He returns to US and reunites with Garfunkel for promotional appearances.

1966 Jan *The Sound Of Silence* tops US chart for 2 weeks and sells over a million, but struggles in UK, which is a disappointment to Simon, who regards UK as a spiritual home.

Mar Debut album *Wednesday Morning 3:AM* is re-promoted and reaches US #30, while their newly-recorded album, *Sounds Of Silence*, including the "electric" re-mix of *The Sound Of Silence*, makes US #21. Both earn gold disks. *Homeward Bound* hits US #5, while The Bachelors' cover of *The Sound Of Silence* hits UK #3 (after the original has failed to score – Simon is not amused, as he makes clear in interviews).

Apr *Homeward Bound* is the duo's UK chart debut, hitting #9, while *Sounds Of Silence* (with *Homeward Bound* added) reaches UK #13.

June *I Am A Rock*, from the album (and originally recorded solo by Simon on 1964's *The Paul Simon Songbook*) hits US #3.

July *I Am A Rock* makes UK #17, while The Cyrkle's cover version of Simon's *Red Rubber Ball* hits US #2.

[5] Duo arrives in UK for promotional visit. Simon contracts tonsilitis, and some dates are cancelled.

Sept *The Dangling Conversation*, a Simon song about deteriorating relationships (and the duo's first track to feature strings), reaches US #25. It fails to chart in UK, as will the duo's next 4 US hit singles.

Dec *A Hazy Shade Of Winter* peaks at US #13. (The Bangles' 1987 revival will hit US #2.) *Parsley, Sage, Rosemary and Thyme*, which includes *The Dangling Conversation* and the duo's new arrangement of traditional *Scarborough Fair/Canticle*, hits US #4, earning a gold disk.

1967 Mar [18] Simon & Garfunkel begin a short 4-date UK tour at the Royal Albert Hall, London.

Apr *At The Zoo* reaches US #16, while Harper's Bizarre cover Simon's *59th Street Bridge Song (Feelin' Groovy)* (from *Parsley, Sage, Rosemary And Thyme*), making US #13 and UK #34.

June [16] Duo appears at Monterey International Pop Festival, CA.

Aug *Fakin' It*, with oblique references to Donovan and (instrumentally) to The Beatles' *Strawberry Fields Forever*, reaches US #23. B-side *You Don't Know Where Your Interest Lies* becomes the rarest Simon & Garfunkel CBS track. (After its deletion, it is never reissued on album or in any other form.) Duo is commissioned to supply music for Mike Nichols-directed movie "The Graduate".

1968 Apr *Scarborough Fair/Canticle* climbs to US #11. Originally featured on *Parsley, Sage, Rosemary and Thyme*, it is also featured in "The Graduate". Meanwhile, the soundtrack album from "The Graduate" (which stars Dustin Hoffman and Anne Bancroft) tops US chart for 9 weeks, earning a gold disk. Alongside incidental music by Dave Grusin, the album features 5 Simon & Garfunkel tracks, of which only *Mrs. Robinson* is a new song.

May *Bookends*, compiling new Simon songs with the duo's recent hit singles and a new, fuller version of *Mrs. Robinson*, tops US chart for 7 weeks, replacing the movie soundtrack album, and selling over a million in US.

June *Mrs. Robinson* tops US chart for 3 weeks and is a million-seller.

July *Mrs. Robinson* restores duo to UK Singles chart, hitting #4. They play sold-out concerts at London's Royal Albert Hall. (During their time in UK, they walk out on BBC1 TV's "Top Of The Pops", when go-go girls dance to their record.)

Aug *Bookends* tops UK chart for 5 weeks.

Sept *Parsley, Sage, Rosemary and Thyme* is re-released in UK and reaches UK #13.

Nov Soundtrack album *The Graduate* is released in UK to tie in with the film's UK release and hits #3. Duo's debut album *Wednesday Morning 3:AM* is also belatedly issued in UK, reaching #24.

1969 Feb 4-track EP *Mrs. Robinson* hits UK #9.

Mar [12] *Mrs. Robinson* wins Record Of The Year and Best Contemporary Pop Performance Vocal, Duo Or Group Of 1968 and *The Graduate* wins Best Original Score Written For A Motion Picture Or A TV Special Of 1968 at the 11th annual Grammy awards.

May New Simon song, *The Boxer*, hits US #7 and UK #6. Duo follows it with a US tour, between lengthy sessions for the next album, only interrupted by Garfunkel's acting commitments.

Nov [30] They host their first television special. The original sponsor AT&T pulled out after realizing the show's obvious political theme.

1970 Feb *Bridge Over Troubled Water* hits US #1 for 6 weeks and UK #1 for 3. The album of the same title is released and rapidly also tops both US and UK charts (in US for 10 weeks and in UK for 41 weeks in 8 separate runs over an 18-month period). This puts the duo in the very rare company of acts who have topped US and UK Singles and Album charts simultaneously. Among the tracks is a revival of The Everly Brothers' *Bye Bye Love*, recorded live on tour at a concert in Ames, IA. (Relations between the 2 have become increasingly strained throughout the reported 800 hours it has taken to complete recording of the album with, among other things, Garfunkel objecting to Simon's song *Cuba Ci, Nixon No* and Simon becoming frustrated by his partner's film commitment interruptions. By the time the album is released, the duo has effectively split.) Simon agrees to continue as a solo artist on CBS, but on his own terms. Garfunkel's first solo project is acting in Mike Nichols' black comedy war drama movie "Catch 22".

May From the album, *Cecilia* hits US #4 and is another million-seller, while folk singer Julie Felix's cover of *El Condor Pasa (If I Could)* (Simon's arrangement of a traditional tune from the Andes) makes UK #19. Also released this month is "Hair" actress/singer Marsha Hunt's version of *Keep The Customer Satisfied* which reaches UK #41.

Oct Duo's own version of *El Condor Pasa (If I Could)* reaches US #18.

1971 Mar [16] Simon & Garfunkel sweep the 13th annual Grammy awards, as *Bridge Over Troubled Water* wins Record Of The Year, Song Of The Year, Best Contemporary Song, Best Arrangement Accompanying Vocalists and Best Engineered Record and *Bridge Over Troubled Water* wins Album Of The Year. (Later in the year, Simon will lead a songwriting workshop at New York University.)

1972 Apr They reunite for a one-off concert in aid of Presidential candidate Senator George McGovern, at New York's Madison Square Garden.

Aug Compilation album *Simon & Garfunkel's Greatest Hits* hits US #5 and UK #2. It includes live versions of some unreleased tracks.

Oct Taken from the compilation, *For Emily, Whenever I May Find Her* reaches US #53. B-side *America* makes US #97 and UK #25.

1973 Oct [16] *Bridge Over Troubled Water* is the first record played on the UK's first commercial radio station, Capital Radio.

1975 Oct [18] Simon & Garfunkel reunite on US NBC TV show "Saturday Night Live".

Dec After some years of successful solo careers, the duo sings Simon's *My Little Town*, which is included on the current solo album by each partner, and also hits US #9 as a single (though it fails to chart in UK).

1977 Oct [18] They appear together (in tuxedos) at the Britannia Music Awards in London where, due to a technical fault with TV cameras, they have to perform *Bookends/Old Friends* for 6 takes. At the awards (a one-off event celebrating the Queen's Silver Jubilee) *Bridge Over Troubled Water* single and album are voted the Best International (Non-UK) Album And Single Released Between 1952 And 1977.

1978 Mar Garfunkel's *Watermark* includes a re-make of Sam Cooke's *Wonderful World* featuring Simon and James Taylor on guest vocals.

1981 Sept Garfunkel's *Scissors Cut* features Simon on Jim Webb-written song *In Cars*.

[19] Duo reunites for a concert in New York's Central Park. Over 400,000 attend the performance, which is recorded and filmed for subsequent record release and TV/video showing.

Nov UK compilation *The Simon & Garfunkel Collection* hits UK #4.

1982 Apr Double live *The Concert In Central Park* is released by Geffen Records and hits both US and UK #6, earning a gold disk.

[19] They announce a further reunion, to tour overseas.

May From the live album, a revival of The Everly Brothers' *Wake Up Little Suzie* reaches US #27.

June [8] They open a 9-date European tour (which will end June 19 with sold-out shows at London's Wembley Stadium), and at the Hippodrome d'Auteuil in Paris, France. (The tour will show the international Simon & Garfunkel audience to be as fervent as ever, but plans for a further US leg will falter as personality rifts again come to a head and they will return to solo projects.)

983 July [19] Duo embarks on another US reunion tour, at the Rubber Bowl in Akron, OH. (It will be a major success and a new Simon & Garfunkel album, *Think Too Much*, is planned as a follow-up, but they will drift apart during recording and the album will appear as Simon's solo *Hearts And Bones*.)

990 Jan [17] Simon & Garfunkel are inducted into the Rock'N'Roll Hall Of Fame at the 5th annual dinner at the Waldorf Astoria, New York.

CARLY SIMON

964 Apr Sarah Lawrence College-educated Carly (b. June 25, 1945, New York, NY) and older sister Lucy, daughters of Richard L. Simon, co-founder of Simon & Schuster publishers, form singing duo The Simon Sisters, playing the campus circuit and folk clubs including New York's Gaslight and Bitter End, where they are seen by record executive Dave Kapp. Kapp signs them to his label where they have a minor hit (US #73) with *Winkin' Blinkin' And Nod* and cut 2 albums (*The Simon Sisters* and *Cuddlebug*).

966 The Simon Sisters split when Lucy marries. Carly moves to France.

967 She returns to US and meets Bob Dylan's manager Albert Grossman. She signs a management deal as Grossman hopes to promote her as a female Dylan.
Sept Simon records 4 tracks with producer Bob Johnston, but she argues with Grossman over her career direction and the songs are not issued, including a version of Eric Von Schmidt's *Baby Let Me Follow You Down*, with revised lyrics by Dylan and Bloomfield and members of The Band backing Simon. She meets Jacob Brackman, film critic for *Esquire* magazine and the 2 begin to write songs together.

969 Having spent much of the past 2 years singing jingles and making demos, Simon meets Jac Holzman, founder of Elektra label, via a mutual friend and pop entrepreneur Jerry Brandt.

970 Holzman signs Simon to the label.

971 Apr Debut album *Carly Simon*, produced by Holzman, enters US chart, eventually reaching #30. It features lyrics by Brackman and, taken from it, *That's The Way I've Always Heard It Should Be* hits US #10.
[6] After a Simon performance at the Troubadour in Los Angeles, CA, James Taylor goes backstage to meet her.
Nov *Anticipation* peaks at US #13. (It will later be used for an ad on US TV.) Second album *Anticipation*, also produced by Paul Samwell-Smith and recorded at Morgan studios in Willesden, North London, is released, reaching US #30.

972 Mar *Legend In Your Own Time* makes US #50.
[14] Simon wins Best New Artist at 14th annual Grammy awards.
Nov *You're So Vain* tops US chart (and will hit UK #3), earning a gold disk. (The song causes considerable conjecture over the identity of its subject. It seems unlikely to be backing vocalist Mick Jagger.)
[3] Simon marries James Taylor in her Manhattan apartment. That evening she joins him on stage, where he announces their union.
Dec *No Secrets* hits US #1 and UK #3. It is her first album produced by Richard Perry, who tries to give her voice a harder rock edge. (It will remain her most successful album.)

973 Mar *The Right Thing To Do* reaches both US and UK #17.

974 Jan *Hotcakes* hits US #3 and UK #19. Again produced by Perry, it includes backing vocals by husband Taylor and features their first song written together, *Forever My Love*.
Mar *Mockingbird*, a duet with Taylor on Charlie & Inez Foxx's 1963 US #7, hits US #5 and UK #34.
May *I Haven't Got Time For The Pain* peaks at US #14. *Playing Possum*, again produced by Perry, hits US #10.
June *Attitude Dancing* reaches US #21.
Aug *Waterfall* stalls at US #78.
Oct *More And More* falters at US #94.
Nov *The Best Of Carly Simon* reaches US #17.
Dec [24] Simon goes carol singing with Linda Ronstadt, Joni Mitchell and James Taylor in Hollywood, CA.

976 June *It Keeps You Running*, a cover of The Doobie Brothers' hit, makes US #46. *Another Passenger*, produced by Ted Templeman and with Brackman as co-writer, reaches US #29.

977 July *Nobody Does It Better* is issued as theme from James Bond movie "The Spy Who Loved Me". The song, co-written by Marvin Hamlisch and Carole Bayer Sager, hits US #2 and UK #7.

978 Apr *Boys In The Trees*, produced by Arif Mardin, hits US #10. *You Belong To Me*, written with Doobie Brother Michael McDonald over a telephone, hits US #6.

[19] Simon joins Bruce Springsteen, Jackson Browne, The Doobie Brothers and others in petitioning President Carter to end nuclear power in US. (It precedes her forthcoming involvement in the "No Nukes" project.)
Aug Another Simon and Taylor duet, a cover of The Everly Brothers' 1958 US #10 *Devoted To You*, reaches US #36.
Nov [2] Simon guests on *I Live In The Woods* in a concert at Jones Hall, Houston, TX, recorded for future Burt Bacharach album *Woman*.

1979 June *Spy* reaches US #45, and will be Simon's last for Elektra. *Vengeance* peaks at US #48.
Sept [19] Simon joins other anti-nuclear musicians singing with Graham Nash, John Hall and Taylor, on the first of a 5-night series of Musicians United For Safe Energy (MUSE) concerts at New York's Madison Square Garden. (The show is recorded for *No Nukes*.)

1980 July *Come Upstairs*, Simon's first for Warner Bros., makes US #36. *Jesse*, from the album, climbs to US #11.
Oct [4] During a nationwide tour to promote *Come Upstairs*, Simon collapses with exhaustion on stage in Pittsburgh, PA. (Over the next few years, Simon develops an increasing fear of live performance.)

1981 Sept *Torch* is released. A collection of standards from the 20s, 30s and 40s, it makes US #50.

1982 July Written and produced by The Chic Organization (Bernard Edwards and Nile Rodgers) and taken from film "Soup For One", *Why* hits UK #10, but stalls at US #74.

1983 Aug On Will Powers' UK #17 *Kissing With Confidence*, Simon provides lead vocals on the Lynn Goldsmith pseudonymous novelty hit.
Sept *Hello Big Man* reaches US #69, while taken from it, *You Know What To Do* makes US #83.

1985 June *Tired Of Being Blonde* stalls at US #70.
Sept *Spoiled Girl*, her only album for CBS/Epic, fails to chart. She appears in film "Perfect", in which she tips water over John Travolta.

1986 Nov *Coming Around Again*, her first single for Arista, reaches UK #12. (B-side *Itsy Bitsy Spider* features the vocal debut of her daughter.) Produced by Samwell-Smith, the song is from Jack Nicholson/Meryl Streep film "Heartburn".

1987 Jan [24] *Coming Around Again* reaches US #18.
May *Coming Around Again* reaches US and UK #25.
June [20] *Give Me All Night* peaks at US #61.

1988 Feb [20] *All I Want Is You* peaks at US #54.
Aug At the annual Martha's Vineyard Celebrity Auction, one of the featured items is a private performance of 1 song by Simon in the home of the winning bidder. Simon sings 3 songs for $26,000 each for 2 men, unable to outbid each other.
Sept *Greatest Hits Live* makes US #87 and UK #49. The album is recorded live in front of invited guests at the harbor in Gay Head, Martha's Vineyard, MA, for HBO special "Carly In Concert – Coming Around Again". Now married to Jim Hart, after her 1983 divorce from Taylor, Simon starts work on soundtrack to movie "Working Girl".

1989 Apr [15] *Let The River Run*, theme to "Working Girl", makes US #49.
June Reissued *Why* peaks at UK #56.
Sept [2] Simon signs copies of her to-be-published children's book *Amy And The Dancing Bear* at the Bunch O' Grapes book store in Vineyard Haven, MA.

1990 Feb [21] *Let The River Run* wins Best Song Written Specifically For A Motion Picture Or For Television at the 32nd annual Grammy awards at the Shrine Auditorium, Los Angeles. (It will also go on to win an Oscar for Best Song.)
Apr [15] "Carly In Concert: My Romance" airs on HBO-TV with guests Michael Brecker and Harry Connick Jr.
May [12] *My Romance*, like *Torch* a standards album, makes US #46.
Oct [27] *Have You Seen Me Lately?*, featuring 11 new Simon songs and guests including sister Lucy and Judy Collins, makes US #66.
Nov Simon's publishes second children's book, *The Boy Of The Bells*.

1991 Jan [31] Simon makes a rare television appearance on NBC TV's "Late Night With Letterman".
Mar *You're So Vain* is reissued in UK to coincide with its extensive TV use on Robert Campbell-conceived Dunlop Tyres ad.

PAUL SIMON

1958 Following US chart success with friend Art Garfunkel as Tom & Jerry, Simon (b. Paul Frederick Simon, Oct.13, 1941, Newark, NJ), his father Louis a bassist in orchestras on Arthur Godfrey and Jackie Gleason TV shows, his mother Belle a music teacher, and having his first copyrighted song *The Girl For Me* in 1955, cuts solo single *True Or False* for same label, Big records, under the name True Taylor, but it flops.

1959 Simon attends Queens College in New York to study English. He makes money cutting demos for music publishers, having been introduced to contacts by fellow demo-maker Carole Klein (later Carole King). He also adopts the name Jerry Landis to make more solo singles, the first *Anna Belle*, for MGM, is another failure.

1961 Several singles for Warwick Records, including *I Want To Be The Lipstick On Your Collar* and *Play Me A Sad Song*, fail to sell, before Simon moves (still, at this time making more money from demo work than his own releases) to Madison Records where he records as Tico and Tico & The Triumphs.

1962 **Jan** *Motorcycle* by Tico & The Triumphs reaches US #99 on Amy Records, which has acquired Madison and Simon's contract. He makes another 2 Tico singles for Amy, neither of them hits. (Some songs from this time are credited to Simon/Landis, the Simon being Paul's brother Eddie.)

1963 **Jan** As Jerry Landis again, *The Lone Teen Ranger*, on Amy, reaches US #97. (He also writes and produces for others, including Ritchie Cordell, The Fashions and Dotty Daniels, and begins to play Greenwich Village clubs like Gerde's Folk City at night, while still plugging songs to publishers during the day. (Later in the year, while at law school, he teams up again with Garfunkel (completing a Math degree at Columbia University), and they perform folk-style material for the first time as Simon & Garfunkel.

1964 Dropping out of law school, Simon travels to UK (joined during summer vacation by Garfunkel), where he plays the folk circuit, and is befriended by London social worker Judith Piepe, with whom he lodges. He records a solo single for UK independent label Oriole Records, still using the name Jerry Landis, *He Was My Brother*, written about a friend killed during the US civil rights disturbances. (It is credited to Paul Kane in US, where it is issued by Tribute Records.)

1965 **Jan** After the US failure of the first Simon & Garfunkel album *Wednesday Morning, 3:AM*, Simon returns to UK, where, with Judith Piepe, he gains some work on BBC radio, contributing songs to a series of Piepe's commentaries on the daily religious series "Five To Ten". He also plays the UK folk circuit, with fellow Americans Tom Paxton, Carolyn Hester and Buffy St. Marie.
May Thanks to his US Columbia contract, Simon is able to record solo album *The Paul Simon Songbook* (showing Simon and Piepe on the sleeve), for UK CBS. (It contains solo acoustic versions of several songs which will later reappear on the next duo album. The solo album is not a big seller and will be deleted at Simon's own request in 1979.) While in UK, he also works with other singer/songwriters, including Jackson C. Frank and Al Stewart.
Dec When Simon & Garfunkel's *The Sound Of Silence* hits US chart, Simon is contacted by producer Tom Wilson and returns to US, to re-form the duo (which will have 5 years of huge international success).

1969 Tensions arise between Simon & Garfunkel during the lengthy recording sessions for *Bridge Over Troubled Water*, and they decide to go their separate ways once the project is completed.

1970 **Feb** While the single and album *Bridge Over Troubled Water* are #1 worldwide, the duo splits. Simon agrees to continue as a solo artist on CBS, but under his own terms.
Apr Simon teaches a class in songwriting and record making for a semester at New York University.
Aug [6] Simon takes part in an anti-war festival at New York's Shea Stadium, 25 years after the bombing of Hiroshima.

1971 He writes songs for, and then records (partly in Jamaica) his first post-duo solo album.

1972 **Mar** *Paul Simon* hits US #4, earning a gold disk, and tops UK chart for a week. Among the guest players is violinist Stephane Grappelli. The album is co-produced by Simon & Garfunkel's former co-producer and engineer, Roy Halee. Taken from it, *Mother And Child Reunion*, a track recorded in Jamaica (and, according to Simon, about a dish of egg and chicken) hits US #4 and UK #5.
May *Me And Julio Down By The School Yard*, also from the album, reaches US #22 and UK #15.
Aug *Duncan*, a third single from the album, makes US #52.

1973 **May** [6] Simon begins his first solo tour since his break with Garfunkel, in Boston, MA.
June *There Goes Rhymin' Simon* hits US #2 and UK #4, earning a gold disk. Again, it features many guest musicians.
July From the album, *Kodachrome* hits US #2 and is a million-seller. Another track, *Take Me To The Mardi Gras* hits UK #7 (with *Kodachrome* relegated to UK B-side because of the BBC's refusal to play songs which mention commercial brand names).

Oct Gospel-styled *Loves Me Like A Rock*, recorded with The Dixie Hummingbirds, hits US #2 and is another million-seller, also reaching UK #39.

1974 **Jan** *American Tune*, from *There Goes Rhymin' Simon*, makes US #35.
Apr Live album *Paul Simon In Concert/Live Rhymin'* peaks at US #33 but fails to chart in UK. It was recorded on tour the previous year, and features some of the guests from the previous studio set. (Simon spends the rest of this year writing and recording.)

1975 **Oct** *Gone At Last*, a gospel-style duet with Phoebe Snow, backed vocally by The Jessy Dixon Singers, reaches US #23, and is a taster for the long-in-production new album.
Dec *Still Crazy After All These Years*, Simon's most jazz-flavored set yet, made with top session crew, tops US chart, selling over a million, and hits UK #6. Among the tracks is Simon & Garfunkel's duet *My Little Town* (also included on Garfunkel's new album), which hits US #9 as a single. Lyrically, the album contains references to his recently failed marriage (Simon and first wife Peggy are now divorced).

1976 **Feb** Taken from the album, *50 Ways To Leave Your Lover* tops US chart for 3 weeks, selling over a million, and makes UK #23.
Mar Simon wins Album Of The Year and Best Male Pop Vocal Performance for *Still Crazy After All These Years* at the 18th annual Grammy awards.
May Title song from *Still Crazy After All These Years* reaches US #40, while Simon is on a lengthy international tour to promote the album (which includes a BBC TV special).

1977 **Jan** [19] Simon participates in the Inaugural Eve Gala Performance for President-elect Jimmy Carter.

1978 **Jan** *Slip Slidin' Away* hits US #5 and makes UK #36. It is also one of 2 new songs on compilation album *Greatest Hits, Etc.*, which is a million-selling album, reaching US #18 and UK #6. (The other new song is *Stranded In A Limousine*.) Simon makes his acting debut in Woody Allen's movie "Annie Hall".
Mar Simon and James Taylor provide guest vocals on Art Garfunkel's revival of *(What A) Wonderful World*, which reaches US #17.
[22] The Rutles' movie "All You Need Is Cash", in which Simon makes a cameo appearance, airs on NBC TV. (He will make occasional appearances on NBC TV's "Saturday Night Live", performing both solo and with Garfunkel (and once, with George Harrison) for the late-night comedy show, and will also be best man at producer Lorne Michaels' wedding.) NBC TV will also air "The Paul Simon Special".
Apr [1] The Philadelphia Furies, a soccer team co-owned by Simon, Peter Frampton, Mick Jagger, and Rick Wakeman, loses its first match of the North America Soccer League 3-0 to the Washington Diplomats.

1979 **Feb** [15] Simon signs to Warner Bros. (partly for the chance to undertake his own movie project), paying CBS $1.5 million to release him from his contract. He also begins a suit against CBS for non-payment of royalties.
Mar He begins work on screenplay for his movie "One-Trick Pony".

1980 Simon devotes most of the first half of the year to the movie: he writes the script and songs for it, and also directs and acts in the production. When the film is completed, Simon embarks on a major US and UK concert tour.
Sept *Late In The Evening*, taken from "One-Trick Pony", hits US #6 and reaches UK #58. Soundtrack album *One-Trick Pony*, treated by fans and reviewers as a new Paul Simon album rather than a movie soundtrack, reaches US #12 and UK #17.
Oct [1] Movie "One-Trick Pony" opens in US (and will be only a moderate success). Included are brief appearances by The B52's and a specially re-formed The Lovin' Spoonful.
Nov Title song *One-Trick Pony* makes US #40.
[6] Simon begins a UK tour at the Hammersmith Odeon, London, his first live appearance in UK for 5 years. He buys the audience a drink – a gesture which costs him £1,000 a night.

1982 **Apr** [19] Simon & Garfunkel announce a reunion (though it will be mainly for nostalgic live concerts).

1983 **Feb** *The Blues*, a duet with Randy Newman, reaches US #51.
Aug [16] Simon marries long-time girlfriend, actress Carrie Fisher.
Dec *Hearts And Bones* peaks at US #35 and UK #17. The set is salvaged from what was to be a new Simon & Garfunkel album on Geffen, and guests include composer Phillip Glass. From it, *Allergies* reaches US #44.

1984 Simon begins work on a new album which will take him to South Africa to record both vocal and instrumental groups.

1985 **Jan** [28] Simon joins the all-star line-up for recording of USA For Africa's *We Are The World*.
Feb He begins recording in Johannesburg, South Africa.

Oct *Graceland* hits US #3, earning a platinum disk, and tops UK chart for 5 weeks. It is chiefly inspired by South African dance music, both traditional and electric, and features the group Ladysmith Black Mambazo (which, as a result of this exposure, becomes an international act, with Simon later co-producing 2 of its Warner Bros. albums). The album also includes contributions from Linda Ronstadt, The Everly Brothers and Los Lobos (who later threaten to sue if their name isn't credited on composer credits). From it, *You Can Call Me Al* hits UK #4 and initially US #44 (but will re-chart at US #23 on re-promotion in mid-1987). Song's promo video features comedy actor Chevy Chase.

Dec Also from the album, *The Boy In The Bubble* reaches UK #26.

987 Jan [10] Title song *Graceland* makes US #81.

[30] Simon holds a press conference in London to state that both the ANC and the UN have removed him from their blacklists (originally imposed after he broke the boycott on recording in South Africa).

Feb [9] Simon wins Best International Solo Artist at the sixth annual BRIT Awards at the Grosvenor House, London.

Mar [21] *The Boy In The Bubble* stalls at US #86.

Apr Simon plays UK dates at the Royal Albert Hall, London, and is picketed by anti-apartheid protestors. Guests on stage include husband and wife Hugh Masekela and Miriam Makeba. (Simon will play Zimbabwe, Africa, later in the summer, where TV film and best-selling home video "The Graceland Concert" will be shot.)

May [23] *You Can Call Me Al* reaches US #23.

988 Mar [2] *Graceland* is named Record Of The Year at the 30th annual Grammy awards.

Sept [13] John Cougar Mellencamp appears with Paul Simon on US NBC TV's "Coca Cola Presents Live: The Hard Rock".

Nov Compilation album *Negotiations And Love Songs, 1971-1986* reaches UK #17 and US #110.

989 June Simon embarks on 15-city tour of Europe and Russia.

July [12] Disney announces at a press conference that their cable network will air Shelley Duvall-produced "Mother Goose Rock'N' Rhyme", in which Simon will appear as Simple Simon, with Garfunkel as the Rhymeland bartender, among others.

Sept [24] Simon closes the 15th anniversary NBC TV "Saturday Night Live" special.

990 Feb [12] Simon, along with Bruce Springsteen and Don Henley is invited on stage by Sting, backed by Herbie Hancock and Branford Marsalis, for a jam at the Rainforest Foundation and the Environmental Media Association fundraiser in Beverly Hills, CA.

June Part of an international delegation in Czechoslovakia to monitor its elections, Simon participates in a concert in Prague's Old Town Square in front of an estimated 10,000 people.

Aug [30] Simon plays a benefit concert at Deep Hollow Ranch, Montauk, for the preservation of Montauk Point Lighthouse, near his Long Island home, singing *Sea Cruise* with Billy Joel.

Oct *The Obvious Child* reaches UK #15.

[27] Parent album *The Rhythm Of The Saints*, based around Brazilian rhythms and musicians, enters UK chart at #1, and will hit US #4.

991 Jan [4] Simon begins "Born At The Right Time" tour in Tacoma, WA.

[5] *The Obvious Child* stalls at US #92.

He donates at least $15,000 from the proceeds of his Phoenix, AZ, concert on Jan.19, to help get a paid state holiday honoring the Rev. Dr. Martin Luther King Jr.

May [12] Simon appears by satellite from Manchester at "The Simple Truth" concert for Kurdish refugees at Wembley Arena, London.

SIMPLE MINDS

im Kerr (vocals)
harlie Burchill (guitar)
ike McNeil (keyboards)
ohn Giblin (bass)
el Gaynor (drums)

977 Nov Johnny & The Self Abusers, a Glasgow, Scotland, septet featuring 3 guitarists, split on the day of their first single *Saints And Sinners'* release on Chiswick. Members of the band divide according to musical interests to form 60s-flavored Cuban Heels and more modern, experimental Simple Minds.

978 Feb Simple Minds debut at Glasgow's Satellite City club. Line-up is Kerr (b. July 9, 1959, Glasgow, Scotland), Burchill (b. Nov.27, 1959, Glasgow), Brian McGee (drums) and Duncan Barnwell (guitar), all ex-Self Abusers.

May Now joined by McNeil (b. July 20, 1958) who has previously played keyboards with a variety of local bands, and Derek Forbes

(bass) ex-Subs, the band records a 6-song demo at Glasgow's Ca Va studios. This comes to the attention of Ian Cranna (then contributor to UK music paper **New Musical Express**, later manager of Orange Juice) and Edinburgh record store owner Bruce Findlay. Band gigs heavily in Scotland, including a residency at Glasgow's Mars bar.

Nov Barnwell quits. Remaining quintet records another demo at Ca Va, subsequently releasing through Edinburgh indie label, Zoom (run by Findlay and licensed to Arista). The deal means Arista retains control of Simple Minds regardless of their own commitment to Zoom.

1979 Jan Band, now with settled line-up of Forbes, MacNeil, Kerr, Burchill and McGee, begins recording debut album at the Farmhouse studios, Amersham, Bucks.

May Group enlists the services of John Leckie, whose production work with Magazine had impressed it, and records debut album *Life In A Day*. It reaches UK #30 in its first week of release, spending a further 5 weeks retreating. Title track reaches UK #62.

They spend the rest of the year gigging extensively in UK and Europe, with 2 appearances on BBC2 TV's "Old Grey Whistle Test" (including a session shot live at New York's Hurrah club during their first US visit in Oct.) and recording a second, more experimental album.

1980 Jan *Real To Real Cacophony* is released. According to a reviewer it is probably the most uncommercial album ever released by Arista.

Feb The album fails to chart, as does single *Changeling*. Zoom folds, and Simple Minds continue on the main Arista label. Findlay joins business lawyer, Robert White, to form Schoolhouse Management (which will handle Simple Mind's future affairs).

Aug [26] Group supports The Skids at Hammersmith Palais, London.

Sept *Empires And Dance* charts for 3 weeks, reaching UK #41. It impresses Peter Gabriel who invites the group to open for him on a lengthy European tour.

Oct As *I Travel* fails to chart, the band looks for a new record deal.

1981 Feb Arista releases *Celebrate* which also fails. Simple Minds have negotiated their departure from Arista, renouncing their rights to back royalties, and sign to Virgin. They enter the studio with new heart, recording a prodigious amount of material.

May First release on Virgin, *The American*, reaches UK #59.

Aug *Love Song*, from a forthcoming album, makes UK #47.

Sept Simple Minds release 2 albums *Sons And Fascinations* and *Sister Feelings Call*, both produced by Steve Hillage, in an unusual double package, initially made available as a limited-edition double album, and subsequently released separately. The double album peaks at UK #11 during a 7-week stay.

McGee quits, citing exhaustion, to be replaced by ex-Zones drummer Kenny Hyslop.

Nov *Sweat In Bullet* stalls at UK #52.

1982 Jan 2 days after recording a new single for Apr. release, the band sets off on a European tour.

Feb Arista releases a compilation of early Simple Minds tracks, *Celebration*, which makes UK #45. *I Travel* is reissued, but fails to chart.

Apr *Promised You A Miracle*, from the next album, peaks at UK #13 in an 11-week stay. Hyslop quits, to be replaced first by Mark Ogletree, then Mel Gaynor (b. May 29, 1959), veteran sessioneer for the likes of Tina Charles, The Nolan Sisters, etc.

Aug *Glittering Prize* reaches UK #16.

Sept *New Gold Dream (81, 82, 83, 84)*, produced by Steve Walsh, is released with work from all 3 drummers, although Gaynor's contributions predominate. The album confirms Simple Minds' increasing popularity, spending a year in the UK Album chart, peaking at UK #3. Band begins a sold-out UK tour.

Oct Having bought the entire Arista Simple Minds back catalog, Virgin reissues all 4 albums.

Nov Third single from *New Gold Dream*, *Someone Somewhere (In Summertime)* makes UK #36. Its 12" release includes *King Is White And In The Crowd*, a BBC radio/session track recorded for the David Jensen program.

1983 Feb Simple Minds begin to make an impression in US, where *New Gold Dream* begins a 19-week stay on chart, reaching #69.

Nov *Waterfront*, marking the group's first collaboration with producer Steve Lillywhite, makes UK #13.

1984 Jan *Speed Your Love To Me* featuring Kirsty MacColl on guest vocals peaks at UK #20.

Feb Steve Lillywhite-produced *Sparkle In The Rain* begins a 57-week stay on UK chart, and is Simple Minds' first UK #1 album, while reaching US #64. (Lillywhite has been introduced to Kerr via mutual friend U2's Bono.)

Mar *Up On The Catwalk* reaches UK #27.

[13] A UK tour is cancelled after Kerr falls ill at end of the opening night in Birmingham, W.Midlands.

May Simple Minds play 8 consecutive nights at London's Hammersmith Odeon, tying with Elton John's 1982 record. John Giblin replaces Forbes on bass.

[5] Kerr marries Chrissie Hynde, following which Simple Minds support Hynde's Pretenders on US tour.

1985 Apr Simple Minds achieve a breakthrough in US with Keith Forsey and Steve Chiff-written *Don't You Forget About Me*, from the soundtrack to US "brat-pack" movie "The Breakfast Club". Their first release that is not self-penned, it had been offered to Billy Idol and Bryan Ferry. It hits US #1, spending 22 weeks on chart (rewarding their US record company who were responsible for its inclusion in the film), and UK #7, spending more than half a year on UK chart.

May Soundtrack *The Breakfast Club* includes the Simple Minds cut, the only album which will feature the hit.

July [13] Simple Minds perform at Live Aid in Philadelphia, PA. Their song *Ghostdancing* is dedicated to Amnesty International, an organization for which they tour later in the year.

Aug A consistent seller, *Don't You Forget About Me* re-enters at UK #61.

Oct Group's new UK #1 album, *Once Upon A Time*, will earn platinum status during an 82-week chart stay. (Released through A&M contract in US, it will hit US #10 in Mar.1986.) Anthemic *Alive And Kicking* hits UK #7 and US #3.

Dec Band begins an extensive world tour.

1986 Jan *Sanctify Yourself* hits UK #10.

Mar *All The Things She Said* hits UK #9.

[15] *Sanctify Yourself* reaches US #14.

Apr [20] The combined Simple Minds/Rod Stewart soccer XI beat Pepperdine 2-0.

May [31] *All The Things She Said* reaches US #28.

June [22] Simple Minds top the bill at the Milton Keynes Bowl Pop Festival, Bucks.

Aug [12] The final date of a world tour in Paris, France, is recorded for future live album release.

Nov A live version of *Ghostdancing* reaches UK #13.

1987 June Third successive UK platinum album *Live In The City Of Light*, a double live set recorded in Sydney, Australia, and Paris, enters UK chart at #1 and will rise to US #96.

July *Promised You A Miracle* makes UK #50, taken from the live album.

1988 June [11] Group plays "Nelson Mandela's 70th Birthday Party" at Wembley Stadium, London, much to the displeasure of Scottish MP Nicholas Fairburn who describes Kerr and fellow performer Annie Lennox as "left-wing scum". They record *Mandela* which they pledge not to release, which is aired on UK radio.

1989 Feb *Belfast Child*, produced by Trevor Horn and based on traditional song "She Moved Through The Fair", tops UK chart for 2 weeks. (At 6 mins. 39 secs., it becomes the second longest UK #1 behind The Beatles' *Hey Jude*.)

Apr *This Is Your Land* reaches UK #13.

May [13] *Street Fighting Years*, concentrating on non-personal themes including Belfast, ecology and anti-apartheid issues, enters UK chart at #1 and goes on to peak at US #70.

[15] Lengthy world tour begins in Italy. They will not perform at the scheduled Murrayfield stadium, Edinburgh, Scotland, date due to Kerr's objection to the venue's administrators allowing Scottish rugby players to attend the sport's centenary celebrations in South Africa.

July [23] UK tour leg starts at Rounday Park, Leeds, W.Yorks., and will end at Wembley Stadium, London, on Aug.26.

Kick It In reaches UK #15.

Dec EP *The Amsterdam EP*, including Simple Mind's version of Prince's *Sign Of The Times*, reaches UK #18. Following the end of their world trek, Kerr and Birchill retreat to Amsterdam to begin writing for their next album. A series of personnel upheavals has left the pair as the only permanent nucleus of Simple Minds.

1990 May Virgin Video releases "Verona", a live performance film taped on the band's last world tour.

June They enter their own highland studio in Scotland to begin recording with Steve Lipson helming production. New line-up includes band stalwart Gaynor on drums, Malcolm Foster on bass and session player Peter Vitesse on keyboards.

Oct [12] Virgin Records release *Themes: Volume 1*, the first of 4 CD only mini box sets each of which includes 4 disks devoted to chronologically recalling all of Simple Minds' 12" single releases. *Themes: Volume 2, ...3*, and *...4* will be released, 1 a week, for the following 3 weeks.

1991 Jan Band completes recording and mixing in London and Los Angeles studios.

Mar *Let There Be Love* trailers parent album *Real Life*.

Apr World tour opens in US, set to reach UK and Europe in Aug.

SIMPLY RED

Mick Hucknall (vocals)
Sylvan Richardson (guitar)
Fritz McIntyre (keyboards)
Tony Bowers (bass)
Chris Joyce (drums)
Tim Kellett (horns)

1984 Manchester-based band The Frantic Elevators, focused around singer/writer Hucknall (b. June 8, 1960, Manchester, Gtr.Manchester), raised by his father, a barber, and his aunt Nellie, an ex-local club DJ and art college student, since 1980, splits after releasing several singles on local UK labels, including *You Know What (Eric's)*, *Searchin' For The Only One* (Crackin' Up), *Voices In The Dark* (TJM) and *Holding Back The Years* (No Waiting), between 1979 and 1983. Hucknall forms a new band, Simply Red, with the initial line-up of David Fryman, Sherwood, Ojo and Mog, named after his distinctive red hair.

1985 Group signs a worldwide deal with Elektra Records, after Seymour Stein of US Sire has shown earlier interest, and begins recording in Amsterdam, Holland, with its new line-up Hucknall, Richardson (guitar), McIntyre (keyboards), Kellett (trumpet) and ex-Duritti Column members Bowers (bass) and Joyce (drums).

July Debut single dance-aimed *Money's Too Tight (To Mention)*, a cover of The Valentine Brothers 1983 UK #73, reaches UK #13. Group supports James Brown in concert in London.

Sept *Come To My Aid* makes UK #66.

Oct Debut album *Picture Book*, produced by Stewart Levine, and showcasing Hucknall's gifted and distinctive soul vocal range, reaches UK #34.

Nov Ballad *Holding Back The Years*, a re-recording of a Frantic Elevators song, reaches UK #51, despite 4 different format releases.

1986 Mar Moody *Jericho* climbs to UK #53 and the band embarks on its first US tour.

July *Holding Back The Years* is reissued in the UK now hitting #2 as worldwide sales top the million mark. *Picture Book* reaches US #16.

[12] *Holding Back The Years* tops US chart for 1 week. It was written by Hucknall with ex-Frantic Elevator Neil Smith, when Hucknall was 19.

Aug *Open Up The Red Box* makes UK #61.

Oct [4] *Money's Too Tight To Mention*, reissued as US follow-up although originally released in Aug.1985, reaches US #28.

1987 Mar *The Right Thing* reaches UK #11. New Alex Sadkin-produced album *Men And Women* hits UK #2 and US #31. The album, including songs by Cole Porter, Sly Stone and Bunny Wailer, is banned in Singapore because of "crude lyrics" in *The Right Thing*. Debut album *Picture Book* picks up renewed sales and now hits UK #2. Band adds new members, Aziz Ibrahim (guitar), replacing Richardson, Ian Kirkham (sax) and Janette Sewell (vocals).

May [16] *The Right Thing* reaches US #27.

June *Infidelity*, co-written by Lamont Dozier, reaches UK #31.

July *Maybe Someday* fails to chart.

Dec *Ev'rytime We Say Goodbye*, a Cole Porter revival previously issued by Simply Red as a bonus track on 12" version of *The Right Thing*, reaches UK #11, and features guest cellist Eleanor Morris.

1988 Feb [17] Group embarks on UK tour at the RDS Hall, Dublin, Eire, set to end Mar.16 at the NEC Birmingham, W.Midlands.

Mar *I Won't Feel Bad* peaks at UK #68.

1989 Jan Soul ballad *It's Only Love* reaches UK #13. UK tabloid **Daily Mirror** publishes article criticizing supposedly left-wing Hucknall for living as a tax exile in Milan, Italy.

Feb [25] Parent album *A New Flame*, produced by Levine and recorded in Montserrat, West Indies, enters at UK #1, for the first of 4 weeks. It also features tracks penned by Hucknall with Lamont Dozier and The Crusaders' Joe Sample. Simply Red, with new guitarist Heitor T.P. replacing Ibrahim (vocalist Sewell is no longer with the band), embarks on major world tour.

Mar [25] *It's Only Love* peaks at US #57.

Apr Remake of Harold Melvin & The Bluenotes' soul classic *If You Don't Know Me By Know* hits UK #2.

June *A New Flame* reaches US #22 during a 39-week residence.

July Title track *A New Flame* reaches UK #17.

[15] *If You Don't Know Me By Now* hits US # for 1 week, their second

US chart-topper.
Oct Ballad *You've Got It* makes UK #46.

1990 Feb [21] *If You Don't Know Me By Now* wins Best Rhythm & Blues Song at the 32nd annual Grammy awards at the Shrine Auditorium, Los Angeles, CA.

1991 Simply Red begins recording fourth album with producer Stewart Levine in Milan.

SIOUXSIE & THE BANSHEES

Siouxsie Sioux (vocals)
John McGeoch (guitar)
Steve Severin (bass)
Kenny Morris (drums)

1976 Sept [20] Bromley, Kent, punkette Siouxsie (b. Susan Dallion, May 27, 1957, London) takes part in the 100 club Punk Festival in London, with Sid Vicious on drums, Steve Havoc on bass and Marco Pironi on guitar. Their live set, featuring Siouxsie reciting The Lord's Prayer, lasts 20 mins. Band splits immediately. (Havoc will revert to the name Steve Severin, Vicious will join The Sex Pistols, and Pironi will join The Models before becoming Adam Ant's songwriting partner in Adam & The Ants.)
Dec [1] Siouxsie appears with The Sex Pistols on UK TV show "Today". Morris joins The Banshees on drums.

1977 Feb [24] Pete Fenton joins on guitar.
July [2] John McKay replaces Fenton.
Oct [20] After Johnny Thunders & The Heartbreakers' Rainbow theater gig, at which The Banshees are support act, Siouxsie and Morris are arrested and detained overnight at Holloway Road Police Station. They are fined £20 each for obstruction and released the following morning.
Nov Band sings *Make Up To Break Up* on its debut UK TV appearance.
[29] They record a session for John Peel's radio show.

1978 June [9] Group signs to Polydor Records.
[21] Siouxsie & The Banshees appear with The Clash, The Sex Pistols and Generation X in Don Lett's film "Punk Rock Movie". (Group was filmed for Derek Jarman's "Jubilee" but the clip was never used.)
Sept After much word-of-mouth and media interest, debut single *Hong Kong Garden* hits UK #7.
Oct [11] Band starts first major UK tour, with Nico and Human League as support.
Dec *The Scream*, produced by the band and Steve Lillywhite, reaches UK #12.

1979 Apr [7] Group plays a charity concert for MENCAP and is later faced with a £2,000 bill for seat damage.
[28] *The Staircase (Mystery)* peaks at UK #24.
July *Playground Twist* climbs to UK #28.
Sept *Join Hands* reaches UK #13. Morris and McKay leave midway through a tour, and after 5 days of panic, the others are temporarily joined for the balance of the dates by Pete "Budgie" (formerly with The Slits) on drums, and Robert Smith (on loan from The Cure) on guitar.
Oct [3] Siouxsie is hospitalized with hepatitis.
[29] *Mittageisen (Metal Postcard)* makes a disappointing UK #47.

1980 Jan [16] With Smith committed to The Cure, John McGeoch (moonlighting from Magazine) joins temporarily on guitar.
Apr *Happy House*, produced by band and Nigel Gray, makes UK #17.
June *Christine* makes UK #24.
July McGeoch joins on guitar full-time (but at first still "unofficially", so that he can continue with other projects).
Aug *Kaleidoscope* hits UK #5.
Oct Band tours US for the first time.
Nov *Israel* climbs to UK #41.

1981 Feb Group embarks on 11-date UK tour.
Mar Severin produces Altered Images' *Dead Pop Stars*.
June *Spellbound* makes UK #22.
[18] The Banshees play their first Iron Curtain concert in Yugoslavia before embarking on what they state will be their last UK tour.
July *Juju* hits UK #7.
Aug *Arabian Nights* reaches UK #32, while the band is on a major 30-date UK tour.
[10] Group plays a charity concert for the Disabled Children's International Games.
Oct Siouxsie and Budgie start a spin-off project as The Creatures, recording *Mad-Eyed Screamers*, which makes UK #24.
Dec Compilation album *Once Upon A Time* reaches UK #21 and is also issued as a video collection. Group tours again in US.

1982 June *Fire Works* reaches UK #22. Siouxsie contracts laryngitis and is ordered to rest her voice for 6 months.
Oct *Slow Dive* makes UK #41.
Nov *A Kiss In The Dreamhouse*, produced by Mike Hedges (and including the band's first recordings with string accompaniment) reaches UK #11. Smith is borrowed from The Cure again for the tour to promote the album when McGeoch falls ill. (Without returning, McGeoch will announce within a few weeks that he has left the group, apparently dissatisfied with Siouxsie's attitude.)
Dec *Melt*, a double A-side with the French-language Christmas song *Il Est Né Le Divin Enfant*, makes UK #49.

1983 Most of the first half of the year is spent on solo/spin-off projects, as Siouxsie and Budgie record The Creatures album *Feast*, while Severin and Smith (who has stayed on as a Banshee in addition to his Cure commitments) form The Glove. Both projects will be released on The Banshees' newly-formed Wonderland Records, through Polydor.
May The Creatures reach UK #21 with *Miss The Girl*.
Aug Their follow up *Right Now*, originally recorded by Mel Torme as the B-side to his 1963 *Comin' Home Baby* hit, makes UK #14.
Sept [6] Group plays a concert in Italy for the communist party.
Oct A revival of the Lennon/McCartney song *Dear Prudence* gives the group its biggest UK single success, hitting #3.
[31] Band plays first of 2 concerts at the Royal Albert Hall, London, which are recorded for live album release (second is Nov.1).
Dec Live double album *Nocturne*, is the first album release on the new Wonderland label. It reaches UK #29.

1984 Apr *Swimming Horses* makes UK #28.
May Smith leaves to concentrate on The Cure and is replaced on guitar by John Carruthers (ex-Clock DVA).
June *Dazzle* peaks at UK #33. *Hyena* reaches UK #15, as the band appears in a Channel 4 TV special.
July *Hyena*, released in US by Geffen Records, becomes the group's first US success, at #157.
Nov EP *Overground*, featuring string-backed (courtesy of The Chandos Players) renditions of songs like *Overground* and *Placebo Effect*, makes UK #47.

1985 Oct Band plays a month-long UK tour, after 2 attempts at beginning a new studio album with 2 different producers, Bob Ezrin and Hugh Jones. Siouxsie spends much of the tour with a leg in plaster, after dislocating a kneecap on stage at London's Hammersmith Odeon.
Nov *Cities In Dust* reaches UK #21.

1986 Jan Group guests in film "Out Of Bounds".
Mar *Candy Man* reaches UK #34.
May *Tinderbox*, produced by the band with Steve Churchyard, reaches UK #13.
July *Tinderbox* makes US #88.

1987 Feb A cover of Bob Dylan's *This Wheel's On Fire*, originally a UK hit for Julie Driscoll and The Brian Auger Trinity, reaches UK #14.
Mar Carruthers leaves, to be replaced by John Klein (ex-Specimen) and Martin McCarrick joins on keyboards. *Through The Looking Glass*, a set of cover versions, reaches UK #15.
Apr *The Passenger*, a revival of an Iggy Pop song, makes UK #41.
Through The Looking Glass peaks at US #188.
July Band makes a one-off live London appearance at the Finsbury Park "Supertent".
Aug *Song From The Edge Of The World* reaches UK #39.

1988 Aug *Peek A Boo* shows a shift in the group's musical direction and peaks at UK #16.
Sept *Peepshow* reaches UK #20, as the group begins another UK tour.
Oct *The Killing Jar* makes UK #41.
Dec [3] *The Last Beat Of My Heart* peaks at UK #44 as *Peek A Boo* makes US #53 and parent album *Peepshow*, on Geffen, climbs to US #68.

1989 Oct The Creatures' *Standing There* makes UK #53.

1990 Mar [20] The Creatures make their North American live debut in Toronto, Canada.

SIR DOUGLAS QUINTET

Doug Sahm (vocals, guitar)
Augie Meyers (organ)
Jack Barber (bass)
Johnny Perez (drums)
Frank Morin (horns)

1964 Sahm (b. Nov.6, 1941, San Antonio, TX), having recorded *A Real American Joe* as Little Doug for Texas label Sarg in 1955, and turned down a chance to join the "Grand Ole Opry" in order to finish school, spends some years in local bar bands and forms Sir Douglas Quintet, with Morin, Meyers, Barber and Perez.

1965 **May** Band signs to Huey Meaux' Tribe label, and *She's About A Mover*, with a British-beat Vox organ riff from Meyers, climbs to US #13.

July *She's About A Mover* reaches UK #15.

Aug Similarly-styled follow-up *The Tracker* fails to chart.

Nov [5] Group appears on commercial TV's "Ready Steady Go!" and gigs during 2-week stay in UK.

1966 **Mar** *The Rains Came* reaches US #31. Debut album, *The Sir Douglas Quintet*, is released, to limited interest.

As the year progresses, the initial novelty of the Quintet wears off, and with a drug bust in Texas hanging over him, Sahm breaks up the band and moves to California.

1968 Sahm cuts *Honkey Blues* with Morin and session musicians, as Sir Douglas Quintet + 2.

1969 Sahm re-forms the original Quintet, with Harvey Kagan replacing Barber, and George Rains replacing Perez, and the band signs to Mercury's Smash label.

Mar Smash debut *Mendocino* makes US #27.

Mendocino peaks at US #81.

Aug *Dynamite Woman* reaches US #83.

1970 **June** *Together After Five* is popular in Europe. *1+1+1=4* is issued.

1971 *Return Of Douglas Saldana* is released (the last on Smash), but goes unnoticed.

1973 **Mar** Sahm breaks up band again to go solo, and *Doug Sahm And Band* on Atlantic makes US #125. Produced by Jerry Wexler and Arif Mardin, it includes contributions by Bob Dylan (*Wallflower*) and Dr. John.

1974 He links with Creedence Clearwater Revival's rhythm section on *Groover's Paradise* for Warner Bros.

1976 Sahm, with the quintet's original producer, Meaux, records *Rock For Country Rollers* on Dot.

1977 Live album, *Live Love*, is released in US on Meyers' Texas label.

1979 Sahm appears in film "More American Graffiti".

1980 *Hell Of A Spell* is released, without success, on Takoma label.

1981 **Feb** Group re-forms again, with original members Sahm, Meyers and Perez joined by Alvin Crow (guitar, vocals), Speedy Sparks (bass) and Shawn Sahm (guitars, vocals) for *Border Wave*, a new wave flavored comeback on Takoma (Chrysalis in UK), produced by Craig Leon and Cassell Webb. Despite the contemporary sound, it makes only US #184.

1988 Having spent most of the 80s touring, Sahm forms a new group, The Almost Brothers, with guitarist Amos Garrett and ex-Blasters pianist Gene Taylor.

1990 **Aug** Sahm and Meyers team with country singer Freddy Fender and accordionist Flaco Jiminez to form The Texas Tornados, releasing *Texas Tornados*.

THE SISTERS OF MERCY

Andrew Eldritch (vocals)
Gary Marx (guitar)
Ben Gunn (guitar)
Craig Adams (bass)

1980 Band, initially studio bound, is formed in Leeds, W.Yorks., with Oxford University-educated Eldritch, Marx, and a drum machine named Doktor Avalanche. Debut single *The Damage Done* is released on their own independently-distributed Merciful Release label. In order to play live, Eldritch and Marx recruit Gunn and Adams. They tour, as support to Nico, The Birthday Party, The Clash and The Psychedelic Furs.

1982 **Apr** Second release *Body Electric*, on Leeds-based Confederacion Nacional de Trabajo label, sells well to a growing cult following and gets good UK music press reviews.

June Band arranges a distribution deal for Merciful Release with York-based Red Rhino, part of independent distributor The Cartel. While touring UK, The Sisters record a BBC Radio 1 session for "The John Peel Show".

Oct Another Leeds group, The March Violets, is signed to Merciful Release, and the bands begin a UK tour together.

Nov A row between the 2 bands flares up and The Violets leave the label to form their own Rebirth Records. The Sisters Of Mercy release *Alice* which climbs the UK Independent chart.

1983 **Mar** *Anaconda* fails.

May 5-track EP *Reptile House* hits top of the Independent charts and sells on export.

June Gunn leaves after disagreements within the band and is replaced by Wayne Hussey, who has worked with Pauline Murray, Dead Or Alive and ska-punk group The Walkie Talkies.

Oct After the release of *Temple Of Love* the group signs a distribution deal with WEA.

1984 **June** *Body And Soul* reaches UK #46.

Oct *Walk Away*, written by Eldritch and Hussey, also makes UK #46.

1985 **Feb** *No Time To Cry* peaks at UK #63.

Apr Debut album *First And Last And Always* reaches UK #14, with impressive sales in the North of England.

More problems arise in the group; Eldritch's lifestyle causes him health problems and Marx, overshadowed by Hussey, refuses to attend soundchecks. On a European tour, Eldritch issues an ultimatum – either Marx leaves or he does. Marx leaves. A concert at London's Royal Albert Hall is filmed (and will be released on video as "Wake" – the title, many assume, alludes to the last Sisters Of Mercy concert. Immediately afterwards the group announces its decision to split. (Hussey and Adams will form The Mission, and Eldritch moves to Hamburg, Germany.

1986 **July** Amid legal tangles over the use of The Sisters Of Mercy name, Eldritch releases *Gift* as The Sisterhood. It manages a 1-week stay on UK chart at #95.

1987 **Oct** Eldritch and Patricia Morrison (ex-Gun Club) return as The Sisters Of Mercy, and *This Corrosion* hits UK #7.

1988 **Mar** The new Sisters' second single, *Dominion*, reaches UK #13. *Floodland* hits UK #9 and will make US #101.

June *Lucretia My Reflection* makes UK #20.

1990 **Oct** [20] With its new line-up of Eldritch, ex-Gen X and Sigue Sigue Sputnik Tony James, ex-All About Eve Tim Bricheno (b. July 6, 1963, Huddersfield, W.Yorks.) and Andreas Bruh, first recording in over 2 years *More* reaches UK #14.

Nov [2] *Vision Thing* peaks at UK debut #11.

Dec [15] *Vision Thing* climbs to US #136.

SLADE

Noddy Holder (guitar, vocals)
Dave Hill (guitar)
Jimmy Lea (bass, piano, violin)
Don Powell (drums)

1964 Hill (b. Apr.4, 1952, Fleet Castle, Devon) and Powell (b. Sept.10, 1950, Bilston, W.Midlands) play in Wolverhampton band, The Vendors, with Johnny Howells (vocals), Mickey Marston (guitar) and Dave Jones (bass). They do not record commercially, but make a 4-song demo EP.

1965 The Vendors become The 'N Betweens and record under their new name, with session drummer Bobby Graham producing. The results, only released in France on Barclay label EPs, include versions of The Sorrows' *Take A Heart* and Rufus Thomas' *Can Your Monkey Do The Dog*. Meanwhile, Holder (b. Neville Holder, June 15, 1950, Walsall, W.Midlands.) is guitarist and backing vocalist in Wolverhampton's Steve Brett & The Mavericks, and plays on their Dec.1965 Columbia single *Chains On My Heart*.

1966 Holder and Lea (b. June 14, 1952, Melbourne Arms, Wolverhampton, W.Midlands) join Hill and Powell in The 'N Betweens when the others leave, thus completing the future Slade line-up.

Nov The 'N Betweens cover The Young Rascals' *You Better Run* on Columbia; the group's last release under this name.

1969 **Feb** After playing mostly covers (Motown, Beatles, ska) on the Midlands club circuit, they move to London. Now named Ambrose Slade, they are seen at Rasputin's club by Chas Chandler, ex-The Animals, who launched Jimi Hendrix's career in UK. Chandler becomes their manager/producer and, in an attempt to cash in on first UK skinhead cult, dresses them in boots, braces and short-cropped hair. He arranges a recording contract with Fontana.

Apr Ambrose Slade releases its only album under that name, *Beginnings*. It sells poorly (as does *Genesis/Roach Daddy*, issued in May).

Oct At Chandler's suggestion, the band shortens its name to Slade for next Fontana release, *Wild Winds Are Blowing*, but it fares no better.

1970 **Mar** *The Shape Of Things To Come*, a cover of a US hit by Max Frost and The Troopers, is the band's last Fontana single, and again fails, despite a grand launch to press and media at London's Bag O' Nails club.

Sept Debut Polydor release, *Know Who You Are*, also fails.

Nov *Play It Loud* is released, but fails to chart.

1971 **June** *Get Down And Get With It*, a revival of a Bobby Marchan song, best known via Little Richard's version, reaches UK #16.

Nov [14] Follow-up *Coz I Luv You* hits UK #1 for 4 weeks. (The band are playing a pub gig at the Black Prince in Bexley, Kent, the day the record hits #1.) It is the first of 6 chart-toppers and a 5-year run of top 20 hits, all penned by Holder and Lea. It also launches the distinctive trademark of personalized spellings of titles.

Dec [24] Group plays a Christmas Eve party gig at London's Marquee.

1972 **Feb** *Look Wot You Dun* hits UK #4.

Apr *Slade Alive* hits UK #2 (and remains on UK chart for over a year).

May [10] Group begins its first major headlining UK tour, supported by Status Quo, in Bradford, W.Yorks.

July *Take Me Bak 'Ome* tops UK chart for a week.

Sept *Mama Weer All Crazee Now* hits UK #1 for 3 weeks.

Oct *Take Me Back 'Ome* is Slade's first US chart entry, at #97, while *Slade Alive* makes US #158.

Dec *Gudbuy T'Jane* hits UK #2, behind Chuck Berry's *My Ding-A-Ling*.

1973 **Jan** *Slayed* tops UK chart for 3 weeks, as *Mama Weer All Crazee Now* makes US #76.

Feb *Slayed* reaches US #69.

Mar *Cum On Feel The Noize* hits UK #1 for 4 weeks, confirming Slade with the most successful run of UK hit singles achieved by a group in the post-Beatles era.

Apr *Gudbuy T'Jane* makes US #68.

June *Skweeze Me Pleeze Me* tops UK chart for 3 weeks, while *Cum On Feel The Noize* stalls at US #98.

July [4] Powell is badly injured in a car crash, in which his girlfriend Angela Morris is killed. (He will be hospitalized for 6 weeks, and will suffer memory problems as a result of his head injuries for some months. He will return to his drumkit, eventually fit again.)

Oct *Sladest* tops UK chart for 3 weeks, and makes US #129. *My Friend Stan* hits UK #2, behind Simon Park Orchestra's million-selling *Eye Level*.

Dec *Merry Christmas Everybody*, recorded in New York during a US tour, enters UK chart at #1, staying on top 5 weeks. After selling over a quarter million copies in its first day, it becomes group's biggest single, selling over a million in UK (it will re-chart every Christmas 1981-86).

1974 **Mar** *Old, New, Borrowed And Blue*, is band's third consecutive UK #1 album, as US-only *Stomp Your Hands, Clap Your Feet* makes US #168.

Apr *Everyday* hits UK #3.

July *Bangin' Man* also hits UK #3. Slade spends the rest of the year working on its feature film, "Flame".

Oct Hymnal *Far Far Away*, an early taster of "Flame" soundtrack, hits UK #2.

Dec Soundtrack album, *Slade In Flame*, hits UK #6 as movie opens in UK. Title is name of a mid-60s band which Slade portrays in the film (which also stars Tom Conti, Alan Lake and UK DJs Tommy Vance and Emperor Rosko).

1975 **Mar** *How Does It Feel* reaches UK #15, ending a run of 12 Top 5 hits.

May *Thanks For The Memory (Wham Bam Thank You Mam)* hits UK #7.

July *Slade In Flame* makes US #93.

Sept [12] The group's movie "Flame" has its first US showing, in St. Louis, MO. (It will make little impression in US.)

Dec *In For A Penny* reaches UK #11.

1976 **Feb** *Let's Call It Quits* also peaks at UK #11.

Mar *Nobody's Fool* makes UK #14. Group leaves Polydor for manager/producer Chandler's own label, Barn Records.

1977 **Feb** Debut Barn single *Gypsy Roadhog* peaks at UK #48.

Apr *Burning In The Heat Of Love* fails to chart.

Nov A rock medley of 2 early Elvis Presley items, *My Baby Left Me/That's All Right Mama* reaches UK #42.

1978 **Mar** *Give Us A Goal* shows Slade's affinity with UK soccer terraces, but fails to chart.

Nov *Rock 'N' Roll Bolero* and *Slade Alive, Vol.2* fail to chart in UK.

Dec Lea and brother Frankie form The Dummies as a sideline from Slade, releasing 3 singles, without chart success.

1979 The last 3 Barn singles, *Ginny Ginny* (May), *Sign Of The Times* (Oct.) and *Okey Cokey* (Dec.) all fail. *Okey Cokey* is reissued a month later by RSO label, but fares little better. There is also an unsuccessful album, *Return To Base* (Oct.).

1980 **June** Slade reappears on another Chandler label, Six Of The Best, which specializes in 6-song 12" EPs. Tracks include *Night Starvation* and *When I'm Dancin' I Ain't Fightin'*.

Oct *Slade Alive At Reading 80*, a 5-track EP recorded at the year's Reading Rock Festival, Berks., and released on Chandler's Cheapskate label, reaches UK #44, the group's first Singles chart entry for 3 years.

Nov Polydor's TV-advertised *Slade Smashes* reaches UK #21.

Dec A live version of *Merry Christmas Everybody*, recorded at Reading Festival, makes UK #70.

1981 **Feb** *We'll Bring The House Down* hits UK #10, the group's first Top 10 for 6 years.

Mar *We'll Bring The House Down* reaches UK #25.

Apr *Wheels Ain't Comin' Down* stalls at UK #60.

Sept *Lock Up Your Daughters*, the group's first single in a newly-signed deal with RCA, reaches UK #29.

Nov *Till Deaf Us Do Part* makes UK #68.

1982 **Mar** [19] Group begins an 11-date UK tour at Apollo theater, Oxford, Oxon. It will end Apr.2 at Colston Hall, Bristol, Avon.

Apr *Ruby Red* peaks at UK #51.

Dec *(And Now The Waltz) C'Est La Vie* makes UK #50, with a live version of seasonal favorite *Merry Christmas Everybody* on the B-side, in competition to Polydor's annual reissue of it. Live album, *Slade On Stage*, makes UK #58.

1983 **Sept** US heavy metal group Quiet Riot hits US #5 and makes UK #45 with a copycat revival of *Cum On Feel The Noize*, which restores the memory of Slade. (The new wave of US glam-metal bands is influenced by the pop-metal and gaudy image of UK bands like Slade and Sweet – for whom the US audience was unreceptive in the early 70s.)

Dec Slade produces one of its catchiest and most commercial singles, *My Oh My*, pitched at an ideal tempo for TV-massed swaying and scarf-waving, which it receives on "Top Of The Pops" and other shows. It hits UK #2, behind The Flying Pickets' *Only You*. *The Amazing Kamikaze Syndrome* makes UK #49.

1984 **Mar** *Run Run Away*, a more rock-oriented follow-up, hits UK #7.

May US album, *Keep Your Hands Off My Power Supply*, containing *Run Runaway*, reaches US #33.

June Polydor releases another hits compilation, *Slade's Greats*, which makes UK #89. *Run Runaway* reaches US #20, their biggest US hit.

Aug US follow-up, *My Oh My*, reaches US #37. Meanwhile, Quiet Riot's second Slade cover, *Mama Weer All Crazee Now*, makes US #51.

Nov *All Join Hands* makes UK #15.

1985 **Feb** *Seven Year Bitch* stalls at UK #60.

Apr *Myzsterious Mizter Jones* (a return to title misspelling) makes UK #50. *Rogues Gallery* reaches UK #50.

May *Little Sheila* makes UK #86.

Dec TV-advertised *Crackers: The Slade Christmas Party Album*, reaches UK #34; extracted *Do You Believe In Miracles* makes UK #54.

1987 **Feb** *Still The Same* makes UK #73.

May *You Boyz Make Big Noize* (a title suggested by the tea lady at the recording studio) makes UK #98.

1988 **Dec** Slade returns with a revival of Chris Montez' 1962 hit *Let's Dance*. (Subsequently the band members go their separate ways – Holder presents a rock revival show on Piccadilly Radio, Hill records a solo album, Lea produces heavy metal band Chrome Molly and Powell becomes an antique dealer.)

SLY & THE FAMILY STONE

Sly Stone (vocals, keyboards, guitar)
Freddie Stone (guitar)
Cynthia Robinson (trumpet)
Jerry Martini (saxes)
Rosemary Stone (vocals, piano)
Larry Graham (bass guitar)
Greg Errico (drums)

1966 DJ on Oakland, CA, station K-DIA and producer (The Beau Brummels, Bobby Freeman) Stone (b. Sylvester Stewart, Mar.15, 1944, Dallas, TX), having earlier formed The Stoners with Robinson (b. Jan.12, 1946), forms The Family Stone in San Francisco, adding brother Freddie (b. June 5, 1946), sister Rosemary (b. Mar.21, 1945) and cousin Graham (b. Aug.14, 1946, Beaumont, TX). The Family Stone starts gigging in bars and clubs in Oakland.

1967 Their iconoclastic collision of funk, jazz, rock and anarchic humor, soon tagged "psychedelic soul", extends their following to the city's emergent psychedelic movement. Group signs to Epic and releases *A Whole New Thing*.

1968 **Apr** *Dance To The Music* hits US #8.

May *Dance To The Music* reaches US #142.

July *Life/M'Lady* peaks at US #93.

Aug *Dance To The Music* hits UK #7.

Sept [11] Arriving in London to begin a tour, UK Customs find cannabis in Graham's possession.

BBC TV cancels a scheduled appearance and a week later the band leaves UK without having performed.

Oct *M'lady* makes UK #32.

Dec *Life* reaches US #195.

1969 **Feb** *Everyday People* hits US #1 for 4 weeks.

Mar *Everyday People* makes UK #36, while B-side *Sing A Simple Song* climbs to US #89.

May *Stand!* reaches US #22.

June *Stand!* makes US #13, and becomes the group's first gold disk. *I Want To Take You Higher*, B-side of *Stand!*, peaks at US #60.

July [3-6] For the first time, rock performers take part in the Newport Jazz Festival at Newport, RI. Sly & The Family Stone are featured on the bill with Led Zeppelin, James Brown and others.

Aug Band performs *I Want To Take You Higher* at the Woodstock Festival. Press reports suggest several members of The Family Stone have drug problems, and the band acquires a reputation for failing to show at scheduled gigs.

Oct *Hot Fun In The Summertime* hits US #2.

1970 Feb *Thank You (Falettinme Be Mice Elf Agin)* coupled with *Everybody Is A Star* hits US #1.

June Reissued *I Want To Take You Higher* makes US #38.

Nov *Greatest Hits* is released, hitting US #2 and bringing the group its second gold disk.

Dec By year end, the increasingly unreliable Stone has missed 26 of his scheduled 80 live appearances and is in mortgage trouble on the house he has bought in Los Angeles from John Phillips of Mamas And The Papas fame.

1971 Sept [4] **The New York Times** reports that Stone's Hollywood landlord is suing him for $3 million, claiming his building is inundated with "loud, noisy and boisterous persons" and he wants Stone to leave.

Dec *Family Affair* hits US #1 in 5 weeks, staying on top for 5 weeks. *There's A Riot Goin' On* also tops US chart.

1972 Jan *Family Affair* reaches UK #15. Graham leaves the group (to form Graham Central Station) and is replaced by Rusty Allen. Errico leaves to be replaced by Andy Newmark, and saxophonist Pat Ricco joins.

Mar *Runnin' Away* peaks at US #23. *There's A Riot Goin' On* makes UK #31.

May *Runnin' Away* reaches UK #17. *Smilin'* peaks at US #42.

Nov [25] Despite an impressive bill including Sly & The Family Stone, Los Angeles radio station K-ROQ's "The Woodstock Of The West" only attracts 32,000 to its 100,000-seater Los Angeles Coliseum.

1973 June *Fresh* hits US #7.

Sept *If You Want Me To Stay* makes US #12.

Dec *Frisky* peaks at US #79.

1974 Feb Graham Central Station's eponymous debut album makes US #48.

May Graham Central Station's *Can You Handle It?* makes US #49.

June [5] Stone marries Kathy Silva on stage before a gig at New York's Madison Square Garden.

Aug *Small Talk* picturing Stone, Silva and baby Sylvester Bubb Ali Stewart on the sleeve, reaches US #15. *Time For Living* makes US #32.

Oct [30] Silva files for divorce. Graham Central Station's *Release Yourself* makes US #51.

Nov *Loose Booty* is Sly & The Family Stone's last chart entry at US #84.

1975 Jan [16] Sly & The Family Stone begin a 6-night stand at New York's Radio City Music Hall. Attendances at the 8-date residency are less than one-third full.

Aug Graham Central Station album *Ain't No 'Bout-A-Doubt It* makes US #22 and goes gold. His *Your Love* reaches US #38.

Nov *High On You*, credited to Stone as a solo, makes US #45. Graham Central Station's *It's Alright* peaks at US #92.

1976 Jan Stone files for bankruptcy.

Mar Instrumental *The Jam* from Graham Central Station makes US #63.

June Graham Central Station's *Mirror* reaches US #46.

1977 Apr Graham Central Station's *Now Do U Wanta Dance* makes US #67.

1978 July Now credited as Larry Graham & Grand Central Station, album *My Radio Sure Sounds Good To Me* reaches US #105.

1979 July Graham's last album with Grand Central Station, *Star Walk*, reaches US #136.

Nov Sly & The Family Stone *Back On The Right Track* makes US #152.

1980 June Graham's solo album *One In A Million You* enters US chart on its way to #27 and a gold certification. Ballad title track also goes gold, hitting US #9.

Nov Graham's *When We Get Married* makes US #76.

1981 Mar Stone is featured on George Clinton and Funkadelic's *The Electric Spanking Of War Babies*.

Aug Graham's *Just Be My Lady* makes US #46.

Sept His *Just Be My Lady* reaches US #67.

1982 July Graham's *Sooner Or Later* peaks at US #142. Single of same name makes UK #54.

1983 Aug Graham's *Victory* makes US #173.

1984 Bobby Womack, having persuaded Stone to seek treatment for his drug addiction, invites him on a 2-month US tour.

1986 Reports say Stone has kicked his drug addiction and that several record labels are interested in signing him. There is also talk of an album with George Clinton.

Dec [27] Jesse Johnson's *Crazay*, featuring Sly Stone, makes US #53.

1987 Jan [29] Stone helps launch "Fight For Literacy Day" in California. *Family Affair* is reissued on CBS dance label Upfront.

1989 Nov Stone is arrested in Bridgeport, CT, and returned to Los Angeles.

Dec [1] Stone is sentenced to 55 days after pleading guilty to a misdemeanor charge of driving under the influence of cocaine.

[14] Stone pleads guilty in Santa Monica, CA, to 2 counts of possession of cocaine. He is sentenced to spend 9-14 months in a drug rehabilitation center, placed on 3 years probation and ordered into anti-drug program as alternative to county jail by Superior Court Judge Robert Altman. Charges stem from arrests in 1986 and 1987.

THE SMALL FACES

Steve Marriott (vocals, guitar)
Ronnie "Plonk" Lane (bass)
Jimmy Winston (organ)
Kenny Jones (drums)

1965 June Group is formed in London when Lane (b. Apr.1, 1946, Plaistow, London) and ex-Outcasts Jones (b. Sept.16, 1948, Stepney, London), who originally met while in the Army cadets and renewed their acquaintance in a Stepney pub, playing in a pub trio with Winston (b. James Langwith, Apr.20, 1945, Stratford, London), and looking for a strong singer or guitarist, find both in Marriott (b. Jan.30, 1947, Bow, London), whom they meet working in a music shop in East Ham, London. In showbiz since age 12 as an actor (appearing in the London production of "Oliver" and UK radio and TV plays and shows), he has cut a solo single (*Give Her My Regards* for Decca in 1963). They adopt the name Small Faces because of their lack of height and the Mod connotations of "Face". All are R&B fans, and they pitch the group directly at the Mod/R&B scene recently opened up by The Who.

Oct Signed to Decca, their debut is Ian Samwell-written/produced *Whatcha Gonna Do About It*, which borrows its rhythm structure from Solomon Burke's *Everybody Needs Somebody To Love* and adds some sawing pop-art guitar. It reaches UK #14.

Nov [1] Winston leaves, to be replaced by Ian McLagan (b. May 12, 1945, Hounslow, London), who comes recommended via a glowing review in **Beat Instrumental** magazine of his playing in Boz & The Boz People. At the same time, follow-up single *I've Got Mine* just misses the chart, and the group begins live work (notably in a residency at London's West End Cavern club, off Leicester Square) to build a firm following on which to launch subsequent disks.

1966 Mar *Sha La La La Lee*, written by Kenny Lynch and Mort Shuman, hits UK #3.

May *Hey Girl*, which hits UK #10, is the group's first Marriott/Lane-composed chartmaker.

[1] Group takes part in the annual **New Musical Express** Poll Winners Concert at the Empire Pool, Wembley, London.

June *The Small Faces* hits UK #3, staying on chart for 6 months.

[10] Marriott collapses while performing on commercial TV's "Ready Steady Go!" Group cancels the following week's gigs.

July [29] Band performs at the sixth annual National Jazz & Blues Festival, Windsor, Berks.

Aug [12] The Small Faces begin Radio England's "Swingin' 66" tour with Crispian St. Peters, Wayne Fontana, Neil Christian and Geneveve, at the Odeon cinema, Lewisham, London. Tour ends Aug.25 at Gaumont cinema, Southampton, Hants.

Sept Group has its first #1 when another Marriott/Lane song, *All Or Nothing*, tops UK chart for a week (deposing The Beatles' *Yellow Submarine/Eleanor Rigby*).

[25] Group plays a concert at Regal cinema, Gloucester, Glos., after a 2,000 signature petition to perform there is presented to them.

Oct [15] They begin a 20-date twice-nightly UK tour with The Hollies, The Nashville Teens, Paul & Barry Ryan, Paul Jones and others, at ABC cinema, Aldershot, Hants. Tour will end Nov.6 at City Hall, Newcastle.

Dec *My Mind's Eye*, again written by Marriott and Lane, hits UK #4 at Christmas (part of its melody is lifted from Christmas carol *Angels From The Realms Of Glory*). Already aware that Decca is trying to push a more polished version of the group on record than that seen in its raucous, stomping live gigs, they are amused when Decca releases a rough mix of the single instead of a more polished take – apparently in error.

1967 Mar *I Can't Make It* reaches UK #26, after which the group announces it is to leave Decca for Andrew Oldham's Immediate label.

[3] Group begins a 32-date twice-nightly UK tour with Roy Orbison,

P.P. Arnold, Paul & Barry Ryan and others, at Finsbury Park Astoria, London. Tour will close Apr.9 at ABC cinema, Romford, Essex.
May Decca releases a final single *Patterns* but, with no promotion from the group, it fails to chart.
[7] Group participates in the annual **New Musical Express** Poll Winners Concert at the Empire Pool, Wembley, London.
June Compilation *From The Beginning*, on Decca, reaches UK #17.
July *Here Comes The Nice* (with some oblique drug references, in tune with the rock mood of the time) reaches UK #12 and *Small Faces* also peaks at UK #12.
[8] Andrew Loog Oldham takes over the group's management from Robert Wace.
Aug [26] They appear at the Festival Of The Flower Children at Woburn Abbey, Beds.
Sept *Itchycoo Park*, the band's most elaborate and experimental production yet, with phased drums and spacey harmonies, hits UK #3.
[2] Group participates in TV spectacular to launch color television in Germany.

968
Jan *Tin Soldier*, another complex production, hits UK #9. *Itchycoo Park* is the group's first US hit single, peaking at #16. Group tours Australia with The Who (both groups are thrown off an aircraft for rowdy behavior while preparing to fly between Australian gigs).
Mar *There Are But Four Small Faces* makes US #178.
Apr *Tin Soldier* peaks at US #73.
May *Lazy Sunday*, eschewing the psychedelic tendencies of the 2 previous Lane/Marriott-penned singles, is a loping good-time rocker in Ray Davies/Kinks style, with Marriott vocalizing in an exaggerated cockney accent. Their biggest UK hit since *All Or Nothing*, it hits #2.
June Concept album, *Ogden's Nut Gone Flake*, tops UK chart for 6 weeks. One side features tracks linked by comedian Stanley Unwin, while the album's round cover (representing the lid of the Ogden's tobacco tin) is a gimmick selling point. Group subsequently refuses to play most tracks from the it when performing live.
Aug *The Universal*, almost free-form in approach, reaches UK #16.
Oct *Ogden's Nut Gone Flake* peaks at US #159. The Small Faces begin a UK package tour with The Who and Joe Cocker.
[19] Peter Frampton of The Herd sits in on guitar at a Small Faces gig, and strikes up a rapport with Marriott. (They begin to make plans to form a new group (which will become Humble Pie); Marriott in particular wants to gain rock credibility, aware of the teen tag still attaching to The Small Faces despite their more recent progressions.)

969
Jan [14] Group makes its US debut at the Fillmore East, New York.
Feb Marriott leaves and The Small Faces disband. Lane, Jones and McLagan stay together (to link up in June with guitarist Ron Wood (b. Ronald Wood, June 1, 1947, Hillingdon, London) and vocalist Rod Stewart (b. Roderick David Stewart, Jan.10, 1945, Highgate, London), and re-launch their career as The Faces.
Mar The final "new" Small Faces single, *Afterglow (Of Your Love)* (coupled with heavy rock spoof *Wham! Bam! Thank You Ma'm*), makes UK #36. Double *The Autumn Stone* is released at the same time, summarizing the group's career via both old and new material.
[8] Group plays its final show at Springfield theater, Jersey.

972
Aug *Early Faces*, compiled as a cash-in on the success of The Faces, and actually containing Small Faces Decca tracks, makes US #176.

973
Mar US reissue of *Ogden's Nut Gone Flake* reaches US #189.

976
Jan *Itchycoo Park* is reissued in UK, picks up strong airplay, and makes Top 10 for the second time, hitting #9.
Apr *Lazy Sunday*, also reissued on the strength of the previous success, makes US #39.
June Spurred by the interest in the group's old hits, Marriott (who has just disbanded Steve Marriott's All-Stars after a long US tour) re-forms the group, with Jones and McLagan rejoining, but Lane declining. Rick Wills comes in on bass instead.

977
Apr [13] Group begins its 11-date reunion tour of UK with a show in Sheffield, S.Yorks. (Group's resurrection has only been officially announced in Mar. though they have been rehearsing for some months while contractual wrangles were worked out.)
Aug *Playmates* by the new line-up fails to chart.
Sept Second UK tour is undertaken to promote the album, with Jimmy McCulloch (ex-Paul McCartney's Wings) temporarily on guitar.

978
May Group splits again after recording the material for a second album. (Jones will join The Who after Keith Moon's death, Wills will move to US to join Foreigner, McLagan will become a member of The Rolling Stones' augmenting road band and Marriott will continue to lead R&B groups into the 80s, mostly in small clubs and pubs.)
Sept *78 In The Shade* fails to chart, and – unlike The Small Faces

material of the 60s – is quickly forgotten.

1983
Sept [20] A benefit concert is held at London's Royal Albert Hall for Ronnie Lane, now suffering from multiple sclerosis. The superstar line-up includes Eric Clapton, Jeff Beck, Steve Winwood and Jimmy Page. (There will be intermittent charity benefits throughout the 80s as Lane continues to battle the disease.)

1991
Apr [20] Marriott dies in a fire in his 16th-century cottage in Arkesden, Essex.

PATTI SMITH

1969
Smith (b. Dec.30, 1946, Chicago, IL), having moved with her family from New Jersey to Paris, then to London and New York, starts a small local newspaper before working for **Rock** magazine.

1970
She spends much of her time writing poetry and meets Village Oldies record store clerk Lenny Kaye, who has previously recorded as Link Cromwell (and in 1973 will compile the legendary compilation album *Nuggets* for Elektra records).

1971
Feb Smith invites Kaye to accompany her poetry readings on guitar. They play support to Andy Warhol/Velvet Underground follower Gerard Malanga, at St. Mark's church, New York. She begins to write for rock monthly **Creem**.

1972
May A professional and personal relationship develops with playwright Sam Shepard, while she works as the opening act for artists at Mercer Art center for $5 a night. One of the bands she supports is The New York Dolls. 2 volumes of her poetry will be published (**Witt** and **Seventh Heaven**) by year's end.

1973
She re-units with Kaye for more readings at Le Jardin in New York, while a piano player, Richard (DNV) Sohl, also joins. They play in an "improv" style. Todd Rundgren's *A Wizard A True Star* includes a dedication to Patti Lee Smith, who had earlier nicknamed him "Runt".

1974
June Smith records *Hey Joe/Piss Factory* for Robert Mapplethorpe's Mer label. Initially released locally, Sire Records picks it up for nationwide release.
After dates at the Whiskey, Los Angeles, CA she recruits new guitar player, Ivan Kral. She plays a 3-week stint at New York's CBGB's and invites the club DJ, Jay Dee Daugherty, to play drums. He stays and The Patti Smith Group is formed.

1975
Jan [1] Smith participates in New York poetry project "New Year's Day Extravaganza" with Yoko Ono.
Group signs to Arista Records.
Dec Debut album *Horses* is released, produced by John Cale. Cale and Smith differ over musical direction, with Cale preferring more improvization. The album includes cover versions of *Gloria* and *Land Of A Thousand Dances*, as well as references to rock idols Jimi Hendrix and Jim Morrison. It makes US #47.

1976
Apr A censored version of *My Generation* is released as a single.
May [16-17] Group makes its UK debut at the Roundhouse, Chalk Farm, London, supported by The Stranglers.
Oct The Patti Smith Group tours Europe.
Dec *Radio Ethiopia* makes US #122.

1977
Jan Smith breaks vertebrae in her neck as she falls off stage at a gig in Tampa, FL, supporting Bob Seger, and she needs 22 stitches.
Sept The full version of *My Generation* is released on a 12" format.

1978
Apr *Because The Night*, co-written with Bruce Springsteen, hits UK #5 and US #13. (It is the first time that Springsteen's name appears in the Top 20 Singles chart.) Parent album *Easter*, produced by Jimmy Iovine, reaches UK #16 and US #20.
Aug [27] The Patti Smith Group plays the Reading Festival, Berks., while *Privilege (Set Me Free)* makes UK #72.

1979
Feb *Babel*, Smith's fifth book of poetry, is published.
May *Wave* makes UK #41 and US #18. Produced by long-time friend, Rundgren, called in by Arista to encourage her to record again, it will be her last album in 9 years. It includes minor hit *Frederick, Dancing Barefoot* (UK #63) and a cover of The Byrds' *So You Wanna Be A Rock'N'Roll Star*.

1980
Mar [1] She marries former MC5, Fred "Sonic" Smith. (Smith retires from rock world, occasionally emerging for ad-hoc poetry readings.)

1988
July Living in Detroit raising her 2 children Jesse and Jackson, Smith comes out of retirement with *People Have The Power* and *Dream Of Life*, produced by Fred Smith and Jimmy Iovine. Both Sohl and Daugherty are still with her. The album reaches US #65 and UK #70.

1990
June [3] Ex-Patti Smith Group member Richard Sohl dies of a cardiac seizure in Long Island, New York, age 37.

THE SMITHS

Morrissey (vocals)
Johnny Marr (guitar)
Andy Rourke (bass)
Mike Joyce (drums)

1982 **May** Marr, a veteran of several Manchester, Gtr.Manchester-based bands, looking for a lyricist for his tunes, meets Morrissey (b. Stephen Patrick Morrissey, May 22, 1959, Manchester), the son of a hospital porter and a librarian, whose book **James Dean Isn't Dead** has been published by locally-based Babylon Books, and who has been UK president of The New York Dolls fan club.

Nov Morrissey and Marr form The Smiths with local musicians Rourke and Joyce (b. June 1, 1963, Manchester).

1983 **Apr** Group signs a one-off single deal with London-based independent label Rough Trade, after turning down Manchester-based Factory Records, interested in them following popular local gigging. (Most early shows have featured Morrissey paying tribute to his various influences/obsessions: a bunch of gladioli, often tucked into the seat of his trousers, representing Oscar Wilde, and a hearing aid in tribute to early 50s vocalist Johnnie Ray. He also styles much of his appearance, and hairstyle, on his favorite vocalist Billy Fury, recently deceased.)

May Debut single *Hand In Glove* benefits from considerable pre-release anticipation, and tops UK Independent chart.

[18] A group session is broadcast on BBC Radio 1's "John Peel Show".

July Group signs a long-term deal with Rough Trade, in the face of potentially more lucrative offers from major companies, and plays London's Hammersmith Palais, supporting Altered Images.

Dec Second single *This Charming Man*, in a sleeve picturing French actor Jean Marais, is UK national chart debut and reaches #25, spurred by an appearance on BBC TV's "Whistle Test". Morrissey writes an article in weekly UK rock magazine **Sounds** in appreciation of his favorite girl singer, Sandie Shaw.

1984 **Feb** Released to coincide with a 20-date UK tour, Marr/Morrissey-penned (as will be all Smiths hits) *What Difference Does It Make* reaches UK #12. Picture sleeve shows actor Terence Stamp in film "The Collector", but when Stamp objects to the use of such an ancient shot, it is replaced by a similarly-posed picture of Morrissey. (Morrissey, meanwhile, moves from Manchester to London, and contracts laryngitis, which causes cancellation of some tour dates.)

Mar Group's debut album *The Smiths*, in a sleeve depicting Joe Dallesandro in Warhol's film "Flesh", hits UK #2.

May Backed by The Smiths, Sandie Shaw reaches UK #27 with her version of *Hand In Glove*. Morrissey, although not featured on this release, expresses in UK music press his admiration both for Shaw and other 60s female singers.

June *Heaven Knows I'm Miserable Now* is their highest-charting single, hitting UK #10 (despite some major chains' refusal to stock it because of objections to the lyrics of B-side *Suffer Little Children*, after complaints from relatives of victims in UK's 60s Moors Murders case). *The Smiths*, released in US on Sire, makes US #150. Band undertakes another UK tour, and headlines Greater London Council's "Festival For Jobs".

Sept *William, It Was Really Nothing* reaches UK #17. On a brief US visit, the band plays the Danceteria in New York.

Nov Welsh live dates are followed by a tour in Ireland, while low-priced album *Hatful Of Hollow*, a collection of BBC radio session tracks and B-sides, hits UK #7.

1985 **Feb** *How Soon Is Now?* makes UK #24. (It will subsequently provide the backing for a jeans UK TV commercial and become heavily sampled in Soho's 1990 hit *Hippychick*.)

[23] *Meat Is Murder* enters UK chart at #1, displacing Bruce Springsteen's *Born In The USA*. (Group begins 5-week UK tour the next day, supported by fellow Manchester band James.)

Mar *Shakespeare's Sister* climbs to UK #26.

[18] Band's concert at the Apollo theater, Oxford, Oxon, is recorded by the BBC. (A live album is mooted, though the tracks are eventually released on various single B-sides.)

Apr Rourke and Joyce play on *Incense And Peppermints* the first single by The Adult Net, a band formed as a sideline by Brix Smith, guitarist with The Fall and wife of its leader, Mark E. Smith. (Both will continue to work with The Adult Net on subsequent projects.)

May *Meat Is Murder* climbs to US #110.

July Extracted *That Joke Isn't Funny Anymore* makes UK #49.

Oct *The Boy With The Thorn In His Side*, showcasing Marr's familiar jangling guitar work, reaches UK #23.

1986 **Feb** Band appears with New Order and The Fall in the "From

Manchester With Love" concert at the Royal Court theater, Liverpool, Merseyside.

Apr Band adds a second guitarist, Craig Gannon.

June *Big Mouth Strikes Again* reaches UK #26. It is taken from *The Queen Is Dead*, which hits UK #2 behind Genesis' *Invisible Touch*.

Aug *Panic* makes UK #11, while *The Queen Is Dead* makes US #70.

Nov *Ask* reaches UK #14. Marr is injured in a car crash, forcing the band to cancel an appearance at an Artists Against Apartheid benefit at London's Royal Albert Hall.

Dec Gannon leaves (and band plays what will be its last live shows).

1987 **Jan** *Shoplifters Of The World Unite*, despite its controversial lyrics, reaches UK #12.

Mar Compilation *The World Won't Listen* hits UK #2 (behind *The Phantom Of The Opera* London cast album). It is announced that The Smiths will sign to EMI Records when their current Rough Trade contract expires.

Apr Originally recorded for a John Peel BBC Radio 1 session, *Sheila Take A Bow* hits UK #10.

May US double compilation album *Louder Than Bombs* on Sire is imported in to UK by Rough Trade and, despite its price, reaches UK #38. It also climbs to US #63.

Aug *Girlfriend In A Coma* reaches UK #13. Unusually for The Smiths (who had once vowed never to get involved with promo videos), it is supported by a video – featuring a solo Morrissey. It fuels speculation that there will soon be no group for EMI to release. It becomes apparent that Marr and Morrissey are finding it difficult to work together (Morrissey is upset by Marr's frequent guitar "moonlighting" with Billy Bragg, Bryan Ferry and others), but several weeks will elapse before the official announcement of a split, and the news that Morrissey will sign with EMI as a solo artist.

Oct *Strangeways, Here We Come*, (referring to a prison in Manchester) hits UK #2, behind Michael Jackson's *Bad* and is their final album.

Nov *I Started Something I Couldn't Finish* reaches UK #23, following which Morrissey moves to EMI. (Marr will continue working with acts like Bryan Ferry, Paul McCartney and Talking Heads, before becoming involved with The Pretenders, while Rourke and Joyce remain with The Adult Net.)

Dec *Last Night I Dreamt That Somebody Loved Me*, from *Strangeways*, makes UK #30, while *Strangeways Here We Come* reaches US #55.

1988 **Mar** Morrissey's debut solo single *Suedehead* on EMI's reactivated HMV label hits UK #5. Its promotion includes a video showing Morrissey at play in James Dean's hometown. Simultaneously, his solo album *Viva Hate*, recorded with producer Stephen Street (and with assistance from another Manchester musician, Vini Reilly of Durutti Column), enters UK Album chart at #1, and will make US #48 through his US Sire record deal.

June [11] Marr plays guitar in Midge Ure's all-purpose back-up band at "Nelson Mandela's Birthday Party" at Wembley Stadium, London.

[18] Morrissey's second single *Everyday Is Like Sunday* hits UK #9.

Sept A live Smiths album, *Rank* (recorded in Oct.1986 at a concert at the National Ballroom, Kilburn, London), hits UK #2 (and US #77), behind Kylie Minogue's *Kylie*.

Oct Strange Fruit Records releases a 12" EP featuring The Smiths' May 1983 BBC "John Peel Show" session. (Amid rumors that Marr will re-form a new version of The Smiths, probably with Rourke and Joyce and even with Morrissey, the guitarist is currently working with The Pretenders.)

1989 **Feb** [11] Morrissey's *The Last Of The International Playboys* hits UK #6.

Apr Marr is announced in the new line-up of Matt Johnson's The The, and is prominent on the act's new album *Mind Bomb*, though the liaison will once again prove temporary.

[29] Morrissey's *Interesting Drug* hits UK #9.

Nov [25] Seance-themed *Ouija Board, Ouija Board* reaches UK #18 for Morrissey.

1990 **May** [5] Morrissey's *November Spawned A Monster* peaks at UK #12 debut.

[19] Electronic, an ad hoc teaming of Marr, The Pet Shop Boys' Neil Tennant and New Order's Bernard Sumner, make US #38 with *Getting Away With It*, having made UK #12 in Jan.

Oct [20] *Piccadilly Palare* reaches UK #18 for Morrissey.

[27] Once again referencing the characters Julian and Sandy from early 60s BBC Radio comedy shows "Beyond Our Ken" and "Round The Horne" (as has recent single), *Bona Drag* hits UK #9.

Dec [1] Morrissey's *Bona Drag* makes US #59.

1991 **Feb** [23] Morrissey's *Our Frank* reaches UK #26.

Mar [16] Much of it co-penned with ex-Fairground Attraction's Mark

Nevin, Morrissey's *Kill Uncle*, featuring ex-Madness keyboardist Mark "Bedders" Bedford and produced by that band's collaborators Clive Langer and Alan Winstanley, debuts at UK peak #8.

[30] *Kill Uncle* makes US #52.

Apr [13] Morrissey's *Sing Your Life* makes UK #33.

SOFT CELL
Marc Almond (vocals)
David Ball (keyboards)

1978 Almond (b. Peter Marc Almond, July 9, 1959, Southport, Merseyside) leaves college in Southport and moves to Leeds polytechnic to study Fine Arts, where he meets Ball (b. May 3, 1959, Blackpool, Lancs.).

1979 **Oct** Both fans of Northern Soul music, Almond and Ball form a duo, with Ball writing music for Almond's theatrical pieces, and Almond penning lyrics to Ball's instrumentals. With the addition of slide and film special effects, handled by Steven Griffith, they become Soft Cell.

Dec Soft Cell plays its first gig, at Leeds polytechnic.

1980 **June** 4-track EP *Mutant Moments*, featuring 4 joint compositions, is recorded in a local studio (the session and pressing of 2,000 copies paid for by Ball).

Sept [6] Coinciding with release of the EP on its own Big Frock label, Soft Cell plays with great success to a 5,000-plus audience at the Futurama 2 Science Fiction Music Festival in Leeds. The EP, meanwhile, attracts the attention of Some Bizzare Records boss Stevo who invites the duo (Griffith and the multi-media accessories have now dropped out) to contribute a track to his projected compilation album of new synthesizer-based "futurist" acts. *The Girl With The Patent Leather Face* is recorded on 2-track equipment at practically no cost.

1981 **Mar** Stevo negotiates a deal for both Soft Cell and Some Bizzare with Phonogram, which includes a £1,000 advance for the duo, and distribution of compilation album *Some Bizzare Album* (which makes UK #58). Duo's first Some Bizzare single *Memorabilia*, produced by Mute Records' Daniel Miller, is released, without charting.

July At London's Advision studios, Soft Cell resurrects little-known (though long a cult favorite on the UK Northern Soul circuit) Gloria Jones track *Tainted Love*, written by ex-Four Preps and Piltdown Men member Ed Cobb and produced by Mike Thorne.

Sept *Tainted Love* tops the UK chart for 2 weeks, and will become the year's biggest-selling single, also hitting #1 in a score of other territories around the world.

Dec *Bedsitter* hits UK #4, while the duo's debut album *Non-Stop Erotic Cabaret*, recorded in New York with Thorne, hits UK #5. **Billboard** magazine names Soft Cell New Wave Band Of The Year.

1982 **Jan** *Tainted Love* re-charts in UK, reaching #43.

Feb *Say Hello, Wave Goodbye* hits UK #3. Duo follows with a lengthy UK club tour. (After it, Ball will return to Leeds for several months, where he will write the album for next album, leaving Almond to do solo work, for which he becomes Marc & The Mambas, a pseudonym used prior to his Soft Cell days. Keyboards player Annie Hogan assists Almond.)

[24] *Tainted Love* wins Best British Single at the first annual BRIT Awards at the Grosvenor House, London.

June *Torch* hits UK #2, behind Adam Ant's *Goody Two-Shoes*. Mini-album *Non-Stop Ecstatic Dancing*, featuring New York-recorded dance remixes of several of the duo's tracks, hits UK #6.

July *Tainted Love* charts for third time in UK, reaching #50, and hits US #8, having been climbing US chart since Jan. (It will set a new longevity record on the Hot 100, its 43 weeks being the longest consecutive chart run by a single.)

Aug *Non-Stop Erotic Cabaret* reaches US #22, while *What*, another Northern Soul revival (the original by Judy Street), hits UK #3.

Sept *Non-Stop Ecstatic Dancing* makes US #57.

Oct Almond experiments with a different musical direction via *Untitled*, released under the name Marc & The Mambas. It couples original material with revivals of songs by Jacques Brel, Lou Reed and others, and makes UK #42.

Dec *Where The Heart Is* reaches UK #21. Marc & The Mambas (Almond, Hogan, bass player Tim Taylor and others) play the Theatre Royal, Drury Lane, London.

1983 **Jan** *The Art Of Falling Apart*, recorded in New York previous Sept., hits UK #5. It is packaged with a free 12" Jimi Hendrix tribute disk, containing Soft Cell's versions of *Hey Joe*, *Purple Haze* and *Voodoo Chile*.

Mar *Numbers/Barriers* reaches UK #25. Duo plays another UK tour, while *The Art Of Falling Apart* makes US #84.

June Ball scores the music for a stage revival of Tennessee Williams'

play "Suddenly Last Summer".

Aug Despite scathing reviews (and a chain store ban because of allegedly obscene lyrics), double album *Torment And Toreros* by Marc & The Mambas makes UK #28. Almond's group now includes a string section, all-girl trio The Venomettes (one of whom, Ginny, marries David Ball).

Oct Soft Cell's *Soul Inside* reaches UK #16.

Nov Ball releases solo album *In Strict Tempo*, with guest vocals from Genesis P. Orridge of Psychic TV. It fails to chart.

Dec Almond and Ball announce the end of Soft Cell as they complete a final album together, and play a last US tour.

1984 **Jan** Duo's final UK live dates are a farewell series at the Hammersmith Palais, London.

Feb *Down In The Subway*, extracted from final album, makes UK #24.

Mar Final Soft Cell album *This Last Night In Sodom* reaches UK #12.

June Almond has his first solo success with *The Boy Who Came Back*, reaching UK #52.

Sept Follow-up *You Have* makes UK #57. Almond takes part in a week-long festival at the Bloomsbury theater, London, which celebrates the work of French Writer George Bataille. (A mini-album of material from this, *Violent Silence*, will be released in French-speaking territories in 1986, and imported in to UK.)

Nov Containing both the solo singles, *Vermin In Ermine*, credited to Marc Almond & The Willing Sinners (3 former Mambas and 3 new musicians), makes UK #36. *Tenderness Is A Weakness* is extracted, but fails to sell.

1985 **Feb** *Tainted Love* charts for the fourth time, making UK #43.

May Almond sings guest vocals with Jimmy Somerville on Bronski Beat's medley of *I Feel Love/Love To Love You Baby/Johnny Remember Me*, which hits UK #3.

Aug *Stories Of Johnny*, Almond's first release away from Phonogram, through Virgin, brings his biggest solo success to date, at UK #23.

Oct *Stories Of Johnny* reaches UK #22, while extracted *Love Letters* (with Westminster City School Choir guesting) makes UK #68. Almond follows its release with a European tour, including UK dates.

1986 **Jan** *The House Is Haunted (By The Echo Of Your Last Goodbye)*, a Mel Torme number, makes UK #55.

Feb Almond and The Willing Sinners play a series of dates in Japan.

June *A Woman's Story*, a revival of a Cher song (allegedly recorded after Almond heard the original playing in a London taxi), makes UK #41. (The 12" version is a multi-track EP, subtitled *Some Songs To Take To The Tomb*, and includes revivals of Procol Harum's *A Salty Dog* and Johnnie Ray's *The Little White Cloud That Cried*, among others.)

Oct *Ruby Red* makes UK #47.

Dec Soft Cell compilation album *The Singles Album* reaches UK #58.

1987 **Feb** Almond's *Melancholy Rose* creeps to UK #71.

Apr *Mother Fist And Her Five Daughters*, again credited to Marc Almond & The Willing Sinners, makes UK #41. Extracted title track stalls at UK #93.

June He duets guest vocals on Sally Timms' *This House Is A House Of Tears* (an Almond composition).

Nov Almond compilation album *Singles* is released, without charting. Following this, his contract with Virgin expires and a new deal is signed with EMI's Parlophone label. The Willing Sinners have now been replaced by new backing group La Magia, though Annie Hogan still remains from the original Mambas, as do Billy McGee and Steve Humphreys from The Sinners.

Dec Almond plays a series of sell-out Christmas concerts at the Astoria, London.

1988 **Sept** *Tears Run Rings*, on Parlophone, reaches UK #26.

Oct [8] *The Stars We Are* makes UK #41.

Nov Almond's *Bitter Sweet* climbs to UK #40.

1989 **Jan** [28] Almond tops UK chart with *Something's Gotten Hold Of My Heart*, duetted with Gene Pitney.

Feb [18] *Tears Run Rings* peaks at US #67, while parent album *The Stars We Are* climbs to US #144.

Apr Almond's *Only The Moment* makes UK #45.

1990 **Mar** Almond's *A Lover Spurned* reaches UK #29.

May [19] Almond's *The Desperate Hours* makes UK #45.

June [16] Parent album, co-produced by Stephen Hague, *Enchanted*, climbs to UK #52.

July Ball re-emerges as one half of East-West label act Grid, whose modern dance debut *Floatation* makes UK #60.

Oct Grid's *Beat Called Love*, aided by drum-thumping dance video, peaks at UK #64.

1991 **Apr** Remixed updates of selected Soft Cell singles by Ball are included on Soft Cell/Marc Almond Parlophone UK retrospective *Memorabilia – The Singles*, while extracted *Say Hello – Wave Goodbye '91* remix has made UK #38 (Mar.23).

JIMMY SOMERVILLE

1984 Somerville (b. June 22, 1961, Glasgow, Scotland) links with Steve Bronski (b. Feb.7, 1960, Glasgow) and Larry Steinbachek (b. May 6, 1960, London), who evolve an electronic dance music style on their twin synthesizers, to form Bronski Beat in London, with Somerville's falsetto vocals the outstanding feature. The trio signs to London Records via its own Forbidden Fruit label.

June [23] Bronski Beat's debut *Smalltown Boy*, highlighting alienation felt by a provincial homosexual, hits UK #3.

Oct [6] *Why?* hits UK #6 and parent album *The Age Of Consent* #4.

Dec Somerville announces his intention to leave because of his dislike of the star treatment the band is getting but is persuaded to stay.

1985 **Jan** [19] A revival of Gershwin's *It Ain't Necessarily So* makes UK #16.

Feb Somerville is fined £50 at London's Bow Street Magistrates' Court for gross indecency.

Mar *Smalltown Boy* is Bronski Beat's only US chart single at #48.

[4] *The Age Of Consent*, a reference to UK sex laws, hits US #36.

May [11] A hi-energy revival of Donna Summer's *I Feel Love*, in a medley with Summer's *Love To Love You Baby* and John Leyton's *Johnny Remember Me*, hits UK #3. It jointly credits ex-Soft Cell singer Marc Almond, who duets with Somerville. Somerville subsequently leaves to work with keyboardist Richard Coles (b. June 23, 1962, Northampton, Northants.), an ex-student of the Royal School of Church Music who has occasionally played on stage with Bronski Beat, and with whom Somerville has worked on a documentary film. They first name themselves The Committee, then discover the name is already in use and decide upon The Communards, named after the French Revolutionaries of 1871. Bronski and Steinbachek recruit John Jon (Foster), from Newcastle, Tyne & Wear, band Bust, as the replacement Bronski Beat vocalist.

Sept Bronski Beat's mini-album *Hundreds And Thousands*, consisting mostly of dance remixes of tracks from the first album, makes UK #24.

Oct The Communards sign to London Records in UK and debut with *You Are My World*, which establishes their sound, a variation on Bronski Beat's dance-oriented keyboard arrangements, again highlighting Somerville's falsetto voice. It reaches UK #30.

1986 **Jan** [25] They play on the first of 7 dates on "Red Wedge" tour of UK, starting at the Apollo theater, Manchester, Gtr.Manchester, with Paul Weller and Billy Bragg, in support of UK Labour Party. For this and later stage work, the duo recruits its regular backing band of (mainly female) session players. (Bronski Beat's *Hit That Perfect Beat*, featured in film "Letter To Brezhnev", is the group's first single to feature John Jon's lead vocals. It hits UK #3.)

Apr Bronski Beat's *Come On, Come On* reaches UK #20.

May Bronski Beat's *Truthdare Doubledare* climbs to UK #18.

June The Communards' *Disenchanted* reaches UK #29.

Aug Bronski Beat's *Truthdare Doubledare* makes US #147.

Sept [13] The Communards' dance-styled revival of Thelma Houston and Harold Melvin's hit *Don't Leave Me This Way* tops UK chart for 4 weeks and is the year's second-biggest UK single, selling 750,000 copies. It features Somerville duetting with Sarah-Jayne Morris, who becomes a regular on-stage duettist/back-up vocalist.

Oct *Communards*, containing the chart singles, hits UK #7.

Nov John Jon leaves Bronski Beat. (Group will remain inactive in 1987 and into 1988. Different reports have them splitting from London Records and breaking up altogether.)

Dec The Communards' *So Cold The Night* hits UK #8, helped by a European tour which is followed by major London dates.

1987 **Jan** *Communards* makes US #90.

Feb A remake of first single, as *You Are My World '87*, makes UK #21.

Mar [7] *Don't Leave Me This Way* is their first US success, reaching #40.

Sept *Tomorrow*, extracted from forthcoming *Red*, peaks at UK #23.

Oct Second Communards album *Red* hits UK #4.

Nov Revival of Gloria Gaynor's hit *Never Can Say Goodbye*, taken from *Red* and arranged similarly to *Don't Leave Me This Way*, hits UK #4.

1988 **Feb** [20] *Never Can Say Goodbye* peaks at US #51 as *Red* makes US #93.

Mar *For A Friend*, dedicated to Coles and Somerville's friend Mark Ashton, who died of AIDS, reaches UK #28.

June Another pro-gay song *There's More To Love* reaches UK #20, and proves to be the last Communards success as Somerville contemplates a solo future.

Oct Jonathan Hellyer takes over as Bronski Beat's lead vocalist.

1989 **Sept** Somerville guests on noted US dance producer Arthur Baker's album.

Dec Somerville reaches UK #14 with a remake of Francoise Hardy's *Comment Te Dire Adieu*.

1990 **Jan** [20] Somerville's remake of Sylvester's *You Make Me Feel (Mighty Real)* hits UK #5.

Feb [3] Somerville's debut solo album *Read My Lips* reaches UK #29.

Mar [31] Somerville's *Read My Lips (Enough Is Enough)* makes UK #31.

May [5] *Read My Lips* peaks at US #192.

Oct Somerville, now living in San Francisco, CA, contributes *From This Moment On* to *Red Hot + Blue*, an anthology of Cole Porter songs to benefit AIDS education.

Nov [24] Somerville's reggae-tinged cover of The Bee Gees' *To Love Somebody* hits UK #8.

1991 **Jan** [5] Somerville's *The Singles Collection 1984-1990*, of material from his Bronski Beat, Communards and solo phases, hits UK #4.

SONNY & CHER

1957 Sonny Bono (b. Salvatore Bono, Feb.16, 1935, Detroit, MI), having moved to Hollywood in 1954, at first working at the Douglas Aircraft factory on an assembly line, becomes a record-packer at Specialty Records.

May He writes *High School Dance*, B-side of Larry Williams' hit *Short Fat Fanny* and *You Bug Me Baby*, the B-side of Williams' *Bony Maronie* on Specialty. He also pens Don & Dwedy's *Koko Joe*, subsequently recorded by The Righteous Brothers. (Sonny later has his own single on the label, *Wearing Black*, under the name Don Christy, and will become a writer, producer and A&R man at Specialty.)

1960 After Specialty has curtailed most of its operations, he will record for 2 years as Sonny Christie and Ronny Sommers for an assortment of labels, with no success.

1962 Sonny co-writes *Needles And Pins* with Jack Nitzsche, which is recorded by Jackie DeShannon and makes US #84. (It will be an international hit for The Searchers in 1964, topping UK chart and reaching US #13.) Nitzsche introduces Bono, now working as promotion man for Record Merchandizing who distribute Philles, to producer Phil Spector, and he begins to work for him as a general assistant and West Coast promotion man – gaining much as a producer by witnessing Spector at work in the studio.

1963 Cher (b. Cherilyn Sarkasian La Pierre, May 20, 1946, El Centro, CA), having moved to Los Angeles primarily to act, meets Sonny at Aldo's Coffee Shop, next to radio station K-FWB and, through his introduction, becomes a session singer for Spector, doing back-ups for The Ronettes. She also begins to sing as a duo with Sonny, and as Caesar & Cleo they release *The Letter* on Vault Records, arranged by Harold Battiste (with whom they will later work at Atco). Meanwhile, The Righteous Brothers record Bono's song *Koko Joe*, written in 1951.

1964 Sonny and Cher marry in Tijuana, Mexico, a year after his divorce from Donna Lynn, whom he married in 1954. After much prompting from Sonny, Spector agrees to record Cher as a soloist, but only 1 single is cut: *Ringo I Love You* on Spector's Annette label, under the pseudonym Bonnie Jo Mason. With borrowed money, Sonny produces a Cher session himself at RCA studios in Hollywood, but it emerges as another duet after Cher has an attack of studio nerves and asks him to sing with her. 4 tracks are recorded, and after sounding out Spector as to their worth, Sonny sells them to Reprise Records, which issues them under the Caesar & Cleo name as 2 (initially unsuccessful) singles, *Baby Don't Go* and *Love Is Strange*.

1965 Atlantic's Ahmet Ertegun is impressed by *Baby Don't Go* and, learning that they have no contract with Reprise, offers a recording deal. They are signed to Atlantic's Atco subsidiary (which does not affect Cher's solo deal with Imperial). They decide to use their own names and debut as Sonny & Cher with *Just You* – again to no initial success.

July *I Got You Babe*, written and produced by Sonny (almost issued as B-side of *It's Gonna Rain* until he persuades Ertegun otherwise) shoots to US #1, holding for 3 weeks and selling over a million. Their eye-catching, hippy dress style and long hair immediately bring them notice on TV appearances. (Bono is refused admission to New York's Americana hotel, because of his mode of dress.)

[31] They arrive amid much publicity in UK for a first promotional visit, which helps *I Got You Babe* to top UK chart for 2 weeks. (They also film segments for a future TV special "Sonny & Cher In London".)

Aug [5] Duo makes its only public UK appearance at the 100 club in London's Oxford Street.

[6] They appear on ITV's "Ready Steady Go!"

Sept Sonny releases a solo single, partially-autobiographical *Laugh At Me*, inspired by an occasion when Sonny was barred entrance to Martoni's restaurant in Hollywood, because of his attire, which hits US #10 and UK #9, while Spector-produced Bonnie & The Treasures' *Home Of The Brave*, with Sonny & Cher on back-up vocals, reaches US #77.

Oct *Baby Don't Go* is reissued by Reprise, re-credited to Sonny & Cher, and hits US #8 and UK #11. *Just You*, repromoted by Atco, also charts in US, reaching #20. Debut album *Look At Us* hits US #2 and UK #7.

Nov *But You're Mine*, follow-up to *I Got You Babe* makes US #15 and UK #17, while Vault reissues *The Letter*, which reaches US #75.

Dec A second solo by Sonny, *The Revolution Kind*, peaks at US #70.

966 Feb The Sonny & Cher clothing line comes on sale at department stores throughout US, including bell-bottom and blouse outfits and bobcat vests ranging from $8 to $18.

Mar Duo starts work on debut film "Good Times" at Paramount studios. A revival of *What Now My Love* reaches US #16 and UK #13.

Apr [2] They bill-top at the Hollywood Bowl, with Jan And Dean, The Mamas And The Papas, The Turtles, Otis Redding, Donovan and Bob Lind, with all proceeds going to the Braille Institute.

June *Have I Stayed Too Long* makes US #49 and UK #42. It is taken from *The Wondrous World Of Sonny And Cher*, which makes US #34 and UK #15.

Aug [26] They make their UK concert debut at a benefit at the Astoria theater, Finsbury Park, London.

Sept [14] Sonny & Cher have a private audience with Pope Paul VI in Rome, Italy.

Oct *Little Man*, in an arresting gypsy-style arrangement by Sonny, reaches US #21 and UK #9.

Nov *Living For You* makes US #87 and UK #44.

967 Jan [1] They become the first pop duo to ride on a float at the New Year's Day Rose Bowl Parade in Pasadena, CA.

Feb Uptempo *The Beat Goes On* (later revived by Vanilla Fudge) is the duo's last major Atco success, hitting US #6 and reaching UK #29.

Mar [17] They begin a 10-day East Coast tour.

Apr [7] "Good Times" opens in Chicago, IL.

May *A Beautiful Story* reaches US #53.

June *Plastic Man* peaks at US #74.

Sept *It's The Little Things* makes US #50.

Oct Compilation *The Best Of Sonny And Cher* reaches US #23, as they make a guest appearance on US TV's "The Man From U.N.C.L.E."

Dec They open in cabaret at the Eden Roc hotel, Miami Beach, FL.

968 Jan Their final Atco hit is *Good Combination*, which reaches US #56.

Aug [4] Duo plays the Newport Pop Festival in Costa Mesa, CA, alongside Canned Heat, Steppenwolf, The Grateful Dead, The Byrds, Jefferson Airplane and others.

969 Mar [4] Daughter Chastity is born in Cedars of Lebanon hospital, Los Angeles.

A second movie, "Chastity" (titled after their daughter's name) is only moderately successful.

970 With hit singles no longer coming despite sporadic releases as a duo, they move to the cabaret scene, appearing regularly in Las Vegas in an act which mixes comedy with music. They sign a new recording deal, covering both the duo's and Cher's solo work, with Kapp Records, a subsidiary of MCA.

971 Aug [1] They begin a highly successful TV series, "The Sonny And Cher Comedy Hour" on CBS, which mixes songs and comedy with star guests, based on format of the club/comedy act they have perfected.

Dec Bolstered by the popularity of the TV show, *All I Ever Need Is You* hits US #7, while *Sonny And Cher Live* makes US #35.

972 Feb *All I Ever Need Is You* hits UK #8.

Apr *A Cowboy's Work Is Never Done* hits US #8. It is taken from *All I Ever Need Is You*, which reaches US #14.

Aug *When You Say Love*, which makes US #32, is taken from a Budweiser beer ad on US TV.

973 Apr MCA (having absorbed Kapp label) releases 2 Sonny & Cher singles during the year; but only *Mama Was A Rock And Roll Singer, Papa Used Write All Her Songs* charts, making US #77. It is the duo's last hit together.

974 Jan The final 2 singles by Sonny & Cher are released by Warner Bros. but neither charts.

Feb [20] Cher files for divorce from Sonny.

June [26] Sonny and Cher's divorce is finalized. (She will marry Gregg Allman 2 days later, and in turn file for divorce from Allman 9 days after that.)

Sept [22] "The Sonny Comedy Revue" premieres on ABC TV.

1976 Feb Following on from a Cher solo TV series on CBS, the network replaces it with a new version of "The Sonny And Cher Show" (which will run until mid-1977).

1980 While Cher is recording for Casablanca, Sonny reappears on the scene as an actor, in both big-screen and TV movies (as he will continue to do throughout the 80s).

1987 Nov [14] Sonny & Cher sing *I Got You Babe* for the first time in 10 years on NBC TV's "Late Night With Letterman".

1988 Sonny appears in movie "Hairspray".

Apr Cher wins the Best Actress Oscar at the Academy Awards for her performance in movie "Moonstruck".

[12] In the same week, Sonny is elected Mayor of Palm Springs. (As Cher continues to star in both film and music, Sonny will become a controversial Mayor. He is also now a restaurant owner, in partnership with his fourth wife.)

SOUL II SOUL

Jazzie B (rap shepherd)
Nellee Hooper (arranger)
Philip "Daddae" Harvey (miscellaneous)

1982 North London friends Jazzie B (b. Beresford Romeo, Jan.26, 1963), British-born of Antiguan immigrants and educated at Holloway Boys Secondary school, London, and Harvey begin offering their services to the emerging UK dance club scene, making available PAs, sound systems and DJs under the name created by Harvey, Soul II Soul. Initially traveling to events on public transport, they evolve to hold their own warehouse raves mainly at Paddington Dome, under the King's Cross arches, London. Becoming major dance event organizers and providers, their soul collective grows to marketable status.

1985 Hooper, a member of Bristol mixing crew Massive Attack, and ex-The Wild Bunch crew, having already cut *The Look Of Love* as a hip-hop number, rents Soul II Soul equipment for a gig in London. When he meets Jazzie B, a furious row erupts over a misunderstanding concerning who should be DJ. The 2 subsequently become firm friends and Hooper joins the growing Soul II Soul ranks.

1986 With a keen commercial eye and ear, Soul II Soul begins a fixed Sunday night residence at the Africa Centre, Covent Garden, London, where all their club, event and sound system efforts will develop.

1987 Following a demo recording, featuring the cut *Fairplay*, helmed by Hooper and Jazzie B, who has rejected piano lessons at an early age and concentrates now on creating music ideas for those around him to perform, Soul II Soul secures a deal with Virgin subsidiary 10 Records.

1988 As the Soul II Soul collective relocates to the Fridge club, Brixton, London, many of its members are involved in the current pirate local radio station movement, particularly Jazzie B who hosts a show on soon to be legal KISS-FM. Soul II Soul has now sprouted offshoot fashion, particularly T-shirts, and accessory success which lead to the opening of 2 Soul II Soul shops in London, one in Camden followed by another in Tottenham Court Road.

Fairplay, featuring Rose Windross on vocals, stalls at UK #63.

Follow-up *Feel Free*, featuring Do-reen, performs moderately at UK #64.

1989 Apr Breakthrough disk, *Keep On Movin'* hits UK #5. Featuring Soul II Soul fixture Caron Wheeler on lead vocals, the single mixes a spacious reggae feel with a unique and hallmarking dance shuffle rhythm which will spawn dozens of imitations over the next 2 years, and itself provide the distinctive rhythm drive to their own next 2 hits.

[22] Debut album *Club Classics Volume One*, combining a myriad of dance/reggae/hip-hop/soul elements is released. Featuring dozens of permanent and temporary Soul II Soul collective members, it will become regarded as a prototype project and will launch the group (and Jazzie B's oft quoted ethos: "A smiling face, a thumping bass for a happy face") worldwide.

June [24] Extracted, but remixed *Back To Life (However Do You Want Me)*, again co-written and sung by Wheeler hits UK #1, becoming a UK summer dance anthem.

July [15] *Club Classics Volume One* finally hits UK #1 on its way to multi-platinum success.

Sept [9] Already a US R&B #1, *Keep On Movin* reaches US #11.

Dec [9] Further honing Jazzie B's trademark rhythm section, *Get A Life* hits UK #3. (Wheeler has already left the line-up and will go on to a successful solo career with RCA in UK, EMI in US.)

[12] *Back To Life (However Do You Want Me)* hits US #4 as album, released in US as *Keep On Movin'* on Virgin America rises to US #14.

1990 Jan Increasingly in demand as producers and arrangers, Jazzie B and Hooper arrange Sinead O'Connor's international chart-topper *Nothing*

SOUL II SOUL cont.

Compares 2 U. (They also make contributions to albums by The Chimes, Fine Young Cannibals and Neneh Cherry.)

Feb [21] Having been awarded 3 American Music Awards and 4 British DMC Dance Awards, Soul II Soul wins Best R&B Performance By A Duo Or Group With Vocal for *Back To Life* and Best R&B Instrumental Performance for *African Dance* at the 32nd annual Grammy awards at the Shrine Auditorium, Los Angeles.

Mar [8] Group is voted Best New Foreign Band in **Rolling Stone** magazine's 1989 Critics Awards.

[14] Soul II Soul wins R&B/Urban Contemporary Album Of The Year, Group, Duo Or Band for *Keep On Movin'*, R&B/Urban Contemporary Song Of The Year and Best R&B/Urban Contemporary Single, Group, Duo Or Band for *Keep On Movin'* at the fourth annual Soul Train awards at the Shrine Auditorium.

May [5] Now overseeing 2 Soul II Soul shops, the Silent Productions company (recording Victoria Wilson-James, Marcia Lewis, Lamya and Jimmy Polo, all for projected release on proposed new label), Soul II Soul Visions video and film company, a fan club and a talent agency, with their own record company in the pipeline, Jazzie B, Hooper and Daddae launch second recording phase of Soul II Soul with *A Dream's A Dream*, featuring Wilson-James, which hits UK #6.

[12] *Get A Life* makes US #54.

June [2] *Volume II: 1990 A New Decade* debuts at UK #1 and will make US #21 at the end of the month. It once again aggregates a large number of singers, DJs, arrangers and musicians, including South African unit Shikisha, hip-hopper Fab 5 Freddie, UK sax master Courtney Pine and female vocalists Kym Mazelle, Razette and Jazzie B's cousin Marcie Lewis.

July [14] *A Dream's A Dream* makes US #85.

[26] US tour begins in Dallas, TX.

[18] Jazzie B suffers back injuries in a 7-car pile-up that sends 31 people to hospital in Illinois, causing cancellation of North American tour.

Sept [17-18] Soul II Soul plays Wembley Arena, London, during nationwide UK tour.

Dec [1] *Missing You*, with soulstress Kym Mazelle reaches UK #22.

1991 **Apr** [12] Jazzie B launches new record label Funki Dred at the Café Royal, London. A joint venture with Motown, early signings include Kofi and Lady Levi.

JOE SOUTH

1958 South (b. Feb.28, 1940, Atlanta, GA), an accomplished guitarist since age 11, and working in a country band with steel guitarist Pete Drake at age 15, has his first success with novelty *The Purple People Eater Meets The Witch Doctor* – a cash-in on 2 recent million-selling novelty hits by Sheb Wooley and David Seville. It reaches US #47, but proves impossible to follow up, so he hones his skills as a songwriter, initially setting poems written by his mother to music.

1961 **Aug** He becomes a DJ on a country music radio station in Atlanta but continues to record sporadically. *You're The Reason*, on Fairlane label, reaches US #87 (eclipsed by Bobby Edwards' US #11 version on Crest).

1962 **Nov** As a session guitarist on the Atlanta studio scene, he begins to place his own songs with local acts, and writes The Tams' *Untie Me*, which peaks at US #60. He also plays guitar on several sessions by Tommy Roe.

1965 **Aug** South produces his close friend, Atlanta-based singer Billy Joe Royal, who is signed to Columbia/CBS. Royal's debut, South's composition *Down In The Boondocks*, hits US #9 – South's first Top 10 success as a writer.

Oct *I Knew You When*, a second South song by Royal, reaches US #14 (while *Down In The Boondocks* makes UK #38). Royal's album, titled after the first hit, climbs to US #96; it is produced by South, and he writes 6 of the 12 tracks, including the 2 hits and Royal's next (US #38) single, *I've Got To Be Somebody*.

1967 **Oct** While doing session work for CBS as a guitarist (on Simon & Garfunkel's *The Sound Of Silence*, to which he helps add a rock backing track to original acoustic arrangement), South continues to work with Royal, and writes and produces *Hush*, which Royal takes to US #52.

1968 **Sept** *Hush* is covered, in a heavier arrangement, by Deep Purple, and this time hits US #4 and is South's first million-selling composition. Meanwhile, he signs to Capitol Records as a vocalist, debuting with his own song *Birds Of A Feather*, which is a regional success but does not make US Hot 100.

1969 **Mar** South's first album, **Introspect**, featuring 11 of his own songs, makes US #117. Taken from it, *Games People Play* becomes a major hit, reaching US #12. At the same time, Johnny Rivers covers South's *These*

Are Not My People (also from the album), reaching US #55.

Apr *Games People Play* hits UK #6, but will be South's only UK success.

July Reissued *Birds Of A Feather* stalls at US #96.

Oct *Don't It Make You Want To Go Home* reaches US #41. It co-credits South's group The Believers: Tommy South (drums, back-up vocals), Barbara South (keyboards, back-up vocals), Eddie Farrell (bass, back-up vocals) and Pee Wee Parks (back-up vocals).

1970 **Feb** *Walk A Mile In My Shoes*, also featuring The Believers, reaches US #12. It is taken from *Don't It Make You Want To Go Home*, a collectio of 14 more of his own songs (including his own versions of *Hush* and *Untie Me*), which climbs to US #60.

Mar [11] South wins 2 Grammy awards for *Games People Play*, voted Best Contemporary Song and Song Of The Year For 1969.

Apr *Children* peaks at US #51.

Oct Compilation *Joe South's Greatest Hits*, with the cream of tracks from his previous 2 albums, makes US #125.

1971 **Feb** Country singer Lynn Anderson covers South's *Rose Garden* (from *Introspect*) and has a million-seller with it, hitting both US and UK #3 (This will become one of South's most-covered compositions, with Elvis Presley, among many others, also cutting it.)

Dec *Fool Me* makes US #78, and will be South's last hit single. Though his songs continue to attract prolific cover versions, he drops out of th busy work schedule which has given him such a high profile for 2 years, feeling a need for rest from the pressures. He is also affected by the death of his brother Tommy – a member of The Believers. (He will not attempt to maintain further commercial success as an artist, and moves to Maui, Hawaii, for 3 years. Later albums *So The Seeds Are Growing*, *Midnight Rainbows* and *To Have, To Hold And To Let Go* (the latter 2 on Island label, to which he moves on returning to mainland US in 1975) will fail to chart, and he will slip into obscurity. Rhino releases the best of South's work on CD in 1990.)

SPANDAU BALLET

Gary Kemp (guitar)
Martin Kemp (bass)
Tony Hadley (vocals)
John Keeble (drums)
Steve Norman (rhythm guitar, sax, percussion)

1969 **Oct** [16] Gary Kemp (b. Oct.16, 1960, Islington, London) is given his first guitar by his parents. He later plays 2 songs at his primary school prize-giving day, and the attending Bishop of Stepney is so impressed that he gives Kemp a tape recorder (which he will use in writing song during the coming years).

1970 Kemp brothers Gary and Martin (b. Oct.10, 1961, Islington, London), both set to attend Owens Grammar school, Islington, also take lessons at Anna Scher's children's theater for acting.

1974 Hadley (b. Anthony Patrick Hadley, June 2, 1959, Islington, London), having had vocal lessons for some years, wins a talent contest singing Gary Puckett's *Young Girl*.

1975 Martin Kemp, excelling at soccer, trains with Arsenal Football club.

1976 Gary Kemp fails his "A-level" examinations, and starts a power pop group The Makers with Owens Grammar school friends Hadley, Keeble (b. July 6, 1959, Islington, London), Norman (b. Mar.25. 1960, Islington, London) and Richard Miller.

1978 **Apr** Hadley features in photo-love story "Sister Blackmail" in UK **My Guy** girls' magazine.

1979 Gary Kemp and ex-schoolmate Steve Dagger revive the failed Makers under a new name, which becomes Spandau Ballet. Hadley, Keeble, Norman and Martin Kemp (later bassist but cannot yet play bass) all join, while Dagger becomes manager.

Nov [17] Inspired by frequent Soho, London, night-clubbing at The Blitz, Billy's Le Kilt and Le Beate Route, Spandau Ballet invites 50 friends to an Islington studio to hear new songs.

Dec At a Steve Strange Blitz club party, Island Records boss Chris Blackwell offers to sign the band. Dagger rejects the overture, and hire a lawyer to organize a label of their own.

1980 **Mar** [7] Setting their own "new romantic" style (with emphasis on clothing, make-up and clubs), Spandau Ballet, now wearing kilts, selects unusual one-off live dates to intrigue the music media, including a gig at the Scala cinema, London.

[13] Band is filmed at the Scala cinema for inclusion on "Blitz Kids" club scene documentary on ITV show "20th Century Box".

Apr Having formed its own Reformation label, the group signs a deal to license its releases and company to Chrysalis Records.

July [26] Band plays aboard H.M.S. Belfast, a Second World War cruiser moored on the River Thames in London.

Dec Debut single *To Cut A Long Story Short*, well marketed, stylishly packaged (as will be all the early releases) and much anticipated after the "buzz" and music press interest around the band, hits UK #5.

981 **Feb** *The Freeze* reaches UK #17.
Mar *Journey To Glory*, Richard James Burgess-produced, hits UK #5.
Apr Band visits US to spread the "New Romantic" style – playing New York's Underground club, with a collection of UK fashion designers.
May *Musclebound* hits UK #10.
Aug Danced-aimed *Chant #1 (I Don't Need This Pressure On)*, made with help from UK funk outfit Beggar & Co., hits UK #3.
Nov *Paint Me Down* makes UK #30.

982 **Jan** Gary Kemp and Burgess work on actress/comedienne Pamela Stephenson's EP *Unusual Treatment*.
Feb *She Loved Like Diamond* peaks at UK #49.
Mar *Diamond* reaches UK #15.
Apr Group begins a UK tour in Edinburgh, Scotland.
May *Instinction*, from *Diamond*, remixed as a single by Trevor Horn, hits UK #10.
Oct *Lifeline*, produced by Swain and Jolley, hits UK #7.

983 **Mar** *Communication* reaches UK #12.
Apr Gary Kemp-penned ballad *True* tops the UK chart in its second week of release, and spends 4 weeks at #1.
May *True* tops the UK chart for a week.
July Now a major live attraction, Spandau Ballet play at London's Royal Albert Hall, Sadlers Wells theater and Royal Festival Hall.
Aug *Gold*, extracted from *True*, hits UK #2, held off the top by KC's *Give It Up*. (The song will be used by BBC TV as the theme for its Olympics coverage.)
Oct *True*, belatedly, is US chart debut, hitting #4, while album of the same title reaches US #19.

984 **Jan** *Gold* makes US #29.
Feb [21] Spandau Ballet wins the Sony Trophy For Technical Excellence at the 3rd annual BRIT Awards at the Grosvenor House, Mayfair, London.
Apr *Communication* peaks at US #59.
June *Only When You Leave*, taken from the band's forthcoming album, hits UK #3.
July *Parade* hits UK #2, held from the top by Bob Marley's *Legend*.
Sept *I'll Fly For You* hits UK #9, *Only When You Leave* makes US #34.
Oct *Parade* makes US #50. From it, *Highly Strung* reaches UK #15.
Nov [25] Group takes part in the all-star session for Band Aid's *Do They Know It's Christmas?*, which will end the year at UK #1. Hadley takes one of the lead vocal lines.
Dec *Round And Round* peaks at UK #18.
[4] Group plays the first of 6 nights of major concerts at Wembley Arena, London .

985 **Feb** Band sues Chrysalis for release from its contract, claiming that a lack of consistent US success is due to the label's inefficient promotion of it in US. (The dispute means that no new material can be released by Spandau Ballet until legal matters are resolved.)
July [13] Spandau Ballet appears on the Live Aid bill at Wembley Stadium, London.
Nov Chrysalis releases compilation *The Singles Collection*, without the band's co-operation. It hits UK #3, aided by TV promotion – which also angers the group.

986 **Jan** [25] Gary Kemp appears solo on the Labour Party "Red Wedge" UK tour, which opens in Manchester, Gtr.Manchester.
Apr [26] The Kemp brothers and Norman all escape serious injury when the car (driven by Norman) in West Berlin, Germany, crashes.
May Freed from its Chrysalis deal, the group signs their Reformation label to CBS.
July *Fight For Ourselves* reaches UK #15. (Band makes it a condition of the new CBS contract that its records are not released in South Africa.)
Nov *Through The Barricades*, recorded in France, hits UK #7. The ballad title track hits UK #6.

987 **Feb** *How Many Lies*, also from the album, peaks at UK #34.
June [5-6] Gary Kemp appears at the 5th annual "Prince's Trust Rock Gala" at the Wembley Arena.

988 **May** The Kemp brothers attend the Cannes Film Festival, where they announce officially that they are to play the notorious 60s London gangland leaders Ron and Reggie Kray in a movie "The Krays".
July *Raw* reaches UK #47, the group's first release since early 1987.

989 **Sept** *Be Free With Your Love*, penned by Gary Kemp, makes UK #42, while parent album *Heart Like A Sky*, co-produced with Gary Langan, reaches UK #31. (Much to the chagrin of the band, who undertake a UK

tour to promote the release, between Dec.14 and Mar.6, 1990, CBS will not release the album in the US, which will ultimately result in termination of the CBS contract.)

1990 **Mar** Gary Kemp, with Jimmy Somerville and others, support Artists Against The Poll Tax. Group becomes inactive as each member views further Spandau Ballet projects with differing enthusiasm.

THE SPECIALS

Jerry Dammers (keyboards)
Terry Hall (vocals)
Neville Staples (vocals, percussion)
Lynval Golding (guitar)
Roddy Radiation (guitar)
Sir Horace Gentleman (bass)
John Bradbury (drums)

1977 **July** Band is formed in UK by Dammers (b. Gerald Dankin), Golding and Gentleman (b. Horace Panter) as The Coventry Automatics, who attempt to forge a punk/reggae fusion, with only marginally successful results. When they start to delve back to the rougher pre-reggae Jamaican ska form, the sound gels.

1978 The line-up expands to include Hall (b. Mar.19, 1959) and Staples (initially a roadie) on vocals, a drummer named Silverton and guitarist Radiation (b. Rod Byers). Group is known as The Coventry Specials for a while, before settling as The Special AKA.
June After attracting the attention of Joe Strummer, the band plays UK national dates as support on The Clash's "On Parole" tour. Clash manager Bernie Rhodes also manages the band, moving it to London for rehearsals in Camden Town, which last for many weeks and this leads to Silverton leaving. Convinced that this approach is wrong, Dammers splits from Rhodes and takes the band back to Coventry, where new manager Rick Rogers takes over.

1979 Dammers conceives the idea of the group recording on its own independent label. £700 is borrowed to pay for recording Dammers-penned *Gangsters*, a tribute to Prince Buster's ska classic *Al Capone*.
Mar Bradbury joins on drums, in time to play on the *Gangsters* session. Because the group cannot afford to record a B-side, Golding suggests to his friend, guitarist Neol Davies, that they use instrumental track *The Selecter*, which Davies has cut with Bradbury on drums, and local trombonist Barry Jones. (This is credited to "The Selecter", though Davies will not form the actual group until the single is selling.)
Apr Dammers makes use of his art college background to design a label. The name 2-Tone comes from his black-and-white creation. A deal is made with Rough Trade in London, which presses 5,000 copies of the single and arranges distribution.
July With the single attracting interest and sales, approaches are made by major record companies. Chrysalis signs The Special AKA and agrees to an autonomous 2-Tone label to be given a budget and marketed by Chrysalis, releasing at least 6 singles a year. All The Special AKA members, and their managers, become 2-Tone directors.
Sept *Gangsters*, taken over by Chrysalis, hits UK #6. Abridging its name to The Specials, the group tours UK with newly-formed Selecter and 2-Tone's other signing, London group Madness. Veteran trombonist Rico Rodrigues (b. Oct.17, 1934) joins The Specials, while trumpeter Dick Cuthy is added for tour work.
Oct [19] The Specials, Madness and The Selecter embark on the 2-Tone UK tour at the Top Rank, Brighton, E.Sussex.
Nov Debut album *Specials*, produced by Elvis Costello, hits UK #4, while a revival of *A Message To You, Rudy* hits UK #10.
Dec [28] Group performs alongside The Who and The Pretenders at the third of 4 concerts in aid of the People of Kampuchea, at London's Hammersmith Odeon.

1980 **Jan** Live EP *The Special AKA Live*, containing 4 revivals of 60s/early 70s ska and reggae hits, plus original song *Too Much Too Young* (which captures the airplay), tops the UK chart for 2 weeks.
[25] A 6-week US tour by the group opens at New York's Hurrah club, ending in 4 sold-out dates at the Whiskey A-Go-Go club in Los Angeles, CA., where many fans pose in "2-Tone" black-and-white clothing.
June *Rat Race* hits UK #5.
[4] Group embarks on 13-date "Seaside Specials" tour at Tiffanys, Great Yarmouth, Norfolk, ending June 19 at the Guild Hall, Portsmouth, Hants. They then tour Japan and Belgium.
July Golding is beaten up after leaving a Modettes gig at the Moonlight club.

Sept [13] A UK fall tour opens at the Riviera Lido, St. Austell, Cornwall, with 2-Tone act The Swinging Cats as support group.
Oct *Stereotype* hits UK #6, while the band's second album, *More Specials*, produced by Dammers and Dave Jordan at Horizon studios, Coventry, hits UK #5. It moves away from the band's ska roots, into what Dammers describes as "lounge music" – much of it coming from his fascination with film soundtrack music.
[16] The UK tour ends in Birmingham, W.Midlands, having played a month of English dates, and 2 in Scotland at Glasgow and Edinburgh. (At a date in Cambridge, Cambs., Dammers and Hall have been arrested and charged with incitement to violence, after trouble in the audience causes them to stop the show. They will be fined £1,000 in court in Jan.)

1981 Jan *Do Nothing* hits UK #4. A proposed US tour is cancelled by Dammers, who is suffering from exhaustion.
[9] Dammers and Hall are fined £400 each in Cambridge, after being convicted of using threatening words and behavior at an earlier gig.
Feb *Dance Craze*, a concert movie based around the music of The Specials and the 2-Tone stable, is released. The soundtrack album, featuring songs by the bands appearing in the film, hits UK #5.
July Haunting social-commenting *Ghost Town* tops the UK chart for 3 weeks, its lyric topical as riots flare in several UK inner-city areas.
Nov [2] Group fragments. Vocalists Staples, Hall and Golding leave to form Fun Boy Three (they will release 2 albums and have 5 UK hit singles before splitting in 1983, with Hall subsequently forming Colourfield and then 1990 trio Terry, Blair & Anouchka). Byers forms his own rockabilly group, Roddy Radiation & The Tearjerkers, while Panter also leaves, initially joining a religious sect, and later re-emerging in General Public. Dammers re-forms the group and reverts to the earlier name of The Special AKA. He and Bradbury alone remain from the earlier line-up, while Gary McManus (bass), John Shipley (guitar) and 3 vocalists – Rhoda Dakar (ex-The Bodysnatchers), Stan Campbell (ex-The Selecter) and Egidio Newton (ex-Animal Nightlife) join.

1982 Feb Fellow 2-Tonee Rhoda, listed with The Special AKA, makes UK #35 with *The Boiler*.
1983 Sept *Racist Friend*, the first release by the new line-up, makes UK #60.
1984 Apr *Nelson Mandela*, an anthem demanding freedom for the ANC leader imprisoned in South Africa, hits UK #9, but will become a global chant throughout the decade at relevant supportive gatherings.
June *In The Studio* reaches UK #34. Long in preparation in the studio, it carries a purposely ironic title.
1985 Mar The members of Special AKA take part, along with Madness, UB40, General Public and The Pioneers, in recording *Starvation*, a new version of an old Pioneers song released to raise funds for Ethiopian famine relief. Released on Madness' Zarjazz label, it reaches UK #33.
1986 Apr [23] Dammers forms Artists Against Apartheid in a meeting at Donmar Warehouse, London.
June [28] Dammers and Artists Against Apartheid organize an anti-apartheid concert in London, featuring Elvis Costello, Peter Gabriel, Boy George, Sade, Sting, Billy Bragg, Hugh Masekela, and others. The audience numbers 250,000.
1988 June [11] Dammers is the prime mover behind "Nelson Mandela's 70th Birthday Party" concert, held at Wembley Stadium, London, and seen all over the world via TV. Artists performing include Dire Straits, Whitney Houston, Stevie Wonder, Simple Minds, Tracy Chapman, and many others. The Special AKA's *Nelson Mandela* is the show's anthem, and, retitled *Nelson Mandela (70th Birthday Remake)*, is reissued in UK.

THE (DETROIT) SPINNERS

Bobbie Smith (vocals)
Phillipe Wynne (vocals)
Billy Henderson (vocals)
Henry Fambrough (vocals)
Pervis Jackson (vocals)

1961 Aug The Detroit-based US group, signed to Harvey Fuqua's Tri-Phi label, an associate of Motown Records, debuts with *That's What Girls Are Made For*. It is also the label's first release, and features Fuqua on lead vocals.
Nov *Love (I'm So Glad) I Found You* also features Fuqua, and peaks at US #91.
1965 Aug *I'll Always Love You* is released on Motown, and reaches US #35.
1967 G.C. (George) Cameron joins the group as lead singer.
1970 Oct After a lengthy period without success, Motown transfers the group to its V.I.P. subsidiary in search of new impetus. Stevie Wonder

produces *It's A Shame*, which does the trick, reaching US #14.
Nov *2nd Time Around* makes US #199.
Dec Group is dubbed The Motown Spinners in UK to avoid confusion with well-known Liverpool, Merseyside, folk group The Spinners. With this billing, *It's A Shame* is UK chart debut, at #20.
1971 Jan Follow-up on V.I.P., again produced by Wonder, is *We'll Have It Made*, which stalls at US #89. Following this, the group leaves Motown in search of a new deal. Both Stax and Avco Embassy are interested, but Aretha Franklin, a long-time friend of the group in Detroit, puts them in touch with Atlantic, to which they will sign before the end of the year. Prior to this, Cameron leaves to pursue a solo career at Motown, and is replaced by Wynne as lead vocalist.
1972 Nov Producer Thom Bell, always an admirer of The Spinners, produces them when he is contracting productions in Philadelphia for Atlantic. Debut single is soul ballad *How Could I Let You Get Away?*, but B-side *I'll Be Around* is superior and more commercial, and steals the airplay until it is made A-side by default. It hits US #3, and is the group's first million-seller.
1973 Mar Follow-up *Could It Be I'm Falling In Love*, produced again by Bell (as will be all The Spinners' Atlantic output until 1979), is a second millon-seller, hitting US #4.
May Cashing in on their current success, Motown reissues 1968 track *Together We Can Make Such Sweet Music*, which makes US #91. A Motown compilation *The Best Of The Spinners*, makes US #124.
June Debut Atlantic album *Spinners* reaches US #14, going gold, while *One Of A Kind (Love Affair)* is group's third consecutive gold single, and peaks at US #11. The Spinners also finally re-chart in UK, as *Could It Be I'm Falling In Love* makes UK #11. The change of label has meant a change of UK name for the group, now known as The Detroit Spinners.
Sept Linda Creed's socially-conscious *Ghetto Child* reaches US #29.
Nov *Ghetto Child* hits UK #7.
1974 Mar *Mighty Love* makes US #20.
May *Mighty Love* reaches US #16, the group's second gold album.
June *I'm Coming Home*, taken from the album, climbs to US #18.
Oct After the group has been the opening act for Dionne Warwick on a 5-week summer theater tour taking in Las Vegas, NV, Bell suggests a duet between her and the group - not a contractual problem, since Warwick is signed to Atlantic's associate label Warner Bros. The result is *Then Came You*, a million-seller which tops US chart - the first #1 hit for either side of the partnership (but the duetting is not carried on to any subsequent singles).
Nov *Love Don't Love Nobody* reaches UK #15, while *Then Came You* peaks at UK #29.
1975 Feb *New And Improved*, which includes the duet with Warwick, hits US #9 and earns the group another gold disk.
Apr *Living A Little, Laughing A Little*, makes US #37.
May *Sadie* reaches US #54.
Oct *They Just Can't Stop It (Games People Play)* puts The Spinners back in US Top 10, hitting #5 and earns another gold disk - as does album *Pick Of The Litter*, which includes the single and hits US #8.
1976 Feb *Love Or Leave* makes US #36, and double *Spinners Live!* US #20.
Aug *Wake Up Susan* reaches US #56.
Oct *Happiness Is Being With The Detroit Spinners* makes US #25, and is their last gold album.
Dec *The Rubberband Man* is a further million-seller, and hits US #2 for 3 weeks (behind Rod Stewart's *Tonight's The Night*). It also reaches UK #16 - the group's first UK hit for 2 years.
1977 Wynne leaves for a solo career, and is replaced by John Edwards (b. St.Louis, MO), having filled in for him on live shows since 1973.
Feb *Wake Up Susan* reaches UK #29.
Apr *You're Throwing A Good Love Away* makes US #43.
May A 4-track UK EP, tied in to a UK tour, coupling earlier hit *Could It Be I'm Falling In Love* with 3 album tracks, makes UK #32. Meanwhile, UK compilation *Detroit Spinners' Smash Hits* (with sleeve notes by Paul Gambaccini) peaks at UK #37, and *Yesterday, Today And Tomorrow* reaches UK #26.
June [10-11] The Spinners take part in third San Diego KOOL Jazz Festival, CA.
Oct *Heaven And Earth (So Fine)* is minor US hit at #89.
1978 Jan *Spinners 8* climbs to US #57.
June Compilation *The Best Of The Spinners* makes US #115.
Aug *If You Wanna Do A Dance* reaches US #49. This is the group's last Bell-produced hit single.
1979 June *From Here To Eternity* stalls at US #165.
1980 Mar Group teams with new producer Michael Zager, who records them on a version of The Four Seasons' *Working My Way Back To You*

blended in a medley with a new song of his own, *Forgive Me Girl*. It hits US #2, giving the group its final million-selling single, while parent album *Dancin' And Lovin'* makes US #32.

Apr *Working My Way Back To You/Forgive Me Girl* is their all-time biggest seller in UK, and only UK #1, topping chart for 2 weeks.

June *Body Language* reaches UK #40.

July A second medley in similar new-plus-old style, blending a revival of Sam Cooke's *Cupid* with *I've Loved You For A Long Time*, hits both US and UK #4.

Aug *Love Trippin'*, which includes the *Cupid* medley, makes US #53.

1981 Mar Another medley, of *Yesterday Once More/Nothing Remains The Same*, reaches US #52.

Apr *Labor Of Love* peaks at US #128.

1982 Jan *Can't Shake This Feelin'* stalls at US #196.

Mar *Never Thought I'd Fall In Love* creeps to US #95.

1983 Jan A revival of Willie Nelson standard *Funny How Time Slips Away* is the group's final US hit single, making #67, while *Grand Slam* is the last chart album, peaking at US #167.

1984 July [14] Former group member Phillipe Wynne dies.

1986 Aug [5] The Spinners take part in the "Rock'N'Roll Special" at Meadowlands, East Rutherford, NJ, with The Righteous Brothers, Frankie Valli & The Four Seasons and Tommy James & The Shondells.

1988 May [14] The Spinners participate in Atlantic Records' 40th anniversary show at New York's Madison Square Garden, as they continue to tour regularly.

SPIRIT

Randy California (guitar, vocals)
Jay Ferguson (vocals)
John Locke (keyboards)
Mark Andes (bass)
Ed Cassidy (drums)

1966 Dec California (b. Randy Wolfe, Feb.20, 1951, Los Angeles, CA), his stepfather Cassidy, always shaven-headed, (b. May 4, 1931, Chicago, IL) and Locke (b. Sept.25, 1943, Los Angeles), form Spirits Rebellious in Los Angeles. Locke has played 4 years with Cassidy in New Jazz Trio, while Cassidy and California have been in The Red Roosters in 1965, prior to going to New York for session work.

1967 Trio recruits the 2 other ex-Red Roosters, Ferguson (b. John Ferguson, May 10, 1947, Burbank, CA) and Andes (b. Feb.19, 1948, Philadelphia, PA), and shortens the name to Spirit.

1968 Apr Signed to Lou Adler's new Ode label, the group releases *Spirit*, critically rated as a progressive rock masterpiece. It climbs to US #31, staying on chart for 8 months.

1969 Mar *The Family That Plays Together* reaches US #22, their highest album chart placing. *I Got A Line On You*, extracted from it, is their first US hit single, reaching #25.

Oct *Clear Spirit* reaches US #55.

1970 Mar *1984*, taken from *Clear Spirit*, reaches US #69.

Sept First release on Epic is *Animal Zoo*, which charts briefly at US #97.

1971 Feb *The 12 Dreams Of Dr. Sardonicus*, generally considered their most accessible work, only reaches US #63.

June California leaves for UK to play solo, while Andes and Ferguson depart to form Jo Jo Gunne, with Matt Andes (guitar) and Curly Smith (drums), which signs to Asylum Records.

1972 Apr *Feedback*, recorded by Cassidy and Locke with newly-joined Texas guitarist Chris Staehely and his bassist brother Al, reaches US #63, after which Cassidy and Locke also leave, and a totally non-original Spirit tours UK.

May Jo Jo Gunne's *Run Run Run* reaches US #27 and UK #6 - its only chart single. *Jo Jo Gunne* makes US #57, but does not chart in UK.

Sept California releases solo album *Captain Kopter And The Fabulous Twirlybirds*, which fails to chart.

1973 May Jo Jo Gunne's *Bite Down Hard* makes US #75, featuring Jimmie Randall on bass in place of departed Mark Andes.

Aug Compilation album *The Best Of Spirit* peaks at US #120.

Oct *Mr. Skin* stalls at US #92.

1974 Jan Jo Jo Gunne's *Jumpin' The Gunne* peaks at US #169. Cassidy and California re-form Spirit as a trio, with Barry Keene on bass, and sign to Mercury Records.

Dec Final Jo Jo Gunne album *So...Where's The Show?* reaches US #198. Ex-Spirit member Chris Staehely plays guitar on it in place of Andes.

1975 June Locke rejoins the group for double album *Spirit Of '76* on Mercury, which reaches US #147.

1976 Mark Andes rejoins, bringing his brother Matt from Jo Jo Gunne on

guitar, for *Son Of Spirit*, which does not chart.

June [18] *The 12 Dreams Of Dr. Sardonicus* goes gold with a half million US sales, 6 years after release.

Aug *Farther Along* reaches US #179.

[29] Group plays a reunion concert at Santa Monica, CA, with Neil Young guesting for the encore version of Bob Dylan's *Like A Rolling Stone* – though California almost throws him off at first.

1977 Apr Group's last Mercury album, *Future Games (A Magical Kahvana Dream)*, includes "Star Trek" dialog, but not Locke or the Andes brothers, who have departed, Mark Andes to join Firefall. It fails.

1978 Feb Locke joins Nazareth for a US tour.

Apr Ferguson, having stayed with Asylum as a soloist after the demise of Jo Jo Gunne, hits US #9 with *Thunder Island*.

Spirit tours UK.

1979 Jan Spirit's live album *Live*, recorded on stage in Germany, is released in US on its own Potato label, and in UK on Illegal Records.

June Ferguson reaches US #31 with solo *Shakedown Cruise*.

1981 Apr Rhino Records in US releases Spirit's *Journey To Potatoland*, a project from the early 70s, rejected by Epic as lacking commercial potential. It reaches UK #40 on Beggars Banquet Records – Spirit's only UK chart entry.

June [16] California and Cassidy, with keyboardman George Valuck, perform on BBC TV's "The Old Grey Whistle Test" followed the next night by a one-off gig at London's Hammersmith Odeon.

1982 Mark Andes joins Heart.

1984 Feb Spirit reunites as a 5-piece, releasing re-recorded *1984*.

Mar *Spirit Of '84/Dream The Thirteenth Dream*, on Mercury Records, features the reunited line-up on re-cuts of old songs *Fresh Garbage*, *I Got A Line On You* and *1984*, plus some new material.

1989 California and Cassidy begin touring again with Mike Nile on bass and Scott Monahan on keyboards, as a recording deal with IRS materializes.

SPLIT ENZ

Tim Finn (vocals, piano)
Phil Judd (vocals, guitar)
Eddie Rayner (keyboards)
Wally Wilkinson (guitar)
Mike Chunn (bass)
Paul Crowther (drums)
Noel Crombie (spoons, design)

1972 Oct Group forms in Auckland, New Zealand, as Split Ends, with Finn (b. June 25, 1952), Judd, Chunn, Miles Golding and Michael Howard.

1973 Mar Their first tour, around colleges and universities, is followed by a New Zealand tour supporting John Mayall.

Apr First single *For You* is released on Vertigo Records.

Sept Band makes the final of the New Zealand NZBC TV "New Faces" talent show, giving their startling image nationwide coverage, and a major brewery offers them touring sponsorship on the pub circuit.

1975 Mar Band moves to Australia and changes name to Split Enz.

May They sign to Mushroom Records, and first album *Mental Notes*, is recorded in Australia. Group supports Roxy Music in Sydney, and sparks interest from guitarist Phil Manzanera.

1976 May Band moves to UK, where Manzanera produces *Second Thoughts* (mainly upgraded re-recordings of songs from the first album).

1977 May During a US tour Judd leaves and is replaced by Finn's 18-year-old brother Neil (b. May 27, 1958, Te Awamutu, NZ). Wilkinson, Chunn and Crowther also leave to be replaced by Englishmen Nigel Griggs (b. Aug.18, 1949) and Malcolm Green (b. Jan.25, 1953) shortly before their third album *Dizrhythmia* is released.

1978 Group tours UK, usually as a support act. Judd rejoins, then quits again as Chrysalis drops the group. They return to Australia after recording *Frenzy* and re-sign with Mushroom. *I See Red* hits Top 10 in Australia and New Zealand.

Oct Split Enz plays **Time Out** magazine's "10th Anniversary Concert" in London.

1979 Sept After spending most of the year touring, the band releases *True Colours*.

1980 A&M Records offers the group a worldwide contract on the strength of the album. Led by Neil Finn's catchy single *I Got You*, *True Colours* becomes the group's best-selling album. Chrysalis releases retrospective album *Beginning Of The Enz*.

Aug *I Got You* reaches UK #12 and US #40. *True Colours* is released in gimmick formats, including different color sleeves and the first commercial use of laser-etched vinyl. It peaks at UK #42 and US #40 during a 6-month chart run.

SPLIT ENZ cont.

1981 **Mar** *Waiata* (the title Maori for "song", "party" or "celebration") is released.
May Neil Finn's *History Never Repeats* makes UK #63. *Waiata* enters US charts and peaks at #45 during a 19-week run.

1982 **May** Green leaves shortly after *Time And Tide* is released.
June *Time And Tide* enters US chart, peaking at #53. In UK, *Six Months In A Leaky Boat* is banned by BBC in the event that it might refer to the British fleet preparing to engage Argentina in the Falklands War.

1983 Group celebrates its 10th anniversary with a concert in Te Awamutu, New Zealand.
Sept Tim Finn's solo album *Escapade* peaks at US #161.

1984 **Aug** *Conflicting Emotions* makes US #137.

1985 As Tim Finn announces he is leaving the group to go solo (on Virgin), he marries actress Greta Scacchi. After the mini-album *See You Round*, Neil Finn and Hester form a new group with Nick Seymour.

1986 Tim Finn's second solo album, *Big Canoe*, fails to chart, despite a US tour with Tony Levin, Alex Acuna and Rick Marotta. Neil signs to Capitol Records and moves to Los Angeles to work with Mitchell Froom, calling his new band Crowded House, with Paul Hester and Nick Seymour, a reference to life at his Los Angeles residence.

1987 **Apr** [25] Crowded House debut, *Don't Dream It's Over*, hits US #2. *Crowded House* makes US #12, and will spend rest of the year on chart.
June *Don't Dream It's Over* reaches UK #27.
July [25] *Something So Strong* hits US #7.
Sept [12] *World Where You Live* peaks at US #65.

1988 **June** [11] Paul Young sings *Don't Dream It's Over* at "Nelson Mandela's 70th Birthday Party" at Wembley Stadium, London.
Aug Crowded House's *Temple of Low Men* reaches US #40, while extracted *Better Be Home Soon* makes US #42.

1989 **Aug** [3] Tim Finn embarks on major North American tour, supporting 10,000 Maniacs, in Vancouver, Canada, set to end Oct.7, Princeton, NJ.

1991 **Feb** [14] Crowded House previews its new line-up, with Tim Finn joining Neil Finn, Paul Hester and Nick Seymour, at a Los Angeles radio station KIQQ-FM gig on board a boat off the Californian coast.

DUSTY SPRINGFIELD

1960 Springfield (b. Mary O'Brien, Apr.16, 1939, Hampstead, London), ex-member of UK vocal trio The Lana Sisters, with her brother Dion O'Brien and friend Tim Field, forms The Springfields, a folk and country music-based vocal/guitar trio. She adopts new stage name Dusty Springfield, while Dion becomes Tom Springfield. They begin working in folk clubs.

1961 **May** Signed to Philips Records, the trio's debut *Dear John* fails to chart.
Sept *Breakaway* makes UK #31.
Dec Christmas song *Bambino* reaches UK #16. Debut album *Kinda Folksy* is released, and they are named Best UK Vocal Group in **New Musical Express** readers' poll, on the strength of 2 minor hits.

1962 **June** Field leaves and is replaced by Mike Pickworth, who changes name to Mike Hurst.
Sept *Silver Threads And Golden Needles*, having failed to chart in UK, reaches US #20.
Nov *Dear Hearts And Gentle People* is US follow-up and makes #95.

1963 **Mar** *Island Of Dreams* hits UK #5.
Apr *Say I Won't Be There* also hits UK #5, as the group tours UK supporting US visitors Del Shannon and Johnny Tillotson.
Aug The Springfields' *Come On Home* reaches UK #31, their last hit.
Sept [24] Group announces that it is to split, and that Dusty Springfield will be signing a solo deal with Philips.
Oct [11] Group plays its farewell concert at the London Palladium. (After the split, Hurst will become a record producer, most notably for Showaddywaddy in the 70s, while Tom Springfield will write such hits as *The Carnival Is Over* and *Georgy Girl* for The Seekers, and in the early 70s will launch Springfield Revival.)
[20] Springfield makes her solo debut at a concert for British troops stationed in Germany.
Nov [8] She begins first solo tour, with The Searchers, Freddie & The Dreamers, Brian Poole & The Tremeloes and Dave Berry, in Halifax, W.Yorks.

1964 **Jan** Dusty's solo debut is a change from pop/folk to more Motown-style music and *I Only Want To Be With You* hits UK #4. The Springfields appear in UK movie "It's All Over Town" (a cameo slot filmed before their break-up), singing *If I Was Down And Out*, which is also released as a final Springfields single.
[1] *I Only Want To Be With You* is the first record played on new BBC TV show "Top Of The Pops".

[29] Springfield begins a 29-date twice-nightly UK package tour, with The Swinging Blue Jeans, Bobby Vee and Big Dee Irwin at the Adelphi theater, Slough, Berks., set to end at the Empire theater, Liverpool, Merseyside, on Mar.29.
Mar *Stay Awhile*, in similar style to her debut, reaches UK #13, while *I Only Want To Be With You* makes US #12.
Apr She tours Australia with Gerry & The Pacemakers.
May Debut album *A Girl Called Dusty* hits UK #6, as *Stay Awhile* climbs to US #38.
July Bacharach/David-written *I Just Don't Know What To Do With Myself* hits UK #3.
Aug *Wishin' And Hopin'*, another Bacharach/David song, from the debut album is chosen as US single and hits #6. (A version by The Merseybeats charts in UK at the same time.) She visits US briefly to record some tracks in New York.
Oct US-only *All Cried Out* makes US #41.
Nov [14] Springfield embarks on 21-date UK package tour, with Herman's Hermits, Dave Berry & The Cruisers and Brian Poole & The Tremeloes, at the Granada theater, Edmonton, London, set to end on Dec.6 at the Gaumont theater, Hanley, Staffs.
[29] *Losing You* hits UK #9.
Dec [9] Springfield leaves for South African tour, stipulating that she will only perform in front of non-segregated audiences.
[14] She plays for a multi-racial audience at a cinema near Cape Town.
[15] Officials from the South African Minister of the Interior serve her with deportation orders and she leaves South Africa the next day.

1965 **Feb** *Your Hurtin' Kinda Love* halts at UK #37.
Mar [25] Springfield begins a 12-date twice-nightly UK package tour, with The Searchers, Heinz, The Zombies, special guest star Bobby Vee and others, at the Odeon theater, Stockton-on-Tees, Cleveland, set to end Apr.10 at the Sophia Gardens, Cardiff, Wales.
Losing You stalls at US #91.
Apr [11] She takes part in an all-star cast at the annual **New Musical Express** Poll Winners concert at the Empire Pool, Wembley, London.
[14] Springfield guest on ITV's "The Bacharach Sound" with Dionne Warwick and The Searchers among others.
[21] "The Sound Of Motown", an ITV special featuring The Supremes, Martha & The Vandellas, Stevie Wonder, Smokey Robinson & The Miracles and The Temptations and hosted by Springfield, airs on ITV.
May [19] Springfield pulls out from opening of 6-week summer show at the Winter Gardens, Bournemouth, Dorset, because of illness.
[30] She goes to Harley Street specialist to gain a medical ruling on whether she will be fit to open in her summer show next Monday. (Cleo Laine deputizes for her during first 2 weeks of the engagement.)
July Uptempo *In The Middle Of Nowhere* hits UK #8.
Aug She flies to the Virgin Islands for a complete rest and cancels all engagements.
Sept [17] Springfield appears on "Ready Steady Go!", her first TV appearance since her illness.
Oct *Some Of Your Lovin'*, a ballad with vocal backing by Madeleine Bell and Doris Troy, hits UK #8.
Nov *Everything's Coming Up Dusty* hits UK #6, as she appears in the Royal Variety Show in London.

1966 **Feb** Uptempo *Little By Little* reaches UK #17.
Apr *You Don't Have To Say You Love Me*, an Italian song (which had been that country's entry for the San Remo Song Festival) with new English lyrics by Simon Napier-Bell and Vicki Wickham, tops UK chart and is her all-time best-selling single.
May [1] Springfield appears on a star-studded bill at the annual **New Musical Express** Poll Winners Concert at the Empire Pool, Wembley.
July Goffin/King ballad *Goin' Back* hits UK #10, as *You Don't Have To Say You Love Me* hits US #4.
Aug [18] BBC TV series "Dusty" airs for the first time.
Oct Another ballad, *All I See Is You*, hits UK #9 and US #20.
Nov Compilation album *Golden Hits*, rounding up her singles successes to date, hits UK #2.
[3] Springfield makes US night club debut at Basin Street East, New York, amidst complaints that the support acts, Los Vegas and The Buddy Rich Orchestra and a host of celebrities introduced to the audience, mean Springfield waits more than 3 hours to make her debut.
Dec [23] Springfield opens in "Merry King Cole" at the Empire theater, Liverpool.

1967 **Jan** She records 2 movie theme songs, *The Corrupt Ones* for "The Peking Medallion" and *The Look Of Love* for James Bond movie "Casino Royale".
Mar *I'll Try Anything* reaches UK #13 and US #40.

Sting

Ike & Tina Turner

T. Rex

June *Give Me Time* makes UK #24 and US #76.

July [7] Springfield begins 3-week season at New York's Copacabana.

Sept [19] Second season of BBC TV's "Dusty" comes to a close.

Nov *The Look Of Love*, from "Casino Royale", is her last hit on Philips in US, reaching #22. *Where Am I Going* peaks at UK #40.

Dec *What's It Gonna Be* reaches US #49.

'68 May [8] 9-week "It Must Be Dusty" series airs for the first time on ITV.

[19] Springfield performs at the Royal Variety TV show with Tom Jones, Long John Baldry and others.

Aug *I Close My Eyes And Count To Ten* hits UK #4.

Sept *I Will Come To You* fails to chart. Now signed to Atlantic records in US, she travels to Memphis, TN, to record an album with the label's Southern session men.

Nov [24] Springfield guests on CBS TV's "Ed Sullivan Show".

'69 Jan *Son Of A Preacher Man*, recorded in Memphis, hits UK #9, and US #10, while *Dusty ... Definitely* makes UK #30.

Mar *Don't Forget About Me* reaches US #64, while B-side *Breakfast In Bed* makes US #91.

Apr *Dusty In Memphis*, from the Memphis sessions and recorded in less than a week (later considered one of her finest), is released and is her first album not to chart in UK.

[28] Springfield guests on US TV's "Joey Bishop Show", followed by a 10-day North American tour, accompanied by King Curtis.

May *The Windmills Of Your Mind*, the theme song from film "The Thomas Crown Affair", reaches US #31.

July A version of Tony Joe White's *Willie And Laura Mae Jones* climbs to US #78.

Sept *Am I The Same Girl*, covering Barbara Acklin's US #79 and Young-Holt Unlimited's instrumental version *Soulful Strut*, a US #3, peaks at UK #43.

Nov [30] She appears with David Bowie, Grapefruit and The Graham Bond Organization, at "Save Rave '69", a benefit show in London for the magazine **Rave**.

Dec *A Brand New Me*, written and produced in Philadelphia, PA, by Gamble and Huff, reaches US #24.

70 Mar *Silly, Silly Fool* stalls at US #76, her last US Singles chart entry.

Sept A revival of The Young Rascals' *How Can I Be Sure* makes UK #37, and is her last UK hit single for 9 years.

'72 She leaves UK to live in Los Angeles, CA.

Nov *See All Her Faces* fails to chart.

'73 May *Cameo*, released on Philips in UK and Dunhill in US, fails.

'74 She begins recording her second Dunhill album *Longings* (but it will not be released).

Mar *What's It Gonna Be* is her last new release for Philips in UK. She becomes a session singer in Los Angeles, almost signing to Rocket Records.

'75 She sings back-up vocals on recording sessions by Anne Murray.

'78 She attempts a recording comeback, signing new dual deals, with Mercury in UK and United Artists in US.

Feb *A Love Like Yours* and *It Begins Again* are produced by Roy Thomas-Baker. The album is critically acclaimed, but is only a moderate seller, making UK #41.

'79 May *Living Without Your Love* also fails to chart.

Nov *Baby Blue*, on Mercury, reaches UK #61 – her first UK chart single since 1970.

'80 She signs to 20th Century Records in US, releasing only 1 single *It Goes Like It Goes*, the Oscar-winning song from "Norma Rae".

Oct [7] She makes her first New York stage appearance in 8 years, at the Grande Finale club.

'83 *White Heat*, an electronic dance-flavored set on US Casablanca, despite some US critical plaudits, is not released in UK.

'84 Mar A Dusty Springfield/Spencer Davis duet, re-working old William Bell/Judy Clay hit *Private Number*, is released in UK on Allegiance Records.

'85 Aug She returns to UK to promote her new single *Sometimes Like Butterflies*, released on Peter Stringfellow's Hippodrome label, but it finds little success.

'87 Aug The Pet Shop Boys invite Dusty Springfield to guest on their single *What Have I Done To Deserve This*, which is a worldwide hit.

Sept She sings guest vocals on Richard Carpenter's single *Something In Your Eyes*.

Dec *I Only Want To Be With You* is re-issued to tie in with Springfield's brief appearance in a UK soft drink TV ad. The single is backed by her 1968 recording of *Breakfast In Bed* (which will be a hit in 1988 for UB40 & Chrissie Hynde).

'88 Jan Compilation *The Silver Collection* on Philips reaches UK #14.

Feb [8] She makes a rare TV appearance with The Pet Shop Boys at the BPI annual awards ceremony from London's Royal Albert Hall, performing *What Have I Done To Deserve This*.

[20] *What Have I Done To Deserve This?* hits US #2.

Dec Springfield teams with US singer B.J. Thomas to record *As Long As We Got Each Other*, used as the theme to hit US TV sitcom "Growing Pains".

1989 Mar *Nothing Has Been Proved*, penned and co-produced by The Pet Shop Boys and featured in the film "Scandal", reaches UK #16.

Dec Uptempo *In Private*, also written and co-produced by The Pet Shop Boys, reaches UK #14, following an appearance on ITV's "The Dame Edna Experience".

1990 May *Reputation* makes UK #38.

July [7] *Reputation*, with 4 tracks written by The Pet Shop Boys, a remake of the Goffin/King song *I Want To Stay Here* and 2 tracks produced by Dan Hartman, reaches UK #18.

Nov *Arrested By You* stalls at UK #70.

BRUCE SPRINGSTEEN

1963 Having tried drumming unsuccessfully at an early age, Springsteen (b. Bruce Frederick Joseph Springsteen, Sept.23, 1949, Freehold, NJ), son of Adele and Douglas Springsteen, as a teenager buys a guitar for $18 from a local pawn shop and begins to learn songs from the radio. (He will be influenced by Elvis Presley, Chuck Berry and, later on, by The Beatles and The Rolling Stones.)

1965 Already composing his own songs, Springsteen discovers sister Ginny's boyfriend George Theiss has a vacancy in his high school band, The Castiles. Springsteen passes 2 auditions for group manager 32-year-old Tex Vineyard. With the band practising every day after school, Vineyard, an unemployed factory worker, secures The Castiles constant gigs at school dances, YMCA parties and clubs around New Jersey areas Red Bank, Long Branch and Asbury Park.

1967 Aug Having recorded 1 demo, *That's What You'll Get*, The Castiles play their final gig at Off Broad Street coffee house, Red Bank. Springsteen moves to live in nearby Asbury Park and joins short-lived trio Earth. He also begins spending many evenings at the Upstage club, a popular local hangout for aspiring musicians, where he meets Vini Lopez, Southside Johnny and Steve Van Zandt.

1969 Springsteen forms new band Child from club members, which changes name to Steel Mill when they realize another Child already exists. Managed by Tinker West, the group begins constant local gigging, and also a mini club-tour of California, which attracts good press reviews.

1971 Steel Mill splits. (3 members, drummer Lopez, keyboardist Danny Federici and bassist Van Zandt will join Springsteen's future backing E Street Band.) Springsteen forms Dr. Zoom & The Sonic Boom, a collection of Asbury Park musicians not currently affiliated to other line-ups. It plays only 3 dates, as summer performing is seriously interrupted by Asbury riots.

Sept Springsteen starts 10-piece group, The Bruce Springsteen Band, with a horn section and girl singers. After only 2 dates, the line-up is cut to David Sancious on keyboards, Garry Tallent on bass, Van Zandt (now on guitar), Lopez and Federici, while Asbury saxophonist Clarence Clemons also joins.

1972 May Springsteen auditions for aspiring producers Mike Appel and Jim Cretecos and, after returning from an unsuccessful solo trip to California, signs a long-term management contract with Appel's Laurel Canyon Promotion Company, on a car hood in an unlit parking lot. Appel arranges an audition for Springsteen in front of CBS/Columbia A&R head John Hammond who is impressed and arranges a further audition for Columbia colleagues at the Gaslight club, Greenwich Village, New York.

June [9] Despite difficulties between an aggressive Appel and the label, Springsteen signs a worldwide long-term 10 album CBS deal for an advance of $25,000 with a $40,000 recording budget. Springsteen quickly re-forms The Bruce Springsteen Band (now without Van Zandt) against the wishes of CBS which sees him as a solo folk performer. Undaunted, Springsteen takes the band into the studio to record his first album in 3 weeks.

1973 Jan Debut album *Greetings From Asbury Park* is released. Selected as a priority by CBS head Clive Davis, critics are encouraged to think of Springsteen as the new Dylan. Despite a lengthy club tour and a 10-date support role for CBS headliners Chicago (criticized as a misconceived disaster), the album only sells 25,000 copies. Relations between artist's management and CBS worsen.

Feb Springsteen's *Blinded By The Light* disappears without trace.

May While Davis is fired, Springsteen plays the CBS Records Annual Convention in San Francisco prior to recording second album.

Nov *The Wild, The Innocent And The E. Street Shuffle* is released. It proves popular with rock critics who pay particular attention to native ballad *Asbury Park Fourth Of July (Sandy)*. A 6-city club tour fails to ignite sales, even though Springsteen and the band are now seasoned live performers, commonly playing 2-hour sets. Ernest Carter replaces Lopez as the backing group are named The E Street Band – after the road where Sancious' mother lives in Belmar, NJ.

1974 May Band plays 3 nights at Charley's club in Harvard Square, Cambridge, MA. One of them is attended by influential rock critic, 26-year-old Jon Landau who writes for **Rolling Stone** and Boston-based **The Real Paper**, and is suitably impressed, particularly by Springsteen's first live performance of new song *Born To Run*.

[22] After seeing a second date in Cambridge, Landau is moved to write: "I saw rock and roll future – and its name is Bruce Springsteen." The often misquoted sentence immediately sparks intense promotion ideas at CBS and snowballs further similar reviews by other critics. CBS re-promotes the first 2 Springsteen albums as a long-term friendship develops between the artist and Landau.

Aug [3] Springsteen & The E Street Band open for Anne Murray at the Schaefer Festival, NY. It is the final gig in the line-up for Carter and Sancious who are replaced by drummer Max Weinberg (b. Apr.13, 1951) and pianist Roy Bittan.

Nov With production indecision delaying the third album, Springsteen asks Landau to help, which he unofficially does.

1975 Feb Landau becomes co-producer of the new album and invites Steve Van Zandt to relink with Springsteen to provide a rockier edge to the current recordings. Appel, also co-producing with Springsteen, is unhappy with Landau's involvement.

Apr UK act The Hollies shorten earlier Springsteen song to *Sandy*, peaking at US #85.

July His first 2 releases finally chart, *Greetings* making US #60 and *The Wild, The Innocent* reaching US #59.

Sept [6] Third album *Born To Run* is released and immediately hailed as a rock classic. It will hit US #3, while the title cut simultaneously climbs to US #23. Springsteen and the band begin their first national tour, a 40-date "Born To Run" trek which gains sensational reviews.

Oct [27] In an unprecedented move, both **Time** and **Newsweek** magazines feature cover stories on Springsteen. Many other critics feel that the hype machine is out of control.

Nov At Los Angeles, CA, gig, Springsteen meets Phil Spector. The arrangement of the title track from *Born To Run* was credited as a tribute to the producer. Spector invites Springsteen to a Dion session, and he plays 2 dates at London's Hammersmith Odeon, his first UK performances, as part of a European tour also taking in Stockholm and Amsterdam. As *Born To Run* makes UK #36, many people, including Springsteen, are outraged by CBS hype which features bill posters of the famous (misquoted) Landau review. A theater hoarding announces "At last London is ready for Bruce Springsteen."

Dec Appel tapes 3 concerts for a planned live album. Only cut which will officially emerge is festive *Santa Claus Is Coming To Town*, which highlights a special live rapport between Clarence Clemons and Springsteen.

1976 Jan Follow-up *Tenth Avenue Freeze Out* peaks at US #83.

Feb Van Zandt produces *I Don't Want To Go Home* for Southside Johnny & The Asbury Jukes, including Springsteen song *The Fever*.

Mar Springsteen enlists the help of Landau and lawyer Mike Mayer in looking at his original Appel contract. Appel is seeking to renegotiate a management contract with Springsteen who realizes for the first time that he only receives 3½% of wholesale album sales as opposed to Appel's 14%.

Apr Band begins a US tour as Manfred Mann's Earth Band's cover of Springsteen's *Spirit In The Night* makes US #97 (it will re-chart a year later to make US #40).

[29] At 3am, after a gig in Memphis, Springsteen, Van Zandt and publicist Glen Brunman ask a Memphis cab driver to take them to Elvis Presley's Graceland home. Springsteen climbs over the wall. A security guard assumes he is just another crank fan and apprehends him.

May [14] Appel's Laurel Canyon company sends Springsteen an outstanding payment check for $67,368.78.

July [2] Appel legally informs Springsteen that he must not use Landau as a producer on his fourth album.

[27] Springsteen counters with writs alleging fraud and breach of trust by Appel.

Aug He plays a 1-week engagement in Red Bank, NJ, to earn money

during the legal dispute.

Sept He opens another lengthy tour, at the Coliseum, Phoenix, AZ.

1977 Jan Manfred Mann's Earth Band's cover of Springsteen's *Blinded By The Light* tops US chart (having hit US #6 6 months earlier).

May [28] After several legal flurries, an out-of-court settlement is reached with Appel. He reportedly wins substantial monies, but Springsteen is free to seek new management and make his own decisions.

June [1] Springsteen and Landau begin legal recording under a renegotiated deal with CBS at Atlantic studios, Manhattan, NY.

July Always a prolific songwriter, Springsteen gives *Fire* to New York rockabilly Robert Gordon and *Because The Night* to Jimmy Iovine who producing a Patti Smith album in the next door studio (the song will reach US #13 and UK #5).

1978 May [23] Prefacing the finished album, Bruce Springsteen & The E Street Band return to stage work at Shea's Buffalo theater. The beginning of another lengthy series, the performances now extend to hours with the inclusion of many cover versions.

June [3] Springsteen plays Long Island's Nassau Coliseum – his first New York appearance in 2 years.

Darkness On The Edge Of Town is finally released and hits US #5 and makes UK #16, while *Prove It All Night* makes US #33 (he will be without a UK chart single until 1980).

Sept *Badlands* peaks at US #42.

Dec The Pointer Sisters follow Gordon and record *Fire*, hitting US #2 (and UK #34 in Mar.1979).

1979 Jan [1] A 7-month tour ends in Cleveland after 109 shows in 86 cities all sell-outs including dates at New York's Madison Square Garden.

Mar Band enters the Power Station to record a new album.

Apr During hi-jinks with comic Robin Williams and Springsteen's girlfriend Joyce Heiser, Springsteen damages a leg in a motorbike accident at home, forcing him to take a 3-month break.

May Tapes for a new album leak out of the studio, aiding increasing pirate/bootleg operations.

June [3] Springsteen & The E Street Band are joined by Rickie Lee Jones and Boz Scaggs for a jam session on stage at the Whiskey A-Go-Go in Los Angeles, at the wedding reception of his lighting man Mark Brickman.

July Greg Kihn cuts Springsteen's *For You* on his album *With The Naked Eye* while The Knack record his *Rendezvous*.

Aug CBS and Springstein file a suit in Los Angeles against 5 bootleggers, seeking $1.75 million in damages.

Sept [23] On his 30th birthday, Springsteen plays the Musicians United For Safe Energy (MUSE) concert at New York's Madison Square Garden at Jackson Browne's invitation. Springsteen performs on condition that no politicians are present and that photographer Lynn Goldsmith is also barred (Goldsmith had sold private pictures of Springsteen taken during their brief 1978 tour affair). Springsteen is strongly featured in subsequent *No Nukes* triple album and film.

Oct Springsteen re-enters the studio to work on a new album.

1980 Nov Double album *The River* is released, trimmed from an original choice of 60 songs, and set to hit US #1 and UK #2, spending over a year on both charts. Extracted *Hungry Heart*, with unavailable elsewhere B-side *Held Up Without A Gun* hits US #5 and makes UK #4.

[3] "The River" tour begins in Ann Arbor, MI, with the live set now extended at some dates to 4 hours and including popular encore medley of Mitch Ryder songs which will remain a long-term habit.

1981 Mar *Fade Away* peaks at US #20.

[19] After initially postponed dates caused by ill-health, he returns to UK for first dates since 1975, opening with 2 nights in London.

May Gary U.S. Bonds releases *Dedication* (US #27 and UK #43) produced by Springsteen and containing 4 of his songs including *This Little Girl* (US #11, UK #43) and *Jolé Blon* (US #65, UK #51). Springsteen will also convert backing vocals on the album to live assistance on selected Bonds' dates.

[11] Springsteen finishes a 32-date European tour in Paris, France.

June Title track from *The River* makes UK #35.

Oct 1975-recorded *Santa Claus Is Comin' To Town* is included on CBS various artists' album *In Harmony*, released in aid of Children's Television Workshop and children's charities. It becomes a seasonal radio favorite.

1982 Jan Sessions for a new album begin at Springsteen's home and in the studio – they will dominate the next 2 years of his career.

July Second Springsteen-produced Gary U.S. Bonds album *On The Line* is issued (US #52, UK #55), including US #21 *Out Of Work*. Springsteen gives *From Small Things (Big Things One Day Come)* to UK rocker Dave Edmunds, but it will fail to chart.

Sept With little fanfare, Springsteen releases *Nebraska*, a solo set of acoustic compositions recorded by Springsteen and his band at Power Station on a 4-track home tape recorder. It hits both US and UK #3 but no singles will be issued from it. The original home recordings also feature new songs including *Working On The Highway* and the first electric version of future hit *Born In The USA*.

1983 Springsteen spends the year writing and recording over 100 new songs for selection on his next project. With no live dates, he also drives extensively throughout US.

1984 **Apr** Van Zandt leaves The E Street line-up amicably and sets up Little Steven & The Disciples Of Soul.

May Following a near 2-year wait, new material emerges with *Dancing In The Dark*, helped on its way to hit US #2 and UK #28 by his first formal video, directed by Brian De Palma. Previously shy of the device, his only celluloid promotion has been a live clip of popular number *Rosalita*.

June New album *Born In The USA* is released to become his most successful multi-platinum album. It will spend over 2 years on both US and UK charts, hitting US #1 on each. The "Born In The USA" tour debuts in St. Paul, MN, with Nils Lofgren replacing Van Zandt on guitar. It is Springsteen's first live work since "The River" tour and will take in Europe, Australia, US, Canada and Japan. It also features his first female backing singer, Patti Scialfa, ex-Southside Johnny & The Asbury Jukes. *Born To Run* now makes UK #17.

Oct *Cover Me* hits US #7 and will reach UK #16.

Dec Title cut *Born In The USA*, already an anthemic live number re-identifying Springsteen's harder image, hits US #9.

1985 **Jan** [25] Springsteen contributes a lead vocal to USA For Africa's *We Are The World* benefit disk. He will also donate popular live cut (previously unreleased) *Trapped* for **USA For Africa** (the track was recorded on Aug.6, 1984 at Meadowlands, East Rutherford, NJ, and is part of extensive live recordings accompanying the "Born" tour). Meanwhile, *Dancing In The Dark* is re-promoted in UK, hitting #4.

Feb Ballad *I'm On Fire*, supported by his first concept-acted video begins a 5-month US chart stay on its way to hit #6.

[26] *Dancing In The Dark* wins Best Rock Vocal Performance, Male at the 27th annual Grammy awards.

Mar Reissued *Cover Me* makes UK #16 as US close-harmony cover band Big Daddy's unrecognizable version of *Dancing In The Dark* makes UK #21.

May [13] Springsteen marries model/actress Julianne Phillips at Our Lady of the Lake church, Lake Oswego, OR.

June As *Glory Days* hits US #5, the tour reaches UK amid unprecedented ticket demand, with sell-outs at 72,000-attendee dates at Wembley Stadium, London. Double A-side *I'm On Fire/Born In The USA* hits UK #5 as all 7 Springsteen albums either re-enter or enter UK chart simultaneously (*The Wild* peaks at #33, while *Greetings* makes #41).

Aug *Glory Days* reaches UK #17 as sixth extract from album *Born In The USA*, *I'm Goin' Down* hits US #9.

Oct [2] "Born In The USA" tour ends at Los Angeles' Coliseum.

Nov Springsteen contributes lead vocals to Artists United Against Apartheid single *Sun City* and appears in a video alongside its inspirator, Little Steven Van Zandt (US #38, UK #21).

Dec Festive *Santa Claus Is Coming To Town/My Hometown* hits UK #9.

1986 **Jan** [25] Still from *Born In The USA*, *My Hometown* hits US #6.

Feb Lee Iacocca reportedly offers Springsteen $12 million to license *Born In The USA* for a series of Chrysler commercials. Springsteen rejects the offer.

[10] Springsteen wins Best International Solo Artist at the fifth annual BRIT Awards at the Grosvenor House, London.

Mar Always concerned at the quality and quantity of live bootleg recordings, Springsteen has ensured that many of the "Born In The USA" dates have been taped to add to other live recordings of the past 10 years for future release. Over 200 album bootlegs are freely available on the market.

Sept [25] Springsteen joins U2 on stage during the group's concert in Philadelphia, PA.

Nov [29] Having performed over 500 shows in the past decade, he releases personally-compiled unprecedented 5 album live set *Live 1975 – 1985*, reflecting the performance glory which has so endeared his live act to his dedicated followers. Dominated by his latest stadium concerts, the set includes 4 never available Springsteen performances: instrumental *Paradise By The Sea*, his versions of *Because The Night*, *Fire* and new *Seeds* taped at Los Angeles' Coliseum in Sept.1985. Produced by Landau, Springsteen and Chuck Plotkin and compiled from 21

concerts, it enters US chart at historic #1 and hits UK #4.

Dec [27] From it, *War*, a cover of Edwin Starr's 1970 US #1 hit accompanied by a live video, hits US #8 and makes UK #18.

1987 **Jan** [21] Springsteen performs *Oh, Pretty Woman* with its composer Roy Orbison at the second annual Hall Of Fame dinner.

Feb [28] *Fire* makes US #46 and UK #54.

May Live *Born To Run* reaches UK #16.

Aug [21] Springsteen gigs at the Stone Pony.

[22] Springsteen joins Levon Helm & His All Stars on *Lucille* and *Up On Cripple Creek* at the Stone Pony, Asbury.

Oct [17] New studio album, the most subdued *Tunnel Of Love* enters UK chart at #1, while *Brilliant Disguise* makes UK #20.

[22] Springsteen attends memorial service for John Hammond at St. Peter's church in New York, singing Dylan's *Forever Young*.

[31] Springsteen and members of The E Street Band play halloween gig at McLoone's Rumrunner, Sea Bright, NJ, performing much of the *Tunnel Of Love* album for the first time and an acoustic version of *Born To Run*.

Nov [6] Springsteen jams with The Fabulous Greaseband at an open day at the school near his home in Rumson, NJ. They sing *Carol*, *Lucille*, *Stand By Me* and *Twist And Shout*.

[7] *Tunnel Of Love* tops US chart.

[20] Springsteen joins Bobby Bandiera's band on stage at the Stone Pony, singing *Carol*, *Little Latin Lupe* and others.

[21] *Brilliant Disguise* hits US #5.

Dec *Tunnel Of Love* makes UK #45.

[7] He performs *Remember When The Music* at a memorial concert for Harry Chapin at Carnegie Hall, New York, with Paul Simon, Harry Belafonte and others.

[13] At Madison Square Garden, NY, Paul Simon-organized benefit for homeless children, Springsteen joins Billy Joel, Lou Reed and James Taylor vocally backing Dion on *Teenager In Love* before playing an acoustic version of *Born To Run*.

1988 **Jan** Springsteen plays selected acoustic gigs in aid of Harry Chapin Memorial Fund and begins a 6-week period of rehearsals with The E Street Band for an upcoming tour.

[20] Springsteen inducts Bob Dylan into the Rock'N'Roll Hall Of Fame at the annual dinner at the Waldorf Astoria, New York.

Feb *Tunnel Of Love* hits US #9.

[25] "Tunnel Of Love Express" tour of US opens at the Centrum, Worcester, MA, set to end May 23.

Mar [2] *Tunnel Of Love* wins Best Rock Vocal Performance, Solo at the 30th annual Grammy awards.

Apr [23] *One Step Up* reaches US #13.

May Natalie Cole covers previous Springsteen B-side *Pink Cadillac* hitting #5 in US and UK.

June [11] Springsteen's European tour begins at the Stadio Communale, Turin, Italy.

[21] UK leg of "Tunnel Of Love Express" tour opens at Aston Villa Football Club ground, Birmingham, W.Midlands.

July *Tougher Than The Rest* reaches UK #13.

[3] During his second show in Stockholm, Sweden, Springsteen announces the planned Amnesty "Human Rights Now!" tour.

Aug [3] European leg of tour ends at the Nou Camp football stadium, Barcelona, Spain.

[30] Julianne files for divorce, following photographic newspaper evidence of close relationship between Springsteen and Patti Scialfa.

Sept [2] Springsteen participates in the opening concert at Wembley Stadium, London, of "Human Rights Now!" Amnesty International 6-week world tour with Sting, Peter Gabriel, Tracy Chapman and Youssou N'Dour, set to end Oct.15 in Buenos Aires, Argentina. Springsteen contributes *I Ain't Got No Home* and *Vigilante Man* to the Woody Guthrie/Leadbelly tribute album *Folkways: A Vision Shared*

Oct *Spare Parts* makes UK #32.

1989 **Jan** [18] Springsteen sings *Crying* as a tribute to Roy Orbison who has died the month before at the Rock'N'Roll Hall Of Fame dinner at the Waldorf Astoria, New York.

He reaches an out-of-court settlement with Julianne Phillips which reportedly prevents her revealing details of their marriage to the press or in book form.

Feb Video compilation "Bruce Springsteen – Video Anthology 1978-88" is released. It features 100 mins. of clips up to *Spare Parts* and is an instant best-seller in US and UK.

Mar [1] The Springsteen's divorce decree is finalized.

[10] Springsteen makes a surprise appearance on stage with The Mighty Hornets, a local band at Mickey Rourke's Los Angeles club,

Rubber, singing *See See Rider*.

June [30] After having jammed at Nils Lofgren and Neil Young concerts earlier in the month, Springsteen joins Jackson Browne on stage at Bally's, Atlantic City, for *Stay*, *Sweet Little Sixteen* and *Running On Empty*.

Aug [11] Springsteen joins Ringo Starr on stage at the Garden State Arts Center, Holmdel, NJ, for 4 numbers (*Get Back*, *Long Tall Sally*, *Photograph* and *With A Little Help From My Friends*.) Actor John Candy also makes an appearance on tambourine.

Sept [13-14] Springsteen records *Viva Las Vegas* at One On One studio in North Hollywood, CA, for **The Last Temptation Of Elvis**, a charity album organized by Roy Carr of the **New Musical Express** to raise funds for the Nordoff-Robbins Music Therapy charity. His rhythm section comprises Ian McLagan on keyboards, Bob Glaub on bass and Jeff Porcaro on drums.

[22] On eve of his 40th birthday, Springsteen joins Jimmy Cliff on stage at the Stone Pony to sing *Trapped*, the Cliff-penned track Springsteen featured on the album **We Are The World**.

[23] Springsteen celebrates his birthday at the McLoone's Rumrunner with The E Street Band and Little Steven. Editors of Springsteen fanzine **Backstreets** publish a book on the Boss' 40th birthday.

[29] Springsteen, traveling from Los Angeles on a motorbike, drops in at Matt's Saloon in Prescott, AZ, and jams with the house combo Mile High Band for about an hour, singing *Don't Be Cruel*, *I'm On Fire*, *Route 66* among others. (A few weeks later, Springsteen will send Matt's barmaid Brenda Pechanec $100,000 to pay her hospital bills.)

Nov [13] **Newsweek** and **People** both run stories stating that Springsteen has told the members of The E Street Band they are no longer needed.

1990 **Jan** [15] Official announcment is made that Patti Scialfa is pregnant.
[17] Springsteen attends the annual Rock'N'Roll Hall Of Fame dinner at the Waldorf Astoria hotel in New York. He joins the traditional jam at the end of the proceedings, joining John Fogerty on stage and then taking part in an ensemble version of *Long Tall Sally*.

Feb [12] Springsteen joins Jackson Browne, Don Henley and Paul Simon, for a jam at a benefit concert for Sting's Rainforest Foundation and the Environmental Media Association fundraiser in Beverly Hills, CA. After the show, Springsteen repairs to Los Angeles' China club where he joins Bruce Hornsby, Don Henley, Sting and Branford Marsalis for a 45-min. impromptu set.

Mar [1] Springsteen and Bob Dylan join Tom Petty on stage at the latter's Inglewood Forum, CA, concert. (The RIAA certifies **Born In The USA** has reached sales of 12 million.)

Apr Springsteen and Tom Waits sing *Jersey Girl*, *Stand By Me* (Springsteen) and *Fever* (Waits) at Chuck Plotkin's marriage to Jersey girl Wendy Brandchaft at Michael's restaurant, Santa Monica, CA.

June Springsteen gives rap group 2 Live Crew permission to sample *Born In The USA* for their single *Banned In The USA*.

July [25] Son Evan James Springsteen is born at Los Angeles' Cedars-Sinai medical center, weighing in at 7lb.9oz.

Nov [16] Springsteen joins Jackson Browne and Bonnie Raitt for an acoustic concert to raise money for the Christic Institute, a non-profit group that is waging a lawsuit accusing the US Government of sanctioning illegal arms sales and drugs trafficking to finance covert operations during the Iran-Contra affair. The concert, which raises more than $600,000, is Springsteen's first official concert appearance since his participation in the Amnesty International World Tour.

1991 **Jan** [20] Springsteen and Weinberg reunite at McLoone's Rumrunner, taking part in a benefit for local singer Jim Faulkner, who is recovering from a stroke.

SQUEEZE

Chris Difford (vocals, guitar)
Glenn Tilbrook (vocals, lead guitar)
Jools Holland (keyboards)
Harry Kakoulli (bass)
Paul Gunn (drums)

1974 **Mar** Difford (b. Nov.4, 1954, London) meets Tilbrook (b. Aug.31, 1957, London) when he answers Difford's music paper ad requesting band members for a new group. With the recruitment of Holland (b. Julian Holland) and Gunn, Squeeze is formed, taking its name from a Velvet Underground album.

1976 They sign with Miles Copeland's BTM label and management company. Gunn is replaced by Lavis, and Kakoulli joins on bass.

1977 **Jan** *Take Me I'm Yours*, scheduled for release by BTM, is withdrawn.

July EP *Packet Of Three*, on Deptford Fun City Records, is produced by John Cale. They sign to A&M worldwide, becoming the company's first "new wave" signing since The Sex Pistols.

1978 **Apr** *Take Me I'm Yours*, on A&M, reaches UK #19. Debut album **Squeeze**, produced by Cale, fails to chart. Band makes its first visit to US but has to change name temporarily to UK Squeeze to avoid confusion with a US band called Tight Squeeze.

June *Bang Bang* peaks at UK #49.

Aug They play the Reading Festival, Berks.

Nov *Goodbye Girl* reaches UK #63.

1979 **Mar** Second album **Cool For Cats** produced by John Wood, makes #4

Apr *Cool For Cats* hits UK #2, kept from the top by Art Garfunkel's *Bright Eyes*.

June *Up The Junction* also hits UK #2, this time blocked by Tubeway Army's *Are "Friends" Electric?*

Sept *Slap And Tickle* makes UK #24.

Nov Festive *Christmas Day* fails to chart.

1980 **Mar** *Argy Bargy*, again produced by Wood, and featuring new bassist John Bentley, makes UK #32. *Another Nail In My Heart* reaches UK #17

Apr Group begins its fourth US tour.

May *Pulling Mussels From A Shell* reaches UK #44.

July [28] They perform at the Dalymount Festival, Dublin, Eire, with The Police and U2.

Aug After returning to UK, Holland quits the group. (He supports The Police on tour and makes a documentary with them for UK TV, which leads him to become a co-host of Channel 4 TV show "The Tube" 1982-87. He will also front his own band The Millionaires and host a late 80s US TV rock series, ending the decade as the new host for BBC TV's "Juke Box Jury" revival.) He is replaced by Paul Carrack (ex-Ace).

Nov [30] Squeeze and Elvis Costello perform a benefit concert at the Top Rank club in Swansea, Wales, for the family of Welsh boxer Johnny Owen, who died from injuries sustained during a world title bout in Las Vegas, NV.

1981 **Mar** Tilbrook teams with Elvis Costello for one-off *From A Whisper To A Scream*.

May **East Side Story**, co-produced by Elvis Costello and Roger Bechirian, makes UK #19. *Is That Love* climbs to UK #35.

Aug Soulful *Tempted*, with Carrack on lead vocal, reaches UK #41 and US #49.

Oct Country-flavored ballad *Labelled With Love* hits UK #4. Prior to its release Carrack leaves to join Carlene Carter's band. Ex-Sincero Don Snow replaces him.

1982 **Apr** *Black Coffee In Bed*, with guest vocals from Elvis Costello and Paul Young, reaches UK #51.

May *Sweets From A Stranger* makes UK #37.

June Group tours US, where it sells out New York's Madison Square Garden.

July *When The Hangover Strikes* fails to chart.

Oct Alan Tarney-produced *Annie Get Your Gun* makes UK #43.

Nov Group announces a split and plays what will be its last show at the 3-day Jamaica World Music Festival at the Bob Marley Performing Center near Montego Bay. Compilation album **Singles 45's And Under** is released, and hits UK #3.

1983 **Feb** "Labelled With Love", a musical based on Difford and Tilbrook songs, opens in Deptford, London. They decide to stay together and write. They also work with Helen Shapiro, Billy Bremner (ex-Rockpile), Paul Young and Jools Holland. Lavis joins Chris Rea's band.

1984 **July** Difford and Tilbrook release eponymous album, produced by Tony Visconti and E.T. Thorngren, which makes UK #47, while *Love's Crashing Waves* makes UK #57.

1985 **Jan** [14] Squeeze re-forms for a charity gig at a pub in Catford, London. The reunion becomes permanent (other commitments allowing). Line-up is Difford, Tilbrook, Holland and Lavis with Keith Wilkinson on bass.

Mar *The Last Time Forever* peaks at UK #45.

Sept *Cosi Fan Tutti Frutti*, produced by Laurie Latham, reaches UK #31 and US #57.

1986 **Apr** [28] Holland and Lavis are involved in a car crash returning to London from Plymouth after performing in a charity concert for a drug and alcohol rehabilitation center. Lavis breaks an arm.

1987 Squeeze embarks on another successful US tour spurred by renewed US chart activity, including sold-out Madison Square Garden concerts in New York.

Aug *Hourglass* reaches UK #17.

Sept **Babylon And On**, featuring additional keyboard player ex-Soft Boy Andy Metcalfe, reaches UK #14 and US #36.

Oct [17] Taken from it, *Trust Me To Open My Mouth* stalls at UK #72.
Dec [5] *Hourglass* reaches US #15.

'88 **Feb** [13] *853 5937*, also from the album, makes US #32.

'89 **Oct** Produced by Tilbrook with Eric "E.T." Thorngren, *Frank* makes US #113 (having already peaked at UK #58), while Difford, Tilbrook, Holland, Lavis and Wilkinson embark on extensive US tour, set to end Dec.11 at the Universal Amphitheater, Universal City, CA.

'90 **Jan** Holland again leaves group to devote more time to TV work, while Squeeze prepares to support Fleetwood Mac on US tour.
Apr *A Round And A Bout* makes UK #50.
May [5] Holland solo *World Of His Own* climbs to UK #71.
[30] Group supports Fleetwood Mac on the US leg of "The Mask" tour in Portland, OR, set to end at Jones Beach, Wantagh, NY, on Aug.2.
June [23] *A Round And A Bout* makes US #163.

'91 Band begins recording debut album via new recording contract with Warner Bros., with sessions produced by Tony Berg.

ISA STANSFIELD

'84 Having met Andy Morris and Ian Devaney in a Rochdale, Gtr.Manchester, school musical and started her musical career at age 15, Stansfield (b. 1965), who has grown up in Rochdale, forms Blue Zone, with her 2 friends (once married, Stansfield also lives with Devaney for 2 years), pooling their financial resources to build their own self-contained studio.

'86 Honed as a soul-funk outfit, Blue Zone signs, via its own fledgling Rockin' Horse label, to Arista Records, and begins slowly to record its debut album *Big Thing*, around self-penned pop dance songs. (3 singles, all featuring Stansfield's lead vocals, *Jackie*, *On Fire* and *Thinking About His Baby*, will be released, but none will chart.)

'89 **Apr** UK dance production duo Matt Black and Jonathan Moore invite Stansfield to contribute her soulful voice to their own Coldcut's third single (after Morris and Devaney have worked on their previous hit *Stop This Crazy Thing*), *People Hold On* dance-soul composition, which reaches UK #11. Its success confirms the interest being shown in Stansfield as a solo artist by ex-Wham! manager and Big Life owner Jazz Summers, who signs her. Devaney and Morris continue to back the soulstress will full writing and production support.
Sept Written by Devaney/Morris/Stansfield, but produced as a one-off by the Coldcut team, debut solo single *This Is The Right Time* reaches UK #13, released on Arista via the Big Life label.
Nov [11] Instant airplay nugget, *All Around The World* hits UK #1 for the first of 2 weeks, highlighted by Stansfield's soul-filled vocal performance. It will go on to chart-top in over 10 other territories.
Dec [2] Her debut solo album *Affection* debuts at UK peak #2. Entirely written by the ex-Blue Zone trio, and produced (bar the Cold-cut) by Devaney and Morris, who also play all instruments except an additional trumpet on *The Love In Me*, it will go on to sell over 4 million copies worldwide and launch the singer as a major new soul star. (Part of her affable image includes the constant donning of a variety of hats on her UK TV appearances; she has in the past been a presenter of ITV's pop show "Razzamatazz".)

'90 **Feb** [6] Stansfield collects the Variety Club Of Great Britain Recording Artist Of 1989 honor at their annual awards lunch in London.
[17] *Live Together* hits UK #10.
[18] She wins Best British Newcomer at the ninth annual BRIT Awards at the Dominion theater, London.
[20] Stansfield is presented to the US media at an Arista pre-Grammy dinner at the Beverly Hills hotel, Beverly Hills, CA.
Mar [17] Stansfield participates in the "That's What Friends Are For" benefit, alongside labelmates Whitney Houston, Dionne Warwick, The Four Tops and Daryl Hall & John Oates among others, celebrating Arista Records 15th anniversary and raising money for AIDS charities.
Apr [2] Stansfield, Devaney and Morris collect the Best Contemporary Song Award for *All Around The World* at the annual Ivor Novello Awards lunch held at the Grosvenor House, Mayfair, London.
[7] *All Around The World* launches Stansfield's US career, hitting #3 (it will also top US R&B chart, with Stansfield becoming only the second white artist to achieve that feat.)
[18] 1-month UK leg begins at the start of her "All Around The World" global tour in Liverpool, Merseyside, set to end May 14 at the Queen Elizabeth Hall, Oldham, Gtr.Manchester.
May [12] *Affection* hits US #9 on the day after her first US tour begins, on its way to RIAA platinum ratification.
[19] UK EP release *What Did I Do To You* reaches UK #25.
June [22] She is named Best Newcomer at the annual Nordoff-Robbins

Music Therapy charity awards lunch at London's Grosvenor House.
July [18] Stansfield participates in the annual Prince's Trust Rock Gala at the Wembley Arena, London.
[28] US follow-up *You Can't Deny It* reaches US #14.
Sept [18] European dates re-start, set to climax London's Wembley Arena, at the end of Oct.
Oct [6] Belated US issue of *This Is The Right Time* reaches US #21, while Stansfield contributes her version of *Down In The Depths* to **Red, Hot + Blue**, an anthology of Cole Porter updates, released to benefit AIDS awareness.

1991 **Feb** [10] Stansfield wins Best British Female Artist at the 10th annual BRIT Awards and, despite a prior request from organizer Jonathan King not to do so, she is the only winner who mentions the Gulf War in her acceptance speech.
[20] She guests on NBC TV's "Late Night With Letterman".
Mar [7] Stansfield wins Best New Female Singer in the annual **Rolling Stone** Critic's Picks 1990 music awards.
May [12] Stansfield appears live at "The Simple Truth" concert for Kurdish refugees at Wembley Arena, London.

RINGO STARR

1969 **Feb** [20] "Candy", an Italian/French film adaptation version of Voltaire's "Candide", in which Starr, famous as The Beatles' drummer (b. Richard Starkey, July 7, 1940, Liverpool, Merseyside) appears as a Mexican gardener, premieres at Kensington's Odeon cinema, London.

1970 **Jan** [27] Starr guests in NBC TV's "Rowan & Martin's Laugh-In".
Feb [22] "The Magic Christian", in which Starr appears as Youngman Grand, the adopted son of the world's richest man, Sir Guy Grand, played by Peter Sellers, premieres in New York.
Apr *Sentimental Journey* hits UK #7 and US #22. The commercial value of being an ex-Beatle going solo is exemplified by this George Martin-produced selection of standards, including *Night And Day* and *Bye Bye Blackbird*. Starr claims "I did it for me mum!" Arrangers on the album include The Bee Gees' Maurice Gibb, Elmer Bernstein, Johnny Dankworth, Les Reed and Quincy Jones.
June [30] Starr flies to Nashville, TN, to begin recording tracks for forthcoming album.
Oct Nashville album *Beaucoups Of Blues* makes US #65. Using songs commissioned from top C&W writers and produced by pedal steel guitarist, Pete Drake, and engineered by Elvis Presley's guitarist, Scotty Moore, it features top country musicians, including Jerry Reed, The Jordanaires (Elvis Presley's backing vocalists) and Charlie Daniels.
Nov [28] *Beaucoups Of Blues* peaks at US #87.

1971 **Apr** [25] Starr appears live on BBC TV "Cilla" show.
June [5] Self-penned *It Don't Come Easy*, featuring guitar work from producer George Harrison and Stephen Stills, hits both UK and US #4, as he begins filming "Blindman".
Aug *It Don't Come Easy* is certified gold.
[1] Starr appears with Eric Clapton, Bob Dylan, Billy Preston, Leon Russell and others at the George Harrison-organized "Concert For Bangla Desh".
Nov [10] Frank Zappa's film "200 Motels", in which Starr has the dual roles of Larry The Dwarf and Frank Zappa, premieres in New York.
[15] "Blindman", a spaghetti western in which he plays an outlaw called Candy, premieres in Rome, Italy.

1972 **May** [13] Harrison-produced *Back Off Boogaloo* hits UK #2 and US #9.
Nov Starr appears as Uncle Ernie in Lou Reizner's all-star album of The Who's *Tommy*.
Dec [14] "Born To Boogie", a film of T. Rex in concert and Starr's debut as director, premieres at the Oscar 1 cinema in London.

1973 **Apr** [12] "That'll Be The Day", in which Starr plays a teddy boy, premieres at the ABC2 cinema, Shaftesbury Avenue, London.
Sept [18] Starr buys Tittenhurst Park from John and Yoko Lennon.
Nov [24] *Photograph*, co-written with Harrison, hits UK #8 and US #1. *Ringo* hits UK #7 and US #2. It is produced by Richard Perry and includes Beatles' contributions (notably Lennon's *I'm The Greatest* which features all but McCartney).

1974 **Jan** [26] With Harry Nilsson on "shoo-wops" and a kazoo vocal by Paul McCartney *You're Sixteen*, a cover of Johnny Burnette's 1960 US #8 hit, hits US #1 and UK #3.
Apr [7] BBC Radio 1 airs Starr's personal musical favorites in "My Top Twelve".
[27] *Oh My My* hits US #5.
Dec *Goodnight Vienna*, again produced by Perry and using top LA session men, reaches UK #30 and hits US #8.

1975 **Jan** [11] A cover of The Platters' 1955 smash *Only You* makes UK #28 and hits US #6. It will be his last UK hit single.

Apr [5] *No No Song*, written by Hoyt Axton, hits US #3.

[28] Starr guests on NBC TV's "The Smothers Brothers Comedy Hour".

July [12] *It's All Down To Goodnight Vienna* makes US #31. Starr appears as the Pope in Ken Russell's film "Lisztomania".

[17] Starr and his wife Maureen are divorced.

1976 **Jan** [17] Greatest hits album *Blast From Your Past* reaches US #30.

[25] He joins Bob Dylan on stage for his "Night Of The Hurricane II" benefit concert for boxer Ruben "Hurricane" Carter at the Houston Astrodome, TX.

Mar [10] Starr signs with Polydor in the UK and Atlantic in the US.

Oct *Ringo's Rotogravure*, another all-star session this time produced by Arif Mardin, makes US #28.

Nov [6] *A Dose Of Rock'N'Roll* reaches US #26.

[25] Starr appears with a host of stars performing *I Shall Be Released* at The Band's "The Last Waltz" farewell concert.

1977 **Feb** [12] A cover of Bruce Channel's 1962 US chart-topper *Hey Baby* stalls at US #74.

Nov [12] *Ringo The 4th* peaks at US #162.

Dec "Scouse The Mouse" is released, with Starr in the title role of this children's story written by British actor, Donald Pleasence.

1978 **Apr** [25] TV special "Ringo", a musical adaptation of "The Prince And The Pauper" narrated by Harrison, airs on US TV. (Ratings released the following week show that it finished 53rd out of 65 programs.)

May *Bad Boy* peaks at US #129. A collection of cover versions, it includes The Supremes' *Where Did Our Love Go* and Gallagher & Lyle's *Heart On My Sleeve*. He appears in Mae West's last film "Sextette", with Timothy Dalton and Tony Curtis.

1979 **Apr** Starr has life-saving intestinal operation in Monte Carlo.

May [19] Starr teams with McCartney and Harrison to play at Eric Clapton's wedding reception.

June [8] Starr drums on NBC TV's "Midnight Special".

Sept [3] He plays on Jerry Lewis' annual Muscular Dystrophy telethon.

Nov [28] His Los Angeles, CA, home is destroyed by fire.

1980 **Feb** [18] Starr begins filming "Caveman" in Durango, Mexico, where he meets future wife, actress Barbara Bach.

May [19] Driving to a party in South-West London, Starr and Bach are involved in a serious car smash less than a half mile from where Marc Bolan has been killed. Although their car is a write-off, they are not seriously hurt.

1981 **Apr** [27] Starr and Barbara Bach marry.

Nov *And Smell The Roses* reaches US #98. McCartney and Harrison contribute and Van Dyke Parks produces a new version of *Back Off Boogaloo* for the album, featuring a medley of Beatles and Starr songs.

Dec [12] Starr guests on BBC TV's "Parkinson" chat show, as *Wrack My Brain* makes US #38.

1983 **Nov** [6-7] Judith Krantz's "Princess Daisy", in which Mr. and Mrs. Starr appear, airs on US TV.

1984 **July** [4] He guests at 2 Beach Boys gigs in 1 day, an afternoon show in Washington, DC, and an evening show in Miami, FL.

Oct [9] Children's series, "Thomas The Tank Engine And Friends", narrated by Starr, premieres on ITV. (It will become a worldwide hit.)

Nov Mr. and Mrs. Starr appear in Paul McCartney's film "Give My Regards To Broad Street". Starr's *Old Wave*, co-produced with Joe Walsh, is released in Canada and Germany only.

Dec [8] Starr guests on NBC TV's "Saturday Night Live".

1985 **Jan** [18] "Water", in which Starr guests with Harrison and Clapton, premieres in London.

[22] He becomes a father-in-law when son Zak marries Sarah Menikedes, although he is not aware of it at the time.

Mar [11] Starr films a cameo appearance for Bill Wyman's video "Willie & The Poor Boys".

Sept [7] He is the first Beatle to become a grandfather when his son Zak and his wife Sarah have a daughter, Tatia Jayne.

Oct [21] Starr takes part in the Carl Perkins' Channel 4 TV special "Blue Suede Shoes", with Eric Clapton, Dave Edmunds, Harrison and others, recorded at Limehouse studios in London. (The program is shown at Christmas and subsequently released on video.)

Dec [9] Starr appears as the Mock Turtle in a US TV production of "Alice In Wonderland".

[14] Starr and son Zak both contribute to the Artists United Against Apartheid album, from which *Sun City* makes US #38 and UK #21.

1986 **Sept** [24] Second "Thomas The Tank Engine" series premieres on ITV.

1987 **June** [5-6] Starr takes part in the Prince's Trust Rock Gala at Wembley

Arena, London. He sings *With A Little Help From My Friends*.

Sept [26] Starr's co-owned restaurant The London Brasserie opens in Atlanta, GA.

1988 **Jan** [20] He attends the third annual Rock'N'Roll Hall Of Fame dinner with Harrison and Yoko Ono, celebrating The Beatles induction.

Feb He appears in a video for Harrison's hit *When We Was Fab*.

Mar [3] Starr and Harrison appear on ITV chat show "Aspel & Co."

Aug Reports emanate from US that Starr, Harrison and Jeff Lynne are forming a group and will tour.

Oct [11] The Starrs begin treatment for an alcohol abuse problem in Tucson, AZ.

1989 **Jan** Starr contributes a version of *When You Wish Upon A Star* to the Walt Disney album *Stay Awake*.

Feb Starr hosts US TV's weekly show "Shining Time Station" playing 18" tall Mr. Conductor, a revamp of his "Thomas The Tank Engine" clips. (The show will be nominated for an Emmy.)

Mar [5] He contributes to *Spirit Of The Forest* ecology benefit single.

[27] Starr records *Act Naturally* with country star Buck Owens at Abbey Road studios in London.

Apr Rhino Records in US releases compilation album *Starrstruck: Ringo's Best 1976-83*.

June [13] Starr joins Bob Dylan on stage at the latter's Les Arenes, Frejus, France, concert.

[20] Starr announces a comeback tour with his All-Starr Band, comprising Dr.John, Billy Preston, Joe Walsh, Rick Danko, Levon Helm, Nils Lofgren, Jim Keltner and Clarence Clemons, and later that evening guests on NBC TV's "Late Night With Letterman".

July [23] Ringo Starr & His All-Starr Band begin 30-date "Tour For All Generations" North American trek (the first by a Beatle in 13 years), at the Park Central Amphitheater, Dallas, TX, set to end Sept.4 at the Greek theater, Los Angeles.

[26] Starr succeeds in temporarily blocking release of a Chips Moman-produced album because of his dissatisfaction in his own performance. In his lawsuit, Starr contends that the recording quality was not up to standard because Moman brought alcoholic beverages into the sessions. Atlanta's Fulton County Superior Court Judge Clarence Cooper presides over case.

Aug [11] Springsteen joins Starr on stage for 4 numbers (*Get Back, Long Tall Sally, Photograph* and *With A Little Help From My Friend*.) at the Garden State Arts Center, Holmdel, NJ. Actor John Candy also makes an appearance on tambourine.

Oct [14-15] Starr gives party in Cannes to celebrate 1 year of sobriety.

[30] Starr and his band begin a 7-date Japanese tour at the Rainbow Hall, Nagoya, set to end Nov.8 at the Yokohoma Arena.

Nov [15] He testifies in Atlanta to block the release of the 1987 Chips Moman album. He wins permanent court order blocking its release.

1990 **Jan** [5] Judge Cooper rules that Moman hands over recording in exchange for $74,000 in expenses.

Mar [22] Starr with Lynne, Petty, Walsh and Keltner record *I Call You Name* as part of John Lennon tribute to be held in Liverpool on May 5.

Apr [12] Starr dubs the voice of the cartoon Ringo Starr in Fox-TV's "The Simpsons".

STATUS QUO

Francis Rossi (guitar, vocals)
Rick Parfitt (guitar, vocals)
Alan Lancaster (bass)
John Coghlan (drums)

1962 Lancaster (b. Feb.7, 1949, Peckham, London) and friend Alan Key join their Beckenham comprehensive school orchestra, playing trombone and trumpet respectively and also form a trad jazz combo. This evolves into a beat group, with Lancaster on bass and Key and his friend Rossi (then calling himself Mike, b. Francis Dominic Rossi, Apr.29, 1949, Forest Hill, London) playing guitars. Classmate Jess Jaworski is talked into trading in his new guitar for a Vox organ and joins the group when Key quits. With a friend playing drums, they make their live debut at the Samuel Jones sports club in Dulwich. After adding permanent drummer Coghlan (b. Sept.19, 1946, Dulwich, London), they call themselves The Spectres.

1964 After regular working men's club appearances, local gasfitter Pat Barlow offers to manage them and secures the act a Monday night residency at the Café des Artistes in London's Brompton Road. He also arranges a gig on the same bill as The Hollies, which doubles as an audition for a place as a Butlins holiday camp resident group.

1965 They accept a 4-month Butlins summer contract. Jaworski decides to continue his education and is replaced by Roy Lynes (b. Oct.25, 1943, Redhill, Surrey). They also meet Parfitt (b. Richard Harrison, Oct.12, 1948, Woking, Surrey), who is playing holiday camps. (He will join the group 2 years later.)

1966 Songwriter Ronnie Scott introduces the group to John Schroeder, Pye Records' recording manager.

July The Spectres sign to Piccadilly, licensed to Pye.

Sept Their first single, a version of Leiber & Stoller's *I (Who Have Nothing)*, fails.

Nov Lancaster's *Hurdy Gurdy Man* is a second unsuccessful single.

1967 Feb The last single as The Spectres is *We Ain't Got Nothin' Yet*.

Mar The Spectres change name to Traffic Jam at the same time as Steve Winwood forms Traffic, and release *Almost But Not Quite There*.

Nov At Barlow's suggestion, the group name-changes to Status Quo, and is signed to Pye label.

1968 Feb *Pictures Of Matchstick Men*, with Parfitt in the group, hits UK #7, while the group is working as Madeline Bell's backing band and with Barlow still part-time manager.

Apr Follow-up *Black Veils Of Melancholy* is released.

[5] Group begins a 28-date twice-nightly UK tour with Gene Pitney, Amen Corner, Don Partridge, Simon Dupree & The Big Sound and others, at the Odeon theater, Lewisham, London, set to end May 7 at the Granada theater, Walthamstow, London.

Aug *Pictures Of Matchstick Men* reaches US #12, prompting a US tour.

Sept Debut album *Picturesque Matchstickable Messages* is released but fails to chart. In addition to the singles, it includes covers of The Bee Gees' *Spicks And Specks*, The Lemon Pipers' *Green Tambourine* and Tommy Roe's *Sheila*.

Oct *Ice In The Sun*, co-written by singer Marty Wilde, hits UK #8 and peaks at US #70. Band is currently promoted with smartly chic outfits.

1969 Jan [24-25] Group takes part in all-night "Midnite Rave – Part 2" with Love Sculpture, Gun, Joe Cocker, Aynsley Dunbar and others.

Mar [16] US tour opens in Philadelphia, PA.

Apr Status Quo supports Gene Pitney on a UK tour. Group's act mixes its pop sound with its later 12-bar blues sound.

May Ballad *Are You Growing Tired Of My Love* peaks at UK #46.

Oct *Spare Parts* fails to chart as the members decide to grow their hair and change musical direction.

1970 July Boogie-tinged *Down The Dustpipe* reaches UK #12 as Lynes quits the band.

Aug *Ma Kelly's Greasy Spoon* is released. Blues-based, it includes *Junior's Wailing*, a cover of a song by blues band Steamhammer, which will become one of the group's most popular live tracks.

Dec *In My Chair*, penned by Rossi and group tour manager Bob Young (who will co-write many of the group's future hits), makes UK #21.

1971 June Follow-up *Tune To The Music* begins 3-year chart absence.

Nov Final Pye album, *Dog Of Two Head*, is released.

1972 Jan As the band leaves the label, it begins building a solid cult following on the club circuit, playing a heavier brand of blues and boogie, and signs to Phonogram's new rock subsidiary, Vertigo.

May [10] Status Quo begins a UK tour in Bradford, W.Yorks., as support to Slade.

July Group receives critical and popular acclaim at the British Great Western Festival in Lincoln, Lincs. (and Reading Festival in Aug.).

1973 Jan Debut Vertigo album *Piledriver* is self-produced and enters UK chart, set to hit #5. Status Quo has now defined its classic long-haired image on stage initiating a heads down, no-nonsense act, which sets the style and pose for a myriad of UK heavy metal groups, none of whom will be so successful for so long.

Feb *Paper Plane* hits UK #8, as Status Quo tours Australia supporting Slade.

May *Mean Girl*, from the last Pye album, reaches UK #20.

June Pye album *The Best Of Status Quo* peaks at UK #32.

Oct Vertigo single *Caroline*, written in 1970, hits UK #5. Self-produced album *Hello*, with ex-Herd member Andy Bown guesting on keyboards, enters UK chart at #1.

1974 May *Break The Rules* hits UK #8 as parent album *Quo* hits UK #2.

1975 Jan *Down Down* is Status Quo's only UK Singles chart-topper.

Mar *On The Level* hits UK #1. Pye releases *Down The Dustpipe*, featuring 1970-71 material, on its Golden Hour label. It reaches UK #20, as group embarks on a 2-month US tour.

Apr *Status Quo* is the group's only US chart album, reaching #148 during a 7-week stay.

June 3-track live EP *Roll Over Lay Down* with *Gerdundula* and *Junior's Wailing*, hits UK #9. (Sleeve notes are provided by UK DJ John Peel.)

1976 Mar *Rain* hits UK #7, as parent album *Blue For You* hits UK #1, helped by Phonogram's marketing deal with Levi's jeans (a Status Quo

trademark), which sees the record advertised in 6,000 clothes shops. (It is one of the first sponsorship tie-ups between the commercial world and rock music in UK.)

[28] After an incident at Vienna airport, Rossi, Parfitt and Lancaster are arrested. Lancaster is charged with assaulting an airport official and the other 2 with resisting arrest. (They are released on bail.)

July [24] Group tops a bill featuring Hawkwind, Curved Air, The Strawbs and Budgie, at Cardiff Castle, Wales.

Aug *Mystery Song* hits UK #11.

Oct The Rolling Stones' mobile studio is brought to Glasgow's Apollo theater to record 3 concerts. Tickets for the shows have sold out within hours. Former Herd keyboardist Andy Bown joins the live line-up.

1977 Jan *Wild Side Of Life*, reviving Tommy Quickly's 1964 hit and produced by ex-Deep Purple bassist Roger Glover, hits UK #9. In Vienna, the 3 Status Quo defendants plead guilty to a reduced charge of obstructing the police and are fined a total of £3,200.

Mar *Status Quo – Live* hits UK #3. Band begins a world tour that will take it to Europe, the Far East, Australia and New Zealand.

Nov John Fogerty's *Rockin' All Over The World*, is released for UK leg of the tour, hitting UK #3. (When Status Quo performs it on BBC TV show "Top Of The Pops", Lancaster, now semi-resident in Australia, is substituted by a life-size string puppet, discreetly playing bass in the background.) *Rockin' All Over The World*, with Pip Williams co-producing, hits UK #5.

1978 For tax reasons, Status Quo will not reside in UK throughout the year. It tours Australia, followed by a studio visit to Hilversum in Holland to record album *If You Can't Stand The Heat*.

Aug [26] Band makes its only UK appearance of the year, headlining the Reading Rock Festival, Berks.

Sept *Again And Again* reaches UK #13.

Nov *If You Can't Stand The Heat* hits UK #3.

Dec *Accident Prone* makes UK #36, as Status Quo starts work on a new album in Hilversum.

1979 Oct *Whatever You Want* hits UK #4, while parent album *Whatever You Want* hits UK #3. UK media is beginning to criticize the band's supposed 3-chord rock limitations.

Dec Rare ballad *Living On An Island* reaches UK #16.

1980 Mar *12 Gold Bars* hits UK #3.

Oct *Just Supposin'* hits UK #4 as extracted *What You're Proposing* hits UK #2.

1981 Jan *Lies* reaches UK #11.

Mar *Never Too Late* hits UK #2. Extracted *Something 'Bout You Baby I Like* hits UK #9.

[6] Status Quo begins a UK tour in St. Austell, Cornwall.

Oct *Fresh Quota*, a rarities album from the PRT label, spends a week at UK #74.

Dec *Rock'N'Roll*, a ballad from *Just Supposin'*, hits UK #8.

1982 Coghlan leaves during recording for a new album in Montreux, Switzerland, to concentrate on his own band, Diesel. He is replaced by Pete Kircher (b. Folkestone, Kent), ex-Honeybus and The Original Mirrors.

Apr *Dear John* hits UK #10, while *1982* is the group's fourth UK chart-topper.

[23] Group begins UK tour.

May Group plays a BBC-televised show at the Birmingham NEC, attended by the Prince and Princess of Wales – all the proceeds go to the Prince's Trust charity. (The show is also recorded for a live album.)

June *She Don't Fool Me* makes UK #36.

Nov *Caroline*, recorded live at the NEC, Birmingham, reaches UK #13. *From The Makers Of ...*, a 3-album set including a live album from the NEC, as well as a selection of hits on both Pye and Vertigo, hits UK #4.

1983 Lancaster relocates to Australia and suggests the other members follow. Rossi and Parfitt decline and Lancaster continues to play with Status Quo on a loose basis.

Sept *Ol' Rag Blues* hits UK #9.

Nov *A Mess Of The Blues* peaks at UK #15.

Dec *Back To Back* hits UK #9.

1984 Jan Displaying its lightest pop side yet, *Marguerita Time* hits UK #3. Band begins UK-billed "The End Of The Road Tour".

June *Going Down Town Tonight*, fourth single from *Back To Back*, reaches UK #20.

July [21] Group ends its UK tour topping the bill at Milton Keynes Bowl, Bucks., filmed for later video release.

Aug A Dutch import album, *Live At The NEC*, reaches UK #83.

Nov A revival of Dion's *The Wanderer* hits UK #7. Lancaster quits the line-up.

STATUS QUO cont.

Dec Vertigo packages a second TV-advertised album *12 Gold Bars*. It reaches UK #12.

1985 Parfitt records an unissued solo album, while Rossi works with Bernard Frost on *Modern Romance (I Want To Fall In Love Again)*, which makes UK #54, and *Jealousy*.

July [13] Lancaster rejoins Status Quo to open the Live Aid spectacular at Wembley Stadium, London. They set the tone for the event by opening with *Rockin' All Over The World*.

By the time the group has gone back to the studio, Lancaster has taken out an injunction to stop the others playing without him as Status Quo. (Court eventually sides with Rossi and Parfitt.) Group fails to release a single during the year, breaking a run of achieving a Top 20 hit each year since 1973, and Kircher also quits the line-up.

1986 **May** Status Quo re-emerges with Dave Edmunds-produced *Rollin' Home*, which hits UK #9. Line-up is now Rossi, Parfitt, Bown, bassist John Edwards and drummer Jeff Rich.

July [11-12] Status Quo supports Queen for 2 nights at Wembley Stadium.

Aug *Red Sky* hits UK #19.

Sept *In The Army Now* hits UK #7.

Nov *In The Army Now*, penned by German pop-writers Bolland and Bolland, hits UK #2.

1987 **Jan** *Dreamin'* reaches UK #15.

1988 **Apr** *Ain't Complaining* makes UK #19.

June *Who Gets The Love* peaks at UK #34 as parent album *Ain't Complaining* reaches UK #12.

Sept *Running All Over The World*, a revised jogging version of *Rockin' All Over The World* altered for Sport Aid, makes UK #17.

Dec *Burning Bridges (On And Off And On Again)*, their 39th consecutive chart single, hits UK #7. In terms of chart records, Status Quo are now the most successful UK group ever, leading The Rolling Stones (with 34 hits) and The Hollies (with 31). Band ends a major UK tour, portraying itself as a non-drink and non-drug-taking group, after several recent newspaper stories relating a wild-living past.

1989 **Oct** *Not At All* makes UK #50.

Dec *Perfect Remedy* stalls at UK #49.

1990 **Oct** *Anniversary Waltz Part 1*, a medley of rock'n'roll standards in non-stop Quo style, hits UK #2 as compilation album *Rockin' All Over The Years* also hits UK #2.

1991 **Feb** [10] Group is honored with Outstanding Contribution To The British Music Industry at the 10th annual BRIT Awards at the Dominion theater, London, and celebrates by disrobing regulation black tie formal wear to reveal traditional jeans'n't-shirt uniform.

TOMMY STEELE

1956 **July** Steele (b. Thomas Hicks, Dec.17, 1936, Bermondsey, London), having served 4 years as a pantry boy, lift boy and assistant steward for the Cunard shipping line, and having sung semi-professionally while ashore, including stints as guitarist with C&W group Jack Fallon & The Sons Of The Saddle, and a UK tour playing second guitar behind bluesman Josh White, is singing at the 2 I's coffee bar in Soho, London, at the start of a month-long leave the day after his ship has docked, when he is approached by photographer and PR man John Kennedy, who sees potential in his singing style and youthful looks. Kennedy is working for manager/agents Roy Tuvey and Geoff Wright, who have already spotted Steele, but after disagreements over financial matters, Kennedy splits from them and teams with Larry Parnes, who is willing to finance Steele's launch while Kennedy handles management. They persuade him to leave the Merchant Navy and sign to them as a professional (they also promise his parents that if nothing comes of his career within a few months, they will not hold him to any contract).

Aug Kennedy renames him Tommy Steele, felt to be a "sharper" name than Hicks' own. He launches him on the live circuit in ways calculated to gain publicity; performing at high class, high-profile debutantes' balls, and at the plush Stork Rooms in London's West End. It all makes major (favorable) press copy.

Sept George Martin at EMI Records rejects Steele, but Decca A&R man Hugh Mendl is enthusiastic: he becomes Decca's first rock signing.

Oct Debut recording is *Rock With The Caveman*, written by Steele, with Mike Pratt and Lionel Bart. The backing session musicians are mostly jazzmen, led by saxophonist Ronnie Scott, but credited as "The Steelmen" on the disk.

[15] He makes his UK TV debut performing the single on Jack Payne's "Off The Record" show.

Nov *Rock With The Caveman* reaches UK #13. His earnings shoot up from £7 a week 6 months previously, to £700 a week.

[5] He makes his bill-topping debut at the Empire theater, Sunderland,

Tyne & Wear.

Dec [7] A bona fide group of Steelmen (including Roy Plummer on guitar and Alan Stewart on sax) is put together to back him on stage, and he begins live work in earnest (debuting at London's Finsbury Park Astoria), to fan hysteria reminiscent of that being generated by Elvis Presley in US. Meanwhile, second single *Elevator Rock* fails to chart, but is allowed to die when Steele covers current US #1 hit, *Singing The Blues* by Guy Mitchell.

1957 **Jan** Both Mitchell's and Steele's versions of *Singing The Blues* top the UK chart, the latter replacing the former for a week, and then being deposed by it again. This is Steele's biggest UK hit. Meanwhile, his first major cabaret engagement is at London's Café de Paris.

Feb He has a cameo role (as a coffee bar singer) in UK thriller movie "Kill Me Tomorrow". A starring role in a semi-autobiographical feature film, "The Tommy Steele Story", is also announced.

Mar Steele also covers Mitchell's follow-up, *Knee Deep In The Blues* (written, like *Singing The Blues*, by Melvin Endsley), but Mitchell hits UK #4 and Steele makes UK #15.

May [3] Rapidly-made low budget film "The Tommy Steele Story" is released in UK. (It will be a UK box office success, released in US as "Rock Around The World".)

July *Butterfingers*, another Steele/Pratt/Bart song, included in the movie, hits UK #8.

Aug Steele's cover of Andy Williams' *Butterfly* is one of 6 tracks by various artists on EP *All-Star Hit Parade, No.2*, which reaches UK #15.

Sept Double A-side *Water, Water/Handful Of Songs*, from "The Tommy Steele Story" hits UK #5. (*Handful Of Songs* is also the theme for his TV shows, and for many years will be Steele's signature tune.) He writes and sings the theme song for another UK film, "The Shiralee", which reaches UK #11.

Oct He begins filming his second movie, "The Duke Wore Jeans". In UK music paper **New Musical Express** annual readers' poll, Steele is named runner-up to Elvis Presley as World Musical Personality.

Nov *Hey You* makes UK #28. Steele appears in the Royal Variety Show in London.

Dec He appears in pantomime for the first time, playing in "Goldilocks" in Liverpool, Merseyside.

1958 **Mar** Calypso-flavored *Nairobi*, released while Steele is touring South Africa, hits UK #3.

May *Happy Guitar* reaches UK #20.

June Steele becomes engaged to dancer Anne Donati. Kennedy and Parnes try to keep this quiet, believing it will adversely affect his teen following, but already his career has moved from rock'n'roll singer to versatile family entertainer. (Marty Wilde – another Larry Parnes protege – arrives on the scene in mid-summer, and Cliff Richard in mid-fall, and teenage fans switch to them.)

Aug Steele covers Tony Bennett's US hit *The Only Man On The Island*, reaching UK #16.

Nov [15] Steele and his backing group The Steelmen part company.

Dec He covers Ritchie Valens' first US release *Come On Let's Go*, hitting UK #10, while Valens' original fails to chart in UK. Steele begins another pantomime season in "Cinderella".

1959 **Aug** A cover of Freddy Cannon's *Tallahassie Lassie* just outsells the original in UK – Cannon reaches UK #17, but Steele makes #16 – while B-side *Give Give Give* also charts at UK #28.

Sept Steele tours Australia, earning £100,000 from a 10-week stint.

1960 **Jan** He stars in UK comedy film "Tommy The Toreador", with Sid James and others. From it, Pratt/Bart/Roy Bennett-penned children's favorite *Little White Bull* hits UK #6.

June [18] Steele marries his fiancee Anne at St. Patrick's church, Soho Square, London.

July A pure Cockney music hall song, *What A Mouth*, hits UK #5.

Dec Seasonal *Must Be Santa* makes UK #40.

1961 **Aug** *The Writing On The Wall*, a cover of a US Top 5 hit by Adam Wade, reaches UK #30 and is Steele's last chart entry. (He will continue to record for Decca for a year, and will cover Brook Benton's *Hit Record* which fails, before switching to Columbia for more sporadic recordings. Steele will leave the record world behind him during the early 60s, and become an international star of stage and film musicals. His movie successes will include "Half A Sixpence", "The Happiest Millionaire" and "Finian's Rainbow". He will also triumph on stage in "Half A Sixpence" in London and on Broadway in 1963/64, at the Old Vic, London, as Tony Lumpkin in "She Stoops To Conquer" and in self-directed "Hans Christian Andersen" and "Singing In The Rain" at the London Palladium 10 and 20 years later – well removed from his groundbreaking role as the prototype UK rock star and teen idol.)

STEELY DAN

Donald Fagen (vocals, keyboards)
Walter Becker (bass)
Jeff "Skunk" Baxter (lead guitar)
Denny Dias (rhythm guitar)
Jim Hodder (drums)

1967 Fagen (b. Jan.10, 1948, Passaic, NJ) and Becker (b. Feb.20, 1950, New York, NY) meet as students at Bard's college in upstate New York.

1969 They leave college (only Fagen graduates – in English literature) and begin trying to sell songs they have written there, with little success. Intent on a musical career, they cut a low-key film soundtrack for an early Richard Pryor movie, "You Gotta Walk It Like You Talk It" (which will not be released on disk until the late 70s). Despite its failure, it leads to another movie project, a dance video starring Becker's mother, for which they are paid $1,500.

1970 Still writing and trying to sell songs to Brill Building publishers in New York, Becker and Fagen answer an ad in **Village Voice** newspaper from guitarist Dias who is looking for "musicians with jazz chops". They join Dias' band, Demian, and record demos in his basement.

1971 Having sold, through Richard Perry, *I Mean To Shine* for recording on a Barbra Streisand album, Becker and Fagen quit Demian to join Jay & The Americans, who sing on Brill Building demos and on the New York live circuit. With the band, they meet producer Gary Katz (a 3-year partner in Cloud Nine Productions with Richard Perry) and guitarist Baxter, a communications major from Boston University, and a veteran of band Ultimate Spinach and The Holy Modal Rounders.
Nov Katz is offered the house producer's job at ABC-Dunhill Records in Los Angeles, CA. He accepts on condition that Fagen and Becker are hired as staff writers, and all parties agree.

1972 **Apr** After only 6 months, the songwriting contract is cancelled and replaced by Dunhill with an offer for Becker and Fagen to record their own compositions. Katz gathers session help from Dias, Baxter, drummer Hodder (ex-Bead Game) and others, including David Palmer (ex-Middles Class), who handles vocals.
June The name Steely Dan is taken from William Burroughs' novel **The Naked Lunch** (in which it refers to a steam-powered dildo), and work begins on a debut album.

1973 **Feb** *Can't Buy A Thrill* reaches US #17, as *Do It Again*, taken from it, hits US #6.
Apr Palmer departs (to resurface in The Big Wha-Koo on ABC), and Fagen reluctantly takes over lead vocals.
May *Reeling In The Years*, also from the first album, reaches US #11.
Aug *Show Biz Kids* peaks at US #61.
Sept *Countdown To Ecstacy* makes US #35, earning second gold disk, but yields no major hit singles. They tour US with 2 girl backing vocalists, Jenny Soule and Gloria Granola, temporarily in line-up.
Nov *My Old School*, taken from the album, peaks at US #63.

1974 **Apr** A first UK tour is interrupted by Fagen's throat infection, and only 5 of 12 dates are completed. The visit boosts newly-released *Pretzel Logic* to become the band's UK debut chart album, at #37. (On its return to US, the band will play only a selection of Californian dates.)
June *Pretzel Logic* hits US #8, and is the band's third gold album.
July [4] Following an Independence Day gig at Santa Monica Civic Center, Becker and Fagen retire from live work (for 3 years).
Aug [3] With little prospect of further work with Steely Dan, Baxter leaves to join The Doobie Brothers (with whom he has toured before), and Hodder also leaves. Jeff Porcaro replaces the latter on drums, while Michael McDonald joins on keyboards (both have augmented the group on tour, with extra vocalist Royce Jones). Meanwhile, *Rikki, Don't Lose That Number* becomes band's biggest-selling US single, hitting #4.

1975 **May** *Katy Lied* reaches both US and UK #13, and is another US gold disk. (The near-complete recording was almost ruined by faulty studio equipment – which caused producer Katz to storm out of ABC for Warner Bros.) Following its recording, McDonald leaves to join The Doobie Brothers, Porcaro returns to sessions (and will eventually form Toto), while Dias also leaves to move into session work. They are not replaced: Steely Dan will nucleus around Becker and Fagen, with numerous session men on album recordings.
June *Black Friday*, about the 1929 stock market crash, taken from *Katy Lied*, makes US #37.
Sept Debut album *Can't Buy A Thrill* belatedly charts in UK at #38, as does *Do It Again*, at UK #39.

1976 **June** *The Royal Scam* reaches US #15, earning another gold disk, and (following a European promotional tour) peaks at UK #11.
July *Kid Charlemagne*, from *The Royal Scam*, peaks at US #82.

Oct *The Fez*, also from the album, makes US #59.

1977 **Jan** UK-only release, taken from *The Royal Scam*, *Haitian Divorce*, climbs to UK #17, and is Steely Dan's best-selling UK single.
Mar [31] ABC, irritated by the duo's endless perfectionism in the studio, has set this date for delivery of the next album. (Becker and Fagen will miss it by months.)
Nov *Aja* hits US #3, earning a first platinum disk as a million-seller. It is also the first Steely Dan album to hit UK Top 10, at #5, and first release by Becker and Fagen officially as a duo.

1978 **Feb** [23] Duo wins a Grammy award for *Aja*, named the Best-Engineered Non-Classical Recording.
Mar *Peg*, extracted from *Aja*, reaches US #11.
June *Deacon Blues*, also from *Aja*, makes US #19. (Its title will inspire the name for 80s Scottish group, Deacon Blue.)
July *FM (No Static At All)*, taken from the soundtrack of movie "FM", reaches US #22.
Aug *FM (No Static At All)* makes UK #49.
Sept *Josie*, a final single from *Aja*, climbs to US #26.

1979 **Jan** Double compilation *Greatest Hits* reaches US #30, becoming another million-seller, and makes UK #41. It includes a new song, *Here In The Western World*, and is the first of several Steely Dan compilations.
Mar Taken from the compilation, *Rikki Don't Lose That Number* reaches UK #58.

1980 Duo signs to Warner Bros. and begins work on *Metal Leg*, until it is pointed out that Steely Dan still owes an album to MCA Records, ABC's new owners.

1981 **Jan** *Gaucho*, on MCA, hits US #9, becoming their third (and last) platinum album. It makes UK #27.
Feb *Hey Nineteen*, from *Gaucho*, hits US #10 (their first US Top 10 hit for 6 years).
Apr Also from *Gaucho*, *Time Out Of Mind* makes US #22, and is the duo's final US hit single.
June [21] The duo announces its split, but not ruling out working together as Steely Dan again at some future time. (Each begins work on solo projects: Becker as a producer and Fagen as a solo act.)

1982 **July** Retrospective *Steely Dan Gold* makes US #115 and UK #4.
Nov Fagen's *The Nightfly*, on Warner Bros., reaches US #11 and UK #44. The album is an account of a night at a fictional jazz radio station, W-JAZ, with Fagen as the DJ, known as The Nightfly.
Dec From *The Nightfly*, *I.G.Y. (What A Beautiful World)* reaches US #26.

1985 **May** China Crisis album *Flaunt The Imperfection* which hits UK #9, is produced by Becker. It also contains 3 UK hit singles.
Nov TV-promoted compilation *Reelin' In The Years – The Very Best Of Steely Dan* makes UK #43.

1987 **Feb** Ex-model Rosie Vela's A&M debut album *Zazu* is produced by Gary Katz, who persuades both Becker and Fagen to play on it, leading to speculation about a reunion.
Oct Another TV-promoted compilation album, *Do It Again – The Very Best Of Steely Dan*, reaches UK #64.

1988 **Apr** Fagen takes time off from being music editor for US movie magazine **Premiere** to release *Century's End*, taken from the movie soundtrack of "Bright Lights Big City".

1990 Fagen, resident in New York and organizing occasional live package shows, including featuring Michael McDonald, Patti Austin and Phoebe Snow on the same bill, and Becker, in demand as a producer working from his own Hawaii studio, begin working together again, although both deny that a Steely Dan reunion will result.

STEPPENWOLF

John Kay (guitar, vocals)
Michael Monarch (guitar)
Rushton Moreve (bass)
Goldy McJohn (organ)
Jerry Edmonton (drums)

1967 Kay (b. Joachim F. Krauledat, Apr.12, 1944, Tilsit, Germany), Monarch (b. July 5, 1950, Los Angeles, CA), Moreve (b. 1948, Los Angeles), McJohn (b. May 2, 1945, US) and Edmonton (b. Oct.24, 1946, Canada) form as The Sparrow in Canada. (Kay has been in Canada since 1958, when he arrived with his parents after escaping from East Germany.) After recording unsuccessful single *Tomorrow's Ship* for Columbia, the group relocates to California and is noticed playing at a coffee house in Venice Beach. It signs a new recording deal to Dunhill Records and, at producer Gabriel Mekler's suggestion, the name is changed to Steppenwolf (taken from the Herman Hesse novel). After some early recordings and gigs, Moreve is replaced on bass by John Russell Morgan.

1968 **Jan** Debut album *Steppenwolf* is released, together with a single reviving Don Covay's *Sookie Sookie*. The single fails to chart, but album slowly climbs as the group's hard rock live reputation spreads. (It will hit US #6 when *Born To Be Wild*, the second single extract, becomes a smash.) Album also contains band's anti-drug song *The Pusher*, which becomes an on-stage anthem.

Aug *Born To Be Wild*, penned by Dennis Edmonton (aka Mars Bonfire) and featuring the lyric "heavy metal thunder", hits US #2 for 3 weeks behind The Young Rascals' *People Got To Be Free*, and sells over a million copies, earning a gold disk. (It will become the archetypal biker song when used in film "Easy Rider" a year later.)
[4] Group plays the Newport Pop Festival in Costa Mesa, CA, alongside Canned Heat, Sonny & Cher, The Grateful Dead, The Byrds and others.

Nov *Magic Carpet Ride* hits US #3 and is the group's second consecutive million-selling single. It is taken from *Steppenwolf The Second*, which also hits US #3 and earns a gold disk.

Dec [28] Band plays the Miami Pop Festival in Hallendale, FL, to 100,000 people. The 3-day bill includes The Grateful Dead, Marvin Gaye, Chuck Berry, The Turtles, Joni Mitchell and many more.

1969 **Mar** *Rock Me*, notable for its lengthy polyrhythmic drum/percussion break, hits US #10. It also features in sex-spoof film "Candy", for which they write and perform the songs (premiered in US a month earlier).

Apr *At Your Birthday Party*, which includes *Rock Me*, hits US #7. Monarch and Morgan leave the band, and are replaced by Larry Byrom (b. Dec.27, 1948, US) on guitar and Nick St. Nicholas (b. Sept.28, 1943, Hamburg, Germany) on bass.

May *It's Never Too Late* breaks run of Top 10 singles, making US #51.

June *Born To Be Wild* is the group's only UK chart entry, at #30.
[20] They play Newport 69 festival in Northridge, CA, with Jimi Hendrix, Joe Cocker, The Byrds, Creedence Clearwater Revival and others.

Aug *Early Steppenwolf*, a live recording from 1967 when the group was still known as The Sparrow (and including a marathon early 21 min. version of *The Pusher*), reaches US #29. Film "Easy Rider" uses Steppenwolf's *The Pusher* and *Born To Be Wild* as the soundtrack for its opening scenes.

Sept *Move Over* (the first notice of the band's later concern with political matters) makes US #31.

1970 **Jan** Politically-oriented *Monster* reaches US #17, earning a third gold album, while the title track climbs to US #39.

May Double live *Steppenwolf Live* hits US #7 (earning another gold disk), while *Hey Lawdy Mama* peaks at US #35.
[24] Group embarks on short UK tour at Fairfield Hall, Croydon, London.

June St. Nicholas leaves, and is replaced by George Biondo (b. Sept.3, 1945, Brooklyn, New York, NY).
[26] Band appears in UK's Bath Festival Of Blues And Progressive Music, at Shepton Mallet, Somerset, together with Led Zeppelin, The Byrds, Donovan, Frank Zappa, Santana and many more.

Aug [6] Steppenwolf takes part in a 12-hour anti-war rock festival at New York's Shea Stadium, alongside Paul Simon, Janis Joplin, Johnny Winter and others.

Sept *Screaming Night Hog* reaches US #62.

Dec *Steppenwolf 7* reaches US #19 and earns a gold disk, while *Who Needs Ya* makes US #54.

1971 **Apr** Another anti-drug song, *Snow Blind Friend*, makes US #60, while compilation *Steppenwolf Gold*, rounding up the hit singles to date, reaches US #24 and earns the band's final gold album.

May Byrom is replaced on guitar by Kent Henry.

Aug *Ride With Me* peaks at US #52.

Nov *For Ladies Only* makes US #54 while the extracted title track reaches US #64.

1972 **Feb** [14] Kay formally announces the group's dissolution in a press conference at the Hollywood Holiday Inn, CA, explaining: "We were locked into an image and style of music and there was nothing for us to look forward to." (The group has been trapped by its own success, turning over $40 million in disk sales for Dunhill.) The day is declared "Steppenwolf Day" in Los Angeles by the mayor Sam Yorty, commemorating the group's retirement.

May Kay's solo album *Forgotten Songs And Unsong Heroes*, on Dunhill, makes US #113 and provides him with his only solo hit single, a revival of Hank Snow's *I'm Movin' On*, which reaches US #52. Edmonton and McJohn form their own band, Manbeast, without notable success.

Aug Steppenwolf album *Rest In Peace*, compiled from earlier material, reaches US #62.

1973 **Mar** Another compilation, *16 Greatest Hits*, creeps to US #152.

July Kay's solo album, *My Sportin' Life*, anchors US chart at #200.

1974 **Feb** Kay re-forms Steppenwolf, with McJohn, Edmonton, Biondo and ex-Flying Burrito Brothers' guitarist Bobby Cochran, and the band is signed to Mums label.

Oct *Slow Flux*, on Mums, reaches US #47. Extracted *Straight Shootin' Woman* is the band's final US hit single at #29, as McJohn is replaced by Wayne Cook.

1975 **Oct** *Hour Of The Wolf*, released on Epic, regains some of the band's old spirit, but Kay's material is generally considered weaker than his early songs. It is the band's last chartmaker, at US #155.

1976 Steppenwolf splits again. (Monarch will join heavy metal band Detective.)

1978 Kay records solo *All In Good Time* for Mercury, without success.

1980 Kay puts together a new band, which tours US as John Kay & Steppenwolf.

1981 **July** [1] Moreve is killed in an auto accident in Los Angeles.

1987 **Oct** *Rock & Roll Rebels*, on the Qwil label and credited to John Kay & Steppenwolf, peaks at US #171.

1988 **Sept** Kay and a re-formed Steppenwolf release *Rock & Roll Rebels*.

1990 **June** New Kay & Steppenwolf album *Rise And Shine* is released on IRS, as the band begins regular US touring.
(*Born To Be Wild* is used in UK TV ad for Shell petrol/gas stations.)

CAT STEVENS

1965 Stevens (b. Steven Georgiou, July 21, 1947, Soho, London), son of a Greek London restaurateur and a Swedish mother, begins spare-time songwriting and singing in a folk/rock style while studying at Hammersmith college, London.

1966 **July** He is heard performing at the college by ex-Springfields member, now record producer, Mike Hurst. Though he has been planning to leave for US to work, Hurst is sufficiently excited by the young student's songs and voice to organize a recording session, at which they cut self-penned *I Love My Dog*. This impresses Tony Hall at Decca, who signs him (now renamed Cat Stevens) as first act on new Deram label, designed to be a showcase for progressive young UK talent.

Nov *I Love My Dog* is debut single and reaches UK #28, aided by strong pirate radio airplay.

1967 **Feb** Highly commercial orchestrally-arranged *Matthew And Son* hits UK #2 (behind The Monkees' *I'm A Believer*) and heightens his reputation as a songwriter. (He is already attracting cover versions – The Tremeloes' first hit without Brian Poole is a version of his *Here Comes My Baby*, at UK #4.)

Mar [31] Stevens embarks on 24-date UK package tour with The Walker Brothers, Engelbert Humperdinck and The Jimi Hendrix Experience, at Finsbury Park Astoria, London. Tour will end Apr.30 at Granada cinema, Tooting, London.

Apr *I'm Gonna Get Me A Gun* (publicized by some gun-toting pictures which Stevens will later disown) is another commercially strong combination of unusual lyric and string arrangement, and hits UK #6. Entirely self-written debut album, *Matthew And Son*, hits UK #7 at the same time.

June Former Ikette P.P. Arnold's cover of Stevens' *The First Cut Is The Deepest* reaches UK #18.

Aug *A Bad Night* reaches UK #20.

Dec *Kitty* makes UK #47 as second album, *New Masters*, fails to chart.

1968 **Feb** *Lovely City* does not chart. Stevens is unavailable to promote it. He contracts tuberculosis and is hospitalized. 2 more singles, *Here Comes My Wife* and *Where Are You* are issued without success while he is convalescing, completing his Deram contract.

1969 Originally reported to be writing a musical, Stevens spends the last months of his recuperation honing more sensitive and less commercial songs, having intensely disliked the whirlwind pop star trappings of his initial rise to fame.

1970 **July** He signs to Island Records in UK and A&M in US, and *Mona Bone Jakon*, produced by ex-Yardbird Paul Samwell-Smith, showcases a new, more serious singer/songwriter style. It makes UK #63.

Aug *Lady D'Arbanville*, taken from the album and dedicated to ex-girlfriend, actress Patti D'Arbanville, hits UK #8.

Sept Jimmy Cliff's cover of Stevens-written and produced *Wild World* hits UK #8.

Dec *Tea For The Tillerman*, featuring his original of *Wild World* reaches UK #20.

1971 **Apr** *Wild World* is US chart debut, reaching #11. *Tea For The Tillerman* follows it and hits US #8 (it will remain charted for 79 weeks in US and earn Stevens his first gold disk). *Mona Bone Jakon* also belatedly charts in US, at #164.

May Double album, combining the first 2, *Matthew And Son/New Masters*, belatedly sells the Deram material in US, reaching #173.

Aug *Moon Shadow*, from his next album, makes US #30 (and UK #22 a few weeks later).

Oct *Teaser And The Firecat* hits UK #3 and US #2, earning a gold disk. It will stay on chart for 93 weeks in UK and 67 weeks in US. The sleeve features his own artwork, and he also produces a short animated film with the same title as the album, later to be screened at gigs.

Nov *Peace Train*, extracted from the album only in US, hits US #7.

1972 **Jan** Also from the album, Stevens' interpretation of Eleanor Farjeon's children's hymn *Morning Has Broken*, with Rick Wakeman playing piano, hits UK #9.

Feb Compilation *Very Young And Early Songs* is released on Deram in US, reaching #94.

May *Morning Has Broken* hits US #6. Stevens contributes to the soundtrack of Hal Ashby's cult movie "Harold And Maude".

Sept He begins a 31-date tour of US and Canada at the Shrine Auditorium, Los Angeles, CA, backed by an 11-piece orchestra (and supported by folk/blues singer Ramblin' Jack Elliott) to a sold-out crowd of 6,500.

Nov *Catch Bull At Four*, which broadens his instrumentation by using Alun Davies (guitar), Jean Roussel (piano), Alan James (bass) and Gerry Conway (drums), with Stevens himself playing synthesizer on some tracks, hits UK #2 and tops US chart for 3 weeks, earning a further gold disk.

1973 **Jan** Different singles are extracted from *Catch Bull* in UK and US. *Can't Keep It In* reaches UK #13, while *Sitting* reaches US #16.

Aug *Foreigner* hits both UK and US #3, and earns a further gold disk. 1 side is devoted to *Foreigner Suite*, a long and lyrically profound piece indicating Stevens' increasing involvement with philosophical and religious concerns. His live appearances dwindle, and he becomes more reclusive and rarely interviewed. Extracted *The Hurt* makes US #31, but does not chart in UK. He is now living in Brazil, having left UK for a year's tax exile. The money he would have lost to the UK taxman, he donates to Unesco and other charities.

Nov [9] He makes his US network TV debut on ABC TV's "In Concert" show, a 90-min. special taped at the Hollywood Bowl.

1974 **May** *Buddah And The Chocolate Box*, Stevens' sixth US gold disk, hits UK #3 and US #2. *Oh Very Young*, taken from it, hits US #10, but fails to chart in UK (where Island does not promote his singles heavily, being keen to maintain Stevens as its best-selling album act).

Sept A revival of Sam Cooke's *Another Saturday Night* reaches UK #19, and hits US #6 a few weeks later.

1975 **Jan** *Ready* climbs to US #26.

Aug Compilation *Greatest Hits*, rounding up his Island/A&M singles, hits UK #2 and US #6, and earns another gold disk. *Two Fine People*, included on the compilation, reaches US #33 but fails in UK.

Nov He tours Europe with a 5-piece backing band (including a Brazilian percussionist) and a female back-up vocal group, performing in an elaborate and specially-constructed stage set.

Dec [11] UK leg of his tour begins at the Liverpool Empire, Merseyside, ending at the Hammersmith Odeon, London, Dec.20.

1976 **Jan** *Numbers* reaches UK #13, but is his first Island album not to chart in UK. His most complex and lyrically involved album, it proves inaccessible to many devotees of his light earlier touch.

Mar *Banapple Gas* makes US #41.

1977 **Apr** Rod Stewart's cover of Stevens-penned *First Cut Is The Deepest* reaches US #21 (and subsequently UK #1).

June *Izitso* reaches UK #18 and hits US #7, Stevens' last gold disk.

July *(Remember The Days Of The) Old School Yard*, on which Stevens duets with Elkie Brooks, is his last chart single in UK, making #44, and climbs to US #33.

1978 **Jan** Instrumental *Was Dog A Doughnut* peaks at US #70.

1979 **Feb** *Back To Earth* fails to chart in UK but makes US #33, while *Bad Brakes* peaks at US #84. Some take the album title to mean a return to his earlier, earthier pop concerns, but it signifies a return from international celebrity to private person, as he retires from all aspects of making music. By this time, he has totally committed himself to the Muslim faith and life, and changes his name to Yusef Islam.

Sept [9] He marries Fouzia Ali at Kensington Mosque, London.

1981 He finances the establishment of, and begins to teach at, a Muslim school in North London. (He also has the Greek flag removed from the sleeve artwork of his *Greatest Hits*.) Officially confirming he has left

show business for good, he auctions all trappings of his pop career, including his gold disks, and donates the money to his current work.

1985 **Jan** Compilation *Footsteps In The Dark*, combining tracks from his 9 Island/A&M albums with 3 additional songs, makes US #165.

July Rumors persist that Yusef is to appear at Live Aid, and is even willing to go on stage as Cat Stevens.

1987 **June** The Pet Shop Boys' worldwide hit *It's A Sin* has a melody closely based on *Wild World*'s (Stevens is reportedly more flattered than annoyed), while US band 10,000 Maniacs revive his *Peace Train*.

1988 **June** Maxi Priest hits UK #5 with a revival of *Wild World*.

1989 **Feb** US radio stations urge people to burn Stevens' albums after he expresses public support for Muslim proclamation requiring death sentence for author Salman Rushdie.

1990 **June** Yusef is barred from entering Tel Aviv, Israel, turned away with his 8-year-old son Mohammed, as an "undesirable".

Nov Yusef visits Iraq and successfully secures the release of a number of UK Muslims held hostage by the Gulf crisis.

SHAKIN' STEVENS

1968 Stevens (b. Michael Barratt, Mar.4, 1948, Ely, Wales), one of 12 children, whose chief childhood musical influence has been 50s rock'n'roll records owned by his elder brothers, begins playing the Cardiff, Wales, club circuit with a rock'n'roll revival band, The Sunsets.

1970 **Jan** After gaining a strong reputation on the UK rock revival circuit, Shakin' Stevens And The Sunsets sign a recording contract with EMI's Parlophone label, and record album *A Legend* with producer Dave Edmunds, at Rockfield studios, Wales. It fails to sell, as does a revival of Big Al Downing's *Down On The Farm*, and EMI drops the group.

1971 A second one-off deal, with CBS, produces another unsuccessful album, *I'm No J.D.*

1973 Popular as a live attraction in Europe, the group signs to Dutch label Dureco for an album (and amid many successful European tours, will continue to record for Dutch labels like Dynamo and Pink Elephant until 1976).

1976 **Apr** *Jungle Rock*, released on Mooncrest, fails to sell against Hank Mizell's UK #3 version. It is the group's final single, as The Sunsets split shortly afterwards.

1977 Stevens is 1 of 3 actors (with P.J. Proby and Tim Whitnall) signed to play Elvis Presley at various stages of his life in the Jack Good musical "Elvis" on London's West End stage. (The show runs for 19 months and wins a theater award as Best Musical Of 1977.)

Apr Stevens is signed as a soloist to Track Records, but in spite of his West End success, 3 singles and a first solo album, *Shakin' Stevens*, fail to chart over a 12-month period with the label.

1978 He becomes a UK TV regular, alongside Lulu, Alvin Stardust and others, in Jack Good's revival of his late 50s rock show "Oh Boy", and features in Good's "Let's Rock" in US. He also signs with manager Freya Miller.

Aug Stevens is signed to the Epic division of CBS, working with producer Mike Hurst. First Epic single *Treat Her Right* does not chart, and neither do 2 follow-ups, revivals of Jody Reynolds' *Endless Sleep* and The Classics IV's *Spooky*.

1980 **Mar** *Hot Dog*, taken from debut Epic album *Shakin' Stevens Take One!*, finally gives him a UK Singles chart debut at #24, while the album makes UK #62. Produced by Hurst (his last work with Stevens), the album features "musical co-ordination" and remixing by Stuart Colman, who also plays bass as part of the 8-man backing group (which includes Albert Lee on lead guitar).

Sept Colman takes over production on *Marie Marie*, a cover of a song by US rockabilly band The Blasters, which reaches UK #19.

1981 **Mar** [28] A revival of Stuart Hamblen's *This Ole House* (a 1954 UK #1 for Rosemary Clooney) is given a sharp rock arrangement by Colman and proves to be Stevens' major breakthrough, topping the UK chart for 3 weeks.

Apr *This Ole House*, with rock revival band Matchbox, hits UK #2.

May *You Drive Me Crazy*, an original song by Ronnie Harwood, hits UK #2 for 4 weeks (behind Adam And The Ants' *Stand And Deliver*).

Aug Budget album *Shakin' Stevens*, a compilation of early material, makes UK #34.

[1] A revival of Jim Lowe/Frankie Vaughan 1956 hit *Green Door* tops the UK chart for 4 weeks.

Oct Stevens' first slow-tempo hit revives Irma Thomas' *It's Raining*, and hits UK #10.

Nov *Shaky*, including the 3 recent hits, tops the UK chart for a week.

1982 **Jan** [30] *Oh Julie*, his first self-penned hit, tops the UK chart for a week.

May *Shirley*, a revival of an obscure 60s John Fred & The Playboy Band track, hits UK #6.

Sept Uptempo *Give Me Your Heart Tonight* reaches UK #11.

Oct *Give Me Your Heart Tonight* hits UK #3.

Nov Stevens revives one of Jackie Wilson's early R&B-rockers, *I'll Be Satisfied*, and hits UK #10.

Dec *The Shakin' Stevens EP*, spotlighting a seasonal revival of Elvis Presley's *Blue Christmas*, hits UK #2, held from the top by Rene & Renato's *Save Your Love*.

1983 Aug Stevens switches producers to Christopher Neil, and a revival of Ricky Nelson's 1959 hit *It's Late* makes UK #11.

Nov *Cry Just A Little Bit*, an original composition by Bob Heatlie, hits UK #3, while parent album *The Bop Won't Stop* makes UK #21.

1984 Jan Stevens teams with fellow Welsh vocalist Bonnie Tyler, to revive Brook Benton and Dinah Washington's 1960 US Top 10 hit *A Rockin' Good Way (To Mess Around And Fall In Love)*. Credited to Shaky And Bonnie, it hits UK #5.

Apr *A Love Worth Waiting For* hits UK #2 for 2 weeks, behind Lionel Richie's *Hello*.

May Stevens' only US chartmaker is *Cry Just A Little Bit*, which reaches US #67.

Sept Dennis Linde's song *A Letter To You* hits UK #10.

Nov Compilation *Greatest Hits*, anthologizing 18 singles from *Hot Dog* up to date, hits UK #8.

Dec Self-penned *Teardrops* hits UK #5.

1985 Mar *Breaking Up My Heart*, another Heatlie song, reaches UK #14.

Nov Stevens reunites with his original producer Dave Edmunds for a revival of *Lipstick, Powder And Paint*, a mid-50s US R&B hit for bluesman Joe Turner, which makes UK #11. Edmunds-produced album of the same title reaches UK #37.

Dec [28] Heatlie-penned *Merry Christmas Everyone*, produced again by Edmunds, tops the UK chart in Christmas week, his fourth UK #1.

1986 Feb *Turning Away* makes UK #15.

Nov *Because I Love You*, again produced by Neil, reaches UK #14.

Dec *Merry Christmas Everyone* re-charts, making UK #58.

1987 Aug Stevens' revival of Gary Glitter's *A Little Boogie Woogie (In The Back Of My Mind)* makes UK #12. It is co-produced by Mike Leander, Glitter's former producer.

Oct *Let's Boogie*, Stevens' first album after an unusually long hiatus, makes UK #59. From it comes his first revival of a Motown oldie, The Supremes' 1964 million-seller *Come See About Me*, which reaches UK #24, and marks a reunion with Stuart Colman.

Dec Self-produced (with Carey Taylor) revival of Emile Ford's 1959 million-seller *What Do You Want To Make Those Eyes At Me For?* and in an almost identical arrangement, hits UK #5.

1988 Aug A revival of The Detroit Emeralds' mid-70s soul hit, *Feel The Need In Me*, reaches UK #26.

Oct *How Many Tears Can You Hide?* makes UK #47.

Dec Stevens has a rare ballad hit with a revival of Bing Crosby/Grace Kelly oldie *True Love* at UK #36, while *A Whole Lotta Shaky* peaks at UK #42.

[31] As one of the most successful performers of the 80s, Stevens appears on the 25th Anniversary edition of BBC TV's "Top Of The Pops", singing his first chart-topper *This Ole House*.

1989 Feb [18] Incongrously produced by Art Of Noise's J.J. Jeczalik, *Jezebel* stalls at UK #58.

May *Love Attack* restores him to UK Top 30 at UK #28. During the past decade Shakin' Stevens has accumulated no less than 26 Top 30 hits, unsurpassed by any other act.

1990 Mar The run continues as Pete Hammond-produced *I Might* reaches UK #20. 3 further less successful Hammond helmed singles during the year – *Yes I Do* (#60), *Pink Champagne* (#59) and *My Cutie Cutie* (#75), together with Telstar-issued album *There's Two Kinds Of Music: Rock'N'Roll* (#65), indicate that Shaky's fans may have now grown up.

AL STEWART

1962 Stewart (b. Sept.5, 1945, Glasgow, Scotland), after learning guitar alongside Robert Fripp (later to found King Crimson), plays his first live gigs as lead guitarist in a rock/pop band, Tony Blackburn (future UK DJ) & The Sabres, in Bournemouth, Dorset (having moved from Scotland with his widowed mother at age 3, and subsequently attended public school until dropping out).

1965 Strongly influenced by Bob Dylan, he becomes immersed in modern folk music and starts to write his own songs, performing at London area folk club venues like Bunjies and Les Cousins. He also temporarily

shares a flat in the East End with visiting folk duo Simon & Garfunkel.

1966 Aug His first recording, *The Elf*, inspired by his reading J.R.R.Tolkein's **The Lord Of The Rings** a one-off on Decca, sells 496 copies.

1967 Sept Signed to CBS in UK, he releases debut album *Bedsitter Images*, which has mostly introspective songs for voice and guitar, backed by orchestral arrangements. CBS mounts a concert at London's Royal Festival Hall presenting Stewart with a complete group and orchestra as back-up. His more usual shows are still one-man affairs, and he becomes a popular fixture on the college circuit, where his self-analytical, sometimes acidic, and occasionally controversial lyrics are widely appreciated.

1968 July [6] Stewart takes part in the Woburn Music Festival, Beds.

1969 Jan *Love Chronicles* (with Jimmy Page on guitar) has an 18-min. title track which includes the word "fucking", preventing airplay. It is Stewart's first US release, and his only one on CBS/Columbia.

Dec UK music weekly **Melody Maker** votes *Love Chronicles* Folk Album Of The Year in its annual survey.

1970 Apr *Zero She Flies* is Stewart's UK chart debut, reaching #40.

May [22] Stewart plays at the Queen Elizabeth Hall, London.

1972 Feb *Orange* shows musical influences outside the folk troubadour style of his first 3 albums, but is not a success.

1973 Dec [23] Stewart plays at Alexandra Palace, London, with Renaissance, Wishbone Ash and Vinegar Joe.

1974 Mar Stewart makes his first major US tour accompanied by members of just-disbanded group Home.

June *Past, Present And Future*, a concept album tracing historical events, with inspiration from the book **The Centuries Of Nostradamus**, does not chart in UK, but released via a new US deal with Janus Records, makes US #133.

1975 Apr *Modern Times* reaches US #30. He tours US again, with a backing band consisting of Gerry Conway, Pat Donaldson, Simon Nicol and Simon Roussell.

1977 Feb Stewart signs a new recording deal with RCA in UK. *Year Of The Cat*, produced by Alan Parsons (and rejected a year earlier by Virgin boss Richard Branson, who was offered the album for a £5,000 advance), reaches UK #37, but hits US #5, selling over a million to earn a platinum disk. Extracted title track makes UK #31, his only UK chart single. It is also his US Singles chart debut and, aided by strong US airplay, hits #8.

May *On The Border*, from *Year Of The Cat*, reaches US #42.

1978 Nov A new US label deal with Arista Records precedes *Time Passages* also produced by Parsons. It reaches UK #38 (on RCA) but hits US #10, earning another platinum disk. It is another of his albums to eschew romantic songs in favor of time-capsule pieces concerned with specific historical events.

Dec Title song from *Time Passages* hits US #7.

1979 Mar *Song On The Radio*, again from *Time Passages*, makes US #29.

1980 Oct *24 Carrots* reaches UK #55 and US #37, while, from it, *Midnight Rocks* peaks at US #24, and is Stewart's last US hit single.

1981 Dec Double album *Live/Indian Summer*, consisting of 3 sides of live material and one from the studio, makes US #110.

1984 June *Russians And Americans* makes UK #83.

1988 After 4 years of legal problems which restrict his creativity, Stewart releases *License To Steal* on Enigma Records, on which he suggests that lawyers should be subject to limited nuclear warfare.

1989 Resident in Los Angeles, CA, since 1976, Stewart returns to UK for one-off performance at the Cambridge Folk Festival.

1991 Apr [17] While EMI promotes Stewart retrospective album *Chronicles ... The Best Of Al Stewart*, he embarks on 19-date UK tour starting at the Municpal Hall, Colne, Lancs., set to end May 13 at the Leas Cliff Hall, Folkestone, Kent, his first such venture in 15 years.

ROD STEWART

1961 Stewart (b. Roderick David Stewart, Jan.10, 1945, Highgate, London), of Scottish parents who moved to London, having attended William Grimshaw school, Hornsey, with Ray and Dave Davies and Pete Quaife (who will achieve success as The Kinks), signs as an apprentice with professional soccer team Brentford Football Club. After 3 weeks, tired of little more than polishing other players' boots, he quits, heading for Europe, where he becomes a busker. (He is deported from Spain for vagrancy.) He returns to UK, becomes a beatnik and attends CND's Aldermaston marches.

1963 He joins Birmingham, W.Midlands-R&B band The Five Dimensions as vocalist and harmonica player. The band plays throughout UK, backing singer Jimmy Powell, who records a single for Pye on which Stewart plays blues harp.

964 Stewart performs the same duties for Long John Baldry & The Hoochie Coochie Men, who have just signed with United Artists Records. Baldry had heard Stewart singing, while waiting for a train at Twickenham station.
Aug Decca Records staff producer Mike Vernon sees Stewart perform at London's Marquee club, and signs him to a solo deal.
[6] Stewart makes his UK TV debut on "The Beat Room", with The Hoochie Coochie Men.
Oct Debut single *Good Morning Little Schoolgirl*, despite an appearance on ITV show "Ready Steady Go!", fails to chart. The Hoochie Coochie Men split, and Stewart joins The Soul Agents.

965 He joins Steampacket, a group formed by Giorgio Gomelsky, with Stewart sharing vocals with Baldry and Julie Driscoll with Brian Auger (keyboards), Rick Brown (bass) and Mickey Waller (drums) in the line-up.
July Steampacket supports The Rolling Stones and The Walker Brothers on a UK tour, and records an album (which will not be released until the 70s).
Nov Stewart signs a solo deal with EMI, releasing *The Day Will Come*, on Columbia. He appears in UK TV documentary "Rod The Mod", a 30-min. portrait of a typical mod.

966 **Mar** Steampacket splits. Stewart joins The Shotgun Express with Peter Bardens (keyboards), Beryl Marsden (vocals), Peter Green (guitar), Dave Ambrose (bass) and Mick Fleetwood (drums).
Oct Band releases 1 single, *I Could Feel The Whole World Turn Around* and appears at the Richmond Rhythm & Blues Festival.
Dec Stewart joins The Jeff Beck Group.

967 **Apr** The Jeff Beck Group makes UK #14 with *Hi Ho Silver Lining*.
Aug Group plays the 1967 National Rhythm & Blues Festival at Windsor, Berks.

968 **Feb** Stewart sings vocals on the B-side, *I've Been Drinking*, of Beck's hit version of Eurovision song contest entry *Love Is Blue*.
Mar Stewart releases *Little Miss Understood* for Immediate Records, but it fails to chart.
June [22] The Jeff Beck Group makes its US debut at the Fillmore East, New York, at the start of a tour.
Sept Group album *Truth* hits UK #8 and US #15. Stewart strikes up a friendship with guitarist Ron Wood.

969 **June** Stewart appears with The Small Faces at Cambridge University as Quiet Melon.
July Beck Group album *Cosa Nostra – Beck Ola* reaches UK #39 and US #15.
Oct The Jeff Beck Group splits and Stewart turns down the chance to join US band Cactus. He stays in UK and joins The Faces (now without the "Small" adjective), who sign to Warner Bros. He also signs a solo deal with Phonogram, and will run his group and individual careers simultaneously until The Faces split. (Stewart is advanced £1,000 to record his solo debut.)
Nov *An Old Raincoat Won't Ever Let You Down*, comprising a mixture of originals and cover versions, fails to chart in UK, but makes US #139. The Faces play on the album.

970 Stewart records guide vocals for Python Lee Jackson's *In A Broken Dream*, for which he is paid enough to buy seat covers for his car. (When the record is released and becomes a hit, Stewart's vocal has not been replaced, but he receives no credit.)
June *Gasoline Alley* reaches UK #62 and US #27.
Oct [1] He begins a 28-date US tour at Goddard college, Plainfield, VT.

1971 **June** *Every Picture Tells A Story* tops UK chart for 6 weeks and US chart for 4 weeks.
Sept Tim Hardin-ballad *Reason To Believe* reaches UK #19. DJs flip the record, and *Maggie May* becomes A-side.
Oct *Maggie May* tops UK and US charts for 5 weeks. (Stewart tops both UK and US Singles and Album charts in the same week.)
Dec *(I Know) I'm Losing You* reaches US #24.

1972 **Mar** *Handbags And Gladrags*, written by Mike D'Abo, makes US #42.
Aug *Never A Dull Moment* hits UK #1 for 2 weeks and US #2.
Sept *You Wear It Well* tops UK chart.
Oct Python Lee Jackson's *In A Broken Dream* hits UK #3, having already climbed to US #56, while *You Wear It Well* reaches US #13.
Dec Double A-side *Angel* (a Jimi Hendrix song) and *What Made Milwaukee Famous* (a hit for Jerry Lee Lewis) hits UK #4 and US #40.
[9] Stewart sings *Pinball Wizard* in a special stage production of "Tommy".

1973 **May** Re-released *I've Been Drinking*, credited to Jeff Beck and Rod Stewart, reaches UK #27.

Aug Compilation *Sing It Again Rod* tops UK chart and makes US #31.
Sept *Oh No Not My Baby*, reviving Manfred Mann's 1964 hit, hits UK #6 as revival of Sam Cooke's *Twisting The Night Away* makes US #59.
Nov *Oh No Not My Baby* makes US #59.

1974 Stewart begins a world tour with The Faces.
May Stewart guests on the Scotland World Cup Football Squad's album *Easy Easy*. He duets with soccer star Denis Law on *Angel*.
Oct *Farewell*, backed with a medley of *Bring It On Home To Me* and *You Send Me*, hits UK #7. Parent *Smiler* tops UK chart, and reaches US #13.
Dec *Mine For Me*, written for album *Smiler* by Paul McCartney (along with Elton John and Bernie Taupin's *Let Me Be Your Car*), stalls at US #91. Stewart signs to Warner Bros., after a legal dispute over whether Phonogram or Warner has the rights to his solo releases.

1975 **Mar** [5] Stewart meets Swedish actress Britt Ekland at a party in Los Angeles, CA, and embarks on a highly publicized love affair. He announces that he is setting up permanent residency in US, and applying for citizenship.
July Press reports claim that Stewart owes the UK taxman over £750,000. On a trip to UK, Stewart refuses to leave the international departure lounge to avoid setting foot in UK.
Aug *Atlantic Crossing* hits UK #1 and US #9. The set is produced by Tom Dowd in Muscle Shoals, AL, using the famed rhythm section, which includes Steve Cropper and Donald "Duck" Dunn.
Sept *Sailing*, penned by Gavin Sutherland, tops UK chart.
Nov Reviving Motown classic *This Old Heart Of Mine*, Stewart hits UK #4 with his first release on Riva Records, set up by his manager Billy Gaff. *Sailing* makes US #58.
Dec The Faces, inactive for some time, finally split.

1976 **May** Compilation album *The Best Of Rod Stewart* makes US #90.
June *Tonight's The Night (Gonna Be Alright)* hits UK #5. (The song is mostly banned because of its subject matter, the seduction of a virgin.)
July *A Night On The Town*, recorded in Los Angeles with top session players David Foster, John Jarvis, Steve Cropper and "Duck" Dunn, hits UK #1 and US #2.
Aug BBC TV documentary series "Sailor" adopts *Sailing* as its theme, sung by the crew of H.M.S. Ark Royal. It becomes the unofficial anthem of the Royal Navy.
Sept *The Killing Of Georgie (Parts 1 and 2)*, a 2-part saga about the death of a gay friend in New York, hits UK #2.
Oct *Sailing*, reissued because of the TV documentary, hits UK #3. A special based on *A Night On The Town* airs on UK TV.
Nov *Tonight's The Night* tops US chart for 7 weeks.
Dec *Get Back*, featured in Lou Reizner's film "All This And World War II" utilizing covers of Lennon/McCartney songs, reaches UK #11. A reissue of *Maggie May* makes UK #31.

1977 **Apr** A revival of Cat Stevens-penned *First Cut Is The Deepest* reaches US #21.
May Coupled with *I Don't Want To Talk About It* as a double A-side, *First Cut Is The Deepest* tops UK chart for 4 weeks, holding off The Sex Pistols' *God Save The Queen*.
July *The Killing Of Georgie* makes US #30. Compilation album *The Best Of Rod Stewart* reaches UK #18.
Oct *You're In My Heart (The Final Acclaim)* hits UK #3.
Nov *Foot Loose And Fancy Free* hits UK #3 and US #2 as Stewart begins a major tour with a band comprising long-term musical associate Jim Cregan (guitar), Gary Grainger (guitar), Billy Peek (guitar), Phil Chen (bass) and Carmine Appice (drums).

1978 **Jan** *You're In My Heart (The Final Acclaim)* hits US #4.
Feb Hot-rocking *Hotlegs/I Was Only Joking* (featuring a reference to *Maggie May*) hits UK #5.
Apr *Hotlegs* reaches US #28.
June Stewart, pursuing his love of soccer, hits UK #4 with *Ole Ola (Muhler Brasileira)*, with the Scottish World Cup Football Squad. (After Scotland fails to qualify for second round, drawing 1-1 with Iran, it speedily drops down the chart.) *I Was Only Joking* makes US #22.
Dec *D'Ya Think I'm Sexy*, written by Stewart and Appice, tops UK chart. (Songwriter Jorge Ben will later sue, claiming it is based on his *Taj Mahal*.) *Blondes Have More Fun* hits UK #3 and tops US chart.

1979 **Jan** [9] The "Music For UNICEF" concert, to celebrate the International Year Of The Child, takes place in the General Assembly Hall of the United Nations in New York. Rod Stewart sings *D'Ya Think I'm Sexy?*, donating the royalties from the song to UNICEF.
[10] NBC TV airs "A Gift Of Song - The Music For UNICEF Concert".
Feb *Ain't Love A Bitch* makes UK #11 as *D'Ya Think I'm Sexy* hits US #1.
Apr [6] Stewart marries Alana Hamilton, ex-wife of actor George Hamilton, in Beverly Hills, CA.

May *Blondes (Have More Fun)* stalls at UK #63.

June *Ain't Love A Bitch* reaches UK #22.

[21-28] Stewart finishes a 4-month US tour with 6 performances at the Forum, Ingelwood, CA.

Nov *Rod Stewart's Greatest Hits* tops UK chart and reaches US #22.

1980 **Feb** *I Don't Want To Talk About It* makes US #46. (Written by Crazy Horse member Danny Whitten, Everything But The Girl's version will re-chart in UK in 1988, and Stewart himself will re-record it in 1990.)

May *If Loving You Is Wrong (I Don't Want To Be Right)* reaches UK #23.

Nov *Foolish Behavior* hits UK #4 and US #12. Extracted *Passion* makes UK #17.

Dec Self-penned ballad *My Girl* reaches UK #32.

1981 **Feb** *Passion* hits US #5.

Mar *Somebody Special* stalls at US #71.

Nov *Tonight I'm Yours (Don't Hurt Me)* hits UK #8. Parent album *Tonight I'm Yours* hits UK #8 and US #11.

Dec *Young Turks*, aided by a gang dancing video, reaches UK #11 and hits US #5.

1982 **Mar** Stewart covers Ace's hit *How Long*, but it peaks at UK #41. It will be his last chart single for Riva. *Tonight I'm Yours (Don't Hurt Me)* reaches US #20.

Apr [26] He is mugged in Los Angeles, while standing next to his car.

May *How Long* makes US #49.

July Stewart records Burt Bacharach and Carole Bayer Sager's *That's What Friends Are For* for Henry Winkler/Michael Keaton film "Night Shift". (Dionne Warwick & Friends will subsequently take the song to the top of US chart.)

Nov Double album *Absolutely Live* reaches UK #35 and US #46.

1983 **June** *Body Wishes*, his first for Warner Bros., hits UK #5 and US #30.

July *Baby Jane* tops UK chart, as prelude to UK tour; it makes US #14.

Sept *What Am I Gonna Do (I'm So In Love With You)* hits UK #3.

Oct *What Am I Gonna Do (I'm So In Love With You)* makes US #35.

Dec *Sweet Surrender* reaches UK #23.

1984 Stewart and his wife Alana separate.

June *Infatuation* makes UK #27, while parent album *Camouflage* hits UK #8 and US #18.

July *Infatuation* hits US #6.

Sept A revival of *Some Guys Have All The Luck* reaches UK #15.

Oct *Some Guys Have All The Luck* hits US #10.

1985 **Jan** A revival of Free's *All Right Now* stalls at US #72. Stewart headlines 2 nights at the world's largest rock festival, Rock In Rio, in Rio de Janeiro, Brazil.

July Stewart pairs with old friend Jeff Beck to release a version of The Impressions' *People Get Ready*, from Beck's *Flash*. It makes US #48.

1986 **Apr** *Sailing* makes UK #41, with all royalties going to the bereaved families and survivors of the Zeebrugge Ferry Disaster.

June *Love Touch*, produced by Mike Chapman and from Robert Redford/Debra Winger film "Legal Eagles", reaches UK #27.

July *Every Beat Of My Heart* hits UK #2.

Aug *Love Touch* hits US #6.

Sept *Another Heartache*, co-written by Bryan Adams, makes UK #54 and US #52.

Nov *Every Beat Of My Heart* stalls at US #83. *Love Touch*, produced by Bob Ezrin, hits UK #5, and titled *Rod Stewart* in US, it reaches #28.

1987 **July** [25] *Twistin' The Night Away*, a new version of his 1973 US #59 and used in the Dennis Quaid/Martin Short film "Innerspace", stalls at US #80.

1988 **June** *Out Of Order*, produced by Duran Duran's Andy Taylor and Chic's Bernard Edwards, reaches UK #11 and US #20. Songwriting assistance comes from Simon Climie, whose *Love Changes Everything* Stewart has previously turned down. Extracted *Lost In You* reaches UK #21 and US #12.

Aug *Forever Young* stalls at UK #57.

Oct *Forever Young* reaches US #12, helped by a video co-starring Stewart's son by current girlfriend Kelly Emberg.

Dec Third single from *Out Of Order*, *My Heart Can't Tell You No* begins a 6-month US chart stay to hit #4.

1989 **Feb** Stewart hosts the annual American Music Awards at the Shrine Auditorium, Los Angeles.

[25] "South Of The Border Tour" starts in Mar Del Plata, Argentina.

Apr [8] 450 fans are injured trying to rush the stage at a concert at Monterrey, Mexico.

May Belated UK release *My Heart Can't Tell You No* peaks at #49 as his ex-wife Alana applies for increased alimony. Retrospective video collection "Rod Stewart & The Faces" is released in UK.

[31] Stewart embarks on 39-date US tour in New Haven, CT, set to end

July 31 at the Hollywood Bowl, Los Angeles.

June [3] Stewart fail to show up for Boston radio station W-XKS birthday concert because of voice problems. DJ Sunny Joe White extracts promise from Stewart to re-book.

[20] He begins 6-week US concert tour at Columbus, OH, having toured intermittently for over a year.

July [29] *Crazy About Her* reaches US #11.

Aug [5] Stewart fulfills his promise to White performing a charity concert at the Wang Center, Boston, in aid of the American Cancer Society, in memory of Terry Fox. (*Never Give Up On A Dream* is written about Fox.)

Nov Recut with Ronald Isley, updated version of *This Old Heart Of Mine* makes UK #51, while *The Best Of Rod Stewart* hits UK #3.

Dec Definitive solo and group retrospective boxed-set *Storyteller/The Complete Anthology: 1964-1990* makes US #54.

1990 **Jan** [16] Charles Falterman, who slipped and fractured his kneecap at a Apr.22, 1989 Lafayette, IN, Stewart concert, files lawsuit against the singer, alleging that his kicking soccer balls into the audience caused the crowd to "react almost as an uncontrollable herd of animals".

[27] Trevor Horn-produced cover version of Tom Waits' *Downtown Train* hits US #3.

Feb *Downtown Train* hits UK #10, following a performance of the song at the BRIT Awards, held at the Dominion theater, London.

May [19] *Downtown Train/Selections From Storyteller*, with extracted cuts from the *Storyteller* box-set, reaches US #20.

[26] *This Old Heart Of Mine*, a duet with Ronald Isley reviving Stewart' own cover of The Isley Brothers original, hits US #10.

Sept Stewart sings *Hot Legs* at a benefit for AIDS Project Los Angeles a the Wiltern theater, Los Angeles.

Nov [13] Patricia Boughton of Utica, MI, files lawsuit in Oakland County Circuit Court, Pontiac, MI, alleging that she suffered a rupture tendon in her middle finger and a possible break after Stewart kicked a football into the crowd during a June 22 concert at the Pine Knob musi theater, East Troy, WI.

Dec *It Takes Two*, an update of Marvin Gaye & Tammi Terrell's Motown classic, now duetted with Tina Turner, mainly for blanket coverage as the latest UK Pepsi commercial theme, hits UK #5.

[15] Stewart marries model Rachel Hunter in Beverly Hills Presbyterian church.

1991 **Feb** Kelly Emberg, who lived with Stewart 1985-90, files $25 million palimony suit in Los Angeles Superior Court.

Mar [23] *Rhythm Of My Heart*, new album's lead-off track, hits UK #3.

Apr [1] Elton John crashes Stewart's Wembley concert, dressed to look like Stewart's new bride Rachel Hunter. (She helps John with his make-up.)

[6] *Vagabond Heart* debuts at UK #2 peak, behind *Eurythmics' Greatest Hits*.

May [4] *Rhythm Of The Heart* hits US Top 10 at #8, still climbing, as parent album *Vagabond Heart* continues to rise.

[12] Stewart appears by satellite from Switzerland in "The Simple Truth" concert for Kurdish refugees at Wembley Arena, London.

STING

1971 While at teacher training college (having played bass with The Ronnie Pierson Trio on board Princess Cruises liners), Gordon Sumner (b. Oct.2, 1951, Wallsend, Newcastle, Tyne & Wear) plays in semi-professional jazz-rock bands, Earthrise, Phoenix Jazz Band and River City Jazz Band.

1972 Now teaching under-9s at St. Paul's first school, Cramlington, Sumner joins The Newcastle Big Band, which makes a locally-distributed album on which he plays bass. He is nicknamed Sting by Newcastle jazz player Gordon Soloman, because of his yellow and black hooped T-shirt, reminiscent of a bee.

1974 He plays in another local band, Last Exit.

1975 Last Exit releases *Whispering Voices*, on which Sting plays bass and sings lead on both sides.

1977 **Jan** Sting joins The Police (as both lead singer and bass player until 1984). Signing a publishing deal with Virgin, he will pen all their hits.

1978 **Sept** With many acting roles in TV ads behind him, he begins filming "Quadrophenia", based on The Who's album, playing character Ace.

1979 **Nov** Movie "Quadrophenia" opens nationwide in US. (He also appears in UK TV movie "Artemis '81".)

1980 **Sept** Chris Pettit's film "Radio On", with Sting appearing as Just Like Eddie, premieres in US.

1981 **May** "The Secret Policeman's Other Ball", in which Sting sings an acoustic version of The Police hit *Roxanne*, opens in US cinemas.

1982 June [27] An out-of-court settlement is reached between Sting and Virgin Music over contract concerning the copyright to Sting's early songs, originally signed in 1977.

Aug *Spread A Little Happiness*, from the soundtrack of TV film "Brimstone And Treacle" in which he stars as Martin, is his first solo single, making UK #16. He also records cover versions of *Tutti Frutti* and *Need Your Love So Bad* for *Party Party* soundtrack.

Sept Sting's first solo single, a revival of *Spread A Little Happiness* from soundtrack of "Brimstone And Treacle", makes UK #16. It will be the start of an increasingly successful solo career.

Sting splits from his actress wife, Frances Tomelty.

1984 Feb [28] *Brimstone And Treacle* wins Best Rock Instrumental Performance at the 26th annual Grammy awards.

Nov [25] Sting contributes a vocal lead to Band Aid's *Do They Know It's Christmas?*.

Dec A film of Frank Herbert's novel **Dune**, with Sting starring as Feyd Rautha, opens in US.

1985 Jan With The Police now effectively disbanded, he holds auditions for a new group in New York, looking for top jazz talent.

Feb His backing group Blue Turtles Band is formed, with Sting (vocals, bass), Darryl Jones (bass), Kenny Kirkland (keyboards), Omar Hakim (drums), Branford Marsalis (various brass, woodwind), Wynton Marsalis (trumpet) and Dollette McDonald and Janice Pendarvis (vocals). It debuts at the New York Ritz.

Mar Phil Collins' *No Jacket Required* features a Sting duet on *Long Long Way To Go*.

June He sings the intro on Dire Straits' *Money For Nothing*, UK #4 and US #1 single, which he co-writes with Mark Knopfler. Sting's *If You Love Somebody Set Them Free* makes UK #26, as debut album **The Dream Of The Blue Turtles**, recorded at Eddy Grant's Blue Wave studio in Barbados, is released, set to top UK chart and hit US #2. Sting contributes to Miles Davis' *You're Under Arrest*.

July [13] He plays Live Aid with Phil Collins and Branford Marsalis.

Aug *Love Is The Seventh Wave* makes UK #41. *If You Love Somebody Set Them Free* hits US #3. "The Bride", in which Sting stars as Frankenstein, premieres in US.

Sept [13] Sting begins his first solo tour in San Diego, CA.

The film of David Hare's play "Plenty", with Sting co-starring opposite Meryl Streep and Sam Neill, opens nationwide in US.

Oct *Fortress Around Your Heart* hits US #8.

Nov *Russians*, aided by black and white Godley & Creme video, makes UK #12. Director Michael Apted's film of Sting and his band before and during his concert tour in Paris, France, titled "Bring On The Night", opens in US. Sting sings *Mack The Knife* on A&M various artists compilation *Lost In The Stars*, an anthology of Kurt Weill's work.

Dec *Love Is The Seventh Wave* reaches US #17.

1986 Feb Jazz-tinged *Moon Over Bourbon Street* makes UK #44.

Mar [1] *Russians* reaches US #16.

June Live double album **Bring On The Night** is released to accompany the documentary, which has been edited from 350,000' of film.

[11] The Police reunites at an Amnesty International concert in Atlanta, GA, performing 5 songs.

[28] Sting takes part in Jerry Dammers-organized Artists Against Apartheid concert on Clapham Common, London, with Elvis Costello, Peter Gabriel, Billy Bragg, and others, before an estimated audience of 250,000.

July [21] Police begins recording for the follow-up to *Synchronicity*, but abandons the sessions soon after, as Sting insists on pursuing solo musical and acting interests.

Nov "A Conspiracy Of Hope" tour begins in US with Sting, Bryan Adams, Bob Dylan, Peter Gabriel, Tom Petty and U2.

[14] **Conspiracy Of Hope**, in aid of Amnesty International and with contributions from Sting, Peter Gabriel, Elton John and Steve Winwood, is released.

1987 Feb [24] "Bring On The Night" wins Best Music Video, Long Form at the 29th annual Grammy awards.

July Sting joins former musical associate Eberhard Schoener in an evening of songs by Bertolt Brecht and Kurt Weill in Hamburg, Germany. He plays Umbria Jazz Festival, Italy, with The Gil Evans Orchestra.

[2] Sting continues recording in Montserrat during his mother's funeral.

Nov *We'll Be Together* makes UK #41. **Nothing Like The Sun**, with guests, Andy Summers, Eric Clapton, Mark Knopfler, Rubén Blades and Branford Marsalis, hits UK #1 and US #9.

Dec [5] *We'll Be Together* hits US #7.

Sting contributes *Gabriel's Message* to the Special Olympics Christmas album **A Very Special Christmas**.

1988 Jan [20] Sting begins a 46-date US tour in Tampa Bay, FL.

Feb *An Englishman In New York*, about UK exile Quentin Crisp, falters at UK #51.

[8] **Nothing Like The Sun** is named Best British Album at the seventh annual BRIT Awards at London's Royal Albert Hall.

Mar *Be Still My Beating Heart* peaks at US #15.

[2] **Bring On The Night** wins Best Pop Vocal Performance, Male at the 30th annual Grammy awards.

[29] His US tour ends in Portland, OR.

Apr *Fragile* peaks at UK #70 and is not issued in US. A mini-album of Spanish versions of songs from the last album, for the South American market, is released. Sting contributes George Gershwin's *Someone To Watch Over Me*, the theme to Ridley Scott's thriller of the same name.

May *An Englishman In New York* stalls at US #84.

June [11] Sting opens "Nelson Mandela's 70th Birthday Party" concert with *If You Love Somebody Set Them Free*.

Aug Sting plays the title role on Stravinsky's "Soldier's Tale", released on his own Pangaea label. Ian McKellen plays the narrator and Vanessa Redgrave the devil, with the London Sinfonietta. Sting writes the music for Quentin Crisp documentary "Crisp City".

Sept Ballad *They Dance Alone* from **Nothing Like The Sun**, written as a protest to Peruvian leader General Pinochet, fails to chart in UK. Sting's *Englishman In New York* is used as the title track to Daniel Day Lewis film "Stars And Bars". (Sting's own movie appearances in 1988 include "Stormy Monday" and "Julia Julia".)

[2] Sting joins Bruce Springsteen, Tracy Chapman, Peter Gabriel and Youssou N'Dour on Amnesty International's "Human Rights Now!" world tour.

Nov A compilation of Sting clips, "The Videos", is released.

Sting contributes *I Can't Say* to Rubén Blades' **Nothing But The Truth**.

1989 Mar Sting donates a track to the ecological album **Greenpeace Rainbow Warriors**.

Apr He undertakes an international promotional tour of interviews to publicize the plight of the Kayapo Indians to help save their Brazilian rainforest homeland.

[4] He wins an Ivor Novello award in London for Best Song Musically & Lyrically for politically conscious *They Dance Alone*.

June Press reports that Sting and Paul McCartney are to lead UK BBC radio campaign to raise listeners' awareness of environmental issues.

Sept Sting opens in "The Threepenny Opera" at Washington's National theater.

Dec [5] He is a keynote speaker at the second annual Human Rights Award ceremonies at Faneuil Hall, Boston, MA, where he presents $30,000 award to 4 young activists in Chinese student movement.

1990 Feb [12] Sting, backed by Herbie Hancock and Branford Marsalis, invites Bruce Springsteen, Paul Simon, Jackson Browne and Don Henley on stage for a jam at the Rainforest Foundation and the Environmental Media Association fundraiser in Beverly Hills, CA. After the benefit, Sting, Springsteen, Henley, Marsalis and Bruce Hornsby repair to Los Angeles' China club for 45-min. impromptu set.

July [29] Daughter Eliot Pauline born in Pisa, Italy.

Aug Curious Ben Liebrand remix update in Soul II Soul-style of *Englishman In New York* reaches UK #15.

1991 Jan [19] Sting hosts NBC TV's "Saturday Night Live", as *All This Time*, from forthcoming **The Soul Cages**, reaches UK #22.

Feb [1] Sting kicks off "Soul Cages" world tour in San Francisco, CA.

[2] **The Soul Cages** debuts at UK #1.

Mar [9] Second UK extract *Mad About You* peaks at UK #56.

[10] His concert at Carnegie Hall raises $250,000 for The Rainforest Foundation.

[16] *All This Time* hits US #5.

[23] **The Soul Cages** hits US #2.

Apr [21] Sting's European tour leg debuts at the City Hall, Newcastle, Tyne & Wear. The 59-date trek will end July 14 at an open concert at the Milton Keynes Bowl, Bucks.

May [12] Sting appears by satellite from Holland in "The Simple Truth" concert for Kurdish refugees at Wembley Arena, London.

THE STONE ROSES

Ian Brown (vocals)
John Squire (lead guitar)
Peter Garner (bass)
Alan "Reni" Wren (drums)

1980 Brown (b. Sale, Gtr. Manchester) and Squire (b. Nov.24, 1962, Sale), having been brought up 2 doors apart on Sylvan Avenue, Sale, and attended Altrincham Grammar school together, form The Patrol, lined-up as Andy Cousens (vocals), Brown (bass), Simon Wolstencroft, ex-The Smiths (drums) and Squire (lead guitar) playing local colleges and clubs. Squire and Brown move to Hulme in central Manchester and mix with Smiths member Johnny Marr's friends.

1983 The Patrol changes to English Rose, inspired by a Jam track from *Setting Sons*. Wolstencroft is temporarily replaced by a man known as Wazza. Brown spends much of his time being a "scooter boy" while Squire takes a number of jobs including set-making on a TV adaptation of "The Wind In The Willows".

1984 Hitching around Europe, Brown meets a Scandinavian promoter in Germany who guarantees the band gigs in Sweden. Brown returns to the UK and hastily reassembles the band with himself now as vocalist and comprising Cousens, switched to guitar, Squire and new members Garner (bass) and drummer Wren, whom Squire and Brown have known since age 11, fighting with him at the Belle Vue speedway track. Rejecting the name The Angry Young Teddy Bears, they travel to play 5 gigs in Sweden as The Stone Roses, a combination of their earlier name and The Rolling Stones, their favorite band.

1985 **June** The Stone Roses perform at the latest of their own Manchester-held middle-of-the-night warehouse parties and begin spray-painting the city with the band logo.
Aug Group signs to small local independent label Thin Wine which issues unsuccessful 12" single *So Young* produced by legendary Mancunian music figure Martin Hannett. Further sessions with the producer prove unfruitful.

1986 Band links with manager Garth Evans, a local club owner. Cousens quits to join The Hight as the group seeks a more commercial direction, influenced not least by Creation band Primal Scream.

1987 **June** The Stone Roses release *Sally Cinnamon*, a one-off 12" for the FM Revolver label, which is praised, but does not sell beyond Manchester.
Sept They perform at Sefton Park, Liverpool, Merseyside, with The La's at a 1-day indie-fest. Wren is currently moonlighting as a kissogram girl and Garner is replaced by old band friend Mani (b. Nov.16, 1962).

1988 **Oct** Rough Trade pulls out of an expected label deal, so New Order's Peter Hook-produced *Elephant Stone* is licensed with the band to Andrew Lauder's new Silvertone Records. The Stone Roses are fast becoming the darling of the alternative music press and late night UK radio.
Dec Band performs at the Central London polytechnic with Chameleons' offshoot The Sun & The Moon.

1989 **Feb** [23] During UK tour, which has included dates at Manchester's Hacienda, London's Powerhaus and Hull's Unity club, The Stone Roses perform at a much praised gig at the Middlesex polytechnic, while *Made Of Stone*, written about Brown's hitch-hiking days, hits UK Independent chart at #4.
May Critically raved debut album *The Stone Roses* is released on Silvertone. Produced mainly by John Leckie, it initially makes UK #32, but will re-chart 5 times in the next 12 months.
July [29] Group performs before a sold-out 6,000 capacity audience at the Empress Ballroom, Blackpool, Lancs., to be followed by European dates and 4 further sell-outs in Japan.
Nov The Stone Roses are heard for only 45 secs. on BBC TV's arts program "The Late Show", when the volume of their performance blows BBC studio fuses.
[18] Capacity 8,000 show to see band play Alexandra Palace, London.
Dec [2] Together with The Happy Mondays, now revered as leaders of the new wave of the Manchester rock scene, Stone Roses hit UK #8 with bass funk laden *Fool's Gold*, double A-sided with *What The World Is Waiting For*, later to be sampled by Run DMC. By coincidence, both The Roses and The Mondays have made their BBC TV "Top Of The Pops" debuts on Nov.30.

1990 **Jan** As *The Stone Roses* re-enters UK chart set to peak at #19, band vents its anger in growing dispute with old label FM Revolver by making a paint attack inside the company's office causing £23,000 of damage. The label has made a video without the group's permission or approval, to re-promote *Sally Cinnamon*, which re-enters at UK #46.

Mar [4] At fan-attended court case, the band is fined £3,000.
[17] Silvertone begins reissuing the group's 3 label singles: *Made Of Stone* re-charts at UK #20.
[27] Stone Roses perform to a fanatical 30,000 capacity crowd at Spike Island, Widnes, Cheshire.
[30] As US college radio begins picking up on the band's UK success, *She Bangs The Drums* now makes UK #34.
July [14] After a lengthy recording absence, newly released *One Love* hits UK #4 in its first week.
Sept To the growing displeasure of the band, Silvertone reissues *Fool's Gold/What The World Is Waiting For* (UK #22), perhaps in the knowledge that the band is now the most sought after signing for a major label. Months of courting by nearly every big company will result in Silvertone and The Stone Roses entering into lengthy litigation over their recording and license obligations. Initial moves by Silvertone will prevent the band from even entering a recording studio until well into 1991.

THE STRANGLERS

Hugh Cornwell (vocals, guitar)
Dave Greenfield (keyboards)
Jean-Jacques Burnel (bass)
Jet Black (drums)

1974 **Oct** The Guildford Stranglers are formed in Chiddingford, Surrey, originally as a trio comprising chemistry graduate and ex-science teacher Cornwell (b. Aug.28, 1949, London), one-time jazz drummer and ice cream salesman Black (b. Brian Duffy, Aug.26, 1958) and Burnel (b. Feb.21, 1952, London), son of French parents, and a history graduate from Bradford University. Group signs with Albion management.
1975 **May** Greenfield joins on keyboards after answering an ad placed by the band as a "soft-rock group" in **Melody Maker**, replacing Swedish guitarist Hans Warmling. A sax player, recruited at the same time, lasts for just 3 days, and the band decides to remain a quartet.
1976 **May** [17] After a year on the road in minor club gigs, The Stranglers make their major venue debut supporting Patti Smith at London's Roundhouse.
[19] 7-date UK tour begins at Birmingham's Bogarts, W.Midlands, ending May 28 at the Gaiety theater, Leicester, Leics.
July [4] Group plays the American bicentennial show at the Roundhouse, with The Ramones and The Flamin' Groovies.
Sept They support Patti Smith on a UK tour (followed by a UK tour on their own through Oct. and Nov.).
Dec [17] Group signs a recording deal with United Artists, one of the earliest new wave band contracts.
1977 **Jan** [30] Supporting The Climax Blues Band at London's Roundhouse, the group's performance is cut short by a power turn-off after Cornwell reveals his "F**k" T-shirt on stage. (The Greater London Council has warned the management that its performance regulations would not allow this display.)
Feb Group-penned debut single *(Get A) Grip (On Yourself)*, produced by Martin Rushent, makes UK #44 (after being accidentally omitted from the chart by compilers BMRB in its first week of release) while the group is playing live dates in Europe.
Mar The Stranglers record their first live session for "The John Peel Show" on BBC Radio 1, after completing a UK mini-tour.
Apr Group plays again at London's Roundhouse, with The Jam and Cherry Vanilla. First album *The Stranglers IV: Rattus Norvegicus*, recorded in 6 days, hits UK #4.
May Another UK tour begins, lasting into June. Some dates are cancelled when local councils and venue bookers begin banning punk-associated groups.
June Band backs Celia Collin, a female singer found by its manager Dai Davies, who has sung live with them at London's Nashville, on a revival of Tommy James & The Shondells' *Mony Mony*, credited as Celia And The Mutations. It does not chart.
July *Peaches/Go Buddy Go* hits UK #8. (The A-side is banned by the BBC for "offensive lyrics", so the B-side is promoted equally. Group play it on their first major TV appearance, on BBC TV's "Top Of The Pops".)
Aug *Something Better Change/Straighten Out* hits UK #9. Burnel is drafted into the French army for military service, but escapes it by providing proof of his permanent residency in UK.
Sept [1] The Stranglers begin a major UK tour, following with another European tour.
Oct *No More Heroes* hits UK #8, while the album of the same title, again produced by Rushent, hits UK #2.

Nov Group plays a short residency at London's Roundhouse, supported by The Dictators. The act is taped for later live album use.

[22] The Stranglers perform on the first night of the 3-week Hope & Anchor Front Row Festival in Islington, London.

978 Feb *Five Minutes* makes UK #11.

Mar [16] Group opens its first US tour (moving on to Canada, Iceland, Scandinavia, and down through Europe).

May *Nice'N'Sleazy* makes UK #18.

June *Black And White*, including *Nice'N'Sleazy*, hits UK #2, supported by a UK tour.

Sept A high-speed, keyboard-driven revival of Bacharach/David's *Walk On By* makes UK #21. Jazzman George Melly guests on B-side *Old Codger*.

Oct Group plays London's Battersea Park with Peter Gabriel (with strippers performing during *Nice'N'Sleazy*), before beginning a series of one-off shows in London using pseudonyms to beat local council bans.

979 Mar Live album *Live (X Cert)*, from a variety of concert appearances, hits UK #7.

Apr Burnel releases solo album *Euroman Cometh*, which makes UK #40. He also undertakes a solo tour.

June Group records a new album in Paris, France, co-producing the tracks with Alan Winstanley (who had engineered previous recordings), and also headlines the Loch Lomond Festival in Scotland.

Aug [18] The Stranglers perform at Wembley Stadium, London, with AC/DC, Nils Lofgren and headliners The Who.

Sept *Duchess*, from the forthcoming album, makes UK #14.

Oct *The Raven*, the first pressing featuring a 3-D sleeve picture, hits UK #4. Cornwell also releases an album, *Nosferatu*, in collaboration with Robert Williams, but it fails to chart.

Nov *Nuclear Device (The Wizard Of Aus)*, taken from *The Raven*, reaches UK #36, as the band tours UK again.

Dec 4-track EP *Don't Bring Harry* makes UK #41.

980 Jan [7] Cornwell is found guilty of possession of heroin, cocaine and cannabis. He is fined £300, and sentenced to 3 months' imprisonment in Pentonville prison, London.

Mar [21] Cornwell is sent to Pentonville after losing the appeal against his drug conviction.

Apr *Bear Cage* makes UK #36.

[25] Cornwell is released from prison. (The story of his time spent there will be told in his book **Inside Information**.)

June *Who Wants The World* reaches UK #39.

[21] The Stranglers are arrested in Nice, France, after allegedly inciting a riot when a concert at the university is cancelled because a generator has not been supplied for electrical power. (Black will chronicle this event in his book **Much Ado About Nothing** – the group members are fined in a Nice court later in the year.)

981 Feb *Thrown Away* makes UK #42. It is the group's first release on Liberty Records (as parent company EMI renames United Artists).

Mar Self-produced *Themeninblack*, also on Liberty, hits UK #8.

Nov *Let Me Introduce You To The Family* peaks at UK #42, as the group tours UK to promote forthcoming album *La Folie*.

982 Feb Melodic waltz-time *Golden Brown*, with an arresting harpsichord arrangement, proves to be The Stranglers' most popular single, hitting UK #2 behind The Jam's *A Town Called Malice*.

Mar *La Folie*, which includes *Golden Brown*, makes UK #11.

May Title track *La Folie*, sung by Burnel in French, makes UK #47.

Aug *Strange Little Girl* hits UK #7.

Oct Album *The Collection 1977-1982*, a 14-track singles anthology compiled as a final EMI album, makes UK #12. Hassles with the label in 1982 ensure that The Stranglers will not re-sign to Liberty as their first contract expires (they have tried to move to Phonogram but an EMI injunction prevented it).

Nov Band signs a new recording deal with Epic.

983 Jan *European Female* hits UK #9, while parent album *Feline*, the first for Epic, hits UK #4.

Feb Band plays a UK tour in support of the album.

Mar *Midnight Summer Dream*, from the album, makes UK #35.

May [5] *Golden Brown* is named Most Performed Work Of 1982 at the Ivor Novello Awards lunch at the Grosvenor House, Mayfair, London.

Aug *Paradise*, also from *Feline*, reaches UK #48.

[27] Group plays the Reading Rock festival, Berks., before embarking on a tour of Europe.

Dec Burnel and Greenfield release the album, *Fire And Water*, which reaches UK #94.

984 Oct *Skin Deep*, a trailer for the forthcoming album, makes UK #15.

Nov *Aural Sculpture*, produced by Laurie Latham, makes UK #14.

Dec *No Mercy*, extracted from *Aural Sculpture*, peaks at UK #37.

1985 Feb *Let Me Down Easy*, also from the album, reaches UK #48. A UK tour of major venues includes 5 nights at London's Dominion theater.

Sept Cornwell's solo single *One In A Million*, recorded for Epic's associated Portrait label, fails to chart.

1986 Sept *Nice In Nice* precedes the new Epic album, and reaches UK #30, while Liberty release *Off The Beaten Track*, a compilation of rare earlier tracks, makes UK #80.

Nov *Always The Sun* makes UK #30. It is taken from Latham-produced *Dreamtime*, which reaches UK #16.

Dec *Big In America*, also from the album, peaks at UK #49.

1987 Mar *Shakin' Like A Leaf* makes UK #58.

May *Dreamtime* peaks at US #172.

1988 Jan After a lengthy absence from recording, the group's revival of The Kinks' *All Day And All Of The Night* hits UK #7.

Mar *All Live And All Of The Night*, combining on-stage recordings from 1987 with the recent studio-recorded hit single, makes UK #12.

May Cornwell, signed solo to Virgin, releases solo *Another Kind Of Love*, which makes UK #71, and *Wolf*, which makes UK #98.

1989 Jan As part of a current inexplicable UK trend, *Grip '89 (Get A) Grip (On Yourself)* remixed update makes UK #33, issued by EMI.

Feb Same label releases *The Singles*, an incomplete anthology, which stalls at UK #57.

1990 Feb Remake of ? & The Mysterians' *96 Tears* reaches UK #17.

[19] The Stranglers undertake their final tour with the current line-up throughout UK until Mar.21.

Mar [17] Tenth album *10*, produced by Roy Thomas Baker, reaches UK #15.

Apr [21] *96 Tears* follow-up *Sweet Smell Of Success* stalls at UK #65.

1991 Feb [2] Unable to resist the temptation, Epic releases *Greatest Hits 1977-1990*, which climbs to hit UK #9. (Extracted reissues *Always The Sun* and *Golden Brown* make UK #29 and UK #68 respectively.) The Stranglers audition for a new vocalist as founding member Cornwell announces that he has achieved all he wanted to with the group, and leaves amicably.

THE STRAY CATS

Brian Setzer (guitar, vocals)
Lee Rocker (double bass)
Slim Jim Phantom (drums)

1979 Trio is formed in Long Island, New York, by 3 former schoolfriends with a taste for rough-edged 50s rockabilly. Early gigs, mostly featuring revivals of Eddie Cochran and Gene Vincent numbers, are on a part-time basis, since Setzer (b. Apr.10, 1960) is also a member of New York rock band The Bloodless Pharoahs. When the latter group splits, he joins Rocker (b. Leon Drucher, 1961) and Phantom (b. Jim McDonnell, Mar.20, 1961) full-time, and they begin to put together their own traditionally-styled new material.

1980 July Group moves to UK, with manager Tony Bidgood, but on arrival in London find previously-booked gigs and accommodation unavailable. Rather than returning home, they persist in getting themselves on the London club circuit (helped by Keith Altham's PR office, which is also their first London home), where well-received performances quickly attract good UK music press coverage and record company interest.

Sept [29] They perform at London's Rainbow as the opening act for Elvis Costello.

Oct With interest from several labels, the group signs to Arista Records in UK.

Dec Debut single, double bass heavy *Runaway Boys*, written by Setzer, hits UK #9.

1981 Feb *Rock This Town*, again penned by Setzer, also hits UK #9.

Mar *Stray Cats*, mostly produced by Dave Edmunds, hits UK #6.

May *Stray Cat Strut* reaches UK #11. (Group will spend much of the rest of the year on tour, selling out in UK, Europe and Australia, and also playing support dates to The Rolling Stones in US.)

July The Stray Cats team with Dave Edmunds for a remake of George Jones' 1964 US Country #3 *The Race Is On*, which makes UK #34.

Nov *You Don't Believe In Me* peaks at UK #57. It is taken from the group's second album *Gonna Ball*, self-produced in Montserrat with the aid of Hein Hoven, which makes UK #48.

1982 July Band signs a US recording deal with EMI America Records, and plays a 3-month US tour in an effort to succeed at home.

Nov *Built For Speed*, a US compilation from earlier UK albums, hits US #2 for 15 consecutive weeks, held from the top by Men At Work's

THE STRAY CATS cont.

Business As Usual and then Michael Jackson's *Thriller*. It earns a platinum disk, selling over 2 million copies.

Dec Bolstered by heavy MTV video play, *Rock This Town* finally debuts the group on the US Singles chart, hitting #9.

1983 **Feb** *Stray Cat Strut* hits US #3.

May [28] Group co-headlines the first day of the 3-day US 83 Festival in San Bernardino, CA, with The Clash and Men At Work.

Aug Band's last UK hit single is Setzer's *(She's) Sexy And 17*, which makes UK #29.

Sept Group's third and last album, *Rant'N'Rave With The Stray Cats*, produced again by Edmunds, peaks at UK #51.

Oct *(She's) Sexy And 17* hits US #5, while *Rant'N'Rave With The Stray Cats* makes US #14.

Dec *I Won't Stand In Your Way* climbs to US #35.

1984 **Feb** *Look At That Cadillac* peaks at US #68. Band splits shortly after, as Setzer tries for solo fame, staying with EMI America to record *The Knife Feels Like Justice*.

Mar [20] Phantom marries actress Britt Ekland on his 23rd birthday.

1985 **Oct** Rocker and Phantom form a new trio with David Bowie's ex-guitarist Earl Slick, naming themselves Phantom, Rocker And Slick, signing to EMI America for eponymous album, which makes US #61.

1986 **Apr** Setzer solo *The Knife Feels Like Justice* reaches US #45.

Oct Stray Cats' *Rock Therapy* makes US #122.

1987 Setzer plays Eddie Cochran in the Ritchie Valens biopic "La Bamba".

1988 **July** Setzer releases Dave Stewart-produced solo album *Live Nude Guitars* for EMI Manhattan, which makes US #140.

Sept Trio reunites for a 35-date US tour. (Recording sessions for a new album with original producer Edmunds will follow.)

1989 **Feb** [11] Lee Rocker marries Deborah at the Bel Age hotel, Los Angeles.

Apr Reunion album released by EMI *Blast Off* peaks at US #111.

Oct [18] Group plays Las Vegas, NV, during a short US tour.

1990 **Apr** [18] Rocker and wife Debbie become parents to Justin Eliot in Los Angeles. By year's end, a new Stray Cats album is expected, to be completed under the production of Nile Rodgers.

THE STYLE COUNCIL

Paul Weller (vocals, guitar)
Mick Talbot (keyboards)

1983 After the break-up of The Jam, Weller (b. John Weller, May 25, 1958, Woking, Surrey) joins Talbot (b. Sept.11, 1958, London), ex-late 70s London mod band The Merton Parkas and Dexys Midnight Runners' offshoot The Bureau, to concentrate on soul/jazz-based music which is closest to their hearts, and sign to The Jam's former label, Polydor.

Mar Debut single *Speak Like A Child* hits UK #4.

May [1] The Style Council plays its first live gig, part of the "May Day Show For Peace And Jobs" at Liverpool Empire, Merseyside.

June *The Money-Go-Round* reaches UK #11. Duo plays another live gig at the Brockwell Park YNCD Festival in London, and a week of recording sessions in Paris, France, follows.

Aug EP *Paris*, featuring *Paris Match* and *Long Hot Summer*, hits UK #3.

Nov *Solid Bond In Your Heart*, originally planned as the final Jam single, reaches UK #11. (Duo's Solid Bond recording studio, near Marble Arch, London, is named after this.) The Style Council appears at the "Big One" peace show at London's Victoria Apollo theater, with Dee C. Lee (ex-back-up singer with Wham! and later a solo artist) as a vocalist. In US, mini-album *Introducing The Style Council* (not released in UK but featuring tracks from early UK singles) makes #172.

1984 **Mar** Debut album *Café Bleu*, with guests including Tracy Thorn of Everything But The Girl (on a new version of *Paris Match*), hits UK #2, and will stay on UK chart for 38 weeks. Meanwhile, from the album, *My Ever Changing Moods* hits UK #5.

[12] The Style Council plays its first full UK concert date, at the Gaumont theater, Southampton, Hants., followed by 7 similar gigs, billed as "Council Meetings".

May *My Ever Changing Moods*, a slightly amended version of *Café Bleu*, is released on Geffen in US, and reaches UK #56.

June *Groovin'*, a maxi-single with joint lead tracks *You're The Best Thing* and *Big Boss Groove*, hits UK #5. Title track from US album *My Ever Changing Moods* is the group's first US hit single, peaking at #29.

July US follow-up, soul ballad *You're The Best Thing*, makes UK #76.

Sept [7] Weller appears in a concert at London's Royal Albert Hall, with Wham! and other acts, to benefit the strikers involved in the UK coal mining dispute.

Oct *Shout To The Top* hits UK #7.

Nov [25] Weller takes part in the recording of Band Aid's *Do They Know It's Christmas?*, at Sarm studios, London.

Dec *Soul Deep*, inspired by the UK coal miners strike, is released under the name The Council Collective, including guests Jimmy Ruffin and Junior. Royalties go jointly to the support group Women Against Pit Closures, and taxi driver David Wilkie's widow, killed in the dispute.

1985 **May** *The Walls Come Tumbling Down* hits UK #6.

June *Our Favourite Shop* tops the UK chart for a week, during a 22-week chart run.

July *Come To Milton Keynes* makes UK #23. *Internationalists* is released in US on Geffen, and climbs to #123.

[13] The Style Council plays on the Live Aid bill at Wembley Stadium, London.

Oct *The Lodgers* reaches UK #13.

1986 **Jan** [25] The "Red Wedge" tour, featuring The Style Council and several other acts with left-wing inclinations (Billy Bragg, Junior, and The Communards), and designed to encourage support among young voters for UK's Labour Party, opens in Manchester, Gtr. Manchester.

Feb Weller closes his record label Respond Records, which achieved moderate success for new acts including Tracie and The Questions.

Apr *Have You Ever Had It Blue*, written for Julien Temple-directed movie "Absolute Beginners", makes UK #14. Live album *Home And Abroad* hits UK #8.

Dec Weller and Dee C. Lee are married.

1987 **Jan** *It Didn't Matter* hits UK #9.

Feb *The Cost Of Loving*, with guest vocalists Curtis Mayfield and The Valentine Brothers, hits UK #2.

Mar *Waiting* peaks at UK #52. The group's 30-min. movie "JerUSAlem", a satire of the pop world and The Style Council's relationship with it, is released as a cinema support feature and on home video.

May Group returns to Polydor in US for *The Cost Of Loving*, which makes US #122.

Nov *Wanted* reaches UK #11.

1988 **Apr** Weller is reported to be selling Solid Bond studios.

June *Life At A Top People's Health Farm* reaches UK #28. Weller and his wife Dee have a son.

July Despite constant rumors of a split, the group releases *Confessions Of A Pop Group*, which reaches UK #15 and US #174. *How She Threw It All Away*, taken from it, makes UK #41.

1989 **Feb** *Promised Land*, a cover of concurrently released original by Joe Smooth, reaches UK #27.

Mar Style Council career retrospective *Singular Adventures Of The Style Council* hits UK #3, with TV advertising assistance.

May Curious 1989 remix *Long Hot Summer* stalls at UK #48.

1990 **Mar** Weller and Talbot split. Weller will return with the Paul Weller Movement within 12 months.

THE STYLISTICS

Russell Thompkins, Jr. (lead vocals)
Herb Murrell (vocals)
Airrion Love (vocals)
James Dunn (vocals)
James Smith (vocals)

1968 Group is formed in Philadelphia, PA, when members of 2 earlier vocal groups, The Percussions (Murrell and Dunn) and The Monarchs (Thompkins (b. Mar.21, 1951, Philadelphia), Love and Smith), join up.

1969 *You're A Big Girl Now*, written by road manager Marty Bryant and back-up band member Robert Douglas, is recorded for Philadelphia independent label Sebring Records, and becomes a local hit.

1971 **Feb** A year of steady East Coast US sales for the single attracts the attention of Avco Embassy Records, which signs the group and reissues *You're A Big Girl Now*, providing a US chart debut at #73.

July Group is teamed with Philadelphia-based producer Thom Bell at Sigma Sound studios, and his songwriting partner Linda Creed. First collaboration is *Stop, Look, Listen (To Your Heart)*, which makes US #39, and establishes The Stylistics' forte: rich, soft-soul ballads, given an extra edge by Thompkins' ethereal high tenor.

1972 **Jan** *You Are Everything*, again written by Bell and Creed (as is virtually all the group's material for 2 years) hits US #9, the first of 5 million-selling singles. (It will be revived as a UK Top 10 hit in 1974 by a Diana Ross and Marvin Gaye duet, as will *Stop, Look, Listen (To Your Heart)*.)

Apr *Betcha By Golly, Wow* hits US #3, earning a gold disk. The group's eponymous debut album, containing all the singles to date, also goes gold as it reaches US #23.

July Socially-conscious *People Make The World Go Round* peaks at US #25. Meanwhile, *Betcha By Golly, Wow* is the band's first UK hit at #13.

Oct Following a US coast-to-coast tour, the group visits UK for the first time, and US bases in Germany.

Dec *I'm Stone In Love With You*, taken from the second album, hits US #10 and UK #9, and is another US million-seller. (It will also be a UK Top 10 hit for Johnny Mathis in 1975.)

1973 Jan *Stylistics: Round 2* makes US #32, and is a second gold album.

Apr *Break Up To Make Up*, from the second album, hits US #5 and earns another gold disk. It peaks in UK at #34.

June A revival of Bacharach/David-penned Dionne Warwick hit *You'll Never Get To Heaven* reaches US #23.

July Different track from second album, *Peak-A-Boo*, climbs to UK #35.

Dec Group's first uptempo hit is Bell and Creed's *Rockin' Roll Baby*, which peaks at US #14. It is extracted from the album of the same title, which makes US #66, and is the final album collaboration between The Stylistics and Thom Bell.

1974 Feb *Rockin' Roll Baby* hits UK #6.

June Belatedly extracted from the third album, and featuring Love's deep baritone lead for much of the song, rather than Thompkins' familiar tenor, *You Make Me Feel Brand New* is the group's biggest US hit, and their fifth and last million-selling single. It hits US #2 for 2 weeks (behind Bo Donaldson & The Heywoods' *Billy, Don't Be A Hero*).

July Avco teams the group with the veteran writing/production team of Hugo (Peretti) and Luigi (Creatore), with arranger Van McCoy, for *Let's Put It All Together*, which, like subsequent recordings, takes them away from Philadelphia and to Media Sound studios in New York. It reaches US #14, their third (and last) US gold album.

Aug *Rockin' Roll Baby* is, belatedly, group's first UK chart album, reaching #42. It charts mainly due to inclusion of *You Make Me Feel Brand New*, which repeats its US success by hitting UK #2.

Sept Title song from *Let's Put It All Together* reaches US #18.

Oct *Let's Put It All Together* makes UK #26.

Nov *Let's Put It All Together* hits UK #9, while *Heavy Fallin' Out*, taken from the second Hugo/Luigi-produced album, peaks at US #41.

Dec *Heavy* reaches US #43.

1975 Feb *Star On A TV Show* makes US #47 and UK #12.

Mar *Heavy* is re-titled *From The Mountain* in UK and given a different sleeve design (both considered out of keeping with the group's UK image). It reaches UK #36.

Apr Compilation *The Best Of The Stylistics* reaches US #41 but tops UK chart for 2 weeks (and will return to #1 for 5 weeks in May and 2 weeks in Aug.), spending 63 weeks on chart. It is the best-selling album of the year and the biggest-selling ever in UK by a black act.

May *Thank You Baby*, the title track from the forthcoming album, stalls at US #70. *Sing Baby Sing* is extracted in UK, hitting #3.

July *Thank You Baby* makes US #72.

Aug Taken from the album, *Can't Give You Anything (But My Love)* peaks at US #51, but tops UK chart for 3 weeks, the group's biggest UK hit single. At the same time, *Thank You Baby* hits UK #3 (*The Best Of The Stylistics* being #2 at the time).

Dec *You Are Beautiful* climbs to US #99 and UK #26, and is the group's last album for Avco Embassy. *Na Na Is The Saddest Word*, taken from it, hits UK #5.

1976 Jan Extracted *Funky Weekend* makes US #76.

Mar *Funky Weekend* hits UK #10. (A string of singles will continue to be major UK hits while making minor or no impression in US. The split from Bell and subsequent loss of the soft Philly soul sound is cited as a factor for the US decline: under Hugo and Luigi, the group's material has become more brashly orchestrated, and more obviously middle of the road, losing much of the R&B radio station market in US.)

Apr Title track from *You Are Beautiful* reaches US #79, and is The Stylistics' last US chart single.

[4] Group begins 11-date UK tour with Brook Benton at the De Montfort Hall, Leicester, Leics. Tour will end at Wolverhampton Civic Hall, W.Midlands, after 2 shows at London Palladium on Apr.9 and 10.

May Group revives Elvis Presley's *Can't Help Falling In Love* (written by Hugo and Luigi, with long-time collaborator George David Weiss) as a UK single, and it hits #4.

July Hugo and Luigi form their own H&L label, taking The Stylistics with them. *Fabulous*, on H&L, reaches US #117 (though no further releases by the group on the label will chart in US), and makes UK #21.

Sept *16 Bars*, extracted from *Fabulous*, hits UK #7.

Oct Second compilation album, *The Best Of The Stylistics, Vol.2* tops UK chart for a week.

Dec EP *You'll Never Get To Heaven*, coupling the earlier US hit with 3

---

later tracks, is marketed in UK as a single, and makes #24.

1978 Apr The overnight domination by disco music of the R&B music scene finally puts The Stylistics out of commercial favor in UK. Their final chart single is *7,000 Dollars And You*, which makes UK #24.

1980 Dec After 2 quiet years of mainly club work, the group signs to TSOP Records, a division of Gamble and Huff's Philadelphia International. *Hurry Up This Way Again* makes US #127 after a 4-year chart absence. (There are no Stylistics hit singles on TSOP. With almost a decade's-worth of mostly ballad-slanted hit repertoire behind them, The Stylistics will continue to command nightclub and occasional TV work all around the world, particularly in UK, where they will remain frequent cabaret visitors throughout the 80s.)

STYX

Dennis DeYoung (vocals, keyboards)
Tommy Shaw (lead guitar)
James Young (guitar)
Chuck Panozzo (bass)
John Panozzo (drums)

1964 Group is formed in Chicago, IL, as The Tradewinds, by neighbors DeYoung (b. Feb.18, 1947, Chicago), the twin Panozzo brothers (b. Sept.20, 1947, Chicago) and guitarist Tom Nardini. They play regular gigs on the Chicago bar/club circuit, and shorten their name to TW4 in 1965 to avoid confusion with New York's *A Lonely Town* Trade Winds (actually songwriters Anders and Poncia).

1969 Oct Group's base becomes Chicago State University where DeYoung and the Panozzos enrol. Nardini leaves, and TW4's new guitarist is fellow student John Curulewski.

1970 Young (b. Nov.14, 1948, Chicago), who has been playing with a rival band, joins the quartet, and the new line-up begins more musical experiments, with classical/rock fusions, and electronic trickeries, all of which find favor on college dates.

1971 A demo comes to the attention of Wooden Nickel label, which offers the band a recording deal.

1972 Wooden Nickel's Bill Traut renames them Styx (after many other names have been rejected), after the mythological river of the dead. Debut album *Styx* follows, but only sells around their live performances.

Oct *Best Thing* makes US #82, mainly on Chicago-area sales and airplay.

1973 *Styx II* is released, again initially without charting, though DeYoung's song *Lady* picks up Chicago airplay. Group members quit their day jobs and begin regular touring further afield, to create a wider following.

1974 Feb Third album *The Serpent Is Rising* creeps to US #192.

Nov *Man Of Miracles* makes US #154.

1975 Mar *Lady*, still the most popular track on the band's hometown airwaves, is given renewed national promotion as a single, and this time hits US #6. In its wake, parent album *Styx II* reaches US #20, some years after release, and earns a gold disk.

May *You Need Love*, taken from *Man Of Miracles*, stalls at US #88.

Dec Curulewski leaves the band, and a road manager suggests Shaw (b. Sept.11, Montgomery, AL) as a replacement, having seen him play guitar with a Chicago group named Ms. Funk. A week after auditioning, Shaw joins.

1976 Mar Needing a bigger and more commercial label, the group signs to A&M Records in Los Angeles, CA, debuting with *Equinox*, which peaks at US #58 and earns a second gold disk.

Apr First A&M single, *Lorelei*, taken from the album, makes US #27. Derek Sutton becomes the band's manager, restructures its business affairs and organizes the first nationwide tour.

Nov *Crystal Ball*, the first with Shaw, makes US #66, again earning a gold disk.

Dec From the album, *Mademoiselle* peaks at US #36.

1978 Jan *Come Sail Away* hits US #8.

Feb Parent album *The Grand Illusion* hits US #6 and is the group's first platinum album (having had a significant release date: 7.7.77.).

Apr *Fooling Yourself (The Angry Young Man)*, also from *The Grand Illusion*, makes US #29.

Nov *Blue Collar Man (Long Nights)* reaches US #21, while *Pieces Of Eight* hits US #6.

1979 June Double A-side *Sing For The Day/Renegade* makes US #16. A US national poll by Gallup reveals that Styx is now the most popular rock band with 13-19-year-olds.

Nov *Cornerstone* is UK chart debut, reaching #36.

Dec *Cornerstone* hits US #2, earning a third platinum while, taken from it, DeYoung's ballad *Babe* tops US chart for 2 weeks, and is a million-seller – their all-time best-selling single. (The released version is a scarcely-embellished reissue of DeYoung's original demo, which proves superior-sounding to attempted re-recordings.)

1980 **Jan** *Babe* hits UK #6.

Feb *Why Me* reaches US #26.

Apr *Borrowed Time* peaks at US #64.

June [20] Group plays the Hammersmith Odeon, London.

1981 **Jan** [16] Styx begins a 110-date 6-month North American tour in Miami, FL.

Feb *The Best Of Times* makes UK #42, while parent album *Paradise Theater*, a concept album, hits UK #8.

Mar *The Best Of Times* hits US #3.

Apr *Paradise Theater* tops US chart for 3 weeks, the band's fourth platinum album.

May *Too Much Time On My Hands*, also from the album, hits US #9.

Aug *Nothing Ever Goes As Planned* peaks at US #54.

1983 **Mar** *Kilroy Was Here*, another concept album, makes UK #67.

[11] Band begins a major venue "Kilroy Was Here" US tour in San Diego, CA, which will continue through the year, with a theatrical stage act built around the album, in which costumed band members have roles and dialogue, in addition to playing the music. (Not everybody rates the idea and some dates do not sell out.)

Apr *Mr. Roboto* hits US #3, becoming the band's second million-selling single, while parent album *Kilroy Was Here* also hits US #3, and is a fifth million-selling album.

June *Don't Let It End*, taken from *Kilroy Was Here*, stalls at UK #56.

July *Don't Let It End* hits US #6.

Sept *High Time* makes US #48.

1984 **May** Double live album *Caught In The Act* climbs to US #31 and UK #44, following which DeYoung and Shaw will both pursue solo recording projects for A&M (putting Styx on extended hold).

June *Music Time*, from the live set, makes US #40.

Nov Solo chart debuts come simultaneously, as DeYoung's *Desert Moon* hits US #10, and Shaw's *Girls With Guns* reaches US #33.

Dec DeYoung's *Don't Wait For Heroes* stalls at US #83, while his album *Desert Moon* climbs to US #29; Shaw's *Girls With Guns* makes US #50.

1985 **Jan** *Lonely School*, Shaw's second solo single, peaks at US #60.

Oct Shaw's *Remo's Theme (What If)*, from film "Remo: The Adventure Begins", makes US #81.

Dec Shaw's *What If* peaks at US #87.

1986 **Apr** [26] DeYoung's *Call Me* peaks at US #54 as parent album *Back To The World* makes US #108.

July [5] DeYoung's *This Is The Time*, from film "The Karate Kid Part II", stalls at US #93 despite promotion from the movie.

1988 **Mar** [12] Shaw's *Ever Since The World Began* peaks at US #75.

Dec DeYoung's *Boomchild* is released, failing to chart.

1990 Shaw teams with Ted Nugent to form new band Damn Yankees.

May [19] Damn Yankees' *Coming Of Age* peaks at US #60.

Oct [27] Re-formed Styx, with Glen Burtnik in Shaw's place, make US #80 with *Love Is The Ritual*, from comeback album *End Of The Century*.

Nov [3] Styx' *End Of The Century* makes US #63.

1991 **Jan** [12] Damn Yankees' *High Enough* hits US #3 as parent album *Damn Yankees* climbs to #26, helped by major North American tour with Bad Company.

Feb Styx' *Show Me The Way* begins chart climb into US Top 10, fuelled by patriotic sentiment because of the Gulf War. Its chart appearance means that Styx joins an elite club of acts who have secured Top 10 hits under each of the last 4 US presidents.

DONNA SUMMER

1968 Summer (b. LaDonna Gaines, Dec.31, 1948, Dorchester, MA), after singing with some Boston-based rock groups, tests for an understudy part in "Hair" on Broadway, but is offered instead a leading role in the production of the musical in Munich, Germany. (She will remain in "Hair" for a year and a half, also doing some modelling and studio back-up singing in Germany.)

1971 She moves to Austria when offered parts in Vienna Volksoper's productions of "Porgy And Bess" and "Showboat", and also marries Austrian actor Helmut Sommer (keeping an anglicized version of his surname after they are divorced).

1973 While performing in Germany in "Godspell", she begins regular work as a session singer at Munich's Musicland studios, where she meets owner/producer Pete Bellotte and his partner Giorgio Moroder, and records for their Oasis label. *Hostage* and *Lady Of The Night* are European hits, but not released in US or UK.

1975 She records *Love To Love You Baby*, an erotic love song with a disco beat and inspired by the success in Europe of reissued *Je T'Aime ... Moi Non Plus* by Jane Birkin and Serge Gainsbourg. Moroder mixes a 17-min. version with Summer's overtly suggestive breathy sighs and groans. Neil Bogart of US Casablanca Records sees commercial potential in the track, which he licenses and issues in its full version to discos and in edited form as a single.

1976 **Feb** *Love To Love You Baby* hits US #2 behind Paul Simon's *50 Ways To Leave Your Lover* (earning a gold disk) and UK #4, while Summer's debut album of the same title reaches US #11 and UK #16. She begins a 2-month US tour, and is also divorced from her first husband.

June Second album *A Love Trilogy* makes US #21 and UK #41, while *Could It Be Magic*, based on a Chopin melody and taken from the album, makes US #52 and UK #40.

July *Try Me, I Know We Can Make It*, also from *A Love Trilogy*, stalls at US #80.

Dec *Four Seasons Of Love* peaks at US #29.

1977 **Jan** Taken from it, *Spring Affair* makes US #47, while swaying *Winter Melody*, also from the album, reaches UK #27.

Mar *Winter Melody* makes US #43.

July *I Feel Love*, a disco song built over a mesmeric electronic sequence rhythm, tops the UK chart for 4 weeks, selling over a half million copies. It is taken from *I Remember Yesterday*, which hits UK #3.

Sept *I Remember Yesterday* reaches US #18, while *Down Deep Inside*, the theme song from Nick Nolte/Jacqueline Bisset-starring film "The Deep", hits UK #5.

Oct Title cut *I Remember Yesterday* reaches UK #14. This is on GTO Records, original UK licensee of Summer's recordings, whereas *The Deep* theme is on Casablanca, which now takes up new recordings. (For 6 months, singles are released in competition by both labels.)

Nov *I Feel Love*, extracted as a US single following its UK success, hits US #6, and becomes Summer's second US gold single.

1978 **Jan** *I Love You*, on Casablanca, makes US #37 and hits UK #10, taken from disco fairy tale concept album *Once Upon A Time*, which makes US #26 and UK #24. Meanwhile, *Love's Unkind*, on GTO, hits UK #3.

Feb GTO compilation album *Greatest Hits* hits UK #4.

Apr *Rumour Has It* makes US #53 and UK #19.

May [17] Film "Thank God It's Friday", a disco-oriented Casablanca/Motown co-production, in which Summer features as a singer attempting to make the big time, premieres in Los Angeles, CA.

July *Last Dance*, Paul Jabara-penned and taken from "Thank God It's Friday", hits US #3, earning another gold disk, but stalls at UK #51. (It will earn an Oscar at the 1979 Academy Awards as Best Film Song.)

Nov [11] A revival of Jim Webb's *MacArthur Park* (originally a 1968 hit by actor Richard Harris) tops the US chart for 3 weeks, becoming another million-seller, and hits UK #5. It is taken from the studio side of double album *Live And More*, with 3 sides of Summer recorded in concert. The album simultaneously tops the US chart for 1 week and makes UK #16.

1979 **Jan** [9] The "Music For UNICEF Concert", to celebrate the International Year Of The Child, takes place in the General Assembly Hall of the United Nations in New York. Summer sings *Mimi's Song*, donating the royalties from the song to UNICEF.

[10] NBC TV airs "A Gift Of Song – The Music For UNICEF Concert".

Feb [15] Summer wins Best Rhythm & Blues Vocal Performance, Female for *Last Dance* at the 21st annual Grammy awards. *Last Dance* also wins Best Rhythm & Blues Song.

Mar *Heaven Knows*, from *Live And More*, and recorded with trio Brooklyn Dreams, hits US #4 (another gold disk) and makes UK #34.

Apr [9] *Last Dance* wins an Oscar for Best Original Song at the 51st annual Academy Awards.

June *Bad Girls* tops the US chart for 6 weeks and reaches UK #23, while extracted *Hot Stuff* tops the US chart for 3 weeks and reaches UK #11, Summer's first platinum single, selling over 2 million copies in US.

July [14] The title song *Bad Girls* tops the US chart for 5 weeks (her second platinum single), and makes UK #14.

Nov A third single from *Bad Girls*, *Dim All The Lights*, hits US #2, earning a gold disk, and peaks at UK #29. Summer duets with Barbra Streisand on Paul Jabara and Bruce Roberts' *No More Tears (Enough Is Enough)*, which tops the US chart for 2 weeks while *Dim All The Lights* is still in the Top 5. It earns a further gold disk in US and hits UK #3.

1980 **Jan** Double compilation album *On The Radio – Greatest Hits – Volumes I And II*, anthologizing Summer's hits up to the Streisand duet, tops the US chart for 1 week and reaches UK #24. Meanwhile, Summer sues her manager Joyce Bogart and husband Neil Bogart's Casablanca Records for $10 million, alleging "undue influence, misrepresentation and fraud". The label releases her from her contract.

Feb [27] Summer wins Best Rock Vocal Performance, Female for *Hot Stuff* at the 22nd annual Grammy awards.

Mar *On The Radio*, a new song extracted from the compilation album, hits US #5 (another gold disk) and peaks at UK #32.

June [19] Summer is the first act signed by David Geffen to his new Geffen label.

July *Sunset People*, issued only in UK by Casablanca, reaches UK #46.
[16] She weds Bruce Sudano of Brooklyn Dreams, and former member of Alive 'N Kickin', 1970 *Tighter Tighter* hitmakers, in Los Angeles.

Oct Summer's final Casablanca single *Walk Away* makes US #36.

Nov *The Wanderer*, her Geffen debut, hits US #3 (earning her last gold single), and creeps to UK #48. *The Wanderer* makes UK #55. Another Casablanca compilation album, *Walk Away – Collector's Edition (The Best Of 1977-1980)*, makes US #50.

1981 Jan Having become a born-again Christian a year earlier, she includes the first lyric messages of her new-found faith on *The Wanderer*, which reaches US #13. Taken from it, *Cold Love* reaches US #33 and UK #44. (Later born-again pronouncements, in public rather than on record, will cause more controversy – notably when she nominates gays as sinners, and AIDS as a divine ruling.)

Apr *Who Do You Think You're Foolin'*, from the album, makes US #40.

1982 Aug After a lengthy recording hiatus, *Love Is In Control (Finger On The Trigger)* hits US #10 and makes UK #18.
[11] Summer and husband Sudano have a daughter, Amanda Grace.

Sept *Donna Summer*, Quincy Jones-produced, reaches US #20 and UK #13.

Nov From the album, a hymnal revival of Jon & Vangelis song *State Of Independence*, with Summer joined by an all-star chorus including Michael Jackson, Lionel Richie, Kenny Loggins, Dionne Warwick, James Ingram and Stevie Wonder, makes US #41 and UK #14.

1983 Mar *The Woman In Me* makes US #33 and UK #62.

Aug *She Works Hard For The Money* hits US #3 and makes UK #25, while the album of the same title hits US #9, and reaches UK #28. (These releases on Mercury, sister label to Casablanca, are part of a contractual deal whereby Summer delivers an album owed at the time of severing her former contract. After this, she returns to Geffen.)

Oct *Unconditional Love*, with back-up vocals from UK group Musical Youth, makes UK #14 and US #43.

1984 Jan *Stop, Look And Listen* makes UK #57, while *Love Has A Mind Of Its Own*, duetted with Matthew Ward of gospel group 2nd Chapter Of Acts, makes US #70.

Feb [28] Summer wins Best Inspirational Performance for *He's A Rebel* at the 26th annual Grammy awards.

Oct *Cats Without Claws* makes US #40 and UK #69. Taken from it, *There Goes My Baby*, reviving The Drifters' 1960 hit, makes US #21.

Nov *Supernatural Love*, also from *Cats Without Claws*, stalls at US #75. (Following this, she will concentrate on her Christian activities and family life.)

1985 Feb [26] Summer wins Best Inspirational Performance for *Forgive Me* at the 27th annual Grammy awards.

1987 Aug [27] Summer embarks on a US and European tour in Concord, CA, her first US tour since 1983.

Oct [3] Summer's first single in 3 years, Brenda Russell-penned *Dinner With Gershwin*, makes US #48, while parent album *All Systems Go* peaks at US #122.

Nov *Dinner With Gershwin* reaches UK #13.

1988 Jan Title cut of recent album, *All Systems Go* stalls at UK #54.

1989 Mar Lead-off single from sessions with UK hitmaking songwriting/production team Stock/Aitken/Waterman, *This Time I Know It's For Real*, hits UK #3. Parent album *Another Place And Time* enters UK chart, making #17.

June *I Don't Wanna Get Hurt* hits UK #7.
[24] *This Time I Know It's For Real* hits US #7, as parent album *Another Place And Time* reaches US #53.

Sept *Love's About To Change My Heart* makes UK #20 but only US #85.

Nov [25] Fourth extract *When Love Takes Over You* stalls at UK #72, while parent album title ballad cut remains unreleased.

1990 June Now a keen artist, Summer exhibits her neo-Primitive paintings and lithographs in Beverly Hills, CA. She sells 75 pieces for as much as $38,000 each.

Nov Warner Bros. issued *Best Of Donna Summer* reaches UK #24, while remixed version of *State Of Independence* makes UK #45.

SUPERTRAMP

Richard Davies (vocals, keyboards)
Roger Hodgson (guitar)
John Helliwell (saxophone)
Dougie Thomson (bass)
Bob C. Benberg (drums)

1969 Band is formed in UK as the result of sponsorship from young Dutch millionaire Stanley August Miesegaes, known as Sam, whom Davies (b. July 22, 1944) has met in Munich, Germany, while playing in a band named The Joint. Davies recruits other players through a UK music paper ad, offering a "genuine opportunity" to form a new band. Bass player Hodgson (b. Mar.21, 1950), Richard Palmer (guitar), Dave Winthrop (b. Nov.27, 1948) (sax) and Bob Miller (drums) are recruited. Originally to have been named Daddy, the group follows Winthrop's suggestion and takes its name from W.H. Davies' book **The Autobiography Of A Supertramp**, published in 1910.

1970 Aug Signed to A&M Records, the band releases its eponymous debut album, with a reception at the Revolution club in London.
[27] Supertramp plays on second day of UK's Isle of Wight Festival.

1971 July New members Kevin Currie (drums) and Frank Farrell (bass) replace Miller and Palmer, while Hodgson moves over to lead guitar, for **Indelibly Stamped**, which also fails to chart. Supertramp and sponsor Sam split, with the latter absolving the group of some £60,000-worth of owed equipment and recording costs. The other players also depart, leaving just Davies and Hodgson.

1973 Aug Helliwell (ex-Alan Bown), Thomson and Benberg (b. Robert Siebenberg), ex-Bees Make Honey, join the group and Thomson takes charge of the group's business affairs.

1974 Dec *Crime Of The Century*, written and recorded in Southcombe (a farmhouse in Somerset, in which A&M has installed the band), and produced by Ken Scott, hits UK #4.

1975 Jan [23] Group begins a 10-date UK tour at the City Hall, Sheffield, S.Yorks. It will end Feb.9 at Colston Hall, Bristol, Avon.

Mar *Dreamer*, taken from the album, makes UK #13, while the album makes US #38.

May *Bloody Well Right*, also from the album, reaches US #35. Group tours US for the first time.

Nov [13] Band begins major 30-date UK tour, with Joan Armatrading, at Colston Hall, Bristol, ending Dec.20 at the Kursaal, Southend, Essex.

Dec *Crisis? What Crisis?*, again produced by Scott, with the group's now-familiar electric piano rhythm-based tracks, topped by the distinctive and contrasting dual vocals of Hodgson and Thomson, is released and reaches UK #20.

1976 Jan *Crisis? What Crisis?* makes US #44.

1977 May Band produces itself on *Even In The Quietest Moments ...*, which reaches UK #12 and US #16.

July *Give A Little Bit*, taken from the album, climbs to UK #29.

Aug *Even In The Quietest Moments ...* reaches US #16, while *Give A Little Bit* makes US #15.

1978 Mar A re-promotion of the group's 1970 debut album *Supertramp* makes US #158.

1979 Apr *Breakfast In America* hits UK #3, and will become their most successful and enduring album. Extracted *The Logical Song* hits UK #7.

May *Breakfast In America* tops US chart for 6 weeks, earning a platinum disk.

June *The Logical Song* hits US #6.

July The title song from *Breakfast In America* hits UK #9.

Sept *Goodbye Stranger*, also from the album, reaches US #15.

Nov *Goodbye Stranger* makes UK #57.
[29] Group's concert at the Pavilion in Paris, France, is recorded for live album release.

Dec *Take The Long Way Home*, the final extract from *Breakfast In America*, hits US #10.

1980 Oct Double live *Paris*, recorded at the Pavilion in 1979, hits UK #7.

Nov A live version of the band's early hit *Dreamer*, taken from *Paris*, climbs to US #15, as the album hits US #8, earning a gold disk.

Dec Also from the album, live *Breakfast In America* peaks at US #62.

1982 Nov *Famous Last Words* hits UK #6, while extracted *It's Raining Again* makes UK #26. This is Supertramp's last album with Hodgson, who leaves to go solo. Band remains a quartet.

Dec *Famous Last Words* hits US #5, earning a gold disk, while *It's Raining Again* makes US #11.

1984 Mar *My Kind Of Lady*, taken from *Famous Last Words*, reaches US #31.

Oct Hodgson's debut solo album (also for A&M) is *In The Eye Of The Storm*, which climbs to UK #70 (and US #46, 2 months later).

SUPERTRAMP cont.

1985 **June** Supertramp's first post-Hodgson album, *Brother Where You Bound*, tighter and more R&B-rooted than earlier ones, makes UK #20.
July *Brother Where You Bound* reaches US #21, while *Cannonball*, taken from it, makes US #28.
Sept Group makes a North American tour to promote the album, beginning in Chicago, IL.

1986 **Mar** 6-month US tour comes to an end.
Oct Compilation album *The Autobiography Of Supertramp* hits UK #9. Hodgson briefly rejoins the group for a short promotional stint.

1987 **Oct** Supertramp album *Free As A Bird*, produced by the band, mixed by Tom Lord-Alge and recorded at Davies' own Los Angeles studio, peaks at UK #93. An instrumental addition is a full horn section.
Nov *Free As A Bird* peaks at US #101, but includes a surprise US Dance chart hit, *I'm Begging You*, which does not cross over. Meanwhile, Hodgson's second solo album *Hai Hai* makes US #163. It includes, also released as a single, and a lyrical counterpoint to his earlier composition *Breakfast In America*.

1988 **Aug** *The Logical Song/Breakfast In America* appear as an A&M CD single.
Oct *Supertramp Live 88* is released.

THE SUPREMES

Diana Ross (lead vocals)
Mary Wilson (vocals)
Florence Ballard (vocals)

1959 A female vocal trio is formed by Detroit manager Milton Jenkins, to complement his male group The Primes (later to become The Temptations) on stage, comprising Wilson (b. Mar.6, 1944, Greenville, MS), Ballard (b. June 30, 1943, Detroit, MI) and Betty Travis. They are joined by Ross (b. Mar.26, 1944, Detroit), brought in by Paul Williams of The Primes to help fill out the original trio's sound.

1960 As The Primettes support The Primes on Detroit club dates, Travis leaves to be replaced by Barbara Martin, then the group dissolves as Ballard's and Martin's parents persuade them to concentrate on high school grades. Wilson and Ross perform as a duo before the quartet re-forms and is signed briefly to LuPine Records after Smokey Robinson (a neighbor of Ross) fails to interest Motown's Berry Gordy Jr. in the girls (though they do some studio work for him, backing Marvin Gaye and others).
Dec Martin leaves again as Gordy decides to sign the group. He requests a name-change, and Ballard chooses The Supremes (initially much disliked by Ross and Wilson). *I Want A Guy* is issued as their first US single, but flops.

1961 **July** [21] Second single *Buttered Popcorn*, with Ballard singing lead, is released in US (and will also fail).

1962 **Aug** *Your Heart Belongs To Me* is their US chart debut, reaching #95.
Oct [16] The Supremes begin a 2-month US Motown Records package tour with labelmates Marvin Gaye, The Miracles, Mary Wells and Little Stevie Wonder, in Washington, DC.
Nov [19] The Motown package tour begins a 10-day run at New York's Apollo theater in Harlem.

1963 **Jan** *Let Me Go The Right Way*, written by Gordy, makes US #90.
Aug *A Breath Taking Guy*, penned by Smokey Robinson, makes US #75.

1964 **Jan** A Holland/Dozier/Holland song, uptempo dancer *When The Lovelight Starts Shining Through His Eyes*, is the group's Top 30 breakthrough, reaching US #23.
Mar *Run, Run, Run*, penned by the same trio, stalls at US #93.
June Group begins a US tour on Dick Clark's "Caravan Of Stars", alongside Gene Pitney, The Shirelles, Brenda Holloway, and others.
Aug *Where Did Our Love Go* (written by Holland, Dozier and Holland for, but rejected by, The Marvelettes) tops US chart for 2 weeks, and is the group's first million-seller.
Sept *Where Did Our Love Go* is The Supremes' UK chart debut, at #3.
[13] Trio appears in Murray The K's 10-day "Rock'N'Roll Spectacular" at New York's Fox theater, Brooklyn, on a bill including Motown labelmates The Temptations, Marvin Gaye, The Miracles and Martha & The Vandellas.
Oct *Baby Love*, also by Holland/Dozier/Holland, hits US #1 for 4 weeks and is a second million-seller. *Where Did Our Love Go* hits US #2, staying charted for 89 weeks.
[30] Group appears in the T.A.M.I. show, a stage spectacular videotaped for US TV and UK movie release, alongside The Rolling Stones, The Beach Boys, Marvin Gaye, James Brown, and others.
Nov The Supremes become the first all-girl group to hit UK #1, when *Baby Love* tops UK chart for 2 weeks.
Dec *Come See About Me*, by Holland/Dozier/Holland and taken from the album to compete with Nella Dodds' version (a minor US hit on Wand Records), tops US chart for a week, but is deposed by The Beatles' *I Feel Fine*. Meanwhile, **Meet The Supremes** hits UK #8 and *A Bit Of Liverpool*, featuring covers of UK group hits, makes US #21.
[27] Trio makes its debut on US TV's "Ed Sullivan Show".

1965 **Jan** *Come See About Me* replaces The Beatles *I Feel Fine* for a further week at US #1, and is their third consecutive million-seller.
Feb *Come See About Me* makes US #27.
Mar Again the trio deposes The Beatles as Holland/Dozier/Holland' *Stop! In The Name Of Love* replaces Lennon/McCartney's *Eight Days A Week* at US #1 for 2 weeks.
[20] The Supremes arrive in London to take part in the Motown package tour which helps launch the label's identity in UK (all previous releases having been licensed on UK labels like London, Oriole and Stateside), with labelmates Martha & The Vandellas, The Miracles, The Temptations and Stevie Wonder.
Apr *The Supremes Sing Country, Western And Pop* makes US #79 while *Stop! In The Name Of Love*, the first single released on UK Tamla Motown label, hits UK #7. The trio's characteristic hand-movement choreography for the song is worked out during rehearsals for UK TV "Ready Steady Go!".
June *Back In My Arms Again* tops US chart for a week, the trio's fifth consecutive US #1 single and million-seller. In UK, it makes #40 while *We Remember Sam Cooke*, featuring songs associated with the recently-deceased Cooke, makes US #75.
July [29] The trio opens for 3 weeks at New York's Copacabana club.
Aug *Nothing But Heartaches* reaches US #11 but fails to chart in UK.
Sept *More Hits By The Supremes* hits US #6.
Oct [10] The Supremes appear again on US TV's "Ed Sullivan Show", introducing *I Hear A Symphony*.
Nov *I Hear A Symphony* tops US chart for 2 weeks (deposing The Rolling Stones' *Get Off Of My Cloud*) and is a million-seller.
Dec Live album *The Supremes At The Copa*, a recording of their club act at New York's Copacabana, reaches US #11.

1966 **Jan** *I Hear A Symphony* makes UK #39.
Feb *My World Is Empty Without You* hits US #5, and is a further million-seller, but fails in UK.
Apr *I Hear A Symphony* hits US #8.
May *Love Is Like An Itching In My Heart* hits US #9. (Though not a UK hit, it will become a classic dance record on the UK Northern Soul scene in the mid-70s.)
Sept *You Can't Hurry Love* hits US #1 for 2 weeks, selling million-plus, and UK #3. (Phil Collins' 1982 revival of it will be a million-seller.)
Oct *The Supremes A' Go-Go* tops US chart for 2 weeks, deposing The Beatles' *Revolver*. It is the trio's first #1 album.
Nov *You Keep Me Hangin' On* tops US chart for 2 weeks, selling over a million.
Dec *The Supremes A' Go-Go* makes UK #15, while *You Keep Me Hangin' On* hits UK #8.

1967 **Jan** [6] The Supremes begin recording an album of Disney tunes. (The project is shelved before release and only *When You Wish Upon A Star* appears.)
Mar *Love Is Here And Now You're Gone* tops US chart for a week (a further million-seller) and makes UK #17. It is taken from *The Supremes Sing Holland-Dozier-Holland*, which hits US #6.
Apr After Ballard, unhappy about her role in the group, starts to become unreliable, missing concerts in New Orleans and Montreal, Canada, Cindy Birdsong (b. Dec.15, 1939, Camden, NJ) of Patti LaBelle & The Bluebelles is auditioned as a stand-in.
[29] Birdsong makes her Supremes stage debut at the Hollywood Bowl, at a benefit show for the United Negro College Fund and UCLA School of Music, which also features The 5th Dimension, Johnny Rivers, and others.
May *The Happening*, theme from the Anthony Quinn film of the same name, becomes The Supremes' 10th US #1 (in 13 releases), for 1 week.
June *The Happening* hits UK #6, while *The Supremes Sing Motown* (a re-titling of US album *The Supremes Sing Holland-Dozier-Holland*) makes UK #17.
July *The Supremes Sing Rodgers And Hart* makes US #20. During a Las Vegas club engagement at the Flamingo, Ballard is dismissed from the group and fired from Motown (the label flies her back to Detroit, where she is hospitalized with exhaustion). Birdsong steps in, but Gordy announces that lead singer Ross is to be elevated to featured status in preparation for a solo career, and the group will henceforth be credited as Diana Ross & The Supremes.
Sept *Reflections*, the first release with the new billing (and also one of

Motown's first experiments with "progressive" backing music elements, having a characteristically 1967 swirling "psychedelic" intro), hits US #2 (behind Bobbie Gentry's *Ode To Billie Jo*), selling a million, and UK #5.

Oct Double compilation album *Diana Ross And The Supremes' Greatest Hits* tops US chart for 5 weeks, while *The Supremes Sing Rodgers And Hart* makes UK #25.

Dec *In And Out Of Love* hits US #9 and UK #13.

1968
Jan Trio plays a short nightclub season at London's Talk Of The Town. Among those who catch the opening of the act are Paul McCartney, Cliff Richard and Michael Caine. They also appear on UK TV's "Sunday Night At The London Palladium".

Feb Compilation album *Diana Ross And The Supremes' Greatest Hits* (reduced from the US double album to a 16-track single album for UK) tops UK chart for 6 weeks.

[3] TV special "The Supremes Live At The Talk Of The Town" airs on UK BBC TV.

[29] Ex-Supreme Ballard marries Thomas Chapman in Detroit.

Mar Ballard signs to ABC Records as a soloist. (She will record 2 solo singles, the first *It Doesn't Matter*, but neither will sell.)

Apr UK-recorded live album *Live At The Talk Of The Town* hits UK #6, while *Forever Came Today*, the last Supremes single written and produced by Holland/Dozier/Holland (who will leave Motown to set up their own successful Invictus and Hot Wax labels), reaches both US and UK #28.

June *Reflections* peaks at US #18.

July *Some Things You Never Get Used To*, written and produced by Ashford & Simpson, makes US #30 and UK #34, while *Reflections* makes US #30.

Aug Rumors that Ross is shortly to leave The Supremes are reported in both US and UK press.

Oct Live album *Live At London's Talk Of The Town* peaks at US #57, while album *Funny Girl*, featuring the group's versions of songs from the show, makes US #150.

Nov *Love Child*, a social-conscience song team-written by Pam Sawyer, Frank Wilson, Deke Richards and R. Dean Taylor tops US chart for 2 weeks after the trio premieres it on TV's "Ed Sullivan Show". It deposes The Beatles' *Hey Jude* and is another million-seller.

[19] The Supremes appear before the Queen at the Royal Variety Show in London. Ross does an unrehearsed between-songs monologue urging racial tolerance, which is rapturously applauded.

Dec *Diana Ross And The Supremes Join The Temptations* hits US #2, while *Love Child* makes US #15.

1969
Jan *Love Child* reaches US #14, while a revival of Madeleine Bell's *I'm Gonna Make You Love Me*, duetted with The Temptations and taken from the 2 groups' joint album, is a million-seller, hitting US #2 (behind Marvin Gaye's *I Heard It Through The Grapevine*).

Feb *I'm Gonna Make You Love Me* hits UK #3, while *Diana Ross And The Supremes Join The Temptations* tops UK chart for 4 weeks and *Love Child* hits UK #8. Meanwhile, *T.C.B.*, again with The Temptations, and featuring the soundtrack of the 2 groups' TV spectacular of the same title, tops US chart for a week.

Mar *I'm Livin' In Shame* (said to have been inspired by Lana Turner film "Imitation Of Life") hits US #10.

Apr A revival of The Miracles' *I'll Try Something New*, with The Temptations (from *T.C.B.*), makes US #25.

May *I'm Livin' In Shame* makes UK #14, while *The Composer*, penned by Smokey Robinson, makes US #27.

June *No Matter What Sign You Are* makes US #31.

July *Let The Sunshine In* makes US #24, while The Supremes/Temptations album *T.C.B.* reaches UK #11 and *No Matter What Sign You Are* makes UK #37.

Aug *No Matter What Sign You Are*'s B-side, *The Young Folks*, charts in US at #69.

Sept A revival of The Band's *The Weight*, duetted with The Temptations, peaks at US #46.

Oct A revival of The Miracles' *I Second That Emotion*, again with The Temptations, makes US #18.

Nov *Together*, a third set with The Temptations, makes US #28.

Dec *Someday We'll Be Together*, produced and co-written by Johnny Bristol, tops US chart for a week and sells over a million. It is The Supremes' 12th and last US #1 (and their last single together before Ross departs for a solo career), and the last #1 of the 60s. It is taken from *Cream Of The Crop*, the last studio set from the Ross-led line-up, which reaches US #33.

[21] Ross & The Supremes make their last TV appearance together on

US TV's "Ed Sullivan Show", singing *Someday We'll Be Together*.

1970
Jan *Someday We'll Be Together* makes UK #13, as *On Broadway*, soundtrack to a Supremes/Temptations TV special, makes US #38.

[14] Diana Ross & The Supremes make their final live appearance together at Las Vegas' Frontier hotel. (Ross will leave the following day, having introduced her replacement Jean Terrell (b. Nov.26, 1944, Texas), the sister of boxer Ernie Terrell, on stage.)

Feb Compilation album *Diana Ross And The Supremes Greatest Hits, Volume 3*, continuing the hits anthology from the earlier double album, makes US #31, while *Together* with The Temptations makes UK #28.

Apr Group's billing reverts back to The Supremes for *Up The Ladder To The Roof*, the first release featuring Terrell on lead vocals, which hits US #10. Group is now working with producer Frank Wilson, who has co-written the song with Vincent DiMirco. *Why (Must We Fall In Love)*, with The Temptations (and featuring Ross), makes UK #31.

May *Up The Ladder To The Roof* hits UK #6.

June Double live album *Farewell*, by Diana Ross & The Supremes, a recording of the trio's final concert on Jan.14, peaks at US #46.

July *Right On*, the first featuring Terrell, reaches US #25.

Sept *Everybody's Got The Right To Love*, from the album, makes US #21.

Nov *The Magnificent 7*, recorded with The Four Tops, peaks at US #113, while The Supremes' *New Ways But Love Stays* makes US #68.

Dec From the album, *Stoned Love*, produced and co-written by Frank Wilson, hits US #7, giving the new line-up its first million-seller. Meanwhile, a revival of Ike & Tina Turner's *River Deep, Mountain High*, with The Four Tops (from *The Magnificent 7*), reaches US #14.

1971
Feb *Stoned Love* hits UK #3.

June *Nathan Jones* reaches US #16, while *The Magnificent 7*, with The Four Tops, hits UK #6.

July *River Deep, Mountain High* peaks at UK #11, while The Supremes' *Touch*, with sleeve notes written by Elton John, makes US #85 and *The Return Of The Magnificent Seven*, again with The Four Tops, climbs to US #154. The duetted *You Gotta Have Love In Your Heart*, taken from it, makes US #55.

Sept *Nathan Jones* hits UK #5 (and will be revived by Bananarama in 1988) and *Touch* makes UK #40, while title cut stalls at US #71.

Nov [12] Group begins 13-date UK tour at Regal theater, Edmonton, London, set to end Nov.29 at the Brighton Dome, E.Sussex.

Dec *You Gotta Have Love In Your Heart*, with The Four Tops, makes #25 on UK chart.

1972
Jan *Dynamite*, with The Four Tops, makes US #160.

Mar *Floy Joy*, written and produced by Smokey Robinson, reaches US #16 and hits UK #9.

June Birdsong leaves, to devote more time to home and marriage. She is replaced by Lynda Lawrence. *Floy Joy* reaches US #54 while, from it, another Robinson song, *Automatically Sunshine*, makes US #37.

July *Automatically Sunshine* hits UK #10, the group's last Top 10 hit. (The song will reappear in a UK TV ad for Persil Automatic washing powder in 1987.)

Sept *Your Wonderful, Sweet Sweet Love* makes US #59.

Nov *I Guess I'll Miss The Man* (from Broadway musical "Pippin") stalls at US #85.

Dec *The Supremes* written/produced by Jimmy Webb makes US #129.

1973
May *Bad Weather*, produced and arranged by Stevie Wonder, makes UK #37.

June *Bad Weather* spends 1 week at US #87. It is the group's last recording to feature Terrell; she leaves shortly after and is replaced by Scherrie Payne (b. Nov.14, 1944, Detroit, MI).

1974
July Triple compilation album *Anthology (1962-1969)* reaches US #66.

Sept *Baby Love* is reissued in UK and re-charts, making #12. It is their last UK hit single.

1975
July *The Supremes* peaks at US #152.

1976
After Laurence has left and Birdsong has returned temporarily, the third slot is filled by Susaye Greene.

Feb [21] Following hard times, including a lost $8.7 million lawsuit against Motown and separation from her husband, which left her on welfare, Ballard dies, aged 32, at Mount Carmel Mercy hospital, Detroit, from a heart attack brought on by coronary thrombosis.

July *High Energy* makes US #42, while extracted *I'm Gonna Let My Heart Do The Walking* makes US #40 (after the group has been absent from the Singles chart for 3 years).

Dec *You're My Driving Wheel* stalls at US #85, and is their final US hit single. Wilson, the final original member, leaves and is replaced by Karen Jackson. (Motown sees little commercial potential left in the group and it will disband. Wilson will later perform with new back-up singers as Mary Wilson & The Supremes.)

1977 Sept TV-promoted UK compilation album *Diana Ross And The Supremes' 20 Golden Greats* tops UK chart for 7 weeks.

1981 Dec [20] Musical "Dreamgirls", supposedly based on the story of The Supremes, opens on Broadway at the Imperial theater.

1983 May [16] Wilson and Birdsong are reunited with Ross as The Supremes on the Motown 25th anniversary US NBC TV spectacular.
June The Supremes with Wilson tour US on an oldies package with Frankie Valli & The Four Seasons, The Righteous Brothers, The Four Tops and The Association.

1984 Wilson writes a book telling her own history of the group, **Dreamgirl: My Life As A Supreme**.

1986 June *25th Anniversary* makes US #112.

1988 Jan [20] The Supremes are inducted into the Rock'N'Roll Hall Of Fame at the third annual dinner at the Waldorf Astoria, New York.
Dec As Bananarama, now claiming to be the most successful girl trio in rock history, revive *Nathan Jones* in UK Top 20, the most successful girl trio in rock history The Supremes are set for compilation album chart revival through Motown's planned *Love Supreme*.

SWEET

Brian Connolly (vocals)
Andy Scott (guitar)
Steve Priest (bass)
Mick Tucker (drums)

1968 Jan Ex-members of Wainwright's Gentlemen, Connolly (b. Oct.5, 1949, Hamilton, Scotland) and Tucker (b. July 17, 1949, Harlesden, London) form Sweetshop with Priest (b. Feb.23, 1950, Hayes, London) and Frank Torpey on guitar.
Feb Sweetshop's live debut is at Hemel Hempstead Pavilion, Herts.
July Debut single is *Slow Motion*, on Fontana, which fails to chart.
Aug Group makes its first radio broadcast on UK BBC Radio 1's "David Symonds Show".
Sept A move to EMI's Parlophone label for *Lollipop Man* sees minimal sales. (2 more Parlophone singles will also fail to chart in 1970, before the label drops the group.)

1970 Torpey is replaced by Scott (b. June 30, 1951, Wrexham, Wales), who has moved to London after his most recent band Elastic Band has split up. Group abbreviates its name to Sweet.

1971 Jan Group makes its UK TV debut, on juvenile pop show "Lift Off". New recording deal is signed with RCA, and Sweet links with producer Phil Wainman.
May Wainman-produced Nicky Chinn/Mike Chapman composition *Funny Funny* is UK chart debut, reaching #13.
July *Co-Co* hits UK #2, held from the top by Middle Of The Road's *Chirpy Chirpy Cheep Cheep*.
Oct *Alexander Graham Bell* makes UK #33, while *Co-Co* is US chart debut at #91.

1972 Mar *Poppa Joe* makes UK #11. It begins a series of Chinn/Chapman-penned glam pop confection UK hits which makes the band "Top Of The Pops" regulars on UK TV, and encourages its ever more way-out visual image, with flamboyant costumes, make-up and glitter.
May Group is taken to court in Belgium, by a town objecting to earlier Sweet concert which involved the use of an allegedly pornographic film clip.
July *Little Willy* hits UK #4. The slight double entendre is exploited by the group (and its audience), especially on live ballroom dates. (Later, for what is considered an overtly sexual stage act, the group is banned from UK Mecca dancehall circuit.)
Oct *Wig Wam Bam* hits UK #4. It is played on TV in American Indian costume and warpaint-like make-up.

1973 Jan *Blockbuster*, using one of the most familiar riffs in rock music (the same one as David Bowie's *The Gene Genie*, which sits at #2 below it), tops UK chart for 5 weeks. Like all Sweet hits, it has a hard rock band-composed B-side.
May *Hellraiser* hits UK #2, behind Dawn's *Tie A Yellow Ribbon*. In US, *Little Willy* gives the band its biggest success, hitting #3 and selling over a million.
Aug *The Sweet* makes US #191.
Sept *Ballroom Blitz* enters UK chart at #2, held off the top by Simon Park Orchestra's *Eye Level*.

1974 Jan *Teenage Rampage* is third in a row UK #2, behind Mud's *Tiger Feet*.
May Band begins its first UK tour, while *Sweet Fanny Adams* makes UK #27 – the group's only UK chart album during the 70s. In contrast to the singles, this is entirely self-written.
July *The Six Teens* hits UK #9, while *Blockbuster* makes US #73.

Dec Group splits from Chinn and Chapman, to write and produce itself, and attempts to find greater international rock credibility.

1975 Apr Group-penned *Fox On The Run* hits UK #2, behind The Bay City Rollers' *Bye Bye Baby*.
Aug *Action* reaches UK #15.
Sept Band begins 3-month US tour, which heralds its greatest period of US success.
Oct *Ballroom Blitz* hits US #5, a year after its UK success. *Desolation Boulevard*, having failed in UK, reaches US #25, earning a gold disk.

1976 Jan *Fox On The Run* hits US #5, and is a second million-selling single, while *Lies In Your Eyes* makes UK #35.
Apr *Action* makes US #20, while entirely group self-penned *Give Us A Wink*, recorded in Munich, Germany, reaches US #27.

1977 May *Off The Record* makes US #151.
Aug *Funk It Up (David's Song)*, not issued as a UK single, makes US #88. Group retires to Clearwell Castle in Wales to write another album later moving to France to record it.

1978 Feb After a 2-year UK Singles chart absence, band leaves RCA following 3 flop singles, and signs to Polydor. *Love Is Like Oxygen*, featured in Joan Collins movie "The Bitch", hits UK #9. Sweet tours US for the first time in 4 years.
June *Love Is Like Oxygen* hits US #8, while parent album *Level Headed* makes US #52.
Aug Also from the album, *California Nights* makes US #74. It is the band's last US hit single (having failed in UK).

1979 May *Cut Above The Rest* makes US #151. Connolly leaves to go solo. (Priest takes over as lead vocalist with Gary Moberley joining on keyboards. Connolly will later form The New Sweet, with no original members.)

1980 Apr *Give The Lady Some Respect* and *Water's Edge* both fail.

1981 Group tours with new guitarist/keyboardist back-up, but finds no recording success, and splits after release of *Identity Crisis*.

1984 Oct Retrospective compilation *Sweet 16 – It's... It's... Sweet's Hits*, on UK independent label Anagram, reaches UK #49.

1985 Feb Also on Anagram, segued *It's It's The Sweet Mix*, put together from original hits (*Blockbusters, Fox On The Run, Teenage Rampage, Hellraiser* and *Ballroom Blitz*) by UK club DJ/remixer Sanny X, reaches UK #45. Amid the interest this creates, the group re-forms briefly, with Paul Mario Day (ex-Wildfire) replacing Connolly and keyboardist Phil Lanzon (ex-Grand Prix).

1988 Scott tours UK with pub-rockers Paddy Goes To Holyhead.

1990 Group re-forms with Scott and Tucker and releases *Live At The Marquee* on Maze Records, before embarking on tours of UK and US.

THE SWINGING BLUE JEANS

Ray Ennis (lead guitar, vocals)
Les Braid (bass)
Ralph Ellis (rhythm guitar, vocals)
Norman Kuhlke (drums)

1958 May Group forms from the nucleus of 2 Liverpool, Merseyside, skiffle groups who come first and second in a talent contest at Liverpool's Empire theater. The 4 who decide to regroup to play rock'n'roll rather than skiffle are Ennis (b. May 26, 1942, Liverpool,), Ellis (b. Mar.8, 1942, Liverpool), Braid (b. William Leslie Braid, Sept.15, 1941, Liverpool) and Kuhlke (b. June 17, 1942, Liverpool); they name themselves The Bluegenes.

1961 Mar [21] Holding a regular Tuesday night residency at Liverpool's Cavern club, The Bluegenes host the first appearance of a new group at the club, The Beatles.

1962 They hold residencies at Liverpool's Mardi Gras and Downbeat clubs, becoming synonymous with these venues much as The Beatles do with the Cavern.

1963 Changing name to more commercial-sounding Swinging Blue Jeans, the group is among many from Liverpool to gain a recording contract in the wake of The Beatles' early success, signing to EMI's HMV label.
July Debut single *It's Too Late Now* reaches UK #30.
Sept *Do You Know* fails to chart.
[29] Group begins a 13-week series "Swingtime", sponsored by jeans manufacturers Lybro, on Radio Luxembourg.
Dec [7] The Beatles, appearing on BBC TV show "Juke Box Jury", vote the group's new single a hit. A raucous revival of Chan Romero's *Hippy Hippy Shake*, it is a long-time stage favorite with the group.
Group appears in an episode of BBC TV's police drama series "Z Cars" as a Merseyside beat group, singing *Hippy Hippy Shake*.

1964 Jan *Hippy Hippy Shake* hits UK #2, behind The Dave Clark Five's *Glad All Over*.

[6] Group embarks on 12-date twice-nightly "Group Scene 1964" UK package tour with The Rolling Stones, The Ronettes, Dave Berry & The Cruisers and Marty Wilde & The Wildecats, at the Granada cinema, Harrow, London. Tour ends at Bristol's Colston Hall, Avon.
Feb [29] They begin a 20-date twice-nightly UK package tour with Gene Pitney, Billy J. Kramer And The Dakotas and Cilla Black, at the Odeon cinema, Nottingham, Notts.
Apr Similarly-styled revival of Little Richard's *Good Golly Miss Molly* reaches UK #11, while *Hippy Hippy Shake* is US debut, climbing to #24.
[26] Group appears at the **New Musical Express** Poll Winners Concert, with The Beatles, The Dave Clark Five and others, at the Empire Pool, Wembley, London.
May [9] Band starts a 21-date twice-nightly UK tour supporting Chuck Berry, with Carl Perkins, The Animals, The Nashville Teens and others, at the Finsbury Park Astoria, London. Tour ends May 29 at Southend's Odeon cinema, Essex.
June *Good Golly Miss Molly* makes US #43, and *Hippy Hippy Shake* reaches US #90.
July More subdued cover of Betty Everett's *You're No Good* hits UK #3.
Aug *Promise You'll Tell Her*, a self-penned but undistinctive number, fails to chart. *You're No Good* peaks at US #97.
Oct Group's first UK album, *Blue Jeans A-Swingin'*, is released (the earlier US album having been a compilation of singles/EP tracks) but sells poorly.
Dec *It Isn't There* also fails.
1965 While continuing to work and tour regularly, the group's music on record loses the pulse of the UK music scene as it moves on from Merseybeat into a tougher R&B stance. 2 singles, *Make Me Know You're Mine* and *Crazy 'Bout My Baby* (with a version of *Good Lovin'*, a million-seller for The Young Rascals in 1966, on the B-side), are released, but without success.
1966 Feb A revival of Dionne Warwick's *Don't Make Me Over* provides the group's first success for 18 months. It reaches UK #31, but The Swinging Blue Jeans will not chart again.
[17] Ellis leaves the group and is replaced by Terry Sylvester from The Escorts, who makes his debut with the band in Bolton, Gtr.Manchester. Only weeks later, Braid also departs, and another ex-Escort, Mike Gregory, replaces him.
1967 Aug Group covers Herman's Hermits' US hit *Don't Go Out Into The Rain*, but it fails.
1968 June In an effort to re-define the group's image, follow-up *What Have They Done To Hazel?* is credited to Ray Ennis And The Blue Jeans, and released on Columbia (EMI having closed HMV as a pop label). When this fails too, Sylvester leaves (to join The Hollies 6 months later) and the group splits.
1973 Ennis re-forms the group with a new line-up, to capitalize on the nostalgic success of events like Herman's Hermits/Gerry & The Pacemakers/Searchers "British Re-Invasion" tour of US. Group finds solid club and cabaret bookings, as well as playing on oldies tours in UK and Europe (particularly popular in Scandinavia). *Brand New And Faded*, plus a remake of *Hippy Hippy Shake* on independent Dart label fail to make much impression. (With a name still striking a chord with adult audiences who were teenagers in 1964, The Swinging Blue Jeans will continue to work as a successful club nostalgia act into the 80s.)

.REX

Marc Bolan (vocals, guitar)
Steve Peregrine Took (percussion)

1965 Nov [12] After a teenage career as a male model, among other things, and being spotlighted by **Town** magazine as one of the leaders of the mod scene, Bolan (b. Mark Feld, Sept.30, 1947, Hackney, London) changes his performing name from Toby Tyler to Marc Bolan and, now signed to Decca, performs his first single *The Wizard*, on commercial TV's "Ready Steady Go!".
[23] He makes his second TV appearance on "Five O'Clock Funfair".
1966 June Second single *The Third Degree* is released.
Nov Bolan links with new producer Simon Napier-Bell (also The Yardbirds' manager), and records third single *Hippy Gumbo* for EMI (another failure), plus many other tracks which will only emerge in 1974 after he achieves fame.
1967 May He signs to Track Records and joins South London psychedelic group John's Children as guitarist/harmony vocalist, along with Andy Ellison (vocals), John Hewlett (bass) and Chris Townson (drums).
Sept John's Children breaks up after 3 unsuccessful singles, and Bolan forms the acoustic duo Tyrannosaurus Rex, with percussionist Took.

1968 Feb Duo signs new recording deal with producer Tony Visconti, for release on EMI's Regal Zonophone label.
Mar [21] They appear at the Royal Albert Hall, London, supporting Donovan, in a concert in aid of Imperial College charity carnival.
May Debut Tyrannosaurus Rex single *Debora* reaches UK #34.
July *My People Were Fair And Had Sky In Their Hair, But Now They're Content To Wear Stars On Their Brow* makes UK #15.
[6] Duo takes part in the Woburn Music Festival, Beds.
Sept *One Inch Rock* reaches UK #28.
Nov *Prophets, Seers And Sages, The Angels Of The Ages* is issued in UK. Duo makes its TV debut on "John Peel In Concert".
1969 Jan *Pewter Suitor* is released.
June Third album *Unicorn* reaches UK #12.
Aug *King Of The Rumbling Spires* spends 1 week at UK #44, and is the group's first record to feature Bolan playing electric guitar.
Oct Following a poorly received US tour, Took leaves and is replaced by Mickey Finn.
1970 Jan *By The Light Of The Magical Moon* is released by the new duo in UK, but does not chart.
Mar *A Beard Of Stars* peaks at #21 in UK.
May [25] Duo plays the Electric Garden, Glasgow, Scotland, at the end of a short Scottish tour.
Aug Bolan, Visconti, David Bowie and Rick Wakeman release an impromptu UK single *Oh Baby*, under the name Dib Cochran & The Earwigs. It fails to sell, but will later be an in-demand collectors' rarity.
Oct Visconti shifts label outlet for his productions from Regal Zonophone to Fly Records in UK. After much urging from his producer, Bolan abbreviates his group name to T.Rex, and releases *Ride A White Swan*, which climbs steadily to hit UK #2 at the year's end.
Nov [28] At a Roundhouse, Dagenham, Essex, gig, The Turtles' Howard Kaylan joins the duo on stage.
Dec T.Rex expands to a quartet with the addition of Steve Curry on bass, and Bill Legend on drums (in fact Bill Fifield, but known to Bolan as Legend because he was recruited from the Mickey Jupp-led group, Legend.) *T.Rex* peaks at UK #13, in a chart residency lasting 6 months.
1971 Feb *Ride A White Swan* is US chart debut at #76.
Mar *Hot Love* tops UK chart for 6 weeks.
June *Hot Love* peaks at US #72, while *T.Rex* edges in at #188.
July *Get It On* tops UK chart for 4 weeks, and will become Bolan and T.Rex's biggest international hit.
Aug Compilation album *The Best Of T.Rex*, largely composed of tracks by Tyrannosaurus Rex, reaches UK #21.
Oct *Electric Warrior*, first album by the 4-piece group, is released.
Nov As Bolan decides to leave Fly Records for a new deal, the label issues album track *Jeepster* (never intended by Bolan for single release) in UK, and it leaps to #2.
Dec *Electric Warrior* tops UK chart for 6 weeks, and reaches US #32.
1972 Jan [1] Bolan signs new deal with EMI, to release records in UK on his own T.Rex Wax Co. label.
Feb *Telegram Sam*, the first EMI release, tops UK chart for 2 weeks.
Mar *Bang A Gong (Get It On)* is Bolan's biggest US hit, at #10. The title amendment has been necessary in US because the group Chase has had a Top 30 hit with a different song titled *Get It On* in mid-1971. T.Rex plays 2 sold-out concerts at the Empire Pool, Wembley, London, to audiences of 100,000, while being filmed by Ringo Starr for Apple documentary film on the group's success, "Born To Boogie". Double album reissue coupling *My People Were Fair ...* and *Prophets, Seers And Sages* by Tyrannosaurus Rex tops UK chart for a week, while a single reissue twinning *Debora* and *One Inch Rock* hits UK #7.
May *Metal Guru* ("It's about a car," says Bolan) tops UK chart for 4 weeks as the country is afflicted by "T.Rextasy". In US, *Telegram Sam* peaks at US #67. *Bolan Boogie*, on Fly, compiling the hits up to *Jeepster*, tops UK chart for 3 weeks.
July Newly-recorded *The Slider* hits #4 in UK (reputedly selling 100,000 copies in 4 days), and also becomes the group's most successful US album, peaking at #17.
Sept *Children Of The Revolution* hits UK #2.
Dec Movie "Born To Boogie", featuring T.Rex, is premiered in London. *Solid Gold Easy Action* peaks at UK #3, while another double reissue album coupling *Unicorn* and *A Beard Of Stars* charts briefly at #44.
1973 Mar *Twentieth Century Boy* hits UK #3, while *Tanx* makes #4, and also reaches US #102.
June *The Groover* reaches UK #4 - T.Rex's 10th and final UK Top 5 hit.
July Jack Green joins the group on additional guitar, and 3 girl back-up vocalists are recruited, including US soul singer Gloria Jones, who will become Bolan's girlfriend.

T.REX cont.

Aug *Blackjack* is issued in UK under the name Marc Bolan With Big Carrot, but does not chart.

Nov Compilation album *Great Hits* (an anthology from *Telegram Sam* onwards) peaks at UK #32.

Dec *Truck On (Tyke)* reaches UK #12.

1974 Jan Davy Lutton replaces Legend on drums and Gloria Jones starts to play keyboards on stage, as T.Rex plays first major UK tour in 2 years. [28] Band ends tour at the Odeon cinema, Birmingham, W.Midlands.

Feb *Teenage Dream* reaches UK #13. This is the first release on which the group's name is amended to Marc Bolan and T.Rex.

Mar *Zinc Alloy And The Hidden Riders Of Tomorrow* reaches UK #12 as Bolan parts company with his long-time producer Visconti.

Apr Bolan leaves UK for several months' tax exile in Monte Carlo.

June Tracks recorded as demos in 1966 with Simon Napier-Bell finally gain commercial release in UK via Track Records, as *The Beginning Of Doves* and maxi-single *Jasper C. Debussy*. Neither charts.

July *Light Of Love* reaches UK #22.

Nov *Zip Gun Boogie* makes UK #41.

Dec Mickey Finn and Jack Green leave the group, while Dino Dines joins on keyboards.

1975 Feb *Bolan's Zip Gun* is released in UK, sells poorly and does not chart.

July *New York City* restores Bolan to UK Top 20, reaching #15.

Sept Rolan, son of Bolan and Gloria Jones, is born in London.

Oct *Dreamy Lady* (credited to T.Rex Disco Party) reaches UK #30.

1976 Mar *Futuristic Dragon* and single *London Boys* are released in UK, charting at #50 and #40 respectively.

July *I Love To Boogie* becomes Bolan's last UK Top 20 hit, reaching #13.

Oct *Laser Love* makes UK #41. It features Bolan with a T.Rex made up of session men like Miller Anderson (guitar) and Herbie Flowers (bass), the last group survivor from the major hit years, bassist Steve Curry having now also left.

Nov The session players also make up the final touring line-up of T.Rex, accompanying Bolan on a charity date at London's Drury Lane Theatre Royal, followed by a UK tour which has punk band The Damned as support act.

1977 Jan Bolan and Gloria Jones issue duet revival of The Teddy Bears' *To Know Him Is To Love Him* in UK, but it does not chart and later becomes another collectors' item.

Mar [20] The final live T.Rex gig takes place at the Locarno in Portsmouth, Hants.

Apr *The Soul Of My Suit* makes UK #42, while *Dandy In The Underworld*, Bolan's final album to be issued in his lifetime, reaches #26. (The album title track will be issued as a quick UK follow-up single and flop completely.)

Aug *Celebrate Summer* fails to chart in UK, making it Bolan's second consecutive miss. Meanwhile, he begins a stint as a guest pop journalist, writing a weekly column in UK magazine **Record Mirror**, and also hosts a series of 6 weekly Wednesday late-afternoon UK TV shows, called "Marc". Guests include David Bowie, who sings a live duet with Bolan on one show.

Sept [16] After a long night out at a London club, Bolan and Gloria Jones are on their way home when, at 5am, their car (driven by Jones) leaves the road at a bend on Barnes Common, London, and crashes into a tree. Jones is badly injured, and Bolan is killed, 2 weeks shy of his 30th birthday.

1978 Apr *Crimson Moon* is the first posthumous Bolan release and, though it does not chart, begins a sequence of reissues and releases comprising previously unheard material which will still be in full flood a decade after his death. (In all, 5 singles will chart in UK posthumously: the EP *Return Of The Electric Warrior* (May 1981 – #50), *You Scare Me To Death* (Sept.1981 – #51), a reissue of *Telegram Sam* (Mar.1982 – #69), a medley of hit extracts titled *Megarex* (May 1985 – #72) and *Get It On* (May 1987 – #54). 5 albums: *Solid Gold* (July 1979 – #51), *T.Rex In Concert* (Sept.1981 – #35), *You Scare Me To Death* (Nov.1981 – #88), *Dance In The Midnight* (Sept.1983 – #83) and *Best Of The 20th Century Boy* (May 1985 – #5) – will also be posthumous UK chart entries.)

1980 Oct [27] Bolan's first performing partner Steve Peregrine Took dies from asphyxiation.

1985 May Definitive greatest hits package, *Best Of The 20th Century Boy* hits UK #5 and an accompanying video collection also confirms Bolan's enduring popularity.

1989 Feb UK video company, Channel 5, releases a compilation of Bolan's 70s TV appearances: "Marc", while his albums begin CD release in US.

TALK TALK

Mark Hollis (vocals, guitar, keyboards)
Paul Webb (bass)
Lee Harris (drums)

1977 Having left in his second year of studying child psychology at Sussex University and inspired by the current UK punk movement, Hollis (b. 1955, Tottenham, London) begins writing songs, relocating in London. His brother Ed, manager of Eddie & The Hot Rods, secures Hollis studio time backed by Island Records, keen to hear a demo tape. The company signs Hollis' band, The Reaction.

1978 The Reaction releases only 1 single, *I Can't Resist*, but also records *Talk Talk* (which only appears on Beggars Banquet punk compilation album *Streets*).

1979 The Reaction folds and Hollis is mainly supported by his wife, Flick.

1981 Ed Hollis brings in 2 musicians he is currently working with to record new demos with brother Mark: drummer Harris and bassist Webb, friends since schooldays and ex-various Southend R&B bands. They are joined by keyboardist Simon Bremner. Rehearsals on Hollis compositions go well and Talk Talk is formed. Hollis signs a publishing deal with Island Music, which provides 6 months' studio money. Keith Aspden leaves his job at Island Music to manage the group.

Sept They make their first live appearance in London.

Oct BBC Radio 1 DJ David "Kid" Jensen attends Talk Talk's debut gig and invites them to record a radio session.

Nov Impressed by demos produced by Rolling Stones producer Jimmy Miller, EMI signs Talk Talk.

1982 Feb While debut album is recorded, first single *Mirror Man* appears but fails to chart.

Apr *Talk Talk* single makes UK #52 as the band supports Duran Duran on UK tour. Both groups are currently using EMI nominated Colin Thurston as albums producer.

July As *Today* reaches UK #14, synthesizer-based debut album *The Party's Over* with all songs penned or co-penned by Hollis peaks at UK #21, as the group embarks on first headlining UK tour.

Aug Talk Talk begins a US visit behind Elvis Costello & The Attractions.

Oct *Talk Talk* stalls at US #75 as debut album makes US #132.

Nov UK re-issued *Talk Talk* now rises to UK #23.

1983 Mar The only chart record of the year is *My Foolish Friend* at UK #57. In what will become a familiar band practice, Talk Talk retreats for an entire year to prepare a new album. Bremner leaves, but his replacement becomes an invisible fourth member: Tim Friese-Green arrives to co-write with Hollis, play keyboards and produce the new songs.

1984 Jan *It's My Life* peaks at UK #46.

Feb Anthemic synthesizer-driven *It's My Life* peaks at UK #46, but repays its £250,000 cost by earning a gold disk in every other European territory.

Apr *Such A Shame* makes UK #49, as the band begins a European tour, with dates in Belgium, Holland, Italy and Germany.

May Helped by a Steve Thompson US remix, *It's My Life* rises to US #31, while parent album spends 5 months on chart peaking at US #42.

Aug *Dum Dum Girl* falters at UK #74. Follow-up *Such A Shame* stalls at US #49.

Oct A remix album, *It's My Mix*, featuring 6 cuts from first 2 Thompson-mixed albums, emerges from EMI Italy and becomes a UK import favorite.

1985 Jan Talk Talk plays San Remo, Italy, TV festival. Hollis and the band retreat again to work with Friese-Green on the next project.

1986 Jan Piano led *Life's What You Make It* is released and becomes their biggest hit in 4 years at UK #16.

Feb [15] *Life's What You Make It* makes US #90.

Mar *The Colour Of Spring* hits UK #8, their most successful release eventually going gold, and will peak at US #58. Written and produced by Hollis and Friese-Green, it features Steve Winwood playing organ on 2 tracks, and is another big European success.

Apr As *Living In Another World* makes UK #48, Talk Talk begins a major world tour.

May Ballad *Give It Up* peaks at UK #59, with no US follow-ups.

1987 While a further remix mini-album emerges from EMI Greece, the band retreats to the studio, this time keener to avoid synthesizer-based music. Hollis is enthusiastic to experiment in more abstract songwriting form. Together with his wife, Flick and their 2 children, he also moves from London to rural Suffolk, while Webb and Harris relocate to North London.

988 **Sept** Now diverted from EMI main label to UK Parlophone, fourth Talk Talk album, *Spirit Of Eden*, 14 months in the making, is issued featuring 6 extended tracks. Confirming its less commercial style, EMI issues a statement that, according to Hollis' wishes, a single will not be extracted. Album peaks at UK #19, as single *I Believe In You*, an anti heroin song, is released but fails to chart, and a US release is pondered.
Oct Talk Talk announces it will not tour to promote the album due to complexities of reproducing *Eden*'s sound, which includes a mini-orchestra and the Chelmsford Cathedral Choir.

989 Relationships between band and label deteriorate to the point of legal confrontation. Band signs to Polydor.

990 Prior to debut Polydor releases, EMI begins remixing and reissuing their Talk Talk catalog: *It's My Life* (May – UK #13), *Life's What You Make It* (UK #23) and the album *Natural History: The Very Best Of Talk Talk*, which hits UK #3 in June, during a 5-month chart residence – a video collection of the same title will also sell strongly.

TALKING HEADS

David Byrne (guitar, vocals)
Tina Weymouth (bass)
Jerry Harrison (keyboards)
Chris Frantz (drums)

974 **Sept** Having first met in Sept.1970 as freshmen students at the Rhode Island School of Design, Byrne (b. May 14, 1952, Dumbarton, Scotland), Weymouth (b. Martina Weymouth, Nov.22, 1950, Coronado, CA) and Frantz (b. Charlton Christopher Frantz, May 8, 1951, Fort Campbell, KY), form a trio after Frantz and Weymouth graduate, and move to New York. (Byrne has earlier played in Baltimore in a duo called Bizadi, while Frantz has been in The Beans, who had a residency at New York's Electric Circus in 1970. Since their student days together, the 2 have also played (Oct.1973-June 1974) in The Artistics, a Rhode Island quintet playing mainly 60s covers, plus Byrne/Franz/Weymouth composition *Psycho Killer*.)
Oct They begin rehearsing, living together in a Chrystie Street garret on Manhattan's Lower East Side, and obtain day jobs.

975 **May** After rejecting names like The Portable Crushers and The Vague Dots, Talking Heads is found in an old issue of "TV Guide".
June Following an audition by Hilly Kristal, owner of New York's CBGB's club (which stand for "Country, Bluegrass and Blues and other Music for Urban Gourmets"), the group is given its first gig, supporting The Ramones.
Oct Sire Records boss Seymour Stein sees the band and offers a recording deal, which is initially rejected.
Dec First TV appearance is in "Rock From CBGB's", on a Manhattan cable network.

976 **Apr** Harrison (b. Jeremiah Harrison, Feb.21, 1949, Milwaukee, WI) sees the band playing in Boston, MA, and expresses his wish to join. (He has been a member of Jonathan Richman And The Modern Lovers 1970-74, later studying at Harvard and working in computers in Boston.)
July Group headlines CBGB's bicentennial concert.
Sept Harrison plays with them for the first time, at the Ocean club in Lower Manhattan. He does not join immediately, having enrolled in an architecture course at Harvard.
Nov After considering recording offers from Arista, CBS, RCA and Beserkley Records, the trio signs with Stein at Sire.
Dec Debut single *Love Goes To Building On Fire*, produced by Tony Bongiovi, fails to chart.

977 **Jan** Group plays a mini-tour of US North-East (plus Toronto, Canada), with Harrison joining in dates at Boston and Providence.
Feb Harrison, having completed his Harvard degree in architecture, becomes a full-time member. Work on an album begins with Bongiovi.
Apr [24] Band begins its first European tour, supporting The Ramones in Switzerland, France, Holland and UK.
May [14] Talking Heads play a night headlining on their own at London's Rock Garden, where they are seen by Brian Eno, who develops what will be a lasting professional relationship with Byrne.
June [6] Group supports The Ramones at London's Roundhouse, returning to US the next day.
[18] Frantz and Weymouth marry in Maysville, KY.
[23] Group supports Bryan Ferry at New York's Bottom Line club.
July Debut album is completed, despite disagreements between the group and producer Bongiovi.
Oct While the band is on a 38-day promotional tour of East Coast and Mid-West clubs and colleges, *Talking Heads '77* enters US chart (for a 6-month stay), peaking at #97.

Dec [2-18] Band plays its first West Coast tour, taking in San Francisco and Los Angeles, CA.

1978 **Jan** [9] Talking Heads return to Europe for a 27-day tour of France, Holland, Belgium, Germany and UK, this time as headliners. Support acts include XTC in Europe and Dire Straits in UK.
[31] Band makes UK TV debut, on BBC's "The Old Grey Whistle Test".
Feb *Psycho Killer*, originally performed by Byrne and Frantz in The Artistics, is the group's first Singles chart entry, at US #92. *Talking Heads '77* spends a week on UK chart at #60.
Mar Group records in the Bahamas, with Eno producing.
May They make a 2-week tour of North-East US, before playing in Europe (including 1 UK show in London).
July *More Songs About Buildings And Food*, produced by Eno, reaches UK #21, while the group is on tour in UK.
Nov *More Songs About Buildings And Food* makes US #29.

1979 **Jan** A revival of Al Green's *Take Me To The River* reaches US #26.
June After completing a new album, the band plays its first Pacific tour, taking in New Zealand, Australia, Japan and Hawaii.
Aug A US tour opens to promote the new album, with a slot in the Dr. Pepper festival in New York's Central Park.
Sept *Fear Of Music*, again produced by Eno, reaches US #21 and UK #33. Group plays the Edinburgh Festival in Scotland, alongside Van Morrison and The Chieftains. (Touring continues through Europe, with 8 more UK dates, until the end of the year.)
Nov *Life During Wartime* makes US #80.

1980 **Jan** Group returns home after an exhausting tour, and all 4 take a rest from Talking Heads projects. Byrne records *My Life In The Bush Of Ghosts* with Eno.
July After completing a new album, the band considers touring again, but feels extra musicians are needed to do justice to the new material. Harrison recruits several players with whom he has been working on other projects in New York and Philadelphia.
Aug [23] Talking Heads makes its live debut in the expanded line-up at the Heatwave festival in Toronto, Canada, along with Elvis Costello, Rockpile, The Pretenders and others. The augmenting musicians are Busta "Cherry" Jones (bass), Donette MacDonald (back-up vocals), Bernie Worrell (keyboards), Steven Scales (percussion) and Adrian Belew (guitar).
[27] The 9-piece band plays again, at Wollman Rink in New York's Central Park. (This and the Canadian gig were designed to be the only showcases for the larger band, but Sire Records says it will support a tour.)
Nov *Remain In Light*, recorded in the Bahamas where the larger line-up has been playing live, peaks at US #19 and UK #33.
Dec [1-2] Group plays 2 UK shows at London's Hammersmith Palais and Odeon, during a European tour. New Irish band U2 is support act.

1981 **Mar** *Once In A Lifetime* reaches UK #14, while Byrne and Eno's *My Life In The Bush Of Ghosts* reaches UK #29 and US #44.
May *Houses In Motion* stalls at UK #50. At the end of another major tour, the band members disperse to work on individual projects.
July Frantz and Weymouth's spin-off funk group The Tom Tom Club (including Weymouth's 2 sisters sharing vocals, plus Steve Scales on percussion, Alex Weir on guitar and Tyron Downie on keyboards) hits UK #7 with *Wordy Rappinghood*.
Sept [22] "The Catherine Wheel", a ballet choreographed by Twyla Tharp, featuring Byrne's music, premieres at the Broadhurst theater on Broadway, New York. (Ballet will be shown in Mar.1983 on PBS TV.)
Oct The Tom Tom Club's *Genius Of Love* reaches UK #65, while the group's eponymous album makes US #23 and UK #78.
Nov Harrison records solo album *The Red And The Black*.
Dec Concert at Pantages theater in Hollywood, CA, is recorded for future *Stop Making Sense* release.

1982 **Jan** *Genius Of Love* by The Tom Tom Club tops US Disco chart as Byrne's album of music from "The Catherine Wheel" makes US #104.
Feb Byrne produces The B52's *Mesopotamia*.
Apr The Tom Tom Club's *Genius Of Love* crosses over to make US #31.
May Double album *The Name Of This Band Is Talking Heads*, a compilation of live performances and out-takes, reaches US #31 and UK #22. Group tours US and Europe as an 8-piece.
July [13] Band plays at the Wembley Arena, London, with The Tom Tom Club as support act.
Aug Tom Tom Club's *Under The Boardwalk* reaches UK #22.
Sept [3-5] Talking Heads plays the US Festival, financed by Apple Computers founder Steven Wozniak, in San Bernardino, CA, to 400,000 people, along with Jackson Browne, The Cars, Fleetwood Mac, The Grateful Dead, Eddie Money, Police, Santana, and many others.

TALKING HEADS cont.

Nov [4] While the group is in Nassau, the Bahamas, recording at Compass Point studios, Weymouth gives birth to son Robert.

1983 **Feb** Byrne produces UK trio The Fun Boy Three's *Waiting*.
July Self-produced *Speaking In Tongues* makes US #15 and UK #21.
Aug Jonathan Demme-directed movie "Stop Making Sense", a filmed account of Talking Heads on tour, premieres. It includes Byrne performing a version of *Psycho Killer* backed only by a cassette recorder rhythm track.
Sept The Tom Tom Club album *Close To The Bone* reaches US #73.
Oct *Burning Down The House* hits US #9, their biggest hit single to date.

1984 **Jan** *This Must Be The Place (Naive Melody)* makes US #62 and UK #51.
Apr [4] Byrne begins recording solo album at One On One studios in Hollywood, CA.
Oct *Stop Making Sense*, recorded alongside the filming of a concert at Hollywood's Pantages theater in Dec., reaches US #41 and UK #37, staying on chart for 81 weeks.
Nov A cover of The Staple Singers' *Slippery People* stalls at UK #68.

1985 **Jan** Byrne stages a solo show, illustrating (with slides) a journey across US, titled "The Tourist Way Of Knowledge", at the New York Public theater.
July *Little Creatures* makes US #20 and hits UK #10. Harrison produces Milwaukee's Violent Femmes' *The Naked Leading The Blind*, while Frantz and Weymouth work on a third Tom Tom Club album.
Sept *And She Was* begins a 5-month US chart stay, but climbs no higher than #54. Byrne releases solo *Music For The Knee Plays*, a series of musical vignettes linking longer scenes from Robert Wilson's epic opera "The Civil Wars".
Nov *Road To Nowhere*, aided by an innovative video, brings Talking Heads its only UK Top 10 success, hitting #6.

1986 **Feb** *And She Was* reaches UK #17.
May [3] Some 5 years after giving the group its first UK chart success, *Once In A Lifetime* makes US #91, following its exposure in film "Down And Out In Beverly Hills" (although this single has the live version from *Stop Making Sense*).
July Movie "True Stories", written and conceived by Byrne, premieres. A *True Stories* soundtrack from the film and a separate album of songs from it played by Talking Heads, are both released.
Sept *Wild Wild Life* makes UK #43.
Oct *True Stories* reaches US #17 and hits UK #7.
Nov Byrne/Robert Wilson's work "The Knee Plays" premieres in New York.
Dec [6] *Wild Wild Life* reaches US #25.

1988 **Apr** *Naked*, recorded in Paris with producer Steve Lillywhite (and assistance from guitarist Yves N'Djock and keyboardist Wally Badarou) and then completed in New York, makes US #19 and hits UK #3. Band disperses for a sabbatical to work on individual projects.
May Harrison's *The Casual Gods* (also the name of his 13-member backing group) appears almost immediately, and makes US #78.
Aug Byrne appears live with David Bowie in London, while *Blind* peaks at UK #59.
Sept The Tom Tom Club plays a 3-week stint at New York's CBGB's. Lou Reed and Debbie Harry make special guest appearances. Harrison's *Rev It Up*, taken from *Casual Gods*, creeps to UK #90.
Oct The Tom Tom Club's third album *Boom Boom Chi Boom Boom*, produced by Frantz and Weymouth, is released (following the duo's production work earlier in the year with Bob Marley's son Ziggy, which resulted in the latter's hit album and single *Conscious Party* and *Tomorrow's People*). Group (with guitarist Mark Roule and keyboards player Gary Posner) plays UK club tour.

1989 **Apr** Tom Tom Club's *Boom Boom Chi Boom Boom* makes US #114.
June [9] Byrne and wife Adele Lutz become parents to a daughter, Malu Valentine.
July [5] PBS TV airs Byrne's Brazilian music "Ilé Aiyé (The House Of Life)" as part of its Alive From Off Center summer season.
[18] Group makes its first appearance since the 1984 "Stop Making Sense" tour when Byrne and Harrison join Weymouth and Frantz during a Tom Tom Club gig at the Ritz, New York.
Oct [2] Byrne embarks on world tour in Japan, while Byrne album *Rei Mo Mo* peaks at US #71 and UK #52.
Nov [1-2] Byrne performs in New York during the US leg of his tour.

1990 **June** [23] Harrison's Casual Gods' *Walk On Water* climbs to US #188.
Aug Frantz, Harrison and Weymouth, waiting for Byrne's next Talking Heads move, participate in a low-key coast-to-coast US tour as part of a CBGB's new wave, now veteran retrospective package, also including other acts which played the seminal venue, including The Ramones and Deborah Harry.

Sept [25] Byrne opens a full lecture series "Speaking Of Music & Other Things" at the New School for Social Research in New York.
Oct Byrne contributes *Don't Fence Me In* to *Red Hot + Blue*, an anthology of Cole Porter songs to benefit AIDS education.

1991 **Mar** Byrne and folk veteran Richard Thompson perform an acoustic set together for Channel 4 TV "Rock Steady" at the Town Crier Pub, Pawling, New York.
Apr Byrne releases his third collection of Brazilian music, this time concentrating on "forro", called *Brasil Classics 3*.

JAMES TAYLOR

1963 Taylor (b. Mar.12, 1948, Boston, MA), the second of 5 children in a musically talented family, having spent his childhood between Chapel Hill, NC, and Milton Academy, Milton, MA, meets Danny Kortchmar in Chilmark, Martha's Vineyard, MA, where they win the local hootenanny contest.

1964 He joins older brother Alex's rock band, The Fabulous Corsairs, but shortly after commits himself to the McLean psychiatric hospital in Belmont, MA, suffering from severe depression. During his 10-month stay there, he starts writing songs.

1966 **July** He moves to New York and joins Kortchmar's The Flying Machine. They play clubs in Greenwich Village before splitting the following spring.

1968 In an attempt to overcome heroin addiction, Taylor moves to London's Notting Hill. At Kortchmar's suggestion, Taylor takes a demo tape to Apple Records A&R man Peter Asher.
Nov Asher signs Taylor.
Dec Debut album *James Taylor* is released. Unable to kick his addiction, Taylor returns to US, and enters Austin Riggs mental hospital in Stockbridge, MA.

1969 **July** Taylor makes his live debut at Los Angeles, CA's Troubadour, but his career is halted when he breaks both hands in a motorbike accident.
Dec He signs to Warner Bros. and moves to California to work with Asher on a new album. (Asher becomes his manager and will produce most of his future output.)

1970 **Mar** *Sweet Baby James* enters US chart to hit #3 (and a 2-year run).
Oct *Fire And Rain* makes US #3. *Sweet Baby James* is certified US gold. Debut album *James Taylor* is released in US, reaching #62.
Nov *Fire And Rain* reaches UK #42. *Sweet Baby James* enters UK chart, where it stays for over a year and hits #7.
Dec *Carolina In My Mind* peaks at US #67.

1971 **Feb** Euphoria Records releases *James Taylor And The Original Flying Machine – 1967*, which makes US #74.
Mar Taylor stars in Monte Hellman's film "Two Lane Blacktop" with Dennis Hopper, Warren Oates and The Beach Boys' Dennis Wilson. He begins a sell-out 27-city US tour as *Country Road* makes US #37.
[1] Taylor is featured on the cover of *Time* magazine.
Apr [6] After a performance by Carly Simon at the Troubadour in Los Angeles, James Taylor goes backstage to meet her.
May *Mud Slide Slim And The Blue Horizon* enters US and UK charts to hit #2 and #4 respectively.
July Carole King-penned *You've Got A Friend* tops US chart for 1 week.
Aug *Country Road* climbs to US #37.
Oct *You've Got A Friend* hits UK #4.
Nov *Long Ago And Far Away*, with harmony vocal contribution from Joni Mitchell, makes US #31.

1972 **Mar** [9] Taylor plays a benefit concert with many others for presidential candidate George McGovern at Los Angeles' Forum.
[12] Taylor wins Best Pop Vocal Performance, Male for *You've Got A Friend* at the 14th annual Grammy awards. The song wins its writer Carole King the Song Of The Year grammy.
Nov [3] Taylor marries Carly Simon in her Manhattan apartment. He plays New York's Radio City Music Hall that evening and announces the happy event to his audience.
Dec *One Man Dog*, with contributions from Carole King, Linda Ronstadt, Carly Simon and Taylor's brothers Alex and Hugh and sister Kate, hits US #4 and makes UK #27.

1973 **Jan** *Don't Let Me Be Lonely Tonight* reaches US #14.
Feb *One Man Parade* peaks at US #67.

1974 **Mar** Taylor duets with wife Carly Simon on Inez & Charlie Foxx's hit *Mockingbird*, which hits US #5 and reaches UK #34.
Apr [30] Taylor begins a month-long US tour in Moorehead, MN. The tour will end at the Nassau Coliseum, Uniondale, NY.
June *Walking Man*, produced by David Spinozza, makes US #13.
July [13] He starts a 3-week tour, accompanied by his band The

Manhattan Dirt Riders and special guest Linda Ronstadt.

Dec [24] Taylor and Simon join Linda Ronstadt and Joni Mitchell, singing Christmas carols on the streets of Hollywood.

975 Apr [30] Taylor begins a month-long US tour in Indianapolis, IN. The tour will end with 3 nights at New York's Carnegie Hall.

May *Gorilla*, produced by Russ Titelman and Lenny Waronker, hits US #6. Taken from it, a cover of Marvin Gaye's 1965 smash *How Sweet It Is* hits US #5.

July [2] Taylor begins a month-long US tour to promote *Gorilla*.

Nov He makes two short US tours while *Mexico* makes US #49.

976 May *In The Pocket*, again produced by Titelman and Waronker, peaks at US #16.

Sept *Shower The People* reaches US #22.

Dec Aware that Taylor is to leave the company, Warner releases *Greatest Hits*. It reaches US #23 and goes platinum. Taylor signs to CBS/Columbia Records.

977 July His cover of Jimmy Jones' 1960 smash *Handy Man*, and first CBS/Columbia album, *JT*, from which it is extracted, are produced by Asher and both hit US #4. The album goes platinum.

[26] Taylor ends a 22-date tour of the US in Pine Knob, Clarkston, MI.

Oct Taylor produces, plays guitar and sings on sister Kate's CBS/Columbia debut, a cover of Betty Everett's 1964 US #6 *It's In His Kiss (The Shoop Shoop Song)*. It makes US #49.

Nov Taylor begins a brief tour of California and Hawaii, including 4 nights at the Pantages theater, Hollywood, CA.

Dec *Your Smiling Face* reaches US #20. Country singer George Jones releases a cover of *Bartender's Blues* by Taylor, who contributes backing vocals.

978 Feb [23] Taylor wins his second Best Pop Vocal Performance, Male for *Handy Man* at the 20th annual Grammy awards. Peter Asher wins Best Producer Of The Year grammy.

Mar Taylor joins Paul Simon to sing on Garfunkel's *What A Wonderful World*, which reaches US #17. *Honey Don't Leave LA*, the third single from *JT*, peaks at US #61.

Apr Taylor and over 40 performers petition President Carter to end US commitment to nuclear power.

May *Kate Taylor*, produced by brother James and on which he plays and sings, is released.

July CBS/Columbia issues the original Broadway cast album *Working*, a musical based on the life of Studs Terkel. It contains 3 Taylor songs: *Millworker*, *Brother Trucker* (his own versions will appear on *Flag*) and *Un Mejor Dia Vendra*.

Sept A second duet with Carly Simon, a version of The Everly Brothers' 1958 hit *Devoted To You*, makes US #36.

979 May *Flag* enters US chart, to hit #10.

July Taken from it, *Up On The Roof*, a cover of The Drifters' Goffin/King-penned 1962 smash, hits US #28.

[3] Taylor begins a 25-date US summer tour, including 5 nights at Los Angeles' Greek theater, in Memphis, TN. The tour will end Aug.17 at the Greek theater, Berkeley, CA.

Sept [19] Taylor performs in the first of 5 Musicians United For Safe Energy (MUSE) concerts at New York's Madison Square Garden. The shows are filmed and recorded under the *No Nukes* banner and feature Jackson Browne, The Doobie Brothers and Bruce Springsteen.

Dec Live triple album *No Nukes* is released, featuring Taylor solo on 2 songs and others with The Doobie Brothers, Carly Simon and John Hall. It makes US #19.

980 July [19] The "No Nukes" film documentary premieres in New York.

Aug [3] Taylor begins a 23-date US tour in Memphis, TN. It will end Aug.30 at the Merriweather Post Pavilion, Columbia, MD.

Sept [24] All-star album *In Harmony*, recorded for children's TV show "Sesame Street", is released. The Taylor and Simon families feature on most of the tracks. *Jelly Man Kelly* is co-written with daughter Sarah. (The album will win a Grammy for Best Children's Recording.)

981 Feb [11] Taylor begins a 5-week US tour at the Holiday Star theater, Merrillville, IN.

Apr [25] A 47-date US tour opens at the Greek theater, Berkeley, CA as *Dad Loves His Work* hits US #10. The tour, which will include 8 sold-out shows at the Savoy, New York, will end July 4 at Belmont race track, New York.

May [2] *Her Town Too*, a post-divorce themed bitter sweet ballad and duet with J.D. Souther, makes US #11. (Souther will join tour's first leg.)

June *Hard Times* peaks at US #72.

Sept [4] Singing *Brother Trucker*, Taylor appears as a truck driver in PBS TV's "Working". (The show will be broadcast in early 1982.)

[11] Taylor begins a 17-date tour of Japan and Australia in Osaka, Japan. The tour will end Oct.10 in Adelaide, Australia.

Oct [13] On his return to the US, Taylor stops off in Hawaii, where he performs a sell-out show at the 12,000-seat NBC Arena in Honolulu.

1982 Feb [1] 30-date US tour starts at Front Row theater, Cleveland, OH.

June [9] Taylor appears with Jackson Browne and Linda Ronstadt in a "Peace Week" benefit concert at the Nassau Coliseum, Uniondale. (3 days later he will take part in another benefit in New York's Central Park in front of approximately 1 million people.)

July [14] Taylor begins a 37-date US tour in Columbia, MD.

1983 Aug [1] A 25-date US tour begins at the Blossom Music Center, Universal City, CA.

1984 Apr [4] Taylor begins the first of 3 separate US tours lasting until Sept., a 23-date trek which will end in Dallas, TX.

Aug [1] He begins his second tour in Cincinnati, OH. Randy Newman joins Taylor on the 29-date tour.

1985 Jan [12] Taylor makes the first of 2 appearance at the Rock In Rio festival, Rio de Janeiro, Brazil.

Dec *That's Why I'm Here*, Taylor's first album in 4 years and his first self-produced effort, with help from engineer Frank Filipetti, is released. The album, which features guests Joni Mitchell, Don Henley, Graham Nash, David Sanborn, The Brecker Brothers and Deniece Williams, reaches US #34 as a cover of Buddy Holly's *Everyday* peaks at US #61. He duets with country singer Ricky Skaggs on Christmas song *New Star Shining*, for his album.

1986 Mar [28] Taylor embarks on 4-date UK tour, his first in 15 years, at the Hammersmith Odeon, London.

1987 Apr A 16-track UK-only compilation *Classic Songs* makes UK #53.

1988 Mar *Never Die Young* makes US #25.

Apr [23] *Never Die Young* climbs to UK #80.

June Taylor appears in UK, before embarking on a major US tour during the summer. He duets on brother Livingston's *City Lights*.

1989 Sept [11] Taylor plays "House The Homeless" benefit concert at Harvard Stadium, Cambridge, MA.

1990 Feb Taylor sings at the Cathedral of St. John the Divine, New York with Paul Simon, Roberta Flack and Placido Domingo at a celebration for Czech President Vaclav Havel.

June Taylor embarks on major US summer tour.

1991 Feb Taylor guests on new Atlantic recording artist Marc Cohn's self-titled debut effort.

THE TEARDROP EXPLODES

Julian Cope (vocals, bass)
Michael Finkler (guitar)
Paul Simpson (keyboards)
Gary Dwyer (drums)

1978 Oct Named after a **Marvel** comic caption, The Teardrop Explodes forms from remnants of several Liverpool, Merseyside, bands. Cope (b. Oct.21, 1957, Bargoed, Wales), ex-The Crucial Three with Ian McCulloch (later of Echo & The Bunnymen) and Pete Wylie (later of Wah!), moves on to The Mystery Girls and The Nova Mob before joining Finkler and Simpson in A Shallow Madness.

Nov The Teardrop Explodes plays its first concert at Liverpool's seminal venue Eric's.

1979 Feb Group's first disk, EP *Sleeping Gas*, is released by Zoo Records.

June Simpson leaves to study, and is replaced by Dave Balfe, ex-Lori & The Chameleons and co-owner of Zoo. *Bouncing Babies* is released.

Aug The Teardrop Explodes plays at all-day open air concert in Leigh, Gtr.Manchester, with A Certain Ratio, Echo & The Bunnymen, Joy Division and OMD. An estimated 300 people witness the event.

1980 Feb *Treason (It's Just A Story)*, written by Cope with McCulloch, is the group's third single.

July Alan Gill, ex-Dalek I Love You, replaces Finkler, who leaves to go to college. Zoo signs a distribution deal with Phonogram Records.

Aug Group signs to Phonogram subsidiary Mercury.

Oct First Mercury release *When I Dream* reaches UK #47. Balfe leaves and is replaced by Jeff Hammer. *Kilimanjaro* is released, reaching UK #24 during a 35-week chart stay.

1981 Feb *Reward*, with added trumpet from "Hurricane" Smith, hits UK #6.

Mar *Kilimanjaro* is reissued to include *Reward*.

Apr Group's third single *Treason (It's Just A Story)* is remixed, climbing to UK #18.

Aug *Ha, Ha, I'm Drowning* and *Poppies In The Field* are scheduled for release, but Cope objects and some 30,000 copies are withdrawn.

Sept *Passionate Friend* reaches UK #25. Cope reorganizes the band as all but Dwyer depart. Alfie Agius, ex-Interview, briefly joins on bass while Troy Tate, ex-Shake, arrives on guitar. Balfe rejoins taking

Hammer's place (who will later join The Stray Cats). Cope becomes frontman, and switches from bass to rhythm guitar.

Nov Second album *Wilder* reaches UK #29, while *Colours Fly Away* peaks at UK #54.

Dec Club Zoo opens in Liverpool with help from the band.

1982 Jan After Agius leaves, ex-Sincero Ron Francois joins on bass.

Mar 3 Teardrop Explodes tracks are featured on the various artists compilation album *To The Shores Of Lake Placid*.

June *Tiny Children* makes UK #44.

July Francois and Tate quit, making it a trio of Cope, Dwyer and Balfe.

Nov Cope splits the band on its fourth anniversary. Balfe joins The Dumbfounding Two before forming his own management company and the Food label, while Dwyer remains temporarily with Cope.

1983 Mar Group's final single *You Disappear From View* makes UK #41.

Nov Remaining contracted to Mercury Records, Cope returns as a soloist on *Sunshine Playroom*, which peaks at UK #64.

1984 Mar First solo album *World Shut Your Mouth* reaches UK #40.

Apr From the album, *The Greatness And Perfection Of Love* makes #52.

Sept Cope releases a one-off single, *Competition*, on independent UK label Bam Caruso, under the pseudonym Rabbi Joseph Gordan.

Nov Completing his contractual obligation to Mercury, *Fried* makes UK #87 for 1 week. Cope retreats, allegedly with a drug problem.

1985 Feb Belated release of Cope's *Sunspots* on Mercury fails to chart.

June Reissue of Teardrop's biggest hits *Reward/Treason* is released.

1986 Oct Cope signs to Island Records and releases *World Shut Your Mouth*, the same title as his earlier album (although the song was not included on the album). It reaches UK #19 and raises his profile considerably, not least with an appearance on BBC1 TV's "Top Of The Pops".

1987 Feb *Trampolene*, taken from his imminent new album, reaches UK #31.

Mar Mini-album *Julian Cope* makes US #109. Third solo album *Saint Julian* (the title a reference to a tobacco brand, with allusions to his own cult status) reaches UK #11 and US #105.

Apr [4] *World Shut Your Mouth* stalls at US #84.

Eve's Volcano (Covered In Sin), taken from the album, makes UK #41.

1988 Sept *Charlotte Anne* makes UK #35.

Oct [9] Cope embarks on a 3-week UK tour.

My Nation Underground makes UK #42.

1989 Jan A revival of The Vogues' *5 O'Clock World* makes UK #42.

June *China Doll* makes UK #53.

1990 Apr [14] Teardrop Explodes' *Everybody Wants To Shag*, collecting rare old material and out-takes and released on Fontana, peaks at UK #72, though extracted *Serious Danger* and *Count To Ten And Run For Cover* fail to score.

1991 Feb [23] Cope's solo career continues as *Beautiful Love*, aided by dolphin-playing promo clip, peaks at UK #32 in advance of parent *Peggy Suicide*, a 73 min., 19 track project.

Sept Cope's first volume of autobiography, **Head On**, assessing the period 1977-82, is published.

TEARS FOR FEARS

Curt Smith (vocals, bass)
Roland Orzabal (guitar, keyboards)

1980 Smith (b. June 24, 1961, Bath, Avon) and Orzabal (b. Roland Orzabal de la Quintana, Aug.22, 1961, Portsmouth, Hants), having first met at age 13 when Smith inducted guitar-playing Orzabal into his school band in Bath, both join Graduate, a 5-piece pop/ska band influenced by the current 2-Tone sound, also including Steve Buck, Andy Marsden and John Baker. Signed to Pye's Precision label in UK, and produced by Tony Hatch, Graduate has a near-hit with *Elvis Should Play Ska* and cuts *Acting My Age*, as well as 3 unsuccessful singles (though they gain some popularity in Spain).

1981 After Graduate splits, Smith and Orzabal stay together and record demos of 2 Orzabal songs – *Suffer The Children* and *Pale Shelter* at David Lord's studios in Bath, experimenting with synth-pop. Duo's name comes from Arthur Janov's book, **Prisoners Of Pain**, concerned with Primal Therapy: confronting fears in order to eliminate them (or shedding "tears for fears"), which Orzabal has read in 1978. Demos of their first 2 songs interest Phonogram A&R man Dave Bates, who signs them to Mercury label, initially only for the 2 releases.

Nov First single *Suffer Little Children* is issued, without charting. Manny Elias (drums) and Ian Stanley (keyboards) join for live work.

1982 Mar *Pale Shelter* is released.

Nov *Mad World*, produced by Chris Hughes (early Adam And The Ants drummer), hits UK #3, and the band plays its first UK tour as support to The Thompson Twins.

Dec Group is named Most Promising New Act Of 1982 in **Smash Hits** magazine poll, and signed to a management deal with Paul King.

1983 Feb *Change* hits UK #4.

Mar *The Hurting*, further inspired by Janov's theories and produced by Hughes, hits UK #1 in its second week on chart, and will remain charted for 65 weeks in UK.

May *Pale Shelter* is reissued in a remixed version included on the album, and hits UK #5. Meanwhile, the band's US chart debut is with *The Hurting*, which peaks at US #73.

Aug *Change* is first US Singles chart entry, climbing to #73.

Dec *The Way You Are* reaches UK #24.

1984 Sept *Mother's Talk* reaches UK #14.

Dec Anthemic *Shout* hits UK #4, becoming one of 1984's top-sellers.

1985 Mar *Songs From The Big Chair*, also produced by Hughes, and featuring both keyboardist Stanley and drummer Elias, hits UK #2. Containing only 8 tracks, it will eventually go triple-platinum in UK.

Apr *Everybody Wants To Rule The World* hits UK #2, behind USA For Africa's *We Are The World*.

May Group ends a major headlining UK tour at London's Royal Albert Hall, before setting off on 18-month world concert trek.

June *Everybody Wants To Rule The World*, written by Orzabal, Smith and Hughes, tops US chart for 2 weeks, aided by a heavy-rotation video on MTV, and earns the group a gold disk.

July *Songs From The Big Chair* tops US chart for 5 weeks, turning platinum with sales over a million while, in UK, *Head Over Heels*, taken from the album, makes UK #12.

Aug *Shout* becomes their second consecutive US chart-topping single (and million-seller), holding #1 for 3 weeks.

Sept Band's first 2 singles, *Suffer The Children* and *Pale Shelter*, are reissued in UK in their original forms, charting at #52 and #73.

Oct *I Believe (A Soulful Re-Recording)*, a new version of a track from the album, reaches UK #23.

Nov *Head Over Heels* hits US #3.

1986 Feb [10] *Everybody Wants To Rule The World* wins Best British Single at the fifth annual BRIT Awards at the Grosvenor House, London. *Everybody Wants To Rule The World* briefly re-charts in UK at #73.

May [24] *Mother's Talk*, belatedly issued as a US single in a remixed version, makes US #27.

June *Everybody Wants To Run The World*, a re-written version of *Rule The World* with lyrics relating to Sport Aid's "Race Against Time", is used as theme tune for Sport Aid Week and the worldwide fun run, raising funds for African famine relief. It hits UK #5.

Nov Smith retreats from an exhausting 2 years to renovate a new house he has bought with wife Lynn, while Orzabal does the same with his wife Caroline in Chalk Farm, London.

1987 Jan Orzabal, now recognized as main songwriting force in Tears For Fears, starts work on new material with keyboardist Nicky Holland.

1988 Jan Smith gains substantial damages against UK newspapers **The Daily Star**, **The Sun** and **The News Of The World** over their stories in Oct.1986 allegedly revealing antics from his schooldays in St. Albans, Herts. (Smith had never even been to St. Albans. He gives the out-of-court settlement to his mother to buy the council flat in which she lives.)

Feb Smith and Orzabal begin work yet again in London on **Big Chair** follow-up with David Bascombe after lengthy sessions with Langer and Winstanley and then Chris Hughes have proved unsatisfactory. The featured musicians are Seattle, WA-born Oleta Adams, who the duo had discovered in Hyatt Regency restaurant, the Peppercorn Duck club, in Kansas City, MO, on their last US tour (they will subsequently write and produce songs for her May 1990 debut album *Circle Of One*), Manu Katche (drums), Neil Taylor (guitar), Pino Palladino (bass), Carole Steele (percussion) and Simon Clark (keyboards).

June [11] Smith participates in "Nelson Mandela's 70th Birthday Party" concert at Wembley Stadium, London, taking time off from recording the new album.

1989 July [15] Smith, Orzabal and Bascombe oversee the final mix of the new album at London's Mayfair studios.

Sept Beatles-celebrating *Sowing The Seeds Of Love* hits UK #5.

Oct [7] Parent album *The Seeds Of Love*, costing over £1 million to record, enters UK chart at #1, where it stays for a week.

[28] *Sowing The Seeds Of Love* hits US #2 and *The Seeds Of Love* US #8.

Nov *Woman In Chains*, featuring Phil Collins on drums and Adams on vocals, reaches UK #26.

1990 Feb [3] *Woman In Chains* makes US #36, as they tour US with Deborah Harry as their support act.

Mar [3] *Advice For The Young At Heart* makes UK #36.

[8] Group wins Best Video and Best Album Cover categories in the annual **Rolling Stone** Readers' Picks 1989 music awards.

[24] *Advice For The Young At Heart* climbs to US #89, as Oleta Adams' *Rhythm Of Life* peaks at UK #52.

May [30] Group begins major North American tour in Memphis, TN.

991 **Feb** [2] Masquerading as Johnny Panic & The Bible Of Dreams, Orzabal and Bascombe release single , also named *Johnny Panic & The Bible Of Dreams*, a re-recording of a Tears For Fears B-side (from *Advice For The Young At Heart*).

May UK specialist label Sequel issues early Graduate songs on CD.

TELEVISION

Tom Verlaine (vocals, lead guitar)
Richard Lloyd (rhythm guitar)
Richard Hell (bass)
Billy Ficca (drums)

971 Bassist/vocalist Hell (b. Richard Myers, Oct.2, 1949, Lexington, KY) forms his first group, The Neon Boys, in New York with ex-boarding-school friend Verlaine (b. Thomas Miller, Dec.13, 1949, Mt. Morris, NJ), who renamed himself after the French poet, and drummer Billy Ficca. Neither The Neon Boys nor later trio Goo Goo lasts.

973 **Dec** New Jersey guitarist Lloyd, after seeing a Verlaine solo gig, suggests they form a group. Verlaine calls up Hell, Ficca returns from his blues band job and Television is formed.

974 **Mar** Television makes its live debut at New York's Townhouse theater, and picks up a sufficient following in the New York underground for Verlaine to convince the owner of CBGB's club to feature live bands, thus establishing an important base for the city's new wave of music. Verlaine plays guitar on Patti Smith's first single, *Hey Joe/Piss Factory*, and collaborates with Smith on a book of poetry, **The Night**.

975 Brian Eno produces demos for the band for Island Records but the label does not sign them up. Hell leaves, replaced by Fred Smith. (Hell will later form The Heartbreakers with ex-New York Doll Johnny Thunders.) Television records *Little Johnny Jewel*, on its own Ork records (named after ex-manager William Terry Ork), selling enough copies to attract major record company attention.

976 Hell leaves The Heartbreakers and forms backing unit The Voidoids with Marc Bell on drums and Ivan Julian and Robert Quine on guitars. Television's EP *Blank Generation*, released on Stiff in UK, brings the group UK attention. It signs to Elektra Records.

977 **Feb** Debut album *Marquee Moon*, a critical success but with poor sales in US, is enthusiastically received in UK and makes #28.

Apr *Marquee Moon* reaches UK #30.

May [21] Group opens a US tour supporting Blondie.

Aug *Prove It* makes UK #25.

Sept Hell & The Voidoids album *Blank Generation* is released on Sire Records. (Hell tours UK with The Clash, and will sign to UK label Radar. He replaces Bell (who left to join The Ramones) with Frank Mauro in The Voidoids.)

978 **Apr** *Foxhole* makes UK #36.

May Television album *Adventure* hits UK #7. Its US sales are promising but it fails to chart.

Aug Group splits. (Smith will play with Blondie; Verlaine will go solo.)

979 **Sept** Verlaine releases solo album *Tom Verlaine* for Elektra, without success.

Dec Lloyd releases *Alchemy*, but career efforts are hampered by drug-related problems.

981 **Oct** Second Verlaine album *Dreamtime*, released through Warner Bros., reaches US #177.

982 **May** Verlaine releases *Words From The Front*. Hell releases *Destiny Street* on independent Red Star label with Fred Maher on drums.

Nov Hell makes his film debut in "Smithereens". (He will semi-retire from music and work as a journalist.)

984 **Sept** After a long silence, Verlaine releases *Cover*, on Virgin, and *Five Miles Of You* and *Let Go The Mansion*.

985 **Nov** Lloyd, having overcome his drug problems, releases *Field Of Fire*. He plays well-received comeback gigs but soon returns to obscurity.

987 **Feb** Phonogram revives the Fontana label for Verlaine's album *Flash Light*. 3 singles are released from the album, but all fail to sell, leaving the album with a 1-week chart stay at UK #99.

Mar *Cry Mercy Judge* fails to make UK Top 75. Verlaine plays a well-received gig at London's Town & Country club (but will slip out of the picture once more).

990 Lloyd is a featured member of John Doe's backing band on his album *Meet John Doe*.

THE TEMPTATIONS

Eddie Kendricks (vocals)
Otis Williams (vocals)
Paul Williams (vocals)
Melvin Franklin (vocals)
David Ruffin (vocals)

1960 Initially known as The Elgins, the group forms from members of The Primes and The Distants, both based in Detroit, MI. The Primes consisted of Kendricks (b. Dec.17, 1939, Birmingham, AL) (ex-Cavaliers, who has also formed all-girl group The Primettes to play with The Primes), Paul Williams (b. July 2, 1939, Birmingham) and Cal Osborne, and were formed in Birmingham. The Distants included Franklin (b. David English, Oct.12, 1942, Montgomery, AL), Otis Williams (b. Otis Miles, Oct.30, 1949, Texarkana, TX), Franklin's cousin Richard Street (b. Oct.5, 1942, Detroit), Albert Harrell and Eldridge Bryant. After The Distants have failed with *Come On* on Northern label, Street and Harrell leave (Street will later join The Temptations) and Kendricks and Williams are invited to join the remaining Distants to form The Elgins. (Kendricks has originally moved to Detroit after forging his brother's signature on an $82 income tax refund cheque.)

1961 The Elgins are signed by Berry Gordy Jr. to his new Motown subsidiary Miracle Records.

Aug Group is renamed The Temptations (a suggestion from Otis Williams) for their first single *Oh Mother Of Mine*.

1962 Bryant leaves after the failure of second single *I Want A Love I Can See* (now on Gordy label, where group will remain throughout its tenure with Motown) and is replaced by Ruffin (b. Jan.18, 1941, Meridian, MS). They begin working with writer/producer Smokey Robinson.

1964 **Apr** Robinson's song *The Way You Do The Things You Do*, with Kendricks on lead vocals, is The Temptations' first US hit, making #11.

June *Meet The Temptations* reaches US #95.

July *I'll Be In Trouble* makes US #33.

Sept [13] They appear in Murray The K's "Rock'N'Roll Extravaganza" at New York's Fox theater, Brooklyn, with Marvin Gaye, Martha & The Vandellas, The Supremes, The Searchers and The Ronettes.

Oct *Girl (Why You Wanna Make Me Blue)*, produced by Norman Whitfield, peaks at US #26.

1965 **Mar** Ruffin takes over lead vocal on *My Girl*, written and produced by Robinson. It tops US chart for a week, selling a million, and makes The Temptations the first male Motown group to have a #1 hit. In UK, *My Girl* makes #43, as the group arrives in London to play on the Motown package tour with labelmates Martha & The Vandellas, The Supremes and Little Stevie Wonder.

May *It's Growing*, another Robinson song, reaches US #18 and UK #45. It is taken from *The Temptations Sing Smokey*, which makes US #35.

Aug *Since I Lost My Baby* makes US #17.

Nov *My Baby* climbs to US #13 as B-side *Don't Look Back* makes US #83.

Dec *Temptin' Temptations* reaches US #11.

1966 **Apr** Robinson's final production for the group, *Get Ready*, makes US #29 and tops R&B chart.

July Norman Whitfield and Brian Holland take over production for *Ain't Too Proud To Beg*, which reaches US #13 again topping R&B chart.

Aug *Ain't Too Proud To Beg* is their first UK Top 30 hit, peaking at #21.

Sept *Gettin' Ready* makes US #12.

Oct *Beauty Is Only Skin Deep* hits US #3 and R&B #1, while also making UK #18.

Dec *(I Know) I'm Losing You* hits US #8 and R&B #1, while *Getting Ready* is group's first UK chart album, reaching #40.

1967 **Jan** *(I Know) I'm Losing You* makes UK #19.

Feb Compilation album *The Temptations' Greatest Hits* is the group's first US Top 10 album, peaking at #5. In UK, it makes #26.

June Whitfield is now the group's sole producer. *All I Need* hits US #8 and R&B #1 while *Temptations Live!* hits US #10.

July *Temptations Live!* makes UK #20.

Aug [10] Group debuts at the Copacabana with a 2-week stint.

Sept *You're My Everything* hits US #6 and UK #26, as *With A Lot O' Soul* hits US #7.

Nov *(Loneliness Made Me Realize) It's You That I Need* reaches US #14, while *With A Lot O' Soul* makes UK #19.

1968 **Jan** *The Temptations In A Mellow Mood*, which includes some Broadway standards, makes US #13.

Feb Written by Whitfield and Barrett Strong, ballad *I Wish It Would Rain*, taken from *Mellow Mood*, hits US #4 and R&B #1.

Mar *I Wish It Would Rain* makes UK #45. (The Whitfield/Strong writing team will provide the group with their next 13 hits.)

June *I Could Never Love Another (After Loving You)* reaches US #13, tops R&B chart, and peaks at UK #47, while *The Temptations Wish It Would Rain* (which shows them on the sleeve in a desert wearing Foreign Legion uniforms) climbs to US #13.

July Ruffin, after pushing for a change of the group's sound to a deeper soul style, leaves and signs to Motown as a soloist. He is replaced by Dennis Edwards (b. Feb.3, 1943, Birmingham, AL), who has sung with gospel group The Golden Wonders and with Motown's The Contours.

[9] The Temptations make their first appearance without Ruffin at the Valley Forge Music Fair, PA.

Aug *Please Return Your Love To Me* reaches US #26, and is the last single in the familiar Temptations style.

Sept Ruffin sues Motown for $5 million, alleging company has put him in peonage by blocking his making recordings and live appearances.

Dec 10-day revue begins in Detroit with The Temptations, Stevie Wonder, Gladys Knight & The Pips, Edwin Starr and Bobbie Taylor.

1969 Jan Whitfield's ideas for a different direction for the group first take shape on *Cloud Nine*, which has Edwards on lead vocal and adapts the "psychedelic soul" style pioneered by Sly & The Family Stone. It hits US #6 and R&B #2 (and will win Motown's first Grammy award, as Best Group R&B Performance). Meanwhile, the group teams with The Supremes on *Diana Ross & The Supremes Join The Temptations*, which hits US #2. Taken from this is a duetted revival of Madeleine Bell's hit *I'm Gonna Make You Love Me*, which hits US #2, behind Marvin Gaye's *I Heard It Through The Grapevine*.

Feb *T.C.B.*, the soundtrack of a TV special of the same title featuring The Supremes and The Temptations, tops US chart for a week, while the group's own album, *Live At The Copa*, makes US #15. It is the first album to feature Edwards.

Mar *Runaway Child, Running Wild*, a similar sound to *Cloud Nine* with a further socially-conscious lyric, hits US #6 and R&B #1. *Get Ready*, not a hit on original UK release, is reissued and hits UK #10.

[12] *Cloud Nine* wins Best R&B Performance By A Duo Or Group, Vocal Or Instrumental Of 1968 at the 11th annual Grammy awards.

Apr A revival of The Miracles' *I'll Try Something New*, duetted with Ross & The Supremes, reaches US #25.

May *Cloud Nine* hits US #4.

[10] Band plays at a Masquerade Ball at the White House in Washington, DC, as guests of Tricia Nixon.
Don't Let The Joneses Get You Down, again dealing with social issues, reaches US #20 and R&B #2.

Sept *Cloud Nine*, belatedly issued in UK (it was originally considered "too progressive"), reaches UK #15. Album of the same title makes UK #32. Meanwhile, the TV soundtrack album *The Temptations Show* peaks at US #24.

Oct *I Can't Get Next To You*, which has each member of the group singing lead in succession, tops US chart for 2 weeks, selling over a million, while a revival of The Band's *The Weight*, with Ross & The Supremes, makes US #46.

Dec *Puzzle People*, including *I Can't Get Next To You*, hits US #5, while *Together*, with Ross & The Supremes, makes US #28.

1970 Jan TV soundtrack album *On Broadway*, featuring The Temptations and The Supremes performing show tunes, reaches US #38.

Feb *Psychedelic Shack* hits US #7 and R&B #2 while *I Can't Get Next To You* reaches UK #13 and *Puzzle People* makes UK #20.

May *Psychedelic Shack* hits US #9.

June *Ball Of Confusion (That's What The World Is Today)* is another million-seller, hitting US #3 (and R&B #2).

July *Psychedelic Shack* makes UK #33 and the album of the same title reaches US #56.

Sept Live album *The Temptations Live At London's Talk Of The Town*, recorded in UK, reaches US #21.

Oct *Ungena Za Ulimwengu (Unite The World)* continues the formula of recent hits with sound and lyric, but peaks at US #33. Whitfield decides on a change of pace for the next release. Meanwhile, *Ball Of Confusion* is the group's highest-placed UK single to date, hitting #7.

Nov Compilation *The Temptations' Greatest Hits, II* reaches US #15.

1971 Jan *The Temptations' Greatest Hits, II* makes UK #35.

Apr With Kendricks on lead vocal, *Just My Imagination (Running Away With Me)*, a slow ballad in the group's traditional style, tops both US pop and R&B charts for 2 weeks, becoming another million-seller.

June *Just My Imagination (Running Away With Me)* hits UK #8. Kendricks leaves for a solo career (like Ruffin, staying with Motown). Paul Williams is also forced to quit the group because of poor health

(he has an alcoholism problem and a serious liver complaint). They are replaced by Damon Harris (b. July 3, 1950, Baltimore, MD) and ex-The Distants' Street.

July *The Sky's The Limit* including *Just My Imagination*, makes US #16

Aug *It's Summer*, from the album, peaks at US #51.

Dec *Superstar (Remember How You Got Where You Are)* makes US #18. By year's end, Kendricks has left band to begin a solo career, which has kicked off with a week's residence at the Apollo theater, Harlem, NY.

1972 Feb *Superstar (Remember How You Got Where You Are)* peaks at UK #32

Mar *Solid Rock* makes both US and UK #24.

Apr *Take A Look Around*, from *Solid Rock*, reaches US #30 and UK #13

July *Mother Nature* stalls at US #92.

Dec *Papa Was A Rollin' Stone*, edited from an 11-min.-plus album track with Edwards on lead vocal, tops US chart for a week, selling over a million. (The instrumental section of the song on the single's B-side will win a Grammy as Best R&B Instrumental.) *All Directions*, containing the full version, hits US #2.

1973 Feb *Papa Was A Rollin' Stone* peaks at UK #14, and *All Directions* at UK #19.

Apr *Masterpiece* hits US #7 and R&B #1, while the album of the same title also hits US #7.

July *The Plastic Man*, from *Masterpiece*, peaks at US #40 as the album reaches UK #28.

Aug [17] Paul Williams, in ill health since leaving the group in 1971, though he has continued to supervise the group's choreography, is found dead in his car. (In financial and matrimonial troubles as well as having serious health problems, he has shot himself in the head.)

Sept *Hey Girl (I Like Your Style)* makes UK #35.

Oct *Law Of The Land*, issued as single in UK but not US, makes UK #41

Nov Triple compilation album *Anthology* makes US #65.

1974 Jan *Let Your Hair Down* reaches US #27, while parent album *1990* makes US #19.

Feb Group wins Best Group R&B Performance for *Masterpiece* at the 16th annual Grammy awards.

May *Heavenly* climbs to US #43.

July *You've Got My Soul On Fire* makes US #72, (and is the group's last single to be produced by Whitfield for nearly 10 years).

1975 Feb *Happy People*, with new producer Jeffrey Bowen, makes UK #40.

Mar *A Song For You* reaches US #13.

June *Shakey Ground* makes US #26.

Aug *Glasshouse* reaches US #37. Damon Harris leaves the group and is replaced by Glenn Leonard.

1976 Feb *Keep Holding On* makes US #54. It is taken from *House Party*, which peaks at US #40.

June *Wings Of Love* reaches US #29.

July *Up The Creek (Without A Paddle)* creeps to US #94.

Oct *The Temptations Do The Temptations*, on which the group cuts members' own compositions, reaches US #53.

1978 Jan Without Edwards, who leaves to go solo and is replaced by Louis Price, The Temptations sign a new deal with Atlantic. *Hear To Tempt You*, produced by Norman Harris and Brian Holland, and mostly written by Ron Tyson (who will join the group in 1983) creeps to US #113, but with no hit singles. Group, out of the public eye at a time when new disco acts abound on the charts, settles into steady work on the club and cabaret circuits.

Nov *Bare Back* also on Atlantic, makes R&B #46 but fails to cross over

1980 June Berry Gordy, having lured the Temptations back to Motown, writes and produces their first Top 50 hit in 5 years. Edwards returns to sing the lead and *Power* makes US #43. Album of the same title reaches US #45.

1981 Oct *Aiming At Your Heart* makes US #67, while parent album *The Temptations* reaches US #119.

1982 June *Reunion* and its accompanying tour sees the brief return of Ruffin and Kendricks to the group. Album reaches US #37, while extracted *Standing On The Top, Part 1* makes US #66 and UK #53. It is written and produced by, and features, Rick James.

1983 New member Ron Tyson, a successful writer and producer, joins the group, which appears on NBC TV's Motown 25th anniversary show. A team-up on the show with The Four Tops, during which they trade medleys of oldies, leads to a joint international tour.

Apr *Love On My Mind Tonight* peaks at US #88, while *Surface Thrills* makes US #159.

1984 May Group is reunited with Whitfield for *Sail Away*, which makes US #54. *Back To Basics* climbs to US #152.

Dec *Treat Her Like A Lady*, with new lead vocalist Ali-Ollie Woodson (who has replaced Edwards), reaches UK #12. Parent album *Truly For*

You makes US #55 and UK #75.

985 **Feb** *Treat Her Like A Lady* peaks at US #48.

Oct Ruffin and Kendrick (having dropped the "s" at end of his name, although it will re-appear at a future juncture) join Daryl Hall & John Oates at the re-opening of New York's Apollo theater. They perform The Temptations' classics *The Way You Do The Things You Do* and *My Girl*, which reach US #20 and UK #58 as a medley titled *A Nite At The Apollo Live!*. Album from which the tracks come, *Live At The Apollo With David Ruffin And Eddie Kendrick*, makes US #21 and UK #32.

Dec Ruffin and Kendrick contribute to the all-star Artists United Against Apartheid combine, with *Sun City* making US #38 and UK #21.

986 **Feb** *Touch Me* makes US #146.

May *25th Anniversary* climbs to US #140.

Aug *To Be Continued* peaks at US #74.

Nov [8] *Lady Soul* makes US #47.

[15] The Temptations appear on US TV show "227" performing *Get Ready* and *Lady Soul*.

987 **July** The Temptations back Bruce Willis on his version of *Under The Boardwalk*, which hits UK #2 and US #59.

Aug *Papa Was A Rollin' Stone* is given an updated remix for the UK dance market, and climbs to UK #31.

Nov With Edwards back in line-up, *Together Again* makes US #112.

Dec Signed as a duo to RCA, Ruffin and Kendricks issue *Ruffin And Kendricks*, which makes US R&B #60, with extracted single *I Couldn't Believe It* reaching #14 on US R&B chart.

988 **Feb** Nearing the end of their third decade, The Temptations release *Look What You Started*, which makes UK #63.

989 **Jan** [18] The Temptations are inducted into the Rock'N'Roll Hall Of Fame at the fourth annual dinner at the Waldorf Astoria in New York.

Oct *All I Want From You* peaks at UK #63. It is taken from current Motown album *Special*, which rises up US R&B survey to #25.

990 The Temptations sing *Get Ready* with help from Candice Bergen, Delta Burke, Dixie Carter, Jean Smart and Gerald McRaney to promote CBS TV programs.

Mar As a duo, Kendricks and Edwards release *Get It While It's Hot*, co-penned by Jermaine Jackson, on A&B Records.

991 **May** [14] The Temptations contribute *Shake Your Paw* to jazz label GRP's Garfield tribute album *Am I Cool, Or What?*

June [1] Ruffin dies in Philadelphia of a drugs overdose.

0CC

Graham Gouldman (vocals, guitar)
ric Stewart (vocals, guitar)
ol Creme (vocals, guitar)
evin Godley (vocals, drums)

963 All 4 are members of groups in Manchester's booming beat scene. Creme (b. Lawrence Creme, Sept.9, 1947, Manchester, Gtr.Manchester) and Gouldman (b. May 10, 1945, Manchester) rehearse regularly as members of The Sabres and The Whirlwinds respectively. Brian Franks, a member of The Sabres introduces his cousin Godley (b. Oct.7, 1945, Manchester) to Creme, who immediately strike up a rapport, having made their debut at Manchester's Heaton Park Youth Club in 1960. Stewart (b. Jan.1, 1945, Manchester) is a member of Jerry Lee & The Staggerlees.

964 **Apr** Stewart joins Wayne Fontana & The Mindbenders who enjoy success in UK and US with major hits including *The Game Of Love* and *Um Um Um Um Um Um*. Godley and Creme begin studying graphic design at art college.

June Gouldman's group signs to HMV label releasing an unsuccessful cover of Buddy Holly's *Look At Me* with Creme-penned B-side *Baby Not Like Me*.

965 **Feb** Gouldman forms The Mockingbirds, with Godley on drums. They sign to Columbia label and begin a regular spot as warm-up band for UK BBC1 TV's "Top Of The Pops", transmitted from Manchester. Gouldman's first song for the group *For Your Love*, written during his lunchbreak while working at a gentlemen's outfitters, Bargains Unlimited in Salford, is rejected by Columbia, but becomes a major hit for The Yardbirds. The Mockingbirds release a clutch of singles which all flop but for The Yardbirds Gouldman writes *Heart Full Of Soul* and *Evil Hearted You*. The Hollies hit with his *Bus Stop* and *Look Through Any Window*, and Herman's Hermits enjoy a string of Gouldman-penned songs including *No Milk Today*.

Oct The Mindbenders split from Wayne Fontana and have a major hit with *A Groovy Kind Of Love*.

966 **Feb** Gouldman attempts a solo career again, signing to Decca for *Stop*

Or Honey I'll Be Gone, but without success. Gouldman debuts on Decca with *Stop! Stop! Stop!* and writes song for Connie Francis movie "When The Boys Meets The Girls".

Nov Gouldman pens *Pamela Pamela* for Wayne Fontana based on an idea for a stage production by Godley & Creme.

1967 **Mar** Another Gouldman single *Bony Maronie At The Hop* by studio aggregate Manchester Mob fails.

Apr Gouldman writes a track for The Mindbenders' *With Woman In Mind* called *Schoolgirl*, which is released as a single but is banned by UK BBC on grounds of suggestive lyrics.

1968 **Feb** Gouldman signs to RCA but 3 singles and an album *The Graham Gouldman Thing*, co-produced by Gouldman and John Paul Jones (later of Led Zeppelin) all fail to chart.

Mar Gouldman steps in as a temporary replacement for Bob Lang in The Mindbenders.

Aug He writes the group's last single *Uncle Joe, The Ice Cream Man*.

Nov After The Mindbenders split, Stewart and Gouldman invest in Inter-City recording studio in Manchester, renamed Strawberry by Stewart, from The Beatles song *Strawberry Fields Forever*.

1969 **Sept** Godley and Creme, having been working as designers for Pan Books on cut-out books based around films such as "The Railway Children" and "The Charge Of The Light Brigade", sign a contract with ex-Yardbirds manager Giorgio Gomelsky's short-lived Marmlade label and release *I'm Beside Myself*, billed as Frabjoy and Runcible, with Gouldman and Stewart playing on the session, bringing together the future members of 10cc for the first time.

Oct Gouldman spends time in New York as a staff writer for Kasenatz-Katz production team which specializes in creating "bubblegum" music for teenagers. Gouldman writes and sings lead vocal on *Sausalito (Is The Place To Go)* as Ohio Express. He also writes *Have You Ever Been To Georgia* which is a hit for a number of artists.

Nov Kasenatz-Katz books Strawberry studios for 3 months as UK branch of its operation. Gouldman and Stewart call in Godley and Creme to help on the sessions and the fledgling members of 10cc embark on a marathon bout of writing, producing and playing on records which are released worldwide under different names. Godley and Creme pen a minor US hit (under the name Crazy Elephant) *There Ain't No Umbopo*, while Gouldman writes and sings on a million-seller in France for Freddie & The Dreamers, *Susan's Tuba*.

1970 **Aug** With money from Kasenatz-Katz work, the group re-equips Strawberry studios and writes heavy rhythmic African-styled *Neanderthal Man*, to test out the new equipment. When Dick Leahy of Philips Records hears the test tape he offers the group £500 as an advance. The disk sells over 2 million copies worldwide, hitting UK #2 and US #22, under the name Hotlegs. 2 further singles and an album *Thinks: School Stinks* fail and a spot on a Moody Blues tour is cancelled when The Moody Blues' John Lodge goes down with a viral infection.

1971 The 4 concentrate on writing, producing and playing on a variety of sessions at Strawberry studios (including records by soccer teams Manchester City and Leeds United, John Paul Jones' hit *The Man From Nazareth*, and writing the material for *Space Hymns* by a central heating salesman from Sheffield called Ramases, who believes he is a reincarnation of an Egyptian god). Their most successful venture is in reviving Neil Sedaka's career with work on his albums *Solitaire* and *The Tra La La Days Are Over* and singles *That's When The Music Takes Me*, *Standing On The Inside*, *Dimbo Man* and *Our Last Song Together*.

1972 They record demos of *Donna* and *Waterfall* and Jonathan King, an old friend of Stewart's, signs them to his UK label. He names them 10cc (after the average male ejaculation 9cc, adding 1cc to indicate they are above average).

Oct *Donna*, a Godley & Creme pastiche of 50s US pop, hits UK #2. Group makes its UK TV "Top Of The Pops" debut.

Nov Follow-up *Johnny Don't Do It*, another 50s pastiche, but a teen death song, sinks without trace.

1973 **June** Group's first UK #1 hit is with jail-riot song *Rubber Bullets*, despite little radio play because of the British Army's controversial use of rubber bullets in N.Ireland.

Aug [26] 10cc makes its stage debut at the Douglas Palace Lido, Isle of Man, at the beginning of a UK tour.

Sept *The Dean And I* hits UK #10 as parent *10cc* makes UK #36.

Oct *Rubber Bullets* is the group's US chart debut, at #73.

1974 **Feb** [21] Group begins its first US tour at Club Richard, Atlanta, GA.

Mar [14] Godley is taken ill and the tour is cancelled.

May [28] A rescheduled US tour begins.

June *Sheet Music*, continuing the group's innovative writing style with subject matter ranging from a talking bomb to voodoo, hits UK #9 and makes US #81.

July *Wall Street Shuffle* hits UK #10.

Aug [23] 10cc plays UK's Reading Festival, Berks.

Sept [1] Group begins a UK tour.

Oct *Silly Love* makes UK #24.

1975 Feb They sign to Phonogram in deal allegedly worth $1 million plus.

Mar *The Original Soundtrack* hits UK #4 and US #15.

[5] Group embarks on another UK tour at Leeds University, W.Yorks. Tour will end Mar.26 at the Liverpool Empire, Merseyside.

May *Life Is A Minestrone* hits UK #7.

June *I'm Not In Love* hits UK #1 and US #2, where it will stay for 3 weeks, behind 3 different #1s. (Group was reticent about releasing this plaintive Stewart-sung ballad, with a multiplicity of overdubbed backing vocals, but UK airplay forces its release and radio listeners will consistently vote it into all-time Top 10 lists in coming years.) *10cc – The Greatest Hits* hits UK #9 and climbs to US #161.

July Group appears at Cardiff Castle, Wales, supported by Steeleye Span and Thin Lizzy.

Oct 10cc begins a third US tour, and appears on The Moody Blues' Justin Hayward and John Lodge's *Blue Guitar*.

1976 Jan *Art For Art's Sake* hits UK #5, but stalls at US #83.

Feb *How Dare You?* hits UK #5 and makes US #47.

[7] Group begins a 14-date UK tour at Edinburgh's Usher Hall, Scotland, ending Feb.22 at Birmingham Odeon, W.Midlands.

Apr *I'm Mandy Fly Me* hits UK #6 and reaches US #60.

Aug [21] Group appears at UK's Knebworth Festival, Herts., with The Rolling Stones.

Oct Godley and Creme announce they are quitting the group to develop a new musical instrument – the "Gizmo", a guitar attachment which can hold notes and create orchestral sounds for a long period. They plan to record a single showcasing its effect, but recording leads to a triple album *Consequences* and a long-term duo career. Gouldman and Stewart carry on with 10cc and open Strawberry South studio in a former cinema in Dorking, Surrey. They become a trio when drummer Paul Burgess joins full time after working on previous tours.

1977 Jan *Things We Do For Love* hits UK #6.

Apr *Things We Do For Love* hits US #5.

May *Good Morning Judge* hits UK #5 as parent *Deceptive Bends*, with Stewart and Gouldman playing all instruments, hits UK #3 and makes US #31. Group begins a UK tour, adding Stuart Tosh on drums, Rick Fenn on guitar and Tony O'Malley on keyboards.

June *People In Love* makes US #40.

Sept *Good Morning Judge* peaks at US #69.

Dec Double live *Live And Let Live*, from the May tour, highlighting *Deceptive Bends* and Stewart/Gouldman compositions from the classic 10cc era, reaches UK #14 and US #146.

1978 Mar Duncan Mackay joins on keyboards.

Sept *Dreadlock Holiday* hits UK #1. The reggae song is inspired by Justin Hayward's experience on holiday in the Caribbean. *Bloody Tourists* hits UK #3 and makes US #69.

Nov *Dreadlock Holiday* makes US #44.

1979 Feb *For You And I*, from John Travolta/Lily Tomlin film "Moment By Moment", stalls at US #85.

July Gouldman makes UK #52 with the title theme to Farrah Fawcett film "Sunburn".

Oct *Greatest Hits 1972-1978* hits UK #5, but stalls at US #188.

1980 Apr *Look Hear?* makes UK #35 and US #180. Gouldman releases music from the animated feature album *Animalympics* (and will later produce The Ramones and Gilbert O'Sullivan.) Stewart writes music for French film "Girls" and produces Sad Café.

1982 Apr Stewart teams with Paul McCartney to play on the latter's *Tug Of War*, and appears in the group line-up for the video of McCartney's hit *Take It Away*.

Aug *Run Away* is the group's final chart single at UK #50. (It is the only 1 to chart from 11 releases since *Dreadlock Holiday*.)

1983 Oct *Windows In The Jungle* makes UK #70, after which the group splits. (Gouldman will have some success as one half of Wax, with Andrew Gold.)

1986 Apr Wax's *Right Between The Eyes* peaks at UK #60.

May [10] *Right Between The Eyes* makes US #43.

1987 Aug Wax's *Bridge To Your Heart* reaches UK #12.

Sept 10cc hits are included on *The Changing Faces Of 10cc And Godley And Creme* which hits UK #4. Wax's *American English* peaks at UK #59.

10,000 MANIACS

Natalie Merchant (voices)
Robert Buck (guitars)
John Lombardo (guitars)
Steven Gustafson (bass)
Jerry Augustyniak (drums)
Dennis Drew (keyboards)

1981 Jan Gustafson and Drew join Still Life whose line-up already includes Buck. They begin performing local gigs, playing mostly cover versions of late 70s UK new wave acts including Joy Division and Gang Of Four. Merchant, who has met Gustafson in 1980 when he is running the campus radio station with Drew at the Jamestown Community College, Jamestown, NY, where she is studying, joins. Band, also augmented by Lombardo, changes its name, mistakenly taking it from a B-movie horror-pic "2,000 Maniacs".

1982 Extended to a 6-piece, 10,000 Maniacs add folk and country influences. They release a 5-track EP, *Human Conflict Number Five*, on their own Christian Burial Records, which sells mainly at their concerts. The tracks are recorded as projects for the sound engineering program at the State University of New York at Fredonia.

1983 Now including drummer Augustyniak and commuting between London and New York, the band releases debut album *Secrets Of The Ching*, again on its own US label and distributed throughout a US East Coast tour. The album is licensed for independent UK distribution and tops the relevant chart, while New York-based Englishman Peter Leak becomes the group's manager.

1984 Band signs a worldwide recording deal with Elektra.

1985 *The Wishing Chair* is released. Recorded at Livingstone studios in London, it is produced by Joe Boyd. Comprised entirely of songs written by Merchant and Lombardo, it receives rave critical reviews in US and UK, but fails to chart.

1986 July Founding member Lombardo quits, and the 4 remaining males will construct music around Merchant's lyrics. (Lombardo, after a period of silence, will re-emerge with a debut album on Rykodisc, with guests Augie Meyers and Ronnie Lane, before teaming with Mary Ramsey as John & Mary, releasing *Victory Gardens* in 1991.)

1987 June 10,000 Maniacs tour behind R.E.M. in US.

July [29-30] Band performs at the Cambridge Folk Festival, Cambs.

Aug *In My Tribe*, produced by Peter Asher, is released and is again highly rated by critics. It tops the US college charts, becoming a student favorite (and will climb to US #51 in Sept.1988).

Nov 10,000 Maniacs begin a successful UK tour.

1988 Feb Merchant performs a solo showcase at London's Donmar Warehouse, preceding a similar low-key set by Tracy Chapman.

June *Like The Weather* reaches US #68.

Oct *What's The Matter Here* makes US #82.

1989 May [20] Second Asher-produced set, *Blind Man's Zoo* begins 12-week US chart stint during which it peaks at #44 and UK #18. Extracted *Trouble Me* will also reach US #44, while *Eat For Two*, Merchant's observations on pregnancy will become a hot modern airplay track, as group embarks on major US tour.

Nov [3] *Rubáiyát*, Elektra's 40th anniversary compilation, to which group contributes a cover of Jackson Browne's *These Days*, makes US #140.

[10] *Hope Chest*, a repackaging of tracks from the first 2 10,000 Maniacs projects, now released by Elektra, peaks at US #102. Also known as "The Fredonia" recordings, it collects 14 recordings between 1982-83, newly remixed by Joe Barbaria.

1991 Apr [20] 10,000 Maniacs take part in the "Earth Day 1991 Concert" at Foxboro Stadium, Foxboro, MA, with Billy Bragg, Jackson Browne, Rosanne Cash, Bruce Cockburn, Bruce Hornsby & The Range, Indigo Girls, Queen Latifah, Ziggy Marley, Willie Nelson and others.

TEN YEARS AFTER

Alvin Lee (guitar, vocals)
Leo Lyons (bass)
Chick Churchill (keyboards)
Ric Lee (drums)

1965 Aug Group forms in Nottingham, Notts., as The Jaybirds, when Alvin Lee (b. Dec.19, 1944, Nottingham) and Lyons (b. Nov.30, 1943, Standbridge, Beds.), who have been in a trio of the same name which has played clubs in Hamburg, Germany, team with Ric Lee (b. Oct.20, 1945, Cannock, Staffs.) from Nottingham group The Mansfields. They

play hard, guitar-based R&B around the North of England club circuit.
Band moves to London, playing a 6-week stint as stage band for play "Saturday Night and Sunday Morning", then backing The Ivy League on tour.

66

Nov They contact Chris Wright of Chrysalis agency with a view to management, and he takes them on. Churchill (b. Jan.2, 1949, Mold, Wales) joins, and the band changes its name to Ten Years After (following a single Marquee gig as The Blues Yard).

67

Oct Signed via Chrysalis to Decca, the band's debut album *Ten Years After* is released on new "progressive" Deram label, without charting and no single accompanies it. (Band will release very few singles, particularly in UK, during its album-dominated career.)

68

Oct Their chart debut live album *Undead*, makes UK #26 and US #115.

69

Feb [28] US tour begins at the Fillmore East in New York.

Mar *Stonedhenge* hits UK #6 and peaks at US #61.

July Ten Years After participates in the Newport Jazz Festival at Newport, RI – the only occasion that rock bands play at the festival.

Aug [15] Band plays the Woodstock Festival in US, where Alvin Lee's lightning guitar technique proves a festival-stopper. Success of the act here has much to do with Ten Years After's subsequent US acceptance (the band will play much of its 8 months per year touring US). Lee's 11-min. guitar trip on *I'm Going Home* is filmed for film "Woodstock".

Oct *Ssssh* hits UK #4 and US #20.

70

May *Cricklewood Green* hits UK #4 (band's most successful UK album, staying charted for 27 weeks) and US #14, while *Love Like A Man*, extracted from it, peaks at US #98.

Aug *Love Like A Man* is the band's only UK singles chart entry, hitting #10. It couples the studio album cut of the song with a long B-side live version which plays at 33rpm.

71

Jan *Watt* hits UK #5 (last big-selling UK album) and makes US #21.

Sept [18] Group begins first UK tour in 18 months at the Coliseum, London.

Nov *I'd Love To Change The World* reaches US #40. It is taken from *A Space In Time*, which introduces electronics as a counter to the guitar, and is band's biggest-selling US album, reaching #17 and earning a gold disk for a half million sales. In UK, where the band's chart presence is fading, it peaks at #36. It is their first album released via a new deal with CBS/Columbia in US and Chrysalis Records in UK.

72

Jan *Baby Won't You Let Me Rock'N'Roll You* reaches US #61.

May Compilation *Alvin Lee And Company*, rounding up early tracks, is released by Deram in US and makes #55.

Oct *Rock'N'Roll To The World* makes UK #27 and US #43.

Dec *Choo Choo Mama* stalls at US #89, ending the band's short run of hit singles.

73

July Double live *Recorded Live* makes UK #36 and US #39.

74

Feb Lee records *On The Road To Freedom* with US gospel singer Mylon LeFevre, plus guest players Steve Winwood, Jim Capaldi, George Harrison and Ron Wood. It reaches US #138. Churchill releases solo *You And Me*, which does not chart.

Mar After most of a decade on the road, including 28 lucrative but grueling US tours, Lee decides that Ten Years After has run its useful course, and it breaks up.

[22] Band plays its final UK concert, at London's Rainbow.

June Act's last album, *Positive Vibrations*, makes US #81 but fails to chart in UK.

Sept Lee forms Alvin Lee & Co., initially a one-off band to play the gig which is recorded as *In Flight*, and then an augmented unit to tour promoting it.

75

Feb Double live *Alvin Lee & Co: In Flight* reaches US #65.

July Ten Years After regroups for one-off farewell US tour (40 dates through July and Aug.).

Sept Lee's solo *Pump Iron!* makes US #131.

76

Mar Lee forms another version of Alvin Lee & Co. for a UK/European tour, and to record tracks for an album (which is not released).

78

Feb After an inactive year, Lee forms 3-piece Ten Years Later, with Tom Compton on drums and Mick Hawkesworth on bass, and signs to RSO Records.

July Ten Years Later's *Rocket Fuel*, credited to Lee, makes US #115.

79

June Ten Years Later's *Ride On*, again credited to Lee, makes US #158.

80

May Ten Years Later splits, but Lee is only off the road for a few weeks before he puts together The Alvin Lee Band with Steve Gould (guitar), Mickey Feat (bass) and Tom Compton (drums). The band tours and cuts *Freefall* for Atlantic Records and makes US #198. (He will continue to tour with short-lived backing groups throughout the early-mid 80s.)

86

Lee's *Detroit Diesel* with Lyons from Ten Years After and George Harrison, makes US #124.

1988 German promoter asks original band to reform for 4 festivals in Germany.

1989 **Oct** [1] US tour begins as *About Time*, produced by Terry Manning and released on Chrysalis, makes US #120.

THE THE

Matt Johnson (vocals, guitar)

1980 **July** East Londoner Matt Johnson, having played in bands since age 11, including rock outfit Road Star, and having left school at 16, eventually to work for a music publisher in London where he meets Colin Tucker and John Hyde, with whom he forms alternative music outfit The Gadgets, forms the The, with Keith Laws. Through cartoonist friend Tom Johnstone, the duo enlists the production help of Wire's Graham Lewis and Bruce Gilbert on their debut demo. The results interest 4AD indie label boss Ivo Watts, who releases debut one-off single *Controversial Subject*.

1981 Laws loses interest in the project, and Johnson, now with Johnstone and drummer Peter Ashworth, returns to the studio to record 2 further tracks, *Time Again For The Golden Sunset* and *The River Flows East In Spring*, subsequently taping an entire album, now planned as a solo project for Johnson. He releases the resulting album *Burning Blue Soul* under his own name on 4AD, but will revert to The The for all future releases.

1982 **Dec** Now signed to Some Bizzare, label boss Stevo has secured licensing deal for The The to CBS/Epic Records, which releases *Uncertain Smile* (following the unsuccessful and unreleased project *The Pornography Of Despair*), featuring Squeeze member Jools Holland on piano. It reaches UK #68.

1983 **Feb** Follow-up *Perfect* fails to chart, as The The plays 5 nights at the Marquee club, London.

Nov *Soul Mining*, based entirely around Johnson's ideas, songs and production, but featuring Holland, Zeke Monyaka and Thomas Leer, makes UK #27, after *This Is The Day* reaches UK #70, its 12" featuring cuts from *Pornography Of Despair* sessions. Album will go UK gold.

1984 **June** 4AD Records re-releases his 1980 solo album *Burning Blue Soul*, but with new sleeve artwork by longtime girlfriend Fiona Skinner.

1985 During a period of introspection and songwriting in preparation for his next album, Johnson contributes new The The track, *If You Can't Please Yourself, You Can't Please Your Soul* to Some Bizzare compilation, *Flesh And Bones*.

1986 When *Sweet Bird Of Truth* is due for release, CBS/Columbia fails to promote it (the song's story of a US fighter pilot lost in Arab territory is close to current world affairs in Libya). The label is also advised to take down the US flag at its London offices for fear of a Libyan bomb attack. Further problems with a censored sleeve hinder its chart progress.

July *Heartland* is also controversial, but reaches UK #29.

Sept Politically critical *Infected* is released as an album, with a full-length video and accompanying book illustrated by Johnson's brother, Andy Dog, who designs all The The releases covers, after 2 years in the making. Johnson used 62 musicians, 3 producers and 5 video directors filming in 4 different countries. With extensive promotion, the album reaches UK #14 and *Infected* single makes UK #48. Johnson announces that The The will not be touring to support the project.

1987 **Jan** *Slow Train To Dawn*, featuring Neneh Cherry on backing vocals, peaks at UK #64.

Mar *Infected* makes US #89.

May *Sweet Bird Of Youth* makes UK #55.

1989 **Apr** *The Beat(en) Generation*, introducing ex-Smith Johnny Marr as a new The The member, reaches UK #18 and becomes a hot US college airplay track.

May *Mind Bomb* hits UK #4, and will make US #138 as The The embarks on a major world tour, its first.

July *Gravitate To Me* peaks at UK #63.

Oct [7] *Armageddon Days Are Here* stalls at UK #70.

1990 **Mar** [7] The The, comprising Johnson, Marr and ex-ABC's James Filer (bass) and David Palmer (drums), ends North American tour at the Wiltern theater, Los Angeles, CA.

1991 **Mar** [2] EP *Shades Of Blue* makes UK #54.

THEM

Van Morrison (vocals)
Billy Harrison (lead guitar)
Jackie McCauley (piano)
Alan Henderson (bass)
Patrick McCauley (drums)

1963 Group is formed in Belfast, N.Ireland, with Morrison (b. George Ivan, Aug.31, 1945, Belfast), Harrison (b. Oct.14, 1942, Belfast), Henderson (b. Nov.26, 1944, Belfast), Eric Wrixen (piano) and Ronnie Mellings (drums). One of the first R&B/beat groups in N.Ireland (dominated by conservative "showbands"), it builds its reputation as a strong live act during a residency in the R&B club at Belfast's Maritime hotel.

1964 **July** Wrixen leaves to join The Wheels and Mellings quits to become a milkman. McCauley brothers Jackie (b. Dec.14, 1946, Coleraine, N.Ireland) (piano) and Pat (b. Mar.17, 1944) (drums) replace them. Group moves to London and signs to Decca.
Sept Debut single *Don't Start Crying Now* fails to chart, but sells well in Belfast.

1965 **Feb** Aided by "Ready Steady Go!" TV appearances, *Baby Please Don't Go*, a sharp R&B version of a blues standard, hits UK #8. Like most later recordings, it is made without much contribution from the band's own players; the producers Tommy Scott and Bert Berns back Morrison on vocals with session men like Jimmy Page on guitar and Peter Bardens on piano. B-side, little-played in UK at the time, is Morrison-penned *Gloria*, a riff-driven group favorite which frequently develops live into a 20-min. jam. It becomes an anthem to the US emerging garage band generation: basic repertoire alongside *Louie Louie*. (It will be Them's most enduring number and one of the most influential records of the 60s, despite lack of early chart success.)
Apr *Here Comes The Night*, written and produced by Berns (writer of *Twist And Shout* and *Hang On Sloopy*), hits UK #2. It is Them's biggest, but last, UK success. (Berns, an American working in London, cut *Here Comes The Night* the previous Nov. with Lulu. It made UK #50. He will work extensively with Them, mainly because he is impressed with Morrison as a vocalist. After this hit, he will return to US to launch his own Bang label, bringing success to The Strangeloves, The McCoys and many others.) *(The Angry Young) Them* is released in UK, but does not chart. Group heard is mostly Morrison and session men, which causes the disillusioned McCauley brothers to quit and form their own similar R&B band, The Belfast Gypsies. Harrison leaves to work for the Irish post office. Bardens joins for a while, and John Wilson (b. Nov.6, 1947) comes in on drums.
[11] Band plays at the **New Musical Express** Poll Winners Concert at the Empire Pool, Wembley, London. Morrison's distinctive vocals are the focus of Them's live appeal, which otherwise suffers from a lack of visual image due to the ever-changing line-up.
May *Gloria* charts for a week at US #93, selling mostly in California, where it hits Top 10 in some West Coast cities.
June Morrison-penned *One More Time* fails to chart in UK.
July *Here Comes The Night* reaches US #24.
Aug *(It Won't Hurt) Half As Much*, written by Berns, is another UK chart failure.
Sept *Them* makes US #54.
Dec *Mystic Eyes*, a Morrison-penned, harmonica-led rave-up from the album makes US #33. Group line-up has now semi-stabilized as: Morrison, Henderson, Wilson, Jim Armstrong (b. July 24, 1944) on guitar, and Ray Elliott (b. Sept.13, 1943) on piano and saxophone. Group's second album credits this quintet.

1966 **Jan** *Them Again*, mixing R&B standards with some originals, fails to chart in UK. Wilson leaves and is replaced on drums by Terry Noone.
Apr Band (with Dave Harvey on drums) tours US, playing mainly California dates, including the Fillmore in San Francisco, and the Troubadour in Los Angeles.
May Aided by the group's live presence, *Gloria* climbs to US #71, but a US cover by The Shadows Of Knight hits US #10. *Them Again* reaches US #138.
June Them's return to UK coincides with the release on Decca of a cover of Paul Simon's *Richard Cory*. It fails to sell, and the group splits. Morrison returns to Belfast. (He will play some gigs with friends including Eric Bell, later of Thin Lizzy, before flying to US at Berns' invitation to sign to Berns' Bang label and begin a successful solo career. Them will re-group in Los Angeles in 1967, in its final line-up but with Belfast vocalist Ken McDowell in Morrison's place. 2 US albums on Tower label will appear in 1968 without charting, and the group will continue until the early 70s, re-recruiting some of its earliest

members for a while but without further success.)

1972 **Aug** Double *Them Featuring Van Morrison*, a compilation of Decca material, reaches US #154.

THIN LIZZY

Phil Lynott (vocals, bass)
Scott Gorham (guitar)
Brian Robertson (guitar)
Brian Downey (drums)

1969 Group is formed in Dublin, Eire, by Lynott (b. Aug.20, 1951, Dublin, Eire, of Brazilian and Irish parents), at 3 sent to live with his grandmother in Crumlin, Dublin and at 16 joining covers band Black Eagles and Downey (b. Jan.27, 1951, Dublin), who have been at school together and have played variously or together in Skid Row, Sugar Shack and Orphanage (whose version of *Morning Dew* was a success in N.Ireland). They recruit Bell (b. Sept.3, 1947, Belfast, N.Ireland), earlier briefly with Them, whom they have met while in Orphanage, and start to play gigs around N.Ireland, sometimes fly-posted as "Tin Lizzie".

1970 **Nov** Alerted by the group's Irish reputation as a strong live act, Decca's A&R man investigates, and signs Thin Lizzy to the label. Trio moves to London to play club gigs, but UK debut at the Speakeasy club in London is not a success.

1971 **Apr** Debut album *Thin Lizzy* is released by Decca, and fails to chart. Trio tours with Arrival and Worth, but dates are poorly attended.

1972 **Mar** *Tales From A Blue Orphanage* also fails.

1973 **Feb** *Whiskey In The Jar*, a guitar riff-driven rock version of a folk tune, is a surprise UK hit, at #6.
May *Randolph's Tango* fails to chart.
Sept *Vagabonds Of The Western World* (not including *Whiskey In The Jar*, which the band disowns) has a heavier rock stance but still fails.
Dec [18] Group returns to N.Ireland after a short tour of Germany and Denmark.

1974 **Jan** Bell leaves to stay in Ireland. Gary Moore, ex-Skid Row with Lynott, is recruited as guitar replacement. (He will only stay for 4 months before leaving to join Jon Hiseman's Colosseum.)
May Guitarists Andy Gee (ex-Steve Ellis' band) and John Cann (ex-Bullitt) are brought in for an already-contracted tour of Germany.
June Full-time guitarists Brian Robertson (b. Sept.12, 1956, Glasgow, Scotland) and Scott Gorham (b. Mar.17, 1951, Santa Monica, CA) join.
Aug A new recording deal is signed with Phonogram's progressive rock label, Vertigo.
Oct Debut Vertigo single *Philomena* and *Nightlife* are released, but neither charts.
[4] New line-up makes its stage debut, at Aberystwyth University, Wales, and follows with a UK club and college tour.

1975 **Mar** Lynott contracts hepatitis.
June Group tours UK, including a major headlining gig at London's Roundhouse.
July [12] Thin Lizzy and 10cc headline an open-air festival at Cardiff Castle in Wales.
Sept *Fighting* is the group's first chart album, at UK #60. It includes *Still In Love With You*, with guest vocalist Frankie Miller. Band tours UK again to promote the album.
Nov *Wild One* is released, without success.

1976 **Mar** [5] Group begins a 15-date UK tour at Sheffield University, S.Yorks., which will end Mar.20 at Liverpool Stadium, Merseyside.
July *Jailbreak* is the band's breakthrough, hitting UK #10 in a 50-week chart run, and also US chart debut, reaching #18 and earning a gold disk. From it, *The Boys Are Back In Town* hits UK #8 and US #12.
Aug Extracted title song from *Jailbreak* makes UK #31.
Oct *Cowboy Song* is the band's second (and last) US chart single, at #77.
Nov *Johnny The Fox* reaches UK #11 and US #56.

1977 **Jan** Robertson is forced to leave after his hand is badly cut following a brawl at London's Speakeasy club. He is unable to play on a 10-week US tour supporting Queen, and Gary Moore returns to replace him.
Feb *Don't Believe A Word*, from *Johnny The Fox*, reaches UK #12.
May Moore returns to Colosseum (from which he has been "on loan") and Robertson, having recovered and toured with Graham Parker & The Rumour deputizing for Brinsley Schwarz, rejoins Thin Lizzy for the recording of *Bad Reputation* in Toronto, Canada.
July Group headlines the Reading Festival, Reading, Berks.
Sept *Dancin' In The Moonlight (It's Caught Me In The Spotlight)*, taken from *Bad Reputation*, reaches UK #14.
Oct *Bad Reputation* hits UK #4 and makes US #39.
Nov Group plays a UK tour (ending with 2 dates at London's

Hammersmith Odeon in Dec.).

978 **June** Double live album *Live And Dangerous* hits UK #2 (and will stay on UK chart for 62 weeks). From it, live medley *Rosalie/Cowgirl's Song* reaches UK #20.
Aug Robertson quits again, to form Wild Horses; Moore rejoins again.
Sept Double live album makes US #84.

979 **Mar** *Waiting For An Alibi*, from the group's next album, hits UK #9.
May *Black Rose (A Rock Legend)* is their second consecutive UK #2 album, held from the top by *The Very Best Of Leo Sayer*. Meanwhile, Moore's solo single on MCA, *Parisienne Walkways* hits UK #8. Moore plays guitar on the disk, with Lynott as guest vocalist.
July *Do Anything You Want To* reaches UK #14, while *Black Rose (A Rock Legend)* makes US #81.
[17] Moore is sacked by the band's management during a US tour. He is replaced by ex-Slik and Rich Kids (and future Ultravox) guitarist Midge Ure.
[28] Group appears at the "World Series Of Rock" concert at Cleveland Stadium, OH, along with Journey, Ted Nugent and Aerosmith.
Aug Ure, never intended as a permanent guitarist in the band, stays with it for a tour of Japan after the US visit, before leaving for Ultravox.
Nov *Sarah* reaches UK #24.
[12] Guitarist Snowy White (ex-Pink Floyd live band) replaces Ure.

980 **Feb** [13] Lynott marries Caroline Crowther, daughter of UK TV personality Leslie Crowther.
Apr Lynott releases his first solo single, *Dear Miss Lonely Hearts*, making UK #32.
May Lynott's solo album *Solo In Soho* reaches UK #28.
June *Chinatown*, the title track from the group's forthcoming album, reaches UK #21.
July Lynott's solo *King's Call*, a tribute to Elvis Presley, makes UK #35.
Oct *Chinatown* hits UK #7. From it *Killer On The Loose* hits UK #10. (Its lyrics cause controversy in the wake of the Yorkshire Ripper killings.)
Dec *Chinatown* peaks at UK #120.

981 **Mar** Lynott's solo *Yellow Pearl* makes UK #56.
Apr TV-promoted compilation *Adventures Of Thin Lizzy* hits UK #6.
May EP *Killers Live*, including *Bad Reputation, Are You Ready* and *Dear Miss Lonely Hearts*, reaches UK #19.
Aug *Trouble Boys* peaks at UK #53.
Dec *Renegade* halts at UK #38. This is the last album to feature White, who leaves for a solo career (and spell with Whitesnake), and is replaced by ex-Tygers Of Pan Tang guitarist John Sykes.

982 **Jan** Lynott's solo *Yellow Pearl* is reissued, this time climbing to UK #14, when it is selected as the new theme tune to BB1 TV's "Top Of The Pops". It also appears on his second solo album, *The Philip Lynott Album*, which does not chart.
[20] Lynott appears with Rick Derringer and Charlie Daniels in a UNICEF benefit show at the Savoy hotel, New York.
Mar *Hollywood (Down On Your Luck)*, from *Renegade*, peaks at UK #53. In US, *Renegade* climbs to #157.
Apr [22] Group begins an 8-date UK tour which will end May 1 at London's Dominion theater.

983 **Mar** *Thunder And Lightning*, the group's final studio set, featuring new member Darren Wharton on keyboards, hits UK #4. Taken from it, *Cold Sweat* reaches UK #27.
May Extracted title song from *Thunder And Lightning* reaches UK #39.
June *Thunder And Lightning* makes US #159.
Aug Band splits, Lynott feeling that it has become predictable and directionless. Final chart single, *The Sun Goes Down*, peaks at UK #52.

84 **Dec** Double *Life – Live*, recorded live before the split, reaches UK #29. Its tracks feature all ex-Thin Lizzy guitarists in spotlighted roles.

85 **Feb** The double live album creeps to US #185. Grand Slam, a group including Lynott and Downey, fails to secure a recording deal. Lynott goes solo again to cut unsuccessful *Nineteen*, with Paul Hardcastle producing (but not the same song as the latter's own hit of that title).

86 **Jan** [4] Lynott dies of liver, kidney and heart failure and pneumonia. (Following an overdose, he has been in a coma for 8 days.) He is buried in Howth, his grave overlooking Dublin Bay.
May [17] Thin Lizzy re-forms for a one-off date at the Self Aid concert in Dublin, its act a tribute to Lynott, with Bob Geldof handling vocals.

91 **Feb** [16] Following UK #40 placing for Jan. release *Dedication*, 13-track *Dedication – The Very Best Of Thin Lizzy* hits its UK peak at #8.

THE THOMPSON TWINS

Tom Bailey (vocals, keyboards)
Joe Leeway (percussion)
Alannah Currie (vocals, saxophone, percussion)

1977 Aspiring classical pianist Bailey (b. June 18, 1957, Halifax, W.Yorks.), having met friends Leeway (b. 1957, London) and John Hadd at teacher training college, initially ignores these associations and forms The Thompson Twins (named after 2 characters in Hergé's cartoon **Tin Tin**), with guitarists Peter Dodd and John Roog in Chesterfield, Derbys.

1978 They move to London with Hadd as agent and link up with drummer Chris Bell. Equipped with a van and a PA, they begin constant London gigging in pubs and clubs with the pledge that they can play anywhere, anytime (whi h they do for 2 years), active not least for the "Rock Against Racism" cause.

1980 **May** Group's first release, *Squares And Triangles*, is on its own independent Dirty Discs label.
July [21] Group plays at the Hope & Anchor pub in London.
Nov Another independent label, Latent, releases *She's In Love With Mystery*, which becomes a UK Independent chart-topper. Bailey begins dating Currie (b. Sept.20, 1959, Auckland, New Zealand).

1981 **Feb** Band signs to Arista Records in UK and first release on the Tee label, *Perfect Game*, fails to chart.
June Ex-Japan saxophonist Jane Shorter is recruited to help Bailey, Dodd, Roog and Bell record debut album **A Product Of ...**, which sees *Animal Laugh* extracted as a single.
Aug During a tour to promote releases, Currie joins the band on percussion. Old friend Leeway, until now a roadie, is also invited by Bailey to join after the group buys him a pair of bongos.
Sept *Make Believe* is released.

1982 **Jan** Shorter is fired. Bassist Matthew Seligman (ex-Soft Boys) is recruited as Bailey becomes frontman.
Mar *Set*, produced by Steve Lillywhite, is promoted by live performances and makes UK #48. Taken from it, *In The Name Of Love* becomes a hot US club hit (#1 on Dance chart). *Set* is released in US as *In The Name Of Love* and reaches US #148.
Apr After a successful UK university/college tour, a US visit is offered. Manager Hadd turns it down, firing Bell, Dodd, Seligman and Roog. Bailey and the record company realize The Thompson Twins as a trio is the way ahead. (Seligman will play live with David Bowie while Bell will join Spear Of Destiny, Specimen and Gene Loves Jezebel.)
May After *Runaway* is released without success, Arista drops the Tee subsidiary and releases all future product on the main label.
Oct First Arista disk *Lies* makes UK #67, starting a string of chart hits.

1983 **Jan** Relying on Bailey's songwriting skill, *Love On Your Side* hits UK #9.
Mar *Quick Step And Side Kick*, produced by Alex Sadkin in Nassau with Grace Jones guesting, hits UK #2. It is released in US as *Side Kicks* and will peak at #34 after a 25-week run. *Lies* reaches US #30, aided by good club and dance support.
Apr *We Are Detective* hits UK #7 and features Currie's vocals for the first time.
May *Love On Your Side* makes US #45.
July *Watching* makes UK #33.
Nov *Hold Me Now*, introducing a firm slow style, hits UK #4.

1984 **Feb** *Doctor Doctor* hits UK #3. Third album *Into The Gap* hits UK #1. (In US it will be on chart for over a year and hit #10 after 6 months.)
Mar *You Take Me Up* hits UK #2.
June *Sister Of Mercy* reaches UK #11.
July *Doctor Doctor* reaches US #11 while the group is on a world tour.
Sept *You Take Me Up* makes US #44.
Nov *Lay Your Hands* reaches UK #13. US-only release *The Gap* peaks at #69. Bailey contributes keyboards on Foreigner's future #1, *I Want To Know What Love Is*.

1985 **Mar** Having toured endlessly for 2 years, and now writing and producing a new album, Bailey falls sick through exhaustion. Current live work is suspended and US producer Nile Rodgers is recruited to complete the project.
July Bailey recuperates in time for the group's appearance at Live Aid concert in Philadelphia, PA. Madonna joins them for their set, which includes a version of The Beatles' *Revolution*.
Aug Anti-drug themed *Don't Mess With Doctor Dream* reaches UK #15.
Sept Nearly a year after its UK success, *Lay Your Hands On Me* hits US #6, and is included on *Here's To Future Days* which hits UK #5. Also from it, *King For A Day* reaches UK #22.
Dec A cover of *Revolution* peaks at UK #56.

1986 **Feb** *Here's To Future Days* reaches US #20.

Mar [22] *King For A Day* hits US #8.

Sept [13] The Thompson Twins' title track for newly-released Tom Hanks/Jackie Gleason movie "Nothing In Common" makes US #54.

Dec Leeway, frustrated with growing internal friction, quits the group leaving Bailey and Currie as The Thompson Twins. (Currie is made honorary Cultural Ambassador for New Zealand.)

1987 Jan Major tour dates are postponed as Currie goes through serious personal problems and re-scheduled UK gigs are cancelled.

Mar Following promotion at Montreux Music Festival in Switzerland, first single as a duo, *Get That Love*, peaks at UK #66.

May *Close To The Bone*, produced by Rupert Hine, makes UK #90 for 1 week and peaks at US #76.

[16] *Get That Love* makes US #31.

June *Long Goodbye* is the first UK single for 5 years not to chart.

1988 Apr Currie and Bailey have their first child.

Sept *Greatest Mixes*, a collection of hits and remixes, makes US #175.

Oct A remix of *In The Name Of Love* makes UK #46.

1989 Oct *Big Trash*, first fruits of a major new recording contract with Warner Bros., makes US #143.

Nov [18] *Sugar Daddy* reaches US #28.

1990 Mar [24] Stylus TV-advertised *The Greatest Hits*, reaches UK #23.

1991 Mar Bailey travels to New York to remix second Warner Bros. album, tentatively titled *Queer*.

THREE DOG NIGHT

Danny Hutton (vocals)
Cory Wells (vocals)
Chuck Negron (vocals)
Mike Allsup (guitar)
Jimmy Greenspoon (organ)
Joe Schermie (bass)
Floyd Sneed (drums)

1968 Group is formed in Los Angeles, CA, by Hutton (b. Sept.10, 1946, Buncrana, Eire, and raised in US), an ex-freelance producer and a session singer with Hanna-Barbera Productions, who has had a solo hit (US #73 in 1965) with self-penned (and produced) *Roses And Rainbows*. After auditioning unsuccessfully for The Monkees, he conceives the idea of a rock group with a triple lead singer line-up and enlists Wells (b. Feb.5, 1944, Buffalo, NY), whom he has produced for MGM as a member of The Enemies, and Negron (b. June 8, 1942, The Bronx, New York, NY), who has previously recorded as a soloist (without success) for CBS/Columbia. The backing quartet of Greenspoon (b. Feb.7, 1948, Los Angeles, CA), Sneed (b. Nov.22, 1943, Calgary, Canada), Allsup (b. Mar.8, 1947, Modesto, CA) and Schermie (b. Feb.12, 1945, Madison, WI) is assembled from a variety of background influences, from Los Angeles session work to country, gospel and backing José Feliciano. Group name derives from an Australian expression (in the outback, the colder the night, the more dogs you sleep beside to share warmth: coldest is a 3-dog night).

Nov Signed to Lou Adler's Dunhill label, group records eponymous debut album with producer Gabriel Mekler, mainly comprising cover versions. (Group's forte will always be personalized versions of outside writers' material, which sees the group running against the grain of most late 60s/early 70s rock, but results in it being early champions of writers like Randy Newman, Harry Nilsson, Laura Nyro and Leo Sayer.) First single *Nobody* fails to chart.

Dec [28] Group appears at the Miami Pop Festival in Hallendale, FL, to 100,000 people, on a bill with Chuck Berry, Fleetwood Mac, Country Joe & The Fish, Joni Mitchell, Canned Heat and many more.

1969 Apr From debut album, a revival of *Try A Little Tenderness*, based on Otis Redding's 1967 soul version, is group's first US chart single, at #29.

June A Harry Nilsson song, *One*, the last single taken from *Three Dog Night*, hits US #5 and is group's first million-seller. During a 62-week chart stay, the album climbs to US #11 and will be the first of 12 consecutive gold albums.

Sept Group's version of *Easy To Be Hard* (from rock musical "Hair") hits US #4, earning the second gold single. It is taken from *Suitable For Framing*, which reaches US #16 and sells over a half million copies in US during 74 weeks on chart.

Nov Also from the album, cover of Nyro's *Eli's Coming* hits US #10.

1970 Jan *Captured Live At The Forum*, recorded on stage in Los Angeles, hits US #6.

Mar Bonner/Gordon's gospel-styled *Celebrate* reaches US #15.

June Group's first #1 is a revival of Randy Newman's *Mama Told Me (Not To Come)*, previously cut by Eric Burdon as an album track. It holds #1 for 2 weeks and is the third million-selling single. It is also included on *It Ain't Easy*, produced by Richard Podolor (who had engineered the previous album), which hits US #9.

Sept *Mama Told Me (Not To Come)* is band's UK chart debut, hitting #3 (It will have no consistent UK chart success.)

Oct *Out In The Country*, also from *It Ain't Easy*, reaches US #15.

Dec *One Man Band*, from the band's next album, reaches US #19.

1971 Jan *Naturally* makes US #14 and earns another gold disk.

Apr Closing track from *Naturally*, *Joy To The World* (first presented to group by its composer Hoyt Axton via a rendition in the recording studio) is their second US #1, holding for 6 weeks (despite Axton himself reportedly being disappointed by it). With sales over 2 million it is the biggest-selling single of 1971 in US, and also the biggest seller both for the group and for Dunhill Records. Meanwhile, compilation *Golden Bisquits*, rounding up singles to date, hits US #5.

June *Joy To The World* makes UK #24, group's second and final UK hit.

July On tour in Europe, group hears the reggae arrangement of *Black And White* by Greyhound (then UK #6) and determines to record it.

Aug Russ Ballard's song *Liar* (originally cut by Ballard's group Argent) hits US #7.

Dec *An Old Fashioned Love Song*, written by Paul Williams, hits US #4 and is the group's fifth million-selling single. It is taken from *Harmony*, which hits US #8.

1972 Feb Also from the album, *Never Been To Spain*, another Axton song (and later performed live by both Tom Jones and Elvis Presley) is a further million-seller, hitting US #5.

Apr *The Family Of Man* reaches US #12.

Sept Group has its third (and final) US #1 and sixth million-selling single with *Black And White*, the song expressing racial harmony heard in Europe the previous summer (though written in 1955 by Earl Robinson and David Arkin, in response to the 1954 US Supreme Court ruling banning segregation in US schools). It is included on *Seven Separate Fools*, which hits US #6.

Dec *Pieces Of April*, written by Dave Loggins, peaks at US #19.

1973 May Double live *Around The World With Three Dog Night*, recorded on various worldwide tour dates, reaches US #18.

June [20] Group appears on 20th anniversary special of Dick Clark's "American Bandstand" on US TV, along with Little Richard and Paul Revere & The Raiders.

July *Shambala* hits US #3, becoming their seventh million-selling single. Schermie leaves, and is replaced on bass by Jack Ryland. A new keyboards player, Skip Konte, also joins, making the group 8-piece.

Nov *Cyan*, including *Shambala*, peaks at US #26, but earns a gold disk for a half million sales.

Dec *Let Me Serenade You*, from *Cyan*, reaches US #17.

1974 May Group covers Leo Sayer's chart-topper *The Show Must Go On*, hitting US #4. It is group's final million-selling single and is also on album *Hard Labor*, which reaches US #20.

Aug *Sure As I'm Sittin' Here* makes US #16.

Nov *Play Something Sweet (Brickyard Blues)* peaks at US #33.

1975 Feb Compilation *Joy To The World – Their Greatest Hits* reaches US #15, and is last of the group's 12 consecutive gold albums.

July [3] On the opening night of a US tour, Negron is arrested in his hotel room in Louisville, KY, and charged with cocaine possession. (The charge will be dropped in court in Oct., on the grounds that the warrant used for the arrest was issued on "unfounded information".)

Aug Dunhill is absorbed into parent company ABC, and group's first album on the new label, *Coming Down Your Way*, peaks at US #70. From it, Dave Loggins' song *'Til The World Ends* is group's final US Singles chart entry, peaking at #32.

1976 May *American Pastime* stalls at US #123, despite continuing success i live work. Immediately after, Hutton leaves and is replaced by new vocalist Jay Gruska. 3 former members of Rufus, Al Ciner, Ron Stocker and Denny Belfield, join the expanded backing band, as the band becomes more a cabaret soul revue but splits before making any more recordings.

1981 June After varied solo work (Hutton has produced new wave bands i Los Angeles, including Fear), group re-forms for live work in US, around the original vocal nucleus of Hutton, Negron and Wells.

1983 Sept Three Dog Night's *Joy To The World* receives exposure again whe featured in movie "The Big Chill".

1989 Aug Various group members appear in court to fight for the rights to the band name for the purpose of touring.

TIFFANY

1984 13-year-old Tiffany (b. Tiffany Renee Darwish, Oct.2, 1971, Norwalk, CA) visits producer George Tobin and sings country songs in his office. He is impressed by her raw talent and becomes her manager, producer and general mentor.

1986 She signs a worldwide contract with MCA Records, through Tobin's production company.

1987 **Sept** *Tiffany* is released and promoted across US on a "School Spirit Tour" with The Jets.
Oct [8] Tiffany appears on NBC TV's "Tonight" show.
Nov [7] First single from the album, a remake of Tommy James & The Shondells' *I Think We're Alone Now*, tops US chart. Further promotion, prior to returning to school for her junior year, includes the "Tiffany Shopping Mall Tour '87". It involves 3 shows each weekend in busy US shopping malls where Tiffany performs free for passing consumers. This innovative idea generates enormous media interest including a popular spot on NBC TV's "Tonight" show. (She will return to high school in Norwalk, to begin her junior year.)

1988 **Jan** *I Think We're Alone Now* is released in UK and tops UK chart. Tiffany arrives to great media hoopla but fails to find any malls.
[23] *Tiffany* hits US #1.
Feb [6] Ballad *Could've Been* also tops US chart as *Tiffany* hits UK #5.
Mar *Tiffany* is confirmed quadruple platinum (4 million units) in US. Tiffany runs away from problems with her mother Janie Williams to her grandmother in La Mirada, CA. *Could've Been* hits UK #4.
Apr *I Saw Him Standing There*, a gender-amending remake of The Beatles' 1964 US #14 smash, hits US #7.
[2] A court gives Tiffany's aunt a temporary custody order to become the teenager's guardian.
June *I Saw Him Standing There* hits UK #8. The court issue is resolved. Janie Williams resumes guardianship over her daughter and royalties already due to Tiffany are placed in trust.
July *Feelings Of Forever* makes US #50 and UK #52.
Dec [10] Second album *Hold An Old Friend's Hand* is released, set to reach US #17 and UK #71, while extracted *All This Time* will hit US #6, and *Radio Romance* reaches UK #13.

1989 **Jan** [25] Tiffany is presented with a platinum disk for *Hold An Old Friend's Hand* in a shopping mall in Los Angeles.
Feb *All This Time* makes UK #47, while *Radio Romance* peaks at US #35.
Apr [4] She sings the national anthem on opening day of the baseball season at Anaheim Stadium.
Sept [12] A Los Angeles Superior Court judge orders Jeff Deane Turner of Santa Cruz, CA, to stay at least 200 yards away from Tiffany. The defendant, described as an obsessed fan, had written numerous letters to the singer, including one which states "that God wants us to be together".

1990 Tiffany plays the voice of Judy Jetson in "Jetsons: The Movie", and contributes 3 songs. She begins work on her third MCA album with producer Maurice Starr, projecting the teen star, now separated from Tobin and with New Kids On The Block manager Dick Scott, at a more mature audience.
Dec Third album *New Inside*, with New Kid On The Block Donnie Wahlberg guesting, and extracted single, the Diane Warren-penned *Here In My Heart* are released, but neither charts.
[23] Tiffany sings at Fort Campbell, KY, home of the 101st Airborne Division's Screaming Eagles, before a crowd of 4,000 children, whose parents are serving in Saudi Arabia.

1991 **Feb** [10] Tiffany joins with nearly 100 celebrities in Burbank, CA to record *Voices That Care*, a David Foster and fiancee Linda Thompson Jenner-composed and organized charity record to benefit the American Red Cross Gulf Crisis Fund.
Mar [9] Tiffany appears in Fox TV's "Totally Hidden Video".

THE TOKENS

Hank Medress (tenor vocals)
Jay Siegel (baritone vocals)
Mitch Margo (tenor vocals)
Phil Margo (bass vocals)

1955 Group is formed as The Linc-Tones at Lincoln high school, Brooklyn, New York, by Medress (b. Nov.19, 1938, Brooklyn) and Neil Sedaka, the other members being Eddie Rabkin and Cynthia Zolitin, and performs at hops and dances.

1956 Siegel (b. Oct.20, 1939, Brooklyn) replaces Rabkin, and group records *I*

Love My Baby for small Melba label, to only minor local interest.

1958 Sedaka leaves to develop his songwriting career and signs to RCA as a soloist. Zolitin also departs. Medress and Siegel draft in replacements and become Daryl & The Oxfords for a year, to little success.

1959 **Dec** Margo brothers Phil (b. Apr.1, 1942, Brooklyn) and Mitch (b. May 25, 1947, Brooklyn) join and group is renamed The Tokens.

1960 **July** The Margos and Medress write *Tonight I Fell In Love*, a determined effort to create a hit song. Group records it privately, then hawks it around New York record companies.

1961 **May** Sold as a one-off to Morty Kraft's Warwick label, *Tonight I Fell In Love* climbs to US #15. The Tokens audition for producer/songwriters Hugo (Peretti) and Luigi (Creatore) at RCA.
Oct RCA debut is a revised version of Paul Campbell's African folk-based *Wimoweh*, one of the group's audition songs, for which Hugo and Luigi, with songwriting partner George Weiss, have written English lyrics, re-titling it *The Lion Sleeps Tonight*.
Dec *The Lion Sleeps Tonight* tops US chart for 3 weeks, earning a gold disk for million-plus sales. Additional vocalist Joseph Venneri joins the group to fill out the sound for live appearances.

1962 **Jan** *The Lion Sleeps Tonight* reaches UK #11, the group's only UK success. Meanwhile, it signs a production deal with Capitol, independent of its recording contract with RCA, and sets up its own company, Big Time Productions, in New York.
Feb Follow-up *B'Wa Nina*, a similar pseudo-African blend, peaks at US #55 while debut album *The Lion Sleeps Tonight* makes US #54.
Mar Only weeks after The Tokens' hit, Scottish folk/pop singer Karl Denver takes *Wimoweh* in its traditional form to UK #4.
July *La Bomba*, a re-working of Ritchie Valens' hit *La Bamba*, makes US #85.

1963 **Mar** The group's first major production success is with The Chiffons' *He's So Fine*, which tops US chart. (Several other Chiffons' production successes will follow.)
Aug *Hear The Bells* stalls at US #94, and is The Tokens' last hit on RCA.

1964 **Sept** Group forms its own B.T. Puppy label (B.T. standing for Big Time), debuting with The Four Seasons-influenced *He's In Town*, written by Goffin and King, which climbs to US #43. (The Rockin' Berries' cover hits UK #3.)

1966 **Apr** *I Hear Trumpets Blow*, written by the group, reaches US #30, and is its final hit on its own label.
May *I Hear Trumpets Blow* creeps to US #148.
Aug The Happenings, a vocal quartet from Paterson, NJ, is signed to B.T. Puppy, and produced by The Tokens on a revival of The Tempos' *See You In September*, which hits US #3. (There will be 7 more Tokens-produced Happenings US hits over the next 2 years, including another #3 with *I Got Rhythm*.)

1967 **May** The Tokens are signed to Warner Bros., and reach US #37 with a revival of Steve Lawrence/Matt Monro's ballad hit *Portrait Of My Love*.
Aug *It's A Happening World*, also on Warner, peaks at US #69 while B.T. Puppy album *Back To Back* offering a side apiece by The Tokens and The Happenings, makes US #134.

1969 **Dec** After a lean period, group resurfaces on Buddah Records with *She Lets Her Hair Down (Early In The Morning)*, an adaptation of a Silvikrin TV commercial jingle which it has also performed. It reaches US #61.

1970 **Mar** Final Tokens hit single, again on Buddah, is a revival of The Beach Boys' *Don't Worry Baby*, peaking at US #95. The group also records an album for Buddah, *Both Sides Now*, which includes remakes of most of its earlier hits but does not chart.
Oct Medress leaves group to concentrate on production and begins a new string of successes in collaboration with Dave Appell, producing Tony Orlando-led group Dawn. (The group is named after Dawn Siegel, daughter of Tokens' member Jay.) The Tokens continue performing as a trio.

1972 **Mar** Medress produces a new version of *The Lion Sleeps Tonight* by Robert John, which hits US #3 and is also a million-seller.

1973 **Oct** Siegel and the Margo brothers, signed to Atco under the new name of Cross Country, reach US #30 with a harmony update of 1965 Wilson Pickett hit *In The Midnight Hour*. (This is their only success and they will split a year later, moving into various production and writing areas, Phil Margo into movie work, acting and writing screenplays.)

1981 **Oct** [3] Several years after group has quietly dissolved, Margo, Margo, Medress and Siegel are reunited for a final reunion/farewell show as The Tokens, at Radio City Music Hall, New York.

1982 **Mar** *The Lion Sleeps Tonight* is updated by UK group Tight Fit with an 80s dance beat, and hits UK #1.

1988 **Aug** The Tokens, reformed by Siegel, revive *The Lion Sleeps Tonight* in contemporary style for small Downtown label.

THE TORNADOS

Alan "Tea" Caddy (lead guitar)
George Bellamy (rhythm guitar)
Roger Lavern (keyboards)
Heinz Burt (bass guitar)
Clem Cattini (drums)

1961 **Sept** London-based session musicians Caddy (b. Feb.2, 1940, Chelsea, London), Bellamy (b. Oct.8, 1941, Sunderland, Tyne & Wear), Lavern (b. Roger Jackson, Nov.11, 1938, Kidderminster, Hereford & Worcs.), Burt (b. July 24, 1942, Hargin, Germany) and Cattini (b. Clemente Cattini, Aug.28, 1939, London) are recruited by independent UK producer Joe Meek. Cattini and Caddy are ex-members of Johnny Kidd's Pirates, while Burt is a protege of Meek, who feels his teutonic good looks will give the group's visual image a focus. Meek uses them as session men to back his solo artists on record and plans to record them as an instrumental group with a prominent keyboard sound to challenge The Shadows' guitar-led grip on the instrumental market.

1962 **Feb** After playing first live dates supporting singer John Leyton, group becomes Billy Fury's onstage backing unit, playing on record sessions for Meek behind Leyton, Don Charles, Michael Cox and Alan Klein.
Apr Meek records The Tornados on his instrumental composition *Love And Fury* (a deliberate reference to their stage "boss"), and signs them to Decca. Released as their debut single, it fails to chart.
July They accompany Fury during his summer season at the Windmill Theatre, Great Yarmouth, Norfolk.
Aug Inspired by the recently-launched (July 10) Telstar communications satellite, Meek writes instrumental *Telstar*, tailored to The Tornados' style, with futuristic sound effects.
Oct *Telstar* tops UK chart for 5 weeks. (It will sell 910,000 in UK.)
Dec *Telstar* tops US chart for 3 weeks, the first single by a UK group ever to do so. The chart-topping pattern is repeated worldwide with sales over 5 million.

1963 **Jan** Burt leaves to go solo as a vocalist, using his first name Heinz, but Meek remains his producer. He is replaced on bass by Chas Hodges of The Outlaws, then by Tab Martin.
Feb *Globetrotter*, a Meek tune with *Telstar*-clone sound and arrangement hits UK #3, making it the third instrumental in UK top 5. (*Diamonds* by Jet Harris and Tony Meehan displaced The Shadows' *Dance On* at #1.) *Telstar*, a US-only release, climbs to #45.
Mar Martin leaves to form another Meek-produced group, The Saints (who back Heinz on stage). Brian Gregg, ex-Johnny Kidd's Pirates, replaces him. *Ridin' The Wind*, is released in US and peaks at #63.
Apr *Robot* makes UK #17, while the group appears in UK pop movie "Just For Fun", playing *All The Stars In The Sky*.
May First Heinz single *Dreams Do Come True* (later recorded by The Tornados as an instrumental album track) is from UK film "Farewell Performance", in which Heinz features and which has a score by Meek.
June Soundtrack album *Just For Fun* reaches UK #20. *The Ice Cream Man* reaches UK #18.
July EP *Tornado Rock* is released. A departure from their usual sound, it contains revivals of rock classics *Ready Teddy*, *My Babe*, *Long Tall Sally* and *Blue Moon Of Kentucky*.
Aug Lavern, Bellamy and Gregg leave for solo and session work, and are replaced by Jimmy O'Brien, Brian Irwin and Ray Randell.
Sept Heinz, long an ardent Eddie Cochran fan, hits UK #6 with tribute song *Just Like Eddie*, written by Meek.
Oct The Tornados' *Dragonfly* makes UK #41. They appear with Billy Fury on *We Want Billy!*, recorded live on stage.
Dec *Country Boy* by Heinz makes UK #26, but his solo album *Tribute To Eddie* does not chart. The Tornados split with Fury.

1964 **Jan** The Tornados' first UK album *Away From It All* fails to chart. The once revolutionary sound of the group is now, in the context of Merseybeat and Beatlemania, out of date. Caddy leaves and is replaced by Stuart Taylor from Screamin' Lord Sutch's group.
[3] Group undertakes its final engagement with Billy Fury in Amsterdam, Holland.
Feb *Hot Pot* fails to chart followed by *Monte Carlo* and *Exodus* (released by Decca in Apr. and Aug.)
Mar Heinz reaches UK #26 with *You Were There*.
Oct On Columbia, Heinz makes UK #39 with *Questions I Can't Answer*.

1965 **Jan** Also on Columbia, The Tornados release *Granada*, with no success.
Feb Cattini, the last remaining original Tornado, leaves to become drummer and leader of Division Two, the touring band behind UK hitmakers The Ivy League. (He will move to constant session work, drumming on records by most major UK names of the 60s and 70s.)

Mar Heinz reaches UK #49 with *Diggin' My Potatoes*. (He will move into cabaret work, before fading from sight and later returning in 70s rock'n'roll revival shows.)
Apr Cattini releases *No Time To Think* as the Clem Cattini Orchestra.
May [21] Band re-forms as Tornados '65, releasing *Early Bird*, named after another communications satellite, on Columbia.
Sept Group records theme from TV puppet adventure "Stingray".

1966 **Aug** Following 2 more non-chart singles, *Pop Art Goes Mozart* and *Is That A Ship I Hear?*, The Tornados (who have had fluctuating personnel since Cattini left) disband, mostly moving to studio session work.

1967 **Feb** [3] Joe Meek dies (on the eighth anniversary of Buddy Holly's death), apparently from self-inflicted shotgun wounds to the head.

TOTO

Bobby Kimball (lead vocals)
David Paich (keyboards, vocals)
Steve Lukather (lead guitar)
Steve Porcaro (keyboards, vocals)
David Hungate (bass)
Jeff Porcaro (drums, percussion)

1978 Group is formed in Los Angeles, CA by 6 noted sessionmen: brothers Jeff (b. Apr.1, 1954, Los Angeles) and Steve Porcaro (b. Sept.2, 1957, Los Angeles), sons of jazz percussionist Joe Porcaro, their boyhood friend Paich (b. June 25, 1954, Los Angeles), son of bandleader/arranger Marty Paich, who has previously played in Rural Still Life with Jeff, and Hungate (b. Los Angeles), Lukather (b. Oct.21, 1957, Los Angeles) and Kimball (b. Robert Toteaux, Mar.29, 1947, Vinton, LA.), with whom the first 3 have co-performed for several years, behind acts including Jackson Browne, Aretha Franklin and Barbra Streisand, and as back-up band on Boz Scaggs' hit albums *Silk Degrees* and *Down Two Then Left* in 1976 and 1977. The Toto name is partly a simplification of lead singer Kimball's real surname, partly after the dog in "The Wizard Of Oz".

1979 **Jan** Debut single *Hold The Line*, written by Paich, hits US #5, selling over a million, while eponymous first album, produced by Toto, hits US #9, and also becomes a million-seller, securing an enthusiastic AOR (adult oriented rock) live following. Recorded in Hollywood, 8 of the 10 cuts are written by Paich.
Mar *I'll Supply The Love*, taken from the album, makes US #45, while *Hold The Line* is UK chart debut at #14.
Apr *Toto* peaks at UK #37.
June *Georgy Porgy*, with guest vocals by soul songstress Cheryl Lynn, makes US #48.
Dec Hard rock follow-up *Hydra*, produced by the band with Tom Knox, makes US #37, earning a gold disk.

1980 **Mar** *99*, from the second album, reaches US #26. (All band members will remain highly respected and in-demand writers and session musicians in between Toto projects and will individually contribute to much of the best-selling mainstream US music of the 80s.)

1981 **Feb** Self-produced *Turn Back* makes US #41.
1982 **July** *Toto IV* is the group's most successful album, hitting US #4 and selling over a million. From it, *Rosanna* (a tribute to Lukather's girlfriend, actress Rosanna Arquette) stays at US #2 for 5 weeks, behind both Human League's *Don't You Want Me* and Survivor's *Eye Of The Tiger*, and is also a million-seller.
Sept *Make Believe*, also from *Toto IV*, reaches US #30.

1983 **Feb** *Africa*, written by Paich and Jeff Porcaro, tops US chart for a week, and is another million-seller. It also hits UK #3.
[23] Toto dominates the 25th annual Grammy awards, winning 6 awards: Record Of The Year, Best Vocal Arrangement For Two Or More Voices and Best Instrumental Arrangement Accompanying Vocal (all for *Rosanna*) and Album Of The Year, Best Engineered Recording and Producer Of The Year (the group itself) for *Toto IV*.
Apr *Rosanna*, reissued in UK as follow-up to *Africa*, reaches UK #12.
May Ballad *I Won't Hold You Back* hits US #10.
July *Waiting For Your Love* peaks at US #73, while *I Won't Hold You Back* makes UK #37.

1984 Hungate leaves, to be replaced on bass by third Porcaro brother Mike (b. May 29, 1955, Los Angeles). Shortly after, Kimball also departs for a solo vocal career, and is replaced by Dennis "Fergie" Fredericksen (b. May 15, 1951). (Kimball will re-emerge in Frank Farian-masterminded heavy group Far Corporation, which hits with a carbon copy revival of Led Zeppelin's *Stairway To Heaven*.)
Aug Toto is commissioned to write the theme for the 1984 Los Angeles Olympic Games.
Dec *Stranger In Town* climbs to US #30, but parent album *Isolation*

peaks at US #42 and UK #67.

85 **Jan** Band members are instrumental in helping to record the backing track for the historic USA For Africa recording. The group's wholly instrumental soundtrack album from science fiction movie "Dune" (on which the group is accompanied by the Vienna Symphony Orchestra) receives poor reviews, and struggles on the chart at US #168.
Feb *Holyanna* peaks at US #71.

86 **Nov** *Fahrenheit*, the first to feature new singer Joseph Williams (who has previously recorded a solo album for MCA and has been a backing singer for Jeffrey Osborne) makes US #40 and UK #99. It also features guest appearances from Miles Davis, Michael McDonald, Don Henley and others.
[22] Taken from it, ballad *I'll Be Over You*, written by Lukather with Randy Goodrum, reaches US #11.

87 **Feb** [14] *Without Your Love*, taken from *Fahrenheit*, makes US #38. Keyboardist Steve Porcaro quits the line-up and is not replaced, but will continue to contribute in a reduced capacity.

88 **Apr** *The Seventh One*, with almost identical album cover to the first release, makes US #64 and UK #73. Guest vocalists include Jon Anderson and Linda Ronstadt. Consistent with the previous 6 albums, there is at least 1 cut named after a woman: *Pamela*, which is extracted as a single and reaches US #22.

90 After a lengthy period of silence, Toto, now comprising Paich, Lukather and Jeff and Michael Porcaro, returns with new lead vocalist Jean-Michel Byron. Forthcoming album, *Past And Present 1977-1990*, features 4 new tracks with Byron's vocals.
Sept [18] Toto begins 16-date European tour at the Forest National, Brussels, Belgium. It will end Oct.9 at London's Hammersmith Odeon.
[22] *Past To Present 1977-1990* makes US #153.

TRAFFIC

Steve Winwood (vocals, keyboards, guitar)
Dave Mason (vocals, guitar)
Chris Wood (flute, saxophone)
Jim Capaldi (drums, vocals)

967 **Apr** [2] Winwood (b. May 12, 1948, Birmingham, W.Midlands) leaves The Spencer Davis Group at the height of its success after 3 years and forms a new band with 3 friends from UK Midlands: former Spencer Davis roadie Mason (b. May 10, 1947, Worcester, Hereford & Worcs.), ex-Sounds of Blue player Wood (b. June 24, 1944, Birmingham) and Capaldi (b. Aug.24, 1944, Evesham, Hereford & Worcs.), who has played with Mason in The Hellions. Signed to Island Records, they cut a debut single, then retreat to a cottage in rural Berkshire, to rehearse, write and prepare their first album.
July *Paper Sun*, written by all 4 group members, and with lead vocal by Winwood, hits UK #5.
Sept *Paper Sun* makes US #94 for 1 week, as the group makes its live debut in Oslo, Norway.
Oct *Hole In My Shoe*, penned by Mason and featuring his lead vocal, hits UK #2. (It will also be a UK #2 hit 17 years later in a spoof revival by Neil from the "Young Ones" TV series.)
[4] Group embarks on UK tour, with The Young Rascals, at Finsbury Park Astoria, London.
Dec [29] Mason leaves after differences of musical opinion with Winwood and goes to US to play initially with Delaney & Bonnie before working solo. He is not replaced and Traffic continues as a trio. Meanwhile, *Here We Go Round The Mulberry Bush* hits UK #8; it is the theme from UK movie of the same title, a romantic teen drama starring Barry Evans and Judy Geeson. Traffic's *Utterly Simple* is also heard on the film's soundtrack, with contributions from The Spencer Davis Group and others. Group also appears in The Beatles TV fantasy "Magical Mystery Tour".

968 **Jan** Album *Mr. Fantasy* hits UK #8.
Mar *No Name, No Face, No Number*, from the album, makes UK #40, and will be group's last UK hit single.
May Mason rejoins group to contribute to sessions for second album.
June *Mr. Fantasy* (which has a different track content from the UK release, and includes *Paper Sun* and *Hole In My Shoe*), reaches US #88.
[10] Group plays the Zurich rock festival in Switzerland, with Jimi Hendrix and Eric Burdon & The Animals.
Sept *Feelin' Alright*, from the forthcoming album, fails to chart.
Oct Mason quits for the second time.
Nov *Traffic* hits UK #9. Its most-aired track, *You Can All Join In*, is not released as a UK single (though sells well on import from Europe), but its wide exposure helps boost album sales.

1969 **Jan** Traffic splits as Winwood leaves to join Eric Clapton, Rick Grech and Ginger Baker in Blind Faith. Keyboards player Wynder K. Frog (Mick Weaver) joins Capaldi, Mason and Wood, and they briefly become Wooden Frog, but split after just 2 months of rehearsal. *Traffic* reaches US #17.
[7] Capaldi and Wood both attend Winwood's first gig with Blind Faith, a free concert in London's Hyde Park.
July Having failed to chart in UK, *Last Exit*, recorded as a farewell package before the split, reaches US #19.

1970 **Feb** After the demise of Blind Faith, and having spent a month with Ginger Baker's Airforce, Winwood records a solo album. Capaldi and Wood join the sessions and, with the results working well, it is decided to make it a Traffic album. The original producer, Guy Stevens, drops out early on. Meanwhile, compilation *Best Of Traffic*, rounding up hit singles and tracks from earlier albums, reaches US #48.
June [14] Mason breaks a lengthy spell of solo touring in US to join Eric Clapton's Derek & The Dominos for their first UK live shows.
Aug Rick Grech (b. Nov.1, 1946, Bordeaux, France), ex-colleague with Winwood in Blind Faith and Airforce, joins on bass. Mason, signed in US as a soloist to Blue Thumb Records, reaches US #22 with his debut album *Alone Together* (recorded with help from Capaldi, Leon Russell, Delaney & Bonnie, and others), also earning his first gold disk.
Sept *John Barleycorn Must Die* reaches UK #11 and hits US #5, the group's biggest US success and first gold disk. From Mason's album, his solo version of *Only You Know And I Know* (which will be a US Top 20 hit by Delaney & Bonnie a year later) reaches US #42.
Oct *Empty Pages*, from *John Barleycorn Must Die*, makes US #74.
Dec Mason's *Satin Red And Black Velvet Woman* stalls at US #97.

1971 **Apr** Group returns from an inactive winter spent in Morocco, having ostensibly been writing a movie score (for "Nevertheless", starring Michael J. Pollard) which has fallen through. Mason has teamed with Mama Cass Elliot, formerly with The Mamas And The Papas, and their duetted album *Dave Mason And Cass Elliot* makes UK #49.
May For new recordings and in preparation for UK and US tours, group expands its line-up, adding Ghanaian percussionist Reebop Kwaku-Baah and Derek & The Dominos' drummer Jim Gordon (freeing Capaldi for more vocal spotlights). Mason also returns for a few months, and is present on live recordings which produce *Welcome To The Canteen*.
June Double compilation album *Winwood*, bringing together The Spencer Davis Group, Blind Faith and Traffic tracks which have Winwood on lead vocals, reaches US #93. It is not released in UK.
Nov *Welcome To The Canteen* makes US #26, while live single from it, a revival of The Spencer Davis Group's *Gimme Some Lovin'* with Winwood reprising his lead vocal, reaches US #68.
Dec Grech leaves (later to join KGB), while Mason quits and Gordon returns to session work in US.

1972 **Jan** *The Low Spark Of High Heeled Boys*, made before the break-up of the last line-up (though after Mason's departure) fails to chart in UK but hits US #7, and becomes the band's second gold disk. *Rock'N'Roll Stew (Part 1)* makes US #93. Winwood contracts peritonitis and his illness and recuperation render Traffic inactive for a while. Capaldi fills the time recording a solo album in Muscle Shoals, AL, while Mason records another solo album. Group embarks on a US tour with replacements Roger Hawkins and David Hood joining current line-up of Winwood, Capaldi, Wood and Rebop.
Apr Capaldi's *Oh How We Danced* makes US #82 and extracted *Eve* peaks at US #91, while Mason's half-studio, half-live album *Headkeeper* reaches US #51.
Nov Muscle Shoals drummer and bassist Roger Hawkins and David Hood, who played with Capaldi at the beginning of the year, are invited to Jamaica to record Traffic's next album, with Winwood, Capaldi, Wood and Kwaku-Baah still in the main line-up.

1973 **Mar** *Shoot-Out At The Fantasy Factory* is another UK chart failure, but hits US #6 and earns the band's third gold disk.
May Mason's solo live album *Dave Mason Is Alive!* makes US #116.
June Hawkins and Hood remain with Traffic for a world tour, while keyboards player Barry Beckett is also recruited to fill out the stage sound on tour. Several tour gigs are recorded for a future live album.
Aug [23] In mid-tour, the group headlines UK's Reading Festival.
Sept After the tour, Kwaku-Baah, Hood, Hawkins and Beckett all return to session work, and the 3 principals rest for 2 months.
Nov Bass player Rosko Gee (formerly with Gonzales) joins to augment the trio for some UK live dates (and will stay for the last year of the group's life).
Dec Double live *Traffic – On The Road*, recorded on the world tour,

reaches UK #40 and US #29, while Mason switches labels to CBS/Columbia and makes US #50 with *It's Like You Never Left*, which features guest appearances by Graham Nash and Stevie Wonder.

1974 **July** Compilation of Mason's Blue Thumb recordings, *The Best Of Dave Mason* makes US #183.

Aug *It's All Up To You*, a Capaldi solo, reaches UK #27.

Sept *When The Eagle Flies*, Traffic's final recording together, reaches UK #31 and is the group's last UK chart album. Meanwhile, Capaldi's solo *Whale Meat Again* creeps to US #191.

Nov *When The Eagle Flies* hits US #9, earning the group's fourth and final gold disk. They complete a US tour, then decide to split to pursue individual careers.

Dec Mason's solo album *Dave Mason*, on Columbia, reaches US #25 and earns his second gold disk.

1975 **Feb** Capaldi's solo *It's All Right* makes US #55.

Mar A revised version on Blue Thumb of compilation album *The Best Of Dave Mason At His Best* after the substitution of one track, peaks at US #133.

May Compilation album *Heavy Traffic* makes US #155.

Oct Follow-up compilation, *More Heavy Traffic*, creeps to US #193.

Nov Capaldi's solo revival of oldie *Love Hurts* hits UK #4 and reaches US #97, where a competing version by UK group Nazareth hits US #8, selling over a million. Meanwhile, Mason's album *Split Coconut*, with guest appearances by Manhattan Transfer, David Crosby and Graham Nash, reaches US #27.

1976 **Feb** Capaldi's solo album *Short Cut Draw Blood* peaks at US #193.

1977 **Jan** Mason's solo live double album *Certified Live* climbs to US #78.

June Mason's *So High (Rock Me Baby And Roll Me Away)* makes US #89 while his *Let It Flow* reaches US #37 and earns a gold disk.

July Winwood begins his solo career with album *Steve Winwood*, which reaches UK #12 and US #22.

Nov Mason's *We Just Disagree*, from *Let It Flow*, is his biggest solo single success, reaching US #12.

1978 **Feb** *Let It Go, Let It Flow* by Mason makes US #45.

Mar Mason plays the California Jam 2 rock festival in Ontario, CA, alongside Santana, Aerosmith, and others.

July Mason becomes the sixth act to have a US hit single with The Shirelles 1961 chart-topper *Will You Love Me Tomorrow*, reaching US #39. It is taken from his *Mariposa De Oro*, which peaks at US #41.

Aug [26] Mason takes part in the Canada Jam Festival, a spinoff from California Jam, with The Doobie Brothers, The Commodores, and others.

Nov Yet another Blue Thumb repackage of early solo material, *The Very Best Of Dave Mason*, peaks at US #179.

1980 **July** The last solo hit single by Mason is *Save Me*, peaking at US #71. It comes from his final chart album *Old Crest On A New Wave*, which makes US #74. (He will continue to work in US and in the following year will be heard singing Miller Beer ads on US radio.)

1983 **June** After some time spent in South America, Capaldi is signed to Atlantic for solo *Fierce Heart*, which climbs to US #91. Taken from it, *That's Love* makes US #28.

July [12] Chris Wood dies of liver failure after a lengthy illness, in London.

Sept *Living On The Edge* by Capaldi reaches US #75. (Like Mason's, his career will wane, while Winwood's will soar to peaks beyond those achieved by Traffic.)

RANDY TRAVIS

1979 Travis (b. Randy Bruce Traywick, May 4, 1959, Marshville, NC) is already a country music veteran, having formed a duo with his brother at age 10, moved to Charlotte, NC when 16, where he has won a talent contest at Country City USA club and subsequently become one of the venue's regular performers under the wing of its own (and Travis' subsequent manager) Lib Hatcher, when he makes his recording debut for local Paula Records, cutting *Dreamin'* and *She's My Woman*, produced by Joe Stamford.

1981 Travis relocates to Nashville, TN, where he concentrates on songwriting, earning a living initially as a cook and washer-up. (Later he will become a country performer, again at the invitation of Hatcher, who has by now opened a Nashville club.)

1985 He signs to Warner Bros., and makes his label debut recording *Prairie Rose* for inclusion on movie soundtrack album *Rustler's Rhapsody*.

Sept First solo Warners release *On The Other Hand*, immediately showcasing Travis' smooth deep-throated earthy baritone vocal quality, makes US Country #67.

1986 **Feb** Second outing *1982* hits US Country #6.

June Reissued Paul Overstreet/Don Schlitz-written *On The Other Hand* is the first of many US Country chart hits for Travis.

Aug [9] Parent album *Storms Of Life* tops US Country chart on its way to US #85. Heralded as one of the pioneering albums for the new country movement, which will find increasing sympathy from the rock and pop markets, it is produced by Kyle Lehning and contains songs and musical contributions from the cream of Nashville's talent.

Oct *Diggin' Up Bones* also hits US Country top spot, as Travis wins Country Music Association's Horizon Award for the Most Promising Newcomer Of The Year, the first of many CMA honors.

1987 **Feb** Fourth extract *No Place Like Home* hits US Country #2.

May Travis visits Europe for a US forces tour, the first time he has been outside US.

June [20] *Always & Forever* hits US Country #1 for the first of 40 weeks, and will also reach US #19, selling over 2 million copies. It includes 4 US Country #1 hits and confirms Travis as the leading new country artist, whose young good country looks boost his success and belie the maturity of his exceptional voice.

1988 **Mar** [2] Travis wins Best Country Vocal Performance, Male for the album *Always & Forever* at the 30th annual Grammy awards. The ceremony, acknowledging the growing popularity of the new country movement, includes performances by its 3 brightest stars, Steve Earle, Dwight Yoakam and Travis.

June Travis performs at the Royal Albert Hall, London, at the beginning of his first headlining UK tour, as *Forever And Ever, Amen* peaks at UK #55.

Aug [27] *Old 8 x 10*, featuring a familiar line-up of guest musicians and songwriters, and again produced by Lehning, hits US Country #1 and will reach US #35 and UK #64. Once again, it will spawn country single chart-toppers: *Honky Tonk Moon*, *Deeper Than The Holler* (scribed by Overstreet and Schlitz), and *Is It Still Over?*

1989 **Jan** [30] Having recently swept the board of another CMA Awards ceremony, Travis wins Country Male Vocal, Single for *I Told You So* and Album for *Always & Forever* at the 15th annual American Music Awards.

Feb [22] Travis collects his second Best Country Vocal Performance, Male honor for the album *8 x 10* at the 31st annual Grammy awards.

Nov [4] *It's Just A Matter Of Time*, an update of Brook Benton's 1959 US #3, recorded initially for producer Richard Perry's labor of love *Rock, Rhythm & Blues*, hits US Country #1 in the same week that other parent album *No Holdin' Back* achieves the same on the Album survey, having already made US #33.

Dec US only-issued festive collection of chestnut covers and new country songs, *An Old Time Christmas*, peaks at US #70.

[23] In **Billboard**'s The Year In Music survey, *Old 8 x 10* is named Top Country Album and Travis, Top Country Artist.

1990 **May** *Always & Forever* is voted Country Album Of The Decade by **Billboard** magazine.

[5] Travis contributes *Nowhere Man* to the "John Lennon Tribute Concert", held at the Pier Head Arena in Merseyside to celebrate the former Beatle's songs.

Nov [3] Travis' sixth platinum album *Heroes And Friends* peaks at US #31. It comprises 12 duets with "artists who have been heroes to me most of my life and over the past few years ... have now become friends", namely Dolly Parton, Willie Nelson, Merle Haggard, Vern Gosdin, Loretta Lynn, B.B. King, George Jones, Kris Kristofferson, Tammy Wynette, Clint Eastwood, Conway Twitty and Roy Rogers.

Dec [4-8] Travis, who spends the best part of every year on SRO tours performs 5 consecutive dates at Bally's, Las Vegas, NV.

[22] In **Billboard**'s The Year In Music survey, Travis is once again named Top Country Artist and *No Holdin' Back* is named Top Country Album.

1991 **Feb** [10] Travis joins with nearly 100 celebrities in Burbank, CA, to record *Voices That Care*, a David Foster and fiancee Linda Thompson Jenner-composed and organized charity record to benefit the American Red Cross Gulf Crisis Fund. (Travis will participate in several of the US TV networks' "Welcome Home" to the troops celebrations.)

[28] Travis' embarks on US tour in Huntsville, AL, with support act, rising country star Alan Jackson.

Mar [7] Travis is named Best Country Artist in the annual **Rolling Stone** Readers' Picks music awards.

[8] Travis issues a statement confirming that he has been living with his manager Lib Hatcher for some years, in response to a claim by the **National Examiner** that he is gay.

[9] He guest stars, as himself, on NBC TV sitcom "Down Home".

THE TROGGS

Reg Presley (vocals)
Chris Britton (guitar)
Pete Staples (bass),
Ronnie Bond (drums)

1964 Group forms as The Troglodytes in Andover, Hants, comprising Tony Mansfield, guitar, lead vocals, Dave Wright, guitar, and ex-apprentice bricklayers Presley (b. Reginald Ball, June 12, 1943, Andover – he will not use the name Presley until 1966) on bass and Bond (b. Ronald Bullis, May 4, 1943, Andover), in school band The Emeralds, on drums.

1965 Mansfield and Wright leave the group, and are replaced by Britton (b. June 21, 1945, Watford, Herts.) and Staples (b. May 3, 1944, Andover), both ex-Andover group Ten Foot Five. Staples plays bass, so Presley, with initial reluctance, becomes lead vocalist in Mansfield's place. This new line-up is spotted and signed by The Kinks' manager Larry Page, after he witnesses their very basic live rendition of The Kinks' *You Really Got Me*. (This rawness will always be the key to The Troggs' individuality.)

1966 **Feb** [11] Group abridges its name to The Troggs, and debut single Presley's song *Lost Girl*, leased by Page to CBS, is released.
Apr *Wild Thing*, by US writer Chip Taylor and cut (obscurely) in US by The Wild Ones, is sent to Page by his US publishing associate. The group thinks the lyric corny but, once the heavy, innuendo-laden arrangement is worked out, it is recorded in a rapid session, with an unusual ocarina solo in place of a whistling passage on the US original.
May Ball changes his name to Reg Presley (which, as anticipated, gets him press notice once the record is climbing) as the single is released via a new deal between Page's production company Page One and Fontana label. Following UK TV slots on "Thank Your Lucky Stars" and "Top Of The Pops", *Wild Thing* hits UK #2.
July *Wild Thing* tops US chart for 2 weeks, selling over a million. Because of a US rights dispute, it is released in US on both Fontana and Atco labels. Fontana shares the same B-side as the UK release, but Atco couples *Wild Thing* with the UK follow-up, *With A Girl Like You*.
Aug Presley's composition *With A Girl Like You*, cut in slightly lighter, but similar, style to *Wild Thing*, tops UK chart for 2 weeks. Group's debut album *From Nowhere ... The Troggs* hits UK #6.
Sept Fontana issues *With A Girl Like You* in US, but since half the US buyers of *Wild Thing* already own the track, it halts at US #29.
Oct [1] Group begins 33-date "Star Scene 66" twice-nightly package tour, with The Walker Brothers and Dave Dee, Dozy, Beaky, Mick & Tich, at Granada cinema, East Ham, London. Tour ends Nov.13 at Finsbury Park Astoria, London.
Page launches his own Page One label in UK and *I Can't Control Myself*, Presley-penned, hits UK #2. Meanwhile, *Wild Thing* climbs to US #52.
Nov *I Can't Control Myself*, also a dual-label release in US, reaches #43.

1967 **Jan** Another Chip Taylor song, *Any Way That You Want Me* (also a US hit 3 years later for Evie Sands), hits UK #8.
Feb [17] Band begins a 28-date UK tour, with Gene Pitney, David Garrick, Sounds Incorporated, The Loot and Normie Rowe & The Playboys, at Finsbury Park Astoria. Tour ends Mar.19 at the Coventry theater, W.Midlands.
Mar Chanted *Give It To Me*, also Presley-penned, reaches UK #12, while *Trogglodynamite* hits UK #10.
Apr [1] Page announces he is imposing a "ban in reverse": he is forbidding The Troggs to play London dates, because of illegal-drug publicity the city's music venues are receiving. (The date of the ban appears to be significant.)
May [10] Group makes its first overseas tour; a 5-day visit to Italy.
June *Night Of The Long Grass*, a deliberate change of sound with a hint of psychedelia in lyric and arrangement, makes UK #17.
[30] A High Court injunction prevents band from engaging anyone other than Page One Records to act as its managers, agents or representatives, after it tries to leave the label.
Aug *Hi Hi Hazel* (a minor UK hit the previous year for soul singer Geno Washington) peaks at UK #42, while compilation *Best Of The Troggs* reaches UK #24, and is the group's last UK chart album.
Nov *Love Is All Around*, a ballad with merely a hint of *Wild Thing*'s jerky rhythm, hits UK #5.

1968 **Mar** *Little Girl* reaches UK #37, and is The Troggs' last UK chart entry. (The band will continue live work for another year on UK club and college circuits.)
May *Love Is All Around* hits US #7.
June LP *Love Is All Around* makes US #109.

1969 **Mar** A year after Britton originally planned to leave, the group splits.

(Presley and Bond will both record solo singles, *Lucinda Lee* and *Anything For You* respectively, but without success. Britton will cut unsuccessful *As I Am*.)

1972 Presley and Bond re-form the group with Britton and Staples replaced in the line-up by Richard Moore and Tony Murray, for college and club dates in UK and in France, Holland and Germany, where a following for the usually outrageous stage act remains strong. A studio tape made during sessions in their later days at Page One also surfaces in bootleg form under the title *The Troggs Tapes*, its main interest being West Country foul language as the group struggles with the attempted creation of a hit. This revives interest in The Troggs, particularly in US.

1973 **Nov** [16] Group guests on David Bowie's first US TV special, "The 1980 Floor Show", taped earlier at London's Marquee club, and aired on NBC TV's "Midnight Special".

1975 **Jan** The Troggs, reunited with Page, cut a revival of The Beach Boys' *Good Vibrations* for his Penny Farthing label. Reviews are more amused than scathing but it fails to chart.
Nov Group revives The Rolling Stones' *(I Can't Get No) Satisfaction*, again without success.

1976 Group is on a nostalgia tour of US when Sire label releases compilation *Vintage Years*, containing The Troggs' 60s hits.
July Penny Farthing releases *The Troggs Tapes* (which capitalizes on bootleg tape title, but has nothing to do with it). Rhythm guitarist Colin "Dill" Fletcher has now made the group a quintet. (The inherent unmusicality of The Troggs is cited as an influence by many punk groups, and Los Angeles band X revives *Wild Thing* on disk.)

1980 Signed in US to Basement records, group releases *Live At Max's Kansas City*, recorded at the New York club. (With a cult following which is apparently undying, the group will continue regular live work in US and UK into the 80s.)

1989 **Apr** [27] Group appears at a concert at the City Hall, Sheffield, S.Yorks., in aid of the Hillsborough soccer disaster.

1990 *Wild Thing* is extensively aired on UK TV as theme for a Lion Bar chocolate ad.

THE TUBES

"Fee" Waybill (vocals)
Bill "Sputnick" Spooner (guitar)
Vince Welnick (keyboards)
Rick Anderson (bass)
Michael Cotten (synthesizer)
Roger Steen (guitar)
Prairie Prince (drums)
Re Styles (vocals, guitar)
Mingo Lewis (percussion)

1975 Establishing a reputation as San Francisco, CA's prime theatrical rock band, The Tubes, formed in Phoenix, AZ and led by ex-drama student Waybill (b. John Waldo, Sept.17, 1950, Omaha, NE) sign to A&M Records, using the advance to produce more extravagant stage shows.
Aug Al Kooper-produced debut *The Tubes*, featuring the band's anthem *White Punks On Dope*, makes US #113.

1976 **June** *Young And Rich*, produced by Ken Scott, makes US #46.
Aug *Don't Touch Me There*, with Waybill in the guise of glam-rock star "Quay Lewd", peaks at US #61.

1977 **June** *The Tubes Now* reaches US #122.
Nov Group tours UK for the first time and a live performance ban in Portsmouth, Hants, does not hinder *White Punks On Dope* chart peak at UK #28.

1978 **Mar** Double live *What Do You Want From Live* reaches US #82 and UK #38.
May [9] While on a UK tour, Waybill falls off stage and breaks a leg. They have to cancel 7 nights at London's Hammersmith Odeon. The BBC's film of the incident shows him apparently wielding a chainsaw.

1979 **Mar** Band fills large venues but is unable to translate live popularity into disk sales. With *Remote Control* they announce that future emphasis will be on the latter. With Todd Rundgren producing, the album reaches US #46.
May *Prime Time* makes UK #34.
June *Remote Control* reaches UK #40.

1980 They begin recording follow-up album, *Suffer For Sound*, but it's release is blocked by A&M.
Aug Band appears in Olivia Newton-John/Gene Kelly-starring movie "Xanadu".

1981 **July** A&M drops the band and it signs to Capitol, which releases *Completion Backwards Principle*, produced by Canadian David Foster.

It becomes The Tubes' highest charting album to date at US #36.

Aug Uncharacteristic ballad, *I Don't Want To Wait Anymore* makes US #35 and UK #60.

1982 June While The Tubes are touring UK, a publicity stunt involving young girls dancing on the back of a flat-bed truck in London's Tottenham Court Road results in Waybill's arrest for obstruction.

Sept A&M releases *T.R.A.S.H. (Tubes Rarities And Smash Hits)*, of hits and out-takes, which peaks at US #148.

1983 May *Outside Inside*, including guest appearances from Earth, Wind & Fire's Maurice White and The Motels' Martha Davis, reaches US #18 and UK #77.

July Group's first US Top 10 hit is *She's A Beauty* at #10.

Aug *Tip Of My Tongue* makes US #52.

Oct *The Monkey Time* peaks at US #68.

1984 Nov Waybill releases solo *Read My Lips* which makes US #146.

1985 Mar *Piece By Piece* charts briefly at US #87.

1986 Mar *Love Bomb*, reuniting the group with producer Rundgren, makes US #89.

May PMI Video releases "The Tubes Video" which captures the band performing *White Punks On Dope* and *Mondo Bondage*.

Oct XTC's *Skylarking* is recorded at The Tubes' own Sound Hole studio in San Francisco.

1988 Apr Waybill appears on Richard Marx's eponymous debut album.

1990 Welnick replaces Brent Mydland in The Grateful Dead. Waybill's *Meeting Half The Way* is featured on *Nobody's Perfect* soundtrack on the Sisapa label.

IKE & TINA TURNER

1951 Ike Turner (b. Izear Turner, Jr., Nov.5, 1931, Clarksdale, MS), son of Baptist minister Izear Luster Turner, Sr., a self-taught musician who has backed local bluesmen Robert Nighthawk and Sonny Boy Williamson on piano, is a DJ at Clarksdale's W-ROX, which leads to recording work with his band Kings Of Rhythm, formed at high school. Their *Rocket 88*, recorded at Sam Phillips' Sun studio in Memphis, with lead vocal by sax player Jackie Brenston, hits R&B #1 (and will often be cited as the first rock'n'roll record).

1952 Moving to session guitarwork and production, Ike will play on sessions by B.B. King, Howlin' Wolf (both of whom he recruits for Modern Records in Los Angeles, having become a roving R&B talent scout for the label around the South), Johnny Ace and others, as well as touring with his band, until 1956.

1956 The Kings Of Rhythm have settled in a club in East St. Louis, MO, where Ike first meets Tina (who at this time is still Anna Mae Bullock, b. Nov.26, 1939 Brownsville, TN) and her older sister Alline. Deserted by their mother and later their father into the care of relatives before their teens, the sisters have moved to St. Louis to work and are regulars at R&B clubs. She has been singing since childhood in church and junior talent contests, and repeatedly asks Ike if she can sing with his band, but he is not interested. One evening at the club, after the drummer has offered the microphone to her sister, who is unwilling to sing, she takes it and jumps on stage with the group. She and Ike begin dating and she becomes a regular guest vocalist.

1958 Ike and Tina are married and, at Ike's suggestion, she takes the stage name Tina Turner.

1960 Their first record as Ike & Tina Turner comes about by accident when the session singer booked to record Ike's *A Fool In Love* fails to show and Tina steps in.

Oct Already an R&B success, *A Fool In Love* is the duo's first crossover hit, reaching US #27. Ike's band becomes The Ike & Tina Turner Revue and 3 female backing singers, The Ikettes, are incorporated to support Tina, around whom the show's routines revolve – she is now a striking and uninhibited live performer.

Dec *I Idolize You* makes US #82 and R&B #5.

1961 Sept *It's Gonna Work Out Fine* is their first US Top 20 hit, reaching #14 (and R&B #2).

1962 Jan *Poor Fool* makes US #38 (and R&B #4).

Feb Without Tina, The Ikettes and the band record *I'm Blue (The Gong Gong Song)*, which Ike leases to Atco. It makes US #19.

Apr *Tra La La La* reaches US #50 (and R&B #9).

July *You Should'a Treated Me Right* makes US #89 and is the duo's last pop hit for Sun Records. (A pattern of R&B successes that do not always cross over is developing: The Ike & Tina Turner Revue will be one of the most popular acts of the 60s on the R&B tour circuit, but will only consistently break to wider audiences towards the end of the decade.)

1964 Oct *I Can't Believe What You Say (For Seeing What You Do)* reaches US #95 while the duo is signed to Kent label.

1965 Feb They move to Warner Bros. on the strength of the recent hit single No Singles chart entries will follow on Warner, but *Live! The Ike And Tina Turner Show*, a recording of their highly-rated stage act at the Skyliner Ballroom, Fort Worth, TX, makes US #126.

Apr Ike records The Ikettes again for Kent's sister label Modern and their *Peaches'N'Cream* climbs to US #36.

Nov The Ikettes' follow-up *I'm So Thankful* peaks at US #74.

Dec They film a segment for the "TNT Award Show" TV program with Joan Baez, Bo Diddley, The Byrds, Ray Charles, The Lovin' Spoonful, The Ronettes, Roger Miller, Petula Clark and Donovan.

1966 Jan While moving around in one-off record deals with independent labels like Innis and Pompeii, they meet producer Phil Spector, who offers Ike $20,000 dollars to put Tina under a production contract. (Spector admires Tina's voice, but is underwhelmed by Ike's production of her records, so the payment is part of a condition that Ike takes no part in the sessions.) Songwriters Jeff Barry and Ellie Greenwich are called in to pen songs, with Spector, for Tina.

Mar [7] Tina records her vocal on *River Deep, Mountain High* after Spector has already spent over $22,000 creating the "Wall Of Sound" backing track.

June Released on Spector's Philles label, *River Deep, Mountain High* climbs no higher than US #88. (This apparent rejection of what he regards as one of his finest productions is given as a major factor in Spector's shutdown of Philles immediately afterwards, and his short-term retirement from production.)

July By contrast, *River Deep, Mountain High* is a major UK success (the duo's first), hitting #3. Warner Bros. releases an earlier track, *Tell Her I'm Not Home*, in UK and this too charts, reaching #48. After years as an R&B enthusiasts' act in Europe and UK, the Turners are suddenly considered major stars – though still restricted to the R&B circuit in US.

Sept [23] They begin 12-date "Rolling Stones '66" UK tour with headliners The Rolling Stones and The Yardbirds, Long John Baldry and others, at London's Royal Albert Hall. The tour ends Oct.9 at the Gaumont theater, Southampton, Hants. They also appear on ITV's "Ready Steady Go!".

Oct *River Deep, Mountain High*, coupling Spector productions with new Ike Turner-produced versions of oldies by the duo, makes UK #27.

Nov Spector-produced UK (but not released in US) follow-up from the same sessions as *River Deep*, a revival of a Martha & The Vandellas B-side, *A Love Like Yours*, reaches UK #16.

Dec Group performs Christmas week at the Galaxy in Hollywood.

1967 Apr [2] Group embarks on 8-day promotional visit of US.

1969 Feb *River Deep, Mountain High* is reissued in UK, and reaches #33.

May Duo signs a 2-album deal with Blue Thumb Records, cutting mainly blues-based material, and also a longer-term contract with Minit. A revival of Otis Redding's *I've Been Loving You Too Long* on Blue Thumb peaks at US #68 and *I'm Gonna Do All I Can (To Do Right By My Man)*, on Minit, reaches US #98. Blue Thumb album *Outa Season* makes US #91.

June [20] Ike & Tina Turner participate in the 3-day Newport '69 Festival.

Aug *The Hunter*, on Blue Thumb, peaks at US #93, while live Minit album *In Person*, recorded at Basin Street West, reaches US #142.

Oct *River Deep, Mountain High*, finally released in US on A&M after 3 years, peaks at US #102.

Nov Second Blue Thumb album *The Hunter* makes US #176.

[7] Duo supports The Rolling Stones on a US tour, which opens in Denver, CO.

1970 Jan Ike's composition *Bold Soul Sister*, a final single on Blue Thumb, peaks at US #59.

Apr A version of The Beatles' *Come Together* (on Minit) reaches US #57.

June *Come Together* makes US #130.

Aug A revival of Sly & The Family Stone's *I Want To Take You Higher* is their first hit on Liberty, which has absorbed Minit. It reaches US #34 (and will become a highlight of the Turners' live act). The Ike & Tina Turner Revue guests on important US TV shows like Ed Sullivan's and Andy Williams'. They also pick up lucrative work in Las Vegas, NV casinos. By the end of the year Ike has built his own Bolic Sound recording studio in Inglewood, CA.

1971 Mar An R&B-style revival of Creedence Clearwater Revival's *Proud Mary* is their first US Top 10 hit, at #4, and first million-selling single. It is taken from *Workin' Together*, which is their biggest-selling album to date in US, peaking at #25. (Despite a hugely successful European tour, neither single nor album produce similar chart results in UK.)

June A revival of Jesse Hill's *Ooh Poo Pah Doo* (on United Artists, as Liberty Records has now become) reaches US #60.

Sept Double live album *Live At Carnegie Hall/What You See Is What You Get* reaches US #25 and is the duo's first gold album, selling over a half million copies in US.

Dec *'Nuff Said* makes US #108.

1972 **Mar** *Up In Heah* reaches US #83.

Aug *Feel Good* makes US #160.

1973 **Oct** Tina's composition, stomping *Nutbush City Limits* reaches US #22 and hits UK #4.

1974 **Jan** *Nutbush City Limits* makes US #163.

Apr [22] Tina begins filming in the role of the Acid Queen in The Who's film "Tommy".

Dec *Sexy Ida* reaches US #65.

1975 **June** Ike Turner-penned *Baby Get It On* reaches US #88, and is the duo's last hit single together. (Behind the scenes, all is not well with the couple domestically: Tina will later claim to have been regularly beaten and kept a prisoner in the house by her husband.)

Oct On the strength of her Acid Queen performance in "Tommy", Tina records a solo album, *The Acid Queen*, which reaches US #155.

1976 Strengthened by her newfound Buddhist faith, Tina walks out on Ike and in July they are divorced. While he continues to produce at his studio (where he will be arrested after rigging electronic equipment to make long distance telephone calls without charge), she has 4 children to support. After depending for a time on food stamps, she recruits a band and plays cabaret gigs. (She is still a far bigger draw in Europe than in US.)

1979 Late in the year Tina meets Roger Davies, a young Australian promoter trying to make it in the US music business. She has no recording deal, is playing the cabaret circuit, and is half a million dollars in debt.

1980 Tina teams with Davies, who makes changes in her band and books her into less middle-of-the-road-oriented clubs (with the occasional Las Vegas stand to pay the bills). Record company interest is minimal, partly because Ike's difficult reputation lingers with Tina.

1981 Tina's career prospects brighten again as she supports The Rolling Stones on tour. Late in the year Davies has a call from Virgin Records in UK to say that Ian Craig Marsh and Martyn Ware of Heaven 17 and the British Electric Foundation want Tina to sing The Temptations song *Ball Of Confusion* on their album of choice revivals, *Music Of Quality & Distinction*. With its electronic backdrop, it is not the kind of rock she now wants to record, but the finished track brings her renewed notice as an active vocalist.

Dec [18] Tina supports Rod Stewart at a Los Angeles Forum concert, broadcast live by satellite around the world.

1982 Davies works out a new solo recording deal with Capitol/EMI. Meanwhile, Ike's studio is destroyed by fire and rumors indicate he has a serious cocaine problem.

Apr [9] Tina begins comeback at Hammersmith Odeon, London.

Dec Davies promotes a series of Tina Turner dates at the New York Ritz, building up a guest list of notables – though aware that management changes at Capitol during the year have left the company less enthused about its new signing, and that she seems in danger of being dropped. David Bowie resolves the problem. He is just signed to EMI (Capitol's parent company), and its top executives from around the world have been invited to a listening party for his forthcoming *Let's Dance*. When Bowie announces to the party that he is moving on to see his "favorite singer" Tina Turner, EMI's executives follow and witness a storming comeback show. (She will stay with Capitol.)

1983 **Dec** Marsh and Ware-produced version of Al Green's *Let's Stay Together* is Tina's first Capitol single. It hits UK #6, with her UK profile raised by packed dates at London's the Venue and an appearance on Channel 4 TV's "The Tube".

1984 **Mar** *Let's Stay Together* reaches US #26, as various writer-producers, including Rupert Hine and Terry Britten, are brought in to collaborate on a first Capitol album. It is recorded at UK sessions spread over just 2 weeks, while her revival of The Beatles' *Help!* reaches UK #40.

[27] Tina begins a UK tour at St. Austell's Coliseum, Cornwall.

Apr She opens as support on Lionel Richie's "Can't Slow Down" tour.

July First release from the album sessions is *What's Love Got To Do With It?*, written by Britten and Graham Lyle (ex-Gallagher & Lyle), which hits UK #3.

Aug *Private Dancer* hits US #3 and UK #2 (and will stay in US Top 10 until May 1985 and sell over 10 million copies worldwide).

Sept As the tour with Richie finishes, *What's Love Got To Do With It* tops US chart for 3 weeks, selling over a million. It is her first #1 hit, and sets a new record for length of time between an act's first US Hot

100 entry and first #1 record – 24 years. On the same day the single hits #1, she seals a deal with Australian director George Miller to appear in his third "Mad Max" movie, with Mel Gibson. (Miller had called offering her a part quite unaware of "Mad Max 2" being one of her favorite films). She performs at a series of McDonalds sales conventions (booked a year earlier in the penniless days). Meanwhile, *Better Be Good To Me*, from *Private Dancer*, reaches UK #45.

Nov *Better Be Good To Me* hits US #5.

Dec Title track *Private Dancer*, penned by Mark Knopfler with Jeff Beck handling the lead guitar part, reaches UK #26.

1985 **Jan** She plays the Rock In Rio festival, at Rio de Janeiro, Brazil, along with Rod Stewart, Queen, Whitesnake and AC/DC.

[28] Tina takes part in the recording of USA For Africa's *We Are The World*.

Feb [26] *What's Love Got To Do With It?* wins Record Of The Year, Song Of The Year and Best Female Vocal Performance and *Better Be Good To Me* wins Best Female Rock Vocal at the 27th annual Grammy awards.

Mar Title song from *Private Dancer* hits US #7 – her third consecutive US Top 10 hit from the album.

[14] Tina plays Wembley Arena, London, as her revival of Ann Peebles' *I Can't Stand The Rain* peaks at UK #57.

May *Show Some Respect* peaks at US #37.

June Movie "Mad Max: Beyond Thunderdome" is released. Tina's performance as Aunty Entity is striking, and leads to further film offers. (She reportedly turns down Steven Spielberg's offer of a role in "The Color Purple" 3 times.) Meanwhile, her European tour is breaking records, and the original 8 dates in Germany are extended to 30.

July [13] She appears on the Live Aid bill in Philadelphia, PA, where she duets raunchily with Mick Jagger.

Aug *We Don't Need Another Hero (Thunderdome)*, from *Mad Max: Beyond Thunderdome* soundtrack, hits UK #3.

Sept *We Don't Need Another Hero (Thunderdome)* hits US #2, behind John Parr's *St. Elmo's Fire*.

Oct A second soundtrack single, *One Of The Living*, reaches UK #55.

Nov *It's Only Love*, a duet with Canadian rocker Bryan Adams (on his label A&M), reaches UK #29.

Dec *One Of The Living* reaches US #15.

[8] Tina wins an award as Best Actress from the NAACP for her role in "Mad Max: Beyond Thunderdome".

1986 **Jan** Duetted *It's Only Love* makes US #15.

June [20] Tina participates in the Prince's Trust concert in London, alongside Eric Clapton, Elton John and Bryan Adams.

Aug [28] Tina receives her star on Hollywood Walk Of Fame outside Capitol Records' headquarters.

Sept *Typical Male*, from her forthcoming album, reaches UK #33.

Oct *Typical Male* hits US #2, behind Cyndi Lauper's *True Colors*. *Break Every Rule* hits UK #2.

Nov *Two People*, also from *Break Every Rule*, makes UK #43, while the album hits US #4, earning a platinum disk for million-plus sales.

1987 **Jan** *Two People* reaches US #30.

Mar [4] Tina embarks on her "Break Every Rule" world tour in Munich, Germany. (It will break box office records in 13 countries.) Financial backing is provided by her corporate sponsors, Pepsi, for whom she films a "live" commercial. *Break Every Rule* has now hit #1 in 9 territories.

Apr *What You Get Is What You See* reaches UK #30 and US #13.

May [23] *Break Every Rule* peaks at UK #74.

June *Break Every Rule* makes UK #43.

Aug US leg of the tour begins.

1988 **Jan** [16] On the South American tour leg, Tina plays to 180,000 people in the Maracana Arena, Rio - the largest audience ever assembled for a single performer.

Mar Live version of Robert Palmer's *Addicted To Love* makes UK #71.

[28] "Break Every Rule" world tour comes to a close after 230 dates in 25 countries (playing to 3 million fans) in Osaka, Japan.

Apr Double concert album *Live In Europe* hits UK #8 but only US #86.

May Video "Rio '88" featuring live footage filmed in Brazil is released.

July Ike Turner, sentenced to a year's imprisonment for possession and transportation of cocaine, begins work on *My Confessions*, an autobiographical set to be released on Starforce label.

1989 **Jan** [18] Tina inducts Phil Spector into the Rock'N'Roll Hall Of Fame at a dinner at New York's Waldorf Astoria.

Apr [11] *The Best*, featuring an Edgar Winter sax solo, reaches US #15 and will become a natural commercials anthem for a number of products over the next 2 years.

June She recreates her Acid Queen role in "Tommy" for Los Angeles

charity event as part of The Who's reunion tour. She also completes the Paris/Los Angeles recording of her album *Foreign Affair*.
July Ike begins serving 4-year prison sentence at the California Men's Colony, San Luis Obispo, CA.
Sept *The Best*, first single from new album with a video directed by Lol Creme, hits UK #5.
[30] *Foreign Affair* enters UK chart at #1, and will rise to US #31.
Nov [4] *The Best*, with a sax solo Edgar Winter, reaches US #15.
[26] Tina celebrates her 50th birthday at the Reform club with Eric Clapton, Mark Knopfler, Bryan Adams, Duran Duran and others.
Dec Ballad *I Don't Wanna Lose You* hits UK #8.

1990 Jan [16] Ike Turner is convicted in his absence of driving under the influence of cocaine and being under the influence of cocaine. A Santa Monica jury is deadlocked on 2 felony cocaine charges, forcing a mistrial on those counts.
Mar *Steamy Windows*, penned by Tony Joe White, reaches UK #13, having already made US #39.
Apr [27] Tina Turner opens the European leg of her 121-date "Foreign Affair" World tour in Antwerp, Belgium.
June [28] She plays Palace of Versailles during part of European tour. She becomes the first woman to play there. (Pink Floyd are the only other act to have played there, in 1988.)
Aug *Look Me In The Heart* makes UK #31.
Oct *Be Tender With Me Baby* reaches UK #28.
Nov [4] "Foreign Tour" world tour ends in Rotterdam, Holland, having been seen by more than 3 million people.
Dec *It Takes Two*, an update of Marvin Gaye & Tammi Terrell's Motown classic, now duetted with Rod Stewart, mainly for blanket coverage as the latest UK Pepsi commercial theme, hits UK #5.

1991 Jan [17] Ike & Tina Turner are inducted into the Rock'N'Roll Hall Of Fame at the sixth annual dinner at the Waldorf Astoria in New York.

THE TURTLES

Howard Kaylan (vocals, sax)
Mark Volman (vocals, sax)
Al Nichol (guitar, piano, vocals)
Jim Tucker (guitar)
Chuck Portz (bass)
Don Murray (drums)

1963 Kaylan (b. Howard Kaplan, June 22, 1947, New York, NY), Nichol (b. Mar.31, 1946, Winston Salem, NC), Tucker (b. Oct.17, 1946, Los Angeles, CA) and Portz (b. Mar.28, 1945, Santa Monica, CA) add sax player Volman (b. Apr. 19, 1947, Los Angeles) to their Westchester, Los Angeles, high school swift band The Crossfires, and change its name to The Crossfires. Playing popular surf instrumentals, the new line-up wins several Battle of the Bands competitions, earning a residency at Redondo Beach's Revelaire club, run by DJ Reb Foster, then at Hollywood's Red Velvet club. Debut single is surf instrumental *Fiberglass Jungle*, on local small label Capco Records.

1964 "British Invasion" influence (they frequently impersonate UK groups to gain gigs) inspires them to dispense with surf instrumentals, and Volman and Kaylan switch from saxes to vocals. As a change of pace, they play some folk music dates at high schools as The Crosswind Singers, gradually electrifying the material as the folk-rock style begins to bite nationally.

1965 Ted Feigen, co-owner of new Los Angeles label White Whale, approaches the group at a gig and offers a recording deal, though a change of name is thought advisable. Manager Reb Foster suggests The Tyrtles (having seen The Byrds around town), but the eventual compromise is The Turtles.
Sept A driving version of Bob Dylan's *It Ain't Me Babe* hits US #8.
Nov Debut *It Ain't Me Babe* reaches US #98, while follow-up single, P.F. Sloan's *Let Me Be* (chosen by the band in preference to his offered *Eve Of Destruction*) makes US #29.

1966 Mar *You Baby*, another Sloan song, reaches US #20.
June *Grim Reaper Of Love*, penned by Nichol and Jim Pons, peaks at US #81 while *You Baby*, recorded hurriedly between tours, fails to chart. Murray quits the band, to be replaced by John Barbata (b. Apr.1, 1946, New Jersey), ex-drummer with surf band The Sentinels. Portz also leaves shortly afterwards, replaced first by former Californian State Diving finalist of 1961 Chip Douglas, ex-Modern Folk Quartet and currently playing with Gene Clark, then by Jim Pons (b. Mar.14, 1943, Santa Monica, CA), ex-The (*Hey Joe*) Leaves.
Nov *Can I Get To Know You Better?* stalls at US #89.

1967 Mar *Happy Together*, written by Gary Bonner and Alan Gordon and

acquired when The Turtles are playing New York's Phone Booth club, tops US chart for 3 weeks and is a million-seller.
Apr *Happy Together*, the band's UK chart debut, reaches UK #12.
June Another Bonner/Gordon song, in a romping good-time arrangement, *She'd Rather Be With Me* hits US #3 and earns the band's second gold disk. *Happy Together* reaches US #25.
July *She'd Rather Be With Me* hits UK #4 while the group is on a UK tour. Tucker leaves, and is not replaced.
Sept *You Know What I Mean*, a mid-tempo ballad, reaches US #12.
Dec *She's My Girl*, with a hint of psychedelia, reaches US #14.

1968 Jan Compilation *The Turtles! Golden Hits* is the group's biggest-selling album, hitting US #7 and earning a gold disk for a half million sales.
Mar *Sound Asleep*, the first single produced by the band itself, makes US #57.
July Nilsson song *The Story Of Rock And Roll* (with the composer on piano) peaks at US #48.
Nov *Elenore* hits US #6 and UK #7 (and will be The Turtles' last UK hit). It is taken from jokey concept album *The Turtles Present The Battle Of The Bands*, which peaks at US #128.
Dec [28] The Turtles take part in the 3-day Miami Pop Festival at Hallendale, FL.

1969 Mar *You Showed Me*, originally recorded by The Byrds, pre-*Mr. Tambourine Man*, and resurrected by The Turtles on *Battle*, is extracted to hit US #6.
May [10] Band plays the White House as guests of Tricia Nixon. (Stories circulate concerning Kaylan and Volman allegedly snorting cocaine on Abraham Lincoln's desk.)
Barbata leaves (later to join Jefferson Airplane) and is replaced by John Seiter, ex-Spanky & Our Gang.
July *You Don't Have To Walk In The Rain* reaches US #51.
Oct *Love In The City* stalls at US #91.
Nov The Kinks' Ray Davies produces *Turtle Soup*, which reaches US #117.
Dec Judee Sill's *Lady-O*, the last official Turtles single, reaches US #78.

1970 May Compilation *The Turtles! More Golden Hits* reaches US #146.
June Band refuses to complete *Shell Shock* because of growing displeasure with White Whale, which retaliates by issuing *Eve Of Destruction* (from the first album) as a single. It spends 1 week at US #100, while the band dissolves amid dissension within its own ranks, as well as with the label. Kaylan and Volman, (with Pons following), accept Frank Zappa's invitation to join The Mothers Of Invention. They first appear on *Chunga's Revenge*, billed as The Phlorescent Leech & Eddie, because of legal restraint against using their names.

1971 Having befriended Marc Bolan when Tyrannosaurus Rex supported The Turtles on a US tour, Kaylan and Volman assist on Bolan's new T. Rex material, singing back-up vocals on albums *T. Rex* and *Electric Warrior*, and on hit singles *Hot Love* and *Get It On (Bang A Gong)*.
June With Zappa, they record live *Fillmore East, June 1971*.
Aug [7] At UCLA, Zappa records live *Just Another Band From LA*, the last to feature Kaylan and Volman, who leave to record as Flo (Volman) and Eddie (Kaylan). The duo also appears in Zappa's movie "200 Motels" and performs on the soundtrack album.

1972 *The Phlorescent Leech And Eddie*, on Reprise, is recorded with Pons, Aynsley Dunbar, Don Preston and Gary Rowles (ex-Love). Duo also sings back-up vocals on John Lennon's *Some Time In New York City*.

1973 *Flo & Eddie* is released; the duo having shortened its name to this.

1974 Weekly radio show, "Flo And Eddie By The Fireside", goes into national syndication in US.

1975 Jan Double anthology *Happy Together Again: The Turtles' Greatest Hits*, compiled and annotated by Kaylan and Volman, and including rare and unissued material as well as the hits, reaches US #194. Meanwhile, Flo & Eddie change labels, releasing *Illegal Immoral And Fattening* on CBS/Columbia.

1976 *Moving Targets* is released, including a new version of The Turtles' *Elenore*. Volman and Kaylan buy the rights to the group's name. Nicol moves to Arcata, CA, for the hippy life and Pons heads film department of the New York Jets football team, then signs publishing deal with Chappell in Nashville, TN.

1980 Volman and Kaylan sing back-up vocals on albums by Blondie (*Autoamerican*) and Alice Cooper (*Flush The Fashion*).

1981 After a period as guest vocalists and producers, the duo releases *Rock Steady With Flo And Eddie* on Epiphany, recorded in Jamaica with top reggae artists.

1982 Rhino Records in US begins a reissue program of the entire Turtles catalog, releasing all albums, including rare *Wooden Head*, various compilations and much previously unavailable material – all with full assistance from Kaylan and Volman. A new touring version of The Turtles, based around the duo, hits the road for a successful series of nostalgia gigs.

'87 Rhino issues unreleased *Shell Shock*, abandoned at the end of the group's White Whale career.

'88 Rhino releases 4 Turtles former hits on a 3" CD EP.

'89 **July** Volman and Kaylan sue De La Soul for $1.7 million for sampling part of *You Showed Me* as backing track for *Transmitting Live From Mars*.

U2

Bono (vocals)
The Edge (guitar)
Adam Clayton (bass)
Larry Mullen Jr. (drums)

'76 Dublin school boy band, featuring Bono (b. Paul Hewson, May 10, 1960, Dublin, Eire), The Edge (b. David Evans, Aug.8, 1961, Wales), Clayton (b. Mar.13, 1960), Mullen Jr. (b. Oct.31, 1961, Dublin) and Dick Evans, forms as Feedback at Mullen's parents' home, in response to Mullen's note on Mount Temple high school notice board. Playing mainly cover versions at small-time local engagements, the group changes name to The Hype and, with Dick Evans' departure to form The Virgin Prunes, to U2. (Hewson has adopted the name Bono from a billboard, advertising a hearing aid retailer, Bono Vox.)

'78 **Mar** [30] After playing pub and club gigs in Dublin, U2 wins a talent contest sponsored by Guinness at the Limerick Civic Week. Still in their final year at school, they win £500 and the chance to audition for CBS Ireland (through contest adjudicator A&R man Jackie Hayden) at the Keystone studios. Already managed by Paul McGuinness, U2 secures live support slots for The Stranglers and The Greedy Bastards.
Sept Hayden arranges for **Record Mirror** journalist Chas de Whalley to record further demos at the Windmill Lane studios, Dublin, which leads to signing with CBS Ireland (UK does not take up the option).
[18] Band poses backstage after a gig at Dublin's Project Arts Centre, holding gun and pistol replicas.

'79 **Sept** Having built considerable Irish fan support, following an RTE Radio 2 Irish demo session tape broadcast, U2 finally releases EP *U2:3*, featuring *Out Of Control*, *Stories* and *Boy – Girl*. Only available in Ireland, it tops the chart.
Dec U2 plays its first UK dates to little interest. Miscredited as "V2" at the Hope & Anchor pub in London, only 9 people show to watch them.

'80 **Jan** U2 wins 5 categories in Irish music magazine **Hot Press'** annual poll.
Feb As *Another Day*, produced by Whalley, also hits #1 in Ireland, U2 plays sell-out gigs in its home territory.
Mar After more promising UK dates attended by A&R employee Bill Stewart, UK label Island signs the band (it remains on CBS in Ireland).
May Debut Island single, *11 O'Clock Tick Tock* is released, produced by Martin Hannett, but fails to chart in UK.
[22] A UK tour opens at the Hope & Anchor to coincide with release of *11 O'Clock Tick Tock*. It will end at the Half Moon, Herne Hill, London, on June 8.
July [28] Group participates in the Dalmount Festival, Dublin with The Police and Squeeze.
Aug *A Day Without Me* is released.
Oct *I Will Follow* is released in both UK and US, but charts in neither.
Nov Debut album *Boy*, produced by Steve Lillywhite, and recorded at the Windmill Lane studios, Dublin, fails to chart. (The boy featured on the front cover is Peter, a brother of Virgin Prunes vocalist Guggi.) U2 performs its first US dates, a 3-week club tour on the East Coast.
Dec Constantly gigging, U2 supports Talking Heads on a UK tour, having recently played in Belgium and Holland.

'981 **Feb** Prior to embarking on a major US tour, the group headlines at London's Lyceum Ballroom. It also appears on UK BBC TV's "The Old Grey Whistle Test".
Mar *Boy* climbs to US #63.
Apr US tour closes with gigs at New York's Palladium and the Civic Center, Santa Monica, CA.
June Band returns to UK to perform at London's Hammersmith Palais.
July *Fire*, recorded during US tour break at Compass Point studio, Nassau, Bahamas, is the group's UK chart debut at #35.
Aug *Boy* belatedly makes UK #52.
Oct [1] U2 begins an 18-date UK tour.
Gloria makes UK #55, supported by a video shot at Dublin docks.
Nov Parent album *October*, produced by Lillywhite and again

recorded at the Windmill Lane studios, Dublin (their long-term professional base), reaches UK #11 and US #104, as U2 begins fresh round of US dates.

1982 **Jan** U2 performs its first Irish tour for over a year, with a finale at Dublin's RDS.
Mar [17] U2 plays a St. Patrick's Day gig at the Ritz, New York.
Apr Following a sold-out UK tour, *A Celebration* (not available on album) makes UK #47.
June U2 enters Windmill Lane to spend the rest of the year recording new songs.
Oct During a concert in Belfast, N.Ireland, Bono introduces new song *Sunday Bloody Sunday*. (Written by The Edge, its "peace in Northern Ireland" message becomes a live focal point for the band in coming years and highlights links between lyrics and politics.)

1983 **Feb** *New Year's Day*, boosted by a snow-bound video, hits UK #10 as parent album *War*, their last with Lillywhite, climbs to US #12. U2 begins a 27-date sell-out UK tour.
Mar *War* enters UK chart at #1.
Apr U2 begins a 2-month US arena tour while *Two Hearts Beat As One* reaches UK #18.
May [4] Debut US chart single *New Year's Day* peaks at #53, as remaining US dates draw superlative reviews and large crowds.
[28] U2 takes part in the 3-day US Festival in San Bernadino, CA.
Aug U2 headlines Irish open-air rock festival "A Day At The Races", in front of 25,000 people at Dublin's Phoenix Park.
Nov First live album *Under A Blood Red Sky*, produced by Jimmy Iovine, is released simultaneously with same-titled video. It hits UK #2 and begins a climb to US #28. Recorded in Boston, MA, Germany and at the Red Rocks festival in Colorado, it becomes the most successful live album ever, but does little to offset the growing number of U2 bootleg recordings.
Dec U2 performs its first gigs in Japan.

1984 **Jan** [28] *I Will Follow* makes US #81.
July Bono duets with Bob Dylan on *Blowing In The Wind* at Dylan's concert at Slane Castle, Eire.
Aug U2 performs first concerts of new world tour in New Zealand and Australia. Band establishes its own Mother Records to showcase the recordings of unsigned talent (mostly Irish). The label's first release is In Tua Nua's *Coming Thru'*. Run by Fachtra O'Ceallaigh, Mother will also sign, usually on a one-record basis, bands including Cactus World News, Tuesday Blue, Operating Theatre, Painted Word, The Subterraneans and Hothouse Flowers.
Sept Now produced by Brian Eno and Daniel Lanois, new studio album *The Unforgettable Fire* hits UK #1 and US #12 as extracted *Pride (In The Name Of Love)*, dedicated to Martin Luther King Jr., hits UK #3.
Nov [25] Bono contributes a lead vocal part to Band Aid's *Do They Know It's Christmas?*, while Clayton plays bass. Both are in London on UK stage of ongoing tour, including 2 SRO dates at Wembley Arena.
Dec [15] *Pride (In The Name Of Love)* makes US #33.

1985 **Feb** [25] U2 begins its first full US arena tour following sold-out European dates, in Dallas, TX.
Apr [1] U2 headlines at New York's Madison Square Garden as **Rolling Stone** magazine honors the group as The Band Of The 80s.
May *The Unforgettable Fire* hits UK #6.
June [22] Band bill-tops at "The Longest Day" concert at the Milton Keynes Bowl, Bucks., in a series of summer European festival dates.
[29] U2 returns to Eire to perform in front of 55,000 audience at Dublin's Croke Park.
July [13] U2 plays the fund-raising Live Aid spectacular at Wembley Stadium, Wembley, London, being introduced transatlantically by Jack Nicholson in Philadelphia, PA. US import album *Wide Awake In America*, a live studio collection of 5 cuts, makes UK #11. (Title track is the only previously unreleased track.)
Oct Released as an EP in US, *Wide Awake In America* reaches US #37.
Nov Bono appears on Little Steven-organized Artists United Against Apartheid single and video *Sun City* (UK #21 and US #38). He also sings the closing number, *Silver And Gold*, on the accompanying album, recorded with The Rolling Stones' Keith Richard and Ron Wood.

1986 **Jan** Bono is a featured vocalist on Irish folk group Clannad's *In A Lifetime*, which reaches UK #20.
Feb U2 wins Best Band, and Best Live Aid Performance in **Rolling Stone**'s 1985 Readers' Poll.
Mar U2 resumes world touring (which will include performing on Amnesty International's 25th anniversary tour).
May [17] U2 joins other Irish rock acts to play Self Aid in Dublin, to raise funds for the unemployed.

June [4] Amnesty International's "A Conspiracy Of Hope" 2-week US tour begins, featuring U2, Sting, Peter Gabriel, Bryan Adams and Lou Reed at Cow Palace, San Francisco, CA.

Aug Band enters the studio, with Eno and Lanois, to record a new album. (The Edge also records soundtrack album *The Captive* with Irish songstress Sinead O'Connor.)

Sept [25] U2 is joined on stage by Bruce Springsteen during a concert in Philadelphia, PA.

1987 **Feb** U2 begins a 110-date arena venue world tour.

Mar [21] *The Joshua Tree* enters UK chart at #1, going platinum in 48 hours, the fastest selling album in UK chart history to date.

[27] Group films a video for *Where The Streets Have No Name* in downtown Los Angeles, CA, drawing a crowd of thousands.

[28] *With Or Without You* hits UK #4.

Apr [2] U2 embarks on another world tour, beginning in Arizona. With changed US chart eligibility, mini-album *Wide Awake In America* now makes US #100.

[25] *The Joshua Tree* tops US chart, staying there for 9 weeks.

[27] U2 makes the cover of **Time** magazine with the headline "U2: Rock's Hottest Ticket".

May [16] *With Or Without You* becomes U2's first US #1. With music by U2 and lyrics by Bono, it is typical of their songwriting format. An immediate airplay and sales smash, it stays on top for 3 weeks.

[27] European leg of world trek opens in Rome, and is set to end Aug.8 in Cork, Eire.

I Still Haven't Found What I'm Looking For, with a video filmed on the streets of Las Vegas, NV, hits UK #6.

Aug *Where The Streets Have No Name*, accompanied by a performance video filmed on top of a Los Angeles building, hits UK #4.

[8] *I Still Haven't Found What I'm Looking For* tops US chart.

Sept [10] North American leg of world tour resumes at the Nassau Coliseum, Uniondale, NY, the first of 50 dates.

Nov [7] *Where The Streets Have No Name* reaches US #13. Book **Unforgettable Fire: The Story Of U2** hits UK book best-seller lists. Written by Eamon Dunphy, it was originally authorized by the band who later withdrew their support having negotiated unsuccessfully to change the text, which is claimed to be inaccurate.

[18] U2 opens for itself at Los Angeles' Coliseum as country/rock outfit The Dalton Brothers.

Dec U2 contributes *Christmas (Baby Please Come Home)* to Jimmy Iovine's charity album **Special Christmas**.

1988 **Jan** [23] *In God's Country* makes US #44, after making UK #48 on import.

Feb [8] U2 receives Best International Group award at the British Record Industry Awards ceremony at London's Royal Albert Hall.

[20] *The Joshua Tree Singles* spends 1 week on UK chart at #100.

Mar [2] Band wins Album Of The Year and Best Rock Performance By A Duo Or Group With Vocal for *The Joshua Tree* at the 30th annual Grammy awards at Radio City Music Hall, New York.

Apr Band works in Los Angeles, recording new album tracks and overseeing post-production of their forthcoming live documentary movie "Rattle And Hum".

Sept U2 contribute *Jesus Christ* to Woody Guthrie/Leadbelly tribute album **Folkways: A Vision Shared**, and Bono and The Edge make contributions to Roy Orbison comeback album **Mystery Girl**.

Oct [8] *Desire* becomes U2's first UK #1 single.

[16] U2 performs at the "Smile Jamaica" live TV fund-raiser for the Hurricane Gilbert disaster fund, at London's Dominion theater, playing 4 cuts from *Rattle And Hum*. They are joined on stage by Keith Richard and bill-topper Ziggy Marley.

[22] Double album *Rattle And Hum*, produced by Jimmy Iovine, (the title taken from U2 song *Bullet The Blue Sky*), capturing live performances from the past 2 years and including rare studio songs, hits UK #1 (with record ship-out figures).

[27] U2's film "Rattle And Hum" receives its world premiere in Dublin. It was directed by Philip Joanou, whose brief was to "follow the 'Joshua Tree' tour and make a film".

Nov U2 plays "Smile Jamaica" benefit gig at London's Brixton Academy and is joined on stage by Keith Richard.

[12] *Rattle And Hum* tops US chart.

[26] *Desire* hits US #3.

Dec *Angel Of Harlem*, recorded at the legendary Sun studios, Memphis, TN, hits UK #9.

Group is featured singing *Maggie's Farm* on **Live For Ireland**, a compilation which also features Elvis Costello and Van Morrison.

Dec *Rattle And Hum* gains multiplatinum status for 2 million sales.

1989 **Feb** [11] *Angel Of Harlem* reaches US #14.

[13] Band wins Best International Group at the eighth annual BRIT Awards at London's Royal Albert Hall.

[22] U2 wins Best Rock Performance By A Duo Or Group With Vocal for *Desire* and Best Performance Music Video for "Where The Streets Have No Name" at the 31st annual Grammy awards.

Apr *When Love Comes To Town*, with blues legend B.B. King hits UK #
[29] *When Love Comes To Town* peaks at US #68.

May [10] Bono and wife Alisa's daughter Jordan is born.

June [4] Bono joins Bob Dylan on stage in Dublin for encores of *Knockin' On Heaven's Door* and *Maggie's Farm*.

[24] *All I Want Is You* (with U2's version of *Unchained Melody*) hits U #4, as 23-date Australian tour, the group's second, opens in Perth.

July [15] *All I Want Is You* makes US #83.

Aug [6] Clayton is arrested in Dublin for marijuana possession and intent to supply the drug to another person.

Sept [1] Clayton's marijuana conviction is waived in exchange for paying $34,500 to the Dublin Women's Aid & Refuge Centre.

[6] U2 and B.B. King win Best Video From Film award at the sixth annual MTV Music Video Awards ceremony at the Universal Amphitheater, Los Angeles.

[10] NBC TV broadcasts first annual International Very Special Arts Festival, featuring U2, Kenny Rogers, Mikhail Baryshnikov, Lauren Bacall and Michael Douglas, from the lawn of the White House. The festival celebrates accomplishments of physically and mentally handicapped artists from around the world.

[12] Band begins a 5-week, 19-date Australian tour in Perth, followed by 9 further concerts in New Zealand and Japan.

Dec [31] Band's New Year's Eve gig at Dublin's Point Depot is broadcast live throughout East and West Europe.

1990 **Feb** [6] The Royal Shakespeare Company production "A Clockwork Orange 2004", an adaptation of Anthony Burgess' **A Clockwork Orange** with music by The Edge, opens in London.

Mar [8] Bono wins Best Songwriter and Sexiest Male Rock Artist and Adam Clayton wins Best Bassist in the annual **Rolling Stone** Readers' Picks 1989 music awards.

May [26] The Chimes' cover of *I Still Haven't Found What I'm Looking For* hits UK #6.

June Mullen pens official Eire World Cup soccer team's song.

Oct U2 contribute *Night And Day* to **Red Hot + Blue**, an anthology of Cole Porter songs to benefit AIDS education and travel to Berlin, Germany to film promo clip with director Wim Wenders.

Dec [1] U2's "Night And Day" video is featured in hour-long TV special of "Red Hot + Blue" on International AIDS Day.

UB40

Ali Campbell (lead vocals, rhythm guitar)
Earl Falconer (bass)
Robin Campbell (lead guitar, vocals)
Mickey Virtue (keyboards)
Brian Travers (saxophone)
Jim Brown (drums)
Norman Hassan (percussion)
"Yomi" Babayemi (percussion)

1979 **Feb** After 6 months of rehearsal, UB40 (named after the number on a UK unemployment benefit form) debuts at the Horse and Hounds in King's Heath, Birmingham, W.Midlands, sharing the bill with new local band, The Au Pairs. Most of the group have known each other for up to 10 years and several have attended art school together. Ali (b. Alastair Campbell, Feb.15, 1959, Birmingham) and Robin Campbell (b. Dec.25, 1954), sons of Scottish folk singer Ian Campbell, have sung with 2 other brothers in a barbershop quartet and been reggae fans since childhood. After only 1 more gig, Babayemi is deported to Nigeria by immigration authorities. The group and its manager, ex-encyclopedia salesman Simon Woods, contact local producer Bob Lamb, an ex-member of Birmingham reggae band The Locomotive (1968 hitmakers with *Rudi's In Love*) who owns an 8-track studio, to make some demos. Before the first sessions, reggae toaster/singer Astro (b. Terence Wilson, June 24, 1957, Birmingham) joins the group which now includes Earl Falconer (b. Jan.23, 1959, Birmingham), Michael Virtue (b. Jan.19, 1957, Birmingham), Jim Brown (b. Nov.20, 1957) and Norman Hassan (b. Jan.26, 1957, Birmingham). Their big break comes when The Pretenders' Chrissie Hynde sees their live show and offers a support slot on The Pretenders' 1979/80 UK tour. Despite major label interest, the group signs to Graduate, run by David and Susan Virr from their record shop in Dudley, W.Midlands. The deal gives them total control but no advance monies – resulting in debts at the outset of their career.

1980 **Apr** A-side of the group's first release is *King* (a dedication to Martin Luther King), but radio picks up on the catchy B-side *Food For Thought*. It tops Independent chart for 3 months before hitting UK #4. Recorded in Lamb's studio, it sells over a half million copies. Major record company pressure intensifies during the tour with The Pretenders.
July Follow-up *My Way Of Thinking*, backed with Randy Newman's *I Think It's Going To Rain Today*, hits UK #6.
[26] UB40 supports Police at the Rockatta De Bowl, Milton Keynes, Bucks.
Sept First album, *Signing Off*, recorded by Lamb in 8-track, hits UK #2 (and will stay on chart for 71 weeks).
Nov *The Earth Dies Screaming* hits UK #10.
Dec UB40 leaves Graduate, apparently due to Graduate deleting anti-apartheid *Burden Of Shame* from the South African release of the album. Group sets up its own DEP International company. After concerts in Europe and Ireland, it tours UK and appears on a Christmas bill at the Birmingham NEC, W.Midlands.

1981 **June** *Present Arms*, the first album on DEP International, hits UK #2, spending 38 weeks on chart. Initial copies of it come with a free 12" single containing 2 instrumentals, *Don't Walk On The Grass* and *Dr. X* (a reworking of the album's title track). The tracks are produced by the band's sound engineer, Ray "Pablo" Falconer, brother of bassist Earl. *Don't Let It Pass You By/Don't Slow Down* makes UK #16.
Sept *One In Ten*, a commentary on UK unemployment figures, hits UK #7. UB40 plays benefit gigs for those arrested during UK inner-city riots of the summer, which lead to UB40 being banned from venues in some cities. Group begins a major international tour.
Oct *Present Arms In Dub*, dub reworking of the album, makes UK #38.

1982 **Feb** *I Won't Close My Eyes* makes UK #32. B-side features Astro as a toaster and is a highlight of UB40's UK tour.
June *Love Is All Is Alright* makes UK #29 and hits #1 in Zimbabwe, for 3 weeks.
Sept Funk-tinged *So Here I Am* reaches UK #25. *The Singles Album*, a collection of the group's Graduate singles, makes UK #17.
Oct *UB44* hits UK #4, despite some negative reviews.

1983 **Feb** *I've Got Mine* makes UK #45 (their poorest chart position to date).
Mar *UB40 Live* reaches UK #44.
Sept *Red Red Wine*, their first UK #1 hit, tops chart for 3 weeks. (Group claims it was unaware the song was a Neil Diamond composition and had picked it up from Jamaican singer Tony Tribe's 1969 version.) *Labour Of Love*, a collection of classic songs given reggae covers, hits UK #1 and stays on chart for 18 months. It is supported by a short film, similarly titled, directed by Bernard Rose together with latest UB40 recruit Brian Travers (b. Feb.7, 1959, Birmingham, W.Midlands).
Nov *Please Don't Make Me Cry*, reviving Winston Groovy's original, hits UK #10.
Dec Jimmy Cliff's *Many Rivers To Cross* reaches UK #16.

1984 **Mar** [31] *Red Red Wine* makes US #34, the group's first US hit single.
Apr *Cherry Oh Baby* reaches UK #12. *Labour Of Love* reaches US #39.
Oct *If It Happens Again* hits UK #9 and *Geffrey Morgan* hits UK #3.
Dec *Riddle Me* peaks at UK #59. Group plays concerts for the Greater London Council, which is fighting off dissolution by the Government. *Geffrey Morgan* makes US #60.

1985 **Feb** UB40 joins Madness, Special AKA, General Public and The Pioneers to record *Starvation* (the profits go to the Ethiopian appeal).
May *I'm Not Fooled* peaks at UK #79.
Aug Ali Campbell and Chrissie Hynde's duet on a reggae version of Sonny & Cher's *I Got You Babe*, hits UK #1 for 1 week. The video for it is filmed by Jonathan Demme at a concert at Jones Beach, Long Island, NY, during one of UB40's 3 1985 US visits.
Sept *Baggariddim*, consisting of dub versions of tracks from the previous 2 albums, with toasters like Dillinger and Sister V guesting, reaches UK #14. In a trimmed-down version in US, *Little Baggariddim*, makes #40, while *I Got You Babe* (also included on the mini-album) makes US #28.
Dec *Don't Break My Heart*, taken from the free 12" issued with the album, hits UK #3.

1986 **July** *Sing Our Own Song*, an expression of solidarity with black activists in South Africa, hits UK #5.
Aug *Rat In The Kitchen*, featuring US label boss Herb Alpert on guest trumpet, hits UK #8 and makes US #53.
Oct *All I Want To Do* makes UK #41.

1987 **Jan** Single *Rat In Mi Kitchen* reaches UK #12.
May *Watchdogs* makes UK #39.

June Live Russian visit rockumentary "UB40: CCCP" is released by Virgin Video.
Sept *CCCP: Live In Moscow* climbs to US #121.
Oct *Maybe Tomorrow* reaches UK #14. "The Best Of UB40: Volume 1", a collection of video hits linked by Travers-directed "Fat Family" sketches, becomes a video best-seller.
Nov Virgin Records releases TV-advertised *The Best Of UB40 Vol.1* for the Christmas market. It hits UK #3. Falconer's Volvo turbo goes out of control and hits a wall, killing his brother Ray. The discovery of twice the legal limit of alcohol in Earl's bloodstream leads to charges.

1988 **Feb** UB40 guests on UK #17 Afrika Bambaataa hit *Reckless*.
June Second UB40/Chrissie Hynde collaboration, a version of reggae standard *Breakfast In Bed*, hits UK #6. Band completes filming of short film "Dance With The Devil", featuring Ali Campbell in the lead role as a trickster and a host of guest artists including Hynde, Robert Palmer and UK TV soap "Crossroads" actor Paul "Benny" Henry.
July A week before the group's world tour (set to last for 12 months) is due to start, a Birmingham Crown Court judge jails Earl Falconer for 6 months on charges from the car accident. Group is forced to use stand-in bassist at short notice. Newly-recorded *UB40* with sleeve painting by UK artist Steve Masterson, reaches UK #12.
[11] UB40 performs at "Nelson Mandela's 70th Birthday Party" at Wembley Stadium, London.
Sept *Where Did We Go Wrong* reaches UK #26.
Oct [15] *Red Red Wine* tops US chart while *Labour Of Love* (which contains the single) reaches US #14 and *UB40* makes US #44. Band is on major US tour when *Red Red Wine* (originally a 1984 US #34 peak) hits the top. It has been resurrected by a Phoenix, Arizona DJ who begins heavy airplay rotation of the disk following its performance at the Nelson Mandela concert.

1989 **June** *I Would Do For You* makes UK #45.
Nov A remake of The Chi-Lites' *Homely Girl* hits UK #6.

1990 **Feb** [3] *Here I Am (Come And Take Me)* makes UK #46 as *Labour Of Love II* peaks at US #69.
Parallel video release of "Labour Of Love II" is released by Virgin.
Apr [14] *Kingston Town* hits UK #4.
May [19] *Labour Of Love II*, featuring sleeve design by Barry Kamen, hits UK #3. It proves to be another multi-platinum collection of the band's interpretations of oldies.
July [8-9] UB40 ends 50-city North American arena tour with 2 shows in San Diego, CA.
Aug [1] Band is deported from the Seychelles after police uncover marijuana in their hotel room. They choose deportation over the other option, a mandatory 3-year jail term.
[18] *Wear You To The Ball* makes UK #35.
Nov [17] Teaming with Robert Palmer, a cover of Dylan's *I'll Be Your Baby Tonight* hits UK #6.
Dec [1] *Impossible Love* makes UK #47.
[15] *The Way You Do The Things You Do* hits US #6.

ULTRAVOX

John Foxx (guitar, lead vocals)
Billy Currie (synthesizer, piano)
Chris Cross (bass, synthesizer)
Warren Cann (drums)

1973 Foxx (b. Dennis Leigh, Chorley, Lancs.) recruits Cross (b. Christopher St. John, July 14, 1952, London), who has moved from London to join Preston, Lancs. band Stoned Rose, to form new band Tiger Lily.
Apr They add Cann (b. May 20, 1952, Victoria, Canada) on drums and Steve Shears on guitar. With Roxy Music as chief musical inspiration, they begin live gigs and demos.
Aug First significant gig is at London's Marquee club supporting The Heavy Metal Kids.
Oct Currie (b. Apr.1, 1952, Huddersfield, W.Yorks.) joins on keyboards.

1975 **Mar** Group records Fats Waller's *Ain't Misbehavin'*, (for an X-certificate film of the same title, which flops) coupled with *Monkey Jive* on small Gull label. (It will be reissued on Dead Good Records in Aug.1980.)

1976 **July** After trying a series of names, including The Zips, The Innocents, London Soundtrack and Fire Of London, they become Ultravox.
Aug Group signs to Island Records and spends rest of the year writing and rehearsing its debut album. First product is *The Wild, The Beautiful And The Damned* which is featured on an Island sampler album.

1977 **Feb** Debut single *Dangerous Rhythm*, from upcoming album, is issued.
Mar *Ultravox!*, co-produced by ex-Roxy Music Brian Eno, is released

and is critically well received.

Oct *Rockwork* and parent album *Ha! Ha! Ha!* are issued; neither charts.

1978 Feb *Retro*, a live 4-track EP, is released. Band travels to Germany to record with Conny Plank. Prior to the sessions, Shears leaves, to be replaced by Robin Simon, ex-Neo.

Aug Group performs at the Reading Festival, Berks. (billed second to The Jam), and 5 consecutive dates at London's Marquee.

Sept Plank-produced *Systems Of Romance* is issued; it does not chart.

Dec [26] Original line-up plays 2 last UK dates at London's Marquee.

1979 Jan Island Records drops the group.

Mar After some weeks of final gigs in US, Foxx leaves for a solo career on returning to UK. Cann works with New Zealand singer Zaine Griff, while Currie and Simon play with Gary Numan and Magazine respectively, and Cross writes songs with his brother. Apart from Foxx, the members still wish to continue with Ultravox, and look for a new singer and guitarist.

Apr Guitarist/singer Midge Ure (b. James Ure, Oct.10, 1953, Gambusland, Glasgow, Scotland) joins. He has been with Currie in Visage and was in Salvation, which became UK teenybop try-outs Slik. (In 1976, after teaming with The Bay City Rollers' producers Bill Martin and Phil Coulter, they become brief pop sensations, hitting UK #1 with *Forever And Ever*. Ure left in 1977 and then teamed with ex-The Sex Pistols' Glen Matlock in The Rich Kids.) While the group works on new material, Ure stands in for Brian Robertson in Thin Lizzy.

Nov New line-up plays 4 UK gigs, starting at Eric's, Liverpool, Merseyside, to prepare for a US tour the following month.

1980 Jan Foxx, having created his own MetalBeat label, releases *Underpass*, which makes UK #31 as parent album *Metamatic* reaches UK #18.

Mar Foxx's 4-track EP *No One Driving* makes UK #32.

Apr Ultravox, signed to Chrysalis, releases *Sleepwalk*, the group's first single with Ure. It reaches UK #29 while Island issues *Three Into One*, a compilation of the best of the 3 albums for the label.

July *Vienna*, the group's first album with Ure and for Chrysalis, hits UK #3 during a 72-week chart stay. Foxx's *Burning Car* makes UK #35.

Aug [2] Group begins a UK tour at the Drill Hall, Lincoln, Lincs. [24] They play at Tiffanys as part of the Edinburgh Rock Festival.

Oct Ultravox's *Passing Strangers* peaks at UK #57, as *Vienna* is US debut at #164.

Nov *Burning Car*, by Foxx, makes US #51.

1981 Jan Grandiose ballad *Vienna* attracts heavy UK airplay, hitting UK #2, held off the top by Joe Dolce's novelty *Shaddap You Face*.

Mar Island releases 3-track EP *Slow Motion*, which makes UK #33.

June *All Stood Still* hits UK #8.

Aug *The Thin Wall*, recorded earlier in the year in Germany with producer Plank, reaches UK #14. Foxx makes UK #40 with *Europe After The Rain*.

Sept *Rage In Eden* hits UK #4.

Oct Foxx's second album *In The Garden* reaches UK #24.

Nov Ultravox's *The Voice* peaks at UK #16, while *Rage In Eden* makes US #144.

1982 June Ure releases solo Chrysalis single, *No Regrets*, which hits UK #9. (He will produce Steve Harley, Atrix and Modern Man, while also working with Visage.)

Sept Ultravox reaches UK #12 with *Reap The Wild Wind*.

Oct *Quartet*, recorded in Montserrat with George Martin producing, hits UK #6.

Nov *Hymn* reaches UK #11.

1983 Mar *Visions In Blue* reaches UK #15.

Apr [30] Group achieves its only US single success with *Reap The Wild Wind* which makes US #71. Parent album *Quartet* peaks at US #61.

June *We Came To Dance* reaches UK #18.

July Ure's *After A Fashion* with Japan bassist Mick Karn makes UK #39.

Oct *Monument – The Soundtrack* hits UK #9. Foxx's *The Golden Section* reaches UK #27.

1984 Feb *One Small Day* reaches UK #27.

Apr *Lament* hits UK #8.

May *Dancing With Tears In My Eyes* becomes Ultravox' first UK Top 10 record in 3 years, hitting UK #3.

June *Lament* climbs to US #115.

July Extracted title track, *Lament*, reaches UK #22.

Oct *Love's Great Adventure* reaches UK #12.

Nov Chrysalis issues a retrospective album of its Ultravox recordings, *The Collection*, which hits UK #2. Ure is approached by Bob Geldof to write a song to be recorded by an all-star band to raise funds for the starving people of Ethiopia.

Dec [15] *Do They Know It's Christmas?*, is recorded by Band Aid. (It

enters UK chart at #1 and will become the UK's biggest-selling single.)

1985 July Continuing his efforts with Geldof to raise money to ease famine in Africa and especially Ethiopia, Ure is active behind the scenes in organizing the Live Aid spectacular, at which he also performs.

Sept Ure's solo *If I Was* tops UK chart, as Ultravox remains quiet.

Oct Ure's *The Gift* hits UK #2. Foxx's *In Mysterious Ways* spends 1 week on UK chart at #85.

Nov *That Certain Smile* reaches UK #28.

Dec Ure begins his first solo tour, with Zal Cleminson, ex-The Sensational Alex Harvey Band, on guitar and Kenny Hyslop (with whom Ure has worked in Slik), on drums.

1986 Feb Ure's *Wastelands* makes UK #46.

June His follow-up *Call Of The Wild* reaches UK #27.

Oct Group album *U-Vox* hits UK #9, as *Same Old Story* makes UK #31.

Nov *All Fall Down* reaches UK #30.

1988 June [11] Ure assembles the band for "Nelson Mandela's 70th Birthday Party" concert.

Sept Ure's *Answers To Nothing* reaches UK #30, as the title track makes UK #49.

Nov *Dear God* peaks at UK #55.

1989 Feb Ure album *Answer To Nothing* rises to US #88.

Mar [11] Ure's *Dear God* peaks at US #95.

1991 Jan Currie solo album *Stand Up And Walk* emerges on UK independent label Hot Food.

THE UNDERTONES

Feargal Sharkey (vocals)
John O'Neill (guitar)
Damian "Dee" O'Neill (guitar)
Michael Bradley (bass)
Billy Doherty (drums)

1975 Nov Band is formed by 5 friends in Londonderry, N.Ireland, playing pop covers in local pubs. Line-up remains the same throughout band's existence.

1977 Band begins to perform more of its own songs and makes a demo which is rejected by Stiff, Chiswick and Radar Records.

1978 Aug After a period of playing regional gigs during which their act and repertoire are finely honed, The Undertones are spotted and recorded by Belfast independent label Good Vibrations Records.

Sept Punk-tinged debut release *Teenage Kicks* receives UK airplay from BBC DJ John Peel, which brings A&R interest from UK labels.

Oct Band flies to London to play "Top Of The Pops" as the record climbs the chart. They are still without a manager, so Sharkey (b. Aug.13, 1958) negotiates a 5-year deal with Sire Records. Sire reissues *Teenage Kicks* (only 7,000 copies were pressed on Good Vibrations).

Nov *Teenage Kicks* reaches UK #31 in a 6-week chart run. The band begins its first UK tour with The Rezillos, who split halfway through and leave The Undertones to continue the tour alone.

1979 Feb *Get Over You* makes UK #57.

May *Jimmy Jimmy* is first UK Top 20 hit at #16. Debut album *The Undertones* is released and climbs to UK #13, the sleeve inspired by The Who's *My Generation* 1965 debut.

July A re-recorded version of *Here Comes The Summer*, extracted from the album, makes UK #34. While it is on the chart, the group plays its first US tour, supporting The Clash.

Oct *You've Got My Number (Why Don't You Use It?)* peaks at UK #32.

1980 Jan Band goes to Holland with producer Roger Bechirian to record second album.

Apr *Hypnotised* is released and becomes their biggest-selling UK album, hitting #6. *My Perfect Cousin* is their biggest UK hit single at #9, aided by UK Subuteo boardgame-featuring promotion video.

July Extracted *Wednesday Week* charts at UK #11.

Aug The Undertones tour US again, this time as headliners, but they fail to chart there and remain cult favorites. A headlining European tour follows.

Oct Dissatisfied with lack of chart progress outside UK, the band does not renew its Sire contract but sets up its own label, Ardeck Records, through EMI.

1981 May New UK single *It's Going To Happen* and album *Positive Touch* are released displaying a widening of approach and more sophistication than earlier aggressive work. Album charts at UK #17 and single peaks at UK #18.

July Rapid UK follow-up *Julie Ocean* makes #41.

1982 Feb *Beautiful Friend* is issued in UK but fails to chart.

Oct *The Love Parade* also fails to chart.

1983 Mar *The Sin Of Pride* makes UK #43 but has no hit singles to keep it on chart.

June Group disbands and EMI marks the split by reissuing *Teenage Kicks*. It makes UK #60.

Dec 30-track compilation *All Wrapped Up*, issued as a memorial to the band, charts at UK #67. Sharkey, always the group's main focus, joins ex-Depeche Mode and Yazoo writer/keyboardist Vince Clarke for The Assembly one-off single, *Never Never*, which hits UK #4, then announces plans to continue as a solo act.

1984 Oct Invited to be first act on Madness' Zarjazz label, Sharkey has band backing him on his solo *Listen To Your Father*, which reaches UK #23.

Dec [7] He performs in a benefit concert for Ethiopia at London's Royal Albert Hall, organized by Save The Children Fund, along with Nick Heyward, Julian Lennon, Mike Rutherford of Genesis and others.

1985 July Sharkey signs to Virgin, and debut *Loving You* makes UK #26.

Nov He tops UK chart for 2 weeks with *A Good Heart*, written by Maria McKee of US group Lone Justice. *Feargal Sharkey*, produced by Dave Stewart of Eurythmics, makes UK #12.

1986 Jan *You Little Thief*, taken from the album (and first promoted in UK by Sharkey on a live TV slot from a Virgin airliner flying over London on Christmas Day) hits UK #5.

Feb [6] While Sharkey is touring UK and performing in Sheffield, his mother Sybil and sister Ursula, visiting friends in Londonderry, N.Ireland, are held at gunpoint for 4 hours by terrorists but eventually released.

Apr *Someone To Somebody* makes UK #64. Sharkey separates from his wife and moves to Los Angeles, CA to re-start his career. *A Good Heart* makes US #74 as parent album *Feargal Sharkey* reaches US #75.

1988 Jan *More Love*, Sharkey's first recording for over 18 months, makes UK #44, though parent album *Wish* will fail to score when issued in Apr.

1991 Mar New campaign is launched with self-penned ballad *I've Got News For You*, which begins immediate UK chart rise.

USA FOR AFRICA

1984 Dec UK superstar line-up group Band Aid, assembled by Bob Geldof, hits UK #1 with *Do They Know It's Christmas?*, released to raise funds to help feed starving people in Ethiopia and elsewhere in Africa. It sells over 3 million copies in UK alone, and Geldof suggests that the music industry, on a worldwide basis, could raise over $500 million.

[20] Inspired by Geldof's efforts, music veteran Harry Belafonte conceives the idea for a US fund-raiser for the same cause. He calls management and TV production company head Ken Kragen, who in turn calls Lionel Richie.

[21] Richie's wife Brenda spots friend Stevie Wonder in their local store and asks him to contact her husband about the idea. Meanwhile, Kragen asks Quincy Jones to produce the project, and Jones secures the help of Michael Jackson.

1985 Jan While Kragen establishes the United Support of Artists Foundation (with himself as president and Jackson, Richie, Belafonte, Jones and Kenny Rogers on the board of directors) and as major stars are quietly invited to participate, he enlists the financial and organizational abilities of Marty Rogol who has already run fund-raisers with Harry Chapin and Rogers. Kragen also invites Barrie Bergman, head of large US record retailers Record Bar, to organize a committee to ensure that all retail profits from any product will go to the USA For Africa fund.

[28] Kragen has decided to record the USA For Africa disk on the night of the American Music Awards when a concentration of top artists will attend. Following the AMA celebrations at 10.00pm, 45 artists arrive at the A&M studios, Hollywood, CA, greeted by the warning from Jones to "check your ego at the door". The song to be recorded, *We Are The World*, has been written by Jackson and Richie in just 2 hours, following 3 days of preparation. It is arranged, produced and engineered by Jones, Tom Bahler and Humberto Gatica. Inside the studio, a strip of named tape for each performer has been stuck on the floor forming a semi-circular ensemble. Those chosen for lead vocals will be later grouped close to one of 6 microphones, as their efforts will be recorded after the choruses have been taped. (Geldof sings as part of the chorus, with a host of stars.) This in turn follows the instrumental tracks, recorded earlier by Jones. The end result features 21 solo vocal segments which are, in order of appearance, Lionel Richie, Stevie Wonder, Paul Simon, Kenny Rogers, James Ingram, Tina Turner, Billy Joel, Michael Jackson, Diana Ross, Dionne Warwick, Willie Nelson, Al Jarreau, Bruce Springsteen, Kenny Loggins, Steve Perry, Daryl Hall, Huey Lewis, Cyndi Lauper, Kim Carnes, Bob Dylan and Ray Charles. Prince has been invited, but fails to show. (He will contribute a song to

the subsequent album.) A video team tapes the historic event resulting in 75 hours of footage, later edited to promote the song. After 10 hours, only Richie and Jones remain, putting the final touches to an extraordinary record.

Feb While efforts are made to ship the disk as soon as possible, Kragen decides on CBS/Columbia for its free manufacturing and distribution (all major record companies have offered the same). Meanwhile, Jim Mazza at EMI suggests Kragen organize the release of an album of unreleased tracks from some participating USA For Africa artists.

Mar [7] 800,000 copies are distributed to record stores nationwide in US. (Within 2 days they have been sold and re-orders are flooding in.)
[23] *We Are The World* enters US chart at #21. (It will hit #1 by Apr.13, where it will stay for 4 weeks. It also hits UK #1, tops charts in most Western territories and sells 7.5 million copies in US alone.)

Apr [4] Columbia ships 2.7 million copies of *We Are The World* in US. Rush-released, donated cuts are from Springsteen, Prince (4 *The Tears In Your Eyes*), Huey Lewis & The News, Chicago, Turner, The Pointer Sisters, Rogers, Perry, USA For Africa and Northern Lights. (Inspired by USA For Africa, a Canadian effort under the banner Northern Lights is organized. The track is *Tears Are Not Enough*, produced by David Foster and featuring Bryan Adams, John Candy, Corey Hart, Dan Hill, Gordon Lightfoot, Joni Mitchell, Anne Murray and Neil Young, among others.) The album will spend 3 weeks at US #1 and reach UK #31.
[5] At 3.50pm GMT, over 5,000 radio stations worldwide unite for 7 mins. 2 secs. as *We Are The World* is aired.
[20] USA For Africa Foundation's legal counsel, Jay Cooper, claims that bootleg merchandise, particularly T-shirts, is appearing in many US cities. Authorized merchandisers, Winterland, take measures to clamp down on the pirates.

May [16] An initial cheque for $6.5 million in royalties is handed to Kragen by Columbia executive Al Teller. Associated and combined sales from the song, album and merchandise will exceed $50 million.

June [10] First airlift of supplies is flown to Africa for relief.
[14] With various local fund-raising efforts still gathering momentum, video distributor RCA/Columbia ships "We Are The World – The Video Event" to swell USA For Africa funds further. Company president Robert Blattner signs an agreement with Richie to ensure that all profits from the $14.95 video are donated directly to the foundation.

RITCHIE VALENS

1952 At Pacoima Junior High, Valens (b. Richard Steven Valenzuela, May 13, 1941, Pacoima, Los Angeles, CA) builds a solid-body electric guitar (which he will use until success pays for a Fender Stratocaster), after learning to play acoustic Spanish guitar (right-handed, despite being left-handed) 2 years earlier. Surrounded by Mexican music (with Mexican-Indian parents), he has been music-obsessed since an early age – initially Chicano folk, then R&B, and eventually Little Richard-style rock'n'roll.

1957 Nov He joins The Silhouettes, a Mexican band which includes a Japanese tenor sax player and 2 Afro-Chicanos. He sings R&B and rock'n'roll numbers with the group, and is so popular that he becomes its frontman.

1958 May He auditions for Bob Keene, owner of Hollywood-based Del-Fi label, after being seen at an American Legion dance in San Fernando, CA by a Del-Fi talent scout. Keene decides to record him. The first session produces *Come On, Let's Go*, for which he has a riff worked out, but no lyrics, so he makes up the words on the spot. Coupled with Leiber/Stoller's *Framed* (also recorded by The Coasters), it is released with his name shortened to Ritchie Valens.

Aug Valens begins his first US tour during which he befriends Eddie Cochran and appears singing *Come On, Let's Go* on Dick Clark's "American Bandstand" TV show.

Oct *Come On, Let's Go* has a 13-week US chart run, peaking at #42 as he finishes touring (in UK Tommy Steele's cover hits #10). On his return to Los Angeles, Valens records *Donna*, written for his high school sweetheart Donna Ludwig. For the B-side, Keene suggests updating a traditional Mexican wedding song which, sung in Spanish, becomes *La Bamba*.

Dec [5] Valens returns to his old school, to play a concert which is recorded by Keene. He films a cameo slot for Alan Freed's movie "Go, Johnny, Go", lip-synching his *Ooh My Head*.
[25] After a second "American Bandstand" appearance, he plays a 10-day run with Cochran, Bo Diddley and The Everly Brothers in Alan Freed's Christmas Show at New York's Loew's State theater, as both sides of his second single (*Donna* and *La Bamba*) race each other up the

US chart, *La Bamba* initially in the lead.

1959 **Jan** Valens records tracks for an album and joins "The Winter Dance Party" tour through the upper Mid-West in icy weather.

Feb [2] *La Bamba* reaches US #22.

[3] After a show at Clear Lake, IA, Buddy Holly charters a plane to take them to the next venue. Holly's guitarist Tommy Allsup gives up his seat to Valens, and bassist Waylon Jennings gives his to The Big Bopper. Minutes after take-off, the plane crashes in a frozen corn field, killing all on board. *Donna* hits US #2 and is a posthumous million-seller.

Mar *Donna* charts in UK at #29 for 1 week, overtaken by Marty Wilde's cover which hits #3.

Apr *Ritchie Valens* makes US #23 and *That's My Little Suzie* peaks at US #55.

July *Little Girl* reaches US #92. (Further singles and 2 albums – *Ritchie*, made up from the remainder of his unissued studio tapes, including some guitar instrumentals, and *Live At Pacoima Junior High School*, from the Dec.1958 concert – will be released by Del-Fi over the following 12 months, but neither will chart. Valens' songs will be covered by many artists, and his influence as a pioneer of "Chicano rock" will endure despite his short career.)

1985 Manuel Velasquez, artist and counselor for the Community Youth Gang Services, honors Valens with a mural at Pacoima Junior High.

1987 Taylor Hackford's biopic "La Bamba", with Lou Diamond Phillips playing Valens, attracts a new audience and Los Lobos hit US and UK #1 with their interpretation of *La Bamba* featured on the movie soundtrack.

Sept *The Best Of Ritchie Valens* makes US #100.

1990 **May** [11] Valens is honored posthumously with the dedication of a star on the Hollywood Walk Of Fame.

VAN HALEN

David Lee Roth (vocals)
Eddie Van Halen (guitar)
Michael Anthony (bass)
Alex Van Halen (drums)

1973 Roth (b. Oct.10, 1955, Bloomington, IN), who has attended a child guidance clinic as a child, suffering from hyperactivity, having moved to Pasadena, CA, with his parents in 1972 (his father is a surgeon), joins local rock band The Red Ball Jets, while Alex Van Halen (b. May 8, 1955, Nijmegen, Holland) and his brother Eddie (b. Jan.26, 1957, Nijmegen), whose family has moved to Pasadena from Holland in 1965, and who have learnt drums and guitar respectively, form their latest outfit The Broken Combs. The Van Halens meet Roth and decide to form heavy rock covers combo Mammoth, playing local club circuit.

1974 They link with Snake bassist Anthony (b. June 20, 1955, Chicago, IL).

1975 Now established as the loudest and heaviest band in the Los Angeles area, they reject name Rat Salade and settle on Van Halen. With a growing live reputation, they open for groups including Santana, UFO and Sparks, mostly at the Gazzari on Los Angeles' Sunset Strip.

1976 While playing at Los Angeles' Starwood, having been booked there by Rodney Bingenheimer who in turn had seen them on the California bar circuit, Van Halen impresses Kiss bassist Gene Simmons, who offers to produce a demo tape of live numbers including *Runnin' With The Devil* and *House Of Pain*, but it is rejected by all major labels. A songwriting pattern is emerging with Roth writing lyrics and the other members creating the music.

1977 Again playing at the Starwood club, Van Halen, led as much by Eddie Van Halen's impressive guitar work as by Roth's outrageously extrovert stage antics, is spotted by Warner Bros. producer Ted Templeman, who persuades label boss Mo Ostin to sign the band. The contract allows Van Halen to retain full artistic control and includes paternity insurance clauses.

1978 **Feb** Debut album *Van Halen*, produced by Templeman, is released and will hit US #19, with sales over 2 million.

Mar [3] Van Halen embarks on its first US tour at the Aragon Ballroom, Chicago, with contracts insisting that M&M confectionery provision does not include the brown ones.

[25] Roth's overt performance receives national media attention and Van Halen's cover of The Kinks' *You Really Got Me* makes US #36.

May [20] *Runnin' With The Devil* peaks at US #84 and, supported by a first UK tour behind Black Sabbath, makes UK #52. *Van Halen* rises to UK #34.

1979 **Apr** *Van Halen II*, produced by Templeman, has taken only 6 days to record. It will hit US #6 (and UK #23) on its way to 5 million sales.

[7] Group plays the California Music Festival at Los Angeles' Memorial Coliseum.

[8] Van Halen begins a 10-month world tour, transporting over 22 tons of equipment. At some gigs, Roth invites all fans to backstage parties as media concentrates increasingly on alleged drug-taking and wild rock'n'roll celebration.

[13] Roth collapses on stage in Spokane, Washington, DC.

June Van Halen headlines the UK leg of the world tour.

July [4] *Dance The Night Away* reaches US #15. As US dates resume, the group hires lookalikes to parachute into Los Angeles's Anaheim Stadium as a prelude to the gig.

Oct [6] Roth lyric-led *Beautiful Girls* stalls at US #84.

1980 **Apr** *Women And Children First* hits US #6 and UK #15, and will earn platinum disk . Van Halen's annual tour begins, now titled "Invasion".

June Roth breaks his nose and has multiple contusions and concussion during recording of Italian TV special, colliding with hanging stage lights during the execution of a flying squirrel leap.

[28] *And The Cradle Will Rock* stalls at US #55.

1981 **Apr** [11] Eddie Van Halen marries actress Valerie Bertinelli.

May *Fair Warning* hits US #6 and makes UK #49. Like each Van Halen album, it outsells its predecessor.

1982 **Apr** [17] *(Oh) Pretty Woman*, reviving Roy Orbison's 1964 hit, reaches US #12.

May Fifth album *Diver Down* is released; it will hit US #3 and UK #36.

June Van Halen hires Francis Ford Coppola's soundstage at Los Angeles's Zoetrope studios to try out its new touring sound system.

July As *Dancing In The Street* makes US #38, "Hide Your Sheep" tour begins at Steve Wozniak's US Festival in San Bernardino, CA.

Oct [22] "Van Halen Day" is declared in Worcester, MA.

1983 **Feb** In place of a cancelled UK visit, Van Halen embarks on its first South American tour playing Uruguay, Venezuela, Brazil and Argentina.

Apr Eddie Van Halen is acclaimed for his guitar work on Michael Jackson's *Beat It* US #1. (Eddie completed the session work free of charge, as a favor.)

May [28] Band is paid $1 million (the largest fee ever) to play a single concert, at the second US Festival in San Bernardino. The organizers need an audience of 750,000 to break even – only 300,000 show.

Dec [31] *1984* is released on New Year's Eve at the band's insistence.

1984 **Feb** *1984* hits US #2 and UK #15 (despite a ban in some UK outlets due to baby smoking cover shot). It marks the band's first major use of synthesizers and includes its live favorite from 1976, *House Of Pain*.

[25] *Jump*, written by all band members, tops US chart for 5 weeks. The promotional video, according to Roth, cost $6,000 to record on home 16mm equipment.

Mar Despite BPI imposing a £6,000 fine on UK Warner Bros. for hyping the single, *Jump* hits UK #7.

[21] Kurt Jefferies of Phoenixville, PA, wins a "Lost Weekend With Van Halen" competition out of more than 1 million entrants.

May *Panama* falters at UK #61.

June [2] *I'll Wait* reaches US #13.

Aug Van Halen plays the Monsters Of Rock festival at Castle Donington, Leics.

[18] *Panama* makes US #13.

Sept UK act Aztec Camera records an acoustic ballad version of *Jump* as B-side to *All I Need Is Everything*.

Oct As president of his own "Jungle Studs" club, Roth plans a trip to Papua New Guinea.

Nov [24] *Hot For Teacher* peaks at US #56.

1985 **Feb** Always the central focus of the band Roth, still with the band, releases debut solo single, with the help of The Beach Boys' Carl Wilson, a cover of their *California Girls*. With predictably babe-filled video, it hits US #3, but only UK #68.

Mar Roth's solo album *Crazy From The Heat* (on Warner Bros.) peaks at US #15 and UK #91.

June [1] A long-time fan of Al Jolson, Roth's medley of *Just A Gigolo* and *I Ain't Got Nobody* reaches US #12, as Roth confirms that he is quitting Van Halen.

Sept Ted Templeman bets Roth that he can't drive his 1951 Mercury Lowrider from Los Angeles to New York in 3 days in time for the MTV awards. In typical Roth style, he arrives minutes before the show is due to start.

1986 **Feb** Eddie and Alex ignore Warner Bros.' advice not to use the Van Halen name with Roth gone.

Apr [26] *5150* tops US chart.

May [17] *Why Can't This Be Love* hits US #3, featuring new lead singer

Sammy Hagar (b. Oct.13, 1947, Monterey, CA) as Roth's replacement. (Hagar's most recent solo success has been *I Can't Drive 55* which will be incorporated into future Van Halen dates.)

June First Hagar-featured disk, *Why Can't This Be Love* hits UK #8 as parent album *5150*, New York's Police code for the criminally insane and the name of Eddie Van Halen's own recording studio, hits US #1 and reaches UK #16 . It has been recorded at Eddie's studio in his Hollywood Hills home.

July Roth releases further cover versions on mini-album *Eat 'Em And Smile* which hits US #4 and UK #28 and includes Sinatra's *That's Life*.

[19] Van Halen's *Dreams* makes US #22 and peaks at UK #62.

Aug [30] Roth's *Yankee Rose* reaches US #16, as he begins a 10-month tour at Hampton, VA, with a band comprising Steve Vai (guitar), Billy Sheehan (bass) and Gregg Bissonette (drums).

Oct [4] Van Halen's *Love Walks In* makes US #22.

[18] Roth's *Goin' Crazy* peaks at US #66.

Dec [6] *That's Life* falters at US #85.

[20] Linda Duke claims she suffers "acoustic trauma" at Roth's Los Angeles Forum concert.

987 Mar [14] Hagar's solo single *Winner Takes All* from Sylvester Stallone movie "Over The Top", peaks at US #54.

June Hagar continues a parallel solo career with *Sammy Hagar* which makes US #14. From it, *Give To Live* reaches US #23 and *Eagles Fly* peaks at US #82.

988 Jan While vacationing on Turtle Island off the Australian coast, Eddie Van Halen suffers from 105°F temperature having been bitten by a mosquito.

Feb Roth's third solo album, *Skyscraper* (featuring a front cover photograph of him hanging on to the side of a mountain) is released, hitting US #6 and UK #11.

Mar Extracted *Just Like Paradise* hits US #6 and UK #27.

May His follow-up *Stand Up* stalls at US #64.

[27] Van Halen returns to live work after a 2-year break, opening its "Monsters Of Rock" tour at the Alpine Valley Music theater, Troy, WI. Featuring 4 other heavy metal acts (Scorpions, Dokken, Kingdom Come and Metallica), it is the most ambitious HM package tour ever attempted. With 250,000 watts of sound at 20 all-day festival concerts, the events are mostly under-attended and some lose money.

June Van Halen album *OU812*, featuring Hagar lyrics and vocals, peaks at UK #16, but in less than a month hits US #1. It is produced by long-time band associate Donn Landee.

July Roth's *Damn Good/Stand Up* stalls at UK #72.

Aug Roth plays the Monsters Of Rock Festival at Castle Donington, as Van Halen releases first single from the album, *When It's Love*, which hits US #5 and UK #28.

Sept [29] Band begins a 45-city US tour.

Nov Roth returns to UK for selected dates including Wembley Arena, London, as *California Girls* is reissued.

Dec Van Halen's *Finish What Ya Started* reaches US #13.

989 Mar [18] *Feels So Good* reaches US #35.

Oct [15-16] Eddie Van Halen and Anthony participate in the first World Music Invitational pro/am celebrity golf tournament at Stonebridge Ranch in Dallas, TX.

990 May Group plays at the opening night of their recently-purchased 350-seater Cabo Wabo Cantina restaurant and bar in Cabo San Lucas, Mexico.

Dec [17] Group files a federal law suit against rap act 2 Live Crew, alleging they used a riff from *Ain't Talkin' 'Out Love* for their *The Funk Shop* without permission, seeking $300,000 for copyright infringement and unfair competition.

991 Jan [19] Roth's *A Lil' Ain't Enough*, from his forthcoming album, makes US #32.

[26] *A Little Ain't Enough* enters UK chart at peak #4.

Feb [16] *A Little Ain't Enough* reaches US #18.

[22] Roth's 32-date European leg of his world tour opens in Glasgow, Scotland.

Mar [16] Wolfgang, a son to Eddie and Valerie Van Halen, is born at St. John's hospital, Santa Monica, CA.

Apr [26] Roth's North American leg of his world tour opens at the Centrum, Worcester, MA.

LUTHER VANDROSS

973 Vandross (b. Luther Ronzoni Vandross, Apr.20, 1951, New York, NY), his father a crooner, his mother a gospel singer and his sister a member of 50s group The Crests, having been influenced by the soul music of the early 60s and formed his first group with friends, guitarist

Carlos Alomar and Robin Clark, while still at William Howard Taft high school in The Bronx, becoming Listen My Brother, a musical theater workshop that performs at the Apollo theater, Harlem, and appearing on the first episode of TV show "Sesame Street", studies music briefly after the group breaks up in the early 70s and disappears into a succession of day jobs. He then spends 2 semesters at Western Michigan and has also worked as an S&H Green Stamp defective-merchandise clerk.

1974 Alomar, working with David Bowie, invites Vandross and Clark to Philadelphia's Sigma Sound studios for the recording of album *Young Americans*. Bowie is impressed with the pair and invites Vandross to arrange all the vocal parts. He also sings backing vocals on most of the tracks as well as contributing the song *Fascination*.

1975 Vandross and Clark join Bowie on the "Young Americans" tour, with Vandross also becoming the opening act. Vandross' *Everybody Rejoice (A Brand New Day)* is included in forthcoming movie *The Wiz*. (The song will later be used in a Kodak commercial.) Bowie introduces Vandross to Bette Midler for whom he performs vocals on her album *Songs For The New Depression*. (Producer Arif Mardin will later use Vandross for sessions with Ringo Starr, Carly Simon, Chaka Khan, Donna Summer, Barbra Streisand and Average White Band.)

1976 Royalties from *Everybody Rejoice* allow Vandross to record more of his songs with a newly-formed vocal group. Cotillion Records signs the band and calls it Luther. Vandross' style does not mesh with the disco flavor of the times and both the group's albums, **Luther** and **This Close To You**, fail to interest, but *It's Good For The Soul* and *Funky Music (Is A Part Of Me)* are both Top 40 R&B hits.

1977 Without a recording contract, Vandross earns a living as a session vocalist and jingles singer (some of his credits include AT&T, Burger King, Kentucky Fried Chicken, Miller Beer, featuring an all-star choir of Ashford & Simpson, Roberta Flack and Teddy Pendergrass, Pepsi-Cola, Seven-Up and the US Army).

1978 June Quincy Jones enlists Vandross' vocals for his album *Sounds ... And Stuff Like That!!*. He duets with Patti Austin on *I'm Gonna Miss You In The Morning* and Gwen Guthrie on *Takin' It To The Streets*.

Dec He also sings back-up vocals on Chic's *Le Freak* and Sister Sledge's *We Are Family*.

1979 Nov Vandross arranges the vocals on Barbra Streisand and Donna Summer's smash *No More Tears (Enough Is Enough)*. (By the end of the decade, Vandross has been voted MVP Background Singer 3 years in a row for his commercial work.)

1980 May Vandross is main vocalist for debut album *The Glow Of Love* by disco group Change, which will earn a gold disk. He is also the featured singer on Change's 2 hits *Searchin'* and *The Glow Of Love*. Vandross signs to Epic in a deal which allows self-production freedom.

1981 Roberta Flack sings his song *You Stopped Lovin' Me* from movie "Bustin' Loose" and invites him to tour with her.

Sept *Never Too Much*, Vandross' first solo record, is released. It will reach US #19 on its way to platinum sales.

Nov [28] Vandross has first solo hit with *Never Too Much*, which reaches US #33.

1982 Aug Vandross produces Aretha Franklin's *Jump To It*.

Oct Soul-drenched *Forever, For Always, For Love* is released, and will reach US #20, Vandross' second platinum disk.

Dec [4] Vandross reaches US #55 with *Bad Boy/Having A Party*.

1983 Nov He produces Dionne Warwick's *How Many Times Can We Say Goodbye* (UK title: *So Amazing*).

[12] His duet with Warwick on the ballad title track makes US #27.

Dec *Busy Body* enters the US chart. It will reach US #32 and earn a third consecutive platinum disk.

1984 Jan *Busy Body* makes UK #42.

May [12] *Superstar*, a reworking of the Leon Russell classic, stalls at US #87.

1985 Apr *The Night I Fell In Love* peaks at UK #19 and US #19.

May [25] *'Til My Baby Comes Home* reaches US #29.

1986 Sept [20] Uptempo *Give Me The Reason*, from movie "Ruthless People", makes US #57.

Nov *Give Me The Reason* enters the UK chart. It will hit UK #9 and spend over a year on the chart.

[29] *Give Me The Reason* tops US R&B chart, and will reach US #14.

1987 Jan [17] *Stop To Love* tops US R&B chart.

Feb *Never Too Much* belatedly makes UK #41.

[14] *Stop To Love* reaches US #15.

[24] Vandross performs live at the 29th annual Grammy ceremonies. He is nominated in the Best R&B Vocal, Male category, but loses to James Brown.

Mar [24] Vandross and Dionne Warwick co-host the first annual Soul Train Music Awards at the Hollywood Center Television studios, CA.

Apr He produces *It's Hard For Me To Say* for Diana Ross' **Red Hot Rhythm & Blues**.

May [9] Vandross' duet with Greogry Hines, *There's Nothing Better Than Love*, makes US #50 and tops US R&B chart.

June [8] Vandross' drummer, Yogi Horton, leaps to his death from a 17th-floor hotel window, having told his wife he is tired of living in Vandross' shadow.

[18] Vandross cancels 2 sell-out concerts in Phoenix, AZ as a protest to Governor Mecham's rescinding of the Martin Luther King public holiday.

July *Forever, For Always, For Love* reaches UK #23.

1988 Jan On its second reissue *Give Me The Reason* reaches UK #26.

Feb Vandross wins Favorite Male Soul and Favorite Male R&B Artist categories at the 15th annual American Music Awards.

May *I Gave It Up (When I Fell In Love)* reaches UK #28.

July Duet with Gregory Hines, *There's Nothing Better Than Love* stalls at UK #72.

Sept [28] Vandross begins a 3-month "The Heat" US tour with Anita Baker in Washington, DC.

Oct *Any Love*, produced (as all previous albums) by Marcus Miller, enters the UK chart at #3 and hits US #9, as the title track makes US #44 and UK #31.

Nov [5] *Any Love* tops US R&B chart.

[26] *Any Love* tops US R&B chart.

1989 Jan [3] Vandross sings *Love Won't Let Me Wait*, a cover of Major Harris' 1975 US #5, on first edition of Fox TV's "Arsenio Hall Show".

Feb *She Won't Talk To Me* makes UK #34.

Mar [18] *She Won't Talk To Me* reaches US #30.

[31] Vandross plays the first of 2 nights at Wembley Arena, London.

Apr *Come Back* peaks at UK #53.

Oct Remixed *Never Too Much* reaches UK #13.

Nov *The Best Of Luther Vandross – The Best Of Love* reaches US #26 and UK #14.

1990 Jan *Here And Now* makes UK #43. (Vandross has sung the song at the wedding, broadcast live, of Sharyn Gillyard and Michael Haynes of New York, who had won WBLS-FM's "Wedding Of A Lifetime" contest.)

[22] Vandross wins Favorite Soul/R&B Male at the 17th annual American Music Awards.

Mar [14] Vandross wins Best R&B/Urban Contemporary Single/ Male for *Here And Now* at the fourth annual Soul Train Awards at the Shrine Auditorium, Los Angeles. He also co-hosts the event with Patti LaBelle and Dionne Warwick.

Apr [21] *Here And Now* hits US #6.

Nov Vandross produces *Who Do You Love?* for new Whitney Houston album **I'm Your Baby Tonight**.

Dec [1] He is named Best Male Artist for **The Best Of Luther Vandross** at the 23rd annual NAACP Image Awards at the Wiltern theater, Los Angeles.

1991 Feb [10] Vandross joins with nearly 100 celebrities in Burbank, CA to record *Voices That Care*, a David Foster and fiancee Linda Thompson Jenner composed and organized charity record to benefit the American Red Cross Gulf Crisis Fund.

[20] Vandross wins Best R&B Vocal Performance, Male for *Here And Now* at the 33rd annual Grammy awards at Radio City Music Hall, New York.

Apr [27] *Power Of Love/Love Power*, from forthcoming album **Power Of Love**, debuts at US #63.

VANILLA FUDGE

Mark Stein (vocals and organ)
Vince Martell (guitar)
Tim Bogert (bass)
Carmine Appice (drums)

1966 Bogert (b. Aug.27, 1944, Richfield, NJ) and Stein (b. Mar.11, 1947, Bayonne, NJ), who have been playing in Rick Martin & The Showmen, form their own group, The Pigeons. Martell (b. Nov.11, 1945, New York, NY) joins as lead guitarist, and Appice (b. Dec.15, 1946, New York) replaces the original drummer.

Dec Renamed Vanilla Fudge, the quartet is one of the few East Coast groups to join ranks with acid rock West Coast movement, with a style it will describe as "psychedelic-symphonic rock" (a central element of which is slowed-down rearrangements of other artists' hit singles).

1967 July [22] Signed to Atlantic Records, group makes its New York debut at the Village theater (soon renamed the Fillmore East) with The Byrds and The Seeds. Debut single, a version of The Supremes' *You Keep Me Hangin' On*, hits US #6 and makes UK #18.

Sept Debut album **Vanilla Fudge** hits US #6 (and will make UK #31 2 months later). It includes elongated versions of The Beatles' *Eleanor Rigby* and *Ticket To Ride* and Cher's *Bang Bang*.

1968 Feb *Where Is My Mind* peaks at US #73.

Mar **The Beat Goes On** reaches US #17. A concept set, it is ambitiously presented as a musical record of the past 25 years. Title track professes to include the entire history of music in 12 mins. playing time.

July **Renaissance** makes US #20.

Oct *Take Me For A Little While*, from the album, peaks at US #38.

Dec Also from **Renaissance**, a cover of Donovan's *Season Of The Witch* reaches US #65.

1969 Mar **Near The Beginning** (1 side studio, the other live) makes US #16. Taken from it, *Shotgun* peaks at US #68.

July Vanilla Fudge takes part in 3-day Seattle Pop Festival at Woodenville, WA, with The Byrds, The Doors, Led Zeppelin and more.

Oct Band's *Rock And Roll* makes US #34.

1970 Internal dissent leads group to disband. Appice and Bogert form heavy metal band Cactus, before joining Jeff Beck in Beck, Bogert & Appice. Stein forms Boomerang and Martell leaves the music world.

1982 Vanilla Fudge re-forms and releases **Greatest Hits**.

1984 Aug Vanilla Fudge re-forms again and records **Mystery** for Atlantic subsidiary Atco. It fails to chart.

1988 June Band re-forms once more for Atlantic Records' 40th Anniversary celebration.

STEVIE RAY VAUGHAN

1968 Having recently seen Cream and heavily influenced by an Albert King tape, 14-year-old Vaughan (b. Oct.3, 1954, Dallas, TX), the son of an asbestos plant worker and a secretary at a ready-mix cement factory, plays guitar for the first time. Hooked on blues, he will play for local teen school outfits, including The Chantones, Nightcrawlers and Blackbird.

1972 Having dropped out of high school in his senior year, Vaughan follows his older brother, by 3 years, Jimmie to Austin, TX. Jimmie has left home in 1966 to tour with The Chessmen and will tutor his brother and invite him to join several bands during Stevie's Austin apprenticeship. (Jimmie will go on to form The Fabulous Thunderbirds in 1979 with vocalist Kim Wilson.)

1974 Performing consistently on the Texas club circuit, Vaughan joins Austin blues outfit The Cobras (before forming similar music aimed Triple Threat in 1977).

1981 Taking its name from the Otis Rush blues track, Vaughan recruits Tommy Shannon, a veteran of Johnny Winter's band circa 1970, on bass and Chris Layton on drums to form Double Trouble after Triple Threat disbands. (The Rolling Stones' Mick Jagger will see a video of the group in concert, which will lead to a New York nightclub appearance at his request.)

1982 Now augmented by keyboardist Reese Wynans, Double Trouble is signed to Epic Records by A&R veteran talent scout John Hammond Sr., who has seen them performing at the annual Montreux Jazz Festival in Switzerland. Vaughan also comes to the attention of David Bowie, who invites him to make a major guitar contribution to his current Nile Rodgers-produced recording of **Let's Dance** album.

1983 July Always projected as Stevie Ray Vaughan & Double Trouble, debut release **Texas Flood** begins US chart ascendancy to #38, ultimately selling over 500,000 copies, spurred by near constant cross-country touring which band will maintain throughout its history.

1984 Feb [28] Stevie Ray Vaughan & Double Trouble feature prominently in the 26th annual Grammy awards, with (unsuccessful) nominations in the Best Rock Instrumental (*Rude Mood*) and Best Traditional Blues Recording (*Texas Flood*) categories.

June Second album **Couldn't Stand The Weather**, displaying a tougher edge than its predecessor, begins US chart climb to #31, where it will be his first platinum album for 1 million sales. It includes the first of 2 cover versions he will perform of Jimi Hendrix' *Voodoo Chile*, which will receive a Grammy nomination.

Dec By year's end, Vaughan is voted Best Electric Blues Player, while the recent album is confirmed Best Guitar Album in **Guitar Player** magazine. He is also awarded Entertainer Of The Year and Instrumentalist Of The Year by The Blues Foundation.

1985 Feb [26] Stevie Ray Vaughan & Double Trouble share the award with

Ultravox

U2

Van Halen

Stevie Wonder

The Walker Brothers

The Who

Sugar Blue, Luther Johnson and others for Best Traditional Blues Recording at the 27th annual Grammy awards, for their contribution of the track *Flood Down In Texas* to the Atlantic blues collection *Blues Explosion*.

Oct Jazz-tinged third album *Soul To Soul* is released, set to make gold US #34. During their album-supporting US tour, Vaughan will be voted Best Electric Blues Player by **Guitar Player** magazine and receive another Grammy nomination for Best Rock Instrumental for the extract *Say What*.

'86 During a year of continued live performing, including a return to the Montreux Jazz Festival, Vaughan, suffering from an ongoing drug and alcohol abuse problem, falls off stage in London and spends a month in rehabilitation in an Atlanta, GA hospital. He will also complete co-production of Lonnie Mack's comeback album *Strike Light Lightning*.

'87 Feb Double package performance album, *Live Alive* peaks at US #52, featuring the Grammy nominated track *Say What*.

May Vaughan's interpretation of The Chantays' *Pipeline* is featured in the movie soundtrack to "Back To The Beach", and will receive a Grammy nomination for Best Rock Instrumental at the 30th annual awards ceremony held next year.

'89 July Fifth Epic album, *In Step*, produced by Jim Gaines, and Vaughan's first studio effort for 4 years, begins gold sales rise to US #33, and will bring Vaughan his UK chart debut at #63. Vaughan & Double Trouble concurrently embark on US tour with Jeff Beck.

Dec By year's end, Vaughan has been inducted into **Guitar Player** magazine's "Gallery Of The Greats".

'90 Feb [21] *In Step* wins Best Contemporary Blues Recording at the 32nd annual Grammy awards at the Shrine Auditorium, Los Angeles, CA.

Mar [14] Vaughan is named Musician Of The Year and Musician Of The Decade at the ninth annual Austin Music Awards, held at the Palmer Auditorium, Austin, TX.

June [8] Vaughan & Double Trouble begin North American "The Power And The Passion Tour" with Joe Cocker at the Shoreline Amphitheater, Mountain View, CA, set to end July 22 in Vancouver, Canada.

July He completes recordings of a forthcoming album *Family Style*, with his brother Jimmie, produced by Nile Rodgers at studios in Memphis, TN, Dallas and New York.

Aug [27] During a US tour, Vaughan is killed when the helicopter in which he is traveling to Chicago, IL, following a concert at the Alpine Valley Music Center, East Troy, WI, which ended with a jam including Vaughan, his brother Jimmie, Eric Clapton, Robert Cray, Buddy Guy and Phil Palmer, crashes in thick fog into the side of a man-made ski hill. (Also killed are Clapton's agent Bobby Brooks, his bodyguard Nigel Browne, the tour manager Colin Smythe and the pilot Jeffrey Brown.)

[31] At his memorial service held in the Laurel Land Memorial Park, Oak Cliff, Dallas, Jackson Browne, Bonnie Raitt and Stevie Wonder sing *Amazing Grace*.

Sept *Couldn't Stand The Weather* becomes Vaughan & Double Trouble's first RIAA certified million-seller 6 years after release.

[22] Previously charting *In Step* peaks at US #75.

Nov [10] The Vaughan Brothers album *Family Style* hits US #7 (and UK #63). It features Jimmie singing a rare vocal on 1 cut, while Stevie had recorded the lead on the remaining songs.

[24] The Vaughan Brothers' *Tick Tock* peaks at US #65.

'91 Feb [20] *D/FW*, a track from *Family Style* wins Best Rock Instrumental Performance and *Family Style* wins Best Contemporary Blues Recording for The Vaughan Brothers at the 33rd annual Grammy awards, held at Radio City Music Hall, New York.

BOBBY VEE

'58 Inspired by Buddy Holly's *That'll Be The Day*, Vee (b. Robert Thomas Velline, Apr.30, 1943, Fargo, ND) forms The Shadows at Central high school in Fargo, with brother Bill, Bob Korum and Jim Stillman. They play mainly instrumentals, with a few Holly and self-penned vocal items by Vee.

'59 Feb [3] The Shadows answer a request over local radio station K-FGO for a group to fill in on visiting "Winter Dance Party" one-night show in Fargo (which Holly, The Big Bopper and Ritchie Valens, who died in a plane crash in the early hours, would have played). They appear second on the program, performing *Bye Bye Love* and *Long Tall Sally*, wearing matching outfits which they bought that afternoon.

[14] Local promoter Bing Bingstrom, who was in the "Winter Dance

Party" audience, has offered to find The Shadows some paying gigs. Their first is a Valentine Day dance, earning $60.

June [1] Group pays $500 to record its own session at Soma Records' studio, Minneapolis, and cuts Vee-penned *Suzy Baby* and group instrumental *Flying*.

July Soma issues the single, to major success in Minneapolis and surrounding areas. Group tours radio stations around Iowa and North Dakota, and sales spread. After a San Diego, CA, station starts to play it, *Suzy Baby* attracts the attention of Liberty Records, which buys the master and releases it nationally. Band experiments with adding a pianist to expand the live sound, and hires Bob Zimmerman, who is spending the summer in Fargo. (He calls himself Elston Gunn at the time – the name will later change to Bob Dylan.) He plays 2 gigs with The Shadows, but his repertoire proves a compatibility problem. He is paid $30 and asked to leave.

Sept *Suzy Baby* makes US #77. Liberty signs the group, and also Vee himself to a separate deal as a soloist. (Liberty will do little on record with the group but it will back Vee on tour until 1963.)

1960 Apr Pairing him with producer Snuff Garrett, Liberty has Vee cover Adam Faith's recent UK chart-topper *What Do You Want?* (which is also in Holly-influenced style), but it stalls at US #93.

Oct After an album session at Norman Petty's studio in Clovis, NM (where most of Holly's hits had been recorded), Garrett tries Vee (against the singer's wishes) on R&B oldie The Clovers' *Devil Or Angel*. His first major success, it hits US #6. (B-side, a similar revival of Ivory Joe Hunter's *Since I Met You Baby*, makes US #81).

Dec [23] He begins a week at New York's Brooklyn Paramount theater, in Clay Cole's Christmas Rock'N'Roll show, alongside Neil Sedaka, Dion, Bo Diddley and many others.

1961 Jan Garrett is offered material from Don Kirshner's Brill Building Aldon Music stable for Vee, and *Rubber Ball*, co-written by Gene Pitney, hits US #6, becoming his first million-seller.

Feb *Rubber Ball* is his UK chart debut, hitting #4 after holding off a Top 10 cover version by the established Marty Wilde.

Mar A John D. Loudermilk song, *Stayin' In* makes US #33 while B-side revival of The Crickets' (post-Buddy Holly) *More Than I Can Say*, peaks at US #61. He has his first Album chart success with second album *Bobby Vee*, which reaches US #18.

May *More Than I Can Say*, promoted as UK A-side, hits UK #4.

June *How Many Tears*, the first of a run of Carole King/Gerry Goffin songs recorded by Vee, makes US #63.

[25] He appears on Alan Freed's outdoor rock show at the Hollywood Bowl, together with Jerry Lee Lewis, Brenda Lee, The Shirelles, and others.

Sept Goffin and King's *Take Good Care Of My Baby* becomes Vee's all-time most successful single, topping US chart for 3 weeks, and selling over a million. Meanwhile, *How Many Tears* hits UK #10.

[30] 2,000 teenage fans, members of the California Racquet Club in Cheviot Hills, Los Angeles, CA, fete Vee on "Bobby Vee Afternoon".

Nov *Bobby Vee Sings Hits Of The Rockin' '50s* peaks at US #85.

Dec *Run To Him* penned by Goffin with Jack Keller, hits US #2 (behind The Tokens' *The Lion Sleeps Tonight*). The B-side, Goffin/King's *Walkin' With My Angel*, makes US #53.

1962 Jan Despite a universal thumbs-down from the "Juke Box Jury" panelists on UK BBC TV, *Run To Him* hits UK #6. (For a while it is available in UK on 2 labels, as London Records' UK licensing agreement with Liberty runs out, and the US label launches in its own right through EMI.)

Feb *Take Good Care Of My Baby* makes US #91, and hits UK #7. Vee appears on UK national radio ("Easy Beat") and TV ("Thank Your Lucky Stars").

[9] Vee begins 15-date twice-nightly UK tour with Tony Orlando, Clarence "Frogman" Henry, The Springfields and others, at Doncaster Gaumont, S.Yorks. Tour will end Feb.25 at the Winter Gardens, Bournemouth, Dorset.

Mar *Please Don't Ask About Barbara*, issued in UK to coincide with tour, peaks at UK #29, while *Hits Of The Rockin' '50s* reaches UK #20.

Apr *Please Don't Ask About Barbara* reaches US #15. (B-side *I Can't Say Goodbye* has already made US #92 in Feb.)

July *Sharing You*, a Goffin/King song in similar style to *Run To Him*, hits US #15 and UK #10.

Aug *Bobby Vee Meets The Crickets* (Holly's ex-backing group, at this point consisting of Sonny Curtis, Jerry Allison, Glen D. Hardin and Jerry Naylor, is also recording for Liberty) makes US #42, while *A Bobby Vee Recording Session* peaks at US #121. Vee appears in cameo slot, singing *At A Time Like This* (which he has recorded in UK at EMI), in Billy Fury-starring film "Play It Cool".

Oct *Punish Her* reaches US #20. (B-side *Someday (When I'm Gone From You)*, taken from the album with The Crickets, made US #99 in Sept.)

Nov *Bobby Vee Meets The Crickets* is his most successful album in UK, hitting #2, behind UK group The Shadows' *Out Of The Shadows*. Vee makes lengthy UK tour with The Crickets, throughout Nov.

Dec Compilation *Bobby Vee's Golden Greats* reaches US #24, while seasonal *Merry Christmas From Bobby Vee* makes US #136. *A Forever Kind Of Love*, recorded in UK during the summer with producer Norrie Paramor, reaches UK #13 (having not been issued in US as a single – while the US has not had *Punish Her*).

1963 **Jan** *The Night Has A Thousand Eyes*, from the movie "Just For Fun" (in which he has a cameo role, singing 2 songs), hits US #3 and becomes another million-seller.

Feb *A Bobby Vee Recording Session* hits UK #10.

Mar *The Night Has A Thousand Eyes* hits UK #3.

Apr *The Night Has A Thousand Eyes* makes US #102.

May Compilation *Bobby Vee's Golden Greats* hits UK #10, while *Charms* reaches US #13.

June *Bobby Vee Meets The Ventures*, pairing the singer with Liberty's top guitar instrumental group, makes US #91.

July *Be True To Yourself* makes US #34. (B-side *A Letter From Betty* peaks at US #85.) *Bobby Tomorrow*, a reversal of *Charms*, which is relegated to UK B-side, makes UK #21. It will be his last UK hit single.

Oct *The Night Has A Thousand Eyes* reaches UK #15.

Nov [8] He begins US tour with Dick Clark's "Caravan Of Stars" package, in Teaneck, NJ. Sharing the bill are Brian Hyland, The Ronettes and Little Eva, among others.

Dec *Yesterday And You (Armen's Theme)* climbs to US #55. (B-side *Never Love A Robin* creeps to US #99.)

1964 **Feb** *Stranger In Your Arms* peaks at US #83.

[29] Vee begins 29-date twice nightly UK package tour with Dusty Springfield, The Searchers and Big Dee Irwin at Adelphi cinema, Slough, Berks. Tour will end Mar.29 at the Liverpool Empire, Merseyside.

Apr *I'll Make You Mine* makes US #52.

[11] On tour again in UK, Vee appears on BBC radio show "Saturday Club", with The Searchers, Adam Faith and Gerry & The Pacemakers.

June *Bobby Vee Sings The New Sound From England!*, featuring Merseybeat arrangements and recent UK hits (plus *She's Sorry*, written as a straight imitation of The Beatles' *She Loves You*), reaches US #146. Vee tours US with The Rolling Stones.

July *Hickory, Dick And Doc* climbs to US #63.

1965 **Jan** *(There'll Come A Day When) Ev'ry Little Bit Hurts* stalls at US #84 (B-side *Pretend You Don't See Her* having peaked at US #97 in Dec.)

Feb *Cross My Heart* creeps into US Hot 100, at #99. It is his last single with producer Garrett (B-side is titled *This Is The End*); the 2 cease working together by mutual consent.

Mar [25] Vee begins 12-date twice-nightly UK package tour, with Dusty Springfield, The Searchers, Heinz, The Zombies and others, at the Odeon cinema, Stockton, Cleveland. Tour will end Apr.10 at the Sophia Gardens, Cardiff, Wales.

June *Keep On Trying*, recorded in UK with George Martin producing, makes US #85.

1966 **July** *Look At Me, Girl* peaks at US #52.

1967 **Sept** Folk-tinged ballad *Come Back When You Grow Up*, produced by Dallas Smith and pairing Vee with The Strangers, hits US #3 and is his final million-seller.

Oct *Come Back When You Grow Up* reaches US #66.

Dec A cover version of Kenny O'Dell's *Beautiful People* makes US #37 (1 place ahead of the original).

1968 **Mar** *Maybe Just Today* reaches US #46.

May A medley of 2 oldies, Smokey Robinson's *My Girl* and Goffin/King's *Hey Girl* makes US #35. *Just Today* peaks at US #187.

Sept *Do What You Gotta Do*, reviving The Four Tops hit, makes US #83.

Dec *I'm Into Lookin' For Someone To Love Me* stalls at US #98.

1969 **Aug** *Let's Call It A Day Girl* makes US #92.

1970 **Dec** As Liberty Records becomes United Artists Records, *Sweet Sweetheart* peaks at US #88 and is also his last US chart entry.

1972 In a conscious effort to break from his earlier style and image, Vee releases *Nothing Like A Sunny Day* under his real name. A laid-back country/rock-styled package along the lines of Rick Nelson's Stone Canyon Band material, it has a small combo backing (including pedal steel guitar). Among the tracks is a slowed-down re-creation of *Take Good Care Of My Baby*. It does not chart, but is critically well received.

1980 **May** Compilation *The Bobby Vee Singles Album* hits UK #5,

demonstrating the nostalgic appeal of his early 60s recordings.

1985 **Mar** A regular on the oldies touring circuit in US, Vee tours UK on a nostalgic package with contemporaries Del Shannon and Rick Nelson.

1988 **May** Vee makes another oldies tour of UK, again with Shannon and also Brian Hyland. (Vee will continue to tour US and UK, making an annual appearance at the Buddy Holly Memorial concert held in either Fargo or Clear Lake.)

SUZANNE VEGA

1975 Vega (b. Aug.12, 1959, New York, NY), half Puerto Rican, having grown up in a Hispanic neighborhood of New York, is encouraged by her father, a novelist, to attend the New York High School of Performing Arts (of "Fame" fame) where she studies dance and begins composing songs with the guitar.

1977 While working as an office receptionist during the day, she performs her own compositions on the quiet New York folk circuit, including Folk City, the Speakeasy and the Bottom Line.

1983 She meets lawyer Ron Fiernstein and engineer Steve Addabbo, who offer to manager her. Together, they form publishing units Waifersongs and AGF Music Ltd.

1984 **July** *New York Times* review of a recent performance calls Vega: "one of the most promising talents on the New York City folk circuit".

Dec Encouraged by increasingly glowing receptions, A&M signs her to a worldwide recording deal.

1985 **Jan** She begins 3 months of taping 10 of her own compositions for her first album at Celestial studios, New York.

Apr Debut album *Suzanne Vega* is released to universal critical acclaim. She is viewed as the first of many new folk female stars of the late 80s. Produced by Addabbo and ex-Patti Smith guitarist Lenny Kaye, the album will spend 27 weeks on chart, climbing to US #91, and will achieve double gold status in UK (where it reaches #11).

May With UK reaction breaking faster, Vega takes her band, including Marc Shulman (guitar), Sue Evans (drums), Mike Visceglia (bass), Anton Sanko (keyboards) and Stephen Ferrare (percussion) on a European tour. Vega performs at the Royal Albert Hall, and the Prince's Trust benefit at Wembley Arena, London.

1986 **Jan** From the debut album, *Small Blue Thing* peaks at UK #65.

Mar *Marlene On The Wall* is first major chart single, reaching UK #21.

June New recording *Left Of Center* makes UK #32, with the help of one of the earliest CD single release formats. With Joe Jackson featured on piano, the song is included on the current John Hughes film soundtrack *Pretty In Pink* but will not appear on a Vega studio release.

Nov [18-19] As a climax to a successful touring year in Europe (and a larger US folk circuit) Vega plays selected UK venues including 2 sold-out dates at London's Royal Albert Hall. They are filmed for BBC TV showing and later video release.

1987 While writing songs for her second album, Vega contributes 2 compositions for a forthcoming Philip Glass album *Songs From Liquid Days* – 1 will be sung by Janice Pendarvis, the other by Linda Ronstadt. *Luka*, already a UK #23, becomes her first major US hit, peaking at #3 and earning a Grammy nomination.

May *Solitude Standing*, again produced by Addabbo and Kaye, will benefit from the international success of *Luka* and hit US #11 and UK #2. Vega begins 11-month "Suzanne Vega World Tour 87", beginning in UK and Eire (traveling to US and Canada in July and Aug., including sold-out nights at New York's Carnegie Hall, and returning to Europe in the fall, following first visits to Japan and Australia).

July *Tom's Diner* peaks at UK #58.

Sept [12] *Solitude Standing* makes US #94.

1988 **Aug** UK CD-only EP is released featuring *Luka* and *Left Of Center*.

Oct Vega contributes the title track to Disney compilation *Stay Awake* for A&M Records.

1989 **July** Vega begins work on third album with beau Anton Sanko using makeshift studio assembled in their apartment.

1990 **Feb** Hugh Padgham mixes the album in New York.

Apr [28] Third album *Days Of Open Hand*, recorded at New York's Skyline studios with a band comprising Sanko, Visceglia, Shulman and Frank Vilardi (drums), hits UK #7.

May [19] *Book Of Dreams*, with Shawn Colvin on backing vocals, peaks at UK #66 as parent album *Days Of Open Hand* makes US #50.

June [9] D.A.Pennebaker film documentary on Vega airs on VH1, and subsequently on UK BBC2 TV.

[11] Vega begins a North American tour in Washington, DC.

Aug [11] UK remixers DNA hit UK #2 for 3 weeks with *Tom's Diner*. The sampling duo have "borrowed" the cut, adding a repetitive dance rhythm track, releasing it initially as a bootleg, only to have it signed up by A&M (with whom Vega is still contracted). She is reported to be initially appalled, though the DNA hit will outperform all of her own original creations from her current album.

Oct [2] Vega begins the second leg of her North American tour in Atlanta, GA, at the conclusion of a European tour.

THE VELVET UNDERGROUND

Lou Reed (vocals, guitar)
Sterling Morrison (bass, guitar)
John Cale (bass, keyboards, viola, vocals)
Nico (vocals)
Maureen Tucker (drums)

1964 Cale, (b. Dec.4, 1940, Garnant, Wales), in New York on a Leonard Bernstein scholarship, has been performing in avant-gardist La Monte Young's ensemble The Dream Academy, when he meets Reed (b. Mar.2, 1943, New York, NY) at a party. Reed plays Cale demos of his songs and the 2 decide to form a band. Reed brings in Morrison, while Cale adds his neighbor Angus MacLise on percussion. They play mostly free gigs under a variety of names. As The Primitives, they release several singles for Pickwick. (The Velvet Underground is taken from the title of a pornographic paperback.)

1965 Mutual friends draw them to the attention of artist Andy Warhol who becomes the group's manager. He decides that Nico (b. Christa Paffgen, Cologne, Germany), who is singing at the Blue Angel Lounge, New York, should join the group. The rest of the band are less enthusiastic and MacLise abruptly leaves for Nepal. (He will die there of malnutrition in 1979, aged 41.) He is replaced by Tucker.
Nov [11] The Velvet Underground debuts live as the opening act for The Myddle Class at a high school dance in Summit, NJ.

1966 Early in the year they begin a residency at Cafe Bizarre in Greenwich Village. They become the house band of Warhol's Factory and then the musical component of his multi-media show "The Exploding Plastic Inevitable". Band signs to MGM's Verve label.

1967 Jan Group plays a week-long series of concerts at the Montreal World Fair, Canada.
Mar Debut album *The Velvet Underground And Nico*, is released, reaching US #171. Reed takes control of the band and dispenses with Nico and Warhol. (Nico will record a collection of covers for solo album *Chelsea Girls*.)

1968 Jan *White Light, White Heat*, recorded in a day at the end of a tour, charts for 2 weeks at US #199.
Mar Clashes between Reed and Cale come to a head, and Cale leaves. Bassist Doug Yule, ex-Boston folk-rock group The Grass Menagerie, replaces him.

1969 Apr *The Velvet Underground*, recorded in Los Angeles, is released. Atlantic Records signs the band after MGM drops it. Cale produces Nico's solo album *Marble Index*.

1970 June Group returns to New York for a month's residency at Max's Kansas City club. Tucker is pregnant, and Yule's brother Billy deputizes.
Aug *Loaded* is released. Reed, having left the band to go solo, complains that it has been remixed without his knowledge. Band tours the East Coast with Yule on lead vocals with singer Walter Powers added to the line-up.

1971 Willie Alexander joins the band in place of Morrison, who leaves to teach English at the University of Texas in Austin. Tucker leaves shortly thereafter and moves to Phoenix, AZ. to raise a family. Yule will keep The Velvet Underground name (until 1973), recording *Squeeze*, an almost solo effort, released in UK only. (He will join West Coast band American Flyer in the mid 70s.) Nico releases *Desertshore*, with Cale again producing.
Oct [8] Group embarks on 8-date UK tour at Birmingham University, W.Midlands, set to end Oct.28 at Bristol University, Avon.

1972 Atlantic releases *Live At Max's Kansas City*, taken from fan Brigit Polk's cassette recording of the group's last gig with Reed.

1974 Double live album *1969 – The Velvet Underground Live*, released on Mercury, contains previously unrecorded songs. Reed, Cale and Nico play an impromptu "reunion" concert in Paris, France, which is filmed.
June [1] Nico joins Cale at his London concert (recorded for *June 1st, 1974*). Performance leads to the recording of Nico/Cale album *The End*.

1979 Apr Film "Rock'N'Roll High School", satirizing US 50s teen movies, uses The Velvet Underground's *Rock And Roll* in its soundtrack.

1980 Tucker releases a home-recorded single, *Playin' Possum*, for Spy Records.

1981 Nico's *Drama Of Exile*, containing Reed and Bowie covers, is released.

1982 Tucker releases *Playin' Possum*.

1983 Nico releases live mini-album *Do Or Die*.

1985 Polydor releases a remixed album of previously unreleased material as *V.U.*, which makes US #85 and UK #47. While recording himself, Cale brings Nico into the studio to record *Camera Obscura*.

1986 May Polydor UK releases The Velvet Underground box set titled *Another View* as Tucker releases EP *MoeJadKateBarry*.

1988 July [18] Nico, having spent several years living in Manchester, Gtr.Manchester, with poet John Cooper Clarke, dies of a brain hemorrhage, having fallen off her bicycle while on holiday in Ibiza.

1989 Sept Tucker releases *Life In Exile After Abdication*. (She has been working at a Georgia Wal-Mart discount store warehouse, and has asked for leave to record the album, and quits when she is refused permission.) Lou Reed and Sonic Youth guest on album, which magician Penn Jellette, of Penn and Teller, helps finance on the 50 Skidillion Watts label.

1990 June The original group plays together for the first time since 1969 as they attend the opening of the Cartier Foundation's Andy Warhol retrospective at Jouy en Josas, outside Paris, France, and perform *Heroin*.
Dec Tucker performs at St.Ann's church, New York.

THE VENTURES

Nokie Edwards (lead guitar)
Don Wilson (guitar)
Bob Bogle (guitar, bass)
Howie Johnson (drums)

1959 Wilson (b. Feb.10, 1937, Tacoma, WA) and Bogle (b. Jan.16, 1937, Portland, OR) are working as tuckpointers (mortar removers) for a building construction company in Seattle, WA, when they start to play as a duo at local dances and hops.

1960 Jan Edwards (b. May 9, 1939, WA), initially playing bass, and Johnson (b. 1938, WA) join, and the quartet names itself The Versatones, with Wilson's mother Josie as manager.
Feb After recording some tracks at Custom Recorders in Seattle, they release *Cookies And Coke* on their own label, Blue Horizon.
Apr Second Blue Horizon single, this time with a version of Johnny Smith's *Walk Don't Run*, is pressed in small quantities, with the group name changed to The Ventures. They take the disk to The Fleetwoods' manager Bob Reisdorff, who runs local Dolton label. He turns it down, so they try DJ acquaintance, Pat O'Day, who has a show on K-JR in Seattle, and he plays it after each news bulletin. Reisdorff, hearing the disk on the radio, reconsiders and buys the master of *Walk Don't Run* and the group (in a deal carefully negotiated by Josie Wilson which gives the group artistic control over its releases via Blue Horizon Productions, with Reisdorff and Wilson named as joint producers).
Aug Released nationally, *Walk Don't Run* hits US #2 (behind Elvis Presley's *It's Now Or Never*) and becomes a million-seller. Because Dolton is marketed nationally by Liberty Records, The Ventures' recording operations are moved to Los Angeles, CA, where Liberty has its studios, and the group cuts a debut album, mainly consisting of its versions of other acts' instrumental hits.
Oct *Walk Don't Run* hits UK #8, in a close race with a UK cover version by The John Barry Seven.
Dec A revival of standard *Perfidia*, given the same guitar treatment as *Walk Don't Run*, reaches US #15.

1961 Jan Debut *The Ventures* reaches US #11 while *Perfidia* hits UK #4.
Mar *Ram-Bunk-Shush*, a 1957 hit for R&B organist Bill Doggett, reaches US #29 and UK #45.
May Another revived oldie, *Lullaby Of The Leaves*, peaks at US #69 and UK #43 (it is The Ventures' last UK chart entry).
Aug *Another Smash!!!* reaches US #39.
Sept *(Theme From) Silver City*, played with Hank Levine's orchestra, makes US #83.
Nov *Blue Moon*, recently a vocal million-seller by The Marcels, is put through its guitar paces to US #54.

1962 Mar *Twist With The Ventures*, containing instrumental versions of Twist hits, reaches US #24. (It is the first and most successful of a series of Ventures albums intended as music for dancing to.)
Sept *Lolita Ya-Ya*, the theme from film "Lolita", makes US #61. Meanwhile, following an auto accident, Johnson, although not physically injured, feels the need to rest and leaves the group. He is replaced on drums by Mel Taylor (b. New York, NY).

1963 Jan Historically notable for being the first single recording to use fuzz-box guitar, *The 2,000lb Bee* peaks at US #91.

Feb *The Ventures Play Telstar And The Lonely Bull*, which contains covers of those 2 and several more instrumental hits, is the group's biggest-selling album, hitting US #8, and earning a gold disk for a half million sales. Edwards, who has been sharing lead guitar on record and stage for some time, officially takes over on lead, with Bogle switching to bass.

June *Surfing*, a cash-in on the current California surf instrumental boom (which has gained much of its original inspiration from The Ventures), reaches US #30. Group teams with Liberty artist Bobby Vee for part-vocal, part-instrumental *Bobby Vee Meets The Ventures*, which peaks at US #91.

July Blue Horizon Productions contract clause expires and Josie Wilson drops out of production. Group loses automatic creative control over its releases.

Oct *Let's Go!*, headed by a cover of The Routers' hit, makes US #30.

1964 Mar The last Ventures album produced by Reisdorff, *The Ventures In Space*, combining original material with versions of science fiction movie themes, reaches US #27. (Keith Moon of The Who will later quote this as one of his favorite albums.)

Aug The Ventures' new, updated arrangement of *Walk Don't Run*, now under the title of *Walk Don't Run '64*, with ideas borrowed liberally from The Chantays' *Pipeline* and other surf instrumentals, hits US #8. *The Fabulous Ventures* with new producer Dick Glasser makes US #32.

Nov An update of Richard Rodgers' *Slaughter On 10th Avenue* makes US #35. It is taken from *Walk Don't Run, Vol.2* (also featuring *Walk Don't Run '64*), which makes US #17.

1965 Feb *Diamond Head*, another surf-style instrumental, makes US #70.

Apr *The Ventures Knock Me Out!* reaches US #31.

Aug Live *The Ventures On Stage*, recorded at concerts in Japan and US, peaks at US #27. (Group's first visits to Japan coincide with first mass availablity of electric guitars in Japan, and The Ventures become the model guitar group to the Japanese. Over the next 10 years, although little of it will feed back to the West, the group runs a parallel career in Japan, where its popularity is on a par with The Beatles'. Regular tours and dozens of albums recorded specifically for the Japanese market keep a vast demand satisfied. Their collaboration with Japan's emerging pop culture is such that The Ventures write many tunes designed for Japanese writers to add lyrics in their own language.)

Sept *Play Guitar With The Ventures* is an instructional album, with 4 tunes (including *Walk Don't Run*) repeated over with lead, rhythm or bass guitar parts missing, and the instructions to enable the guitar-learning listener to fill the part with his own instrument and play along with The Ventures. The album makes US #96 and stays on chart for 13 weeks.

Nov Joe Saraceno takes over as group's producer for *The Ventures A Go-Go*. An anthology of instrumental dance tunes, it makes US #16.

1966 Mar Group competes with Johnny Rivers on *Secret Agent Man*, the theme from TV series "Secret Agent" (a re-titling of UK series "Danger Man"), starring Patrick McGoohan. Rivers' vocal version hits US Top 10 while The Ventures make US #54.

Apr Group cashes in on another TV craze with *The Ventures/Batman Theme*, which makes US #42.

1967 Apr Band shares vogue for psychedelic sounds with a mainly cover-version *Guitar Freakout*, which reaches US #57.

Oct *Golden Greats By The Ventures* (not a compilation of their own, but a collection of other acts' hits) reaches US #50 and, in a 44-week chart stay, earns another gold disk.

1968 June Edwards leaves for solo work and is replaced on lead guitar by Jerry McGee.

1969 May The Ventures hit US #4 with *Hawaii Five-0*, the theme from the police TV series starring Jack Lord, which is another million-seller. The group is now a quintet, having added keyboards player Johnny Durrill (ex-The Five Americans).

June *Hawaii Five-0* reaches US #11, earning group's third gold disk.

July A revival of Percy Faith's 1960 million-seller *Theme From A Summer Place*, taken from the album, reaches US #83 but is the group's last chart single.

1970 Jan *Swamp Rock* reaches US #81.

Nov Double *The Ventures' 10th Anniversary Album* makes US #91.

1972 Edwards returns to the group, McGee having left to join Delaney & Bonnie's band.

Mar *Joy/The Ventures Play The Classics*, makes US #146, and is the last Ventures US chart album.

1981 After many years concentrating on their still-buoyant Japanese market, The Ventures record, in US, *Surfin' And Spyin'* (written by Charlotte

Caffey of The Go-Gos). It is distributed mainly around the Californian surf music revival circuit, where they play live shows to huge acclaim. (The line-up is back to a quartet: Bogle, Wilson, Edwards and Taylor.)

THE VILLAGE PEOPLE

Victor Willis (lead vocals)
David Hodo (vocals)
Felipe Rose (vocals)
Randy Jones (vocals)
Glenn Hughes (vocals)
Alex Briley (vocals)

1977 Group is formed by Jacques Morali, a French producer working in US, after seeing costumed young men in New York gay discos. He conceives the idea of a group visually representing 6 American male stereotypes: the cowboy, the Indian, the policeman, the biker, the G.I. and the construction worker. He hires actor/singers to perform his tailor-made disco songs behind lead singer Willis. The name represents Greenwich Village, New York, from which the inspiration has come. Via his Can't Stop Productions, Morali signs the group to Casablanca Records in US and Mercury/Phonogram worldwide, and will produce and co-write (usually with Willis and Henri Belolo) all the material.

Oct Eponymous debut album is released, reaching US #54. In an 86-week chart stay, it will go gold with sales over a half million.

Dec A disco hit in US, the group's first single *San Francisco (You've Got Me)* makes UK #45.

1978 May Group is heard on the soundtrack of Casablanca/Motown-produced disco movie "Thank God It's Friday", singing gay anthem *I Am What I Am* and *Hollywood*.

Aug *Macho Man* reaches US #25 and, despite its self-consciously (though a tongue-in-cheek feature of subsequent singles also) gay idiom, sells over a million copies to earn a gold disk. The album of the same title makes US #24, staying on chart for 69 weeks to top a million sales and earn a platinum disk.

[26] Group performs in Ontario, Canada, at the first Canada Jam festival, to 80,000 people, sharing the bill with The Commodores, Kansas, Earth, Wind & Fire, Dave Mason and Atlanta Rhythm Section.

1979 Jan *Y.M.C.A.*, a disco smash with the ultimate tongue-in-cheek camp lyric, hits US #2 and sells more than 2 million copies, earning a platinum disk. In UK, it tops the chart for 3 weeks, selling 150,000 copies in one day at its peak, with eventual UK sales of almost 1,300,000 (1 of UK's top 25 all-time best-sellers).

Feb *Cruisin'*, which includes *Y.M.C.A.*, hits US #3 (another platinum disk) and makes UK #24.

Apr *In The Navy* (which the US Navy considers using as a recruitment song until its full implications are pointed out) hits US #3, again selling over a million, and UK #2.

May *Go West*, featuring *In The Navy*, hits US #8 (the group's third consecutive platinum disk) and reaches UK #14.

July Title track from *Go West* reaches US #45 and UK #15.

Sept Billy Connolly makes UK #38 with a comedy version of *In The Navy*, retitled *In The Brownies*.

Dec *Ready For The 80s* peaks at US #52, the group's final US hit single. Double *Live And Sleazy*, coupling a live album with a studio set, makes US #32 and earns the group's final gold disk. Willis leaves, and is replaced as lead singer by Ray Simpson, brother of Valerie Simpson (of writer/producer/performing duo Ashford And Simpson).

1980 Sept *Can't Stop The Music* reaches UK #11. Group co-stars with Valerie Perrine and Bruce Jenner in movie of the same title, crammed with its (and others') music, which flops. Soundtrack album climbs to US #47.

1981 Aug Group signs to RCA but *Renaissance*, an attempt to change its visual image with the stereotype macho men disappearing in favor of smooth New Romantic types, peaks at US #138, its last US chart entry.

1982 Simpson leaves and is replaced by Miles Jay. With the fading of disco as a major commercial pop genre, the group loses its niche in the marketplace and disappears.

1985 Feb A renewed version of the group proves outdated and only spawns UK #59 *Sex Over The Phone*.

GENE VINCENT

1955 May Vincent (b. Vincent Eugene Craddock, Feb.11, 1935, Norfolk, VA) leaves US Navy with a serious leg injury, after a motorcycle accident as a despatch rider. His broken bones do not heal properly because of too-rapid use and he spends several months in hospital. By the end of the year the leg is still in a plaster cast.

956 **Feb** [11] Vincent marries 15-year-old Ruth Ann Hand. (The marriage will not last.)

Mar Vincent hangs out at his local WCMS radio station, and occasionally sits in with the house band, The Virginians. Among the songs he sings is *Be-Bop-A-Lula*, purchased for $25 from fellow hospital patient Donald Graves. WCMS DJ "Sheriff" Tex Davis notices the young singer and arranges for him to make a demo tape containing that song, *Race With The Devil* and *I Sure Miss You*.

Apr Davis sends the demo to Ken Nelson of Capitol Records, who is on the look-out for another Elvis Presley. Vincent is signed to the label, after entering the label's "Elvis Soundalike Sweepstakes".

May [4] Nelson arranges for a recording session at Owen Bradley's Nashville studio, using the same demo band: guitarists Cliff Gallup and Willie Williams, bass player Jack Neal and drummer Dickie Harrell, who become The Blue Caps. The 3 demo songs are re-recorded, with *Woman Love*.

June *Woman Love* is the first Gene Vincent & The Blue Caps release, but B-side *Be-Bop-A-Lula* enters the US chart.

[4] Vincent & The Blue Caps play first live gig, at Myrtle Beach, NC.

July *Be-Bop-A-Lula* hits US #7, bringing a sudden demand for extensive live work.

[28] They make their first US national TV appearance on NBC's "Perry Como Show".

Aug *Woman Love* is banned by UK's BBC because of its suggestive lyrics, but *Be-Bop-A-Lula* climbs to UK #16.

Sept Williams quits The Blue Caps and is replaced by Paul Peek in time for a 2-week residency in Washington, DC.

Oct *Blue Jean Bop* reaches US #16 (Vincent's only US Album chart entry). Follow-up single *Race With The Devil* peaks at US #96 but makes UK #28. The strain of performing aggravates Vincent's leg (still in a plaster cast). He ignores medical advice to slow down, and he and The Blue Caps go to Hollywood to film a slot performing *Be-Bop-A-Lula* for movie "The Girl Can't Help It". (The bottom of his plastercast is disguised as a shoe by the studio's make-up department.)

Nov *Blue Jean Bop* climbs to US #49 and makes UK #16.

Dec Gallup, who left The Blue Caps before the Hollywood movie, but returned to play on the recording of a second album, leaves for good, taking his influential and original guitar sound with him. (The line-up changes frequently and there will be 6 different versions of The Blue Caps in 2 years.)

957 **Jan** Vincent spends 3 weeks in a Norfolk hospital for treatment to his injured leg. He is also prevented from live work while a legal wrangle over management is cleared up.

June Vincent has a metal leg brace (which he will wear for the rest of his life) fitted in place of his plaster cast. The new touring version of The Blue Caps (with drummer Harrell the only original) proves successful with lead guitarist Johnny Meeks.

Sept *Lotta Lovin'* climbs to US #13. He makes an ecstatically-received tour of Australia with Eddie Cochran and Little Richard.

958 **Jan** *Dance To The Bop* reaches US #23 after being performed on US TV's "Ed Sullivan Show". (It will be Vincent's last US hit.)

Mar Vincent and the band appear in teen movie, "Hot Rod Gang" (UK title: "Fury Unleashed"). They record in Hollywood, with Vincent's friend (since touring together twice in 1957) Eddie Cochran moonlighting on (uncredited) backing vocals on the sessions.

Apr Vincent begins a US West Coast tour which is followed by a 40-date trip around Canada. Vincent has trouble holding his group together, due to the exhausting pace on and (allegedly) off-stage, which has players constantly leaving to rest or keep from going crazy. These worries and a growing list of non-hit records take their toll on Vincent (who becomes increasingly moody and unreliable – particularly to DJs and the media – and begins to drink heavily).

May He gets married for the second time, to Darlene Hicks.

Nov After a year without hits and with only low-paid Los Angeles, CA live gigs, The Blue Caps split when Vincent abandons his group in mid-tour because he is unable to pay them 3 weeks' back wages. The Musicians Union withdraws his union card, and he moves with his new wife to the North-West, playing local gigs with pick-up bands.

959 **June** Vincent meets and works with guitarist Jerry Merritt. With a new band, they play one of the first-ever rock tours of Japan, where they are enthusiastically welcomed.

Aug Regaining his card, Vincent returns to Los Angeles and records *Crazy Times*, with Merritt on guitar and session men like Sandy Nelson on drums and Jackie Kelso on sax. The album meets little success at a time when the US record industry is looking for clean, inoffensive pop

stars. After more low-key live work, he moves to Europe at the invitation of promoter Larry Parnes and UK TV producer Jack Good.

Dec [5] Vincent arrives in UK, where his reputation remains high despite 3 years without hits, and receives an enthusiastic welcome from fans at London airport.

[6] He makes his UK live debut at Tooting Granada, London, as a guest on Marty Wilde's show.

Vincent appears on UK TV rock show "Boy Meets Girls", headlined by Wilde. In US Vincent was urged to tone down his image, but TV producer Jack Good persuades him to dress entirely in black leather and to emphasize his limp. Good gives him a residency on "Boy Meets Girls", and the image of the tortured black leather rock rebel is created. He plays to a rapturous reception at the Paris Olympia, France, and well-received dates at military bases in Germany.

1960 **Jan** *Wild Cat* makes UK #21. Vincent plays a 12-date UK tour. Eddie Cochran flies to UK at Parnes' invitation to co-headline a 12-week tour with him.

[16] Vincent and Cochran appear together on "Boy Meets Girls".

Feb While touring in Scotland, Vincent has a kilt and tam o'shanter made in Craddock tartan.

Mar *My Heart* reaches UK #16.

Apr [17] The car taking Vincent and Cochran to London airport at the end of the UK tour in Bristol, crashes, killing Cochran. With a broken collarbone, broken ribs and further damage to his leg, Vincent also suffers psychologically from the death of his closest professional friend.

May [11] After a short spell in hospital and a rest in US, Vincent returns to UK to make his first UK recording, at EMI's Abbey Road studio in London. Backed by The Beat Boys (with Georgie Fame on piano), he cuts *Pistol Packin' Mama*.

July *Pistol Packin' Mama* makes UK #15. *Crazy Times* peaks at UK #12 (his only UK chart album).

1961 **May** He tours South Africa for the first time, playing with The Mickie Most Band.

July To coincide with another UK visit, *She She Little Sheila*, recorded in 1959 at album *Crazy Times* sessions, is released and reaches UK #22.

Sept *I'm Going Home*, recorded in London with backing by UK group Sounds Incorporated, makes UK #36 (his last UK hit single despite impressive live form).

1962 **Mar** [31] He begins a UK tour with Brenda Lee at the Brighton Essoldo, E.Sussex, and performs *Spaceship To Mars*, accompanied by Sounds Incorporated (and dressed in white rather than his customary all-black leathers), in UK pop movie "It's Trad, Dad!"

July [1] Vincent stars at Liverpool's Cavern club, on a bill featuring up-and-coming local group The Beatles.

Nov [21] He begins UK tour with Adam Faith. Tour ends Dec.9 at the De Montfort Hall, Leicester, Leics..

1963 **Jan** Vincent marries for the third time, to English girl Margaret Russell.

Apr [22] His recording contract with Capitol expires, and is not renewed. The last recording is an inferior remake, at Abbey Road with Charles Blackwell's orchestra, of *Be-Bop-A-Lula*.

1964 **Mar** [20] He begins UK tour, with Carl Perkins, on a package headlined by The Animals.

Oct *Shakin' Up A Storm*, recorded in London, is issued on EMI's Columbia label.

Dec [31] Vincent flies back to US to spend Christmas with his parents.

1965 **Mar** [17] He enters the Royal National Ear, Nose & Throat hospital, Gray's Inn Road, London for an emergency operation.

July He begins a 3-month UK seaside summer season at South Pier theater, Blackpool, Lancs., backed by UK group The Puppets. Vincent is divorced from his English wife and married to South African singer Jackie Frisco.

Dec Vincent is ordered to pay £675 to manager Don Arden for breach of contract.

1966 **July** He records in a country style for Challenge Records in Los Angeles. (*Bird-Doggin'* will be released in UK only in 1967.)

1969 **Sept** [13] Vincent performs at the Toronto Rock'N'Roll Festival, Canada, with several of his contemporaries and newer acts like The Doors and John Lennon's Plastic Ono Band. He is overshadowed by performances from Chuck Berry and Jerry Lee Lewis. He returns to tour UK, backed by The Wild Angels, and is the subject of UK BBC TV documentary, "The Rock'N'Roll Singer."

1970 **Feb** *I'm Back And I'm Proud*, mixing rock and country, is released on Dandelion label, run by lifelong Vincent fan and UK BBC radio DJ John Peel. Critically rated, it fails to chart.

Apr He signs in US to Kama Sutra Records and records 2 country albums, *Gene Vincent* and *The Day The World Turned Blue*, which are well reviewed but poor sellers. His personal life declines. Lack of commercial success and ever-present management and ex-wife problems cause constant depression, accentuated by heavier drinking, which adversely affects his previously consistent stage image. His fourth wife leaves him.

Sept He makes a chaotic UK tour.

[1] He records 5 songs at BBC Radio studios in Maida Vale, London, with backing by UK band Kansas Hook.

[12] Having returned to US to scrape some money together, Vincent dies in hospital in Newhall, CA from a bleeding ulcer, aged 36. (The most eloquent tribute – apart from covers of *Be-Bop-A-Lula* by major artists like John Lennon, and widespread aping of his leather-clad tough rocker image – will be Ian Dury's 1977 song *Sweet Gene Vincent*.)

BOBBY VINTON

1960 Vinton (b. Stanley Robert Vinton, Apr.16, 1935, Canonsburg, PA), the son of a band leader, having formed his own big band in high school, played trumpet in similar groups while at Duquesne University and in the US Army, puts together a band of his own once out of the service. They are engaged to play as a back-up and featured outfit on a Dick Clark "Caravan Of Stars" US tour. On a tour stop in Pittsburgh, PA, Vinton records a single for local DJ Dick Lawrence, who intends to place it with a label. Epic Records passes on the disk, but is interested in Vinton's band and he is signed to a 2-album contract. He then embarks on "The Fall Edition Of The Biggest Show Of Stars For 1960" US tour providing the musical accompaniment for Chubby Checker, Brenda Lee, Fabian and Jimmy Clanton.

1962 Apr Neither band album having sold, Vinton is to be dropped, but is owed a recording session by Epic. Rather than a band arrangement, he records country-style version of a song found on a demo, *Roses Are Red*.

July *Roses Are Red* tops US chart for 4 weeks, selling over a million (Epic's first #1 hit), and Vinton's recording contract is renewed. Although he will do further big-band work and feature his trumpet live, on disk he will stick to the middle-of-the-road vocal slot which *Roses Are Red* has established for him.

Aug *Roses Are Red* reaches UK #15, beaten by a cover version from UK's Ronnie Carroll which hits #3.

Sept *Roses Are Red* hits US #5.

Oct *Rain Rain Go Away*, from the album, reaches US #12. It is in competition with another Vinton single, *I Love You The Way You Are*, on Diamond label (his 1960 recording, which Lawrence has dusted off and sold to the label after *Roses Are Red*'s success). It reaches US #38.

1963 Jan Double A-side *Trouble Is My Middle Name/Let's Kiss And Make Up* reaches US #33/#38.

Apr A revival of Johnnie & Joe's *Over The Mountain (Across The Sea)* makes US #21.

June *Blue On Blue*, submitted by Burt Bacharach for Vinton, hits US #3 and earns his second gold disk.

Sept *Blue Velvet* (a 1951 hit for Tony Bennett) tops the US chart for 3 weeks, earning another gold disk. Album of the same title, on which all the songs are concerned with the color blue, hits US #12.

Dec [7] The Beatles, appearing on BBC TV show "Juke Box Jury", vote Vinton's new single *There! I've Said It Again* a miss. (8 weeks later, the group's *I Want To Hold Your Hand* will knock the song off the top of the US chart, marking the beginning of The Beatles' dominance of the American pop scene.)

1964 Jan *There! I've Said It Again* (a revival of a 1945 Vaughn Monroe hit, recorded by Vinton in 1 take) tops US chart for 4 weeks (holding The Kingsmen's *Louie Louie* at #2). It earns Vinton's fourth gold disk and reaches UK #34 – his second and final UK hit.

Mar *My Heart Belongs To Only You* hits US #9 while *There! I've Said It Again*, containing both the title track and the new single, hits US #8.

June *Tell Me Why* reaches US #13.

Aug *Tell Me Why* climbs to US #31.

Sept *Clinging Vine* makes US #17.

Nov Compilation *Bobby Vinton's Greatest Hits* reaches US #12, earning a gold disk for a half million sales.

Dec Self-penned *Mr. Lonely*, originally recorded alongside *Roses Are Red* and used as a track on the album of that title, is belatedly released after an earlier cover version by Buddy Greco has failed. It tops US chart for a week and is another million-seller.

1965 Feb *Mr. Lonely* reaches US #18.

Apr A revival of Lee Andrews & The Hearts' 1957 doo-wop classic *Long Lonely Nights* reaches US #17.

June *L-O-N-E-L-Y*, Vinton's third single in a row with the word in the title, peaks at US #22.

July *Theme From Harlow (Lonely Girl)*, from Carroll Baker movie "Harlow", peaks at US #61.

Oct Protest song *What Color (Is A Man?)* makes US #38.

1966 Jan Vinton returns to his most romantic style on *Satin Pillows*, which reaches US #23.

Mar A cover of Ken Dodd's UK million-seller *Tears* peaks at US #59.

1967 Jan *Coming Home Soldier* hits US #11.

Nov Billy Sherrill becomes Vinton's producer for *Please Love Me Forever*, which reprises his *There! I've Said It Again* style and hits US #6

1968 Feb *Just As Much As Ever* (a hit for Nat "King" Cole) reaches US #24 while *Please Love Me Forever* makes US #41.

Apr Vinton revives Bobby Vee's 1961 chart-topper *Take Good Care Of My Baby*, but it peaks at US #33.

Aug Another revived 1961 Goffin/King song, Tony Orlando/Billy Fury hit *Halfway To Paradise*, makes US #23.

Dec Vinton's revival of *I Love How You Love Me* (a 1962 Phil Spector-produced US #5 hit by The Paris Sisters) hits US #9. It sells over a million, earning his sixth gold disk.

1969 Feb *I Love How You Love Me* reaches US #21.

May Another revived oldie, The Teddy Bears/Peter And Gordon hit *To Know You Is To Love You*, makes US #34.

1970 Mar His version of *My Elusive Dreams* (a country duet hit by David Houston and Tammy Wynette) reaches US #46.

1972 Apr *Every Day Of My Life* makes US #24.

Aug A revival of Bryan Hyland's 1962 original, *Sealed With A Kiss* reaches US #19.

1974 Nov After over a decade with Epic, Vinton signs a new recording deal with ABC Records, and returns to original producer, Bob Morgan. The result is his first million-selling single for 6 years, *My Melody Of Love* (partly sung in Polish – a bow to his own ancestry), which hits US #3.

1975 Jan ABC album *Melodies Of Love* reaches US #16, earning a gold disk. Vinton begins a syndicated weekly musical variety show on US TV. (It will air until 1978.)

Apr A disco-style revival of *Beer Barrel Polka* reaches US #33.

July Vinton revives Elvis Presley's *Wooden Heart* and it makes US #58

1976 June Vinton's version of *Save Your Kisses For Me*, a cover of Brotherhood Of Man's UK million-seller (and winner of 1976 Eurovision Song Contest), stalls at US #75.

1980 Jan After another quiet period, Vinton, signed to Tapestry label, makes US #78 with *Make Believe It's Your First Time*.

1986 Sept Vinton's version of *Blue Velvet* is used as theme for movie of the same title.

1989 Dec Sergiusz Mikulicz, head of Poland's radio and TV ministry, approves the playing of Vinton's *Santa Must Be Polish* on state radio.

1990 Vinton cuts *What Did You Do With Your Old 45s* on new album *Timeless*.

Oct Vinton, living in semi-retirement in California and still earning considerable income from occasional US cabaret engagements, unexpectedly hits UK #2 (though widely touted as #1 on UK's network singles chart) as *Blue Velvet* in its original 1963 form benefits from UK TV commercial exposure for Nivea face cream.

Nov Hastily packaged Epic album *Blue Velvet* peaks at UK #67 while *Roses Are Red (My Love)* reissue stalls at UK #71.

JOHN WAITE

1975 Waite (b. July 4, 1954, Lancaster, Lancs.) is already a veteran of a number of bands when he is invited by the manager of UK rock act The Babys, which already includes guitarist Mike Corby (b. July 3, 1955, UK), guitarist Wally Stocker (b. Mar.17, 1954, UK) and drummer Tony Brock (b. Mar.31, 1954, UK) to join the group as its bassist, vocalist and co-songwriter. Waite, who has played bass, harmonica and sung vocals since age 14, has formed short-lived outfit Graf Spee whilst studying graphic design at Lancaster Art College before briefly relocating to West Hampstead to live in a 10' x 8' room during which he is 3-month recruit of rock unit England, having left Lancaster wrongly accused by the local police of involvement in a jewel robbery. After a brief stint in another rock outfit, The Boys, based in Cleveland, OH, at the instigation of an England colleague, Waite has returned once again to London and, having joined The Babys, fronts an expensive Mike Mansfield-directed promo video which, even without a traditional audio demo tape, secures the group a lucrative (Waite describes it as "elephant dollars") contract with Chrysalis.

1976 During its 5-year history, Waite will co-write and sing on the majority of Babys' hits which are projected firmly at the American market (they will only make UK #45 in Feb.1978 with *Isn't it Time*). While personnel change will see Jonathan Cain (b. Feb.26, 1950, Chicago, IL) replace Corby in 1977 and Ricky Phillips join as a main bassist allowing Waite to feature more prominently up front in 1979, The Babys will garner 8 Chrysalis US chart singles (1977's *If You've Got The Time* #88 and their biggest hit, the power ballad *Isn't It Time* #13, 1978's *Silver Dreams* #53, 1979's *Every Time I Think Of You* #13 and three final entries in 1980, *Back On My Feet Again* #33, *Midnight Rendezvous* #72 and *Turn And Walk Away* #42. US album successes begin with *The Babys* #133 and *Broken Heart*, both released in 1977, 1979's *Head First* #22, 1980's *Union Jacks* #42 and the final *On The Edge* #71. (Many producers will cut their teeth on these projects, including Ron Nevison and Keith Olsen.)

980 Dec [9] The day after John Lennon's murder in New York, Waite, performing with The Babys in Cincinnati, OH, on the group's farewell US tour is pulled off stage by a member of the audience, damaging the cartilage in his knee and forcing him to complete his last Babys project on crutches.

981 With The Babys officially split (Cain will travel on to Journey, Stocker will join Air Supply) and the retrospective *Anthology* climbing to US #138, Waite returns to the UK and spends 6 months writing songs at his Lake District home, recently bought with his girlfriend.

982 July Still signed to Chrysalis, Waite's debut solo album *Ignition*, recorded in New York, is released, set to reach US #68, where he, both as a solo artist and group member, will remain most popular.

984 July Following a period of semi-retirement, Waite, newly inked to EMI America, issues *No Brakes*, co-produced with David Thoener and Gary Gersh. It will eventually hit US #10, and is released at a time when Waite is appearing as a hairdresser in the hit US ABC TV series "Paper Dolls", co-starring Morgan Fairchild.

Sept [22] Extracted ballad *Missing You*, featuring Waite's powerful rock vocal over an Andy Summers' recalling rhythm guitar pick, co-written by Waite about his relationship with his Lake District belle, hits US #1 and will also hit UK #9.

Nov *No Brakes* peaks at UK #64, his first and only native album score as either a solo or group act, while US follow-up *Tears* makes US #37.

985 Feb Third extract *Restless Heart* peaks at US #59.

Apr Resurrected from his debut album and now featured in the movie soundtrack to "Vision Quest", *Change* makes US #54.

Sept As Waite embarks on a lengthy US tour, *Mask Of Smiles* begins chart rise to US #38, while lead-off single *Every Step Of The Way* heads to US #25.

Nov *Welcome To Paradise* stalls at US #85.

986 July [17] While he is recording a new album at the Right Track studios, New York, with producer Frank Fillipetti, *If Anybody Had A Heart*, chosen for the "About Last Night" Rob Lowe/Demi Moore-starring movie soundtrack compiled by Bones Howe, makes US #76.

Aug [1] Co-written with Bon Jovi collaborator Desmond Child, *These Times Are Hard For Lovers* peaks at US #53, while parent album *Rover's Return*, named after the pub featured in Waite's favorite UK TV soap opera "Coronation Street", climbs to US #77, and features Maria Vidal on guest vocals.

Oct [10] Extracted *Don't Lose Any Sleep* stalls at US #81. Without a major hit since 1984, Waite leaves EMI America.

988 Reunited with ex-Babys Phillips (bass) and Cain (keyboards), Waite forms a rock supergroup with Cain's Journey colleague, guitarist Neal Schon (b. Feb.27, 1954, San Mateo, CA). Together with drummer Dean Castronova, Bad English, based around a hard rock AOR Waite vocal-led style, signs to CBS/Columbia Records to cut its debut album.

989 Aug [26] Bad English's chart debut, rock-driven *Forget Me Not* makes US #45.

Nov [11] Power ballad, written by Diane Warren, *When I See You Smile*, highlighted by Waite's soaring rock vocal, hits US #1 for 2 weeks, while eponymous debut album *Bad English*, produced by Richard Zito, climbs to US #21 and gold sales.

990 Mar [10] *Price Of Love*, co-written by Waite and Cain, hits US #5. [21] Group embarks on major US tour, supporting Whitesnake, in Pensacola, FL.

Apr [28] Fourth extract *Heaven Is A Four Letter Word* peaks at US #66.

June [29] US tour comes to an end in Weedsport, NY.

Aug [18] *Possession* reaches US #21.

OM WAITS

972 Having joined The Systems soul group at high school and sung and played professionally in his late teens and early twenties on accordian and piano in San Diego and Los Angeles bars and dives, Waits (b.

Dec.7, 1949, in the back of a taxi cab in the parking lot at Murphy Hospital, Pamona, CA), now a popular local performer on Los Angeles blues and rock club circuit, is spotted by Asylum Records at the famous Troubadour haunt, playing his own subterranean brand of songs.

1973 Debut album *Closing Time*, produced by Jerry Yester, is released. It arouses critical acclaim and low sales, but prompts opening live slots for Charlie Rich and Frank Zappa.

1974 The Eagles cover Waits' *Ol' 55* for *On The Border* which reaches US #17. It becomes Waits' first compositional success though he will later claim "the only good thing about an Eagles LP is that it keeps the dust off your turntable". He teams with producer Bones Howe for second effort *Heart Of Saturday Night*. Tracks reveal a hardened, throaty vocal-style suggesting a legendary lifestyle of "liquor, girls, liquor and more liquor".

1975 Nov Waits, after 5 years of different motels, settles on permanent residence at the Tropicano motel in West Hollywood where he has a piano installed in the kitchen. He releases live double *Nighthawks At The Diner*, which enters US chart at #164, and has the word "nighthawk" tattooed on his right arm.

1976 Nov *Small Change* is released and makes US #89. It features a mixture of original jazz blues with lush "bad lives and broken heart" ballads. Constant US touring keeps chart-interest alive.

1977 Oct *Foreign Affairs*, featuring duet with Bette Midler, makes US #113.

1978 June Waits begins an acting career with a bit part in Sylvester Stallone's "Paradise Alley".

Nov *Blue Valentine* peaks at only US #181, despite featuring some-time girlfriend, Rickie Lee Jones, on the cover.

1980 Oct Waits records his final album for Asylum, *Heartattack And Vine* which charts at US #96. It features *Jersey Girl* which will become an integral part of Bruce Springsteen's live sets throughout the decade. Waits is quoted saying: "I'm so broke I can't even pay attention."

1981 Dec [31] He marries Irish playwright, Kathleen Brennan, whom he met while working on the soundtrack to Francis Ford Coppola film "One From The Heart", at the Always and Forever Wedding Chapel, Manchester Boulevard, Los Angeles.

1982 After 18 months' work, the soundtrack album is released through CBS/Columbia. It is Waits' final work with producer Bones Howe and the end of a certain musical style for the songwriter. The soundtrack receives an Oscar nomination.

1983 Having made various cameo acting appearances since 1978, including "Wolfen", "Stone Boy" and "One From The Heart", Waits features in "The Outsiders", with Matt Dillon, and Coppola's "Rumblefish". Asylum releases 3 compilations during the year: double *The Asylum Years*, *Bounced Check*, which includes 2 previously unreleased songs, and *Anthology*.

July Rickie Lee Jones records Waits' composition *Angel Wings* on her 10" mini-album *Girl At Her Volcano*, which reaches US #39.

Oct Waits' daughter Kellesimone is born. His debut for Island Records, *Swordfishtrombones* makes US #167 and UK #62. It is the first of 3 concept albums loosely based around *Frank's Wild Years*, a featured track, and marks a serious change of musical direction which Waits describes as "sounding like a demented parade band".

1984 He appears in another cameo role in Coppola's film "The Cotton Club" and contributes a cover version of *What Keeps Man Alive* to an A&M Kurt Weill tribute *Lost In The Stars*.

1985 June Waits moves from Los Angeles to New York, claiming "it's a great town for shoes".

Sept Son Casey Xavier is born. Waits' first-choice name, Senator Waits, is rejected by Kathleen.

Oct He undertakes sold-out US and European tour to promote second Island album *Raindogs*, which makes UK #29. Guest musicians on the release include Keith Richards (whom Waits claims is "a relative I met in a lingerie shop"), while boxing legend Jake La Motta appears in the video for single *Downtown Train*.

1986 June His musical "Frank's Wild Years", written with his wife, opens at the Steppenwolf Theater Company in Chicago and later moves to New York. He plays a jailbreaking, unemployed disk jockey in his first starring role in black and white film "Down By Law".

1987 Sept *Frank's Wild Years*, featuring many songs from the musical, completes trilogy started in 1983. It makes UK #20 but only US #115.

Nov Waits visits UK to perform songs from the musical and others at sell-out concerts which receive ecstatic reviews.

1988 He contributes *Heigh-Ho (The Dwarfs' Marching Song)* for Disney compilation of favorites, *Stay Awake*. He begins work on *Big Time* and a new film project in Montana. This follows his successful portrayal of a dying street-bum in the Nicholson/Streep movie "Ironweed".

Looking to the future, Waits insists that his gravestone epitaph read: "I told you I was sick."

Oct *Big Time*, recorded live in America and Europe, peaks at US #152, and spends a week on UK chart at #84.

1989 Waits sings end title theme to Al Pacino/Ellen Barkin thriller "Sea Of Love", reviving Paul Phillips' 1959 US #2, and continues acting career, starring in "Cold Feet" with Keith Carradine and Sally Kirkland.

1990 Jan [27] Waits has his biggest success as a writer when Rod Stewart hits US #3 with *Downtown Train*.

Mar [3] *Downtown Train* hits UK #10.

Apr [10] Waits' lawsuit against Frito-Lay and Tracy-Locke for using a Waits-soundalike in radio ads for Doritos chips begins. Los Angeles jury will award Waits $2.475 million in punitive damages. Waits says, "Now by law I have what I always felt I had . . . a distinctive voice."

THE WALKER BROTHERS

Scott Engel (vocals)
John Maus (vocals)
Gary Leeds (drums)

1964 Aug Trio comes together in Los Angeles, CA, after Leeds, drumming for P.J. Proby, befriends Engel and Maus when they are playing bass and lead guitar with The Dalton Brothers, the resident band at Gazzari's club on Sunset Boulevard, Los Angeles. Leeds (b. Sept.3, 1944, Glendale, CA), a drummer since his early teens, studied at the Aerospace Technology School in New York (having to quit after a leg injury), co-founded The Standells in Los Angeles in 1963 but left after the first 2 singles to join first Johnny Rivers and then P.J. Proby and visited UK during Proby's launch on a Jack Good TV show. Engel (b. Noel Scott Engel, Jan.9, 1944, Hamilton, OH) having made some solo singles for minor California labels in his teens and learned double bass at high school, majored in music and switched to electric bass to join instrumental group The Routers, playing on its 1963 hit *Let's Go* and follow-up *Make It Snappy*. Maus (b. Nov.12, 1943, New York, NY), a child actor at age 12 in TV series "Hello Mum" with Betty Hutton, moved to the West Coast, already with pseudonym John Stewart, and teamed up with Engel after being cast as brothers in a TV play.

Oct They make their first recordings with producers Jack Nitzsche and Nik Venet (ex-Capitol Records, to which The Dalton Brothers were contracted). 4 titles are recorded and a deal signed with Mercury Records' Smash label. They appear in a cameo slot in teen movie "Three Hats For Lisa". Leeds is keen to return to UK, having seen the potential for success while touring with Proby. Jack Good also advises the trio to launch itself in London.

1965 Feb Trio arrives in UK, with Barry Clayman and Maurice King as managers, and impresses Johnny Franz, A&R man of Mercury's UK counterpart Philips Records.

Mar US-recorded uptempo *Pretty Girls Everywhere*, with Maus on lead vocal, is debut single but does not chart.

[26] The group makes its UK TV debut on "Ready, Steady, Go!"

May [22] They make their live UK debut at the Odeon cinema, Leeds, W.Yorks., deputizing for The Kinks.

June Dramatic ballad *Love Her*, reviving an Everly Brothers Barry Mann/Cynthia Weil B-side, reaches UK #20. Another of the tracks made with Venet in Los Angeles, with Nitzsche arrangement, establishes trio's lush, orchestrally-backed hit style, highlighting Engel's rich lead vocals. The Walker Brothers begin to play live in the UK, with Engel and Maus laying aside bass and guitar to front the act on vocals and backing band The Quotations is formed around Leeds.

Sept Amid regular slots on "Ready Steady Go", *Make It Easy On Yourself*, a revival of Jerry Butler's 1962 US #20, which Franz produces in similar style to that established by *Love Her*, tops UK chart. The Walker Brothers become major teen favorites, constantly pictured in magazines and subject to hysterical female audiences at live gigs.

Nov *Make It Easy On Yourself* reaches US #16. A show at London's Finsbury Park Astoria is last before UK work permits are renewed.

1966 Jan *My Ship Is Coming In*, a cover of US soul singer Jimmy Radcliffe's original, hits UK #3 and debut album *Take It Easy With The Walker Brothers* hits UK #4. Leeds, who for contractual reasons cannot sing or play on the trio's records, signs as solo singer to CBS.

Feb *My Ship Is Coming In* peaks at US #63.

[12] Leeds makes his solo debut on UK TV show "Thank Your Lucky Stars", promoting *You Don't Love Me*, issued on CBS under the name Gary Walker, which reaches UK #26.

[27] Trio appears on UK TV's "Ready Steady Go" broadcast live from La Locomotive club in Paris, France.

Mar *The Sun Ain't Gonna Shine Anymore*, originally recorded in 1965 b Frankie Valli of The Four Seasons, tops UK chart for 4 weeks.

[19] Leeds is kidnapped by students raising money for the Harrow Technical College Rag Fund. He is taken to a tube station at 4am and left to be collected – 4 days later he hands over £50 to the charity.

[25] Trio begins 31-date twice-nightly UK tour with Roy Orbison, Lul and others at London's Finsbury Park Astoria. Tour Will end May 1 at the Coventry theater, W.Midlands.

[29] Maus receives concussion as group is mobbed entering their hote in Chester, Cheshire. They are unable to perform the next night in Wigan, Gtr. Manchester. Engel is also confined to bed with concussion

Apr [3] Group spends 2 hours in a Leeds police station, before being escorted to gig.

May *The Sun Ain't Gonna Shine Anymore* peaks at US #13. It is their las US hit single. Capitol in UK releases *I Only Came To Dance With You* as by Scott Engel and John Stewart; it is actually a relic of their days in The Dalton Brothers.

[1] The Walkers perform at the **New Musical Express** Poll Winners Concert at the Empire Pool, Wembley, London.

June Another Gary Walker solo release, *Twinkie Lee*, reaches UK #26.

[12] Group makes its London Palladium Show debut.

July [8] "Ready, Steady, Go!" airs a special on the group.

Aug *(Baby) You Don't Have To Tell Me* reaches UK #13.

Sept *Portrait* hits UK #3.

Oct A revival of Gene McDaniels' *Another Tear Falls* reaches UK #12.

[1] Group begins 33-date twice-nightly show with The Troggs, Dave Dee, Dozy, Beaky, Mick & Tich and others, at Granada cinema, East Ham, London, ending Nov.13 at Finsbury Park Astoria, London.

Dec *Deadlier Than The Male* (the theme from film of the same title) peaks at UK #34. EP *Solo Scott – Solo John* displays the 2 vocalists' individual talents. Engel and Maus are growing increasingly irritated by each other's company, both off and on stage. The consequent pressures start to pull the trio apart as hit singles lessen in impact.

1967 Jan [20] Engel is placed under sedation after plane group is taking to Australia returns to Heathrow airport after developing engine trouble A tour of Australia and the Far East with Roy Orbison, The Yardbirds and others, follows, opening at Sydney Stadium, Australia. 17 teenage girls are taken to hospital after collapsing in the 90°F heat.

Feb A cover of Lorraine Ellison's *Stay With Me Baby* reaches UK #26.

Mar [31] Trio embarks on what will be its last UK tour, a 24-date package with Cat Stevens, Jimi Hendrix and Engelbert Humperdinck, at Finsbury Park Astoria, London. Tour will close Apr.30 at Tooting Granada, London.

Apr *Images* hits UK #6.

[2] Group tops the bill on "London Palladium Show".

May [3] At end of concert at Tooting Granada, London, they announce intention to split because of growing internal incompatibilities.

[14] Fans of the trio march from Baker Street station to Maida Vale apartment of manager Barry Clayman, where Maus has been living, to protest the breaking up of the group.

June [1] Maus makes live solo debut at Palais Des Sports, Paris, France.

[4] Maus plays the Olympia, Paris, while The Walker Brothers' reviva of The Ronettes' *Walking In The Rain* reaches UK #26.

[25] Leeds joins a star-studded team of backing vocalists at recording of The Beatles' *All You Need Is Love* on the "Our World" TV show.

July [25] Engel is taken to St. John & Elizabeth hospital, London, suffering from head injuries after a fall in Regent's Park.

Aug Maus has the first post-group solo hit. Released under the name John Walker, *Annabella* reaches UK #24. (He will not be able to maintain his UK chart profile and will return to California. Leeds will drop completely out of sight but will continue to reside in UK.)

Oct Compilation *The Walker Brothers' Story* hits UK #9, but its sales are overshadowed by Engel's first solo album *Scott*, released as by Scott Walker, which hits UK #3.

1968 Jan *Jackie* by Scott Walker, a dramatic version of Jacques Brel's song with a controversial lyric which guarantees it little airplay, reaches UK #22. Trio reunites for a one-off tour of Japan (live album from it will be released in UK 19 years later by Bam Caruso Records).

Apr Leeds' new band Rain, comprising John Lawson (bass), Joey Molland (lead guitar) and Paul Crane (rhythm guitar), embarks on firs UK tour with The Kinks, The Tremeloes and The Herd.

May *Scott 2*, like its predecessor a mixture of songs by an eclectic batch of "quality" composers with a large proportion of Jacques Brel numbers, tops UK chart.

June *Joanna*, a romantic ballad by Scott Walker which he professes to dislike, is his biggest UK solo hit at #7.

Oct [4] Engel embarks on 14-date UK solo tour with The Love Affair, The Paper Dolls and others, at Finsbury Park Astoria, London. Tour ends Oct.20 at the Coventry theater, W. Midlands.

9 Jan [10] Maus is injured in an auto crash.

Mar A Scott Walker weekly UK TV show on BBC1, mostly a straight showcase for his singing, begins a 2-month run.

Apr *Scott 3* hits UK #3.

July *Lights Of Cincinnati* is Engel's last solo hit single as Scott Walker. It reaches UK #13 but *Scott Walker Sings Songs From His TV Series*, with a strong MOR slant, hits #7. (Scott Walker will follow his "brothers" out of the charts, despite recording albums regularly, and will spend most of his time in seclusion, making live appearances with little notice once or twice a year. His non-charting albums will be *Scott 4* and *'Til The Band Comes In*, self-penned under the name Noel Scott Engel in 1970; film theme set *The Moviegoer* in 1972; *Any Day Now*, anthologizing favorite songwriters, in 1973; and 2 country-tinged sets for CBS, *Stretch* and *We Had It All*, in 1974.)

Sept Maurice King sues Engel, alleging breach of contract.

75 Jan Leeds releases *Hello How Are You*, produced by The Hollies' Allan Clarke, on United Artists.

Aug Against all expectations, trio reunites and signs to GTO Records in UK.

76 Feb A revival of Tom Rush's *No Regrets*, performed in the trio's traditional dramatic style, hits UK #7 and newly-recorded album of the same title makes UK #49.

Sept *Lines* fails to chart, as does parent album of the same title.

78 July *Nite Flights* breaks new ground by containing material written entirely by the trio and is more avant-garde in approach and arrangement than any previous Walker Brothers album. It does not chart. *The Electrician*, written by Engel, also fails to sell. After this, trio does not record together again.

84 Mar [31] Scott Walker solo *Climate Of Hunter*, on Virgin, peaks at UK #60, though the singer himself remains in almost total seclusion.

87 July Engel appears in UK black-and-white TV and cinema ad for Britvic soft drinks, in a cameo role as his 60s persona. Also in the ad are 60s contemporaries Sandie Shaw, Georgie Fame, Dusty Springfield and Dave Dee, among others.

90 Aug *After The Lights Go Out – The Best Of 1965-1967* and Scott solo *Boy Child – The Best Of 1967-1970* are released in UK on Fontana, as reappraisal of trio's career becomes fashionable.

JUNIOR WALKER & THE ALL-STARS

Junior Walker (sax, vocals)
Willie Woods (guitar)
... Thomas (organ)
James Graves (drums)

61 4 high-school friends form jazz/R&B-styled band to play the South Bend, IN, club circuit. Group leader is Earl Bostic-influenced saxophonist Walker (b. Autry DeWalt II, 1942, Blythesville, AR), called Junior by his stepfather. Group name arises from an occasion when, as they perform a jazz number at a club, a customer shouts out "these guys are all stars" and they dub themselves The All-Stars.

62 Band is heard in a club by Johnny Bristol, who recommends it to Harvey Fuqua in Detroit. He signs Walker and Co. to his Harvey label, and they release 3 singles through the year.

64 After Fuqua's labels are absorbed into Berry Gordy's Motown conglomerate, Junior Walker & The All-Stars are re-signed by Gordy, and placed on Soul label. First single for it also fails to chart.

65 Jan Playing a benefit show in Benton Harbor, MI, Walker sees 2 teenagers dancing an unfamiliar dance they call the Shotgun. Walker pens a booting dance tune with that title in his motel room and records it back in the studio in Detroit.

Mar Record takes off immediately and tops US R&B chart for 3 weeks.

Apr *Shotgun* crosses over and hits US #4, becoming a million-seller.

July A celebration of another dance, *Do The Boomerang* reaches US #36.

Aug First Soul label album, *Shotgun* makes US #108.

Sept *Shake And Fingerpop*, in a similar dance groove to the first 2 singles, reaches US #29.

Nov B-side of *Shake And Fingerpop*, slow, more jazz-influenced *Cleo's Back*, wholly instrumental, unlike the previous hits, peaks at US #43.

66 Feb Another instrumental in almost identical style, *Cleo's Mood* reaches US #50.

Mar [15] *Shotgun* is nominated for Best R&B Recording Of 1965 at the 8th annual Grammy awards, but is beaten by James Brown's *Papa's Got*

A Brand New Bag.

Apr *Soul Session* makes US #130.

June *(I'm A) Road Runner* reaches US #20.

Sept A revival of Marvin Gaye's *How Sweet It Is (To Be Loved By You)* reaches US #18 and also debuts Walker on UK chart at #22. *Road Runner* peaks at US #64.

Dec Another revival of a Motown classic, Barrett Strong's *Money (That's What I Want) Part 1*, makes US #52.

1967 Mar *Pucker Up Buttercup*, a return to *Shotgun* style, reaches US #31.

Aug *Shoot Your Shot* makes US #44.

Oct *"Live!"* peaks at US #119.

1968 Jan A mellower than usual single, reviving The Supremes' *Come See About Me*, reaches US #24.

Oct *Hip City, Pt.2* makes US #31.

Dec [28] Group plays the Miami Pop Festival in Hallendale, FL, alongside Chuck Berry, Marvin Gaye, Three Dog Night, Fleetwood Mac and many others.

1969 Feb *Home Cookin'* peaks at US #172, while its extracted title track makes US #42.

May Reissue of *(I'm A) Road Runner* reaches UK #12.

Aug *Greatest Hits*, a compilation of hit singles to date, makes US #43, while new single *What Does It Take (To Win Your Love)*, with a lengthy, distinctive sax intro from Walker, is group's biggest success since *Shotgun*, hitting US #4 and selling over a million.

Nov *What Does It Take (To Win Your Love)* reaches UK #13.

Dec *These Eyes*, a cover of a hit by Canadian rock band Guess Who, reaches US #16, as group starts production liaison with Johnny Bristol.

1970 Feb *What Does It Take To Win Your Love* stalls at US #92.

Mar *Gotta Hold On To This Feeling*, from the album, reaches US #21.

Aug *Do You See My Love (For You Growing)* makes US #32.

Oct *A Gasssss* peaks at US #110.

1971 Jan A revival of Neil Diamond's *Holly Holy* reaches US #75.

Aug *Rainbow Funk* stalls at US #91.

Sept *Take Me Girl, I'm Ready*, extracted from the album, makes US #50.

1972 Jan *Way Back Home* peaks at US #52.

Feb *Moody Jr.*, Walker's final US Album chart entry, makes US #142.

June Atmospheric semi-instrumental *Walk In The Night* makes US #46.

Sept [8] Group takes part in the Jazz & Blues Festival, Ann Arbor, MI, a tribute to blues pianist Otis Spann, alongside Muddy Waters, Howlin' Wolf, Bobby Bland and others.

Walk In The Night reaches UK #16.

1973 Feb *Take Me Girl, I'm Ready*, belatedly issued in UK, makes #16.

July Another belated release, *Way Back Home*, peaks at UK #35.

1977 Feb [9] Walker participates in ABC TV's "American Bandstand's 25th Anniversary Special", as part of an all-star house band including Chuck Berry, Johnny Rivers and Steve Cropper of Booker T. & The MG's.

1981 Sept Foreigner's *Urgent*, featuring a blistering sax solo from Walker, hits US #4, as Walker continues what he does best – playing live.

WAR

Lonnie Jordan (keyboards, vocals)
Howard Scott (guitar, vocals)
Charles Miller (saxophone, clarinet)
B.B. Dickerson (bass, vocals)
Harold Brown (drums, percussion)
"Papa Dee" Allen (keyboards, vocals)
Lee Oskar (harmonica)

1969 Band forms from remnants of early 60s Long Beach, CA, group The Creators, who became Night Shift and were only successful on the local circuit. As Night Shift, Jordan (b. Leroy Jordan, Nov.21, 1948, San Diego, CA), Scott (b. Mar.15, 1946, San Pedro, CA), Miller (b. June 2, 1939, Olathe, KS) and Brown (b. Mar.17, 1946, Long Beach, CA), with bassist Peter Rosen, are backing football star turned soul singer Deacon Jones, when noted by ex-The Animals lead singer Eric Burdon, harmonica player Oskar (b. Oskar Levetin Hansen, Mar.24, 1946, Copenhagen, Denmark) and producer Jerry Goldstein, who are looking for a blues-based black band to accompany Burdon.

June Burdon, Oskar and the band meet at Goldstein's home and decide to work together with Goldstein as producer. The name War is chosen as being in stark contrast with current peace preoccupations in music and therefore memorable. Shortly after, Rosen dies from a drug overdose, and ex-Creators bassist Dickerson (b. Morris Dickerson, Aug.3, 1949, Torrance, CA) replaces him, while Allen (b. Thomas Allen, July 18, 1931, Wilmington, DE) also joins on keyboards to make it a 7-piece instrumental unit. Burdon is already signed to MGM, and the new team continues with the label.

1970 Band tours US, then moves to UK and Europe.
July War jams with Jimi Hendrix in an impromptu session at Ronnie Scott's jazz club in London.
Aug Debut album *Eric Burdon Declares War* reaches US #18. Taken from it, group-composed *Spill The Wine* hits US #3 and sells over a million, to earn a gold disk. The album also contains musical tributes to Roland Kirk and Memphis Slim, and a version of John D. Loudermilk's much-revived *Tobacco Road*.
Oct *Eric Burdon Declares War* makes UK #50.
1971 **Jan** *They Can't Take Away Our Music* reaches US #50. It is taken from double album *The Black Man's Burdon*, which makes US #82.
Feb The album makes UK #34, and another European tour follows but Burdon drops out, exhausted, and returns to Los Angeles, CA. Band completes all contracted dates on its own and, at tour's end, it is decided not to continue partnership with Burdon. Group's manager Steve Gold negotiates new recording deal with United Artists Records.
May *War*, the debut without Burdon, creeps to US #190.
June [30] Band plays the Hollywood Bowl in United Artists' "99 Cent Spectacular", a low entry-price showcase for the label's new acts.
Sept *All Day Music*, written by Goldstein and the band, makes US #35.
1972 **May** *Slippin' Into Darkness* also reaches US #16, spending 22 weeks on chart and selling over a million to give the band its first "solo" gold disk. The track is an edited version of a cut on *All Day Music*, which also peaks at US #16, and is the band's first gold album (selling over a half million copies).
Aug [19] Group plays on the first edition of NBC TV's "Midnight Special", performing *Slippin' Into Darkness*.
1973 **Jan** *The World Is A Ghetto* reaches US #7 and is another million-seller.
Feb *The World Is A Ghetto*, written by the band and produced by Goldstein (he and the group have formed their own Far Out production company, which leases all recordings to UA), tops US chart for 2 weeks, becoming its second gold album. It includes a 10-min. version of the title track and 13-min. *City, Country, City*.
Apr *The Cisco Kid*, from the album, hits US #2, the band's third consecutive million-selling single.
Sept *Gypsy Man* hits US #8. It is taken from *Deliver The Word*, which hits US #6 and earns another gold disk.
1974 **Jan** Also from *Deliver The Word*, *Me And Baby Brother* reaches US #15.
May Double live album *War Live!* reaches US #13.
July Instrumental *Ballero*, from the live album, climb to US #33.
1975 **Aug** *Why Can't We Be Friends?* hits US #8, becoming band's fifth gold album, while title track hits US #6 and sells over a million. (Song is beamed into space to US and Russian astronauts during the summer 1975 link-up in Earth orbit.)
Nov Sparse Latin funk track *Low Rider*, also from *Why Can't We Be Friends?*, hits US #7.
1976 **Feb** Group signs a new deal for UK distribution with Island Records and *Low Rider* is its UK chart debut, reaching #12.
July *Me And Baby Brother*, belatedly issued in UK as follow-up, reaches UK #21. Oskar has solo success with US #29 album *Lee Oskar*. (2 further solo albums, *Before The Rain* (US #86) and *My Road Our Road* (US #162) will chart in 1978 and 1981.)
Sept *Summer* hits US #7, and is another million-seller. Group writes and performs the music for Krishna Shah's movie "The River Niger", starring Cicely Tyson and James Earl Jones.
Oct Compilation *Greatest Hits*, rounding up all the successful singles, hits US #6. Band's biggest-selling album, it earns a platinum disk for a million-plus sales. Meanwhile, War and United Artists are at loggerheads (or with "philosophical differences", as the statements quote) over matters of direction and marketing of the band's music. The agreed solution is that the band's production company will move elsewhere, but will deliver a final album to UA, to be a departure from the mainstream for release on subsidiary Blue Note jazz label.
1977 **Jan** ABC Records releases *Love Is All Around*, a collection of old early tracks recorded with Burdon 1969-70. It reaches US #140.
Aug *L.A. Sunshine*, the rare appearance of a single on Blue Note (and a sampler for new album) peaks at US #45.
Sept Double album *Platinum Jazz*, the set owed to UA, makes US #23 and earns a gold disk.
1978 **Feb** Band's Far Out Productions signs new deal with MCA Records. First MCA release, *Galaxy*, reaches US #15, while title track makes US #39 and UK #14. Alice Tweed Smyth joins on additional vocals.
Apr *Hey Senorita*, from *Galaxy*, reaches UK #40. Dickerson leaves and is replaced on bass by Luther Rabb.
Aug War's soundtrack album from film "Youngblood", a drama of

ghetto gang warfare, reaches US #69.
1979 **May** *The Music Band* peaks at US #41, earning War's final gold albu[m]. Group adds Pat Rizzo on horns and Ron Hammond on percussion.
1980 **Jan** *The Music Band 2* reaches US #111.
1982 **Apr** Band moves labels again, signing to RCA for *Outlaw*, which reaches US #48. *You Got The Power*, taken from the album, reaches US[?] #66 and UK #58. Smyth leaves.
July Title track from *Outlaw* makes US #94.
1983 **July** RCA album *Life (Is So Strange)* reaches US #164.
1985 **Apr** *Groovin'*, a revival of The Young Rascals' 1967 chart-topper, lea[ses] by the band and Goldstein to UK independent R&B music label Bluebird Records, makes UK #43.
1987 **July** Goldstein launches band's own Lax label in UK. First release is updated remix of *Low Rider* on 12"-single, which makes UK #98, as *T[he] Best Of War ... And More* peaks at US #156.
1988 **Aug** [30] Allen dies of cerebral hemorrhage while on tour.

JENNIFER WARNES

1956 Warnes (b. Seattle, WA), having been raised in Orange County, CA, makes her professional debut wrapped in the US flag singing *The Sta[r] Spangled Banner*, accompanied by 300 accordians.
1967 **Feb** Warnes, as Jennifer Warren, becomes a regular on US CBS TV's "The Smothers Brothers Comedy Hour". One of the show's writers, Mason Williams invites Warnes to duet with him on *Cinderella Rockefella* for his album *The Mason Williams Ear Show*.
1968 **Nov** [22] West Coast production of "Hair", in which Warnes stars a[s] Sheila, opens at Los Angeles, CA's Aquarius theater.
1969 Now a veteran of the Los Angeles folk scene, gaining a reputation fo[r] singing Canadian poet Leonard Cohen's songs, Warnes signs to Warner Bros. Records.
1972 She releases her first album *Jennifer* for Reprise, produced by John C[?] and featuring songs by Jackson Browne, Jimmy Webb, Donovan and Barry Gibb.
1975 Warnes signs to Arista Records.
1977 **May** *Jennifer Warnes*, produced by Jim Ed Norman and Jim Price, makes US #43.
1978 **Mar** Peter McCann-penned *Right Time Of The Night* hits US #6.
Sept *I'm Dreaming* makes US #50.
1979 **Aug** *Shot Through The Heart*, self-produced with Rob Fraboni, make[s] US #94.
Nov *I Know A Heartache When I See One* reaches US #19.
1980 **Jan** A revival of Dionne Warwick's 1963 Bacharach/David-penned h[?] *Don't Make Me Over* peaks at US #67.
Apr [14] Warnes' ballad *It Goes Like It Goes*, from Sally Field film "Norma Rae", wins an Oscar for Best Original Song at the annual Academy Awards.
May *When The Feeling Comes Around* makes US #45.
1981 **Dec** *One More Hour*, written by Randy Newman for his score to mov[ie] "Ragtime", receives an Oscar nomination.
1982 **Jan** *Could It Be Love*, 1 of 3 new tracks from otherwise retrospective *Best Of Jennifer Warnes*, makes US #47.
Nov *Up Where We Belong*, a duet with Joe Cocker from Richard Gere film "An Officer And A Gentleman", tops US chart for 3 weeks.
1983 **Feb** *Up Where We Belong* hits US #7.
[23] *Up Where We Belong* wins Best Pop Performance By A Duo Or Group With Vocal Of 1982 at the 25th annual Grammy awards.
Apr [11] Cocker and Warnes perform *Up Where We Belong* at the Academy Awards. It wins an Oscar for Best Original Song.
Nov *All The Right Moves*, a duet with Chris Thompson from movie o[f] same name, stalls at US #85.
1987 **Jan** Warnes, the first signing to new Cypress label, releases *Famous Blue Raincoat*, featuring only Leonard Cohen songs and self-produce[d] with Roscoe Beck. It makes US #72.
July Warnes is one of the featured friends on "The Black And White Night – Roy Orbison And Friends", a filmed concert with Orbison backed by Bruce Springsteen, Elvis Costello, James Burton, Tom Wai[ts] and many others. Warnes duets with country singer Gary Morris on *Simply Meant To Be*, penned by Henry Mancini with George Merrill a[nd] Shannon Rubicam (husband and wife writers of Whitney Houston's *I Wanna Dance With Somebody* and *How Will I Know*), for Bruce Willis/Kim Basinger film "Blind Date".
[25] *First We Take Manhattan* spends a week on UK chart at #74.
Aug *Famous Blue Raincoat* makes UK #33.
Nov [28] Warnes' duet with Bill Medley, *(I've Had) The Time Of My Life*, from film "Dirty Dancing", tops US chart and hits UK #6.

1988 Mar [2] *(I've Had) The Time Of My Life* wins Best Pop Performance By A Duo Or Group With Vocal of 1987 at the 30th annual Grammy awards.
Apr [11] Warnes is awarded her third Oscar as *(I've Had) The Time Of My Life* wins Best Original Song.

1991 Feb Currently signed to Private Music, Warnes' latest cameo appearance is on UK songstress Tanita Tikaram's third album *Everybody's Angel*.

DIONNE WARWICK

1960 After singing in the New Hope Baptist church choir in nearby Newark, NJ, from age 6, Warwick (b. Marie Dionne Warrick, Dec.12, 1940, East Orange, NJ), daughter of Chess Records' gospel promotion department head, is a regular performer, playing piano with The Drinkard Singers gospel group, managed by her mother. She forms The Gospelaires, with sister Dee Dee, cousin Cissy Houston and friend Doris Troy, and they sing in churches throughout New York and New Jersey. Warwick enrols at Hartt College of Music in Hartford, CT, and to pay for her tuition The Gospelaires work as back-up singers at the Apollo, Harlem, New York and on New York studio pop and R&B recording sessions.

1961 July While working with The Gospelaires on a Leiber/Stoller-produced session for The Drifters', Warwick is first heard by composer Burt Bacharach and then partner Bob Hilliard, whose song *Mexican Divorce* The Drifters are cutting. Later, on a break from college, Warwick contacts Bacharach, who invites her to become the regular singer on demos he and lyricist partner Hal David are making of their songs for playing to record companies.

1962 Via demos made for Scepter Records' group The Shirelles, Warwick begins regular studio back-up work for the label's acts, including Chuck Jackson and Tommy Hunt, and is signed to Scepter as a solo vocalist, with Bacharach and David as writers and producers.

1963 Jan She leaves college and makes her debut single *Don't Make Me Over*. Written (as will be virtually all her Scepter output) by Bacharach and David, it reaches US #21.
Apr *This Empty Place* peaks at US #84 (its B-side is *Wishin' And Hopin'*, later successfully revived by Dusty Springfield and The Merseybeats). Marlene Dietrich introduces Warwick on her debut at the Olympia theater in Paris, France.
Aug *Make The Music Play* makes US #81.

1964 Feb *Anyone Who Had A Heart* hits US #8. In UK, it makes #42, eclipsed by Cilla Black's #1 cover version.
May *Walk On By*, rush-released in US and UK to prevent cover versions, and promoted by Warwick on UK TV shows during a promotional visit, marks her UK breakthrough, hitting #9.
[30] Warwick makes her UK TV debut on BBC TV's "Top Of The Pops", during a week long radio and promotional tour.
June *Walk On By* hits US #6, becoming her first international million-seller while *Presenting Dionne Warwick* reaches UK #14.
Aug *You'll Never Get To Heaven (If You Break My Heart)* (which will be revived later by The Stylistics) reaches UK #20.
Sept *You'll Never Get To Heaven (If You Break My Heart)* makes US #34 while B-side *A House Is Not A Home* (theme from the movie of the same title) peaks at US #71, in competition with a version by Brook Benton.
Oct *Reach Out For Me* reaches UK #23.
Nov *Reach Out For Me* reaches US #20 and *Make Way For Dionne Warwick* peaks at US #68.
[9] While on UK tour, Warwick is slightly injured in an auto accident in Glasgow, Scotland, causing cancellations of tour dates.
[28] She makes her second appearance on ITV show "Thank Your Lucky Stars", with The Isley Brothers.
Dec [1] She flies back to US after recording album at Pye's London studios with Bacharach. (Warwick is named Top Selling Female Vocalist Of The Year by NARM.)

1965 Mar *The Sensitive Sound Of Dionne Warwick* peaks at US #107.
[29] Warwick begins a 2-week stint in cabaret at London's Savoy hotel.
Apr *Who Can I Turn To*, from musical "The Roar Of The Greasepaint – The Smell Of The Crowd", peaks at US #62.
[2] Warwick guests on the first ever "Ready, Steady Goes Live!"
[10] She is a guest panellist on BBC TV show "Juke Box Jury".
[14] She appears on ITV show "The Bacharach Sound" with Dusty Springfield, The Searchers and others.
May An uncharacteristic uptempo R&B single, *You Can Have Him* peaks at US #75 and UK #37.
Aug *Here I Am*, from Bacharach/David-penned soundtrack of movie "What's New Pussycat?", makes US #65. (Its B-side is Warwick's original recording of *(They Long To Be) Close To You*, which will be a

million-seller 5 years later for The Carpenters.)
Nov *(Here I Go Again) Looking With My Eyes* peaks at US #64.

1966 Jan *Are You There (With Another Girl?)* makes US #39.
Feb *Here I Am* makes US #45.
May Live album *Dionne Warwick In Paris*, recorded on stage at the Olympia, peaks at US #76, while *A Message To Michael*, a gender-switched revival of Bacharach/David's hit by both Lou Johnson and Adam Faith as *A Message To Martha (Kentucky Bluebird)*, hits US #8.
June Compilation *Best Of Dionne Warwick* hits UK #8.
Aug *Trains And Boats And Planes* (a 1965 UK hit for Bacharach himself and a US and UK hit by Billy J. Kramer) reaches US #22.
Nov *I Just Don't Know What To Do With Myself*, an album cut covered as a UK hit by Dusty Springfield in 1964, reaches US #26.

1967 Jan *Another Night* makes US #49, as Warwick begins a 4-month European tour.
Feb *Here, Where There Is Love* reaches US #18 and UK #39, and earns Warwick's first gold album. It contains her version of *Alfie*, the film theme which has hit for Cher and Cilla Black the previous year.
June *On Stage And In The Movies* peaks at US #169.
[10] Warwick appears at the 2-day Fantasy Faire And Magic Mountain Music Fest in Mt. Tamilpais, CA, with an audience of 15,000. She is billed alongside The Miracles and several of California's new breed of rock bands including The Doors and Jefferson Airplane.
July After strong airplay as an album track, *Alfie* is released as a single and reaches US #15, while B-side *The Beginning Of Loneliness* peaks at US #79. She makes her West Coast cabaret debut at the West Side Room, Los Angeles, CA.
Sept *The Windows Of The World* makes US #32.
Nov *The Windows Of The World* reaches US #22.
Dec From the album, *I Say A Little Prayer* hits US #4.

1968 Jan *Dionne Warwick's Golden Hits, Part One* hits US #10.
Feb *I Say A Little Prayer*, with B-side movie theme *(Theme From) Valley Of The Dolls*, penned by André and Dory Previn, recorded at the suggestion of the film's star Barbara Parkins, becomes Warwick's biggest double-sided chartmaker of her career, and a million-seller in US alone. Issued in UK as an A-side, *(Theme From) Valley Of The Dolls* reaches UK #28.
Apr *Valley Of The Dolls* hits US #6 and earns a gold disk.
May *Do You Know The Way To San José*, taken from the album, and written by Bacharach/David, hits US #10 while B-side *Let Me Be Lonely* peaks at US #71.
June *Valley Of The Dolls* hits UK #10 while *Do You Know The Way To San José* hits UK #8.
Sept *Who Is Gonna Love Me?* makes US #33. Its B-side revives Warwick's original *(There's) Always Something There To Remind Me* (a 1964 hit for Sandie Shaw and Lou Johnson) and peaks at US #65.
Dec *Promises Promises*, from Bacharach/David's Broadway musical of the same title, reaches US #19.

1969 Jan *Promises Promises* reaches US #18.
Mar *This Girl's In Love With You*, from *Promises, Promises* (and a gender-switch revival of Herb Alpert's million-seller of the previous summer) hits US #7.
[12] *Do You Know The Way To San José* wins Best Contemporary Pop Vocal Performance, Female Of 1968 at the 11th annual Grammy awards.
May *Soulful*, recorded in Memphis, TN with producer Chips Moman, reaches US #11.
June *The April Fools*, theme from Jack Lemmon/Catherine Deneuve film of the same title, makes US #37. Warwick makes her own film acting debut in "Slaves", a historical drama, opposite Stephen Boyd and Ossie Davis. (She also sings the movie's theme song.) The next time she acts it will be in a guest-starring role with Isaac Hayes in an episode of "The Rockford Files".
Sept *Dionne Warwick's Greatest Motion Picture Hits* makes US #31 and earns a gold disk while *Odds And Ends* reaches US #43.
Nov A revival of The Righteous Brothers' *You've Lost That Lovin' Feelin'* reaches US #16.
Dec Compilation *Dionne Warwick's Golden Hits, Part 2* reaches US #28.

1970 Feb *I'll Never Fall In Love Again*, from "Promises Promises" (a UK hit for Bobbie Gentry in 1969), hits US #6.
Apr [13] Warwick makes a sole European appearance at the Royal Albert Hall, London.
May *Let Me Go To Him* makes US #32.
June Compilation albums *Greatest Hits Vol.1* and *Greatest Hits Vol.2* make UK #31 and #28 respectively. In US, *I'll Never Fall In Love Again* reaches #23.

Aug *Papier Maché* makes US #43.

Nov *Make It Easy On Yourself*, a revival of Bacharach/David's 1962 hit for Jerry Butler, makes US #37.

[26] She appears in NBC TV special with Andy Williams, The Supremes, Bobbie Gentry, Henry Mancini, Burl Ives, Tennessee Ernie Ford and Pearl Bailey.

1971 **Jan** *Very Dionne* makes US #37 while, taken from it, *The Green Grass Starts To Grow* reaches US #43.

Mar [16] Warwick receives her second Grammy, as *I'll Never Fall In Love Again* is named Best Contemporary Vocal Performance, Female Of 1970 at the 13th annual Grammy awards.

Apr *Who Gets The Guy* makes US #57.

Aug *Amanda*, from soundtrack *The Love Machine*, stalls at US #83, and is Warwick's last hit single on Scepter. She signs to Warner Brothers.

Dec Double album *The Dionne Warwicke Story*, featuring live versions of her hits, makes US #48. (A numerologist advises Warwick to suffix an "e" (for husband Bill Elliot) to her name to bring her luck. For a short period, she changes the spelling of her surname on all billing, to include the extra "e" in Warwicke, but will revert back to its original form.) (Husband Elliot, who she married in the early 60s, and by whom she has 2 sons, Damon and David, will die in the early 70s.)

1972 **Mar** *Dionne*, her debut on Warner, peaks at US #54 while, from it, *If We Only Have Love* stalls at US #84. This hit marks the end of her long collaboration with Bacharach and David, who will no longer write for her when they also split professionally. Warwick sues the duo, alleging the breaking of a contractual obligation.

Apr *From Within*, with reissued Scepter material, makes US #169.

1973 **Feb** Second Warner album *Just Being Myself*, teaming her with Holland/Dozier/Holland peaks at US #178 and, like most of Warwick's Warner albums, fails to spin off a hit single. (Her vocals are added to tracks already used by Freda Payne and Honey Cone.)

1974 **Oct** *Then Came You*, duetted with The Spinners, tops the US chart for a week, selling over a million. It is the first chart-topper for both Warwick and the group. (The Spinners have been her opening act on a 5-week theater tour during the summer and producer Thom Bell has suggested her voice would blend well with the group's lead singer Phillipe Wynne and Bobbie Smith.)

Nov *Then Came You* reaches UK #29.

1975 **Mar** *Then Came You*, including the duet with The Spinners, peaks at US #167.

1976 **Jan** *Track Of The Cat*, produced by Thom Bell and mostly written by him and Linda Creed, makes US #137.

Feb From the album, *Once You Hit The Road* stalls at US #79.

1977 **Mar** Double live album *A Man And A Woman*, on which Warwick duets with Isaac Hayes, released on his Hot Buttered Soul label, makes US #49 and coincides with the opening of a joint US tour by the 2.

1979 **Jan** Her Warner Brothers contract expired, Warwick signs to Arista Records and drops the "e" from the end of her name. She also completes her masters degree in music.

Oct *I'll Never Love This Way Again* hits US #5 and sells over a million. It is taken from her debut Arista album *Dionne*, produced by labelmate Barry Manilow, which reaches US #12 and, in over a year's stay on chart, will sell a million.

1980 **Feb** *Déjà Vu*, also from *Dionne*, reaches US #15.

[27] Warwick wins Best Pop Vocal Performance, Female for *I'll Never Love This Way Again* and Best R&B Vocal Performance, Female for *Déjà Vu* at the 22nd annual Grammy awards.

Apr *After You*, theme from the film of the same title, and also produced by Manilow, peaks at US #65.

Sept Warwick hosts the first season of the US syndicated-TV pop show "Solid Gold". (She refuses to return for the second season, unwilling to co-host with country singer Tanya Tucker. She returns in 1984 through to 1986.)

Oct *No Night So Long* and the extracted title song both reach US #23.

Dec *Easy Love*, also from the album, peaks at US #62.

1981 **July** Double album *Hot! Live And Otherwise*, which has 3 live (recorded at Harrah's in Reno, NV) and 1 studio-recorded side, makes US #72. From it, Michael Masser-produced *Some Changes Are For Good* peaks at US #65.

1982 **June** *Friends In Love* makes US #83 while the title song, a duet with Johnny Mathis, reaches US #38.

Dec *Heartbreaker*, produced by The Bee Gees' Barry Gibb with Albhy Galuten and Karl Richardson, and mostly co-written by Gibb (apart from revived oldie *Our Day Will Come*) reaches US #25 and hits UK #3, while the title track, written by The Bee Gees and with Barry Gibb on backing vocals, hits UK #2.

1983 **Jan** *Heartbreaker* hits US #10 while UK follow-up, The Bee Gees-penned ballad *All The Love In The World*, hits UK #10.

Feb *Yours*, another Bee Gees composition, peaks at UK #66.

Apr *Take The Short Way Home*, written by Gibb and Galuten, is Warwick's 50th US hit single, making US #41.

May UK compilation *The Collection* reaches UK #11.

June A reissue of *I'll Never Love This Way Again*, taken from *The Collection*, peaks at UK #62.

Nov *So Amazing* makes UK #60.

Dec *How Many Times Can We Say Goodbye*, (the US title of *So Amazing*) produced by Luther Vandross, peaks at US #57 as the title song, a duet with Vandross, reaches US #27.

1984 **Nov** Warwick contributes to Stevie Wonder's soundtrack album for movie "The Woman In Red", which hits US #4 and UK #2.

1985 **Jan** [28] Warwick takes part in the recording of the all-star charity single *We Are The World* by USA For Africa, which will top charts throughout the world.

Feb *Without Your Love*, containing duets with Barry Manilow, Glenn Jones and Stevie Wonder and reuniting her with Burt Bacharach, stalls at UK #86.

Mar In US, the album is given the alternative title *Finder Of Lost Love* and peaks at US #106.

Nov *That's What Friends Are For*, written by Bacharach and his wife Carole Bayer Sager for 1982 film "Night Shift" and originally sung by Rod Stewart, is revived initially to provide a duet for Warwick and Stevie Wonder. When it is decided to donate its profits to the American Foundation For AIDS Research, Warwick asks first Gladys Knight and then Elton John to add vocal parts. The song is released as a single, credited to Dionne Warwick & Friends, and reaches UK #16.

Dec *Friends* reaches US #12.

[12] She receives a star on Hollywood's Walk Of Fame.

1986 **Jan** [18] *That's What Friends Are For* tops the US chart for 4 weeks, selling over a million. All company and artists' profits from it are given to AIDS charities, and it will be the year's best-selling single in US.

[25] *That's What Friends Are For* tops US R&B chart.

Feb [25] Warwick presents her cousin Whitney Houston with the Grammy for Best Pop Vocal Performance, Female at the 28th annual Grammy awards. (She announces the setting up of the Warwick Foundation to find a cure for AIDS.)

Mar [29] *Whisper In The Dark*, from *Friends*, peaks at US #72.

1987 **Feb** [24] *That's What Friends Are For* wins Song Of The Year and Best Pop Performance By A Duo Or Group With Vocal at the 29th annual Grammy awards.

Mar Warwick co-hosts (with Luther Vandross) the First Annual Soul Train Music Awards at the Hollywood Center television studios.

Aug *Love Power*, a duet with Jeffrey Osborne, peaks at UK #63.

[29] *Love Power* reaches US #12. Parent album *Reservations For Two*, containing duets with Kashif, Howard Hewett (ex-Shalamar), Osborne, Smokey Robinson and June Pointer of The Pointer Sisters, makes US #56.

Sept [23] The city of New York honors Warwick for her work in raising $1 million for AIDS research.

Nov [21] *Reservations For Two*, from the album of the same title and duetted with Kashif, peaks at US #62.

1988 **Mar** Warwick duet with Howard Hewett, *Another Chance To Love*, makes #42 on US R&B chart.

Sept Warwick sings *Champagne Wishes And Caviar Dreams*, the theme for the sixth season of Robin Leach's US TV show "Lifestyles Of The Rich And Famous".

1989 **Nov** Warwick/Jeffrey Osborne duet *Take Good Care Of You And Me* makes #46 on US R&B chart.

1990 **Jan** [14] TV show "Dionne And Friends" premieres on US cable stations.

[20] *Greatest Hits 1979-1990* peaks at US #177.

[27] Compilation *Love Songs* hits UK #6.

Feb Motown releases *Forgotten Eyes*, a charity single featuring 100 artists including Warwick. (All proceeds from the record will go to benefit Retinitis Pigmentosa International.)

Mar Melba Moore's *Lift Up Every Voice And Sing*, on which Warwick guests with Anita Baker, Bobby Brown, Howard Hewett, Freddie Jackson, Jeffrey Osborne, and Stevie Wonder, to benefit the NAACP United Negro College Fund, and sickle cell anemia research, is released on Capitol.

[17] Warwick joins her Arista labelmates in the company's "That's What Friends Are For" 15th anniversary concert at Radio City Music Hall, which will raise more than $2 million, the proceeds going to the

Gay Men's Health Crisis and other AIDS organizations.
Sept [15] *Dionne Warwick Sings Cole Porter* peaks at US #155.

THE WATERBOYS

Mike Scott (vocals, guitar)
Anthony Thistlethwaite (sax, multi-instrumentalist)

1981 Scott (b. Dec.14, 1958, Edinburgh, Scotland), a veteran of unsuccessful UK bands including DNV, Funhouse, The Red & The Black and Another Pretty Face, who were signed to Virgin for 4 months in 1980, has relocated from his native Edinburgh, where he has studied English and Philosophy at Edinburgh University, to London in the late 70s and set up a fanzine, **Jungleland**, inspired by the Bruce Springsteen song, for which he has interviewed The Clash and The Only Ones among others, and now forms his latest project, The Waterboys with sax player Thistlethwaite (b. Aug.31, 1955, Leicester, Leics.). They sign to the fledgling Ensign label.
Dec They begin recording their debut album with sessioneers Kevin Wilkinson, Ray Massey, Norman Rodger, Nick Linden and Steven Tayler at the Redshop studio, London and the Farmyard studio, Little Chalfont, Bucks., through Nov.1982.

1983 **Feb** *The Waterboys* fails to chart as does extracted Rupert Hine-produced *A Girl Called Johnny*, song written by Scott about Patti Smith, who he met in London in 1978.
Apr Having answered an ad placed by Scott in **Sounds** looking for a "guitarist into Iggy Pop", keyboardist Karl Wallinger (b. Oct.19, 1957, Prestatyn, Wales) joins The Waterboys in time to contribute to the second album recording sessions. His experience in indie outfits The Invisible Body Club and Out and working at a music publishers, makes Wallinger a keen participant on piano, organ, percussion and vocals.
May The Waterboys make their TV debut on BBC TV's "The Old Grey Whistle Test".

1984 **June** [18] *A Pagan Place*, also featuring current Waterboy Kevin Wilkinson on drums, makes UK #100. It is entirely written and produced by Scott and attracts much critical praise.

1985 **Mar** Band enters the Townhouse studio in London to begin 5 months of recording. It becomes apparent during the sessions that Wallinger, himself full of creative energy, wants an increasingly active role. In addition to songwriting, he also co-arranges tracks and becomes a multi-instrumentalist on the project.
Oct Third album *This Is The Sea* is released, set to make UK #37, a critical and commercial breakthrough.
Nov While Scott moves to take up permanent residence in Eire, extracted anthem *The Whole Of The Moon* reaches UK #26.

1986 As Scott confirms, Wallinger quits the band "pregnant with World Party". Wallinger stays within the Ensign family and establishes his own act, World Party, over which he has complete creative control. (Group will go on to secure hit albums, including 1987's *Private Revolution* and 1990's *Goodbye Jumbo*.) Scott begins recording a new Waterboys album, but eventually scraps the project in favor of concentrating on his new interest in Irish celtic and gaelic music.

1987 Still with Thistlethwaite, Scott has met Irish fiddle player Steve Wickham and invited him to join The Waterboys and record folk-jig album, which will be musically termed "raggle-taggle".

1988 **Oct** The resulting *Fisherman's Blues*, recorded mainly in the dining room at the Spiddal House, Spiddal County, Galway, Eire, reaches UK #13, and will make US #76 during a half-year chart stay. The album includes an update of Van Morrison's *Sweet Thing*, a track titled *World Party*, which will become a popular US college cut and Scott-penned *Strange Boat*, which will subsequently be recorded by Tom Jones.

1989 **Jan** During a UK tour with full raggle-taggle Waterboys line-up, title track *Fisherman's Blues* makes UK #32.
July Following a US visit, *And A Bang On The Ear* peaks at UK #51.
Sept Still based on the west coast of Eire, Scott produces an unreleased album by traditional celtic players Steve Cooney and Seamus Begley, recorded in a pub in Dingle Bay.

1990 **May** During recording of the fifth album with Thistlethwaite and Scott. now augmented by double bassist Trevor Hutchinson, Colin Blakey (flute, organ) and Sharon Shannon (accordian, fiddle), Wickham leaves the line-up and will join Dublin folk unit The Texas Kellys.
June Scott marries Irene Keough in Dublin (she was the studio manager at the Windmill Lane complex in Dublin where early *Fisherman's Blues* tracks were recorded). A dance update of *The Whole Of The Moon* by Little Caesar peaks at UK #68.
Sept [2] Co-produced by Scott and Barry Beckett, *Room To Roam* hits UK #5 as The Waterboys embark on a major UK tour, focused in a rock

direction with a live line-up including US drummer Ken Blevins, Hutchinson and helmsmen Scott and Thistlethwaite.
Nov [10] *Room To Roam* peaks at US #180.

1991 **Apr** [13] In a period of hip reappraisement of the band, *The Whole Of The Moon*, reissued as a trailer to a greatest hits package, *Best Of The Waterboys '81-'90*, hits UK #3.

MUDDY WATERS

1943 Waters (b. McKinley Morganfield, Apr.4, 1915, Rolling Fork, MS), having moved to Chicago from a plantation in Clarksdale on the Mississippi Delta where he grew up, is introduced by fellow bluesman, Big Bill Broonzy, to the South Side clubs and bars where he begins to develop a strong local reputation. He has begun learning the guitar in 1937, cutting his first records *I Be's Troubled* and *Country Blues* for the American Library of Congress 4 years later. He earns a living for the next 3 years driving a truck for a venetian blind manufacturer.

1945 Chicagoans Leonard and Phil Chess sign Waters to their Aristocrat Records label, where he begins work as a sideman for other artists.

1948 After working as a sideman at Columbia Records, Waters moves back to Aristocrat to record his first own-name single *I Can't Be Satisfied*.

1949 He records *Screamin' And Cryin'*, followed by *Rollin' And Tumblin'*.

1950 Aristocrat is renamed Chess. Waters' first single on Chess is *Rollin' Stone* which features the group he will use on many of his best releases over the next decade (Little Walter (harmonica), Otis Spann (piano) and Jimmy Rogers (second guitar); bass player and composer, Willie Dixon, will be another regular in the line-up).

1951 Waters' first big national R&B success is *Louisiana Blues*. (Between now and 1958, he will have a further 11 national R&B hits, of which the most successful will be *She Moves Me* (1952), *Hoochie Coochie Man* (1954), *Mannish Boy* (1955), *I've Got My Mojo Working* (1957) and *Close To You* (1958).)

1958 Waters on his first UK tour makes a big impression on white London bluesmen, Cyril Davies and Alexis Korner, who will be pioneers of UK's emergent R&B movement. (By the end of the decade, the mass black American audience for the blues will largely disappear, favoring the more sophisticated R&B/soul styles. Waters will be able to avoid the limbo into which many US bluesmen are cast thanks to marketing initiatives by Chess, who successfully project him as an albums artist, selling increasingly to white audiences.)

1961 **Sept** Live *Muddy Waters At Newport* introduces him to the mainstream jazz audience.

1963 **Oct** [18] Waters plays at the American Negro Blues Festival at the Fairfield Hall, Croydon, London, with Memphis Slim, Sonny Boy Williamson and Willie Dixon.

1964 **May** *Muddy Waters Folk Singer*, a solo acoustic album, gives him a new folk following. Waters is championed by UK R&B/beat groups, including The Rolling Stones and The Yardbirds, and re-issued albums of his 50s singles start selling to a new generation of fans.

1965 **June** [17-20] Waters takes part in the first New York Folk Festival at Carnegie Hall, New York.

1966 **Apr** Waters makes his first Los Angeles, CA, appearance in 10 years, at the Troubadour.

1968 **May** *The Super Super Blues Band*, with Bo Diddley and Howlin' Wolf, is released, followed by 2 controversial "psychedelic" albums: *Electric Mud*, which reaches US #127, and *After The Rain*.
Sept [2] Waters appears at 3-day Sky River Rock Festival and Lighter-Than-Air Fair, in Sultan, WA, with Santana, The Grateful Dead, Country Joe & The Fish, The Youngbloods and others.

1969 **Oct** *Fathers And Sons*, featuring white US bluesmen Paul Butterfield and Mike Bloomfield, climbs to US #70.

1972 **Mar** [14] *They Call Me Muddy Waters* wins Best Ethnic Or Traditional Recording at the 14th annual Grammy awards.
July *The London Sessions* is released.

1973 **Mar** [3] *The London Muddy Waters Session* wins Best Ethnic Or Traditional Recording at the 15th annual Grammy awards.
Oct [11] A serious car accident, in which 3 people are killed, forces Waters into semi-retirement for 2 years.

1976 **Feb** [28] *The Muddy Waters Woodstock Album* wins Best Ethnic Or Traditional Recording at the 18th annual Grammy awards.
Nov [25] His first major live appearance following the accident is at The Band's farewell "Last Waltz" concert in San Francisco. He performs *Mannish Boy*.

1977 **Mar** Bluesman and rock star, Johnny Winter, signs Waters to his Blue Sky label, producing Waters on 2 albums, *Hard Again*, which makes US #143, and *I'm Ready*, which peaks at US #157.

1978 **Feb** [23] *Hard Again* wins Best Ethnic Or Traditional Recording Of

MUDDY WATERS cont.

1977 at the 20th annual Grammy awards.
Third Blue Sky set, *Muddy Waters Live* is released.
Aug Waters is invited to play at a White House picnic organized by President Jimmy Carter.

1979 **Feb** [15] *I'm Ready* wins Best Ethnic Or Traditional Recording Of 1978 at the 21st annual grammy awards.

1980 **Feb** [27] Consistent recognition for Waters' dominance of the blues is confirmed as he collects his sixth Grammy, for Best Ethnic Or Traditional Recording Of 1979 for *Muddy "Mississippi" Waters Live* at the 22nd annual Grammy awards.

1981 **May** *King Bee* reaches US #192.

1982 He plays a concert in Miami with guest Eric Clapton.

1983 **Apr** [30] Waters dies of a heart attack at home in Chicago.

1987 **Jan** [21] Waters is inducted into the Rock'N'Roll Hall Of Fame at the second annual induction dinner at the Waldorf Astoria, New York.

1988 **July** Waters receives posthumous UK success when *Mannish Boy* reaches UK #51 through exposure on a Levi 501 jeans TV commercial.

WET WET WET

Marti Pellow (vocals)
Graeme Clark (bass)
Tom Cunningham (drums)
Neil Mitchell (keyboards)

1982 Clark (b. Apr.15, 1966, Glasgow, Scotland), Cunningham (b. June 22, 1965, Glasgow) and Mitchell (b. June 8, 1967, Helensborough, Scotland), having formed a group while attending Clydebank high school, Glasgow, approach Mark McLoughlin (b. Mar.23, 1966, Clydebank, Scotland) to front as vocalist and, as The Vortex Motion, plays Clash cover versions, with its first gig at Clydebank community center. McLoughlin changes his name to Marti Pellow and the group settles on Wet Wet Wet as a name, taken from a line in Scritti Politti song *Getting Having And Holding*.

1984 **Dec** Having gigged locally in Scotland all year, the group meets Elliot Davis who becomes its manager. Together they establish their own label, The Precious Organisation, and record a demo tape which they send to major record companies in London.

1985 From their demo alone, 9 major companies compete to sign them. Dave Bates, A&R at Phonogram wins, but only after guaranteeing that the manager will receive a monthly supply of Whiskas cat food – a small sign of faith. Phonogram proposes a string of producers, including Stephen Hague and John Ryan, who do not suit the band's white soul aspirations, but eventually allows the group to record a session with its choice, Al Green production maestro Willie Mitchell.

1986 **Jan** Debut TV performance is on UK music show "The Tube".
[17] Group begins 6-date tour at Liverpool University, Merseyside, their first dates outside Scotland.
June Band records several tracks with Mitchell in Memphis, TN. Despite creative satisfaction on both sides, Phonogram refuses to use material for debut album. Increased promotion work includes sessions for Glasgow's Radio Clyde and an appearance at London's Royal Albert Hall for a Greenpeace charity concert.

1987 **Apr** Group and management insist that remixed demo of *Wishing I Was Lucky* is released as debut cut. It hits UK #6, with Phonogram conceding defeat on trying to force production ideas on the group.
June Prior to their own headline tour, the group undertakes a supporting role on Lionel Richie UK dates.
Aug *Sweet Little Mystery* hits UK #5.
Sept Debut album *Popped In Souled Out* enters UK chart at #2. (Recorded in Apr. with another American producer, Michael Baker, it will hit UK #1 in 1988.)

1988 **Feb** *Angel Eyes (Home And Away)* hits UK #5.
[8] The group wins Best British Newcomer at the seventh annual BRIT Awards at the Royal Albert Hall, London .
Mar Group travels to New Orleans, MS., to film the video for *Temptation*, which reaches UK #12.
May [21] Remake of The Beatles' *With A Little Help From My Friends*, from *Sgt. Pepper Knew My Father* released to raise funds and awareness for the Childwatch charity, tops UK chart, as a double A-side with Billy Bragg's *She's Leaving Home*. (It is the only instance of 2 covers of the same Beatles song topping the charts – Joe Cocker's version hit the summit in Nov.1968.)
June [5-6] As plans to release an EP of the Mitchell Memphis sessions are shelved, the group maintains a high profile, taking part in the sixth annual Prince's Trust Rock Gala at the Royal Albert Hall, London, singing *Twist And Shout*.

[11] They sing *Wishing I Was Lucky* at "Nelson Mandela's 70th Birthday Party" concert at Wembley Stadium, London, while undertaking more sold out UK dates.
[25] *Wishing I Was Lucky*, on the newly re-activated Uni label, peaks at US #58. Both Van Morrison and Squeeze reach out of court settlements when lyrics are "found" in *Sweet Little Mystery*, from Morrison's *Sense Of Wonder* and *Angel Eyes* and Squeeze's *Heartbreaking World*.
July *Popped In Souled Out* peaks at US #123.
Nov *The Memphis Sessions* hits UK #3.

1989 **Apr** [19] Group participates in a Prince's Trust Rock Gala at the London Palladium with Paula Abdul, Erasure, Debbie Gibson, T'Pau and others.
Oct *Sweet Surrender* hits UK #6.
Nov Second album *Holding Back The River* hits UK #2.
Dec Ballad *Broke Away* reaches UK #19.

1990 **Mar** Title cut *Hold Back The River*, about alcohol abuse, makes UK #31.
May [5] Wet Wet Wet sing *I Feel Fine* at the "John Lennon Tribute Concert" at the Pier Head Arena in Merseyside to celebrate the songs of Lennon. (Proceeds go to John and Yoko-established Spirit Foundation.)
July [18] Group takes part in the annual Prince's Trust Rock Gala at Wembley Arena.
Aug Double A-side *Stay With Me Heartache/I Feel Fine* reaches UK #30.

WHAM!

George Michael (vocals)
Andrew Ridgeley (guitar)

1975 Michael (b. Georgios Panayiotou, June 25, 1963, Finchley, London) and Ridgeley (b. Jan.26, 1963, Windlesham, Surrey) meet each other on first day of term at Bushey Meads comprehensive school.

1979 Together with Ridgeley's brother, Paul, David Austin and Andrew Leaver, Michael and Ridgeley form ska-based band, The Executive, which gigs locally but disbands within 18 months.

1981 Concentrating on songwriting and rehearsing for demos at home, the duo has already written *Careless Whisper* and *Club Tropicana*. Ridgeley is unemployed, Michael has several casual jobs and both enjoy the hectic London nightclub scene, where they create the Wham! name and image and are inspired to write *Wham Rap! (Enjoy What You Do?)*.

1982 Hiring a Portastudio for £20, Wham! records demos of *Wham Rap!*, *Come On!*, *Club Tropicana* and *Careless Whisper* in Ridgeley's parents' front room. Record companies are universally uninterested. Duo is introduced to ex-Phonogram employee, Mark Dean, who recently established small dance-based label Innervision. Through a loan-arrangement with CBS, he offers Wham! a contract which will later prove highly restrictive.
Apr Wham! signs publishing contract with Morrison/Leahy Music Group. Club appearances to promote debut single *Wham Rap!*, with new girl recruits Shirlie Holliman and Mandy Washburn (soon replaced by Diane Sealey (Dee C. Lee)), fail to lift it into UK Top 100.
Oct *Young Guns (Go For It)* is released and enters UK chart, but will take 2 months to hit UK #3. It is helped by a startling dance performance on BBC TV's "Top Of The Pops".

1983 **Feb** Re-release of *Wham Rap! (Enjoy What You Do?)* hits UK #8. Wham! is joined by session players Dean Estus, Robert Anwai and Anne Dudley, to record *Bad Boys*, the first release written solely by Michael.
May *Bad Boys* hits UK #2, accompanied by a black and white video which Michael describes as the lowest point in Wham!'s career.
July Experiencing serious difficulties with Innervision, Wham! seeks management assistance from 60s pop entrepreneur, Simon Napier-Bell.
[9] Debut album *Fantastic* enters UK chart at #1, while its fourth single, *Club Tropicana* hits UK #4. Michael assumes control of musical elements, particularly writing and producing, with Ridgeley concentrating on style, image, visuals and direction.
Aug First Wham! concert tour is announced, sponsored by Fila sportswear. Prior to its start, Michael flies to Muscle Shoals studios in Alabama to record solo version of *Careless Whisper* with Jerry Wexler. Sessions are instructive but unsuccessful and Michael decides to re-record the song in London with help of keyboardist Andy Richards for later release. *Bad Boys*, poorly promoted, stalls at US #60.
Oct Dee C. Lee leaves to join The Style Council, replaced by singer/dancer, Pepsi (later to realize success with co-backing performer Shirlie). "Club Fantastic" tour is launched in Aberdeen, Scotland.
Nov With a major legal battle looming, Innervision releases a mix of album cuts titled *Club Fantastic Megamix*. Although Wham! denounces the single in UK press, it climbs to UK #15.

84 Jan Wham! visits Japan on promotional tour.

Apr Released from wrangle with Innervision, Wham! is signed to Epic. Michael is busy writing and producing new songs, one of which, *Wham! Shake* is rejected by Ridgeley.

May First Epic release *Wake Me Up Before You Go Go*, inspired by a note Ridgeley left lying in his bedroom, hits UK #1.

June Michael flies to Miami, FL to shoot solo video for *Careless Whisper*. Ridgeley receives much publicized plastic surgery to his nose.

Aug *Careless Whisper* is released in the UK as a solo by Michael, despite co-writing credit with Ridgeley. It hits UK #1 and is Epic's first UK million-seller, earning a platinum disk. Michael dedicates the ballad to his mother and father, "5 minutes in return for 21 years". It will top charts around the world over the next 6 months.

Sept *Wake Me Up Before You Go Go* is released in US and takes 10 weeks to top *Billboard* survey. Michael and Ridgeley, in the South of France to record second album, with Michael assuming full responsibility in all areas and Ridgeley providing quality control, advice and guitar-work, meet Elton John and develop a long-term friendship.

Nov [17] *Make It Big*, which includes *Careless Whisper*, is released to phenomenal worldwide success and hits UK and US #1. *Fantastic* also charts at US #83.

Dec A world tour starts at Whitley Bay Ice Rink, Northumberland. Michael is featured singing on Band Aid's Christmas chart-topper *Do They Know It's Christmas?*, which prevents Wham!'s own *Last Christmas* from hitting the top spot.

85 Jan *Last Christmas* is changed to double-A with *Everything She Wants*. It holds UK #2 position for another 4 weeks, and earns a platinum disk, one of the last few million-selling singles in UK chart history. *Careless Whisper* is released in US, this time as "Wham! featuring George Michael". It becomes their second US chart-topper and earns a gold disk. World tour continues throughout Australia, Japan and US.

Feb [11] Wham! wins Best British Group at the fourth annual BRIT Awards at the Grosvenor House, London.

Mar *Everything She Wants* begins climb to US #1 and Michael receives Songwriter Of The Year award at prestigious Ivor Novello Ceremony, London, the youngest ever recipient.

Apr Wham! is first western pop group invited to perform live in China, following lengthy negotiations between Napier-Bell and the Chinese Government.

[7] Wham! plays 10,000-seater Workers' Gymnasium in Beijing.

May Michael, becoming increasingly independent musically, performs duets with Smokey Robinson and Stevie Wonder at Motown celebration in New York.

July While Ridgeley fund-raises and performs backing vocals, Michael sings *Don't Let The Sun Go Down On Me* to Elton John's piano accompaniment at Live Aid, Wembley, London. Wham! undertakes stadium tour of US.

Aug *Freedom* hits US #3, breaking a run of 3 consecutive US chart-toppers.

Nov Michael records backing vocals on new Elton John album *Ice On Fire*, while latest Wham! single *I'm Your Man* tops UK chart. Privately, Michael and Ridgeley, still very close friends, decide that Wham! will split in 1986.

Dec Michael features on 4 Top 20 records in UK Christmas chart: *I'm Your Man*, re-entered *Last Christmas* (UK #6), Band Aid's *Do They Know It's Christmas?* and as backing vocalist on Elton John's *Nikita*.

86 Feb [1] *I'm Your Man* hits US #3.

[10] Duo are honored for their Outstanding Contribution To British Music at the fifth annual BRIT Awards at the Grosvenor House, London.

Apr Michael releases second solo single, ballad *A Different Corner*, which hits UK #1 and US #7. It coincides with official announcement that Wham! is to quit as a band having achieved far more than its original goals. They simultaneously dissolve management links with Napier-Bell.

June [28] Final Wham! single is 4-track EP, featuring double-A *The Edge Of Heaven/Where Did Your Heart Go*. It tops UK chart in the same week as Wham!'s farewell concert "The Final" is performed in front of 72,000 fans at Wembley Stadium, London.

[19] *The Final*, a best of hits compilation, hits UK #2, behind Madonna's *True Blue*.

Aug The US postscript, the greatest hits package *Music From The Edge Of Heaven* hits US #10. Michael actively pursues solo career, while Ridgeley concentrates on a future of semi-retirement, unsuccessful motor racing and acting. Both continue solo contracts with Epic Records.

Nov [1] *Where Did Your Heart Go*, written and originally recorded by Was (Not Was), makes US #50.

Dec Re-promotion of *The Final* as a boxed set, complete with Wham! pencil, paper pad and poster, revives its UK chart fortune for the festive season. *Last Christmas*, re-issued a second time, makes UK #45.

1990 May Ridgeley makes recording comeback with debut solo *Son Of Albert* (US #130). Much criticized by the press, extracted *Shake* stalls at US #77 and UK #58.

1991 Jan Wham! reunites briefly at George Michael's Rock In Rio festival performance when he is joined on stage by Ridgeley for several numbers.

BARRY WHITE

1960 White (b. Sept.12, 1944, Galveston, TX), having lived since infancy in East Side Los Angeles, singing in church choir and learning a variety of instruments in his early teens, after troubles in high school which sent him to the Reese school, a center for incorrigible youth, joins Los Angeles R&B quintet, The Upfronts, which records for Lummtone Records, without success.

1964 Feb Bob And Earl's *Harlem Shuffle*, arranged by White for Rampart label, makes US #44. He also plays keyboards on many small label R&B recording sessions, while performing solo in Los Angeles clubs.

1966 Jan Earl Nelson of Bob And Earl reaches US #14 under the pseudonym Jackie Lee with *The Duck*, and White tours with him as drummer and road manager.

1967 He becomes involved in A&R for Mustang Records in Los Angeles, writing and producing for Felice Taylor, whose *It May Be Winter Outside* reaches US #42 and *I Feel Love Comin' On* makes UK #11.

1968 While working for Mustang, White discovers female vocal trio Love Unlimited (sisters Glodean and Linda James, and Diane Taylor) from San Pedro, CA. He becomes their manager and producer.

1972 May Having signed Love Unlimited to UNI Records, White produces its *Walkin' In The Rain With The One I Love*, which reaches #14 in both US and UK and sells over a million. (His own voice is heard in the "telephone break" midway through the disk.) The trio's *Love Unlimited* makes US #151. He also launches, with Larry Nunes, his own production company, Soul Unlimited Productions (originally MoSoul, which was felt too similar to Motown).

Dec White signs himself, his production house, and Love Unlimited to newly re-launched 20th Century Records.

1973 June White records as a soloist for the first time, in a variation of Isaac Hayes' style of deep, intimate vocals in lush orchestral arrangements. Debut album *I've Got So Much To Give* reaches US #16 while extracted *I'm Gonna Love You Just A Little More, Baby* hits US #3 (earning a gold disk for a million sales) and makes UK #23.

Sept Title song *I've Got So Much To Give* reaches US #32.

Dec Love Unlimited's revival of Felice Taylor's *It May Be Winter Outside* peaks at US #83.

1974 Jan White's second album *Stone Gon'* makes US #20, as extracted *Never, Never Gonna Give You Up* hits US #7 and earns a gold disk.

Feb *Never, Never Gonna Give You Up* reaches UK #14, while Love Unlimited's *Under The Influence Of...* hits US #3 and goes gold. The trio's *It May Be Winter Outside* is its second and last UK hit single, reaching #11. Also taken from the Love Unlimited album is instrumental *Love's Theme*, a dance piece played by a White-conducted 40-piece orchestra. On the album it serves as the lengthy (8 min.) introduction to the trio's vocal track *I'm Under The Influence Of Love* but, after it becomes a hit with disco DJs, White releases it as a single with the musicians credited as The Love Unlimited Orchestra. It tops the US chart, earning a gold disk, and hits UK #10.

Mar White's *Honey Please, Can't Ya See* makes US #44 while his album *Stone Gon'* reaches UK #18.

Apr *Rhapsody In White*, an instrumental set by The Love Unlimited Orchestra and featuring *Love's Theme*, hits US #8 and makes UK #50.

May Love Unlimited's *I'm Under The Influence Of Love*, the vocal "sequel" to *Love's Theme* (and another song originally recorded by White with Felice Taylor) makes US #76.

June Title track, The Love Unlimited Orchestra's *Rhapsody In White*, peaks at US #63.

Aug *Together Brothers*, soundtrack to the film of the same title performed by The Love Unlimited Orchestra (and including 2 vocal tracks by White and Love Unlimited), reaches US #96.

Sept White's *Can't Get Enough Of Your Love, Babe* hits US #1 for 1 week (his third million-selling single) and UK #8.

Oct *Can't Get Enough* tops the US chart for a week, and is his biggest-selling album.

Nov *Can't Get Enough* is also White's biggest album seller in UK, where it hits #4.

Dec *You're The First, The Last, My Everything*, taken from *Can't Get Enough*, tops the UK chart for 2 weeks. Love Unlimited Orchestra's *White Gold* reaches US #28; Love Unlimited's *In Heat* makes US #85.

1975 **Jan** *You're The First, The Last, My Everything* hits US #2 (his fourth gold single) behind Elton John's *Lucy In The Sky With Diamonds*, while Love Unlimited's *I Belong To You* reaches US #27 and is the trio's final hit single. White marries Glodean James from Love Unlimited.

Apr White's *What Am I Gonna Do With You?* hits UK #5 and US #8 while The Love Unlimited Orchestra instrumental track *Satin Soul* makes US #22.

June *Just Another Way To Say I Love You* reaches US #17 and UK #12. Extracted *I'll Do For You Anything You Want Me To* makes US #40 and UK #20.

Dec Compilation *Greatest Hits* reaches US #23 and UK #18.

1976 **Jan** *Let The Music Play* hits UK #9 and reaches US #32.

Feb Love Unlimited Orchestra instrumental *Music Maestro Please* reaches US #92.

Mar White's *Let The Music Play* makes UK #22.

Apr *You See The Trouble With Me* hits UK #2 (held from the top by Brotherhood Of Man's *Save Your Kisses For Me*). *Let The Music Play* makes US #42.

July *Baby, We Better Try To Get It Together* stalls at US #92.

Sept *Baby, We Better Try To Get It Together* reaches UK #15.

Nov Love Unlimited Orchestra's *My Sweet Summer Suite* reaches US #123 and is the group's last chart album. Extracted title makes US #48.

Dec White's *Don't Make Me Wait Too Long* reaches UK #17. *Is This Whatcha Wont?* makes US #125.

1977 **Feb** The Love Unlimited Orchestra's US Singles chart swan song is *Theme From King Kong*, a disco variation of the movie theme, which peaks at US #68.

Mar *I'm Qualified To Satisfy* makes UK #37. Love Unlimited's *He's All I've Got* (on White's own new Unlimited Gold label) makes US #192.

Apr Compilation *Barry White's Greatest Hits Vol.2* reaches UK #17.

Oct *It's Ecstasy When You Lay Down Next To Me* makes UK #40.

Nov *It's Ecstasy When You Lay Down Next To Me* hits US #4, becoming his fifth and last solo gold single. It is taken from *Barry White Sings For Someone You Love*, which hits US #8 and is also a million-plus seller, earning a platinum disk.

1978 **June** *Oh What A Night For Dancing* makes US #24.

Dec *Barry White The Man* peaks at US #36 (earning another platinum disk in 6 months on chart) while extracted *Your Sweetness Is My Weakness* peaks at US #60 and is his last US hit single.

1979 **Jan** White's revival of Billy Joel's 1978 hit *Just The Way You Are* reaches UK #12 (but is not issued as a US single).

Feb *The Man* (including *Just The Way You Are*) makes UK #46.

Apr *Sha La La Means I Love You* peaks at UK #55.

May White moves to his own Unlimited Gold label (which he has signed to CBS Associated Labels for distribution) with *The Message Is Love*, which peaks at US #67.

Sept *I Love To Sing The Songs I Sing*, a swan song release from 20th Century, makes US #132.

1980 **Apr** [11] White receives an honorary degree in Recording Arts and Sciences from UCLA's Faculty club.

Aug *Barry White's Sheet Music* reaches US #85.

1982 **Oct** *Change* peaks at US #148.

1985 **Dec** TV-promoted compilation *Heart And Soul*, anthologizing White's major hits of the 70s, makes UK #34.

1987 **Oct** After a rest from recording, during which he has updated his home studio R.I.S.E. (Research In Sound Excellence) in Sherman Oaks, CA, to state-of-the-art 80s specifications, White signs a new recording deal with A&M Records. With a new group of musicians – keyboard players Jack Perry and Eugene Booker (White's godson) and guitarist Charles Fearing (ex-Ray Parker Jr.'s Raydio) – he produces *The Right Night And Barry White*, which makes UK #74.

Nov *The Right Night And Barry White* peaks at US #159 while *Sho' You Right*, taken from the album, reaches UK #17 and US #14.

1988 **Jan** *For Your Love (I'll Do Most Anything)* makes US R&B #27 while a re-mixed reissue of *Never Never Gonna Give You Up* makes UK #63.

July Compilation *The Collection*, a new anthology of White's 20th Century singles, hits UK #5 as he plans a UK tour.

Dec *The Man Is Back!* reaches #24 on US R&B chart, and extracted *Super Lover* makes #34 on US R&B chart.

1990 **Mar** [14] White joins El DeBarge, James Ingram and Al B. Sure! at the fourth annual Soul Train Music Awards at the Shrine Auditorium, Los Angeles, singing *The Secret Garden*, a track which features the 4 soloists from Quincy Jones' *Back On The Block*.

May [25] White embarks on a major US tour in St. Louis, MO, set to end on Aug.1 in San Carlos, CA, with the 30-piece Love Unlimited Orchestra.

June [2] *The Man Is Back!* makes US #148.

1991 **Feb** [23] Re-promoted best of *The Collection* makes UK #28.

WHITESNAKE

David Coverdale (vocals)
Bernie Marsden (guitar)
Micky Moody (guitar)
Neil Murray (bass)
David Dowle (drums)

1976 **Mar** Coverdale (b. Sept.22, 1949, Saltburn-by-the-Sea, Cleveland), the son of a steel-worker, leaves Deep Purple following a disastrous UK tour, after which the band itself splits up. Contractual ties make it impossible for him to work live or record solo in UK during the forseeable future, so he moves to Germany with his family, writing material for future use while legal complexities are being untangled.

1977 **May** Solo album *Whitesnake*, a set of rock ballads, is released in a snakeskin-style sleeve, but fails to sell in a UK market dominated by the punk explosion. (Coverdale, still in Germany, has recorded his vocals in Munich over backing tracks cut in UK.)

1978 **Jan** His enforced exile over, Coverdale returns to UK to form a band to promote his second solo album *Northwinds*, again split-recorded between London and Germany. He recruits sessioneers who have provided his backing tracks: ex-Juicy Lucy Moody (guitar), ex-Babe Ruth Marsden (guitar), Murray (bass), Brian Johnston (keyboards) and Dowle (drums).

Feb [23] As David Coverdale's Whitesnake, the band begins its debut UK tour at Nottingham's Sky Bird club.

Mar *Northwinds* is released, without charting.

June With Pete Solley replacing Johnston on keyboards, the band records 4-track EP *Snake Bite*, highlighted by a revival of Bobby Bland's 1974 soul classic *Ain't No Love In The Heart Of The City* (which will become a Coverdale stage favorite). Released by EMI International at budget price on white vinyl, the EP is the band's chart debut, reaching UK #61.

Aug Coverdale's ex-Deep Purple colleague Jon Lord joins on keyboards, replacing Solley who is not keen to tour (and will become a successful producer).

Sept *Lie Down (A Modern Love Song)* is taken from the band's forthcoming album, but fails to chart.

Oct [26] Lord plays his first gig with Whitesnake at Newcastle, Tyne & Wear, on a tour to promote the first full group album.

Nov *Trouble* makes UK #50.

[23] Tour ends at Hammersmith Odeon, London, and is recorded for a live album.

1979 **Mar** *Time Is Right For Love*, from *Trouble*, is issued in UK to tie in with a headlining charity show (at London's Hammersmith Odeon on Mar.3, in aid of the Gunnar Nilsson Cancer Treatment Campaign). (Most of the first half of this year is spent touring overseas.)

July Ex-Deep Purple drummer Ian Paice replaces Dowle.

Aug [26] Band plays UK's Reading Festival, Berks.

Oct *Love Hunter* (on which Dowle plays throughout) reaches UK #29. It has a sleeve illustrating a naked woman astride a gigantic snake, which is over-stickered in some territories, including US.

Nov *Long Way From Home*, a 33rpm maxi-single also including 2 live tracks, makes UK #55.

1980 **Mar** Band plays its first tour of Japan, where live album *Live At Hammersmith*, recorded in 1978, is first released.

May *Fool For Your Loving*, a new Coverdale/Moody/Marsden composition, becomes the first major Whitesnake hit single, reaching UK #13.

June [24] Band plays Hammersmith Odeon (again recorded for album use), on a UK tour to support new album *Ready An' Willing*, which hits UK #6.

July Taken from the album, *Ready An' Willing (Sweet Satisfaction)* makes UK #43.

Aug Band headlines the Reading Festival.

Sept Released on Mirage label, *Ready An' Willing* marks band's US chart debut, peaking at #90 while *Fool For Your Loving* makes US #53.

Oct Whitesnake develops its initial US success with several months of US touring, supporting AC/DC, Jethro Tull, and other major names.
Nov A live version of *Ain't No Love In The Heart Of The City*, from the June Hammersmith Odeon show, makes UK #51, while double live album *Live In The Heart Of The City* (combining both the 1978 and 1980 Hammersmith Odeon gigs) hits UK #5, selling over 300,000 copies in the UK alone.

1981 Jan Live *Live In The Heart Of The City* (in US a single album with just the 1980 gig) makes US #146.
May *Come An' Get It* hits UK #2 while, from it, *Don't Break My Heart Again* reaches UK #17.
June *Come An' Get It* makes US #151 while second extract, *Would I Lie To You*, makes UK #37. On another UK tour to promote the album, the band sells out 5 nights at the Hammersmith Odeon.
Aug Band headlines Monsters Of Rock festival at Castle Donington, Leics., (completing its UK live work for the year, before returning to the recording studio, where sessions will be abandoned).
Oct After a tour of Germany leads to friction within the band. Whitesnake is put on indefinite hold. Coverdale devotes time to nursing his sick daughter. Lord completes a solo album, while Murray and Paice play with Gary Moore (and will later join his band).

1982 Coverdale reassembles Whitesnake without Marsden, Murray and Paice. He invites Cozy Powell (drums) to join, while Lord and Moody remain, and recruits Mel Galley (guitar) and Colin "Bomber" Hodgkinson (bass). The previous year's unfinished recordings are salvaged, with Coverdale re-recording the vocals and Galley overdubbing fresh guitarwork.
Nov *Here I Go Again*, from the forthcoming album, makes UK #34.
Dec *Saints'N'Sinners*, comprising the revamped tracks from a year earlier, hits UK #9.

1983 Aug Band again headlines the Monsters Of Rock festival, at Castle Donington, its only UK live appearance of the year (which is filmed by EMI for release on home video). *Guilty Of Love*, from a new studio album in progress, produced by Eddie Kramer and released to tie in with the festival appearance, makes UK #31. (Shortly after, Coverdale will fire his producer and re-cut all the remaining album vocals. The strain will prove too much, and he will collapse from exhaustion.)
Nov Moody leaves the band prior to a year-end tour, and Hodgkinson follows him. The latter is replaced be a returning Murray, while new guitarist is ex-Thin Lizzy and Tygers Of Pan Tang member John Sykes.

1984 Jan *Give Me More Time*, from the forthcoming album, reaches UK #29.
Feb *Slide It In* hits UK #9, as the group opens a 17-date tour of the British Isles in Dublin, Eire (ending with a show at London's Wembley Arena).
Mar While on tour in Germany, Galley breaks his arm.
Apr *Standing In The Shadow*, taken from *Slide It In*, makes UK #62.
May Lord leaves the band to join re-forming Deep Purple.
July With a change of US label to Geffen Records, *Slide It In* reaches US #40 as Whitesnake tours US supporting Dio.
Aug Group tours Japan, with Richard Bailey filling Lord's keyboards slot on stage. Another US tour follows, supporting Quiet Riot.

1985 Jan Whitesnake participates in world's largest rock festival Rock In Rio, Brazil.
Feb *Love Ain't No Stranger*, belatedly from *Slide It In*, makes UK #44.
Oct Whitesnake starts work on a new album with producer Mike Stone, in Vancouver, Canada. Coverdale, Murray and Sykes are joined by Aynsley Dunbar on drums and Don Airey on keyboards.

1986 Jan Sykes leaves the album sessions to fly home when his former Thin Lizzy colleague Phil Lynott dies. Coverdale, meanwhile, is having major problems with his voice, caused by an abcessed sinus infection, which bring the sessions to a halt. Stone suggests a substitute vocalist, and is fired.
Apr With a deviated septum diagnosed, Coverdale is forced to have an operation and rest his voice.
Aug Coverdale returns to the studio with new producer Keith Olsen to finish the album. Dutch guitarist Adrian Vandenburg and keyboardist Bill Cuomo help out, along with Mark Andes and Denny Carmassi from Heart.

1987 Apr Finally completed, *Whitesnake 1987* hits UK #8 while extracted *Still Of The Night* makes UK #16. For touring to promote the album, Coverdale puts together a new line-up of Whitesnake, retaining Vandenburg on guitar, and adding Vivian Campbell (guitar), Rudy Sarzo (bass) and Tommy Aldridge (drums).
June *Whitesnake 1987* hits US #2, the band first million-seller and first platinum disk. (The album will sell over 10 million copies worldwide.)
[20] Whitesnake plays the 10th Annual Texas World Music Fest, with Boston, Aerosmith, Poison and others, at the beginning of a world tour.
July [18] *Still Of The Night* makes US #79 while *Is This Love*, a Coverdale/Sykes composition also from the album, hits UK #9.
Aug Group begins a US tour supporting Motley Crue.
Oct [10] *Here I Go Again*, originally a track on the 1982 album *Saints'N'Sinners* (and a UK #34 hit single at the time), now re-cut with new backing track under Coverdale's vocal (during the late 1986 album sessions, at Geffen Records' suggestion), tops the US chart for a week. [30] Group begins a headlining US tour (through to Dec.6).
Nov Re-recorded *Here I Go Again* hits UK #9.
Dec [19] *Is This Love* hits US #2 (unable to dislodge George Michael's *Faith*). Coverdale co-stars in the song's promo video with actress Tawny Kittaen.

1988 Feb *Give Me All Your Love*, a re-recorded version of a track from the album, featuring the new band, reaches UK #18.
Mar [19] *Give Me All Your Love* makes US #48.
Dec Campbell leaves due to reported "musical differences". No replacement is announced, but the remaining quartet begins recording an album for mid-1989 release at Coverdale's home in Incline Village, Lake Tahoe, NV. Vandenburg injures his wrist while practicing the piano. Steve Vai takes his place.

1989 Feb [17] Coverdale marries Tawny Kitaen in Bel Air, CA.
June Tour dates are cancelled when Coverdale develops laryngitis.
Nov Produced by longtime associate Keith Olsen and mixed by Mike Clink, *Slip Of The Tongue*, featuring 9 Coverdale/Vandenberg compositions, hits UK #10 and US #10.
Dec Re-recorded 1980 UK #13, *Fool For Your Loving* makes UK #43. [23] *Fool For Your Loving* makes US #37.

1990 Feb [2] Whitesnake, now comprising Coverdale, Steve Vai, Adrian Vandenberg, Rudy Sarzo and Tommy Aldridge, begins its latest world trek, opening in Fairfax, VA.
Mar [10] *The Deeper The Love* reaches US #28.
June [2] *Now You're Gone* stalls at US #96.
Aug [18] Group headlines the Monsters Of Rock festival at Castle Donington.

THE WHO

Pete Townshend (guitar)
Roger Daltrey (vocals)
John Entwistle (bass)
Keith Moon (drums)

1959 Townshend (b. May 19, 1945, Chiswick, London), Entwistle (b. Oct.9, 1944, Chiswick) and Phil Rhodes form The Confederates (sometimes also known as The Aristocrats and The Scorpions) while still at Acton County Grammar school. Townshend comes from a musical background (his father Cliff a sax-playing member of RAF dance band The Squadronaires and his mother a singer with the Sidney Torch Orchestra). He is determined to become a pop star and spends most of his time studying guitar. Entwistle is an accomplished musician studying piano and playing french horn with the Middlesex Youth Orchestra.

1961 They leave school. Townshend goes to art college – the classic training for British 60s rock stars. Entwistle becomes a civil servant.

1962 Daltrey (b. Mar.1, 1945, Hammersmith, London), an ex-pupil of Acton County Grammar school, invites Entwistle to join his band, The Detours. Townshend soon follows on rhythm guitar, leaving Daltrey to switch to vocals. Semi-professional drummer Doug Sandom, who is 10 years older than the others, also joins.

1963 Group supports a wide range of artists from Wee Willie Harris to The Rolling Stones. Material ranges from covers of James Brown to Bo Diddley.

1964 Group meets freelance publicist, Pete Meaden, who introduces them to the blossoming world of "mod" in London. (A youth cult in reaction to rockers who revelled in motorbike oil and rock'n'roll; mods were opposite, dressed and behaved well, held steady jobs, rode scooters but indulged in drugs.) He molds them into the mod band. Sandom leaves the band and various drummers fill in. During a gig at Acton Town Hall, a drunk man, dressed completely in ginger with a Wayne Fontana haircut, sits in on drums during an interval. His wild style clicks with the band and Moon (b. Aug.23, 1947, Wembley, London), a former Carroll Levis discovery, becomes their drummer. Meaden changes their name to The High Numbers (a mod term for style), and secures a record deal with Fontana.
July *I'm The Face*, a re-write of Slim Harpo's *Got Love If You Want It* with lyrics by Meaden, is released on Fontana but fails.

Sept Film director Kit Lambert, looking for a group to appear in a film, goes to a High Numbers gig. He and his partner, Chip Stamp (brother of actor Terence), take up group management paying off Meaden with £500. They make a promo film of a gig and work on the group's style. The abiding image of the group destroying its equipment originates at its regular venue, the Railway hotel, Harrow, where the ceiling is so low that Townshend's swinging- guitar style takes chunks out of it until one evening the top of his guitar neck disappears, leading to complete destruction of the instrument, with crowds arriving weekly to witness the mayhem.

Nov Lambert changes the group's name to The Who (a name they had used before) as he is worried that posters featuring The High Numbers give the image of advertising a bingo session. Group begins a Tuesday night residency at the Marquee club as The Who-Maximum R&B.

1965 Jan Group's demo is rejected by EMI, but expatriate American producer, Shel Talmy, shows interest and secures a contract with Brunswick. His reputation is based on his hits with The Kinks and his hard-edged raw production sound. Townshend's *I Can't Explain*, is selected for a single and Talmy augments The Who with leading session man, Jimmy Page, to bolster Townshend's guitar, and The Ivy League to provide high backing voices.

Feb Group makes its US vinyl debut with the release of *I Can't Explain* on Decca.

Apr 2 months after its release, *I Can't Explain* hits UK #8 and US #93.
[2] First radio appearance on BBC Radio's "The Joe Loss Pop Show".

June *Anyway Anyhow Anywhere* is released. Townshend describes it as "anti-middle age, anti-boss class and anti-young marrieds". Its melange of feedback causes US label Decca to return the master-tape claiming it to be faulty. It hits UK #10, as ITV's "Ready Steady Go!" adopts it as its theme tune.

Aug [6] The Who plays on the opening day of the fifth annual National Jazz & Blues Festival with Manfred Mann, Rod Stewart and The Yardbirds at the Richmond Athletic Ground, London.

Nov My Generation hits UK #2 (reaching US #74 in Feb.1966). It establishes a landmark in rock history in reflecting the thoughts of a generation. *The Carnival Is Over* by The Seekers prevents it from reaching UK #1. Daltrey threatens to leave the group after onstage bust-ups and Boz Burrell (later of Bad Company) is lined up to take over, but Daltrey stays. He is quoted as saying "when I'm 30 I'm going to kill myself, 'cos I don't ever want to get old".

Dec Debut album *My Generation* hits UK #5. With The Beatles' and The Rolling Stones' debuts, it becomes the final piece of the triumvirate of British rock music, invading international markets.

1966 Jan The Who appears on ABC TV's "Shindig!"
[5] Group appears on first BBC "The Whole Scene Going" teenage mag series.

Feb [4] They play the first of 6 concerts over the weekend as a rehearsal for the group's first bill-topping UK tour starting Mar.25, with The Fortunes, The Merseys and Screaming Lord Sutch.

Mar Townshend produces The Cat's *Run Run Run* on Reaction.
[9] Polydor Records are served with an injunction, preventing any more copies of *Substitute* being sold or distributed, until court hears complaint from group's former manager Shel Talmy. Polydor circumvents injunction by pressing new B side to *Substitute*. New B side *Waltz For A Pig* are session musicians under the name of The Who Orchestra.
[18] Injunction lifted, Polydor reverts to original B-side. Group breaks with Brunswick and signs to Robert Stigwood's newly-formed Reaction label.

Apr [1] Group star in "Ready Steady Allez-Oops!" from the Locomotive in the Moulin Rouge, Paris, France.
[4] Judge grants injunction restraining the group from recording for the moment.
[14] Tour with The Spencer Davis Group opens at the Gaumont, Southampton, Hants.
Substitute, on Reaction, hits UK #5. Brunswick releases *A Legal Matter* which makes UK #32. Talmy, represented by Quentin Hogg, sues the group (and gets a royalty on The Who's next 5 years of recorded output).

May [1] The Who performs at the **New Musical Express** Poll Winners Concert at the Empire Pool Wembley, London.
[20] Townshend and Daltrey go on stage at the Rikki Tik club, Newbury, Berks., with a stand-in bassist and drummer when Entwistle and Moon fail to show up. When they arrive during the show, Townshend hits Moon over the head with his guitar during *My Generation*, causing a black eye and a cut on his leg, which requires 3

stiches. Moon informs the press that he and Entwistle are going to leave to form a duo. He rests in London nursing home, but will rejoin The Who a week later.

July Allen Klein and Andrew Oldham take over management.
[30] They take part on the second day of the sixth annual National Jazz & Blues Festival, Windsor, Berks., with The Yardbirds, Chris Farlowe and The Move.

Sept [7] UK one-niter tour starts at Ipswich Gaumont, Ipswich.

Oct *I'm A Boy* hits #2 while Brunswick releases *The Kids Are Alright* which makes UK #41. Group appears on "Ready Steady Go" UK TV special.

Nov The "Ready Steady Go" performance is re-recorded in studio and released on The Who's only EP *Ready Steady Who* as a tribute to the program. Tracks include *The Batman Theme, Bucket T* and *Barbara Ann,* the latter covers of The Beach Boys. Brunswick, meanwhile, releases *La La La Lies*. Neither disk charts.

Dec *A Quick One* hits UK #4 (US #67 in May 1967 as *Happy Jack*). Townshend breaks with musical convention pre-dating *Sgt. Pepper* by linking songs into a mini-opera called *A Quick One While He's Away,* laying the ground for their grand opus *Tommy.*

1967 Jan *Happy Jack* hits UK #3 (US #24 in June).
B [25] The Who makes its US stage debut as part of Murray The K's Easter show "Music In The 5th Dimension" at the RKO Radio theater, New York.

Apr [8] The Who begins a 12-day tour of Germany.

May *Pictures Of Lily,* inspired by a picture of vaudeville star Lily Bayliss hanging on a wall in Townshend's girlfriend's house, hits UK #4 (US #51 in Aug.), released on newly-formed offshoot from Polydor called Track (which Lambert and Stamp run).
[29] Moon collapses during recording session and is rushed to St. George's hospital. (It is announced that he will be unable to play for at least 2 weeks, and for UK dates Julian Covey deputizes on drums.)

June The Who plays the Monterey International Pop Festival, CA.
[25] Moon takes part in the live recording of The Beatles' *All You Need Is Love* on the "Our World" global TV show.
[30] Group records *The Last Time* and *Under My Thumb* as a tribute to The Rolling Stones. With Entwistle honeymooning on the QE 2, Townshend plays bass.

July [14] Band begins its first US tour, as support to Herman's Hermits and The Blues Magoos in Seattle, WA, set to end Sept.8.

Aug Group releases covers of The Rolling Stones' *The Last Time/Under My Thumb* as a gesture of support to imprisoned Mick Jagger and Keith Richard. It makes UK #44.

Sept The Who appears on "The Smothers Brothers" US TV show. Moon overdoes a flash powder explosion in his drum kit which leaves Townshend with singed hair and damaged ears. Moon is cut on the leg by a broken cymbal while fellow guest, Bette Davis, faints into Mickey Rooney's arms.

Oct [25] The Who begins a UK tour at Sheffield City Hall with The Tremeloes, Traffic, Herd and Marmalade.

Nov *I Can See For Miles* hits UK #10 and US #9 (first US Top 10 hit).
[19] Group plays the Hollywood Bowl, CA, during a US tour.

1968 Jan *The Who Sell Out,* with tracks linked by commercial radio ads, reaches UK #13 and US #48.

Feb [21] The Who begins a 6-week US tour in San Jose, CA, set to end Mar.30 at the Westbury Music Fair, NY.
[22-24] They play at the Fillmore West, San Francisco, and become the highest paid act ever at that venue.

Mar While in Los Angeles, they record a "Little Billy" jingle for the American Cancer Society in US on radio stations, dissuading children from taking up smoking, at Gold Star studios.

May *Call Me Lightning* makes US #40.

June *Dogs* climbs to UK #25. Townshend becomes enamored of the teachings of Meher Baba, an Indian Perfect Spiritual Master, which will profoundly alter his life and his writing of *Tommy.*

Sept *Magic Bus* makes US #25.

Oct *Magic Bus, The Who On Tour* reaches US #39.

Nov *Magic Bus* makes UK #26.
[8] They begin a UK tour with Joe Cocker & The Grease Band, Crazy World Of Arthur Brown, The Mindbenders at the Granada theater, Walthamstow, London.

Dec [11-12] Group performs at "The Rolling Stones Rock And Roll Circus".

1969 Apr *Pinball Wizard* hits UK #4 and reaches US #19. It is released as a curtain-raiser to *Tommy,* which BBC Radio 1 DJ Tony Blackburn describes as "sick".

May *Tommy* is given a press launch at Ronnie Scott's club with The Who performing the double album in full. The story is of a deaf, dumb and blind boy, a genius or wizard at pinball who is elevated to prophet status and then turned on by his followers.

June *Tommy* hits UK #2 and US #4. The Who begins a major US tour performing the opera in its entirety.

The Who open "The Magic Circus" in Hollywood Palladium with Poco and The Bonzo Dog Doo Dah Band.

July Townshend produces Thunderclap Newman's UK #1 *Something In The Air*. He writes an unreleased tribute to the recently deceased former Rolling Stone Brian Jones, *A Normal Day For Brian, A Man Who Died Everyday*.

Aug [9] They take part in the ninth National Jazz & Blues Festival at Plumpton Racecourse near Lewes, Sussex, with Yes, King Crimson and The Strawbs.

The Who's performance at Woodstock is critically regarded as one of its greatest, capturing the image of a generation. They perform with Bob Dylan at the Isle of Wight festival, using one of the largest sound systems ever erected in UK. A notice on the speakers warns the audience not to come within 15'. *I'm Free* reaches US #37.

Sept [29] They begin a series of concerts at Fillmore East, New York.

Oct [5] They appear on CBS TV's "Ed Sullivan Show".

Dec Band begins tour of European opera houses to perform "Tommy".

1970 Jan Moon, a non-driver, accidentally runs over and kills his chauffeur Neil Boland, when trying to escape from a group of skinheads outside a club in Hatfield, Herts.

May *The Seeker* reaches UK #19 and US #44.

June *Live At Leeds*, recorded at the University, hits UK #3 and US #4.

[7] They perform "Tommy" at New York's Metropolitan Opera House.

Aug Taken from the live album, a cover of Eddie Cochran's classic *Summertime Blues* reaches UK #38 and US #27.

Nov *See Me, Feel Me* climbs to US #12.

1971 Aug *Won't Get Fooled Again* hits UK #9 and reaches US #15.

[31] During a US tour, security guard George Byrington is stabbed to death at The Who's concert at Forest Hills, New York.

Sept *Who's Next* is their first UK chart-topper. It hits US #4.

Oct Entwistle is the first group member to achieve solo success with *Smash Your Head Against The Wall* (at US #126).

Nov [4] Group opens new rock venue the Rainbow, Finsbury Park, London, performing 3 nights.

Dec *Let's See Action* climbs to UK #16, as *Behind Blue Eyes* makes US #34. Greatest hits album *Meaty Beaty Big And Bouncy* hits UK #9 and US #11.

1972 Group takes time out from recording and touring to concentrate on solo projects releasing just 1 single during the year.

July *Join Together* hits UK #9.

Aug Moon appears as a nun in Frank Zappa's film "200 Motels" and as J.D. Clover, a drummer with a group backing Billy Fury, in film "That'll Be The Day".

Sept *Join Together* reaches US #17.

[18] They top the bill at the open-air "Rock At The Oval" concert at the Kennington Oval, London with The Faces, Mott The Hoople, Atomic Rooster, Quintessence and others.

Oct Townshend releases first solo album *Who Came First* which reaches UK #30 and US #69.

[28] The United States Council For World Affairs adopts *Join Together* as its anthem.

Nov Entwistle's second solo album *Wistle Rymes* peaks at US #138.

Dec An all-star cast performs a fully orchestrated "Tommy" with The Who at the Rainbow. Lou Reizner releases an all-star cast version of *Tommy* with orchestration and Daltrey in the central role. It hits US #5.

1973 Jan *Relay* makes UK #21 and US #39. Masterminded by Townshend, Eric Clapton makes his comeback at the Rainbow after his heroin addiction.

Apr Daltrey opens a barn studio. One of his first clients is singer/songwriter Leo Sayer, who co-writes songs with Dave Courtney for Daltrey's debut solo album *Daltrey*. It reaches UK #45.

May Daltrey's *Giving It All Away* hits UK #5, but peaks at US #83.

June Entwistle solo album *Riger Mortis Sets In* reaches US #174.

Sept Daltrey's *I'm Free* reaches UK #13.

Oct *5:15* makes UK #20.

Nov *Quadrophenia* hits #2 in both UK and US. Inevitably compared with *Tommy*, it relates the story of Jimmy, an adolescent mod on a spiritual search. The use of sound effects on the album created a problem as most FX libraries kept only mono recordings so The Who had to record every effect, including bribing the driver of a UK rail

train to blow his whistle when leaving Waterloo Station. Moon collapses during a concert after his drink is spiked with horse tranquilizer. 19-year-old Scott Halpin from the audience volunteers to replace him on drums for the remaining 3 numbers.

Dec *Love, Reign O'er Me* peaks at US #76.

[2] Group is arrested in Montreal and spends 6 hours in cell after wrecking hotel suite. Band agrees to pay £1,400 compensation in return for the management not to press charges.

1974 Feb *The Real Me* reaches US #92.

Apr Shooting begins on film "Tommy" directed by Ken Russell and starring The Who with Oliver Reed, Ann-Margret, Jack Nicholson and Elton John among others.

[14] Townshend makes his live solo debut at London's Roundhouse.

June The Lambert/Stamp partnership breaks up and Bill Curbishley unofficially takes over as manager. (Lambert will die after a fall at his mother's house in Fulham Apr.1981.)

Oct *Odds And Sods* hits UK #10 and US #15. It is a collection of unreleased material compiled by Entwistle. Moon appears in film "Stardust", the follow-up to "That'll Be The Day".

1975 Feb [21] Entwistle starts a 5-week US tour with his band Ox in Sacramento, CA.

Mar Film soundtrack album *Tommy* makes UK #21. Entwistle album *Mad Dog* peaks at US #192.

[1] Daltrey celebrates his 30th birthday.

May Moon releases his only solo album *Two Sides Of The Moon*.

July Daltrey's *Ride A Rock Horse* reaches UK #14 and US #28.

Aug Daltrey stars in the title role of Ken Russell's film "Lisztomania".

Oct *The Who By Numbers* hits UK #7 and US #8. Moon becomes a UK "lollipop man" to promote a road safety campaign for a zebra crossing outside Battersea Primary school.

Nov Daltrey's *Come And Get Your Love* makes US #68.

1976 Feb *Squeeze Box* hits UK #10 and US #16.

Mar [9] A US tour is cancelled when Moon collapses during a performance at The Boston Garden, Boston, MA. Tour is rescheduled.

May [31] The Who's concert at Charlton Athletic Football Club enters **Guinness Book Of Records** as the loudest performance (at 120 decibels) by a rock group.

Oct Compilation album *The Story Of The Who* hits UK #2.

[9-10] The Who plays the Oakland Stadium, CA sharing the bill with The Grateful Dead.

Nov *Substitute* re-released in the wake of the album hits UK #7.

1977 May Daltrey's *Written On The Wind* makes UK #46.

July Daltrey's album *One Of The Boys* peaks at UK #45 and US #46.

[23-24] The Who plays at Oakland Stadium.

Oct Townshend, with Ronnie Lane, releases *Rough Mix*, which makes UK #44 and US #45. Daltrey's *Avenging Annie* stalls at US #88.

Dec [15] Band plays the first of 2 "behind closed doors" concerts for its fan club members at Shepperton TV studios, UK. The show is filmed for use in "The Kids Are Alright" film documentary.

1978 Aug *Who Are You* reaches US #18.

[5] Pete Meaden commits suicide.

Sept [8] Keith Moon dies of an overdose of Heminevrin prescribed to combat alcoholism, in the same Park Street apartment as Mama Cass had died 4 years earlier. **The Times** obituary describes Moon as "among the most talented rock'n'roll drummers in contemporary music". *Who Are You* hits UK #6 and US #2.

Nov *Who Are You* climbs to US #14.

1979 Jan Despite the group's claim that Moon is irreplaceable, ex-Small Faces and Faces drummer, Kenney Jones (b. Sept.16, 1948, London), takes over. He begins a 3-month crash course learning Who material. John "Rabbit" Bundrick (b. TX) is unofficially added to the line-up on keyboards.

May [2] The new line-up makes its debut at the Rainbow, as film "Quadrophenia" premieres. Based on the original album, it is directed by Franc Roddam and creates new interest in The Who.

June *The Kids Are Alright*, a compilation of live cuts tying in with the documentary feature film of the same name directed by The Who, makes UK #26 and hits US #8.

July *Long Live Rock* peaks at UK #48 and US #54.

Aug [18] The Who plays Wembley Stadium, London, with AC/DC, Nils Lofgren and The Stranglers.

Oct Soundtrack album *Quadrophenia* reaches UK #23 and US #46. Daltrey appears in horror film "The Legacy".

Nov *5:15* makes US #45.

Dec [3] A concert at Riverfront Coliseum, Cincinnati, OH, turns into disaster when 11 members of the audience are trampled to death after a stampede to claim unreserved seats.

[28] Group plays the "Concert For Kampuchea" at London's Hammersmith Odeon.

1980 Apr Townshend's solo *Rough Boys* makes UK #39.

[30] Film "McVicar", with Daltrey in title role, premieres in London.

May Townshend's *Empty Glass* makes UK #11 and hits US #5.

June Townshend's *Let My Love Open Your Door* peaks at UK #46.

Aug Soundtrack album *McVicar* makes UK #39 and US #22. Taken from it, *Free Me* climbs to UK #39 and US #53. Townshend's solo *Let My Love Open Your Door* hits US #9.

Oct Daltrey's *Without Your Love* makes UK #55 and US #20. Townshend's *A Little Is Enough* reaches US #72. Virgin re-releases long-deleted album *My Generation*, which makes UK #20.

Nov *Rough Boys* reaches US #89.

1981 Mar *Face Dances*, the first to be recorded by the new line-up, and produced by Bill Szymczyk, hits UK #2 and US #4.

Apr *You Better You Bet* hits UK #9 and US #18.

May *Don't Let Go The Coat* makes UK #47 and US #84.

Oct Entwistle's *Too Late The Hero* reaches US #71.

1982 Mar Daltrey's *Best Bits* peaks at US #185.

July Townshend's *All The Best Cowboys Have Chinese Eyes* makes UK #32 and US #26.

Aug Townshend's *Uniforms (Corps D'Esprit)* climbs to UK #48.

Sept Final Who studio album *It's Hard* reaches UK #11 and hits US #8.

Oct *Athena* makes UK #40 and US #28.

Dec [17] Group performs the last gig of its North American farewell tour at Maple Leaf Gardens, Toronto, Canada. It is filmed for TV.

1983 Jan *Eminence Front* makes US #68.

Feb [8] Townshend wins a Lifetime Achievement award at the second annual BRIT Awards at the Grosvenor House, London.

Mar Townshend solo album of Who demos and unfinished work *Scoop* reaches US #35.

Dec [16] The Who officially splits.

1984 Mar Daltrey's *If Parting Should Be Painless* climbs to US #102. His *Walking In My Sleep* makes UK #62 and US #56.

Nov *Who's Last* documenting The Who's final concert makes UK #48 and US #81.

1985 July [13] The Who re-forms for one-off appearance at Live Aid concert in London.

Oct Daltrey's *After The Fire* makes UK #50 and US #48.

Nov Daltrey's *Under A Raging Moon* makes UK #52, while Townshend's *White City* makes UK #70 and US #26.

Dec Townshend contributes to the Artists United Against Apartheid album, with its extracted single *Sun City* making US #38 and UK #21.

1986 Jan [11] Daltrey's *Let Me Down Easy* peaks at US #86.

[18] Townshend's *Face The Face* reaches US #26.

Mar Daltrey's *Under A Raging Moon* makes UK #43.

Nov Townshend's *Pete Townshend's Deep End Live!* makes US #98.

1987 Apr [4] Townshend's *Another Scoop* spends 1 week at US #198.

July Daltrey solo *Can't Wait To See The Movie* fails in UK and US.

1988 Feb [8] The Who is honored for its Outstanding Contribution To British Music at the seventh annual BRIT Awards at London's Royal Albert Hall. *My Generation* re-charts in UK at #68.

Mar Greatest hits package on album and video, *Who's Better, Who's Best* hits UK #10.

1989 Jan [18] Townshend attends the Rock'N'Roll Hall Of Fame dinner at New York's Waldorf Astoria to induct The Rolling Stones.

Apr Daltrey completes work as the street singer in forthcoming film of Bertolt Brecht's "The Threepenny Opera".

June [21] Group plays a warm up show for "The Kids Are Alright Tour: 1964-1989" at Glen Falls, NY, with additional musicians, Steve "Boltz" Bolton (lead guitar), John "Rabbit" Bundrick (keyboards) and Simon Phillips (drums).

[24] Entwistle, Townshend and Daltrey reunite to play in Toronto, Canada, scene of their final concert in 1982, at the start of a sold-out 25-city North American tour. The tour includes songs from Townshend's just released new album *The Iron Man* (based on Poet Laureate Ted Hughes' children's story, and featuring John Lee Hooker (Iron Man), Nina Simone (The Dragon), Daltrey and Entwistle, and 2 new tracks with The Who line-up.

[27] "Tommy" is performed at Radio City Music Hall, New York, by Rock'N'Roll Hall Of Fame in aid of Nordoff-Robbins – its first performance in 19 years.

Aug [17] Townshend smashes his hand during a concert at the Tacoma Dome, WA. He is treated for cuts on his finger and palm at St. Joseph hospital in Tacoma after injuring himself doing a windmill

guitar riff during *Won't Get Fooled Again*.

[24] The Who perform "Tommy" at Universal Amphitheater, Universal City, CA, with Elton John (The Pinball Wizard), Steve Winwood (The Hawker), Patti LaBelle (The Acid Queen), Phil Collins (Uncle Ernie) and Billy Idol (Cousin Kevin), in aid of charity.

[30] During a concert at the Oakland Coliseum, Townshend presents a $10,000 check to hard-of-hearing fellow musician Kathy Peck's non-profit Hearing Education Awareness Of Rockers.

Sept [3] Tour ends at Cotton Bowl, Dallas, TX.

Oct [23] Band plays first of 4 concerts at the Wembley Arena, London.

1990 Jan [17] The Who are inducted into the Rock'N'Roll Hall Of Fame at the fifth annual dinner at the Waldorf Astoria in New York.

July [26] Daltrey wins $272,000 settlement after suing the Home Farm who he claims were responsible for deaths of up to 500,000 fish at his Iwerne Springs trout farm in Dorset in Aug.1986.

KIM WILDE

1980 Wilde (b. Kim Smith, Nov.18, 1960, London), daughter of 50s UK hitmaker Marty Wilde, has been singing backing vocals on her father's live appearances since leaving art school, when she records a demo with her brother Ricky, who is a production deal with Mickie Most's RAK Records. Most, attracted by her vocals and visual appeal, signs her to RAK. Her mother Joyce Smith, ex-The Vernons Girls, becomes her manager, while Most reportedly puts £250,000 of RAK's money into launching and developing her as a major act.

1981 Mar Debut single *Kids In America*, written by Ricky and produced by him and Marty, hits UK #2 for 2 weeks.

May *Chequered Love* hits UK #4. Wilde does no UK touring to promote this or other early singles, relying on videos and TV appearances, stating that she will need to strengthen her voice to do a satisfactory live performance with a band.

July Debut *Kim Wilde*, mostly written by her brother and including the 2 earlier singles, hits UK #3, and stays on chart for over 3 months.

Aug Taken from it, double A-side *Water On Glass/Boys* reaches UK #1

Dec *Cambodia* reaches UK #12.

1982 Mar She announces in a magazine interview a desire to write her own material, but for the moment continues to cut her brother's songs.

May *View From The Bridge* makes UK #16. *Select* reaches UK #19.

Aug RAK announces that in 18 months, Wilde has sold over 6 million disks worldwide – more than her father achieved during his 14-hit UK (just 2 in US) chart career. *Kids In America*, following a deal with EMI America, reaches US #25. *Kim Wilde* peaks at US #86.

Oct *Child Come Away* makes UK #43. Wilde begins a European tour which includes sell-out dates. (In Germany, her glamorous image has her nicknamed "The Bardot Of Rock".)

1983 Feb [8] Wilde wins Best British Female Artist at the second annual BRIT Awards at Grosvenor House, Mayfair, London. (She soon moves from the family home to a flat in London.)

Aug *Love Blonde* reaches UK #23.

Nov *Dancing In The Dark* peaks at UK #67. *Catch As Catch Can* spends a week in UK chart at #90.

1984 May Wilde signs a new contract with MCA.

Nov MCA debut *The Second Time* reaches UK #29, and *Teases And Dares* peaks at UK #66.

Dec *The Touch* makes UK #56.

1985 Jan Her US MCA debut is Marty and Ricky's *Go For It*, which peaks at US #65, while *Teases And Dares* stalls at US #84.

Apr Rockabilly-flavored *Rage To Love*, remixed by Dave Edmunds, reaches UK #19.

May RAK releases a retrospective singles collection, *The Very Best Of Kim Wilde*, which peaks at UK #78.

1986 Aug [29] A Kim Wilde mini-dress is sold at Christie's Rock Memorabilia auction in London for £400.

Nov *Another Step* charts briefly at UK #73.

Dec After a year out of the record-buying public's eye (though she has done some live performances in Europe) Wilde's version of The Supremes' 1966 million-seller *You Keep Me Hangin' On* hits UK #2. It is also a big hit in most of Europe, where she has almost reached superstar status.

1987 Apr Wilde performs on the Ferry Aid single *Let It Be*, for the victims of the Zeebrugge ferry disaster, which hits UK #1. She sings at the AIDS benefit concert at Wembley, London, performing Elton John's *Sorry Seems To Be The Hardest Word* with Marty and Ricky Wilde.

May Wilde duets with UK soul singer Junior on *Another Step (Closer To You)*, which hits UK #6.

June [6] With heavy airplay and rotation on MTV, *You Keep Me Hangin' On* tops the US chart for a week, making Wilde only the fifth UK female artist to achieve a US #1. She gets a telex from Lamont Dozier, one of the song's writers, congratulating her. *Another Step* makes US #40.

Aug *Say You Really Want Me*, accompanied by a controversial video which eliminates Wilde's girl-next-door image, reaches UK #29, despite its talented production team of Rod Temperton, Richard Rudolph and Bruce Swedien.

[15] *Say You Really Want Me* makes US #44.

Sept Reissue of *Another Step*, in a new sleeve and with a bonus record of singles remixes, reaches UK #73.

Dec She teams with comedian Mel Smith (as Mel And Kim) on a remake of Brenda Lee's *Rockin' Around The Christmas Tree* (all proceeds go to Comic Aid charity). It hits UK #3.

'88 May *Hey Mr. Heartache*, written by Ricky and Marty Wilde and recorded at the family's home studio in Hertfordshire reaches UK #31.

June *Close* hits UK #8.

July Wilde supports Michael Jackson in Europe and UK on his 1988 "Bad" world tour.

Aug Dance-styled *You Came* hits UK #3.

Oct *Never Trust A Stranger* hits UK #7.

[22] *You Came* makes US #41 as *Close* peaks at US #114.

Dec Ballad *Four Letter Word* hits UK #6.

'89 Mar *Love In The Natural Way* makes UK #32.

'90 Apr Co-written by Kim and Ricky, *It's Here* makes UK #42.

May Parent *Love Moves*, produced by her brother, peaks at UK #37.

June Extracted *Time* stalls at UK #71, as US hits are proving elusive.

DENIECE WILLIAMS

'67 Having grown up in a religious environment, singing in the gospel choir at a local church, Williams (b. Deniece Chandler, June 3, 1951, Gary, IN), working in a record store while still at Tolleston high school, sings (on the recommendation of the store owner) for a rep from provincial Chicago record label, Toddlin' Town, which signs her and releases *Love Is Tears*, the first of a number of singles, with only limited local success.

'69 Williams goes to Baltimore Morgan State College and becomes a nurse, moonlighting as a nightclub singer. She enrols at Purdue University, marries and has 2 children, Ken and Kevin.

'71 Stevie Wonder hears Toddlin' Town recordings and invites Williams to Detroit to audition for his backing vocal group, Wonderlove. She gigs with them for a month but gets homesick and returns to Chicago Mercy hospital. Wonder persists and Williams becomes a permanent member of Wonderlove, contributing on support spot of The Rolling Stones' 1972 tour. During the next 3 years, she also contributes Wonderlove vocals to Wonder's albums, *Talking Book* (1972), *Innervisions* (1973), *Fulfillingness' First Finale* (1974) and *Songs In The Key Of Life* (1976).

'75 Nov Williams leaves Wonderlove to settle in California and concentrate on a solo career. She writes, records and sends demos. One comes to the attention of Earth, Wind & Fire leader, Maurice White, who arranges her signing to Columbia/CBS.

'76 Nov Debut solo album *This Is Niecy* is released. Produced by White, it immediately scores in soul circles (US #33) and first hit single *Free* follows at US #25. She embarks on 6-month period of touring, supporting Earth, Wind & Fire at major US and UK venues.

'77 Apr *Free* hits UK #1 and promotes *This Is Niecy* to UK #31.

Aug *That's What Friends Are For* hits UK #8, with Williams performing at a Royal Command Performance before the Prince of Wales.

Nov Second album *Songbird* is released. It reaches US #66 but fails in UK. A stray cut *Baby Baby My Love's All For You* makes UK #32.

'78 Mar Williams teams with her childhood heart-throb, Johnny Mathis, to record duet *Too Much Too Little Too Late*. Radio and public find it irresistible. It hits US #1 and UK #3, providing a first ever chart-topper for Mathis with his first duet. Williams makes extensive UK promotion visit including a live spot on BBC TV's "Val Doonican Show".

Apr Williams and Mathis perform in front of the Prince of Wales and Princess Anne in a concert in aid of the World College Fund.

July *That's What Friends Are For*, all Mathis/Williams duets, reaches US #19 and UK #16. It includes follow-up cover of Gaye/Terrell classic *You're All I Need To Get By*, which makes US #47 and UK #45. Compositions by Williams now begin to be covered by acts which will include Frankie Valli, The Whispers, The Emotions and Merry Clayton.

'79 Aug Williams signs to Maurice White's new ARC label (through Columbia) and *When Love Comes Calling* is released. It is produced by

David Foster and Ray Parker Jr., but falters at US #96. *I've Got The Next Dance* reaches only US #73, and Williams will have no further UK attention for 5 years.

1981 Apr Written and produced with Thom Bell (Stylistics, Delfonics, Spinners), a new mature soul direction is realized on *My Melody*.

Aug *My Melody* reaches US #74, extracted ballad *Silly* makes US #53.

1982 Apr The second Bell collaboration *Niecy* makes US #20, aided by her biggest hit for 6 years, a remake of The Royalettes' 1965 hit *It's Gonna Take A Miracle* which reaches US #10.

1983 Apr Returning to mainstream Columbia, *I'm So Proud* charts for 19 weeks, but slows to peak at US #54.

1984 Jan Williams re-unites with Mathis to record 2 duets. A cover of Major Harris' *Love Won't Let Me Wait* fails, but new song *Without Us* becomes popular theme tune to top-rated US TV series "Family Ties".

Feb Hugely successful film soundtrack containing a Williams cut *Footloose* is released and makes US #1 and UK #7.

May [26] Extracted *Let's Hear It For The Boy*, written by Dean Pitchford and Tom Snow, hits US #1 and will hit UK #2 and becomes an international smash. It has taken Williams only 20 mins. to record.

June Hastily prepared *Let's Hear It For The Boy* makes US #26. A second single from the album, *Next Love* reaches only US #81.

1986 *Hot On The Trail* fails to chart.

1987 Feb [24] Williams wins Best Soul Gospel Performance, Female Of 1986 with *I Surrender All* and with Sandi Patti Best Gospel Performance By A Duo Or Group, Choir Or Chorus Of 1986 with *They Say* at the 29th annual Grammy awards. (Williams' success will move to the specialist market, scoring with *Never Say Never* (#6) and *I Confess* (#24) on the US R&B chart.

1988 Mar [2] *I Believe In You*, from *Water Under The Bridge*, wins Best Gospel Performance, Female at the 30th annual Grammy awards.

July Retreating further to gospel roots, she releases specialist inspirational *So Glad I Know* on Sparrow label.

Oct [29] *I Can't Wait* peaks at US #66, as parent album *As Good As It Gets* makes #48 on US R&B chart.

1989 Dec *Every Moment* peaks at #55 on US R&B chart.

HANK WILLIAMS

1935 Williams (b. Hiram Williams, Sept.17, 1923, Mount Olive West, AL), son of Elonzo and Lillian Williams, learns the rudiments of blues music from an itinerant black street singer Tee-Tot (Rufus Payne) in Georgiana, AL. He also wins first prize in a songwriting contest with *WPA Blues*.

1937 Williams moves with his family to Montgomery, AL, and makes appearances on country radio stations WCOV and WSFA where he is dubbed "The Singing Kid". He forms first group with Smith "Hezzy" Adair as Hank And Hezzy's Driftin' Cowboys and begins a long apprenticeship playing the tough honky tonk circuit.

1938 He spends a number of years drifting from job to job working in a rodeo, traveling medicine show and in the shipyards of Mobile, AL, where he meets his future wife Audrey Guy.

1942 He makes his first recording *I'm Not Coming Home Anymore* at Griffins Radio Shop, Montgomery, AL.

1944 Dec [15] Hank and Audrey marry at a filling station, and she becomes a singing member of his regular touring outfit The Drifting Cowboys.

1946 Sept [14] Williams and wife travel to Nashville, TN, to meet songwriter Fred Rose of the famed Acuff/Rose publishing house which he had formed in 1942 with country star Roy Acuff. Williams signs a songwriting agreement and offers demos to singer Molly O'Day. She scores hits with *Six More Miles* and *When God Comes And Gathers His Jewels* which begin to establish Williams' name.

Dec [11] With Oklahoma group, The Wranglers, he records *Wealth Won't Save Your Soul* and *When God Comes And Gathers His Jewels* for Al Middleman's Sterling Records which although not successful leads him to cut 4 more songs for the label.

1947 Jan Sterling releases *Calling You*, backed with *Never Again (Will I Knock On Your Door)*.

Mar [6] As a result, Rose secures the interest of the newly formed MGM Records which signs Williams to the label.

1948 Apr The Alabama Journal reports that *Move It On Over*, Williams' 1947 MGM debut recording has now sold over 100,000 copies.

Dec [22] Williams records one of his biggest hits, *Lovesick Blues*, at the Herzog studio, Cincinnati, OH. Song originates from the 1922 musical "Oooh Ernest!"

1949 May [26] Randall Hank Williams is born in Shreveport, LA. *Lovesick Blues* reaches US #24 nationally and tops **Billboard**'s Folk Record chart for 16 weeks.

June [11] Williams makes his debut at the Grand Ole Opry in Nashville, and receives an unprecedented total of 6 encores. (The Opry had been originally established by radio station WSM as the WSM Barn Dance on Nov.28, 1925. It became the Grand Ole Opry in 1927 when WSM became an NBC affiliate and followed a highbrow Musical Appreciation Hour. Station director George D. Hay made the announcement, "For the past hour we have been listening to music taken largely from Grand Opera but from now we will present the Grand Ole Opry." The name stuck, giving country listeners a certain pride in their own defintion of their music and thus the Ryman Auditorium inherited a new name.) Williams tours US bases in Germany later in the year as part of an Opry package.

1950 Jan He begins a series of recordings as Luke The Drifter. With songs that consist of moral monologues the pseudonym is adopted by MGM to clearly differentiate the releases from Williams' usual material.

1951 Apr *Cold Cold Heart* reaches US #27. (Tony Bennett will top the pop charts with a cover version later in the year. Other songs become pop hits for Jo Stafford (*Jambalaya*) and Joni James (*Your Cheatin' Heart*).
May [21] Williams is admitted to the North Louisiana Sanitarium suffering from acute alcoholism. Williams has regularly resorted to alcohol and narcotics to ease severe back pains which are now analyzed as a birth defect, spina bifida occulta.
Aug [15] He joins one of the largest variety tours ever mounted in the US, the Hadacol Tour (promoting a medicinal compound) appearing alongside celebrities such as Bob Hope, Jack Benny, Jimmy Durante and Milton Berle.
Sept *Hey Good Lookin'* reaches US #29.

1952 Jan [29] He performs at the Mosque, Richmond, VA, in a state of near collapse due to the combined effects of drink and drugs.
May [29] Hank and wife Audrey divorce.
Aug [17] Williams is arrested for drunken behavior at the Russell hotel, Alexander City, AL.
Sept [20] To restore his live credibility he begins the first of weekly Saturday night appearances on the Louisiana Hayride for a fee of $250 a week. *Jambayala* makes US #20.
Oct [18] He marries Billie Jean Jones in Minden, LA.
[19] The couple repeat their wedding vows twice for a paying public after the 3pm and 7pm shows that Williams performs at the New Orleans Municipal Auditorium.
[31] He is admitted to hospital in Shreveport, LA, suffering from acute alcoholic intoxication.
Dec [11] Discharging himself from hospital, he is arrested and imprisoned for drunken behavior. Despite being in a rapidly deteriorating condition, Wiilams fulfils many live engagements meeting hostile crowds who are appalled by his drunkeness. The ominously titled *I'll Never Get Out Of This World Alive* reaches US #20.
[30] He flies to Charleston, WV, for a gig but bad weather grounds his flight in Knoxville, TN.
[31] 17-year-old Charles Carr drives William's Cadillac from Montgomery, AL, as they set out out for a New Year's Eve gig at the Memorial Auditorium, Canton, OH. Highway patrolman Swann Kitts books Carr for speeding near Rutledge, TN, and suggests to the driver that his back seat passenger looks dead. Carr continues driving.

1953 Jan [1] At 5.30am Carr stops for directions in Oak Hill, WV. Outside a Pure Oil service station he realizes Williams' body feels cold and calls the police. Patrolman Howard Jamey confirms the death. A piece of paper is clutched in Williams' right hand. It reads, "We met, we lived and dear we loved, then comes that fatal day, the love that felt so dear fades away. Tonight love hathe one alone and lonesome, all that I could sing, I love you you (sic) still and always will, but that's the poison we have to pay." An autopsy conducted at Oak Hill hospital gives cause of death as heart failure. At the time of his death, age 29, Williams is the most successful artist in country music history. At Canton Memorial Auditorium a spotlight is shone on the stage curtain as a weeping audience listen to The Drifting Cowboys perform *I Saw The Light* behind the drapes.
[4] Williams' funeral service is held at the City Auditorium, Montgomery, AL. Roads leading into the city are choked as 20,000 mourners throng the streets. Williams leaves no will and for the next 20 years his estate will be wrangled over by his mother, and his 2 wives, who will both begin touring as Mrs. Hank Williams. Billie Jean removes herself from the estate squabbles after receiving a $30,000 settlement from Williams' mother Lilly.
Feb *Kaw-Liga* reaches US #23.
Mar *Your Cheatin' Heart* reaches US #25.

1954 Billie Jean marries country singer Johnny Horton (who will die in a car

crash in 1960).

1961 Nov [3] Williams becomes the first artist elected to the Country Mus Hall Of Fame.

1964 A film biography is released called "Your Cheatin' Heart" with Georg Hamilton in the title role. It is later withdrawn after Billie Jean sues an wins a libel case claiming the film presents her as a lewd woman. Han Williams Jr. sings his father's songs for the screen biography and will later become a major force in country music, in his own right.

1965 Aug *Father And Son* reaches US #139. Hank Jr's vocals are dubbed in with those of his father to create a duet effect.

1969 June *Songs My Father Left Me* reaches US #164. Hank Jr. adds music to lyrics written by his father.

1973 Williams receives the Pioneer Award from the Academy Of Country Music.

1975 Audrey dies 2 weeks after a court decides that Billie Jean was Willian legal wife at his death.

1983 Feb [23] *Your Cheating Heart* is inducted into the NARAS Hall Of Fan at the 25th annual Grammy awards.

1987 Jan [21] Williams is posthumously inducted into the Rock'N'Roll Ha Of Fame at the second annual dinner at New York's Waldorf Astoria.

1988 Mar [2] Williams is honored by the NARAS at the 30th annual Grammy awards with a Lifetime Achievement Award, noting that Williams was "(posthumously) a pioneering performer, who proudly sang his songs so honestly and openly, capturing completely the joys and sorrows and essence of country life, and whose compositions helped create successful careers for various singers who followed him

1990 Feb [21] *There's A Tear In My Bear*, a posthumous collaboration with Hank Williams Jr., (which was promoted via an ingenious video whic brings the "ghost" of Williams Sr. to the modern day Williams Jr.) win Best Country Vocal Collaboration at the 32nd annual Grammy award at the Shrine Auditorium, Los Angeles.
Dec Polydor Records releases a definitive box set of Williams' work, the 84-song *The Original Singles Collection ... Plus*.

1991 Sept [17] Hank Williams Jr. unveils a life-size bronze statue of his father, erected in the Montgomery city car park.

JACKIE WILSON

1950 Wilson (b. Jack Leroy Wilson, June 9, 1934, Detroit, MI), while at high school in Detroit, wins American Amateur Golden Gloves Welterweight boxing title by posing as an 18-year-old under the name Sonny Wilson. He is set for a boxing career, but his mother persuades him to finish school and develop his singing talent instead. He joins The Ever Ready Gospel Singers, and sings with R&B quartet The Thrillers (alongside Hank Ballard) once he completes school and goes to work at a car assembly plant.

1951 Wilson is discovered in a talent show at Detroit's Paradise theater, by Johnny Otis who mentions him to Billy Ward, vocal teacher and leade of successful doo-wop group Billy Ward & The Dominoes. Ward note Wilson's vocal talent and later hires him as a back-up singer. (In the meantime, Wilson records *Danny Boy* on a one-off single for Dizzy Gillespie's Dee Gee label, without success.)

1953 Apr Wilson's own idol Clyde McPhatter, The Dominoes' lead singer, fired from the group (and will shortly form The Drifters), and Ward invites Wilson (who has toured with the group) to replace him as lead tenor vocalist. (He is to sing lead on 2 years' worth of the group's recordings on King and Federal labels, one of which, *Rags To Riches*, hits R&B #3 in early 1954.)

1956 June After leaving King/Federal and recording briefly for Jubilee, Ward & The Dominoes are signed to major label Decca.
Sept Wilson sings lead on *St. Therese Of The Roses*, The Dominoes' firs Decca single, and the group's first US pop chart hit, peaking at #13. It his last recording with the group.

1957 Despite The Dominoes' popularity and his own high status among other vocalists (Elvis Presley raves about his stage performance of *Don't Be Cruel* on the preserved tape of the Dec.1956 Sun Records Presley/Carl Perkins/Jerry Lee Lewis jam session), Wilson is feeling stifled as an individual since, because of group's billing and the fact he sings lead, audiences believe him to be Ward. Encouraged by Al Green a Detroit publisher and agent who becomes his manager, Wilson leave to go solo and signs to Brunswick Records, a Decca subsidiary, to wor with producer/orchestra leader Dick Jacobs in New York.
Sept [8] His solo career begins with release of *Reet Petite (The Finest Girl You Ever Want To Meet)* (co-written by Berry Gordy Jr., future founder of Motown, and Tyran Carlo, a pseudonym for Wilson's cousin Billy Davis), on Brunswick.

Nov Uptempo *Reet Petite* is a moderate solo chart debut in US, at #62.

1958
Jan *Reet Petite* hits UK #6.

May Contrasting (but also penned by Gordy/Carlo) dramatic ballad *To Be Loved* makes both US and UK #23.

Sept Gordy-penned *We Have Love* stalls at US #93.

Oct Wilson's first album, *He's So Fine* , is released but fails to chart. (He will not have a US chart album until 1962.)

Dec *Lonely Teardrops* tops US R&B chart for 7 weeks – both his and writer Gordy's first chart-topper.

[25] Wilson begins a 10-day residency in Alan Freed's Rock'N'Roll Spectacular at Loew's State theater, New York, alongside 16 other acts including Eddie Cochran, Bo Diddley and The Everly Brothers.

1959
Feb *Lonely Teardrops* is Wilson's first US Top 10 hit, at #7, selling over a million copies to earn his first gold disk.

Apr [22] Freed's film "Go Johnny Go", in which Wilson appears singing *You Better Know It*, premieres in US.

May *That's Why (I Love You So)* reaches US #13.

Aug *I'll Be Satisfied* (which UK rocker Shakin' Stevens will revive in the 80s) reaches US #20. It is his last hit penned by Gordy/Carlo.

Oct *You Better Know It* (premiered earlier in the year in "Go Johnny Go") makes US #37, and spends a week at R&B #1.

1960
Jan *Talk That Talk* makes US #34 (hitting top 3 on R&B chart). Wilson is now managed by Nat Tarnopol, former assistant to the late Al Green, who steers both his recordings and live performances (which include engagements at major Hollywood, CA, Las Vegas, NV, and New York nightclubs) towards the majority white middle-class audience.

May Wilson's second million-seller is double A-side *Night* (which hits US #4, and is an almost operatic rendition of a ballad set to the melody of *My Heart At Thy Sweet Voice* from Camille Saint-Saens' "Samson And Delilah") and *Doggin' Around* (a blues groover which reaches US #15). *Doggin' Around* also hits US R&B #1 for 3 weeks and is issued as UK A-side with *The Magic Of Love* on the B-side, the classical adaptation of *Night* being felt likely to fall foul of a BBC ban (academic, since it fails to sell in UK).

Aug Another double A-side, *(You Were Made For) All My Love* reaches #12 and *A Woman, A Lover, A Friend* makes US #15 and R&B #4 for 4 weeks. He also releases one of his most acclaimed albums, **Jackie Sings The Blues**.

Sept *(You Were Made For) All My Love* makes UK #33.

Nov *Alone At Last*, its melody based on Tchaikovsky's "Piano Concerto #1 in b flat", hits US #8 while B-side *Am I The Man* makes US #32.

Dec *Alone At Last* makes UK #50, and will be Wilson's last UK chart entry for over 8 years. In US, he is voted Entertainer Of The Year by **Cash Box** magazine.

1961
Feb *My Empty Arms*, another classical adaptation (from Leoncavallo's "On With The Motley") hits US #9 and B-side *The Tear Of The Year* makes US #44 and is reissued as a UK A-side after *My Empty Arms* is deleted at time of release for similar reasons as *Night*.

[15] Wilson is shot by Juanita Jones, a female fan who invades his New York apartment and demands attention. Her gun (with which she has threatened to shoot herself) goes off as he tries to disarm her, and leaves him with a stomach wound and a bullet lodged in his back. He is rushed to Roosevelt hospital.

Mar [31] Wilson is discharged from hospital, with bullet still lodged in a not dangerous, but not easily-operable, spot.

Apr *Please Tell Me Why* reaches US #20 and B-side *Your One And Only Love* makes US #40.

July *I'm Coming Back To You* reaches US #19 and B-side *Lonely Life* makes US #80.

Sept *Years From Now* makes US #37 while B-side *You Don't Know What It Means* (co-written by Wilson) peaks at US #79.

Nov *The Way I Am* makes US #58 as B-side *My Heart Belongs To Only You* peaks at US #65.

1962
Jan [21] Wilson appears on US TV's "Ed Sullivan Show".

Feb *The Greatest Hurt* reaches US #34 and B-side *There'll Be No Next Time* makes US #75.

Apr *I Found Love*, a duet with Linda Hopkins co-written by Wilson and Alonzo Tucker, stalls at US #93.

May *Hearts* makes US #58.

July *I Just Can't Help It*, also by Wilson/Tucker, peaks at US #70.

Oct *Forever And A Day* makes US #82.

Nov *Jackie Wilson At The Copa*, recorded at New York's Copacabana, is Wilson's first US chart album, reaching #137.

1963
Apr Wilson/Tucker-penned *Baby Workout*, a strong R&B dance performance with big band-type arrangement and a contrast to his ballads, hits US #5.

May *Baby Workout* tops US R&B chart for 3 weeks, while album of the same title reaches US #36.

June A revival of Faye Adams' *Shake A Hand*, in another duet with Linda Hopkins, makes US #42.

Aug *Shake! Shake! Shake!*, continuing the dance groove of *Baby Workout*, reaches US #33.

Oct *Baby Get It (And Don't Quit It)* makes US #61.

1964
May *Big Boss Line* stalls at US #94.

Aug *Squeeze Her – Tease Her (But Love Her)* peaks at US #89.

1965
Mar A return to middle-of-the-road ballads with traditional Irish *Danny Boy* falters at US #94.

Aug *No Pity (In The Naked City)*, Wilson's last hit co-written with Tucker, makes US #59.

Oct *I Believe I'll Love One* creeps to US #96.

1966
Jan *Think Twice*, a duet with LaVern Baker on a revival of Brook Benton's 1961 hit, reaches US #93.

Dec Carl Davis-produced *Whispers (Gettin' Louder)*, cut in Chicago rather than New York, moves Wilson into the emerging soul field and reaches US #11. (Davis will continue as Wilson's producer.)

1967
Jan *Whispers* makes US #108.

Feb *Just Be Sincere* reaches US #91; its B-side *I Don't Want To Lose You* peaks at US #84.

May *I've Lost You* reaches US #82.

Oct Wilson finally scores his third million-selling single with *(Your Love Keeps Lifting Me) Higher And Higher*, which hits US #6 (and tops R&B chart for a week).

Dec *Since You Showed Me How To Be Happy* reaches US #32 as *Higher And Higher* makes US #163.

1968
Mar A revival of Jerry Butler And The Impressions' *For Your Precious Love*, on which Wilson sings with Count Basie's band, reaches US #49.

May *Chain Gang*, also with Basie, creeps to US #84.

June Wilson/Basie collaboration **Manufacturers Of Soul**, including the 2 hit singles, peaks at US #195.

Sept *I Get The Sweetest Feeling*, co-written by arranger Van McCoy, reaches US #34.

Nov A revival of standard *For Once In My Life* reaches US #70.

1969
June Unsuccessful in UK on its original release, *(Your Love Keeps Lifting Me) Higher And Higher* reaches UK #11 – Wilson's first UK chart entry since *Alone At Last* in 1960.

1970
May *Let This Be A Letter (To My Baby)* reaches US #91.

1971
Dec *Love Is Funny That Way* stalls at US #95.

1972
Mar *You Got Me Walking*, written by Eugene Record of The Chi-Lites, reaches US #93, and is Wilson's final US hit single.

Sept A reissue of *I Get The Sweetest Feeling* hits UK #9.

1975
May Double A-side reissue of *I Get The Sweetest Feeling/Higher And Higher* makes UK #25.

Sept [29] Wilson has a heart attack while singing *Lonely Teardrops* in a Dick Clark revue at the Latin Casino in Camden, NJ. Hitting his head as he falls, he lapses into a coma, suffering severe brain damage due to oxygen starvation. (He is hospitalized and will recover consciousness, but with all faculties, including speech, impaired. Barry White and The Spinners will be among those who perform benefits to raise money for his care.)

1978
Mar [15] Wilson's *That's Why (I Love You So)* is included on the soundtrack of movie "American Hot Wax", based on the life of DJ Alan Freed, which premieres in US.

1984
Jan [21] Wilson dies, having been immobile and in permanent care since his heart attack. His funeral is held at Chrysler Drive Baptist church in Detroit, where Wilson once sung gospel music; The Four Tops, The Spinners and Berry Gordy Jr. all attend.

1986
Dec Wilson's first single *Reet Petite*, reissued in UK and promoted via an inventive model-animation video, dethrones The Housemartins' *Caravan Of Love* to top UK chart at Christmas for 4 weeks, 29 years after its original release, this time selling over 700,000 copies.

1987
Jan [21] 3 years to the day since his death, Wilson is inducted into the Rock'N'Roll Hall Of Fame at the annual ceremony held at the Waldorf Astoria hotel in New York.

Mar A third UK reissue of *I Get The Sweetest Feeling* is follow-up to *Reet Petite* and hits UK #3.

July *Higher And Higher* reaches UK #15.

WILSON PHILLIPS

Chynna Phillips (vocals)
Carnie Wilson (vocals)
Wendy Wilson (vocals)

1973 Carnie Wilson (b. Apr.29, 1968, Los Angeles, CA), who has already made her vocal debut at age 2, on The Beach Boys' *This Whole World* from their *Sunflower* album, her sister Wendy (b. Oct.16, 1969, Los Angeles, CA), daughters of Beach Boy Brian Wilson and his ex-wife Marilyn Rovell, record their first (unreleased) song together *Take Me Out To The Ballgame* as The Satellites with childhood friend Chynna Phillips (b. Feb.12, 1968, Los Angeles, CA), daughter of The Mamas & The Papas' singers John and Michelle Phillips. The 3 girls will remain friends and all attend Santa Monica Montessori school.

1986 Owen Vanessa Elliot, daughter of late Mamas & The Papas' singer Cass Elliot, having been raised in Northampton, MA by her aunt, a singer in her own right, Leah Kunkel, goes to California to seek acting work where she links with her cousin Chynna, who is already gaining roles, including parts in the movies "Some Kind Of Wonderful", "Caddyshack II", "Say Anything" and most notably will star as Roxanne Pulitzer in the TV movie "Roxanne: The Prize Pulitzer". Together, they start looking at a career in music and hit upon an idea to record an anti-drug single featuring the offspring of 60s musicians. Phillips contacts the Wilson sisters who suggest recording a song by another pair of Wilson sisters, Ann and Nancy, of Heart: *Dog And Butterfly*, which they practice with Elliot.

1987 The foursome take their demo to veteran producer Richard Perry who, after hearing them harmonize on a version of Stevie Nicks' *The Wild Heart* points them to the studio. It becomes clear that Elliot's vocals do not gel in the unit and her cousin asks her to leave them as a trio. (Elliot will subsequently be snapped up by MCA for a solo deal.) Perry continues to demo the girls, enlisting the songwriting assistance of Glen Ballard.

1988 Perry hawks the unnamed trio's demo around the Los Angeles record labels, though only SBK production company, through Charles Koppelman and Artie Mogull, shows enthusiasm, and finances further recordings. Subsequent interest from companies, including MCA and Warner Bros. is rejected by the singers, who also extricate themselves from Perry. He has tried to project them in a Pointer Sisters direction, and through a deal will receive over $200,000 on royalty points from their debut album. New SBK offshoot, SBK Records enters the bidding arena and signs the trio, installing Ballard as producer of album tracks to be recorded at Studio Ultimo in Los Angeles and which will be finished by spring 90. (During this period, Phillips will meet up with her father for the first time in 8 years, while at the 1989 Capitol Records Grammy party, the Wilson sisters will meet up with their father for only the second time in 8 years, a reunion not planned by Brian Wilson's constant companion Eugene Landy.)

1990 **Apr** [24] Wilson Phillips (they have finally settled on their band name after rejecting 40 others including *Gypsy* and *Leda*) make their network TV debut on NBC TV's "Late Night With Letterman".
May [27] The week-long 19th Tokyo Song Festival begins in Tokyo, Japan. Group wins the festival's Grand Prize with their performance of *Hold On*. This is followed by a promotional tour of Japan and Australia.
June [9] Following a carefully orchestrated marketing plan by SBK promotion man Daniel Glass, airplay friendly/close harmonizing debut smash *Hold On*, written by Phillips and Ballard with additional lyrics by Carnie Wilson, hits US #1, and is certified gold by the RIAA. (25 years earlier to the day, The Beach Boys were at #1 with *Help Me Rhonda*.)
[30] *Hold On* hits UK #6.
July [6] Trio begins a 35-city US tour, supporting Richard Marx, at The Concord Pavilion, Concord, CA.
Aug [4] Debut album, *Wilson Phillips*, with 6 of the 10 songs written or co-written by Wilson Phillips and featuring contributions from Joe Walsh, Little Feat's Bill Payne and Toto's Steve Lukather, hits US #2, after a steady rise, on its way to 5 million US sales, but unable to penetrate MC Hammer's grip on the pole position with *Please Hammer Don't Hurt 'Em*. (*Wilson Phillips* has already hit UK #7 in July). It will also sell a further 2 million copies worldwide.
Sept [15] Further harmonizing *Release Me* also hits US #1, having peaked at UK #36 on Aug.25, the trio's second certified gold single.
Oct Wilson Phillips have to cancel some tour dates as Phillips undergoes minor throat surgery.
Nov [2] During promotion trip to UK, Wilson Phillips appears on BBC TV talk show "Wogan".

[16] Trio guests on ABC TV's "Into The Night With Rick Dees".
[17] *Impulsive*, penned by Steve Kipner/Clif Magness, makes UK #42.
[26] Trio wins Hot 100 Single category with *Hold On* at the 1990 **Billboard** Music Awards Show in Santa Monica, CA.
Dec Trio turns down a support slot on Michael Bolton's planned 1991 Spring tour.
[22] *Impulsive* hits US #4, as **Billboard** magazine confirms band as Top Singles Act and Top Pop Singles Artist – Duo Or Groups for 1990. Wilson Phillips end the year with 27 consecutive weeks in the US Top 10 Album chart, an achievement not bettered since The Supremes in 1967 with their *Greatest Hits*.

1991 **Jan** [29] Wilson Phillips sing an acoustic medley of their hits at the American Music Awards at the Shrine Auditorium, Los Angeles.
Feb [20] Wilson Phillips are beaten out in all 4 categories in which they have been nominated at the 33rd annual Grammy awards at Radio City Music Hall, New York.
Apr [20] Fourth extract from debut album, *You're In Love* tops US chart.

JOHNNY & EDGAR WINTER

1959 Albino guitarist/vocalist Johnny Winter (b. John Dawson Winter III, Feb.23, 1944, Leland, MS) cuts his first single *Schoolday Blues* on Dart label in Texas, as Johnny & The Jammers.

1968 After several years playing Chicago clubs in groups like Black Plague (with brother Edgar) and Gene Terry & The Down Beats, Johnny forms his own group, with brother Edgar (b. Dec.28, 1946, Beaumont, TX) on keyboards, Tommy Shannon on bass and John Turner on drums. They are recruited as regular group at New York's Scene, after owner Steve Paul reads an effusive article about Johnny's blues guitar playing in **Rolling Stone** magazine. Paul also becomes Johnny's manager.

1969 **Feb** Johnny signs to CBS/Columbia, on a 5-year, $300,000 contract.
May Imperial Records releases a one-off album, *The Progressive Blues Experiment*, which makes US #49. Recorded some time earlier, it is released in competition with the first Columbia album.
June Columbia debut album *Johnny Winter* reaches US #24.
[20] He takes part in the 3-day Newport 69 Festival, in CA.
[27] Johnny Winter plays at a festival at the Mile High Stadium, Denver, CO, before 50,000 people.
July [3] He particpates in Newport Jazz Festival on Rhode Island, RI.
Aug [30] He plays to 120,000 people at the 3-day Texas International Pop Festival at Dallas International Motor Speedway.
Oct *The Johnny Winter Story*, a compilation of early tracks cut during his days in Chicago and released by GRT Records, peaks at US #111.

1970 **Jan** Columbia album *Second Winter* makes US #55, while a revival of Chuck Berry's *Johnny B. Goode*, taken from it, makes US #92. (The album is a double, but only 3 sides have material, the fourth is blank.)
Apr [17] He tops London's Royal Albert Hall bill with Flock and Steamhammer.
May *Second Winter* is his UK chart debut, at #59.
June After appearing on his brother's album *Second Winter*, Edgar signs to CBS/Columbia and *Entrance*, featuring Edgar on almost all instruments, makes US #196.
July [3-5] Johnny plays at the 3-day Atlanta Pop Festival at the Middle Georgia Raceway in Byron, GA, to 200,000 people, with Jimi Hendrix, Jethro Tull, B.B. King and others.
Aug [6] Johnny participates in an anti-war 12-hour festival at New York's Shea Stadium, alongside Paul Simon, Janis Joplin, Steppenwolf and many others.
Oct *Johnny Winter And*, featuring Edgar and Rick Derringer's group The McCoys as back-up band, makes US #154.
Nov *Johnny Winter And* reaches UK #29.

1971 **May** Live album *Johnny Winter And/Live*, consisting mainly of rock and R&B standards, played by the same line-up as the previous album, reaches US #40 and UK #20, while a cover of The Rolling Stones' *Jumpin' Jack Flash* on a single makes US #89. (Johnny's increasing heroin dependency forces him out of action for a period following an early 1971 tour.)
June Edgar forms the brass-based group White Trash, featuring Floyd Radford (guitar), Bobby Ramirez (drums), George Sheck (bass), Mike McLellan (trumpet, vocals), Jon Smith (saxophone) and Jerry La Croix (lead vocals, saxophone). Group's debut album *Edgar Winter's White Trash* makes US #111.

1972 **Feb** *Keep Playin' That Rock'N'Roll* by White Trash makes US #70.
May White Trash's double live album *Roadwork* reaches US #23 while extracted revival of Otis Redding's *I Can't Turn You Loose* peaks at US

#81. (Edgar disbands White Trash shortly after to form rock band The Edgar Winter Group, which includes ex-Van Morrison sideman Ronnie Montrose (guitar), Chick Ruff (drums) and Dan Hartman (bass).

July [24] White Trash's drummer Bobby Ramirez is killed in a brawl in a Chicago bar. (Drug problems keep Johnny Winter musically inactive through this year.)

73 **Jan** *They Only Come Out At Night*, the first by The Edgar Winter Group, produced by Derringer, hits US #3, earning a gold disk.

Apr Johnny Winter returns to record with the (deliberately) ironically-titled *Still Alive And Well*, which reaches US #22.

May *Frankenstein*, an instrumental by The Edgar Winter Group, tops the US chart for a week, selling over a million. It has originally been B-side of *Hangin' Around*, until airplay prompted Columbia to turn the single over. The title *Frankenstein* comes from the fact that the track is heavily cut, patched and edited from the original master.

June *Frankenstein* reaches UK #18.

July [15] Edgar Winter performs at the White City, London with Sly & The Family Stone, Canned Heat, Lindisfarne, Barclay James Harvest and the JSD Band.

Oct *Free Ride*, also from *They Only Come Out At Night*, reaches US #14 and features a driving acoustic guitar. (It will be the band's last major hit; Montrose will leave to form his own eponymous group. He will be replaced first by Jerry Weems, then by the group's producer Derringer.)

74 **Jan** Edgar Winter Group's *Hangin' Around* makes US #65.

Feb Johnny Winter is one of the celebrities attending the opening of New York's Bottom Line club.

Apr His album *Saints And Sinners* peaks at US #42.

June 96 people are arrested after trouble in the audience of an Edgar Winter concert at the Omni in Atlanta, GA.

Aug Edgar's *Shock Treatment*, with Derringer on lead guitar, reaches US #13, earning a gold disk, while solo *River's Risin'* makes US #33.

Nov *Easy Street*, by The Edgar Winter Group, stalls at US #83.

75 **Jan** *John Dawson Winter III* makes US #78, his first release on new CBS-distributed Blue Sky label.

July *Jasmine Nightdreams*, a solo album by Edgar, also on Blue Sky, makes US #69.

Nov *The Edgar Winter Group With Rick Derringer* peaks at US #124.

76 **Apr** Johnny's *Captured Live!* makes US #93. Hartman and Derringer leave Edgar's group. (Hartman will become first a disco artist, with a major hit in *Instant Replay*, then a successful solo performer with more mainstream material like *I Can Dream About You*, and a producer for James Brown and others.)

July The Winter brothers combine for *Together*, a collection of live tracks and revivals, which makes US #89.

77 **Mar** Johnny produces acclaimed comeback *Hard Again* for blues legend Muddy Waters and tours as a member of his group.

Sept Johnny returns to his roots for *Nothin' But The Blues*, which makes US #146.

78 **Sept** Johnny's *White, Hot And Blue* makes US #141. It will be his last US chart entry for 6 years.

79 *The Edgar Winter Album* is released.

80 Edgar recruits a new band, including Jon Paris (bass) and Bobby Torello (drums), for *Raisin' Cain*, which fails.

81 *Standing On Rock* is Edgar's final album. (He will concentrate on session work for Meat Loaf, Dan Hartman, Bette Midler and others.)

84 **Aug** Johnny's *Guitar Slinger*, on independent blues label Alligator Records, makes US #183.

85 **Oct** His album *Serious Business* on Alligator makes US #156.

87 **Sept** [12-13] Johnny plays 15th San Francisco Blues Festival.

88 **Nov** [5] He ends a 23-date US tour at the Riverwalk Blues Fest in Fort Lauderdale, FL, part of the live promotion for his new album *Winter Of '88*, released on Voyager Records through MCA.

89 Edgar plays a sax on Tina Turner's *The Best*.

90 **Apr** [18] Johnny embarks on major US tour in Columbus, OH, while Edgar continues to tour with Rick Derringer.

STEVE WINWOOD

63 Winwood (b. May 12, 1948, Birmingham, W.Midlands) joins The Spencer Davis Group as vocalist, guitarist and keyboardist at age 15.

67 **Apr** He leaves The Spencer Davis Group and forms Traffic.

74 Between 2 incarnations of Traffic, he has also been a member of Blind Faith and Ginger Baker's Airforce. His first solo album would have been *Mad Shadows* in mid-1970, but it was released as Traffic's *John Barleycorn Must Die* after Jim Capaldi and Chris Wood helped him record it, and Traffic re-formed. Under his own name in June 1971,

double album *Winwood*, a compilation of tracks featuring him with his previous bands, reached US #93.

Dec After Traffic has dissolved following a US tour in support of *When The Eagle Flies*, Winwood retires home to Gloucestershire, where he builds his own Netherturkdonic studio. (He will spend the next 2 years quietly experimenting, while also working on sessions for others, notably fellow Island label acts like Sandy Denny, The Sutherland Brothers and Toots and The Maytals.)

1976 **Oct** Winwood joins Michael Shrieve to guest on Stomu Yamashta's *Go*, which makes US #60. He appears with Yamashta in a concert at London's Royal Albert Hall.

1977 **July** His solo album *Steve Winwood* is released just as punk is getting into its commercial stride in UK and is dismissed by some reviewers as passe. From it, *Midland Maniac* which features Winwood playing all instruments, reaches UK #12.

Oct *Steve Winwood* makes US #22.

1978 While not active in live work, he decides to cut an album on which he will fill every role, playing all instruments, producing and engineering. (It will take over 2 years to complete *Arc Of A Diver*.)

1981 **Jan** *Arc Of A Diver*, with music by Winwood and varied lyric contributions from Will Jennings, Vivian Stanshall and George Fleming, reaches UK #13. Extracted *While You See A Chance*, Winwood's first solo single, makes UK #45. Winwood's contract with Island has expired and the album's success enables him to negotiate a new deal on favorable terms, including gaining all the publishing rights to his earlier material.

Apr *Arc Of A Diver* hits US #3, earning a gold disk for a half million sales, and *While You See A Chance* hits US #7.

June US follow-up single, the title song from *Arc Of A Diver*, reaches US #48.

Nov *There's A River*, the last extract from the album, fails to chart.

1982 **Aug** *Talking Back To The Night*, made in a similar way to (though much faster than) the previous album, with Winwood playing everything but collaborating (with Jennings, who moves from Nashville to UK to co-write) on the songs, hits UK #6.

Sept *Still In The Game*, from *Talking Back To The Night*, reaches US #47 having failed in UK, while the album makes US #28.

Oct Synthesizer-driven *Valerie*, from the album, reaches UK #51.

Nov *Valerie* peaks at US #70.

1983 Winwood contributes songs to the soundtrack *They Call It An Accident*.

Apr [30] His manager Andy Cavaliere dies in New York after a heart attack, aged 36.

Sept [20] He appears at the ARMS benefit concert for multiple sclerosis-suffering former Faces member Ronnie Lane, at London's Royal Albert Hall, alongside Eric Clapton, Jeff Beck, Jimmy Page and others. (He also undertakes a short US tour with this charity line-up.)

1986 With his marriage to first wife Nicole in difficulties (the couple will divorce during the year), Winwood moves to New York, and, renouncing 1-man recording, makes *Back In The High Life*, with producer Russ Titelman and local musicians. 5 of its 8 songs are again collaborations with Jennings.

July *Higher Love*, featuring guest vocals from Chaka Khan, reaches UK #13. It is taken from *Back In The High Life*, which hits UK #8.

Aug [30] *Higher Love* tops the US chart for a week.

Sept *Back In The High Life* hits US #3, earning a platinum disk, while *Freedom Overspill*, also from the album, peaks at UK #69.

Nov [22] *Freedom Overspill* reaches US #20.

1987 **Jan** [18] Winwood marries Eugenia Grafton in Nashville, TN. (The couple will commute between Nashville and Winwood's UK farm.)

[24] *Back In The High Life Again* peaks at UK #53.

Feb [24] *Higher Love* wins Record Of The Year and Best Pop Vocal Performance, Male Of 1986 at the 29th annual Grammy awards. (These complete his Island contract and, with the singer a hot property following his 1986 successes, the label is outbid. He signs a new deal with Virgin Records, reported as being worth $13 million, and carrying a royalty rate of 18%.)

Apr [18] *The Finer Things* hits US #8.

Aug [15] *Back In The High Life Again* reaches US #13.

Oct In UK, Island reissues, from its retrospective compilation, Winwood/Jennings composition *Valerie* (a minor hit in late 1982, but subsequently remixed), which reaches UK #19.

Nov Compilation *Chronicles* reaches UK #12 and US #26.

Dec [19] *Valerie* hits US #9.

1988 **Mar** [12] *Talking Back To The Night*, extracted from *Chronicles*, makes US #57.

June *Roll With It*, the title song from his first album for Virgin, makes UK #53. Winwood promotes the album with an appearance at the Montreux Rock Festival in Switzerland, televised worldwide.

July *Roll With It*, recorded in Dublin and Toronto and co-produced by Winwood and Tom Lord Alge, hits UK #4. Most of the songs are Winwood/Jennings collaborations, but *Hearts On Fire* is co-written with ex-Traffic's Jim Capaldi.

[7] Winwood begins a 2-month US tour, backed by a band recruited in Nashville, and sponsored by a brewery. (It will be followed by a European tour.)

[30] *Roll With It* tops the US chart for 4 weeks, the longest of the year.

Aug [20] *Roll With It* also hits US #1 for a week, going platinum.

Oct [29] Ballad *Don't You Know What The Night Can Do?*, helped by its exposure on a Michelob beer TV commercial, hits US #6.

1989 Jan [28] *Holding On* reaches US #11.

Apr [22] *Hearts On Fire* peaks at US #53.

Aug [24] Winwood plays The Hawker in a charity production of Pete Townshend's "Tommy" at the Universal Amphitheater, Universal City, CA, with Elton John as the Pinball Wizard, Patti LaBelle as The Acid Queen, Phil Collins as Uncle Ernie and Billy Idol as Cousin Kevin.

1990 Dec [1] *Refugees Of The Heart* reaches US #28.

[22] *One And Only Man* reaches US #18.

BILL WITHERS

1967 Withers (b. July 4, 1938, Slab Fork, WV), having spent 9 years in the US Navy, then worked as a mechanic for Ford and IBM while writing songs in his spare time, moves to California and has a day job at the Lockheed Aircraft Corporation. He slowly saves $2,500 to pay for studio time to make demos of his songs, but gets little response.

1970 He is working in a factory manufacturing jumbo jet toilet seats, and learning the guitar, when he meets Booker T. Jones, ex-Booker T. & The MG's and now recording, writing and producing in Los Angeles for A&M Records. Jones, impressed by Withers' latest material, aids him in getting a recording deal with A&M-distributed Sussex Records.

1971 June [26] On the release of his first album, Withers makes his first professional live appearance, in Los Angeles, CA.

Sept Withers' debut album the soul drenched *Just As I Am*, produced by Jones, climbs to US #39 as extracted (self-penned) *Ain't No Sunshine* hits US #3, selling over a million.

Dec *Grandma's Hands*, also from the album, makes US #42.

1972 Mar [14] *Ain't No Sunshine* wins Best R&B Song at the 14th annual Grammy awards.

July [8] Self-produced *Still Bill* hits US #4, earning a gold disk while, extracted self-penned *Lean On Me* hits US #1 for 3 weeks, his second million-selling single.

Oct Also from the album, *Use Me* hits US #2 and is another million-seller. Meanwhile, *Lean On Me* is his UK chart debut, reaching #18. (*Ain't No Sunshine* did not sell in UK and Michael Jackson's album track cover version was extracted as a UK single, hitting the Top 10.)

1973 Jan *Let Us Love* makes US #47.

Mar *Kissing My Love* reaches US #31.

June Double live *Bill Withers Live At Carnegie Hall* reaches US #63.

July *Friend Of Mine* reaches US #80.

Withers and his actress wife Denise Nicholas (currently starring in ABC TV's series "Room 222") become parents for the first time.

1974 May *'Justments* (a title based on a phrase frequently used by his grandmother, who partially raised him) reaches US #67 while, from it, *The Same Love That Made Me Laugh* reaches US #50.

1975 Jan *Heartbreak Road* makes US #89.

May Compilation *The Best Of Bill Withers* reaches US #182. This is his last release on Sussex, with which he is now in legal dispute. Soon afterwards, Sussex folds and Withers signs a new deal with CBS/Columbia (which will also purchase his earlier Sussex material for reissue).

Dec Columbia debut album *Making Music* reaches US #81.

1976 Feb *Make Love To Your Mind*, from *Making Music*, reaches US #76.

Nov *Naked And Warm* stalls at US #169.

Dec *Mud* hits UK #7 with a cover of *Lean On Me*.

1977 Dec *Menagerie* reaches US #39, earning Withers a second gold album.

1978 Feb *Menagerie* reaches UK #27 while, from it, *Lovely Day* reaches US #30 and hits UK #7.

1979 Apr *'Bout Love* reaches US #134.

1981 May Grover Washington Jr.'s *Just The Two Of Us* featuring Withers on vocals, hits US #2 (behind Sheena Easton's *Morning Train (Nine To Five)*), and is a million-seller. (Withers' own recording career is quiet but he is

an eagerly-sought guest vocalist.) Compilation *Bill Withers' Greatest Hits* (which includes *Just The Two Of Us*) reaches US #183.

1982 Feb [24] *Just The Two Of Us* wins Best R&B Song at the 24th annual Grammy awards.

1984 Oct Ralph McDonald's *In The Name Of Love*, with Withers on guest vocal, reaches US #58.

1985 June *Oh Yeah!* peaks at UK #60. It is taken from *Watching You, Watching Me*, which reaches UK #60.

1987 Mar [21] A revival of Withers' song *Lean On Me* by Sacramento, CA-based quintet Club Nouveau, tops the US chart (earning a gold disk) and hits UK #3. Withers sends a telegram to the group thanking and congratulating them.

1988 Mar [2] *Lean On Me* wins Best R&B Song at the 30th annual Grammy awards.

Sept *Lovely Day*, remixed with new instrumental and rhythmic additions by Dutch DJ Ben Leibrand, hits UK #4. His *Greatest Hits* al re-charts, making UK #90.

[18] On the strength of his remixed hit, Withers travels to UK to play London's Hammersmith Odeon, where he is introduced on stage by son Todd.

Dec Withers returns to UK for a full national tour, as a reissue of *Ain No Sunshine* makes UK #82.

WIZZARD

Roy Wood (vocals, guitar)
Rick Price (bass)
Hugh McDowell (cello)
Nick Pentelow (saxophone)
Mike Burney (saxophone)
Bill Hunt (keyboards, French horn)
Keith Smart (drums)
Charlie Grima (drums)

1972 July Wood (b.Ulysses Adrian Wood, Nov.8, 1946, Birmingham, W. Midlands), having embarked on a new venture with guitarist Jeff Lynne (b. Dec.30, 1947, Birmingham), after their Birmingham group The Move has had its last hit (UK #7 in May) with *California Man*, originally the Wood-Lynne project but now called the Electric Light Orchestra (ELO), which hits UK #9 with its first single, *10538 Overtur* loses interest in the concept and announces the formation of his new group, Wizzard.

Aug Wizzard debuts at London's Wembley Rock'N'Roll Festival, on mismatched bill with Chuck Berry and Bill Haley.

1973 Jan Debut single *Ball Park Incident* hits UK #6. The Move's contract with EMI/Harvest officially has 2 years to run, but the company continues with both splinter groups.

Apr Wood writes, produces and plays on *Farewell*, a single by UK children's TV presenter Ayshea.

May *See My Baby Jive* tops UK chart, as Wood's multi-colored hair an clothes become part of Wizzard's image.

June *Wizzard Brew* reaches UK #29.

Aug Wood solo *Dear Elaine* reaches UK #18. (B-side *Songs Of Praise* was shortlisted for previous year's UK Eurovision Song Contest entry

Sept *Angel Fingers* tops UK chart. Wood's solo album *Boulders* reach UK #15.

Nov *Boulders* makes US #173. (Wizzard will never achieve US chart success.)

Dec Harvest celebrates Christmas with Wizzard's *I Wish It Could Be Christmas Every Day*, which hits UK #4, and Wood's *Forever*, which hit UK #8. (*I Wish It Could Be Christmas Everyday* will re-chart at Christma 1981 (#41) and 1984 (#23).)

1974 Wood begins year in poor health. The demands of touring and recording lead to ulcers and he is advised to slow down.

May Wizzard signs to Warner Bros. and first single *Rock'N'Roll Winte (Looney's Tune)* hits UK #6.

July Wood's solo *Going Down The Road* reaches UK #13.

Aug *This Is The Story Of My Love (Baby)* makes UK #34. *Introducing Eddy And The Falcons* reaches UK #19. Each track on the album is in the style of a 50s rock'n'roll hero: Gene Vincent, Duane Eddy, Cliff Richard, Del Shannon, etc.

Nov Wizzard begins unsuccessful US tour.

1975 Jan Featuring Wood's favorite new instrument, the bagpipes, *Are Yo Ready To Rock* hits UK #8.

May Wood's solo *Oh What A Shame*, on Jet label, reaches UK #13.

Oct Wizzard's management refuses to finance second US tour; band splits.

Nov Wood's second album, *Mustard*, is released. Despite vocal contributions from Phil Everly and girlfriend Annie Haslam, it flops. It is subsequently repackaged as *Roy Wood The Wizzard*.

1976 Wood signs to EMI/Harvest, Warner and Jet at the same time, with little idea which he is most bound to. He also has managerial difficulties.
Mar On Jet, *Indiana Rainbow*, credited to Roy Wood's Wizzard, is drawn from planned *Wizzo* (which will never be released). The Beach Boys release *It's OK*, on which Wood and 2 other members of Wizzard had played during their 1974 US tour.

1977 **Apr** Wood re-emerges with The Wizzo Band. Its *On The Road Again* features contributions from Led Zeppelin's John Bonham, Andy Fairweather-Low and original Move vocalist Carl Wayne. Album is deleted soon after release and band ceases. Wood will write and produce for other acts, including Darts, and forms a live band, The Helicopters, as well as releasing several unsuccessful singles.
Sept Warner Bros. releases Roy Wood's Wizzo Band's *Super Active Wizzo*, featuring Wood with new line-up of Bob Wilson (guitar), Rick Price (pedal steel, guitars), Paul Robbins (vocals, keyboards), Graham Gallery (bass), Billy Paul (saxes) and Dave Donovan (drums).

1979 *On The Road Again* is released in US and Germany as a Wood solo.

1982 **July** Speed Records releases a compilation album of Wood's work with The Move and beyond, *The Singles*, which reaches UK #37.

1983 Wood sings *Message In A Bottle* on *Arrested*, a collection of The Police songs performed by various rock musicians and the Royal Philharmonic Orchestra.

1985 He signs to Legacy Records.

1986 **Mar** Wood joins other Birmingham musicians including Robert Plant, ELO and The Moody Blues for "Heartbeat '86" benefit gig.
Nov He helps out Doctor & The Medics with their version of Abba's first hit, *Waterloo*, which reaches UK #45.

BOBBY WOMACK

1959 The Womack Brothers, consisting of Bobby (b. Mar.4, 1944, Cleveland, OH), Cecil, Curtis, Harris and Friendly Jr., become popular favorites on the gospel circuit and, while touring, meet Sam Cooke & The Soul Stirrers.

1960 **June** While continuing his career with his brothers, Bobby Womack is recruited by Cooke as a guitarist in his band.

1961 Cooke signs The Womack Brothers to his own SAR label, as The Valentinos and The Lovers.

1962 **Sept** *Lookin' For A Love* is an R&B hit and charts at US #72. It is quickly followed by *I'll Make It Alright* which reaches US #97. Chart success prompts a support slot on James Brown's US tour.

1964 **July** *It's All Over Now* is The Valentinos' final chart entry together (US #94). Written by Bobby, it will later become a worldwide smash for The Rolling Stones (at UK #1 and US #26), with whom Bobby will develop a long-term relationship.

1965 **Feb** Following the murder of Sam Cooke in Dec.1964, Bobby marries his widow, Barbara. He embarks on an unsuccessful stint on Him label and starts a period of heavy session work. As a guitarist, he will contribute to recordings for artists including King Curtis, Ray Charles, Joe Tex, Wilson Pickett, The Box Tops, Aretha Franklin, Dusty Springfield and Janis Joplin.

1966 As a songwriter, Womack begins writing hits for Wilson Pickett, who will cover 17 Womack songs over 3 years, including *I'm A Midnight Mover* (US #24) and *I'm In Love* (US #45).

1968 **Sept** Following brief stints at Chess and Atlantic, Womack signs to Minit label for his first solo success at US #52 with *Fly Me To The Moon*, taken from debut solo album of the same name, which makes US #174.

1969 **Jan** An R&B cover of The Mamas & The Papas classic *California Dreamin'*, also from the album, makes US #43.
Dec *How I Miss You Baby* reaches US #93.

1970 **May** *More Than I Can Stand* (US #90) is his final Minit hit. Divorce from Barbara coincides with his meeting R&B superstar, Sly Stone. Together they become immersed in a drugs and groupie wilderness which will dominate their lives throughout 70s.

1971 **May** A one-off live recording *The Womack Live* (actually recorded some 3 years earlier at the California club, Los Angeles, CA) is released on United Artists' subsidiary Liberty and reaches US #188.

1972 **Jan** Debut single for UA *That's The Way I Feel About Cha* makes US #27 and promotes sales for simultaneously released *Communication*, which reaches US #83.
June *Woman's Gotta Have It* reaches US #60 and *Understanding* makes US #43.

Sept A cover of Neil Diamond's *Sweet Caroline (Good Times Never Seemed So Good)* charts at US #51.
Dec B-side *Harry Hippie*, popular Womack live number, makes US #31.

1973 **Jan** He completes film soundtrack for "Across 110th Street", starring Anthony Quinn. The album makes US #50, while title track single reaches US #56.
July Beginning a trilogy of albums which will all be recorded in Memphis, *Facts Of Life* achieves US #37 and includes *Nobody Wants You When You're Down And Out*, which makes US #29.

1974 **Mar** Simultaneous release of new Memphis album *Lookin' For A Love Again* reaches US #85 and title song *Lookin' For A Love* gives Womack his biggest career hit at US #10.
June He produces long-time friend, Rolling Stone Ron Wood's debut album *Now Look*, which reaches US #118.
July *You're Welcome, Stop On By* makes US #59.
Dec UA releases *Bobby Womack's Greatest Hits* which shows signs of his career slowing up (US #142).

1975 **May** *Check It Out* reaches US #91 with only 3 weeks on the survey. Taken from *I Don't Know What The World Is Coming To*, it is his final UA chart single.

1976 **Jan** Critics pan new *Safety Zone* and it only climbs to US #147.
Mar [6] Womack plays the Hammersmith Odeon, London, during a short UK tour.
May Final United Artists album *B.W. Goes C&W* is released. The label dumps Womack after his attempt to go country (original working title of album is, according to Womack, *Move Over Charley Pride And Give Another Nigger A Chance*).
Sept He signs a new deal with CBS/Columbia who releases his final Memphis recording, *Home Is Where The Heart Is*, which fails to chart.

1978 **July** *Pieces*, the second CBS/Columbia effort, again fails. The murder of his brother, Harry, compounds Womack's depression as he retreats further into drugs.

1980 **Nov** Currently without a contract, Crusader Wilton Felder enlists Womack as his lead vocal assistance on single and album, both titled *Inherit The Wind*. The album reaches US #142; the single makes UK #39, his first artist chart entry in UK.

1981 **Dec** Recovered from narcotics, Womack returns triumphantly with *The Poet*, released on small California soul label, Beverly Glen. It becomes a best-selling R&B album and reaches US #29.

1982 Womack takes label owner, Otis Smith, to court claiming that he is receiving no royalties. Consistently claiming throughout his career that, like James Brown and many other black artists, he has been short-changed, tempers flair as Womack punches Smith in the courtroom.

1984 **Apr** With legal wrangles finally over, Womack is free to release second part of Poet project, *The Poet II*. A one-off album deal with Motown, it reaches US #60 and becomes the first UK Album chart entry at #31.
June As Womack undertakes major US tour, a duet from *Love Has Finally Come At Last* with Patti LaBelle climbs to US #88, while *Tell Me Why* makes UK #60.
Dec He organizes benefit concert for Sly Stone, now seeking rehabilitation and visits UK for a mini-tour. Brother Cecil begins scoring hits as one-half of Womack & Womack, with his wife, Linda. As Sam Cooke's daughter, she now becomes Bobby Womack's sister-in-law, having previously been his step-daughter.

1985 **Feb** Womack renews his connection with Felder for the latter's second album *Secrets* which makes US #91 and #77 in UK, where Womack unites with Altrina Grayson for *(No Matter How High I Get) I'll Still Be Lookin' Up To You*, which reaches UK #63.
Sept He signs a million-dollar recording contract with MCA worldwide. First release, soul album *So Many Rivers*, makes UK #28.
Oct *I Wish He Didn't Trust Me So Much*, taken from the album, reaches UK #64.
Nov *So Many Rivers* makes US #66.
Dec [14] Artists United Against Apartheid, comprising 49 artists including Womack, makes US #38 and UK #21 with *Sun City*.

1986 **June** The Rolling Stones invite Womack to contribute guitar and vocals on their new album *Dirty Work*. He is prominent as co-vocalist with Jagger on *Going Back To Memphis*.
July *Womagic* is released but fails to chart.

1987 **Nov** Having recently recorded a cover version of UK band Living In A Box's *Living In A Box*, the album *Womagic* is deleted and replaced by new album *The Last Soul Man*, including the single, 2 other new cuts and the majority of tracks on *Womagic*. Neither charts.

1989 **Aug** Womack guests with Ben E. King, Wilson Pickett, Don Covay, Darlene Love, Marvis Staples and Ellie Greenwich on *What Is Soul?*

from Paul Shaffer's *Coast To Coast*. (He will also guests on *Want Of A Nail* from Todd Rundgren's *Nearly Human*.)

Dec *Ain't Nothin Like The Lovin' We Got*, a duet with Shirley Brown, makes #46 on US R&B chart.

1990 Jan *Save The Children* peaks at #83 on US R&B chart.

June [22] Womack, a regular visitor to the UK, plays at the Hammersmith Odeon, London.

STEVIE WONDER

1960 Blind since birth, Wonder (b. Steveland Judkins, May 13, 1950, Saginaw, MI), a member of the Whitestone Baptist Church Choir with his mother, 4 brothers and sister, is recommended by friend John Glover (with whom he has formed a duo) to Glover's cousin Miracle Ronnie White, who takes Wonder to meet Motown Records' president, Berry Gordy, and producer, Brian Holland. Gordy signs the child prodigy to a long-term contract with Tamla label.

1962 Aug [16] First single, credited to Little Stevie Wonder, *I Call It Pretty Music (But The Old People Call It The Blues)*, featuring Marvin Gaye on drums, is released, but fails to chart.

Oct [16] Wonder, after making his live debut at Detroit, MI's Latin Quarter club, begins a 2-month Motown Records package tour in Washington, DC with Marvin Gaye, The Miracles, The Supremes and Mary Wells.

1963 May [21] A Stevie Wonder concert is recorded in Detroit for forthcoming *12 Year Old Genius*.

Aug Fourth single, *Fingertips – Pt. 2* sells over a million and tops the US chart, the first live record to do so. *Recorded Live – The 12 Year Old Genius* tops the US chart. Wonder becomes the first artist to top the Hot 100, R&B Singles and Album charts simultaneously. Meanwhile, he enrols at the Michigan School for the Blind in Lansing, now unable to continue at Fitzgerald school in Detroit because of his success.

Nov *Workout Stevie, Workout* reaches US #33.

Dec [26] Wonder visits UK for promotional spots on ITV shows "Ready, Steady, Go!" and "Thank Your Lucky Stars".

1964 Feb [5] Wonder appears on CBS TV's "Ed Sullivan Show".

Apr *Castles In The Sand* makes US #52.

July *Hey Harmonica Man* reaches US #29. Wonder drops his "Little" prefix. He makes his movie debut in teenpix "Bikini Beach" and "Muscle Beach Party".

1965 Mar [18] Wonder and other Motown artists fly to London, for recording of ITV's hour-long "The Sound Of Tamla Motown" show.

[20] The Motown review opens 21-date twice-nightly UK package tour at the Finsbury Park Astoria, London, with Wonder, Martha & The Vandellas, The Miracles, The Supremes and The Temptations with special UK guest stars Georgie Fame & The Blue Flames, set to end on Apr.12 at the Guildhall, Portsmouth, Hants.

Oct *High Heel Sneakers* makes US #59.

1966 Jan [21] Wonder flies to London for his third UK tour.

Feb *Uptight (Everything's Alright)* hits US #3 and R&B #1, selling over a million.

Mar *Uptight* reaches UK #14, his UK chart debut.

May *Nothing's Too Good For My Baby* reaches US #20.

June *Up Tight Everything's Alright* is released, making US #33.

Sept A revival of Bob Dylan's *Blowin' In The Wind*, duetted with Henry Cosby, hits US #9 and makes UK #36.

Nov Wonder begins a 3-week European tour at the Titan club, Rome, Italy.

Dec *A Place In The Sun* hits US #9.

1967 Jan *A Place In The Sun* reaches UK #20.

Feb *Down To Earth* enters the US chart, rising to #92.

Apr *Travlin' Man* makes US #32. (B-side *Hey Love* will make US #90 in May.)

July *I Was Made To Love Her* hits US #2 and is a million-seller.

Aug *I Was Made To Love Her* hits UK #5. Parent album *I Was Made To Love Her* will make US #45.

Nov *I'm Wondering* reaches US #12 and UK #22.

1968 Jan Wonder graduates from Michigan State School for the Blind in Lansing, MI.

Apr *Greatest Hits* is released and will make US #37 and UK #25.

May *Shoo-Be-Doo-Be-Doo-Da-Day* hits US #9 and makes UK #46.

Aug *You Met Your Match* reaches US #35.

Sept *Stevie Wonder's Greatest Hits* makes UK #25.

Nov Wonder, credited as Eivets Rednow, reaches US #66 with *Alfie*, a piano instrumental. (He also records an instrumental album under this reversal of his own name.)

Dec An updating of standard *For Once In My Life* hits US #2, behind Marvin Gaye's *I Heard It Through The Grapevine*, and is another million-seller.

1969 Jan *For Once In My Life* hits UK #3, as parent album *For Once In My Life* heads for US #50.

Mar *I Don't Know Why* makes US #39.

[7] He embarks on an 18-day UK concert tour.

Apr *I Don't Know Why* reaches UK #14.

May [5] Wonder meets President Nixon at the White House and is presented with the President's Committee on Employment of Handicapped People's "Distinguished Service Award".

July *My Cherie Amour*, B-side of *I Don't Know Why*, hits US #4 and tops a million sales.

Aug *My Cherie Amour* hits UK #4 as parent *My Cherie Amour* rises to US #34.

Dec *Yester-me, Yester-you, Yesterday* hits US #7 and UK #2. *My Cherie Amour* reaches UK #17.

1970 Jan [10] Wonder is awarded 1969 Show Business Inspiration Award by Fight For Sight, which promotes research into eye diseases.

Mar *Never Had A Dream Come True* reaches US #26 and hits UK #6.

Apr *Stevie Wonder Live* makes US #81.

Aug *Signed Sealed Delivered I'm Yours* hits US #3 and reaches UK #15 as *Signed Sealed And Delivered* is released, set to make US #25.

Sept [14] Wonder marries Syreeta Wright, a former secretary at Motown Records. He will co-write and produce several hits for her.

Nov *Heaven Help Us All* hits US #9 and reaches UK #29.

1971 May [13] On his 21st birthday, Wonder receives all his childhood earnings. Despite having earned in excess of $30 million, he receives only $1 million. (His renegotiations with Motown result in the formation of autonomous Taurus Productions and Black Bull Publishing companies.)

We Can Work It Out, a revival of Lennon/McCartney's song, reaches US #13 and UK #27. *Where I'm Coming From*, written by Wonder and Syreeta, makes US #62.

July *Never Dreamed You'd Leave In Summer* makes US #78.

Aug [17] Wonder sings at the funeral of the legendary King Curtis, fatally stabbed in New York City.

Oct *If You Really Love Me*, again written with Syreeta, hits US #8.

Nov *Greatest Hits, Vol.2* makes US #69.

1972 Jan [13] Wonder begins UK tour at Hammersmith Odeon, London. Tour ends Feb.2 at Manchester Odeon, Gtr.Manchester.

Feb *If You Really Love Me* reaches UK #20. *Greatest Hits Vol.2* makes UK #30.

Mar *Music Of My Mind*, recorded with synthesizer specialists Robert Margouleff and Malcolm Cecil, reaches US #21.

June [3] Wonder begins a 50-date 8-week tour as support to The Rolling Stones in Vancouver, Canada.

July *Superwoman (Where Were You When I Needed You)* reaches US #33.

Aug [30] Wonder joins John and Yoko Lennon for "One On One" benefit for Willowbank hospital at New York's Madison Square Garden.

Sept *Keep On Running* stalls at US #90.

Nov *Talking Book* hits US #3.

1973 Jan *Superstition*, written for Jeff Beck, tops the US chart, selling over a million, and reaches UK #11.

Feb *Talking Book* reaches UK #16.

May *You Are The Sunshine Of My Life* tops the US chart, becoming another million-seller.

June *You Are The Sunshine Of My Life* hits UK #7.

Aug Rufus' *Tell Me Something Good*, Wonder-inked, hits US #3.

[6] While traveling from Greenville to Durham during a US tour, Wonder is seriously injured in a car accident near Winston-Salem, NC. (He suffers multiple head injuries and lies in a coma for 4 days.)

[18] *Higher Ground* tops **Billboard**'s Soul charts.

Sept *Innervisions* hits US #4, selling over 1 million, and UK #8.

[25] Wonder makes his first post-accident appearance jamming on *Honky Tonk Women* with Elton John at the Boston Garden, MA.

Oct *Higher Ground* hits US #4 and reaches UK #29.

Nov [9] Wonder receives Nederlands Edison Award for *Talking Book*.

1974 Jan *Living For The City* hits US #8 and UK #15.

Mar Wonder plays his first US concert since his accident at Madison Square Garden. He is joined on stage by Roberta Flack, Eddie Kendricks, Sly Stone and Wonderlove, and sells out concerts at the Rainbow theater, London.

[2] Wonder wins Grammys in 4 categories: Best Pop Vocal Performance, Male (for *You Are The Sunshine Of My Life*), Best R&B

Song and Best R&B Vocal Performance, Male (both for *Superstition*) and Album Of The Year (for *Innervisions*) Of 1973 at the 16th annual Grammy awards.

May *He's Misstra Know It All* hits UK #10.

June *Don't You Worry 'Bout A Thing* reaches US #16.

Sept *Fulfillingness' First Finale* tops the US chart for 2 weeks and hits UK #5.

[13] Wonder begins a US tour at Nassau Coliseum, Long Island, NY.

Nov *You Haven't Done Nothin'*, with The Jackson 5 on back-up vocals, hits US #1 and UK #30.

[22] "Stevie Wonder Day" is celebrated in Los Angeles.

1975 Feb *Boogie On Reggae Woman* hits US #3 and UK #12.

Mar [1] Wonder again wins 4 Grammys: Best Pop Vocal Performance, Male and Album Of The Year (both for *Fulfillingness*), Best R&B Vocal Performance, Male (for *Boogie On Reggae Woman*) and Best R&B Song (for *Living For The City*) at the 17th annual Grammy awards.

[6] Wonder is awarded the NARM Presidential Award "in tribute to a man who embodies every facet of the complete musical artist: composer, writer, performer, recording artist, musician and interpreter through his music of the culture of his time . . ."

Apr Minnie Riperton's *Lovin' You*, written by Wonder, tops the US chart. Having recently moved to Manhattan, Wonder and new companion Yolanda Simmons parent a daughter, Aisha Zakia.

May [10] Wonder headlines a concert in front of 125,000 people at the Washington Monument to celebrate "Human Kindness Day". Wonder performs in Jamaica with Bob Marley & The Wailers.

1976 Jan [25] Wonder joins Bob Dylan and Isaac Hayes for the Night Of The Hurricane II" benefit show for convicted murderer, boxer Ruben "Hurricane" Carter in the Houston Astrodome.

Stevie Wonder Home For Blind And Retarded Children opens, confirming ongoing personal interest in a wide number of charity and human rights causes.

Apr [14] Wonder and Motown Records announce the signing of a $13-million-dollar contract renewal – the largest negotiated in recording history to date.

Oct Double album *Songs In The Key Of Life* debuts at US #1, where it stays for 14 weeks, and hits UK #2.

1977 Jan *I Wish* hits US #1 and UK #5, and is another million-seller.

Feb [19] Wonder is named Producer Of The Year, *Songs In The Key Of Life* wins Album Of The Year and Best Pop Vocal Performance, Male and *I Wish* is named Best R&B Vocal Performance, Male at the 19th annual Grammy awards.

May *Sir Duke*, a tribute to Duke Ellington, is a further million-seller, topping the US chart and hitting UK #2, behind Deniece Williams' *Free*.

Sept *Another Star* makes UK #29.

Oct *Another Star* reaches US #32.

1978 Jan *As* makes US #36.

1979 Feb *Pops We Love You*, a tribute to Berry Gordy's father on his 90th birthday, with Diana Ross, Marvin Gaye and Smokey Robinson, reaches US #59 and UK #66. Compilation *Looking Back* makes US #34.

Apr The Wonders become parents to daughter, Kita Swan Di.

[27] Wonder makes a surprise appearance, performing *Sir Duke*, at a Duke Ellington tribute at UCLA's Royce Hall, Los Angeles.

Nov Double *Journey Through The Secret Life Of Plants* hits UK #8.

Dec [2] Wonder, accompanied by the National Afro-American Philharmonic Orchestra, performs material from *Journey Through The Secret Life Of Plants* at New York's Metropolitan Opera House.

Send One Your Love hits US #4 and UK #52 as parent album *Journey Through The Secret Life Of Plants*, the soundtrack for a documentary film of the same title, hits US #4.

1980 Feb *Black Orchid* peaks at UK #63.

Mar *Outside My Window* makes both US and UK #52.

Sept [1] Wonder returns for a UK tour after a 6-year absence, including 6 sold-out Wembley Arena dates.

Oct Marley-inspired *Master Blaster (Jammin')* hits UK #2, behind The Police's *Don't Stand So Close To Me*.

Nov *Hotter Than July*, dedicated to Martin Luther King Jr., hits US #3 and UK #2. (Wonder will conduct a campaign to have King's Jan.15 birthdate celebrated as a US national holiday. After marches on Washington in 1981 and 1982, he will have his wish granted in 1986.)

Dec *Master Blaster (Jammin')* hits US #5.

1981 Jan *I Ain't Gonna Stand For It* hits UK #10.

Mar *I Ain't Gonna Stand For It* reaches US #11.

May *Lately* makes US #64 and hits UK #3.

June Wonder contributes to gospel singer Andrae Crouch's *I'll Be Thinking Of You*.

Aug *Happy Birthday* hits UK #2, behind Shakin' Stevens' *Green Door*.

[15] Wonder gives his *Hotter Than July* gold disk to Tami Ragoway, whose boyfriend had been shot and killed returning home after Wonder's concert at Los Angeles' Forum.

1982 Mar *That Girl* hits US #4 and makes UK #39.

May *Ebony And Ivory*, a duet with Paul McCartney recorded in Montserrat, West Indies, tops US and UK charts, selling over a million. *Stevie Wonder's Original Musiquarium 1* hits UK #8. It is a compilation album spiced with new tracks.

June [6] Wonder participates in "Peace Sunday: We Have A Dream" anti-nuclear rally at the Rose Bowl, Pasadena, CA, with Jackson Browne, Crosby, Stills & Nash, Bob Dylan, Linda Ronstadt and others. *Do I Do* hits UK #10 while *Stevie Wonder's Original Musiquarium 1* hits US #4.

July *Do I Do* reaches US #13.

Oct *Ribbon In The Sky* makes US #54 and UK #45.

Dec *Used To Be*, a duet with Charlene, reaches US #46.

1983 May [7] Wonder plays tennis while hosting NBC TV's "Saturday Night Live".

Aug Wonder sings on and co-writes Gary Byrd's *The Crown*, which hits UK #6 as a 12"-only single.

1984 Jan He guests on Elton John's *I Guess That's Why They Call It The Blues*.

June Wonder begins a UK and European tour.

Sept *I Just Called To Say I Love You* (taken from soundtrack *The Woman In Red* which hits UK #1 and UK #2) tops the UK chart for 6 weeks, selling more than 1 million copies – it is Wonder's first solo UK #1, and one of the 10 best-selling UK singles of all time.

Oct *I Just Called To Say I Love You* tops the US chart.

Nov Wonder guests on Chaka Khan's US and UK hit *I Feel For You*. Compilation *Love Songs – 16 Classic Hits* reaches UK #20.

Dec *Love Light In Flight* makes UK #44.

[24] Wonder is given the key to the city of Detroit. (He will later announce plans to run for Mayor.)

1985 Jan Self-explanatory *Don't Drive Drunk* peaks at UK #62.

[28] Wonder participates in the recording of USA For Africa's *We Are The World*.

Feb *Love Light In Flight*, also from *The Woman In Red*, reaches US #17.

Mar [25] *I Just Called To Say I Love You* wins the Oscar for Best Song at the annual Academy Awards ceremony. Wonder dedicates the award to Nelson Mandela.

[26] South African radio stations ban the playing of all Wonder's records in response to his Mandela tribute.

July Wonder plays harmonica on Eurythmics' *There Must Be An Angel (Playing With My Heart)* UK chart-topper.

Sept *Part-Time Lover* hits UK #3 as parent album *In Square Circle* hits UK #5. He writes and plays *She's So Beautiful* with vocal by Cliff Richard for the album of Dave Clark's *Time*. Released as a Richard single, it reaches UK #17.

Oct *In Square Circle* hits US #5.

Nov *Part-Time Lover* becomes the first single to top the US pop, R&B, adult contemporary and dance/disco charts. *Go Home* peaks at UK #67.

Dec *I Just Called To Say I Love You* re-enters UK chart at #64.

1986 Jan Wonder joins Elton John and Gladys Knight as Dionne Warwick's guests on US #1 *That's What Friends Are For*.

[15] To celebrate the first observance of Martin Luther King Jr.'s birthday as a US national holiday, Wonder organizes concerts in Washington, New York, and Atlanta.

Feb *Go Home* hits US #10.

[25] *In Square Circle* wins Best R&B Vocal Performance, Male Of 1985 at the 28th annual Grammy awards.

Apr [12] *Overjoyed* reaches US #24 and UK #17.

June *Land Of La La* makes US #86.

[17] Wonder begins a US tour to promote *In Square Circle* in Seattle.

July [31] Wonder is nominated for an Emmy for his appearance in top-rated NBC TV's "The Cosby Show".

1987 Jan *Stranger On The Shore Of Love* peaks at UK #55.

Feb Wonder announces a boycott of the state of Arizona, until Governor Evan Meacham reinstates Martin Luther King Jr.'s birthday as a state holiday. (Several other artists support his boycott.)

[24] Wonder wins Best Pop Performance By A Duo Or Group With Vocal with Dionne Warwick, Elton John and Gladys Knight for *That's What Friends Are For* at the 29th annual Grammy awards.

Mar Wonder records anti-drug song, *Don't Pass Go* in an audio visual experiment, linking Nile Rodgers in a New York studio with Quincy Jones and Wonder in his own Los Angeles studio Wonderland 3,000 miles away.

Aug Wonder begins a UK and European tour.

Sept During an 8-day stint at London's Wembley Arena, fan Barry Betts answers Wonder's request to help courier a tape of a new song, *Get It*, to Michael Jackson in Los Angeles.

Oct *Skeletons* peaks at UK #59.

Nov *Characters* makes UK #33.

[28] *Skeletons* tops US R&B chart.

Dec [5] *Skeletons* reaches US #19 and hits R&B #1, having faltered at UK #59. *Characters* reaches US #17.

[19] *Characters* tops US R&B chart.

1988 Feb [2] *You Will Know* peaks at US #77.

Mar [5] *You Will Know* tops US R&B chart.

May Wonder begins European tour. (Paul Young joins him on *Birthday*.)

[28] *Get It*, a duet with Michael Jackson, makes US #80 and UK #37.

June [4] Wonder/Julio Iglesias duet *My Love* peaks at US #80.

[11] Wonder, despite having synthesizer programs stolen, plays at "Nelson Mandela's 70th Birthday Party" at Wembley Stadium.

Aug Wonder's duet with Julio Iglesias, *My Love* hits UK #6, after stalling at US #80. He plays an 8-date series of concerts at New York's Radio City Music Hall, as he prepares for a US tour.

1989 Jan [18] Wonder is inducted into the Rock'N'Roll Hall Of Fame at the fourth annual dinner at the Waldorf Astoria in New York.

Mar *With Each Beat Of My Heart* reaches #28 on US R&B chart.

Apr Wonder confirms his backing for the proposed Rhythm Radio Group pitching for a new station franchise in London.

May He begins a European tour including sold-out dates at major UK venues and stadium dates in East Europe.

[13] Wonder celebrates his 39th birthday on stage at the Wembley Arena, London, joined by Paul Young during an encore. Belated release of *Free* from *Characters* makes UK #49.

June Wonder becomes the first Motown act to play Eastern bloc countries. He donates the royalties from *Characters* to the Polish Foundation for the Handicapped.

[17] Wonder sings *Happy Birthday* at the centenary celebration of the Eiffel Tower in Paris, France.

1990 Jan [6] Wonder plays at the Los Angeles Forum to raise funds for the Inner City Foundation for Excellence in Education.

[15] He donates the proceeds to his concert at the Beacon theater, New York to aid the homeless.

Feb [21] Wonder sings *We Can Work it Out* in a tribute to Paul McCartney, being honored with a Lifetime Achievement Award at 32nd annual Grammy awards.

Apr [3] Los Angeles Urban League honors Wonder with Whitney M. Young Jr. Award, given to individuals who have made significant contributions in advancing civil and human rights for African Americans and other minorities.

[23-24] He guests with Patti Austin, James Taylor, Phoebe Snow and Take 6 for Special Olympics Africa at Carnegie Hall, New York.

Aug [31] Wonder sings *Amazing Grace* with Bonnie Raitt and Jackson Browne at memorial service for Stevie Ray Vaughan in Oak Cliff, Dallas, TX.

Oct [26] Whitney Houston presents Wonder with the Carousel Of Hope award from the Children's Diabetes Foundation at a benefit at the Beverly Hilton hotel, CA.

Nov [15] Wonder is honored by Recording Artists Against Drunk Driving receiving its Honorary Global Founder's Award for *Don't Drive Drunk*.

Dec [23-24] Wonder performs at the Tokyo Dome, Japan.

1991 Mar Spike Lee commissions Wonder to pen soundtrack for his new movie "Jungle Fever", putting on hold his own *Conversation Pieces* album.

WORLD PARTY
Karl Wallinger

1983 Apr Having drifted through a series of bands, including Zero Zero, Invisible Body Club and funk outfit Out, Wallinger (b. Oct.19, 1957, Prestatyn, Wales), primarily a keyboardist, answers an ad in **Sounds** magazine, posted by The Waterboys' Mike Scott, looking for a guitarist who is "into Iggy Pop". Auditioning successfully, Wallinger joins the line-up in time for its UK TV debut on BBC TV's "The Old Grey Whistle Test", and will record and perform with the band for 2 albums. Wallinger, the youngest of 4 children. whose first group experience was in Quasimodo in 1976, with pre-Alarm members, has moved to London in the late 70s and worked for ATV/Northern Songs music

publishers as a royalties analysis clerk before becoming the musical director of the (then Tracey Ullman-starring) "Rocky Horror Picture Show" in the West End.

1986 Wallinger leaves The Waterboys, frustrated in his desire for complete creative control and forms World Party based entirely around his own ideas, songs, musical and production skills. "Pregnant With World Party," as Scott will later claim, Wallinger is invited to retain links with Ensign to whom The Waterboys are contracted, and moves from London to the rural escapism of his Woburn, Beds., home The Old Rectory, where he establishes his own studio to record debut album.

1987 Feb Ecology awareness promoting *Ship Of Fools* makes UK #42.

Mar [21] Edited from over 2 hours of songs, including non-released version of Prince's *Pop Life* and John Lennon's *Across The Universe*, World Party debut *Private Revolution*, heavily themed on environmental issues and on which Wallinger produces and plays all instruments, except saxophone by Waterboy Anthony Thistlethwaite, violin by new Waterboy Steve Wickham and vocal help from new labelmate, Irish singer Sinead O'Connor, makes UK #56 and US #39, where the act is an instant success particularly on the college circuit.

Apr [25] With its extended US title, *Ship Of Fools (Save Me From Tomorrow)* reaches US #27.

May World Party undertakes extensive UK, European and US tours, which will take up the rest of the year.

1988 Jan 3 Wallinger-assisted tracks appear on O'Connor's debut album *The Lion And The Cobra*.

1989 Mar [6] Wallinger joins Peter Gabriel, Annie Lennox, The Edge and others for the *Greenpeace – Rainbow Warriors* album launch in Moscow, USSR.

While meticulously recording his second World Party album, Wallinger inks a management agreement with Cavallo, Ruffalo & Fargnoli, the US team which handles Prince.

1990 May [19] Critically raved and ecology-heavy *Goodbye Jumbo* makes UK #36 and begins slow US chart rise as World Party, with current touring line-up of Dave Catlin-Birch (guitar), Guy Chambers (keyboards), Max Edie (synthesizers) and Chris Sharrock (drums), sets off on a series of 4 alternate European and US live treks. Featuring O'Connor on backing vocals for *Sweet Soul Dream*, the album, once again edited from 70 mins. of music onto a 53 mins. 38 secs. set also includes appearances from Jeff Trott, Chris Whitten and Steve Wickham.

July [7] Extracted world-saving *Message In The Box*, which World Party will perform live at the forthcoming MTV Video Awards, makes UK #39.

Aug [18] *Goodbye Jumbo* peaks at US #73.

Sept [15] *Way Down Now* stalls at UK #66.

Dec [3] Band performs previously postponed gig at the Corn Exchange, Cambridge, Cambs., originally scheduled Oct.13.

[6] World Party participates in the Reims Music Festival, France.

1991 June 9-track World Party EP *Thank You World*, to include a cover version of the Beatles' *Happiness Is A Warm Gun* is due to be released.

XTC
Andy Partridge (guitar, vocals)
Colin Moulding (bass, vocals)
Barry Andrews (keyboards)
Terry Chambers (drums)

1977 Sept Partridge (b. Malta), Moulding and Chambers, all ex-members of Swindon, Wilts., based Star Park rock band, changing name to Helium Kidz at the height of the punk boom, are joined by ex-King Crimson keyboard player Barry Andrews. Having earlier auditioned for CBS Records, XTC signs to Virgin.

Oct EP *3-D* is released.

1978 Jan *White Music*, recorded in a week, makes UK #38, as the band is linked to the current popular UK new wave movement.

Feb *Statue Of Liberty* is released.

May *This Is Pop*, produced by Robert John Lange, is released.

Nov *Are You Receiving Me?* is an unsuccessful prelude to *Go Two* which reaches UK #21.

1979 Jan Andrews quits the band on its return from a 10-date US mini-tour. (He teams with Robert Fripp to form The League Of Gentlemen and to record as a soloist for Virgin.) The rest of the band approach long-time friend Dave Gregory as a replacement.

May *Life Begins At The Hop* peaks at UK #54. Andrews' first solo *Town And Country* is released.

July Band tours Australia, New Zealand and Japan.

Aug Third album *Drums And Wires* makes UK #34 as the band begins a brief UK tour.

Nov *Making Plans For Nigel* reaches UK #17.

'80 Feb Partridge releases John Leckie-produced solo *Takeaway/The Lure Of Salvage* under the name of Mr. Partridge. *Drums And Wires* climbs to US #176.

Mar *Wait Till Your Boat Goes Down* is released.

Sept Double A-side *Generals And Majors/Don't Lose Your Temper* makes UK #32. *Black Sea* reaches UK #16.

Oct *Towers Of London* makes UK #31.

Nov *Take This Town*, from "Times Square" movie soundtrack, released.

'81 Feb [21] *Sgt. Rock (Is Going To Help Me)* reaches UK #16. *Black Sea* reaches US #41.

Mar *Respectable Street* fails to chart, partly due to its ban on BBC radio for reference to Sony.

Group begins a tour of Venezuela, and will also tour US, the Middle East, South-East Asia and Australia during the year.

'82 Feb [20] *Senses Working Overtime*, their biggest success, hits UK #10.

[27] Double album **English Settlement**, produced by Hugh Padgham, hits UK #5.

Mar Partridge collapses on stage in Paris, France, from exhaustion.

Apr [10] *Ball And Chain* peaks at UK #58. Partridge collapses again (with a stomach ulcer), having given himself less than a month to recover from his earlier illness. He later claims it is "a phobia about being in front of people". A tour is cancelled and Chambers leaves.

May *No Thugs In Our House* is released.

[22] **English Settlement** makes US #48.

Nov Partridge announces the band will never play live again.

[20] *Waxworks – Some Singles (1977-1982)* peaks at UK #54.

'83 May *Great Fire* is released.

July *Wonderland* is released.

Aug *Mummer*, featuring songs written during Partridge's convalescence, makes UK #51. Pete Phipps (ex-Glitter Band) plays drums on tracks on which Chambers does not appear. Refusal to promote the album with live work causes friction between the band and Virgin. Geffen releases the album in US where it climbs to #145.

Oct *Love On A Farmboy's Wages* makes UK #50.

Nov XTC, as The Three Wise Men, releases *Thanks For Christmas*. Partridge begins producing other acts including Peter Blegvad (ex-Slapp Happy).

'84 Mar *Mummer* makes US #145.

Oct *The Big Express* makes UK #38 and US #178. Extracted *All You Pretty Girls* peaks at UK #55.

'85 Apr Mini-album *The Dukes Of Stratosphear: 25 O'Clock* is released by the group's psychedelic alter-ego, The Dukes Of Stratosphear.

'86 Oct *Skylarking*, produced by Todd Rundgren at his own Woodstock, NY studio and The Tubes' Soundhole studios in San Francisco, CA, stalls at UK #90. It will spend over 6 months on US chart, reaching #70 in 1987.

'87 Aug The second Dukes Of Stratosphear project, *Psonic Psunspots* and CD-only compilation *Chips From The Chocolate Fireball* are released. Remaining a trio, they continue to work as a studio band only, releasing both XTC and alias issues, including Partridge's singles as Buster Gonad and The Jolly Josticles.

'89 Feb *Mayor Of Simpleton* makes UK #46.

Mar [11] *Oranges And Lemons* reaches UK #28 and makes US #44, the group's most successful US album to date.

May [20] *The Mayor Of Simpleton* peaks at US #72.

'90 Nov Partridge-produced *Hands Across The Ocean*, released by the Mission, reaches UK #28.

HE YARDBIRDS

eith Relf (vocals, harmonica)
aul Samwell-Smith (bass)
hris Dreja (guitar)
m McCarty (drums)
nthony "Top" Topham (guitar)

'63 Relf (b. Mar.22, 1943, Richmond, London), Samwell-Smith (b. May 8, 1943, Richmond, London), Dreja (b. Nov.11, 1945, Surbiton, London), McCarty (b. July 25, 1943, Liverpool, Merseyside) and Topham (b. 1947), having met in local groups in the burgeoning London area R&B scene, come together at the Kingston Art School, London, initially as The Metropolitan Blues Quartet. They play pubs and clubs in the local Richmond area, before moving on to bigger London clubs. They take over the residency from The Rolling Stones at Giorgio Gomelsky's

Crawdaddy club. Topham leaves to return to college and is replaced by Eric Clapton (b. Eric Patrick Clapp, Mar.30, 1945, Ripley, Derbys.).

Dec Group is recorded backing Sonny Boy Williamson on UK tour.

1964 Feb Gomelsky takes demos to various labels. Decca turns them down, feeling it already has too many R&B bands. Group signs to EMI's Columbia label and cuts 3 songs at its first recording session.

[28] They play the first Rhythm & Blues Festival at the Town Hall, Birmingham, W. Midlands.

June Debut single, a revival of Billy Boy Arnold's *I Wish You Would*, fails to chart but gets exposure on TV and in pop press.

Sept Relf is rushed to hospital with a perforated lung.

Oct Despite a BBC ban, a revival of Don & Bob's R&B standard *Good Morning Little Schoolgirl* makes UK #44.

Dec Debut album, recorded live at the Marquee club in London, is *Five Little Yardbirds*.

[24] Group opens in "The Beatles Christmas Show" at London's Hammersmith Odeon. (Songwriter Graham Gouldman sees them, and writes *For Your Love* with them in mind. Clapton hates the song so much, he will leave the band.)

1965 Mar *For Your Love* is group's first major hit, at UK #3.

[13] Clapton leaves. He joins John Mayall's Bluesbreakers and Jeff Beck (b. June 24, 1944, Wallington, London) replaces him.

Apr [30] Group begins 21-date twice-nightly UK package tour, supporting The Kinks with Goldie & The Gingerbreads and others, at Adelphi cinema, Slough, Berks., ending May 23 at Gaumont cinema, Derby.

June *Heart Full Of Soul*, also written by Gouldman, hits UK #2. *For Your Love* hits US #6, while album *For Your Love* reaches US #96.

[20] Group supports The Beatles at the Olympia, Paris, France.

July [17] Group fails to turn up for a gig at the Birdcage, Southampton, Hants. The promoter announces his intention to ban them from nearly 50 clubs in South-East England.

Aug [6] The Yardbirds play on the opening day of the National Jazz & Blues Festival at the Athletic Ground, Richmond.

Sept *Heart Full Of Soul* hits US #9.

[2] Group is scheduled to fly to New York to start TV and radio tour, but is delayed because of work permit problems.

[23] They sing *Heart Full Of Soul* on US TV's "Shindig". Also featured is Raquel Welch singing *Dancing In The Street*.

Oct Double A-side *Evil Hearted You/Still I'm Sad* hits UK #3.

Nov [18] Group begins 16-date twice-nightly UK tour, with Manfred Mann, Paul & Barry Ryan, Inez & Charlie Foxx and others, at ABC cinema, Stockton, Cleveland, to end Dec.6 at Slough Adelphi.

[22] They miss the first show at Bradford Gaumont, after they are stranded on M1 motorway in a blizzard with a puncture.

Dec *I'm A Man* reaches US #17, and *Having A Rave Up With The Yardbirds*, including tracks from UK live album, makes US #53.

[15] Group begins 6-week US tour.

1966 Jan Fontana in UK releases *The Yardbirds With Sonny Boy Williamson*, recorded live in Dec.1963.

Mar *Shapes Of Things* hits UK #3.

Apr [1] Group stars in "Ready Steady Allez-Oops!" from the Locomotive in the Moulin Rouge, Paris.

[9] Beck collapses on stage during a gig in Marseilles, France. He is admitted to hospital with suspected meningitis. It is a false alarm, and he resumes playing with the band Apr.16 at Southport, Merseyside. *Shapes Of Things* reaches US #11, as group ends 5-year management agreement with Gomelsky. Simon Napier-Bell becomes new manager.

May [1] The Yardbirds take part in the annual **New Musical Express** Poll Winners Concert at the Empire Pool, Wembley, London. Relf's first solo, a cover of Bob Lind's *Mr. Zero* is released.

June Samwell-Smith leaves for a career as a producer; his replacement is UK session guitarist Jimmy Page (b. Apr.9, 1944, London). Dreja moves to bass, while Page shares lead duties with Beck. *Over Under Sideways Down* hits UK #10.

[21] Page makes his debut with the band at the Marquee in London.

July *Over Under Sideways Down* reaches US #11. Band releases its first studio album *Yardbirds*, which makes UK #20.

Aug [5] Group begins US tour in Minneapolis, MN. Tour ends Sept.4 in Honolulu, HI.

[22] Group guests on Dick Clark's "Where The Action Is" TV show.

Sept album *Over Under Sideways Down* makes US #52.

[23] The Yardbirds start the 12-date "Rolling Stones 66" tour with The Rolling Stones, Ike & Tina Turner, Long John Baldry and others, at the Royal Albert Hall, London. Tour ends Oct.9 at the Gaumont theater, Southampton.

Oct [28] Group embarks on a Dick Clark tour with Sam The Sham & The Pharaohs, Brian Hyland and others. Beck departs after first 2 gigs, to form a band with Rod Stewart and Ron Wood. Group continues as a 4-piece. *Happenings Ten Years Time Ago* makes UK #43.

Dec *Happenings Ten Years Time Ago* reaches US #30.

1967 Jan Columbia pairs the band in the studio with producer Mickie Most (but there will be no more UK hits), for first recordings as a 4-piece.

[22] Group begins tour of Australasia and Far East with Roy Orbison and The Walker Brothers at the Sydney Stadium, Australia.

Mar [11] After a disastrous opening night at the Granada cinema, Mansfield, Notts., Beck's new group pulls out of The Spencer Davis Group/Hollies tour. The Tremeloes replace them.

May [8] The Yardbirds appear at the Cannes Film Festival to coincide with their appearance in the film "Blow Up", playing *Stroll On*.

The Yardbirds' Greatest Hits reaches US #28, while Most-produced *Little Games* makes US #51.

Aug A cover of Manfred Mann's UK hit *Ha Ha Said The Clown* reaches US #45.

Sept Album *Little Games* makes US #80.

Nov *Ten Little Indians*, written by Harry Nilsson, makes US #96. Group successfully stops release of album *Little Games* in UK, though it appears in US despite their opposition.

Dec Group flies to New York for a gig at Madison Square Garden.

1968 Mar [30] The Yardbirds allow recording of a US gig at Anderson theater, New York, for possible release as live album by their US label, Epic, but retain final approval of the project. (On hearing the tapes, they convince the label not to issue it.)

July [7] Group splits. (Page forms The New Yardbirds (later to become Led Zeppelin), Dreja becomes a photographer. Relf and McCarty plan their own bands. Relf and sister Jane will form the nucleus of the first version of Renaissance.)

1970 Oct Compilation *The Yardbirds Featuring Performances By Jeff Beck, Eric Clapton, Jimmy Page* peaks at US #155.

1971 Epic releases the Mar.1969 concert album, but it is withdrawn when Page, now with Led Zeppelin, serves an injunction.

1975 Relf joins Armageddon.

1976 May [14] Relf dies, aged 33, electrocuted while playing guitar at home.

1977 McCarty joins Illusion.

1982 The Yardbirds' 1963 sessions with Sonny Boy Williamson are released on album, in Spain.

1983 June Dreja, McCarty and Samwell-Smith reunite for gigs at the Marquee club, London. Trio, augmented by John Fiddler as lead vocalist, forms new band, Box Of Frogs, and signs to Epic Records.

1984 June Box Of Frogs' *Back Where I Started* is released.

1989 McCarty, Eddie Phillips (ex-Creation), Ray Phillips (ex-Nashville Teens), Don Craine and Keith Grant (ex-Downliners Sect) form the British Invasion All-Stars, releasing *Regression*.

YAZOO

Alison Moyet (vocals)
Vince Clarke (keyboards)

1982 Jan Keyboard/synthesizer whizz Clarke (b. July 3, 1961), having left Depeche Mode after writing 3 hit singles and much of the group's first album, is looking for a singer to work with when he answers an ad placed by "Alf" Moyet (b. Genevieve Alison Moyet, June 18, 1961, Basildon, Essex) for a "rootsy blues band". Moyet has been a vocalist with UK Southend R&B acts like The Vicars and The Screaming Abdabs.

May *Only You*, on independent Mute label, which also handles Depeche Mode, hits UK #2.

July Follow-up *Don't Go* hits UK #3.

Sept Yazoo tours UK to promote debut album *Upstairs At Eric's*, which hits UK #2 in its week of entry. Moyet begins to write for the duo, which launches itself in US with a New York performance.

Oct *Situation* (UK B-side of *Only You*) reaches US #73. Duo has to go under the name Yaz in US, where a small record company has already registered the name Yazoo.

Nov *Upstairs At Eric's* peaks at US #92.

Dec *The Other Side Of Love* reaches UK #13.

1983 Feb [8] Duo wins Best British Newcomer at the second annual BRIT Awards at the Grosvenor House, London.

Mar *Only You* peaks at US #67.

June *Nobody's Diary* hits UK #3. It is announced that Yazoo will break up after completion of a second album, currently being recorded.

July [16] *You And Me Both* enters UK chart at #2 (behind Wham!'s

Fantastic), but rises to hit #1 the following week.

Sept *You And Me Both* peaks at US #69. (Both will go on to be successful: Moyet as a solo performer and Clarke as the instrumental half of 2 more Mute Records duos, Assembly and Erasure.)

YES

Jon Anderson (vocals)
Steve Howe (guitar)
Tony Kaye (keyboards)
Chris Squire (bass)
Bill Bruford (drums)

1968 June Anderson (b. Oct.25, 1944, Accrington, Lancs.) meets Squire (b. Mar.4, 1948, London) in a club in Soho, London. Anderson has worked in beat group The Warriors, who released 1 single for Decca in 1964, and has cut 2 solo singles for Parlophone in 1967. Squire has been in The Syn, which has recorded for Deram. They are joined by Kaye, ex-Federals, Bruford (b. May 17, 1948, London), ex-Savoy Brown and guitarist Peter Banks, also ex-The Syn, to form Yes.

Nov [26] They open Cream's farewell concert at London's Royal Albert Hall (which leads to a residency at London's Marquee).

1969 June Signed to Atlantic, first release *Sweetness* makes little impact.

Nov Debut album *Yes* features re-workings of The Beatles' *Every Little Thing* and The Byrds' *I See You*.

1970 Feb [7] Yes supports The Nice at the Royal Festival Hall, London.

Mar Banks is replaced by guitarist Steve Howe (b. Apr.8, 1947, London), who has played with The Syndicats, The In Crowd, Tomorrow and Bodast. (Banks will later form Flash.)

[21] Howe makes his first London appearance with the band at Queen Elizabeth Hall.

Aug *Time And A Word* makes UK #45.

1971 Apr *The Yes Album*, produced by Eddy Offord, hits UK #7 and is US chart debut at #40.

Aug Kaye leaves to form Badger, replaced by Rick Wakeman (b. May 18, 1949, London), ex-Strawbs, to give more flamboyant keyboard style.

Sept [30] Group begins 23-date UK tour at the De Montfort Hall, Leicester, Leics., ending Oct.28 at the Guildhall, Southampton, Hants.

Dec *Your Move* makes US #40 as *Fragile* hits UK #7 and US #4. It is the group's first album to feature the artwork of Roger Dean, who creates the Yes logo and the distinctive sci-fi fantasy style of future sleeves.

1972 Jan [14-15] Yes plays 2 nights at the Rainbow theater, London.

Feb [15] Group begins its third US tour at Providence, RI.

Apr *Roundabout* reaches US #13.

Aug Bruford quits to join King Crimson, and is replaced by ex-Plastic Ono Band and Happy Magazine drummer Alan White (b. June 14, 1949, Pelton, Durham).

Sept A revival of Paul Simon's *America* makes US #46, as *Close To The Edge* hits UK #4 and US #3.

Dec *And You And I (Part II)* makes US #42.

1973 Feb Wakeman releases solo *The Six Wives Of Henry VIII*, which hits UK #7 and US #30.

May 3 album set, *Yessongs*, of live shows from the previous year, hits UK #7 and US #12. (A movie is later released with the same name.)

Dec *Tales From Topographic Oceans* becomes first album to qualify for gold disk on ship-out sales.

1974 Jan Double album *Tales From Topographic Oceans*, based on the Shastric scriptures, tops UK chart for 2 weeks and hits US #6.

Feb [18] Yes plays the first of 2 nights at New York's Madison Square Garden.

May Wakeman's solo *Journey To The Centre Of The Earth* tops UK chart and hits US #3.

June [8] Wakeman announces he is leaving the band.

July Wakeman is admitted to hospital with suspected coronary pain.

Aug [18] Ex-Refugee member Patrick Moraz (b. June 24, 1948, Morges, Switzerland) replaces Wakeman.

Nov *Relayer* hits UK #4 and US #5, with *The Gates Of Delirium*, based on Tolstoy's **War And Peace**, on side 1. Movie "Yessongs" is released.

1975 Mar *Yesterdays*, including tracks from the first 2 albums, reaches UK #27 and US #17.

Apr Wakeman hits US #2 and US #21 with *The Myths And Legends Of King Arthur And The Knights Of The Round Table*.

Nov Solo albums by Howe (*Beginnings* – UK #22 and US #63) and Squire (*Fish Out Of Water* – UK #25 and US #69), both have chart success, as Yes takes much of the year off from group activities.

1976 Mar White makes UK #41 with *Ramshackled*.

Apr Moraz's eponymous solo album makes US #28 and US #132. No

Earthly Connection, by Wakeman, hits UK #9 and US #67.

July Anderson's *Olias Of Sunhillow* hits UK #8 and US #47.

Nov Band re-forms, with Wakeman rejoining, taking Moraz's place. (Moraz will join The Moody Blues in 1978.)

1977 **Feb** Wakeman's music for 1976 Innsbruck Winter Olympics, *White Rock* makes UK #14 and US #126.

July Moraz solo *Out In The Sun* makes UK #44.

Aug *Going For The One* tops UK chart for 2 weeks and hits US #8. Group plays a week of sell-out performances at Madison Square Garden, the Coliseum, New Haven, CT, and the Boston Garden, Boston, MA.

Sept *Wonderous Stories* hits UK #7.

Nov *Going For The One* reaches UK #24.

Dec Wakeman has support from Squire and White for *Criminal Record*, which reaches UK #25 and US #128.

1978 **Sept** *Don't Kill The Whale* makes UK #36 as parent album *Tormato* hits UK #8 and US #10.

1979 **June** Wakeman's solo *Rhapsodies* makes UK #25 and US #170.

Nov Howe's second solo album *Steve Howe Album* reaches UK #68 and US #164.

1980 **Feb** Anderson teams with Greek keyboardist Vangelis Papathanassiou as Jon & Vangelis for *I Hear You Now*, which hits UK #8. Parent *Short Stories* hits UK #4.

Mar In an unexpected move both Anderson and Wakeman leave the band after an attempt to record a new album is abandoned.

May *Jon & Vangelis* makes US #125.

[18] The 2 members of Buggles, Trevor Horn (b. July 15, 1949), on vocals and guitar and Geoff Downes on keyboards, join Yes.

Aug The first release with the new line-up, *Drama* hits UK #2 and US #18. (1 of the tracks (and US single) *Into The Lens* is later re-recorded by Buggles as *I Am A Camera*.)

Sept Jon & Vangelis' *I Hear You Now* peaks at US #58.

[4-6] Group sells out more shows than any other in history when it plays 3 nights at New York's Madison Square Garden.

[18] Wakeman embarks on solo tour at Newcastle City Hall,Tyne & Wear, through to Oct.2 at the Guildford Civic Hall, London.

Nov Anderson's solo *Song Of Seven* reaches UK #38 and US #143.

1981 **Jan** Double live *Yesshows*, recorded between 1976 and 1978, reaches UK #22 and US #43.

Apr [18] Group's break-up is officially confirmed when Squire and White join ex-Led Zeppelin members Robert Plant and Jimmy Page in rehearsals, which eventually come to nothing.

June Wakeman's *1984* reaches UK #24.

July Jon & Vangelis' *The Friends Of Mr. Cairo* hits UK #6 and peaks at US #64.

1982 **Jan** Jon & Vangelis hit UK #6 with *I'll Find My Way Home*.

Mar Buggles re-form. (Downes will leave to form Asia with Howe.)

June *I'll Find My Way Home* stalls at US #51 as Anderson's solo *Animation* makes UK #43 and US #176.

Sept *Classic Yes* makes US #142. Squire and White form new band Cinema. They invite South African guitarist Trevor Rabin to join. Kaye also later joins. They cut several tracks with Rabin on vocals but, dissatisfied with the results, the group approaches Anderson to join. Band, now virtually Yes, changes name from Cinema.

1983 **July** *He Is Smiling*, by Jon & Vangelis, peaks at UK #61. Parent *Private Collection* reaches UK #22 and US #148.

Oct Yes comeback single, *Owner Of A Lonely Heart*, released on Atlantic subsidiary Atco, reaches UK #28. It takes a new direction musically, abandoning the "pomp-rock" tradition in favor of newer "producer-pop" sounds as defined by Horn. Horn decides against joining the band, but remains producer.

Nov *90125*, named after its international catalog number, makes UK #16 and hits US #5.

1984 **Jan** *Owner Of A Lonely Heart* tops the US chart.

Mar *Leave It* reaches UK #24.

Apr *Leave It* reaches US #24.

July *It Can Happen* peaks at US #51.

Aug Jon & Vangelis' *State Of Independence* (later to perform better as a Donna Summer cover version) peaks at US #67 as compilation *The Best Of Jon And Vangelis* makes UK #42.

Oct Wakeman teams with Kevin Peek for *Beyond The Planets*, which climbs to UK #64.

1985 **Feb** [26] Yes wins Best Rock Instrumental Performance for *Cinema*, a track from *90125*, at the 27th annual Grammy awards.

Dec Anderson releases seasonal *3 Ships* featuring a mix of new songs with traditional carols.

1986 **Mar** Issued in US 4 months earlier, live mini-album *9012 Live: The Solos* makes UK #44.

Apr Anderson provides guest vocals on Mike Oldfield's *Shine*.

May Anderson contributes vocals to Tangerine Dream's *Legend*, which makes US #96.

July [12] GTR, a 5-piece UK rock band with Steve Howe, ex-Genesis Steve Hackett and Max Bacon, reaches US #14 with *When The Heart Rules The Mind*. Parent album *GTR* reaches US #11.

Sept [6] GTR's *The Hunter* makes US #85.

1987 **May** [16] Wakeman's *The Gospels* spends a week on UK chart at #94.

Oct [3] *Love Will Find A Way* peaks at UK #73 as new album *The Big Generator* makes UK #17 and US #15.

[20] Yes begins a 2-month US tour at the Civic Center, Peoria, IL.

Nov [28] *Love Will Find A Way* reaches US #30.

1988 **Feb** [6] *Rhythm Of Love* makes US #40.

Aug Anderson's solo *In The City Of Angels* is released.

Nov Anderson joins Steve Harley and Mike Batt on charity single *Whatever You Believe*.

1989 **June** Anderson, Bruford, Wakeman & Howe's *Brother Of Mine* peaks at UK #63.

July *Anderson Bruford Wakeman Howe* reaches UK #14 and US #30.

[29] Anderson, Bruford, Wakeman & Howe begin 36-date US tour at the Mud Island Amphitheater, Memphis, TN. The tour will end Sept.11 in Concord, CA.

1991 Fully re-formed Yes, now over-riding recent legal disputes over use of band name, and including Hare, Kaye, Anderson, Squire, White and Wakeman, embarks on "Yesshows", a lengthy world tour which will include UK dates at the Birmingham NEC, W.Midlands, June 25 and London's Wembley Arena June 28-29.

May During the band's comeback world tour, new Arista album *Union* is released.

NEIL YOUNG

1965 Having spent 3 years playing the Canadian and border folk club circuit as Neil Young & The Squires, during which time he met fellow musician Stephen Stills, Young (b. Nov.12, 1945, Toronto, Canada) drives to Los Angeles in his 1953 Pontiac hearse to link with Stills. This follows a 1 disk stint with Detroit band, The Mynah Birds, whose lead singer is Rick James.

1966 **Mar** Stills, Young and Richie Furay form electric folk band Buffalo Springfield which begins 2 years of overnight US success.

1968 **May** [5] Buffalo Springfield plays it final gig in Long Beach, CA.

1969 **Jan** Signed to Reprise as a solo, Young releases unsuccessful debut *Neil Young*, with session help from Jack Nitzsche and Ry Cooder.

May With hastily-formed backing band Crazy Horse (Danny Whitten on guitar, Ralph Molina on drums, Billy Talbot on bass and producer arranger Nitzsche), Young releases follow-up *Everybody Knows This Is Nowhere*, which begins a long climb to US #34 (to earn a gold disk).

July [25] Young plays his first concert with Crosby, Stills & Nash at New York's Fillmore East. He is asked to join the trio initially for live work (but will record with them over the next 20 years).

1970 **Mar** Crosby, Stills, Nash & Young release debut *Déjà Vu*, which will become the year's best-selling US album and confirm each member as a rock superstar.

June *Cinnamon Girl*, from Young and Crazy Horse, rises to US #55 in the wake of CSN&Y's popularity. Young is working on the soundtrack to movie "Landlord" and is also having a studio installed underneath his Topanga Canyon, CA home. He pens *Ohio* for CSN&Y, about the recent Kent State University killings.

Sept Although continuing to tour with CSN&Y, Young releases solo *After The Goldrush* which climbs to hit US #8 and UK #7. It features Crazy Horse members, and Nils Lofgren and Stills.

Dec *Only Love Can Break Your Heart* makes US #33.

1971 **Jan** [6] Young returns to Canada to perform at the Queen Elizabeth theater, Vancouver, Canada.

Apr *When You Dance I Can Really Love* stalls at US #93.

Aug Young, still touring with CSN&Y, begins work on scoring music for his movie "Journey Through The Past." He also splits from wife Susan and begins a relationship with actress Carrie Snodgress.

1972 **Mar** Fourth solo album *Harvest* is released and will hit both US and UK #1. An acoustic set, it includes US #1 and UK #10 *Heart Of Gold* and orchestral-backed ballad *A Man Needs A Maid* written about Snodgress. The album also features James Taylor and Linda Ronstadt.

June *Old Man* makes US #31.

July On a one-off union with Graham Nash, *War Song* peaks at US #61.

Sept [8] Snodgress gives birth to a son, Zeke.

Nov Double album *Journey Through The Past*, chronicling live recordings with Buffalo Springfield, CSN&Y, The Stray Gators and Crazy Horse, is released and will make US #45. Only new song is side 4's *Soldier*.

[18] Crazy Horse member, 29-year-old Whitten, dies from a heroin overdose.

1973 **Jan** [5] Young begins a 3-month 65-city US tour with The Stray Gators.
[23] Young stops in the middle of New York concert to announce accord had been reached for Vietnam peace.

Mar Young & The Stray Gators play a sold-out date at New York's Carnegie Hall.

Apr [8] Young's autobiographical documentary film "Journey Through The Past" premieres to mixed reactions at the US Film Festival in Dallas, TX.

Aug Young mixes all the tracks for his future *Tonight's The Night*, with songs recorded throughout the year with new Crazy Horse line-up Molina, Talbot, Lofgren and Ben Keith.

Sept [20] Young & Crazy Horse open Los Angeles' Roxy theater, the first of 4 nights.

Oct *Time Fades Away*, featuring more collaboration from guests David Crosby and Graham Nash, begins a rise to US #22 and UK #20.

1974 **June** Young is persuaded to reunite with CS&N to embark on a major US tour which grosses $8 million.

Aug [3] CSN&Y top the bill, ahead of The Beach Boys, Joe Walsh, Jesse Colin Young and The Band in their last 70s gig together.
Walk On peaks at US #69 as parent album *On The Beach* is released and will reach US #16 and UK #42. It includes later Young-favored 9-min. *Ambulance Blues*.

1975 **July** Dedicated to Danny Whitten and a late CSN&Y roadie Bruce Berry, *Tonight's The Night* is issued. Recorded "live" in the studio with no overdubbing, it will reach US #25 and UK #48.

Oct [13] Young undergoes a successful throat operation.
Dec *Zuma* reaches UK #44 and US #25. Its closing song unites CSN&Y on *Through My Sails*.

1976 **Oct** Young links with Stills to release *Long May You Run* (US #26 and UK #12). With 5 Young songs and 4 by Stills, they are backed by the Stills-Young band, Joe Lala, Jerry Aiello, George Perry and Joe Vitale.

Nov [25] Young takes part in The Band's farewell "The Last Waltz" Thanksgiving Day concert at San Francisco's Winterland, singing *Helpless* with Joni Mitchell and joining in an all-star cast on *I Shall Be Released*, directly after concluding a 6-week US tour.

1977 **July** *American Stars'N'Bars* is released, reaching US #21 and UK #17. It includes unissued studio tracks from the past 3 years and vocal spots by Emmylou Harris, Linda Ronstadt and Nicolette Larson.

Nov [11-13] Young celebrates his 32nd birthday performing with 24-piece Gone With The Wind band at the Miami Music Festival of the Arts in front of 125,000 people.

Dec 3-disk compilation *Decade* makes US #43 and UK #46. It chronicles Young's work from Buffalo Springfield, CSN&Y and solo material.

1978 **Oct** As *Comes A Time* is released, hitting US #7 and UK #42, Young and Crazy Horse embark on a major "Rust Never Sleeps" tour. It has replaced earlier project "Human Highway", a live documentary film including Cleveland-based new wave act Devo.

Nov He plays sold-out dates at New York's Madison Square Garden.

1979 **Mar** With harmony vocal by Nicolette Larson, *Four Strong Winds*, written by Ian Tyson, peaks at US #61 and UK #57.

July [11] Film "Rust Never Sleeps" premieres in Los Angeles. It is directed by Young under the pseudonym Bernard Shakey and is released simultaneously with an album of the same name, which will hit US #8 and UK #13. 1 side of the album is electric, the other features acoustic numbers, all backed by latest Crazy Horse line-up, Lofgren (guitar), Keith (pedal steel and keyboards), Bruce Palmer (bass), Molina (drums) and Joe Lala (percussion).

Nov Title cut *Rust Never Sleeps (Hey, Hey, My My (Into The Black))* stalls at US #79.

Dec Double live *Live Rust* reaches US #15 and UK #55. New York magazine **The Village Voice** names Young "Artist Of The Decade".

1980 **Nov** Dispensing with Crazy Horse and recruiting top session help, including The Band's drummer Levon Helm, Young releases *Hawks And Doves*, which will reach US #30 and UK #34.

1981 **Nov** Young's 17th album *Re-ac-tor* reaches US #27 and UK #69 and is his last for Reprise label.

1982 **Jan** *Southern Pacific* peaks at US #70 as "Human Highway" movie, starring Dean Stockwell, Russ Tamblyn and Devo is released.

Aug Young and Crazy Horse begin European and Australian tours.

1983 **Jan** *Trans*, his first for Geffen Records and recorded in Hawaii, reaches US #19 and UK #29.

Feb *Little Thing Called Love* peaks at US #71.

Mar [4] Young collapses from exhaustion during his US tour.

Sept Unexpected rockabilly *Everybody's Rockin'*, credited to Neil Young & The Shocking Pinks, makes US #46 and US #50.

Dec The David Geffen Co. seeks $3 million in punitive and exemplary damages plus compensation from Young in a Los Angeles Superior Court. The suit alleges that Young provided albums "which were not commerical in nature and musically uncharacteristic of Young's previous records".

1985 **Sept** *Old Ways* makes US #75 and UK #39.

1986 **Aug** *Landing On Water* is released, making US #46 and UK #52, but with no hit singles.

1987 **July** *Life* peaks at US #75 and UK #71.

Sept [19] Young participates in Farm Aid II benefit with John Cougar Mellencamp, Joe Walsh, Lou Reed and others at the University of Nebraska's Memorial Stadium.

1988 **May** *This Note's For You*, with 9-piece Bluenotes on reactivated Reprise label, makes US #61 and UK #56. The accompanying video, featuring Michael Jackson-lookalike with hair on fire (as Pepsi commercial) is initially banned on US TV.

Nov After a 14-year gap, Young reunites with CS&N to record *American Dream*, which will reach US #16 in 1989.

1989 Various artists album *The Bridge: A Tribute To Neil Young*, an album of Neil Young songs (*After The Goldrush* by The Flaming Lips, *Helpless* by Nick Cave) with a portion of the proceeds going to the Bridge School, a San Franciscan special-education facility.

Aug At end of set at Greek theater, Los Angeles, Young is joined by Crosby and Nash to perform *Ohio*.

Sept [6] "This Note's For You" wins Best Video Of The Year at the sixth annual MTV Music Video Awards ceremony at the Universal Amphitheater, Los Angeles.

Oct *Freedom* reaches US #35.

1990 **Mar** [8] *Freedom* is chosen **Rolling Stone** 1989 Critics' Award for Best Album.

Apr [16] Young participates in the "Nelson Mandela – An International Tribute To A Free South Africa" concert at Wembley Stadium, London.

Oct Young is joined by Elvis Costello, Jackson Browne, Edie Brickell, Chris Isaak and Steve Miller at his fourth annual Bridge School benefit held at the Shoreline Amphitheater near San Francisco, CA. *Ragged Glory* makes US #31 and UK #15.

1991 **Feb** Young embarks on US tour with Social Distortion and Sonic Youth.

PAUL YOUNG

1976 While serving an apprenticeship at Vauxhall car plant, Young (b. Jan.17, 1956, Luton, Beds.), having been encouraged by his parents, Doris and Tony, to play piano at school (at age 14 changing to learn the bass), has played in 2 local bands, one of which is locally popular Kat Kool and The Kool Kats.

1977 He forms rock group Streetband, with Roger Kelly, John Gifford, Mick Pearl and Vince Chaulk (from Mr. Big) and signs to Logo Records.

1978 **Nov** *Toast*, B-side of *Hold On*, produced by Chaz Jankel, makes UK #18 on the strength of its novelty appeal. Young loses his voice for the first time.

1979 **Sept** Streetband splits up after 4 singles and 2 albums (*London* and *Dilemma*) fail. Some members, including Young as lead vocalist, form 8-piece group Q Tips.

1980 **Jan** Gaining a reputation as a live combo, Q Tips opens for US band The Knack at London's Dominion theater.

May Group signs to Chrysalis UK.

Aug *Q Tips* charts for 1 week at UK #50. (This will be Q Tips' only chart appearance despite a string of covers including *Tears Of A Clown* and *Love Hurts*.)

1982 **Sept** After playing over 700 gigs in 2 years, the band quits following the release of *Live At Last*. Young signs a solo deal with CBS.

Nov He releases debut single *Iron Out The Rough Spots* which fails. A production association with Laurie Latham is established.

1983 **Jan** He releases an unsuccessful cover of Nicky Thomas' hit *Love Of The Common People* and assembles a backing group called The Royal Family, with ex-Q Tips and songwriting partner, Ian Kewley (keyboards), Mark Pinder (drums), Pino Palladino (bass), Steve Bolton (guitar) and backing vocalists Maz and Kim (The Fabulous Wealthy Tarts).

July A cover of Marvin Gaye's *Wherever I Lay My Hat (That's My Home)* is nominated **New Musical Express** single of the week and shoots to UK #1. *No Parlez*, featuring his first 3 singles and covers, including Joy Division's *Love Will Tear Us Apart*, also hits UK #1.

Sept Young begins his first headlining solo UK tour with The Royal Family.

Oct *Come Back And Stay* hits UK #4. *Wherever I Lay My Hat (That's My Home)* reaches US #70.

Nov *Love Of The Common People* is re-released and hits UK #2.

984 Jan He completes an 8-city US tour.

Feb [21] Young is named Best British Newcomer at the third annual BRIT Awards at the Grosvenor House, London.

Mar [17] He takes part in the second annual Prince's Trust Rock Gala at the Royal Albert Hall, London.

Apr *No Parlez* peaks at US #79 and *Come Back And Stay* makes US #22.

June *Love Of The Common People* reaches US #45. Non-stop touring takes in Australia and Japan as *No Parlez* heads towards world sales of 7 million.

July *No Parlez* achieves triple platinum status in UK.

Aug Young's voice goes for second time and a 2-month rest is ordered. *Retrospective Streetband Featuring Paul Young* is released on Cambra Records.

Sept Fabulous Wealthy Tarts leave The Royal Family, as does guitarist Bolton. A new singing trio is added to the backing group: George Chandler, Tony Jackson and Jimmy Chambers.

Nov A UK tour begins as his cover of Ann Peebles' *I'm Gonna Tear Your Playhouse Down* hits UK #9.

Dec *Everything Must Change* is his first self-written hit at UK #9.

985 Feb [11] Young wins Best British Male Artist at the fourth annual BRIT Awards at the Grosvenor House, Mayfair, London.

Mar In search of US success, Young covers Hall & Oates' *Every Time You Go Away*. (It will hit US #1 in July and UK #4.)

Apr Second album *The Secret Of Association* hits UK #1 and makes US #19.

July *Tomb Of Memories* makes UK #16 as he prepares for a 6-month world tour.

[13] Young duets with Alison Moyet, singing *That's The Way Love Is*, in the Live Aid concert at Wembley Stadium, London.

Sept *I'm Gonna Tear Your Playhouse Down* peaks at US #13.

986 Jan [11] *Everything Must Change* peaks at US #56.

Feb [10] Young wins Best British Music Video for "Every Time You Go Away" at the fifth annual BRIT Awards at the Grosvenor House.

June [20] Young participates in the fourth annual Prince's Trust Rock Gala at the Wembley Arena, with Paul McCartney, Elton John, Tina Turner and Phil Collins.

Oct Young concentrates on his own compositions and *Wonderland*, from the forthcoming album, peaks at UK #24.

Nov *Between The Fires* is released in UK and US. It hits UK #4 but charts briefly, and peaks at US #77. Taken from the album, *Some People* makes UK #56.

Dec [13] *Some People* peaks at US #65.

987 Feb Young moves to Jersey for tax purposes as third extract from *Between The Fires*, *Why Does A Man Have To Be Strong* reaches UK #63, and begins an 18-month period of relative inactivity, devoting much of his time to his young daughter, who he names Levi, after The Four Tops' lead singer.

Young takes part in the annual Prince's Trust Rock Gala, duetting with Phil Collins on *You've Lost That Lovin' Feelin'*.

988 June [11] He takes time off from recording a new album to sing a cover of Crowded House's hit *Don't Dream It's Over* at "Nelson Mandela's 70th Birthday Party" at Wembley Stadium.

990 May Revival of The Congregation's 1971 UK #4 *Softly Whispering I Love You* reaches UK #21.

June Fourth solo album *Other Voices* hits UK #4 and will make US #142 in Sept.

July *Oh Girl*, reviving The Chi-Lites classic, reaches UK #25.

Oct [6] *Oh Girl* returns Young to US prominence, hitting #8, as MC Hammer's remake of another Chi-Lites' classic, *Have You Seen Her?*, is also charted. *Heaven Can Wait* stalls at UK #71.

991 Young duets with Clannad on a version of *Both Sides Now*, featured in Blake Edwards' film "Switch".

THE (YOUNG) RASCALS

Felix Cavaliere (vocals, keyboards)
Eddie Brigati (vocals, percussion)
Gene Cornish (guitar)
Dino Danelli (drums)

1964 Feb Group forms as a trio, comprising ex-Joey Dee & The Starliters Cavaliere (b. Nov.29, 1944, Pelham, New York, NY), Brigati (b. Oct.22, 1946, Garfield, NJ) and Cornish (b. May 14, 1945, Rochester, NY), in Garfield, and first gigs as a rock/R&B trio are at local Choo Choo club. Shortly after, Danelli (b. July 23, 1945, New York), an old friend of Cavaliere's (they have been in Sandu Scott & Her Scotties together) who has played jazz with Lionel Hampton and in various New York and Las Vegas club house bands, joins on drums. Quartet becomes The Rascals.

July The Rascals become the resident band at the Barge, a floating, fashionable nightclub off Southampton, Long Island, NY. A 45-min. act of familiar and self-penned R&B, interspersed with rock oldies, is honed, with the group wearing choirboy shirts and knickerbockers.

Aug New York promoter Sid Bernstein becomes interested in the group, and takes over as manager. He turns down offers from Red Bird and Phil Spector's Philles Records, and signs them (now as The Young Rascals and minus the uniforms) to Atlantic for a $10,000 advance.

1965 Aug [15] They play on The Beatles bill at Shea Stadium, New York. They then play a 4-week engagement at New York's Harlow club.

1966 Jan Debut single *I Ain't Gonna Eat Out My Heart Anymore*, written by Pam Sawyer and Lori Burton, and heavily supported (due to the group's overtly black sound) by R&B radio stations, reaches US #52.

Apr *Good Lovin'* (a Rudy Clark/Artie Resnick song, originally an R&B hit for The Olympics in 1965) tops US chart for a week, and is group's first million-seller.

July *You Better Run*, first self-penned A-side (by Cavaliere and Brigati), reaches US #20. Debut album *The Young Rascals*, heavy on R&B cover versions from the group's stage act, reaches US #15. (It will earn a gold disk in an 84-week chart stay.)

Oct Cavaliere's composition *Come On Up* makes US #43.

Nov [29] Group arrives in UK for brief visit which will include appearances on "Ready, Steady, Go!" and "Saturday Club" and a live appearance on Dec.1 at Blaises, London, before flying to Paris, France, on their way home to the US.

1967 Mar *I've Been Lonely Too Long*, another Cavaliere/Brigati collaboration with a Motown dance feel (aiding it considerably on R&B chart), makes US #16. *Collections* reaches US #14, and is group's second gold album.

May *Groovin'*, the first self-produced by the group (with assistance from Atlantic's Tom Dowd and Arif Mardin), signals a move towards a more uniquely Young Rascals sound than their R&B, fusing Latin influences and a cool jazz sensitivity. Written by Cavaliere and Brigati (and a euphemism for Sunday afternoon sex, according to the former), it tops US chart for 4 weeks, selling 2 million copies.

July *Groovin'* is group's UK chart debut, hitting #8.

Aug *A Girl Like You* hits US #10 and makes UK #37 (the group's UK chart swan song).

Sept *Groovin'*, featuring the previous 2 singles and the forthcoming release, hits US #4 and earns group's third gold album.

Oct *How Can I Be Sure* is another change of pace, inspired by romance in Cavaliere's life (he will marry shortly), wrapped in a loping arrangement with French accordian and strings. It hits US #4.

[4] Group embarks on UK tour, with Traffic, at Finsbury Park Astoria, London.

1968 Jan Psychedelia-inflected *It's Wonderful* reaches US #20. Group has become absorbed in the "Summer Of Love" philosophy, and Cavaliere adopts Indian philosopher Swami Satchidananda as his guru, with the whole group becoming involved in the latter's Integral Yoga Institute.

Mar On tour in Florida, the group's trailer breaks down outside Fort Pierce, and The Young Rascals encounter heavy anti-rock and racist harassment from rednecks. In response to this, they announce they will play no further live bills which do not include at least 1 black act.

Apr *Once Upon A Dream*, an effects-laden concept album in *It's Wonderful*-style, hits US #9. While on tour, Cavaliere is admitted to San Diego hospital, CA with an internal complaint keeping him hospitalized for 2 weeks. Remaining West Coast dates are cancelled.

May Group persuades Atlantic to drop the "Young" from its name, and *A Beautiful Morning* appears as by The Rascals. Their third million-selling single, it hits US #3.

Aug *People Got To Be Free* tops US chart for 5 weeks, becoming their fourth and last million-selling single. Written by Cavaliere and Brigati, the song is the former's reaction to the assassinations of Martin Luther King and Robert Kennedy earlier in the year.

Sept Compilation *Time Peace/The Rascals' Greatest Hits* tops US chart for a week. It earns a gold disk for a half million sales and will stay on chart for 58 weeks.

Dec *A Ray Of Hope*, the last Rascals A-side co-written by Brigati and Cavaliere, is a deliberate sequel to *People Got To Be Free*, and is dedicated to Senator Edward Kennedy (who responds with an appreciative letter to the group). It reaches US #24.

1969 **Mar** *Heaven*, penned by Cavaliere (as are the remainder of the group's chart hits) in waltz-time, makes US #39.

May Double *Freedom Suite* reaches US #17. Included is wholly instrumental *Music Music*, a new departure for the group.

June *See* reaches US #27.

[20] The Rascals play the 3-day Newport 69 Rock Festival at Northridge, CA, alongside Jimi Hendrix, Jethro Tull, Creedence Clearwater Revival and many others.

Oct *Carry Me Back* reaches US #26.

1970 **Jan** [28] Group takes part in a 7-hour benefit concert at New York's Madison Square Garden, along with Judy Collins, Peter, Paul & Mary, and others, for the Vietnam Moratorium Committee.

Feb *See* makes US #45 while, from it, *Hold On* peaks at US #51. The album is the last to feature Brigati, who leaves following a lengthy period of dissension within the group.

Aug Gospel-flavored *Glory Glory*, with vocal backing from The Sweet Inspirations, peaks at US #58.

1971 **Mar** *Search And Nearness* charts for just 1 week at US #198. It is the last album to feature Cornish, who leaves after it is recorded. He and Brigati are replaced by Buzzy Feiten (guitar) and Robert Popwell (bass). Classically-trained vocalist Ann Sutton also joins, expanding the line-up to a quintet. Its contract expired, the group leaves Atlantic for a $1 million-plus offer from CBS/Columbia.

July *Love Me* creeps to US #95, the group's only Singles chart entry on Columbia, and its final US Top 100 single. It is taken from debut Columbia album *Peaceful World* which makes US #122.

1972 **May** *The Island Of Real* stalls at US #180. Soon after, group disbands.

Dec Cornish and Danelli form Bulldog, with John Turk (vocals and keyboards), Eric Thorngren (guitar) and Billy Hocher (bass). Signed to Decca, they chart in US with *No* (#44) and *Bulldog* (#176), but this initial impetus is not followed up, and the group will split. (Brigati is engaged mostly on session work, while Cavaliere concentrates on production, notably with Laura Nyro.)

1974 Cavaliere signs to Bearsville Records as a solo artist, releasing Todd Rundgren-produced *Felix Cavaliere*, which does not chart.

1975 **Sept** Second Cavaliere solo *Destiny* also fails to sell.

1976 Brigati records *Brigati* for Elektra with his brother David, including a disco-style version of *Groovin'*.

1978 **May** Cornish and Danelli are reunited in Fotomaker and with Atlantic. *Where Have You Been All My Life* peaks at US #81, *Fotomaker* at US #88.

Dec Fotomaker's *Miles Away* makes US #63, but is group's last chart success. (2 further albums, *Vis A Vis* and *Transfer Station*, will follow in 1979 before the band splits.)

1980 **Apr** Cavaliere has his only solo hit with *Only A Lonely Heart Sees*, on Epic, which makes US #36. It is taken from *Castles In The Air*, which does not chart.

1982 Danelli joins Steve Van Zandt's Little Steven & The Disciples Of Soul.

1988 Without Brigati, group re-forms for a "Good Lovin' 88" US tour. (*Good Lovin'* has recently been featured in a highly-rated episode of US TV series "Moonlighting".)

1989 Danelli and Cornish sue Cavaliere to prevent him from calling his band The Young Rascals. New York judge rules that Danelli and Cornish can call themselves The New Rascals and Cavaliere "formerly of The Young Rascals."

THE YOUNGBLOODS

Jesse Colin Young (guitar, bass, vocals)
Jerry Corbitt (guitar, vocals)
Banana (keyboards, guitars)
Joe Bauer (drums)

1964 Young (b. Perry Miller, Nov.11, 1944, New York, NY), is working as a folk singer in New York when he meets singer/writer Bobby Scott, who helps him strike a one-off deal with Capitol to record solo *The Soul Of A City Boy*.

1965 Young moves to Boston, MA, to play the club circuit. His second solo album, *Youngblood*, on Mercury, like the first does not chart. He teams

with Corbitt (b. Tifton, GA), to form The Youngbloods, recording for Mercury. Banana (b. Lowell Levinger, 1946, Cambridge, MA) from The Trolls and ex-jazz drummer Bauer (b. Sept.26, 1941, Memphis, TN) join

1966 Group performs as a house band at New York's Café A-Go-Go, signing to RCA after Young has cleared his Mercury contract. (Mercury will release *Two Trips*, made up of existing recordings, in 1970.)

1967 **Feb** *Grizzly Bear* is taken from the group's eponymous debut RCA album, and peaks at US #52. Album also includes the group's trademark song, the Dino Valenti-penned *Get Together*.

Apr *The Youngbloods* reaches US #131.

Oct *Get Together* reaches US #62. *Earth Music* is released without charting. Corbitt leaves for a solo career and the group continues as a trio and moves to Marin County, CA.

1968 **Sept** [2] Group appears at 3-day Sky River Rock Festival and Lighter-Than-Air Fair, in Sultan, WA, with Santana, The Grateful Dead, Muddy Waters, Country Joe & The Fish and others, including Dino Valenti as a soloist.

1969 **Sept** *Get Together*, is used as the theme for the National Council Of Christians And Jews, and becomes a major seller, hitting US #5. Group is scheduled to sing it on NBC TV's "Tonight" with Johnny Carson, but walks off the set after being unhappy with the technical arrangements. *Elephant Mountain* makes US #118.

1970 **Mar** In UK, where The Youngbloods have made no impact, *Get Together* is covered by The Dave Clark Five as *Everybody Get Together* and hits US #8.

May *Darkness, Darkness* is a disappointing follow-up, reaching US #86.

June Group signs to Warner Bros. in a new deal which allows it to form its own label, Raccoon.

Oct RCA starts repackaging of the group's earlier work with *The Best Of The Youngbloods*, which reaches US #144.

Nov First Raccoon label album *Rock Festival*, a mixture of live and studio material, reaches US #80.

1971 Michael Kane joins on bass, allowing Young to revert to guitar.

Aug *Ride The Wind*, consisting of material recorded live in New York in 1969, reaches US #157. *Sunlight*, another compilation of earlier tracks, makes US #186.

Dec *Good 'N' Dusty*, consisting of oldies covers, reaches US #160.

1972 **Apr** After the group disbands, Young's solo *Together* reaches US #157. Banana releases *Mid Mountain Ranch* (as Banana And The Bunch), and Bauer releases experimental *Moonset*. (Bauer and Banana will team with Kane to form the band Noggins, and release an album, *Crab Tunes*. Young will produce solo albums for Michael Hurley. Corbitt will produce Don McLean's debut *Tapestry*).

Dec The last group album *High On A Ridgetop* reaches US #185.

1973 **Dec** Young solo *Song For Juli* reaches US #51. It is released on Warner Bros.; the Raccoon label no longer exists.

1974 **Feb** Reissue of Young's 1964 *The Soul Of A City Boy* reaches US #172. Though scoring no more hit singles, Young will have a consistently successful US solo chart career with a string of hit albums: *Light Shine* (#37 June 1974); *Songbird* (#26 May 1975); *On The Road* (#34 May 1976); *Love On The Wing* (#64 Apr.1977); *American Dreams* (#165 Dec.1978).

1979 **Sept** Young appears with Bruce Springsteen, Jackson Browne and The Doobie Brothers and others, in anti-nuclear MUSE (Musicians United For Safe Energy) concerts at Madison Square Garden, New York (later on album and film *No Nukes*).

1988 **Sept** Young re-records *Get Together* for the soundtrack of film "1969".

FRANK ZAPPA

1956 Zappa (b. Francis Vincent Zappa, Dec.21, 1940, Baltimore, MD), having moved with his parents to California in 1950, and begun to write songs and to play drums and guitar in high school bands, meets Don Van Vliet (b. Jan.15, 1941, Glendale, CA) (later Captain Beefheart) at Antelope Valley high school in Lancaster, CA, and they form The Blackouts.

1958 **June** Zappa graduates from high school, and begins to play with various bands gigging around the bar circuit.

1960 He writes a soundtrack for B-movie "The World's Greatest Sinner".

1962 Zappa and Collins, a member of East Los Angeles' doo-wop group Little Julian Herrera & The Tigers, write *Memories Of El Monte*, a tribute song to doo-wop, recorded by The Penguins. Released on Art Laboe's Original Sound label (for which Zappa does regular work), it becomes a classic of the genre.

1963 The fees for another B-movie soundtrack (western "Run Home Slow") enable Zappa to finance his own Studio Z in Cucamonga, CA. It has already been equipped with specially-designed 5-track recording equipment by Zappa's electronics expert friend Paul Buff. He continues to gig with local bands like The Masters and The Soul Giants, several of whom record one-off singles at Studio Z.

'64 Studio Z is closed down after Zappa is arrested and given a 10-day jail sentence in San Bernardino Prison (plus 3 years probation). (He has cut, for a much-needed $100, a mock-pornographic tape for a vice squad officer posing as a used car salesman.) He moves to Los Angeles and puts together The Muthers from the remains of earlier band The Soul Giants, comprising Zappa (guitar), Ray Collins (vocals), Elliott Ingber (guitar), Roy Estrada (bass) and Jimmy Carl Black (drums).

'65 Group is offered a management contract by Herb Cohen and begins a residency at the Whiskey A-Go-Go club. Name is amended to The Mothers.

'66 **Jan** MGM Records' producer Tom Wilson, more interested in the group's R&B strengths than its musical social satire, signs The Mothers to MGM's jazz/R&B Verve label, for a $2,500 advance.
July Verve prevails upon Zappa to expand the group's name to The Mothers Of Invention for debut album, a double set titled *Freak Out*.

'67 **Feb** After a lot of underground media promotion (much of it by Zappa), double album *Freak Out!* climbs to US #130, during a 23-week chart stay.
July *Absolutely Free* makes US #41.
Aug Ian Underwood joins on saxophone.
Sept [23] The Mothers Of Invention, backed by a 15-piece orchestra, make their UK debut at London's Royal Albert Hall.

'68 **Feb** [14] Zappa anounces that The Mothers Of Invention are to make a film documentary on the band, "Uncle Meat".
Mar *We're Only In It For The Money*, with a sleeve which parodies The Beatles' *Sergeant Pepper's Lonely Hearts Club Band*'s and mocks the hippy psychedelia of 1967, reaches US #30. The Mothers play a lengthy residency at Garrick theater in Greenwich Village, New York.
Apr [12] Group plays at the US Record Industry's NARAS annual dinner in New York, with a performance which pokes barbed fun at the assembled diners.
June *Lumpy Gravy*, the first released under Zappa's own name rather than The Mothers Of Invention, is a largely instrumental and partially orchestral sound collage. It peaks at US #159.
July *We're Only In It For The Money* makes UK #32.
Oct [25] Group plays 2 concerts at London's Royal Festival Hall.

'69 **Jan** *Cruising With Ruben And The Jets*, credited to the group of the title, but by a thinly-disguised Zappa & Mothers, peaks at US #110 and is a pastiche of doo-wop.
Apr Compilation *Mothermania/The Best Of The Mothers* makes US #151. Compiled by Zappa, it fulfills his contractual obligation to Verve. He launches Bizarre/Straight Records in partnership with manager Cohen, distributed by Warner Bros. (He will produce non mainstream acts like Captain Beefheart, The GTO's and Wild Man Fischer.)
May Zappa begins to lecture on the US college circuit, speaking in New York, Los Angeles and elsewhere on themes like "Pigs, Ponies and Rock'N'Roll".
June Double *Uncle Meat*, billed as "the soundtrack for a movie you will probably never get to see" (though not actually a soundtrack recording) reaches US #43.
[27] Group plays the Denver Pop Festival at Mile High Stadium, with Jimi Hendrix, Creedence Clearwater Revival, and others, to 50,000 people.
Aug [20] Zappa disbands The Mothers Of Invention at the end of a short tour of Canada, reportedly "tired of playing for people who clap for all the wrong reasons" (and also because of the heavy expenses of keeping the large band on the road). (Zappa will only re-group musicians for recording purposes initially.)
He moves back to Los Angeles and marries second wife Gail (who will be the mother of Zappa's sons, Dweezil and Ahmet Rodan, and daughters, Moon Unit and Diva).
Dec *Hot Rats*, released under Zappa's own name on Bizarre and featuring guest appearances by Captain Beefheart and violinist Jean-Luc Ponty, makes US #173.

'70 **Mar** *Hot Rats* hits UK #9, as The Mothers Of Invention mostly instrumental *Burnt Weeny Sandwich* reaches US #94 and UK #17.
Aug The Mothers Of Invention are re-formed as a performing unit, featuring Zappa and Underwood with newcomers George Duke (keyboards), Jim Pons (bass) and Aynsley Dunbar (drums) with ex-Turtles Howard Kaylan and Mark Volman on vocals.
Oct *Weasels Ripped My Flesh*, also by The Mothers, makes UK #28, having reached US #189 in July. It is a combination of unissued live

and studio material from the previous 3 years.
Dec Zappa solo *Chunga's Revenge* peaks at US #119 and UK #43.

1971 **Feb** Zappa is forced to cancel a UK concert at London's Royal Albert Hall with the Royal Philharmonic Orchestra: venue officials declare the libretto "200 Motels" (the score of which is to have been featured) obscene and refuse to have it played. Undaunted, Zappa makes movie "200 Motels", a fictionalized "documentary" of The Mothers, in UK's Shepperton studios, with guest appearances by Ringo Starr and Keith Moon of The Who, and others. (Critical and audience response to the film will be muted.)
June [6] John Lennon and Yoko Ono jam on stage with Zappa at the Fillmore East in New York – Lennon's first stage appearance since 1969 (the show is recorded for Lennon's *Some Time In New York City*).
Aug Live *The Mothers/Fillmore East – June 1971* climbs to US #38.
[7] The Mothers Of Invention play UCLA, Los Angeles, the show being recorded for future release as *Just Another Band From L.A.*
Nov Double soundtrack *Frank Zappa's 200 Motels*, on United Artists, reaches US #59.
Dec [3] Band is performing at Montreux Casino, Switzerland, when the venue burns to the ground (as recounted in Deep Purple's *Smoke On The Water*). Nobody is hurt, but The Mothers lose $50,000-worth of equipment in the blaze, which is reputedly started by a hippie listening to the music on the casino roof.
[10] At a concert by The Mothers Of Invention at London's Rainbow theater, Zappa is pushed off stage into the orchestra pit by the jealous boyfriend of an ardent female Zappa fan. He breaks a leg and ankle in several places and suffers a fractured skull. (Recuperation will involve 9 months in a wheelchair and 3 more in a surgical brace.)

1972 **May** The Mothers' *Just Another Band From L.A.* makes US #85.
Sept Solo instrumental *Waka/Jawaka – Hot Rats* makes US #152.

1973 **Dec** The Mothers' *Over-Nite Sensation*, Zappa's first release on his new DiscReet label, makes US #32 and is his first gold disk for a half million sales.

1974 **July** Solo *Apostrophe* (with a guest appearance by ex-Cream bassist Jack Bruce) hits US #10 (Zappa's only US Top 10 disk) and earns his second gold disk.
Nov Live *Roxy And Elsewhere* reaches US #27. *Don't Eat The Yellow Snow*, from *Apostrophe*, makes US #86.

1975 **Aug** In an out-of-court settlement, Zappa regains ownership of all masters originally recorded for Verve, plus a $100,000 cash payment covering unpaid royalties.
Sept *One Size Fits All* reaches US #26.
Nov *Bongo Fury*, with Mothers and Captain Beefheart, makes US #66.

1976 Zappa sues ex-manager Cohen and Warner Bros. to gain full control of the early albums of which he has recovered the tapes from MGM/Verve. He cuts distribution ties with Warner.
Aug He produces Grand Funk's *Good Singin', Good Playin'* for MCA, which reaches US #52.
Dec *Zoot Allures* makes US #61.

1978 **May** Double live *Zappa In New York* reaches US #57 and UK #55.
Nov Instrumental *Studio Tan* reaches US #147. This is the first of 3 instrumental albums delivered by Zappa to Warner to fulfil contractual obligations – all 3 are released on DiscReet despite Zappa's own severance from the label.

1979 **Feb** Instrumental *Sleep Dirt* peaks at US #175.
Mar Double *Sheik Yerbouti* reaches US #21 and UK #32.
May *Dancin' Fool*, a disco parody from *Sheik Yerbouti*, makes US #45.
June Instrumental *Orchestral Favorites*, Zappa's final release on DiscReet, reaches US #169.
Oct *Joe's Garage, Act I* reaches US #27 and UK #62.

1980 **Jan** Double *Joe's Garage, Acts II & III* reaches US #53 and UK #75. Zappa also releases the concert animation movie "Baby Snakes".
June [17-18] Zappa plays 2 dates at the Wembley Arena, London.

1981 **May** Double live *Tinsel Town Rebellion*, the first release on Zappa's new Barking Pumpkin label, reaches US #66 and UK #55.
Oct Double *You Are What You Is* reaches US #93 and UK #51.

1982 **Mar** Zappa's 2 elder children Moon Unit and Dweezil reportedly form their own band Fred Zeppelin, which comes to little.
June *Ship Arriving Too Late To Save A Drowning Witch* reaches US #23 and UK #61.
Sept *Valley Girl*, featuring daughter Moon Unit rapping in the artificial dialect and idioms of San Fernando Valley's spoiled-stupid female teens, reaches US #32.

1983 **Feb** [9] Zappa conducts San Francisco Music Players at the city's War Memorial Opera House, in works by Edgar Verese and Anton Webern.
May *The Man From Utopia* makes US #153 and UK #87.

1984	**Oct** *Them Or Us* makes UK #53.
1985	On his own Barking Pumpkin label via mail order, Zappa releases a 7-album boxed set containing remixed versions of the 5 Verve albums , plus a "Mystery Disk" of unreleased material from the early-mid 60s.
1986	**Jan** *Frank Zappa Meets The Mothers Of Prevention* peaks at US #153.
	Mar Zappa appears in NBC TV's "Miami Vice".
1987	**June** Zappa is relieved of his role as guest host on US TV's "The Late Show" after a disagreement with producers over the choice of guests.
1988	**Mar** [2] Zappa wins Best Rock Instrumental for *Jazz From Hell* at the 30th annual Grammy awards.
1990	**Jan** [22] Zappa meets with Czech president Vaclav Havel in Prague, Czechoslovakia.
	Feb [26-28] Zappa guest hosts on the cable-TV Financial News Network's "Focus" series. He interviews Havel for the program. Zappa reports "he told me he liked my records, especially *Bongo Fury*."

THE ZOMBIES

Colin Blunstone (vocals
Rod Argent (keyboards)
Paul Atkinson (guitar)
Chris White (bass)
Hugh Grundy (drums)

1963	**Mar** Group is formed by Argent (b. June 14, 1945, St. Albans, Herts.), Blunstone (b. June 24, 1945, Hatfield, Herts.), Grundy (b. Mar.6, 1945, Winchester, Hants.) and Atkinson (b. Mar.19, 1946, Cuffley, Herts.), while still at St. Albans Grammar school. Original bass player is Paul Arnold, who leaves to concentrate on exam work (and will later qualify as a doctor).
	Sept White (b. Mar.7, 1943, Barnet, Herts.) joins on guitar, and group rehearses and writes its own material in a room over a store owned by White's father. They begin playing local gigs at colleges and rugby clubs, making their first major public appearance at Watford Town Hall, Herts.
1964	**Jan** Group wins a "Herts Beat" competition for the region's new bands, organized by London newspaper **The Evening News**. Prize is an audition with Decca Records.
	June Decca signs group to 3-year recording contract, more on the strength of Argent's and White's original material than its carefully-prepared demo of standard *Summertime* (which will be re-recorded for first album).
	July They leave school (with 50 GCE "O-level" and "A-level" passes between them) and turn professional, signing with manager Tito Burns as debut single *She's Not There* is released in UK.
	Sept *She's Not There*, distinguished by a minor-key subtle jazzy arrangement and Blunstone's breathy vocal, gains wide airplay and reaches UK #12.
	Oct Follow-up *Leave Me Be*, written by White in identical style but lacking a commercial hook, fails to chart.
	Dec *She's Not There* hits US #2 and sells over a million, bringing offers of US work.
	[25] After a 3-day wrangle with US immigration authorities, who initially ban the group from playing (despite international union agreement) because of concern over the number of UK groups "invading" US to work, The Zombies play 10 days of New York concerts in Murray The K's Christmas show, alongside The Shangri-Las, The Nashville Teens, The Shirelles and others. The rest of the proposed tour is cancelled.
1965	**Feb** *Tell Her No* is US follow-up and hits #6. It also makes UK #42, but is the last Zombies UK hit single.
	Mar *The Zombies* makes US #39.
	[25] Group begins 12-date twice-nightly UK package tour, with Dusty Springfield, The Searchers, Heinz, special guest Bobby Vee and others, at the Odeon cinema, Stockton, Cleveland. Tour ends Apr.10 at the Sophia Gardens, Cardiff, Wales.
	Apr *She's Coming Home* peaks at US #58 as group tours US for first time, supporting Herman's Hermits on a 34-day Dick Clark "Caravan Of Stars" trek. Meanwhile *The Zombies – Begin Here* is released in UK.
	July [15] A 25-day US tour with The Searchers opens in Chicago, IL, as *I Want You Back Again* stalls at US #95.
1966	**Feb** [10] Laurence Olivier/Keir Dullea film "Bunny Lake Is Missing", in which group makes a cameo appearance singing *Nothing Is Changed, Remember You* and *Just Out Of Reach*, opens at London's Leicester Square Odeon.
	June *Indication* fails to chart. Despite plenty of still-lucrative touring work, mainly in Europe and the Far East (Japan and The Philippines

	where occasional hits are still coming), group is disenchanted with Decca over a lack of development of its recording career and Decca's reluctance to allow another album.
1967	**Mar** A revival of Little Anthony & The Imperials' *Goin' Out Of My Head* is group's 10th, and final, Decca release.
	June Decca contract expires, with no interest in re-signing from either side. Group signs to CBS, where more artistic freedom is promised, a label and group co-finance the making of *Odessey And Oracle* (an apparently deliberate misspelling of the first word), produced by Argent and White.
	Sept *Friends Of Mine* is first single from the CBS sessions, followed by *Care Of Cell 44*.
	Dec Group splits, spurred by Blunstone and Atkinson who are both wearied by a lack of acceptance, particularly in UK. Blunstone leaves the music business for an insurance office job, but will decide to return as a soloist within the year.
1968	**Apr** *Odessey And Oracle* and single *Time Of The Season* are released CBS despite group's demise. Album is positively reviewed and single finds airplay in UK, but neither charts. (Album is not scheduled for US release, until Blood, Sweat & Tears' leader Al Kooper, who also records for CBS, badgers the label to do it justice. Kooper contributes a sleeve note to US version, which is put out hesitantly on subsidiary Date label, normally reserved for soul releases.)
	June US group The People reaches US #14 with White's song *I Love You*, originally cut by The Zombies as B-side of unsuccessful *Whenever You're Ready* in 1965. This prompts a reissue of original as a US A-side.
1969	**Jan** Blunstone signs to Deram and records a new version of original Zombies' hit *She's Not There* with baroque string arrangement, under the pseudonym Neil MacArthur. It reaches UK #34.
	Mar Following a gradual build-up of radio support (which will become huge and translate into nationwide sales), *Time Of The Season* hits US #3 and is group's second million-seller. Offers from US flood for a Zombies re-formation, including a deal offering $20,000 for a single concert. All are resisted, though Argent does agree, while in the process of assembling his own new band Argent, to complete some further recordings as The Zombies (with an interim group comprising himself (vocals, keyboards), Jim Rodford (bass), Hugh Grundy (drums) and Rick Birkett (guitar) with Chris White co-producing) to make up planned album of unreleased material (which does not appear).
	Apr *Odessey And Oracle* makes US #95.
	May Recently completed *Imagine The Swan* is issued as a US single.
	July *If It Don't Work Out*, another recent "Zombies" track completed Argent (originally cut as a demo for Dusty Springfield), is final US single. Several bogus groups are touring US under The Zombies' name cashing in on *Time Of The Season*'s success; these are eventually litigated to a halt. Group itself has now split for solo pursuits: Atkinson and Grundy will work in A&R for CBS, Blunstone will return as a successful soloist, White and Argent become partners in production, while the latter also founds the successful 70s band Argent.

ZZ TOP

Billy Gibbons (guitar, vocals)
Dusty Hill (bass, vocals)
Frank Beard (drums)

1963	Gibbons (b. Dec.16, 1949, Houston, TX) receives a Gibson Melody Maker guitar and a Fender Champ amplifier for his birthday. He forms a succession of local Houston bands including The Saints, The Coachmen and The Ten Blue Flames. Meanwhile, Hill (b. 1949, Dallas, TX), hanging out mainly in blues clubs becomes a friend of guitar great Freddie King and joins East Dallas band The Deadbeats with his older brother.
1964	Beard (b.1949, Frankston, TX), age 15, marries Irving high school sweetheart at a shotgun wedding – the union soon dissolves. He takes up drumming.
1967	The Hill brothers form Warlocks, who release one-off singles on Paradise and Ara labels. Beard joins the line-up. Gibbons forms The Moving Sidewalks, a psychedelia band which has a local hit with *99th Floor*.
1968	Warlocks changes name to American Blues (and will record 2 unsuccessful albums).
	June The Moving Sidewalks open for The Jimi Hendrix Experience, having released *Flash*.
1969	As both bands split, Gibbons auditions for members for a new band, ZZ Top. Beard is enlisted as drummer and, through him, Hill joins.

Gibbons has also linked with promotion man Bill Ham who becomes the band's long-term manager. ZZ Top releases first single *Salt Lick* on small Scat label.

1970 With a US-only deal signed with London Records, which unsuccessfully reissues *Salt Lick*, ZZ Top records debut **ZZ Top's First Album**. Extracted single *Shakin' Your Tree*, it fails to sell beyond Texas. Band begins a 7-year period of near non-stop touring, which will provide the base for increased sales in coming years. (It will open for many acts including Janis Joplin, Humble Pie, Ten Years After and Mott The Hoople.) Early dates focus strongly in the Texas, Louisiana and Mississippi areas, where it develops a large cult following.

1971 By year's end, Ham has booked ZZ Top into more than 300 venues.

1972 **May** *Rio Grande Mud* makes US #104, as the band supports The Rolling Stones on a US visit.

July *Francene* makes US #69. Band attracts an audience of 100,000 to its "ZZ Top's First Annual Texas Size Rompin' Stompin' Barndance Bar-B-Q" in Austin, TX.

1973 **Aug** *Tres Hombres* will hit US #8 and earn a gold disk. Band is currently opening for Alice Cooper.

1974 **May** Documenting a famed whorehouse, *La Grange* makes US #41.

1975 **May** Half-studio, half-live album *Fandango!* hits US #10 as **Newsweek** magazine reports ZZ Top has outdrawn Elvis Presley in Nashville and broken Led Zeppelin's attendance record in New Orleans.

July Debut UK chart entry is *Fandango!* which climbs to UK #60.

Sept From the album, *Tush*, the band's future long-term live encore, makes US #20.

1976 Group begins "ZZ Top's Worldwide Texas Tour" including 100 US dates and first concerts in Europe, Australia and Japan. Renowned for touring excess, 75 tons of equipment are transported together with a Texas State-shaped stage and live buffalo, steer and snakes. The trek will gross over $10 million.

Nov *It's Only Love* makes US #44.

1977 **Feb** *Texas* rises to US #17. Exhausted from the tour, the band begins a 2-year vacation: Beard visits the Caribbean, Hill goes sailing in the Pacific and Gibbons travels to Europe and Madagascar.

Apr B-side of *It's Only Love, Arrested While Driving Blind* makes US #91.

1978 **Feb** Interim album **The Best Of ZZ Top** stalls at US #94. It is their final release on London label.

1979 **Nov** Band signs to Warner Bros. Both Gibbons and Hill have stopped shaving and now sport long beards, unlike clean-shaven Beard. The frontmen will develop these growths as the beards become integral to ZZ Top image for the next 10 years. As Warner Bros. reissues all ZZ Top's London albums, new *Deguello* is released, peaking at US #24. It features the Wolf Horn section (actually Hill and Gibbons).

1980 **Mar** As serious touring resumes, *I Thank You* makes US #34.

July *Cheap Sunglasses* stalls at US #89.

1981 **Aug** *El Loco* makes UK #88 and will make US #17.

Oct *Leila* makes US #77.

1982 Band enters the studio to record a new album, adding synthesizers to their familiar Texan boogie-rock style.

1983 **Apr** *Eliminator*, recorded at Ardent Recording studios in Memphis, TN, is released and will hit US #9, earning a platinum disk, and UK #3 during a 135-week chart stay.

May Primed for MTV airplay, the band releases an accompanying video to current single *Gimme All Your Lovin'*. The first of a memorable trilogy, directed by Tim Newman, it features common ZZ Top images like stocking-clad models, heroic story-lines and striking ZZ Top car and keyring. Constant TV showing helps the disk to US #37.

Aug Second in the trilogy, *Sharp Dressed Man* makes US #56 and *Gimme All Your Lovin'* makes UK #61.

Nov [19] The first of many, "Gimme All Your Lovin'" receives **Billboard**'s Best Group Performance Video award at a ceremony in Pasadena, CA.

Dec *Sharp Dressed Man* reaches UK #53.

1984 **Mar** As the worldwide "Eliminator" tour sells out, *TV Dinners* makes UK #67.

July *Legs* hits US #8.

Nov *Gimme All Your Lovin'*, reissued in UK, hits UK #10.

1985 **Jan** [1] Hill accidentally shoots himself in the stomach. (He recovers after surgery.)

Sharp Dressed Man, again re-released, makes UK #22.

Mar *Legs* reaches UK #16.

July Now a UK chart fixture, Warner Bros. assembles EP *Summer Holiday*, including *Tush*, *Got Me Under Pressure*, *Beer Drinkers & Hellraisers* and *I'm Bad, I'm Nationwide*, which makes UK #51.

Oct From the new album, *Sleeping Bag* begins a climb to hit US #8 and

UK #27, aided by a Steve Barron-directed video clip.

Nov *Afterburner* repeats the *Eliminator* formula and heads towards US #4 and UK #2.

Dec [3] "Afterburner Tour" opens in Toronto, Canada, the first of a non-stop 212-date worldwide venture with increased tonnage and special effects.

1986 **Feb** *Stages* makes UK #43.

Mar [8] *Stages* peaks at US #21.

May [17] Ballad *Rough Boy* rises to US #22 and reaches UK #23.

Aug [30] *Velcro Fly* (with promo film now directed by Danny Kleinman) reaches US #35 and peaks at UK #54. (*Afterburner* is certified multi-platinum with 3 million US sales.)

Sept [12] Group begins a 29-date European leg of the world tour in Stockholm, Sweden.

Oct [23] At the end of European leg, ZZ Top completes a fourth sold-out date at Wembley Arena, London.

1987 **Jan** [12] **Pollstar** name ZZ Top the #1 concert draw of 1986.

Mar [21] "Afterburner" tour ends in Honolulu, HI with 40 pounds of confetti blasted into audience. (Band is now free to resume vacation.)

Oct [10] ZZ Top announces that it has made an advance booking for the first passenger flight to the Moon.

1988 Group spearheads a drive to raise $1 million for permanent Muddy Waters exhibit at the Delta Blues Museum in Clarksdale, MS.

1989 Gibbons unveils "Cadzzilla" automobile designed with Larry Erickson at Chevy's in New York.

1990 **June** [23] *Doubleback*, from movie "Back To The Future Part III", reaches US #50.

Sept *Eliminator* is RIAA certified 7 million.

Oct [1] Group begins North American tour in Canada.

[20] ZZ Top plays a benefit concert at the Cotton Bowl, Dallas, to help raise funds for the Texas Special Olympics, their first US gig in 4 years.

Nov [17] *Recycler* hits US #6.

1991 **Jan** [4] ZZ Top continues its North American tour in New Orleans. [5] Group is honored before its Memphis gig at a reception given by Governor Ned Ray McWherter for its help in raising money for the Delta Blues Museum in Clarksdale.

Feb [23] *Give It Up* stalls at US #79.

Apr [13] *My Head's In Mississippi* enters at UK peak #37.